International Directory of
COMPANY HISTORIES

International Directory of

COMPANY HISTORIES

VOLUME 9

Editor
Paula Kepos

StJ

St James Press

Detroit   London   Washington D.C.

Library of Congress Catalog Number: 89-190943

British Library Cataloguing in Publication Data

International directory of company histories. Vol. 9
I. Paula Kepos
338.7409

ISBN 1-55862-324-8

Printed in the United States of America
Published simultaneously in the United Kingdom

The trademark **ITP** is used under license.

Cover photograph courtesy of Foto Marburg / Art Resource, NY.

10 9 8 7 6 5 4 3 2 1

CONTENTS _____

Preface . . . . page ix
List of Abbreviations xi

Company Histories

PREFACE

International Directory of Company Histories provides detailed information on the development of the world's largest and most influential companies. To date, *Company Histories* has covered more than 1800 companies in nine volumes.

Inclusion Criteria

Most companies chosen for inclusion in *Company Histories* have achieved a minimum of US$500 million in annual sales. Some smaller companies are included if they are leading influences in their industries or geographical locations. State-owned companies that are important in their industries and that may operate much like public or private companies also are included. Wholly owned subsidiaries are presented if they meet the requirements for inclusion.

St. James Press does not endorse any of the companies or products mentioned in this book. Companies that appear in *Company Histories* were selected without reference to their wishes and have in no way endorsed their entries. The companies were given the opportunity to participate in the compilation of the articles by providing information or reading their entries for factual accuracy, and we are indebted to many of them for their comments and corrections. We also thank them for allowing the use of their logos for identification purposes.

Entry Format

Each entry in this volume begins with a company's legal name, the address of its headquarters, its telephone number and fax number, and a statement of public, private, state, or parent ownership. A company with a legal name in both English and the language of its headquarters country is listed by the English name, with the native-language name in parentheses.

Also provided are the company's earliest incorporation date, the number of employees, and the most recent sales figures available. Sales figures are given in local currencies with equivalents in U.S. dollars. For some private companies, sales figures are estimates. The entry lists the exchanges on which a company's stock is traded, as well as the company's principal Standard Industrial Classification codes. American spelling is used, and the word ''billion'' is used in its American sense of one thousand million.

Sources

The histories were compiled from publicly accessible sources such as general and academic periodicals, books, annual reports, and material supplied by the companies themselves. *Company Histories* is intended for reference use by students, business people, librarians, historians, economists, investors, job candidates, and others who want to learn more about the historical development of the world's most important companies.

Cumulative Indexes

An Index to Companies and Persons provides access to companies and individuals discussed in the text. Beginning with Volume 7, an Index to Industries allows researchers to locate companies by their principal industry.

ABBREVIATIONS FOR FORMS OF COMPANY INCORPORATION

A.B.	Aktiebolaget (Sweden)
A.G.	Aktiengesellschaft (Germany, Switzerland)
A.S.	Atieselskab (Denmark)
A.S.	Aksjeselskap (Denmark, Norway)
A.Ş.	Anomin Şirket (Turkey)
B.V.	Besloten Vennootschap met beperkte, Aansprakelijkheid (The Netherlands)
Co.	Company (United Kingdom, United States)
Corp.	Corporation (United States)
G.I.E.	Groupement d'Intérêt Economique (France)
GmbH	Gesellschaft mit beschränkter Haftung (Germany)
H.B.	Handelsbolaget (Sweden)
Inc.	Incorporated (United States)
KGaA	Kommanditgesellschaft auf Aktien (Germany)
K.K.	Kabushiki Kaisha (Japan)
LLC	Limited Liability Company (Middle East)
Ltd.	Limited (Canada, Japan, United Kingdom, United States)
N.V.	Naamloze Vennootschap (The Netherlands)
OY	Osakeyhtiöt (Finland)
PLC	Public Limited Company (United Kingdom)
PTY.	Proprietary (Australia, Hong Kong, South Africa)
S.A.	Société Anonyme (Belgium, France, Switzerland)
SpA	Società per Azioni (Italy)

ABBREVIATIONS FOR CURRENCY

DA	Algerian dinar	Dfl	Netherlands florin
A$	Australian dollar	NZ$	New Zealand dollar
Sch	Austrian schilling	N	Nigerian naira
BFr	Belgian franc	NKr	Norwegian krone
Cr	Brazilian cruzado	RO	Omani rial
C$	Canadian dollar	P	Philippine peso
DKr	Danish krone	Esc	Portuguese escudo
E£	Egyptian pound	SRls	Saudi Arabian riyal
Fmk	Finnish markka	S$	Singapore dollar
FFr	French franc	R	South African rand
DM	German mark	W	South Korean won
HK$	Hong Kong dollar	Pta	Spanish peseta
Rs	Indian rupee	SKr	Swedish krona
Rp	Indonesian rupiah	SFr	Swiss franc
IR£	Irish pound	NT$	Taiwanese dollar
L	Italian lira	B	Thai baht
¥	Japanese yen	£	United Kingdom pound
W	Korean won	$	United States dollar
KD	Kuwaiti dinar	B	Venezuelan bolivar
LuxFr	Luxembourgian franc	K	Zambian kwacha
M$	Malaysian ringgit		

International Directory of
COMPANY
HISTORIES

ACKERLEY COMMUNICATIONS, INC.

Ackerley Communications, Inc.

800 Fifth Avenue
Suite 3770
Seattle, Washington 98104
U.S.A.
(206) 624-2888
Fax: (206) 623-7853

Public Company
Incorporated: 1975 as Northwest Communications, Inc.
Employees: 926
Sales: $187 million
Stock Exchanges: American
SICs: 7312 Outdoor Advertising Services; 7319 Advertising
Nec; 7941 Sports Clubs, Managers & Promoters; 4832
Radio Broadcasting Stations; 4833 Television Broadcasting
Stations

Ackerley Communications, Inc. is a diversified communications company involved in outdoor and airport advertising, radio and television broadcasting, and professional basketball. With 10,150 billboards located in Florida, Massachusetts, Oregon, and Washington, the company is the largest operator of outdoor advertising in each of the markets it serves. As the largest operator of airport advertising displays in the United States, Ackerley Communications owns and operates 5,160 displays in 129 airport terminals throughout the country. It owns five television stations in New York, Colorado, California, and Washington, and three radio stations in Florida and Washington. The company also owns the Seattle Supersonics, a National Basketball Association franchise.

By the early 1960s, the advertising industry had begun to attract hopeful entrepreneurs intent on profiting from the billboard properties that dotted the nation's landscape. The inertia that had characterized the industry in the late 1950s ended when a group of investors purchased one of the nation's largest billboard interests, General Outdoor Advertising, and then proceeded to sell off several of its markets. Prior to the break-up of General Outdoor, billboard properties had rarely changed hands and the opportunities to enter the field had, consequently, been limited. As more properties became available, interested parties began purchasing them, hoping to capitalize on what many viewed as a low-cost, high-margin investment. One of

these hopeful entrepreneurs who envisaged the profit potential in the industry was Barry A. Ackerley.

During this time Ackerley was working in New York, selling advertising space for the magazine *Better Homes & Gardens* and hoping for greater opportunity and a faster path to success. Lacking the necessary capital to enter into the business immediately, he nevertheless was encouraged by the possibilities and returned to his native state of Iowa to work for an outdoor advertising firm, Stoner Outdoor Advertising. Soon after his relocation to Iowa in 1964, he approached a wealthy family in Wichita, Kansas, and asked for their financial assistance in acquiring billboards. The family agreed and, as a minority shareholder in the venture, Ackerley purchased billboards in Fresno and Bakersfield, California. Over the next four years, Ackerley purchased additional billboards in San Francisco, Oakland, and San Jose, California.

By 1968, the billboards in northern California had generated enough income to provide Ackerley with the start-up capital he had lacked in New York five years earlier. He sold his interest in the venture back to his benefactors and, with a new partner, parlayed the proceeds toward the establishment of an outdoor advertising company, Golden West Outdoor Advertising. Golden West, under Ackerley's management, operated properties in Sacramento, California, and in Colorado until 1974, when Ackerley purchased his partner's share in the company and then sold the billboards in Sacramento, thereby becoming the sole owner of the Colorado market. These Colorado properties were not to remain with Ackerley long, however. Shortly after he had gained complete control of Golden West, he sold the company to Gannett Company, an outdoor advertising firm that would soon be one of Ackerley's main competitors.

With the money garnered from the sale to Gannett, Ackerley, after a brief return to the Northeast to work for an advertising firm, relocated to Seattle, Washington, in 1975 and purchased Seattle-based Foster & Kleiser from Metromedia Inc. and Obie Outdoor Advertising based in Eugene, Oregon. The acquisition of these two Northwest outdoor advertising companies formed the initial components of Ackerley's new company, named Northwest Communications, Inc. initially, and renamed Ackerley Communications, Inc. the following year.

From 1975 on, Ackerley no longer entertained the idea of selling any of his assets. His penchant for acquiring companies at a rapid rate led to his precipitate rise in the outdoor advertising industry, and while it also left his company in debt throughout most of its existence, for Ackerley, this was not necessarily a precarious position. By acquiring company after company and recording the consequent deductions allowed for interest payments and asset depreciation, Ackerley kept his taxable income at a minimum. Accordingly, his company rarely posted substantial earnings and often operated without showing any profits, but still continued to expand. Rather than gauging his company's success by monitoring the rise or decline in net income, the traditional barometer of a company's financial status, Ackerley relied on the amount of cash flow his company recorded. By maintaining a sufficient level of cash flow (the income from operations before depreciation, amortization, and interest are charged) Ackerley could continue to enlarge his holdings while his company appeared to teeter on the edge of failure.

In its inaugural year, Northwest Communications recorded revenues totaling $6.6 million, giving Ackerley enough bargaining power to persuade the First National Bank of Chicago into financing the purchase of additional properties in Florida the following year. After securing a foothold in the Florida market, Ackerley next purchased billboard displays in Massachusetts in 1978 and then began plans to diversify his business interests. In 1980, he purchased Hart Advertising Company, a St. Louis-based operator of airport advertising displays. The Hart acquisition gave the company, now known as Ackerley Communications, Inc., advertising displays in 36 U.S. airport terminals, marking the company's initial move into airport advertising. A year later, Ackerley augmented his investment in airport advertising by purchasing the Winston Network's TDI subsidiary, which operated advertising displays in nearly 50 airport terminals.

After establishing a solid presence in both the airport and outdoor advertising markets, collectively known as "out-of-home media," Ackerley next explored the broadcasting industry for further expansion opportunities. In 1982, the company purchased ABC-TV affiliate WIXT-TV in Syracuse, New York, from WIXT Television Inc. for $13.8 million. Eight months later, Ackerley Communications acquired KKTV, a CBS-TV affiliate serving the Colorado markets of Colorado Springs and Pueblo. Before the end of 1983, the company purchased yet another television station, KPWR-TV, since renamed KGET, the NBC-TV affiliate in Bakersfield, California.

By the end of 1983, Ackerley Communications owned television stations affiliated with each major television network, 11,000 billboard displays in Washington, Oregon, Florida, and Massachusetts, and advertising displays in 86 airport terminals. The company's all important cash flow had more than doubled in the previous four years, from $9.5 million to $22.3 million, and Ackerley stood ready to acquire additional businesses. That year the company also entered into a line of business that would facilitate the move from advertising on billboards to television stations: in November, Ackerley announced he had entered a definitive agreement with Seattle SuperSonics Corp., owned by FNI Corp., to purchase the Seattle Supersonics basketball franchise of the National Basketball Association for $21 million.

In less than ten years, Ackerley had built and led Ackerley Communications toward enviable success and had demonstrated an ability to acquire any company he deemed worthy of inclusion in his growing empire. Ackerley's acquisitive talents, however, failed him on two occasions in the year following the purchase of the Seattle SuperSonics. First, his bid to acquire a fourth television station, unaffiliated KZAZ in Tuscon, Arizona, was rejected, presumably because Ackerley Communications did not boast a large reservoir of cash. The second attempted acquisition was far more disheartening. Ackerley offered $156 million to buy the Des Moines Register & Tribune Company, the addition of which would more than double the revenues of his existing company. Recording $88.5 million in revenues for 1983, Des Moines Register & Tribune owned *The Des Moines Register,* the *Daily Sun* in Jackson, Tennessee, as well as two rural newspapers in Iowa. In addition to these principal compo-

nents, the company also owned two television stations in Hawaii and Illinois, and three radio stations in Oregon and Wisconsin. Even more appealing, the company's properties also included a 14.3 percent ownership in Cowles Media, publisher of *The Minneapolis Star and Tribune.* The deal, however, was never seriously considered by the newspaper company. Industry pundits cited Ackerley's lack of newspaper experience as a possible reason for the failed bid and others speculated that, given Ackerley's holdings in broadcasting, he was only after the company's television stations, and would sell the newspaper once he had acquired it. Ackerley attempted to mollify the owners of the Des Moines company by stating that he had no intention of breaking up the company, telling *The Wall Street Journal,* "Look at our history. We only buy. We never sell," but conceded that the chairperson of the Des Moines company, "won't even return my phone calls." Although Ackerley Communications was the third largest outdoor advertising company in the United States and the largest airport advertiser, critics contended that Ackerley had overestimated his position within the media industry. The newspapers were sold to Gannett Company, publisher of *USA Today* and the owner of a vast number of billboard displays, for $200 million in early 1985.

Despite the discouraging setback, Ackerley continued to expand and diversify, making an entrance into radio broadcasting during this time. Following the purchase of the Seattle Super-Sonics, Ackerley acquired his first radio station, KJR-AM, in May 1984 for $5.8 million. Purchased from Metromedia Inc., the same company Ackerley had purchased Foster & Kleiser from in 1975 to launch Northwest Communications, the addition of the 5,000 watt radio station soon gave Ackerley Communications the synergism within its operations that had been lacking once the basketball team was acquired. KJR, regarded as a pioneer in developing the "Top 40" music format, was converted into a sports talk station and by 1987 had obtained the broadcasting rights to the SuperSonics games. Now, with the addition of KJR, Ackerley could employ his billboards to advertise the SuperSonics broadcasts on KJR, which at once incorporated the three separate business segments composing Ackerley Communications.

Once all three of these business lines were working together, Ackerley set forth to increase his holdings in both out-of-home advertising and broadcasting. In 1985, Ackerley purchased unaffiliated KVOS-TV, located in Bellingham, Washington, and primarily serving the Vancouver, British Columbia, market. A month after the KVOS acquisition, Ackerley purchased the two radio stations owned by the Des Moines Register & Tribune Company, KGON-FM, a 100,000 watt station, and KFXX-AM, a 50,000 watt station, both of which served Portland, Oregon. By this time, a discernible pattern had developed in Ackerley's acquisitions. Almost without exception, broadcasting properties were acquired in markets where Ackerley had already established a considerable presence in the outdoor advertising market. Accordingly, as Ackerley continued to augment his television and radio assets, the markets that his broadcasting interests served mirrored the markets served by his outdoor advertising properties. This integration of his business segments enabled Ackerley to offer advertisers a multimedia package with a guaranteed audience, a set-up that was much more attractive to advertisers who typically had to negotiate for each advertising format.

With this strategy driving the company's acquisitions, Ackerley purchased KCBA-TV, an independent station affiliated with the Fox Broadcasting network and serving Salinas-Monterey, California, in 1986. The following year, KLTX-FM, a 100,000 watt station in Seattle, was added to the growing list of Ackerley Communications' broadcasting properties. Two years later, in early 1989, before his company publicly offered shares of stock for the first time in the fall, Ackerley acquired WBOS-FM in Boston, Massachusetts, for $19.3 million and $16.9 million worth of outdoor advertising properties in southern Florida.

By this time, the company's aggressive expansion had produced a large debt—$222 million at the end of 1989—but this was nothing new for Ackerley Communications. The cash generated by the outdoor and airport advertising operations was sufficient to service the debt and fund additional acquisitions, such as the purchase of WAXY-FM, a 100,000 watt radio station serving Miami-Fort Lauderdale, Florida, in 1990. But, as the company entered the 1990s and the nation experienced economic recession, Ackerley's losses exponentially increased, becoming too large even for a company accustomed to operating in the red. In 1990, Ackerley Communications recorded a loss of $14.5 million, and by the following year the figure had increased to $39.1 million. Ackerley responded to this downturn by cutting costs, increasing the efficiency of the company's operations, and selling two of his radio stations, WBOS-FM in Boston and KFXX-AM in Portland, in 1992. By early 1993, the company had rebounded, posting its first profit for a full year since 1981.

As Ackerley Communications attempted to build upon the $3.2 million it earned in 1992, its prospects appeared bright. The Seattle SuperSonics reached the Western Conference finals during the 1992–93 season, a feat expected to boost the company's earnings in fiscal 1993, and its return to posting profits after an eleven-year hiatus bodes well for the future. The company had to contend, however, with the burgeoning movement against the erection of billboards, an issue it has fiercely challenged in the courts. Assuming legislation will not eliminate the underpinnings of Ackerley's communications empire, Ackerley Communications should continue to dominate each of the markets it is involved in.

Principal Subsidiaries: Ackerley Communications of Florida; Ackerley Communications of Massachusetts; Ackerley Communications of the Northwest; KVOS-TV; WIXT-TV; KKTV-TV; KCBA-TV; KGET-TV; WAXY-FM; KLTX-FM; KJR-AM; KGON-FM; Seattle Supersonics.

Further Reading:

''Ackerley Agrees to Buy Seattle Basketball Team,'' *The Wall Street Journal,* November 2, 1983, p. 19.

''Going Public Via the Back Door,'' *Marple's Business Newsletter,* November 21, 1984, pp. 2–3.

Lee, Gordon, ''Recent Ventures Turn Spotlight on Ackerley Firm,'' *Puget Sound Business Journal,* March 4, 1985, p. 6.

Pierce, J. Kingston, ''Battlin' Barry,'' *The Weekly,* February 13, 1985, pp. 36–41.

Roberts, Paul, ''The Last Tycoon,'' *The Weekly,* May 30, 1990, pp. 38–42.

Virgin, Bill, ''Ackerley Has First Winning Year Since '81,'' *Seattle Post-Intelligencer,* January, 22, 1993, p. B2.

Zonana, Victor F., ''Ackerley's Drive to Expand Media Firm Is a Factor in Bid for Des Moines Register,'' *The Wall Street Journal,* December 7, 1984, p. 24.

—Jeffrey L. Covell

Advanced Technology Laboratories, Inc.

22100 Bothell Everett Highway
Bothell, Washington 98041-3003
U.S.A.
(206) 487-7000
Fax: (206) 485-6080

Public Company
Incorporated: 1969
Employees: 1,896
Sales: $323.7 million
Stock Exchanges: NASDAQ
SICs: 3845 Electromedical Equipment

Advanced Technology Laboratories, Inc., (ATL) is one of the leading diagnostic ultrasound imaging companies in the world, serving customers in over 80 countries through a network of direct subsidiaries and independent distributors. Ultrasound employs high frequency sound waves to create an image of the body's soft tissues, organs, and fetal anatomy, as well as enabling the display of blood flow characteristics. As an innovator in the ultrasound imaging industry, ATL has contributed significantly to the advancement of ultrasound technology and the fabrication of ultrasound equipment, which medical facilities utilize to avoid more invasive and costly procedures.

Founded in 1969, ATL did not enter the medical ultrasound industry until 1974, the year a transfer of technology from the University of Washington in Seattle enabled the company to begin manufacturing products for hospitals and physicians. This connection with the University of Washington was the first such tie with the academic community and was a relationship ATL would cultivate in the future and rely on for assistance in pioneering new products. Being on the vanguard of new technology was essential to ATL's business, as it found itself in a fiercely competitive and rapidly growing market that allowed only those companies using the latest technological advances to survive. ATL thrived during its first decade of business, using its ties with academia and investing in its own research to quickly rise to a leading position in the ultrasound industry.

In fact, growth had come so quickly for the company that it was unable to keep pace with its success in a systematic manner. By the end of the 1970s, the facilities used to manufacture, market,

and administrate its business had expanded to the extent that the efficacy of the company's operations was somewhat hampered. ATL's 14 buildings were scattered throughout two communities east of Seattle, Washington, and its warehouse was situated ten miles from its manufacturing plants. Nevertheless, it would be several years before the facilities were consolidated, and ATL's haphazard expansion did reflect its success, which had not gone unnoticed by those looking for a way to enter the ultrasound market.

The Squibb Corporation, a manufacturer and marketer of a broad line of health care and consumer products, was one company piqued by ATL's initial success. In the late 1970s, Squibb was involved in a diversification plan that called for a move into the medical equipment market, and the acquisition of ATL appeared to be the answer for such an entrance. In December 1979, Squibb purchased ATL for $60 million and formed a medical equipment subsidiary within which ATL operated. As part of Squibb's diversification efforts, Spacelabs, Inc., a manufacturer of patient monitoring systems, was also acquired shortly after the purchase of ATL, and for the next decade Spacelabs was grouped with ATL.

Spacelabs was formed in 1958 as an independent company to assist the National Aeronautics and Space Administration (NASA) in its bid to launch astronauts in space. Initially, the company developed monitoring devices to assess the life functions of test pilots and astronauts, then, in 1968, it began manufacturing equipment for intensive care and coronary units in hospitals. Like ATL, Spacelabs flourished in the 1970s, attracting the attention of Squibb in the latter part of the decade. Two months after Squibb purchased ATL, it acquired Spacelabs for $34.4 million, and, along with another company Squibb had formed, Squibb Medical Systems, the medical equipment subsidiary began operations.

Under Squibb's management, the robust performance records and rapid expansion enjoyed by both Spacelabs and ATL during the 1970s slowed considerably, particularly in ATL's case. ATL's decline was largely attributable to a drop in capital investments and an insufficient allocation of funds toward research and development. For a company whose success had been predicated on consistently incorporating technological advances into its products, the absence of funds to fuel further technological development caused the company to fall behind its competitors, and its performance suffered. Spacelabs experienced a similar reduction in capital investments, but fared better than ATL, as observers began to question whether Squibb was genuinely committed to its new business segment.

In 1985 ATL's diffused assortment of buildings was replaced with a more centralized complex to increase the efficiency of its operations. Questions concerning Squibb's commitment to ATL still hounded Squibb's leadership, however, and some financial analysts began to predict that Squibb would sell ATL. Nevertheless, Squibb's chief executive officer, Richard M. Furlaud, hoped the establishment of a new, consolidated headquarters for ATL would put to rest the doubts of the investing public. When asked about Squibb's level of commitment to ATL and what the new complex meant for the relationship between ATL and Squibb, Furlaud responded to the *Seattle Times,* ''I believe it [ATL] is going to be very successful and play a key role in the future of Squibb . . . and I don't think anybody will have to ask that question anymore.'' Despite Furlaud's optimism, ATL and its medical equipment counterparts racked up combined losses of $37 million for the year, as the subsidiary continued to struggle for profitability. Less than a year after Furlaud had attempted to assuage the anxieties concerning ATL's future, Squibb announced plans to spin off Spacelabs, Squibb Medical Systems, and ATL to Squibb shareholders.

The spin-off of the subsidiary was part of a general plan initiated by Squibb in 1984 to divest itself of less profitable, non-pharmaceutical operations. Before the decision was announced, the corporation had achieved remarkable results in developing a new heart drug, Capoten, which underscored the strength of its primary line of business—the development and distribution of pharmaceutical drugs—and the weakness of its less successful operations. Accordingly, 96 percent of the three medical equipment companies' stock was distributed to Squibb shareholders in January 1987, and a holding company for the former subsidiary was created, named Westmark International Inc.

First, Westmark needed new leadership, and after an extensive executive search failed to produce a suitable candidate, the president of Squibb, Dennis C. Fill, opted to assume the stewardship of the reorganized company. Fill, who had been largely responsible for Squibb's success in the development of Capoten, inherited an organization riddled with problems stemming primarily from ATL's lackluster performance over the past several years. Customers had recently begun to complain about the quality and reliability of ATL's products, a consequence of the scarcity of resources appropriated for research and development. Unable to pursue experiments employing digital technology, the newest breakthrough in ultrasound products, the company was overrun by its major competitors, Acuson Corp., Hewlett-Packard, and Toshiba. To exacerbate matters, these rival companies were better financed than ATL and enjoyed greater research and development budgets, which further widened the technological gulf between ATL and the rest of the industry. As a whole, the subsidiary had generated sales of $243.8 million in 1986, the year before it was spun off from Squibb, and was still recovering from the $37 million it had lost in 1985. The prospects for the company were bleak and some industry pundits claimed Fill had taken the helm of a ''rapidly sinking ship.'' However, once the companies were returned to a more entrepreneurial environment, unfettered by the directives of Squibb, and needed changes were effected, the newly formed Westmark slowly began to produce positive results.

Despite the losses incurred by the companies, Squibb left its former subsidiary in relatively good shape for recovery. Westmark was granted $50 million in working capital, which Fill immediately earmarked for the company's research and development budget, and nearly $40 million of debt was cancelled by Squibb. To expedite the company's return to the forefront of ultrasound and patient monitoring technology, an esteemed scientific advisory council was formed that included Nobel laureate Dr. Paul Berg of Stanford Medical School. In addition to increasing research and development spending by over 20 percent, Fill also closed a factory in Tempe, Arizona, in

an attempt to streamline the company's manufacturing operations. In its first year of operating independently from Squibb, Westmark's sales climbed to $291.8 million, but the company still suffered a $7.2 million loss. Partly to blame for the year's loss were several difficulties with patents for Westmark's products and some production problems. Nevertheless, once these were rectified, the company began posting profits. In 1988, sales climbed to $365.2 million, and the company's net income surged into the black, reaching $10.7 million.

This remarkable turnaround was chiefly attributable to the more sophisticated products Spacelabs and ATL produced after the spin off from Squibb. The emphasis Fill placed on research and development had enabled the two companies to catch up to their competitors, and now they were successfully competing for market share. ATL, which accounted for over 60 percent of Westmark's revenues, was, by this time, immersed in the development of ultrasound products utilizing the latest all-digital technology. By mid-1989, ATL had introduced Ultramark 9, the result of its efforts toward developing digital ultrasound equipment, and the sales generated by the company increased markedly. ATL had also designed its products to be utilized for a broad range of medical specialties, including cardiology and obstetrics, an advantage its products held over those of Acuson and Hewlett-Packard. Sales for the year were $438.7 million, and net income shot up to nearly $20 million, as both ATL and Spacelabs once again found themselves in a dominant position within the medical equipment market. Spacelabs controlled a 17 percent share in the patient monitoring market, running a close second to Hewlett-Packard, and the technology used in ATL's recently introduced Ultramark 9 was expected to become the industry standard.

In 1991 ATL unveiled a new product employing digital ultrasound technology that was regarded by the medical industry as a significant advance in the applicability of ultrasound diagnoses. Using ''high definition imaging,'' the new product, manufactured under the Ultramark 9 line, enabled medical personnel to view a sharper, more detailed image of various body tissues and organs than existing ultrasound products allowed. The advent of high definition imaging provided a considerable boost to ATL's revenues, as physicians, clinics, and hospitals found the new Ultramark 9 to be a cheaper, yet more powerful tool in the diagnoses of internal disorders. Selling for approximately $250,000, the high definition imaging system approached the scanning quality of magnetic resonance imaging systems, which sold for more than $1 million. With roughly 70 percent of ATL's $279.7 million in revenues generated by the Ultramark 9, Westmark's revenues increased to $504.7 million, and its net income climbed to nearly $23 million.

In June 1992, Westmark's board of directors decided to split its two subsidiaries apart. Under the terms of the arrangement, shareholders in Westmark were distributed all outstanding common stock of Spacelabs on a one-for-one basis. Westmark then adopted the name of Advanced Technology Laboratories, Inc. Both companies had been operating independently since they had been separated from Squibb, so the dissolution of Westmark did not represent a dramatic change for either company. Rather, the division of the two companies was a testament to their remarkable success since 1987. Now strong enough to operate as independently traded companies, both Spacelabs and

ATL had secured a leading position in their respective markets. Fill became president of ATL and led the company toward its promising future. By this time, ATL commanded a 28 percent share in the estimated $2 billion global radiology market and held a ten percent share in the $1 billion to $2 billion a year specialized ultrasound market.

ATL's investment in research and development should continue to fuel the company's growth. Its high definition imaging ultrasound products are regarded as the best in the industry, which gives the company an appreciable advantage over its competitors. However, the effects of the Clinton administration's decisions concerning health care reform may hinder sales, as hospitals and clinics await the full ramifications of a national health care plan. In August 1993, ATL laid off 240 workers to mitigate losses incurred by the company as a result of a decline in sales from such uncertainties. Nevertheless, barring any further losses, ATL should continue to lead the ultrasound market into the future.

Further Reading:

"Bedside Processors Handle Intensive Care in Hospitals," *Electronics,* September 5, 1974, pp. 29–31.

Bishop, Jerry E., "Digital Ultrasound Is Seen as Major Diagnostic Advance," *Wall Street Journal,* April 17, 1991.

Buck, Richard, "ATL No Longer Victim of Its Own Success, Ultrasonic Scanners Keep Company Rosy," *Seattle Times,* July 29, 1985, p. D9.

Ciavola, Gina, "Westmark Thinks Two Firms Are Better Than One," *Washington CEO,* May 1992, pp. 14–15.

Day, Connie, "A Man for All Seasons," *Washington CEO,* January 1993, pp. 18–22.

Healy, Tim, "Westmark Hits the Mark," *Seattle Times,* January 7, 1992, p. E3.

Heberlein, Greg, "New Company Will Be Formed from Three Squibb Subsidiaries," *Seattle Times,* July 9, 1986, p. B4.

——, "Westmark Story Is a Tale of Woe," *Seattle Times,* July 28, 1990, p. A15.

Markey, Keith A., "Westmark Int'l," *Value Line Investment Survey,* December 25, 1987, p. 236.

Matthee, Imbert, "Layoffs at ATL Outrage Labor Officials," *Seattle Post-Intelligencer,* August 26, 1993, p. B7.

Milburn, Karen, "Westmark Considering Spinning Off Subsidiaries," *Seattle Times,* February 13, 1992, p. C3.

Parks, Mike, "Has Dennis Fill Found His Perfect Job at Last," *Business Week,* September 21, 1987, p. 76.

Siwolop, Sana, "Westmark International: Up, Up . . . ," *Financial World,* May 15, 1990, p. 20.

"Spacelabs Buys into Bellevue's First Medic," *Seattle Times,* December 29, 1987, p. F1.

"Spacelabs May Be Sold as Result of the Death of Founder this Year," *Wall Street Journal,* November 29, 1979, p. 6.

"Spacelabs, Squibb Set $34M Merger," *Electronic News,* February 18, 1980, p. 50.

"Spacelabs, Trinity to Make Interface for Monitor Data," *Modern Healthcare,* February 15, 1984, p. 86.

"Squibb to Spin Off Medical Systems," *New York Times,* July 10, 1986, p. D4.

"These Health-Care Stocks Can Prosper Even in the Face of Cost Cutting," *Money,* July 1990, p. 55.

"Westmark International," *Fortune,* June 19, 1989, p. 148.

Wynter, Leon E., and Allen, Frank, "Squibb to Spin Off Lack Luster Medical Electronics Line," *Wall Street Journal,* July 10, 1986, p. 33.

—Jeffrey L. Covell

Alcatel Alsthom Compagnie Générale d'Electricité

54, rue La Boetie
75008 Paris
France
(1) 40-76-1010
Fax: (1) 40-76-1400

Public Company
Incorporated: 1898 as Compagnie Générale d'Electricité
Employees: 200,000
Sales: Ffr 160.08 billion
Stock Exchanges: Paris Amsterdam Antwerp Basle Brussels
    Geneva Zurich
SICs: 6719 Offices of Holding Companies, nec; 4899
    Communications Services, nec.

With operations in more than 100 countries, Alcatel Alsthom Compagnie Générale d'Electricité was the second-largest company in France in 1993. After almost a century as Compagnie Générale d'Electricité, the conglomerate changed its name in 1991 to reflect its two primary subsidiaries, Alcatel N.V. and GEC Alsthom. Alcatel, which brings in about 60 percent of the group's sales, was the world's largest manufacturer of telecommunications equipment, systems, and cables. GEC Alsthom, a 50/50 joint venture with Great Britain's GEC plc, was one of Europe's top power and transportation concerns. It constituted about 20 percent of the group's annual sales, and was known for the development of France's high-speed Trains a Grand Vitesse. Alcatel Alsthom Compagnie Générale d'Electricité also held publishing and nuclear interests in the early 1990s.

Compagnie Générale d'Electricité (CGE) was created in 1898 through the combination of two electric generating companies and a light bulb manufacturer. The merger, engineered by Pierre Azaria, formed one of Europe's pioneer electric power and manufacturing companies, with interests in electric utilities in France and abroad.

During the first half of the 20th century, CGE expanded its electrical equipment manufacturing through acquisitions. The most important of these were: Société Francaise des Cables Electriques Bertrand-Borel, merged in 1911; Atelier de Construction Electrique de Delle, acquired in 1912; and Cie Générale d'Electro-Ceramique, purchased in 1921. The growth

led CGE into building and equipping electric power plants as well as manufacturing the cable used for the distribution of electricity.

In the 1920s CGE entered into a joint venture with its primary French competitor, Thomson-Brandt (an electronics manufacturer later renamed Thomson). The creation of the new concern, a light bulb manufacturer called Cie des Lampes, was encouraged by the French government, which would involve itself in CGE's affairs in varying degrees over the course of the 20th century.

During the 1930s CGE diversified through the acquisition of construction and civil engineering companies and added batteries to its line of electrical products. By World War II, CGE was a diversified manufacturer of electrical equipment, a primary supplier to utilities, and itself an important distributor of electricity. The French government nationalized CGE as part of its effort to coordinate resistance to the German attack. But when the country came under Nazi occupation in 1941, the business was taken over by the invaders and run by collaborators. Unfortunately, this made CGE's factories regular targets of Allied bombs. After the war, all of France's electric utilities were nationalized, but the remainder of CGE's operations returned to private management. The company's traumatic experience under government control led it to reduce its dependence on government contracts.

CGE played a key role in the postwar redevelopment of the French economy. The company diversified into home appliances, telephone equipment, and industrial electronics, and expanded its traditional businesses in the manufacture of electric utility equipment, especially cables. By the end of the 1950s, CGE was a conglomerate with over 200 subsidiaries and the bureaucratic inertia that came with such a far-flung enterprise.

A reorganization in the 1960s formed six primary business groups: power generation, engineering, telecommunications, cable and wire, raw materials, and other products. In 1966 the conglomerate acquired a large construction company, the Société Générale d'Entreprises. In the late 1960s the French government enforced a restructuring of the country's entire electrical engineering industry. The government felt that the industry would run better if Thomson-Brandt's large Alsthom subsidiary, which manufactured power generating equipment and constructed power plants, were transferred to CGE. CGE, in turn, was enjoined to shift its data processing and appliance businesses to Thompson.

The new arrangement seemed to work out well at first: France enjoyed a period of rapid growth during the 1970s. CGE expanded its telecommunications interests with the purchase of Alcatel, a French communications pioneer established in 1879. Alcatel had introduced high-speed, high-capacity digital switching exchanges in 1970. The new division was combined with CGE's existing telecommunications group, CIT, to form CIT Alcatel. The conglomerate's General Contracting group became one of Europe's top construction companies with the acquisition of a controlling interest in Sainrapt et Brice. CGE merged its Alsthom group with Chantiers de l'Atlantique, a top shipbuilding company, to form Alsthom-Atlantique, in 1976.

During the 1980s CGE consolidated its manufacturing and service operations in two broad areas: communications and energy. Communications included: public network switching, transmission, business communications, and cable manufacture. Energy included power generation, transmission and distribution, railway transport, and battery manufacture. Over the course of the decade, several major acquisitions were made, and non-core businesses were divested.

After Francois Mitterand's administration re-nationalized CGE in 1982, the company acquired the electrical equipment operations of Sprecher & Schub and the railroad business of Jeumont-Schneide. The 1983 transfer of Thomson's telecommunications operations to CGE made the latter company the fifth-largest telephone equipment manufacturer in the world.

When conservative Jacques Chirac was elected prime minister of France, the political pendulum swung away from nationalization. In 1986 CGE returned to private control with a US$1.9 billion initial public offering—one of the largest stock offers in French history. Pierre Suard became chairman and CEO. He sought to remake CGE as an international conglomerate run by a cosmopolitan management team. He eschewed France's renowned cultural pride by making English the official working language at CGE's Paris headquarters.

Suard was praised for his skill with acquisitions and divestments, which he began to apply as soon as the company was privatized. CGE increased its energy holdings with the purchase of a 40 percent stake in Framatome—a nuclear power company—and sold unsuccessful operations in markets like televisions and personal computers.

One analyst called the conglomerate's 1986 purchase of a majority interest in the European telephone equipment operations of the United States's ITT Corp. "the most important development in CGE's modern history." ITT's operations were combined with CGE's CIT Alcatel subsidiary to form Alcatel N.V., the world's second-largest telecommunications company. CGE owned 55.6 percent of the new multinational operation, which was registered in Holland with headquarters in Brussels. ITT held 37 percent of Alcatel, and the remainder was split between Belgium's Société Générale and Credit Lyonnais, a French bank. Alcatel N.V. became the hub of CGE's strategy as a privatized company. From 1980 to 1990 the group's telecommunications business grew from US$9 billion annually to US$27.6 billion.

A 1987 acquisitions spree diversified CGE into pumping systems, batteries, nuclear boilers, and publishing. CGE also formed joint ventures with the United States' Intermagnetics General Corp., Ferro Corp., and Exide Electronics during the year.

The 1989 merger of CGE's Alsthom power and transportation subsidiary with the United Kingdom's General Electric Company's Powers System Division formed GEC Alsthom N.V., a 50/50 joint venture. CGE increased its ownership to 61.5 percent later that year through an internal consolidation of two major subsidiaries, Compagnie Financiere Alcatel and Alsthom. CGE also acquired 15 energy, transportation, and communications companies during that year alone.

Suard was acclaimed for his ability to integrate these new divisions' management, research, and manufacturing into the overall group scheme. He also emphasized research and development, spending about eight percent of total sales, or US$2.3 billion, in 1990 alone.

During the 1990s CGE focused on forging strategic alliances with foreign companies. It was hoped that the joint ventures would maximize the partners' research and development efforts and give CGE entree to local markets. In 1990 the conglomerate formed a joint venture with Fiat S.p.A. that gave CGE control over the telephone transmission business of Fiat's Telettra S.p.A. subsidiary. The two parent companies exchanged shares (Fiat received six percent of Alcatel and Alcatel secured three percent of Fiat), and Telettra was merged with Alcatel's existing Italian operations. The new venture was 75 percent owned by Fiat and 25 percent owned by Alcatel N.V. This complex deal was carefully observed by the European Commission, which used its authority over cross-border business alliances to regulate transactions between the two companies.

From 1985 to 1990 alone, CGE's sales doubled, from Ffr 71.94 billion to Ffr 143.90 billion. As the company grew, its net income on sales followed suit, increasing from 1.1 percent in 1985 to 2.9 percent in 1990.

During 1990 Suard decided to change CGE's name, which was often mistaken in the global marketplace for the United States' GE (General Electric Corp.) or the United Kingdom's GEC (General Electric Co.). In fact, the French entity was prohibited from using its initials in some markets because of this type of confusion. Although not particularly well known in the United States, the Alcatel division had by this time overtaken AT&T as the world's largest manufacturer of telecommunications equipment. The Alsthom name was well known in heavy electrical engineering, especially for the development of France's Trains a Grande Vitesse. These two subsidiaries had also grown to become the primary businesses of CGE by 1990. As of January 1, 1991, CGE's name was changed to Alcatel Alsthom Compagnie Générale d'Electricité, and the conglomerate was commonly known as Alcatel Alsthom.

Suard hoped to parlay the company's more cosmopolitan name into an increased global presence: in 1991, 80 percent of Alcatel Alsthom's business was still focused in Europe. Efforts were concentrated on Asia (especially China), the Pacific Rim, and Latin America. The People's Republic of China represented a substantial opportunity for growth, because its 1.16 billion population needed the three services Alcatel Alsthom was prepared to provide: communications, energy, and transportation. Although the country's limited infrastructure and politically inspired five-year plans held up progress, by 1991 GEC Alsthom was China's primary provider of power, and Alcatel had a 40 percent share of the country's public communications equipment market. By 1992, sales to China contributed 5 percent of Alcatel Alsthom's total sales.

Alcatel also targeted the substantial U.S. telecommunications equipment market, which purchased 40 percent of the world's telephone equipment. Alcatel acquired America's number-three supplier, Rockwell International Corporation's telephone transmission equipment division, for US$625 million in 1991. When combined with the company's existing Alcatel Network Systems subsidiary, the purchase brought Alcatel's share of the U.S. market to 15 percent, a distant second to AT&T's 58 percent stake. Alsthom also penetrated the U.S. market when it formed a consortium to build a TGV-type high-speed rail system linking the major cities of Texas in the early 1990s.

The new Alcatel 1000 telecommunication system, developed to provide high-speed data and image transmission and high-density television capability, as well as conventional telephone functions, was launched in 1991. Alcatel also became the first European company to test its cellular phone system that year.

Alcatel Alsthom purchased two more telecommunications and power cable manufacturers, Canada Cable & Wire Company and Germany's AEG Kabel A.G., in 1991 and formed a "Space Alliance" with two European companies, Aerospatiale and Alenia, and the Loral Corporation of New York. The cooperative venture formed the world's second-largest supplier of satellite equipment.

Alcatel Alsthom slowed its acquisitions pace in 1992, but bought out ITT's 30 percent stake in Alcatel N.V. for US$3.7 billion in cash and a 7 percent share of Alcatel that spring. The transaction made ITT one of Alcatel's primary shareholders.

By the early 1990s, Alcatel Alsthom controlled 80 percent of France's telephone transmission business. The company had also captured 20 percent of Germany's telephone equipment market, second only to the venerable Siemens A.G. In 1993 Alcatel Alsthom commanded 23 percent of the worldwide market for telephone line transmission. Unlike other segments of the telephone equipment business, this highly profitable trade had grown on strong demand for high-capacity fiber-optic cables. Whereas other electronics companies were hard hit by the global recession of the early 1990s, Alcatel Alsthom suffered slower growth, rather than an actual decline. The company hoped to expand into the development of software for telecommunication switching and transmission in the 1990s.

Principal Subsidiaries: Alcatel N.V. (Netherlands, 69.6%); GEC Alsthom N.V. (Netherlands, 50%); Cegelec; Ceac (48.3%); Framatome (44.1%); Sogelerg; Occidentale Forest Industries (United States); COF; Groupe Express; Hoche Friedland (50%); SEPA; Electro Bail (60%); Locatel (99.7%); CGE Maroc (Morocco, 50%); Alcatel Alsthom Recherche; Aurelec; Cie Immobiliere Meridionale; Civelec; Electro Banque; Opagep; Samag; Soficim; Societe Immobliere Kleber Lauriston; Cemilec. The holding company has subsidiaries in Austria, Australia, Belgium, United Kingdom, Canada, Italy, Mexico, United States, Spain, Norway, Switzerland, Taiwan, Germany, and in more than 75 other countries around the world.

Further Reading:

"Alcatel Alsthom: Power Play," *Economist,* August 3, 1991, pp. 65–66.
"ITT Sells Its 30% Alcatel N.V. Stake for $3.7 Billion for $600 Million Gain," *Wall Street Journal,* July 6, 1992, p. 16(E).
Mason, Joanne, "Giants Ride Out the Crisis," *International Management,* January/February 1993, pp. 26–59.
Morant, Adrian, "Exploring New Markets from the Inside Out," *Telephone Engineer & Management,* August 1, 1991.
Neher, Jacques, "A French Giant Stalks U.S. Telephone Market," *New York Times,* November 25, 1991, p. D1(L).
"Net Income Increased 20% to $1.13 Billion Last Year," *Wall Street Journal,* April 9, 1992, p. A11(E).
Stallmann, Linda, "Top 50 European Electronics Companies: Sales Were Up, but Profits Nosedived," *Electronic Business,* October 21, 1991.

—April S. Dougal

Allied Signal Engines

P.O. Box 5217
Phoenix, Arizona 85010
U.S.A.
(602) 231-1000
Fax: (602) 231-5045

Wholly Owned Subsidiary of Allied-Signal Corporation
Incorporated: 1936 as Aircraft Tool and Supply Company
Employees: 4,200
Sales: $520.0 million
SICs: 3724 Aircraft Engines and Engine Parts

Allied Signal Engines evolved from the Garrett Corporation, one of the nation's leading manufacturers of aircraft power systems and engines. Garrett became a leading supplier of cabin pressurization systems and auxiliary power units after World War II. This enabled the company to branch into turbine engines and other systems for a variety of aircraft.

The enterprise, now known as Allied Signal Engines, provides a major component for nearly every major aircraft, including the 747, MD-11, the A300 series, C-5 Galaxy, and Fairchild Metro.

Company founder Cliff Garrett gained entry into the aviation industry with the help of his mother. Garrett's mother had babysat for Ken Jay, who grew up to found the Lockheed Aircraft Company. In 1928, when Garrett's mother asked Jay to help her son secure a job, Garrett soon became Lockheed's 29th employee.

Garrett showed up for work with his own set of crude tools. At first, Garrett's supervisor sought to keep Garrett away from the company's airplanes, assigning him to the stockroom and keeping him busy running errands. However, this did little to dampen Garrett's love for flying.

In 1929, a growing aviation conglomerate called Detroit Aviation took over Lockheed. Unwilling to remain with the company after its acquisition, Ken Jay, Allan Lockheed, and the company's chief designer, Jack Northrop, elected to leave Lockheed. Northrop and Jay later established their own firm, the Avion Corporation, and Cliff Garrett followed them to the new company. However, he was forced to resign several months later because of ill health.

After selling the Avion Corporation to Bill Boeing's United Aircraft combine, Northrop and Jay established yet another company, the Northrop Corporation, as a division of Douglas Aircraft. They invited Garrett back to work for them, placing him in charge of production, and eventually purchasing.

Northrop later sold his share in the company to Douglas, and established another company—his fourth—where he could develop a radical flying wing aircraft without interference from Douglas.

During his employment at Lockheed, Northrop, Boeing, and Douglas, Cliff Garrett realized that there were no companies specifically engaged in the business of supplying the growing aircraft industry. Many of the specialized components each company needed had to be developed and manufactured in-house. Responding to the need for suppliers, Garrett left Douglas in 1936, and on May 21 of that year established the Aircraft Tool and Supply Company. The small business served initially as a sales representative for Cleveland Pneumatic, B. F. Goodrich, and several other suppliers.

Each day, Garrett made the rounds, visiting Westinghouse, Consolidated, Douglas, Lockheed, Vultee, and several other fledgling aircraft manufacturers. As the company's reputation grew, the board (which included Northrop and Jay) decided to change the company's name to the Garrett Supply Company.

By 1937 Garrett's operations had outgrown their one-room office and took over a lease on a warehouse where inventory could be maintained. During this time, Garrett added several more clients, including Ryan Aeronautical, North American Aviation, and four oil equipment companies.

By January 1938, many of the companies that Garrett represented had established their own sales offices in southern California. Garrett's substantial sales of their products had helped them determine that the growing aircraft industry in and around Los Angeles represented a valuable market. In order to stay in business, Garrett needed a product line, and rather than marketing other company's wares, he decided to develop and manufacture his own line of patent-protected products. This necessitated another change in the company's name, this time to the Garrett Corporation on August 18, 1938.

The new company's first products included seamless tubing and, later, an oil cooler and cabin pressurization systems. Drawing on personal experience, Garrett stressed the importance of quality manufacture in each of his products; as his older brother Stirling was killed in a plane crash, he resolved that no one should have to die because of a faulty part.

The Garrett Corporation was responsible for several innovations in the industry. First, Garrett found a vitally important product in cabin pressurization. He knew that aircraft operated most efficiently at high altitudes where there was little oxygen. In order to carry passengers in comfort, compressed air would have to be pumped into an airtight aircraft. To develop these systems, Garrett established a separate business called Airesearch Manufacturing. Then Garrett engineers developed an intercooler that regulated the temperature of air drawn into an aircraft engine for maximum operating efficiency. This was followed by an oil cooler, which performed a similar function.

When the company outgrew its warehouse, Garrett built a new factory on a 20-acre bean field in Glendale, California. In an attempt to diversify the company's product line, Garrett acquired the Northill Company, a marine products manufacturer, in 1940.

During this time, hostilities in Europe had escalated into war. The French and British, unable to build their own war implements quickly enough, placed several orders with American manufacturers. As a major supplier of aircraft parts, Garrett naturally saw a rapid increase in the volume of its business. When the U.S. military began its own armament program, demand grew even more.

Garrett was forced to add a third shift in order to satisfy orders from Boeing, Douglas, Lockheed, and North American, as well as from the navy and several other customers. With conscription depleting its workforce, Garrett relied on more women to fill job openings. After the Japanese attack on Pearl Harbor, military planners implored manufacturers to establish factories away from the coasts, where they might be vulnerable to enemy attack. In need of additional factory space, Garrett complied and built its next factory in Phoenix.

As war production went into full gear, it became difficult for Garrett to secure the precision machine tools it needed to expand production. Nevertheless, the company managed to turn out a vast array of aviation products for bombers, fighters, and cargo transports.

By 1944 Allied victory was imminent, and Garrett began planning for the postwar period by seeking new nonmilitary markets for the company's products. Certain that aircraft manufacturers would see the growth of a massive new airline industry, Garrett began a public relations campaign to build demand for air travel.

With the application of jet engines, which were introduced at the end of World War II, Garrett faced a new challenge. Cabin air provided by jet turbine engines was much warmer than that provided by turbochargers on piston engines. In order to maintain its position in the cabin pressurization market, the company would have to develop an air cooling system. Garrett's AiResearch group, as it was now called, developed an entire line of turborefrigeration products that not only cooled jet air, but also engine oil.

Garrett's work on turbine systems brought it into a new market. The company began development of a small independent gas turbine engine to supply cabin pressure, power for heating, air conditioning, and de-icing systems, as well as to drive an electrical generator. This device, separate from aircraft engines, became known as the auxiliary power unit, or APU.

After the war, Garrett was buoyed by sales of products for Convair's B-36 bomber and other aircraft. While this work provided millions of dollars in revenue and enabled the company to avoid the huge layoffs that were common after the war, the Phoenix plant was forced to close.

Garrett funnelled significant funding to the APU and other aircraft systems, emphasizing the company's role in the engine business. By designing a variety of small gas turbines, the company gained experience in an area that had been the sole province of automotive companies. Furthermore, Garrett continued to develop turbochargers, which compressed air for more efficient operation of piston engines at high altitudes. The company supplied superchargers for two leading airliners, the Convair 240 and Lockheed Constellation.

Garrett established a subsidiary called AirSupply to represent the products of 150 different manufacturers. Primarily a sales organization, AirSupply was the successor to Cliff Garrett's original aviation supply enterprise. Another subsidiary, the AiResearch Aviation Service Company, refurbished interiors of war surplus aircraft, providing them with facilities useful to the travelling business executive. With business back on a steady upswing, Garrett reopened its Phoenix plant and won a listing on the New York Stock Exchange.

In 1951 the company received a $36 million U.S. Navy order for auxiliary engines, starters, and controls. This necessitated further expansion at Phoenix, which provided the capacity to supply a larger number of commercial airliner projects. Garrett provided starters and other systems for the Lockheed Electra, the complete line of Convair aircraft, and Douglas's DC-8 jetliner.

The company began an acquisition spree in 1954, taking over a variety of engineering, sales, and service companies. In the process, it established offices in New York, San Francisco, Toronto, and Belmar, New Jersey, as well as in Japan, the United Kingdom, and Switzerland.

Producing at least one significant part or system on every airplane under development, Garrett established a new million-square-foot factory in Torrance, California. The company also created an industrial division that provided turbochargers for construction machinery, railroad locomotives, and even oil pipeline pumping stations.

In the early 1950s, Cliff Garrett's health began to deteriorate. After a three-year leave of absence, the founder suffered a stroke in 1955. In order to place the company under firm leadership and assure orderly executive succession, the company's board appointed Bill Whitehead president and moved Garrett into the new position of chairman.

Garrett returned to work in 1956, a somewhat less patient and more suspicious man. He deeply resented being pushed out of the presidency and felt that Whitehead was trying to take over the company. As his demeanor became more disagreeable, Garrett won Whitehead's resignation at a board meeting in October 1957 and was reinstated as president.

Despite the corporate upheaval, Garrett's company remained on track throughout the 1950s. The enterprise had diversified into a wide range of aviation, naval, and industrial projects and had maintained its leading position in the aircraft supply business. With growth came the ability to attract a large corps of talented engineers, whose work provided tremendous synergies. The various Garrett businesses were invited to tackle new problems encountered with ever-faster jet aircraft, more efficient engine systems, and complex new armaments. Garrett's GTC85 gas turbine was the company's first engine to be employed as a stand-alone power plant, and three GTC85s drove the McDonnell Little Henry jeep helicopter.

By 1960 Garrett gas turbines, cabin pressurization systems, air conditioners, and flight control systems were aboard the Convair 880, Lockheed Super Constellation, Vickers Viscount, Sud Aviation Caravelle, Douglas DC-8, and Boeing 707. The company had also developed the first inflatable airliner evacuation slides.

While the company struggled to reduce its reliance on increasingly short-term military contracts, the commercial markets were slowing down. At this juncture, on June 22, 1963, Cliff Garrett died, giving rise to a battle for control of the company.

At a board meeting five days after Garrett's death, a group led by Eddie Ballande wrested control from director Walker Brownlee, who subsequently resigned. The company was under firm management, but weakened by the death of its founder and the boardroom battle. At this point Ted Berner, chair of Curtiss-Wright, suggested a merger of his company with Garrett.

Curtiss-Wright emerged from World War II as one of the largest aircraft companies in the world, but allowed its leading position to deteriorate thereafter by neglecting to invest in new products and technologies. In Garrett, Berner saw the opportunity to acquire hundreds of talented engineers and thousands of successful products.

When Garrett's president, Harry Wetzel, refused the offer, Curtiss-Wright launched a thinly veiled hostile bid for the company. Wetzel enlisted the help of Russ Green, a close friend and official with Signal Oil & Gas. Through Green, Wetzel persuaded Signal to buy up enough Garrett shares to deny Curtiss-Wright a controlling interest. A few weeks later, Curtiss-Wright upped its bid for Garrett from $50 per share to $57, and Garrett's institutional investors considered selling. At this time, Wetzel began looking for a merger to help it stave off Curtiss-Wright's takeover. He was surprised to learn that Signal was interested, and stipulated that Garrett would refuse the merger if it was not guaranteed managerial autonomy. Both companies agreed to each other's terms, and the merger was consummated on January 20, 1964.

Garrett's work in valves and control systems won it a role in more than 20 missile projects and led to the company's involvement in the space program. From its experience with pressurized environmental systems in aircraft, Garret was selected to develop similar systems for the Mercury, Gemini, and, eventually, Apollo space programs. This included the construction of test chambers, rocket controls, and even space suits. Garrett also made a move into the turbine propulsion market in 1963, developing a 575-horsepower turbine called the TPE331, which won a place on Beechcraft, Aero Commander, and Mitsubishi aircraft.

By the late 1960s, Garrett developed a more powerful TFE731 engine, rated at 3,500 pounds of thrust. One variant served as an APU for the DC-10, while another became the propulsion system for the Dassault Falcon 10 and Learjet 35. A second engine, rated at 9,000 pounds of thrust, was the ATF3, which didn't gain certification until 1981.

Garrett also made a brief foray into mass transit systems, participating in the development of systems in San Francisco and New York. The company's products found an ever-widening number of applications, including retrofit turbocharger kits for automobiles, inflatable military hospitals, nuclear containment systems, and emergency beacons.

By 1966, Garrett had turned around its flagging business and turned in $359 million in revenue for its parent company, which changed its name to The Signal Companies in 1968 to better reflect its own diversification.

During this time, the city of Los Angeles attempted to evict Garrett from its prime real estate near Los Angeles International Airport. Garrett strongly resisted its relocation, which would have cost more than $100 million. After years of maneuvering, including an attempt to condemn the property, the city gave up.

Garrett's earlier work on the space program had given it a lead in the promising new storage technology, cryogenics, which involved super-freezing gases for storage in much smaller vessels. While this had obvious applications on space missions, commercial markets also began to emerge for airline galley refrigeration and natural gas storage.

The company continued to lead the market in APUs. Garrett power units were aboard the Boeing 727 and 747, BAC One-Eleven, Douglas DC-9, and Fokker 28. Garrett also was chosen to build systems for the American supersonic transport, a project which was cancelled in 1970.

During the 1970s, the volume of Garrett's military work grew steadily. The company produced a variety of environmental, flight, and power control systems for Lockheed's C-5 Galaxy, F-14, F-15 and F-16 fighters, and the B-1 bomber. Garrett's TPE331 and TFE731 found a place on a wide range of medium-size aircraft—a market that had been overlooked by jet engine giants General Electric and Pratt & Whitney. Despite a brief problem with gearshaft cracks on the TFE731 (solved by torque adjustments), these engines were chosen to power the Cessna Citation, British Aerospace 125 and Jetstream, and Swearingen Merlin. Variations on these engines served as APUs for a new generation of jetliners, including the Airbus 300 and 310, and Boeing 757 and 767. Other systems were used as uninterruptable power sources for air traffic control networks.

Garrett's experimental work included construction of a Mach 7.7 ramjet, while space projects included motors for the lunar rover and environmental control systems for the space shuttle. Garrett also teamed with Boeing and General Electric to test new gas/electric rapid transit trains. The company produced turbochargers for a wider range of cars in 1978, which led to the formation of an automotive group in 1980.

That year, with the election of Ronald Reagan as president of the United States, defense budgets skyrocketed. As a supplier of systems to the country's largest defense companies, Garrett was overwhelmed with work. While many new product lines were established, the core of the company's business remained environmental and flight control systems and APUs—the 25,000th of which was delivered in 1983.

In 1984 Garrett formed a partnership with Allison to develop an engine for the Army's general purpose light helicopter. The company also teamed with Rolls-Royce on a marine propulsion system for the navy.

Perhaps most important, Garrett formed a joint operation with General Electric called CFE. This company developed a 6,000-pound thrust engine called the CFE738 for the medium-size airliner market, an industry segment neither company had fully exploited.

In 1985 Signal merged with the Allied Corporation. Now part of a $17 billion company, Garrett's operations were soon divided into an engine division and an APU group, and included some assets of Bendix Aerospace, which Allied had acquired in 1983.

Garrett continued to operate as a separate subsidiary of Allied-Signal. Toward the end of the 1980s, the organization loaded much of its $200 million research and development budget into the improvement of its existing engines, rather than launching new designs. This was not only more economical but has served to maintain the company's reputation as the market leader in the small engine market.

In 1992 Allied Signal reorganized, reducing its 5,300-person work force by ten percent. In 1993 Allied Signal Propulsion Engines and Allied Signal Auxiliary Power were integrated into a single organization called Allied Signal Engines.

Allied Signal Engines remained the market leader in small aircraft engines, APUs, and a variety of other aviation products. Despite the reduction in defense spending, the company is well positioned to maintain its dominance in commercial markets.

Further Reading:

"Garrett Engine," *Air Transport World,* April 1992, pp. 37–38.
"Garrett Engines: Still Growing with Technology," *Business & Commercial Aviation,* June 1991, pp. 64–70.
Schoneberger, William A., and Robert R. H. Scholl, *Out of Thin Air, Garrett's First 50 Years,* Phoenix: Garrett Corporation, 1985.

—John Simley

Allison Gas Turbine Division

P.O. Box 420
Indianapolis, Indiana 46206-0420
U.S.A.
(317) 230-2000
Fax: (317) 230-3562

Wholly owned subsidiary of General Motors Corporation
Incorporated: 1915 as the Indianapolis Speedway Team
  Company
Employees: 7,000
Sales: $820 million
SICs: 3724 Aircraft Engines & Engine Parts; 3511 Turbines
  & Turbine Generator Sets

The Allison Gas Turbine Division of the General Motors Corporation is one of the largest manufacturers of aircraft engines for medium-sized aircraft. While not as large as companies like Pratt & Whitney, Rolls-Royce, or General Electric, Allison has played an important role in the development of aviation. Its engines have been found on aircraft including the Lockheed P-38, C-130 Hercules, Curtiss P-40, Lockheed F-94, and Convair 580.

The company's founder, James A. Allison, was born in Michigan in 1872. After growing up in Indiana, he made the acquaintance of a bicycle manufacturer-turned-automobile-salesman named Carl Fisher. In 1904 the two established a small agency for marketing concentrated acetylene gas. Despite frequent explosions, acetylene was extremely popular among the growing number of automobile manufacturers in and around Indianapolis, who used the gas to fuel their headlamps. Allison and Fisher changed the name of the company in 1906 to Prest-O-Lite, after their product's ability to light quickly.

Allison developed an active interest in automobiles and in 1909 purchased $72,000 worth of farmland, where he established the Indianapolis Motor Speedway Company. Allison held his first 500-mile race at this track in 1911. Allison was later persuaded to establish his own racing team, and in 1915 he incorporated an automobile shop called the Indianapolis Speedway Team Company. Allison funded the shop with his substantial profits from Prest-O-Lite.

In 1914 Prest-O-Lite Co., Inc., hired Dr. George Curme to develop a synthetic alternative to acetylene that was less prone to explode. In the course of his work, he consulted with engineers at Prest-O-Lite's main competitors, Linde and Union Carbide. Allison and Fisher later sold a controlling interest in Prest-O-Lite to Union Carbide, but retained large interests in both firms. Meanwhile, in 1920, Curme's team stumbled upon ethylene glycol, which Union Carbide marketed as a radiator coolant called Prestone.

When the United States entered World War I in April 1917, Allison volunteered the use of his growing Speedway company for the manufacture of military hardware. Due to its experience with automotive products, the company was assigned contracts to build tractors, tanks, superchargers, and, most importantly, Liberty aircraft engines. These 12-cylinder water-cooled behemoths were unsuitable for the light aircraft then being built, but served to establish Allison's name among the members of the government's Aircraft Production Board. After the war Allison sold all his racing interests and moved to Florida, where he became an important figure in local society. While active in real estate and charitable causes, he remained committed to building a better aircraft engine.

In the process of building a derivative of the Liberty for marine propulsion, Allison discovered a way to improve the Liberty's crankshaft and rod bearings, which frequently failed. In 1920 he established a new company for this business called the Engineering Company. Allison won a contract to retrofit the army's stock of the engines, and during the 1920s the bearing business contributed a major portion of the company's receipts. Allison later sold bearings to Wright Aeronautical and Rolls-Royce.

From his experience with the Liberty, Allison discovered a fundamental problem with aircraft power plants, in that engines operated more efficiently at significantly higher speeds than propellers. The solution lay in a reduction gear; however, machining such a gear proved extremely difficult, since the slightest inaccuracy in alignment would pit or completely shred the teeth off the gear. Allison eventually perfected a two-speed reduction gear, and sold it as an adjunct to the Liberty and to newer engines built by Wright and Curtiss. The company also built superchargers, which enable engines to operate more efficiently by compressing the air drawn into an engine's cylinders.

After Allison died of pneumonia in 1928, the company's chief engineer, Norman Gilman, decided to put the company up for sale. Offers from Wright and Consolidated Aircraft were rejected because they merely planned to close the business after raiding it of its patents and engineers. Gilman agreed to an offer from the Detroit-based Fisher & Company. Ninety days later, Fisher's parent company, General Motors, took direct control of the enterprise.

The acquisition of Allison was just one part of a grander scheme by GM President Alfred P. Sloan. Ever since Charles Lindbergh's triumphant flight across the Atlantic in 1927, investors had poured millions of dollars into aviation stocks. Huge vertical monopolies were being formed, and Sloan decided that GM should have a place in this new transportation industry.

In 1929 General Motors established large or controlling interests in Bendix Aviation, the Fokker Aircraft Corporation of America, General Aviation, North American Aviation, Eastern

Air Transport (Eastern Airlines), and Transcontinental Air Transport and Western Air Express (which became TWA). In Allison, General Motors had an experienced engineering firm with an important new engine, an 800-horsepower design called the V1710, under development.

A significant improvement over the Liberty, the V1710 entered the market at the worst time. The stock market had collapsed, and both Wright and Pratt & Whitney had entered the market with lighter air-cooled engines. Gilman decided to upgrade the engine with a supercharger, but the conversion took nearly seven years and was punctuated with numerous failures. Meanwhile, the Wright Cyclone and Pratt & Whitney Wasp gained a stranglehold on the market. Nevertheless, during the period that the V1710 was being altered, the engine was tested on a number of experimental aircraft, including the Curtiss XP-37 and Bell XFM-1 Airacuda. By 1939 the engine had won a place on the Lockheed P-38 and Curtiss P-40.

In Europe, meanwhile, the French and British had begun a massive armament program to counter the growing military power of Germany. Having outstripped their own manufacturers' ability to supply aircraft, they placed tremendous numbers of orders with American companies. Boosted by this demand, Allison had orders for more than 4,000 V1710s by May of 1940.

General Motors knew that additional orders for the V1710 would soon come from the U.S. War Department. It wisely transformed Allison into an engineering shop, under the assumption that its engines could be manufactured by its other subsidiaries, Chevrolet, New Departure, Hyatt Bearing, AC, Delco, Packard, Antioch, Harrison, and Inland.

Allison turned out 48 V1710s in 1939, a number that climbed to 6,433 in 1941. During the same period, employment grew from 600 to 4,000. By 1942, after the United States became directly involved in World War II, Allison built several new plants and began a scramble to recruit and train qualified workers. While the United Auto Workers had won the right to represent workers in other GM divisions during the 1930s, it was unable to organize Allison until 1943, when the company's payroll exceeded 23,000 employees.

Drawing on its parent company's experience with mass production, Allison managed to speed the production of V1710s by reducing the number of separate components from 7,000 parts to just 700. The company also completed a larger 2,000-horsepower engine called the V3420. This engine powered B-19 and B-39 bombers, as well as a number of PT boats. By April 1945, the month that the government cancelled all future orders with Allison, the company had supplied engines for more than 10,000 P-38s and nearly 18,000 P-40s. All that remained was the grim task of laying off 90 percent of the work force and converting back to a peacetime economy.

Alfred Sloan established a postwar plan for GM's aviation interests as early as 1942. When the time came to act on it, Sloan decided that Allison would suffer if GM were to manufacture aircraft in competition with its division's customers. As a result, GM divested all of its aviation companies, including the airline companies, Bendix and North American. Fisher Aircraft personnel were transferred to Allison. Sloan had not counted on labor action in relation to the wartime wage freezes. The UAW struck GM—and Allison—for five months until March 1946. While it may have been devastated by the peace, Allison emerged from the war with experience in an important new product, the jet engine.

When the British came to the United States shopping for aircraft in 1940, they were also looking for a company that could develop a gas turbine designed by the British inventor Frank Whittle. The War Department awarded funding only to Westinghouse, General Electric, and Allis Chalmers, because they had experience with steam turbines and presumably would provide no competition to Rolls-Royce after the war.

But because General Electric lacked the resources to turn out the huge number of jet engines forecast, it enlisted Allison as a manufacturer. The war ended before GE could get a jet engine into production, but it maintained its subcontracting arrangement with Allison.

During the late 1940s, Lockheed, Grumman, and Martin built a series of aircraft that used a total of 15,525 GE-designed, Allison-built J33 jet engines. When Allison was asked to build GE's new J35, it was so busy that it had to pass the work on to Chevrolet. By the time General Electric had developed its J47, the government had terminated its wartime industrial coordination responsibilities. Fearful of turning General Motors into a competitor, GE canceled its partnership agreement with Allison.

Allison began development of a more powerful J71 jet engine with the same dimensions as the J35, hoping to win retrofit as well as new business. But while Allison jet engines saw a great deal of action in Korea, America's first jet war, the company accepted the military's request for new turboprop engines. The move would put Allison in third place behind General Electric and Pratt & Whitney (which acquired Westinghouse's licenses), but it would also guarantee Allison a leading position in the turboprop market.

The company developed two designs, the T38 and T40, that were jet-powered propeller engines. Enormously complex, they provided the power and fuel efficiency to drive large aircraft, such as cargo planes and, more importantly, the new generation of big airliners. Able to drive two counter-rotating propellers, the T40 appeared on numerous experimental aircraft, including the Convair XP5Y and XFY-1 "Pogo Stick," a vertical take-off and landing aircraft. For commercial markets, Allison built a T38 derivative called the T56. This model was standard on a variety of Lockheed aircraft, including the L-188 Electra and Convair 340, 440, and 580.

With jet engines, Allison's J71 won a place on the Lockheed F-94, and was tested on several other models. But by 1955, General Electric and Pratt & Whitney had achieved an insurmountable lead in powering bombers and new jetliners, such as the Boeing 707 and Douglas DC-8.

Allison gained a leading position in helicopter propulsion in 1958, when it was chosen to power the army's LPH reconnaissance vehicle. The company built nearly 4,000 T65 turboshafts for Hughes and Bell helicopters during the mid 1960s.

Meanwhile, Rolls-Royce, which hoped to gain a larger share of the American market, suggested a manufacturing partnership with Allision. The two companies decided to adapt the Rolls-Royce Spey engine into a new engine for Boeing's new 727 jetliner. However, the AR963 engine they built lost out to Pratt & Whitney's JT8D, mainly because Eddie Rickenbacker—president of launch customer Eastern Airlines—knew Pratt & Whitney's management personally.

Allison and Rolls-Royce got a second shot at a successful partnership when the air force asked that the Spey be built to military specifications for the Vought A-7 Corsair. The second derivative, the TF41, made it into the air. But by 1970, cracks in the turbine's spacer rings were shown to be the cause of several A-7 crashes. The problem was quickly resolved, but not without expense to Allison's reputation. Allison lost its momentum in the jet engine market, not because of its problems with the TF41, but because it had no engine ready to follow it.

Rolls-Royce asked to participate in the development of Allison's new RB211 turbofan in 1966. However, Allison backed out of the deal because it couldn't resolve the cost projections. Five years later, problems with the RB211 plunged Rolls-Royce into bankruptcy and nearly ruined its main customer, Lockheed.

Allison, it seemed, was destined to stay in the turboprop business. But the company's main commercial customers, Convair and Lockheed, lost their market to Boeing and Douglas jetliners. All that remained was the cargo and military business.

The T56 engine powered a growing number of C-130 Hercules cargo planes and P-3 Orion and Grumman E-2 reconnaissance craft. To keep this business, Allison borrowed a practice from GM EMD railroad locomotive division. The company routinely overhauled its engines to spot and correct problems and keep track of their performance. This not only kept the engines in the air, it also greatly enhanced customer satisfaction.

From its experience powering the Regulus, Snark, Matador, and Mace missiles during the 1950s, Allison bid successfully to build a rocket casing for the Thiokol Minuteman missile. This work later earned the company a position in the Apollo space program, building propulsion components.

On September 1, 1970, GM Chairman James M. Roche announced the merger of Allison and Detroit Diesel, a manufacturer of large engines that was in need of Allison's excess factory space. Allison, it was thought, was in rapid decline and would benefit from a consolidation.

The new Detroit Diesel Allison Division (DDAD) was given responsibility for developing a roadworthy gas turbine intended to compete with conventional truck engines. GM hoped the project, which dated back to 1958, would create a greater cohesion in the division. But when the Arab oil embargo of 1973–74 rendered gas-guzzling, jet-powered trucks obsolete, the project's GT404 engine was converted for military use.

The oil crisis created a massive new market for oil field helicopter services, as domestic oil exploration went into high gear. At one point, DDAD was building 2,000 250-T63 derivatives a year. This production greatly bolstered the company's position in the helicopter engine market. In a competition to build engines for the new Boeing Vertol heavy lift helicopter in 1973, DDAD defeated General Electric.

Despite this business, DDAD continued to decline. General Motors' prejudice toward automobiles and its resistance to increasingly costly research and development over a period of 20 years badly eroded the group's position. The merger of Allison and Detroit Diesel created few synergisms. Deep divisions remained as employees in both organizations resisted the combination.

In 1981 GM broached the idea of selling DDAD to Garrett AiResearch. Disinterested, Garrett bid too low. But six other suitors lined up, including United Technologies, TRW, and Rolls-Royce. A consulting group suggested that GM could revive the group if it merely put someone in charge who knew the turbine business. Dissatisfied with the offers it was receiving, GM drafted Blake Wallace, a veteran of Garrett, General Electric, and Pratt & Whitney, to run DDAD.

Wallace declared that the division would only succeed if it chose to excel in its current markets and get back into the commercial and military markets it had allowed to slip away. He resolved to boost investment in research and development and product support, modernize operations, and bolster the marketing organization. Finally, he tackled Allison's unfortunate relationship with Detroit Diesel by splitting the organization back in two in May 1983.

The first market tackled by the newly independent Allison was its money-spinning mainstay, helicopters. The company developed a series of upgraded derivatives of its 250 engine for Bell, Augusta, McDonnell Douglas, and even the Soviet manufacturer Kasmarov. Allison also built a new T406 turboprop for the navy's tiltrotor V-22 Osprey, and won new sales of its 501 gas turbines for jet boats and other marine applications.

In an effort to get back into the commercial transport business, Allison formed a partnership with arch rival Pratt & Whitney to develop a jet-powered propeller engine called a propfan. Allison's experience with counter-rotating propeller systems was essential to the project. But while the highly efficient engine worked, the market for propfans disappeared when airline companies' acquisition budgets evaporated and fuel prices plummeted.

In October 1988 Allison and Garrett were selected to develop engines for a new light helicopter. The two companies produced the T800 engine. While successful, the engine's sales prospects were hurt by military budget cuts. Allison had a second go at commercial markets in 1989, when GMA 2100 turboprop was selected to power the Saab 2000 airliner. The engine, which drove six-bladed propellers like the propfan, was a direct outgrowth of the earlier project.

Blake Wallace's remake of Allison placed the company on much more solid ground. But as General Motors struggled to stave off market share losses in its automobile business, the parent company elected to spin off those companies that were not immediately related to the core business.

Despite tremendous investments in Allison and the company's good prospects, GM decided in 1992 to put Allison back on the auction block. The substantial sums GM had spent reviving Allison, it was thought, would be favorably reflected in the company's purchase price. By late 1993, however, no buyer had been found.

Further Reading:

Kaplan, Ellen, ed., *In the Company of Eagles,* Stanford, Connecticut: Pratt & Whitney, 1990.

Mattera, Philip, *Inside U.S. Business: A Concise Encyclopedia of Leading Industries,* Homewood, Illinois: Dow Jones-Irwin, 1987.

Propulsion, Cincinnati, Ohio: GE Aircraft Engines, 1991.

Sonnenberg, Paul, and William Schoneberger, *Power of Excellence,* Malibu, California: Coastline Publishers, 1990.

—John Simley

Ames Department Stores, Inc.

2418 Main Street
Rocky Hill, Connecticut 06067-2598
U.S.A.
(203) 257-2000
Fax: (203) 563-8234

Public Company
Incorporated: 1958
Employees: 23,000
Sales: $2.8 billion
Stock Exchanges: New York
SICs: 5311 Department Stores

Ames Department Stores, Inc., is one of the largest American discount retailers, with more than 300 stores located in 14 Northeastern states. The company originally made its mark selling low-priced goods in rural areas or small towns where few competing stores were located. After decades of profitability and steady growth, Ames exploded in size in the 1980s when it began buying up other discount retail chains. Its largest purchase, of nearly 400 Zayre stores, coincided with a downturn in the economy of its core states and drove the company into bankruptcy. After shedding more than half its properties, Ames emerged from bankruptcy, determined to rebuild its profitability.

Ames was founded in 1958 when two brothers, Milton and Irving Gilman, opened a general store in an old mill in Southbridge, Massachusetts. The Gilmans took the name of their store from the name of its site's old tenant, the Ames Worsted Textile Company. In starting out their business, the Gilmans sought to fill a niche in the retail industry that had hitherto been ignored. They did so by opening a discount store in a rural area where there were no other large, competing stores around. When this formula proved profitable, the Ames company was incorporated in 1962.

Ames expanded steadily, concentrating its growth in the Northeast. In January of 1972, fourteen years after its founding, Ames made its first major acquisitions: the Joseph Leavitt Corporation and the K & R Warehouse Corporation. Six years later, the company continued its expansion through acquisition when it purchased the Davis Wholesale Company for $1 million, bringing 13 W.T. Grant general stores into the company fold. The purchase of Neisner Brothers, Inc., followed ten months later

for $38 million. Neisner Brothers, which was in Chapter 11 bankruptcy and reorganization, operated 32 stores in New York and Florida. Their acquisition brought the number of stores Ames had acquired during the 1970s to 47; however, the company soon closed ten stores in the New York area.

In each of its acquisitions, Ames bought a retailer when the company was struggling. Ames then worked to turn around its operations, and proved largely successful in this endeavor. The company brought in merchandise made by well-known manufacturers and sold it in bright, well-organized settings. Prices were kept low all the time, rather than being set high and then reduced for periodic sales. For advertising, the company relied on direct mail sent to carefully selected shoppers who lived near Ames stores. In some cases, this formula succeeded in raising sales by as much as 50 percent.

By 1981, Ames was operating 115 discount stores, in a chain that ran from Maine to Maryland. In addition, the company ran 20 variety stores, most of which were located in Florida. Five discount stores and one variety store had been opened in the last year. All of the company's retail properties were located in small towns or near highways that were easily reached by people living in the surrounding areas. Ames had stuck to its original rural orientation, eschewing heavily industrialized areas and places where one company employed almost all the inhabitants. About 55 percent of the company's sales came from hard goods, and the rest were in soft housewares and apparel.

In order to maintain its policy of offering brand names at discount prices, Ames maintained tight control over its overhead and interest payments. These policies enabled the company to establish an unbroken record of profitability since its inception, and eight straight years of growing sales and earnings. Ames ended 1981 with sales of $400 million, nearly one-half of which were accumulated in the last quarter of the year, when Christmas sales enhanced retailers' results.

The company relied on enhanced sales of hard goods such as housewares, automotive supplies, and hardware to power its growth and added departments featuring furniture, flowers and plants, cosmetics, toys, and sports equipment. The quality of Ames's women's clothing and accessories was upgraded, and the company also moved to bring its jewelry sales operations more firmly under its own control. To continue its upward path, Ames began a process of renovating its stores, in hopes of improving its sales per square foot of retail space. In March 1981, the company remodeled its original Massachusetts store, adding one-fifth more display space for higher quality goods and new products. These modifications resulted in a sales increase of one-quarter. After this success, the company embarked on a program to update its other properties, scheduling two more stores for overhauls in the next nine months, and eight others for renewal in 1982.

Ames returned to its policy of growth through acquisition in 1984 when it bought KDT Industries, Inc. for $28.5 million. Like past Ames purchases, this company was an organization in distress. Some of its properties had been sold to pay creditors, leaving 42 King's department stores, and $98 million in tax credits. At the end of that year, Ames could look back on a promising pattern of growth, as sales rose more than 25 percent to $822 million, and earnings climbed 43 percent, to $28.5 million.

Reassured by these positive results, the company made a more risky purchase the next year: Ames paid $196.5 million in April 1985 for the G.C. Murphy Company, a discount department store chain based in Pennsylvania. With this move, the company doubled its sales, to $1.7 million, and in one stroke became a powerhouse in retailing. This expansion came at a price, however, as Ames's debt grew temporarily to 80 percent of the company's worth. By purchasing Murphy, Ames moved its operations into 14 additional states.

Within three months of its purchase of Murphy, Ames closed or sold 130 of the chain's unprofitable stores in an effort to make its unwieldy purchase profitable. In addition, the company began the process of converting the Murphy stores to the Ames model, as it reconfigured operating systems, methods, and procedures. This process proved difficult and time-consuming, and it temporarily distracted the company's management from aggressive growth in its other stores. In the spring of 1986, Ames brought its clothes for the warmer months to stores late in the selling season and as a result was forced to mark down much of the merchandise, depressing earnings for that period.

Despite this setback Ames planned further expansion, plotting a 12 percent growth for each year left in the decade. These ambitions were stymied in the following year, as Ames experienced unusually high "shrinkage"—retailing jargon for losses due to theft and embezzlement of goods, as well as poor inventory control and pricing mix-ups. Ames ended 1987 with $34.2 million in profits.

Nine months later Ames agreed to make its largest and most ambitious purchase to date, pledging $800 million to acquire the discount stores division of the Zayre Corporation, based in Framingham, Massachusetts. With this move, Ames doubled its number of stores for the second time in three years to become the third-largest American discount store operator. The newly combined companies estimated sales of $5.39 billion in their 736 total stores. For its money, Ames got 392 stores located in the Northeast, the South, and the Great Lakes states. While Ames already operated in many of these areas, its stores were primarily located in rural areas, while Zayre's strength was in urban zones. Although the Zayre purchase enabled Ames to begin operating stores in such promising markets as Florida and Illinois, overall, the move was a risky one. The Zayre properties were sold below their theoretical value as a result of their recent history of large losses. "I love to buy when its unfashionable and everything is in disarray," Ames's chairman told the *Wall Street Journal* at the time.

Because the Zayre name was so well known in the areas where it operated, Ames planned to keep the name for a certain period of time while it converted the stores to the more efficient Ames operating standards, which included a large number of refurbished store properties, lower prices and less reliance on sales to move merchandise, and a smaller selection of goods in some departments. Initially, the company also planned to retain all Zayre personnel, although, ultimately, it estimated that 10 to 15 percent of Zayre's unprofitable stores would be closed.

In the first month of 1989, Ames began to implement these plans, closing 77 discount department stores, 74 of which were Zayre stores that had been racking up annual losses of $20 million. To further streamline itself and sharpen its focus on its largest and most recent purchase, Ames sold off its G.C. Murphy properties in August 1989 to E-II Holdings, owned by the Riklis family, for $77.6 million. In this way, Ames hoped to concentrate its efforts on discount retailing, shedding its variety store operations, which fit in less well with the company's overall profile than Ames executives had anticipated. In addition, the sale of the Murphy properties allowed the company to pay off some of the high interest debts incurred in the purchase of Zayre. After these reductions, Ames became the nation's fourth-largest discount retailer, with 693 stores in 20 states running from the Northeast, out to Illinois, and then down to the South.

These moves helped Ames to incorporate its new properties more fully into the company. However, the decision whether to change the name of the Zayre stores still had to be made. Zayre had its own history as one of the oldest and best-known American retail chains. In deference to this heritage and to the brand loyalty of many of Zayre's urban customers, Ames announced in February 1989 that the company would not change the names of 61 profitable inner city Zayre stores to "Ames." Eight months later, however, on October 26, 1989, it did reopen 254 other old Zayre stores as refurbished Ames stores. Improvements included new paint, better lighting, and more attractive displays, as well as a computerized cash register system meant to speed up transactions and improve inventory control. The grand reopening was supported by a multimillion dollar television advertising campaign featuring the slogan, "We grew up with better values." In addition, the company planned further renovations of these stores in the near future.

Among the most pressing tasks in consolidating Zayre and Ames operations was merging management staffs. The company closed Zayre's Massachusetts office and moved its employees to the Ames headquarters located outside Hartford, Connecticut. Zayre's management corps was cut in half, and the company's 23 regional offices were reduced to seven. This transition was made much more quickly than originally planned, in seven months rather than a year and a half. As a result of this speed, Ames expected to quadruple its savings from this paring down, to $40 million.

Despite this unexpected gain, Ames's profits remained low because sales for the spring quarter of 1989 proved disappointing. The company was forced to post a loss for the first half of the year. As the economy of the Northeast, where nearly half the company's stores were located, further slowed, Ames gradually saw its high hopes for its Zayre stores grow dimmer. Although sales in its old Ames stores rose, returns at its Zayre properties went into a slump, dropping off by 15 percent. By the end of Ames's third quarter, continuing difficulties with Zayre caused a further loss of $7 million, bringing to nearly $28 million the total for the year.

Growing desperate, Ames opened its stores on Thanksgiving day, in hopes of boosting sales. Nevertheless, it appeared that Zayre's traditional core of customers was eschewing the remade stores. Zayre shoppers were used to stores open 24 hours a day, which Ames eliminated as a cost-cutting measure. In addition, Zayre brought customers into stores with periodic deep discount sales, which were heavily promoted in newspapers and mailed circulars. Along with these items, racks and bins of marked-down items were found in the stores. Ames store policy eliminated deep discounts in favor of steady, everyday low prices, to which it hoped customers would adjust. Although this kept profit margins higher, the company's prices proved uncompetitive in a discount department store bargain war. In addition, Ames switched Zayre's apparel merchandise from inexpensive but fashionable items to basic goods, alienating traditional Zayre customers. The company's elimination of the Zayre credit card and its lack of heavy advertising also cut into sales.

Despite the poor results from the Zayre stores, Ames executives were resolved to stick with their original plan of converting the stores to the traditional Ames model. "The philosophy is working," the chairman of the company told the *Wall Street Journal*. "It has worked for half our business. It's going to work for the other half." This optimism, however, proved ill-founded, as company results continued to worsen. In early 1990 Ames closed an additional 15 old Zayre stores, most of which were located near other Ames outlets. When unexpectedly poor sales made it impossible to pay for past purchases, Ames found itself unable to buy needed merchandise from its suppliers. The company ended the year with losses of $228 million.

By late April 1990 Ames was staggering from continued poor sales at its Zayre operations, as well as the debt burden brought on by the large purchase and the costs of converting stores. Manufacturers were refusing to ship the company merchandise, and bankers were refusing to lend it any more money. Finally, on April 25, 1990, Ames was forced to file for bankruptcy, seeking protection from its creditors in Chapter 11 reorganization. Shortly after this, the company's chairman resigned. A specialist in retail corporate turnarounds replaced him and began the long process of digging Ames out of the hole created by its Zayre purchase. As a result of its bankruptcy filing, Ames suspended all advertising for four weeks, hoping to get the pipeline of merchandise moving again. In addition, the company was able to secure a $250 million loan from a New York bank that allowed it to make essential cash outlays, such as meeting its payroll and paying utility bills.

Among the first steps taken by Ames in this predicament was the closing of an additional 221 stores, a reduction of one-third of its store base. In doing so, the company let 18,000 employees go. Most of the stores, which together had lost nearly $50 million in the previous year, were located in the Midwest and South. Liquidating these properties allowed Ames to raise $210 million from its sold-off inventory. Despite this gain, the company, now being run by a new team of managers, reported a $538 million loss for operations over the first half of 1990. Additional cost-cutting measures were announced in 1991, as Ames continued to work on a plan to pay off its creditors under the watchful eye of the bankruptcy court. In October the com-

pany announced that it would close 77 more stores and lay off 4,500 more employees after the holiday season.

In 1992 Ames began to wrap up its negotiations with its creditors in an effort to finalize a plan for reorganization to present to the bankruptcy court. In January the company submitted a tentative plan for reorganization to the court. In March hearings were delayed because disputes over the nature of the company's final payments to creditors remained unresolved. In September, Ames submitted an amended reorganization plan to the court that included an additional set of store closings. In order to help raise $325 million in cash to pay its creditors, Ames elected to shutter 60 stores in 12 states, costing 3,500 workers their jobs.

In December 1992 continuing weak results and large operating losses caused Ames's board of directors to oust the company's chairman, brought in at the time it had filed for bankruptcy to turn the company around. The company had introduced a policy of offering deeply discounted items to bring customers into stores, with the expectation that, once in a store, people would also buy higher priced items. Instead, however, the company found that shoppers were "cherry picking" bargains and then leaving, causing Ames to report losses of $91.4 million over its third quarter of 1992. As losses for November continued to mount, despite a relatively high sales volume, the company asked for another delay in the consideration of its reorganization plan.

Finally, on December 20, 1992, a bankruptcy judge approved Ames's plan to leave Chapter 11. Ten days later, the company consummated the plan and formally emerged from bankruptcy. The new Ames operated 309 stores in 14 states, a drastic reduction from its peak of 678 stores. To finance its operations, the company had arranged a $210 million letter of credit from its bankers. It planned to use this money to upgrade and replenish the merchandise of its remaining stores. As Ames moved into the mid-1990s, its managers vowed to concentrate on basic discount retailing and to rebuild the company's strength through slow, steady growth and customer service. In this way, the once solid retailer hoped to return to the profitability it had enjoyed for decades before its dramatic, and, as it turned out, overly ambitious, growth.

Principal Subsidiaries: Ames Transportation Systems, Inc.; AMD, Inc.; Ames Realty II, Inc.; Zayre New England Corporation (50%); Zayre Central Corporation (50%).

Further Reading:

Byrne, Harlan S., "Ames Department Stores, Inc.," *Barron's,* October 16, 1989.
Campanella, Frank W., "Small-Town Merchant," *Barron's,* December 28, 1981.
Driscoll, Lisa, "The Fix-It Doctor with a Rough Bedside Manner," *Business Week,* October 29, 1990.
King, Resa W., "Now Ames Is a Big-League Retailer," *Business Week,* June 10, 1985.

—Elizabeth Rourke

AMETEK

AMETEK, Inc.

Station Square
Paoli, Pennsylvania 19301
U.S.A.
(215) 647-2121
Fax: (215) 296-3412

Public Company
Incorporated: 1930 as American Machine and Metals, Inc.
Employees: 6,200
Sales: $770 million
Stock Exchanges: New York Pacific
SICs: 3829 Measuring & Controlling Devices, Nec; 3621
Motors & Generators; 8650 Electrical, Electronics,
Instrumentation Industries; 8670 Machinery Industry; 8600
Manufacturing Industries; 3086 Plastics Foam Products.

AMETEK, Inc. is a global manufacturer and marketer of precision instruments for the aerospace, trucking, petroleum refining, and food processing industries, as well as a major small motor producer for business machines, computers, copiers, and floor care machines. The company's U.S. Gauge division is the world's largest manufacturer of gauges, while the Microfoam division is the only producer in the world of recyclable polypropylene (plastic) foam sheeting. Furthermore, the company was rapidly becoming a national leader in water filtration systems and products. A small regional firm at the outset, AMETEK over the years has directed its operations into the global market, acquiring plants in Italy, Germany, Great Britain, Denmark, and Mexico, and exporting products to over 90 countries worldwide.

By March 1930, several months after the stock market crash, AMETEK's predecessor, the Manhattan Electric Supply Company, had fallen into bankruptcy, and stockholders decided to establish a new company in which the Manhattan electric firm would be included. The new firm, American Machine and Metals, was listed on the New York Stock Exchange as AME, which for many years thereafter served as the abbreviated company name.

AME consisted of several companies, including the Troy Laundry Machinery division in East Moline, Illinois, Haliwell Electric in New York City, and the Trout Mining Company in Phillipsburg, Montana. One year after AME's formation, the Manhattan Electric Supply Co. proved to be ill-fitted to the group and was sold by the end of 1931. In its place, the Tolhurst Machine Works of Troy, New York, which showed a small profit despite the national economic conditions, was brought into the AMEfold. AME headquarters were located on Wall Street, and the company's first president was Philip G. Mumford, under whose leadership the company managed to survive the Depression years, although it operated in the red for well over a year.

By 1932, the worst year of the Depression, AME began to show a slight profit, reporting overall assets of nearly $5 million. With the New Deal inaugurated the following year and massive government orders flowing into the economy, AME's business showed marked improvement. By 1935, AME was profitable. Perhaps because the firm was born of the Depression, the company took its social responsibilities seriously: its 900 employees received benefits and incentives and were a factor in the company's rapid recovery. At the end of fiscal year 1935, AME was able to pay its stockholders their first dividends.

The onset of war in Europe in 1939 brought about significant growth for AME. During this time, the U.S. government began looking for businesses that could be transformed rapidly into manufacturers of critical war material, should the country become involved in the war. One of those selected was the East Moline branch of AME, which in 1941 converted its production towards the war effort, turning out laundries for ships and fans for tanks. By war's end, the company's Tolhurst division was manufacturing centrifuges—rotating machines used to separate substances of unequal densities—that helped produce the new miracle medicines of the war, penicillin and sulfa drugs.

Like many American companies, AME's growth during the war years was phenomenal, enabling stockholders to consider further acquisitions. Their choice in terms of future growth proved excellent: the United States Gauge company in New York. The purchase was finalized in 1944 for the price of $3 million in cash. This division employed twice the number of people that had begun work at AME in 1930. Considering the importance of U.S. Gauge in the postwar years, this purchase marked a turning point in the history of the company that would contribute to a transformation in its identity.

After a period of impressive growth and sales, AME experienced a slump during the immediate postwar years. Mumford, having guided the company through tough times, stepped down as president in 1948 and was replaced by the energetic, younger John C. Vander Pyl. Soon thereafter, the company's business increased, chiefly because of the demands of the Cold War. Tensions turned into open hostilities in Korea in 1950, and for the next several years the demands of confronting communism kept the U.S. economy almost as prosperous as the World War II years.

Annual sales for AME in 1955 stood at $30 million, making the company a comparably small player among the giants of American industry. Nevertheless, stockholders' dividends had increased annually, and in 1955, they once again approved a worthy acquisition: the purchase of Lamb Electric for $34 million. Like U.S. Gauge, Lamb Electric would become one of the most important components of AME and would enable the company to make the transition from the manufacture of simple machinery to more technologically advanced products.

By the early 1960s, AME's principal operations had changed significantly from the traditional manufacture of heavy machinery and mining ventures. Trout Mining of Montana had been divested in 1958, and with the additions of U.S. Gauge and Lamb Electric, the company was producing a wide variety of precision components and electric motors for small appliances. In recognition of the company's new focus on smaller, more technologically refined products, stockholders approved the company's name change from American Machine and Metals to AMETEK, Inc., a changeover that allowed the firm to retain AME as its stock trading symbol.

Rapid expansion followed, and new plants, among the first to boast central air conditioning, were constructed. In 1965, with the acquisition of Mansfield and Green, Inc., AMETEK was launched into the lab instruments business. The accession of Dr. John H. Lux as president of the firm in 1966 also vitalized the company. Under Lux, managers were required to visit company plants and get to know the employees and business firsthand, a strategy that boosted employee morale and contributed to company growth. In 1967, the first water filtration equipment business of the company, Plymouth Products, was acquired. Furthermore, Lamb Electric branched out into the manufacture of computer and photocopier motors. By 1980, sales had reached $400 million, and three years later, AMETEK for the first time made it into the rankings of the Fortune 500 companies, with a reputation as a manufacturer of highly advanced products and materials.

In 1988, stockholders approved a major restructuring of AMETEK, which resulted in the divestment of a dozen unrelated industries. As a result, AMETEK became much more streamlined with a sharper focus. Henceforth, the company consisted of three principal entities: Electro-mechanical, Precision Instruments, and Industrial Materials. Moreover, AMETEK expanded its markets globally, with exports accounting for an increasingly larger proportion of sales revenues. These changes proved timely as trade barriers were collapsing in much of the world, and free market economies were on the rise in Eastern Europe, Russia, and China. With a diverse array of products, the company would not suffer should any one of them fail in the marketplace.

In 1993, under chairperson and CEO Walter E. Blankley, AMETEK consisted of 33 manufacturing facilities and 14 divisions across the country and abroad. Of its three principal operating segments, the Electro-mechanical Group, which included Lamb Electric, represented more than 40 percent of company sales. Its market was global, with over 25 percent of its sales derived from overseas. To enhance this division, AMETEK acquired three Italian electric motor companies that gave the company a base on the European continent. The Electro-mechanical group produced a wide variety of electric motors, chiefly for floor care appliances, computers, copiers, medical equipment, and high efficiency heating units. As a producer of small appliances, the Electro-mechanical Group became a global leader in the early 1990s, increasing its sales 24 percent in 1992, despite an economic recession in the United States.

The second principal segment of AMETEK was the Precision Instruments Group, to which U.S. Gauge belonged as did Aerospace Products, acquired by AMETEK in 1989 as the company's only major subsidiary. Manufacturing advanced measuring and monitoring devices for the aerospace industry, this group of companies generated nearly 40 percent of company sales in 1993. However, of all AMETEK's operations, Precision Instruments suffered the most from the 1990s recession, primarily due to cutbacks in military spending and financial difficulties in the commercial airlines industry, areas on which Precision Instruments relied for nearly half of its sales. Nevertheless, the division manufactured a wide variety of products and expected to make up for its losses by exploring new markets. For example, demand for instrument panels for the heavy truck industry increased as did the need for measuring and monitoring devices in Europe, where air pollution standards have become increasingly stringent. Furthermore, industry analysts project that by the turn of the century, most airplanes will need modernization and repair, renewing business opportunities in the airline industry. AMETEK's acquisitions of Debro Messtechnik GmbH in Germany and AMETEK Denmark A/S testify to the broadening of the market for precision instruments.

AMETEK's third major segment, Industrial Materials, contributed approximately 20 percent of sales in 1993. Among the great variety of items produced by this group were specialty metals, heat exchangers, feather weight foam sheet packaging material, drinking water filters and treatment systems, and high temperature resistant plastics and textiles. Plymouth Products, in Sheboygan, Wisconsin, was the group's leading producer of kitchen and bathroom water filtration products, demand for which was expanding rapidly. Such important acquisitions as the Kleen Plus Company in Milwaukee and AMETEK Filters (formerly Eurofiltec) in Billingham, England, are expected to position AMETEK as a global leader in the water filtration enterprise. Furthermore, Industrial Materials was the only producer in the world of low density polypropylene foam packing material and a leader in heat exchanger technology, aimed at recovering waste energy from boilers more efficiently.

Growing concern for the environment at home and abroad has prompted AMETEK to produce and market environmentally safe products. Water filtration became a major growth enterprise for AMETEK when the state of Wisconsin certified its water filtration products as 99.9 percent free of the parasite that polluted Milwaukee's drinking water in 1993. In addition, the Haveg manufacturing facility, in the Industrial Materials group, became the world's biggest producer of silica yarn, a suitable replacement for asbestos. The Microfoam division of Industrial Materials produced plastic furniture packing that not only was recyclable but was made without Chloroflourocarbons, another first for AMETEK. High efficiency furnaces that utilize the type of high temperature motor blowers produced by AMETEK were increasing in popularity in the early 1990s.

A broad range of products, attention to international marketing opportunities, and new product development for a safer environment are regarded as AMETEK's strengths and should provide the company with growth and profitability in the future.

Principal Subsidiaries: Aerospace Products, Inc.

Further Reading:

"Ametek Buys Bruner Filter Line," *The Wall Street Journal,* December 1, 1992, p. C14, C20.

"Ametek, Inc.," *The Wall Street Journal,* May 13, 1993, pp. B6, B12.

Annual Report: AMETEK, Inc., Paoli, Pennsylvania: AMETEK, Inc., 1992.

Reisch, Marc, "Environmental Push Pays Off for Packaging Firm," *Chemical & Engineering News,* February 3, 1992, pp. 14–15.

"Unique Recycling Idea Could Save Millions," *Modern Materials,* December 1992, p. 12.

Young, P. K., "Ametek—Company Report," *Shearson Lehman Bros., Inc.,* March 26, 1993.

—Sina Dubovoj

Applied Power, Inc.

P. O. Box 325
Milwaukee, Wisconsin 53201
U.S.A.
(414) 781-6600
Fax: (414) 783-3790

Public Company
Incorporated: 1910 as Applied Power Industries, Inc.
Employees: 3,020
Sales: $357 million
Stock Exchanges: New York
SICs: 3492 Fluid Power Valves and Hose Fittings; 3621
    Motors and Generators; 3545 Machine Tool Accessories

Applied Power, Inc., is the nation's leading manufacturer of hydraulic products for use in industry and construction. With four business units, the company supplies a variety of tools and machines to manufacturers in a number of fields. Established around the turn of the century, Applied Power now sells its products in markets across the globe.

Applied Power was founded in 1910 in Milwaukee, Wisconsin. The company got its start as the American Grinder and Manufacturing Company, a producer of hand grinders that sharpened tools used in agriculture and other fields. The company's advertisements claimed that its products were suitable for use in "Ship Yards, Construction Work, Lumber Camps, Mining and Engineering, Signal and Line Repair Work, Machine Shops, Garages, etc." When the United States entered World War I, American Grinder began to manufacture water and oil pumps for use in engines that powered trucks and other military vehicles. At the end of the war, the company decided to continue its manufacture of these products, offering them to the general automotive market that was then beginning to take root and grow.

By the end of its first decade, American Grinder had expanded its line to include hand tools as well as pumps, a move made at the behest of the company's distributor. For this new line, American Grinder chose the trade name "Blackhawk," in reference to the Blackhawk Army Division, which had fought with distinction in World War I. The line's logo featured an arrowhead with the silhouette of an Indian and the slogan "Service, Quality, Finish." Many of the tools sold, such as sets of socket wrenches in different sizes, were designed for use in automobile repairs.

After American Grinder chose to call its engine pumps and mechanic's tools Blackhawk, this trade name began to establish a reputation in the automotive field. In 1925 American Grinder officially changed its company name to Blackhawk, and, shortly thereafter, the company sold off its line of tool grinders, as it reoriented itself towards the automobile industry. Eventually, however, Blackhawk water pumps were made obsolete, as car manufacturers began to include this equipment in their vehicles as a matter of course. After discontinuing its pump operations, Blackhawk sought out a business to replace them. In 1927 the company purchased a small hydraulic jack manufacturer, the Hydraulic Tool Company, in Los Angeles, California, which fit the bill. After acquiring these operations, Blackhawk marketed the Hydraulic Tool Company's products under the Blackhawk trade name.

As Blackhawk grew, its products gained a wider reputation, and its trade name became known across the country. In the late 1920s, Blackhawk expanded its line further when a snowplow manufacturer asked the company to help it develop a hydraulic pump to replace the hand winch then used to raise and lower the plow. In response to this request, Blackhawk developed a hydraulic system, made up of a hand pump, a long bending hose, and a hydraulic cylinder, which it marketed under the name Power-Packer. This line was soon expanded to include other remote-control hydraulic systems for use in different kinds of equipment. By the end of the 1920s, the company's logo—placed on its expanded line of products—had evolved to feature an Indian's profile in a large feathered headdress, placed inside an abstract representation of an arrowhead.

In the mid-1930s Blackhawk further expanded its product offerings when it used the technology developed for use in snow plows to make products for the collision repair market. Calling this line "Porto-Power," Blackhawk marketed hydraulic tools to be used in repairing auto bodies. The Porto-Power line featured a set of pumps and cylinders, with a variety of attachments that could be used to perform different pulling, pushing, and straightening tasks to fix damaged cars. In the late 1930s, Blackhawk marketed its Porto-Power line of products to a wider pool of customers, offering them for use in industrial and construction fields, through various distributors. The company tailored its products to different tasks and industries, creating special pumps and cylinders that could be used as building blocks for different applications.

In 1955 Blackhawk sold off its original line of hand tools, as its business evolved away from that area into more complicated systems. Late in that decade, the company decided to further restructure itself to provide more definition for each of its different parts. The two lines of products, Blackhawk and Power-Packer, became separate business units within the company. In 1960 the company's industrial and construction lines were set apart and given the name Enerpac in an effort to strengthen their identity within their respective markets.

Also in 1960, Blackhawk began an effort to expand its markets beyond the borders of the United States. Although its products had long been sold in other countries through importers and distributors, Blackhawk began to set up its own direct overseas operations, to both sell and manufacture goods. Its first targets for growth were the United Kingdom and continental Europe.

In 1961 Blackhawk changed its corporate name to Applied Power Industries, Inc. in an effort to better reflect the different aspects of its operations. In the 1960s, the company expanded through acquisitions of other companies in its field. In January of 1966, it bought Rivett, Inc., and two years later, Applied Power purchased Branick Manufacturing, Inc. In 1969 the company acquired the Big Four division of the Studebacker Company. In May of 1970, Applied Power added the operations of the Bear Manufacturing Company, and later that year, the company added another business unit to its corporate profile, taking over the Marquette Corporation. This company was a maker of diagnostic systems and service equipment, including products designed especially for use with batteries, for automobiles.

Also in 1970, Applied Power increased its geographical scope further when it opened a subsidiary in the Netherlands. This trend continued the following year, when Applied Power made a number of purchases which increased its international holdings. The company acquired Bear Equipment & Services, Ltd., of Scarborough, Canada, and renamed it Applied Power Automotive Canada, Ltd. In addition, Applied Power bought 80 percent of two French companies, Matairco, which eventually became a separate business unit of its parent company, and Société-Hydro-Air S.a.r.L. Three years later, Applied Power completed its acquisition of these properties, increasing its stake in them to 100 percent. In January of 1973, Applied Power Industries clarified its name to Applied Power, Inc.

Following the simplification of its name, Applied Power also streamlined its corporate structure. In the mid-1970s, the company fine-tuned its operations, shedding businesses that did not fit with its larger corporate identity, or that were not as profitable as others. In 1975 the company sold Hydralique Gury S.A. to a group of French investors for $2.1 million. Five years later, the company divested itself of its Bear Wheel Service and Marquette Engine Diagnostic Equipment Product Lines, reaping $8 million.

In 1981 Applied Power added the last of its major brand groups when it purchased Electro-Flo, Inc. This company supplemented Applied Power's Power-Packer unit in providing specialized hydraulic products for use in the manufacture of other kinds of heavy equipment. Electro-Flo used electronic controls of hydraulic systems to enable precise movement and positioning of machinery. Electro-Flo technology, which included microprocessors, flow control valves, and electronic sensors, was used in the precise laying of asphalt by road-reconditioning equipment and in the movement of booms on materials-handling machinery.

By 1985, Applied Power's 75th year in business, the company had become a solid operation closely held by the members of its founding family. Lacking new blood, the company had begun to stagnate. While its operations returned a steady profit, the company had ceased growing. In an effort to remedy this situation and increase Applied Power's financial returns, company leaders brought an outside executive aboard, hiring Richard G. Sim,

a former General Electric Company executive, as president and chief executive officer.

Among the first steps taken in the mid-1980s were a series of acquisitions. The company bought half of the Toyo Hydraulic Equipment Company, of which it already owned the other half, and also added Electro-Hydraulic Controls, Inc., for which it paid $2.6 million in cash. In 1986 Applied Power divested itself of one of its core businesses—and the line of products with the longest heritage of any made by the company—when it sold its Blackhawk automotive division to the Hein-Werner Company for $9.3 million. One year later, in August of 1987, the newly defined Applied Power offered stock to the public for the first time, tendering 1.8 million shares. With the proceeds from this sale, the company moved to reduce part of the debt it had amassed through its long string of acquisitions. At the end of 1987, Applied Power reported a loss of $1.6 million.

In 1988 Applied Power returned to its roots, re-entering the field that had launched the company decades before, when it purchased a manufacturer of hand tools, Garner-Bender, Inc., for $31.4 million. This company was subsequently renamed GB Electrical, Inc. The next year, Applied Power made its most ambitious purchase to date, when it engineered the hostile takeover of the Barry Wright Corporation for $147 million. This purchase doubled the size of Allied Power and increased its debt six-fold. Barry Wright, an ailing manufacturer based in Watertown, Massachusetts, made equipment for use in computer rooms and devices that controlled vibration. The company's earnings had dropped in the previous year from $8.4 million to $1.3 million as its sales stagnated. Applied Power's executives hoped that their acquisition could come to dominate certain niche markets profitably. Such previous successes helped Applied Power notch sales of $245 million in 1989, up from $100 million just four years earlier.

In integrating Barry Wright with the rest of its operations, Applied Power faced a challenging task—it sought to streamline Barry Wright's product line and cut its manufacturing costs. The first of the new acquisition's units to face the ax was Barry Wright's specialized office supplies division, called Wright Line. This business was severed from Applied Power in early 1992 at a loss of $33 million. This loss followed a year of lackluster results in 1991, when earnings fell to $12 million, hurt by the overall high costs of absorbing the Barry Wright operations and by a general recession. As a maker of tools for use in construction, Applied Power was hurt in particular by the slump in that industry. While its GB Electrical unit and its Enerpac operations continued to contribute strongly, another company unit, Apitech, which had been recently inaugurated to develop high-tech valves and other equipment to improve automobile suspensions, continued to eat up millions of dollars in research and development costs.

This trend continued in 1992, as Applied Power reported a loss of $24.4 million. In an effort to strengthen its positions, Applied Power reorganized certain aspects of its operations, altering the structure of its Barry Controls division in California and changing the nature of its Power-Packer operations in Europe. In addition, the company moved forward aggressively in foreign markets, purchasing the remaining portions of its joint venture operations in Mexico and Germany. Anticipating dramatic growth in Asia, Applied Power hired a new executive to run its Asian operations in Korea and Japan, with the intention of intensifying marketing efforts in those countries.

This thrust toward foreign markets continued in 1993, as Applied Power entered into a joint project with the Detec Design and Industrie Company in Germany to manufacture hydraulic products. As the company moved into the mid-1990s, its history of solid performance within its niche markets boded well for its continued viability and profitability.

Principal Subsidiaries: Applied Power International, Ltd.; GB Electrical, Inc.; Enerpac, Inc.; Power-Packer, Inc.; Barry Controls, Inc.

Further Reading:

Byrne, Harlan S., ''Applied Power: Struggling Past a Big Acquisition,'' *Barron's,* October 12, 1992.

—Elizabeth Rourke

TV Asahi

Asahi National Broadcasting Co., Ltd.

Asahi National Broadcasting Company, Ltd.

1-1-1 Roppongi
Minato-ku, Tokyo 106
Japan
(03) 3587-5111
Fax: (03) 3586-6369

Public Company
Incorporated: 1957 as Nippon Educational Television
Employees: 1,300
Sales: ¥177.7 billion (US$1.6 billion)
Stock Exchanges: Tokyo
SICs: 4833 Television Broadcasting Stations

The Asahi National Broadcasting Company, or TV Asahi, as it is more commonly known, is one of Japan's largest national television networks. TV Asahi's largest shareholders are the *Asahi Shimbun* newspaper; Toei, a television and movie production house; and Obunsha, a publishing company. Because Japanese broadcasting laws prevent the dominant cross-ownership schemes that exist in other industries, none of these companies can be said to control TV Asahi.

A unique provision of Japanese television regulation prevents any network from owning or controlling more than one broadcast station. By contrast, in the United States, broadcast regulations allow networks to operate up to five stations. As a result, network growth in Japan is especially dependent on affiliates, of which TV Asahi has 20, covering 90 percent of Japan's population.

The network was established in November 1957 and was the first to broadcast a combination of educational programming, dramas, game shows, and sports events. A company, Nippon Educational Television (NET), was created to operate the network, funded largely by government money and associated with *Asahi Shimbun,* one of Japan's largest and most respected newspaper publishing groups.

Much of NET's early staff came from Nikkei Shimbun Toei, a movie company and theater business, and from competing networks. *Asahi Shimbun* provided NET with several presidents after 1969. On-air personalities were recruited from other broadcasting companies or were developed internally.

NET began broadcasting on February 1, 1959, on a partial schedule, though few families owned televisions at the time. The network's morning programming consisted of children's television shows that concentrated on teaching history, math, language, and science. Afternoon and evening shows concentrated on general audiences with variety shows and other entertainment with broad appeal.

Initially, broadcasting was limited to Tokyo and a few other urban areas. NET became a nationwide commercial network in April 1961, when a web of affiliates was established throughout Japan. Despite its wide coverage, NET was not considered a major network primarily because there were few VHF stations operating at the time that were able to cover areas outside Tokyo.

Japan's other networks made the conversion to color broadcasting between 1960 and 1965. In order to avoid being relegated to a minor status, NET began color broadcasting in November 1967. During this period, NET altered its programming to expand its entertainment and variety shows and began including as many commercials as other stations. The network also began Japan's first live morning news show, which ran from 1965 to 1993.

NET remained on the forefront of technological advances during the 1960s through its daily live satellite feeds from the United States for its *Morning Show,* which enabled NET to create a commercially competitive news division. Rather than merely read the news from America, or wait more than a day for film footage to arrive by airplane, NET was capable of running film from America almost as soon as it was shot. In addition, NET established a reputation as the most internationally minded network in the 1960s by acquiring the rights for U.S. boxing championships, the Indianapolis 500, and the Daytona 500. NET's coverage of the Apollo missions were considered Japan's most extensive.

In November 1973 NET was formally licensed by the Post of Telecommunications Ministry as a station of general programs. This designation stiffened competition with Japan's other large networks: Fuji Television, Tokyo Broadcasting, and Nippon Television.

In April 1977, NET concluded an exclusive deal to broadcast the Moscow Olympics in 1980. This was a major coup for NET, which invested heavily in the competition. Unfortunately, six months before the Olympic games, Soviet troops occupied Afghanistan. In protest, the United States, Japan, and several other countries boycotted the competition. Since the Japanese athletes were not present, the network's coverage of the Olympics was a commercial failure.

A month after its successful bid to cover the Olympics, NET changed its name. As part of an effort to lose its association with educational television and adopt a newer, more commercial image, NET became the Asahi National Broadcasting Company.

"Asahi" is a popular corporate name in Japan. In addition to *Asahi Shimbun,* there is an Asahi Brewery and Asahi Pentax. None of these companies are related; Asahi means "rising sun." The name Asahi was chosen for NET primarily because of the company's close association with the *Asahi Shimbun.*

The newspaper had become increasingly involved in the network, particularly during its conversion into a general audience commercial network. More than just another medium of communication, Asahi National Broadcasting had become an important investment and a valuable source of earnings for the newspaper.

In October 1977, TV Asahi, as the network was commonly called, had enormous success with its broadcast of the American miniseries *Roots*. Though the network had consistent ratings success in the 1960s with such shows as the U.S.-made *Rawhide, The Little Rascals,* and TV Asahi's own *Morning Show, Roots* captivated the Japanese viewing audience and enabled TV Asahi to trounce its competitors in the ratings.

Asahi's programming formula remained the same for the remainder of the 1970s and well into the 1980s. Some of the most expensive shows produced by Japanese networks were TV Asahi's traditional Japanese dramas or "Samurai Dramas" (though the name was misleading). In general, most commercial stations of the day lacked the budget to produce their own high-cost shows and thus many programs were imported from the United States.

In April 1982, TV Asahi concluded a deal to air news programs from the U.S.-based Cable News Network (CNN). The Japanese language version of CNN proved successful and provided incentive for Asahi to develop additional news porgrams of its own. More than a year later, in October 1985, TV Asahi hit the airwaves with *News Station,* a revolutionary show with a unique approach to the news. After considering several anchormen, the show's creator, Kyuemon Oda, decided that conventional news readers were merely talking heads and opted for a more dynamic anchor.

The network settled upon Hiroshi Kume, a popular game show host from the TBS network. Casting Kume in this role, it was said, was comparable to asking the often outrageous David Letterman to anchor the NBC News in place of the staid Tom Brokaw. Some network officials seriously doubted whether or not Kume would be able to transfer his popularity from other shows to *News Station.* Kume was intense and fast-paced. It took many people a long time to get used to his opinionated delivery of the news and quick detours into a talk-show format. But his personality prevailed, and, perhaps because of his unusual style, his popularity began to rise. Though *News Station* was primarily a traditional news show, each edition included a 15-minute in-depth look at a particular subject drawn from areas as diverse as nature and politics.

Within months *News Station* became the most popular show in Japan, which some compared to CBS Television's market-leading program *60 Minutes* (whose host Mike Wallace, incidentally, also was once a game show host). *News Station* buoyed the network and provided it with considerable advertising revenue. These revenues were plowed back into production of the 80-minute news show, further strengthening its position in the market and triggering an intense competition among the major networks for the 10 p.m. slot. In fact, TBS created a copy-cat version of *News Station* in 1988 using a former NHK anchorperson and was badly defeated; the network cancelled the show within a year.

News Station led TV Asahi to create a string of other news shows around its new flagship series. A powerful line-up of news programs was developed, beginning with a 90-minute show at 5:30 a.m., a half-hour update at 11:30, and a standard format 60-minute evening news program at 6 p.m., followed by *News Station* at 10. The rapid expansion of news coverage further allowed TV Asahi to develop strong links with CNN, which had become a highly respected news organization in just a few short years.

TV Asahi hires about 50 new people each year, mostly recent graduates from universities in Tokyo. The network employed 1,350 people by the early 1990s and staffed 23 overseas bureaus that enabled Asahi to cover events almost anywhere in the world. To guard against the development of an entrenched population of employees, TV Asahi did not maintain regular employment contracts with its employees. A great many staff members were technically freelance writers, production assistants, camera operators, and other workers, whose contracts could be terminated almost immediately.

Along with the the newspaper organization *Asahi Shimbun,* the television and film production house Toei was also a major investor in TV Asahi. Through the Toei, Sochiku, and Toho film companies, TV Asahi became a partner in several film projects, including Shochiku's *Merry Christmas, Mr. Lawrence,* starring British singer David Bowie. After a banner year with films in 1985, TV Asahi broke even in 1986. But, as its investment in the production industry has increased, TV Asahi's returns also have grown.

Another popular show, *Tetsuko's Room,* began airing in 1975. An afternoon talk show, *Tetsuko's Room* is hosted by former actress Tetsuko Kuroyanagi. Like Kume, Kuroyanagi was a dynamic and unconventional host who had discussed moving or taboo subjects with over 1,500 Japanese and foreign guests by the early 1990s.

Other successful programs have included prime-time detective series, which have garnered 25% of the country's ratings, as well as Saturday evening feature-length dramas that have reached 26–28% of the audience. Considering competition from eight channels and three satellite channels, these ratings are impressive.

Similar to the now-defunct practice in the United States in which one sponsor would purchase all the advertising slots in a given show, TV Asahi's *News Station*'s advertising is bought by Dentsu. In order for an advertiser to receive airtime on the show, it has to go through Dentsu for its ads. Since many Japanese corporations simultaneously use 2 or more advertising agencies, this is not considered an unusual practice. Through this system, Dentsu, who co-created the show with TV Asahi, takes sole responsibility for finding the show's sponsors.

In April 1989, after building a heliport and employing helicopters for news gathering, TV Asahi began satellite news gathering (SNG) to facilitate live feeds between the company's studios at Roppongi in Tokyo and news bureaus throughout the country. SNG has helped the network reach mountainous and rural areas of Japan; it has also facilitated much of their news gathering. In August 1991, TV Asahi began using A-Star, a trans-Pacific satellite owned by Intelsat.

While TV Asahi maintains 20 affiliates in Japan, its competitors operate as many as 30 affiliates each, affording them greater market penetration. In an effort to cater to the English-speaking segment of the market in Japan, TV Asahi became involved in a cable television venture called Japan Cable Television, or JCTV. JCTV was established to pipe English-language and other special programming to hotels and other large customers. As pay-per-view and other programming began to develop, cable service was expanded to the residential market.

JCTV's penetration remains low, however, and is not likely to grow substantially, despite the rise of satellite-based direct broadcast systems, which were introduced in Japan in 1991. This may be due in part to the fact that there is no market for culturally targeted programming because Japan is culturally homogeneous. More likely, the less than stellar growth is because of the technical difficulties of outfitting large cities like Tokyo with cable systems and extending service to highly mountainous areas.

In preparation for direct broadcasting, in which signals are beamed directly from satellites to viewers' televisions, TV Asahi has laid its own plans for the new medium. An existing system reserves two channels for the non-profit NHK network, while a third is controlled by Japan Satellite Broadcasting, a consortium of 195 companies in which TV Asahi is a participant. In the future, as capacity is expanded, TV Asahi is likely to apply for its own direct broadcast channel.

With direct broadcasting, JCTV is likely to be relegated to an all-premium-channel format in order to remain profitable. With capacity for many channels, viewers may be given the option of using JCTV to see non-broadcast movies and specials, much as HBO and Showtime operate in the United States. With five major networks already in operation in Japan (including NHK), TV Asahi remains the smallest of the commercial operations. *News Station,* however, remains immensely popular.

Further Reading:

"TV Asahi in Its 4th Decade," *Variety,* March 28, 1990.
"About TV Asahi," Company Document; Annual Report, 1992.

—John Simley

ascom

Ascom AG

Belpstrasse 37
CH-3000 Bern 14
Switzerland
(31) 999 11 11
Fax: (31) 999 45 33

Public Company
Incorporated: 1987
Employees: 16,982
Sales: SFr 3.37 billion (US$2.31 billion)
Stock Exchanges: Basel Zurich Geneva

Ascom AG is Switzerland's largest telecommunications company. Ascom manufactures and distributes a wide array of telecommunications equipment, including switching and transmission equipment, mobile radio systems, corded and cordless telephones, cellular telephones, fax machines, hearing aids, coin and card-operated telephones, pneumatic-tube mailing systems, and automatic teller machines. Endeavoring to emerge from the protected Swiss market in order to become a worldwide presence in the telecommunications industry, the company staked its future on the corporate network sector of the industry.

Ascom was formed from the 1987 merger of Switzerland's three largest telecommunications industries. Hasler Holding AG (founded in 1852), Autophon AG (founded in 1922), and Zellweger Telecommunications AG had flourished for years serving the Swiss Post, Telephone, and Telegraph (PTT). Autophon, based in Solothurn, specialized in standard as well as mobile phones, and the Bern-based Hasler produced switching systems, electronics, and telex machines. Prior to the merger Hasler and Autophon had expanded steadily. Autophon's sales had grown on average 17 percent annually from 1981 to 1985; Autophon's 1986 sales were SFr 800 million, while Hasler reported SFr 850 million.

By the 1980s, however, the PTT was expected to liberalize its market, and Hasler, Autophon, and Zellweger joined forces in an effort to adapt to the changing Swiss and global communications industry. The two companies merged operations July 1, 1987, and the merger was effected retroactively to January 1 of that year. The new company had annual sales of SFr 2 billion ($1.17 billion), 13,000 employees, and produced about two thirds of Switzerland's telecommunications equipment.

From its inception Ascom sought to lessen its dependence on the Swiss market, which accounted for 70 percent of sales, and increase sales and manufacturing outside the country. To this end, in 1988, the company purchased the New Jersey-based Rockaway Corporation, which manufactured mail-handling equipment. By the end of that year the company's revenues were SFr 2.42 billion, and profits reached SFr 49.7 million—profits having increased by 20.8 percent. The following year sales had increased ten percent to SFr 2.64 billion, and foreign sales accounted for 36 percent of the total. However, net earnings had increased only 3.1 percent and cash flow by only five percent.

In 1990 Ascom acquired a majority position with the German energy-systems company Frako GmbH, and it assumed management responsibilities for the French service-automation company Monétel. In 1990 sales (42 percent of which were outside Switzerland) were SFr 3 billion, cash flow was SFr 249 million, and net profit reached SFr 52 million.

Ascom's position as a mid-sized company long dependent on government contracts and struggling against multinational giants in an ever-globalizing market, led to the company's focus on continued improvements and innovations. Leonardo E. Vannotti, appointed chief executive officer in 1991, felt that Ascom's survival in a European telecommunications industry dominated by such powerhouses as Ericsson, Alcatel, and Siemens depended on establishing a niche in the market. He decided to focus on the sector known as corporate networks, in which all of a company's telecommunications are integrated, thus providing workstation-to-workstation connectivity. The company estimated that the market for corporate networks would grow nine percent annually through the 1990s (making it the fastest growing sector in the industry), when 60 to 70 percent of all personal computers would be connected to networks. The company foresaw the international market growing more than fourfold to $165 billion by 2010.

Ascom found the cornerstone of this strategy in Timeplex, a highly regarded subsidiary of the U.S. computer company Unisys. Ascom was able to take advantage of the difficult position of Unisys, which was struggling to raise cash to service heavy debt payments, to acquire its Timeplex subsidiary. Unisys had purchased the Woodcliff, New Jersey-based Timeplex three years earlier for stock valued at $300 million; it sold the subsidiary to Ascom for $207 million in September 1991 (although it was to continue to market Timeplex products through a joint-marketing agreement). Sales at the unit were around $250 million in 1990.

Timeplex, founded in 1969, had been at the forefront of providing private backbone communications networks. The company eventually began offering an array of products to unify local area and wide area communications, including innovating routing, circuit, and frame switching technology. By the time it was purchased by Ascom, Timeplex was considered a world leader in the industry, with a market consisting principally of large industrial and service companies in the United States and Europe. Timeplex also sold equipment to such public network clients as AT&T, U.S. Sprint, France Telecom, and British Telecom. A full 55 percent of its business was outside the

United States, and the company was concentrating its efforts in growing markets such as Eastern and Western Europe, Asia, and Latin America.

The newly named Ascom Timeplex, Inc. became the centerpiece of Ascom's Corporate Networks Division, bringing together Ascom's advanced research and development with the networking strength of Timeplex. "The future trend is clearly where technology provides the same links for data and voice," Vannotti told the *Wall Street Journal*. Through the acquisition, Ascom would build its U.S. presence, and Ascom Timeplex would further its image as an international internetworking company. The acquisition also demonstrated Ascom's desire to be a major player in corporate networking. During this time, Ascom Timeplex began developing asynchronous transfer mode (ATM) technology, which combined voice, data, video, and image transmissions, allowing for interactive, integrated communications.

Another part of Vannotti's strategy to increase Ascom's presence was through the creation of alliances with other firms. Interested primarily in its synchronous digital hierarchy (SDH) transmissions equipment, Ascom entered a joint venture with the Swedish firm Ericsson in late 1991. The agreement called for Ascom to contribute the business operations of its transmissions-system division, while Ericsson would supply the hardware. The venture was to initially target the Swiss PTT as competition, but plans were to use Ericsson's extensive global network to expand. Through the agreement, Ericsson gained access to the Swiss PTT while Ascom gained access to the expensive SDH technology. Ascom held a 60 percent stake in the venture, Ascom Ericsson Transmission Ltd., which started operations June 1, 1992.

Ascom's sales in 1991 rose three percent to SFr 3.05 billion, with cash flow reaching SFr 282 million. Net profits reached SFr 54.3 million, but due to a change in accountancy procedure 1991 figures were not comparable to earlier years' figures.

Ascom experienced a difficult year in 1992, when it lost SFr 46 million and its stock did not pay a dividend. Problems were cited at its cable television business in Germany as well as its mobile radio business, where internal reporting procedures proved inadequate and outside auditors discovered the shortfall. The loss came less than a month after a letter to shareholders predicted a SFr 25 million profit. Furthermore, economizing at the Swiss PTT resulted in Ascom's orders being cut by 20 percent. These moves hastened the company's decision to look more aggressively at other markets, especially in the private sector, and its stated goal was to increase sales outside Switzerland to 70 percent of its total. However, Switzerland's rejected entry into the European Economic Area (EEA) in December 1992 complicated the company's ease of access to other European markets.

Ascom's poor performance in 1992 led to a structural reorganization toward the end of that year. Thus, in an effort to achieve "a stronger focus on private sector customers," and to create "an organization that was more transparent to those inside and outside," the number of divisions was cut from six to four, and the corporate management committee was pared from 12 to seven. The company's four new divisions included corporate networks (the company's core division producing enterprise networks, private branch exchanges, and cordless communications systems); telecom terminals (which handled corded and cordless telephones, fax machines, and mobile radio transceivers, and served mainly national telecom companies and large corporations); public networks and mobile radio (which served primarily the public sector with transmission and switching equipment); and diversified operations (which covered those activities not directly related to telecommunications, such as automatic teller machines, pay telephones, hearing aids, and franking machines).

Other efforts were made to trim costs. A factory in Estavayer-le-Lac was to close at the end of the year and further payroll cuts, largely in Switzerland, were planned. Ascom also shed its mail processing business, the Hasler KM8 Company, in a sale to Bell & Howell.

In 1992 Ascom Timeplex won several important orders, including a $16-million contract with the Federal Reserve Bank in Chicago to integrate its communications systems so as to connect its check processing, wire transfer, and automated clearinghouse services into a single nationwide network, bringing together the information from each of the reserve's twelve branches. This was Ascom Timeplex's largest contract to date. Another important contract included providing networking equipment to the Shanghai (China) Posts & Telecommunications Administration, worth $1.2 million.

In early 1993 Ascom announced a joint venture with LK Products, a subsidiary of the Finnish firm Nokia, to develop its position in the worldwide SAW (surface acoustical wave) components market. SAW components are intelligent chips used in mobile communications and optical transmission. Ascom was to contribute the design, development, and manufacturing of the technology, while Nokia was to distribute and market the product and handle the day-to-day operations of the new company, Advanced SAW Products, based in Neuchatel, Switzerland.

Principal Subsidiaries: Ascom Business Center AG; Ascom Hasler AG; Ascom Telematic AG; Ascom Timeplex Inc. (U.S.)

Further Reading:

"Ascom Expects Sales Gains, Improved Cash Flow for '92," *Wall Street Journal Europe,* May 26, 1992, p. 18.
"The Ascom Holding Annual Report," Bern: Ascom Holding, 1992.
Ascom's Sales Jump 10%," *Financial Times,* January 30, 1990, p. 25.
Collier, Andrew, "Ascom Timeplex Sees Future in ATM," *Communications Week,* August 30, 1993, p. 25.
——. "Ericsson Forming Swiss Venture in Move on Transmission Gear," *Electronic News,* December 9, 1991, p. 15.
——. "Timeplex Takes Aim at Internetworking," *Electronic News,* January 20, 1992, p. 16.
——. "Unisys Sells Timeplex to Foreign Firm, *Electronic News,* June 17, 1991, p. 1.
Dullforce, William, "Ascom Sales Rise in Line with Forecast," *Financial Times,* June 7, 1990, p. 35.
——. "Swiss Telecommunications Companies Plan Merger," *Financial Times,* December 22, 1986, p. 17.
Karpinski, Richard, "Timeplex Sale Boosts Vendor's Local Exchange Focus," *Telephony,* June 17, 1991, p. 9.

Lapreta, Laura, "Ascom Is Seen Returning to Profitability in '93, Though It May Be 'Difficult Year,' " *Wall Street Journal Europe,* May 6, 1993, p. 5.

"Nokia Forms Joint Venture," *Cellular Business,* March 1993, p. 10.

Rodger, Ian, "Ascom Loses Swiss Status Under Ownership Rules," *Financial Times,* May 26, 1992, p. 20.

——. "Ascom Puts Lack of Control as Reason for Loss," *Financial Times,* May 6, 1993, p. 24.

Suder, Margaret, "Ascom's Chief Plots Ambitious Strategy," *Wall Street Journal Europe,* February 18, 1993, p. 4.

—C. L. Collins

ASK Group

ASK Group, Inc.

2440 W. El Camino Real
Mountain View, California 94039-7640
U.S.A.
(415) 969-4442
Fax: (415) 962-1974

Public Company
Incorporated: 1972 as ASK Computer Systems
Employees: 2,400
Sales: $432 million
Stock Exchanges: New York
SICs: 7372 Prepackaged Software

The ASK Group, Inc. is a producer of software for use in business settings, primarily manufacturing. With 91 offices in 15 countries around the world, ASK maintains a significant share of the market it pioneered and once dominated. Built on the strength of one program, the company expanded dramatically in the 1990s through two major acquisitions.

ASK was started in 1972 by Sandra and Ari Kurtzig, a couple living in California. Sandra Kurtzig had quit her job as a marketing specialist with a unit of the General Electric Company, and invested $2,000 of her and her husband's savings in starting up a new company in the second bedroom of their home. The two formed the name of their fledgling venture by taking the initials of their names, Ari and Sandra Kurtzig, as their corporate moniker.

Initially the Kurtzig's firm developed software for various business applications. In 1974 they incorporated their endeavor, but it was not until four years later, in 1978, that the Kurtzigs came up with a product that would allow their company to grow dramatically. This innovation was a program for use on a Hewlett-Packard mini-computer that permitted small manufacturing companies to control the operation of an entire factory. With ASK's program, companies could plan such aspects of their business as the purchase of materials and production schedules. In the past, these tasks could only be performed on very large mainframe computers. ASK's product, called "ManMan," an abbreviation for manufacturing management, had a six-figure cost and was aimed at small and medium-sized manufacturers. To reduce the cost of its program to businesses with sales of less than $10 million a year, ASK also offered its software on a time-sharing basis. For a smaller, monthly fee,

companies were able to rent a terminal to run the program on a central computer owned by ASK.

ManMan was an instant success, and with its take-off came a sharp rise in revenues and earnings for ASK. As a result of this hit program, ASK was able to sell stock to the public for the first time in 1981. Within two years, Sandra Kurtzig's personal stake in the company was worth $67 million, as ASK had come to dominate the market for information systems geared toward manufacturers. In order to insure continued growth and maintain the company's entrepreneurial spirit, ASK directed nearly half of its research and development budget toward the creation of new products.

In March of 1983 ASK made its first acquisition, purchasing a privately held software company called Software Dimensions, Inc., for $6 million. This company designed microcomputer based programs with business applications to be used with personal computers. Its best selling product was Accounting Plus, a phenomenally successful program that pulled in earnings of $250,000 on sales of $3 million in 1983 alone.

After taking over Software Dimensions, Kurtzig renamed it ASK Micro. To further increase sales of Accounting Plus and provide revenues for ASK to undertake a retooling of ManMan that would allow it to run on personal computers, the company launched an aggressive program to push Accounting Plus. ASK hired sales personnel to supplement the distributors who were already handling sales of the program, but this strategy backfired when previous sellers of Accounting Plus became insulted and hostile. In addition, the company's overhead on the program soared as a result of its enlarged payroll. Finally in June of 1984, Kurtzig announced that she was shutting down ASK Micro, at a cost of $1 million, and auctioning off the rights to Accounting Plus. Regarding this fiasco, in which the company also failed to transform ManMan for use on the personal computer, Kurtzig told *Business Week,* "We have our fingerprints all over the murder weapon" that killed Software Dimensions.

Despite the failure of ASK Micro to move ASK into the smaller-computer market, the company continued to try to make its product available more cheaply, to a broader array of businesses. As technological advances made computing power less and less expensive, ASK struggled to keep its market share from being eroded by competitors offering similar services in less cumbersome formats.

By the fall of 1984, ASK planned to offer a version of its original product, ManMan, for about one-third of its previous price. This was possible as a result of the introduction of lower-priced minicomputers from Hewlett-Packard and the Digital Equipment Corporation (DEC), the two hardware manufacturers for whose products ASK had developed software. Because of the continuity between the old and new lines of machines, ASK was able to market its product less expensively, with very few adjustments or alterations necessary. In this way, the company hoped to protect its market share with smaller companies to which it had once offered time-share facilities. In addition, ASK planned to market its original product more aggressively to middle-range manufacturers. ASK estimated that almost four-fifths of these potential customers had yet to be tapped.

Despite these efforts, by 1985, ASK had started to see its fortunes falter, as an overall decline in spending by its customers hurt the company's returns. In the midst of this dismaying financial news, in February Kurtzig and her family members also began selling off large blocks of their stock holdings in the company, a move that later resulted in a shareholder lawsuit. In August Kurtzig sold off additional shares of ASK.

This reduction in ownership of the company was indicative of a larger withdrawal on Kurtzig's part from more and more of ASK's day to day operations. Beginning in March of 1984, Kurtzig had gradually begun to relinquish her duties at ASK to a deputy. That year she named Ronald W. Branniff president of the company, and in 1985 he took over her post of chief executive officer as well. Kurtzig attributed her declining interest in the business to family pressures, along with other factors. Divorced from her husband, with whom she had founded ASK, Kurtzig was trying to raise her two sons, who were aged 12 and 9 at the time. She had grown tired of the constant pressure to spend time on her business, and the unending glare of publicity that resulted from her status as a leading woman in the high technology industry. "I felt guilty about all the attention I got, became tired of being the news," Kurtzig later told the *Wall Street Journal.* "It all became very wearisome."

In the wake of Kurtzig's departure from active participation in the company, ASK hired managers with backgrounds in running large businesses, as the company passed out of its entrepreneurial stage and became a more solidly entrenched major player. Although the company remained profitable, its level of earnings and sales dipped in 1986, falling to $5.89 million on revenues of $76 million. These figures improved in the following year, and ASK acquired the NCA Corporation for $43 million in cash in August of 1987.

Despite these small advances, it gradually became clear that ASK was losing ground to its competitors. Slowly ASK's business had grown stale. The company's atmosphere changed, however, as a host of new managers were brought in to run its operations. ASK began to concentrate the bulk of its energy on designing products for the minicomputer, largely ignoring the growing workstation market.

In its research and development activities, ASK began to focus nearly all of its resources on upgrading and improving existing products. Work on new products virtually ground to a halt. This overall caution, described in a *Wall Street Journal* article as a "toe in the water approach," made impossible any real breakthroughs that would result in continued market leadership. ASK had lost its entrepreneurial edge, and its primary position in its field, as its managers grew distant from their employees and lost contact with the actual nature of the business.

In the meantime, Kurtzig had spent her time traveling, writing her autobiography, and dabbling in investment in other technology companies. Eventually she found herself frustrated and bored. In mid-1989 the ASK managing board approached Kurtzig and asked her to resume an active role in the company, and she accepted their invitation, despite the fact that she had formally resigned as chairman of the company, severing all official ties just a few months earlier.

Among the first signs of Kurtzig's return was ASK's purchase of Data 3 Systems, a privately owned competitor that made manufacturing software. ASK paid $18.7 million for the company, whose products were designed for use on IBM hardware, a natural complement to ASK's products for other computers. In addition to this complementary expansion, Kurtzig began to revamp the way her old company had been run. She reconfigured existing products, shifted personnel, and tried to alter the pervading spirit of the enterprise. She changed such minor but important details as the quality of the food and beer at the company's Friday evening celebrations in an effort to reconnect upper level management with the company's employees. She also began attending many meetings at all levels of ASK to keep her finger on the pulse of the company's operations.

As part of this effort, Kurtzig had research and development workers rate their bosses, and those who scored low were dismissed, while those whose efforts won praise were given more responsibility. She abolished bonuses for upper-level management that left out low-level workers, convinced that they detracted from team spirit at the company. In addition, Kurtzig recruited managers with entrepreneurial experience.

In addressing ASK's product line, Kurtzig moved to simplify the company's programs and insure that they could be used with a broader array of computers and databases. In addition to its attempts to make inroads into the IBM market, the company also set its sights on products manufactured by Sun Microsystems. To market its products, ASK began exploring second party distribution channels, rather than the direct sales it had relied on in the past. In addition, ASK moved to tap the international market by opening offices in Europe and Asia. These efforts combined to give ASK a successful final year of the 1980s, as the company posted earnings of $13.5 million.

In 1990, ASK made another significant acquisition, purchasing the Ingres Corporation, a software manufacturer that had been suffering declining financial fortunes. In order to finance this move, ASK entered into an unusual four-way financing arrangement, taking on significant capitalization from the Hewlett-Packard Company and the Electronic Data Systems Corporation (EDS), a subsidiary of General Motors. This unorthodox arrangement elicited alarm from some of ASK's stockholders, notably one man who held ten percent of the company's shares and who announced that he would try to have the company's managing board ousted at the next shareholders meeting. Despite this glitch, Kurtzig's arrangement proceeded as planned. The deal called for 30 percent of ASK to be sold to Hewlett-Packard and EDS for a total of $60 million, which in turn enabled ASK to pay $110 million for Ingres.

In this way, Kurtzig was able to unite several components in partnership with ASK that were essential for the company's success. ASK already made use of Ingres software in its own work, linking the accounting and manufacturing departments of its clients to its own database. Hewlett-Packard made the hardware upon which much of ASK's software ran, and the company resold Hewlett-Packard products as part of its software packages. Both Hewlett-Packard and EDS had strong histories of involvement with manufacturing businesses, and this heritage promised to open up more potential markets for ASK.

Kurtzig told the *Wall Street Journal* at the time of the purchase of Ingres that she considered the deal "a home run." This good news provided a counterpoint to ASK's mediocre results over the past several quarters, indicative of a lull in business while the company tried to bring new products to market. With its new purchases, ASK had moved beyond its original scope, as a software company that catered to manufacturers, to become a much larger, global, diversified company. The unified ASK and Ingres group expected yearly revenues of $400 million. Upon beginning the merger of its acquisition into its operations, ASK announced that 270 jobs, or 12 percent of Ingres' workforce, would be eliminated, because they overlapped with operations provided by ASK. The company ended 1990 with revenues of $206 million.

In the early 1990s, ASK concentrated on the development and introduction of new products, designed to provide communication between different computer systems and programs. In 1992 the company also introduced ManMan/X, an updated version of its original manufacturing management program, with 27 nodules.

In 1992 ASK was restructured to better reflect the nature of its operations. The company was renamed the ASK Group and was now comprised of three separate business groups—ASK Computer Systems, Data 3, and Ingres. In addition to this structural reshuffling, ASK underwent a significant shift in top management when Kurtzig appointed a new president and once again retired, retaining only the title of chairman.

The reconfigured ASK, again under new leadership, ended 1992 with an increase in revenue of more than 23 percent, which was offset by write-offs that caused an overall loss for the year of $44 million. With significant partnerships in place and a history of domination in its market for manufacturing-related software, ASK appeared to be on solid footing as the company faced the challenging environment of the computer industry in the 1990s.

Further Reading:

"ASK Computer's Search for a Strategy," *Business Week,* August 27, 1984.

Gupta, Udayan, "ASK Co-Founder Is Proving You Can Go Home Again," *Wall Street Journal,* May 30, 1990.

—Elizabeth Rourke

Associated Grocers, Incorporated

3301 South Norfolk Street
Seattle, Washington 98119-5648
U.S.A.
(206) 762-2100
Fax: (206) 764-7731

Private Company
Incorporated: 1934 as Associated Grocers Co-operative
Employees: 1,400
Sales: $1.09 billion
SICs: 5141 Groceries—General Line; 5147 Meats & Meat
Products; 5143 Dairy Products Except Dried or Canned;
5122 Drugs, Proprietaries & Sundries; 5148 Fresh Fruits
& Vegetables; 5142 Packaged Frozen Foods

Associated Grocers, Incorporated, a grocery wholesaler providing retail support and distribution services to approximately 160 independent grocers operating about 320 stores, is the largest privately held company in the state of Washington. It delivers over 4.5 million pounds of fresh and nonperishable foods each day to retail customers in Washington, Oregon, Alaska, Hawaii, and more distant destinations such as Samoa and Guam.

After the stock market crashed in 1929 and sent the U.S. economy spiraling downward, businesses that had managed to survive the tumultuous economic conditions still faced years of difficult recovery. The economic climate had still not improved by 1934 when eleven independent grocers in Seattle, Washington, banded together to form Associated Grocers Co-operative. Although it was not the first time businesses with similar interests had created a cooperative to help stave off the harmful effects of the Depression, the formation of Associated Grocers did mark one of the first instances in which grocers united to share resources and to create an organizational structure to oversee their well-being. The eleven grocery stores, mostly smaller, street-corner operations, commonly known as "mom and pop" stores, joined together through the assistance of Harry Henke Jr., a corporate lawyer in Seattle. The stores also solicited the help of J. B. Rhodes, a supermarket executive working in San Francisco, to lead the newly formed cooperative.

With a starting capital of $8,325, Associated Grocers initially provided grocery products to the individual, independent stores, enabling them to compete with the larger chain stores that relied on centralized distribution centers and possessed larger reservoirs of cash. Accordingly, the cooperative provided a buffer for the independent grocers against their better-financed competition and, in effect, enabled them to pool their resources in order to survive the debilitating times. Since the cooperative was owned by the grocers, a portion of the profits earned by Associated Grocers from the sales to the grocers were returned to the grocers in the form of patronage dividends.

In its first year of operation, Associated Grocers fared well. Revenues totaled $1.27 million for the year, and the cooperative was becoming stronger as more grocery stores joined and it became better able to keep the independent grocer competitive in an industry increasingly dominated by large chain stores. Four years after its inception, in 1938, Associated Grocers constructed a 41,800 square foot warehouse in Yakima, Washington, to complement the cooperative's warehouse in Seattle and accommodate its burgeoning clientele. The facility in Yakima, a community east of Seattle in central Washington, was established as a branch warehouse to fulfill the needs of member grocery stores near the facility. By establishing branch warehouses, Associated Grocers reduced transportation costs to stores located outside the immediate service area of its Seattle warehouse and was able to transport the merchandise in a shorter time, particularly important for the perishable products that member stores required.

When the United States entered World War II in 1941, a scarcity of some grocery products resulted, but the affects of the shortage were mitigated by Associated Grocers' ability to provide competitively priced merchandise to its customers. In addition to supplying its member stores with merchandise, the cooperative also began offering services intended to help the independent grocer's position in the marketplace. For example, Associated Grocers became one of the first wholesalers in the nation to offer retailers a complete pricing service, allowing member stores access to the prices other stores charged for products and keeping member stores apprised of competitive pricing in their market. By 1942, the cooperative had outgrown its main warehouse in Seattle, and a new warehouse was built to accommodate the cooperative's members, which by this time had increased from the original 11 stores to 260 independent grocers.

After World War II, business accelerated, fueled by a postwar boom that increased Associated Grocers' customer base considerably. By 1952, the cooperative had 600 members, operating stores in Washington, Oregon, Alaska, and the Hawaiian islands. In addition to the warehouse in Seattle and the branch warehouse in Yakima, which had been enlarged by 11,000 square feet in 1948, the cooperative also opened nine "cash and carry" branches to supply both member and nonmember stores. Independent stores that did not belong to Associated Grocers could buy merchandise at these cash and carry outlets, but did not receive the cooperative's patronage dividends. Since Associated Grocers opened for business eighteen years earlier, the cooperative had returned an average of nearly $155,000 per year in patronage dividends for a total of $2.7 million. Sales now stood at $33 million, and Associated Grocers once again found itself in need of additional warehouse space as well as more modern equipment and facilities to effectively service its members.

In a much heralded event in the local press, Associated Grocers completed construction in 1952 on a $2.2 million warehouse that at once answered the increasing needs of the cooperative. Located on a 26-acre plot, the site was comprised of four buildings, including the warehouse. The warehouse featured a large loading dock to receive and dispatch merchandise to and from its fleet of trucks and 235,000 square feet of space sheltered by a nine-acre roof. Included in this large area were a series of curing rooms, to store fruit until ripened, and a separate area for frozen foods. The complex also included a building used to service and repair warehouse equipment and the cooperative's fleet of trucks, which by this time consisted of 100 trucks and trailers. Another building was devoted solely to the repair and maintenance of the tires used on the cooperative's vehicles. This distribution complex provided more than ample space to service Associated Grocers increasing membership, and additional land surrounding the new buildings offered the opportunity for the cooperative to further expand.

While the cooperative continued to expand its operations, store membership did not dramatically increase beyond the 600 stores belonging to the cooperative in 1952. Rather, growth came from an increase of services to members and in the size of the stores they operated, which in turn helped Associated Grocers realize future gains in revenues. Following the completion of the warehouse complex, a new department was created to manage drugs and sundries, and in 1953 the cooperative recorded nearly $39.5 million in sales and returned $455,417 in patronage dividends. Two years later, Associated Grocers management began looking for a way to assist its members in financing major remodeling projects and new store construction. Many wholesale grocery concerns had been assisting their members in financing new store construction recently, approximately 25 percent of the wholesale industry engaged in this activity, and Associated Grocers sought to extend the service to its members. With an initial investment of $50,000, the cooperative formed a wholly owned subsidiary named Market Finance Co. that enabled member stores to borrow the requisite funds to relocate their stores, construct new stores, or complete preapproved remodeling projects. The amount of the loans was generally limited to $50,000, for which the retailers were charged six percent simple interest. Market Finance was advanced the money from banks at a lower interest rate than charged to the retailer, with the difference between the two rates financing the subsidiary's operating expenses. Not designed to earn a profit, the subsidiary was, nevertheless, a financial success. Within two years, roughly 25 percent of the cooperative's members had applied for financing through Market Finance, amounting to over $1 million in loans.

The addition of these services would figure prominently in the company's business strategy during the 1960s. By this time, competition from the larger, better-financed retail chains had intensified, as large supermarkets began to dominate the markets in which Associated Grocer member stores operated. Consequently, a large number of mom and pop stores were forced out of business, giving way to new stores that occupied sites as large as a city block. During this era of decline for small grocery stores, Associated Grocers increased the services it provided to its members, helping them with store decor, establishing electronic ordering systems, and supplying them with innovative packaging methods. However, these efforts were not enough to keep some of the smaller stores in business, and the cooperative's membership dwindled. By the end of the decade, the effect of these losses impelled Associated Grocers to seek new leadership.

The cooperative's new president, Bert Hambleton, was elected in 1971. Hambleton, who had spent 21 years with grocery and retailing chains in Ohio and Illinois before joining Associated Grocers, accepted the position with some reluctance. As he later recalled, "The operation was in deep trouble when I came in. . . . When the board first offered me the job I turned them down because I didn't think the company was going to survive." However, under Hambleton's leadership, lasting changes were made that reinvigorated Associated Grocers' position in the wholesale industry. Throughout the cooperative's offices, computers were brought in to improve the efficiency and accuracy of all facets of operations, from the management of the warehouses to market research. Cooperative-owned dairy and egg farms were established, creating a stable supply of dairy products for the independent grocers, and the organizational structure of the company was revamped to give its operations a configuration more characteristic of a corporation rather than a cooperative. The changes implemented by Hambleton were successful. When he assumed control of Associated Grocers, revenues were $150 million and earnings were less than $1 million. By the end of the decade, revenues had climbed to $625 million, and the dividends paid to the cooperative's members totaled $8 million.

The mounting pressure put on independent grocers continued into the 1980s, as such giants in the industry as Safeway Stores competed for customers with Associated Grocers member stores. While the cooperative had increased its market share from below 20 percent to greater than 25 percent during the 1970s, it needed to further penetrate the markets in which it operated. A supermarket development subsidiary was formed in 1981 to manage the financing and development of stores for Associated Grocers members, tasks that had clogged the cooperative's administration operations, consuming as much as 60 percent of its time. Utilizing the cooperative's computers, the subsidiary conducted site analyses and demographic studies that enabled independent stores to enter markets before other commercial and residential development. Although riskier in nature, this method proved successful in allowing Associated and its members to compete for sites with the chain store operators.

In 1985, Associated Grocers purchased 25 stores located in Washington from Lucky Food Stores, a retail chain operating in 30 states. Lucky had been unable to efficiently operate the stores from its distribution and manufacturing centers in California, so the cooperative purchased the 23 supermarkets and two discount outlets and sold the stores to independent grocers in an effort to increase the number of stores under its purview. The addition of the Lucky stores, as well as an agreement with Pacific Gamble Robinson to supply 88 grocery stores, gave Associated Grocers 406 stores. Largely due to the association with Pacific Gamble, revenues had increased by 20 percent since 1984 to reach approximately $900 million.

Later that year, Associated Grocers initiated negotiations with United Retail Merchants Stores Inc., a wholesale grocery distributor operating in eastern Washington, to effect a merger.

The proposed merger would join United Retail's distributing facilities with those of Associated Grocers to lend greater efficiency to the two wholesalers' purchasing and distribution operations and enable Associated Grocers to more fully utilize its warehouse space. Associated Grocers' board of directors approved the proposal, voting unanimously in favor of uniting United Retail's approximately $400 million in revenues with the cooperative's $900 million. However, United Retail backed out in early 1986. Aggressively seeking the merger, Hambleton at one point had offered to step aside if his departure would facilitate the union, but his efforts were to no avail. One month after United Retail made their announcement, Hambleton, who had been stunned by the decision, opted for early retirement and was succeeded by Donald Benson, Associated Grocers' executive vice-president of finance.

Although the collapse of the deal with United Retail in 1986 was discouraging, the year was generally good for Associated Grocers' management. Through the assistance of the cooperative, independent grocers experienced a resurgence during this time due to their new focus on customer service. Stores were now being remodeled much more frequently, the merchandise was becoming more diverse, and the stores' management began orienting their marketing and products to the residents living in proximity to the particular store. These adjustments enabled Associated Grocers to match Safeway's market share for the first time, which was a combined 72 percent for the two companies. By attempting to appeal to as many different types of customers as possible and generating more sales per square foot, Associated Grocers members increased their profits and the cooperative, in turn, collected the rewards of a revitalized business. By 1990, Associated Grocers was the largest privately held company in Washington, and revenues surpassed the $1 billion mark.

As Associated Grocers entered the 1990s, a two-month strike was effected by its workers. Increased costs resulting from the strike cut into the cooperatives earnings, which dropped from $4.2 million to $3.5 million, and the cooperative's patronage dividends fell from $14.7 million to $10.7 million. Nevertheless, Associated Grocers' performance rebounded in 1991, as the dividends climbed back up to $13.5 million, and earnings jumped to $5.2 million on revenues of $1.1 billion.

The considerable growth Associated Grocers achieved in revenues during the 1990s prompted management to consider offering shares in the cooperative publicly. Whether Associated Grocers remains a privately held company or goes public, independent grocers are still expected to benefit from the added strength the cooperative provides.

Principal Subsidiaries: Market Food Service; Market Advertising.

Further Reading:

"AG Is the Largest Private Firm in State," *The Seattle Times,* May 21, 1993, p. C7.
"Associated Grocers Co-op Fetes New Plant," *The Seattle Times,* August 17, 1952, p. 48.
"Associated Groceries Is State's Top Private Firm," *The Seattle Times,* March 11, 1991, p. B5.
"Associated Grocers to Buy Lucky Stores," *The Seattle Times,* October 24, 1985, p. D1.
Blake, Judith, "Groceries Going All Out to Win Back Customers," *The Seattle Times,* August 2, 1989, p. C1.
Dwyer, Kevin, "Billion Dollar Baby," *Washington CEO,* March 1991, pp. 28–29.
"Eleven Groups Associated in Western Area," *The Seattle Times,* August 17, 1952, p. 50.
"Grocers' Co-op Sets New Sales Record," *The Seattle Times,* December 8, 1953, p. 35.
Mahoney, Sally Gene, "Associated Grocers May Merge with Spokane Merchant Group," *The Seattle Times,* December 10, 1985, p. C4.
——. "Lucky Pullout Almost Complete," *The Seattle Times,* November 12, 1985, p. B1.
——. "URM Calls off Merger with Associated," *The Seattle Times,* January 8, 1986, p. D4.
"Northwest Supers Finally Cash in on ATMs," *Supermarket Business,* January 1985, p. 6.
Pucci, Carol, "Bagging More Customers: Independent Grocers Alter Image to Get Growing Share of the Market," *The Seattle Times,* December 7, 1986, p. E1.
Sharpe, Gary, "Development Financing Grocery Company's Big Ticket," *Seattle Business Journal,* February 15, 1982, p. 6.
Warren, James R., *A Century of Seattle's Business,* Bellevue: Vernon Publications Inc., 1989.
"Wholesaler Sponsored Financing Strengthens Washington Independents," *Progressive Grocer,* December 1956, pp. 51–55.

—Jeffrey L. Covell

AST Research Inc.

16215 Alton Parkway
P.O. Box 19658
Irvine, California 92713-9658
U.S.A.
(714) 727-4141
Fax: (714) 727-9355

Public Company
Incorporated: 1980
Employees: 4,000
Sales: $944.10 million
Stock Exchanges: New York
SICs: 3571 Electronic Computers

AST Research Inc., is the third-largest American manufacturer of personal computers based on the industry standard microprocessing chip. In its short history, the company has grown dramatically from a small endeavor started by three friends, to a major power in the computer business, with markets throughout the world.

The story of AST's genesis is a classic tale of a California computer company that was started on a shoe-string and rocketed to wealth and prominence on the strength of technological innovation. The company was founded by Thomas C. K. Yuen, who talked two friends into taking on extra jobs as computer consultants in 1979. The three pooled their spare cash—a total of $2,000—and started the company they named with the initials of the their first names. Albert C. Wong, Yuen's old roommate from Orange Coast College, contributed the "A"; Safi U. Qureshey, who had met Yuen while working at minicomputer maker Computer Automation, Inc., contributed the "S"; and Thomas Yuen, the son of a Hong Kong textile company limousine driver, contributed the "T."

In the spirit of equality, the three friends, all immigrants who had been trained as engineers, drew straws to determine who would take what office in the new company. Qureshey, originally from Pakistan, became president; Wong, from Hong Kong, became secretary; and Yuen took over the post of treasurer. The company was incorporated in 1980, but it was not until 1981 that the three principals of AST had an idea for their first product.

That idea was sparked by IBM's introduction of the first personal computer, or PC. AST's founders saw a need for a means to upgrade the computers so that such options as a larger memory could be added. Accordingly, the company designed circuit boards that could be installed in the IBM PC's that would allow for additional functions. By the end of 1981 the tiny company had produced its first shipment of these items. Although the check AST received in payment for its first sale bounced, the next payments did not, and the company's fortunes took off on the strength of its one good idea.

In recalling this period in AST's business, Yuen later commented in *Business Week,* "It became like a fairy tale. Every month, sales doubled." Needing more financing to keep up with demand, AST turned to banks for money. When the fledgling operation was turned down, the founders each took out second mortgages on their homes and raised $50,000. This investment paid off in 1983, when AST's sales soared to $13 million. After venture capitalists invested an additional $2.4 million in AST, the company grew large enough to justify a public offering of shares in 1984. In June the company offered two million shares to the public.

Following this milestone, AST's fortunes were bolstered by the introduction of further add-on products for the IBM PC and IBM-compatible PC's. Most successful among these was Six-PakPlus. After its introduction in 1983, sales grew dramatically. That same year the company also entered a marketing agreement with IBM, which permitted the giant computer maker to resell AST's products.

In March of 1985 AST formed its first international division, opening AST Far East, Ltd. to facilitate the manufacture of its products in Hong Kong. By this time the company's offerings ranged from adaptor boards that allowed PC's to interact with other computers, to graphics facilities, to a hard disk drive for the Macintosh. Driven by demand for these innovative products, AST's revenues doubled in just a year, to reach $138.6 million. Earnings had risen 233 percent over the last twelve months, to reach $19 million. With these funds, AST made a number of acquisitions. In March of 1986, the company bought Camintonn, a computer memory manufacturer, and in May AST purchased the National System Company, a French computer wholesaler, subsequently forming AST France.

Despite AST's history of rapid growth, however, the company's initial operations were coming to an end. With the introduction of more powerful PC's, the need and demand for AST's peripheral products was inevitably waning. In response to this circumstance, AST was forced to lay off seven percent of its workforce in July of 1986. Faced with the decline of its original market, and the need for continued growth, AST's founders decided that the obvious next step was to begin manufacturing their own PC's. This was a risky move because the PC market was crowded with powerful competitors, among them IBM, Compaq, Leading Edge, and NEC.

In late October, 1986, AST introduced five IBM-compatible PC models, and the following month, the company announced a $2 million print ad campaign to support its new products. AST planned to promote its Premium/286 PC, along with its laser printer and laser scanner, as a package that provided desktop publishing, outperforming its competitors while selling for less money.

AST also continued to aggressively push its geographical expansion. In addition to its French operations, the company opened European subsidiaries in the United Kingdom, Germany, Canada, and Australia. By 1987, one-quarter of AST's revenues came from overseas sales.

In an attempt to stay ahead of its fierce competition, AST put its emphasis on cutting-edge technology. When the introduction of a higher-capacity microchip, the Intel Corporation's sophisticated 80486 chip, was announced, AST followed close behind with a computer design that used this new technology. The company's offering debuted on October 19, 1987.

Despite this advance, however, AST experienced some rough times. In June of 1987 the company delayed shipment of a new product for use with IBM computers, and the following month, AST cancelled a planned stock offering. Then in November the company was sued by IBM, which was aggressively seeking to protect its PS/2 trademark from infringement, because AST had used the name in an advertising campaign that boasted "PS/2 Memory. Our Name Says It All." The company chose to settle out of court in the matter.

In addition, AST's rapid growth had slowed. The company's net income for 1987 was only $13 million, less than half what the company had made the year before. AST's PC offerings, despite their many virtues, were not special enough to set them apart from the welter of competitors. In an attempt to remedy the company's woes, AST undertook a reorganization. In June of 1988 the company merged its data communications group with its systems product group. To maintain pace with the industry standard, AST also set about developing its own version of the newer OS/2 computer operating system, along with communications software based upon it.

July of that year saw AST introduce 5 new models of its Premium workstation family, and three months later, two other products in this line were introduced. In September AST announced its first national network television ads, to be broadcast during the Summer Olympics. This effort, which cost $2.2 million, made up a significant portion of the company's $12 million advertising effort. AST hoped that the ads would raise consumer awareness of the company's brand name. To make the most of this effort, AST planned to tie in the Olympics campaign with posters, pins, and highlights videos, to be distributed to computer dealers.

By the end of the year it seemed that these efforts had paid off, as sales rose 100 percent from the previous twelve month period to reach $412.7 million. AST had become the third-largest seller of IBM-compatible computers, behind only IBM itself and the Compaq Computer Corporation. Despite this gain, however, all-important revenue growth had reached a plateau.

Tiring of the company's struggles, one of AST's three cofounders, Albert Wong, left the company after a particularly virulent fight with Thomas Yuen in late 1988. By early 1989 AST's fortunes had soured to the extent that the company reported its first ever quarterly loss, which totaled $8.9 million. AST had failed to anticipate that the introduction of a new

microprocessor chip, the Intel 80386, would make its models based on the old chip obsolete. As sales slowed, products were stockpiled in warehouses, and the company's costs continued to grow. The blow AST suffered as a result of its failure to innovate quickly enough and stay at the cutting edge of technology was not a lesson the company's leaders forgot quickly.

In an effort to streamline itself and stem the tide of red ink, AST laid off six percent of its employees, letting 120 people go in January of 1989. "Everything," Yuen later recounted in *USA Today*, "was negative." The company took further steps to return to financial health. In April the Camintonn acquisition was sold off to the unit's managers, and AST also divested itself of its Apple Macintosh product lines, which were purchased by Orange Micro. With these moves, the company was able to refocus its efforts on its core business of IBM-compatible PC's.

By the fall of 1989 the company was showing signs of a turnaround, as AST introduced a new line of computers with a feature that its previous models had lacked. Invented in response to the rapid advance of technology, and called "cupid architecture," this design innovation allowed computer buyers to upgrade their machines easily by switching one circuit board inside the computer. AST made this possible by isolating the aspects of a computer that were likely to become obsolete, the microprocessor and memory chips, on one circuit board that could be easily removed and replaced. In this way, customers did not have to worry about improvements in speed and processing power making their unit obsolete. Although many customers were not expected to actually make the move to an upgrade, observers lauded AST's strategy as a great marketing ploy, since it removed the impetus to delay a computer purchase. The cupid architecture design innovation also allowed AST to introduce updated computer models to the market more quickly than its competitors, and helped keep the cost of new technology down. In this way, the company was able to underprice its rivals by ten to sixty percent.

In April of 1990 AST announced that it had developed a computer to imitate Japanese competitor NEC Corporation's PC 9801. AST planned to try and sell this machine in the Japanese market, dominated by NEC. This risky move, which lacked the safety net of possible U.S. sales, was an attempt to tap into the vast Japanese market for business computers, second in size only to America. "It's one of those huge, untapped markets for aggressive overseas companies," Qureshey told the *Wall Street Journal* at the time.

The machine AST planned to market in Japan was called the Dual SX/16, and it was capable of running software written for NEC machines as well as IBM machines. AST set out to implement its usual strategy of offering more features on its Japanese product than its competitors did, while also charging a lower price. In addition, to encourage acceptance of the product by Japanese consumers, the company planned to sell its wares under various Japanese trade names that would be familiar to customers.

This move came as part of AST's overall push to make up for lost U.S. market share with heavy overseas expansion. A key aspect of this was the company's entry into foreign markets frequently overlooked or ignored by other U.S. computer makers. AST peddled its products in the former Soviet Union, for example, supporting its sales with Russian-language advertising, and computers were also sold on the Indian subcontinent.

As a result of these and other efforts, AST's financial outlook was steadily improving in the early 1990s. Support from the financial community came as the company's share price grew nearly 260 percent in 1990, keeping pace with growing sales and earnings. As AST solidified its position as the third-place IBM compatible computer maker, the company's sales neared the billion-dollar mark.

In April of 1991, as a result of AST's aggressive pricing, Compaq and its competitors cut their prices, indicating that AST's policies were having an impact on the industry as a whole. By this time, the company's original business, add-on circuit boards for PC clones, had shrunk to make up just seven percent of its business. In its place, AST had become a force to reckon with in the PC industry due to its unusual strategy of selling computers both under its own name through a network of thousands of dealers and under the brand names of other companies, including Texas Instruments and Digital Equipment Corporation.

In addition, the company maintained its technical edge, announcing advances in its own products in order to keep up with innovations in technology. For instance, AST unveiled a new product based on the new industry standard microprocessor, the Intel 486SX, just one day after the new chip was introduced. As the overall American economy entered a recession, AST was able to cater to companies seeking bargains in their computer purchasing. In a big coup, AST won a contract from AT&T to supply more than 1,600 notebook computers to its sales corps. By spring of 1991 the company was selling its low-priced products to 65 percent of the *Fortune* 500 companies. As growth in the domestic market and in overseas operations continued, AST opened a fourth manufacturing plant to supply its products to vendors.

By mid-1992, however, fierce competition in the computer industry had started to slow AST's growth, and the company began to consider various forms of restructuring in order to keep its costs as low as possible. In a surprising move Thomas Yuen announced in June that he would be leaving the company and would be replaced, in effect, with an ally of the last original member of the troika, Safi Qureshey. Under its sole leader, AST then set out to maintain its position in an industry undergoing widespread upheaval.

A staple of the company's business philosophy was to keep pace with technological developments, and accordingly, in November of 1992 AST announced that it would produce a notebook computer that exploited the capabilities of Intel's new i486SL, a chip designed for portable models. With this chip and its faster processing rate, notebook computers would have a longer battery life. AST called its entry into this segment of the PC market the Powerexec 4/25SL Colorplus.

The company's commitment to technological innovation continued in 1993, when AST announced that it would enter the pen computing market with its shipments of the PenExec "PenTop" notebook computer, which used a cordless stylus to enter data on a screen. AST had created this product as a joint venture with its competitor Tandy's Grid unit, and the product was manufactured by that company's TE Electronics unit. Later that summer, AST announced that it had purchased these two parts of Tandy for $160 million, causing the company to incur a loss for that financial quarter.

Despite this temporary financial setback, AST's position as the third-largest producer of IBM-clone PC's appeared solid. In a brief time, the company had grown from a three-man operation to a major player in the computer industry, its growth driven by innovative products and constant attention to technological advances. As the computer industry continued to evolve, AST appeared to be well prepared to meet the continuing challenges of its market.

Principal Subsidiaries: AST Research Deutschland GmbH (Germany); AST Europe Ltd. (England); AST Research (Far East) Ltd. (Hong Kong); AST Research, Inc. (Canada); AST Research ANZ Pty. Ltd. (Australia); AST Research, Inc. (China); AST Research (Switzerland) S.A.; AST Research Japan (K.K.); AST Taiwan Ltd.; AST Research France S.A.R.L.; AST Research Italia S.r.l.

Further Reading:

Armstrong, Larry, "This 12-Year-Old Has Come of Age," *Business Week,* May 6, 1991.
Rebello, Kathy, "Computer Maker Earns Leading Role," *USA Today,* May 13, 1991.

—Elizabeth Rourke

ATARI®

Atari Corporation

1196 Borregas Avenue
Sunnyvale, California 94089
U.S.A.
(408) 745-2000
Fax: (408) 745-4306

Public Company
Incorporated: 1972
Employees: 507
Sales: $127 million
Stock Exchanges: New York
SICs: 3571 Electronic Computers; 3944 Games, Toys &
    Children's Vehicles; 7372 Prepackaged Software

The Atari Corporation is a manufacturer of video games and home computers that pioneered the industry of video entertainment. The company's history has been beset by a series of successes and defeats. The company made money from arcade games, then nearly went bankrupt; it took on new life and astronomical profits in the early 1980s, only to see its industry crash once again, leaving the company to rebuild slowly under different management.

Atari was founded by Nolan Bushnell in 1972. Bushnell had first become interested in computer games as an engineering student at the University of Utah. After graduation, he worked as a researcher in a Silicon Valley firm, and there he developed his first electronic game, called Computer Space, in 1971. Although this game, like all the other fledgling products before it, was not a commercial success, Bushnell used $500 to start a company with a friend anyway, naming it Atari, a term from the Japanese game of *go* used to politely alert opponents that they are about to be overrun.

Bushnell's second game was a revolutionary development, in that it was far simpler than other games had been. Called "Pong," it was an electronic version of ping pong, played on a screen with a vertical line down the middle, and two sliding paddles that batted a blip back and forth. The company first marketed a coin-operated version of this game in 1972, for use in arcades. Since the game could be played by two people in competition with each other, Pong was a dramatic departure from the solitary skills of pinball, and it changed the nature of arcade games.

Unfortunately, Atari was unable to reap the rewards of this advance, since dozens of competitors quickly duplicated the game and grabbed a large portion of the market. Within two years of Pong's introduction, its inventors had sold only ten percent of the machines in existence.

Atari channeled the profits it had made into ventures that turned out to be shortsighted and nonproductive. The company wasted half a million dollars on an abortive attempt to market its products in Japan. In addition, it sunk resources into an attempt to open game arcades in Hawaii. Although Atari introduced a series of new games to follow Pong, formulated in the company's informal, unstructured atmosphere, none caught on as its first offering had.

Video games for use in the home had first been introduced by Magnavox in 1972, and Atari decided that a logical next step would be to introduce a home version of Pong, to be played on a television screen. Short of funds, the company worked out an arrangement with Sears, Roebuck & Company for the retailer to buy all 100,000 of the devices that Atari manufactured, as well as helping out with funding for Atari's inventories, to guarantee delivery. In the fall of 1975, the home version of Pong was introduced.

Clearly, Atari needed further funds to expand. Rather than sell stock to the public, the company decided to look for a buyer. In 1976, after four months of legal wrangling complicated by a lawsuit filed against Bushnell by his first wife, Atari was sold to Warner Communications Inc., for $28 million. Of this, Pong's inventor collected about $15 million.

By the next year, however, Atari's problems had moved beyond funding. The company's products at the time could be used to play only one game, and consumers were beginning to feel that the novelty of playing that one game had worn off. In late 1977, however, Atari's researchers introduced the Video Computer System, or VCS 2600, which used a semiconducter chip in a programmable device. With this product, the customer gained versatility. Any number of games could played on cartridges, which were inserted into the set like cassette tapes.

Introduced shortly before the big Christmas selling season, the new games initially failed to conclusively dislodge the old, single-purpose products. In addition, the company had come up against steep competition from several of its competitors, who had also introduced multipurpose video game equipment. Throughout 1978, Atari saw its new product languish on the shelves.

This disappointing news was compounded by administrative confusion at company headquarters. Original Atari employees felt no loyalty toward their new bosses, and top administrators also disagreed with some of Warner's key decisions. After a chaotic budget meeting in New York, Bushnell was ousted from his position as chair of the company.

In his place, executives with backgrounds at large companies were installed, and procedures and practices at Atari became much more businesslike. In an effort to sell off some of the backlogged inventory of slow-moving games that the company had built up, Atari launched a $6 million advertising campaign in the last seven weeks of 1978, designed to clear out inventory and make way for new products.

The strategy worked. At the important, industry-wide Consumer Electronics Show in January of 1979, store owners demanded more products to sell. Over the next twelve months, Atari was able to sell all of the game devices it manufactured.

In addition to its game operations, Atari ambitiously branched out into the hotly competitive personal computer field, introducing two models, dubbed the Atari 400 and the Atari 800. These were intended for the home rather than office market. In the company's second year of operation in this field, it lost about $10 million on sales of twice that amount.

With the start of the 1980s, however, Atari's successes in the video game field more than made up for its losses in other areas, as its growth and profits shot up. In January 1980, Atari began an effort to shift the emphasis of the video game industry away from holiday-generated sales, to prove that people were willing to buy video games all year round. To do this, Atari introduced four new video game cartridges late in the first month of the year. The tactic was successful, and demand for the company's product continued to build. By the end of the year, Atari had sold all of the video game machines that it had manufactured. Among its biggest selling cartridges was Space Invaders, an adaptation of a coin-operated arcade game originally designed in Japan.

Atari's arcade operations were also going strong. In 1980, the company introduced Asteroids to compete with the Space Invaders arcade game, which was produced by another company. Atari's version proved to be a popular alternative. By the end of the year, 70,000 of the units had been shipped. Overall, revenues from coin-operated games reached $170 million, up from $52 million the year before. In addition to its arcade business, in 1980 Atari also began to explore the market for its products overseas. The company's overall revenues had more than doubled in just one year, topping $415 million, and its operating income had increased by five times.

Because the sale of video cartridges was extremely profitable, Atari introduced new games at a steady pace, releasing titles at the rate of one per month. In 1981, with demand running at feverish pitch, the company decided to ration its product. More than one million cartridges of Space Invaders had been sold. All in all, with its competitors falling by the wayside, Atari was the world's largest producer of video games, holding 80 percent of the American market. At the end of 1981, the company had sold more than $740 million worth of video game equipment and cartridges. In addition, its home computer operations had become profitable, and Atari products dominated the sales of low-priced machines.

To protect its strong market position in the video game field, Atari also began an aggressive effort to shut down video game pirates by taking legal action against them. In November 1981, the company won an important case against a company that was selling a copycat "Centipede" game.

Although Atari was aggressive in introducing lucrative new software, it lagged behind in marketing new hardware. Essentially, the company had not followed its introduction of the Video Computer System with a second, more sophisticated generation, except to produce a remote-control model, known as Touch Me, that cost $100 more than the basic set.

The introduction of a Pac-Man cartridge in the spring of 1982, however, helped to stave off these concerns, as the company estimated that it would sell nine million of the games, to reap over $200 million in that year alone. Pac-Man was a breakthrough game, attracting many women and families to the video game market for the first time, and thereby expanding the industry's consumer base. In the fall of that year, Atari also took steps to update its game equipment, introducing a more elaborate version of its game machine, which sold for $350. It also quadrupled its sales of personal computers. In general, Atari poured tens of millions of dollars into research and development, in an effort to stay out in front of the competitive industry.

Despite these efforts, however, by the end of 1982, Atari's rise in the industry, which many had believed would continue indefinitely, had been checked. Competition in the video games industry had expanded dramatically, as new companies rushed into the lucrative field. Now, Atari faced more than 30 other game makers, some of which had lured away the company's top game designers, a damaging loss in a field where innovation was suddenly as important as distribution. On December 8, 1982, Atari's corporate parent, Warner Communications, announced that previous sales estimates would not be met because of "unexpected cancellations and disappointing sales during the first week of December," as the *New York Times* reported at the time. In the wake of this sudden news, the company's stock value dropped precipitously, and several Atari executives were later investigated for insider stock trading, since they had sold off large blocks of stock just before the announcement.

Following this setback, Atari announced in February 1983, that it would fire 1,700 American workers in order to move manufacturing facilities to Hong Kong and Taiwan. This move set off a wave of protest. In the financial community, it was taken as the sign of a company adrift, since Atari had hired 2,500 new U.S. workers just the year before in a campaign to build up its domestic production capacity, only to undo itself a short time later.

In addition, Atari found itself being challenged by competitors in its home computer business. In May 1983, the company reduced the price of its outmoded 400 computer by two-thirds, from $299 to $100. By the end of its first quarter, losses overall had reached $46 million. In an effort to restore some of the original creative luster to Atari, the company announced an agreement with ousted founder Nolan Bushnell to sell consumer versions of the coin-operated games he was developing in his new business.

By September 1983, quarterly losses had reached $180.3 million, and its nine-month losses reached $536.4 million. The company ended the year with overall losses of $538.6 million on sales of $1.12 billion, half its previous year sales of $2 billion.

To stem Atari's losses, Warner brought in a new head executive who fired more than half the company's 10,000 employees. Nevertheless, costs could not be brought in line with revenues, and the company needed an infusion of further funds to pay for research on new products. Unable to support this continuing drain on its resources, Warner Communications began to look for a buyer for its failing subsidiary. In July 1984, the company announced that it had agreed to sell all Atari operations, with the exception of the small coin-operated arcade video game business and a new telecommunications venture, called Ataritel, to Jack Tramiel, a businessperson who had made his reputation as the head of Commodore International Limited, a computer company. The price for Atari was $240 million.

Three days after purchasing the company, Tramiel began his own aggressive effort to cut costs, laying off hundreds more employees and taking steps to collect outstanding funds owed to the company. Unable to sell unwanted video game cartridges, Atari dumped truckloads of them into a landfill in New Mexico. Tramiel installed three of his sons in top management positions, brought in former associates to fill other key spots, and made plans to raise funds through the sale of stock to the public. To Tramiel, Atari was poised to become a computer manufacturer to rival his previous company, despite the fact that its extant computer offering, the 800XL, was outmoded and less powerful than its competitors.

In January 1985, Atari unveiled two new lines of home computers, the XE series—an improved version of the old 800XL made cheaper by a reduction in the number of components and renegotiated contracts with suppliers—and the ST line—a cut-rate imitation of the Apple Macintosh, that used a color screen, fancy graphics, and a mouse in an effort to move in on the market for Apple computers in the home. By July, the 520-ST had started to make its way into stores. The computer arrived past schedule, with no advertising to announce its presence, and no software to demonstrate its capabilities. Many machines in the first shipment didn't work at all because microchips inside had been shaken loose in transit. Nevertheless, with a price of $799, the product initially seemed to have found a receptive public, with a large percentage of sales taking place in Europe.

Despite this good news, Tramiel continued to run Atari in crisis mode. The company's U.S. staff had shrunk to 150, and in May 1985, executives agreed to have one-third of their salaries withheld indefinitely. The company finished out 1985 posting a loss of $26.7 million.

By 1986, the industry in which Atari originally made its mark, video games, was beginning to show signs of life once again. This time, however, product lines were led by sophisticated, expensive Japanese equipment, sold by companies such as Nintendo and Sega. Atari re-entered the field with its old machine, the VCS 2600, which sold for only $40, and also introduced the 7800, a more advanced unit, which sold for twice as much. The company also began a modest advertising campaign for these products for the first time in two years. By the end of the year, these efforts, combined with Atari's home computer sales, had resulted in profits of $45 million, on sales of $258 million. With these strong results, the company was able to offer stock to the public for the first time in November 1986.

With these funds, Atari increased its advertising budget in support of new products it introduced. In 1987, the company began to market a clone of IBM's PC, priced at under $500, as well as a more sophisticated video game console, in addition to introducing products for the desktop publishing field. In October 1987, Atari purchased the Federated Group, a chain of 62 electronics stores based in California and the Southwest, for $67 million. Tramiel hoped that the stores could provide a good distribution outlet for Atari products, and he put his youngest son in charge of the chain. Operating in a depressed area of the country, however, Federated continued to lose money, and the company was forced to shut the stores after just one year.

At the end of 1987, Atari held 20 percent of the American video game market and relied on foreign sales of its home computers, which remained unpopular in the United States, for a significant portion of its income. Overall, the company earned $57 million, on sales that neared $500 million.

The following year, Atari once again allied itself with its founder, Nolan Bushnell, agreeing to market video games that he had developed. Furthermore, the company announced another big advertising push, in an effort to ensure that the video game crash that had threatened Atari in the early 1980s would not recur. Atari also turned to the courts in December 1988, charging that Nintendo's licensing policies monopolized the market. These moves reflected the continuing lack of demand for Atari's home computer products in the United States, as the company, hampered by its image as a toymaker rather than a high-tech powerhouse, fought for part of this highly competitive market.

In January 1989, Nintendo followed up Atari's suit with a countersuit charging copyright infringement, and by the end of the year, the dispute had reached the U.S. House of Representatives, whose subcommittee on anti-trust echoed Atari's charges. In November 1989, Atari continued its push into the game market by introducing a portable video game player called Lynx, which sold for $200, to compete with Nintendo's popular Game Boy. The company finished out the year with earnings of $4.02 million.

In the spring of 1990, Atari introduced its Portfolio palmtop personal computer. Early the following year, the company came out with a revamped, color Lynx product, and several months later it introduced new notebook computers. Despite these advances, however, Atari was in trouble. Sales of its home computers in Europe began to flag as the company faced increased competition, and in 1991 foreign sales collapsed. In the video games field, Atari's efforts to challenge Nintendo through legal means had been rebuffed, and the company was unable to regain significant market share from its Japanese competitors. By the first quarter of 1992, losses over a three-month period had reached $14 million.

In September of 1992, Atari took steps to stem its losses by cutting its research and development expenditures in half and closing branch offices in three states. The company hoped that the introduction of new products, such as the Falcon030 multimedia home entertainment computer would help to revive its fortunes. In addition, the company was working on a more sophisticated video game machine, called the "Jaguar." Nevertheless, 1992 ended with a loss of $73 million.

As Atari began to ship its Falcon030 system to stores in small numbers in early 1993, the company's fate was unclear. Decidedly, it was experiencing another severe downturn, and whether it could again rise to the challenge and become profitable remained to be seen.

Principal Subsidiaries: Atari (Benelux) B.V.; Atari Taiwan Manufacturing Corporation; Atari Computer Corporation; Atari Microsystems Corporation.

Further Reading:

Bernstein, Peter W., "Atari and the Video-Game Explosion," *Fortune,* July 27, 1981.

Hector, Gary, "The Big Shrink Is on at Atari," *Fortune,* July 9, 1984.

Machan, Dyan, "Cheap Didn't Sell," *Forbes,* August 3, 1992.

Petre, Peter, "Jack Tramiel Is Back on the Warpath," *Fortune,* March 4, 1985.

Shao, Maria, "There's a Rumble in the Video Arcade," *Business Week,* February 20, 1989.

——. "Jack Tramiel Has Atari Turned Around—Halfway," *Business Week,* June 20, 1988.

"Video Games Are Suddenly a $2 Billion Industry," *Business Week,* May 24, 1982.

"What Sent Atari Overseas," *Business Week,* March 14, 1983.

—Elizabeth Rourke

Automatic Data Processing, Inc.

One ADP Boulevard
Roseland, New Jersey 07068-1728
U.S.A.
(201) 994-5000
Fax: (201) 994-5495

Public Company
Incorporated: 1949
Employees: 21,000
Sales: $2.2 billion
Stock Exchanges: New York Chicago Pacific Philadelphia
    Boston
SICs: 7374 Data Processing & Preparation; 7372
    Prepackaged Software; 8721 Accounting, Auditing &
    Bookkeeping

The undisputed number one paymaster to the nation, Automatic Data Processing, Inc. prepares the paychecks for one out of seven American workers. The company, widely known as ADP, is also a leading supplier of stock quotation systems, handles the back-office processing for many securities brokers, and provides a variety of computerized services to auto dealers as well as claims service support for auto insurers and repairers.

The multibillion dollar operation owes its start to the fact that when the bright and innovative Henry Taub graduated from New York University in 1947, he was still shy of his 20th birthday, and thus more than a year away from eligibility for the CPA exam. Consequently, Taub, who had worked part-time for a small Manhattan public accounting firm while a commuter student at NYU, became a full-time employee. The work entailed keeping the books for dozens of small businesses, coupled with lots of handholding.

Taub soon became aware that preparing payrolls and maintaining the necessary supporting data were a major headache for smaller employers. Social security was as yet less than a dozen years old, and income tax withholding had only started during World War II. All in all, payroll accounting was becoming steadily more demanding.

So, in 1949, with the support of two business acquaintances, Taub opened a company to provide that specialized service. He called his new business Automatic Payrolls, Inc. As he readily recalled later, the "Automatic" defined the service only from the point of view of the client, who was spared many burdensome tasks; on the company's side, automation started with little more than an adding machine. Taub also noted the deeper significance of the carefully chosen name. In his hometown of Paterson, New Jersey, an old-line textile center where the automation of looms had long been a major issue, "automatic" carried the connotation of "an advanced form of work."

From a small office in Paterson, Taub solicited accounts in the surrounding area, often utilizing public transportation to pick up time sheets and return the finished payroll. During this time, Taub's company didn't handle the clients' money; signing the checks or placing cash in the pay envelopes was left for the employer to do on site. In 1951, Taub's younger brother Joe joined the organization, specializing in administrative functions for the next 25 years.

In 1953 the third member of Automatic Payroll's long-time guiding trio came aboard. He was Frank R. Lautenberg, the son of a Paterson textile worker. Three years older than Henry, Lautenberg served in Europe during World War II then earned an economics degree at Columbia University and became a sales trainee for Prudential Insurance. The local Prudential office was in the same Paterson building as Automatic, and he and the Taubs met occasionally at a nearby coffee counter. Since most of Lautenberg's life insurance sales calls took place in the evening, he found time to solicit business for Automatic during the day, and after a while joined the company full-time.

Henry Taub recollected: "We formed an effective trio, with complementary strengths—me in accounting, Joe in organization, and Frank in marketing—and very compatible in personality and business style." Eventually, Lautenberg succeeded Henry Taub as chief executive in 1975 and held that job until his election as U.S. senator from New Jersey in 1982. Henry Taub then became the company's honorary chairperson while remaining an active director and chairing the executive committee.

The young company kept adding customers in northern New Jersey and the New York City area, but progress was moderate. By the June 1957 fiscal year, operating revenues had grown to $150,000; profits for the entire year, however, were a mere $964. One factor was the switch that year from manual bookkeeping machines to an early IBM computer. Lautenberg later told *Investor's Reader* magazine that the punch card computer system "damned near killed us. It wasn't a very good improvement. Then we started developing techniques that enabled us to start working with computers."

With the new equipment, Automatic Payrolls also branched into some general data processing services such as analytical reports covering sales, costs and inventories, questionnaire tabulation, and even the maintenance of bowling league statistics. In 1959 the Taubs set up a separate company, Automatic Tabulating Services, to handle the general data processing business. Then, in June 1961, in preparation for going public, the payroll and tabulating companies were merged into the newly named Automatic Data Processing. At the time, ADP had about 200 payroll clients, including the cast and crew of the Broadway hit *My Fair Lady* and 30 general processing customers.

With only a modest $419,000 in revenues and $25,000 in net profits for the June 1961 year, ADP was very much of a "penny stock" when the first 100,000 shares were offered to the public in September 1961 at $3 a share. Henry Taub reflected: "Those first dozen years were our incubation period. We learned how to operate what was essentially a brand-new business." When it emerged from the incubator, ADP was set to mature. Starting with its first quarter as a public company, ADP managed an unbroken string of double-digit earnings per share growth—a string that encompassed 128 quarters as of the end of the 1993 fiscal year. Meantime, each share bought for $3 in 1961 had multiplied into 144 shares worth more than $7,000 by 1993.

Just prior to offering its stock on Wall Street, ADP went to Wall Street to drum up business. Encouraged by a couple of brokerage houses that were already payroll clients, ADP opened an office in downtown Manhattan in July 1961 to process "back office" data such as customer trade confirmations and related reports—the start of what was to become ADP's second most important line.

Buoyed by strong internal growth after going public, ADP was ready to speed its development through aggressive use of acquisitions by the mid-1960s. Since then, it acquired more than 100 companies or corporate units. However, management stressed that these acquisitions should serve as "catalysts" and not as "our main engine of growth." As Josh S. Weston, who joined the company in 1970 and became CEO in 1982, explained to security analysts, acquisitions were intended "to telescope time and risk in helping us pursue a strategic direction that we wanted to pursue anyway."

The acquisition drive got under way in 1965 when ADP broadened its brokerage business with the addition of Brokerage Processing Center and shortly thereafter expanded its payroll service with Payrolls for Industry of Long Island. Then, in 1967, Miami Beach-based Computer Services of Florida was purchased. This represented a significant geographic breakout, since ADP had effectively been limited to customers that could be served by its local pickup and delivery facilities, except for a handful of payroll clients whose requirements permitted mail communication (computer transmission of payroll data and checks was not yet possible). The Florida beachhead was followed by a flurry of other east coast acquisitions. Thereafter, the company acquired or established its way into other parts of the nation. By 1972 it operated centers in 20 cities from which it paid over one million people.

That year ADP acquired CSI Computer Systems of Cincinnati, which helped about 500 car dealers with their paper work. This led ADP into its third major line, which it called Dealer Services. Since then ADP vastly expanded both the concept and scope of these services. By 1993 it served more than 7,000 North American car and truck dealers, while 1,000 European dealers were added with the 1992 acquisition of Germany's Autonom Computer. While Autonom served primarily German GM/Opel dealers, ADP planned to add more European cars and countries.

In North America, ADP clients represented roughly one-third of all dealerships while accounting for over half of vehicle sales. Many used ADP-supplied computers and programs that elimi-nated preprinted forms—after blank sheets were inserted into the printer and pertinent data was entered, completed invoices emerged. Other programs handled scheduling for the repair shop or kept track of all data on showroom visitors (including their preferences and dislikes) to give sales staff a better shot at closing a deal. Some of the software used to show potential financing and insurance costs came under FTC attack in 1991 for allegedly making financing the car through the dealer seem cheaper than paying cash; ADP, while insisting that the pro-financing claims were "standard industry practice," agreed to remove the challenged segment. All in all, even though, as chairperson Weston quipped to stockholders in 1992, the U.S. auto industry nowadays "seldom has one good year in a row," ADP steadily increased its dealer business, which accounted for roughly 12 percent of total ADP revenues.

With the acquisition of Itel Corp.'s Autadex division in 1980, ADP began developing another auto-related business line, now known as Automotive Claims Services. Through a huge data base maintained in Ann Arbor, Michigan, that cataloged the components of virtually every model produced since 1970, adjusters and repair shop operators could instantly obtain detailed repair estimates, including parts and labor. In 1985 ADP added a Vehicle Valuation Service for cars that were stolen or "totaled." It also started a parts service showing price and availability of private brand and salvage yard parts. Moreover, in 1993, ADP undertook a minority investment in National BioSystems, which evaluated medical costs of accident victims.

Claims Service, whose clients included most of the major insurance companies, brought in about five percent of ADP revenues in the early 1990s. Since that time, it received less emphasis. In 1993, the "Other" group, which, along with Claims, counts such minor activities as network, general accounting, and wholesale distribution, as well as overseas payroll services (mostly Britain and the Benelux countries), registered six percent of revenues as opposed to nine percent in fiscal 1992. However, the "Other" contribution may have been somewhat understated because this category was also the place for certain corporate accounting adjustments.

Strongest growth in the early 1990s was in Brokerage Services, which produced 23 percent of fiscal 1993 revenues. ADP processed over one-fifth of the trades executed on Wall Street each day. Nevertheless, these back-office functions were eclipsed by ADP's presence in the front office. In 1983 ADP bought GTE's Telenet Information Services, which put it into stock quote machines, and three years later it acquired the Bunker Ramo quote machine operations. ADP was therefore in the forefront of the industry revolution that replaced "dumb terminals" with intelligent work stations that provided each individual broker not only with current stock quotations and market news but instant access to client account records, background data, and analysts' opinions on securities, as well as offering the capability to enter orders electronically. By 1991 ADP was the top provider of such information services. Some infringement disputes with previous industry leader Quotron (which became a Citicorp subsidiary in 1986) were settled in 1993 when, as part of a deal in which ADP bought Quotron's overseas stock quotation business, ADP obtained a permanent license to certain Quotron stock information software.

ADP entered the proxy distribution business in 1989. This segment sent out stockholder reports and proxy statements to investors whose stock was held in "street name" by brokerage houses, and then processed the returned proxy votes. In 1992 ADP acquired another major proxy distribution company, Independent Election Corp. of America. However, while the ADP service was directed at individual customers of brokerage houses, Independent dealt with large institutional holders. The difference in client groups and operating systems slowed the integration of the two proxy units, and, while net results were beneficial, this generated some embarrassing problems during the 1993 proxy season. ADP remained confident, however, that the glitches would be overcome, and the company was set for a smooth 1994 season.

By far the largest ADP business, with 59 percent of total revenues in 1993, remained what is now called Employer Services. The broadened title reflected the fact that, beyond payroll-related work, this sector offered such services as job costing, labor distribution analysis, management reporting, unemployment compensation management, human resources information, and personnel benefit services. In 1993, the core of this operation paid more than 16 million employees of some 275,000 employers and prepared all the related W-2 forms and other required reports, as well as all sorts of internal personnel reports for the employer. More than 75 percent of the payroll clients also used ADP's tax filing service (started in 1982) in which ADP handled the actual submission of tax payments to all levels of government. During this time, over 95,000 clients submitted their payroll by computer. ADP was also able to arrange the laser printing of paychecks on site, while an increasing number of payments were electronically deposited directly to the employee's designated bank account.

While traditional banking institutions were a major competitor for payroll services, ADP gradually acquired such payroll businesses, often arranging for the bank to remain the up-front marketing agent while ADP operated the service. The largest such acquisition (indeed, ADP's largest single acquisition ever) was the takeover of Bank of America's 17,000-client, $110 million revenue payroll business in May 1992. Interestingly, this deal was concluded just one month after Bank of America completed the merger of Security Pacific, another California banking giant whose payroll business had been acquired by ADP eight years earlier.

While ADP started out "helping those who couldn't help themselves" when it came to payroll automation, and it continued to derive about half its payroll revenues from firms with under 100 employees, large "national accounts" with over 1,000 employees were increasingly shifting to ADP from in-house installations. Here ADP benefitted from the almost universal belt-tightening mode at most major corporations, which became willing to outsource nonstrategic functions. Furthermore, the constant growth and change in regulations on both the federal and local level required unending adjustment in payroll software programs, and many companies found it easier to leave the adjusting to a specialist like ADP. The same logic applied in adjusting a program to fit all the many jurisdictions in which a national company retained employees. Furthermore, ADP offered great flexibility. For instance, it could take in ready stride the requirements of clients like H&R Block, whose payroll,

depending on the time of the tax year, fluctuated from 2,000 to 65,000 employees.

For all its business lines ADP set certain criteria. In order to realize economies of scale, the company preferred computing services that could be mass marketed and mass produced. ADP stipulated that its services should induce long-term client relationships with repetitive revenues, and should require enough specialization and know-how to raise barriers to entry by competitors and exit by clients.

Josh Weston also looked for what he called "a silent third force"—a set of conditions that provided a relatively uniform framework within which ADP could design its products. Thus, the IRS and the wage and hour laws set an overall pattern for wage payments, the SEC and the stock exchanges regulated the handling of securities transactions, and the auto manufacturers informed franchised dealers how to keep their records.

ADP also maintained, "it is a prime criterion for us in either starting up or later staying in a business that we think we have an excellent chance to be number one in that particular business." In September 1993 Weston told security analysts that ADP was assessing potential opportunities in four new data service markets, any one of which, if entry through a suitable acquisition could be arranged, might develop into a fourth major ADP line. The company's presumed target would be volume in the $200 million-plus range, or more than double the Claims Service peak.

Since the mid-1980s, ADP also actively engaged in "pruning," which it defined as having "sold, shrunken, or milked" various product lines or businesses that no longer, according to Weston, "fit our long-term strategic objectives." Among others, ADP sold a computerized tax processing business, its electronic funds transfer operation that serviced automatic teller machines, and its interest in a Brazilian payroll company. It also planned to simply shrink some businesses "where a smaller ongoing operation gives ADP a better return" than selling it, especially when a unit might continue to generate cash that could build up other operations. And while counting on outsourcing by other companies to feed its growth, ADP also used outsourcing when appropriate. Thus, in 1990 it arranged for IBM to take over the maintenance of its stock quote terminals.

Throughout its existence, ADP has used highly conservative accounting, with a strong cash position, low debt, and quick depreciation, allowing it to move into technologically advanced replacements without incurring big write-offs of the displaced equipment. This operating scheme permitted the longest string of consecutive earnings advances on the New York Stock Exchange, where the company arrived in 1970. ADP crossed the billion dollar mark in revenues in 1985 and topped $2 billion in fiscal 1993 when earnings reached a record $294 million. Dividends, while fairly conservative, were raised each year since payments started in 1974. Furthermore, the company was also convinced that room existed for further progress. In 1993, ADP noted that it still had only about a 15 percent penetration of the payroll market nationally and even in its New York-New Jersey home area only about 25 percent.

Insisting that ADP push toward continually higher goals, Weston cited the example of the pole vaulter who, even after all competitors have been eliminated, is made to try for ever higher jumps until he fails to clear the bar three times. Only after the inevitable final failure is the vaulter brought to the winner's stand. As Weston sought to inspire his company to ever greater efforts with the pole vault analogy, he concluded: "Since they're going to be recognized as winners anyway, asking them to jump an inch higher isn't dirty pool."

Principal Subsidiaries: ADP Credit Corp.; Brokerage Processing Center; Computer Services of Florida; CSI Computer Systems; Telenet Information Services; Independent Election Corp. of America.

Further Reading:

"Automatic Data Processing Hews to Winning Formula," *Wall Street Journal,* December 24, 1992.
"Payroll Specialist" *Investor's Reader,* July 26, 1972.
"Presentation on Automatic Data Processing by Josh Weston, Chairman and CEO, to The New York Society of Security Analysts," Roseland, New Jersey: Automatic Data Processing, Inc. September 13, 1990.
"They Make Money Paying Us," *Forbes,* January 4, 1993.
Weston, Josh, "Soft Stuff Matters," *Financial Executive,* July/August 1992.

—Henry R. Hecht

AutoZone, Inc.

3030 Poplar Avenue
P.O. Box 2198
Memphis, Tennessee 38101-9842
U.S.A.
(901) 325-4600
Fax: (901) 325-5122

Sales: $1.2 billion
Employees: 15,000
Founded: 1979 as Auto Shack
Stock Exchanges: New York
SICs: 5531 Automobile & Home Supply Stores

AutoZone is a chain of 783 auto parts stores that stretches across 23 states. Dedicated to serving the needs of the amateur mechanic, the company expanded remarkably quickly after its inauguration in Arkansas by an experienced retailer. With a premium on customer service as a touchstone of its corporate philosophy, AutoZone has become a major player in the automotive aftermarket in little more than a decade.

AutoZone was founded in 1979 by Joseph R. Hyde III as a division of Malone & Hyde, Inc., a wholesale food business founded by Hyde's grandfather in 1907. Joseph Hyde III had entered the family business at the age of 22 immediately after his graduation from college. His contribution was to develop a line of specialty retail chains. He began with drug stores, founding Super D Drugs at age 26, and then moved on to sporting goods stores, supermarkets, and finally, auto parts stores.

Hyde's first entry into this market came on July 4, 1979, when he opened his premier store in Forrest City, Arkansas. He named the outlet Auto Shack. The company had 25 people on its payroll at that time. To support further expansion, Hyde opened a 12,000-square-foot warehouse in Memphis, and by the end of the first year, seven more stores in Arkansas and Tennessee had made their debut.

The idea behind Auto Shack was straightforward. The company aimed to provide a wide selection of auto parts at a low price to "Do-It-Yourselfers"—what it referred to as the DIY market. In addition to these customers, the company identified a pool of potential buyers as "Shade Tree Mechanics," people who worked on other people's cars in their spare time as a source of extra income, and "Buy-It-Yourselfers," customers who bought parts and then hired others to install them, lacking the expertise to do so themselves.

To serve these customers, Auto Shack sought to establish quality and expert advice from employees as a hallmark of its business plan. In addition, the company sought to locate its stores in the neighborhoods where people who worked on their cars lived and to keep its stores open at hours when its customers were not otherwise occupied at work. Initially, this meant that many Auto Shack stores stayed open all night. Auto Shack stores were clean and bright, and the company emphasized friendly, helpful service. Company chairman Hyde himself spent one-quarter of his time visiting Auto Shack stores, garbed in a company uniform with name tag, to keep an eye on operations and to encourage employees to do their best.

In its second year of operation, Auto Shack added 23 more stores, branching out into five more states: Alabama, Kentucky, Missouri, Mississippi, and Texas. By this time, the company had started to hit its stride; it would go on to open a new store, on average, once a week, every week, for its first ten years in business. Before opening a new outlet, Auto Shack's research analysts spent thousands of hours looking at appropriate sites. The company's intended customer base was lower or middle-income men between the ages of 18 and 49. The company's ideal customer was a man who, both as a hobby and an economic necessity, spent a lot of time working on his car to keep it running much longer than ordinarily expected. Auto Shack estimated that the ever-rising cost of a new car, both in raw dollars and as a percentage of the average family's income, was a strong incentive for a large portion of the population to enter the market for replacement auto parts.

In addition, Auto Shack took note of the business practices of other successful retailing establishments of the South such as Wal-Mart, on whose corporate board Hyde sat for seven years. By selling a large volume of goods in a high number of stores serviced by central distribution centers, Auto Shack was able to keep its costs and prices low, providing the chain with a tremendous competitive advantage over smaller operations. In addition, the bright, modern, clean store interiors were a stark contrast with the dark, grimy aura some auto junk yards and other used car parts outlets projected.

By 1981 Auto Shack had opened 45 stores, and by the following year the tally was up to 74 stores, all within its core southern markets. By 1982 Auto Shack's Memphis warehouse had expanded to 96,000 feet, growth made necessary by the increasing number of Auto Shack outlets.

In 1983 Auto Shack expanded its size, maintaining 139 stores, and its geographical scope, adding outlets in Georgia, Arizona, Illinois, and Louisiana. By the following year, the number of Auto Shacks reached 200, and openings in Florida and South Carolina pushed the company's tally of states to 13. In addition, two more distribution centers were opened to serve the increasingly far-flung Auto Shack operations. Facilities in San Antonio and Phoenix brought the company's total warehouse space to 320,000 square feet.

In 1984 the leaders of Auto Shack's corporate parent, Malone & Hyde, decided that the company's stock was undervalued in the stock market. To milk the most value out of their properties,

Hyde and his fellow executives decided to take the properties private in a leveraged buy-out. To do this, they enlisted the help of the investment banking firm Kohlberg Kravis Roberts & Company, (known as KKR), which engineered the withdrawal of Malone & Hyde from the stock market. KKR was compensated with large blocks of Auto Shack stock. In effect, KKR became the owner of Auto Shack at this time.

Despite its new corporate status, Auto Shack continued to grow at a dramatic rate. In 1985 the company opened an additional 68 stores, moving into North Carolina. Along with its standard format stores, Auto Shack also inaugurated an Express Parts Service that rushed auto parts to customers who called in over a toll-free phone service line. In this way, the company was able to offer services to parts of the country that were not yet served by an Auto Shack store.

Auto Shack took another step toward upgrading customer service in 1986, when it instituted a life-time warranty on 42,000 separate parts that it offered. The company's philosophy on what products to offer was closely tied to its research into what customers desired. For some types of goods, Auto Shack stocked a wide variety of nationally known brands. Motor oil fell into this category. Surveys indicated that Auto Shack customers had a strong preference for private label oils, being more concerned about the perception of guaranteed quality than the lowest price.

For many other goods, however, research indicated that customers simply wanted the cheapest price possible. In general, this criteria applied to more expensive car parts, where brand names were little known. Auto Shack developed its own sources for these products, eliminating the middleman and the additional costs that a distributor brought. In this way, the company was able to offer a less expensive product to its customers. On this level, Auto Shack was structured like a vertically integrated business, although it had not taken on the complications of a manufacturing operation. The company's supply lines were directed by product managers, who visited factories and worked closely with suppliers to insure quality control on various parts. The company's high volume of sales made it possible for specialized efforts such as this to be efficient. In addition, Auto Shack's advertising department participated in the efforts to define and upgrade products, and then attempted to win new customers for them.

By 1986 these practices had allowed Auto Shack to expand to 339 stores in 15 states, as New Mexico was added. A new warehouse was also opened in Greenville, South Carolina. The company's telemarketing operation, Express Parts, logged its one millionth call, and an additional service, an Electronic Catalogue, was brought on line on October 1, 1986, at the company's Bellevue store in Memphis, Tennessee. This database, installed throughout all the company's stores, eventually grew to contain more than four million entries on parts for over 15,000 vehicles.

In 1987 Hyde divested himself of all parts of his family business, Malone & Hyde, except Auto Shack, the fastest-growing unit. For the first time, Auto Shack stood alone, apart from its corporate parent. As a symbol of its new identity, and to give the company's stores a slightly more upscale image than the word

"shack" implied, Auto Shack's name was changed to Auto-Zone. The company announced that this new moniker would apply to all 390 stores.

This process of conversion began in the following year. An outlet was opened under the new name in Enid, Oklahoma, marking the company's entry into yet another state. Overall, AutoZone had 470 stores in 16 states by the end of 1988, and served a total of 47.7 million customers in that year alone. In June 1988 the company unveiled its own line of auto products, developed by its product managers, under the trade name "Duralast."

The number of AutoZone customers for these and other products rose to more than 51 million by 1989, the year of the company's tenth anniversary. AutoZone sales topped $500 million. By this time, AutoZone had become the third-largest American auto parts retailer. To continue to build this growth, the company advertised aggressively on television, on radio (airing ads in Spanish and Navajo, as well as English), and in newspapers.

In a symbolic gesture, AutoZone opened its 500th outlet, a store in Hobbs, New Mexico, on July 4, the precise date it had opened its first store ten years earlier. By the end of the year, 14 more stores had been added and all of the store facilities were known by the company's updated name.

Under this name, AutoZone diversified its outlets to include regular stores and Superstores. The first of these larger outlets was opened in Memphis, Tennessee. The usual AutoZone store filled about 5,400 feet and cost $200,000 to construct, while the larger version cost about $70,000 more, and stocked about 5,000 more items. More than 50 Superstores had been opened by the middle of 1989. The largest of these, located in New Halls Ferry, St. Louis, Missouri, boasted a 17,368-square-foot selling floor.

By 1990 AutoZone had expanded into two additional states, opening stores in Utah and Indiana, for a total of 539 outlets. The company also broke ground for a distribution center in Lafayette, Louisiana, to serve its expanded geographical operations, and introduced another line of its specially manufactured items, Deutsch filters. In addition, AutoZone opened its first 8,100-square-foot prototype store, in Santa Fe, New Mexico.

In April 1991 AutoZone ended its tenure as a privately held company when it re-entered the public market, as shares were offered for sale on the New York Stock Exchange. The 3.2 million shares offered produced a large paper profit for the company's primary owner, Kohlberg Kravis Roberts & Company. Under the structure of the stock offering, KKR retained its ownership stake in AutoZone, as investment partnerships run by KKR retained 68 percent of the company after the public offering. AutoZone managers kept 16 percent of the company, and former managers retained another six percent, leaving ten percent for the public at large. With the ten percent of stock offered, AutoZone reduced bank and mortgage debt, and also invested in general company operations.

In the five months following AutoZone's stock offering, the price of the company's shares rose dramatically, fueled by enthusiasm for the company's rapid growth and financial prospects. In September 1992 KKR announced that it would sell an additional 2.3 million shares of AutoZone to the public in an effort to increase the company's financial liquidity and reduce the swings in the prices of its stock.

While AutoZone's financial fate was being determined on Wall Street, the company's operations and expansion continued apace. Its fifth distribution center, in Lafayette, Louisiana, was opened in 1991, as were an additional 53 stores, including the first outlets in Colorado.

Also in 1991, AutoZone introduced an electronic Store Management System that allowed prices to be bar-coded and scanned at check-out counters, thus speeding up customer transactions. In addition, the system allowed electronic credit card and check approval. It refined inventory control, and automated in-store accounting procedures.

In December 1991 AutoZone held its first shareholders' meeting, at which the company was able to announce that gross revenues had increased more than 20 percent in the previous year, to reach $818 million. Net income rose to $44 million, an increase of 89 percent.

Relying on demographics, which indicated that the Midwest contained a large pool of blue-collar workers who worked on their cars both as a hobby and to save money, AutoZone began to plot its expansion into this new area of the country. In 1992 the company upped its number of stores to 678, and made its first move into Wisconsin. Company sales topped $1 billion for the first time, allowing the company to continue its string of store openings without going into debt. More openings were made in another Midwest state, Michigan, in 1993. To distribute products to its new customers, the company opened a warehouse center in Danville, Illinois, its seventh such facility.

In 1993 the company's growth potential seemed virtually limitless. With stores spread across the southern United States, reaching up into the Midwest, the company serves a core group of customers by continued adherence to a proven merchandising formula. With more than a decade of spectacular growth behind it, AutoZone shows no signs of breaking down in the near future.

Further Reading:

AutoZone, Inc. Annual Reports, Memphis, TN: AutoZone, Inc., 1991–1993.
AutoZone, Inc. *Tune-In* newsletters, Memphis, TN: AutoZone, Inc., 1989–1992.
Neumeier, Shelley, "AutoZone," *Fortune,* December 2, 1991.

—Elizabeth Rourke

Avnet Inc.

80 Cutter Mill Rd.
Great Neck, New York 11021
U.S.A.
(516) 466-7000
Fax: (516) 466-1203

Public Company
Incorporated: 1955 as Avnet Electronics Supply Co., Inc.
Employees: 7,100
Sales: $2.24 billion
Stock Exchanges: New York
SICs: 5065 Electronic Parts and Equipment, Nec; 3674
    Semiconductors and Related Devices

Avnet Inc. is the largest distributor in North America of electronic components and computer products for industrial and military customers. The company consists of three major product groups: Electronic Marketing, Video Communications, and Electrical and Industrial. The Electronic Marketing Group handles assembly, processing, and marketing of electronic and electromechanical components and computer products for industrial and military clients. This group accounts for about 85 percent of Avnet's sales, with more than half the group's sales generated by its Hamilton Hallmark division. Avnet Computer Group accounts for about 15 percent of group sales. The Video Communications Group handles assembly and marketing of television signal processing and audio equipment, including home satellite antennas. The Electrical and Industrial Group distributes electrical insulation, magnet wire, electrical equipment, seals, electrical motors and parts, and industrial maintenance products. Its Freeman Products company manufactures and sells trophy components, engraving supplies, plastic injection moldings, and zinc diecastings.

Avnet, like other electronics distributors, buys components in volume from suppliers and stocks and resells them to original equipment manufacturers (OEMs). The distributors operate as a sales force for the suppliers, reaching OEMs the suppliers cannot reach cost-effectively. Although nearly 1,100 electronics distributors operate in the United States, the five largest account for more than half of the total distribution volume.

Avnet's predecessor was a small distributor of radio replacement parts founded by Charles Avnet in 1921 in lower Manhattan. Avnet and other entrepreneurs set up small parts jobbing operations in the basements or back rooms of their parts stores on Courllandt Street in New York to sell ham radio parts to ships and hobbyists in the early days of radio broadcasting, before commercial, battery-powered radios were available. "Radio rows" sprang up in New York and other major cities, and Avnet and the other dealers sold parts and made repairs, first on ham radios, and then as manufacturing developed, on commercial sets. As radio manufacturing grew, parts distribution also took off. During the 1930s, Avnet's company also manufactured automobile antennas and car radio kits.

When World War II started, radio parts became important to the war effort. Since production of home radio sets was prohibited, radio shop owners began selling parts to government and defense contractors instead of consumers. During this time, Charles Avnet and his son Lester established Avnet Electronic Supply Co.

After the war, the company concentrated on buying and selling surplus electronic and electrical parts. A significant contract with Bendix Aviation Corporation helped Avnet's sales soar, and the company opened a second warehouse in Los Angeles, soon becoming an authorized jobber and assembler of electrical connectors for Bendix. In 1955, the company incorporated as Avnet Electronics Supply Co., Inc., and by the end of the year Avnet had sales of $1 million and a net loss of $17,000. In 1958, the company became Avnet Electronics Corp.

At the same time, other companies that would become key elements in Avnet's development were being launched; some of their founders would go on to become top executives at Avnet. In 1948, Leon Machiz and partner Seymour Schweber invested $3,000 each to start Life Electronics Sales, which sold surplus connectors. The company prospered, but eventually the two split up, and Machiz founded Time Electronics. With the start of the space program in the late 1950s, Avnet, Time Electronics, and the other electronic distributors thrived.

Anthony Hamilton, a buyer for Lear, Inc., went into business for himself in 1957 as a GE-franchised distributor of tantalum capacitors. Sales for Hamilton Electro Sales reached over $1 million in the first year and more than doubled the next year. In Texas, a Westinghouse manager, Jack Turpin, opened Hall-Mark, which first became a Motorola franchise. Many other distribution companies also opened all over the country.

In 1960, Avnet made its first acquisition, British Industries Corporation, and gained a listing on the New York Stock Exchange. That year, Avnet had sales of more than $4 million and net income of $1 million. Avent's acquisitions during this time included Hamilton Electro Corporation in 1962, Fairmount Motor Products Co, Inc. in 1963, and Valley Forge Products, Inc. in 1964. Under the agreement between Avnet and Hamilton, the companies remained autonomous; Hamilton bolstered Avnet's strong connector business with semiconductor technology and, in turn, Hamilton expanded its program nationwide.

In 1964, Avnet Electronics became Avnet, Inc. to reflect its diversification into other areas, including audio turntables and electric motors. Upon the death of Charles Avnet that year, Lester became the company's president and chairperson. Other executive roles were filled by Simon Sheib, who became an Avnet director and the treasurer of British Industries Corp.,

Avnet's first acquisition. Anthony Hamilton, the president of Hamilton Electro, was made an Avnet director and company vice-president. Net sales in 1964 reached $57.5 million with earnings of $3 million.

The 1960s continued to be a period of acquisition, and Avnet purchased Guarantee Generator & Armature Co. in 1965, Channel Master Corporation in 1967, and Brownell Inc., Carol Wire and Cable Corporation, and Machiz's Time Electronic Sales in 1968. Regarding the Time Electronic acquisition, some claimed a conflict of interest, as Time Electronic was a distributor for Cannon, while Avnet distributed for rival Bendix. To accommodate the two rival suppliers, Machiz and Avnet kept their two companies separate and independent.

By the end of the 1960s, Avnet was among the top three electronics distributors in the nation with diversified interests in five areas: electronic marketing, consumer products, wire and cable, automotive, and electrical and engineering.

Lester Avnet died in 1970 and was succeeded by Simon Sheib as chair and chief executive officer. With the country in a recession, 1970 was a tough year for Avnet. The company also struggled to absorb the many acquisitions of the previous decade, and net earnings dropped. Avnet arranged new financing, cut overhead, and eliminated dividends for a year. Sheib and Hamilton also combined Avnet Electronics with Hamilton Electro to form Hamilton/Avnet, which along with Time Electronics, became Avnet's Electronic Marketing Group, headed by Anthony Hamilton. Under Hamilton's leadership, the Electronic Marketing Group became the first nationwide electronic components distributor and the first to distribute semiconductors, integrated circuits, and microprocessors.

In 1971, after two years of declining earnings, Avnet experienced an increase in earnings. This turnaround was accomplished in part by eliminating the profit drain caused by Channel Master's OEM color picture tube business. While consumer products had been the leading segment of Avnet's business for decades, in the early 1970s, the Electronic Marketing segment came on strong, and by 1973 it accounted for the highest sales in the company. Company officials attributed this in part to the consolidation of the Hamilton Electro and Avnet Electronics divisions. Earnings for the year were $21.7 million. During this period, Intel Corp., a new company that had brought out the first microprocessor, signed Hamilton/Avnet as a distributor, thus providing the opportunity for Avnet to become involved in the computer business.

Avnet's sales soared, reaching $225 million in 1974. The next year, however, recession and backlogs brought huge sales and earnings declines in the entire industry. Most distributors, including Avnet, were overstocked, as suppliers met monthly quotas by shipping to distributors. Most severely affected by recession at Avnet were its two leading groups—consumer products and electronic marketing.

During 1975, however, not only did the company recover, but it showed record earnings of more than $35 million. That year, Hamilton/Avnet and supplier Intel entered the hi-tech systems market, and Avnet was soon also selling computer peripherals and then complete systems and software. In 1979, Avnet hit the $1 billion mark in sales and had profits of $54 million, with the

Electronic Marketing Group accounting for almost $30 million of those earnings. In 1980, Hamilton became chair and CEO of Avnet when Sheib died. The following year, Avnet acquired peripherals distributor Loonam Associates and a 50 percent share of Computer SuperStores. Two years later, Avnet was generating sales of $1 million a day in computer-related products.

However, in the early 1980s the country was once again experiencing economic recession, and earnings for the Electronic Marketing Group declined. In 1982, Avnet sold its wire and cable businesses. Nevertheless, confident that its new computer lines would prove profitable, the company purchased Sertech and FMI in the custom chip and microcircuitry businesses and set up Avnet Development Labs to develop satellite and cable TV equipment.

During the 1980s, CEO Hamilton, known as a superb salesperson, helped Avnet become the leading industrial distributor in the United States because of his innovative approach to the industry. Hamilton led Avnet until he died of cancer in 1988 at the age of 64, and he was succeeded by Machiz.

The early years of Machiz's term were challenging. The industry was caught in another nationwide recession, which called for new strategies. Like other major distributors, Avnet substantially reduced its inventories to save money. Through centralization of inventories eliminating redundant facilities and personel, it cut inventory costs from $567 million in September 1988 to only $457 million two years later. It continued to cut inventory in 1991 by another $20 million to $30 million.

Machiz also made plans to further cut operating costs by centralizing operations—setting up hub locations and shifting personnel from branch office operations to field sales support positions. Although Hamilton/Avnet had split its organization into computer systems and electronics in 1988, Machiz conceded the next year that the restructuring was not well timed and had proved more costly than expected. By 1993, however, Avnet had streamlined its distribution system from about 100 storage facilities to three mega-warehouses in order to serve its more than 130,000 customers. Inventory in those facilities was computer controlled, as was purchasing.

Avnet also announced plans to merge its Avnet Computer Technologies Inc. and Hamilton/Avnet Computer divisions, closing about 20 branches and laying off management and support personnel. The decision was triggered by sluggish demand for systems and vendors' unhappiness with their product lines being split between two operations.

With customers reducing the number of suppliers they dealt with, product quality and service became a major concern in the industry. In 1989, Avnet instituted quality programs to improve customer service and boost profits. Improved service was expected to cut down on returns and the higher operating costs incurred when mistakes were made.

By 1992, the ten largest distributors in the country controlled 71 percent of the market, up from 58 percent in 1980. Avnet had endured several years of disappointing financial performance but came back in 1992 with $1.76 billion in sales. That performance accounted for an 18 percent share of the U.S. electronic components distribution market. Sales by its Electronic Marketing Group accounted for 80 percent of Avnet's earnings and revenues.

In 1993, Avnet acquired Hall-Mark Electronics Corporation, a rival distributor, for more than $344.6 million. Hall-Mark was the third largest distributor in the country—behind Avnet and Arrow Electronics Inc.—and, through its Allied Electronics division, was among the largest catalog distributors of electronic components in the United States. Avnet predicted that combined sales of Avnet and Hall-Mark would top $3 billion in 1993. With this acquisition, Hamilton/Avnet, the largest member of Avnet's electronic marketing group, and the largest Avnet subsidiary, combined with comparable operations at Hall-Mark to form Hamilton Hallmark. Hall-Mark Computer Products was to operate as a subsidiary in the Avnet computer group, while continuing to function as a separate unit. With the addition of Hall-Mark Computer Products, Avnet's computer group gained new franchises, including Hewlett-Packard; Avnet already had franchises for Digital Equipment, Intel, NCR, Seagate, and Okidata.

Machiz considered the merger an important strategic move because manufacturers now expected higher levels of technical sales support along with a full array of value-added services. The special skills and technology needed to fill the manufacturers' requirements were only available to the best capitalized companies, according to Machiz. So the Hall-Mark acquisition gave Avnet the opportunity to strengthen its position in the marketplace, increase its customer base, and improve penetration of key markets in the United States and Mexico. The acquisition also made Avnet the only U.S. distributor to carry all of the top five American semiconductor lines.

The electronics components industry in the United States was enjoying a healthy expansion period that industry experts expected to last at least until the end of the century; large distributors were expected to benefit the most. Furthermore, Avnet was divesting itself of unsuccessful product lines and reducing its cost structure, making its future even more promising.

Avnet's Time Electronics business, which distributed connectors to military/aerospace and industrial original equipment manufacturers, was hurt by cuts in military spending in the early 1990s. To offset those losses, Time focused more of its energies on commercial distribution with good results.

During this time, many suppliers and customers wanted Avnet to have a stronger European presence, and during an 18-month period in the early 1990s, Avnet acquired three European distributors: F.H. Tec Composants of France, Nortec AB of Scandinavia, and Access Group, a British semiconductor distributor. In early 1993, Avnet acquired Electronic 2000 AG, which did business in Germany, Austria, and Switzerland, and announced its intention to acquire Adelsy, an Italian electronic components distributor. Although 90 percent of Avnet's 1992 revenues came from domestic sales, Machiz restated his commitment to global expansion, anticipating that the bulk of the company's growth through the end of the century would come from international trade. Because distribution in Europe was not nearly as centralized as in the United States, Machiz saw great opportunity to improve service and cut costs of overseas operations. He predicted that Avnet would reach $1 billion in international sales by the end of the century.

Principal Subsidiaries: Hamilton Hallmark; Avnet Computer Group; Time Electronics Inc.; Allied Electronics Inc.; Avnet E2000 (Germany); Avnet Access (UK); Avnet Composants (France); Avnet Nortec (Scandinavia); Avnet Adelso (Italy); Channel Master (U.S. and U.K.); Brownell Electro; Mechanics Choice.

Further Reading:

Bambrick, Richard, "The Barons of Distribution," *Electronics News,* January 25, 1982, Sec. 2, pp. 78 81.
"History of Distribution," *1983 Annual Report,* Great Neck, New York: Avnet, Inc., 1983, pp. 6–8.
McCreadie, John, "Avnet Takes Progressive Stance to Build Profits," *Electronic Business,* October 30, 1989, p. 70.
Rayner, Bruce C. P., "Avnet, Other Distributors Getting into the Groove," *Electronic Business,* October 16, 1989, pp. 199–202.

—Wendy J. Stein

Barnett Banks, Inc.

50 North Laura Street
Jacksonville, Florida 32202
U.S.A.
(904) 791-7720
Fax: (904) 791-7166

Public Company
Incorporated: 1930 as Barnett National Securities Corp.
Employees: 18,752
Sales: $3.27 billion (1991)
Stock Exchanges: New York
SICs: 6712 Bank Holding Companies; 6022 State
    Commercial Banks; 6021 National Commercial Banks

In 1993 *Business Week* magazine called Barnett Banks, Inc.,
"Florida's most dynamic bank." Jacksonville-based Barnett
was Florida's largest financial institution at the time, holding
the majority of single-family-home mortgages, 27 percent of the
state's deposits, and a large percentage of consumer loans. It
ranked 20th among banking organizations nationwide. Although Barnett had only entered Georgia's market in 1986, it
had become that state's ninth-largest bank by the early 1990s.
The holding company had 32 banks and 7 non-banking affiliates
in 235 cities, with over 600 offices in Florida and Georgia by
1993.

In 1877 banker William Boyd Barnett, his wife, and two sons
Bion and William D. moved from Hiawatha, Kansas, to Jacksonville, Florida. The Barnett boys hoped a mild southern
climate would benefit their mother's health. They could not
have known that their father would found what would become
Florida's largest bank. William B. established The Bank of
Jacksonville on May 7, 1877. By the end of the year, the
institution boasted $35,000 in capital. In 1888 the establish-
ment's name was changed to The National Bank of Jacksonville. The burgeoning bank outgrew its original building in 1897
and moved to a new headquarters the following year.

Son Bion became president of the family enterprise in 1903
after his father died. The family name became part of the
corporate culture in 1908, when the bank emerged from a reorganization as Barnett First National Bank of Jacksonville. The
growing institution marked its 50th anniversary by moving into
yet another new headquarters. When Bion celebrated the occa-

sion in 1927, he proudly recounted that the family-owned institution had endured epidemics, fire, freezes, and financial panics.

But an even bigger challenge loomed on the bank's horizon.
When some of Florida's financial institutions failed in the wake
of the 1929 stock market crash, the relatively secure Barnetts
formed Barnett National Securities Corporation, a bank holding
company. The new entity quickly acquired and reopened three
banks that had failed. Later, when President Franklin Roosevelt
scheduled a bank holiday for March 5, 1933, Barnett's officers
used an ingenious strategy to prevent a run on deposits. On
March 4, the bank hauled out all of its cash in denominations of
one-, five-, ten-, and twenty-dollar bills—nothing larger. All the
teller windows were opened, and employees were instructed to
count out each withdrawal slowly. As customers at the end of
the lines saw their friends and neighbors leaving the bank with
large bundles of bills, their confidence in the bank's liquidity
was restored, and many went home.

With its headquarters in the state capital, a military town,
Barnett First National's growth paralleled the city's development during World War II. And in the postwar era, when
Florida became a retirement haven, immigrating seniors
brought their savings and pensions to the state's financial institutions. Barnett stock was sold on a limited basis to the public
beginning in the mid-1950s, and in 1962 the shares were listed
on the Over-the-Counter Exchange.

Jacksonville attorney Guy W. Botts joined Barnett First National as president in 1963. He hoped to transform the essentially local entity into a statewide banking institution. The
vehicle for this metamorphosis was Barnett's 30-year-old holding company subsidiary, Barnett National Securities Corporation. Although Florida's unique banking law restricted Barnett
First National Bank from acquiring additional banks, when
Barnett National Securities became the group's parent company
in 1966, it was empowered to purchase other banks. Over the
course of the four years before 1970, the reorganized entity
acquired eight local banks and opened a ninth in Jacksonville.
Each of these subsidiary banks was a separate corporation composed of a single full-service banking office. Botts' strategy
worked so well and quickly that the holding company changed
its name to Barnett Banks of Florida, Inc., in 1969 to reflect its
statewide influence.

During the 1970s Barnett established the state's first credit card
franchise. The Barnett Computing Co. subsidiary was subsequently created to facilitate credit transactions. This expensive
undertaking helped the parent develop chainwide computerization before its competitors. The company founded many of its
nonbanking subsidiaries during this decade. In 1971 the Barnett
Mortgage Company subsidiary was formed, and many of the
company's subsidiary banks were renamed "Barnett Banks."
Barnett Winston Company, an investment vehicle, was formed
in 1972; Barnett Investment Services, Inc., Barnett Leasing
Company, and Barnett Banks Trust Company, N.A., began
operations the following year. Barnett also became the southeast's first bank to be listed on the New York Stock Exchange in
the early 1970s.

Charles E. Rice became Barnett's president in 1972. He had
been president of First National Bank of Winter Park, the first

bank acquired in 1966 by the Barnett holding company. Rice led the second wave of acquisitions—by 1975 Barnett controlled the largest number of banks of any holding company in Florida and had a market share of deposits of at least five percent in the state's eight largest cities; Barnett ranked second only to Southeast First National Bank of Miami. These acquisitions were made in spite of the brutal national recession of the mid-1970s and the Florida real estate crash. Barnett was duly proud that it had been able to pay quarterly dividends throughout this period, which promotional literature described as the "most severe financial crisis since the Great Depression."

As Barnett recovered in 1976, Florida's lawmakers revised laws that had prohibited branching. In 1977, the first year it was allowed (and coincidentally, Barnett's centenary), Barnett began to consolidate its more than three dozen individual banks and to open new offices. Four branches were launched that year, and nine more opened in 1978. Barnett worked to "blanket" Florida with branches: from 1978 to 1988, 230 branches were built.

Barnett grew much faster than its in-state competitors, and it was able to garner a dominant share of the market. The institution's strong position prepared it for the deregulation of the banking industry and the advent of regional interstate banking, which Florida's lawmakers approved in 1985. Unlike many of its rivals, Barnett was able to withstand the assault from outside banks—of Florida's top 15 banking companies in 1980, all but four were acquired by 1988.

And Barnett did not just hold its own. In 1986 the bank moved into neighboring Georgia with the purchase of First National Bank of Cobb County, a metropolitan Atlanta institution. Barnett dropped "of Florida" from its name, becoming Barnett Banks, Inc., in 1987. By the early 1990s, Barnett had made enough acquisitions to be Georgia's ninth-largest bank.

As interest rates dropped precipitously in the late 1980s and early 1990s, bank customers in all ranks sought higher-interest alternatives to standard savings. Barnett launched the Emerald group of mutual funds in 1988 to keep those customers "inside the Barnett family." And as the baby-boomer generation began to reach trust and private banking minimum income and net worth levels, competition to win their accounts intensified. Barnett joined a movement to merge trust and private banking. Prior to this time, private bankers had concentrated on gathering deposits, and trust departments had managed clients' investments. But in the 1990s many banks focused on providing their most affluent customers with a service-, rather than product-oriented, approach. The merger of these two departments provided the convenience desired by customers and encouraged officers in the two departments to share contacts.

Barnett was the subject of a class action suit in 1990 that charged that Barnett Equity Securities had distorted or failed to disclose vital information to investors. The case was settled out of court in 1992 through the issue of $1.25 million in common shares to the plaintiff class.

In 1991 the company announced that it would acquire CSX Commercial Services, a student loan holder, from CSX Corp. The $1 billion unit's name was changed to BTI Services. Barnett became the Florida student loan system's "Lender of Last Resort." Under sponsorship of the state's guarantor agency, the Office of Student Financial Assistance, Barnett distributed loans to students who had been denied by at least two banks.

Barnett purchased United Savings of America, a failed Florida thrift, in February of 1992. That May, Barnett also agreed to buy the 144 branches of First Florida Banks, the state's last large independent bank, for $800 million. While some analysts criticized the purchase as too expensive, Barnett justified the acquisition in terms of "synergies and data center consolidation," according to a 1992 *Computerworld* article. It hoped to consolidate and convert the two banks' check processing systems from a paper-intensive operation to one based on new imaging technology. The technology stored an electronic image of each financial document, so that a printout with over a dozen "checks" per page could be sent to the customer, rather than the physical checks themselves. Besides saving storage costs for customers (especially businesses) and banks, imaging reduced postage costs and streamlined the work flow. Barnett had already begun testing of Unisys Corp.'s InfoImage check processing imaging system at three of its check processing centers, and hoped to reap a return of 15 percent to 18 percent on its investments in the new technology.

Barnett's intricate and far-flung network of computerized branches, automatic teller machines, and offices was assaulted, along with the rest of south Florida, by Hurricane Andrew on August 24, 1992. Barnett's first challenges were to protect assets, locate employees, and try to conduct business at the affected branches. The bank had warehoused cash in anticipation of the storm, and had stockpiled 10,000 gallons of fuel at strategic locations for emergency generators. Barnett's disaster plan also included contracts with vendors to provide new ATMs, satellite dishes, and other emergency equipment. Contracted security officers provided 24-hour protection, and company recovery efforts were coordinated through a central command that worked with the Florida governor's office to set up temporary banking locations in the hardest-hit areas. Most major bank branches in the affected areas were reopened less than two weeks after Andrew struck.

Barnett was considered one of the more progressive banking firms in terms of employee child care and health benefits. In 1992 *Working Mother* magazine ranked Barnett Banks, Inc., among the 100 best companies for employees who were parents. The corporation had a child care center at its Jacksonville headquarters and arranged for discounted child care for employees at 600 branch offices. Barnett also established an on-site medical clinic to make health care services more convenient to employees. And while many U.S. businesses resisted passage of 1993's Family Leave Act, Barnett already had a similar policy in place.

By 1993, Barnett enjoyed deep market penetration within its home state: the institution's chief retail executive, Thomas B. Johnson, bragged that Florida offices were within ten minutes of 96 percent of the state's population. And although the company had itself grown through acquisitions, it found itself the frequent subject of takeover speculation. The lucrative and still-growing Florida market was one of the U.S. banking industry's most attractive. Analysts reasoned that such regional banks as

First Union Corp., NationsBank Corp., Sun-Trust Banks Inc., and Wachovia Corp. would try to acquire Barnett if the federal government lowered barriers to national banking during the 1990s. Barnett defended itself against such threats by maintaining high earnings and a high stock value.

Principal Subsidiaries: Barnett Bank of Alachua County NA; Barnett Bank of Central Florida NA; Barnett Bank of Highlands County NA; Barnett Bank of Jacksonville NA; Barnett Bank of the Keys; Barnett Bank of Lake County NA; Barnett Bank of Lake Okeechobee; Barnett Bank of Lee County NA; Barnett Bank of Manatee County NA; Barnett Bank of Marion County NA; Barnett Bank of Martin County NA; Barnett Bank of Naples; Barnett Bank of North Central Florida; Barnett Bank of Palm Beach County; Barnett Bank of Pasco County; Barnett Bank of Pinellas County; Barnett Bank of Polk County; Barnett Bank of South Florida NA; Barnett Bank of Southwest Florida NA; Barnett Bank of the St. Johns; Barnett Bank of the Suncoast NA; Barnett Bank of Tallahassee; Barnett Bank of Tampa NA; Barnett Bank of The Treasure Coast; Barnett Bank of Volusia County; Barnett Bank of West Florida; Barnett Bank of Atlanta; Barnett Bank of Fayette County; Barnett Bank of Southeast Georgia NA; Barnett Bank of Southwest Georgia; Barnett Banks Insurance Inc.; Barnett Banks Trust Co. NA; Barnett Card Services Corp.; Barnett Mortgage Co.; Barnett Recovery Corp.; Barnett Securities Inc.; CreditQuick Inc.; Creditquick Finance Co.

Further Reading:

Brammer, Rhonda, "Good Banks, Bad Banks," *Barron's,* September 9, 1991, p. 14.

Danielson, Arnold G, "Southern Banking: Life after NationsBank," *Bank Management,* September 1991, pp. 14–18.

DeGeorge, Gail, "A Southern Belle Not Looking for Suitors," *Business Week,* August 9, 1993, p. 65.

Freer, Jim, "Pacesetters Merging Trust with Private Banking," *United States Banker,* November 1992, pp. 51–54.

Hammond, Jairus K., "Regional Bank Reports: Good and Not So Good," *The Commercial and Financial Chronicle,* May 5, 1975, p. 8.

"High Rates Plus Rising Loans Equal Peak Net for Barnett Banks of Fla.," *Barron's,* September 11, 1978, pp. 39, 41.

"A Highflier Hits a Storm," *Business Week,* June 30, 1975, pp. 88–89.

Hoffman, Thomas, "Barnett Banks on IS Merger," *Computerworld,* June 8, 1992, p. 94.

"Investing in a Sales Culture," *Bank Management,* June 1993, pp. 30–37.

Jordahl, Gregory, "Banks Check Out Imaging," *Inform,* September 1991, pp. 20–23.

Marcial, Gene G., "The Hungry Eyes Looking at Barnett Banks," *Business Week,* March 29, 1993, p. 81.

Radigan, Joseph, "Sue You Blues," *United States Banker,* August 1992, p. 50.

Schram, Jamie, "Student Loans: Making the Grade?," *United States Banker,* August 1991, pp. 34–38.

Spooner, Lisa, "Golden Years Rich with Marketing Potential," *Bank Management,* June 1991, pp. 32–38.

—April S. Dougal

Bell and Howell Company

5215 Old Orchard Road
Skokie, Illinois 60077
U.S.A.
(708) 470-7100
Fax: (708) 470-9425

Private Company
Incorporated: 1907
Employees: 5,707
Revenues: $670 million
SICs: 3579 Office Machines; 7389 Business Services

Bell and Howell Company is one of the leading suppliers of equipment and services for information related services and products, including optical equipment, electronic instrumentation, business equipment, educational publishing, technical training, and micrographics. From the time of its original involvement in motion picture technology at the beginning of the twentieth century, the company has been at the forefront of technological development in the industry.

During the early years of the century, when Chicago was the center of the motion picture industry, Donald J. Bell worked as a projectionist in theaters around northern Illinois, where he became well acquainted with the equipment used for showing movies. As his interest in films and equipment grew, a friend helped secure him permission to use the machinist tools in the power house of Chicago's Northwestern Railway, where Bell remodeled an Optoscope projector and later modified a Kinodrome Projector. Bell met Albert S. Howell at the Crary Machine Works, where many of the parts for projectors were manufactured.

Howell was born in Michigan and traveled to Chicago to work in a machine shop that built and repaired motion picture projectors. In 1906 he applied for his first patent, a device that improved framing for 35mm Kinodrome motion picture projectors. With Bell's experience as a movie projectionist, contacts in the movie industry, and ready cash, and Howell's inventive genius and mechanical aptitude, the two men decided to start their own business. Incorporated with a capitalization of $5,000 in February 1907, Bell and Howell Company entered the business of manufacturing, jobbing, leasing, and repairing machines.

During its first year of business, over 50 percent of the new company's business involved repairing movie equipment made by other manufacturers. What made the company famous, however, was its development of equipment that addressed the two most important problems plaguing the movie industry at the time: flickering and standardization. Flickering in the early movies was due to the effects of hand-cranked film, which made the speed erratic. Standardization was needed as divergences in film width during these years made it nearly impossible to show the same film in any two cities within the United States. By 1908, Bell and Howell refined the Kinodrome projector, the film perforator, and the camera and continuous printer, all for the 35mm film width. With the development of this complete system, and the company's refusal to either manufacture or service products of any other size than the 35mm width, Bell and Howell forced film standardization within the motion picture industry.

In 1910, the company made a cinematograph camera entirely of wood and leather. When the two men learned that their camera had been damaged by termites and mildew during an exploration trip in Africa, they designed the first all metal camera. Introduced in 1912, the design 2709 soon garnered the reputation as "the most precision film mechanism ever made" and was produced for 46 continuous years. Following the relocation of the motion picture industry from Chicago to Hollywood, Bell and Howell's first movie camera was used in southern California in 1912. By 1919, nearly 100 percent of the equipment used to make movies in Hollywood was manufactured by Bell and Howell Company.

With business expanding rapidly, the number of employees at Bell and Howell increased from 18 to 85 over a few years. In 1914, Bell and Howell decided to permanently locate its offices on Larchmont Avenue in Chicago. In the midst of the company's success, however, internal problems began to emerge. While Howell supervised production, Bell acted as a company salesperson, a job that required many long trips. In order to meet the needs of a growing business during his absences, Bell hired Joseph McNabb as both bookkeeper and general manager in 1916. When Bell returned from one of his trips, he discovered that McNabb had made drastic changes in the operation of the company. While confronting McNabb, Bell accused Howell of acting as McNabb's accomplice. Bell gave them their last paychecks and fired them.

The following day, McNabb and Howell returned to the office and offered to purchase Bell's holdings in the company. McNabb brought with him Rufus J. Kittredge and Charles A. Ziebarth. Kittredge, McNabb's father-in-law, was head of a label manufacturing firm, and Ziebarth had been a former employee at Bell and Howell and a superintendent at the Chicago laboratory of the American Film Company. Both men had significant capital to invest in the company and years of management experience.

The purchase of Bell's interests in Bell and Howell amounted to $183,895. Having contributed an initial investment of $3,500 a little over ten years earlier, Bell was satisfied with the purchase price. Nevertheless, as he left, Bell told McNabb that the company was "a milked cow." Bell moved first to New York and then to California and was never again associated with the company except in name. With Bell's resignation as director and chairperson, four new officers were elected: Rufus Kittredge as president, Albert Howell as vice-president, Joseph McNabb as treasurer, and Charles Ziebarth as secretary.

By the 1920s, Bell and Howell's business was widely dispersed; two-thirds of all revenue came from the sale of cameras, camera accessories, punches, pilots and dies, and perforators. Hollywood was still equipped with mostly Bell and Howell products, and net sales had increased from $10,000 in 1907 to $338,500 by 1923, while profits were erratic. Nevertheless, the company opened branch offices in both New York and Los Angeles, and a new building was established in Hollywood.

Bell and Howell had expanded into the amateur movie market in 1919 when the company began developing 17.5mm equipment. In 1921 McNabb and Howell were invited to Rochester, New York, by George Eastman of Eastman Kodak to observe the experiments using 16mm reversal material. McNabb and Howell were impressed with the results and redesigned all the company's 17.5mm equipment to use the 16mm film. In 1923 Bell and Howell manufactured the first spring-driven 16mm camera, beating Eastman Kodak by two years. The demand for this camera was so great that, even at a price of $175, it was on back order until 1930. Over the next 20 years, almost two-thirds of all company developments were in the amateur field, and Bell and Howell equipment became prized for its lifetime guarantees.

Kittredge resigned as president in 1923, remaining to chair the board of directors until 1930. McNabb succeeded his father-in-law as president and led the company through the prosperity of the 1920s. Bell and Howell's growth necessitated larger facilities. Accordingly, the plant on Larchmont was doubled in size, and the company also opened its Rockwell Engineering Laboratory. From 1923 to 1929, the firm's net sales increased annually with a high point in 1925 when the percentage of profits to sales reached 39.9 percent.

After the financial collapse on Wall Street in 1929, Bell and Howell was forced to adapt its products and change its price structure to meet the economic conditions of the Great Depression. Net sales decreased between 1930 and 1933, and the company was operating at a deficit in 1932.

In spite of this financial setback, the company's department of product development and improvement remained highly active. In 1932, the Filmosound 16mm sound-on-film projector was introduced, and the company pioneered a zoom lens called the "Varo." Also that year, the automatic production printer as well as the motor drive and magazines on Eyemo cameras first appeared. Both a 16mm and 8mm perforator were manufactured in 1934, along with the 16mm continuous sound printer and the 8mm projector. In 1935, both the spool camera and the Bell and Howell developing machine were produced, while the turret camera and a title writer were brought to market in 1938. The following year, the 35mm non-slip sound printer was introduced. As a result of these product developments, Bell and Howell net sales rose to $2.7 million in 1936 and $4.8 million by 1939. Disappointingly, however, net profits generally remained unchanged.

The fortunes of the company improved dramatically with the onset of World War II. Contracts were made with the U.S. Army, Navy, and Air Force for defense materials. During these years, Bell and Howell developed the gun camera used to assess the accuracy of machine guns, the retriflector sight used in B-29 bombers, the flight simulator employed in training pilots, bombardiers, and navigators to use radar, and an adaptation of the Eyemo camera for military purposes. By 1945, sales amounted to $21.9 million, the highest in the company's history, while the number of employees increased to over 2,500.

The war years also ushered in changes for the company's management and employees. Howell resigned as chief engineer in 1939, and was appointed to chair the board of directors, where he served until his death in 1951. Charles Ziebarth remained with the company until his death in 1942. One year later, Bell and Howell created the Bell and Howell Employees Trust to provide for the retirement of its workers, and in the spring of 1945 the company decided to go public.

At the end of the war, Bell and Howell experienced a sudden drop in production for war materials, losing government contracts worth $9 million in 1945. Even though the company retooled its manufacturing lines for civilian products and introduced 12 new items from 1947 to 1949, including the Foton camera and various microfilm equipment, Bell and Howell was hit hard by a 40 percent decline in sales for the U.S. photographic industry. Net sales decreased from over $21 million in 1945 to $13 million in 1949, and the number of employees dropped by 30 percent.

One fortunate occurrence during these years was the purchase of the microfilm division of Pathe Manufacturing Company in 1946. This purchase provided the company with new product lines of microfilm equipment, including recorders, readers, and automatic feeders. Two years later, the Microfilm Division was selling products to Harris Trust, Firestone, Federal Reserve Bank of Chicago, and Continental Illinois National Bank.

After a long tenure as president of Bell and Howell, Joseph McNabb died in January of 1949 and was replaced by his hand-chosen successor Charles Percy. Percy, a graduate of the University of Chicago, had held a variety of positions in the company beginning in 1938. When he assumed the position of president and chief executive office at Bell and Howell, he was 29 years old.

The new president represented a marked departure from the past in both administration and public relations. As owner and president, McNabb had run the company as he chose; his word on financial matters and product development was final. Percy, on the other hand, was the first among equals in a newly created executive committee. Charged with the responsibility of making recommendations on policy, salaries, promotions, dividends, acquisitions, and a host of other issues, Percy did not possess sole authority to make decisions. In addition, not many people outside Bell and Howell knew who McNabb was or what he did. When the company went public, it was clear there was a need for someone with a flair for dealing with the media. Percy's speeches, interviews, and articles over the years of his presidency led to a rise in personal prestige and, consequently, a comparable rise in public esteem for Bell and Howell.

During the 1950s, the company continued to emphasize development and expansion of its product line, which eventually included inexpensive amateur equipment, tape recorders, and hi-fi phonographs. In 1951, Bell and Howell was awarded its first Oscar by the Academy of Motion Picture Arts and Sciences for technical achievement. Four years later, the 16mm Filmo 70 camera was adapted for Admiral Richard E. Byrd's journey to the South Pole. Other developments included the electric eye camera in 1956 and the first zoom lens to fit 8mm projectors in 1957.

Under Percy's direction, Bell and Howell also initiated an aggressive acquisition strategy. Its first purchase was the Three Dimension Company, a manufacturer of stereo equipment, slide projectors, and tape recorders. DeVry Corporation, a projector company, was also purchased during this time. The Inserting and Mailing Machine Company, maker of equipment for mail order firms, insurance companies, and banks, was acquired in 1958. With the purchase of Consolidated Electrodynamics Corporation, a research and development firm involved in aviation equipment, control systems, and electronic instrumentation, Bell and Howell sales increased to $114 million by 1960, while its staff grew to 7,590.

In 1960, the company's International Division was reorganized. Major acquisitions, manufacturing contracts, and licensing agreements during this time led to the sale and servicing of Bell and Howell products in 99 countries around the world. The success of the International Division was indisputable: in 1963 cumulative sales from the division jumped an amazing 67 percent over the previous year.

Increasingly active in public life and service, Percy resigned as president in 1963 but remained as chairperson until he was elected to the U.S. Senate in 1966. Peter G. Peterson assumed Percy's responsibilities in 1963 and became company chair when Percy relinquished that title. Since 1958, Peterson had served as the company's executive vice-president, head of the Photo Products Division, and chair of the Bell and Howell corporate research board.

Continuing Percy's strategy of expanding the company's product lines through acquisitions, in 1966 management purchased DeVry Technical Institute, Inc., a training school for students in motion pictures, radio, television, and electronics. The following year, Charles E. Merrill Publishing Company was acquired, as was KEL Corporation, a manufacturer of radio communications equipment. New products were also coming from Bell and Howell's own research and development programs. A thermal spirit copier-duplicator was developing in 1964, and a Super 8mm movie camera was completely automated and introduced in 1965. One year later, a zoom lens system was designed for the Surveyor I spacecraft, and language materials that facilitated instruction in speech correction and remedial reading were developed in conjunction with Bell and Howell Language Master equipment.

Under Peterson, the company's accomplishments rivaled those recorded during Percy's leadership. Developments in photographic equipment and business machines, work in software materials for the educational field, expansion into space exploration technology and instrumentation, and the growth of the international operation led to a 1970 sales figure of $297.7 million with net profits of approximately $11 million. However, profit margins for many products were much lower than expected, and the aggressive diversification strategy resulted in an assortment of entirely unrelated holdings—over 20 divisions were offering products and services that ranged from high-tech vocational classes to military binoculars.

In January 1971, Peterson joined the Republican administration of President Nixon and was soon appointed Secretary of Commerce. His successor was Donald N. Frey, who held a Ph.D. in metallurgical engineering from the University of Michigan and represented the first engineer to hold the position of chief executive officer at Bell and Howell. Charged with the responsibility of pruning the company into a more efficient and profitable shape, Frey got rid of Bell and Howell's movie camera business and its consumer products business, including its trademark sound/slide projectors and famous 8mm cameras, as well as a host of other marginally profitable businesses. He then made microimagery and mail sorting, two previously tangential operations, the focus of Bell and Howell's product development.

By the early 1980s, Frey was confident he had turned the company around; from 1983 to 1984 operating earnings increased 33 percent to $24.6 million, and sales grew 11 percent to $679.2 million. Bell and Howell's mail-handling equipment operation and its vocational schools, especially DeVry Institute of Technology, expanded and generated significant sales. Furthermore, Bell and Howell had received Academy Awards for its motion picture program tape punch and modular film printer in 1975 and 1981, respectively. However, the company's microimagery division, which provided nearly 30 percent of the company's total sales, had developed into a "cash cow" with a projected annual sales growth rate of five percent; the market for microfilm had reached its peak and was saturated with competing products. Moreover, Frey had mistakenly held on to many businesses long after they had lost their profitability. Most importantly, however, by 1986 Frey had made 37 acquisitions, only one of which he could point to with satisfaction. Despite Bell and Howell's growing financial problems, compounded by 15 years of continuous acquisitions and divestitures and the high turnover of its management, Frey predicted that his restructuring strategy would succeed.

In 1986, however, Gerald Schultz, trained as the successor to Frey, was named president of the company. And, as revenues stalled in 1988 at $600 million, Schultz became part of the management group that joined forces with Texas financier Robert M. Bass to undertake a $678.4 million leveraged buyout of Bell and Howell. Contributing $82.3 million of the funds for the buyout, Bass assumed control of the company, appointed Schultz chief executive officer, and privatized the entire operation. After the acquisition, the company immediately began to sell what it described as "non-core" businesses in order to raise the money necessary to pay off the buyout debt. In September 1989, the company sold its textbook publishing division, Merrill Publishing, formerly one of its core businesses, for $260 million to MacMillan, Inc.

Schultz resigned at the end of September 1989, fueling speculation about the disagreement over product development between himself and Bass. In 1990, William J. White, formerly president and CEO of Whitestar Graphics, Inc., a business forms company, was hired by Bell and Howell as its new chief executive. As Bass and White worked together, Bell and Howell slowly developed into an information management business, with an emphasis on manufacturing mail processing systems and providing micrographics services as a republisher of newspapers, periodicals, dissertations, and books on microfilm. Once an illustrious example of innovation in the motion picture industry, Bell and Howell faced several challenges as it strove to become a prosperous information management business in the 1990s.

Further Reading:

Robinson, Jack, *Bell and Howell Company: A 75-Year History,* Chicago: Bell and Howell, 1982.

Simon, Ruth, "What, All Kidding Aside, Is New," *Forbes,* October 20, 1986, pp. 88–91.

Toy, Stewart, and Zachary Schiller, "Bob Bass May Have to Settle for a Quick Profit on This One," *Business Week,* October 9, 1989, pp. 48–50.

—Thomas Derdak

Best Buy Co., Inc.

7075 Flying Cloud Drive
P.O. Box 9312
Eden Prairie, Minnesota 55437
U.S.A.
(612) 947-2200
Fax: (612) 947-2422

Public Company
Incorporated: 1966 as Sound of Music Inc.
Employees: 16,000
Sales: $2.1 billion
Stock Exchanges: New York
SICs: 5722 Household Appliance Stores; 5731 Radio, TV &
   Electronics Stores; 5734 Computer & Software Stores;
   5735 Record & Prerecorded Tape Stores; 5946 Camera &
   Photographic Supply Stores

One of two powerhouses among consumer electronics retailers, Minnesota-based Best Buy Co., Inc., dominates the central U.S. market through a network of more than 150 stores in 18 states. The company's arch-rival is Virginia-based Circuit City, with $3.6 billion in sales and strongholds on both the east and west coasts. By 1993 both superstore titans had virtually vanquished the remaining competition, which included such former number two retailers as Highland Superstores (forced to liquidate) and Dixons Group's Silo Holdings (forced to downsize and sell to Fretter Inc.). Best Buy's recent growth has been nothing short of spectacular. From 1989 to 1992 corporate sales rose annually by 23 percent, while the industry as a whole expanded by a yearly average of just 3 percent. From 1992 to 1993 revenues catapulted for the first time beyond the $1 billion mark, from $929 million to $1.6 billion, for an increase of 74 percent. During this same period, net earnings soared 107 percent to just under $20 million. Although Circuit City is a significantly larger and more stable company in the eyes of investors, with a history of wider profit margins and negligible debt, it is Best Buy that has generated the most excitement on Wall Street. For the first half of 1991, Best Buy outshone all other New York Stock Exchange stocks in percentage appreciation. However, with excitement comes volatility: in 1993 the stock nearly doubled within a three-month period but then dropped by 10 percent in a single day in mid-November. Part of this roller coaster pattern is due to Best Buy's increasingly heated battle with Circuit City, which has many analysts wary. In the notoriously competitive

industry of consumer electronics, Best Buy has proven itself an expert player. The only question that remains is whether two giants can remain healthy at the top of the heap, as each tries to usurp market share within the other's established domain.

Best Buy is the brainchild of the company's founder, chairman, and CEO, Richard M. Schulze. In 1966 Schulze and a partner opened Sound of Music Inc. in an attempt to capture a share of the Twin Cities' home and car stereo retail market. First year sales reached $173,000. Four years later Schulze bought out his partner and proceeded to expand his retail chain; his product line, however, was limited to audio components until the early 1980s. Then, according to an Executive of the Year cover story for *Corporate Report Minnesota,* Schulze said, "the lights began to turn on." Writer S. C. Biemesderfer explained: "Schulze had come to realize that there wasn't much of a future in a market glutted with vendors, serving a shrinking audience of 15- to 18-year-olds with limited resources." His ability to alter the course of his company was enhanced by a week-long management seminar he attended in 1981. Departing the seminar as a "reformed controller," Schulze saw the dynamic possibilities that lay ahead and turned them into reality.

His first step was to expand Sound of Music's offerings to include appliances and VCRs. Schulze saw sales quickly climb. In 1982 revenues reached $9.3 million; the following year the company renamed itself Best Buy and firmly oriented itself toward an older, broader, and more affluent customer base. Then, in 1984, Schulze took another major step by introducing the superstore format and quickly capturing 42 percent of the local market. At the time the company operated just eight stores in the Midwest, but by 1987 this number had tripled, while sales and earnings had spiraled upward to $239 million and $7.7 million, respectively. In addition to greatly expanded warehouse size and product offerings, the superstore format meant significantly smaller margins in order to maintain its good service-low prices image.

Of course Best Buy was not alone among upstart chains during the 1980s in capitalizing on the superstore format and such hot-ticket consumer items as VCRs. "But after a raft of these chains went public," wrote Mary J. Pitzer in 1987, "they expanded rapidly and began colliding head-on. As a result, many companies took a beating on profit margins and are now gravely wounded." It was, in a very real sense, the best of times and the worst of times for Best Buy. Although sales had practically doubled to $439 million in fiscal 1988, net earnings had declined by 64 percent. Price wars were the chief culprit, and they were still escalating to a frenzied pitch in Best Buy's core Twin Cities market, which Highland had boldly entered in early 1987.

For a while, both companies benefited from market share increases, if not profit gains, by the battle. Then, finally, a saturation point was reached, with too many stores in the same area competing for the same dollars. According to Biemesderfer, "Rumor had it that, as Best Buy limped into the fall of 1988 Schulze tried to sell his company to Sears and failed because of his demands for certain perks." Biemesderfer went on to write that "Schulze denies the allegation, but to this day, even his backers question his version of the story." Schulze's own explanation was that "At no point in time were there ever any concerns or fears about the future of the company. . . . Our discussion with Sears Roebuck was simply an attempt to understand the interest they would have in supplying capital necessary to grow the company independently.''

Despite the earnings downturn in fiscal 1989 (net profits for the year ending March 31 slumped 26 percent, to just $2 million), and the looming presence of Highland, revenues were still climbing, albeit more slowly. In Schulze's mind, the key to regaining the momentum of the mid-1980s was to stand out from the competition, for the average customer recognized little difference among superstores, with their discount prices, multiple-step purchase processes, commissioned salespeople, and ubiquitous service plan and extended warranty packages. Schulze's answer? Concept II stores.

The unveiling of Best Buy's first Concept II stores in 1989 was the culmination of a daring new advance by Schulze. The idea behind Concept II was that the traditional superstore format was largely out of sync with the needs or preferences of most shoppers. Shoppers were entering electronics discount stores with only a limited need for sales help and a desire for hassle-free buying (no service plan contracts, no waiting for merchandise from the back room, no switching from counter to counter). Thus the revamped Best Buy stores would feature well-stocked showrooms averaging around 36,000 square feet; fewer salespeople; more self-help product information; Answer Centers, for those requiring personal assistance; and one-stop purchasing. As a veteran Best Buy analyst, quoted by Biemesderfer, has proclaimed: ''Concept II is the most innovative thing to happen in this industry—ever.'' The revenue Best Buy sacrificed in de-emphasizing service plans was compensated for by lowered employee costs. Stores without commissioned sales help were now able to operate at two-thirds of the work force required in the past.

In April 1991, even before Best Buy had gotten around to converting its 10 Twin Cities stores, loss-ravaged Highland exited the metropolitan area, conceding defeat and closing all six of its stores there. Best Buy itself reported a loss of $9.4 million for fiscal 1991, but this was due to a $14 million change in its method of accounting for extended service plans. From fiscal 1992 to fiscal 1993, Best Buy reported ''the best financial performance in the company's 27-year history.'' In addition to its stunning increases in revenues and earnings, the fast-growing retailer opened 38 new stores and saw comparable store sales (sales from stores open at least 14 months) increase by 19.4 percent.

During the calendar year 1993, Best Buy opened 9 more stores in Chicago, for a total of 23, to solidify its leadership position in the Midwest and also entered the key Circuit City markets of Atlanta and Phoenix with an additional 13 stores. Numerous other openings, including a small number of megastores

(40,000- to 50,000-square-foot self-service warehouses emphasizing the emerging growth lines of prerecorded music and computers), brought Best Buy's tally to 151 stores by year-end 1993. At that point, the only internal factor seriously saddling the company was a hefty 43 percent debt-to-capital ratio. However, Best Buy's ''push'' distribution system, in which products are automatically shipped to outlets based on computer analysis of past sales trends; its rapid turnover time; and its expectation of rising sales per store indicated that the company could hold its costs while continuing to expand.

Its greatest concern for the future was the bottom line impact of Circuit City's latest moves. Just as Best Buy had looked to the outer corridors of the country, Circuit City had looked inward. It, too, had embraced Chicago, where price wars began anew. The Virginia company also had plans to enter Kansas City, Missouri, and the Twin Cities in 1994. Whether the two would be able to operate side-by-side for long was unknown. Whatever the case, the stakes were high, not only for the companies but for related retailers and manufacturers. Such high-image manufacturers as Mitsubishi had already retreated from both store chains, complaining of poor price and sales support. And, wrote Berss, ''the last thing retailers need this Christmas—the biggest selling period of the year—is a price war. But that's what they're getting.'' The obvious winner in all of this? The consumer, by sheer happenstance. Then again, maybe it's by design.

Further Reading:

Apgar, Sally, ''Best Buy Planning to Spend $5 Million to Upgrade Stores in Twin Cities Area,'' *Star Tribune,* March 31, 1993, p. 1D; ''Best Buy Files for New Stock Offering,'' *Star Tribune,* April 21, 1993, p. 1D.

Berss, Marcia, ''High Noon,'' *Forbes,* December 20, 1993, pp. 44–45.

''Best Buy Co.,'' *Wall Street Journal,* January 9, 1992, p. B8.

''Best Buy Inc.,'' *Chain Store Age Executive with Shopping Center Age,* December 1992, pp. 64, 66.

Biemesderfer, S. C., ''Laughing Last (Executive of the Year: Richard M. Schulze),'' *Corporate Report Minnesota,* January 1992, pp. 33–42.

Kennedy, Tony, ''Best Buy Predicting Flat Earnings for First Half,'' *Star Tribune,* June 17, 1993, p. 3D; ''Sales at Best Buy Coincide with Rally of Its Stock,'' *Star Tribune,* July 9, 1993, pp. 1D, 7D.

Marcotty, Josephine, ''Best Buy Co. Stock Takes a Beating as Possible Price War with Circuit City Looms,'' *Star Tribune,* November 12, 1993, pp. 1–2D; ''Best Buy Earnings Soar 114 Percent for Quarter,'' *Star Tribune,* December 17, 1993, p. 4D.

Pitzer, Mary J., ''Electronics 'Superstores' May Have Blown a Fuse,'' *Business Week,* June 8, 1987, pp. 90, 94.

Sullivan, R. Lee, ''Appealing to the Technophiles,'' *Forbes,* April 27, 1992, pp. 52, 54.

—Jay P. Pederson

Bindley Western Industries, Inc.

4212 W. 71st Street
Indianapolis, IN 46268
U.S.A.
(317) 298-9900
Fax: (317) 297-5372

Public Company
Incorporated: 1968
Employees: 450
Sales: $2.9 billion
Stock Exchanges: NASDAQ
SICs: 5122 Drugs, Proprietaries & Sundries

Twenty-five years after starting his operation in borrowed basement space, Bill Bindley has built Bindley Western Industries, Inc. into the fifth-largest distributor of pharmaceuticals, health care products, and beauty aids in the United States. One of the owner's most gratifying moments came in 1990 when *Fortune* magazine recognized the company as second best in the country in revenue-per-employee. That year Bindley Western took in a little more than $2 billion in sales and employed 429 people, resulting in $4.7 million per employee.

In 1865 Bindley's great-grandfather founded E.H. Bindley & Company. Located in Terre Haute, Indiana, the company provided pharmaceuticals to independent corner drug stores. By 1941, the year Bill Bindley was born, Bindley Company was thriving as a small, well-respected drug wholesaler to local hospitals and apothecaries.

After graduating from Purdue University in 1961 with a degree in industrial management, Bindley decided against joining the family business and signed on as a management trainee with Brunswick Corporation. Not long afterward, he switched firms and began working in the finance department of Controls Company of America where he remained until 1965. The same year, at his father's request, Bindley finally joined the management team of the family business.

Recognizing the beginning of a new era of chain drug stores and the myriad possibilities for expanding the family operation, Bindley approached his father for support for his ideas. However, the father was more conservative than the son and refused to allow him to use the family resources for any risky ventures that might threaten the stability of the company.

Bindley accepted his father's decision, but after three years with the family firm, he began to tinker with ways to create his own company. Unable to convince his family to provide him with start-up capital and unable to borrow money from local banks, Bindley decided to raise the needed cash on his own. By mortgaging his house and selling some equity in a real estate development in Aspen, Colorado, Bindley was able to raise $50,000. He asked his father if he could use the basement of the family's company building in Terre Haute and opened Bindley Western Industries with an employee, a truck, and a driver.

Even though both Bindley and his family were in the same business and potential competitors for the same market, there was no resentment between him and his father. In fact, the two men reached an amiable agreement: Bindley's enterprise would exclusively target the burgeoning new market of wholesale drug distribution to chain stores, while the family business would continue the tradition of selling to the local, independent drug stores.

Bindley's family was acquainted with Bud Hook, the president of Hook's Drug Stores during that time, and a stroke of good luck allowed Bindley to study Hook's purchasing methods as well as which items he chose to warehouse. Bindley devised a plan to purchase pharmaceuticals at a lower price, provide better service, and better turn-around time. He soon signed a contract with Hook, and Bindley Western Industries had its first major customer.

In 1973, Bindley Western had grown large enough to move from the basement in Terre Haute to corporate office space in Indianapolis. The founder had established a market niche for his company by implementing a simple strategy—take over the service load for pharmaceutical manufacturers and reduce the price of purchasing drugs by allowing chains to buy products from Bindley Western on a more cost-effective basis than if the manufacturer itself handled shipping, replenishing inventory, and warehousing. By 1975 the company had reached $100 million in sales.

One crucial factor in the company's success was its ability to develop technology in order to help its customers manage inventory, reduce lead time, and make pharmaceutical purchases more efficiently. No drug manufacturer, even if it were willing and able to sell directly to drug stores and hospitals, could match the rates of Bindley Western and other distributors. In spite of the fact that profit margins were very thin, the company's automated distribution system allowed it to become the lowest-cost provider in the industry. With a growing reputation as the most efficient wholesale distributor in the pharmaceutical industry, long-term relationships were established with companies such as Hooks, Eckerd, Rite-Aid, Revco and CVS. In 1977 Bindley Western entered the ranks of the top ten drug wholesalers in the United States.

When his father retired in 1979, the family decided to sell E.H. Bindley and Company. Since the business was no longer run by relatives, Bindley felt released from the constraints of competing with his own family. As a result, he began to develop his firm into a full-service pharmaceutical wholesaler. With approximately $15 million in capital expenditures, Bindley Western began distributing non-perishable foods and health and beauty aids in addition to selling wholesale drugs. The time had also come to expand the firm's markets from chain drug stores to independents and other retailers.

In fifteen years Bindley Western grew from $50,000 in startup capital to sales of $440 million. In 1983 the company went public and revenues began to soar with internal growth. Other positive factors were an industry compounded growth rate of 15 percent since 1980, the increasing reliance of manufacturers on drug wholesalers, and the aging of America. Soon Bindley Western was the fifth-largest drug wholesaler in the country.

The transition from a private to a public company, and the demands of an accelerated growth rate, forced a turnover in upper management in the early 1980s. Many of the individuals who were with the firm from the beginning no longer fit into the management style suitable to a larger firm. Much more problematic, however, was the FBI investigation that started in 1985. Three employees of the company, two of whom were designated board members, were accused of "illegal drug diversion" and of accepting kickbacks from vendors in return for placing orders with those vendors.

The FBI determined that there were no other individuals involved in criminal behavior besides the three employees initially identified and declared the company itself free from blame. The charge of illegal drug diversion was proved wrong; the individuals had bought drugs from legal secondary suppliers. However, they were found guilty of accepting kickbacks and avoiding income tax. Fired by Bindley Western in the summer of 1985, two of them went to prison and the third committed suicide

Bindley Western stock dropped dramatically from $17 to $6 per share. Financial analysts wondered how the company, and Bindley himself, would deal with the scandal. As sales continued to grow—from $626 million in 1985 to $1 billion in 1987—Bindley Western's stock began to recover slowly. Since no customers had been lost during the crisis, and the company's ability to provide efficient service continued unabated, business resumed as usual. Yet the investment community remained wary. Finally Bindley realized that the company's reluctance to reveal information during the drug diversion scandal had been a public relations fiasco. Bindley Western immediately implemented a credibility campaign that was aimed at rehabilitating the company's image and reassuring the investment community.

With the acquisition of Stamford Drug Group in 1987, Bindley Western aggressively entered the direct store delivery market of the wholesale pharmaceutical industry. Direct store delivery includes sales to supermarkets, hospitals, independent drug stores, health maintenance organizations, and home health care sites. Comprising all the sales outside the chain warehouse market, the growth of direct store delivery sales also produced profit margins from three to six times higher than drug store sales did, leading to a consistent streak of higher annual earnings. As the company inaugurated a coast-to-coast distribution network the same year, Bindley Western was proud to announce that it had surpassed the $1 billion sales mark.

The wholesale drug industry experienced rapid consolidation from 1982 to 1992, and by the end of the ten-year period, seven firms, including Bindley Western, controlled 80 percent of the $40 billion market. By employing coast-to-coast distribution networks and centralized data processing, these firms have tried to build economies of scale in order to offset razor-thin profit margins.

Bindley Western exemplifies many trends in the pharmaceutical industry. In 1990, the company posted $2 billion in sales, but net earnings of $9.7 million. In 1992, the company reported sales of $2.9 billion, while net earnings increased to $12.8 million. High profit margins are not endemic to the wholesale drug industry, but with cutting-edge technology and distribution efficiency, Bindley Western created substantial earning potential.

Automation contributes to the company's distribution efficiency. Computerization enables Bindley Western to keep the number of its employees low while providing the tools necessary to replace inventory without high warehousing costs. The days when a customer picks up the phone and calls to place an order are long gone. At Bindley Western, placing an order involves communication through the use of hand-held, portable, electronic ordering equipment. Larger customers communicate by means of a mainframe-to-mainframe computer network, and all payments are done by means of electronic fund transfers. And due to the efficiency of the company's inventory system, it doesn't have to stock large quantities of products. By maintaining a smaller inventory which turns over 30 times a year—in contrast to the industry average of eight—Bindley Western significantly reduces the costs related to warehousing in its fourteen sites across the United States.

Continually searching for new and more profitable markets, in 1992 Bindley Western focused on alternative care delivery. The market for alternative care involves shipping pharmaceuticals, such as new biotechnology drugs, to places other than drug stores or hospitals. A new AIDS drug will be shipped directly to an individual's home, while innovative cancer drugs will be shipped directly to the cancer clinic that makes the request. The acquisition in March of 1993 of a Florida-based pharmaceutical wholesaler that sells dialysis and cancer drugs over the phone, Charise Charles Ltd., fit into this market strategy.

Bindley Western, along with the entire drug industry, suffered when newly elected U.S. President Bill Clinton attacked pharmaceutical companies by accusing them of profiteering, a scheme that involves increasing drug prices much higher than the rate of inflation. Although most drug companies denied the charge, Clinton's accusations raised the issue of a federal control on drug prices. Such legislation would have an adverse effect on Bindley Western because the majority of the company's revenue comes from prescription drug sales.

The owner was nevertheless optimistic about the company's future as Bindley Western Industries celebrated its twenty-fifth anniversary in 1993. Bindley predicted that health care reform would help his firm more than hurt it, especially if Clinton included prescription drug coverage as part of the minimal package of nationwide health insurance benefits. This would translate into larger sales for drug wholesalers, a scenario Bindley envisioned with hope.

Further Reading:

Hamilton, Dennis, ''Managing the Margins,'' *Indianapolis C.E.O.,* June 1991, Reprint.

Neumeier, Shelley, ''Bindley Western Industries,'' *Fortune,* September 23, 1991, p. 122.

Shaffer, David, ''Bindley Western Looks to the Future,'' *Indianapolis Star,* May 2, 1993, Business Section, pp. 1–2.

—Thomas Derdak

BISSELL

BISSELL, Inc.

P.O. Box 1888
Grand Rapids, Michigan 49501
U.S.A.
(616) 453-4451
Fax: (616) 453-5203

Private Company
Incorporated: 1883
Employees: 2,500
Sales: $320 million
SICs: 3589 Service Industry Machinery Nec; 3635
   Household Vacuum Cleaners

BISSELL is best known for its line of mechanical carpet cleaners. These devices, which predate electrical vacuums by 50 years and continue to defy obsolescence, helped build BISSELL into a diversified homecare company. In addition to carpet sweepers, BISSELL Homecare manufactures deep cleaning machines, vacuums, and cleaning agents. The BISSELL Graphics division designs, manufactures, and markets a wide range of custom printed business forms, specialty tags, labels, and other printed products. Finally, the BISSELL Healthcare division markets over 8,000 patient-assist, rehabilitation, orthopedic treatment, and therapeutic products.

The BISSELL carpet sweeper was developed in 1876 by Melville R. Bissell, who operated a crockery store with his wife, Anna, in Grand Rapids, Michigan. The Bissells received most of their fragile glass and china shipments in crates packed with sawdust, which often spilled onto the floors in their shop. In sweeping up the wood shavings, Mr. Bissell kicked up dust that got into his rugs, prompting him to invest in a carpet sweeper. These devices, which had been available since 1858, used floor wheels to drive rotating brushes that swept dirt out of the pile in rugs. While not perfect, they were infinitely more effective than brooms.

Bissell purchased a model called the "Welcome," but he noted several deficiencies in the design, and endeavored to develop a better model. The BISSELL design also used floor wheels to drive a brush, but on an improved reduction gear. The bristles bent slightly as they brushed through the carpet. When they rotated off the floor, they sprung whatever debris was in their path up into a compartment. The dirt could be emptied by simply opening the top of the box and shaking it over a garbage can.

Soon, many of the shop's patrons were asking where they could buy this carpet sweeper, which they had seen work so effectively on sawdust, and Bissell began to wonder if his carpet sweeper was a marketable product. Anna Bissell had no doubt about the product. She eloquently noted that because Americans were clean in mind and body, the carpet sweeper would serve the cause of responsible living while reducing the strain and drudgery of housekeeping.

Melville Bissell couldn't deny his wife's logic, or the many customers asking about the sweeper. Beginning to see the device as nothing less than a revolution in housekeeping, Bissell cleared a space on the second floor of their crockery store for an assembly shop, where he supervised a small staff of workers. His wife collected brushes from cottage industry homemakers who were enlisted to assemble them.

The Bissells conducted their own sales visits, choosing to distribute their product through housewares retailers rather than through door-to-door salesmen. It took several months, but Anna Bissell succeeded in getting skeptical shopkeepers to purchase and display the carpet sweeper.

The device performed well in in-store demonstrations, and word of mouth quickly established a strong demand for the product. Soon the Bissells were turning out thirty carpet sweepers a day and shipping them to retailers throughout Michigan, the Midwest, and Eastern states.

The Bissells stumbled onto an effective new sales tool when a young BISSELL bookkeeper named Claude Hopkins suggested a change in the sweeper's sales brochure. He argued that schematic diagrams and other mechanical details were of less interest to the consumer than the fashion aspects of the product. Hopkins's brochure focused on the "*golden* maple, *opulent* walnut and *rich* mahogany" used to make the BISSELL sweeper.

The company's directors feared that Hopkins's approach undersold the technological superiority of the product: every aspect of the sweeper was patented, and the company vigorously sued those who infringed on its design. But they couldn't deny the fact that Hopkins drastically boosted sales of the carpet sweeper. Inspired, Hopkins drew up a pamphlet promoting a limited edition of the device made from vermilion, a rare and exotic wood transported out of the jungles of India on the backs of elephants and floated to port on rafts. The stunt produced more sales in six weeks than the company had been able to muster in a year. Hopkins, who developed the strategy of promoting the carpet sweeper as a Christmas gift, later joined a Chicago advertising agency, where he built a career as one of the first masters of his art.

Melville and Anna Bissell incorporated their company in 1883, and built a new factory for making carpet sweepers. They also bought out two competitors, the Michigan Carpet Sweeper Company and the Grand Rapids Carpet Sweeper Company, but only to raid them of their managerial talent.

Soon after the new five-story BISSELL plant was completed, it was leveled in a fire. Melville Bissell mortgaged his entire personal fortune, including his home and his stable of horses, to finance a reconstruction. Shortly after production resumed, it was discovered that the factory's entire output was defective. In order to protect the brand name, Bissell ordered the recall of every defective model, at a cost of more than $35,000.

The BISSELL name had become so well established by 1889, and had such a strong reputation for quality, that few competitors dared to challenge it. But tragedy struck that year when Melville contracted pneumonia and died at the age of forty-five. When Anna Bissell took control of the company, she became one of America's first female executives.

After taking over for her husband, Anna decided to build BIS-SELL into an international brand. The company already had agencies in 20 foreign countries, but its penetration was light. Even though Europeans were more meticulous housekeepers, they had fewer carpet sweepers than Americans.

BISSELL salesmen in England held public demonstrations of the product, gently proving that the carpet sweeper could clean even the most delicate rugs. The big break came when Queen Victoria allowed the BISSELL sweeper to be used in her palace. Following the royal example, thousands of English homemakers ordered their own sweepers. Soon the practice of carpet sweeping became known generically as "Bisselling."

Anna Bissell remained head of the company into the 1920s, when a new threat to the business emerged. Household electrification swept aside gas lights, hand cranks, and foot pedals and paved the way for hundreds of new appliances, including the vacuum cleaner. Bissell, however, remained confident that the public would not overcome its fear of the strange new power source for many years. She recognized electric vacuum cleaners as unforgiving monstrosities that were capable of shredding frail carpets and expensive Oriental rugs. Many models shorted out through misuse, causing terrifying flashes and even fires. BISSELL's greatest asset at this point was the carpet sweeper's well-established position in the retail network. By contrast, vacuum cleaners were sold by door-to-door salesmen, who had reputations as boisterous, imposing cheats.

As better models were developed, vacuum cleaners were accepted in more homes. In addition, vacuum manufacturers gradually eased their way into retail channels, where they made the BISSELL carpet sweeper look ancient by comparison. In order to avoid losing its place in the market, BISSELL introduced its own electric vacuum cleaner, with motorized brushes and a fan blade for sucking up dust. BISSELL vacuum cleaners, like others on the market, were loud and clumsy and kicked up dust.

Convinced that a market remained for the carpet sweeper, BIS-SELL continued to make improvements to its product line. Earlier innovations included better bearings and a handle that adjusted the sweeping pressure on the brushes. With a design that debuted in 1928, the cleaner automatically adjusted the height of the brushes to different surfaces.

Melville Bissell, Jr., took control of the company from his mother by this time. During the Great Depression, few people had money to spend on an expensive electric vacuum, so they opted for the BISSELL carpet sweeper. As demand for vacuums weakened, causing many manufacturers to go out of business, BISSELL decided to discontinue building electric models.

Bissell believed that the carpet sweeper had a unique place in the home. Where electric vacuums could be used for heavy duty cleaning, the carpet sweeper would be favored for quick touch-ups, in the same way a broom might be used to sweep up a small mess. To reinforce a peaceful coexistence between the two devices, BISSELL emphasized the ease and convenience of using the carpet sweeper instead of a vacuum cleaner for small jobs around the home, and for cleaning the patio, the pool area, and the cottage. There was a place in every home for the lightweight, inexpensive, and portable carpet sweeper.

World War II naturally curtailed production of consumer products. At BISSELL, the raw materials for making a carpet sweeper, including rubber, aluminum, and wood, were diverted for military production. As a manufacturing organization, BIS-SELL was melded into the military procurement system and given the task of building a variety of light industrial implements.

After the war, with newfound prosperity and a rapidly increasing standard of living, vacuums became a fixture in every home. In England, the practice of carpet cleaning became known as "Hoovering." The company re-established its European franchise by building—or in some cases rebuilding—factories and distribution facilities in Britain, France, Germany, Ireland, and Switzerland. To these were added sites in Canada and Australia, making Bissell a truly international name.

Melville Bissell III, a nephew of Melville Jr., took over leadership of the company in 1953. Unlike his uncle, this Melville Bissell was determined that the Bissell name should stand for more than just mechanical carpet sweepers. He saw the company's market as "floor care," and later, complete home care. Bissell was aware that the carpet sweeper was effective only for topical dirt. Conventional vacuum cleaners, which BISSELL had continued to avoid, could only brush up dirt in the top quarter-inch of a carpet. A more thorough cleaning, down to the nap of a carpet, would require wet shampooing. He ordered the development of a new product called the Shampoomaster, a non-electric device that used only water and detergent. The Shampoomaster was manufactured from 1957 to 1967 and during those years was promoted ahead of BISSELL's carpet sweeper.

The company's revenue grew five-fold over this period, but only because of a burst in demand for the carpet sweeper. Sales of the Shampoomaster floundered because few homes were large or consistently dirty enough to warrant shampooing. The device was discontinued, and the company turned back to its traditional carpet sweeper line. In addition, in 1960 BISSELL had introduced the "stick vac," a lightweight vacuum that could be handled like a broom. The BISSELL stick vac competed with similar models built by vacuum cleaner manufacturers Regina and General Electric. BISSELL also acquired the Ohio-based Wood Shovel and Tool Company in 1965. The firm manufactured more than 300 different garden implements, but after only three years all but the company's snow shovel line was spun off.

In 1970 BISSELL purchased a Swiss electric shaver company. But when European currencies were allowed to float in 1973, manufacturing costs skyrocketed. BISSELL sold all of the company's assets, but kept an electric motor technology which was developed into a headlight wiper motor for BISSELL's French subsidiary RIAM S.A. In 1971 BISSELL entered the printing industry by taking over the Michigan Tag Company, which was renamed BISSELL Printed Products. A second firm, Imperial Business Forms, was acquired by BISSELL, and was followed by two more firms, Atlas Tag & Label and Marion Manufacturing, all of which are now part of BISSELL Graphics.

John M. Bissell, a cousin to Melville III, assumed leadership of the company in 1971. Unlike Melville, he believed that the company should not risk losing the business it knew first: floorcare. In his mind, the center of that business was the carpet sweeper. Based on that business, BISSELL focused its acquisitions on new ways to protect and grow its floorcare business. BISSELL purchased the Penn Champ Company, a manufacturer of aerosol cleaners and fabric shampoo, in 1974. Hoping to provide retailers with an entire family of BISSELL floor care products, the company developed another token line of vacuum cleaners and in 1980 re-introduced the carpet shampoo concept, but as a simple household wet extraction device called The Carpet Machine.

In 1981 BISSELL rolled out a second wet carpet cleaner called "It's Magic." The product contained no pump (the part most likely to fail on such devices), but drew its water pressure from a sink faucet. While the wet carpet cleaner filled out the BISSELL line, it performed below expectations and was phased out of production.

Resuming its diversification in 1976, BISSELL purchased Venturi, Inc., a manufacturer of plant foods and other organic products. In 1978 BISSELL purchased the Atlantic Precision Works, a manufacturer of kitchen warming trays, and relocated the factory from New York to Grand Rapids. BISSELL later added two other companies to the operation, Slip-X Safety Treads, a bathroom mat maker, and the E&B Company, which made flag poles and clothesline supports. Eventually BISSELL sold off all of these operations.

BISSELL acquired the Fred Sammons Company of Chicago in 1982. Involved in the manufacture of self-help aids for the disabled community, Sammons sold primarily to institutional markets until a new Enrichments line was established for individuals. To support sales of these products, BISSELL created a small network of retail stores under the same name, which it placed in shopping malls. By the early 1990s, Sammons products were largely sold via direct-mail catalogs.

BISSELL's diversification was necessary, not because of weakness in the floor care segment, but because the floor care market had stagnated. John Bissell told the *Grand Rapids Press,* "If we're going to achieve the growth rate we want, we'll have to do it through acquisitions." BISSELL acquired Chicago-based Maxi Vac, Inc., a maker of wet/dry vacuum cleaners, in 1982, boosting its manufacturing and research capabilities in the deep cleaning market. In 1985 BISSELL introduced a three-in-one vacuum cleaner, intended for use on stairs and on the second level of homes, where a heavy vacuum cleaner would be less practical and more cumbersome. In 1992 the company rolled out a new carpet shampoo device called the BISSELL Promax (since renamed Powerlifter due to a copyright battle with Hoover). This was followed a year later by another product with more attachments and capabilities, called the BISSELL Big Green Clean Machine.

The BISSELL Big Green Clean Machine was promoted through the much-maligned but effective medium of the "infomercial." While the ad harkened back to the sweeper demonstrations of the 1880s, BISSELL risked damaging its good name in such an ad. Nevertheless, the infomercial gave the BISSELL Big Green Clean Machine a more successful launch than other mediums might have. In fact, a smaller version of the device, the BISSELL Little Green Clean Machine, was introduced the same way in October 1993.

While the deep cleaning machines replaced the carpet sweepers as the core BISSELL business, the carpet sweeper remained a large portion of BISSELL's business. The sweeper continued to be promoted as an essential accessory to be used daily, like a broom, to sweep up small messes before they are stepped on and ground into carpet. By contrast, the use of a vacuum was portrayed as a greater household chore.

Despite competition from Royal and Hoky, BISSELL maintained a commanding lead in the market for carpet sweepers in the early 1990s. The company accounted for about 70 percent of domestic carpet sweeper market and about 40 percent of the international market. In addition, BISSELL manufactured carpet cleaners and a variety of carpet and upholstery cleaning products.

Principal Subsidiaries: BISSELL Ltd. (Canada); Penn Champ, Inc.; Barcolene, Inc.; BISSELL Homecare (Overseas), Inc.; BISSELL Housewares (England); BISSELL S.A. (France); BISSELL Ireland; BISSELL-Sabco (Pty) Ltd. (Australia).

Further Reading:

"Bissell, Inc. Finds Niches—and Grows," *Grand Rapids Press,* June 2, 1985, p. G1.
"The Bustling Business of Bissell," *Michigan Business,* September 1984, pp. 40–42.
"More 'Filth' on TV," *Advertising Age,* February 3, 1992, p. 10.
Powers, David Cleary, "Bissell Carpet Sweepers," *Great American Brands,* New York: Fairchild Publications, 1981.

—John Simley

Blockbuster Entertainment Corporation

One Blockbuster Plaza
Fort Lauderdale, Florida 33301
U.S.A.
(305) 832-3000
Fax: (305) 832-3901

Public Company
Incorporated: 1982 as Cook Data Services
Employees: 37,000
Sales: $2.1 billion
Stock Exchanges: New York, London
SICs: 7841 Video Tape Rental; 6794 Patent Owners and
   Lessors

Blockbuster Entertainment Corporation is the world's largest movie video rental store chain, with over 3,000 outlets in 10 nations. Founded in Texas as an alternative to small, local operations with limited selection, the company branched out in the early 1990s to include other elements of the entertainment industry, including family entertainment centers and music retailing.

Cook Data Services, Inc., was founded in 1982 by David Cook to supply computer software services to Texas's oil and gas industry. When the industry went bust, the company was left without a strong customer base. Cook was searching for another source of revenue when his wife, Sandy, a big movie fan, suggested the video rental business.

Looking into the industry, Cook learned that the video rental field was highly fragmented. Most stores were relatively modest family operations that carried a very small selection of former big hit movies. Providing a large selection of movies required a large investment of capital, since distributors typically charged approximately $70 per tape. In addition, tapes were generally not displayed, but kept behind the counter to discourage theft, and had to be fetched and laboriously signed out before the customer could leave. Cook saw that operations could be greatly streamlined by a computerized system for inventory control and check out, something his software background had prepared him to develop.

After Sandy Cook had conducted several months of research into the video rental industry, David Cook sold his oil and gas software business to its managers, and entered the movie rental

business. In October 1985 Cook opened the first Blockbuster Video outlet in Dallas. With 8,000 tapes, covering 6,500 titles, it had an inventory many times larger than its nearest competitor. In addition, tapes were displayed on shelves throughout the store, like a bookstore, so that customers could pick them up and carry them to the front desk for check out. A magnetic strip on each video and sensors at the door discouraged theft. Computers were used to keep track of inventory, and a laser scanning system, which used barcodes on the tapes and on members' cards, simplified and reduced the time involved in conducting transactions.

The first Blockbuster store was an immediate hit. The Cooks discovered that the public had a much greater appetite for renting video movies than they had previously suspected. People were interested not just in seeing hit movies they had missed in the theaters, but also in a broad variety of other features.

By summer 1986, Cook had expanded the Blockbuster concept to three additional stores. To reflect the different nature of the company, Cook Data Services became Blockbuster Entertainment Corporation in June 1986. In September, the company set out to raise money for further expansion with an initial stock offering. However, days before the sale was to take place, a financial columnist wrote a damaging article citing Cook's background in the oil industry and questioning the company's know-how in the video field. The article caused the equity offering to be cancelled, and without this infusion of cash Blockbuster began to run out of money. The company finished 1986 with a loss of $3.2 million.

In February 1987, however, Cook sold a third of Blockbuster to a group of three investors, who were all former associates at another company, Waste Management, Inc. Wayne Huizenga had co-founded Waste Management, which grew to be the largest garbage disposal business in the world, in 1972 and served as its president and chief operating officer until 1984, when he retired. John Melk, the president of Waste Management's international division, was first to invest in a Blockbuster franchise. Joined by Donald Flynn, the chief financial officer of Waste Management, the group invested $18.6 million in Blockbuster stock.

With this move, Cook surrendered future control of Blockbuster, and Huizenga became the dominant voice in determining the company's future. Where Cook had envisioned growth through franchising, selling Blockbuster's name and computer system to individual entrepreneurs, Huizenga foresaw growth through company ownership of stores. In April 1987, two months after the men from Waste Management bought into Blockbuster, Cook left the company.

By June 1987 Blockbuster owned 15 stores and had franchised 20 others. With this base, Huizenga set out to transform Blockbuster into the industry's dominant player. He kept most of Cook's policies, such as store hours from 10 a.m. to midnight every day, a three-day rental policy, which encouraged customers to rent more than one tape at once, and a broad selection of titles. Despite conventional wisdom that the video tape rental business was heavily dependent on hits, 70 percent of Blockbuster's rental revenues came from non-hit movies, which had the added benefit of being less expensive to purchase from distributors. In addition, Blockbuster's management decided to eschew revenue from X-rated adult films, opting instead for a family environment.

With these policies in place, Blockbuster set out on a program of aggressive expansion. The company began to buy back franchised operations hoping to franchise stores only in areas where the population was too small to support several stores, with a goal of 60 percent company-owned Blockbuster outlets. In addition, Huizenga began to buy up chains of video stores that already dominated their local markets, using this as a shortcut to quick expansion. In March 1987 Blockbuster bought Southern Video Partnership as part of this policy. Two months later, it purchased Movies To Go, Inc., of St. Louis, for $14.5 million.

To support its expansion, Blockbuster established six regional offices, including a distribution center in Dallas that prepared tapes to be placed in stores. By the end of 1987, Blockbuster was operating 133 stores, and had become the country's fifth-largest video chain in terms of revenue. Sales had risen from $7.4 million in 1986 to $43.2 million in 1987, despite the half-million dollar price tag for building new stores.

Blockbuster continued its ambitious expansion program in 1988. In March, the company purchased Video Library, Inc., for $6.4 million plus stock. The following month, Blockbuster made a deal with the United Cable Television Corporation (UCTC) to open 100 franchised stores over the next two and a half years. In addition, UCTC purchased 5 percent of Blockbuster's stock for $12.25 million. By November, this stake had risen to 20 percent. With 200 stores, Blockbuster had become the largest video rental chain in the country. At the end of the year, the company's number of stores had risen to 415.

In January 1989, Blockbuster finalized its purchase of Las Vegas–based Major Video, Inc., the country's fourth-largest video rental chain, for $92.5 million. It also purchased Oklahoma Entertainment, Inc. The following month brought the purchase of Vector Video, Inc., and Video Superstores Master Limited Partnership, which, with 106 stores, had been Blockbuster's largest franchisee. By June, 1989, two years after Huizenga's takeover, the company ran 700 stores. Sales had tripled, profits nearly quadrupled, and the value of the company's stock had risen sevenfold.

Despite these gains, in April 1989 Blockbuster's efforts to buy up other chains with stock suffered a setback when an analyst at a large stock brokerage issued a report condemning what he considered to be the company's misleading accounting practices. In calculating its earnings, Blockbuster spread out the costs of purchasing video store chains and building new stores over a forty-year period, and also spread out the cost of buying large numbers of hit tapes over three years, much longer than tapes retained their value. In addition, the company relied on one-time-only franchise fees for 28 percent of its revenue. Despite this criticism, Blockbuster declined to change its accounting practices, and the company's stock price eventually regained its former level.

In November 1989, Blockbuster's largest shareholder, the United Artists Entertainment Company, announced that it would sell its 12 percent holding in the company, having previously sold its 28 franchised Blockbuster stores, in an effort to streamline its business holdings. Worries that the video rental industry was reaching a saturation point cast doubts on Blockbuster's ability to keep opening stores indefinitely.

One response to this concern was to look to markets outside the United States for growth. Accordingly, original investor Melk was dispatched to start up a British subsidiary, with the company's first foreign store to be opened in South London. Blockbuster's management continued to maintain that since the video "superstore" concept was open for anyone to copy, it needed to grab market share as fast as possible in order to exploit its ground-breaking concept. Carrying out this philosophy, the company opened its 1,000th store before the end of 1989.

To increase business, Blockbuster embarked on a $25 million ad campaign, and also undertook joint promotions with fast food outlets such as Domino's Pizza and McDonald's. In addition, the company accelerated foreign expansion, augmenting its operations in Britain, and planning for operations in Australia and the rest of Western Europe. In the United States, the chain had opened its 1,200th store by June 1990, and new outlets opened at a rate of one a day.

In October 1990, Blockbuster announced plans to cooperate with Den Fujita, the company that ran McDonald's franchises in Japan, in the development and franchising of video rental stores in that country. The following month, Blockbuster made its largest acquisition to date, when it acquired Erol's, a large video store chain with 200 outlets on the East Coast and in the Midwest, for $30 million, including cash, notes, and debt assumption.

Although Blockbuster continued its strong pace of new store openings in 1990, the slowing growth of the video rental industry was becoming more evident. Though the company's earnings grew an astronomical 114 percent in 1988, they had shrunk to a still-impressive 93 percent rate of growth in 1989, followed by rate of 48 percent in 1990. In keeping with this trend, first quarter financial results for 1991 were disappointing. Huizenga blamed the Gulf War for keeping people interested in television news instead of rented videos. In early May, Cox Communications, one of the company's franchisers, announced that it would sell all 82 of its Blockbuster stores.

Faced with a rapidly maturing industry, Blockbuster began to expand its offerings to maintain profitability. The company began to offer video game equipment and Sega Genesis video games at some of its stores. The company considered selling audiocassettes and compact disks. Further, Blockbuster also acquired the right to market tapes of the 1992 Olympic games.

In a further effort to encourage rentals, the company launched an advertising campaign themed "Win in a Flash," and made an agreement with the Showtime cable network for a joint promotion. In August 1991, Blockbuster dropped its rental price for hit movies for the first three months after their release, and shortened the time they were taken out, as a further step to raise earnings. In an effort to insure that the company would be just as good at running video stores over the long haul as it was at opening them, Blockbuster hired more senior executives with long-term experience in the retail field.

In addition to these efforts to increase earnings in the United States, Blockbuster increased its foreign efforts. Along with its operations in the United Kingdom and Japan, the company found markets in Europe, Australia, and Latin America. With 30 stores already established in Britain, Blockbuster announced in November 1991 a large expansion in that country, designed to make it the nation's number one video rental chain. Further foreign involvement came later that month, when Philips Electronics N.V., a Dutch firm, agreed to invest $66 million in the company. As a result of this partnership, Blockbuster said that it would market Philips's newly introduced interactive compact disk systems and software in its stores. Five months later, Philips purchased an additional six million shares to raise its investment to $149 million.

To streamline its corporate management, Blockbuster bought a large office building in Florida and consolidated the company's five regional offices. As Wall Street pundits continued to predict that Blockbuster's success was short-lived, and that the video rental industry would be made obsolete by new technologies, Blockbuster's system wide sales of $1.5 billion in 1991 earned $89 million. By the end of the year, the company had opened stores in Japan, Chile, Venezuela, Puerto Rico, Spain, Australia, New Zealand, and Guam.

In further overseas expansion, Blockbuster bought Citivision PLC, the largest video rental chain in Britain, for $135 million, in January 1992, anticipating that this property would provide valuable exposure in the United Kingdom, and a jumping-off point for further European growth. The company hoped that through joint ventures international operations would contribute a quarter of revenues by 1995. With 952 stores in 9 foreign countries, Blockbuster began to intensify its efforts to expand both in products and geographically.

In October 1992, Blockbuster embarked on a series of agreements that were designed to expand the company's operations beyond its core movie rental business. Blockbuster bought Music Plus and Sound Warehouse from Shamrock Holdings, a California company, for $185 million. One month later, Blockbuster entered into an agreement with Virgin Retail, a British conglomerate that began as a record store, to set up "megastores" in the United States, Europe, and Australia. In December 1992, the first such store in the United States opened in Los Angeles, the precursor to a network of stores which Huizenga envisioned not only renting videos, but also selling and renting music, computer programs, and games, and containing high-tech "virtual reality" entertainment arcades. It also hoped to improve on the traditionally low profits of music retailing by adding other, more profitable products.

By 1993, the distinctive bright blue and yellow Blockbuster logo adorned more than 3,400 video stores worldwide, about one-third of them overseas. Late in January of that year, Blockbuster branched out further, paying $25 million for a one-third, controlling share in Republic Pictures, a movie and television production and distribution company based in Hollywood. Re-

public's most valuable asset was its film library of television shows and films, including several John Wayne movies and the hit television series "Bonanza."

In March 1993 Blockbuster purchased 48.2 percent of Spelling Entertainment, a producer of popular television shows with a large library of past programs.

In addition, Blockbuster began construction of a prototype family entertainment center in Florida, as the company explored ways to integrate Wayne Huizenga's professional sports teams, the Florida Marlins and a hockey team, into its operations. With its ever-growing number of corporate activities, Blockbuster has pursued diversification to complement its success in the video movie rental business.

Principal Subsidiaries: Blockbuster Videos, Inc.; Movies to Go, Inc; Blockbuster Distribution Corporation; Blockbuster Management Corporation; Blockbuster Computer Systems, Inc.; Blockbuster Credit Corporation; Video Library, Inc.; Major Video Corporation; Vector Video Corporation; Video Superstores Venture, L.P.

Further Reading:

Chakravarty, Subrata N., "Give 'em Variety," *Forbes,* May 2, 1988, pp. 54–56.
Calonius, Erik, "Meet the King of Video," *Fortune,* June 4, 1990, p. 208.
Castle, Steven, "Wayne's World," *Robb Report,* February 1993.
Carlson, Gus, "The Next Disney," *Miami Herald,* March 14, 1993, p. 1K.
DeGeorge, Gail, "Blockbuster's Grainy Picture," *Business Week,* May 20, 1991, pp. 40–41.
DeGeorge, Gail, "The Video King Who Won't Hit 'Pause,'" *Business Week,* January 22, 1990, pp. 47–48.
DeGeorge, Gail, "They Don't Call It Blockbuster for Nothing," *Business Week,* October 19, 1992.
Engardio, Pete, and Fine, Antonio N., "Will This Video Chain Stay on Fast Forward?" *Business Week,* June 12, 1989, pp. 72–74.
Govoni, Stephen J., "Blockbuster Battles the Shorts," *CFO,* December 1991.
Katel, Peter, "New Kid on the Block, Buster," *Newsweek,* January 11 1993.
Miller, Michael, "Coming Soon to Your Local Video Store: Big Brother," *Wall Street Journal,* December 26, 1990, p. 9.
Savitz, Eric J., "An End to Fast Forward?" *Barron's,* December 11, 1989, pp. 13, 43–46.
Silverman, Edward R., "Global Go-Getters," *International Business,* October 1992.
"USA/UK Blockbuster Strikes from Home Base," *Sunday Times,* November 10, 1991.
Walsh, Matt, " 'Rent Things,' " *Florida Trend,* March 1993.
Whitford, David, "The Predator's Ball Club," *M,* June 1992, pp. 80–85.

—Elizabeth Rourke

Bob Evans Farms, Inc.

3776 South High Street
P.O. Box 07863
Columbus, Ohio 43207-0863
U.S.A.
(614) 491-2225
Fax: (614) 492-4949

Public Company
Incorporated: October 28, 1953 as Bob Evans Farm Sales, Inc.
Employees: 19,000
Sales: $653.2 million
Stock Exchanges: NASDAQ
SICs: 5812 Eating Places; 2013 Sausages and Other Prepared Meat Products

Bob Evans Farms, Inc. owns and operates nearly 300 full service, family restaurants in 19 states. The company also operates 11 plants across the Midwest, Southwest, and Southeast, which produce and distribute fresh and fully cooked sausage products, as well as fresh deli-style salads, to consumers throughout the United States. At the heart of its distribution system are Bob Evans Farms driver-salespersons who deliver many varieties of food products, including: roll sausage, Italian casing, dinner links, Brown 'n' Serve sausage, Smoked and Kielbasa sausage, Sausage and Ham Burritos, and fully cooked Sausage 'n' Biscuits and Ham 'n' Cheese 'n' Biscuits.

Bob Evans Farms got its start when founder Bob Evans began preparing farm fresh sausages for the 12-seat, 24-hour restaurant—the Bob Evans Steak House—he opened in 1946 in Gallipolis, Ohio. While the restaurant was a success, the difficulty Evans experienced in obtaining high quality sausage prompted him to start making his own from hogs raised on the farm. Favorable reports from his customers, many of whom were truck drivers who bought 10-pound tubs of the sausage to take home to their families and friends, prompted Evans to take some time away from his restaurant and concentrate on building a business to distribute the sausage products. He delivered the product himself and operated his sausage business only during the cool months of the year when storage was possible. Eventually distribution was expanded to grocery stores, and, as the popularity of his sausage grew, Evans invited grocery store managers to come to the family farm, known as the Homestead, in Gallia County to witness the sausage-making process.

The Homestead, where Evans and his wife Jewell raised their six children, was once an inn and stagecoach stop and is now on the National Register of Historic Places. Visitors may hike or ride horses on the farm's 1,100 acres of rolling hills or visit the farm's museum and authentic log cabin village. Craft fairs and other special events are held at the farm on many weekends during the tourist season, which runs from Memorial Day weekend through Labor Day weekend.

In 1953, a group of friends and family recognized the growing demand for Bob Evans Farms Sausage and became business partners. When a packing plant in Xenia, Ohio, came up for sale, the partners, led by founding chairperson Emerson E. Evans, bought it and went into the sausage business on a larger scale. Sausage distribution was expanded into southwestern Ohio. The Xenia plant not only allowed for increased production of Bob Evans Farms Sausage, but also gave many of the company's current top management their start in the business.

By 1957, 14 delivery trucks delivered fresh Bob Evans Farms Sausage overnight to central and southern Ohio outlets, and by 1963, when the company went public, the sales territory covered most of Ohio. The first move out of Ohio was into Michigan in 1964. In conjunction with that year's introduction of sausage into Detroit, the company opened a third sausage plant in nearby Hillsdale, Michigan. As the company expanded west, Galva, Illinois—a concentrated hog producing area—became the site of Bob Evans Farms' fourth sausage production plant in 1974.

As the reputation of Bob Evans Farms Sausage grew, and more people began coming to his farm, Evans built another restaurant in the area in 1962. The success of the Sausage Shop encouraged the company to open the first of what would become the Bob Evans restaurant chain in 1968. A further incentive to opening a restaurant was to maintain consistent returns for shareholders amid the ups and downs of the sausage business. Located in Chillicothe, Ohio, the pilot restaurant featured a design reminiscent of the farm, including a red exterior with white trim, which would eventually serve as the model colors for the entire Bob Evans chain. The restaurant's first menu, however, was not quite as successful as the building design. The Chillicothe restaurant was initially intended as a fast-food outlet featuring sausage sandwiches, hamburgers, french fries, and milk shakes. When business started to decline, a team of employees, including top management, closed the restaurant for one weekend, redesigned the interior as a sit-down, full service facility, hired waitresses, put in a new menu, and reopened with great success.

Bob Evans Restaurants were initially known for their hearty breakfasts, available at the restaurants at all hours of the day. However, the company's reputation for high quality breakfasts began to overshadow the lunch and dinner hours, and some restaurants were so slow after two o'clock p.m. that they had trouble keeping staff. In response to this problem, management sought to develop and refine its menu to meet changing consumer tastes and lifestyles. To build the dinner business, platters of charbroiled ribs, chicken, and catfish were added, nightly dinner specials were offered, and advertising targeted both adults and families with children. Moreover, a greater variety was eventually introduced into the Bob Evans dinner menu, including such dishes as veal parmesan, spaghetti with meat sauce, and the Mexican-inspired Skillet Breakfasts and taco salad. Bob Evans was also active in promoting healthier menus by introducing a new summer menu with lighter, health-oriented foods such as grilled chicken salad, egg substitutes, and a new skillet breakfast line.

In June 1991, the company established Bob Evans foodservice division, which sold food products directly to distributors and institutions. Items such as gravies, burritos, sausage and biscuit sandwiches, soups, ham, and specialty sausages were sold to convenience stores, restaurants, and non-commercial foodservice segments. In fiscal 1993, the food products segment made up 30 percent of sales for Bob Evans Farms. Bob Evans had established a position of market leadership in sausage products and a major competitive advantage based on the direct-store delivery system. The company distributed many types of sausage produced at its manufacturing plants, and its products gained a reputation for premium quality based on whole-hog ingredients, proprietary recipes, and unparalleled freshness. With a fleet of trucks making deliveries to over 14,000 grocery stores each week, Bob Evans had a unique ability to place refrigerated products on grocery store shelves within 24 hours of making the products, circumventing the distributors and chain warehouses.

In order to maintain its market share and market success, the food products segment introduced many new items. For customers looking for products lower in fat, Country Lite Sausage was test marketed in Chicago, St. Louis, Buffalo, Houston, and Dallas in the early 1990s, and was soon available in much of the company's marketing territory. Plans were also underway to enter the gourmet food market as several new items were in development and were slated for testing in the mid-1990s.

Several other new products included bratwurst, Italian dinner links, and smoked sausage. Moreover, Bob Evans Harvest Salads were targeted to consumers looking for a high-quality prepared item. The Harvest Salad line included tuna salad, macaroni salad, Italian pasta salad, and others. Testing has been expanded into the Pittsburgh and Buffalo/Rochester, New York markets. This salad line complemented the sausage business, since sausage volumes were highest in the fall, while the salad business was at its best in the spring and summer.

The Bob Evans Farms food products division grew not only through new products but also through acquisitions. Owens Country Sausage, based in Richardson, Texas, was purchased by Bob Evans Farms on January 16, 1987, in a stock transaction worth nearly $16 million. Bob Evans Farms acquired all Owens's outstanding common stock in exchange for shares of Bob Evans Farms stock. Until the Bob Evans Farms acquisition, Owens was a privately held company.

Owens Country Sausage was founded in 1928 by the late Clifford Boyce Owens, and was chaired by his son, Jerry Owens, in the early 1990s. Selling a variety of food products in the Southwest, Owens offered a new market for Bob Evans Farms and provided the company with a wealth of opportunities for restaurant expansion. The first Owens Family Restaurant, in Irving, Texas, retained the Owens name, but resembled the Bob Evans design and menu concept. In 1993 there were thirteen Owens Family Restaurants in the Dallas/Fort Worth area and plans called for more sites in the future.

Bob Evans Farms acquired Mrs. Giles Country Kitchens—a food production company operating in Lynchburg, Virginia—on September 13, 1991 from an affiliate of the Campbell Soup Company. Mrs. Giles, founded by Zena Giles in 1933, produced refrigerated deli salads and distributed most of its products in bulk, unbranded, to delicatessens around the United States. In May 1992, Bob Evans Farms upgraded several of the Mrs. Giles recipes and marketed them under the Bob Evans brand in Columbus and Cincinnati, Ohio.

Another acquisition occurred in March 1992, when Bob Evans Farms bought Hickory Specialties, Inc. Hickory specialized in charcoal products, grills, liquid smoke seasonings, and application systems. The company had two major divisions, Nature-Glo Charcoal and Zesti Smoke Flavor. Nature-Glo produced several lines of grills (under the Champion brand) as well as charcoal, hickory, and mesquite wood smoking chips. The charcoal and smoking chips were sold under the Mr. Quick, Old Hickory, and Mountain Hardwood names. The company also manufactured the Jack Daniel's line of charcoal and smoking chips. The company patented technology to produce a new line of gas grill briquets that provide a hickory or mesquite flavor. The Zesti Smoke Flavor division produced liquid smoke flavorings to the meat-packing and the processed food industries. Major customers included Nabisco, Kraft, Carnation, and Heinz. The commercial flavor products were used in the manufacture of such items as potato chips, pet foods, nuts, pharmaceuticals, smoked hams, and barbecue sauces.

Bob Evans continued its growth in foodservice sales as it increased its product line and marketed its products to more schools, hotels, convenience stores, and other foodservice customers. Regarding this area as one of great growth opportunity, the company has been committed to actively pursuing such additional sales. Management's long-term goal remains for the food products division to generate 40 percent of total revenues.

In the early 1990s, Bob Evans Farms management realized that in order to enhance future growth while retaining the commitment to quality, the company had to diversify. Although it developed a strong network of restaurant and sausage operations through a coordinated marketing and expansion strategy, the company needed to minimize dependence on the breakfast business and sausage products. The sausage business remained subject to volatile hog costs and, due to health concerns, continual declines in U.S. pork consumption. For this reason the company increasingly emphasized new developments in its restaurant business. Consequently, the restaurant segment generated approximately 70 percent of total revenues in fiscal 1993, up from approximately 52 percent in 1982.

In April 1992, Bob Evans opened its first Cantina del Rio, a Mexican-style restaurant and bar, in Columbus, Ohio. Bob Evans's entry into the Mexican food market was well planned. The Mexican food business was the fastest growing segment in the restaurant industry in 1991 at 18.3 percent. In order to create a quality restaurant and menu, Bob Evans chose Phillip Torres, the owner of the successful Guadalajaran Mexican Grille and Bar (located in Houston, Texas) to head the operations. Management was pleased with the initial results and anticipated further success because of the restaurant's atmosphere and recipes. Six more Cantina del Rios were scheduled to open in the Midwest in fiscal 1994.

Further expansion of the restaurant business included the development of Bob Evans General Store and Restaurants. Designed to recall the country stores of the mid-1800s, the stores were constructed of red oak and wooden pegs and featured ceiling-high shelves displaying country crafts and homemade goods. The adjacent restaurants featured gift shops that sold pottery and other craft goods, a restaurant with a new country-style menu, and an in-house bakery. The first General Store and Restaurant opened in April 1991 near Kings Island Amusement Park in Mason, Ohio, and over the next three years seven more went into operation. Intended for high-traffic sites near tourist attractions, resorts, and junctions of interstate highways, the Restaurants and General Stores were in direct competition with Cracker Barrel Old Country Stores, another restaurant and gift shop chain whose territory Bob Evans attempted to break into.

Another development in the restaurant segment was the launching of the Bob Evans "Smalltown" Restaurants. "Smalltown" outlets were smaller versions of the traditional Bob Evans family restaurants, featuring 90 percent of the chain's traditional menu and targeting locals in cities of 15,000 to 30,000 residents, many of whom used to travel up to 50 miles to enjoy a Bob Evans meal. The first unit was opened in Bellefontaine, Ohio, in spring 1993. This 3,200-square-foot, 96-seat version of the traditional restaurant was expected to provide a boost to the company as it was less expensive to build and operate than traditional Bob Evans Restaurants and should allow the company to expand to smaller towns where building a traditional restaurant would not have been feasible. Targeting sites near Wal-Mart discount stores, prime areas of small town traffic, Bob Evans expects to open ten of these restaurants in fiscal 1994.

While the new restaurant concepts were certainly in the spotlight during the early 1990s, Bob Evans realized that the traditional Bob Evans and Owens Family Restaurants were the strength of the company. These restaurants generated average unit sales of $1.6 million annually, and all were company owned, with no plans to franchise. Bob Evans owned the buildings and equipment at every location and owned the land for nearly all sites. For these reasons the company focused on several strategies to improve these restaurants.

First, as part of its long-term strategy, Bob Evans was involved in a continual remodeling, renovating, and redesigning plan. All existing units, on a three-year basis, were given new coats of paint and were furnished with new carpeting and drapes. About every eight years the company purchased new furniture as well as new kitchen equipment. Renovation or remodeling costs per unit run approximately $50,000 to $75,000.

Beginning March 4, 1991, a new Bob Evans prototype restaurant was unveiled, from a design featured in an Indianapolis restaurant. The new design was larger, consisting of 5,500 square feet, compared with 5,000 square feet in the original building. The dining room had more than half of the 150 seats designed for non-smoking customers, a large foyer was added, and the restrooms were moved to the front of the building for the customers' convenience. While the new prototype featured an interior decorated in oak wood and light country colors, the Bob Evans style of food and logo remained the same.

Another pivotal change at Bob Evans was the enhancement of the restaurant manager position. As a result of the 1990 management restructuring, managers received higher compensation, stock options, and better training. Unit managers were given greater autonomy and increased accountability for the performance of their individual units. Managers were encouraged to localize their operations—from menu items to service strategies and in-store decorative accents—reflecting the taste of the community served, and were asked to send new product ideas and management approaches on to headquarters.

These company innovations resulted in a sharp decline in management turnover and an improvement in customer satisfaction. Bob Evans continually strove to enhance its benefit packages, providing medical coverage and paid holidays and vacations. Consequently, hourly employee turnover in 1993 was about half of the 300 percent industry average. In return, the company expected a commitment from its employees. Each new management employee underwent comprehensive training, including a 14-week program for new Bob Evans Restaurant managers, which helped to ensure that Bob Evans's standards of quality were upheld.

Another strategy aimed at enhancing the profitability of the restaurant segment and heightening customer satisfaction was the development of a point-of-sale (POS) computer system which increases accuracy and efficiency in the restaurants. This highly specialized computer program handled customer orders and inventory, tracked sales trends, monitored buying patterns by region and unit, and kept a tally of store costs. In 1993, the POS system was operational in approximately 60 Bob Evans Restaurants and all of the Cantina del Rios. The company planned to eventually install the system in all of its restaurants.

Furthermore, Bob Evans implemented a silent shopper program, in which anonymous shoppers visited each restaurant four times a month, evaluating the stores' employees, service, food, value perception, and cleanliness. The results of the evaluations were reviewed by the company's operations management and then communicated back to each restaurant's management team.

An internal task force was also organized to supervise the emendation of nutritional labels on all packages to meet new FDA regulations. A costly undertaking, the task force should help ensure that the project is completed in the most efficient and cost-effective manner.

A final strategy designed to improve the profitability of the restaurant segment concerns branding, or highlighting a food manufacturer's brand name product on a menu. According to Roger Williams, senior vice president of marketing for Bob Evans Farms in 1993, branding had a two-fold function—it made a quality statement about the restaurant, and it provided a service for the manufacturer. William noted that extensive branding at Bob Evans was "absolutely positive." Bob Evans menu's featured Quaker oatmeal, Smucker's jelly, Fleischmann's Egg Beaters egg substitute, 100% Pure Florida Orange Juice, in addition to the company's own branded Bob Evans Farms sausages.

Analysts expected Bob Evans Farms to remain at the high end of the midscale restaurant segment and to hold as a market leader in the sausage business. Although the company has grown extensively over the years, its commitment to quality and "down on the farm" hospitality remained a top priority.

Principal Subsidiaries: BEF Holding Co., Inc.; Owens Country Sausage, Inc.; Mrs. Giles Country Kitchens, Inc.; Hickory Specialties, Inc.; BEF Aviation Co., Inc.

Further Reading:

Bob Evans Farms, Inc. Annual Reports, Columbus, Ohio: Bob Evans Farms, Inc., 1992–93.

Elder, Martin, "Bob Evans Wins the Heartland," *Restaurant Business,* February 10, 1988, pp. 128–32.

McKenna, Peter, "Cheaper Goods Haven't Hurt," *Restaurant Business,* July 20, 1992, pp. 110–14.

Scarpa, James, "Branding," *Restaurant Business,* October 10, 1991, pp. 145–61.

Yanez, Luisa, "Food Fight on the Interstate," *Restaurant Business,* September 20, 1992, p. 50.

—Carol Kieltyka

B O R L A N D

Borland International, Inc.

1800 Green Hills Road
P.O. Box 66001
Scotts Valley, California 95067-0001
U.S.A.
(408) 439-4736
Fax: (408) 439-9273

Public Company
Incorporated: 1983
Employees: 986
Sales: $482.5 million
Stock Exchanges: New York
SICs: 7372 Prepackaged Software

Borland International, Inc., is the world's third-largest personal computer software company. Founded by a French math teacher who emigrated to America, Borland initially made its mark as a retailer of inexpensive tools for computer programmers, then moved into the market for corporate software. Through its streamlined and unorthodox management style, as well as two major acquisitions, the company grew to rival the largest firms in its field.

Borland was founded in 1983 by Philippe Kahn, who taught mathematics at the University of Nice and Grenoble. Kahn left France for the United States in 1982 with $2,000 in savings and settled in Silicon Valley in California. Unable to get a job because he was an illegal alien, Kahn decided to start his own company to market a software program he had developed. He named the company after seeing a television advertisement starring Frank Borman, the chairman of Eastern Airlines. Kahn thought "Borman" sounded authentically American, so he adopted it for his company, changing the name slightly to avoid confusion or legal difficulties.

Borland's early prospects looked questionable. Among the company's first employees were a former Japanese restaurant manager, a cocktail waitress, and a salesman who had last peddled Campbell Soups in Mexico. Borland employees later described their early business practices as "barely on the right side of the law" in a *Wall Street Journal* interview. Kahn preferred to think of them as ingenious. Short of money for office equipment, for instance, the company printed up impressive letterhead stationary and sent letters to manufacturers asking to evaluate their products for possible distribution. Dozens

of pieces of computer equipment and supplies came flooding in, which Borland used as unofficial loans until the company was better funded.

Unable to attract investment from venture capitalists, Kahn contributed the remnants of his own savings to the new enterprise and rounded up $18,000 from other sources. The company rented a two-room office over a Jaguar garage for $600 a month. In these cramped quarters, Kahn and his employees refined the design for Turbo Pascal, a computer program that made programming in Pascal, a complicated computer language, easier and faster. Turbo Pascal was intended for sale to computer programmers, primarily students in classes from high school through graduate school. After six months, the product was ready to be sold.

Kahn and other Borland employees began to market Turbo Pascal during the day, taking orders, and then filled those orders at night. They priced Turbo Pascal at $49.95, making the cost low enough that the program would be attractive to a wide spectrum of buyers. Soon, Borland found that its product was being purchased by programmers who worked in corporations, as well as students and computer enthusiasts.

Borland's second product was developed in-house as a tool for company employees to simplify their work. Programmers and salespeople found it cumbersome to switch completely out of one computer program and into another when they wished to perform some simple task, such as jotting down an idea or looking up an address. To make this unnecessary, the company designed a desktop organizer, which contained a calculator, a notepad, a perpetual calendar, and a phone directory. This software was loaded into a computer's memory and then could be called up at any time while another program was in use. In June 1984 Borland named this device "Sidekick," and began to sell it to computer users outside the company. As with Turbo Pascal, the company kept the price of the product low to appeal to a wide variety of customers, charging just $49.95 for the package. Sidekick won immediate acceptance, surprising its makers with its popularity. By the end of 1984, the desktop organizer had become one of the three best-selling pieces of software on the market. With this boost, Borland's sales for 1984 reached $10 million, and profits were $1.7 million.

With this success came rapid expansion. The company added new employees and changed offices twice to accommodate its growth. By early 1985, Borland had 100 workers and a 30,000-square-foot headquarters office. By June 1985 company sales were running at $2 million a month, and Kahn had acquired a reputation as the court jester of Silicon Valley for his lavish parties, garish clothing, and impromptu saxophone solos.

In the following year, Borland solidified its reputation as one of the fastest-growing companies in the computer software field. In March 1986 the company introduced Turbo Prolog, a program that used artificial intelligence to allow the creation of expert systems on IBM PCs. At the end of that month, Borland also introduced a modified version of its Sidekick program for the Apple Macintosh computer. After announcing profits of $8 million for the fiscal year ending in April 1986, Borland purchased Singular Software, the maker of a software line for the Macintosh, in July. Four months later, the company made another acquisition when it bought the Click On Worksheet spreadsheet program from T/Maker. At that time, Borland also announced plans to start a new division dedicated to scientific and engineering software.

In June 1986 Borland announced that it would offer shares to the public on the London Unlisted Securities Market, avoiding the high fees associated with selling stock in the United States. By September the company had raised $25 million to fuel further expansion. By March 1987 Borland's sales had reached $29.2 million, and its pre-tax profits were $4.7 million.

Four months later, Borland made its biggest acquisition to date when it agreed to purchase privately held Ansa Software in a stock swap worth $29 million. On the surface, Borland and Ansa were very different companies. Ansa's main product was a high-priced database management program called Paradox, which retailed for $725 and had yet to make its developer profitable. Borland hoped that the merger of the two companies would help to upgrade its own operations in areas where they were weak. Rather than continue to rely on its telemarketing-based operations for sales to individuals, for instance, Borland hoped to make use of Ansa's more sophisticated sales force to peddle both companies' products to large corporations.

Just one month later, Borland unveiled its Quattro spread-sheet program, which was designed to compete with the Lotus Development Corporation's best-selling 1-2-3 spreadsheet. Despite the fact that Lotus had a virtual lock on this enormous market, Borland asserted that Quattro was faster than its competitor's offering and would also carry a lower price. This product was the first of several planned introductions in the field of business applications programs, moving Borland away from its smaller core of original customers, most of whom were programmers, and toward companies. Attracting companies as customers meant Borland would be competing with the large market leaders in the software industry. Kahn hoped to enlarge his company by following "the Honda way." For him, this meant a business strategy of getting into a market with low-priced goods and then expanding market share with more sophisticated and expensive products, in the same way that the Japanese car maker had acted.

To support this move, Borland introduced its first advertising campaign. In addition, the company moved to reorganize its corporate structure on a more formal and professional level, adding several key posts, including a chief financial officer. These efforts came as Borland's initial torrid corporate growth had started to slow. The company earned only $1.8 million in profits for the fiscal year ending in March 1988, leaving it far behind the industry leaders it aspired to join.

Borland's move into the corporate software market continued in June 1988, when the company introduced Sprint, a word-processing program for use on IBM and IBM-compatible computers. At that time, Borland also purchased the programs of Surpass Software Systems, Inc., allowing it to incorporate technology from its rivals' products into its own Quattro spreadsheet program. By August 1988 Borland's efforts in the corporate software market had started to show some results. Quattro had sold more than 125,000 copies in the nine months since it had been introduced, helped by a Borland promotion that of-

fered the product to previous customers at just $79. Monthly sales of Paradox had doubled and had reached 3 to 4 percent of the data-base market since Borland had purchased its maker. Sprint, Borland's word-processing program, had become a best-seller in France, with more than 25,000 copies sold.

Despite these gains, at the end of August 1988, Borland announced that it would lay off 13 percent of its workforce in an effort to bring costs in line with its earnings. At this time, the company also underwent further restructuring, moving its marketing and sales departments away from sales of its programs through catalogues and direct mail to dealer sales.

In the following year, one of Borland's competitors turned the tables on the company. In July 1989, Microsoft announced that it would market a low-cost challenger to Turbo Pascal, Borland's first product.

Two months later, Borland intensified its head-to-head competition with another big software seller when it released Quattro-Pro, a spreadsheet program that was designed to mimic and supplant Lotus 1-2-3 to an even larger extent than earlier versions. Borland's product was more powerful than 1-2-3 and could also be run on older computers with smaller memories. The company hoped to convince corporate customers to buy Quattro-Pro rather than a Lotus upgrade. To persuade them further, Borland introduced an extremely aggressive pricing strategy, as it had earlier done with its Paradox program. Just as Borland had offered Paradox to its competitor Ashton-Tate's dBase customers for $150, rather than its usual price of $725, the company offered Quattro-Pro to former Lotus buyers for just $99, hundreds of dollars less than rivals' prices. In addition, Borland introduced a novel marketing concept, selling its mainstream business products through direct mail campaigns, which kept the costs attributed to dealers or other middlemen low or nonexistent. Following these moves, late in 1989, Borland sold stock to investors in the United States for the first time.

By June 1990 Borland had sold more than 200,000 copies of its Quattro-Pro spreadsheet program, and the company had started to make real progress in eroding the market share of giant Lotus, some of whose programs were plagued by bugs and glitches. One study reported that sales of Quattro-Pro were matching those of one Lotus version, as Borland won converts in small- and medium-sized companies.

In July 1990 the success of Borland's introduction of Quattro-Pro prompted a law suit from its intended target, Lotus. Charging that Borland had infringed its copyright on its software, Lotus sought to make the company alter its product, which accounted for 15 percent of company revenues. As a counter-move, Borland sued Lotus in California, hoping to get a favorable judgment. The possibility that Borland would lose this suit cast a shadow over the company's future as the case wended its way laboriously through the courts.

By the end of 1990, Borland's Quattro-Pro shipments had reached 50,000 a month, and the company attained a market share of about 20 percent. In addition, sales of the company's Paradox database program had also improved, doubling to about 20 percent of the market. By March 1991 Borland had seen its revenues double and its earnings rise to $11.8 million over the last twelve months.

On the basis of this growth, in July 1991, Borland took a further step toward becoming a major player in the software market when it agreed to purchase one of its biggest competitors, the Ashton-Tate Corporation, for $439 million. Ashton-Tate's primary product was dBase, a database program that had once dominated the market but had started to lose ground after the company introduced a version of the program riddled with flaws. With the purchase of Ashton-Tate, Borland became the industry leader in database software and one of the top five personal computer software firms overall.

To make its acquisition profitable, Borland moved quickly to bring its own stream-lined management style to the less efficient Ashton-Tate, cutting costs by cutting employees. These measures proved expensive, and Borland was forced to take a charge against its earnings to counteract them. The company ended the year with a loss of $110.4 million. In addition, Borland's purchase of Ashton-Tate brought the company face to face with the integration of two incompatible software programs, because the two companies' offerings could not interact. Despite these obstacles, however, Borland's two database programs retained control of 50 percent of the market, worth $300 million in sales, through the spring of 1992.

Having bought its way into the big-time with its purchases of the makers of Paradox and dBase, Borland saw programs for use with the Windows operating system as the next big opportunity in the software field. Using a new software development tool called C++, which used object-oriented programming to break tasks down into smaller, more manageable parts, Borland sought to bring Paradox for Windows and Quattro-Pro for Windows to market before its competitors got too far ahead.

In July of 1992, Borland suffered a legal setback when a Massachusetts judge ruled in its long-standing copyright infringement dispute with Lotus that it had illegally copied part of the larger company's program. Anxious to take the case to an appeals court, where it believed it would receive a more sympathetic hearing, Borland announced in August that it had removed the feature in question from its Quattro-Pro product.

In September 1992 Borland began offering Quattro-Pro software adapted for Windows at a reduced rate with its older spreadsheet program, as the company attempted to address customer concerns about the economics of switching between programs. In its database business, Borland's share of the market, which had grown to 65 percent, began to be eroded by the company's postponement of its introduction of Windows versions of Paradox and dBase and by low-priced products introduced by such competitors as Microsoft.

Further bad news came at the end of 1992, when Borland announced that it would lay off 350 employees and take a $35 million charge against its earnings. The company planned to consolidate research and development activities in order to control costs. Three months later, Borland finished out its fiscal year with a loss of $49.2 million on sales of $464 million. In an effort to return to profitability in 1993, Borland introduced a new version of its dBase product, which nevertheless was not adapted for use with Windows. With a decade of striking growth behind it, Borland faced a broad array of new challenges as it peered into the future of the software industry.

Principal Subsidiaries: Borland/Analytica, Inc.; Borland California, Inc.; Borland International Ltd. (UK); Borland International S.A.R.L. (France); Borland GMBH (Germany); Borland International Software, Inc., (Canada).

Further Reading:

Bellew, Patricia A., ''In the Silicon Valley, L'Enfant Terrible Is Also L'Enfant Riche,'' *Wall Street Journal,* June 4, 1985.

Brandt, Richard, ''Borland the Barbarian,'' *Business Week,* July 1, 1991.

——, ''Lotus the Copycat Killer Pounces Again, '' *Business Week,* July 16, 1990.

——, ''Software's Bad Boy Has His Eye on the Big Time,'' *Business Week,* August 8, 1988.

Churbuck, David, ''The Next Microsoft?'' *Forbes,* April 27, 1992.

Rebello, Kathy, '' 'This Has to Be Borland's Worst Nightmare,' '' *Business Week,* April 6, 1992.

Schwartz, Evan I., ''Ashton-Tate Is Not an Active Force Anymore,'' *Business Week,* July 22, 1991.

Shaffer, Richard A., ''Why Borland Is Doing Well,'' *Forbes,* December 24, 1990.

Tracy, Eleanor Johnson, ''Hit Software from an Alien Entrepreneur,'' *Fortune,* February 18, 1985.

—Elizabeth Rourke

Bramalea Ltd.

1867 Yonge Street
Toronto, Ontario M5C 2Y9
Canada
(416) 366-3200
Fax: (416) 359-0076

Public Company
Incorporated: 1957 as Bramalea Consolidated Developments
  Ltd.
Employees: 2,100
Sales: $838.3 million
Stock Exchanges: Toronto

Bramalea Ltd. is a real estate company that develops and manages properties throughout North America. Its income-producing properties include shopping centers, office buildings, and residential and industrial holdings. The company also had extensive holdings in hotels, which were put up for sale in the early 1990s.

The origins of the company go back to Bramalea Consolidated Developments Ltd., first established on December 11, 1957. The new company's avowed aim was to build a self-contained city 12 miles west of Toronto, the biggest urban center in southern Ontario. The all-inclusive community was to house 70,000 people between Malton and Brampton, two small towns whose names the company combined to form Bramalea. The vision for North America's biggest satellite city belonged to James Sihler, a doctor in southern Ontario. He talked some of his business contacts, and eventually some British merchant bankers, into backing the project.

The bulk of the new company's land holdings were purchased from Bayton Holdings Ltd. in 1958 and 1959, at a cost of $1.18 million. The plots of land themselves held mortgages worth $5.52 million. Bramalea was first listed on the Toronto Stock Exchange in August 1960, and over the next five years, the company bought up properties and property development companies. In 1966 the company sold off a 40 percent stake in Victoria Property and Investment Co. Ltd. A year later, Bramalea sold its 50 percent interest in Braemar Apartments Ltd., based in St. Catherines, around 70 miles south of Toronto.

Also in 1967, Bramalea consolidated its wholly owned subsidiaries, Bramalea Construction (Peel) Ltd. and Bramalea Shop-

ping Centers Ltd., within the parent company. Then, in November of that year, the company incorporated another subsidiary, Bramalea General Contracting (Peel) Ltd.

By January 1968, Bramalea had established a land development division to oversee the parent company and its other land divisions. In May 1969, the company formed a joint venture with Hengran Developments Ltd. to develop land at Unionville, Ontario, cited to be named Village in the Valley. In 1975 Bramalea bought out the stake held by Hengran for just under $4.1 million.

In 1970 Bramalea ventured into the British property market after establishing Bramalea Overseas Developments Ltd., another wholly owned subsidiary. A year later, the company formed Bramalea Wescorp Developments Ltd., in equal partnership with Wescorp Industries of Vancouver, British Columbia. The new venture was to manage properties held in western Canada.

Bramalea's first significant expansion as a property developer occurred after 1972, when the company was bought by two Toronto lawyers, Dick Shiff and Ken Field. Shiff and Field received financial support from Benjamin Swirsky, a Toronto accountant and lawyer. Rising inflation beginning in this period boosted the value of the company's land holdings, adding to Bramalea's bottom line and making further investments more appealing.

Shiff's and Field's management styles were very different. Shiff, who became chairperson and CEO of Bramalea, was known as a conservative and somewhat tight-fisted corporate lawyer, while Field, Bramalea's president, was more impulsive and outgoing. Swirsky, who became a director of Bramalea in 1976 as well as a major shareholder, offered the company his financial expertise.

One of the trio's first big property deals was the 1975 purchase of a raft of office buildings and hotels from Trizec Corporation Ltd. for $102 million. The real estate was mainly in western Canada and featured 75 percent ownership of the Hyatt Regency hotels in Toronto and Vancouver. In 1978, the hotel in Toronto was renamed the Four Seasons Hotel.

In June 1976, the company's name was shortened from Bramalea Consolidated Developments Ltd. to Bramalea Ltd. This followed an earlier consolidation of the following subsidiaries under the parent company: Bramco Developments Ltd., Bramalea Leasing Corporation Ltd., Bramalea Management Corporation Ltd., The Greater Cedarwood Development Corporation Ltd, Bramalea Office Buildings Ltd., Amberlea Developments Ltd., and Co-Chuk Investments Ltd.

Building a strong investment portfolio in rental income producing properties became Bramalea's business strategy during the late 1970s. The success of this strategy was made evident in 1979 when total revenues for the company reached $138.3 million, up from $112.4 million the year before.

However, by 1980 the company was beginning to feel the effects of a sluggish North American economy, attended by high interest rates and reduced retail spending. As Richard Shiff noted in the company's 1979 annual report: "Our overall profitability is, of course, affected by the high cost of borrowed funds. This situation will continue, and perhaps worsen in the current year.''

In 1981 the company faced recessionary conditions by unloading non-core holdings amid a high interest rate climate. First to be sold that year was Five Oaks Holdings Ltd., followed by Village in the Valley. Subsequently, Bramalea Developments (U.S.) changed its name to Bramalea Inc.

Nevertheless, during this time the company announced plans to develop four city blocks in Dallas, Texas, building "Main Center," a project of some three million square feet of new commercial and retail real estate. Furthermore, in Denver plans were unveiled for "Trinity Center," a two million square foot development comprising a 50-story tower and a companion 28-story building. Bramalea continued to build and manage shopping centers, which had become the company's single largest source of rental income and earnings.

Hard times for rival property concerns offered Bramalea opportunities to buy faltering companies, including Coseka Resources Ltd., a gas and oil company in which Bramalea bought a 27 percent interest for $85.4 million. By January 1982, the company had bumped that stake up to 36 percent, and, by August, Bramalea held a controlling 52.6 percent interest in Coseka.

Also that year, Bramalea began work on a 30 acre office and retail development in Culver City, near the Los Angeles Airport. This development called for eight separate buildings to hold more than 1.64 million square feet of new space. Earnings for Bramalea fell sharply in 1982, being posted at $7.6 million, down from $12.6 million recorded a year earlier. The decline stemmed from industrial, retail, and commercial tenants scaling back on expansion plans as well as a record number of business bankruptcies driving up vacancy rates across North America.

In turn, general economic uncertainty drove down the number of new housing developments and purchases by first-time residential buyers. Furthermore, growing energy conservation and lowered oil and gas consumption during the recession affected the performance of Coseka Resources, of which Bramalea held a 62.9 percent interest by mid-1983.

In 1984 Bramalea became the target of interest from rival property developer Trizec Corporation, based in Calgary. That year, Trizec Equities Ltd. bought an initial 18 percent stake in Bramalea for $160 million. A year later, they raised their stake to 31 percent after buying 3.53 million Bramalea shares at $20 each from Richard Shiff and his family. The rival also maintained an option to increase that stake to 43 percent. Trizec shareholders then had a one-third stake in a rival property developer with more than $2 billion worth of assets in its portfolio. Specifically, Bramalea held more than 20 million square feet of retail, commercial, and industrial real estate in 95 buildings across North America. In addition, Bramalea was a community developer and home builder, and, through Coseka Resources Ltd., had oil and gas interests. The influence of Trizec's interest in Bramalea was felt almost immediately. In August 1986, Bramalea sold almost its entire Canadian shopping center holdings to Trizec for $578.7 million, representing a net gain for Bramalea of $221.2 million.

The orchestrated profit made when Trizec purchased the Canadian holdings allowed Bramalea to refinance and restructure Coseka Resources, suffering during this time by the steeply falling price of oil on the world market. In February 1986, Bramalea suspended exploration by the company and closed the U.S. office to reduce overheads. The company was then able to write down its steep loss from gas and oil exploration to the amount of $280 million.

The shopping mall shuffle between the two companies continued when Bramalea purchased a subsidiary of Trizec, which owned 30 Canadian shopping centers, in 1986. In effect, Bramalea was buying back the shopping malls it had just unloaded as well as several of Trizec's shopping centers. To fund the deal, the company offered Trizec 18.5 million shares in Bramalea at $25 each, increasing Trizec's ownership of Bramalea to 61 percent.

Bramalea's two-step transaction with Trizec lead to the formation of Trilea Centers Inc., a wholly owned subsidiary, to manage its newly purchased retail shopping mall properties. By now, Trizec's hold over Bramalea was tightening. It installed Gordon Arnell to head Trilea, angering Kenneth Field, who resigned as co-chief executive of Bramalea and sold his share in the company for $80 million.

While Trizec gained control of Bramalea, it lost in Shiff and Field the creative force responsible for building up the company from 1973 to 1986. For Trizec, this meant a greater involvement in and responsibility for Bramalea's growth, which Trizec didn't necessarily anticipate. Furthermore, management at Trizec wasn't content with being forced to part with its prized shopping center portfolio to make way for Trilea. Several disputes ensued, including one involving which computer system should be used to manage the shopping malls. While Bramalea claimed ownership of the malls, Trizec argued that as the controller of Bramalea, its equipment should predominate.

During this time, Benjamin Swirsky was named president of Bramalea. The company's business strategy focused on drawing rental income from commercial assets like office buildings and shopping centers, and relying less on housing and land sales. The idea was to manage properties that produced long-term income, rather than looking for quick profits through property sales. Expanding rental income would come in part through renewing leases in prime properties in a buoyant economy when rents were likely to rise. But the strategy really hinged on developing or acquiring new properties.

By 1988 Bramalea's property portfolio had reached 40 million square feet of industry, commercial, and retail space, in addition to its giant housing and land banks. Plans were announced that year to boost the portfolio to 60 million square feet over the next five years. During this period of unprecedented expansion, Trilea Centers purchased a 34 percent interest in J.D.S. Investments Ltd. by acquiring 288,000 common shares worth $30 million in the regional shopping center and office building concern, based mostly in Toronto. A month later, in January 1989, Bramalea paid $250 million to purchase the U.S.-based Marlborough Development Corporation, a house builder in the southern California region.

Benjamin Swirsky exuded confidence over Bramalea's break-neck pace of growth, stating in the company's 1989 annual report: "We have a clear perception of Bramalea's growth potential. Our strategy is to select key markets where we can concentrate our expertise and effort. We know these local markets very well and the opportunities they offer."

In 1990 the company posted revenues of just under $1.2 billion, and profits of $64 million. However, during this time Bramalea had amassed more than $5 billion in debt to fund its expansion, and, like every other major North American property developer, the company soon confronted the worst global recession experienced since the Great Depression.

By the middle of 1990, Trizec recognized that Bramalea was in trouble. Swirsky was replaced as president by Marvin Marshall, a specialist brought in from Houston-based Cullen Center Inc., a Trizec subsidiary. Marshall was faced with the challenge of selling as many Bramalea assets as possible in order to bring the company out from under a $5 billion pile of debt.

Selling more than $1 billion worth of assets a year in a buyer's market proved a difficult task. Marshall sought to keep Bramalea from landing in the bankruptcy court, laden as it was with a daunting loan repayment schedule. Just in 1992 alone, Bramalea was forced to refinance $633 million in debt.

Among the prized properties put on the block early on was the Hyatt Regency Hotel in Vancouver, going for $95 million, and a three-quarters stake in the Four Seasons Hotel in Toronto. Early sales included a half-stake in One Queen Street East, a 403,000 square foot building in downtown Toronto. The deal, concluded in May 1991, involved the Ontario Teachers' Pension Plan Board as buyer.

Marshall also shook up the Bramalea management. In February 1991, he brought on board Paul Campbell, a one-time manager under Marshall at Cullen Center and a former president of Campeau Corporation, a struggling Toronto-based property development concern. In April, Frank Graham, a one-time chief financial officer with Coca Cola Beverages of Canada, was appointed Bramalea's chief financial officer. By the summer of that year, more than 350 employees, or 12 percent of Bramalea's staff, were laid off.

Asset sales eventually arrived. An office building in Toronto, land holdings in Brampton, Ontario, and a nearby shopping center went for $90 million. And in November 1991, the company announced that it had sold a 50 percent lease on the Scarborough Town Center, outside Toronto, for around $140 million. In February 1992, the company announced a common share offering, by which Bramalea's equity base was increased to $935 million at the half-year mark, against a figure of $884

million held at October 31, 1991. However, these funds were not enough. Bramalea suspended all dividend payments on the company's common shares and postponed payment of interest due June 30, 1992, on the 10.2 percent debentures maturing in 1999.

The company's restructuring plan also called for Trizec to forgo all its dividend and interest payments and to approve a plan to convert loans to equity. Among the properties to be put on the block for sale were its Edmonton office buildings, a 50 percent stake in major Canadian shopping malls, most of what it owned in Ottawa, and four out of twelve office buildings in Toronto. The company was also to sell 50 percent interests in office buildings in Dallas and Oakland, as well as commercial land sites in Atlanta, Chicago, and Los Angeles.

In July 1992, despite Bramalea's efforts to conserve cash, declining revenue and cash flow again threatened to throw Bramalea into bankruptcy court. Bramalea defaulted on an interest payment of $4.4 million, and the grace period on the default expired on July 30 of that year.

Well-timed asset purchases by parent company Trizec saved Bramalea from bankruptcy. In September 1992, an agreement was reached between Bramalea and its creditors on its restructuring plan. The company would continue to sell its assets where possible, defer interest payments, and exchange debt for equity.

Analysts began to wonder how long Trizec would continue to help Bramalea stay afloat. A partial response came in late November 1992 when Bramalea required a $38.6 million financing commitment. Trizec balked and the commitment came instead from Carena Developments Ltd. of Toronto, which owns 40 percent of Trizec.

Principal Subsidiaries: Bramalea Urban Properties Group Inc.; Marlborough Development Corporation; Trilea Centers Inc.; Perez Bramalea Ltd.; Bramalea Wescorp Developments Ltd.; Bramalea Leasing Corporation Ltd.; Bramalea Management Corporation Ltd.; The Greater Cedarwood Development Corporation Ltd; Bramalea Office Buildings Ltd.; Amberlea Developments Ltd.; Co-Chuk Investments Ltd.

Further Reading:

"Bramalea Riding Out Housing Slump," *Globe and Mail,* February 28, 1991.
"The Bronfire of the Vanities?" *Business Week,* August 10, 1992.
"How Bramalea's Dream Became a Nightmare," *Globe and Mail,* November 7, 1992.
"Mall Owners Get Retail Warning," *Financial Post,* December 5, 1991.

—Etan Vlessing

Brauerei Beck & Co.

Am Deich 18–19
2800 Bremen 01
Germany
(421) 509 40
Fax: (421) 509 46 67

Private Company
Incorporated: 1873
Employees: 4,257
Sales: DM 1.30 billion (US$762 million)
SICs: 2082 Malt Beverages

Brauerei Beck & Co. is the world's largest exporter of beer, accounting for more than one-third of the total exports of the beverage from Germany. Sold in 140 countries, the company's products have long been the most widely recognized beers from a nation known for its breweries. Indeed, Beck's beer cases are labeled with the phrase ''Found on Five Continents.'' Even in its highly competitive German home market, Beck's claims the highest brand awareness and largest distribution of any beer. The privately held firm also benefits from holdings of glass manufacturing concerns and a bottling concession with Coca-Cola Co.

The original breweries that today comprise the corporate entity of Beck & Co. have roots that reach back to medieval times in Bremen, a major port on the Weser River. The city-state of Bremen was an important member of the Hanseatic League, a powerful federation formed by German merchants in the Middle Ages for trading and defense. Bremen's merchant class tightly controlled Northern European shipping and commerce for two centuries and influenced it for many more.

One of the largest exports out of the Bremen harbor during the Middle Ages was beer from the city's breweries, of which there were more than 300. As early as the thirteenth century, this beer was exported to Scandinavia, England, and Holland, and in 1489 the city's breweries formed the Bremen Brewers' Society to regulate the production and export of the beverage. As foreign markets clamored for Bremen's beers in subsequent centuries, competition increased, and only the brewers whose products consistently withstood long sea journeys survived. By 1870 only 30 of the original 350 members of the Bremen Brewer's Society remained, including the Beck Brewery, which had altered the chemical formulation of its beer to produce a

heavy barley ale that survived the rigors of the trade routes. Until modern brewing technology was developed in the nineteenth century, this type of ale was a standard Beck product.

In the late nineteenth century, prominent Bremen business leader Lueder Rutenberg incorporated the company that is today known as Brauerei Beck & Co. after the Beck brewery was merged with two other local breweries, Bierbrauerei Wilhelm Remmer and Hemelinger Aktienbrauerei. In 1921 Beck & Co. formed a cooperative agreement with another Bremen brewery, the Brauerei C. H. Haake & Co. Control of the market was divided between Beck & Co. and Haake, with Brauerei Beck & Co. agreeing to produce beer for the export market under the brand name of Beck's, while Haake-Beck Brauerei AG would sell its products under the names Haake-Beck, Remmer, and Hemelinger in the domestic German market. Haake-Beck Brauerei was later made a subsidiary of Beck & Co., making Brauerei Beck the largest privately owned brewery in Germany.

The location of Beck & Co. in the port city of Bremen contributed to its success and played an influential role in many outward aspects of the firm. Bremen's status as a major player in North European commerce facilitated Beck's delivery to several foreign ports. The reputation of the Bremen brewers solidified the beer's potential to hold and maintain increasing shares of foreign markets. Although the beer was at first shipped in the traditional barrels, Beck & Co. began exporting bottles sheathed in straw and packed in weighty wooden crates to withstand high seas.

In its advertising Beck & Co. features an important aspect of its history—the Reinheitsgebot, or Purity Law, enacted by the Bavarian Court of Duke Wilhelm IV in 1516. The law specified that only malted barley, yeast, hops, and water could be used in beer brewed in Germany for the German market. German beer exporters stress this law in citing the long tradition of excellence of German beers, but not all brew their export beer in compliance with the statute. All of Beck's beers, according to the company's literature, contain only hops grown in the nearby Tettnag and Hallertau regions, water from Geest-area springs and the reservoirs of the Harz mountains, and a particular strain of yeast cultivated for decades by the brew masters at the Bremen plant.

Each year the city of Bremen holds the Schaffermahl, a formal dinner held in mid-February that dates back to the sixteenth century when the Haus Seefahrt Foundation established the gathering to raise money for needy sailors. Prominent guests gather in the city hall, smoke traditional white clay pipes, and dine on a meal of dried fish and smoked pork. The most important part of the dinner, however, is the beer brewed by Beck & Co. especially for the occasion and drunk from pewter tankards. This is a version of the company's original Seefahrtsbier, the extremely strong quaff that could withstand long sea voyages.

The evolution of lager beers (''lager'' being German for ''to store'') was spurred by technological developments, including research into yeast cultures and fermentation as well as the invention of refrigeration. In bottom-fermented beer, the yeast sinks to the bottom, which makes for a clearer beer that is less likely to sour, but which needs to be stored and cooled longer than top-fermented ales. Beck & Co., like the other major German breweries, began producing lager beers late in the nineteenth century.

Because of its chemistry, beer had a relatively short shelf life, until modern brewing and storing methods improved matters. Beck & Co. has continually invested in state-of-the-art brewing facilities, applying technological innovations to improve product quality. For instance, Beck & Co. managed to greatly reduce the oxygen count of its product to give it a longer shelf life. Beck & Co. was also one of the first breweries to use the modern keg. These have been improved by using stainless steel containers as well as a hygienic tap system that helps lengthen the amount of time beer can be stored and reduces the risk of contamination involved in pouring draft beers.

Today Beck & Co. is the last brewer remaining in the city of Bremen. However, the brand name of Beck's is found only on bottles exported out of Germany; the company's Haake-Beck, Remmer, and Hemelinger lines are brewed specifically for domestic consumers. These three brands retain their vestigial names to help differentiate them in a large and diverse home market and remind drinkers of Bremen's long brewing history. Each of them, while targeting different domestic markets, also represents a distinct product, reflecting the dissimilar tastes of Germans for their beer. Haake-Beck's beer is distributed throughout all of Germany, while the Hemelinger and Remmer brands are part of the tradition of local specialty beers found in and around Bremen. Also carrying the Remmer brand name is a light beer with a lower alcohol and calorie content that is distributed throughout Germany.

On the international market, Beck & Co. attempts to appeal to the widest range of tastes while still adhering to German brewing standards. The Beck's beer sold in North America, for instance, is a much lighter version of a traditional German brew. Here, the products found under the Beck's label, in addition to the flagship lager, include Beck's Dark, Beck's Light, and Haake-Beck. These are imported by Dribeck Importers Inc. of Greenwich, Connecticut, a subsidiary founded in 1964.

Although there are several thousand breweries producing regional beers, Beck & Co. is one of the few that distributes throughout all of reunified Germany. The fall of the Berlin Wall in 1989 opened up a huge new market of consumers for German companies. Beer brewed in the former East Germany by state-owned breweries was poor in quality due to a shortage of raw materials and antiquated machinery. Frequently adulterated with corn or rice, East German beer required additives to enhance shelf-life and therefore did not meet Reinheitsgebot standards.

Shortly after trade between the two Germanies was fully reestablished, Beck & Co. began selling its products in the former East German states and achieved remarkable gains in sales, due in part to the novelty of West German beer among consumers there. In April of 1991 Beck & Co. acquired the Rostocker Brauerei VEB, formerly a state-owned company in Rostock, a port on the Baltic Sea. Although Beck & Co. had to invest heavily to upgrade the brewery's equipment, it gave the company an excellent position from which to target the East German market, brewing a new and improved Rostocker for East Germans consumers. In addition, the geographical location of the newly acquired brewery permitted easier access for exports of Beck's beer to areas within the former Soviet Union. By 1992 Beck's products were sold in most of the former Eastern Bloc countries.

Consumers around the globe are drawn to import beers for their sophisticated edge. Beck & Co. has sought to position itself as part of a centuries-old tradition of German brewing excellence, stressing both the company's longevity and the quality of its product. In the 1980s, however, a North American trend toward moderation in alcohol consumption had a significant impact on import sales, while a weakened U.S. dollar also made it difficult for foreign companies such as Beck & Co. to keep prices low. Competition in the beer market became fierce as consumers' palates became more discriminating. The company's inroads into Eastern Europe did help offset the decrease in import sales by its Dribeck subsidiary in the United States. In addition, Brauerei Beck & Co. expected a unified Germany to provide great opportunity for expansion and profit.

Principal Subsidiaries: Nienburger Glas GmbH & Co. KG (92%); Bremer Erfrischungsgetraenke-GmbH; Rostocker Brauerei GmbH; Haake-Beck Brauerei AG (95.17%); Dribeck Importers Inc. (U.S.A.).

Further Reading:

Anderson, Will, *From Beer to Eternity: Everything You Always Wanted to Know About Beer,* Lexington, MA: Stephen Greene Press, 1987.

''Beck's Counts Itself Among German Gems,'' *New York Times,* November 21, 1992, p. D19.

''Bulging Beck's,'' *Food and Beverage Marketing,* April 1992, p. 43.

Dennis, Darienne L., ''How About a Beer?'' *Fortune,* August 1, 1988, p. 8.

Fahey, Alison, ''Party Hardly,'' *Adweek's Brandweek,* October 26, 1992, pp. 24–25.

Finch, Christopher, *Beer: A Connoisseur's Guide to the World's Best,* New York: Abbeville Press, 1989.

Gorman, John, ''Beer Lovers Spread the Word: Beck's,'' *Chicago Tribune,* May 17, 1985, sec. 3, pp. 1–2.

Hemphill, Gary A., ''Imports: A Taste of Reality,'' *Beverage Industry,* September 1989, pp. 1–26.

Jackson, Michael, ed., *The World Guide to Beer,* New York: Prentice-Hall, 1977.

—Carol Brennan

Bristol-Myers Squibb Company

Bristol-Myers Squibb Company

345 Park Avenue
New York, New York, 10154
U.S.A.
(212) 546-4000
Fax: (212) 546-4020

Public Company
Incorporated: 1900 as Bristol-Myers Company
Employees: 52,600
Sales: $11 billion
Stock Exchanges: New York
SICs: 2834 Pharmaceutical Preparations; 2844 Perfumes,
     Cosmetics

Bristol-Myers Squibb Company is the second largest pharmaceutical company in the world and is also recognized worldwide as a major producer and distributor of such consumer products as toothpaste and drain opener. The merger between Bristol-Myers Company and the Squibb Corporation, two large and successful firms with compatible operations, occurred during the late 1980s, when competitive pressure and the increasing cost of research led many pharmaceutical firms to seek business partners in order to survive.

Bristol-Myers was founded in 1887 by two former fraternity brothers, William McLaren Bristol and John Ripley Myers. They each invested $5,000 in the Clinton Pharmaceutical Company, a failing drug manufacturer based in New York, and their small operation began selling medical preparations by horse and buggy to local doctors and dentists. For the first few years the company struggled due to insufficient capital and the new owners' lack of understanding of how drugs were made. The firm relocated from Clinton to Syracuse, New York, in 1889 to improve its shipping capability, and then moved again, ten years later, to Brooklyn for easier access to its expanding base of customers in Pennsylvania and New England.

In 1898 the company's name was changed to Bristol, Myers Company. One year later John Ripley Myers died. To help the company grow, the firm increased its sales force, referred to as "detail men," and began shifting its attention from physicians to wholesale and retail druggists who were now recognized as primary suppliers of medication.

In 1900 the firm incorporated and modified its name, replacing the comma with a hyphen. The same year, Bristol-Myers Company made its first profit and entered the market for specialty products. Sales of such Bristol-Myers items as Sal Hepatica, a laxative mineral salt, and Ipana toothpaste, the first such product to contain a disinfectant, grew rapidly between 1903 and 1905. Strong demand caused several changes in the company's operation, including the creation of an export department to handle international orders and the opening of new manufacturing facilities in Hillside, New Jersey.

In 1915 Henry Bristol, William Bristol's oldest son, became general manager. Henry was joined in 1928 by his brothers, William Jr. and Lee, who handled manufacturing and advertising, respectively. During the recession that followed World War I the company discontinued its line of "ethical," or prescription, drugs to focus production on its two best-selling specialty products and other toiletries, antiseptics, and cough syrups. Bristol-Myers also moved to its present location in Manhattan at this time. The shift in product focus was accompanied by a new emphasis on advertising directed toward consumers rather than doctors and dentists. Bristol-Myers sponsored a radio show featuring a group called the Ipana Troubadours, and introduced the slogan "Ipana for the Smile of Beauty; Sal Hepatica for the Smile of Health."

The company became a part of Drug, Inc., a large, newly formed holding company, in 1928. Drug, Inc., produced proprietary drugs and other medications and also operated a large retail chain. Bristol-Myers continued to grow and advertised heavily during the Great Depression, launching several new and successful consumer products. Other operations affiliated with Drug, Inc., did not fare nearly as well, however, and the holding company disbanded in 1933.

Upon the outbreak of World War II, Bristol-Myers again became a manufacturer of ethical pharmaceuticals. It mass produced penicillin for the Allied armed forces through its Bristol Laboratories subsidiary, which had been previously acquired under the name of Cheplin Laboratories. Bristol Laboratories' experience in the process of fermentation—which was required to make its primary product, acidophilus milk—was easily converted to the manufacture of the antibiotics. This led to the firm's formal re-entry into the ethical drug area and enabled it to take advantage of the growing demand for antibiotics after the war.

The company continued to grow over the next decade, assisted by television advertisements. In 1957 Henry Bristol became chair of the board and was succeeded as president and chief executive officer by Fredric N. Schwartz, the former head of Bristol Laboratories. Assisted by Gavin K. MacBain, the company's treasurer who later assumed the position of chairperson, Schwartz acquired several smaller, well-managed companies in growing industries. The new subsidiaries grew quickly with help from Bristol-Myers's research and marketing expertise. These acquisitions included Clairol, a maker of hair coloring products, purchased in 1959; Drackett, a household products manufacturer, acquired in 1965; and Mead Johnson, which produced infant formula and children's vitamins, purchased in 1967. Clairol had already made marketing history as a result of the popular advertising campaign "Does she or doesn't she? Hair color so natural only her hairdresser knows for sure!"

Richard Gelb, the son of Clairol's founder, reluctantly joined Bristol-Myers after the acquisition to head the Clairol operation. Gelb was given a wide berth in managing Clairol and did so well that he was promoted to executive vice-president and then to president under chairman Gavin MacBain. Gelb became president just as Bristol-Myers's growth flattened out. A string of new-product failures during the late 1960s drained finances and depressed stock value. In 1972 Gelb was appointed chair and CEO. He initiated a comeback over the next decade by spending $400 million advertising the company's most popular brands and by expanding its line of health care products. This growth was accomplished in part through the acquisitions of Zimmer Manufacturing Company, a producer of orthopedic and surgical products, in 1972, and of Unitek Corporation, a dental equipment supplier, in 1978.

Under Gelb's leadership, Bristol-Myers was able to shift gears quickly in response to market changes. When concern over the use of fluorocarbons threatened the spray deodorant market in the mid-1970s, the company increased advertising of its Ban roll-on deodorant. This strategy vaulted Ban into the top-selling spot and increased the sales of all other roll-on products by 75 percent in one year.

Soon thereafter, however, the company suffered a major marketing setback with its Clairol products. In 1977 the National Cancer Institute reported a link between an ingredient used in hair colorants, 2-4 DAA, and cancer in laboratory animals. Bristol-Myers disputed these findings at first but later introduced a new line of hair coloring products and reformulated the original line without the ingredient in question.

Bristol-Myers's continued attention to health-care research was also a major factor in its resurgence. Beginning in the late 1970s Bristol-Myers began to use cash generated by its consumer-products business to fund the research and development of additional drugs beyond its antibiotics and synthetic penicillins. Several new areas were explored, including cardiovascular agents and anticancer drugs.

At the time, Bristol-Myers was the only pharmaceutical company to invest in anticancer drugs, because growth potential appeared small. The company obtained the marketing rights to several anticancer drugs developed by the National Institutes of Health and other research institutions, universities, and drug companies, and was well positioned when this market took off. Between 1974 and 1980 Bristol-Myers launched 11 new drugs for treatment of cancer and other diseases. Although none of these products was a breakthrough drug, combined they contributed over $200 million in sales to the company by 1980. This growth occurred despite the company's relatively small research budget.

The company was already an experienced marketer of over-the-counter (OTC) analgesics. Its Excedrin and Bufferin brands had accounted for one-quarter of the total market for nonprescription pain relievers until the early 1960s, when an OTC version of Johnson & Johnson's Tylenol—a nonaspirin product—took a significant percentage of Bristol-Myers's market share. In the mid-1970s Bristol-Myers challenged Johnson & Johnson with Datril, a nonaspirin product priced lower than Tylenol. Johnson & Johnson responded quickly, lowering the price of Tylenol.

In 1981 the company settled a series of ten-year-old antitrust suits alleging that Bristol-Myers and Beecham Group, a British pharmaceutical company, had improperly obtained a patent on the antibiotic ampicillin. The suits also accused the firms of engaging in restrictive licensing practices, which had resulted in excessive charges to hospitals, wholesalers, and retailers.

The following year a series of product tampering incidents occurred involving various over-the-counter analgesic products, including Bristol-Myers's Excedrin capsules. The company responded to new Food and Drug Administration (FDA) regulations in 1983 with tamper resistant packaging for its capsule products.

In 1984 Bristol-Myers signed an agreement with Upjohn which enabled it to introduce Nuprin, a new nonprescription form of ibuprofen pain reliever. The agreement gave Bristol-Myers the means to take on Tylenol once again. It also pitted the firm against American Home Products, which already sold a pain reliever under the Anacin brand and was planning to launch a new ibuprofen-based product called Advil.

At this time, Bristol-Myers entered the market for drugs used to treat anxiety and depression. The company licensed the rights to products manufactured by foreign firms while continuing to invest heavily in its own pharmaceutical research and development. The firm had reorganized its internal research operations and, in 1984, built a multimillion dollar research facility in Wallingford, Connecticut. Two years later Bristol-Myers received FDA approval to market its own tranquilizer product, BuSpar, which did not produce many of the negative side effects of other antidepressant drugs already on the market.

In 1986 the firm became enmeshed in the complex acquisition of Genetic Systems Corporation (GSC), a Seattle-based biotechnology company. GSC was founded in 1980 by a group of entrepreneurial microbiologists who teamed up with Syntex Corporation, a drug company, to manufacture and market tests for sexually transmitted diseases. Three years later the partners formed another venture, Oncogen, to manufacture products for cancer treatment, and in 1985 they offered Bristol-Myers an opportunity to invest in the operation. Later that year, after a Bristol-Myers competitor, Eli Lilly & Company, acquired Hybridtech, a leading producer of monoclonal antibodies, Bristol-Myers negotiated an agreement with GSC management to buy GSC and Oncogen, unaware that GSC had negotiated a similar deal with Syntex two months before. After threatening a lawsuit, Syntex elected to withdraw its offer for GSC in exchange for a $15 million compensation package provided by Bristol-Myers and for marketing rights to selected GSC and Oncogen products. Bristol-Myers sold GSC to Sanofi, a French pharmaceutical firm, in 1990.

In June 1986 a second incident of tampering with capsule-type pain relief products caused two deaths in the Seattle area. This incident led Bristol-Myers to recall its Excedrin capsules nationwide. It soon withdrew all of its nonprescription capsule products from the market, including Comtrex cold relief medication. The capsules were replaced with the caplet, a specially coated, capsule-shaped pill. With this action, Bristol-Myers became the second company in its industry, after Johnson & Johnson, to end the sale of OTC medication in capsule form.

In an attempt to establish a stronger position in the field of coronary care, Bristol-Myers negotiated an agreement in March 1987 to acquire SciMed Life Systems, a manufacturer of coronary balloon angioplasty catheters and other disposable products for treating cardiovascular disease. Two months later Bristol-Myers withdrew its offer after SciMed was sued by Eli Lilly & Company for patent infringement.

Bristol-Myers continued to grow as a manufacturer of prescription pharmaceuticals, lessening its dependence on consumer products by focusing on acquired immune deficiency syndrome (AIDS) research. Since both cancer and AIDS research are virology-based, this area was a natural fit for the company. In 1987 Bristol-Myers obtained an exclusive license to produce and test two new AIDS drugs, dideoxyadenosine (DDA) and dideoxyinosine (DDI). It also received FDA approval to test an experimental AIDS vaccine on humans.

In November 1989 Bristol-Myers merged with Squibb Corporation. Squibb had been established in 1858 and was among the oldest U.S. pharmaceutical companies. Over half of Squibb's sales were generated by pharmaceuticals, and the company also owned a profitable cosmetic business. The two firms had similar corporate cultures. The merger also brought together two chief executives, Gelb and Richard M. Furlaud of Squibb, who had been friends for 25 years and had discussed the idea of a merger occasionally over the previous three years.

As part of the merger agreement Richard Gelb became chairman and chief executive officer of the combined company, while Furlaud, his counterpart at Squibb, became president and headed up the company's pharmaceutical business. Squibb benefited from Bristol-Myers's biomedical research capabilities and established presence in consumer health products. This market was becoming increasingly important to Squibb, since several competitors were already negotiating agreements to market their prescription drugs in OTC forms to consumers. In Squibb, Bristol-Myers obtained a new source of prescription drugs with strong sales potential, particularly in the cardiovascular area, and a sizable budget to add to its own continuing research operation.

The merger, which united the twelfth and fourteenth largest companies, was not without tension. By December 1990, 2,000 employees—four percent of the total workforce—had been laid off, and Bristol planned to close 60 pharmaceutical plants worldwide. Closings of six of 18 consumer products plants were scheduled through 1993. Nevertheless, the merger gave Bristol an important worldwide presence, thanks to Squibb's strong position in Europe, the world's largest drug market.

Bristol-Myers Squibb Company is comprised of four major product areas with significant global growth potential: pharmaceuticals, consumer products, medical devices, and nutritionals. The company's pharmaceutical products include cardiovascular and anticancer drugs, anti-infective agents, drugs for treating the central nervous system, diagnostic imaging agents, and dermatological products which are marketed through the company's Westwood Pharmaceuticals subsidiary. As the population ages and health care costs continue to increase, Bristol-Myers Squibb's goal is to develop new pharmaceutical products that will reduce hospitalization and keep health care expenses down.

The company markets over 140 consumer brands, including nonprescription medicines, vitamins, skin care preparations, toiletries, beauty aids, and household items. Its medical devices division serves the orthopedics market with such products as artificial hip and knee replacements, and also supplies various items needed for ostomy procedures, wound and burn care, and other surgical specialties.

The second-largest maker of infant formula in the world, Bristol-Myers Squibb Company also manufactures products for people of all ages requiring nutritional support. In 1989 the company negotiated an agreement with Gerber Products Company to manufacture and market Gerber Baby Formula directly to U.S. consumers. Controversial advertising for this product touched off a boycott of the company's line of formula products by a group of pediatricians who felt that Bristol-Myers Squibb was attempting to discourage breastfeeding and to compromise physicians' influence in baby formula selection.

As it entered the 1990s, Bristol-Myers Squibb's goal was to achieve the top spot in world pharmaceutical sales by the year 2001. The company received FDA approval for its cholesterol-lowering drug, Pravachol, in 1991. Company executives predicted that Pravachol, which helps offset the effects of heart disease and allows some patients to forego surgery, would become a billion dollar drug.

Bristol-Myers Squibb also had several other drugs in various stages of development. One important and promising drug in development was Videx, used to fight AIDS. Another important development was Taxol, an anticancer drug made from the bark of the Pacific yew tree. The FDA gave the company the go-ahead in early 1993 to market Taxol to ovarian cancer patients. However, in February 1993, the U.S. Subcommittee on Regulation, Business Opportunities, and Energy accused Bristol-Myers Squibb and several other pharmaceutical companies of overpricing, pointing to Taxol's price of six to eight thousand dollars per complete treatment. However, the company maintained that the price was not excessive, and declined to supply the subcommittee with the data used to set the price.

By the end of the first quarter of 1993, sales at Bristol-Myers Squibb had increased four percent or $2.8 billion. During that quarter, two committees of the U.S. Food and Drug Administration gave the go-ahead to new uses of two of the company's existing products: Capoten, for use by patients who had suffered a heart attack, and Megace, for treatment of anorexia and HIV-related weight loss. At the same time, generic drug makers began working on a non-branded version of Capoten, whose patent is due to expire in 1995.

In January 1993, Bristol signed a contract with Mead Johnson, establishing a joint venture to produce and sell Enfamil and Enfapro infant formulas in Guangzhou, China. Nevertheless, the main focus of research at Bristol-Myers Squibb remains in anti-cancer drugs. Company scientists seek to develop drugs that will kill cancerous cells with fewer side effects in the patient.

The future of Bristol-Myers Squibb Company is dependent upon continued product leadership on an international basis in each of its highly competitive core businesses, as well as a continuing commitment to research and development of new products. Several forces—including an aging population, an increasing percentage of women in the full-time workforce, and a growing number of nontraditional households—are expected to create needs that will have a strong influence on the company's consumer products business.

Further Reading:

Bristol-Myers Company Special Report: The Next Century, New York: Bristol-Myers Company, 1987.
Bristol-Myers Squibb Company Annual Reports, New York: Bristol-Myers Squibb Co., 1988–92.
"Bristol-Myers Squibb Gets an Okay on Taxol," *Chemical Marketing Reporter,* January 4, 1993, p. 3.
"Bristol-Myers Squibb Reports Results," *PR Newswire,* April 21, 1993.
Hager, Bruce, "Marriage Becomes Bristol-Myers Squibb," *Business Week,* December 3, 1990, pp. 138–39.

—Sandy Schusteff
updated by Marinell Landa

British Vita PLC

Oldham Street
Middleton, Manchester M24 2DB
United Kingdom
(061) 643-1133
Fax: (061) 653-5411

Public Company
Incorporated: 1966 as British Vita Company Ltd.
Employees: 12,746
Sales: £635.95 million (US$947.57 million)
Stock Exchanges: London
SICs: 2822 Synthetic Rubber; 2823 Cellulosic Manmade
   Fibers

British Vita PLC is involved in the manufacture and processing of a wide assortment of polymers, including cellular foams, synthetic fiber fillings, specialized and coated textiles, and polymer compounds and moldings. Their products are marketed to the furniture, transportation, apparel, packaging, and engineering industries. The company is also involved in the licensing of advanced technical processes.

Founded with £100 by Norman Grimshaw in 1949, the company first began business as Vitafoam Ltd. in Oldham. Its primary business was the manufacture of foam cushions and mattresses. Vita's first regional foam conversion plant was opened at High Wycombe, approximately 30 miles northwest of London, in 1954. The main office was moved to Middleton in 1957, and the company acquired Liverpool Latex the same year. By 1960 Vita established its first foreign division when operations commenced in Rhodesia (now Zimbabwe). Another plant opened in Nigeria in 1962.

Vita's history is one of aggressive mergers and acquisitions that have allowed the company to expand its product base and market. The company was incorporated as British Vita Company Ltd in 1966, the same year that J. Mandelberg, a maker of coated fabrics and flame laminating, was acquired. Throughout the 1960s, Vita worked to diversify its product line, adding polyether foam, pvc foam, carpet underlay, general rubber molding, and coated fabrics. In 1967 the company celebrated its listing on the London Stock Exchange.

By 1968 Vita had 15 operations throughout the United Kingdom involved in the manufacturing of latex, polyurethane and polyvinyl foams, precision mold and pattern making, footwear components, fabric coating and laminating. Its foreign holdings were expanding as well, and in 1971 British Vita International Ltd was formed to supervise the overseas operations. During the 1970s, Vita began to decentralize its operations and adopted new methods to cut costs and increase efficiency. At the same time, the company was expanding its foreign holdings into Australia, Canada, Indonesia, New Zealand, Japan, and Egypt.

Vita's management team has been singled out for its longevity and stability. Fernley Parker joined the company in 1954 and rose steadily through the ranks as corporate secretary, finance director, and chief executive officer before serving as chairman for ten years. He retired from the board in 1987 but remained involved in the company as chairman of British Vita Pensions Trust Limited. Robert McGee succeeded Fernley Parker as chief executive officer in 1975 and again as chairman in 1988. McGee had spent virtually all of his business career with Vita. He was hired in 1955 and was appointed to the board in 1972. Rod Sellers, McGee's successor as chief executive officer, had been with the company since 1971. Vita's deputy chief executive officer, Frank Eaton, was likewise a long-term employee of the company. Eaton was hired in 1958 and was appointed to the board in 1975.

In 1978 Vita acquired Libeltex and Portways, both fiber manufacturers, and Caligen, a foam manufacturer. For the next five years, the company concentrated on developing its fabric knitting and finishing operations. During the 1980s, Vita continued to acquire companies that allowed it to increase its holdings. The European market was expanded through the acquisition of Tramico in France, Isofel in Spain, and Koepp/Veenendaal in Germany and the Netherlands. A joint venture with Viktor Achter, an automotive fabric firm, resulted in the formation of Vita-Achter. The industrial products division was expanded with the acquisition of three firms: PEC Plastics, Inversale, and Rubber Latex Limited. The latter is now known as Vita Liquid Polymers in the United Kingdom and as RLA Polymers in Australia.

During 1987 Vita further expanded its operations through acquisitions, the building of new plants, and the implementation of innovative production procedures. The German-based Metzeler Schaum group and Royalite Plastics, with operations in Scotland and Italy, were added to the Vita conglomerate. The company formed a new division, Engineering Thermoplastics, enlarged its coated fabrics operation, and began to manufacture staple fibers.

Vitafoam introduced combustion-modified high resilience foams in 1988. That same year, ICOA group of Spain and the UK-based Rossendale Combining Company were acquired. Acquisitions in 1989 included Esbjerg Thermoplast in Denmark; Alpha Flock, a manufacturer of fiber for electrostatic spraying in the United Kingdom; and Ball & Young Adhesives, a UK-based maker of rubber carpet underlays. Vita also purchased one-third of the Spartech Corporation, a manufacturer of engineering thermoplastics in the United States. A series of smaller acquisitions the following year allowed Vita to further strengthen its fiber processing, thermoplastic engineering, laminating, and foam operations.

In 1991 Vita made more inroads in the U.S. marketplace with the acquisition of a portion of Leggett & Platt in Missouri, which became Vitafoam Incorporated, with foaming plants in High Point, North Carolina, and Tupelo, Mississippi. In 1992 the Libeltex subsidiary obtained Sporta Vadd and its two fiber-processing operations, and Norman BV, a 100-year-old foam mattress manufacturer in the Netherlands, became part of Vita Interfoam. Yet another foam mattress company, Oost BV and its subsidiary, Sanaform BV, were acquired later the same year.

Although the company continued to enjoy growth and prosperity, Vita was faced with many of the same problems other businesses endured in the early 1990s. The economic recession in the United Kingdom slowed production. Increased competition from Italy and the restructuring of the automotive industry in Germany also affected Vita's growth in France and Germany. In addition, environmental regulations placed new restrictions on manufacturers, requiring them to modify some equipment. In 1993 Vita was forced to dispose of ICOA in a management buyout. Further restructuring was planned for Metzeler Laminados, one of the two remaining Spanish operations. The prolonged drought in Africa affected profits in the Zimbabwe companies. However, the company remained optimistic about its growth potential and credited improvements to its manufacturing and quality systems as well as innovative product development as reasons for its continued success.

Acquisitions continued in 1993 with the purchase of Pre-Fab Cushioning in Canada and Nabors Manufacturing in the United States. In France, Vita acquired Pullflex, specialist foam converters, and the Gaillon Group, a Lyon-based manufacturer of thermoplastics. A subsidiary was formed in Poland with construction underway on a new factory for foam manufacturing and converting.

Principal Subsidiaries: Ball & Young Ltd.; British Vita Investments Ltd.; Caligen Foam Ltd.; Kay-Metzeler Ltd.; Royalite Plastics Ltd.; The Rossendale Combing Company Ltd.; Vitacom Ltd.; Vitafoam Ltd.; Vitamol Ltd.; Vita Industrial Polymers Ltd.; Vita Liquid Polymers Ltd.; Vita International Ltd.; Vita Services Ltd.; Vita-tex Ltd.; Caligen European BV; Deutsche Vita Polymere GmbH; Draka Interfoam BV; ICOA SA; ICOA France; ICOA Levante SA; Isofel SA; Koepp AG; Ledikanten-en Matrassen Fabriek Oost BV; Lebeltex AB; Libeltex GmbH; Libeltex NV; Metzeler Laminados Iberia SA; Metzeler Mousse SA; Metzeler Plastics GmbH; Metzeler Schaum GmbH; Morard Europe SA; Norma Boxmeer BV; Poly-Kunstoffverarbeitung GmbH; Radium Foam BV; Radium Latex GmbH; Roon SA; Royalite Plastics SRL; J.Schmidt Schaumstoffe GmbH; Tramico SA; Unifoam AG; Veenendaal en Co BV; Veenendaal Schaumstoffwerk GmbH; Vitafoam Europe BV; Vita Interfoam BV; Vita Polymers Denmark A/S; Vita Polymers Europe BV; Vita Polymeres France SA; Vitafoam CA Ltd.; Vitafoam Inc.; BTR-Vitaline Ltd.; Emotex Trading Company Ltd.; Vita-Achter Ltd.; Vita Cortex Holdings Ltd.; Spartech Corporation; Taki-Vita SAE; Vita Inoac Ltd.; Vitafoam Nigeria PLC; Vitafoam Products Canada Ltd.

Further Reading:

Rooney J., et al, *UK Portfolio Perspective—Topical Report,* Lehman Brothers Limited, January 29, 1993.

—Mary McNulty

Budget Rent a Car Corporation

4225 Naperville Road
Lisle, Illinois 60532-3662
U.S.A.
(708) 955-1900
Fax: (708) 955-7799

Private Company
Incorporated: 1960
Employees: 10,400
Revenues: $2.2 billion
Stock Exchanges: New York
SICs: 7514 Passenger Car Rental

In the early 1990s the Budget Rent a Car Corporation ranked as the world's third largest car and truck rental system, with company-owned and franchise operations in more than 110 countries and in all 50 of the United States. The company has grown steadily throughout its 35-year history and has solidified its position within the increasingly important service sector. Though the company was founded as a service to "budget-minded" leisure travelers, Budget has recently increased its selection of available automobiles and has made considerable inroads into the business market. The company operates a fleet of approximately 232,500 cars and trucks from more than 3,200 locations including 825 airports in over 100 one hundred countries.

Budget was founded in Los Angeles in 1958 when Morris Mirkin opened a small rental car company for personal renters seeking an inexpensive automobile. The company consisted of Mirkin and his wife; together they managed a fleet of ten cars, originally available at the rate of four dollars a day and four cents a mile. By 1960, Mirkin had established the Budget Rent a Car Corporation and laid the foundation for a system of corporate and licensee-owned operations.

Budget maintained a tight market focus on value-oriented leisure travelers throughout the 1960s and 1970s. The company grew by more than 20 percent every year in the leisure market during its first two decades. In addition to consumer markets, Budget began to develop policies and programs designed for smaller businesses and medium-sized corporate accounts, and the car renter moved into limited national accounts. Following an industry-wide trend, much of Budget's rental business grew to revolve around national and international airport locations.

Budget remained a predominantly franchise-operated rental company until the late 1970s. As the rental firm planned for a shift in focus as it headed into the 1980s, it began to experience turbulent times. The company's franchising business formula propelled much of Budget's growth and commanding position in certain markets during its first 30 years. With the initiation in 1983 of a program to convert from a franchising to an operating company, however, the company began to fidget with their winning formula. The change in management policy was attributed to the company's desire to ensure greater efficiency and consistency in service, communications, and procedures throughout its expanding, worldwide system of rental agencies. The decision, however, meant breaking from Budget's history of concentrating on the interests of smaller businesses and medium-sized corporations. These changes, along with the repeal of the federal investment tax credit in 1986, signaled the restructuring of Budget's management. Repeal of the tax credit law meant that owners of the rental-car companies were no longer the recipients of tax exemptions for new car purchases.

The company underwent a complete change in ownership in 1986 when the New York-based investment firm Gibbons, Green, Van Amerongen purchased Budget for over $200 million in a leveraged buyout. Twenty-nine percent of Budget's stock was purchased just one year later in a public offering. In early 1989, Beech Holdings Corp.—a holding company comprised of Budget management, Ford Motor Co., and Gibbons, Green, Van Amerongen—purchased 100 percent of Budget stock for $333 million.

Budget, like all U.S. rental companies, routinely upgrades its fleet, selling older cars and supplanting them with newer models. Consistent with nationwide trends in the U.S. car rental industry, Budget entered into purchasing agreements with a major U.S. automaker, in this case Ford, which had gained non-voting stock in Budget in the 1989 sale to Beech Holdings Corp. Following the reorganization under Beech Holdings, Budget replaced its entire U.S. fleet (composed of Ford and Lincoln-Mercury models) every six months. In addition, much of Budget's rental fleet was upgraded to include more luxury vehicles.

Business travelers comprise car rental companies' largest customer base: fewer than 2.5 million frequent business travelers account for nearly 50 percent of all car rentals at U.S. airports, the industry's most important market. Following the restructuring of Budget's management in 1989, the company began a concerted drive toward gaining more corporate and *Fortune* 500 accounts with the goal of further penetrating that business market. By 1991, Budget was the primary or secondary provider of rental vehicles to 210 of the *Fortune* 500. Instrumental to this shift in the company's focus was William N. Plamondon, who was promoted to senior vice president of marketing in 1989 and named executive vice president and general manager, North America in December of 1990. In 1993, Plamondon became Budget's president and chief executive officer.

Budget's drive to gain blue chip accounts was linked to the company's 1980s campaign to gain corporate control over its franchised licensees. With greater corporate control, Budget could guarantee the availability of more luxury automobiles and services, such as the availability of cellular phone service in rental cars, that were targeted toward business travelers. These changes culminated in late 1990 when Budget gained corporate control over its largest licensee, Diversified Services of Fort Lauderdale, Florida. The buyout gave Budget direct access to seven additional high-traffic airport sites, including key locations in Los Angeles and Florida—the two largest car rental markets in the United State Budget's acquisitions in domestic markets were paralleled by a similar expansion in foreign car rental markets during 1990 and 1991.

While many major car rental companies experienced a downturn in foreign operations during 1991 because of the Persian Gulf War, Budget did not. In fact, Budget executive Bob Wilson insisted in the May 23, 1991, *Travel Weekly,* "The big story for Budget over the last two years is its corporately acquired locations in Europe—the U.K., Belgium, France, Spain—where Budget owns the outlets rather than franchising them." In line with the company's domestic policy of corporate-run outlets, Budget's foreign rental outlets provided the same corporate-designed services and automobiles tailored to business clients.

In recent years, Budget Rent a Car has followed a growing trend in service-oriented companies to make use of newly developed information technologies. Budget pursued new communications developments in an effort to integrate their car rental system into a growing, computerized "info-environment" and designed a diverse range of interactive services which allowed customers to access information concerning Budget's rental services. Initial services of this sort centered on the availability of telephone information lines, but soon expanded to include on-line information services as well.

In 1990, Budget introduced Remote Transaction Booths (RTB's) into several major North American cities. The RTBs operate very much like automatic bank teller machines, allowing clients with a driver's license and a major credit card to rent from high-activity locations such as hotels and shopping malls. In 1991, Budget introduced Point to Point Directions to twenty-seven of its airport locations. The multilingual system offers customers directions to any city address within the airport's metropolitan area—a function traditionally fulfilled by service representatives at the rental counter.

In 1992, Budget considered a joint development project between itself, Hilton Hotels, Marriott Corporation and AMR Information Services called Intrico. The venture originally aimed at development of a reservations information network called Confirm that would be used by the hotel and car rental companies. Budget announced its decision to drop out of the system's development in July of 1992 because of the project's uncertain future.

The car renter began contracting with TML Information Services Inc., a New York company that performs searches of driver-history databases in an effort to cut liability insurance costs. The rental company determines whether a renter constitutes a "high risk" based on information from TML's computers and, if so, refuses the company's rental services. TML Information Systems, Budget's link to the driver-history databases, accesses Florida, Maryland, New York, and Ohio record keeping systems, and is also seeking access to records in other states.

Budget Rent a Car stands in a solid position to expand its services worldwide. With the increased reliance of U.S. automakers on rental fleets for domestic sales, Budget and other rental companies face a relatively steady future—unless used car markets fail to absorb the rapid turnover of rental fleet cars. Currently, the rental car industry purchases approximately 10 percent of cars made by American companies. In addition, Budget's increased corporate control over its worldwide operating outlets puts the company in a position of greater flexibility in the face of changing customer and corporate needs.

Further Reading:

"Rental-Car Industry: A Tumultuous Giant," *Automotive News,* March 27, 1989.
"Car Rental Companies Checking Records," *Detroit Free Press,* October 8, 1993.
"Car Rental Terminal," *Fortune,* November 5, 1990.
"Budget Acquires Largest Licensee," *Travel Weekly,* September 3, 1990.
"Car Rentals on Rebound After War," *Travel Weekly,* May 23, 1991.
"Budget Mapping," *Travel Weekly,* July 15, 1991.

—Thomas Bohn

BARD

C.R. Bard Inc.

730 Central Avenue
Murray Hill, New Jersey 07974
U.S.A.
(908) 277-8000
Fax: (908) 277-8240

Public Company
Incorporated: 1923
Employees: 8,850
Sales: $990 million
Stock Exchanges: New York
SICs: 3841 Surgical and Medical Instruments; 3842 Surgical
    Appliances and Supplies

C.R. Bard Inc. is a developer and manufacturer of surgical and medical instruments, including cardiovascular and urological equipment and general health care products. Bard markets these products worldwide to hospitals, extended care facilities, and home care professionals. A pioneer in the health care industry, Bard developed presterilized instruments and the concept of complete sterilized disposable surgical trays. The company was also a pioneer in angioplasty, a technique using a tiny balloon to unclog arteries so that more blood may be pumped to the heart.

C.R. Bard Inc. was founded by Charles Russell Bard, an American importer of French silks as well as the exclusive distributor of a nineteenth-century European medicine purported to relieve urinary discomfort. In 1907 Bard began distributing a recently invented uretal catheter for a French firm, J. Eynard, his European connections enabling him to market the catheter in the United States. Bard's involvement with medical products expanded in 1915 when he became partners with Morgan Parker, who had invented a new scalpel. Parker provided the patents, Bard provided office space and $500, and Bard-Parker Co. Inc. was begun.

During World War I, imported scalpels became scarce, and demand for the Bard-Parker scalpel soared. After the war, however, Bard and Parker disagreed over manufacture of the scalpel. While Parker wanted the company to manufacture the instrument, Bard wanted to continue to subcontract for manufacture with a company in Ohio. The two partners could not resolve their differences, and in 1923 Parker bought out Bard's interest in the partnership for $23,000. Bard-Parker later be-

came a division of Becton Dickinson & Company, a medical instruments manufacturer.

Bard formally incorporated as C.R. Bard in 1923, continuing to distribute Eynard catheters and other urological devices. His health failing, however, Bard hired John Frederick Willits as his sales manager. Willits, a former sales manager for a medical book publisher, understood that Bard would eventually turn over the business to him.

Bard kept his word and sold the business to Willits and accountant Edson L. Outwin in 1926 for $18,000. Willits, the older of the two men, became president of the company, and Outwin became vice-president and treasurer. Although Willits and Outwin borrowed the money to buy C.R. Bard, within a year, they were able to repay the loan with profits from the company. Bard became a company consultant until his retirement in 1932. He died in 1934.

Outwin, Willits, and James Vassar, the company's first full-time salesperson, hired by Bard in 1923, visited their sales regions twice a year and were on the road for 12 to 14 weeks at a time. Willits covered the West Coast, Outwin the Southeast and Mid-Atlantic states, and Vassar the rest of the United States and part of Canada. In 1929, the company added another sales representative, Willits' son Harris, to cover the upper Midwest, New York, and Canada. During this time, the four men sold the company's line of urological instruments directly to practicing urologists.

In 1934, Dr. Hobart Belknap, an Oregon doctor and Bard customer, published an article in the *Urological Cutaneous Review* presenting his idea for a balloon-type instrument to control secondary bleeding in cases in which no suprapubic opening existed. Davol Rubber Co. of Providence, Rhode Island, developed a device based on Belknap's idea. During this time, American Anode, a division of B.F. Goodrich of Akron, Ohio, also developed devices based on Belknap's idea for Dr. Frederick E. B. Foley of St. Paul, Minnesota. Extensive litigation ensued for the patent for the device, until Davol and Goodrich agreed to cross-license each other's product. The generic name for the instrument became the Foley catheter. Since Bard was already the exclusive distributor of Davol's other catheters, it also began distributing the Foley catheters. Sales of Foley catheters took off when Harris Willits discovered that a surgeon in Flint, Michigan, was using the Foley on a routine basis as a retention catheter for post-operative patients.

In 1940, Germany's invasion of France halted all shipments of Eynard instruments from France to C.R. Bard in the United States. Bard added American-made catheters to its line when Norman Jeckel founded the United States Catheter and Instrument Corporation to manufacture the first American woven catheter which he had developed. However, when the United States entered World War II in 1941, the U.S. military had first priority for purchase of the USCI catheters, limiting supplies and Bard's ability to meet the demand of civilian customers.

In 1945, Outwin and John Willits switched positions at the company, with Outwin becoming company president and Willits vice-president. Harris Willits became a member of the board of directors. Furthermore, a 150 percent increase in the company's net sales since 1935 led to the addition of two more sales positions. Net sales increased between 1945 and 1947 as a result of new urological procedures and the increase in the population of urologists and patients.

The soaring sales also necessitated a move to bigger headquarters. Bard commissioned a 5,400 square foot building to be constructed in Summit, New Jersey, and in March 1948, the company moved there from its Madison Avenue offices. That fiscal year, net sales rose to above the $1 million mark, and 18 employees were added. Bard quickly outgrew its new facility, and, as more space was needed for one-the-premises packaging, Bard purchased the property next door to its facility.

During the 1950s, net sales grew more than 400 percent, and the number of employees increased to 200. While in 1940 more than 85 percent of its products had been imported, by the 1950s the company's products were all made in the United States. During this time, Willits resigned as chairperson, and Outwin took his place. Harris Willits then became Bard's president.

In 1958, Bard introduced its products in presterilized packages. Initially the company sent its packaged goods to an outside laboratory for sterilization. However, packaging was soon sterilized in Bard's own laboratories. The introduction of presterilized products cut down on costs for hospitals and reduced the risk of contamination. The introduction of ready-to-use disposable products led to a contract with Resiflex Laboratory, Inc. to market Resiflex's disposable drainage tubes with the tradename Bardic. Bard also contracted with Deseret Pharmaceutical Company, Inc. to distribute its new intravenous tube tradenamed Bardic-Deseret Intracath. This soft, plastic tube could be placed in the patient's vein for intravenous feeding, eliminating the need to retain a steel needle for feeding.

The decade of the 1960s brought remarkable growth. Net sales increased by $42 million, reaching $51 million in 1969. The number of employees increased from 200 to 2,200. In 1961, the company moved its headquarters to a 50,000 square foot building in Murray Hill, New Jersey. The company expanded its product line by marketing cardiological, radiological, and anesthesiological products, in addition to urological devices. By 1969, Bard owned 14 plants and was manufacturing 75 percent of the 6,000 products it sold.

Bard became a public company in the 1960s when the Outwin family sold their stock on the over-the-counter market. Chairperson Edson Outwin, however, retained his own personal shares, representing a 2.5 percent interest in the company. Outwin remained chairperson until 1966, when he resigned due to ill health. Harris Willits then became chairperson, and Outwin was named chairman emeritus. In 1968, Bard stocks were traded on the New York Stock Exchange for the first time.

Bard's thriving international mail order business led to the formation of two new corporations in 1963. Bard-Davol Inc., located in England and owned equally by C.R. Bard Inc. and Davol Rubber Inc., began producing surgical and hospital supplies for the United Kingdom. Bard-Davol International, headquartered in Bard's Murray Hill, New Jersey, offices, was responsible for all other export trade. A year later, Bard formed C.R. Bard Limited, headquartered in Toronto, specifically to handle distribution in Canada.

Bard's first in-house manufacturing began in 1964 with the molding and assembling of medical plastic tubing. Bard began making its own intravenous tubes and disposable surgical masks when Bard's and Deseret's association ended on friendly terms.

Bard bought USCI in 1966 after a 25-year association with this leading producer of urological instruments and cardiovascular products. USCI was a well-respected and innovative company, whose founder, Norman Jeckel, had collaborated with Nobel Prize winner Andre Cournand to develop the first intravenous heart catheter. USCI scientists had also collaborated on the development of artificial arteries and dacron grafts.

In 1968, the MacBick Company of New England and Lowndes Products Inc. of Easley, South Carolina, also became part of the Bard corporation. MacBick designed and manufactured hospital supplies and equipment, including mobile carts, work stations, and disposable presterilized patient care items. Lowndes produced underpads, diapers, mattress covers, surgeons' caps and masks, and other products for the medical market.

Once again, Bard found itself in need of more space because of its expanded packaging and in-house sterilization operations. As a result, the company doubled the size of its headquarters and built a 172,000 square foot manufacturing plant, also in Murray Hill. With the completion of the new plant, the company consolidated all of its New Jersey manufacturing and product assembly operations.

Bard also began manufacturing its own extruded tubing at this plant. By 1982, it was producing 14,000 miles of extruded tubing rather than purchasing it from outside vendors. Bard also expanded by building a 100,000 square foot plant in Covington, Georgia, to produce Foley drainage trays and clean catch kits.

During the 1970s, Bard made several acquisitions as its business rapidly grew. The company acquired Homer Higgs Associates, Inc. of Fairfield, New Jersey, a distributor of convalescent and home care products, and Burnett Instruments Co., Inc. of Lawrence, Kansas, a manufacturer of disposable instruments, orthopedic and physiotherapy products, and electronic heat and related products for hot compress therapy. LeMoyne & Grant Inc., of Montreal, Canada, which produced mobile stretchers, also became part of Bard during this time. Furthermore, Med-Econ Plastics of California, a maker of disposable plastic respiratory products, was acquired in 1972, as well as Sani-Pac Corp. of New York, manufacturers of bed pads and adult diapers. Two years later, Bard acquired a company that made suction collection instruments, Deaton Medical Co. of Oklahoma.

Acquisitions continued throughout the decade, including American Membrane Corp. of California—which held a license from the federal government to develop a membrane for kidney dialysis—and William Harvey Research Corp. of California, the developer of the disposable bubble oxygenator and cardiotomy used in open-heart surgery. Bard also acquired Medical Device Laboratory, Aerway Laboratories Inc., and MI Systems, Inc. By 1976, Bard was distributing 13,000 products.

In 1979, Bard obtained the sole rights to manufacture and sell the Gruntzig catheter. This device, with a small balloon at the tip, could be used to open up artery walls by pressing fatty deposits against the walls. This device and procedure, called angioplasty, became a well-accepted alternative to the more costly and riskier heart bypass surgery. In using the Gruntzig catheter, the surgeon inserted a long wire through the femoral artery near the groin and up through the patient's arteries to the clogged arteries of the heart. A tiny balloon at the end of the wire was then inflated, compressing the fat against the walls of the artery and opening the passage to allow more blood to flow to the heart.

The 1970s brought growth in Bard's international operations as well. Bard entered into joint ventures with companies in Japan and Denmark, and it acquired Brazilian company Rossifil Industria Produtos Plasticos Ltda, a producer of intravenous administration, blood collection and transfusion sets.

In the late 1970s, Robert H. McCaffrey was elected CEO and George T. Maloney was elected president and chief operating officer. Harris Willits retired from his honorary chair in 1979. He died in 1992.

Bard's growth prompted the company to decentralize in 1980, forming divisions based on product lines, including urological, cardiopulmonary, implants, cardiology and radiology, medsystems, electro/medical, home health divisions, and international divisions. Divisions designed and carried out their own product development, working with medical specialists.

The 1980s brought another healthy growth spurt for Bard. During the early 1980s, Bard continued to expand by purchasing Davol Inc. and Davol International from International Paper Co. This acquisition was significant as Davol manufactured Foley catheters, still Bard's single largest selling product. Bard also acquired Shield Healthcare Management Inc., Catheter Technology Corp. and the assets of Radi Medical Systems AB.

Some acquisitions sent the company in new directions. The purchase of Automated Screening Devices Inc., which produced a blood pressure monitoring system, moved Bard toward more technologically advanced products. Bard also entered the orthopedic implants arena by becoming the sole distributor in the United States and Canada of the orthopedic line of German firm Waldemar Link GmbH & Co.

By the late 1980s, the company operated domestic plants in 12 states and Puerto Rico and plants or offices in several foreign countries, including Canada, Mexico, Australia, Japan, Hong Kong, India, Singapore, as well as most countries in Europe and Great Britain. In 1990, McCaffrey retired, and Maloney became president and CEO. Shortly after that, William H. Longfield was named company president.

During this time, Bard faced some challenges regarding its coronary balloon angioplasty catheters. In 1990 the company had to temporarily withdraw its catheters from the market, pending approval from the Federal Drug Administration (FDA),

after modifications were made to the devices. While catheter sales for that year were virtually nonexistent, Bard re-entered the angioplasty market in April 1991.

In the 1990s, Bard began to focus more carefully on its major markets, selling those divisions incidental to their main focus of development of single-patient-use products for diagnosis and treatment for the urological, cardiovascular, and surgical markets. In 1990, the company sold its Shield Healthcare Centers subsidiary to a subsidiary of Kobayashi Pharmaceutical Co. of Japan and also sold its MedSystems infusion pump division to Baxter International.

In 1992, Bard had net sales of more than $990 million, a 13 percent increase over 1991 sales of $876 million. The company attributed the sales increase in part to its re-entrance into the balloon angioplasty market following FDA approval of several of Bard's designs. Furthermore, the company looked forward to a healthy sales increase from the marketing of an implant from Collagen Corp. that would combat urinary incontinence. The product was available in several foreign countries, and FDA approval was pending in the United States in 1992.

Although in 1992 Bard was best known for its urological products—its Foley catheter was the leading device for bladder drainage—its largest product group was cardiovascular care devices, which contributed about 40 percent of the company's net sales. Competition in the health care industry was intense in the early 1990s, and Bard depended on its reputation for reliable products and service and innovative research and design. Bard continued to work closely with medical and health care specialists to develop new products or improve existing products. However, like many other health care companies and institutions, Bard was uncertain about the direction health care reform would take during President Bill Clinton's administration. Bard's management continued to view technology as an important component in improving the patient's quality of life and continued to develop new and improved products, with FDA approval critical to the company's growth.

Principal Subsidiaries: Bard Access Systems, Inc.; Bard Canada Inc.; Bard Cardiopulmonary, Inc.; Bard Devices, Inc.; Bard Implants, Inc.; Bard International, Inc.; Bard Shannon Limited (Ireland); BCP Puerto Rico, Inc.; CRB Delaware, Inc.

Further Reading:

Annual Report, Murray Hill, New Jersey: C.R. Bard Inc., 1982, 1992.
Bard World, Volume 2, Number 4, 75th Anniversary Edition, Murray Hill, New Jersey: C.R. Bard Inc., 1982.
Kindel, Stephen, "A Deadly Probe," *Financial World,* December 11, 1990, pp. 52–4.
Weiss, Gary, "Despite a Tough Blow, Bard Is Up and Swinging," *Business Week,* November 19, 1990, p. 128.

—Wendy J. Stein

research in beer making through its Carlsberg Laboratory, and supported Danish history and the arts through the establishment of several museums. The Carlsberg Foundation today controls a 51 percent interest in Carlsberg A/S.

Tuborg was founded in 1873 by a group of Danish businessmen headed by Phillip Heyman. The Tuborgs Fabrikker first included a glass factory and a sulfuric acid works, but Heyman spun off all but the brewery in 1880. Tuborg's Green Label pilsner quickly established a strong reputation in Denmark. By 1894 Tuborg was the major partner in an affiliation of 11 Copenhagen breweries.

Carlsberg and Tuborg signed an operating agreement as early as 1903, stating that they would share profits and deficits and contribute equally to financing new plants and installations. The two brands dominated the Danish beer market. Though Danes were dedicated beer drinkers, the market was relatively small, as the total Danish population was only around five million people. Carlsberg and Tuborg eventually decided to expand their sales outside the country. After World War II, the two breweries began intensive marketing campaigns abroad. As a result, their exports tripled between 1958 and 1972, and the two companies established breweries in other European countries and in Asia. To reinforce their growing export presence, Carlsberg and Tuborg combined under one name in 1970, becoming United Breweries Ltd.

United Breweries continued to expand its business by penetrating foreign markets. One of its most important markets was Great Britain. In 1970 the company set up a partnership with the British beer maker Watney to build a lager brewery at Northampton. This was United's biggest operation outside Denmark. By 1975 the Carlsberg brand lager produced there accounted for about 14 percent of British lager sales. The Grand Metropolitan group took over Watney in 1972, and in 1975 it sold its 49 percent interest in Carlsberg U.K. back to United Breweries, leaving the Danish parent with 100 percent control. Grand Metropolitan continued to distribute Carlsberg lager through its 7,500 pub outlets.

United Breweries took a different tack with its Tuborg brand, however. The largest British brewer, Bass Charington, distributed Tuborg, which was at first all imported directly from Denmark. Tuborg was then brewed under license at four Bass breweries, but that agreement ended in 1981. United took back independent control of Tuborg marketing in Britain, hoping to increase sales. The company also intensified its drive to market Tuborg internationally, and in 1981 licensed a Hungarian brewery to produce the lager there.

United Brewery's two main brands were available in almost every European capital by the mid 1980s. About 70 percent of United's beer was sold abroad, through direct exports, through licensed foreign breweries, or through breweries that the company owned. Despite its growing success in Europe, Asia, and Africa, United faced problems in its native Denmark. That country ranked eighth in the world in per capita beer consumption, and United had an 80 percent market share, but sales were stagnant. United worked under a fixed price system in Denmark, where it sold its products for the same price everywhere, regardless of volume. Some Danish supermarkets began to fight

Carlsberg A/S

Vestervaelledvej 100
DK-1799 Copenhagen V
Denmark
(45) 33 27 33 27
Fax: (45) 33 27 47 11

Public Company
Incorporated: 1970 as United Breweries, Ltd.
Employees: 13,800
Sales: DKK 14.96 billion (US$2.23 billion)
Stock Exchanges: Copenhagen
SICs: 2082 Malt Beverages

Carlsberg A/S is one of the world's largest brewing companies. Its two principal brands, Carlsberg and Tuborg, are the leading beers in Denmark, and are also two of the most widely sold beers in the global market. Over half the brewery's sales come from outside Denmark. The company operates brewing facilities in Singapore, Malawi, Germany, Italy, Hong Kong, Cyprus, and a number of other countries, and maintains licensing agreements for distribution of its brands in others, so that Carlsberg and Tuborg can be found in 140 different countries altogether. Carlsberg A/S has interests in a few businesses outside brewing as well. Most notably, the company owns Royal Copenhagen A/S, makers of renowned fine porcelain, silverware, and glassware. Other companies owned by Carlsberg produce bottles, milling technology, wine, and spirits, and develop food processing and quality control equipment.

Carlsberg A/S was formed from the merger of two venerable Danish breweries, Carlsberg and Tuborg. The original Carlsberg brewery was founded in Copenhagen in 1847 by Captain J. C. Jacobsen. The Captain was interested in brewing technology, and he studied modern brewing methods extensively before he opened his shop, which he named for his son Carl. His constant work to improve the quality of his beer soon made his lager very popular. Carl Jacobsen carried on his father's passion for beer making, and he studied brewing both in Denmark and abroad before taking his place in the family business in 1871. Carl eventually established his own brewery, called New Carlsberg. New Carlsberg and Old Carlsberg were united in 1906, as both father and son willed their breweries to a charitable foundation J. C. Jacobsen had established in 1876. The Carlsberg Foundation assumed the running of the breweries, carried on scientific against what they considered United's monopolistic practices, by slashing beer prices to less than wholesale. United resorted to threatening to halt deliveries of Carlsberg and Tuborg to stores that discounted. Another problem with the Danish market was that younger drinkers were increasingly turning to wine. In an effort to win back its young customers, United entered into a distribution agreement with American brewer Anheuser-Busch to sell its Budweiser brand in Denmark. Younger people were interested in American imports, and more apt to experiment with a new brand than older drinkers. Anheuser-Busch also began to import the Carlsberg brand to the United States for United.

United Breweries diversified somewhat in the 1980s. It formed Carlsberg Biotechnology in 1983, and acquired interests in firms that made such things as ventilation plants and fishing industry equipment. The company acquired 83 percent of a German brewery in 1988, the Hannen Brauerei GmbH, and also bought Vingaarden A/S, a Danish wine and spirit maker. A separate financial branch, Carlsberg Finans A/S, was established in 1989 to manage the parent company's stock portfolios and pension funds. But by end of the 1980s, the company decided to sell off much of its non-beverage business. United Brewery's name had been changed in December 1987 to Carlsberg A/S in order to give the firm a more distinct business profile. The renamed company consolidated its operations and gradually began to pare down its work force to cope with what it perceived to be a mature beer market. Sales grew steadily throughout the 1980s, from DKK 6.31 billion in 1982 to DKK 10.48 billion in 1990.

Carlsberg A/S continued to make strategic investments in international markets in the 1990s. The company acquired a controlling interest in Unicer, the largest brewery in Portugal, in April 1991. Carlsberg subsequently sold its stake in a Spanish brewery, Union Cervecera, which had been losing money. Guinness bought out Carlsberg's 60 percent share, and then Carlsberg acquired 10 percent of Guinness's interest in a larger Spanish brewery, La Cruz del Campo S.A. Carlsberg also moved to secure its crucial British market by forming an alliance with Allied-Lyons, a large brewing and wholesale company. Britain provided almost half of Carlsberg's worldwide profit by the early 1990s, and competition among brewers there had become increasingly stiff. Previous to the 1991 merger with Allied-Lyons, Carlsberg had only a 4 percent share of the British beer market, with 1990 sales of £1.31 billion. The new firm, a 50–50 joint venture called Carlsberg-Tetley P.L.C., had an 18 percent market share, just behind market leaders Bass, with 23 percent, and Courage, with 21 percent. The alliance gave Carlsberg access to Allied's six breweries, its strong distribution network, and a larger brand portfolio. Carlsberg had to wait almost a year for the British antitrust agency to approve the deal, but when Carlsberg-Tetley began operations in early 1993, it had a secure place among the top three British brewers.

The situation in Britain, where three large companies including Carlsberg-Tetley controlled about two-thirds of the beer market, seemed a model to Carlsberg for what the global market was becoming. Global consumption of beer for 1991–92 was down, reflecting the European economic recession, and competition escalated among increasingly large international brewing companies. Carlsberg continued to strengthen its ties with for-

eign breweries, as it anticipated negative growth in beer consumption in the 1990s. Some of Carlsberg's slow growth in Europe was offset, however, by increased sales in Asia. Carlsberg had become the leading international beer brand in the Far East by the early 1990s, and Singapore, Malaysia, and Hong Kong were particularly good markets for the company. Carlsberg A/S also had modest sales in South Korea, Japan, Indonesia, and Nepal. Carlsberg's subsidiary Danbrew worked on construction of a Carlsberg brewery in Thailand in the early 1990s, and by 1992 Carlsberg beer was introduced to China and Sri Lanka.

In Denmark, Carlsberg undertook a major restructuring of its beer production facilities. In 1992 the company began to phase out its Tuborg brewery and transferred production to two other existing plants, in the interest of long-term operating economy. Carlsberg had been cutting its work force since the mid 1980s, and this move further reduced the company's personnel. Carlsberg took another significant action concerning its home market in 1992, acquiring 80 percent of A/S Dadeko, the company in charge of the bottling and sale of Coca-Cola, Fanta, Sprite, and other soft drinks in Denmark.

Carlsberg A/S achieved steady growth in sales and profits through the 1980s and into the 1990s, but by the end of 1992, the company acknowledged that it might be facing a period of reversal. Beer was a mature and highly competitive market in Europe, and the economic downturn flattened beer consumption. In spite of favorable sales in Asia, Carlsberg prepared for bad times ahead. The company invested DKK 805 million in its production plants and equipment in 1992, more than half of that in Denmark, in order to increase productivity and reduce future operating costs. Though it prepared for some drop in profits, Carlsberg A/S had a long history of solid expansion, based almost entirely on its expertise in brewing and marketing its brands of beer. Carlsberg had not veered from its original business, and this conservative strategy had promoted two Copenhagen breweries to become one of the world's largest beer producers. With such demonstrated strength, one would expect Carlsberg to weather any low period satisfactorily.

Principal Subsidiaries: Carlsberg Brewery Limited (UK); Hannen Brauerei GmbH (Germany); Industrie Poretti S.p.A. (Italy; 50%); Unicer-Uniao Cervejeira, S.A. (Portugal; 31%); Carlsberg Malawi Brewery Limited (49%); Carlsberg Brewery Hong Kong Limited (50%); Carlsberg Marketing (Singapore) Pte. Ltd. (50%); Fredericia Bryggeri A/S; Wiibroes Bryggeri A/S; A/S Dadeko (79%); A/S Rynkeby Mosteri; Vingaarden A/S (81%); Royal Copenhagen A/S (79%); Danbrew Ltd. A/S; J.C. Bentzen Industri A/S; Carlsberg Finans A/S; A/S Kjobenhavens Sommer-Tivoli (45%).

Further Reading:

Barnes, Hilary, "Improvement at Danish Brewer," *Financial Times,* November 27, 1979, p. 34; "United Breweries Holds Dividend, Plans Scrip," *Financial Times,* November 25, 1987, p. 28.

"Bass and Tuborg End Lager Agreement," *Financial Times,* April 6, 1981, p. 4.

"Brewers in the Snug Bar," *Financial Times,* October 23, 1991, p. 22.

"Brewers Merging British Operations," *New York Times,* October 23, 1991, p. D3.

"Brewing up a Qualified Success," *Marketing,* October 31, 1991, p. 16.

"Carlsberg A/S Reports and Accounts," Copenhagen: Carlsberg A/S, 1992.

Gooding, Kenneth, "Grand Met. Ends Brewing Link with Carlsberg," *Financial Times,* September 13, 1975, p. 10.

"Lager Clout," *Marketing,* March 8, 1990, p. 35.

Navarro, Valerie, ". . . While A-B Gets Ready to Bring Bud to Denmark," *Advertising Age,* February 3, 1986, pp. 40–42.

Rawstorne, Philip, "Allied and Carlsberg to Merge UK Beer Interests," *Financial Times,* October 23, 1991, p. 1.

Ridlake, Suzanne, "Beer Giants Merge," *Marketing,* October 24, 1991, p. 2.

—A. Woodward

Cascade Natural Gas Corporation

222 Fairview Avenue North
Seattle, Washington 98109-5312
U.S.A.
(206) 624-3900
Fax: (206) 624-7215

Public Company
Incorporated: 1953
Employees: 466
Sales: $152.46 million
Stock Exchanges: New York
SICs: 4924 Natural Gas Distribution

Cascade Natural Gas Corporation is a gas distribution company that serves more than 100,000 customers in nearly 90 communities located throughout Washington and Oregon. Cascade primarily serves the smaller communities in this region, eschewing the more densely populated cites, such as Seattle, Tacoma, and Spokane.

In the early 1950s, business leaders and public officials in the Pacific Northwest initiated a campaign to bring natural gas to the region to replace gas and other fuels that had been steadily rising in price over the past 20 years. As an alternative fuel, natural gas afforded additional benefits beyond its cheaper cost to both industrial and residential users. Scientists by this time had discovered over 25,000 industrial applications for natural gas, a form of fuel featuring greater combustion efficiency and requiring neither storage facilities nor vaporization and atomization processes. Residential customers were attracted to the convenience and cleanliness of natural gas. In an attempt to tap into this burgeoning demand for natural gas, five gas companies serving 15 communities in Washington, Oregon, and Idaho, merged in 1953 to form Cascade Natural Gas Corporation. The five companies, Bellingham Gas Co., Bremerton Gas Co., Wenatchee Gas Co., Northwest Cities Gas Co., and Consolidated Gas Co., possessed combined assets of $2.67 million and served between 10,000 and 11,000 customers. Stewart Matthews was selected as the corporation's first president and C. Spencer Clark as its board chairperson.

From the corporation's outset it only attempted to secure those markets located outside large population centers, focusing on smaller, rural communities scattered throughout the region. Natural gas came to the area predominately from the Peace River area of northern British Columbia in Canada and the San

Juan Basin fields in Colorado and New Mexico, both of which Cascade drew from, although it relied more heavily on the gas originating from Canada. This dependence on Canadian gas, a source that would support the corporation's supply for much of its existence, was not the only connection between the newly formed consortium of gas companies and Canada. One of the principal backers of the merger was Pacific Petroleums Ltd., a Canadian company that held roughly 25 percent of Cascade's outstanding stock during it first year.

By the end of 1954, Cascade had reached an agreement with Pacific Northwest Pipeline Co. to provide a two-way supply of natural gas from the fields in Canada and in the San Juan Basin. Once the corporation had established primary and supplementary sources of natural gas, plans and financing were arranged to enlarge its area of service. At this time, Cascade was distributing gas to 17 communities in Washington, Oregon, and Idaho, and by 1955 eight additional communities in the region became Cascade customers. To bolster its customer base, Cascade, in early 1956, launched an expansion program totaling approximately $20 million to be spent over the next several years, as the corporation hurriedly sought to meet the increasing demand occasioned by a rapidly growing population.

However, by 1959 the number of customers served by Cascade had increased only marginally. A merger with Oregon Natural Gas Co. that year gave Cascade a total of 14,000 customers, only several thousand more than the original consolidation of gas companies produced six years earlier. The boost provided by this acquisition, which helped Cascade reach $9 million in revenues for the year, did, however, demonstrate the gains that could be made by purchasing additional companies. Four months after Cascade merged with Oregon Natural, in early 1960, it announced another merger, this time with Pacific Natural Gas Corp., which served communities throughout Washington. Pacific Natural initially operated as a wholly owned subsidiary of Cascade, with O. Marshall Jones, who had by now succeeded Matthews as Cascade's president, supervising Pacific Natural's operations. After two years, the merger was completed and the stocks between the two companies were traded on a share for share basis.

The infusion of Pacific Natural's business yielded the first appreciable growth Cascade had experienced since its inception. By 1962, the corporation served over 20,000 customers located in 52 rural communities. Cascade had withdrawn from the utility market in Idaho several years earlier to concentrate solely on the Washington and Oregon markets, which provided more than enough business for the corporation to manage. Throughout the region, natural gas distributors were raising their capital expenditures to meet the growing demand engendered by an increasing population, economic expansion, and the wide acceptance of natural gas by both residential and industrial consumers. Cascade shared in the vitality of the industry, connecting an average of 5,000 customers annually to its service during the early 1960s. In fact, from 1960 to 1964, Cascade experienced a dramatic surge in growth, more than doubling its number of residential customers from 16,074 to 33,834, and increasing its commercial and industrial users from 4,682 to 7,555. A large part of this growth was attributable to Cascade's success in convincing potential customers to switch to natural gas, a conversion made more attractive to residential clients by an innovative service the corporation provided. Cascade offered to install and maintain natural gas appliances in a customer's home for a monthly charge of $2, a service at that time not offered by the corporation's competitors. As a result, revenues soared during this period from $9 million in 1959 to $20.3 million in 1964, solidifying Cascade's position in Washington and Oregon, and providing a foundation from which Cascade could expand its business.

Although the growing demand for natural gas augured well for Cascade's expansion plans, some uncertainties were developing in regard to the corporation's supply of fuel. Since 75 percent of the natural gas consumed in the Pacific Northwest had to be piped in, Cascade was largely dependent on Pacific Northwest Pipeline Co., which controlled the only two sources of natural gas to the region. This in itself posed no immediate concerns to Cascade, and, in fact, the price Pacific Northwest Pipeline charged for Cascade's supply had just begun to stabilize in recent years, facilitating the corporation's efforts toward meeting the heightened demand for fuel. Problems did arise, however, when the U.S. Supreme Court ordered the owner of Pacific Northwest Pipeline, El Paso Natural Gas Co., to relinquish its control of the pipeline. This ruling, the effects of which were still undetermined in 1964, raised some doubts as to the availability of natural gas in the Pacific Northwest, and Cascade's management became convinced that the amount of fuel eventually allocated to Pacific Northwest Pipeline would be insufficient to supply the corporation's needs, or at least would upset the stability of natural gas prices.

As a hedge against whatever resulted from El Paso Natural's sale of Pacific Northwest Pipeline, Cascade purchased Garfield Gas Gathering Co. in 1965. The acquisition of Garfield Gas created Cascade's Colorado-Utah division, giving the corporation valuable natural gas holdings in northwestern Colorado and equally important sales contracts to supply natural gas companies, located outside Cascade's territory, with fuel. In addition to the $1.2 million Cascade paid for Garfield Gas, it also spent $7 million to construct 120 miles of pipeline from Colorado to Utah and began developing reserves of natural gas along the route that would eventually deliver fuel into the corporation's distribution areas.

The exponential rise in revenues from 1960 to 1964 continued after the acquisition of Garfield Gas. In 1965, Cascade recorded $21.7 million in sales, the majority of which was garnered from industrial users. Industries within Cascade's territory had converted to natural gas at a steady rate and by now accounted for 56 percent of the corporation's sales. The remainder of the corporation's business was roughly divided between commercial and residential customers. By this time, the corporation supplied nearly 30 percent of the residential market in the Pacific Northwest and anticipated increasing its share up to 80 percent by adding 5,000 to 6,000 new customers annually. Encouraged by its remarkable success over the previous five years and desirous of reaching its optimistic prognostications, Cascade continued to invest in expansion, spending $7 million on capital improvements after constructing the Utah-Colorado pipeline.

The following year, in 1966, revenues shot up to $25.3 million and an additional 7,000 customers were connected to Cascade's service, exceeding the projections the corporation set the previous year. By now, Cascade served over 46,000 customers lo-

cated in 67 Washington and Oregon communities, enough of a presence to rank the corporation as the fourth largest natural gas distributor in the northwest. Cascade continued to court residential customers by offering an "all gas rate" to those households using natural gas in space heating, water heating, and one other appliance. This offer encouraged greater natural gas usage by both new and existing customers, enabling Cascade to realize gains in revenues without necessarily having to increase its customer base. Although a shortage of new customers was not an immediate concern of Cascade's, when the population boom did subside, and Cascade was no longer able to rely on a robust influx of new residents, greater usage by existing customers would continue to invigorate revenues. By the end of 1966, 25 percent of Cascade's residential customers qualified for the all gas rate and nearly 17 percent used natural gas for more than two appliances.

While strides were being made in Cascade's residential business, its industrial segment, which still accounted for over half of the corporation's revenues, was experiencing difficulties resulting from the divestiture of El Paso Natural's Pacific Northwest Pipeline Co. By 1967, this situation had created delays in the supply of natural gas from Canada and, consequently, Cascade was forced to switch its industrial users to an interruptible supply of natural gas in order to provide a consistent supply of fuel to its residential and commercial users. Revenues were negatively affected by the drop in industrial usage, but two years earlier Cascade had anticipated such problems might occur and continued to invest in the exploration of supplementary sources of natural gas to mitigate any further losses incurred from a vacillating supply. In addition to the money spent on natural gas development and the expansion of its distribution system, which totaled approximately $15 million since the purchase of Garfield Gas, Cascade had also diversified into mineral processing and mineral exploration by this time. The corporation held a substantial interest in a pilot plant involved in the extraction of magnesium and other commercial chemicals from olivine—a mineral found in abundance near Cascade's service area in northwestern Washington—and had been granted mineral permits providing access to over 4,000 acres of land in northeastern Washington.

Since the acquisition of Oregon Natural Gas Co. in 1959, Cascade had grown at an enviable pace, nearly tripling the number of customers it served. In order to meet the demand of this growing clientele, which numbered 56,000 by 1968, Cascade spent a considerable amount of money to construct additional facilities and broaden its distribution network to service the 70 communities in Washington and Oregon that composed the corporation's territory. The majority of these capital expenditures had been financed through loans and, consequently, Cascade had accrued a large debt by the end of the 1960s. When the population boom in the Pacific Northwest began to wane by the end of the decade, the debt borne by the corporation started to chip away at its earnings, and Cascade started to look for a way to ameliorate its financial position. By 1971, it became apparent that the only way to augment Cascade's revenues was to increase its rates. The increase in rates, the first increase to raise the corporation's rate of return since 1958, lifted the corporation's revenues by $5.5 million, enabling Cascade to sufficiently service its debt for the present time and fund additional capital expenditures.

By the end of the 1960s, however, the years of dramatic growth were over for Cascade. From 1968 to 1980, Cascade added 26,000 customers, nearly half as many as were added from 1959 to 1968. Part of the reason for the decline in new customers was attributable to the stabilization of the population growth within Cascade's territory, while other conditions peculiar to the Pacific Northwest natural gas industry as a whole contributed toward a general decline in business. In 1973, the same year Cascade's stock was first traded on the New York Stock Exchange, water seepage into key natural gas fields in Canada, the primary source of Cascade's supply, reduced the supply of natural gas to the Pacific Northwest by as much as 25 percent. Once again, Cascade's industrial customers bore the brunt of the natural gas shortage, convincing some of the users to switch to residual fuel oil. Hampered by an inconsistent supply and losing business as a result of the decline in popularity of natural gas, Cascade responded by streamlining its operations. Three years after the Canadian supply was reduced, Cascade sold its Colorado-Utah division to Mountain Fuel Resources, Inc. for approximately $8.5 million.

Although revenues during the early and mid-1970s climbed steadily, Cascade's net income did not respond in kind. In 1975, the corporation posted $91 million in sales and recorded $4.1 million in net income, but the following year its net income dropped to $2.5 million on sales of $106 million. This pattern continued into the late 1970s until 1978, when Cascade's net income reached a nadir of $2.3 million from $116 million in revenues. Nevertheless, by the following year Cascade had effected a remarkable turnaround, increasing its revenues by nearly 30 percent to $150 million and reporting roughly $5 million in net income. This resurgence was largely due to the rising cost of oil, as OPEC wielded its control over the oil market and drove many of those who had converted to residual oil back to natural gas. Appliance dealers, for the first time in years, began stocking gas appliances, convinced that the public's fear of natural gas shortages had dissipated, and Cascade once again returned to connecting a substantial number of customers to its service.

As Cascade entered the 1980s, a growing shortage of electrical energy helped buoy the corporation's business even further. In an effort to boost their generating capacities during peak periods of usage, electrical utilities used natural gas as fuel for their turbine generators, a costly method for the utilities and one that was financially beneficial for Cascade. Moreover, the conservation of electrical energy by both industrial and residential consumers engendered additional business for Cascade, as natural gas became the preferred choice of those seeking an alternative energy source. By 1984, revenues had grown to nearly $234 million, and earnings had climbed to $7.6 million, a level of performance Cascade would soon be unable to match.

In 1986, Northwest Pipeline Co., Cascade's longtime source for natural gas, was forced to shut down its natural gas lines in accordance with stipulations associated with deregulation. While Northwest Pipeline negotiated with the Federal Energy Regulatory Commission to arrive at an equitable solution, Cascade's financial condition suffered. For the year, revenues dropped to $146 million, and net income plummeted to $1.1

million. A final agreement between Northwest Pipeline and the federal regulatory body was finally reached in 1988, by which time Cascade's financial condition had improved with revenues rising to $157 million and earnings reaching $5.5 million.

As Cascade charts its course in the 1990s, the result of the Northwest Pipeline agreement bodes well for the future. Under the provisions of the agreement, Cascade was able to purchase ancillary supplies of natural gas at a lower price than the average cost of Northwest Pipeline's gas. Analysts speculated that this reduction in price, in addition to the stabilization of the corporation's supply of natural gas and the luxury of supplementary sources, would enable Cascade to offer a competitively priced and stable energy source to industrial, commercial, and residential consumers in the Pacific Northwest in the future.

Further Reading:

"Big Board Adding 3 Stocks, Amex Slates One This Week," *Wall Street Journal,* June 18, 1973, p. 29.
"Cascade Gas Financing Is Completed," *Seattle Daily Journal of Commerce,* January 13, 1956, p. 1.
"Cascade Natural Gas Corp., Pacific Natural Plan Merger," *Seattle Times,* February 16, 1960, p. 22.
"Cascade Natural Gas Corp.," *Puget Sound Business Journal,* July 24, 1989, p. 16.
"Cascade Natural Gas Corp.," *Wall Street Journal,* June 19, 1978, p. 15.
"Cascade Natural Gas Files Petition to Increase Rates," *Wall Street Journal,* June 4, 1971, p. 30.
"Cascade Natural Gas Has Record Profits," *Seattle Times,* February 4, 1988, p. B1.
"Cascade Natural Gas: New Growth," *Marple's Business Newsletter,* April 2, 1980, pp. 2–3.
"Cascade's Profits Down: Warm Temperatures Cited," *Seattle Times,* April 22, 1987, p. B2.
Doran, H. V., "Cascade Assures Its Future Gas Supply," *Investment Dealers' Digest,* January 31, 1966, pp. 30–31.
"Financing Plans for Gas Distribution Being Arranged," *Seattle Daily Journal of Commerce,* January 19, 1955.
Flynn, Dan, "Cascade Hopes Natural Gas Will Lure Relocating Industry," *Seattle Business Journal,* April 30, 1984, pp. 6–7.
"Gas Firms' Merger Is Now in Effect," *Seattle Daily Journal of Commerce,* August 30, 1962, p. 1.
"Gas Firms Slate Merger," *Seattle Times,* March 5, 1954, p. 38.
"Merger Plans of Five Gas Firms Told," *Seattle Times,* December 8, 1953, p. 27.
"Mountain Fuel Resources Acquires New Division, *Pipeline and Gas Journal,* October 1976, p. 8.
"Natural Gas Distribution Plan Offered," *Seattle Daily Journal of Commerce,* August 27, 1954, p. 1.
"Operations of Cascade Natural Gas Fueled by Growth in the Northwest," *Barron's,* December 25, 1967, pp. 22, 27.
"Oregon Gas Firm Merges with Cascade," *Seattle Times,* October 27, 1959, p. 19.
"Successful Year for Cascade," *Investment Dealers' Digest,* March 28, 1966, p. 29.
"The Economy . . . ," *Seattle Times,* January 31, 1985, p. E1.
Troxell, Thomas N. Jr., "Despite Canada," *Barron's,* March 10, 1980, pp. 42, 46.
Willatt, Norris, "West Coast Gas," *Barron's,* October 26, 1964, pp. 11, 22, 24.

—Jeffrey L. Covell

Century Telephone Enterprises, Inc.

P.O. Box 4065
Monroe, Louisiana 71211-4065
U.S.A.
(318) 388-9500
Fax: (318) 388-9602

Public Company
Incorporated: April 30, 1968
Employees: 2,827
Sales: $418 million
Stock Exchanges: New York
SICs: 4813 Telephone Communications except Radiophone;
    4899 Communications Service Nec.

Century Telephone Enterprises, Inc., is one of the few remaining large independent telephone companies in the United States. The company operates more than 250 telephone exchanges in 14 states. In addition, Century operates a formidable collection of cellular telephone franchises in Michigan, Louisiana, Arkansas, Arizona, Mississippi, Minnesota, New Mexico, Texas, and Wisconsin.

The history of Century is rooted in the family of William Clarke Williams, a former manager of the Ozona Telephone Company in West Texas. In 1921, shortly after accepting a job in the payroll department of Southern Bell in Monroe, Louisiana, Williams married Marie Hill, a former teacher and operator for the Mertzon Telephone Company in Mertzon, Texas.

Williams purchased the Oak Ridge Telephone Company near Monroe from F. E. Hogan, Sr. The Williamses moved the company's switchboard into their home, where Marie Williams worked as an operator. Assisted by two young girls, Mrs. Williams switched calls around the clock, except for a five hour break on Sundays for church. The family also maintained two phone booths in their front parlor for people who did not have a telephone. Each month, Mrs. Williams would manually write the bills for each of the company's 75 customers and send her son Clarke on his bicycle to collect on them.

As these were the early days of telephony, as many as ten customers commonly shared a single line. Parties were distinguished only by a unique ringing pattern, but anyone was free to pick up on someone else's line and listen in. Each line consisted of a single wire that ran from the switchboard, to several phone

sets. A second wire connected the telephone to the ground. To improve transmission during dry weather, subscribers frequently had to pour water on the ground line.

The Oak Ridge Telephone Co. was leased to a relative and William and Marie Williams moved to nearby Oak Grove, where Marie became chief operator of the telephone company and William become district manager of a rural electric power co-op district. In 1946 William and Marie gave the Oak Ridge Telephone Company to their son, Clarke.

At this time, the Bell companies had begun to introduce dial systems, which enabled callers to reach a party without the intervention of an operator. Enthused at the prospect of automating the small system, Clarke Williams secured an agreement for the $3,500 such a system would cost. Eight months later, when the Kellogg device arrived by train, Williams returned to the bank only to learn that the elderly loan officer who had promised him the loan had died. The bank's officers refused to honor the dead banker's promise.

A family acquaintance and former banker named Joe Sydney Carter intervened with a personal loan to Williams, enabling him to haul the switch home and begin installation. The dial system proved so reliable for Williams that he decided to buy and upgrade a second telephone company, located in Marion, Louisiana. Upon purchase of the Marion Telephone Company, Clarke and Marie moved to Marion to begin operating the Oak Ridge and Choudrant systems as well as the Marion telephone system.

In 1948 Clarke Williams and his father-in-law, George Lee, went to negotiate the purchase of another company in Plain Dealing, Louisiana, for Lee. When they arrived, however, they learned that its proprietor had just died. Rather than turn around, the two managed to contact the owner's son and later emerged with an agreement to buy the Plain Dealing Telephone Company on credit.

In Plain Dealing, the previous owner did not want to build lines outside the city limits. The rural customers built the lines from the city limits to their homes. When the customers did not keep the lines in working condition, he simply cut the wires at the city limits. When a state commissioner came to demand that Williams and Lee observe their obligation to universal service outside the city limits, Lee countered that they could only afford it if they could tear out the private lines. The commissioner agreed, and service outside the city was restored.

According to a company publication entitled *Centuryan,* Clarke Williams's father had earlier suffered a severe stroke that left him unable to speak. Shortly before he died in 1957, the elder Williams advised his son to spend all the life insurance proceeds on new telephone businesses. Williams and Lee began searching for new telephone companies located contiguously to companies they already owned. This would enable them to handle toll calls between more locations and economize on maintenance.

The first company they investigated buying was in Junction City in southern Arkansas. Though located in another state, the franchise served an area adjacent to one of Williams's companies. A few weeks later they found a second, considerably larger company in northern Arkansas. By 1962 they had acquired both companies, and a third contiguous property.

George Lee died in 1965. The loss of an effective and trusted manager led Williams to consider new forms of organizing his growing company. In 1968, with 15 telephone companies in the enterprise, he decided to form a holding company and take it public. The new company, called Central Telephone and Electronics, and headquartered in Monroe, Louisiana, was formed on April 30, 1968. It was renamed Century Telephone Enterprises, Inc., in 1971.

Williams brought in two new managers: Marvin Hill, a former engineer with Stromberg-Carlson, and Ken Conrad, whose Breaux Bridge Telephone Company had earlier been acquired by Century.

Small telephone companies throughout the United States went up for sale during the 1970s, largely because descendants of the families that operated them held no interest in the tiny operations. A moratorium on acquisitions by Bell companies meant that many were eventually taken over by larger independent companies such as General Telephone and Consolidated Telephone. Several other smaller independents were involved in the consolidation of the industry at this time. Rochester Telephone, TDS and particularly Century among them, grew very quickly from these seemingly insignificant acquisitions.

During the 1970s, Century expanded into neighboring Arkansas and acquired telephone properties in Wisconsin and Michigan. The company's most significant acquisition during this period came in 1972, when it took over the La Crosse Telephone Corporation of La Crosse, Wisconsin. La Crosse Telephone was larger than any of the company's other properties and instantly established Century as a major independent telephone company.

On October 24, 1978, Century Telephone Enterprises, Inc., gained a listing on the New York Stock Exchange. This afforded the company the recognition and access to funding it needed to continue growing. Century had a well-established reputation among independent companies. While other buyers were known for instant lay-offs and other severe tactics, Century was respected for its dedication to existing management and employees. This reputation served Century well, as many small companies chose to deal only with Clarke Williams. By the 1980s the number of independent telephone companies in the United States had declined from 7,500 to about 1,500. Century emerged as one of the largest independent telephone companies in the nation.

Just as Century was one of the first small companies to introduce dial service, it also became one of the first to implement digital switching. These switches, more closely related to computers, replaced older electromechanical devices that were prone to break down. The introduction of digital switching also brought Century customers a variety of new network capabilities, such as call forwarding, call waiting, and three-way calling.

In 1984 the Justice Department finally won its 70-year antitrust battle with AT&T. One of the areas that opened up for competition was the cellular telephone business, which was still in its infancy at that time. Century bid for licenses to operate cellular systems in numerous areas. In those especially important areas where the company's bids had been unsuccessful, Century offered to purchase the licenses from the winning bidders.

As in the wire-line past of the business, Century understood that contiguous properties could provide numerous operating economies and more efficient concentration of resources. Cellular licenses for vast rural expanses, when grouped together, held as much potential as the more hotly contested urban licenses. This was particularly true of rural areas with busy interstate highways.

Century was one of the first companies to develop cellular operations. As a result, when other companies began to show interest in the market, prices for licenses were bid up to astronomical levels. Not only have Century's cellular operations grown into extremely valuable assets, they are also profitable.

The company also started a paging service as part of its Century Cellunet cellular communications group. The rapid growth of Century's cellular operations, particularly between 1985 and 1987, raised concerns that the company could easily be targeted for a hostile takeover. Rather than loading the company with debt, a common but dangerous defense strategy, Century took the unusual action of granting four votes to each shareholder who owned the company's stock for more than four years. The strategy was later augmented to 10 votes for each shareholder of record prior to May 1987.

The action brought a lawsuit from Mario Gabelli, a financier who owned 14 percent of Century's shares, almost all of which had been purchased after 1987. The suit was dismissed, and Century succeeded in concentrating voting power through the company's employee stock ownership plan. The result was employee control of 40 percent of Century's voting rights.

Williams's only son, Clarke, Jr. was slated to follow his father and grandfather as head of Century. However, the younger Williams was afflicted with Hodgkin's Disease. In 1989, after serving as Century's president for six years, Clarke, Jr. suffered a cerebral hemorrhage. He returned to work briefly, but later took disability retirement.

That same year Century took over the operations of Universal Telephone, a company with 48,000 access lines in 5 states and licenses to operate cellular systems in 19 markets. The $90 million acquisition was Century's largest to date. In 1992 Century acquired the Ohio operations of Centel Corporation, a company serving 64,000 lines, mostly in the growing suburban Cleveland area. The $135 million deal significantly boosted Century's position in the industry and increased its total access lines by 20 percent, to more than 425,000.

Century subsequently added several more smaller companies, building upon the company's contiguous property "clustering" strategy. These clusters comprised important rural areas which, unlike the saturated urban areas controlled by the Bell companies, had much higher potential for growth.

Its strongest growth in the early 1990s was in Michigan, where it controlled cellular licenses for almost the entire state. Its second-largest concentration of cellular properties was in northern Louisiana and southern Arkansas, including Texarkana, Shreveport, and Monroe. Century also owned cellular interests in a huge area covering southeastern Colorado, western New Mexico, and northern Arizona. In the years since the divestiture of AT&T, telephone stocks were one of the highest-growth sectors in American industry, and Century led the pack.

With the early retirement of Clarke Williams, Jr., it appeared that the eventual retirement of his father would end the Williams family leadership of Century. The man most often cited as a possible successor to the elder Williams was Glen F. Post III, the company's vice chairman, president, and CEO.

If Post succeeded Clarke Williams as chairman, it was expected that he would maintain the conservative, low-debt policies that have made Century the seventh largest non-Bell telephone company. Safely insulated from the prospect of a hostile takeover in the early 1990s, it appeared that Century was well-positioned to concentrate its energies on the development of its service areas and strategic acquisitions of other promising ones.

Principal Subsidiaries: Century Cellunet; Century Business Communications, Inc.; Century Telecommunications, Inc.; Century Service Group, Inc.; Century Supply Group, Inc.; Interactive Communications, Inc.

Further Reading:

Centuryan, Monroe, LA: Century Telephone Enterprises, Inc., March 1981.
Century Telephone Enterprises, Inc. Annual Reports, Monroe, LA: Century Telerphone Enterprises, Inc., 1990–92.
''Company Profile,'' Monroe, LA: Century Telephone Enterprises, Inc., May 1993.
''Company Watch,'' *Financial World,* September 15, 1992, pp. 12–13.
''Minding its Own Business,'' *Forbes,* February 17, 1992, pp. 110–111.

—John Simley

Chemical Waste Management, Inc.

Chemical Waste Management, Inc.

3001 Butterfield Road
Oak Brook, Illinois 60521
U.S.A.
(708) 218-1500

Public Company (77 percent owned subsidiary of Waste
    Management, Inc.)
Incorporated: 1978 as a wholly owned subsidiary of Waste
    Management, Inc.
Employees: 6,800
Sales: $1.5 billion
Stock Exchanges: New York
SICs: 4953 Refuse Systems; 5093 Scrap & Waste Materials

Chemical Waste Management, Inc., (CWM) is America's largest provider of hazardous waste removal services. The company provides transportation, recycling, treatment, and disposal services for chemical and low-level nuclear products of both government and industry at 40 facilities spread across the United States and Mexico.

CWM was first formed in 1975 as a subsidiary of a much larger waste-disposal firm, Waste Management, Inc. This company was created in 1956 when a number of small trash haulers in Illinois and Florida banded together to form one company; this new entity subsequently grew by acquiring other local operations. In 1971 this company went public as Waste Management, Incorporated.

At the start of 1971, Waste Management purchased the Calumet Industrial Development (CID) disposal facility, a landfill located south of Chicago in the Calumet City area. This marked the company's first foray into the handling of hazardous wastes. Three years later, Waste Management finished work on a 3,750-square-foot laboratory space at the CID site. This enabled the company to better analyze and track chemical wastes buried there.

In 1975 Waste Management separated its chemical waste management operations from the rest of its businesses, forming Chemical Waste Management as a separate division of the company. At the same time, it moved to consolidate all of its chemical waste disposal activities in the Chicago area. A further step in this direction was taken in March 1975, when the company began operation of an acid neutralization plant at its

CID site. This allowed it to process wastes from the steel industry, as well as other waste materials, in liquid form.

In the following year, CWM's operations came under more comprehensive government regulation when the U.S. Congress passed the Resource Conservation and Recovery Act, the country's first complete set of regulations detailing how hazardous wastes should be managed. With these national guidelines in place, CWM reorganized a year later to place its business on a national footing, expanding beyond its base in the Midwest.

In 1978 CWM was restructured once again, to be incorporated as a wholly owned subsidiary of Waste Management, Inc. The company began its nationwide expansion in earnest, buying up waste disposal facilities across the United States. Among CWM's acquisitions at this time were sites in Emelle, Alabama; Lake Charles, Louisiana; Vickery, Ohio; and Port Arthur and Corpus Christi, Texas. In addition, the company announced that it would invest $1.5 million in equipment to reclaim solvent and paint sludge.

The following year CWM bought a facility in Kettleman Hills, California, extending its reach to the West Coast. In its first twelve months of operations, the company reported revenues of $49.7 million. In 1980 the Federal Resource Conservation and Recovery Act took effect, and CWM's facilities received interim status under the new law, which allowed it to continue treating and disposing of chemical wastes. Among the jobs the company was selected to perform was the burial of all remaining chemical stocks of the Silvex Company. CWM was hired to complete this task by the federal government's Environmental Protection Agency (EPA). As a result of this and other contracts, CWM's revenues reached $84.9 million by the end of 1980.

In 1981 CWM diversified its activities, forming an Environmental Remedial Action division (abbreviated ENRAC), to clean up contamination at hazardous waste sites. This branch of CWM was designed to provide government and industry with specialists available around the clock to take care of spill emergencies and the renovation of abandoned chemical dumps. In addition, CWM made an agreement with the Ashland Chemical Company, a leading chemical distributor, to provide chemical waste collection and disposal services to companies that generated chemical wastes nationwide. The idea was to meet the needs of the many businesses that generated a relatively small quantity of hazardous substances, but were nonetheless obligated to comply with a welter of complicated federal, state, and local regulations governing the disposal of all such substances. Under the agreement with Ashland, that company would provide help with documentation, pick-up, and delivery of chemical wastes, and then CWM would provide verification of the nature and quantity of the wastes received, along with analysis, treatment, and disposal or reclamation of the substances. The company planned to undertake these activities at its 18 fully certified facilities throughout the country. This service was launched in October 1981.

In addition to this initiative, CWM opened its Technical Center in Riverdale, Illinois. This facility served CWM as a centralized laboratory for the analysis of chemical wastes. By the end of 1981, company revenues had risen to $119.1 million.

In the next year, CWM was selected for yet another EPA job, when its ENRAC unit was chosen to handle the cleanup of a contaminated site called MIDCO I, located near Gary, Indiana. This job was the first project of the Superfund program, which the government had set up to mitigate the worst cases of environmental pollution.

In December 1982 the company's ENRAC unit also began work on the Seymour Recycling Center, in Seymour, Indiana, another Superfund site, whose cleanup was privately funded. CWM moved men, materials, equipment, and mobile laboratories onto the site in preparation for the removal of 60,000 55-gallon drums holding both solid and liquid toxic and flammable substances, many of which were rusted, damaged, or leaking. In addition, the site contained 98 large storage silos and significant quantities of contaminated topsoil. The company expected the project to take about a year to complete, for which it would be paid $7.7 million.

In addition to these undertakings, CWM also made a number of improvements and acquisitions to increase its capabilities. In April 1982 the company brought on line its Consumer Aerosol Destruction plant, at its Calumet City site. The company bought Solvent Resource Recovery, Inc., in West Carrollton, Ohio, which enabled it to recycle chemical wastes for the first time. In addition, CWM purchased Chem-Nuclear Systems, Inc., operators of a hazardous waste management operation in Arlington, Oregon. This unit would later become a subsidiary of CWM.

In September 1982 CWM also announced that it had entered into a joint agreement with two other companies to form Environmental Systems Corporation, an entity created for the express purpose of cleaning up the chemical wastes left at a site previously owned by the Lakeway Chemical Company, near Muskegon, Michigan. The company planned to treat contaminated soils and water on the site as well as materials created by the continuing operation of the companies that had taken possession of the site. It planned to use five different techniques to dispose of the wastes, all certified by the EPA and Michigan Department of Natural Resources.

In 1983 CWM continued its string of acquisitions by buying Trade Waste Incineration, Inc., located in Sauget, Illinois. This gave the company the capability of burning hazardous waste for the first time. In addition to this land-based site, the company also purchased Ocean Combustion Services, which owned an ocean-going incinerator vessel. The *Vulcanus I,* bought in January 1983, was registered in Liberia. Originally built as a tanker, it had been converted for incineration purposes in 1972. In May 1983, after two test burns monitored by the EPA, the ship demonstrated that its destruction rate for PCBs and other contaminants was higher than 99 percent. It was subsequently sent to Singapore for re-fitting of some of its equipment.

CWM's other waste incinerator ship, the *Vulcanus II,* also managed by its Ocean Combustion Services unit, was built for incineration purposes in West Germany, and was completed in November 1982. It operated out of Antwerp, burning European wastes, by 1983. In July 1983 CWM applied for EPA permission to use its two ships to burn wastes generated in the United States.

This move came as CWM formulated an internal policy forbidding the burial of liquid wastes, two years before federal regulations made this illegal. In addition, in further efforts to enhance compliance with regulatory structures, the company formed its own Environmental Compliance program of internal auditors based at each of its waste disposal sites.

Despite these efforts, in July 1984 CWM found itself the object of an EPA order to accelerate its cleanup of a hazardous waste landfill in Lowry, Colorado, near Denver. The company was ordered to remove all hazardous substances in drums and ship them to a new and more appropriate site, rather than try to contain them at their old home.

Also in 1984, CWM bought SCA Services, Inc., and in doing so took over the management of four additional hazardous waste treatment sites in Chicago; Model City, New York; Newark, New Jersey; and Fort Wayne, Indiana. During this time, the federal government updated and tightened its regulations concerning the treatment and disposal of hazardous wastes. As a result of these new laws, a majority of the nation's former waste handling facilities were forced to close, since they failed to comply with new standards. Since all of CWM's sites passed inspection, they were allowed to continue operation. CWM anticipated a much larger market, given the far smaller number of competitors left. Counteracting this boon, however, was a rash of fines assessed by the EPA for waste disposal violations at many of CWM's sites. The company was assessed a $600,000 fine for improper storage of PCBs in Emelle, Alabama. CWM's facility at this location, with 2,400 acres, was the nation's largest toxic waste dump. The company was then hit with a $6.8 million penalty for violations at its Vickery, Ohio, facility, followed by another $2.5 million assessment for continued misconduct at the same site. In addition, the company paid $4 million as a result of problems at its Kettleman Hills center. CWM shuffled its management in an effort to improve its rate of compliance with EPA regulations.

In October 1986, CWM offered stock to the public for the first time, when Waste Management, Inc., its corporate parent, offered 19 percent of the company's worth on the New York Stock Exchange. Following this move, the company acquired the Oil and Solvent Process Company, which boasted facilities to recycle solvents in Azusa, California, and Henderson, Colorado. In addition, CWM entered the booming market for asbestos cleanup. To help clients reduce the amount of hazardous waste they produced, CWM also formed a division of consultants, available to advise industrial concerns on reduction of their waste stream.

In May 1986 CWM suffered a setback in its efforts to commence use of its ocean-going incinerator vessels, *Vulcanus I* and *Vulcanus II.* Although the EPA had six months earlier tentatively approved a test-burn of 700,000 gallons of PCB-contaminated oil off the coast of New Jersey, subsequent public hearings produced widespread objections and the tests were postponed indefinitely.

Despite this setback concerning ocean-going operations CWM continued to invest in other aspects of its technological capabilities. In 1987 the company purchased a 49 percent interest in TITISA, an operation located in Tijuana, Mexico, that recovered solvents and blended fuels. This was CWM's first move into international operations. In addition, the company moved into the field of wastewater treatment, introducing a prototype of PO*WW*ER, an on-site aqueous cleansing service, at its Lake Charles, Louisiana, center.

In 1988 CWM made a number of acquisitions that complemented its own operations and also moved aggressively into a number of areas new to the company. CWM bought a part of HAZCO International, Inc., a company that helped industries dispose of small quantities of hazardous waste. The company also purchased a part of Tracker Services, Inc., as well as Inland Pollution Control, of Rockland, Massachusetts, marking its first move into the New England market. In addition, the company bought 49 percent of Brand Companies, Inc., the country's largest asbestos cleanup operator, for $50 million, and merged its operations in this field with those of its partner. In a more traditional vein, CWM began construction on a fourth hazardous waste incinerator at its Saugus, Illinois, center. This device, which doubled the plant's incineration capabilities, was designed to burn contaminated soil, much of which was expected to come from EPA Superfund sites. The company also began to build a new incinerator in Fort Arthur, Texas.

Moving into a new area, CWM used X*TRAX, a patented solvent extraction system, to treat low level radioactive wastes, mixed with other hazardous substances, at the federal Energy Department's Oak Ridge National Laboratory in Tennessee. Later that year, the company's Chem-Nuclear Systems subsidiary won a contract to operate three facilities for refinement of low-level radioactive wastes from 14 states.

In 1989 CWM continued to win big contracts for its services. The company snagged a $48 million job cleaning up the 44 sites that made up the Denver Radium Superfund project. In addition, the company was assigned to oversee collection and disposal of waste from the Exxon *Valdez* oil spill.

In an effort to garner additional government contracts, CWM formed Chem-Nuclear Environmental Services, Inc., which focused on the cleanup tasks necessary at former Department of Energy and Department of Defense installations. In response to an EPA contract to dispose of dinoseb, a banned pesticide, CWM opened a Memphis transfer station, its fourth, to collect the substance before treatment.

In 1990 CWM diversified its activities further, purchasing two engineering and consulting firms, Sirrine Environmental Consultants and Enwright Environmental Consulting Laboratories, both based in Greensborough, South Carolina, to seek out clients in the private sector. In addition, it continued to buy companies whose activities meshed with its own, and it increased its stake in Brand Companies, Inc., its asbestos operation, to 55.9 percent.

CWM maintained its aggressive pace of acquisitions in 1991, adding four new operations, entering one joint venture, and buying out its Mexican partner. Despite these gains, however, the company suffered a series of setbacks. In February 1991 an explosion at its hazardous waste incinerator in Calumet City, south of Chicago, shut the plant down and eventually yielded a $3 million fine for falsifying records and sloppy practices.

On a broader level, the general recession in the American economy reduced the amount of waste produced by many industrial concerns, as they cut back on overall operations. In addition, tighter budgets caused some potential clients to postpone expensive cleanup jobs. In addition, CWM was assessed a $3.1 million penalty by the EPA in December 1991 because of the failure of its big No. 4 incinerator unit at its Sauget site in Southern Illinois to pass air quality emissions tests. Four months later, the EPA barred CWM from burning any more Superfund waste at Sauget because the air pollution problems had not been resolved. Between September 1990 and July 1991 CWM suffered a total of $7.8 million in federal and state fines for improper practices at its Calumet City facility alone. CWM's legal difficulties continued in 1992, as the company came under criminal investigation for possible violations of environmental laws on one of its cleanup jobs and faced another six government fines exceeding $100,000 each.

In addition to these regulatory ills, CWM was threatened by movements to limit or end interstate transfer of hazardous wastes. Efforts to limit such transfers were particularly strong in Alabama, where CWM operated the enormous Emelle hazardous material landfill and storage facility. The company received some relief from this threat in 1992, when the U.S. Supreme Court ruled in its favor and allowed interstate shipping of hazardous wastes under the Commerce Clause.

Also in that year, CWM increased its activities in Mexico and began work on another project at Oak Ridge, Tennessee. As part of a continuing reorganization involving its parent company, CWM consolidated its environmental restoration efforts into CWM Remedial Services, Inc., which was designed to provide services to both national and local customers, and also restructured itself to spin off its on-site hazardous waste disposal operations to a new company, of which it became part owner.

Despite these shifts, CWM's core activities of collecting and disposing of hazardous wastes remained secure and profitable. With ever-widening environmental awareness, and no end of chemical waste disposal needs in sight, the company's future appears secure.

Principal Subsidiaries: The Brand Companies, Inc. (56%); Rust International, Inc. (58%); Chem-Nuclear Systems, Inc.; SCA Services., Inc.; EWM Federal Environmental Services, Inc.

Further Reading:

Bailey, Jeff, "Waste Management Plans Public Offer of 20% Stake in Its Foreign Operations," *Wall Street Journal,* March 20, 1992.
——, "Chemical Waste Is Investigated; Shares Decline," *Wall Street Journal,* April 2, 1992.
Fass, Susan, "Ships to Burn Hazardous Waste," *Journal of Commerce,* August 5, 1983.
"Hazardous Waste Cleanup Begins at Seymour Site," *Journal of Commerce,* December 15, 1982.
Richards, Bill, "EPA Orders Unit of Waste Management To Begin Tests at Big Dump in Alabama," *Wall Street Journal,* April 5, 1988.
Taylor, Robert E. "EPA Denies Waste Company's Request To Burn Toxic Wastes Off New Jersey," *Wall Street Journal,* May 29, 1986, p. 10.
"Three Companies Form $20 Million Waste Project," *Journal of Commerce,* September 29, 1982.

—Elizabeth Rourke

Chiles Offshore Corporation

1400 Broadfield Boulevard
Suite 400
Houston, Texas 77084-5133
U.S.A.
(713) 647-0100
Fax: (713) 647-0931

Public Company
Incorporated: 1987
Employees: 420
Sales: $44.45 million
Stock Exchanges: American
SICs: 1381 Drilling Oil & Gas Wells

Chiles Offshore Corporation is an international provider of offshore contract drilling and well workover services for major and independent oil and gas companies. Chiles owns and operates a fleet of offshore drilling rigs, providing new well drilling services as well as workover or enhancement and maintenance services for existing wells. The bulk of the company's drilling activities are conducted in the U.S. Gulf of Mexico and offshore near Nigeria on tracts leased by the company's customers.

Chiles Offshore informally traces its corporate lineage to the 1946 formation of Chiles Drilling Company, a supplier of contract drilling services for oil and gas companies operating in southern Texas. In 1980 Chiles began operating in the U.S. Gulf of Mexico through various limited partnerships, including Chiles Offshore, Inc. and other predecessor companies.

In 1980, 32-year-old William E. Chiles became president and chief operating officer of Chiles Offshore at a time when several drilling companies were setting up shop in the U.S. Gulf region. In 1981 C. Ray Bearden, at the age of 34, joined the company as vice-president of operations.

In April 1987, with energy prices stabilizing and the market for drilling services improving after a two-year lull, the company was incorporated as Chiles-Alexander International, Inc., with seven jackup drilling rigs and two platform rigs. The following year, the company sold its two platform rigs, ending the year with a fleet of seven jackup rigs. Chiles finances took a beating its first full year, with the company losing $7.2 million on annual sales of nearly $29 million.

Losses continued to mount in 1989, and, after a trio of quarterly deficits in December of that year, the company began a four-month-long refinancing program, which included the establishment of a $35 million line of credit with a Norwegian bank. The company also initiated a private placement of additional common stock, receiving a net income of $48.6 million, which helped Chiles post its first annual profit in 1989 and earn $7.7 million on sales of $27.2 million.

Through the private placement of stock, control of 80 percent of Chiles passed into the hands of three companies which had been involved with Chiles-Alexander since 1987. Those companies included P.A.J.W. Corporation, a firm wholly owned by Gordon Getty of the former Getty Oil Company; OMI Investments Inc., a division of the diversified and publicly held OMI International Corporation which controlled one of the largest oil tanker operations in the United States; and Anders Wilhelmsen, a Norwegian shipping company which gained a 14 percent interest in Chiles as part of what became a 23 percent foreign investment in the drilling firm.

As part of the company's refinancing program, the operating subsidiary, Chiles-Alexander Offshore, Inc., was merged into the parent company, and by March 1990 all outstanding shares of Chiles preferred stock were reclassified into common stock. With the oil service and drilling stock markets gaining momentum, the company changed its name to Chiles Offshore Corporation in April 1990, and the following month went public in order to finance a rig fleet expansion and refurbishing program. Chiles earned $64.6 million through an offering of 5.7 million shares of common stock, and with additional loans totaling more than $60 million, the company acquired ten used jackup drilling rigs and one used semi-submersible drilling rig in four separate 1990 purchases adding up to more than $128 million.

During its first year as a public corporation, Chiles operated exclusively in the U.S. Gulf of Mexico, where natural gas represented the greatest potential for discovery. During the winter of 1990, however, slumping natural gas prices forced several smaller and independent oil concerns to suspend drilling plans, and the losses Chiles anticipated from the expansion of its rig fleet were magnified. Decreased demand for drilling services contributed to a 1990 fourth quarter loss of $1.8 million and a loss for the year of $2.7 million, despite an increase in annual revenues which nearly doubled to $50.4 million.

With the slump in drilling activity in the U.S. Gulf region, Chiles began seeking overseas work and branching into the international arena. In February 1991 the company formed the wholly owned subsidiary, Chiles Offshore International, Inc., to operate one of the company's jackup drilling rigs offshore near Trinidad. That month the company also formed Chiles Offshore Africa, Inc., another wholly owned subsidiary, for the purpose of providing services offshore near West Africa.

During mid-1991 Chiles relocated one of its rigs to Trinidad, where it had a drilling contract with Royal Dutch/Shell, and secured additional loans to modify drilling rigs earmarked for West Africa. By September 1991 Chiles had joined a mass exodus out of the U.S. Gulf region which had been prompted by low natural gas prices, a rapidly declining availability of drilling jobs, and a highly competitive bidding arena.

During the last six months of 1991 Chiles redeployed four rigs to offshore Nigeria, three of which traveled by a single heavy-lift ship in one of the industry's largest rig transfers ever. By the end of the year Chiles had five rigs working in Nigeria and a sixth rig en route to West Africa.

During 1991 Chiles sold four of its rigs, including its semi-submersible rig and three of its platform rigs, for a total of $44 million. Despite the income from rig sales and increases in annual revenues which climbed to 52.7 million in 1991, however, Chiles lost $25.8 million for the year. The auditor's report in Chiles 1991 annual report noted that "the industry conditions which contributed to these losses . . . continue to deteriorate. In addition, the company will not be able to remain in compliance with certain terms and covenants" of its loan agreements. The company's losses, stemming from dismal market conditions in the Gulf of Mexico and up-front costs to modify and move rigs to international markets, led the company's auditors to conclude that there was "substantial doubt as to the Company's ability to continue as a going concern."

By the end of 1991 Chiles Offshore had a long-term debt of more than $75 million, with sizable loan payments scheduled for 1992. In December 1991 the company secured waivers on some of its loan covenants which had been violated after Chiles total debt to total assets ratio fell below a stipulated level. For the year, Chiles lost more than $25 million on revenues of $52.7 million.

The company began 1992 with four rigs operating under contract in West Africa, five rigs under contract in the U.S. Gulf of Mexico, and five rigs inactive, including one rig awaiting work offshore near Trinidad.

In March 1992 the company formed the wholly owned subsidiary Chiles Offshore Mexico, Inc. to pursue drilling opportunities in Mexico and South America. By the end of the month the company faced a quarterly loss of $3.32 million, and again fell into technical default on certain loan covenants.

During the first part of 1992 rapidly deteriorating industry conditions forced Chiles to take cost-cutting measures, and as the company's rigs came off contract they were cold stacked, or placed in inactive status, with idle rigs moved to a single U.S. Gulf of Mexico location and their separate drilling crews replaced by a single, smaller maintenance crew. By the end of April, seven of the company's rigs located in the Gulf were taken out of active status. Furthermore, during the second quarter of 1992, Chiles closed its Lafayette, Louisiana, field office and reduced the number of its shore-based employees by about 30 percent. Despite these moves to cut its overhead, the company found itself in technical default on loan agreements in both April and May 1992.

With its financial situation deteriorating and a second quarter loss of $24 million looming, the company announced several changes in the company's management. William E. Chiles resigned as president, chief executive, and a member of Chiles corporate board, and was replaced by C. Ray Bearden, vice-president of operations for Chiles Offshore and its predecessors since 1981. Marc Leland was replaced as chairperson by Winthrop A. Wyman, chief executive officer of OMI Petrolink Corporation. In addition, Robert F. Fulton, vice-president and chief financial officer since 1991, was elected to the company's board and named a senior vice-president, replacing Mark Keller who resigned in the management realignment. As a result of the management shakeup, Chiles Offshore also expanded its board from six to eight members with the new board including a representative from each of the three major limited partnership companies, OMI, Anders Wilhelmsen, and P.A.J.W.

In early July 1992 Chiles again fell into technical default on loan agreements. The new management team responded by requesting a four-month deferral of $7 million worth of late loan payments in order to buy time to reschedule Chiles long-term debt obligations and complete a corporate recapitalization plan.

By November 1992 conditions in the drilling market had improved, allowing Chiles to reactivate two of its stacked rigs and to relocate its rig near Trinidad to the U.S. Gulf of Mexico. That month Chiles staged a secondary offering that resulted in the sale of 22.2 million shares of common stock. The offering, coming at a time when natural gas stocks were shifting back into the public's favor while gas prices were hitting a seven-year high, netted the company $28.3 million. About half of the stock sold in the secondary offering was acquired by Chiles' three principle limited partners.

The 1992 stock offering allowed Chiles to reduce its long-term debt by $17.3 million, bolster its working capital fund by $11 million, and keep Gulf of Mexico offshore drilling operations from sinking. At the time of the offering half of Chiles Offshore's 14 rigs were cold stacked, while one rig was stacked offshore near Trinidad. Only six rigs were working, two in the Gulf of Mexico and four offshore near Nigeria.

For the 1992 year Chiles lost $31.8 million on declining sales of $44.4 million, with the company's four rigs in West Africa accounting for 71 percent of the Chiles revenues for the year. Nevertheless, the company closed the year in significantly stronger financial condition, having improved its working capital position from a negative $50 million to a positive $19 million and reduced its total debt from $75 million at the beginning of the 1992 to $49 million by year-end. The company also had rescheduled its loan repayments, which were spread out through 1997.

The company entered 1993 with a rig fleet of 14, and, as of March 1993, three of the company's 14 rigs were operating offshore near Nigeria while five were contracted in the U.S. Gulf of Mexico. A ninth rig was available for work, while the company's five remaining rigs stacked in either West Africa or the U.S. Gulf.

For the first quarter of 1993 Chiles lost $3.7 million, with those losses stemming largely from costs to reactivate two rigs expected to begin work in the summer of 1993. During the middle of 1993 the company announced that 12 of its 14 rigs would be working by year-end as a result of increased drilling activity worldwide.

As Chiles moved towards the mid-1990s, the company's strategy was to pursue drilling opportunities both in the U.S. Gulf of Mexico and in international markets, with Bearden predicting profitability for Chiles if market conditions continued to improve in the U.S. Gulf of Mexico. Regardless of developments in the U.S. Gulf, Chiles anticipated ongoing dependance on its operations in Nigeria, where demand for drilling was expected to remain relatively stable.

Despite signs of improvement in the drilling market, Chiles future remained uncertain as it neared mid-decade. The company believed it had adequate working capital to do business and make loan payments through 1994, but its ability to make timely debt payments and secure other needed cash requirements beginning in 1995 hinged largely on industry conditions, which in previous recent years had been highly volatile.

Principal Subsidiaries: Chiles Offshore International, Inc.; Chiles Offshore Africa, Inc. (Cayman); Chiles Offshore Mexico, Inc.

Further Reading:

Calkins, Laurel Brubaker, "Oil Rigs Exit Gulf in Record Numbers," *Houston Business Journal,* September 2, 1991, Section 1, p. 1.
Chiles Offshore Corporation Annual Report, Houston: Chiles Offshore Corporation, 1992.
Gill, Douglas, "Financing Strategies," *Oil and Gas Investor,* April, 1991, pp. 65–69.
McNamara, Victoria, "Chiles Offshore Corp. Makes Public Stock Offering," *Houston Business Journal,* April 16, 1990, Section 1, p. 15.
Payne, Chris, "Drillers Go to Wall Street as Gas Prices Rise in Gulf," *Houston Business Journal,* October 19, 1992, Section 1, p. 1.
Solomon, Caleb, "Chiles Offshore Expects to Report Fourth-Period Loss," *The Wall Street Journal,* March 1, 1991, Section A, p. 4F.

—Roger W. Rouland

Chips and Technologies, Inc.

CHIPS and Technologies, Inc.

2950 Zanker Rd.
San Jose, California 95134
U.S.A.
(408) 434-0600
Fax: (408) 434-9315

Public Company
Incorporated: 1985
Employees: 281
Sales: $97.9 million
Stock Exchanges: OTC NASDAQ Midwest SE
SICs: 3674 Semiconductors and Related Services; 7372
Prepackaged Software; 7373 Computer Integrated Systems
Design

Founded in 1985, CHIPS and Technologies, Inc., supplies advanced semiconductor devices to the worldwide personal computer industry. The company pioneered the concept of implementing discrete system functions in highly integrated chipsets. CHIPS' product portfolio includes CRT and flat-panel graphic controllers, graphics accelerators, desktop video devices, integrated communications ICs and system logic CHIPsets. CHIPS' products are found in a wide range of systems from compact portables to high-performance desktop computers.

CHIPS operates its sales activities out of its corporate headquarters in San Jose, California, and out of regional and district offices located in Norcross, Georgia, and Schaumburg, Illinois. The company or its subsidiaries maintain branch offices in Paris, France; Munich, Germany; Taipei, Taiwan; and Berkshire, England. In addition, CHIPS has appointed 23 independent manufacturer's representative organizations, 10 domestic distributors, and 27 international representative/distributors.

The company's product portfolio includes a family of circuits and chipsets integrating the system logic of microcomputer systems compatible with IBM PCs; a family of graphics controller circuits and chipsets for CRTs and flat panel displays that provide compatibility with industry standards for computer graphics display, including IBM's Video Graphics Array (VGA); a family of interface circuits for serial and parallel port communications, PC-to-mainframe communications controllers, and bus interface protocol control for various add-in cards; and a family of circuits for various forms of mass storage control. In the early 1990s, the company began focusing on

single-chip systems in order to exploit anticipated growth in hand-held and sub-notebook computers.

When Gordon Campbell founded CHIPS in 1985, his main objective was to develop more cost-effective methods of designing and producing microcomputer systems components for a rapidly growing market. Campbell was already well versed in the industry. Before embarking on the CHIPS venture, he served as president and CEO of SEEQ Technology, Inc., a publicly held company that he and four other Intel Corp. employees founded to address growing needs for high density circuits. He also held marketing experience as a major accounts manager for Intel's non-volatile and bipolar memories, as well as sales, management, and engineering positions at major semiconductor manufacturers. With this expertise and a well-chosen staff, Campbell entered the highly competitive semiconductor industry of the mid-1980s.

CHIPS introduced innovative products that provided systems designers with higher levels of circuit integration and the ability to produce marketable products more quickly. The company pioneered the use of Large Scale Integration (LSI) and Very Large Scale Integration (VLSI) semiconductor chips to integrate PC sub-systems based on Small Scale Integration (SSI) and Medium Scale Integration (MSI) semiconductors. VLSI design and engineering techniques figured into the company's first successful products. In 1985 CHIPS introduced the first integrated system logic chipset for computers compatible with IBM PC/AT system architecture. The five-chip AT CHIPSet integrated 63 of the 94 logic circuits in the AT system board into a compact and cost-effective chipset. PC makers could depend on the chipset to make smaller system boards with faster 80286 microprocessors using significantly fewer chips than previously possible, at a lower cost.

The early success of CHIPS was also secured by its products for graphics capabilities. The company designed an integrated chipset for enhanced graphics that replaced over 20 SSI and MSI circuits on the AT-compatible Enhanced Graphics Adapter (EGA) with only four chips. With the EGA CHIPSet, leading add-in board manufacturers were able to design, produce, and rapidly bring to market EGA-compatible graphics cards that outperformed IBM's EGA at less than half the price, according to CHIPS 1987 annual report. When IBM introduced its PS/2 family of computers with "VGA" graphics, an extension of the EGA architecture with slightly higher resolutions, more colors, and more extensive display modes, CHIPS followed suit with its VGA-compatible chip and bus interface circuit that enabled PC AT-compatibles to upgrade from EGA to VGA.

CHIPS also tapped a growing market for increasingly complex communications and mass storage controls. The company identified the need for easier access to large data bases and the importance of connectivity between shared laser printers, file servers, electronic mail, and other forms of on-line communications. Demand virtually exploded for communications interface products such as modems, devices linking mainframes to terminals, and local area networks (LANs). In late 1986, CHIPS introduced two StarLAN circuits that consolidated many of the primary functions of the StarLAN serial interface board and StarLAN Bug controller board. Following this initial encoder/decoder, the company developed other communications products, including a single chip permitting PC-to-mainframe compatibility.

From the beginning, CHIPS applied many of its technological advances toward the development of still more advanced products. The company developed a powerful array of mainframe-based design tools to assist in the system integration, compaction, and physical layout of its microcomputer-specific circuit designs. Using a proprietary computer aided engineering (CAE) system, designers were able to apply macrofunctional partitioning, a procedure in which systems designs were subdivided into large functional blocks that could be manipulated or combined with other macrofunctions to form highly integrated components. Formatted in an extensive mainframe library, the functional blocks could be interconnected according to designer's specifications. With these CAE tools, CHIPS was able to achieve a quicker design-to-market cycle for its components, as well as lower costs for better-tailored designs.

By 1987, the company drew on its advanced CAE system to offer system design services to customers desiring complete systems solutions. With CHIPS' Design Services Operation, major customers could count on the company's support in integrating its VLSI chipsets and other components into entire, customized systems.

In addition to innovative chip design, CHIPS initiated new manufacturing strategies. The company led the industry in the general move away from private foundry facilities and toward the use of high-volume, contract semiconductor foundries around the world. In addition to cost leverage, the practice helped pair specific projects with specific foundry specialties and capacities. In 1990 the company also commenced "die-buy" programs in which semiconductor die were purchased from strategic suppliers of bulk silicon and packaged by specialist packaging vendors. Costs were saved over the conventional route of purchasing fully tested, finished products from outside suppliers.

With solid footing in design and manufacturing established from the start, CHIPS experienced healthy growth into the late 1980s. In 1987, net sales exceeded $80.2 million, up from $12.7 million the year before; and net income grew to $12.9 million, up from $1.5 million. Such financial growth fueled advances on various fronts. The company introduced the industry's first AT/386 CHIPSets, attracting major corporate accounts, including Hewlett-Packard Co., NEC Corporation, and Tandy Corporation. In addition, CHIPS introduced the first IBM PS/2 Model 30-compatible single chip after negotiating license agreements with the computer giant. For a company that had traditionally reverse-engineered chips without patent licenses, licensing with IBM marked a new tack. "Because of the number of patents for the PS/2, it may be difficult to design chips without a license," explained Ron Yara, a vice president for CHIPS, in an October 1987 article for *PC Week.*

Placing a shining cap on the 1980s, the company reported record growth for fiscal 1989. Net sales for the year reached $217.6 million, an increase of 54 percent over the $141.5 million posted for 1988. Net income for the year rose to $33.0 million, up from $22.1 million the previous year. Stockholders received a 38 percent return in equity totaled $105.4 million on June 30, 1989, up from $66.6 million at the end of 1988. Reflecting its outstanding financial management within the semiconductor industry, CHIPS received INSTAT's 1988 "Kachina" Award.

In the early 1990s the PC market became an extremely volatile and competitive arena characterized by price slashing, consolidation, turmoil in distribution sectors, and general malaise linked to a sluggish world economy. CHIPS suffered intense pricing pressure across its entire product line, including new products. Price erosion in the company's core logic chipset business was particularly severe. According to the market research firm In-Stat, Inc., prices for core 16-bit and 32-bit system logic declined 19.4 percent in 1991. Such a decline contrasted sharply with the tremendous surge in business that CHIPS experienced when its PC/CHIP business took off in 1989. A key factor contributing to CHIPS' market decline was the rapid ascent of Advanced Micro Devices, Inc., (AMD) as a viable second-place supplier of microprocessors after Intel Corp. By 1992, with $150 million in assets, CHIPS would have a hard fight against the $4.7 billion Intel and $1.2 billion AMD.

The growing profits that CHIPS had enjoyed in the late 1980s diminished into losses in the early 1990s. In 1990, the company reported record net sales of $293.4 million, a 35 percent increase over the $217.6 million in net sales for fiscal 1989. Net income, however, declined 11 percent to $29.3 million. By 1991, figures looked even less promising: the company reported a net loss of $9.6 million, or 71 cents a share, on sales of $225.1 million. By 1992, net sales declined 37 percent to $141.1 million. Gross margins eroded from $82.5 million or 36.7 percent in fiscal 1991 to $17.0 million or 12.0 percent in fiscal 1992.

Reflecting its declining sales, CHIPS' cash position fell from $37.6 million at June 30, 1991, to $14.2 million a year later. On July 16, 1992, CHIPS announced a $23 million financing package that included a private placement of over $10 million in convertible promissory notes and reconfirmed bank lines of $13 million. The company also expected a tax refund of over $25 million from carrying back its operating losses over the preceding years.

In addition to increased competition over market share, the early 1990s saw rising tension over intellectual property. The industry leader, Intel Corp., increasingly turned to lawsuits to protect its products from competitors like AMD and CHIPS. According to Drew Peck, analyst for Donaldson, Lufkin & Jenrette Securities Corp., a New York investment bank, firms wishing to compete against Intel in the microprocessor business would have to contend with a complex mixture of legal and technical issues in order to position their products in a standards-oriented market. On one hand, a company might try to exactly duplicate a standard chip, thereby risking lawsuits defending patent design. On the other hand, a company might design an altogether new solution, incompatible with the existing standard, but capable of performing the same tasks. Most competitors, including CHIPS, tried to compromise between these two options to introduce products that conformed to industry standards but depended on unique design features to perform additional tasks.

CHIPS' new products released in 1992—such as its Itel pin-compatible 38600SX and 386DXZ chips and a line of SX and DX chips requiring a modified socket—followed this formula. They were designed to be both "fully compatible" yet "innovative and improved" at the same time. With a unique feature called SuperState, CHIPS also tried to maximize compatibility between different hardware and software combinations, thus attracting systems designers to the convenience of CHIPS components.

Despite CHIPS' efforts to avoid accusations of imitation by including innovative features, Intel engaged the company in a drawn-out legal suit. When Texas Instruments, Inc., considered licensing a PC core processor from CHIPS in 1992, Intel tried to prevent the move by asking the court to stop CHIPS from transferring its technology. In a letter to stockholders from CHIPS 1992 annual report, Gordon A. Campbell, president and CEO, summarized the Intel situation: "CHIPS continues to vehemently reject Intel's lawsuit claiming CHIPS' processor products violate Intel's patents. Intel's litigation has so far met with failure in the face of CHIPS' defense."

On other fronts, CHIPS' found itself defending its own patents against competitors. In September 1991 the company asked the International Trade Commission to ban the sale and import of IBM-compatible chipsets made by OPTi Computer, Eteq Microsystems, Elite Microelectronics, and Sun Electronics because they allegedly infringed on patents held by CHIPS. In August 1992 CHIPS and OPTi reached a settlement wherein OPTi acknowledged its infringement on page interleave patents and certain memory controller products and agreed to pay an undisclosed sum to CHIPS. CHIPS agreed that OPTi could continue to sell key controller products without further claims of past infringement. The other companies reached similar agreements.

With slipping sales profits and legal complications regarding intellectual property in the early 1990s, CHIPS emphasized development of new and truly innovative products to restore growth. From 1990 to 1991, the company increased its research and development spending by 16 percent. Select new products reflected the company's dedication to innovative change. In 1990 the company introduced Single Chip AT Controller (SCAT) technology, by which the functionality previously found in chipsets could be integrated into one chip. In turn, integrating several SCAT chips, the company introduced the Entry-Level Enhanced AT (ELEAT) CHIPSet, a platform incorporating systems logic, graphics, data communications, mass storage, and BIOS. Also in 1990, CHIPS developed the Multi-Processor Architecture Extension (M/PAX) product line, providing hardware that supported multiple micro-processors working together for symmetrical multiprocessing (SMP). SMP reduced processor wait time and increased the capabilities of advanced systems.

In 1992 CHIPS introduced several additional products and made new strategic alliances. In June 1992 Trion computers—a joint design and engineering effort between CHIPS and ComputerLand, Inc.—unveiled a new module incorporating CHIPS' Super38605DX microprocessor. The module permitted users to upgrade 386-based computers to 486-based performance at an extremely competitive cost. That same month, CHIPS intro-

duced its 82C481 True Color Graphics Accelerator, a single chip solution to increase graphics performance in Windows, OS/2, and CAD environments. The company also introduced its WinCHIPS CHIPSet, a system solution combining logic and graphics improvement for most popular PC systems. When Epson American Inc. introduced a PC using the accelerator, the firm noted a tenfold improvement in Windows performance over comparable Super VGA PCs, according to a June 1992 *PC Week* article.

Also in 1992, CHIPS completed several joint ventures to exploit growing demand for smaller, portable computer systems. In November the company collaborated with Logitech, Inc., to create a low-cost pen-based computer hardware design for a new class of mass-market, pen-based computers. Also in November, CHIPS announced an agreement with Lexmark International, Inc., to design, manufacture, and market a new class of low-cost, sub-notebook computers featuring significantly improved panel quality, keyboard technology, and battery life.

In 1993, CHIPS continued to offer money-saving performance boosters for the PC market. In June of that year, the company introduced a new system-logic chipset that greatly reduced the design and manufacturing costs of 486-based PC/AT compatible systems. "We are providing a price-performance value that let OEMs put 486 systems on retailer shelves for the same selling price as today's entry-level 386 systems," said S.S. Chao, product manager for systems logic at CHIPS, in a company news release. The company also introduced a new graphic user interface (GUI) accelerator to deliver high-end performance at a mainstream market price. The Wingine DGX overcame the limitations of existing GUI systems depending on dynamic random access memory (DRAM) by introducing a proprietary caching scheme called XRAM.

These and other products helped distinguish CHIPS as a viable player in the increasingly cutthroat computer market of the 1990s. In a May 1992 article for *PC Week,* securities analyst Drew Peck gave CHIPS a 50–50 chance of resuscitating its expiring business growth with its new products. "The products are very strong," he said.

Beginning in 1992, the company also began a vigorous program of cutting costs and focusing on specific, profitable products. From June 30 to November of 1992, the company reduced its head count by 20 percent, with plans to further reduce the number by 20 percent through staff reductions and attrition. Marketing and design efforts were also directed at single chip systems for emerging computers and embedded control markets, placing high hopes on the emergence of hand-held computers.

CHIPS also responded to growing world markets by expanding international offices. After recording 67 percent of net sales to foreign customers in 1992 (70 percent in fiscal 1991), such measures were in order. European headquarters were established in Neuchatel, Switzerland, and overseas design centers were opened in Munich and Taipei. In addition to seven direct sales offices in the United States, CHIPS operated branch offices in Taipei, Taiwan; Seoul, Korea; and Munich, Germany. Markets were also serviced throughout Japan, Korea, Taiwan,

Hong Kong, Singapore, China, India, Israel, Great Britain, France, Germany, Italy, Scandinavia, and North America.

In 1993, CHIPS showed preliminary signs of recovering financial stability. Net loss narrowed to $4.09 million for the quarter ending March 31, compared to a loss of $10.3 million the previous year. Paired with the company's restructuring plan, hopes for worldwide economic stimulus, and the truly innovative nature of CHIPS' products, the future looked ''possibly comfortable,'' or PC in the industry lingo.

Principal Subsidiaries: Chips and Technologies Taiwan, Inc.; Chips and Technologies Korea, Inc.; Chips and Technologies, GmbH; Chips and Technologies Japan K.K.; Chips and Technologies Texas, Inc.; Chips and Technologies, S.A.; Chips and Technologies J.V. (Cyprus) Ltd.

Further Reading:

Bourassa, Barbara, ''C&T Restructures to Trim Expenses,'' *PC Week,* November 23, 1992, p. 3.

Burke, Steven, ''Troubled C&T Bets on New Products: Cash-Poor Chip Vendor Is Counting on 386 Deals with PC Makers,'' *PC Week,* May 4, 1992, p. 147.

Chips and Technologies Corporate Background, San Jose: Chips and Technologies, Inc., 1985.

''CHIPS and Technologies Inc. Settles Lawsuit Against OPTi,'' *Business Wire,* August 18, 1992.

''New Products Using Chips and Technologies Inc.'s Super39605DX CPU,'' *PC Week,* June 29, 1992, p. 26.

Ristelhueber, Robert, ''Chips Stops $50M x86 Processor Development,'' *Electronic News,* August 10, 1992, p. 4.

Schroeder, Erica, ''Graphics Prices Fall as Chips Proliferate,'' *PC Week,* June 28, 1993, p. 37.

Spiegelman, Lisa L., ''Chip Makers Negotiate with IBM to License PS/2 Patents,'' *PC Week,* October 27, 1987, p. 1.

''Texas Aims to License Chip Technology,'' *PC User,* p. 18.

Wilkinson, Stephanie, ''Competitors Emerge Despite Litigation Threat: Advanced Micro Devices Inc. and Chips and Technologies Inc. Clone the Intel 80386 Chip,'' *PC Week,* November 11, 1991, p. S5.

—Kerstan Cohen

Chris-Craft Industries, Inc.

600 Madison Avenue
New York, New York 10022
U.S.A.
(212) 421-0200
Fax: (212) 935-8462

Public Company
Incorporated: 1928 as National Automotive Fibers, Inc.
Sales: $332 million
Employees: 1,000
Stock Exchanges: New York Pacific
SICs: 4833 Television Broadcasting; 3081 Unsupported
   Plastics Film & Sheet; 3086 Plastics Foam Products; 2299
   Textile Goods, Nec; 3089 Plastics Products Nec

Chris-Craft Industries, Inc., is the owner and operator of eight television stations across the United States, with a significant market share in the greater New York and Los Angeles areas, which are the country's two largest TV markets. Two of these stations are affiliated with networks, while six are independent. As a result, Chris-Craft is the second largest independent broadcaster in the nation, and the sixth largest TV broadcaster overall. In addition to its television division, which produces over ninety-five percent of the company's revenues, Chris-Craft also has an Industrial Division which manufactures plastic flexible films and contamination control plastic bag products, fiber carpet underlay, and insulation.

Chris-Craft Industries bears virtually no resemblance to the company from which it originated, National Automotive Fibers, Inc., which was founded in 1928 in Detroit. National Automotive Fibers manufactured upholstery, interior trim and carpeting, plastic products, and foam rubber for major Detroit automakers, especially Chrysler, Ford, and Studebaker-Packard. The company's present name was adopted two years after it had acquired the famous Chris-Craft boat manufacturer in 1960, and was retained even after the company divested itself of its boat manufacturing interest in 1981. The company still leases the name to the boat manufacturer.

National Automotive Fibers was successful, but remained a relatively minor supplier to the automobile industry. It had acquired the Montrose Chemical Company of San Francisco in the 1940s, but the company nevertheless remained almost wholly dependent on the automobile industry, and its revenues reflected those of the auto industry, often fluctuating wildly.

National Automotive Fibers, Inc., operated during and after World War II with moderate success, but in 1956 its fortunes changed dramatically when the company lost over $1 million on sales of $46 million. However, the company had attracted the attention of Paul V. Shields, senior partner of the Wall Street investment firm Shields & Co., who had determined that the company's troubles resulted from overdependence on the auto industry. Shields acquired National Automotive Fiber in a bold takeover move, trimmed it of marginally profitable products, and diversified its operations.

While sales revenues of National Automotive dropped to $23 million a year later, profits rose to a record $1 million, and by 1960, the firm (then called NAFI to emphasize its new identity as a diverse manufacturer) had accumulated assets of $10 million. By then NAFI had entered into oil and gas operations, as well as TV and radio broadcasting.

NAFI's financial health provided the means to acquire the Chris-Craft Company, a boat manufacturer worth $50 million. Chris-Craft was privately owned by the descendants of its founders, Christopher Columbus Smith and his brother Henry. During the 1880s the Smiths were backwoodsmen in St. Clair County, Michigan, who depended on duck hunting for a living. The ancestors of today's well-known pleasure boats were the Smiths' simple rowboat, built for cruising the St. Clair River.

The two brothers supplemented their incomes by acting as field guides for wealthy businessmen and professionals from Detroit, who vacationed fifty miles away in the unspoiled, natural environment of St. Clair County. To the brothers' surprise, these tourists admired the simple, sturdy lines of the Smiths' homemade vessels. Soon they found themselves selling the boats to eager buyers. In 1884 they built a boat house, and soon boatbuilding supplanted the business of hunting.

Fifteen years later, business was booming in the Smith boat house on the St. Clair River in Algonac. From simple duck boats the brothers had expanded their product line to include canoes, rowboats, and even a few sailboats. So successful were they that the Smith's business had become the town's major industry. The first gasoline-powered boat on the Great Lakes was a Smith craft, as were the fastest speed boat and the world's first hydroplane. By 1930 the boat making firm was called Chris-Craft Corporation, and at the time of its acquisition by NAFI in 1960, was the largest manufacturer of small boats in the world.

The acquisition of Chris-Craft involved a great deal of negotiation because the company's president, Harsen Smith, was opposed to the sale. Harsen's objections were rooted in his strong loyalty to the company and an urge to maintain its dynastic heritage. Harsen controlled only about 25 percent of the company, however, and the rest of the Smith family was in favor of selling. The company's valuation at approximately $50 million came as a huge surprise to the family and afforded them the opportunity to be selective in choosing a buyer.

On January 18, 1960, Joseph Flannery, who was the assistant to NAFI's president, Paul Shields, happened to encounter Owen

Smith, Chris-Craft's majority stockholder, at a boat show in New York. Owen Smith indicated his amenability to Chris-Craft's sale, and a series of high level negotiations began, with the reluctant Harsen Smith the recipient of competing offers between NAFI and a rival bidder, Brunswick Corporation.

Within one month of the chance meeting between Owen Smith and Joseph Flannery, NAFI had arranged a complicated buyout of Chris-Craft with a sale price of $40 million. The sale was predicated on Shields's willingness to agree to a "hands-off" management style with Chris-Craft.

The arrangement worked, for the 1960s proved to be the most successful period in the company's history—so successful, in fact, that in 1962, NAFI's stockholders agreed to change the company's name to Chris-Craft Industries, Inc., in order to capitalize on the division's success.

While the success of Chris-Craft's marine operations would eventually decline, the stimulus it injected into the parent company was enormous. Virtually all identification with the old National Automotive Fibers company disappeared, except for the manufacture of some carpet fiber, insulation, and chemical products. NAFI's annual revenues had stabilized long ago, thanks to Paul Shields' diversification strategy.

Throughout the 1960s, the Baldwin-Montrose chemical manufacturing company had invested increasingly in Chris-Craft, until it became Chris-Craft's biggest stockholder. Herbert J. Siegel was the chairman of Baldwin-Montrose who led a takeover of Chris-Craft, completed in 1968. Siegel remained chairman of Chris-Craft from 1968 into the 1990s.

In 1968 Chris-Craft headquarters moved from Oakland, California, where they had been since 1962, to New York. Siegel set about streamlining and re-organizing the company, which consisted of three main operations: the Boat Division; the fast growing Television Broadcasting Division with TV stations in Los Angeles, Minneapolis–St.Paul, and Portland, Oregon; and the small Industrial Division, consisting of Montrose Chemical of California (the world's largest producer of DDT until the federal government banned it in 1972) and Chris-Craft Industrial Products, Inc. Their combined sales for 1968 were $89 million.

The 1970s and 1980s saw the divestment of the Boat Division and Chris-Craft Industries' continued expansion into television broadcasting. During the 1970s Chris-Craft invested in Paramount, which provided Chris-Craft ownership of United Television, Inc.. In 1983 Warner Communications, Inc., later Time-Warner, Inc., in an attempt to avert a hostile takeover by

Australian investor Rupert Murdoch, welcomed Chris-Craft's investment in the company, enabling it to become Warner's biggest stockholder.

The Chris-Craft-Warner venture led to the formation of BHC Communications, a seventy percent owned public subsidiary of Chris-Craft. BHC owned and operated all eight of Chris-Craft's TV broadcasting stations, and was the parent company of United Television, Inc. The remaining thirty percent was owned by Time-Warner, the world's biggest media company.

In the early 1990s Chris-Craft continued to expand into the television broadcasting arena, acquiring Pinelands, Inc., in August 1992 for $313 million. Pinelands owned WWOR-TV, an independent station which broadcasted in a tri-state area that included the second most important television market in the country, New York City.

Chris-Craft's sales declined during the recession of the early 1990s, but by 1992 they had increased 16 percent over 1991, to $332 million. With its six independent and two network-affiliated TV stations, Chris-Craft had become the nation's sixth largest television broadcaster and the second largest independent television producer in the country. During the early 1990s Chris-Craft's stations reached approximately 20 percent of the households in the United States. The far smaller Industrial Products Division of the company manufactured packaging films, contamination control products, carpet fibers, and insulation, and was experiencing vigorous growth and expansion in the United States as well as in Europe with sales of over $1 million.

Principal Subsidiaries: 70% BHC Communications (New York, NY); Chris-Craft Industrial Products, Inc. (Gary, IN).

Further Reading:

"BHC Communications (Acquires Pinelands, Inc.)," *Wall Street Journal,* August 24, 1992, p. B4(W), p. B4(E).

"FCC Clears a Chris-Craft Unit to Buy WWOR-TV," *New York Times,* August 20, 1992, p. D4(L).

"Little Movement in Top 25 (Chris-Craft Increased Its Reach from 11% to 18%)," *Broadcasting & Cable,* March 22, 1993, p. 29.

"Paul V. Shields Group Acquires Control of Automotive Fibers," *Wall Street Journal,* September 24, 1956, p. 7.

"Pink Pick-Ups (Claster Television in Deal with Chris-Craft/United TV Stations for 'Pink Panther' Cartoon Show)," *Broadcasting & Cable,* January 25, 1993, p. 101.

Rodengen, Jeffrey L., *The Legend of Chris-Craft,* Fort Lauderdale: Write Stuff Syndicate, 1988, 294 p.

—Sina Dubovoj

Circuit City Stores, Inc.

9950 Mayland Drive
Richmond, Virginia 23233-1464
U.S.A.
(804) 527-4000
Fax: (804) 527-4187

Public Company
Incorporated: 1949 as Wards Company
Employees: 16,362
Sales: $3.27 billion
Stock Exchanges: New York
SICs: 5731 Radio, Television & Electronics Stores; 5722
  Household Appliance Stores

Circuit City Stores, Inc., is the nation's leading retailer of consumer electronics, with more than 250 stores located throughout the United States, primarily in the Southeast and West. The company, based in Virginia, pioneered the concept of the electronics superstore, providing a broad variety of products in a cavernous setting. In perfecting this formula, the company became the dominant marketer in many of the areas into which it expanded.

Circuit City was founded by Samuel S. Wurtzel, an importer-exporter who owned a business in New York. Wurtzel had sold his business and was vacationing in Richmond, Virginia, in 1949 when he went to get a haircut, and, while chatting with the barber, learned that the first commercial television station in the South would shortly go on the air in Richmond. Learning this, Wurtzel got the idea that it would be a good business proposition to open a store to sell television sets, reasoning that sales in the area would increase because of consumer interest in the new station's local broadcasts.

Wurtzel moved his family to Richmond and opened a store named "Wards," an acronym of its founder's family's names: "W" for Wurtzel, "A" for his son Alan, "R" for his wife Ruth, "D" for his son David, and "S" for his own name, Samuel. In addition, Wurtzel took a partner, Abraham L. Hecht. From its base in retailing televisions, Wurtzel soon branched out his business to include other home appliances. Within ten years, the business had expanded to encompass a chain of four stores, all of which were located in Richmond. Combined sales volume was about $1 million a year.

In 1960 Wards started to expand in another direction, as it began to operate licensed television departments within larger discount mass merchandisers in different areas of the country. The company ran television and other audio equipment sales operations in G.E.M., G.E.S., and G.E.X. stores. In the following year, Wards offered stock to the public for the first time, selling 110,000 shares in the company for $5.375 through a Baltimore stock broker.

In 1962 Wards increased its commitment to customer service by implementing a new service plan that included a free loan of a television set if a customer's television could not be repaired in the home. Two years later, the company opened its fifth television and appliance store, in Richmond's Southside Plaza Shopping Center. This, along with the company's earlier stock offering, signaled a period of quick expansion for the company.

In 1965 Wards made its first moves to grow through acquisition. The company purchased the Richmond Carousel Corporation, a discount department store in Richmond, from the T.G. Stores company. By taking over this company, Wards moved into the sale of automotive supplies, gasoline, household supplies, clothing, and children's toys, as well as appliances. In addition, in September 1965 Wards purchased Murmic, Inc., a Delaware company that operated hardware and housewares sales areas in department stores located in the Southeast.

The following year, Wards opened its sixth Virginia store, this one located in the Walnut Mall Shopping Center in Petersburg. Each of the company's stores featured 5,000 to 8,000 square feet of space in which to display and sell televisions, audio equipment, and other household appliances. With the additional revenue from this facility, company sales reached $23 million. Also in 1966, one of Samuel Wurtzel's sons, Alan, a lawyer, returned to Richmond to take a role in the family business, in preparation for eventually taking over the reins from his father.

In 1968 Wards offered additional stock to the public, selling 1,700 shares on the American Stock Exchange. With the revenue generated by this offering, in May 1969 the company purchased Custom Electronics, Inc., an outfit that sold audio and hi-fi equipment. The company owned four stores in the Washington, D.C. area, as well as a mail-order audio supplies operation called Dixie Hi-Fi, and also ran nine stereo departments in department stores located in an area stretching from Mobile, Alabama, to Albany, New York. Five months later, Wards continued its rapid expansion in the Mid-Atlantic states by buying the Certified TV and Appliance Company of Virginia Beach, Virginia, which operated three stores in the Tidewater area. The company also opened an additional Carousel store in the Richmond area.

One month later, Wards branched out from its familiar geographical area and its core business of appliance retailing when it purchased The Mart, located in Indianapolis, Indiana. This company had as one of its major components the tire retailing operations of the Rose Tire Company and its affiliates, but it also sold televisions, appliances, and furniture. In its furthest geographical leap, Wards also signed a contract to operate licensed television departments in Zody's Department Stores in Los Angeles.

The company's rapid expansion continued in 1970. Wards bought Woodville Appliances, Inc., which ran five television and appliance stores in Toledo, Ohio. Also in the Midwest, it acquired the operations of the Frank Dry Goods Company, which ran a television, appliance, and furniture store in Fort Wayne, Indiana.

By this time, Wards' rapid growth had brought it to a new era, and this was symbolized in 1970 by the transfer of power from the founders of the company to a younger generation. Samuel Wurtzel, its founder, stepped down as president, although he remained chairman of the board, and Abraham Hecht, his partner, retired. In their stead, Alan Wurtzel was named president of the company.

Among the first moves made by the new president was the opening of two specialty stores in Richmond, called Sight 'N Sound, that sold only audio equipment. These outlets were designed to take advantage of the boom in demand for high-tech stero equipment.

In 1972 Alan Wurtzel, still president, assumed the responsibilities of Chief Executive Officer of Wards. In an effort to eliminate weaker areas of the company, he closed the Franks of Fort Wayne store that Wards had purchased two years earlier, and also shut down three stores formerly run by Certified in Virginia. Following this consolidation, the company began to expand in the next year. Five audio stores were opened: three in the east, in Washington D.C., Richmond, Virginia, and Charlottesville, Virginia; and two in California. In the following year, Wards began to suffer the adverse effects of its rapid expansion and diversification into areas not related to its core business of television and appliance retailing. In 1974 the company lost $3 million on overall sales of $69 million. In an effort to stem the red ink, Wurtzel withdrew Wards from areas in which it was not turning a profit, such as tire sales. In addition, Wards was losing a large amount of money on its licensed appliance departments in three discount department store chains that were doing very badly. To cut its losses, the company began to move out of its leased audio and television operations in department stores, retaining only its involvement in the California Zody's stores.

In a shift in direction, Wards also closed two of its original stores in Richmond, opting instead to risk half the company's net worth opening a $2 million electronics superstore. With this move, Wards began to shift its focus from appliances in general to the growing market in consumer electronics. The company called its pioneering venture "The Wards Loading Dock." With 40,000 square feet, the warehouse store displayed and sold a very large selection of video and audio equipment and major appliances. This enormous facility, with its exceptionally broad offerings of more than 2,000 products, enabled Wards to take a strong lead against its competitors. In addition, the superstore's high volume of sales meant that the company could afford to offer lower prices than its smaller competitors, as well as such amenities as home delivery and in-store repairs. In this way, by locating its stores in medium-sized markets otherwise served only by smaller, mom-and-pop operations, Wards was able to exploit growing consumer interest in new electronics products. The successful superstore concept became the innovation upon which Wards built its future growth.

Also during this time, Wards expanded its Dixie Hi-Fi line of discount audio stores, adding nine new properties. In the next year, as its Richmond superstore showed promising returns, Wards began to streamline its operations. The company sold its four Woodville television and appliance stores in Toledo, Ohio, and also shuttered four of its five Mart stores in Indianapolis. In addition, the company shed its two Carousel stores in Richmond.

Two years later, in 1977, anticipating that the boom in stereo sales would eventually slow, Wards began to broaden the offerings of its Dixie Hi-Fi and Custom Hi-Fi discount audio equipment stores, transforming them into full-service electronics specialty markets. With this new concept, Wards changed the name of the stores to "Circuit City," opening six of the new facilities in the Washington, D.C., area. With 6,000 to 7,000 square feet of space, the new stores featured video and audio equipment made by well known brand names, as well as in-store service capabilities and a pick-up area for people to load purchases into their cars.

To shift its operations toward the Circuit City concept, Wards continued to streamline in 1978. The company left the mail order electronics business, which it ran under the name "Dixie," and also closed its four Richmond Sight 'N Sound stores. In the following year, the company continued its progress toward large retail outlets, opening a second Wards Loading Dock in Richmond. The company ended 1979 with $120 million in sales.

In 1981 Wards made its first incursion into a significant and challenging new market when it merged with the Lafayette Radio Electronics Corporation, which ran eight consumer electronics stores in the New York City metropolitan area. The company paid $6.6 million for the bankrupt retailer, earning $36.5 million in tax credits as a result of the acquisition, a benefit that observers predicted would drive up its own earnings. Lafayette's reputation within the highly competitive New York market was that of a small specialty seller that provided obscure, high-priced brand-name goods to hi-fi hobbyists. Wards faced an uphill battle in its struggle to broaden the chain's appeal and return it to profitability, especially since other New York electronics retailers routinely discounted items 50 percent or permitted haggling over the price of their products.

At the same time that Wards moved into the New York market, the company began to expand its Loading Dock super-store concept in the geographical areas where it already had a presence. Capitalizing on its other name, the company christened its new outlets Circuit City Superstores. The first four stores under this name opened in Raleigh, Greensboro, Durham, and Winston-Salem, North Carolina. In the following year, Wards simplified the naming of its outlets by changing the names of its Richmond Wards Loading Dock stores to Circuit City Superstores.

By 1982 Wards was operating four retail chains, including Circuit City stores, larger Circuit City Superstores, its Lafayette properties in New York, and its operations in Zody discount stores in California. Altogether, the company ran 100 outlets, twice the number it had owned just seven years earlier. Eighty percent of Wards' revenue was derived from sales of consumer electronics, while the company reaped solid profits from its marketing of Sony Betamax videocassette recorders and Pioneer stereo equipment. In Washington, D.C., Wards' Circuit City stores held the largest market share, garnering 11 percent of the sales of consumer electronics. By the end of 1983, Wards' pattern of consistent growth through its marketing decision to emphasize large retail outlets had led to sales of $246 million for the fiscal year.

As a sign of its shifting identity, Wards changed its corporate name to Circuit City Stores, Inc., in 1984. At this time, its stock was also listed on the New York Stock Exchange for the first time. Although the leadership of the company changed hands—Alan Wurtzel stepped up to the post of chairman of the board, to be succeeded by Richard Sharp—its basic direction did not. Sharp's background was in computers, not retailing, and he had first come into contact with Circuit City when he installed a computer system to control sales and inventory in some of its stores. Under Sharp, the company continued to consolidate its operations in very large stores, replacing regular Circuit City stores with Circuit City Superstores. This process began in Knoxville, Tennessee; Charleston, South Carolina; and Hampton, Virginia.

These stores, some of which contained nearly an acre of floor space, used their grand scope to bring a theatrical flair to retailing consumer electronics. The stores featured solid walls of television sets, all tuned to the same channel. Customers entered by walking past the service department, a visible symbol that the company serviced what it sold. The stores were laid out like baseball diamonds, and customers were led around the displays by a red tile walkway. Particularly popular items were located at the back of the store, to encourage impulse purchasing on the way. By 1984 Circuit City was operating 113 stores, which made it the leading specialty retailer of brand name consumer electronics. The company's growth continued briskly, fed by innovative new electronics products such as cordless telephones, microwave ovens, and videocassette recorders (VCRs), for which initial demand was high. Its Superstores contributed the largest part of its earnings, while the company's New York operations continued to lose money. To fuel continued growth, Circuit City further expanded its operations. In 1984 the company planned a large expansion around Atlanta and opened 15 new stores in Florida. In locating stores, Circuit City adhered to a policy of clustering them together in the same geographic area, which allowed for economies of scale in advertising and promotion.

In 1986 Circuit City took the final step in consolidating its operations. The company closed down its 15 unprofitable stores in the New York area, run under the Lafayette name, after a five-year, $20 million struggle to crack this tough market. In addition, Circuit City withdrew from its arrangement with the 50-store Zody's discount department store chain in California. This low-rent retailer, which had long been suffering financial troubles, provided an inhospitable home to Circuit City's operations, and contributed no earnings to its bottom line. Instead, the company decided to put the resources previously used to run these operations into further Circuit City Superstores, concentrating expansion in the Southeast and in California, where it

planned to open its own free-standing stores. In moving into a new area, Circuit City methodically set out to win the lion's share of sales in that market. The company typically opened a large number of very large stores all at once, advertised heavily, and distributed products efficiently.

These efforts bore fruit in February 1987, when Circuit City's annual sales hit the $1 billion mark for the first time, driven in large part by the demand for VCRs, which also pushed up demand for new televisions and other audio equipment. The company faced a challenging future, however, as demand for this core product cooled and competition from other electronics superstores heated up. Despite these adverse circumstances, by 1988 the company owned 105 stores, 32 of which were located in California.

Armed with the nation's largest market share, Circuit City planned to add 20 new outlets. Among these new outlets were several that featured a new format. Called Impulse, these stores were tested by the company in Baltimore, Maryland; Richmond, Virginia; and McLean, Virginia. These stores, designed for malls, sold small electronic products for personal use or to be given as gifts. Three years later, the company announced that its test of this concept had been successful, and that it planned to open 50 more such outlets.

By 1989 Circuit City's profits had tripled in just three years to reach $69.5 million, despite a general recession in the consumer electronics retailing industry. Observers attributed the company's success to strong management and a merchandising formula that had been honed and refined for many years. That formula was further adjusted in 1989 when Circuit City began opening mini-Superstores in markets too small for a full-fledged massive outlet. Claiming that the mini-store offered the same service and selection as a larger outlet, the company opened a test site in Asheville, North Carolina. By the following year, sales overall had hit $2 billion, and earnings were up as well.

Performance continued strong into 1993, when Circuit City shocked observers by announcing that it would test the idea of selling used cars as it searched for future areas of growth. Whether the company perseveres in this field, it had built a solid reputation for growth and efficiency in its core consumer electronics field that should continue to serve it well in the years to come.

Principal Subsidiaries: Carmac.

Further Reading:

Andrews, Edmund L., "Struggling for Profits in Electronics," *New York Times,* September 10, 1989.

Brown, Paul R., "Some People Don't Like to Haggle," *Forbes,* August 27, 1984.

Carpenter, Kimberly, "Circuit City Lays An Egg And Hatches A Strategy," *Business Week,* April 21, 1986.

Cochran, Thomas N., "Circuit City Stores, Inc.," *Barron's,* January 2, 1989.

Foust, Dean, "Circuit City's Wires Are Sizzling," *Business Week,* April 27, 1992.

Merwin, John, "Execution," *Forbes,* April 18, 1988.

—Elizabeth Rourke

Citicorp

399 Park Avenue
New York, New York 10043
U.S.A.
(212) 559-1000

Public Company
Incorporated: 1812 as the City Bank of New York
Employees: 89,000
Assets: $213.70 billion
Stock Exchanges: New York Midwest Pacific London
    Amsterdam Tokyo Zurich Geneva Basel Toronto
    Düsseldorf Frankfurt
SICs: 6712 Bank Holding Companies; 6021 National
    Commercial Banks; 6035 Federal Savings Institutions

Citicorp, a holding company and the parent of Citibank, is one of the largest financial companies in the world. Often compared to the Bank of America, Citicorp has consistently out-performed Bank of America and other financial institutions and is regarded as the leading bank in the United States. At a time when the U.S. budget deficit has led to the transfer of enormous amounts of American capital to foreign banks—particularly Japanese banks—Citicorp has remained highly competitive, even in international markets.

Citicorp has its origin in the First Bank of the United States, founded in 1791. Colonel Samuel Osgood, the nation's first postmaster general and treasury commissioner, took over the New York branch of the failing First Bank and reorganized it as the City Bank of New York in 1812. Only two days after the bank received its charter, on June 16, 1812, war was declared with Britain. The war notwithstanding, the City Bank was for all intents and purposes a private treasury for a group of merchants. It conducted most of its business as a credit union and as a dealer in cotton, sugar, metals, and coal, and later acted as a shipping agent.

Following the financial panic of 1837, the bank came under the control of Moses Taylor, a merchant and industrialist who essentially turned it into his own personal bank. Nonetheless, under Taylor, City Bank established a comprehensive financial approach to business and adopted a strategy of maintaining a high proportion of liquid assets. Elected president of the bank in 1856, Taylor converted the bank's charter from a state one to a national one on July 17, 1865, at the close of the Civil War.

Taking the name National City Bank of New York (NCB), the bank was thereafter permitted to perform certain official duties on behalf of the U.S. Treasury; it distributed the new uniform national currency and served as an agent for government bond sales.

Taylor was the treasurer of the company that laid the first transatlantic cable, which made international trade much more feasible. It was at this early stage that NCB adopted the eight-letter wire code address "Citibank." Taylor died in 1882 and was replaced as president by his son-in-law, Percy R. Pyne. Pyne died nine years later and was replaced by James Stillman.

Stillman believed that big businesses deserved a big bank capable of providing numerous special services as a professional business partner. After the panic of 1893, NCB, with assets of $29.7 million, emerged as the largest bank in New York City, and the following year it became the largest bank in the United States. It accomplished this mainly through conservative banking practices, emphasizing low-risk lending in well-secured projects. The company's reputation for safety spread, attracting business from America's largest corporations. The flood of new business permitted NCB to expand; in 1897 it purchased the Third National Bank of New York, bringing its assets to $113.8 million. That same year it also became the first big American bank to open a foreign department.

Far from retiring or diminishing his influence within NCB, Stillman nonetheless began to prepare Frank A. Vanderlip to take over senior management duties. Stillman and Vanderlip, who was elected president of the bank in 1909, introduced many innovations in banking, including travelers' checks and investment services through a separate but affiliated subsidiary (federal laws prevented banks from engaging in direct investment, but made no provision for subsidiaries).

Beginning in the late 1800s, many U.S. businessmen began to invest heavily in agricultural and natural-resource projects in the relatively underdeveloped nations of South and Central America. But government regulations prevented federally chartered banks such as NCB from conducting business out of foreign branches. Vanderlip worked long and hard to change the government's policy and eventually won in 1913, when Congress passed the Federal Reserve Act. NCB established a branch office in Buenos Aires in 1914 and in 1915 gained an entire international-banking network from London to Singapore when it purchased a controlling interest in the International Banking Corporation, which it gained complete ownership of in 1918.

In 1919 Frank Vanderlip resigned in frustration over his inability to secure a controlling interest in the company, and James A. Stillman, the son of the previous Stillman, became president. NCB reached $1 billion in assets, the first American bank to do so. Charles E. Mitchell, Stillman's successor in 1921, completed much of what Vanderlip had begun, creating the nation's first full-service bank. Until this time national banks catered almost exclusively to the needs of corporations and institutions, while savings banks handled the needs of individuals. But competition from other banks, and even corporate clients themselves, forced commercial banks to look elsewhere for sources of growth. Sensing an untapped wealth of business in personal banking, in 1921 NCB became the first major bank to offer interest on savings accounts, which it allowed individual customers to open with as little as a dollar. And in 1928 Citibank began to offer personal consumer loans.

The bank also expanded during the 1920s, acquiring the Commercial Exchange Bank and the Second National Bank in 1921, the People's Trust Company of Brooklyn in 1926, and merging with the Farmers' Loan and Trust Company in 1929. By the end of the decade, the "Citibank" was the largest bank in the country, and through its affiliates, the National City Company and the City Bank Farmers' Trust Company, it was also one of the largest securities and trust firms.

In October 1929 the stock market crash that led to the Great Depression caused an immediate liquidity crisis in the banking industry. In the ensuing months, thousands of banks were forced to close. NCB remained in business, however, mainly by virtue of its size and organization. But in 1933, at the height of the Depression, Congress passed the Glass-Steagall Act, which restricted the activities of banks by requiring the separation of investment and commercial banking. NCB was compelled to liquidate its securities affiliate and curtail its line of special financial products, eliminating many of the gains the bank had made in establishing itself as a flexible and competitive full-service bank.

James H. Perkins, who succeeded Mitchell as chairman in 1933, had the difficult task of rebuilding the bank's reputation and its business (it had fallen to number three). He instituted a defensive strategy, pledging to keep all domestic and foreign branches open and to eliminate as few staff members as possible. Perkins died in 1940, but his defensive policies were continued by his successor, Gordon Rentschler.

As a major American bank, NCB was in many ways a resource for the government, which depended on private savings and bond sales to finance World War II. The bank followed its defensive strategy throughout the war, amassed a large government bond portfolio, and continued to stress its relationship with corporate clients. Unlike its competitors, NCB was so well placed in so many markets by the end of the war that it could devote its energy to winning new clients rather than entering new markets. Sixteen years after Black Tuesday, NCB had finally regained its momentum in the banking industry.

The bank changed direction after the death of Gordon Rentschler in 1948 by moving more aggressively into corporate lending. In 1955, with assets of $6.8 billion, NCB acquired the First National Bank of New York and changed its name to the First National City Bank of New York (FNCB), or Citibank for short.

Citibank used its bond portfolio to finance its expansion in corporate lending, selling off bonds to make new loans. By 1957, however, the bank had just about depleted its bond reserve. Prevented by New Deal legislation from expanding its business in private savings beyond New York City, Citibank had nowhere to turn to for more funding. The squeeze on funds only became more acute until 1961, when the bank introduced a new and ingenious product: the negotiable certificate of deposit.

The "CD," as it was called, gave large depositors higher returns on their savings in return for restricted liquidity, and was intended to win business from higher-interest government bonds and commercial paper. The CD changed not only Citibank but the entire banking industry, which soon followed suit in offering CDs. The CD gave Citibank a way to expand its assets—but at the same time required it to streamline operations and manage risk more efficiently, since it had to pay a higher rate of interest to CD holders for the use of their funds.

The man behind the CD was not FNCB's president, George Moore, nor its chairman, James Rockefeller, but Walter B. Wriston, a highly unconventional vice-president. Wriston, a product of Wesleyan University and the Fletcher School, had worked his way up through the company's ranks since joining the bank in 1946. Having made a name for himself with the CD, Wriston was later given responsibility for revamping the company's management structure to eliminate the strains of Citibank's expansion. Like Vanderlip more than 50 years before, Wriston advocated a general decentralization of power to permit top executives to concentrate on longer-term strategic considerations.

In an attempt to circumvent federal regulations restricting a bank's activities, in 1968 Citibank created a one-bank holding company (a type of company the Bank Holding Company Act of 1956 had overlooked) to own the bank but also engage in lines of business the bank could not. Within six months, Bank of America, Chase Manhattan, Manufacturers Hanover, Morgan Guaranty, and Chemical Bank had also created holding companies.

Citicorp made no secret of its intention to expand, both operationally and geographically. In 1970 Congress—recognizing its error and concerned that one-bank holding companies would become too powerful—revised the Bank Holding Company Act of 1956 to prevent these companies from diversifying into traditionally "non-banking" activities.

Wriston, who was promoted to president in 1967 and to chairman in 1970, continued to press for the relaxation of banking laws. He oversaw Citibank's entry into the credit card business, and later directed a massive offer of Visa and MasterCharge cards to 26 million people across the nation. This move greatly upset other banks that also issued the cards, but succeeded in bringing Citibank millions of customers from outside New York state. The bank failed, however, to properly assess the risk involved. Of the five million people who responded to the offer, enough later defaulted to cost Citicorp an estimated $200 million.

In an effort to gain wider consumer recognition, the holding company formally adopted "Citicorp" as its legal name in 1974, and in 1976 First National City Bank officially changed its name to "Citibank." The "Citi" prefix was later added to a number of generic product names, Citicorp offered CitiCards, CitiOne unified statement accounts, CitiTeller automatic teller machines, and a host of other Citi-things.

Citicorp performed very well during the early 1970s, weathering the failure of the Penn Central railroad, the energy crisis, and a recession without serious setback. In 1975, however, the company's fortunes fell dramatically. Profits were erratic due to rapidly eroding economic conditions in Third World countries. Citicorp, awash in petrodollars in the 1970s, had lent heavily to these countries in the belief that they would experience high growth and faced the possibility of heavy defaults resulting from poor growth rates. In addition, its Argentine deposits were nationalized in 1973, its interests in Nigeria had to be scaled back in 1976, and political agitation in Poland and Iran in 1979 precipitated unfavorable debt rescheduling in those countries. Shareholders soon became concerned that Citicorp, which conducted two-thirds of its business abroad, might face serious losses.

In its domestic operations, Citicorp suffered from a decision made during the early 1970s to expand in low-yielding, consumer-banking activities. Although New York usury laws placed a 12 percent ceiling on consumer loans, Citibank bet that interest rates would drop, leaving plenty of room to make a profit. But the oil shock following the revolution in Iran sent interest rates soaring in the opposite direction: Citicorp lost $450 million in 1980 alone. In addition, Citibank purchased $3 billion in government bonds at 11 percent, in the belief that interest rates would continue a decline begun during the summer of 1980. Again, the opposite happened. Interest on the money Citibank borrowed to purchase the bonds rose as high as 21 percent, and the bank lost another $50 million or more.

One investment that did not go awry, however, was the company's decision to invest $500 million on an elaborate automated teller network. Installed throughout its branches by 1978, the ATMs permitted depositors to withdraw money at any hour from hundreds of locations. Not only were labor costs reduced drastically, but by being first again, Citibank gained thousands of new customers attracted by the convenience of ATMs.

Citicorp raised the profitability of its commercial-banking operations by de-emphasizing interest-rate-based income in favor of income from fees for services. Successful debt negotiations with developing countries cut losses on debts which would otherwise have gone into default. And as a result of the 1967 Edge Act and special accommodations made by various states, Citicorp, until then an international giant known domestically only in New York state, was able to expand into several states during the 1980s. Beginning with mortgages and its credit card business, then savings and loans, and then banks, Citicorp established a presence in 39 states and the District of Columbia. Internationally, the company expanded its business into more than 90 countries. Some of this expansion was accomplished by purchasing existing banks outright.

Wriston, after 14 years as chairman of Citicorp, retired in 1984, shortly after the announcement that Citicorp would enter two new businesses: insurance and information. He was succeeded by John S. Reed, who had distinguished himself by returning the "individual" banking division to profitability.

In May 1987 Citibank finally admitted that its Third World loans could spell trouble and announced that it was setting aside a $3 billion reserve fund. Losses for 1987 totaled $1.2 billion, but future earnings were much more secure. Citibank's move forced its competitors to follow suit, something few of them were able to do as easily—Bank of America, for example, wound up selling assets to cover its reserve fund.

As Citicorp entered the 1990s, the United States' biggest bank faced perhaps its most challenging period since its founding. A faltering economy, coupled with unprofitable business loans—particularly in the commercial real estate market—led to serious financial difficulties which threatened the bank's existence. Year end statistics for 1990 revealed a twenty-year low for Citicorp's share price, which eventually fell to $8. Citicorp's ratio of core capital to total assets stood at 3.26 percent, considerably lower than the minimum four percent which regulators instituted as the standard requirement in 1992. The company was operating on an expenses-to-revenue ratio of 70 percent, which prompted immediate cost-cutting efforts in nearly all expendable (non-core) business operations. Third quarter financial statements for 1991 reflected the impact of restructuring charges, asset write-downs, and additions to reserves necessary for coverage of non-performing loans: Citicorp reported an $885 million loss. For the first time since 1813, shareholders did not receive their 25 cents a share quarterly dividend. Citicorp was in desperate need of reorganization.

Chairman John Reed described this period of great instability as "tough, demanding," and a time of "turnaround." Widely viewed as a slow-moving and analytical visionary, Reed appeared to many to be unable to maneuver the ailing bank out of its mounting difficulties. Critics blamed Citicorp's loan crisis on Reed's efforts during the mid 1980s to expand in the international market and overextend credit to real estate developers like Donald Trump. Reed silenced his critics, however, with the successful implementation of a two-year, five-point plan aimed at improving capital strength and operating earnings to offset future, but imminent, credit costs.

Of primary importance in the recovery process were cost-cutting measures, growth constraint, and disciplined expenses and credit quality—considered the control aspects of the banking industry. Staff cuts for the two-year restructuring period resulted in the layoff of more than 15,000 employees—including many in senior management positions. Expenses were also trimmed as Citicorp consolidated its U.S. mortgage service and insurance service operations, as well as its telecommunication resources.

Nearly half of Citicorp's third-quarter $885 million loss was affected by the write-down of its $400 million investment in Quotron Systems, Inc. Citicorp bought the stock quotation service for $680 million in 1986 at a time when the company was hoping to expand in the information business. Since the acquisition, Quotron had been losing contracts with major Wall Street firms such as Shearson Lehman and Merrill Lynch. Quotron Systems, Inc., could not compete with the updated technology of its rival, Automatic Data Processing (ADP). In 1992 Citicorp sold two Quotron divisions to ADP, the leader in the computer services market.

To help raise the projected $4 to $5 million in capital under the five-point plan, Citicorp sold its marginal operations in Austria, Italy, and France; abandoned its efforts in the United Kingdom; and offered $1.1 billion of preferred equity redemption cumulative stock (PERCS).

Although Citicorp relinquished some if its weaker holdings in Europe, it continued to expand and improve operations in the Asian/Pacific region. New branches were opened in Mexico, Brazil, Japan, Taiwan, South Korea, and Australia. Such selective investing produced growth in earnings of up to 30 percent. From September 1991 to September 1992, Citicorp obtained $371 million in net income from consumer banking in the developing world, exceeding earnings in the Japan, Europe, and North America (JENA) unit of global finance.

Citicorp continues its commitment to international core business, capital growth, and credit stability as it cautiously proceeds through a successful recovery period. Though circumstances called for conservative action in the early 1990s to compensate for severe losses, Citicorp remains a pioneer in the banking industry. No other bank is attempting to run a worldwide consumer-banking business. Citibanking in Europe affords customers with the only multi-country interconnected retail bank, offering Citicard Banking Centers that accept deposits, permit account transfers, and dispense cash—a package of services unique to European Automatic Teller Machines. Citibank originated the use of credit cards featuring revolving credit, photo identification, and risk-adjusted pricing. A newly developed credit card program linked with Ford Motor Co. rewards cardholders with credit toward the purchase of a new automobile.

Citicorp's innovative approach and aggressive global marketing strategy, in addition to a reorganization that emphasized revenue over profit, have enabled it to maintain the number one ranking among bank holding companies. It appears that this trimmer, more focused, and more disciplined consumer bank will remain highly competitive in the future.

Principal Subsidiaries: AMBAC; Citicorp Diners Club; Quotron Systems; Transaction Technology, Inc.; CapMac (Capital Markets Assurance Corp.); KKB Bank A.G.; Citicorp Mortgage Inc.; Citibank Canada; Citibank Espana; Citibank Italia; Citibank Belgium; Citicorp International Trading Co.; Citibank (Maryland), N.A.; Citibank (Nevada), N.A.; Citibank (South Dakota), N.A.; Citibank (Florida), N.A.; Citibank; (New York State) Citibank; (Arizona) Citibank; (Utah) Citibank (Maine), N.A.; Citibank Delaware.

Further Reading:

Leindorf, David and Donald Etra, *Ralph Nader's Study Group Report on First National City Bank,* New York: Grossman, 1973.
Citibank, Nader and the Facts, New York: Citibank, 1974.
"Citicorp Battling Back," *The Economist,* April 25, 1992, pp. 84, 86.
Cleveland, Harold van B. and Thomas F. Huertas, *Citibank 1812–1970,* Cambridge, Massachusetts: Harvard University Press, 1985.
Egan, Jack, "The Fight to Stay on Top," *U.S. News & World Report,* December 30, 1991/January 6, 1992, pp. 70–71.
Hutchison, Robert A., *Off the Books,* New York: William Morrow and Company, 1986.
Lee, Peter, "Is Citi Back from the Dead?," *Euromoney,* December 1992, p. 30.
Meeham, John and William Glasgall, "Citi's Nightmares Just Keep Getting Worse," *Business Week,* October 28, 1991, pp. 124–25.

—updated by Edna M. Hedblad

The Coleman Company, Inc.

250 North St. Francis
Wichita, Kansas 67202
U.S.A.
(316) 261-3211
Fax: (316) 261-3153

Public Company
Incorporated: 1900 as the Hydro-Carbon Light Company
Sales: $491.9 million
Employees: 2,513
Stock Exchanges: New York
SICs: 3648 Lighting Equipment, Nec; 3589 Service Industry
   Machinery, Nec

The Coleman Company, Inc. is one of the most famous and successful manufacturers of camping equipment and outdoor recreational products. The well-known Coleman lamp was invented by 1909 and the lantern in 1914, and since that time over 45 million of the lanterns have been sold throughout the world. Coleman is the market leader in pressurized lighting, cooking, and heating appliances for camping, and it has created a loyal consumer following for a broad range of insulated food and beverage containers, sleeping bags, backpacks, tents, canoes, portable electric lights, and other recreational accessories.

The founder of the company, William Coffin Coleman, was born to a young couple who migrated west to Kansas from New England in 1871. Coleman became a schoolteacher in Kansas and later entered the University of Kansas Law School. Shortly before receiving his degree, however, Coleman ran out of money, and he became a traveling typewriter salesman. Traveling across the southern part of the United States, he found himself in Brockton, Alabama, a poor coal mining community with dirt streets and wood sidewalks.

According to company lore, as Coleman was taking an evening walk down one of the town's streets, he noticed the intense white glow of a lamp in a drug store window. The lamp, which was powered by gasoline, was so bright that even with his bad eyesight Coleman was able to read under it easily. Since most people at that time used flickering gaslights, smoky oil lamps, or dim carbon filament light bulbs, Coleman immediately saw the lamp as an important step forward.

Coleman arranged to sell this new type of lamp for the Irby-Gilliland Company of Memphis, and traveled to Kingfisher, Oklahoma, to begin his new venture. Unfortunately, he had only sold two lamps at the end of the first week. The lack of sales dismayed him, but he soon discovered that another salesman had previously sold dozens of lamps to the town's shopkeepers. Since the lamps could not be cleaned, they clogged with carbon deposits which snuffed the light out after a short time. The salesman had left a bit too quickly, and the shopkeepers felt swindled.

Unable to sell his lamps, Coleman hit upon the idea of leasing them for $1 per week and servicing them himself. If the lamps failed, the customer did not have to pay. Revenues skyrocketed. In order to remain competitive almost all the town's shopkeepers purchased his lighting service. The business flourished as Coleman reinvested profits and branched out into neighboring communities. Not long afterward, he founded the Hydro-Carbon Light Company.

With the demand for his lamps and lighting service increasing, Coleman received $2,000 from his two brothers-in-law for an eight percent interest in the company. In 1902 requests for his lighting service were so numerous that he decided to move the business to Wichita, Kansas, and establish a permanent headquarters. One year later, Coleman bought the rights to the Efficient Lamp, improved its design, and began selling it as the Coleman Arc Lamp. Ever on the lookout for original ways to market his lamps, in 1905 Coleman arranged for the Arc Lamps to provide the lighting for a night football game.

By 1909 Coleman had invented a portable table lamp with a gasoline tank designed as a small fount with a flat base. Bug screens were later added to protect the mantles during outdoor use. In 1914 the company developed the Coleman gasoline lantern for use in inclement weather. When World War I broke out, the Allies requested U.S. wheat and corn to replenish their food supplies. Realizing the need for a reliable, bright, and portable light for farmers carrying out the tasks necessary to aid the Europeans, the American government declared the Coleman lamp essential for the wartime support effort and provided Coleman with both money and materials to produce the lanterns. During World War I, the company made over one million lamps for American farmers.

The company grew steadily in the 1920s. Although electricity came to the smaller towns across the United States, most rural areas had to wait. Coleman thus found its largest markets in rural areas, with ever-increasing sales of gasoline stoves, used both as camp stoves and cook stoves, and lamps and lanterns. The company also established international operations with a manufacturing plant and headquarters in Toronto. Locating an office in Canada was a smart move on the part of Coleman, since the British Commonwealth gave preferential tariffs and duties to products made in member nations. By the end of the 1920s the reputation of the Coleman lantern was firmly established, and various accounts of its use were reported: Admiral Byrd used the lantern on his trip to the South Pole; on Pitcairn Island the descendants of British mutineers from the *Bounty* and their Tahitian families illuminated primitive homes with Coleman lanterns; and Coleman lantern-lit runways in the Andes made emergency landings possible.

The company was not entirely successful in developing new products and markets. During the late 1920s, Coleman made a line of waffle irons, coffee percolators, toasters, and electric irons. Coleman could not, however, compete with Westinghouse Electric Corporation and General Electric Company and withdrew these product lines quickly. William Coffin Coleman (known as W. C. to the rest of the company) designed a coffee maker for restaurants and hotels. Although it brewed excellent coffee, the machine was complicated to handle and difficult to clean. It was commercially unsuccessful and the company halted its production.

Coleman was hit very hard when the stock market crashed in 1929. During the next two years, the Great Depression severely affected almost every industry in the nation. The demand for Coleman products declined rapidly, mainly due to the searing poverty and inability of many people in rural areas to purchase anything other than food. Inevitably, the company experienced financial losses, but a good working relationship with a number of banks helped Coleman to overcome the worst years of the depression. In 1932 the company's sales totaled a mere $3 million, but a small profit was made.

After Franklin Delano Roosevelt was elected to the U.S. presidency in 1932, he launched a massive program for rural electrification, and Coleman was faced with a decline in its market for gasoline stoves and lights. However, Coleman found two potentially profitable markets, oil space heaters and gas floor furnaces, and by the end of the decade the company was the leading manufacturer of both products. At the same time, Coleman's portable stove and lantern business was making headway in the camping equipment market, and the international operation was beginning to reap significant profits. In 1941 the company reported annual sales of $9 million.

When World War II began, Coleman was called upon to manufacture products for the various branches of the American armed services, including 20-millimeter shells for the army, projectiles for the navy, and parts for the B-29 and B-17 bombers for the air force. In June 1942 the company was notified by the Army Quartermaster Corps with an urgent request—field troops needed a compact stove that could operate at 125 degrees above and 60 degrees below zero, was no larger than a quart bottle of milk, and could burn any kind of fuel. Moreover, the Army wanted 5,000 of the stoves delivered in two months.

Coleman worked non-stop to design and manufacture a stove to the army's specifications. The end product was better than the army had requested: the stove could work at 60 degrees below and 150 degrees above Fahrenheit; it could burn all kinds of fuel; it weighed a mere three and one-half pounds; and it was smaller than a quart bottle of milk. The first order for 5,000 units was flown to American forces involved in the November 1942 invasion of North Africa. Ernie Pyle, the famous World War II journalist who wrote about the common man's experience in the war, devoted 15 articles to the Coleman pocket stove and considered it one of the two most important pieces of non-combat equipment in the war effort, the other being the Jeep.

When the war ended, Coleman's business boomed. Since the company had been manufacturing products for the armed services during the war, there was an enormous backlog of demand for its regular products, which had been off the market. Sales rose to $34 million by 1950, while profits also substantially increased. At the start of the decade, there were four main divisions of Coleman products: oil space heaters accounted for 30 percent of sales; gas floor furnaces, also at 30 percent; camp stove and gasoline lantern sales at 20 percent; and military contracts to supply Boeing Co. with airplane parts for the B-47 bomber at 20 percent.

In the early 1950s, Coleman was the leader in sales in each of its civilian product lines. At the end of the decade, however, sales for oil heaters and gas floor furnaces alone dropped a whopping 85 percent, and by 1960 the company suffered an overall loss of 70 percent in sales volume. The U.S. military had also phased out Coleman's contracts for airplane parts. In response, Coleman developed its camp stove and lantern products into an extensive line of camping equipment. The company's portable ice chests and insulated jugs quickly became leaders in the field of outdoor recreation products. Coleman also expanded its line of oil, gas, and electric furnaces to manufacturers of mobile homes, and began designing air conditioning equipment and furnaces for on-site homes.

During the 1960s, Coleman continued to expand its product lines in the field of camping, adding sleeping bags, tents, and catalytic heaters; Coleman soon became the leading manufacturer of camping equipment. Growing along with the mobile home industry, Coleman supplied 40 percent of the specialized furnaces and 50 percent of the air conditioning equipment for mobile homes. Sales grew from $38 million in 1960 to $134 million by 1970, and during the same period net profits increased dramatically from $278,000 to $7 million.

The two leaders of the company were Sheldon Coleman, who replaced his father as chairman of the board in 1941, and Lawrence M. Jones, a longtime employee of Coleman who possessed a doctorate from Harvard University. Sheldon had hired Jones as president of the company in 1964, and the two men collaborated on product development and market strategy. Their joint effort resulted in the manufacture of adjustable backpack frames, a compact cooler, a small backpack stove, canoes made from a petroleum-based substance that created a quieter ride than aluminum, Crosman air guns, and camping trailers. In 1977 Coleman's success continued unabated, with sales reaching $256 million. The company's outdoor recreation business seemed to be recession-proof, and profits from its mobile home products kept increasing.

For more than three-quarters of a century, Coleman had worked hard to establish and maintain a reputation for high quality products sold at reasonable prices. This reputation paid off handsomely during the 1980s as both profits and sales increased steadily. According to *Fortune,* however, the Coleman family, who owned 25 percent of the company's stock, began withdrawing profits rather than reinvesting for product development and market expansion. Sheldon Coleman, Jr., replaced his father as chairman of the board in 1988, and only one year later he decided to privatize the company in order to reap an even larger profit—the pension plan of the company was overloaded by approximately $30 million.

New York financier Ronald Perelman purchased Coleman for $545 million in 1989 through his company MacAndrews & Forbes Holdings Inc. Together, Perelman and Jones sold the heating and air-conditioning business, shut down an obsolete factory, and implemented a strategy that improved efficiency and ultimately reduced inventory costs by $10 million.

Through a comprehensive restructuring of its operations lines, the company increased productivity significantly in 1991, and Coleman's sales reached $346 million by the end of the year. In 1992 sales increased to $491 million, proof that the company's concentration on manufacturing products in growing recreational markets was paying off. With Perelman's knack for streamlining a company and getting the most production out of its employees, and Jones's intimate acquaintance with what the company did best, Coleman appeared poised for a very prosperous future.

Further Reading:

Coleman, Sheldon, and Lawrence Jones, *The Coleman Story: The Ability to Cope with Change,* New York: Newcomen Society, 1976, pp. 1-28.
Dumaine, Brian, ''Earning More By Moving Faster,'' *Fortune,* October 7, 1991, pp. 89–94.

—Thomas Derdak

Comdisco, Inc.

6111 North River Road
Rosemont, Illinois 60018
U.S.A.
(708) 698-3000
Fax: (708) 518-5854

Public Company
Incorporated: 1971
Revenues: $2.2 billion
Employees: 2,087
Stock Exchanges: New York
SICs: 5045 Computers and Computer Peripheral Equipment
and Software; 7379 Computer Related Services

Comdisco is one of the most impressive entrepreneurial success stories of the 1970s and 1980s; it has grown from a one-man operation into one of the world's largest companies for selling and leasing used computers. With its disaster recovery services for computer users and its foray into the field of supplying high-technology medical equipment, the company is preparing for the computer needs of the 21st century.

The founder of Comdisco, Ken Pontikes, a first-generation American of Greek ancestry, began working before the age of 11 in his father's grocery store on the south side of Chicago. While a teenager, he worked as a redcap at Union Station, hauling luggage to save for tuition at Southern Illinois University. After graduation, he worked for IBM selling punch card equipment.

Working for IBM during the mid-1960s, Pontikes noticed a new and highly promising market beginning to emerge. Large corporations were becoming increasingly reliant on computers and computer technology, but most of these firms hesitated to spend the large amounts of money needed to buy equipment that might become obsolete overnight. In order to meet this growing demand, in 1969 Pontikes started the Computer Discount Corporation. With a capitalization of $5,000, the company opened as a broker/dealer of IBM mainframe computers and soon afterward began leasing the same equipment.

Pontikes was enormously successful—one year later the company's revenues amounted to approximately $1 million, and he had hired two employees. The owner believed that he was providing a valuable service, that this service was cost-effective, and that he had a solid customer base upon which he could rely. As the demand for using computers on a short-term basis grew, the newly renamed Comdisco's revenues began to soar. By 1973 the company reported over $24 million in revenues.

During its early years, Comdisco held an enviable strategic position within the highly competitive computer market. When IBM announced a new line of computers, most companies in the computer business suffered due to head-on competition with the dominant firm in the marketplace, but Comdisco actually benefited from IBM's technological advancements. Immediately after IBM's announcement, a sales freeze would occur as users delayed the decision to buy while they waited for the new equipment. As a consequence, the prices on computers dropped sharply. At this point, Pontikes started buying inventory and preparing for the inevitable scenario: IBM's delivery schedule stretched out over a number of years, and users would likely be scrambling for the computer equipment they needed for the interim.

Comdisco's success entailed some risks, however. In 1974 the company suffered its only loss to date when Intel Corporation dumped $250 million worth of IBM System 360 computers into the resale market only a few months after Pontikes struck a deal to purchase hundreds of System 360 computers. The loss amounted to a bit less than $1 million and taught Pontikes a lesson about the volatility of the market. After that time, he kept Comdisco's inventory at less than two months' sales—approximately $20 million worth of computer equipment.

Leasing companies sometimes run risks when they offer their customers lenient lease terms and at the same time overestimate the residual value of the equipment—the value and selling price of the computer after the lease has expired. If the leasing company is unable to sell the equipment for its residual value as stated in the company's books, then it suffers a loss on the leasing transaction. Computer leasing is particularly risky because equipment values are at the mercy of lightning-quick changes in technology. For two decades after the loss in 1974, Comdisco only changed its residual estimates three times. Every one of those occasions required an increase in residual estimates.

In 1975 Comdisco's earnings rebounded, and revenues surpassed $47 million. One year later, Comdisco Financial Services, Inc., was established to finance its customers' leasing of IBM computer equipment and other non-computer goods. Comdisco Financial Services not only arranged financing for a new IBM computer but also assisted customers in disposing of their old equipment. By offering such services, the subsidiary grew rapidly.

With business booming due to the success of its leasing and resale activities, soon Comdisco sales offices were opened in Texas, Minnesota, California, Massachusetts, Connecticut, Florida, and Michigan; overseas branches were opened in France, Switzerland, and West Germany. By the end of the decade, Comdisco employed 186 people and revenues had reached the $225 million mark.

Developing new ventures that augmented Comdisco's main computer leasing business, Pontikes created Comdisco Disaster Recovery Services in 1980. Pontikes intended to open numerous disaster relief centers around the country to aid subscribers with computer and office equipment when their own machines were out of service due to flood or fire damage, loss of power, or some other catastrophe. Along with the disaster relief services, customers had the option of leasing "shells"—empty rooms with controlled temperatures and numerous wall sockets so they could use Comdisco's inventory to recreate their own computer and office machine configurations. Over a few years, Comdisco opened DRS offices in Chicago, the Dallas-Ft. Worth area, northern California, and a "super center" in Carlstadt, New Jersey.

With revenues over $500 million and earnings more than $51 million in 1983, Pontikes decided to use some of the excess cash to enter the arbitrage business. In 1984 he established Comdisco Equities, Inc., a subsidiary engaged in high-risk stock speculation of possible takeover targets, and hired Martin A. Weinstein of Salomon Brothers to direct the operation. The owner was convinced that the complicated computer deals his company had put together in the recent past had prepared the way for entering the world of fast-paced, highly speculative arbitrage. In the same year, Comdisco's leasing activities hit an all-time high, and new international sales offices were opened in both the United Kingdom and the Netherlands.

The Internal Revenue Service and the Securities and Exchange Commission began investigating Comdisco's tax shelters. The company used shelters to raise money toward the purchase of computer equipment. When Comdisco bought a computer from IBM, they leased it to a customer. The company then took the lease to a bank and collected the present value of the lease payment, which was approximately 90 percent of the computer's original cost. The customer paid back this nonrecourse loan, and the transaction greatly reduced the company's risk. Comdisco still owned the computer after the money was collected from the bank and was free to sell the equipment, with the accompanying tax benefits, as a tax shelter. This resulted in a second payment, normally an up front cash payment of approximately 16 percent of the equipment's cost. In the eyes of the IRS, Comdisco was paid up front for the lease of the loan. Accordingly, they considered this money, and not the revenues over the entire term of the lease, to be taxable. Pontikes referred to the IRS inquiry as a "nonissue," but the proposed assessments amounted to $200 million. In 1987 the company finally reached an agreement with the IRS on the audit of its 1983 and 1984 income tax returns.

The dispute with the IRS did not slow Comdisco's growth. Although the company discontinued its arbitrage business due to a net loss of nearly $80 million following the stock market crash of 1987, revenues grew to $1.3 billion, and earnings were at a record level of $92 million by 1988. Comdisco opened new domestic sales offices in Denver, Pittsburgh, and St. Louis, while international offices were established in Belgium, Italy, Spain, Japan, and Finland. New Comdisco Disaster Recovery Service sites opened in Montreal, Los Angeles, Bridgeport, and St. Louis, accumulating more than $10 million in pre-tax earnings.

In 1988 Comdisco entered the field of medical equipment leasing, an area that many financial analysts predicted would ultimately generate more revenue than computer equipment leasing. With medical technology advancing at speeds comparable to the computer industry, and with costs skyrocketing, hospitals saw leasing as a cost-effective alternative to purchasing. Comdisco started with leasing high-tech medical machines such as magnetic resonance scanners and computerized tomography. Two years later, high-technology medical equipment leasing amounted to over 50 percent of Comdisco's new financing.

Comdisco's sales force expanded 17 percent in 1987 and 45 percent in 1988. Pontikes encouraged his sales force to be both aggressive in finding new business and creative in discovering ways to meet the needs of its customers. In 1989, for example, when the William Wrigley Jr. Company planned to relocate its data processing center, a Comdisco representative solved a potentially expensive and complicated logistical problem by first arranging to install duplicate computer equipment in the new location and then arranging to take the original computer equipment. In 1989 a hardworking, but hardly exceptional, sales employee could make up to $125,000, the majority of which came from commissions. Pontikes noted that he was inclined to offer handsome rewards to employees who made exceptional contributions toward Comdisco's growth.

Revenue increased to $1.9 billion by 1990, helped by a significant contribution from the Comdisco Disaster Recovery Services, which experienced an average annual growth rate of 44 percent for the previous five years to total $118 million in sales by 1990. During the same year, Comdisco also formed a joint venture with Nomura, Babcock, & Brown to develop a foray into gas and oil technology and prospects. Yet 1990 signaled the first setback in the company's financial performance. Continuing losses in Comdisco's European operations, user uncertainty and changes affecting the mainframe product market, increasing price competition in leasing markets, and excess personnel led to a 21 percent decline in company earnings from continuing operations over the previous year.

A slow rate of growth in both the United States and many foreign economies and the effects of a recession were exacerbated by the IBM Corporation, which filed a suit against Comdisco accusing the company of disassembling the computer systems owned by its credit subsidiary in order to sell and lease the parts. Comdisco admitted to dismantling IBM systems when it replaced equipment the large manufacturer had already leased to customers, but Pontikes argued that reconfiguring parts was common practice in computer leasing and that, most importantly, his company always returned comparable parts and equipment to IBM when the lease was over. In interviews, Pontikes maintained that the actual reason IBM was bringing suit against Comdisco was to increase his company's operating costs so that IBM itself could gain a larger market share in both the primary and secondary leasing businesses.

Defending itself vigorously against IBM's challenge, Comdisco incurred extensive legal fees during 1991. Although revenues reached $2.2 billion in 1992, the company was adversely affected by the sluggish economy, and earnings from continuing operations declined. In light of these persistent difficulties, Pontikes initiated an organizational restructuring, established a litigation reserve to fight the IBM suit, and issued preferred stock to strengthen the company's capital structure. Pontikes's strategy stabilized Comdisco, with both revenues and earnings slightly lower in 1993. The phenomenal rate of growth the company experienced during its early years, however, appeared to be over.

Further Reading:

Stillwell, Newcomb, ''We Learned Our Lesson Good,'' *Business Week,* May 11, 1981, pp. 140–42.

Slutsker, Gary, ''Trader's Revenge,'' *Forbes,* January 27, 1986, p. 80.

Therrien, Lois, ''Comdisco Takes a Hand in Another Risky Game,'' *Business Week,* May 9, 1989, p. 108.

—Thomas Derdak

CONVERSE®

Converse Inc.

1 Fordham Road
North Reading, Massachusetts 01864
U.S.A.
(508) 664-0194
Fax: (508) 664-7268

Wholly Owned Subsidiary of Interco Incorporated
Incorporated: 1908 as Converse Rubber Company
Employees: 2,700
Sales: $180 million
SICs: 3149 Footwear, Except Rubber, Not Elsewhere
    Classified

Converse Inc. tapped the enormous success of its canvas All Star basketball shoe to become the largest U.S. manufacturer of athletic footwear. The Converse All-Star basketball shoe was the first in the industry, and by the early 1990s, more than 500 million pairs, in over 56 colors and styles, had been sold in over 90 countries worldwide. In addition, the company diversified into varied rubber products and full lines of athletic shoes for tennis, cross-training, team sports, running, walking, and children's recreation. Starting in the 1970s, Converse faced a new wave of competitive, high-performance athletic shoe brands such as Nike and Reebok. The company also changed ownership in an increasingly hostile corporate environment: in 1972 Converse was purchased by Eltra Corp.; in 1979 ownership shifted to Allied Corp., a diversified manufacturer of industrial products; and after spinning off as a private company in 1981, Converse was acquired by Interco Inc. in 1986. After Interco Inc., emerged from Chapter 11 Bankruptcy proceedings in the fall of 1992, Converse continued aggressive marketing and design initiatives aimed at reclaiming center court.

The origins of Converse Inc. date back to 1908, when Marquis M. Converse founded the Converse Rubber Co. in Malden, Massachusetts with a capital investment of $250,000. Converse had gained extensive retail experience as a general manager of one of Boston's largest department stores as well as at Beacon Falls Rubber Shoe Co. He started his own firm after Beacon was absorbed by U.S. Rubber, and within one year of its founding, the Converse Rubber Company had integrated 350 employees into a full production team in a new plant. In September of 1909, the company hired Edward F. Casey, who would rise from a sweeper's position to a directorship and vice-presidency,

contributing so much to rubber footwear production in his 57-year career that became known as "Mr. Converse." By 1910, the company had expanded its plant to produce 4,000 pairs of boots and rubbers daily.

The young company experienced a dramatic increase in success after its 1917 introduction of the Converse canvas All Star, one of the world's first basketball shoes. The game of basketball was still in its infancy, having been invented by James Naismith in 1891 at the International Young Men's Christian Association Training School. All Star's rapid ascent was spurred by the reputation and marketing savvy of the basketball star Charles "Chuck" H. Taylor, who joined the Converse sales force in 1921 to become the brand's first player endorser. From a town outside of Columbus, Indiana, Taylor progressed from high school directly to a career in basketball, even though professional teams were still not established. After playing for barnstorming basketball teams including the Buffalo Germans and the Akron Firestones, Taylor joined Converse's Chicago sales office in 1921. He traveled around the country selling the shoe and promoting the sport in basketball clinics. In 1968, a year before his death, Taylor was inducted into the Naismith Memorial Hall of Fame.

The original Converse Rubber Company soared beyond the scope of its 1908 designs until 1929 when it fell into bankruptcy. Control of the company passed on to Mitchell B. Kaufman, who had been serving as president of Hodgman Rubber Company since 1925. After Kaufman's untimely death a year later, his successor, Albert Wechsler, operated the company for the Kaufman estate until 1933, when a depressed economy and reduced profits prompted yet another takeover.

The 1933 purchase of the company by the Stone family began a 39-year period of family ownership during which Converse became a market leader. After providing protective footwear, special-purpose boots, parkas, and other equipment for the American Armed Services during World War II, the Stones concentrated on rapid growth toward civilian ends. In 1946, the company's Granite State Division in New Hampshire began operation of two large plants that continued in operation until 1979. In 1953, Converse established the Coastal Footwear Corporation in Canovanas, Puerto Rico. Converse brand lines were further expanded with the 1961 acquisition of the Tyer Rubber Company and the 1964 acquisition of the Hodgman brand of sporting goods equipment. The company also opened a new factory in Presque Isle, Maine, in 1967 and purchased the Bristol manufacturing company in Rhode Island in 1969.

By the early 1970s, Converse had diversified beyond footwear to provide numerous industries—textile, plastic, automotive, paper, paper converting, photocopying, and leather processing—with products ranging from hockey pucks to teethguards, sports and industrial boots, and rubber compounds for specific applications. Sales were delegated to three separate divisions: Sporting Goods, Footwear, and Industrial.

The Stone family dynasty ended in 1972, when Converse was purchased by the Eltra Corporation. That same year, the footwear division of B. F. Goodrich Co. was acquired, adding a modern manufacturing plant in Luberton, North Carolina, and a large distribution center in Charlotte, North Carolina, which remained the hub for Converse distribution as the company continued to expand.

By the late 1970s, factors including increased foreign competition, soaring labor and overhead costs, and a weak domestic economy forced the company to pare down operations, consolidate, and increase efficiency. The Hodgman line was sold and the Malden and Andover plants closed, followed by the Granite State Division. Sales divisions, which had traditionally been divided between sporting goods and footwear, were consolidated into one team.

Converse changed hands once again in 1979. Under the ownership of Allied Corporation, the brand would achieve unprecedented sales and profits. By 1982, however, the giant chemical conglomerate underwent a restructuring and moved out of the consumer products business. Though Converse produced 12 million pairs of sports shoes a year and had become the leader in basketball footwear, Allied put the company up for sale.

Through the combined efforts of a group of senior managers, Converse spun off from its parent to become a privately owned and operated entity. The group, led by Richard B. Loynd, president of Allied's Eltra Corporation of which Converse was part, and John P. O'Neil, Converse president, negotiated the purchase of Converse division from Allied for approximately $100 million. By 1983 Converse stock was available on the NASDAQ national market.

Facing growing pressure of foreign imports, Converse moved to develop export business to international markets. In 1984, for example, the company signed separate agreements with Moon-Star Chemical Corp., Mizuno Corp., and Zett Corp. to handle the manufacture, distribution, and sale of Converse footwear in Japan. With the opening of an office and warehouse in Osaka in 1984 and plans to develop new shoes specifically for the Japanese market, Converse anticipated that "within three years, [it] will be a leader in the distribution of athletic footwear in Japan," according to company president John P. O'Neil. Between 1987 and 1988, Converse's international business increased by more than 60 percent. One driving force behind such growth was the building of direct company operations in key European, Asian, and North American locations, in addition to licensed distributors in over 90 countries worldwide.

Converse also faced competition from other domestic shoe companies. Since the early 1970s, the introduction of high-performance, leather athletic shoes strained Converse's leading position with its simple, canvas classic. By January of 1986 The New York Times reported that "Nike of Beaverton, Ore., maker of Air Jordan basketball shoes, appears to outrunning such competitors as Reebok International Ltd., Converse Inc. and Hyde Athletic Industries."

Consequently, Converse diversified to become a full-line athletic shoe operation. By the mid-1980s, Converse running shoes had become popular. Sales of tennis shoes, including the popular Jimmy Connors leather model, increased 400 percent in 1983 alone. By the 1990s, the Converse brand was associated not only with the famous Chuck Taylor All Star line, but with other fashion canvas shoes and footwear for all major sports played by all age groups.

To ensure continued development of innovative and well-designed footwear, Converse invested in an advanced-technologies lab staffed by a 70-member research and development team. Upon its completion in the early 1980s, it was one of only two in-house, biomechanical footwear labs in the country. The facility included work stations equipped with powerful computers, robots, and testing systems.

In addition to designing the most effective shoes possible, Converse enhanced its reputation by sponsoring major basketball organizations and events worldwide. Converse was the first company ever named the official shoe of the National Basketball Association. Valid from 1985 to 1995, the contract granted the company permission to use the NBA name in all advertising and promotions, and to manufacture shoes with logos of NBA teams or other affiliations. Converse also supplied merchandise to cheerleaders and ball retrievers throughout the league.

Converse was also a sponsor of USA Basketball since its inception in 1975. The Colorado Springs-based group was responsible for selecting national teams to represent the country in various international competitions and served as a class A member of the United States Olympic Committee. After 1977, Converse was contracted as the official shoe of USA Basketball, which agreed to "use [its] best efforts to outfit players in Converse shoes," according to Jeffrey Orridge, assistant executive director for corporate and legal affairs for the sports group, in a September, 1992 article in The American Lawyer. That agreement later caused legal conflicts, as USA Basketball team members including Michael Jordan held contracts with competing shoe companies such as Nike. Requiring players to wear Converse shoes introduced ethical and legal problems that had to be carefully resolved.

With the globalization of basketball, Converse increased its overseas contacts. In 1988, the company signed a sponsorship for the World Association of Basketball Coaches (WABC), located in Rome, Italy, and responsible for over 50 clinics worldwide. In February 1990, the company began a five year, seven figure contract as the sponsor of the Federation Internationale de Basketball (FIBA). Founded in 1932 and based in Munich, Germany, FIBA included 176 member countries and approximately 119 million registered players. Its competitions included the European Championship Club Cup Final and the European Championship for both men and women.

Converse also competed in the Olympic Games. Though the brand provided Olympic footwear every year since 1936, in 1984 it became the first footwear supplier ever chosen to officially represent the games. The honor was not cheap: Converse paid the Los Angeles Olympic Organizing Committee (LAOCC) $4 million and spent an additional $3.5 million for national television advertising. Total promotional costs approached the $10 million mark.

Ever since Chuck Taylor served as its first player endorser, Converse has continued to promote its footwear through high-profile sports celebrities and athletes. By 1990, the brand had contracted endorsements with over 14 pros representing 11 different teams across the United States. In addition, company statistics showed that 21 percent of all professional basketball players wore Converse shoes.

In the case of basketball endorser Earvin "Magic" Johnson, Converse received more publicity than it may have bargained for. In 1979, Johnson was enlisted as an official company endorser until 1994. By the late 1980s, Johnson showed dissatisfaction with the deal, which placed him in the top income echelon of Converse endorsers but yielded less than other top endorsers for some other leading brands. After Converse filed suit against the player for failing to comply with his long-term endorsement contract in 1987, matters were temporarily resolved.

When Jordan won the NBA's most valuable player award, Converse created a 30-second highlight piece of his best moves in the NBA tournament filmed in slow motion to the accompaniment of "Amazing Grace." And in 1990, the brand allotted a quarter of its $40-million advertising campaign to launch its Magic Johnson footwear and apparel line. After the player announced that he had tested HIV positive in the winter of 1991, Converse aired a $1 million public service campaign called "Magic's Athletes Against AIDS." Yet in 1992, old friction resumed with Johnson's public statements that Converse marketing was outdated and that he was terminating his contract before the official date. "Converse as a company is stuck in the '60s and '70s. They think the Chuck Taylor sneaker days are still here," Johnson told reporters in Monte Carlo after the U.S. basketball team practiced for the Olympics. "I've been trying to get out for years," he added.

Despite Johnson's criticism, Converse moved into the late 1980s and early 1990s with new and innovative marketing strategies aimed at regaining lost market share. In 1985, the brand paired two rival coaches—Denny Crum from the University of Louisville Cardinals and Joe B. Hall of the University of Kentucky Wildcats—on one poster to promote the Converse brand. Other promotional strategies included free trial shoes at the 1985 Sports & Runners Expo in Boston; environmental sponsorship of the Windstar Foundation of Snowmass, Colorado; and sponsorship of the Hoop-It-Up three-on-three basketball tour, bringing the game of American streetball to 13 European cities and to youth groups at home.

In the late 1980s, Converse stressed advertising and promotional campaigns to compete with such brands as Nike, Reebok, L.A. Gear, and Keds. Even under the financial strain of its bankrupt parent, Converse garnered an effective creative team at its New York agency, Ingalls Quinn and Johnson, which developed a hit campaign featuring NBA Rookie of the Year Larry Johnson dressed up as his basketball-playing "grandmama." In her new, light Converses, the ad proclaimed, grandmama could blow by you "faster than a passing thought. She'll eat point guards for lunch and pick her teeth with a power forward."

In October 1986, Converse was acquired by Interco Incorporated, a broad-based manufacturer and retailer of consumer products and services primarily in the areas of footwear and furniture products. Citing doubt regarding Interco's future profitability, *Standard & Poor's* placed the company on Credit-Watch. Nevertheless, Converse announced record sales for fiscal 1987, breaking the $315 million barrier and representing a 36 percent increase over 1986.

In January 1991, however, *Standard & Poor's* doubts proved justified. Interco filed for relief under Chapter 11 of the federal bankruptcy laws. Until it emerged from bankruptcy proceedings in the autumn of 1992, support for rapidly slipping Converse brands was limited to a dangerously low budget.

Interco's 1992 financial restructuring, however, freed up new funds for Converse investments and marketing plans. In June of that year, Converse's advertising team at Ingalls startled Madison Avenue by pulling up stakes and moving across town to Houston, Effler & Partners Inc. The $25 million Converse account followed along one day later. Houston took off with a new generation of ads to sell new shoes. In 1993, Converse introduced its Run 'N' Gun, featuring a patented React cushioning device with a combination of gas and gel built into the heel to absorb shock and provide additional maneuvering control. After some critics objected to the shoe's name as too violent, Converse changed it to Run 'N' Slam.

Houston also designed a 30-second television spot featuring Kevin "KJ" Johnson of the Phoenix Suns, with music by pop group En Vogue. "It's a hip, upbeat, funky commercial," said Converse spokesperson Jennifer Murray, in a March 7, 1993 article for the *Chicago Tribune*. The spots primarily targeted cable channels such as the Black Entertainment Network and MTV.

With its continued series of vivacious and entertaining ads for Converse, Houston bordered on becoming known as a "hip, upbeat, and funky" advertising agency. In a 1993 campaign for the new AeroJam shoe, the agency again played off Larry Johnson's "grandmama" theme. While grandmama performed staggering jumps and dunks in her AeroJams, Johnson narrated: "There was an old lady who lived in a shoe. . . . And that shoe let her do things that no man could do." KJ and Grandmama returned in a series of highly effective, award-winning commercials.

These and other aggressive promotional programs began to pay off for Interco's shoe business. Footwear group sales by Florsheim and Converse for the second quarter of 1993 were $162.1 million compared to $146.2 million in the same period of the previous year. From its early days as a basketball shoe innovator, Converse grew into one of the world's largest manufacturers of athletic footwear. Over the years, the brand adapted to changing market trends, as evidenced in its repositioning of the classic Chuck Taylor All Star from the basketball court to the fashion-oriented street. After the 1980s, however, the brand faced unprecedented competition and drastic losses in market share. Yet Converse entered the 1990s financially optimistic, as its parent company emerged from bankruptcy and its new line of high-performance shoes allured both consumers and advertising professionals. From canvas and rubber sneakers for barnstorming teams to computer-designed footwear promoted by multimillion dollar endorsement and marketing budgets, Converse was meeting the changing needs of athletes and consumers alike.

Further Reading:

Bidlake, Suzanne, "Converse Steps Away From Plan to Launch Across Europe; Athletic Footwear Manufacturer," *Marketing Publications Ltd.* (England), April 19, 1990, p. 2.

Carter, Leon H., "Timeout; Bird Won't Fly From Converse," *Newsday*, July 26, 1992, p. 19.

"Converse and 'Grandmama' Hoop-It-Up For the First Time in Boston," *PR Newswire*, July 16, 1993.

"Converse Announces Record Sales," *Business Wire*, May 11, 1988.

"Converse Basketball Goes Global With NBA Stars," *PR Newswire*, July 7, 1993.

"Converse Inc. Press Kit," North Reading, Massachusetts: Converse Inc., 1993.

"Converse Launches Environmental Program with the Windstar Foundation," *PR Newswire*, June 27, 1991.

"Converse Purchase," *PR Newswire*, March 4, 1982.

"Converse Seizes 100 Pairs on N.C. Fakes, Goes to Court," *Footwear News*, August 13, 1984, p. 20.

"Converse Signs Mizuno, Zett and Moon-Star for Japanese Sales and Distribution," *Business Wire*, January 26, 1984.

Farley, Maggie, and Bob Ryan, "Magic Kicking Converse," *The Boston Globe*, July 23, 1992, p. 45.

Farley, Maggie, "The $25 Million Heist; Ingalls' Biggest Ad Account Gets Away," *The Boston Globe*, July 12, 1992, p. 45.

"Interco Files For Chapter 11 Reorganization," *PR Newswire*, January 25, 1991.

Jankowski, Dianna, "Boston Expo Crowd Belies Running's Decline," *Footwear News*, April 22, 1985; "Converse Lab Tackles Many Problems," *Footwear News*, November 12, 1984, p. 28.

"Kevin Johnson Demands Grudge Match With Grandmama and Larry Johnson Puts the Rock in the Hole in Converse TV Ads," *PR Newswire*, March 8, 1993.

Lee, Sharon, "Converse Shoots for Fashion," *Footwear News*, March 5, 1990, p. 34.

Palmer, Thomas, "If Converse Can't Pay, Will Its Stars Leave?" *The Boston Globe*, March 9, 1991, p. 15.

Rattray, Jim, "Converse Sues Magic Johnson," *United Press International*, December 4, 1987.

Rifkin, Glenn, "The Machines of a New Sole," *The New York Times*, February 10, 1993, p. D7.

"Spreading the Action; Converse Betting on Magic Ads—$10 million Worth," *Footwear News*, February 12, 1990, p. 106.

Vartan, Vartanig G., "A Brisk Pace Is Set by Nike," *The New York Times*, January 21, 1986, p. D12.

Wessling, Jack, "Converse Improves Productivity," *Footwear News*, February 13, 1984, p. 126; "Converse Inks Big Name in College Basketball," *Footwear News*, January 21, 1985, p. 33.

Yerton, Stewart, "Dream Job With the Dream Team," *The American Lawyer*, September, 1992, p. 40.

—Kerstan Cohen

Coopers &Lybrand

Coopers & Lybrand

1251 Avenue of the Americas
New York, New York 10020
U.S.A.
(212) 536-2000
Fax: (212) 536-3035

Private Company
Incorporated: 1898 as Lybrand, Ross Bros. & Montgomery
Sales: $5 billion
Employees: 65,000
SICs: 8721 Accounting Auditing & Bookkeeping Services;
  4110 Accountants; 8305 Professional Services Nec

Coopers & Lybrand, one of the oldest accounting firms in the United States, offers a wide range of professional financial and consulting services to thousands of prominent companies and financial institutions in more than 120 countries around the world. Unlike many other accounting firms, Coopers & Lybrand emerged from the 1990s recession unscathed and has retained its position among the top American accounting firms.

Accounting practices were necessitated by the increasingly complex and sophisticated needs of businesses during the early nineteenth-century Industrial Revolution. Accounting as a profession emerged over several decades in the United States, and by 1898, the year in which Coopers & Lybrand was founded, there was not yet a single school of accounting. Furthermore, the only texts available were British and these often failed to address American problems and practices.

Accountants therefore received their training on the job, initially as bookkeepers, the most able and talented ones trained by their supervisor in accounting practices and procedures. This was the route taken by the four American founders of Coopers & Lybrand: William M. Lybrand, brothers T. Edward Ross and Adam A. Ross, and Robert H. Montgomery. All had worked in the same firm of Heins, Lybrand & Co. in Philadelphia and had received the same training; all four would be active in establishing accounting as a profession. The Ross brothers, Adam and Edward, were pioneer members in 1897 of the Pennsylvania Association of Public Accountants, one of the few professional associations for accountants in the country. During this time, a British accounting firm known as Cooper Bros. & Co., founded by William Cooper, was celebrating its 44th anniversary. Nearly sixty years later, the American and the British firms would merge into Coopers & Lybrand International.

The four American employees of the Heins office pooled their resources, and on January 1, 1898 they opened a two-room, two-desk business in Philadelphia. Until 1973, the company would be known as Lybrand, Ross Bros. & Montgomery. Hours were extremely long, almost always beyond the official nine hours per day, Monday through Friday. For many years, young men hired by the firm would receive $7 a day and were expected to work evenings and be on call during weekends.

From the start, the firm had a reputation for high professional standards, which the four partners attributed to the example of their former chief, John Heins. Also from the start, clients were plentiful. Outside of his regular accounting duties, Adam A. Ross, who as an apprentice in Heins' office had taken part in the first regular audit of a bank by a public accountant in Philadelphia's history, lobbied for state legislation mandating certification for public accountants, a cause that his brother and partner, T. Edward Ross, would also espouse. Partners in the firm also gave lectures in accountancy in the evenings and were hard at work persuading the University of Pennsylvania to establish a night school in accountancy, which finally happened in 1902. Robert Montgomery undertook the first American textbook on accountancy, published in 1905, while also that year Lybrand contributed several articles to the new *Journal of Accountancy,* establishing the principles of the accounting profession. That was just the beginning of the many contributions the four partners would make over the years to the professionalization of their field.

Barely two years after the firm of Lybrand, Ross Bros. & Montgomery was founded, it was already necessary to move into larger facilities in Philadelphia. By 1902, the firm's first brand office in New York City was established, followed by another in Pittsburgh in 1908. In its first forays into tax consulting, the company assisted in the drafting of the first federal income tax law in 1913, and a member of the firm, Walter Staub, wrote a seminal essay, *Income Tax Guide,* explaining the pending tax legislation. In 1917 Mongtgomery published the classic (and continuously updated until 1929) *Income Tax Procedure 1917.* When the author established a tax practice in the New York office in 1918, he was immediately besieged by anxious customers.

In 1919, Lybrand, Ross Bros. & Montgomery decided to expand their company into the District of Columbia. During the year and a half in which the United States participated in World War I, Montgomery served on Bernard Baruch's War Industries Board in Washington and also on the Board of Appraisers of the War Department; other firm members served on the Liberty Loan committee and engaged in other war efforts.

By the end of the war, the professionalization of accountancy and its indispensability to the country's economic structure, were established. The greatly expanded firm of Lybrand, Ross Bros. & Montgomery, pacesetters in the accounting profession, were demanding college degrees of their job applicants. Because of the paucity of accounting schools at universities and colleges, the firm was willing to take on college graduates with little or no background in accounting, subjecting them, once hired, to a rigorous two-year night school program of training. Accounting being an exclusively male profession during this time, the company hired only men.

During the 1920s, the firm experienced rapid expansion. Branches were established in the center of the vital automobile industry, Detroit, in 1920, and as far away as Seattle. In 1924, when the firm merged with the accounting company of Klink, Bean & Co., offices opened in Los Angeles and San Francisco. Also that year, an office was established in Berlin, Germany, followed by a Paris office in 1926 and a London office in 1929, the year of the stock market crash. This would mark the beginning of the firm's globalization that would eventually result in branches in over 120 countries worldwide.

The Great Depression was both bane and blessing to the accounting firm of Lybrand, Ross Bros. & Montgomery. The greatly expanded firm, employing hundreds of staff, was faced with shrinking business opportunities as financial institutions and corporations collapsed and went bankrupt. On the other hand, throughout the country and more importantly, on Capitol Hill, the crash was blamed on the lack of independent auditing of the stock exchange. With a new president installed in 1933, Congress established the Securities and Exchange Commission, the regulatory agency for public corporations and the stock exchange, which resulted in a plethora of auditing activities for the firm. The company also became involved in New Deal projects, serving, for instance, as independent auditors for the Tennessee Valley Authority after 1944. Throughout the Depression years, expansion of the company continued, with branch offices opening up in Illinois, Texas, and Kentucky. In 1935, Robert Montgomery became the president of the prestigious American Institute of Accountants.

During World War II over four hundred employees of Lybrand, Ross Bros. & Montgomery served in the armed forces. These accountants in uniform, along with 18 administrative assistants, received entertaining newsletters from the company wherever they were stationed; in the end, six members of the firm lost their lives in the conflict. Remarkably, the London and Paris branches of the firm stayed open for business throughout the war, with only the Berlin office having closed down in 1938.

By its fiftieth anniversary in 1948, the company employed nearly 1,200 staff members and 56 partners. The professionalization of accountancy by then was complete; the role of accountants in business and government unquestioned. The company's evolution in the postwar years therefore would be marked by an enormous expansion in the company's array of services and the continued internationalization of the firm.

Lybrand, Ross Bros. & Montgomery emerged from the war one of the largest accounting firms in the United States. Times were changing, however, and no accounting firm could afford to restrict itself to traditional auditing and accounting services. In 1952, the firm entered a new arena when it started a management consulting service for its clients in the banking and big business world. This was the first of what would become a wide array of consulting services as well as information services and special software packages with the advent of personal computers. While these services by no means supplanted traditional auditing and accounting, they had a significant impact on the firm. By 1974, the firm was the first to establish a career track in accounting for those with computer expertise.

The year 1957 marked the establishment of the European Common Market. Soon thereafter, a merger resulted in Coopers & Lybrand International, consisting initially of the firm's Canadian and British branch firms. While all foreign branches of the firm would bear the name Coopers & Lybrand, the company in the United States retained its original name, Lybrand, Ross Bros. & Montgomery, until 1973. That year, the firm's management decided in favor of adopting a single name for the entire global network of branch companies, which by then were located on all five continents. While the firms, in over 120 countries, remained autonomous, they shared common goals and policies.

Since 1971, Coopers & Lybrand headquarters have remained in the hub of the financial and business world, New York City, with an important office and political action committee located in Washington, D.C. By 1977, Coopers & Lybrand was ranked the third largest accounting company in the United States and was still among the "Big Six" accounting firms by 1993. In 1981, Coopers & Lybrand became the first American accounting firm to establish a foothold in China. The following year, the company played an important role in the breakup of the $115 billion telephone monopoly, AT&T. Despite the severity of the 1990s recession, Coopers & Lybrand did well—with a 2.5 percent growth in revenue in 1991, the worst year of the recession—partly due to its rapid adaptation to the changing needs of business and a lack of dependency on the domestic marketplace. With the fall of communism in eastern Europe, Coopers & Lybrand opened offices in Hungary, Poland, Czechoslovakia, Berlin, and Russia, and remains one of the few American firms to do business in eastern Europe. Consequently, the company secured a foothold in an area of the world that is likely to become profitable in the next century.

Further Reading:

Bedrosian, Linc, ''The Art of Accounting: CPAs Move Beyond Bean Counting to Assume Greater Roles,'' *BusinessWest,* March, 1993, p. 13.

Boys, Peter, ''What's in a Name: Update (Names of Accounting Firms),'' *Accountancy,* March 1990, p. 132.

Cassidy, Tina, ''Brain Drain at Coopers,'' *Boston Business Journal,* February 8, 1993, p. 1.

''Coopers & Lybrand: Foundation for Tomorrow,'' Coopers & Lybrand, 1991.

''Coopers & Lybrand International,'' *The New York Times,* January 14, 1993, p. C6.

''Coopers in TV Land,'' *CPA Journal,* March 1993, p. 8.

The Early History of Coopers & Lybrand, 1898–1948, New York: Garland, 1984 reprint.

Elliott, Stuart, ''Coopers & Lybrand (Accounts),'' *The New York Times,* November 25, 1992, p. C17, D18.

Felsenthal, Edward, ''Coopers Wins Suit,'' *The Wall Street Journal,* March 2, 1993, pp. B10–11.

Lawyer, Gail, ''Largest Accounting Firms in the Metro Area (Metropolitan Washington Area),'' *Washington Business Journal,* March 19, 1993, p. 30.

Woo, Junda, ''Big Six Accounting Firms Join Forces for Legal Change (Firms Want Protection From Shareholders of Client Companies),'' *The Wall Street Journal,* September 1, 1992, p. B7.

                                                              —Sina Dubovoj

Corporate Software Inc.

275 Dan Road
Canton, Massachusetts 02021
U.S.A.
(617) 821-4500
Fax: (617) 821-5688

Public Company
Incorporated: 1983
Employees: 1,000
Sales: $301 million
Stock Exchanges: NASDAQ
SICs: 5045 Computers and Computer Peripheral Equipment
   & Software; 7379 Computer Related Services, Nec

Corporate Software Inc., a public company that planned to go private in 1994, is a leading provider of software and other related computer services to large corporations in the United States and Europe. Corporate Software distributes more than 20,000 products for IBM-compatible or MacIntosh PCs and also offers a wide selection of support services, including training, implementation, and integration of programs.

Morton Rosenthal started Corporate Software in November 1983 with Christopher D. Robert, a sales manager from Data General Corp., and Donald Boudreau, an executive at Child World Inc. Robert became company president, Boudreau treasurer, and Rosenthal chairperson and CEO.

Upon graduating from college Rosenthal had started his own business selling photographs of rock stars for record albums. He eventually sold the business, earned an MBA, and worked for software companies before starting Corporate Software. According to *Business Week* magazine, Corporate Software's growth is as much due to Rosenthal's "ebullient showman" personality as his business talents.

Rosenthal was 34 years old when he invested $30,000 of his own money and $450,000 from private investors in his belief that big companies would pay more for software if they received extra service in return. Within four years, Corporate Software's revenues soared to almost $60 million with profits of $1.86 million. The company had a better rate of growth than many of the software developers whose wares it was distributing.

When the three men started the business, they bundled software and services together. Companies that spent $3,000 a quarter could call a hotline staffed by 25 troubleshooters. Larger buyers received a monthly newsletter on disk providing overviews of new technology and products, tips, and advice on system management problems. The biggest spenders, $60,000 or more, received in-house seminars as well as customized newsletters on disk that contained information about the products they used most. Other value-added services included monthly purchase activity reports, quarterly newsletters, biannual guide lists and reviews, and trial copies of new software. Corporate Software's clients were spending about five percent more than they would pay discounters for software programs, but with the increasingly complex world of computers, large companies regarded the service was worth the extra money.

Corporate Software's business expanded so quickly that it outgrew office space only four months after it had moved in. During its second year of business, the company grossed more than $24 million and had a growth rate of more than 20 percent a month, according to company officials.

When it began, Corporate Software was one of only a few resellers that sold directly to end users. According to Robert, most distributors were reluctant to sell to end users because that might alienate their primary outlets, such as large retail chains and other dealers. However, because these retailers depended on only a handful of bestselling software packages and did not research other packages, they did not meet the needs of the corporate buyer. According to *PC Week,* Corporate Software might more accurately be called a "specialized corporate reseller" than a distributor.

From the start, Corporate Software did business only with volume buyers, mostly Fortune 1,000 companies; it did not service individuals or small businesses and did not stock game, home education, or small business software. Its customers were businesses with full-time data processing departments, a mainframe, and a relatively large number of personal computers. Its services were tailored specifically to the needs of large corporations.

Corporate Software sold only IBM-compatible software in its first year, emphasizing products that were not necessarily bestsellers but that met a specific business need. Before listing any software in Corporate Software's catalog, product managers evaluated it and presented it to a three-person review board. Approved products were then assigned to a product category, and product managers were expected to stay current on new software in their categories. By the second year, the company also began selling expansion cards and modems and was considering carrying minicomputer and mainframe products.

According to an interview with Rosenthal in 1985, about 75 percent of the staff spent at least half of their time talking to customers. Its services included presale consulting, demonstration floppy disks, evaluation copies, and technical support. It also supplied users with a monthly newsletter and a semiannual software guide. Company president Christopher Robert described Corporate Software's combination of services as rare, even though each of the services itself was not unusual. At that time, Corporate Software stocked about 350 software products.

In 1987, Corporate Software went public with financial support of $916,000 from Hambro International Venture Fund and $466,000 from General Electric Venture Capital Corp. Corporate Software raised $9 million on an offering of one million shares. Company insiders retained 48 percent control of Corporate Software, and Rosenthal's initial investment was now worth $4 million. The company's sales had grown from $1.7 million in 1984 to $14.7 million in 1985 and to more than $32 million in 1986. It had 11 sales offices and 160 employees.

In 1989, Corporate Software expanded its staff from 308 employees to 425 employees. Most of the increase was in sales personnel as the company opened new offices and foreign subsidiaries. It had 20 domestic sites by the end of the year, and, at that time, Robert resigned as Corporate Software president to become president and CEO of Epoch Systems Inc., a manufacturer of optical-disk file servers. Rosenthal became company president in addition to his other functions as CEO and chairperson. In 1990, European sales grew by 73 percent, providing 37 percent of the company's total revenues; North American sales grew 33 percent in 1990.

As computer systems became more complex, service was becoming even more vital. However, support lines were labor intensive and labor expensive. Corporate Software also established a network lab—an expensive operation—to duplicate clients' configurations and figure out how LAN-smart an application would be.

By 1991, product support specialists were responding to more than 170,000 calls annually. Corporate Software was serving about 42 percent of the Fortune 1,000 in the United States and more than half of the Financial Times 100 in England. Its largest suppliers were software companies Microsoft and Lotus, both of which had brought out many new products within the previous two years.

In 1991, Corporate Software altered its support policies in response to changes within many corporations it served or had targeted. Traditionally, the company combined software and support services and charged five to ten percent more than its competition, targeting information center managers who both purchased equipment and software and provided support for their companies. With many companies dividing purchasing and support services internally, Corporate Software also separated those functions. To attract new clients, Corporate Software began selling software only to high-volume, price-conscious clients, and support services were priced separately. The company also started offering support service to business users rather than only to support staff at client companies as the companies introduced complex new software systems.

For its first service provided on an extra-cost basis Corporate Software teamed up with Microsoft to help large companies switch to Microsoft's new Windows software. Windows allowed PC users to control their machines by using a mouse and pointing at an icon or menu, similar to the MacIntosh computer. Microsoft's Windows products accounted for 25 percent of sales for Corporate Software in 1991 while two years earlier it had posted almost no revenue from Windows.

The fee-based program was based on a pilot program Corporate Software had conducted, which followed the problems that fourteen specified companies encountered as they moved into the new Windows graphical user interface. To ease conversion phase pressures felt by corporate computer support departments, to which the PC users usually turned with problems, program users could call Corporate Software directly with their Windows questions.

Corporate Software also added telemarketing to its sales strategy for reaching mid-sized companies in 1992. Salespeople still called on large corporate clients, however, and their staff included 35 salespeople in North America and 30 in offices in England, France, Germany, and their newest office in Belgium. Corporate Software became one of the largest software resellers in Europe with market shares of between seven and 16 percent in those countries in which it operated. The company's share of the domestic corporate market was estimated at ten to 15 percent.

In 1992, company vice-president Stephen D. R. Moore became president while Rosenthal continued as chairperson and CEO. Co-founder and chief operating officer Donald Boudreau retired. That year, Corporate Software also announced it would compete more aggressively for business by setting up customized, cost-plus price lists so that a high-volume product would have a lower mark-up than items that sold only occasionally. The company also set up a bid desk to handle large, price-sensitive orders.

Corporate Software was facing stiff competition from many types of vendors including other value-added resellers, mail order firms, computer superstores, hardware manufacturers, and software manufacturers themselves. Corporate Software, however, continued to stress its support and systems integration services.

Corporate Software was looking at a healthy sales revenue and profit in the first part of the decade because of the increased power and versatility of new hardware, resulting in the development of more powerful software, such as upgraded versions of Microsoft Windows, Excel, and Lotus 123. Corporations, however, were facing an increasingly confusing PC-environment. While computers had become inexpensive, facilitating decisions regarding which hardware to purchase, software choices, unless carefully made, could lead to incompatibility within the company. Corporations found themselves in need of professional advice in order to monitor costs and to ensure compatibility and return on investment.

With frequent product upgrades and the introduction of portable computers, corporate licensing issues during this time became more problematic. Traditionally, software companies issued one license for each computer and user, a policy that became increasingly difficult to apply or enforce because of the networking and portability of PCs. Corporations became concerned about the potential for licensing violations. Although software developers responded with many options for licensing, this made the issue even more complex, and businesses were hungry for assistance from resellers and systems integrators. In response to the difficulties of dealing with licensing agreements and upgrades, Corporate Software added asset management to its inventory of products and services. With this value-added service, Corporate Software said it would handle license negotiations, track software usage, conduct audits for licensing compliance, and duplicate disks and documentation for site license compliance.

In the early 1990s, many new software distributors were competing with Corporate Software. Discounters were also adding more services, making competition even more intense. Even though increased competition was slowing Corporate Software's growth, which had been so phenomenal during its early years, the company was nevertheless regarded as well positioned to help businesses through the PC software maze.

Further Reading:

Hammonds, Keith H., "When Big Companies Need a Hand to Hold," *Business Week,* February 29, 1988, pp. 73–4.

Humphrey, Charles, "Bundled 'Value-Add' Sparks Corporate Software," *PC Week,* September 11, 1989, p. 11

Lyons, Daniel, "New Breed of Software Resellers Aim to Make the Complex Simple," *PC Week,* April 26, 1988, p. 144.

Zarley, Craig, "Corporate Distributors," *PC Week,* April 1, 1986, p. S27.

—Wendy Stein

COUNTY·SEAT®
THE JEAN STORE

County Seat Stores Inc.

17950 Preston Road
Suite 1000
Dallas, Texas 75252-5638
U.S.A.
(214) 248-5100
Fax: (214) 248-5214

Private Company
Incorporated: 1973
Employees: 3,500
Sales: $500 million
SICs: 5651 Family Clothing Stores

County Seat is one of the nation's largest mall-based specialty retailers of casualwear for teens and young adults. With more than 630 jean stores in 46 states, it is the seventh largest "single concept" retailer. Jeans and jean jackets account for more than 50 percent of the company's sales in 1993, with shirts, shorts, t-shirts, socks, belts, fashion jewelry, and other accessories accounting for the rest.

The first County Seat store opened in Minneapolis in 1973. Beginning as an offspring of the grocery store chain Super Valu Stores, County Seat was intended as a budget-priced chain of stores offering casual clothes for the entire family, with about 3,500 square feet per store. The stores featured Levi jeans and other Levi apparel and had a distinct country western look with a rustic wood decor. That decor predominated for 12 years, as the chain slowly grew.

In 1984, Carson Pirie Scott and Company, the second largest department store chain in Chicago, acquired the County Seat's 275 stores. The following year, it brought in a management team headed by Barry J.C. Parker as chief executive officer. Parker had begun his retail career at F&R Lazarus in 1971 as a buyer, became vice-president and general merchandise manager of the Children's Place in 1975, and eventually became that company's chief financial officer and senior vice-president of finance and systems. Richard H. Gundy, who had 28 years experience in retailing, became County Seat's senior vice-president and general merchandise manager in 1984, and was promoted the following year to executive vice-president of merchandising and marketing.

Parker and his team retained the name of the store and the core merchandise theme—jeans—but almost everything else about County Seat changed. The company took on a new look and an aggressive expansion drive. During the next three years, 374 stores were added. The new stores used glass and matte black fixtures for a contemporary look and used colorful signs and rock music to appeal to young people for whom shopping had become recreational. Most of the existing stores were also remodeled so that County Seat stores across the nation were easily identifiable and familiar.

Furthermore, the new management team targeted a narrower clientele—high school and college age shoppers, the largest of the markets of the original County Seat stores. According to Parker, the store doubled the average price of merchandise and drastically changed its merchandising. He called the new County Seats a more youthful version of rival chain, The Gap. County Seat began selling only premium brands of jeans—Levi, Girbaud, and Guess. Although denim remained a staple, the stores also began offering fashion merchandise and even developed private labels: Nuovo jeanswear, Shore Club activewear, and Cotton Cargo sportswear. The average sale increased to about $42. By 1989, there were 415 County Seat stores mostly located in malls of at least 500,000 square feet.

To control costs during this period of rapid growth, County Seat purchased the technology necessary to track construction expenses and negotiate prices competitive for the specific region. The program computed average square foot costs for each subcontractor trade by region and based on costs for projects completed during the previous 12 months.

When P. A. Bergner and Co., a Milwaukee-based midwestern department store chain, acquired Carson Pirie Scott and Company in a hostile takeover in 1989, the new owners retained the department store divisions but sold off other businesses under the Carson Pirie Scott umbrella. A management team, led by Parker, and partially financed by Donaldson, Lufkin & Jenrette Securities Corporation investment group, acquired County Seat in late 1989. Parker became president and chair of the board as well as chief executive officer.

Unlike many other chains which encountered serious financial problems following leverage buyouts, County Seat continued to expand and profit. County Seat management attributed its continued success to its nearly recession-proof market of teens and also to the strength of the chain. The management team had already been running the company very successfully for several years before the buyout, so they had made many of the strategic moves necessary for their long-term success. The new owners did not have to sell off assets, revamp operations, or bring a new management team on board.

According to Parker, who had doubled sales since taking over in 1985, the teen market was less vulnerable to recession and was often the last market to be negatively affected by the economy. This was attributed to the three major reasons young people replace their clothes: they outgrow them, they wear them out, or their tastes change. This translated into high turnover of merchandise for County Seat. While County Seat's competition, The Gap and the Limited clothing stores began to target older customers, County Seat management remained focused on the

14-to-22-year-old market. Their major sales periods remained back-to-school season in late summer and the holiday season in December. Parker also cited private labels as a reason for their success; private labels offered County Seat cost controls and high margins.

By 1990, County Seat owned and operated 492 stores in 39 states. Stores were located from the Rocky Mountains to the East Coast and from Florida to Washington D.C. The greatest concentration of stores was in Illinois, Texas, and Florida. Sales revenue was $330 million.

Within the next few years, County Seat expanded into New York and New Jersey, and increased its presence in the Washington D.C. area. It also established stores on the northern Pacific coast and had targeted southern California, New Mexico, Nevada, Utah, and Idaho as important expansion markets.

The chain traditionally has done little advertising other than participating in ads sponsored or required by the malls and advertising back-to-school clothes in *Rolling Stone, Seventeen,* and other youth magazines. For the most part, however, the chain relied on colorful point-of-sale graphics.

Looking to the future, County Seat built its own 152,000-square-foot distribution center near Minneapolis, Minnesota, which could service as many as 800 stores. County Seat saved on time and labor costs by generally distributing items that were pre-ticketed and packaged by the vendors. The company considered its weekly store deliveries unique in the retail industry, maintaining that the short delivery time allowed the company to adjust inventory frequently to maintain tight control over inventory for individual stores and the chain.

County Seat anticipated healthy increases in sales through the end of the century as demographic studies showed that the 14-to-22-year-old population would continue to increase. The nation's more than 34 million young people were spending more than $16 billion annually on clothing purchases. Teens do their shopping in the malls, according to County Seat research, and the company expected its growth to continue with the growth of regional malls. Although some industry experts were pessimistic about the future of malls, County Seat remained confident, predicting that malls would remain very much alive as a "healthy environment for the youth of America."

Further Reading:

"County Seat Press Kit," Dallas: County Seat, 1993.
"County Seat Builds with Store Data System," *Chain Store Age Executive,* November 1988, p. 104.
King, Kit, "Baby Boomers Step Aside," *Dallas Apparel News,* August 1991, p. 18.

—Wendy J. Stein

Crate&Barrel

Crate and Barrel

725 Landwehr Road
Northbrook, Illinois 60062
U.S.A.
(708) 272-2888
Fax: (708) 272-5366

Private Company
Incorporated: 1962
Employees: 2,500
Sales: $225 million
SICs: 5719 Miscellaneous Home Furnishings Stores; 5712
  Furniture Stores; 5947 Gift, Novelty, and Souvenir Shops

Crate and Barrel is an innovative nationwide chain of retail home furnishings stores. Although not among the largest companies in its industry, Crate and Barrel receives a great deal of attention and is widely regarded as a trendsetter in style and retail display. A Crate and Barrel store typically serves as a stockroom and a showroom at the same time. Housewares are displayed in large quantities, often stacked like items in a supermarket, and are bathed in dramatic lighting. The company, which also goes by the corporate name Euromarket Designs Inc., is based in Northbrook, Illinois, a suburb of Chicago. Crate and Barrel currently has about 47 retail outlets, five of which sell primarily furniture. Furniture accounts for roughly 15 percent of the company's sales. A significant share of sales also comes from the company's catalogue operations.

Crate and Barrel was founded in 1962 by Gordon and Carole Segal. Gordon Segal had recently graduated from Northwestern University and was working as a real estate agent, while Carole was a schoolteacher. According to company lore, Gordon was inspired to open a store while doing the dishes at home one day. While he stood admiring the beauty of the piece of imported German china dripping in his hand, Segal mulled the fact that reasonably priced but classy items for the kitchen were not readily available to the Chicago consumer. With the St. Lawrence Seaway newly opened, the Segals got the idea to have European goods shipped straight to Chicago, where they could be sold directly to the public. In this way, importers and wholesalers could be bypassed, allowing the fledgling merchants to keep prices in check. With their life savings of $12,000, plus $5,000 borrowed from Gordon's father, a successful Chicago restaurateur and caterer, the Segals went into business in spite of their complete lack of experience in either importing or retailing.

The first Crate and Barrel store was opened in a former elevator factory in Old Town, an area of Chicago in the process of gentrification. The store was put together in a mere two weeks. By opening day, Crate and Barrel consisted mainly of a big room, one employee, and a bunch of merchandise. Even the cash register had not yet arrived. With no tables or display cases available, the goods, mainly plates, glassware and cookware, were stacked on overturned packing crates and barrels. From the necessity of the company's humble beginning came the chain's now-household name. The Segals' inexperience showed in the first few months of operation. In the first month, the store sold $8,000 worth of merchandise. The following month, however, this figure was cut in half. Sales fell by 50 percent again the month after that.

As customers began to discover Crate and Barrel, the Segals became interested in a broader range of products than those that they had seen and used personally and had had shipped in quantity to Chicago. In 1964, they took their first European buying trip in order to make direct contact with the independent and often small craftspeople and manufacturers that would be the sources of their merchandise for years to come. Another key to the company's early survival was Gordon Segal's ability to concoct unique and advantageous leasing agreements with landlords. For example, in 1965, as the first Crate and Barrel was thriving in the Old Town location, the company found itself faced with the possibility of losing its lease. Segal was able to patch together a deal with the landlord in which Crate and Barrel would build a new home and rent it back from the landlord. Under the agreement, Crate and Barrel would then purchase the building in 15 years. 1965 also marked the departure of Carole Segal from the operation. The driving force in the company's early stylistic innovations, Carole left to attend graduate business courses, as well as study gourmet cooking. In 1979, she started a store of her own called Foodstuffs, a high-end food store with a merchandising approach similar to that of Crate and Barrel.

In 1966, Segal and Lon Habkirk, a designer who would remain affiliated with the company for at least twenty more years, traveled to Boston to study a store called Design Research. Design Research, the creation of architect Ben Thompson, dealt in imported housewares and furniture. In Design Research, Segal saw the clean, modern, Euro-look that he sought for his store, and was heavily influenced by Thompson's unorthodox retail approach. Design Research, however, sold expensive and rare items, and had trouble turning a profit in spite of a high dollar per square foot sales ratio. Segal realized that Crate and Barrel must focus more on keeping prices lower through volume buying. His goal was to keep prices 30 percent to 40 percent lower than those of similar merchandise at other retail outlets by keeping profit margins low and importing goods directly from the manufacturer.

By 1968, Crate and Barrel had annual sales of around $500,000. That year, a second store was opened at the Plaza del Lago shopping center in Wilmette, an upscale suburb of Chicago. As the company grew, Crate and Barrel began to face the problem of developing a reliable management team in an industry with traditionally low pay and high employee turnover. Segal's solution was to hire young college graduates into sales positions with the explicit goal of eventually moving them into management roles. Segal also aimed to create an environment conducive to keeping employees around, partly by expanding only to cities that were hospitable to workers, avoiding rough-and-tumble markets like New York. This strategy paid off handsomely in employee loyalty. In 1970, for instance, a core of new staff members was brought on board. 15 years later, nearly two-thirds of this group held senior executive positions with the company.

Oak Brook, another affluent Chicago suburb, became home to Crate and Barrel's third store in 1971. By the middle of the 1970s, the chain was beginning to receive widespread attention for its unique marketing style and the quality of its wares. This attention was boosted by the 1975 opening of a new store at a highly visible location on Michigan Avenue in Chicago. Over the course of the next few years, Crate and Barrel began its nationwide expansion, propelled by its sterling reputation among the growing class of young adults with money to spend, otherwise known as "yuppies." The first non-Chicago markets into which the chain expanded were Boston and Dallas, and the stores were usually placed in upscale malls. Soon thereafter, San Francisco and Washington D. C. were added to the list. In 1981, Crate and Barrel tried its hand at retail furniture sales for the first time. One of the company's Boston stores was converted into a furniture outlet at that time. This Boston location was used as a test subject as Segal considered the possibility of expanding further into furniture retailing. This way, he could experiment with different approaches and product lines without risking a heavy commitment to the furniture business. Ten years later, furniture sales were contributing about one-fifth of the company's revenue.

In 1983, Crate and Barrel raised $7 million through Harris Bank industrial revenue bonds to finance a new 136,000-square-foot complex in Northbrook, Illinois, another suburb of Chicago. The complex would house the corporate headquarters and a central warehouse. The chain had grown to 17 stores by 1985. That year, these stores generated about $50 million in sales and employed 600 workers (twice as many during peak periods). Revenue was growing at a rate of 20 percent a year. The merchandise sold at Crate and Barrel stores across the United States was supplied by about 350 different manufacturers, many of them small independents. Of these, 250 were located overseas. In addition, the company had developed a vibrant mail-order operation, which by this time was processing about 3,000 pieces each day.

In the middle part of the 1980s, Crate and Barrel found that the tastes of its customers had become somewhat more expensive. This was most apparent in the furniture operations. When the company first began to sell furniture, the emphasis was on glass, chrome, and black leather, in keeping with the clean, basic look of its tabletop merchandise. It soon became clear that its young, relatively affluent constituency wanted more classic, comfortable furniture and was willing to pay higher prices for it. This trend away from sleek and toward warm then seeped into the kitchen, where the demand for painted dinnerware and hand-decorated glassware began to increase. Meanwhile the catalogue business continued to thrive. Although the mail-order

operation was costly to run (50,000 orders a year were required just to break even), direct mail had the helpful side effect of boosting in-store sales. In fact, sales at the stores generally grew by as much as 20 percent during a month that immediately followed a catalogue mailing.

Crate and Barrel doubled its sales over the next few years, passing the $100 million mark in 1989. By this time, the chain was 27 stores in size. Los Angeles and Houston had been added to the carefully selected group of markets into which Crate and Barrel had ventured. The company's second furniture store was launched in 1989, this time on home turf, as an extension of its Plaza del Lago store in Wilmette, Illinois. The Wilmette furniture store was an immediate hit, generating $1,000 in sales per square foot, triple what was considered good in an industry that was in the midst of a lengthy slump. The success of the Wilmette furniture operation led to the announcement later that year of a second planned furniture outlet in the Chicago area, this one an expansion of the chain's Oakbrook Center accessories location.

In 1990, Crate and Barrel opened a new flagship store on a ritzy stretch of Michigan Avenue in Chicago. The building was designed by John Buenz, whose firm (Solomon Cordwell Buenz & Associates) had been designing Crate and Barrel stores since 1976. The exterior of the four-story, 45,000-square-foot structure showed lots of glass and metal, reflecting the clean, modern feel of the standard Crate and Barrel interior. Two floors of the new outlet were to be devoted to furniture. This was a bold move, in light of the fact that furniture had not been sold successfully on this pricey stretch of Michigan Avenue for many years, including failed attempts by such well-known retailers as John M. Smyth and Marshall Field's. For that year, sales were about $150 million. 1990 also marked the closing of the oldest operating Crate and Barrel store, the 5,000-square-foot outlet on Wells that had opened in 1965 just down the street from the original Old Town store. This store was replaced by a new 10,000-square-foot location about a mile away, to be used primarily as an outlet for end-of-season and close-out merchandise.

By the early 1990s, Crate and Barrel had tapped into the Minneapolis and San Diego markets with new store locations. Four new stores were added in 1991, bringing the chain's total to 34. The company had over 1,000 employees by this time. Merchandise sold at the various Crate and Barrel stores came from at least 25 different countries, although most of the furniture was manufactured in the United States. In 1992, the company entered the Florida market for the first time, opening stores in Palm Beach Gardens and Boca Raton. Sales at Crate and Barrel reached $170 million that year.

Although many stores sell more dishes and sofas than Crate and Barrel does, few are as well respected among retail chains. Crate and Barrel's reputation for quality and class results from a combination of elements: a unique presentational style whose success has bred a legion of mimics; a steady plan for growth that is ambitious in scope while modest enough in its rate to succeed; and a keen insight into the evolving tastes of its target market, not to mention an ability to put merchandise that matches those tastes on the shelves. Virtually every decision that Segal and his company have made seems to have worked.

As long as the company remains in his control, Crate and Barrel seems likely to continue its winning ways.

Further Reading:

Barnhart, Bill, and Sallie Gaines, ''Fewer Fish in the Barrel?,'' *Chicago Tribune,* December 5, 1984, sec. 7, p. 1.

Carroll, Margaret, ''Segals Create Barrel of Fun While Selling,'' *Chicago Tribune,* February 12, 1986, sec. 3, pp. 1–2.

Collins, Lisa, ''Crate Gets Respect—A Customer at a Time,'' *Crain's Chicago Business,* November 26, 1990, p. 20.

Collins, Lisa, ''Crate Expectations Fuel Furniture Push,'' *Crain's Chicago Business,* April 22, 1990, p. 1.

Gapp, Paul, ''Made to Order,'' *Chicago Tribune,* October 21, 1990, sec. 13, p. 14.

Gruber, William, ''Crate and Barrel Plans for Florida and More,'' *Chicago Tribune,* July 22, 1991, sec. 4, p. 2.

Kahn, Joseph P., ''On Display,'' *Inc.,* November, 1985, pp. 110–122.

McNamara, Michael D., ''Crate and Barrel Set to Launch Furniture Store in Chi. Area,'' *HFD,* April 10, 1989, p. 20.

Palmeri, Christopher, ''Stanley, This Is What I Want to Do,'' *Forbes,* January 20, 1992, pp. 90–92.

Strangenes, Sharon, ''The Gambler,'' *Chicago Tribune,* August 26, 1990, sec. 15, p. 1.

—Robert R. Jacobson

Crédit Lyonnais

1, rue des Italiens
F-75009 Paris
France
(1) 42 95 70 00
Fax: (1) 42 95 14 30

State-Owned Company
Incorporated: 1863
Employees: 70,000
Sales: FFr3.2 billion (1991; US$548 million)
SICs: 6021 National Commercial Banks

As one of France's three largest banks, Crédit Lyonnais provides a full range of commercial banking and financial services domestically and worldwide. Known for its innovations in deposit banking, global expansion, and, in particular, its aggressive acquisition strategies, the bank has become a well established presence in the industry.

Crédit Lyonnais was created to fulfill a need in France for a bank that would accept small deposits during the expansion of the Second Empire, when the country needed an infusion of capital. The city of Lyons, with its rich and long-established banking tradition and the residents' desire to become independent of Parisian tutelage, was favorably suited to the formation of such a bank. The legal pathways were made clear by a May 23, 1863 law permitting the establishment of businesses without governmental authorization. The active personality of 39-year-old Henri Germain was also an important element in the bank's foundation. The son of a prosperous Lyons family, he had been a lawyer, stockbroker, silk merchant, and mine manager before launching Crédit Lyonnais and becoming its first president. Of the bank's 20 million francs of capital (40,000 shares at 500 francs each), Germain became the biggest shareholder with 2,150 shares. On July 6, 1863, 200 businessmen met in the presence of a notary in Lyons to finalize a charter for Crédit Lyonnais, and on July 26, the bank opened for business at the Palais du Commerce in Lyons.

In its first years, Crédit Lyonnais operated as a deposit bank and served the needs of local business. However, sudden losses in a dye factory in Lyons deterred further direct participation in businesses. Germain's edict that the amount of all deposits and current accounts be equaled by liquid capital for immediate reimbursement became not only the rule at Crédit Lyonnais, but at all deposit banks. Such policy became influential in the bank's increasing reputation for reliability and security, as it expanded both in France and abroad.

By 1865, Germain had married into a Paris family and assumed a seat in the French parliament. A newly established branch of Crédit Lyonnais in Paris became increasingly more important, and Germain traveled regularly between Lyons and Paris. With the beginning of the Franco-Prussian War in 1870, Germain moved some of the bank's assets to London, creating Crédit Lyonnais's first foreign branch. During the Commune of 1871, a provisory office was installed at Versailles. Germain's active participation in negotiations over the financial clauses of the Frankfort treaty, which ended the Franco-Prussian War, reflected his growing influence in the financial community and helped to assure that his business went on as usual after the war. As a parliamentarian, Germain was much in the public eye and was suggested as a candidate for Finance Minister, but his attentions remained fixed on Crédit Lyonnais.

During the 1870s, Germain acquired some capital for expansion in Paris, southeastern France, and abroad. The construction in 1878 of a new, ornate building on Boulevard des Italiens to house the central Paris branch, which became known as a "temple of finance," signaled the ultimate dominance of Paris over Lyons in the bank's future. Branches were also established in Aix-en-Provence, Nice, and Montpellier, among other cities in the southeast of France. The international network of branches, which would become fundamental in the history of the bank, began as offices added in Constantinople and Alexandria in 1875, Geneva and Madrid in 1876, and Vienna in 1877. The establishment of a branch in St. Petersburg represented the first instance in Russia of a bank operating under its foreign name. The New York branch opened in 1879 on Broadway, but subsequently closed its doors at a loss in 1882 due to high American federal government taxes. By 1882, 30 offices had opened in Paris alone, as well as others in Bordeaux, Toulouse, and Reims.

The recession of 1882 and the loss of confidence in the Banque de l'Union Générale, due to speculation, put a halt to Crédit Lyonnais's expansion. However, the crisis of its fellow bank helped establish Germain's policy of maximum reimbursement of deposits in the face of the numerous withdrawals which took place, and confidence in Crédit Lyonnais grew. In 1888, the bank's prestige suffered somewhat due to the failure of its investment in the Panama Canal project. Nevertheless, that year Crédit Lyonnais played a substantial role in the 500 million franc loan to Russia, and these foreign loans became a specialty of the bank, although they were sometimes criticized for diverting French capital abroad. Crédit Lyonnais's business showed no signs of slowing from the late nineteenth century to the First World War, a period that became known as the company's "Belle Époque." The bank invested in real estate during this time, notably in Paris and on the Cote d'Azur, while also taking part in loans to foreign governments after the liberation of territory in 1870. From 1882 to 1900, branches increased from 110 to 189 with offices added in Moscow, Jerusalem, Madrid, and Bombay.

From 1901 to 1913, total assets rose from 1,700 million to 2,830 million francs. Despite the suspension of Russian government loans at the onset of the Russo-Japanese War, and the circulation of pamphlets by radicals claiming that Crédit Lyonnais's foreign branches were political centers of reactionary propaganda, the bank's prosperity did not wane. Germain died in 1905, but not before witnessing Crédit Lyonnais overtake Lloyd's and Deutsche Bank as first in the world in total assets, a ranking it maintained until 1920. Even Vladimir Lenin deposited his money at Crédit Lyonnais while in exile in France. The central office in Paris, designed by the architect Bouwens and completed in 1913, symbolized the worldwide power and prosperity of Crédit Lyonnais, at a time when the Federal Reserve Act had only just allowed U.S. banks to expand overseas.

With the outbreak of World War I, Crédit Lyonnais's supremacy was threatened. The war years saw weaker bank leadership and declining public confidence, in light of the bank's limited liquidation of accounts. With the complete cancellation of the Russian debt, due to the revolution in that country, came strong discontent among Russian clientele whose deposits were lost. In Petrograd, the Bolsheviks liquidated all private banks, Crédit Lyonnais included, and replaced them with the Bank of the People. Elsewhere, some 135 branches, now located in occupied territory, had limited or stopped services. The bank evacuated assets from Paris upon the German advance in the spring of 1918.

The postwar period of 1920 to 1929 was one of economic difficulty for Crédit Lyonnais, which for the first time in 40 years lost its premier position in the world to Société Générale. Furthermore, the bank faced economic inflation, which depleted its assets as well as those of its clientele, and competition from new, smaller banking establishments. As a result of the low salaries it now offered, the bank experienced a massive employee strike in the summer of 1925, and, four years later, one fifth of Crédit Lyonnais was bought out by the Berlin bank Mendelssohn. By 1928, deposits at Crédit Lyonnais were once again increasing. Due to a refined strategy for its foreign branches, an increase in new branches in France, and stronger leadership, Crédit Lyonnais was once again able to overtake Société Générale as the bank with the most assets in France. The bank withstood the Great Depression despite closing a few foreign branches and the death of the Madrid director in the Spanish Civil War. However, the company had to cut 18 percent of its staff in the face of a 20 percent drop in profits.

At the outbreak of World War II, a 32-car train was used to evacuate 500 tons of stocks, bonds, and securities from Paris for safekeeping. In much of France, with the exception of the Alsace and Moselle regions, normal operations continued against great odds. Many Crédit Lyonnais directors and employees were killed in bombings or in combat during the Liberation. By 1944, normal relations were reestablished in Africa, and the bank retook possession of its offices in the Alsace and Moselle areas. All overseas offices were entirely reunified the following year. Most importantly for Crédit Lyonnais and the three other largest French deposit banks, the banking industry in France was nationalized after the Liberation. On January 1, 1946, Crédit Lyonnais shares were taken over by the government, and the bank remained a commercial company subject to common regulations in force for all private banks. Eduard Escarra, the bank's former general manager, became president after several years of transition.

Due to protective legislation and less competition, Crédit Lyonnais experienced a successful postwar period. Expansion occurred in Latin America and Africa, after decolonization, as well as in Iran and Lebanon. During this time, Crédit Lyonnais became one of the frontrunners in the application of banking technology and was the first bank to install automatic teller machines in 1956 and to introduce the Carte Bleue credit card in 1967. From 1966 onward, the French government created favorable conditions for a new cycle of expansion and innovation in the banking industry. In 1967, legislation to institute a "mixed bank" was passed, which effectively allowed for the bringing together of business banks and deposit banks. In addition, certain regulations overseeing the opening of branches were revoked. The merger in 1966 of BBCI and CNEP, the third and fourth largest French banks, into the Banque Nationale de Paris, made Crédit Lyonnais second in France. However, this merger stimulated a dynamic competition between Banque Nationale de Paris, Société Générale, and Crédit Lyonnais.

Favorable legislative conditions were accompanied by an increase in the number of Crédit Lyonnais branches, which rose from 828 to 1,905, as well as employees, which increased from 29,000 to 47,000, in the years 1967 to 1974. The central office in Paris was renovated, and a branch was opened in 1973 at La Défense, the business district on the west side of Paris, to help decongest operations downtown. Another period of internationalization began in the early 1970s, pushing Crédit Lyonnais back into the ranks of the world's ten largest banks. Branches were opened in Tokyo in 1970 and in Singapore, Sydney, and New York the following year. In South America, Crédit Lyonnais helped form Banco Frances e Brasileiro in Brazil. It formed a consortium during this time with Germany's Commerzbank, with Italy's Banco di Roma, and later with Spain's Banco Hispano Americano to offer medium-term Eurocurrency loans. Crédit Lyonnais became the first western bank to obtain representation in Moscow in 1972.

However, such expansion at times proved difficult to direct, and social unrest proved detrimental to the bank. In 1968, a general strike led by a Trotskyist caused the central office to close for ten days. Another long strike occurred in 1974, expanding to include other banks in the industry. In 1976, the bank's president, Jacques Chaine, was killed near the central office by a labor movement fanatic.

In 1982, France's socialist president, Francois Mitterand, completed the steps that nationalized the country's banking industry. Crédit Lyonnais, however, had already been nationalized for 36 years, and when a more conservative government returned briefly to power between 1986 and 1988, the new president of Crédit Lyonnais, Jean-Maxime Léveque, began to prepare the bank for privatization. He guided Crédit Lyonnais into dealings in securities and helped create Clinvest, the bank's investment arm in 1987. Such measures were subsequently halted by the return of the socialists to power in 1988.

That year, Jean-Yves Haberer, the former head of the Paribas merchant bank, assumed the bank's presidency. His leadership of Crédit Lyonnais was based on a commitment to the development of marketing and automated banking, more active cooperation with businesses, the development of European and international network strategies, and a unified European market. The bank took an extremely aggressive approach to expansion under Haberer, buying brokerage firms, financial service companies, and other banks, as well as non-bank assets. In 1990, Crédit Lyonnais took control of Thomson-CSF's finance operations subsidiary, Altus Finance, thereby bolstering profits. In 1992, the bank increased its stake in the Irish leasing and banking company Woodchester Investments to 48 percent. Crédit Lyonnais also acquired 20 percent of Aerospatiale from the French government after providing money for the development of new aircraft and missiles.

The bank had implemented its aggressive strategy in an effort to position itself for the 1993 opening of a single European market. In fact, Jean-Yves Haberer's organization of Crédit Lyonnais was that of a pan-European bank. In 1989, the company had established Crédit Lyonnais Europe, a wholly owned subsidiary, to consolidate the company's various European commercial banking units. Crédit Lyonnais's acquisitions, including Germany's Bank fur Gemeinwirtschaft in December 1992 and several in Spain and Italy, increased the size of its operations beyond the minimum required to operate successfully in the European community. In the early 1990s, the bank was planning to enter the market in eastern Europe when political conditions became more favorable. In November 1991, Crédit Lyonnais was the lead manager of Spain's 13-year French franc six billion issue, which underlined the growing importance of the French franc sector of the Eurobond market. The deal, and its outstanding size and maturity, made Crédit Lyonnais the lead bookrunner for French franc Eurobonds.

In addition to concerted efforts at European expansion, Crédit Lyonnais's policy included a program of international expansion to transform itself into a universal bank, along the German model. As of 1993, Crédit Lyonnais was close to opening offices in China and was one of only several foreign banks awarded licenses to operate branches in Vietnam.

However, along with the aggressive policy of acquisition and expansion under Haberer came several bad loans and growing debt. While profits in 1990 had increased 20 percent from the previous year, Crédit Lyonnais's first half 1992 earnings fell by almost two-thirds, as bad loans forced the bank to nearly double its loan provisions. The bank had several high profile debtors, including the late Robert Maxwell, the former Soviet Union, the developer Olympia & York, and Giancarlo Parretti, who borrowed $1 billion through the bank's Dutch branch to take over Metro–Goldwyn–Mayer in 1990. Parretti's inability to turn MGM around led to a suit removing him from the board. A Delaware court found him guilty of breaking a government contract and ordered him to relinquish control of MGM-Pathe Communications to Crédit Lyonnais in 1992. The loan to Parretti was the bank's biggest liability in the early 1990s, dragging down its profits and stock prices.

In May 1993, France's newly elected conservative government announced a sweeping privatization program, involving 21 large, state-controlled companies, including AirFrance, Renault, and Crédit Lyonnais. The selloff was to take place in the fall 1993 on a company-by-company basis. Unlike a similar program carried out between 1986 and 1988, no limit was placed on foreign acquisition of shares. Among those expected to look at Crédit Lyonnais were other large European institutions that, like Crédit Lyonnais, wanted to create pan-European institutions.

By the 1990s, Crédit Lyonnais had a domestic network of approximately 2,400 branches, over 700 offices in Europe, and 800 across the rest of the world. Faced with an uncertain future involving debts, growing European unification, and privatization, the bank's response has been traditionally enterprising. Crédit Lyonnais was likely to continue operations in the twenty-first century with its typical dedication to innovation and concerted worldwide expansion.

Principal Subsidiaries: Altus Finance (68%); Arnault et Associés (29.5%); Banco Comercial Espanol (Spain; 97.8%); Banco Continental (Chile; 88.3%); Banco Francês e Brasileiro SA (Brazil; 53.9%); Clinvest; Crédit Lyonnais Europe SA; Crédit Lyonnais USA; International Moscow Bank (12%); Société Rhodanienne Mobilière et Immobilière; Union de Banques Arabes et Françaises (40%); Union des Assurances Fédérales; Woodchester Group (Ireland; 48%).

Further Reading:

Bouvier, Jean, *Le Crédit Lyonnais de 1863 à 1882,* Paris: S.E.V.P.E.N., 1961.
Dagneau, Jacques, *Les Agences Regionales du Crédit Lyonnais, Années 1870–1914,* New York: Arno Press, 1977.
Histoire du Crédit Lyonnais, New York: Crédit Lyonnais, 1993.
Un Siècle d'Economie Française 1863–1963, Paris: Crédit Lyonnais, 1963.
Labasse, Jean, *Les Capitaux et la Région,* Paris: A. Colin, 1955.
Riding, Alan, "France is Selling 21 Big Companies," *The New York Times,* May 27, 1993, p. C1.
Rivoire, Jean, *Le Crédit Lyonnais,* Paris: Cherche midi, 1989.

—Jennifer Kerns

CRÉDIT NATIONAL

Crédit National S.A.

45 Rue Saint Dominique
75700 Paris
France
(1) 45 50 90 00
Fax: (1) 45 55 89 58

Public Company
Incorporated: 1942
Employees: 1,405
Stock Exchanges: Paris
SICs: 6021 National Commercial Banks

Crédit National S.A. is a French commercial bank specializing in medium and long-term financing for French businesses. Unable to accept deposits, the bank raises its funds through bond issues and borrowing. Crédit National manages loans and grants made by French government to foreign governments. The bank's chairperson and two vice-chairs are named by the French president, and its board of directors retains two censeurs, representing the government and named by the Minister of Finance. Crédit National's net profits rose by 9.1 percent in 1992 to Ffr 585.9 million.

Crédit National was formed by an act of parliament after World War I. Since large areas of France had served as battlegrounds in that costly and devastating war, a special government commission had been convened to study ways to finance the rebuilding of the "territories affected by the invasion." The commission's report, which found that existing French banks were unable to raise the enormous sums needed, prompted the creation of Crédit National on July 7, 1919, which was approved by parliament on October 10, 1919. In addition to providing funds for the reconstruction effort, the bank was called on to make loans available to small and medium sized French businesses, which for some time had lacked adequate capital.

During this time, the idea of state-owned, nationalized institutions was not yet popular, and the decision was made to create a private enterprise that would serve the state. Thus, from the beginning, Crédit National was a private company in whose direction the government never directly participated—except that its chairperson and two vice-chairs were appointed by the French president.

To raise sufficient funds to process the reparations payments, Crédit National issued bonds—at a five percent rate for 75 years—worth Ffr 100 million, divided in 200,000 shares. By the end of 1919, the bank had raised Ffr 4 billion. A similar issue followed the next year, and a series of bond issues, at various lengths and rates, followed through 1924, by which time the bank had raised more than Ffr 25.5 billion, or more than 30 percent of the total estimated war damages. Although the bank's original task was to be limited to industrial and commercial enterprises, by 1920 its role was expanded to handle the claims of property and agricultural damages. By 1925 market conditions kept the bank from being able to issue more bonds, and it was granted Ffr 1 billion by the state. Much of this was from monies received from Germany as war reparations. The role of Crédit National thus evolved into service mainly as a paying agent for the state.

Concurrently, in order to create, develop, or renew French industrial and commercial concerns, Ffr 500 million was designated to be lent, for a minimum of three and a maximum of ten years. Crédit National's role as a lending institution was carefully circumscribed by law. It could neither receive deposits in cash, nor make loans other than those for which it was created, nor handle operations normally undertaken by the existing banking system. While Crédit National issued the loans, interest rates were fixed by the government, which also set the conditions of the loans. Four-fifths of the total 500,000 francs advanced for this purpose was to go those areas which had suffered during the war, mainly in the northern and eastern parts of the country. Furthermore, loans were not to exceed Ffr 2 million to the same borrower. The bank's first loan was to a company in the Meuse region in the northeast to finance the reinstallation of a hydroelectric plant, for Ffr 150,000, in 1920. By 1928 the government no longer limited such loans to specific areas and increased the maximum to Ffr 5 million.

By 1933 most of the claims had been settled. In all, more than 1.8 million accounts were handled by Crédit National, which had paid out more than Ffr 32.6 billion in cash and Ffr 31.3 billion in short-term and long-term loans. During this time, Crédit National developed an efficient system with which to handle the huge volumes of documentation used to verify the claims and the number of payments made.

As Crédit National eventually outgrew its original task, the government asked the bank to help develop French economic activities overseas. In 1929 the government approved a project allowing the bank to extend its long-term lending to all of the country's colonies, protectorates, and mandated territories. Low-interest, long-term loans were paid, though most were to help areas which had fallen victim to natural disasters. To administer these loans, Crédit Colonial, a subsidiary, was created in 1935. Economic as well as political considerations made it difficult for the subsidiary to adequately serve the needs of France's overseas possessions, however, and Crédit Colonial was dissolved by law December 31, 1958. It had loaned a total of over Ffr 591 million.

The government also called on the bank to raise capital for large public works projects used to combat the high unemployment of the 1930s and, in response, Crédit National issued bonds in 1937 and 1938. Encumbered by its efforts to settle war reparations, however, the bank grew slowly in the 20 years after its creation.

The onset of World War II once again saw the bank called to distribute damage payments, by a new law passed October 11, 1940, four months after Paris fell under Nazi occupation. In November 1940 a law was passed introducing three representatives (censeurs), named by the General Assembly, to "consult" the board of directors. Another law was passed in March 1941 which called on lenders, including Crédit National, to issue state-backed loans to businesses engaged in providing necessities, in an effort to keep the economy functioning. In June 1941 the maximum length for loans was extended to 15 years and the total loan amount increased to Ffr 25 million; in 1943 limits were extended to 20 years and Ffr 30 million. The wartime government passed further laws directing funds to be advanced to businesses to revive economic activity (1940), as well as to film producers (1941) and to national and local sports associations (1942).

However, the burden of raising the funds and paying out claims was made immeasurably more difficult by the war. A series of six bond issues followed from 1941 through 1946, as well as an issue in dollars in 1947, and a final issue in francs in 1950. In total these efforts raised Ffr 100 billion, a small fraction of the funds needed to meet damage payments, and the amount outstanding was paid by the French treasury.

Furthermore, although the funds the bank raised were not large, the multitude of laws governing their payment made payment and recordkeeping a complicated task. From 1941 through 1968, Crédit National made more than 13 million payments of more than Ffr 34 billion. At the height of the process more than 7,000 payments were made a day by more than 800 agents. Over 52 million documents were handled which, by 1968, covered more than over five miles of shelves. The enormity of the task—especially after World War II, during which almost no area of France was spared—spurred some dissatisfaction among those who felt the process moved too slowly or felt denied what was owed them.

Much of the government's postwar reconstruction effort was focused on rebuilding key industrial sectors, and Crédit National gave priority to those industries. In 1946 the government instituted a plan to recover the production levels of 1929—with a 25 percent increase proposed by 1952—in certain priority industrial sectors, such as coal, electricity, cement, transportation, and agricultural machinery. The bank was allowed to control its interest rates, and the amount it was allowed to loan to each business from its own funds was raised from Ffr 150 million to Ffr 250 million in 1955. These measures allowed Crédit National to concentrate on making long-term loans to business; these loans grew from Ffr 55 billion in 1950 to Ffr 240 billion in 1958. Its loans to medium-term bank refinancing activity grew from Ffr 149 billion in 1950 to Ffr 435 billion in 1958.

In 1955 the French government created the Economic and Social Development Fund (FDES) to more directly stimulate the private sector to meet reconstruction objectives, via large state subsidized loans. Representatives from Crédit National and other financial institutions joined with government ministers on special lending committees to direct economic policy. In 1959 the French franc was devalued, and henceforth, the bank's financial figures represented "new" francs.

The bank was also used to stimulate French business overseas. The French government passed a law in 1960 to increase loans to foreign public service projects guaranteed by their governments. In exchange for these loans, such projects were expected to commission work from French businesses and industries. In 1967, hoping to increase the country's exports, French government emended the law so that loans could be made directly to foreign countries. Crédit National made a series of loans, on behalf of the government, to such countries as Chile, Vietnam, Greece, Cambodia, Lebanon, Mexico, and India. From 1962 to 1968, Ffr 554 million was paid out by the bank for the state.

In the mid-1960s the government again decided to use the FDES program to directly support French business, and Crédit National participated actively in distributing these loans. By 1965 total loans were at Ffr 1.4 billion, and by 1968 they had reached Ffr 4 billion. To stimulate the economy during the recession of the mid-1970s, the government made available huge subsidies on capital expenditure projects. After 1975 Crédit National dominated in the distribution of these loans.

By 1985, however, the period of government intervention in the economy was perceived as coming to an end, and state funding for its program of subsidized loans was substantially cut. Crédit National's long-time role as adviser and financial agent of the state became obsolete as the era of deregulation arrived. After 1987 the bank no longer distributed state subsidized loans, and was forced to address the changing financial situation by diversifying. While Crédit National's clients had largely been large industries, the bank now sought out the service sector. By 1987, the bank's clientele as well as its financing options had changed significantly. That year nearly 40 percent of its loans were made to service companies, up from 12 percent during 1982–84, and 30 percent of its customers were companies with less than 500 employees.

Crédit National also began to acquire interests in other businesses during this time. In 1987, it acquired a majority position of the Dupont-Denant stockbrokerage firm, and the following year, it acquired Alfi Gestion, an investment-fund management firm. Crédit National increased its new credit agreements by 25 percent in 1988 to Ffr 33.3 billion. Moreover, the bank created the Financière Saint Dominique subsidiary, a holding company that provided equity and quasi-equity financing.

In the late 1980s Crédit National entered the real estate market in a further effort to diversify. The difficult economic period that commenced in 1989, causing the number of business failures to increase 40 percent between 1989 and 1992, affected some of the bank's activities more than others. In 1989 the bank's net profits soared 59.5 percent over the previous year's, but dropped the following year by 27.8 percent, to Ffr 499 million. Nevertheless, Crédit National remained committed to its real estate activities.

In 1991 the bank initiated a three-year plan to increase its long term and specialized financing from Ffr 90 billion to Ffr 102.3 billion, as well as to increase its return on capital from ten to 15 percent. By this time, Financière Saint Dominique had evolved into one of the continent's major providers of investment capital, carrying five percent of the European market, and had achieved listing on the Paris stock exchange. However, Moody's Investors Service lowered its long-term ratings of the bank and its Interfinance Crédit National NV subsidiary from double-A-2 to double-A-3, citing the company's diversification into riskier ventures.

In 1992 the bank's Banque Saint Dominique subsidiary (acquired in 1987 as Banque CSIA) lost Ffr 85 million; it stock was delisted and its national and international trading activities were suspended while it was reorganized. However, one of Crédit National's other recent acquisitions fared much better; by 1991 Financière Saint Dominique held five percent of the European market, with investments totaling around Ffr 1.1 billion in 1992.

Crédit National continued its efforts to strengthen its presence in certain foreign markets, but avoided the eastern European market. In late 1992 the bank joined with Elettrofinanziaria Spa (Elfi) to purchase the newly privatized household appliance maker Thomson Electroménager, a former subsidiary of Thomson S. A. In order to effect the purchase, Crédit National and Elfi created a holding company, Brandt Electroménager, of which Crédit National retained a 34 percent interest. The purchase was concluded in January 1993, and the companies reportedly paid Ffr 2 billion for Brandt.

Crédit National's presence in the United States was represented by its subsidiary, ABM Corporation, a mortgage-backed securities trader. In 1992 the subsidiary's net income was $2.5 million, with $648 million in securities outstanding.

Principal Subsidiaries: Alfi Gestion (66%); Banque Saint Dominique; Dupont-Denant; Financière Saint Dominique.

Further Reading:

Crédit National: 1919–1969, Crédit National, Paris, 1969.
Crédit National Annual Report, Paris: Crédit National, 1992.
"Crédit National Forecasts 7% Rise in Banking Income," *Wall Street Journal Europe,* June 10, 1992, p.12.
"Crédit National Group, Crédit National," Company Document, Paris: Crédit National, 1992.
Crédit National Records 9% Rise," *Financial Times,* p. 28.
Gay, Pierre-Angel, "Le Groupe Italien Elfi Constitue Sa Nouvelle Entité Brandt Electroménager," *Le Monde,* p. 22.
Graham, George, "Crédit National Advances Due to Rise in Activity," *Financial Times,* March 22, 1990, p. 33.

—C.L. Collins

Crompton & Knowles Corp.

One Station Place
Metro Center
Stamford, Connecticut 06902
U.S.A.
(203) 352-5400
Fax: (203) 353-5424

Public Company
Incorporated: 1900 as Crompton & Knowles Loom Works
Sales: $530 million
Employees: 2,300
Stock Exchanges: New York
SICs: 2865 Cyclic Organic Crudes Dyes & Pigments; 2869 Industrial Organic Chemicals, Nec; 3559 Special Industry Machinery, Nec; 2842 Specialty Cleaning Polishing; 2099 Food Preparations, Nec; 3559 Special Industry Machinery, Nec; 2800 Chemicals & Allied Products

Crompton & Knowles Corporation is a medium-sized company whose business is divided into three highly specialized areas: dyemaking, the manufacture and marketing of extrusion equipment and components (for processing of plastics), and the production of flavors, food colorings, and fragrances for the food processing and pharmaceutical industries. Crompton & Knowles is one of the largest dye producers in America for the textile and related industries and the sole supplier of 40 percent of the dyes it makes.

Crompton & Knowles's roots lie in the cotton weaving industry, one of the first enterprises to be mechanized in western Europe in the late eighteenth century. William Crompton was a New England businessman who originated an improved loom, which he began manufacturing and marketing in the town of Worcester, Massachusetts, in 1837. For the next four decades, the Crompton Loom Works was practically without competitors, and it steadily prospered. Toward the end of this exclusive reign, Lucius J. Knowles, another New England businessman, developed an improved version of the textile loom in 1862, whereupon he too established his own company, L. J. Knowles & Bros., in the town of Warren, Massachusetts.

There was no bad blood between the two competitors until 1879, when Knowles decided to move his manufacturing establishment to Crompton's hometown of Worcester. The next eighteen years witnessed fierce rivalry between the two firms, both

of which meanwhile developed many improvements in their respective looms, perhaps because of the intense pressure of competition. Finally, in 1897, the two companies took the surprising but sensible step of merging into the Crompton & Knowles Loom Works. The new company prospered and expanded; by 1907 it had opened offices and warehouses in Philadelphia and in Charlotte, North Carolina. In time, Crompton & Knowles, whose mainstay was the manufacture and marketing of the textile loom, became renowned for the production of multi-color weaving machines, which were exported all over the world. By World War II, the company was one of the largest textile machinery manufacturers in the world.

Meanwhile, the Neversink Dyeing Company, a business that would add an important dimension to the Crompton & Knowles firm in future decades, operated in Reading, Pennsylvania. Founded by Nathan Althouse, this company became one of the biggest textile dyeing facilities in the nation by World War I. Unfortunately, as the war in Europe progressed, the company was increasingly deprived of dyestuffs. To relieve this crisis, the firm began manufacturing its own dyes. By the end of the war, the company had changed so much that it adopted a new name, the Althouse Chemical Company, and thereafter it emphasized research into new and improved dye products for natural textiles as well as for the increasingly popular synthetic fabrics.

The Crompton & Knowles Loom Works continued to produce and sell its famous textile machines until the advent of the World War II, when traditional production gave way to fulfilling military needs. With the return to civilian production in 1945, Crompton & Knowles's work force stood at 3,000, nearly 800 more than the present-day firm with its greater productive capacities and far greater sales revenues. The company continued to manufacture its textile machines well into the early 1950s.

While there was still strong demand for the textile machinery in the early 1950s, it became apparent that the company's future success depended on diversification rather than reliance on only one major commercial product. In 1954 the firm branched off into the dye and chemical business with the purchase of the Althouse Chemical Company. The purchase laid the foundations for the manufacture of dyestuffs, which would eventually become the company's most important enterprise.

Crompton & Knowles continued to manufacture textile weaving machines, and through most of the 1960s the textile machinery division was the company's biggest in terms of sales revenues. However, diversification continued, and other enterprises gradually dwarfed the textile machinery business. The process drastically altered the company's identity and size. In 1956 stockholders changed the name of the company from Crompton & Knowles Loom Works to Crompton & Knowles Corporation; the company ceased manufacturing textile looms altogether by 1981.

Further expansion took place in 1969, when Crompton & Knowles established its first European subsidiary, Crompton & Knowles Tertre, a dye and chemical company in Belgium; this was followed in 1971 with the acquisition from Ciba Chemical & Dyestuff Company of Intracolor, another dye and chemical enterprise that further strengthened Crompton & Knowles's dye manufacturing base. Seven years later, the Harshaw Chemical Company's dye business was bought up in Lowell, North Carolina.

When the Du Pont Company exited the dye business in 1979, Crompton & Knowles was waiting eagerly in the wings to purchase its holdings, which included the high-quality Sevron dye products. The range of Crompton & Knowles's dyestuffs expanded significantly. Two years later, the company bought the rights from the Du Pont company to manufacture Dybln dyes for polyester and cotton textiles. Crompton & Knowles acquired and absorbed other dye and chemical businesses, becoming in the process a leader in the domestic dye business.

The company's dye and chemical business had expanded so much, that by the early 1980s, Crompton & Knowles supplied dyes and chemicals to a variety of industries including paper, leather, printing ink, and heat transfer printing establishments, in addition to the textile and garment industry.

Over the years, dye and chemical operations became the company's biggest division and its mainstay. In 1960, the company diversified further into the manufacture of flavors, food colorings, and fragrances for the food processing and drug industries, the company's second major operation. In that year, Crompton & Knowles acquired the Bates Chemical Company, founded in 1923 when the federal government first certified food colorings. Crompton & Knowles expanded even further in this direction when it acquired the American Flavor & Fragrance Company in 1980. Still, the firm was not considered a major player in the flavor/fragrance market until 1988, the year it acquired the Ingredients Technology Corp. of Pelhem, New York, as a major subsidiary.

A third significant operation was added to the company in 1961 with the purchase of the Davis-Standard Company, a major manufacturer of plastic processing, or extrusion, machinery and systems, marking the origins of present-day Crompton & Knowles's multi-million dollar extrusion machinery business. This purchase added a great variety of products to Crompton & Knowles's inventory. Within two decades, the company had not only survived but altered its identity significantly, expanding from the production of only one major commercial product, to hundreds of diverse products and three principal operations.

By the mid-1980s, Crompton & Knowles was the last remaining U.S. dye producer and marketer, one of the largest as well, marketing its products to Europe, Latin America, and Asia. It was also a leading provider of dyes to the clothing and hosiery businesses in North America. How and why this company succeeded—increasing sales revenues 15 percent during the worst year of the recession in the early 1990s—had much to do with the dynamic leadership of its president and CEO Vincent Calarco. When he came on board in 1985, the company had not fully recovered from the economic downturn of the early 1980s. Calarco expanded the company's business by buying up dye operations that large companies, such as Du Pont and Allied Chemical, were unloading. By the early 1990s, Crompton & Knowles had a healthy eight percent share of the worldwide market in dye products, and had strengthened its own dye business, especially in carpeting and clothing. Moreover, Crompton & Knowles became the sole producer of at least 40

percent of its own dye products, making it the most influential dyestuff producer and marketer in North America. Under Calarco's management, the company's specialty process equipment and controls division gradually moved out of the cable business and into the far more lucrative medical tubing, food packaging, and blow molding equipment fields, which were ignored or underestimated by bigger competitors. Calarco also led Crompton & Knowles further into international business endeavors.

In the early 1990s, 75 percent of Crompton & Knowles's sales came from its specialty chemicals division. As a leading manufacturer of dyestuffs in North America, the company furnished dyes to both the textile and industrial markets. The company's wide range of industrial dyes and chemicals were used for paper and leather products including shoes and luggage. Its textile dyes and chemicals were used in knit and woven clothing, carpets, draperies, and automotive furnishings, including seat belts. Company technicians and specialists produced a variety of chemical intermediates (essential to the making of dyes) for the textile industry as well as a steady stream of artificial flavor, color, and fragrance ingredients to the food and drug industries, a small but growing business that was part of the specialty chemicals division. Flavor substances, including seasonings, were marketed to the food processing and beverage industries, and increasingly to the pharmaceutical industry as well, especially for coated tablets and flavored medicines. Fragrance formulas were in great demand by the household products industry, most often for floor care and cleaning products.

Approximately one quarter of Crompton & Knowles's sales derived from the specialty process equipment and controls division. This division manufactured and marketed a variety of extrusion machines and systems and blow molding equipment (usually attached to extruders), which processed plastic products such as sheeting for cars, appliances, sports equipment, and film. Specially designed extrusion systems recycled plastics, a technology that was found to be increasingly in demand by companies and communities alike.

On the eve of the twenty-first century, Crompton & Knowles had evolved a significant international business. The acquisition in 1969 of a subsidiary in Tertre, Belgium (present-day Crompton & Knowles Europe SA) was the company's first step toward major overseas expansion and penetration of the European market. In 1991 the company purchased ICI Colours in Oissel, France, from a major British chemical firm. In one stroke, this acquisition doubled Crompton & Knowles's productive capacity in Europe, making the company a major player in the European dye and chemical markets. In the 1990s, worldwide sales of Crompton & Knowles's products in the Latin America, Europe, and Asia reached record levels, constituting approximately one third of sales revenues.

By the early 1990s, the U.S. dyestuff market had become a $1 billion industry. Only a handful of dye manufacturers produced over 50 percent of the world's dyes, and competition was intense. With its increasing international presence and diverse businesses, Crompton & Knowles was poised to become a global leader in the dye and chemicals fields.

Principal Subsidiaries: Crompton & Knowles Europe SA (Belgium); Crompton & Knowles France SA (France); Ingredient Technology Corp.

Further Reading:

"C & K Operation Net Up 21% in Quarter," *Daily News Record,* January 29, 1993, p. 10.
Labate, John, "Crompton & Knowles," *Fortune,* July 12, 1993, p. 100.
Morris, Kathleen, "Crompton & Knowles: Playing the Niches in Slumping Markets," *Financial World,* November 12, 1991, p. 16.

Reingold, Jennifer, "Niche Rich: Crompton & Knowles Hunts for Treasure in Staid Markets—and Strikes Gold," *Financial World,* June 22, 1993, p. 56.
"Bright Acid Dyes," *Textile World,* March, 1992, p. 64.
"Crompton & Knowles Corp. to Purchase a Unit of Imperial Chemical Industries PLC," *Wall Street Journal,* May 11, 1992, p. B3.
"Crompton & Knowles Corp.," *Wall Street Journal,* December 16, 1992, p. C11.

—Sina Dubovoj

Crystal Brands, Inc.

Crystal Brands Road
Southport, Connecticut 06490
U.S.A.
(203) 254-6200
Fax: (203) 254-6252

Public Company
Incorporated: 1970
Employees: 4,900
Sales: $589 million
Stock Exchanges: New York
SICs: 2329 Men's and Boys' Clothing Nec; 2339 Women's,
   Misses', and Junior's Outerwear Nec; 5611 Men's and
   Boys' Clothing and Accessory Stores; 5621 Women's
   Clothing Stores

Crystal Brands, Inc., manufactures and merchandises sports-wear, costume jewelry, and accessories under some of the industry's best-known brand names, including Gant, Izod, Evan-Picone, Monet, and Trifari. Crystal Brands started operations November 1, 1985, after having been divested from General Mills. It began its life with a handful of well-known brand names, the most recognized being Izod/Lacoste, which General Mills had acquired in 1968.

The Lacoste shirt was first marketed in the United States by David Crystal, Inc. The shirt and its distinctive "alligator" emblem (really a crocodile) was named after the French tennis player Jean Rene Lacoste, who, during the 1920s, earned the nickname "le crocodile," connoting as much his distinctive profile as his style of play. Lacoste broke with tradition by playing in short-sleeved knit shirts instead of then-customary dress-shirts. He started to market his shirts with a crocodile emblem embroidered over the left breast, and in 1950 Lacoste entered the U.S. market by licensing his all-cotton shirts to David Crystal, Inc., a New York-based manufacturer of dresses, suits, and other apparel marketed under a variety of names, including Izod. The shirts were initially available only in white; after several years, in an attempt to broaden the shirts' appeal beyond the tennis court, colors were introduced. Further, the company linked the Lacoste name with its own Izod brand to give it an air of class and style. (The name Izod originally belonged to a British tailor whose clients included the royal family, and who eventually sold his name and thus the right to

use the phrase "By Appointment—Shirtmaker to the King" to David Crystal, Inc.) In 1968, to make the garment easier to care for and to further widen its market, the company started producing the shirt in a double-knit fabric of dacron polyester using a pique stitch. That year the company was bought by General Mills. Two years later Crystal Brands, Inc., was incorporated, its operations part of various divisions and subsidiaries of General Mills.

The Lacoste shirt surged in popularity in the late 1970s with the advent of the "preppy" look. Sales rose from 1979, and its peak year was 1982, when sales hit $450 million. Quickly, however, the shirt became the victim of its own success. General Mills, using the "commodity" approach that it used with cereal, proceeded to saturate the market with merchandise. The market was flooded with both officially licensed products and low-priced knockoffs available at street vendors' stalls and discount outlets. The brand invariably lost its upscale cachet, and combined with the rapid waning of the "preppy" look, sales and profits began to fall precipitously. By 1984, problems with the apparel division—known as the General Mills Fashion Group—contributed to the end of General Mills 22-year run of earnings increases. The company decided to jettison the Fashion Group, which had cost the company $80 million, as well as its also-struggling toy division (which became Kenner Parker Toys, Inc.).

Shares of Crystal Brands, Inc., began trading on the New York Stock Exchange on November 1, 1985. The following week holders of General Mills stock received one share of Crystal Brands stock for every five General Mills shares they owned.

Crystal Brands was to be headed by Richard Kral, who had joined General Mills several years earlier after having served for 22 years at the well-regarded apparel manufacturer Warnaco, Inc. Kral recruited other Warnaco veterans to join him. Crystal started with several established brand names in addition to Izod/Lacoste. Monet, the jewelry company acquired by General Mills in 1968, was seen as the company's recession-proof bright spot, making up almost half of all department store costume jewelry sales. Ship 'n Shore apparel, a well-known name with a lackluster image, survived by providing blouses to private labels; it accounted for about a quarter of sales. Crystal also provided clothing to Sears Roebuck & Co. and J.C. Penney Co.

General Mills handed Crystal Brands not only brand-name products with strong name recognition, however. Crystal also carried over high-selling, general, and administrative expenses, which in 1986 were 30.5 percent of sales. Crystal owned and leased a series of manufacturing plants and distribution facilities, many established at the peak of Izod/Lacoste brand's popularity, when General Mills had increased production capacity as well as support staff. Crystal also inherited a top-heavy management structure, partly created to sustain the high-growth levels of 1979–1982 and partly a legacy of General Mills' bureaucracy, where decisions were made by committee. This system is perhaps well suited to the slow-moving food business, but it is clumsy in the fast-changing fashion market. Crystal lost $43.4 million in fiscal 1985.

Kral quickly set out to both streamline management to make Crystal more responsive to the market and to find profitability at reduced sales levels. The previously autonomous Izod/Lacoste, Monet, and Ship 'n Shore lines were brought under tighter control. Inventory was cut and drastic cost-reduction measures were taken. Kral also tried to get a handle on administrative costs and to this end moved company headquarters from its expensive New York City offices to Southport, Connecticut, in 1986.

Turning around the fortunes of Izod/Lacoste, which accounted for about half of sales, was clearly a priority. Crystal decided to try to increase the brand's sales by reestablishing the aura of exclusivity that was responsible for so much of its previous success (as well as the success of its chief rival, Polo by Ralph Lauren) and that had subsequently been eroded by overselling. To do this, the company trimmed its distributors list, favoring the better department stores and specialty stores, and eliminating mass merchants. To gain retail space, the product line was expanded to include jackets, trousers, and swimwear, all adorned with the alligator logo. To win and sustain the consumer's attention, the company started to showcase the apparel at in-store "shops," spaces set aside within a retailer that featured the Izod and Izod/Lacoste line exclusively. The shirt tried to position itself between Ralph Lauren's Polo and private labels.

Crystal also set out to increase earnings by adding to its roster of well-established labels. In April 1988 Crystal bought the jewelry merchandiser Trifari, Krussman & Fishel, Inc., for $66 million. Trifari's line of jewelry featured color and contemporary styling, and along with the Trifari brand came the popular Marvella line of pearl costume jewelry. These lines complemented Monet's, which emphasized classic styling and was known for its "look of the real." With this acquisition Crystal became the leading manufacturer and marketer of quality costume jewelry.

In December of that year Crystal acquired privately owned Palm Beach Holdings for $95 million, and with it an impressive list of names, including Evan-Picone, John Weitz, Polo by Ralph Lauren for Boys, Calvin, and Palm Beach. With this acquisition Crystal entered the tailored clothing and formal wear markets, a move analysts saw as a defensive maneuver taken to shake off a rumored takeover attempt. Palm Beach, which had sales of $404.5 million in 1987, doubled Crystal's revenues.

Izod/Lacoste seemed to briefly revive, and the in-store shops (there were 47 by 1988) helped increase sales. The Gant brand of men's and boys' sportswear, using the same in-store shop concept, performed well, as did the Salty Dog label, a line of casual, relaxed sportswear developed in 1985 to appeal to a younger market. The Evan-Picone line was redefined using the same "quality over quantity" approach that appeared to be working for Izod/Lacoste.

Crystal stock, which had started trading in 1985 at around $19, hit a peak in 1989 at $37 a share. Sales reached $857.2 million and earnings achieved their high of $28.9 million in 1990, but Crystal's good fortune proved to be short-lived. Crystal had undertaken its aggressive and costly expansion, which had been financed with debt, just as the apparel market and the economy as a whole began to weaken in 1989. By 1991 reorganization was necessary, and in July of that year Crystal announced a $49.9 million restructuring. It set about consolidating facilities, shuttering unprofitable lines (it had already divested its Ship 'n Shore line in January of the previous year), selling or leasing office space, and cutting staff.

Along with these moves, Crystal again shifted its marketing strategy for Izod/Lacoste. Industry analysts estimated that shirt sales in 1990 were between $125 and $150 million (not including sales from its outlet stores), and, in an attempt to increase volume, Crystal decided to change the focus from prestige to value. The names Izod and Lacoste were separated, creating an alligator-less knit shirt emblazoned with the name Izod, which was to sell for about 30 percent less than the traditional version (which sold for $42.50 and was to be labeled Chemise Lacoste). These attempts at mass-merchandising made it plain that Crystal was trying to find a place in the market for its knit shirt. In retrospect it was seen that Crystal had tried to recreate Izod/Lacoste's upscale appeal just as the wider market had indeed turned the product into a "commodity" item, with no-name varieties widely available for much less (at the time, fully 30 percent were sold through discount outlets). With the slowdown of the economy, consumers sought value and were much less impressed with designer names than they had been in the 1980s.

Crystal sought to catch up with the cost-conscious consumer by increasing quality for price points, especially in the Gant and Salty Dog labels. The company's problems were exacerbated by a sharp downturn in jewelry sales, which historically did well in recessions as consumers increasingly looked to costume jewelry rather than their more expensive counterparts. Furthermore, the company had delivery problems that antagonized retailers. Crystal lost $71.4 million in 1991 on sales of $862.9 million.

The recession, as well as a decrease in white-collar jobs and a trend to more relaxed office wear, severely affected men's tailored clothing sales. In April 1992 Plaid Holdings Corp. announced that it intended to buy Crystal's Palm Beach and Calvin Clothing divisions. Crystal thus exited the men's and boys' tailored clothing and formal wear business less than five years after it had entered it. The company gained $55 million; $40 million was used to pay down debt and $15 million was used for working capital purposes. The agreement was signed in October.

The Palm Beach sale couldn't stop the flow of red ink, however. Although it had been able to sign a new agreement with lenders in February, Crystal could not cover expenses. Unable to find a lender to extend its credit line, Crystal announced in July that it was selling its 50 percent interest in Lacoste Alligator S.A. to the other 50 percent owner, Sporloisirs S.A., thus ending its exclusive license to make and market alligator-labeled products in the United States, Canada, and the Caribbean as of June 1993. Sporloisirs S.A. was a unit of Chemise Lacoste, the French company that had been originally founded to market the shirts. Crystal was to gain $31.5 million in the transaction, $30 million of which was to be paid in cash. Crystal continued to own the Izod trademark, however.

The company's financial position worsened, and in August it suspended its cash dividend. In September Crystal hired a firm that specialized in corporate turnarounds to aid in reorganization. In November Richard Kral resigned as chairman and chief executive officer. Upon news of his resignation Crystal stock closed up 12.5 cents, reaching $2.625. Wall Street was not optimistic about Crystal's prospects.

By year's end Crystal entered into a new credit agreement, which carried heavy terms, with virtually all the company's assets to be used as collateral. Cost-reduction programs were implemented companywide, and new management was brought in at all levels. In April 1993 Crystal announced that it was organizing the three jewelry companies—Monet, Trifari, and Marvella—by combining them.

Final sales results for 1992 were $589 million, and losses totaled $75.3 million. The company stated that it did not have enough capital to cover expenses and that additional sell-offs of businesses or assets would perhaps be necessary to meet its credit agreements.

Principal Subsidiaries: Crystal Apparel, Inc.; Crystal Brands Ltd. (Hong Kong); Empire Textile Corp.; Five Star Products, Inc.

Further Reading:

Agins, Terry, "Izod Lacoste Gets Restyled and Repriced," *Wall Street Journal,* July 22, 1991, p. Bl.

"The Alligator Returns After Being Left for Dead," *Adweek's Marketing Week,* January 2, 1989, p. 44.

Crystal Brands, Inc., Annual Report, Southport, CT: Crystal Brands, Inc., 1991.

The Crystal Brands Story, Southport, CT: Crystal Brands, Inc.

Gellers, Stan, "Clothing Industry Wonders: Who's Next?" *Daily News Record,* April 23, 1992, p. 1.

Gerlin, Andrea, "Crystal Brands Plans to Sell Stake in Lacoste Alligator," *Wall Street Journal,* July 14, 1992, p. B7.

Houston, Patrick, and Mary J. Pitzer, "Can the General Mills Babies Make It on Their Own?," *Business Week,* November 18, 1985.

Lebow, Joan, "Alligator's New Turf Is Crystal Clear," *Advertising Age,* March 9, 1987, p. 74.

Marcial, Gene G., "Crystal Is Shining Even Brighter Now," *Business Week,* December 12, 1988.

Meadus, Andrea, "Crystal's Jewelry Units Merge," *Women's Wear Daily,* April 9, 1993, p. 9.

"Resignation at Crystal," *Wall Street Journal,* November 5, 1992, p. B16.

Sager, Elizabeth, "Tracking the Alligator," *Barron's,* September 29, 1986.

—C. L. Collins

Darigold, Inc.

635 Elliot Avenue West
P.O. Box 79007
Seattle, Washington 98119
U.S.A.
(206) 284-7220
Fax: (206) 281-3456

Private Company
Incorporated: 1918 as United Dairymen's Association
Employees: 1,700
Sales: $881 million
SICs: 2021 Creamery Butter; 2022 Cheese—Natural &
    Processed; 2023 Dry, Condensed & Evaporated Dairy
    Products; 5143 Dairy Products Except Dried or Canned;
    5451 Dairy Products Stores

Darigold, Inc. is the processing and marketing arm for a cooperative of dairy farmers, known as Darigold Farms, in Washington, Oregon, California, and Idaho. Through Darigold, Inc.'s 12 processing facilities and 19 sales and distribution branches, the milk produced by Darigold Farms' 1,300 members is manufactured into over 1,500 dairy and related products. Darigold, Inc. operates as a 99 percent owned subsidiary of Darigold Farms, while Dairy Export Company, Inc., which manages seven retail farm stores in Washington, Oregon, and Idaho, functions as a wholly owned subsidiary of Darigold, Inc. These three components form what is informally known as the Darigold organization. As the second largest privately held company in Washington and the fifth largest dairy cooperative in the United States, the Darigold organization has provided milk, butter, cheese, and other dairy products to generations of Pacific Northwest residents.

The predecessor of Darigold, Inc., the United Dairymen's Association (UDA), was formed in 1918 in an attempt to address some of the difficulties inherent in the industry. One of the challenges facing the dairy industry involved maintaining an equilibrium between supply and demand. Although cows produced milk at a consistent rate, the dairy market was not as predictable. When demand declined, dairy farmers were often saddled with surplus milk. With nowhere to sell the excess milk once the market was sated, the dairy farmer's only option was to wait for demand to increase. Consequently, five dairy cooperatives in the Pacific Northwest banded together to form the UDA.

In the period between the establishment of Washington's first creamery in 1880 and the creation of the UDA, the dairy industry had grown dramatically. By 1909, Washington was the nation's third largest producer of condensed milk and ranked 13th and 15th in the production of butter and cheese, respectively, outpacing the indigenous demand. This overabundance of milk accorded the creameries with an appreciable advantage over the dairy farmers. Able to adjust the amount of milk they purchased to the shifting needs of their customers and generally dictate the price they paid for the milk from the dairy farmers, the creameries control over the fate of independent dairy farmers impelled some of the farmers by the turn of the century to form dairy cooperatives, such as the UDA, to more effectively market their milk. Furthermore, in 1918, the situation was exacerbated by the continuing growth of the dairy industry and the cyclicality of the dairy market.

The UDA, in its effort to serve as a marketing federation for the cooperatives, hired the services of Seattle food broker Umberto M. Dickey to develop distant markets in which UDA members could sell their dairy products. The relationship between Dickey and the UDA would prove to be of great significance in the legacy of the Darigold name. In 1925, at a summer picnic for UDA affiliated members, a prize was offered for the best suggestion of a brand name for the cooperative's dairy products. The name Darigold was selected as the winner and, by the following year, Dickey, who owned Consolidated Dairy Products Company (CDP), had registered his use of the Darigold trademark in the United States and six other countries in Europe, North America, and Asia. In 1930, Dickey sold CDP to his customers, the dairy farmers of the UDA. Established as a wholly owned subsidiary, the addition of CDP, which would continue to be led by Dickey until 1939, provided members with a new processing and marketing operation and extended the Darigold trademark to all UDA affiliates.

A year before Dickey sold his company to the UDA, he had constructed a new processing plant and purchased American Creamery and Bradner & Co and Mutual Creamery Company. Prior to the addition of the two creameries and the completion of the plant, a $300,000 building that could manufacture two million pounds of butter a year, CDP was strictly a jobbing concern, purchasing dairy products from other manufacturers and then selling them to retailers. The addition of the processing plant, however, enabled the company, for the first time, to provide distribution, processing, and marketing services to the 12,500 farms that shipped their products to CDP.

During the decade that followed the acquisition of CDP, the UDA expanded its membership and territory in its perpetual drive to give dairy farmers additional markets to sell their milk and dairy products. While creameries still held a decided advantage against the dairy farmers, the expansion during the 1930s bolstered the farmer's bargaining power. By the beginning of World War II, the UDA represented approximately 40 independent groups of dairy farmers, which included roughly 40,000 small dairy farm members throughout Washington, Oregon, Idaho, and Montana. The development of these ancillary markets would soon be required to support the prodigious increase in dairy production during the war. Washington's total herd during these years rose to an unprecedented high of 331,000, a record that would stand for decades to follow when the average number of cows ranged between 200,000 and 240,000.

Russell J. Waltz, who had been instrumental in CDP's expansion during the 1930s as a sales manger and general manager, succeeded Dickey as president of CDP in 1939, a position he would hold for the next 20 years. Under his stewardship, CDP made significant advances during the 1950s, acquiring companies both in California and abroad. In 1950, a butter packaging and distribution facility was opened in Los Angeles that also distributed cheese and dry milk under the Darigold label. Six years later, CDP solidified its presence in southern California, constructing an office and warehouse building in Los Angeles that provided storage, cutting, and packaging facilities for cheese and butter products. CDP also opened a branch in San Jose, California to sell cheese and butter. During this time, CDP tapped into a growing trend in the dairy industry by making several acquisitions in Washington. After 1950, ice cream and frozen dairy products supplanted butter as the principal use of fluid whole milk in the manufacturing of dairy products. In order to capture this new market, CDP, in 1952, purchased three dairy plants, Alpine Dairy & Ice Cream Co., Apex Dairy, and Issaquah Creamery Co. Financed by member dairy farmers, who now numbered 50,000, the new dairy plants added cottage cheese and ice cream to CDP's product line, representing the first time these two products were sold under the Darigold name. In 1957, CDP entered the international dairy market by acquiring an evaporated and condensed milk production facility in the Philippines.

By the end of the 1950s, the markets in which northwest dairy farmers could sell their milk had broadened considerably through the concerted efforts of the UDA and CDP. No longer confined to supplying local markets or overly dependent upon creameries to purchase their milk, the member dairy farmers now could rely on markets as far away as Asia to sell their dairy products. As the marketing and processing organization for the farmers, CDP also prospered. While in 1928, a year before it constructed its processing plant, CDP had posted sales of $7 million, by 1959, at the end of Waltz's tenure as president, revenues had climbed to $53 million.

E. E. Pedersen, a Darigold employee since 1929, replaced Waltz as president in 1959. While the company headed into the 1960s with new leadership and a solid position in the regional dairy industry, the industry was undergoing several changes that would transform the way in which CDP operated in the future. CDP's regional presence would be called upon to help the dairy farmers keep pace with the changing times, as the dairy industry evolved from a consortium of local organizations to larger, regional organizations. Several factors led to this shift, the first of which was the decline in popularity of home milk delivery. Large supermarkets began to attract more customers, chipping away at home delivery service, and, consequently, the ways in which milk was retailed needed updating. Another significant change occurred in the processing plants themselves, as improvements in processing technology allowed the dairy plants to package and process a greater amount of products in a shorter time. Furthermore, improvements in the interstate highway system quickened the delivery time of dairy products and enabled larger container trucks to increase the size of shipments they hauled. Responding to such changes in the dairy market, CDP

enlarged and modernized its fluid milk processing plant in Seattle in 1962, which decades later would still stand as the largest fluid milk plant in the Pacific Northwest.

CDP's new fluid milk plant also served new cooperatives that were being formed in the industry. In 1961, eight UDA cooperatives involved specifically in the Seattle fluid milk market merged to form Northwest Dairymen's Association (NDA), which would years later become Darigold Farms. Associations similar to the NDA were formed throughout the Pacific Northwest during this period; many of these new associations would later join the Darigold organization. In 1966, five dairy cooperatives in Oregon and southern Washington joined Mayflower Farms, which 15 years later would merge with the NDA. In 1968, three cooperatives in southwestern Idaho united to form Dairymen's Creamery Association, which would eventually merge into the Darigold organization.

In 1971, Pedersen's 12 year tenure at CDP came to a close. His replacement, Louis Arrigoni, who would lead CDP for the next 19 years, had figured prominently in CDP's expansion during the 1950s, especially in the establishment of the plants in Los Angeles and Manilla, and had also been a key contributor in the modernization of the fluid milk plant. During Arrigoni's first decade of leadership, UDA cooperatives continued to consolidate, bracing themselves against the deleterious economic conditions of the 1970s. Farm prices plummeted during the early and mid-1970s, prompting Congress to increase the price the government paid for surplus dairy products, which resulted in a dramatic increase in production, particularly in the West. As they had so often done in the past, dairy farmers and the cooperatives to which they belonged reacted to the unsettling conditions by joining together. By the end of the decade, the Pacific Northwest dairy industry was comprised of several large dairy associations, the result of roughly 80 years of cooperatives banding together.

In 1981, Mayflower Farms, representing dairy cooperatives in Oregon, merged with the NDA, making the NDA a genuine, regional cooperative. As such, the NDA began playing a much larger role in the industry, and, consequently, diminishing the role of the UDA as the preeminent cooperative. Three years later, the Darigold name, which had adorned many of the dairy products manufactured in the Pacific Northwest since 1926, was adopted as the official name of CDP. Renamed Darigold, Inc., the processing, sales, and marketing organization continued to work in concert with the NDA. As part of this effort to reinforce the dairy farmer's ownership of the Darigold brand, the NDA, in 1989, changed its name to Darigold Farms, finally bringing the Darigold brand name and the Darigold dairy farmers together officially.

As Darigold, Inc. and Darigold Farms entered the 1990s, they represented the largest agricultural cooperative in Washington. With revenues of $725 million in 1990, Darigold, Inc. processed and marketed dairy products for Darigold Farm's 1,150 dairy farmers. Of these revenues, 40 percent were generated from the sale of packaged milk products sold under the Darigold label, while 20 percent were garnered from bulk sales to other dairy processors.

The remaining 40 percent of the organization's revenues resulted from the sale of dairy commodities, including powdered milk, butter, cheese, and whey. This portion of Darigold's business suffered sluggish sales during the economic recession of the early 1990s, cutting into the organization's earnings. Although sales increased from $642 million in 1989 to $725 million in 1990, earnings dropped from $17.2 million to $11.9 million. To halt this slide in earnings, Darigold's new president Wesley E. Eckert, who had managed the organization's plant in the Philippines during the late 1960s and early 1970s, began to look toward acquisitions to diversify the cooperative's markets.

In 1990, Darigold made an offer to purchase Washington Cheese Co., but the two parties were never able to agree on terms, and the offer was dropped. Later in the year, Darigold began construction of a $22 million milk processing plant, which, when completed, processed over two million pounds of milk a day into various dry milk products. The following year, Idaho's largest dairy cooperative, Dairymen's Creamery Association, created during the consolidation of cooperatives in the 1960s, merged with Darigold Farms, boosting its membership to 1,400 dairy farmers.

As Darigold planned for the future, the 1995 Farm Bill loomed as a significant issue. The Farm Bills of 1985 and 1990 lowered the federal support price of milk, and Darigold expected the 1995 bill to further reduce government assistance. The antici-pated removal of federally-funded agricultural programs could forestall the cooperative's recovery from the economic recession of the early 1990s; earnings continued to drop in 1993. Nevertheless, Darigold's longevity in the volatile dairy industry—its decades of experience in responding to change—should serve the company well should it face further challenges in the future.

Principal Subsidiaries: Dairy Export Company, Inc.

Further Reading:

"Alpine Dairy Group May Sell to Consolidated," *The Seattle Times,* May 20, 1952, p. 29.

Darigold Farms Annual Report, Seattle: Darigold Farms, 1993.

Denne, Lorianne, "Darigold Plans for Dairy Farming's Unsure Future," *Puget Sound Business Journal,* November 19, 1990, pp. 9–10, 30.

"Seattle Dairy Firm to Expand in California," *The Seattle Times,* June 17, 1956, p. 55.

Stewart, Betty, "A Factory That Makes 12,500 Farmers Arise at 4 A.M.," *The Seattle Times,* December 1, 1929, p. 9.

"U.M. Dickey Business Leader, Dies," *The Seattle Times,* October 26, 1959, p. 31.

"Waltz Retires as President of Dairy Firm," *The Seattle Times,* February 22, 1959, p. 15.

—Jeffrey L. Covell

Day & Zimmermann Inc.

1818 Market St.
Philadelphia, Pennsylvania 19103
U.S.A.
(215) 299-8000
Fax: (215) 975-6806

Private Company
Incorporated: 1916
Employees: 12,500
Sales: $600 million
SICs: 8711 Engineering Services; 8741 Management
    Services; 8712 Architectural Services; 8742 Management
    Consulting Services

Day & Zimmermann Inc., among the nation's 300 largest privately owned firms, oversees a wide variety of engineering and management projects through its three divisions: engineering and construction, defense systems, and management services. D & Z, Inc., the 2,500-employee engineering and construction group, served as construction manager for dozens of city airports around the country, built a plant for Pepperidge Farms Inc., built and operated a recycling plant in New Jersey, and managed construction of the Alamodome sports complex in San Antonio, Texas. The 5,000-employee management services group provided security personnel for nuclear plants, federal installations, and large companies, including General Electric, the Philadelphia Power Com.'s nuclear power plants, and Los Alamos National Laboratory in New Mexico. Day & Zimmermann's defense systems group, with 4,500 employees, ranked among the nation's 100 largest U.S. military contractors, operating munitions plants for the military and providing millions of tons of ammunition annually. This division provided about 40 percent of the company's revenues.

Day & Zimmermann traces its ancestry back to two companies: Dodge and Day, founded in 1901, and H.L. Yoh Company, founded in 1940. In 1901, two young men just out of college joined forces to start their own company. Charles Day, an electrical engineer, and Kern Dodge, a mechanical engineer, formed Dodge & Day and were hired to modernize machine tool drives for Link-Belt Engineering Company of Philadelphia, Pennsylvania. The following year, Jeansville Iron Works hired the young firm to help update its facilities by converting belt-driven machine tools to motor driven ones, designing power

plant steam heating and electrical systems, and supervising installation of machine foundations and equipment. In 1903, Dodge & Day won a contract from Westinghouse Electric and Manufacturing Company to evaluate new equipment. In 1905, Dodge & Day added an architectural department and construction force. By the following year, the firm needed more work space and moved from its offices at the Link-Belt Company to facilities in downtown Philadelphia.

The company continued to grow, expanding its services to include electric railway engineering and construction and expanding its territory to include North Carolina as well as its home base of Pennsylvania. John Zimmermann, a former classmate of Day, joined the firm in 1907, bringing his expertise in finance and operations, and, in 1910, the firm's name was changed to Dodge, Day & Zimmermann. The company's long history of contracting services to the U.S. government began during this time, when the government hired the company to evaluate efficiency at naval yards. In 1912, Dodge resigned, and the company's name was again changed, to Day & Zimmermann, under which it was incorporated in 1916.

During the 1920s, as U.S. involvement in World War I became inevitable, Day & Zimmermann's services were in demand to help companies convert their facilities to wartime production. Charles Day also became a member of the Council of National Defense, which was formed to advise the government on the mobilization of U.S. resources in the event of war. The United States entered World War I in April 1917, and the following year Day & Zimmermann took over design, engineering, and construction supervision of the army's giant quartermaster terminal in Philadelphia.

Another project Day & Zimmerman had taken on in Philadelphia during this time had to be postponed until the end of the war. The city had hired the firm to build the 685-foot Bensalem Bridge, an important part of the city's proposed traffic network. The war interrupted construction, and by the time construction was resumed, inflation had doubled the cost of labor and materials. Nevertheless, Day & Zimmermann fulfilled the terms of its original contract, completing construction and absorbing immense losses that nearly bankrupted the company. The company eventually recovered and continued to accept new work from the city; the Day & Zimmerman name appeared on many bond issues proposed by the city for engineering and construction projects.

In the late 1920s, Day & Zimmermann formed Penn Central Light & Power and the Municipal Service Company as umbrella organizations under which to operate electric utilities and rail transportation services in the eastern part of the country. For a short time, Day & Zimmermann became a subsidiary company when John Zimmermann became president of United Gas Improvement Company, the state's largest utility company, bringing Day & Zimmerman under its umbrella. This lasted only a year, however. In 1928, W. Findlay Downs and Nicholas Roosevelt bought Day & Zimmermann back from UGI and reestablished it as an independent, privately-held company offering consulting, engineering, and management services.

Day & Zimmermann weathered the 1929 stock market crash and the Depression that followed, to a large extent because of its involvement in utility projects, including construction of electric transmission lines to support rural electrification following the completion of Boulder Dam.

By the late 1930s, the U.S. economy was recovering, and the threat of another world war was imminent. Day & Zimmermann designed and built a 1.5 million square foot aluminum reclamation area in Cressona, Pennsylvania, which it would operate during World War II to produce artillery for the U.S. Navy. Other wartime contracts included design and construction of the Iowa Ordinance Plant, which was built in a record 11 months and operated by Day & Zimmermann during the war years. During peak production years during the war, the company employed 18,000 men and women.

In 1951, the company began its operation of the Lone Star Army Ammunition Plant in Texarkana, Texas. The plant encompassed 16,000 acres, contained more than 900 buildings, and was serviced by 160 miles of roads, 40 miles of railroad, 90 miles of electrical distribution service, 45 miles of water mains, and 25 miles of sewers. Day & Zimmermann continued to operate the plant for over 40 years, and during this time, in 1965, the plant was awarded a presidential citation for outstanding contribution to greater economy and improvement in operations.

During the 1950s, Day & Zimmermann undertook projects all over the country and abroad, including a feasibility study of Lincoln Center in New York and a survey of electrical power requirements in the Republic of Vietnam. By the end of the decade, Day & Zimmermann was operating four major departments: reports, industrial engineering, management service, and engineering design and construction.

In 1961, Day & Zimmerman was acquired by the engineering firm of H.L. Yoh Company for about $2.5 million, creating one of the largest technical firms of its kind in the United States with 3,300 employees. The H.L. Yoh Company was founded in 1940 by Harold L. Yoh for the purpose of war production and training. Yoh was the son of Ohio farmers whose ancestors had emigrated from Holland in the 1700s. Upon graduation from the Wharton School in 1929, he became a partner in a tool-designing firm. After 11 years, he formed the company that bore his name, and, largely because of his determination, the firm grew quickly. By 1953, the engineering division employed more than 500 engineers, draftspeople, architects, and industrial planners.

Upon acquiring Day & Zimmerman, Yoh decided to retain the name of the larger company, with H.L. Yoh Company becoming a subsidiary. In the four years following Yoh's acquisition, the company more than doubled in size, employing more than 8,000 people involved in evaluation, planning, engineering, construction, ordnance development, and management. Day & Zimmermann continued to do substantial work for the U.S. military. In 1967, at the request of the Navy, the company provided engineering, procurement, and construction services for two airfields in Thailand to support U.S. operations in southeast Asia. The next year, the company completed modernization projects at the Philadelphia and Portsmouth naval shipyards.

The 1970s brought further expansion. Day & Zimmermann opened the Kansas Division to operate the Army's munitions plant in that state. Moreover, the company acquired Cole*Layer*Trumble Company, one of the largest mass appraisal companies, and MDC, which became part of Day & Zimmermann's infrastructure services division. Also during this time, Day & Zimmermann was hired as the construction inspector for the $50-million Veterans' Stadium complex in Philadelphia.

Further projects included conducting a property valuation of the entire railroad system of Penn Central Transportation Company, when that rail company declared bankruptcy; the project, which amounted to a $2.1 billion valuation, was ongoing until the early 1980s. Under contract for the U.S. Railway Association, Day & Zimmerman developed a system plan for the government-sponsored ConRail. After serving as project manager for the new airport terminal in Charlotte, North Carolina, the company played a key role as master contractor in the three-year modernization program for the U.S. Postal Service and supervised more than 300 architectural and engineering firms throughout the eastern region of the postal system.

The 1970s also brought a change of ownership. Yoh Sr., who had run Day & Zimmermann since its acquisition in 1961, retired and sold the company to his son, Harold L. "Spike" Yoh, Jr.—who had worked with his father since 1958—and five other executives who offered $16 million for the company, outbidding two other investor groups. Upon retirement from Day & Zimmerman, the senior Yoh moved to Florida, where he bought a restaurant; he died in 1976, a year after selling Day & Zimmerman.

Growth through acquisition and internal expansion continued into the 1980s. In a joint venture with the Frank E. Basil Company, the Day & Zimmermann/Basil Corporation began operating the Hawthorne Plant, an army facility in Nevada. Located on 236 square miles and featuring more than 2,800 buildings, the plant represented the largest ammunition storage depot in the world, housing 400,000 tons of ammunition. In the early 1990s, with the cessation of the Cold War, Day & Zimmermann personnel would also become responsible for demilitarizing much of the munitions stockpiled at the Hawthorne Plant.

Day & Zimmermann helped to staff a Du Pont office and provided further management through its Day Engineering division in the 1980s. The acquisition of SEACOR in 1982 gave the company the necessary marine engineering skills to serve naval and commercial ship operators. Acquisitions later in the decade included the Wagner Group, Delta Associates, NPS Energy Services and NPS, Inc., Aquidneck Data Company, and Barry Services.

In 1983, the company's property appraisal services were retained by the state of West Virginia for a state-wide property revaluation. A year later, Day & Zimmermann introduced a new technique for mass real estate appraisal—Landisc—which utilized both computer and laser-video technology to create a property image useful to the tax assessors, police and fire departments, and real estate offices. Other services in this area included analysis of hardware and software needs of clients, training, disaster planning, offsite backup storage, and computer time sharing, as well as public education programs to support assessors as they conducted revaluations.

At the onset of the 1990s, Day & Zimmermann restructured, forming D & Z, Inc. to coordinate efforts in engineering, design, construction, operation, and maintenance, and SEACOR Services, Inc. to manage international and base support projects. During this time, Day & Zimmermann provided a wide range of services to foreign and domestic clients of military, industrial, and municipal natures. Yoh Jr. continued to head the company and was the principal owner; his fellow investors from the 1976 buyout eventually retired and sold their interests to him. The company was owned by Yoh and one other executive who held less than a ten percent interest.

Day & Zimmermann's roots were in pioneering engineering techniques, and it continued to modernize engineering techniques in the 1990s. Engineers helped manufacturers to incorporate statistical process controls, computer-integrated manufacturing techniques, and vision-capable robotics in order to streamline the production process. The company also designed air circulation and filtration systems to meet stringent requirements for contamination control in the manufacture of foods, beverages, and health care products.

Despite cuts in defense spending, Day & Zimmermann continued to contract work with the U.S. military and its allies. The company was involved in demilitarizing and destroying obsolete weaponry; making conventional ammunition items from primers and detonators to fully-assembled bombs and missiles; and providing clients in other countries with consulting services in setting up manufacturing systems.

Day & Zimmermann also looked forward to continued nonmilitary contracts with the federal government. A new $40 million, five-year contract with the Resolution Trust Corporation called for Yoh's company to appraise the thrift's furniture and equipment inventories.

With governments at all levels taking a serious look at the condition of the nation's infrastructure, Day & Zimmermann looked forward to continued growth by providing services for the expansion of roads, railroads, bridges, water and sewer works, and airports. For more than 50 years, Day & Zimmermann had served as a consulting engineer on many water and sewer authorities, and its services included construction management support services, and direct contact operation services. Day & Zimmermann was also a leading consultant on airport construction, having worked for more than 90 airports or airline

clients. Its services included noise abatement studies, economic analysis, and environmental impact statements.

In rail transportation, the company provided systems integration services and assistance with improvements to control systems and equipment. The company also developed a program management oversight concept for the Urban Mass Transportation Administration to help its staff evaluate major transit projects and determine the efficiency of their use of federal grant money.

The nation's growing concern for the environment also fueled growth at Day & Zimmermann. The company worked on technology for plastics recycling, often in conjunction with state, county, and municipal governments, to reduce the amount of solid waste being hauled to landfills around the country. Furthermore, the company worked with Rutgers University to turn waste products into carpet, containers, construction materials, and automotive parts.

For owner and chief executive officer "Spike" Yoh, the company's key values were safety, quality, and integrity; he maintained that "without those three values we have nothing." Of course, a fourth key, profits, was also necessary, and continued growth was essential to the company's success, according to Yoh. He told the *Philadelphia Inquirer,* "If I have one problem, it is making sure we grow. Whether we want to or not, I say we have to grow." Attributing much of the company's success to its talented staff, Yoh maintained that it was important to find openings at the top for the brightest, and the way to ensure that was through growth.

Principal Subsidiaries: D & Z, Inc.; Life Sciences International; H. L. Yoh Company; Cole*Layer*Trumble Company/ Landisc Systems; Lone Star Division; Kansas Division; Munitions Technology Division; Systems Engineering Associates Company; NPS Energy Services, Inc; Day Data Systems; Protection Technology.

Further Reading:

Binzen, Peter, "This Family Firm has Grown Up a Lot, But it's Not Done Yet," *Philadelphia Inquirer,* January 6, 1992, p. 3D.
Day & Zimmermann Inc., A History of Quality and Excellence, Philadelphia: Day & Zimmermann Inc., 1993.

—Wendy J. Stein

Dell Computer Corp.

9505 Arboretum Blvd.
Austin, Texas 78759-7299
U.S.A.
(512) 338-4400
Fax: (512) 338-8700

Public Company
Incorporated: 1984
Employees: 4,700
Sales: $2.01 billion
Stock Exchanges: NASDAQ
SICs: 3571 Electronic Computers

Dell Computer Corp. is the fifth largest personal computer company in the United States and holds a 3.5 percent share of the world market. The company manufacturers a wide variety of computer hardware, which it sells primarily through direct marketing. In addition, Dell has begun selling software and other peripheral PC equipment through catalogues.

Dell was founded by Michael Dell, who started selling personal computers out of his dorm room as a freshman at the University of Texas in Austin. Dell bought parts wholesale, assembled them into clones of IBM computers, and sold them by mail order to customers who did not want to pay the higher prices charged by computer stores. The scheme was an instant success. He was soon grossing $80,000 a month, and in 1984 he dropped out of school to found Dell Computer.

At the time, the PC industry was dominated by large firms like IBM, while smaller, lesser-known mail order firms sold IBM clones at a steep discount. Dell used low-cost direct marketing to undersell the better-known computers being sold through such high-overhead dealer networks. Dell placed ads in computer magazines, gearing his merchandise to buyers who were sophisticated enough to recognize high quality merchandise at low prices. Customers placed orders to Dell by dialing a toll free number. As a result of these methods, Dell's computers became the top brand name in the direct mail market.

Dell achieved sales of $6 million its first full year in business, approaching $40 million the next year. Dell hired former investment banker E. Lee Walker as president in 1986 to help deal with his firm's explosive growth. By 1987 Dell held a dominant position in the mail-order market, but it was clear that the firm

had to move beyond mail order if it was to continue growing. To accomplish this goal the firm needed a larger professional management staff, and Dell hired a group of marketing executives from Tandy Corp., another maker of low-cost PCs. The group built a sales force able to market to large corporations and put together a network of value-added resellers, who assembled packages of computer components to sell in specialized markets.

The Tandy team soon helped raise gross margins to 31 percent, up from 23 percent a year earlier. Rather than merely undercutting the prices of competitors, they set prices in relation to the firm's costs. The new marketing department soon ran into trouble with Michael Dell, however. Battles erupted over advertising budgets and the number of salespeople required for corporations and resellers. While Dell believed that the new team did not understand direct selling and was trying to create a traditional marketing department with an overly large sales force, the Tandy group alleged that Dell lacked the patience to wait for the sales force to pay off. By early 1988, most of the Tandy group had resigned or been forced out.

Regardless, the firm continued growing rapidly, opening a London office that sold $4 million worth of computers during one month in 1988. Dell also formed a Canadian subsidiary. Early in 1988 the firm formed various divisions to raise its profile among corporate, government, and educational buyers. With reported sales of $159 million in 1987, the firm went public during this time, selling 3.5 million shares at $8.50 a share.

The firm faced several challenges, however. Announcing their own clone of IBM's new PS/2 computer system well before it was actually ready, Dell later had trouble reproducing important aspects of the PS/2's architecture, and the computers were delayed significantly, embarrassing the young company. Furthermore, Dell faced competition from several Japanese manufacturers, which were offering IBM clones at low prices. Further, having had trouble meeting demand, Dell used money raised from its stock offering to expand capacity and warehouse space, leaving the company with little cash. When it overestimated demand during the fourth quarter of 1988, the firm suddenly had no cash and warehouses full of unsold computers.

Dell responded to the increasing competition by increasing the level of technical sophistication in its computers. Half of its 1988 sales came from PCs using the Intel Corp.'s 80386 microprocessor, the most powerful PC chip at the time, and the company began producing file servers using the sophisticated Unix operating system. Dell also hired computer scientist Glenn Henry away from IBM to work on product development. Scrapping the company's first attempts at cloning IBM's PS/2, Henry initiated new plans for producing clones. Henry built Dell's research and development staff from almost nothing to 150 engineers, who began working on ways to combine the function of several chips onto one chip. When Intel released its 486 microprocessor, Dell began speeding to market the computers that could use it. Another of Henry's goals was high-quality graphics, which required better monitors and special circuit boards. By mid-1989 Dell had finished initial attempts at graphics hardware, giving it inroads into the higher-end of the PC market.

Despite these advances, Dell still had a research and development budget of $7 million, compared with the hundreds of millions spent by larger competitors like IBM. Dell's share of the PC market was only 1.8 percent, but it was still growing rapidly. U.S. sales for 1989 reached $257.8 million, while sales in Britain increased to $40 million and a branch in western Germany realized the break-even point.

Dell considered itself as much a marketing company as a hardware company, and its sales staff played an important role in its successes. Dell's sales personnel trained for six weeks or more before taking their seats at the phonebanks, and, along with their managers, they held weekly meetings to discuss customer complaints and possible solutions. In addition to fielding questions and taking orders, sales staff were trained to promote products. They helped buyers customize orders, selling them more memory or built-in modems. Orders were then sent to Dell's nearby factory where they were filled within five days. The telemarketing system also allowed Dell to compile information on its customers, helping the firm spot opportunities and mistakes far more quickly than most other PC companies.

In 1990 Dell set up subsidiaries in Italy and France and began selling some computers through large computer stores, whose high-volume low-margin strategy complemented Dell's established operations. The firm was making important corporate inroads as well, developing client/server computing systems with Andersen Consulting, for example, and introducing powerful servers using the Unix operating system. As a result, 40 percent of Dell's $546 million in 1990 sales came from the corporate world, up from 15 percent in 1987. Dell became the sixth largest PC maker in the United States—up from number 22 in 1989—and retained a staff of 2,100. Furthermore, the company's emphasis on customer satisfaction paid off, as it was rated number one in J. D. Powers & Associates first survey of PC-customer satisfaction.

That year, however, Dell manufactured too many memory chips and was forced to abandon a project to start of line of workstations. As a result, 1990 profits fell 65 percent to $5 million, despite the doubling of the firm's sales.

Also during this time, the traditional PC market channels were in flux. With a recession dampening sales, PC makers engaged in a furious price war that resulted in slumping profits nearly across the board. Compaq, IBM, and Apple all had profit declines or were forced to lay off employees. Furthermore, Compaq filed a lawsuit against Dell, which it eventually won, claiming that Dell's advertising made defamatory statements against Compaq. Nevertheless, the economic recession actually benefited Dell. While customers had less money, they still needed PCs, and they purchased Dell's inexpensive but technologically innovative IBM clones in record numbers. Consequently, annual sales shot up toward $1 billion.

In the early 1990s, notebook-sized computers were the fastest growing segment of the PC market, and Dell devoted resources to producing its first notebook model, which it released in 1991. The following year it introduced a full-color notebook model and also marketed PCs using Intel's fast 486 microchip.

As the PC wars continued, Compaq, which had been a higher-priced manufacturer stressing its quality engineering, repositioned itself to take on Dell, releasing a low-end PC priced at just $899 and improving its customer services. The new competition affected Dell's margins, forcing it to cut its computer prices by up to $1,400 to keep its market share. Dell could afford such steep price cuts because its operating costs were only 18 percent of revenues, compared with Compaq's 36 percent. The competition also forced Dell away from its attempts to stress its engineering. Dell executives began speaking of computers as consumer products like appliances, downplaying the importance of technology. Reflecting this increased stress on marketing, Dell began selling a catalogue of computer peripherals and software made by other companies; it soon expanded into fax machines and compact discs. Dell's database, containing information on the buying habits of over 750,000 of its customers, was instrumental in this effort.

Toward the end of 1992 Dell's product line experienced technological difficulties, particularly in the notebook market. In 1993 quality problems forced the firm to cancel a series of notebook computers before they were even introduced, causing a $20 million charge against earnings. The firm was projected to hold a 3.5 percent share of the PC market in 1993, but Digital Equipment Corporation, whose focus was minicomputers, nevertheless topped Dell as the biggest computer mail order company. To fight back against Compaq's inexpensive PC line, Dell introduced its Dimensions by Dell line of low-cost PCs. Sales for the year reached $2 billion, and Dell made a second, $148 million stock offering.

With price wars continuing, Dell cut prices again in early 1993 and extended the period of its warranty. However, increased competition and technical errors had hurt Dell, and despite growing sales, the firm announced a quarterly loss in excess of $75 million in 1993, its first loss ever. Dell attributed many of the problems to internal difficulties caused by its incredible growth. It responded by writing down PCs based on aging technology and restructuring its notebook division and European operations.

Like most of its competitors, Dell was hurt by an industry-wide consolidation taking place in the early 1990s. The consolidation also offered opportunity, however, as Dell fought to win market share from companies going out of business. Dell moved aggressively into markets outside of the United States, and by 1993, 36 percent of its sales were abroad.

Further Reading:

Forest, Stephanie Anderson, "PC Slump? What PC Slump?" *Business Week,* July 1, 1991, p. 66.
Kelly, Kevin, "Michael Dell: The Enfant Terrible of Personal Computers," *Business Week,* June 13, 1988, p. 61.
——, "Dell Computer Hits the Drawing Board," *Business Week,* April 24, 1989, p. 138.
Pope, Kyle, "For Compaq and Dell Accent Is on Personal in the Computer Wars," *Wall Street Journal,* July 2, 1993, p. A1.
Jones, Kathryn, "Bad News for Dell Computer," *New York Times,* July 15, 1993, p. C3.

—Scott M. Lewis

Deloitte & Touche

Deloitte & Touche

10 Westport Road
P.O. Box 820
Wilton, Connecticut 06897-0820
U.S.A.
(203) 761-3000
Fax: (203) 834-2200

*Private Wholly Owned Subsidiary of Deloitte Touche
   Tohmatsu International*
Founded: 1989
Employees: 16,500
Sales: $4.5 billion
SICs: 8721 Accounting, Auditing & Bookkeeping; 8742
   Management Consulting Services

Deloitte & Touche is the fourth largest public accounting firm in the world, one of the prestigious Big Six accounting firms that dominate public accounting. The firm of Deloitte & Touche was created as a result of the 1989 merger between two of what were then the "Big Eight" accounting firms—the firm of Touche Ross and the firm of Deloitte, Haskins, and Sells. The two firms were roughly the same size before the merger; the newly combined Deloitte & Touche could boast of revenues of nearly five billion dollars, with clients such as General Motors, Procter & Gamble, Nabisco, Sears Roebuck and Company, and other Fortune 500 companies.

Deloitte & Touche provides professional services including accounting, auditing and tax services, and management consulting through 15,300 professionals in more than 100 U.S. cities. A private partnership, Deloitte & Touche is also part of Deloitte Touche Tohmatsu International, a global leader in professional managerial consulting services with 56,000 professionals in 108 countries. The Tohmatsu name comes from Tohmatsu Avoiki & Sanwa, Japan's largest audit firm, which was part of Touche Ross at the time of the merger in 1989.

The 1989 merger between Touche Ross and Deloitte, Haskins, and Sells was thought by many industry experts to be an unlikely match, despite the fact that the accounting industry is one with a long history of mergers and acquisitions—over the years more and more partners have become concentrated in a shrinking number of firms. For the last half century, however, eight firms had dominated public accounting; these firms were dubbed the "Big Eight" by *Fortune* magazine. But the genealogy of Deloitte & Touche looks much like a large family tree stretching back over 100 years to the rise of the multinational corporation and its need for standardized accounting procedures.

Each of the two predecessor firms to Deloitte & Touche has a long history of growth. For example, Deloitte, Haskins and Sells traces its history back to the mid-1800s in England, when William Welch Deloitte devised the double entry accounting system to help the Great Western Railway to deal with its large capital stock. In those days, as companies grew, due to their size and complexity, new problems were presented over how to depreciate fixed capital. For example, some imagined that as the cost of replacement of locomotives rose, then the value of a firm's assets rose by the same amount, ignoring depreciation. The system devised by Deloitte solved this problem and was instrumental in the passage in 1844 of the Joint Stock Banking Act in England, which required firms to provide balance sheets and income statements. A number of leading firms were established at this time, including Deloitte in 1845 and Price Waterhouse. Changes in tax legislation, such as the introduction of an income tax in the United States in 1913, were critical for the growth of accounting as a profession. Thus, as Archibald Richards points out in his historical account of the company, the evolution of accounting as a profession can only be understood in the context of the developing business community. In other words, accountancy became indispensable to any well-run business, and the practice of accountants has roughly paralleled business trends.

Deloitte has evolved for this entire period, moving with the needs of business. For example, in the late 1970s and early 1980s Deloitte began offering administration services for 401(k) retirement plans for companies. Using leased software, Deloitte administered 20 investment funds, offered myriad services for participants, and provided consultants in such areas as legal issues, plan design issues, employee communications, and compliance issues. The service was set up nationwide and administered through regional consulting offices in over 15 offices with a staff of over 250 people. The company also moved increasingly toward management consulting.

The origins of Touche Ross, the other partner in the Deloitte Touche marriage, can also be traced back to England. Founded in 1899, the firm initially provided services needed by investment trust companies. Starting with a staff of 11 that included only two accountants, the firm grew rapidly through directorships, receiverships, and reconstruction, rather than by additional audits. The 1930s were rough years for the company, but by the end of World War II, the firm had a staff of 67 total and was called George A. Touche & Co., then a small- to medium-sized firm. Expansion continued in America, Canada, and overseas, both through internal expansion and by merger. The firm eventually assumed its position as one of the Big Eight.

By the 1970s Touche Ross was the third largest accounting firm in the United Kingdom. By 1972 the firm included 74 offices, 450 partners, and 5000 staff in America and, through Touche Ross International, offices in 45 countries.

Prior to the merger of 1989, Touche Ross had a reputation as the "most scrappy" and "least stuffy" member of what was then known as the Big Eight, while Deloitte, Haskins and Sells was known as the industry's "creaky old man." Touche made headlines when two of its employees were accused of insider trading. In 1989 three accountants in the firm's London office were charged with having profited from information obtained illegally from a Touche audit of a British industrial conglomerate.

Also contributing to the instability of the pre-merger period was a problem that large accounting firms shared; that is, many of the economic disasters of the 1980s, specifically leveraged buyouts and the savings and loan scandal, took place under the watch of Big Eight accounting firms. With Deloitte's corporate culture, thought to be slow and steady, and Touche's reputation as an aggressive auditor, many at the time thought the marriage of Deloitte and Touche to be one of strange bedfellows. But under the lead of J. Michael Cook and Ed Kangos at Touche, the firms were able to hammer out a merger agreement.

Besides, both firms, had Fortune 500 clients locked up: Touche had Chrysler while Deloitte had General Motors; Touche had retail giants Sears, Macy's, Litton Industries, and Pillsbury while Deloitte had the Wall Street buyout powerhouse of Kohlberg Kravis Roberts as well as Kimberly Clark, Monsanto, and Procter and Gamble. After the merger, the Deloitte contingent largely took control of the new firm, with long-time Deloitte chief J. Michael Cook taking over as Chairman and Chief Executive Officer. Cook was a life-long Deloitte employee who, in 1986, at the age of 43, had become chairman of Deloitte, Haskins, and Sells. The merger took place the same year that another major merger between Big Eight firms, Ernst & Whinney and Arthur Young, reduced the Big Eight to the Big Six.

Competition had created an environment where the accounting industry was no longer a bunch of bookkeepers but a broad-based consulting practice serving a network of multinational organizations that included corporate, governmental, and financial institutions. This created the background for Deloitte's involvement in the S&L fiasco—with a pressure to retain clients so strong that by the 1980s, a government accounting office study of 11 bankrupt thrifts found that a number of accounting audits, including some completed by Deloitte, Haskins and Sells, failed to meet professional standards. The long held view that these accounting firms played a disinterested neutral advisory role was burst asunder. The competition for clients had obviously intensified in the deregulated savings and loan environment of the 1980s.

Most recently, as the company moves further into the 1990s, it has ventured into complementary services with data processing applications to ease out of the slide in its management consulting business, while still trying to recover from its ill-fated involvement (along with other Big Six firms) in the disastrous S&L slide. This effort, coupled with the recession at the beginning of the decade, made the period a difficult one for Deloitte & Touche. In the glory days of management consulting of the 1980s, when mergers and acquisitions were running wild, Deloitte & Touche had reported double digit annual growth rates in its consulting business. In 1991, however, Deloitte's New York consulting business plunged 30 to 40 percent, due mainly to the slumping financial services sector.

In response to the slump, Deloitte slashed its own costs, or as Alan Breznick, writing in *Crain's* in 1992 put it: "Instead of just cutting other people's jobs these days, high-priced management consultants are cutting their own for the first time." Deloitte also began revamping its other business services as well and in turn cut its consulting rates.

To expand its management consulting services, Deloitte & Touche entered into an operating agreement with Software 2000 of Hyannis, Massachusetts, to offer customers complementary services. The agreement combined Deloitte's personnel and training knowledge with Software 2000's software expertise. The software products were installed in Deloitte's joint technology centers in New York and Charlotte, North Carolina, and offer software applications such as audits, tax management, and consulting services for various management problems.

In other software ventures, Deloitte & Touche joined with Brightwork Development and Egghead Discount Software in July 1992 to provide a software license auditing service to find and eliminate illegal software copies. The service costs $10,000 to $30,000 for a 500 workstation site. The need for the service was apparent since, in 1991 alone, the Software Publishers Association collected $3 million in litigation involving pirated software. In another venture in July 1992, Deloitte launched Microcomputer Asset Management Services, which will also help companies comply with software-licensing laws.

Deloitte & Touche's revenues rose sharply over 1991, with gross revenues for the year of $2 billion, 50 percent of which was derived from environmental risk management consulting services—manufacturing plant audits, waste minimization plans, regulatory and public policy analysis, risk financing, and design of management systems, among other services. Deloitte & Touche's international parent, Deloitte Touche Tohmatsu International, also had a big year, reporting global fee income up seven percent to $4.8 billion (U.S. dollars) in fiscal year ending September 1992.

In the late 1980s and early 1990s, however, the company continued to devote a substantial portion of its resources to settling matters related to the S&L crisis. In December 1992 the firm, according to chairman and Chief Executive Officer J. Michael Cook, began negotiating with the federal government to resolve an estimated $1.4 billion in claims from the failure of the federally insured thrifts. In general, many of the Big Six were accused of negligent auditing practices that may have overstated the value of failing thrifts. The settlements for the allegedly faulty audits are under negotiation with the federal government regulators (Resolution Trust Corporation). It remains to be seen whether or how much the firm's legal liability from the S&L situation will weigh it down in the future.

Deloitte & Touche appears to be diversifying its business and will undoubtedly continue to remain a formidable presence in public accounting. It keeps adding new partners and has launched a program to accelerate the promotion of women to the level of partner. While other firms have started similar programs, Deloitte & Touche's is considered more comprehensive than those of other companies.

Deloitte & Touche's risk management consulting services continued to grow as well, posting a 12.7 percent increase in revenues to $13.3 million for 1992. Overseas growth is also being fueled; the government of Russia has enlisted the aid of an international group of western advisors, including Deloitte & Touche, to guide it through its privatization program. The firm is also seeing growth prospects in Asia, especially Korea. Growth, however, was slower in the company's more traditional financial services businesses like insurance program reviews, but the company noted that these areas were expected to rebound.

Further Reading:

"Agency Sues 2 Audit Firms," *New York Times National Edition*, March 7, 1992.

Breznick, Alan, "Big Six Consultants Called to Account Deloitte & Touche," *Crain's New York Business*, February 23, 1992.

"Deloitte & Touche Offers Software-Auditing Service," *PC-Week*, July 20, 1992.

"Deloitte & Touche Risk Management Consulting Services Division Posts 1992 Gross Revenues of $13.3 Million," *Business Insurance*, March 8, 1993.

"Deloitte Wants More Women For Top Posts in Accounting," *Wall Street Journal*, April 28, 1993.

Jones, Edgar, *Accountancy and the British Economy 1840–1980: The Evolution of Ernst & Whinney*, London: B.T. Batsford, Ltd., 1981.

Kettle, Sir Russell, *Deloitte & Co., 1845–1956*, New York: Garland Publishing Inc., 1982.

Moskowitz, Milton, et al, *Everybody's Business: A Field Guide to the 400 Leading Companies in America*, New York: Doubleday, 1990.

Richards, Archibald B., *Touche Ross & Co. 1899–1981: The Origins and Growth of the United Kingdom Firm*, Touche Ross & Co., 1983.

Stevens, Mark, *The Accounting Wars*, New York: Macmillan Publishing Company, 1985.

——, *The Big Six: The Selling Out of America's Top Accounting Firms*, New York: Simon & Schuster, 1991.

Rees, David, "Merged Accounting Firms See Shakeups Rather Than Benefits," *Los Angeles Business Journal*, May 20, 1991.

"Russia Has Enlisted the Aid of an International Group of Western Advisers to Guide it Through Privatization," *Oil and Gas Journal*, August 3, 1992.

"S&L Agency Sues Deloitte, Peat Marwick, Seeking Total of $250 Million in Damages," *Wall Street Journal*, March 9, 1992.

"Software 2000 Signs with Big-6 Firm," *Midrange Systems*, February 18, 1992.

Stevens, Mark, *The Big Eight*, New York: Macmillan Publishing Company, Inc., 1981.

Swanson, Theodor, *Touche Ross: A Biography*, Touche Ross & Co., 1972.

Woo, Junda, "Big Six Accounting Firms Join Forces For Legal Change," *Wall Street Journal*, September 1, 1992.

—John A. Sarich

Digi International Inc.

6400 Flying Cloud Drive
Eden Prairie, Minnesota 55344
U.S.A.
(612) 943-9020
Fax: (612) 943-5330

Public Company
Incorporated: 1985 as DigiBoard, Inc.
Employees: 204
Sales: $57.8 million
Stock Exchanges: NASDAQ
SICs: 3577 Computer Peripheral Equipment Nec; 7373
   Computer Integrated Systems Design

Digi International Inc. is one of America's fastest growing computer companies and is known for its unusual product line, which includes hardware and software products that enable as many as 512 computer users to work off a single, desktop personal computer. By equipping workers with dummy terminals, rather than full-fledged PCs, and allowing them to communicate through a single computer, rather than over an expensive local area network, Digi (pronounced ''Didgy'') can set up an office network at a fraction of the cost of a conventional system. In 1993 an article in the Minneapolis-St. Paul newspaper *City-Business* commented, ''If Digi International's growth curve were a mountain, a climber would have a hard time scaling it.'' In fact, since its inception, Digi has managed an annual growth rate of more than 90 percent.

The company was created in 1985 by a former rocket scientist named John Schinas. After working for GTE Sylvania during the 1960s, Schinas joined the Massachusetts Institute of Technology as a researcher. There he developed computer software used to guide the Apollo lunar module in its moon landings and rendezvous with the orbiting command module. Schinas later moved across Boston to work for Raytheon, where he wrote software programs for air traffic control systems. He also helped develop the first shared-access computer system for *The Washington Post,* enabling writers and editors to convert news copy directly into page layouts.

After leaving Raytheon, and working for a couple of years at Stearns Computer Systems, Schinas joined Digigraphic Systems (now called DSC Nortech), a manufacturer of computer

circuit boards and assemblies. Digigraphic was struggling in a depressed market, and after its restructuring in 1985, the company elected to abandon some of its major circuit board lines, including those that allowed computer terminals to share a single processor.

Schinas, then a group vice-president, strongly disagreed with the move and tendered his resignation. He purchased the company's inventory of circuit boards, some test equipment, and machinery for $400,000, raising the cash through a second mortgage and from friends. He then sold off the product inventory, earning a small pool of cash, and hired a some software engineers to develop improved boards, while he set up a new company called DigiBoard.

During this time, the 286 chip was developed. This chip, combined with a UNIX operating system for personal computers, enabled a single controller to take over thousands of simple functions from the CPU, or ''brain box'' in a conventional personal computer. This, in turn, meant that a single CPU could serve several computer terminals at the same time. Such a network proved useful for standard interoffice communication, basic computing functions, and sales and inventory work. It was also cheaper to set up than local area networks, or LANs, pioneered by companies such as Novell, which required a CPU at each work station.

To Schinas, LANs seemed an inefficient use of resources. Few applications required so much computing power, and because the market for such simple applications was enormous, it was clearly more economical to have several workstations share a single CPU. Schinas then made a daring assumption: he decided that, in their rush to sell computers, manufacturers such as IBM, Compaq, Apple, and DEC would ignore the simplicity of the 286 chip application, preferring to market LAN systems consisting of several terminals each equipped with a CPU. Schinas decided to develop a system that could compete with LANs.

The DigiBoard system, known as the PC8 input-output, or ''I/O,'' system, required the installation of three items: a circuit board to perform the function of serving several computer screens and keyboards, the software to govern these functions, and the wiring needed to connect everything. The system's major selling point was its low cost. Customers could either equip their offices with several $4,000 computers, or use Schinas' system consisting of a single $4,000 computer and several $250 terminals.

Many computer manufacturers refused to market the PC8 system, fearing that it would cut into computer sales. Furthermore, for larger companies such as Novell the DigiBoard system represented a threat to their commanding presence in the growing LAN market. In order to get his product to market, Schinas hired Mykola Moroz, a former purchasing executive at Digigraphics. Drawing on his experience in both computer systems and marketing strategy, Moroz established a series of distribution channels, including magazine classifieds and the few computer retailers then in existence.

Wary of competition, Schinas sought to hold down costs at DigiBoard. Rather than manufacturing its product himself, he elected to farm out the work to local subcontractors. This enabled DigiBoard to concentrate on new product development and marketing. In another attempt at holding down costs, Digi-Board located its offices in an unfinished $2 per square foot factory space, where engineers had to contend with noisy ceiling furnaces and occasional fuel oil leaks.

DigiBoard ended its first year in operation with impressive total sales of $1.5 million. After losing $260,000 in 1986, the company made a million dollar public offering the following year, and sales grew to $3.5 million. During this time, faster and more complex personal computers were developed, robbing LAN architectures of their comparative strengths. Customers could do more with a single CPU than ever before, and at rapidly dropping prices. All this activity in the market helped Digi-Board to garner sales of $7.8 million in 1988, enabling Schinas to repay those who invested in his venture.

Thinking in terms of a global market, Schinas launched a second public offering in October 1989 under a new parent organization called Digi International. The offering reaped $11 million, and shares in the company were publicly traded on the NASDAQ. Digi finished 1989 with sales of $14.6 million. The following year, the company acquired PC Research, a software developer, and a division of Progressive Computing that developed ISDN technologies, which allowed tremendous amounts of data to be sent over conventional telephone lines. Sales in 1990 topped $23 million.

However, as the market continued to grow, so did the competition. From a host of smaller companies, Arnet Corporation emerged as Digi's chief competitor. When Arnet's founder announced his intention to retire in 1990, he purposely sought out Schinas, hoping Digi would offer to buy out the company. With its product line and facilities, Arnet was a good match for Digi, which acquired the company for $5 million on March 1, 1991.

By this time, Digi had moved into a new office complex in Eden Prairie, Minnesota, and had established a manufacturing facility in nearby St. Louis Park. Furthermore, on July 8, 1991, the company opened a German sales subsidiary in Köln.

The rapid growth in computing power, driven by a revolution in computer chips, continued to broaden the potential applications for Digi's I/O systems. New versions of the PC8 were introduced that enabled phone banks to handle hotel and ticket reservations and product orders.

In the early 1990s, the U.S. economy, weakened by years of deficit spending and short-term business strategies, slipped into a prolonged recession. Corporate budgets were cut drastically, and capital purchases, including those for computer equipment, were deferred indefinitely. Computer companies such as Dell, Apple, DEC, and Compaq suffered huge declines in sales, while IBM and Wang were devastated. Digi suffered a less profound blow, however, buoyed by the fact that its systems came into demand as cheaper alternatives to LANs.

The company also gained greater marketing strength through a series of distribution agreements. The Digi product line was incorporated into larger systems sold by IBM, NCR, Bell Labs, MCI, Honeywell, and GTE Data Services. Later, distribution channels were established through Bell Atlantic and BellSouth.

In 1991, Digi had about 20 percent of the market for multi-user systems, then valued at about $200 million annually. However, growth in this market had topped out, and, in order to maintain its sales, Digi decided to break into the market for LAN systems, which were less of a competing technology than ever.

Digi established manufacturing agreements with Novell and Microsoft, in which Digi LAN products were integrated with those of established LAN operating systems. Digi later expanded its LAN technologies into the wide area network, or WAN, market, in which computer systems in different locations are linked by telephone wires.

Digi completed a third stock distribution in September 1991, generating an additional $23 million in capital. This enabled the company to create a telecommunications group to develop and market high-speed data communications equipment. The following year, Moroz succeeded Schinas as chief executive of the company. Schinas retained his position as chairperson, establishing a smooth path of transition for his eventual retirement.

Digi acquired another competitor, Stargate Technologies, in April 1993. This company manufactured a variety of alternative software systems for the I/O and LAN market. Also that year, Digi made its first major entry into the ISDN market with a new PC IMAC product line using the Novell NetWare and Microsoft LAN Manager and Windows systems. The system simplified the commands needed by a computer user to establish and administer a high-speed data connection over telephone company ISDN lines.

In 1993, Digi International held a leading 25 percent market share of the I/O market and had established a strong position in the LAN and WAN connectivity markets. The company's systems were distinguished by their software, a command-intensive system that eliminated the need for large hardware adjuncts, making it easily—and inexpensively—adaptable to existing computer systems.

Digi International has frequently been noted for its rapid growth and good management. In 1990 Schinas told *Minnesota Ventures,* "Management by consensus is the biggest problem in U.S. corporations. It detracts and draws away from the abilities of creative people. Companies are afraid to make mistakes, and fear strangles you. It makes you impotent." Schinas attributed his company's success not so much to the quality or innovation of its products, but rather to its looser style of management.

Principal Subsidiaries: DigiBoard Inc., FSC; Arnet Corp.; Stargate Technologies, Inc.; DigiBoard GmbH (Germany).

Further Reading:

"DigiBoard Gets Serious About ISDN," *PC Week,* June 29, 1993.
"Digi International," *CityBusiness* (Minneapolis-St. Paul), January 1, 1993, p. 6.
"Digi International," *Fortune,* March 11, 1991, p. 96.
Digi International Inc. Annual Report, Eden Prairie, MN: Digi International, 1992.
"Digi International Investor Fact Sheet," Company Document, Summer 1993.

"Digi to Enter LAN Market," *Communications Week,* October 14, 1991, pp. 14–16.

"John Schinas," *Minnesota Ventures,* November/December 1990, pp. 46–49.

"Minnesota's Best Entrepreneurs: John Schinas," *Minnesota Ventures,* August 1991.

"The New Minnesota Computer Industry," *St. Paul Pioneer Press,* March 22, 1993, p. D1.

"Survivor," *Corporate Report Minnesota,* September 1992, p. 115.

"The Tightwad and the Rocket Scientist," *Forbes,* November 8, 1993, pp. 222–23.

"Unconventional Wisdom," *Corporate Report Minnesota,* December 1990, p. 50.

—John Simley

Dime Savings Bank of New York, F.S.B.

589 Fifth Avenue
New York, New York 10017
U.S.A.
(212) 326-6170
Fax: (212) 326-6194

Public Company
Incorporated: 1859
Employees: 2,190
Assets: $8.77 billion
Stock Exchanges: New York
SICs: 6035 Federal Savings Institutions

Dime Savings Bank of New York ("the Dime") is a full-service bank offering a wide variety of financial services, mostly residential property loans but also commercial real estate and consumer loans. The Dime operates over 40 banking offices in the New York City area. In the early 1990s the bank had assets totalling over $8 billion and was presided over by Richard D. Parsons, the first African American to lead a large thrift of Dime's size. During the Savings and Loan (S&L) crisis of the 1980s, Dime suffered high delinquencies on home loans. Following a capital restructuring plan at the hands of federal S&L regulators, the Dime turned a profit in 1992 for the first time in five years.

The Dime has a history dating back to 1859, when it was founded as a state-chartered mutual savings bank (owned by its depositors). It wasn't until 1983 that the Dime became a federally chartered mutual savings bank and FDIC member; in 1986, the Dime became a public corporation.

Up until the late 1970s, savings and loan banks were heavily regulated in the types of loans they could offer and the interest rates they charged; for example, commercial lending was limited by New York State law to five percent of a savings bank's assets, and mutual savings banks were restricted by New York State law to only offering home mortgages. Thus, most firms merely had to function profitably within heavily prescribed limits. Smooth growth from low-risk home mortgages worked well for the Dime in the booming postwar housing market.

By 1978 Dime had 11 offices in the New York area and $4 billion in deposits. But the U.S. economy was stagnating at this

time (compared to the 1950s and 1960s) and, in 1977 and 1978, Dime began a series of mergers. In October 1977 the bank bought Mechanics Exchange Savings Bank. In 1978 Dime merged with Citizens Savings & Loan Association (which had $98 million in deposits and five offices), also of New York. Both Dime and Citizens were mutuals (i.e., owned by their depositors), so, in merging, they merely pooled their assets and liabilities. Dime subsequently also merged with Mechanics Exchange Savings in Albany ($245 million in deposits) and First Federal Savings & Loan Association of Port Washington, New York ($116 million in deposits).

By 1980, Dime was New York's second largest savings bank and continued to expand through acquisition, now into the suburban New York market. Upon acquiring Union Savings Bank (assets of $232 million), the $5 billion Dime was within a "few million dollars" of Bowery Savings Bank, New York's largest savings institution.

During the late 1970s, fundamental changes were also occurring in the regulation of financial services. The new laws allowed thrifts to enter markets other than home mortgages, leading to fierce competition within the industry and with other large financial institutions. The potential for growth was enormous, but the risks were also much greater. Soon savings banks were offering credit cards, car loans, and other commercial loans, allowing them the room to compete more effectively with commercial banks. The Dime moved quickly into this competitive foray.

Dime continued its expansion, buying out Westchester County Savings & Loan, with Westchester becoming the Westchester Division of Dime ($30 million in deposits with three offices in Westchester County). Prior to this expansion, Dime had eleven offices in Brooklyn, Manhattan, Nassau, and Suffolk Counties (totalling $4.6 billion in deposits) and no offices in Westchester County.

In addition to its expansionary moves through acquisition, the Dime was moving into new technology and capitalizing on its services through new delivery methods. By 1984, with $6.1 billion in deposits, Dime began utilizing automated teller machines (ATMs), entering into a joint venture with Automatic Data Processing Inc., and Electronic Banking Systems, a marketing firm, to operate ATMs in General Corporation's Pathmark food store chains. Dime had previously operated small branches in food stores. However, much more profit was possible with the application of ATM technology than was generated through Dime's old extended delivery system, and the high levels of customer traffic, convenient locations, and long hours made food stores ideal locations for ATMS.

In 1986 Dime went public, becoming a federally chartered stock savings bank. Dime issued 22,425,000 common shares of stock at $17.75 per share; 4,397,895 shares were offered to deposit account holders, borrowers, trustees, officers, and employees of the Dime, and 18,027,105 shares were sold publicly.

By 1988, the Dime had assets of $11.46 billion and 55 branches in eleven eastern states. Dime acquired Starpointe Savings Bank of Somerset, New Jersey, for $63 million, establishing Dime's first consumer banking presence in New Jersey. (It had previously been limited to mortgage banking in the state.)

Instrumental in the deal was the bank's new president and chief executive officer, Richard Parsons, formerly a partner at the New York law firm of Patterson, Belknap, Webb, & Tyler. The deal made Dime the third largest thrift in New York state and the eighteenth largest in the nation, with 52 retail banking offices in New York state and eleven mortgage offices in New York, Connecticut, New Jersey, and Florida. At the end of 1989, Dime had $12.4 billion in assets. As a result of the deal, Starpointe changed its name to Dime Savings Bank of New Jersey.

By the late 1980s, many S&Ls had extended themselves too far, making real estate loans to questionable borrowers. Over 500 S&Ls had fallen victim to insolvency (with taxpayers financing their return to solvency) and, in 1989, losses for the industry were said to have been growing at a rate of $15 billion per year. Dime was left with huge losses on some 1500 defaulted mortgages. By the end of the decade, the Dime had weathered the S&L crisis, but its profitability had plummeted. Parsons was assigned the task of navigating the Dime out of its troubles. Despite its weak capital position, Dime was considered one of the strongest thrifts on the East Coast.

The goals Parsons outlined for Dime were diversification, cost restructuring, and acquisition. Parsons noted that savings banks like Dime were now competing with large banks. (In fact, Dime's foremost competitor was Citibank.) Because the rules of the game had changed so substantially and competition had increased, Parsons concluded that only expansion into new lines of business and new geographic markets could guarantee survival and high profitability for Dime.

In attempts to cut costs, in February 1992 Dime eliminated 400 jobs (about 15 percent of its staff), and turned to outsourcing of many office activities. About one-third of the bank's back-office activities (including check printing, check processing, and distribution of checking and mortgage statements) were farmed out to Nationar, a processing firm based in New York. This step alone reduced Dime's overhead by approximately $11 million a year. The company also restructured its top management, shedding its chief financial officer, head of foreclosed real estate, chief service quality executive, and senior mortgage official.

Despite these measures, Dime lost $40 million in the first nine months of 1991. And, with a deficient risk-based capital ratio, a legal requirement for thrifts, the Dime continued to be under the careful scrutiny of federal regulators. Dime had to contend with both satisfying federal regulators from the Office of Thrift Supervision on its capital improvement plan, as well as the possibility that regulators would force the company into a merger with a stronger institution. Dime continued to be troubled by non-performing assets, mostly overdue mortgages and foreclosed homes (which made up 10.8 percent of its assets as of September 1992, up from 1.65 percent in 1987). Nonetheless, Dime continued to write new mortgages of $1.5 billion in 1992, up from $250 million in 1991. The company hoped to hit the $3 billion mark by 1994. But three straight years of heavy losses

(including over $140 million in losses in 1990 alone) continued to put a drag on growth prospects.

The Dime's new lending strategy focused on safe loans and included a tactic referred to as wholesale mortgage lending. By buying a sizeable portion of new loans from other companies, Dime hoped to achieve geographic diversification of its loans without the expense of opening more branches. While some analysts considered this a high risk strategy, since the purchasing company is far removed from knowing its borrowers, Dime argued that costs of these loans are low and that they would only deal with well-established lenders.

After a record loss of $237.4 million in 1991, Dime earned a profit in 1992, its first recorded profit since 1987. From 1987 to 1993, Dime sold twelve of its branches and reduced its staffing from 3,700 to 1,900 employees. In late 1992, regulators approved Dime's capital improvement plan. As part of its capital restructuring, Dime reduced its assets to $8.8 billion from $12 billion. All of these moves helped to increase its profit rate.

In May 1993, Dime sold the eight branches of its subsidiary in New Jersey to First Fidelity Bancorp. Dime was thus left with 34 remaining branches in what it called its core markets of New York City.

Principal Subsidiaries: Garden Management Co., Inc.; Mide Advertising, Inc.; Northeast Appraisals, Inc.; Pinebrook Development Corp.; R.M.B., Inc.; Medford Associates, Inc.; Midway Holdings, Inc.; UPH Corp.; Virginia Drive Corp.; DNJ Agency, Inc.; Granny Road Land Corp.; 114 Park Drive South Corp.; Pembroke and Livingston, Inc.; Plainview Inn, Inc.; TDA Securities, Inc.

Further Reading:

"Dime Savings Bank Agrees to a Merger with New York S&L," *Wall Street Journal,* July 12, 1978.

"Dime Savings Bank Organizes Division for Commercial Loans," *Wall Street Journal,* December 17, 1980.

Slater, Karen, "3 Major BHCs May Bid for Big New York Thrift," *American Banker,* January 8, 1982.

Weinstein, Michael, "Trio Plans to Install ATMs in Markets: New York Thrift, Data Processor, Marketing Firm Team Up," *American Banker,* February 22, 1984.

Thompson, Kevin D., "Turning On a Dime: The B.E. Interview," *Black Enterprise,* February 1989.

O'Henry, Sheila, "Outsourcing Solutions to the DP Puzzle," *Bankers Monthly,* July 1991.

McNatt, Robert, "At Dime, Thrift Problems of Another Kind," *Crain's New York Business,* December 29, 1991.

"Chastened Dime Renews Home Lending," *American Banker,* February 26, 1992.

"Dime Savings Plans to Cut 400 Jobs," *American Banker,* February 26, 1992.

McNatt, Robert, "Dime Savings' Fate in Regulators' Hands," *Crain's New York Business,* April 12, 1992.

LedBetter, James, "Rudy: Soft on Dime? Giuliani Transition Chief Smokes Out Boston Tenants," *Village Voice,* November 16, 1993.

—John A. Sarich

Dole Food Company, Inc.

31355 Oak Crest Drive
Westlake Village, California 91361
U.S.A.
(818) 879-6600
Fax: (818) 879-6973

Public Company
Incorporated: 1894 as the Castle & Cooke Co., Inc.
Sales: $3.4 billion
Employees: 50,000
Stock Exchanges: New York Pacific
SICs: 0174 Citrus Fruits; 5148 Fresh Fruits and Vegetables;
   5149 Groceries & Related Products, Nec; 2033 Canned
   Fruits & Vegetables; 2034 Dehydrated Fruits, Vegetables,
   Soups; 2024 Ice Cream & Frozen Desserts; 6552
   Subdividers & Developers, Nec

The Dole Food Company, Inc., is the world's largest producer
and distributer of pineapple and a global leader in the processing and marketing of a wide variety of fruits, nuts, and vegetables. The company's real estate interests, managed through its
80 percent-owned subsidiary, Castle & Cooke Co., Inc., represent a significant sideline, as do two luxury resorts in Hawaii
owned and operated by Dole.

Christopher Columbus first brought pineapples from the Caribbean to Europe, where they were called "ananas," a corruption
of the Indian word "nana," or aromatic. However, the English
referred to the fruit as pineapple, finding it similar in appearance
to the pine cone and as juicy and crisp as an apple. For centuries,
pineapples remained expensive delicacies.

In the 1880s, English seaman Captain John Kidwell decided to
try mass marketing pineapple, and after disappointing attempts
to cultivate the wild Hawaiian variety, he opted to import a
Florida pineapple known as the "smooth Cayenne." However,
the fresh pineapple had to be shipped thousands of miles to
market, which took several weeks, with no refrigeration.

While Kidwell never made a successful business from commercially grown pineapple, James Drummond Dole did. A 21-year-
old graduate of Harvard, Dole arrived in Hawaii in 1899. His
cousin, Sanford B. Dole, an influential politician who became
governor of the newly acquired territory of Hawaii, encouraged
James's ambition to market pineapple commercially.

By 1901 James Dole had acquired 60 acres of land 18 miles
north of Honolulu, in Wahiawa, and had formed the Hawaiian
Pineapple Company. His groves of smooth Cayenne pineapples
were ready to be harvested two years later. Rather than trying to
export the fresh fruit, Dole decided to market his pineapple in
cans. He established his cannery near his pineapple groves,
allowing him to achieve the best results by canning soon after
harvesting the ripened produce. The Hawaiian Pineapple Company packaged and marketed nearly 2,000 cases of canned
pineapple in 1903.

Two years later Dole was shipping 25,000 cases of canned
pineapple. The company's success was facilitated by a new
railroad constructed between Wahiawa and Honolulu, as well as
by the fact that ample, cheap labor was available, allowing the
company to keep its costs low. In addition, Dole persuaded the
American Can Company to establish a manufacturing plant next
to his cannery. For Dole, this eliminated the expense of importing cans from the mainland, so that vast quantities of pineapple could be processed quickly and cheaply. However, the
company's increased supply depended on a corresponding demand, and, outside of residents on the California coast, few
Americans had ever seen, much less tasted, pineapple. Furthermore, the company's existing market was already approaching
saturation.

In 1911 engineer Henry Ginaca, an employee of the Hawaiian
Pineapple Company, invented a machine that could process 100
pineapple cylinders a minute. Such production facilities enabled
the company to market its produce in much of the United States.
Developing a successful marketing strategy became a high
priority for the company during this time.

Together with several smaller companies also involved in the
processing of pineapple, Dole financed an advertising blitz in
the mainland's magazines and newspapers, promoting canned
pineapple products under exotic, foreign brand names, such as
Ukelele and Outrigger. As a result, demand increased significantly. Toward the end of World War I, in 1918, Dole's
Hawaiian Pineapple Company was producing one million cases
annually and had gained a reputation as the largest processor of
pineapples in the world. During this time, Dole purchased more
land in order to expand his business.

By the mid-1920s Castle & Cooke Ltd., a Hawaiian real estate
and land development company established in 1851, had become the dominant stockholder in Hawaiian Pineapple. Also
during this time, surplus supply compelled Dole and other pineapple growers to pool their resources to mount an even bigger
national advertising campaign than they had before the war.
Using the new medium of radio, the company aired advertising
using slogans such as "It Cuts with A Spoon—Like a Peach"
and "You Can Thank Jim Dole for Canned Pineapples." As a
result, sales and profits increased dramatically.

However, with the onset of the Great Depression, the company's sales declined and its advertising budget was depleted.
The introduction of a new product, pineapple juice, was unsuccessful due to the company's inability to successfully promote
it. In the first nine months of 1932, Hawaiian Pineapple lost
over $5 million, and the principal stockholders, Castle &
Cooke, took over Dole's company. Thereafter the Hawaiian

Pineapple Company became Castle & Cooke's principal business, and while Dole's name was affixed to the company's products in 1934, Dole himself was relegated to an essentially powerless role.

Nevertheless, the new owners managed to reverse the downward trend of the Hawaiian Pineapple Company. With greater financial resources at its disposal, the company launched a major advertising campaign for pineapple juice, boosting sales and putting the company back on a profitable footing by 1936. Sales of pineapple juice were also facilitated by the end of Prohibition, as the company promoted pineapple juice as a mixer for liquors, particularly gin.

The company continued to report healthy profits over the next two decades. By the 1950s Americans were spending more on food than any nation on earth, and food companies were quickly expanding their markets to accommodate demand. Castle & Cooke introduced several new pineapple products during this time, including both fresh and canned pineapple, processed in chunks and slices or crushed, in addition to expanding their markets to include bananas, citrus fruit, macadamia nuts, vegetables, and even tuna.

Given the tremendous diversification of Dole products, advertising became critical to ensuring the company's dominance in the marketplace. First, in order to capitalize on public recognition of the Dole brand name, Castle & Cooke decided to use it on the labels of several of its non-pineapple food products. Also, television became an important medium, and by the 1960s James Dole's dream of making pineapple as familiar as apples and oranges had been realized.

During the 1970s and 1980s, Dole took advantage of the increasing demand for nutritious foods, advertising its products as healthy additions to the diets of adults and children. During this time, the company introduced Dole canned pineapple in a "lite," low calorie, natural juice. In the early 1990s, Dole launched a major, multimedia advertising campaign accompanied by the slogan "How'd You Do Your Dole Today?" to encourage consumers to eat more vegetables and fruit, including pineapple, regularly. As a result of its effective advertising, Dole has maintained the biggest market share of pineapples and bananas in North America.

In 1991, under chairperson and CEO David H. Murdock, Castle & Cooke's stockholders voted to use the Dole name to represent all of their fruit and vegetable operations, reorganizing under the name Dole Food Company, Inc. The Castle & Cooke name was retained solely for the company's real estate business, which became a subsidiary of Dole Food, with operations in Hawaii, California, and Arizona. No longer dependent on pineapple as its sole source of profits, the Dole Food Company conglomerate produces a variety of fresh and packaged foods and beverages. The product line includes canned, frozen, and dried fruits, fruit juices and beverages, 30 different types of vegetables, and a variety of nuts. In the early 1990s, ice cream bars were added to the list of Dole food products. The company also retained interests in beer processing in Honduras, sugar refining in Hawaii, and tropical flower marketing in the Philip-

pines. In addition to the individual consumer, Dole's market has been expanded to include other food processors, who use Dole products as ingredients.

Expansion into international markets has also been important to the company. While Dole products have the leading market share in the United States, Canada, Mexico, and Japan, the company has also gained a significant share of the European market. In 1989 a division of Dole Foods was established in London, poised to take advantage of imminent changes in the European common market. Since 1991, Dole's international growth strategy has included expansion into eastern Europe, South Korea, and the Middle East, where eight branch offices have been opened. In 1993 Dole was operating in more than 70 countries worldwide. Furthermore, Dole has established important manufacturing centers in Thailand and the Philippines.

Dole has survived several fluctuations in the market and remains the most widely recognized brand of canned fruits and vegetables in North America and the world. The company's continued success depends on its ability to penetrate international markets as well as to provide an increasingly health conscious public with the produce they demand, two areas in which the company has excelled.

Principal Subsidiaries: Castle & Cooke Company, Inc. (80%)

Further Reading:

Cleary, David Powers, *Great American Brands,* New York: Fairchild, 1981.
"Dole Food Co. (Plans to Branch Out to Eastern Europe)," *New York Times,* November 23, 1991, pp. N19, L37.
Dole Food Company Annual Report, 1991.
"Dole Food Posts Lower Profit," *Los Angeles Times,* June 27, 1992, p. D2.
"Dole Fresh Fruit Company," company document, 1992.
"Dole PSA Aimed at Kids' Market," *Supermarket News,* March 23, 1992, p.37.
Elliott, Stuart, "Public Service Spots Produced by Dole," *New York Times,* March 6, 1992, pp. D5, C5.
"Facts On: Dole Fresh Pineapple," company document, 1992.
"The History of Dole," company document, 1992.
Horovitz, Bruce, "L.A. Ad Shops Going after Dole's Account, Lord, Dentsu and Partners, Inc.," *Los Angeles Times,* March 9, 1991, p. D2.
Ishikawa, Lisa, "Pining Away (Dole Food Co. Hawaiian Div. Closes Canning Operations," *Hawaii Business,* August 1992, p. 35.
Koeppel, Dan, "Dole Wants the Whole Produce Aisle: Branded Fruits and Vegetables are Turning the Nation's Supermarkets into Dole Country," *Adweek's Marketing Week,* October 22, 1990, p. 20.
Petruno, Tom, "Why Dole Offers More Than Just a Bit of Appeal," *Los Angeles Times,* October 11, 1991, p. D3.
Reinhold, Robert, "After Long Affair, Pineapple Jilts Hawaii for Asian Suitors (Pineapple Industry in Hawaii Coming to an End)," *New York Times,* December 26, 1991, pp. A1.
White, Todd, "LA Firms Warily Eye Vietnam Trade Possibilities," *Los Angeles Business Journal,* December 7, 1992, p. 10.
Zwein, Jason, "Pineapples, Anyone? (Dole Food Operations)," *Forbes,* November 27, 1989, p. 286.

—Sina Dubovoj

Dr Pepper/7Up Companies, Inc.

8144 Walnut Hill Lane
Dallas, Texas 75231-4372
U.S.A.
(214) 360-7000
Fax: (214) 360-7980

Public Company
Incorporated: 1988
Employees: 900
Sales: $658.7 million
Stock Exchanges: New York
SICs: 2086 Bottled & Canned Soft Drinks and Carbonated
   Water

While the best-known names in soft drink manufacturing are Coca-Cola and Pepsi, the third-place manufacturer in the $46.6 billion market is Dr Pepper/7Up Companies, Inc. The result of a 1988 merger of two former rival soft drink manufacturers, today Dr Pepper/7Up Companies, Inc., is the largest non-cola soft drink producer in the world.

Dr Pepper, the elder brand, was invented in Waco, Texas, at Morrison's Old Corner Drug Store. In 1885 a young pharmacist who worked for Morrison's, Charles C. Alderton, experimented on his own soft drink. He mixed phosphorescent water, fruit juice, sugar, and other ingredients to produce a new soft drink unlike any tasted before. With Morrison's approval, Alderton offered the drink to the store's customers. One of these jokingly called the concoction "Dr. Pepper's drink"—for Dr. Charles Pepper, the disapproving father of a woman Morrison had been courting, suggesting that Pepper might be flattered.

The name and the soft drink, with its tart, yet sweet flavor, became popular locally, and in 1887 Morrison offered beverage chemist Robert S. Lazenby the opportunity to participate in the marketing and development of this new product. After sampling "Dr Pepper's drink," Lazenby agreed to go into partnership with Morrison to produce the beverage at his Circle A Ginger Ale Company, also in Waco. Alderton, the drink's inventor, dissociated himself from Dr Pepper, opting instead to turn his talents to the pharmaceutical trade.

The new product, "Dr. Pepper's Phos-Ferrates," was available only in soda fountains until 1891, when the manufacturers began bottling the beverage. With Lazenby handling the busi-

ness end, Dr Pepper became a top seller in and around Texas. Expansion was inevitable, and Lazenby sought a marketing opportunity to introduce Dr Pepper to the world.

The ideal forum was the 1904 World's Fair, held in St. Louis. Lazenby and his son-in-law, J. B. O'Hara, demonstrated their product there, providing samples of Dr Pepper to some of the approximately 20 million World's Fair visitors. Incidentally, the 1904 exhibition also showcased other innovations, including the ice-cream cone and buns for hot dogs and hamburgers. Dr Pepper's success encouraged Lazenby and Morrison, who founded the Artesian Manufacturing and Bottling Company, which would eventually be renamed the Dr Pepper Company; by 1923, headquarters were moved from Waco to Dallas, Texas.

Around 1920, while Dr Pepper was growing in favor, C. L. Grigg, an advertising veteran of 30 years, had formed the Howdy Company in St. Louis, Missouri. The company was named for the Howdy orange-flavored soft drink Grigg had developed, but the CEO had other ideas—specifically, to invent a new flavor of beverage. For two years, Grigg tested different combinations of lemon and other flavors. By the mid-1920s he had settled on a distinctive lemon-lime formula and in 1929 the Howdy Company introduced the soda to the general public.

Grigg and company were confident of their invention's appeal. As an early sales bulletin noted, consumers "are tired of the insipid flavors, and the aftertaste of the heavy synthetic flavors is more objectionable.... So in [our beverage] we have provided seven natural flavors so blended and in such proportions that, when bottled, it produces a big natural flavor with a real taste that makes people remember it."

The only thing that might have stood in the way of the drink's early success was its name, "Bib-Label Lithiated Lemon-Lime Soda." Griggs derived the new and much simpler name, 7Up, from the beverage's "seven natural flavors." The new name first appeared on the bottle later in 1929; it retains that name today. Interestingly, the "7" is spelled out only in corporate communications. The beverage sold well, and the new name made it easy for consumers to remember. In 1936, the Howdy Company became the 7Up Company, and by the 1940s its product became the world's third-largest selling soft drink.

Although what distinguished both drinks from the rest of the market was unique flavor, neither beverage was marketed simply as a refreshment. Indeed, both Dr Pepper, whose name still retained the period at this time, and 7Up were promoted as health drinks in their first decades. Dr Pepper's famous slogan "Drink a bite to eat at 10, 2 & 4" capitalized on the idea that one typically experienced an energy slump during those hours; a serving of Dr. Pepper would presumably provide the energy boost needed to make it through the day. At the same time, 7Up boasted in ads that it "energizes . . . sets you up, dispels brain cobwebs and muscular fatigue."

The fortunes of both companies grew during World War II, with Dr Pepper able to go public in 1946, while the postwar period saw the Baby Boom, which produced an unprecedented number of soft drink consumers. In their marketing efforts, both beverage companies sought to appeal to this lucrative market. Dr Pepper, for instance, became a regular sponsor of the hit teen show "American Bandstand," while 7Up became noted for its "uncola" campaign of the late 1960s, which capitalized on the individualistic tendencies of young people by distancing 7Up from the cola market.

More recent advertising efforts have avoided the so-called "cola wars" of the 1980s, focusing instead on what makes Dr Pepper and 7Up different. Dr Pepper ads declare the soft drink is "just what the Dr ordered," while Diet Dr Pepper is "the taste you've been looking for." 7Up introduced an animated character, "Spot," derived from the its long-used logo, a large 7 with a red spot in the middle, that revitalizes the "uncola" theme that worked so well in the 1970s.

Both companies spent years testing and introducing new products while refining existing ones. Both Dr Pepper and 7Up brought out "diet" versions by the early 1970s, and as of the early 1990s, the Dr Pepper lineup consisted of Regular, Diet, Caffeine-Free, and Diet Caffeine-Free versions; 7Up had Regular, Diet, Cherry, and Diet Cherry.

While Dr Pepper was traded on the New York Stock Exchange until 1984, when it was taken private in a leveraged buyout, 7Up was a privately owned family business that did not avail itself to public trading until 1967. The two companies joined forces on May 19, 1988, when a merger of holding companies formed the Dr Pepper/7Up Companies, Inc. The combined market strength of the two companies created a stronger contender in the soft drink market, against Coke and Pepsi.

Corporate headquarters are in Dallas, home of Dr Pepper; manufacturing and research facilities are in St. Louis, where 7Up got its start. Dr Pepper is manufactured under the name Dr Pepper USA and is the company's number-one seller, providing approximately 40 percent of total revenue. 7Up USA accounts for 32 percent of the company's sales. Both brands are bottled by independent bottling agents and sold nationwide, primarily in supermarkets, grocery and convenience stores, and other retail outlets.

The Dr Pepper/7Up Foodservice unit, a separate division of the company, handles "fountain" sales selling Dr Pepper and 7Up to restaurants and to corporate customers for vending machines and cafeterias. Fountain sales account for 19 percent of total sales. Customers have included McDonald's, Burger King, Taco Bell, 7-Eleven, Hardee's, and Wendy's. Through a licensing agreement with Cadbury Beverages, the company also provides food service operators offering Dr Pepper/7Up products

the option to sell such brands as Sunkist, Canada Dry, and Tahitian Treat soft drinks.

Another eight percent of the company's sales comes from a wholly owned subsidiary, Premier Beverages, which was formed in 1981 after Dr Pepper Company purchased the rights to Welch's soft drinks. Under its new management, Welch's expanded its product line to include more fruit-flavored soft drinks to complement its Sparkling Grape Soda, which ranked as the number one grape-flavored soft drink in 1992.

In addition to the familiar Welch's name, the Premier product lineup also includes IBC Root Beer, a regional favorite in the Midwest and South. IBC was founded by the former Independent Breweries Company of St. Louis during the height of prohibition, when root beer was a popular alternative to alcoholic drinks. Today, IBC Root Beer is still sold in old-fashioned bottles. The remaining one percent of Dr Pepper/7Up's sales comes from foreign distribution, primarily in Japan, Canada, and Holland. Internationally, company beverages are sold under such brand names as Salute and Big Red.

In 1990 Dr Pepper/7Up entered the sport drink field with Nautilus Thirst Quencher. Like rival Gatorade, Nautilus is promoted as a high-electrolyte, energy-producing beverage to revive athletes. But Nautilus also stood out in its debut as the only major brand sport drink sweetened entirely by aspartame (the artificial sweetener marketed under the name NutraSweet).

With 12 percent of the total soft drink market, Dr Pepper/7Up Companies, Inc., has sought to expand its influence in America and worldwide. The St. Louis research and development plant boasts a completely automated syrup production facility that produces approximately 180 flavors for both company products and numerous private labels. Other manufacturing plants are located in Canada, the United Kingdom, and Japan.

Principal Subsidiaries: Premier Beverages; Dr Pepper/Seven-Up Foodservice.

Further Reading:

"Annual Report," Dr Pepper/Seven Up Companies, Inc., 1992.
"Dr Pepper/Seven Up," Standard NYSE Stock Reports, vol. 60, no. 62, sec. 6, entry no. 771U, Standard & Poors Corp., March 31, 1993.
"Dr Pepper/Seven Up Companies, Inc., The Nation's Third Largest Soft Drink Company," Dr Pepper/Seven Up Companies.

—Susan Salter

Duracell International Inc.

Berkshire Industrial Park
Bethel, Connecticut 06801
U.S.A.
(203) 796-4000 or (800) 243-9540
Fax: (203) 778-9016

Public Company
Incorporated: 1935 as P.R. Mallory & Company
Employees: 7,900
Sales: $1.5 billion
Stock Exchanges: New York
SICs: 3691 Storage Batteries

Duracell International Inc. is the world's largest manufacturer and marketer of alkaline batteries. The parent company of the United States-based Duracell Inc., Duracell International markets the brand Duracell, under the same name, around the world and controls 79 percent of the U.S. consumer battery market. Its only real competitor is Eveready, which, with Duracell, combines for about 80 percent of the alkaline battery market worldwide. Known as P.R. Mallory for decades after its founding in 1935, the company's name was changed in 1978 when it was acquired by Dart Industries. Since that time, Duracell has been involved in numerous acquisitions and mergers, including one of the largest leveraged buyouts (LBOs) of the 1980s. Best known for batteries, Duracell also makes a variety of electrical and electronic components used by manufacturers of consumer durables and many related products bought by industry, various government agencies, and consumers.

P.R. Mallory originated the Duracell brandname in 1935. The battery component of Mallory's business grew steadily throughout the post-World War II period, reflecting the booming economy and the rapidly growing market for consumer durables and electronic consumer goods, some of which would require battery power. Later, in the 1980s, as electronic technology shifted to the "cellular age," Duracell would adapt its products accordingly, producing smaller cells to meet this now booming technology.

Although sales were growing, the company's business also closely tracked the business cycle because sales of many of its products were at the mercy of consumer buying power—itself a function of wages and earnings. For example, from the early 1960s into the mid-1970s sales grew strongly (the average

annual rate was five percent from 1963 to 1972); however, company profits reflected the recession of the mid- and late-1960s, with earnings per share hitting a peak of $2.34 in 1966 before falling sharply with the recession. With the beginning of the deep recession in mid-1973, company earnings began to fall sharply.

Mallory's profit margins were respectable in that price-competitive climate, but were under constant pressure. The boom of 1972 allowed the firm to boost sales of electrical and electronic items to industry, complementing consumer sales. Specifically, makers of appliances bought Mallory components to satisfy the growing retail demand for household items, such as laundry units, electric and gas ranges, and dishwashers, among other consumer durables. The company saw this expansion of consumer durables, in particular, as a basis for long-term growth.

The strong growth in consumer durables generated an expanding volume of sales and, thus, economies of scale in production, meaning lower unit costs, higher profit margins, and some insulation from price wars. Therefore, even as the U.S. economy left the fast-growth path of the 1960s and Mallory's margins fell, it was able to weather the downslide of demand that accompanied the recession of 1973. The company's debt load was small, and, although most of its market was domestic, it was well positioned to take on the foreign firms using their low production costs to make headway into the U.S. market in the late 1970s.

In 1977, *Fortune* magazine ranked Mallory as the 507th largest company, with $323 million in sales and profits of $10 million (which put it in the 170th position). Most of the company's sales were to individual consumers and to makers of consumer durables. Industry accounted for the rest of Duracell's sales, mostly electrical contacts, welding products, and special metals for the automotive, power generating, aerospace, and communications industries. Mallory was also a supplier of batteries of all sizes to the military, and its Duracell batteries were used in everything from hearing aids to military communications equipment. Brand building was essential during this time; the company's ad campaign focused on the use of batteries in toys, and the "copper-top" image it created would be very successful in promoting the "long life" of Duracell batteries.

The battery is essentially an undifferentiated product, and niches in the market were primarily established through advertising. To a certain extent, before the 1980s, the technology included transistor batteries and photo and watch batteries. Since the early 1980s, however, Duracell and Eveready have been primarily selling general purpose batteries where image is the only means to promote differentiation.

The company was bought by Dart Industries in 1978, becoming Duracell Inc. and kicking off what would be a tumultuous two decades of mergers and acquisitions. Many deals transpired in the 1980s, including one of the largest leveraged buyouts in history.

The 1978 takeover was launched by Dart CEO and president C. Robert Kidder, who had come to Dart from Ford. Mallory fought the takeover but eventually settled on Dart's offer of $46 per share, making the total acquisition worth $215 million. At the time, Mallory was being hit hard by competition from

Energizer and Panasonic. Kidder had joined Dart as vice-president of Planning and Development and made the recommendation that Dart acquire Mallory in order to add more consumer business to Dart. After gaining control over Mallory, Dart divested several of Mallory's subsidiaries but kept and promoted Duracell.

Shortly thereafter, Kidder joined Duracell as a vice-president based in Europe, where company growth was slower. Within one year, Kidder was promoted by Chairman Pete Viele to vice-president of sales and marketing for Duracell U.S.A. Kidder would be credited with the forward-looking strategy of creating the "cordless Duracell home" of cellular phones and pocket computers and, most importantly, recognizing the need to capture this market. This market shift points to the unique, and perennial, technological parameters of a profitable battery business—companies can't just invent new battery products without an established application for their use. Thus, Duracell's success has been highly dependent on energy technologies, especially in the 1980s and 1990s, built into cellular telephones, camcorders, pocket computers, and other innovations.

By 1980 the company was again on the market, this time as part of a deal between Kraft Inc. and Dart. Kraft, which was owned by Phillip Morris at the time, merged with Dart, owner of Duracell. This marriage would last until 1986, when Dart and Kraft split, with Kraft keeping Duracell.

Two years later Duracell was taken over by the investment banking firm of Kohlberg Kravis Roberts (KKR) in what would be one of the largest leveraged buyouts of the 1980s. The central players, Jerome Kohlberg Jr., Henry R. Kravis, and George R. Roberts, raised $62 million to buy out 35 companies between 1976 and 1989, including Duracell. The purchase price for Duracell was $1.9 billion in 1988. Kidder and the management team that organized the buyout from Kraft became 30 percent owners, Kidder was named president and CEO of Duracell, Inc., and the new Kidder team devised a particular marketing and restructuring strategy for the newly independent firm.

At the time, the KKR buyout was viewed as very successful in that, compared to other LBOs, there were no assets sold and no large layoffs. Increased research and development spending, prudent debt management, and cost cutting measures led to an increased market position for the KKR-controlled Duracell. The buyout was hailed by some as KKR's most successful LBO. Of course Duracell also benefited from the increase in battery demand in the United States as well. Duracell and its major rival, Eveready, together controlled 75 percent of the $3 billion a year market. Another key factor in the success of the LBO was the fact that most of the growth of the business had shifted to long-lasting alkalines (from zinc batteries) so that alkalines accounted for 80 percent of Duracell's revenues in 1989.

In addition, the new marketing strategy for the streamlined company emphasized marketing the Duracell brand around the world, including such new products as Lithium Manganese Dioxide batteries and the Copper Top Tester, a package that allowed consumers to test the power of batteries. These marketing commitments were part of the buyout agreement. The commitment to the fierce mass marketing campaign paid dividends as Duracell distribution became vast—"We're in mass mer-chandising, food, drug, jewelry, and hardware stores, catalogue showrooms, 7-Elevens, and the Price Club, to name a few," said Kidder.

The LBO firm KKR had a reputation for piling on debt as part of its takeovers, and the future of Duracell was uncertain in spite of its strong marketing position. To maintain a healthy cash flow, and as part of the takeover agreement, they sold two plants. Further, shortly after the buyout, KKR took Duracell public in May 1989, and the share values rose from $15 to $20 in the first hour of trading. KKR made a $1.1 billion paper profit, and Kidder made a handsome paper profit as well. KKR still controlled 61 percent of the company's stock while institutions held some 36 percent. Operating profits in the second quarter of 1990 rose 13 percent over the previous year to $194 million.

Back in the battery market, Duracell was closing the gap on market leader Eveready Battery; Eveready held 60 percent of sales in 1986, but by 1989 Eveready's share had fallen to 42 percent and Duracell made a significant gain, to a 36 percent share. Duracell challenged Germany's Varta internationally and in 1988 captured almost half of Europe's alkaline market, despite aggressive advertising by European battery makers, who spent $25 million on advertising that year.

As part of its advertising strategy, Duracell hired the high-profile advertising agency Ogilvy & Mather to promote its new battery tester product. Whereas previous Duracell ads focused on the toy market, these television spots showed people, for example, at a bridal shower, unable to capture the event on film or operate any appliances because their batteries were dead. Of course, had they purchased the Duracell's Tester, they would have known beforehand that the batteries were dead. Promoted as "another Tester-monial," the spots used nonactors in everyday situations where batteries are essential. The spots were very successful.

Each year, as part of its marketing strategy, Duracell's higher spending on advertising has continued to pay off. Worldwide sales in 1991 were close to $1.5 billion and netted a 43 percent share of the U.S. alkaline market. As of the early 1990s, Duracell was outsold in the U.S. market only by Ralston Purina and was challenged in Europe only by Varta, which is Europe's one major rival to the North American heavyweights.

As Duracell moved into 1993, the unbridled growth of the modern "cellular society"—telephones, computers, compact disc players, and power tools—brought double-digit growth to the battery industry and to Duracell. Today the consumer battery market is one of small batteries with more power than ever, with narrow, smaller penlite-type and mini-penlites taking over two-thirds of the market, squeezing out the traditional C and D battery lines. Duracell is also a leader in the new alkaline manganese battery, whose longer life—up to six times that of zinc carbon—more than compensates for its higher price. Zinc-chloride batteries seemed to be ready to take over the market in the early 1980s but were overcome by the longer-lasting, lower-cost alkaline cell.

As the market for zinc and alkaline cells began to reach its limits in a global market, new challenges faced Duracell in its battle with the largest players in the battery industry. According to International Management in 1993, this intense struggle showed no sign of slowing down. One issue that surfaced is recyclability, notably in Europe, adding another dimension to the competitive struggle. For example, the throwaway image of nonrechargeable batteries has provoked concern about the environment, with the European Commission, in 1989, giving battery makers a choice—eliminate dangerous metals (notably cadmium and mercury) or collect batteries for recycling. Although some companies, such as Varta, moved to make batteries mercury-free, some made the case that the costs associated with recycling outweighed the environmental benefits. In some cases, companies have cooperated to deflect costs—Europile, the consumer battery makers association, includes Duracell, and Duracell's Richard Leveton chairs the Europile environment committee.

The rechargeable market was also revived, with companies trying to balance the higher costs of new technology with the potential gains from new markets. Duracell, for example, began supplying nickel-metal hydride cell phone batteries to Fujitsu and launched a consumer version of the same product in the early 1990s. Although Duracell has cooperated with other industry leaders on such issues as recyclability and the environment, intensified competition continued in the core markets. In one effort to reap the benefits of new product development, Duracell entered into a joint research project with competitor Varta (Germany) and Toshiba. The company hoped to expand into new products and new geographical markets, especially in Asia. In any case, the ever-present competitive warfare of the industry exerts continuing pressure on Duracell to innovate and cut costs. As *International Management* summed up in its April 1993 issue: "The struggle for power shows no sign of running down."

Principal Subsidiaries: Duracell Canada Inc.; Duraname Corp. USA; Duracell Danmark A/S (Denmark); Duracell Finland OY; Duracell Holdings (UK) Limited; Duracell Overseas Trading Limited (United Kingdom); Duracell SARL (France); Duracell Batteries Limited (United Kingdom); Duracell Italia Holdings SpA (Italy); Pile Superpila SRL (Italy); Tudor Hellensens Svenska AB (Sweden); Duracell SpA (Italy); Duracell Technologies A.G. (Switzerland); E.P.C.I. SA (Switzerland); NV Duracell Belgium SA (Belgium); NV Duracell Batteries SA (Belgium); Duracell Batteries Sucursal en España (Spain); NV Duracell Benelux SA (Belgium); Duracell Inc.; Duracell Argentina SA; Duracell Australia Pty. Ltd.; Duracell International GmbH (Austria); Duracell do Brazil Industria E Comercia Ltda. (Brazil); Duracell Chile Sociedad Comercio Ltda. (Chile); Duracell Colombia Ltda.; Daimon-Duracell Gmbh (Germany); Duracell Asia Ltd. (Hong Kong); Duracell International Trading KFT (Hungary); Duracell Batery Japan Ltd.; Duracell SA de CV (Mexico); Duracell Nederland BV (Netherlands); Duracell New Zealand Ltd.; Duracell Norge A/S (Norway); Daimon-Duracell (Pilhas) Ltda. (Portugal); Duracell Caribbean, Inc. (Puerto Rico); Duracell (SEA) Pte. Ltd. (Singapore); Duracell Svenska AB (Sweden); Duracell-Hellesens Inc. (Switzerland); Duracellven CA (Venezuela).

Further Reading:

"Duracell Uses Packaging to Sell Lights," *Packaging,* December 1983.
Erickson, Julie Liesse, "Perrin Leads Duracell's Charge," *Advertising Age,* June 26, 1989.
Farnham, Alan, "What's Sparking Duracell?" *Fortune,* July 16, 1990.
Huhn, Mary, "Batteries and Boxer KO the Competition," *AdWeek,* November 12, 1990.
Lazo, Shirley A., "Speaking of Dividends," *Barron's,* March 1, 1993.
Levine, Bernard, "Dart-Mallory Accord Seen Mirroring Cap Firms' Woes," *Electronic News,* December 11, 1978.
"Mallory's Profits Sparkle," *Financial World,* November 7, 1973.
Oliver, Joyce Anne, "Duracell CEO Charged Up About His Company," *Marketing News,* November 11, 1991.
Shipman, Alan, "Power Struggle: The World's Battery Makers Are Fighting Over an Expanding Market as Consumer Demand and Environmental Concerns Put the Combatants on Their Mettle," *International Management,* April 1993.
Tilsner, Julie, "Duracell Looks Abroad for More Juice," *Business Week,* December 21, 1992.

—John A. Sarich

E-Systems, Inc.

6250 LBJ Freeway
P.O. Box 660248
Dallas, Texas 75266-0248
U.S.A.
(214) 661-1000
Fax: (214) 661-8508

Public Company
Incorporated: 1964 as LTV Electrosystems, Inc.
Employees: 18,600
Sales: $2.1 billion
Stock Exchanges: New York London
SICs: 3812 Search Navigation and Aeronautical Systems;
  3679 Electronic Components, Nec

E-Systems, Inc. is one of the leading defense electronics companies in the United States. This diversified company designs, develops, produces, and services high technology systems, especially surveillance, verification, and aircraft ground-land navigation equipment, primarily for defense applications around the world. The company also develops electronics programs and systems for business, industrial, and nondefense government programs and agencies. Much of E-Systems' business serves the government national security market, with more than two-thirds of its business falling within the two primary areas of intelligence and reconnaissance command, control, and communications. The company includes five divisions and four wholly owned subsidiaries.

The company's definition of electronic warfare includes "timely detection, identification, location, and tracking of the electromagnetic emissions associated with foreign communications and weapons systems," and refers to strategic systems for intelligence, reconnaissance and surveillance applications, tactical systems relating to electronic countermeasures, and jamming and deception devices. The company's command, control, and communications segment includes communications equipment as well as command and control systems to process data for analysis and decision making. The company develops and produces a wide range of systems, including air traffic control systems for the Federal Aviation Administration and communications systems for NATO. The guidance, controls, and navigation segment develops and manufactures flight controls for commercial and military aircraft, including missile steering and tracking systems. The aircraft maintenance and modification area provides specialized service for aircraft of all types, both military and commercial.

E-Systems' predecessor company was created in December 1964 when the LTV Temco Aerospace division of Ling-Temco-Vought Inc. formed LTV Electrosystems, Inc. as a wholly owned subsidiary. In April of the following year, LTV Electrosystems became a publicly-held subsidiary and was listed as an over-the-counter stock. During the summer of that year, it acquired from its parent nearly all of the operating properties of LTV Military Electronics Division (known as the Garland Division), Continental Electronics Manufacturing Company, and Continental Electronics Systems, Inc. It also opened a new facility in South Carolina as an adjunct to its Greenville Division. Sales for 1965 were almost $81 million, with net earnings of $2.1 million.

During the period from 1965 to 1972, the company focused on expansion. A series of acquisitions began during this time that included such companies as Memcor, Inc., Pickard & Burns Electronics, the Eagle Transport Company. However, overly rapid growth led to large debt and deteriorating profits, and the company was forced to divest itself of some companies, only a year or two after acquiring them, to cut costs and rid itself of marginal operations that could not promise high enough return for the financial risk involved. In 1969, a Memcor plant and most of the assets of Continental Electronics Manufacturing Company were sold because of low profits.

By 1970, the company had returned to profitability; it had net sales of almost $200 million with earnings of $2.8 million, up from the previous year's net loss of $4 million. LTV Electrosystems acquired American Standard Inc.'s Melpar Division in 1970 and established a new Commercial Services Division in Greenville to perform heavy structural modification and maintenance for the airlines. In 1971 LTV Electrosystems acquired Hamilton Watch Company's Electronics division and established a new domestic international sales company known as Electrosystems Export Company. Nevertheless, after unloading several of its acquisitions, employment in 1970 was down to 7,000 from a high in 1968 of more than 11,000.

In 1972, E-Systems emerged as an independent, publicly owned corporation, headed by John W. Dixon, who had served as LTV Electrosystems' president and chief executive officer since 1969. During its first year as a public company, sales reached $156 million, and, with $34 million spent on research and development, total company assets amounted to $90 million. The company employed 5,500 employees, 26 percent of whom were engineers, scientists, and technicians. The entire company occupied less than three million square feet of floorspace.

The 1970s was a decade of reorganization and acquisition for the newly renamed E-Systems Inc. In 1973, the company formed its Aircraft Systems Group through consolidation of its Greenville and Donaldson divisions and the newly acquired Serv-Air, Inc. Serv-Air maintained, modified, and supported all National Aeronautics and Space Administration (NASA) aircraft flown by the astronauts at the Johnson Space Center in

Houston. That year, E-Systems also consolidated its Montek, Garland, and Melpar divisions with the newly-acquired TAI, Inc. to form the Electronics Systems Group. TAI was an engineering firm providing consulting services for the construction of telecommunications networks around the world. E-Systems further acquired a major product line called Digicom from GTE Sylvania to augment the company's data systems capabilities. Offices in Korea and Brazil were opened in addition to an international office at the Dallas headquarters.

In 1973, E-Systems' Greenville Division began providing depot maintenance, logistics support, and special modifications for aircraft belonging to the U.S. Air Force's Special Air Mission Fleet. This important contract provided service for aircraft used by the president of the United States, the vice-president, and cabinet members.

In 1974, the Memcor Division became the basis for the newly formed Production Electronics Group. During this time, E-Systems acquired Electronic Communications, Inc. and Air Asia Co., Ltd. of Taiwan from Air American, Inc. In 1976, the company formed an Energy Technology Center for research on developing practical uses for solar energy. The Commercial Division was established in 1978, and merged with the TelSat-Com Division the following year.

By the mid 1970s, E-Systems was the world's top supplier of military radios and large earth station antennas for satellite communications as well as one of the top technical consultants for microwave telecommunications systems. E-Systems' business consisted of about 55 percent defense contracts and 45 percent international, industrial, and other nondefense contracts. The company was investing considerable research and development funds in digital techniques, microminiaturization, surface acoustic wave devices, digital processing, and voice and video compression.

E-Systems began its participation in the automation of air traffic control in 1981 with the development and production of the Flight Service Automation System (FSAS) for the Federal Aviation Administration. By 1990, the system included an extensive nationwide network of 400 computers and 3,000 display terminals involving 18,000 airports. It provided general aviation pilots with weather briefings and navigation advisories and assisted them with the filing of flight plans. Updated replacement systems for FSAS provided extensive use of satellite technology and color displays for windowing weather graphics and textual data.

E-Systems had record sales of $827 million in 1983 and booked new orders amounting to more than $900 million. The company's Garland Division was awarded a $31 million contract by McDonnell Douglas Corporation to upgrade the U.S. Air Force F-4G aircraft with a system to suppress enemy surface-to-air missiles and anti-aircraft artillery systems. The system utilized special electronic warfare equipment along with anti-radiation missiles and conventional weapons. This contract substantially increased the importance of the company's electronic warfare product area. That year *Fortune* magazine rated E-Systems first among company's known for high returns to investors over the past ten years.

The company substantially increased its research and development budget in 1984, concentrating heavily on defense electronics; electronic warfare; and command, control and communications. Over the following year, more than 65 percent of the company's sales were generated by electronic warfare equipment and systems, and sales and new order bookings were at an all time high. E-Systems expanded many of its facilities, opening a total of 264,000 square feet of automated production and engineering facilities at the Communications Manufacturing Division in St. Petersburg, Florida, and the Garland Division. It also added 240,000 square feet of engineering and administrative space at ECI in St. Petersburg and Melpar, based in Falls Church, Virginia.

In 1986, for the first time in its history, E-Systems had sales of more than $1 billion. By this time, employment was at 15,000 with 45 percent of the employees engaged as engineers, scientists, and technicians. The company occupied more than 5.6 million square feet of floor space; research and development expenditures were at a record $211 million; and company assets totaled over $600 million.

This was also the last full year in which John W. Dixon served as chair and chief executive officer. Dixon stepped down in 1987 to become Chairman Emeritus, and was succeeded by David R. Tacke. Under Tacke, the company outbid Lockheed and General Dynamics to develop an important new program known as the Joint Service Imagery Processing System (JSIPS). JSIPS was a transportable ground station for multisensory processing and dissemination of national strategic and tactical imagery. E-Systems also completed a mammoth processing system utilizing high speed programs able to process information at a rate of four billion bits per second and store more than one and a half trillion bits. Analysts compared the processing of this amount of data to processing the contents of the Library of Congress in an average work day. The system, which could take up to an acre of floor space, provided information to top military and civilian defense officials.

In the international arena, E-Systems sold its Taiwanese-based subsidiary Air Asia, after finding it incompatible with the rest of the company's business. The company next entered into a joint venture with the West German company GROB TFE to develop the EGRETT-1, a single-engine, turboprop aircraft. E-Systems was responsible for the plane's aircraft systems integration, which could be adapted for commercial communications, environmental protection activities, or scientific applications such as geophysical surveys. In 1990, E-Systems entered into TELOS, a joint venture with German partners formed for the operational maintenance and logistics support of EGRETT aircraft programs. E-Systems considered this EGRETT program an important opportunity through which to develop its international marketplace, which the company considered a big growth area despite the difficulties in exporting sensitive high technology.

Tacke served as head of the company only until spring 1989, when E. Gene Keiffer, the former president and chief operating officer became chair and CEO of E-Systems. That year the company acquired Engineering Research Associates, located in Vienna, Virginia, a technology leader in the field of high-frequency surveillance systems.

Also during this time, the company was continuing its work on high performance, high speed computer systems and software, applying Very High Speed Integrated Circuit, Monolithic Microwave Integrated Circuit, and Gallium Arsenide technologies to specialized military systems. E-Systems developed artificial intelligence applications for defense systems, as well as specialized systems and programs for speech processing, digital imagery enhancement, and data base management. The company also explored the field of neural networking, which allowed computers to recognize and analyze patterns of information. Work continued in the area of mass data storage as well as the development of a robotic, mass storage library system using cassettes instead of computer tapes. Furthermore, the company became involved in research concerning new ways to apply fiber optic technology to defense systems.

E-Systems acquired HRB Systems Inc. from Hadson Corp. in 1990 for $65 million, half the price Hadson had paid only two years before. Hadson attributed HRB's decreased market value and declining sales to the end of the Cold War. E-Systems CEO Keiffer, however, thought the investment was a good one, observing that the new acquisition would complement and expand E-Systems' position in the advanced intelligence and reconnaissance systems marketplace. HRB designed and developed signal collection, processing, and analysis systems and was based in State College, Pennsylvania, with about 1,300 employees.

Also in 1990 E-Systems finally settled a criminal and civil lawsuit involving its production of radios for the U.S. Army. The radios were supplied by E-Systems' Memcor division, which had been providing tactical radios to the Army for more than 15 years and at one time had been the world's leading producer of such equipment. In 1985, the Army terminated for default two contracts with Memcor totaling about $19 million. Following the cancellation, E-Systems was forced to shut down Memcor, laying off most of the division's employees. The company appealed the Army's terminations and also filed a $13-million claim against the Army. In early 1988, the federal government informed E-Systems that it was initiating a criminal investigation to determine whether the company had violated any procurement regulations associated with the cancelled contracts. The government charged that three managers and a supervisor at the Memcor plant had neglected to report test failures and repairs as required and, moreover, created fake documents on untested radios. Several former E-Systems employees were indicted for the test falsifications; E-Systems plead guilty to the charges and agreed to pay $4.6 million in fines. (The former comployees were acquited of the criminal charges.) In addition, as part of the settlement, E-Systems agreed to drop its suit against the government. Payment of the fines enabled E-Systems to continue to do business with the U.S. government.

In 1993, as the Cold War ended and eastern and western Germany became unified, Germany announced a freeze on defense contracts, a move that affected profits at E-Systems. The EGRETT project was scrapped for both financial and political reasons; analysts estimated that the contract would have brought in between $600 million and $1 billion for E-Systems through the end of the decade.

Consequently, E-Systems began to focus increasingly on commercial and industrial markets over the next few years, emphasizing the adaptation of leading edge technologies for existing systems and applying those technologies in new ways to serve nonmilitary purposes. The company sought wider distribution of its robotic data storage system, EMASS, developed for use by defense and intelligence agencies for storing massive amounts of data on tape cartridges. Major oil companies had purchased the systems to keep track of seismic data, but E-Systems was still having difficulty breaking into other information-intensive industries. In 1993 E-Systems entered into agreements with IBM, Conves, and Cray Research to help market the system. IBM agreed to include the EMASS system along with other data storage systems it marketed.

Other nondefense projects included a contract with the California Department of Forestry and Fire Protection to operate and maintain the state's 31 aircraft in support of the its wildfire suppression program. Furthermore, the U.S. Department of Education established a $16 million contract with E-Systems for a national student loans and grants database. The company had previously won a data processing contract for the government's Stafford Loan program, formerly known as the Guaranteed Student Loan program. In the medical field, a new E-Systems unit, E-Systems Medical Electronics, Inc., worked to promote the company's image-processing, distribution, and storage technology, acquiring Advanced Video Products, Inc., a Massachusetts-based medical electronics company, in the process.

Nevertheless, U.S. Defense Department and military work continued to generate the bulk of E-Systems' income. During 1992, the company's Serv-Air division received a contract from the Army, expected to generate more than $600 million over four years, to operate and manage activity for the Special Operations Command by providing maintenance, repair, logistics support, systems engineering, and system modifications for military helicopters, avionics equipment, and communications equipment. In early 1993, E-Systems received a $64 million contract to provide two Learjet instrumentation systems and to train pilots and maintenance workers and provide spare parts supplies as well as operator and maintenance manuals. This contract was expected to generate as much as $400 million with its renewal options.

In an E-Systems annual report of the early 1990s, management observed that "in an environment of reduced U.S. forces abroad, reconnaissance, intelligence collection, and signal processing become even more important." E-Systems speculated that the industry could become more competitive as other defense contractors sought to replace lost programs by entering E-Systems' niche in reconnaissance and surveillance, communications, and special aircraft integration. Company officials expected that international sales would be the company's greatest source of growth in years to come as other nations assumed more responsibility for their own security. They also predicted that nonmilitary contracts would account for ten percent of business by the end of the 1990s.

Principal Subsidiaries: E-Systems Medical Electronics, Inc.; HRB Systems, Inc.; Serv-Air, Inc.; Engineering Research Associates, Inc.

Further Reading:

"E-Systems Agrees to Buy Defense Unit from Hadson Corp." *Wall Street Journal,* August 30, 1990, p. C19.

E-Systems Annual Reports, Dallas, Texas: E-Systems, 1965–1992.

"E-Systems Inc. Pleads Guilty to Fraud," *Wall Street Journal,* August 28, 1990, p. B4.

"Federal Grand Jury Indicts 4 Employees of E-Systems Inc.," *Wall Street Journal,* August 2, 1990.

"Germany Freezes Defense Contracts," *Wall Street Journal,* February 4, 1993, p. A14.

—Wendy J. Stein

Eckerd Corporation

8333 Bryan Dairy Road
Largo, Florida 34647
U.S.A.
(813) 397-7461
Fax: (813) 398-8369

Public Company
Incorporated: 1986 as Jack Eckerd Corporation
Employees: 38,000
Sales: $3.8 billion
Stock Exchanges: New York
SICs: 5912 Drug Stores and Proprietary Stores; 5995 Optical
  Goods Stores

Eckerd Corporation operates a chain of about 1,700 drug stores primarily in the Sunbelt states, and a chain of Eckerd Optical centers and Visionworks stores in five southeastern states and Washington, D.C. The company also operates a large photo processing enterprise with all stores offering photo-finishing services and more than 400 stores operating mini-labs with one-hour Express Photo service. In 1989, Eckerd Corp. acquired Insta-Care Pharmacy Services, which provided prescription drugs and medical consulting services to long-term care health care facilities in six states.

Eckerd drugstores traces its history to the days when Jack Eckerd's father, J. Milton Eckerd, launched one of the country's first drugstore chains in Erie, Pennsylvania. Jack began working for his father's company during the Depression. He learned the business from the bottom up, despite his father's warning, "You're going to work longer and harder than anyone else, and you're not going to make too much money."

In the 1950s, Jack Eckerd became interested in a new concept being used in drugstores—self-service. In 1952, Jack left his father's chain to purchase three struggling drugstores in Tampa and Clearwater, Florida. Using the self-service concept, he turned the three stores into financial successes.

According to friends and family, the Jack Eckerd chain became successful because of Eckerd's honesty, hard work, dedication, and people-oriented philosophy of management. He told one interviewer, "I made up my mind I would never do anything, if I could help it, that wasn't in the best interest of the customers, the employees, and the stockholders." His wife Ruth wrote that

he could not drive by one of his stores without going in to talk to the employees. He himself said that understanding employees and making decisions based on fairness were essential to his success. He called his employees his company's greatest asset.

Eckerd tried to keep in touch with employees and listen to their suggestions because they were the ones who came in contact with the customers. To foster a sense of family, Eckerd sent personally-signed birthday cards to all employees throughout the chain, stopping this practice only when the employee rolls grew to 8,000.

Eckerd drew attention when he successfully challenged Florida's "fair trade law," which prohibited retailers from reducing prices below those charged by other retailers in the state. Eckerd successfully argued before the Florida Supreme Court that the law was unconstitutional and that he had the right to provide discounts to increase his share of the market. Discount pricing and other customer-pleasing strategies such as senior citizen discounts and two-for-one prints of processed film helped make the Eckerd chain a success.

In 1959, Publix markets, a southern grocery chain, offered Eckerd the opportunity to build drugstores next to five of its supermarkets in strip shopping malls. Eckerd borrowed $1 million and committed to a 15-year lease on each of the stores. Eckerd took his company public in 1961 as Eckerd Drugs of Florida and then went on to buy a string of other southeastern drugstores and other businesses. In 1966, Eckerd bought Old Dominion Candies (which he sold in 1972); in 1968, he purchased Jackson's/Byrons, a junior department store chain based in Miami that was renamed J. Byrons; and in 1969, he acquired the Gray Security Service and the food-service supplier Kurman Company. In 1970, Eckerd bought Brown's Thrift City Wholesale Drugs and Mading-Dugan Drugs. He also purchased Eckerd Drugs Eastern and Ward Cut-Rate Drug in 1973. In 1977, he bought Eckerd Drugs of Charlotte, North Carolina, a store that his father had started and then sold, along with other stores, to his son-in-law in the 1930s. With this purchase, all Eckerd drugstores were now owned by Jack Eckerd.

During the 1970s, Jack Eckerd made a number of unsuccessful bids for public office. He lost his first race when he ran in a primary election for governor of Florida in 1970. In 1974, he won the Republican nomination to run for the U.S. Senate but lost the election. Eckerd ran for governor again in 1979 but once again lost his bid for elected office. Eckerd only held public office when President Gerald Ford named him head of the General Services Administration (GSA) in 1975. During his tenure at the GSA, Eckerd turned over chairmanship of the company to Stewart Turley, who remained chairman of the board more than 15 years. Eckerd returned to the company as a member of its board in 1979.

In 1980, Eckerd Drugs strengthened its presence in Texas by acquiring Sav-X drugstores of Abilene and 40 Sommers Drug Stores. Eckerd also entered the video market by acquiring American Home Video, which owned the Video Concepts stores. Eckerd sold both the video concern and J. Byrons stores in 1985.

Jack Eckerd became a hero in the Christian press in the mid-1980s when he ordered *Playboy, Penthouse,* and *Hustler* magazines and other "questionable books" off the shelves of Eckerd Drugs stores, calling them "America's family drugstores." According to the *Christian Herald*, Eckerd also led a drive, through lobbying and public pressure, to convince other drugstore chains to "stop selling pornography."

The late 1980s brought a shakeup in management when the corporation was in danger of being seized in a hostile takeover. To block the hostile takeover, Eckerd sold his shares in the company to a management investment group in a leveraged buyout. Merrill Lynch Capital Partners negotiated the leveraged buyout of the Eckerd Drugs company by its managers for $1.2 billion. The buyout left Merrill Lynch and affiliates with 58 percent share of the company, and Eckerd Drugs was once again a private company, named the Jack Eckerd Corporation. Jack Eckerd's sale of his shares brought him $36 million.

Eckerd is well-known for his philanthropic work, especially the $10 million he donated to Florida Presbyterian College, which was renamed Eckerd College in 1971. He had also been active in prison work, chairing a private-sector board to oversee prison industries in Florida. After the sale of his company shares, he continued to donate money and energy to various causes, especially his Eckerd Family Youth Alternatives, which operated in seven states and sponsored wilderness programs for troubled youths. By the early 1990s, it had more than 850 employees and a budget of more than $20 million, and Eckerd served as board chairman.

The management buyout brought a new look to the drug chain, as the company spent $20 million a year to remodel more than 250 stores each year. The late 1980s also brought some massive closings and purchases. Eckerd Corp. shut down 45 of its least profitable stores and sold eleven of its Tulsa, Oklahoma stores. On the other side of the ledger, however, it bought 32 Shoppers Drug Mart Stores located in Florida and also opened 50 new stores. The company also expanded its optical and photofinishing services by adding 79 Express Photo mini-labs and more than 20 Visionworks stores.

When Revco drugs declared bankruptcy in 1990, Eckerd immediately acquired 220 of its stores, and engaged in protracted negotiations to acquire the remaining stores in the Ohio-based chain. Eckerd chairman Stewart Turley saw Revco and Eckerd as very compatible, given the similarity of size and the fact that geographically they complemented each other: half of Revco's stores were located in states in which Eckerd operated, but the other half were located in the Midwest, which would extend Eckerd's market. The merger of Revco and Eckerd would also have given Eckerd more clout in the prescription market. With competition tight for the third-party payment plans of government, unions and company medical plans, volume was the key to prescription profits. If Eckerd became the largest drugstore chain, it could offer lower prices and become more attractive to third-party clients.

Eckerd's offer for Revco was worth almost $779 million, pushing challenger Rite-Aid out of the running. Most creditors were now backing Eckerd's plan, which also called for turning Revco headquarters into a regional office and closing about 250 Revco stores. However, a last-minute re-organization plan by Revco promised to save thousands of jobs and keep most

Revco stores open, quashing Eckerd's bid. Revco agreed to pay Eckerd $7.5 million to cover the expenses generated by the bidding process. When Revco came out of bankruptcy in mid-1992, however, speculation continued that it would again be put on the block by its managers and creditors and that Eckerd and RiteAid were still interested in owning the Revco chain.

According to *Florida Trend* magazine, however, Eckerd's numbers look rather dismal: long-term debt was more than $1 billion in 1992. Since the 1986 leveraged buyout, shareholder equity dropped from $478.5 million to a deficit of $265.5 million. The company lost $300 million between 1987 and 1992, and in four of those years operating profits did not even cover interest expenses. In the spring of 1993, Eckerd negotiated a refinancing deal with two banks, allowing it to simplify its debt structure and save considerably on interest and dividend costs. The company announced that the refinancing also would support expansion plans.

Eckerd Corp. owned 1,692 stores in 13 states as of 1993. More than 540 Eckerd drugstores were located in Florida, 475 in Texas, almost 200 each in North Carolina and Georgia, more than 100 in Louisiana, and fewer than 100 in South Carolina. There were also Eckerd stores scattered throughout Tennessee, Mississippi, Oklahoma, New Jersey, Alabama, Delaware, and Maryland. Express Photo shops were located in 405 of these stores. Prescription drugs and over-the-counter drugs accounted for more than half of the company's revenues, with prescription drugs showing tremendous growth.

In 1992, the chain launched plans to increase its cosmetics and fragrance sales by adding new upscale product lines. It also consolidated its corporate structure, reducing operating regions from eight to six, and cutting about 600 headquarter and field office jobs to reduce the number of bureaucratic layers between stores and top management.

The expansion of beauty aids sales and consolidation of operations came at a time when Eckerd, as well as other drugstore chains, were facing intense competition from mass merchandisers such as Wal-Mart Stores, which were carrying more health and beauty aids that were traditionally bought at drugstores. The drugstores had already lost business to supermarkets and were being forced to become more like corner convenience stores by carrying more foods and beverages. According to Eckerd chairman Stewart Turley, chain stores such as Eckerd must have core departments, especially prescriptions, photoprocessing, and greeting cards. Eckerd, as well as other chain drugstores, also began offering free home delivery for elderly customers and young parents. In August of 1993, Jack Eckerd Corporation returned to the public arena as the Eckerd Corporation. The company is listed on the New York Stock Exchange.

Further Reading:

DeGeorge, Gail, "A Drugstore Cowboy Rides to Revco's Rescue," *Business Week,* January 27, 1992, p. 35.

deTorok, Judy, "Jack Eckerd," *Tampa Bay Business,* January 10–16, 1988, p. S5.

Hagy, James, "A Miracle Drug for Jack Eckerd," *Florida Trend,* February 1992, pp. 49–51.

—Wendy J. Stein

Eddie Bauer Inc.

15010 Northeast 36th Street
Redmond, Washington 98052-5317
U.S.A.
(206) 882-6100
Fax: (206) 882-6383

Wholly Owned Subsidiary of Spiegel Inc.
Incorporated: 1920 as Eddie Bauer's Sports Shop
Employees: 8,500
Sales: $1 billion
SICs: 5699 Miscellaneous Apparel & Accessory Stores; 5941
    Sporting Goods & Bicycle Shops; 5719 Miscellaneous
    Home Furnishing Stores; 5947 Gift, Novelty & Souvenir
    Shops; 5961 Catalog & Mail-Order Houses

Eddie Bauer Inc., a mail-order and storefront retailer of outdoor apparel, sporting goods, and home furnishings, is one of the fastest growing retail businesses in the country. As the largest specialty outdoor merchandiser in the United States, Eddie Bauer boasts 272 stores in virtually every major market in the United States and Canada and receives a considerable amount of business through its catalog sales.

Created by the son of Russian immigrants, Eddie Bauer Inc. began as a tennis racquet stringing business in Seattle, Washington. While his parents would eventually play a significant role in the development of Eddie Bauer Inc., Eddie Bauer initially drew upon his childhood years on Orcas Island, a sparsely populated island near Seattle, as the inspiration for what would eventually become a billion dollar retail business.

Those early years were spent fishing, hunting, and trapping on the wooded island, imbuing Bauer with a love of the outdoors. When his family moved to Seattle in 1912, Bauer was 13 years old and looking for work. He immediately gravitated toward the only full-line sporting goods store in the city, Piper & Taft, and landed a job as a stock boy. Over the years, Bauer watched and learned, eventually becoming adept at making guns, fly rods, and golf clubs. In addition to these talents, Bauer also developed considerable skill in stringing tennis racquets, winning the world speed championship, while in a display window at Piper & Taft's, by stringing 12 racquets in just over three-and-a-half hours. Still in his teens, Bauer had already gained the attention of Seattle's sporting community. He was often referred to in local newspapers for killing the biggest elk, or catching the

most fish, or for winning rifle- and pistol-shooting competitions. This local recognition would serve Bauer well when, in 1919, with $25 in his pocket and $500 borrowed on a 120-day loan, he rented 15 feet of wall space in a gun shop for $15 a month and began stringing racquets on his own. In this venture, Bauer enjoyed immediate success, stringing enough racquets to accumulate $10,000 within his first year. Encouraged by his initial success, Bauer arranged for credit from a bank and opened his own shop, Eddie Bauer's Sports Shop, in 1920, the predecessor of Eddie Bauer Inc.

In addition to his renowned racquet stringing abilities, Bauer also offered golf equipment and trout fishing flies during his first year of business, and the 20-foot storefront quickly became a haven for sporting enthusiasts throughout the Pacific Northwest. Bauer's success during these nascent years was largely due to his reputation as an experienced outdoorsman and his active participation in the sporting community. He worked at his store from February through August each year, then hunted and fished for steelhead throughout the winter. During these sojourns in the wild, he field tested all of the equipment he sold in his stores, which, after the first year, included an array of outdoor equipment and clothing. Two years after he opened for business, this firsthand knowledge of his stock enabled him to offer an unconditional guarantee of satisfaction on all of the products sold in his store, a rarity for retail businesses during the 1920s. Bauer also promoted sporting activities in his spare time, increasing the public's awareness of such sports as skiing by importing Norwegian hickory skis and persuading Norwegian skiers to come to the Pacific Northwest to help foster growth in the sport.

By 1924, Bauer had added a complete selection of fishing tackle, firearms, and skeet and trap equipment to his store and renamed it Eddie Bauer's Sporting Goods. Customers continued to flock to Bauer's store, lured by his unconditional guarantee and his knowledge of the outdoors. Eddie Bauer's Sporting Goods had quickly become a favorite place for outdoorsmen to outfit themselves for a wide variety of sporting endeavors. With a large and loyal clientele, Bauer's future success appeared as guaranteed as the products he sold, but, in the coming years, Bauer's position as a successful operator of a local sporting goods store would be elevated to a height not imagined even during the optimistic 1920s.

Bauer's success had been predicated on his experience and interest in sporting equipment, so it was fitting that the innovation that would eventually launch his company into the upper echelon of the outdoor apparel industry came as a result, at least in part, of his desire to improve sporting equipment. In the late 1920s, Bauer attempted to improve the consistency of flight in badminton shuttlecocks. He imported premium feathers from Europe and developed a method utilizing buckshot that achieved the desired results. In 1930, his design was patented and eventually adopted for use in the badminton world championships.

While investigating which type of feather would improve the flight of shuttlecocks, Bauer came across goose down, reminding him of an uncle who had once extolled the virtues of goose down's insulating quality. Years earlier, Bauer's uncle, a Cossack fighting in Manchuria during the Russo-Japanese war, had worn a coat lined with goose down to stave off the 50 degrees below zero winter weather. Bauer, who had suffered through many cold winters fishing and hunting in the mountains near Seattle, decided to use goose down to make a coat for himself. After designing and sewing a quilted goose down jacket for himself, Bauer discovered the truth of his uncle's story, and soon was making down jackets for a few of his friends. The popularity of these jackets led Bauer to patent his design and begin production of America's first quilted, goose down insulated jacket in 1936. Called the "Skyliner" and selling for $34.50, the jacket was an immediate success, particularly with Alaska bush pilots, and led to the production of a wide assortment of garments with different quilting styles. Starting with ten seamstresses in 1936, Bauer needed 125 by 1940 to meet the voracious demand for his quilted jackets. By this time, Bauer had secured a virtual monopoly on the insulated jacket market, employing as many seamstresses as his rapidly expanding business required and purchasing all the European and North American goose down he wanted.

This supply of goose down, however, ended just as Bauer's quilted down garments began to attract orders through the mail. When the United States entered World War II in 1941, the war production board requisitioned all of the goose down supply on the market and froze Bauer's existing supply. No longer able to purchase or use goose down, he was relegated to using eiderdown as a replacement, a substitution that negatively affected his sales. It appeared as if his flourishing retail trade had been swept away from him, but whatever losses Bauer incurred as a result of the government's seizure, he more than made up for them by providing goose down products to the United States Army Air Corps. At first, Bauer provided the military with sleeping bags and snowshoes and binders, which he sold at retail prices, and eventually his business with the government increased considerably. Using the war production board's goose down, Bauer manufactured 25,000 flight suits and nearly 250,000 sleeping bags for Air Corps flight crews and those fighting in the frigid Aleutian campaign. In order to satisfy the military's needs, Bauer constructed a production factory, invested roughly $200,000 in specially built machinery, and hired 400 power sewing machine operators to work in three shifts, seven days a week. This prodigious wartime production salvaged what otherwise could have been a recessive period for Bauer's company and, more important, it also carried the Eddie Bauer name across the nation. All of the garments Bauer manufactured for the military had the Eddie Bauer label stitched on them, the only garments during the war that carried the manufacturer's private label.

Although Bauer's civilian business slackened during the war, he continued to advertise in order to create a demand for his products when the war ended. Once it did, he steeled himself for an immediate return to the prosperous days of the late 1930s. Expectations now ran higher, however, considering the tremendous strides in name recognition the company had made as a result of the war, so Bauer introduced a new way to bring his products to the public. In 1945, just as many of those who had worn Eddie Bauer products during the war were returning home, Bauer issued the company's first mail-order catalogs. Although the introduction of the catalogs represented a significant landmark in Eddie Bauer Inc.'s history, a more pressing concern during these immediate postwar years

overshadowed their import. Bauer's company seemed in danger of failing.

In order to fill the demands of his contract with the Air Corps, Bauer had invested in equipment that could only serve his production needs during the war. Both the profits and the machinery were temporary, so, once the war ended, Bauer was left with the machinery and nowhere to sell it, leaving him in a precarious situation. As he would later recall, "We were stuck with the machinery and I lost practically everything I owned, down to where I had to start all over again." To assist with this rebuilding process, Bauer entered into a partnership in 1951 with William F. Neimi Sr., a friend with whom Bauer hunted and fished, and together they strengthened the company by placing an emphasis on the mail-order side of the business and concentrating on producing a larger selection of products. From this point forward, until the 1970s, Bauer's company would be primarily a mail-order business. Before the end of the decade, Bauer would close his stores in Seattle and rely almost exclusively on purchases made through the mail, with the only retail sales being generated by a factory store in Seattle.

The changes made by Bauer and Neimi worked. By mailing catalogs to potential customers and outfitting those outdoorsmen who came to the factory in Seattle, the company generated $1 million in sales in 1960. Although Bauer's financial position had seemed bleak 15 years earlier, the widespread recognition of the Eddie Bauer name had always remained secure. And now a new generation of potential customers were being introduced to the Eddie Bauer line of products through the catalogs arriving in the mail. By this time, Bauer's company used nearly half of the world's supply of northern goose down and had outfitted every American expedition to the Himalayas over the previous ten years. When mountain climbers needed to train for assaults on the towering peaks in the Himalayan range, they often selected the mountains in proximity to Seattle as suitable sites. By the 1960s, a visit to Bauer's factory store became a natural stop for climbers needing clothing and equipment, which further bolstered the nation's recognition of the Eddie Bauer name. When James W. Whittaker became the first American to reach the top of Mount Everest in 1963, he wore an Eddie Bauer parka, slept in an Eddie Bauer sleeping bag, and used Eddie Bauer gear, as did the entire expedition. Three years later, Bauer's company outfitted the American Antarctic Mountaineering Expedition, and it continued to produce the preferred gear for expeditions to follow in later years.

In 1968, Eddie Bauer retired and sold his company to a group of Seattle investors. These investors, however, were undercapitalized, so after three years of operating the company and two unsuccessful attempts to make Eddie Bauer Inc. a public company, they sold it to General Mills, Inc. for a reported $10 million. What General Mills received was still essentially a mail-order business. Since Neimi and Bauer had decided in 1951 to concentrate almost entirely on revenues garnered through mail-order purchases, the company's retail sales had been limited to the products sold from its factory store. It was this segment of Eddie Bauer's business General Mills wanted to fortify.

It was several years, however, before the disparate merchandising philosophies of the two companies would effectively join together and even longer until Eddie Bauer obtained consistent leadership. From 1975 to 1978 the company went through four presidents, until finally settling on James J. Casey, who had joined Eddie Bauer three years earlier. At this time, the state of Eddie Bauer's product line was still in flux, as General Mills attempted to reshape its subsidiary's market appeal. Six months after Casey assumed leadership of the company, he maneuvered it away from a merchandising failure that had added golf and tennis apparel to the company's product line. For customers inured to a product line whose reputation had been built on manufacturing down parkas and outfitting expeditions to the Antarctic, the shift was a difficult one to make, and potential customers went elsewhere when purchasing items for warmer climes. Although General Mills continued to struggle with the specialty outdoor market niche, it had increased the number of Eddie Bauer retail locations. By the end of the decade, there were 16 retail stores and plans in place to double that figure. In General Mills first year of ownership, Eddie Bauer posted $11 million in sales, and, with the boost in sales provided by the additional stores, sales climbed to $80 million, ranking the company second only to L.L. Bean in the specialty outdoor market. The disparity between retail and catalog sales disappeared, with half of the total revenues generated by the stores, and 14 million catalog customers accounting for the remainder.

By 1984, the changes initiated by General Mills had substantially altered the image Eddie Bauer projected to its customers. Apparel now generated approximately 70 percent of the retail store revenues, and much of it did not resemble the clothing worn by members of a Mount Everest expedition, or even the clothing worn by weekend adventurers camping in the woods. Tents, backpacks, and fishing rods had slowly begun to disappear from the shelves of the company's stores and were replaced with oxford cloth shirts, lamb's wool sweaters, and other items uncharacteristic of the rugged, expedition outfitter. With 41 stores located in Canada and the United States, the company broadened its appeal—enough for Ford Motor Co. to begin production of the Eddie Bauer Bronco II—and attracted a more diverse clientele. The expansion of the retail side of the business represented a move toward greater growth for the mail-order segment as well. In 1983, Eddie Bauer mailed 14 million catalogs, and, by the following year, 30 million catalogs were sent to potential customers, two million of which were printed in French to accommodate the company's burgeoning clientele in Canada. Plans called for further expansion of the company's retail business, some 60 stores over the next five years. To lead the company toward this goal, a switch in leadership was made. In 1984, Michael Rayden replaced Casey and began separating retail, mail-order, and manufacturing into three distinct divisions.

By 1988, Eddie Bauer had 57 retail stores located in the United States and Canada. But just as General Mills was announcing further plans to augment Eddie Bauer's retail holdings, the corporation put Eddie Bauer up for sale along with another specialty clothing chain it owned, Talbots, in a bid to divest itself of all non-food related businesses.

Speigel Inc., a catalog marketer of apparel, home furnishings, and other merchandise agreed to buy Eddie Bauer for $260 million, roughly equal to the sales the company generated at the time of its purchase. Wayne Badovinus was selected to lead Eddie Bauer and, over the next two years, 100 stores were added to the retail chain, bringing total sales up to $448 million. In 1991, Eddie Bauer's first "Premier" store was opened in Chicago, which housed all of the company's recently introduced specialty product lines. "All Week Long," Eddie Bauer's collection of women's sportswear and casual attire, first introduced as a catalog business in 1987, had evolved into a retail business by 1991 with the opening of its first store in Portland, Oregon, and now was part of the Premier store concept. Also included in the Premier stores were "The Sport Shop at Eddie Bauer," featuring custom-built fishing rods, reels, and fishing flies, and "The Eddie Bauer Home Collection," which sold a wide assortment of indoor and outdoor furnishings. The addition of these specialty retail concepts, each first introduced in 1991, marked another dramatic leap in revenues. In the three years since Speigel had purchased Eddie Bauer, the parent company had witnessed an increase in revenues from roughly $260 million, to nearly $750 million, occasioned primarily by the dramatic increase in Eddie Bauer's retail business. This expansion continued after 1991, giving the company 265 retail stores by the end of 1992.

Since 1920, the Eddie Bauer name has evoked several images. What once represented fishing tackle, guns, and mountaineering equipment, stood for durable, comfortable apparel in the 1990s. As Eddie Bauer planned for the future, with its new image and new products, and pursued its goal to establish a store in every major North American market, its product lines appeared to remain as strong as the Eddie Bauer name.

Further Reading:

"Eddie Bauer Catalog Sidesteps Recession Doldrums," *Direct Marketing,* November 1983, p. 72.

"Evolution of a Down-Wear Retailer," *New York Times,* March 12, 1981, p. D4.

Palmeri, Christopher, "Indoor Sportsman," *Forbes,* March 29, 1993, p. 43.

"REI, Eddie Bauer Expand," *Chain Store Age Executive,* August 1987, pp. 46–47.

"Retreat, Hell: Four Contrarians Who Hear Opportunity Knocking," *Business Week,* January 14, 1991, p. 64.

Ricketts, Chip, "Eddie Bauer's Southern Expansion Push Includes Metroplex," *Dallas Business Journal,* February 26, 1990, p. 3.

Schwadel, Francine, and Richard Gibson, "General Mills Is Putting Up for Sale Talbots, Eddie Bauer Clothing Chain," *Wall Street Journal,* January 8, 1988, p. 4; "General Mills to Sell Last Retail Units, Talbots and Bauer, for $585 Million," *Wall Street Journal,* May 19, 1988, p. 4.

Schwadel, Francine, "Waters Resigns From General Mills, Pursues Purchase of Units He Managed," *Wall Street Journal,* January 11, 1988, p. 32.

Spector, Robert, "Eddie Bauer's New Look," *The Weekly,* January 2, 1985, pp. 20–22; "Eddie Bauer: The Man Behind the Name," *Pacific Northwest Magazine,* May 1983, pp. 61–64.

Warren, James R., "Eddie Bauer's Guarantee Was Key to Firm's Success," *Seattle Business Journal,* June 13, 1983, pp. 6–7.

—Jeffrey L. Covell

Edison Brothers Stores, Inc.

501 North Broadway
P.O. Box 14020
St. Louis, Missouri 63178-4020
U.S.A.
(314) 331-6000
Fax: (314) 331-7500

Public Company
Incorporated: 1929
Employees: 21,100
Sales: $1.51 billion
Stock Exchanges: New York
SICs: 5661 Shoe Stores; 5621 Women's Clothing Stores;
5611 Men's and Boys' Clothing Stores; 5812 Eating
Places

Edison Brothers Stores, Inc., is a leading retailer, specializing in apparel, footwear, and entertainment. Begun as a shoe store in Atlanta, Georgia, in 1922, Edison stores (under many different names) now dominate many regional shopping malls, with some malls having six or more Edison-owned stores. Edison Brothers Stores, Inc., now comprises the Edison Menswear Group, the Edison Footwear Group, 5–7–9 Shops, Edison Brothers Stores International, and Edison Brothers Entertainment. The company owns and operates 1,883 apparel stores including J. Riggings, JW/Jeans West, and Oaktree; 766 footwear stores including Bakers/Leeds, Wild Pair, and Sacha London; and 138 entertainment units including Dave & Buster's, Time-Out, and Space Port. Currently the company's expansion is focused on its menswear chains and its large-space entertainment centers.

The Edison brothers got their start in the early 1920s. On October 28, 1922, Sam, Harry, Mark, Irving, and Simon Edison opened their first shoe store, called Chandlers, in Atlanta. Although there was relatively little variation in footwear styles at that time, the Edisons' new store sold stylish women's shoes for six dollars. This one-price policy was an industry standard since other chains discovered that the practice sped up sales.

Although their business began small, the Edison brothers certainly had extensive connections to the shoe business. Their father, a Latvian immigrant, had been a small business owner in Europe and later in Atlanta before working as an agent for a Boston shoe manufacturer. Prior to their initial collaborative

business effort, all of the Edison sons had connections to footwear sales. In 1920 Sam and Mark Edison were running two shoe stores, and that same year Irving and Simon began a ladies' boot shop. Harry Edison is credited with the idea of getting all of his brothers together to start the first Chandlers store.

The Edisons' first store was an immediate success, with their low prices attracting customers from many markets, including Atlanta's upper class. In addition, with swift marketing sense, the Edison brothers quickly capitalized on the heightened fashions of women's shoes after World War I. They bought a large stock of high-style shoes on credit, and the shoes sold quickly, netting the nascent partnership a profit of $282,000 in their first year in business.

Growth was fast and furious and the brothers opened their second store, called Baker's, the next year. Baker's shoes were geared toward a lower priced market than the original Chandler's store. Then they set up another Chandler store in New Orleans after picking up a good site at a low price. In 1926 the Edison Brothers' partnership incorporated in Georgia (with $150,000 of paid-in capital), becoming Edison Brothers Stores, Inc. (EBS). Stores were opened in Nashville and Louisville, and by 1928 the Edisons had a chain of 12 Chandler stores stretching throughout the Midwest and southeast and as far west as San Antonio, Texas.

As profits grew throughout the 1920s, competition in the industry intensified. Price warfare became the order of the day, but the Edisons were able to expand their operations in both the Baker's and Chandler shops, and, by 1929, sales in their 17 stores totaled more than $3 million. In order to expand beyond the limits of their earnings, and hesitant to continue to expand their already over-leveraged borrowing position, the company went public in 1929 (issuing $950,000 of common and preferred stock) and moved its headquarters from Atlanta to St. Louis. The funds enabled them to add fourteen more Baker's and three more Chandler stores in 1929. The company was in a good position to weather the unforeseen economic collapse of the 1930s.

The onset of the Great Depression, while slowing profit growth considerably as demand collapsed, did not stop Edison from expanding its operations throughout the 1930s, even with prices falling drastically. With heavier emphasis on the Baker's shoes, which were lower in price, the Edisons were in a relatively good competitive position overall. They even opened a new chain called Burt's, which sold a line of $2.88 shoes. Thus, with shoes in three differently priced markets, the Edison Brothers were diversified and in fair good shape compared to their competitors. Overall, during the period from 1930 to 1938, the company added an average of a dozen stores per year while only closing a few.

The Edison Brothers continued to apply their retailing wisdom and rarely picked unprofitable markets. In addition to the cost-cutting behavior necessary for any successful business, the Edisons operated their stores under different names, thereby avoiding confusion with local competition. For example, on the West Coast, where a C. H. Baker shoe chain already existed, Edison called its medium-priced stores Leed's.

Expansion continued for the company in the early 1940s and was bolstered by government wartime spending. Sales at the 168 stores rose to $45 million in 1942, but the entry of the United States into World War II brought rationing, including rationing of shoes and shoe leather—up to 40 percent of the nation's supply of sole leather was slated for military use—and other market restrictions. To combat this smaller shoe market, Sam Edison put in a line of millinery, called the "Casual Hat Bar Operation," but this failed to revive profitability as overall sales fell below $40 million and two stores failed. By 1945 the sales drought had passed, and sales reached $53 million. In 1946, with the war over and rationing lifted, sales jumped to $65 million as pent-up spending power was unleashed and new style demands pushed women to replenish and update their shoe wardrobes. Sales stabilized around $70 million by 1947–48, and upward pressure on prices—from slowly rising leather costs and demand pressures—led some to suspect the Edisons of collusive inflationary pricing practices. Edison's comptrolling Vice-President Alfred T. Leimbach pointed out, however, that leather costs more than doubled in the years surrounding World War II, and Edison's profit margins actually declined over the period.

In 1948 Edison Brothers, Inc., opened its first store in a shopping mall, posting sales of $75 million during the year. That same year saw the opening of Edison's 200th store, after 25 years in business. Just nine years later, Edison opened its 300th store, and in 1958 sales shot above $100 million. Harry Edison was named chairman of the board, and Irving Edison was elected president of the company. Edison also entered into the New York City market with a Bakers store on 34th Street.

By the mid 1960s, Edison stores were continuing to achieve record sales and profit growth. Sales in 1964 were growing at a rate of ten percent, and the four main Edison store chains, Baker's, Chandler's, Leed's, and Burt's reported a net income of $1.15 per share, up from $1.04 per share from the year earlier. By 1966 Simon Edison was named chairman, and he continued the Edison policy of opening and acquiring new stores and closing unprofitable stores. Edison opened 20 stores in 1965 and closed 13 (with 515 stores total in operation at that time). The company also expanded its business, operating women's accessories shops and moving into children's shoes (which were being sold in 60 of the company's 515 stores). Overall, from 1960 to 1965, the company closed 46 stores and replaced them with more productive units.

By 1968 Irving Edison retired, and his son, Bernard Edison, became president of Edison Brothers. Store expansion continued as the Edisons acquired Jeans West, a chain of pants stores with sales of $7.5 million. In 1970 EBS acquired 5–7–9 shops, a future mainstay in the Edison store stable. Wild Pair, a shoe store that featured "look-alike" or "unisex" shoes designed for young people, opened its first stores in Houston and Tucson in 1972, as total Edison sales topped $290 million.

Shoe styles were becoming dressier at this time, and this was a good sign for Edison's growth prospects. Boots became more popular among men, and more informal wear also became popular. A devalued dollar helped the export market and cut down import competition, and production in the industry in general expanded. Competition led to greater concentration,

however, as the number of U.S. shoe manufacturers shrunk from 721 in 1964, to 581 in 1967, to 481 in 1971. Edison stores remained near the top of the shoe and apparel retailing business.

Although it took Edison 40 years to get 500 stores, only ten more years were needed to reach 1,000, accomplished in 1973. Julian Edison, son of Mark Edison, took on the duties of president of the shoe division, but it was the non-shoe component of the business that made the most rapidly increasing contribution to the growth of sales—by 1972, non-shoe sales were 28.6 percent of corporate sales. One major non-shoe venture was Edison's acquisition of Handyman Home Improvement Centers, a San Diego-based chain of eight do-it-yourself hardware and building materials stores. Since then, they have spread as far as Texas and into Oregon. Also in 1971, Edison added another non-shoe business: United Sporting Goods, a four-unit chain based in Los Angeles. Fashion Conspiracy, a San Diego operator with 127 stores selling women's junior wear, was also acquired.

During the same period, Edison's existing major chains, Chandler's, Baker's, Leed's, and Burt's, covered much of the price spectrum of the shoe market up to where luxury prices begin. Baker's and Leed's continued to do well with fashion shoes priced under $15, while Burt's prices were even lower. According to Edison, the idea was to seek high volume by covering lower price ranges with trendy footwear, accepting the risks of inventory going out of fashion any moment while foregoing the high margins of the luxury/high fashion range.

Diversification continued, but the shoe market began to stagnate in the mid-1970s. Imports grabbed a bigger share of the market and Edison Brothers Stores' competition such as Brown Group Inc., Interco Inc., and Melville Corp. diversified through acquisition as well. EBS's earnings growth performance remained strong through the late 1970s mainly due to its diversification and reliance on its non-shoe business. Shoe and apparel still accounted for 76 percent of sales volume and 86 percent of net income, with the rest coming from hardware and building materials operations. Per share net income was up 25 percent in 1976, with no sign of letup into the 1980s.

EBS soon became the largest retailer of women's shoes. In 1979, just six years after opening its 1,000th store, Edison opened its 2,000th store. Among the new stores in the late 1970s was Oaktree, which opened its first store in Houston in 1976. By 1983, sales surpassed the $1 billion mark; Andy Newman, son of Julian Edison, became president of the shoe division; and Martin Sneider became president of the company's rapidly growing apparel division. Sneider was the first non-Edison to hold a top management position at EBS. The shoe and apparel divisions moved into a newly completed corporate headquarters building in St. Louis, so that they could share information between them.

By 1985 more changes in the corporate officers were under way. Andy Newman was elected chairman, and Martin Sneider became president of the company as Bernard Edison retired. The Edison family, nonetheless, maintained control of over 30 percent of the company's stock. The mid-1980s would be a time of reorganization and rethinking of a long term strategy as the company fell on hard times. According to some sources, Edison began to fall behind by squandering its competitive position in the malls, with many of its original stores needing remodeling. Further, the Handyman Home Improvement Centers unit was losing money, prompting EBS to sell off its assets, one share for four EBS shares. Edison's 2,475 stores posted a loss in the first half of 1987 of $10.8 million, following a profit of $9.2 million in 1986, and its rate of return on equity fell from 27.9 percent to 15.4 percent.

Despite declining profitability, EBS continued to pursue growth by acquisition, acquiring the J. Riggings division of U.S. Shoe Corporation, with more than 200 stores operating as part of what is now the Edison Menswear Group. Edison then turned around and sold off 14 of its less profitable Fashion Conspiracy women's apparel stores to Wisconsin ID, Inc. These acquisitions and sales were part of an overall fierce cost-cutting campaign designed to reduce overhead and restore greater profitability. This also involved a massive capital investment project to remodel its more established store lines as well.

As part of the company's new strategy, Edison president Martin Sneider made what some called a highly risky maneuver: taking the company away from women's wear and into a risky young men's market. By joining the world of men's fashion, Edison faced heightened competition from stores such as The Gap. Edison purchased the 200 J. Riggings stores, along with two other men's chains, Jeans West and OakTree, for their growth potential. J. Riggings sells moderately priced suits and sports jackets to an older clientele. Jeans West featured casual wear and were called JW stores. OakTree sold low priced urban trendy wear with designer labels.

Edison Brothers Stores also spent $3 million in 1985 and $20 million overall (from 1985 to 1987) to remodel its older stores. Sneider's restructuring plan has paid off handsomely for EBS in less than three years. Earnings had peaked in 1983 at $46 million and sales had stalled at around $1 billion. Sneider's plan helped Edison develop niches in men's fashion, and overall profits recovered. By 1987 Sneider's Edison Brothers, Inc., turned a $21 million loss to a $36 million profit. Stock prices rose as well.

Edison Brothers Stores continued to acquire profitable enterprises: 200 Foxmoor Stores; 120 Webster/Zeidler and Zeidler stores; 39 Harry's Big and Tall stores; a small chain of Repp Ltd. big/tall/athletic menswear stores. EBS also opened its first store in Mexico. The company started Edison Brothers International, a new division to handle foreign buying offices in Hong Kong, Taiwan, and Bangkok. They also opened a $10 million facility near Los Angeles to ease distribution for products.

In another competitive move, Edison Brothers Stores, Inc., expanded into the business of mall-based entertainment centers, a business strategy designed to attract people to shopping malls for purposes other than shopping and to bring more families to the malls for whole day outings. EBS started its entertainment division with the acquisition of Dave & Buster's restaurant/entertainment complexes and grew with the acquisition of Time-Out and Space Port family entertainment centers. By 1991 Edison Brothers became the exclusive U.S. distributor for Virtuality, the first application of virtual reality technology accessible to the general public, in malls. Virtuality is a type of computer game software, for use in video arcades, where participants wear helmets containing screens that show three-dimensional computer-generated images. The helmets also block out the real world so that the user is immersed in this virtual world. EBS operated ten Virtuality centers across the country.

Edison's most publicized move in this area came when Paramount Pictures licensed the use of the television series *Star Trek: The Next Generation* to the company for use in its virtual reality centers. Edison's largest virtual reality project was called Exhilarama, a 40,000 square-foot family arcade. Executives of EBS expressed confidence that the arcade would attract families to malls.

Further Reading:

Abelson, Reed, "Companies to Watch: Edison Brothers Stores," *Fortune,* November 6, 1989.

Bryant, Adam, "Beam Me Up. I'm Out of Change," *New York Times,* September 29, 1992.

"Edison Bros. Stores Boasts Stylish Growth in Earnings," *Barron's,* July 24, 1978.

"Edison Brothers Says 1965 Profit Rose 10%," *Wall Street Journal,* January 13, 1966.

"Edison Brothers Stores: How Five Sons of an Immigrant Peddler Built Up the Largest Chain of Women's Shoe Stores in the U.S.," *Fortune,* February 1948.

Marshall, Christy, "A Retailer On a Role: Edison Brothers Positioned for Growth," *St. Louis Sun,* December 15, 1989.

McGrath, Roger, "Virtuality Puts Retailer on New Plane," *Advertising Age,* February 22, 1993.

Pacey, Margaret D., "Better Foot Forward: Shoe Makers Have a Good Deal Going for Them," *Barron's,* January 24, 1972.

Reilly, Patrick M., "Edison Bros. Plans a New Enterprise in Virtual Reality," *Wall Street Journal,* September 25, 1992.

"The Retailer Speaks: How Edison Is Lighting Up the Young Men's Biz," *DNR,* September 2, 1991.

"Selling Shoes without a Store: Edison Brothers Markets through Subsidiaries," *Financial World,* January 1, 1974.

"Sixty Years of Progress: Highlighting Edison Brothers Stores," St. Louis, MO: Edison Brothers Stores, Inc., 1982.

VandeWater, Judith, "Edison Brothers Widens Its Teen-age Appeal," *St. Louis Post-Dispatch,* May 28, 1990.

Von Koschembahr, John, "Getting a Boot Out of Diversifying," *Financial World,* March 1, 1978.

—John A. Sarich

EGGHEAD SOFTWARE®
North America's Software Eggsperts®

Egghead Inc.

P. O. Box 7004
22011 S.E. 51st Street
Issaquah, Washington 98027
U.S.A.
(206) 391-5160
Fax: (206) 391-0880

Public Company
Incorporated: 1988
Employees: 2,600
Sales: $664.8 million
Stock Exchanges: NASDAQ
SICs: 5734 Computer and Software Stores

Egghead Inc. is the largest retail vendor of personal computer software. The firm markets software programs to individual consumers as well as corporations, and offers detailed training in the use of its products.

Victor D. Alhadeff founded Egghead in 1984. Alhadeff had been involved in an oil and gas limited partnership until a drop in prices drove him out of business in 1983. Shopping for software later that year he found that salespeople at computer stores spoke in technical jargon that often confused the average customer. Alhadeff had sold shoes while in college, and with this retail experience, he decided that he could sell software far more effectively using traditional customer-friendly methods.

Using $50,000 of his own money along with $1 million from local investors—including Paul Allen, a co-founder of Microsoft Corp.—Alhadeff opened his first Egghead store in Bellevue, Washington. From the beginning, Egghead made an effort to make computer software less intimidating to the average consumer, projecting a warm image through the store mascot, a cartoon character named Professor Egghead. Salespeople received intensive training in order to become familiar with a wide range of software and explain it in simple terms. Egghead carried a wide range of software, as many as 1,300 titles, while its warehouse maintained a further 1,000. Customers were allowed to take software home for a 30-day trial period, and stores had up to four computers available for in-store demonstrations. Furthermore, Egghead featured extremely low prices, sometimes 40 percent off the list price.

With its unique approach to software retailing, Egghead's sales rose quickly, and it soon was adding new stores. Corporate customers accounted for a major percentage of Egghead's sales, and the company established a large direct-sales force in 1985. Soon it was selling to Fortune 500 companies like IBM and Boeing. Despite its growth, Egghead kept its costs down, investing its savings in new stores. The firm's quick growth attracted attention and investor interest. Some investors were cautious, however, due to a controversy surrounding the bankruptcy of Alhadeff's previous company, against which several investors filed suit claiming Alhadeff had misled them about the company's finances.

In 1987 Egghead prepared to go public. The offering was called off at the last minute, however, when the U.S. stock market fell dramatically in October of that year. Alhadeff instead raised $25 million in credit from the U.S. Bank of Washington, and several million more from private investors, including Prudential Venture Capital, for a total of $47 million in venture capital invested in Egghead. Egghead's sales came to $77.5 million in 1987, nearly doubling sales of the previous year. Perhaps more importantly, the firm had profits of $2 million, after losing nearly $1 million in 1985 and 1986. However, in the rapidly changing computer industry, the firm faced new competitors. B. Dalton Books was expanding its Software Etc. division, which had over 100 boutiques, many of them in the bookstores, and Babbages Inc., carrying similar merchandise, doubled its stores in 1987 to 58.

By early 1988 Egghead operated 107 stores in 13 cities and maintained $40 million of software inventory. In June 1988 Egghead finally went public, with an initial offering of 3.6 million shares at prices above 50 times the firm's 1987 earnings. Egghead used nearly $24 million raised in the offering to add about 100 new stores and put the rest into working capital. In one nine-month period, 64 new Egghead stores were opened as the chain tried to saturate the market before it was filled by competitors. As a result of this growth, Egghead stores and corporate sales staff accounted for about ten percent of U.S. software sales in 1988.

Despite annual sales climbing toward $350 million, however, profits declined due to the swiftness of expansion. In addition to opening the new stores, Egghead added 60 salespeople to the direct sales staff of 132. That meant an addition of 1,600 total employees in one year, and new salespeople required extensive training. As a result, the firm's administrative and selling costs doubled in a year and its operating margins sunk from 4.5 percent in 1988 to about 3.7 percent in 1989. Egghead tried to obtain maximum profits from its low margins by getting volume discounts from software manufacturers. That meant increasing inventory, however, which was both expensive and risky in an increasingly unstable software market.

This tumult lead to two straight years of losses for Egghead, and the company was forced to close 29 stores to cut costs. With large volumes of software flowing quickly through its warehouses, control over Egghead's inventory system slipped and theft increased. In 1989, in the midst of this period, Alhadeff hired Stuart Sloan and Matthew Griffin to help turn around the company. Sloan, who became chief executive officer, had a background on Wall Street, where he had led the leveraged buyout of Quality Food Centers Inc. in 1986. Griffin, who replaced Alhadeff as chairman, had made millions in real estate. The two put internal controls into effect that made each store manager responsible for the performance of his or her store. Retail store managers were sent monthly profit-and-loss statements for their stores, while district managers were sent statements for their areas. Furthermore, Sloan and Griffen refocused company efforts on selling software directly to corporate customers, who accounted for 60 percent of sales. The moves strengthened Egghead's bottom line.

During this time, however, a new rival was emerging: chains of computer superstores that matched or beat the prices of Egghead's software and also sold computer hardware. Egghead responded by strengthening its promotional machinery. When Microsoft's MS-DOS 5 operating system came out, Egghead promoted it extensively, and sold it for $39.99, which was 60 percent lower than the $99.95 list price. Seeking to take advantage of its higher level of customer service, Egghead invested $3 million into training its sales experts. It also added 300 items to the store's inventory, increasing the selection in the average store to 1,600 items.

By 1990 Egghead was profitable again, with sales of $519 million and profits of $15.4 million. However, a growing recession was affecting the sale of personal computers as well as PC software, and computer superstores were becoming more popular. Furthermore, hardware manufacturers were beginning to offer free software with hardware purchases, circumventing software retailers altogether. As software became more standardized and easier to use, Egghead's customer service became a less significant advantage, and other retail outlets, such as bookstores and office supply stores, began to stock software. Attempting to boost sales, Egghead began promoting and licensing business applications by Computer Associates, the country's second largest software firm. It signed a $3.5 million

contract with SalePoint Systems to shift its point-of-sales (POS) software to IBM's OS/2 operating system. The POS system linked the firm's stores, distribution centers, and headquarters. Most software products were bar coded by version when the firm received them, helping its sales and distribution.

By the end of 1991 the firm had 205 stores in 20 states and sales of $665 million. It remained profitable, with earnings of $15.7 million. As Egghead continued to expand rapidly, opening 12 stores and closing two during the first quarter of 1992, earnings again declined. Furthermore, the company made a costly error when it overstocked Microsoft's new Windows 3.1 software, predicting heavy demand that never appeared, in part because several computer manufacturers had already loaded the program onto their hardware as an added feature. Egghead fought back with an aggressive marketing campaign and planned to open between 20 and 40 stores by the summer of 1993.

Software industry price wars intensified during 1992, driving margins still lower, and Egghead brought in a new management team in early 1993. Timothy E. Turnpaugh, previously vice-chairman and operations manager at Seafirst Bank in Seattle, became president and chief executive. Griffin, who had resigned the year before, was replaced by Richard P. Cooley, a director and retired chairman at Seafirst.

Further Reading:

"Over Easy," *The Economist,* October 3, 1992.
Hafner, Katherine M., "Selling Software High and Low: Two Winning Formulas," *Business Week,* February 29, 1988.
Jerenski, Laura, "Soft in the Head?" *Forbes,* March 6, 1989.
Scholl, Jaye, "Scramble for Egghead," *Barron's,* May 16, 1988.
Yang, Dori Jones, and Stephanie Anderson Forest, "Egghead Scrambles Back," *Business Week,* July 29, 1991.

—Scott M. Lewis

84 Lumber Company

P.O. Box 8484
Eighty Four, Pennsylvania 15384
U.S.A.
(412) 941-8497
Fax: (412) 941-9867

Private Company
Founded: 1956
Employees: 3,500
Sales: $900 million
SICs: 5211 Lumber and Other Building Materials; 5031
   Lumber, Plywood and Millwork

84 Lumber is the largest, privately owned retailer of building materials in the United States, with more than 365 lumberyards in 31 states.

The history of 84 Lumber is primarily the story of entrepreneur Joseph A. Hardy, Sr., whose business philosophy consisted primarily of "nothing fancy." Hardy opened his first 84 Lumber store in 1956 in Eighty-Four, Pennsylvania, near Pittsburgh, and soon became renowned for his frugal approach to sales and management. As he built more stores, he continued to pay cash for land and facilities which typically had no heating or air conditioning systems since that would have increased overhead costs.

Hardy's example sent a message to company employees, whom he preferred to call "associates" in order to foster a sense of family working towards a common goal. The plain, no-frills stores conveyed the company's commitment to keeping costs down for its target market of skilled do-it-yourselfers and small contractors. Hardy told *Do It Yourself Retailing* magazine, "We want the pickup truck crowd. We want the guy who backs his truck up, smashes the bumper into the loading dock and says, 'Let's get going'."

Hardy continued as owner and president of 84 Lumber for almost 30 years, working in the lumber yards, visiting each store, and talking with the associates. Although he strove to maintain his image as a small-town, small business owner, his interests were diversifying during this time. He acquired real estate in several states and began collecting artwork, including paintings by Norman Rockwell, Pablo Picasso, Andy Warhol, and others. In 1983, Hardy spent $170,000 to purchase an

English lord's title and an additional $58.1 million to acquire and renovate Nemacolin, a 550-acre retreat in southeastern Pennsylvania. Hardy's daughter Maggie took charge of the resort, which soon featured a spa, five restaurants, and a golf course.

While Hardy focused on new interests and enterprises, the character of 84 Lumber changed as the stores began to stock non-lumber items in order to compete with such home improvement superstores as Home Depot, which were taking market share away from lumber yards. The company also ordered a 200-store expansion. However, rapid expansion and diversification of products resulted in a drop in earnings from $52 million in 1987 to less than half of that two years later. Hardy responded by slowing his expansion plans and even closing some stores. Furthermore, Hardy's oldest son, Joe Hardy, Jr., who had served as executive vice-president and had run the company for several years, was found to be in the early stages of multiple sclerosis. When his father decided that his son was not up to the task of running the company, Joe Jr. left in anger to run his own real estate development company. A rapid succession of top executives at 84 Lumber ensued, and the company continued to lose its focus, targeting "yuppie" consumers rather than its traditional market of contractors and do-it-yourselfers.

In 1990, chief operating officer Jerry Smith joined 84 Lumber. In an effort to refocus the company, he drafted a mission statement clarifying the goals and values of the company and communicating its character to associates, vendors, and consumers. The mission statement said, in part, that "84 Lumber is dedicated to being the low-cost provider of lumber and building products to residential builders, residential remodelers, and dedicated do-it-yourselfers, while adding value to our products through trained, knowledgeable and motivated associates." The company further hoped to gain an edge through personalized service, inventory maintenance and competitive prices, and growth and strong leadership. Associates began carrying laminated business-card size copies of the mission statement in their pockets, while messages posted throughout company buildings and in an employee newsletter reminded associates of company goals and plans.

In 1991, Hardy reclaimed a more active role as head of the company and designated his daughter Maggie as his heir-apparent to the company presidency. He halted the expansion plans and recommitted the company's merchandising efforts to the lumber business. But the increasing number of home improvement superstores were still an impediment to 84 Lumber's growth. Hardy's response was to diversify into do-it-yourself home and kitchen design centers. In 1991, 84 Lumber opened 24 new kitchen design centers which featured state-of-the-art computer technology for designing kitchens and baths.

In its approach to materials purchasing, 84 Lumber opted to switch to a centralized system for its hundreds of lumber yards during this time. The company had tried unsuccessfully to implement such a system in the mid-1970s, but had quickly returned to regional and store purchasing. Regional buying had allowed more market awareness since inventory could be tailored to the specific store in response to customer demand and new markets. However, this splintered purchasing structure also meant loss of bulk buying power. Furthermore, the lack of coordination with company headquarters also meant dead inventory in stores and wide discrepancies in prices each region or store paid for its products. When company management decided to institute centralized purchasing, it also moved operations, accounts payable, and sales from the store and regional levels and centralized them at company headquarters. A team of "purchasing managers" was formed from former store managers familiar with operations at the store level. Purchasing managers developed expertise in specific product categories. While vendors had not been in the habit of making site visits to 84 Lumber stores, with the new arrangement, they were encouraged to train 84 Lumber sales associates and aid them in merchandising. Stores adopted vendor suggestions for improving efficiency.

The company also invested in new computer technology to upgrade communications and information management, so that each night, daily sales data from each store could be sent to the company headquarters by telephone modem. This daily information became the basis for purchasing. The operations department could now keep in close communication with each store through biweekly bulletins and telephone calls twice a day. The company made communication with store managers a priority, making sure that they were kept up-to-date on any changes or additions to product lines. Despite the centralization of many functions, company executives maintained that store managers and associates still had significant input into product and promotion decisions.

The company continued to purchase wood in the United States and in Canada. About one-third of its stores were served by railroad, some with direct rail service right to the yard. Other 84 Lumber stores were supplied through reload centers, where freight from a rail car was loaded onto trucks or further rerouted by rail. This latter practice allowed the company to reduce inventory at a single 84 yard by splitting railcar loads among several yards rather than sending an entire carload to one yard. The reload centers also allowed the company to send both lumber and plywood to its lumber yards. A reload center in Aurora, Illinois, served 84 Lumber yards as far east as Ohio and as far south as St. Louis, Missouri; Charleston, West Virginia; and Charlotte, North Carolina.

In 1991, Hardy turned over 40 percent of the 84 Lumber stock to Maggie. At 25 years old, she faced a tough challenge as she joined her father at company headquarters. Although she had no college degree and her only business experience was in manag-

ing the Nemacolin Woodlands Golf, Spa, and Conference Center, she assumed a position that outranked top executives familiar with the lumber business. However, Hardy maintained that Maggie, the youngest of his five children, displayed more of an aptitude and interest in business than her older siblings.

The following year, the 84 Lumber Company pursued an extensive training and development program, requiring every associate to attend the "84 University" program to learn about new products and sharpen their sales skills. In 1992, 84 Lumber opened a new management training center and dormitory in Eighty-Four, Pennsylvania, and throughout the year store managers and other employees from all over the country attended three-day training sessions.

In 1992, 84 Lumber launched a new concept entitled 84 Affordable Homes Across America, a line of do-it-yourself home-building kits. Hardy was willing to double the company's long term debt to $80 million to back the new enterprise, which consisted of 30 home models in a price range of $39,900 to $59,900 (not including the cost of the lot). Included in the price were all the supplies necessary for the structure itself as well as the costs of excavation, plumbing, wiring, and heating.

Some critics predicted failure for the new home kits, speculating that not many people were likely to have the skill or the determination to build their own home themselves, even from a kit. Nevertheless, Maggie Hardy predicted that the model homes business would reach sales levels equal to those of the stores within ten years. Furthermore, Maggie and her father were predicting growth in the coming years through expansion of the chain of stores and from the home kits, which, according to Maggie Hardy, had no competition.

Further Reading:

Johnson, Walter E., "Life at 84 Lumber," *Do It Yourself Retailing,* February 1992.
Mallory, Maria, "The Lord of 84 Lumber Co. Is Back Behind the Counter," *Business Week,* June 22, 1992, pp. 80–1.
Stern, Gabriella, "More Daughters Take the Reins at Family Businesses," *Wall Street Journal,* June 12, 1991, p. B2.
"Two Views of Decentralized Purchasing," *Building Supply Home Centers,* November 1989, pp. 52–6.

—Wendy J. Stein

Ernst & Young

787 Seventh Avenue
New York, New York 10019
U.S.A.
(212) 830-6000
Fax: (212) 586-3121

Private Company
Incorporated: 1989
Employees: 70,000, including 6100 partners
Sales: $5.4 billion
SICs: 8721 Accounting, Auditing & Bookkeeping

Ernst & Young is the second largest public accounting firm in the world. The firm was formed in 1989 when the third largest accounting firm at the time, Ernst & Whinney (based in Cleveland, Ohio), merged with the sixth largest firm, Arthur Young (headquartered in New York), forming what, at the time, was the world's largest accounting firm. Ernst & Young currently stands as one of the "Big Six" accounting firms that dominate the accounting business. A private partnership, Ernst & Young is owned by its senior partners.

The roots of Ernst & Young can be traced back well over 100 years to the formation of the auditing business and the development of generally accepted accounting practices, rules that became increasingly necessary with the rise of the multinational corporation and the intrusion of complicated taxes into private business. A far cry from the basic bookkeepers of early accountancy, Ernst & Young provides tax auditing services primarily to the world's largest corporations. In fact, in recent years, the firm has increasingly moved into the business of management consulting, providing guidance to clients in such areas as risk management, mergers and acquisitions, and recent trends in worker-management relations such as Total Quality Management.

Although touted as a merger, the evidence suggests that the 1989 transaction that created the firm Ernst & Young was, in fact, an acquisition in disguise, with the stronger Ernst & Whinney swallowing up the floundering Arthur Young practice. Arthur Young had established a strong reputation over many years, although it was generally seen as a cautious and stodgy practice. But by the 1980s, after much of its traditional audit practice started to collapse and massive leveraged buyouts became an increasingly common practice in the business world,

Arthur Young had difficulty competing in the cut-throat environment of the accounting arena.

Historically, the accounting business has seen increasing numbers of partners concentrated in a decreasing number of firms. In this respect, the birth of Ernst & Young in 1989 was the natural outcome of the cycle of competition that breeds concentration and expansion, thus leading to further rounds of competition. But for over one-half of a century previous to the creation of Ernst & Young, eight firms had dominated the accounting business. The elite group was dubbed the "Big Eight" by *Fortune* magazine.

Following two major mergers in the 1980s (the Ernst & Young deal and the merger the same year between Deloitte, Haskins & Sells and Touche Ross), the "Big Eight" became the "Big Six." All of the "Big Six" are private partnerships, meaning that all are owned by the firm's senior executives, which also means that none of the firms are required to report their profits.

The Ernst & Young merger created a firm with 6100 partners and two Chief Executive Officers, Ray Groves from Ernst & Whinney and William Gladstone from Arthur Young. The newly formed firm had world revenues in 1989 of $4.27 billion, and its total sales eclipsed that established by a merger in 1987 of Peat Marwick and KMG Main Hurdman.

Prior to the 1989 merger, each of the two firms had enjoyed rich histories. Both rose from very small beginnings by capitalizing on the enterprise potential of accounting in its early years. Pioneer Arthur Young founded and headed the original Arthur Young firm back in 1895 in Kansas City after breaking from an earlier union of the firm of Stuart and Young in Chicago. In 1896 Young formed the firm of Arthur Young and Company with his brother Stanley, but by 1906 Young had completely terminated his unsatisfactory partnership with Stuart. Arthur Young and Company flourished for many years, slowly developing its reputation as "old reliable" for auditing, adding more and more partners throughout the years.

The other half of the marriage, Ernst & Whinney, can be traced back on a family tree to 1906, when the firm of Ernst & Ernst was founded by a partnership between Alwin C. Ernst and his older brother, Theodore C. Ernst. The firm was based, and continues to be based, in Cleveland, Ohio. The firm took on its first additional partners in 1910 and from there the family tree expanded by immense and unforeseen proportions. By 1913, when income taxes began to be levied in the United States, the need for accountants began to swell dramatically. By the 1980s the firm had become one of the largest members of the Big Eight. In one of its more publicized actions, Ernst & Whinney's audit paved the way for the 1979 government bailout of the Chrysler Corporation.

Meanwhile, the Arthur Young firm endured a rocky decade in the 1980s. Long known for its reliable auditing practice and a clean, conservative interpretation of tax law, the company image was tarnished by events of the 1980s, many in the area of the emerging national savings and loan scandal. For instance, Arthur Young was sued for $560 million for allegedly allowing Western Savings Association of Dallas to overstate its net worth by more than $400 million. In 1988 the Bank of England sued

Arthur Young and collected $44 million after a bank that Young audited collapsed.

In contrast to the struggles of Arthur Young prior to the merger, Ernst & Whinney's business had thrived, with its management consulting practice growing faster than its audit and tax practice. In fact, at the time of the merger, consulting fees accounted for 24 percent of Ernst & Whinney's revenues while only 17 percent of Arthur Young's revenues came from consulting. There was a strong motive for merger coming from international competitive pressures as well. The stage was set for a potential union of the two companies.

In general, both firms thought that the merger represented a comparative advantage for each. While both had heavy hitters for clients, Arthur Young's clients were mostly investment banks and high-tech firms on the East and West Coasts, while Ernst & Whinney had more health care and manufacturing industry clients concentrated in the Midwest and South. Internationally, Arthur Young had more clients in Europe, while Ernst & Whinney had established a presence in the Pacific Rim countries. Arthur Young's clients included American Express, Mobil, and Texas Instruments, while Ernst & Whinney had BankAmerica, Time, Inc., and Eli Lilly.

There was a conflict at the time of the merger over each firm's "cola" clients. A conflict of interest existed in that PepsiCo had been an Arthur Young client since 1965, while Coca-Cola had been an Ernst & Whinney client since 1924. Coca-Cola forced the firm to dump PepsiCo, as Ernst & Young noted that Coca-Cola had been a client for a longer time and that Coke's annual audit fee was $14 million, a much higher figure than Pepsi's $8.8 million audit fee.

The actual merger in 1989 was essentially viewed as a smart competitive move, although some observers thought the merger might be difficult due to perceived differences in management styles, with Ernst & Whinney governed from the top and Arthur Young favoring a more decentralized management system. At the time of the merger Ernst & Whinney had 1,276 partners and 14,739 total personnel in 118 U.S. offices as well as 3,159 partners and 35,600 total personnel in 89 countries. The smaller Arthur Young had 829 U.S.-based partners and 10,652 total U.S. personnel in 93 offices; worldwide they had 2,900 partners and 33,000 total personnel in 74 countries.

In one of its first business decisions following the merger, Ernst & Young began to move into computer-aided software engineering. This step reflected Ernst & Young's diversification into management systems and strategic planning services for businesses. Under the general heading of Development Effectiveness, these services capped a string of moves into computer-aided software engineering. The general thrust of the project incorporates management consulting, Total Quality Management, and process innovation. The process innovation services are sold worldwide, primarily to the insurance and banking industries.

But as the newly formed firm faced the 1990s it was steeped in the controversy surrounding the crisis of the savings and loan industry. Ernst & Young's audits of 23 failed savings and loans were investigated by the Office of Thrift Supervision (OTS) under a subpoena issued in June 1991. OTS was formed by the federal government to recover losses from accounting firms that should have discovered improprieties during S&L audits and to impose fines on auditors for violations of accounting rules. Some of the thrifts that Ernst & Young audited included the failed Charles Keating's Lincoln Savings & Loan (Irvine, California), Silverado Banking (Denver, Colorado), Vernon Savings & Loan (Vernon, Texas), and Western Federal Savings & Loan (Dallas, Texas), all of which experienced total losses of over $5.5 billion. The OTS subpoena required that Ernst & Young surrender one million documents from its work for the 23 failed S&Ls.

Several judgments were rendered against Ernst & Young in connection with the investigation. In July 1992, for instance, the firm paid a fine of $1.66 million to settle accusations that it helped Charles H. Keating, Jr. (of Lincoln Savings & Loan) deceive the federal government about the health of his failing S&L. Moreover, former Ernst & Young partner Jack D. Atchison's license was suspended for four years by the Accounting Board of Arizona. He was accused of helping persuade five U.S. senators to intervene with federal regulators on Keating's behalf. In connection with this settlement, Ernst & Young paid $63 million to settle charges of wrongdoing in the Keating affair. Ernst & Young did not admit guilt, however, and the claim was paid largely by insurance. In total, some $204 million in fines were paid in this civil suit.

In another settlement, Ernst & Young paid $400 million to the federal government in compliance with a federal ruling against the company. The settlement secured recovery of losses attributable to audit failures. In addition, the settlement avoided huge litigation costs and assured that future audits of insured institutions would be conducted according to the highest professional standards. With potential claims that could have mounted to an estimated $1 billion, the ruling relieved Ernst & Young of concerns regarding future penalties involving S&L auditing improprieties. Ernst & Young also agreed to change its accounting practices and ensure that its partners meet federal guidelines for working with federally insured financial institutions. Some of Ernst & Young's partners have been barred from doing such work and recent changes in banking laws require accounting firms to be legally responsible for sharing with regulators reports prepared for bank management.

Despite these troubles, Ernst & Young has remained strong, with a substantial increase in revenues in 1992. Sales from Ernst & Young's risk management and actuarial services group rose 7.4 percent from 1990 to 1991, from $9.5 million to $10.2 million. The company garnered an increasing number of clients, and their involvement in large projects such as municipal insurance and environmental risk management consulting continued to grow. Revenues in risk management consulting went from $10.3 million in 1991 to $10.9 million in 1992. This increase reflected a growing market for these kinds of services. Moreover, major restructuring is taking place in hospitals and in the health care industry in general, creating a need for consultants.

But the traditional Ernst & Young mainstay, auditing, still fared quite well in the new firm's early years. By 1992, in fact, Ernst & Young performed the most audits of large publicly held multinational companies. It audited 3,231 companies with a total value audited of $10.228 trillion (based on asset figures for financial companies and sales for all other firms audited).

Further Reading:

Berton, Lee, "Arthur Young, and Ernst Firm Plan to Merge," *The Wall Street Journal*, May 19, 1989.

Burton, J.C., ed., *Arthur Young and the Business He Founded,* New York: Arthur Young & Company, 1948.

"Entrepreneurial Services: Ernst & Young's Territory," Emerson's Professional Services Review, November, 1991.

"E&W, AY, DH&S, and TR Financial Data Creates Public Stir," Emerson's Professional Services Review, March, 1990.

"E&Y: The Masters of Total Quality Management," *Emerson's Professional Services Review*, March, 1992.

Ernst & Ernst: A History of the Firm, Cleveland: Ernst & Ernst 1960.

"Ernst & Young: Driving For Specialization and Service Integration Leadership," *Emerson's Professional Services Review*, March 1990.

"Ernst & Young Settles Lincoln Savings Case," *New York Times*, July 15, 1992.

Jones, Edgar, *Accountancy and the British Economy 1840–1980: The Evolution of Ernst & Whinney*, London, B.T. Batsford, Ltd., 1981.

Labaton, Stephen, "$400 Million Bargain for Ernst," *New York Times*, November 25, 1992.

Law, Donald M., "Business Tycoon Arthur Young Loved Life In Aiken At Crossways," *Aiken Standard*, April 19, 1987.

Moskowitz, Milton, et al, *Everybody's Business: A Field Guide to the 400 Leading Companies in America*, New York: Doubleday, 1990.

Stevens, Mark, *The Accounting Wars*, New York: Macmillan Publishing Company, 1985.

——, *The Big Eight*, New York: Macmillan Publishing Company, Inc., 1981.

——, *The Big Six: The Selling Out of America's Top Accounting Firms*, New York: Simon & Schuster, 1991.

—John A. Sarich

Estée Lauder Inc.

767 5th Avenue
New York, New York 10153
U.S.A.
(212) 572-4200
Fax: (212) 572-6745

Private Company
Incorporated: 1946
Employees: 10,000
Sales: $2 billion
SICs: 2844 Toilet Preparations

Founded in 1946 by Estée Lauder and her husband Joseph, Estée Lauder Inc. is the largest privately owned cosmetics company in the United States, accounting for 30 to 50 percent of overall department store sales of cosmetics and fragrances. The company has five divisions: the original Estée Lauder line, including skin treatment and fragrances; Aramis, a group of men's toiletries; Clinique, a hypoallergenic line; Prescriptives, an upscale line; and Origins, a botanical treatment line designed to appeal to the environmentally conscious consumer. According to a statement by Leonard Lauder in the *New York Times* in 1982, the company enjoyed a compounded annual growth rate of 20 percent during its first three decades of operation.

Estée Lauder was born Josephine Esther Mentzer in Corona, Queens, New York, in 1908, the ninth child of Rose and Max Mentzer who emigrated from Hungary. Regarding her childhood, Lauder has been quoted as saying, "I loved to make everyone up. . . . I was always interested in people being beautiful, . . . who look like they have a cared-for face."

Lauder was first inspired to enter the business of cosmetics when her uncle, John Schotz, a chemist from Hungary, established New Way Laboratories in Brooklyn in 1924. Her uncle's products included a Six-in-One Cold Cream, Dr. Schotz Viennese Cream, and several perfumes. Lauder got her start by selling these products in New York City and then, from 1939 to 1942, in Miami Beach as well.

In 1944 Lauder began working in various New York salons and smaller department stores, selling her own product line from behind a counter. Of that original line, three skins creams were her uncle's creations. Lauder also sold a face powder, an eye shadow, and a lipstick called Just Red. Soon the entrepreneur

was spending Saturdays selling her products on the floor in Bonwit Teller department store on Fifth Avenue. Lauder's next goal was to get her items into Saks Fifth Avenue. Lauder convinced the Saks buyer that there was a demand for her products after a successful lecture and demonstration at the Waldorf Astoria persuaded customers to line up outside for more product information. A notable detail from the lecture highlighted what would remain a classic Estée Lauder characteristic over the years; the fledgling cosmetics dynamo was selling lipsticks in upscale metal cases at a time just after World War II when most lipsticks were packaged in plastic.

The year Estée Lauder got started, women's cosmetics was a $7 million business in the United States. The Saks connection helped Lauder achieve a reputation that would allow her to sell her products nationally. Beginning in the late 1940s, Estée Lauder travelled the country, making personal appearances in specialty and department stores and training staff in proper sales techniques. She made impressions on influential people early on, securing a spot in I. Magnin's of San Francisco, a store well-respected in the retail trade. I. Magnin's carried her products exclusively in the San Francisco area until the late 1970s. During these early years, Lauder met buyers all over the country and others in the business who would later help her achieve success.

Against the advice of their lawyer, Lauder and her husband entered full-scale into an industry known for extreme market swings and short-lived endeavors. Joseph Lauder worked every day at the small space they had rented, while their oldest son, Leonard, delivered to Saks and other stores on his bicycle.

One technique, now standard in the cosmetics industry, which Estée Lauder pioneered was the gift-with-purchase tactic. Lauder offered free items to bring the customer back for more. Later, the offer was made when a customer bought an item of a certain price. Lauder's gift-with-purchase gained her a loyal following and established her business. Over the decades, however, this standard practice would be responsible for the markedly low profit margin in the cosmetic industry as a whole, and her company in particular.

Early in the 1950s the Lauders, with $50,000 saved from business profits, looked for an advertising representative. After learning that the amount was hardly enough to finance a full-scale campaign, Estée chose to begin advertising with the help of Saks Fifth Avenue direct mail. During this time Lauder reunited with a fragrance executive she had met a decade earlier in order to develop a perfume. Following the examples of Helena Rubenstein and Elizabeth Arden, who had both made their starts in skin care and then moved on to fragrances, Lauder developed a bath oil with a fragrance that lasted for 24 hours. She called the bath oil Youth Dew and introduced it in 1953 at $8.50 a bottle.

With Youth Dew Estée Lauder became an overnight success. "Middle America went bananas for it," stated former employee Andy Lucarelli, as quoted in *Estée Lauder: Beyond the Magic.* Youth Dew sales reached an unprecedented volume of 5,000 units a week in the mid-1950s. Furthermore, sales of skin care products increased due to the popularity of Youth Dew. Thirty years later, the fragrance still had sales of $30 million world-wide.

In 1958, 24-year-old Leonard Lauder joined the company. That year he married Evelyn Hausner, a Vienna-born schoolteacher who would later rise in the company and eventually take over for Estée Lauder herself, making appearances as company spokesperson.

In the early 1960s, Estée Lauder joined Rubenstein, Arden, Revlon, and Cosmetiques in the race to develop a skin care cream like the European products that were becoming popular during this time. Estée Lauder's Re-Nutriv—a careful blend of 25 ingredients—was introduced in a well-orchestrated marketing program typical of most Estée Lauder ventures. Advertisers were careful not to make specific claims regarding the product's ability to revitalize skin or eliminate wrinkles, as such claims could get a cosmetics company into regulatory trouble. A full-page *Harper's Bazaar* ad simply read: "What makes a cream worth $115.00?" The expensive product generated lots of free press for the company.

Estée Lauder Inc. developed an identifiable image in the 1960s. Since the company couldn't afford color ads, they used black-and-white photos instead. Moreover, in 1971, model Karen Graham began portraying the serene, elegant "Estée Lauder look," a role she would fulfill for 15 years. Graham's identification with Estée Lauder was so successful, many people thought she was Estée Lauder herself.

Through the early 1960s, company sales climbed to $14 million. Lauder had by then gathered a small, talented staff that included Ida Steward, from Bristol-Myers; June Leaman, from Bergdorf Goodman; and Ira Levy, a recent graduate of UCLA—all of whom remained with the company for decades.

In 1964 the company introduced Aramis, a trendsetting male fragrance blended of citrus, herbs, and spice for a woodsy scent. Revlon promptly began to compete by launching its own fragrance for men, known as Braggi. Following the deaths of cosmetic leaders Helena Rubenstein and Elizabeth Arden (in 1965 and 1966, respectively), competition increased between giant Charles Revson's Revlon and Estée Lauder.

The introduction of the Clinique line in 1968 firmly established Estée Lauder's success in the cosmetics industry. Clinique's first exposure came via an interview between *Vogue* veteran Carol Phillips and dermatologist Norman Orentreich entitled "Can Great Skin Be Created?" The article, published in the August 15, 1967 edition of *Vogue*, elicited outstanding reader response. Soon thereafter Phillips accepted an offer from Leonard Lauder to join the company and lead the development of the new Clinique line. From the development stage to full-scale introduction, Clinique was designed to be more than just an allergy-tested line of products. Rather, it cultivated an image as a well researched and medically sound line of products produced in laboratories. The first 20 salespeople were given the title of "consultants"; they were rigorously trained and given white lab coats to wear. Sales counters were brightly lit, products were packaged in clinical light green boxes, and a chart allowed customers to determine which Clinique products fit their particular skin type. As stated in the September 26, 1983

Business Week, "Clinique helped fuel a tenfold expansion of the big cosmetics company."

By 1968, sales for privately-owned Estée Lauder, at $40 million, financed a move to new corporate headquarters in the General Motors building, which was completed in 1969. The company was also able to support the Clinique venture, which lost approximately $3 million over the first seven years. Such patient financing became a trademark of Estée Lauder launches. By 1975 the Clinique line had become profitable, prompting competition from Revlon. Through a hasty and ultimately unsuccessful introduction of a product line designed to compete with Clinique, Charles Revson made an important discovery. Estée Lauder held a significant influence over department store buyers, who generated customer loyalty through the exclusive sale of her products. Revlon products, on the other hand, were available at lower price discount centers and inspired no such loyalty.

After 12 years with the company, the founders' oldest son Leonard was named president of Estée Lauder Inc. in 1972. Leonard Lauder focused on maintaining good relations with store buyers. His methods ensured a systematic, goal-oriented method of selling company merchandise, coordinating the advertising levels for various product lines and the quality and quantity of store space to be devoted to those Lauder products. Estée Lauder, board chairperson, spent mornings working at home and afternoons at the office in the General Motors building. Joseph Lauder oversaw production at the Melville, Long Island, plant.

The challenge faced by Estée Lauder in the 1970s was to increase its overall presence while building on its respectable reputation. The company's private, family-controlled ownership gave it the flexibility to respond rapidly, when necessary, to industry trends and competition. Through the 1970s, such quick maneuvering was necessary as the company faced increased competition in the fragrance industry. Revlon scored a huge success with the mass-marketed fragrance "Charlie" in 1973, as did Yves Saint Laurent's "Opium," launched in Paris in 1977 and brought to the United States the following year.

During this time, Lauder had been working on a subtler version of its original Youth Dew fragrance. Noting the success of Opium, Lauder launched both Soft Youth Dew and a spicier, oriental version called Cinnabar in the fall of 1978. Due to the simultaneous introduction of the closely related products, some questions concerning the company's marketing plans were raised. Both retail buyers and consumers were confused over whether Cinnabar was a version of Youth Dew or a new product. Ronald Lauder commented, as quoted in the September 15, 1978 *Women's Wear Daily,* that the company would "continue to market both [fragrances]," and would "probably decide after Christmas which way to go." While the marketing approach was muddled, the privately-owned company proved that it could react quickly in an aggressive market.

A new skin-care line in the style of an upscale Clinique was introduced in 1979. The Prescriptives line was promoted as even more high-tech, with one-hour makeup and fashion consultations included as part of the program. When Prescriptives met with a lukewarm reception, the company regrouped to revise the approach. Estée Lauder's other divisions were challenged as well, as competition extended to the relatively slow market for men's fragrances.

In 1978, sales of the Estée Lauder line were approximately $170 million. Clinique sales stood at $80 million, and the Aramis line, which had developed into over 40 products, had estimated sales of $40 million. Men's products, though the lowest in revenue, were growing at a rate of 18 percent a year. Several men's fragrances were launched in lower-priced markets. With the widely successful 1978 debut of Ralph Lauren's Polo, Estée Lauder Inc. was prompted to consider launching a new men's product. JHL, named after Joseph Lauder, was introduced in 1982, and, like other Lauder products, was marketed as a more expensive and upscale fragrance. Sales clerks requested business cards from customers in order to send them free samples, and an elegant counter display was developed for promotional items.

In 1982 Estée Lauder Inc. became involved in a legal dispute, charging Harco Graphics, Inc., Harry Aronson, and Spencer Press, Inc., with fraud, commercial bribery, and conspiracy. Asking for $5 million in damages, the company alleged that Harco Graphics had rendered false invoices for Lauder products amounting to $1 million to Spencer Press, who billed Lauder for the expenses. Stephen V. Juda, a former director of graphics arts purchasing at Estée Lauder, was also named in the case.

In executive changes in 1982 Leonard Lauder, president of the company, was also named chief executive officer. Ronald Lauder, another son of the founders and executive vice president, became chair of international operations; the division comprised half the company's sales volume, though less of it profits. The changes did not affect Estée Lauder's active chairmanship or Joseph Lauder's management of the company plants.

By 1983, Estée Lauder Inc. reached a billion dollars in sales, and was recognized as the premier cosmetics company. The company underwent several more executive changes. Ronald Lauder left active management to join the Reagan administration as Deputy Assistant Defense Secretary. Joseph Lauder died in January 1983. The family bought Mr. Lauder's stock for $28 million, at a price the IRS would later charge was undervalued, leaving the company liable for $42.7 million in taxes. The Lauders' lawyer countered that shareholder agreements from 1974 and 1976 controlled the price of the shares, since the stock of the family-owned company couldn't be sold.

Just as Estée Lauder reached a billion dollars in sales, its closest rival, Revlon—which had watched the Lauder empire grow from infancy—experienced a first-ever drop in sales, to $1.2 billion. While still formidable, Revlon no longer had the guidance of its leader, Charles Revson, who died in 1975.

Unlike Revlon, which touted its large number of product introductions, Estée Lauder took a more careful approach. Clinique added only 12 new products since its inception, most of which were still being sold after 15 years. Estée Lauder's sole product launch in 1983, Night Repair, reportedly had years of research and development invested in it. Night Repair advertising copy claimed that the product was "a biological breakthrough" which "uses the night, the time your body is resting, to help speed up the natural repair of cells damaged during the day."

Dr. Norman Orentreich, the dermatologist consulted in the groundbreaking 1967 *Vogue* interview preceding the introduction of Clinique, offered a different view. As quoted in the September 1984 issue of *Drug & Cosmetic,* Orentreich stated, "there is no topical preparation affecting the outermost layer of the stratum corneum that the FDA will allow [one] to call a cosmetic that will work." Such objections did not impair sales; in fact, Night Repair went on to become a top seller in the Estée Lauder line.

The company's increasing investment in laboratory research and development proved successful, as indicated by the sales of the Clinique line and Night Repair. As reported in the September 26, 1983 *Business Week,* Leonard Lauder stated that "growth in 1983 R & D expenditures will be twice the company's sales increase."

In 1990, in a widely reported company change, Robin Burns was brought in to replace Robert J. Barnes as chief executive of Estée Lauder Inc. Barnes, who held the position for 26 years, remained with the company as a consultant for the international division. Robin Burns started her career as a fabric buyer for Bloomingdale's at age 21 in 1974, joining the staff at Calvin Klein Cosmetics Corporation in 1983. Burns was instrumental to the introduction of the fragrances Obsession and Eternity during her seven-year tenure, turning the $6 million company into a $200 million success story. Leonard Lauder was quoted in the January 12, 1990 *Women's Wear Daily* as commenting that "Calvin told me, 'No matter what you've heard about her, she's ten times better.'"

Officially taking over in May 1990, Burns revived the image of several Estée Lauder fragrances by the end of the year. Hoping to make the company's flagship Estée Lauder line more accessible by implementing changes in its advertising, Burns oversaw production of ads that featured Paulina Porizkova (the model representing the company's entire line since 1988), suggesting that a more friendly, less remote countenance would have a wider appeal for consumers. Furthermore, Burns opted to give the company's White Linen scent its own representative, model Paul Devicq.

Similarly, the Aramis line was reinvigorated with a campaign designed to reach a younger male audience. Ad spending was increased by 40 percent, and print ads, traditionally placed in the magazines *Fortune* and *Esquire,* were moved instead to *Rolling Stone, Cosmopolitan,* and *GQ.* Televisions spots were switched from news programs like *60 Minutes* to comedy programs like *In Living Color,* which attracted young people.

Prescriptives branched out in the 1990s with the introduction of All Skins, makeup formulated for working women of different ethnic backgrounds. Nearly all cosmetics companies had been criticized for ignoring large segments of the population for too long. By mid-1992 All Skins was attracting 3,800 new customers a month.

In 1990 the company formed a new corporate division, Origins Natural Resources Inc., which catered to public concern for the environment. Recycled paper was used for product packaging and company correspondence, makeup shades emphasized natural skin tones, and animal products such as lanolin and petroleum-based active ingredients were not used in the makeup formulations. Origins was also offered via freestanding boutiques in Cambridge, Massachusetts, and Soho, Manhattan, which proved to be the new division's top-selling locations.

William Lauder, grandson of the founders, headed the Origins division. His statement, quoted in the July 13, 1990 *Women's Wear Daily,* summarized the contemporary Estée Lauder mission: "We are trying to rewrite the book on how a cosmetics company operates and thinks in the 21st century." The company's new approach included gearing more merchandise toward consumers of all economic backgrounds and a commitment to communicating with a growing international audience in addition to a wider variety of American consumers.

In January 1992 Daniel J. Brestle, the president of Prescriptives who had brought that division from a shaky start to $70 million in sales, was named president of Clinique Laboratories USA. The founders' two sons, Leonard and Ronald, continued to play active roles in the executive lineup. Leonard remained president and chief executive officer of Estée Lauder Inc., while Ronald continued as chairperson of both the international and Clinique divisions. Evelyn Lauder, Leonard's wife, oversaw new product development as senior corporate vice president. By 1992 Evelyn Lauder had gradually taken on Estée's role as company spokesperson as the founder made fewer appearances.

Commenting on Estée Lauder's success in the industry in the July 13, 1990 *Women's Wear Daily,* Leonard Lauder summarized the Estée Lauder philosophy. The founder's son and chief executive stated, "We think in decades. Our competitors think in quarters."

Further Reading:

Appelbaum, Cara, "Just Who Is an Aramis Man?" *Adweek's Marketing Week,* September 30, 1991.
Bird, Laura, "Estée Lauder Pulls Whiz Kid Burns Away from Calvin Klein," *Adweek's Marketing Week,* January 15, 1990.
Born, Pete, "Lauder Readies Origins Brand, First in Decade," *Women's Wear Daily,* July 13, 1990.
Deutschman, Alan, "Nudes for Lauder?" *Fortune,* March 12, 1990.
Duffy, Martha, "Take This Job and Love It," *Time,* August 6, 1990.
Edelson, Sharon, "Lauder's Populist Message," *Women's Wear Daily,* February 7, 1992.
"Estée Lauder Appoints Brestle to Head Clinique," *Women's Wear Daily,* January 27, 1992.
Fallon, James, "Estée Lauder Goes to Oxford," *Women's Wear Daily,* September 6, 1991.
Harting, Joan, "Lauder's Cinnabar Exudes Oriental Mystique," *Women's Wear Daily,* September 15, 1978.
Israel, Lee, *Estée Lauder: Beyond the Magic,* New York: Macmillan, 1985.
Kogan, Julie, "What Smell Success?" *Working Woman,* November 1982.
Langway, Lynn, "Common Scents," *Newsweek,* February 6, 1978.
"Lauder and Two Units Suing Printing Company for Fraud," *Women's Wear Daily,* April 16, 1982.
"Lauder's Success Formula," *Business Week,* September 26, 1983.
"Launch Fever," *Women's Wear Daily,* August 9, 1991.
Lloyd, Kate, "How to Be Estée Lauder," *Vogue,* January 1973.
"Looking for Deep Pockets," *Forbes,* January 21, 1991.
Salmans, Sandra, "Estée Lauder: The Scents of Success," *New York Times,* April 18, 1982.
Schwartz, Judith D., "Estée Lauder Uses Bubbling Water to Win Consumers for Time Zone," *Adweek's Marketing Week,* February 5, 1990.
Sloan, Pat, "Burns Reshaping Lauder," *Advertising Age,* November 26, 1990.
Strom, Stephanie, "The Lipstick Wars," *New York Times,* June 28, 1992.
Warren, Catherine, "Estée and Joe," *Women's Wear Daily,* January 7, 1983.
Watters, Susan, "Lauders Fight IRS Ruling over Father's Inheritance," *Women's Wear Daily,* June 14, 1991.

—Frances E. Norton

Fairchild Aircraft, Inc.

P.O. Box 790490
San Antonio, Texas 78279-0490
U.S.A.
(210) 824-9421
Fax: (210) 820-8656

Private Company
Incorporated: 1936 as Fairchild Engine & Airplane
   Corporation
Employees: 1,000
Sales: $580 million
SICs: 3721 Aircraft

Fairchild Aircraft, Inc. is an unlikely survivor of the modern aircraft industry. The company was nearly ruined during the 1980s by acrimonious factions within its boardroom and rescued from bankruptcy by investor Carl Albert, but Fairchild emerged as a mere shadow of its former self. The company was once one of America's leading aircraft manufacturers, building a line of successful commercial and military designs.

The original Fairchild company was established in 1936 as a holding company for the aircraft interests of Fairchild Camera founder Sherman Fairchild. While its Ranger Aircraft Engine subsidiary produced engines for the navy, Fairchild participated in the aviation market largely as a subcontractor during World War II. After the war, Fairchild sought new opportunities in the growing aircraft industry, but was hampered by a lack of capital and engineering talent. Nonetheless, the company turned out a successful cargo design called the C-82. It sought to extend its work in this area by developing a second, larger design, the C-119 ''Flying Boxcar,'' but lost the manufacturing competition to the Kaiser-Frazier company. While Fairchild was awarded a subcontract for the C-119 and a subsequent design called the C-123, its employees' resentment for Kaiser was reflected in their work. Furious with Fairchild's performance, the air force virtually shunned the company.

Fairchild turned instead to commercial designs. It established an arrangement with the Dutch airplane builder Fokker to build versions of its popular F-27 airliner. The company also began development of its Goose guided missile system. Unable to sell either design, Fairchild fell into a deep crisis that lasted from 1958 through 1960. Sherman Fairchild returned from retirement to head the company briefly, and was successful in repairing

damaged relations with the government and returning financial discipline. He was replaced in 1961 by Edward G. Uhl, an engineer.

Uhl's first actions as head of Fairchild were to fire several executives, slash costs, and switch the company from product diversification to technology diversification. Uhl was convinced that Fairchild's greatest weakness was its lack of engineering talent. Rather than spend years building a capable staff, Uhl began an acquisition campaign that included the Hiller Aircraft Company in 1964. The following year, Uhl found an opportunity to buy a financially distressed manufacturer with an army of good engineers. On September 30, Fairchild took control of the Republic Aviation Corporation, a military aircraft manufacturer based in Farmingdale, on New York's Long Island.

Republic Aviation was founded in 1931 by a Russian immigrant named Alexander P. Seversky. A graduate of the Russian naval academy and military aeronautics school, Seversky learned to fly and during World War I was Russia's leading fighter ace. In 1917, while Seversky was in Washington, D.C. to procure aircraft, the Bolsheviks seized power in Russia. Seversky and several in his delegation elected to stay in America.

Seversky worked as a consulting engineer and test pilot, and developed a solid-fuel shore bombardment rocket for the navy. In 1922 he perfected a bomb sight device, which he sold to the U.S. government for $50,000, and used the payment to establish the Seversky Aero Corporation. Rather than building aircraft, Seversky concentrated on improved structures, landing gear, and air-to-air refueling systems.

The Great Depression took a heavier toll on the aviation industry than on others. Seversky's was one of hundreds of aeronautics firms that were forced into bankruptcy in 1931. The company was rescued by the financier Paul Moore, who reorganized the enterprise as Seversky Aircraft Corporation. Moore retained Seversky as president, and took on Alexander Kartveli—an associate of Seversky's and also a Soviet immigrant—as an engineer.

Seversky and Kartveli worked feverishly to perfect the concept of a single-skin all-metal aircraft. The result of their work was the SEV-3, a floatplane fitted with retractable wheels. This design failed to win a volume order, but served as a necessary step in developing additional all-metal aircraft. Seversky succeeded in selling a subsequent trainer model, the BT-8, to the government. Lacking a factory, Seversky Aircraft was forced to subcontract its manufacturing business to the Kirkham Engineering Company in Farmingdale, New York.

In 1935 Seversky Aircraft was forced to terminate its manufacturing agreement with Kirkham Engineering when the Colombian government failed to pay an installment. Seversky collected his half-finished aircraft and completed assembling them at an abandoned warehouse nearby. At this site, Seversky began work on the P-35, another derivative of his original design. The P-35 won a government design competition against the Curtiss P-36 Hawk, bringing in a badly needed order for seventy-seven aircraft. Seversky had difficulty overcoming several shortcomings in the P-35, including a jam-prone starter, leaky fuel tanks, and faulty landing gear. The company lost $70,000 on the order and the following year lost an order to Curtiss for 210 additional aircraft.

Seversky's over-enthusiastic drive to sell aircraft, his disdain for Curtiss, and his difficult personality caused his company to become increasingly alienated from the American military establishment. As Seversky's reputation grew, his company's business declined. He was forced to turn to a greater number of export customers, including the Soviet Union and Japan, which held tenuous regard for human rights and even proprietary aircraft designs.

Seversky converted the P-35 to a racer and struck up a relationship with the aviatrix Jacqueline Cochrane in an attempt to win recognition for the aircraft's performance. The design won several races, but failed to win more sales. Most of the government's P-35s were stationed in the Philippines and were later destroyed during the Japanese invasion of that country.

Hoping to reduce his company's reliance on military sales, Seversky spent tremendous sums on the development of a large five-propeller passenger craft. But by 1939 Paul Moore had enough of Seversky. That year, while the founder was on a sales mission to England, the company's beleaguered board of directors voted to oust Seversky and install its own candidate, W. Wallace Kellett, as president of the firm. Seversky was given $80,000 and retired into a more distinguished career as a columnist.

Kellett slashed the payroll from 500 to 185 employees and later won a lucrative Swedish export order. With a $10 million backlog, the company was profitable for the first time. Hoping to rid the company of its bad name, the board voted to change the company's name to Republic Aviation.

Alexander Kartveli remained with the firm and was instrumental in designing its next fighter, the P-47 Thunderbolt. A clear improvement over the lightly armed P-35, the P-47 was the first fighter capable of providing uninterrupted air cover for American bombers between Britain and Germany. As a result, the P-47 secured a leading role for Republic during World War II. Republic Aviation, still located in Farmingdale, grew to employ more than 32,000 workers, a great many of whom were women. By 1944, Republic was turning out 20 P-47s a day.

With the end of the war drawing near, the company began planning for much leaner times. Fearing the loss of its military contracts, Republic hoped to convert a new high-altitude reconnaissance craft it had developed into a civilian airliner. The four-engine RC-2 Rainbow was as sleek as a missile, and its speed was unrivaled, but the two launch customers, Pan American and American Airlines, lost interest after learning the airliner's cost. A second project for the civilian market was the RC-3 Seabee. Conceived of as a family sedan floatplane, the Seabee suffered from a collapse in public interest in private aviation. After only about 1,000 Seabees were built, Republic abandoned the civil aviation market.

British and American manufacturers quickly began development of jet aircraft after Germany's Me-262 fighter jet appeared during the final months of the war. Under Karveli's direction, Republic began work on its own jet design, the F-84 Thunderjet. Fitted with an Allison J-35 engine, the F-84 first flew in 1946.

The Thunderjet was capable of air-to-air refueling and carrying nuclear bomb payloads. The design saw heavy action during the Korean War, and by 1953 more than 7,000 were turned out for the Air Force and several foreign air services.

While the F-84 proved to be a formidable fighter bomber, its development took a heavy toll on Republic. Costs were so high that the company only narrowly avoided bankruptcy. Nevertheless, having demonstrated its ability to build a great jet, Republic won further government funding for an experimental rocket-powered version, the XF-91, and a successor to the F-84, the F-105 Thunderchief. The Thunderchief matched or outperformed all competing designs during the mid-1950s, including the North American F-86 and Lockheed F-104. The multi-role F-105 was the U.S. Air Force's standard fighter bomber throughout the 1950s, and more than 800 were built. During the late 1950s, the company began development of a ramjet-powered fighter called the XF-103. Capable of speeds in excess of 3,000 miles per hour, the titanium fighter was deemed too expensive by the Air Force and was canceled.

When President Kennedy took office, Defense Secretary Robert McNamara attempted to rein in aircraft development costs by ordering development of a fighter bomber suitable for use by both the Air Force and Navy. This strategy caught Republic by surprise. As Boeing Co., General Dynamics Corp., and Grumman Corp. scrambled to meet the call, Republic found itself simply unprepared to develop such a design. Like Martin Aircraft some years before, Republic elected to concentrate its resources on space projects. The company was chosen to make space suits and build satellites and rocket engines, but despite these efforts, Republic was unable to secure a lasting position in the space industry.

By the time production of the F-105 ended in 1965, Republic was left only with a few subcontracting arrangements, including building aft sections of McDonnell's F-4 Phantom. With all but 3,700 employees laid off and in dire need of financial backing, Republic was acquired by the new Fairchild-Hiller company. As a division of Fairchild-Hiller, Republic afforded its parent company a better relationship with the military. By 1966, Fairchild-Hiller's finances had become strong enough that it was able to bid for the acquisition of another distressed airplane builder, the Douglas Aircraft Co.

While Fairchild-Hiller lost out to McDonnell Aircraft on that bid, it retained a strong interest in commercial aircraft. As a result of its close relationship with Fokker, the company began negotiations to manufacture the Dutch company's new F-28 jetliner in the United States under license. However, the partnership was later terminated with a $30 million write-off when sales of the Fokker-Fairchild F-228 failed to materialize.

The Republic Aviation Division won valuable subcontracts to manufacture parts for Boeing Co.'s 747 and supersonic transport, or SST. Republic also won a design competition to develop a vertical take-off and landing fighter jet with the German company Entwicklundring Sud. Unfortunately, both the SST and the fighter were later canceled.

In a 1969 design competition with McDonnell-Douglas Corporation, Republic lost a highly profitable contract for the F-15. Many considered Republic's design to be vastly superior, but

McDonnell-Douglas maintained an extremely competent lobbying organization. In addition, the Pentagon had just awarded the F-14 Tomcat to Grumman, located in Bethpage, a scant nine miles from Republic. In the world of political "horse trading," two major contract awards for the same congressional district would never be tolerated.

In 1971 the company had changed its name to Fairchild Industries and was looking to acquire another aircraft manufacturer with excess capacity—and located away from the East Coast. In November of that year the search ended with the Swearingen Aircraft Company. At the time it was acquired by Fairchild, Swearingen was little more than a design shop with a small manufacturing facility located in San Antonio, Texas. The company was founded in 1959 by a talented aircraft designer named Ed Swearingen, Jr. Originally a one-man operation, the Swearingen Aircraft Company was established solely for the purpose of modifying twin-engine Queen Air business craft, built in Wichita by Beech Aircraft. Unlike other aircraft modifiers, Swearingen did not merely add new fixtures and controls. Instead, he replaced the Queen Air's original fuselage with one of his own design. Swearingen marketed the rebuilt aircraft under the name Merlin.

During the 1960s, Swearingen incorporated further enhancements on the Queen Air, which he sold as the Merlin II and Merlin IIB. Swearingen sold a total of 115 Merlins. By 1970 Swearingen had so radically altered the original Beech design that he decided to build the craft from scratch. He called the new business craft the Merlin III, but also developed a commuter airline version called the Metro.

While Swearingen went deeply into debt to finance production of the new craft, the project gained the attention of Fairchild. Seeing the opportunity to buy into a promising civilian craft at the earliest stage, Fairchild negotiated a deal to buy out Swearingen. The San Antonio facility remained in operation for several more years as Fairchild Swearingen until the founder's name was eventually dropped.

In 1972 Fairchild Republic won a competition to produce a new ground attack aircraft, the A-10 Thunderbolt. This unusual craft, called Warthog by the pilots who flew it, was designed not to fly against other aircraft, but against tanks and artillery. Heavily armored, the A-10 carried a powerful 30mm rapid fire cannon that could destroy a tank in half a second. The A-10 was extremely maneuverable, able to snoop around trees and loiter at low altitudes for hours. The air force, addicted to flashy supersonic fighters, wanted no part of the project, but with no other anti-tank alternative, production of the A-10 began. The air force was obligated to maintain the craft. In battle, the A-10 would be under the direction of the army.

Hoping to remain a step ahead of cancellation, Fairchild immediately began searching for another civilian project in which to invest profits from the A-10. The company studied a number of designs with Sweden's Saab-Scania, settling on a 34-passenger twin-prop called the SF-340. Fairchild and Saab agreed to develop and manufacture the airliner jointly and to coordinate sales efforts.

In 1982, with A-10 production nearing the end of its cycle, Fairchild won a second contract to produce the T-46 jet trainer for the air force, but air force officials were so incensed by the presentation of a mock-up when a finished version was due, they requested a full review of the company. They found Fairchild unable to control costs or affect engineering discipline because the company's senior executives were waging a pitched battle for control of the company, and driving it into complete disarray.

After Fairchild delivered the last of 700 A-10s in 1984, the company was unable to cover rising costs on the T-46. No longer able to support the SF-340 project, Fairchild bailed out after building only 96—half what was needed to break even. The divided management attempted to steer the company into the communications and space industries (the company built numerous space components, including the Space Shuttles' tail fins), but when the air force canceled the T-46 in 1987, it sounded the death knell for the Republic division. Republic's Farmingdale site was sold to a shopping mall developer in 1988, and many of its employees moved to Grumman.

In July of 1987 Fairchild restructured its operations and sold its San Antonio operations to Los Angeles-based GMF Investments, headed by renegade board director Gene Morgan. Fairchild continued to collect small contracts for updated versions of the Metro from the air national guard and a handful of commuter airlines. After a while, its president and two other executives were fired for "philosophical differences" with Morgan. After a boardroom showdown in January of 1990, Fairchild declared bankruptcy. It remained under Chapter 11 supervision until August 15, when a former Fairchild customer named Carl Albert bid for the company.

Albert had purchased many Fairchild Metros during his career as head of the Wings West commuter airline. As a one-time customer, he knew how to sell them. When the AMR Corporation bought out Wings West, Albert had $42 million to spend. Later that year, Albert and a group of investors organized Fairchild Aircraft Incorporated, and acquired the airplane builder for $66.4 million. They immediately laid plans to rebuild the company, riding their bets on a newer, more versatile Metro III.

Months later, the A-10 proved itself in battle in Kuwait, destroying 1,000 tanks, 1,200 artillery pieces, and 2,000 military vehicles. Some Warthogs returned from battle with as much as 20 feet of wing missing, tails shot off and gaping holes in the fuselage. The effectiveness and incredible resilience of the craft forced many in the Pentagon to rethink their earlier treatment of Fairchild. The company sold its rights to the aircraft to Grumman before closing its Farmingdale plant.

Under Carl Albert, Fairchild emerged as a financially sound company—and the only consistently profitable small aircraft manufacturer. The company manufactured derivatives of its successful new Metro 23, including passenger, cargo, military, and aerial surveillance versions.

Principal Subsidiaries: Fairchild Aircraft Services Co.; Merlin Express, Inc.

Further Reading:

"A-10 Warthogs Damaged Heavily In Gulf War . . . ," *Aviation Week & Space Technology,* August 5, 1991, pp. 42–3.

Bright, Charles D., *Jet Makers,* Lawrence, Kansas: Regents Press of Kansas, 1978.

"Carl Albert, Chairman of Fairchild Aircraft Corp.," *Air Transport World,* August, 1991, p. 99.

"Company on the Make," *Magazine of Wall Street,* February 4, 1967. pp. 13–51.

"Fairchild, General Dynamics Team to Develop New Surveillance Aircraft," *Aviation Week & Space Technology,* August 31, 1992, p. 59.

"Fairchild Industries' Continuing Quest," *New York Times,* October 31, 1979, p. D1.

"Fairchild Industries, Inc.," *Moody's Industrial Manual 1977,* p. 601.

"New Fairchild Venture Seeks Joint Venture Partners," *Aviation Week & Space Technology,* May 20, 1991, pp. 65–6.

"Setting Loose the Hogs of War," *Fortune,* February 25, 1991, p. 56.

Stoff, Joshua, *The Thunder Factory,* Osceola, Wisconsin: Motorbooks International, 1990.

—John Simley

Federated DEPARTMENT STORES, INC.

Federated Department Stores Inc.

7 West 7th Street
Cincinnati, Ohio 45202
U.S.A.
(513) 579-7000
Fax: (513) 579-7185

Public Company
Incorporated: 1929
Employees: 56,421
Sales: $7.08 billion
Stock Exchanges: New York
SICs: 5311 Department Stores

Federated Department Stores, Inc. is one of America's largest operators of premier retail chains, with over 220 department stores in 26 states. Retail divisions in the group include: Abraham & Straus/Jordan Marsh, Bloomingdale's, The Bon Marche, Burdines, Lazarus, Rich's/Goldsmith's, and Stern's. The current combination of stores was formed in the late 1980s, when Federated Department Stores, Inc. and Allied Stores Corporation were acquired and merged by the Campeau Corporation. The heavily leveraged merger caused the new group to file for Chapter 11 bankruptcy in 1990. The reorganized Federated Department Stores, Inc. emerged from bankruptcy in February 1992.

Federated Department Stores, Inc. was organized in Columbus, Ohio, in 1929 as a holding company for founding members F&R Lazarus & Company, its subsidiary Shillito's, and Abraham & Straus department stores. The Federated group was formed and led by Fred Lazarus, Jr., whose namesake company was the dominant retail store in Columbus. F&R Lazarus was created by Fred's grandfather, Simon. The elder Lazarus, a Jewish refugee of religious persecution in Germany, founded the men's clothing store in 1851. Shillito's, a Cincinnati-based store acquired by F&R Lazarus in 1928, was founded in 1830. While Shillito's was the oldest store west of the Allegheny Mountains, it ranked only fourth among Cincinnati stores by the time it was purchased by Lazarus. Within a year under the management of the Lazarus family, Shillito's sales grew by over 50 percent, and within a decade, the store had regained the top spot in its urban market. The other founding member of Federated, Abraham & Straus (A&S), was founded in 1865 in

Brooklyn, New York. It would grow to become the group's sales and profits leader by the mid-twentieth century.

Bloomingdale's joined the Federated group in 1930, a year after Federated was organized. This revered name in retail had been founded in 1872 by Lyman and Joseph Bloomingdale on New York's east side. Although the brothers had chosen an area of the city that was underdeveloped at the time, Bloomingdale's reputation for carrying unique merchandise brought more and more patrons to the store. The department store carried European imports as early as 1886 and quickly became a leader in home furnishings.

During the 1930s, Fred Lazarus, Jr. earned a reputation for innovation that made his family "the first name in retail," according to a 1961 *Forbes* article. In the late 1920s, "Mr. Fred" instituted an administrative division of labor that placed department managers in charge of buying and selling all of the merchandise in their particular department. This brought a spirit of entrepreneurship to the individual departments in each store. In 1934, Lazarus revolutionized retail clothing sales when he adopted a French merchandising technique in which apparel was arranged according to size, rather than by color, price, or brand. The system became an industry standard. In 1939, Mr. Fred was a key figure in convincing President Roosevelt to move the Thanksgiving holiday to the fourth Thursday of November. The calendar change extended the Christmas shopping season, giving retailers more time to sell at their busiest time of year.

Federated stores helped their customers during the Great Depression by extending credit and establishing a reputation for community involvement in times of crisis. The Federated organization helped support its divisions throughout the Great Depression by sharing their risks and benefits. The loosely-defined coalition worked so well that, by the end of World War II, the holding company was making more money than it could profitably reinvest in existing stores.

With the threat of fierce competition from suburban shopping centers, Federated reached a turning point at which it had to decide whether to break up or form a central organization geared towards expansion. Chairperson Fred Lazarus, Jr., whose chain had contributed substantially to the success of Federated, pushed for a stronger organization, which he achieved in June 1945. Federated's main office was moved to Cincinnati, and the central management team worked to capture a leading role in the retail revolution of the postwar era. Although the holding company's leadership took a more aggressive role in corporate administration after 1945, divisional autonomy remained a hallmark of the Federated organization for decades.

Federated "boomed" along with the postwar population of the 1950s through expansion and acquisition. In 1956, Burdines, of Miami, became a division of Federated through an exchange of common stock. Rikes' and Goldsmith's, the largest department stores in Dayton, Ohio, and Memphis, Tennessee, respectively, were purchased in 1959. Over the course of the decade, sales at Federated's 50 main stores and 32 branches increased over 100 percent, and the group became the United States' largest, most profitable department store company. Its members included the most prestigious department store chains in almost any given metropolitan area: Foley's of Houston, Sanger's in Dallas, and Filene's of Boston. The haute couture reputation of Federated's stores carried a high price, which translated into the high profit margins that accounted for much of the corporation's success.

Growth continued in the 1960s: by mid-decade, Federated's annual sales topped the $1 billion mark. Sales increased 250 percent from 1960 to 1970, reaching $2 billion by 1970. Ralph Lazarus succeeded his father, Fred Lazarus, Jr., as chair and chief executive officer of Federated in 1967. He had worked his way up through the corporate ranks, from salesperson to general merchandise manager, vice-president for publicity, executive vice-president, and finally president by 1957. In 1965, Federated purchased Bullock's and I. Magnin, two upscale department stores based in California. The Federal Trade Commission forced a consent decree on Federated as a result of the purchases, so that the company was prohibited from acquiring any more department stores until 1970.

Since the company's expansion by acquisition was limited, Ralph Lazarus led Federated into the supermarket industry in 1968 with the purchase of Ralph's Industries, a West Coast supermarket chain that served upper-income markets. The chain had 65 stores that contributed ten percent of Federated's total sales by the end of the decade. Federated also got into mass merchandising during the 1960s, with the creation of Gold Circle discount stores in 1968. The small Gold Circle chain totaled five stores in Columbus and Dayton at the end of the decade.

However, Federated's success was not uninterrupted. In 1971, the group sold its Fedway chain to a competitor, Dillard Department Stores, for $6 million in cash. Fedway had been created in 1951 to take advantage of southward population shifts. Its stores represented a new direction for Federated, a move into the small, but burgeoning markets of the "sunbelt": Texas, Arizona, and California. Fedway peaked in the mid-1960s with 11 stores and over $30 million in annual sales. After that point, the chain was overcome by larger, more experienced retailers like Sears & Roebuck, Montgomery Ward, and J.C. Penney. By the time it was liquidated, Fedway's sales volume had dwindled to $13 million, and the chain had shrunk to six stores.

The Federated chain grew dramatically in the 1970s. Net income increased from $91.1 million in 1970 to $277.7 million in 1979, and sales nearly tripled during that time to $6.3 billion. The growth was stimulated by a $2.2 billion acquisition spree that almost doubled the group's number of stores to over 350 units. This growth was doubly astonishing in light of punishing recessions that cycled throughout the 1970s. Part of Federated's enduring success stemmed from the fact that most of its upper-class clientele was not as badly affected by economic downturns as working class shoppers.

The group made a pivotal acquisition in 1976 when the purchase of Rich's Inc. gave it a foothold in southeastern retail. The $157 million stock trade gave Federated a 109-year-old, Atlanta-based institution with 11 department stores, three Rich's II boutiques, and 11 Richway discount stores in Atlanta, Birming-

ham, Alabama, and Charlotte, North Carolina. The Rich's chain gained the financial backing of America's largest department store chain, with resources that promised to expand the division throughout the south.

Federated also expanded its established chains more aggressively. In 1976, Bloomingdale's opened its first full-line store outside the New York market, in a suburb of Washington, D.C. Bullock's, I. Magnin, Burdine's, and other divisions were also planning regional and cross-country branches far from their traditional metropolitan markets. For example, Bullock's, based in Los Angeles, moved into Arizona in 1977. I. Magnin planned to add five new stores and go national between 1976 and 1980. Filene's, a Boston store, moved into New Hampshire, and Cincinnati-based Shillito's had three stores in Kentucky by 1977. New stores were built 20 percent smaller than usual to squeeze more profits from less space. Federated's tradition of divisional autonomy gave way to more centralized supervision.

But Federated's growth was countered by troubled divisions throughout the 1970s. In the early years of the decade, Federated's biggest unit and dollar producer, the original Abraham & Straus store in Brooklyn, pulled the entire A&S division down. Some of the division's problems were out of its control, like a demographic shift that eroded its traditionally affluent customer base. As middle-class Brooklynites escaped to the suburbs, they were replaced by an impoverished population with little interest in A&S's pricey merchandise. Many of the new residents were also drawn to a large regional mall just miles away. Furthermore, the chain's management had neglected its 100-year-old, 1.5 million square foot Brooklyn store. By 1973, both sales and profits at A&S had leveled off, and two years later, A&S's pretax profits slid a disturbing 45 percent. The chain launched a comprehensive remodeling in an attempt to recapture its middle-income shoppers.

Ralph's, the 98-unit Los Angeles-based supermarket chain, faltered throughout most of the decade as well, as management made a lukewarm commitment to that competitive industry. Although Ralph's was recognized as one of the country's most productive, enterprising food stores, it fell victim to costly price wars in California in 1976 and 1977. The grocery chain eventually withdrew to its home region, closing 18 stores after failing in northern California.

Federated's long-running attempts to diversify into mass merchandising, which began in the 1960s, reaped uninspiring results in the 1970s. Gold Circle, which was projected to grow into a 200-unit upscale discounter, had only 42 units by 1981. It had run into trouble after it expanded into California with seven stores in 1976 and 1977. Prior to the expansion, the chain had been limited to Cleveland, Columbus, Cincinnati, and Rochester, New York. High startup costs and no profits in the western units disappointed Federated officials, who had underestimated the competition that came from K Mart and Target. By the end of the decade, Gold Circle was slated to retreat from the California market entirely.

Two industry trends also threatened Federated's dominant position in retail. Specialty stores started to broaden their appeal, attracting increasingly more upscale shoppers. At the same time, Sears, J.C. Penney, and other mass merchandisers were enhancing their stores to attract more affluent shoppers. Federated felt the squeeze between these two forces: the company's 1979 profits stagnated at $179.9 million, even though sales had increased ten percent to $5.4 billion.

When Howard Goldfeder was elevated from president to CEO, succeeding Ralph Lazarus in 1981, he set demanding return-on-investment quotas as a prerequisite to further expansion. Furthermore, he instituted seven new strategies to induce Federated to retake its position as a retail innovator. These included: enlarging market share through more aggressive promotions and deeper inventories; renovating key units in major markets; expanding department stores into the high-growth sunbelt; cultivating new divisions; ensuring lower management turnover; repositioning and expanding Ralph's supermarkets; and disposing of or merging less profitable units.

Nevertheless, some industry analysts criticized Federated, and especially Goldfeder, for attempting to dominate too many segments of the retail industry. While rivals Dayton-Hudson and R. H. Macy's sharpened their focus on either mass merchandising or upscale retail, Federated spread its investments and profit margins among a wide range of concepts. As the decade wore on, Federated's return-on-equity stagnated, and its stock price dwindled. By the late 1980s, the company was ripe for a hostile takeover; it wasn't strong enough to command a high stock price, yet it was not weak enough to be beyond help.

In 1988, Federated was acquired by Campeau Corporation. Subsequently, Federated's Bullock's and I. Magnin divisions were sold to competitor R. H. Macy Corp., and the Foley's and Filene's divisions were sold to other retailers. Furthermore, the headquarters of Allied Stores Corporation was moved from New York to Cincinnati to be consolidated with Federated. Allied had been founded in 1935 to succeed Hahn Department Stores, Inc., a holding company that managed Boston's Jordan Marsh stores, among others. Allied had been instrumental in the establishment of the United States' first regional shopping center in 1950, and had acquired the Stern Brothers and Block's department stores over the course of its history.

Campeau Corporation's Robert Campeau had acquired Allied for $3.6 billion in a 1986 hostile, debt-financed takeover. Then he borrowed $6.5 billion—97 percent of the purchase price—to buy Federated in 1988. Campeau had scheduled his 1989 debt payments according to profit projections of $740 million. However, Federated only made $372 million that year, and Campeau's creditors clamored for the $627 million that was due them. On January 15, Federated and Allied filed the second largest nonbank bankruptcy on record and the largest, most complex restructuring in the retail trade.

During the course of the two-year reorganization, Federated and Allied merged and cut all ties with Campeau Corporation. More than 40 stores were liquidated. Federated traded $8.2 billion in debt for $850 million in cash, plus $2.8 billion in new debt and 92 million shares of new stock valued at $2.3 billion. Over $2 billion of the debt was forgiven, but the new Federated was still stuck with $3.5 billion debt on its balance sheet. The new entity boasted 220 department stores in 26 states and annual sales of

about $7 billion. A new CEO, Allen Questrom, led the reorganization. He had been instrumental in the turnaround of Federated's troubled Rich's division in the 1980s and was hailed as one of the top leaders in retailing of the 1990s.

Together with Federated president James A. Zimmerman, Questrom instituted cost-cutting measures that benefited Federated and its customers in the first months after the reorganization. SABRE, a data processing system, and FACS, the credit services operation, helped centralize sales, credit, and inventory tracking while promoting economies of scale. The merger of the background operations of Abraham & Straus and Jordan Marsh saved Federated $25 million per year without disrupting either chain's image. Part of the savings realized by these measures was passed on to the choosier shopper of the 1990s. Some industry observers cited Questrom's commitment to GMROI (gross margin return on investment), a new, but reliable performance measurement for department stores, as another reason for high confidence in the new Federated.

Within months of its rise from bankruptcy, Federated made one of Wall Street's largest initial public offerings of 1992. The group had planned to offer 40 million shares and use the proceeds to pre-pay a chunk of its long-term debt, but was pleasantly surprised when applications for 50 million shares poured in, thus enabling the company to generate more than $500 million. In 1992, Federated prepaid almost $1 billion of its debt. During the first six months of 1993, the company was able to retire $355 million of its most expensive bonded debt. The interest savings permitted Federated to increase its 1993–96 budget for store renovations and openings by $461 million to $1.2 billion.

In January 1994 Federated was attempting to purchase R. H. Macy & Company, which had been in bankruptcy, by acquiring a large portion of Macy's debt. The merger would require bankruptcy court approval, however.

Principal Subsidiaries: Abraham & Straus/Jordan Marsh; Bloomingdale's; The Bon Marche; Burdines; Lazarus; Rich's/Goldsmith's; Stern's.

Further Reading:

"Bloomingdale's Celebrates a Century," *Stores,* November 1972, p. 10.
Chakravarty, Subrata N., "Federated Chooses Not to Choose," *Forbes,* April 8, 1985, pp. 82, 86–87.
Cobleigh, Ira U., "Federated Department Stores, Inc." *The Commercial and Financial Chronicle,* July 31, 1969, p. 393.
"Fadeout for Fedway," *Dun's,* October 1971, p. 60.
"Federated: Blue Chip Retailer," *Financial World,* March 22, 1972, p. 6.
"Federated's Push to Improve Profitability," *Business Week,* July 6, 1981, pp. 44–46.
"Federated: The Most Happy Retailer Grows Faster and Better," *Business Week,* October 18, 1976, pp. 74–77, 80.
Feinberg, Phyllis, "Federated Finesses Recession," *The Commercial and Financial Chronicle,* October 27, 1957, pp. 1, 3.
"The First Family of Retailing," *Forbes,* March 15, 1961, pp. 19–22.
Jereski, Laura, "Damn the Torpedoes," *Forbes,* June 10, 1991, p. 66.
Klokis, Holly, "Retailing's Grande Dame: Cloaked in New Strategies," *Chain Store Age Executive,* March 1985, pp. 18–20.

Loomis, Carol J., "The Biggest, Looniest Deal Ever," *Fortune,* June 18, 1990, pp. 48–72.

"Optimism at Federated," *New York Times,* May 24, 1993, p. D3.

"Ralph Lazarus of Federated," *Stores,* January 1974, pp. 2–3.

Reda, Susan, "Staying in Tune: Allen Questrom, Chairman and CEO, Federated Dept. Stores," *Stores,* September 1992, pp. 18–24.

Rosenberg, Hillary, "Life Among the Ruins," *Institutional Investor,* June 1990, pp. 92–94+.

"A Southern Bastion Falls to Federated," *Business Week,* July 26, 1976, pp. 43–44.

"This Peacock Won't be Tomorrow's Feather Duster," *Forbes,* June 15, 1957, pp. 24–33.

"Where 'Beautiful People' Find Fashion," *Business Week,* September 2, 1972, pp. 44, 45.

Zinn, Laura, and Michele Galen, "Short Chapter, Happy Ending," *Business Week,* February 10, 1992, pp. 126–127.

—April S. Dougal

Fieldcrest Cannon, Inc.

326 E. Stadium Drive
Eden, North Carolina 27288
U.S.A.
(919) 627-3000
Fax: (919) 627-3109

Public Company
Incorporated: 1953 as Fieldcrest Mills, Inc.
Employees: 17,000
Sales: $1.21 billion
Stock Exchanges: New York
SICs: 2211 Broadwoven Fabric Mills, Cotton; 2221
   Broadwoven Fabric Mills, Manmade Fiber and Silk; 2269
   Finishers of Textiles, Nec; 2273 Carpets and Rugs; 2281
   Yarn Spinning Mills

Fieldcrest Cannon, Inc. is one of the leading producers of household textile products in the United States. Upon the purchase by Fieldcrest Mills of competing Cannon Mills Co., the emergent Fieldcrest Cannon became a dominant force in the home textile industry.

FIELDCREST MILLS

The early histories of both Fieldcrest Mills and Cannon Mills center on determined industrialists. Fieldcrest started with aspiring empire-builder Benjamin Franklin Mebane, who launched an ambitious plan to open one mill a year in and around 600 acres of land he had purchased in Spray, North Carolina, in 1893. By 1905 he owned six mills in the area, renamed Eden (after a surveyor's comment that it resembled the garden of Eden). Mebane had gone to Chicago retailer Marshall Field for help in financing his plan, and after Mebane started having trouble repaying his debt, Field decided to take over. By 1910 Field had gained voting control of Mebane's Spray Water Power & Land Co. and had installed new managers; by 1912 the takeover was complete and the company had become a subsidiary of Marshall Field & Co. Field invested in improvements and expansion projects for the subsidiary, which was renamed the Thread Mills Company. In 1916 the company acquired a 1,600-acre site near Martinsville, Virginia, for a huck (flat weave) and terry towel plant and employee housing; the facility in the newly created community of Fieldale, started operation in 1919. It would continue operating into the 1990s.

In 1935 the mills were reorganized. Previously part of Marshall Field's wholesale division, they became part of the manufacturing division, and sales departments distributed their products nationally at both wholesale and retail levels.

During World War II shortages hampered the mills' ability to meet consumer demand. Nevertheless, they did produce a variety of goods for the armed services, including silk cartridge cloth, camouflage net, parachute cloth, and mosquito netting. In 1947 the division's name was changed to Fieldcrest Mills, to clearly identify them with the nationally advertised products that it manufactured.

By 1953 Marshall Field & Co. was eager to expand its stores, especially in the emerging suburban landscape. To raise enough capital, the company sold its mill operations (including its carpet mills, which manufactured the well-respected Karastan brand of carpets) to Amoskeag Co. Fieldcrest Mills, Inc., was incorporated in September of that year; its sales were $39 million.

Amoskeag Co., an investment trust based in Boston, also owned the Bangor & Aroostoock Railroad in Maine and various real estate and mining interests. Amoskeag, in turn, was controlled by the Dumaine trust, a family trust organized by F.C. Dumaine, Sr., a textile mill baron who had become the head of Amoskeag in 1905. Upon his death in 1951 stewardship for the trust passed to his son F.C. Dumaine, Jr., who had started working for Amoskeag in 1922. By 1961 sales had reached $77 million, and the following year Filedcrest became a publicly owned company, with Amoskeag holding about 40 percent of the stock. In 1967 Fieldcrest was listed on the New York Stock Exchange.

Fieldcrest grew through the mid-1960s via a series of acquisitions and improvements, and by 1967 those costs totaled $82.3 million. At that time the Fieldcrest division, which produced blankets, bedspreads, sheets, and towels, comprised 65 percent of the company's sales, while the Karastan division, which produced Karastan and Laurelcrest carpets, contributed 20 percent. Sales that year were $175.3 million.

Fieldcrest produced goods under its own name as well as private labels, with customers Sears, Roebuck & Co. and J.C. Penney accounting for almost 15 percent of total sales. Fieldcrest's strength came from strong showing of its medium- and upper-priced lines, which made up almost two-thirds of total sales. These lines, carrying the Fieldcrest label, appeared primarily in department stores—its Royal Velvet towels, introduced in 1954, were known for their luxury. The lower priced St. Marys brand was sold through mass merchandisers.

The twentieth anniversary of Fieldcrest Mills, Inc., in 1973, saw sales reach $290 million and annual growth since 1961. By 1977 volume had grown to $417 million. Profits had generally followed this upward trend as well. During this time, Fieldcrest tried to meet the growing consumer demand for more fashionable styles for bed and bath products, entering the "designer" sweepstakes. In 1976 it introduced its first designer line, the Halston collection, and the following year a Geoffrey Beene line was introduced, as well as the Carleton Varney line for the St Marys brand. The market responded favorably, and Fieldcrest saw a 43 percent gain in its bed and bath products in 1976–77. Carpet sales also increased, due to a boom in housing as well as an aggressive promotional program and a successful entry in the contract carpeting market. Halston rugs were introduced in 1977.

That year the company formed a 50 percent joint venture with the Bank of Ireland and P.J. Carroll & Co. Ltd.—Fieldcrest Ireland, Ltd.—to build and operate a Fieldcrest towel plant in Kelkenney, Ireland, in an attempt to penetrate the European market.

Profits crested at $24.8 million on sales of $517.7 million in 1979. Thereafter sales began to slide, falling to $10.4 million in 1982 on sales of $492 million. The recession had affected the company's performance, but other mills proved able to sustain earnings during that period. Market analysts pointed to ill-conceived and expensive expansion attempts; Fieldcrest had spent $100 million expanding or updating its facilities between 1978 and 1981. Furthermore, Fieldcrest had responded to a surge in blanket sales in 1977 and 1978 due to unusually cold winters and high energy costs by modernizing its blanket mill in Eden for $40 million, but blanket sales had begun declining after 1978. The plant in Ireland closed in 1982 after high inflation in that country priced the towels out of the European market, and Fieldcrest lost $8 million.

Most troubling for Fieldcrest were attempts by other manufacturers to encroach upon its ensconced and lucrative position at the head of the premium towel market. Fieldcrest had decided to aggressively expand its St. Marys line, and this triggered attempts by J.P. Stevens, West Point-Peppernell, and, notably, Cannon Mills to move into the upper end of the market. Cannon added a Royal Touch towel to its Royal Family line that directly competed with Fieldcrest's Royal Velvet. Fieldcrest found itself defending its territory at the top, where the profits were highest, while trying to advance farther at the other end of the market. As the recession took hold, the rounds of discounting began and inventory was reduced.

Amoskeag Co., whose earnings were largely sustained by those of Fieldcrest, grew concerned, and in 1982 the chief executive of Amoskeag, Joseph Ely II, was brought in to head Fieldcrest. He had served as a board member since 1976. In December of that year, Fieldcrest wrote off its half of a Canadian joint venture, Crossley Karastan Carpet Mills, Ltd., which had lost $1.2 million in 1981.

Soon thereafter, Fieldcrest shifted its marketing strategy. Instead of trying to increase profits through high volume of its lower end products, it sought to broaden its range of items built around the Fieldcrest name. By reemphasizing the Fieldcrest lines, which it had neglected to update while the effort had been on the designer lines, the company chose to retain profits and avoid price cuts at the expense of expanding its market share. Fieldcrest was the only towelmaker that continued to use its name solely with its premium products; Cannon Mills, for example, sewed its name into all of its towels, regardless of the price category. Fieldcrest promised department stores carrying its line that they had the protected use of its name, thereby hoping to seal their loyalty and expand its carriage trade. Fieldcrest also hoped to grow its private-brand business, of which Sears was its biggest customer, contributing $75 million in sales in 1983.

In 1986 Fieldcrest took the bold step of acquiring Cannon Mills, which it purchased for $321 million. With that acquisition, Fieldcrest, which became Fieldcrest Cannon, Inc., gained 12,900 employees, 12 plants, and 14 sales offices, thus doubling its size and becoming the country's fifth largest publicly held textile company.

CANNON MILLS, CO.

Towards the end of the nineteenth century, James William Cannon, a 35-year old partner and manager of a general store, became intrigued with the textile business and decided to open a cotton mill. He raised $75,000 and built a mill in Concord, North Carolina, which started business in 1887 as the Cannon Manufacturing Company. Cannon also managed the plant. He evidently brought some knowledge of the retail business with him when he decided to put his name on the fabric that his mill manufactured, reasoning that sales could only increase if customers could ask for a product by name. The popularity of "Cannon cloth" spread throughout the south, and thus the Cannon retailing philosophy was born.

Realizing that the south had no towel manufacturing plants, Cannon opened a mill that produced huck towels in 1894 and another mill that made terry towels four years later. In 1906 Cannon bought a 600-acre parcel of land, previously a cotton plantation, and started developing the community that became Kannapolis. The mills there started operation in 1908 and were able to produce more towels than any other group of mills, due in part to automatic terry looms. The mills also produced a variety of "gray goods" such as cotton cloth and woman's hosiery.

By 1916 Cannon had decided to try to market as well as manufacture his products, and so a new sales force, Cannon Mills, Inc., was established in New York City. James Cannon died in 1921 at which time he controlled 12 mills with over 15,000 employees and an estimated $40 million in annual sales. Kannapolis was considered a "model mill city," and its mills could turn out 300,000 towels daily. His youngest son, Charles Cannon, who had quit college at the age of 19 to start work in his father's mills and had become a vice-president at the age of 23, became the company's president.

Charles "Mr. Charlie" Cannon ran the company for the next 50 years. Under his stewardship, Cannon Mills maintained its dominant position in the U.S. towel market, regularly producing half of all towels purchased. It also carried one-fifth of the sheeting business. Much of Cannon Mills' success was due to the very high efficiency of its mills, which were virtually all within a 20-mile radius of one another, affording close supervision; only a few steps separated the back door of the CEO's office from Plant No. 1. The company's production was vertically integrated, from the spinning of the cotton to the finished product.

In 1923 Cannon had the Cannon name sewn into all of its towels, becoming the first company to do so. By unabashedly identifying with what had been seen as purely a "commodity" product, Cannon was to develop an intense brand loyalty among consumers, who came to identify the Cannon name with affordability and quality. Cannon, unlike other mills, used its name on its top-of-the line goods as well as its more affordably priced items. Most of Cannon Mills' products were distributed through mass merchandisers.

Cannon's tenure was marked by an entrenched fiscal conservatism. He made no effort to diversify, eschewing the idea of growth for growth's sake. While Cannon was in control the company did not acquire any long-term debt. Furthermore, Cannon's reign over Kannapolis—which remained unincorporated—also reflected his paternalistic style. Kannapolis had no mayor, town council, or legal charter. Cannon Mills paid for the community's police and fire services and was responsible for its water and sewerage system, trash collection, and street maintenance. It also owned approximately 1,600 houses that were rented to mill employees. Moreover, Cannon owned virtually all the property within the one-square-mile business district. In the 1930s Charlie Cannon returned from a business trip to Williamsburg so impressed by its colonial architecture that he had facades for the business district constructed to mimic their colonial style, and downtown Kannapolis was thus transformed into a Georgian village. A massive sign on the edge of town, lighted by 1,800 bulbs and visible from the highway and the railroad, proclaimed that Cannon Mills was the "World's Largest Manufacturer of Towels." After the war, the sign was altered to read "Leading Manufacturer of Towels" and updated with neon.

In 1927 Charlie Cannon brought his company to the New York Stock Exchange, becoming the first southern mill owner to do so. The following year he consolidated the mills into a single entity, the Cannon Mills Co.

In the 1930s Cannon Mills started manufacturing sheets. For many years Charlie Cannon resisted turning out sheets in anything but white. Over time they became more colorful, but prints were disdained, except for one featuring a tightly closed rosebud introduced in 1953. "It took another 13 years to get that rosebud opened," a marketing vice-president told *Forbes*.

In 1962 Cannon Mills was removed from the New York Stock Exchange, when Charlie Cannon refused to solicit proxies from all of the company's shareholders, preferring to solicit only those who held voting stock. Cannon felt the required disclosure of information was intrusive and unnecessary. At that time the Cannon family and relatives held 40 percent of the voting stock and 27 percent of the total stock.

Charlie Cannon died in 1971 after suffering a heart attack at his office. At that time Cannon Mills owned 17 plants and employed 24,000 workers, the largest employer in the Carolinas. The population of Kannapolis was 36,000, ten percent of which lived in company housing. Sales in 1971 reached $323 million. Cannon left no long-term debt and over $60 million in cash and marketable securities. The Cannon name was recognized by a remarkable 90 percent of consumers. However, growth had been very slow—in the five years prior to Cannon's death, sales figures had increased only two percent a year.

The Cannon neon sign remained unlit after Cannon died, but Cannon Mills stock soared on Wall Street as investors believed that new management would fully take advantage of the company's cash-rich, debt-free position. Nevertheless, Charlie Cannon's hand-picked successor, Don Holt, continued his mentor's

policies of neither diversifying nor broadening its market appeal. As other mills were bringing in well-known designers to update their look, Cannon continued to resist. "We have the Cannon name. We don't need designers' names," the president of Cannon's merchandising subsidiary told *Forbes* in 1972.

For much of the 1970s Cannon was able to hold onto its share of the towel market, although its sales growth barely matched the rate of inflation and was far outstripped by its competitors. In 1975 its earnings were less than those of 1965, $2.66 a share, although its sales volume had grown 42 percent since that year to $395 million. A new chairperson, Harold Hornaday, was installed, who conceded to *Forbes* that "the times require that Cannon be more market oriented." Nonetheless, Hornaday hesitated to change strategies as its share of the sheet market dropped from 20 to 15 percent. Sales in 1979 reached $609 million. In that year, Cannon was reinstated to the New York Stock Exchange, having given voting rights to all public shareholders and begun publishing more detailed annual reports. Hornaday, however, was asked to leave in October 1980 after several embarrassing missteps led to Cannon's first money-losing quarter in over a decade.

Cannon attempted vigorously to catch up with its competitors, under the youthful leadership of its next chairperson, Otto Stolz. The company diversified into the manufacture of various items for kitchen and bath, including mats and rugs. Luxury fabric designer Robin Roberts was also signed on to create a fashionable and upscale line of sheets and towels. Cannon had difficulty changing its old-fashioned image, however, and its share of the towel market fell to below 35 percent.

Cannon Mills was to experience dramatic change in 1982, after David Murdock, a self-made millionaire and takeover artist from California, disclosed his intentions of acquiring the company. Charlie Cannon's son William was the first to sell, and the other trustees followed his example. After the $413 million leveraged buyout, Murdock took the company private.

Murdock set out to aggressively alter the way Cannon did business. As other mills were reporting slowing growth or declines, Murdock's Cannon sought to increase sales by updating the company with a glamorous and trendy image. The design department was doubled in size, its manager released, and most of the existing towels and sheets discontinued. The Japanese designer Issey Miyake and the Swedish designer Katja were hired to create their own lines. A racy advertising campaign was launched featuring various celebrities between Cannon sheets with the tag line "Two of the most famous names in America sleep together." Towels were marketed at all price levels, including a line that competed directly with Fieldcrest's Royal Velvet. Efforts were also made to expand profits at the mass merchandisers; to that end an agreement was signed with the producers of the nighttime soap opera *Dynasty* so as to produce a Dynasty collection, patterned after the sets used on the show.

Murdock quickly invested $200 million in upgrading mill equipment. Furthermore, he immediately laid off several hundred employees; mill workers who lived in company-owned homes were informed they would have to buy their houses or leave. And Murdock spent $30 million to raze businesses, move homes, build a highway, and refurbish the Georgian business district so as to turn it into "Cannon Village," a factory-outlet shopping mall.

Despite Murdock's attempts to invigorate Cannon with splashy designs and heavy advertising, Cannon continued to lose money. The import-battered market had led to further layoffs (reaching 3,000), the closing of three mills, and a $31 million drop in exports. Under these conditions the Amalgamated Clothing & Textile Workers Union (ACTWU) attempted to organize Cannon employees, which culminated in a vote in October of 1985. The union had failed previously, most recently in 1974 in a 44 to 56 percent vote. Murdock, by that time seeking a buyer for Cannon, fought the union in a venomous campaign in which he jetted frequently into Kannapolis, touring the factories and shaking hands with virtually all of the company's 10,000 employees. The movement to unionize was defeated in a 37 to 63 percent vote.

Several months later, in January 1986, Murdock sold approximately 75 percent of Cannon Mills to Fieldcrest Mills for $321 million. He retained the real estate holdings, which included most of the commercial real estate in downtown Kannapolis, worth approximately $100 million, as well as several other mills. The sale to Fieldcrest did not mark the end of Murdock's involvement with Cannon or the union, however. Murdock had also left Kannapolis with around $25 million from the Cannon pension fund, which had been terminated shortly before the sale was consummated. In October 1986 the ACTWU filed suit, charging that Murdock had mishandled the funds and thus violated his fiduciary duties as a trustee of the plan.

The point of contention was Murdock's use of the funds while he was battling for control of Occidental Petroleum. Murdock had started acquiring Occidental stock in 1981. In February 1982 he was elected as a director of that company under conditions which barred him from acquiring more than five percent of its stock. Late in that year the Cannon pension fund began to purchase Occidental stock, which by 1984 accounted for 7.8 percent of the fund's holding. In 1984 Occidental repurchased its stock from Murdock-controlled entities—including the Cannon pension fund—with a $60 million premium attached. After the fund was terminated late in 1985, the fund's excess assets—including the profits from the Occidental deal—were folded back into Murdock's other entities. The union's suit charged that Murdock had used the funds to either "greenmail" or take over Occidental, as opposed to managing the funds for its participants and beneficiaries, and that he had used the funds similarly in actions against Kaiser Cement. The case was settled out of court in 1989 for a reported $1 million.

Upon the liquidation of the pension plan, Murdock invested the funds with Executive Life Insurance of California. The company, which had invested heavily in junk bonds underwritten by Michael Milken of Drexel Burnham Lambert during the 1980s, suffered sharp losses after the junk bond industry collapsed in 1990. In April 1991 state regulators seized its assets, and monthly pension payments were cut by 30 percent. In August, Murdock announced he would "personally pay all Cannon retirees the full amount of reduction they suffered." The payments were to be in the form of personal checks and were to compensate for the shortfall from May 1 to September 30, when full payments were to resume.

FIELDCREST CANNON, INC.

The acquisition by Fieldcrest of Cannon catapulted the company to the number one position in the towel and blanket market and the number three spot in the sheet market. Observers wondered how Fieldcrest and Cannon, two textile powerhouses with very different market strategies, would work together, especially on the retail floor. Its various lines seemed poised to compete against each other for market share and counterspace. Fieldcrest's flagship brand still prevailed in the department stores, where Cannon's Royal Family line competed against it. Cannon was the number one brand at the discounters, where Fieldcrest's St. Marys always placed behind Cannon's Monticello line. Fieldcrest had chosen to not expand its market share to avoid price cuts, while Cannon had elected to cut prices to generate sales. Fieldcrest executives felt that it was best to keep the lines separate to hold onto precious counterspace as the retail industry consolidated. Fieldcrest had also quickly moved out some of Cannon's management team, replacing them with Fieldcrest staffers. Some observers felt that Fieldcrest lost much-needed experience with high-volume, low-margin mass merchandising.

Less than one year after the purchase of Cannon, Fieldcrest bought Bigelow-Sanford, Inc., a manufacturer of residential and industrial contract carpeting. Bigelow-Sanford had been purchased by a group of its executives in 1981, who in turn sold it to Fieldcrest in December 1986 for $129 million—$4 million in cash and 460,727 shares of Fieldcrest common stock. After the acquisition Fieldcrest merged Bigelow-Sanford with its Karastan division and dismissed the Bigelow-Sanford executives. Soon thereafter, DuPont introduced its Stainmaster fiber, which was enormously popular but proved to be very difficult to dye into the carpet colors that consumers wanted. Lacking knowledgeable staff at the top of its carpet operations and still heavily in debt from its acquisitions, Fieldcrest committed to big capital outlays in an attempt to master the process.

In 1987 Fieldcrest lost $3.7 million on sales of $1.4 billion, and much of the loss was attributed to problems with Bigelow-Sanford. By 1988 Fieldcrest announced that it wanted out of the carpet business altogether and was looking for a buyer. Profits rebounded to $11.3 million that year and reached $23.4 million in 1989. In 1990 the economic downturn exacerbated internal problems, and the company posted a $38-million loss on $1.24 billion in sales. The company's stock value, which had peaked in 1986 at $43, dropped to below six dollars per share.

Several analysts pointed to chairperson Ely as directly responsible for the company's troubles. They cited an overly rapid expansion financed with heavy debt commitments, an exorbitant price paid for Cannon, ill-timed cotton purchases, and difficulties with Bigelow-Sanford. Moreover, critics reasoned that Ely had been able to remain at Fieldcrest as long as he had by virtue of his position as treasurer of the Dumaine trust, holding ultimate power over an elderly board on which remained several members from F.C. Dumaine, Sr.'s, time.

Fieldcrest underwent a series of cost-cutting measures in 1990 under its new chairperson, James Fitzgibbons, which included reducing its workforce by 1,700, discontinuing its unprofitable automatic blanket operations, and unloading inventory. Unable to find a buyer for its rug and carpet division, the company consolidated those operations and was able to turn a profit in 1991. That year Fieldcrest as a whole was able to claim $3.2 million in profit, although sales were $1.21 billion, less than those of 1990. Income in 1992 exceeded that of the previous year, aided by lower cotton prices and higher sales. In mid-1992 the company refinanced its loan agreements, reducing its interest payments. Nevertheless, Fieldcrest had experienced lower sales from 1988 to 1992, largely because of a decline in carpet and rug sales from $371.1 million in 1988 to $235.5 million in 1992. Total sales in 1992 were $1.22 billion.

In January 1993 Amoskeag announced that it was considering selling off its shares of Fieldcrest, disclosing that the Dumaine trust was reviewing its own investment in Amoskeag. At that time the Dumaine trust owned approximately 76 percent of the voting power of the equity of Amoskeag, and Amoskeag controlled about 80 percent of the voting stock and 30 percent of the equity of Fieldcrest. Some of the trust's beneficiaries had criticized the trust's management, but the Dumaine heirs had no say in the management of the trust unless Amoskeag failed to provide a dividend, which was largely furnished by Fieldcrest. Long-simmering dissension and rivalry ruptured into several legal battles attempting to break the trust, each of which ultimately failed. Some industry analysts noted that in the several years prior, Fieldcrest had invested in a major modernization program, which would ultimately make the company a more attractive acquisition.

Principal Subsidiaries: Fieldcrest Mills, International, Inc.; Delaware Valley Wool Scouring Co., St Marys, Inc.; Encee, Inc.; Cannon Mills International, Ltd; Cannon Mills International Sales Corp.

Further Reading:

Ames, Elizabeth, and Marc Frons, "There Are Two David Murdocks— and Both Are Used to Getting Their Way," *Business Week,* January 28, 1985, pp. 88–90.

"Amoskeag May Sell Its Majority Stake in Fieldcrest," *Wall Street Journal,* January 29, 1993.

Anreder, Steven S., and David A. Hoddeson, "Fieldcrest Mills Spins Stylish Profits Pattern," *Barron's,* June 3, 1968.

Burck, Charles G., "Reveille at Cannon Mills," *Fortune,* January 26, 1981, pp. 68–76.

Campanella, Frank W., "Fieldcrest Mills Enjoys Smart Advance in Profits," *Barron's,* December 11, 1978, pp. 44–45.

Chernoff, Joel, "Union Charges Misuse of Assets," *Pensions & Investment Age,* October 13, 1986, p. 1.

Clune, Ray, "Union Vote in Dispute at Fieldcrest Cannon," *Daily News Record,* August 23, 1991.

Coletti, Richard J., "Fieldcrest: Stains on the Carpet," *Financial World,* October 18, 1988, p. 16.

Engardio, Pete, "Why David Murdock Is So Afraid of a Union," *Business Week,* October 14, 1985, p. 43.

Feldman, Amy, "Changing the Sheets," *Forbes,* February 3, 1992.

"Fieldcrest Buys 80% of Cannon," *Textile World,* January 1986, pp. 22–23.

"Fieldcrest Cannon Annual Report," Eden, NC: Fieldcrest Cannon, 1992.

"Fieldcrest Cannon Will Stay in the Carpet Biz," *Textile World,* January 1989, p. 28.

"Fieldcrest: Profit-Blazing Un-Textile Firm," *Textile World,* June 1979, pp. 53–118.

"Fieldcrest: Saving Its Name for a Luxury Image," *Business Week,* January 9, 1984, pp. 112–13.

Hackney, Holt, "Fieldcrest Cannon: Turnaround at Last?" *Financial World,* April 16, 1991.

Heins, John, " 'I Just Make Ideas Happen'," *Forbes,* October 26, 1987, pp. 33–35.

Hussey, Allan F., "Capital Gains: Heavy Outlays Pull Fieldcrest Out of Earnings Slump," *Barron's,* January 23, 1984, pp. 54–55.

Jaffe, Thomas, "One Rude Awakening," *Forbes,* October 25, 1982, p. 116.

Jenkins, J., "Barony in Carolina: The Town that Towels Built," *The Nation,* May 12, 1956, pp. 405–07.

Lappen, Alyssa A., "Thank You, Mr. Ely," *Forbes,* December 12, 1988, pp. 100–02.

"Living in the Past," *Forbes,* June 1, 1975, pp. 46–47.

MacIntosh, Jeane, "Full Cannon Pensions Set," *Home Furnishings Daily,* August 19, 1991.

Marcial, Gene G., "White Sale at Fieldcrest Cannon," *Business Week,* March 19, 1990, p. 107.

"The Passing of Mr. Charlie," *Forbes,* July 15, 1972, pp. 22–24.

Peckenham, Nancy, "Out in the Cold at Cannon Mills," *The Nation,* September 16, 1991, pp. 298–302.

Saunders, Dero A., "Frederic Dumaine: Upstreaming the Profits," *Forbes,* July 13, 1987, pp. 258–62.

"Sleeping with the Stars Pays Off for Cannon," *Business Week,* September 24, 1984, pp. 67–68.

Tasini, Jonathan, "Playing with Pension Funds: What's the Limit?" *Business Week,* November 12, 1986, p. 89.

Troy, Colleen, "Leading Separate Lives," *Home Furnishings Daily,* November 16, 1987, p. 1.

—C. L. Collins

Fingerhut Companies, Inc.

4400 Baker Rd.
Minnetonka, Minnesota 55343
U.S.A.
(612) 932-3100
Fax: (612) 932-3181

Public Company
Incorporated: 1978
Employees: 8,500
Sales: $1.60 billion
Stock Exchanges: New York
SICs: 5961 Catalog and Mail-Order Houses

With an active customer base of 13 million people and 1992 revenues of $1.6 billion, Fingerhut Companies, Inc. is the third largest catalog marketer in the United States. However, in the specialized field of targeted direct-mail marketing, handled by the core business of Fingerhut Corporation, Fingerhut is an undisputed leader. Other business units include Figi's Inc., a Marshfield, Wisconsin-based catalog marketer of specialty foods and gifts; USA Direct Incorporated, an infomercial marketer of proprietary products; and Montgomery Ward Direct L.P., a joint venture catalog marketer formed in late 1991 to build on the strengths of both Fingerhut and general merchandise giant Montgomery Ward.

At the center of Fingerhut is Chairman and Chief Executive Officer Ted Deikel, the son-in-law of company founder Manny Fingerhut. From the recession crisis of mid-1974 through the early 1980s, Deikel presided over the Minnesota-based marketer, initiating such valuable corporate strategies as a nearly fool-proof plan for recognizing, adapting to, and remaining profitable through new economic downturns. After American Can Company's purchase of Fingerhut in 1979, the executive assumed the additional responsibility of overseeing other American properties, including music merchandiser Pickwick International (then owner of Minnesota retail powerhouse Musicland). By 1983, however, Deikel was ready to build his own marketing organization from scratch. The result was Plymouth, Minnesota-based CVN Companies, an enormously successful pioneer of the cable home shopping industry. From $63.7 million in sales in 1984, CVN expanded to $683 million in sales in 1989. In October of that year, CVN merged with Pennsylvania-based competitor QVC Network. Deikel, $42 million richer

from the deal, was searching for a way to continue his partnership with top CVN managers, who together possessed a wealth of experience in merchandising and general operations. A singularly golden opportunity presented itself virtually next door, at Deikel's former employer, Fingerhut.

Since at least 1986, according to Lee Schafer, Deikel had been discussing the possibility of acquiring Fingerhut with his fellow managers. By that time American Can—eventually renamed Primerica—was beginning to redefine itself as a diversified financial services company and simultaneously considering selling off some of its interests, including Fingerhut. The situation intensified from late 1986 into 1987, when Deikel was in direct contact with his friend Gerald Tsai Jr., then chairman of Primerica, about possible business alliances as well as the sale of Fingerhut. Tsai's price of more than $1 billion for the mail-order subsidiary was deemed excessive by Deikel and there the matter rested. Schafer postulated that "Tsai's determination of Fingerhut's price was based less on an analysis of its value than on Primerica's own pressing financial need." Then came Primerica's acquisition of Smith Barney, the October 1987 stock market crash, and Sanford I. Weill's purchase of Primerica. Fingerhut was once again for sale and, as its revenues stalled in 1983 and 1989, it became more and more of a bargain for the right investor under the right circumstances. Just weeks before the CVN-QVC merger, senior management at Fingerhut had resigned. This paved the way for a deal between Deikel and Weill in which a Deikel-led management group would be installed before the end of 1989 and 28 percent of the Primerica subsidiary spun off to the public the following year. Since that time, Fingerhut's picture has been particularly rosy, as Deikel and his team have pursued aggressive strategies to approach 15 percent annual growth in both sales and earnings.

Fingerhut originated in 1948 as a small concern far removed from the world of sophisticated multimedia marketing and high finance. At that time William Fingerhut, the son of Jewish immigrants, was producing and selling automobile seat covers out of his Minneapolis garage to augment the family-run sewing business. William's new enterprise held enough promise—much factory upholstery was then notoriously susceptible to tears and stains—to accommodate his brother, Manny, an exasperated manager of a used-car lot. Aided by four other employees, the Fingerhut brothers saw gross sales during their initial years together that approached $100,000 annually. The "brainstorm that ultimately transformed the company into a big-time operation," wrote Arthur M. Louis, belonged to Manny, who handled sales and bookkeeping.

In 1949, after receiving a mail-order solicitation to purchase neckties, Manny envisioned expanding the seat business far beyond the local car dealer and car buyer market. Fingerhut's new market would be car owners across the United States, all of whom could be reached by mail. Before fully implementing his plan, the younger Fingerhut hired an advertiser to produce an eye-catching circular, which the entrepreneur then mailed to 100 new car owners spread throughout Minnesota. From this first test market, Fingerhut received eight orders, many times over the necessary response for a successful mailing. Within three years, Manny had reoriented the entire business (now grossing nearly a million a year) to mail-order marketing, acquiring lists of new-car buyers, state-by-state, as he went. Unfortunately, Louis noted, "William Fingerhut had been wary of Manny's bold experiment form the start, and when it worked so well he became resentful. . . . The relationship between the brothers became tense, and in 1954 William angrily withdrew from active participation in the business." (The elder Fingerhut eventually sold his share of the company in 1969 for $12.5 million.)

During the mid-1950s the company faced its first crisis when Detroit auto makers introduced vinyl and nylon, fabrics far more durable than previous ones, in their new car models. Fingerhut responded by switching entirely to the production of transparent plastic seat covers, which allowed the car owner both to preserve and display the modern upholstery beneath. The 1950s also saw the company expand its offerings to include towels, dishes, electric drills, and car coats. This last item was so successful that it launched the company firmly into manufacturing as well as merchandising. By the mid-1970s Fingerhut Corporation's product list encompassed some 40 items, a select dozen of which were manufactured internally and responsible for nearly 50 percent of overall sales.

Although a good product mix was certainly crucial to the company's years of continuing growth, even more so was Fingerhut's modus operandi of targeting and maintaining its core market of lower-middle-income consumers. Market research showed that this buying group was most likely to shop by mail and, by logical extension, most likely to buy the many low-cost goods offered by Fingerhut. Coupled with Fingerhut's enticement of free gifts with every purchase and installment credit at department store rates, this made for a powerful sales and marketing formula. Crowning everything was Fingerhut's development and maintenance of a large and dependable customer list, a strategy that would ensure long-term corporate health.

Following the watershed year of 1969, when the company went public in an immensely successful initial offering, Fingerhut was at the top of its game—the biggest complete mail-order marketer in the country. Then came fiscal 1974, when rising mailing, manufacturing, and interest costs; declining real incomes; mounting inventories; and price controls seriously threatened the company's future. In a management shakeup, newly installed president Deikel took charge of domestic operations and focused on a number of key areas, including cost-cutting, boosting company morale, and rethinking product mailings. Two of the most important steps Deikel took were phasing the company out of manufacturing and calling for pinpoint marketing, in which customers would be segmented by their buying preferences. (By the 1980s Fingerhut's database and corresponding mailings had become so advanced that virtually every customer represented a specialized market, thus earning the company the title of perhaps "the ultimate niche company" from *In Search of Excellence* author Thomas J. Peters).

Another positive outcome of the 1974 recession was Fingerhut's development of a multi-step contingency plan to deal with future recessions. The plan involves tracking declines in orders from "solo" product mailings and rises in preshipment cancellations (if certain percentages are reached, a recession is at hand); responding to such key declines and rises by raising credit standards, reducing sales to marginal customers, and increasing sales to core customers; and changing its product

mix. By the last months of 1979, a new recession was in sight and Fingerhut was able to implement its plan. The company's ability to reap a profit increase of ten percent in the second quarter of 1980, while other retailers and mail-order houses suffered profit declines ranging from 18 percent to 43 percent during the same period, immediately placed Fingerhut in the limelight. In a November 1980 article for *Fortune,* Herbert Meyer reported: "As word of Fingerhut's triumph has spread, Deikel and his colleagues have begun to receive inquiries from executives throughout U.S. industry and from economists about what Fingerhut's data are saying now. Understandably, the Fingerhut crew is rather enjoying the attention."

Ironically, it was Deikel's retailing genius that caused non-retailing conglomerate American Can Company (Primerica) to absorb Fingerhut in 1979. Despite difficulties related to Primerica's later plans to divest, Fingerhut did manage to flourish through much of the 1980s. As of 1986 the company ranked alongside Spiegel and behind retailing giants Sears, Roebuck & Co. and J.C. Penney Company, Inc. in catalog sales and was growing at a rate of 20 percent annually.

Since Primerica's 1990 offering—part of a full divestiture plan that was completed in January 1993—Sears has departed the catalog industry and Fingerhut has shown especially strong growth in both sales and net income. Under Deikel, the company has also demonstrated that it is a business true to its origins, capable of doing year-in and year-out what it does best—servicing the customer—while remaining open to change as new possibilities and challenges arise. In addition to expanding its product offerings to attract a wealthier customer group (both through Fingerhut Corporation and Montgomery Ward Direct), Fingerhut has placed considerable emphasis on growth opportunities within USA Direct, its infomercial subsidiary. As the company's 1992 Annual Report pointed out, the infomercial business is intimately tied to Fingerhut's direct-mail marketing. Those products that have the best chance of selling via TV (food dehydrators, juicers, exercise equipment, and floor cleaners) are marketed there first, then through follow-up advertisements in company catalogs and circulars, and finally through retail stores under royalty contract. Two of the most popular of Fingerhut's infomercial-to-retail market products have been the Body By Jake exercise machine and the Bissell Big Green carpet-cleaning machine. Telemarketing and TV revenues for 1992 accounted for nine percent of all corporate sales, double the amount achieved in 1991.

Of course, not everything Fingerhut touches turns to gold or is of long-term benefit to the company. In 1993 plans to sell food catalog subsidiary Figi's and close-out merchandiser C.O.M.B., both money losers, continued. (The sale of C.O.M.B. to Damark International was agreed to in principal in June 1993.) Still, the company appears unstoppable and perhaps this is due to its visionary leader. In the 1992 report, cutely covered in corrugated cardboard, a serene and contemplative Deikel is juxtaposed with Theodore Gall's sculpture "Man in a Box." Just as the man is testing his boundaries, so, too, must Fingerhut, explains Deikel. "We must be innovative in all areas and not be constrained by perceived boundaries. We must 'expand the box' and reach new levels of excellence."

Principal Subsidiaries: Figi's Inc.; Fingerhut Corporation; Montgomery Ward Direct L.P.; USA Direct Incorporated

Further Reading:

Andrews, Edmund L., "New Realities, New Rules," *New York Times,* October 27, 1991, p. F12.

Apgar, Sally, "Fingerhut Will Try to Sell Figi's; Fourth-Period Earnings up 31%" *Star Tribune,* January 15, 1993, p. 1D.

"Damark International Inc.," *Wall Street Journal,* June 23, 1993, p. C14.

"Fingerhut Lays Off 200 in St. Cloud," *Star Tribune,* January 1, 1993, p. 3D.

"Fingerhut Stock Sold by Primerica," *Star Tribune,* January 8, 1993, p. 3D.

Gelbach, Deborah L., "Fingerhut Corporation," *From This Land: A History of Minnesota's Empires, Enterprises, and Entrepreneurs,* Northridge, CA: Windsor Publications, 1988, p. 303.

"Herman (Sonny) Schwartz, Former Fingerhut President, Dies," *Star Tribune,* December 12, 1993, p. 4B.

Jaffe, Thomas, "Thumbs up on Fingerhut?" *Forbes,* January 21, 1991, p. 124.

Kennedy, Tony, "TV Unit of Fingerhut Companies is Pursuing Possibility of Being a 24-Hour Shopping Channel," *Star Tribune,* December 1, 1993, pp. 1D, 8D.

Louis, Arthur M., "Dead-Letter Days for Fingerhut," *Fortune,* November 1974, pp. 184–90.

Meyer, Herbert E., "How Fingerhut Beat the Recession," *Fortune,* November 17, 1980, pp. 102–04.

"Minority Stake in Fingerhut To Be Offered, Firm Says," *Wall Street Journal,* March 20, 1990, p. A20.

Norris, Eileen, "Fingerhut Gives Customers Credit," *Advertising Age,* March 6, 1986, p. 19.

"Primerica's Fingerhut Initiates an Offering of Six Million Shares," *Wall Street Journal,* April 26, 1990, p. C19.

Roberts, Johnnie L., "Bribery Claims at Fingerhut Are Investigated," *Wall Street Journal,* May 20, 1993, pp. B1, B11.

Rosenthal, Thomas M., "The Last Straw for Fingerhut Corporation," *Global Trade,* October 1988, pp. 16, 18.

Schafer, Lee, "Why Ted Deikel Returned to Fingerhut," *Corporate Report Minnesota,* August 1990, pp. 49–52; "Fingerhut Companies, Inc.," *Corporate Report Minnesota,* November 1990, p. 101.

—Jay P. Pederson

First Fidelity Bank, N.A., New Jersey

550 Broad Street
Newark, New Jersey 07102
U.S.A.
(201) 565-3200
Fax: (201) 565-6055

Wholly Owned Subsidiary of First Fidelity Bancorporation
Employees: 6,010
Assets: $11.9 billion
SICs: 6021 National Commercial Banks

First Fidelity Bank is regarded as one of the most stable and reliable financial institutions in the United States. With a distinguished history dating back to 1812, encompassing numerous banking panics, a civil war, two world wars, and the Great Depression, First Fidelity has developed into one of the preeminent banks on the eastern coast of America.

In 1811 the charter for the Bank of the United States expired, and one year later the New Jersey state legislature enacted the Bank Act of 1812, authorizing charters for six state banks located in Newark, Camden, Elizabeth, Morris, New Brunswick, and Trenton. With William S. Pennington as its first president and 13 state appointed directors, many of them heroes of the Revolutionary War, the State Bank of Newark opened for business on June 1, 1812. The first day's total receipts amounted to $18,081.62.

Only 18 days later, the United States declared war on Great Britain. The economy boomed during the war, and many government contractors traveled to Newark to procure much-needed war materials. The sudden increase in business led the bank to move two blocks south from its original location to a larger location on the corner of Broad and Mechanic streets. As a result of its prosperity, the bank's directors approved a four percent dividend on April 1, 1813, and made plans for an additional four-and-a-half percent to be distributed by the end of the year. From that time forward, the bank always paid a yearly dividend.

While the bank continued to prosper through 1814, due to the growing demand for factories to expand and provide more war supplies, the war went poorly for the United States. When the treaty of Ghent was signed in 1814 and hostilities between

America and Britain ended, the economy suddenly fell into a bitter depression with many factory closings, high unemployment in the cities, and numerous bank failures.

However, the State Bank of Newark was largely unaffected by the depression after the war, and began to quicken its pace of development as the city of Newark once again prospered. During this time, Newark became well known as one of the state's great produce markets. Southern businessmen began to travel to the city to consult with northern industrialists. By 1832, the Morris Canal was shipping large amounts of coal, iron, and even more produce, and industrial development was spurred on by the growth of railroads connecting Newark to Jersey City, Trenton, and Philadelphia.

Yet, by 1836, the financial situation across the country was once again discouraging. For years many banks in the new western territories issued notes or currency at will, incurred huge debts, and speculated in land sales. When President Andrew Jackson issued a declaration that all payments for public land sales be in specie, or hard money, the value of paper money fell precipitously and a financial panic followed. The State Bank of Newark, feeling the effects of the panic, suspended specie payments one year later.

William S. Pennington, the bank's first president, had resigned shortly after his appointment to run a successful campaign for governor of New Jersey. His successor, Elias Van Arsdale, Sr., served with distinction until he died in 1846. Caleb Carter, a director of the bank and owner of a carriage business, agreed to serve for a brief time until Elias Van Arsdale, Jr., assumed the presidency of the bank. The son of Van Arsdale Sr. helped steer the State Bank of Newark through several profitable and calm years until his death in 1854. The next president of the bank was not as lucky.

Samuel Meeker became president of the State Bank of Newark soon after Van Arsdale Jr. had died. Then, for the third time in its history, the bank felt the effects of a financial panic. Banking institutions throughout the country were suspending specie payments due to rash speculation and defaulted loans. The State Bank joined all other New Jersey banks in suspending its specie payments on October 14, 1857. Before the year was over, many manufacturers and shop owners in Newark declared bankruptcy, and soup kitchens soon sprung up throughout the city.

As the economy gradually improved, the bank resumed its specie payments in December, but soon a more threatening situation arose—civil war. With more than two-thirds of their sales made to southern businesses, merchants in Newark were distressed over the deteriorating relations with the South. Supporters of Abraham Lincoln were not surprised, therefore, when the city voted against him. But after the bombing of Fort Sumter in 1860, and once Newark merchants began to receive orders for war materials from Washington, sentiment for supporting the Union cause ran high.

One week after the Civil War started, the State Bank of Newark provided $50,000 to Governor Charles Olden to help the Union effort. The bank also increased its federal bond holdings from $102,000 to $607,000, and in 1864 it loaned the city of Newark $25,000 to pay volunteers who substituted for war draftees. The bank prospered during the war, and by 1864 net gains after dividends totaled $25,000.

The State Bank of Newark was directly affected by the National Bank Act, signed in 1863 by President Lincoln. Enacted in order to bring some cohesion to the nation's banking system, the legislation authorized the government to supervise banks and provided for a currency circulation guaranteed by the federal government. Under this law the State Bank of Newark was granted a national charter, and on August 1, 1865, began the day's business as The National State Bank of Newark. Along with a new name, the bank had a new president. Charles S. Macknett replaced Samuel Meeker, who had died in Pisa, Italy, while on a tour of Europe.

After the Civil War, assets at National State increased gradually each year until 1872 when the banking industry suffered from the new trend of mortgage financing. With its conservative management, however, the bank was able to avoid the problems that led to the collapse of many noted New York and New Jersey banking firms. By 1884, bank records reported 12 full-time employees whose annual wages ranged from $4,000 to $264.

From 1864 to 1893, National State had three presidents: Charles S. Macknett, Theodore Macknett, and John J. Jube. When James F. Bless was appointed president in 1893, the country was again in the midst of a depression. However, National State was largely unaffected and, under Bless's leadership, could report that assets rose from approximately $2 million in the 1880s to nearly $3.4 million by 1900.

The extremely conservative management style of the bank had helped it weather five depressions—including the financial panic of 1907—and the directors pointed with pride to their bond holdings in such stable companies as the Essex Passenger Railway Company and the East Tennessee, Virginia, and Georgia Railroad. However, this type of financial management did not generate much new business. In 1910, National State Bank reported assets of close to the amount reported ten years earlier. Still more distressing for National State, Newark banking rival Union National Bank reported assets surpassing $16.9 million.

After 18 years as president, Bless was replaced by William I. Cooper in 1911. An ex-clerk who had worked his way up in the institution, Cooper was determined to expand the bank's business while maintaining its reputation for stability. Helped by the boom in the production of war products brought on by World War I, the bank's assets rose from $3.9 million in 1911 to over $7 million by 1920.

National State grew slowly but steadily through the 1920s; in accordance with its conservative management policy, it refused to involve itself in market speculation. Thus when the New York Stock Exchange collapsed in October 1929, National State did not suffer any ill effects. In fact, Cooper proudly reported in the annual report of 1930 that assets had risen to $10.7 million.

The banking industry had changed dramatically over the years and the era of the "family bank" had vanished. No longer serving the needs of a limited number of local or regional customers, banks had developed into highly structured and sophisticated institutions. Accordingly, after Cooper died in 1931, the directors sought to replace him with someone who could help realize these developments at National State. W. Paul Stillman was a natural choice. Stillman started his career in New York as a runner with the Hanover National Bank. After serving in the Navy during World War I, he worked as a national bank examiner in Newark and was subsequently a manager of the Newark Clearing House. Vice-president of Fidelity Union Bank before he became president of National State, Stillman was just 34 years old.

Under Stillman's leadership the bank's resources rose to over $24 million by 1937. Yet Stillman was not satisfied with merely retaining old accounts, and he aggressively sought new ones. This strategy began to pay off, and by 1940 the bank showed resources of almost $38 million. When World War II arrived, National State grew by providing long-term credit and loans to expanding industry and business.

The end of the war brought a change in the lifestyles of many Americans. Convinced by powerful advertising that the luxuries of life were necessities, people were willing to pay on credit for these items. Government-insured mortgages provided veterans with the opportunity to build new homes, and the age of the automobile brought a sharp increase in requests for auto loans.

Even though National State's assets had grown to more than $80 million by 1948, the bank remained on the periphery of American banking and life, refusing to grant mortgages or provide personal loans. As the demand for credit continued to increase, Stillman decided to enter the mainstream in one dramatic move. In 1949 National State merged with Merchants and Newark Trust Company, producing combined assets of over $115 million. Just as important, the merger brought National State its first branch office as well as its first mortgage, personal, and installment loans.

On June 1, 1950, National State merged with Orange First National Bank in order to provide it with a presence in the growing suburban areas surrounding Newark. On December 1, 1950, a merger with United States Trust Company was also completed and added seven more branches. In less than 18 months, National State grew from one of the smallest banks to one of the largest in the state. Its assets were over $168 million.

Throughout the 1950s, National State pursued a strategy of expansion through mergers. In 1955, Lincoln National Bank consolidated with National State; in 1956 and 1957, the Irvington Trust Company, First National Bank of Milburn, and Citizens National Bank and Trust Company of Caldwell were also acquired. The most significant merger took place in 1958 when the venerable Federal Trust Company came into the fold. By the end of the decade, National State's combined assets amounted to more than $418 million, and it ranked as the second largest bank in New Jersey.

William H. Keith replaced Stillman as president in 1961, while the latter remained as chair and chief executive of the bank. One year later, on its 150th anniversary, National State had almost 1,000 employees working at its headquarters and 21 branch offices, and over half a billion dollars in assets. To reflect its new prominence, the board of directors changed the bank's name to First National State Bank of New Jersey.

When Keith died in 1966, Robert R. Ferguson, Jr. was elected president of First National. Ferguson had a distinguished career at Federal Trust before its acquisition, and he immediately implemented an aggressive strategy of growth and expansion. Under Stillman's and his direction in 1969 the bank formed a parent company, First National State Bancorporation, in order to begin a program of statewide growth, and also laid the foundation for First National's involvement in interstate banking.

Stillman served as chairman of the Bancorporation and Ferguson as its president and chief executive, having assumed this position in 1973. Continuing its strategy of creating a large, statewide retail branch system, by the end of the decade the Bancorporation had expanded into every sector of the state. This system gave First National a substantial commercial banking-retail business.

During the early part of the 1980s, the merger of First National Bank of South Jersey and First National Bank of New Jersey increased assets to $6.4 billion. In 1984, the largest merger in the banking industry to date brought together Fidelity Union Bancorporation with First National to create First National State Bancorporation with assets of $10 billion. Renamed First Fidelity Bancorporation in 1985, it acquired Morris County Savings Bank of Morristown one year later, and in 1988 Fidelcor, Inc., based in Philadelphia, was merged. The merger of First Fidelity and Fidelcor created a super-regional interstate banking corporation with customers throughout the Philadelphia area and the state of New Jersey. Through these major mergers and corporate reorganization, First Fidelity became one of the 25 largest banking companies in the United States, with over $28 billion in assets.

Following the change of name and merger with Fidelcor, First Fidelity Bank, N.A., New Jersey, became the lead bank in the corporation's new lineup of commercial banking affiliates in New Jersey and Pennsylvania. This bank, with over $8 billion in assets of its own, was the largest commercial bank in New Jersey.

Having guided the bank through some of the most dramatic changes in its history, Ferguson retired and was replaced by Hal Pote. Under Pote's direction the bank agreed to some unwise commercial loans, and losses in revenue began to mount. Soon the board of directors was informed that the bank's capital ratio had declined severely, and this led directly to the resignation of Pote. Ferguson was asked to return and serve on an interim basis until a suitable replacement could be found.

In February 1990, the board of directors hired Anthony Terracciano as chairman, president, and chief executive. Terracciano had worked at Chase Manhattan Bank for 23 years, where he rose to the position of vice-chairman. In 1987, as president and chief operating officer of Mellon Bank, he helped Frank Cahouet solve the problems that were plaguing the Pittsburgh bank. When Terracciano arrived at Fidelity he immediately began to slash operating costs. In two years he reduced the workforce by some 20 percent, eliminating 6,000 jobs, introduced a new and more efficient standardized process for the bank's loan underwriting program, and contracted General Motors's Electronic Data Systems to handle the bank's computer operations. Within three years, Terracciano reduced operating expenses from 70 to 57 percent of revenue.

Seeking to expand the bank's assets, Terracciano also began to purchase failed financial institutions from the FDIC and RTC. He acquired a number of thrift and commercial banking institutions with nearly $10 billion in deposits at bargain prices, including the former City Federal Savings Bank, First National Bank of Toms River, and the Howard Savings Bank of Livingston, New Jersey. Terracciano's skillful implementation of his strategy to decrease Fidelity's cost structure while increasing its asset base made Fidelity both the dominant and the most profitable bank in New Jersey, as well as expanding its market share in southeastern Connecticut, eastern Pennsylvania, and Westchester County, New York.

Further Reading:

Forty-Nine Feet on Broad: The Story of the First 150 Years of the National States Bank of Newark, New Jersey, New Jersey: The National State Bank of Newark, 1962.
"A Brief History of First Fidelity," *First Fidelity Journal,* Vol.6, No. 2, December 1992.
Schifrin, Matthew, "The Early Bird," December 7, 1992, *Forbes,* pp. 168–69.

—Thomas Derdak

Fisons plc

Fison House, Princes St.
Ipswich, Suffolk IP1 1QH
England
(04) 73-232525

Public Company
Incorporated: 1843 as James Fison and Sons
Employees: 14,336
Sales: £1.23 billion (US$2.34 billion)
Stock Exchanges: London
SICs: 6719 Offices of Holding Companies Nec; 2833
   Medicinal Chemicals and Botanical Products; 2834
   Pharmaceutical Preparations; 3829 Measuring and
   Controlling Devices Nec; 2879 Pesticides and Agricultural
   Chemicals Nec

In 1993 Fisons plc was the world's third-largest manufacturer of scientific instruments and ranked among the world's 60 largest pharmaceutical concerns. While Fisons was still involved in horticultural products in 1993, it had announced plans to dispose of those operations. The British company's over-the-counter (OTC) pharmaceutical products include the European vitamin brand Sanatogen, and its prescription drugs are comprised of asthma treatments Tilade and Intal; respiratory drugs Aarane and Tipredane; Nasalcrom for hayfever; and Dopacard, a heart drug. Fisons's scientific equipment division concentrates primarily on the manufacture and distribution of spectrometers in North America and Europe. In addition, the company's Greenmaster and Evergreen brand lawn products, Origins organic composts, and Gro-bags soil are well-known British trademarks of the Horticulture division.

Fisons plc began as a flour mill and bakery founded by James Fisons in Barningham, England, in the late eighteenth century. In 1789 a son, also named James, started a maltings business that expanded into Stowmarket and Thetford, two river towns that helped the family businesses expand.

James Fison and Sons was formed in 1808, and by 1840 the firm was recording £100,000 in annual sales. Later that decade, the family entered the developing field of fertilizers and moved the business's headquarters to Ipswich. Within a few years, Fisons had built a manure works and was producing its own sulfuric acid. As fertilizers became the company's primary business, pesticides based on sulphur were added to the product mix.

In 1895 the company was split into two parts: James Fison and Sons and Joseph Fison and Co. During World War I, Fisons helped make explosives, but the company returned to fertilizer by the end of the war to buoy dwindling food production. When fertilizer prices plunged after the war, the two Fison companies, along with two others with which they had recently merged, were reunited to form Fison, Packard, Prentice and Co. (Fisons) in 1929.

During the 1930s, Fisons began to expand through acquisitions. The company's most significant addition was the Anglo-Continental Guano Works Ltd., which doubled the size of Fisons. Anglo-Continental was a budding conglomerate with a pharmaceutical subsidiary, Genatosan; Fisons was thus brought into that lucrative market. Fisons's acquisitions continued throughout the 1930s, and by 1939, with 39 subsidiaries, it was the largest fertilizer company in Great Britain.

During World War II Fisons felt the pressure of both a manpower shortage and increased demand for fertilizers. Some of the company's manufacturing plants were bombed as well. The company name was shortened to Fisons Ltd. for marketing clarity in 1942, and it emerged from the war with nearly two-thirds of Great Britain's fertilizer market.

Fisons made more acquisitions after the war's end, first purchasing Wiffen and Son, a fine chemicals manufacturer. The new subsidiary became part of Fisons's chemicals and biologicals division, headed by Genatosan. The Wiffen acquisition included the Loughborough Glass Company, which would later develop into Fisons's Scientific Equipment division. The purchase of Pest Control Limited during the 1950s brought Fisons into agrochemicals, a market that was closely related to the fertilizer business. Fisons hoped to capitalize on the two fields' common research, development, and distribution methods.

In 1968 researchers at Genatosan discovered disodium cromoglycate (DSCG), which was developed as the branded antiallergenic Intal. The drug differed from its competitors because it was a prophylactic, whereas others were taken after the onset of allergic symptoms. Intal sales boosted the pharmaceutical division's profits from £1.14 million in 1968 to £2.43 million in 1970 and £5.6 million in 1973.

By 1971 Fisons had organized its many subsidiaries into four divisions: Fertilizers, Agrochemicals, Pharmaceuticals, and Scientific Equipment. The company developed these primary businesses through acquisitions as well as product and market expansion. Acquisitions were focused geographically in Europe, Australia, and the United States.

Fertilizers contributed 50 percent of the conglomerate's annual sales at that time, and Fisons fought to maintain a competitive edge in Great Britain's fertilizer market: 80 percent of the division's sales were in its home country. But the supply side of this division was hamstrung, since its primary ammonia supplier was also its primary competitor, Imperial Chemical Industries plc. During the first half of the 1970s, Fisons tried to remedy this situation by increasing its bulk buying in global markets, especially patronizing Morocco. Morocco increased its prices six-fold in 1973, though, and other suppliers quickly followed suit. At the same time, U.K. price controls held fertilizer prices below the world market price for ammonia, effectively eliminating Fisons's fertilizer profits.

Fisons's Agrochemicals group also ran into trouble during the 1970s, when it lost a valuable customer, Ciba-Geigy Ltd. Fisons tried to support this group by increasing capital investments, especially in the United States. The company also boosted research and development funds, but since most of this division's efforts focused on creating substitutes for products that were already on the market, Fisons lacked a strong selling suit.

During the 1970s, anti-allergens comprised between 60 and 70 percent of the Pharmaceutical division's sales, but Intal had only captured 6.1 percent of the anti-allergy market, which was led by Glaxo's Ventolin. After a decade of research, the division was dealt a serious blow when Fisons decided not to market its new drug, Proxicromil, a successor to Intal, because it was found to cause cancer in animals. With Intal's nonrenewable patents set to run out in 1982, the Pharmaceutical division's prospects were not good.

In 1972 the Scientific Equipment Division was spun off from the Pharmaceutical division, and acquisitions in Germany and Australia, as well as the purchase of Britain's Gallenkamp, helped Fisons become Great Britain's top scientific equipment manufacturer. But many of Gallenkamp's contracts were with the government, universities, and hospitals, many of which cut their expenditures in the recessionary 1970s.

Fisons's Horticulture division was separated from the Agrochemical division in 1977. It produced and marketed amateur and professional gardening products, and its strengths were in peat-based products, especially the popular and well-established Fisons Gro-Bags—self-contained, nutritionally balanced soil sacks. The peat operations were extended with a new plant in Yorkshire and the acquisition of Howlett's, a company with peat reserves in Cumbria and Scotland. Although it was a new focus for Fisons, horticulture was actually one of the company's most secure businesses by the end of the 1970s. It was vertically integrated and held commanding shares of the markets in which it operated: 50 percent of the lawn fertilizer market; 20 percent of the solid fertilizer market; 30 percent of the peat market; and 12 percent of Great Britain's weed and pest control business.

Throughout the 1970s, Fisons had gone into debt to make a nebulous reorganization and prop up its historical focus—fertilizers—just as competition and global consolidation in this market eroded profits. At the same time, high interest rates and inflation dug into the profits Fisons managed to earn through its other operations. By 1980 Fisons's prospects looked dim. The Fertilizers division was operating at a loss; Agrochemicals could not hope to compete with the research and development outlays of bigger competitors; the Scientific Equipment division was suffering from government cutbacks; horticulture was a small, underdeveloped business; and the Pharmaceuticals division, a primary profit-maker, had suddenly lost its only long-term growth product. Fisons was on the verge of bankruptcy.

John Kerridge was promoted to chief executive officer (CEO) from executive director in mid-1980 and given the task of reversing Fisons's downward spiral. He began the reformation by cutting costs, closing down four production units and three

farms in the Fertilizer division, then eliminating more than 1,000 positions in the group. Fisons's corporate headquarters were moved from high-rent London back to Ipswitch, and economizations were made in the Scientific Equipment division as well. Kerridge's most fundamental change was the sale of the Fertilizer division to Norsk Hydro a.s. in 1982 for £59 million. The divestment was a radical change for Fisons and involved the disposal of what had been the foundation of the company for more than a century, as well as the division with the most sales. The troublesome Agrochemicals division was sold the following year to Schering A.G. for £60 million.

These divestments left Fisons with three primary businesses: Pharmaceuticals, Horticulture, and Scientific Equipment. The pharmaceutical group was expanded with the 1980 purchase of Great Britain's Charnwood Pharmaceuticals, Australia's Orbit Chemical Pty. Ltd. in 1982, and Italy's Intersint in 1983. Great Britain's Weddel Pharmaceutical was acquired in 1983 and merged with Charnwood, which would specialize in generic drugs.

Fisons's Horticultural operations were expanded geographically through a joint venture with Canada's Western Peat Moss in 1980, and the acquisition of Langley Peat North Ltd. of Alberta in 1983. These purchases gave Fisons access to large peat supplies and the North American market. The British operations were supplanted with the acquisition of Webb and Bees seed operations from Shell Holdings (U.K.) Ltd. in the early 1980s.

The Scientific Equipment division grew through the addition of Watson Victor, a New Zealand distributor of laboratory equipment, in 1982. Haake-Butler Instruments, of which Fisons owned 67 percent, was subsequently founded in the United States. Overall, Kerridge's fundamental changes improved Fisons's balance sheet dramatically: the corporation went from making annual interest payments of £13 million in 1980 to having no net borrowings in 1983. Fisons was even secure enough to make a successful stock offer of £28 million that year.

The Pharmaceutical division's continued heavy research and development expenditures resulted in two new drugs: DSCG-based Opticrom, released in 1984, and Tilade, a new asthma treatment, introduced in 1986. This division acquired Laboratorios Caesen, of Spain, in 1984, and Bracco de Mexico in 1986.

Kerridge was made chairman in 1984, and he clarified the strategy he had been using to turn Fisons around: "We wish to operate in industries of inherent attractiveness, which have potential for growth and a record of profitability of successful participants, [and] we wish to be in clearly defined business segments where Fisons can reasonably aspire to being an effective competitor by virtue of its size and its financial and managerial resources." The company would no longer operate on the fringes of its chosen markets, as it had in the 1970s. For example, Fisons concentrated on the horticulture and scientific equipment markets, which were not yet consolidated or dominated by a single powerful company; Fisons hoped to be the corporation that would eventually be the leader.

Fisons burst onto the U.S. market for scientific equipment, which was home to 40 percent of the world's research activity, with the acquisition of Curtin Matheson Scientific Inc. (CMS) in 1984. CMS was the United States' second-largest distributor of scientific equipment. Fisons also purchased United Diagnostics Inc. and Pacific Hemostasis Laboratories Inc., which were combined with CMS to give the latter manufacturing capacity. By the beginning of 1985, Fisons's Scientific division was the third-largest organization of its type in the world, and the largest outside the United States.

Fisons continued to grow, acquiring in 1985 Murphy Chemical, which helped widen the Horticulture division's portfolio of products, extend marketing in Europe and North America, and shore up Fisons's peat supplies. Later in the decade, the Horticulture division would sell its 50 percent share of Asef-Fison B.V. to its joint-venture partner, DSM Agro Specialties B.V. In 1986 Fisons bought Applied Research Laboratories, a leading manufacturer of scientific equipment with global marketing capacity, and two years later it purchased Union Scientific Limited, a Hong Kong company.

Several important acquisitions were also made by the Pharmaceutical division in the late 1980s. Italchimici S.p.A., an Italian firm, and Pennwalt Corporation's pharmaceutical division, a U.S. manufacturer of ethical and over-the-counter drugs, were purchased in 1988. A French company, Gerbitol S.A., brought expertise in cardiovascular medicine, antibiotics, and dietary supplements to the division in 1989. In all, with the help of its significant 1980s acquisitions, Fisons's pre-tax profits increased by an average 56 percent per year to £230 million (US$410 million). The corporation's market capitalization rose from £40 million in 1980 to £3 billion in 1990.

The 1990 purchase of VG Instruments, a manufacturer of mass spectrometers and surface analysis instruments, more than doubled Fisons's output of analytical instruments and catapulted the Scientific Equipment division to the number three spot in the global marketplace. It looked as if Fisons had launched its second consecutive decade of growth and prosperity. By the end of 1991, however, it was clear that problems in the Pharmaceutical division had dragged the entire company down. Late that year, Fisons revealed that two of its important new drugs, Opticrom for hay fever and Imferon for anemia, had been recalled from the U.S. market after the Food and Drug Administration (FDA) denied approval of the company's British factories. According to a 1992 *Economist* article, the FDA's routine check of Fisons's U.K. factory revealed warehouses with holes in their outside walls; poor record keeping; and "the possibility of rodent, insect or avian activity in the [transport] containers." Fisons's pre-tax profits for 1991 dropped 17 percent to £190 million, and the company faced required investments of more than £25 million to bring its British factory up to U.S. standards.

John Kerridge resigned "on health grounds" in mid-January of 1992 and was temporarily replaced by Patrick Egan. In April of that year, Egan became chairman and Cedric Scroggs was selected as chief executive officer. The new leaders decided to sharpen Fisons's focus on pharmaceuticals and scientific equipment by divesting its OTC drug and horticultural businesses.

In November of 1992, Fisons agreed to sell its North American OTC drug operations to Swiss drug concern Ciba-Geigy Ltd.

for £92 million (US$60.3 million). This segment represented approximately 50 percent of Fisons's global consumer health division sales and 40 percent of that group's profits. Egan and Scroggs recognized that the British company lacked the resources and marketing influence necessary to compete in the American consumer drug market.

Fisons's new management forged a joint development and marketing agreement with Allergan Inc., a U.S. opthalmic company, early in 1993. The arrangement called for Fisons's 400 U.S. salespeople to co-market Allergan's opthalmic drug Acular. The U.S. company's sales force, in turn, would help market Fisons's opthalmic treatment Opticrom. The arrangement presumed that Opticrom would be re-registered by the FDA. By early 1993, Fisons had made significant improvements in its Opticrom factory, but new FDA inspections had still not resulted in approval late in the year.

Fisons suffered yet another setback when it hastily suspended development of an asthma medicine, tipredane. The company had been banking on the new drug to bolster its core respiratory business in the late 1990s. Tipredane had been licensed by Fisons from Bristol-Myers Squibb Co. and was in the midst of unsuccessful clinical trials in more than a dozen countries. The failure of tipredane left Fisons with only one new drug, remacemide—an epilepsy treatment—in development.

In May of 1993 Fisons sold its North American horticulture business to a consortium led by Macluan Capital Corp. of Vancouver for US$60 million in cash and used the proceeds to reduce its debt. Fisons also planned to sell the remainder of its Horticulture division as soon as an opportunity arose. In July the company sold its consumer health products business in Australia and New Zealand to Warner-Lambert for about US$23 million. The sale included the Rosken line of therapeutic skin-care products.

Despite Fisons's early 1990s efforts to bolster its pharmaceutical business, some analysts insisted that the company had neither the research and development strength nor the marketing clout necessary to compete in an ethical pharmaceutical business that demanded frequent discovery of innovative medicines. Observers predicted an imminent merger or takeover for Fisons.

Principal Subsidiaries: VG Instruments Group Ltd.; Fisons Pty. Ltd. (Australia); FSE Pty. Ltd. (Australia); Fisons (Bangladesh) Ltd. (51%); Atlantic Chemical corp. Ltd. (Bermuda); Fisons Corp. Ltd. (Canada); Fisons Horticulture Inc. (Canada); Fisons A/S (Denmark); Laboratories Fisons SA (France); SCAD-Fisons SA (France); Fisons Arzneimittel GmbH (Germany); Gebruder Haake GmbH (Germany); VG Instruments GmbH (Germany); Fisons Italchimici S.p.A. (Italy); Carlo Erba Strumentazione S.p.A. (Italy); Fujisawa-Fisons KK (Japan; 65%); Asef BV (Netherlands); Fisons BV (Netherlands); Fisons Pharmaceutical (Pty.) Ltd. (South Africa); Fisons AG (Switzerland); ARL Applied Research Laboratories SA (Switzerland); Fisons Corp. (United States); Applied Research Laboratories Inc. (United States); Curtin Matheson Scientific Inc. (United States); Kevex Instruments Inc (United States); VG Instruments Inc. (United States).

Further Reading:

Finlay, Paul N., "How Fisons Managed Its Turnaround," *European Journal of Marketing,* vol. 22, pp. 103–117.

"Firm's Horticulture Business to Be Sold for $60 Million," *Wall Street Journal,* May 19, 1993, p. A11.

"Fisons Stock Tumbles as Drug Maker Halts New Medicine's Trials," *Wall Street Journal,* April 7, 1993, p. A10.

"Fisons to Sell Some Operations in Canada, U.S. to Ciba-Geigy," *Wall Street Journal,* November 27, 1992, p. A6.

From a Corner of Suffolk to the Four Corners of the Earth, Ipswich, England: Fisons plc, 1984.

"Full Circle," *The Economist,* January 18, 1992, p. 69.

Moore, Stephen D., "U.K.'s Fisons and Allergan Link up to Develop, Sell Opthalmic Products, *Wall Street Journal,* February 5, 1993, p. B3A.

—April S. Dougal

Fleet Financial Group, Inc.

50 Kennedy Plaza
Providence, Rhode Island 02903
U.S.A.
(401) 278-5879
Fax: (408) 278-5801

Public Company
Incorporated: 1791 as Providence Bank
Employees: 27,500
Sales: $46.93 billion
Stock Exchanges: New York
SICs: 6712 Bank Holding Companies; 6021 National
   Commercial Banks

The Fleet Financial Group, Inc., is one of the largest bank
holding companies in the United States. Although its lending
operations are national in scope, the company's constituent
institutions are concentrated mostly in New York, New Hampshire, Rhode Island, Maine, Connecticut, and Massachusetts.
As a bank holding company, Fleet offers a wide variety of
financial services, including personal and corporate banking,
lending, leasing, and real estate and investment services.

Fleet was formed over a period of 200 years through the amalgamation of dozens of smaller local banks and savings institutions. As a result, the company has an extremely complex but
rich heritage. The earliest predecessor of the Fleet companies
was the Providence Bank, which was established in Rhode
Island in 1791 by a shipping merchant and former Congressional representative named John Brown. He had tried to found a
bank seven years before, in the waning years of the War of
Independence, but failed to inspire the trust of investors. As it
was, the Providence Bank was only the fifth bank to be established in the newly created United States of America.

In 1803, Elkanah Watson, who had been an apprentice in the
shipping business under Brown, established his own financial
institution, the State Bank of Albany. Watson had served as a
soldier under George Washington and as an emissary to Benjamin Franklin in France. Rather than pursue politics, Watson
built on his experience with Brown's shipping company and
moved to Holland, where he studied the Dutch canal system. In
1792, after having returned to America, Watson organized a
number of inland water transportation systems, including the
Western Inland Lock Navigation Company. He continued in

these ventures for another eleven years, at which time he re-
ported having a dream about opening a bank. The next morning
Watson immediately began drawing up papers to establish the
State Bank of Albany. Watson headed the bank until his death in
1842. Throughout its history, the State Bank of Albany financed
transportation projects, including the formation of the New
York Central Railroad Company, the construction of the Great
Western Turnpike (now U.S. Route 20), and a portion of the
Erie Canal.

A third predecessor of Fleet Financial was established in 1886
by Samuel Pomeroy Colt, a young man who had been raised by
his uncle and namesake, Samuel Colt, inventor of the Colt
revolver. After earning his law degree, the younger Colt began a
successful career in Rhode Island state politics. He founded the
Industrial Trust Company in 1886 as a vehicle for his commercial activities, which included an interest in the National India
Rubber Company. While in Europe some years later, Colt noted
the European system of branch banking, a system that enabled a
bank to conduct business in several areas of a city or county. He
brought this idea back to Rhode Island and between 1900 and
1908 purchased 29 smaller banks throughout Providence, with
the aim of converting them into branches of his Industrial Trust
Company.

Thus, by the early twentieth century, the Providence National
Bank, the State Bank of Albany, and the Industrial Trust Com-
pany had been established and were prospering. All three institutions survived the Panic of 1907, a disastrous run on banks
that collapsed the American banking system. Colt's Industrial
Trust was the first of the three, and the first bank in Rhode
Island, to join the new Federal Reserve system. The Providence
Bank, which became a national bank in 1865, recorded its first
acquisition in 1926, when it took over the operations of the
Merchants National Bank, then the largest financial institution
in Rhode Island.

The banks plunged into dire straits in 1929, after the stock
market crashed. The sequence of bankruptcies destroyed companies and banks alike and continued despite federal seizure of
bank assets. Fortunately, the economies of Rhode Island and
upstate New York were primarily—and robustly—maritime
and agrarian, enabling the banks to remain solvent. In fact, the
State Bank of Albany succeeded in growing during this difficult
period by taking over a number of troubled competitors.

The banks remained stable throughout the 1930s, but were
quickly drawn into a war mobilization economy in 1941. When
war broke out later that year, the banks became essential
sources for government investment in new factories. At the end
of the war in 1945, there was tremendous demand for housing,
food, and other goods, and a ready supply of workers returning
from combat. The growing volume and velocity of money
flowing through the economy fueled the growth of the banks.

However, new demands were put on banks when the areas they
served became saturated. Unless they could expand geographically, the banks' growth would be tied only to local average
income growth. Providence National boosted its geographical
coverage in 1951 by merging with another major Providence
bank, the Union Trust Company. A year later, the company
changed its name to Providence Union National Bank and

Trust. In 1954, this company completed another merger, this time with the company founded by Samuel Colt, the Industrial Trust Company. The new institution took the name Industrial National Bank, but continued to operate under the original Providence Bank's 1791 charter. The company remained strongly involved in lending operations to the local jewelry industry, an area in which it specialized.

Industrial National formed its own holding company, Industrial Bancorp, in 1968 (thereby launching the modern fashion of spelling bank with a "c"). The creation of this holding company permitted the institution to skirt regulatory restrictions in the 1956 Bank Holding Company Act that would have precluded the Industrial National Bank from conducting a range of nonbank financial services. The company gained a listing on the New York Stock Exchange on September 18, 1968. Industrial Bancorp changed its name to the Industrial National Corporation in 1970, and began its diversification in 1972, when it purchased New York-based Ambassador Factors. A year later it took over the Southern Discount Company of Atlanta. In 1974 the company acquired Mortgage Associates, a mortgage banking group headquartered in Milwaukee. The man behind Industrial National's diversification strategy was John J. Cummings, Jr., who believed that there was no justification for perpetuating the distinction between banking and traditionally nonbank financial services.

The State Bank of Albany began a similar transformation in 1972, when it took over the Liberty Bank of Buffalo. Liberty had been established in 1882 as the German-American Bank, but adopted the new name in 1918 amid public opposition to anything "German" during World War I. In fact, the bank was a wholly American-owned institution and had nothing to do with Germany or the war. With this transaction, the State Bank of Albany created a holding company called the Union Bank of New York.

In 1975 a former insurance executive named Peter D. Kiernan assumed leadership of Union Bank, emphasizing the need for better service. Like Cummings, Kiernan hoped to expand the Union Bank's scope of operations through acquisition. In 1982 he changed the company's name to Norstar Bancorp. He engineered Norstar's acquisition of the Utica-based Oneida Bank & Trust Company and carried out the first interstate bank merger in nearly 30 years by acquiring the Northeast Bankshare Association of Maine. In 1983 the company formed the Norstar Bank of the Hudson Valley by acquiring and merging the Sullivan County National Bank, Rondout National Bank, and Highland National Bank. The Norstar Bank of Long Island was formed by the merger of the Hempstead Bank, Peninsula National Bank, and Island State Bank. Later that year the Oneida National Bank and the State Bank of Albany were merged to form the Norstar Upstate Bank Group.

Cummings also branded his company with a new name, adopting the moniker Fleet Financial Group in 1982. He considered the company's various divisions to be like a fleet of ships, all working in support of one another. The maritime name was popular in Rhode Island, where the local economy depended on fishing and shipping. Cummings retired later that year and was succeeded by the decidedly gruff J. Terrence Murray. As chairman and CEO, Murray continued Fleet's rapid expansion in

order to build the "critical mass" it would need to compete with bigger banks in New York and California. By 1985 the company had 322 offices in 33 states and four foreign countries. That year, after fighting regulatory and legal battles, Fleet established *de novo* banks in Boston and Hartford. It also acquired First Connecticut Bancorp and Merrill Bankshares, a major Maine bank that had been established in Bangor in 1903.

Meanwhile, Norstar acquired the 102-year old Security Trust Company in 1984 and the Bank of Maine a year later. In 1986 the company established Norstar Trust. After nearly 200 years of operation, Fleet and Norstar began crowding each other's territory. Murray and Kiernan began informal discussions about merging the two companies.

However, Murray was distracted by a painful investigation of its mortgage lending operation, in which regulators charged that Fleet had taken unfair advantage of the state-run Rhode Island Housing & Mortgage Finance Corporation. The agency had become a major Fleet customer, and, it was charged, Fleet's relationship with the bank had become so cozy that Fleet's loan officers were allowed to use agency loans to enrich themselves. More than 250 loans were granted to Fleet employees, and one even went to Murray's in-laws. But an investigation exonerated Murray and concluded that only 11 of the loans were improper. Still, the debacle exposed Fleet's capacity for corruption and, more importantly, its lack of effective senior management oversight.

Murray was also suffering from his growing reputation as a ruthless "downsizer." Indeed, many of the institutions acquired by Fleet were inefficiently run companies with poorly administered data systems. One way in which Fleet was able to derive greater productivity from its acquisitions was to consolidate their administrative positions into Fleet's existing staff and fold their diverse computer operations into Fleet's own system. This necessitated firing hundreds of redundant employees, but dramatically increased the profitability of the company's operations.

Driven by increasing competition from the Bank of Boston and the Bank of New England, Murray and Kiernan finally engaged in serious merger talks in 1987. The merger of Fleet and Norstar was announced January 1, 1988. Although Fleet acquired Norstar for $1.3 billion, Norstar's Kiernan was named chairman and CEO of the new company, which was called the Fleet/Norstar Financial Group. The merger mania continued in 1988 as Fleet/Norstar acquired the New Hampshire-based Indian Head Banks and began consolidating banking operations in Maine. Kiernan died suddenly on September 14, and, six days later, Murray was appointed to succeed him.

Early in 1989 it was revealed that the widespread slump in property values and poor federal oversight of the real estate industry had caused a serious banking crisis. Hundreds of financial institutions were saddled with billions of dollars in bad debt. One of these was Fleet/Norstar's chief competitor, the Bank of New England. BNE's crisis began in 1986 when it outbid Fleet for the Conifer Group, a Massachusetts real estate lender. Conifer's portfolio was a shambles, riddled with failed or shaky deals. Ironically, in losing its bid for Conifer, Fleet avoided a ruinous liability that, in the end, caused BNE to be seized by the Federal Deposit Insurance Corporation.

By 1990, the FDIC was eager to dump BNE and offered exceedingly generous guarantees against its liabilities. Fleet/Norstar badly wanted to bid for BNE, but lacked the capital of leading contenders like BankAmerica and the Bank of Boston. The leveraged buy-out firm Kohlberg Kravis Roberts also wanted to bid for BNE, but regulators soured on the idea of turning New England's second largest bank over to a group of corporate raiders. It became apparent that Murray and KKR's Henry Kravis needed each other, KKR for its money and Fleet/Norstar for its banking expertise. The two groups battled over the terms of their $625 million bid until just five minutes before the FDIC's deadline. To everyone's surprise, the Fleet/Norstar-KKR bid won.

Murray immediately launched into BNE's cost centers, consolidating its data centers with those of Fleet/Norstar and firing nearly half of BNE's 11,000 employees. What remained was a bank with $15 billion in assets, the most extensive retail branch network in the region, and a large number of stable business loans. Within a year, Fleet/Norstar had rehabilitated BNE and turned a number of nonperforming loans back to the FDIC. The failed bank, which *Business Week* said had the allure of a toxic waste dump, was profitable sooner than anyone would have imagined.

The BNE takeover enabled Fleet to surpass the Bank of Boston as the largest bank in New England. It also is the nation's second-largest mortgage banker and its largest student loan processor. As a result of the BNE deal, KKR owns a nonvoting 15.7-percent share of Fleet.

Fleet/Norstar reverted to its old name, Fleet Financial Group, in 1992. With much of the real estate crisis and the Northeast's economic recession behind him, Murray began thinking about further expansion. Unable to wrest further growth out of the region, Murray intimated that Fleet might next turn its attention to the midwest and mid-Atlantic states.

Principal Subsidiaries: Fleet Bank (Long Island); Fleet Bank, N.A., (Connecticut); Fleet Bank—New Hampshire; Fleet Bank—Rhode Island; Fleet Bank of Maine; Fleet Bank of Massachusetts; Fleet Bank of New York; Fleet Bank of New York, N.A.; AFSA Data Corp.; Fleet Associates; Fleet Brokerage Securities; Fleet Credit Corp.; Fleet Factors Corp.; Fleet Finance Corp.; Fleet Investment Advisors, Inc.; Fleet Investment Services; Fleet Mortgage Group; Fleet/Norstar Securities; Fleet Services Corp.; RECOLL Management Corp.

Further Reading:

"Fleet Financial, to Lessen Realty Woes, May Sell Third of Non-Performing Assets," *Wall Street Journal,* September 17, 1992, p. A3.
"Fleet/Norstar Financial Group, Inc.," *Barron's,* September 11, 1989, p. 20.
"Fleet's Ship Comes In," *Business Week,* November 9, 1992, p. 104.
"Right Time, Right Place, Right Price," *Business Week,* May 6, 1991, pp. 26–29.
"Terry Murray's Regional View," *Industry Week,* November 11, 1985, p. 66.
"Unbankerish Banker," *Forbes,* July 16, 1984, pp. 123–27.
"Who Was Minding the Shop?," *Forbes,* March 10, 1986, p 135.

—John Simley

FlightSafety International, Inc.

Marine Air Terminal
LaGuardia Airport
Flushing, New York 11371
U.S.A.
(718) 565-4100
Fax: (718) 565-4134

Public Company
Incorporated: 1951 as Flight Safety, Inc.
Employees: 2259
Sales: $267.9 million
Stock Exchanges: New York
SICs: 8299 Schools and Educational Services Nec; 3699
   Electrical Equipment and Supplies Nec

FlightSafety International, Inc. (FSI) is the largest provider of pilot training services to the general aviation, corporate, military, and commercial airline markets. The company also trains operators of ships, electrical utilities, and steam generating plants, and manufactures flight simulators, operating 132 simulation centers worldwide that offer simulator equipment, visuals, and training courses. An estimated 36,000 pilots a year are trained by FSI, which has long-term contracts with 23 aircraft manufacturers; while nearly half of FSI's business comes from upgrading the skills of corporate pilots, the company also trains commercial and commuter airline pilots and holds contracts with the U.S. military. A mainstay on the *Forbes* magazine list of "Best 200 Small Companies," FSI is highly profitable, and its competitive position was strengthened when it acquired the flight simulator subsidiary of the McDonnell Douglas Corporation. Its major competitors include the major commercial airlines, which often operate their own extensive simulation training centers.

The need for the kinds of services that FSI provides can be traced to the fact that an estimated 65 percent of airline accidents may be attributed to human error. Independent providers of pilot training emerged due to cost considerations as well; simulator training was far less expensive and, of course, less risky than doing the training in the aircraft itself. FSI founder Albert Ueltschi tells a story of teaching an army pilot, in 1939, how to do snap rolls in an open cockpit plane. Apparently, when the plane rolled, Ueltschi's seat broke free from the plane, and he was unable to get his parachute open. Nevertheless, he was

able to walk away from the accident. The flight training his company would offer would be far less risky. Flight simulators would enable pilot trainees to practice both normal and emergency procedures under controlled conditions.

FSI got in on the ground floor of an emerging airline industry in the 1940s and 1950s. In 1942, Albert Ueltschi hired on with Pan American Airlines, operating 'flying boats' that flew out of Flushing Bay. Four years later he began working as the personal pilot for Pan Am founder Juan Trippe. At that time, corporations were buying up military planes left over from World War II and converting them for their own private uses. However, many of the pilots did not have any specific training on the planes they were being hired to fly. Sensing the opening of a profitable business specializing in flight training, Ueltschi started Flight Safety Inc. in 1951.

Initially, Ueltschi was strictly a service provider, hiring moonlighting pilots from the major commercial airlines to train pilots flying private planes for corporate executives. Training was generally done in the clients' aircraft, along with some instrument trainers rented from United Airlines. Operating out of Pan Am's LaGuardia Terminal, some early clients included Eastman Kodak, Burlington Industries, National Distillers, and other companies that required training for the pilots of their corporate fleets—the dominant segment of airline traffic at the time. Perceiving that a demand might later exist for updated training services, Ueltschi mortgaged his house to assist in establishing FlightSafety, Inc.

The company grew by stops and starts, and, with the firm's future uncertain, Ueltschi kept his job at Pan Am. He would keep his job as Trippe's personal pilot for 17 years. Using his salary at Pan Am for living expenses, Ueltschi plowed all of FSI's profits back into the company. This high rate of reinvestment strategy was vital to keeping the company afloat in its early years and eventually led to large profits and strong sales growth.

But the early years were difficult. Ueltschi went heavily into debt and took some big risks to get the company off the ground. For instance, he raised $69,750 in investment capital by convincing some of his early clients to put up the money as prepayment for five years of training services for the crews of their corporate fleets. This gave Ueltschi the cash, without the debt load, to buy his first Link Trainer. The Link Trainer, a flight simulation machine used by the army in the 1930s and later to train pilots during World War II, was a mechanically controlled flight trainer designed to teach mail-carrying pilots how to "fly blind" on an instrument panel. A modern version of this original model is still used by FSI.

After nearly 20 years, FSI achieved stable growth rates, and Ueltschi's growth prospects and markets hinged largely on his success at training pilots. Essentially, he had to convince aircraft manufacturers that he could do a better job of training pilots for their own aircraft than they could themselves, and for less money. Prior to the development of the "training industry," the aircraft manufacturers had generally included the cost of initial flight training in the price of a new plane. Gradually, the manufacturers looked toward specialization on production and opportunities arose for companies like FSI to develop and specialize in the training business. For example, companies like Learjet realized, after a couple of bad accidents, that they should specialize in production and design and leave the training to experts. Learjet, in fact, became the first corporate jet manufacturer to sign up with FSI. FSI set up a training center with a Learjet flight simulator at the company's factory, providing initial and updating of training of pilots for new models.

This success led to other contracts with the airline manufacturers, and by the late 1970s Ueltschi's company had signed similar deals with 12 other plane makers, including Airbus Industrie in France. The business arrangement was the same for all clients: Flight Safety provided the initial training for the buyers of the new planes and trained their pilots at both a company training center and using simulators near the manufacturing facilities. Furthermore, pilots returned periodically for refresher courses, thereby creating more revenue and new markets for the company.

Flight Safety had become very successful, allowing Ueltschi to take the company public in 1968, although he maintained control of 34 percent of its outstanding common stock. From 1973 to 1977 the company's revenues rose by an average annual compound rate of 22 percent and earnings by 35 percent. Return on equity was 23.2 percent in 1978, and its stock price nearly doubled that year.

Markets were also expanding rapidly for Flight Safety. Even the commercial and commuter airlines, which largely trained their own pilots, began to give some of their spillover business to the company. In addition, to ensure a steady supply of simulators, with demand growing for training services, Flight Safety purchased its own simulation systems division out of Tulsa, Oklahoma. The division built simulators for use by Flight Safety as well as for sale to the airlines.

With the large growth in new business in the 1970s Ueltschi changed the name of his company, adding 'International' to create FlightSafety International, Inc. The company grew continuously from the late 1970s, virtually unimpeded. Continuing his high reinvestment policy, Ueltschi invested in a marine simulator at LaGuardia Airport to train operators of supertankers, or natural gas carriers. Ueltschi then launched agreements with 16 companies, including Texaco, to train ship crews.

With the company in solid competitive position at the onset of the 1980s, Ueltschi was poised to take further risks. Moreover, the aviation industry was expanding rapidly, pulling much of the airline services industry up with it. FSI branched out into military pilot training and, later, began to challenge commercial airlines for a portion of their pilot training market.

In 1984, the company successfully competed for an Air Force contract. The Air Force had begun to contract out flight training at Fort Rucker in Daleville, Alabama. To get a jump on the competition, Ueltschi bought land right next to the base and installed a flight simulator. With this move Ueltschi usurped the contract bidding process and immediately won business from the nearby base. By the time the official contract competition was underway, FSI easily won the contract.

During this time, FSI had virtually monopolized the corporate pilot training market, prompting its main competitor, Singer

Company (whose SimuFlite division runs a training center in Dallas, Texas), to sue FSI in 1984 for anticompetitive practices. Singer's suit claimed that FSI maintained too close a relationship with airplane manufacturers, allowing FSI to overtake the industry and exclude others from entering the market. However, Singer eventually dropped the suit.

Competition in the 1980s came mainly from the airline companies as FSI focused on the commercial airlines market. In order to penetrate the passenger airlines market, FSI needed to convince the commercial carriers that it would be cost effective to purchase training services rather than to train pilots in-house. One of FSI's first moves into commercial industry pilot training was launched in 1989 through an agreement with Trans World Airlines (TWA). This new venture would make FSI the main source of trained pilots for TWA. Working out of a St. Louis-based training center, FSI began its Advanced Flight Crew Training Program. This project was part of a major capital spending program aimed mainly at the commuter aircraft training market. Furthermore, as government and the military further privatized, FSI won more contracts. The MarineSafety International and PowerSafety International Divisions also expanded. Record earnings in 1989 reflected the boom: revenues were up $168.15 million, and net income grew 29 percent to $46.7 million.

As FSI entered the 1990s, it seemed to maintain its hold over the flight training industry with more than 100 simulators around the world and close connections with virtually all airplane manufacturers to train their customers. The company had a healthy cash flow and annual earnings growth of more than 15 percent from 1986 through 1990.

The commercial airlines also seemed to have realized the cost cutting potential of specialization by tapping FSI to conduct flight crew training. The cost benefits of specialization and the concomitant need for increasingly more sophisticated training, as well as the traditionally more favorable aspects of the use of simulators, all worked in FSI's favor. Furthermore, insurance companies writing policies for the airlines began to reduce premiums on those pilots who attended refresher courses to keep in top form on the latest equipment. All these factors pointed toward an increasing demand for flight training.

FSI not only sold its services to carriers in the United States but also to airlines in Europe and Asia. By early 1992 the company prepared to tap into the Latin American airline carriers markets. According to James Waugh, FSI's vice-president of marketing, the company was able to support Latin American carriers that had not achieved the critical mass necessary to support in-house training facilities. To support this move, FSI began relocating several transport category full-flight simulators to a newly acquired Miami site to serve the Latin American airlines that were upgrading their fleets. In addition, FSI continued its practice of opening up simulators near manufacturing plants. For example, the company opened a training center, equipped with Boeing simulators, near a Boeing plant in Seattle.

Competition intensified in the early 1990s, and FSI and its main competitors are depending on price wars in recessionary times. The increasing trend toward contracting out of airlines' technical services bodes well for FSI's future commercial carrier business as more airlines seek services in general, and specifically crew training, from outside contractors. Furthermore, while most labor union agreements have previously kept such services in-house, the airlines have successfully applied leverage over new agreements to slash costs by contracting out. FSI has evolved along with this trend, seizing an increasing share of the crew training business. In fact, the share of FSI's revenues from commercial and commuter airlines customers rose steadily throughout the early 1990s. With this shift in focus, the company looked to build new facilities close to airline markets, largely near airports.

FSI has expanded its business worldwide and rapidly increased its share of the commercial airline business. In fact, 20 percent of FSI's revenues were derived from airline contracts of U.S., European, and Asian airlines. At its Vero Beach, Florida, facility, FSI trained pilots for Air Afrique, All Nippon Airways, Asiana Airlines of Korea, Swissair, Australia's Tyrolean Airways, Air France affiliates Air Inter and UTA, and others. FSI also signed a contract with Taiwan's China Airlines to develop a cockpit resources management training system. Further solidifying FSI's competitive position was the purchase of the visual systems division of McDonnell Douglas. This would allow FSI more direct control over the production of visual systems as well. Pointing to its capital expansion plan (which called for development of not only the Miami training center but also centers in Texas, Arizona, and Hong Kong), its solid cash flow position, and its large orders from government agencies, analysts considered FSI well positioned to continue its lead in the industry.

Principal Subsidiaries: Flightsafety International, Inc., Flight-Safety Services Corp.; FlightSafety International, Inc., Simulation Systems Division; MarineSafety International, Inc.; Ma-rineSafety International Rotterdam B.V. (The Netherlands; 51%); InterSystems Leasing, Inc.

Further Reading:

Feldman, Joan M., "Airlines Lighten the Load," *Air Transport World,* November 1992.

"FlightSafety International Will Invest over $150 million in Development and Training Facilities," *Wall Street Journal,* September 21, 1992.

"FlightSafety Marches into Europe," *Interavia Aerospace World,* October 1992.

"FlightSafety Orders MDC Vital VII Systems," *Flight International,* September 15, 1992.

Kernstock, Nicholas C., "FlightSafety Rides Boom in Airline, Military Training to Record Earnings," *Aviation Week & Space Technology,* November 27, 1989.

"McDonnell-Douglas Agrees to Sell Image Display Unit to Flight-Safety," *Aerospace Daily,* November 25, 1992.

McKenna, James, "FlightSafety Moves Simulators to Miami Facility to Serve Latin American Airlines," *Aviation Week & Space Technology,* June 1, 1992; "FlightSafety Sees Airlines as Important Growth Market," *Aviation Week & Space Technology,* September 2, 1991.

Meeks, Fleming, "The Pilots' Pilot," *Forbes,* November 13, 1989.

Morner, Aimee L., "Training Pilots of Corporate Jets is Down-to-Earth Business," *Fortune,* May 22, 1978.

Pacey, Margaret D., "Ground Support Take-Off: Aviation Specialists Prosper by Servicing Planes, Training Staff," *Barron's,* June 5, 1972.

Phillips, Edward H., "Business Flying: Costs, Limits of Flight Training Prompt," *Aviation Week & Space Technology,* October 17, 1988.

"A Simulating Experience: FlightSafety International Lead in Market for Flight-Training Services Could Boost Stock Value," *Forbes,* January 20, 1992.

Zipser, Andy, "Fond of FlightSafety," *Barron's,* December 3, 1990.

—John A. Sarich

Florsheim Shoe Company

130 South Canal Street
Chicago, Illinois 60606-3999
U.S.A.
(312) 559-2500
Fax: (312) 559-7470

Division of Interco Inc.
Incorporated: 1892 as Florsheim & Company
Employees: 6,000
Sales: $210 million
SICs: 3143 Men's Footwear, Except Athletic

Florsheim Shoe Company manufactures and sells one of the world's best-known brands of dress shoes for men. In recent years, casual shoes have also been included in the company's line, which contains a total of over 300 styles. Florsheim shoes are sold at the 300 Florsheim Shoe Shops and by about 3,000 unaffiliated Florsheim dealers nationwide. Florsheim is a division of the St. Louis-based Interco Inc., which also owns Converse, the athletic shoe maker. Interco went into bankruptcy in 1991, after going nearly $2 billion in debt fighting off a takeover attempt. Interco's bankruptcy ended in mid-1992. About half of Florsheim's 6,000 employees work in the United States, where the company has production facilities in southern Missouri and southern Illinois. In addition to its line of classic men's dress shoes, Florsheim markets several specialized shoe types. Shoes in the company's Florsheim Comfortech line weigh half as much as traditional dress shoes and feature a special insert with shock absorbing air bubbles. The Florsheim Outdoorsman line contains rugged casual shoes and boots that are water resistant and insulated for warmth, and the Florsheim Imperial line includes dress shoes with other special comfort features.

The company was founded under the name Florsheim & Co. in 1892. Milton Florsheim, the company's founder, sought to produce high quality men's dress shoes at a moderate price, and he opened his first factory in Chicago. The first Florsheim shoes were made by Milton and his father, Sigmund Florsheim. Florsheim's distribution system was established in the company's infancy. The company provided support for entrepreneurs who wished to set up stores that would sell Florsheim shoes retail. In this way, Florsheim shoes began to go on sale in small towns throughout the United States.

Florsheim expanded its distribution system in the early part of the twentieth century. Wholesale distribution was set up in several metropolitan areas. Company-owned retail outlets were also established in several cities. These stores were large enough to display and sell the entire line of Florsheim shoes and became the company's flagship operations. In 1929, the company began manufacturing woman's shoes. By 1930, there were five Florsheim factories in Chicago. The shoes were sold through 71 retail outlets, either wholly or partly owned by the company, as well as through nearly 9,000 dealers not directly affiliated with the manufacturer. The company had 2,500 employees by this time.

After approaching $3 million in net income in 1929, Florsheim, like most companies dependant on retail sales, was hurt badly by the onset of the Great Depression. By 1931, the company's net income had shrunk to $717,000. As the Depression eased up somewhat in the second half of the 1930s, net income hovered around the $1 million mark, and sales began to slowly climb once again, reaching $9.4 million in 1940.

Despite its size, Florsheim was still very much a family operation in the 1930s. Aside from Milton Florsheim, the company's two highest ranking officers in 1930 were his sons, Irving and Harold, who had joined the business in 1914 and 1920, respectively, after graduating from Cornell University. Two other Florsheims, Louis and Felix, also sat on the board of directors. In addition to its business successes, the Florsheim family was also prominent in the art world, both as patrons and artists. Helen Florsheim, Irving's wife, had a distinguished career as a sculptor. In 1936, Milton Florsheim died and was replaced as head of Florsheim Shoe Co. by Irving. Sales at Florsheim stalled once again in the mid-1940s, hovering around $17 million. In 1946, Irving Florsheim ascended to the position of chairperson, leaving the company's presidency to his brother Harold.

By 1949, Florsheim's sales were $25.3 million. At that time, there were 82 wholly or partly owned Florsheim retail outlets, and another 4,500 unaffiliated stores that sold Florsheim shoes. The bulk of Florsheim's manufacturing was still taking place at the company's Chicago plants, principally the original facility near Chicago's Loop and two others on the northwest side of the city. In 1953, Florsheim was purchased by International Shoe Company (now called Interco), the largest shoe manufacturer in the world, for about $21 million. Three years later, Florsheim's status was changed from that of a subsidiary to a division of Interco. Florsheim was still run autonomously, however, with Harold Florsheim in charge of the division.

Florsheim quickly became International's most important unit. In fact, in its first decade as part of International, Florsheim thrived, increasing its sales nearly every year, while the parent company struggled for the most part. Between 1953 and 1963, Florsheim's sales doubled. By the end of that period, Florsheim was contributing an impressive 58 percent of International's earnings, while generating only about a quarter of its sales. Florsheim was the overwhelming leader among producers of better shoes for men (with prices of at least $20 per pair), controlling over 70 percent of that market. The company's success had much to do with Harold Florsheim's marketing innovations, as well as with the company's wise refusal to dilute its line with cheaper shoes, which could increase sales but would also trim its profit ratios.

Florsheim's operations were again expanded in the mid-1960s. Facilities at Cape Girardeau, Missouri, were enlarged, and, in 1966, 39 new company-owned retail outlets were added, bringing the total number of stores to 238, while the number of outside dealers selling Florsheim shoes reached 5,000. Furthermore, a new Florsheim plant was opened in Anna, Illinois, and soon thereafter one of that facility's units was converted for the additional production of women's shoes, which were sold through Interco's Thayer-McNeil chain of retail stores. Harold Florsheim became company chairperson in 1966. He held this position until his retirement three years later, and remained active in the company for several years before his death in 1987.

In 1971, two new Florsheim manufacturing facilities were launched, bringing the company's total to 14. Retail stores run by the company sold about 25 percent of the shoes produced in these plants. By the end of that year, there were 546 Florsheim outlets, and, of these, 75 were Thayer-McNeil Shoe Salons, where Florsheim's women's line was sold. The following year, 36 more stores were added, including seven Thayer-McNeils. However, later in the 1970s, Florsheim began to phase out its production of women's shoes. Although the company continued to operate its Thayer-McNeil stores, wholesale women's operations were cut out completely, and all outside retail accounts for women's shoes were discontinued.

During this time, an influx of imported shoes began to cripple the American shoe industry. By 1978, the number of U.S. workers in the industry was cut in half to 30,000. Furthermore, between 1980 and 1985, the share of imported men's shoes sold in the United States rose from 44 to 70 percent. As a response to this trend, Florsheim shifted more of its production to foreign countries, where labor was considerably less expensive. About 200 people were put out of work in 1986, when Florsheim closed its Poplar Bluff, Missouri, factory, a plant that had been in operation for 40 years. Despite this industry-wide downturn, Florsheim reintroduced women's shoes to its product line in 1986.

In 1985, Ronald Mueller took over as head of Florsheim. Mueller had worked for the company since 1951, when, at age 15, he was employed as an assistant window dresser. Under Mueller, Florsheim began to experiment with an electronic retailing system called the Florsheim Express Shop. The Express Shop was an interactive computerized system allowing stores to order shoes through a terminal connected to the warehouse at the company's Chicago headquarters, which maintained an inventory of 1.5 million pairs of shoes. The system allowed the customer to view the shoes on a video monitor, and to select any style or size in the 250-style Florsheim line. The buyer then received the shoes via UPS within a week. The test placements of the Express Shop were a clear-cut success. By mid-1987, the terminals were in place at 200 stores.

By the beginning of 1988, 336 Florsheim Express Shops were in operation in 16 states, and the company set a goal of maintaining a total of 2,000 Express Shops. Stores with the terminals installed generally showed increases of 15 to 33 percent in sales. During that year, Interco consolidated its International Shoe Company division into Florsheim, moving its operations into Florsheim's Chicago headquarters. Toward the end of the 1980s, there were actually fewer Florsheim stores, about 250 total, but these stores garnered more sales. This was partly due to a broadening of the Florsheim line to include casual and athletic shoes for the first time in the company's history, including the Florsheim Comfortech line, which incorporated elements of athletic and walking shoes into a dress shoe design. Many stores that had to supplement their inventories with lower priced casual shoes were now able to carry stock composed entirely of Florsheim products. In 1989, Florsheim stores that carried the company's comfort shoe line showed a ten percent increase in sales over the stores that did not.

Meanwhile, Florsheim continued to cut its production costs by moving more of its manufacturing overseas. Between 1986 and 1989, the portion of the company's shoes made in the United States shrank from 80 to less than 50 percent. In 1988 and 1989, nine Florsheim and International Shoe Co. factories in the United States were shut down, leaving only four domestic facilities in operation, all located in Missouri and southern Illinois. In 1990, the company began developing a franchising program, in which smaller stores were opened under franchise agreements in secondary markets (initially Council Bluffs, Iowa, and Clarksville, Tennessee), while the company continued to operate its own stores in the major market areas. Florsheim also began to withdraw from its leased shoe department arrangements in other stores due to their unimpressive sales volume.

Around this time, testing was begun on in-store sales at some well established chains, particularly Kuppenheimer's discount men's clothing stores and Sears, Roebuck & Co. outlets. The Sears test was a huge success, and in 1990, the company announced that Florsheim footwear boutiques would be opened at 100 Sears locations, replacing the regular men's shoe departments of stores in Chicago, Detroit, Milwaukee, southern California, New Jersey, New York, and Connecticut. The boutiques would include electronic Express Shop kiosks, which by this time numbered over 500 nationwide.

In 1991, Interco filed for Chapter 11 bankruptcy. Interco had been starved for cash since fighting off a 1988 takeover attempt by the Rales brothers through their private investment firm, City Capital Associates. That battle saddled Interco with a debt of $1.9 billion, which it sought to reduce by selling off or liquidating most of its holdings. Florsheim was one of the few parts of Interco left intact. In spite of Interco's problems, Florsheim remained active in the early 1990s. Two new shoe styles were introduced in 1991. One of them, the Bantam Walking Shoe, was an attempt to tap into the popular walking shoe market that had long been dominated by such brands as Rockport and Reebok. The Florsheim Comfortech Imperial was a new spin on Florsheim's traditional top-of-the-line Imperial, adding its patented Flor-Flex cushioning and heel padding.

A joint venture was also launched in 1991 with a Mexican investor to sell Florsheim shoes in Mexico. Although this project was reasonably successful, it too was sold off the following year by the cash-poor parent company. Florsheim made another international move in 1991, establishing a wholly-owned subsidiary in Italy, the company's most important European market. That year, the company focused on sales abroad, and was able to increase its exports by 35 percent.

Domestically, the alliance with Sears continued to pay off handsomely. A presence in such a widespread chain helped Florsheim increase its market share significantly. The arrangement also helped Sears, which benefitted from the presence of products with a reputation for high quality in its stores.

Although dress shoes remained Florsheim's principal product in the early 1990s, an overall shrinkage of the U.S. market for dress shoes prompted the company to focus more on casual footwear. Florsheim courted younger buyers in its attempt to beef up sales, unveiling a new, more modern, brass plate logo to replace its longstanding shield logo. Furthermore, the company hired popular sports commentator John Madden to endorse Florsheim shoes in media spots, a move which resulted in increased sales for the Comfortech line. The share of Florsheim's sales contributed by Comfortech (which sold an estimated one million pairs) grew from less than five percent to 23 percent in the four-year period ending in 1992.

The century old Florsheim Shoe Company possesses a far greater brand name recognition than any of its competitors. Although increasingly fewer pairs of dress shoes are being purchased in the United States, a trend that will likely continue, Florsheim is expected to increase its share of those shoes sold for a long time. Florsheim's ability to successfully expand during its parent company's bankruptcy is regarded by many as evidence of its solid grounding in its industry.

Further Reading:

Goldenburg, Jane, "Casuals, Athletic Lines Add to Florsheim Punch," *Footwear News,* January 9, 1989, p. 1; "Florsheim Puts Thumbs Up For Video Buying System," *Footwear News,* January 11, 1988, p. 10.

Gruber, William, "Florsheim Success Work of 'Sole' Man," *Chicago Tribune,* April 6, 1987, sec. 4, p. 4.

Howard, Tammi, Florsheim Mulls Reentry into Women's Wholesale," *Footwear News,* March 25, 1985, p.1.

"Interco: Making Big Strides," *Financial World,* February 9, 1972, p. 5.

"Interco Strides Toward Third Successive Peak," *Barron's,* April 17, 1967, p. 29.

Lassiter, Dawn, "Harold Florsheim Dies at 87; Industry Pioneer," *Footwear News,* February 9, 1987, p. 2.

Lazarus, George, "Florsheim Sees Good Fit in Franchising Venture," *Chicago Tribune,* February 6, 1990, sec. 3, p. 4.

"Nepotism: Good & Bad," *Forbes,* July 15, 1964, pp.32–33.

Randle, Wilma, "Florsheim Works to Capture Heart and Sole of Younger Men," *Chicago Tribune,* August 6, 1990, sec. 4, p. 1.

Rooney, Ellen, "Florsheim Grows Beyond Dress Shoe Foundation," *Footwear News,* August 31, 1992, p. 2; "Florsheim, Sears Team Up With Boutique Operations," *Footwear News,* September 10, 1990, p. 4.

Schechter, Dara, "Florsheim, Converse at Interco Still," *Footwear News,* January 16, 1989, p. 1.

Schmeltzer, John, "Florsheim Steps Forward While Parent Company Treads Water," *Chicago Tribune,* May 4, 1992, sec. 4, p. 1.

Waterman, Phil, "Interco Strides Toward Ninth Straight Peak Year," *Barron's,* February 21, 1972, pp. 26–28.

Wessling, Jack, "Florsheim Expanding Its Electronic Retailing," *Footwear News,* June 29, 1987, p. 2; "Int'l Shoe Name May Be Dropped," *Footwear News,* March 21, 1988, p. 1.

—Robert R. Jacobson

Four Seasons Hotels Inc.

1165 Leslie Street
Toronto, Ontario
Canada M3C 2K8
(416) 449-1750
Fax: (416) 441-4414

Public Company
Incorporated: 1961
Employees: 19,500
Revenues: $878.9 million
Stock Exchanges: Toronto Montreal
SICs: 7011 Hotels, Motels

Four Seasons Hotels Inc. is regarded as the most prestigious and opulent hotel chain in the world. Hotel lobbies typically feature Venetian chandeliers, antique tables, and Kirman rugs. Management at each hotel keeps meticulous records of hotel guests, and on return visits, guests are greeted by name, booked into the room with their favorite view, and provided with their preferred type of pillow and shampoo.

Four Seasons Hotels was founded by Isadore Sharp. Sharp's father, Max, emigrated from Poland to Palestine in 1920, where he helped build one of the first kibbutzim. Relocating to Toronto five years later, Max worked for a few years as a journeyman plasterer; he married and began a family that would include his son "Issy" and three daughters. Drawing on his home renovation experience, Max soon began purchasing houses, repairing and decorating them, and then selling them at a profit. Issy Sharp had lived in 15 houses by the time he was 16 years old.

Issy Sharp attended Toronto's Ryerson Polytechnical Institute and won high marks in architecture while distinguishing himself in athletics. After graduating, he worked alongside his father building small apartment buildings and houses. Determined to build a hotel on his own, Sharp struggled for five years to find the money in order to fulfill his dream. Unable to convince banks and venture capitalists that his hotel would succeed, Sharp finally turned to his brother-in-law, Eddie Creed, owner of a high fashion emporium in Toronto, and Creed's best friend, Murray Koffler, founder and chair of the Shoppers Drug Mart chain. These two men contributed $150,000 each to Sharp's project.

Still requiring over $700,000 in capital, Sharp approached one of his father's business acquaintances, Cecil Forsyth, who managed the mortgage department at Great West Life Insurance Company. Sharp's plan was to raise the rest of the necessary funds through a mortgage. Skeptical of Sharp's business acumen, Forsyth initially refused the application. However, he eventually yielded to Sharp's persistent requests, agreeing to provide the rest of the money.

Sharp's hotel cost nearly $1.5 million to establish and featured 126 rooms that would garner premium prices. Opening on the first day of spring in 1961, the Four Seasons Motor Hotel was an immediate success. Despite the hotel's location in a downtown Toronto area known for its prostitutes and indigent population, patrons were attracted to the structure's casual but upscale atmosphere, as well as its innovative inner courtyard surrounding a swimming pool. Soon the employees of the Canadian Broadcast System, located across the street, adopted the hotel as their after work watering hole, signalling the beginning of the hotel's celebrity association.

From the time the Four Seasons opened for business, Sharp created a climate that fostered professionalism and devotion among his employees. He initiated a profit-sharing plan, scheduled two "stress breaks" every day, and paid his front desk clerks twice the average rate, asserting their importance in providing the public with its first impression of the hotel. One of the more notable examples of employee dedication involved Roy Dyment, a bellboy at Four Seasons since 1967. Dyment discovered that a dignitary had left his briefcase behind after checking out, and he felt responsible since he hadn't placed the briefcase in the limousine trunk. When the worried guest phoned from Washington, stating that the material in the briefcase was essential for an upcoming meeting, Dyment purchased a plane ticket at his own expense and delivered the briefcase personally.

Sharp's second venture in the hotel business proved even riskier than his first. Launched in 1963, Toronto's Inn on the Park was built on 17 acres in a desolate area north of the city, where the only nearby business was a large garbage dump. Short $1 million before the start of construction, Sharp and his father again approached the obdurate Cecil Forsyth, this time for a loan. Forsyth, impressed by Sharp's instant success with the motor hotel, didn't hesitate in providing the money. Despite its location, Sharp's second hotel was also successful, and the area he had chosen for the 569-room resort hotel quickly grew into a sprawling corporate suburbia.

Next, Sharp sought to establish a hotel overlooking London's historic Hyde Park. In doing so, he ignored market research indicating that a new luxury hotel in that location would have trouble competing with such established first class hotels as the Dorchester, Claridge, and Savoy. Sharp opened his 227-room Inn on the Park in 1970. Despite its higher rates and the overcrowded market, the Inn on the Park enjoyed a 95 percent occupancy rate and became one of the most profitable hotels in the world. Its small size, luxurious appointments, and impeccable service were all elements that had become Sharp's personal trademark.

In the early 1970s, Sharp began developing hotels in smaller, less urban areas. He opened an inn in Belleville, Ontario, whose population was 35,000, and spent a year operating a resort in Nassau. Shortly thereafter, he built a luxury condo hotel in Israel that was marginally profitable but experienced difficulties maintaining staff, owing largely to the Israeli draft for military service. Plans for hotel projects in Europe were postponed due to disagreements with potential partners from Paris and Athens; when construction finally started on a hotel in Rome, workers kept uncovering Roman artifacts, and preservationists were able to block further construction on the site. Hoping to develop residential and office buildings in both Canada and Florida, Sharp was continually thwarted by civic officials, who placed restrictions on commercial development.

Undismayed by his setbacks, in 1972 Sharp approached the Sheraton division of ITT Corporation and proposed a joint Four Seasons-Sheraton partnership. The result was the Toronto Four-Seasons Sheraton, a 1,450-room establishment whose first year of operation was plagued by cost overruns, disagreements with city building inspectors, and a singles event which resulted in a temporary suspension of the hotel's liquor license. Although Sharp was hired as assistant manager of the property, he had no real authority to make decisions. In 1976, he finally sold his 49 percent interest for $18.5 million and decided to return to what he did best: developing and operating mid-sized hotels that catered to the luxury market.

That year Sharp purchased his first American property, The Clift, an elegant but aging hotel in San Francisco. Moreover, he opened the Four Seasons Hotel in Vancouver, and, one year later, won a bidding war to manage the new Ritz-Carlton in Chicago. In 1978, Sharp bought a property from Hyatt Hotels in Toronto and remodeled it to suit the Four Seasons style. This Four Seasons Hotel offered service to the wealthy, who frequented Yorkville, Toronto's most exclusive shopping district. In 1979, the Four Seasons Hotel in Washington began operations, and a short time later Sharp opened the first of several hotel and resort properties in Texas. One of Sharp's most successful moves came in 1981 with The Pierre, a landmark hotel in New York frequently cited as one of the best in the city. With a multimillion dollar renovation, The Pierre developed into a showcase of Four Seasons' style and service.

Many hoteliers, Sharp included, followed Conrad Hilton's strategy of managing properties rather than owning them. From 1980 to 1985, Four Seasons opened hotels with a value of over $500 million at a cost of only $15 million. Nevertheless, Four Seasons also owned many properties, and in the early 1980s Sharp initiated an expensive renovation drive of the hotels in which it was owner or part-owner. By 1982, the hotel chain had approximated $116 million in long-term debt.

In order to lessen this debt, Four Seasons began selling its assets. Between 1980 and 1985, nearly $31.2 million worth of assets were sold, including equity in Montreal, Toronto, and San Francisco. Nevertheless, Four Seasons continued to manage these hotels under long-term contracts. When Sharp, Creed, and Koffler, the three original investors, created a new company

to manage such non-hotel assets as development property and a laundry, another $22 million in debt was eliminated. The company's final tactic was to apply $30 million of an initial $60 million raised from a stock offering to reducing the remainder of the debt. Through these three moves, Four Seasons' debt-equity ratio was reduced to a comfortable 1:1 ratio by 1986.

When Four Seasons first publicly issued shares in the company in 1969, stock shares climbed as high as $22. However, after the erratic management and declining profits of the early and mid-1970s, Four Seasons stock had plummeted to only four dollars per share by 1977. Sharp and his partners then decided that it was in their best interest to turn Four Seasons into a private company. In 1985, when they decided to take Four Seasons public again, both Creed and Koffler retained an eight percent stake in the company but sold $8.5 million worth of stock. Sharp agreed to the public offering on the condition that a class of "multiple voting shares" be created for him. As a result of this arrangement, Sharp tightened his grip on Four Seasons; while the public had one vote for each share, Sharp's multiple voting shares carried 12 votes for each share. With a 29 percent share of Four Seasons equity and 83 percent of the votes, Sharp planned to thwart any takeover threat in the future.

During the late 1980s, Four Seasons began examining the world's financial centers, such as Tokyo, Paris, and Frankfurt, for development sites. Expansion proceeded slowly as Sharp wanted only premium locations and refused to settle for less. From 1988 onward however, the acquisition, development, and building of properties was rapid.

By 1992, with the acquisition of Regent International Hotels Limited, a leading operator of luxury hotels in Asia and Australia, Sharp had created the largest network of luxury hotels in the world. Together Four Seasons and Regent International Hotels own and operate 45 medium-sized luxury properties and resorts in 19 countries around the world. In 1992 and 1993, Four Seasons opened hotels in Bali, Milan, and London. New construction and development was ongoing in Singapore, New York, Mexico City, Paris, Berlin, Jakarta, and Prague, and resort properties were under development in Hawaii and California.

With a 1:1 employee-guest ratio, gourmet cuisine, and sumptuous decor resulting in accolades from such diverse publications as *Consumer Reports, Mobil Travel Guide* and *Conde'Nast Traveler Magazine,* Sharp nevertheless strove to improve his properties. His goal was to transform the name Four Seasons into a common phrase for high-quality hotels, and, during the early 1990s, he believed this goal was well within his reach.

Further Reading:

"Issy: Quality Innkeeper—Quality Gentleman," *Report on Business Magazine,* June 1986, pp. 612.
Kummer, Corby, et al., "Does Isadore Sharp Run the Best Hotels Anywhere?" *Connoisseur,* February 1990, pp. 72–76.
Olive, David, "Puttin' on the Ritz," *Report on Business Magazine,* June 1986, pp. 28–35.

—Thomas Derdak

Franklin/Templeton Group of Funds

Franklin Resources, Inc.

777 Mariners Island Blvd.
San Mateo, California 94404
U.S.A.
(415) 312-3000
Fax: (415) 312-3832

Public Company
Incorporated: 1969
Employees: 3,000
Assets: $87 billion
Stock Exchanges: New York
SICs: 6282 Investment Advice; 6719 Holding Companies,
Nec

California-based Franklin Resources, Inc. is the nation's largest manager of municipal funds and one of the nation's fastest-growing and largest mutual fund companies. Although Franklin is a public company, nearly half of its stock is owned by the two brothers who lead the company, Charles and Rupert Johnson. With its purchase of Templeton, Galbraith & Hansberger Ltd. in 1992, Franklin controlled more than $87 billion in assets.

Franklin Resources began as a small fund business founded in 1947. When Charles B. Johnson took over from his father in 1957, the company managed assets of about $2 million. With a staff consisting of Johnson and one other employee, the company slowly began to grow. Much of Franklin's success has been attributed to Charlie Johnson's shrewd recognition that even the world of investment services could benefit from proper marketing—that is, by designing products for specific markets and then promoting those products appropriately to reach the target markets. Some industry insiders have suggested that Franklin was more important as a marketing success than for its investment success.

Franklin Resources went public in 1971. While a stock market crash in 1973–74 nearly wiped out the company, it bounced back stronger than before. Johnson started one of the first funds specializing in gold stocks; the fund gained momentum in the late 1970s as inflation rose. Franklin offered a succession of new fund products during the 1980s, a decade in which the percentage of families investing in mutual funds grew from six to about 25 percent. By the end of the decade, Franklin was running 73 funds.

In the early 1980s, while other fund companies anticipated a rush for equity funds, Franklin maintained that the action would be in fixed income funds. Franklin pioneered mortgage-backed securities and single-state municipal bonds. Franklin's $14.2 billion Franklin U.S. Government Securities Fund was the nation's first fund to invest in Government National Mortgage Association bonds. Then Johnson introduced the $14.3 billion California Tax-Free Income Fund, the first tax-free state bond fund in the United States; income from this fund earned by California residents was not subject to state or federal income tax. With high state income taxes and falling interest rates, the timing on this new product could not have been better. Investors were taking their money out of money funds and looking to invest in tax-free yields instead. By 1984, the state fund had grown to $825 million, doubling the assets that Franklin managed to $2 billion. By 1990, these two funds would account for half of Franklin's $49 billion in mutual fund assets.

During the mid-1980s, while other companies were starting overseas funds, Franklin continued to offer U.S.-based funds to U.S. buyers. Like many other investment companies, Franklin also planned to offer credit cards, consumer loans, and insured certificates of deposit. Furthermore, Franklin bought a real estate syndicate for $11 million. By this time, the company had become a real family business. Charles and his brother Rupert owned 40 to 50 percent of company stock. Four other family members also worked at Franklin, including Harvard M.B.A., Charles E. Johnson, and two of Charles's other children.

In 1987, while stocks were rising, Franklin stocks slipped, but when the market crashed in the fall, Franklin barely dropped, and its low-risk funds became a popular place to protect savings. The following year, Franklin announced that it would open an Adjustable-Rate Mortgage Securities Fund, which would still protect the investor's principal but would also pay higher returns on investment. Franklin funds remained conservative investments.

While most funds did little advertising directly to consumers, Johnson believed strongly in the power of advertising Franklin's funds. During the 1980s, Johnson dramatically increased the advertising for his fast-growing company and its funds. Unlike Fidelity Investments, the nation's largest mutual fund company, Franklin sold its funds through broker-dealers rather than directly to investors. In 1990, Franklin began a print ad campaign to make sure its name was familiar to investors and potential investors. Johnson told *Forbes* magazine, "Our feeling was that name recognition was important." Johnson even hired quarterback Joe Montana to peddle funds on television ads. Johnson noted that a celebrity such as Montana would reach people who ordinarily might not even pay attention to an ad for financial services.

In the 1990s, Franklin was looking for opportunities abroad. In 1992, it was able to gain an immediate presence abroad through acquisition of another major player in the mutual funds market—Templeton, Galbraith & Hansberger Ltd., a mutual funds management company. Franklin Resources acquired Templeton for $913 million and was thereby elevated from fifth to fourth place on the mutual-funds companies list in the United States. The only larger mutual funds companies were Fidelity Investments, Merrill Lynch, and Vanguard Group. Franklin alone already controlled $69 billion in assets, and the purchase of Templeton gave Franklin management combined assets of almost $90 billion. The sale also meant that Franklin could sell Templeton's overseas funds to U.S. shareholders and sell its own funds in the foreign market Templeton had established. The sale of Templeton to Franklin was the largest transaction ever involving an independent mutual fund company.

Franklin decided to operate Templeton as a separate subsidiary. Although Franklin and Templeton funds had little in common, they were excellent complements to one another. Templeton 80-year-old founder John Templeton, renowned in investment circles for his ability to pick stocks, told *The Wall Street Journal*, "The two organizations fit like a hand in a glove." They both sold their funds through brokers and financial planners and charged an up-front sales fee; Templeton emphasized equities, while Franklin stressed fixed-income funds; and Templeton mostly managed global funds while Franklin generally managed U.S. funds. Officials predicted that shareholders soon would be able to move funds between the two without penalty to diversify their holdings. At the time of the transaction, John Templeton's stock in his company was valued at $440 million, and he was expected to continue as an adviser to Franklin-Templeton.

Although the price for acquiring Templeton was high, Franklin was well positioned to handle it, having almost no debt at the time, $370 million in cash and other liquid assets, and financial backing from Chemical Bank and Hellman & Friedman. John Templeton and other Templeton shareholders were also willing to invest $75 million in the merger by buying restricted Franklin stock. The Templeton company also had the advantage of being based in the Bahamas where the tax rate on profits was far lower than that in the United States.

Franklin's negotiating team was headed by Charles E. Johnson, oldest son of Franklin's president and chairperson, Charles B. Johnson. The younger Johnson saw the acquisition as a key move, since he believed that any company that wanted to remain an important player in the fund market had to "go global." Johnson, senior vice-president and head of corporate development, was expected to lead the company when his father retired.

According to a 1992 *Business Week* article, the fund industry had grown 500 percent in the previous ten years. During that time, Franklin's total assets under management grew 3,000 percent, and its stock price skyrocketed by more than 42,000 percent, with much of this growth on a diet of fixed-income funds—U.S. government securities and municipal bonds. Franklin's staff also grew from 26 to more than 3,000 employees.

The immense profits of the 1980s had also prompted an excessive fee lawsuit against Franklin. Two shareholders, filing their suit in 1987, accused Franklin of charging excessive fees for managing its Franklin U.S. Government Securities Fund. This was the first excessive fee suit involving a bond mutual fund to go to trial, although five other suits had been filed—and dismissed—for excessive fees involved in management of money market mutual funds. In 1990, a judge dismissed the complaint against Franklin after a six-day trial, noting that the only main arguments presented by the plaintiffs was that Franklin "simply made too much money managing that fund." The judge ruled that Franklin's after-tax profit was "reasonable," and that the plaintiffs "failed to prove that Franklin realized economies of scale as the fund increased in size, or that economies of scale, if realized, were not shared with investors."

Fiscal problems in California caused some concern for mutual fund companies in the early 1990s. Franklin managed the $12 billion California Tax Free Income Fund, the nation's largest tax-exempt bond mutual fund, and the company was confident that few if any of the riskier bonds—known as Mello-Roos bonds—would default. However, Franklin remained the largest holder of Mello-Roos bonds, which were sold to finance infrastructure development in new communities in the state. According to *The Wall Street Journal*, Mello-Roos bonds did not trade often and were not rated by credit-rating companies; a default could send holders hurrying to sell. Franklin therefore remained cautious in its California investments.

According to financial experts, the dramatic growth that Franklin enjoyed in the 1980s would be difficult to maintain in the 1990s. While the company had earnings growth of 65 percent per year in the 1980s, earnings and asset growth were down to eight percent in 1990, a respectable growth rate for most companies but slow compared to the rapid growth that investors had enjoyed in the previous decade. Nevertheless, in the early 1990s, Franklin's growth rate was expected to continue at ten to 12 percent a year.

Further Reading:

Clements, Jonathan, "Mutual Funds: Templeton Sets Sale of Funds to Franklin," *The Wall Street Journal*, August 3, 1992, p. C1.
——. "Publicly Traded Mutual Funds Rake in Money," *The Wall Street Journal*, April 29, 1991, p. C2.
Heins, John, "All in the Fund Family," *Forbes*, September 8, 1986, p. 248.
Laderman, Jeffrey M., "Humdrum, Humble—And Now a Real Heavyweight," *Business Week*, August 17, 1992, p. 30.
Raghavan, Anita, "Mutual Funds: Fiscal Clouds Darken California Municipal Bond Funds," *The Wall Street Journal*, November 29, 1991, p. C1.
Stodghill, Ron, "John Templeton Unplugs the Stock Ticker," *Business Week*, August 17, 1992, p. 31.

—Wendy J. Stein

The Gates Corporation

900 Broadway
P.O. Box 5887
Denver, Colorado 80217
U.S.A.
(303) 744-1911
Fax: (303) 744-4000

Private Company
Founded: 1911
Employees: 17,000
Sales: $1.45 billion

The Gates Corporation is one of the largest privately held companies in the United States with sales of more than $1.4 billion from automotive and industrial rubber products, formed-fiber products, automotive accessory-drive systems, and petroleum property development. Its Gates Rubber Company, the largest of its subsidiaries, generates about 75 percent of the company's total revenues and is considered the world's largest non-tire rubber company.

The Gates Corporation traces its origins to 1911, when Charles Gates Sr. bought the Colorado Tire and Leather Company in Denver, Colorado. Gates had originally headed west in 1904 after graduating from the Michigan College of Mining and Technology. He took a job as a mining superintendent near Tin Cup, Colorado, but upon hearing of a gold strike in Nevada, he headed there and was hired as a mine engineer for the Nevada United Mines Company. In 1910, he settled in Denver, married, and started looking for a business to buy. The *Denver Post*'s classifieds listed three companies for sale: a manufacturer of soap, a manufacturer of toilet paper, and a mail order company that sold tire covers. Charles, age 33, and his wife Hazel, bought the Colorado Tire and Leather Company for their entire combined savings of $3,500.

The business consisted of a one-room shop with a typewriter and one 18-year old employee. The company's only product was the Durable Tread tire cover, a studded leather band that attached to the car tires to extend the life of the tires. The former owner of the Colorado Tire and Leather Company had shown the Gateses stacks of invoices, promising a healthy profit every month. After buying the company, however, Charles and Hazel Gates found they had been tricked. The piles of invoices represented not one month but several months worth of orders, many of which were withdrawn when the company changed hands.

Furthermore, the company had incurred a significant debt and along with the invoices were several bills. Undaunted, Charles managed to persuade his brother John, an engineer, to join the company too.

Although the tire covers proved a worthy product, only about 5,000 cars were in use in Denver in 1911. The Gateses were selling a product that had too small a local market for the company to survive, let alone thrive. The two brothers launched an aggressive sales campaign through direct mail to reach the automobile users back east. In eighteen months, the business had 18 employees and showed a profit of $200.

The power of advertising again helped Gates to expand its product line. The Colorado Tire and Leather Company became the largest halter manufacturer in the west after the Gates brothers persuaded Buffalo Bill Cody to try the horse halters the company made from leather scraps. Buffalo Bill's testimonial boosted sales, even though the halters cost twice as much as those of the competition.

Over the next few years, Gates introduced other new products, including car fan belts, blowout patches, and emergency boots for tires. But by 1914, a new material was being introduced into many products—rubber—and it was the perfect material for car tires, belts, and hoses because of its flexibility, adhesion, and durability. Gates abandoned leather tire covers and embraced the new technology, introducing retreads made of fabric and rubber.

Colorado Tire and Leather Company soon outgrew its rented space. The Gateses invested $15,000 in the construction of a small two-story building to accommodate the company. The second floor was used for halter production, and the first floor housed the company's offices and production facilities for the Half-Sole, a retread made of rubber fabric that could be cemented to a worn tire. The Half Sole became one of the company's biggest successes.

In 1917, the company's name was changed to the International Rubber Company to reflect its new direction. That year John Gates developed the first rubber and fabric V-belt for use in the automobile. His first version of this car part was made of twine dipped in rubber cement, coated with fabric, and vulcanized in a mold, providing a superior product to the simple, hemp rope then in use on car radiator fans. The V-belt would remain a mainstay of the Gates company.

Gates's company was busy during the first World War. The government classified the Half Sole as a priority product due to the rubber it conserved. After the war, however, the price of rubber dropped from $1.25 to 15 cents a pound, and the Half Sole protective cover became obsolete as tires became inexpensive to manufacture. In 1919, the Gates brothers were forced to develop a new product to take the place of the Half Sole, and the company began manufacturing balloon tires. That year the company was again renamed as The Gates Rubber Company.

During 1920 Gates faced several challenges. Economic recession left tire manufacturers with huge inventories of tires, which they had stockpiled because of the low cost of rubber, and now they were forced to cut prices and operating costs. Despite the poor economy, Charles Gates decided to market a new tire it had developed. The revolutionary Super Tread, so named because of its wider, heavier tread that increased mileage, was introduced during this time, and while tire sales dropped 35 percent nationwide, tire sales for the Gates company increased 40 percent in 1921. Meanwhile, Gates's company developed and marketed belts in 20 sizes to fit most cars on the market. The introduction of the car generator during this time caused sales of the Gates V-belt to nearly double. Towards the end of the decade, Gates introduced molded rubber goods such as hydraulic seals and also began manufacturing garden hoses and radiator hoses.

When the stock market crashed in 1929 and the economy plummeted, Gates managed to remain profitable. Moreover, the company increased its focus on marketing, putting more representatives out in the field to drum up business. The Gates Rubber Company weathered the Great Depression, and, in fact, by 1934, had 2,500 employees, annual sales of $13 million, and a position as the sixth largest rubber company in the United States. The company was manufacturing more than 4,000 rubber products, which Gates called "necessary accessories to essentials," items that people would need despite national events or the ups and downs of the economy.

When the country became involved in World War II in 1941, Gates's products were essential. As men left for military service, hundreds of women began working in the company factories to help meet the wartime demand for belts, tires, and other parts for military vehicles. However, when the Japanese captured Singapore and the Dutch Indies, U.S. access to natural rubber was virtually cut off, with the country having only about six months worth of rubber stockpiled. To sustain the war effort, the rubber industry needed hundreds of thousands of tons of scrap rubber to recycle. Although Americans across the country undertook a great rubber collection drive, even taking the tires off their cars and donating rubber boots and raincoats, the nation needed still more rubber.

During this time, synthetic rubber had been developed and produced, but only in small laboratory quantities. In response to the country's need, U.S. rubber companies, including Gates, joined forces to form the Copolymer Corporation to manufacture synthetic rubber. Charles Gates's son, Charles Jr., spent three years at this company as an assistant chief engineer. During the war years, research was also ongoing in the development of synthetic fibers such as rayon and nylon.

The postwar years were prosperous for the country and Gates Rubber. Demand was high for new products. Between 1946 and 1954, sales at Gates increased from $59 million to $82 million. The company, which by this time employed a staff of nearly 5,500, was the world's largest manufacturer of V-belts and the sixth largest rubber company in the United States. Gates had expanded from a one-room shop to a 53-acre complex with more than 30 buildings.

In 1954, Gates opened its first plant outside of Denver in Brantford, Ontario. In 1958, a second plant outside of Denver was opened, this time in Sioux City, Iowa. Other facilities followed in Toluca, Mexico; Nashville, Tennessee; Cleveland, Ohio; and Charlotte, North Carolina. The company also built a $1-million addition in Denver and tripled the size of its plant in Canada. In 1960, Gates opened a tread rubber plant in Chicago and acquired a metal sheave plant in Wichita, Kansas.

Charles Gates Sr. died in 1961 at the age of 83. His son, Charles Jr., then 40, succeeded him as company president and chairperson. Pointing out that the company's hose and belt market was already mature and was unlikely to grow very rapidly in decades to come, Charles Gates Jr. set about diversifying the company's operations.

Gates referred to his early years as president as his "gunslinging years," during which he made some very diverse acquisitions: a cattle and guest ranch called the A Bar A, Inc., an automated egg farm, a trucking company, an aviation service, and a mutual funds business. In 1967, he acquired the Learjet Corporation, which was in serious financial trouble. Although Gates had to sink millions into the crippled company, he turned the company around after about 18 months, and Learjet remained profitable for many years.

Gates also acquired 3,000 acres in Colorado Springs, Colorado, and formed the Gates Land Company to oversee development of a planned community called Cheyenne Mountain Ranch. The community included housing developments, industrial and business parks, a conference center and resort, and retail shopping.

Although many of Gates's efforts were unsuccessful, he did establish The Gates Rubber Company as an international business. Ventures included Gates South Africa; belt and hose plants in Belgium, Scotland, Germany, France, Spain, Brazil, Canada; and joint ventures in Venezuela, Korea, and Japan. Domestic expansion continued, with plants in Rockford and Galesburg, Illinois; Elizabethtown, Kentucky; Moncks Corner, South Carolina; Jefferson, North Carolina; Siloam Springs, Arkansas; Iola, Kansas; Boone, Iowa; Charleston, Versailes, and Poplar Bluff, Missouri; and Red Bay, Alabama. In 1970, Gates undertook a Japanese joint venture, Unitta Company, Ltd., to manufacture synchronous belts for automotive and industrial customers. Business increased when the Japanese automakers switched to the manufacture of belt-driven overhead cam engines. Domestic expansion also continued, with plant openings in Rockford, Illinois; Elizabeth, Kentucky; and Wichita Falls, Texas. Furthermore, the company introduced new, smaller, and more efficient plants in Kansas, Arkansas, North Carolina, Missouri, and Alabama.

The company's growth was halted when the United States entered an economic recession in the early 1970s. During this time, the Gates Rubber Company had plans to retool its tire plants to produce radial tires, which were taking over the tire industry. The recession forced a tough decision: rather than retool, Gates withdrew from the tire market.

However, new opportunities also arose. In 1970 Gates scientists produced a completely sealed lead-acid rechargeable battery, the first commercially viable battery of this type. The new Gates Energy Products division was introduced to produce these batteries. This Gates company grew rapidly once the U.S. economy recovered from the recession. In 1987 Gates acquired General Electric's battery business, and by 1990, Gates Energy Products had sales of more than $182 million. The division offered a complete line of nickel-cadmium, nickel-hydrogen, and sealed-lead batteries for consumer, industrial, and aerospace use. In 1990, Gates brought out a nickel metal-hydride rechargeable battery for use in communications and computers.

Gates' most successful battery product became its line of sealed-lead rechargeable consumer batteries used in many handheld appliances. However, in 1993, Gates announced it would sell its nickel-based battery operations to Eveready Battery Co. due to disappointing sales figures.

In 1980, Gates sales topped $1 billion. Two years later, The Gates Corporation was established as the parent company to all other Gates operations. The company also acquired Imperial Eastman hydraulic coupling facilities in Great Britain and France. In 1983, Gates acquired Murray Rubber Company and from that purchase created Gates Molded Products. Gates Data Products Division was also formed that year to produce electronic equipment components. However, this business was discontinued in 1985.

The following year, Gates Formed-Fibre Products was established with the purchase of a division of Albany International Corporation. Some of its Automotive products included molded trunk parts for GM, Nissan, and Mazda, carpeted door panel inserts for Ford Motor Company, as well as other trim panels and fabric-covered surfaces. In 1992, this company grossed $54.5 million.

In 1986, Gates undertook a $20-million expansion of its facilities in Elizabethtown, Kentucky, to produce its Poly Chain GT belts. The company also purchased the Uniroyal Power Transmission Company which had five plants and more than 1,700 employees. With this acquisition, Gates became the world's largest synchronous/timing belt maker.

The Gates Rubber Company subsidiary was also expanding during this time. In 1987, it acquired Industrias Vulca S.A. of Spain and the V-belt operations of Gates' former Spanish licensee, Firestone Hispania, as well as Scandura's industrial matting and sheeting operation in Scotland. In 1990, the rubber division opened another V-belt plant in Spain and a synchronous belt plant in Scotland. The following year, it completed a belt plant and began production in a joint venture in South Korea.

A new division was launched in 1988 when Gates purchased Spun Steel, Inc., renaming it Gates Power Drive Products, Inc. The division produced pulleys, idlers, tensioners and mounting brackets, and accessory drive systems. Headquartered in Michigan and operating one U.S. plant and three facilities in Canada, the power drive division was a major supplier to U.S. automakers. Sales in 1993 totaled about $90 million. Furthermore, products from this company were being introduced to markets in Europe and the Pacific Rim. The division was also working with The Gates Rubber Company in a new center in Germany to introduce original equipment Gates products to European automakers.

By 1993, The Gates Corporation had 17,000 employees, with about 9,000 working in the United States. The company operated 46 plants and 35 distribution and service centers. Its products were marketed by a network of more than 150,000 dealers, distributors, and representatives in more than 100 countries. The Gates Rubber Company alone had facilities in 14 foreign countries.

Another economic recession in 1991 halted sales growth again for The Gates Corporation, largely because of declining car sales among Japanese and American automakers whom Gates supplied. In 1992, Gates showed some increase in sales although recovery from recession was slow. Total revenue was $1.45 billion, with sales of $1.09 billion from The Gates Rubber Company, an increase of a little more than seven percent over the previous year. Like many other companies in the United States, the Gates companies pointed to skyrocketing health care costs as a major problem severely affecting its earnings.

In the early 1990s executives at The Gates Corporation considered foreign growth vital to the prosperity of the company. In 1992, Gates Corporation operations included 11 facilities in four Latin American countries; eight facilities in six countries in the Asia/Pacific region; 19 facilities in eight European nations; and three facilities in Canada.

In 1992, Gates Rubber Company's manufacturing operations in 14 foreign countries accounted for almost half of the company's total sales. Gates Rubber's international president L.G. Estenfelder remarked that without these foreign operations, the company would not have achieved its high level of export sales. Although many Americans argued that building overseas plants took jobs away from American workers, Estenfelder told *Colorado Business Magazine* that those foreign plants enabled the company to establish a strong presence in those markets and were the key to building exports. He also asserted that "we haven't nearly exhausted our international growth potential."

Gates Rubber Company considered Asia and Latin America, in particular, to be areas offering opportunity for the company in the years to come. Gates Korea secured adoption of its synchronous belts by all four Korean car companies in 1992, its first full year of operation. This division also began supplying a new belt to the North American automotive replacement market. Unitta, Gates's joint venture in Japan, was ready to supply automatic belt tensioners to the Japanese automotive original equipment markets and to increase its sale of high-temperature longer lasting synchronous belts. Gates was also one of only nine Japanese members of Nissan Motor Company's exclusive supplier association. The Gates facility in Toluca, Mexico, began producing and shipping its first Micro-V belts to U.S. markets in the early 1990s. Al Stecklien, Gates Rubber Company's president of Asia/Pacific and Latin America operations, predicted that "Gates has an exciting future in both Asia and Latin America. These are two of the fastest-growing regions in the world where our presence will increase as we continue to invest in technology and increased capacity."

Principal Subsidiaries: The Gates Rubber Company; Gates Formed-Fibre Products, Inc.; Gates Power Drive Products, Inc.; Gates Land Company; A Bar A, Inc.; Cody Energy, Inc.

Further Reading:

The Gates Story, Denver: The Gates Corporation, 1990.
The Gates Corporation Annual Report, Denver: The Gates Corporation, 1992.
Reed, Carson, "L.G. Estenfelder: President Gates Rubber Co. International Division," *Colorado Business Magazine,* November 1990, p. 17.

—Wendy J. Stein

GE Aircraft Engines

1 Neumann Way
Cincinnati, Ohio 45215-6301
U.S.A.
(513) 243-6136
Fax: (513) 786-1568

Wholly Owned Subsidiary of the General Electric Company
Incorporated: 1941
Employees: 29,100
Sales: $7.37 billion
SICs: 3724 Aircraft Engines and Engine Parts; 3519 Internal
  Combustion Engines Nec

The GE Aircraft Engines unit of the General Electric Company is the world's leading manufacturer of aircraft propulsion systems. The company attributes its success in the industry to heavy investment in research and development, stringent quality control, and excellent customer relations. GE Aircraft Engines is also one of the nation's top exporters, supplying engines for a wide range of commercial and military aircraft, boats, hydrofoils, and industrial power generators.

One of more than a dozen independently managed divisions of General Electric, GE Aircraft Engines traces its origins to 1901, when its parent company began development of steam turbine systems. These turbines maximized the extraction of energy from steam pressure by using a series of fan blades to drive power generators. As a leader in electric power generation, General Electric adapted the turbine concept to accept other forms of pressurized energy. In 1903 GE scientist Dr. Sanford Moss developed America's first gas-powered turbine, regarded by some as the ancestor of the jet engine.

During World War I, the aircraft industry recognized the need for light engines that could provide the same power as larger models. During this time, many planes were unable to climb and maneuver at altitudes above 5,000 feet, and many simply stalled, their engines unable to function effectively at high altitudes, where the air was thinner. In 1919, drawing on its experience with turbine compression systems, GE developed a supercharger, which took energy from the rotation of a piston engine's crank shaft and used it to compress the air in the engine's cylinders. This enabled conventional engines to burn more fuel and increase their power. By 1939 superchargers had become a necessary part of advanced aircraft, and GE had become an important manufacturer of these devices.

The leading engine builders during this period were Pratt & Whitney, whose Wasp engine dominated the industry, and Curtiss-Wright, manufacturer of the Cyclone engine. GE's experience with aircraft propulsion was strictly limited to turbo-compression systems; the company had never built an aircraft engine. However, their inexperience would later prove to be a tremendous asset.

In 1939 British inventor Frank Whittle successfully tested a revolutionary new type of gas turbine. This engine used a series of fan blades to compress air into a combustion chamber. A high-grade fuel was then detonated in this chamber, causing enormous pressure. The gases from the detonation were channeled through a tailpipe, where they passed additional fan blades that drove the compressor fans at the front of the engine. In the process, the gases expelled through the tailpipe produced enormous amounts of thrust. Whittle's engine was capable of propelling an aircraft at speeds nearly double those of even supercharged, piston-powered aircraft.

Realizing that a similar engine was under development in Germany, the British sought to gain an advantage in the war by being the first to develop a jet aircraft. However, Britain's leading engine builder, Rolls-Royce, was swamped with orders for piston engines and unable to devote full attention to Whittle's engine. So the British turned to the United States with an offer to license development of Whittle's engine. Concerned about the competition that Rolls-Royce would face after the war, the British government stipulated that top U.S. manufacturers Pratt & Whitney, Curtiss-Wright, and Allison not be awarded the license. Rather, they opted to select the licensee from three companies whose emphasis was on the research and development of turbine engines and not on manufacturing: Allis Chalmers, Westinghouse, and GE.

GE created a separate engine division within its supercharger group in October 1941, and shortly thereafter it won a contract to develop the Whittle engine. The engine unit established design and production facilities at Lockland, Ohio; Lynn, Massachusetts; and Schenectady, New York. Dr. Moss was called out of retirement to aid in the construction of the jet engine.

The first of the company's designs, the GE I-A, was built and successfully tested six months later. The engine was matched to the Bell Aircraft XP-59A, which made its first flight in October 1942. Unbeknownst to GE and Rolls-Royce, however, German engineers had successfully flown their own jet aircraft two years earlier.

While the I-A could generate great thrust, it guzzled fuel, vibrated badly, and contained parts that wore out quickly. GE continued to improve the engine, hoping to develop a model that would be practical for aerial combat.

The first American jet suitable for combat didn't emerge until after the war, when GE's I-40/J33 engine was matched with the Lockheed P-80 Shooting Star. The company also developed the T31, its first turboprop—or jet-powered propeller—engine. This engine was the first from GE to incorporate an axial flow compressor, as opposed to the traditional centrifugal compressor.

By 1946 the axial flow design had been incorporated into a new engine, the J35. Able to produce 4,000 pounds of thrust, the J35 was chosen to drive the Boeing B-47 and Northrop B-49 flying wing. Allison, with whom GE maintained a close relationship, acquired licenses to build the J33 and J35 that year.

But when the government's carefully orchestrated coordination of the industry ended, GE terminated its technological partnership with Allison and began work on a new design, the J47. This 5,000-pound thrust engine powered the North American F-86 and B-45 and helped UN forces maintain air superiority over Russian-built MiG jet fighters during the Korean War.

Westinghouse lost its competitive edge in jet engines when it proved unable to adapt to changes specified by the Navy, losing millions of dollars in potential contracts. Stepping in to take its place was Pratt & Whitney, a major subcontractor to Westinghouse that was eager to enter the jet engine market.

While the GE staff, now under veteran Harold Kelsey, was busy developing its J73, with 7,000 pounds of thrust, Pratt & Whitney began work on a 10,000-pound engine, the J57/JT3. This engine immediately established Pratt & Whitney as a major force in jet propulsion, particularly after it was chosen to power Boeing's massive new B-52 bomber.

GE introduced a new high-performance J79 engine in 1953. This engine powered the Convair B-58, Lockheed F-104, and McDonnell F-4 Phantom. Unlike Pratt & Whitney's J57, the J79 was designed for supersonic flight aboard lighter strike fighters and bombers.

While GE and Pratt & Whitney were the leading jet makers, their products were not yet in direct competition. This changed when airline companies began voicing demands for passenger jetliners. As Boeing, Douglas, and Convair scrambled to build such an aircraft, the engine makers began adapting their military designs for civilian markets. GE hoped to build a commercial derivative of its J79 but was unable to offer the engine in time for Boeing, whose 707 was introduced in 1954 with Pratt & Whitney JT3 engines. Furthermore, a year later, Douglas chose the JT3 for its DC-8.

Finally, in 1956, GE's CJ805 was ready to be marketed. At the time, however, the only available launch customer was Convair, whose 880 and 990 jetliners entered the market well after Boeing and Douglas had begun deliveries for the massive orders they had received. GE's future in commercial aviation was thus tied to a manufacturer whose airline markets were in decline and whose jetliner had arrived too late to garner significant sales. Furthermore, Pratt & Whitney ensured its leading position in commercial jet propulsion in 1964, when its JT8D engine was chosen to power the new Boeing 727 and Douglas DC-9. Without a position in the commercial market, GE was forced to abandon jetliners.

Nevertheless, the company had achieved success in other markets. Its jet engines were chosen to power missiles, helicopters, hovercraft, speedboats, and auxiliary power generators. GE also developed a J85 series that became a popular engine for smaller private jets.

Gerhard Neumann was put in charge of GE's engine group in 1961. He immediately took steps to centralize administrative and other divisional functions, as well as to promote greater teamwork. The engine division would again be reorganized in 1968, becoming an autonomous business with Neumann as its chief executive officer. Due to the company's strong research capabilities, GE won contracts to build several special engines, including a nuclear-powered jet engine—although this project was later cancelled over concerns for public safety in the event of a crash.

When the Air Force put out specifications for a new triple-sonic high-altitude bomber in 1963, GE was chosen to develop the engines. In order to produce the 30,000 pounds of thrust required, the company sought to develop the use of boron as a fuel for its J93 engine. Although problems during development necessitated the return to conventional fuels, the J93 was a success, enhancing GE's reputation as a hypersonic engine manufacturer.

When Boeing began work on its supersonic transport, or SST, it turned to GE to build the engines. GE developed a derivative of the J93, called the GE4, that could generate nearly 70,000 pounds of thrust and propel the SST at up to 1,800 miles per hour. Nevertheless, the SST project was eventually cancelled after skyrocketing development costs caused airlines to lose interest in supersonic flight.

Among the most important contracts awarded GE during this time involved developing the engines for Lockheed's enormous C-5 Galaxy cargo transport in 1965. This project required GE to develop a more efficient type of turbofan engine. Existing turbofans used a jet engine to drive a large front-mounted fan blade, and nearly half the air drawn into the engine bypassed the combustion chamber and was channeled out the rear for additional thrust. For the C-5, GE developed the TF39 turbofan, which had a bypass ratio of eight to one and produced 41,100 pounds of thrust. The turbofan was not only more efficient than conventional turbojets, it was quieter and perfectly suited for subsonic flight. Furthermore, the GE TF39 turbofan engine had applications in the commercial market. However, Pratt & Whitney again beat GE to the important commercial contracts, supplying the 747 jumbo jetliner with its own turbofan engine, the JT9D, in 1969.

Nevertheless, GE's commercial derivative of the TF39, the CF6, was chosen to power McDonnell Douglas's DC-10 jumbo jet in 1971 as well as Airbus's A-300 in 1974. GE finally had a basis for building a reputation within the commercial airline market. In 1975 Boeing offered the CF6 as an option for the 747. GE had formed a joint venture affiliate with the French engine manufacturer SNECMA the year before. The new company, called CFM International, was created to combine the strengths of each company in areas of engine technology. And as a multinational company, with manufacturing facilities in Evendale, Ohio, and Villaroche, France, it had a better chance of gaining sales in both the United States and Europe. The new company's CFM56 engine was chosen to upgrade the DC-8 and military versions of the 707, and became the standard engine on Airbus's A320.

In addition to supplying the fixed-wing aircraft industry, GE was a successful supplier of engines to the maritime and oil field equipment markets. Furthermore, the company excelled in developments in helicopter propulsion. GE built several turboshaft engines, including the T64, T700, and CT7, for such helicopters as the Boeing CH-46, Sikorsky UH-60, and McDonnell Douglas AH-64 Apache.

In the market for fighter jet engines, GE was chosen to develop an engine for the North American Rockwell B-1 bomber. Its F101, however, was cancelled in 1977, along with the B-1, after the Carter administration expressed concern over the waning utility of the strategic bomber.

In the late 1970s, GE got another chance to overtake Pratt & Whitney when that company's F100 engine repeatedly failed qualification tests. After winning a place on McDonnell Douglas's F-15 in 1970, the F100 fell further and further behind schedule, and, in 1979, GE was asked to provide an alternative. GE combined aspects of the F101 with another model called the F404—developed for the F-18 and the Stealth Fighter—to produce the F110. While Pratt & Whitney was busy fixing its F100, the GE F110 gradually overtook the fighter market. The F110 gained a place on the F-14, F-15, and F-16 and eventually won 75 percent of the F100's market.

Moreover, when the Reagan administration put the B-1 bomber back on order in 1981, the F101 was implemented. The first of 100 B-1s became operational in 1985. A second engine, the F118, was chosen for the B-2 Stealth Bomber, still under development at the time.

Having laid the foundation for GE's ascension in the aircraft engine market, Gerhard Neumann retired in 1977. He was succeeded by Fred McFee, who served for three years as head of the group and was replaced by Brian Rowe, a Briton who came to GE from DeHavilland in 1957.

In an effort to win market leadership from Pratt & Whitney, Rowe instituted a four-part plan that emphasized technology, modernizing facilities, customer service, and international operations. Rowe's plan for the engine division served as a model for GE as a whole, whose new chairman Jack Welch called for a wider transformation of the company. Focusing on eliminating waste and raising profitability, he declared that any GE division not first or second in its market would be spun off.

The efforts to improve products and processes at GE was of great benefit to the aircraft engine group. The success of the CF6, the F110, and the company's partnership with SNECMA posed a serious threat to Pratt & Whitney. Although second in its market, GE consistently registered higher sales growth than its competitor, and had a more complete line of engines in production. Pratt & Whitney had grown complacent during its 15-year reign with the JT8D and JT9D, and its excellent relationship with aircraft manufacturers, airline companies, and the government deteriorated. In 1986 GE overtook Pratt & Whitney in sales, and despite Pratt & Whitney's concerted efforts to win back the customers it had lost, it was unable to wrest its former position back from GE.

GE also benefitted from the rapid expansion in defense spending during the Reagan administration and growth in the commercial airline market. Defense spending was scaled back in 1989, however, and serious losses in the airline industry resulted in the cancellation of aircraft orders. Furthermore, Pratt & Whitney developed two new engines, the PW2000 and PW4000, aimed at winning customers over from GE's CF6 and CFM56. When Boeing introduced its new 757, it chose Pratt & Whitney engines.

Nevertheless, GE continued to lead the market. In 1987 the company formed a second partnership with Garrett called the CFE Company, which developed the CFE738 turbofan for the medium jet market. Later, the CFM56 was chosen to power a new "stretch" version of Boeing's 737.

During this period airline companies began to press for the development of a more efficient propjet. GE and Pratt & Whitney built jet engines whose turbines drove two rear-mounted counter-rotating propellers. While slightly slower than conventional engines, this "propfan" was twice as efficient as turbofans. Boeing and McDonnell Douglas began developing two new twin-propfan designs, the 7J7 and MD-91. After two years, miserable profitability among airline companies and plummeting fuel prices eliminated the demand for propfans. GE continued work on this revolutionary engine, but with very low priority.

In 1987 the General Electric Company launched a new corporate identity program to coincide with its ongoing reorganization. As a result, the Aircraft Engine Business Group received a new name, GE Aircraft Engines. The newly renamed group marked a milestone in marine propulsion that year, when the U.S.S. Leyte Gulf became the 100th Navy cruiser to enter service, powered by an LM2500, the marine derivative of the TF39/CF6. In fact, LM2500 engines were common power plants on a series of marine vessels, including destroyers, aircraft carriers, and frigates, as well as hydrofoils and off-shore oil platforms.

The company's work force peaked in 1989, with 42,000 employed at GE Aircraft Engines. However, with the slowdown in military and commercial sales, the division cut its employment to 30,000 in 1993. Nevertheless, GE Aircraft Engines continued to dominate its numerous markets. In response to the government's request for an Advanced Tactical Fighter, GE developed a new F120 engine that was to be tested against Pratt & Whitney's F119. The winning design was expected to be worth more than $1 billion in sales. In the early 1990s, Boeing and McDonnell Douglas began work on new super twinjets, for which GE Aircraft Engines began developing a turbofan called the GE90. Rated for 75,000 to 95,000 pounds of thrust, the engine was slated to become available in 1994. Furthermore, the company's CF6 was developed for a variety of applications in commercial aircraft.

Further Reading:

Biddle, Wayne, *Barons of the Sky,* New York: Simon & Schuster, 1991.
General Electric, *Propulsion,* Cincinnati: GE Aircraft Engines, 1991.
General Electric, *Eight Decades of Progress,* Cincinnati: General Electric Company, 1990.
"GE's Aircraft-Engine Unit to Cut 3,900 Jobs This Year," *New York Times,* February 27, 1993, p. 35.
Mattera, Philip, *Inside U.S. Business: A Concise Encyclopedia of Leading Industries,* Homewood, Illinois: Dow Jones-Irwin, 1987.

—John Simley

continue its expansion, aided by its concentration on the higher-price market and effective advertising campaigns, while larger, overextended competitors such as Firestone struggled.

By 1929 General was operating 14 retail stores and had garnered 1.8 percent of the tire market. In 1931, while the Great Depression weakened many smaller rubber firms, General, which had become a leader in the industry, was able to purchase two additional companies, Yale Tire and Rubber and India Tire and Rubber. Although General's command of 2.7 percent of tire sales in 1933 represented a much smaller market share than Goodyear's 30 percent sales figure, General was considered an important player because of its specialization in higher-priced tires. The effects of the Great Depression did, however, prompt General to diversify its holdings. During the 1930s the firm began investing in local radio stations, and, in 1942, it bought the Yankee Network, a Boston-based chain of radio stations.

During World War II General, like other tire companies, switched part of its production to meet defense needs. The firm produced motors and rockets in Ohio, West Virginia, and California and acquired Aerojet, a missile manufacturer. A plant General had built in Indiana to make mechanical goods was converted to the production of aviation and other military supplies. The war also led to an increase in synthetic rubber production, which would have applications in civilian sectors after the war.

General was among several medium-sized tire firms that expanded immediately after the war, fueled by a boom in car sales. The company purchased Pennsylvania Rubber and 45 percent of Mansfield, another rubber company. General's media division also received a boost during this time, with the establishment of television as an important source of information and entertainment in many American homes. General's Boston networks began television broadcasting in 1948.

In 1950 the onset of the Korean War disrupted supplies of natural rubber, leading to U.S. government quotas on rubber consumption over the next two years. This prompted an increase in the production of synthetic rubber, which soon became the primary raw material in U.S. rubber production. General built a synthetic rubber plant in Odessa, Texas, in 1955. By 1960 tubeless tires had been introduced into the market, and synthetic fibers such as nylon and rayon were being used by tire makers as bonding agents.

During this time, General continued to expand its line of retail stores, which increased from 72 stores in 1955 to 164 in 1961. The company also continued to diversify. Having maintained its Aerojet subsidiary after World War II, General started an industrial products division that manufactured plastic and metal parts for aircraft and electric appliances. Furthermore, in 1956 the firm bought a majority interest in A. M. Byers, a manufacturer of steel pipe and wrought iron. General's media holdings were also enhanced through the company's purchase of television stations in New York, Los Angeles, and Memphis. In 1955 General purchased RKO Pictures from Howard Hughes for $25 million. RKO's stock of 750 feature films was thereby made available to General's television stations, which aired many of these films. Although General sold RKO's movie business

GenCorp Inc.

173 Ghent Rd.
Fairlawn, Ohio 44333-3330
U.S.A.
(216) 869-4200
Fax: (216) 869-4211

Public Company
Incorporated: 1915 as General Tire & Rubber
Employees: 13,900
Sales: $1.94 million
Stock Exchanges: New York
SICs: 3764 Space Propulsion Units & Parts; 3825 Instruments to Measure Electricity; 3489 Ordnance & Accessories Nec; 3089 Plastics Products Nec

GenCorp is a leading manufacturer of aerospace and defense products, including rocket motors and bombs. Through its several divisions, the company also produces plastics as well as automotive and satellite communications equipment.

GenCorp began as General Tire & Rubber, a company founded in 1915 by William O'Neil. O'Neil had served as a dealer at the Firestone Company until 1911, when he became dissatisfied with a reduction in his sales territory and left to form his own company, Western Tire and Rubber, which focused on the manufacture of tire repair materials. In 1915 O'Neil moved his operation from Kansas City to Akron, Ohio, where his father, Michael O'Neil, owned a department store. The O'Neils established General Tire and Rubber with $200,000 in capital, mostly from Michael, who became company president, while William became general manager. The two hired several Firestone managers to help manage the new business.

General initially manufactured repair materials, beginning the production of tires in 1916. By 1917 the firm was expanding its factory and dealership network and embarking on its first advertising campaign. A difficult time for tire makers began at the onset of World War I, as the rubber supply was diminished, and General Tire, along with its competitors, had trouble meeting dealer demand. Immediately after the war, the industry boomed, and 1919 saw record highs in tire sales. However, the gains realized by the industry were shortlived. An economic recession in 1920–21 hurt tire sales, and although the cost of raw materials plummeted, tire makers entered into a price war that proved damaging to the industry. Nevertheless, General managed to in 1958, its RKO-General subsidiary remained in radio and television.

In 1960, company founder William O'Neil died, and his sons assumed control of General. Jerry O'Neil ran the tire business in Akron, while Thomas O'Neil ran RKO-General in New York and John O'Neil served as General's chief financial officer in Washington D.C. Industry observers later claimed that the operations of Thomas, Jerry, and John lacked coordination and long-term vision, which would contribute to several challenges for General in the 1960s.

In 1965 RKO-General's Los Angeles station's license renewal was opposed by the Federal Communications Commission. Charges that the station's programming was unworthy of retaining its broadcasting license resulted when Thomas O'Neil began cutting back on his programming budget, maintaining that his focus was on making money, rather than achieving high ratings. Problems also ensued at the company's Boston station, where RKO-General was accused of pressuring the company's suppliers to advertise on the RKO stations. While these cases were being appealed, alleged misconduct at General Tire became public. General was accused of maintaining a secret slush fund, which made payoffs to people involved in the overthrow of Chile's Allende government, and of making illegal political contributions in the United States. A special investigation by the Securities and Exchange Commission listed $41 million in questionable transactions by General and its subsidiaries. The RKO licensing hearings became embroiled in these alleged improprieties.

A decline in the tire business following the oil embargo of 1974 added to the firm's difficulties. During this time, General made one-third of its tire sales directly to U.S. auto companies, and when those companies began to struggle from the effects of Japanese competition, General's profits declined. In fact, when General's profits fell to $82 million in 1979, representing a decrease of 29 percent, RKO became the company's leading contributor and was responsible for a record 43 percent of the company's profits. In 1981 General was the fifth-largest U.S. tire maker, but tire making operations were so troubled that the company began selling off its other operations. Cablecom General Inc., a cable television operation, was the first to go, selling for $105.8 million. A tire plant in Akron was then closed down as were seven retreading plants, while the Aerojet subsidiary sold several of its industrial companies. During this time, Jerry O'Neil took on General's rubber unions to win concessions necessary to make the firm's tires competitive.

General also struggled to improve its tires, signing technical agreements with Germany's Continental Gummi-Werke and Japan's Toyo Tire & Rubber Co. While the firm had once been a leading manufacturer of truck tires, the quality of its truck radials was surpassed by that of rivals during the 1970s. In 1976 General tires maintained 17 percent of the truck market, but that figure fell to 12 percent over the next five years. In 1980, while its tire sales approached $1.5 billion, General saw profits of less than $10 million.

In 1982, RKO lost the license for its Boston television station. Nevertheless, the company's Los Angeles station was allowed to retain its license, and the New York station was saved when Congress voted to grant it a five-year license on the condition that it be moved to New Jersey. In an effort to increase the popularity of its networks, RKO began spending more to secure the rights to rerun popular television series.

In 1983 Jerry O'Neil announced that he would be succeeded as chief executive by a non-family member, Warren J. Hayford, who was slated to lead a restructuring of General into a holding company called GenCorp. However, one year after joining the company, and the day after the plan was to be announced, Hayford resigned over differences with the O'Neils. Nevertheless, the restructuring went forward, and Aerojet, RKO, and General's tire, industrial products, chemicals, and plastics divisions all became subsidiaries of the holding company.

Aerojet's business grew rapidly during the 1980s, partially as a result of the Reagan administration's defense buildup. Aerojet received large contracts for the MX missile and several air force projects, as well as $146 million in Strategic Defense Initiative contracts.

In 1985 Bill Reynolds, a former TRW Inc. executive, was named chief executive of GenCorp. A graduate of Stanford University's M.B.A. program, Reynolds immediately introduced formal strategic planning and other professional management techniques. He also began dealing with some of GenCorp's recurring problems, such as continuing litigation over its Los Angeles and Memphis television stations, California pollution problems, an Algerian breach-of-contract lawsuit, and the significant losses incurred by Denver-based Frontier airlines, of which GenCorp owned 45 percent.

Reynolds soon announced a restructuring that involved selling the Los Angeles and New York television stations as well as the firm's stake in Frontier. The price of television stations was climbing rapidly, and the FCC had just relaxed its requirements for license transfer, making the sales more attractive. WOR New Jersey was sold to MCA for $387 million in early 1986, while KHJ-Los Angeles was sold to Walt Disney for $320 million in early 1987. The firm used the money to buy back large segments of its stock, partly to guard against takeover attempts. The restructuring had an immediate positive effect, with GenCorp achieving sales of $3.1 billion and profits of $130 million in 1986, its best results in years.

During this time, GenCorp management decided to concentrate on its defense operations rather than reinvest in its original tire business. Consequently, the company sold General Rubber & Tire to Germany's Continental AG for $660 million. General Tire and Continental already had technical and production links, and Continental wanted to expand further into the United States. Furthermore, this move helped GenCorp resist a $2.2 billion hostile takeover attempt by The Wagner & Brown Investment Group and AFG Industries Inc., which together already owned nearly ten percent of GenCorp. As the two companies had hoped to retain GenCorp's tire business and sell its aerospace and entertainment operations, GenCorp's sale of General Tire helped to discourage the takeover.

Further GenCorp cutbacks included the sale of RKO Bottling to IC Industries for $395.5 million and the shedding of its RKO properties. GenCorp received $32.7 million for its two Washington, D.C. radio stations, $750,000 for its Memphis radio station, $12.6 million for WAXY–FM, Florida, and $39 million for television station WHBQ in Memphis, purchased by Adams Communication. The firm had profits of $210 million in 1989 on $1.94 billion in sales.

Despite the selloff of General Tire and its concentration on aerospace, GenCorp remained active in the automobile market through its GenCorp Automotive affiliate. In 1988 GenCorp Automotive formed GTY Tire with Yokohama Tire and Toyo Tire & Rubber to manufacture radial tires in the United States. It also opened a $65 million plant in Indiana to manufacture reinforced plastic auto parts. In 1990 the affiliate formed GKK Automotive with Japanese firm Kurashiki Kako to sell vibration-control parts.

GenCorp's Aerojet subsidiary continued to meet with success in its work on propulsion systems, including gel propellants for rocket engines. In the early 1990s, Aerojet was bidding on such projects as the manufacture of the main engine for the Advanced Launch System sponsored by the National Aeronautics and Space Administration and the U.S. Department of Defense.

As the United States experienced an economic recession in the early 1990s, GenCorp made several moves to counteract declining sales. In 1992, the company restructured its debt, leading to a significant reduction in interest payments. Despite lower profit margins during this time, GenCorp had become a more focused, stronger company and was poised to explore a broad range of opportunities as the economy recovered.

Principal Subsidiaries: Aerojet-General; GenCorp Automotive; GenCorp Polymer Products; GTY Tire.

Further Reading:

Dworkin, Peter, "The O'Neil Brothers' $350-million Hassle with the FCC," *Fortune,* April 21, 1980.

French, Michael, J., *The U.S. Tire Industry,* Boston: Twayne, 1991.

"General Tire Changes More Than Its Name," *Business Week,* January 30, 1984.

"General Tire: Pondering Spinoffs to Make the Most of Its Assets," *Business Week,* September 7, 1981.

"General Tire: Searching Again for a Driver to Map the Road to Growth," *Business Week,* February 13, 1984.

Schiller, Zachary, "GenCorp Isn't All in the Family Anymore," *Business Week,* June 24, 1985.

——. "Is It Just Beginner's Luck at GenCorp," *Business Week,* November 25, 1985.

—Scott M.Lewis

General Signal Corporation

One High Ridge Park
Stamford, Connecticut 06904
U.S.A.
(203) 357-8800
Fax: (203) 329-4328

Public Company
Incorporated: 1904 as General Railway Signal Company
Employees: 14,700
Sales: $1.6 billion
Stock Exchanges: New York
SICs: 3663 Radio & T.V. Communications Equipment; 3823
  Process Control Instruments; 3612 Transformers Except
  Electronic

The General Signal Corporation is the leading manufacturer of
equipment and instruments for process control, and electrical
and industrial technologies. General Signal was founded in
1904 in New York as the General Railway Signal Company and
primarily operated as a railway supplier. The company diversified its product base, most notably in the 1960s, and grew
steadily into the 1980s when, after a foray into the world of
high-tech semiconductor manufacturing, it ran into overwhelming competition and ended up going back to its more traditionally profitable markets.

The company's current operations are divided into three basic
product sectors: process control, electrical controls, and industrial technology. The process control unit is the largest of the
company's operations, with 38 manufacturing facilities in 15
states and eight foreign countries producing industrial mixers,
pumps, valves, and instrumentation for the waste, wastewater,
chemical, and paper industries. The electrical controls division
operates 33 manufacturing facilities in 15 states and four foreign countries, producing fire protection systems and signaling
products for the construction, electrical utility, computer, and
industrial markets. The industrial technology sector produces
related products for the semiconductor, telecommunications,
automotive, and transit industries.

The origins of the company go back to June 13, 1904, the date
the General Railway Signal Company was founded in New
York. For most of its history, the company supplied control
equipment to the railroad industry. General Railway sold products that were instrumental in automation, warehousing, switch

yards, and other aspects of the railroad business; the company's
equipment was designed to help carry cargo over America's
railroads faster, more reliably, and at a lower cost. With the
diversification of the transportation industry, General Railway
moved into related markets, such as mass transportation rail
lines, and became a leader in transportation supply.

During the 1950s, sales in railroad supply remained around $20
million per year (while profits grew, albeit slowly), and the
company took on a new CEO and chairman, Nathan R. Owen.
Owen had been a partner in a venture capital firm, J. H. Whitney
& Company, when it merged one of its holdings, Regina Corporation, into General Railway. Regina manufactured household
floor-care appliances while, of course, General Railway was
still solidly in the railroad equipment business. One of Owen's
tasks was to forge a company "in between" General Railway
and Regina Corporation.

In 1960 the firm made strong profits, but the potential for
growth was limited by the fact that the railroads were its main
markets. Owen, who had been the leader of numerous corporate
takeovers, often targeted electronics companies that specialized
in related transportation industries, marine and military air traffic controls, which led to spin-offs that could be applied to
related areas. General Railway could achieve benefits from its
merger with New York Air Brake Company, supplier of brake
systems to railroads, which was a perfect complement to General Railway's control systems. Air Brake's expertise in pneumatic and hydraulic control systems dovetailed nicely with
General Railway's electrical and electronic controls as well.

The company doubled in size between 1960 and 1962. By 1963
the company had diversified enough to drop "Railway" from
its name, taking on its present name, General Signal Corporation. Still a respected supplier to the railroad industry, much of
the company was converted to the manufacture of specialty
control devices that could be adapted to many purposes, notably
pollution control, mass transit systems, and medical and educational facilities. By the mid-1960s, more than 50 percent of the
company's sales were in these areas. The mix of businesses
created by Owen was 20 percent water treatment plants and
industrial process controls, 27 percent transportation controls,
18 percent building controls and protection devices, 16 percent
home appliances, 13 percent fluid power controls, and 6 percent
defense electronics, with each division yielding profits in proportion to its share of the company's revenues. From 1963 to
1970, sales and earnings grew every year. More than 80 percent
of the water treatment plants in the United States used some of
General Signal's equipment and controls.

Expansion and diversification continued through acquisition
and internal expansion. Some major acquisitions included ACF
Industries Electronics Division, later renamed Avion Electronics Inc.; the company was sold two years later when it lost $1.8
million. In all, General Signal picked up eight companies between 1961 and 1966, focusing on the areas of electronics and
electrical equipment.

At that time, General Signal still sold nearly half of its output to
the railroads, but as transportation diversified and as mass
transit systems and new highways were being built, General
Signal diversified to meet the growing demand for infrastruc-

ture. The company reaped markets from federal government programs to build schools and hospitals, as the federal government shifted spending away from the Vietnam War and increased spending for social needs at home. General Signal got a piece of federal spending on water pollution control ($1 billion in fiscal year 1971) and medical facilities ($2.8 billion). The federal government at that time committed $5 billion over five years for mass transit alone.

Owen dubbed his flexible product line "social capital goods" to reflect his "manufacture of specialty control devices that can be adapted to many purposes, notably pollution controls, mass transit, and medical and educational facilities." Social spending by the federal government was clearly instrumental in General Signal's growth in the 1960s. The company landed a contract in 1969 in New York City to supply over $1 million in controls for new subway cars.

Other markets were growing as well into the 1970s. From 1970 to 1974, net sales more than doubled, going from $206 million to $470 million; net income rose from $9.4 million to $20.6 million in 1974. The product mix changed slightly over this period as some of the firm's operations grew while other unprofitable operations were sold off. General Signal's home appliance operation, most notably Elektrik Broom and other floor care items (which made up only 10 percent of the firm's sales), in the red to the tune of $1.7 million, was sold off as consumer demand fell off during recessionary times. Mobile controls (12 percent of revenues), a line that included hydraulic valves, pumps, and motors and other forged parts experienced growth, buoyed by strong demand for fluid power controls for mining and agricultural equipment.

David Kimball took over the company from Owen in 1974, with optimistic prospects. In total, General Signal had made over twenty-seven deals in the previous two decades. Markets were growing and federal government contracts in particular continued to be important markets for the three key parts of General Signal's business—transportation controls, life safety, and building controls (including detection, parking systems, power distribution, and safety and building controls). Government contracts also supported environmental and industrial process controls, which were tied to petroleum, petro-chemicals, and chemical and mining activities. The water controls segment, including waste water systems and controls, benefited from a portion of the $9 billion of federal funds earmarked for municipalities. General Signal's wastewater market continued to be strong—80 percent of all installations included one or more of General Signal's products.

One of General Signal's biggest transit deals at the time was a contract to supply transit controls for the Washington, D.C., Metro System in the late 1970s, a $42 million potential deal. They also won contracts for mass transit controls in other cities and other municipal traffic systems as well. By 1980 General Signal was one of the fastest growing conglomerates, with assets of more than $260 billion and sales of $1.5 billion. The firm went into the utilities industry, acquiring Leeds & Northrup, a leader in utility controls. The acquisition reaped large benefits for General Signal, with an increased demand for electricity and the conversion from oil to coal requiring a new set of controls.

General Signal was shifting into high-technology industries, becoming the Silicon Valley's third largest supplier of equipment for producing electronic chips. In 1980, 20 percent of the company's revenues were derived from high tech fields. Moving strongly into this area, General Signal hoped that suppliers of production machinery would need their services as companies sought to automate more of the manufacturing process.

In support of the move into high tech, General Signal acquired several other companies, most notably Xynetics, a leader in probing machines used to test microcircuits, and Kayex, a leader in the $20 million silicon crystal market whose furnaces were used to convert silicon for use in electrical chips. These purchases brought General Signal's "chip" revenue to $100 million. Its purchase in 1988 of the GCA Corporation, a large chip maker, had a profound effect on the company's direction. GCA was best known for a new technology called the XLS stepper, a semiconductor manufacturing machine that put the circuit pattern on a chip. In all, between 1982 and 1988 Owen and Kimball spent $260 million on technology for General Signal, planning to make machines for all the major stages of chip manufacture. At the time of the GCA purchase, General Signal was lauded for keeping this technology in the United States.

In support of the U.S. semiconductor industry, the federal government had poured money into GCA and other Silicon Valley companies through Sematech, the American Semiconductor Industry Consortium, in order to keep the technology from being controlled by Japanese-owned companies Nikon and Canon.

Even government subsidies, however, could not save the industry or GCA. The semiconductor division of General Signal lost over $100 million from 1984 through 1988. Once the largest semiconductor chip maker, GCA now held a meager four percent of market share, (and the company lost $4 million in 1990). Competition in the industry during the decade was fierce, and GCA lost the war to Canon Inc. and Nikon Corp. As a result, General Signal's total revenues remained flat in the late 1980s.

General Signal faced on ongoing struggle to recover from defeat at the hands of its competitors. The decline of GCA led the firm to try to return to its successful "low-tech" roots. Edmund Carpenter took over the company in 1988 and started the retrenchment needed to revive the company. He immediately lopped off over $200 million in assets and reduced costs by cutting his work force by 20 percent and introducing strict inventory control methods in order to reduce turnover time. The reforms were limited as Carpenter was hemmed in by a debt load of $395 million (which was 47 percent of total capital), so he had limited financial flexibility. He did succeed in scaling back the high-tech division and went in the direction of basic process control, which was pushed up to 80 percent from the 50 percent share of the total revenues it had in 1987. General Signal's net income hit bottom in 1990 when it lost $13 million.

By the end of the 1980s, the company's core business, industrial and electrical controls, was hurting as well. The recession in the early 1990s reduced demand for the valves and pumps used to regulate and control the flow of material used to make paper, chemicals, cement, and other manufacturing products. The fourth quarter of 1990 showed a 33 percent decline in earnings in electrical controls, though by 1991 things picked up a bit.

Competition and restructuring reduced General Signal's semiconductor business from 41 percent of the company's business in 1988 to 25 percent of sales in 1990. The company as a whole showed signs of growth. In 1992 capital goods orders improved and orders increased for restoring the infrastructure. By the end of the year, the company made a major acquisition, picking up Ryken Tube Group, a producer and distributor of a variety of automotive tubular parts. With this addition to the General Signal stable, net income rose 12 percent in the fourth quarter of 1992 compared with one year prior. Revenues over the same period increased 4 percent to $408 million. Any profit growth over the year was largely attributed to higher margins for instrumentation, pumps, and heat treating business as well as acquisitions in the electrical controls unit.

Longer term restructuring continued. The company cut costs by shedding workers, consolidating its management, and keeping a close eye on inventory and payables. General Signal expected an increase in domestic sales and new product sales as well as in electric and process control groups. They also expected increased demand for high vacuum pumps and industrial valves used to rebuild municipal and industrial infrastructure.

Finally, General Signal, having tried to shed its ailing semiconductor company, GCA, finally shut the company down in May of 1993. The move left Canon and Nikon (which controlled 80 percent of the market) with control over the semiconductor industry. GCA had been kept alive largely through the efforts of Sematech, in an attempt to keep the industry out of complete Japanese corporate control. In fact, some concern was expressed by the National Security Council that the lack of a "pure domestic" microlithography supplier would be hazardous to American national security. In any case, unable to compete and unable to find a buyer, General Signal shut GCA down and took an $85.6 million charge for the fourth quarter of 1992. The remaining American firms in the market entered into joint operating agreements with Canon. Under a Sematech agreement, the Silicon Valley companies agreed to share new improvements with Canon and divide up the markets, with the Silicon Valley getting the U.S. and Korean markets and Canon getting Japan and Asia.

Principal Subsidiaries: Assembly Technologies Inc.; DeZurik Inc.; Dielectric Communications; Drytek Inc.; Dual-Lite Inc.; Edwards Company Inc.; General Signal Corporation Aurora Pump; General Signal Corporation Edwards Systems Technology Division; General Signal Corporation Electroglas Division; General Signal Corporation GFI-GENFARE; General Signal Corporation GS Electric; General Signal Corporation General Signal ThinFilm Company; General Signal Corporation Hevi-Duty Electric; General Signal Corporation Kinney Vacuum Company; General Signal Corporation Lindberg Blue M; General Signal Corporation Lindberg Division; General Signal Corporation OZ/GEDNEY Company; General Signal Corporation Sola Electric; General Signal Corporation Stock Equipment Company; General Signal Corporation Technology Industries; General Signal Corporation Warren G-V Inc.; Hevi-Duty/Nelson Electric; Kayex Corporation; LIGHTNIN; Leeds and Northrup Company; Midwest Electronics Industries Inc.; O-Z Gedney Company Inc.; Tau-tron Inc.; Telecommunications Technology Inc.; Telenex Corporation; Xynetics Inc.

Further Reading:
"Can General Signal Escape Its High-Tech Hell?" *Business Week,* March 18, 1991.
"General Signal—Peak Earnings," *Barron's,* April 14, 1975.
Hoddeson, David L., "All Along the Line: Demand Is Mounting for Every Kind of Railroad Equipment," *Barron's,* April 8, 1963.
Lubove, Seth, "Dog With Bone," *Forbes,* April 13, 1992.
"Out to Clean Up if Peace Comes: General Signal Corp. Is Set for a Post-Vietnam Drive to Cure Ills Such as Pollution," *Business Week,* October 3, 1970.
Uttal, Bro, "Knighthood Is Still in Flower at General Signal," *Fortune,* October 6, 1980.

—John A. Sarich

Genuine Parts Company

2999 Circle 75 Parkway
Atlanta, Georgia 30330
U.S.A.
(404) 953-1700
Fax: (404) 956-2212

Public Company
Incorporated: 1928
Employees: 19,700
Sales: $4.02 billion
Stock Exchanges: New York
SICs: 5015 Motor Vehicle Parts—Used; 5085 Industrial
   Supplies; 5112 Stationary & Office Supplies; 5021
   Furniture

Genuine Parts Company is the largest automobile parts supplier in the United States, providing parts to more than 6,000 retailers across the country and in areas of Canada. The company maintains close ties with the National Auto Parts Association (NAPA), owning approximately 75 percent of the trade association's member distribution centers. After selling only auto parts for almost 50 years, Genuine diversified into industrial replacement parts and office supplies in the mid-1970s. Although supplying auto parts remains the company's focus, a significant portion of Genuine's business comes from the sale of industrial parts and office products.

Genuine Parts was founded by Carlyle Fraser in 1928 when Fraser bought a small auto parts store in Atlanta. The store had six employees and capital of $40,000 when he acquired it. Sales reached $75,000 the first year, although the store lost about $2,500. Independent garages for car repair were spreading with incredible rapidity, providing Genuine with a swiftly growing market for its parts. Genuine bought auto parts from manufacturers like Tenneco and sold them to parts stores, called jobbing houses, that sold them to the independent garages. From the beginning, Genuine pushed swift, reliable service as a way to outflank the competition. The firm also used its relationship with the NAPA, the trade association co-founded by Fraser. NAPA set standards and sold parts to jobbers.

Genuine's business was in some respects helped by the Great Depression. Many people could not afford to buy new cars, so they held onto aging automobiles and bought the replacement parts needed to repair them when they broke down. In 1936,

about $2 was spent on parts for the average one-year-old car, whereas a three-year-old car required $10 in parts. During the 1930s, company sales went from $339,000 to $3.18 million.

Genuine continued to grow during World War II. Consumers again held onto their older cars, sometimes having little choice because auto makers were devoting much of their capacity to the war effort. By the same token, the War Production Board only allocated resources to parts manufacturers to build "functional" parts for cars. This restriction meant, for instance, no fenders or door hardware were available to sell to those needing them. With auto sales slacking, the average vehicle was 7.28 years old in 1946, compared with 4.77 years old in 1941 before the United States entered the war. As a result, $19 in parts were bought for the average car in 1945. In the year of its 20th anniversary in 1948, the company had $20 million in sales.

With the prosperity of the 1950s and the increasing number of families with two cars, Genuine expanded at a tremendous pace. It opened NAPA operations in Boston in 1950, in Omaha in 1955, in Jacksonville and Miami in 1956, in Denver in 1957, and in Minneapolis in 1959. By 1962 the firm owned 97 retail stores and 12 warehouses along the east coast and in the South and had annual sales of about $80 million. Rebuilt parts accounted for 15 percent of sales. Although it still bought parts from manufacturers, Genuine did some parts rebuilding itself, including clutches, brake shoes, and pumps. To increase its slice of that business, in 1968 the firm acquired Atlanta-based John Rogers Co., a rebuilder of auto engines. In 1969 Genuine diversified out of the auto business for the first time, buying Beck & Gregg Hardware Co., a 103-year-old distributor of home appliances, building goods, and sports products.

By the late 1960s, Genuine was a nationwide distributor, supplying 2,500 independent jobbers and owning 33 of the 55 NAPA distribution centers, which then served 4,000 jobbers throughout the United States. Its first parts under its own brand name were introduced in 1966. Genuine also supplied parts for trucks, tractors, power boats, and power tools.

The OPEC oil embargo in 1973 played havoc with the auto parts market. With the rise in gasoline prices, consumers drove less and needed fewer auto parts in the short term. However, the oil shortage also led to recession in 1973 and 1974. Car owners held onto their older cars, driving up sales and prices of auto parts in the longer term. Nearly 90 million cars were being driven in the United States, and approximately 60 percent of them were over three years old, making them likely candidates for car parts. An increasing number of these vehicles were small cars, whose parts tended to wear out faster than those of bigger cars. Although cars were being driven for fewer total miles than ever before, more of those miles were in urban areas, resulting in greater wear on the parts. Do-it-yourself sales soared, and mass marketers like Sears Roebuck and J.C. Penney began increasing parts orders from distributors. Genuine's sales reached $500 million in 1973, twice as much as its nearest competitor, APS; however, that figure represented just two percent of the fragmented auto parts market.

Auto parts were becoming more elaborate and expensive as a result of technology advances and stricter pollution standards. In 1975, attempting to diversify, Genuine picked up a wholesale office supplies firm, S.P. Richards Co. In 1976, under the leadership of CEO Wilton Looney, Genuine also expanded into the industrial parts business. Looney believed that industrial parts would be recession-proof in the same way that auto parts were: during recessions industrial firms would buy replacement parts for existing machinery rather than replacing it with new equipment. In 1979 the firm bought a Michigan-based industrial parts distributor to expand that part of its business.

In 1978 Genuine installed a computerized point-of-sale system for billing customers, tracking inventories, and automatically ordering replacements for parts that were sold. The system, developed with Data General Corp., cost $24,000 to $30,000 per complete system, and grew to include 900 jobbers by 1982. This system gave Genuine an important advantage over competitors, because no other independent distributor could match the services Genuine could offer.

Genuine's sales reached $1.6 billion in 1981, of which 63 percent came from the distribution of parts, 22 percent came from industrial replacement parts, and 8 percent from office-supply products. The firm had 55 U.S. distribution centers for auto parts and four in western Canada, selling to about 5,200 jobbers, of which it owned about 350. Genuine ran six distribution centers and 160 branches for industrial parts, selling to 50,000 customers. Office supplies were being sold to over 5,000 retailers in 15 states. Genuine's leading item overall was spray paint used for touch-ups, which accounted for eight percent of sales. Exhaust products, filters, hoses and belts, and batteries accounted for between three and six percent of sales each.

The number of vehicles in the United States continued to rise, reaching 160 million by the end of 1981, with an average age of 6.5 years. Parts for imported cars accounted for only about ten percent of inventory, despite rapidly growing import sales in the United States. Since the imported parts broadened inventory, the trend to buy imports was seen as increasing Genuine's advantage against smaller, less-well-financed competitors.

In 1982 Genuine bought General Automotive Parts Corp. of Dallas in a stock swap valued at about $250 million. General Auto had stores in 12 states in the southwest, north, and central regions of the United States. Genuine was also opening about five outlets a year, most in major cities. To better supply them, it opened NAPA distribution centers in Dallas, Houston, and San Antonio in 1983, and Portland, Maine, in 1984.

A recession hit the United States in 1982 and hurt Genuine's supposedly recession-proof industrial parts business. The recession was severe enough to temporarily shut down some factories, and closed factories do not buy parts. As a result of its diversification, about 35 percent of Genuine's sales came from operations other than auto parts, up from ten percent ten years earlier.

NAPA was an increasingly important part of Genuine's business. NAPA's 72 distribution centers sold parts to 5,200 NAPA jobbers, who sold parts to local mechanics. Genuine owned 55 of the distribution centers, and 350 of the 5,200 jobbing sites. Genuine therefore had 85 percent of NAPA's sales, although that accounted for only five percent of the nationwide market for replacement parts. About 85 percent of Genuine's 100,000 auto and truck parts bore the NAPA brand name. Genuine used its NAPA connection to give it leverage over the 5,200 NAPA jobbers. If a jobber began buying less than 85 percent or so of its parts from Genuine, the firm might open another NAPA shop in the same area. If jobbers kept Genuine happy, they would find little direct competition and excellent service. Genuine delivered parts overnight to most of its customers, enabling them to keep their inventories, and thus costs, low. Genuine began refurbishing its image in the mid-1980s, raising awareness of the NAPA brand name and redesigning its stores. Most of the firm's nearly 500 stores installed brighter lighting, updated the layout of sales floors, and added a blue and yellow color scheme that drew attention to the NAPA logo.

Replacement part sales sagged in mid-1980s, barely keeping pace with inflation. Car and truck sales had slumped in 1982 and 1983, meaning fewer cars needed parts several years later. Cars were being built better and generally started to need replacement parts after four years rather than three. Customers increasingly brought their cars back to their dealers for repairs, and the dealers got parts directly from the manufacturers. As Japanese cars steadily acquired U.S. market share, parts suppliers were slow to begin carrying them in sufficient numbers. Warm winters in 1988 and 1989 were partly to blame for the drop in sales as well because alternators, batteries, and other parts tended to fail during very cold weather. At the same time, Genuine's competition was heating up. Specialty shops like Midas and Jiffy Lube were expanding rapidly, and retail chains were increasing their automotive operations.

To help compensate, Genuine tried to increase its efficiency and started a new marketing campaign. Genuine signed agreements with Midas, Montgomery Ward, and others to supply some of their auto parts. To make jobbers aware that it carried foreign parts, Genuine put out a catalogue focusing on imported car parts. By 1990 most of the 6,000 retailers who bought parts from Genuine were connected by computer to one of the firm's 64 NAPA distribution warehouses. In addition to getting parts to jobbers quickly, Genuine used the computer system to keep track of who was selling how many parts and why.

Changes in the auto industry did have some benefits: if cars needed parts less often, the parts continued to increase in cost, with some costing twice what they had 20 years earlier. At the same time, Genuine's other businesses continued to grow at higher rates. Sales for the industrial group were $547 million in 1988, with profits of $35.7 million. Office product sales came to $450 million, with profits of $36.7 million. Nevertheless, the auto parts industry was in many ways traditional. Genuine remained strictly a distributor, avoiding the retail market for fear of alienating its customers by competing with them.

In late 1993 Genuine strengthened its industrial parts business by acquiring Berry Bearing Company for about $300 million worth of stock. Bearings were seen as a stable seller in a recessionary economy as firms delayed purchases of new equipment. With the U.S. auto market in constant flux, Genuine could take nothing for granted. However, its size and savvy in the still unconsolidated auto parts industry would continue to make it a formidable competitor.

Principal Subsidiaries: Balkamp Inc.; Davis & Wilmar Inc.; Motion Industries, Inc.; S.P. Richards Company; Genuine Parts

Holdings Ltd. (Canada); Oliver Industrial Supplies; Berry Bearing Company

Further Reading:

"As Good As New," *Barron's,* November 3, 1969.
"Auto Par Puzzle," *Business Week,* February 7, 1942.
Byrne, Harlan S., "Genuine Parts Co.," *Barron's,* November 20, 1989.
Byrne, Jon A., "A Nasty Little Shock," *Forbes,* October 25, 1982.

"Genuine Parts," *Business Week,* August 25, 1934.
Gordon, Mitchell, "In High Gear," *Barron's,* March 22, 1982.
Judge, Paul C., "Thrives on Breakdowns," *New York Times,* September 20, 1990.
Pacey, Margaret D., "Nearly Recession-Proof," *Barron's,* April 11, 1974.

—Scott M. Lewis

Georgia Gulf Corporation

400 Perimeter Center Terrace
Suite 595
Atlanta, Georgia 30346
U.S.A.
(404) 395-4500
Fax: (404) 395-4529

Public Company
Incorporated: January 1, 1985
Employees: 1,128
Sales: $779.4 million
Stock Exchanges: New York
SICs: 2821 Plastics Materials & Resins; 2812 Alkalies &
  Chlorine; 2869 Industrial Organic Chemicals Nec

Georgia Gulf Corporation is a major manufacturer of several highly integrated lines of commodity chemicals and polymers including aromatic, natural gas, and electrochemical products. Established in 1984 as a leveraged buy-out of Georgia-Pacific Corporation, a large forest products manufacturer, Georgia Gulf began as an extremely successful corporation and was able to take advantage of increases in the demand for salt- and petrochemical products.

The assets that form Georgia Gulf Corporation today were built up by Georgia-Pacific Corporation over a period of 14 years. In 1971, Georgia-Pacific established the first of several chemical plants, phenol/acetone and methanol manufacturing facilities at Plaquemine, Louisiana. Both products are used to make plywood and a wide variety of granulate, wood fiber boards.

Georgia-Pacific added a caustic/chlorine plant at Plaquemine in 1975. Salt mined from large salt domes located nearby is converted into salt brine. Electricity is passed through the solution and chlorine, caustic soda, and hydrogen are formed. Chlorine is used in pulp and paper manufacturing and to make vinyl chloride monomer (VCH), an intermediate to vinyl or plastic resins. Caustic soda, the coproduct of chlorine, is key to the manufacture of aluminum and pulp and paper as well as being a key element in the production of other chemicals.

Later that year a polyvinyl chloride (PVC) resin plant was completed at the site. This facility converted purchased VCM into vinyl resins. These resins are one of the most widely used plastics today and can be found in pipe, window frames, siding, flooring, shower curtains, bottles, medical tubing, and many other end-use products. The vinyl resin facility positioned Georgia-Pacific to eventually produce value-added vinyl compounds.

In 1978, Georgia-Pacific added an ammonia plant adjacent to the methanol plant. This enabled the company to use excess hydrogen, a by-product of the methanol and chlorine manufacturing processes, in the production of ammonia, a key ingredient in the manufacture of fertilizers.

The company built a cumene facility in Pasadena, Texas, in 1979. Cumene, a petroleum product made from benzene and propylene, is used to make phenol and acetone. In addition to resin adhesives, phenol is also a precursor to high performance plastics used in automobiles, household appliances, electronics, and protective coating applications. Acetone is a precursor to methyl methacrylate, which is used to produce acrylic sheeting and in surface coating resins for automotive and architectural markets. It is also an intermediate for the production of engineering plastics and several major industrial solvents.

Georgia-Pacific again expanded the Plaquemine complex in 1979 to include sodium chlorate production. Along with chlorine, the uses for sodium chlorate are primarily industrial. It has major applications in the bleaching process for pulp and paper, and it is also an ingredient in blasting agents, explosives, and solid rocket fuels. In 1980 the Plaquemine facility began producing its own VCM, which integrated the company from raw material to finished vinyl resins.

The company's chemical operations were extended to the northeastern United States in 1981, when Georgia-Pacific purchased an phenol/acetone facility in Bound Brook, New Jersey. Two years later, the company added three resin compounding facilities producing specialty resins. The addition of these plants, in Tennessee, Mississippi, and Delaware, further integrated Georgia-Pacific's vinyl resins into value-added products.

Many companies, spurred on by growth in chemical markets, simply overbuilt capacity, and the limits of this expansion were not discovered until recessionary pressures had already shrunk the market. Companies were left with massive production facilities, but few sales. Georgia-Pacific was no different. After several years of consideration, the company decided to spin off the chemical operations and return its focus to core businesses in the paper and lumber industries.

The first group to organize a plan to take over Georgia-Pacific's chemical interests consisted of five senior executives of the operation, led by James R. Kuse, a senior vice president of Georgia-Pacific who had been in charge of the division for several years.

Kuse and his associates risked long and successful careers with Georgia-Pacific, and set out to raise the necessary capital. Together, the group managed to collect the asking price of $275 million, representing about 20 percent of the asset value. These assets included some of the most technically advanced and efficient plants in the industry.

Having succeeded in making the deal, the owners needed a name for the new company. Locating its headquarters in Atlanta, the name Georgia was linked with Gulf, which represented the company's substantial assets in Louisiana and Texas.

Georgia Gulf came into existence as a privately owned company on January 1, 1985. The first priority of Kuse and his team was to lower costs and increase sales. Already in possession of a viable, integrated chemical enterprise, Kuse only needed a recovery in his company's markets.

This began only months after Georgia Gulf came into existence. The recession ended and demand made its way back through the production cycle to the products manufactured by Georgia Gulf. In fact, demand was so strong that the company's plants operated at more than 90 percent of capacity.

Very strong sales provided an unforecasted increase in available funds, almost all of which were devoted to paying down the company's substantial debt. The debt, which was a result of the leveraged buyout, was not planned to be eliminated until about 1992, but the strength of sales growth virtually eliminated the debt four years later.

This placed the company in an excellent position to go public. The initial offering of 8 million shares on the NASDAQ went off successfully in December of 1987. The following November, Georgia Gulf gained a listing on the New York Stock Exchange, and was listed on the *Fortune 500*. During 1987, Georgia Gulf shares recorded a 183 percent return.

Through this period of economic growth, Georgia Gulf captured market share as it was one of the low-cost producers due to the efficiency of its operations. In addition, falling oil and natural gas prices helped to further strengthen Georgia Gulf's financial position. Georgia Gulf closed its Bound Brook facility in 1987, later relocating the plant to Pasadena, Texas, where it was closer to raw materials.

With the debt nearly eliminated, Georgia Gulf began to expand by acquiring Freeman Chemical Corporation headquartered in Port Washington, Wisconsin. With six plants, Freeman added a new line of polyurethane specialty resins and brought revenues of up to $1 billion. Also that year, Georgia Gulf purchased the Great River Oil and Gas Corporation, a Louisiana-based petroleum company. Great River provided Georgia Gulf with a potential source for hedging future supplies of natural gas. Georgia Gulf also diverted significant operating income toward the repurchase of shares. The repurchase program was initiated in 1987 and continued for three years.

In 1989, Jerry Satrum, a team member of Kuse's 1985 purchase of the Georgia-Pacific assets, succeeded Kuse as president of the company. Kuse remained chairman and CEO until 1990, when Satrum took over as CEO.

1990 was an extremely difficult year for Georgia Gulf. Although the company had virtually no debt and was well-positioned to weather the anticipated economic downturn, the company was forced to defend itself from a hostile takeover. The takeover attempt, which began in July 1989, was brought to a resolution through a plan of recapitalization, which the stock-holders approved in April 1990. The recapitalization plan was a combination of cash distributions, senior subordinated notes, and a new issue of common stock. The company borrowed approximately $746 million and used $65 million from the sale of Freeman Chemical to fund the recapitalization.

The emphasis, therefore, necessarily shifted to sales growth and cost reduction. Already one of the most efficient companies in the chemical industry, there were few costs to cut. While lean, Georgia Gulf still managed to trim nearly 300 jobs.

On the other side of the equation, sales growth was tied directly to the economy, which continued to languish through 1991 and, when recovery seemed imminent, "double-dipped" in 1992. Sales, which hit an all-time high of $1.1 billion in 1989, decreased, with the sale of Freeman, to $932 million in 1990, $838 million in 1991, and $779 million in 1992.

While sales were depressed, Georgia Gulf continued to operate efficiently, maximizing opportunities. By all accounts the company succeeded in preserving itself through the recession, although it was saddled with substantial debt.

In early 1993, demand had begun to recover in the key vinyl resins market. In addition, the provisions of the federal Clean Air Act came into force, dictating the use of cleaner fuels that should increase demand for methanol, which can be used as an oxygenate for gasoline. Forecasted demand for these and other products was projected to remain steady for about three years, during which time the company's debt burden could be reduced.

In an attempt to de-emphasize the sharp effects of the American markets on its business, Georgia Gulf intensified an effort to boost export sales in 1992. This was made more difficult by lingering weaknesses in the world economy. Still, the company managed to make significant sales in European and Asian markets.

If these conditions persist, Georgia Gulf will be able to service its debt obligations and maintain profitability. The company made significant progress in this direction in 1992, reducing its debt from $726 million in 1990 to $444 million in 1992.

Georgia Gulf remains a leader in its various markets, with an annual production capacity of eight billion pounds of caustic soda, chlorine, sodium chlorate, vinyl chloride monomer, vinyl resins and compounds, cumene, phenol, acetone, and methanol. While this makes Georgia Gulf one of America's 30 largest chemical companies, the enterprise continues to be heavily concentrated in a closely related series of markets that remain particularly vulnerable to the business cycle.

As a result, periods of recession are likely to have a negative effect on sales and earnings. Conversely, recoveries are likely to be strong and sustained for periods of several years. During such a period, the company may be expected to devote a slightly lower proportion of its earnings to debt reduction and concentrate on development of product lines closely tied to its core products.

Principal Subsidiaries: Great River Oil and Gas Corporation.

Further Reading:

Finotti, John, "The Gold Mine Georgia-Pacific Gave Away," *Business Week,* May 9, 1988, p. 106D.

"Georgia Gulf Corp.," *Wall Street Transcript,* May 9, 1988, pp. 89, 390.

"Georgia Gulf Corp. +182.1%," *Institutional Investor,* March 1988, pp. 79–80.

Georgia Gulf Corporation, Atlanta: Georgia Gulf Corporation.

Georgia Gulf Corporation Annual Reports, Atlanta: Georgia Gulf Corporation, 1986, 1989, 1991, 1992.

Georgia Gulf: Positioned to Serve, Atlanta: Georgia Gulf Corporation.

McCosh, John, "Solo Success Story at Georgia Gulf," *Atlanta Business Chronicle,* April 13, 1987, p. 3A.

Research: Ideas for Today's Investors—Georgia Gulf, San Francisco: Research Magazine, Inc., 1989.

Sweitzer, Letitia, "Rave Reviews for Georgia Gulf," *Business Atlanta,* December 1988, pp. 40–41.

—John Simley

Georgia-Pacific Corporation

133 Peachtree Street, Northeast
Atlanta, Georgia 30303
U.S.A.
(404) 521-4000
Fax: (404) 521-4581

Public Company
Incorporated: 1927 as Georgia Hardwood Lumber Company
Employees: 60,000
Sales: $12.67 billion
Stock Exchanges: New York Tokyo
SICs: 2421 Sawmills & Planing Mills—General; 2435
     Hardwood Veneer & Plywood; 2611 Pulp Mills; 2657
     Folding Paperboard Boxes

Georgia-Pacific Corporation is a leading manufacturer and distributor of building products, industrial wood products, pulp, paper, packaging, and chemical products. Although it eventually came to own or control over six million acres of timberland throughout North America, the company did not hold the title to a single tree for the first 24 years of its existence. Instead, Georgia Hardwood Lumber Company began operation in 1927 in Augusta, Georgia, as a hardwood lumber wholesaler with $12,000 in start-up funds provided by its founder, Owen Cheatham.

During its first decade in business, the company began lumber manufacturing in addition to its wholesaling activities. Cheatham focused on expanding the company's milling capabilities in the southern United States, a strategy that allowed it to become the largest supplier of lumber to the U.S. Army during World War II. The company's purchase of a plywood mill in Bellingham, Washington, in 1947 coincided with plywood's growing popularity in the construction industry and gave the company a strong competitive advantage.

Additional plywood mills in Washington and Oregon were purchased in 1948, as well as another plywood plant in 1949, to support this growing business area. The company changed its name in 1948 to Georgia-Pacific Plywood & Lumber Company to reflect more accurately its geographic and operational expansion.

In 1951 the company changed its name again, to Georgia-Pacific Plywood Company. Cheatham gradually developed a reputation as an industry maverick. Over the next six years, he conducted a $160 million timberland-acquisition program in the western and southern United States. To finance this program, he borrowed heavily from banks and insurance companies expecting that the proceeds gained from the timber in the future would more than cover the required return on their investment. In order to be closer to these newly purchased resources, the company moved its headquarters from Georgia to Olympia, Washington, in 1953 and then again to Portland, Oregon, the following year.

Over the next decade Cheatham used his financing model several times to acquire additional forest acreage and manufacturing facilities, including Coos Bay Lumber Company and Hammond Lumber Company in 1956. That same year the company's name was changed, for the third time since its founding, to Georgia-Pacific Corporation. Subsequent purchases of Booth-Kelly Lumber Company in 1959 and W. M. Ritter Lumber Company in 1960 took the company to the number-three position in its industry.

The company's unorthodox approach to growth was evident in other areas as well. It opened a kraft pulp and linerboard mill in Toledo, Oregon, in 1957 and its first resin adhesive plant at Coos Bay, Oregon, in 1959. The latter manufacturing operation was intended at first to supply the resin required for the company's plywood-production business but gradually grew large enough to supply resin to other plywood manufacturers as well. Georgia-Pacific was also one of the first manufacturers to use wood by-products rather than timber in pulp production. The company continued to pioneer in the development of plywood products, eventually shifting away from the traditional use of Douglas fir to a process using less-expensive southern pine. This wood previously had been considered inappropriate for use in plywood because of its high resin content.

During the 1960s Georgia-Pacific embarked upon another series of acquisitions by buying several lumber and paper companies across the country. These included Crossett Lumber Company in 1962; Puget Sound Pulp and Timber Company, Vanity Fair Paper Mills, St. Croix Paper Company, and Fordyce Lumber Company in 1963; Bestwall Gypsum Company in 1965; and Kalamazoo Paper Company in 1967. After building its first corrugated-container plant in Olympia in 1961, the company added a series of additional manufacturing facilities for lumber, paper, and chemical products over the course of the rest of the decade.

Upon Cheatham's death in 1970, Robert B. Pamplin, who had worked with Cheatham since the company's inception, became chairman and chief executive officer. Although the company's building-products business benefited from the housing boom of the early 1970s, its paper and pulp interests struggled due to low prices and sluggish demand. To bolster its manufacturing operations, the firm expanded production of two new building materials, polyvinyl chloride (PVC) and particle board, the former through a joint venture with Permaneer Corporation. Georgia-Pacific opened its own PVC manufacturing plant in 1975. When the cost of oil increased soon afterward, however, the company's prices for its PVC-molding products proved to be too high to compete effectively with wood moldings, resulting in significant losses.

It was also during this period that the firm was required by the Federal Trade Commission (FTC) to defend its acquisition of 16 small firms in the South that supplied the company with 673,000 acres of the southern pine used to make plywood. Charging that the acquisitions tended to create a monopoly, the FTC issued a consent order in 1972 that forced Georgia-Pacific to divest 20 percent of its assets. This step resulted in the formation of a spin-off company called Louisiana-Pacific Corporation. The order also prohibited the firm from acquiring any other softwood plywood companies, and imposed restrictions on timberland purchases in the South for five years and on plywood mill acquisitions for ten years.

A slump in the housing industry in 1973 and 1974 depressed the company's lumber and plywood business. Georgia-Pacific continued to post record profits, however, due largely to the growth of its chemical, pulp, and paper operations. These areas experienced slowdowns as well by the middle of the decade. Nevertheless, the company moved forward in its long-range program to increase manufacturing capacity across the board. It expanded through vertical integration into the production of additional chemicals derived from wood wastes, such as chlorine, phenol, and methanol. The 1975 acquisition of Exchange Oil & Gas Corporation enabled the company to become more self-sufficient by developing its own reserves of important raw materials required for the operation of its chemical plants.

In 1976 president Robert Flowerree succeeded Robert Pamplin as chairman and chief executive. A 25-year Georgia-Pacific veteran, Flowerree had been instrumental in taking the company into the chemical business. He was also considered to be more cautious than his predecessors. Under his leadership, the firm expanded its building products to include roofing materials, which it began to produce in a converted paper mill.

By 1978 the company was drawing three-quarters of its sales from the southern and eastern United States. This shift away from the West was instrumental in the decision to move the headquarters of the firm back to Georgia, 150 miles away from its original location in Atlanta. The relocation caused many employees to leave the company, and several senior executives chose to retire rather than make the move. This shift left the firm vulnerable at a critical time, particularly in the growing chemical area.

The dawning of the 1980s brought with it another housing slump, but Georgia-Pacific was able to use its chemical business to maintain overall growth. Its plywood products, however, were slowly losing competitive ground to new and cheaper materials, such as waferboard and oriented-strand board, which were being manufactured and sold aggressively by such firms as Louisiana-Pacific and Potlatch Corporation. Until then, Georgia-Pacific had not placed significant emphasis on these materials, with only one plant producing waferboard and another producing oriented-strand board. Most of its capital expenditure was directed instead toward upgrading existing facilities and buying timberlands.

In 1982 T. Marshall Hahn Jr., who had succeeded Flowerree as president in 1976, became chief operating officer. When he became chairman and chief executive officer one year later, following Flowerree's early retirement, he faced several serious problems. Demand for paper was strong, but only in the area of higher-quality products, not in the basic linerboard and kraft paper sectors in which Georgia-Pacific concentrated. Although an upturn in the construction industry augured well for the company's building products business, the high interest rates on the debt the firm had used to fund expansion severely limited its freedom to take advantage of opportunities in that area. Furthermore, its chemical business, once the firm's star division, fell on hard times as sales dropped significantly. This business was sold to Georgia Gulf Corporation in 1984, followed by the sale of Exchange Oil & Gas in 1985. The company retained its specialty chemicals business, which continued to deliver good returns.

Hahn instituted a series of measures designed to get the company back on its feet. These included reviewing the health of its assets, improvement of cost controls and productivity, and continued investment in areas such as the pulp and paper business, which could insulate the company from future economic calamities and provide a hedge against cyclical upturns and downturns in the various industries in which the company operated. In 1984 Georgia-Pacific acquired a linerboard mill, several corrugated container plants, and over 300,000 acres of forest from St. Regis Corporation. It converted two paper plants to the production of higher-margin products, such as light-weight bleached board and white paper used by copiers and computer printers. It also successfully expanded a wood products mill in South Carolina and a plant in Florida to produce lattice and fencing materials, which were in heavy demand.

In 1986 the company entered another area of the paper market through the introduction of Angel Soft bathroom tissue. By the end of 1987 Georgia-Pacific's tissue and towel operation, combined with its production of linerboard, kraft, and fine papers, enabled the company to achieve higher profitability in paper products than in wood products for the first time in its history, despite tough competition from major consumer products companies such as the Procter & Gamble Company.

Other elements of Hahn's turnaround strategy included further decentralization of the company's operations, which forced plant managers to compete with each other for capital funds, and the addition of several building materials distribution centers nationwide to capitalize on the growing trend toward remodeling and do-it-yourself projects.

During the last few years of the decade, the company made further acquisitions. These included U.S. Plywood Corporation and selected assets of the Erving Distributor Products Company in 1987, and Brunswick Pulp & Paper Company and American Forest Products Company in 1988. Its most controversial purchase, however, commenced in 1989 with an offer to buy Great Northern Nekoosa Corp of Connecticut, a competing producer of pulp, paper, containerboard, lumber, and plywood.

Originally incorporated in 1898 as the Northern Development Company but soon renamed Great Northern Paper Company, the predecessor to Great Northern Nekoosa had begun producing newsprint in 1900. By 1924 it was manufacturing corrugated paper and a decade later began a gradual transition from wrapping paper to business paper production. The company expanded its pulp and paper operations over the next 40 years.

In 1970 the Great Northern Paper Company and the Nekoosa Edwards Paper Company merged to become Great Northern Nekoosa Corporation. Great Northern Nekoosa acquired several firms subsequently to enhance the company's manufacturing and distribution capabilities, including Heco Envelope Company in 1973; Pak-Well in 1975; Leaf River Forest Products in 1981; Barton, Duer & Koch, and Consolidated Marketing, Inc. in 1982; Triquet Paper Company in 1983; Chatfield Paper Company in 1984; J&J Corrugated Box Corporation and Carpenter Paper Company of Iowa in 1986; Owens-Illinois's forest products company in 1987; and Jim Walter Papers in 1988.

Great Northern Nekoosa was a particularly attractive candidate for acquisition because of its depressed stock price. Georgia-Pacific saw the combination of the two companies as an opportunity to achieve economies of scale and other cost savings. In Hahn's opinion the acquisition would enable Georgia-Pacific to add manufacturing capability at less expense than by building its own plants. On the other hand, Great Northern Nekoosa viewed Georgia-Pacific's $3.74 billion bid as a hostile takeover attempt. It attempted to halt the proposed buyout with a series of lawsuits and an extensive search for another buyer. All of these measures failed, however, and the purchase was completed in March 1990. Georgia-Pacific assumed a significant amount of debt as a result, but was able to eliminate part of the burden through the subsequent sale of several mills and some timberland to Tenneco, the John Hancock Mutual Life Insurance Company, and the Metropolitan Life Insurance Company.

With its hard-fought acquisition of Great Northern Nekoosa complete, Georgia-Pacific held market leadership positions in containerboard, packaging, pulp, and communication papers and was a major producer of related products, such as tissue, kraft paper, and bleached board. The most significant threat to the company's continued growth would be the economy's effects on its key business areas. Although the firm's diversification into paper and pulp manufacturing was intended to help its survive cyclical downturns in lumber and housing construction, its new business areas were also highly cyclical in nature, with peaks and valleys lagging only months behind those occurring in lumber and housing.

Paper prices fell soon after Georgia-Pacific closed the Great Northern Nekoosa deal, but true to plan, the declining paper market was offset by record profits in the company's building products division, which posted profits of $432 million in 1990 despite low levels in housing starts. Georgia-Pacific was also able to reduce a significant amount of the $8 billion debt it saddled through its Great Northern Nekoosa purchase, thanks to the company's healthy cash flow. Despite these favorable signs, net income fell to $365 million in 1990, down from $661 million in 1989.

Prices of Georgia-Pacific shares on the New York Stock Exchange fell almost 50 percent in 1990 in response to investors' fears that the company might be acquiring too much debt. To ease this concern, the company took out a two-page ad in national magazines to convey the message that the company had significant cash flow to pay down its debt and had laid the groundwork for a strong future.

Despite Georgia-Pacific's intentions, profits took a dive in 1991 when the bottom dropped out of both the building materials and pulp and paper markets. The company reported a net loss of $151 million, compared to profits of over $3 million the preceding year. Georgia-Pacific continued to rely on its substantial cash flow to pay shareholders and pay down its debt in 1991.

In 1991 the company also reorganized its building products division along product lines, as opposed to its previous method of management along geographical lines. It also completed the expansion of its Ashdown, Arkansas, paper mill with the addition of the world's largest and fastest paper machine. A.D. (Pete) Correll, who joined Georgia-Pacific's paper division in 1988 after being wooed from his position at the Mead Corporation, was elected president and chief operating officer.

Despite its continuously healthy cash flow and record-breaking profits in its building products division, the company posted losses again in 1992. In response to the recession, which continued to affect Georgia-Pacific's key businesses, management chose to focus on keeping costs down and reducing debt in 1992.

Georgia-Pacific did this by paring down its "non-strategic" assets in early 1993, selling its Butler Paper distribution operations (acquired as part of its purchase of Great Northern Nekoosa) to Alco Standard Corporation and its roofing manufacturing business to GAF Corporation in March 1993. Proceeds of both sales, estimated at nearly $225 million, went to further reduce the company's debt.

When Georgia-Pacific announced in January 1993 that Correll was to succeed Hahn as its chairman and CEO, the company's financial outlook began to look brighter. Housing starts were on the rise again, and lumber production remained far below demand. Lumber prices had been rising to record highs since October, and industry analysts expect the growth to continue. Georgia Pacific had grown to become the largest supplier of building lumber in the United States and was perfectly poised to benefit from improvements in the economy.

The pulp and paper market, however, remained in a slump, causing some to question the wisdom of the Great Northern Nekoosa takeover. While Correll admitted that in the short term the purchase may not have seemed like such a good idea, he firmly believed that the investment would pay off substantially once paper industry cycles began to climb again. Demand for the company's pulp and paper products is affected by the overall production capacity of the industry, as well as by economic factors such as currency exchange rates and conditions in foreign markets.

Principal Subsidiaries: American Forest Products Company; Ashley, Drew & Northern Railway Company; Brunswick Pulp & Paper Company; California Western Railroad; Fordyce and Princeton R.R. Company; G-P DISC, Inc.; Georgia-Temp. Inc.; Georgia-Pacific Export, Inc.; Georgia-Pacific Foreign Sales Corporation; Georgia-Pacific Leasing Corporation; Georgia-Pacific Paper Sales, Inc.; Gloster Southern Railroad Company; Great Northern Nekoosa Corporation; Hudson Pulp & Paper Corporation; Phoenix Athletic Club, Inc.; Saint Croix Water Power Company (Canada); The Sprague's Falls Manufacturing

Company; St. Croix Water Power Company; Superwood Corporation; Superior Fiber Products, Inc.; Thacker Land Company (57%); U.S. Plywood Corporation; XRS, Inc.

Further Reading:

"The Best of Everything," *Forbes,* March 15, 1977.

Calonius, Erik, "America's Toughest Papermaker," *Fortune,* February 26, 1990.

Gold, Jackey, "Culture Shock," *Financial World,* February 20, 1990.

Norvell, Scott, "Southern Comfort for a Timber Giant," *New York Times,* March 23, 1993, sec. 3, p. 6.

Reier, Sharon, "New Math vs. Old Culture," *Financial World,* March 22, 1988.

Roots, Atlanta, Georgia: Georgia-Pacific Corporation, 1988.

Wiegner, Kathleen K., "A Tale of Two Companies," *Forbes,* March 6, 1978.

—Sandy Schusteff
updated by Maura Troester

Glaxo Holdings PLC

Lansdowne House
Berkeley Square
London W1X 6BP
England
(071) 493-4060

Public Company
Incorporated: 1972
Employees: 37,083
Sales: £4.10 billion (US$6.09 billion)
Stock Exchanges: New York London
SICs: 2834 Pharmaceutical Preparations

One of Britain's most esteemed companies, Glaxo Holdings PLC is one of the world's largest pharmaceutical entities, second only to Merck & Co., Inc. Glaxo manufactures prescription drugs in over 40 plants throughout the world. The company was transformed from a moderate-sized health care conglomerate into a fast-growing pharmaceutical colossus as a result of the development of the anti-ulcer drug, Zantac. Zantac captured over half of the world's market for anti-ulcer medication and soon became the largest-selling prescription drug in the world. Glaxo executives are quick to refute any suggestion that the company's future depends solely on the strength of one product. Instead they point to Glaxo's long history in drug innovation, its strong emphasis on research and development, and new products soon to be released on the market.

Glaxo began as a merchant trader. After a New Zealand partnership between Joseph Nathan and his brother-in-law was dissolved in 1873, the English-born entrepreneur started an independent company under the name Joseph Nathan & Company. Importing and exporting goods ranging from whalebone to patent medicines, Joseph Nathan prospered. He eventually returned to London in order to supervise his growing business there, while his sons remained in Wellington to manage the company activities in New Zealand.

While on a purchasing trip in London, one of the Nathan sons discovered an American process to dry milk. After securing the rights to this process, the company began production of dried milk at Bunnythorpe factory in New Zealand. Research on the sanitary quality of the milk soon caught the attention of the medical establishment; sales of the product, however, proved disappointing. The most promising market emerged in infant food. Thus, production of Glaxo baby food products began.

Alec, the youngest Nathan son, moved from New Zealand to London to supervise an expansion of the baby food business there. Much of the sales momentum Alec thereafter achieved is attributed to his *Glaxo Baby Book,* a practical guide to child care. In it could be found the Glaxo slogan, "Builds Bonnie Babies," which would soon become famous. Only a year after the product registered its first impressive sales figures, Joseph Nathan died and the chair passed to his son Louis. Sales continued to grow, and within a relatively short period of time Glaxo Baby Foods had become an important U.K.-based manufacturer.

By the outbreak of World War I production demands compelled the company to build a more modern facility and to hire new staff. Ernest Rose joined the company to supervise manufacturing processes, and Harry Jephcott was placed in charge of Glaxo's rudimentary laboratory. With the completion of Glaxo House, the company's new headquarters, Jephcott's laboratory grew and employed a staff of eight scientists including two women.

In the years that followed, Harry Jephcott moved up the ranks from chemist to company chair. Born in 1891, the son of a train driver, Jephcott received his education in pharmacy. When first hired by the Nathan family he was regarded as "Alec's folly," but he quickly proved his worth and became indispensable to Glaxo's success. As a top executive he was known for his firm leadership and business acumen—a perfect complement to Alec Nathan, who tended to focus on worker welfare. Jephcott's accomplishments eventually were rewarded with a knighthood.

Glaxo Baby Foods sales continued to grow in the years following World War I, and the company expanded into such markets as India and South America. Jephcott's 1923 visit to the International Dairy Congress in Washington, D.C. soon changed the course of Glaxo's history. There he observed Professor Elmer V. McCollum's and Dr. Theodore Zucker's original work in identifying and extracting vitamin D. Recognizing the huge market potential in fortifying Glaxo products with this anti-rachitic, Jephcott persuaded the company's directors to secure a process license. After achieving an immediate success with vitamin D fortified products, Glaxo moved on to produce a pharmaceutical item, Ostelin Liquid, Britain's first commercial vitamin concentrate. Ostelin products eventually included a comprehensive line of vitamin preparations.

In the 1930s Glaxo's major advancements included the production of Adexolin (vitamins A and D) and Oster-milk, a retail version of Glaxo's vitamin fortified milk that soon surpassed the pharmaceutical version in sales. Because of increased business overseas, the company built a factory in India, established a company in Italy, and secured distributorships in Greece, Malaya, and China. In an effort to strengthen the company's increasing activity, Glaxo's pharmaceutical department was organized into a separate subsidiary called Glaxo Laboratories Ltd.

During World War II, the company concentrated on producing pharmaceuticals for the war effort, including anesthetics, penicillin, and a variety of vitamin supplements. After the war Glaxo began the mass production of penicillin in earnest, using the American process of deep fermentation. During this time, several long-time Glaxo employees retired. Harry Jephcott became chairperson of the company upon Alec Nathan's retirement. Ida Townsend, Glaxo's successful export manager, joined the board in 1947, the company's first woman director. Changes also occurred in the company's structure: Glaxo's parent company, Joseph Nathan & Company, was dissolved, and Glaxo became an independent public company. All Joseph Nathan's diversified interests, from butter importing to fencing exporting, were sold to finance Glaxo's growth.

By far the most important of Glaxo's postwar achievements was the isolation of vitamin B12. Along with their American counterparts at Merck, who had achieved the same feat virtually simultaneously, Glaxo had made a major advance in the treatment of pernicious anaemia. Of similar magnitude was Glaxo's synthesis of the hormone necessary for the treatment of hypothyroidism.

In the 1950s Glaxo grew through acquisition and consolidation. The company acquired both a chemical and a medical supply subsidiary and established an independent veterinary department to meet the increasing demand for animal pharmaceuticals. Through a merger Glaxo joined forces with Allen & Hanbury's, one of Britain's oldest pharmaceutical manufacturers. Britain's first commercial cortisone product emerged from Glaxo's laboratories during this time. The discovery of sisal as an abundant source of an important steroid led to the commercial synthesis of a series of corticosteroids.

Glaxo's growth continued into the 1960s. To monitor this growth, the directors formed a new parent company, Glaxo Group Limited. Jephcott assumed the title of chairperson for the holding company. In 1963 he retired from this position, becoming Glaxo's first honorary president, and the physicist Sir Alan Wilson assumed the chair. Glaxo's scientists worked to develop Betnovate, a new corticosteroid. Through a licensing agreement with Schering U.S.A., a pharmaceutical company engaged in original research in corticosteroids, Glaxo developed a production process essential to the manufacture of the drug.

During the next decade, Beecham, an industry competitor, attempted the largest takeover in British history by making an unfriendly bid for Glaxo. To protect its independence, Glaxo management sought to increase its holdings through a merger with a company of similar interests. Thus Glaxo and Boots, another competitor, planned to combine their company resources. Yet neither the takeover nor the merger ever happened. The Monopolies Commissioners ruled against the proceedings on the grounds that innovation declines as companies grow above a certain size. In the wake of the aborted takeover attempt, the company was renamed Glaxo Holdings.

In 1973 Sir Alan Wilson retired and Austin Bide, a long time Glaxo employee, assumed the titles of chairperson and chief executive officer. Other changes during the 1970s included the establishment of a U.S. subsidiary. Domestic consolidation brought all Glaxo's UK operations under one holding company. In pharmaceuticals Glaxo's innovative research in cephalosporins resulted in the development of Zinacef.

Near the end of the 1970s Glaxo suffered from the effects of inflation. Citing Glaxo's continuing dependence on export trade, its failure to expand significantly beyond the British and Commonwealth markets, and its persistent reputation for poor marketing decisions, city analysts projected slower growth in

the company's future. What industry observers did not foresee was the release of a drug destined to become highly successful throughout the world. Zantac, Glaxo's tradename for its anti-ulcer drug ranatidine, was still in testing during this time. However, based on the emerging results of these tests, Glaxo knew that Zantac was ready to present a competitive challenge to SmithKline's Tagamet, then the preeminent anti-ulcer medication and best-selling drug in the world.

Soon after Austin retired as chief executive officer, Zantac was launched in several European markets with a high degree of success. Paul Girolami, a long time Glaxo employee who had formerly served as Group Financial Director, assumed Sir Austin's position. Over the next several years Girolami established himself as the architect of Zantac's marketing policy in the United States and Japan. In a joint venture with Hoffmann-La Roche, the Swiss pharmaceutical concern responsible for developing the world's two best-selling tranquilizers, Glaxo introduced Zantac to the U.S. market.

By 1984 Zantac had captured 25 percent of the new prescription market. Glaxo announced plans to build a $40 million plant in North Carolina to manufacture the drug in the United States. Joseph J. Ruvane, Jr., president of Glaxo's U.S. company, claimed Glaxo would become one of America's top ten pharmaceutical firms. The company's actively traded shares increased in price from £2.40 a share in 1980 to £10.25 after a two-for-one split. By the end of the decade, Zantac captured more than half of the world market in its class and became the largest-selling prescription drug in the world. The company employed a unique marketing strategy in 1981: it developed strategic partnerships with drug companies around the world to get an edge in each market. From 1980 to 1988, Glaxo's sales nearly tripled, and in 1989 profits soared 13 percent over the previous year to L1.14 billion, ensuring the company's role as the second-largest pharmaceutical company worldwide.

Over the next few years, however, Glaxo's status declined somewhat. A wave of drug company mergers in 1989 left the company fourth in worldwide sales. The company was reorganized that year, and CEO Bernard D. Taylor was replaced by Ernest Mario, formerly head of U.S. operations. Zantac sales plateaued by the start of the 1990s, when newly formulated anti-ulcer drugs threatened its commanding share, and some industry analysts doubted the company's ability to maintain its lead in new drug introductions.

In 1990, Glaxo announced worldwide regulatory trials for its new anti-migraine drug, Imigran (or sumatriptan, generically). Moreover, Zofran Injection, an important new treatment for the prevention of nausea and vomiting in cancer patients receiving chemotherapy, was approved by the United States Food and Drug Administration early in 1991. Within just over a year, the drug was available in most of the world's markets and registered sales of L259 million in Glaxo's 1991–92 fiscal year.

Glaxo tried to capture some of the entrepreneurial energy of smaller companies through joint ventures. In 1991, Glaxo entered into an agreement with Gilead Sciences Inc. In exchange for about $20 million, Glaxo purchased an equity stake in the company and its potential for creating anti-cancer drugs. The company also sold its interests outside of prescription drugs and increased its research and development allocations. One such development, Ceftazidime, an injectable antibiotic, received a strong market reception in Japan.

Zantac's arrival in Japan had involved major competition in the form of an anti-ulcer drug discovered by the Japanese Yamanouchi Company. The company's difficulties in Japan continued in the early 1990s. Corporate executives cited frequent price reductions and registration delays as impediments to greater success in this, the second-largest market in the world. Glaxo did penetrate the Chinese, Eastern European, and Russian markets in the early 1990s, opening a factory in China and establishing branches and companies in many former Communist bloc countries.

By 1992, Glaxo had captured 3.7 percent of the world's pharmaceutical market, and marked its twelfth year of continuous growth. Profits, however, did not maintain the same pace, having been eroded by research, marketing, and infrastructure costs. At the same time, Glaxo was threatened by competition from Wellcome PLC, a rival that was able to launch more than a dozen drugs during the 1980s and early 1990s, including Zovirax, a herpes treatment, and Retovir, a drug to combat AIDS. Glaxo has been able to retaliate with the introduction of new asthma and hypertension treatments, in limited markets, but has yet to launch a product that could duplicate Zantac's success. Industry observers and the company's directors remain confident, however, that Glaxo's continuing success will be generated by its long history of developing noteworthy pharmaceuticals and effectively marketing them.

Principal Subsidiaries: Glaxo Group Ltd: Glaxo Group Ltd. (U.K.); Eschmann Bros. & Walsh Ltd. (U.K.); Evans Medical Ltd. (U.K.); Farely Health Products Ltd. (U.K.); Glaxo Animal Health Ltd. (U.K.); Glaxochem Ltd. (U.K.); Glaxo Group Research Ltd. (U.K.); Glaxo Operations UK Ltd.; Glaxo Pharmaceuticals Ltd. (U.K.); Glaxomed Ltd. (U.K.); W. H. Deane (High Wycombe) Ltd. (U.K.); Macfarlen Smith Ltd. (U.K.); Glaxo Export Ltd. (U.S. and U.K.); Matburn (Holdings) Ltd. (U.K.); Glaxo Inc. (U.S.); Glaxo India Ltd. (40%); Glaxo Korea Co. Ltd. (50%); Glaxo Nigeria PLC (40%); Chongqing Glaxo Pharmaceuticals Ltd. (50%).

Further Reading:

Feinberg, Phyllis. "Creating Joint Ventures for David and Goliath," *Corporate Cashflow,* May 1991, pp. 57–58.

Foster, Geoffrey. "How to Make Yourself Wellcome," *Management Today,* July 1992, pp. 68–71.

Gerrie, David. "Can Marketing Keep Glaxo in Pole Position?" *Marketing (UK),* October 18, 1990, pp. 24–25.

"Glaxo Goes It Alone," *Chief Executive,* June 1990, pp. 22–25.

Reekie, Duncan W. *The Economics of the Pharmaceutical Industry,* London: Macmillan, 1975.

Rosenberg, Jack, and Cynthia Starr. "New Drugs of 1990," *Drug Topics,* January 21, 1991, pp. 31–43.

Savitz, Eric J. "Glaxo's Headaches: A Remarkable Drug Company Faces Some Challenges," *Barron's,* June 17, 1991, pp. 8–9, 18–22.

"Science and Technology: Glaxo's Headaches," *Economist (UK),* November 17, 1990, pp. 111–112.

Sheeline, William E. "Glaxo's Goal: New Wonder Cures," *Fortune,* v.120, November 6, 1989, pp. 101–108.

Teitelman, Robert. "Staying Power," *Financial World,* April 4, 1989, pp. 28–30.

—updated by April S. Dougal

Global Marine Inc.

777 N. Eldridge Road
Houston, Texas 77079
U.S.A.
(713) 596-5100
Fax: (713) 531-1260

Public Company
Incorporated: 1953
Employees: 1,500
Sales: $260.3 million
Stock Exchanges: New York
SICs: 1381 Drilling Oil & Gas Wells; 1311 Crude Petroleum
& Natural Gas

One of the largest offshore drilling firms in the world, Global Marine Inc. drills oil and gas wells and produces crude petroleum and natural gas.

Global Marine was founded in 1953 as an offshore drilling venture formed by four small oil companies. The future of offshore drilling looked bright throughout the 1950s. War in the Middle East and new U.S. government import restrictions lead to great need for domestic oil production, and petroleum firms were scouring the Gulf of Mexico. The situation changed dramatically in 1958 when the state of Louisiana and the federal government became embroiled in a dispute over the ownership of the tidelands where oil companies were drilling. During the fight lease sales dried up, and the number of drilling rigs in U.S. coastal waters fell from 120 to 40. By this time, Global's major shareholders were Aerojet-General Corp. and Union Oil Co. of California. With the offshore-drilling market tumbling, a group of employees led by engineers Robert F. Bauer and Almeron Field bought Union's share of the company.

Within a few years the dispute was settled, and market conditions changed for the better. Global grew rapidly, going public in 1962. By the mid-1960s it was one of the world's biggest offshore drilling firms, with rigs off the coast of Alaska, Nigeria, Australia, Libya, California, and Louisiana and in the Persian Gulf and the North Sea. The firm was not an oil company and did not sell oil. Global rented its rigs and crews to oil companies for offshore drilling. By 1965 the firm's revenues reached $21.5 million, and all of its rigs were rented for two or more years in advance.

Offshore drilling had not existed until the late 1940s, and rig designs were rapidly becoming more sophisticated, able to work in deeper waters for longer periods, with greater comfort for the crew. While other firms worked on shallow-water platforms using a "jack-up" design, Global put its resources into building a fleet of self-propelled vessels that drilled though wells in their center. The firm believed these vessels had greater speed and flexibility.

With its core business doing well, Global branched into related fields. Through its subsidiary Global Engineering Company it began training crews and inspecting ships for the U.S. Navy. It also installed a secret underwater testing site for the Navy's Polaris missiles. Through another subsidiary it engaged in long-range weather forecasting, usually for other companies involved in ocean exploration. It took core samples of the ocean floor for the National Science Foundation, raised shrimp in Hawaii, and mined for gold off Alaska. Along with other offshore oil companies, Global began to engage in its own oil exploration. It bought interests in the Canadian Arctic and North Sea, where some petroleum companies had found oil. It continued to build drilling vessels, owning 12 by the middle of the 1970s. Sales grew as its fleet expanded, reaching $89 million by 1974.

At about this time, worldwide publicity was briefly turned on Global Marine when it participated in a controversial attempt to raise a Soviet submarine off the floor of the Pacific Ocean, along with the Central Intelligence Agency and Howard Hughes's Summa Corporation. The submarine broke in half as it was raised.

Despite its growing sales and fleet, Global faced trouble because of its heavy reliance on self-propelled vessels, the wisdom of which some industry analysts questioned. The vessels were less stable than other types of rigs in rough seas, and since they cost more to build, they cost more to rent. Because other types of rigs were judged better suited to the North Sea and Gulf of Mexico, Global missed many of the jobs it might have won. As a result, it lost money in 1976 and 1977. Further, it owned one of the oldest fleets in its industry. Finally in 1979, with oil prices rising, Global ordered 17 jack-up rigs for $400 million, to better compete for jobs in shallow waters. To finance its expansion, Global borrowed heavily, leaving it with a 4-to-1 debt-to-equity ratio.

At first this seemed a wise plan. Global's revenues grew from $91 million in 1976 to $456 million in 1982. It paid off substantial amounts of its debt and ordered eight more rigs, to further modernize its fleet. However, oil prices collapsed in the following years, and with an oversupply of natural gas as well, rig rates plummeted by more than 50 percent between 1981 and 1983. In 1983 one of the firm's drillships, the *Glomar China Sea,* sank in a typhoon off the coast of China, killing its entire crew of 84. In 1984 Global had to make a $120 million interest payment on its new rigs, at a time when half of its rigs were leased under break-even contracts. President C. Russell Luigs slashed spending and cut exploratory drilling. The firm made stock and bond offerings to raise cash. Its debt-to-equity ratio nevertheless remained at 2-to-1.

The market remained soft and Global lost $560 million between 1984 and 1986, forcing it to file for bankruptcy protection in 1986. Daily rates on its rigs had fallen from a peak of $50,000 during the early 1980s to $12,000 by 1986, while 75 percent of its drilling fleet stood idle. Sales dropped from $454 million in 1982 to $225 in 1986. Global's suspension of $20 million a month in interest payments prior to its bankruptcy essentially saved the company. Luigs gambled that Global's creditors would not foreclose. Global owed about $1.1 billion to a consortium of eight creditors, and many felt they would be more severely hurt by selling the firm's assets than by giving it a chance to recover.

Global's financial situation was extremely complicated because it had borrowed using specific company assets, usually drilling rigs, as collateral for specific loans. But each rig was financed at different times by different creditors for different interest rates, and this lead to difficulty in coming up with a reorganization plan acceptable to enough of its creditors. The largest creditor was the U.S. Maritime Administration, which had guaranteed $200 million of Global's debt through federal programs geared toward reducing U.S. dependence on foreign oil.

Drilling picked up somewhat in 1987, but Global still had only about half of its rigs active, mostly in the Gulf of Mexico, while a worldwide oversupply of drilling rigs kept prices low. The firm continued to lose money ($155.6 million in 1988 alone) as it struggled to reorganize.

Global emerged from bankruptcy in early 1989. Ironically, it was again one of the strongest offshore drilling firms. Many of its competitors had also gone bankrupt and had not yet reorganized. Global had dealt with its financial problems, at least temporarily, and it now had one of the largest, most modern, and efficient fleets in the industry. It also had reduced its costs, cutting its workforce to 1,500 from over 3,000 in 1985, and hiring more lower-paid foreign workers. Its creditors traded two-thirds of the firm's debt for ownership of over 90 percent of the company. Over the next three years, Global only had to pay one year's interest on its remaining $446 million in debt. Meanwhile, the market had picked up somewhat. Nearly all of Global's rigs were at work, and the day rate had risen to about $26,000. Yet overall it remained a difficult time, alleviated only briefly in 1990 when oil prices rose in response to Iraq's invasion of Kuwait.

Under these conditions, Global was able to cut its debt by another $60 million by the end of 1991, aided by the terms of its new debt service agreement. However, company officials felt that this would not be enough to avoid a fiscal crisis by 1995. They resolved to recapitalize Global and cut its debt further. The firm sold one of its smaller jackup rigs for $18 million, and used the money to lessen its debt. The firm's policy was to retire rigs that were becoming obsolete. It therefore retired the Glomar Biscay semi-submersible rig and the Glomar Atlantic drillship, reducing the average age of its fleet to about ten years. The Biscay was sold for scrap, while the Atlantic was purchased for use outside the drilling industry. Global sold 26 million shares of common stock and $225 million of senior secured notes. These moves decreased Global's total debt by $142 million.

These financial successes not withstanding, 1992 was another difficult year for Global. The average utilization rate for its rigs declined from 86 percent in 1991 to 78 percent in 1992, while the average day rate fell to $27,600 from $29,300. The North Sea market became particularly weak. The natural gas market also softened, and sales at Challenger Minerals Inc., the firm's oil and gas subsidiary, fell to $19 million, down from $28 million in 1991. The firm sold an additional 3.9 million shares of stock in January 1993, raising another $7.8 million.

Principal Subsidiaries: Applied Drilling Technology, Inc.; Challenger Minerals, Inc.; Global Marine Drilling Company.

Further Reading:

"Contract Drillers Tap a Money Field," *Business Week,* March 13, 1965.
Field, Alan M., "Staying Afloat," *Forbes,* October 6, 1986.
"Global Marine Borrows, Slashes Rates—and Sticks Its Neck Out Further," *Business Week,* December 19, 1983.
"Global Splash," *Barron's,* April 25, 1966.
Ivey, Mark, "Global Marine: Pumped Up by Kuwait," *Business Week,* October 29, 1990.
"Now All Global Marine Needs Is a Market," *Business Week,* March 13, 1989.
Stuart, Reginald, "Global Marine Searches World for Undersea Riches," *New York Times,* March 20, 1975.
Vogel, Todd, "Missing the Boat for the Ship," *Forbes,* November 15, 1975.

—Scott M. Lewis

H&R BLOCK®

H & R Block, Incorporated

4410 Main Street
Kansas City, Missouri 64111
U.S.A.
(816) 753-6900
Fax: (816) 753-5346

Public Company
Incorporated: 1955
Employees: 4,200
Sales: $1.4 billion
Stock Exchanges: New York Pacific Midwest
SICs: 7291 Tax Return Preparation Services; 7375
   Information Retrieval Services; 7372 Repackaged
   Software; 7363 Help Supply Services

The name of H & R Block, Incorporated, has become synonymous with the business of preparing income tax returns, and justifiably so. The company is far and away the largest in this field; 20 percent of the Americans who hire someone to prepare their taxes for them, which translates to 10 percent of all Americans who file tax returns, turn to H & R Block. In the late 1970s the company began an acquisition spree, thanks to its substantial cash reserves and paucity of long-term debt. It diversified into computer information and temporary personnel services through its CompuServe Incorporated and INTERIM Services, Inc., subsidiaries, respectively.

H & R Block was founded in Kansas City, Missouri, by Henry and Richard Bloch. The two brothers had followed slightly different paths: Henry Bloch had received his degree in math at the University of Michigan and served as a bomber crewman during World War II, whereas Richard studied economics at the University of Pennsylvania's Wharton School of Finance. In 1946, while still in their early 20s, Henry and Richard teamed up and formed in their hometown a business services company called United Business. They offered bookkeeping, collections, advertising, and other forms of assistance to local businesses. Tax preparation was one of those services, but the Bloch brothers considered it so marginal that they offered it free of charge to their customers. Within eight years, they were running the largest bookkeeping firm in Kansas City. They also made a sideline out of preparing individual tax returns for people who worked in the building in which they were headquartered.

Preparing individual returns might have remained a mere sideline if the Internal Revenue Service (IRS) had not stopped offering such assistance to the public in 1955. Ironically, Henry and Richard Bloch wanted to get out of that line of work at the time, feeling that it was distracting them from their core operations for little profit. However, one of their individual clients, an advertising salesman for the *Kansas City Star* named John White, persuaded them to give tax preparation more of a try—and to take out two advertisements in his newspaper. On the first day that the ads ran, the Blochs found their office flooded with customers.

32 years later, Henry Bloch would recall: "I can distinctly remember thinking, 'This tax thing is tremendous—it is really going to help our accounting business, what with the advertising and the referrals and all.' But it had the opposite effect. . . . Because my brother and I began devoting so much of our time and energies to the tax side, we didn't give our business clients the type of service they wanted. . . . We found that they were quitting on us."

Therefore, the Bloch brothers divested their accounting business by selling it to their employees. They reincorporated in 1955, setting up shop under the H & R Block name, and devoted themselves to preparing tax returns for the little guy full time. The Bloch brothers also chose to deliberately misspell their last name in christening their new venture. Two similar, though distinct, reasons for why they did this have been given. According to one story they dropped the "h" in favor of the more phonetic "k" to make sure people wouldn't mispronounce the name; in another, they simply assumed that people would misspell it phonetically anyway.

However they felt about the new company's name, customers were quick to pony up for its services. In its first year H & R Block generated $20,000 in revenues, enough to pique the Blochs' interest in expansion. In 1956 they opened seven storefront offices in New York City to see if they could duplicate their success. These new offices generated $67,000 in revenues in their first year, but the Bloch brothers grew homesick for Kansas City and didn't want to stay in the Big Apple or shuttle between the two cities to keep tabs on business in both. Anxious to sell, they agreed to hand over their New York operations to two local accountants for only $10,000 and a percentage of future revenues. For that, H & R Block would be hailed as a pioneer in franchising, even though, as Henry Bloch later admitted, the company more or less backed into it. "When we first franchised," he said, "we didn't even know what the word meant."

The company's first experience in franchising would also turn out to be an unhappy one. Concerned by unscrupulous practices on the part of the New York franchisees, H & R Block would initiate legal action against them in 1964, charging violation of the company's pricing and advertising arrangements. The two parties settled out of court in 1966, and as a result H & R Block bought back the franchises for over $1 million.

More immediately, however, the New York experiment proved to the Bloch brothers that tax preparation would be a viable business outside of their hometown. In 1957 H & R Block opened offices in Topeka and Columbia, Missouri. The next year, it added offices in Des Moines, Oklahoma City, and Little Rock to the roster. From there, the company grew at a dazzling rate. It went public in 1962, and by 1967 it could boast of having nearly 1,700 offices in 1,000 cities in 44 states. During the 1967 tax season H & Block estimated that it would prepare a total of 2.5 million tax returns by the April 15th filing deadline. The company operated only 35 percent of these offices itself; the rest were franchised. At first, franchises were granted for a mere two percent of gross receipts. "We didn't sell franchises; we gave them away," Henry Bloch would later recall. "An employee would come in and ask us to help him open an H & R Block office in Chicago or Detroit or someplace. We gave him a little spending money and loaned him enough to rent a store and buy some desks. These guys were on their own, and in almost every case they have become wealthy men." In the 1960s, however, H & R Block wised up and raised its price to ten percent, then about 30 percent of gross receipts.

Of course, the company needed legions of trained personnel to keep up with such rapid expansion. In many respects, this proved to be a more substantial problem than drawing customers. To cope with it, H & R Block set up its own training program, which operated more or less as a trade school for tax preparers. In exchange for a small fee, trainees would enroll in an eight-week course taught by company managers. At the conclusion of the course, trainees might receive employment with the company, but they were also free to work for competitors or use their expertise on their own returns. In 1967, for instance, over 10,000 students enrolled in H & R Block's tax school, but less than half of them went to work for the company at the conclusion of the course. Even so, H & R Block gained 5,000 new employees to staff its storefronts that year.

The tax preparers themselves were and still are seasonal employees, the demand for their services being limited to the first four months of the year. Many of them are housewives, retirees, or people with day jobs looking for a second source of income. In recent years, the company has drawn many working mothers, who like the flexible hours that come with the job. Until H & R Block began diversifying out of its core business in the late 1970s, tax preparers constituted the vast majority of company employees. Despite the seasonal nature of the job, most of them return the next year for another round of grappling with the IRS. In 1987 Henry Bloch stated that 75 percent of the company's preparers come back the following year, no doubt because the company rewards its veterans with higher commission rates.

With a virtual headlock on its market, no capital costs except for the leases on its storefront offices and a few dollars for furniture and coffee, and labor costs limited to a fixed percentage of revenues, H & R Block proved wildly successful in the 1960s. In an average year, profits increased by 50 percent over the previous year. In 1969 and 1971, however, changes in the federal tax code reduced the overall number of taxpayers, thus shrinking the company's customer base. Even worse, in 1972 the IRS went to war against tax preparation firms. It cracked down on fraudulent preparers, resumed helping taxpayers prepare their returns, and launched a massive advertising campaign encouraging them not to use commercial preparation services. The IRS campaign, aided by the press, succeeded in tarring legitimate preparation services like H & R Block as well as dishonest ones. That year, the company's profits fell for the first time in its history.

The IRS campaign eventually collapsed after some public relations debacles of its own. After IRS Commissioner Johnnie Walters declared that the 1040 form was so simple a fifth-grader could complete it, his claim was subjected to various acts of scrutiny that proved it was far more complex than that. An experiment conducted by the *Wall Street Journal* also suggested that the IRS' preparers were no more reliable than most commercial services. H & R Block not only weathered the firestorm but came out of it in better shape than before, because the IRS' crusade had weeded out its weaker competitors. It was, in fact, the only profitable tax preparation firm of consequential size left in the nation. H & R Block solidified its overwhelming position in 1972 when it opened outlets in 147 Sears department stores—an entirely appropriate move for a company that Richard Bloch had once described as "the Sears, Roebuck of taxes."

Once the crisis had passed, the company found itself faced with a happy dilemma, one that the Bloch brothers had begun to contemplate in the late 1960s. Because its capital costs were so small for a business of its size, and because most of its revenues came in the form of cash, H & R Block had been able to accumulate vast cash reserves. It also found itself unburdened by long-term debt. Because the tax preparation business seemed ready to mature and slow its rate of growth, it was only logical that the company should diversify through acquisition to keep its revenues pumped up. H & R Block spent most of the 1970s searching for likely acquisition targets, but was limited by a lack of companies that were both available and potentially profitable, and also by Henry Bloch's reluctance to pull the trigger. "A guy told me that two out of three acquisitions fail," he said in 1974. "I just don't want to make a mistake the first time out."

H & R Block finally took its first major plunge in 1978, when it acquired Personnel Pool of America, a temporary personnel agency specializing in health care, for $22.5 million. The move seemed to make sense, as H & R Block already had some expertise regarding temporary personnel; after all, the core of its workforce at the time was made up of temps. Indeed, the acquisition worked out well: In two years, Personnel Pool of America jumped from the sixth-largest to the third-largest company in the temporary help field.

The 1980 acquisition of CompuServe also proved quite successful. H & R Block paid $23 million for the information services company, which provided computer time-sharing for corporations and government agencies. Soon after it was acquired by H & R Block, however, CompuServe entered the burgeoning field of providing such information services as software forums, electronic bulletin boards, electronic mail, and interactive games for personal computer users. In doing so, it made its new parent company look positively brilliant. CompuServe's earnings tripled between 1983 and 1985 and its subscriber base quadrupled. It was growing so fast that CompuServe chairman and co-founder Jeffrey Wilkins resigned in 1985 when H & R Block refused to allow him and some of his managers to purchase CompuServe stock. Wilkins subsequently headed an investor group that offered to buy CompuServe for $72.5 million, but H & R Block refused to sell. Wilkins' departure may have seemed like a setback to H & R Block, which considered it wise to keep its acquisitions' existing management teams intact, but CompuServe continued to grow without him. By the early 1990s it could boast of 1 million subscribers, making it the largest commercial on-line service.

Also in 1980, the Bloch brothers entered into a joint venture with Ohio attorney and entrepreneur (as well as son-in-law of U.S. Senator Howard Metzenbaum) Joel Hyatt, who wanted to set up his own chain of discount law offices patterned after the Los Angeles-based firm of Jacoby & Myers. Hyatt's idea was to tap into the same middle-income market for basic legal services, but to stake out his own geographic territory before Jacoby & Myers could expand beyond its California base. He had opened nine offices between 1977 and 1980, when H & Block approached him with the idea of partnership. For Hyatt, such a deal would provide him with the capital he needed for rapid and widespread expansion. The two parties set up a separate company called Block Management to operate Hyatt Legal Services in order to comply with American Bar Association rules forbidding anyone but lawyers to directly own a law firm. H & R Block took an 80 percent stake in the company, with Hyatt and his other partners taking the remaining 20 percent.

Both parties in this deal hoped that H & R Block's marketing resources would boost Hyatt Legal Services past archrival Jacoby & Myers. However, before long they realized that the synergies they had expected to create between tax preparation and legal services simply weren't happening. In 1987 H & R Block sold its interest in Block Management to Joel Hyatt for $20 million in what was described as a friendly parting of ways.

The 1985 acquisition of Path Management Industries, a business seminar company, also proved that, for all of Henry Bloch's prudence, H & R Block's touch was not always golden when it came to acquisitions. The 1988 postal rate increase hurt Path Management by hiking the cost of its direct-mail advertising, and the recession of the late 1980s depressed sales. Having paid $35 million for the company, H & R Block sold it to American Management Association in 1990 for $20 million.

In the meantime, Richard Bloch had become less involved with the running of the company after he was diagnosed with lung cancer in 1978. Bloch battled his illness successfully, but after his recovery he devoted much of his time to sponsoring cancer research and treatment. He retired in the early 1980s. At about the same time, Henry's son Thomas began to work his way up through the ranks. Tom Bloch became president and COO in 1988, and in 1992 he succeeded his father as CEO.

Of course, the business of preparing tax returns had remained profitable for the company. Tax preparation did in fact represent a mature line of business for H & R Block in the 1980s, and the company's rapid diversification reduced its contribution to the overall bottom line to just over half of total earnings by the decade's end. But when the IRS began allowing electronic filing of tax returns in 1986, it opened up a brand-new opportunity for H & R Block. The opportunity to receive an early refund inspired many who prepared their own returns to come to H & R Block to file electronically. Providing the service was relatively easy for the company, because it used CompuServe's existing communications links to transmit the returns through cyberspace. H & R Block also began offering advances on refunds through agreements with several different banks. In return for a service charge, a participating bank would loan the amount of the refund to an H & R Block client, accepting direct deposit of the refund check as repayment. Electronic filing gave the company's core business a needed boost; within five years it was handling an annual volume of 4.3 million electronic returns—nearly two-thirds of all returns filed electronically.

For all the adventures that it encountered in the 1980s, H & R Block entered the 1990s still in the market for acquisitions. In 1991 it purchased Interim Systems, a temporary personnel agency, for $49.5 million and merged its assets with those of Personnel Pool of America. The resulting merged subsidiary was then renamed INTERIM Services. As of early 1994, H & R Block was planning the sale of INTERIM through an initial public offering and had recently made the acquisition of MECA Software, Inc.

Without a doubt, the business odyssey of the Bloch brothers has been an astoundingly successful one. Richard Bloch once compared his company to Sears, and a journalist once called it "the McDonald's of tax preparation"; the fact that neither analogy seems absurd is a testament to H & R Block's standing in its part of the service economy. All three of these companies have dominated their respective markets so thoroughly that they have not only become synonymous in the public mind with what they sell, but their names have entered the annals of American popular culture. It is also impressive that the company has managed to maintain a steep earnings curve through successful acquisitions now that its core business has begun to mature. As long as taxes remain one of the two great certainties of life, and as long as the company continues to choose its diversifications carefully, the odyssey of H & R Block should continue to be successful.

Principal Subsidiaries: H & R Block Tax Services, Inc.; CompuServe, Incorporated; INTERIM Services, Inc.

Further Reading:
Ellis, James E., "H & R Block Expands Its Base," *Business Week,* April 29, 1991.
Karp, Richard, "The Bewilderment of Henry Bloch," *Dun's Review,* September 1974.
"Storefront Tax Service Earns a Good Return," *Business Week,* March 25, 1967.
"Taxman Henry Bloch," *Inc.,* December 1987.

—Douglas Sun

HAL Inc.

1164 Bishop Street
Honolulu, Hawaii 96813
U.S.A.
(808) 835-3001
Fax: (808) 835-3015

Public Company
Incorporated: 1929 as Inter-Island Airways Ltd.
Employees: 2,702
Sales: $365 million
Stock Exchanges: American Pacific
SICs: 4512 Air Transport—Scheduled; 4513 Air Courier
  Services; 6719 Holding Companies Nec

HAL Inc. is the holding company established in 1982 for the acquisition of Hawaiian Airlines Inc., a regional and international airline engaged in the transportation of passengers and cargo over routes that primarily cover the six islands of the state of Hawaii. The airline also serves cities on the U.S. mainland including Los Angeles, San Francisco, Seattle, and Anchorage, Alaska. Hawaiian Airlines also flies to the South Pacific and provides passenger charter services worldwide from its home base, Honolulu. The first to offer inter-island air travel, the company has survived 63 years and by 1993 carried an estimated five million passengers annually. The company provides service to 14 international and domestic destinations and to the pacific region, including Tahiti and American Samoa.

HAL Inc. is largely a formal legal entity set up to purchase Hawaiian Airlines. The history of the airline began in 1929 when Inter-Island Airways Ltd. was founded in Honolulu, Hawaii. At that time, Inter-Island Airways was the first company to offer scheduled flights between the six Hawaiian Islands. Inter-Island launched its inaugural flight to Maui and the Big Island of Hawaii, out of Honolulu's John Rodgers Airport, on November 11, 1929 using two eight passenger Sikorsky S-38 amphibian planes. This was the beginning of three weekly round trips between Honolulu and the two other islands. By 1935, Inter-Island moved to modernize its fleet as aviation technology advanced quickly. The company added larger, 16 passenger Sikorsky S-43s to accommodate increased traffic and newly authorized inter-island airmail service.

By 1941, Inter-Island changed its name to Hawaiian Airlines and added 24 passenger DC-3s to its fleet. The company was

under military control during World War II and, after receiving the very first air cargo certificate issued by the U.S. Civil Aeronautics Board, provided an aerial lifeline to Hawaii's neighbor islands. The DC-3 would be a mainstay of the company's fleet for years, and the company would also fly charters for tour operators and the Military Airlift Command in the late 1950s through the early 1960s.

The business grew steadily into the 1960s and became a leader in the inter-island air transport market. Hawaiian Airlines continued to expand its capacity to meet the growing demand, introducing new routes and improved service, as well as the Convair 340, which provided Hawaii with its first pressurized, air conditioned, cabin service. To expand their fleet further, in 1958, it purchased a long-range four-engine DC-6 aircraft for the military charter transpacific flights the company was starting.

With the expanding market base, revenues increased to around $10 million in 1960, representing substantial growth over the previous year. Profitability was fueled by lower costs and by a fare increase approved by the Civil Aeronautics Board. Further markets were opened as Hawaiian Airlines started still more routes, flying three jets between the Hawaiian islands and the West Coast in 1961. Also during this time commercial jet service was being established, resulting in increased air traffic to and from Hawaii. This meant not only expanded market potential for Hawaiian Airlines, but potential competition as well.

Hawaiian Airlines succeeded in attracting a large share of this growing tourist industry on the mainland, and the booming U.S. economy, with the greater purchasing power that followed World War II both for tourism and for cargo, provided a rising market tide that benefited all carriers. Closer to their home base, Hawaiian Airlines reduced travel time between the Hawaiian islands to 20 to 30 minutes. This was made possible by Hawaiian's introduction of the first pure jet inter-island aircraft, the McDonnell Douglas DC-9, which became the backbone of Hawaiian Airline's mixed inter-island fleet.

The company was profitable enough that, by the mid-1960s, it was attracting competition. By the time of the 1978 deregulation of the airline industry, Hawaiian Airlines was one of three companies that controlled the state's inter-island traffic. The industry was fiercely competitive, with Hawaiian Airlines sharing the market with Aloha Airlines and Mid-Pacific Airlines, an aggressive low-cost carrier with 21 percent of the market. With deregulation, an increase followed in the number of direct flights by mainland carriers between the West Coast and the outer islands of Hawaii. In response, Hawaiian Airlines looked to longer term strategies as the company faced competitive challenges from big companies such as United Airlines, which began serving Oahu and Maui with non-stop flights from Los Angeles and San Francisco, and American Airlines, which put a flight in service from Los Angeles and Dallas/Fort Worth to Maui. Aloha Air was also operating new lines to Guam and Taipei and shipping cargo from Taipei to Honolulu.

Company leaders at the time expected that the increase in tourists coming to the islands from the mainland would also mean that more tourists would be traveling within the six islands. Thus, they felt secure in their ability to compete, given their control of inter-island travel. The company's preeminence, along with its long-term cost reduction strategies, ensured that Hawaiian Airlines wouldn't suffer losses of market share and revenues in a rapidly growing market. But, of course, they didn't expect the growth in tourism to continue indefinitely, and they looked to other markets and strategies as well.

One major competitive move at the time involved the company's airport on Maui. Hawaiian Airlines had owned and operated an $8.5 million airport built in the pineapple and cane fields of western Maui near the Kaanapoli and Kapalua resorts. Seeking to avoid competition in inter-island transport from large carriers such as United and American, the company chose to relocate this airstrip closer to the resorts, in order to provide more direct service. The new 3,000 foot airstrip on leased land was developed in 1984.

In another competitive move, the company entered the long-haul charter business and operated four McDonnell Douglas DC-8-60 series aircraft for several charter companies. Their entire fleet by 1985 consisted of four McDonnell Douglas MD80s, two DC-9-50 series aircraft, and five de Havilland Dash 7s for use on inter-island routes. Four DC-8 60 series aircraft based in Honolulu and Niagara Falls, New York, were used for charter operations. The leased charter aircraft were operated through routes that included San Francisco to Honolulu and Maui; Honolulu to Seattle and London weekly round trips; and a weekly San Francisco to Paris round trip.

While the company was able to capitalize on the boom years of the 1960s and 1970s, the 1980s proved tumultuous, unstable, and largely unprofitable. During the 1980s, despite its growing revenues and markets, Hawaiian Airlines became known as a high cost carrier with a reputation for poor quality and unreliable service. Thus, while its sales grew consistently over the decade, its profits continually stagnated and declined. Not only was the airline forced into strict retrenchment, but it also spent a large portion of its earnings on advertising and promotion to overcome its reputation for poor quality.

Throughout the 1980s, the total number of visitors to the islands increased at a rapid rate, but there was also a change in the travel patterns of these visitors. Previously, many travelers visited several islands during trips to the state, but in the 1980s a larger number of repeat visitors visited only one or two islands during their stay. As a result, inter-island traffic remained flat even though overall visitors to the islands increased. Many experts thought that the increase in direct mainland to outer-island service would displace much of the inter-island business. However, company leaders at Hawaiian Airlines maintained that in the long run the increase in passengers could only be beneficial to the company, since this phenomena would ultimately lead to spinoffs of passengers to the home-based inter-island carriers.

Although the company was correct in its speculations about the market, this did not necessarily translate into larger profits. The number of tourists, notably from Japan, and an increase in tourist investment, again notably from Japanese investors who poured money into hotels and restaurants, led to increasing revenues. From 1982 to 1988, company revenues more than tripled, reaching $354 million in 1988. During this period, the total number of visitors to the islands rose from 4.2 to 6.1 million, with Japanese visitors accounting for the bulk of that growth. However, competition was fierce, and Hawaiian Airlines lost control over its costs while the quality of its services declined. In essence, Hawaiian Airlines' cost structure couldn't bear the weight of the price wars. As a result, the company experienced positive profits in only two of the seven years from 1982 to 1988, losing a total of $31 million dollars over the period, including $7.4 million loss for the first quarter of 1989. Hawaiian Airlines, which was thought to be critical to the state's tourism industry, flirted with bankruptcy.

During this time, Hawaiian Airlines, now wholly owned by HAL Inc., opened some new markets worldwide, including, in 1984, service to Pago Pago, American Samoa, and Nuku'alofa, Tonga. To support this expansion, they acquired five Lockheed L-1011 wide body aircraft the following year. On June 12, 1985 HAL opened wide body jet service between the west coast and Hawaii with daily flights to Los Angeles. Daily flights between Hawaii and San Francisco and Seattle started in January 1986. Service to Western Samoa soon followed.

But with increased traffic and expanded use of their existing fleet, maintenance costs rose even higher, doubling between 1986 and 1988, and quality of service and reliability declined, the result of wear and tear from frequent short hops and general depreciation of its already aging fleet. After awhile the firm was left with much of its aircraft out of commission for routine maintenance. Consequently, flight time suffered; by March 1989, only two-thirds of its inter-island flights ran on time, compared with 85 percent for its chief competitor, privately held Aloha Airlines, which had been solidly profitable for around six years.

During this time, Robert Magoon Jr., a 53 percent shareholder in the company, took over the presidency from Paul Finazzo and elevated Albert Wells, the former senior vice-president, to chief operating officer. Magoon moved quickly to restructure costs and improve maintenance. On-time performance improved to 91 percent for inter-island routes, and the airline also began offering heavily discounted fares. However, the airline's costs continued to be high, and its price cuts resulted in heavy losses. Wells conceded at the time, "Maybe we've overdone it on discounts." While the company's load factor of 65.2 percent was one of the highest, it had one of the lowest possible yields per passenger. The company's 30 plane fleet was mostly leased and leveraged, and many of its markets were saturated, most notably the San Francisco and Los Angeles to Honolulu route, while its routes to Australia and New Zealand were heavily regulated, further limiting its profit potential. As a result, the company was again up for sale in 1989. But with its reputation for low quality, as well as its poor performance in the 1980s, Magoon had a tough time finding a buyer.

By January 1990, former major league baseball commissioner Peter Ueberroth and an investor group led by J. Thomas Talbot, after long negotiations, completed a $37 million takeover of HAL, Inc. Ueberroth's group moved quickly to slash costs and increase output. In its first move after the takeover, HAL chair and CEO John Ueberroth, brother of Peter, launched a debt conversion into equity to deal with cash flow problems and boost confidence in its stock, which was at a historically low price. The new owners also began a competitive cost-cutting strategy, giving them room to undercut competitors' prices and expand markets—in fact, they went so far as to cut fares to 68 percent of their competitors' rates. The strategy was not an unmitigated success, however. HAL was still struggling and unable to win back much of its market share. Takeover again loomed.

Other worldwide events were affecting the airline market as well. As the United States attacked Iraq in the Persian gulf, travel demand was cut in general. Fuel prices rose temporarily, which contributed to HAL's loss of $13.3 million in the third quarter of 1990 after a small profit of $300,000 in the third quarter of 1989. Its stock price continued to nosedive; stock that had been priced at $38 in early 1959 fell to a little over $20 at the end of 1989, and then collapsed to around $7 in the middle of 1990.

In December 1990, Northwest Airlines agreed to acquire key pacific routes from HAL along with a 25 percent stake in the company. Northwest paid $20 million to HAL for five routes, including a potentially lucrative route between Hawaii and Fukuoka, Japan, a minority stake in the company, and a $7 million loan which would provide a much needed cash infusion to HAL.

Cost cutting continued. HAL implemented a ten percent cut in wages across the board. The company also cut expenses in all operating categories except promotions, advertising, and sales, in which costs increased by 50 percent as HAL tried desperately to live down its reputation as an unreliable company. In addition, HAL streamlined its fleet to two to four kinds of aircraft in order to cut maintenance expenses and to get rid of excess capacity.

Despite these moves toward increased cost efficiency, 1991 was not a good year as HAL's market share declined to 60 percent from 33 percent. Once the dominant local and regional carrier, HAL's biggest problem, according to company executives, was its inability to deal with its image problem—despite more advertising and improved services and promotional offers. For example, HAL offered a free ticket to anyone who waited in a check-in line or had a flight delayed more than ten minutes. Chairperson John Ueberroth claimed 98 percent on-time performance in 1992 but felt frustrated by the firm's inability to attract customers, exclaiming at the time, "Word of mouth takes a while to get around." By March 1992, market share rebounded to 45 percent.

By the end of 1992 losses abated, but the company was still in the red, with a net loss of $98.5 million or $33.49 a share in 1991, compared to a net loss of $121.3 million or $55.60 a share in 1990. Revenues were also up by seven percent to $365 million from $341 million over the same period.

HAL still sought to revive its mainland routes. It cut fares by 50 percent on its Honolulu-Los Angeles routes and increased capacity and ran full flights while other airlines reduced services. By the end of the second quarter of 1992, traffic on HAL's mainland-Honolulu flights grew at an accelerating rate, and capacity utilization was pushed up to a profitable level—an estimated 88 percent.

As the company moved into 1993, it turned a profit, its first in six years. Furthermore, it was beginning to recover its reputation for good service and safety. In fact, Hawaiian Airlines was rated as one of the ten best U.S. airlines by readers of *Conde Nast Traveler,* the international travel and hospitality publication. As the only airline able to provide single-carrier service from the western United States and the South Pacific to each of Hawaii's islands, Hawaiian Airlines began to expect a profitable future and long-term growth. The airline and its holding company survived the competitive warfare brought on by deregulation and emerged a major player in a more concentrated and centralized airline industry.

Principal Subsidiaries: Hawaiian Airlines, Inc.

Further Reading:

Beauchamp, Marc, "What's Hawaiian for Rotten Management," *Forbes,* June 26, 1989.
"Hawaiian Airlines: A Brief History," Hawaiian Airlines News Release, August 1993.
Jokiel, Lucy, "Meanwhile, at Hawaiian Air . . . ," *Hawaii Business,* February 1990.
Nomani, Asra Q., "Northwest Air to Acquire 25% of Hawaiian Air," *Wall Street Journal,* December 11, 1990.
Smith, Bruce A., "Hawaiian Carriers Revise Inter-Island Service Plans," *Aviation Week & Space Technology,* August 20, 1984.
Yin, Tung, "Hawaiian Airlines Struggles to Win Back Local Fliers: New Owners Gamble on Reduced Fares to U.S. Mainland to Stem Losses," *Wall Street Journal,* June 10, 1992.

—John A. Sarich

HEI

Hawaiian Electric Industries, Inc.

Hawaiian Electric Industries, Inc.

900 Richards Street
Honolulu, Hawaii 96813
U.S.A.
(808) 543-5662
Fax: (808) 543-7966

Public Company
Incorporated: 1891 as Hawaiian Electric Company
Employees: 3,286
Sales: $1.03 billion
Stock Exchanges: New York
SICs: 4911 Electric Services; 6035 Federal Savings
   Institutions; 4449 Water Transportation of Freight, Nec;
   6719 Holding Companies, Nec

Hawaiian Electric Industries (HEI) is a diversified electric utility holding company formed in 1983. HEI's principal subsidiary is the Hawaiian Electric Company (HECO), which serves five of Hawaii's six major islands and 95 percent of the state's total population. By the early 1990s, HEI's nonutility subsidiaries consisted of a federal savings bank, a maritime freight transporter, and a residential real estate developer. The majority of HEI's income was generated by the electric utility and the savings bank.

Hawaiian Electric Company was incorporated in Honolulu on the island of Oahu during the reign of the republic's last monarch, Queen Liliuokalani, in 1891. Her predecessor, King David Kalakaua, had been instrumental in the introduction of electricity to the island in the 1880s. Kalakaua was a progressive leader who had learned of Thomas Edison's revolutionary electrical experiments and visited the inventor at his Menlo Park, New Jersey, laboratory in 1881.

By the time HECO was created, there were several private electrical generators in operation on Oahu, including one at the monarchy's Iolani Palace that provided light for the streets of downtown Honolulu and almost 800 private residences. Jonathan Austin, a community leader and the driving force behind the founding of HECO, formed the joint stock company in 1891 to supply light and power to Honolulu. The company was incorporated with William W. Hall as president and Austin as treasurer. At that time, HECO customers were charged a flat rate of 50 cents per light per month and 20 cents per 1,000 watts per month.

In 1891 King Kalakaua died of a stroke, and agitation for union with the United States intensified after Queen Liliuokalani ascended to the throne. Pro-annexation forces deposed the queen and formed a provisional government in 1893. By 1895, Hawaii had become a Territory of the United States.

In 1893 HECO was awarded an exclusive ten-year franchise, wherein HECO paid the government 2.5 percent of its gross earnings from all electric light and power furnished to consumers and agreed to bring power to everyone in the district of Honolulu who requested service. Jonathan Austin died in 1893; he was replaced as treasurer by William Hall, and Hall's vacant presidency was filled by William G. Irwin.

The company expanded rapidly during the remaining years before the turn of the twentieth century, focusing on adding services and augmenting its customer base. HECO purchased the generator at Iolani Palace and moved it into a larger powerhouse. The new, coal-fired plant was equipped with a 150-horsepower Ball engine and generator and two 45-kilowatt Edison dynamos. Before the advent of the electric refrigerator, the company used its excess capacity to manufacture ice, beginning in 1894. HECO extended light and power service to Waikiki in 1897 and used the proceeds from additional stock offers to buy a 2,000-volt generator. That year, HECO was also able to pay its first dividend, which amounted to five percent of the company's $350,000 capitalization.

Just before the turn of the century, HECO president Irwin and another manager resigned, prompting a reorganization of the company's upper level management positions. From that time until 1943, HECO's day-to-day affairs were directed by a general manager, while the president's responsibilities resembled those of a board chairman. Alonzo Gartley was selected as the new general manager, and Frederick Macfarlane became president.

HECO opened the twentieth century with the acquisition of the People's Ice and Refrigeration Company, its largest competitor in that industry, for $75,000. The merger increased the company's capitalization to $500,000, but fostered a monolithic image of HECO in the eyes of the press and the general public. The acquisition of People's Ice brought more management changes in 1902, when John A. McCandless, a partner in the ice company, succeeded Frederick W. Macfarlane as president of HECO. By this time, the company's flat rates for electric power had been increased to $1 for each 16-candle power lamp in use until midnight, and $1.25 for those who kept their lights on after 12:00 p.m.

When HECO's franchise from the provisional government ran out in 1904, the company requested a new contract from the United States government. Congress traded rate reductions for a perpetual franchise. By 1906, HECO had registered over 2,500 customers, who used 500,000 kilowatts of electricity annually. Use had grown with the invention of electric fans and irons, the expansion of government offices after annexation, and the construction of the island's first major hotel, the Moana. HECO responded to the increased demand by switching from coal to oil as a fuel source, which saved the company $17,000 annually. The company increased its capacity with the installation of Hawaii's first steam-driven turbine, a 750-kilowatt steam turbo-generator, in 1908. The new generator was augmented with a 1,500-kilowatt unit in 1910 and a 2,500-kilowatt unit in 1913.

In 1910 Alonzo Gartley left the post of general manager and was replaced by president McCandless's son-in-law, Harry M. Hepburn. The company continued to extend its electric network to residential districts in outlying areas of Oahu.

At the same time, however, momentum was building to bring the increasing powerful utility under public regulation. Led by W. R. Castle (who, not coincidentally, was an executive of the Honolulu Gas Company), anti-HECO forces accused the electric company of charging exorbitant rates. General manager Hepburn responded to the accusations by noting two recent rate cuts. The utility's opponents introduced a bill to the territorial legislature that called for the creation of a Public Utilities Commission (PUC) and an end to HECO's government-sponsored monopoly on electric power.

The legislature passed the bill, but when Hawaii's governor vetoed it, the bill was returned to the legislature, where anti-HECO representatives won out in 1913. HECO president McCandless and his two brothers sold their controlling interest in the company for over $500,000 and resigned their posts. Their shares were purchased by Richard and Clarence Cooke, who became president and secretary, respectively, and Frank C. Atherton, who became HECO's treasurer. Frank E. Blake succeeded Hepburn as general manager. Ironically, this forced change brought increased prosperity to HECO: Cooke and Blake, who would stay with the company for 28 and 14 years, respectively, immediately slashed rates and ended the flat rate payment schedule. The lower rates brought a large influx of new customers and revenues.

This increased demand led HECO to develop a network of substations in 1914 that facilitated the distribution of power from the main plant to Honolulu's burgeoning suburbs. In 1915, the company also opened a merchandising department that sold electric appliances, like the newly introduced refrigerator. Within five years, this division's profits topped $60,000.

In 1922 HECO added a 10,000-kilowatt generating unit, continuing the expansion of electrification to more isolated regions in the mountains of Oahu. But in 1923, just as these new customers became accustomed to the modern convenience, a severe storm struck. Heavy rain and high winds uprooted trees and downed power lines, causing $100,000 damage to the island, $10,000 of which was borne by HECO. But repairs were accomplished quickly, and the company was even able to bring another 10,000-kilowatt Westinghouse condensing turbo-generator on line that year.

The company's next major project helped beautify Honolulu through the development of an underground conduit system. HECO further enhanced Hawaii's capitol when it constructed a new headquarters in 1927. The Spanish Colonial-style building was later nominated to the National Register of Historic Places as one of the most elegant buildings in the state.

HECO was insulated from the stock market crash of 1929 that defined the decade of the 1930s for most of the rest of the world. By 1931, the company claimed 40,650 residential customers and profits nearing $100,000. HECO had also just made one of its largest capital investments—$1.5 million—for a new plant that was equipped with a 20,000-kilowatt turbo generator. The 1930s saw the modernization of several of HECO's older generators with the installation of more efficient "topping turbines." These units significantly increased the pressure exerted by HECO's existing boilers, which simultaneously increased efficiency and generating capacity. These and other improvements brought the company's total capital investments to almost $3 million in the early 1930s.

General Manager Frank Blake retired in the middle of the decade and was replaced by his son-in-law, Leslie H. Hicks. Hicks continued to expand capacity with a new 7,500-kilowatt turbo-generator on the shores of Pearl Harbor. A second unit with 15,000 kilowatts of capacity was built in 1940. The power plants helped HECO meet the increasing needs of U.S. military establishments and growing sugar and pineapple plantations. Richard Cooke's presidency ended with his passing at the age of 57. He was succeeded by older brother and HECO secretary, Clarence.

Although Hawaii and HECO were largely unaffected by the first World War, World War II landed the territory in the middle of the Pacific theater. After Pearl Harbor came under surprise attack on December 7, 1941, Honolulu was placed under a strict blackout and the government spent over $300,000 to reinforce HECO's primary power plants against further air attacks. But even the total blackout did not lessen the need for electric energy. With U.S. troops working around the clock on the island, the company built two 44,000-volt lines to service primary military bases. HECO power plants furnished more than one million kilowatthours of electricity each day at the height of the war effort.

The outbreak of war coincided with the first attempts at unionization at HECO. In 1941, HECO employees John Hall, John Hendrick, and Walters Eli established the Hawaiian Electric Union to lobby for higher wages, sick leave, and paid vacations and holidays. Later that year, the National Labor Relations Board certified the International Brotherhood of Electrical Workers (IBEW) to represent HECO's trades and crafts personnel. The first labor agreement was drafted in 1942, but it was not until 1943 that trades and crafts employees began to join the IBEW. The early years of the management-union relationship were marred by hostile negotiations. Talks grew so rancorous that union leaders petitioned for municipal ownership of the utility in 1943. The movement was soon quelled, however, and management-labor relations were soon normalized.

The year 1943 also saw the end of HECO leadership by the Cookes and the Athertons when Clarence Cooke died after a 32-year association with the company and Frank Atherton retired from the Board after 36 years of service. Leslie Hicks was named president, and the corporate hierarchy was reorganized so that the position was made responsible for daily operations.

The wartime blackout was lifted in May 1944 and martial law ended that fall. Over the course of the war, HECO's kilowatt-hour sales had grown from less than two million to more than 12.5 million kilowatthours. Income for the same period had climbed from $5.3 million to $9.3 million, and generating capacity had jumped from 82,500 kilowatts to 117,500 kilowatts. Pressure on the system was relieved with the 1944 construction of a 42,000-kilowatt unit at the Honolulu power plant and a 50,000-kilowatt unit at the Waiau plant in 1945.

Although many of the troops left Hawaii at the end of the war, the territory's economy had been transformed. Beginning with the postwar era, Hawaii's economy was dominated by military spending, tourism, and construction. Construction of the $30 million Ala Moana Shopping Center, for example, took over a decade, from 1952 to 1966. It was soon recognized as one of HECO's biggest projects—the shopping center was larger than downtown Honolulu, and cables had to be run underground in reclaimed swampland.

HECO also undertook two expansion projects in the 1950s. The company built a new power plant on the Honolulu waterfront in 1954. The 116,000-kilowatt plant was named after HECO president, Leslie Hicks. New technologies, like a high-capacity (138-kilovolt) line and hydraulic-powered booms that did the heavy work of placing utility poles, helped HECO expand its service area to the relatively undeveloped northeast side of Oahu, across the Koolau mountain range.

These three large projects spanned from 1959 to 1963 and cost HECO $56.8 million. Hawaii became the 50th state of the United States in 1959. The political change helped bring HECO to the attention of the investment community. Hicks retired that year, and was succeeded by Ralph Johnson.

After seven years of research into population growth and residential and industrial expansion, HECO started construction of a new power plant at Kahe Point in West Oahu. Kahe was powered by the state's first reheat steam turbine generator, which cost $16 million. The plant was brought on line with a generating capacity of 86,000 kilowatts, and a second unit with the same capacity was started up in 1964. By the early 1990s, the Kahe plant had six units with a total generating capacity of 648,000 kilowatts and a total cost of $184 million. The expansion helped HECO keep up with demand, which more than doubled during the 1960s.

HECO sold a subsidiary, the Honolulu Electric Supply Company, for $3.79 million in the early 1960s and reinvested the proceeds in technical improvements. In 1964, the company initiated a microwave communications system and an automatic dispatch system (ADS) for control and efficiency. In 1966 Russell Hassler succeeded Ralph Johnson as president when Johnson died unexpectedly. With plans for more expansion underway, HECO made its first public stock offering of $90 million in 1965, then invested the proceeds in its physical plant. The first stage of HECO's 138-kilovolt Halawa Valley station, which would become the utility's largest transmission station, was in operation by 1967.

Acquisition also helped HECO grow in the 1960s. In 1968, the company purchased Maui Electric Company in a friendly take-over, and in 1970 it acquired Hilo Electric Light Company (later known as Hawaii Electric Company), which produced electricity for the "Big Island" of Hawaii. That year, HECO converted its two oldest plants, at Honolulu and Waiau, to low sulfur oil. Though the fuel was more expensive, it reduced air emissions. After three years as president, Russell Hassler died and was succeeded by Lewis W. Lengnick. Lengnick remained president for four years, when he retired and was replaced by Carl H. Williams in 1973.

The early 1970s were marked by the oil crisis, when the cost of fuel oil increased almost one-third from 1970 to 1971. HECO filed for its first rate increase in 17 years in 1971, and despite widespread public opposition, the PUC permitted a 5.9 percent increase the following year. The cost of fuel oil continued to increase throughout the decade, from under $2.50 per barrel in 1970 to $42 per barrel in 1981. HECO's only labor strike occurred in 1973 and lasted two weeks.

In 1980, Carl Williams retired and C. Dudley Pratt, Jr. took over. The following year, the islands of Kauai and Oahu were battered by Hurricane Iwa: 97 percent of HECO's customers lost power at the height of the storm, and it took the company two weeks to restore the entire system. The utility used "rolling blackouts," wherein customers had electricity cut off for an hour every two hours for five to six days, to manage demand while customers were brought back on line. Much of the physical plant was rebuilt to withstand hurricane-force winds. Two other island-wide blackouts in the 1980s left the island without power for half-days. The first, triggered by a fire, occurred in 1983, and another resulted from a transformer explosion the following year.

Following an industry trend, HECO applied to the PUC to form a holding company as a vehicle to diversify the electric company's interests, which would help the company weather periods of low utility profits yet shelter it from bad investments. The reorganization was approved in 1983, and HECO became a subsidiary of Hawaiian Electric Industries, Inc. (HEI). The ensuing years saw the creation and/or purchase of several endeavors: HEI Investment Corp. (1984); Hawaiian Electric Renewable Systems (a wind farm; 1985); Malama Pacific Corporation (real estate); Hawaiian Tug & Barge (inter-island freight; 1986); Hawaiian Insurance Group (1987); and American Savings Bank's Hawaii branches (1988). By far HEI's largest acquisition, American Savings Bank soon provided one-fourth of the holding company's annual income. Dudley Pratt was replaced by Harwood D. Williamson as president and CEO of HECO in 1990, and Robert F. Clarke was appointed president of Hawaiian Electric Industries.

HEI's rapid growth was halted by two events. First, electricity demand increased dramatically in the final years of the 1980s, soaring 5.6 percent in 1988 alone. Having invested in diversification for most of the decade, HEI was unprepared for the pressure on its electrical systems. The company scrambled to purchase power from independents as customers, politicians, and regulators complained of rotating blackouts, restricted use, and frequent outages. In 1991, for example, the entire island of Oahu was totally blacked out during routine maintenance. The blackout lasted 12 hours, but the backlash raged on during the early 1990s. HEI hoped to inaugurate a five-year, $1 billion capital improvements program in 1992. The program intended to add capacity and transmission and distribution capabilities throughout the service area.

Then, on September 11, 1992, Hurricane Iniki's 160-mile-per-hour winds devastated the island of Kauai. Although it was the only island to which HEI did not supply power, HEI's Hawaiian

Insurance Group (HIG) had sold many islanders hurricane insurance, and 98 percent of HIG's policyholders filed claims, which totaled $300 million. The claims bankrupted HIG, leaving the insurer with a negative net worth of $80 million. HEI abandoned the company, leaving it to a guaranty fund supported by the insurance industry. It was one of the largest insurance insolvencies in the state's history. Early in 1993, Hawaii's insurance regulators brought suit against the holding company, charging breach of fiduciary duty, misrepresentation, and negligence.

HEI's planned $1 billion capital improvements campaign was halted by the news of HIG's insolvency. In the last quarter of 1992, HEI's stock fell ten percent, and Standard & Poor's floated the idea of downgrading both HEI's and HECO's ratings. HEI put off a stock offer planned for early 1993 that would have furnished funds to start the capital improvements program.

Principal Subsidiaries: Hawaiian Electric Co., Inc.; HEI Investment Corp.; Malama Pacific Corp.; Hawaiian Tug & Barge Corp.; HEI Diversified, Inc.

Further Reading:

''Ho'ike #1,'' July 1993, pp. 1–12.
''Insurance Regulators Sue Hawaiian Electric Over Former Unit,'' *Wall Street Journal,* April 13, 1993, p. A8.
''Legacy of a Royal Vision,'' *Hawaii: The Electric Century,* 1991, pp. 127–75.
Rose, Frederick. ''Hawaiian Electric Drops Insurance Unit as Claims from Hurricane Iniki Mount,'' *Wall Street Journal,* December 7, 1992, p. B2.
''Hawaiian Electric Still Seeking Shelter from the Storm,'' *Wall Street Journal,* December 15, 1992, p. B4.

—April S. Dougal

Helmsley Enterprises, Inc.

60 East 42nd Street
New York, New York 10022
U.S.A.
(212) 687-6400
Fax: (212) 880-0637

Private Company
Incorporated: c. 1938 as Dwight, Voorhis & Helmsley
Employees: 13,000 (estimate)
Sales: $1.70 billion (estimate)
SICs: 2099 Food Preparations Nec; 5812 Eating Places; 6361
   Title Insurance; 6512 Nonresidential Building Operators;
   6531 Real Estate Agents and Managers; 7011 Hotels and
   Motels

Beleaguered as it has been since Leona Helmsley's 1989 indictment and eventual conviction on charges of tax fraud, Helmsley Enterprises, Inc., is still one of the largest real estate companies in the country. Through a labyrinth of subsidiaries, it owns some 13,000 hotel rooms nationwide, over 100,000 apartments, and approximately 100 million square feet of commercial space. A significant portion of this empire is situated atop some of the priciest land in the country, namely Manhattan. The company's most prestigious cash cow is the Empire State Building, which it leases and manages but does not own. Among Helmsley's prominent holdings are its hotels, which include the 14-unit Harley chain—spread throughout the East, Midwest, and South—and the New York group consisting of the Helmsley Park Lane, the New York Helmsley, the Helmsley Middletowne, and the Helmsley Windsor.

Until the late 1980s, the crown jewel of the Helmsley fold was the inordinately lush 55-story Helmsley Palace (since renamed The New York Palace), located at Madison Avenue and 50th Street. Ironically, this was one of the few Helmsley properties not solely owned by Helmsley founder Harry Brakmann Helmsley and his wife, Leona, whom he married in 1972. Because of this, and because of what even the mainstream media have called Leona Helmsley's "Queen of Mean" tactics, the Palace became the Achilles' heel that brought about Leona's downfall.

The genius behind the phenomenal success of Helmsley Enterprises was—and is—Harry Helmsley. In its pre-gossip column, pre-tabloid, pre-Leona days, the Helmsley name was synonymous with the best, biggest, and brightest in New York real

estate. And the word, handshake, and vision of Harry Helmsley was what the company's development was founded upon.

Helmsley was born in the Bronx, New York, in 1909 to a family of modest means. Following graduation from high school in 1925, he obtained a job with the small Manhattan real estate brokerage of Dwight, Voorhis and Perry, serving first as a mail room clerk for 12 dollars a week. The brokerage specialized in buying, selling, leasing, and managing buildings in low-rent neighborhoods. Helmsley was soon elevated to the role of rent collector in the Hell's Kitchen district. "That's how he learned the city from the street up," recalled a Helmsley-Spear Inc. executive in a 1988 *Crain's New York Business* article.

Around the time of the 1929 stock market crash, Helmsley began free-lancing; that is, though he had no money of his own and his firm had none to spare, he began snatching up prime foreclosed properties by convincing banks the investments were sound and that he would manage the properties for them. During the 1930s Dwight, Voorhis benefited enormously from Helmsley's negotiating and managerial talents, and by the end of the Great Depression the young realtor was both a partner and chief spokesman for the firm, whose name was changed to Dwight, Voorhis & Helmsley and then Dwight-Helmsley, Inc.

Helmsley took his first major stride toward self-made billionaire status in 1938 when he assumed ownership—rather than management—of his first property, a ten-story office building on East 23rd Street between Fifth and Madison avenues. The property was scheduled to foreclose, and Helmsley used that informational leverage to acquire the $100,000 mortgage for a mere $1,000 down payment (all that Helmsley then had). *New York* contributor Nicholas Pileggi quoted Helmsley on the circumstances of the deal: "The mortgage at the time was 3 percent, and it cost me $3,000 a year . . . and I remember I had a hard time, but I was confident that I would be able to turn the building around. I was in the management business. . . . I watched the building's expenses, such as fuel, electricity, and the payroll. I made sure that there wasn't one extra man on the staff. One extra employee could cost $3,000 in those days, and that made the difference as to whether I could pay the mortgage." Shortly after World War II, Helmsley sold the building for $165,000. He had built his nest egg and earned himself a reputation as a fair, though tight-fisted, operator.

Even before the sale, Helmsley was busy leveraging his abilities and testing his hunches through several other deals. According to Richard Hammer in *The Helmsley's: The Rise and Fall of Harry and Leona,* "His goal was to build Dwight-Helmsley into a major force in New York real estate and in the process turn himself into a mover and a shaker." Foreseeing a postwar boom in the midst of World War II, Helmsley began to seek out bargain properties located close to Grand Central Station and other major commuter terminals. As before, he lacked the cash necessary to purchase them, but he discovered that he could retain part-ownership in exchange for signing away his five percent commission. Helmsley further sweetened these deals by contracting for the management of the buildings, which ensured him and the firm—now essentially owned by him—an ongoing stream of income.

In 1949, wrote Jeanie Kasindorf in *New York,* "Harry Helmsley entered the big time." The impetus was Helmsley's meeting with Lawrence Wein, a highly successful real estate lawyer. Wein had become an expert at the tax and legal strategies of buying and selling properties. What he lacked was the knowledge and experience that Helmsley so obviously possessed, that of selecting the choicest pieces of New York real estate and negotiating the best possible prices. Wein offered Helmsley an informal partnership that amounted to a pioneering venture in real estate syndication, which later became a common practice in the hybrid form of the Real Estate Investment Trust, or REIT.

Real estate syndication involves assembling groups of passive investors to buy properties otherwise unaffordable by the principal investors, with the ultimate goal of seeking a high rate of return for all involved. During the next 30 years, Wein and Helmsley created nearly 100 such syndicates, with Helmsley putting up little if any of his own money while generally reaping high profits and lucrative management fees. One of the most complex—and certainly the most famous—of the Wein-Helmsley deals was the sale-and-leaseback of the Empire State Building involving Prudential, which was eventually completed in 1961.

Two other realtors in the Dwight-Helmsley firm, Alvin Schwartz and Irving Schneider, were also making a name for themselves and the company in the New York market. Around the time that Helmsley began teaming with Wein, Schwartz left the firm to join Spear and Company, which specialized in managing office buildings and was owned by Schwartz's uncles. In 1955 Helmsley was flush with syndication revenues and seized an opportunity to reunite with Schwartz, whom he valued, by purchasing Spear and Company for half a million dollars.

Helmsley renamed the expanded concern Helmsley-Spear, which within a decade or so would become one of the city's foremost brokerages. Helmsley himself won early recognition in 1958 when he was named Realty Man of the Year by his peers. Helmsley-Spear (later subsumed by Helmsley Enterprises) gained its prominence by first acquiring the well-respected Charles F. Noyes Company, which was used to expand Helmsley's portfolio in lower Manhattan. The later purchase of Brown, Harris, Stevens was equally important, for this venerable firm brought Helmsley into the arena of rental and cooperative apartment sales and management. However, well-publicized legal battles that arose from Helmsley's repeated attempts to convert residential complexes, such as the Parkchester in the Bronx, into condominiums later soured the mogul on this real estate area.

After fashioning Helmsley-Spear into the largest real estate management company in the United States by 1970, Helmsley turned his attention to the luxury hotel business, which he had first been exposed to years back when he purchased the St. Moritz with Wein. Despite his unquestionable achievements, Helmsley was still known disparagingly "in real estate circles," according to Milton Moskowitz in *Everybody's Business: A Field Guide to the 400 Leading Companies in America,* "as a frugal operator, a landlord who would 'take a schlock property and run it as a schlock property forever.' " In an effort to undo this reputation and to build something from the ground up, Helmsley announced his plans to open the Park Lane Hotel, which was to be the first new luxury hotel built in New York City in a decade. On the heels of the Park Lane's hugely successful opening came Helmsley's divorce from his first wife and his marriage to Leona Roberts, an ambitious New York realtor who had already made her first million and had been hired by Helmsley to work at Brown, Harris, Stevens.

Leona allegedly exerted an enormous and increasingly detrimental influence over Helmsley, who up until that time was a retiring Quaker unaccustomed to palatial living or, for that matter, underhanded business dealings. Although he was still being hailed in 1980 by *New York* magazine as "by far the most successful real-estate man in New York today," with an estimated $5 billion empire, Helmsley was nearing the end of his reign. It was this same year that Leona was installed as president of Helmsley Hotels.

In her new position, Leona Helmsley oversaw the construction of Helmsley Palace, which Harry financed through a limited partnership with Leperq, deNeuflize and Company. The initial estimated cost of the Palace was $73 million, but Leona's numerous embellishments, and a layer of hidden costs that unduly benefited such Helmsley subsidiaries as Deco Purchasing Company (nominally headed by Leona's son from a former marriage), brought the total to $110 million by the time of its opening in 1981. When Harry Helmsley sought an additional $20 million from the Leperq investment group to help cover the overrun, he was met with firm rejection. In 1983 the Leperq group won a $3.5 million judgment against Helmsley for excessively high commissions charges related to Deco. Ironically, this same year Leona became chief executive of all Helmsley hotel operations.

In a devastating critique, Tom Shachtman commented in *Skyscraper Dreams: The Great Real Estate Dynasties of New York:* "Leona's vision involved spending, not creating, and her business decisions were principally negative. Once she took the empire in hand, there were no purchases of outstanding properties, but a considerable decline in the maintenance of those Helmsley properties in New York and Miami that were not her main focus, and a steady exodus of competent middle-rank employees from Helmsley-Spear [the brokerage hub of the empire] who felt that the organization Harry Helmsley had created no longer had a future." The impotency of the Helmsley empire was noticeably hinted at in a 1983 *Forbes* article, which mentioned Harry's grandiose but long-unimplemented plan to top the 1,454-foot Sears Tower of Chicago with a new skyscraper in his own beloved Manhattan.

Were it not for the Helmsleys' purchase of Dunnellen Hall, an $8 million country estate outside Greenwich, Connecticut, all might have been well. The purchase date of June 20, 1983, marked the beginning of a massive scheme, orchestrated by Leona, to defraud minority shareholders in the Palace and other Helmsley properties. In essence, the Helmsleys financed all of the remodeling of the estate, which approached astronomical proportions, through existing Helmsley subsidiaries. In addition, from 1983 to 1985, as the Leona Helmsley trial would later uncover, the Helmsleys evaded more than $4 million in state and federal income taxes. Many cited unadulterated greed as the reason for the scheme, but the amount the Helmsleys appeared to have gone to such great lengths to save paled in comparison to the actual taxes of more than $240 million the couple paid to the government during roughly the same period.

Whatever the case, the aging Harry Helmsley was declared unfit to stand trial in 1989. Following a final appeal of her conviction, Leona began her prison term on April 1, 1992; in the summer of 1993, she was announced eligible for parole as early as January 1, 1994. Meanwhile, as an abbreviated *Forbes 400* notice dated October 18, 1993, put it: "Harry still collecting receipts on empire while marking time, but estimated worth over $1 billion."

No clear successor to the Helmsley empire has been named or is likely to be named, especially given the untimely death of Leona's son, Jay Panzirer. At one point, Schwartz and Schneider were said to have retained the option of buying Helmsley-Spear upon the death of Helmsley, but the Helmsley estate, according to *Forbes* and insiders, is to go to the Quakers. As for the New York Palace, Robert Selwitz reported in *Hotel & Motel Management* that a coup d'etat by the limited partners occurred and that Interstate Hotels Corp., the nation's largest Marriott Hotels franchiser, would manage the property until a buyer could be found. Harry Helmsley once remarked that: "Real estate is the best game around—and when you're ahead in the game, you like to keep playing." Perhaps after Leona's release it will become clear that the game is over for the Helmsleys and that new players must be found.

Principal Subsidiaries: Brown, Harris, Stevens, Inc.; Deco Purchasing Co.; Albert M. Greenfield & Company; Harley Hotels Inc.; Helmsley Hotels Inc.; Helmsley-Noyes Co., Inc.; The Helmsley Palace Hotel; Helmsley-Spear Conversion Sales Corp.; Helmsley-Spear, Inc.; Helmsley-Spear of Illinois, Inc.; National Realty Corp.; Owners Maintenance Corp.; John J. Reynolds, Inc.; Security Title & Guaranty Co.

Further Reading:

Amster, Robin, "Helmsley Conviction Should Have Little Impact on Hotel Empire," *Travel Weekly,* September 21, 1989, p. 30.

Bagamery, Anne, " 'I Notice Everything,' " *Forbes,* March 16, 1981, p. 164.

Barnfather, Maurice, "Has Success Spoiled Harry Helmsley?," *Forbes,* July 20, 1981, p. 94.

Brandt, Harris, "Did Leona's Ad Persona Win Her a Trip up the River?," *Advertising Age,* April 27, 1992, p. 32.

Hammer, Joshua, "Once upon a Time It Was All Harry's," *Newsweek,* August 21, 1989, pp. 50–51.

Hammer, Richard, *The Helmsley's: The Rise and Fall of Harry and Leona,* New York: New American Library, 1990.

"Harry Brakmann Helmsley," *Forbes 400,* October 18, 1993, p. 156.

"Harry Helmsley in 'Let's Make a Deal,' " *Nation's Business,* October 1980, pp. 55–58.

Kasindorf, Jeanie, "Leona and Harry: Money and Love," *New York,* October 3, 1988, pp. 41–49.

"Mr. Empire State Strikes Back," *Forbes,* April 11, 1983, pp. 180–181.

Moskowitz, Milton, editor, "Helmsley," *Everybody's Business: A Field Guide to the 400 Leading Companies in America,* New York: Doubleday, 1990, pp. 130–131.

Pierson, Ransdell, *The Queen of Mean: The Unauthorized Biography of Leona Helmsley,* New York: Bantam Books, 1989.

Pileggi, Nicholas, "The Men Who Own New York," *New York,* May 19, 1980, pp. 26–33.

Selwitz, Robert, "Queen Ousted; Helmsley Palace on the Market," *Hotel & Motel Management,* October 5, 1992, pp. 1 and 21.

Shachtman, Tom, *Skyscraper Dreams: The Great Real Estate Dynasties of New York,* Boston: Little, Brown and Company, 1991.

Sommerfield, Frank, "Inevitable Fall," *Crain's New York Business,* May 23, 1988.

Teinowitz, Ira, "Helmsley Not Talking About Ads," *Advertising Age,* December 18, 1989, p. 44.

Waters, Harry F., "A Queen on Trial," *Newsweek,* August 21, 1989, pp. 46–51.

Winters, Patricia, "Leona Exits Helmsley Ads," *Advertising Age,* February 26, 1990, pp. 4 and 59.

—Jay P. Pederson

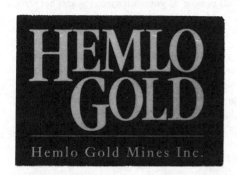

Hemlo Gold Mines Inc.

Suite 2902
1 Adelaide Street East
Toronto, Ontario M5C 2Z9
Canada
(416) 982-7116
Fax: (416) 982-7388

Public Company
Incorporated: 1987
Employees: 449
Revenues: C$211.9 million
Stock Exchanges: Toronto Montreal American London
SICs: 1041 Gold Mining

Hemlo Gold Mines is one of the most important and lowest cost gold producers in North America. The company owns and operates two mines with high gold reserves: the Golden Giant Mine located near Marathon, Ontario, and the Silidor Mine close to Rouyn-Noranda, Quebec. From these mines alone, Hemlo produced 492,100 ounces of gold in 1992. The company also has promising development properties in northeastern Ontario and in Montana, and is actively exploring additional mining sites in Australia and South America.

Like the proverbial pot of gold at the end of the rainbow, the Hemlo area in northwestern Ontario has been regarded for centuries as a land of riches. As early as 1535, French explorer Jacques Cartier was told by native North Americans of a gleaming, lustrous metal found in the North. During their trip in 1665, *coureurs de bois* Radisson and Groseilliers reportedly traded for gold with the local tribes, and in 1869 a native prospector and guide, Moses PeKong-Gay, found gold nuggets in the Hemlo region.

In 1945, storekeeper Harry Ollman and native prospector Peter Mogeg discovered gold, and one year later guide Moses Figher and geologist Trevor Pages staked ground around what is known today as the Williams claim. Prospector Roy Newman and geologist Bob Schaaf came close to becoming millionaires when they found gold in the area during 1974. Even though adventurers, explorers, prospectors, and geologists staked numerous claims and mining companies worked the ground in search of the precious metal, no one was able to locate the quartz rock veins in which Canadian gold is usually embedded.

The gold that was found during these attempts did not have the grade to be commercially profitable.

Not finding gold, most of the prospectors and geologists eventually gave up on Hemlo, but Don McKinnon and John Larche remained patient—and became millionaires. Larche had quit school at 15 and gone to work in the gold mines near the Porcupine River in Timmins, Ontario. He worked for short periods in automobile and airplane plants before he turned to prospecting full time. Larche, with a wife and four children, had once gone for 18 months without earning any money. McKinnon also left school at an early age and moved to Timmins from Cochrane, Ontario. In Timmins he supervised lumber crews for a paper company before leaving to become a prospector.

Both men had studied the Hemlo area for almost 20 years: Larche grubbing the ground with a tractor and backhoe and McKinnon grubbing by means of mining publications, geological surveys, and public and corporate reports. When claims in the area that both men coveted reverted to the Crown in December of 1979, they immediately acted on the opportunity.

Relying on their research and intuition, they began by staking a claim in the traditional manner. A prospector brings an ax, compass, and four-foot-long post with the information about the claim attached to it, or he cuts a tree to the same proportions in the northeast corner of his 40-square-acre claim. Then the prospector cuts down the trees in his path as he paces to the three corners of his "grubstake." While McKinnon watched, Larche marched the 460 paces for each quarter mile that enclosed their claim.

With the cost of drilling 1,500 feet into the ground for samples at a prohibitive $25 to $30 per foot, McKinnon and Larche lacked the money to work the land themselves, but they did not want to sell the claim outright either. The only alternative was to find a mining company that might be interested in funding an exploratory site. When the men began to search for an investor, they discovered that the history of geologists' reports on the Hemlo area weighed heavily against them.

After pounding on the doors of big exploration companies without any results, the two men met David Bell. An independent geologist who had had an eye on the Hemlo area for some time, Bell was eager to sink his drill into the claims staked by McKinnon and Larche. Bell had a theory that no one considered before, namely, that within the Hemlo area there was no quartz rock. According to Bell, the reason for this was due to the fact that the gold was scattered throughout volcanic sediment in wide and fine amounts—similar to the deposits in some of the richest goldfields in Africa.

Bell suggested the men look for a "junior." A junior provides enough money for exploration in the hope that a major mining company will eventually take over the entire operation and give the prospectors a share of the profits. Bell soon found Vancouver businessman Murray "The Pez" Pezim. Pezim told Bell he could raise enough money for exploration through a junior called Corona Resources. For a negligible amount of cash, shares of stock, and a 1.5 percent royalty on every ounce of smelted gold for each of them, Larche and McKinnon gave up their claims at Hemlo to Corona Resources.

In January of 1981, Bell started drilling his first hole near the Trans-Canada Highway. Unable to find high grade gold-bearing material even after 70 holes, he continued drilling with Pezim's encouragement. Turning toward the southwest and away from the highway, Bell drilled at different depths and tried different angles. Finally, on hole 76 at an angle of 50 degrees and a depth of 336.5 feet, Bell found a sample that graded .29 ounces of gold per ton. On May 7, 1981, Bell had made one of the most important discoveries in the history of North American mining. With an additional $20 million from Pezim to help continue digging, by hole 120 Bell had delineated a 250,000 ton deposit grading out at .25 ounces a ton.

News of the discovery jarred the mining companies into action. Teck Corporation reached an arrangement with Corona to take over the development of the claim, and Long Lac Mineral Exploration purchased properties adjacent to Corona's. Goliath Gold Mines and Golden Sceptre Resources, two exploration companies based in Vancouver, also optioned a number of claims. In 1982 Bell moved his drill from the Corona properties and started working the ground on Goliath's and Golden Sceptre's purchases. His drilling program resulted in finding what is now called the Golden Giant mine, with an estimated deposit of 6.5 million tons grading at .25 ounces of gold per ton.

A short time later, one of the largest mining companies in Canada, Noranda Mines Ltd., reached an agreement with Goliath and Golden Sceptre. For a 50 percent interest in their claims, Noranda agreed to provide $290 million to finance all capital expenditures, construct the mine, and complete the exploration project. In 1983 Noranda, Golden Sceptre, and Goliath purchased one-quarter of an adjoining claim from Teck-Corona's Operating Corporation's David Bell mine for the site of the shaft and surface facilities.

Site clearing and building of the mine were initiated in April of 1983. Construction of the mine and mill went quickly and the first bar of gold bullion was poured on April 6, 1985. During the early months of 1987, the interests in the Golden Giant mine held by Noranda, Goliath, and Golden Sceptre were merged into one company, Hemlo Gold Mines Inc. At the same time, the new company struck an agreement with Noranda that allowed it to draw on Noranda's expertise in mine management, exploration, marketing, and technical research. In October 1987, less than five years after the original agreement had been signed to develop the claim, Hemlo announced its first dividend.

From 1985 until the end of 1991, the Golden Giant mine produced 2,300,000 ounces of gold. In 1991 alone, a record 443,400 ounces of gold at an average operating cost of $126 was produced at the mine. In 1992 Golden Giant produced 492,100 ounces of gold, nearly 5 percent more than the previous year, at an average cost of $113 per ounce. Proven and probable

reserves estimated during the same year figured to include an additional 5,300,000 ounces of gold sufficient for another thirteen years of mining. Management estimated an annual production rate of 360,000 ounces for the mine's remaining life.

Hemlo acquired a 55 percent interest in the Silidor Mine, located in northwestern Quebec, and as part of the acquisition from Noranda, it became operator of the mine in May of 1991. During the last eight months of 1991, Hemlo's share of production from the Silidor mine totaled 25,900 ounces, and operating costs averaged $287 per ounce of gold. Hemlo estimated that its share of production from the mine would average 35,000 ounces of gold per year, and projected in 1992 that six years remained in the life of the mine.

In addition to the Golden Giant and Silidor mines, Hemlo had two projects under development which were estimated to provide nearly two million ounces to the company's reserves. At a projected average operating cost of less than $180 per ounce, these two sites had the potential of adding 150,000 ounces of gold to Hemlo's annual production by 1996. The New World Project in Montana, in which Hemlo owned a 60 percent interest, was projected to have an annual production of 80,000 ounces of gold by 1996. Hemlo had a 55 percent direct and indirect interest in the Holloway Joint Venture located in northeastern Ontario, and its share for the company promised another 70,000 ounces by 1995.

The men that set off one of the largest staking rushes in North America remained involved in mining. Geologist David Bell turned his attention to exploring sites in western Europe, South America, and Australia, while maintaining an office in Hamilton, Ontario. McKinnon used the proceeds from his share in the claims to buy a house in Guelph, a farm in Timmins, a cottage in Peterborough, and a winter home in Florida. After his work with Larche, he became involved in projects in the Mishibishu area about 100 miles south of Hemlo. John Larche served two terms as president of the Prospectors and Developers Association of Canada during the late 1980s, but suffered severe injuries from a plane crash in 1991, from which he was fortunate enough to recover. He had ongoing exploration projects in British Columbia and other areas in North America. Clearly, each of these men benefited enormously from the interest they received in the gold recovered by Hemlo Gold Mines Inc.

Further Reading:

Anderson, Scott, "Greening of a Giant," *Canadian Mining Journal,* May 1991.
Mining Life, summer 1992, pp. 12–42.
Skillings, D. N., Jr., "Hemlo Gold Mines Inc. Marks Further Gold Production Record in 1990 at its Golden Giant Mine in Ontario," *Skillinas' Mining Review,* April 6, 1991, pp. 2–4.

—Thomas Derdak

The Hertz Corporation

225 Brae Boulevard
Park Ridge, New Jersey 07656
U.S.A.
(201) 307-2000
Fax: (201) 307-2644

Private Company
Incorporated: 1967
Employees: 18,000
Revenues: $2.8 billion
SICs: 7514 Passenger Car Rental; 7359 Equipment Rental &
    Leasing Nec

The Hertz Corporation is the world's largest car rental company, handling approximately 25 million rentals worldwide with over 5,000 locations in 130 countries and a fleet of 420,000 vehicles, including 230,000 vehicles in the United States. Through its subsidiary Hertz Equipment Rental Corporation, the company also rents construction and industrial equipment to contractors and industrial and government markets. Hertz's claim management subsidiary is a leading third-party administrator, while Hertz Technologies, Inc. provides telecommunications services to corporations. The oldest company in the car rental industry, Hertz has experienced many changes in ownership since it was founded. It is currently owned by Ford Motor Co. (which has a 49 percent controlling interest), Volvo North America Corporation (which holds 26 percent), Commerzbank A.G. (5 percent); and Hertz management (with the remaining 20 percent).

The origins of the company date back to 1918, the year that Walter L. Jacobs, a 22-year-old car salesman with a fleet of a dozen Ford Model Ts, started a small car rental business in Chicago. Within five years, Jacobs expanded his operations to the point where the business was generating annual revenues of about one million dollars through a fleet of 600 cars. In 1923 Jacobs sold the company to John Hertz, the head of Yellow Cab and Yellow Truck, although Jacobs remained with the company, serving as the chief operating officer. Hertz held the DriveUrSelf System, to which he would add his name, for all of three years before including it as part of the deal to sell Yellow Truck to General Motors Corp.

General Motors kept the business until selling it to the Omnibus Corporation in 1953. The following year Omnibus changed its

name to The Hertz Corporation, and a stock offering was made on the New York Stock Exchange, where the company's shares remained until 1967. Also in 1954 the newly public Hertz itself bought Metropolitan Distributors, a pioneer in New York truck leasing and the largest truck rental business at the time, with a fleet of 4,000 trucks. The purchase was made for $6.75 million in cash. Walter Jacobs, who was president of the company until his retirement in 1960, commented at the time that the acquisition "rounds out Hertz operations by providing in New York City the largest single truck rental operation in existence." Leon C. Greenbaum, the president of Metropolitan, became vice-chairman of the Hertz Board of Directors. The acquisition brought the total Hertz fleet to 15,500 trucks and 12,900 passenger cars.

By 1960 the market for rental cars was rapidly expanding, complementing the expansion of air travel into the consumer market and the rapid growth of the travel industry in general. Despite the influx of new firms into the industry, Hertz retained the number one position throughout the 1960s. Much of the success was attributed to the expertise and guidance of rental car veteran Walter Jacobs, who was recognized as being "the maven of the car rental business," knowing how to buy and sell cars expertly in order to build and maintain a profitable rental car fleet.

In 1967 ownership of Hertz was again altered, this time in a merger/stock swap deal. The new association was with Radio Corporation of America (RCA)—while Hertz became a wholly owned subsidiary (though the company operated as a separate entity with its own management and board of directors), Hertz stockholders received RCA stock in return. Leon Greenbaum, who was chairman of Hertz by this time, became a director of RCA.

The relationship with RCA continued until 1985, when RCA decided to focus on its more traditional product lines and sold Hertz to UAL, Inc., owner of United Airlines, the largest airline in the country. UAL ostensibly planned to combine Hertz with United and its Westin Hotel Co. subsidiary in order to make UAL the most formidable travel corporation in the world. The deal was expected to, but did not actually, face resistance from federal government anti-trust scrutiny, and once closed, it joined the three leaders in their respective competitive industries. Since United also invested in travel agencies, UAL clearly meant to overlap nearly all travel services "from reservation to check-in to baggage handling," according to Richard J. Ferris, chairman of UAL. One striking aspect of the deal, according to some analysts, was that during a time of great leveraged buyouts, it did not involve any investment bankers. In the meantime UAL was concerned that it might find itself the target of a takeover.

In 1987 UAL changed its name to Allegis, Inc. Later that year Allegis was involved in a hostile takeover, and Frank A. Olson, the chairman and CEO of Hertz, was named to those positions at Allegis. Olson, who was still leading the company in the early 1990s, joined Hertz in 1964 and helped to build the company's fleet to 350,000 rental cars.

As part of a restructuring plan in which UAL (the Allegis name was dropped) divested itself of its non-airline holdings, Hertz was sold yet again. In a $1.3 billion deal that was completed in December of 1987, Allegis sold Hertz to Park Ridge Corporation, an investor group that was formed expressly to acquire Hertz and included Ford Motor Co. and some Hertz executives. In the buyout, Ford obtained 80 percent of the equity and Hertz management received the remainder. Of the $1.3 billion in necessary capital, $520 million was provided by Ford while the balance was borrowed. After UAL's transition, Frank Olson gave up the chairman and CEO positions of that company, although he remained a member of the board of directors.

After the sale there was some speculation that Ford might want to eventually take Hertz public, a move that had proved profitable in other leveraged buyouts at the time. Buyout groups would make an acquisition and hold it for a short time then sell shares to the public at a sizable profit. More importantly for Ford, the buyout was undoubtedly a strategic move. Hertz had been buying 65,000 vehicles a year from Ford domestically and 15,000 overseas. In fact, Ford's share of Hertz's vehicle orders, about 50 percent, would increase and thereby help Ford maintain its market share even though Hertz would still buy cars from other makers. Although auto sales to rental car companies are not particularly profitable (since rental cars are generally low profit margin), Ford ostensibly thought the move would allow it to keep rivals out and preserve its strong relationship with the rental companies. Put more pointedly by David Healy, an auto industry analyst at Drexel, Burnham, Lambert, "They bought it to keep Hertz out of the hands of Chrysler."

At the same time it was completing its takeover of Hertz, Ford was also trying to keep a distance from some serious legal problems being faced by the car rental company. In August of 1988 Hertz pleaded guilty to defrauding more than 100,000 insurance companies and other third parties by overcharging for repairs that resulted from collisions with Hertz vehicles. It was charged that Hertz, in some instances, had claimed for damages when repairs were not made and, in other instances, paid discounted wholesale rates for car repairs, while charging the retail rates to the parties involved. Although it was noted that such rental car companies as Avis, Budget, and Alamo also followed the practice of charging retail repair costs, according to *Business Week* Hertz failed to disclose to those concerned that they would be billed for repairs at "prevailing retail rates." Hertz agreed to pay $13.7 million in restitution and $6.35 million in fines, "the largest fine ever imposed upon a corporation in a criminal consumer fraud case," according to Andrew J. Maloney, U.S. attorney for the Eastern District of New York.

In addition to this history-making legal settlement, Hertz's parent company, Park Ridge Corporation, faced change in 1988 as well. The Volvo North America Corporation, a subsidiary of AB Volvo of Sweden based in Rockleigh, New Jersey, became an investor in Park Ridge, paying $100 million in cash to Ford in exchange for a 20 percent interest in the joint venture. Park Ridge Corporation was later merged into The Hertz Corporation so that the investors, who retained their equity positions, owned the company directly.

Meanwhile, the competitive battle between the major car rental companies continued to rage. In January of 1992 Hertz and Avis, Inc. reached a settlement after Hertz brought suit against its competitor, accusing them of false advertising. Avis had received the Alfred Award given to the "best car rental company" by Gralla Publications' *Corporate Travel*. Hertz's suit questioned the validity of the magazine's readers poll. In the settlement, Avis was enjoined from further advertising its receipt of the Alfred Award.

In another legal battle, a federal judge in New York City upheld a newly enacted city ordinance that prohibited rental companies from imposing "resident-based" rates, but at the same time barred the city from putting the law into effect. Specifically, Hertz was charging residents of the boroughs of Manhattan, the Bronx, Brooklyn, and Queens higher rates when cars were rented locally. Hertz argued that the increased rates covered what it called the excessive liability costs faced by the company when renting to residents of these boroughs. The U.S. Court of Appeals reversed the U.S. District Court ruling and remanded the case for trial. Hertz continues to charge residence-based rates in New York, while the court continues its stay of the law at issue, effectively barring the city from stopping Hertz's practice.

Competition remained fierce among the top five car rental companies in the early 1990s, and many analysts likened the ensuing price wars to those of the airline and hotel industries, whose markets certainly complement the rental car business. In addition to price cutting, Hertz offered various promotional strategies to expand its product base. One strategy, for example, allowed customers to earn mileage in the frequent flyer programs of such airlines as American, Northwest, United, and U.S. Air as well as gain points in Mariott's Honored guest program. In a cost-cutting maneuver in early 1993, Hertz arranged for IBM to provide the company with some information technology services. Through its Integrated Systems Solutions Corp. unit, IBM agreed to provide some software applications and support of the IBM mainframes at Hertz's Data Center in Oklahoma City, Oklahoma, over the next five years.

Since 1950, when the company began expansion into Europe, Hertz has also been an international firm. In the early 1990s the company began franchise operations at the airport in Tirana, Albania, marking that nation's first rental car company as well as the presence of Hertz in all of the Eastern European countries. In addition, Hertz had operations in Russia and was also represented in Africa, Asia, and Latin America.

Hertz, the oldest car rental company still in business, remained the market leader while facing stiff challenges from four major competitors—Avis, National, Budget, and Alamo—into the 1990s. With an expanding rental car market and a solid competitive position that includes the backing of Ford and Volvo, Hertz was expected to continue holding the industry's top spot.

Principal Subsidiaries: Hertz Equipment Rental Corporation; Hertz International Ltd.; Hertz Claim Management Corporation; Hertz Technologies, Inc.

Further Reading:

Buder, Leonard, "Hertz Admits Use of Fraud in Bills for Auto Repairs," *New York Times,* August 5, 1988.
"Hertz Is Doing Some Body Work—On Itself," *Business Week,* February 15, 1988.

Cole, Robert J., "United Airlines Set to Buy Hertz from RCA in $587 Million Deal," *New York Times,* June 18, 1985.

Halper, Mark, "Hertz Mulls Outsourcing Rescue," *Computerworld,* June 22, 1992.

Harler, Curt, "How Hertz Makes Its Call Center #1," *Communications News,* November, 1992.

"The Hertz Corporation," Park Ridge, New Jersey, Public Affairs Department, The Hertz Corporation, January, 1993.

Magenheim, Henry, "Car Rental Firms Expect a Boost From Air Fare Restructuring," *Travel Weekly,* May 11, 1992.

Moskowitz, Milton, et al, eds., *Everybody's Business: A Field Guide to the 400 Leading Companies in America,* New York, Doubleday, 1990.

"Hertz Corp. Plans Acquisition Here," *New York Times,* December 4, 1954.

Ross, Philip E., "Volvo to Get 20% of Hertz Parent," *New York Times,* June 23, 1988.

Salpukas, Agis, "Ford Leads Group Deal for Hertz," *New York Times,* October 3, 1987.

"Hertz Warns That Car Rental Fees Could Rise," *New York Times,* November 11, 1992.

Ruggless, Ron, "Operators Woo Foreign Tourists With Hertz's Help," *Nation's Restaurant News,* April 12, 1993.

Thomas, Charles M., "Hertz Pays Record Fine: Pleads Guilty to Defrauding Consumers," *Automotive News,* August 8, 1988.

"Judge in New York Upholds Law Barring Surcharge by Hertz," *Wall Street Journal,* April 1, 1992.

McDowell, Edwin, "Pricing Plans Shift at Hertz and Alamo," *Wall Street Journal,* May 5, 1992.

"IBM Reaches Pact With Hertz," *Wall Street Journal,* March 31, 1993.

—John A. Sarich

Hubbell Incorporated

584 Derby Milford Road
Orange, Connecticut 06477
U.S.A.
(203) 789-1100
Fax: (203) 799-4333

Public Company
Incorporated: 1905 as Harvey Hubbell Incorporated
Employees: 5,159
Sales: $786.1 million
Stock Exchanges: New York
SICs: 3643 Current-Carrying Wiring Devices; 3645
    Residential Lighting Fixtures; 3585 Refrigeration &
    Heating Equipment

Hubbell Incorporated is one of the largest and most respected manufacturers of electrical wiring and other instrumentation in the United States. For many decades, Hubbell maintained a modest and unassuming business manufacturing the important products invented by its founder, Harvey Hubbell II. A correspondent for *Forbes* told his readers in 1977 that "unless you are reading this on safari, there is probably a Harvey Hubbell invention within six feet of you right now." The company remained strongly focused on such products until the 1960s, when it embarked on a diversification program. While nonconsumer electrical products remain its core business, the company has also gained footholds in the manufacture of telecommunications equipment and high voltage cables.

Hubbell bears the name of inventor and businessman Harvey Hubbell II. Born in Connecticut in 1859, he graduated from high school and began working for companies that manufactured marine engines and printing machinery. During this time, he accumulated several ideas for new inventions, and in 1888 he set out on his own, opening a small manufacturing facility in Bridgeport, Connecticut. Hubbell's first product was taken from his own patent for a paper roll holder with a toothed blade for use in stores that sold wrapping paper. This cutter stand became a tremendous success; it was a common feature of retail stores that used wrapping paper in the early 1900s and remained in wide use into the late twentieth century.

Hubbell also designed and built a series of new and improved machine tools during his early years in business. In the early 1890s, he began to consider the opportunities presented by

Edison's new electric light bulb, and the fruits of his work would secure both the future of his company and his place in history. On a visit to New York City, Hubbell came upon a penny arcade, featuring several electrically operated games which, although popular with customers, caused maintenance headaches. Every day, the janitor had to detach each of the power supply wires for the games from separate terminals in the wall so that he could move them and sweep the floor underneath. After he was done, he faced the tedious task of reconnecting the wires, making sure that each one went into the proper terminal—the consequence of not doing so being a short circuit. Watching the janitor gave Hubbell the idea for an electrical plug in which the wires were permanently attached in their proper sequence, so that devices could be easily detached and reattached to their power sources. Hubbell built a prototype, which he tested with the help of the janitor, and later patented it. The two-pronged electrical plug that is so common today is a direct descendant of this innovation. In 1896 Hubbell patented a light bulb socket with an on/off pull chain, another invention in use to this day.

In 1901 Hubbell published a 12-page catalogue that listed 63 electrical products of his company's manufacture, and four years later his company incorporated as Harvey Hubbell, Incorporated. In 1909 the company began constructing a four-floor factory and office building that would become the first building in New England made of reinforced concrete.

As electricity became the power source of choice in the United States, Hubbell's company did its best to keep up. Its 1917 catalogue was 100 pages long and listed over 1,000 electrical products, including 277 different types and sizes of light bulb sockets. One important product was a toggle light switch, which Hubbell had invented to replace the old two-button switch. A line of 288 heavy-duty "Presturn" products marked the company's entry into industrial electrical products. In the 1920s, the company produced a line of low-voltage devices for use by farmers who had not tapped into higher-voltage urban electrical grids. Also during this time, Hubbell developed a device that locked streetlamp and household light bulbs firmly in place, filling a need in cities where new trolley cars were producing vibrations that loosened bulbs and caused them to fall out of their sockets.

Harvey Hubbell died in 1927 and was succeeded as president of the company by his son, Harvey III. The 26-year-old Hubbell had been trained as an electrical engineer and was already at work for the family firm. Under Harvey Hubbell III, the company went public in 1936—a timely move considering that, during the later years of the Great Depression, some employees occasionally had to accept company stock in lieu of pay. He also proved his business acumen by establishing a network of independent distributors to help market and disseminate the company's products, a system that would help offset the low profile that the company has traditionally kept.

During World War II, much of the company's capacity was devoted to manufacturing electrical components for the military, including battery-charging systems for the M-4 Sherman tank. Hubbell also opened a plant in Lexington, Kentucky, in part to meet demand for its military products and also because its original factory in Connecticut was considered vulnerable to air attack.

After the war, the Hubbell company shifted its focus back to making products for the civilian economy. It custom designed and produced electrical devices for the luxury ocean liner *United States,* which was launched in 1952 and required electrical wiring that would resist the corrosive effects of salt air while fitting into narrow stateroom partitions. At the end of the 1950s, the company began to ponder the benefits of diversification. Until that point, Hubbell had always been a conservative company with a reputation for making high quality products that sold for higher than average prices. Its narrow range of products, however, limited opportunities for growth and left it vulnerable to cyclical ups and downs. Even with its strong desire to diversify, however, Hubbell chose its targets carefully and did not stray far from its field of expertise. In 1962 it acquired Kellems, a Connecticut-based manufacturer of mesh grips, cord connectors, and wire management products. In 1963 it bought Grelco, an English company that made industrial controls, the California-based Shalda Lighting, and the Chicago-based Ralco Manufacturing. Hubbell later merged Grelco into its British subsidiary, Harvey Hubbell Limited. In 1966 Hubbell purchased Euclid Electric, which it later renamed Hubbell Industrial Controls. The following year, Harvey Hubbell Limited acquired Watford Electric & Manufacturing, solidifying its presence as a producer of industrial controls in Great Britain.

Harvey Hubbell III died in 1968 and was succeeded as CEO by George Weppler, who became the first non-Hubbell to run the company in its 80 years of existence. Under Weppler, the pace of Hubbell's acquisition campaign was maintained. In 1969 the company acquired Kerite, a Connecticut-based manufacturer of high voltage electrical cables used mainly by utility companies and railroads. The next year, it acquired Steber Lighting to augment its light fixtures business. In 1972 Hubbell entered the telecommunications equipment field when it purchased Pulse Communications, a Virginia-based manufacturer of voice and data signal processing components. Also that year Hubbell acquired Southern Industrial Diecasting. Moreover, the company established a presence in South America with its Brazilian subsidiary, Harvey Hubbell do Brasil, after acquiring H. K. Porter do Brasil in 1973 and Metal-Arte Industrias Sao Paolo in 1974.

Weppler was succeeded by Robert Dixon in 1975. Dixon had spent twelve years studying electrical and mechanical engineering in night school and was a firm believer in Hubbell's odyssey through diversification and expansion. "If we had stayed only in the wiring business, our numbers would look better but we wouldn't be as strong," he told a *Forbes* correspondent in 1982, adding that "I even question whether we'd still be independent." Under Dixon, Hubbell acquired Hermetic Refrigeration, a Phoenix-based remanufacture of air conditioning compressors, in 1976. In 1978 it purchased Ohio Brass, which made insulation and surge arrestor for high voltage electrical equipment, as well as mining equipment. In 1981 the company spun off Harvey Hubbell do Brasil, and picked up Arrestor, an American manufacturer of switch, junction, and outlet boxes and electrical fittings.

By this time, Hubbell's diversifications had produced mixed results. On the one hand, the company's original wiring and light fixture business accounted for a disproportionate share of profits into the 1980s, a sign that acquired companies were not proving terribly lucrative despite the fact that Hubbell had made few outright missteps. On the other hand, Hubbell generated record profits every year from 1961 to 1983. In 1961, the company posted a relatively modest $22 million in sales; in 1981 sales reached $445.8 million. Robert Dixon retired as CEO in 1983 and was succeeded by Fred Dusto, who presided over the final acquisitions of Hubbell's long spree: Miller Lighting and Killark Electric Manufacturing, both purchased in 1985. In 1986 the company shortened its name to its current form.

Dusto retired in 1987 and was succeeded by George Ratcliffe, who had once served as the company's chief counsel. Under Ratcliffe, Hubbell spent aggressively on upgrading and automating its capital equipment as well as on research and development. This reinvestment produced profit margins higher than those of its competitors during the 1980s, as the company was able to cut labor costs and also sell innovative products that commanded relatively high returns. Hubbell also made further acquisitions during this time. In 1991 it purchased Westinghouse's Bryant Electric division, which made wiring devices for industrial applications. In 1993 Hubbell acquired Hipotronics, a manufacturer of high-voltage cables, test and measurement equipment, and E. M. Weigmann and Co., Inc., a manufacturer of industrial enclosures.

Although Harvey Hubbell II is not widely remembered today, his inventions were instrumental in facilitating and disseminating the pioneering work of more famous inventors such as Edison and Westinghouse. Similarly, the company that Hubbell founded has labored for over a century without widespread recognition for the company's name or products. Nevertheless, the success of its products, which people use and rely upon daily, signalled profitable years ahead for Hubbell.

Principal Subsidiaries: Bryant Electric, Inc.; Hipotronics, Inc.; Hubbell Premise Wiring, Inc.; Hubbell Canada Inc.; Harvey Hubbell Ltd.; Harvey Hubbell, S.E. Asia Ltd.; The Kerite Co.; Arrestor Incorporated; Killark Manufacturing Co.; Hubbell Industrial Controls, Inc; Hubbell Plastics, Inc.; The Ohio Brass Co.; Hubbell-Bell, Inc.; Hubbell Lighting, Inc.; Pulse Communications, Inc.

Further Reading:

"Crossed Currents," *Forbes,* July 5, 1982.
Hannon, Kerry. "Live Wire," *Forbes,* November 14, 1988.
"Harvey Hubbell, Harvey Hubbell," *Forbes,* August 1, 1977.
Hubbell 100: Second Century of Solutions, Hubbell Incorporated, Orange, 1988.

—Douglas Sun

IMI plc

P.O. Box 216, Witton
Birmingham, W. Midlands B6 7BA
England
(021) 356 4848

Public Company
Incorporated: 1962 as Imperial Metal Industries Ltd., a
   wholly owned subsidiary of Imperial Chemical Industries
   plc
Employees: 17,500
Sales: £1.01 billion (US$235.63 million)
Stock Exchanges: London
SICs: 6719 Offices of Holding Companies Nec; 3366 Copper
   Foundries; 3365 Aluminum Foundries; 3494 Valves and
   Pipe Fittings Nec; 3446 Architectural and Ornamental
   Metalwork; 3498 Fabricated Pipe and Pipe Fittings

IMI plc—formed in 1962 under the name Imperial Metal Industries Ltd., a wholly owned subsidiary of British conglomerate Imperial Chemical Industries plc (ICI)—is a major international manufacturer of advanced and high technology products in four areas: Building Products, Drinks Dispense, Fluid Power, and Engineering. The company has more than 100 subsidiaries with major plants in Great Britain, North and South America, continental Europe, and Australia. IMI sales rebounded to cross the £1 billion pound mark in 1992, but the company's profits declined 7 percent from 1991 to 1992, to £68 million.

IMI's Building Products Group produces copper tubes and fittings, castings, hot-water cylinders, electronic controls, and heat exchangers. The Drinks Dispense Division manufactures food and beverage dispensing and cooling systems and food service equipment, as well as material handling machinery for the dairy and bakery industries. IMI's Fluid Power operations encompass the production of pneumatic systems and components, cylinders, miniature valves, vacuum equipment, and specialized computer software. The Special Engineering group, finally, is something of a catch-all for IMI; it includes such prospective ventures as nuclear safety and aerospace equipment, minting, nickel plating, and sporting ammunition and equipment. In the early 1990s, IMI was also involved in computing and land development.

The largest company in the IMI group is Kynoch Metals, a copper processor that had been acquired by ICI in 1926. George

Kynoch & Co. was founded during the mid-nineteenth century by George Kynoch as an ammunitions manufacturer. After World War I, the company merged with Nobel Industries, and from 1918 to 1926 this new entity diversified into a range of metals businesses. ICI acquired Kynoch as an afterthought; the chemicals giant was primarily interested in Nobel. Regardless of the "historical accident," as *The Economist* phrased it in 1966, the parent company allowed and encouraged its Metals Division to expand.

By the time IMI was transformed into a subsidiary in 1962, its primary business activities were non-ferrous metals, zip fasteners, sporting ammunition, heat exchangers, and other engineering products—a general area comprised of ICI's peripheral business activities. IMI was the only part of ICI to be set up as a separate financial entity, perhaps foreshadowing its eventual divestment.

After its formation, IMI embarked on a strategy of vertical integration and horizontal diversification through the acquisition of companies that were either buyers of the group's products or whose activities were closely related to those of IMI. Significant acquisitions in the early 1960s included Yorkshire Imperial Metals and Wolverhampton Metal (Holdings) Ltd., a refiner and smelter of metal and a supplier to the group. Several subsidiaries were established by the group to develop new lines of business. IMI diversified into hot water cylinders with the 1965 purchase of Range Boilers Limited. That same year, IMI buttressed its zip fastener interests against intensifying competition from Japanese companies by merging its Lightning Zip Fasteners operations in the United Kingdom, France, West Germany, and Austria with those of the Opti Group of companies in West Germany, the Netherlands, and Great Britain to form the LF/Opti Group. IMI held 50 percent of the new company, which soon began to expand geographically.

In 1966 ICI elected to offer ten percent of IMI's shares on the open market. The move acknowledged two factors: first, that IMI's business had little to do with ICI's main focus, and second, that if IMI was to continue to expand, it would have to generate the necessary funds itself.

When Rolls-Royce, a primary customer of IMI, collapsed in 1970, IMI diversified into fluid power with the acquisition of Enots Limited in 1971 and Norgren Shipston International Limited and the United States' C.A. Norgren Co. in 1972. The purchase of two French companies, Mecafrance S.A. and Mapegaz-Remati S.A., brought IMI into production of special valves and formed the origins of IMI's Special Engineering group.

ICI sold its remaining 62 percent interest in IMI in 1977. By that time, IMI had more than 100 operating subsidiaries and employed over 32,000 people throughout the world. The company's sales topped £404 million, over one-third of which came from overseas trade.

During the 1980s, IMI shifted away from commodities production in favor of added value finished products. The Building Products Group evolved from IMI's Kynoch Metals core business. But instead of marketing "midstream" metals in strip, sheet, rod, or wire form, IMI moved its production "downstream" to sell finished products like tube, pipe, and fittings.

IMI exited the rolled metals industry in 1990 and acquired A.W. Cash Valve, an American producer of heating and plumbing controls, in 1991.

IMI got into the business of drinks dispense through the 1982 acquisition of The Cornelius Co., a U.S. business that had participated in joint ventures with IMI in Europe. This division was promoted into a full-fledged part of IMI with several acquisitions, including MK Refrigeration Group and Cannon Conveyor Systems Inc. in 1990 and Remcor Products in 1991.

The Fluid Power division of IMI was diversified in the 1980s to include pneumatic products. The 1986 purchase of Webber Electro Components plc and the acquisition of AB Westin & Backlund's pneumatic division bolstered this segment of IMI's business.

IMI also divested several businesses over the course of this rather low-key refinement of its operations into four key groups. In 1987 the company disposed of its 60 percent interest in Anderson Greenwood (Australia) Pty., Ltd., its 50 percent share in Silverton Engineering Holdings (Pty.) Ltd., and its share of Mapegaz-Remati S.A. The company received £13.5 million cash for its sale of IMI Yorkshire Imperial Plastics Ltd. the following year and disposed of IMI Hayes Metals Ltd. as well.

IMI's sales peaked in 1989 at £1.08 billion. At that time, 47 percent of the company's sales were concentrated in the United Kingdom, and 27 percent came from the rest of Europe. A global recession has enforced a steady decline in the company's sales and profits since that year. The Building Products group was hit especially hard; in 1992, its sales declined for the third consecutive year, from £404 million in 1989 to £305 million. The division's profit margin dropped two points to seven percent. IMI's Special Engineering profits also declined dramatically, from 10.7 percent in 1989 to 5.1 percent in 1992.

IMI's Drinks Dispense division, however, had a record year in 1992, with profits increasing by 25 percent to £28.6 million on sales of £230 million. Much of the profits growth resulted from increased market share, productivity improvements, and a full year of operations for the division's newest addition, Remcor. Fluid Power recovered slightly from a 1991 dip in sales, but its profits were cut in half from 16.8 percent in 1989 to 8.1 percent in 1992. IMI anticipated and prepared for a recovery from the early 1990s recession by increasing its research and development budget and capital expenditures. The company also worked to increase its overseas operations, especially in the United States, where a slow but steady recovery was underway.

Principal Subsidiaries: IMI Yorkshire Copper Tube Ltd.; Irish Metal Industries Ltd.; YIM Scandinavia A.B. (Sweden); IMI Yorkshire Fittings Ltd.; Anson Cast Products Ltd.; IMI Cash Valve Inc. (United States); R. Woeste & Co. ''Yorkshire'' GmbH (Germany); Raccor Orleanais S.A. (France); S.A. Eclipse N.V. (Belgium); A + F Epuletgepesz (Hungary; 90%); Yorkshire Fittings Pty. Ltd. (Australia); IMI Titon Ltd. (New Zealand); IMI Waterheating Ltd.; IMI Range Ltd.; IMI Pactrol Ltd; IMI Rycroft Ltd.; IMI Scott Ltd.; IMI Santon Ltd.; IMI Air Conditioning Ltd.; IMI Reginers Ltd.; IMI Wolverhampton Metal Ltd.; Wolverhampton Abrasives Ltd. (67.5%); IMI Cornelius (U.K.) Ltd.; IMI Cornelius Europe Ltd.; MK Refrigeration Ltd.; Gaskell and Chambers Ltd.; IMI Cornelius Inc. (United States); Remcor Products Company (United States); Cannon Equipment Co. (United States); Cannon Equipment West Inc. (United States); Cannon Conveyor Systems Inc. (United States); Carmun International Inc. (United States); Cumberland Corporation (United States); IMI Cornelius (Pacific) Ltd. (Hong Kong); IMI Cornelius Brasil Ltda.; IMI Cornelius Deutschland GmbH (Germany); IMI Cornelius España S.A.; IMI Cornelius Benelux N.V.; IMI Cornelius Osterreich GesmbH (Austria); IMI Cornelius Hellas S.A. (Greece); Imi Cornelius Italia Srl; MK Refrigeration (Ireland) Ltd.; IMI Cornelius Australia Pty. Ltd. (Australia); IMI Cornelius (New Zealand) Ltd.; IMI Fluid Power International Ltd.; Norgren Martonair Ltd.; Norgren Martonair GmbH (Germany); Norgren Martonair Europa GmbH (Germany); Norgren Martonair Druckluftsteuerungen GmbH (Austria); S.A. Norgren Martonair N.V. (Belgium); Norgren Martonair AS. (Denmark); Norgren Martonair S.A. (France); Norgren Martonair (Ireland) Ltd.; Norgren Martonair S.p.A. (Italy); Norgren Martonair B.V. (Holland); Norgren Martonair A.S. (Norway); Norgren Martonair S.A. (Spain); Norgren Martonair A.B. (Sweden); Norgren Martonair A.G. (Switzerland); Walter A.G. (Switzerland); Watson Smith Ltd.; Webber Electro Components Ltd.; Norgren Co. (United States); Norgren Martonair do Brasil Ltda.; Norgren Martonair (Canada) Inc.; Norgren de Mexico S.A.; IMI Norgren Martonair Pacific Pte. Ltd. (Singapore); Norgren Martonair Pty. Ltd. (Australia); Norgren Martonair (Hong Kong) Ltd.; Norgren Martonair Pneumatics (Singapore) Pte. Ltd.; Norgren Martonair (N.Z.) Ltd. (New Zealand); IMI Titanium Ltd.; IMI Titanium France S.A.R.L.; IMI Titanium Inc. (United States); IMI Yorkshire Alloys Ltd.; IMI Dreh Ltd.; IMI Bailey Birkett Ltd.; Mecafrance S.A.; Mecafrance (Deutschland) GmbH; MCF Controls Inc. (United States); Control Components Inc. (United States); Conax Buffalo Corporation (United States); IMI Marston Ltd.; IMI Marston Inc. (United States); Eley Ltd.; Eley Hawk Ltd.; Eley Americas Inc. (United States); IMI Components Ltd.; IMI Birmingham Mint Ltd.; IMI Amal Ltd.; Bailey Gill Products Ltd.; SJ & E Fellows Ltd.; IMI Computing Ltd.; IMI Computing Inc. (United States); Brook Street Computers Ltd.; Redwood International Ltd.; Uniplex Ltd.; Uniplex Integration Systems Inc. (United States); Uniplex GmbH (Germany); Uniplex S.A.R.L. (France); Uniplex Italia S.r.L.; Uniplex Pacific Pty. (Australia); IMI Property Investments Ltd.; Holford Estates Ltd.; Witton Estates Management Services Ltd.

Further Reading:

''Floating Metals Off,'' *The Economist,* March 5, 1966, p. 931.
History and Business of IMI, Birmingham, England: IMI plc, 1977.

—April S. Dougal

International Flavors & Fragrances Inc.

521 West 57th Street
New York, NY 10019-2960
U.S.A.
(212) 765-5500
Fax: (212) 708-7147

Public Company
Incorporated: 1909 as Morana, Inc.
Employees: 4,242
Sales: $1.13 billion
Stock Exchanges: New York
SICs: 2869 Industrial Organic Chemicals Nec

International Flavors & Fragrances Inc. has been a leader in the fiercely competitive flavor and fragrance industry since 1958, when it debuted under its present name. A strictly business-to-business operation, IFF routinely provides individually tailored fragrances for a host of products ranging from fine perfumes like Calvin Klein's Eternity to scents used in laundry detergents. More unusual IFF fragrances in the closely guarded vault housing about 80,000 formulas include the fresh aroma of new-mown grass (used on a paper strip inside a golf magazine) and the garbage- and urine-tinged odor in a Smithsonian Institution exhibit intended to resemble a slum. Though fragrances have traditionally been the backbone of IFF's bottom line, their flavorings divisions were healthy enough to have reached $378 million by early 1991. Among the company's clients in this area of business are Kraft General Foods, which employs IFF artistry in many of its products, and McDonald's, whose salad dressings receive their flavors from IFF laboratories.

International Flavors and Fragrances traces its origins back to the 1909 incorporation of Morana, Inc. in New York City. In 1920 Morana was taken over by a young man who would build the business into one of the foremost companies in the industry. Arnold Louis Van Ameringen arrived in the United States from Holland in 1917 on his way to represent a Dutch fragrance manufacturer known as Polak-Schwarz. However, Van Ameringen's job security did not stand the test of distance. Before a year had passed he was fired for suggesting a now-common American practice—a profit-sharing plan for employees. Undaunted, Van Ameringen opened his own fragrance and flavor supply business the following year. After merging this

firm into Morana, Van Ameringen decided in the mid-1920s to boost sales by persuading manufacturers of bar soaps and detergents to add fragrances to their products. Several adopted this suggestion, and found that the new ingredient caused their sales to soar. Van Ameringen's business prospered along with theirs, growing large enough by 1929 to warrant merging the company with the operations of William T. Haebler, in whose honor he renamed the company Van Ameringen-Haebler, Inc.

American workers quickly recognized the new company as a good place to be employed. At Van Ameringen-Haebler, the boss had an open-door policy, and bonuses, always promptly paid, ranged between six and nine percent of annual salaries. Employees, especially the highly trained and hard-to-come-by perfumers, were encouraged to settle into the company for the long term. In return, Van Ameringen asked that absolute secrecy about formulas be maintained at all times in order to prevent competitors from copying original ideas. As a private concern, Van Ameringen was also able to keep the company's financial details under wraps.

Despite Van Ameringen's best efforts, however, secrecy was not always easy to maintain. In the unauthorized biography *Estee Lauder: Beyond the Magic,* author Lee Israel maintained that Van Ameringen was romantically involved with Lauder and that he was responsible for the "Youth Dew" fragrance that brought her such fame after its 1953 introduction. Israel also noted that Van Ameringen gave Lauder extended credit—a favor that culminated in a corporate friendship that has spanned several decades.

Van Ameringen-Haebler's sales in 1958 were $28.4 million, of which a scant ten percent came from the company's flavor formulas. In an effort to expand both manufacturing and marketing in this segment of the business, Van Ameringen merged the company with a European manufacturer primarily concerned with flavors, offering broad access to the American fragrance market in return. Called Polak & Schwarz Essencefabricken of the Netherlands, Van Ameringen's new partner was a company he knew well—the same one that fired him in 1917.

The new venture, named International Flavors and Fragrances Inc., proved an instant success, and immediately found such broad markets in the European food industry that new facilities in Holland, Switzerland, France, and Brazil were added to augment the company's older American factories. Within two years foreign manufacturers of cake mixes, pharmaceutical products, gelatin desserts, candies, and soft drinks were using IFF flavorings at a rate that brought the division's sales figures to 35 percent of the $34.2 million total in 1960.

It was clearly time to go public. Offered over the counter, the first shares went on sale in October 1961. At about the same time, Arnold Van Ameringen decided to step down as president so that he could devote himself to raising funds for mental health causes, although he continued to serve as chairman of the board until his death in 1966. Van Ameringen chose as his successor Henry Walter, the man who had been his trusted legal counsel for years.

A rather eccentric man, Henry Walter was daring enough to brave Manhattan's rush-hour traffic on a bicycle and, even as the head of a fragrance company, to wear red suspenders brandishing hand-embroidered skunks. Although Walter could boast a law degree from Columbia University plus almost 30 years of legal practice, he had little knowledge of the fragrance and flavor business, to which he often referred as the "sex and hunger trade." However, Walter firmly took the IFF helm and made sure to imprint his own corporate style on his staff without delay. Just as Van Ameringen had done, Walter also made secrecy his top requirement. In one 1963 action, he chose to emphasize this mandate by suing the Cott Beverage Corporation—which had just employed a former IFF employee as their new director of research and information—maintaining that IFF's formulas for ginger ale and several other soda flavors had been usurped. The outcome of the case was never publicized, but the action itself was enough to convince employees that Walter meant business.

Other changes made the company more visible as an international concern. Walter made it a rule to use local workers in every foreign facility, allowing him to mention in the company's 1966 annual report that only four Americans were currently working in IFF's overseas plants. Being in closer touch with non-Americans also brought the company reliable information about local tastes in fragrances. The company learned that women in warmer climates preferred to use perfumes with a higher fragrance content (though not necessarily a stronger type) than their counterparts in cooler climates, and European men preferred after-shaves that were more highly scented than those used by American men. By the end of 1965 the close attention to cultural differences had paid off handsomely—fully 51 percent of sales came from overseas markets.

Walter allocated generous amounts of corporate income ($5.8 million in 1967) to flavor and fragrance research, and he himself made sure that few innovations in other companies escaped his notice. Especially interesting to him was a process of inking by microencapsulation invented by National Cash Register to replace messy carbons. A man quick to note the far-reaching potential of any industrial novelty, Walter soon licensed the process, and it was not long before IFF was producing scent strips for children's "scratch-'n-sniff" books and perfume samples for magazines. By mid-1966 these new products had stimulated demand enough to send a daily average of $60,000 worth of fragrance compounds flowing from the company's Manhattan headquarters. In addition, at the end of 1970 the fragrance markets for both toiletries and detergents had brought sales figures to $102.7 million, and such customers as Revlon, Procter & Gamble, and General Mills were relying heavily on IFF. Characteristically, Walter celebrated by allocating $8.4 million for the research that was keeping the company out in front of the competition.

If Henry Walter's big push during the 1960s had been expansion, his equally great ambition in the 1970s revolved around cost-cutting. The advertising budget, potentially very large in a company concerned with fragrances, could be kept to skeletal levels because IFF was a business-to-business concern, rather than a retail marketer. A few trade-journal ads usually sufficed and were used for direct mail together with the company's annual report, the cost of which was pared to $1 per copy.

In 1970 S. J. Spitz, a veteran of the chemical industry, joined Walter's staff as chief operating officer. Spitz was well known

for cost-cutting, and together he and Walter managed their 2,671-strong staff with economy and precision.

By 1973 the company's 50 salesmen (20 in the United States and 30 in Europe) were handling both flavors and fragrances, and producing an average turnover of $3 million per annum each. Even the perfumers came under new scrutiny. In most companies, perfumers were precious and carefully handled assets, but at IFF bonuses were cut to the bone, and there was now a new rule that employees leaving the company were barred from their share of profits, even if the money had been earned during their tenure. Complaints about the new regime left Walter unmoved. "When a company gets beyond a certain point," he told *Dun's Review* in 1974, "you cannot run it in the old paternalistic way."

In the early 1970s IFF was secure in a fragrance division that was still producing 75 percent of the bottom line, and Walter was elated about the new popularity of men's toiletries as well as the growing profitability of air freshener products. However, the calm was interrupted in 1973 by the oil embargo, which quadrupled prices of all oil-based ingredients and encouraged other suppliers to raise theirs to match.

By the end of the decade, despite a client list that included Lever Bros. and Colgate-Palmolive, it was impossible to ignore a fragrance market growth rate which had slowed, both domestically and overseas, from 16 percent to 8 percent. In addition, tough competition was another cause for concern. By the late 1970s most top couturiers and cosmetics houses were at least assumed to be regular IFF customers. However, their loyalty was no guarantee of sales growth; these same clients usually invited several fragrance suppliers to submit samples for any new fragrance.

While all fragrance contracts were lucrative, a deal on a potentially expensive perfume could command a very high level of profit. Unwilling to compromise IFF's claims in this area, Walter gladly paid his chief perfumer, Bernard Chant, a 1982 basic salary of $230,000 plus bonus for supervising 40 staff members and dreaming up new ideas. But Chant's considerable creativity could not stem the ominous downward spiral. By 1980 sales figures reached $448.3 million, rising just 1 percent in 1981 to reach $451.1 million. The following year net sales sank to $447.9 million as a result of both a recession and a strong dollar overseas that affected the company's foreign markets.

Always a man who tied his company's developments to events in the outside world, Walter turned his attention to the growing world population and its burgeoning need for food. He noted that the agricultural industry was rising to the challenge with improved fertilizing techniques and freezing methods, and in other food-service areas, the microwave oven was also being increasingly used to bring food to the world's tables in record time. Walter also observed that such advances were not without their downside. The new fertilizers and freezers often came with high price-tags, and the broadening spectrum of foods being produced frequently lacked flavor.

Once he had decided to concentrate on developing his share of the flavor market, Walter gave his experienced research team the green light. Thanks to the generous research budget ($30.6 million in 1980, rising to almost $35 million by 1985) IFF now reaped handsome dividends. The company made full use of the worldwide trend towards healthier eating and drinking by developing beverages that contained little or no caffeine, breads and pizzas with sharply reduced salt, and flavorful cheese products containing little or no fat. At the same time, new consumer interest in ethnic foods brought a need for complex flavoring blends, and a taste for more sophisticated and lower-fat desserts broadened the flavor market further. The flavor segment of IFF's business contributed a healthy 38 percent of total sales by the end of 1984.

Fragrance research also received close attention during these years. Henry Walter had long held the view that fragrances might carry the psychological benefit of mood elevation. As a first attempt to find answers, he had long ago sponsored a study by leading sex experts Masters & Johnson, who were trying to determine the effect of fragrance on sexual behavior; he encouraged his scientists to find scents which might discourage overeating, relieve stress, or bolster sexual excitement.

In mid-1985 both CEO S. J. Spitz and Chairman Henry Walter decided to retire. Into the top spot stepped former senior vice-president Eugene P. Grisanti, a Harvard-trained lawyer with 24 years of experience with IFF. Grisanti got off to a brisk start. His first act was to streamline management by eliminating the position of CEO and giving the vice-presidents of the flavors and fragrance divisions more decision-making responsibility. Next, he instituted a teamwork concept among his New York- and Paris-based product development units, who were now encouraged to cut costs and effort by working closely together. Grisanti also carried on the Walter tradition of a generous research budget, which by 1990 had reached $54 million. Grisanti directed this money partly toward such "bread-and-butter" projects as the development of exactly the right beef-fat flavor for McDonald's low-cholesterol fries and partly toward innovative research into covering bad odors. By the end of 1992 IFF sales figures had reached $1.10 billion, up from $962.90 million in 1990, despite the recurrent recession that brought thousands of layoffs and forced consumers to compromise on important purchases.

Principal Subsidiaries: International Flavors & Fragrances Inc. (The Netherlands); International Flavors & Fragrances G.m.b.H. (Germany); International Flavours & Fragrances Ltd. (England); International Flavors & Fragrances A.G. (Switzerland); International Flavors and Fragrances, Inc. (France); Aromatic Holdings Limited (Ireland); Destilerias Adrian & Klein (Spain); International Flavors & Fragrances (Hong Kong); Auro Tech, Inc.

Further Reading:

"A. L. van Ameringen Dies at 74; A Crusader for Mental Health," *New York Times,* January 5, 1966, p. 31.

Commercial and Financial Chronicle, October 30, 1961, p. 1843.

"A Cook's Tour of IFF Operations with Marketer Hinrichs," *Industrial Marketing,* September 1970, p. 55.

"IFF Shaking Inventory Blues," *Commercial & Financial Chronicle,* July 26, 1976, p. 2.

"IFF: The Sweet Smell of Success," *Forbes,* October 15, 1973, p. 34.

"International Flavors Elects Walter," *New York Times,* December 12, 1962, p. 13.

"International Flavors: Funding Far-Out Ideas for Future Growth," *Business Week,* November 12, 1984, p. 129.

"International Flavors Joins Big Board Today," *New York Times,* March 2, 1964, p. 41.

Israel, Lee, *Beyond the Magic,* New York: MacMillan, 1985.

Karp, Richard, "The Big 'If' at IFF," *Dun's Review,* March 1974, p. 52.

Margetts, Susan, "Sex, Hunger—and IFF," *Dun's Review,* November 1969, p. 95.

McCoy, Frank, "International Flavors Smells Like Money Again," *Business Week,* April 18, 1988, p. 70.

Mendelson, Alan Mark, "Dollars from Scents," *Barron's,* March 31, 1980, p. 39.

Nemy, Enid, "In the World of Fragrance, Reputations Rest on the Nose . . ." *New York Times,* February 11, 1993, p. C2.

Roman, Monica, "Beef-Fat Flavor May Not Sound Glamorous, But . . . ," *Business Week,* March 11, 1991, p. 70.

Smith, Lee, "Adventures in the Sex and Hunger Trade," *Fortune,* August 9, 1982, p. 47.

"A Sweet Little Business," *Forbes,* October 1, 1963, p. 41.

"The Sweet Smell of Success," *Magazine of Wall Street,* August 3, 1968, p. 18.

"U.S. Charges 7 Firms Over $29 Million Cost to Clean Waste Site," *Wall Street Journal,* July 17, 1992, p. A6.

—Gillian Wolf

ISUZU

Isuzu Motors, Ltd.

26-1 Minami-Oi 6-chome
Shinagawa-ku
Tokyo 140
Japan
(03) 5471-1111
Fax: (03) 5471-1043

Public Company
Incorporated: April 9, 1937 as Tokyo Motors, Inc.
Employees: 13,051
Sales: ¥1.14 trillion (US$103.5 billion)
Stock Exchanges: Tokyo, Osaka, Nagoya
SICs: 3711 Motor Vehicles and Car Bodies; 3713 Truck and
    Bus Bodies; 3714 Motor Vehicle Parts and Accessories

Isuzu Motors is best known for its line of spunky little automobiles and trucks. In the United States, the company is noted for an advertising campaign featuring a lying spokesman named ''Joe Isuzu,'' who makes incredible claims about the product. While the campaign was a tremendous success, the products represented by it were not. In 1991 Isuzu decided to completely bail out of the passenger car market and concentrate only on building trucks. This decision has a great deal to do with the global strategy of General Motors Corp. (GM), which owns a third of Isuzu. Under the plan, Isuzu becomes something of a manufacturing subsidiary of GM, building small trucks and components for distribution by the American company. Despite Isuzu's relatively small position globally (the company's sales in America are almost too small to rank), it is the sixth-largest automotive manufacturer in Japan. Unlike larger competitors, Isuzu does not have a successful franchise across the market. Therefore, while Isuzu has a very narrow product line, it remains one of the largest producers of trucks in the world.

Isuzu Motors has its origin in a 1916 diversification plan undertaken by the Tokyo Ishikawajima Shipbuilding and Engineering Company. The company, established after the Meiji Restoration to build heavy ships on Ishikawajima Island near Tokyo, hoped to insulate itself from cyclical downturns in the shipbuilding industry. Tokyo Ishikawajima initiated the venture as a partnership with the Tokyo Gas and Electric Industrial Company, which had the engineering expertise necessary to design vehicles. In fact, Tokyo Gas produced its first vehicle, the Type A truck, in 1918, using engines from Tokyo Ishikawa-

jima. The partnership manufactured a variety of designs under license from the English firm Wolseley, including the model A9 car, which went into production in Japan in 1922. In 1929 the enterprise was separately incorporated as Ishikawajima Automobile Manufacturing, Ltd.

The company developed an air-cooled diesel engine in 1934. Its pioneering efforts in this area established the automotive group as a leader in diesel technologies during the 1930s. Through its association with Tokyo Ishikawajima and Tokyo Gas, the company became a supplier to the military. Under a government mobilization scheme in 1937, the automotive interests of Tokyo Ishikawajima and Tokyo Gas were formally merged into a new company called Tokyo Motors. Mass production of the air-cooled diesel engine began that year.

In 1938 Tokyo Motors began production of a truck under a new nameplate, Isuzu—Japanese for ''50 bells.'' By this time, however, the military had gained control of the government and launched a war against China. As a result, Tokyo Motors came under government production plans, and much of its output was earmarked for the military. In 1939 Tokyo Motors developed a new diesel model, the DA40, representing another advance in the company's diesel technologies. But by 1942, the United States and Britain were at war with Japan over interests in Asia. With the war raging and the economy operating under emergency conditions, the operations of Tokyo Motors were split up in order to affect greater rationalization of the automotive industry. The company's truck business was spun off into a new company called Hino Heavy Industries (later Hino Motors). Tokyo Motors continued to operate as a frame manufacturer, but resumed production of engines in 1943.

A year later, Japan was exposed to bombing raids. As a military resource located in a major industrial center, Tokyo Motors was exposed to these raids. The company's production was completely disrupted until the war ended in September of 1945. Yet Tokyo Motors was quick to recover from the war and resumed production before the end of the year. In 1946 the company introduced a new diesel truck called the TX80. This product helped Tokyo Motors fund major investments in its facilities and expand the scope of its product research.

The company changed its name to Isuzu Motors, Ltd. in 1949. Like many other Japanese companies that had emerged from the war, Isuzu went back into the business of supplying the military, but this time the customer was the American army. These large, stable supply agreements were instrumental in helping Isuzu recapitalize and grow. The company became an important resource for the Americans, particularly in late 1950, after hostilities erupted on the Korean Peninsula. Isuzu supplied a variety of trucks and other industrial products to the forces fighting North Korean aggression, helping to further advance the company's position in the diesel engine market. After an armistice was concluded in 1953, Isuzu re-established licensing agreements with the British. The company signed an agreement to build automobiles designed by the Rootes Group (now called Talbot, and part of the French firm PSA). Under the terms of the agreement, Isuzu manufactured the Hillman Minx.

In 1959 Isuzu introduced a new two-ton N-series truck called the Elf. This was followed in 1961 by an attempt to equip an

Isuzu automobile with a small diesel engine. While economical and reliable, the diesel Bellel car was uncomely, noisy, and, ultimately, a commercial failure. Consumers clearly favored a more cosmopolitan, if less practical, car. In 1962 Isuzu opened a new factory at Fujisawa. With expanded production capacity, the company introduced the Bellett automobile in 1963, followed by the Florian model in 1967. The next year, Isuzu rolled out the sporty two-door 117 Coupe, a luxury model resembling the Ford Mustang. In 1970 Isuzu introduced two new trucks, the medium-size Forward (named for its forward control) and a 12-ton diesel model.

While Isuzu was a recognized leader in the truck market, its rapid development of new models had left it financially weakened. When it appeared to the company's bankers that the market would be unable to support Isuzu's new product line, they began negotiations with the company's competitors, hoping to arrange a merger of Isuzu with a more stable firm. While companies such as Fuji Heavy Industries, Mitsubishi Corporation, and Toyota Motor Corporation were probably approached, it was General Motors that emerged with the greatest interest in Isuzu. The automotive giant was impressed with Isuzu's promise in export markets in the United States and Asia and hoped to include the company in its own global strategies. In 1971 General Motors purchased a 34.2-percent share of Isuzu. As part of its marketing tie-up with General Motors, Isuzu's KB pickup truck was sold through GM dealerships in the United States beginning in 1972. In 1974 General Motors employed Isuzu to manufacture the Kadett, a model designed by its German Opel subsidiary, under the Isuzu nameplate as the Bellett Gemini.

Isuzu introduced a fuel-efficient direct-injected diesel engine in 1974 in two new truck models, the Forward SBR and Forward JBR. Rising fuel prices made these models especially popular with inflation-weary consumers in Japan. General Motors saw the fuel efficiency of Isuzu models as a distinct competitive advantage in the American market. In 1976 it began importing the Gemini into the United States as the Buick Opel. Few consumers suspected that the German design, sold through the dealerships of an American company, were actually manufactured in Japan. But, as GM had suspected, the Gemini/Opel was an attractive alternative to gas-hungry American models, particularly as a second household car. In this role, the car displaced competitors such as Toyota, Datsun, and Volkswagen. Isuzu gained additional growth in the American market with a diesel-powered pickup sold in the United States as the Chevrolet Luv beginning in 1977. Also that year, Isuzu delved back into the diesel car market in Japan with a new Florian sedan.

The energy crisis took a rising toll on GM models in the United States, including those built by Isuzu. A rising consumer revolt against little, underpowered vehicles such as the Opel, Ford Pinto, and Gremlin placed Isuzu in a declining market at the wrong time. Despite a short-lived rise in fuel prices in 1979, the Isuzu product line fell increasingly out of step with American tastes. Dismayed by the poor quality of many American models, consumers were drawn to Toyota, Honda Motor Co., and Nissan in growing numbers.

Isuzu's production for General Motors declined steadily from 1979 to 1981. Responding to what it felt was a loss of synergy with GM, Isuzu established its own dealer network in the United States, American Isuzu Motors, Inc., which technically operated in competition with GM at the wholesale level. Commensurate with the formation of the new group, Isuzu undertook a complete design change of its Luv truck. General Motors' Chief Executive Officer Roger Smith laid a bombshell on Isuzu chairman T. Okamoto in a landmark 1981 meeting. He announced that Isuzu had lost its favorable potential as a global partner for GM. But rather than abandon their partnership, Smith asked Okamoto to help GM buy a stake in Honda, one of Japan's fastest growing auto manufacturers.

Okamoto was stunned by the sudden change of events, but could not refuse the request of Isuzu's single largest shareholder. Ultimately, Honda expressed no interest in an alliance with General Motors, seeing its own prospects for global growth as excellent even without such a partnership. General Motors settled instead for a five percent stake in Suzuki Motors—a small consolation. General Motors may have intended to use this new partnership to leverage Suzuki against Isuzu, hoping the two companies would compete for the right to supply GM. Whether or not that was the case, General Motors had little choice but to expand its relationship with Isuzu. The company established new contracts with GM, building a model called the Storm under an entirely new nameplate, Geo. Once again part of General Motors' international strategy, Isuzu built new joint production facilities in the United Kingdom and Australia. Isuzu also concluded a long-term marketing agreement with Suzuki and Yanase & Company, under which Isuzu provided parts for assembly by Suzuki.

In an effort to raise consciousness of the Isuzu name and boost sales of the company's trucks in the United States, Isuzu launched a revolutionary ad campaign featuring the comedian David Leisure. The performer was portrayed as a spokesman named Joe Isuzu who made outrageously false claims about Isuzu products. A series of subtitles provided factual corrections as well as punch lines to Leisure statements. The campaign could easily have failed had it not been for the comedian's wry delivery and obviously contrived smile. In one ad, Joe Isuzu concludes by saying, "May lightning strike me if I'm lying." At this point the actor is incinerated by a blinding light, leaving only a puff of smoke. Seconds later, the irrepressible spokesman falls out of the air and into the bed of an Isuzu truck. The ads were very effective in promoting Isuzu and launching Leisure's career, but they had only a limited impact on Isuzu's sales. (The company experienced no gain in passenger car sales.) The situation was exacerbated by appreciation of the yen, in effect, artificially raising the price of Isuzu products.

To eliminate the effect of currency fluctuations and stabilize product demand forecasts, Isuzu began studying the possibility of locating a factory in the United States. Other Japanese manufacturers, including Toyota and Honda, had already established American factories. But for Isuzu, the start-up costs were high and the company's sales volumes were too small to justify the badly needed move. Fortunately for Isuzu, Subaru, the automobile manufacturing subsidiary of Fuji Heavy Industries, suffered the same problem. The two companies operated in slightly different areas of the American market, so a joint venture between them was plausible. Isuzu and Subaru agreed to jointly build a factory in Lafayette, Indiana in 1987. The facility went into operation two years later, providing Isuzu with a steady supply of American-built vehicles for distribution through its American sales organization.

Isuzu's export sales surpassed three million units in 1986, but again, much of this growth occurred in Asian markets and was accounted for in truck sales. That year, Isuzu formed a joint venture with Kawasaki Heavy Industries called IK Coach, Ltd. to manufacture coach bodies. Building on its Asian franchises, Isuzu established a subsidiary in Thailand to manufacture engines and a joint venture in Australia with General Motors the following year. These efforts helped to establish Isuzu as the world's largest truck manufacturer (on a per-unit basis) in 1987. The company marked several technological advances that year, including the development of a ceramic Adiabatic Engine and the NAVI electronically controlled transmission system, which was the first of its type.

Isuzu completed several other joint business arrangements in 1990, including an agreement with P.T. Gaya Motor of Indonesia to build pickup trucks in that country. This factory joined Isuzu plants in other developing country markets, including Thailand, Malaysia, and Egypt. The company also entered into agreements to market Isuzu's multipurpose vehicles in Japan through the Jusco Car Life Company, and to handle sales of GM Opel models and Volvo trucks in Japan. These expansion efforts helped Isuzu to maintain its position as the world's largest truck maker. But the company's balance sheet indicated a high price for this leadership. The company lost $500 million in 1991 and was faltering financially.

This deeply concerned General Motors, which was unable to abandon its investment in Isuzu due to plummeting market value. Isuzu was GM's main source of imported light commercial vehicles and heavy trucks, and 37.5 percent of its shares were held by the American company. Isuzu continued to lose money into 1992, prompting the company's board to appeal to General Motors for help. As a condition, GM asked that one of its strategic planning experts, Donald T. Sullivan, be installed as executive vice president of operations, with responsibility for revamping Isuzu's business, engineering, and manufacturing plans. This was an unprecedented move. No Japanese manufacturer had ever involved a non-Japanese speaking manager in such a high position, nor given an American such wide-ranging latitude to rewrite the business plan.

Sullivan's first moves were to raise production at the company's Subaru-Isuzu Automotive facility in Indiana. He slimmed down the Isuzu's line of commercial vehicles, hoping to realize greater production efficiencies from fewer models and eliminate cannibalization within the product line. In a retrenchment strategy virtually unknown in Japan, Sullivan summarily reduced capital budgets by 12.5 percent, hoping to eliminate waste through budget-induced cost savings. Stopping short of employee layoffs, a tactic that was seen to breed only employee disloyalty in Japan, Sullivan ordered a reduction in Isuzu's temporary work force. Perhaps most dramatic was Sullivan's conclusion that Isuzu was not profitably competitive in the automobile market. Rather than continue to invest huge sums in an unpromising segment of the market, Sullivan recommended that Isuzu exit the automobile market and concentrate on what it did best. For Isuzu, this came down to only three products: trucks, recreational vehicles, and engines.

These efforts appeared to have a positive effect on Isuzu's business, stemming losses while reversing a gradual decline in sales. The actions taken by Isuzu under the tutelage of Donald Sullivan have once again placed Isuzu thoroughly within General Motors' global strategy. However, the company's future depends on its ability to perform well as a quasi-division of General Motors and to mark gains in the sales of its own products, principally in the United States. Chief among these are the F-series (Forward) medium-duty trucks, the C-series heavy trucks, tractor trucks, and N-series (Elf) pickups.

Principal Subsidiaries: Isuzu Motors Finance Co., Ltd.; Isuzu Real Estate Co., Ltd.; Kinki Isuzu Motor Sales Co., Ltd.; Shatai Kogyo Co., Ltd.; Isuzu Motors Overseas Distribution Corp.; I.K. Coach Co., Ltd.; Automotive Foundry Co., Ltd.; Jidosha Buhin Kogyo Co., Ltd.; Tokyo Radiator Manufacturing Co., Ltd.; Tokyo Isuzu Motors, Ltd.; TDF Corp.; Zexel Corp.; Daikin Manufacturing Co., Ltd.; American Isuzu Motors, Inc. (USA); Isuzu Motors America, Inc. (USA); Isuzu Truck of America, Inc. (USA); Subaru-Isuzu Automotive Inc. (USA); IBC Vehicles, Ltd. (England); Convesco Vehicle Sales GmbH. (Germany); Isuzu Motors Co. (Thailand) Ltd.; Automotive Manufacturers (Malaysia) Sdn. Bhd.; P.T. Mesin Isuzu Indonesia; Isuzu-General Motors Australia, Ltd.; General Motors Egypt S.A.E.

Further Reading:

"Isuzu Motors, Ltd.," *The Directory of Multinationals 1993,* New York: Groves Dict Music, 1993, pp. 699–700.
"Isuzu Motors, Ltd.," *Hoover's Handbook of World Business 1993,* Austin, TX: Reference Press, Inc., 1993, pp. 280–281.
The Isuzu Way, Tokyo: Isuzu Motors Ltd., 1992.

—John Simley

ITEL

Itel Corporation

2 North Riverside Plaza
Chicago, Illinois 60606
U.S.A.
(312) 902-1515
Fax: (312) 902-1573

Public Company
Incorporated: 1967 as SSI Computer Corp.
Employees: 5,300
Sales: $1.68 billion
Stock Exchanges: New York
SICs: 5065 Electronic Parts & Equipment, Nec; 5063
   Electrical Apparatus & Equipment, Wiring Supplies &
   Construction Materials; 7359 Equipment Rental &
   Leasing; 3678 Electronic Connectors; 4741 Rental of
   Railroad Cars; 4011 Railroads, Line-Haul Operating; 4111
   Local & Suburban Transit; 4789 Transportation Services,
   Nec; 1629 Heavy Construction, Nec

Itel Corporation is a diversified transportation and logistics
company. Its principal business operations are divided between
the following subsidiaries: Anixter Distribution and ANTEC
are leading U.S. suppliers of wiring system products for voice,
data, and video communications as well as for the transmission
of electrical power; Itel Container is the world's largest intermodal container lessor; and Itel Rail Corp. is a leading lessor
and manager of railcars in the United States and a manager of
several shortline railroads and rail car maintenance facilities.
Anticipating growth potential in data networking and cable
industry, Itel shifted primary emphasis to its Anixter and AN-
TEC units in the early 1990s. The company also made minority
investments in other enterprises ranging from energy to real
estate.

Itel was founded in 1967 by San Francisco businessmen Peter
Redfield and Gary Friedman, primarily as a leasing company
for computer systems. With $72,000 of their own capital, the
partners raised $10 million in equity from Fireman's Fund
Insurance Company. They hired a staff of aggressive young
businesspersons to develop innovative, intricate, and often risky
financial mechanisms. Itel set industry records by achieving $1
billion in revenues in its first 12 years.

Such growth was largely attributable to the computer leasing
business. After investing $90 million in IBM System/360 com-

puters, Itel leased the systems, with accessories, at highly competitive prices made possible by careful financial planning. Itel
found equity investors willing to put up 20 percent of the cost of
a computer in exchange for depreciation and investment tax
credits. Lenders covered the other 80 percent. In the end, the
lessee paid the lenders and equity investors for the cost of the
machine—at rates below those available directly from IBM—
while Itel earned a fee and interest in the residual value of the
computer. By 1979, Itel had written $1.7 billion in leases on
IBM-compatible equipment, second only to IBM itself.

In addition to computer leasing in the 1970s, Itel experienced
rapid growth in a variety of other financial services. Itel Air, for
example, leased and sold aircraft to realize a pretax profit of $13
million in its second year of operation. Itel Capital was formed
to extend leases on less expensive equipment ranging from
machine tools to boilers and minicomputers. Highlighting the
company's penchant for innovative leasing deals, a security
analyst speculated in an October 8, 1979 article for *Fortune*
magazine: "They would have started making portable toilets if
the cost were a least $1 million each and they were leasable."

The company also began extensive investment in railcar and
intermodal container leasing, starting with the 1968 acquisition
of SSI Container Corp. Other related expansion included the
June 1970 formation of SSI Trailer Corp.; the February 1973
organization of SSI Navigation, Inc.; the November 1973 acquisition of M.J.B. Management Corp. and subsidiary Transportation Management Services, Inc.; and the May 1975 formation of
SSI Rail Corp. to lease freight cars into the U.S. Rail System.

Further growth occurred in the area of transportation services,
primarily rail transportation. In July 1977, Itel acquired
McCloud River Railroad Co., a short-line railroad in California,
and its Wisconsin division, the Ahnapee and Eastern Railroad
Co. In November 1978, Green Bay & Western R.R. Co. was
also acquired.

Itel's rapid growth translated into an unusually flamboyant
corporate style. The fact that revenues had grown at a compound annual rate of 48 percent from 1972 to 1979 manifested
itself in everything from plush offices embellished with Persian
rugs and *objects d'art* to sporty company cars. Company drinking fountains featured Perrier water, and January annual meetings were lavish: a seven-day Caribbean cruise, costing the
company $1.5 million, was arranged for 1977, while the follow-
ing year, 1,200 employees were flown to Acapulco. Salaries
were also generous; young managers typically received salaries
of $100,000 in addition to attractive stock plans. Compensation
for Peter Redfield, president and CEO, surpassed $600,000.

Such opulence came into strong relief against a backdrop of
financial difficulties beginning in the mid-1970s. In 1976, when
IBM introduced its System/370, the value of Itel's substantial
inventory of System/360's plummeted. Redfield and Friedman
managed to compensate for the loss by switching accountants
and selling off a subsidiary. While it seemed that the company
had learned a lesson—to avoid owning a large stock of data
processing equipment—another breach in that maxim caused
irreversible damage just a few years later.

In 1977, Itel contracted National Semiconductor Corp. and
Hitachi, Ltd., of Japan to build central processing units inter-

changeable with those made by IBM. In 1978, Itel shipped over 200 of its systems, called Advanced Systems, and booked an operating profit of $73 million. Projecting continued success, the company signed long-term purchase contracts with its two suppliers and increased its marketing force by 80 percent.

In case sales of its Advanced Systems were not as bullish as planned, Itel had arranged a seemingly foolproof insurance policy with Lloyd's of London. Between 1975 and 1978, Lloyd's insured Itel against losses in the event a lessee might return a computer before termination of the agreed lease. In essence, Itel was insured against technological change that might render obsolete its leased computers.

Despite insurance coverage, technological change arrived quickly, adversely affecting sales of Itel's Advanced Systems. Widespread industry speculation suggested that IBM was planning to launch a new line of machines for the first quarter of 1979 (the IBM 4300 Series). Customer uncertainty regarding IBM's plans put much anticipated business on hold. In addition, the wait for IBM's announcement stifled sales in Itel's System/370 business as well as its recent $10 million investment in minicomputers from Data General. Itel's first quarter report for 1987 showed a loss of $4.4 million in overall computer operations.

Even with reduced sales, Itel was committed to long-term purchase agreements with its computer manufacturers. While Hitachi had agreed to cut back on deliveries, National Semiconductor refused to do the same. Sales remained flat, and inventories of Advanced Systems swelled to around $45 million. Such pressures were exacerbated by delays in insurance adjustments by Lloyd's. By August 1980, Lloyd's had paid only $8.4 million of $21.5 million in claims. In an attempt to raise cash, Itel began selling assets, including a railcar manufacturing plant, eight ships, an information service for stockbrokers, and even the corporate airplane. Despite $175 million raised, the second-quarter report for 1979 showed a $60 million deficit. Itel's board demanded decisive changes in management and business strategy.

Immediately following the disastrous second-quarter report, Itel's executive committee decided to dissolve the office of the president, which had earned the acronym, "OOPS," by disillusioned management. Within a week, Redfield was forced to resign, shortly followed by Friedman. Thomas S. Tan, formerly head of transportation services, was named president and chief operating officer. The position of CEO remained empty until the March 1980 appointment of James Maloon. In a strategy to reverse losses, Maloon focused operations on Itel's railcar and container leasing divisions as the core of renewed business.

By February 1981 Itel's annual revenues had shrunken to roughly $210 million, and its debt had swelled to $1.3 billion. On January 1 the company sought protection under Chapter 11 of the bankruptcy code. When it emerged two years and eight months later, Itel was a mere shadow of the computer-leasing giant of the 1970s. Whereas $661 million in revenue netted $21.5 million from computer leasing in 1978, Itel earned $19.4 million on $83 million in revenues in the first half of 1983. After leading the company through the restructuring plan as chairperson, president, and chief executive officer, Herbert Kunzel

passed command to a post-reorganization team headed by William P. Twomey.

Reorganization did not bring immediate success. By 1984, Itel's core business was in railcar and container leasing, markets that were still in the throes of a three-year slump. After emerging from bankruptcy, the company faced $317.5 million in secured debt and $217.5 million in notes. Interest payments alone in the first nine months of 1984 amounted to $60 million, contributing to a net loss of $6.7 million.

With its finances in the red, Itel drew the attention of Samuel Zell, an entrepreneur with a reputation as a wildly successful turnaround artist for distressed real estate and undervalued, publicly held companies. Zell's knack for resurrecting dead real estate operations had earned him the name "Grave Dancer." His entrepreneurial zest began with investments in foreclosed student housing at the University of Michigan law school in Ann Arbor, Michigan. Within 20 years, he had amassed holdings reportedly worth $2.5 billion, ranging from stakes in Mississippi River excursion business to mobile home manufacturing. By 1985, Zell was chair and general partner of the Equity Financial and Management Company, a privately owned real estate management company based in Chicago. He was also chairperson of Great American Management and Investment Inc. (GAMI), a diversified real estate investment company that was emerging from bankruptcy when Zell took it over in 1980.

In 1983, Zell began acquiring shares in Itel's common stock and common stock warrants, of which he owned 22 percent by early 1985. Despite management's initial objections, Zell's growing interests in Itel won him a board seat in November 1984. After the resignation of Twomey, Zell was elected as Itel's chair and CEO in April 1985. In October of that year, Rod Dammeyer moved from his post as senior vice-president and chief financial officer for Household International Inc. to assume the presidency of Itel. Dammeyer and Zell immediately began a restructuring plan to revive Itel.

In March 1985 Itel increased its interest in Great Lakes International Inc., a marine dredging company, to approximately 18.7 percent. In January 1986 all remaining outstanding shares of Great Lakes were acquired. With the passage of the "Deep Ports" bill in 1986, $2 billion in federal funds were allotted to the redredging of port areas around the United States. Great Lakes revenues rose 61 percent to $172 million, with two deep port contracts in 1986 alone.

On December 23, 1986, Itel acquired 98 percent of Anixter Bros. Inc., a supplier of wire and cable to the communications and cable television fields, for about $500 million. On January 14, 1987, Anixter became a wholly owned subsidiary of Itel and reported gains of 23 percent to $835 million.

A program of aggressive acquisitions continued through the late 1980s. Between 1986 and 1987 revenues jumped from $288.7 million to $1.27 billion. In March 1987, the company purchased the container fleet and certain related assets of Flexi-Van Leasing Inc., for approximately $235 million. Combined with Itel Containers International Corp., the fleet combined approximately 370,000 TEUs (20-foot equivalent units) of equipment and over $500 million in assets. To manage these and other assets, Itel formed Itel Transportation Services, an umbrella organization for the company's $700 million investments in railcar leasing, short-line railroads, and container leasing businesses.

Other acquisitions continued at a rapid pace. In August 1987, Itel acquired approximately 20,000 railcars and related assets from Evans Asset Holding company for about $300 million. With the January 1988 purchase of Xtra Corp's container fleet for approximately $130 million in cash and stock, Itel increased its stakes in ocean shipping. Then in September of that year, Itel acquired from The Henley Group, Inc. its Signal Capital operations and Henley's stock positions in two major transportation companies, Santa Fe Southern Pacific Corp. and American President Cos. Ltd., for a total of $1.2 billion. Signal Capital was engaged in diversified financing activities, including railcar leasing through its Pullman Leasing division. Pullman's 30,000 railcars combined with Itel Rail's fleet of 43,000 railcars to make Itel the largest railcar leasing company in North America.

Itel's railcar leasing and railroad businesses escalated during this time. In October 1988, Itel Rail purchased the B.C. Hydro Rail Freight Division, a 141-mile line in southwestern British Columbia. Itel Rail built its first new maintenance facility in Dothan, Alabama, in 1989. Optimizing access to multiple customers, the company situated its shop on Itel's Hartford & Slocomb Railroad, linked to the CSX, Norfolk Southern, and Atlanta & Saint Andrews Bay railroads.

Preparing for new growth in European transportation opportunities, Itel purchased about 35 percent of Grand Transport Systems of Great Britain in March 1990. A leading European lessor of marine container chassis equipment, Grand Transport operated lease fleets in Germany, the Netherlands, France, Denmark, and Belgium. Itel hoped to gain exposure and firsthand knowledge about transportation and distribution industries in Europe.

By 1989, having rebounded as one of the nation's fastest growing companies, Itel began trading on the New York Stock Exchange after an eight-year absence. Placement on the "Big Board" reflected Itel's tremendous growth since its 1985 restructuring: during a four-year period, revenues rose 730 percent to $1.6 billion, gross cash flow increased to $371 million from $90 million, and total assets more than quadrupled to $4 billion in 1988.

To accommodate such rapid growth, Itel greatly expanded its nationwide network of distribution centers in the late 1980s and early 1990s. In June 1989, the company acquired Paul Jeffrey Company, Inc., with five distribution centers comprising over one million square feet of space. One year later, Itel raised its number of distribution centers to 38 with the acquisition of Dornbush Group of Atlanta. By 1993, Itel boasted in its annual report of a "hub and spoke" distribution system, with inventory stored in state-of-the-art facilities throughout the United States, Canada, the United Kingdom, and Continental Europe.

In the early 1990s, Itel took aggressive steps to lower its debt burden. In a January 1990 move to reduce funding costs, Itel and Chemical Bank worked out a scheme whereby a special purpose subsidiary, Itel Rail Funding Corp., would use railcars and leases belonging to Itel as collateral behind a debt issue. Itel would sell fixed-rate leases on 6,500 rail cars to the subsidiary,

which would then sell securities to investors, who would be repaid interest and principal from payment received on the leases. For additional protection of investors, Itel would also sell the actual railcars to the subsidiary.

Itel made several other moves to reduce debt. In December 1990, the company sold its intermodal container leasing assets to General Electric Capital Corp. for approximately $825 million, stunning analysts and employees. In March 1991, Itel sold its investment in American President Companies, Ltd. for $79.2 million. Then in June 1991, Itel sold substantially all of the assets and business of Itel Distribution Systems, Inc. for approximately $32 million. In October 1991, it continued the trend, selling Great Lakes Dredge & Deck Company to Blackstone Capital Partners L.P. for approximately $165 million in cash. And in January 1992, Itel Rail Corp. agreed to lease its entire fleet of 70,000 railcars to GE for a period of 12 years at $150 million per year. While many employees at Itel's San Francisco-based subsidiary would lose their jobs, proceeds from the deal were used to pay off high-cost debt.

With raised capital, diminished debt, and new management, Itel took steps in the early 1990s to focus the company on the rapid growth of two major operating business units, Anixter Distribution and ANTEC. Anixter specialized in wiring systems products for data, voice, video, and multimedia networks, as well as power applications. ANTEC was formed as a stand-alone business in 1991 to develop new potential in the cable television (CATV) and broader telecommunications industry. By 1993, Itel had developed international markets for the two divisions. Anixter added offices in Kuala Lumpur, Hong Kong, and Taiwan to its existing Pacific Rim operations in Singapore, Melbourne, and Sydney. Other opportunities were explored in Southeast Asia, Latin America, the Middle East, and Eastern Europe, while business in Western Europe—France, Germany, Italy, Norway, Portugal, Spain, Switzerland—and Mexico, Australia, and Singapore, virtually exploded from 1989 to 1992.

By 1993, Anixter and ANTEC showed positive growth. Their combined operating income before amortization and extraordinary items was $18.8 million in the first quarter of 1993, up from $15 million in the same period the year before. Yet Itel as a whole incurred substantial, albeit less, losses for the same quarter, reporting a net loss of $6.6 million or $.023 a share of first-quarter 1993, compared with a net loss of $12.9 million or $.041 a share in 1992. Itel's new focus on Anixter and ANTEC would have to continue to foster rapid growth for the company to establish itself firmly in the 1990s. Samuel Zell, the CEO and reputed "Grave Dancer," still faced several challenges in attempting to resuscitate an ailing enterprise. Yet Paul Merrion, in an April 15, 1991 article for *Crain's Chicago Business*, suggested that Zell might better be described as a "high-wire artist," struggling to sustain Itel by expanding cyclical businesses and selling assets during a recession. Whether raising the dead or crossing a tight-rope, Zell and Itel faced challenges into the 1990s.

Principal Subsidiaries: Itel Rail Corp.; Anixter Bros., Inc.

Further Reading:

"Can Itel Survive Without Chapter 11?" *Business Week,* October 3, 1983, p. 52.

Chesler-Marsh, Caren, "Chemical's Plan for Itel to Reduce Funding Costs," *The American Banker,* January 29, 1990, p. 24.

Gilpin, Kenneth N., "Largest Shareholder Will Be Itel's Chairman," *The New York Times,* February 5, 1985, p. D2.

"Itel Agrees to Purchase Signal Capital Operations from The Henley Group, and Henley's Stock in 2 Companies," *Business Wire,* July 27, 1988.

"Itel Completes Chapter 11 Reorganization," *Business Wire,* September 19, 1983.

Itel Corporation Annual Report, Chicago: Itel Corp., 1992.

"Itel Names Dammeyer Chief Executive Officer as Part of Continued Transition of Company," *PR Newswire,* November 20, 1992.

"Itel to Purchase Anixter Bros. Deal for Wire, Cable Supplier to Exceed $500 Million," *Chicago Tribune,* November 21, 1986, p. C3.

Johnson, Tracy, et al., "Unpaid Bills; Itel Goes Bust," *Fortune,* February 23, 1982, p. 19.

Merrion, Paul, "Secretive Sam Zell Scouts Acquisitions for Hungry Itel," *Crain's Chicago Business,* March 10, 1986, p. 1.

——. "Zell's Itel Needs its Own Workout; Grave Dancer Finds Problems Close to Home," *Crain's Chicago Business,* April 15, 1991, p. 17.

"Moody's Downgrades Itel Corp and Units," *Reuters,* September 18, 1990.

Muth, Mark, "Itel Struggles to Stay on Its Feet in Technological Storm," *Christian Science Monitor,* December 30, 1980, p. 14.

Nelson, Eric, "Pending Itel Sale for $825 Million Stuns Observers," *San Francisco Business Times,* October 22, 1990, p. 5.

Pelline, Jeff, "Itel Rail Lease Deal May Cost 220 S.F. Jobs," *The San Francisco Chronicle,* January 4, 1992, p. B1.

Strazewski, Len, "Itel Takes Opportunistic Tack in Latest Acquisition Quest," *Crain's Chicago Business,* May 30, 1988, p. 18.

Uttal, Bro, and Shawn Tully, "The Lease Is Up on Itel's Lavish Living," *Fortune,* October 8, 1979, p. 106.

Wise, Deborah, "The Insider Looming Over Itel," *Business Week,* January 28, 1985, p. 98.

—Kerstan Cohen

JWP Inc.

Six International Drive
Rye Brook, New York 10573-1058
U.S.A.
(914) 935-4000
Fax: (914) 935-4179

Public Company
Incorporated: 1966 as Jamaica Water Supply Company
Employees: 22,000
Sales: $3.6 billion
Stock Exchanges: New York
SICs: 1731 Electrical Work; 1796 Installing Building
    Equipment Nec; 4953 Refuse Systems

JWP Inc. is a transnational technical services firm that specializes in the areas of systems engineering, facilities management, information systems, and environmental management systems. JWP is involved in the construction, installation, and maintenance of cost-control systems for Fortune 1000 companies, institutions, and governments. The firm has 220 offices worldwide on all continents except Australia.

Begun in the mid-1960s as a water supplier to Long Island and Queens, New York, JWP transformed itself through acquisition. By the start of the 1980s, JWP was the nation's largest computer reseller and the biggest electrical and maintenance contractor. Essentially, clients use JWP to help increase productivity and decrease costs by upgrading their facilities through, for example, more efficient communication and computer systems. JWP designs, installs, and supports these technical systems.

Through its myriad subsidiaries, JWP also contracts for general electrical systems, electrical power systems, heating and air conditioning systems, ventilation and duct work, plumbing and piping, computer and computer peripherals, wire and cable lines, and telephone equipment, among other services. Today, water systems sales account for less than two percent of JWP's sales, while facilities management (66 percent) and information systems (32 percent) dominate the company's business. With a heavy debt load accumulated in the 1980s and 1990s, the company recently announced that it would apply for Chapter 11 bankruptcy protection.

JWP Inc. was launched in 1966 as the Jamaica Water Supply Company and, for much of its early history, was the primary provider of water to Nassau County, Long Island, and Queens,

New York. The company thus functioned for many years as a regulated monopoly, with low but stable profits and regulated prices. The company began to branch out in the mid- to late-1960s and henceforth was exposed to the instabilities of the marketplace. As it diversified its product lines, JWP experienced many ups and downs in its bottom line.

The company changed its name often between 1966 and 1986, the year it adopted its present name, JWP Inc. This 20-year period was marked by extreme instability, and not in name only. From 1966 to around 1970, the company expanded by buying up other water companies. For example, in 1966 the firm acquired the entire capital stock of Sea Cliff Water Company. In 1968 they acquired most (80 percent) of Orbit International Inc. of San Juan, Puerto Rico.

With this accumulation through acquisition of other water companies, the firm was ready to make its first significant move out of the water business. Founder Martin Dwyer expressed the frustration with the water business at the time, stating, "Private companies have no place in an urban area." Limited by public regulation, he sought to diversify into specialized construction, utility type operations, telephone systems, and electric lighting. In support of this shift in business focus, the company's most significant move was its 1971 acquisition of the Welsbach Corporation, a Philadelphia-based electrical contracting concern. Welsbach also installed street lighting and traffic control systems. Welsbach was merged into Jamaica Water, and the company took on the name Welsbach in 1974. Welsbach had a profit of $659,000 in 1969, and thus helped push Jamaica's bottom line out of the red. Jamaica's acquisitions throughout the late 1960s also led the firm to take on an increasingly expanding stock of debt, and, with interest rates rising, the company's cash flow was severely threatened. Combined with the severe recession of 1973 and 1974, the company went from a stable water utility company to near bankruptcy in the mid-1970s.

In 1978 Andrew T. Dwyer, the son of founder Martin Dwyer, was put in charge of the ailing company. It took Dwyer and his associates several years to fend off complete collapse. They restructured the cost structure of the company to increase cash flow, and in the process, removed some of the debt burden that was dragging down the company's growth prospects. To begin with, Dwyer sold off many of the money-losing ventures (including many of the non-utility holdings). He also began a complete retrenchment of the water utility component of the company (which at the time comprised 50 percent of the company's business) and set his sights on diversification, offering JWP's sophisticated and technologically advanced plumbing and piping systems technology for other applications.

Dwyer's stated goal at the time was to transform the company once again, this time using its already developed strengths in developing large computer systems, equipment, and office maintenance as a base. He started development of heating ventilation and air conditioning systems maintenance and other systems involved in operating high rise buildings in New York City. "The technologies needed to merge," Dwyer said, and his company set up building systems whereby one box could control fire, alarm, energy management, and security systems. By the mid 1980s, in New York City, JWP maintained everything from electric signs in Times Square to printing presses at the *New York Times*.

This general strategy continued to yield positive results as JWP adapted existing technologies to diverse applications. As Dwyer reflected in November of 1991: "We tried to identify those markets where there was a need for sophisticated equipment." The result was phenomenal growth for the company in the 1980s, as the company once again completed a fundamental, and profitable, shift in its focus. Dwyer's first specific target was the fastest growing segment of the economy in the 1980s, the financial services sector. He aimed at providing all the technical services support required to create high tech and efficient trading rooms for Wall Street giants such as Merrill Lynch & Co, Inc., including installation and maintenance of air conditioning, telephones, wiring, cables, and computers. Clients also included Morgan Stanley, Goldman Sachs, and Salomon Brothers. From here, JWP branched out further, installing energy management systems for Sears and computer rooms for Hewlett-Packard.

In the wake of these very successful endeavors, Dwyer's JWP won big contracts with DuPont and also began providing services to hospitals and utilities, including Illinois Bell. One of the largest contracts was a six and one half year, $468 million contract to convert New York City's sludge to fertilizer pellets to be marketed nationally. From solid waste management and conversion plants, JWP developed and marketed security systems and electrical networks. The company expanded overseas during this time as well.

The company grew not only in the rapidly expanding market for technical services and the decentralized management style implemented by Dwyer, but also through smartly managed acquisitions. Dwyer acquired Forest Electric in 1986 and Dynalectric in 1988 to broaden the company's electrical services repertoire. The acquisition of University Industries in 1988 got them into the West Coast mechanical services market. To crack the international market, JWP acquired Drake & Skull Holdings, a British electrical and mechanical services company. Dwyer's JWP gobbled up two dozen companies from 1984 to 1987, generating scale economies out of mergers and getting a jump on the competition in the high tech end of the technical services industry. "We are continually migrating to the higher technology side of the business," Dwyer said, "that's where the margins are better, the growth greater, and the competition a lot smarter." The company's name was officially changed to JWP in 1986.

The successes of these acquisitions were phenomenal. In fact, from 1980 until the end of 1991, JWP enjoyed 48 quarters of uninterrupted growth. The company grew from 400 employees working out of five offices in 1980 to over 21,000 employees in 195 offices in 1990. Successful diversification went hand in hand with the company's move away from water sales as its dominant market. The stable water sales, which made up over 50 percent of the company's total revenues in 1980, declined to less than two percent in 1990, while total net income grew from a loss of $495,000 in 1980 to $59.3 million profit in 1990. At the start of the 1980s JWP was a $40 million water utility that had lost money for eight straight years and was on the brink of bankruptcy. By 1990 the company was a $3 billion technical services company. Compound growth from 1985 through 1989 was 179 percent, and JWP became the dominant maintenance firm in New York. Sales from 1981 to 1986, for example, went from $42 million to $379 million, and net income rose from $1.7 million to $13.5 million.

With the company's expansion into high tech applications, JWP was increasingly getting into the business of setting up computer systems. Thus, it was a natural outgrowth of the company to begin selling the computers to its clients. In 1990 this new avenue of growth for JWP meant the purchase of Neeco, Inc., a desktop computer systems sales company which operated out of Canton, Massachusetts. In its most important recent acquisition to date, the firm bought Businessland in early 1991, a move that was considered a natural extension of the firm's experience in selling electrical systems. This deal pushed total revenues from $744.6 million to $944.9 million. From the Businessland acquisition, Dwyer created JWP Businessland Inc., a division of JWP Information Services, which had sales of $1.8 billion worldwide and which operated through its own retail outlets.

While the 1980s were a decade of unprecedented growth, the early 1990s saw near bankruptcy and collapse. Contributing to the decline of JWP was a commercial construction slump, price wars, and intensified competition in the personal computer component of the business, and of course, the burden of servicing a huge debt accumulated during the boom years of acquisition in the 1980s. JWP's high debt-equity ratio in particular (1.2 to 1.0) caused great concern. Profits fell to around $40 million for 1990 and 1991 as the company struggled through the recession that plagued those years. By the fourth quarter of 1992, however, losses were as great as $265 million.

The company's highly leveraged position threatened its very existence, prompting some drastic action to restructure the company's debt. Meanwhile trouble brewed elsewhere. In April 1992, in their water business, complaints about high rates charged for water were lodged against JWP's water subsidiary, Jamaica Water Supply Co., which still served homes in Queens and Nassau County. JWP eventually sold the unit as part of the corporate restructuring and not, they said, in response to the consumer complaint controversy.

In October of 1992, David Sokel presented to the board evidence of what were alleged to be widespread accounting improprieties, confirming the charges of shareholders, and then he resigned as president of the company. More restructuring decisions led to the sale of ten or more businesses (including the sale of four environmental businesses to Wheelabrator Technologies, Inc., for about $69 million) in order to raise $250 million as the company focused on its traditionally more lucrative mechanical and electrical services. These moves helped raise needed cash to deal with the heavy debt load, which at one point was said to be as large as $485 million.

In a major debt restructuring move, in July of 1993 JWP sold its Information Services subsidiary to an investment group in a deal releasing JWP from about $210 million of the company's more than $300 million in outstanding debt. In 1993 Andrew Dwyer resigned as chairman of the board of JWP, and Edward Kosnik was elected to the post.

Expansion continued, notably on the international front; international operations generated about $1 billion in revenue in 1992. Coupled with the debt restructuring, long-term growth prospects brightened. In 1991 JWP acquired Comstock Canada, the largest electrical and mechanical services firm in Canada, with twelve offices in Canada and $200 million in sales. Furthermore, the Businessland project did business in Canada, the

United Kingdom, Germany, and France, selling its interactive personal computer system integrated to complement its international facilities management. JWP also expected growth in new markets in transportation projects, pharmaceutical, and biotechnology facilities. The most promising general source of demand for JWP's services lay in the fact that, in general, businesses found it increasingly cheaper to "outsource" the kind of services that JWP provided.

Despite its demonstrated resiliency, JWP announced in October of 1993 that it would file for Chapter 11 bankruptcy protection, after nearly a year of negotiating a financial restructuring with its creditors. Under the proposed debt restructuring and capitalization plan, JWP's creditors, a group of fifty bankers, insurance companies, and equity funds, exchanged $484 million of the company's debt for $180 million of new debt and 100 percent control of JWP's equity. The new debt was to be paid from the proceeds of asset sales.

Principal Subsidiaries: Azco Modular Structures Corporation; Dynalectric Company; Enviro-Gro Technologies; Hetra Computer and Communications Inc.; J.C. Higgins Corp.; JWP Energy Products Inc.; JWP Gowan Inc.; JWP Guzovsky Electrical Corp.; JWP Inc. IK Electric Company; JWP Information Services; JWP Mechanical Services Inc.; JWP Network Services; JWP Telecom Inc.; JWP Welsbach Electric Corporation; JWP West; Jamaica Water Supply Company; Kirkwood Dynalectric Company; Lera Electric Company Inc.; R and C Corporation.

Further Reading:

"Accord Is Signed to Sell Information Services Unit," *New York Times,* July 17, 1993.

Cook, James, "If at First You Don't Succeed," *Forbes,* June 29, 1987.

Emmett, Arielle, "JWP: Lean, Mean Business Machine," *Computerworld,* June 15, 1992.

Gilpin, Kenneth N., "JWP's Bankruptcy Plan Will Put the Creditors in Control," *New York Times,* October 12, 1993.

"Jamaica Water Agrees to Acquire Welsbach for About $10.2 Million," *Wall Street Journal,* May 28, 1969.

"Jamaica Water Links With Welsbach; to Get 49% It Doesn't Own," *Wall Street Journal,* October 15, 1970.

"JWP Completes Sale of Four Businesses for about $69 Million," *Wall Street Journal,* October 19, 1992.

Lueck, Thomas J., "Private Owner to Sell L.I. and Queens Water Utility," *New York Times,* April 21, 1992.

Pacey, Margaret D., "Thirst for Acquisitions: Investor-Owned Water Works Grow by Swallowing Municipal Ones," *Barron's,* February 15, 1971.

Pollack, Andrew, "JWP Gains Control of Businessland," *New York Times,* August 6, 1991.

Quickel, Stephen W., "By Leaps and Bounds," *Business Month,* March, 1989; "Ghostbusters: What Are Big Corporations Afraid Of? Buying and Installing Complex Systems," *Financial World,* March 20, 1990.

Steinberg, Jacques, "Water Utility of a Thousand Faces," *New York Times,* November 2, 1991.

Zweig, Jason, "Roller Coaster: JWP Sold Just Water Until Andy Dwyer Arrived. Now the Utility Is Diversified, but Not Very Profitably So," *Forbes,* August 3, 1992.

—John A. Sarich

Keyes Fibre Company

301 Merritt 7
P.O. Box 5317
Norwalk, Connecticut 06856
U.S.A.
(203) 849-4140
Fax: (203) 849-4133

Wholly Owned Subsidiary of Van Leer Holding Inc.
Incorporated: 1903
Employees: 1,600
Sales: $204 million
SICs: 2449 Wood Containers, Nec; 2499 Wood Products,
  Nec

Best known for its Chinet brand disposable dinnerware, the Keyes Fibre Company ranks among the United States's top 50 producers of wood products. The company's output focuses on products for food service and retail distribution. The Chinet line includes disposable plates of varying sizes and shapes made from paper pulp, paper napkins, dinner and luncheon size plastic flatware, and paper dinnerware in holiday themes. In addition to disposable dinnerware, Keyes manufactures egg and fruit packaging, cup carriers, fluorescent tube packaging, and over 400 other wood pulp products. Keyes (sounds like "eyes") was a family-run company from 1903 to 1927. As the company prepared for its centenary, its parent was Van Leer Holding, Inc.

The origins of the Keyes Fibre Company date back to the mid-nineteenth century, when inventor Martin Keyes was born in Lempster, New Hampshire. He started work at his father's saw and grist mill at a young age. His inventive capacity became evident in his youth, and led him to keep pencil and paper on hand in order to write or draw ideas at any time. The habit would prove invaluable to the creation of the Keyes Fibre Company. Keyes's entire career would involve the paper business, especially "papier-mache" (which in French means "chewed paper").

There are two corporate fables regarding the origins of the sturdy, yet disposable paper dishes that were the precursors to Chinet. One recounts that inventor Martin Keyes saw workers at a veneer plant in New York eating their lunches on pieces of maple veneer, and that their impromptu plates got him thinking about disposables. The other story recounts that Keyes' mother

urged her enterprising son to improve upon the pressed wood pie plates that were available at the turn of the century. Before Keyes' invention, there were inexpensive plates stamped from a heavy paper stock, but these weak, absorbent disposables were unreliable. At first, Keyes tried to steam veneer into plates, but he later arrived at a plan to form wood pulp with a mold. Carrying out that plan took at least two years: the inventor had to develop a machine that would mash the pulp and mold, dry, and package the plates. Once he had done so, he ran into another problem.

When Keyes filed to patent his machine, he was notified that the process was already patented. Realizing that someone had stolen his idea, Keyes sued to prove that the paper plate machine originated with him. Although the original patent seemed unchallengeable at first, Keyes was able to enter his daily diary as evidence in the case. The journal unquestionably recounted the progression of the machine from concept to reality. Martin Keyes won the case on the strength of his diary and acquired the basic patent that provided the basis for the development of Chinet brand plates.

Keyes convinced a friend who owned an iron works to build a prototype of his invention in 1902, and rented space in a pulp mill in Shawmut, Maine for his first test run. His original plate machine was displayed for many years at Keyes Fibre's headquarters. Despite difficulties in finding a supplier who could sell him wood pulp of just the right consistency, Keyes was able to incorporate the Keyes Fibre Company in Shawmut, Maine to produce paper pie plates in 1903. The inventor's two brothers-in-law, William Brooks and E. H. Allyn, along with investors Albert B. Page, Edward Lawrence, William Brooks, and Nathan Heard were the original stockholders of the Keyes Fibre Company's initial capitalization of $150,000. Keyes received 1,000 of the company's first 1,500 shares in exchange for allocating his primary patent, three other pending patents, and any subsequent inventions having to do with the manufacture of articles from wood or other pulp, to the company. With the memory of the near-theft of his intellectual property still fresh in his mind, Keyes quickly employed a designer to create a logo for the new company. The star with a "K" inside was registered in 1904 and symbolized Keyes Fibre through the twentieth century.

Keyes fully expected his employees to live up to his own stringent work ethic, as evidenced by an anecdote recounting the construction of the first company-owned mill. The president's right-hand man, Bert Williamson, asked to have November 3, 1903 off so that he could get married. Knowing that construction of the new mill was scheduled to begin on November 4, Keyes gave Williamson one day of vacation, but required him to be back on the job at 7:00 A.M. on the fourth.

The company's first shipment of pie plates went out in the summer of 1904, but Keyes' mill was forced to close the following spring as a result of cost competition. As the founder had expected, Keyes Fibre's plates were indeed better than their predecessors, but they also cost twice as much as alternatives. Stock in the company fell from $100 per share to $10 per share. After cutting prices drastically and applying all his personal finances to the business, Keyes was able to resume production of his unique product late in 1905. Sales of the company's pie plates benefitted from a well-known tragedy, when an entire shipment was sold in San Francisco, where the earthquake and fire of 1906 had created high demand for disposable dishes.

When Keyes Fibre's pulp supplier was abruptly closed down in 1907, the president scrambled to find another site for his business. Martin Keyes considered sites in Massachusetts, New York, and Maine, finally settling on a location in Maine. Keyes's first consumer product, a "picnic package" with different sized plates, was introduced shortly after the Keyes Fibre Company was moved to Waterville, Maine in 1908. By 1910, the company's sales topped $160,000 and profits totaled almost $16,000.

From 1903 to 1911, Keyes Fibre's pie plates were sold through Charles Brown, a shareholder and distributor. Brown had promoted the products under his own trade name, but Keyes sought to publicize his own name and thereby establish a distinctive reputation. In 1911, Keyes Fibre started a 36-year relationship with the John M. Hart Company, a national sales agency, to distribute all of Keyes' products under the company trademark. The new arrangement immediately boosted sales to such a level that production could not keep pace.

When Martin Keyes died in 1914, his son-in-law, Dr. George G. Averill, succeeded him. Keyes had convinced Averill to leave his medical practice and join the company in 1911. Averill led the company for over a decade. In 1915, Keyes Fibre's daily capacity exceeded two million pieces, and a waterproof plate was developed. A four-for-one stock split highlighted the following year. Pulp shortages in the latter half of the decade threatened production and pricing, until 1920, when Keyes Fibre had its own mill built at the original corporate site in Shawmut, Maine. Sales began to decline in the mid-1920s, and Keyes' dissatisfaction with the Hart sales agency grew proportionately to its expanding product backlog.

Then, in 1926, Keyes Fibre's directors discovered that John Hart had secretly been cooperating with former employee Merle Chaplin to devise significant, patentable improvements on the original Keyes process. This new competition and the drop in sales coincided with the expiration of Keyes' original patents. The threat to the company was serious, and Dr. Averill employed several tactics to keep control of the company in the family. In March 1927, Hart and Chaplin offered their five new patents and other inventions in exchange for 3,000 Keyes shares. Averill negotiated to purchase enough shares to maintain his majority, then presented the deal to Keyes Fibre's shareholders, who rejected it. One month later, Averill offered Hart and Chaplin $200,000 for their patents, but the old-fashioned "corporate raiders" refused his offer.

Mid-year, Hart, Chaplin, and several investors formed the Rex Pulp Products Company to compete with Keyes. But after struggling to locate a plant, the competitors made Averill and the Keyes stockholders one last offer: $4.5 million to purchase the company outright. The stockholders agreed, and the deal was completed by the end of the year. Realizing the value of the Keyes name, the officers of the Rex Pulp Products Company assumed the historic name for the newly formed company. Walter Wyman, Maine's most prominent industrialist, was elected president and John Hart was second-in-command.

The new management pushed to diversify from Keyes's product line of varying sizes of pie plates and butter dishes, and by the end of the decade, ice cream dishes, drinking cups, and the smooth-finished line of paper dinnerware called Chinet were added. Chinet's smooth, moisture-resistant finish was devised by Walter Randall, who developed a distinctive drying process for the molded plates.

The business prospered until two years after Keyes's takeover reorganization. The stock market crash of October, 1929 signalled the onset of the United States's worst economic depression. With more than ten million workers unemployed nationwide, Keyes Fibre had trouble maintaining sales. By 1933, the company was over $850,000 in debt and made every effort to meet payroll and other crucial expenses. Keyes Fibre seemed destined to become a casualty of the Depression when, in 1934, the federal government amended the national bankruptcy act. The new provisions allowed companies that were solvent for the long run, but temporarily in distress, to petition a United States District Court for permission to reorganize without bankruptcy. Keyes became one of Maine's first corporations to utilize the new amendment, and emerged from the reorganization with Walter S. Wyman as president. Wyman served in that capacity until 1942, when he was succeeded by Dwight S. Brigham.

Keyes was able to develop several new products despite the depression and its effects. In 1930, the company introduced disposable cake circles, and in 1931, Keyes entered the highly competitive egg packaging field. The company's purchase of Australian, Belgium, Canadian, British, South African, and other patents for egg containers helped launch it into international licensing of Keyes Fibre patents and processes. The company first licensed Martin Keyes's patents for molded paper pulp items to companies in Canada, Denmark, Holland, and Finland in 1936.

Keyes contributed to the United States's World War II effort by taking advantage of its patented KYS-ITE fibrous plastics process, which was developed in the late 1930s. KYS-ITE was used primarily to manufacture plastic cafeteria-style serving trays, which were in high demand when war rationing limited the use of rubber and aluminum, traditional tray materials. The company also manufactured shell caps, pistol grips, and valve wheels during World War II. The company's plastics production would broaden to include salad bowls, cups and saucers, and tracks for window frames, before the plastics division of Keyes's business was sold in 1970. The company's hourly employees were unionized in 1942, when the Star Local 449 of the International Brotherhood of Pulp, Sulphite and Paper Mill Workers was established.

The war's end saw Keyes enjoying the United States' general prosperity: in 1945, the company built a new $1.3 million plant in Hammond, Indiana, and in 1947, Keyes purchased its longtime, closely related sales organization, the John M. Hart Company. Renamed Keyes Fibre Sales Corporation, the service was operated as a subsidiary until 1956, when it was absorbed by the parent.

Wallace Parsons, who had risen from assistant to the vice-president (1927) to general manager (1928) and then vice-president (1942), became president of Keyes Fibre in 1951. Just six years later, Ralph H. Cutting succeeded Parsons. Cutting had been a clerk in the engineering department in 1928, rose to purchasing agent in the following year, and was made assistant treasurer in 1942. By 1945 he had advanced to treasurer and general manager, in 1951 he became vice-president and general manager, then in 1957 he advanced to the presidency.

Keyes Fibre became much more directly involved in the international promotion and distribution of its products in 1962, when it acquired 50 percent of Canadian Keyes Fibre Company, Limited, of Nova Scotia. One year after that acquisition, Keyes commenced subsidiary Norwegian operations to serve markets in Scandinavian countries and the United Kingdom. Late in 1964, the parent company purchased the vast majority of Societe Vendeenne des Embalages, a French licensee. The acquisition doubled Keyes Fibre's capacity and broadened its product line. By 1975, Keyes Fibre had subsidiaries or affiliates in the Republic of Ireland, Mexico, Australia, Belgium, Venezuela, Italy, and Great Britain. There were licensees of the company in Argentina, North Ireland, New Zealand, and South Africa.

Keyes Fibre's domestic net sales and total net income doubled from 1964 to 1974, while the company's total number of employees only increased by nine percent. This efficiency encouraged the company to invest in geographic expansion, and by the mid-1970s, Keyes boasted six American plants in Maine, Indiana, California, Washington, and Louisiana. In 1975, Keyes purchased Huntsman Container, a manufacturer of polystyrene foam hinge-lid containers, food service "takeout boxes," and Tuff Stuff brand disposable dinnerware, which grew to become America's second-most-popular brand of foam plates.

But Keyes did not neglect its original brand of disposable dinnerware. In 1965, the company changed the Chinet trademark to script lettering when the product was moved into the consumer market. The company was able to claim that there was "virtually no comparable product on the market" as late as 1968. Chinet became very popular with institutional food service markets like hospitals, colleges, and industrial cafeterias because it promoted labor and equipment cost savings and eliminated breakage and pilferage losses. Skyrocketing labor costs in the 1960s and 1970s made disposables even more attractive.

When the United States' first wave of popular environmentalism swelled in the 1970s, Keyes responded by announcing that 33 percent of its fibre usage came from waste paper and cartons. The use of post-consumer content in food service products was prohibited by the Federal government, but Keyes was able to incorporate the reused fibre into packing materials for non-food applications. Keyes also showed its "greenness" by introducing Tree Start, a wood-fibre cup that provided a "complete growing medium" for tree seedlings.

Keyes was purchased for the second time in its history in 1978 by Arcata National Corp. in a transaction valued at $87 million.

Based in Menlo Park, California, Arcata was a printing and redwood products concern. Under Arcata's leadership, Keyes opened a new Chinet plant in Alabama in 1979, and doubled its apple tray manufacturing capacity in Wenatchee, Washington, to 180 million trays per year at a cost of $3.2 million the next year. Just three years later, Keyes Fibre was sold again, this time to Royal Packaging Industries Van Leer B.V. and its American subsidiary, Van Leer Holding. Based in Amstelveen, Netherlands, the Van Leer group was a global manufacturer of industrial containers with operations in over 30 countries. By the third time it was purchased, Keyes boasted annual sales of almost $230 million.

Foreseeing tough times ahead for plastics, Keyes sold its Huntsman Container subsidiary and converted all of its production to recycled content in the 1980s. Even food service items, like Chinet, contained 100 percent pre-consumer recycled content. The supplies came primarily from milk carton plants, which sold their unusable stock to Keyes. The 1988 sale of Huntsman Container to Fripp Fibre, a Canadian concern, was particularly fortuitous. In the early 1990s, the Environmental Defense Fund convinced McDonalds Corp. to discontinue the use of polystyrene containers. Plastic food service items, which could not be burned or composted, lost favor with some consumers, and may come under fire from the federal government in the future. Concerns about disposal grew more pressing as consumers become more aware of the environmental impact of their purchases.

After Keyes became a subsidiary of Van Leer, its annual results were grouped with those of the parent company. In the late 1980s and early 1990s, Keyes has concentrated on international activities, especially on manufacturing and selling Keyes process machines to licensees around the world, and expanding its activities in Europe, where pressboard plates still dominate the disposable dinnerware market. The company has a foothold in these markets, where its rough-mold products have been in use since the 1930s.

Further Reading:

"Arcata National Corp., Keyes Fibre Co., Sign Agreement on Merger," *Wall Street Journal,* August 14, 1978, p. 5.

"Arcata to Sell Unit and Sees After-tax Loss of $70 Million," *Wall Street Journal,* December 10, 1981, p. 19.

Cyanamid Paper, "A World Leader in Wood-pulp Products: Keyes Fiber Company," *Dylines,* July 1975, pp. 1–2.

"Keyes Fibre Company," *Wall Street Transcript,* September 23, 1968, p. 14432.

"Keyes Fibre Company," *Wall Street Transcript,* February 21, 1977, p. 46275.

Marriner, Ernest C. *Dishes from Molded Pulp: A History of the Keyes Fibre Company,* Keyes Fibre Company, 1963.

——. "Pulpwood to Pie Plates—The Keyes Fibre Story," *Down East: The Magazine of Maine,* March 1964, pp. 6–15.

Miller, Cyndee. "Chinet Maker Launches PR Drive to Promote Composting," *Marketing News,* July 5, 1993, pp. 14, 18.

—April S. Dougal

King World Productions, Inc.

1700 Broadway
New York, New York 10019
U.S.A.
(212) 315-4000
Fax: (212) 582-9255

Public Company
Incorporated: 1964
Employees: 474
Sales: $503 million
Stock Exchanges: New York
SICs: 7822 Motion Picture & Tape Distribution; 4833
   Television Broadcasting Stations

King World Productions, Inc., is the leading syndicator of television programming. The success of the game shows *Wheel of Fortune* and *Jeopardy!* and of *The Oprah Winfrey Show* have catapulted King World to a position of power in the television industry in the 1980s, altering the traditional relationship between television stations and syndicators. Charles King, the founder of King World Productions, began as a syndicator of radio programs in the 1930s, and was associated with such celebrities as Rudy Vallee and Gloria Swanson. Beset by financial troubles and seeing the money-making potential in television, King redirected his skills into the new medium, working for other distribution companies until 1964, the year he created King World. The first show distributed by King World was *The Little Rascals,* a black-and-white slapstick comedy series featuring the characters Alfalfa, Buckwheat, and Spanky. As a syndicator, King bought distribution rights on the reruns and leased them to television stations, keeping one-third of the licensing fees.

When Charles King died in 1973, his company was experiencing difficulties due to the steadily decreasing demand for black-and-white programming, among other reasons. King's children took on the responsibility of reviving King World, with Michael King as president and chief executive officer, Roger King as chairman of the board, and Robert, Diana, Richard, and Karen King in other executive positions. As chief operating officer, Stuart A. Hersch was the only member of the King World board who was not a member of the King family. Through an agreement with Colbert Television Sales, the Kings began selling the game shows *The Joker's Wild* and *Tic-Tac-Dough.* They en-

joyed moderate success with these, but also sought a show that could challenge industry leaders *Family Feud* and *Entertainment Tonight.*

While research into demographics and audience preferences is utilized by virtually all enterprises related to radio and television, King World has been able to capitalize on its research extremely effectively. The company has its own team of researchers and frequently commissions data from outside agencies. This aspect of King World is seen as a pivotal element in its success.

Extensive research into the television ratings published by Nielson and Arbitron indicated that *Wheel of Fortune,* which was running on NBC during the day, had potential for high ratings in the evenings despite the fact that three previous attempts to syndicate it had failed. Based on the children's game "hangman," the game show was created by Merv Griffin. With Pat Sajak acting as host, the show enjoyed a small but loyal following. In 1982 King World struck a deal with Griffin to syndicate the game show. Under the agreement, King World distributed the show to stations for cash and barter, that is, air time to sell to advertisers. King World's Camelot Entertainment was formed to sell the commercial time, initially 30 seconds per episode. For the first season, King World could find stations to carry the game show in a few large cities including Detroit, Providence, Buffalo, and Columbus, but not New York, Los Angeles, or Chicago. Strong ratings, however, came quickly, and the show was soon showing in all the major markets.

One of the most peculiar aspects of the *Wheel of Fortune* story was the flurry of media attention given to Vanna White, a former model who joined Pat Sajak to turn the letters on the game board. Although White hardly said a word during the show, her popularity skyrocketed, with her face appearing on magazine covers and her autobiography becoming a best-seller. While the Vanna White sensation might have seemed arbitrary, it was largely orchestrated by King World. The company produced thousands of promotional spots featuring White, each customized to the local station running *Wheel of Fortune.* She was flown to cities across the United States to make public appearances, waving from parade floats and judging look-a-like contests. According to an article in *Marketing and Media Decisions,* "The syndicator has meticulously and shrewdly marketed her, making her into a business and an insurance policy for the continued success of the show."

Wheel of Fortune eventually became the most successful television program in syndication history. *Jeopardy!,* the second most successful show, followed in September 1984. Another Merv Griffin production, *Jeopardy!* is a revival of a popular 1960s quiz show in which contestants give "questions" to "answers" in a variety of categories. Alex Trebek hosted the new edition. Although it wobbled during its first season, as soon as researchers at King World discovered that the contestant buzzer was annoying audiences, they were able to rectify the situation, and *Jeopardy!* soared in the ratings.

In October 1984, King World Productions went public. At this point, Robert King left the company, selling his piece of it for $1.7 million. With the two most successful syndicated shows on the air, the company could afford to negotiate with television stations from a position of power. The company pressed for three- and four-year contracts with the stations, and if they were refused, they would take the shows directly to the stations' competitors. King World balanced these aggressive tactics, however, by offering customized market research including a ratings analysis of each station in the market, demographic statistics, and recommendations for scheduling, earning the company a reputation as a supportive partner. Furthermore, King World financed and produced commercials to promote its programming. In general, this sort of assistance facilitated the cooperation of the stations, but at least one station, WCPX in Orlando, Florida, bristled under King World's negotiating style, and in 1985 they filed suit, claiming the syndicator demanded that they carry other King World programming if they wanted the *Wheel of Fortune*. A federal judge threw out the suit, citing insufficient evidence.

According to a 1985 article in *Forbes,* the boom in the television syndication industry, which King World was well positioned to take advantage of, was the result of two factors: the rise of independent stations as opposed to networks, and the shorter life-span of the average network series, which meant fewer shows fit for syndication. At the same time, television syndication was considered by some a risky proposition, with some commentators seeing its rapid growth as a temporary phenomenon. King World needed an unending string of hits in order to continue expanding. Although its first two ventures were undeniably major victories, the chances of accurately predicting audience preference every time, even with the aid of a research staff, were next to impossible.

King World's first disaster was a show called *Headline Chasers* starring veteran game show host Wink Martindale, who first came in contact with King World when it was distributing his *Tic-Tac-Dough.* Combining the missing letter aspect of the *Wheel of Fortune* with a test of contestants' knowledge of current events, the game show was produced by Merv Griffin, whom Martindale contacted at the suggestion of Michael King. Unlike the *Wheel of Fortune* and *Jeopardy!,* *Headline Chasers* debuted on network television as a King World production without previous exposure. The company gave the show a long time to get off the ground, but it never did.

In the daytime talk show ratings, the *Donahue* show, starring silver-haired host Phil Donahue and distributed by Multimedia, had held the number-one position for twelve years until King World decided to find a personality to challenge Donahue. This type of telecast, like soap operas, is primarily aimed at female viewers. The Kings selected Oprah Winfrey as their challenger. Winfrey had recently moved from Baltimore to Chicago to host *A.M. Chicago* on that city's WLS-TV, and she played a supporting role in the 1986 movie *The Color Purple,* directed by Steven Spielberg. On the eve of the National Association of Television Program Executives conference, where the Kings would be pitching the *Oprah Winfrey Show* to television stations, she received the nomination for an Academy Award for Best Supporting Actress. In September 1986, *Oprah* debuted nationally.

With Winfrey's charisma, born of sincerity and common-sense wisdom, the show overtook *Donahue* in its first year. As Winfrey's popularity grew, she formed her own company, Harpo Productions, to produce the talk show starting in 1988.

The success of *The Wheel of Fortune, Jeopardy!,* and *Oprah* meant tremendous growth for King World. Revenues climbed from $81 million in 1985 to $476 million in 1991, a year when the three major networks lost a grand total of nearly $500 million. King World International was formed to distribute programming around the globe; as of 1992, 26 countries broadcast versions of *The Wheel of Fortune.* With three shows in the top ten syndicated programs, King World began to take chances when introducing new shows. According to analyst Paul Marsh, quoted in *Broadcasting* magazine in December 1992: ''When King World starts a new show it's not like they need to make a lot of capital expenditures or add sales staff.... Effectively they get a free swing at the plate every time.''

After *Oprah,* King World went down swinging with nearly every new program. *Nightlife,* a 1986 talk show hosted by stand-up comedian David Brenner and produced by Motown, did little to dent the ratings of Johnny Carson's *Tonight Show.* Industry insiders cited this as a notoriously difficult time slot on the schedule due to the loyalty of Carson's following. The same year, King World brought out the daytime magazine *True Confessions* and the *Rock & Roll Evenings News,* neither of which lasted into the next season. *The Laugh Machine,* produced by George Schlatter, debuted in 1987 and also yielded disappointing ratings. In March of that year, Roger King was arrested for possession of cocaine, and in September, Stuart A. Hersch resigned from the company. Stephen W. Palley was named to take over the position as chief operating officer.

In December 1988, King World purchased the television station WIVB, Buffalo's CBS affiliate, from Howard Publications, Inc., for $100 million. The station had been losing money, and this trend continued after King World acquired it. In 1991 WIVB lost $7.8 million, and the company took action to restructure the debt. In January 1989, King World introduced *Inside Edition,* the first show that the company produced on its own. During this time, the news magazine programs that were appearing on every channel were seen as a new breed in the genre: investigative reporting with less bite than the established CBS program *60 Minutes* presented in a more lively, upbeat style. *Inside Edition,* hosted by Bill O'Reilly, did little at first to distinguish itself from the more popular *Hard Copy* or *A Current Affair,* but King World tinkered with the format, and the show began to climb in the ratings.

Of all of King World's failed programming, perhaps the most devastating loss was *Candid Camera,* a re-make of Allen Funt's classic show starring Dom DeLuise, which debuted in 1991. Based on the statistics, the syndicator had high expectations for its performance in the ratings. When plans for the show were announced, King World stock shot up into the mid-30s; when the program failed, the price fell down into the mid-20s.

King World continued to introduce new shows, relying on extensive market research to determine what might succeed. King World's first foray into children's programming was in 1992, with the animated *Wild West C.O.W.-Boys of Moo Mesa,* from the creators of the Teenage Mutant Ninja Turtles. In September 1993, the company debuted *The Les Brown Show,* a talk show featuring the popular motivational speaker, and the news magazine *American Journal,* anchored by Nancy Glass.

Further Reading:

Duffy, Susan, "All This and *Candid Camera,* Too," *Business Week,* January 21, 1991.

Foisie, Geoffrey, "King World: A Growth Stock Gets Bigger," *Broadcasting,* December 7, 1992.

"King World on Top of Game Show Hill," *Advertising Age,* January 16, 1986.

Paskowski, Marianne, "Prize Packagers," *Marketing and Media Decisions,* March 1987.

Trachtenberg, Jeffrey A., "The Other Green Revolution," *Forbes,* April 8, 1985.

—Mark Swartz

KnowledgeWare®

KnowledgeWare Inc.

3340 Peachtree Road N.E.
Atlanta, Georgia 30326
U.S.A.
(404) 231-8575
Fax: (404) 364-0522

Public Company
Incorporated: 1979 as Database Design, Inc.
Employees: 840
Sales: $128.8 million
Stock Exchanges: NASDAQ
SICs: 7372 Prepackaged Software

KnowledgeWare Inc. specializes in one of the most popular and fastest growing segments of the computer software industry, computer-aided software engineering, or CASE. Much more complex than word processing programs, CASE systems are used by computer professionals for development of applications ranging from payroll to financial management. CASE tools can also be used to customize, modify, or speed up existing programs. As a result, they can greatly increase the efficiency of computer systems and the profitability of the companies that use them.

KnowledgeWare was founded by James Martin in Ann Arbor, Michigan, in 1979. The company, originally called Database Design, Inc., began operations relatively early in the history of software engineering. Computers at that time were generally large, expensive, and slow, and the market for software programs was limited to corporate and institutional customers.

The company's original line of business was consulting, offering client companies logical data modeling services, as well as two software packages, called Information Planner and Data Designer, which were introduced in 1982. These systems used graphics tools organized around an instruction repository, referred to as an encyclopedia.

Database Design also developed a DOS-based system modeling package in conjunction with the accounting consultancy Ernst & Young. This product, called Information Engineering Workbench, or IEW, enabled programmers to quickly and easily build customized programs to handle a variety of specialized financial management tasks. Gradually the company built up a clientele. To better reflect its graduation from consulting into

software engineering, Database Design changed its name to KnowledgeWare.

During this period, Minnesota Vikings quarterback Fran Tarkenton was wrapping up his distinguished career in professional football and beginning a new career as a public speaker. The articulate athlete began giving motivational speeches before employees of corporations, and his colorful and surprisingly effective message for building teamwork inspired greater enthusiasm and raised productivity. During his tours of the corporate circuit, Tarkenton discovered that many companies were crippled to a great extent by the inadequate state of their computer systems. This prompted him to hire a team of programming experts in order to market the additional services of management consulting and troubleshooting for companies with unstable or poorly managed computer systems. Tarkenton named his enterprise Tarkenton Software, Inc., and the new company soon began marketing a COBOL code generator product developed by his engineers. Tarkenton made it clear that his role at the company was that of productivity consultant, not programmer. Nevertheless, some executives dismissed his company as the whim of a retired athlete who didn't even understand the business he was in.

In 1985 Tarkenton decided to merge his small enterprise with a firm that was better established in the market. He soon discovered James Martin's KnowledgeWare, whose software "workbenches" were in great demand. In turn, Tarkenton Software's Gamma code generator provided the back-end coding and testing component that KnowledgeWare needed to enhance its own product line.

When the two firms combined operations later that year, KnowledgeWare adopted Tarkenton's Atlanta headquarters as its new home. Tarkenton eventually retired from productivity consulting and became a senior executive at KnowledgeWare, representing the company to clients that included DuPont and Grumman. This enabled Martin to devote his full attention to the engineering group.

The company's IEW software product walked programmers through a series of customized functions, allowing them to choose individual command sequences and quickly customize a complete, error-free, and often highly complex computer program. These computer-assisted software engineering, or "CASE," programs contained options developed directly from customer requests, often specifically articulated by system operators.

KnowledgeWare quickly established a powerful reputation in the industry. Large companies with thousands of employees and increasingly complex accounting needs found CASE programs essential to maintaining financial order. Furthermore, they appreciated the flexibility of the programs, which allowed them to tailor the programs to their own needs.

In 1988, KnowledgeWare introduced its first desktop-based code generator, called IEW/Construction Workstation. The system enabled customers to analyze business requirements, design new applications, and write new code for mainframes, using only a personal computer.

Hundreds of new clients were drawn to KnowledgeWare, including Caterpillar and Martin Marietta. These clients each paid more than $200,000 for multiple copies of KnowledgeWare's CASE workbench. KnowledgeWare also sparked the interest of IBM, which saw KnowledgeWare as a potentially lucrative business partner as well as a catalyst for sales of its own products. Since KnowledgeWare's popular CASE programs were run on IBM computers, the company, it was hoped, would inspire customers to purchase or retain IBM computers.

KnowledgeWare was the largest and fastest-growing CASE company in the market, and IBM, which produced its own CASE programs, was determined to latch on to the company and ally its product line with KnowledgeWare's. In August 1989, IBM purchased an 8.7 percent stake in KnowledgeWare for $10.5 million. Not legally anticompetitive, the deal helped preserve IBM's position in the market.

With such a powerful vote of confidence, KnowledgeWare became popular on Wall Street. The company seized the opportunity by launching a public offering of 1.7 million shares, representing 15 percent of the company. The sale generated $20 million. Tarkenton personally sold 150,000 shares, netting $1.9 million.

A month after IBM's investment in KnowledgeWare, the latter company's programs were incorporated into IBM's AD/Cycle mainframe CASE product. A few months later, KnowledgeWare introduced its Application Development Workbench, or ADW, program, which garnered the "analysts choice" award from *PC Week* magazine. At the time, ADW was the only CASE system that was compatible with IBM's popular new OS/2 system. IBM customers who wanted to use ADW first had to upgrade their systems to OS/2, providing IBM with the increased sales it had hoped for.

In 1990, KnowledgeWare doubled its sales over the previous year to $92.3 million, representing a four-year growth rate of 1,700 percent. Profits rose by 54 percent, to $9.8 million. On paper, IBM's investment in KnowledgeWare was an instant success.

However, the partnership was derailed later that year when KnowledgeWare introduced a new software product called ADW/MVS. This system used a repository that closely resembled one under development by IBM. Rather than risk incurring a lawsuit from IBM, KnowledgeWare pulled ADW/MVS out of distribution. However, IBM's similar software system, AD/Cycle, met with flat sales, and while IBM could handle the losses, KnowledgeWare had bet its entire future on a projected steady stream of revenue from ADW/MVS. The failure of this product put other joint marketing arrangements with IBM into disarray, denying the company an important sales channel. Furthermore, these failures amplified doubts about KnowledgeWare's other products.

Nevertheless, by March 1991, total sales of ADW reached 25,000, and sales of IEW reached 34,000. Despite its trouble with IBM, KnowledgeWare posted a profit of $5.3 million on sales of $40.3 million during the fourth quarter of 1991. These results were augmented by the company's introduction of the RAD Workstation, Documentation Workstation, and a Japanese-language version of ADW.

KnowledgeWare grew quickly by acquisition in 1991. In January, the company took over UDM Technology, a processing tool designer. In May the company added Quinsoft, and in August it acquired Language Technology. Soon thereafter, Tarkenton announced that KnowledgeWare would attempt to buy out IntelliCorp.

Tarkenton's acquisition campaign was aimed at maintaining the company's earlier sales growth and beefing up its product line. However, KnowledgeWare's president Terri McGowan and financial director Don Ellis reportedly advised against further expansion. Tarkenton, fearing that McGowan and Ellis had become overly cautious, asked for their resignations in September and proceeded with the business of acquiring IntelliCorp.

The bid for IntelliCorp failed, however, as KnowledgeWare announced bleak financial results for 1991. With a deficit of $4.9 million and sales down by ten percent, the company was unable to counteract some of the negative effects of both its acquisitions and the nationwide economic recession. Furthermore, the company faced increased competition from Texas Instruments, whose CASE program, Information Engineering Facility, reportedly worked more smoothly than KnowledgeWare's IEW and ADW.

During this time, KnowledgeWare stock plummeted from $43 to $19 a share. When it was revealed that some of the company's senior executives, including Tarkenton, had cashed in lucrative stock options only months before their decline in value, a lawsuit was filed charging that the management team had profited at the expense of shareholders. The court found that Tarkenton and the others were protected by a new Securities and Exchange Commission rule allowing investors to sell their options at the time that they were awarded. However, while the executives were cleared of charges of impropriety, the scandal proved a public relations disaster.

Nevertheless, during this time Tarkenton's acquisitions were paying off for KnowledgeWare. The technologies assembled through the acquisitions allowed KnowledgeWare engineers to develop a new product, the Legacy Workstation, and move the company further into client/server technology with Construction Workstation-GUI. The company would later strengthen its position in client/server technology by acquiring two more companies, Viewpoint and Computer and Engineering Consultants, Ltd.

By January 1992, KnowledgeWare had reversed its losses, in part due to a massive employee layoff. Still, sales in the second quarter again fell, this time to $1.3 million, down 57 percent from the previous year. During this time, *Computerworld* magazine reported that Flashpoint, the company's first product in the client/server market, was inferior to a competing product from Massachusetts-based Powersoft.

To avoid losing its edge in the client/server market, KnowledgeWare acquired another leader in the technology, Matesys Mathematics, a French company with a profitable operation based in Silicon Valley. The $12 million acquisition brought Matesys' Objectview program into the KnowledgeWare product family.

To improve service and support, KnowledgeWare formed an Application Development Solution Services division and expanded its distribution channels to include systems integrators. Furthermore, the company established an international presence by taking over Ernst & Young's CASE distribution operation in Europe and setting up an international sales division. KnowledgeWare also acquired Ernst & Young's CASE business in Australia in December of 1993.

KnowledgeWare showed surprising resilience in the face of adversity and continued to explore new markets regardless of increased competition. Despite the interruption in the company's perfect record of earnings growth in the early 1990s, KnowledgeWare remained a highly respected, if closely watched, leader in the industry.

Principal Subsidiaries: KnowledgeWare Worldwide, Inc.

Further Reading:

"A Football Star Scores in One of Software's Hottest Games," *Business Week,* November 20, 1989, p. A138.

"IBM to Purchase Stake in Firm," *Electronic News,* August 24, 1989, p. 6

"KnowledgeWare: A Worst-CASE Scenario?," *Information Week,* February 17, 1992, p. 30.

"KnowledgeWare Executive Biographies," Company Document, October 1992.

"KnowledgeWare to Buy Client/Server Firm," *ComputerWorld,* January 25, 1993, p. 15.

"Pressure Weighs on KnowledgeWare," *Computerworld,* March 2, 1992, p. 53.

"Tarkenton Turns Computer Jock," *Fortune,* September 24, 1990, p. 211.

—John Simley

KOHL'S

Kohl's Corporation

N54 W13600 Woodale Drive
Menomonee Falls, Wisconsin 53051
U.S.A.
(414) 783-1640
Fax: (414) 783-4043

Public Company
Incorporated: 1988
Employees: 12,890
Sales: $1.01 billion
Stock Exchanges: New York
SICs: 5311 Department Stores; 6719 Holding Companies

Kohl's Corporation is one of the 12 largest department store chains in the United States, with 90 outlets in Wisconsin, Minnesota, Illinois, Indiana, Michigan, Ohio, Iowa, and South Dakota. The number of stores in the chain more than doubled between 1986 and 1992, when management took the company private. The chain maintains low retail prices through low cost structure, limited staffing, and progressive management information systems, as well as the economical application of centralized buying, distribution, and advertising. This "Kohl's concept" has proved successful in both small and large markets, and in strip shopping centers, regional malls, and free-standing venues.

Management purchased the chain's 40 stores in 1986 from BATUS Inc., the American division of BAT Industries plc. The parent was formed when James Buchanan Duke, founder of the American Tobacco Co., expanded his U.S. tobacco empire to Great Britain. His encroachment on the British market sparked a trade war, provoking several British tobacco companies to join forces as the Imperial Tobacco Group plc. Imperial succeeded in squelching Duke's British effort, then moved to invade the U.S. market. Taking the threat seriously, Duke negotiated a pact with Imperial Tobacco that formed the British-American Tobacco Co. Ltd. (BAT) in 1902 to manufacture and market the two companies' blends and brand names. When the U.S. Supreme Court found that BAT was a monopoly, it compelled American Tobacco to annul its territorial agreement with Imperial and divest its interest in BAT. Imperial kept its 33 percent interest in the company until 1972.

Following a tobacco industry trend, BAT began to diversify in the 1960s, purchasing several famous perfume houses. In the 1970s, the company formed an American subsidiary, BATUS

Inc., and began to acquire retail department stores. Wisconsin-based Kohl's Food and Department Stores, purchased in 1972, were the British conglomerate's first acquisition in this arena. Within a decade, BATUS had the nineteenth-largest retail holdings in the United States, including Gimbles, Saks Fifth Avenue, and Marshall Field & Co. BATUS invested expansion capital into two of its acquisitions, Saks and Kohl's.

By the mid-1980s, BATUS had more than doubled the number of Kohl's outlets to 34, but the chain was an anomaly in the upscale retail group with its "value-oriented," "bargain-basement" positioning. BATUS sold the food segment of Kohl's to Great Atlantic and Pacific Tea Co. (A&P), and began divesting its retail businesses in 1986. That year, Kohl's management team took the chain's 40 stores in Wisconsin and Indiana private. They spent the following three years refining the "Kohl's concept": moderately-priced, quality apparel for middle-income families.

The concept incorporated several factors. To set itself apart from mass merchandisers and discounters and become a specialty department store, over 80 percent of Kohl's merchandise carried national brand names recognized for quality. Kohl's also prided itself on stocking "narrow, but deep merchandise assortments," especially where advertised specials were concerned. At the same time, Kohl's eschewed the high-end and designer merchandise that characterized upscale department stores. The chain dropped low-volume, low-margin departments like candy, sewing notions, and hard sporting goods in favor of higher margin goods like linens and jewelry.

Kohl's was able to price its merchandise more competitively by maintaining a low cost structure. The company kept consumer prices low and margins relatively high through lean staffing, state-of-the-art management information systems, and operating efficiencies that resulted from centralized buying, advertising, and distribution. Promotional and marketing partnerships with vendors also helped hold down overhead. For example, many of Kohl's 200 vendors utilized electronic data exchange (EDI) to submit advance shipment notices electronically, which made ordering more efficient. The chain used aggressive marketing and promotional events to position Kohl's as the "destination store." Once customers arrived, management hoped the stores' convenient layouts, clear signage, and centralized checkouts would encourage high store productivity.

Kohl's most impressive growth spurt began in 1988, when management and The Morgan Stanley Leveraged Equity Fund II, L.P. formed Kohl's Corporation and acquired Kohl's Department Stores. That same year, Kohl's purchased 26 MainStreet department stores from Federated Department Stores, which expanded the chain geographically into the Detroit, Minneapolis/St. Paul, Chicago, and Grand Rapids, Michigan, metropolitan areas. The chain continued to grow internally as well, posting 8 percent to 10 percent store-for-store gains in 1989, 1990, and 1991 despite a recessed retail environment. From 1988 to 1992, Kohl's sales increased from $388 million to $1 billion.

Kohl's did not stop there: in 1992, the corporation prepared for further growth by expanding and upgrading its distribution facilities, automating merchandise handling, and making a public stock offering to finance projected openings of 14 to 16 additional stores annually. Kohl's enlisted the help of consultant group SDI Industries of Pacoima, California, to manage the automation and expansion of the chain's ten-year-old distribution center. The center, which supplied Kohl's stores with 98 percent of their merchandise, was expanded to 500,000 square feet, enough capacity to service 120 stores. Automation was achieved at a cost of $9.7 million. Completed in 1993, it encouraged higher productivity and lower turnaround time, and allowed vendors to send advance ship notices electronically and to pre-ticket merchandise. A second 650,000-square-foot distribution center was under construction in Findley, Ohio.

Kohl's advanced toward the 120-store mark with the opening of eight new stores in 1992, expanding its geographical reach to Ohio. While the chain added Iowa and South Dakota to its roster in 1993, management planned to open most new outlets in existing and neighboring markets to continue to take advantage of advertising, purchasing, transportation, and other efficiencies that ensued from its regional focus.

Principal Subsidiaries: Kohl's Department Stores.

Further Reading:

Arbose, Jules, and Daniel Burstein, "BAT Moves beyond Tobacco," *International Management,* August 1984, pp. 17–20.

"BATUS Battles Chilly Retail Climate," *Chain Store Age General Merchandise Trends,* June 1985, p. 62.

Brookman, Faye, "Kohl's Updates DC," *Stores,* January 1992, pp. 142, 144.

"Earnings Soar at Kohl's in the Third Quarter," *Daily News Record,* December 18, 1992, p. 10.

"Kohl's First $1 Billion," *Discount Merchandiser,* March 1993, p. 12.

Robins, Gary, "Lin Allison Keeps Kohl's on the Leading Edge," *Stores,* August 1991, pp. 54–58.

"Rain Falls on Gimbels' Parade," *Chain Store Age Executive,* August 1986, pp. 59–61.

Rublin, Lauren R., "Taylor-Made Portfolio," *Barron's,* June 22, 1992, pp. 16–20.

—April S. Dougal

Lands' End, Inc.

1 Lands' End Lane
Dodgeville, Wisconsin 53595
U.S.A.
(608) 935-9341
Fax: (608) 935-4260

Public Company
Incorporated: 1963 as Lands' End Yacht Stores
Employees: 6,500
Sales: $734 million
Stock Exchanges: New York
SICs: 5961 Catalog & Mail-Order Houses

Lands' End, Inc. sells traditionally styled, casual clothing through its catalogue, which is known for its folksy, chatty style. The company's emphasis on quality merchandise and customer service has made it a leader in the mail-order marketing field. Based in rural Wisconsin, Lands' End has grown steadily since its inception as a seller of sailing equipment for racing boats.

Lands' End got its start in 1963 when Gary Comer, a successful advertising copywriter with Young & Rubicam who had long pursued a love of sailing in his spare time, decided to pursue his long-standing dream of opening his own business. Comer quit his job of ten years, and, with $30,000 in initial funds, started a company that made sails and sold other marine hardware. The company set up shop in a storefront at 2317 North Elston Avenue, along the Chicago River in the city's old tannery district.

In 1964, Comer produced a catalogue offering Lands' End's goods through the mail. The first booklet, entitled "The Racing Sailors' Equipment Guide," was black and white, had 84 pages, and featured a variety of technical-looking sailing implements on its cover. In a printer's error, the company's name was rendered "Lands' End," with the apostrophe in the wrong place, in the catalogue. Since Comer couldn't afford to have the piece re-printed, he decided to simply change the name of the business to correspond with the brochure. Lands' End began filling orders from its basement. The company shipped out orders the day they were received, and unconditionally guaranteed all that it sold.

In a subsequent catalogue, Comer put his copy-writing skills to work in an innovative, customer-friendly format. The text in the Lands' End publications, rather than being dry, technical, and brief, had a casual, engaging, informative, and sympathetic air to it. Customers were put at ease reading it and came to feel that they had developed a personal relationship with the company that had produced the catalogue and the items that filled it. Comer is credited with originating the concept of the "magalogue," in which pictured items for sale are surrounded and cushioned by appealing text and illustrations.

Lands' End's customers began to look to the company for more than just technical sailing gear, and many felt comfortable writing to the company to ask about purchasing foul weather gear and duffel bags. In response, Lands' End added a small clothing section to the catalogue, featuring rainsuits, canvas luggage, shoes, sweaters, and some other clothing. The catalogue's name was accordingly altered to, simply, the "Lands' End Catalogue." Items sold in the clothing portion of the catalogue soon became the company's most profitable offerings.

Throughout the 1960s, Lands' End continued to sell sailing equipment and related items through its catalogue. In 1970, Lands' End's mail order business had grown large enough to merit computerization of its inventory and sales operations. Lands' End made its first foray into the world of manufacturing something other than sailing equipment in 1973, when the company began to make its own duffle bags. The next year, Lands' End also began to market its own brand of rainsuit, a two-piece outfit worn by sailors in foul weather. In 1975, the company came out with its first all-color catalogue, which featured 30 pages of sailing equipment and 2 full pages of clothing. By the following year, the company had decided to shift its emphasis to the sale of clothing and canvas luggage, and the quotient of non-nautical equipment had risen to include 8 pages displaying duffel bags, and three pages of clothing, including a men's chamois-cloth shirt.

In the spring of 1977, Lands' End issued its first catalogue that paid serious attention to clothing, with 13 out of 40 pages dedicated to dry goods. In addition, Lands' End introduced its own line of soft luggage, called Square Rigger. Following these innovations, sales for the year reached $3.6 million. After 1977, Lands' End phased out the sailing equipment aspect of its operation altogether, retaining the rugged, reliable, and traditional nature that sailing implied, and applying it to a broader variety of clothing. In 1978, the company introduced its first button-down Oxford-cloth shirt, heralding the move to offerings of solid, conservative, basic clothing upon which it would build its future.

Lands' End also began to shift its operations from its Chicago base to a small town in rural Wisconsin called Dodgeville. Comer chose this location for his growing enterprise because, as he noted in a piece of promotional literature, "I fell in love with the gently rolling hills and woods and cornfields and being able to see the changing seasons." In addition to the intangible spiritual benefits of life on the land, the move enabled Lands' End to ultimately locate the bulk of its operations in the middle of a cornfield in rural Wisconsin, an area in which costs were extremely low. The company began this shift when it moved its Chicago warehouse to an empty garage in Dodgeville in 1978.

Lands' End's operations were also shifting in another significant way during this time, as the company moved from filling orders by mail to filling orders by phone. Lands' End had brought its first toll-free 800-number on line, and operators were standing by to take customer calls by the middle of 1978. With this shift, Lands' End incorporated another point of contact with the customer into its operation, and the company stressed politeness and customer service in its operators, a continuation of the message it strove to portray in its catalogue. Calls were answered within a ring and a half, and operators were permitted to chat with customers for as long as it took to make a sale.

Lands' End further transferred operations to Dodgeville in 1979, when it opened an office in a pre-existing strip mall, while it broke ground for an office building and an accompanying 33,000-square-foot warehouse in a Dodgeville industrial park. In the following year, the company moved into its new space on "Lands' End Lane." By this time, the clothing section of its catalogue had grown further, and Lands' End's 800-number service had been expanded to accommodate customers 24 hours a day. Interested in gaining more control over the quality of the clothes it sold, the company began to recruit employees who were knowledgeable about fabric and the manufacture of clothing.

In addition to its new facilities in Dodgeville, Lands' End also opened an outlet store in Chicago, just one block from its original location, to sell the goods that made up excess inventory if catalogue sales of a particular item were not as brisk as expected. Further physical expansion took place the following year, in 1981, when Lands' End began work on a 40,000-square-foot addition to its warehouse in Wisconsin. The company also broke ground on a plant to manufacture its own line of soft luggage in West Union, Iowa.

To further support its burgeoning sales and reputation, Lands' End embarked on a national advertising campaign in 1981. The purpose of this effort was to make customers aware of the Lands' End business philosophy, and associate its name with service, value, and quality. The company used the expression "direct merchant" to describe its relationship, as a manufacturer and distributor, with the customer.

In the next year, Lands' End followed up this effort with a significant investment in computerization, as the company introduced on-line customer sales and ordering to speed up processes. Efficient use of computers was a keystone of Lands' End's program for success, and soon computer systems enabled operators to provide customers with a wealth of information at the touch of a finger.

In addition, Lands' End continued to expand its warehouse facilities as it started construction on an additional 126,000-square-foot warehouse across the street from its original Dodgeville facilities. Moving into this facility in 1983 required the unloading of 8,000 boxes of goods so that the company's new automated sorting system could be made operational. By this time, a nationwide boom in mail-order shopping was begin-

ning to take off, and Lands' End saw its sales and earnings start to grow.

In an effort to exploit Americans' increasing willingness to shop by phone using their credit cards, Lands' End introduced a line of fancier clothing for men and women in 1983, under the name Charter Club. Instead of cotton and wool, these products were manufactured from Italian silks and other luxury fabrics. This line soon had its own catalogue of offerings.

In 1984, Lands' End passed another landmark on the way to becoming a full-fledged manufacturer when its logo was registered as a U.S. trademark. By the following year, demand for Lands' End goods had increased to the point where the company was able to begin issuing monthly as opposed to seasonal catalogues. In addition, Lands' End broke ground on yet another warehouse addition.

In 1986, Lands' End discontinued its Charter Club line of dressier clothing, despite the fact that it was profitable, in an effort to maintain the company's culture and focus on solid, traditional, no-nonsense clothes. "When they started shooting photographs of models in London, I said, 'That's it, enough,' " Comer later told Fortune. His conception of the company was more straightforward, he explained. "I picked things that I liked, and over the years people interested in the same sorts of things gathered around," he said, explaining Lands' End's growth.

By 1986, growth had brought Lands' End profits of more than $14 million on sales topping $200 million. At that point, after several years of phenomenal advances, the company sold stock to the public for the first time, offering 1.4 million shares at $30 a piece. In the following year, shares of Lands' End began to be traded on the New York Stock Exchange, as the company racked up earnings of about $15 million.

Also in 1987, in response to customer requests, Lands' End introduced a line of children's clothing. Within a year it had yielded sales of almost $15 million. By 1988, Lands' End had built up a loyal core of catalogue shoppers. The company shipped nine million booklets a month, full of homey straight talk about classic casual clothing, for a total of 80 million pieces mailed a year. To take the orders generated by this promotional literature, Lands' End also spent heavily on technology to improve its customer service, adding new sorting, packaging, and sewing equipment (for alterations). In addition, the company broke ground on an additional phone center in a town about 30 miles from Dodgeville, Cross Plains, Wisconsin. With this facility, Lands' End planned to add 100 new employees to its payroll.

At the end of the year, the company also opened a small retail outlet in Dodgeville to sell its clothes. Although Lands' End had no intention of branching out from the mail order business into conventional retail, the company had discovered that people felt so at home with the places and people depicted in the Lands' End catalogue that they frequently got in their cars and drove to Dodgeville on vacation to see the place for themselves. After customers began wandering into Lands' End's corporate offices looking to buy turtlenecks and sweatshirts, the company opened a small store to serve them.

After a blockbuster year in 1988, Lands' End's revenues had nearly doubled in the time since its first stock offering, rising to $456 million for the fiscal year ending in January, 1989. Two months later, however, the company was forced to announce its sharpest drop in earnings ever. Although sales had continued to grow, costs had grown at a much steeper rate. Confident that sales would continue strongly after 1988, the company had amassed a large inventory of merchandise. When sales slowed, it was forced to send out a large number of additional catalogues in an attempt to win new customers. This campaign proved to be extremely costly, adding about $2 million to the company's promotional budget. This cost promised to rise further as the post office implemented a 17 percent hike in third class mailing rates.

In addition, Lands' End found itself hurt by the stodgy reputation of its merchandise, as competition in the catalogue sales field heated up. In particular, the company lost ground to Eddie Bauer, a marketer of rugged outdoor gear. Lands' End needed to update and freshen its offerings without alienating old customers who appreciated the company's solid, traditional goods.

Lands' End's outdated offerings continued to damage its profitability throughout the start of 1990, and the company posted a two-thirds drop in profits in the first quarter of that year. Concerned that Lands' End and its rival L.L. Bean might have grown so large that they had glutted the market for their type of merchandise, industry watchers predicted further declines at the company. In response to its falling profits, Lands' End began to increase the amount of new merchandise that it offered in its catalogue. Whereas the previous two years' catalogues had featured first eight and then 11.5 percent new items, 1990 issues had 15 percent and 18 percent new products. Among the additions were sunglasses, children's swimsuits, and clothing and bedding for infants.

In May, the company began to market "Mom Packs," combinations of merchandise packed together to be presented as Mother's Day gifts. In addition, Lands' End introduced three new specialty catalogues: Buttondowns and Beyond, which featured tailored clothing for men; Coming Home with Lands' End, with products for the bed and bath; and in August, 1990, a separate catalogue just for children called Kids.

In the following year, Lands' End began its first attempt to expand its market beyond the borders of the United States. In typical company style, Lands' End invited its customers to participate in this new push by asking them to send in the names of their relatives who lived overseas. Then, Lands' End began to mail a catalogue to possible customers in the United Kingdom.

By March, 1992, the company's efforts to improve profitability had started to pay off, as Lands' End reported a one-third rise in profits for the quarter. Overall, earnings over the last year had nearly doubled, to reach $28.7 million. Building on this strength, the company continued its physical expansion, opening a third phone center in Reedsburg, Wisconsin, which brought to 1,000 the number of operators Lands' End employed. In addition, Land's End launched a print advertising campaign, in addition to the promotional materials contained in its catalogue. At the end of 1992, the company reported continued financial strength, earning profits of $33.5 million. The company continued its move into foreign markets, opening a phone center and distribution facility in the United Kingdom in the fall of 1993. With its strong reputation for quality and its steady course of business growth, Lands' End appeared to be charted for further smooth sailing in calm seas.

Principle Subsidiaries: Lands' End (United Kingdom); The Territory Ahead.

Further Reading:

Berg, Eric N., "Standout in the Land of Catalogues," *New York Times,* December 8, 1988.
Bremner, Brian, "Lands' End Looks a Bit Frayed at the Edges," *Business Week,* March 19, 1990.
Caminiti, Susan, "A Mail-Order Romance: Lands' End Courts Unseen Customers," *Fortune,* March 13, 1989.
Schwadel, Francine, "Lands' End Stumbles as Fashion Shifts Away from Retailer's Traditional Fare," *Wall Street Journal,* April 27, 1990.

—Elizabeth Rourke

Lever Brothers Company

390 Park Avenue
New York, New York 10022-4698
U.S.A.
(201) 871-3443
Fax: (212) 906-4411

Wholly Owned Subsidiary of Unilever United States Inc.
Employees: 4,462
Sales: $2.19 billion
SICs: 2841 Soap and Detergent; 2034 Dried and Dehydrated
   Fruits, Vegetables

Lever Brothers Company is one of the largest manufacturers of
soaps and detergents in the United States. It is well known for
such famous brands as Sunlight dish detergents; Wisk, Surf, and
"all" laundry detergents; and Caress, Dove, Lifebuoy, and
Lever 2000 soaps. Lever Brothers is a subsidiary of the Anglo-
Dutch Unilever group, which includes more than 500 companies and has sales of more than $43 billion annually.

Lever Brothers Company has its roots with William Hesketh
Lever, an English grocer. Beginning in 1874, Lever's wholesale
grocery business had been marketing a soap made specially for
them called Lever's Pure Honey. By the 1880s, Lever had
concluded that he had expanded the grocery business as much
as he could, and he looked for another enterprise. He decided to
market soap. As a child, his first job in his father's grocery store
had been to cut and wrap soap. He knew the importance of a
brand name that he could register for exclusive use and chose
the name "Sunlight." At first he contracted with various soap-
makers to manufacture "Sunlight," which he then packaged
and marketed. In the mid-1880s, raw materials were cheap and
workers plentiful, and Lever decided to set up his own soap-
making plant.

Arranging a loan to start the factory as a branch of his family's
wholesale grocery business, William and his brother James
began production. By January 1886, the plant was producing
twenty tons of soap a week using the "recipe" for Sunlight
soap (made from oils rather than tallow) that the Lever Brothers
had perfected. Two years later, the plant had a capacity of 450
tons a week. Glycerine was a lucrative byproduct of the soap-
making process, and by the end of 1886, Lever Brothers also
had a glycerine factory. At first Lever was selling locally, then
its market branched out to include Scotland, Holland, Belgium,

South Africa, and Canada. In 1888, with the success of Sunlight, William Lever went looking for a new site for his company, which had been operating from leased facilities. He
bought land on the banks of the Mersey River where he built
Port Sunlight. Over a period of years, he bought almost 330
acres.

At first Lever manufactured only Sunlight soap. In 1894,
though, he introduced Lifebuoy soap, a household soap with
carbolic acid as a disinfectant. The new product also used up the
residual oils left over from production of Sunlight. In 1899,
Lever's company also began producing "Lux" soap flakes.

Lever opened a small office in New York in 1895 to handle U.S.
sales of Sunlight and Lifebuoy soaps. In 1898, Lever acquired a
small soap factory in Cambridge, Massachusetts, the company's
first manufacturing operations in the United States. A few years
later, the company acquired a factory in Philadelphia. The
Cambridge plant did business throughout New England, and the
Philadelphia plant distributed to the rest of the country. During
the early years in America, neither Lifebuoy nor Sunlight sold
well. Americans preferred large bars of soap because they
seemed like a better value than the small tablets of Sunlight.
Lever was more successful with its sales of "Welcome" soap,
which satisfied Americans with its larger size. Sales of Lifebuoy
soap and Lux finally started to take off, but Sunlight never did
catch on in the United States.

Sales of Lever products in America were growing largely due to
the management of Francis A. Countway, who headed U.S.
operations for Lever Brothers. Beginning in 1912, he guided
Lever Brothers American business for more than 25 years. He
understood American marketing and Americans' peculiar preferences, and gradually he persuaded the British owners that
selling soap to Americans was very different than selling to
Europeans.

In 1919, Countway reorganized the company. Recognizing that
the markets outside of New England needed to be tapped, he
divided the United States into ten sales territories. He gave up
on Sunlight ever being a success in the United States and
successfully promoted Lux, Rinso, and Lifebuoy as the
mainstays of the company until 1925, when Countway launched
Lux toilet soap. Lever had not been very successful selling
directly to retailers, so Countway also brought the wholesaler or
jobber into the marketing process.

Between 1920 and 1925, sales rose from 21,000 tons to more
than 40,000 tons. Lever's American concern was finally becoming a success. By 1929, it had become the third-largest soap and
glycerine manufacturer in the United States. Competition was
strong among the top three soap manufacturers: Procter &
Gamble, Colgate-Palmolive-Peet, and Lever Brothers. Lever
Brothers had given up on Sunlight, but Lifebuoy and Welcome
were selling well due to heavy promotions which included gifts,
special displays, demonstrations, and even door-to-door visits.
But it was Lux that became its greatest success.

Lux had been touted as a soap suitable for washing woolen
fabrics. But newer, more delicate fabrics were becoming available at low prices by 1913, and Countway began advertising
Lux as a high quality soap that was suitable for even the most
delicate fabrics. By 1919, Lever was selling a million and a half

cases of Lux; its 1913 sales had been 3,000 cases. The introduction of Rinso soap powder was also successful, with sales rising from 64,000 cases in 1919 to 800,000 cases four years later. Lifebuoy sales had soared from 84,000 cases in 1913 to 550,000 cases in 1923.

Meanwhile, the parent company in England was in the midst of negotiations that would soon make Lever Brothers of America a subsidiary of a newly formed partnership. In 1929, after years of talks, Lever Brothers Ltd. and Holland's Margarine Unie finalized a deal to become Unilever. They remained two companies with two sets of shareholders and two headquarters but one board of directors. Unilever Public Limited Company (PLC) was based in London and Unilever NV (Naamloze Vennootschap, meaning limited-liability company) was based in Rotterdam. Although legally distinct, they operated as one company.

Lever Brothers Company in the United States continued to fight for market share. While sales of Lux had surged in the 1920s, its growth had slowed down in the 1930s. But Lifebuoy was going strong, and Rinso powder sales rose from two million cases in 1929 to more than six million a decade later because of its suitability for use in the new electric washers that were being installed in many American homes.

Procter & Gamble was enjoying great success with its Crisco shortening; that product brought in nearly half of the company's profits in the early 1930s. Countway thought Lever Brothers could take advantage of the lard substitute market as well. Delaying direct sales to consumers, Countway entered the market with artificial lard sold to bakeries. When the Depression brought low prices for lard and butter, the market for lard substitutes dropped. It was not until 1936, when the country was in the midst of a serious shortage of real lard, that Lever Brothers brought out its Spry shortening in the United States. By 1939, after a massive cross-country campaign to demonstrate uses of Spry, the new product had reached sales of 50,000 tons. In three years, Spry sales had reached about 75 percent of the sales of Crisco, which had been on the market since 1910.

Lever Brothers sales increased between 1929 and 1934, despite the Depression. This may have been due to Americans' high regard for cleanliness, making soap a necessity rather than a luxury. Between 1929 and 1939, U.S. sales for Lever Brothers increased from $39 million to more than $91 million, and profits more than doubled, from $3 million to more than $7 million. During the 1940s, the company diversified further than soaps and lard substitutes. In 1944, Lever entered the oral hygiene market when it acquired the large Pepsodent Company, manufacturer of toothbrushes and tooth-cleaning products. In 1948, it acquired the John F. Jelke Company, a manufacturer of margarine.

Synthetic detergents were gradually taking over markets for soap products in almost all but the toilet soap segment, where it was difficult to develop a synthetic that did not leave a ring around the bathtub. Lever's Dove, a synthetic toilet soap, finally met with success when it was introduced in the 1950s, but it was a costly product. Synthetic soaps caused an environmental problem because they formed huge collections of foam in rivers and sewer systems. Lever Brothers, like other soap manufacturers, worked to overcome this problem, finally developing more biodegradable detergents.

In 1957, Lever Brothers acquired the Monsanto Chemical Company's line of "all" detergents, which included Concentrated "all," Liquid "all" and Dishwasher "all." This transaction resulted in an anti-trust suit by the U.S. Department of Justice which charged Lever Brothers with restricting competition by acquiring that piece of Monsanto which manufactured low-suds synthetic detergent, a product similar to one that Lever already made. Lever Brothers won the suit, arguing that rather than restricting competition, it was protecting it since both Lever's and Monsanto's products were losing money due to competition with "larger rivals" like Procter & Gamble. Lever Brothers Company successfully argued that if the businesses remained separate, eventually the larger rival would wipe both of them out, and that the acquisition of Monsanto's detergents was actually helping to preserve a competitive marketplace.

Advertising dollars tended to spell the difference among several like products that essentially differed only by scent or color. Procter & Gamble spent massive amounts of money on advertising and promotion and controlled 45 percent to 50 percent of the household products market. Competition from Lever Brothers remained weak until the 1980s. Outside the United States, however, Lever's parent organization, Unilever, was the leading manufacturer of detergents and margarine.

Low profitability was what had plagued Lever Brothers through the 1970s, according to Michael Angus, then Unilever PLC's vice-chairman and head of Unilever's North American operations. He was sent to the States to turn Lever Brothers around. He told *Fortune* magazine in 1986 that Lever Brothers "was in a vicious cycle caused by low profitability." Low profits caused managers to cut costs, such as advertising, which produced lower market shares, lower volumes, and higher production costs. In addition, research and development resources had been reduced as management tried desperately to stay profitable.

Angus kept only the "best" corporate officers at Lever Brothers, letting many others go. He tackled the margarine business first, which was losing vast amounts on Imperial and Promise brands. He shut down outmoded plants and, for a time, contracted with Beatrice Co. to manufacture margarine for Lever. With the savings from shutting down plants and warehouses, Angus was able to begin updating Lever's margarine factories and promoting other products more aggressively. With the acquisition of the Beatrice operations Shedd's Food Products Company in 1984 and J. H. Filbert in 1986, Lever became the leading margarine company in the United States, ahead of Nabisco and Kraft. The acquisitions added production, food service, and private label operations. In 1985 Unilever spent $50 million to expand the laboratories and research staff at its Edgewater, New Jersey, research center.

Lever Brothers launched a string of new products in the mid-1980s. Both Sunlight automatic dishwashing detergent and Snuggle fabric softener managed to win 15 to 20 percent of U.S. markets. Lever also expanded its marketing of Surf powder detergent to compete with Procter & Gamble's Tide. Lever Brother's revenues shot up to $2.1 billion, a 55 percent increase over three years.

With the company becoming more diversified in the 1980s, Unilever reorganized Lever Brothers, forming three separate divisions: Household Products Division, Foods Division, and Personal Products Division. Following the acquisition of Chesebrough-Pond's Inc. by Unilever, Lever's Personal Products Division was transferred to this company. Lever's Foods Division was spun off into its own operating unit, called Van den Bergh Foods, in 1989. Following these changes, Lever Brothers became solely a soap and detergent company.

Lever was now in a position to face Procter & Gamble more confidently in the household products division. Lever already had a winner with Wisk, first in the heavy-duty liquid laundry detergent market. Introduced in the 1950s, Wisk was largely unchallenged until Procter & Gamble marketed Liquid Tide in the mid-1980s.

In 1990 Lever Brothers introduced some innovative products, including Lever 2000—an "all-in-one" deodorant and moisturizing soap for the whole family—and Wisk Power Scoop, a superconcentrated laundry detergent. According to company literature, an ingredient in the detergant called lipase "unlocks the fatty matter that 'glues' dirt to fibers, making dirt linger in clothes." Lever also brought out a liquid Dove and "all" Free: Clear, which contained no perfumes or dyes.

In 1990 the company also began using recycled plastic in its packaging, publicly committing to use 25 to 35 percent post-consumer recycled resins in half the bottles it sold in the United States. It also touted its Wisk Power Scoop as a step in the right environmental direction since it used less packaging per load than ordinary detergents. Lever announced that its new Packaging Development Center in Owings Mills, Maryland, was actively pursuing packaging that supported its environmental policy.

Lever Brothers pulled ahead of Procter & Gamble in the toilet soap category in 1991 with Lever 2000. This was the first time Lever had ever overtaken Procter & Gamble in a product category. Lever spent more than $25 million for advertising that year to make Lever 2000 the market leader.

Lever Brothers' winning position in the toilet soap market convinced the company that it could dominate other market segments too. But Procter & Gamble, Dial, and other soap makers began to develop new products or reposition existing ones to capitalize on the market for "all-in-one" soaps. Soap makers collectively spent more than $183 million on advertising in 1991.

Further Reading:

Brown, Andrew, "Unilever Fights Back in the United States," *Fortune,* May 26, 1986, pp. 32–38.
Wilson, Charles, *The History of Unilever,* Vol. 1, London: Cassell & Company Ltd., 1954, 1970.

—Wendy J. Stein

LIN Broadcasting Corp.

5295 Carillon Point
Kirkland, Washington 98033
U.S.A.
(206) 828-1902

Public Subsidiary of McCaw Cellular Communications, Inc.
Incorporated: 1961
Employees: 1,141
Net Revenues: $774.23 million
Stock Exchanges: NASDAQ
SICs: 4812 Radiotelephone Communications; 4833
  Television Broadcasting Stations; 2741 Miscellaneous
  Publishing

LIN Broadcasting Corp. is part of McCaw Cellular Communications, Inc., America's leading cellular telephone group. LIN owns seven network-affiliated television stations in urban markets in Texas, Indiana, Michigan, Virginia, and Illinois. Although LIN was historically a broadcast communications company, cellular operations contributed almost 80 percent of the company's revenues by the early 1990s. The 1990s promised more change at LIN. The company's 1990 merger agreement with McCaw stipulated that, in 1995, the subsidiary's assets would be put up for sale and sold to the highest bidder. And in 1993, American Telephone & Telegraph (AT&T) purchased McCaw Cellular for $12.6 billion in AT&T stock.

LIN Broadcasting Corp. was founded in Nashville, Tennessee in 1961 as a radio broadcasting company. During its first decade, LIN built up a relatively small communications conglomerate dominated by broadcast radio holdings. Under the leadership of Frederick Gregg, Jr., the company purchased WTVP-TV, of Decatur, Illinois, from Metromedia Inc. for $2 million in 1965. LIN went public the following year with its first over-the-counter stock offer. That same year, the company traded $3 million in stock for a controlling interest in Medallion Pictures Corp.'s 375 feature films and cartoons. The company expanded its radio holdings with the purchase of three Houston, Texas stations, KILT-AM and FM and KOST-FM, for $15 million in 1967. LIN also purchased sister radio and television stations WAVY and WAVY-TV, of Norfolk-Portsmouth, Virginia, that year. In 1968, the company acquired the Adonis Radio Corp., an advertising media buyer, to complement its broadcast holdings.

Although most of these early acquisitions focused on broadcast media, LIN also bought into several peripheral businesses during the 1960s, including a chain of national art galleries, a telephone answering and radio paging service, several direct marketing companies, an educational concern, and the Miss Teenage America Pageant. These wide-ranging operations contributed to over $1 million in combined losses in 1967 and 1968, which culminated in dramatic administrative changes at LIN.

The company's leadership crisis began in January 1969, when Martin S. Ackerman's Saturday Evening Post Co. purchased Frederick Gregg, Jr.'s four percent interest in LIN. Some shareholders later charged that the $3.5 million price tag (which topped the stock's market value by $1.5 million) also bought LIN's presidency, chief executive office, and several seats on LIN's board of directors. Ackerman was a financier whose hostile takeover of the Curtis Publishing Co. and its subsidiary Saturday Evening Post Co. had previously sparked four lawsuits. His infamy definitely shortened his tenure at LIN; after five weeks as president and CEO, Ackerman was fired by the broadcast company's board of directors. Joel M. Thrope, a LIN vice-president, became interim president. LIN's leadership crisis had compounded the company's financial troubles; it had operated under three leaders within less than two months, and lost $6.5 million in 1969.

Donald A. Pels was called in to evaluate the situation and make recommendations. He quickly won the board's confidence and was appointed president and CEO in April, 1969. His prescription for LIN called first for the divestment of all the company's non-broadcast business except the Page Boy Inc. radio paging business in metropolitan New York City. The proceeds from the sales were used to cover operating expenses. Second, Pels instituted strict cost controls governing everything from raises to programming. Although LIN would continue to be involved in broadcast radio until the mid-1980s, Pels shifted the company's emphasis from radio to television.

Until 1973, television broadcasting accounted for only about 25 percent of LIN's total broadcast revenues. But after two years of negotiations, LIN made a pivotal acquisition in 1974. The purchase of WBAP-TV, Dallas-Fort Worth from Carter Publications Inc. for $35 million altered LIN's focus from radio to television and set it on a course for higher earnings. After LIN sold four radio stations to Multimedia Inc. for $8.7 million cash in 1975, television accounted for two-thirds of LIN's broadcast revenues. Perhaps more important than the source of revenues, however, was the increased profitability LIN enjoyed after 1975.

LIN changed WBAP-TV's call-letters to KXAS-TV. In 1975, KXAS-TV's first full year with LIN, the parent's revenues increased by half, from $20.85 million to $31.35 million, and earnings leaped 75 percent, from $2.18 million to $3.95 million. The higher profits were due, in part, to rising print ad rates that pushed many local retailers into television advertising. By the end of the decade, local spot advertising contributed about 44 percent of LIN's television revenues. The above-average prosperity of the Dallas-Fort Worth area also boosted KXAS-TV's performance.

Although radio broadcasting accounted for only one-third of LIN's business, it was also profitable in the 1970s. The highlight of this division, KILT-AM/FM, located in Texas, accounted for about 40 percent of LIN's radio revenues. When other stations in the Houston market shifted their programming, this FM outlet was left with only one primary competitor in its album-oriented rock format. The AM station had a good reputation for local news reporting, and both stations outperformed industry averages.

LIN also still held a remnant of its days as a diversified conglomerate: its two-way mobile radio-telephone services in southern Connecticut and Houston contributed almost ten percent of total revenue. Paging seemed promising, but competition from American Telephone & Telegraph Co.'s New York Telephone Co. and New Jersey Bell hurt this small division's profits. In the 1980s, however, this foothold in telecommunications would help lead LIN into the cellular industry. Net income at LIN quadrupled from 1975 to 1980, from $3.95 million to $16.01 million. The company's profits grew at an average rate of 34 percent annually from 1974 to 1979, ranking LIN highest in this category among the United States' largest broadcasters.

LIN continued to concentrate on television broadcasting in the late 1970s and early 1980s. From 1979 to 1984, the company worked to build up its media holdings to Federal Communications Commission (FCC) limits. In 1979, LIN purchased KTVV-TV of Austin, Texas, for about $6 million. The next three years saw the addition of two Milwaukee radio stations (WEMP-AM and WNUW-FM), a Michigan television outlet (WOTV-TV, Grand Rapids), and *GuestInformant* and *Leisureguides,* hardcover magazines distributed in hotels and motels. In 1984, LIN acquired two Indiana television stations (WISH-TV, Indianapolis and WANE-TV, Fort Wayne), bringing its television group to seven. Television still contributed almost 75 percent of LIN's annual revenues, and the company's complement of ten AM/FM radio stations (in Philadelphia; Houston; St. Louis; Milwaukee; and Rochester, New York) contributed another 21 percent. Although radio paging contributed about four percent of LIN's annual sales, the company had already planted the seeds of its transformation into a full-fledged communications company by mid-decade.

LIN entered the then-speculative field of cellular communication in 1982, when it applied for a license from the FCC to operate a cellular mobile radiotelephone system. Governmental regulation of this infant industry created a "duopoly": two licenses were granted for each of the United States' 733 markets. One license was routinely awarded to the local "wireline," or Bell telephone company in each market. "Nonwireline" licenses were awarded to independent entities through hearings and lotteries. The lag between the automatic awards to wireline companies and time-consuming hearings gave traditional phone companies a competitive edge over their independent competitors.

To help speed up the process, many independents made joint applications. In 1983, for example, LIN teamed up with Metromedia Inc. and Cellular Systems Inc. to compete for the New York cellular license. These cooperative ventures helped LIN become the second-largest player in this new industry, with substantial interests in licenses for Los Angeles, Philadelphia,

Dallas-Fort Worth, and Houston. By 1984, LIN was the only company to have significant stakes in the two largest markets, New York and Los Angeles. By 1989, LIN had solidified its position in five important markets, giving it 18.1 million potential customers ("POPs" in cellular market jargon), and making it the seventh-largest cellular company.

Two primary bidders vied for control of LIN's cellular potential: BellSouth Corp., the largest regional wireline company, and McCaw Cellular Communications Inc., the largest nonwireline cellular company. Under its namesake leader, Craig O. McCaw, the latter company had attained the leading position in cellular communications through smart acquisitions and heavy leveraging. McCaw hoped to repeat Theodore Vail's early-twentieth-century consolidation of local telephone companies into American Telephone & Telegraph (AT&T) by merging the United States' 733 independent cellular licensees into a consolidated, national network known as Cellular One. Despite their time advantage, the Bell companies would not be permitted to form a national cellular network, because it would too closely echo AT&T's recently divided monopoly.

By the end of the decade, McCaw had come a long way toward accomplishing his goal: his company held 50 million POPs, 68 percent more than its next-largest competitor, Pacific Telesis Group. Craig McCaw hoped that the addition of LIN's strong positions in the nation's five most important cellular markets would be the company's most significant step toward his goal. But McCaw had to pay a high price to outbid major telephone groups like BellSouth Corp., Pacific Telesis, U.S. West, and Southwestern Bell to acquire LIN. In June, 1989, McCaw bid $120 per share, or $5.9 billion, for the 90 percent of LIN it did not already own. The bid—$275 per POP—was based more on LIN's potential value than its actual worth. In 1988, LIN's actual revenues were only $226 million, and $100 million of that income had come from its broadcast television and publishing businesses. But BellSouth came back with a plan to sell LIN's broadcasting operations and combine the two companies' cellular businesses, thereby capturing the top spot in the cellular industry from McCaw.

After months of vacillating between BellSouth and McCaw, LIN reached an agreement with the latter in December 1989. The merger called for McCaw to pay $154 per share, or $3.4 billion, for a 40 percent share of LIN that raised its stake in the company to 50.1 percent. The agreement stipulated that, in 1995, LIN's assets would be put up for sale and sold to the highest bidder. McCaw had an option to purchase an additional 23 percent of LIN's stock on the open market before the auction, or put all of its interest on the block.

The agreement gave McCaw about five years to turn a profit on its purchase, which looked like quite a feat by the time the sale was settled. McCaw paid $350 per POP in LIN's license areas; it would have had to capture eight percent of those potential customers within ten years just to justify a $200 per POP price. At the time, the cellular industry's penetration rate was just two percent, and LIN had a wireline competitor in each of its markets. To help shift the odds to its favor, McCaw sold six million of LIN's POPs to Contel Cellular for $1.3 billion, leaving it about $2.5 billion in debt. Even so, McCaw and LIN's combined operating cash flow could not cover the parent's debt service.

McCaw planned to upgrade LIN's services and capture more customers in the early 1990s. The company began to upgrade the New York and Los Angeles cellular systems from analog to digital systems, dedicating $150 million to improvements in New York alone. Digital technology promised subscribers improved call quality, increased voice privacy, more portability, better data transmission capabilities, and other advanced features. The conversion to digital also instantly tripled LIN's capacity. LIN hoped to activate digital service for all of its markets by the end of 1994. The addition of information services, like stock quotes, local weather, and traffic reports, also promised to attract more subscribers and extra income. LIN and its customers began to benefit from the corporate affiliation with McCaw by the end of 1992, when the parent's North American Cellular Network (NACN), which linked cellular coverage areas on the United States' two coasts and north to Canada into one system, grew to serve over 2.3 million customers. Craig McCaw's vision was becoming reality.

LIN's annual cellular revenues grew over 400 percent from 1988 to 1992, from $121 million to almost $609 million, completing the transition from a television broadcasting company to a cellular business. Although telecommunications clearly demanded more time, attention, and money, LIN had not abandoned its broadcasting roots. Cash flow for the company's television group increased by 13 percent from 1991 to 1992 to $70 million, as many of LIN's stations reduced their reliance on more costly outside programming to concentrate on local-interest series. By 1992, LIN's longest-held station, KXAS-TV in Dallas-Fort Worth, occupied an important position in the United States' eighth-largest television market.

Any threat that LIN's television interests could be sold to help diminish McCaw's colossal debt was eliminated when AT&T purchased McCaw. McCaw used the proceeds of the sale to pay down a significant portion of its debt. Although the upper-level merger may have been somewhat reassuring, LIN still faced the possibility of fundamental change in 1995, when the question of corporate ownership would again arise.

Further Reading:

"Ackerman Ousted as LIN President," *Broadcasting,* February 24, 1969, pp. 59–60.

"Back to Basics Spells Growing Profits for LIN," *Broadcasting,* November 5, 1979, pp. 44, 48–49.

"Earnings at LIN Broadcasting Appear Solidly on the Beam," *Barron's,* August 16, 1976.

"Fall-out from the Curtis Deals," *Broadcasting,* February 17, 1969.

Gannes, Stuart. "BellSouth Is on a Ringing Streak," *Fortune,* October 9, 1989, pp. 66–76.

Hof, Robert D. "The Cellular Bidding War Will Get Even Hotter," *Business Week,* June 19, 1989, pp. 39–40.

"LIN Broadcasting Corp.," *Advertising Age,* June 27, 1985, p. 41.

"LIN Shifts Its Diversified Holdings," *Broadcasting,* July 22, 1968, p. 50.

"LIN's Script," *Barron's,* April 16, 1979.

Lopez, Julie Amparano. "McCaw Agrees to Acquire LIN for $3.4 Billion," *Wall Street Journal,* December 12, 1989, p. C25.

Meeks, Fleming. "Winning Is Only the First Step," *Forbes,* December 25, 1989, pp. 80–83.

"Two LIN Holders Sue Firm's Former Chief over His Stock Sale," *Wall Street Journal,* April 17, 1969.

—April S. Dougal

Loral Corporation

600 3rd Ave.
New York, New York 10016-2485
U.S.A.
(212) 697-1105
Fax: (212) 661-8988

Public Company
Incorporated: 1948 as Loral Electronics Corp.
Employees: 22,000
Sales: $2.88 billion
Stock Exchanges: Boston Midwest New York Pacific
  Philadelphia
SICs: 3812 Search & Navigation Equipment; 3761 Guided
  Missiles & Space Vehicles; 3674 Semi Conductors &
  Related Devices; 3675 Electronic Capacitors

Loral Corporation is one of the largest electronic warfare companies in the world. Specializing in radar and infrared detection equipment, Loral is also involved in satellite communications. Loral Electronics Corp. was founded in 1948 in New York by William Lorenz and Leon Alpert, who combined the first syllables of their last names to create the name of their company. The young firm initially concentrated its efforts on developing radar and sonar detection methods following World War II, winning contracts for advanced airborne radar systems and U.S. Navy navigation computing. In 1959, with a series of U.S. military contracts under its belt, Loral went public, offering 250,000 shares at $12 each. It used the proceeds to build and equip a new building at its Bronx, New York headquarters.

Loral's newfound capital allowed it to expand and diversify through acquisitions. In 1959, the company purchased Willor Manufacturing Corp., which made stamped metal parts, and the electronic-equipment leasing arm of Allor Leasing Corp. In 1961, Loral formed a division for developing communications, telemetry and space navigation systems for satellites. It also bought American Beryllium Co., Inc., of Sarasota, Florida, for 95,840 shares of stock. American Beryllium was one of the largest precision machiners of beryllium, a lightweight, toxic material that could withstand harsh environments. Under Loral, American Beryllium became a contract manufacturer of components for aerospace guidance systems and nuclear reactors. In 1961, Loral bought Arco Electronics, and in 1963 acquired A & M Instrument Co., Lerner Plastics and Circle Plastics. To

help pay for this expansion, Loral borrowed $15 million from the Massachusetts Mutual Life Insurance Co. in 1965.

Loral's diversity won it a number of military contracts in the late 1960s. The company won a $3.9-million Navy contract for Doppler navigation radar in 1965, and in 1969, a $14-million contract from General Dynamics for advanced electronics for the Air Force F-111, and a $3.9 million contract for airborne countermeasures for the RF4C plane. By the late-1960s, Loral specialized in radar receivers, which identified the signatures of enemy radar systems on missiles and anti-aircraft guns, separating them from the numerous non-threatening signals also present.

Despite its contract successes, Loral's buying spree was hurting the company by the late 1960s. Loral lost $3 million in 1971, and was not always able to make its loan payments. Many of its acquisitions were unprofitable and unrelated to Loral's primary business, earning Loral the reputation of being a company with good engineers and bad management. Lorenz and Alpert were ready to sell half their interest. Robert Hodes, a Loral director, helped bring in troubleshooter Bernard Schwartz to turn the company around. Schwartz, a former accountant, had helped turn around a packaging materials business run by his brother during the mid-1960s, and in 1968 he became the chief strategist in the diversification of Leasco, a computer leasing company.

Schwartz became president and chief executive officer of Loral in 1972 with a $2 million investment that brought him about 11 percent of the company. Alpert and Lorenz resigned from Loral's board and management. Schwartz reduced costs through measures like reducing security at the firm's South Bronx plant. To make certain he understood what his engineers were doing, Schwartz secretly hired a Columbia University Ph.D. candidate to give him lessons in advanced electronics. To help win and keep talented engineers, he began offering stock options. This move helped bring Frank Lanza, a vice-president of the Dalmo Victor division of Textron, to Loral, where he became executive vice-president and engineering chief.

Schwartz renegotiated the firm's loans and quickly sold many of Loral's money-losing acquisitions, concentrating on getting the firm's government contracts back on schedule and within cost. A important project to design a computerized display system for a Lockheed-built U.S. Navy plane was running behind schedule, so Schwartz flew to California to meet with Lockheed officials. He convinced them that Loral could finish the job, and got their backing for the firm's bid to produce the components. But Schwartz realized that the firm's growth depended on their move from building components to building entire electronic-warfare systems.

By late 1973, with the firm's work back on schedule, Loral began looking for ways to expand its markets. An important early victory was the contract to develop the radar-warning receiver for the U.S. Air Force's F-15 fighter plane. To counter NATO warning receivers, the Soviet Union constantly shifted its radar signals, meaning that NATO planes had to have their receivers taken out and rewired to detect the new signals. Loral proposed a system that used computer tape to reprogram the microcomputers in the warning receivers. This could be done in

20 minutes rather than the days or weeks required for rewiring. Actually putting this system into practice took Loral over four years and required an investment of $2 million beyond the $20 million invested by the U.S. government. Loral's system proved successful, and by 1980 had resulted in $400 million in orders.

Electronic warfare gear had been low on lists of defense priorities, but the 1973 Yom Kippur war changed that. Egypt used Soviet radar-guided weapons to shoot down 100 Israeli planes in one week. Israel's American-made fighters did not have the equipment to detect and jam the radar frequencies used by the missiles, which caused NATO countries to increase electronic warfare spending 600 percent over the next seven years. In 1974, Loral began buying again, purchasing Conic, a maker of missile-tracking systems and microwave communications equipment, for $4.5 million. The purchase of Conic, which had profits of $1.1 million in 1973, allowed Loral to lessen its dependence on government contracts.

Another successful mid-1970s deal was a $4.8 million contract with the Belgian air force for an integrated radar system. Loral had no international experience and had never built the tracking and jamming equipment required for an integrated system. Since no single company built all these components, Loral decided to go after the contract, though it faced competition from bigger firms like ITT and Sanders Associates. To increase Loral's chances of winning the contract, Schwartz signed an agreement with MBLE, one of Belgium's biggest electronics houses, that arranged for MBLE to produce part of the system if Loral won the contract. It did. The victory simultaneously made Loral a full supplier of electronic warfare gear and put it on the map of NATO weapons suppliers.

The Belgian radar system had such tight deadlines that Loral actually lost money on the deal, but Loral executives were confident that Belgium would later expand the contract. It did so in 1979, bringing Loral a further $75 million. Other countries soon expressed interest in buying the system. In the late 1970s, Loral sold electronic surveillance systems worth about $200 million to Canada, Britain and West Germany. In each case Loral agreed to share the production with companies in the customer countries to help seal the contract.

In 1979, Loral acquired Frequency Sources Inc. through a stock trade. Frequency made smaller components for electronic warfare and telecommunications systems, and had about $27 million in sales. By the end of the decade, Loral was the largest electronic warfare company in the United States. Loral's successes lead to a significant rise in the price of its stock. As a result, the firm was able to raise $58 million in a January 1980 stock offering. The money was used to make acquisitions and pay for a new $25 million electronics headquarters in Yonkers, New York, intended to help the firm attract talented engineers.

The electronic warfare market continued to grow during the 1980s, fueled by a defense buildup during the Reagan administration, and the Falklands War, during which a $200,000 missile severely damaged a $50 million battle cruiser. Loral made equipment for virtually every electronic warfare system in the U.S. military, including new airborne warning systems. Even so, Loral became the number two electronic warfare company when Dallas-based E-Systems surpassed Loral's $197 million

in electronic warfare sales, though Loral remained far more profitable. It had total sales of $255 million in 1981, with profits of $24 million, and an order backlog of $346 million. The reprogrammable radar receiver for the F-15 had become its biggest program, with 750 sets delivered by 1982, and the likelihood of at least 250 more. The integrated system originally designed for Belgium had been bought by Israel as well. The U.S. government had passed over it, however, in favor of a non-integrated system developed by ITT, Westinghouse, and Itek.

Loral did well partly because it put so much of its resources into improving products before customers were even ready for the improvements, thus meeting or exceeding reliability requirements. It also brought projects in on schedule and without cost overruns by identifying potential problems early on, before they had a chance to mushroom. Because problems usually came from subcontractors, Loral frequently sent personnel to subcontractors to check up on their operations.

Loral's non-defense businesses were also doing well in the 1980s. Its $15 million plastic packaging business was as profitable as its electronic warfare unit, and its $30 million telecommunications business was growing again by 1982 after two slow years. Nevertheless, defense was the firm's major priority, and in 1986 it sold the packaging division to its president while trying to purchase Sanders Associates, which was for sale. Lockheed's bid of $1.18 billion beat out Loral's $980 million offer, but Loral made a major acquisition the following year when it bought Goodyear Aerospace Corp. from Goodyear Tire & Rubber for $588 million. Loral and Goodyear Aerospace already supplied electronics for some of the same military hardware, so integration was expected to be fairly easy.

In 1989, Loral bought the electro-optic division of Honeywell for $58 million. The division, which specialized in guidance systems, had been for sale for a number of years, and many industry analysts felt that Loral had gotten a good price, given the division's annual sales of $130 million. The same year Loral sold the aircraft braking and engineered fabrics divisions of Goodyear Aerospace for $455 million. The buyer was a group headed by Schwartz and included Manufacturers Hannover and Shearson Lehman. The deal raised a few eyebrows and lead to a number of lawsuits, though few felt the price was unfair.

Loral's experience with guidance systems helped it become a leader in flight simulation and training, and in 1989 it won a Special Operations Force training and rehearsal contract worth up to $2 billion over the next 15 years. Loral also won a major contract to supply U.S. Air Force F-16 fighters with radar warning systems in 1989. However, after a complaint from competitor Litton Industries, the U.S. General Accounting Office found that Loral had improperly acquired information on Litton's system. Loral pleaded guilty to three charges and the government awarded a bigger share of the contract to Litton. As a result, Loral took a $10.5 million charge against earnings. Still, profits reached $87.6 million in 1989 on sales of $1.187 billion.

In 1990, with the Cold War over and analysts predicting that defense expenditures would decrease dramatically, many defense companies began downsizing and selling defense-related divisions. Loral, however, felt that regional and ethnic conflicts would replace the superpower standoff. It therefore maintained its commitment to defense, and looked for bargains offered by other corporations.

In July 1990, Loral bought 51.5 percent of Ford Aerospace for $715 million, virtually doubling the size of Loral. Ford Aerospace had $1.8 billion in sales and $120 million in profits in 1989. Its primary focus was the building of commercial and military satellites, an area where Loral had only been a supplier of components and subsystems. The purchase strained Loral's finances, and it quickly sold off parts of the company, recouping about 40 percent of the purchase price.

Some industry observers considered Loral's refusal to downsize risky. The showdown leading to the Persian Gulf war began a few months later, however, and electronic warfare played an important role during the hostilities. In fact, the Tomahawk missiles used in the initial attack on Iraq used Loral computer guidance systems. The missiles received much praise for their accuracy during the war, though post-war analysis muddied the picture somewhat.

In 1991, Loral sold 49 percent of Space Systems/Loral to three European aeronautics firms for $182 million. In 1992, the firm bought 90 percent of LTV's aerospace and missile division for $261 million. Loral won a $202 million contract to supply the U.S. Army with a new anti-tank missile, a $71 million Air Force contract for REACT missiles launch control centers, and a $141 million contract to maintain tethered aerostar radar systems for the Air Force. Loral also worked on its civilian businesses, forming a mobile phone services company called Loral Qualcomm Satellite Services with Qualcomm.

As the mid-1990s approached, Loral was an increasingly strong defense company, though it was trying to diversify into civilian telecommunications markets. It also was working on medical diagnostic imaging and computer-related information management. It was in the process of finishing a three-year layoff of 5,800 employees that further cut costs, resulting in $49 million in severance payments.

Principal Subsidiaries: Loral Electro-Optical Systems; Loral American Beryllium; Loral Conic; Loral International; Loral Randtron Systems; Loral Rolm Mil-Spec Computers; Loral Space Information Systems; Loral Systems Company; Loral Systems Manufacturing Company; Space Systems/Loral.

Further Reading:

Alster, Norm, "Thank You, Saddam," *Forbes,* October 15, 1990.
Chakravarty, Subrata, "Concept Reborn," *Forbes,* June 21, 1982.
Kraar, Louis, "The Brooklyn Boy Who Debugged Loral," *Fortune,* June 16, 1980.

—Scott M. Lewis

Manpower, Inc.

5301 N. Ironwood Road
Post Office Box 2053
Milwaukee, Wisconsin 53201
U.S.A.
(414) 961-1000
Fax: (414) 961-2124

Public Company
Incorporated: 1948
Employees: 6,000 (plus nearly one million temporary
    workers per year)
Sales: $4.125 billion
Stock Exchanges: New York
SICs: 7363 Help Supply Services

Manpower, Inc. is the largest provider of temporary employees
in the world. While they place workers in a variety of fields, the
company's primary achievement has been its placement of
office workers. Their success in this area is due to economic
conditions in the United States and Europe which have been
favorable to the temporary industry, as well as Manpower's
elaborate programs designed to train workers on word processors and other automated office equipment.

Manpower was begun in 1948 by Elmer L. Winter and Aaron
Scheinfeld, two partners in a Milwaukee law firm who saw the
labor shortage that followed World War II as an opportunity to
form a temporary agency. A year earlier, Kelly Services, Inc.,
which would become the second biggest temporary agency, had
formed in Detroit. By 1956, Manpower's reputation was established enough that franchising the company name became profitable. In order to set up a Manpower franchise, an investor
pays an initial fee, attends a training course, and then sets up an
office. The franchisee is responsible for recruiting and placement, as well as paying a percentage of gross earnings to Manpower, while the company provides promotion and management guidance.

Under its founders' charge, Manpower expanded during the
1960s, establishing franchises all over the world, most prominently in Europe, but also in South America, Africa, and Asia.
In 1965, Mitchell S. Fromstein, whose small advertising agency
had been handling the Manpower account, joined its board of
directors. Fromstein's role in the company's development grew
as the company grew. Its acquisitions in the 1970s included

Nationwide Income Tax Service, Detroit; Gilbert Lane Personnel, Inc. of Hartford, Connecticut; and Manpower Southampton
Ltd., which had been one of its franchises. None of these
companies are currently owned by Manpower.

In 1976, the Parker Pen Co. acquired Manpower for $28.2
million. Like Manpower, Parker was a well-known, family-
owned business that had begun in Wisconsin. Where Manpower
had enjoyed a meteoric rise in the 1950s and 1960s, however,
Parker's sales began faltering in the late 1970s due to its failure
to compete with inexpensive writing implements in the marketplace. With Scheinfeld dead and Winter eager to pursue other
personal interests, a buyout of all stock was initiated by
Fromstein and Parker President George S. Parker. Fromstein
bought 20 percent of Manpower's stock and moved up to the
position of president and chief executive.

When Manpower began, it initially concentrated its efforts on
industrial help. Fromstein made changes in this and many other
respects. Practicing a managerial style he says he learned from
Vince Lombardi, the legendary coach of football's Green Bay
Packers, for whom he once wrote speeches, Fromstein is considered responsible for virtually all of the growth and development that Manpower underwent in the 1980s. His innovative
approach to the temporary industry included shifting emphasis
from the factory to the office, recognizing that automated equipment was revolutionizing the way offices operated, and revising
the company's Employment Outlook Survey. The survey, initiated in 1962 to measure the hiring intentions of employers and
published quarterly, was revised with the assistance of the
Survey Research Center of the University of Michigan. Understanding of and sensitivity to its clients needs have become
hallmarks of Manpower under the guidance of Fromstein.

Above all, it has been Fromstein's commitment to take responsibility for training temporary employees, rather than merely
finding places for them to work, which accounts for Manpower's dominance in the industry. In his *Alternative Staffing
Strategies,* David Nye writes, ''Manpower is by no means the
only [temporary] firm involved in training and testing, but its
approach is clearly the most extensive.''

In 1978, when the prospect of a computer that would fit inside
an office, let alone on top of a desk, seemed preposterous,
Fromstein announced that Manpower would invest $15 million
in a computer training program called Skillware. Nye quotes
Fromstein: ''The days when a secretary walking into a new
office could just flip the 'on' button, roll in a fresh sheet of
letterhead, and go are gone.'' An interactive, self-paced program, Skillware enables Manpower employees to develop competence in a variety of tasks. This approach makes temporary
employees more valuable to companies because they require
less on-site training and make a greater contribution to productivity in a shorter time. Since its inception, Skillware has expanded tremendously, and is available for 160 software programs and in nine languages.

The complexion of the job market in the United States and
abroad contributed greatly to the ascendancy of the temporary
industry in the 1980s. Because the cost of providing benefits
rose faster than the cost of providing wages, employers began to
see that, even considering the percentage that had to be paid to

the temporary agency, hiring on a temporary basis was more economical than searching for, hiring, and training permanent workers. It also proved to be an effective way of testing potential permanent workers. Furthermore, the increase in dual-income families increased the appeal of temporary work to parents faced with the high cost of day care. The Bureau of Labor Statistics reported that temporary jobs accounted for one percent of the work force in 1989, doubling the 1980 statistic. Under Fromstein, Manpower was positioned to capitalize on the situation more effectively than were its closest competitors, Kelly and Olsten Corp. Total sales were at $300 million in 1976, the year he joined; by 1991 they reached $3.5 billion.

Manpower's rapid growth meant that it was drastically outpacing the pen sales at Parker. For a time, its profits made up for the pen company's losses, but by February 1986 the unbalance had become too great, despite Parker's efforts at reducing its work force and cutting back on the varieties of pens manufactured. The writing instruments division was sold to a group of investors for $100 million, and Manpower became the name of the parent company.

In 1987, Manpower engaged in an important affiliation with the International Business Machines Corporation (IBM). Under the agreement between the two companies, Manpower would provide on-site training and support services (such as a hotline for computer questions) to buyers of IBM systems. IBM benefitted from having its users more fully acquainted with its systems, and Manpower benefitted from the awareness among these users that its temporary workers are computer literate.

In the same year, Manpower was the target of a hostile takeover in what turned out to be a tangled and complex affair. In August, Antony Berry's Blue Arrow PLC, a British employment-services firm with revenues only one-sixth the size of Manpower's, offered to buy Manpower at $75 per share, for a total of $1.21 billion. Berry, well known in England from his days as a boxer, had terrific success with Blue Arrow since joining them in 1984, taking them from £410 thousand ($725 thousand) in profits to £30 million ($55 million). Manpower stock had been at $62.375 at the time of the offer, but excitement over the bid drove the price up to $78, thereby outrunning the $75 offered by Blue Arrow. In the weeks that followed, Fromstein and Manpower contemplated a return bid on Blue Arrow, considered a joint venture with the Swiss employment firm Adia S.A., threatened to refuse Blue Arrow unless they increased their bid to $90 per share, and publicly denounced Berry's plans for combining the companies, which included implementing an executive search program. This last suggestion infuriated Fromstein, who told the *Wall Street Journal,* "We aren't blind or deaf. If we thought it was an opportunity, we could have done it years ago." Manpower rejected the bid, prompting a shareholder lawsuit on charges that the directors' decision was financially irresponsible.

Three weeks after the initial offer was made, Manpower finally endorsed the Blue Arrow offer at $82.50 per share for a total of $1.3 billion. Under the terms of the sale, Manpower's operations in the United States would continue under the name "Manpower." Fromstein was allowed to stay on as Manpower President and CEO and one of a five-member Blue Arrow board, though by December of 1987, he was fired from this position after a long simmering conflict with Berry became apparent.

Fromstein's separation from Manpower, however, was not long-lasting. In spite of his early successes, Berry proved to be an inept manager. His enthusiasm for sports led Blue Arrow into an expensive and unauthorized investment in a yacht for the America's Cup competition. The stock market crash of October 1987 brought Berry's most substantial impropriety to light. In order to create the funds necessary to purchase Manpower, Berry had secured a loan of $1.3 billion from the National Westminster Bank (NatWest) in England to be repaid from the proceeds of a stock issue. With the bank as underwriters, 38 percent of the shares were purchased by existing Blue Arrow shareholders, leaving the bank the responsibility of selling the rest. According to an article in *Financial World,* potential buyers might have been scared away had they learned of this situation, so NatWest itself purchased 12 percent in order to boost the amount of sold shares to 50 percent, a more respectable figure. Such a purchase was legal, but the underwriters kept it a secret, and once revealed, this was construed as a deliberate attempt to mislead potential investors. A criminal investigation was launched, and by January 1989, top executives at the bank—most notably its chairman, Lord Boardman—were forced to resign and Berry was disgraced on account of his role in the deal and other financial improprieties.

Backed by Manpower's U.S. franchises, Fromstein mounted a successful campaign to regain control of Blue Arrow. Once back at the helm, his first three decisions were to change the name of Blue Arrow to Manpower, sell all businesses that had belonged to Blue Arrow, and to move the company's headquarters back to Milwaukee.

Most Blue Arrow businesses were sold in 1990 and 1991 and the company became a U.S. corporation in 1991. As Manpower entered the 1990s, its major objectives were to continue its policy of staying current with technological advances in the work place, and to further international expansion into previously inaccessible regions, most notably Eastern Europe.

Further Reading:

Berss, Marcia, "You Can Go Home Again," *Forbes,* October 1990.
"Case Study: Blue Arrow PLC and Manpower, Inc.," *Buyouts & Acquisitions,* November/December 1987.
Gilbert, Nick, "Manpower Comes Home," *Financial World,* April 30, 1991.
Jensen, Dave, "Temp and Team Spirit," *Management Review,* October 1988.
Kapp, Sue, "Titan of Service," *Business Marketing,* November 1991.
"Market Outruns Offer by Blue Arrow," *The Wall Street Journal,* August 5, 1987.
Nye, David, *Alternative Staffing Strategies,* Washington, DC: Bureau of National Affairs, 1988.
Walbert, Laura R., "Menpower versus Penpower," *Forbes,* December 19, 1983.
"Winter's Tale," *Finance,* September 1969.

—Mark Swartz

Marion Merrell Dow, Inc.

9300 Ward Parkway
Kansas City, Missouri 64114-0480
U.S.A.
(816) 966-4000
Fax: (816) 966-4001

Public Company
Incorporated: 1964 as Marion Laboratories, Inc.
Employees: 9,808
Sales: $3.32 billion
Stock Exchanges: New York
SICs: 2834 Pharmaceutical Preparations

Marion Merrell Dow is the product of a 1989 merger between Marion Laboratories, once a prosperous pharmaceutical company, and the Merrell Dow pharmaceuticals division of the Dow Chemical Company. At the time of the merger, analysts' expectations of the new company were low, as the patents on Marion's most profitable drugs were nearing expiration, and no new medicines were under development. Despite Marion Laboratories' refusal to allocate the funds necessary to develop new drugs, the company retained its position in the drug industry after the merger, bolstered by Merrell Dow's introduction of several new products to its line.

Marion Laboratories, Inc. was founded by Erwing Marion Kauffman. After serving as an officer in the U.S. Navy during World War II, Kauffman took a job on the sales staff of a pharmaceutical company in Decatur, Illinois. Energetic and aggressive, Kauffman flourished. Within a year his commissions made him the highest paid employee of the company, including the company's president. When the company reduced the size of his territory and trimmed his commissions, Kauffman resigned, starting his own company in 1950 with $4,000 in capital.

Kauffman decided to focus on the manufacture of a calcium supplement made from crushed oyster shells. To keep overhead costs down, he established the business in the basement of his house; during the day he produced and packaged the product and made sales calls, while in the evenings he typed orders and package labels. As his company grew steadily, Kauffman moved the business outside of his home and added a staff of employees, whom he offered both share options and a profit sharing plan. During the 1950s the plan purchased shares in the company, and as the company eventually achieved 40 percent of the $100 million a year market, four Marion employees were able to retire with a net worth of more than $1 million.

Kauffman's company was incorporated as Marion Laboratories, Inc. in 1964, and that year it saw profits of $130,000. During its first decade the new company actively pursued a policy of acquisitions; the fruits of diversification eventually accounted for 40 percent of the company's sales. During this time, the cost of researching and developing new drugs was prohibitive, and, rather than increase its debt load, Marion Laboratories opted to avoid developing original products entirely, saving millions of dollars on product research. Instead, Kauffman sought to establish a niche in the marketplace through existing products. In 1974 the company's research budget stood at zero, and $1.8 million was spent on reformulating and developing products discovered but rejected by other companies. By 1974 earnings on sales were $12 million, and the company enjoyed a 36 percent return on equity.

In 1978 Marion Laboratories established its consumer products division, which introduced Gaviscon, an over-the-counter antacid. Marketed in chewable tablet form, the product provided for the temporary relief of heartburn. It was immediately successful, and accounted for six percent of the company's net sales in 1986.

The company maintained its focus on drugs for the treatment of ailments related to calcium intake. Cardizem, which garnered the largest percentage of net sales—47 percent in 1986—slowed calcium buildup, preventing the artery muscles from being blocked by calcium deposits. Used in the treatment of stable and unstable angina, Cardizem gained the approval of the Food and Drug Administration, which allowed Marion to release Cardizem in tablet form. Competition increased as similar compounds were submitted to the FDA for approval by other companies in the latter part of 1986.

Marion's ulcer drug, Carafate, gained FDA approval in 1982. Providing a new way to treat stomach ulcers, Carafate formed a protective barrier preventing further damage to mucosal tissues, which block the diffusion of gastric acid and pepsin in ulcer craters. The drug posed no threat to healthy tissue where proteins were bound.

Both Carafate and Cardizem originated from research conducted by the Japanese company Tanabe Seiyaku, and Marion paid licensing fees to Tanabe. The mutual interests of both companies grew, and in 1984 they entered into a joint venture to manufacture and market Tanabe products in the United States and Canada.

During the early 1980s, Marion Laboratories marketed: Sivadone, a cream used to prevent infections in cases of second and third degree burns; Ditropan tablets and syrup, a urological agent that treated certain bladder conditions; Nito-Bid Capsules and Ointment, which managed angina pectoris or chest pain caused by insufficient blood flow to the heart; Ard and Bac-T-Screen, which facilitated the identification of bacteria in the blood stream that could cause infection in patients using antibiotics; and Culturette, a disposable, ten-minute culture transport system used by hospitals and clinics to diagnose Group A streptococci. Another product, ToxiLab, a broad spectrum drug detection system, gained popularity as concern about drug abuse in the workplace increased.

In December 1988, Marion Laboratories sold off its Analytical Systems division and purchased the American Biomaterials Corporation, a manufacturer of dextranomer-based wound treatments. In an effort to regain its focus on pharmaceuticals, Marion Laboratories sold its Scientific Products division in April 1989. And then, to strengthen its drug development capabilities, the company purchased a minority interest in U.S. Bioscience.

In July 1989 the company was informed that Merrell Dow, the pharmaceutical division of Dow Chemical, was interested in merging its operations with Marion Laboratories. Merrell Dow had hoped to acquire Marion as early as 1985, but was unable to afford it. Therefore, Merrell Dow offered to purchase a 67 percent stake of Marion.

Marion, with its strong sales network, appeared to be the perfect match for Merrell Dow, which had a strong research and development organization but a weak position in the pharmaceuticals industry. In addition, Merrell Dow's Seldane antihistamine, Lorelco anti-cholesterol drug, Nicorette anti-smoking gum, and Cepacol mouthwash added strength to Marion's flagging product line.

Marion Merrell Dow shares were buoyed by the persistent rumor that Dow was ready to buy up the 30 percent of the company that it did not own. While this never happened, Merrell Dow retired debt from its acquisition of Marion, further bolstering the shares' value.

The new company announced plans for several new drugs, including Perfan, for treatment of congestive heart failure, Targocid antibiotic, and Sabril, an anti-epilepsy treatment. In addition, Marion Merrell Dow introduced Nicoderm, a nicotine skin patch designed to relieve smokers' urge for cigarettes.

None of these, however, was as profitable as Cardizem and Carafate.

In order to further improve its new product development, Marion Merrell Dow acquired a stake in Gensia Pharmaceuticals, which was developing angina treatments. It also licensed five allergy medicines from Immulogic Pharmaceuticals and took over the Canadian Nordic Laboratories and German Henning Berlin company. The company's effort to extend its product line received a boost in 1992, when Cardizem was approved for treatment of angina, as well as hypertension.

After four years as Marion Merrell Dow, the company witnessed a drop in annual growth from 20 percent to less than ten percent. Moreover, the company was forced to abandon Marion's unique position in the industry as primarily a marketer of drugs. In the early 1990s, analysts questioned whether Marion Merrell Dow will be able to convert the synergies of its predecessor companies into a more dynamic and competitive organization.

Principal Subsidiaries: Marion & Company; Marisub, Inc.; Marisub II, Inc.; Merrell Dow Pharmaceuticals, Inc.; Nordic Laboratories, Inc. (Canada).

Further Reading:

"It's a Wedding for Dow and Marion," *Chemical Week,* July 26, 1989, p. 14.
"Marion Laboratories Chronology," Company Document.
"Marion Merrell Dow Chronology," Company Document.
"Marion, Merrell Dow to Merge," *Journal of Commerce,* December 4, 1989, p. A7.
"Marion Merrell Is Forced to Look Beyond Its Standbys," *Wall Street Journal,* November 24, 1992, p. B4.
"Overdose of Pessimism," *Barron's,* December 9, 1991, pp. 12–13.

—updated by John Simley

℘ MARY KAY

Mary Kay Corporation

8787 Stemmons Fwy.
Dallas, Texas
U.S.A.
(214) 630-8787
Fax: (214) 905-5721

Private Company
Incorporated: 1963
Employees: 1,700
Retail Sales: $1.2 billion
SICs: 6719 Holding Companies, Nec; 2844 Perfumes,
   Cosmetics & Other Toilet Preparations

One of the largest cosmetics companies in the United States, Mary Kay Cosmetics, Inc., specializes in the manufacture and direct sale of more than 200 products, including skin creams, cosmetics, and other personal care items. Its direct sales force consists primarily of women who sell full- or part-time through home demonstrations. Mary Kay Corporation is the holding company for the cosmetics firm.

Mary Kay Ash founded the company that bears her name in 1963, after 25 years of direct selling for other companies, beginning in the late 1930s. A direct sales career allowed her the flexibility she needed as a single mother raising three children.

For many years Mary Kay was a sales representative for Stanley Home Products, presenting "home shows" at the residences of customers. She operated as an independent contractor who purchased merchandise from Stanley and then sold it herself. After a slow first year, the next year she had become "sales queen."

She recruited other women as salespeople since Stanley paid a small commission to the recruiter for the sales of each person recruited. She had eventually signed 150 women and received a small percentage of the sales of each. When Stanley insisted that she move to Dallas to develop its market, but would not pay her any commissions for the sales of the women she had recruited in the Houston area, she reluctantly made the move, but in 1959 Mary Kay left Stanley. Soon afterward, she became a representative for World Gift Company, where she quickly became its national training director. After a disagreement with World Gift, she resigned in 1963.

With no full-time occupation, Mary Kay Ash decided to write a book about direct sales, but it became a book on managing people. She began to think about what a "dream company" might look like, and the book waited 20 years to be written and published. She wrote in *Mary Kay on People Management* that her main objectives became to build an organization where the Golden Rule was the guiding philosophy and to "establish a company that would give unlimited opportunity to women." She also said she based her company on three fundamental principles: God first, family second, and career third.

Mary Kay decided on a direct sales company since that was the area with which she was familiar; direct sales would also be appealing to women who could sell part-time and follow a flexible schedule. After deciding on structure, she chose as a product a line of skin care products she had been using for more than a decade.

She had been introduced to the skin care products while she was selling Stanley products at a home party. The hostess, a cosmetologist, was testing these products on her friends. This woman had developed the products from a leather tanning solution her father had formulated, after he noticed how young his hands looked from using the solution every day. Although the cosmetologist marketed the products to her friends, she did not achieve great success in sales. After her death in 1961, Mary Kay bought the formula from the woman's daughter.

Mary Kay and her husband invested their life savings of $5,000 to rent a small office and manufacture an initial inventory of skin care products. They also recruited nine independent sales representatives.

Only a month before the company was to open for business, Mary Kay's husband died, but Mary Kay decided to proceed with the opening. Her 20-year-old son Richard Rogers quit his job and for $250 a month ran the financial and administrative operations. His qualifications consisted of two college marketing courses and his experience as a sales representative for a life insurance company. Within the year, Mary Kay's son Ben moved his family to Dallas, took a pay cut, and went to work for the family company. Daughter Marylyn joined the company later, becoming the first Mary Kay Director in Houston.

Beauty by Mary Kay opened on Friday, September 13, 1963. The products were manufactured by a Dallas company and sold through a network of salespeople, who were called "beauty consultants" and were required to purchase an initial "Beauty Showcase" kit. The beauty consultants were trained on scheduling and conducting Mary Kay parties, or "skin care classes," in private homes. Beauty consultants purchased Mary Kay products at 50 percent below retail and resold them. They also received commissions for sales of salespeople they recruited.

The company tried to differentiate itself from a company that used illegal pyramiding. Unlike pyramid operations, Mary Kay sold its products to all of its consultants for the same 50 percent discount. It also took recruiter bonuses out of company earnings, not out of each sales recruit's earnings.

The company also developed specific guidelines for its salespeople. Emphasis at home parties was on teaching, rather than selling, and the number of guests was held to no more than six.

Delivery and payment on the spot were required, and beauty consultants could not purchase from the company on credit. Mary Kay also limited its product line so that salespeople would be knowledgeable about each product.

Unlike many companies, Mary Kay did not limit sales territories. Beauty consultants could recruit other consultants from anywhere in the world. She also initiated an incentive program which included the use of a pink Cadillac. This famous prize was established in 1967 when a pink Cadillac was awarded to the top sales director. The year after that, five Cadillacs were awarded and the next year, ten. By 1970, the company was awarding 20 Cadillacs. Later, rather than awarding them on a top-seller basis, they were awarded to any sales director reaching a pre-set sales level. By 1993, 6,500 consultants were driving pink Cadillacs or other complimentary cars.

Annual conventions were held to recognize achievement, a practice which quickly became an important public relations event. Among other programs, the conventions featured workshops for husbands of Mary Kay consultants on how to be supportive of their wives' Mary Kay careers.

In the first full year of operation, sales totaled $198,514 and the company had 318 consultants. Soon, more office space was needed and Mary Kay moved to a three-office headquarters with a training room and warehouse space for a total of 5,000 square feet. Within two years, Mary Kay had about 850 beauty consultants selling its beauty products.

After that year, Mary Kay considered franchising to reach a wider market but decided against it because many women would have to turn to men for financing, which would reduce the level of independence which the company had tried to facilitate. Instead, in 1967, the company went public and used the proceeds from the stock to fund its expansion. Mary Kay Cosmetics was the first company on the New York Stock Exchange chaired by a woman.

For the next decade and a half, sales grew at an average of 28 percent per year. However, between 1974 and 1978 sales slowed. To revive them, the company increased compensation rates for consultants. Sales rates once again rose and ranged from 29 percent to 82 percent growth for the next four years.

As sales grew, so did the company's need for space, so in 1969, a new 275,000-square-foot manufacturing facility was built in Dallas. A few years later, four regional distribution centers were constructed and in 1977 a new eight-story headquarters building opened in Dallas. In 1993, the Mary Kay manufacturing facility was the size of three football fields. It also became an FDA-registered drug manufacturing facility, allowing the company to manufacture and distribute over-the-counter drugs such as sunscreen and acne treatment products.

The 1980s brought a reduction of growth as employment opportunities for women grew and more entered the full-time workforce. Between 1983 and 1985, Mary Kay's contingent of sales consultants was cut in half to 100,000. Sales fell from $323 million to $260 million. Fewer women were available to sell the products and fewer were home to buy them.

Mary Kay stock value dropped significantly because of investors' worries about dropping profits. Concerned about how new product introduction and incentive programs were being affected by quarterly disclosure of financial information, Mary Kay and son Richard, Mary Kay's president, decided to take the company private again and bought back all outstanding stock for $315 million. The buyout proved troublesome for Mary Kay because the Internal Revenue Service claimed that for 1983, 1984, and 1985, Mary Kay owed back taxes since the notes that were issued during the buyout should have been considered equity. Mary Kay contended that its interest payment deductions were proper. The matter was settled in 1991 when Mary Kay Corporation paid the IRS $3 million.

In 1989, Mary Kay tried to take over its largest rival, Avon Products, but was unsuccessful. Mary Kay Corporation then joined forces with other investors to form Chartwell Associates, and this group purchased a 19.8 percent share of Avon. The group also controlled two seats on the Avon board. However, Avon blocked the Chartwell coalition from purchasing more stock. Mary Kay announced it was withdrawing from the association in early 1991. However, shortly after that, Chartwell sold most of its shares, leaving Mary Kay and another associate with a 3 percent share of rival Avon.

Despite tax and acquisition troubles, sales started to rise and climbed to $280 million a year after the company became private again. Mary Kay Ash became chairwoman emeritus of Mary Kay Cosmetics in 1987, and Richard became chairman.

The sales force also grew, boasting 220,000 in 1991, an increase largely due to the inducements of larger commissions and bonuses. More consultants, however, were part-timers. Nearly 70 percent of the consultants had other jobs, while prior to the buyout, only 33 percent of the sales force held other jobs.

Mary Kay Cosmetics was included in both the 1984 and 1993 editions of *The 100 Best Companies to Work for in America*. In 1993, Mary Kay also became a Fortune 500 company. The company surpassed $1 billion in retail sales in 1992, distributing more than 200 products through a sales force of more than 250,000 consultants in nineteen countries.

By 1993, the company had more than 300,000 sales people in the United States and abroad selling to nearly 20 million customers. More than half its national sales directors had earned more than $1 million during their Mary Kay careers, and the company was awarding nearly $38 million in prizes every year.

Mary Kay has also responded to growing pressure to improve its environmental practices. In 1989 it was the target of Berke Breathed's satirical "Bloom County" comic strip for testing its products on animals. The company stopped this practice later that year, and it also instituted a company-wide recycling program, having recycled 11 million pounds of material by mid-1993.

The cosmetics market was highly competitive going into the 1990s, and industry growth was expected to hover only around the rate of inflation. Mary Kay Cosmetics, however, was looking to the overseas market for its greatest growth. It had been steadily adding foreign subsidiaries since 1971 when it opened its first international subsidiary in Australia. Mary Kay opened subsidiaries in Canada in 1978, Argentina in 1980, Germany in 1986, Mexico and Thailand in 1988, Taiwan in 1991, and Spain in 1992.

Beauty consultants in many international markets distributed products made in the United States; however, some Mary Kay products were produced in foreign countries for sale in those countries. Some foreign governments required that products be manufactured locally, while in other countries the duties on imports were so high that only local production would make the products affordable. However, samples of all products were sent to the United States for testing.

By 1993, Mary Kay Cosmetics also had representatives in Bermuda, Brunei, Chile, Guatemala, Malaysia, New Zealand, Nor-way, Singapore, Sweden, and Uruguay. The company was considering foreign expansion options, including acquiring a manufacturing plant in Europe.

Further Reading:

Ash, Mary Kay, *Mary Kay,* New York: Harper & Row, 1981, 1987.
——, *Mary Kay on People Management,* New York: Warner Books, 1984.
Byron, Christopher, "Garbage Time," *New York,* April 1, 1991, pp. 16–17.
Farnham, Alan, "Mary Kay's Lessons in Leadership," *Fortune,* September 20, 1993.
Hattwick, Richard E. "Mary Kay Ash," *Journal of Behavioral Economics,* Winter 1987, pp. 61–69.

—Wendy J. Stein

MasterCard International, Inc.

888 7th Avenue
New York, New York 10106
U.S.A.
(212) 649-4600
Fax: (212) 649-5043

Private Company
Incorporated: 1966
Billings: $200 billion
SICs: 6153 Payment Cards, Travelers Cheques, and Travel
Vouchers; 7323 Credit Reporting Services

MasterCard is one of the major credit cards used regularly by
people in the United States, second only in name recognition
and worldwide billings to Visa. By marketing itself to ordinary
men and women, in contrast to Visa's efforts to capture an
upper-income clientele, MasterCard is slowly chipping away at
Visa's market share in both the United States and other areas
around the globe.

In 1951, the Franklin National Bank (presently European American Bank) issued the first modern credit card, which was
accepted by local merchants. Within a short period of time over
100 additional banks started issuing cards. Cardholders paid
their bills upon receipt, and no fee or interest was charged.
Merchants were charged a fee by the issuing bank for any
transaction made on the card. Because these cards could only be
used within a limited geographical region, customer volume
was low and the banks' profits minimal.

The Bank of America, based in California, introduced Bank-
Americard (later Visa) in 1958, and soon developed an extensive network of licensee banks throughout the United States by
licensing a single bank as its local affiliate in each major
metropolitan area. Each of the licensee banks assumed the responsibility for enrolling cardmembers in their particular geographical area, as well as for reaching agreements with merchants to accept the card as payment for merchandise or
services.

At approximately the same time, a group of American bankers
who were not part of the BankAmericard association decided to
organize their own network and accept one another's credit
cards. On August 16, 1966, these bankers formed the Interbank
Card Association (ICA) to organize, manage and oversee the
functions associated with credit card payments, including authorization, clearing and settlement. ICA was the umbrella
organization for Master Charge, whose name was later changed
to MasterCard. In order to identify both merchants and Interbank Card Association members, the symbol "i" was created
and placed on cards and at purchasing locations.

ICA was unlike BankAmericard in that the association was not
dominated by one bank but rather governed by consensus
among its member banks. Committees supported by an extensive staff were set up to operate and supervise the activities of
the association. Besides establishing guidelines for card authorization, clearing and settlement, the Interbank Card Association assumed responsibility for marketing the card, in addition
to providing security and legal representation to protect the
association's trademark. ICA wasted no time in entering the
international market by forming close ties to Banco Nacional de
Mexico (Banamex) in Mexico in 1968, and with Eurocard
International in continental Europe. During the same year, ICA
added the first Japanese members to the association.

In 1973, ICA developed INAS, a centralized computer network
designed to electronically link the acquiring member or merchant to the issuing member or financial institution. This computer network provided the issuer and merchant with the ability
to communicate quickly and directly, and replaced the time-
consuming telephone exchanges once required for authorizations. In 1974, ICA made the magnetic strip an international
standard on all its cards in order to hasten authorization and
reduce fraud. In 1975, a system called INET was introduced to
provide an electronic exchange of transactions among its members, thus reducing the necessity of actually mailing charge slips
by automating the entire transaction process. In 1979, ICA
changed both the name and trademark of Master Charge to
MasterCard in order to reflect the broadening of the association's services beyond the charge card itself. During the mid
and late 1970s, Access Ltd. from the United Kingdom, Standard
Chartered Bank of South Africa, and the first Australian member became part of the association.

All this apparent success notwithstanding, MasterCard's
billings and number of cardholders began to decline with respect to another charge card system, Visa. The board of directors at ICA, dissatisfied with MasterCard's performance, pres-
sured the president, John J. Reynolds, to implement some
changes they believed were long overdue. But Reynolds response was viewed by many board members as less than
satisfactory, and he was asked to resign his position.

In February of 1980 the ICA board of directors appointed
Russell E. Hogg, a former executive at Macmillan Inc. with
extensive experience at American Express Company's Card
Division, as the new president. Taking his cue from the board of
directors, Hogg immediately instituted sweeping changes
within Interbank: he redrew the company's organization chart
and created horizontal reporting lines, thereby encouraging
communication among employees and eliminating the long-
standing classic hierarchical structure to which Reynolds had
adhered; he relocated several of the company's support divisions to St. Louis and placed them under new supervision; he
completely eliminated all jobs dealing with increasing U.S.
members since Hogg believed that the domestic credit card

market was saturated; and he summarily fired eight of the highest level officers in the company.

Even with these changes, Hogg faced an uphill climb in his efforts to turn MasterCard into a frontrunner ready to compete with Visa. Despite the fact that a large majority of U.S. banks who issued credit cards already issued both Visa and Master-Card, Visa clearly had created an international identity for itself. Before changing its name to Visa in 1977, BankAmericard had been issued under approximately 20 names around the world. Yet by 1980, it had consolidated its image and identity under the Visa trademark. MasterCard, on the other hand, not only had difficulty convincing its U.S. members that the name change from Master Charge was beneficial, but also suffered from an identity which was fragmented by affiliates and a myriad number of joint ventures in both Europe and Asia.

Hogg's strategy was to concentrate on developing and expand-ing MasterCard's line of products and services. In 1981, the company introduced MasterCard Travelers Cheques and during the same year brought out the Gold MasterCard card, which was the first attempt by the company at market segmentation. In 1983, MasterCard started its Emergency Card Replacement program and also included a laser hologram on all its cards in order to combat user fraud. Keeping pace with Visa, especially its vast, state-of-the-art, highly sophisticated electronic commu-nications network, was also not an easy task. In 1984, Hogg supervised the launching of Banknet, MasterCard's global packet-switching network that enables its international card acceptance locations to authorize transactions. At the same time, Hogg decided to incorporate INET into Banknet and adapt INAS on the system to more efficiently transmit authorizations from member to member. Like Visa, MasterCard also imple-mented an automated point-of-sale program to improve its authorization system worldwide.

Since affinity cards had been such a huge success in Japan, in 1985 the Card Program Development Group was formed and immediately introduced the MasterCard BusinessCard for the international market. There were now over 120 million Master-Card cardholders throughout the world. In 1986, a MasterCard office was opened in Hong Kong, the first in the Pacific Rim region, and one year later MasterCard arranged to become the first credit card issued in the People's Republic of China. During this time, the company opened a regional office for Latin America in Miami, and both cardholders and members were offered the full range of Banknet services at locations around the world.

In 1988, Hogg purchased Cirrus, the largest automated teller machine (ATM) network in the world, for $34 million. Master-Card also acquired a 15 percent interest in Eurocard Interna-tional. Yet just at the time when the 20th million MasterCard card was issued in the Pacific Rim area, and the first MasterCard card was issued in the Soviet Union, the board of directors at Interbank began to show their displeasure with Hogg's aggres-sive management style. Representing over 28,000 member banks, the ICA board of 25 directors criticized Hogg for spend-ing too much money on unsuccessful projects such as travel vouchers and "smart cards," and accused his management team of providing unreliable data on MasterCard's market share of charge-card billings. Disagreement and competing interests

within the board of directors itself prompted Hogg suddenly to resign in July of 1988.

The board of directors decided to appoint Alex W. Hart as the new chief executive officer and president. A longtime executive vice president at First Interstate Bancorp., with extensive expe-rience in credit card management, Hart began a program to solve some of MasterCard's management problems by estab-lishing regional boards of directors in Europe, Asia, and South America. In 1989, Hart supervised the launching of the Master-Card ATM Network. MasterCard also handled a local settle-ment in Venezuela, the first time the company processed this function outside the United States mainland. At approximately the same time, the company offered the MasterCard Card Pro-cessing Service, which helped members outside the United States begin to issue cards and acquire programs quickly and inexpensively through the use of a microcomputer.

In 1990, the MasterCard ATM Network was combined with CIRRUS to create the MasterCard/CIRRUS ATM Network. This network provided cash access for cardholders of Master-Card at over 50,000 locations worldwide. In addition, Hart negotiated with organizers of the 1990 World Soccer Cup to become the official card for that event; his effort was well repaid since MasterCard was enormously successful in height-ening brand recognition by capitalizing on the sporting event with the largest worldwide audience in 1990. At the same time MasterCom, developed two years earlier to send images of sales slips from one bank to another electronically, was implemented as a global service. Also during the same year, Banknet started to process currency transactions in India.

In 1991 MasterCard introduced Maestro, a worldwide debit system for cardholders of participating institutions including Eurocard International, Eurocheque International, and other ATM networks in the United States. Created in order to com-pete with Visa's Interlink system, both systems are highly sophisticated on-line, point-of-sale debit systems which process authorization, data accumulation, and debiting on an individ-ual's bank account. Both Visa's and MasterCard's debit pro-grams make use of a bank's proprietary debit card. Carrying either one or the other association's mark, the card can be used instead of cash and checks at locations where their mark is displayed. Ordinary retail transactions, such as day-to-day pur-chases at supermarkets, gas stations, and convenience stores, are the primary market for use of a debit transaction.

MasterCard processed its first Maestro debit transaction in August 1992. Interlink, on the other hand, surpassed 120 mil-lion transactions for holders of its debit card by the same time. By the beginning of 1993, Visa's Interlink debit program was far ahead of MasterCard's program: Interlink counted more than 16 million debit cardholders while MasterCard reported only 800,000. Both Visa and MasterCard recognize that banks will only need one debit brand and will not agree to using both, so competition is growing more and more intense between the two companies.

With its aggressive advertising campaign starting in 1991, Mas-terCard is determined to create a higher profile for itself and, in turn, a larger share of credit card billings around the world. Sponsorship of the World Cup in 1994 includes sponsoring 269 matches between 1991 and 1994, and this will certainly contribute to an increased recognition of MasterCard's name and services. Its foray into the credit card market for taxi cab fares is also helping it to become more competitive with Visa and American Express. Indeed, MasterCard is slowly but surely taking over some of Visa's market share.

Chief executive officer and president Alex Hart has revamped ICA's management structure and improved MasterCard's marketing strategy, advertising, program development, and electronic communications network in order for it to more readily compete with the other major credit cards such as Visa, American Express, Discover, Diners Club, and Carte Blanche. Yet the credit card market is saturated in the United States, and new cardholders will be more and more difficult to sign. Even though MasterCard has prepared well for the future, it will have to work diligently to overcome Visa's lead in credit card billings.

Further Reading:

"How a New Chief Is Turning Interbank Inside Out," *Business Week,* July 14, 1980, pp. 109–111.
Miller, Frederic A., "Is MasterCard Mastering the Possibilities?," *Business Week,* October 10, 1988, p. 123.

—Thomas Derdak

Mayo Foundation

200 1st St. S.W.
Rochester, Minnesota 55905
U.S.A.
(507) 284-2511
Fax: (507) 284-8713

Nonprofit Company
Incorporated: 1919 as Mayo Properties Association
Employees: 20,615
Sales: $1.49 billion
SICs: 8062 General Medical & Surgical Hospitals; 8099
Health and Allied Services

The nonprofit Mayo Foundation oversees the largest and most renowned private medical center in the world, the Mayo Medical Center of Rochester, Minnesota. The heart of the center is the Mayo Clinic, a research and treatment leader in cardiology, endocrinology, gynecology, neurology, oncology, orthopedics, urology, and a number of other disciplines. However, the Mayo Clinic is virtually inseparable from two nearby, highly reputed hospitals, Saint Marys and Rochester Methodist, both of which are entirely owned and governed by the Mayo Foundation. Since the mid-1980s, the Mayo Foundation has spearheaded a program to extend the unique Mayo medical system of total patient care far beyond southern Minnesota. Mayo Clinic Jacksonville (in Florida) and Mayo Clinic Scottsdale (in Arizona), both linked via satellite to Mayo Clinic Rochester, are two major outcomes of this nationwide expansion program. The Mayo Foundation also supports the Mayo Graduate School of Medicine, Mayo Medical School, and the Mayo School of Health-Related Sciences.

To visit the 12 - building, pedestrian - subway - linked Mayo "campus" in Rochester—a city of around 70,000 whose local economy is dominated by the health care, hospitality, and computer industries (a major IBM plant is located on the outskirts of the city)—is to understand just how completely the dreams of Mayo's founder, William Worrall Mayo, have been realized. Each year, well over 350,000 patients and their families flock to this medical mecca. Some do so for geographic reasons (80 percent of all Mayo patients are from Minnesota, Iowa, Wisconsin, and Illinois); others, out of long-established habit (U.S. Supreme Court Justice Harry Blackmun, for example, has revisited Mayo each summer for a checkup since serving as the

Clinic's general counsel in the 1950s); and still others, due to a high recommendation from a relative or acquaintance. (Though Mayo still bears the image of a hospital for the elite, it requires no physician referrals or lengthy admissions process; over 95 percent of its patients consistently report that they are "satisfied" or "very satisfied" with the care they have received.) All, without question, visit Mayo secure in the knowledge that it is home to some of the most advanced medical technology and one of the most respected groups of physicians in the world.

Mayo's long, rich history of excellence in medicine extends back to 1863, when Dr. W. W. Mayo of Le Sueur, Minnesota, was appointed examining surgeon of Civil War enlistees for the state's southern district. The district's headquarters were located in Rochester, then a ten-year-old pioneer settlement with a population of less than 3,000. Born and raised in England, Mayo arrived in the United States in 1845 at the age of 26. His first job was that of chemist for Bellevue Hospital in New York City. A string of nonmedical jobs intervened before Mayo became apprenticed to a doctor in Lafayette, Indiana. Harold Severson noted that Mayo studied at the Indiana Medical College in LaPorte. "This put him in a special category, for until the 1860s—and in some sections long afterward—a frontier doctor was almost any man who had the audacity to advertise himself as one."

A bout with malaria in 1854 convinced Mayo that he needed to move to a more congenial climate. Ultimately, the doctor chose St. Paul, though his wife, Louise, was at first hesitant to relinquish her thriving Indiana millinery business. Once the move was completed, however, she quickly launched a new shop that was equally prosperous. Mayo, on the other hand, resisted settling or committing to one line of employment, for he was an inveterate explorer and jack-of-all trades. Nonetheless, his medical calling resurfaced within a year or so, and he decided to become a country doctor in the picturesque town of Le Sueur. Louise agreed to sell her business and follow him.

Mayo supplemented his small and unstable income by farming, running a ferry boat, and serving as local veterinarian and justice of the peace. "All these divergent activities," wrote Helen Clapesattle, "were not such deviations from the Doctor's professional path as they might appear; they helped immeasurably to spread his name and acquaintance up and down the Minnesota Valley." Although always faced with competition, Mayo was able to expand his regular practice across three counties, earning himself in the process a reputation as a skilled and caring doctor.

Despite the attractions of Le Sueur, Mayo perceived more fertile prospects in Rochester after working there for a year, and, in 1864, he again relocated his family. This move marked the end of Mayo's itinerant path and the beginning of Rochester's development into a center for modern American medical knowledge and treatment. Mayo staked his private, home-visit practice upon his own ingenuity, experience, and energetic personality. The clinical thermometer had yet to be invented, and the use of the stethoscope, not to mention anesthetics, was still in its infancy. Antisepsis, the technique of preventing infection, was a lofty and far-off goal; and surgery of any kind was a procedure best avoided, if at all possible. Despite such handicaps, the medical profession was on the brink of rapid advancement, and Mayo, according to Philip K. Strand, shortly became "one of the most respected physicians in Minnesota." This was in no small part due to Mayo's drive for excellence. "A perfectionist who would not tolerate sloppy medicine," says Strand, "[Mayo] went to great lengths to increase his own medical knowledge." After barely five years of successful doctoring in Rochester, he realized that his training was inadequate for the high standards he wished to maintain. Thus, he chose to take several months off from his practice to study in New York with some of the country's top surgeons. Upon his return, Mayo abandoned his primitive microscope in favor of the latest model, which he purchased by mortgaging his house.

In 1880 Mayo attempted his first critical operation, the surgical removal of an ovarian tumor. Only a handful of doctors in the East were then attempting and succeeding at this particular operation. It soon became Mayo's forte. Although still teenagers, Mayo's sons, William Mayo and Charles Mayo, were assisting in the operating room by this time. Dr. Will and Dr. Charlie, as they were later affectionately known, were to become the very essence of the Mayo Clinic. It was their partnership, as much as that with their father, that brought the term Mayos' Clinic into common usage by the turn of the century. There is no doubt that W. W. Mayo greatly guided and influenced his sons to follow in his footsteps. However, wrote Harriet W. Hodgson, "Some think Louise Mayo deserved equal credit for Will and Charlie becoming physicians. An intellectual in her own right, she pursued interests in astronomy and botany, assisted her husband with surgery, applied splints, and listened to patients' complaints when Dr. W. W. was out on a call. . . . Her medical education was gleaned from on-the-job training and persistent study of her husband's textbooks."

Aside from the maturation of the Mayo boys into full-fledged physicians during the 1880s, the decade also marked the beginning of hospitalized care in Rochester. On August 21, 1883, a tornado struck the town, causing widespread injury and havoc. In the aftermath, Mayo sought a place to house and care for the wounded. The most likely spot was the convent operated by the Sisters of Saint Francis, a local teaching order. With poorly trained, volunteer nurses and virtually no management structure, the improvised hospital was chaotic but nonetheless served its immediate purpose. It served another purpose as well: that of convincing convent head Mother Alfred that a permanent hospital should be built by the order to serve the Rochester area. Prior to the tornado, Mother Alfred had actually been approached by St. Paul Bishop John Ireland about founding a hospital, but at the time she rejected the idea because her nuns were educators and not nurses. Now, after witnessing a city-wide emergency and seeing the capable response of W. W. Mayo and scores of volunteers, Mother Alfred became a strong proponent of the plan and beseeched Mayo to oversee the hospital upon its completion. Interestingly, she had difficulty convincing Mayo, for he was keenly aware of the public's perception of hospitals as places where the sick and indigent succumbed to death. Finally, Mayo agreed to the plan, with the stipulation that the Sisters should allot $40,000 for construction expenses. Four years later the first hospital in Rochester—and only the eighth in the entire state—was completed.

A three-story building with 27 beds, this was the original Saint Marys Hospital that, after numerous additions and modern-

izations, grew by its centennial into a thousand-plus-bed facility in which an average of 130 surgeries were performed daily. During its first full year of operation, Saint Marys hospitalized some 300 patients while maintaining an enviably low death rate, attributable in large part to the diligent practice of Dr. Joseph Lister's technique of wet antisepsis. "Eventually," wrote Clapesattle, "the message began to spread throughout the Midwest: Saint Marys Hospital is a place where people go to be healed."

The original Mayo group practice quickly evolved into one in which Dr. Will Mayo (who received his medical degree in 1883) and Dr. Charlie Mayo (who received his five years later) served as the two attending surgeons while Dr. W. W. Mayo functioned as the consulting physician. Of the three, Will demonstrated the greatest ability and concern for handling the Clinic's financial and administrative matters, which from the inception of Saint Marys were remarkably sound. So successful was the Mayo enterprise that two other physicians in the area opened a rival group named Riverside Hospital in 1892. Although it, too, thrived, the Riverside practice was moved to St. Paul within a few years. Around this same time, the Mayo Clinic began attracting outside medical talent. By the turn of the century, the practice numbered eight doctors, two of whom were women.

The tradition of Mayo innovation was already alive during these early days, for W. W. Mayo had instilled in his sons a strong emphasis on continuing medical education and scientific experimentation. This, in turn, resulted in the hiring of uniquely gifted and motivated colleagues who could extend the Clinic's areas of expertise. In effect, the original group of partners assembled by the Mayo brothers represented a new concept in medicine, the multi-specialty group practice. Will Mayo concentrated on diagnosing and treating pelvic and abdominal problems and Charlie Mayo, on eye, ear, nose, and throat ailments. No member of the group was more brilliant, eccentric, or esteemed than Dr. Henry Plummer, a former intern at St. Marys who joined the Clinic in 1901. Considered "no less than a genius" by Dr. Will Mayo for his work with iodine solutions to treat thyroid disease, Plummer is equally revered by Mayo historians for his lasting contributions to the day-to-day operations of the Clinic and Saint Marys. These include such inventions as a compressed-air system to transport internal records; an intra-clinic phone system; an envelope-coding system; and the system of underground walkways that link the Mayo Campus; as well as his architectural masterpiece, the Plummer Building.

By the early 1900s, W. W. Mayo had effectively retired in order to pursue his abiding interests of research, politics, and travel. He died in 1911, just a few months before his 92nd birthday and was paid tribute by the town he had helped to build. Saint Marys was now one of the largest and most advanced hospitals in the United States; more operations were being performed there each year than at any other facility in the country, including the prestigious Johns Hopkins in Maryland. The Mayo Clinic's reputation was now truly international, with famous physicians from Paris, Leipzig, Edinburgh, and elsewhere having made the trek to Rochester to learn first hand from the "country doctors" Will and Charlie Mayo, luminaries in their own right. Both men researched, wrote, and lectured extensively throughout their careers. In 1905 Will Mayo was named president of the American Medical Association; a decade later, Charlie received the same honor. Although vastly different in personality, the two formed a close bond, holding the same ideals of dedicated service and commitment championed by their father.

In 1914 the brothers oversaw the construction of the first building to bear the Mayo Clinic name and the first in the world designed specifically for a group medical practice. Now 75 strong, the Mayo partners were seeing an average of 30,000 patients annually. The following year the independently wealthy Mayo brothers, in an effort to preserve the education and research tradition they had founded, established a nonprofit endowment through the University of Minnesota, which they named the Mayo Foundation for Medical Education and Research. This foundation was funded by nearly $2 million from the brothers' personal savings. Then in 1919, "in an act without precedent in American medicine," according to *Mayo Clinic,* "the two brothers transferred all of the assets of the Mayo Clinic into an endowment to advance medical science [originally named the Mayo Properties Association, this endowment became the Mayo Foundation in 1964]. Thus began Mayo's tradition of giving, an essential part of our position in world medicine." This same year marked the opening of the Mayo Graduate School of Medicine.

From 1919 until 1939, Dr. Will Mayo served as president of the foundation. Among the highlights of this era were the construction in 1922 of a state-of-the-art surgical pavilion, which doubled the capacity of Saint Marys; the establishment in 1923 of a voluntary physicians' association, which ended all proprietary interests by Mayo staff, who now became salaried; the beginning of air transportation to Rochester in 1928; and the public donation of Mayo Foundation House, the former residence of Dr. Will and his wife, so that it might be used as "a meeting place for the exchange of ideas for the good of mankind."

With the deaths of Charles in May and Will in July of 1939, an enormous loss was felt around the country. Harold Severson reported that "messages of condolences poured in from people in all walks of life—from President and Mrs. Franklin D. Roosevelt to a little old woman in Texas who sent a potted plant and a note to Mrs. Charlie Mayo expressing her deep sorrow on the death of the man who had been so kind to her years ago." Harry Harwick, chief administrative officer since 1908, assumed the chairmanship of the Foundation upon Will's death. He presided over a thrilling era of Mayo's development, which included the creation of the first post-anesthesia room (a forerunner of modern intensive care units) in 1942 and the awarding of the Nobel Prize in 1950 to two Mayo researchers for their synthesis of cortisone. Other medical advances—too numerous to chronicle—have continued to keep the Mayo name in the spotlight of world medicine into the 1990s.

Until the mid-1980s, the structure of the Mayo Foundation, including its longstanding alliance with Saint Marys Hospital, remained essentially unchanged. However, with improvements in health care, concurrent declines in patients' average hospital stays, rising medical costs, and tighter governmental controls, there was a much more pressing need for conserving resources and maintaining revenue levels. Thus, the Mayo Foundation, Saint Marys, and a third entity, Rochester Methodist Hospital, entered into negotiations about integrating. On May 28, 1986, their organizational merger was complete and the newly ex-

panded Mayo Medical Center was now the largest nonprofit medical concern in the country. At the time of the merger, combined revenues exceeded half a billion dollars, with pooled assets listed at around $1 billion. One proviso of the agreement was that Saint Marys would retain its separate legal identity as a Catholic hospital and continue to receive support from the Sisters of St. Francis.

As of 1992, the Mayo Foundation had 2,071 hospital beds available for service but only a 61.3 percent hospital occupancy rate, down from 64.5 percent in 1991. Like other hospital alliances around the nation, Mayo continued to monitor and react to the changing dynamics of American health care. In its 1992 *Annual Report,* the foundation noted that "one of the biggest issues facing the United States is healthcare reform. Mayo introduced a set of healthcare policy principles, which emphasize quality, access and cost control that could help guide changes in American healthcare reform and shared these principles with state and U.S. governmental leaders."

Despite Mayo's leadership in this area, the future of U.S. medicine remains clouded. In an October 1993 article for *Forbes,* Marcia Berss posed this question: "If the Clinton health care package passes, U.S. medicine will be subject to a kind of price control. Can a quality provider like the Mayo Clinic survive price control?" Berss never answered the question directly. She noted, however, that "it will be a supreme irony if the impending changes in health care weaken the Mayo, because it already practices many of the things health care reformers would like to see." For his part, Mayo CEO Dr. Robert Waller responded, "Have price controls ever worked? It will stifle capital investment, and what we have to do is develop networks for health care delivery systems." Since the mid-1980s, Mayo has done this. Mayo has also found new sources of income by providing specialized lab services to outside doctors and hospitals and by launching such commercial enterprises as the *Mayo Clinic Family Health Book* and the *Mayo Clinic Health Letter* (which now carries 385,000 subscribers worldwide). In addition, Mayo now actively solicits charitable contributions, whereas in the past it operated as a self-funding organization. In 1992 outside philanthropy to Mayo totalled more than $58 million, approximately the same amount that is spent separately by the foundation each year on education and research. One can only hope that the traditions of the Mayo Foundation will indeed outlast the health reform of the 1990s, for the survival of Dr. Will's motto—"The best interest of the patient is the only interest to be considered"—is riding on the outcome.

Principal Subsidiaries: Minservco, Inc.

Further Reading:

"America's Best Hospitals: 1992 Annual Guide," *U.S. News & World Report,* June 15, 1992.
Berss, Marcia, "Mayo's Dilemma," *Forbes,* October 25, 1993, pp. 72, 74–5.
Clapesattle, Helen, *The Doctors Mayo,* Minneapolis: University of Minnesota Press, 1941, 2nd ed., 1963.
Cope, Lewis, "Shuttle Deploys Satellite for Mayo 'Telemedicine,'" *Star Tribune,* September 13, 1993, pp. 2A, 4A.
Gelbach, Deborah L., "Mayo Clinic," *From This Land: A History of Minnesota's Empires, Enterprises, and Entrepreneurs,* Northridge, CA: Windsor Publications, 1988.

Hodgson, Harriet W., *Rochester: City of the Prairie,* Northridge, CA: Windsor Publications, 1989.

Mayo Clinic, Rochester, MN: Mayo Foundation, 1990.

Severson, Harold, *Rochester: Mecca for Millions,* Rochester, MN: Marquette Bank & Trust Company, 1979.

Strand, Philip K., *A Century of Caring, 1889–1989,* Rochester, MN: Saint Marys Hospital, 1988.

Zemke, Ron, and Dick Schaaf, ''The Mayo Clinic and Hospitals,'' *The Service Edge: 101 Companies That Profit from Customer Care,* New York: New American Library, 1989, pp. 153–56.

—Jay P. Pederson

Mazda Motor Corporation

3-1
Fucho-cho Shinichi
Aki-gun
Hiroshima-ken 730-91
Japan
(082) 282-1111
Fax: (082) 287-5237

Public Company
Incorporated: 1920 as Toyo Cork Kogyo Company
Employees: 29,835
Sales: ¥2.304 trillion (US$2.09 billion)
Stock Exchanges: Tokyo Osaka Nagoya
SICs: 3711 Motor Vehicles and Passenger Car Bodies

Mazda Motors Corporation is the fourth largest manufacturer of automobiles in Japan. As a leader in the small car market, Mazda chose not to follow the example of its chief competitors Honda, Toyota, and Nissan in marketing larger luxury automobiles; rather, the company has achieved its greatest sales from smaller sports cars, particularly a model known in the United States as the Miata. Despite the commercial success of the Miata, however, the company experienced disappointing sales elsewhere in its product line in the early 1990s.

Mazda was organized by Jugiro Matsuda in 1920 as the Toyo Cork Kogyo, or East Sea Cork, Manufacturing, Company. The small enterprise, located in Hiroshima in southern Japan, was initially involved in the manufacture of cork products. In the mid-1920s, however, it expanded its product line to include several machined products. Reflecting this diversification, Matsuda dropped the word Cork from its name in 1927, and in 1929 the company began production of machine tools.

Matsuda believed that the enterprise could only remain successful if it had a truly unique product. To this end, Toyo Kogyo began design work on an unusual three-wheeled truck that proved commercially successful after its introduction in 1931. Furthermore, the company was an early supplier of products to a family of closely linked firms operating under the Sumitomo industrial conglomerate, with whom Toyo Kogyo maintained a close relationship. In 1935 the company began turning out rock drills and gauge blocks, which were of particular interest to Sumitomo, then one of Japan's largest mining concerns. The company supplied Sumitomo—and other companies involved

in the exploitation of resources in Taiwan, Korea, and later Manchuria—with machine tools.

After the seizure of Japanese government by right-wing militarists in the mid-1930s, Toyo Kogyo was drawn into military production. The company produced a variety of products for the Japanese Army, including automotive parts and machinery. The company's management was placed under government authority after the United States declared war on Japan in 1941. Although an important and capable supplier, Toyo Kogyo was not considered a target for strategic bombing. Its operations remained intact until the last days of the war, although its operations were somewhat limited by the increasing lack of access to raw materials.

However, on August 9, 1945 the entire city of Hiroshima was destroyed by an American atomic bomb. Toyo Kogyo was Hiroshima's largest employer, and while the factory was located far enough from the city center to avoid serious damage, many of Toyo Kogyo's employees were not. Soldiers who had worked for Toyo Kogyo before the war returned to Hiroshima skeptical as to whether the city and its businesses could be rebuilt. Nevertheless, by December 1945 Toyo Kogyo was back in business, again turning out the three-wheeled trucks that were the core of its business. With a large commercial operation back in business, and a thriving local economy, Hiroshima was quickly rebuilt. Many workers felt a personal debt to Toyo Kogyo for its role in reviving the war-torn city.

During this time, Jugiro Matsuda retired, designating his son, Tsuneji, as his successor. Tsuneji Matsuda proved to be an extremely capable manager, exemplifying many of the qualities that would come to define the company as a whole: patience, diligence, and dedication to quality and efficiency. Early in his tenure, Tsuneji Matsuda became interested in the manufacture of automobiles, which he saw as essential to modern life in Japan. Indeed, with personal incomes increasing in Japan, automobile production had the potential to generate tremendous profit and lift the company to even greater heights.

In 1954, Toyo Kogyo established a technological agreement with Acme Resin that enabled the company to begin using a new shell molding method. After several years of development, Toyo Kogyo established plans for its first mass-produced automobile, the two-door "Mazda" R360 coupe. Matsuda reportedly chose the car's name for its association with Auda Mazda, the ancient Japanese god of light, as well as for its similarity to the name Matsuda. The R360 made Toyo Kogyo a competitor in the growing consumer automobile market. However, while the company had introduced a viable product, the Mazda lacked one thing: it was not unique.

Matsuda had long known of a virtually abandoned engine technology developed in Germany by the inventor Felix Wankel. Wankel's pistonless engine worked on a revolutionary principle in which a single triangular rotor circulated around a large combustion chamber with a gear at its axis. The rotor, moving orbitally around the gear, compressed air and fuel on one side, where a spark plug ignited the mixture. This drove the rotor around the axial gear, expelling exhaust fumes while setting up the next face of the rotor for another combustion. As the rotor wound its way around the combustion chamber, the gear at its axis was forced to spin. This gear was attached to a clutch and transmission, and from there to a drive shaft. The Wankel engine offered more than mere novelty; by eliminating the in-out-in-out motion of pistons, the Wankel would operate more smoothly and with better performance than a conventional engine.

While successful in a laboratory, the Wankel engine was overlooked by engine makers because no one believed that it could be accurately machined in mass production. Matsuda, however, had great faith in his company's machining techniques, and his engineers assured him that such an engine could be built on a massive scale. Matsuda reached an agreement with NSU/Wankel, the German firm that held a patent for the Wankel Engine, and in 1961 he won an exclusive agreement to develop the engine. Design work commenced, but it took several years to develop a suitable model.

In the meantime, Toyo Kogyo introduced a four-door automobile, the Carol 600, in 1962, and the following year the company's one millionth vehicle rolled off its assembly line. In 1965, Toyo Kogyo produced another new model, the Mazda 800/1000, and completed work on a proving ground at Miyoshi. Also that year, the company established a diesel engine technology agreement with Perkins Services. Branching into the market for light duty trucks, Toyo Kogyo introduced the Mazda Proceed B-series compact pickup truck.

In 1966 the company completed construction of a new passenger car plant at Hiroshima. The following year, this plant began manufacturing the Mazda Cosmo Sports 110S automobile, the first Toyo Kogyo vehicle to be powered by a Wankel rotary engine. This model placed Toyo Kogyo in a truly unique position in the market. The rotary-powered engine gave the company an exclusive product that was smooth riding, quiet, and fast. Nothing produced by Toyo Kogyo's competitors, industry giants Nissan and Toyota, could match it.

Other introductions to the company's automobile line during this time included the Mazda 1000/1200; the rotary-powered R100 Mazda Familia Coupe; the RX-2 Capella; the RX-3 Savanna; and the RX-4 Luce. In 1972, Toyo Kogyo completed its five millionth vehicle, nearly one million of which had been exported. As worldwide sales increased, Toyo Kogyo set up sales organizations in the United States, Canada, Belgium, West Germany, Australia, and Malaysia.

In 1972 Henry Ford flew to Hiroshima to negotiate a license that would allow the Ford Motor Company to begin building rotary engines. Sure that Toyo Kogyo was on to something unique and profitable, however, Matsuda flatly refused to share the Wankel technology. Subsequently, Matsuda launched a bold worldwide marketing campaign in which the rotary engine was touted as the answer to high fuel prices. Consumers showed strong interest in the Mazda product line. To finance an expansion of production capacity, Toyo Kogyo made a huge public equity offering.

The OPEC oil embargo on 1973 sent a shockwave through the world economy. With petroleum prices skyrocketing, consumer demand for energy efficient automobiles increased dramatically. The Mazda's highly efficient rotary engine seemed the perfect alternative to conventional piston-engined automobiles.

However, emissions from the rotary engine exceeded clean air standards in California, the company's largest export market. Adjustments made to clean up the engine came at the expense of fuel economy, which fell to ten miles per gallon. Furthermore, the rotary model was prone to breakdown. Production continued while Toyo Kogyo technicians launched an emergency re-engineering of the Wankel design.

By 1974, amid increasing pressure from the OPEC embargo, Toyo Kogyo managed to stretch the Mazda's mileage rating to 16 miles per gallon, and then 20. But by this time, Honda, Ford, General Motors and Curtiss-Wright had begun development of stratified charge engines that promised greater efficiency than conventional and rotary engines. Moreover, Nissan and Toyota began an all-out war for market leadership in Japan, squeezing out smaller competitors such as Toyo Kogyo and Suzuki.

As consumer interest in the rotary waned, Toyo Kogyo began searching for ways to keep its factories operating nearer capacity. Matsuda negotiated a deal with Ford in which Toyo Kogyo would manufacture Ford's Festiva model at its facilities. Strapped for cash, Toyo Kogyo finally agreed to license its rotary technology—to Suzuki, which used the engine for a new motorcycle.

When the oil embargo was lifted, oil prices and consumer interest in fuel-efficient engines declined rapidly. Improvements in the rotary design were finally perfected, giving Toyo Kogyo the efficient, environmentally friendly engine it needed—about two years too late. While U.S. fuel economy regulations kept Toyo Kogyo in the American market, the company had lost two years fixing the rotary engine, during which time Honda, Ford, and GM had developed their own improved engines, leaving Toyo Kogyo in the middle of a crowded pack.

With nothing other than the rotary engine to distinguish its product line, Toyo Kogyo was forced to quickly develop new models and concentrate on product quality as a competitive factor. The Mazda Familia and Capella 626 were introduced in 1977, followed by the Savanna RX-7 in 1978. By this time Toyo Kogyo had turned out more than ten million vehicles, one million of which were rotary-powered.

Amidst the company's efforts to recover from the debacles of the 1970s, Tsuneji Matsuda retired, leaving his son Kohei Matsuda in charge. The younger Matsuda initially made great progress in shoring up the company's balance sheet. However, in the opinion of the Sumitomo interests, which owned most of Toyo Kogyo's shares and bankrolled its earlier failures, the turnaround wasn't good enough. Sumitomo Bank officers felt that Kohei Matsuda was not adequately preparing the company for the future, and they disagreed strongly with his plans for restructuring the company, which included a wider product line and greater autonomy from Sumitomo management. Eventually, Matsuda was forced to resign his presidency to Yoshiki Yamasaki, a director favored by Sumitomo. The abdication formally ended the Matsuda dynasty at Toyo Kogyo.

The company enjoyed a jump in sales in 1979, when the Iranian Revolution caused a brief oil crisis. Also helping boost sales was the fact that Toyo Kogyo and other Japanese manufacturers had become known in the United States for the high quality of their products; American cars, by contrast, had become known as poorly designed, carelessly built, and overpriced.

In 1979 Ford Motor Company began negotiations to acquire a large stake in Toyo Kogyo, hoping to merge it with its own Japanese subsidiary, Ford Industries. The $135 million deal, completed in November, left Ford with a 24.5 percent share of Toyo Kogyo. The merger paved the way for several new joint ventures between Ford and Toyo Kogyo, in which the Japanese company built small cars and trucks under the Ford nameplate and distributed Ford products in Japan.

In 1980, shedding the last of its failures with the rotary engine, Toyo Kogyo settled a class action suit charging design flaws with early models. Also that year, the Mazda FWD Familia was named car of the year in Japan. Unable to match Nissan and Toyota's large sales staffs, Toyo Kogyo established a string of showrooms across Japan under the name Autorama. Also that year, as it exported its five millionth vehicle, the company set up sales organizations in the United States and Europe. In 1982, Toyo Kogyo established another production plant at Hofu, and in 1983 turned out its 15 millionth vehicle. The following year Toyo Kogyo formally changed its name to Mazda Motors, reflecting the tremendous popularity of its main product line.

Mazda introduced several new automobiles in 1985, 1986, and 1987, including the new versions of the Mazda RX-7 and 626. By 1987 the company had produced 20 million vehicles. Mazda also entered into several joint ventures, including one with Ford and Matsushita for the production of air conditioning systems. Under a second partnership, Mazda manufactured microcars for Suzuki, and under a third, it imported Citroën cars to Japan.

Mazda Motors continued to be led by a committee of Sumitomo bankers, who received input from Ford and Kia Motors, which acquired an eight percent interest in the company in 1983. In 1987, however, Norimasa Furuta, a former official of the Ministry of International Trade and Industry, assumed the presidency of the company.

Under Furuta, Mazda sharpened its focus, developing several new vehicles for specific markets. The Persona and Proceed were developed specifically for the Japanese market, joining the company's mainstay, the 323 Sedan. The MPV minivan, initially intended for sale only in the United States, was later introduced in Japan. Of the company's new vehicles, the MX-5 Miata was undoubtedly the most successful. A small sports car reminiscent of the MGB and Triumph Spitfire, the Miata was marketed in the United States, where it found an appreciative market particularly among young, affluent males. In designing the Miata, Mazda engineers borrowed liberally from the British Lotus and Elan, which they admitted disassembling for reference. Miata sales were brisk and did much to revive the reputation of Mazda in the United States.

While Nissan, Toyota, and Honda created luxury car divisions to compete with American Buicks, Lincolns, and Cadillacs, Mazda continued to specialize in smaller cars and trucks. With Ford as its largest shareholder, Mazda found its marketing niche operating informally as a small car subsidiary of Ford. Mazda established an American production facility in the Detroit suburb of Flat Rock, Michigan, employing American union labor. The company also established a massive sales and research organization in the United States, employing thousands of Americans.

Nevertheless, 80 percent of the vehicles Mazda sold in foreign markets were produced in Japan, saddling the company with extra transportation costs and subjecting it to foreign import restrictions, particularly in Europe. In addition, Mazda maintained five separate dealerships in Japan for Mazda, Ford, and Citroën.

Yoshihiro Wada succeeded Furuta as president of Mazda in 1990. Furuta was given a ceremonial position on the board, joining chairman Kenichi Yamamoto, who headed Toyo Kogyo's rotary development during the 1960s. As it entered the 1990s, Mazda occupied a unique niche in the market, producing a relatively narrow line of midsize cars and small trucks. The stigma of the malfunctioning Wankel rotary engine largely overcome, Mazda remained a major manufacturer in Japan and one of the major brands worldwide precisely because it performed so well in its segment.

Principal Subsidiaries: Mazda Motor Manufacturing (USA) Corp.; Mazda Motors (Deutschland) GmbH.; Mazda Canada, Inc.; Eunos, Inc.; Autozam, Inc.; Mazda Australia Pty. Ltd.; Mazda (North America), Inc.; Mazda Chuhan Co., Ltd.; Kurashiki Kako Company, Ltd.; Mazda Credit Corp.; Mazda Logistic Service Company, Ltd.; Toyo Advanced Technologies Co., Ltd.; Mazda Motor of America, Inc.

Further Reading:

"Family Operation Ends in Toyo Kogyo Shuffle," *Automotive News,* January 30, 1978, pp. 15–16.
"A Ford Acquisition," *Business Week,* July 23, 1979, p. 72.
"History of Mazda Motor Corporation," Company Document.
"Kenichi Yamamoto: Leading by Courageous Example," *Automotive Industries,* February 1986, pp. 46–49.
"Mazda Motor Corporation," *Diamond's Japan Business Directory 1992,* pp. 852–853.
"Mazda Ponders Its Route through a Bumpy Future," *Wall Street Journal,* September 8, 1993, p. B4.
"Mazda's Bold New Global Strategy," *Fortune,* December 17, 1990, pp. 109–11.
"The Rotary Turnabout," *Forbes,* March 1, 1975, p. 46.
"Toyo Kogyo Agrees to Court Settlement on Mazda Complaints," *Wall Street Journal,* February 25, 1980, p. 18.
"When I Was a Lad," *The Economist,* December 23, 1989, p. 70.

—John Simley

McKinsey & Company, Inc.

55 E. 52nd Street
New York, New York 10022
U.S.A.
(212) 446-7000
Fax: (212) 446-8575

Private Company
Incorporated: 1925
Employees: 4,700
Revenues: $1.2 billion
SICs: 8742 Management Consulting Services

McKinsey & Company, Inc. is an international management consulting firm with more than fifty offices in twenty-five countries. One of the five largest consulting services in the United States, it specializes in problem solving and program implementation, primarily for corporate clients. As the top consulting firm offering general management guidance, it works with upper-level management to improve company performance and develop and implement strategies for growth and change. McKinsey has advised many of the Fortune 500 companies in the United States and top corporations in other countries. Its list of clients includes General Motors, PepsiCo, Ford Motor Company, and American Express. Many former McKinsey consultants have gone on to hold high management positions in major companies around the world.

McKinsey and Company was founded in 1925 by James O. McKinsey, an accounting professor at the University of Chicago whose accounting and management writings brought him many consulting jobs on the side. As McKinsey acquired more work, he hired consultants to work for him. For the most part, he hired industrial managers in their mid-forties whom he thought his clients would find credible because of their age and experience. After McKinsey died in 1937, the company continued the hiring practices the founder had instituted.

McKinsey & Company shifted direction in 1950, however, when Marvin Bower became managing director. Bower is credited with molding McKinsey into the successful and world-class company it has become. McKinsey's billings increased from $2 million in 1950 to more than $200 million when Bower stepped down in 1967.

Bower joined the company in 1933, when management consulting was called management engineering. He was a graduate of Harvard Law School and had been working for a prestigious Ohio law firm. As managing director, Bower introduced a radically different approach to hiring consultants: he recruited recent graduates of the country's top business schools. His view clashed with the prevailing view that experience counted far more than education. To Bower, consulting was a "thinking activity," so it required education and smarts even more than experience. Although it took several years for clients to fully accept McKinsey's young M.B.A.s, the firm became the most respected and well known consulting company in the country and, later, in the world. The company continued to hire under the Bower philosophy, even after Bower resigned as managing director in 1967. In recent years, the majority of McKinsey's new consultants have been M.B.A.s with degrees from Wharton, Harvard, Northwestern, and Stanford.

Bower, considered a founder of modern management consulting, considered consulting a profession, not a business, and said he emphasized improving the client's performance rather than making money for McKinsey. To Bower, the client always came first. Bower had a keen eye for recognizing the needs and weaknesses of a company—and its top executives.

By the late 1950s, McKinsey & Company had five offices in the United States. In 1959, it opened its first overseas office in London, at a time when foreign firms were eager to learn American business practices. Hugh Parker, an American educated at Cambridge, was the director of the first overseas office. McKinsey soon opened more offices overseas. While these offices were headed by Americans, they were staffed mostly by local people. During the 1960s and 1970s, McKinsey opened offices in France, Germany, Switzerland, Belgium, Italy, the Netherlands, and Scandinavia, and worked with major European clients such as KLM and Royal Dutch/Shell. More recently, it has opened offices in Japan and Australia.

Over the years, the management of foreign offices shifted; by the late 1980s, a majority of the company's senior partners were foreign, even though many had been educated at American schools. Kenici Ohmae, who headed the Japan office, held a Ph.D. in nuclear engineering from the Massachusetts Institute of Technology (M.I.T.). The Chicago office was headed by Indian Rajat Gupta, who had earned an M.B.A. from Harvard. R. Ronald Daniel led the firm for 12 years, from 1976 to 1988. According to Alonzo McDonald, who served as managing director from 1973 to 1976, the company had grown so large that Daniel was "the last managing director to personally know everyone in the partnership." Daniel had joined the firm in 1957; eleven years later, he was a senior partner managing the company's recruiting program. In 1970, he became the manager of the New York office. In 1976, he was elected managing director by the other partners. While he was managing director, the professional staff grew from 600 to 1,800, and revenues grew to $510 million. Although other firms, such as Bain & Co. and Boston Consulting Group, challenged McKinsey's domination of the general consulting profession, McKinsey remained the firm that many of the Fortune 500 companies turned to for management expertise.

Although McKinsey had helped many businesses become successful, it also took part in business failures; it was impossible to tell, however, if the failures were due to advice from McKinsey consultants or poor implementation of their advice. In the mid-1980s, General Motors Corp. called in McKinsey for reorganization help. McKinsey's plan called for the company to be divided into two divisions, instead of the five divisions into which it was then divided. However, the move resulted in great inefficiency, according to critics, and the company failed to realize any savings in costs or increase in productivity.

In 1988, Ron Daniel stepped down as managing director, and Fred Gluck took his place. Gluck had made a name for himself in the company partly for his work as a McKinsey consultant to giant American Telephone & Telegraph. Gluck was a different breed for the firm, and to some observers, Gluck's election to the post signalled the possibility that it was a new era for the company. According to *Business Week,* the election of Gluck was a reflection of how much McKinsey & Company had changed. "Blue-blooded Harvard M.B.A.s" had dominated the company for decades. But Gluck was an engineer who had been born to a German Catholic family in Brooklyn. Although Gluck did not fit the McKinsey mold, he promised that the company would maintain its traditions of client service and the importance of the company over the individual consultant. Under Gluck, McKinsey, in the tradition of Marvin Bower, continued to hire the "best and the brightest" from the country's top business schools.

Gluck was largely responsible for efforts to disseminate the information that consultants around the world had gathered, making it available to everyone in the firm. Gluck started the company's fifteen "centers of competence," ranging from corporate finance to manufacturing logistics. Each group was urged to issue periodic bulletins concerning the work it was doing. Gluck was also an advocate of increased use of computers to track the more than 1,400 studies the company conducted yearly all over the world, research for which the company had been highly regarded for many years. McKinsey claimed to publish more academic review articles than any competitor company.

McKinsey also continued to conduct many notable pro bono projects for organizations such as the Joffrey Ballet, Pittsburgh Theater, and the University of Texas business school. Its 1992 study of the University of Texas involved a team of fourteen consultants who spent nearly 4,000 hours determining how to overhaul the M.B.A. program to make it more competitive with the leading business schools in the country and more relevant to the real world business environment. This study would have cost the school as much as $1.5 million.

McKinsey was not without its critics, whose comments were directed at the lofty attitudes that McKinsey seemed to claim were its greatest strengths. *Forbes* magazine likened the McKinsey style to that of "an upright old family lawyer or doctor . . . always stressing pride of workmanship," but that its "lofty attitudes" may have been out of sync with the new demand for specialized, technical expertise. The company, however, was determined to continue to provide a "top management prospective."

While other consulting firms had gone public or were sold during the 1980s, McKinsey remained a private and discreet organization. It revealed little about itself and protected the confidentiality of its very powerful clients. The company discouraged cultivating any "stars" in the organization, emphasizing that the firm and its expertise were what the company was selling and individual consultants were members of a McKinsey team.

Although top graduates from the top business schools may not have considered consulting the answer to their dreams, few candidates for jobs at McKinsey ever turned down a job there. For decades it has been an effective stepping stone to management positions in the country's largest corporations. Squads of former McKinsey consultants hold top positions at PepsiCo and American Express. Former McKinsey consultants included Michael L. Ainslie, CEO and president of Sotheby's Holdings, Paul W. Chellgren, president and chief operating officer of Ashland Oil, William B. Ellis, chairman and CEO of Northeast Utilities, Louis V. Gerstner, Jr., chairman and CEO of IBM, Harvey Golub, chairman and CEO of American Express, Michael H. Jordan, chairman and CEO of Westinghouse Electric Corp., C. Robert Kidder, chairman and CEO of Duracell International, Jim P. Manzi, chairman and CEO of Lotus Development, and Robert D. Haas, chairman and CEO of Levi Strauss. Other McKinsey alumni held top positions at General Electric, PepsiCo, Merrill Lynch, and Raychem. The ranks of McKinsey alumni have formed a powerful network of top executives around the world. They call on other McKinsey alumni when they are hiring or when they need information, and they call on McKinsey when they need the services of a consulting firm.

McKinsey's revenues more than doubled between 1987 and 1992, from about $510 million to $1.2 billion, with about 60 percent of those earnings coming from outside the United States. Revenues for McKinsey increased by 14 percent between 1991 and 1992, and outbilled all other management consulting firms in the world except Andersen Consulting, according to *Consultants News,* a newsletter for the consulting industry. But even that second place finish was deceiving because McKinsey's average earnings per professional were $387,000, triple Andersen's average, largely because McKinsey worked mostly with top management and thus commanded more lucrative fees.

By the mid-1990s, the company continued to be run as a loose democracy. The managing partner had no real power over colleagues other than that of persuasion and the responsibility of naming members of the firm to various committees. If a majority of partners did not approve of someone's actions, they would not reelect him. Ownership of the firm has remained in the hands of the partners since Bower started selling some of his shares to younger partners decades ago. Shares have never been traded outside the organization. According to company literature, by maintaining internal ownership, the independence and objectivity of the company has never been compromised because it remained answerable only to its clients, its partners, and its staff.

The organization suffered some problems in the early 1990s when several top partners left the firm, along with teams of consultants, to work for rivals or establish rival firms. It also found itself being left behind in the fast growing area of information technology, and in order to acquire the necessary expertise, it purchased Information Consulting Group in late 1989 from a British firm. Gluck had advocated strongly for the purchase of Information Consulting Group, a 250-person information technology firm based in Washington, D.C. McKinsey said it made the acquisition so that it could better respond to the needs of its clients for whom information technology was becoming very important. By 1993, however, half of the nineteen partners and more than half of the staff left Information Consulting Group for other jobs.

Although McKinsey signaled a change with its appointment of Gluck, it still came under fire from women and minorities for its lack of black partners and its small percentage of women partners worldwide. It was forced to reevaluate a company policy on reimbursement for partners' club memberships when a group of African-American Harvard business school students criticized the company for reimbursing partners for memberships in clubs that discriminated on the basis of race, religion, or gender. McKinsey partners, however, said that the company was committed to employing a diversified work force.

Gluck was expected to step down as managing director in 1994, and insiders speculated that the company might elect its first non-American partner to replace him. However, the main goals and objectives of the company were not expected to change. It would continue to provide nearly half of its work in the fields of strategy, overall organization, and related policy areas, as well as provide advice on improving short-term performance by helping clients turn around profit declines, reorient their product/market strategies, cut costs, and increase productivity. It also would continue to do extensive work in areas important to top management of client companies, such as research and development, finance, sales and marketing, manufacturing and distribution, planning and control, management information, and information technology. McKinsey continued to pride itself on its ability to solve clients' problems in a collaborative effort to integrate new strategies with the existing culture and traditions of the client company.

Principal Subsidiaries: Information Consulting Group.

Further Reading:

Byrne, John A., "Calling in the Consultants—to the Classroom," *Business Week,* November 16, 1992, pp. 92–95.
——, "The McKinsey Mystique," *Business Week,* September 20, 1993.
——,"What's a Guy Like This Doing at McKinsey's Helm?" *Business Week,* June 13, 1988, pp. 82–84.
Merwin, John, " 'We Don't Learn from Our Clients, We Learn from Each Other,' " *Forbes,* October 19, 1987, pp. 122–128.

—Wendy J. Stein

Medco Containment Services Inc.

100 Summit Avenue
Montvale, New Jersey 07645
U.S.A.
(201) 358-5400
Fax: (201) 358-5783

Public Company
Incorporated: 1983
Employees: 9,400
Sales: $2.6 billion
SICs: 5122 Drugs, Proprietaries and Sundries; 5961 Mail
   Order Houses

Medco Containment Services Inc. controls more than 50 percent of one of the fastest growing segments of the health-care industry, the funded mail-order prescription drug trade in the United States. Within ten years of its founding in 1983, it was serving 36 million workers from more than 3,100 client companies. In addition, it was dispensing more than 600,000 prescriptions weekly from its eleven regional distribution centers. Health care and financial experts anticipated that health care reform policies would further enhance Medco's business.

Martin Wygod spent his first 20 years after college in small-scale investment banking and acquisitions, in addition to owning a controlling interest in Porex Technologies Corp. In 1983, with $10 million from the sale of one of his investments, he went shopping for a new challenge. Wygod formed Medco as a holding company so he could buy National Pharmacies for $30 million in cash and Porex stocks. National Pharmacies, owned by APL Corporation, was a vitamin distributor and a small mail-order prescription drug business. It had yearly revenues of about $25 million and profits of about $400,000. Wygod eliminated the vitamin business and built up the mail-order drug business.

Although the Veterans Administration and other nonprofit groups had handled long-term prescriptions by mail for almost 40 years, in 1984 mail-order drugs accounted for only two percent of the prescriptions filled in the United States. But Wygod's timing was perfect. Large corporations were looking for ways to save money on employee drug costs, and mail order was a convenient way to save on long-term prescriptions for the chronically ill patient. Wygod aggressively sought new clients for his mail-order company and quickly signed up corporate-

funded drug benefit plans offered by Alcoa, General Motors, Georgia-Pacific, and Commonwealth Edison Co. By 1992, Medco had more than 1,300 company accounts. Medco grew from 200 employees serving fewer than four million people in 1985 to 6,000 employees serving close to 30 million people in 1993. Within ten years, Medco controlled 50 percent of the prescription mail business nationally, and its revenues were consistently growing by an average of 47 percent a year.

Although Medco was not the first mail-order prescription company, it was the first company that aggressively sold its services to large corporations, labor unions, and health plans. When Wygod bought National Pharmacies, the cost of employee drugs as an employment benefit was rising 15 percent to 20 percent a year, and only five percent of employees were covered by drug plans. By 1991, more than 40 percent were covered.

In 1984, Wygod sought underwriting by Drexel Burnham and sold 20 percent of the company in a public offering. That same year, the company's name was changed to Medco Containment Services Inc. In 1985, Wygod acquired Paid Prescriptions from Computer Sciences Corp. This small company provided plan subscribers with a prescription-drug card that allowed them to purchase drugs at 40,000 drugstores, who then billed the plan sponsors. This acquisition allowed Medco to offer plan participants the ability to fill prescriptions for acute illness at a discount at participating drugstores. While mail-order prescriptions of preferred drugs cost a minimal co-payment of $2, participants could also purchase drugs at a local store for a higher co-payment. This computer network also allowed Medco to gather information on consumer prescription drug spending and sell that information to the nation's largest health plan sponsors.

Walgreen Co. had dominated the mail-order prescription business when Wygod bought National Pharmacies. But Wygod anticipated that Walgreen would not expand that operation because if it did it would be competing against its own local drugstores. Wygod's Medco surged ahead of Walgreen in mail-order operations. It has since taken market share from mail-order drug companies owned by Baxter International and J.C. Penney, as well as retail drugstore chains such as Walgreen and Rite-Aid. Independent retail pharmacists and state pharmacy boards have lobbied to restrict mail-order sales and have even brought legal suits protesting the sending of drugs across state lines, but they have had no success in stopping Medco or other mail-order prescription services.

Medco specialized in maintenance drugs for high blood pressure, arthritis, diabetes, and other chronic diseases. Patients still shopped at local pharmacies for antibiotics and other prescriptions needed for acute illnesses, but chronic ailments which called for regular drug therapy were increasingly being serviced by Medco and smaller mail-order companies. Medco claimed to save at least 20 percent on most prescriptions because it encouraged the use of generic drugs and it could negotiate healthy discounts from manufacturers. In the early 1990s, providing prescription drug coverage cost employers in a Medco-run plan about $167 per employee versus $266 per employee in unmanaged plans.

In late 1990, Medco introduced a controversial program called Prescriber's Choice: for a deep discount from a drug company, Medco would promote that company's drug as the top choice in its category. The Prescriber's Choice program covered many chronic conditions such as hypertension and ulcers, for which there were drugs priced at various levels. When the company believed a physician had ordered a more expensive drug than necessary, a pharmacist reviewed the patient's questionnaire that revealed his/her ailments and other medications. Then the pharmacist contacted the physician and told her about another equally effective but less costly alternative. The physician was free to change the prescription to the less expensive treatment or chose the drug they had originally prescribed. However, statistics showed that more than 40 percent of physicians agreed to rewrite their prescriptions. According to the *Wall Street Journal*, Medco was switching—with doctors' permission—50,000 prescriptions monthly in eight major drug categories. Once Medco had called doctors' attention to the cheaper drug, they often started prescribing that drug for other patients as well.

Ulcers was one of the first categories that Medco addressed with its Prescriber's Choice program. This was an excellent category to choose since patients were repeat customers for refills, sales of ulcer medication were vast, and there were only four similar drugs doctors generally prescribed. Medco negotiated with the makers of the four drugs, Glaxo, SmithKline Beecham, Merck, and Eli Lilly & Co. In the summer of 1991, SmithKline Beecham's Tagamet became Medco's number one choice for ulcer prescriptions. Patients could get any of the other medications, but Tagamet was the most cost-effective because of the volume discount Medco won in exchange for listing that drug as its top choice. Medco accounted for ten percent of the ulcer medication's $3-billion-a-year market. Health plans paid a lower cost for Tagemet and patients paid a lower co-payment for Tagamet than they would for the other medications.

Medco also established a formulary for 18 other categories of medication. Under this plan, Medco listed a small number of medications in each category; Medco would reimburse most of patients' costs if they were using drugs from the Medco listing. Patients, however, had to pay a higher amount for drugs not listed in the formulary. In a formulary Medco established in Massachusetts, the co-payment was $8 for a generic drug, $15 for a brand in the formulary, and $30 for a brand outside the formulary. Medco often ended up recommending older drugs with small market share because the smaller companies tended to cut prices in order to increase their market share.

Although many doctors, retail pharmacists, and drug companies complained about formularies and Medco's Prescriber's Choice, it seemed to be the direction prescription drug distribution would take as managed care gained momentum in the United States. According to Wygod, the Prescriber's Choice program offered cost containment and choice while other formularies offered no choice. In formularies, patients may be reimbursed for only one or two of the drugs prescribed for a particular ailment and all other drugs are excluded. Some experts predicted, however, that by the year 2000, prescription purchases would be decided by committees rather than by individual prescribing physicians. These large buying groups would reduce drug costs since buyers would have volume-purchasing power. Formularies were seen as a means of controlling prescription drug costs by changing physicians' prescribing habits. Formularies listed nonformulary drugs and the recommended cheaper alternatives.

Physicians, pharmacists, and some drug companies pointed out that prescription choices should be made on a therapeutic basis rather than a cost basis, but Medco and other health plans and organizations seemed determined to keep the formularies. Drug companies, especially when their products were not adopted on formularies, argued that cost comparison should not be the only criteria on which to base a choice. They argued that the physician and the health agency needed to look at the overall picture and that some drugs could prevent the need for surgery. They also pointed out that although some drugs might have a higher per-dose cost, the total course of therapy might cost less because fewer doses were needed.

Retail pharmacists complained that they could not get the same price breaks that giant Medco won from manufacturers. Some physicians complained that Medco and other formularies were taking control away from the physician. And some drug companies complained that Medco exercised too much control over the drug market because it had the power to promote one drug over another to the tens of millions of patients it served. Because Medco controlled such a large share of the prescription market, Medco's deals could heavily influence sales of many drug categories and shift the balance from one drug to another. Many drug makers were unhappy about this, but they could not afford to alienate Medco. By 1993, all but a handful of major U.S. pharmaceutical firms had signed on with Medco.

Medco chairman Martin Wygod was one of the five highest-paid CEOs in the United States in 1992, earning a $33-million pay package, much of it in stock options. Wygod told the *Wall Street Journal* that he deserved that immense compensation for making the company "the Wal-Mart of pills." Medco was able to offer medications for 25 percent less than retail pharmacies because of volume discounts and automation that helped each pharmacist or technician process 70 prescriptions an hour, even with each order reviewed for accuracy by two pharmacists.

In 1992, former Citibank President Richard Braddock became CEO of Medco—later resigning in September of 1993—while Wygod retained his position as chairman of the company. The top jobs were split so that Wygod could concentrate on acquisitions and dealings with drug companies while Braddock focussed on operations. Wygod said that Braddock's skills were important for helping the company through a "major growth stage." Braddock also noted that health-care reform could benefit Medco and other companies that stress cost containment.

Medco's growth has been steady and dramatic since its inception in 1984. For five years in a row, Medco's revenues increased an average of 47 percent annually, and its earnings gained an average of 45 percent a year. In 1991, Medco's revenue increased only 35 percent, to $1.81 billion, but its net income leaped 75 percent, to $102 million. In 1992, revenue was above $2 billion. By 1993, more than 100 of the Fortune 500 companies had signed on with Medco.

In 1991, Comnet Corporation, a producer of direct-marketing and health-care software, sold Medco enough stocks to give Medco a 23 percent share. Wygod also became chairman of

Comnet as well as Medco. That same year, Medco launched Medical Marketing Group Inc. to collect data from drugstores and physicians on prescribing patterns and sell the data to drug companies for their promotional or marketing needs. Medical Marketing gathered the information chiefly from IMS America Ltd., a Dun & Bradstreet division that collects data from pharmacies. The balance of Medical Marketing's data came from Medco and the mail-order prescription service of the American Association of Retired Persons (AARP).

In 1991, Medco completed a deal to acquire American Biodyne Inc., a provider of managed mental health services. Medco paid $121 million in Medco common stock. Medco also acquired Personal Performance Consultants, which provided employee assistance programs. In 1991, Medco also established the Medco Foundation and the Rose Foundation to provide prescription drug aid for uninsured and impoverished people.

Health-care related companies were anxiously waiting as American politicians hammered out health-care reform measures in 1993. Medco, however, seemed to be in a good position to benefit from any managed-care program, a likely component of any reform measure. Companies such as Medco, which can provide drugs on a large scale and at a lower price than other outlets, were poised to take advantage of the health care reform legislation and employer and health plan efforts to contain costs.

According to *Forbes,* in 1990, about $10 billion in maintenance drugs were funded by drug benefit plans other than Medicaid, with only $2 billion provided through mail-order services. By 1995, maintenance drug costs would almost triple, according to *Forbes,* and the mail-order share would be about $7 billion. Some drug companies were predicting that by 1995, 60 to 65 percent of all outpatient drugs would by funded. With Medco's 50 percent or higher mail-order market share, it was looking forward to healthy growth for the rest of the decade. Wygod told the *Washington Post* that his goal was to provide "each patient with the right medication at the right time for the right reason— at a price that is affordable to the plan sponsor."

Principal Subsidiaries: Medical Marketing Group; Synetic Inc.; Medco Behavioral Care Corp.

Further Reading:

Anders, George, "Medicine: Pharmacy Chain's Successful Sales Pitch Dismays Some Doctors and Drug Firms," *Wall Street Journal,* February 26, 1993, p. B1.

Mathews, Jay, "Medco's 'Managed Care' Hits the Pharmacy Business," *Washington Post,* February 28, 1993, p. H1.

O'Reilly, Brian, "Rx for Costs: Drugs by Mail," *Fortune,* August 24, 1992, p. 116.

Peers, Alexandra and Michael Siconolfi, "Inside Track: Medco Officials Take Profits from Big Gains," *Wall Street Journal,* January 29, 1992, p. C1.

Rudnitsky, Howard, "Drugs by Mail," *Forbes,* April 15, 1993, pp. 60–61.

Winslow, Ron, "Buyer's Market: Prescribing Decisions Increasingly Are Made by the Cost Conscious," *Wall Street Journal,* September 25, 1992, p. A1.

—Wendy J. Stein

Mitsubishi Motors Corporation

33-8 Shiba 5-chome
Minato-ku
Tokyo 108
Japan
03-3456-1111
Fax: 03-5232-7747

Public Company
Incorporated: 1970
Employees: 26,470
Sales: ¥3.09 trillion (US$28.05 billion)
Stock Exchanges: Tokyo Nagoya Osaka Kyoto Hiroshima
   Fukuoka Niigata Sapporo
SICs: 3711 Motor Vehicles & Car Bodies

Mitsubishi Motors Corporation is Japan's fourth-largest auto manufacturing company. Its line of automobiles includes the Diamante luxury sedan, the midsize Galant sedan, the 300GT sports car, and the company's top-seller, the compact Eclipse. Just over half the cars produced by Mitsubishi are sold inside Japan, where the company operates ten manufacturing facilities. Mitsubishi also maintains plants in the United States, Puerto Rico, Denmark, Germany, Portugal, Australia, New Zealand, Thailand, the Philippines, Indonesia, and the Netherlands. Sales in the United States, though on the decline in recent years, still total about 177,000 vehicles annually. The company's U.S. manufacturing operation is Diamond-Star Motors Corporation, located in Normal, Illinois. Diamond-Star was founded in 1985 as a joint venture with the Chrysler Corporation, but has been owned entirely by Mitsubishi since 1992. Current international joint ventures include the Malaysian-built Proton Saga, and a car built in conjunction with Volvo and the government of the Netherlands, called the Netherlands Car. Mitsubishi also exports automobile engines, including over 400,000 V6s to Chrysler alone in 1992.

Mitsubishi Motors was formed as a wholly owned subsidiary of Mitsubishi Heavy Industries (MHI) in 1970. MHI is the modern incarnation of Mitsubishi Shipbuilding Co. Ltd., which had begun manufacturing automobiles as early as 1917. As the sprawling network of companies under the Mitsubishi umbrella grew in the early part of the century, the Mitsubishi Internal Combustion Engine Co., Ltd., was established in 1920 to manufacture engines for airplanes. This company's name was changed to Mitsubishi Aircraft Co. in 1928. MHI was created in 1934 upon the merger of Mitsubishi Shipbuilding and Mitsubishi Aircraft. After the breakup of the Japanese conglomerates known as *zaibatsu* following World War II, use of the corporate name Mitsubishi was banned for several years. MHI was chopped into three regional sections with the names East Japan Heavy Industries, Central Japan Heavy Industries, and West Japan Heavy Industries. Eventually the forbidden name began to reappear, and in 1964 MHI was reintegrated out of its three fragments. By 1967, MHI's Motor Vehicle Division was producing about 75,000 cars a year. That division was spun off as an independent company in 1970, creating Mitsubishi Motors Corporation. Tomio Kubo, a successful engineer from MHI's aircraft operation, was placed in charge of the new company.

An important part of Kubo's early strategy was to build up the company's volume by emphasizing exports. This was to be done by making connections with well-established foreign companies. Mitsubishi's longstanding association with the Chrysler Corporation began the following year, when Chrysler purchased 15 percent of the company's stock. MHI retained the other 85 percent interest. By 1971, the company was producing 260,000 cars a year. Chrysler quickly began to market Mitsubishi-built cars in the United States. The most important of these was the subcompact sold in the United States as the Dodge Colt and Plymouth Arrow. At home in Japan, Mitsubishi concentrated on producing cars for special niche markets. Among the more successful of these models were the Lancer and the Celeste.

By 1973, annual production had reached 500,000 vehicles. That year, the Mitsubishi Motor Sale Financing Corporation was created to handle financing for the company's domestic sales. Although sales began to stall somewhat at that point due to the oil crisis, the introduction of the Galant in 1976 gave the company a welcome boost. As Mitsubishi's sales in the United States grew, friction began to arise between the company and its American affiliate Chrysler. Company officials felt that Chrysler demanded too much say in Mitsubishi decisions, and the idea of marketing its own cars in the United States gained support. By 1977, Mitsubishi had begun to set up its own collection of Colt dealerships across Europe. Tensions between Mitsubishi and Chrysler grew further around that time, as the two companies began competing head to head in the subcompact car market. As U.S. automakers began making smaller cars, Chrysler unveiled the Omni hatchback, a model aimed at the same market as Mitsubishi's latest Colt model, sold in Japan as the Mirage. In spite of the disagreements, the two companies continued to cooperate, with Chrysler marketing Mitsubishi's cars in the United States and Mitsubishi contributing its advanced engineering know-how to Chrysler. For 1978, Mitsubishi sold a total of 965,300 units, a 17 percent increase over the previous year. Of those, 534,600 were sold in Japan, a 20 percent increase.

Mitsubishi's annual production passed the one million mark in 1980. That year, Mitsubishi Motors teamed up with the Mitsubishi Corporation to purchase Chrysler Australia, subsequently renaming it Mitsubishi Motors Australia Ltd. By 1981, the company had captured eight percent of the Japanese auto market, running neck and neck with Mazda behind industry leaders Toyota and Nissan. Mitsubishi entered the American automobile market under its own name for the first time in 1982. Three models were initially made available to American buyers, all of them fairly upscale: the Starion, a $12,000, turbo-charged sports car; the $7,000 Cordia sedan; and a family sedan called the Tredia, priced at around $6,500. Mitsubishi also began to sell small pickup trucks in the United States, offering vehicles under its own name identical to those already being sold by Chrysler. Under import restraints on Japanese cars, the 30,000 Mitsubishi vehicles sold in 1982 had to come out of Chrysler's annual allotment of around 120,000 cars. Seventy dealers in 22 U.S. markets sold the Mitsubishi line that year.

While the company was making its foray into the U.S. market, sales at home began to sag. In 1983 a new president, Toyoo Tate, was brought in to try to reverse this trend. Tate's early moves included personnel changes in the executive offices, along with a renewed push for more international alliances. One important new connection made was with South Korea's Hyundai Motor Co., of which Mitsubishi purchased a 7.5 percent interest. By 1984 the company's revenue had reached ¥1.17 trillion. During that year, Mitsubishi Motor Sales, a separate corporation that handled domestic auto sales, was absorbed into Mitsubishi Motors.

In 1985 Mitsubishi and Chrysler launched a joint venture called Diamond-Star Motors Corp., named after the corporate logos of the two companies. The twin central Illinois towns of Bloomington and Normal were chosen as the site of the Diamond-Star plant, which was to produce a line of subcompact cars using engines and transmissions imported from Mitsubishi's Japanese facilities. For Mitsubishi, the venture provided a guaranteed source of cars to sell in the United States, the largest automobile market in the world, regardless of any restrictive trade measures that might be enacted by either country involved. By 1987, the company was selling 67,000 cars a year in the United States.

Mitsubishi Motors went public in 1988, ending its status as the only one of Japan's eleven auto manufacturers to be privately held. To pave the way for the shift to public ownership, changes had to be made in the company's stock agreements with both MHI and Chrysler. MHI agreed to reduce its share to 25 percent, retaining its position as largest single stockholder. Chrysler meanwhile increased its holding to over 20 percent. The $470 million in capital raised by the ten percent initial offering enabled Mitsubishi to pay off part of its debt as well as to expand its investments throughout Southeast Asia, where by now it was operating in the Philippines, Malaysia, and Thailand.

Toward the end of the 1980s, Mitsubishi initiated a major push to beef up its presence in the U.S. market. While Japan's quotas allowed the company to export 193,000 cars a year to the United States, two-thirds of those cars were marketed by Chrysler in 1988. In 1989 Mitsubishi pumped its U.S. sales goal up to 130,000 cars, and attacked this goal from several angles. First the company made plans to increase its U.S. dealer network by 40 percent, up to 340 dealers. Mitsubishi also aired its first national television advertising campaign. The company also began to further exploit its relationship with Hyundai, importing the Precis, a carbon copy of Hyundai's popular Excel. Diamond-Star began to pay off with the production of the Eclipse, a sporty car sold by Chrysler as the Plymouth Laser.

For 1989, Mitsubishi's worldwide production, including its overseas affiliates, reached 1.5 million units.

Mitsubishi's American thrust continued into the 1990s. In 1991 the company added a number of models to its line at a time when American companies were delaying their new models and laying off workers due to sluggish sales. Among Mitsubishi's new products was the Diamante luxury sedan. The Diamante, with a price tag of $28,000, was the winner of that year's prestigious Japan Car of the Year award. Part of Mitsubishi's strategy to increase its American market share was to target buyers who were already likely to purchase Japanese or European cars, and offer its vehicles at prices slightly lower than comparable cars in other companies' lines.

Mitsubishi gained another outlet for its cars in 1991 with the acquisition of Value Rent-A-Car. In addition, the company began producing two minivans that year, the Expo and the Expo LRV. Later in 1991, Mitsubishi bought out Chrysler's share of Diamond-Star for around $100 million, with Mitsubishi assuming all of Diamond-Star's debt. The two companies continued to split the operation's output. By this time, Chrysler's interest in Mitsubishi had fallen to about 11 percent. Of the 322,500 Mitsubishi-made vehicles sold in the United States in 1991, 187,500 were marketed under the company's own name. 1991 also brought the preliminary stages of a joint venture with Volvo Car Corporation and the government of the Netherlands to produce cars in that country.

Mitsubishi sold 176,900 vehicles in the United States in 1992, over seven percent less than the company's 1990 peak. Although company profits declined somewhat for that year, Mitsubishi's performance was considerably better than that of its Japanese competitors, all of whom suffered dramatic drops in sales in the face of a weak global economy. Mitsubishi's results were aided by strong sales of its recreational models such as the Pajero, whose sales leaped by 52 percent in the first half of the fiscal year. The company continued to outpace its fellow Japanese automakers going into 1993. With 10.7 percent of the domestic market in hand, Mitsubishi bucked another trend by spinning off a new model at a time when the others were condensing their lines. Focusing on the lower end of the market, Mitsubishi unveiled a new two-door version of the Mirage, to be sold in Japan as the Mirage Asti. The Asti's price of about $8,500 was well below the company's previous bottom end, the $11,430 Mirage four-door sedan. For the fiscal year ending in March of 1993, Mitsubishi's profits declined by 7.9 percent, a modest drop for one of the Japanese auto industry's worst years ever. Foreign exchange losses caused by a rapidly rising yen were blamed for much of the decline.

As all of the Japanese companies continued to lose market share in the United States in 1993, Mitsubishi attempted to gain a foothold in the family sedan market with the introduction of a newly redesigned Galant midsize sedan. The Galant was to be produced in the United States at the company's Normal, Illinois, plant, creating two advantages: assembling it in the United States avoids the inflated price tag the soaring yen would cause; and the Illinois plant, previously operating at only half of capacity, needed the work.

After decreasing its interest in Mitsubishi to less then three percent in 1992, Chrysler announced its decision in 1993 to sell off all of its remaining Mitsubishi shares on the open market. The two companies stated that they would nevertheless continue their close alliance, with Chrysler supplying engines and transmissions for Mitsubishi's Diamond-Star operation, and Mitsubishi marketing Chrysler products in Japan. Although the Japanese automobile industry in 1993 was not thriving as it had ten years earlier, when it appeared unstoppable in the worldwide car arena, Mitsubishi Motors has performed as well as any company in the field in recent years. With the backing of the gigantic extended family of Mitsubishi companies, Mitsubishi Motors' solid position among auto manufacturers seems relatively secure.

Principal Subsidiaries: Diamond-Star Motors Corporation (U.S.A.); Mitsubishi Fuso Truck of America, Inc. (U.S.A.); Mitsubishi Motor Sales of Caribbean Inc. (Puerto Rico); Mitsubishi Motors New Zealand Ltd.; Mitsubishi Motors Europe B.V. (Netherlands); Mitsubishi Motor Sales of America, Inc. (U.S.A.; 82%); Philippine Automotive Manufacturing Corporation (50%); Mitsubishi Motors Australia Ltd. (50%); Mitsubishi Motors de Portugal S.A. (50%); PT Mitsubishi Krama Yudha Motors and Manufacturing (Indonesia; 49%); MMC Sittipol Company, Ltd. (Thailand; 48%).

Further Reading:

Armstrong, Larry, "Mitsubishi Is Souping Up Its Image," *Business Week,* February 27, 1989, p. 56.

Cullison, A.E., "Mitsubishi Eyes Own US Sales Team," *Journal of Commerce,* April 13, 1977, p. 3.

Dodsworth, Terry, "Living with Chrysler," *Financial Times,* November 10, 1977, p. 27.

Furukawa, Tsukasa, "Mitsubishi to Retain Amiable Relationship with Chrysler, It Says," *American Metal Market,* July 5, 1993, p. 8.

Holusha, John, "Mitsubishi's U.S. Car Venture," *New York Times,* October 26, 1982, p. D3.

Kanabayashi, Masayoshi, "Japan's Battered Auto Makers Adopt Mixed Outlook for the Current Year," *Wall Street Journal,* June 1, 1993, p. A9B.

Levin, Doron, "Chrysler Corp., Mitsubishi Set Site for Plant," *Wall Street Journal,* October 8, 1985, p. 2; "Mitsubishi's Big Campaign in U.S.," *New York Times,* April 30, 1991, p. D1.

Maskery, Mary Ann, *Automotive News,* "Japan Niche Prompts a 2nd Mirage," May 17, 1993; "Mitsubishi to Sell Stock in Auto Firm," October 31, 1988, p. 4; "Mitsubishi Sets Sights on Mazda in U.S.," September 21, 1992, p. 21.

Miller, Krystal, "Mitsubishi Restyles Galant to Anchor Line," *Wall Street Journal,* June 23, 1993, p. B1.

"Mitsubishi Motors Posts 27% Decline in 1st-Half Profit," *Wall Street Journal,* November 6, 1992, p. A5A.

—Robert R. Jacobson

Mitsui Petrochemical Industries, Ltd.

Kasumigaseki Bldg.
2-5, Kasumigaseki 3-chome
Chiyoda-ku, Tokyo 100
Japan
(03) 3580-3616
Fax: (03) 3593-0028

Public Company
Incorporated: 1955
Employees: 4,301
Sales: ¥330.83 billion (US$3 billion)
Stock Exchanges: Tokyo Osaka
SICs: 2869 Petrochemicals

Mitsui Petrochemical Industries, Ltd., also known as Mitsui Sekka, is one of Japan's leading petrochemical companies. Mitsui Petrochemical is part of the Mitsui Group, one of the largest of Japan's *keiretsu*—loosely connected groups of corporations interrelated by networks of ownership. Mitsui Petrochemical produces and sells a wide assortment of chemicals used for making plastics, polymers, solvents, and various other synthetic materials. Nearly half of the company's sales are generated by industrial chemicals and basic raw materials. Synthetic resins make up approximately 30 percent of sales. The remainder of company revenues comes from specialty chemicals. Mitsui operates production and research facilities in Yamaguchi and Chiba and maintains district sales offices in Osaka, Nagaya, Fukuoka, Sapporo, and Hiroshima. Its overseas offices are located in New York City, Houston, Düsseldorf, London, Paris, and Beijing. In addition to its own subsidiaries, Mitsui is engaged in joint ventures throughout the world with such well-known companies as DuPont Chemical Company, General Electric Company, and Amoco Corporation.

Mitsui Petrochemical Industries (MPC) was formed in 1955 and was Japan's first integrated petrochemical operation. The family of Mitsui companies out of which MPC grew made up the reconstituted version of the Mitsui *zaibatsu,* one of the largest of Japan's family-run conglomerates. Although the *zaibatsu* were broken up in the aftermath of World War II, their fractured remains were eventually reassembled in the 1950s. Mitsui, which was split into 180 separate entities after the war, started to regroup in 1950, when 27 leaders of former Mitsui companies began coordinating their activities at regular meetings.

During the early 1950s Japan found itself falling behind in a number of high-tech industries, including petrochemicals. The government reacted by passing laws to support research and development in these new industries. Up to that time, the production of organic chemicals in Japan was dependent on coal, carbide, and fermentation processes as sources of raw material. Meanwhile, wartime production of high-octane gasoline in the United States had led to major advances in the U.S. petrochemical industry, which was by then using waste gases from the naphtha-cracking process. In order to modernize its petrochemical operations, Japan began importing technology from the United States and Europe, as well as offering loans and tax breaks to domestic companies interested in utilizing that technology. The first such operation was MPC, which was put together by several Mitsui companies, including Mitsui Chemical, Mitsui Bank, Mitsui Mining, and Toyo Koatsu.

The MPC complex at Iwakuni, located on Hiroshima Bay in the Yamaguchi Prefecture, was opened in 1958. Using naphtha supplied by Koa Oil, MPC began producing ethylene, propylene, polyethylene, and other chemicals. The chemicals were then distributed by Mitsui Bussan, the general trading company. The most significant customer was another Mitsui affiliate, Toyo Rayon, Japan's largest manufacturer of synthetic fibers. As worldwide use of plastics increased, MPC grew quickly. Before the decade had ended, development had already begun on a research complex in Chiba on land reclaimed from Tokyo Bay. In 1960 MPC launched Mitsui Polychemicals Co., Ltd. (later called DuPont-Mitsui Polychemicals Co., Ltd.), a 50–50 joint venture with DuPont. Further construction continued to take place at the company's Iwakuni facility, and in 1962 it was renamed Iwakuni-Ohtake Works. A district sales office was opened in Osaka that year as well.

In October of 1962 MPC was listed on the Tokyo and Osaka stock exchanges for the first time. As the use of plastics continued to skyrocket in the 1960s, the Japanese petrochemical industry thrived. Another subsidiary, Tokyo Polymer Co., Ltd. (later called Mitsui Petrochemical Industrial Products, Ltd.), was formed in 1964. That year, MPC obtained the rights to use Union Carbide Corporation technology to produce materials for the manufacture of injection-molded high density polyethylene beverage cases.

Ethylene production in Japan was climbing sharply in the mid-1960s as the country sought to further reduce its reliance on imports for its manufacturing needs. In 1965 MPC received permission to expand its ethylene capacity by 200,000 metric tons a year. Two more district sales offices were opened the following year, one in Nagoya and the other in Fukuoka. MPC also acquired a major share of Mitsui Fluorochemicals Co., Ltd. (later called DuPont-Mitsui Fluorochemicals Co., Ltd.), a company of which it still maintains half ownership.

Two more joint ventures were launched in 1967. MPC teamed with Texaco to form Sanseki-Texaco Chemicals Co., Ltd., an industrial organic chemical products producer. Ukishima Petrochemicals Co., Ltd. was established that year as a 50–50 venture with Nippon Petrochemicals Co., Ltd. Ukishima produces and sells ethylene, propylene, and other basic petrochemical products. MPC also began manufacturing operations at the company's Chiba Works facility and opened a research center at the Iwakuni-Ohtake Works. In 1968 the company moved its corporate headquarters to Tokyo's Kasumigaseki Building and purchased a one-third interest in Honshu Chemical Industry Co., Ltd., a manufacturer of raw materials for synthetic resins, pharmaceuticals, dyes, and other man-made products. Another district sales office, located in Sapporo, was established the following year.

MPC's fast-paced growth continued into the 1970s. In 1970 the company bought into Tokyo Serofan Co., Ltd., a producer of cellophane and plastic film. MPC came to hold a majority of stock in Tokyo Serofan, which has been operating since 1929. In 1972 MPC combined with two other Mitsui companies, Bussan and Toatsu, for a project in Iran. The three companies, along with the National Petroleum Corporation of Iran and Imperial Chemical Industries, signed a contract for the establishment of a petrochemical complex located in that country. A proposed 1973 joint venture with Hercules Inc. of Wilmington, Delaware, was aborted, however, when antitrust issues were raised by the U.S. Justice Department. Officials maintained that such a venture would restrain competition in the U.S. polypropylene business, in which both companies controlled significant market shares.

In 1974 MPC opened two overseas offices to facilitate its international operations, one in New York City and one in Düsseldorf. In May of that year, the company acquired Tohcello Shoji Co., Ltd., which came to be called New Tohcello Shoji Co., Ltd. This acquisition added another cellophane and plastic film operation to MPC's growing empire. 1974 also marked the start-up of a new plant at the Iwakuni-Ohtake Works capable of producing 5,000 tons per year of hydroquinone, a chemical with photographic applications. The following year, MPC began producing and marketing TPX, the lightest plastic yet developed. The entire business was essentially taken over from Imperial Chemical Industries Ltd., a British company that previously held the worldwide marketing rights for TPX. MPC also obtained from BP Chemicals International Ltd. the necessary technology to produce the monomer used as the raw material for TPX production.

MPC opened its Polymer Technical Center toward the end of 1976. Over the next several years, the company benefitted from several technological breakthroughs that resulted from its own accelerated research and development activities. Joining with Montedison to develop a highly efficient catalyst for use in the production of polypropylene, the company used its new technology to initiate full-scale commercial production of meta-toluidine, a chemical crucial in the production of color photography developers, dyes, and agricultural chemicals. In 1979 MPC was one of four Japanese companies hired by the Chinese government to build plants as part of that country's push to modernize its industrial capabilities.

As the 1970s drew to a close, the Japanese petrochemical industry began to struggle somewhat, due in part to more heated competition from developing countries, increased chemical activity in oil-producing nations, and a rise in the prices of naphtha and other oil-based raw materials. In 1980 MPC sold most of its stake in the Iran venture to Mitsui Bussan, lowering its share from 13 to 5 percent. For the year, MPC saw its sales decline by 2.3 percent to $1.4 billion and its earnings plummet

to $11 million, a decrease of 60 percent. The company did not stop launching new joint ventures, however. MPC teamed up with Amoco Chemicals Corp. of Singapore and Samsung Group that year to open a purified terephthalic acid plant in South Korea. The plant's output provided half the raw material needed by South Korea's entire polyester fiber and textile industry, dramatically reducing the country's reliance on imported materials.

In 1981 Nippon Amorphous Metals Co., Ltd., was formed, with Allied Corporation owning half and MPC sharing the remaining half with three other Mitsui companies. The creation of this company allowed Mitsui to begin marketing Allied's amorphous metals in Asia. Another major joint venture was launched in 1982, with the creation of GEM Polymers, Ltd., 51 percent-owned by General Electric Company. The remaining share was split evenly between MPC and Mitsui Toatsu. GEM Polymers manufactures plastics used in the automotive, electrical, and electronics industries. Also in 1982 MPC formed Mitsui PET-Resin Co., a wholly owned subsidiary.

The joint ventures continued to multiply from there. In 1983 Mitsui Nesseki Polymers Co., Ltd., was founded, with ownership split evenly between MPC, Mitsui Toatsu, and Nippon Petrochemicals. Another new company, Nippon Polyamide Co., was formed that year as an equally owned venture with France's state-owned chemicals group Rhone-Poulenc S.A. Nippon Polyamide was created to produce resins for the auto and electrical goods industries using MPC facilities and Rhone-Poulenc-licensed technology. A year later, MPC launched a joint venture with the Swiss company Ciba-Geigy Ltd. called Nippon Alky Phenol Co., Ltd. The Hiroshima District Sales Office was established in 1984 as well.

MPC research resulted in several commercial successes in the mid-1980s. The company began applying its petrochemical technology to the field of biotechnology, resulting in a number of marketable products. Beginning in 1983, MPC scientists were able to make dyes from plants that had been used medicinally for centuries. The dyes proved hugely successful as ingredients in soaps and cosmetics, such as an award-winning "bio-lipstick." Next, similar cell-culture technology was applied to produce virus-free flower bulbs, enabling MPC to make huge advances in flower-growing efficiency.

For the fiscal year ending in March of 1986, MPC reported net income of $40.2 million on sales of $1.6 billion, a slight increase over the previous year. Several new ventures were initiated during 1986, including Sunrex Industry, a wholly owned subsidiary specializing in man-made fabrics and plastic film, and Mitsui Petrochemicals (America), Ltd., the company's first overseas subsidiary. A second project with General Electric, GEM Chemicals Ltd. (later called GE Plastics Japan Ltd.), was also established during that year. GEM Chemicals produced a chemical called bisphenol A, which is used in epoxy and resins. The following year, MPC opened its Advanced Technology Center at Sodegaura-cho in the Chiba Prefecture. For fiscal 1987, MPC's sales increased modestly to $1.8 billion.

In 1988 MPC once again joined forces with Toatsu and Nippon Petrochemicals to form a new company. The result was Ukishima Polypro Co., Ltd., a polypropylene operation. A year later, the company's second overseas subsidiary, Mitsui Petrochemical Industries (Europa) GmbH, was established. It was based at MPC's existing Düsseldorf office, and additional offices were eventually opened in London and Paris. Also formed that year was Nippon Epoxy Polymers Co., Ltd., a joint venture with Dainippon Ink and Chemicals, Inc., and Asahi Denka Kogyo K.K. MPC followed up with several new projects in 1990, including Chiba Phenol Co., Ltd., a joint venture with Idemitsu Petrochemical. The creation of Chiba Phenol coincided with major increases in phenol production throughout Japan and elsewhere. MPC also purchased the Pathtek Division of Eastman Technology, subsequently creating Mitsui-Pathtek Corporation, based in Rochester, New York.

It was clear by 1991 that Japan's petrochemical industry was entering a difficult period. Around that time, Western companies such as Dow Chemical Co., British Petroleum Company PLC, and Exxon Corporation began entering the chemical arena in Southeast Asia, Japan's most important foreign market. Developing countries located there continued to beef up their petrochemical investments as well. These events, combined with a generally sluggish Japanese economy, created problems for MPC and its competitors. MPC saw its operating profits decline by approximately one-third during this period. The company nevertheless continued investing at a breakneck pace. Its 1991 activities included the formation of two loosely related wholly owned subsidiaries: San-Business Services, Ltd., a provider of welfare programs and general clerical services; and Mitsui Sekka Engineering Co., Ltd., a company specializing in the engineering and construction of industrial and public welfare facilities.

MPC and Exxon announced an agreement in 1992 to work together in commercializing ethylene-based polymers that are made by using advanced technology developed by the two companies. The industry continued to suffer, however, and for fiscal 1992, MPC's sales declined by more than three percent to ¥320 billion. Profits dropped to ¥15 billion, a decrease of about 40 percent. Most of Japan's other chemical companies were showing similarly dismal results. The difficulties being experienced in the Japanese chemical industry led to discussions of a possible merger between MPC and Toatsu; such a marriage within the Mitsui group remained a possibility for the future in spite of antitrust concerns and the ongoing but friendly rivalry between the two companies. Meanwhile, MPC persisted in fearlessly seek out ventures all over the world in hopes of finding markets in which to exploit its advanced research capabilities.

Principal Subsidiaries: Mitsui Petrochemicals (America), Ltd.; Mitsui-Pathtek Corporation (United States); Mitsui Petrochemical Industries (Europa) GmbH (Germany); Nippon Alky Phenol Co., Ltd. (50%); Mitsui PET-Resin Co., Ltd.; Mitsui Petrochemical Industrial Products, Ltd. (75%); Mitsui Sekka Engineering Co., Ltd.; San-Business Services, Ltd.; Chiba Phenol Col, Ltd. (55%); Nippon Epoxy Polymers Co., Ltd. (50%); Tokyo Serofan Co., Ltd. (53.8%); New Tohcello Shoji Co., Ltd.; Tohcello Chemical Co., Ltd.; Sunrex Industry Co., Ltd.; Sun Medical Co., Ltd. (70%); Senshin Industry Co., Ltd.; Hi-Sheet Industries, Ltd.; Sanshin Kako Co., Ltd. (38.7%); Meiwa Apex Co., Ltd. (67%); Kyushu Taiyo Chemical Co., Ltd. (34.75%); Nippon Reform Co. (50%); Sakushin Kogyo Co., Ltd. (50%).

Further Reading:

"Allied Broadens Its Horizons," *Chemical Week,* June 10, 1981, p. 23.
"Call Off Venture Already Called off Demanded in U.S. Suit," *Wall Street Journal,* June 1, 1973, p. 19.
Chynoweth, Emma, "Japan: Gray Skies at Home and Abroad," *Chemical Week,* November 27, 1991, pp. 33–40.
Fujita, Yasuhiro, "R&D Activities of Mitsui Petrochemical Industries, Ltd. in the Field of Biotechnology," *Business Japan,* June 1987, p. 113.
Gross, Neil, "Japanese Biotech's Overnight Evolution," *Business Week,* March 12, 1990, pp. 69–72.
"Hydroquinone for Mitsui Brought Into Production," *Chemical Marketing Reporter,* December 16, 1974, p. 28.
"Mitsui Chemical Units Plan Joint Research, Production and Sales," *Asian Wall Street Journal,* October 29, 1979, p. 14.
"Plastics in Japan: Growth and Diversity," *Modern Plastics,* January 1965, p. 120.
"Resin Operation Started by Mitsui Petrochemical," *Chemical Marketing Reporter,* April 14, 1975, p. 14.
"Rhone-Poulenc S.A., Mitsui Petrochemical Form a Resins Venture," *Wall Street Journal,* August 24, 1983, p. 30.
Roberts, John G., *Mitsui: Three Centuries of Japanese Business,* New York: Weatherhill, 1973.
Smith, Charles, "Mitsui Raises Its Share in Iran Chemical Project," *Financial Times,* March 5, 1980, p. 6.
"Three-Nation Venture Opens Petrochemical Plant in South Korea," *Asian Wall Street Journal,* May 5, 1980, p. 7.
Wood, Andrew, "Exxon/Mitsui in Metallocene Catalyst Linkup," *Chemical Week,* April 29, 1992, p. 12.
Wood, Andrew and Chynoweth, Emma, "Mitsui Toatsu and Mitsui Sekka Confirm Merger Talks," *Chemical Week,* April 29, 1992, p. 28.
Wood, Andrew, "Phenol Expansions East and West," *Chemical Week,* April 18, 1990, p. 9.

—Robert R. Jacobson

Monsanto

Monsanto Company

800 N. Lindbergh Blvd.
St. Louis, Missouri 63167
U.S.A.
(314) 694-1000
Fax: (314) 694-7571

Public Company
Incorporated: 1933 as Monsanto Chemical Company
Employees: 33,797
Sales: $7.8 billion
Stock Exchanges: New York Amsterdam Brussels Chicago
    Frankfurt Geneva London Paris Tokyo Zürich
SICs: 2821 Plastics Materials & Resins; 2834 Pharmaceutical
    Preparations; 3823 Process Control Instruments; 2833
    Medicinals & Botanicals

Monsanto is one of the largest corporations and most important agrichemical concerns in the United States. Innovative products for the agricultural industry—such as bovine somatotropin (BST), used in milk production—as well as for consumer use— such as the fat substitute Simplesse and the artificial sweetener NutraSweet—have contributed to Monsanto's profits and renown for research and development.

Monsanto traces its roots to John Francisco Queeny, a purchaser for a wholesale drug house at the turn of the century, who formed the Monsanto Chemical Works in St. Louis, Missouri, in order to produce the artificial sweetener saccharin. By 1905 John Queeny's company was also producing caffeine and vanillin and was beginning to turn a profit. In 1908 Queeny felt confident enough about his firm's future to leave his part-time job with another drug house to work full time as Monsanto's president. The company continued to grow, with sales surpassing the $1 million mark for the first time in 1915.

While prior to World War I America relied heavily on foreign supplies of chemicals, the increasing likelihood of U.S. intervention meant that the country would soon need its own domestic producer of chemicals. Looking back on the significance of the war for Monsanto, Queeny's son Edgar remarked, ''There was no choice other than to improvise, to invent and to find new ways of doing all the old things. The old dependence on Europe was, almost overnight, a thing of the past.'' Monsanto was forced to rely on its own knowledge and nascent technical ability. Among other problems, Monsanto researchers discovered that pages describing German chemical processes had been ripped out of library books. Monsanto developed several strategic products, including phenol as an antiseptic, in addition to acetylsalicyclic acid, or aspirin.

With the purchase of an Illinois acid company in 1918, Monsanto began to widen the scope of its factory operations. A postwar depression during the early 1920s affected profits, but by the time John Queeny turned over the company to Edgar in 1928 the financial situation was much brighter. Monsanto had gone public, a move that paved the way for future expansion. At this time, the company had 55 shareholders and 1,000 employees and owned a small company in Britain.

Under Edgar's direction Monsanto, now the Monsanto Chemical Company, began to substantially expand and enter into an era of prolonged growth. Acquisitions expanded Monsanto's product line to include the new field of plastics and the manufacture of phosphorus.

By the time the United States entered World War II in 1941, the domestic chemical industry had attained far greater independence from Europe. Monsanto, strengthened by its several acquisitions, was also prepared to produce such strategic materials as phosphates and inorganic chemicals. Most important was the company's acquisition of a research and development laboratory called Thomas and Hochwalt. The well-known Dayton, Ohio, firm strengthened Monsanto at the time and provided the basis for some of its future achievements in chemical technology. One of its most important discoveries was styrene monomer, a key ingredient in synthetic rubber and a crucial product for the armed forces during the war.

Largely unknown by the public, Monsanto experienced difficulties in attempting to market consumer goods. However, attempts to refine a low quality detergent led to developments in grass fertilizer, an important consumer product since the postwar housing boom had created a strong market of homeowners eager to perfect their lawns.

In the mid-1950s Monsanto began to produce urethane foam, which was flexible and easy to use; it later became crucial in making automobile interiors. In 1955 Monsanto acquired Lion Oil, increasing its assets by more than 50 percent. Stockholders during this time numbered 43,000.

Having finally outgrown its headquarters in downtown St. Louis, Monsanto moved to the suburban community of Creve Coeur in 1957. Three years later Edgar Queeny turned over the chair of Monsanto to Charles Thomas, one of the founders of the research and development laboratory so important to Monsanto. Charlie Sommer, who had joined the company in 1929, became president. Under their combined leadership Monsanto saw several important developments, including the establishment of the Agricultural Chemicals division, created to consolidate Monsanto's diverse agrichemical product lines. Monsanto's European expansion continued, with Brussels becoming the permanent overseas headquarters in 1962.

In 1964 Monsanto changed its name to Monsanto Company in acknowledgment of its diverse product line. The company consisted of eight divisions, including petroleum, fibers, building materials, and packaging.

According to Monsanto historian Dan Forrestal, "Leadership during the 1960s and early 1970s came principally from ... executives whose Monsanto roots ran deep." In 1964 Edward O'Neal became chairperson. O'Neal, who had come to Monsanto in 1935 with the acquisition of the Swann Corporation, was the first chair in company history who had not first held the post of president. Another company leader was Edward J. Bock, who had joined Monsanto in 1941 as an engineer. He rose through the ranks to become a member of the board of directors in 1965 and president in 1968. Edgar Queeny, who left no heirs, died in 1968.

Although Bock had a reputation for being a committed company executive, several factors contributed to his volatile term as president. High overhead costs and a sluggish national economy led to a dramatic 29 percent decrease in earnings in 1969. Sales were up the following year, but Bock's implementation of the 1971 reorganization caused a significant amount of friction among members of the board and senior management. In spite of the fact that this move, in which Monsanto separated the management of raw materials from the company's subsidiaries, was widely praised by security analysts, Bock resigned from the presidency in February 1972. After a nine month search, John W. Hanley, a former executive with Procter and Gamble, was chosen as president. Hanley also took over as chairperson in 1975.

Under Hanley, Monsanto more than doubled its sales and earnings between 1972 and 1983. Toward the end of his tenure, Hanley put into effect a promise he had made to himself and to Monsanto when he accepted the position of president, namely, that his successor would be chosen from Monsanto's ranks. Hanley and his staff chose approximately 20 young executives as potential company leaders and began preparing them for the head position at Monsanto. Among them was Richard J. Mahoney. When Hanley joined Monsanto, Mahoney was a young sales director in agricultural products. In 1983 Hanley turned the leadership of the company over to Mahoney. Wall Street immediately approved this decision with an increase in Monsanto's share prices.

During this time, public concern over the environment began to escalate. Ralph Nader's activities and Rachel Carson's book *Silent Spring* had been influential in increasing the U.S. public's awareness of activities within the chemical industry in the 1960s, and Monsanto had responded in several ways to the pressure. In 1964 the company introduced biodegradable detergents, and in 1976, Monsanto announced plans to phase out production of polychlorinated biphenyl (PCB).

In 1979 a lawsuit was filed against Monsanto and other manufacturers of agent orange, a defoliant used during the Vietnam War. Agent orange contained a highly toxic chemical known as dioxin, and the suit claimed that hundreds of veterans had suffered permanent damage because of the chemical. In 1984 Monsanto and seven other manufacturers agreed to a $180 million settlement just before the trial began. With the announcement of a settlement Monsanto's share price, depressed because of the uncertainty over the outcome of the trial, rose substantially.

Also in 1984, Monsanto lost a $10 million antitrust suit to Spray-Rite, a former distributor of Monsanto agricultural herbicides. The U.S. Supreme Court upheld the suit and award, finding that Monsanto had acted to fix retail prices with other herbicide manufacturers.

In August 1985, Monsanto purchased G. D. Searle, the "NutraSweet" firm. NutraSweet, an artificial sweetener, had generated $700 million in sales that year, and Searle could offer Monsanto an experienced marketing and a sales staff as well as real profit potential. Since the late 1970s the company had sold nearly 60 low margin businesses and, with two important agriculture product patents expiring in 1988, a major new cash source was more than welcome. What Monsanto didn't count on, however, was the controversy surrounding Searle's intrauterine birth control device called the Copper-7.

Soon after the acquisition, disclosures about hundreds of lawsuits over Searle's IUD surfaced and turned Monsanto's takeover into a public relations disaster. The disclosures, which inevitably led to comparisons with those about A. H. Robins, the Dalkan Shield manufacturer that eventually declared Chapter 11 bankruptcy, raised questions as to how carefully Monsanto management had considered the acquisition. In early 1986 Searle discontinued IUD sales in the United States. By 1988 Monsanto's new subsidiary faced an estimated 500 lawsuits against the Copper-7 IUD. As the parent company, Monsanto was well insulated from its subsidiary's liabilities by the legal "corporate veil."

As Monsanto entered the 1990s, it faced continued challenges from a variety of sources, including government and public concern over hazardous wastes, fuel and feedstock costs, and import competition. At the end of the 99th Congress, then-President Ronald Reagan signed a $8.5 billion, five-year cleanup superfund reauthorization act. Built into the financing was a surcharge on the chemical industry created through the tax reform bill. Biotechnology regulations were just being formulated, and Monsanto, which already had types of genetically engineered bacteria ready for testing, was poised to be an active participant in that field.

In keeping with its strategy to become a leader in the health field, Monsanto and the Washington University Medical School entered into a five-year research contract in 1984. Two-thirds of the research was to be directed into areas with obviously commercial applications, while one-third of the research was to be devoted to theoretical work. One particularly promising discovery involved the application of the bovine growth factor, a way to greatly increase milk production.

In the burgeoning low-calorie sweetener market, challengers to NutraSweet were putting pressure on Monsanto. Pfizer Inc., a pharmaceutical company, was preparing to market its product, called alitame, which it claimed was far sweeter than NutraSweet and better suited for baking.

In an interview with *Business Week*, senior vice-president for research and development Howard Schneiderman commented, "To maintain our markets—and not become another steel industry—we must spend on research and development." Monsanto, which has committed eight percent of its operating budget to research and development, far above the industry average, may emerge in the 1990s as one of the leaders in the fields of biotechnology and pharmaceuticals that are only now emerging from their nascent stage.

By the end of the 1980s, Monsanto had restructured itself and become a producer of specialty chemicals, with a focus on biotechnology products. Monsanto enjoyed consecutive record years in 1988 and 1989—sales were $8.3 billion and $8.7 billion, respectively. In 1988 the Food and Drug Administration approved Cytotec, a drug that prevents gastric ulcers in high-risk cases. Sales of Cytotec in the United States reached $39 million in 1989.

The Monsanto Chemical Co. unit prospered with products like Saflex, a type of nylon carpet fiber. The NutraSweet Company held its own in 1989, contributing $180 million in earnings, with growth in the carbonated beverage segment. Almost 500 new products containing NutraSweet were introduced in 1989, for a total of 3,000 products.

Monsanto continued to invest heavily in research and development, with seven percent of sales allotted for this area. The investment began to pay off when the research and development department developed an all-natural fat substitute called Simplesse. The FDA declared in early 1990 that the product was "generally recognized as safe" for use in frozen desserts. That year, the NutraSweet Company introduced Simple Pleasures frozen dairy dessert. Monsanto hoped to see Simplesse used eventually in salad dressings, yogurt, and mayonnaise.

Despite these successes, Monsanto remained frustrated by delays in obtaining FDA approval for bovine somatotropin (BST), a chemical used to increase milk production in cows. Opponents to BST said it would upset the balance of supply and demand for milk, but Monsanto countered that BST would provide high-quality food supplies to consumers worldwide.

The final year of the 1980s also marked Monsanto's listing for the first time on the Tokyo Stock Exchange. Monsanto officials expected the listing to improve opportunities for licensing and joint venture agreements.

Monsanto had expected to celebrate 1990 as its fifth consecutive year of increased earnings, but numerous factors—the increased price of oil due to the Persian Gulf War, a recession in key industries in the United States, and droughts in California and Europe—prevented the company from achieving this goal. Net income was $546 million, a dramatic drop from the record of $679 the previous year. Nonetheless, Searle, which had caused considerable public relations scandals and headaches in the 1980s, had a record financial year in 1990. The subsidiary had established itself in the global pharmaceutical market and was beginning to emerge as an industry leader. The Monsanto Chemical Co., meanwhile, was a $4 billion business that made up the largest percentage of Monsanto's sales.

Monsanto continued to work at upholding "The Monsanto Pledge," a 1988 declaration to reduce emissions of toxic substances. By its own estimates, the company devoted $285 million annually to environmental expenditures. Furthermore, Monsanto and the Environmental Protection Agency agreed to a cleanup program at the company's detergent and phosphate plant in Richmond County, Georgia.

The company restructured during the early 1990s to help cut losses during a difficult economic time. Net income in 1991 was only $296 million, $250 million less than the previous year. Despite this showing, 1991 was a good year for some of Monsanto's newest products. Bovine somatotropin finally gained FDA approval and was sold in Mexico and Brazil, and Monsanto received the go-ahead to use the fat substitute, Simplesse, in a full range of food products, including yogurt, cheese and cheese spreads, and other low-fat spreads. In addition, the herbicide Dimension was approved in 1991, and scientists at Monsanto tested genetically improved plants in field trials.

Furthermore, Monsanto expanded internationally, opening an office in Shanghai and a plant in Beijing, China. The company also hoped to expand in Thailand, and entered into a joint venture in Japan with Mitsubishi Chemical Co.

Monsanto's sales in 1992 hit $7.8 million. However, as net income dropped 130 percent from 1991 due to several one-time aftertax charges, the company prepared itself for challenging times. The patent on NutraSweet brand sweetener expired in 1992, and in preparation for increased competition, Monsanto launched new products, such as the NutraSweet Spoonful, which came in tabletop serving jars, like sugar. The company also devoted ongoing research and development to Sweetener 2000, a high-intensity product.

In 1992, Monsanto denied that it planned to sell G. D. Searle and Co., pointing out that Searle was a profitable subsidiary that launched many new products. However, to decrease losses, Monsanto did sell Fisher Controls International Inc., a subsidiary that manufactures process control equipment. Profits from the sale were used to buy the Ortho lawn-and-garden business from Chevron Chemical Co.

In the 1990s, Monsanto expected to see growth in its agricultural, chemical, and biotechnological divisions. In 1993, Monsanto and NTGargiulo joined forces to produce a genetically-altered tomato. The companies expected that the new tomato would be on the market in three to five years.

Principal Subsidiaries: Bolgen NV Collagen Corp.; Monsanto PLC; Monsanto Canada Inc.; Monsanto Electronic Materials Co.; Monsanto Enviro-Chem Systems Inc.; Monsanto Europe S.A.; Monsanto International Sales Co., Inc.; Monsanto Oil Co.; Monsanto (Suisse) S.A.; Nutra Sweet Co.; Ortho Chemical Co.; Polyamide Intermediaries Ltd. (50%); RDI Inc.; G. D. Searle & Co.

Further Reading:

Crisafulli, Patricia, "Monsanto, EPA Resolve Superfund Cleanup," *Journal of Commerce,* April 12, 1991, p. 13A.
Donlon, J. P., "After Restructuring, What?" *Chief Executive (U.S.),* March-April, 1988, p. 50.
Ellis, James E., "Monsanto and the Copper-7: A 'Corporate Veil' Begins to Fray," *Business Week,* September 26, 1988, p. 50.
Forrestal, Dan J., *Faith, Hope, and $5,000: The Story of Monsanto: The Trials and Triumphs of the First 75 Years,* New York: Simon and Schuster, 1977.
Kiesche, Elizabeth S., "Monsanto Cultivates Lawn and Garden Line with Ortho Buy," *Chemical Week,* January 20, 1993, p. 7.
Monsanto Company Annual Reports, St. Louis: Monsanto Company, 1988–92.

—updated by Marinell Landa

Morton International Inc.

100 North Riverside Plaza
Chicago, Illinois 60606
U.S.A.
(312) 807-2000
Fax: (312) 807-2010

Public Company
Incorporated: 1848
Employees: 10,200
Sales: $2.14 billion
Stock Exchanges: New York
SICs: 2891 Adhesives & Sealants; 3479 Metal Coating &
    Allied Services; 2865 Cyclic Crudes & Intermediates;
    2899 Chemical Preparations Nec

Morton International—probably best known for its popular
blue canister of table salt, featuring a raincoat-clad girl with an
umbrella and the tagline, "when it rains, it pours"—is a diversified company maintaining profitable divisions involved in a
wide range of products that include chemicals and automotive
airbags. In 1986 the company, then called Morton Thiokol,
gained notoriety for its part in the explosion of the NASA space
shuttle *Challenger*. The accident precipitated a crisis that
led Morton to spin-off the Thiokol rocket business in 1989.
Both companies now operate as completely independent
enterprises.

Morton began as a small agency distributing salt in the American Midwest, from shipments routed from the eastern seaboard
on the Erie Canal. After the Civil War, the demand for salt kept
pace with the expansion of the meat-packing industry, particularly in Chicago, where both the meat-packing and salt industries became well established. In 1879 a 24-year-old clerk
named Joy Morton joined the agency, and by the age of 30 he
owned it.

Morton soon came to dominate at least a third of the salt market,
becoming the product's only nationwide distributor. Morton
experienced moderate success, maintaining a large share of a
stable and profitable market with few competitors. However, by
the mid-twentieth century, the salt industry had fully matured.
In the 1950s, Morton diversified into specialty chemicals, including bromides, adhesives, dye stuffs, and polymers. In 1965
Morton Industries went public and decided to diversify further.
Its first major acquisition that year was Simonize, a maker of

auto wax and household cleaners. Four years later, Morton
merged with Norwich Pharmaceuticals, which manufactured
prescription drugs as well as such over-the-counter products as
Unguentine, Chloraseptic, and Pepto-Bismol.

However, the Morton-Norwich merger was problematic in that
Morton did not possess the financial resources to revitalize
Norwich. Despite its established product line, Norwich was
slowed in its growth by an inadequate research and development budget; at the time, the marketing of a new drug could
incur costs of $50 million, a figure far exceeding Morton-
Norwich's entire research budget. As a result, from 1969 to
1971, Morton-Norwich's dividends remained negligible, and its
stock shares sold for only eight times dividends, which was low
for pharmaceutical companies. To remedy the situation Morton-
Norwich went into partnership with Rhone-Poulenc, a French
drug manufacturer. In exchange for 20 percent of its stock,
Morton-Norwich received right of first refusal on any of Rhone-
Poulenc's new products. Moreover, Rhone-Poulenc had ample
research facilities.

However, the partnership with Rhone-Poulenc was beset with
difficulties. "We couldn't run our business with those people,"
said Charles Locke, then president of Morton. Moreover,
Rhone-Poulenc was eventually nationalized by French President Mitterand, and decided to sell its stock in Morton-Norwich. The French company did not abide by an earlier agreement to refrain from selling its share of Morton-Norwich to a
single buyer, so Morton-Norwich found itself a potential takeover candidate.

In 1982 Morton sold Norwich and used part of the proceeds to
buy back its stock from Rhone-Poulenc. However, Morton
remained a potential candidate for takeover due to the steady
income from its salt operation. Its stock was selling for $30 a
share, but with only $20 a share cash reserves, the management
at Morton decided to take action. As a result, management
began to look for an eligible specialty chemicals company to
purchase or merge with.

Thiokol, with its 20 percent annual growth rate, was Morton's
prime candidate for a merger. Thiokol controlled 40 percent of
the solid rocket fuels market, and its Texize division manufactured a popular and profitable line of household cleaners that
included the brand Glass Plus. Morton decided that the household products divisions in both companies would complement
one another, and in 1982 the two companies completed the
finalization of their merger.

One year later, however, a severe disagreement arose between
the upper management of each company. As a result, the top
management at Thiokol walked out. Among the defectors was
Robert Davies, president of Thiokol, considered one of the
brightest executives in the aerospace and chemical industries.
Four other high level executives with experience in aerospace either retired or quit when Davies left. Consequently,
Morton's Charles Locke was given complete control of both
companies.

Despite these defections, few industry analysts questioned the
wisdom of the Thiokol-Morton merger. In the first year after the
merger the company posted record earnings. Two years later
earnings per share increased 26 percent. Morton's and Thi-

okol's specialty chemicals divisions were working well together, and the new company offered chemical purification products, metal recovery chemicals, coatings, polymers, and chemicals for the electronics industry. The household products division saw many of its items, including Glass Plus, Yes Detergent, and Spray & Wash, achieve ten to 20 percent market growth in a crowded and highly competitive field. To further strengthen its position in the household products market during this time, Morton Thiokol began to manufacture its own packaging materials, becoming one of the first manufacturers in the industry to do so. In 1985 the household products division was sold to Dow Chemical Company in order to prevent an attempted takeover by that chemical firm.

In the mid-1980s, Morton Thiokol's staff of engineers was gaining acclaim for its work on materials for the aerospace industry, and the company won a contract to produce rocket boosters for NASA's space shuttle *Challenger*. On January 26, 1986, Morton Thiokol engineers are alleged to have approved the launch of the *Challenger* space shuttle, despite the below freezing weather conditions. Seventy-three seconds after lift-off an explosion occurred that destroyed the rocket and killed its crew. The explosion was attributed to the failure of rubber O-rings on Morton Thiokol's rocket boosters.

Morton Thiokol chair Charles Locke shocked the public when, shortly after the accident, he told reporters that "the shuttle thing will cost us ten cents a share." Quoted out of context, the remark nonetheless ensured Locke of a reputation as tactless and insensitive. In 1989, despite performing $400 million worth of redesign work at cost and the resumption of shuttle flights, Morton Thiokol lost a bid for a new booster design to Lockheed. At this point, Locke decided to spin off the Thiokol division.

Before dividing the companies, Locke transferred Thiokol's chemical businesses to the Morton side of the company. Morton also retained Thiokol's promising automotive airbag business. The companies were officially split on July 1, 1989. Morton International, with $1.4 billion in sales and 8,000 employees, remained concentrated mostly in chemicals and salt. But the company also invested nearly $100 million in its airbag business.

Airbags, designed to inflate upon the impact of a car crash, protected drivers from colliding with an automobile's dashboard and windshield. After Mercedes-Benz ordered the first airbag, other auto manufacturers found it to be a competitive advantage. Chrysler incorporated airbags into its designs in 1987, and others followed. The most important development in the airbag market occurred in 1991, when congress passed legislation making airbags mandatory on all new cars. At the time, Morton dominated the market with 55 percent of the market, while its closest competitor TRW held 35 percent.

Morton also actively expanded its chemical operations after its divestiture of Thiokol, taking over the Whittaker Corporation's coatings and adhesives business for $225 million. In taking over this business, Morton integrated vertically into the polyester market. Subsequent acquisitions included the K.J. Quinn and German Iromer Chemie and Sandoz-Quinn Produckte companies, which were added to Morton's Dynachem and Bee Chemical divisions. The company's specialty chemicals business grew to include adhesives, coatings, sealants, electrical chemicals, dyes, sodium borohydride, biocides, tin stabilizers, and laser and semiconductor materials. In late 1991 Morton sold its food and cosmetic colors business to Milwaukee-based Universal Foods in order to concentrate on its industrial dyes operations.

Since the spinoff, Morton managed consistently higher earnings than Thiokol, possibly a result of Morton retaining Thiokol's most promising businesses before the two companies split up. As it approached the twenty-first century, Morton concentrated its investments on high-growth niche markets.

Principal Subsidiaries: Bee Chemical Company; CVD, Inc.; The Canadian Salt Co., Ltd. (Canada); Inagua Transports, Inc. (Liberia); Morton Bahamas, Ltd. (Bahamas); Morton Coatings, Inc.; Morton International, B.V. (Netherlands); Morton International GmbH. (Germany); Morton International, Ltd. (Canada); Morton International, Ltd. (Japan); Morton International S.A. (France); Morton International S.p.A. (Italy); Morton Japan Ltd. (Japan); Morton Overseas, Ltd.; Morton International S.A. de C.V. (Mexico); Morton Yokohama, Inc.; N.V. Morton International S.A. (Belgium); Nippon-Bee Chemical Company, Ltd. (Japan); Toray Thiokol Company, Ltd. (Japan); Toyo-Morton, Ltd. (Japan).

Further Reading:

"After an Aerospace Spin-off, Morton is Ready for an Upswing," *Chemical Week*, May 23, 1990, pp. 14–19.
"A High-Stakes Bet that Paid Off," *Fortune*, June 15, 1992, pp. 121–122.
"Life Beyond Challenger," *Forbes*, September 21, 1987, p. 44.
"Morton Sells Colors Business," *Chemical Week*, August 7, 1991, p. 5.
"Morton Thiokol Completes Spinoff," *Journal of Commerce*, July 6, 1989.
"Morton Thiokol is to Spin Off Chemical Line, *Wall Street Journal*, February 28, 1988, p. A3.
"Morton Thiokol: Reflections on the Shuttle Disaster," *Business Week*, March 14, 1988, pp. 82–91.
"Redemption," *Forbes*, January 7, 1991, p. 307.

—John Simley

**══The══
Musicland
══Group══**

Musicland Stores Corporation

7500 Excelsior Boulevard
Minneapolis, Minnesota 55426-4599
U.S.A.
(612) 932-7700
Fax: (612) 931-2013

Public Company
Incorporated: 1977 as The Musicland Group Inc.
Employees: 10,000
Sales: $1.02 billion
Stock Exchanges: New York
SICs: 3652 Prerecorded Records and Tapes; 5735 Record
and Prerecorded-tape Stores; 5942 Book Stores

The leading specialty retailer in the United States of prerecorded music, movies, and audio and video accessories, Musicland Stores Corporation operates more than 1200 stores in 49
states, Puerto Rico, and the United Kingdom. These include
approximately 870 Musicland and Sam Goody stores (selling
prerecorded home entertainment products, primarily in suburban shopping malls); 300 Suncoast Motion Picture Company
stores (selling video and video-related products, primarily in
metropolitan shopping malls); some 30 On Cue stores (selling a
variety of entertainment products in small town markets); and
around 15 Media Play megastores (selling books, music, videos, and other products to select large-to-mid-size markets).
Although launched as a small independent retailer during the
1950s, Musicland was virtually reborn in 1988 during a highly
leveraged $410 million buyout from owner Primerica. The prin-
cipals of the deal included Musicland chairman Jack W. Eugster
and the Donaldson, Lufkin & Jenrette investment group. So
successful was the 1988 buyout that in 1992 Musicland—still
debt-heavy but now considerably expanded and margin-
strong—was able to float an initial public offering of 16 million
shares priced at $14.50 each in order to pay off senior debt and
continue its ambitious expansion plans. With market share more
than twice the size of its nearest competitor, the Musicland fold
looked to a bright future in the 1990s. In his 1992 letter to
shareholders, Eugster explained: "We see ourselves not only as
industry leaders with the strength, discipline, energy, and organization to make the most of existing opportunities, but as
industry pioneers willing to explore entirely fresh possibilities
for growth. Our goal is to be the most complete multi-media
retailer in the business."

Musicland began humbly enough in 1956 with a single outlet
near downtown Minneapolis. One of the founders, Terry Evenson, had opened his first music store in his hometown of
Cloquet, Minnesota, while still a teenager some eight years
earlier. Following a college education he helped fund by leading
a dance band, Evenson served in the Korean War. He then
resettled in Minneapolis and launched the Musicland business
with partner Grover Sayre, a former member of his band. The
partnership had grown to a chain of six stores by 1963, at which
time Evenson and Sayre decided to sell their interest.

His entrepreneurial streak still alive, Evenson founded a sizable
chain of greeting card stores, which he ultimately sold to
Hallmark. Sayre, on the other hand, remained with Musicland
until 1981. From 1963 until 1968, Musicland was the property
of two St. Louis Park, Minnesota, brothers, Amos and Dan
Heilicher. Veterans of record distribution since the 1930s, the
Heilichers had supplied Evenson with prerecorded music since
his early days in Cloquet. Musicland expanded rapidly to 48
stores under their management before the private concern
merged with Pickwick International, a music and book production, distribution, and merchandising corporation based in New
York with 300 retail outlets. The Heilicher brothers remained in
the Twin Cities to head Musicland's distribution and retailing
divisions.

Then in 1976, according to Mike Langberg, "Amos Heilicher
had a falling out with other members of the Pickwick board and
sold his stake in the company." The year after the break, packaging giant American Can (since renamed Primerica to reflect
its diversification into financial services and other industries)
purchased Pickwick for $102 million (Pickwick's revenues for
the year ending April 30, 1976, totaled $264.9 million). At this
juncture Musicland appeared a clear leader in record retailing,
with approximately 230 stores.

Unfortunately for Primerica, wrote Langberg, "the purchase of
Pickwick was a classic case of bad timing. The recorded music
business lurched into a long slide after 1978, while Primerica—
with little knowledge of retailing in its top executive ranks—
poured money into acquisitions of smaller record store chains
and opening of new stores." Some of the slide was due to the
flash-in-the-pan music phenomenon of disco. The greatest factor, though, was likely the changing demographics of record
buyers: baby boomers were no longer primarily teenagers, the
largest record-buying group by age, but part of an older crowd
fast approaching middle age.

From 1979 to 1983, Ted Deikel managed Musicland and Primerica's other retailing concerns. Deikel's foremost task was to
restructure Pickwick and return it to profitability. It was to
Eugster, hired in 1980 by Deikel, that the arduous job of reshaping an overexpanded Musicland fell. A former Dayton Hudson
and Gap Stores retailing executive, Eugster took several predictable steps over the next few years, including closing more
than 100 poorly located or unprofitable outlets and centralizing
distribution to just two (rather than the previous 18) warehouses. In addition, he sought savings by taking the tiniest and
least obvious of measures, including switching off back room
store lights and shaving the number of paper bag sizes offered to
the customer.

Eugster's greatest contribution came with the introduction of a computerized inventory system that, according to Christopher Palmeri, "remains the standard in the record retailing business." Called Retail Inventory Management (RIM), the two-way system tracked every individual item that left the St. Louis Park warehouse by means of a bar code similar to those for supermarket products. Computerized registers at each retail outlet then scanned the bar codes at the point of sale and relayed the information back to headquarters. The final step in the process involved a computer model that forecasted the optimum levels for all music and video products on a store-by-store basis.

In 1985, because of RIM and Eugster's other managerial improvements, Musicland was back in the black. The transition had been complex and costly, though, for from 1981 to 1984 virtually all of the company's non-retail operations (i.e., wholesale distribution and record production) were curtailed, even while American Can continued to buy up and merge smaller record chains into Musicland. Nonetheless, flush with revenues of $327.5 million and profits of $8.8 million, the subsidiary entered 1986 both comfortable in the knowledge that it was the nation's largest music retailer and hungry for further expansion. In May of that year, plans to acquire California-based Record Bar / Licorice Pizza, a 60-store joint enterprise, for $13 million were announced. When completed, the deal would bring Musicland's tally of stores to 512. Other major developments included the launch of Musicland's first for-sale video specialty store (debuting as Paramount Pictures, Musicland's movie division saw sales grow to nearly 7 percent of all corporate revenues within its first year). Then, in August, American Can announced its plans for an initial public offering of Musicland stock.

The offering was postponed until February 1987, when 19 percent of Musicland was sold by parent company American Can (that same year, American changed its name to Primerica). The IPO was particularly well received due to Musicland's dominant market position and a new upsurge in record-buying among the thirty- and forty-something crowd. Consonant with this trend, Sam Goody, with its more upscale image and emphasis on new-age, jazz, and classical music, made its Twin Cities debut a year later. A discount record chain begun during the Great Depression, Sam Goody was bought by American Can back in 1978. Within ten years, the chain had expanded from 28 to 190 stores, most located either on the West or East Coasts. Next to the original Musicland chain, Sam Goody had become a primary contributor to the company's overall revenues of more than half a billion.

Retailing trends, market dominance, high hopes for video sales, and other positive indices within Musicland's divisions prompted Eugster and a group of fellow investors committed to the company's long-term growth to pursue a daring leveraged buyout (LBO) in August 1988. When the ink was dry, Musicland's new management had decreased Primerica's ownership stake from 81 percent to just 20 percent and also reduced Primerica's role to that of passive investor. Since that time, Musicland has continued its program of aggressive expansion, solidly outdistancing such competitors as Trans World Music, Wherehouse Entertainment, and Tower Records.

In July 1990 the company entertained plans of going public, believing it could raise as much as $96 million in interest-free capital. However, with the Iraqi invasion of Kuwait in August and the subsequent downturn in the stock market, the plan was scrapped. Due to the economic recession, Musicland saw its sales soften and profits stall along with those of other music retailers. "In late November [1991]," according to a January 1992 *Star Tribune* article, "some industry observers speculated that Musicland was hitting rough times when it ended negotiations to buy New York City–based Record World Inc., a chain of 80 music stores, from Chemical Banking Corp." However, such speculation was quelled in February 1992 when Musicland extricated itself from LBO financing pressures by taking the company public in an enormously successful offering. A follow-up *Star Tribune* article from that month cited Ken Salmon, an analyst with C. L. King & Associates. According to Salmon, Musicland's Wall Street appeal, despite both significant internal and external economic pressures, was that: "It's bigger and slightly better in everything—whether it's sales per square foot or operating margins—than any other music company out there. It was not an LBO under stress."

Since the 1992 offering, Musicland has topped the $1 billion mark in sales and redefined itself as a conservatively capitalized company. In addition, holdings by the chief outside investors—Primerica, Donaldson, and Equitable—were cut by 30 to 60 percent. The largest remaining stockholder among the three, Donaldson, saw its interest drop from about 25 percent to 17 percent. In November 1992 Musicland reaffirmed its market-driving reputation by opening its first Media Play store in a suburban strip center in Rockford, Illinois. A 40,000-square-foot prototype (later Media Plays ranged up to 50,000 square feet) competitive with such discounters as Wal-Mart and such multimedia retailers as Kmart's Borders Books & Music, the store is part of a new program to capitalize on the emerging trend of integrated media. "In the new megastore," wrote Palmeri, "customers are encouraged to browse. There is a kids' play section, easy chairs in the travel book section, a cafe in the center of the store. . . . Eugster proudly shows visitors a slide that projects that by 1998 Media Play sales could equal those of the Musicland music stores, suggesting company-wide revenues in the neighborhood of $3 billion."

Although Musicland also faced competition in this area from Virgin Retail, Blockbuster Entertainment, and Tower Records, it "appears to be moving faster and with a broader sweep than its most direct competitors," according to a 1993 *Wall Street* article by Patrick Reilly. Interestingly enough, wrote Martin Pedersen, "With the Musicland and Sam Goody stores accounting for 8 percent of the industry's total music sales, the opening of more Media Play outlets eventually will put the company in the unusual position of competing with itself. "If we don't compete with ourselves," Eugster commented, "somebody else will."

Principal Subsidiaries: Musicland Group Inc.

Further Reading:

Apgar, Sally, "Musicland Plans Stock Offering to Add Stores and Pay Off Debt," *Star Tribune,* January 17, 1992, pp. 1D, 4D.
——, "Musicland Stores Corp. Draws Rave Reviews as It Makes Debut Appearance on Wall Street," *Star Tribune,* February 27, 1992, pp. 1D, 7D.

Cochran, Thomas N., "Musicland Stores Corp.," *Barron's,* August 20, 1990, p. 45.

Goddard, Connie, "Musicland to Open 10 'Full-Media' Stores Around U.S.," *Publishers Weekly,* August 9, 1993, pp. 18–19.

Kennedy, Tony, "Musicland Posts a Loss for the Second Quarter Despite Rise in Revenues," *Star Tribune,* July 15, 1993, p. 2D.

——, "Musicland Stores Will Expand in Minnetonka," *Star Tribune,* August 4, 1993, p. 3D.

Koshetz, Herbert, "Move to Acquire Pickwick Is Made by American Can," *New York Times,* January 20, 1977, p. 57.

Langberg, Mike, "Musicland Plans Initial Public Offering," *Pioneer Press & Dispatch,* November 10, 1986.

——, "Musicland Plays Sweet Tune of Growth," *Pioneer Press & Dispatch,* June 8, 1987.

Mehler, Mark, and Geoff Mayfield, "Management in Leveraged Buy of Musicland," *Billboard,* February 20, 1988, pp. 1, 78.

"Musicland Buyout Approved: Deal Valued at $410 Million," *Billboard,* September 10, 1988.

"Musicland's Big Picture: More Video Sales," *Corporate Report,* July 1990, p. 18.

Paige, Earl, "Acquisition of Calif. Chain Near Completion: Musicland, Record Bar Ink $13-Million Deal," *Billboard,* May 3, 1986, p. 3.

——, "Musicland, MCA Expose Promo Options," *Billboard,* November 28, 1992, p. 63.

Palmeri, Christopher, "Media Merchant to the Baby Boomers," *Forbes,* March 15, 1993, pp. 66, 70.

Pedersen, Martin, "Musicland's New Multimedia Store Tune," *Publishers Weekly,* April 12, 1993, p. 22.

"People: Sam Goody," *New York Times,* December 13, 1977, Sec. 3, p. 5.

Pokela, Barbara, "Musicland Hits Different Note with Area's First Sam Goody," *Star Tribune,* November 21, 1988.

Reilly, Patrick M., "Musicland Plans Media Medley in Superstores," *Wall Street Journal,* July 26, 1993, pp. B1, B4.

—Jay P. Pederson

Nabors Industries, Inc.

515 West Greens Road
Suite 1200
Houston, Texas 77067
U.S.A.
(713) 874-0035
Fax: (713) 872-5205

Public Company
Incorporated: 1978 as Anglo Industries, Inc.
Employees: 3,168
Sales: $286.26 million
Stock Exchanges: American
SICs: 1381 Drilling Oil & Gas Wells; 1389 Oil and Gas
    Field Services

Nabors Industries, Inc., is the largest land drilling contractor in the United States and one of the largest international land drilling contractors, with a fleet of over 200 land drilling rigs operating in most of the significant oil, gas, and geothermal drilling markets in the world. Nabors also provides offshore drilling services through more than a dozen offshore, jackup, and barge rigs, as well as a range of complementary oilfield management, logistics, and engineering services.

Nabors is the amalgamation of several other restructured drilling companies and informally traces its lineage to Anglo-Lautaro Nitrate Corporation, a Chilean nitrate production company formed by Guggenheim family interests in the late 1920s. During the early 1970s the government of Chile repatriated Anglo-Lautaro's mining interests in exchange for several million dollars in cash, and the company began diversifying after changing its name to Anglo Company, Ltd., in March 1972.

Under the direction of Peter Lawson-Johnston, chairman and heir to the Guggenheim family fortune, and Albert Van de Maele, president and chief executive, during the two years following the company's name change, Anglo Company acquired a wide range of businesses. These purchases included Minerec Corporation, a manufacturer of chemicals used in the mining industry; a 50 percent interest in Printex Corporation, a manufacturer of printed circuit boards for the electronics industry; a 25 percent interest in Robert Garrett & Sons, Inc., an investment banking firm; and Motor Parts Industries, Inc., an automotive replacement parts supplier.

In 1974 Anglo entered the contract drilling business when it acquired a 52.6 percent interest in Nabors Drilling Limited of Canada, an independent oil and gas drilling contractor. Nabors Drilling's precursor was the Parker Drilling Company of Canada, which had been organized in 1952 and had been operating in Alaska since 1963. By 1978 Anglo had increased its interest in Nabors Drilling to 99 percent by initiating a number of refinancing and reorganizational moves designed to expand its activities in the contract drilling business.

In order to fund the acquisition of R.L. Manning Company, a Denver-based contract drilling firm, Anglo went public in the spring of 1978 through a two-part offering that included nearly $20 million in subordinated debentures and one million shares of common stock. In May 1978 Anglo Company, Inc., was created to act as a holding company for Anglo Company, Ltd., and its subsidiaries, which included Anglo Industries, Inc., also formed in May 1978. That same month Anglo acquired R.L. Manning for $23.6 million, or about three-quarters of the $30.2 million Anglo eventually raised through its initial public offering.

By the end of 1978 Anglo had a fleet of 49 drilling rigs and had earned $9.9 million on annual sales of $99.7 million, with Nabors Drilling contributing nearly two-thirds of those revenues. By 1979 sales had risen to $145 million, pushing income up proportionately to $14 million. Anglo entered 1980 as a diversified company predominantly engaged in contract drilling for oil and natural gas in Western Canada, Alaska, and the U.S. Rocky Mountains. The company was also marketing oilfield hauling services in Alaska and producing circuit boards and automotive replacement parts through its manufacturing subsidiaries. In 1980 William J. Johnson joined the company as executive vice president and chief operating officer and became president and chief executive the following year when Van de Maele retired. Under Johnson's guidance Anglo expanded its oilfield service operations during the early 1980s by acquiring a handful of small oilfield equipment and supply companies.

In 1981 Anglo sold Printex and diversified into oil and gas exploration through a partnership with National Utilities & Industries Corporation to explore undeveloped land in Texas and Louisiana. Unfortunately, while the company was expanding its range of oilfield operations, an oil glut was developing. The following year, Anglo was forced to slice its 2,500-employee payroll by 1,000. After recording a quarterly loss of $7.8 million in September of 1982 the company suspended its stock dividend. For the year Anglo earned only $444,000, compared to $27 million in 1981.

By early 1983 the company's stock value had plunged from a 1981 high of $35 to about $6. As the shakeout of small drilling firms ensued, Anglo began selling its supply and equipment operations and cutting management pay. The company also secured a short-term borrowing agreement with an $85 million credit line. Anglo lost $41 million during the spring 1983 quarter, spurring Johnson's resignation and a reevaluation of the company's activities. Chosen to help redirect the company and solidify its focus on contract drilling and oilfield services were Allen F. Rhodes, former president of Warren Oilfield Services, who became Anglo president, and Nabors Drilling president K. G. Reed, who became Anglo's senior vice president of operations. The new management team promptly agreed to abandon Anglo's oil and gas exploration venture and accelerate the sale of Anglo's oilfield supply and equipment businesses.

By November 1983 Anglo had sold about two-thirds of its oilfield equipment line, having dealt away its exploration and production business for $14 million. With liabilities of nearly $200 million, that same month the company—which had been renamed Anglo Energy, Ltd., during the early 1980s—filed for reorganization under Chapter 11 of the federal bankruptcy code.

Between November 1983 and mid-1986 Anglo Energy's five subsidiaries, all engaged in oil drilling and transportation, continued to operate outside the jurisdiction of bankruptcy court while the parent operated under bankruptcy protection. During this time Anglo Energy and its creditors both filed several rounds of competing reorganization plans until reaching an accord in April 1986. In August 1986 the company was restructured and emerged from bankruptcy with a new president and chief operating officer, Richard A. Stratton. In January of the following year Eugene M. Isenberg became chairman and chief executive officer and soon initiated a business strategy geared toward developing and expanding Anglo's position in international drilling markets, where there was potential for long-term contracts. In December 1987 Anglo significantly expanded its oilfield service operations when it entered into a 50–50 partnership with Peak Maintenance and Equipment Company to form Peak Oilfield Service Company, an oilfield maintenance, hauling, and construction service firm.

Expenses stemming from discontinued businesses took their toll on Anglo's earnings in 1987, and the company lost $85.9 million on revenues of $28.6 million. In February 1988 Anglo again filed for Chapter 11 protection, invoking a seldom-used section of the U.S. federal code that allowed the company to petition for bankruptcy with a reorganization plan already pre-approved by a majority of its creditors. A month after filing for bankruptcy protection, Anglo sold the assets R.L. Manning Company and bowed out of the Rocky Mountain drilling market.

In May 1988 Anglo again emerged from bankruptcy and through its approved reorganization plan exchanged about $100 million worth of debt obligations for about 30 million shares of new common stock, effectively eliminating the company's liabilities. Debt-free, Anglo was able to borrow on its rig fleet and between late 1988 and 1990 the company made three strategic acquisitions of international drilling companies that were designed to extend Anglo's operations beyond the bounds of Alaska and Canada.

In November 1988 Anglo acquired the Westburne Group of Companies, a Canadian-based drilling and oil transportation contractor with operations in the Middle East, the Far East, North Africa, Southeast Asia, Australia, Canada, and the North Sea. Because a majority of Anglo's business was conducted by Nabors Drilling Ltd. and Nabors Alaska Drilling subsidiaries and because the company wanted to change its moniker to reflect its new management's goals, in March 1989 the company changed its name to Nabors Industries, Inc.

In February 1990 Nabors joined the field of the world's largest drilling companies after paying $58 million to acquire Loffland

Brothers Company and its 53 rigs, which increased Nabors' fleet to more than 100 rigs. Founded in Ohio in 1906, Loffland was the world's oldest contract drilling company and had a reputation for ultra-deep drilling, frontier drilling, and major discoveries, such as its discovery of the huge Prudhoe Bay oilfield on Alaska's North Slope. Loffland also added domestic geothermal drilling operations to Nabors' activities, helped expand Nabors' presence in the North Sea, Canada, the lower 48 states, and the Middle East, and gave Nabors a new presence in Venezuela and the Gulf of Mexico.

In November 1990 Nabors expanded its international and domestic operations further when it purchased Henley Drilling Company, a subsidiary of Hunt Oil Company with 11 rigs operating in Texas, Louisiana, and Yemen. Nabors then merged the operations of Henley and Loffland to create a new subsidiary, Nabors Loffland Drilling Company. Largely as a result of the acquisitions of Henley, Loffland, and Westburne, Nabors annual sales rose between 1988 and 1990 from $56 million to $138 million.

Between 1988 and 1990 Nabors grew not only on land, but on water as well; at the end of 1990, the company controlled about 20 percent of the platform rigs in the British North Sea. Although international operations were expanding, the company's North American operations, which accounted for two-thirds of the company's rigs, were only marginally profitable, particularly in the lower 48 states.

As a result of its ongoing financial struggle to make operations in the lower 48 states pay, Nabors' strategy during the early 1990s included internal growth of its Alaskan operations and redeployment of acquired equipment in North America to such international markets as the Middle East, South America, the Far East, and Central America. By the beginning of 1991 Nabors Industries was operating a fleet of 111 land and offshore rigs in most of the world's major drilling markets and was among the largest international drilling contractors.

In 1991 Nabors began solidifying its position in the service contract market by creating Crest Service Company, which would provide oilfield transportation and construction services in the Middle East and other international frontier drilling markets. Through continuing redeployment of rigs, during 1991 Nabors steadily expanded its presence in the Middle East countries of Yemen and Saudi Arabia, as well as in Venezuela and the British North Sea.

In North America, where financial results continued to hover around the break-even mark, Nabors concentrated on developing new technology with worldwide applications, such as the company's new slim hole drilling rig designed to provide a more cost-effective and efficient means of conducting exploratory drilling in remote and logistically difficult regions. In 1991 Nabors also stepped up efforts to consolidate its corporate activities in Houston, where the company had moved its headquarters a year earlier from New York City. By the end of 1991 Nabors' annual revenues had jumped to more than $240 million, and net income nearly doubled from $14.5 to $27 million.

In 1992 Stratton was named vice chairman and Anthony G. Petrello became president and chief operating officer. The company's presence on the Alaskan North Slope was further solidified that year when Nabors became the first service company to join in a new long-term alliance with the operator of the Prudhoe Bay oilfield. In 1992 international drilling, particularly in Yemen, continued to provide the majority of operational growth for Nabors; revenues climbed to $286.2 million and income rose to $33.7 million. At the close of 1992 Nabors secured a ten-year, fixed-rate financing agreement, providing the company with available capital for further internal expansion efforts and potential acquisitions.

In 1993 Nabors moved closer to its goal of becoming a total drilling service when it acquired the Thistle Group, a provider of platform drilling and testing services. Nabors further expanded its offshore operations that year in the British North Sea, introducing integrated drilling services, including engineering and platform management services. Nabors' international land drilling and service operations also continued to expand, and by 1993 the company was operating a fleet of exploratory, development, workover, and water well rigs in Yemen, while also offering logistical and drill site construction services. That same year the company received its first drilling contract in Russia and extended into 1995 its long-term contract for geothermal drilling in Costa Rica. In 1993 Nabors debuted one of its new slim hole rigs in Venezuela, where the company's operations were expected to become increasingly profitable as a result of new government polices designed to spur oil exploration and production activities.

In June 1993 Nabors became the largest land drilling contractor in the United States after buying out its major domestic competitor, Grace Drilling Company. The $32 million transaction gave Nabors an additional 167 land rigs, which were merged with Nabors' existing 40-rig "Lower 48" fleet. The expanded domestic drilling firm was renamed Nabors Drilling USA, Inc.

Nabors entered the mid-1990s expecting to capitalize on its acquisition of Grace Drilling through an anticipated upswing in domestic natural gas drilling. The company's strategy—used since its 1987 reorganization—was to use the assets of the former services companies it had acquired to maintain and expand upon its position in international and domestic land drilling markets, tapping into their potential for long-term contracts.

Principal Subsidiaries: Nabors Drilling USA, Inc.; Nabors Alaska Drilling, Inc.; Nabors Drilling International Limited; Loffland Nabors Limited (United Kingdom); Nabors Loffland Drilling Company; Nabors Development Corporation; Peak Oilfield Service; Nabors Yemen, Ltd.; Loffland Brothers de Venezuela, C.A.

Further Reading:

Booth, Michael, "R.L. Manning Co. Sell Rigs, Will Close," *Denver Business Journal,* March 28, 1988, Section 1, p. 6.

Brammer, Rhonda, "Blowing in the Wind: The Battered Oil-Service Industry Is Primed for Recovery," *Barron's,* October 28, 1991, pp. 10, 11, 20.

Calkins, Laurel Brubaker, "Competitors Buying Each Other Out in Oilfield Services Industry," *Houston Business Journal,* May 3, 1993, Section 1, p. 21.

Griffin, Judith Fuerst, "Over a Barrel: Falling Oil Prices Pushed Oil Field Work into a Precipitous Decline that Tested the Mettle of Alaska's Oil Field Service Firms," *Alaska Business Monthly,* February 1989, Section 1, p. 30.

Neumeier, Shelley, "Companies to Watch: Nabors Industries," *Fortune,* January 13, 1992, p. 65.

Palmeri, Christopher, "Making a Killing from a Corpse," *Forbes,* September 13, 1993, pp. 70–71.

Percefull, Gary, "N.Y. Firm to Buy Tulsa-Based Driller: Loffland Brothers Getting New Nabors," *Tulsa World,* November 23, 1989, Section B, p. 1.

——, "Loffland to Continue Operations Under Name," *Tulsa World,* February 27, 1990, Section B, p. 5.

—Roger W. Rouland

National Geographic Society

1145 17th Street, N.W.
Washington, D.C. 20036
U.S.A.
(202) 857-7000
Fax: (202) 828-6679

Non-Profit Organization
Incorporated: 1888
Employees: 1,950
Sales: $446.9 million

Founded as a club of distinguished gentlemen devoted to promoting the study of geography, the National Geographic Society is currently the largest educational society in the world and the publisher of one of the world's most widely circulated magazines, *National Geographic.* The company is also involved in book publishing, education, public service projects, and the production of a popular series of television documentaries, but its magazine remains its crowning achievement. Thanks in large part to the efforts of three generations of the Grosvenor family, *National Geographic* has become a staple of American mass culture, so well known that allusions to it are found in such diverse sources as Elizabeth Bishop's poem "In the Waiting Room" and MTV's animated television show "Beavis and Butt-head."

The National Geographic Society was founded in January 1888 in Washington, D.C. by a group of eminent citizens who wanted to promote geographic research and the popular distribution of the results of such research. The charter members of the Society included Alexander Graham Bell; Bell's father-in-law, lawyer Gardiner Greene Hubbard; explorers John Wesley Powell and A. W. Greeley; and scholar George Kennan, uncle of future ambassador to the Soviet Union George F. Kennan. Hubbard was one of Bell's early financial backers and had served as the first president of the Bell Telephone Company, the forerunner of AT&T. He was elected to serve as the Society's first president.

The first issue of *National Geographic* appeared shortly after the Society's founding and was published intermittently until January 1896, when monthly publication began. The early magazine bears little resemblance to the readable, eye-catching *National Geographic* of today. Its articles were written in a dry, academic style and bore titles such as "Geographic Methods in

Geologic Investigation" and "The Classification of Geographic Forms by Genesis," and there were no illustrations. It is not surprising, then, that circulation remained limited, with less than 1,000 subscribers and negligible newsstand sales.

Gardiner Greene Hubbard died in 1897 and was succeeded as president by his famous son-in-law. When Alexander Graham Bell took the helm, he found the National Geographic Society in a precarious financial state, largely because its magazine had failed to provide a strong revenue base. He soon realized that *National Geographic* needed two things: a change in editorial policy that would make it a popular scientific magazine rather than a scholarly journal, and a full-time editor who would manifest the changes he sought. Bell hoped to fill both needs in 1899 when he wrote to his friend, historian Edwin Grosvenor of Amherst College, to ask if either of Grosvenor's sons might be interested in assuming editorship. Gilbert H. Grosvenor, then a 23-year-old prep school teacher in New Jersey, accepted.

Having grown up in Istanbul while his father researched his two-volume history of the Turkish capital, Gilbert Grosvenor had become fascinated with foreign lands and peoples at an early age—but he later confessed that he was also drawn to the job by his desire to be near Bell's daughter Elsie, whom he later married.

Grosvenor proved to be the catalyst behind the immensely successful popularization of the magazine. After studying such classic examples of travel writing as Darwin's *Voyage of the Beagle* and Charles Dana's *Two Year's Before the Mast,* Grosvenor concluded that *National Geographic* articles could be made more readable without sacrificing their educational value. Grosvenor mandated stylistic changes for the magazine: Eliminate academic jargon, keep sentences short and punchy, and replace scholarly formality and detachment with engaging first-person narrative.

Grosvenor also introduced photographs into the magazine, a step that would gain *National Geographic* more recognition than its newly accessible style. He knew well the impact that photographs would have; his father's history of Istanbul, published in 1895, was the first scholarly book published in the United States to make extensive use of photoengravings. Though some critics considered it vulgar to run photos in an academic work, the book sold well. Similarly, Gilbert Grosvenor encountered much opposition from more conservative trustees of the National Geographic Society when the changes that he wished to make became known. He had, however, the firm backing of Alexander Graham Bell, which afforded him the time to prove the editorial merits of his innovations. Skyrocketing circulation (by 1906, the magazine could boast of 11,000 regular subscribers) would confirm his abilities.

Opposition from within the Society's board would soften, too. In December 1904 Grosvenor grew alarmed when the next month's issue was about to go to press with eleven pages blank for want of copy. In that day's mail, however, he found an unsolicited packet containing the first photographs ever taken of the Tibetan capital of Lhasa. Awed by the photos and desperate for material, he used them to fill the blank pages. He later wrote that he expected to be fired for running an eleven-page pictorial spread, but several days after the issue appeared, he was elected a trustee of the Society. Grosvenor ran *National Geographic*'s first color photos in 1910. The magazine remains a pioneer in the journalistic use of photography.

Alexander Graham Bell retired as president of the National Geographic Society in 1903, although he remained a contributor to the magazine and an influential member of the organization until his death in 1922. He was succeeded by a series of short-term chief executives: W. J. McGee served briefly, followed by Grove Karl Gilbert. Willis Moore served from 1905 to 1909. Henry Gannett, a charter member and chief geographer of the U.S. Geological Survey, succeeded Moore and served until his death in 1914. Gannett was succeeded by O. H. Tittman, who resigned in 1919. He was followed by John E. Pillsbury, who served less than a year before his death in December 1919. In 1920 the entire National Geographic Society and its expanding operations became Gilbert Grosvenor's responsibility when he succeeded John Pillsbury as president. Grosvenor remained editor of the magazine, which continued the readable, relatively upbeat, house style that he had created.

In these early years the Society began its sponsorship of high-profile exploratory, archaeological, and naturalistic expeditions. In 1906 it contributed $1,000 to the Arctic expedition led by Commander Robert E. Peary, with whom the Society had a longstanding professional relationship. In 1909 Peary became the first human being to reach the North Pole, and the National Geographic Society has basked in this triumph ever since. Another of its early successes was Yale archaeologist Hiram Bingham's 1912 expedition to Peru, during which the Inca capital of Macchu Picchu was excavated.

As president of the Society, Grosvenor continued its sponsorship of high-profile expeditions. The Society provided financial support for Commander Richard E. Byrd's various Arctic and Antarctic voyages between 1925 and 1930, during which he became the first human to fly to the North and South Poles. Byrd was aided by a special compass designed by Albert Bumstead, the Society's chief cartographer, which used the sun for navigation, since magnetic compasses would not work at the poles. In 1935 it co-sponsored with the U.S. Army Air Corps *Explorer II*, a helium balloon that set an altitude record for an occupied balloon that stood until the dawn of the Space Age. In 1939 the National Geographic Society and the Smithsonian Institution co-sponsored an expedition to southern Mexico during which archaeologist Matthew Sterling uncovered a Mayan stela, an inscribed tablet, that was the oldest known human artifact from the New World.

National Geographic reached the mass readership that its founders had sought, with a circulation of 500,000 at the end of World War I, and the Society continued to expand its activities. In 1922, after receiving a request for geographical information from the National Education Association, the Society launched a weekly publication designed for classroom use, *Geographic School Bulletins*. During World War II, the Society opened its photographic and cartographic archives to the United States military. Its vast library of photographs of foreign countries provided intelligence about infrastructure in enemy-held territory and also helped unveil camouflage when compared with the military's own reconnaissance photographs. The Society's maps of distant lands, which it had been accumulating since

creating its own cartographic department in 1916, also proved valuable. After the war, the Society received a grateful letter from Fleet Admiral Chester Nimitz, one of the war's heroes, who reported that a National Geographic map of the South Pacific saved him considerable difficulty in 1942 when the crew members of the B-17 in which he was flying used it to get back on course after losing their bearings in a storm near Guadalcanal. Further, President Franklin Roosevelt asked the Society for a map, and was so impressed with the encased set that was given him that he later asked for and received a similar set to give to Prime Minister Winston Churchill. Churchill was so pleased with his maps that after the war, when the Society asked him to return the original set for a new and updated set in order to place the originals in the Society's museum, Churchill politely refused.

After the war, with so much of the Earth's landmass already explored and mapped, the Society turned part of its attention to the last remaining frontier: outer space. It co-sponsored with the California Institute of Technology the ambitious Sky Survey, which would produce the Sky Atlas, the first comprehensive photographic map of the heavens. Work on the Sky Survey began in 1949 and was completed in 1956, using the 48-inch "Big Schmidt" telescope at Palomar Observatory in California.

Almost concurrently, the National Geographic Society also began its long and successful association with marine explorer Jacques-Yves Cousteau. The Society sponsored a number of Cousteau expeditions in the 1950s, including the 1956 dive during which he took photographs of the Romanche Trench in the Atlantic Ocean, the deepest point at which photographs had ever been taken. During another National Geographic-sponsored expedition in the mid-1950s, Cousteau shot footage for his Oscar-winning documentary *The Silent World*.

Gilbert Grosvenor retired in 1954 after 34 years as president of the National Geographic Society and 55 years as editor of *National Geographic*. He then became chairman of the Society and was succeeded in his former positions by his old friend and longtime assistant editor, John Oliver La Gorce. La Gorce served for three years, then retired and became vice-chairman of the Society. He was succeeded by Grosvenor's son, Melville Bell Grosvenor. Although his father remained the unquestioned sage of the board of directors, the title of chief executive officer was given to the younger Grosvenor.

As editor of *National Geographic*, Melville Bell Grosvenor expanded the magazine's use of color photography and put a color photo on the cover for the first time. As CEO of the National Geographic Society, he expanded the Society's book publishing operations and also led it into the increasingly ubiquitous medium of television. Film shot by National Geographic photographer had appeared on television since 1955, but always on network programs. Then, in 1958, Grosvenor and longtime staffer Luis Marden decided to produce the Society's own television programs. Three years later, the Society formed its documentary film department. The first Society-produced television special, "Americans on Everest," aired on CBS in 1965.

Gilbert H. Grosvenor died in 1966, and the next year his son retired and became chairman of the Society. In 1970, Gilbert M. Grosvenor, Melville's son, assumed the leadership position at

National Geographic. He had joined the staff straight from Yale after winning the National Press Photographers Award for coverage of President Eisenhower's tour of Asia in 1951. Before long, Grosvenor became the center of controversy by enacting a subtle shift in *National Geographic*'s editorial policy, easing it away from the uniformly upbeat tone and avoidance of sensitive topics that his father and grandfather had maintained. Under Gilbert M. Grosvenor, the magazine ran major stories on racial turmoil in South Africa, communism in Cuba and social conditions in Harlem. Although the board of trustees publicly endorsed Grosvenor's editorship, some directors of the Society were scandalized, and conservative media critics accused *National Geographic* of contracting "a bad case of radical chic." Grosvenor became president of the Society in 1980, leaving the post of editor to his longtime assistant Wilbur Garrett.

Grosvenor took charge of an organization that was, in some ways, the envy of the publishing industry. In 1980 *National Geographic* boasted 10.7 million subscribers and a circulation of well over 30 million. That year, the Society announced a profit of $3 million on revenues of $217 million, yet the Society continued to refer to its annual profit as a "surplus" and its subscribers as "members," genteel terms used by non-profit organizations. The Society retained its not-for-profit status and accompanying tax exemptions even though it published one of the best-selling magazines in the world and ran successful book publishing and television production operations. And when the Society erected a new headquarters building in Washington, D.C., in 1981 at a cost of $30 million, it paid in cash.

The 1980s would not prove entirely kind to the Society, however. Circulation figures and advertising revenues from *National Geographic* remained flat throughout most of the decade. Slowdowns in the economy and increased competition from other popular science magazines presented the greatest threat of decrease in readership since the Great Depression. The Society's television operations received a boost in 1985 when it signed an agreement with cable station WTBS to produce a weekly documentary series, "National Geographic Explorer."

Gilbert Grosvenor had always focused on emerging technologies that could affect the Society's long-term future. In 1981 he speculated openly about the possibility of putting *National Geographic* and publishing books on video discs. In 1990 the Society published a multimedia software package called "GTV" in collaboration with Lucasfilm and Apple Computer. "GTV" was designed for use in middle schools and provided interactive lessons in American history.

The Society represents the established order of the United States—it was founded by eminent men, and in more recent years its trustees have included such notables as Supreme Court Chief Justice Warren Burger, Lady Bird Johnson, Air Force General Curtis LeMay, astronaut Frank Borman, and businessman J. Willard Marriott, Jr. It has gained a reputation for conservatism and cautiousness, yet its hallmark has always been discovery of the unknown, and it has embraced new media and new techniques in publishing. It has brought the far corners of the world to the doorsteps of millions of Americans. As Frank Luther Mott, the eminent journalism historian, once wrote, *National Geographic* compiled "a fabulous record of success, especially since the magazine is founded on an editorial conviction that rates the intelligence of the popular audience fairly high."

Further Reading:

Behr, Peter, "Geographic: The Wealth of Knowledge," *Washington Post,* December 7, 1981.

Conaway, James, "The Geographic's Founding Family," *Washington Post,* December 19, 1984.

Grosvenor, Gilbert H, *The National Geographic Society and Its Magazine,* Washington, D.C.: National Geographic Society, 1957.

Ringle, Ken, "Around the World in 25 Years," *Washington Post,* February 4, 1990.

Sawyer, Kathy, "Change at the Geographic," *Washington Post,* July 17, 1977.

Trueheart, Charles, "Garrett, Grosvenor and the Great Divide," *Washington Post,* May 7, 1990.

—Douglas Sun

N.Y. STOCK EXCHANGE

New York Stock Exchange, Inc.

11 Wall Street
New York, NY 10005
U.S.A.
(212) 656-3000
Fax: (212) 269-4830

Private Company
Incorporated: 1971.
Employees: 1,600
Operating Revenues: $374 million
SICs: 6231 Security & Commodity Exchanges

Founded in 1792 amid the budding financial enterprises of lower Wall Street in New York city, the New York Stock Exchange (NYSE) has evolved into one of the world's foremost securities marketplaces. In order to maintain an efficient and orderly marketplace during rapid growth, the NYSE has both contributed to and complied with wide-ranging securities regulation and innovative trading systems. Following broad initiatives of the Securities and Exchange Commission (SEC) in 1975 and advancements in computer and telecommunications technologies, the securities industry evolved along the lines of a National Market System (NMS), linking the NYSE with other securities exchanges as well as over-the-counter (OTC) and off-exchange markets. In the early 1990s, the NYSE found itself embroiled in industry-wide debate over the future of securities trading. In numerous forums—including the SEC's Market 2000 review—the NYSE spoke out in favor of consistent regulation to best preserve competitive equality and investor protection in the marketplace. Many of the regulatory decisions reached in the late 1990s will affect the scope and shape of the NYSE, and the securities industry in general, into the twenty-first century.

The NYSE took shape in New York City in the 1790s, where merchants and brokers held public auctions and negotiated deals in and around the landmark Tontine Coffee House at the corner of Wall and Water Streets. New York proved a particularly rich market for the government securities which had helped fund the Revolutionary War. As New York commerce evolved, the budding securities market grew accordingly in complexity and scope. On May 17, 1792, two dozen brokers signed the "Buttonwood Agreement," founding the Exchange on lower Wall Street. They agreed to avoid public auctions, to collect minimum commissions on federal bonds (public stock), and to "give preference to each other" in their trading deals.

Following the War of 1812, the stock market experienced unprecedented growth. Increased trade with Britain transformed New York into the leading American port. Private and commercial banks proliferated. Key brokers decided to establish a steady forum—with a fixed location and regular hours—and on March 8, 1817, they adopted a constitution and the name "New York Stock & Exchange Board" (NYS&EB).

The NYS&EB was governed by distinct rules and procedures. Members were elected on the basis of a ballot-style election process. The exchange followed rules regarding sales and delivery procedures, commission rates, and business ethics. Stipulations also controlled absenteeism, distractions during bidding, and even the wearing of hats. Daily trading consisted of members bidding on securities from designated seats, while the President "called" out each stock or bond.

The stock market fed off a flow of new capital from the 1820s to the 1830s. Trading of federal securities financed the construction of roads, bridges, canals, and municipal water, sewerage, and lighting systems. New laws brought governmental charters within closer reach of young companies. Consequently, trading volume at the NYS&EB rose from an average of 100 shares per day in 1827 to 5000 shares per day in 1834. By the late 1830s, however, the securities market followed the overall economy into a slump. British cutbacks in American investment, rampant speculation in land and securities, and the 1836 closing of the federally-chartered Second Bank of the United States culminated in the Panic of 1837. Though it lost the momentum it had gathered in the 1820s and early 1830s, the NYS&EB managed to survive until the down cycle reversed in 1843.

Among the many new issues listed at the Board, railroads accounted for particularly high trading volume in the mid-1800s. Though the first railroad issue—Mohawk & Hudson Railroad—was listed on the Exchange in August of 1830, the rail frenzy reached its pinnacle in the 1850s and 1860s. By the early 1850s, the NYS&EB listed over ten rail companies.

In 1863, the Board changed its name to the New York Stock Exchange (NYSE) and began construction of its first permanent building. Designed by John Kellum in the Italian Renaissance style, the new space accommodated expanded business. The second-floor Board Room was designed to seat the elected members with assigned places from which they negotiated the stock call, held three times daily.

With the end of the Civil War, intense capitalization of American industry spurred unprecedented growth in stock trading and the emergence of new and competing exchanges. In 1869, the NYSE joined forces with two key competitors: the Open Board of Brokers and select representatives from the Government Bond Department. These mergers were accompanied by administrative and organizational changes that would effect the shape of the NYSE over the following century. Trading volume rose substantially to over $3 billion in securities, a figure that was managed by a body of 1060 members, up from 533 before 1867. On October 23, 1868, memberships were made salable, with prices averaging between $7,000 and $8,000. Continuous trading replaced the "call" system.

The latter half of the nineteenth century brought numerous technological advances. Communications between brokers, investors, and different exchanges were catapulted by the development of the telegraph in 1844, the completion of a transatlantic cable in 1866, and, eventually, the development of the telephone, which reduced trading time from roughly fifteen minutes to less than sixty seconds after 1878. The NYSE also benefitted from the 1867 introduction of the first stock ticker. In order to control accuracy and fair distribution of trade information, the NYSE established its own New York Quotation Company to gather transaction data and distribute it systematically to ticker companies.

Despite efforts to control trading, a combination of financial buccaneering and broad economic influences disrupted the securities market in the late 1860s and early 1870s. Reckless gold speculation in 1869, including an attempt by Jay Gould and James Fisk, Jr., to corner the gold market, prompted the U.S. government to sell some of its supplies, precipitating a sharp break in gold and other securities on September 24. The investor calamity earned the name "Black Friday." In September of 1873, the failure of Jay Cooke & Company sparked another major market break that closed NYSE offices for ten days and scared the securities industry until the end of the decade.

By the 1880s, the scope and trading volume of the NYSE reflected the rise of large corporations and industry-wide trusts. The Exchange created an "Unlisted Department" through which shares were traded until a company qualified for regular listing (the department was abolished in 1910). On December 15, 1886, the exchange traded a record 1,200,000 shares. When trading volume reached three million shares in April of 1901, plans were drafted for expanded offices. Completed in 1903, the new Exchange building was designed by George B. Post in the classical-revival manner. To embellish the white marble facade, J. A. Ward sculpted the figures of "Integrity Protecting the Works of Man."

In the early 1900s, the NYSE saw the rise of oil and steel industries and the tremendous financial clout of such magnates as John D. Rockefeller, Henry Clay Frick, and John Pierpont Morgan. On October 23, 1907, monetary inflation and speculation caused a run on banks and a rapid decline in stock prices. Containment of the crisis was largely attributed to Morgan, who organized a consortium of major banks to hold up the market with a subscription of over $25 million. The Panic of 1907 had almost abated when World War I broke out in the summer of 1914, with foreign exchanges closing down in drones. By July, the NYSE stood as the last major exchange to absorb worldwide investor panic. It suspended trading until December 14. When it reopened, military procurements stimulated renewed trading energy that carried the NYSE prominently into the 1920s. To finance the war, large issues of United States Liberty Bonds were traded, attracting new investors.

After the war, the American economy was powered by retail chain stores and massive holding companies which accounted for rapid expansion in new issues, greater volume of trading, and increasing value of listed shares. The NYSE took several measures to maintain order amid the flux of new activity: the Stock Clearing Corporation was established on April 26, 1920, to facilitate transfers of cash and stock between members, banks and trust companies; Exchange membership was increased from 1100 to 1375 in 1929; and the trading floor was physically expanded and updated to handle higher volume. While the market value of all NYSE listed stocks was $27 billion in 1925, it jumped to approximately $90 billion by 1929.

In the late 1920s, financial optimism persisted despite signs of weakening markets in agriculture, real estate, and construction. On October 24, 1929, however, the market underwent its first sharp break, known as "Black Thursday." One week later, on October 29, 1929, the market "crashed." Stock prices dropped 11.7 percent and volume soared to a record 16,410,000 shares. The Dow Jones Industrial Average dropped from 386 to 41.

The United States Congress passed corrective legislation, of which the Securities Act of 1933 and the Securities Exchange Act of 1934 directly influenced the NYSE. The 1933 Act mandated the registration of all new issues of securities with the Federal Trade Commission (FTC) and the full availability of all pertinent information to investors. The later Act created the Securities and Exchange Commission (SEC) to monitor price manipulation, speculation, and unfair practices in all securities exchanges. On October 1, 1934, the NYSE registered with the SEC as a national securities exchange. The NYSE initiated substantial organizational change with the June 30, 1938, election of its first full-time paid president and chief executive officer, William McChesney Martin, Jr. Martin restructured the Exchange's Governing Committee and its entire committee system, and paved the way for stricter self-regulation.

After weathering World War II and assisting the federal government in the sale of seven giant defense loans, the NYSE entered the 1950s with a plan to gain the confidence of new investors. In June of 1953, the Exchange admitted its first member corporation, Woodcock, Hess & Co., expanding on rules that had limited memberships to partnerships. In January of 1954, the Exchange inaugurated a Monthly Payment Plan, in which stocks could be purchased with regular payments. And in February of that year, the push to broaden public ownership fostered a print and radio campaign of public education with the theme: "Own Your Share of American Business."

Starting in the 1960s, a virtual revolution in automated data-processing, information, and communication technology effected every level of Exchange activity, from trading practices to regulation and industry-wide organization. In December of 1964, the "black box" ticker was replaced with a 900-character-per-minute model. The old pneumatic tube system was replaced with computer cards. The Market Data System (MDS), completed in December of 1966, used the latest computer technology to integrate the ticker system, the NYSE Common Stock Index and stock-clearing operations. A joint venture between the NYSE and the American Stock Exchange resulted in the 1972 establishment of the Securities Industry Automation Corporation (SIAC), which provided consulting and development services in automated systems for the entire industry. Improved systems utilized by the NYSE also included the 1976 Designated Order Turnaround (DOT) system to electronically route trade information between the Exchange and member firm offices (the improved SuperDOT system followed), and a computerized Stock Watch system to monitor price fluctuations in listed stocks.

Starting in the early 1970s, major organizational changes affected the NYSE and the securities industry at large. In 1970, public ownership of member firms was approved. Then in February of 1971, the Exchange again called on William McChesney Martin, Jr., to overhaul its constitution, rules, and procedures. Changes following Martin's recommendations were numerous: the NYSE was incorporated as a not-for-profit organization; in July of 1971, member corporations began listing their stock; alternative listing standards attracted foreign-based corporations, and qualified foreign-based brokers were invited to apply for membership; electronic-access memberships were added to physical memberships to expand broker-dealer participation in NYSE markets; and the fixed commission system was abolished in May of 1975. In addition, the Board of Governors was replaced by a Board of Directors in July of 1972; by 1993, the Board consisted of 12 public members, 12 industry members, and two NYSE officers, the chair/CEO and the president/chief operating officer.

With the Securities Acts Amendments of 1975, Congress enacted further changes. A full consolidated tape was introduced to electronically collect and report trades in NYSE listed stocks from all markets in which they occurred. The 1978 inauguration of the Intermarket Trading System (ITS) used computers to connect the NYSE to six other stock exchanges: the American, Boston, Cincinnati, Midwest, Pacific, and Philadelphia. A Composite Quotation System and National Clearance and Settlement System enabled brokers to do comparative shopping between different markets. Those markets grew in number to include, among others, the over-the-counter (NASDAQ) market after 1982.

In the 1980s, the NYSE was influenced by three main trends: the rise of options and financial futures markets; the proliferation of non-Exchange instruments such as limited partnerships, penny stocks, and junk bonds; and the surge of computerized information delivery systems, giving industry professionals unprecedented power to manipulate the market in what the press often called "market games." The first trend was manifest in the August 7, 1980 opening of the New York Futures Exchange (NYFE). All three trends contributed to a bullish market throughout the early 1980s.

The September 21, 1987, record price of $1,150,000 paid for a NYSE membership reflected confidence in the market's strength. Nevertheless, less than six months later the market experienced a sudden downturn. On October 19, 1987, the Dow Jones Industrial Average dropped 508 points, followed a day later by the highest volume day of 608,148,710 shares at the NYSE. In order to reduce record stock-market volume, on October 20 the NYSE curbed the use of its electronic order-delivery system, forcing many traders to turn away orders. The overall turmoil and tremendous loss to investors earned the name "Black Monday." The overall crisis became known as the Crash of 1987.

The Crash of 1987 prompted energetic discussion and planning toward regulatory overhaul of the nation's financial industry. While strategies differed, general consensus supported the basic objectives of national market system legislation: fair competition between market participants; economically efficient and fast execution of customer orders; public access to market information; and the opportunities for investors to interact without broker participation. The exact means of arriving at these objectives remained a subject of heated and ongoing debate. One plan proposed a $1 billion superfund, created with capital advanced by large member firms. In a *New York Times* editorial on October 21, 1987, Lawrence H. Summers suggested that the stock index futures market should be regulated out of existence, as it "increased market volatility by creating huge selling pressure following market declines." Edward A. Kwalwasser, executive vice-president of the NYSE Regulatory Group, proposed a general regulatory structure that would apply the same rules to all securities execution systems. He argued that different regulations too often applied to different trading systems.

Indeed, from the 1980s onward, the NYSE faced growing competition by off-exchange trading in NYSE-listed securities. Customers were increasingly drawn to so-called third-market firms for several reasons: they had no exchange fees to pay, they outperformed regional exchanges, and they could execute orders at incredible speeds, often within seconds. Yet critics cited important disadvantages as well: third-market firms permitted their brokers/dealers to funnel order flow to sources of liquidity that might undermine the primacy of the investor and the capital raising function. In an April 1993 hearing on the Future of the Stock Market, NYSE CEO William Donaldson defended the Exchange against the encroachment of dealer markets. He noted that "the fragmented nature of dealer markets combined with flexibility in the time a trade can be reported makes trade reporting in the dealer market inherently unreliable." Praising the NYSE's combination of computer automation with on-floor communication, Donaldson added that "It's only at the point of sale where we believe that human intelligence and competitiveness must be brought together in executing an order."

In January of 1992, the NYSE began a yearlong series of programs and events in observance of its bicentennial. It also continued its fight to retain any further slippage in its market share, adding policies like the "clean-cross rule" allowing large institutional investors to cross block orders on the floor without interference from smaller public orders. In addition, the NYSE continued to develop international contacts: in November of 1986 it led a Wall Street delegation to China for a symposium on financial markets; in November of 1988 it opened an office in London to facilitate European access to U.S. capital markets; and in October of 1990 the NYSE established an exchange program with the U.S.S.R. (now C.I.S.) Ministry of Finance and Gosbank, the state bank. Where some analysts foresaw a not-too-distant world in which investors would trade directly with each other on personal computers, the NYSE moved into an era in which technology and growing competition would have to be worked and reworked into an efficient and orderly marketplace.

Principal Subsidiaries: New York Futures Exchange (NYFE).

Further Reading:

Anders, George, Cynthia Crossen, and Scott McMurray, "Big Board Curb on Electronic Trading Results in Halt at Stock-Index Markets," *Wall Street Journal,* October 21, 1987, p. 3.
"Demolition on Wall Street; The NYSE Is Gloomy Because the NYSE Is Gloomy," *The Economist,* February 4, 1987, p. 81.

"Excerpt of the Hearing of the Telecommunications and Finance Sub-committee of the House Energy and Commerce Committee," *Federal News Service,* April 14, 1993.

Fadiman, Mark, *Rebuilding Wall Street,* Englewood Cliffs, NJ: Prentice Hall, 1992.

Gardner, Deborah S., *Marketplace: A Brief History of the New York Stock Exchange,* New York: NYSE, 1993.

Jones, Alex S., "Caution in the Press: Was It Really a 'Crash'?" *New York Times,* October 21, 1987.

Feinberg, Andrew, "Blown Away by Black Monday," *New York Times Magazine,* December 20, 1987, pp. 39, 67–71.

Metz, Tim, *Black Monday; The Catastrophe of October 19, 1987 and Beyond,* New York: William Morrow.

New York Stock Exchange Press Kit, New York: NYSE, Inc., 1993.

Schmerken, Ivy, "Off-exchange Trading Chips Away at NYSE Volume," *Wall Street & Technology,* December, 1992, p. 42.

Summers, Lawrence H., "In the Wake of Wall Street's Crash," *New York Times,* October 21, 1987.

"Text of Testimony Prepared for Delivery by Edward A. Kwalwasser, Executive Vice-President Regulatory Group, NYSE, before the Telecommunications and Finance Subcommittee of the House Energy and Commerce Committee," *Federal News Service,* May 26, 1993.

—Kerstan Cohen

newell®

Newell Co.

Newell Center
29 East Stephenson Street
Freeport, Illinois 61032-0943
U.S.A.
(815) 235-4171
Fax: (815) 233-8657

Public Company
Incorporated: 1902 as W. F. Linton Company
Employees: 17,400
Sales: $1.45 billion
Stock Exchanges: New York Midwest
SICs: 3365 Aluminum Foundries; 3469 Metal Stampings;
   3089 Plastic Products; 3429 Hardware; 3951 Pens and
   Mechanical Pencils; 3231 Products of Purchased Glass

Originally founded near the turn of the century to make brass curtain rods, Newell Co. has evolved into a diversified company that manufactures and markets a variety of high-volume brand name consumer products, including hardware and home furnishings and houseware, office, and other products. Newell's hardware, houseware, and office products are sold primarily through mass merchandisers, including discount, variety, chain, and hardware stores, as well as hardware and houseware distributors, home improvement centers, office product superstores, and office product dealers and wholesalers. Each group of Newell's products is manufactured and marketed by a subsidiary or division devoted to a specific product area.

Newell Co. traces its roots to the short-lived W. F. Linton Company, an Ogdensburg, New York, firm incorporated in 1902 to make brass curtain rods. The Linton Company received $1,000 to move the company from Providence, Rhode Island, to Ogdensburg from the Ogdensburg Board of Trade, with the board's president, Edgar A. Newell, signing off on the loan. In 1903 the company went bankrupt and Newell took control of its operations, renaming the firm Newell Manufacturing Company, Inc.

Although he was familiar with sales, Newell had no understanding of manufacturing and, as a result, hired and subsequently fired several general managers between 1903 and 1907. Edgar Newell then hired his son Allan to run Newell Manufacturing and started a new company, Newell Manufacturing Company Ltd. (Newell Ltd.), in Prescott, Canada. Established to capital-

ize on Ogdensburg's location, which made shipments south costly and left Canadian distribution channels more financially attractive, Newell Ltd. purchased a small dockside building in Prescott.

Newell Manufacturing's initial product line was composed exclusively of brass curtain rods, created through a method of tube making that utilized a waterwheel; Newell's was powered by the nearby Oswegatchie River. In 1908 Newell began producing a greater variety of curtain rod shapes after adopting a new, faster, and more adaptable manufacturing process that used roll forming machines. By the end of the decade the Newell companies were employing about 20 people and generating annual sales of about $50,000.

Throughout Newell Manufacturing's second decade, increasing managerial authority was given to Allan Newell, although Edgar Newell retained all voting shares of both Newell companies. In 1912 the domestic company began construction of a new factory, which was completed a year later.

Although Ogdensburg operations were sailing smoothly, by 1912 Newell Ltd. found that curtain rods were not enough to keep its operations afloat. A new manager, Lawrence "Ben" Ferguson Cuthbert, was given a chance to bail out the Canadian plant in return for a 20 percent cut of its gross profits. Between 1912 and 1913 Newell Ltd. acquired the factory it had been leasing and expanded its plating department in order to produce a variety of products, including towel racks, stair nosings, ice picks, and other items requiring a finish of brass, zinc, or nickel. The expanded product line spurred additional sales, and Newell Ltd. soon became profitable.

As war spread across the globe, the cost of brass rose, and Newell hired the Baker Varnish Company to devise a new metal-coating method tailored to Newell's roll forming manufacturing process. By 1917 Newell's curtain rods were being coated with a nontarnishable lacquer. Not only were the new rods cheaper to produce than brass rods, but because they wouldn't tarnish, they were better suited to lace and ruffle curtains.

With its new curtain rod Newell courted and won the business of Woolworth stores, after agreeing to buy out Woolworth's on-hand stock of curtain rods. Newell's first buy-back deal soon paid dividends, boosting sales and helping to establish the company's first long-term relationship with a major national retailer.

In 1920 Edgar A. Newell died and, for the first time, stockholder changes were made at the company. Cuthbert called in his profit-stake from running Newell Ltd., and, after some subsequent legal jousting, the company's stock ownership was resolved. Allan Newell received a 64 percent share in Newell Ltd., and Cuthbert received 33 percent of Newell Manufacturing and 20 percent of Newell Ltd. Albert Newell, Edgar's other son, who had been helping with sales, received 66 percent of Newell Manufacturing and 16 percent of Newell Ltd. Allan Newell was named chairman and president of Newell Manufacturing but bowed out of active affairs with the company, opting for a political life that eventually led him to the New York State Assembly. Albert Newell was also reluctant to be involved with the family business, and management of both companies passed to Cuthbert, who moved to Ogdensburg.

In 1921 Cuthbert, the Newell brothers, and a former Ogdensburg employee named Harry Barnwell each put up $5,000 to start a new curtain rod factory in Freeport, Illinois. The new business, Western Newell Manufacturing Company, was designed to take advantage of local railroad transportation and serve as a western branch of Newell Manufacturing. Barnwell served a brief stint as Western Newell's president before selling his 25 percent stake in the operations to Cuthbert's cousin, Leonard Ferguson, who was recruited to manage the fledgling company. Like Newell Manufacturing, Western Newell began operations with ten employees and initially produced curtain rods in a red brick factory it rented. The company quickly became profitable, and in 1925 a new factory was erected. By 1928 Western Newell's sales had grown to $485,000, more than twice that of Newell Ltd. and about half that of Newell Manufacturing. At the time of the stock market crash in October 1929, Western Newell was producing a wide variety of drapery hardware, including extension curtain rods, ornamental drapery rods, and pinless curtain stretchers.

Despite a dramatic slide in sales that forced the companies to layoff workers and reduce workdays, the Newell companies made it through the Great Depression without dipping into red ink. The bottom of the Depression's well for Newell Manufacturing came in 1933 when that company logged only about one-half of its 1929 level of sales, or $425,000. With a small operational base and modest salaries, Western Newell fared the best of the two American companies during the Depression, and by 1933 the 12-year-old Western Newell, with sales figures 25 percent lower than Newell Manufacturing, had a net income 30 percent greater than the original company. In 1933 Western Newell earned $61,000 on sales of $320,000, whereas Newell Manufacturing earned $47,000 on sales of $425,000. By 1937 Western Newell, under the leadership of Ferguson, had surpassed Newell Manufacturing in both revenues and income, earning $126,000 on sales of $553,000, whereas Newell Manufacturing earned $70,000 on sales of $511,000.

At Cuthbert's suggestion, in the late 1930s the Newell brothers agreed to give Ferguson a small stake in Newell Manufacturing, effectively taking the founding company out of the hands of the Newell family, although the brothers retained rights to voting control through the late 1940s.

Between 1938 and 1939 Newell Manufacturing established a third domestic factory, this one in Los Angeles, and made its first acquisition—Drapery Hardware Ltd. of Monrovia, California (DRACO), a maker of wooden and heavy iron drapery fixtures that was eventually sold to S. H. Kress and other smaller customers. Before the 1930s drew to a close a number of officer changes were made: Cuthbert was named to succeed Allan Newell as president of Newell Manufacturing and Ferguson was named president of Western Newell, although Allan Newell remained president of Newell Ltd. and chairman of all three companies.

During World War II the Freeport factory won a coveted Army/ Navy "E" Award for excellence in wartime production, churning out more than 230 million metallic belt links for machine guns within a two-year period. During the postwar decade the Newell companies enjoyed steady growth, although no new manufacturing plants were started or acquired. In 1954 the

Newell family ceded further power over its namesake companies as complete operational control was given to Leonard Ferguson, who became president of all three Newell companies.

During the early 1960s Newell acquired the rights to additional drapery hardware brands and names, including Angevine and Silent Gliss. In 1963 Ferguson was named chairman and chief executive of the three Newell companies and two years later his son, Daniel C. Ferguson, became president of the companies. Under the leadership of the father and son team, in 1966 all Newell companies were consolidated into one Illinois corporation, Newell Manufacturing Company, with headquarters in Freeport. Under the guidance of Daniel Ferguson, the $14 million family business turned its focus from its products to its customers and initiated a multiproduct strategy designed to boost sales to its existing buyers.

During the 1970s Newell continued to acquire other companies, greatly expanding its product line in the process. In 1968 Newell purchased a majority interest in Mirra-Cote Industries, a manufacturer of plastic bath accessories. In 1969 Newell acquired Dorfile Manufacturing Company, a maker of household shelving, and E.H. Tate Company, which brought the "Bulldog" line of picture hanging hardware into the Newell line of products. During the late 1960s DRACO began phasing out of manufacturing operations and finally closed its doors in the early 1970s. In 1970 the company was reincorporated in Delaware as Newell Companies, Inc. The following year Newell added sewing and knitting accessories to its product line when it acquired The Boye Needle Company, a Chicago-based world leader in knitting needles and crochet hooks, and Novel Ideas, Inc., another maker of do-it-yourself sewing materials.

In April 1972 Newell went public as an over-the-counter stock and that same year initiated an acquisition strategy that would later be replayed in various forms. Newell made an offer to buy EZ Paintr Corporation, a paint and sundries company in which Newell already had a 25 percent stake, and EZ Paintr in turn filed a pair of lawsuits to fight back against a possible takeover. But in February 1973 Newell gained majority control of EZ Paintr after its president and co-founder agreed to sell his family's interest in the paint supply company, a move opposed by EZ Paintr's management. By March 1973 Newell had ousted the EZ Paintr board and Daniel Ferguson had became president of the company, which yielded complete control of its stock to Newell six months later. In 1974 Newell completed another drawn-out acquisition and purchased complete control of Mirra-Cote.

In 1975 Leonard Ferguson died and a descendant of Ben Cuthbert, William R. Cuthbert, was later named chairman. Between 1976 and 1978 Newell expanded its shelving, paint, and sundries offerings and acquired Royal Oak Industries, Inc., Baker Brush Company, and Dixon Red Devil Ltd. (later renamed Dixon Applicators). During the same period the company sold some of its knitting products businesses, including Novel Ideas. In May 1978 Newell acquired 24 percent of the financially-troubled BernzOmatic Corporation, a manufacturer of propane torches and other do-it-yourself hand tools. In February 1979 Newell gained operational control over BernzOmatic after its president, who had earlier sold convertible debentures to Newell, yielded his position to Ferguson and Newell had taken control of the smaller firm's board.

In June 1979, after coming off of its first $100 million sales year, Newell began trading on the New York Stock Exchange. About the same time Newell began targeting a new customer base—the emerging mass merchandisers like K Mart—in order to piggyback on the increasing popularity of such stores.

Newell entered the 1980s riding on the growth of mass merchandisers while continuing to expand and compliment its product line through acquisitions. Between 1980 and 1981 Newell acquired the drapery hardware division of The Stanley Works and Brearley Co., a manufacturer of bathroom scales. In April 1982 Newell acquired complete control of BernzOmatic and in December of that year entered into a $60 million financing and stock purchase agreement with Western Savings & Loan Association, with the S&L paying $18.4 million for a 20 percent stake in Newell, which it gradually sold off to private investors during the next five years.

Through two separate stock deals worth over $42 million, in 1983 Newell acquired Mirro Corporation, a maker of aluminum cookware and baking dishes. In May 1984 Newell increased its number of common stock shares from 14 million to 50 million and later that year through a stock swap acquired Foley-ASC, Inc., a maker of cookware and kitchen accessories. In May 1985 the company changed its name to Newell Co. In June 1985 Newell acquired a 20 percent stake in William E. Wright Company from a group dissenting from the majority, including three board members and the grandson of Wright Company's founder. A few months later Newell raised its stake in Wright, a maker of sewing notions, and by the end of the year Newell had obtained majority control of the company and ousted Wright's board and top officers.

In January 1986 William P. Sovey, former president of AMF Inc., was named president and chief operating officer. Ferguson remained chief executive and was named to the new position of vice chairman. In October 1986 Newell acquired the assets of Enterprise Aluminum, the aluminum cookware division of Lancaster Colony Corporation.

By 1987 Newell had acquired complete control of Wright, which was added to a list of about 30 acquisitions the company had logged since Ferguson had become president. In July 1987 Newell—true to its acquisition formula—paid $330 million to acquire control of Anchor Hocking Corporation and its targeted glassware operations. At the time of the acquisition Anchor, with $758 million in sales, had nearly double the annual revenues of Newell and provided its new parent with brand name tabletop glassware, decorative cabinet hardware, and microwave cookware, with each product line holding a number one or two position in their respective markets. Within a week after the takeover Newell began employing its usual post-acquisition strategy on a large scale, dismissing 110 Anchor employees and closing its West Virginia plant.

Between 1988 and 1989 Newell acquired several small companies that made bakeware, paint sundries, metal closures, cabinet hardware, and aluminum cookware, and sold its Carr-Lowrey specialty glass container business and its William E. Wright/ Boye Needle home-sewing business. In 1989 Newell unsuc-

cessfully tried to buy a 20-plus percent investment in Vermont American, a maker of consumer and industrial tools that turned to another suitor after suggesting Newell would be a disruptive force in its operations.

Newell closed its books on the 1980s having achieved a number of significant financial accomplishments. Between 1987 and 1989 the company's income rose more than $48 million, while during the course of the entire decade sales spiraled from $138 million to $1.12 billion as income ballooned from $7.8 million to $85.3 million. Newell was also listed number 22 on *Forbes* list of the best stocks of the 1980s, having provided a total return to stockholders that averaged 39.5 percent per year.

Newell entered the 1990s as a market leader in Electronic Data Interchange, a computer-to-computer system that allowed Newell customers to place orders electronically. Attempting to once again piggyback on a growing mass merchandiser market— namely the trend to sell office supplies through mass retailers— in 1991 Newell entered the office products business by acquiring two small firms, Keene Manufacturing, Inc., and W.T. Rogers Company.

In 1991 Newell also increased its interests in hardware firms and agreed to invest $150 million in the Black & Decker Corporation in a stock deal giving Newell a 15 percent stake in the hardware company. (The following year Newell backed away from a move to purchase a 15 percent interest in another hardware manufacturer, Stanley Works, which had filed an antitrust suit against Newell.) In 1991 Newell also acquired a six percent stake in the Ekco Group Inc., a maker of houseware products, kitchen tools, and bakeware, which was later sold.

In 1992 Newell became a major force in the office products market. It acquired both Sanford Corporation, a leading producer of felt-tipped pens, plastic desk accessories, storage boxes, and other office and school supplies, and Stuart Hall Corporation, a well-known stationary and school supply business, in two stock swaps totaling more than $600 million. The two businesses combined brought Newell's annual office products sales to $350 million. In 1992 Newell also sold its closures business for $210 million, and the company's books for the year reflected a record $119 million in earnings on a record $1.45 billion in sales.

In a 1992 changing-of-the-guard, Daniel Ferguson bowed out of active management to move up to chairman, replacing the retiring William Cuthbert, and Thomas A. Ferguson (no relation to Daniel and Leonard Ferguson) was named president. Sovey was named to succeed Daniel Ferguson as vice chairman and chief executive. Although the company had another Ferguson in line to run Newell, by 1992 stock dilution had reduced insider control of the company to 15 percent. However, four members of the 11-person board were members of the Ferguson, Cuthbert, or Newell families.

In 1993 Newell—in what could be perceived as a return to its roots—acquired Intercraft Industries, Inc., the largest supplier of picture frames in the United States. As it moved through 1993, Newell's strategy was to continue merchandising an expanding but complimentary multiproduct brand-name group of staples while improving its image as a customer service company through such programs as EDI and shelf restocking services. With Newell selling primarily to leading mass merchandisers and virtually all of Newell's products claiming brand names and positions as market leaders within their respective product groups, Newell entered the mid-1990s in an apparent position to hold onto—if not improve—its status in more familiar markets, such as drapery, hardware, and houseware product areas. At the same time Newell was becoming an emerging force in the office product market, where the trend towards mass merchandising was just gaining momentum.

Further Reading:

Benmour, Eric, "Vermont American Suitor Proves Tenacious," *Business First-Louisville,* August 28, 1989, Section 1, p. 1.

Borden, Jeff, "Newell Makes Its Move," *Crains Chicago Business,* November 25, 1991, p. 46.

Byrne, Harlan S., "Newell Co.," *Barron's,* April 12, 1993, p. 52.

Conley, Thomas P., "The NHMA Report: Electronic Partnerships Provide Bottom-Line Payoffs," *Discount Merchandiser,* January 1993, pp. 45–46.

Cuthbert, William R., *Newell Companies—A Corporate History—The First 40 Years,* Freeport, IL: Newell Co., 1983.

Hackney, Holt, "Strategic Alliances," *Financial World,* October 29, 1991.

Kelly, Kevin, "Newell Isn't Bagging Big Game Anymore," *Business Week,* July 8, 1991, pp. 83–84.

Magnet, Myron, "Meet the New Revolutionaries," *Fortune,* February 24, 1992, pp. 94–101.

Murphy, H. Lee, "Newell Dresses Up Its Image with a Shade-y Acquisition," *Crains Chicago Business,* April 12, 1993, Section 1, p. 7.

O'Connor, Matt, "Simple Secret of Newell's Success: Basic Strategy Pays Off for Consumer Firm," *Chicago Tribune,* July 27, 1987, Section 1, pp. 1, 5.

Pellet, Jennifer, "No Paint, No Gain," *Discount Merchandiser,* March 1992, pp. 74–75.

Pouschine, Tatiana, "The Old-Fashioned Way," *Forbes,* January 6, 1992, pp. 66–68.

Scott, Carlee R., "Newell Plans to Acquire Sanford Corp. in Stepped-Up Move into Office Products," *Wall Street Journal,* November 25, 1991, p. A5 1.

Stouffer, Paul W., "Heading for a Billion: Major Acquisition Bringing Newell Toward a Record Sales Mark, *Barron's,* August 24, 1987.

White, Joseph B., "Workers' Revenge: Factory Towns Start to Fight Back Angrily When Firms Pull Out," *Wall Street Journal,* March 8, 1988, pp. 1, 24.

—Roger W. Rouland

The Nikko Securities Company Limited

3-1, Marunouchi 3-Chome
Minato-Ku
Tokyo 100
Japan
(03) 283-2211
Fax: (33) 283-2470

Public Company
Incorporated: 1944
Employees: 9,943
Revenues: ¥495.89 billion
Stock Exchanges: Tokyo Osaka Nagoya Düsseldorf Frankfurt
   Luxembourg Paris
SICs: 6211 Security Brokers, Dealers and Floatation
   Companies; 6221 Commodity Contracts Brokers and
   Dealers; 6159 Miscellaneous Business Credit Institutions;
   6282 Investment Advice.

The Nikko Securities Company Limited is one of the largest securities companies in the world, and—along with Daiwa Securities Company, Nomura Securities Company, Limited, and Yamaichi Securities Company, Limited—is regarded as one of Japan's "Big Four" investment houses. Troubled in the early 1990s by a scandal involving illegal client reimbursements, Nikko has nevertheless regained its status as a leader in the industry and has sought to expand its business by diversifying operations internationally.

Founded in 1944, Nikko is the youngest of Japan's Big Four securities houses, which collectively transact more than half of the brokerage and investment banking in Japan. Nikko was formed as a merger between the Kawashimaya Securities Company and the Nikko Securities Company, which was at that time part of the Industrial Bank of Japan. The new company could count the long experience of its two predecessors among its assets.

In 1918, Genichi Toyama founded the Kawashimaya Shoten to buy and sell stocks and bonds; two years later his company was incorporated as Kawashimaya Shoten Inc., Ltd. Kawashimaya expanded throughout the 1920s and 1930s, and in 1939 Toyama set up a separate company, Kawashimaya Securities Company, Ltd., as a bond underwriter. In 1943, the business of Kawashi-

maya Shoten was assimilated by the Kawashimaya Securities Company.

The Nikko Securities Company grew out of the securities department of the Industrial Bank of Japan. Although Nikko separated from IBJ in 1920 and operated autonomously on a day-to-day basis, it remained under the ultimate control of the bank. In 1943, Nikko strengthened its position in the markets when it acquired the Kyodo Securities Company, Ltd. A year later, it merged with Kawashimaya, formally separating itself from IBJ and creating the present-day Nikko Securities Company.

Japan's securities markets were in a chaotic state after World War II as stock prices plummeted. In 1945, all trading on the major exchanges was suspended while the Occupation forces restructured the Japanese economy and political system. Because of the forced disintegration of the huge Japanese cartels known as *zaibatsu,* stock ownership became broadly based. Reconstruction called for extensive borrowing, and this need was met by substantial debenture issues. The new Nikko Securities opened during this chaos with 736 employees in 12 offices. It survived by buying and selling securities over the counter at its offices throughout Japan.

In 1948, Japan's Securities and Exchange Law laid the foundation for the reopening of Japan's principal exchanges, allowing the Tokyo Stock Exchange and the other major markets to reopen in 1949. The economy took off in 1951 as a result of increased export demand from United Nations forces, primarily American troops, engaged in the Korean conflict. This boom pulled the Japanese stock market out of a serious slump and heralded the steady growth of the Japanese economy. Nikko's own growth, for the most part, mirrored that of Japan.

In the postwar period, Nikko, along with the other Japanese securities houses, invested heavily in public relations to educate the Japanese people about equity and capital markets. The investment paid off; nearly half of all Japanese became active investors during the 1950s. Nikko established public relations libraries where people could go to keep abreast of the markets. These outreach centers were found in shopping centers, railway stations, even underground on subway concourses. In addition, the company sponsored a television show called "Morning Smiles," which went on the air as the Tokyo Stock Exchange opened and reported trends and developments in the securities markets. Nikko also targeted women in its advertisements and media campaigns, and women became a significant group of investors. According to Nikko founder Genichi Toyama, in the early 1960s "discussions of the market [received] almost as much attention in most Japanese homes as the weather and baseball." Nikko had helped cultivate a nation of avid securities consumers.

Investment trusts became one of the most popular ways for Japanese to invest. Nikko opened the first of its investment trusts in 1951, and by 1957 was managing more than ¥100 billion in subscriptions. The company offered two types of investment trusts. A unit-type trust allowed an investor to purchase a unit for ¥5,000 that would mature in five years. An open-end type resembled the American mutual fund; shares were bought and sold at the market price, which was in turn based on the net asset value at a given time.

With an increasing need for capital in the late 1950s, Nikko established itself abroad to facilitate the flow of foreign capital into Japan. In 1959, Nikko set up an office in New York. This office was primarily a research center until 1965, when it took on new services and was upgraded to subsidiary status. Nikko's main U.S. affiliate in the late 1950s and 1960s was Nikko Kasai Securities Company, a joint venture with Kasai Securities established in 1955 in San Francisco. Nikko Kasai focused on developing an interest in Japanese securities among west coast investors. Nikko continued to expand into key foreign financial centers in the 1960s, opening an office in London in 1964 and in Zurich in 1969.

In 1961, Nikko Securities went public, offering its shares on the Tokyo, Nagoya, and Osaka exchanges. Japanese securities market activity expanded at an incredible rate until 1964, when the economy slipped into one of the most severe recessions of the postwar era. The Japanese government's newly imposed tight monetary controls combined with U.S. restrictions on foreign investment to put a clamp on growth. The resulting drop in stock prices caused a public loss of confidence in the markets.

Some analysts blamed the securities companies for irresponsible, even unethical, behavior in the months leading up to the crisis. They accused the dealers of overzealously pushing securities on investors to avoid getting stuck with issues they had underwritten. As a result of these and other practices, the Japanese Ministry of Finance called for the complete reorganization of the securities industry. Nikko was reviewed and allowed to obtain the new licenses necessary to operate as a securities underwriter and dealer. Top management underwent several major changes: many of the company's managers were replaced by younger executives, nine directors retired, and the 56-year-old Moriatsu Minato, a former director with a strong background in banking, became president. By 1966, the Japanese economy had resumed its extraordinary rate of growth—growth that continued uninterrupted until the oil crisis of 1973.

When the worldwide oil crisis struck, Japanese industry, heavily dependent on imported oil, suffered a terrible blow. More than 11,000 companies went bankrupt during the recession that followed. When the economy recovered, the stunning growth rates of the 1960s and early 1970s leveled off, and slower (though still impressive) growth characterized the second half of the 1970s. This period also saw the development of a more sophisticated bond market. Large government issues beginning in 1975 brought about changes in the capital markets. Japanese companies were in competition with the government for Japanese capital investment.

Nikko responded to this challenge by establishing new offices and subsidiaries around the world. By 1979, Nikko had offices or subsidiaries in Frankfurt, Luxembourg, Paris, Hong Kong, and Singapore in addition to its London and New York operations. Japanese stocks and bonds became increasingly popular overseas, particularly in Europe, and by 1980, Nikko, riding the wave of Japanese industrial strength, was competitive with Europe's largest securities companies.

As countries relaxed their regulations on financial services in the 1980s, the securities industry became increasingly globalized. Nikko's skyrocketing profits reflected those developments. In fact, Japanese securities companies, Nikko included, were soon ranked among the world's largest financial services companies. Domestic competition among the Japanese "Big Four" was fierce. Nikko continued to look overseas for new opportunities. Since the United States represented the largest single market in the world, Nikko resolved to establish itself there.

In the mid-1980s, the Ministry of Finance approved substantial changes in Japan's capital market controls. Japanese securities companies found new opportunities in the new varieties of bonds that were now permitted. European issues of Japanese bonds denominated in yen became very popular. As the yen took on greater significance as a benchmark currency, Nikko further solidified its position in the Euromarkets. The company's progress in the United States, however, was not as spectacular.

Nikko had difficulty penetrating American markets for several reasons. Its primary operations in the United States during the mid-1980s revolved around U.S. treasury bonds. The company was designated a primary dealer in U.S. government securities by the Federal Reserve in 1987, and Japanese investors had a large appetite for U.S. treasury bonds. Since it did not have a base of domestic investors in the United States, Nikko focused on investment banking services rather than brokering. But nearly all the Japanese securities houses were treated with caution by American investors and corporations issuing debt or equities. Nikko had trouble competing with the investment banking services of large U.S. companies like Goldman Sachs, First Boston, or Salomon Brothers.

Furthermore, some analysts considered the Japanese style of management poorly suited to the complex world of investment banking. In Japan, decisions requiring immediate resolution were deferred to top management, and further held up by the consensus approach characteristic of Japanese business. These problems were compounded in October 1987 when the New York stock market crashed and Nikko's mainstay—Japanese investors—were scared out of the markets. Although still committed to entering American markets, Nikko needed to regroup and develop a new strategy.

Nikko set out to diversify its services, purchasing 20 percent of the Blackstone Group in 1988. Blackstone, an American merchant bank, specialized in friendly takeovers, the only kind the Japanese will contemplate. As demand for mergers and acquisition assistance grew in the late 1980s, Nikko's connection with the American company proved an excellent arrangement. Nikko also became heavily involved in swaps, designing an advanced method of valuing swaps called "zero coupon valuation" that was superior in many ways to those used by some of Wall Street's best known investment banks. Nikko also established a presence in the American commodity futures industry in the late 1980s. Through these new services Nikko hoped to attract U.S. customers and broaden its Japanese base.

Nikko was ranked fifth among the world's securities firms in 1988. Along with Japan's other "Big Four" firms, Nikko was designated "omnipotent" by a *Tokyo Business Today* writer. By 1989, Nikko had established 14 subsidiaries and nine representative offices around the world to market, underwrite, and distribute all the securities traded in Japanese markets. The firm had distinguished itself in four primary areas: computerized investment technology, a 100+ branch national network, a strong mergers and acquisitions record, and activity in the high-potential regions of the pacific Rim and southeast Asia.

But Nikko's plans for the future were brought to a halt by upheaval in Japan's major brokerage houses. The Tokyo stock market dropped suddenly in 1990 and continued to decline in 1991. That year, Japan's securities market was rocked by the revelation of *tobashi,* the Japanese practice of reconciling the accounts of favored clients to compensate for stock losses. Analysts estimated that Japan's "Big Four" had reimbursed over 225 favored clients close to $1 billion from the 1990 Tokyo market crash to mid-1991. Nikko and Nomura were also linked to underworld boss Susumu Ishii and his Inagawa-Kai crime syndicate. The revelation of these scandals prompted an extraordinary deluge of public and private censure in Japan that culminated in the resignations of Nikko's and Nomura's top executives. Japanese Finance Minister Ryutaro Hashimoto took a ten percent pay cut for three months in acknowledgment of his office's negligence in regulating the market.

By the end of 1991, Nikko's pretax profits of ¥11.3 ranked it behind the Tokyo offices of two United States firms. Salomon Brothers' and Morgan Stanley's accomplishment was partially ascribed to the bans assessed by the Ministry of Finance on Nikko for their indiscretions. In the final assessment, most of the charges against Nikko were dropped because the firm had not technically broken Japan's vague securities laws.

Despite public disgust over the brokerage scandals, many analysts agreed that the "Big Four" would emerge from the embar-

rassing events of 1991 intact. Nikko hoped to reduce its dependence on the Japanese market in the 1990s by diversifying internationally. The firm worked to build its corporate finance capacity in Europe. And the problems of the parent notwithstanding, Nikko Securities Co. International, a U.S. subsidiary, found success in the derivatives arena and established a strong presence in America's futures markets.

Principal Subsidiaries: The Nikko Securities Co. International, Inc.; The Nikko Securities Co., (Europe) Ltd.; The Nikko Bank (U.K.) plc; Nikko Bank (Switzerland) Ltd.; Nikko Bank (Deutschland)GmbH; Nikko Bank (Luxembourg) S.A.; Nikko France S.A.; Nikko Investment Banking (Middle East) E.C.; Nikko Nederland N.V.; The Nikko Securities Co. (Asia) Limited; The Nikko Merchant Bank (Singapore) Ltd.; The Nikko Securities Co. (Australia) Ltd.; The Nikko Securities Co. Canada, Ltd.; The Nikko Futures (Singapore) Pte., Ltd.; Nikko Capital Services, Inc.; Nikko Espana Sociedad de Valores S.A.; Nikko Italia S.p.A.; Nikko Securities Indonesia; P.T. Nikko Securities Indonesia.

Further Reading:

Baba, Kuniko. "Big Four Chill Doesn't Temper U.S. Growth," *Futures: The Magazine of Commodities & Options,* September 1992, pp. 58–64.
King, Paul. "Japanese Banks in Europe: The New Phase—a More International Approach," *Euromoney,* July 1992, pp. S20–S24.
"Tokyo's Stock Scandal Keeps Growing," *Financier,* August 1991, pp. 31–34.

—updated by April S. Dougal

Nobel Industries AB

Gustav Adolfs Torg 18
Box 16397
S-103 27 Stockholm
Sweden
(08) 613 25 00
Fax: (08) 20 12 05

Public Company
Incorporated: 1984
Employees: 20,000
Sales: SKr 21.48 million (US$2.56 million)
Stock Exchanges: Stockholm, Copenhagen
SICs: 2804 Industrial Chemicals; 2834 Pharmaceutical
   Preparations; 3820 Measuring & Control Instruments;
   2850 Paints & Allied Products; 2891 Adhesives; 3843
   Dental Equipment & Supplies

Nobel Industries AB is one of Europe's leading manufacturers of specialty industrial chemicals, paints, and adhesives. The company has 300 diverse subsidiaries and allied companies under its umbrella, operating in six major categories. Seventy-seven percent of its sales are in markets outside Sweden. Nobel is a world leader in the field of pulp and paper chemicals, mainly through its subsidiary, Eka Nobel AB. This company manufactures chlorine and alkaline products and other special chemicals for the wet-end section of paper manufacturing as well as chemicals for use in the detergent and cleaning product industries, with plants in 12 countries outside Sweden. Nobel Industries' biotechnology division develops and manufactures titanium devices, primarily implants for dental reconstructions. Its major markets are in the United States, Europe, and Japan. In the area of paints and adhesives, Nobel Industries is one of Europe's foremost manufacturers, with market strongholds in Great Britain, Ireland, Belgium, Greece, and Scandinavia. Nobel Industries is also a European leader in the manufacture of industrial coatings. The company's surface chemistry division manufactures and markets ethylene oxide, ethanol and ethylene amines, and cellulose derivatives for applications in surface and colloid chemistry, with major markets in the detergent and cleaning industries. Nobel Industries also operates a pharma-chemicals division, which manufactures fine chemicals used in sun screens, vitamins, pigments, and X-ray contrast agents, and therapeutic chemicals used in the treatment of cardiovascular disease, and gastric, intestinal, and central nervous system dis-

orders. Nobel Industries also included a consumer goods division, making skin care, hair care, and other personal hygiene products, until January of 1992, when this area was divested to Henkel, a German chemical company. Nobel had also long been involved in the armaments business, but the company divested itself of all its defense industry areas by March 1993. One further significant area of operation is Nobel Industries' 87 percent share in Spectra-Physics AB, a company specializing in high-tech measurement using laser, microwave, and infrared technologies.

Nobel Industries was created in 1984 by the merger of a chemical company, KemaNobel, and an armaments maker, Bofors. Both Bofors and KemaNobel had historic ties to Alfred Nobel, the great 19th century Swedish inventor who was the first to discover a way to detonate the flammable liquid nitroglycerin. After inventing the blasting cap in 1863, Nobel founded a company called Nitroglycerin Ltd. the following year and began travelling to set up nitroglycerin plants in Europe and America. He typically exchanged his patent rights for a share in the business, and a network of companies grew bearing the Nobel name. Problems with transport and storage of nitroglycerin caused several deadly accidents over the next few years, until Nobel's 1867 development of the explosive he named dynamite. With the invention of this stable package of nitroglycerine, Nobel's businesses expanded rapidly, and he soon garnered one of Europe's largest fortunes through dividends of his plants in the United States, Britain, Norway, France, Italy, Spain, Finland, Scotland, Austria-Hungary, and elsewhere.

Alfred Nobel died in 1895, having directed that his fortune be used to establish the awards that bear his name. His first company, Nitroglycerin Ltd., continued in the explosives business. In 1965 the company's name was changed to Nitro Nobel, and in 1978 the business was acquired by Swedish industrialist Marcus Wallenberg, who headed a group of companies that included Sweden's largest bank, major airline, leading telecommunications company, a major forest products company, the well-known household appliance maker Electrolux, and the country's second largest auto company. These holdings, controlled directly or indirectly by Wallenberg, were said to account for 25 percent of Sweden's gross domestic product. Wallenberg merged Nitro Nobel with his KemaNord group, and renamed the company KemaNobel.

Bofors, the second company involved in the formation of Nobel Industries, traced its lineage back to 1646, when it was a hammer forge near Karlskoga, Sweden, that by 1894 had become a munitions factory. Alfred Nobel bought Bofors that year, his last acquisition before his death in 1895. Bofors became well known for its howitzer, first sold in 1936. This gun was instrumental to the defense of Britain in World War II. Bofors' subsequent anti-aircraft weapon, the L/70 40mm gun, had strong sales in NATO countries after the war. The RBS 70 anti-aircraft missile was another of Bofors' popular export weapons, along with its 155mm FH 77 mobile howitzer. Because Sweden is a neutral country, Bofors' weapons followed Swedish specifications that they be primarily defensive, and exports were limited by complex government policies. By the mid-1970s about 55 percent of Bofors' weapons and ammunition output went to supply the Swedish defense forces, but that figure declined over the next decade.

Government contracts for armaments made up most of Bofors' profits, but the company had interests in other areas as well. These included a chemicals and plastics division called Bofors Nobel, which specialized in manufacturing chemicals that other companies found too messy to make themselves. Strict pollution laws made many firms unwilling to handle the dangerous wastes often produced by chemical manufacture, and Bofors found a growing market for its services, especially in West Germany and Great Britain. Another division, called Nobel Chematur, contracted chemical engineering ventures, mainly explosives factories. Bofors also produced steel tools and truck axles and made diesel engines. By 1976, however, the company had decided to expand its chemistry areas and divest others in order to establish a firm foundation in just two major industries—armaments and chemicals.

Bofors merged with KemaNobel due to the dealings of a canny Swedish financier, Erik Penser. Penser had dropped out of law school in the mid-1960s, preferring to play poker rather than study, according to a *Business Week* account. He became a broker, then began investing for himself on borrowed money. The Swedish stock market was at a low ebb in the 1970s, but Penser optimistically gambled on a brighter future. The market took a sudden upward swing after a 1982 krona devaluation, and Penser invested his profits in Bofors until he ultimately controlled 40 percent of the company. Next, he set his sights on KemaNobel, the company controlled by Marcus Wallenberg.

Wallenberg, in the meantime, had a lot on his hands. In 1984 he became embroiled in a bitter takeover battle with AB Volvo chairman Pehr G. Gyllenhammar over several major Swedish multinational companies. Penser had already bought up 20 percent of KemaNobel, and while Wallenberg was occupied with Volvo, Penser offered 30 percent above the market price for another 32 percent share of the chemical giant. Wallenberg's investors could not refuse the price. Penser combined KemaNobel with Bofors and named the new entity Nobel Industries. The 42-year old broker now controlled a company with sales of one billion dollars. He installed a friend, Anders Carlberg, as president, while Penser himself moved to England in order to avoid Swedish income taxes.

Nobel Industries expanded rapidly, making many acquisitions. In 1986 the company bought Italian industrial paints company TechnoMax and a Swedish defense electronics firm named Pharos. Nobel also acquired an option to buy Swedish Match, another large chemical company controlled by Marcus Wallenberg. In 1989 the company increased its holdings in its industrial paints division, buying up 60 percent of Italian paint company Colorifico Valtramigna SpA; acquiring a West German adhesives company, Hermanns & Co. GmbH; a Belgian paint company called Trimetal; and the impregnated paper operation of Britain's Catalin. The defense area expanded as well with the acquisition of Philips Elektronikindustrier AB, a defense electronics operation, in addition to the formation of a joint venture with a firm called Telefonaktiebolaget LM Ericsson. Nobel Industries also bought an American electronics company, Automatic Power, an Italian pharmaceutical chemical company, Profarmaco SpA, shares in a British consumer goods company, and several others. Though not all the company's divisions performed equally well, sales and profits were at times stellar.

Profits jumped 54 percent between 1986 and 1987, and in a four-month period in 1988 group earnings increased 83 percent. The adhesives and paints division did particularly well at this time, as did the pulp and paper chemicals area.

When Erik Penser formed Nobel Industries in 1984, armaments sold by Bofors accounted for 34 percent of the new company's total sales as well as 39 percent of its operating profits. Three years later, 80 percent of the company's sales and 43 percent of its profits came from paints, adhesives, explosives, plastics, chemicals, and pulp and paper products. This buoyed the company against declining Swedish defense orders and export sales, which were subject to political oversight. Yet Bofors continued to make some key sales, in the mid-1980s providing Pakistan with $102 million worth of missiles, $83 million worth to Norway, and winning contracts to manufacture guns for Indonesian patrol boats. Dwarfing these sales however was Bofors' contract to provide $1.3 billion worth of 155mm howitzers to India in 1986. Scandal swirled around this deal, however. Sweden's Prime Minister Olof Palme had personally lobbied Indian Prime Minister Rajiv Gandhi for Bofors, and when news leaked out of questionable payments to Indian middlemen to cement the agreement, Gandhi's integrity became suspect. Bofors admitted to making payments of $60 million to unspecified agents, but the company claimed this money was "windup costs" paid to its own Indian representatives. Suspicions that Gandhi or people close to him had profited from the Bofors contract dogged the prime minister in his re-election bid, which he lost in 1989. The managing director of Bofors, Martin Ardbo, also lost his job in connection with the India contract and allegations that Bofors was involved in smuggling arms to Iran.

Although Nobel's president, Anders Carlberg, complained to *Forbes* magazine in 1988 that the Bofors affair was taking too much of his time, the company continued undaunted in its expansion. Earnings in 1988 were four times their level when Nobel Industries was founded, and sales grew 21 percent that year. The company also carried $1.5 billion in debt, but this did not seem to be a cause for concern at the time. After the slew of acquisitions made in 1989, the company went on to purchase the paper chemicals division of British firm Albright & Wilson as well as the bleaching chemicals operations of Stora Kopparbergs Bergslags AB, solidifying Nobel's position as one of Europe's leading producers of chemicals for the pulp and paper industry. The company's consumer goods division paid $107 million to Gillette Company for its European hair and skin care operations, and its Pharos subsidiary acquired an American company, Spectra-Physics Inc., which was the world's leading laser and laser system manufacturer. Renamed Spectra-Physics AB, Pharos also bought a British firm, Continental Microwave. The troubled Bofors unit formed a joint venture company with the Swedish state-owned arms firm FFV. The new company, called Swedish Ordnance-FFV/Bofors AB, controlled virtually all Swedish arms output.

The debt resulting from these acquisitions finally threatened to swamp Nobel in 1991. The company had invested as much as 10 billion krona in 1990, and it was overburdened. On top of this, Nobel had offered an unlimited guarantee to the creditors of a financial service company, Gamlestaden, also owned by Erik Penser. When Gamlestaden failed in the summer of 1991, Nobel could not cover its guarantee. On the verge of financial collapse, Nobel was taken over by the Swedish bank Nordbanken. Penser lost his entire 67 percent holding in Nobel, while trading in Nobel shares was suspended for four days. With Nordbanken as its major shareholder, Nobel recovered, but lost almost $1 billion. To reduce its debt burden, Nobel sold its entire consumer goods division in 1992 to a German chemical group, Henkel. In February of 1992 Nobel divested its 50-percent share of Swedish Ordnance-FFV/Bofors AB, and in March of the following year it sold off its remaining defense electronics business.

The financial crisis had lingering repercussions. As lawsuits involving Gamlestaden dragged on, sales decreased, mainly because of the divestment of the consumer goods division. In addition, the business climate in Europe was dampened by recession, and the Swedish krona was weak. The company prepared for a more difficult time sustaining profitability in the 1990s. But Nobel had a strong industrial foundation, and the company did not expect a repeat of the 1991 fiasco. Rid of its consumer goods and defense divisions, the company had grown more consolidated in its chemical operations. Nobel expected to continue to grow through acquisitions, but to move more cautiously.

Principal Subsidiaries: AB Nobel Industrier Finans; Nobel Paints & Adhesives; Eka Nobel AB; NobelTech AB; Nobel Biotech AB; Dragochem AB; AB Alpinum; NobelTech Systems AB; Berol Nobel Holding AB; Nobel Coatings AB; Casco Nobel Industrial Products AB; Nobel Chemicals International AB; NobelTech Electronics AB; Nettovagen 6 KB; KemaNord Kraft AB; Sicklaverkstader AB; Nobel Koncernservice AB; Spectra-Physics AB (87%); Nobel Finance S.A. (Belgium); Nobel Industries Holding B.V. (Netherlands); Nobel Industries Sweden (UK) Ltd.; Nobel Industries A/S (Denmark); Nobel House S.r.l. (Italy); Nobel Industrier GmbH (Germany).

Further Reading:

"A Tremor of Fear," *The Economist,* November 4, 1989, pp. 47–48.

"Accord Reached to Acquire Unit of Stora Kopparbergs," *Wall Street Journal,* May 18, 1990, p. A6.

"Adhesives and Paints Blaze Trail at Nobel," *European Chemical News,* June 27, 1988, p. 21.

Berss, Marcia, "When Wallenberg Sells," *Forbes,* May 6, 1985, pp. 56–58.

Dullforce, William, "Bofors Sets Its Sights on a New Diversification Target," *Financial Times,* April 2, 1979, p. 10.

"Firm Plans Share Offering to Protect Against Losses," *Wall Street Journal,* August 27, 1991, p. C21.

Gupte, Pranay, "Rhetoric and Reality in the Iranian Arms Trade," *Forbes,* October 19, 1987, pp. 32–35; "Who Got the $60 Million?" *Forbes,* June 27, 1988, pp. 51–52.

"Hit By a Bofors Gun," *The Economist,* July 2, 1988, pp. 30–32.

"Hoist By Its Own Petard," *The Economist,* September 19, 1987, p. 82.

"In the Soup Over Bofors," *The Economist,* October 14, 1989, pp. 37–38.

Jackson, Donald Dale, "While He Expected the Worst, Nobel Hoped for the Best," *Smithsonian,* November 1988, pp. 201–224.

Kapstein, Jonathan, "A Financial Gambler Tries to Trump the Wallenbergs Again," *Business Week,* January 19, 1987, p. 50.

"Nobel Advances," *European Chemical News,* March 30, 1987, p. 21.

"Nobel Industries and Gillette in Deal," *New York Times,* March 31, 1990, p. L 33.

"Nordbanken Leads Bailout of Nobel Unit, Increases Stake to 70%" *Wall Street Journal,* August 28, 1991, p. B6.

"Sweden's Nobel, FFV to Merge Arms Units," *Wall Street Journal,* December 28, 1990, p. 4.

"The Gun That Can Kill at Four Years' Range," *The Economist,* September 9, 1989, pp. 35–36.

—A. Woodward

Nomura Securities Company, Limited

Nomura Shoken Kabushiki Kaisha, 1-9-1
Nihonbashi, Chou-ku
Tokyo 103
Japan
(33) 211-1181
Fax: (33) 278-0420

Public Company
Incorporated: 1925
Employees: 10,200
Assets: ¥976 billion
Stock Exchanges: Tokyo Osaka Nagoya Amsterdam
  Luxembourg
SICs: 6211 Security Brokers, Dealers and Floatation
  Companies; 6221 Commodity Contracts Brokers and
  Dealers; 6159 Miscellaneous Business Credit Institutions;
  6282 Investment Advice.

The Nomura Securities Company, the largest securities firm in Japan, has long been recognized as an industry pacesetter. Since, as *The Economist* has put it, "What Nomura does this morning, the rest of the Japanese securities industry will do after lunch," Nomura has played a key role in the development of the securities industry in Japan. The company has made great strides in the international arena as well. It was the first Japanese company to become a member of the New York Stock Exchange, in 1981, and has seen phenomenal success in the Euromarkets. Despite the numerous scandals that disrupted the Japanese securities market in the early 1990s, Nomura remains Japan's largest securities firm. Since it was established in 1925, Nomura has struggled through many economic and cultural changes in Japan, but it has emerged as a powerhouse not only at home but also in the international securities markets.

Nomura was incorporated in 1925, but its story begins much earlier. In 1872, four years after the Meiji Emperor reclaimed the Japanese throne and began an unprecedented reform campaign, Tokushichi Nomura opened the Nomura Shoten in Osaka, Japan. Nomura was a moneychanger. At that time there was no one single currency in Japan. Various gold, silver, and copper coins were appraised by merchants like Nomura, and their value was dictated by the current market price. But along with the Meiji Restoration came extensive monetary reforms,

and Nomura's business changed rapidly as the Japanese industrial revolution came into full swing.

In 1878, Tokushichi Nomura had a son, Shinnosuke (later called Tokushichi II). In his youth, Shinnosuke Nomura assisted his father in the moneychanging business, but his interests lay in a field which was still quite new to Japan—stock trading. At age 19, after completing his studies at the Osaka Commercial School, Shinnosuke Nomura went to work as an apprentice at a small stock trading shop managed by his brother-in-law. Nomura's apprenticeship was cut short after only a few months when he was conscripted into the Japanese army for three years. When he returned home, however, Nomura resolved to take Nomura Shoten into the stock trading business.

During the 1890s the stock market in Japan was still a somewhat crude affair. Only a few joint-stock companies existed at all. Most shares were held by a handful of rich and powerful businessmen, and government regulation of the exchanges was virtually nonexistent. Price rigging and other corrupt practices gave stock brokers a bad reputation. Shinnosuke Nomura believed that through sound, ethical business practices, Nomura Shoten could win the confidence of investors over the long haul. Under his guidance, the stock trading department of Nomura Shoten was a consistent money maker by the turn of the century.

In 30 years Japan had transformed from a feudal to an industrial country. In 1904 and 1905 Japan fought and won a war against Russia. This victory over a major European power was regarded as signifying Japan's coming of age. The stock markets reflected the optimism which military victory brought and trading volume reached record heights.

In 1906, Nomura Shoten established the first research department at a Japanese financial company. The company also began publishing a daily financial newsletter that year, the *Osaka Nomura Business News*. Nomura's innovations began to attract a great deal of attention. In 1907, Tokushichi Nomura retired, leaving Shinnosuke to run the business. Shinnosuke was known from this time on as Tokushichi Nomura II.

In 1908, Tokushichi Nomura II took a five-month tour of the world's financial centers. When he returned he brought with him many new ideas. He divided the company's research department into four separate divisions: research, statistics, editing, and translation. Furthermore, while in the United States, Nomura saw the positive impact publicity could have on profits, so he began investing a good deal of money in advertising his company's services. Nomura also entered the bond trading and underwriting fields. By the beginning of World War I, Nomura Shoten was regularly participating in underwriting syndicates.

World War I brought a boom to the Japanese economy. Exports to belligerent nations increased dramatically. As Japanese heavy industry floated bonds to finance its rapid expansion, Nomura's business picked up accordingly. After the war the bull market subsided, but Nomura continued to expand. In 1917, Nomura Shoten was reorganized as Nomura Shoten Incorporated. One year later, Tokushichi Nomura II fulfilled a lifelong dream when he opened the Osaka Nomura Bank (now Daiwa Bank). He also set up a securities department to handle bond sales and underwriting. By 1920, regulations on bond trading were relaxed and bonds were sold at the exchanges. The market for securities had come a long way in 30 years.

In 1922, Nomura and Company was established as a holding company for the entire Nomura group, including the Osaka Nomura Bank and Nomura Shoten Inc. Throughout the early 1920s the bond market became increasingly more active, and the securities department of the Osaka Nomura Bank was expanding at a tremendous rate. In order to serve its customers better, the department was separated from the bank.

The Nomura Securities Company, Limited was incorporated on December 25, 1925. The company focused on the bond market and left the stock market alone. Otogo Kataoka, the president of the Osaka Nomura Bank and former head of its securities department, was elected president. Tokushichi Nomura II oversaw the entire operation. The firm began business with 84 employees and offices in Osaka, Nagoya, Tokyo, Kyoto, and Kobe.

The late 1920s were a time of economic difficulties for Japan. In 1927, a major panic rocked the financial community, and 37 banks were forced to close. Two years later the collapse of the New York stock market brought a worldwide depression. The economic difficulties were paralleled by the rise of militant nationalists in Japan.

Under the influence of these political groups, the government began to assume control over the economy. In 1931, Japan set up a puppet regime in Manchuria, and hostilities with China escalated until those two countries were fully at war by 1937. To finance the conflict, the government found it necessary to increase its bond issues. Nomura Securities was one of eight houses allowed to underwrite and sell bonds for the government and corporations. Government control of the bond market, however, pushed investors in the direction of stocks. In 1938, Nomura Securities opened a stock department and became an active dealer in both stocks and bonds.

World War II initially stimulated economic growth in Japan. Stocks and bonds were traded briskly and Nomura, as one of the official dealers, did well. By 1942, Nomura had a 19 percent market share of the bond market, the largest of any securities house. However, a year later Japan's military success was clearly coming to an end and the stock market plunged. Nomura, however, through its bond activities and through the newly authorized investment trust business, managed to expand right up until the end of the war.

The investment trust business was introduced in Japan in 1941 as a way of providing additional funds to finance the war. Nomura was the first company to offer the new form of investment. The decision to enter this new field caused some controversy in the company's boardroom, however. Otogo Kataoka, chairperson of Nomura Securities, was against their entry into the investment trust business. Tokushichi Nomura II, on the other hand, was in favor of entering the new business in full force. His long experience in finance and his knowledge of investment trusts overseas convinced him that the new investment vehicle could prove to be very profitable. The company's almost immediate success in the investment trust area proved him right. Nomura enjoyed a 47 percent market share of the investment trust business between 1941 and 1945. Chairperson Kataoka, having been overruled on such a key issue, resigned.

From 1941 to 1947, Seizo Iida was president of Nomura Securities. Iida had been largely responsible for Nomura's entering the investment trust business. He had begun with the Nomura group in 1922 at the Osaka Nomura Bank and joined Nomura Securities at its founding in 1925. He wrote several books on economic analysis and continually stressed the importance of Nomura's Research Department. Iida left the company in 1947, when the occupation authorities mandated retirement of many top corporate officers of the large family-controlled Japanese industrial groups known as zaibatsu.

After the war, Japan was devastated. It was estimated that one-fourth of Japan's national wealth was wiped out in 1944. Millions of Japanese were homeless. Jobs were scarce, and with six million returning soldiers, the unemployment rate seemed hopeless. The occupation forces began to reorganize the nation's political and economic structure. The 15 largest zaibatsu, of which the Nomura group was one, were broken up to end family control of the Japanese economy. Nomura Securities Company was dissolved and reorganized. Trading on the exchanges was prohibited until 1949. In the meantime, securities companies traded non-defense related industry securities over the counter at their offices. This market was vigorous as people flocked to liquidate their holdings for cash. As industrial reconstruction reached full swing, the bond market picked up. By 1948, Nomura, stressing the individual investor, had captured ten percent of the market, the largest share of any investment house.

Throughout the late 1940s, Nomura built its retail network. In addition to its 15 regular offices across Japan, Nomura set up 19 investment consultant centers in shopping malls and other key locations. These centers were an excellent way for the company to develop new customers. By providing basic information on the stock and bond markets, Nomura attracted customers who might not otherwise have been interested in investing.

In the mid-1950s, the Japanese economy slumped. But the Korean War soon stimulated demand and the economy revived quickly. Japanese exports increased dramatically. The country entered a period of steady growth, and Nomura's profits reflected this trend. In 1951, investment trusts were allowed for the first time since World War II. Nomura focused a great deal of energy on recruiting investors for the trusts and used a number of new techniques for this task. For example, it held a number of "Ladies Savings Investment Seminars" to educate women about the various forms of investing. The company also introduced the "Million Ryo Savings Chest" program, and lent out cash boxes as "piggy banks" which, once full, could be turned in for a share in an investment trust. The idea was to promote securities investment as a form of savings. The program was very successful, and by 1962 more than a million chests had been distributed.

In 1953, Nomura re-established its office in New York, which had been closed since 1936. It also established a Transfer Agency Department, the first in Japan, in 1953. In 1955, Nomura became the first company in Japan to introduce a computer system—a Univac 120. Two years later the company established the Nomura Real Estate Development Company, Ltd. The traditional businesses of Nomura grew as well throughout the decade.

In 1959, Tsunao Okumura was replaced by Minoru Segawa as president of Nomura Securities. Okumura had presided over the company since 1948. He became chairman of the board and remained in that office until 1968. Minoru Segawa had previously served as general manager of the firm. One of Segawa's first important actions was to set up separate companies to handle Nomura's huge investment trust funds. In 1960, the Nomura Investment Trust Management Company and the Nomura Investment Trust Sales Company assumed the management and development duties of Nomura's investment trusts.

Nomura's success continued throughout the early 1960s. In 1961, Nomura passed a milestone when it co-managed the first Japanese stock offering in the United States. The issue of ¥100 million worth of Sony Corporation American depositary receipts (ADRs) sold out in one hour. A year later, Nomura co-managed the first bond issue of a Japanese company in the United States. This $10 million issue for Mitsubishi Heavy Industries was soon followed by $20 million bond issue for Toshiba. Foreign capital poured into Japan, and Nomura cashed in on the increase in investment.

In 1965, Japan was hit by a severe recession, but Nomura's stable position in the marketplace allowed it to weather the storm. Nomura was the only one of the Japanese big four securities houses to record profits for both fiscal 1964 and 1965. Nomura launched one of its most ambitious projects in 1965— the Nomura Research Institute (NRI). Rather than expand its existing research department, Nomura decided to establish an independent research institute which would serve not just Nomura's needs but those of Japan as well. A number of advisors from the Stanford Research Institute in the United States helped Nomura set up the new "think tank." The company's belief that economics and technology would be closely intertwined in the future proved to be correct. NRI remains one of the premier research organizations in Japan.

In 1967, the Japanese government liberalized the capital markets, giving Nomura the opportunity to solicit greater foreign investments. Nomura International (Hong Kong) was established in 1967. In 1968, Kiichiro Kitaura became president. Kitaura was strongly in favor of an international orientation, and under his guidance Nomura continued to strengthen its overseas network. In 1969, Nomura Securities Inc. was incorporated in the United States, and was the first Japanese securities company to become a member of an American stock exchange (Boston).

In 1973, the oil crisis sent shock waves through the Japanese economy. Japanese industry, heavily dependent on imported oil, suffered a major blow and stock prices tumbled. Nonetheless, capital continued to flow into Japan in the 1970s, and as the Japanese government removed further restrictions on foreign investment, began to flow out of the country as well. Nomura established a number of investment trusts based on foreign stocks. By 1973, some half a dozen foreign stocks were listed on the Tokyo Stock Exchange. "Samurai bonds," bonds issued by foreign governments but denominated in yen, became very popular in the first half of the decade. In 1973, Nomura had its own shares listed on the Amsterdam Stock Exchange. Activities in Europe picked up dramatically. Branches in Amsterdam and London were incorporated as a single subsidiary, Nomura Eu-

rope N.V. The Frankfurt office became the headquarters of a separate subsidiary, Nomura Europe GmbH.

During the first half of the 1970s the bond market in Japan began to expand at a tremendous rate. The development of a secondary market for bonds was bolstered by an increase in government, particularly municipal, bond issues. In 1975 bond sales were more than three times what they had been in 1970 and Nomura's profits on bond transactions were up 900 percent. The "bond boom" continued throughout the decade.

In 1978, Setsuya Tabuchi took over as president of Nomura. Tabuchi devoted himself to making Nomura a primary force in the international securities arena, but also stressed the importance of the satisfied customer to the company's continued success. Tabuchi served as president for seven years, and then became chairman of the board. In 1979, the second oil crunch jeopardized economic growth, but unlike the oil crisis of 1973, panic did not set in. High-tech and other export-related companies had growth enough to ensure continued prosperity in the markets. As Nomura entered the 1980s, the Japanese economy was in excellent shape.

In 1981, Nomura's American subsidiary, Nomura Securities International. Inc., became the first Japanese securities company to gain membership on the New York Stock Exchange. As Japan strengthened its position in the world economy, Nomura Securities prepared to do the same. Nomura initiated a "Buy Japan" campaign designed to attract investment from the Middle East, Europe, and the United States and began an intensive, worldwide recruiting campaign to lure the best talent to Nomura's expanding global organization. As new offices and subsidiaries opened in Paris, Sydney, Beijing, Bahrain, Zurich, and Kuala Lumpur, they were staffed by the cream of the crop of local and Japanese personnel. Nomura also maintained its lead in securities-related computer technology. A computerized communications system, COMPASS-III, linked all its international offices by 1985. In 1982, CAPITAL (Computer Aided Portfolio and Investment Total Analysis) began to provide customers with up-to-the-minute market information and analysis. In 1985, the STOCKPORT function of CAPITAL was providing fund managers with quick analyses of the effect certain securities would have on their portfolios.

In the mid-1980s, Japan's Ministry of Finance approved substantial changes in Japan's capital market regulations. The markets were to be less restricted, allowing greater foreign competition and new debt-issuing instruments. Nomura responded by developing new kinds of bonds and by increasing its underwriting activities. Nomura presided over what can best be described as a Euroyen craze. By managing large issues like a ¥50 billion Euroyen bond issue for Dow Chemical and a $100 million forex-indexed issue for IBM Credit Corporation, Nomura established a reputation as a world class securities house. Its success in the Euromarkets was a highlight of Nomura's growth in the 1980s.

In 1985, Yoshihisa Tabuchi was chosen as Nomura's next president. Setsuya Tabuchi (no relation to Yoshihisa), nicknamed "Big Tabuchi" even though several inches shorter than his successor, became chairperson. One year after taking the helm at Nomura, Yoshihisa was named Man of the Year by

Financial World magazine. In many ways the honor was a recognition of Nomura's ascension to the top of the world's securities industry.

Despite Nomura's success in Japan and Europe, the company, along with other Japanese securities houses, had difficulty establishing itself as a major player in the American market. Nomura Securities International operated more or less as an arm of the parent company. Most of its customers were Japanese. The company found it very difficult to compete with large American firms like Salomon Brothers, Merrill Lynch, Morgan Stanley, First Boston, and others who had long-established ties to institutional fund managers and debt issuers. Some analysts blamed the problem on Nomura's lack of decision-making autonomy: all major decisions had to be approved by the Tokyo office, and although Nomura recruited top-notch managers from other investment firms, many stayed only a short time because of a lack of real power to make decisions. Another problem Nomura faced was the traditional, consensus-oriented style of Japanese management. This lesson was brought home when Nomura missed out on the opportunity to participate in a $300 million issue for J. P. Morgan & Company led by Merrill Lynch in 1986 because it could not obtain approval for the action within fifteen minutes. Nomura was embarrassed to have missed the boat, and took steps to remedy this weakness.

In the late 1980s, Nomura Securities International in New York fell upon hard times. The stock market crash of October 1987 wiped out some investors and scared many others out of the market. Bond sales, including U.S. treasury notes, also declined a year later. Although Nomura was the largest and wealthiest securities firm in the world by 1989, it was still having trouble muscling into the U.S. domestic market and was considering acquiring an established American securities firm.

Nomura's staggering success of the 1980s was overshadowed by the scandal ridden 1990s. When the Tokyo stock market dropped suddenly in 1990, Nomura's stock plunged 70 percent from its 1987 summit. The firm's equity underwritings fell from 1,201 in fiscal year 1990 to a scant 12 in the first six months of 1991. While the Tokyo stock market continued to decline in 1991, Japan's top securities firms were embarrassed by public disclosure of *tobashi,* the Japanese practice of reconciling the accounts of favored clients to compensate for stock losses. The government investigated charges that Nomura had improperly covered ¥170 billion in losses suffered by wealthy customers. The company was also linked to Japanese underworld boss Susumu Ishii and his Inagawa-Kai crime syndicate. Finally, Nomura was accused of manipulating Tokyu Corp.'s stock price. Nomura chair Setsuya Tabuchi and president Yoshihisa Tabuchi resigned in disgrace in 1991.

The government did not file formal charges against Nomura because the company had technically not broken any Japanese laws. The lack of regulations and ethics outraged many of the ordinary investors Nomura had worked so hard to cultivate. The scandal, and the government's slow, weak reaction to it, threatened the cooperative relationship between Japan's bureaucrats and businesspeople. Although the investment firm received

light discipline from the government, the sentence from investors and clients was severe: Nomura's trading volume fell from 16.3 percent of the market in 1987 to 5.8 percent by the end of 1991. Earnings amounted to ¥50 billion, ten percent of the 1987 high.

Nomura's new leaders, president Hideo Sakamaki and co-chair Katsuya Takanashi, worked to revive the firm according to a new set of client-driven rules. A comprehensive overhaul of the firm's day-to-day procedures was undertaken. Cost-cutting measures included a five-year phase-out of 2,000 jobs through attrition. Nomura also worked to reduce its dependency on the Japanese stock market and transform its European units into investment banks, rather than "mere brokers." The branches were also granted more autonomy.

Despite the scandals and market troubles, Nomura had several strengths in the early 1990s. The firm remained financially sound, having refrained from investing profits in Tokyo's "roaring bull market" of the 1980s. Nomura's change in corporate culture was reflected in the fact that in 1991, for the first time in Nomura's history, branches were ranked on whether they earned enough to cover their overhead, rather than the total of their commissions. Analysts suggest that perhaps, by returning to the customer oriented ideals of Tokushichi Nomura II, Nomura Securities can regain its financial and ethical reputation.

Principal Subsidiaries: Nomura Research Institute (NRI); NRI Life Science; Nomura Investment Management Co., Ltd.; Nimco Europe Ltd.; Nomura Computer Systems Co., Ltd.; Nomura Operation Services Co., Ltd.; Nomura Business Services Co., Ltd.; Nomura Land and Building Co., Ltd.; Nomura Real Estate Development Co., Ltd.; Nomura China Investment Co., Ltd.; The Nomura Securities Investment Trust Management Co., Ltd.; Nomura Tourist Bureau, Inc.; Japan Associated Mortgage Acceptance Co., Ltd.; Nomura Card Services Co., Ltd.; Japan Associated Finance Co., Ltd.; JAFCO American Ventures Inc.; Jafco International (Asia) Ltd.; Jafco Finance Co., Ltd.; Nomura, Babcock, & Brown Co., Ltd.; Nomura Securities International Inc.; Nomura Securities International Ltd.; Nomura International Finance Plc; Nomura Belgium; Nomura Europe N.V.; Nomura Europe GmbH; Nomura (Switzerland) Ltd.; Nomura France; Nomura Investment Banking (Middle East) E.C.; Nomura International (Hong Kong) Ltd.; Singapore Nomura Merchant Banking Ltd.; Nomura Futures (Singapore) Pte Ltd.; Nomura Australia Ltd.; Associated Japanese Bank (International) Ltd.; P.T. Finconesia.

Further Reading:

Beyond the Ivied Mountains: The Origin and Growth of a Japanese Securities House, Tokyo: Nomura Securities Company, Ltd., 1986.
"How to Grow Strong on Humble Pie," *Economist,* November 23, 1991, pp. 93–94.
Sender, Henny. "The Humbling of Nomura," *Institutional Investor,* February 1992, pp. 49–53.
"Tokyo's stock scandal keeps growing," *Financier,* August 1991, pp. 31–34.

—updated by April S. Dougal

Northern Trust Company

50 South LaSalle Street
Chicago, Illinois 60675
U.S.A.
(312) 630-6000
Fax: (312) 630-1512

Wholly owned subsidiary of Northern Trust Corporation
Incorporated: 1889
Employees: 5,798
Assets: $10.5 billion
SICs: 6021 National Commercial Banks

Not as large as Chase Manhattan, nor as well known as J. P. Morgan, the Northern Trust Company has built a solid reputation on personal trust management. With stable leadership, conservative but sound policies, and the ability to create its own opportunities, this century-old bank is regarded as one of the most reliable banking institutions in the United States.

The Northern Trust Company was founded by Byron L. Smith. Formerly associated with the Hide and Leather Bank and then the Merchants Savings, Loan and Trust Company, Smith left the banking industry in 1885 to devote more time to family business matters. Over the next four years, however, he was frequently called upon by relatives and friends for advice about planning estates and setting up trusts. As the demand from wealthy Chicagoans for his services increased, he decided in 1889 to open a new type of bank.

Because of the previously chaotic nature of banking throughout the United States, Chicago was ripe for a different kind of financial institution. During the nineteenth century the banking industry was unregulated; it lacked any centralized control over bank charters; and individual banks issued hundreds of different paper notes, which flooded the local area and were of questionable value. In 1887 the Illinois state legislature, sensing the potential danger, enacted banking laws that regulated state bank charters and the administration of trusts.

This is the predicament that led Smith to open the Northern Trust Company on August 12, 1889. In one room on the second floor of the Rookery Building, which still stands on the corner of Adams and LaSalle streets, a staff of six opened seven accounts and handled $137,981 of deposits during the first day's

business. By the beginning of the new year, the bank had taken in over $1.5 million in deposits.

Smith provided 40 percent of the bank's original capitalization of $1 million, and counted such businessmen and civic leaders as Marshall Field, Martin A. Ryerson, and Philip D. Armour among the original 27 shareholders. Intimately acquainted with the operations of the bank, these men would personally examine Northern's assets and records at each year's end. On December 31st, they would assemble in the banking room, count all the bank's cash and securities, and greet the new year.

Northern became the first bank in Chicago to advertise its services, first by direct mail and then by ads in the daily newspaper and Chicago City Directory. Smith reasoned that spending significant amounts of cash on newspaper advertising and becoming the first bank in the city to hire an advertising agency would help build confidence in Northern's conservative approach to banking.

During the 1893 Columbian Exposition, held in Chicago to commemorate the 400th anniversary of the arrival of Columbus in the new world, Congress had authorized another Chicago bank to open a branch on the fairgrounds. The exposition had only been open for eight days when the bank failed, and Northern was asked to operate the branch. The exposure bolstered Northern's reputation and increased its international recognition. Despite the panic in the financial industry due to bank closures and industrial insolvencies across the United States in 1893, which, in turn, led to a general economic decline for several years, Northern's fortunes continued to improve. By 1895 deposits totaled $10.5 million.

Declaring its first dividend in July 1896, Northern began to grow rapidly. In 1906 the bank constructed its own building in the center of Chicago's financial district. The architecture of the bank received so much attention that its cornerstone was used to measure the height of all buildings in Chicago. Much fanfare also surrounded the fact that the banking offices were the first in Chicago equipped with "manufactured air," an ancestor of modern air conditioning, and that its telephone system was at the forefront of technology for the era.

The business climate began to change dramatically in the early years of the twentieth century, and Northern was forced to reassess some of its long-standing policies. Since its founding, the bank had only made collateral loans, but now aware that this policy stymied growth, the board of directors approved Northern's purchase of commercial paper in 1912. When the Federal Reserve System was created two years later, reducing the chance of the money panics that plagued the banking industry during the nineteenth century, Northern joined the system and began to provide unsecured lines of credit to its most reputable customers. Within a brief period of time, commercial banking become one of the most important sectors of Northern's business.

A new era was on the horizon when Byron L. Smith died in March 1914 and his son, Solomon A. Smith, took over the reins of the bank. World War I started in August 1914, and stock and bond prices dropped markedly, even though the dollar gained in value against European currencies. When the United States finally entered the war in 1917, Northern acted as a depository for the Alien Property Custodian Act and held over $500 million in enemy assets. During and immediately after the war, Northern sold nearly $30 million in war bonds for the Liberty Bond and Victory Bond campaigns.

Immediately after the war, the American economy muddled through a short period of inflation and slow growth. But by 1922 the "Roaring Twenties" was in full swing, a time when public confidence in the economy was at its highest, and throughout the nation investors were enticed into highly speculative markets. On October 23, 1929, however, the flamboyant decade of the 1920s came to a sudden halt—the stock market crash led to a spectacular drop in prices, employment and production. Banks were hit particularly hard. What had previously been regarded as sound loans could not be collected, and panicking depositors withdrew their funds from banks. As these troubles swept across the country, one bank after another closed.

By mid-1932 the American economy had reached its lowest point ever, and public confidence—especially in the banks—had all but faded away. Two days after his inauguration on March 6, 1933, Franklin D. Roosevelt closed all the banks in the United States. When they reopened a short time later, there was a great deal of uncertainty as to what might occur. Fortunately, the people in line outside the Northern bank offices were there to deposit money instead of withdraw it. In fact, so much money was deposited during the first day that cash had to be stacked in huge piles on the floor.

Northern's conservative policies had served it well during the 1920s. Since it had refused to involve itself in highly dubious stock or bond speculations and had passed up the opportunity for rapid earnings growth, the Northern was able to pay its depositors their money whenever they wanted it. It was therefore no fluke that public confidence in the Northern ran high; more than 10,000 new accounts were opened at the bank in the early 1930s. In 1929 deposits amounted to $56 million; by 1935, deposits had soared to over $300 million. In 1929 there were 335 banks within Cook County; in 1935 there were only 95 left. The Northern Trust was one of the few banks in Chicago that survived the depression without the need for any government assistance.

Near the end of the depression, Northern started to expand its effort to solicit commercial business, particularly in the Midwest. By 1941 nearly half of all the bank's commercial accounts were drawn from outside the Chicago metropolitan area. During World War II, Northern once again took part in the government's war bond drives, and also provided loans for manufacturing war materials under special government programs. The war created more opportunities for the bank; all sectors of its business expanded, and by 1945 the Northern Trust had doubled in size.

The years after World War II brought even greater prosperity to the bank as it continued to expand its services. Still under the direction of Solomon Smith, management at the bank became more aware of electronic data processing and how this new technology would revolutionize the banking industry. During the 1950s, Northern was at the forefront of developing numerous automated banking services, including fully automated financial statements for trust clients, the very first in the industry.

When Solomon Smith died in 1963 and his son, Edward Byron Smith, assumed leadership of the bank, assets totaled more than $1 billion. Near the end of the decade, Northern became the first state-chartered bank from Illinois to open an office outside the United States. Illinois banking laws were revised in order to allow state-chartered banks to open offices abroad, yet strangely prohibited opening branches within the state. Northern's new London office helped expand the bank's services to European customers. The Northern Trust International Banking Corporation, a New York subsidiary created to handle currency transactions for financial institutions abroad, was also established the same year.

The 1970s ushered in dramatic changes not only for Northern Trust but for the banking industry as a whole. Deregulation had two far-reaching effects: First, financial institutions were allowed to pay their depositors interest rates that were competitive with other market rates. Consequently banks began to lose depositors to money market funds offering higher interest rates. Second, many corporations discovered that the commercial paper market was a cost-efficient method of borrowing short-term funds, and thus banks lost their most stable and most profitable earnings asset. As a result of these changes, Northern, like many other banks, was forced to search for new markets.

During the late 1960s, the creation of the Eurodollar market provided American banks with the opportunity to grant foreign loans at a much lower risk than what was ordinarily expected. In 1973 the availability of dollars skyrocketed when the OPEC oil cartel inflated its prices for a barrel of crude oil, and many nations that depended on OPEC oil watched helplessly as their dollar reserves were depleted. The United Nations and many world governments, in order to prevent less developed countries from becoming even poorer, encouraged banks to recycle what came to be known as "petrodollars," by granting loans to these countries. As speculation rose in financial circles as to the prospects of crude oil increasing to $100 a barrel, the more needy nations demanded more and more bank credit.

When oil prices dropped suddenly in the early 1980s, many South American nations realized they could not pay off their enormous bank loans. Northern suffered uncharacteristically high losses, but through aggressive and astute management, loan reserves, and write-offs, the bank was able to restore its asset quality.

In 1971 Northern acquired Security Trust Company, located in Miami, Florida. Additional trust operations were established in Palm Beach, Sarasota, and Naples. In 1982 Northern expanded its services in the state of Florida from trust operations to include a full range of financial services. In 1990 the bank administered trust assets worth over $5 billion in South Florida alone. In 1974 Northern established a trust operation in Arizona, and expanded in 1986 to include full financial services. In 1988 a trust subsidiary was created with offices in San Francisco, Los Angeles, and Santa Barbara, California. In 1989 the acquisition of Concorde Bank in Dallas, Texas, provided Northern with access to business opportunities in one more state. By the end of 1993, the bank has plans for forty-three offices in five states.

The bank created a holding corporation in 1971, the Northern Trust Corporation, for the purpose of future expansion within the state of Illinois. In 1981, when the state finally permitted Illinois banks to acquire banks in Cook and the surrounding counties, Northern immediately took advantage of the law and acquired O'Hare International Bank in Park Ridge, First Security Bank in Oakbrook, and First National Bank of Lake Forest.

With offices in five states, Northern Trust provided many personal financial services, including investment management, securities custody, estate planning and administration, and tax preparation. The bank provided master trust and custody services to foundations, endowments, corporations, and pooled investments worldwide. Northern's cash management and commercial banking services were provided to corporations and financial institutions to help manage cash collections, control cash disbursements, and create information systems needed for the growing complexity of clients' needs.

When Edward Byron Smith retired in 1979, he was succeeded by E. Norman Staub, followed a few years later by Philip W. K. Sweet, and then by Weston Christopherson. When company veteran David W. Fox took over, he was only the seventh chief executive in the bank's existence. This stability, in both leadership and financial policy, enabled the Northern Trust to weather some difficult moments in its history and develop into one of the most trustworthy banks in the United States.

Further Reading:

Fox, David W., *The Northern Trust Company Celebrating 100 Years,* Newcomen Society, 1989, pp. 1–26.
"Northern Trust Opts to Build, Not Buy," *ABA Bank Journal,* March 1990, pp. 54–55.

—Thomas Derdak

Olympia & York Developments Ltd.

2 First Canadian Place
Toronto, Ontario M5X 1B5
Canada
(416) 862-6100
Fax: (416) 862-5349

Private Company
Incorporated: 1969
Sales: C$4.00 billion (US$3.45 billion)
SICs: 6552 Real Property Subdividers and Developers,
    except of cemetary lots

Of the many developers who fell victim to the real estate depression beginning in 1989, none was bigger or more highly respected than Canada's Reichmann brothers, owners of Olympia & York Developments Ltd. (O&Y). Until the market took a turn for the worse in 1989, the Reichmanns enjoyed a career of unbroken and brilliant success, gaining a reputation as financial magicians while assembling the world's largest collection of office buildings and a stock portfolio that included several of Canada's leading corporations. Like most deal makers, however, Paul Reichmann and his brothers were gamblers who kept their interest in the game by continually raising the ante, a strategy that culminated in O&Y's Canary Wharf development in London, the largest office complex ever conceived. Then the real estate market plummeted in 1989. Unable to maintain debt payments, O&Y was forced into Chapter 11 bankruptcy in Canada and the United Kingdom, and its holdings were parceled out among ninety-one lenders who had come to believe the Reichmanns infallible. The final reorganization of assets has not yet been settled, but even if the Reichmanns retain a good chunk of equity their reputation will never be fully repaired.

Albert, Paul, and Ralph Reichmann were born in pre-World War II Vienna to a family headed by Samuel Reichmann, a prosperous merchant. Originally from Hungary, Samuel Reichmann led his family on a series of traumatic escapes from Nazi persecution of Jews, eventually settling in the free port of Tangier, Morocco. There Reichmann built a reputation for wizardry in banking while preparing his children for a life in business. Albert Reichmann, eldest of the three brothers, joined his father's business; Paul Reichmann went on to Talmudic colleges in England. In 1957 Paul joined Ralph Reichmann for another family exodus to Canada, where the two brothers

started a tile import business in a Toronto suburb. An ancient Greek culture enthusiast, Ralph named his venture Olympia Floor & Tile Co. Within a few years, the rest of the Reichmann family joined him.

When the prospering tile company needed a new warehouse, the Reichmanns built it themselves for about half of the contractor's bid. They decided to pursue opportunities in suburban real estate, and began by building more warehouses. The strong economy of the early 1960s provided ample room for expansion in the Toronto real estate market, and the Reichmann family soon became known as a leading local builder of high-quality industrial space. The Reichmanns learned early the importance of streamlined construction practices, developing a knack for money-saving innovations that would later prove to be worth many millions of dollars. Their real estate business was organized in several companies. One of them was called York Developments, and in 1969 the three brothers consolidated their various concerns under the name of Olympia & York Developments Ltd.

The Reichmanns already had established a number of operating principles from which they would never deviate. They were scrupulously honest in their negotiating, earning a reputation as people whose handshake was as good as a contract. They built solid structures on time and under budget, maintained excellent relations with tenants, and came up with ingenious financing packages designed to keep ownership of all properties within the family. The brothers paid close attention to the desires of municipal and state government officials, whose cooperation became increasingly important as the size of their projects grew. The Reichmanns remained devoutly Orthodox, stopping all work by sundown every Friday and on Jewish holidays throughout the year.

In 1965 the brothers demonstrated the last ingredient in their formula for success—a willingness to gamble. When U.S. real estate mogul William Zeckendorf fell on hard times, the Reichmanns seized a chance to buy from him 500 acres of land just outside Toronto for $18 million. After selling off a few parcels to reduce debt, the brothers constructed a series of highly successful office buildings on the site. The Reichmanns were able to build the complex office structures with their usual efficiency, advancing from projects on the Zeckendorf purchase to bigger and more profitable ventures in Ottawa, Calgary, and downtown Toronto.

The brothers were still relatively unknown when they acquired a valuable piece of property in the heart of Toronto in 1973 and announced plans to construct the tallest building in Canada, a 72-story office tower called First Canadian Place. The proposal was considered too grand for Toronto's market in some quarters—its 3.5 million square feet represented a 10 percent increase in the city's available office space—but the Reichmann brothers went to work with their customary ingenuity. They devised a new method of construction in which all activity took place within the building; a complicated network of elevators and turntables moved supplies and men to where they were needed. The Reichmanns estimated that the technique saved up to 2.5 hours of labor per worker every day, a saving that became crucial when the building was slow to lease. Despite the leasing problems, the Reichmanns refused to cut their rents and eventually managed to raise them 350 percent during the four years it took to fill the building. First Canadian Place permanently changed the Toronto high-rise market and became the flagship of O&Y's real estate empire.

Having amassed a net worth estimated at US$1 billion by the time First Canadian was finished in 1976, the Reichmanns began to look farther afield for their next project. In New York City, the National Kinney Corporation was trying to sell a block of eight Manhattan office buildings known as the Uris portfolio. At the time, the city was flirting with bankruptcy and its real estate market was severely depressed. It was not clear whether New York would retain its position as the world's most important business center or slide into a decline. The Reichmanns concluded that, unless New York's recession was permanent, the Uris land alone was worth more than the US$320 million asking price, and in 1977 they used the equity built up in First Canadian Place to finance the deal. Within a few years the glut of Manhattan office space had become a shortage as the local economy roared back to health, and the Reichmanns were able to triple rents while still keeping their eight new buildings nearly full. The Uris acquisition proved to be a tremendous coup for the Reichmanns; their investment of US$320 million grew in five years to an estimated value of US$3 billion, providing an equity base sufficient to launch bigger developments.

O&Y moved on to the World Financial Center at Manhattan's extreme southern tip. The Battery Park site, adjacent to the World Trade Center, had been entangled in political and financial difficulties since it was created out of landfill. In 1980 Olympia joined 11 other bidders in a competition to gain approval for construction and eventually emerged as the winner. World Financial Center was a gigantic project: six buildings with two-thirds as much space as the towering World Trade Center next door, 250,000 square feet of shops and restaurants, and four acres of well-designed public spaces. The project, in which the Reichmanns poured US$300 million of their own money, also provided for the construction of low-cost public housing in the area. The Reichmanns were able to do all of this with money borrowed below prime rate against their Uris properties, and by implementing the same highly efficient construction methods as they had used at First Canadian Place. At the same time, they were erecting another US$750 million of office towers in other U.S. cities, all during a period of severe recession. To land the prestigious tenants the World Financial project needed to assure its success, the Reichmanns took the unusual step of buying the buildings housing the tenants' previous offices in exchange for long-term lease commitments. In this way both American Express Company and City Investing Company agreed to take large blocks of space.

The Reichmanns also had begun buying stock in major industrial corporations. In 1981 the brothers paid C$618 million, most of it, again, borrowed against the Uris properties, for about 90 percent of the stock in Abitibi-Price, the world's largest manufacturer of newsprint paper. They soon added large pieces of MacMillan Bloedel Ltd., another forest-products company; Hiram Walker Resources Ltd., the liquor giant; and also bought into a number of other important Canadian real estate developers. In 1983 the brothers joined forces with Canada's Bronfman family, taking a 13 percent interest in the Bronfman's Trilon

Financial Corporation, a fast-growing diversified marketer of financial services. During the next few years the Reichmanns increased their holdings in Hiram Walker to 49 percent, but in 1986 they lost a bidding war for control of the company and traded their stake for US$360 million in cash and a 10 percent share of its new owner, Allied-Lyons plc of the United Kingdom. More successful was a 1985 bid for Chevron Corporation's 60 percent interest in Gulf Canada Ltd., one of the country's leading oil producers; O&Y's US$2.1 billion offer was accepted, and the brothers have since increased their stake to nearly 75 percent. Finally, in 1987, they took part in a restructuring of Santa Fe Southern Pacific Corporation, buying 19.6 percent of the enormous rail, oil, and real estate concern.

While these were sizable acquisitions by any standard, O&Y's stock portfolio remained secondary to its real estate business, which continued to grow apace as the boom decade of the 1980s drew to an end. Real estate was the premier investment for lenders in the 1980s, and with money readily available new skyscrapers were constructed worldwide at an unprecedented rate. Although many economists predicted that this bull market would soon exhaust itself, the world's most experienced lenders and developers continued building ever larger and more expensive projects. In 1987 the Reichmanns became interested in London's vast Canary Wharf development, a municipal initiative whose goal was the transformation of former docks east of the city into a new corporate office center intended to rival the city's centuries-old business district. Canary Wharf called for the eventual construction of twenty-four buildings containing twelve million square feet of office space to be connected to the city center by new rail and subway links. However, lack of financing halted construction until the Reichmanns agreed in 1987 to pump several billion dollars of their own money into the project and serve as its managing partners. The Reichmanns' reputation as savants reassured other lenders, and development of Canary Wharf finally proceeded, promising no less than a restructuring of London's commercial office market and the possible formation of a new center for business throughout Europe.

The Reichmanns' most lucrative deals had occurred in the middle of real estate recessions (the Uris purchase in 1977 and the World Financial Center in 1980), prompting many observers to admire their courage and foresight when the market strengthened and their projects became gold mines. Canary Wharf, on the other hand, was initiated at the height of a real estate boom which had already enjoyed five years of solid growth. When the bottom fell out in 1989, the Reichmanns found themselves in serious trouble along with the ninety-odd banks and other lenders who had put their faith in the Reichmann mystique. To make matters worse, O&Y was also completing work on 55 Water Street in New York City, the world's largest single office building as measured by square footage, and the brothers had become entangled in the decline of Campeau Corporation, the Canadian retailing conglomerate in which the Reichmanns were major shareholders.

Because O&Y was a private company, the Reichmanns were able to conceal the situation until late 1991, when the company admitted that it could not raise enough cash to "roll over" its commercial borrowings. The vacancy rate on its total holdings of forty-five million square feet was estimated at 17.7 percent, and in April 1992 O&Y called a meeting of its lenders to negotiate a reorganization of debt. In May its Canadian corporation went into Chapter 11 bankruptcy, followed shortly by the UK subsidiary in charge of Canary Wharf. (O&Y's American subsidiary did not enter bankruptcy, however.) Creditors of O&Y Canada (the firm's chief holding company) agreed in January 1993 to a five-year rescheduling of debt payments in exchange for about 80 percent of the company's equity. In effect, its creditors decided that O&Y was worth more as a going concern with the Reichmanns as managers than would be its buildings if sold off piecemeal in a down market. The family would thus retain some equity and limited control of its tattered empire, but with the real estate glut predicted by some to extend past the year 2000, it remained to be seen whether the Reichmanns' slice of the pie would have any tangible value.

Further Reading:

Foster, Peter, ''The $18-Billion Miscalculation,'' *Canadian Business,* June 1992, pp. 30+.

Mason, Todd, and Elizabeth Weiner, ''Inside the Reichmann Empire,'' *Business Week,* January 29, 1990.

Milligan, John W., ''Blind Faith,'' *Institutional Investor,* September 1992, pp. 27+.

Tully, Shawn, ''The Bashful Billionaires of Olympia & York,'' *Fortune,* June 14, 1982.

—Jonathan Martin

OshKosh B'Gosh, Inc.

112 Otter Avenue
Oshkosh, Wisconsin 54901
U.S.A.
(414) 231-8800
Fax: (414) 231-8621

Public Company
Incorporated: 1895 as Grove Manufacturing Company
Employees: 5,904
Sales: $346.2 million
Stock Exchanges: NASDAQ
SICs: 2369 Girls'/Children's Outerwear Nec; 2326 Men's/
 Boys' Work Clothing; 2339 Women's/Misses' Outerwear
 Nec

OshKosh B'Gosh was founded in 1895 as Grove Manufacturing Company, a maker of "hickory-striped" bib overalls worn by railroad workers and farmers. The company is now the largest maker of overalls in the world, manufacturing sizes to fit everyone from a newborn to an adult male. The company was incorporated as the Grove Manufacturing Company in Wisconsin in 1895. Based in Oshkosh, Wisconsin, a town of 50,000 on the Fox River, the company went through several name changes before assuming its unlikely current name in 1937. Its name was changed in 1897 to Oshkosh Clothing Manufacturing, and in 1911 to Oshkosh Overall Company. Company legend attributes the current name to one of the company's former-owners, William L. Pollock, who heard the phrase in a vaudeville skit while he was on a New York buying trip. The company started labeling its bibs "OshKosh B'Gosh" as early as 1911.

The company has been run by one family since Pollock retired in 1934. That year, Earl W. Wyman bought the company with partner Samuel Pickard and over the next few years they rounded out the company's line with painter's pants, work shirts, and denim jackets. By that time, the company had garnered a reputation for manufacturing durable, dependable products. During World War II and the Korean War, OshKosh B'Gosh produced garments for the military, including pants, jungle suits, and underwear. Wyman remained chairman of the board until he died in 1978. Wyman's son-in law, Charles F. Hyde, ran the company until his son, Douglas W. Hyde, took over as CEO in 1992. At that time, members of the Wyman family still controlled over 50 percent of company shares.

In the late 1960s, after decades of producing heavy duty utility clothing sold in men's and boys' clothing outlets around the Midwest, the company stumbled on a discovery. While it had always made pint-sized bibs as a novelty item for boys to wear in order to look like their working fathers, they were not viewed as a serious commodity. That feeling changed when Miles Kimball Co., an Oshkosh mail order house, included a pair of kids' bibs in its catalog and received over 10,000 requests. The company, according to *Forbes,* was "on the verge of discontinuing the small-fry line, but thought better of doing so when it saw the catalog response." Then-President Charles Hyde decided to see if there was an additional market to be tapped, and, following Kimball's lead, sent direct mail solicitations to children's stores around the country. Among the seven items included in the solicitation were overalls, coveralls, painter's pants and caps.

The experiment was a success. The line made its big national break in 1971, according to *Working Woman,* when Bloomingdale's in New York asked to pick up the products. The chain's upscale competitors, including Lord and Taylor, Saks Fifth Avenue, and Nordstrom's, soon followed suit. Despite this initial success, however, Oshkosh did not readily turn its attention from workwear, even though that market was beginning a steady decline. As the major retail chains came like so many suitors to the company's door, offering to pick up the line and requesting a greater range of styles, Charles Hyde was cautious of what could have been a passing fad. As orders for the children's clothes increased throughout the decade, however, the company realized that workwear was a shrinking market and children's overalls would be the company's new source of growth.

At the end of the decade, Hyde increased the company's sales force. And, at the suggestion of then-vice-president Douglas Hyde the company added a little style into its product by dying the overalls bright primary colors and introducing patterns and stripes. As production rose, Charles Hyde made sure that quality—and the company's good name—did not suffer. Through the 1970s, the garments continued to be cut by hand in Oshkosh, Wisconsin.

The year 1979 was a turning point in several respects. Children's clothing then constituted 16 percent of the company's total clothing sales, or $5 million. To accommodate those sales, the company added two new production plants, paid for entirely out of cash flow. In order to raise its profile, the company also launched a national marketing campaign, enlisting the help of Milwaukee advertising agency Frankenberry, Laughlin & Constable. The agency advised them to adopt the tag "The Genuine Article Since 1895," on a blue and yellow patch that would adorn all of the company's products. A few years later, the company took that advice a step further by calling its new group of outlet stores "The Genuine Article" as well. Through the early- to mid-1980s, the company's sales grew exponentially, as the mini-baby boom created a demand for children's products. While children's products amounted for 16 percent of the company's sales in 1979, that percentage better described workwear, the company's former mainstay, by 1988.

In 1981 the company opened a showroom on Seventh Avenue in New York City, the nerve center of the garment business.

That same year, OshKosh began to diversify its product offerings, adding infant wear and knit separates. Over the years, the company has expanded its line to include newborn to children's size 14 clothing, and added dresses, activewear, and swimwear. In addition, the company signed licensing agreements with producers of accessories and clothing items, including hosiery, shoes, hats, sleepwear, outerwear, and woven and knit accessories. In 1985 the company introduced a line of maternity wear, including but not limited to bib overalls, which, the company learned, pregnant women had been buying for years in men's sizes.

Sales in the United States were increasing, but the company began to devote more resources to sales in the southern and southwestern United States. Prior to that, most of their sales were concentrated in the midwest and along the two coasts. The company entered the global marketplace in 1985 by incorporating OshKosh B'Gosh International Sales as its first wholly-owned subsidiary. Through 1985 and 1986, international sales still accounted for only about one percent of the company's total, but the OshKosh name was gaining recognition. In 1986 *U.S. News and World Report* noted that the company was making a splash in London's upscale boutiques. Among the company's satisfied customers were Britain's royal infants, Princes Harry and William, the children of the Prince and Princess of Wales.

In early 1987, Charles Hyde wrote to the company's shareholders that OshKosh was "monitoring very closely major changes taking place in the retail marketplace, changes which seem to be accelerating. Mergers, acquisitions and leveraged buyouts have changed retailers' sourcing strategies and presented us with challenges that we are positioning our marketing forces to meet. In the confused and competitive retail scene—with no consensus on promoting branded or private label apparel, with retailers doing manufacturing and manufacturers doing retailing—the long term outlook must remain unclear." Hyde's comments were prescient, for in the following year, the company itself became a victim both of this uncertainty and of its own runaway growth: from 1977 to 1987, sales increased almost ninefold, to $226 million.

By the late 1980s, according to *Forbes,* "the company was sweating as it struggled to keep up with the growing demands of its retailers and customers. New stores such as Kids 'R' Us, started by Toys 'R' Us in 1984, wanted more product to fill their shelves and were looking for OshKosh supplies." In late 1987 and early 1988, orders for two consecutive seasons strained the company's production and distribution capacities to the limit, and orders arrived late. According to *Forbes,* retailers reported receiving shipments where the tops of matched separates arrived without bottoms. "We were unable to respond quickly enough to take advantage of stronger than anticipated demand for specific styles," CEO Charles Hyde wrote to his shareholders in April, 1988. "External contractors proved harder to line up than usual and the larger design content our Holiday 1987 and Spring 1988 lines caused hitches in our own production that led to some late deliveries and increased production costs. We encountered these combined difficulties at the very moment that the October stock market decline undermined retailers confidence and prompted a few of our customers to cut back or cancel their orders." These problems continued through

the remainder of 1988 and early 1989, so while the company's overall sales figures continued to grow, unit shipments were sluggish and the company's stock valuation fell by half between 1987 and 1988.

"It was at that point," *Forbes* observed, "that Hyde showed his true mettle. Many businessmen would have shrunk from the problems and cut back their businesses." However, using a strategy the magazine called "investing one's way out of trouble," the company moved quickly to remedy the causes of the distribution problems by upgrading and expanding manufacturing facilities. Four new plants were opened, and in the company's OshKosh plant, woven fabric cutting was computerized. The company also opened a new centralized distribution and finishing center in Tennessee. These expanded facilities cut down the company's dependence on outside contractors—which had caused so much of the trouble—to about 80 percent of total sales in 1990, down from 34 percent in 1988.

In view of all of these new challenges, the company also invested in its future growth by retaining an outside management consultant. Based on the consultant's report, in 1990 the company added three new executive positions: president and chief operating officer; vice-president of human resources; and vice-president of management information systems. Under the change, Harry Krogh, formerly president of Interco Inc., became president, Charles F. Hyde's title changed to chairman and chief executive officer and Thomas R. Wyman was promoted to vice chairman. "Both of us have been freed up from the daily operations of the business to concentrate on long-range planning to meet the challenges of a new decade. At the same time a clear and comfortable succession plan is now in place," Hyde wrote of himself and Wyman in March of 1990.

Also in 1989, the company began to turn its attention towards diversification, both geographically and in terms of product offerings for both older and younger consumers. Toward the end of the year, the company started a joint venture with Poron Diffusion, a publicly held company with $130 million in revenues based in Troyes, France. The resulting venture, designed to market both companies' childrens wear throughout Europe, was christened OshKosh B'Gosh Europe, with majority ownership going to OshKosh. "The accord," the *Wall Street Journal* observed at the time, "will position OshKosh to take advantage of the breakdown in trade barriers among European countries in 1992." Through the agreement, OshKosh also acquired its second wholly owned subsidiary, the U.S. operations of the company, which made baby and infant clothing under the well-known Absorba label.

In 1990, the company further advanced its diversification campaign. In April, the company acquired its third subsidiary, Essex Outfitters Inc., which held a long-term licensing agreement to use the Boston Trader brand name for children's clothing. The Boston Trader label is known in adult clothing for its classic casual style, and the children's line—fitting kids age six and older—has a similar look and is sold in higher-end retail outlets. A few weeks later, the company reached an agreement to sell some pieces of the OshKosh B'Gosh children's line in J.C. Penney and Sears Roebuck stores.

The latter agreement constituted more of a change for the company than the former. Throughout the 1980s, the company's children's products were regarded in the same class as Volvos and pricey mineral water: for the consumption of upscale customers. In 1991, *Business Week* noted that when the legendary jeans maker Levi Strauss & Co. began distributing to Sears and Penney's, "R.H. Macy & Co. discontinued its Levi's jeans because it felt their image had been cheapened." Having studied Levi's experience, OshKosh decided to go ahead with the deal for several reasons. First, as Hyde and Krogh told their shareholders in 1991, "the heavy debt loads being carried by some of our major customers [including, according to *Business Week*, the bankruptcy proceedings of Federated Department Stores], as well as Sears' and Penney's repositioning in the retail market" indicated the wisdom of their decision. Second, the company said it would reserve some high-end specialty items for the likes of Saks Fifth Avenue and Bloomingdale's.

In 1991, the company put its succession plan into effect, moving Charles F. Hyde to the position of chairman and his son Douglas W. Hyde, who had been in charge of merchandising for 12 years, to the position of president and chief executive officer. Michael Wachtel became chief operating officer and executive vice-president. Also in that year, the company continued its foreign expansion by beginning operations at a manufacturing facility it had purchased in Choloma, Honduras, the year before, its first plant outside of the United States. Foreign business, including sales through OshKosh B'Gosh Europe, export sales to overseas distributors, and sales by foreign licensees totaled approximately $23 million, an 83 percent increase from the previous year. In addition, the company was moving into new markets in Argentina, Brazil, Chile, Mexico, Taiwan, and Thailand. The company's Essex Outfitters also proved a good investment, with its retail stores and sales to other outlets outperforming expectations.

Overall earnings dropped during 1991 due to a number of factors. The largest burden turned out to be the Absorba line, which the company had purchased only the year before. And, in view of what were seen as weak long-term prospects for the subsidiary, the company decided to take a loss and phase out the label. However, both Essex and Absorba added to the company's administrative expenses. Continued trouble for retail stores also gave sales of men's and women's wear rather mixed results.

The company experienced financial loss in 1992 as well. The nationwide recession reduced overall consumer demand, particularly in the company's largest markets, California and the Northeast. The recession, plus the continued expenses of the Absorba phase-out contributed to a drop in sales figures from the year before. Faced with these problems, the company went to work to improve its main trouble spot, the domestic wholesale business, which continued to be plagued by late deliveries and cost overruns. "Our customers and the marketplace sent a clear message that business as usual could not continue," Douglas Hyde informed shareholders in March, 1993. Responding to the challenge, the company began implementing plans to streamline manufacturing and improve flexibility. The company revamped its central children's wear line by adding a new line of coordinated separates with simple styling which met consumer desire for clothing that was easy to mix and match. They also formed a special design team to make the products of the menswear division more appealing.

The bright part of 1992 was that the company increased its penetration into foreign markets. In September of 1992, it completed the purchase of Poron, S. A.'s share of OshKosh B'Gosh Europe, making it a wholly owned subsidiary of the company. In addition, the company signed an agreement with Berleca Ltd., a Japanese company which would oversee marketing of OshKosh's products in that country. At the end of the year, the company was in the process of forming a new subsidiary, OshKosh B'Gosh Asia/Pacific Ltd., to provide sales and marketing support in that region. Despite its difficulties through the late 1980s and early 1990s, the company has remained on solid financial footing, fortified by its age, its reputation for quality, and its ability to change and adapt to new circumstances.

Principal Subsidiaries: Essex Outfitters, Inc.; OshKosh B'Gosh Europe, S.A.; OshKosh B'Gosh Asia/Pacific, Ltd.

Further Reading:

Abelson, Reed, "Investing One's Way Out of Trouble," *Forbes,* June 11, 1990.
Byrne, Harlan S., "OshKosh B'Gosh Inc.: It's on the Mend After a Costly Distribution Snarl," *Barron's,* June 19, 1989.
Girone, J.A., "OshKosh: Getting Back on Track," *Earnshaw's,* April 1993.
Harris, William, "Fashion Is Fickle," *Forbes,* June 22, 1981.
Jakubovics, Jerry, "OshKosh's Upward Climb," *Management Review,* September, 1987.
Patner, Andrew, "At OshKosh B'Gosh, Childhood's Magic Days Are Past: Clothier for Tots Makes Plans for a Future in which Kids Are Grown," *Wall Street Journal,* March 9, 1989.
Perlick, Gail, "B'Gosh, It's OshKosh: How Humor and Nostalgia Overhauled the Overall," *Working Woman,* August 1987.
Schellhardt, Timothy D., "OshKosh B'Gosh Sets European Venture Through Accord with Poron of France," *Wall Street Journal,* November 8, 1989.
Siler, Julia Flynn, "OshKosh B'Gosh May be Risking Its Upscale Image," *Business Week,* July 15, 1991.

—Martha Schoolman

Pall Corporation

2200 Northern Boulevard
East Hills, New York 11548
U.S.A.
(516) 484-5400
Fax: (516) 484-5228

Public Company
Incorporated: 1946 as Micro Metallic Corporation
Employees: 6,400
Sales: $687.2 million
Stock Exchanges: New York
SICs: 3569 General Industrial Machinery, Nec

Pall Corporation is the world's leading supplier of fine filters and other products used for fluid clarification. The company markets its filters in three major areas: health care, aeropower, and fluid processing.

Pall Corporation traces its origins to the formation of the Micro Metallic Corporation by David Pall in 1946. During World War II, Pall, a Canadian-born chemist, worked on the Manhattan Project, a covert operation in which the American government sought to develop the first atomic bomb. Pall, then 27 years old, helped design a filter to separate uranium 235 from uranium 238. He and his colleagues developed the filter to separate the raw uranium material from the heavier, less stable uranium by sintering—heating to just below melting point—powdered stainless steel and producing a very fine screen. Pall and his company, renamed the Pall Corporation in 1957, remained focused on developing filters for special tasks, and, as technology in other fields emerged, new markets opened up for the company's filters.

In 1950 Pall brought his neighbor, a certified public accountant named Abraham Krasnoff, into the company to help with administration and finance. Krasnoff's organizational skills along with Pall's scientific genius resulted in a successful organization.

In 1958, Pall began developing filters for the aircraft industry. Its first filters were for the American Airlines fleet of Boeing 707s, the technicians for which had resorted to operating their landing gear manually after finding that impurities were causing the hydraulic landing gear system to malfunction. Next, Pall

developed a filter for purifying jet fuel. The company soon became the leading supplier of aircraft filters, and in the 1960s and 1970s, Pall filters were used on most major military aircraft, including helicopters and fighter jets.

In fact, by the late 1970s, Pall had become overly dependent on military and defense industries, and the company sought new markets for its fine filter technology. During this time, Pall was able to provide the emerging semiconductor and biotechnical industries with the finer filters needed in their manufacturing processes.

According to Abraham Krasnoff, who became the company chairperson in 1989, Pall preferred to service niche markets, where manufacturing needs were very specialized and challenging. Accordingly, Pall eschewed the production of filters widely used by individual consumers, such as gasoline or oil filters for cars. Furthermore, once Pall's development of a certain technology was complete, the company usually jettisoned its business in that area. For example, in 1988, Pall sold its compressed air dryer business as well as its facility that produced gas mask filters, as they both became technologically and financially mature units.

Recognizing that the company could not rely solely on the genius of one person—David Pall—the company also focused on building a research and development department. Referring to David Pall, Krasnoff told *Industry Week,* "You can always succeed a good manager, but you can never succeed a genius." Therefore, Krasnoff and Pall set about assembling an impressive array of scientists who would help develop fluid clarification products. Pall spent only about four percent of its sales on research and development, compared to the budgets of some of its chief competitors, such as Millipore, which allotted more than seven percent of sales. The company was able to keep its costs down by focusing solely on fluid clarification, unlike Millipore and other companies, which had diversified their interests and therefore required a wider array of researchers.

Another of Krasnoff's organizational strategies was to assemble a team of scientists known collectively as the company's Scientific Laboratory Services, or SLS, to help test, advise, and communicate with researchers. Krasnoff told *Financial World* that SLS was "a bridge between the leading edge customer and our own marketing and research people."

In order to ensure that supplies and prices remain steady worldwide, manufacturing for each of Pall's product lines was performed in at least two Pall facilities. The size of each facility was limited to no more than 450 employees, fostering a sense of team spirit and familiarity.

Much of the steady growth Pall experienced, measuring about 17 percent annually through the 1980s and into the 1990s, was accomplished through internal growth, not through acquisitions. Pall focused on building new factories and creating subsidiaries throughout the world. Pall faced international competition, but maintained its edge in several markets and managed to dominate almost every niche it carved out for its subsidiaries.

In the early 1990s Pall's health-care products division was the fastest growing segment of the company. In 1992, with sales of

$331.6 million, the division represented almost half of Pall's sales and 60 percent of its operating expenses. It included filters for direct use with hospital patients to provide protection against contamination and infection through blood, breathing, or IV. Blood filters in particular were a high growth area in the first part of the decade with sales estimated to reach $260 million, or 26 percent of total sales, by 1995. Pall's leukocyte filters treated with gamma rays were used to filter out white blood cells, which caused the rejection of platelets during the multiple transfusions necessary for organ donors and recipients, AIDs patients, and those undergoing chemotherapy. David Pall led the team that developed the blood filter, which proved a vital part of the system used for processing whole blood at blood collection sites.

Other Pall health care products included filters to use in diagnostic devices and filters for the manufacture of contamination-free pharmaceuticals, biopharmaceuticals, and biologicals. Moreover, Pall produced electronic instruments for use in testing the filters before and after use. Pall also included food, beverage, and household water filters in its health care segment. Products in this market included filters for the final filtration process of beer, wine, and bottled water and filters used in the production of high fructose corn syrup. Pall entered into an agreement to apply its dynamic microfiltration systems to a series of dairy product applications of Ault Foods of Toronto, Canada.

The company's Aeropower division accounted for sales of $204.7 million in 1992. This division produced fluid clarification filters used to clean hydraulic, lubricating, and transmission fluids for both military and commercial aircraft. Other industrial customers included manufacturers and end users of fluid power equipment and bearing lubrication systems for steel, aluminum and paper mills, and the automobile and aerospace industries. Furthermore, Pall's filters were used by manufacturers of on- and off-road vehicles and construction equipment and machinery for moving earth, as well as having applications in agriculture machinery, oil drilling and exploration, mining, metal cutting, and electric power generation.

Military sales accounted for only ten percent of Pall's sales in 1990, down from 25 percent ten years earlier. During the Persian Gulf crisis involving Operation Desert Shield and Operation Desert Storm, however, military sales went up when Pall supplied $26 million worth of filters to keep sand out of helicopter engines. Furthermore, Pall entered into an agreement with FMC Corporation, a defense and military systems contractor, to provide an industrial air purification method (called Pressure Swing Absorption or PSA) to FMC for most military applications in North America, including foreign military sales. Pall anticipated that this would build a strong base for military sales, which the company expected to slowly increase despite the downsizing of the military occurring in the early 1990s.

The fluid processing market, with sales of $148.8 million in 1992, included service to manufacturers of electronic components, liquid crystal displays, magnetic tape, electric power, film, fiber, chemicals, petrochemicals, oil, gas, paper, steel, and other products in which filters are needed for removing contaminants or particles. Pall worked with several world-renowned scientists to develop new products in this market segment, especially the area of semiconductor technology. Although this was a mature market, research and development was opening new applications for Pall.

Pall's international operations provided about two-thirds of its revenues in the early 1990s. In the mid-1960s Pall had acquired a small English metalworking company run by Maurice Hardy. This initial investment in Hardy's company was Pall's jumping-off point for further overseas expansion. By the time England became a full member of the European Common Market more than a decade later, Pall Europe was generating sales revenues of $9 million. Despite duties imposed by the EEC, 40 percent of Pall's sales were in West Germany, Italy, and Holland, while ten percent were in Scandinavia.

In each country Pall entered, it used roughly the same strategy. It set up a small sales unit, then expanded to include technological and engineering support. It then added distribution to its services. Krasnoff maintained that Pall did not establish foreign facilities to take advantage of lower labor costs, telling *U.S. News & World Report* in 1988 that the three most important rules he had learned about operating overseas were, "Hire competent locals, use competent locals, and listen to competent locals."

In 1991, Pall's sales growth in Europe was at 18 percent, and its growth in Asia reached 31 percent, while its growth in the United States that year was only eight percent. By 1993, Pall was generating about two-thirds of its revenues from foreign markets and had subsidiaries in Brazil, Spain, Germany, France, Singapore, Canada, Japan, Korea, and other nations and was considering further expansion in Japan and the rest of the Pacific Rim. Pall projected that by 1995, as much as 75 percent of its sales could be generated abroad.

In the early 1990s Pall faced intense competition from the Japanese, particularly in the blood filtering market. While Pall controlled about 50 percent of the blood filtering market, its market share was threatened by Asahi, a Japanese chemistry conglomerate worth billions of dollars, and Terumo, a medical equipment manufacturer. Nevertheless, Pall was able to beat these Japanese firms to market with its improved leukocyte filter.

In 1993 Pall looked forward to international growth, particularly in the high-tech areas of ultrafiltration (molecular separation) and dynamic microfiltration. To this end the company sought to form alliances with global operations rather than to acquire them. According to CEO Maurice Hardy, who replaced Krasnoff, a company must have "a multinational and, later, a global operating strategy."

Principal Subsidiaries: Pall Aeropower Corporation; Pall Trinity Micro Corp.; Pall Biomedical Products Company; Russell Associates Inc.; Pall Espana SA (Spain); Pall Europe Corporate Services Ltd. (Great Britain); Pall Puerto Rico Inc.; Pall Industrial Hydraulics Corp.; Pall Trincor Corp.; Nihon Pall (Japan).

Further Reading:

Hardy, Maurice, "Going Global: One Company's Road to International Markets," *The Journal of Business Strategy,* November/December, p. 24–27.

"His Business Knows No Borders," *U.S. News & World Report,* March 7, 1988, p. 52.

Slutsker, Gary, ed., "To Catch a Particle," *Forbes,* January 23, 1989, p. 88–89.

Teitelman, Robert, "Focused Functions," *Financial World,* July 11, 1989, p. 54–55.

—Wendy J. Stein

Pay 'N Pak Stores, Inc.

Public Company
Incorporated: 1961
Employees: 2,200
Sales: $498.4 million
Stock Exchanges: New York
SICs: 2499 Wood Products, nec; 2542 Partitions & Fixtures
Except Wood; 2541 Wood Partitions & Fixtures; 2599
Furniture & Fixtures, nec; 3546 Power-Driven Handtools;
3645 Residential Lighting Fixtures; 3632 Household
Refrigerators & Freezers; 5211 Lumber & Other Building
Materials; 5251 Hardware Stores

Before its 1992 dissolution, do-it-yourself retailer Pay 'N Pak
Stores, Inc. sold a wide variety of products, from electrical and
plumbing supplies to automotive accessories and sporting
goods, and operated as many as 107 stores in 15 states in the
western United States. At one time, Pay 'N Pak was a leading
retailer in the industry, but as the lucrative market attracted
more competitors, the company proved unable to compete and
ceased operations in 1992.

Created in 1961 with the establishment of one plumbing and
electrical supply store in a rural community in Washington
State, Pay 'N Pak expanded rapidly during its first several years,
adding stores throughout western Washington. During these
formative years, Pay 'N Pak enjoyed much success, opening an
average of two stores per year and developing a program to
create Pay 'N Pak franchises that extended as far south as
California. While this early growth provided an important foundation for the company to build on, the first defining event in
Pay 'N Pak's existence came eight years after its inception, in
the form of a merger. The merger, in 1969, combined 14
company stores and five franchise stores with the assets of
Eagle Electric & Plumbing Supply and Buzzard Electrical &
Plumbing Supply. Joined together, the amalgamation of the
three companies comprised 22 stores plus Pay 'N Pak's five
franchised stores, giving the newly formed entity revenues of
more than $15 million. Although the merger increased the num-
ber of stores Pay 'N Pak operated and extended its presence into
eastern Washington, the new management was of greater importance to the future of the company.

The key figure in the new management was David J. Heerensperger, president of Eagle Electric and the largest stockholder in
the merged operations of the three companies. Once the compa-

nies merged, Heerensperger, who had founded Eagle Electric
ten years earlier, took control of the combined operations and
immediately began to initiate changes that had a lasting affect
on the future of Pay 'N Pak. First, he eliminated Pay 'N Pak's
franchise program and its recently-formed modular housing
operation, both of which were experiencing considerable financial difficulties at the time of the merger. Next, Heerensperger
placed a greater emphasis on customer service by hiring a
training director to develop an instructional program which
stressed product knowledge and various installation techniques
used for projects that utilized products sold by Pay 'N Pak.
Employees who underwent such instruction were able to impart
valuable information to Pay 'N Pak customers, a vast majority
of whom were consumers remodeling or repairing their residences without the assistance of professional contractors. This
type of informative salesmanship became a hallmark of Pay 'N
Pak's early success, enabling a customer to purchase the proper
tools and supplies for a particular project and also receive
advice on how the project might best be completed.

The average size of a Pay 'N Pak store in the years following the
merger was 18,000 square feet, with the various products displayed in both bulk quantities and room arrangements. The
company offered a wide array of home improvement products,
including plumbing, electrical, and lighting fixtures, as well as
building materials, cabinets, and appliances. In addition to products that catered to the do-it-yourself market, nine of the company's stores also sold automotive parts and sporting equipment, adding to Pay 'N Pak's appeal. This was particularly
important since Pay 'N Pak stores were located in rural or
suburban areas with populations ranging between 50,000 and
75,000, areas that generally offered a limited selection of
merchandise to neighboring residents. After Heerensperger
made his sweeping changes, the square footage of the stores
increased by 70 percent, with some as large as 33,000 square
feet, lending a ''warehouse feel'' to the stores that encouraged
greater sales.

Greater sales were exactly what Pay 'N Pak produced, as the
effect of the changes made an immediate impact on the financial
health of the company and fueled its expansion. By 1974, Pay
'N Pak operated 48 stores in ten states in the western United
States and experienced a phenomenal increase in its revenues.
Since Heerensperger had assumed stewardship of the company,
revenues had increased 29 percent annually and earnings had
swelled at a faster clip of 34 percent. At this point, Pay 'N Pak
boasted $51.9 million in revenues and was formulating plans to
open six to eight stores per year in the coming years. This
success was partly attributable to the growth in the do-it-yourself home improvement market nationwide. According to research conducted by *Building Supply News,* over $22 billion
was spent per year during this time on products similar to those
sold by Pay 'N Pak, and this figure was expected to increase as
more consumers completed household projects themselves instead of hiring professionals.

Because nearly 75 percent of homeowners nationwide engaged
in remodeling or repair projects, Pay 'N Pak focused their
advertising on consumers and eschewed the professional sector.
Pay 'N Pak's advertising efforts saturated the markets it operated in, employing 37 newspapers in 30 cities and augmenting
those advertisements with tabloids inserted in newspapers to

announce its yearly chainwide sales. The employee training programs that had proven effective were held three times a year, and employees had access to approximately 40 sound and color films detailing the specifications and installation procedures of Pay 'N Pak's products. Thus, with aggressive advertising, a knowledgeable sales staff, and the likelihood of further growth in the do-it-yourself market, especially in the Pacific Northwest, where the economy was growing at a faster rate than the national average, Pay 'N Pak achieved remarkable results in the years immediately following the merger and stood ready to open additional stores to build on this success.

By 1975, Pay 'N Pak had opened an additional six stores, for a total of 54, and increased its revenues to $60 million despite a nationwide recession that caused many retailers to suffer appreciable losses. As a result of the recession, consumers were left with less disposable income, but tended to spend what little they possessed on more prudent expenditures, such as repairing their plumbing or electrical problems themselves. Accordingly, Pay 'N Pak was sufficiently insulated against the economic downturn and was able to post an increase in earnings of roughly 20 percent. Further, housing industry cycles, which negatively affected retailers involved in the building industry at this time, had little impact on Pay 'N Pak's business since lumber accounted for a mere four percent of the company's total revenues.

Even though the market niche Pay 'N Pak had carved for itself served as a buffer against a majority of the pernicious affects of the recession, some of the items the company sold did suffer from a decline in sales. More expensive items, such as appliances, did not generate as much revenue as before the recession, but Pay 'N Pak's line of automotive parts experienced a surge in sales that more than made up for losses. Beyond cutting inventories by $3 million, Pay 'N Pak emerged from the recessionary mid-1970s as a financially stronger company, still looking to expand and possessing the necessary cash flow to finance such growth.

Over the next five years, Pay 'N Pak opened an average of approximately five stores each year and extended its presence into five more western states, giving the company 78 stores in 15 western states by the end of the 1970s. Revenues had also increased during this period, more than doubling from $60 million in 1975 to a robust $138 million in 1980. Heerensperger, who by now was chairman and chief executive officer of Pay 'N Pak, had witnessed a 23 percent annual increase in revenues since he joined the company, growth that was still largely predicated on the superior service its salespeople provided to customers. Retail chains similar to Pay 'N Pak offered their products in warehouse style formats, but operated their stores as self-service establishments, typically hiring part-time help to staff the stores. This lack of qualified sales support on the part of Pay 'N Pak's competitors gave the company a distinct advantage in the do-it-yourself market, establishing it as a haven for consumers who wished to complete home improvement projects but did not possess the expertise.

In 1982, after spending $750,000 to affix new colors and graphics to each store and remodel each bathroom and kitchen room arrangement, Pay 'N Pak eliminated its automotive and sporting goods product lines, which had proven to be low-profit

items. At this time, retailers nationwide were once again reeling from poor financial conditions, as inordinately high inflation rates shrunk profit margins. But Pay 'N Pak's financial position remained strong, buoyed by homeowners forced to remodel their homes instead of moving to new ones and by growth in the building materials retail market, a segment of Pay 'N Pak's business that was expected to double in the next three years. With 90 stores and revenues of $180 million, the company was growing at a prodigious rate and seemed immune to the recessionary periods that affected other retailers.

By 1985, Pay 'N Pak was operating 107 stores and revenues had topped $300 million, a rate of growth indicative of the vitality of the home improvement market, which now was a $50 billion business. Encouraged by the profits that could be gleaned in this lucrative market, many large retailers diversified into the home improvement industry and Pay 'N Pak began to suffer from the proliferation of competitors. Reacting to the increased competition, Heerensperger insisted on maintaining Pay 'N Pak's market share even if it resulted in losses for the company, which was exactly what happened the following year. In 1986, although revenues rose to $333 million, the company's earnings dropped to $8 million from the $10 million posted the previous year. A price war soon developed among the home improvement retailers, which further eroded Pay 'N Pak's earnings, but the company remained true to its promise to uphold its market share, and slashed its prices as well. By this time, in 1987, Pay 'N Pak's market had attracted the attention of a corporate takeover specialist named Paul Bilzerian who attempted a hostile takeover of Pay 'N Pak. Bilzerian's efforts failed, however, due to a management-led buyout of Pay 'N Pak, but the cost of rescuing the company from the takeover drained a considerable amount of its resources and left it saddled with a hefty debt.

Pay 'N Pak now suddenly found itself on the verge of collapse. The company had changed from a rapidly expanding retail chain with an enviable rate of revenue growth to a company that had overextended itself and was unable to successfully compete in a market saturated with competitors. To exacerbate the situation, the price war continued after 1987, as Pay 'N Pak fought to service its debt and operate with reduced profits. This was a losing battle, made more difficult by the company's better-financed competitors. K-Mart Co.'s Builders Square, Service Merchandise Co.'s Home Depot Inc., and HomeClub could sustain the losses induced by the price war, but Pay 'N Pak, with its mounting debts and limited cash flow, could not. The company limped along, losing more money each year, until 1991, when it defaulted on a $12.5 million debt payment. Pay 'N Pak's inability to pay its bankers eventually led the company to file for bankruptcy in September of that same year and it attempted to reorganize under the protective conditions provided by Chapter 11 of the United States Bankruptcy Code.

The United States Bankruptcy judge presiding over Pay 'N Pak's case granted a $100 million debtor-in-possession financing package to the company, enabling it to restock some of its 74 stores, and initiate a new merchandising plan that placed a greater emphasis on home design products. The company opened eight stores with this new concept in early 1992, but just as the new stores opened for business, Pay 'N Pak decided the competition within its territory and the debilitating debt were too much to bear. Less than a year after Pay 'N Pak filed for bankruptcy, it liquidated as much of its inventory as it could and closed the doors to the company's stores by the end of September in 1992, ending 31 years of business in the do-it-yourself industry.

Further Reading:

"Big Retailers Doing All Right," *Seattle Times,* February 16, 1975, p. B8.

Dunphy, Stephen H., "Vast Growth Seen in Do-It-Yourself Market," *Seattle Times,* January 24, 1982, p. D6.

Greenwald, Judy, "Pay 'N Pak: This Home Improvement Chain Poised for Smart Profits Rise," *Barron's,* March 23, 1981, pp. 42, 44.

Jalonen, Wendy, "Pay 'N Pak Dumps Warehouse Style," *Puget Sound Business Journal,* August 10, 1987, p. 1.

——, "Pay 'N Pak in a Tough Battle for Profits," *Puget Sound Business Journal,* December 23, 1985, pp. 1, 8.

Miller, Scott, "Despite Growing Revenues, 1986 Was a Tough Year for Pay 'N Pak," *Puget Sound Business Journal,* September 29, 1986, p. 8.

Parks, Michael J., "Comparative Analysis: N.W. Retail Chains," *Seattle Times,* June 24, 1973, p. D4.

"Pay 'N Pak, Eagle Electric Plan to Merge," *Seattle Daily Journal of Commerce,* February 6, 1969, p. 1.

"Pay 'N Pak Stores, Inc.," *Over-the-Counter Securities Review,* October 1969, p. 68.

"Pay 'N Pak Stores, Inc.," *Wall Street Transcript,* May 6, 1974, p. 36,837.

"Pay N' Pak Winds Down: Vacates Stores This Week," *Seattle Times,* September 28, 1992, p. B3.

Prinzing, Debra, "$100 Million Pay 'N Pak Bailout OK'D," *Puget Sound Business Journal,* November 18, 1991, p. 3.

——, "Pay 'N Pak Goes after a Game-Winning Format," *Puget Sound Business Journal,* July 8, 1991, p. 5.

——, "Pay 'N Pak Seeks Refinancing After Defaulting on Bank Debt," *Puget Sound Business Journal,* June 17, 1991, p. 2.

——, "Pay 'N Pak Seeks Refinancing after Defaulting on Bank Debt," *Puget Sound Business Journal,* June 17, 1991. p. 2.

Stevens, John H., "Pay 'N Pak Will Close with a 12-Week Sale," *Seattle Times,* June 17, 1992, p. A1.

Tibergien, Mark, "Pay 'N Pak Adds Its 48th Store to Retail 'Do-It-Yourself' Chain," *Investment Dealers' Digest,* November 27, 1973, p. 14.

—Jeffrey L. Covell

Pfizer Inc.

235 E. 42nd Street
New York, New York 10017
U.S.A.
(212) 573-2323
Fax: (212) 573-7851

Public Company
Incorporated: 1900
Employees: 40,700
Sales: $7.2 billion
Stock Exchanges: New York London Basle Lausanne Paris
    Brussels Zurich Geneva
SICs: 2834 Pharmaceutical Preparations; 2833 Medical
    Chemicals & Botanical Products

Pfizer Inc. is one of the leading research-based, health care companies in the United States and the world. The company has introduced three major drugs—the antidepressant Zoloft, a cardiovascular agent called Norvasc and an antibiotic called Zithromax. Furthermore, Pfizer's Procardia XL, a treatment for angina and hypertension, became the company's first $1 billion product in the United States. Pfizer's revolutionary developments occurred following almost one hundred years of manufacturing fine chemicals; the development of penicillin eventually led Pfizer to important innovations within the industry.

In 1849 Charles Pfizer, a chemist, and Charles Erhart, a confectioner, began a partnership in Brooklyn to manufacture bulk chemicals. While producing iodine preparation and boric and tartaric acids, Pfizer pioneered the production of citric acid, a product Pfizer continues to market to soft drink companies, using large-scale fermentation technology.

While Pfizer technicians became experts in fermentation technology, across the ocean Sir Alexander Fleming made his historic discovery of penicillin in 1928. Recognizing penicillin's potential to revolutionize health care, scientists struggled for years to produce both a high quality and large quantity of the drug. Experimentation with production became an imperative during the Nazi air raids of London during World War II. In a desperate attempt to solicit help from the community of United States scientists, Dr. Howard Florey of Oxford University travelled to America to ask the U.S. government to mobilize its scientific resources.

Due to their expertise in fermentation, the government approached Pfizer. Soon afterward, Dr. Jasper Kane from the company laboratory began his own experiments. Initially using large glass flasks, Dr. Kane's experimentation then led to deep-tank fermentation. Later, the company announced its entrance into large-scale production with the purchase of an old ice plant in Brooklyn. Refusing government money, the company paid the entire $3 million for the purchase and within four months John McKeen (future chairperson and president) had converted the ancient plant into the largest facility for manufacturing penicillin in the world.

However, early production was not without its difficulties. The first yields of penicillin required constant supervision, and yet quality and quantity remained low and inconsistent. In one of those inexplicable quirks of history, however, a government researcher browsing in a fruit market in Peoria, Illinois, discovered a variant of the "Penicillium" mold on an over-ripe cantaloupe. Using this variant, production suddenly increased from 10 units per millimeter to 2,000 units per millimeter. By 1942 Pfizer divided the first flask of penicillin into vials for the medical departments of the Army and Navy; this flask was valued at $150,000. It was Pfizer penicillin that arrived with the Allied forces on the beaches of Normandy in 1944.

Even as the government controlled production of the drug for the sole use of the Armed Forces, the public, aroused by miraculous results of penicillin, asked Pfizer to release the drug domestically. In 1943 John L. Smith, Pfizer president, and John McKeen, against the explicit regulations of the federal government, supplied penicillin to a doctor at the Brooklyn Jewish Hospital. Dr. Leo Lowe administered what was thought of as massive dosages of penicillin to several patients and cured, among others, a child suffering from an acute bacterial infection and a paralysed and comatose woman. Smith and McKeen, visiting the hospital on Saturdays and Sundays, were witness to penicillin's curative effects on the patients.

Nevertheless, it was not until the end of the war when the federal government realized its mistake in restricting production of the drug. In 1946 Pfizer purchased Groton Victory Yard, a World War II shipyard, in order to renovate it for mass production of the new publicly accessible medicine. This marked Pfizer's first official entrance into the manufacturing of pharmaceuticals. In a few years the five story building, equipped with 10,000 gallon tanks, produced enough penicillin to supply 85 percent of the national market and 50 percent of the world market. In 1946 sales had already reached $43 million.

Competition from 20 other companies manufacturing penicillin soon resulted in severe price reductions. The price for 100,000 units dropped from $20 to less than two cents. Furthermore, while the company could boast ownership of fermentation tanks "exceeded in size only by those in the beer industry," Pfizer's bulk chemical business decreased as former customers began establishing production facilities of their own. Pfizer's instrumental role in developing antibiotics proved beneficial to society, but a poor business venture.

All this was to change drastically under the new direction of president John McKeen. In 1949 McKeen, whose career at Pfizer began the day after he graduated from the Brooklyn

Polytechnic Institute in 1926, was elevated to president and later chair of the company. Already responsible for increasing sales by an impressive 800 percent between 1939 and 1950, McKeen's business acumen became even more evident during the Terramycin campaign. In the postwar years, pharmaceutical companies searched for new broad-spectrum antibiotics useful in the treatment of a wide number of bacterial infections. Penicillin and streptomycin, while helping to expand the frontier of medical knowledge, actually offered a cure for only a limited number of infections. Pfizer's breakthrough came with the discovery of oxytetracycline, a broad range antibiotic that would soon prove effective against some 100 diseases.

The drug's remarkable capture of a sizeable portion of the market was not due entirely to its inherent curative powers. Rather it took McKeen's ability to promote the new drug that actually propelled Pfizer into the ranks of top industry competitors. McKeen's first accomplishment was the timely decision to market the antibiotic under a Pfizer trademark. Thus Terramycin, the drug's chosen name, launched Pfizer into its first ethical drug campaign. Lacking the resources other pharmaceutical companies had to promote their drugs, McKeen announced the "Pfizer blitz" whereby the company's small sales force used an unusual array of marketing strategies.

For the first time, the company circumvented traditional drug distributing companies and began selling Terramycin directly to hospitals and retailers. Pfizer's miniscule detail force (pharmaceutical salespeople) would target one small region at a time and promote their product to every accessible healthcare professional. The sales force left generous samples of the drug at every sales call, sponsored golf tournaments, and ran noisy hospitality suites at conventions. Surprised at the success of this tiny band of salespeople, which would eventually grow into a 4000-man army, industry competitors reluctantly increased their own sales forces and similarly began promoting their products directly to physicians.

Taking the calculated risks of insulting the entire medical community, Pfizer ran lavish advertisements in the conservative *Journal of the American Medical Association.* The ad was greeted with a large degree of reservation and threatened the drug industry's abhorrence of "hard sell" marketing. In an unprecedented move, the company had paid a prohibitive $500,000 to run the multipage ad. In two years the entire Terramycin campaign cost $7.5 million, and Pfizer became the largest advertiser in the American Medical Association's journal.

After twelve months on the market, Terramycin's sales accounted for one-fourth of Pfizer's total $60 million sales. Yet problems with the company's advertising strategy were soon to surface. In 1957, while promoting the reputability of a new antibiotic called sigmamycin, a Pfizer advertisement used the professional cards of eight physicians to endorse the drug. John Lear, science editor of the *Saturday Review,* denounced this advertisement in a scathing attack. Not only were the names of the eight physicians fictitious, Lear claimed, but the code of Pharmaceutical Manufacturers Association prohibited soliciting endorsements from physicians. Moreover, Lear used the Pfizer ad to underscore and criticize what he saw as a trend towards the overprescription of antibiotics, exaggerated claims on drug effects, and concealment of possible side effects.

Pfizer was quick to defend their advertisement. The company upheld the reputability of the ad agency, William Douglas McAdams Inc., a highly respected firm responsible for the Sigmamycin campaign. While defending the drug and the clinical reports supporting the drug's efficacy, Pfizer admitted that the business cards were purely symbolic and therefore fictitious and, as a result, may have been misleading. The company accordingly changed the campaign.

John Lear's final attack on Pfizer expressed an unspoken industry complaint. Not only was it disturbing that such "hard sell" tactics should actually prove successful, but so was Pfizer's status in the industry; as the company's recent past was in bulk chemical production, it was a relative newcomer to the industry of ethical drugs. Lear argued that the young company should have shown respect for the industry's formal and restrained method of conducting business. However, Pfizer was not intimidated by the industry's attitude toward its advertising campaign; it was interested in claiming and maintaining a share of the market. If it meant breaking tradition, it was clear Pfizer was not going to hesitate.

Aside from its modern marketing campaigns, Pfizer was very successful at developing a diversified line of pharmaceuticals. While many companies concentrated their efforts on developing innovative drugs, Pfizer generously borrowed research from its competitors and released variants of these drugs. While all companies participated in this process of "molecular manipulation," whereby a slight variance is produced in a given molecule to develop greater potency and decreased side effects in a drug, Pfizer was particularly adept at developing these drugs and aggressively seizing a share of the market. Thus, the company was able to reduce its dependence on sales of antibiotics by releasing a variety of other pharmaceuticals.

At the same time Pfizer's domestic sales increased dramatically, the company was quietly improving its presence on the foreign market. Under the methodical directive of John J. Powers, head of international operations and future president and chief executive officer, Pfizer's foreign market expanded into 100 countries and accounted for $175 million in sales by 1965. It would be years before any competitor came close to commanding a similar share of the foreign market. Pfizer's 1965 worldwide sales figures of $220 million indicated that the company might possibly be the largest pharmaceutical manufacturer in the United States. By 1980 Pfizer was one of two U.S. companies among the top ten pharmaceutical companies in Europe, and the largest foreign health care and agricultural product manufacturer in Asia.

Pfizer's crowning success to its unorthodox business procedures involved McKeen's quest for diversification through acquisition. While competing companies within the industry preferred to keep between $50 and $70 million in savings, Pfizer not only kept a meager $25 million in cash, but was the only major pharmaceutical to use common equity to borrow capital. "Not to have your cash working is a sort of economic sin," McKeen candidly stated. Between 1961 and 1965 the company paid $130 million in stock or cash and acquired 14 companies.

including manufacturers of vitamins, antibiotics for animals, chemicals, and Coty cosmetics.

McKeen defended this diversification strategy by claiming that prodigious growth had decreased overall profits while competitors, on the other hand, had neither grown nor profited from their conservative investments. Furthermore, Pfizer's largest selling drug, Terramycin, generated only $15 to $20 million a year and therefore freed the company from a dependence on one product for all its profits.

In 1962 Pfizer allotted $17 million for research and that same year McKeen announced plans for his ''five by five'' program which included $500 million in sales by 1965. Obviously, sales would not come from new pharmaceuticals, but from the company's accelerated rate of acquisitions.

McKeen never actually saw the company reach this goal during his presidency. In 1964 sales did surpass $480 million, but the following year Powers replaced McKeen as chief executive officer and president, and inherited a company with almost half its sales generated from foreign markets and wide product diversification from 38 subsidiaries.

For the next seven years Powers continued to preside over the company's comfortable profits and sizeable growth. In the absence of McKeen's style of conducting business, Powers directed Pfizer towards the more conservative and methodical approach of manufacturing and marketing pharmaceuticals.

Powers guided the company in a new direction with an increased emphasis on research and development. With increased funds allocated for research in the laboratories, Pfizer joined the ranks of other pharmaceutical companies searching for the innovative, and therefore profit making, drugs. Vibramycin, an antibiotic developed in the 1960s, was very profitable; by 1981 it generated sales of $250 million.

In the early 1970s Edmund Pratt Jr. stepped in as company chairman and Gerald Laubach took over as Pfizer president. While company assets reached $1.5 billion and sales generated $2 billion by 1977, Pfizer's overall growth was much slower through the period of the late 1970s and early 1980s. Increased oil prices caused comparable increases in prices for raw materials; low incidents of respiratory infections slowed sales for antibiotics; and even a cool summer in Europe reduced demands for soft drinks and, consequently, the need for Pfizer citric acids. All of these factors contributed to the company's slow rate of growth.

In the light of this, the two new top executives significantly changed company strategy. First, funds for research and development reached $190 million by 1981; this marked a 100 percent increase in funding from 1977. Secondly, Pfizer began a comprehensive licensing program with foreign pharmaceutical companies to pay royalties in exchange for marketing rights on newly developed drugs. This represented a noticeable change from the years Powers supervised international operations. Under his directive Pfizer choose to market its own drugs on the foreign market and establish joint ventures or partnerships only if no other option was available.

The two new drugs, one called Procardia, a treatment for angina licensed from Bayer AG in Germany for its exclusive sale in the U.S., and the other called Cefobid, an antibiotic licensed from a Japanese pharmaceutical, promised to be highly profitable items. Furthermore, drugs discovered from Pfizer's own research resulted in large profits. Sales for Minipress, an antihypertensive, reached $80 million in three years, and Feldene, an anti-inflammatory, generated $314 million by 1982.

By 1983 sales reached $3.5 billion and Pfizer was spending one of the largest amounts of money in the industry on research ($197 million in 1983). Pratt, in a final move to shed Pfizer of its former idiosyncrasies, began selling some of its more unprofitable acquisitions.

Interestingly, one Pfizer product acquired through a company acquisition in the 1960s experienced a market rediscovery during the 1980s. Ben Gay, a well established liniment marketed for relief of arthritis pains through the late 1970s, found new patrons in the health-conscious 1980s. Discovering that sales for Ben Gay were increasing when marketed as a fitness aid, Pfizer began an advertising campaign by employing athletic superstars to endorse the drug. This campaign cost the company $6.3 million in 1982.

By 1989, Pfizer operated businesses in more than 140 countries. Net sales that year were $5.7 billion, but net income declined. Research and development expenditures had quadrupled during the 1980s, and Pfizer planned to continue investing heavily in research and development. Procardia XL was launched in 1989, and Diflucan, an antifungal agent, received Food and Drug Administration approval. Globally, Pfizer chalked up $150 million in sales—in 14 countries—of its Plax dental rinse.

Pfizer headed into the 1990s with numerous drugs in development, including preparations in the areas of anti-infectives, cardiovasculars, anti-inflammatories, and central nervous system medications. Net sales in 1990 reached $6.4 billion. Procardia rapidly became the most widely prescribed cardiovascular drug in the United States. Research and development costs rose 20 percent, in keeping with Pfizer's determination to invest heavily in new drugs.

Pfizer International launched 37 new products worldwide in 1990. Sixty additional launches were slated for 1992. Pfizer's antifungal drug, Diflucan, became the world's leading drug of its kind during this time. Sales of Pfizer's newest products accounted for 30 percent of all pharmaceutical sales, up from 13 percent in 1989.

Pfizer entered the decade facing controversy about heart valves produced by Shiley, a Pfizer subsidiary. In 1990, 38 fractures of implanted valves were reported. Pfizer instituted a policy of compensating those with fractured valves.

In 1992, Pfizer received final approval from the Food and Drug Administration for Norvasc, used in treating angina and hypertension. Also in 1992, the company introduced Veri-Lo fat extenders for use in low-fat salad dressings, mayonnaise and sauces. Zithromax, an antibiotic developed to treat out-patient pneumonia, tonsillitis and pharyngitis, also hit the market after FDA approval. Net sales in 1992 were $7.2 billion, with a net income of $811 million, and research and development expenses hit $863 million. Pfizer's chairperson and CEO of 19 years, Ed Pratt, retired and was succeeded by William C. Steere, Jr.

Cognizant of new national developments regarding insurance coverage and health-care cost containment, Pfizer stepped up its visibility in public discussions and planned to advocate comprehensive coverage as a necessary part of any health-care reform package. Pfizer also vowed not to raise prices on any single product by more than 4.5 percent in 1993. Other pharmaceutical manufacturers joined Pfizer in declaring a cap on price increases.

In 1993, Pfizer continued its vigorous research and development activities. The company filed with the FDA for approval of Enablex, an anti-arthritic drug. Other promising drugs Pfizer was developing included Dofetilide, one of a new class of drugs that can make irregular heart rhythms normal; zamifenicin, to treat irritable bowel syndrome; and ziprasidone, for psychotic illness. Researchers at Pfizer were confident that the remainder of the decade would be a time of unprecedented opportunity for innovations and development of new drugs.

Principal Subsidiaries: Radiologic Sciences, Inc.; Shiley Inc.; Valleylab, Inc.; Composite Metal Products, Inc.; Redmond Holding Co.; Pfizer Hospital Products Group, Inc.; Site Realty, Inc.; Pfizer Pigments Inc.; Pfizer Genetics Inc.; American Medical Systems, Inc.; Quigley Company, Inc.; Adforce Inc.; Myerson Tooth Corp.

Further Reading:

Pfizer Inc. Annual Report, New York: Pfizer, Inc., 1989–92.
LaBell, Fran, "Fat Extenders in Salad Dressings," *Food Processing,* May 1992, p. 64.
"Pfizer Joins with Other Drug Makers on Price Control," *Chemical Marketing Reporter,* February 1, 1993, p. 7.
"Pfizer Shareholders are Told Company is Well-Positioned for Growth in Changing Pharmaceuticals Environment," *PR Newswire,* April 22, 1993.
"Pfizer Wins U.S. FDA Approval for Norvasc," *European Chemical News,* August 17, 1992, p. 23.

—updated by Marinell Landa

PINKERTON®
SECURITY & INVESTIGATION SERVICES

Pinkerton's Inc.

15910 Ventura Blvd., Suite 900
Encino, California 91436
U.S.A.
(818) 380-8800
Fax: (818) 380-8515

Public Company
Incorporated: 1850
Employees: 43,000
Revenues: $703.70 million
Stock Exchanges: NASDAQ
SICs: 7381 Detective & Armored Car Services

Pinkerton's Inc. is the country's oldest security firm, providing security guard personnel and investigative services to some of the largest businesses in the United States, including ITT Corp. and Hewlett-Packard Co. During the nineteenth and early twentieth centuries, the company emerged as a leading detective agency whose private investigators became famous for solving crimes involving the country's railroads, banks, and businesses. Since the 1940s, however, Pinkerton's has focused increasingly on security, developing into a business primarily engaged in guarding property; in 1990 more than 98 percent of the company's business consisted of contracts to provide security guards.

The history of the Pinkerton detective agency may be traced to its founder Allan Pinkerton. Pinkerton was born in 1819 in the Gorbals, an impoverished and crime ridden district of Glasgow, Scotland. Soon after the death of his father in 1827, Pinkerton left elementary school to help support his family, achieving the status of journeyman cooper ten years later. During this time, Pinkerton became involved in Chartism, a political movement espousing an independent, democratic Scottish parliament that would provide citizens with voting and property rights. The movement turned violent in the early 1840s, and Pinkerton became known in Glasgow for his activism. When police sought his arrest, he went into hiding for several months and eventually decided to flee the country. In April of 1842 he and his bride, Joan Carfrae, set sail for the United States.

The Pinkertons settled in Chicago, where Allan found work making kegs and barrels for a brewery before establishing his own cooperage in the nearby town of Dundee. According to his biographers, Pinkerton's involvement in detective work began in 1847, when his suspicions regarding some activities he observed on a nearby island resulted in the exposure of a gang of counterfeiters. Soon thereafter, local bankers and shopkeepers began hiring Pinkerton to help them apprehend thieves and counterfeiters, and he was appointed deputy sheriff of Kane County. In addition to his work as a cooper and amateur detective, Pinkerton became involved in the burgeoning abolitionist movement, establishing his home as a stop on the underground railroad from which slaves escaped to freedom in Canada.

After selling their cooperage, the Pinkertons moved back to Chicago in the late 1840s. There Pinkerton served as sheriff of Cook County and was appointed as Chicago's first detective. He quickly became known as an honest and uncompromising law enforcer and a shrewd detective. When the post office experienced a concentration of thefts in the Chicago area, Pinkerton was appointed Special United States Mail Agent in order to help find the source. Pinkerton went undercover, targeted some suspects, and eventually caught one man in the act of stealing envelopes during the sorting process. As a result of his work, Pinkerton became nationally famous. Observing a need for organization in the field of law enforcement, Pinkerton founded his detective agency in 1850.

During this time, the country's policing system consisted primarily of sheriffs and bounty hunters in rural areas and loosely organized and often corrupt police departments in the larger cities. Describing these circumstances, biographer Frank Horan stated in his book *The Pinkertons: The Detective Dynasty That Made History,* "What was needed at the time to fill the niche between the lack of rural law and the incompetence of corrupt urban law-enforcement organizations, was a private police force that could move across local, county, and even state boundaries in the pursuit of criminals. This is what Pinkerton established."

Pinkerton composed a code of ethics for his agency; his *General Principles* outlined several areas in which the agency would not accept contracts, including divorce cases, or cases of a "scandalous" nature, and the investigation of public officials, jurors, or political parties. The Pinkerton agent, furthermore, was forbidden to accept rewards or gratuities not specified in the contract. Many of these rules continued to be honored through the twentieth century.

Setting up business in downtown Chicago, the agency originally employed five detectives and a few administrative personnel. Among Pinkerton's detectives was George Bangs, who became the company's leading detective and general manager. Pinkerton was also the first in the country to hire a woman detective, Kate Warne, who served the agency for several years. Pinkerton, who referred to himself as the company's principal rather than president, hired agents, or operatives, based on their intelligence, perceptiveness, and courage, rather than on experience in detective work. Once hired, operatives received training through dramatizations of crimes as well as lessons in how to assume disguises and play the roles demanded of them.

From the onset, the company flourished and its staff of operatives grew. Focusing on a territory that included Illinois, Indiana, Michigan, and Wisconsin, the agency soon established branch offices in each state. While its chief area of business in the early years was the investigation of train robberies, Pinkerton's agency also worked on cases involving forgery, counterfeiting, and murder. In the 1850s Pinkerton and his agents became known collectively as The Eye that Never Sleeps, in reference to their unrelenting pursuit of criminals.

Also during this time, Pinkerton maintained his commitment to abolition. His home in Chicago was one of the most crucial stops on the underground railroad, and he became a staunch supporter of the renowned abolitionist John Brown, to whom he provided both financial and moral support. During the Civil War, Allan Pinkerton and his agency assumed various roles in the union cause. Operatives traveled undercover in the South, investigating reports of espionage and conspiracy; some operatives were captured and executed by Confederate forces. Convinced that President Lincoln was the target of an assassination plot in Boston in 1861, the Pinkerton Agency persuaded Lincoln to amend his travel plans, providing guards to guarantee his safe passage back to Washington. Whether or not such a plot existed later became a topic of controversy among scholars, some of whom have suggested that Pinkerton fabricated the incident in order to further his reputation. Throughout the war, Allan Pinkerton maintained a close personal association with the union general George McClellan, spending much time in Washington D.C. and at various battle sites and providing McClellan with information on Confederate forces, even suggesting strategies for battle. However, Pinkerton proved a better detective than military advisor.

In the postwar period, as reconstruction began in the South and the country strove to develop more adequate communication and transportation networks, Pinkerton faced a new type of crime. Wiretapping, specifically of Western Union telegraph lines, involved the interception of information which was then falsely relayed to newspapers in major cities, creating sensational stories of mine disasters and bank failures that significantly affected investors on Wall Street and consequently caused financial crises. Wiretappers were then able to take advantage of the declining stock prices prompted by the false reports. Instrumental in dissolving bands of wiretappers, the Pinkerton Agency also prompted Congress to enact laws protecting the wire service as a public utility.

Bank and train robberies also occupied the Pinkerton Agency during the second half of the nineteenth century. Notorious gangs such as the Reno family, Frank and Jesse James, and Butch Cassidy's Wild Bunch were all pursued and most were eventually captured by Pinkerton operatives, who now operated out of offices in the west as well as in New York and Philadelphia. During this time, however, Allan Pinkerton suffered a debilitating stroke, and the great Chicago fire destroyed the agency's headquarters. Although the headquarters were quickly rebuilt, and Pinkerton eventually regained his speech and mobility, national economic crises in the early 1870s strained the agency's finances. Furthermore, the integrity of operatives' expense accounts was brought into question by management and the company's auditors. The period of cost cutting that ensued allowed the agency to remain in business.

The company received an important financial boost during this time in the form of a contract with Franklin Benjamin Gowen, president of the Reading Railroad. After investigating several instances of violence and vandalism, particularly involving railroad equipment in Pennsylvania's coal mining region, Pinkerton suggested further investigation of a group known as the Molly Maguires.

The Molly Maguires was a group formed as a result of disputes between labor and management in the coal mining industry, consisting largely of militant Irish miners attempting to garner safer working conditions and better wages. Increasingly violent demonstrations were staged by the Molly Maguires, and Pinkerton suggested to Gowen that one of his operatives infiltrate the group. Pinkerton chose James McParland for the assignment, and McParland spent nearly three years as a member of the Molly Maguires, reporting to the agency on its activities and plans for violent raids and demonstrations. Towards the end of McParland's service in this capacity, he came under the suspicion of the Molly Maguires and managed to flee the area before he could be harmed. In the late 1870s many of the group's leaders were convicted in court of murder and arson and were sentenced to be hanged.

Allan Pinkerton died in 1884, and his sons William and Robert succeeded him as co-principals of the agency; William directed operations in the West from his office in Chicago, while Robert maintained an office in New York and supervised the eastern operations. During this time the Pinkerton Agency became increasingly involved in the labor wars. Uniformed Pinkerton operatives were hired to help protect property and non-striking workers as well as to provide intelligence to company management. Although the Pinkertons did not technically break strikes, an enmity developed between the agency and the labor union movement. In 1892 more than 300 armed Pinkerton operatives were employed by Carnegie Brothers & Co., Ltd. to help protect their iron works at Homestead, Pennsylvania, near Pittsburgh. The Pinkertons were attacked by gunfire as they tried to reach the Homestead plant via the Monongahela river, and a riot ensued during which the Pinkertons were defeated and run out of the area.

At the turn of the century, Pinkerton began to face competition from the William J. Burns security agency, as well as from improved city police departments and other private agencies then being formed by railroad companies and other businesses. Nevertheless, Pinkerton continued to expand its operations, opening new offices throughout the country, which handled investigations for insurance claims and provided protection at racetracks and public events. Moreover, the firm began investigations into the growing Mafia presence in New York and New Orleans.

Robert Pinkerton died in 1907; his son Allan Pinkerton II took his place as head of western operations. When William Pinkerton died after suffering a heart attack in December of 1923, Allan Pinkerton II assumed the position of principal at the agency. During the 1920s, the Pinkerton Detective Agency expanded its operations both in the United States and abroad. As industry boomed, Pinkerton detectives continued to be hired as factory guards as well as to perform investigations into labor union activities. Also during this time, Pinkerton employees were engaged in resolving cases of armed robbery, particularly those involving banks, a crime that had been facilitated by the growing popularity of the automobile. One of Pinkerton's most famous cases involved the apprehension of the notorious bank robbers Willie Sutton and Marcus Bassett, who were captured and sentenced to life in Sing Sing prison in 1930.

That year Allan Pinkerton II died suddenly. His successor, son Robert II, was initially reluctant to head the agency, preferring to pursue his career as a Wall Street stockbroker. Nevertheless, he gradually adopted the role of principal at the Pinkerton Agency. During the 1930s a Senate subcommittee was convened to examine the practice of investigating labor activities, and in 1937 Congress passed the Wagner Act, which deemed such investigations unlawful as they interfered with the rights of workers to organize. Thereafter, the Pinkerton agency resolved to deny contracts to investigate the organization and collective bargaining tactics of unions. As a result of renouncing this line of work, the company's 1938 earnings dropped to $1.2 million, down from more than $2 million the year before.

During this time, the agency increased its presence in the horse racing industry, which was beset with corruption. Robert Pinkerton personally investigated gambling syndicates, primarily in New York, as well as identifying gangs of "ringers" who fixed races by either altering the appearance of a horse or doping it. Pinkerton was largely successful in his efforts to eradicate crime from the racetrack. However, in doing so he was on several occasions targeted for murder by the syndicates and experienced several near misses.

By 1940, the character of the Pinkerton National Detective Agency had changed significantly. Over the next 20 years, the company's services narrowed in scope, as Pinkerton's provided investigative services for accounting and insurance firms, and the guarding of property became central to its business. During World War II, Pinkerton operatives were hired to guard war supply plants. The company's 1944 gross income topped $4 million, $1.7 million of which represented such wartime work. The company also gained several important contracts in the 1950s and 1960s, including one to provide security guards for the 1964–65 World's Fair in New York. The Pinkerton National Detective Agency became Pinkerton's Inc. in 1965, prompted by its general shift in focus from detective work to security services. Two years later the company went public, and Edward J. Bednarz assumed the presidency, becoming the first non-family member to attain the position. Although its role in police work had diminished, the company prospered, maintaining over 70 branch offices throughout the world by 1968.

In 1983, Pinkerton's was purchased by American Brands for $162 million. Some analysts suggested that Pinkerton's was not likely to fit well with the other businesses in the American Brands conglomeration, which included manufacturers of cigarettes and other merchandise. Nevertheless, the company maintained that with new direction, Pinkerton's would become a profitable part of the conglomerate. In January of the following year Robert McGuire, a former assistant U.S. attorney and police commissioner of New York City, became the company's chairperson and CEO. McGuire sought to increase the company's sales and profits through improved service, particularly through the investigation of white collar crime and embezzlement in big business. McGuire was optimistic, commenting in a *Forbes* article in 1984 that with "reduced police resources

nationwide and intolerable levels of crime," opportunities existed in "executive protection, computer security and the alarm business." Nevertheless, the company's revenues remained flat, and by 1987 Pinkerton reported losses of $11 million on sales of $413 million.

In 1988 Pinkertons came under the leadership of Thomas Wathen, who purchased the company from American Brands for $95 million and merged it with his California Plant Protection (CPP). Wathen had graduated from Indiana University in the late 1950s with a degree in police administration and worked as the security director for a toy company in Los Angeles. There Wathen oversaw the hiring of security guard firms until 1964, when he purchased CPP, a struggling security guard business. Recalling this new venture in a May 1990 article in *Nation's Business,* Wathen observed that his only experience with security guard firms had been as a customer. Consequently, he noted, "I ran the business the only way I could possibly know how to run it, and that's the way the customer would want it to be operated. That gave me a hell of an edge philosophically." Over the next 20 years, Wathen developed CPP into a successful business with annual revenues of $250 million, up from $163,000 in 1964.

Among Wathen's contributions to the security industry was his implementation of extensive training programs for his company's guards. In order to gain certification, guards at CPP took special courses and were expected to perform satisfactorily on written exams. Furthermore, even after being hired, CPP guards underwent psychological tests to ensure the company's employees were well suited to their jobs. Wathen's training programs as well as several screening techniques used to evaluate applicants were incorporated at Pinkerton's after the acquisition.

When Pinkerton's joined CPP, its headquarters was moved from New York to Van Nuys, California, and the entire enterprise was renamed Pinkerton's Inc., reflecting the name long recognized for outstanding police work. One of the most notable changes for the Pinkerton company was effected by Wathen's policy of accepting very few contracts that required armed guards. In 1990 less than two percent of Pinkerton's guards carried guns, and Wathen told *Forbes* at the time, "I don't like guns, dogs, or liability."

In 1989 Pinkerton's combined revenues totaled $605 million. In order to spur further growth, the company began a series of acquisitions. In 1991, Pinkerton's purchased several security guard companies in the United States, Mexico, and Great Britain. Moreover, the company began to diversify its interests, providing clients with investigative services for workers' compensation cases and background checks on prospective employees. Although plans were underway during this time for branching out into the electronic alarm systems business, this idea was soon abandoned in order to cut expenses.

By September of 1991 Pinkerton's was projecting a growth rate of 25 percent for the following year. However, in June of 1992, after selling 48,000 shares of stock reportedly worth $1.26 million, the company acknowledged that earnings had fallen significantly below expectations. During the first half of 1992, the company's operating expenses increased 36 percent to $24.4 million, while its earnings dropped 41 percent to $2.5

million. At that time, Robert J. Berger stepped aside as the company's president, choosing to remain on the board of directors. Soon thereafter, upon learning that Berger and Wathen had sold some of their stock in the company just prior to the financial reports, a group of shareholders filed a lawsuit alleging that Wathen and Berger had deliberately misled investors in order to inflate the company's stock prices.

Despite its legal entanglements, Pinkerton's continued to generate new business, including an $8 million contract to provide security services to Hughes Aircraft Co. in 1992. Industry analysts noted that Hughes, like many other companies, preferred to contract with outside security companies due to the expenses associated with administering to in-house security staffs. By curtailing large acquisitions, consolidating its operations in a new headquarters in Encino, California, and relying chiefly on internal growth, Pinkerton's stood to reduce operating expenses and retain its status as the nation's leading security firm.

Further Reading:

Barrett, Amy, "Feeling a Bit Insecure," *Business Week,* September 28, 1992, pp. 69–72.

Barrier, Michael, "Tom Wathen's Security Blanket," *Nation's Business,* May 1990, pp. 26–30.

Davenport, Carol, "Stick 'Em Up," *Fortune,* July 31, 1989, p. 267.

Horan, James D., and Howard Swiggett, *The Pinkerton Story,* New York: G.P. Putnam's Sons, 1951.

Horan, James D., *Desperate Men: Revelations from the Sealed Pinkerton Files,* New York, Bonanza Books, 1969.

——. *The Pinkertons: The Detective Dynasty That Made History,* New York: Crown Publishers, 1967.

MacNeil, V. "Pinkerton: Security Sleuths Call Van Nuys Home," *Los Angeles Business Journal,* February 5, 1990, pp. 36–7.

Morn, Frank, *"The Eye that Never Sleeps": A History of the Pinkerton National Detective Agency,* Bloomington: Indiana University Press, 1982.

Mullen, Liz, "Security Guard Firms Stake Out Booming Business," *Los Angeles Business Journal,* June 22, 1992, p. 26.

Schlax, Julie, "The New Pinkerton Man," *Forbes,* September 17, 1990, pp. 46–8.

Siringo, Charles A., *Two Evil Isms: Pinkertonism and Anarchism,* reprint, Austin, Texas: Steck-Vaughn Company, 1967.

Trachtenberg, Jeffrey A., "It's a Jungle Out There, Thank Goodness," *Forbes,* September 24, 1984, p. 166.

—Tina Grant

PIONEER.

PIONEER HI-BRED INTERNATIONAL, INC.

Pioneer Hi-Bred International, Inc.

400 Locust St.
700 Capital Square
Des Moines, Iowa 50309
U.S.A.
(515) 245-3500
Fax: (515) 245-3650

Public Company
Incorporated: 1973
Employees: 5,016
Sales: $1.26 billion
Stock Exchanges: National Market System
SICs: 0115 Corn; 0116 Soybeans; 0119 Cash Grains NEC;
    2879 Agricultural Chemicals NEC; 5191 Farm Supplies;
    0181 Ornamental Nursery Products

Pioneer Hi-Bred International, Inc. is the world's largest seed company, with research facilities in 30 countries worldwide. Pioneer develops, produces and markets hybrid corn, sorghum, sunflower, soybean, alfalfa, wheat, canola, and vegetable seeds. The company dominates most of the markets it participates in, holding a 39.6 percent share of the North American seed corn market, and even higher shares in European markets. The company was instrumental in one of the most important genetic accomplishments of American agriculture, the development of hybrid corn. Pioneer has become more involved in the use of biotechnology to speed up the breeding process in the last decade of the twentieth century.

Pioneer was established in 1926 as the Hi-Bred Corn Company under the leadership of Henry Agard Wallace. Before the company was created, it was commonly assumed that a farmer's best-looking corn yielded the highest-producing seeds. Farmers took their handsomest ears to university-sponsored county- and state-wide contests to be judged and used as the following season's seed. But a select group of people questioned the efficacy of this seed-choosing process. One of those forward-looking people was young Henry A. Wallace. At 16, he conducted a field test pitting one of the area's best-looking ears of seed corn against one of the ugliest, and the ugliest ear out-yielded the pretty one. The tassels of corn grown in test fields were removed in order to isolate a hybrid's desirable characteristics. "Detasseling" continued throughout the twentieth cen-

tury, requiring massive numbers of seasonal laborers at Pioneer's seed corn fields.

Studies made during the first two decades of the twentieth century revealed that yield varied greatly with the quality of seed: the seed yielding in the top ten percent outproduced that in the bottom ten percent by an average of 25 bushels per acre. At a time when farmers generally expected to yield about 40 bushels per acre, the disparity was astounding. Unfortunately, the results of these tests would have seriously undermined the university-sponsored "pretty corn" contests and many researchers' findings weren't published.

But Henry Wallace had an advantage over many researchers: his father, Henry C. Wallace, owned a progressive farming newspaper, *Wallace's Farmer*. The Wallace family provided a heritage of farming leadership that helped launch Pioneer: young Henry's uncle had served on President Theodore Roosevelt's first Commission on Life in Rural America, and in 1921, his father was appointed to be U.S. Secretary of Agriculture. Henry A. Wallace inherited the editor's chair at *Wallace's Farmer* that year and got both a forum for his studies and an advertising medium for his seed.

When Henry, his brother Jim, and several partners founded the Hi-Bred Corn Company in Johnstown, Iowa in 1926, it was the first business created for the specific purpose of developing and marketing hybrid seed corn. The joint stock company was established with 200 shares and a $5,000 capitalization. Hi-Bred's first seed crop consisted of 40 acres of hand-planted, hand-picked corn. The company's seed was sold by mail-order through advertising in the family newspaper and profited $33.62 in the first year of sales, 1928. Sales doubled in 1929, prompting Hi-Bred to purchase 80 additional acres and create a Parent Seed Department. Soon, Pioneer's hybrid seeds dominated Iowa corn yield contests. The majority of farmers, who still relied on open-pollinated seed, complained that hybrid corn was too costly and unrealistic to produce and use, so the contests were split into two separate divisions.

The 1930s brought depression to the world economy, and drought, erosion and pestilence to the fields of the Midwest. The brutal growing conditions were both a blessing and a curse for Hi-Bred. Several breeds of corn failed during the harsh drought of 1934, but other lines endured the weather long enough to produce a crop. In comparison with open-pollinated fields, which performed miserably, Hi-Bred was able to show a significant advantage in hybrid corn.

As word of Hi-Bred's relative success spread, demand for the seed increased. To market the product, the company instituted the "farmer-salesman concept," where farmers worked part-time for Hi-Bred and full-time on their own farms. This sales method became an industry standard and was continued throughout the century. These local representatives were familiar to their customers and had first-hand knowledge of the product and its performance. Farmer-salesmen often used eight-pound samples of seed to graphically illustrate Hi-Bred seed's advantages vs. open-pollinated seed. Skeptics soon learned that the commercial seed produced heartier, stronger, more uniform plants and yielded about twenty bushels more per acre. Hi-

Bred's first distributorship was established in the 1930s in the southwest.

Growing competition in the hybrid field prompted the company to distinguish itself from its rivals, and the Pioneer Hi-Bred name was instituted. And even though the company lost money throughout the depression years, remote research operations were expanded to several areas in the Midwest to test seed under varying climactic conditions. Founder Henry A. Wallace left Pioneer in 1933 to follow his father as Secretary of Agriculture. In 1941, he was elected Vice President of the United States under Franklin D. Roosevelt. Fred Lehman, Jr., a founding partner in Pioneer, succeeded Wallace as president of the company.

World War II's profound technological and workforce changes affected Pioneer as well as the rest of the world. While "Rosie the Riveter" took her husband's place in the factories, "Marge the Detassler" roamed Pioneer's corn fields. Pioneer even brought German prisoners of war into the process when labor was scarce. Wartime rationing slowed Pioneer's growth somewhat, but the company was able to expand into Canada, and expand research into cold germination and increased mechanization. Pioneer's eggs and broiler hens became a more significant part of the business during the 1940s as well. By the end of the decade, nearly all farmers had made the transition to hybrid corn seed. With much of the world engaged in war, the United States became the world's granary.

Pioneer chalked up several "firsts" during the prosperous 1950s: the first electronic analysis of research and sales data, the first sorghum hybrid breeding program, and the first attempts at alternative packaging. Research facilities were expanded to Florida and South America, and Pioneer entered into a joint venture with the Arnold Thomas Company to produce alfalfa hybrids. By the end of the decade, corn sales rose to 400,000 bushels per year. The company's upper management clarified the company's four guiding principles in a 1952 booklet titled, "The Long Look." Executive vice-president Jim Wallace and sales director Nelson Earvin noted that Pioneer had always tried to provide quality products, honest product information, strong product promotion and advice to customers.

Farming in America had changed dramatically since Pioneer was created. The number of farms had decreased from 6.5 million to four million, and the number of farmers shrunk from one-fourth of the population to just five percent. When Pioneer first sold corn seed, the average family farm consisted of 150 acres producing a variety of livestock and crops for subsistence and commercial use; by the 1960s, most farmers devoted their 300-acre farms to a single crop. Technological improvements in corn harvesters in the 1960s permitted farmers to shell corn as it was mechanically "picked" and dry and store it on the farm, saving time and money. These advances made new demands on hybrid corn: it had to shell easier and dry faster. Farmers averaged three hours of work per bushel of corn in 1929, but advances in equipment, pesticides, fertilizers, and especially hybridization had shortened that time to six minutes. Higher yields meant higher profits and a better standard of living for many farm families.

Pioneer concentrated on overseas development during the 1960s, establishing joint ventures in Australia, Argentina, and South Africa. And as concerns about overpopulation and global hunger mounted, Pioneer strove for ever higher yields and worked to lengthen the company's growing season by creating its first winter nursery, in Hawaii. The fiftieth state's year-round growing season permitted three crops of seed per year. But with its eyes on foreign development, Pioneer lost market share in America.

By the 1960s, the U.S. hybrid seed corn market was saturated, and had little unit growth, forcing a higher level of competition. DeKalb AgResearch Inc., a rival since the 1930s, pulled ahead of Pioneer in terms of market share. The rival company introduced a revolutionary hybrid that gave it a slender lead in the industry by the end of the decade. But by 1972, each of the seed corn producers held 22 percent of the hybrid seed corn market.

In 1973, Pioneer went public and reorganized its operations. Prior to this time, Pioneer was a federation of geographically-based companies. Each independent dealer purchased its seed from Pioneer's centralized research division, but was responsible for its own operations. The incorporation and reorganization also brought about the formation of the Cereal Seed Division to breed wheat. Pioneer made acquisitions to diversify primarily within the hybrid seed business. The company expanded its alfalfa and soybean seed research with the purchase of the Arnold Thomas Co. and Peterson Soybean Seed Co. The acquisition of NORAND, a computer company, put Pioneer in debt for the first time since 1926, but the parent applied the new subsidiary's hand-held computer technology to field research and sales programs. Pioneer also acquired New Labs, a developer of microbial products that encouraged the formation of silage (feed that is fermented in a silo) and aided animal digestion. Pioneer was reorganized so that central management could assess the company's total value and consolidate its competitive efforts against DeKalb and new entrants into the market by bringing uniformity to policies, pricing, and promotion.

By the mid-1970s, the company faced new competition from chemical and pharmaceutical companies like Ciba-Geigy, Sandoz, Union Carbide, Upjohn, and Pfizer, who all applied their research expertise to the development of new hybrids. But Pioneer's decades of experience in the industry set it far ahead of these new rivals.

Over the course of the 1970s, Pioneer and its primary rival, DeKalb, applied divergent business strategies: DeKalb diversified into oil and gas exploration, mining, irrigation, and other industries, while Pioneer concentrated on developing seed with ever-higher yields. Pioneer's concentration on research and new product development paid off with the development of 3780, a corn hybrid that broke yield records and soon became the company's and the industry's best-seller. Pioneer's timing could not have been better: from 1970 to 1980, unit sales in the overall seed corn industry grew by one-third, and dollar volume tripled. Farmers were willing to pay Pioneer's premium prices for higher yields. At the same time, the United States' seed exports nearly doubled, fueled by technological improvements and increased global demand for food. By the end of the decade, Pioneer had regained the top share of the seed corn market, with 34 percent, and DeKalb's share diminished to 14 percent. Pioneer's sales multiplied five times from 1972 to 1980, to $400 million, and profits grew eightfold, to $53 million.

The United States' 16-month grain embargo in protest of the Soviet Union's invasion of Afghanistan marked the beginning of a difficult decade for American farmers. The 1980–1981 embargo caused grain prices to fall sharply, which precipitated a farm crisis in the United States. Grain surpluses from the embargo combined with a recession to force many farmers into bankruptcy. Others stuck with farming, but reduced their corn acreage to take advantage of government subsidies. A drought in 1983 deepened the downward spiral: corn acreage decreased by 27 percent over the course of the decade, and the U.S. seed corn market shrunk by one-fourth.

On the other hand, however, the Soviet grain embargo encouraged production in the affected countries, creating new markets where there were none before. After the embargo, Pioneer worked to capture these new global customers. The company added "International" to its name to reflect the growing importance of overseas operations. By the end of the 1980s, Pioneer had expanded to 32 countries abroad.

Rivals in the seed corn industry introduced hybrids that closely resembled some of Pioneer's best-selling products in the early 1980s. These low-priced knock-offs were so similar to Pioneer's most popular hybrids that company officials became suspicious of their origin and development. When genetic mapping proved that Holden Foundation Seeds had illegally used Pioneer's proprietary germ plasm to develop their seeds, Pioneer brought suit against the rival company and won. Pioneer instituted stricter controls to protect the company's intellectual property as a result, and has worked to patent many of its products.

Pioneer expanded into biotechnological research in the late 1980s and early 1990s. Biotechnology is a genetic science that seeks to add new traits through gene manipulation rather than the slower process of traditional breeding. This emphasis on research helped Pioneer claim "the best-performing product lineup in the seed industry," as well as over 39 percent of the United States seed corn market by 1992. The company posted record results in the early years of the decade. Earnings rose over 40 percent in 1991 and again in 1992 to $152.16 million in the latter year. But Pioneer officials were cautious about earnings projections for the remainder of the decade. They were acutely aware that the impact of politics and the weather were two unpredictable, yet significant factors that could influence their business at any time. Corn acreage in North America and Europe was expected to drop, reducing the volume of the seed corn market and threatening Pioneer's unit sales. From a global perspective, however, 40 percent of the world's corn acres did not employ hybrids, leaving significant room for expansion of the market. Pioneer expanded its product lines to include relatively new products, including two oilseeds, canola and sunflower, and vegetable seeds. The company hoped to utilize research and marketing to achieve 20 percent return on equity by 1995.

Principal Subsidiaries: Pioneer Overseas Corp.; Advantage Corp.; Endonor Corp.; Green Meadows, Ltd.; Microbial Environmental Services, Inc.; PHI Communications Co., Inc.; PHI Financial Services, Inc.; PHI Insurance Co.; PHI Insurance Services, Inc.; Pioneer Hi-Bred Australia PTY Ltd; Pioneer Hi-Bred Europe Inc.; Pioneer Hi-Bred Ltd; Pioneer Hi-Bred Philippines Inc.; Pioneer Hi-Bred Production Ltd.; Pioneer Hi-Bred Puerto Rico Inc.; Pioneer Overseas Corp. Ltd. (Thailand); Pioneer Seed Co. Pvt. Ltd. (Zimbabwe); Pioneer Vegetable Genetics Inc.; Pioneer Vegetable Genetics Ltd. (90%); Semillas Pioneer S.A.; U.S. Specialty Grains Co.; Ethiopian Pioneer Hi-Bred Seeds Inc. (70%); Grainfield Co., Ltd. (49%); Hibridos Pioneer de Mexicanos S.A. de C.V.; Hibriven Hibridos Venezolanos C.A.; Investigaciones Pioneer S. de R.L. de C.V.; Lesotho American Hi-Bred Seeds (PTY) Ltd (60%); Misr Pioneer Seeds Co. S.A.E. (70%); PT Pioneer Hibrida Indonesia; PHI Biogene Ltd. (40%); Pioneer Agrogenetique Cote D'Ivoire S.A. (99%); Pioneer Argentina S.A.; Pioneer Egypt Inc.; Pioneer Genetique Cameroon S.A.; Pioneer Genetiques S.A.R.L.; Pioneer Hi-Bred Agricultural Technologies Inc. (80%); Pioneer Hi-Bred FSC Ltd; Pioneer Hi-Bred Italia SpA; Pioneer Hi-Bred Japan Co., Ltd. (52%); Pioneer Hi-Bred Korea, Inc.; Pioneer Hi-Bred Magyarorszag K.F.T.; Pioneer Hi-Bred Nederland B.V.; Pioneer Hi-Bred S.A.R.L.; Pioneer Hi-Bred Sementes de Portugal, S.A.; Pioneer Hi-Bred Nigeria Ltd. (70%); Pioneer Hi-Bred Thailand Co., Ltd. (95%); Pioneer Overseas GmbH; Pioneer Overseas Research Corp.; Pioneer Research Co., Ltd. (65%); Pioneer Saaten GmbH; Pioneer Seed Co., Ltd. (65%); Pioneer Semena Holding GmbH; Pioneer Tohumculuk A.S.: Semillas Hibridas Pioneer S.A. (75%); Semillas Pioneer Colombia S.A.

Further Reading:

Davenport, Caroline H. "Sowing the Seeds: Research, Development Flourish at DeKalb, Pioneer Hi-Bred," *Barron's,* March 2, 1981, pp. 9–10, 33.
Pioneer: A History, produced by Pioneer Hi-Bred International, Inc., 60 min., Des Moines, IA, 1992, videocassette.
"Seed Corn's Long, Hot, Bruising Summer," *Business Week,* August 25, 1980, pp. 52, 54, 56.
"A Sustained Harvest," *Forbes,* October 15, 1979, pp. 120, 122.

—April S. Dougal

PITTWAY CORPORATION

Pittway Corporation

200 S. Wacker Drive
Suite 700
Chicago, Illinois 60606
U.S.A.
(312) 831-1070
Fax: (312) 831-0828

Public Company
Incorporated: 1950
Sales: $586.3 million
Employees: 4,500
Stock Exchanges: American
SICs: 3669 Communications Equipment; 2721 Periodicals
   Publishing and Printing

Pittway Corporation is a major distributor of professional fire and burglar alarms, but also has a distinguished reputation as a publisher of trade magazines and directories. The company has undergone several incarnations and shifts in focus to reach its present state. Incorporated in 1950 as the Pittsburgh Railway Company, the firm was originally a subsidiary of the Standard Gas and Electric Company, a public utility holding company formed during the mid-1920s. The Pittsburgh-based company operated numerous street railway and bus companies. In 1957 the board of directors at Standard Gas and Electric voted to dissolve and subsequently convert itself into a closed-end investment company—in accordance with the Investment Company Act of 1940—named Standard Shares. As a result of the dissolution, Pittsburgh Railways became a public company, but Standard Shares, with 42 percent ownership of its stock, retained operating control of the firm.

During the late 1950s, Standard Shares drew the interest of Neison Harris. A year after graduating from Yale University, Harris entered the beauty supply business. In 1944 he set up a company called Toni Co. that manufactured beauty products, such as the first home permanent wave, with his brother Irving. The success of Toni products was so great that the Harris brothers sold their company to Gillette Company in 1948 (when Neison was only 33 years old) for approximately $20 million. For the next 12 years, Neison Harris served as president of Toni and as a member of Gillette's board of directors.

Harris grew disenchanted with Gillette management when it changed Toni's operating structure and product line, and he resigned. Along with his brother Irving and sister June, he purchased stock in Standard Shares until they had a controlling interest. But purchasing Standard was only a means to an end; Harris knew that Pittsburgh Railways was the principle asset of Standard, and it was this company that garnered his interest. With the era of mass private transportation clearly in decline, Harris saw an opportunity to remake Pittsburgh Railways.

Using his family's controlling interest, Harris convinced the board of directors at Standard Shares to redeploy Pittsburgh Railways' assets and diversify into areas more financially promising than bus and trolley car operation. Harris immediately went on a shopping spree and, in April of 1962, acquired G. Barr & Company, a rapidly growing aerosol products packager. A year later, he purchased the Alarm Device Manufacturing Company (Ademco), a leading manufacturer and distributor of burglar and fire alarm equipment. By the time the city of Pittsburgh condemned the streetcar business in 1964, Neison had also bought Seaquist Manufacturing Corporation and the Industrial Publishing Company, a publisher of business directories and trade magazines.

In 1967 Pittsburgh Railways changed its name to Pittway because of the major changes in the direction of its business. Around the same time, company offices were relocated from Pittsburgh to Chicago, where the Harris family resided and directed its operations. With Neison Harris as president of Pittway and Irving Harris chairman of the board at Standard Shares, the two brothers collaborated in developing the core businesses of alarm systems, packaging, and publishing, and also expanded into real estate.

The company's packaging businesses, Barr and Seaquist, grew rapidly during the mid and late 1960s, largely due to the success of pressurized aerosol products. In 1968 management wanted to develop a presence in Europe in addition to entering the growing aerosol pump business. Seaquist subsequently acquired an interest in German aerosol valve manufacturer Perfect-Ventil GmbH and, two years later, purchased the French company Valois, a leading producer of perfume and pharmaceutical valves. The success of Perfect-Ventil impressed the Harris brothers, and they decided to make it a wholly owned subsidiary of Seaquist in 1971.

Pittway continued its diversification strategy by entering the real estate business in 1968. For $2.5 million, the Harris brothers acquired a ten percent equity position in Metropolitan Structures, a high-profile real estate developer in Chicago headed by Bernard Weissbourd. Metropolitan built office buildings, apartment buildings, industrial parks, and shopping centers. Much of the company's work, especially in Chicago, was done in cooperation with renowned architect Ludwig Mies van der Rohe. During the same time, the company also purchased a 50 percent interest in a huge apartment development project on Nuns Island near Montreal.

By the end of the 1960s, Pittway's success was indisputable. The company's four main divisions—the Alarm Device Division, the Barr/Stalfort Division, the Seaquist Division, and the

Industrial Publishing Division—grew from a total sales figure
of $46.4 million in 1965 to $61.8 in 1968, an average annual
increase of ten percent. Earnings for these same divisions grew
from the 1965 figure of $3.8 million to $8.7 million in 1968, an
average annual increase of 31 percent.

For Pittway, the success of the 1960s continued into the 1970s,
mitigated only by minor setbacks. In 1968 Industrial Publishing
acquired Patterson Publishing, and then augmented this purchase with Reinhold Publishing in 1974. These two companies
published highly regarded magazines such as *Hospitality, Progressive Architecture,* and *Air Transport World.* With the acquisition of Penton in 1976, a prestigious publisher of specialized
trade magazines, Pittway's Industrial Publishing became one of
the leading American magazine publishers.

Seaquist, and the entire aerosol filling industry, were hurt by the
negative press which surrounded the banning of fluorocarbons
and aerosols during the mid-1970s. Ecologists accused the
company of making aerosol propellants that destroyed the
ozone layer of the earth's atmosphere. Yet Seaquist's decision
in 1976 to expand into the dispensing cap business kept it in
financial health. A short time later, Seaquist Closures, one of
Seaquist's sub-divisions, rapidly developed into the leader of
what soon became a major packaging market. Around the same
time, Pittway acquired a 35 percent stake in the Pfeiffer Group,
a German producer of pumps for both the pharmaceutical and
perfume industries. As a result of these measures, Pittway was
able to increase its market share in the aerosol filling business
even though sales decreased by 17 percent.

BRK Electronics was purchased in 1970 to add ionization
smoke detectors to the product line at Ademco. With the expansion of the smoke detector business in the early 1970s, BRK
grew exponentially and, by 1975, had developed into a separate
division at Pittway. By 1977 BRK was the largest producer of
residential smoke detectors in the world, with sales peaking
at $84 million and operating profits at $32 million. Ademco
benefitted enormously from the acquisition of BRK and the
growing concern with crime prevention. In 1963, when
Ademco first became part of Pittway, sales and operating profits
were a mere $2 million and $800,000 respectively; by 1981
sales reached $96 million and operating profits had jumped to
$22.2 million.

The early 1980s did not look favorably on Pittway. With the
onset of a recession, BRK Electronics sales fell to $44 million
by 1980 and operating profits decreased to a mere $5 million.
Competition in the mature residential smoke alarm business
pushed the retail price of a smoke detector down from $49 to $9.
In the mid-1980s, however, BRK began to make a comeback
when smoke detector codes spurred the demand for residential
alarm detectors. BRK also expanded its manufacturing base by
designing such products as rechargeable flashlights, timers,
night lights, and fire extinguishers.

The fierce competition in the retail market for alarm equipment
spilled over into the commercial market, and Pittway's Ademco
profits nearly disappeared along with a substantial loss of its
market share. In 1984 Ademco rehauled its distribution policy
to cover items manufactured by competitors as well as those

produced internally. The company also expanded its network of
regional warehouses by acquiring a number of regional alarm
distribution companies. Management then created Ademco Distribution to handle its distribution business. By 1988 sales of
alarm equipment began once again to increase rapidly, and
Ademco Distribution was soon the leader in its field.

Pittway management also decided that Ademco needed to make
a significant investment in advanced alarm system products;
thus the company developed new product lines of control com-
municators, passive infrared motion sensors, short-range radio
devices, and long-range radio systems. A commitment to replacing older factory equipment was implemented, and the
company established a maquila plant in Juarez, Mexico to
provide it with relatively simple but labor intensive alarm components. Slowly Ademco garnered a reputation as a leading
manufacturer of innovative, high-quality alarm systems and
started to reclaim the market share it had lost during the early
part of the decade.

The publishing division of Pittway did not suffer at all during
the 1980s, nor did Seaquist. In fact, Pittway's Penton/Industrial
Publishing Company kept growing and improving its standing
in the national magazine specialty market. In 1985 the company
(now known as Penton) purchased *Millimeter.* In 1987 *American Machinist* and *33 Metal Producing* were also acquired,
along with *Electronics, Electronic Design, Electronic Design
International,* and *Microwaves & RF.* Penton also developed
successful magazines such as *Computer Aided Design* and
Foodservice Distributor internally. While Penton was adding
titles to its growing list of magazines, Seaquist was also busy
with acquisitions. Both Bielsteiner, a German producer of dispensing closures, and SAR, a leading Italian manufacturer of
aerosol pumps, were purchased during the decade, along with
interests in numerous small packaging companies throughout
Europe.

From 1988 to 1993, Pittway and Standard Shares embarked on a
comprehensive restructuring strategy to focus their combined
resources on businesses with the potential for solid and long-
term growth. The Harris family intended to shed unrelated
businesses in an attempt to strengthen the firm's financial position. Led by King Harris, Neison Harris's son, Pittway and
Standard Shares merged in November of 1989 to consolidate
operations under the name of Pittway Corporation. In 1991
Pittway sold Bielsteiner to the Pfeiffer Group. In 1992 the
company sold BRK Electronics and its consumer products
smoke detector and fire extinguisher sub-division, First Alert,
for $92.5 million to the division's management. The same year,
Barr was sold to Canada's CCL Industries. In 1993 Pittway was
given approval to spin off its Seaquist Packaging Group, which
then merged with the Pfeiffer Group to create a new public
company, AptarGroup.

By the end of 1993, Pittway's restructuring strategy left it with
two main businesses, alarm systems and publishing. Ademco
burglar alarms and security systems provided over 70 percent of
company revenues and nearly 80 percent of its operating profits.
The division of Penton Publishing trade magazines provide the
remainder of Pittway's revenues and operating profits. King
Harris views the streamlining of company operations as an

opportunity to bolster Ademco by means of a long-term, carefully conceived acquisition program designed to maintain its position as the leading seller of burglar alarms in the United States. Since Ademco represents most of the company's sales, the success of this program will largely determine the future of Pittway.

Further Reading:

Murphy, H. Lee, "Pittway Sounds the Alarm for Restructuring," *Crain's Chicago Business,* August 17, 1992, p. 34.

"Smoke Detectors: Hot Item in Fall Advertising," *Media Decision,* September 1977, pp. 66–69.

—Thomas Derdak

Pratt & Whitney

400 Main Street
East Hartford, Connecticut 06108
U.S.A.
(203) 565-4321
Fax: (203) 565-8377

*Wholly Owned Subsidiary of United Technologies
   Corporation*
Incorporated: 1925 as Pratt and Whitney Aircraft Company
Employees: 33,000
Sales: $6.9 billion
SICs: 3724 Aircraft Engines & Engine Parts

Pratt & Whitney is one of the largest aircraft engine manufacturers in the world. The company gained a leading position in the piston-driven aircraft engine market during the 1930s and made the transition to jet engines during the early 1950s. Today Pratt & Whitney manufactures only jet engines, while smaller engines and those for propeller aircraft are built by its Canadian sister company, Pratt & Whitney Canada.

Pratt & Whitney was organized principally by Edward Deeds, an Ohio businessman who had earlier founded National Cash Register (NCR) and Dayton Engineering Laboratories (Delco). In the early months of World War I, Deeds predicted that the United States would eventually enter the war and understood that European military products greatly surpassed those manufactured by the United States. He purchased the rights to the venerable Wright Brothers name and built a factory to produce aircraft engines for the coming war effort. Deeds was instrumental in the development of the Liberty engine, a giant, standardized, water-cooled 12-cylinder engine that was unsuitable for the light airframes produced at the time. Despite this fact, Deeds's Wright Company built more than 12,000 Liberties.

At the end of the war, the government cancelled its aircraft procurement program, bankrupting hundreds of manufacturers that had expanded in anticipation of government contracts. Deeds left the market in 1918, selling the Wright Company to Mack Truck, but Frederick Rentschler, Wright's president, maintained the company's role as a government supplier.

In 1924 the government requested development of a lighter air-cooled engine, but Wright's board refused Rentschler's funding request for its design. Rentschler resigned in protest, and months later joined Deeds and engineer George Mead in acquiring an interest in Pratt & Whitney, a gun manufacturer. Pratt & Whitney was founded in 1860 by two former employees of the Colt pistol factory, Francis Pratt and Amos Whitney; the latter was a cousin of Eli Whitney, the gunsmith and inventor of the cotton gin. The small company prospered by selling guns during the Civil War, and later expanded into machine tool production, but the glut of armaments after World War I forced the company to convert its factory into space for drying tobacco.

Investing its war profits, Pratt & Whitney funded George Mead to design a light air-cooled radial engine. If successful, the engine would be built by the newly formed Pratt & Whitney Aircraft. Mead's staff completed the engine, called the Wasp, before the end of 1925. It exceeded all expectations and won a strong recommendation from the head of the Navy's aeronautical section, Admiral William Moffett.

In June 1927, the government opened mail delivery contracts to private airline companies. This caught the attention of aircraft manufacturer Bill Boeing, who used the Wasp engine in his Model 40 aircraft. The combination worked so well that Boeing decided to go into the air mail business. Frederick Rentschler and Boeing, acquaintances since 1918, joined efforts in this and other endeavors, purchasing Pacific Air Transport in 1928.

Late in the summer of that year the two decided to merge their companies with Thomas Hamilton, a Milwaukee propeller maker, and Chance Vought, another aircraft manufacturer. The companies were incorporated on January 19, 1929, as the United Aircraft and Transport Company. Drawing on the tremendous public interest in aviation after Charles Lindbergh's solo flight across the Atlantic, public sale of the company's shares netted more than $14 million. Boeing, Rentschler, Mead, and a small group of investors became instant millionaires.

Rentschler, as United's president, used the company's newfound millions to fund a large-scale acquisition program. Purchases included Standard Steel Propeller; the Northrop design shop; Sikorsky, an amphibian builder; and Stearman, a private airplane builder. He also acquired several airline companies, including Stout Airlines, Varney Airlines, and National Air Transport, a major competitor. Combined with Boeing's existing air services, these companies were later grouped into a single unit called United Air Lines. When the stock market crashed in 1929, many aviation companies closed, but United remained financially secure. Indeed, the Depression facilitated Rentschler's plan to build a conglomeration of airplane manufacturers and suppliers because of these companies' reduced market values.

In 1930 Boeing's designers developed a fast new aircraft called the 247, which was fitted with Mead's newest engine, the Hornet. However, United's pilots balked at the difficult handling of the new craft. Rentschler, over Mead's objections, ordered the 247 to be scaled back. Transcontinental & Western Airways, a forerunner to TWA and competitor to United Air Lines, asked to purchase the Boeing 247, but was told it had to wait until Boeing completed building 60 models for United. In response, TWA invited bids for large scale production of any aircraft that could outperform the Boeing 247. The challenge was met by Donald Douglas, who developed the DC-2, which was powered by Curtiss-Wright's Cyclone engine, a strong rival to the Pratt & Whitney Hornet. By the time Boeing had completed its order for United, Douglas's DC-2 was on the market. The new model eliminated interest in the Boeing 247 and provided Douglas with the capital to incorporate improvements that led to the development of the highly successful DC-3.

In 1934 the government changed its rules regarding air mail delivery, stipulating that no aircraft holding company could qualify for a contract. This prompted Frederick Rentschler to diversify his company to avoid losing its most profitable business. He spun off the unprofitable Boeing Company, but retained Pratt & Whitney, Vought, Hamilton Standard, and Sikorsky under the United Aircraft umbrella.

After the Boeing 247 debacle, Curtiss-Wright, whose Cyclone engine powered the DC-3, was poised to surpass Pratt & Whitney as the nation's leading engine manufacturer. In a major coup, Rentschler won a $15 million engine order for the military, but his insistence on supplying propellers to Japan in defiance of a State Department request led the War Department to abruptly switch the order to another company.

Fortunately for Pratt & Whitney, several French and British delegations placed orders to help their military organizations maintain parity with their German counterparts. The business enabled Rentschler to build new plants and increase employment from 5,200 workers to more than 15,000. Furthermore, after President Franklin Delano Roosevelt called for an industry capable of producing 50,000 aircraft a year, Pratt & Whitney was assigned to supply the U.S. Navy with Wasp and Hornet engines. The company eventually built or leased factory space in seven additional plants, and by 1943 Pratt & Whitney employed 40,000 people. The company's engines powered the Grumman Hellcat, the B-24 bomber, the Vought Corsair, and the Curtiss Commando. By the end of the war, Pratt & Whitney had turned out 129,505 engines and its licensees had produced another 234,114.

At the end of World War II in 1945, the government cancelled more than 85 percent of its orders with Pratt & Whitney, representing more than $400 million worth of business. Rentschler laid off all but 6,000 workers. In the postwar period, Pratt & Whitney's plans included attempting to win support from the U.S. military or foreign governments for development of a jet engine, but the U.S. Navy purported to have no use for jets on its 200-foot carrier decks, and other support was not forthcoming. Rentschler decided to develop a jet engine without government backing, bearing the entire $15 million cost internally. The task was made easier after Pratt & Whitney was asked to build two Rolls-Royce jet engines as a subcontractor. The company built several models used for combat during the Korean War, but none that rivalled models by General Electric, Westinghouse, and Allison.

The company's competitors had built jet engines with up to 4,000 pounds of thrust, and were planning models capable of up to 7,000 pounds. In order to take the lead, Pratt & Whitney had to build an engine capable of producing even higher amounts of thrust. The engine designed to do so, the J57, was introduced in 1953, rated at 13,500 pounds of thrust. It was perfectly suited

for Boeing's new eight-engine B-52 bomber, then under development. The B-52 succeeded, and by 1956 the company was turning out nearly 3,000 jet engines a year. With the success of its J57, Pratt & Whitney was positioned to dominate the civilian aircraft engine market as it had the military.

With the encouragement of Pan Am's chairman, Juan Trippe, Boeing and Douglas began to augment the development of passenger jetliners. When the Boeing 707 and Douglas DC-8 entered service in the late 1950s, they both used Pratt & Whitney engines. This success helped establish Pratt & Whitney's place at the top of the nation's jet engine manufacturers, a position it would retain for 15 more years. The 707 and the DC-8 also provided the funding necessary for the development of another new design, the JT8D. This engine was created specifically for the Boeing 727, but ultimately powered the Douglas DC-9 and Boeing 737.

Pan Am's Trippe stayed involved in aircraft design, approaching Lockheed to modify its C-5 military cargo plane for use as a jumbo jetliner, the 747. Lockheed refused, and when Douglas suggested only a stretched version of its DC-8, Trippe turned to Boeing, which held a losing design for the C-5. Trippe insisted, however, that Boeing take full responsibility for delivering the aircraft on time.

Boeing was sure that any problem with the 747 would likely come from its engines, Pratt & Whitney JT9Ds. Jack Horner, Pratt & Whitney's new chairman, was forced to abide by subcontractor terms and cover Boeing for breach of contract if the engines did not work. Ultimately, the engines performed, and as demand grew for the 747, Pratt & Whitney had a second period of major prosperity, this time from commercial aircraft.

Despite the company's apparent financial success, it was criticized for what was seen as a growing arrogance and lack of focus on customer needs, as well as for having relied for too long on the success its JT8D. Realizing that some of the criticisms were justified, Pratt & Whitney began to pay closer attention to its customers' needs. General Electric began to make quick gains in the market, encroaching on Pratt & Whitney's market share. Pratt & Whitney's new chairman Robert Daniell began a new effort to win back the business the company had lost.

On the military side of the business, Pratt & Whitney provided J58 engines for Lockheed's SR-71 and J75s for the U-2 spy plane. The company's J52 was its military mainstay. In production for 30 years, the J52 was built for the Hound Dog missile in 1960, but later powered a series of naval aircraft. Pratt & Whitney was also asked to design an engine for a dual-purpose fighter-bomber eventually named the F-111. This jet was the brainchild of U.S. Defense Secretary Robert McNamara, who hoped to rein in separate development costs for the Navy and Air Force.

Disagreements between the U.S. Navy and Air Force loaded the plane with so much extra hardware that its performance was compromised, and Pratt & Whitney's engine for the F-111, the TF-30, was unsuccessful. The builders, General Dynamics and Grumman, blamed Pratt & Whitney for not producing a satisfactory engine on time. The F-111 made it into the air years behind schedule, discrediting McNamara and ushering in the era of "fly before you buy" design competitions. When improved, however, the TF-30 was also chosen for use in the Grumman F-14 Tomcat.

Pratt & Whitney's next project, the F-100, rivalled the JT9D, the engine used for the 747, for financial riskiness. Pratt & Whitney won a competition against General Electric to produce the F-100 for the U.S. Air Force and Navy. But after the failure of several prototypes, including one test stand explosion, Pratt & Whitney was liable for a complete and ruinously expensive redesign, without a government safety net.

At the same time, United Aircraft's new chairman, Harry Gray, resolved to lessen the company's reliance on aircraft engines. While Pratt & Whitney contributed 75 percent of United's total revenues, its business provided steadily decreasing margins. Gray subsequently diversified the company and changed its name to United Technologies in 1975. It was Gray and his attorneys who carefully examined Pratt & Whitney's fly-before-you-buy contract with the government and discovered a loophole that obligated the Pentagon to help fund corrections in the F-100. The engine was redesigned with slightly lower specifications and entered production powering McDonnell Douglas's F-15 and General Dynamics' F-16.

But the problems with the F-100 took years to correct, enabling General Electric to step in with an alternative, the F110. This engine powered all of America's leading fighter jets, including the F-15, F-16, and F-14. Eventually, GE's F110 gained 75 percent of the F-100's market. Pratt & Whitney developed new variants of its F-100, and slowly won back a quarter of the business it had lost to GE. It also developed a new engine, the F118, which was chosen to power Northrop's B-2 Stealth bomber.

In the military market, Pratt & Whitney began competing to power the Northrop/Lockheed Advanced Tactical Fighter, or ATF. The company's F119 challenged GE's F120 for an estimated $1 billion supply contract. In the commercial market, the company established an international partnership with the German Motoren und Turbinen Union and Italy's Fiat Avianzione. It developed the PW2037 for Boeing's 757, and the PW4000—designed specifically to compete with GE's CF6—for the 747 and 757.

Pratt & Whitney later formed a second consortium, called International Aero Engines, with MTU, Fiat, Rolls-Royce, and Japanese Aero Engines. The company's V2500 engine was used to power Airbus's A320.

During the mid-1980s, General Electric and Pratt & Whitney began work on jet-driven propeller engines called propfans. While slightly slower than conventional engines, the propfan was twice as fuel efficient as turbofans. Boeing and McDonnell Douglas tested propfans on a 727 and MD-80, and began development of two new twin-propfan designs, the 7J7 and MD-91.

By 1988 competition and deregulation drove commercial airlines into near bankruptcy, while fuel prices dropped. Airlines cancelled orders for hundreds of new aircraft, choosing instead to squeeze a few more years of service out of their existing fleets. As a result, airframe and engine manufacturers were forced to shelve the propfan indefinitely. Despite this, Boeing began planning a larger super twinjet, the 777, intended to compete with the MD-11. Pratt & Whitney's PW4000 was chosen as the launch engine for the 777.

While improvements in quality, increased attention to customers, and continued technological innovation served Pratt & Whitney well, external factors have damaged the company's business. With the end of the Cold War in 1991, defense appropriations in the United States were greatly reduced; at the same time, the number of commercial airlines continued to decline. Pratt & Whitney was forced to reduce its employment levels in 1993, with a goal of 30,000 workers by 1994.

Further Reading:

"United Technologies Goes in for a Little Engine Work," *Business Week,* October 21, 1991, pp. 108–10.
"Pratt & Whitney's Comeback Kid," *New York Times,* February 4, 1992, p. D1.
"United Technologies Posts Big Loss for 4th Quarter, Plans to Cut More Jobs," *Wall Street Journal,* January 27, 1993, p. A3.
"Pratt Could Use a Jump," *Business Week,* February 8, 1993, pp. 26–27.
Fernandez, Ronald, *Excess Profits: The Rise of United Technologies,* Reading, Massachusetts: Addison-Wesley, 1983.
Kaplan, Ellen, ed., *In the Company of Eagles,* Pratt & Whitney: Stanford, Connecticut, 1990.

—John Simley

Premier Industrial Corporation

4500 Euclid Avenue
Cleveland, Ohio 44103
U.S.A.
(216) 391-8300
Fax: (216) 391-0155

Public Company
Incorporated: 1946
Employees: 4,400
Sales: $640.84 million
Stock Exchanges: New York Montreal
SICs: 5065 Electronic Parts and Equipment; 5072 Hardware;
 5063 Electrical Apparatus and Equipment; 3450 Screw
 Machine Products, Bolts, etc.; 3452 Bolts, Nuts, Screws,
 Rivets and Washers; 2842 Polishes and Sanitation Goods;
 2992 Lubricating Oils and Greases; 3429 Hardware, nec;
 3569 General Industrial Machinery, nec; 6719 Holding
 Companies, nec.

Premier Industrial Corporation is one of the United States'
largest broad-line electronics distributors. It has a record of
conservative yet outstanding performance: record earnings in
31 of 33 years as a publicly-traded company, and a balance
sheet with 30 percent cash. Despite more than a dozen acquisitions, Premier Industrial Corporation has never been more than
$13 million in debt.

Premier started out as a distributor of general automotive supplies, but quickly began to focus on specialized, high-margin
parts. In the 1960s, the company diversified into fire-fighting
equipment, lubricants and coatings, and, most significantly,
electronics. During the 1970s, electrical specialty parts became
an increasingly important segment of Premier's business, until
1981, when the division emerged as its primary profit center.
In the last decade of the twentieth century, 70 percent of Premier's revenues and operating profits came from electronics
distribution.

The company was established in 1940 as Premier Automotive
Supply Company when three brothers—Morton, Jack, and Joseph Mandel—bought their uncle's storefront auto parts distributorship for $900. Morton, a 19-year-old college dropout and
the youngest brother, gravitated toward administrative duties,
while his older brothers honed their sales and marketing skills.

In these early years of automotive repair, the Mandels soon
learned of a class of parts that were hard to come by because
they were hard to describe. The brothers would locate a supplier
of these "thingamajigs" and carry them around in cigar boxes
so customers could pick out the part they needed.

In 1946, the company was incorporated as Premier Industrial
Corporation The name change clarified an ongoing shift from
standard automotive parts to specialized industrial maintenance
products. The fledgling company grew relatively slowly during
its first two decades, but cultivated a reputation for first-rate
service and innovation. Even though the company did not
manufacture most of the items it sold, Premier worked with its
suppliers to customize parts for its clients. The company would
even offer to reorganize and resupply a customer's entire inventory of fasteners, including the bins for storing parts. These
early efforts were the foundation of the company's longstanding
"find a need and fill it" philosophy.

The two older Mandels, Joe and Jack, were responsible for
many product and marketing innovations. Joe was instrumental
in making Premier one of the first companies to develop rust-
resistant plating for most of its fasteners. Until then, nuts, bolts,
and screws had been black in color and rusted easily. Fastener
plating soon become an industry standard. The Mandels' marketing tactics were ingenious, if a little primitive by today's
standards: they sewed Premier parts onto felt books for a
display that was much tidier than a cigar box of nuts and bolts.
But by the mid-1950s, Premier's roster of products had grown
to include three divisions: Premier Fastener Co., which sold
screws, nuts, bolts, washers, cotter pins, rivets, and specialty
hardware; Premier Autoware Division, which sold brake parts,
gaskets, fuel pump apparatus, automatic transmission components and repair kits; and the Certanium Alloys and Research
Co., which sold welding equipment and supplies. The display
books weighed so much that some ingenious sales reps attached
wheels to the books, prompting Premier to publish its first
illustrated catalog.

By 1960, when Premier went public, sales revenues stood at
$12.6 million. Sales volume had increased one and one-half
times from 1953 to 1960, and earnings almost tripled during the
same time. Although Premier still did no manufacturing, the
products it purchased from over 300 suppliers were made to
exacting specifications and sold under the company's brand
names. For example, Premier's Supertanium alloy cap screw
had a reputation for strength and durability that earned it a place
in auto racing history. After the death of an Indianapolis 500
driver was traced to a broken fastener, the U.S. Auto Club asked
Premier to supply a more reliable product. In 1960, the company began supplying Supertanium nuts and bolts to Indy drivers at the track's Gasoline Alley. Premier's trademark fasteners
registered an uninterrupted safety record.

After twenty years in business, Premier began to expand its
distribution network and diversify through acquisitions. The
company launched a Canadian division in 1960, and purchased
Akron Brass Manufacturing Co. for $6 million in cash and stock
in 1962. Within two years, this manufacturer of fire-fighting
nozzles, hose controls, couplings and valves completed a new
$100,000 research center in Wooster, Ohio. Akron Brass con-

tributed 20 percent of Premier's sales by mid-decade. In 1964, Premier acquired J.I. Holcomb Manufacturing Co. for $10 million from Butler University. This manufacturer compounded its own cleaners, deodorizers, insecticides, waxes and brushes.

Premier's growth during the 1960s was also fueled by the introduction of new and innovative products. In 1967, Akron Brass expanded into couplings for the petroleum and cement industries while orders for its Turbo-Jet fire-fighting nozzles were backlogged. Akron Brass' sales doubled from 1962 to 1967, and 25 percent of its annual volume came from items introduced during that time. The company's business was augmented with the purchase of Western Fire Equipment Co., a producer and supplier of fire-fighting products for government forestry service agencies, in 1968. Premier's "bread-and-butter" line of industrial maintenance products grew to 10,000 items during this period, and the company's distribution network was expanded through new warehouses in Atlanta and Dallas.

The company's 1968 purchase of Chicago-based Newark Electronics Co. for about $6.5 million marked a turning point for Premier. Newark would eventually bring Premier unparalleled growth, but the Mandels first had to turn their new acquisition around. At the time it was acquired, Newark's operations were characterized by poor organizational structure and uninspired marketing. Premier revamped Newark's management, expanded distribution geographically, and boosted sales efforts. The Mandels also shifted Newark's customer base from original equipment manufacturers (OEMs) to the replacement and maintenance market and dropped the manufacturer's high-volume products to concentrate on niche items. The turnaround temporarily cut into Premier's profits, but proved to be one of the company's best investments.

The recessionary 1970s caused Premier to look inward for continued profitability and growth. In some respects, the company was able to thrive during tough economic times because its customers were more likely to repair equipment—using Premier's maintenance products, of course—than purchase new machinery. Premier's diversified markets of products and customers also shielded it from the vacillations of a particular market or the margin-reducing demands of a specific client or supplier.

Premier was forced to tighten its operations somewhat during the 1970s, introducing tighter inventory controls through an improved computer system, for example. But the nature of the business, not to mention the conservative management of the company, allowed Premier's growth to continue nearly uninterrupted throughout the decade. One key to the company's growth was its ability to expand product lines quickly, yet with relatively low startup costs, by simply finding a high-quality, low-cost supplier.

The Newark Electronics division grew dramatically over the course of the 1970s. By 1977, Newark had 53 branches. By the end of the decade, the number of Newark branches had grown to 120, and the division's contribution to annual profits had increased from 17 percent in 1976 to 32 percent just two years later, and to 42 percent in 1980.

Premier was also able to expand internationally during the decade, establishing operations in the United Kingdom, Holland, Belgium, West Germany and France. By 1975, international sales contributed five percent of the company's annual revenues. The enlargement of Premier's salesforce to 1,200 representatives also helped the company's annual sales to triple over the course of the decade, from $103.16 million in 1970 to $317 million in 1980. Premier's commitment to service and quality allowed it to command premium prices that more than quadrupled the company's net income over the same period, from $6.58 million to $31.3 million.

This decade of internal growth and conservative management gave Premier an enviable balance sheet: only $220,000 in long-term debt and $19.4 million in cash and temporary investments. The Mandels were ready for another round of capital investments and acquisitions in the early 1980s to augment the electronics group. Newark opened 30 new sales branches from 1979 to 1981 and distributed a new catalog. In 1981, the electronics division was enlarged with the purchase of Car-lac Electronic Industrial Sales Inc. of Bohemia, New York, a national distributor of electronic components for OEM and maintenance with sales of $10 million annually. The following year, the company acquired Hoffman Industrial Products Inc. of Farmingdale, New York. This supplier of electrical connectors and terminals with $6 million in annual sales helped make electronics Premier's primary business. The acquisitions continued in 1984, when Premier purchased MCM Electronics of Dayton. This distributor helped Premier penetrate the computer-, television-, and stereo-repair markets, and brought another $8 million in annual sales to the balance sheet. By the mid-1980s, Premier had completed its evolution from a focus on automotive replacement parts to industrial maintenance items to electrical components. The Newark Electronics division had grown to become America's largest broad-line electronics distributor and its catalog was considered the industry "bible."

By 1986, Premier stocked the broadest product line in its industry, with more than 100,000 items and deep inventories that permitted 90 percent of orders to be shipped within 24 hours of placement. In spite of its impressive growth, Premier had retained its reputation for service by providing products quickly and reliably. Frequent internal audits, inspections, and recognition of employees who performed well helped maintain the Mandel's high standards. Customers were willing to pay Premier's premium prices for the service and quality they had come to expect. These high standards—and the premium prices they entailed—had made Premier the most profitable of all the major electronics distributors, even though it was the seventh-largest in terms of sales.

Premier's success and growth brought the Mandel brothers, who consistently owned about 60 percent of the company's stock, a great deal of personal wealth. Their philanthropic efforts garnered local and national recognition. Morton Mandel and Premier were instrumental in the creation of Cleveland's Mid-Town Corridor in 1982. The organization was formed to revitalize a one-square-mile area of downtown through business expansion and new development. Within four years, over 100 companies had located in the area, and the project was recognized with the third annual George S. Dively national award for the promotion of urban development. The Mandels also contributed to local education through the funding of a School of Social Work and a Center for Management of Non-profit Organizations, both at Case Western Reserve University.

As the still-vital Mandel brothers advanced in age, industry observers and analysts began to speculate about succession at Premier, especially about who would follow Morton Mandel, chairman and chief executive officer. They got one hint in 1987, when the company's top management was restructured and two young executives, Philip S. Sims and Bruce W. Johnson, were promoted to executive vice-presidencies. Both men retained their respective duties as treasurer and chief financial officer and head of Newark Electronics. Then, in 1991, Sims was awarded a vice chair on Premier's board, and Johnson was named president-elect. The Mandels planned to retain their 60 percent stock holdings as a valuable family legacy.

Premier glided through a late-1980s, early-1990s recession with predictable ease. By 1991, the company had $226 million in working capital and $52 million in cash and cash equivalents. Premier hadn't made an acquisition since 1984, but planned to expand its Newark Electronics subsidiary into Europe. International sales accounted for ten percent of Premier's annual sales in the early 1990s, and the company hoped to increase that segment to 30 percent by 2003. Premier also hoped to continue its growth through acquisition.

Principal Subsidiaries: D-A Lubricant Co. Inc.; Premier Industrial Corporation (Indiana); Newark Electronics Corp.; Premierco Service Corp.; PIC Corp.; MCM Electronics Inc.; Premier Foreign Sales Corp. Inc.; Premier Fastener Ltd.; Certanium B.V.; Premier Industrial Holland B.V.; Premier Industrial Belgium S.A.; Premier Industrial (UK) Ltd.; N.V. Certanium Services S.A.; Premier Industrial France S.A.R.:.; Premier Industrial Deutschaland GmbH; Premierco Espana S.L.; Premier Industrial Italia S.R.L.

Further Reading:

Byrne, Harlan S, "Premier Industrial," *Barron's,* February 1, 1993, pp. 43–44.

"Feeling Pretty Good: Premier Industrial Is Cheery about the Profits Outlook," *Barron's,* May 11, 1981, pp. 59–61.

Fraker, Susan, "Making a Mint in Nuts and Bolts," *Fortune,* August 22, 1983, pp. 131–133.

Gerdel, Thomas W., "Premier Credits Success to Fast Customer Service," *Plain Dealer* (Cleveland), August 19, 1986, pp. 1C, 5C.

Gleisser, Marcus, "Premier Finds the Need and Fills It," *Plain Dealer* (Cleveland), February 17, 1983, p. 10D; "Premier Weighs Expansion Plans, *Plain Dealer* (Cleveland), January 16, 1986, p. 2E; "Reputation for Service Makes This Premier," *Plain Dealer* (Cleveland), October 10, 1988, p. 6B.

Koshar, John Leo, "Staying in City: Premier Grows along Euclid Ave.," *Plain Dealer* (Cleveland), February 21, 1980, p. 5C.

"New Peak Seems on Tap for Premier Industrial," *Barron's,* November 7, 1977.

"Premier Industrial Boasts Broad Mix and Steady Growth," *Barron's,* June 2, 1975, pp. 40–41.

"Premier Industrial Slated to Maintain Growth Rate," *Barron's,* August 7, 1967, pp. 25, 29.

"Results at Premier Industrial Corp. Head for All-time Highs This Year," *Barron's,* August 1, 1960, pp. 20–21.

Rudolph, Barbara, "Sounds Trite, but so Does 'I Love You,' " *Forbes,* March 1, 1982, p. 66.

Sabath, Donald, "Premier Industrial Looks to Expand Abroad," *Plain Dealer* (Clevcland), October 10, 1992, p. 2F.

Talbott, Stephen, "Companies with Future: Premier Industrial, Pioneer-Standard Find Selling Electronics Parts Promises Solid Growth," *Plain Dealer* (Cleveland), November 23, 1980, p. 1E.

"Wider Scope Pays Off for Premier Industrial," *Barron's,* July 26, 1965, p. 20.

Yerak, Rebecca, "The Premier Saga of the Brothers Mandel," *Plain Dealer* (Cleveland), July 29, 1990, pp. 1E, 4E; "Premier Promotes Longtime Managers in Succession Hint," *Plain Dealer* (Cleveland), October 9, 1991, p. 1H.

—April S. Dougal

Price Waterhouse

1251 Avenue of the Americas
New York, NY 10020
U.S.A.
(212) 819-5000
Fax: (212) 790-6620

Private Company
Incorporated: 1988
Employees: 49,000
Sales: $3.89 billion
SICs: 8721 Accounting, Auditing & Bookkeeping Services;
  8742 Management Consulting Services

Price Waterhouse holds a reputation as the most traditional and dignified of the big six accounting firms. This reputation has helped it attract more Fortune 100 clients than any other accounting firm.

The firm was founded in London in 1850 by Samuel Lowell Price, who wanted to take advantage of England's recent parliamentary laws requiring the examination of a company's financial statements and records. The public accounting profession was growing so rapidly during these years that in 1865 Price took on a partner, Edwin Waterhouse, to help with the expanding business. During the late 1860s and 1870s, while primarily working on arbitrations, bankruptcies, and liquidations, Price and Waterhouse also developed a practice of introducing borrowers to prospective lenders. At this time, many privately-owned businesses were converted to public companies and, consequently, reports on earnings signed by reputable accountants soon became an indispensable ingredient in any firm's prospectus.

As the nineteenth century drew to a close, the firm of Price Waterhouse had garnered a reputation in Britain as one of the leaders of auditing, accounting, and financial consulting services. And, as many of its European clients established operations in the United States, Price Waterhouse sent its own representatives to evaluate the business ventures and opportunities they were financing in order to protect investments and shareholders' interests. Although Price had died in 1887, business in the former colonies was so significant that Waterhouse made the commitment to establish a permanent American presence. On September 1, 1890, the American branch of the company opened an office at 45 Broadway Avenue in New York City.

A talented member of the London staff, Lewis D. Jones, was the first office manager in New York. Faced with developing clients over an enormous territory that included North, Central, and South America, and serving the needs of diverse industries such as brewing, mining, steel, railroad, leather, and packing, Jones soon required an assistant. Another member of the firm from London, William J. Caesar, arrived and opened a Chicago office the following year. Caesar's aggressive style and management ability soon earned him the leadership of the U.S. operation.

At the turn of the century Arthur Lowes Dickinson succeeded Caesar; it was Dickinson who made the United States office a uniquely American firm in both outlook and operation. Rather than continuing the practice of bringing accountants from Britain to serve clients in America, Dickinson focused on hiring native talent. Dickinson also encouraged his employees to develop their professional creativity. This quest to break new ground in accounting methods and procedures led to the firm's creation of consolidated financial statements. After Price Waterhouse consolidated the accounts of U.S. Steel, the method gained industrywide acceptability.

The financial report for U.S. Steel was the very first to include supporting statements and time schedules that reflected significant balance sheet accounts, such as inventories and long-term debt, and to provide information on assets, operating funds, payroll statistics, and additional facts of interest to stockholders. By this method of fair disclosure, Price Waterhouse set the standard for financial reporting at the beginning of the twentieth century. Price Waterhouse was also the first to provide client shareholders with quarterly financial data and, in 1903, while the firm conducted its first municipal audit, it also pioneered efforts to survey the accounting and audit systems of government organizations. These accomplishments drew attention to accountancy and the role of public accountants in a rapidly developing industrialized economy.

As a young accountant working on the Price Waterhouse's audit of Eastman Kodak, George O. May so attracted the attention of George Eastman that Eastman offered him a job. May refused and twenty-odd years later, while Eastman was visiting May's office, Eastman remarked, "What a mistake you would have made had you accepted." May, whom many people regard as the father of the accounting profession in the United States, assumed leadership of Price Waterhouse in 1910.

May opened many new offices throughout the United States, and developed new services for clients. In 1913, immediately after Congress enacted a federal income tax, May initiated a tax practice. He also encouraged the firm to provide services for emerging industries, such as the motion picture and automobile industries. It was under May's stewardship that the firm was contracted to handle the balloting of the Academy Awards in 1935 to assure the honesty of the voting process.

Primarily remembered for his devotion to public service, May campaigned relentlessly during the 1920s for Congress to enact laws stipulating that publicly traded companies adopt standard auditing methods and accounting procedures. May secured the New York Stock Exchange as a client of Price Waterhouse, and his work there in the late 1920s and early 1930s led to the formulation and passage of the Securities Exchange Act of

1934. He retired in 1940 and devoted the remainder of his life to writing about the accounting profession.

During the 1940s, the firm faced its first major crisis. A highly profitable drug wholesaler, McKesson & Robbin, Inc., was the victim of an embezzlement scheme carried out by a senior executive and the man's three brothers. The scheme, extremely complex and carefully conceived, eluded detection by the independent auditors from Price Waterhouse. Although a subsequent investigation indicated that the firm's auditing procedures were in strict compliance with the law and the industry's professional standards, the inability of the auditors to discover the embezzlement was of concern to both the firm and the industry at large.

When senior partner John C. Scobie, a Scotsman with a reputation for being scrupulously honest, became head of the firm, he implemented new auditing procedures which were designed to provide auditors with more access to a client's operations. Scobie's plan was to improve the auditor's ability to evaluate whether accounting data reflected the actual performance of any given company; this, in turn, would enable auditors to provide advice to clients on the many operational factors that influence financial results.

After World War II, overseas expansion and investment by companies previously maintaining a national or even regional profile led to the demand for Price Waterhouse to develop a stronger international organization. During this period, the first U.S. senior partner, Percival F. Brundage, and a native New Zealander, John B. Inglis, acted as co-leaders of the firm. Their strategy was twofold: to initiate broader national and international approaches to serving the needs of clients and to build and improve the firm's operational structure.

In concert with the British arm of the organization, the Price Waterhouse International Firm—which promoted uniform accounting standards for all Price Waterhouse offices around the world—was established in late 1945. A management consulting service, MCS, otherwise known as the systems department, was founded in 1946 as part of the evolution of manual accounting systems the firm had been developing for various clients throughout the years. The importance of electronic data became increasingly obvious during the war, and the leadership at Price Waterhouse was quick to recognize the advent of the computer age. Full-time auditors and data processing professionals were hired to design charts for account and pro forma financial statements, develop accounting and various financial systems, and provide advice on productivity improvements. During these years, Price Waterhouse was called upon more and more to recommend the kinds of systems used to organize and produce financial and management information.

When Brundage resigned as senior partner in 1954 to accept a position in the Eisenhower Administration, John Inglis took over sole command and guided the firm into an era of specialization. Since clients more frequently needed nonauditing services, Inglis created four specialized divisions, including accounting research, international tax, SEC review, and an international department. Following the comprehensive revision of the U.S. tax code in 1954, the tax department developed into one of the most important of the firm. The firm's success was

indisputable—in 1959 its gross income was nearly $28.5 million.

Inglis retired in 1960 and was replaced by Herman W. Bevis, a brilliant theoretician and writer, who garnered a reputation for leading the debates on the controversial issues of the day, such as deferred taxation and investment tax credits. He led Price Waterhouse through an enormous period of expansion. Within the United States, federal, state and local governments became important clients of the firm's services. In the international arena, Price Waterhouse was sought after by many companies to supply information on foreign business practices, taxes, and government regulations, and to help assess the comparability of financial statements. The firm also helped companies such as Toyota and Sony secure capital from American financial markets by making sure their financial statements were in full compliance with the requirements of the Securities and Exchange Commission.

From its earliest days, Price Waterhouse's elite image had helped the firm bring in blue-chip corporations. Oil and steel industry giants had always been high profile clients, and over the years their presence prompted more and more blue-chip companies to want to share in the prestige of the firm. By the time John C. Biegler became U.S. chairman in 1969, Price Waterhouse counted almost 100 of the Fortune 500 as clients.

Yet Biegler's appointment came at a time of dramatic changes not only for Price Waterhouse but for the accounting profession itself. The expanding economy the firm knew since World War II had suddenly vanished, and a creeping inflation and slow national growth ushered in recession. Dramatic drops in the stock market and futures exchanges during 1970 led to a decade of financial instability. Moreover, many of the big eight accounting firms were served with lawsuits from disgruntled owners of failed businesses. These problems led directly to an increased competition for clients among all the accounting firms. As a result, Price Waterhouse could no longer rely on its reputation and high-quality work to secure accounts. In order to compete more effectively for clients, the firm was forced to develop aggressive hard-sell marketing techniques, expand the scope and range of its services, and reduce fees.

When Joseph E. Connor replaced Biegler to lead the firm in 1978, he succeeded in implementing a specific market-driven strategy which had immediate payoffs. Connor developed "industry services groups" which were comprised of specialists with extensive knowledge and experience in various industries. This strategy helped bring in new clients. Expanding services in the firm's traditional areas of tax, audit and management consulting also helped retain many previous clients.

Notwithstanding the success of his strategy, in 1984 Connor met with chairman Charlie Steel and discussed a merger with Deloitte Haskins & Sells, another of the big eight accounting firms, widely known in accounting circles as the "auditors' auditor." The intention behind the merger was to create an organization of such proportions that no other accounting firm could ever again gain a competitive advantage. A letter of intent was signed on October 11, 1984, and, conditional upon the approval of the partners, the merger would take place on January 1, 1985. Yet despite Connor and Steele's confidence in the benefits of such a union, when the balloting was finished the U.S. partners of Price Waterhouse approved while the influential British part of the firm vetoed the merger. For both men, it was a personal and professional defeat. Steel was forced to resign in 1986, while Connor remained as chairman of the U.S. firm until he was replaced in 1988 by Shaun F. O'Malley.

The failure of the proposed merger between Price Waterhouse and Deloitte had raised the possibility of creating a giant accounting firm, and many of the big eight partners discussed little else beside potential mergers. After Ernst & Whinney merged with Arthur Young on June 22, 1989, to create Ernst and Young, within weeks four other firms announced plans to merge: Deloitte Haskins & Sells with Touche Ross, and Price Waterhouse with Arthur Anderson.

The proposed merger between Price Waterhouse and Anderson seemed doomed from the start. The Anderson people thought the new firm should be named Arthur Anderson while the Price Waterhouse people thought it should be named Price Waterhouse; Anderson thought it would be acquiring an auditing practice while Price Waterhouse thought it was acquiring a consulting practice, but neither firm wanted to give the impression that its services were "acquired" by the other; and finally, O'Malley and Anderson's chairman, Larry Weinbach, were new in their positions and just starting to implement development and marketing strategies for their own respective firms. O'Malley and Weinbach agreed to halt merger negotiations after three months.

The year 1990 did not begin auspiciously for Price Waterhouse. In May, a federal judge ordered Price Waterhouse to offer a partnership and nearly $400,000 in back pay to Ann B. Hopkins, who claimed that she had been denied a promotion to partner on grounds of sexual discrimination. In November of the same year, a British bank, Standard Charter PLC, sued the firm for negligence in failing to provide an accurate financial accounting during the acquisition of United Bank of Arizona in 1987. Financial analysts interpreted this latter action as another setback for the accounting industry in the United States: more than $3 billion in damage claims had already been brought against accounting firms by regulatory agencies during the collapse of many savings and loan associations.

Entering the 1990s, Price Waterhouse had been expanding its services to clients. The firm offered accounting, tax, and consulting products and services in relation to information systems technology, corporate finance, financial services, petroleum, public utilities, retailing, entertainment, and other industries. With the highest partner earnings and more blue-chip clients—including IBM, USX, J.P. Morgan, Westinghouse, and Shell Oil—than any of the other big six U.S. accounting firms, the partners at Price Waterhouse may not seem worried about the firm's future. But as its blue-chip client base shows signs of shrinking, and with its sterling image tarnished by two aborted merger attempts, Price Waterhouse will have to fight vigorously for smaller clients and market itself aggressively to survive in the modern world of consulting services.

Further Reading:

Allen, David Grayson, and Kathleen McDermott, *Accounting for Success: A History of Price Waterhouse in America, 1890–1990,* Cambridge, Massachusettes: Harvard Business School Press, 1993.
O'Malley, Shaun F., *Price Waterhouse: 100 Years of Service in the United States,* New York: Newcomen Society, 1990, pp. 1–28.
Stevens, Mark, *The Big Eight,* New York: MacMillan Publishing Co., Inc., 1981, pp. 10–12, 38–42, 70–72.
——, *The Big Six,* New York: Simon and Schuster, 1991, pp. 175–182, 195–199, 236–243.

—Thomas Derdak

PR·Ọ·M·U S ®

C O M P A N I E S

Promus Companies, Inc.

1023 Cherry Road
Memphis, Tennessee 38117
U.S.A.
(901) 762-8600
Fax: (901) 762-8637

Public Company
Incorporated: 1954 as Holiday Inns of America, Inc.
Employees: 23,000
Sales: $1.03 billion
Stock Exchanges: New York
SICs: 7011 Hotels, Motels; 7999 Amusement and Recreation
  Nec

Promus is one of the United States' leading hotel and casino companies, although it is known to the public mainly through its subsidiaries, which include Harrah's, Embassy Suites, Hampton Inns, and Homewood Suites. Until 1990 Promus had been known as the Holiday Corporation, named for its largest subsidiary, the Holiday Inn hotel chain. But that year, the British brewing company Bass plc purchased the hotel chain, prompting the Holiday Corporation to change its name to Promus.

Since that time, Promus has continued to expand in the profitable casino gambling industry (called "gaming" by its proponents) and through a number of niche-market hotel chains. The company's success in these areas has come despite anemic growth in the hospitality industry in general.

Promus got its start after World War II, when the American economy launched into an unprecedented era of growth. With the proliferation of affordable automobiles, cheap gas, and the development of a national highway system, families began taking vacations in their new cars. With encouraging slogans like "See America first," and "See the USA in your Chevrolet," tourists set out to see the corners of the country. Kemmons Wilson, a Memphis-based real estate developer, saw the rise in automobile tourism as an opportunity to create a huge market for a chain of motor hotels, dubbed "motels," to be strategically located along major highways. In 1952 he built the first of these lodges in Memphis and called it Holiday Inn.

Wilson built additional motels along frequently travelled routes and designed them as affordable stopover locations for those on route to their destination. The Holidays Inns used a uniform

color scheme and a trapezoidal neon sign that soon came to signify a clean, comfortable room with few amenities. In fact, many of the hotels shared the same blueprints; thus, customers knew exactly what to expect at each location. To support the growth of the chain, Wilson created a holding company called Holiday Inns of America, Inc., in 1954. The firm managed financing and franchise agreements and worked to maintain uniform standards of cleanliness and service. First-time lodgers were queried on their destinations, allowing Holiday Inn to determine the best locations for additional hotels. It also gave the chain an opportunity to advise travelers of the location of other Holiday Inns along the way.

Holiday Inns of America went public in 1957, assuring the growing company access to private investors. The share issues were well received, helping Holiday Inn to accelerate construction across the country. This vast expansion was made possible by President Eisenhower's massive interstate highway project. Existing mom-and-pop motels, the primary competition for Holiday Inns in the early years, found themselves by-passed by the new freeway systems and went out of business.

In 1963, with hundreds of Holiday Inns now dotting the map, Wilson's company gained a listing on the New York Stock Exchange, giving it access to institutional investors. This allowed Wilson to develop Holiday Inns in other countries and make improvements on existing motels. Restaurants and swimming pools were added. Gradually, the chain shed its motel image in favor of a more upscale roadside hotel.

Wilson, who was credited with inventing the concept of hotel franchising, witnessed the opening of the 1000th Holiday Inn in 1968. A year later, hoping to diversify into related businesses, Holiday Inns of America acquired the Trailways bus company and Delta Steamship Lines. These companies funnelled tourists to Holiday Inns on package deals. After acquiring these companies, the parent company changed its name to Holiday Inns, Inc. Holiday Inns' growth slowed slightly during the 1970s as other hotel chains entered the market. In addition, much of the interstate highway system had been completed, and the market began to level off. The growth of airline traffic also affected Holiday Inn by limiting the number of vacationers and businesspeople who traveled by car. To combat this trend, Holiday Inns were established near airports, where customers could easily catch flights.

Kemmons Wilson retired in 1979 and was succeeded as chairman and CEO by Roy E. Weingardner. He and the company's new president, Michael D. Rose, made the first of many bold shifts in Holiday Inns' growth strategy that year by acquiring a 40-percent interest in River Boat Casino, a gambling operation located next to the Holiday Inn in Las Vegas.

The company also acquired Perkins Cake & Steak, a growing chain of family restaurants formulated on the same strategy as Holiday Inn—identical establishments with similar menus and uniform quality standards. During this time, Weingardner and Rose decided to sell off the Trailways bus business because bus travel had fallen out of favor with travelers.

By far the boldest change in Holiday Inns' strategy came in February 1980 when the company acquired the Harrah's hotel and casino business. Harrah's was established as a bingo parlor in Reno, Nevada, in 1937 by Bill Harrah. At the time Nevada was the only state in the country where gambling was legal. The bingo operation netted Harrah a modest income, which he used to establish a larger operation, Harrah's Club, in 1946.

In 1955 and 1956, Harrah took over several clubs in the town of Stateline, on the Nevada side of Lake Tahoe. In 1959 Harrah expanded his Lake Tahoe operation, adding new games and luxurious parlors that were frequented by the rich and famous. In competition with casino operators in Las Vegas, Harrah rapidly expanded his properties, with an 8500-square foot addition at Lake Tahoe in 1964 and a 400-room hotel tower and club in Reno.

Harrah's company went public in 1971, and the following year it gained a listing on the American Stock Exchange. Offering a beautiful resort destination, premium quality accommodations, gambling, and top name entertainment, Harrah's became synonymous with high living. It was also a terrific investment. Unencumbered by the alleged gangster reputations in Las Vegas, Bill Harrah cultivated a strong reputation for financial responsibility and excellent management.

The listing helped Harrah to finance additional expansions at Lake Tahoe in 1973 and 1976. But Harrah died in 1978, leaving the company with a more consensus-oriented leadership. That year, the company's board elected to build a hotel and casino in Atlantic City, New Jersey, where gambling had recently been legalized. For the first time, Harrah's would compete in the same city as the Las Vegas interests.

Although Harrah's remained profitable, it lacked a strong leader. Concentrated in only three markets and in a narrow line of business, the company needed to diversify. That opportunity came in 1980 when Holiday Inn offered to purchase Harrah's.

In November of that year, Harrah's opened a 506-room hotel in Atlantic City, which included a 44,000-square foot casino. When Michael Rose succeeded Weingardner as CEO of Holiday Inn in April 1981, he spun off the Delta Steamship company and purchased the 60 percent of River Boat Casino the company did not already own. Management of the casino was turned over to Harrah's.

Meanwhile, Holiday Inns' image began to falter and it faced increased competition from chains such as Ramada, Marriott, Hilton, and Hyatt, who were eating away at Holiday's middle-market traveller.

Rather than remake the Holiday Inn image, Rose launched two new hotel chains in an attempt to corner the up-and-coming niche markets. The Embassy Suites chain, featuring only suite-sized hotel rooms, was created in February 1983. Shortly after, the company founded Hampton Inns, a chain of budget hotels. Both chains became operational in 1984. That year the parent company acquired Granada Royale Hometels, another suite chain, and merged it with Embassy. In 1985 it acquired a 50-percent interest in the Brock Residence Inn chain.

Holiday Inns, the parent company, underwent several changes in 1985. Rose, who succeeded Weingardner as chairman in 1983, oversaw the issue of 6.3 million new shares of stock, which were purchased by the corporation. In May, shareholders approved a name change to Holiday Corporation, and in July a new world headquarters in Memphis opened. In November, the Holiday Corporation sold its interest in Perkins to the Tennessee Restaurant Company in exchange for an equity share in the company.

In 1986 developer Donald Trump announced he had acquired five percent of Holiday Corporation shares in an apparent takeover attempt. Trump was drawn by the fact that a 1983 appraisal valued the company at $2.7 billion. While the company's worth had appreciated, its market value was only $1.5 billion. Rose responded with a brutal poison-pill defense. He arranged a leveraged recapitalization in which the company took on a staggering $2.4 billion in new debt—half of it in junk bonds. Two thirds of the money was used to pay a $65-per share dividend, but now Holiday Corporation had a negative net worth of $800 million, rendering it an unattractive takeover target. Trump took the huge dividend, cashed in his stock, and went away.

The recapitalization left Holiday's top managers with a ten percent share of the company (Rose himself held 2.3 percent). The company sold its interest in Residence Inns and opened the new Bill's Casino in Lake Tahoe. In March of 1988 it also founded a fourth hotel chain aimed at extended-stay travellers called Homewood Suites. Harrah's and the company's other new chains were doing very well, but the Holiday Inns group appeared to be doomed.

The Holiday Inn hotels were aging and in need of renovation, which many franchisees could not afford. The hotels' deterioration served to increase the public's perception that the chain was past its prime. Earnings from the division were dropping fast. By contrast, the gambling operations were growing quickly but required additional investment to take advantage of the rising demand. Rose decided to unload the Holiday Inn chain at any cost.

In May 1988 he found a buyer in Bass plc, a UK-based brewing conglomerate seeking diversification. The company sold 13 U.S. Holiday Inns and a number of international hotels to Bass for $475 million. Additional asset transfers continued until the entire Holiday Inn business had been acquired by Bass in January of 1990, for a total of $2.2 billion, much of it in the form of debt assumptions.

In preparation for the transfer, Rose created a new holding company for the non-Holiday Inn assets. This company, established in November 1989, was called "Promus," Latin for "one who serves." When the deal with Bass was completed, Promus became the sole parent company of Harrah's and the three new hotel chains.

Following the sell-off of the Holiday Inn chain to Bass, Promus shareholders were paid a special $30-per share dividend. The company was now a third smaller, with annual revenues of about $1 billion. The sale freed Promus of future costs on more than 1,500 hotels and the suffocating debt it took on to repel Trump, while providing millions of dollars for investment in the Harrah's chain.

No longer worried about cannibalizing business from its Holiday Inn chain, Promus recast its 260-unit Hampton Inns chain from a budget hotel to a middle-market chain, competing directly with Holiday Inn and Courtyard by Marriott. Promus gained its own listing on the New York Stock Exchange in 1990. A year later, the company established a call center in Memphis to handle reservations for the three hotel chains. In addition, Promus acquired a 20-percent interest in KYZ International, a Hong Kong–based hotel management and development company.

Harrah's headquarters were moved from Reno to Memphis in June 1991. At the time, several states legalized some forms of gambling in an effort to lure jobs and increase taxable income. Harrah's, which contributed 85 percent of Promus's total revenues, had an extremely good reputation for solid management. As a result, the company was awarded a franchise for a riverboat casino in Joliet, Illinois.

The legalization of gambling and entry of companies such as Harrah's into conservative areas led to strong opposition from some community organizations. They complained that although gaming provided jobs, it merely redistributed income and did not result in the creation of a product with any economic value. In addition, there were few barriers of entry for those who could least afford to gamble. Others worried about the possible increase in crime in the neighborhoods surrounding the casinos.

To counteract these perceptions, Harrah's insisted that it was a service enterprise, not a manufacturing business. Casinos provided hundreds of spin-off jobs that could revitalize the local economy. Many communities, like Joliet, simply could not afford to lose an employer to another city. The same logic led North Kansas City, Shreveport, and Tunica County, Mississippi, to invite Harrah's to develop riverboat casinos in the early 1990s.

In November 1992, Promus acquired an interest in Sodak Gaming, Inc., a distributor of slot machines and other gambling equipment used on Native American reservations. A month later, the Ak-Chin community in Arizona selected Promus to develop an $18-million casino near Phoenix. Promus's business with Native American interests took off in 1993, as the company negotiated development agreements with a Sioux community in Minnesota and the Poarch Creek community in Alabama. Harrah's also developed plans for casino developments in St. Louis, New Orleans, Southern Indiana/Eastern Kentucky, Northern Kentucky/Southern Ohio, and Windsor, Ontario.

Ironically, Promus's transformation from the parent company of a family hotel chain into a leading international casino operator probably would not have occurred if the company had not been targeted by Donald Trump. The failed raid forced Rose to develop a tight business strategy.

Promus ran into trouble with Bass over its Holiday Inn deal in 1992. Bass sued for a sum in excess of $50 million, charging that Promus withheld information on a Federal Trade Commission probe of Holiday Inns International, a defunct time-share unit that roped consumers into high-pressure sales meetings under the aegis of a contest prize. By late 1993 the suit was still unresolved.

Promus continued to experience stable growth from the three niche-market hotel chains it operates. Most of these were sold to franchisees before the 1990–92 recession, which in turn boosted Promus's earnings. Typically, the company developed a hotel and sold it within three years, deriving investment-free fee income from management contracts.

Promus derives nearly seven-eights of its revenue from middle-market gambling operations. The Harrah's business, still one of the most respected casino businesses in the world, maintains strict managerial discipline and wagering limits aimed not only at protecting customers' losses, but also at maintaining stable earnings.

Principal Subsidiaries: Aster Insurance, Ltd. (Bermuda); Embassy Suites, Inc.; Embassy Suites de Mexico, S.A. (96%); Embassy Suites (Puerto Rico); EPAM Corp.; ESI-Air, Inc.; ESI Development, Inc.; ESI Mortgage Development Corp.; ESI Mortgage Development Corp. II; ESI Equity Development Corp.; GOL (Heathrow), Inc.; Hampton Inns, Inc.; Harrah's (Nevada); Homewood Suites, Inc.; Pacific Hotels, Inc.; Tennessee Restaurant Company (33.2%).

Further Reading:

"Bass Can't Get Comfortable at Holiday Inns," *Business Week,* March 2, 1992, p. 42.
"Corporate Milestones," Memphis, Tennessee: Promus Companies, Inc., 1993.
"Hotel Rooms with a Rosy View," *Business Week,* March 12, 1990, p. 110.
"It's an Ill Wind . . . ," *Forbes,* December 7, 1992, pp. 124–25.
"Promus Companies," *Fortune,* February 11, 1991, p. 110.
"Promus: Fighting for the Middle of the Road," *Business Week,* August 13, 1990, p. 107.
"Rolling the Dice with Promus," *Financial World,* April 2, 1991, pp. 21–22.

—John Simley

QVC Network Inc.

Goshen Corporate Park
West Chester, Pennsylvania 19380
U.S.A.
(215) 430-1000
Fax: (215) 431-6170

Public Company
Incorporated: 1986
Employees: 4,500
Sales: $1 billion
Stock Exchanges: NASDAQ
SICs: 5961 Catalog & Mail Order Houses

QVC Network, Inc. is the nation's largest cable television shopping business, selling a wide variety of merchandise including clothing, jewelry, cosmetics, electronics, and sporting equipment. In 1993, the company's two channels—broadcasting live all day everyday—reached approximately 45 million cable-equipped homes and another three million satellite dish customers. QVC, which stands for "Quality, Value, and Convenience," grew quickly into an industry powerhouse due to increases in cable subscription rates; consumers' growing dependence on mail-order shopping; and advances in telecommunications, allowing the company, with its interactive approach, to integrate computers, television, cable, and telephone lines into an "information superhighway."

QVC Network was founded in July 1986 by Joseph M. Segel, founder of the Franklin Mint Corp., perhaps best known as a mail-order marketer of commemorative coins. According to *Venture Magazine,* QVC Network achieved its rapid success through a combination of quick financing and the founder's ability to seize a ripe moment in the nascent industry. During this time, Home Shopping Network, Inc., was the market leader. Founded in 1977 as a radio shopping program, HSN switched to cable television in 1985 and expanded its operations to three channels. "Like countless others," according to *Venture,* Segel "was watching closely as Home Shopping Network Inc. went public that May. Two months later Segel had organized a management team, formed his own company, and lined up the cable companies and satellite capacity needed to transmit QVC's program—which didn't even exist yet." Among Segel's early backers was Ralph Roberts, chairperson of Comcast Corp., the fourth largest cable operator in the country.

Roberts contributed seed money to QVC and was responsible for persuading other cable companies to carry the shopping channel in return for a stake in QVC.

The company began broadcasting in November, and the programs went on the air full-time in January 1987, transmitted from the company's unassuming headquarters in a West Chester, Pennsylvania, office park. By January 31, 1988, the end of the first full fiscal year, the company had achieved $112.3 million sales. QVC spent the next couple years strengthening its position in TV shopping through acquisitions. In late 1989, it bought out The Fashion Channel, followed by the 1990 purchase of competitor CVN and, in May of the following year, the J.C. Penney Shopping Channel. In this climate the television shopping field narrowed from 20 companies in 1987 to just two major players by late 1992: QVC and the Home Shopping Network.

As QVC gained financial strength, the company also garnered new respectability for its industry, which tended to have a reputation for marketing cheap merchandise. In contrast to the older networks' "fast-paced, hard-sell route, with heavy emphasis on price-cutting and savings," according to *Women's Wear Daily,* QVC took "an intimate, soft-sell approach by using a talk-show format with hosts, placing emphasis on product information more than on price." This approach was enhanced by the network's growing cast of celebrity regulars, who sold their name brand products and took viewer calls. On QVC, daytime soap opera star Susan Lucci sold her hair care system, actress Victoria Jackson promoted her cosmetics, comedienne and talk show host Joan Rivers advertised a line of women's apparel, and Diane Von Furstenburg marketed her moderately-priced silk scarves and clothing. The Parfums International division of the Elizabeth Arden cosmetics company also publicized products on the station.

At the beginning of 1993 founder Joseph Segel retired, passing leadership on to Barry Diller, the former chair of Fox Inc. who, in late 1992, purchased a three percent stake in QVC for $25 million. "Within one week," market analyst Peter J. Sirus remarked to *Women's Wear Daily,* "control of an industry that had been treated largely as the butt of jokes [was] transferred from the original entrepreneurs to some of the smartest and most powerful executives in the media business." Diller, a California native who dropped out of college to pursue a career in show business, eventually rose to prominence as an agent at the William Morris talent agency and at the studios of ABC and Paramount." Diller was chair and chief executive officer of Paramount Pictures from 1974–1984, where he was highly regarded and successful. In the mid-1980s, Diller created Fox Broadcasting, which became a fourth television network to compete with CBS, NBC, and ABC, and quickly achieved a large viewership. Thus, when Diller retired from Fox in early 1992 and resurfaced ten months later as chairperson of QVC, the company became a showcase in the industry for the works of a man widely regarded as a media genius.

Prior to taking over the business, Diller remarked to *Women's Wear Daily:* "There have been a whole series of biases against TV shopping, as there are in the early days of any medium. The challenge is to grow in spite of, or out of, those biases. Every day you have to prove the naysayers an inch wrong, and eventually people will start to say, 'Hey, that's interesting,' and see the applications it could have for them.'' In his first year at QVC, Diller put his words to the test in several areas. First, he raised the awareness of mainstream retailers to the sales possibilities the network could hold for them as a natural extension of in-store and catalogue merchandising. For example, in March 1993, the company signed an agreement with Saks Fifth Avenue to carry the upscale retailer's moderately-priced ''Real Clothes'' house brand. *Women's Wear Daily* observed at the time that the move could be mutually beneficial because it gave QVC ''a quick jolt of upscale credibility, and it puts Saks on the front lines of what some observers see as the distribution wave of the future: electronic selling.'' According to the company, gross orders for the Real Clothes line exceeded $570,000 in the first three months. In addition, in a mid-1993 move that further strengthened the company's fashion sales, QVC introduced a second channel, The QVC Fashion Channel, which, at the end of the year reached over seven million cable-equipped homes.

Concurrently, Diller was working to expand the reach of the company's programming. In April 1993, QVC made its first excursion into broadcasting outside the United States. The company agreed upon plans with Grupo Televisa, S.A., the largest media company in Mexico, to expand QVC's style of electronic retailing throughout the Spanish and Portuguese-speaking world. Grupo Televisa was a sixty year old company with interests in television production and broadcasting, international distribution of television programming, cable television, radio production and broadcasting, music recording, publishing, professional sports promotion, and several other areas. The agreement between QVC and Grupo Televisa was designed to form an electronic retailing program service and related support systems that would serve Mexico, Spain, and Latin America in Spanish, as well as Brazil and Portugal in Portuguese.

Diller's deal with Grupo Televisa prompted a similar agreement in Europe. QVC and British Sky Broadcasting (BSkyB) made plans to form a 24-hour electronic retailing service to be broadcast out of London. BSkyB, according to QVC, was one of the largest pay television services in Europe. The six channel service, launched in February 1989, served about four million homes and was 50 percent owned by Rupert Murdoch's News Corporation Ltd. The joint venture channel would serve the United Kingdom, Ireland, and Europe, with the exception of the Iberian Peninsula.

In July 1993, the company announced that it would launch yet a third shopping channel, called Q2, to go on line in the spring of 1994. The new channel, according to company literature, was ''designed to reach a contemporary audience that hasn't yet become involved with home shopping because they feel it doesn't meet their needs.'' To bring in the new audience, the station intended to address specific consumer issues by featuring segments such as ''finding the computer that's right for you''; ''buying and using a mountain bike''; ''products for life on the road''; ''baby-proofing made easy''; ''creating a bachelor's kitchen''; and ''50 ways to work a little black dress.'' To manage the new channel's development, Diller tapped as president Candice M. Carpenter, a graduate of Stanford University and Harvard Business School, and the former head of Time Life Television and vice-president for consumer marketing at American Express.

In late September 1993, QVC became front page news when it entered into a bidding war with Viacom Inc. for the purchase of Paramount Communications Inc., Barry Diller's former employer and owner of film, television, publishing, and sports franchise concerns. Because of the changing nature of television's capabilities, and the three companies' prominence in television, the hostile bid was viewed as perhaps among the most significant in industry history. While the results of the proposed deal were not resolved by the end of the year, the proposal and the stir it caused signaled more ambitious years ahead for Barry Diller and QVC.

Further Reading:

Betts, Katherine, ''Show and Sell,'' *Vogue,* February 1993.
Fabrikant, Geraldine, ''QVC's Other Bid May Get Less Priority,'' *New York Times,* September 22, 1993.
——. ''TV Shopping Concern Makes Bid as a Battle for Paramount Begins,'' *New York Times,* September 21 1993.
Gordon, Maryellen, ''Shopping by TV: Fashion's Future?'' *Women's Wear Daily,* January 6, 1993.
King, Larry, ''Shopping on the Interactive Highway,'' *Advertising Age,* May 17, 1993.
Roberts, Johnnie L., ''Comcast President Paved Way for Bold Bid by QVC Network,'' *Wall Street Journal,* September 22, 1993.
''Saks-QVC Plan: Sixty Minutes and $400,000,'' *Women's Wear Daily,* March 19, 1993.
Smith, Randall, ''Paramount Bidders Shoot at Each Other's Stock,'' *Wall Street Journal,* September 29, 1993.
——. ''Wall Street Hopes it Hears the Roar of the '80s,'' *Wall Street Journal,* September 22, 1993.
Tapellini, Donna, ''Coming at You Live,'' *Venture,* April 1989. Weintraub, Bernard, ''What's Driving Diller to Play for Paramount?'' *New York Times,* September 22, 1993.

—Martha Schoolman

RR DONNELLEY
& SONS COMPANY

R. R. Donnelley & Sons Company

The R. R. Donnelley Building
77 West Wacker Drive
Chicago, Illinois 60601
U.S.A.
(312) 326-8000
Fax: (312) 326-8543

Public Company
Incorporated: 1890
Employees: 34,000
Sales: $4.19 billion
Stock Exchanges: New York Pacific Chicago
SICs: 2732 Book Printing; 2759 Commercial Printing Nec;
   7372 Prepackaged Software; 7375 Information Retrieval
   Services

R.R. Donnelley & Sons Company is the largest commercial printing firm in the world. Included in its broad range of products are telephone directories, Bibles, books, consumer magazines, and catalogues.

In 1864 Richard R. Donnelley, a 26-year-old saddlemaker's apprentice from Hamilton, Ontario, moved to Chicago. There he established a print shop, called Church, Goodman, and Donnelley—Steam Printers, which became a modest success. When the shop's building and presses were destroyed in the Chicago fire of 1871, leaving Donnelley virtually penniless, he borrowed $20 for a trip to New York, where he managed to get new presses completely on credit. Nevertheless, it took Donnelley nearly two years to get the printing plant fully operational again.

Donnelley was a perfectionist who paid particular attention to both the artistic aspects of printing as well as the trade's scientific developments. His approach resulted in a high quality of printing that won the firm many customers. In a move that proved fortuitous, Donnelley began printing telephone books in 1886, a market that grew astronomically with the importance of the telephone. The firm also pioneered the printing of mail-order catalogues, beginning with such local firms as Sears, Roebuck & Co. In 1890, under the aggressive leadership of Richard's son Thomas E. Donnelley, the firm was incorporated as R.R. Donnelley and Sons. By 1897 the company was so successful that it expanded into larger quarters in another building. After the turn of the century, Donnelley began printing encyclopedias.

Although becoming increasingly mechanized, printing was still very much a craft executed by hand before World War I. Donnelley often hired his employees right out of grade school, putting young workers through the Apprentice Training School he started in 1908, one of the first industrial training programs in the United States. Employees worked their way up through each department, learning all aspects of the printing business.

In 1921 Donnelley opened a printing plant in Crawfordsville, Indiana. The plant was built by local workers, who then helped install the equipment, and were offered jobs and training in how to use the equipment. In 1928 Donnelley began printing one of the first of a new wave of national, mass marketed magazines, entitled *Time.* The following year, the onset of the Great Depression was disastrous for the printing industry, and magazine and newspaper circulations plummeted. However, with contracts like it had with *Time,* Donnelley was able to stay in business.

In 1934 magazine circulations began to increase again. Donnelley foresaw the demand for a larger format for magazines, printed on coated paper, as well as the industry's need to produce these new magazines on tight deadlines. Thus the company began developing the materials and expertise to produce such magazines at a reasonable cost. Donnelley engineers combined a rotary press with smaller printing cylinders with a high-speed folder to increase production from 6,000 to 15,000 impressions an hour. Donnelley researchers, working with ink manufacturers, developed a heat-set process for instantly drying ink at these speeds, using a gas heater built right into the printing press.

During this time, the publishers of *Time* magazine had been considering the development of a picture magazine. Shortly after they heard about Donnelley's new high-speed printing methods they awarded the firm the contract to publish the new *Life* magazine. The first issue came out nine months later, in 1936.

World War II, with its paper shortages and government imposed restrictions on commercial printing, was a difficult time in the industry. After the war, however, printing boomed, quickly becoming a $3 billion-a-year industry. New technologies appeared that promised to revolutionize the industry, including phototypesetting and electronic scanners for platemaking. Donnelley, already the biggest commercial printer in the United States and continuing to grow, quickly invested in such technologies as they came out.

Donnelley went public in 1956 to raise capital for further expansion. By that time the company had over 160 presses, many of them huge and modern, using over 1,000 tons of paper and 20 tons of ink a day. The firm employed 7,500 people; Crawfordsville alone had 1,600 employees. Representing a rare exception in the printing industry, most Donnelley employees did not belong to a union. About 90 percent of Donnelley's executives and supervisors were graduates of the Apprentice Training School and were either college graduates who had gone through a training program or those who had come up through the ranks. The firm's turnover remained low.

The firm's magazine printing business was its most profitable, and nationally distributed periodicals like *Time, Life, Look,*

Sports Illustrated, Farm Journal, National Geographic and *Fortune* accounted for about half of the company's sales. Donnelley's huge mail-order catalogues for Sears, Roebuck & Co. and Marshall Field's accounted for about 17 percent of sales. Donnelley printed over 1,000 telephone directories for subscribers throughout much of the United States, accounting for about 13 percent of its sales. It printed encyclopedias like *World Book, Encyclopedia Britannica* and *Compton's,* as well as corporate reports, the Bible and other religious publications. Donnelley engaged in less glamorous printing as well, such as booklets, pamphlets, menus, and the labels for packages and cans.

Donnelley mailed so many publications every day that the U.S. Post Office had employees working in the company's plants to supervise the vast mailings. Major plants, with total floor space totaling nearly three million square feet, were located in Chicago; Willard, Ohio; and Crawfordsville and Warsaw, Indiana. The firm continued its role as a research and development leader in the industry, spending about $1.6 million a year. In addition to designing mechanical equipment and improving printing materials, Donnelley worked to keep up with cutting-edge electronic and photographic technology. Looking for new technologies was imperative as the costs of labor, material, and equipment were all rising, while intense competition kept prices down.

Having gone public, Donnelley grew by a total of 50 percent between 1954 and 1959, with record sales of $130.1 million in 1959. Despite a depressed economy, sales reached $149.8 million in 1961, with Time Inc. accounting for 29 percent. During the mid-1960s, however, Donnelley's profits leveled off. The firm recovered by 1968 as magazine sales, which accounted for 41 percent of sales, broke out of a slump. By that point Donnelley's hardcover publishing had increased to represent 22 percent of its sales. Retail catalogues also stood at 22 percent.

Printing technology changed rapidly in the late 1960s. Photocomposition, computerized justification, and electronic scanning were changing the way plates were readied, while high-speed offset printing was also changing the process. In 1968 Donnelley bought an RCA Videocomp, which set 4,500 characters of type per second using a cathode ray tube. One Donnelley manager estimated that the machine could set as much type as every hot-metal typesetter in the Midwest. Simultaneously, the firm created a separate photocomposition and electronics division which employed computer programmers and electronic communications specialists instead of production staff.

As type became easier to set, however, the popular magazine market was shrinking. *Look* folded in 1971, taking $15 million of Donnelley's business with it. Also that year, *Life* cut circulation from 8.5 million to 5.5 million. As a result of these losses, Donnelley laid off 700 people, soon cutting an additional 400 people to keep its costs down. Thus, despite its losses, the firm made $24 million in 1971 on sales of $340 million. With magazines suffering, most of Donnelley's growth was coming from catalogs and directories. To keep pace, the firm opened a plant in Lancaster, Pennsylvania, in 1972, exclusively for the printing of phone books for the Mid-Atlantic states. To further offset mass market magazine losses, Donnelley worked to win jobs producing special-interest periodicals, printing 24 such periodicals for Ziff-Davis Publishing alone.

In 1972 *Life* magazine stopped publishing entirely, resulting in a $3 million charge against earnings and further layoffs. Donnelley also lost its contracts with *Fortune* and *American Home.* Fortunately, the company found new customers in *Esquire* magazine, and signed ten-year contracts with *Glamour* and *Mademoiselle,* and a five-year contract with *U.S. New & World Report.* Donnelley's conservative financial practices helped it weather the storm. The firm paid low dividends on its earnings, had net working capital of $90 million, and only $3 million in long-term debt.

In 1974 the firm began shifting away from high quality, four-color, extended runs, which had accounted for most of its work until then. Numerous small publishers were appearing, and publishers were moving toward smaller initial press runs to cut down on remainders and the costs of storage. Publishers instead wanted the ability to quickly reprint books that sold out their first edition. Donnelley was determined to change accordingly. Over the next few years the company installed a short-run plant in Crawfordsville, for producing college, professional, and trade books, and doubled capacity at its Willard, Ohio, plant. In the late 1970s the firm began building a state-of-the-art plant in Harrisonburg, Virginia, to offer overnight delivery to publisher warehouses on the east coast. In the early 1980s, Donnelley increased its shift toward small press runs. It began an aggressive telemarketing campaign in which it contacted numerous small publishers, trying to change its image as a printing house for larger clients only. As a result, by 1983, Donnelley had between 600 and 700 book publishers as customers, and short-run books accounted for nearly 50 percent of unit sales.

Sales grew rapidly, reaching $2.2 billion in 1986. The following year Donnelley purchased Metromail Corp. for $282.6 million. Metromail provided lists to direct-mail marketers, and, as Donnelley already printed and distributed catalogues for direct-mail marketers, the acquisition was expected to complement Donnelley's existing business. It also moved into financial printing, opening a Wall Street financial printing center shortly before the stock market crash of October 1987.

In the late 1980s, Donnelley's expansion went into overdrive, culminating with the purchase of Meredith/Burda Printing for $570 million. Donnelley was also moving rapidly into such information services as computer documentation, with sales of $190 million by 1989 out of total sales for the year of $3.1 billion. The firm used electronic printing techniques and information from Metromail to help its clients gear advertising and editorial content toward different audiences. Furthermore, Donnelley was entering the markets for printing books for children, professional books, and quick-printing, with the purchase of 25 percent of AlphaGraphics, a high-end quick-printing chain.

The firm pushed expansion so hard because it believed that rapidly changing technologies gave it an opportunity to capture large chunks of business from smaller companies that could not afford to keep up. Donnelley's moves into cutting-edge technology were not always successful, however; in 1984 it had made a premature, ill-fated attempt to move into electronic shopping.

With the U.S. economy in recession in 1991, the firm's net income declined about nine percent to $205 million. Donnelley bounced back the following year, however, with total sales of $4.193 billion. During this time, the company acquired Combined Communication Services, a trade magazine printer, and American Inline Graphics, a specialty, direct-mail printer. The firm also continued its expansion outside the United States, opening new offices and plants in The Netherlands, Scotland, Mexico, and Thailand. Furthermore, Donnelley increased its presence in electronic media and on-line services, manufacturing, for example, 350 products for QUE, an imprint of Prentice Hall Computer Books.

Such successes helped to partly offset losses in Donnelley's traditional markets. In early 1993 Sears ceased publication of its 97-year-old catalogue, which Donnelley had printed since its inception. Consequently, Donnelley laid off 660 employees, took a $60 million charge against earnings, and closed its historic Lakeside Press plant. A few months later, Donnelley announced that it would become the printer of the *National Enquirer* and *Star* tabloids. These publications opted to use Donnelley because its advanced printing processes allowed for tighter deadlines and turnaround times of less than 40 hours.

While the printing industry remained fragmented and in constant flux in the early 1990s, Donnelley continued to emphasize its flexibility and focus on the future. Industry analysts predicted continued growth for this leading firm.

Principal Subsidiaries: Metromail Corp.; Meredith/Burda Printing; Alphagraphics (25%); Combined Communications Services; American Inline Graphics.

Further Reading:

"Donnelley Recovers from *Life*'s Death," *Financial World,* May 16, 1973, p. 10.
Kellman, Jerold L., "Donnelley: A Big Printer Looks to Small Publishers and Short Runs," *Publishers Weekly,* January 14, 1983, p. 44.
"R. R. Donnelley & Sons Co.; Presses Shift to High Speed at Commercial Printer," *Barron's,* January 29, 1990, p. 59.
"R.R. Donnelley & Sons Set to Register Profits Gain," *Barron's,* September 25, 1972, p. 27.
"R.R. Donnelley Sees Another Bright Chapter in Continuing Success Story," *Barron's,* April 4, 1960, p. 28.
Waltz, George H., *The House that Quality Built,* Chicago: The Lakeside Press, 1957.

—Scott. M. Lewis

Red Wing Shoe Company, Inc.

River Front Ctr.
Red Wing, Minnesota 55066
U.S.A.
(612) 388-8211
Fax: (612) 388-7415

Private Company
Incorporated: 1905
Employees: 1,200
Sales: $86 million
SICs: 3140 Footwear Except Rubber; 3143 Men's Footwear
    Except Athletic; 3149 Footwear Except Rubber, Nec; 3021
    Rubber & Plastics Footwear

Red Wing Shoe Company, Inc. manufactures durable and comfortable footwear tailored to the needs of specific occupational and recreational activities, from farming to hunting and hiking. Until the 1970s, Red Wing's reputation rested primarily on a wide variety of footwear marketed as "work shoes," emphasizing their practical applications in the workplace. By the mid-1980s, however, as American workers moved increasingly out of industrial and agricultural sectors into service related jobs, the company's scope changed. Under the direction of a new president, William J. Sweasy, and a new generation of management, the company's emphasis shifted from "work shoes" to "shoes for work," a slight semantic change that underscored the company's new commitment to innovative lines of lighter, more comfortable footwear developed to accommodate new work oriented and recreational needs. By the 1990s, Red Wing maintained a workforce of over 1,400 employees and sold over 12,000 pairs per day, both nationally and internationally. In the United States, Red Wing shoes were distributed to 400 Red Wing Shoe Stores (of which 40 percent were company owned) and through approximately 4,800 privately owned shoe stores. International markets had expanded to include over 80 countries by 1992.

Red Wing traces its history to 1905, when German immigrant Charles Beckman closed his retail shoe store and organized the Red Wing Shoe Company with 14 other investors. The young company initially manufactured 110 pairs of shoes per 10-hour day. The brand's steady growth stemmed from the booming industries of farming, logging, mining, blacksmithing, and railroading that represented largely untapped footwear markets. Red Wing tailored its shoes to the demands of specific customer

groups, offering a wide range of shoe sizes and widths to ensure fit, and a constantly growing line of specialized products with different capabilities.

Red Wing innovation in its early years reflected efforts to shod diverse markets. In 1908, the brand offered welt-constructed shoes featuring a leather strip attached to the shoe upper and sewn into the sole. The enhanced comfort and durability of the shoes particularly appealed to farmers, Red Wing's primary customers at the time. Continued demand justified the construction of a four-story factory with a daily output of 450 pairs, four times the 1906 capacity. Then in 1912, the company added the black and brown "Chief" line, commonly known as "the farmer's shoe." In addition to the traditional welt construction of earlier farming shoes, the Chief featured specially tanned, manure-proof leather for longer durability.

Numerous other shoe designs ensured the company's continued success. Red Wing began fulfilling military needs with the onset of World War I, manufacturing in 1918 the regulation Munson U.S. Army Last, designed to "fit all feet" with maximum comfort and durability. After the war, the Munson remained a top seller and influenced other popular shoe designs for over 50 years. In the 1930s, Red Wing moved into a steel toe line designed to provide added toe protection in high risk jobs. That line retained its popularity and developed into several models, one of which even became popular during the punk counterculture fad of the 1970s. Also in the 1930s, the company developed an oil-resistant, highly comfortable design named the "Oil King" boot and adopted primarily by oil field workers. For slightly more elite circles of the era, Red Wing also introduced a men's dress or riding boot dubbed the "Aristo," which served as a model for a women's line of shoes and boots.

The development of rubber added significantly to Red Wing's success in its early decades. In the early 1930s, the company president, J. R. Sweasy, introduced the rubber cord sole to replace the leather norm. His gamble with the new material proved both lucrative and trendsetting. The Gro Cord soles and Goodyear heels used in Red Wing shoes set the standard for a shoe industry that grew to depend almost exclusively on synthetic materials.

In addition to durability, lowered costs figured into Red Wing's new materials. During the Great Depression, synthetic materials helped produce an extremely cost-effective shoe. Model No. 99, named after its price of 99 cents, kept the factory in production during the financial downswing.

Red Wing continued to grow at a healthy rate, and after World War II the company reached national and eventually international markets. War mandated unprecedented volume, as the U.S. government contracted hundreds of combat shoes manufactured to regulation specifications in 239 different sizes and widths. By 1949, when William D. Sweasy took over as company president, Red Wing had proven its reliability in meeting urgent demand under tight supervision. Sweasy turned that strength to civil ends, introducing a company reorganization to place greater responsibility on department heads and develop teams of management specialists in every department. Sweasy also initiated a new distribution strategy in which Red Wing retail stores would open on the west coast and move east over time.

Reorganization paid off quickly. Record profits were achieved in 1952, largely attributable to the No. 877 Irish Setter Sport Boot, which continued to assure Red Wing a strong position in the competitive boot market. The Irish Setter's landslide success was partly responsible for Red Wing's introduction of its Vasque outdoor division in 1965. That division capitalized on the hiking boot craze of the 1970s and went on to include lightweight hiking boots and walking shoes in the 1980s and 1990s.

After continued growth through the 1960s and 1970s, Red Wing responded to trends in market research, changing many of its marketing strategies and brand lines. In an October 1, 1984, *Footwear News* article, Tom McConnell, Red Wing product manager, identified three trends affecting the company: a shift from a rural to a metropolitan workplace; the replacement of a blue-collar workforce with a gray-collar or service related one; and rising numbers of women in the workforce. To service these new markets, Red Wing changed its emphasis and its motto, from "work shoes" to "shoes for work." While the company would continue to offer work and sports boots, product development and marketing efforts in the 1980s increasingly focused on those markets promising the most growth, including footwear for such professions as computer operators, food service technicians, health care workers, and security personnel.

Red Wing's shift in marketing strategy was paralleled by a new corporate tone prompted by an increasingly younger generation of management. In 1984, William J. Sweasy, Jr. assumed the role of president after Arlo "Ole" Jensen retired from the post. Sweasy represented the third generation of his family to serve as a Red Wing executive; his father, William Sweasy, remained CEO. The 33-year-old president ushered in an era of active strategic planning, greater communications, increased line diversity, and new personnel. "Before, the upper management team operated intuitively; they shot from the hip, so to speak," noted one company spokesperson in a 1986 *Footwear News* article. The article emphasized that overall company spirit was not critical of the old management, but favored the new approach in light of changed and emerging business opportunities. In August 1989, William Sweasy became the first company executive from outside the Twin Cities area elected to chair the Better Business Bureau of Minnesota, representing an honor for Red Wing Shoe Company and its new leader.

New management style and brand image also brought new products to Red Wing. Special attention was paid to women's comfort footwear. While over 40 million women held jobs involving substantial standing or walking in the mid-1980s, Tom McConnell told *Footwear News* that "most resources have simply remade men's styles on a scaled-down last." In response, Red Wing introduced Lady Red Wings, incorporating safety toes and lightweight urethane soles in a more feminine, less cumbersome line of shoes. McConnell projected sales of approximately 250,000 pairs, retailing at $40 and up.

In the 1980s, Red Wing also developed its Vasque Outdoor Footwear division, which produced aesthetically appealing walking shoes under the Vasque brand name. While earlier walking shoes had often sacrificed cosmetics for hi-tech features used in running shoes—rubbers, bottoms packages, heel counters, and lacing systems—Red Wing emphasized casual, multipurpose walking shoes in attractive designs. Art Kenyon, divisional manager for Vasque in 1988, told *Footwear News*

"the consumer today really is concerned with cosmetically fine footwear, boots that can function and still look nice." In the early 1990s, Vasque also benefited from the renewed popularity in hiking boots, sales of which had been declining since the 1970s. Despite the downward sales trend, Vasque had continued to create heavy hiking boots for wilderness excursions as well as a variety of lighter styles for casual walkers and fashion customers. Discussing the company's ready position at the time of the hiking boot resurgence, Kenyon—who had by 1991 become president of Vasque—observed: "We came from the mountain down to the mainstream," adding that "the others came up from the gymnasium," in reference to competition from such athletic footwear companies as Nike, Reebok, and New Balance. In 1990, Vasque introduced Kids Klimbers, a line of hiking footwear for children, featuring a "variable fit child growth system" to accommodate quickly growing feet for an extra six months on average, and also incorporating children's tastes into shoe design. The division's hiking boot product line became the fastest growing segment of the Red Wing Shoe Co. during the early 1990s. In 1993, Vasque launched its first line of sports sandals, responding to a popular trend during that time.

In the work shoe arena, Red Wing also explored new directions. Following the demands of consumers who often wore athletic shoes outside the workplace, the company introduced steel toe athletic shoes—two safety-style athletic shoes in black and white. In addition, the company moved toward work shoes made from lighter materials and softer leather. "Our consumers are saying, make it soft but tough," explained Andy Thompson, advertising and promotions manager of Red Wing, in a 1988 *Footwear News* article. Red Wing also developed a group of barnyard acid resistant shoes geared for the farm industry and a "decathlon" sole made from a durable, lightweight, shock resistant, and oil resistant material.

Red Wing's new products were supported with new marketing initiatives. Lady Red Wings appeared in a TV ad campaign that was second only to Acme Boot Co. in terms of market saturation, according to McConnell. Premiering in October 1984, the commercials were computer animated to lend a contemporary feeling to the new line. Red Wing also ran a series of print advertisements featuring a top model in *McCalls, Women's Day,* and *Mademoiselle* magazines and promoting the image of an up-to-date, attractive and fashionable Red Wing clientele.

In the late 1980s, the company began a restructuring of its retail division in order to gain exposure and market penetration. In May 1986 Wes Thies, retail division manager, outlined a two-fold strategy in *Footwear News*. The company's object was to expand the existing specialty store concept and to introduce three prototypes geared to various consumer demographics. The first prototype was aimed at smaller markets with populations between 30,000 and 60,000. The units were designed with a sales area in front and shoe repair shop in back and targeted Red Wing's blue-collar consumers.

Red Wing also emphasized the use of a company newsletter as a marketing tool. The "Red Wing's Shoe News & Views," published monthly, helped a 40-member sales staff communicate product news and company policies with over 6,000 stores.

While the Red Wing newsletter addressed retailers, the company moved to develop more effective means of communicating brand awareness to the public. With the advent of desktop computer power and database marketing, age-old advertising techniques were losing their effectiveness. Stan Rapp, president of CRC Consulting Group in New York, told attendees of the 1992 All-Industry Marketing (AIM) Conference that marketing efforts had to be increasingly individualized as mass advertising rapidly became obsolete. He noted that shoe companies needed to micromarket and draw consumers into a feedback loop by fostering two-way, relationship marketing. In its own variation on such techniques, Red Wing launched a television campaign in the early 1990s in which it sought to foster a relationship with consumers by providing a toll-free number. The commercial claimed that ''our shoes don't wear out,'' providing consumer testimonials and toll free purchasing information. In addition, all customers were sent a note thanking them for their business and a form to rate their salesperson. After six months, each customer received another form to rate the shoes' performance, strengthening a personalized, two-way marketing dynamic.

Red Wing's efforts to adapt to changing markets also included greater emphasis on international growth. By 1990 several brands were being distributed in over 80 countries. Despite the intricacies of dealing with currency fluctuations and of identifying elusive, foreign trends, the market for American footwear exports offered substantial growth potential for Red Wing. Palmer Beebe, one executive instrumental in setting up Red Wing's international department, moved on to run Team America, an export business handling footwear for a consortium of U.S. companies. ''U.S. footwear is underexported,'' Beebe claimed in a July 1991 *Footwear News* article.

As early as 1984, Red Wing had reported that two to three percent of overseas laborers in supervisory positions were company customers. Phil Margolis, director of marketing at the time, projected 25 percent growth over the next few years, citing wider distribution base and increased technology as means of lowering prices to raise foreign sales. By 1990, Census Bureau statistics indicated that the best European customers for American footwear were West Germany, France, Italy, the United Kingdom, and Spain. Other large importers included Canada, Japan, Mexico, Hong Kong, and Saudi Arabia.

The uncertain outcome of a proposed common market in Europe as well as of the North American Free Trade Agreement (NAFTA) overshadowed Red Wing's international activity in the early 1990s. Red Wing's projected expansion in European markets remained uncertain until common market regulations solidified in Brussels.

In addition to international trade concerns, Red Wing faced pressing issues regarding employee health insurance as it entered the 1990s. With medical costs skyrocketing and health care reform a top priority for the Clinton Administration and the press, the company faced several challenges. In 1992, the company encountered astronomical expenses for worker's compensation insurance, a burden that prompted Red Wing—and other Minnesota companies—to look at other states with cheaper policies for future expansion. Even though Red Wing earned a 25 percent discount in 1992 for the job-classification quoted rate, for a positive safety record, premiums still increased 41

percent from 1988 to 1992. In an effort to ease such burdens, the 1992 state legislature changed some benefits and gave broad authority to the Department of Labor and Industry to cut overall costs by 16 percent. Later that year, Rich Chalmers, vice-president of human resources at Red Wing, collaborated with Ron Schiemann, a Minnesota entrepreneur, to conceive a health care purchasing group designed to improve the delivery of heath care and reduce costs for ten employers, including Red Wing Shoe Co., Riedell Shoes Inc. and the City of Red Wing. According to the plan, participating employers would be self insured for a given dollar amount, beyond which re-insurance would take effect. The Chalmers/Schiemann plan was just one of several health care measures that Red Wing considered to best cover its employees.

The decisive factor in Red Wing's continued success remained its servicing of new markets, as it shifted emphasis from ''work shoes'' to ''shoes for work'' in a service oriented economy. With Sweasy presiding over new initiatives in marketing and brand development, Red Wing would likely continue its successful promotion of high quality footwear.

Principal Subsidiaries: Vasque Outdoor Footwear.

Further Reading:

Francis, Lorna R., ''Strong Gains Reported in Steel Toe Athletics; Work and Safety shoes,'' *Footwear News,* November 14, 1988, p. 4.

Francis, Lorna R., ''Work and Safety Shoes Make Nick in Fashion Scene; Boot Industry,'' *Footwear News,* November 3, 1986, p. 26.

''Health Care Relief Plan to Unfold in Red Wing,'' *Business Dateline,* July 13, 1992, sec. 1, p. 1.

''How the Once Ugly Duckling Was Turned Into a Swan; Walking Shoes,'' *Footwear News,* April 11, 1988, p. S2.

Howard, Tammi, ''Footwear Sources Jump on Newsletter Bandwagon; Marketing Tools,'' *Footwear News,* May 26, 1986, p. 12.

——. ''Red Wing Giant Waking Up To Get Place in the Sun; Marketing; Shoe Industry,'' *Footwear News,* May 26, 1986, p. 52.

——. ''Red Wing Shifts Marketing to Service-Related Fields,'' *Footwear News,* October 1, 1984, p. 17.

Meyers, Mike, ''Proving a Negative Positively Impossible, Especially When It's About NAFTA Impact,'' *Star Tribune,* May 31, 1993, p. D1.

''Red Wing Shoe Co. Attributes 87 Years of Success To One Word: Service,'' Company Document, Spring, 1992.

Rooney, Ellen, ''Vasque to Celebrate Silver Anniversary,'' *Footwear News,* October 9, 1989, p. 15.

Seckler, Valerie, ''Micromarketing Puts Focus on Individuals; Footwear marketing,'' *Footwear News,* May 18, 1992, p. 2.

St. Anthony, Neal, ''Worker's Comp Irks Blue-Collar Employers; Above-Average Rates Frustrate Companies,'' *Star Tribune,* November 30, 1992, p. D1.

Underwood, Elaine, ''The Competition is Stepping Up For Hiking Boots,'' *Chicago Tribune,* September 9, 1991, p. C6.

''Vasque Debuts Line of Kids' Hiking Boots; Red Wing Shoe Co. Vasque Outdoor Footwear Div.,'' *Footwear News,* November 12, 1990, p. 23.

Watters, Susan, ''Makers Hedge Dollar Bets to Build Export Business; Fluctuating Foreign Currency Deters U.S. Footwear Companies From Exporting,'' *Footwear News,* July 8, 1991, p. 30.

Wilner, Rich, ''Resources Set to Put Sport Sandals in Overdrive,'' *Footwear News,* November 9, 1992, p. 1.

—Kerstan Cohen

Reebok International Ltd.

100 Technology Center Drive
Stoughton, Massachusetts 02072
U.S.A.
(617) 341-5000
Fax: (617) 341-5087

Public Company
Incorporated: 1979 as Reebok U.S.A.
Employees: 4,600
Sales: $3.02 billion
Stock Exchanges: New York
SICs: 5139 Footwear; 5136 Men's/Boy's Clothing; 5137
   Women's/Children's Clothing

Reebok International is one of the world's leading athletic footwear and apparel makers. The company first gained prominence by opening up a new market for athletic shoes—aerobic exercise shoes for women interested in fashion as well as function—and subsequently built upon that success by expanding into other sports and products and by seeking business around the world.

Reebok began its growth into a worldwide enterprise in 1979 when Paul B. Fireman, a marketer of camping and fishing supplies, noticed the products of a small British athletic shoe-maker, Reebok International, at a Chicago sporting goods show. Looking for a business opportunity, Fireman acquired the North American license for the company's products, founding Reebok U.S.A.

The British parent company, the oldest manufacturer of athletic shoes in the world, got its start in the 1890s in Bolton, England, when Joseph William Foster began handcrafting shoes with spiked soles for runners. By 1895 he was the head of J. W. Foster and Sons, Inc., providing shoes to world-class athletes, including the 1924 British Olympic running team. In 1958 two of Foster's grandsons founded Reebok, named after an African gazelle, to manufacture running shoes in Bolton, and this company eventually took over the older firm.

After Fireman acquired the right to sell Reebok products made in Britain in the United States, he introduced three top-of-the-line models of running shoes, with price tags of $60, the highest on the market. Sales topped $1.5 million in 1981, but after two years in the extremely competitive U.S. market, Fireman's

enterprise was out of money, and he sold 56 percent of his fledgling company to Pentland Industries PLC, another British shoe company. Reebok used the infusion of cash to open a factory in Korea, thereby significantly lowering production costs.

The company's fortunes began to change dramatically, however, in 1982 with the introduction of a shoe designed especially for aerobic exercise. Unlike traditional athletic shoes, which were made of unglamorous materials in drab colors, Reebok aerobics shoes were constructed of soft, pliable leather, and came in a variety of bold, fashionable colors. Reebok's Free-style aerobics shoe was the first athletic shoe designed and marketed specifically for women, and it quickly became hugely popular. By selling its shoes to women, Reebok had opened up a new market for athletic shoe sales. This market would continue to expand as women began to wear their comfortable athletic shoes on the street, for daily life. In addition, the company both contributed to and profited from the boom in popularity of aerobics in the early 1980s, sponsoring clinics to promote the sport and its shoes.

In 1983, the year following the introduction of the shoe for aerobics, Reebok sales shot to $13 million. The company had become the beneficiary of a full-fledged fad. By the following year, sales of Reebok shoes had reached $66 million, and Reebok U.S.A. and its corporate sponsor, Pentland Industries, made arrangements to buy out Reebok International, the company's British parent, for $700,000. In addition, the company expanded its offerings to include tennis shoes, although shoes for aerobics continued to make up more than half of Reebok's sales in 1984.

By 1985 Reeboks had gained a large following of trendy young consumers, and the shoe's standing as a fashion item was solidified by the appearance of actress Cybill Shepherd wearing a bright orange pair of Reeboks under her formal black gown at the presentation of the Emmy awards. Such celebrity endorsements, as well as an advertising budget of $5 million, helped to push the company's 1985 sales to more than $300 million, with profits of nearly $90 million. Fireman, Reebok's founder, set up an office in California to help the company stay on top of trends and maintain its shoe's popularity.

In July 1985 Reebok International stock was offered publicly for the first time, selling over the counter at $17 a share. By this time international sales of Reebok shoes were contributing ten percent of revenues. By September the company was unable to meet the continuing high demand for its products and was forced to restrict the number of shoes available to individual stores until it could expand production at its South Korean factories.

Consumers who were able to purchase Reebok shoes were finding that their high price tag did not guarantee high quality, as the shoes' soft leather uppers sometimes fell apart within months. Reebok launched an attempt to improve quality control in 1986, increasing its number of on-site factory inspectors from seven to 27. Although the company's production reached four million pairs a month by mid 1986, a backlog of $400 million in orders existed, and plans were made for further expansion of production capacity. In keeping with this gain, Reebok's advertising budget grew to $11 million, and the company began advertising on television for the first time.

Anticipating an inevitable decline in the popularity of its aerobics shoes—which contributed 42 percent of the company's sales in 1985—as the aerobics trend peaked and slacked off, Reebok moved to further protect its sales position in 1986 by diversifying its product offering. The company began by introducing sports clothing and accessories, limiting sales to $20 million so that growth could be controlled. In addition, the company inaugurated a line of children's athletic shoes, called Weeboks, at the end of 1986. Perhaps the most significant innovation was the introduction of a basketball shoe. In entering this market, Reebok was stepping up its competition with rival athletic shoe makers Nike and Converse, which controlled a large part of the lucrative basketball shoe market. By the end of 1986, revenues from basketball shoes totaled $72 million and made up 8.6 percent of Reebok's total sales.

In June 1986, Reebok was rebuffed in its first attempt to expand through the acquisition of other companies, when Stride Rite Corp., another shoe manufacturer, rejected Reebok's offer. However, Reebok was successful in its negotiations for the purchase of Rockport Company, a leading maker of walking shoes with sales of around $100 million that had gotten its start in the early 1970s. Rather than integrate the new company's operations closely with its own, Reebok maintained a separation between the two, even to the extent of allowing competition.

Later that year, the company was restructured into three areas: footwear, apparel, and international products, in an effort to better manage its growth. Sales tripled in 1986 to reach $919 million, and the company's stock began trading on the New York Stock Exchange at the end of the year.

By the start of 1987, Reebok's backlog of orders for all its lines of shoes had grown to $445 million, indicating that demand for its products continued to be strong. With Fireman, as chairman, receiving record compensation tied to the company's profits, Reebok's growth continued unabated, and the company embarked on a string of purchases of other shoe companies. In March 1987 Reebok made arrangements to buy Avia Group International, Inc., another maker of aerobic shoes, for $180 million. Following this move, the company sold $6 million worth of stock to raise money to help offset the cost of its acquisition, reducing Pentland Industries' interest in the company from 41 to 37 percent. The company's pace in buying other footwear manufacturers did not slow, as Reebok-owned Rockport acquired a bootmaker, the John A. Frye Company, in May 1987. This 125-year-old company, which also marketed hand sewn shoes, had yearly sales of about $20 million. One month later, after forming a Canadian subsidiary, Reebok Canada Inc., Reebok moved through it to purchase the ESE Sports Company, Ltd. Reebok closed out 1987 by finalizing plans to acquire the U.S. division and the U.S. and Canadian rights to the trademark of an Italian apparel company, Ellesse International S.p.A., for $25 million, a more modest version of an earlier plan to acquire the entire company.

In addition to its purchases of other shoemakers and apparel companies, Reebok continued to expand its own offerings in 1987, as part of its effort to maintain and protect its market share by providing a wide variety of products. The company introduced shoes designed specifically for walking, in hopes of establishing a presence in a field that Reebok chairman Fireman believed would be the next fad in fitness, and also began offering volleyball shoes and dressier styles for women. This trend continued in the next year with the introduction of shoes for golf.

In an attempt to shed its reputation as a company noted for fashion products, as opposed to serious high-performance athletic shoes, Reebok entered the fray of high-tech design innovations, an area previously dominated by its competitor Nike, with the introduction of energy return system shoes. At the end of 1987, Reebok held a quarter of the market for basketball shoes and dominated the field in aerobics, tennis, and walking shoes, its new entry.

In 1988 Reebok's long and meteoric rise began to show signs of flagging, however, as the company's historically high profit margins went into a slump. Reebok's strength in the youth market, focused primarily on basketball shoes, was shaken by a massive advertising campaign by competitor Nike, which outspent Reebok by $7 million to $1.7 million in the first quarter of 1988.

In an effort to regain lost ground, Reebok went on the offensive, publicizing its products in several ways. The company gave away shoes to young people known as style makers, and also renovated urban playgrounds. In addition, it sponsored a series of rock concerts to raise money for human rights groups, and in conjunction with this, inaugurated a Reebok Human Rights Award. Starting in August 1988, Reebok also devoted a portion of its $80 million advertising budget to an innovative and esoteric television and print campaign built around the theme, "Reeboks let U.B.U.," which featured people expressing their personalities in unique ways while wearing Reeboks. However, the campaign was unsuccessful, and by the end of 1988, earnings had fallen by one-fifth, on sales of $1.79 billion.

In March 1989 the company unveiled a new $30 million advertising campaign entitled "The Physics Behind the Physique." This push was focused on women, traditionally Reebok's strongest customer base, and connected sweaty physical exertion with sex and narcissism. These relatively rapid shifts in emphasis from performance to fashion and back again began to muddle the consumer's idea of what the company stood for, and Reebok continued to see its portion of the market slip as its sales growth waned. Commentators observed that the company appeared to have lost its focus.

Reebok also underwent a period of turmoil in its administrative and executive structure during this time. In August 1989 the company's head of marketing, Mark Goldston, left after less than a year with the company, and two months later, its president, C. Joseph LaBonte, brought in by Fireman only two years earlier, resigned as well. In addition to these changes at home, Reebok moved to strengthen its international management team at this time.

Reebok sold its Frye boot subsidiary in 1989. The company then made its only purchase outside the footwear and sportswear industries, buying a manufacturer of recreational boats, Boston Whaler, Inc., for $42 million in 1989.

Although Reebok's market share had fallen behind Nike's, to 22 percent by the end of 1989, the seeds of Reebok's resurgence were sown in mid-November with the introduction of "The Pump," a basketball shoe with an inflatable collar around the ankle to provide extra support. Although the expensive shoes made up only a small portion of Reebok's overall sales, the popularity of the new technology lent a sorely missed air of excitement to the company's brand name.

Reacting to its previous difficulties, and continuing challenges in both the fashion and performance shoe markets, Reebok rearranged its corporate structure at the beginning of 1990, splitting its domestic division into two areas, one focusing on performance products and the other on fashion products. A month later, the company further restructured by merging its international and U.S. units into one global business.

Reebok split with its ad agency, Chiat/Day/Mojo, in an effort to regain lost market share. To do so, the company built on its recent success with The Pump technology by expanding The Pump to other lines of footwear, including aerobics, cross-training, running, tennis, walking, and children's shoes. In addition, facing a relatively mature and highly competitive U.S. market for athletic shoes, Reebok looked to foreign markets, which made up a quarter of the company's sales, for further growth.

Results were immediate—overall European sales grew 86 percent in 1991 alone. By 1992 Reebok products were available in approximately 140 countries outside the United States, holding a number one ranking in sales for nine of those countries, including the United Kingdom, Canada, and Australia. U.S. growth stood at less than ten percent. The company needed to project its image as a leader in innovative athletic apparel through products in other sports categories that would display the latest in Reebok technology.

Reebok premiered football and baseball shoes in 1992, and more than 100 players in the major leagues donned its footwear. Marketing momentum increased as Notre Dame's Fighting Irish captured the Cotton Bowl championship on New Year's Day, 1993, sporting the Reebok football shoes supplied them throughout the season. The development of a shoe for basketball players on playground courts—branded the Blacktop—became very successful in 1991. Reebok acquired two other sports apparel manufacturers, consolidating their products with

Reebok's own line of clothing and accessories, sold subsidiaries Boston Whaler and Ellesse, and positioned Reebok, Rockport, and Avia to be the principal operating units of the future. In early 1993 Reebok struck an agreement with golf legend Jack Nicklaus to create a unique line of golf shoes. Reebok also generated tremendous sales with its debut of a casual, non-athletic footwear line called Boks during the fall of 1992.

Reebok took steps to enhance its reputation through sponsorship of targeted sporting events and support of human rights programs. The company became the sponsor of the Russian Olympic Committee through 1996 and the International Hockey Federation Olympic Winter Games for 1994. Reebok's commitment to human rights led to the establishment of the Witness and Volunteer Programs in 1992. In 1993 Reebok increased its budget for a global publicity campaign, estimated at $115 million. During the 1993 SuperBowl, the company aired a 60-second commercial premiering "Planet Reebok," a campaign associating Reebok products with intense competition and high performance. Reebok renewed relations with Chiat/Day/Mojo to promote individual products and began a weekly Top 30 countdown radio program based on the "Planet Reebok" theme.

Principal Subsidiaries: Avia Group International, Inc.; Reebok Canada, Inc.; Reebok International, Ltd.; Rockport Company, Inc.

Further Reading:

Grimm, Matthew, "Deft Reebok Strides into Women's Walking," *Brandweek,* August 24, 1992.
——, "Reebok's Big Idea," *Brandweek,* January 25, 1993.
Pereira, Joseph, "Reebok Trails Nike in Fight For Teens' Hearts and Feet," *Wall Street Journal,* September 23, 1988.
Sloan, Pat, "Reebok Takes Off Around the Planet," *Advertising Age,* January 25, 1993.
"The Sneaker Wars," *Forbes,* March 25, 1993.
Therrien, Lois, "Reeboks: How Far Can A Fad Run?" *Business Week,* February 24, 1986.
Watkins, Linda M., "Reebok: Keeping a Name Hot Requires More Than Aerobics," *Wall Street Journal,* August 21, 1986.
"Where Nike and Reebok Have Plenty of Running Room," *Business Week,* March 11, 1991.
Wulf, Steve, "A Costly Blunder," *Sports Illustrated,* July 6, 1992.

—Elizabeth Rourke
updated by Edna M. Hedblad

Reliance Electric Company

6065 Parkland Boulevard
Cleveland, Ohio 44124-6106
U.S.A.
(216) 266-5800
Fax: (216) 266-7666

Public Company
Incorporated: 1907
Employees: 14,000
Sales: $1.55 billion
Stock Exchanges: New York
SICs: 3621 Motors & Generators; 3679 Electronic
  Components Nec; 3663 Radio & TV Communications
  Equipment

Reliance Electric Company is a manufacturer of large mechanical couplers and electrical motors and drives used in heavy industries from steel and paper mills to coal mines. The company diversified into electronic equipment for the telecommunications industry in the 1970s. Reliance's stock was returned to public equity markets in February 1992 after a thirteen-year absence. The company has more than 250 operating facilities in nine countries as well as a global marketing and distribution network.

Reliance Electric was founded in 1904 in Cleveland, Ohio, as a partnership between two cousins: inventor John Lincoln and industrialist Peter Hitchcock. Lincoln had developed a new and better arc-type light bulb while working with the Brush Development Company. He convinced Hitchcock to use his financial resources to develop, manufacture, and market the bulb. By the time the two formed their partnership, however, the inventor Thomas Edison had announced the development of his incandescent light bulb, rendering null Lincoln's advances of the clearly inferior arc bulb.

The partners were dismayed at this unfortunate turn of events, but Lincoln revealed that he had also been working on a new type of direct current (D-C) motor. Direct current was the primary means of electrification at the time because alternating current was considered dangerous and unpredictable. Lincoln invented the first adjustable speed direct current motor, and Hitchcock fronted the money to begin manufacturing. They shipped their first industrial electric motor in 1905. The two named their new company after the inventor: Lincoln Electric Motor Works.

When Hitchcock died in 1907, Lincoln sold his interest in the company to Charles and Ruben Hitchcock, Peter's sons. The youngest, Ruben, took over the company. Having little business or electrical experience, Ruben sought a new president. He found one in Clarence Collens, a Yale graduate, who stayed with the company in that capacity for the next forty years. Ruben Hitchcock served as executive vice-president. When Collens came on as president, the company was incorporated as Reliance Electric and Engineering Company. There had been some confusion in the Cleveland business community prior to the name change—another electric concern in the area was named Lincoln Electric.

The variable speed motor, or armature shifting motor, as it was known in the trade, was Reliance's only product until 1913. That year, the company's chief engineer, Alex McCutcheon, designed a T-line D-C motor that soon became Reliance's primary product. It was used in many of Cleveland's booming steel mills and was a mainstay of the product line until the early 1950s.

Reliance began to design and manufacture industrial alternating current (A-C) motors in the 1920s, but the company was late to join the race to convert to A-C. A-C generation had been developed around the turn of the century, and came into heavy use in industry by 1910. General Electric Company (GE) and Westinghouse Electric Co. had used the ensuing decade to become well-established producers of industrial A-C motors.

Combined, GE and Westinghouse held 50 percent of the United States' total industrial electric business. As industry leaders, they established the prices that the rest of the market followed. Reliance executives soon realized that they needed to find a niche for their company to remain competitive and profitable. They decided to concentrate on becoming a flexible, timely supplier of industrial motors, emphasizing the applied engineering aspect of the business. To accomplish this conversion, Reliance hired sales representatives with technical knowledge. These representatives would not just sell Reliance products, they would also investigate customers' needs and recommend equipment to get the job done.

One of the salesman, Jim Corey, proved his technical expertise when he received a patent for an adjustable voltage, multi-motor control system for use in the paper and textile industries. Corey was not trained as an electrical engineer. He had started at Reliance as a "blueprint boy," then moved up to become a draftsman, salesman, sales manager, vice-president of sales, and eventually president of the company.

Reliance made its first inroads into the A-C business in 1927 with a modification of the General Electric enclosed fan-cooled motor. The GE model was not well suited for the high-particulate environment found in most automotive factories, so Reliance copied and improved the motor for those specific conditions. A lucrative contract with General Motors for the manufacture of its new Pontiac cars gave Reliance just the push it needed to get established in alternating current motors.

The company grew quickly on the basis of these new technologies, and in 1929, on the eve of the Great Depression, Reliance's sales peaked at about $3 million. The Corey motor helped partially insulate the company from the severe economic downturn, since the textile industry was virtually depression-proof. The introduction of the first electrical variable speed drive package during the 1930s established Reliance's enduring leadership in that facet of the business.

During World War II, Reliance served as a primary supplier of motors to the military, especially the Navy. The company also supplied the motors needed to build hundreds of tanks. This war-related business required and enabled Reliance to build two new Cleveland plants in the 1940s and another in the suburb of Euclid in 1951.

Technological advances, like semi-conductors, transistors, and digital equipment, combined with mergers and acquisitions to drive Reliance's growth in the postwar era. During the 1950s, the company expanded its electrically-based products to include mechanical power transmission products. Reliance acquired the Reeves Pulley Company in 1955 and the Master Electric Company in 1957. These two entities complemented Reliance's established mechanical operations. The company prospered in the late 1950s, and its stock began to be traded on the New York Stock Exchange in 1957. Sales that year neared the $100 million mark. In 1959 Reliance established a Canadian subsidiary, and two years later, it formed a joint venture with a firm in Switzerland.

Mergers and acquisitions continued in the 1960s and 1970s. The Mechanical Group was expanded with the purchase of the Dodge Manufacturing Company in 1967. Dodge and previously-acquired Reeves were then, and remain in the late twentieth century, respected trademarks among power transmission products. That year Reliance also purchased the Toledo Scale Company. 1968 saw the acquisition of Atlanta-based Custom Engineering Corp., and Applied Dynamics, a computer manufacturer, was purchased the following year. With foreign sales of $30 million in 1969, Reliance purchased two European companies to secure its international position.

B. Charles Ames was named president and chief operating officer of Reliance in 1972, and was given the additional duties of chief executive officer four years later. In 1973 Reliance merged with Lorain Products Corp., a suburban Cleveland manufacturer of specialized power equipment for the communications industry. The company made its second acquisition in this field in 1977, with the purchase of Continental Telephone Electronic Co., a producer of telecommunications equipment. The company further shored up its telecommunications business with the purchase of Utility Products Co. of Milwaukee and Federal Pacific Co. of Newark. Kato Engineering, maker of industrial electrical generators, was purchased in 1978. As a result of these acquisitions, Reliance grew steadily over the course of the decade: the company marked its fourth consecutive year of record sales and earnings in 1976, posted profits of $13.4 million on sales of $207.6 million in 1977, and registered record earnings of $64.6 million on sales of $966.2 million in 1979.

In December of that year, the Exxon Corporation purchased Reliance for $1.24 billion. The sale consisted of $72 for each Reliance common share and $201.60 for each share of convertible preferred stock. Exxon, like several of its competitors in the oil industry, sought to use its excess capital to diversify its interests. Exxon was especially hopeful that Reliance would be able to manufacture the oil company's experimental "alternat-

ing current synthesizer," a device that would use current only when needed. Exxon boasted that the alternating current synthesizer, or ACS, could save the United States as much as one million barrels of oil each day. Exxon transferred its ACS Group to Reliance in 1980 so that the subsidiary could apply its electrical engineering expertise and develop, manufacture, and sell a line of variable speed drives using the new technology. By the end of 1981, however, it had become painfully clear that Exxon's ACS projections were exaggerated: the test model was too expensive and unreliable to be manufactured on a large scale. To make matters worse, Reliance posted losses in three of the next four recession-plagued years: $6 million in 1980, $50 million in 1982, and $59 million in 1983. The $31 million profit in 1981 did not come close to balancing the losing years.

Ownership by Exxon had both positive and negative effects on Reliance. There was some apprehension among Reliance's customers as to what the oil conglomerate would do with the motor manufacturer. That uncertainty was exploited by Reliance's rivals as they attempted to undermine customer confidence in the company's staying power. At the same time, Exxon supported Reliance throughout crises that might have devastated the company, had it remained independent during the 1980s. A recession in 1981 and 1982 diminished Reliance's primary markets, including steel and other metals, mining, machine tools, and industrial controls.

Federal Pacific Electric (FPE), which Reliance purchased just months before the 1979 Exxon takeover, turned out to be one of the company's most unfortunate acquisitions. Reliance discovered that FPE had been manufacturing some substandard circuit breakers, its largest line of products, and had deceived Underwriters Laboratory (UL) to get its approval for the critical home and commercial construction markets. As a result, UL withdrew its approval of all FPE circuit breakers, forcing the company to purchase and market others' products. Reliance initiated a costly seven-year, multi-suit litigation against UV Industries Inc., former owners of FPE, which was not concluded until the late 1980s, when Reliance divested the troublesome subsidiary.

The devastating recession, excess capacity, low demand, and intense competition forced the company to close its original plant on Ivanhoe Road in Cleveland in February 1984 and move its operations to more modern facilities in Ashtabula, Ohio, and Shelby, North Carolina. The tough times led to other cutbacks as well. From 1982 to 1984, Reliance eliminated 25 percent of its manufacturing space and 27 percent of its payroll. When a strong recovery forecast for 1986 did not materialize, further economizing was undertaken.

In 1985 Reliance earned $30 million on revenues of $1.67 billion and purchased Inertia Dynamics Inc., a small company headquartered near Hartford, Connecticut. Reliance hoped to combine Inertia Dynamics' expertise in electric clutches and brakes with its own industrial motor and drive technology in order to broaden its product line into copiers, motorized wheelchairs, computer disc drives, and other specialized equipment.

Reliance became the largest industrial motor manufacturer in the United States with the April 1986 purchase of the Medium A-C Motor Division from one of its oldest competitors, Westinghouse Electric Corporation. By the end of that year, Reliance entered a new phase in its ownership status when a group of the company's officers and institutional investors took the company private after six years under Exxon's wing. Led by John B. Morley, president and chief executive officer of Reliance since 1980, the investment group included Citicorp Capital Investors and Prudential Bache Securities, two New York investment firms. Citicorp purchased about 43 percent of the company in the buyout, Reliance management bought an estimated 15 to 20 percent. Prudential assumed about 13 percent, and institutional investors secured the remainder. The $1.35 billion leveraged buyout included two companies Reliance managed for Exxon: Exxon Printing Systems Inc., a startup ink-jet business in Connecticut, and Lionville Manufacturing Inc., an electronic design and production firm near Philadelphia. At the close of the leveraged buyout, 50 to 60 percent of Reliance's business was concentrated in electrical and mechanical sales, 25 percent of revenues came from telecommunications, and the remainder came from Toledo Scale Corp. sales. Although the company's stock was not publicly traded, many of its preferred stock and debt issues were traded on the over-the-counter market, requiring public disclosure of financial figures.

While under Exxon's control, the company had invested over $400 million of its own cash flow into new plants and economized substantially, but it was faced with massive interest charges after the buyout. In 1987 Reliance accumulated sales of $1.17 billion, posted a $4 million profit, and brought down its debt level to $969 million. The company moved to a new headquarters in 1989, following the 1988 sale of a forty-acre parcel of land to a St. Louis developer in exchange for the new building. The move consolidated staff from three buildings into one, thereby lowering some overhead costs, and brought in extra cash (from the sale of the old buildings) that was used to pay the debt from the buyout.

The 1989 sale of Toledo Scale Corp. to Mettler United States Inc., an affiliate of Switzerland's Ciba-Geigy Ltd., and a $24 million 1988 profit on sales of $1.3 billion helped Reliance bring its debt down to about $600 million, half the 1986 level. The significantly lower debt allowed Reliance to pursue more aggressive research and development and growth-oriented strategies, including acquisitions, joint ventures, and licensing contracts.

Several factors combined in the early 1990s to induce Reliance to make a public stock offering in 1992. In 1991 Citicorp indicated its desire to liquidate its 43 percent stake in Reliance common stock. That request led Reliance to hire Goldman, Sachs & Co. and Prudential Bache Securities (which still held 13 percent of Reliance) to help the company find a new primary investor. In November of that year, Reliance entered into preliminary discussions with Siemens Corp. that were expected to result in the acquisition of Reliance by the German company, but the negotiations failed in December. By this time, Reliance's debt had risen to $700 million. Plummeting interest rates prompted the company to refinance its buyout debt in 1992, saving approximately $36 million in interest costs. Reliance executives decided to further reduce debt by taking the company public in February 1992 with an offering of 15.8 million shares of common stock at $19 each. The over $300 million cleared from the sale was used to recover Reliance's outstanding subordinated debentures as part of the plan to recapitalize the company's debt-ridden balance sheet.

On its first day of public trading in more than a decade, Reliance topped the New York Stock Exchange's list of most active traders, with more than five million shares changing hands. Reliance remained cautiously focused on debt-reduction in the early years of the 1990s, thereby justifying a no-dividend policy. In 1992 alone, the company had reduced its debt from $588 million to $375 million, helping it raise its senior debt credit rating given by Standard & Poors to "BBB." Although a persistent recession prevented many of Reliance's traditional customers from making capital investments in the company's engineered products and systems, profits increased modestly from $34 million in 1991 to $48 million in 1992. Reliance dedicated itself to meeting the International Standards Organization's strict ISO 9000 global quality requirements by the end of 1993. The company continued to make significant investments in research and development ($103 million in 1992) to maintain its customer-driven research and fund experiments in new technologies, especially energy-efficient motors. Sales of industrial equipment constituted three-fourths of Reliance's sales in the early 1990s, but company executives still considered telecommunications an important growth vehicle.

CEO Morley hoped to lower Reliance's debt to $250 million, or a debt-to-equity ratio of about 33 percent, in 1993. Profits doubled in the first quarter of that year, perhaps forecasting Reliance's emergence from the nationwide recession.

Principal Subsidiaries: Reliance Electric Industrial Company; Reliance Comm/Tec Corporation; North American Transformer, Inc.; Reliance Motion Control, Inc.; Inertia Dynamics, Incorporated; Reliance Automation Pty. Ltd. (Australia); Reliance Electric GmbH (Austria); Reliance Electrica Ltda. (Brazil); Reliance Electric Limited (Canada); Reliance Electric Scandinavia ApS (Denmark); Reliance Electric S.A.R.L. (France); Reliance Electric (Hong Kong) Limited; Reliance Electric S.p.A. (Italy); Reliance Electric Limited (Japan, 45%); Reliance Electric Service Ltd. (Japan, 45%); Renix Co. Ltd. (Japan, 36.9%); Suntech Company, Ltd. (Japan, 49.2%); Yonjun-Reliance Electric Co. Ltd. (Korea, 55%); Reliance Electric & Engineering Co. S.A. de C.V. (Mexico); Dodge de Mexico s.A. de C.V.; Productos Lorain de Mexico S.A. de C.V.; Reliance Exportel S.A. de C.V. (Mexico); Reliance Electric (Singapore) Pte. Ltd.; Reliance Electric S.A. (Spain); Reliance Electric A.G. (Switzerland); Electro-Craft Limited (United Kingdom); Reliance Electric (UK) Ltd.

Further Reading:

"Reliance Sues UV Industries Trustees in FPE Sale," *(Cleveland) Plain Dealer,* June 27, 1980, 4-D.

"Exxon's Ownership Is Credited with Preserving Reliance's Status," *(Cleveland) Plain Dealer,* February 17, 1987, 5-D.

"Company History and Overview," Cleveland: Reliance Electric Company, [1992].

Conway, John A., "The Little Motor That Couldn't," *Forbes,* February 9, 1987, 8.

Gerdel, Thomas W., "Reliance Electric Sold by Exxon, Remains Here," *(Cleveland) Plain Dealer,* December 12, 1986, 1A, 4A.

——, "Repaying Debt Expands Reliance's Options," *(Cleveland) Plain Dealer,* March 9, 1989, 11-E.

——, "Reliance Developing Capital Plan," *(Cleveland) Plain Dealer,* May 3, 1991, 1-E.

——, "Reliance Chief Sees Bright Future," *(Cleveland) Plain Dealer,* December 25, 1991, 1-F.

——, "Reliance Electric to Continue to Reduce Debt," *(Cleveland) Plain Dealer,* April 16, 1993, 2-E.

Klein, Carrie, "Reliance Electric: Back in Gear," *Financial World,* v. 161, August 4, 1992, 12–13.

"Closing a Dreary Chapter," *Mergers & Acquisitions,* March-April 1987, p. 12.

Phillips, Stephen, "Reliance, Siemens Call Off Buyout Talks," *(Cleveland) Plain Dealer,* December 21, 1991, 1-E.

Picking, J. W., "Recollections and Reflections about Reliance, the Control Division, and Systems," Cleveland: Reliance Electric Company, 1967.

Solov, Diane, "Reliance Electric to Offer Shares to Help Repay Debt," *(Cleveland) Plain Dealer,* March 17, 1992, 7-F.

——, "Investors Receptive to Reliance," *(Cleveland) Plain Dealer,* May 8, 1992, 1-E.

Talbott, Stephen, "Buy-Out Means Independence for Reliance," *(Cleveland) Plain Dealer,* February 17, 1987, 1-D, 5-D.

Wiernik, Julie, "Exxon Offer for Reliance Deemed Fair," *(Cleveland) Plain Dealer,* May 26, 1979, 10-B.

—April S. Dougal

Rheinmetall Berlin AG

Kennedydamm 15-17
Postfach 10 42 61
D-40033 Düsseldorf
Germany
(211) 473-04
Fax: (211) 473-2900

Public Company (65% of shares held by Röchling Industrie
 Verwaltung GmbH, a holding company)
Incorporated: 1889 as Rheinische Metallwaaren- und
 Maschinenfabrik AG
Employees: 16,000
Sales: DM 3.5 billion (US$2.12 billion)
Stock Exchanges: Berlin Düsseldorf Frankfurt Hamburg
SICs: 3592 Carburetors, Pistons, Piston Rings, and Valves;
 3714 Motor Vehicle Parts and Accessories; 3554 Paper
 Industries Machinery; 3565 Packaging Machinery; 3480
 Ordnance and Accessories; 3795 Tanks and Tank
 Components; 2522 Office Furniture, Except Wood

Rheinmetall Berlin AG, the parent company of a group of more
than 60 industrial manufacturing firms, is a leading German
producer in each one of its four primary fields: defense technology, paper and packaging machinery, high-tech automotive
components, and, since 1993, office furniture. For most of its
100-year history, Rheinmetall Berlin and its predecessor corporations have been primarily involved in the weapons industry,
and it was not until the 1980s that the balance of production
shifted to nonmilitary industrial equipment.

The company's founder, Heinrich Ehrhardt, was an industrial
engineer from Zella in central Germany's Thüringen region.
After starting out as a sales representative and completing his
higher education on the side, Ehrhardt worked for a number of
years as an engineer for a cast steel works in Witten, where he
improved the production of train axles. In 1878 the 38-year-old
Ehrhardt founded his own small machine tool factory in Zella.
He quickly attained an excellent reputation as a designer and
industrialist, and the granting of licenses for his patents brought
him into contact with directors of foreign enterprises.

Ehrhardt had become mutual friends with the manager of a
munitions factory, Josef Massenez. When Massenez's company, Hörder Bergwerks- und Hüttenvereins, won a contract
from the War Ministry that it could not fulfill, Massenez offered

it to Ehrhardt in exchange for a commission. Although Ehrhardt
lacked the technical expertise, production capacity, and sufficient capital, he was willing to take the risk. Accepting the job,
Ehrhardt brought together a group of venture capitalist associates and on April 13, 1889, founded Rheinische Metallwaaren-
und Maschinenfabrik AG (Rhine Metalware and Machine Factory Joint-Stock Company), which was registered on May 7 as a
business in Düsseldorf on the Rhine.

At first Ehrhardt was completely occupied with the government
contract, untiringly developing an appropriate manufacturing
method. In December of 1889 production started in rented space
in Düsseldorf. Only three months later the young enterprise had
1,400 employees and supplied the war ministry with 800,000
projectiles a day.

Ehrhardt's ingenuity had paid off. On June 28, 1891, he received a patent for a "technique for simultaneous perforation
and modelling of iron and steel ingots in heated condition."
Having already begun the search for resourceful engineers two
years before while still in Zella, Ehrhardt took his employees'
talents further with the development of seamless tubing for gun
barrels. His company next developed a drawing technique,
which received a patent in April of 1892. Ehrhardt's pressing
and drawing methods for the production of metal tubing and
hollow parts garnered strong sales not only in the military, but
also in the shipping and railroad industries and in gas and water
utilities.

With the completion of his first government contract, Ehrhardt
began construction of Rheinische Metallwaaren- und Maschinenfabrik's own factory in Düsseldorf-Derendorf, to which production gradually shifted. A metal tubing manufacturing facility
and an iron foundry enabled production of nonmilitary products
as well. The expansion of the production programs had led to
increasing needs for steel, so in 1892 Ehrhardt and his son-in-
law Paul Heye acquired a small forge in Rath that they named
Rather Metallwerk Ehrhardt & Heye. In 1896 the forge was
merged into Rheinische Metallwaaren- und Maschinenfabrik as
the Rath division. Thus, Ehrhardt controlled a secure, integrated
output of quality steel and semi-finished products that rendered
him independent from suppliers.

In 1896 Ehrhardt developed a 7.5-cm field cannon into the first
barrel recoil cannon suitable for field service, a significant
technical development at that time. It brought Ehrhardt high
accolades from Norwegian kings, Austrian emperors, and finally German Kaiser Wilhelm II. With this development, Ehrhardt's company was guaranteed great business success.

For the field testing of weapons and ammunition, in 1899
Rheinische Metallwaaren- und Maschinenfabrik took a lease on
a large track of land near the village of Unterlüß in the Lower
Saxony. A small manufacturing facility was also established
there for the production of ammunition and cartridge cases.
In subsequent years the testing grounds were enlarged and
ultimately reached an area of 15 kilometers (km) long and
5 km wide.

Rheinische Metallwaaren- und Maschinenfabrik expanded its
production program and strengthened its market share with its
acquisition in 1901 of Munitions- und Waffenfabrik AG in
Sömmerda in Thüringen. At its factory, Dreysesche Gewehr-

fabrik, Munitions- und Waffenfabrik produced hand weapons, cartridges, and shell fuses. In the following years until the outbreak of World War I, Rheinische Metallwaaren- und Maschinenfabrik's manufacturing operation, partly through further acquisitions, developed considerably.

At the beginning of 1914 the Rheinische Metallwaaren- und Maschinenfabrik factories had nearly 8,000 workers. One year later, following the outbreak of World War I, there were 11,000 employees, and by 1918 the work force had grown to approximately 48,000, including about 9,000 women. Then, with the Armistice in November of 1918, military production came to a sudden standstill. The Düsseldorf enterprise, which had virtually quadrupled its staff during the war years, had to dismiss 22,000 employees.

With the signing of the 1919 Treaty of Versailles, prohibiting Germany from manufacturing large calibre weapons, Rheinische Metallwaaren- und Maschinenfabrik was deprived for a time of a substantial part of its business. Although small and midsized weapons could still be produced—beginning in 1921 it built mid-calibre guns for the navy—the company took a major turn toward building up its nonmilitary production capacity. Steel production at Rath was considerably strengthened in order to support civilian production. Meanwhile, the company was able to stay financially liquid by issuing public bonds, and in 1924 the majority of its stock was acquired by the state.

In the first half of the 1920s agricultural machinery, such as heavy steam-powered ploughs, railroad cars, and locomotive engines, were built in the company's Düsseldorf factories, while precision mechanical apparatus, including typewriters, calculating machines, and principal motor vehicle parts, were assembled at the Sömmerda plant in Thüringen. By 1921 the motor vehicle division had developed into a large and significant business within its industry in Germany. At the beginning of the 1920s the name Rheinmetall began to be used as a trademark.

Ehrhardt continued into old age to direct his creativity towards weapons technology development. In 1922 at the age of 81 he finally retired from Rheinmetall's board of directors and returned to his native Thüringen. He died on November 20, 1928, at age 88.

Meanwhile, Germany's economic crisis had intensified. As a result of the lack of orders, the civilian production division in Düsseldorf began showing losses, and, with the exception of the profitable steam-plough production, production lines gradually ground to a halt. However, Rheinmetall did not suffer as greatly as some other enterprises did. In April of 1933 it acquired another major company facing liquidation, August Borsig GmbH, one of Germany's leading manufacturers of locomotive engines. Two years later the merger led to a new name, Rheinmetall-Borsig AG, and in 1938 the headquarters of the firm moved from Düsseldorf to Berlin.

From the middle of the 1930s, Rheinmetall-Borsig, as with many other industrial enterprises at the time, developed and produced weapons and munitions in response to orders from the Reich War Ministry. Production included machine guns, tank guns, mortars and field artillery, anti-aircraft guns, and railroad guns.

With the outbreak of World War II in September of 1939, Rheinmetall-Borsig restructured itself into a Regular Works and an Affiliated Works. Regular Works comprised the facilities in Düsseldorf, Sömmerda, Unterlüß, and the Borsig plant in Berlin-Tegel, along with separate divisions in Derendorf, Rath, Grafenberg, Halver, Gruiten, and Oberkassel. Affiliated Works consisted of eight facilities that since 1936 had been used as production plants for weapons and munitions. The factories were located in Berlin, Guben and Fürstenberg (Mark Bradenburg), Breslau, and Apolda in Thüringen. By the first year of the war, all ordinance factories came under the control of institutions of the German armed forces. In March of 1940 the newly created Ministry of Armaments and Munitions began to coordinate the arms efforts.

As the war dragged on, the Nazi state demanded ever greater efforts from the industry to increase its weapons production. Demands of the commanders of the navy and air force for technical innovations compelled Rheinmetall-Borsig's research and development department to work under intense pressure. By July of 1944 the company had introduced nearly 20 different weapons systems into the armed forces. Its chief engineer since 1938, Carl Wanninger, was a talented and creative designer who provided a strong stimulus to the development of military technology. An example of the high level of Rheinmetall's research and development was its varied rocket projects, although there was only one rocket production line. At the beginning of the war, the factories of Rheinmetall-Borsig had about 47,000 workers, a number that climbed to 85,000 by October of 1944.

Toward the end of the war, air-raids left their mark on the Rheinmetall plants and impaired production considerably. Thus, numerous production activities of the Düsseldorf facilities were relocated to the central and eastern regions of Germany. Later, factories in Berlin and Sömmerda also prepared themselves to move. In November of 1944 British air-raids caused heavy damage to the factories in Derendorf and Rath. In March of 1945 the last smelting at the foundry in Derendorf took place, as Düsseldorf lay under severe artillery bombardment. Two months later the German Reich capitulated.

Under the occupation of Allied forces, Rheinmetall-Borsig had to give up its armaments production completely. A total production prohibition temporarily ceased all activities, and the company ended the war with a loss of 620 million Reichsmark. Many of Rheinmetall-Borsig's factories were completely dismantled by the Allies; it would not be until the 1950s that it was possible to begin normal business activities.

In order to resume civilian production, Rheinmetall-Borsig was reorganized and reincorporated in 1951. Borsig AG in Berlin and Rheinmetall AG in Düsseldorf were established as separate subsidiary operating companies of the same group management company, Rheinmetall-Borsig AG, a newly incorporated entity. In the following economically difficult years up until 1956, the Rheinmetall group undertook significant rebuilding. A small enterprise of civilian machine manufacture was started up at the company's two main locations, Düsseldorf and Berlin. Production in Düsseldorf centered on loading and transport equipment, while steam boilers and refrigerators were manufactured in Berlin.

On June 23, 1956, the majority share of Rheinmetall-Borsig AG, which had been controlled by the federal government since 1951, was purchased by Röchlingsche Eisen- und Stahlwerke GmbH and would eventually go to the latter's holding company. In August of that same year, the subsidiary Borsig AG was sold off after two eventful decades with Rheinmetall. With Borsig gone, the company was renamed Rheinmetall Berlin AG at the next general shareholders' meeting in November. The Düsseldorf subsidiary Rheinmetall AG became Rheinmetall GmbH in 1957. Soon, with the establishment of the Bundeswehr (federal armed forces), Rheinmetall again took up military productions while also continuing its civilian industrial machine manufacturing activities.

With the acquisition of Benz & Hilgers, a leading manufacturer of bottling and packaging machinery for the food industry, Rheinmetall diversified into packaging technology. Leading the business strategy of increasing nonmilitary industrial production were Chairman of the Board Ernst Röchling, board member Otto Kranzbühler, and veteran board member Otto Paul Caesar, who became chairman in 1968. In subsequent years more small machine manufacturing enterprises were founded or purchased, although they did not justify any change in the corporate structure.

Meanwhile, the military production sector expanded through Rheinmetall Berlin's traditional means of acquisition. In 1970 the company took over a majority share of Nico-Pyrotechnik, which was later transferred to Rheinmetall GmbH. In 1975 Rheinmetall GmbH acquired the munitions manufacturer NWM de Kruithoorn in Hertogenbosch of the Netherlands. Moving beyond guns and ammunition, in 1979 Rheinmetall delivered its first battle tank, Leopard 2, to the Bundeswehr. It was equipped with Rheinmetall's 120 mm smooth-bore gun, a noteworthy technological innovation in NATO (North Atlantic Treaty Organization) tanks.

By 1979 there were approximately 5,700 employees in the Rheinmetall group, bringing in sales of DM 735.5 million (US$401.3 million), 70 percent of which was in military production and 30 percent in industrial equipment manufacturing.

Rheinmetall Berlin tested the limits of its diversification with the 1979 acquisition of Württembergische Metallwarenfabrik (WMF), a manufacturer of such consumer durables as cutlery, silverware, glass, and hotel furnishings. The federal anti-trust commission, however, withheld its approval of the acquisition, and in 1985 WMF was sold off. The later acquisition in 1981 of majority shares in Ganzhorn & Stirn GmbH and Jagenberg AG propelled the Rheinmetall group more decisively in the direction of packaging technology. Ganzhorn & Stirn, subsequently renamed Gasti-Verpackungsmaschinen GmbH, ranked among the leading suppliers of bottle filling and capping machinery for the food industry. Jagenberg is a leading manufacturer of paper treating and converting machinery.

The acquisition of a controlling share in Jagenberg, a move initiated by Hans U. Brauner, chief executive of Rheinmetall Berlin since 1980, also necessitated restructuring the machine manufacturing business of Rheinmetall Berlin. A new independent profit center called Machinery was created at the same administrative level of the military equipment subsidiary Rheinmetall GmbH. The management of this new profit center was to be undertaken by the Jagenberg subsidiary.

The next major acquisition of Rheinmetall Berlin was the 1986 purchase of an 80 percent share of Pierburg GmbH in Neuss, a manufacturer of carburetion systems and motor components. Pierburg's activities were consolidated into the Rheinmetall group's third major business center, Automotive Components. Brauner, having become chairman of Rheinmetall Berlin in 1985, continued to spearhead the company's diversification as a means of balancing financial risk.

In the late 1980s more emphasis was put on research and development. In May of 1986 construction began on a new research and development center in Unterlüß, TZN Forschungs- und Entwicklungszentrum Unterlüß. The facility, which develops applied electronic technologies, is supported by Rheinmetall GmbH, the state of Lower Saxony, and a regional manufacturers' association. Meanwhile, the new subsidiary Pierburg GmbH was developing into an electronic-oriented enterprise in the field of carburetion technology. In 1988 Pierburg introduced the multi-point injection system Ecojet M and a lambda-controlled carburetor, Pierburg Ecotronic. In addition, Jagenberg introduced Jagmatic, a system for controlling squareness in the process of manufacturing paper. Other technological developments of Rheinmetall Berlin at this time included the introduction of compact lasers and automated control systems using five-axis robots in their production processes. By 1992 Rheinmetall Berlin was spending approximately five percent of its income on research and development.

With the 1988 acquisition of the Kampf group of companies, a leading manufacturer of foil machines, Jagenberg entered a new phase in machine construction. Machines for paper processing and rolling, foil-laying, plastic laminating, and packaging became the primary equipment types constructed. The movement toward packaging machinery was reinforced with the 1989 acquisition of Automation und Fördertechnik ELM GmbH, a packaging equipment firm. Acquisitions and careful management contributed to Rheinmetall Berlin's postwar record sales of DM 3.25 billion (US$1.85 billion) in 1988. Pre-tax profit was DM 171.8 million (US$97.82 million), and at the close of that year the group employed 15,465 people.

In the early 1990s the Machinery and Automotive Components sectors suffered as a result of the German and global recession. In 1992 Jagenberg's sales fell 12.6 percent, resulting in a net loss of DM 7.5 million (US$4.8 million), and Pierburg's sales fell 12.8 percent, causing a net loss of DM 6.6 million (US$4.2 million). Both subsidiaries reduced their work forces by 7 percent and 11.6 percent respectively. Consolidated group sales fell 9.8 percent to DM 3.1 billion (US$2.01 billion) with a net income of DM 20.2 million ($12.93 million).

With the end of the Cold War and resulting cutbacks in military spending, not only the group as a whole, but even the Defense Technology subsidiary Rheinmetall GmbH began to look for ways to expand into related nonmilitary technology. In April of 1992 Rheinmetall Berlin established Rheinmetall Machine Vision GmbH, an industrial image processing business with about 140 employees. Rheinmetall GmbH also entered the fields of nonmilitary explosives with the acquisition of Pyrotechnische

Fabrik Oskar Lünig GmbH; propellent chemicals with the acquisition of WNC-Nitrochemie GmbH; and security systems, including video surveillance and metal detectors, with the purchase of Heimann Systems GmbH. Other product developments were in the fields of computerized control and signal systems. In July of 1992 Rheinmetall won a contract for disposal of former East German army ammunition. Also in 1992, Rheinmetall GmbH discontinued its historic Düsseldorf facilities and moved its headquarters to Ratingen.

In March of 1993 Rheinmetall Berlin acquired a 63 percent share in the electronics company Preh-Werke GmbH, which expanded Pierburg's production into the field of electronic components. Preh manufactures digital input systems and control and indicator systems, which are used in automobile heating, ventilation, and air conditioning systems. Preh's sales prior to its acquisition were about DM 220 million (US$141 million), and it employed 2,000 people.

In February of 1993 Rheinmetall Berlin moved into an entirely new field of business with its acquisition of a 75 percent share of Mauser Waldeck AG, Germany's largest manufacturer of office furniture with sales of DM 400 million (US$256 million). This subsidiary, Office Systems, was established as Rheinmetall Berlin's fourth independent business sector and accounted for approximately 12 percent of the group's business. At that time Automotive Components of Pierburg GmbH contributed 28 percent, Machinery of Jagenberg AG 27 percent, Defense Technology of Rheinmetall GmbH 26 percent, and nonmilitary diversifications of Rheinmetall GmbH 7 percent of the group's business. These ratios would undoubtedly change as Rheinmetall Berlin AG continued to be a flexible group of companies prepared to adapt to industry's economic and technological developments.

Principal Subsidiaries: Rheinmetall GmbH; Pierburg GmbH; Jagenberg AG (51.83%); Mauser Waldeck AG (75%).

Further Reading:

"Ausbau zivile Aktivitäten," *Frankfurter-Allgemaine,* April 2, 1992, p. 21.
Ehrhardt, Heinrich, *Hammerschläge: 70 Jahre Deutsher Arbeiter under Erfinder,* Leipzig: K.F. Koehler, 1923.
Rheinmetall -eine Technologie-Gruppe, Düsseldorf: Rheinmetall Berlin AG, 1993.
"Rheinmetall kauft Heimann," *Frankfurter-Allgemaine,* April 2, 1993, p. 20.
Zeittafel 1889–1989, Düsseldorf: Rheinmetall Berlin AG, April 1989.

—Heather Behn Hedden

Riklis Family Corp.

725 Fifth Avenue
New York, New York 10005
U.S.A.
(212) 735-9500
Fax: (212) 735-9450

Private Company
Incorporated: 1980
Employees: 21,000
Sales: $1.5 billion
SICs: 5331 Variety Stores; 5199 Nondurable Goods, Nec;
    General Merchandise

Riklis Family Corp. is a privately-held conglomerate of variety retail businesses that have included Rapid-American Corporation, McCrory Stores, Faberge/Elizabeth Arden, Samsonite luggage, Collagen, Schenley Industries Inc., and E-II Holdings Inc. The company is almost wholly owned by the Riklis family, including Meshulam Riklis and his second wife, singer Pia Zadora, as well as his three children and six grandchildren from a previous marriage. Besides closed ownership, Riklis Family Corp. is private in another fundamental way: Mr. Riklis's deals have been so labyrinthine and secretive that few Wall Street firms or investors have been able to follow them. Fulfilling his reputation as a financial wizard, Riklis combined a penchant for complex financial transactions with $750,000 borrowed in the 1950s to create a multibillion dollar empire. By the 1990s, with substantial losses in McCrory Stores and numerous legal and financial setbacks, some analysts questioned whether the debt that had fostered the company's growth would prove too heavy to bear.

The history of Riklis Family Corp. reflects the unconventional profile of its founder. Meshulam Riklis was born in Turkey in 1923, while his parents were en route from Russia to Israel. He grew up in Tel Aviv, where he graduated from the Herzliya Gymnasia. In 1947, he traveled to Columbus, Ohio, and enrolled in Ohio State University. After receiving a B.A. degree in mathematics in 1950, he taught Hebrew in the Talmud Torah School in Minneapolis. A year later, he joined the investment firm of Piper, Jaffray and Hopwood in Minneapolis as a junior stock analyst.

Riklis quickly demonstrated his insight, talent, and ambition. As a stockbroker, he developed his conglomerate philosophy of paying with debentures and selling for cash. After talking several clients into creating a pool of $750,000, he began a spree of acquisitions that would culminate in the formation of Riklis Family Corp. and would situate him on the *Forbes* list of the 400 wealthiest people in the United States by the 1980s.

By 1956, Riklis had advanced from stockbroker to chairperson and CEO of Rapid Electrotype Company and American Colortype Company. In 1957 he merged the companies and became president of Rapid-American Corp., an office machine, printing, and Christmas-card company. Largely through high-yield debt and stock swaps, he began buying merchandising, tire, apparel, and packaging companies.

In 1960, Riklis acquired 38, and later 50 percent of the stock of United Stores Corporation, a subsidiary of H. L. Green Company, Inc., which had merged McCrory Stores, McLellan Stores, and H. L. Green Stores in 1959. The McCrory-McLellan-Green (M-M-G) relationship resulted in approximately 850 stores with an estimated annual volume of more than $310 million. Within 15 years, M-M-G, renamed McCrory Stores (a subsidiary of McCrory Corporation), would represent the keystone of Riklis Family Corp's variety store business.

The McCrory acquisition brought to Riklis a legacy extending back to 1882, when John G. McCrorey joined the country's earliest variety retailers by opening his first five-and-ten store in Scottdale, Pennsylvania (the 'e' was later removed from his name, allegedly to save costs on the growing number of store signs). The stores offered wide varieties of items at bargain prices, including brooms for ten cents and Boss handsaws at 24 cents each. In 1901, with 20 stores grossing roughly $498,000 a year, McCrory established a New York City headquarters. Operations quickly expanded to 69 stores in 1911 and 128 stores in 1915, when McCrory was incorporated under the laws of Delaware.

In 1922, McCrory Corporation opened one of the world's largest variety stores—two floors with 2,500 lineal feet of counter space—in Brooklyn, New York. The company had expanded to 159 stores with annual sales of $14,400,000.

The 1930s marked significant changes in management and planning. In 1931, John G. McCrory vacated the president's office after nearly 50 years of service and was succeeded by C. T. Green, who had been with S. H. Kress Company for 30 years. Green, and his successors, R. F. Coppedge and R. W. Paul, moved to modernize operations through construction of new stores, personnel training programs, and extended price ranges and merchandise assortments. However, McCrory Corporation and its 203 stores slipped into bankruptcy in 1933.

In 1936 the Morrow Brothers bought the debentures and preferred stock of both McCrory and its competitor, McLellan Stores, which was founded in 1916 and had also declared bankruptcy in 1933. Working through their United Stores Corporation, they negotiated a reorganization wherein they received about 37 percent of the new common stock. Under the direction of R. F. Coppedge, the "dime store" image was elevated with improved facilities and presentation, including more accessible window displays and consumer-friendly color schemes for store interiors. The June 1950 issue of *Chain Store Age* reported that "McCrory had become one of the leaders in the chain variety store field in fashion and ready-to-wear assortments." By 1957, sales reached approximately $112 million and net profit after tax totaled $3.5 million.

In 1958, Albert M. Greenfield, chairperson at Bankers Securities Corporation and Variety Stores Corporation, acquired a large percentage of United Stores Corporation stock. In January 1959, McCory and McLellan, 37 percent owned by United, effected a merger. Then on February 18, 1959, H. L. Green Company, Inc. acquired Greenfield's equity in United Stores Corp. H. L. Green Co. dated back to 1932, when Harold L. Green acquired five retail companies in the limited price field. With its 1959 McCrory-McLellan-Green acquisition, United had control over 850 stores.

Meshulam Riklis appeared on the scene in 1960, when he acquired a significant amount of the stock of United Stores. In 1961, the financier bought full control of the H. L. Green Company, Inc., temporarily taking over as president of McCrory Corp. but soon passing on responsibility to a line of carefully chosen managers. The new officers upgraded existing stores while expanding to new locations. They decentralized and realigned field management and appointed regional and district managers to better control sales and profits. Despite such efforts, M-M-G experienced several difficulties. Profits during the 1962–63 fiscal year were negligible. Declining earnings at McCrory Stores forced Riklis to liquidate all Rapid holdings except 51 percent of McCrory. From 1960 to 1964, the company had gone through four presidents and one acting president, contributing to general malaise and low morale.

This downswing was in part reversed by Samuel Neaman, who assumed the presidency of M-M-G in 1964. In addition to streamlining operations, Neaman focused on incentive plans, increasing salaries across the board and tripling bonuses over 1963. In a 1966 plan to increase efficiency, the company headquarters were moved from New York City to York, Pennsylvania, home of M-M-G's distribution center. The company experienced a dramatic upturn in profits.

Also in 1966 Riklis completed his master's degree in finance at Ohio State University. In an MBA thesis examining the early years of his career, he outlined his strategies for buying companies with borrowed cash. In the thesis, Riklis lauded "the effective use, or rather non-use, of cash." This strategy governed his dealings with McCrory and with the rapidly growing Riklis Family Corp. in general.

M-M-G continued to grow into the 1970s. In 1969 the company purchased 22 superstores in the south. In order to better service small variety chains and independent variety stores, M-M-G established the York Distribution Company (YDC) in 1970. Two years later, Rapid-American Corp. acquired the J. J. Newberry Company and merged it with McCrory Corporation, joining 650 M-M-G stores with 439 Newberry units, including select William Tally House Cafeterias. Renamed G. McNew, the resulting chain was decentralized and broken into six separate subdivisions, referred to as MAC companies.

After severe losses in 1973 and the 1974 resignations of McCrory Corporation's chairperson as well as the G. McNew division's president, the company again moved to stimulate growth. Emphasis was shifted from decentralization to strong central control from the Pennsylvania headquarters. On February 1, 1975, the chain's name was changed from G. McNew to McCrory Stores. In addition, measures were taken to close unprofitable stores, to rehabilitate low budget stores, to monitor and tighten overall efficiency, to launch an aggressive sales program, and to tailor cost-effective distribution in face of escalating transportation costs.

These measures paid off, increasing chain performance and spurring a new round of Riklis acquisitions. Rapid-American Corp., which already held 62.5 percent interest in McCrory Corporation, acquired full control on March 12, 1976. Through the acquisition, Rapid-American operated a total of over 2,000 stores, including 883 McCrory Stores. Later that year, McCrory further expanded by taking over the leases on 15 locations of the beleaguered W. T. Grant Company. Continued expansion included the takeover of eight variety stores from Neisner Brothers in 1980 and the acquisition of 46 S. H. Kress and V. J. Elmore stores from the S. H. Kress Company in 1981.

By the late 1980s, McCrory Stores was again experiencing heavy losses. To address the problem, Riklis retained an elite group of managers, whom he retrained in management, marketing, and sales skills, dubbing them the company's "green berets." From this group Riklis chose 30 members to serve as a squad of shock troops, dubbed "unit 101" after Israeli Industry and Trade minister Ariel Sharon's anti-terrorist unit. These special trainees were sent to McCrory's top 100 stores equipped, among other things, with a powerful incentive plan shared on all company levels: if the company's pre-tax profits were 10.4 per cent, all employees would receive a bonus of seven days pay; 11.4 per cent on sales would yield a bonus of 10 days pay. In June 1989, Riklis rewarded 2,000 McCrory employees and their spouses with a company-paid, two-week tour of Israel, Greece, and Egypt.

Other moves to improve McCrory business included streamlining and consolidating operations. In June 1990, the company's Bargain Time Inc. affiliate moved its main buying office to the McCrory headquarters in Pennsylvania and closed its buying office in Newark, New Jersey.

The 1980s were also marked by a series of new and convoluted financial feats at Riklis Family Corp. Riklis bought out Rapid-American's public stockholders in 1985 but left its debt in public hands. In doing so, he owned 100 percent of the equity in a debt-ridden but cash-generating conglomerate. By 1988, Rapid and McCrory held 23 debt issues totaling $750 million. Though the company's bond rating hovered at CCC, Riklis had little trouble raising approximately $150 million per year to service the debt. Even if McCrory's earnings plunged, as in 1987, other subsidiaries—such as Schenley Industries, Faberge toiletries, and McGregor apparel—provided necessary cash.

Keen on making further acquisitions but short on the necessary assets, Riklis engineered yet another ingenious solution in 1986. In May, he transferred the cash-generating Schenley and Faberge/McGregor assets from Rapid/McCrory to his Riklis Family Corp., paying for them largely in paper: nonvoting, cumulative preferred stock issued by the new Schenley company and the newly merged Faberge/McGregor.

In possession of the Schenley and Faberge/McGregor assets, Riklis was ready to conduct new deals. In 1987, Riklis Family Corp. sold Schenley to the United Distillers plc division of Britain's Guinness plc for $480 million. Schenley Industries Inc., was the sixth largest distributor of spirits in the United States and included in its portfolio Dewar's White Label, the country's leading scotch whiskey.

Like many of Riklis' deals, the Schenley sale did not pass without controversy. The press issued reports that the sale was a result of Riklis' entanglement in Guinness' scandal-ridden 1986 takeover of United Distillers Co. According to a June 19, 1989, *Business Week* article, among other sources, Riklis feared that Guinness would endanger his U.S. distribution of Dewar's whisky. Riklis and Guinness allegedly worked out a deal: Riklis purchased more than five percent of Guinness to help boost the price of stock with which Guinness was acquiring Distillers. In return, Riklis earned an indefinite extension of his Dewar's distribution contract, as well as the U.S. trademark for the whiskey, for a small fee. When Guinness' top managers resigned after the scandal came to light, new executives threatened Riklis with legal action. Even though the subsequent sale of Schenley incurred a pre-tax loss of $46 million, it enabled Riklis to wash his hands of the deal, according to *Business Week*.

In July 1988, an affiliate of the Riklis Family Corporation again attracted media attention with the acquisition of E-II Holdings Inc., a subsidiary of American Brands, Inc. The sale included Culligan International, Samsonite, Samsonite Furniture, Home Fashions, Beatrice Food Ingredients, Frozen Specialties, Lowrey's Meat Specialties, Martha White Foods, and Pet Specialties. Even before Riklis entered the picture, E-II had a turbulent history. In 1987, Chicago entrepreneur Donald P. Kelly launched the company by patching together a group of strong brands including Samsonite. After trying to use E-II to take over American Brands Inc., however, he lost his fledgling company to American Brands. Eager to bail out of E-II's massive debt, American Brands sold the company to Riklis in 1987 for $1.2 billion and assumption of $1.5 billion in debt. Riklis installed his long-time friend Steven Green as CEO of E-II and began a pattern of lopping off debt by selling assets.

E-II bondholders resisted the sale to Riklis, whom they feared was using E-II coffers to prop up ailing Riklis Family Corp. enterprises. They also were wary of Riklis' relatively low credit rating and feared that E-II's rating would sink to the level of its new parent. John Canella, a federal district court judge, ruled their complaint a "moot point," and denied an order barring the transaction. Yet E-II's fears were partly justified. E-II bonds which had sold at 110 percent of their face value fell to about 80 percent after the sale. In addition, many Riklis deals proved less than favorable to E-II interests: in December of 1989, Riklis sold E-II the money-losing Bargain Time Inc. retail chain from McCrory for $170 million plus preferred stock; six months later Bargain Time shut down and dumped its $221 million loss onto E-II's books; and in August of 1990, E-II paid $16 million for a group of California television stations owned by another Riklis affiliate.

The problems intensified, and, outraged by Riklis' alleged use of E-II funds for other interest, bondholders ousted him in 1990.

In July 1992, financier Carl Icahn scuttled Green's restructuring plans for the ailing company, arguing that Green was continuing to serve Riklis' interests. After filing for Chapter 11 in July, E-II announced a plan to sue Riklis for roughly $500 million siphoned out of the company. By April 1993, court rulings were still pending regarding Green's plans for overcoming bankruptcy and legally pursuing Riklis.

During this time, Riklis continued to work deals on other fronts. In October 1988 Riklis entered another segment of retailing with the purchase of Odd Lot Trading, Inc. by OLT-I Corp. and OLT-W Corp., subsidiaries of Riklis Family Corp., for approximately $37.1 million. Odd Lot was a 103-store chain specializing primarily in discounted merchandise.

After several years of negotiating a deal with Unilever PLC, Riklis finally sold its Elizabeth Arden cosmetics company to the consumer products titan in August 1992. With the introduction of Red Door, its first new fragrance since 1930, total retail sales jumped 29 percent, sending Arden in a positive direction under its new parent.

By the early 1990s, the highly leveraged debts supporting Riklis Family Corp. were in danger of losing much of their leverage, ensnaring Riklis enterprises in more setbacks. In 1992, Riklis' Las Vegas casino, the Riviera Hotel, filed for bankruptcy protection after some of its creditors refused to accept a restructuring plan. Riklis was still fighting the bondholder suit filed by E-II Holding Inc. Furthermore, in December of that year, McCrory Corp. announced it would close nearly one-quarter of its 1,000 stores. In February 1992, McCrory missed a payment of $3.37 million in debt securities and hinted that it might file for bankruptcy court protection. "Let's just say that I'm not eating any milk and honey," said Meshulam Riklis in a January 13, 1992, *Business Week* article.

Nevertheless, the story of Riklis Family Corp. was far from over. Known for his resilience and resourcefulness, Riklis would likely find a way to shore up losses, even if it incurred more debt.

Principal Subsidiaries: E-II Holding Corp.; Riklis Holding Corp.; McCrory Stores; Rapid-American Corp.

Further Reading:

"American Brands To Sell Part of E-II," *Reuters,* June 13, 1988.

Cashman, Greer Fay, "The 'Superstars' Have Come," *The Jerusalem Post,* June 8, 1989.

Grover, Ronald, Joseph Weber, and Peter Krouse, " 'Let's Just Say I'm Not Eating Any Milk and Honey,' " *Business Week,* January 13, 1992, p. 38.

"Guinness PLC Buys Schenley," *Business Wire,* September 17, 1987.

Lataniotis, Dolores, "There Are Two Kinds of Money," *Forbes,* July 25, 1988, p. 40.

"Lawsuit Filed On E-II Sale," *The New York Times,* August 5, 1988, p. D12.

Light, Larry, "Did Riklis Play it Straight?" *Business Week,* March 22, 1993, p. 75.

"McCrory Is Expecting To Miss Debt Payment," *The New York Times,* February 15, 1992, p. 39.

"McCrory Stores 100 Year History In Variety Retailing," New York: The Riklis Family Corp., 1982.

"McCrory Stores To Close Affiliate Headquarters," *Reuters,* June 6, 1990.

"Revco Announces Intention To Sell Odd Lot," *PR Newswire,* October 18, 1988.

Rice, Faye, "Elizabeth Arden; Profiting By Perseverance," *Fortune,* January 27, 1992, p. 84.

"Riklis Family Subsidiary To Purchase Odd Lot Trading," *PR Newswire,* October 19, 1988.

Rothman, Andrea, "Riklis' Fancy Footwork May Be Tripping Him Up," *Business Week,* June 19, 1989, p. 86.

—Kerstan Cohen

Riser Foods, Inc.

5300 Richmond Road
Bedford Heights, Ohio 44146
U.S.A.
(216) 292-7000
Fax: (216) 591-2640

Public Company
Incorporated: 1988
Employees: 4,500
Sales: $1.1 billion
Stock Exchanges: American NASDAQ
SICs: 5411 Grocery Stores; 5141 Groceries, General Line;
6719 Holding Companies, Nec

Riser Foods, Inc., a holding company, controls northeast Ohio's largest grocery chain. This leading retail and wholesale food seller and manufacturer is headquartered in a suburb of Cleveland, Ohio. The company was formed in 1988 through the combination of Fisher Foods, Inc.; Rini Supermarkets; Rego Supermarkets; and American Seaway Foods, Inc. The Riser name was arrived at through a combination of three company names: "RI" from Rini, "SE" from Seaway, and "R" from Rego. Riser's wholesale division distributes national brand and private label products to stores in Riser's subsidiary chains and to other retail competitors throughout Ohio and western Pennsylvania. The retail division, composed of 44 stores in northeastern Ohio, includes 42 groceries and two deep discount outlets.

Riser's oldest predecessor, Fisher Foods, Inc., was formed in 1907 as Fisher Bros. Co. by Manning and Charles Fisher. The two brothers moved from New York City to open a market in Cleveland because they heard that the city was growing fast and would need grocery stores. Their expectations were met and exceeded: within two years, Fisher Bros. had opened six additional stores, and by 1916, the chain boasted sixteen stores. The company built a state-of-the-art warehouse to supply its stores in 1923, and became one of the first area chains to open a "complete food store" offering fresh meats in 1928. Fisher Bros.' slogan, "It's Fresher at Fisher's," helped the chain win customers from traditional meat markets.

Even the Great Depression did not impede the grocery chain's growth: in 1930, the company doubled its warehouse capacity. By 1937, the founders had died and left the company to Ellwood

Fisher, Manning's son. Fisher Bros.' gold and green signs adorned over 300 neighborhood stores at the end of the decade. With the advent of increased automobile travel and the interstate system after World War II, Cleveland became more suburbanized, and Fisher Bros. was able to consolidate many of its smaller stores. By 1948, the company had halved its number of stores, but remained Greater Cleveland's largest retail food distributor, with over $63 million in sales.

Fisher did not fare as well when competition intensified in the postwar era. By the mid-1960s, the 75-store chain was losing money on $86 million in annual sales, and held only 12 percent of the metropolitan Cleveland market it had once dominated. In 1965, a group of investors that included two sets of brothers, Carl and John Fazio and Sam and Frank Costa, purchased a controlling interest in Fisher Bros. for an estimated $3.1 million. The investors were all involved in the Stop-N-Shop Super Markets Association, and although at least one Fisher Bros. stockholder fought the sale, it was permitted. The purchase merged Fisher Bros. with the other investors' namesake chains, Fazio and Costa supermarkets.

Carl and Frank Fazio, who had owned six supermarkets before the merger, became chairman of the board and president, respectively. The new owners closed 28 stores and renamed and remodeled others in an effort to revive the languishing Fisher chain. The Fazios had been involved in Cleveland's grocery trade since the 1920s, when the Sicilian immigrants started a fruit and vegetable stand in the suburb of Cleveland Heights. Within three years, the chain was earning $4.5 million, and had regained a 21 percent share of the market.

The renamed Fisher Foods, Inc. made its first venture outside Ohio with the purchase of Chicago's Dominick's Finer Foods for $12 million in stock in 1968. This 18-store chain had been founded by Dominick DiMatteo, Sr., and was owned by Dominick DiMatteo, Jr. That same year, the Fazio's chain was extended to Columbus, Ohio, where it eventually grew to include six stores in Ohio's capitol city. In 1970, Fisher moved into the Warren-Youngstown area of Ohio with eight new stores, and two years later, the company acquired the 46-store Shopping Bag chain, which became Fisher's southern California division.

Fisher had experienced financial growth through strategic consolidation and acquisition during the decade after it changed ownership: the new management closed a total of 58 stores from 1964 to 1975, yet sales grew from $86 million to $1.3 billion during that period, making Fisher's the 26th largest retailer and 13th largest food chain in the United States. By the mid-1970s, Fisher had 197 stores in Ohio, Illinois, and California.

But this expansion was heavily financed, and several factors combined to stunt Fisher's growth in the late 1970s. Wholesale food prices had skyrocketed in 1973 and 1974, and when those prices plateaued, grocery surpluses glutted the market. This surplus, combined with a slowing of population growth in many areas (especially Cleveland) after 1975, forced many store owners to realize that the only way they could increase market share was to lower prices and bring in more customers. Price wars broke out in Los Angeles, Chicago, and Cleveland, but many industry analysts noted that, once the competition ended—or people could not decide which store had the lowest prices—

shoppers returned to their regular stores. To exacerbate the lowered profit margins and increased advertising outlay effected by the price wars, many supermarkets, including those in the Fisher group, were hit with higher labor costs and increased energy expenses during the oil crisis of the late 1970s.

In 1976, Fisher lost its number one spot in the Cleveland food market to Pick-N-Pay, which held a full third of the market. Later in the year, the Costa brothers retired from Fisher Foods' board of directors. Profits dropped another 64 percent in 1977, when the chain's share of the northeastern Ohio market dropped from 29 percent to 26.5 percent.

Fisher's California chain—which, at 46 stores, was still relatively small—was fined $5,000 in Los Angeles for fifteen charges of false advertising and one charge of mislabeling in July 1977. Fisher pleaded no contest, claiming that the infractions all stemmed from oversights, not deliberate deception. This, however, would not be the last time the grocery chain and its officials would be brought to court for charges such as these.

The chain seemed to bounce back somewhat in the last two years of the 1970s, when wholesale prices rose nine percent and ten percent. Fisher began to contend with Pick-N-Pay, regaining 28 percent of the Cleveland market to Pick-N-Pay's 29.1 percent. The grocery chain's profits soared to $9.83 million on sales of $1.45 billion in 1978. That year, the company sold its southern California stores to Albertson's, Inc., of Boise, Iowa for more than $50 million.

In 1979, Fisher turned to warehouse-style stores to save labor and overhead. It opened ten of the groceries, which asked customers to package their purchases with their own shopping bags and used computerized checkouts to cut labor requirements, in Akron and southern Ohio. That year, decades of rumors that the Fazio brothers had trouble working together culminated in the forced resignation of John Fazio as president and CEO. Dominick DiMatteo, Jr. succeeded him as president and three administrators shared the duties of the chief executive office: John's brother, Carl, DiMatteo and Robert G. Everett. John Fazio was Fisher's single largest shareholder, with 12.5 percent of the company's stock. Carl held 12.3 percent.

Although the new administration hoped that the new warehouse stores would help increase profit margins, the initial startup and conversion costs hit Fisher hard in 1979: Moody's Investors Service and Standard & Poor's Corp downgraded the company's long term bonds to "speculative investments" that year because the company could barely cover its debt. The company lost $7 million on sales that declined eight percent that year.

Fisher consolidated its position in the early 1980s, beginning with the closing of all eight Warren-Youngstown stores in the wake of numerous steel plant closings in 1979 and 1980. In the fall of 1980, Fisher also sold six Fazio's in Columbus to Seaway Food Town, Inc., of Maumee, Ohio. The divestments continued in 1981, when Fisher sold its two stores in northern Kentucky and three in Cincinnati. In December of that year, Dominick DiMatteo, Jr. bought back the 71-store Dominick's Finer Foods chain for over $80 million ($74.3 million in cash, and $4 million in stock). The sale of the Dominick's chain contributed the bulk ($20 million) of Fisher's 1981 profits of $21.1 million. The company used the rest of the proceeds of the Dominick's sale to reduce long-term debt from $60 million to $20 million and hoped to strengthen and expand the company's northeast Ohio stores. The sale left Fisher's with 64 components: 57 supermarkets in Ohio, a commercial bakery in Columbus, a doughnut plant in Cincinnati, an ice cream plant, a distribution center, a fruit basket company, a meat commissary, and a produce warehouse.

In the fall of 1981, price-fixing charges were brought against Fisher, contending that the company collaborated with First National Supermarkets, Inc. (parent of Pick-N-Pay stores) and the Association of Stop-N-Shop Stores to price goods below cost and thereby force others out of business. The company was slapped with five multi-million-dollar suits from individuals and companies. Later that same year, a second anti-trust suit was brought against Fisher and others by two nursing homes and a restaurant for fixing wholesale prices. Both cases enumerated infractions in the late 1970s. The first case resulted in the largest consumer class action settlement of a price-fixing case in U.S. history: one million households in seven northeast Ohio counties received $20 in grocery coupons. John Fazio, who was president and CEO of Fisher Foods when the violations occurred, was sentenced to five years of probation beginning in 1982, but his sentence was commuted in 1984.

Consolidation hit closer to home in 1982, when Fisher closed ten Cleveland-area stores. By the end of the year, the chain had been cut to 47 northeast Ohio stores. Management worked to extract concessions from grocery labor unions and concentrated on expanding the Heritage Wholesale Distribution Center that had been started in 1981. In 1983, Carl Fazio retired as chairman and CEO. He was succeeded by Bill J. Nichols, who had served only a few months when Cincinnati businessman Carl Lindner's American Financial Corp. bought 16.5 percent of Fisher's for $10.69 million. The following year, Lindner purchased all of the estimated 900,000 shares owned by Carl Fazio and family for $12.6 million. The acquisition increased American Financial's stake in Fisher Foods to more than 35 percent.

But Lindner had bought into an industry that was struggling with a familiar set of problems. The Cleveland-area market was plagued by decreasing population, high labor costs, new non-union competition, market saturation, and some of the lowest profit margins in the United States. The northeast Ohio market was the ninth largest in the United States: food sales in the 19-county area rose from $2.1 billion in 1973 to almost $4.8 billion a decade later. But population dropped by over 155,000 during that period, and from 1980 to 1982 alone, population in metro-Cleveland's Cuyahoga County dropped 25,400. Some industry observers noted societal shifts that hurt traditional groceries as well, including changing household and work patterns that favored more convenience store shopping and fast food restaurants.

In 1984, Fisher lost $5.5 million. Robert L. Hayden, who became president of the ailing grocery chain in the fall of 1985, tried to convert more stores to warehouse-type markets. By this time, Lindner's American Financial had become Fisher's largest shareholder, with 44 percent of the company's stock. Hayden worked to modernize many of the Fazio stores, and opened six Carl's Superstores and two Jax discount drugstores by 1986. Fisher Foods, the only publicly held grocery in the

Cleveland area, lost $1.95 million that year due to remodeling costs and interest expenses.

In January 1987, Lindner sold his 44.6 percent stake in Fisher to 5300 Ricmond Road Corp., a private company, for $20.6 million. 5300 was a joint venture of American Seaway Foods, Rego's Stop-N-Shop, and Rini's Stop-N-Shop. American Seaway was the Cleveland area's largest food wholesaler, with $380 million in annual sales. American Seaway was formed in 1957 through the combination of four family-owned businesses: Eagle Wholesale, Economy Wholesale, J.F. Sanson and the David Lombardi Co. Rego's and Rini's, also family-owned and operated businesses, had 11 and 10 supermarkets, respectively, in 1987. The latter two chains operated under the advertising umbrella of Stop-N-Shop.

Fisher's new management closed 19 stores within six months of the purchase, and threatened to shutter the entire chain, unless it could negotiate concessions with the United Food & Commercial Workers. In mid-year, Fisher employees rejected, then accepted a compromise that eliminated 800 jobs in favor of maintaining the 42 remaining stores and the jobs they offered.

The 5300 Richmond Road Corp. and Riser proposed the merger of Rini's, Rego's, and Fisher's in the fall of 1987 through an exchange of stock. But the plan had to overcome the specter of price-fixing from the late 1970s. Part of the settlement reached in that case forbade Fisher from exchanging information with Stop-N-Shop or opening a store under the Stop-N-Shop umbrella. The three companies' shareholders and the appropriate federal agencies finally approved the merger in June 1988, after Fisher sold nine more stores in its effort to streamline operations.

The newly organized Riser Foods Inc. consisted of 53 stores: one Fazio's; 11 Rini's Stop-N-Shops; ten Rego's Stop-N-Shops; 18 Rini-Rego Stop-N-Shops; 11 Carl's Superstores; one Food Center Supermarket; and one Supersavers discount drugstore. The combination of American Seaway with Fisher's Heritage Wholesale operations created one of the largest food wholesaling concerns in the Midwest. Anthony C. Rego became co-chairman in charge of administration and joint CEO of the new entity. Charles A. Rini, Sr., headed Riser's retail operations and was named president of Riser, and Michael L. Borstein headed the wholesale operations and served as the other joint CEO.

Fisher lost $27.4 million in 1987 while management struggled to adjust to the new corporate culture. Their first move was to change the nameplate of nine Fazio's to Rini-Rego Stop-N-Shops. The renamed stores reported that sales jumped 20 percent in the first few months of operation under the new name. The Rini-Rego name conveyed a good reputation to replace the infamy Fazio's had earned in some neighborhoods. The new management also tried to infuse Carl's with new vigor, and even opened an 11th store in August 1988, but eventually had to close all the stores.

Riser went public in 1988 on the American Stock Exchange. During 1989, the company sold and subleased eleven stores and closed three others in a continuing austerity plan. The three-man management team tried to pare liabilities by increasing profit margins and reducing inventory. They hoped to use revenue, not loans, to remodel and expand. But a recession that started in the late 1980s and continued into the early 1990s prevented Riser's retail operations from achieving profit goals. During the recession, consumers were more willing to shop around for bargains. They found their deals at competing wholesalers, while discounters like Sam's Club, Kmart, and Twin Valu. The Food Marketing Institute warned grocers that alternative-format stores—including clubs, mass merchandisers and supercenters—would increase their share of the grocery business to 13 percent from six percent by the turn of the century. These low-cost outlets also helped fuel a 3.3 percent decline in food prices in the first few years of the decade.

Riser's responded to the low-cost challenge with its own bulk merchandise. The company's private label helped keep more of the profits in Riser's cash flow as consumers "traded down" to branded products during the recession. Riser capitalized on this trend by expanding its private label line to 500 items and repackaging the products to make them look better. But despite all these efforts, net sales for fiscal year 1991–92 declined 3.6 percent to $979 million, down from $1.022 billion.

Riser sold its unprofitable Food Service Division to Sysco Food Services of Cleveland, Inc. in 1992 and closed yet another retail store. The company also worked to enter more vibrant local markets by purchasing two stores, remodeling two, and replacing an outdated grocery with a larger store of 52,000 feet. Perhaps the most promising division of Riser resulted from the combination of the wholesale warehouses of American Seaway and Fisher, which enabled the company to supply up to 65 percent of a grocery's needs. In January 1992, this division got a lift when a competitor from New York, Peter J. Schmitt, filed for bankruptcy, leaving 85 northeast Ohio and western Pennsylvania supermarkets without a supplier. Riser's wholesale division was able to increase its volume to approximately 500 stores as a result of Schmitt's collapse.

Late in 1992, Riser's groceries held 25 percent of the Greater Cleveland grocery business, a virtual tie with its largest competitor, Finast Supermarkets. Although that year's profits dropped another 16 percent, to $8.12 million, the management planned to raise capital reinvestment for 1993 by about 2.5 percent, to $26.5 million. Riser planned to upgrade supermarkets and bank on the wholesale and food manufacturing divisions. Riser's plan for competing in the retail arena included new advertising, increased customer convenience features, and upgraded store facilities. The company hopes to utilize unique and regionally exclusive concepts to capture an even larger number of Greater Cleveland grocery shoppers.

In July 1993 Riser announced that it had entered into an agreement to purchase various assets of Boston Distributors, including a portion of that company's existing inventory and a 350,000-square-foot warehouse facility in Maple Heights, Ohio. Riser plans to use the acquisition to begin operations of its own health and beauty care and general merchandise warehouse.

Principal Subsidiaries: Fisher Foods, Inc.; Eagle Ice Cream Co.; Rini Holding Co.; Rego Supermarkets, Inc.; Rini-Rego Warehouse Co.

Further Reading:

Clark, Sandra, "Food Fights Heat Up," *Plain Dealer* (Cleveland), October 13, 1992, pp. 1F, 6F.

——, "Riser Foods to Boost Capital Outlay 9.4 Percent in '93," *Plain Dealer* (Cleveland), December 13, 1992, p. 5E.

——, "Riser to Supply 53 More Ohio Supermarkets," *Plain Dealer* (Cleveland), June 26, 1992, p. 1G.

Frisby, Michael K., "Supermarket Firms Face Price-fix Trial," *Plain Dealer* (Cleveland), October 15, 1981, pp. 1A, 5A.

Gerdel, Thomas W., "Fisher Sells 71 Chicago Stores for $100 Million to First Owner," *Plain Dealer* (Cleveland), December 31, 1981, p. 2B.

——, "Grocery Strategies Churn as Sales Sag," *Plain Dealer* (Cleveland), September 23, 1984, pp. 1E, 2E.

Gleisser, Marcus, "Fazios to sell Fisher Foods Stock," *Plain Dealer* (Cleveland), March 8, 1984, p. 5C.

——, "Fisher Foods Described as Strong," *Plain Dealer* (Cleveland), October 12, 1985, p. 3B.

——, "New Yorkers' Efforts Launched Chain," *Plain Dealer* (Cleveland), July 9, 1987, p. 9C.

"Grocers 30 Years Give Faith Credit," *Plain Dealer* (Cleveland), March 15, 1937, p. 2.

Karle, Delinda, "Control of Fisher Foods Sold," *Plain Dealer* (Cleveland), January 13, 1987, p. 1A.

——, "Fisher's Problems Felt Industrywide," *Plain Dealer* (Cleveland), July 13, 1987, pp. 1B, 3B.

——, "Fisher Merger with Rini, Rego Is Proposed," *Plain Dealer* (Cleveland), September 26, 1987, p. 4B.

Koshar, John Leo, "Fisher's Fazio Steps Down," *Plain Dealer* (Cleveland), April 27, 1983, p. 4C.

"L.A. Fines Fisher Foods for False Ads, Mislabeling," *Plain Dealer* (Cleveland), July 21, 1977, p. 3E.

"Q & A," *Plain Dealer* (Cleveland), September 26, 1976, supp., p. 40.

"Riser Broadens Its Sharp Sword of Service," *Tri-State News*, October 1992, pp. 1, 16.

Russel, Mark, "Riser Foods Management Is Optimistic," *Plain Dealer* (Cleveland), July 26, 1988, pp. 1D, 14D.

Talbott, Stephen, "Fisher's Operations Separated; Sale Seen," *Plain Dealer* (Cleveland), November 9, 1984, p. 18B.

Wiernik, Julie, "Fisher Foods Is Pulling Out of Slump," *Plain Dealer* (Cleveland), April 19, 1978, p. 8E.

Woge, Mairy Jayn. "Fazio's, Pick-n-Pay in New Antitrust Suit," *Plain Dealer* (Cleveland), November 13, 1981, p. 1A.

Yerak, Rebecca, "Riser Foods Settles Suit Over Stamps," *Plain Dealer* (Cleveland), August 19, 1989, p. 2E.

—April S. Dougal

Ritz-Carlton Hotel Company

3414 Peachtree Road NE, No. 300
Atlanta, Georgia 30326
U.S.A.
(404) 237-5500
Fax: (404) 261-0119

Private Company
Incorporated: 1983
Employees: 14,000
Sales: $2.9 billion
SICs: 7011 Hotels, Motels

Since the early years of the twentieth century, the name Ritz-Carlton has been synonymous with the luxury hotel, conjuring images of opulent yet elegant furnishings based on designs from Versailles and Fontainebleau, *haute cuisine* in the best French tradition, and meticulous attention to the needs and comforts of its clientele. The Ritz-Carlton Hotel Company in Georgia is known in the hotel industry for its unwavering commitment to the tradition of impeccable service and luxurious ambiance introduced by the man who made the Ritz name famous, Cesar Ritz.

The ambitious child of a poor herdsman, Cesar Ritz was born in 1850 in the small mountain village of Niederwald, Switzerland. One of thirteen children, Ritz left home at the age of 16 to work in the dining room of a hotel in the adjacent town of Brieg. After a few months on the job he was fired, according to his employer, for not possessing even an "aptitude," much less a "flair," for the hotel business. Hired as a waiter in the restaurant of another hotel, Ritz was soon fired once again.

Undismayed, Ritz traveled to Paris, where he worked emptying slops for small hotels. Fired from two more jobs, he finally landed a position at a chic restaurant near the Madeleine and worked his way up from bus boy to manager. At the age of 19 he was asked to become a partner by the owner of the restaurant, yet Ritz politely refused the offer. His ambition was still unsatisfied, but now that he knew what he wanted, he rolled up his aprons and sauntered down the street to the most elegant and famous restaurant of the day, Voisin, an international meeting place for royalty and gourmets. Starting at the bottom as an assistant waiter, Ritz learned how to carve a roast and press duck, how to decant wine, and how to serve food in ways that pleased both the eye and the palate.

It was at Voisin that Ritz developed his instincts for high-quality food and service, and his personal touch began to attract influential customers such as Sarah Bernhardt, Alexandre Dumas the younger, and the Rothschilds. When Germany invaded France and laid siege to Paris in 1871, a food scarcity led the city zoo to butcher its two elephants; Voisin's purchased the trunks of the animals. When Ritz served them in high style, *trompe sauce chasseur* became a gourmet's rage and Ritz himself an overnight sensation in Parisian culinary circles.

A short time later, Ritz left Paris and worked for three years in resort restaurants and fashionable hotels in Nice, San Remo, Rome, Baden-Baden, and Vienna. Good luck now came his way. Ritz was the restaurant manager at Rigi-Kulm, an Alpine hotel renowned for its location and cuisine, when he was informed one cold winter day that the heating plant had broken down and, at almost the same moment, that a group of 40 wealthy Americans were to arrive soon for lunch. Ritz ordered lunch to be served in the drawing room instead of the dining room—it looked warmer because of the large red curtains that framed the room. He directed the waiters to pour alcohol into large copper pots and then set them afire, and bricks were placed in the ovens. The room was warm when the Americans arrived, and each of them was given a brick wrapped in flannel to warm their feet. By the end of the meal, which started with a peppery hot consomme and ended with flaming crepes suzette, the guests were gushing with praise for the young manager.

Reports of Ritz's modest miracle of quick thinking and resourcefulness spread among hotelmen throughout Europe and the United States. When the owner of a large hotel in Lucerne heard the story, he immediately hired Ritz to act as his general manager. The hotel had been losing money steadily for some time, but the 27-year-old former peasant revived the hotel in two years. Here he developed and refined the hotel service and methods that made his name famous. "People like to be served, but invisibly," Ritz once said. And it was Ritz who originated the phrase "The customer is always right." Ritz remembered who preferred Turkish cigarettes, who loved gardenias in their room, and who ate chutney during breakfast. If a diner didn't like the way his meat was prepared, it was immediately whisked away without any questions asked. For Ritz, no detail was too small and no request too big if it meant satisfying a customer.

In 1892, Ritz journeyed to London to manage the Hotel Savoy, an elegant hotel in the midst of a financial crisis. Ritz brought along his lifelong associate, Auguste Escoffier, a chef whom he had met during one of his jobs in Europe. With Ritz devoting his attention to a myriad of details, sometimes roving from room to room remaking beds to assure his guests the most comfortable night's sleep in London, at other times arranging lavish entertainment for important customers, and with Escoffier whipping up gourmet dishes in the kitchen, the Savoy soon became the toast of London's high society. When Alfred Beit, a diamond mogul from South Africa, asked Ritz to arrange a party for him, Ritz flooded the Savoy's main dining room and transformed it into a miniature Venice, with dinner served to guests as they lounged in gondolas serenaded by native gondoliers. At another party, with Cecil Rhodes, James Gordon Bennett, Lord Randolph Churchill, and Gilbert and Sullivan attending, Ritz arranged for Caruso to sing for their evening pleasure. After three years, the Savoy's stock rebounded from a few shillings to 20 pounds a share.

When a quarrel broke out one day between Ritz and the directors of the Savoy, Ritz left the hotel never to return again. Ritz's friends reacted immediately with over 200 telegrams sent to show him their support. The Prince of Wales, a close friend who was later to become King Edward VII, wired the statement, "Where Ritz goes, we follow." With such support from wealthy and influential friends, Ritz decided to pursue a dream he had had for years—to open a hotel of his own that would be the epitome of elegance.

The Ritz Hotel, built in Paris on the Place Vendome, opened for business in 1898. The lobby was small to discourage idlers, and only 225 rooms were constructed for its guests, but furnishings were exquisite and service meticulous to the last detail. Ritz designed a garden to encourage conversation over coffee and tea; he painted the hotel's walls instead of papering them because it was easier to keep clean; he borrowed the overall color scheme for the hotel from a painting by Van Dyck; and, highly innovative for the time, Ritz equipped many of the rooms with private baths. Ritz also established the traditional apparel for hotel personnel: a black tie for the maitre d'hotel, a white tie for the waiter, and brass buttons for the bellhop's uniform. On opening day people came from miles around Paris to walk through the hotel's corridors. And anybody who was anyone during the early years of the twentieth century—from J. P. Morgan to Lily Langtry—either lunched or dined at some time in the Hotel Ritz.

Ritz prepared an elaborate reception and elegant dinner in 1902 in honor of the coronation of his good friend Edward VII. All the arrangements had been finalized when a telegram informed Ritz that Edward was grievously ill and required an operation. With a heavy heart the great hotelier attended to the details of cancellation and then, exhausted from his exertions, collapsed. He revived and redoubled his efforts to please patrons of the hotel, but suffered a physical and mental breakdown in 1911. Never fully regaining his renowned verve and energy for work, for seven years Ritz was a figurehead at his own hotel. In October 1918, as he lay dying, Ritz thought he saw his wife at the bedside and asked her to take care of their daughter. Ritz and his wife had no daughter—the "daughter" was the way both of them referred to Ritz's dream hotel in Paris.

Near the turn of the century, Ritz had arranged to build and operate the Carlton Hotel in London, and, shortly thereafter, opened the Ritz Hotel in Picadilly. At this time, he also organized a group of hoteliers and financiers and created the tricontinental Ritz-Carlton Management Corporation. The purpose of the group was to lease the Ritz-Carlton name, crest, and stationary to interested parties willing to establish a hotel of their own and abide by the service and culinary standards set by Ritz himself. Under the terms of this agreement, one of the most famous of all the Ritz-Carlton Hotels opened in New York in 1910.

The New York Ritz-Carlton was built for $5 million, and its equipment and furnishings cost $750,000 more. Robert Goelet, a businessman, paid $5,000 for use of the Ritz-Carlton name and nurtured the hotel like one of his children. Soft rugs, gilded mirrors, glittering chandeliers, oversized bathtubs, and vials of perfume under the seats of the elevators welcomed and rewarded its rich guests. The hotel immediately became renowned for its superb cuisine—Chef M. Diat created Vichyssoise in its kitchen in 1912. On every floor two waiters were stationed day and night to attend the needs of customers who preferred to eat in their rooms. The hotel was a mecca for the world's richest and most famous people and, for New York society, was host to a seemingly endless stream of balls, cotillions, and receptions. For one coming-out party, its ballroom was decorated with $10,000 worth of eucalyptus trees; at another, live monkeys helped transform the ballroom into a tropical jungle. Joffre, Foch, Clemenceau, Leopold I of Belgium, the Duke of Windsor, Mrs. George W. Vanderbilt, and Charlie Chaplin were all served at the Ritz-Carlton. The New York Ritz-Carlton remained faithful to Cesar Ritz's imperatives—pamper your guests with lavish surroundings and meticulous service.

During the 1920s, the Ritz-Carlton Management Company leased the use of its name to a number of financiers that wanted to build hotels and were also willing to abide by the standards set down by Cesar Ritz. During this decade the Philadelphia Ritz-Carlton, Montreal Ritz-Carlton, Atlantic City Ritz-Carlton, and Boston Ritz-Carlton opened for business. All of these hotels, in their individual manner, carried on the tradition of fashionable sophistication so important to the Ritz name. Yet those who had known Cesar Ritz would say that none of the hotels ever captured the rococo elegance of the Paris Ritz on the Place Vendome.

After Cesar Ritz and one of his sons died in 1918, it was assumed that the remaining son, Charles, would take the place of his father and continue managing the Paris and London hotels under the Ritz-Carlton name. But Charles was more inclined to travel, and even before the death of his father he journeyed to the United States and worked in a New London, Connecticut, hotel. His jobs over the next several years ranged from working as a night manager at the New York Ritz-Carlton to selling Swiss music boxes to department stores. The rather leisurely pace of Charles Ritz's business activities provided him the time to pursue what interested him most—fly fishing. In 1928, his mother made a pilgrimage across the Atlantic to persuade him to return to Paris and work at his father's hotel. He yielded to his mother's urgings, but once in Paris he found that all the top management spots at the hotel were filled, so he worked in the local office of a New York stockbroker. Rather than being disappointed with not working for the hotel, Charles was able to continue developing his expertise in fly-fishing. In fact, he had already launched a secondary career as a designer of fishing rods.

After the crash of the New York Stock Market in 1929, the hotels that bore the Ritz-Carlton name in Europe and America suffered from the onset of a worldwide depression. Though the hotels were able to weather the financial hardship, many of them began to lose the elegant luster they so earnestly and carefully cultivated before the depression. Many millionaires who frequented Ritz-Carlton dining rooms in search of new gustatory delights were no longer millionaires; indeed, the New York Ritz-Carlton even changed its luncheon and dinner menus from French into English hoping that it would result in more customers. The owner and manager of the Boston Ritz-Carlton, realizing he was almost at the point of insolvency, went from room to room turning on the lights in its empty rooms to impress his wealthy father before the old man arrived to discuss terms of a loan for the hotel.

The difficulties luxury hotels experienced during the depression were compounded by World War II. When leisure travel between Europe and America was common in the 1920s and 1930s, many wealthy individuals stayed and dined at Ritz-Carlton hotels. This traffic ceased altogether when the war started in Europe in 1939, and, not surprisingly, Ritz-Carlton hotels suffered as a result. When World War II was at its height, many Ritz-Carlton dining areas and ballrooms on both sides of the Atlantic were used as meeting rooms for military personnel.

Many of the Ritz-Carlton hotels did not survive the combined effects of the depression and World War II. Even though the Paris Ritz celebrated it 50th birthday in 1948 amid diplomats and millionaires drinking champagne, the Philadelphia Ritz-Carlton and Montreal Ritz-Carlton had closed their doors. In 1950, when the New York Ritz-Carlton announced that it would close to make way for a 25-story office building, its former guests protested. The only Ritz-Carlton hotel left in North America was the Boston Ritz-Carlton, and its survival was questionaable.

The London Ritz-Carlton and the Paris Ritz prospered during the 1950s and 1960s by gradually adapting to a new breed of guest—the international businessman. When Charles Ritz became chairman of the board of the Ritz-Carlton Management Company in 1953, most of the old wealth and aristocracy were gone. By 1968, 70 percent of the guests staying at the Paris Ritz were American businessmen on expense accounts. With his success in Paris, Ritz was asked to serve as a consultant to the firm of Cabot, Cabot, and Forbes, purchasers of the Boston Ritz-Carlton in 1964. He also served as consultant to the Ritz-Carlton in London.

The Ritz-Carlton Management Company leased its name to financiers in both Lisbon and Madrid, stipulating that the hotels meet acceptable standards. Although Charles Ritz owned only one percent of the stock in the company, with the remainder held by British and Continental investors, he was the guardian of the hotel's standards; during the late 1960s, the company sued the Ritz in Rome over use of the name because the hotel didn't measure up to those standards.

The hotels operating under the Ritz name in Europe prospered throughout the 1970s, primarily due to the ever increasing presence of international business travelers with corporate expense accounts and a surge in travel by the nouveau riche. Indeed, the company's continued commitment to and cultivation of attentive service to a new generation of guests had the effect of raising revenues for almost all the European operations. The week before Charles Ritz died in July 1976, he was still issuing orders to improve the luxury and elegance that symbolized the Paris hotel.

In 1983, William B. Johnson, a real estate mogul and developer from Atlanta, purchased the rights to the name and the aging Ritz-Carlton in Boston for approximately $70 million. Having already constructed over 100 Waffle House restaurants and numerous Holiday Inns, Johnson turned his attention to the Boston Ritz-Carlton and spent $22 million to restore the hotel to its original condition. He then established a headquarters for his company in Atlanta, the Ritz-Carlton Hotel Company, and began to arrange financing for new hotels around the country, mostly through partnerships between Johnson and other parties.

By 1990, Johnson's Ritz-Carlton Hotel Company operated and managed 28 Ritz-Carlton hotels. Johnson directly owned the hotels in Boston, Buckhead, Georgia, and Naples, Florida; financing for the remainder of the hotels was through partnerships, including those in Australia, Hawaii, and Cancun. The only Ritz-Carlton Hotel that Johnson didn't operate was in Chicago. Built by Four Seasons before Johnson purchased rights to the name, the Chicago Ritz-Carlton is also managed by the rival hotel.

The company won the Malcolm Baldridge National Quality Award in 1992. Chosen by the U.S. Department of Commerce, the Ritz-Carlton Hotel Company is the first hotel company awarded the highly prestigious prize. With 24-hour room service, twice-a-day maid service, complete gymnasium facilities, and menus that continue the tradition of culinary excellence first established by Cesar Ritz, Johnson's company is well prepared for competing with Four Seasons and other hotel groups in the luxury hotel market.

Further Reading:

Kent, George, "The Word for Elegance," *Readers Digest,* 1948, pp. 147–50.
"Why the Ritz Caters to a Business Elite," *Business Week,* August 17, 1968, pp. 56–62.

—Thomas Derdak

Rohr Incorporated

P.O. Box 878
Chula Vista, California 92012-0878
U.S.A.
(619) 691-4111
Fax: (619) 691-2905

Public Company
Incorporated: 1940 as Rohr Aircraft Company
Employees: 9,200
Sales: $1.28 billion
Stock Exchanges: New York
SICs: 3724 Aircraft Engines and Engine Parts; 3764 Space
   Propulsion Units and Parts

Rohr Incorporated is the world's leading manufacturer of aircraft engine parts, including nacelles, cowlings, pylons, and thrust reversers. Rohr controls about 80 percent of the market for these products, which appear on the Boeing, McDonnell Douglas, and Airbus jetliners, as well as C-130, C-5, F-14, and KC-135 military craft. The company also manufactures a variety of other formed metal products, including parts for the Titan IV rocket motor.

The company was named for its founder, Frederick Hilmer Rohr, who was born into an immigrant German family in 1896 and grew up in San Francisco. Rohr served as an apprentice in his father's sheet metal works by day and attended school by night. Upon discharge from the Navy after World War I, Rohr returned to his father's business, now in Fresno, where he developed a stamping process for forming metal trim on building facades.

Rohr and several friends pooled their savings to purchase and restore old war aircraft, including Jennys and DeHavillands, in which they learned to fly. Rohr quit flying when he married in 1920 and left his father's company four years later to establish his own firm, the Standard Steel Works, in San Diego.

When Rohr heard that the nearby Ryan Aircraft Company was searching for a fuel tank supplier, he managed to coax the specifications out of a shop foreman. He returned to Ryan the next morning with a finished product. The foreman was so impressed with the job that he asked Rohr to join the firm as a sheet metal foreman. When Rohr joined the company, Ryan was switching from fabric- and wooden-skinned aircraft to sturdier metal designs.

In 1927, shortly after Claude Ryan sold his company to Thomas Mahoney, an airmail pilot named Charles Lindbergh came by with the unusual request for an aircraft capable of crossing the Atlantic. Rohr did the sheet metal work and built the fuel tanks for the craft, the *Spirit of St. Louis,* which was completed in just 60 days. However, after Lindbergh's flight to Paris, Mahoney moved the Ryan company to St. Louis, leaving Rohr without a job.

Rohr was taken on as a factory manager by the Solar Aircraft Company, which produced parts for the Ford Trimotor as a subcontractor. Solar developed its own craft, an eight passenger model called the MS-1, but it failed to sell in the Depression-era market.

Solar next turned its attention to the manufacture of stainless steel manifolds—a business that sustained the company for years—and even began manufacturing milk cans for dairy farmers. Rohr, meanwhile, perfected a new process for hammering sheet metal, suggested by the method he had used earlier for punching out building trim. Rohr demonstrated his punch-and-die "drop hammer" system for Solar directors, using a form modeled from a toilet seat. When word of the system reached Boeing, Rohr was invited to set up a drop hammer line at Boeing's factory in Seattle.

Rohr served as sheet metal engineer with Boeing until 1935, when the company's chairperson, Claire Egtvedt, suggested that he go into business for himself as a subcontractor. Rohr then returned to San Diego to work for Claude Ryan, who had established a second aircraft company, before finally taking Egtvedt's advice and establishing his own firm. The Rohr Aircraft Company was established on August 6, 1940 and consisted of Rohr, two former Ryan engineers, and a couple of lawyers.

The three-person design team worked out of the garage at Rohr's home for two weeks, designing drop hammers and heat treatment tanks. Already known for his work at Ryan, Solar, and Boeing, Rohr had an easy time gaining an audience at the Consolidated Aircraft Corporation.

Rohr emerged with his first contract, building Sperry bombsights for the LB-30, an early version of the B-24 bomber. Next, Lockheed asked Rohr to build cowlings for the A-28 Hudson bombers it was manufacturing for the British. The sudden rush of business forced Rohr to relocate from a small rented factory space to a new 37,500-square foot complex, and eventually two additional facilities.

Impressed with the company's work on the bombsight, Consolidated asked Rohr to manufacture complete "power packages"—motor mounts, cowlings, plumbing, electrical harnesses and everything else that held a bare engine to a wing—for the PB2Y3 flying boat. This enabled Consolidated to concentrate on building airframes, while leaving the engine mounting to Rohr. When the United States became involved in World War II, Consolidated asked Rohr to build power packages for the B-24, which was by now rolling off assembly lines in droves. Production shot up to 56 power packages a day.

To meet this demand, the company's factory space was expanded to 600,000 square feet. But, in need of even greater space, Fred Rohr took over his father's sheet metal plant in

Fresno. As production rose, and Rohr's employees went off to war, Rohr began hiring female employees. The first woman joined the payroll in May 1942. Only a year later, 55 percent of the work force, now numbering several thousand, were women. By November 1944, with Allied victory imminent, the company employed 13,000 workers. Rohr faced the tremendous dilemma of keeping the enterprise running after the war ended.

Rohr decided that the company was best equipped to manufacture consumer products for the millions of men who would soon be returning home to start families. He entered into merger negotiations with the Detroit-based International Detrola Corporation, a manufacturer of machine tools, radios, washing machines, refrigerators, furniture, and other consumer durables. Detrola's acquisition of Rohr Aircraft, through an exchange of shares, was concluded in July 1945.

A month later, the war ended and the government cancelled all orders for new aircraft. Facing a 90 percent drop in sales, Rohr was forced to lay off all but 500 employees. Fred Rohr was personally opposed to this diversification of his company into products its management did not understand, but he decided that it was the only way to keep the company going.

Just as the company began preparations for building radio cabinets and vacuum cleaners, Boeing returned with an order for a small quantity of aircraft parts. The government wished to retain a strong military deterrent for the Soviet Union, and Boeing bombers were to be a major component of that capability. Boeing also had promising commercial projects, including the 377 Stratocruiser, and a growing number of follow-on military projects that required parts from Rohr.

This work greatly lifted the spirits of Fred Rohr, who felt he had no place running a vacuum cleaner factory. However, he grew impatient with the parent company Detrola during this time. He decided that Detrola, which had changed its name to the Newport Steel Corporation, was entirely too involved in buying, selling, and reorganizing companies, while exhibiting no talent for actually operating them.

Thus, when Newport Steel decided to sell Rohr Aircraft, Rohr made an attempt to buy it. He organized a group of employees and other shareholders who together controlled 100,000 shares of Newport stock. Convincing Boeing to pay in advance for orders it had made and collecting additional cash from the treasury, Rohr presented a buy-out offer to the Newport board. The directors bargained for a higher price, and, when Rohr managed to meet this price, they finally agreed to sell the company to Rohr and his partners. Rohr Aircraft regained its independence on December 7, 1949.

The aircraft industry experienced a sudden burst in orders after war erupted in Korea in 1950, with the prospect of a wider war involving China and the Soviet Union. Rohr was forced to expand once again, but was bound by military strategy to locate a second facility away from its first plant. After considering Salt Lake City, Rohr settled on a site near Riverside, 100 miles north of San Diego.

The company produced large quantities of power packages and other engine parts for Boeing, Convair, and Lockheed. One of the company's largest contracts was for the Lockheed C-130 Hercules transport, awarded in 1954. But Lockheed balked at the prospect of shipping its engines from Pratt & Whitney in Connecticut to Rohr in California, and then to Lockheed's factory at Marietta, Georgia. In order to reduce shipping costs and provide better service to Lockheed, Rohr set up a third plant at Winder, 35 miles from Marietta, where the engines would be assembled. The Winder plant worked so well for Lockheed that Rohr established an engine build up facility for Boeing—supplying aft fuselage section for the 707—at Auburn, Washington, in 1956.

During the 1950s, Boeing, Douglas, and Convair were developing new jet-powered airliners. These jetliners were so popular with airline companies that orders for propeller-driven craft plummeted. However, because the jets were larger and faster than turboprop aircraft, airlines needed fewer of them. This created a sharp decline in demand for Rohr's jet- and piston-engine power packages.

In search of other profitable ventures, Rohr applied its metal forming experience to building large antenna dishes, one of which relayed television coverage of the first moon walk. By 1965, Rohr was one of the country's largest antenna suppliers. The company also began manufacturing hulls for patrol and rescue boats, tugs, and yachts.

Fred Rohr died suddenly of a stroke on November 8, 1965. The company carried on under Burt Raynes, a co-founder of Rohr who had been appointed president of the company two years earlier. Late the following year, Rohr received two huge orders to provide nacelles, struts, and thrust reversers for Boeing's new 747 as well as nacelles and pylons for Lockheed's enormous C-5 Galaxy.

In his determination to spur Rohr's growth, Raynes steered the company into ground transportation, winning a contract to build rail cars for public transit systems in San Francisco and Washington, D.C. In 1971, Rohr purchased the Flxible Company, an Ohio-based bus manufacturer (the company's unusual name resulted from an early trademark battle in which it was denied proprietary rights to the word "flexible").

Next, Raynes organized the purchase of a French hovercraft technology, with the aim of developing intercity transports to compete with trains and aircraft. Rohr also attempted to start up a gas turbine and light-rail people mover division. In other areas, Rohr became involved in postal automation systems, rail car conversion, and the manufacture of gas turbines and prestressed concrete structures.

Rayne's rapid diversification of Rohr's business diluted profits from its aviation business, causing a series of quarterly income losses. Furthermore, quality problems on mass transit systems embroiled the company in an embarrassing legal dispute. Defying his own balance sheet, Raynes continued to paint an optimistic picture. This led to Raynes' firing in February 1976 and subsequent replacement by Fred W. Garry, a former General Electric executive.

Returning to Fred Rohr's philosophy of the core business, Garry immediately began divesting Rohr of all its non-aerospace operations. He dropped the mass transit and light rail operations, the hovercraft, antenna and concrete businesses, the postal unit, and a warehouse automation group. In the process, he slashed the payroll from nearly 8,000 employees to just 3,800.

In 1978, Garry arranged the sale of Flxible to Grumman for $40 million. However, soon after taking over the bus company, Grumman sued Rohr for misrepresenting the quality of the Flxible product line. Nevertheless, the suit had little effect on Rohr's contract to supply engine nacelles for Grumman's F-14 Tomcat Navy fighter.

In 1979, President Carter ordered massive increases in defense spending. In an effort to grab orders, aircraft companies spilled their capacity demand on to subcontractors such as Rohr. Determined not to lose a contract, Rohr's board refused to deny any new business. Unprepared for a deluge of new orders, Rohr's assembly lines became snarled, its warehouses became bloated with inventory, deliveries were delayed, costs soared, and profits plunged. Unable to rein in the overambitious goals set by the board, Garry resigned in protest. He was replaced by director Carl L. Sadler, a former Sundstrand executive, who had helped overcome a similar production mess at that company.

However, much of the damage had already been done. Grumman beat Rohr in a bid to build nacelles for re-engined DC-8s, and Boeing elected to build its own nacelles for its new 767. Ironically, the loss of these contracts made it easier for Sadler to scale down the company's backlog and restore control. Despite its flirtation with disaster, Rohr managed to pull out a profit for several consecutive years. The earlier losses were made up by follow-on work for Boeing and Grumman.

In addition, Rohr's assembly plant in Toulouse, France, established in 1973 to supply the European Airbus consortium, won a contract for that company's A-310 and, later, the A-320. Gradually, Rohr built up 100 percent shares of McDonnell Douglas and Airbus' nacelle business and 50 percent of Boeing's.

Sadler retired in 1982 and was succeeded by Harry Todd, who shared Sadler's strategies and philosophies concerning Rohr. The following year, Rohr won additional follow-on work for the Lockheed C5-B, requiring the establishment of a third assembly plant at Foley, Alabama. During the latter half of the decade, commercial aircraft orders climbed drastically. This necessitated the establishment of new assembly plants at Sheridan and Heber Springs, Arkansas.

During this time, Rohr was transformed from a "build to print" subcontractor into an integrated systems designer. Rather than simply building to a customer's specifications, Rohr was invited to participate in the design process for the components it built. This served to bolster Rohr's 80 percent share of the engine nacelle and power package markets, allowing the company to derive greater profit from those activities.

In October 1987, Rohr purchased the composite bonding operations of the financially troubled Fairchild Aircraft Corporation. The purchase helped Rohr to enter the 1990s with more than $1 billion in sales.

Harry Todd retired in 1990 and was succeeded by Robert Goldsmith. Shortly after Goldsmith took over leadership at Rohr, the company came under investigation by the U.S. Attorney's office for allegedly fabricating results of its parts testing. Goldsmith admitted to deficiencies in the process, and moved to correct them, but maintained that Rohr had engaged in no "purposeful mischief" to defraud the government.

Although Rohr made progress in drawing down debt, controlling costs, and raising profitability, its share price was low, and shareholders were upset with the government's investigation. Moreover, Goldsmith announced his retirement in January 1993 without appointing a successor, leaving Rohr vulnerable to an unwelcome takeover bid.

Board member Jim Kerley was appointed interim chairperson to fill the leadership vacuum, but rumors persisted that Northrop, Martin Marietta, and the Euronacelle consortium had given serious consideration to taking over Rohr. Much of this speculation was put to rest after Martin Marietta took over General Electric's aerospace group instead, and Rohr appointed a new CEO, Robert H. Rau, a former executive with Parker Hannifin, a manufacturer of hydraulic and pneumatic aircraft systems. Under Rau, Rohr began to feel the effects of a widespread cancellation in aircraft orders by failing airline companies. Cuts in defense spending also affected Rohr's business, forcing employment to be trimmed from 12,091 in 1989 to 9,230 in 1992. The government investigation into parts testing had not yet reached a conclusion in 1993.

Further Reading:

"Bidders Look at Rohr as Aerospace Industry Shrinks," *Wall Street Journal,* January 14, 1993.
"A Crucial Year for Rohr's Survival," *Business Week,* February 28, 1977, pp. 86–87.
"Flxibility?" *Forbes,* October 15, 1977, p. 152.
"How Rohr's Move into Transportation Backfired," *Business Week,* January 19, 1976, pp. 46–48.
Rohr Incorporated Annual Report, Chula Vista, CA: Rohr, 1992.
"Rohr on a Roll," *Financial World,* June 13, 1989, pp. 18–19.
"Rohr Taps Robert H. Rau to be President and CEO," *Wall Street Journal,* April 14, 1993, p. B11.
"Soaring Demand Hurts an Overeager Rohr," *Business Week,* April 21, 1980, pp. 59–60.
"The Tough Route from Jets to Rail Cars," *Business Week,* May 1, 1971, pp. 96–99.
"What Doldrums?" *Barron's,* April 25, 1983, pp. 49–50.

—John Simley

Scarborough Public Utilities Commission

1530 Markham Road
Suite 100
Scarborough, Ontario
Canada
M1B 3M4
(416) 292 1530
Fax: (416) 292 3106

Government-Owned Utility
Incorporated: 1920 as Scarborough Public Utilities
   Commission
Employees: 1,235
Sales: C$316.7 million (US$251.9 million)

The Scarborough Public Utilities Commission provides electricity and water to Scarborough, Ontario, a borough of Toronto. Electricity first came to Scarborough in 1892 via the Toronto and Scarborough Electric Railway tracks that ran through the township. In 1906 the Hydro-Electric Power Commission of Ontario was created to supply energy to greater Toronto. Scarborough, with a mostly rural population of 3,426 in 1910, had a lower demand for electricity than the urban Toronto area, so it was not until the Toronto Electric Light Company extended its electric cables to Scarborough that electricity for seven street lights was available in 1908.

Demand grew with time, and in 1912 the Toronto Electric Light Company further extended its wires, but their placement created a problem for nearby residents because they were placed on the same power poles that held lines supplying energy to the electric railway. When a street car passed a home lighted with these wires, the light dimmed measurably, and returned to normal only when the street car had passed well into the distance.

In January 1913, the Scarborough Town Council approved a plan to supply "a municipally owned railway and electric power at a moderate price." In May 1913, the Ontario provincial government gave its approval for the municipal railway proposal. In the summer of 1914, the public first learned the details of the proposed Toronto Northeastern hydro-electric railway. Two years later, construction on the railway began, and concurrently the population of Scarborough grew. This increase led to the construction of new electric power lines, and 74 residential customers received power in their homes for the first time in 1917.

In 1920 administration of the Scarborough hydro-electric system and the water works was handed over to the newly established Scarborough Public Utilities Commission. In 1921 the Commission purchased the distribution rights for all electric energy in Scarborough from the Toronto Electric Light Company, increasing the number of its consumers from 1,433 in 1922 to 2,749 in 1923.

Demand for electricity, known as "load" or "power requirement," is the rate at which electric energy is delivered to customers at any given time. Scarborough's demand remained strong into the 1930s. By 1931 the Commission was serving 4,580 customers through 72 lineal miles of power lines. It bought more than 3,000 horsepower of electricity daily from the Ontario Hydro-Electric Power Commission, which generated energy from hydro-electric plants in northern Ontario. Capital investment for the company in 1931 was $424,691. To secure those funds, the Commission issued debentures to investors, and reinvested operational surpluses.

The depression of the 1930s slowed the Commission's growth. Of the 21,448 people in Scarborough in 1935, approximately one quarter were unemployed or on welfare. Economic strain also stunted the borough's population growth. Ten years later in 1945, 25,482 people lived in Scarborough, up only slightly from a decade earlier.

During World War II, electric power supplied the regional war effort. This boosted the Utility's production and after 1945, veterans who moved to Scarborough created new demand for water and electricity. More than 250,000 people moved to Scarborough in the decade preceding 1955, creating a significant industrial and commercial center north of Toronto. Residential demand for electricity in this decade grew 15-fold. Commercial and industrial demand doubled. In 1955 the Commission's water revenue was $4.04 million, of which $1.4 million came from industrial and commercial customers.

This growth had led to expansion. The store front office the utility had occupied was replaced by a new three-story, 25,000 square-foot office building which opened in 1953. The new headquarters served 28,000 electric and 18,000 water customers, and housed the utility's almost 300 employees. In 1958 the company bought nine acres of land and an office building to house its hydro and water construction and stores department. The population of Scarborough continued to grow rapidly and capital expenditure for the Commission grew to $17.64 million in 1960.

In 1960 the Commission first installed underground power lines in residential subdivisions. Previously, overhead power poles and wires served as carriers of power. By 1965, the new practice became mandatory in Scarborough.

During this period of impressive growth, customers paid less for service despite the fact that the use of electricity and electrical appliances grew with the population. Greater population allowed the Commission to reduce the average charge per household from 4.6 cents per kilowatt hour in 1921 to 1.25 cents in 1966.

This situation changed in the early 1970s, however, because the escalating price of oil on the world market made electricity a more appealing source of energy. For the Commission, demand increased, but national inflation caused production costs to rise, forcing the Commission to raise consumer rates.

In 1973 the company used computerized billing for industrial and commercial customers for the first time. Its goal was to reduce operating costs, thereby forestalling consumer rate increases. Savings aside, in 1974, the Commission reported an 11.5 percent increase in wholesale power costs. This was passed on to consumers in the form of an 11.2 percent rate increase. Still, the company warned of future increases of even greater magnitude due to the stagnant Ontario economy and its growing inflation.

During the same year, the company moved its waterworks meter testing facility. In addition, a new, more powerful computer was installed at the company's headquarters to aid in customer accounting and general business operations. Again, automation aimed at greater cost savings. Despite these efforts, rates increased in 1976. That year, a rise in operating costs of 22 percent led to a 19.6 percent general rate rise. Higher overheads were due in part to an aging waterworks system which suffered growing numbers of main breaks. In addition, the summer in 1976 was wet and cool, yielding decreased water use. During this period, greater energy conservation further bit into projected annual energy use. Electricity consumption in 1977 rose 3.4 percent, much less than the 6 percent projected by the Commission.

To speed up the bill payment system for customers, in 1977 the Commission introduced an automated telephone answering service to record meter readings submitted by residential and commercial users. Total revenue for the Commission in 1977 was $67.7 million, up from $52.6 million recorded a year earlier.

Successive rate increases had led to an increasing number of complaints. In 1978, the company introduced a new computer system to better monitor customer service. The Supervisory Control and Data Acquisition System (SCADA) featured a central location by which engineers could operate the entire electricity and water networks, ensuring maximum reliability at the lowest operating cost.

The Commission also had a public relations challenge in convincing customers to practice conservation, but only when usage fell faster than rates rose would lower monthly utility bills be possible. Initiatives included computerized microfilm work order forms, cash receipts, and customer inquiries. But the company's cost-cutting efforts were met with rising costs and a poor economic outlook. General manager James Curtis said of the utility's situation in 1981: "We continue to produce the lower growth levels being experienced as a result of inflation and the down turn in the economy. With the continued increases in bulk power costs, this lower growth rate puts added pressure on the efforts to hold down rate increases at the retail level."

To encourage greater conservation, in 1981 the Ontario government introduced a program which provided homeowners with low-interest loans and energy audits to encourage lower energy use. The Commission trained employees to visit homes and advise on window and door sealing, insulation, and energy-conscious habits.

In 1983 the Commission leased a new headquarters to ease congestion at existing facilities. Also in 1984, the SCADA computer monitoring system finally came into operation. It comprised 19 individual control cabinets for use by company engineers. They were to check relay settings, analyze equipment breakdowns, and prevent system shut-downs, especially during poor weather.

During 1985, peak power usage by the Commission's customers surpassed 700 megawatts for the first time. This represented a 10 percent increase compared to a year earlier. In 1986 the company provided electricity to 119,442 customers, up two percent, and it had 100,702 water customers, up from 96,754 customers in 1985.

James Curtis retired as general manager of the Commission in 1987. He was replaced by Gordon Murless, who had been assistant general manager and treasurer. Murless retained his treasurer position on the Commission board.

The recovering Ontario economy in 1989 helped the Commission set records in several areas: the number of customers served, electricity kilowatt hour sales and demand, sales of cubic meters of water, and requests for service by commercial and industrial customers. Indeed, the growing use of air conditioners meant the peak demand for electricity in July, traditionally the hottest month of the year, reached record levels. But 1989 was also marked by labor troubles. Employees belonging to the Utility Workers of Canada Union struck in July, and did not return to work until a new collective agreement was signed in October.

A year later, the company introduced computerized meter reading using the Itron Meter Reading System. This eliminated the use of reading sheets. Employees could now quickly read meters, and gather data that went straight into the company's computer bank.

Revenue for the company in 1991 hit $292.9 million, compared with $267.9 million a year earlier. In 1992 Kim Allen replaced Gordon Murless as general manager and treasurer of the Commission. The company was subsequently reorganized into four divisions: Customer Services, Electric, Water, and Corporate Support.

In 1992 revenue for the Commission was $316.7 million, up from $293.9 million a year earlier. Importantly, the 127,387 customers the Commission served that year was down slightly from 128,140 served in 1991, so existing customers were consuming more energy.

Looking to the future, the Commission began a 25 year program to convert its entire 4.16 kV electrical system to a new and more efficient 27.6 kV system. This was intended to replace old, deteriorated cables and meet anticipated customer demand into the next century.

Further Reading:

Bonis, Robert, *Hydro-Electric Power in Scarborough,* Scarborough Public Utilities Commission, Toronto, 1966.

—Etan Vlessing

SCI SYSTEMS, INC. ___

SCI Systems, Inc.

2101 West Clinton Avenue
Huntsville, Alabama 35805
U.S.A.
(205) 882-4800
Fax: (205) 882-4466

Public Company
Incorporated: 1961 as Space Craft Inc.
Employees: 9,512
Sales: $1.05 billion
Stock Exchanges: New York
SICs: 3672 Printed Circuit Boards; 3679 Electronic
   Components, Nec; 7389 Business Services, Nec

SCI Systems, Inc., is one of the world's largest electronics subcontractors. The Fortune 500 company's business is concentrated in government and commercial subcontracting. The commercial division designs, manufactures, markets, and services electronic products and systems for the computer, aerospace, telecommunications, medical, and banking industries. SCI's government division provides data management, instrumentation, communication, and computer subsystems for military and civilian applications. The company has seventeen plants that serve markets in North America, Western Europe, and Asia. SCI cultivated its billion-dollar business by manufacturing and delivering large quantities of high-quality products on time and at prices well below the manufacturing cost of its customers.

SCI was established in Huntsville, Alabama, as a partnership in 1961 by Olin King and several investors. Raised in rural Georgia, King was the son of a Methodist minister and was expected to assume his father's legacy. Instead, King trained as an engineer and went to work for RCA Corp. In 1956 he went to work with Werner Von Braun on the United States' first satellite program, and formed Space Craft Inc. (later renamed SCI) with two associates in 1961. With a total investment of $21,000, the company began operations in the basement of King's home.

Space Craft first manufactured small satellites, but converted to subcontracting when the new Apollo space program was undertaken by NASA. The high standards and state-of-the-art technology demanded by the government prepared Space Craft for the rigors of computer subcontracting. In the first decade of SCI's history, 80 to 90 percent of the company's business came from government contracts. The company produced technical

systems and subsystems for the Saturn/Apollo program and the affiliated Skylab project. SCI started by providing electronic assemblies to NASA's Marshall Space Flight Center for the Saturn IB and Saturn V programs, equipping each Saturn V with over 400 SCI-built assemblies. When the Saturn/Apollo program was abruptly canceled, SCI began work on military missile projects, and earned contracts for the Titan III launch vehicle, Poseidon Fleet ballistic missile, and other military satellite projects.

The Poseidon Program became one of SCI's longest-running government contracts, enduring fifteen years form 1967 to 1983. Over the course of the project, SCI manufactured five types of hardware for the missile. The company's longest government contract was connected with the U.S. Air Force's Titan launch vehicle program, undertaken in 1966. SCI's participation in the program was expected to continue into the twenty-first century.

In the last few years of the 1960s, SCI integrated its manufacturing operations vertically. In 1967 the company formed SCI Metals, Inc., and the following year it formed SCI Plastics, Inc., and acquired Plastel Corp. of Huntsville and Simplex Piston Ring Mfg. Co. of Miami, Florida. In the last year of the decade, SCI purchased Decatur Plastics, Inc., of Decatur, Alabama. Decatur Plastics was divested in 1977, but SCI Metals and SCI Plastics were merged into the parent company in 1972.

In the early 1970s, the company created communications and test gear for Navy and Air Force jet fighters. During the course of the decade, the company diversified its customer base to include private contracts with original equipment manufacturers. SCI had experienced the cyclic, low-margin nature of government subcontracting, but did not wish to abandon the work entirely. The company earned its first commercial contract with computer-giant International Business Machines Corporation (IBM) in 1976. The relatively small contract for subassemblies for IBM desktop terminals that tied into mainframe computers helped SCI get its start in private industry. Thus SCI entered the field of subcontracting, offering manufacturing services to original equipment manufacturers at lower cost and higher quality than OEMs could achieve themselves. By mid-decade, the ratio of government-to-private contracts was about one-to-one. SCI still manufactured communications and test gear for Navy and Air Force jet fighters, but also marketed such diverse products as white blood cell analyzers and coin sorters for private industry. The company had grown to become Huntsville's second-largest private sector employer, with sales of $27.3 million in 1975.

The diversification into private contracts had given SCI capacity in plastic molding, aluminum casting, metal machining and forming, and electronic assembly. By the end of the decade, the company's operations were organized into three divisions: government, computers, and products. SCI had three facilities in Huntsville, and in 1979, the company achieved record sales of $36.8 million.

SCI realized its most significant growth in the 1980s due to three primary factors. First, and most importantly, the company nurtured its contracts with OEMs. SCI also made a commitment to strategic geographical diversification, and began to cater to customers' needs by locating manufacturing facilities near clients' operations. Finally, the company pioneered the surface-mount assembly process, a method that utilized smaller components and mounting devices to achieve space savings and soon became the design standard for the electronics industry.

Soon after IBM decided to compete with Apple Computer Inc. in the personal computing arena in 1981, the computer giant realized that the surface-mount process was expensive and time-consuming to implement. IBM fielded that work out to subcontractors, and chose SCI because of its reputation for high quality, low cost components. The company had recorded only one failure per 50,000 assemblies, and in the mid-1980s, its $12 per-hour labor costs were about half of IBM's. Contracts with IBM provided about 40 percent of SCI's revenue by 1987, and SCI soon became IBM's largest subcontractor.

By the mid-1980s, SCI had become the world's largest electronics subcontractor, and was known as a customer-first company. Its reputation for on-time delivery was illustrated with an anecdote in the *Wall Street Journal* (August 1987): "In 1984, an SCI cargo plane ran out of fuel at 4 a.m. and plunged into the Florida Everglades on its way to . . . 'a big customer' (probably IBM). Mr. King . . . dispatched airboats to fetch the circuit boards, which were rushed to a Florida motel, where SCI technicians tested them for damage. Meanwhile, Mr. King roused some of his slumbering workers, opened the company's Arab, Alabama, plant, and rented another plane. By 10 a.m., SCI delivered enough circuit boards from both the Florida swamp and Alabama to meet the customer's production schedule for that day."

Over the course of the 1980s, the company showed strong growth and steady profits in the ruthless, notoriously low-margin (6 percent pretax) subcontracting industry: by 1987 earnings had increased an average of 35 percent every year from 1981 to 1986, when they reached $13.8 million. But some critics, especially the International Brotherhood of Electrical Workers, felt that this financial success was gained through unfairly low wages. The union tried unsuccessfully during the 1980s to organize SCI's workers. In 1985 a complaint was filed with the National Labor Relations Board charging that the company illegally laid off 250 workers who had union ties and coerced other workers to stay out of the union. The case was settled when SCI paid $83,000 in back wages without admitting guilt. King acknowledged that SCI's wages were low, but pointed out that the company's workers had better benefits than comparably employed workers in the region.

During the 1980s, SCI began to produce on contract some finished products, like computers, computer peripherals, business machines, industrial automation equipment, and medical instruments. At that time, SCI also started to develop its own line of computer-related products, including high-speed rotary printers, microcomputer systems, and microcomputer-based business machines. In 1984 SCI launched a line of microcomputers that were sold to larger companies such as Kodak, who sold the machines as their own. The new business earned pretax margins as high as 20 percent, and helped SCI gain a measure of independence. SCI's government contracts in the 1980s included work with the MX "Peacekeeper" missile program,

wherein the company delivered more than 300 units with a 100 percent rate of acceptance.

By the end of the 1980s, SCI had grown to rank on *Fortune* magazine's list of the United States' 500 largest companies, and had spawned two major subsidiaries: SCI Technology, Inc., and SCI Manufacturing, Inc. The Technology subsidiary controlled the Government and Computer divisions' four facilities, as well as two smaller subsidiaries in Canada and Hong Kong. The Manufacturing subsidiary operated fourteen plants throughout the United States, Western Europe, and East Asia. From 1979 to 1989, sales increased from $36.8 million to $987 million.

SCI surpassed the $1 billion annual sales mark in 1990, but a recession in the early 1990s brought many changes to the computer industry. Many of SCI's customers liquidated their inventories, and those that did not lost market share. Component prices fell, and some customers delayed or canceled orders. Some analysts have criticized SCI's dependence on contracts from IBM because the computer giant could bring SCI's contracts in-house, find another provider, or try to cut into SCI's already slim margins. Although sales increased by almost $200 million from 1989 to 1990, profits dropped from $20.88 million to $2.31 million over the same period. SCI responded to the crisis by working to broaden its customer base and expand its product line.

As the recession deepened in early 1992, SCI's revenues declined 7 percent from 1991 to $1.05 billion, and profits declined to $3.8 million, down significantly from 1991's $12.6 million. But since SCI tended not to have large inventories, it was able to maintain a positive cash flow, and reduce its debt by $111 million. The company totally computerized its purchasing system, and extended on-line data communications from the Huntsville, Alabama, headquarters internationally to the United Kingdom, Mexico, and Ireland. Canada and Asia were added in 1993. SCI looked forward to emerging from the recession with certification according to International Standards Organization's strict ISO 9000 guidelines. The company worked plant-by-plant to bring the United Kingdom, Irish, and Singaporean operations, and eventually all manufacturing plants up to meet this stringent worldwide quality controls. Moving into the mid-1990s, SCI planned to improve efficiency and thereby raise the profit margin and make capital investments in infrastructure.

Principal Subsidiaries: SCI Technology Inc.; Consolidated Communications Corp.; SCI Foreign Sales Inc.; SCI Mex Inc.; Adelatos de Tecnologia S.A. de C.V.; SCI U.K. Holdings Inc.; SCI U.K. Ltd; Sci Holdings Inc.; SCI Development Ltd.; SCI Manufacturing Singapore Pte Ltd; SCI Systems (Thailand) Ltd.; SCI Irish Holdings; SCI Ireland Ltd.; SCI Alpha Ltd; SCI Systems (Canada) Ltd; Cambridge Computer Ltd.; Norlite Technology Inc.; Newport Inc.

Further Reading:

Gilman, Hank, "SCI Flourishes as Main Subcontractor in Electronic Industry," *Wall Street Journal,* August 14, 1987.
Russler, Beth, "Hunstville Firm Is Still Growing," *Birmingham Post-Herald,* September 27, 1976, B5.
Stavro, Barry, "Riding the Tiger," *Forbes,* October 8, 1984, 181, 184.

—April S. Dougal

Shaw

™

Shaw Industries

P.O. Drawer 2128
Dalton, Georgia 30722
U.S.A.
(706) 278-3812
Fax: (706) 226-6654

Public Company
Incorporated: 1967 as Philadelphia Holding Co.
Employees: 19,100
Sales: $1.75 billion
Stock Exchanges: New York Pacific
SICs: 2273 Carpets & Rugs

Since 1987, Shaw Industries—based in Dalton, Georgia, which is also known as "The Carpet Capital of the World"—has been the world's largest carpet manufacturer. The company designs and manufactures about 800 styles of tufted carpet for residential and commercial use. Among the name brands produced by Shaw Industries are Philadelphia, Cabin Crafts, Shaw Commercial Carpets, Stratton, Networx, Shawmark, Evans Black, Salem, and Sutton. The majority of the company's products are made from tufted nylon yarn. The production process, according to the company, involves a series of needles which form loops in a synthetic backing. Approximately 98 percent of carpeting produced today is made with such a tufting process, and approximately 99 percent of carpeting produced in the United States is made from nylon or some other synthetic fiber.

Shaw Industries is run by brothers Robert and J.C. Shaw, who founded the company in 1967. Robert Shaw oversees the day-to-day operations as president and chief executive officer and J.C. "Bud" Shaw serves as chairman of the board of directors. According to a profile in the *Atlanta Journal and Constitution,* the brothers were born in Dalton to the owner of Star Dyeing Co., a subcontractor serving the carpeting industry. As young men, they went their separate ways and left Dalton. Upon their father's death in 1960, the brothers returned home to decide whether to sell or close the business. They did neither, deciding instead to retool their father's company as a supply firm to the industry, which they called Star Finishing Co. The small company—with ten employees and four machines—dyed and finished carpeting for other companies.

The Shaws first entered carpet manufacturing in December 1967, when they acquired the Philadelphia Carpet Company of Cartersville, Georgia. In order to make the purchase, the company incorporated as Philadelphia Holding Co., Inc., but adopted the name Shaw Industries when the company went public in 1971. The company was listed on the American Stock Exchange in March 1972.

The 1970s posed a number of challenges to the young company as it faced the oil embargo, and the consequent energy crisis and inflation. At that time, housing starts slowed and the construction industry suffered. The embargo also affected the availability of petrochemical products used in producing the synthetic carpet yarns. Despite those pressures, the company continued to grow. In June of 1972, the company acquired New Found Industries, Inc., a spinner of fine gauge carpet yarns. In the same year, the company started up its own heat-set and twisting operations for processing the continuous filament nylon yarn used in making shag carpeting. They also built a new carpet finishing plant in suburban Los Angeles, California in order to help supply West Coast markets.

In the 1974 fiscal year, Shaw acquired Elite Processing Co., Inc. of Dalton, Georgia, and Syntex Yarns, Ltd of Calhoun, Georgia. The former purchase allowed the company to increase its capacity for dyeing tufted carpeting, for Elite had newer "beck dyeing" equipment than Shaw then possessed, as well as "TAK" dyeing equipment, which manufacturers use to create designs by sprinkling flecks of dye onto the carpet material. The Syntex acquisition, renamed New Found Yarns, Inc., added approximately 150,000 pounds per week to the company's yarn-producing capacity. That increased capacity added both to Shaw's in-house production and the materials they sold to other producers.

By 1975, however, the energy crisis began to catch up with the company, decreasing orders and backing up inventory. Sales and revenues decreased 11.8 percent, primarily due to downturns in the construction and home furnishing industries. This year was the first and only year when Shaw's revenues declined. In 1976, while inflation continued and housing starts remained sporadic, matters improved for the company, which showed a 16.2 percent increase in sales and revenues, which was offset partially by a decrease in the sales price of the products due to the slow market. At the same time, Shaw Industries was able to spend five million dollars to upgrade and expand its production facilities.

The 1977 and 1978 fiscal years marked a significant change of course for the company, as it consolidated all levels of operations. The company had been producing yarn and providing finishing services for its own products and for those of other manufacturers. During this period, however, it was determined that the New Found Yarns Division did not have sufficient capacity to meet internal demands as well as those of outside buyers, so they discontinued yarn sales. All of the company's other dyeing, printing and tufting manufacturing facilities were set aside exclusively for the company's own use as well. On the administrative side, the company brought senior management together with scheduling, product development, and other support functions in its Dalton offices to make the management structure more efficient. In the course of this restructuring, Bud Shaw, who had been running the Philadelphia Carpet division, assumed a less active role in the corporation's day-to-day operations.

Shaw restructured through acquisitions and sales as well. In 1977, the company acquired the Magee Carpet Company's tufted residential and commercial carpeting operations and sold its own finishing facilities in California. At the end of that fiscal year, it sold its Philadelphia, Pennsylvania carpet-weaving facility to Pennsylvania Carpet Mills, Inc. Neither holding fit into the company's long-range plans, Senior Vice-President for Operations W. Norris Little wrote in a letter to the stockholders, and the two sales "allowed us to concentrate our efforts more fully on our Dalton and Cartersville carpet operations," referring to the company's two major centers of production in Georgia.

Over the next few years, the company continued to consolidate as well as grow in the face of fluctuations in the larger economy which affected the price and availability of raw materials as well as the market for new carpeting. In an industry commonly regarded as cyclical, with its dependence on economic fluctuations and even less controllable factors such as the effect of bad weather on the construction business, the company continued to stay one step ahead.

The next pivotal point in the company's trend toward consolidation came in 1982 at the nadir of the most recent industry cycle. CEO Robert Shaw decided to eliminate the middleman—in the person of outside carpeting distributors—from its sales structure. The company added eight regional warehouses to its original two and expanded its sales force, taking the further gamble of putting the salespeople on salary rather than compensating them through straight commission. In 1982, according to the *Atlanta Journal,* 55 percent of the company's sales were to national or overseas distributors, while 45 percent went directly to retailers. Three years later retailers accounted for 80 percent of sales. In the intervening years, Shaw had become the largest carpet manufacturer in the nation. At the end of 1985, Shaw was the first company ever to sell more than $500 million worth of carpet in the United States in a single year, and that figure was more than double the company's 1982 sales.

In the decade that followed, Shaw's transition to direct sales would be seen as pivotal to its move to world leader. With the benefit of hindsight, analysts could see the change in strategy in more abstract terms. *Fortune* contributor Brian O'Reilly wrote in 1993 that, at that time, "Shaw . . . accepted an unpleasant truth about his industry: Carpets are a commodity." That is to say, brand loyalty and brand-name recognition are practically nonexistent in the industry and price had become the major concern of consumers. Apparently this truth, like so many others, came as no surprise to Robert Shaw, who was called "our Iacocca" by one industry observer. Shaw told the *Atlanta Journal*: "we're not really concerned with the normal cycles in the carpet industry because we're in better control of our marketing strategy through the number of customer accounts we have. . . . We're turning over the inventory at the same rate—even though the regional distribution system is larger. The risk factor you face is running your inventory out of control, whether it's in one place or 12."

In the next few years, Shaw Industries continued to grow, expanding its yarn-spinning capacity to meet the increased demand of its own tufting operations. In 1984, it acquired the spinning facilities of Avondale Mills in Stevenson, Alabama. In 1986, the company followed up by acquiring the spinning facilities of the Candlewick division of Dixie Yarns, Inc., also of Dalton.

Shaw Industries' ownership of facilities at all levels of carpet production is common within the industry, according to a 1986 article in *Barron's.* The practice is known as "vertical integration," and Shaw is one of the best integrated in the business. "The carpet business . . . is affected significantly by trends in fashion, principally color. Many variations in style of tufted carpet are created by the various ways color is applied through dyeing or printing. Shaw's dyeing facilities rate is among the most modern and versatile in the industry," noted *Barron's.* That versatility came in handy in the fall of 1986, according to *Forbes* magazine, when the Du Pont and Monsanto companies "turned carpet retailing on its head with the first genuine technological innovation in carpet fibers in five years." That innovation, as most consumers know by now, was the stain resistant fiber most carpets are sold with today. The breakthrough may have thrown the whole industry for a loop, but Shaw Industries was able to respond quickly, purging its outdated stock and changing over its machinery.

In late 1987, Shaw Industries became the world's largest carpet maker by purchasing the carpet business of West Point-Pepperell of West Point, Georgia, the fourth-largest producer in the country. According to the *Atlanta Journal,* West Point's sales and profits had been hurt by its slow transition to stain-resistant technology and its inability to produce sufficient yarn for the company's own needs. Those, of course, were two areas in which Shaw Industries particularly excelled, especially since it acquired an additional yarn-spinning plant in Thompson, Georgia, earlier the same year. West Point then produced Cabin Crafts carpeting, a well-established brand which had been around since 1932.

With the acquisition of West Point, Shaw's revenues topped $1.2 billion, double its nearest competitor, Burlington Industries. The deal, according to *Forbes,* bolstered Shaw in three relatively weak areas of its business: luxury high-pile carpets, durable commercial carpets, and pricier wool carpets. From 1981 to 1988, Shaw's sales had increased fivefold, and income more than tripled. "We just keep adding the zeros," Chief Executive Robert Shaw told *Forbes.*

In December 1989, Shaw acquired the property, plant, equipment, inventories and businesses of the carpet divisions of the Lancaster, Pennsylvania-based Armstrong World Industries, Inc. Armstrong's carpet business was then the fifth-largest in the country, and its acquisition increased Shaw's share of the domestic market from approximately 14 to 18 percent. The deal included manufacturing plants in Georgia, North Carolina, Tennessee, and Virginia and was viewed by observers as a coup for Shaw.

The company continued to grow through the end of the decade and into the early 1990s. In 1989, the company held 22 percent of the domestic market, sales of $1.2 billion and a 41 percent increase in earnings from the year before. In 1990 an industry analyst told the *Atlanta Journal,* "They're in control of their future and I'm not sure if the people they are competing with can say that." And that control, the company has shown, comes largely from its willingness to put profits back into the company toward the continual updating of equipment. For this reason, *Fortune* estimated, Shaw pays ten percent less for supplies than its competitors, further increasing its edge.

In May of 1992, the company acquired Salem Carpet Mills, Inc., the second-largest publicly held carpet maker, through a merger agreement. According to the company, that move significantly enhanced the company's position in the residential marketplace by adding the Salem and Sutton labels, both well respected in the industry, to their arsenal. During the same year, the company also expanded its commercial product offerings, and its seven-year-old modular tile business, Networx, continued to grow in a difficult market. In July of the same year, the company acquired the polypropylene carpet fiber manufacturing facilities in Andalusia, Alabama and Bainbridge, Georgia from Amoco Fabrics and Fibers Company.

In the early 1990s, the company began to turn more of its attention to international markets. During 1992, the company opened a full-service distribution center in Preston, England to serve its U.K. and European markets. In March of 1993, the company acquired the English company Kosset Carpets, Ltd. of Bradford, England. The largest single-site manufacturer of carpeting in the United Kingdom, it is the producer of the well-known brands Kosset and Crossley. Into 1993, Shaw Industries showed no sign of losing its grip on its dominant market position. As the editor of *Carpet and Rug Industry* Magazine told the *Atlanta Journal* in 1990: "I can easily see Shaw reach-

ing 40 percent [of the market] by 1995. It's the class act in the industry right now."

Further Reading:

Brown, Elicia, "Shaw's Red-Carpet Status," *Financial World,* January 8, 1991.
Burritt, Chris, "Bob Shaw Has Quarterbacked His Carpet Company to No. 1," *Atlanta Journal,* December 22, 1986.
——, "Rug Industry Leader Taking a Giant Step," *Atlanta Constitution,* October 13, 1987.
——, "Shaw Industries Acquires Vacant Thompson Factory for a Yarn Plant," *Atlanta Journal,* August 28, 1987.
——, "West Point Deal Hinged on Several Key Issues," *Atlanta Constitution,* November 11, 1987.
Campanella, Frank W., "Clean Sweep: Record Sales, Earnings Year Shapes Up for Shaw Industries," *Barron's,* December 29, 1986.
Flamming, Douglas, *Creating the Modern South: Millhands and Managers in Dalton, Georgia, 1884–1984,* Chapel Hill: University of North Carolina Press, 1992.
Hannon, Kerry, "Full Speed Ahead and Damn the Stock Market," *Forbes,* January 25, 1988.
Hawkins, Chuck, "Shaw Industries Is on Top, Thanks to Bold '82 Moves," *Atlanta Journal,* March 17, 1985.
Hendrick, Bill, "Top-Performing Georgia Stock of the Eighties Was Shaw Industries," *Atlanta Journal and Constitution,* January 1, 1990.
O'Reilly, Brian, "Know When to Embrace Change," *Fortune,* February 22, 1993.
Poole, Sheila M., "Carpet Maker Rolling Up Profits," *Atlanta Journal,* May 16, 1990.
——, "Shaw to Buy Armstrong Carpet Units," *Atlanta Journal,* November 11, 1989.

—Martha Schoolman

Shearson Lehman Brothers Holdings Inc.

World Financial Center
American Express Tower
New York, New York 10285-0001
U.S.A.
(212) 298-2000
Fax: (212) 619-6726

74% Owned Subsidiary of American Express
Incorporated: 1983
Employees: 31,250
Revenues: $11.18 billion
Stock Exchanges: New York Pacific
SICs: 6211 Security Brokers, Dealers and Floatation
   Companies; 6221 Commodity Contracts Brokers and
   Dealers; 6159 Miscellaneous Business Credit Institutions;
   6162 Mortgage Bankers and Loan Correspondents; 6282
   Investment Advice; 6411 Insurance Agents, Brokers and
   Service

Shearson Lehman Brothers Holdings Inc. is one of the largest investment banking firms in the United States. The company is known for its expertise in mergers and acquisitions, having taken over some 40 firms during its rise to prominence, including such older firms as Hayden Stone, Shearson Hammill & Company, Loeb Rhoades, Hornblower & Company, Lehman Brothers Kuhn Loeb, and E.F. Hutton. Shearson Lehman Brothers is a subsidiary of American Express, which owns 74 percent of the company.

Sanford Weill was Shearson's guiding force through much of its rise to prominence. Beginning his career as a runner for the firm of Bear Stearns, Weill helped form the investment firm of Carter, Berlind, Potoma & Weill in 1960. With some $215,000 in capital, CBPW was a small firm, but Weill's ambition and his genius for melding companies would characterize its growth. In 1965 the firm evolved into Carter, Berlind, Weill and Levitt, Inc., and Weill became chairperson. Two years later, CBWL made its first acquisition, taking over Bernstein Macauley, Inc., a firm that specialized in investment management. This first acquisition had most of the characteristics of later Weill deals— Weill would take over a well-respected firm that had run into trouble and merge it smoothly into his operation, usually cutting back its office employees and keeping its sales representatives.

Frequently, the target firm specialized in an area of investment banking in which Weill's firm was weak.

Weill's next acquisition, in 1970, represented an influential merger unlike anything yet seen on Wall Street. That year CBWL acquired Hayden Stone, a retail brokerage that had grossed $113 million in 1968, five times its gross in 1960, earning significant profits. In the late 1960s, however, like many Wall Street firms, Hayden Stone had difficulties with their administrative functions. The firm, whose business had almost tripled during the decade, had expanded too rapidly, and it was forced by the New York Stock Exchange to cut back on its trading.

When losses accelerated in 1969, and the situation worsened in the first months of 1970, Hayden Stone began to look for a merger partner. CBWL, whose gross revenues that year were only $11 million, emerged as the leading candidate when Walston & Company decided to limit its acquisition to 15 retail offices due to Hayden Stone's lack of capital.

However, several of Hayden Stone's private investors proved more interested in suing the firm than in selling it. Convinced they had been duped into investing, these investors argued that Hayden Stone should be allowed to fail, and that the NYSE should have to pay for the losses, as an example to other firms allowed to remain in violation of NYSE capital rules. The NYSE and CBWL engaged in a furious effort to convince investors to agree to the sale—which included a clause prohibiting them from suing. Eventually the investors agreed to the deal, and Hayden Stone merged with CBWL. This deal also led to several significant reforms in the operations of the New York Stock Exchange. This takeover thrust the firm, now called CBWL-Hayden Stone, into Wall Street's limelight. Weill was able to successfully merge the two companies, and his strict control of the administration helped turn Hayden Stone around and stem losses.

During the recession of the early 1970s, Wall Street suffered along with U.S. industry. Many firms decided their best chance for survival was to join forces, and CBWL-Hayden Stone took advantage of the difficult days of 1973 to acquire H.L. Hentz, another brokerage, and Saul Lerner & Company. Then came its 1974 acquisition of Shearson Hammill & Company, easily the most ambitious takeover Weill had yet attempted. Despite its strong retail sales force, Shearson Hammill had become strapped for cash, and the firm opted to merge with the smaller, but better capitalized, CBWL-Hayden Stone. The two firms became known as Shearson Hayden Stone. The Shearson name was retained for its wide recognition as a major underwriter, one looked to on the biggest deals. Shearson Hayden Stone made two major acquisitions in 1976: Faulkner, Dawkins & Sullivan, a regional brokerage with one of the best research divisions in the industry, and Lamson Brothers, a well-regarded commodities broker.

By 1977, Shearson's holdings were consolidated, resulting in the seventh largest investment banking firm in the country. Its revenues had more than tripled since 1972, to $134 million in 1977, and employees now numbered more than 4,000.

Shearson's growth and success contrasted with the general environment on Wall Street in the mid-1970s. Now legally prohibited from both advising and underwriting a client on a single deal, most firms' overall trading volume dropped significantly. New York Stock Exchange seat prices were down by a factor of ten (by 1976 prices were down to $40,000 a seat), and some were calling for more liberal membership requirements. Furthermore, Wall Street faced increased regulatory pressures from the Securities and Exchange Commission and competition in its traditional fields from a variety of sources. Some companies took to underwriting their own issues. Mergers and bankruptcies had driven the number of New York Stock Exchange member firms down from the 1960s high of 681 to 490. In addition, on May 1, 1975 fixed commissions were eliminated, and price cutting ensued, which further increased the pressure on firms to perform well.

In 1979, Shearson acquired Loeb Rhoades, Hornblower & Company, one of Wall Street's oldest and most successful firms. The takeover of Loeb Rhoades made Shearson second in the investment banking world. Weill's mastery of mergers paid off as he brought the two large firms together. One of the most important aspects of Weill's acquisition policy was to ensure that Shearson kept absolute control of administrative functions, which allowed both firms to run smoothly. Furthermore, Shearson usually incorporated firms very slowly, a kind of patience rarely seen in Wall Street firm mergers.

By 1981, Shearson had averaged a 60 percent yearly increase in profits over the last four years. That year Weill gambled, directing the takeover of the Boston Company, a money management firm. The $47 million takeover was in direct violation of the Glass-Steagall Act, which separated commercial and investment banking after the stock market crash of 1929. While many banks protested the violation of Glass-Steagall, several hoped that it would increase their chances of being allowed to underwrite securities and perform other actions that Glass-Steagall had denied them. Shearson eventually was allowed to keep the Boston Company.

Soon thereafter, Weill approached the American Express Company, suggesting that it take over Shearson. Knowing that a well capitalized partner would serve as a stabilizing factor in uncertain times, Weill also hoped that American Express's capital could help give Shearson more dealmaking power. In addition, American Express and Shearson together would be able to offer customers more services. The potential scope of the combined company was much broader than that of any bank.

However, the $900 million deal had some potential drawbacks. Some felt that Shearson might lose its flexibility when mired in the bureaucracy of a $21 billion company like American Express, making it unable to practice its aggressive strategies. Others remembered American Express's previous venture into the investment banking world, when it bought 25 percent of Donaldson, Lufkin & Jenrette only to see the firm, and the investment, fizzle. Nevertheless, Shearson and American Express fit together rather neatly. Within 18 months of the deal, Shearson had acquired four more companies and its capital had more than doubled.

Shearson did not make another major acquisition until 1984. In May of that year, Shearson acquired Lehman Brothers Kuhn Loeb for $360 million. Only ten months before, Lehman Broth-

ers had reported another in a string of exceptionally profitable years. Then, in a surprisingly short time period, the firm fell apart, due largely to the combined forces of a market downturn in 1984 and an internal power struggle in which Peter Peterson was replaced as chief executive by Lew Glucksman. Acquiring Lehman Brothers established Shearson as a dominant force on Wall Street. It also marked Peter Cohen's coming of age. Cohen, Weill's longtime personal assistant, had taken over as CEO when Weill became president of American Express in 1983.

Between 1984 and 1987, Shearson rode a lengthy bull market smoothly, surviving the insider trading scandal of 1986 better than most. After a period of low activity, the firm saw increased action in 1987. First, in March of that year, American Express sold 13 percent of Shearson to Nippon Life Insurance, a Japanese company, for $508 million. Later that year Shearson went public, with American Express retaining 61 percent of the firm. Then came the stock market crash of October 19, 1987, and Shearson suffered along with the rest of Wall Street. For the year, revenues were flat, at $6.7 billion, and earnings dropped 70 percent, to $101 million. But only two months after the crash, Shearson announced an important deal: the purchase of E. F. Hutton.

Hutton had been in difficulty for some time, and its top officers had debated heatedly before rejecting an offer from Shearson in October 1986. Hutton's fortunes plunged after the crash, so when Shearson returned in late 1987 offering $962 million, Hutton accepted. While the timing seemed poor, coming so soon after a tremendous downturn, Shearson had frequently made its acquisitions during troubled times on Wall Street. The key would be whether Cohen could continue Shearson's tradition of smoothly merging disparate corporate cultures.

After the acquisition, Shearson became Shearson Lehman Hutton and established itself as a retail force second only to Merrill Lynch on Wall Street. But 1988 brought continued problems. In the takeover, Shearson Lehman Hutton laid off 6,000 employees and closed or merged 150 offices. It also absorbed charges of $165 million due to the acquisition.

The firm began 1988 with a strong first quarter, but performance declined throughout the year, and dropped sharply when Kohlberg Kravis Roberts & Company beat Shearson's bid for the right to underwrite the RJR Nabisco leveraged buyout, the largest in world financial history.

Losing the deal damaged Shearson's reputation, as did a scandal at its Boston Company subsidiary in 1988. The firm also suffered setbacks the following year when three of its top officers left Shearson, due to conflicts of personality and strategy with Cohen. Furthermore, in the face of SEC objections, Shearson had to abandon its attempts to sell a new investment instrument, the unbundled stock unit, after only four months. Nevertheless, Shearson advised Time, Inc. in its purchase of Warner Communications, one of the year's biggest deals.

In February 1990, Cohen resigned and was replaced as CEO by American Express's chief financial officer, Howard L. Clark, Jr., a change greeted with relief by many. At the time of Clark's takeover, Shearson was struggling to protect its credit rating, and, following a failed share offering, had hastily announced a rights offering to its common shareholders.

With a plummeting stock price and serious financial and morale problems, Shearson and Clark had their work cut out for them. Clark and American Express CEO James Robinson III worked to reverse the trend that saw Wall Street's second largest firm lose $1 billion in 1989 on junk bonds, real estate, and just plain bad deals. Amex purchased an additional 13 percent of Shearson and injected the ailing subsidiary with more than $1 billion. Robinson and Clark laid off 2,300 employees: Shearson had reduced the workforce by about 15,000 since the 1987 stock market crash. The reorganization was further reflected in the subsidiary's name change to Shearson Lehman Brothers Holdings Inc., with Shearson as a retail investment unit and Lehman Brothers as an institutional investment group. Jonathon Linen, a former Amex card executive, was charged with the retail arm, and the institutional division was headed by Richard Fuld and J. Tomilson Hill III, the former a trader and the latter a banker. Fuld and Hill applied cost cutting measures to their division by firing 20 percent of Lehman Brothers' bankers, merging commercial banking with trading, and combining the mergers and acquisitions department with general corporate finance. Linen diminished fixed costs by closing 110 branch offices and laying off 3,000 administrative employees, which reduced break-even expenses by one-fourth. American Express's customer service ideals were also adopted by the reinvigorated company. Each broker's desk was equipped with a table tent that enumerated the parent's guiding principles. The changes helped SLB raise its tangible net worth from practically nil to $722 million by the end of 1991.

But Shearson Lehman Brothers still faced several challenges. In 1991, 28 percent SLB-owned First Capital Holdings, a California Insurance company, went bankrupt. Shearson worked with California Insurance Commissioner John Garamendi to bring subsidiary First Capital Insurance Co. back to viability. The plan called for SLB to pump $50 million into First Capital and guarantee policies that would be kept up-to-date for five years. In 1997, Shearson planned to be able to acquire the assets and policy holder liabilities of First Capital for just 20 percent of the appraised value. The bankruptcy also brought litigation from First Capital creditors, who accused Shearson of recommending First Capital services to 60,000 Shearson customers despite the knowledge that the undercapitalized insurance company was overloaded with junk bonds. The $300 million lawsuit alleged that Shearson bought into First Capital to shelter itself from shareholder lawsuits. Shearson denied the charges of "gross mismanagement and breach of fiduciary duty."

And when Amex put Shearson's Boston Company subsidiary up for sale in 1992, rumors spread that the parent company was improving SLB's equity-to-assets rating so that it could jettison the brokerage. The $1.45 billion sale of Boston Co. to Mellon Bank Corp. brought Shearson's bond rating closer to an "A," making it a more attractive candidate for acquisition. But Amex CEO Robinson maintained that the credit card company was committed to Shearson Lehman Brothers, although Amex was interested in lowering that commitment to 40 percent.

Principal Subsidiaries: Shearson Lehman Hutton Inc.; Shearson Lehman Brothers International; The Robinson-Humphrey Co., Inc.; Foster & Marshall Inc.; The Boston Co.; The Balcor Co.; Shearson Lehman Mortgage Corp.; Lehman Management Co.; Shearson Asset Management, Inc.; Shearson Lehman Commercial Paper Inc.; Shearson Lehman Money Markets International, Inc.; Bernstein-Macaulay, Inc.; The Ayco Corp.; Shearson Management Inc.; Shearson Equity Management; Shearson Lehman Investment Strategy Advisors, Inc.; Shearson Lehman Global Asset Management Ltd.; Shearson Lehman Hutton Asia Inc.; Shearson Lehman Hutton International, Inc.; Shearson Lehman Hutton Mortgage Corporation; Shearson Lehman Hutton Puerto Rico Inc.; Shearson Lehman Hutton Special Financing Inc.; SLH Asset Management.

Further Reading:

Picker, Ida, "The Robinson Raj at Shearson Lehman Brothers," *Institutional Investor,* August 1991, pp. 57–62.
Spiro, Leah Nathans, et al, "Is Shearson on the Block, Too?" *Business Week,* August 24, 1992, pp. 64–65.
"To the Rescue at Shearson," *Fortune,* November 18, 1991, p. 108.

—updated by April S. Dougal

Silicon Graphics Incorporated

2011 North Shoreline Boulevard
Mountain View, California 94039
U.S.A.
(415) 960-1980
Fax: (415) 961-0595

Public Company
Incorporated: 1982
Employees: 2,568
Sales: $866.6 million
Stock Exchanges: New York
SICs: 3577 Computer Peripheral Equipment Nec; 7372
   Prepackaged Software

Silicon Graphics Incorporated is one of the leading manufacturers of graphics computer systems. Its history may be described as an exemplary, perhaps even archetypal, Silicon Valley success story. Founded by a high school dropout turned college professor, Silicon Graphics capitalized on pioneering technology in 3-D computer graphics to create products used in a wide variety of professions, including engineering, chemistry, and film production. The company combined technological prowess with shrewd management to produce explosive growth; within a decade of its founding, it had entered the Fortune 500.

The story of Silicon Graphics began in 1979, when James Clark, an electrical engineering professor at Stanford University, assembled a team of six graduate students to study the possibilities of computer graphics. Within two years, Clark's team developed a powerful semiconductor chip, which they called the Geometry Engine, that would allow small computers to produce sophisticated three-dimensional graphics simulations previously the domain of large mainframes. Clark patented the Geometry Engine, and in 1982 he and his team left Stanford to found Silicon Graphics.

In 1983 the company released its first products: the IRIS 1000 graphics terminal and an accompanying software interface known as the IRIS Graphics Library. The next year Silicon Graphics released its first workstation, the IRIS 1400, and followed it in 1985 with the IRIS 2400, a workstation with a window manager. These early entries in the IRIS series targeted the middle range of the graphics workstations market—those selling for $45,000 to $100,000—and accounted for over 50 percent of all 3-D graphics workstations sold by 1988. Sales

increased steeply and consistently, reaching $153 million in 1988. Within its first six years, Silicon Graphics had established a secure and lucrative niche for itself in the computer industry.

Silicon Graphics succeeded so brilliantly in its early years in large part because it had introduced a useful product that had drawn relatively little attention from any of its potential rivals. 3-D graphics simulations were extremely useful to mechanical engineers who wanted to assess their designs without having to build prototypes, as well as chemists who used 3-D modelling to study molecules. Workstations like the IRIS series provided power at a relatively affordable price, and major workstation manufacturers like Hewlett-Packard, Apollo Computer, and Sun Microsystems were slow to focus their energies on 3-D graphics, leaving Silicon Graphics without much direct competition.

Observers also credited James Clark's technical skill and entrepreneurial sense for the company's success. The path to Silicon Valley glory was a circuitous one for Clark, who dropped out of high school in Plainview, Texas, after he was suspended for setting off a smoke bomb on a school bus. After a hitch in the Navy, he went back to school, enrolling as an undergraduate at Tulane University. He went on to earn an M. S. in physics from University of New Orleans and a Ph.D. in computer science from University of Utah, where he first became interested in computer graphics. Clark then committed himself to an academic career, holding teaching posts at University of California at Santa Cruz, the New York Institute of Technology, and University of California at Berkeley before coming to Stanford. But along the way, he became disenchanted with the ways of academia. "I had always seen myself as a senior professor at a university," he once told *The Business Journal–San Jose,* "but I think I learned that my strength is making things that work, rather than writing papers. Universities encourage writing a lot of papers." Hence his departure from Stanford and the founding of Silicon Graphics in 1982.

Once he founded the company, Clark displayed the good sense to find his proper role within the operating structure and stick to it. While high-tech companies like Silicon Graphics are often founded by technologists who turn day-to-day operations over to businesspeople, in many cases the companies falter because the technologists remain too closely involved in business affairs, making poor decisions or allowing the technological edge to dull. Soon after Silicon Graphics was born, Clark brought in Edward McCracken, a veteran Hewlett-Packard executive, to run the company as president and CEO while he remained chairperson. Clark concentrated on serving as the company's technology guru, leaving McCracken to take care of the business operations. According to McCracken, this role best suited Clark's temperament: "Jim's not a day-to-day person. He works in his own time frame," he told *The Business Journal— San Jose.* McCracken continued, "He takes complex things and makes it simple. It might take a month, a day, or a year. He gets in these moods for a while where he's almost unavailable. He's most effective when he's in that mood." Clark also used this division of labor to devote more time to outside interests that included ballet, classical music, art, and flying a stunt plane.

A useful blend of high technology and business sense enabled Silicon Graphics to move forward from its early successes. In

1987 it became the first computer company to make use of MIPS Computer Systems' innovative reduced instruction-set chip, or RISC, when it incorporated RISC architecture into its new IRIS 4D/60 workstation. Within several years, most workstations would use RISCs. The company received a boost the next year when IBM agreed to buy Silicon Graphics' IRIS graphics card for use in its own RS/6000 graphics workstations and to take out a license for the IRIS Graphics Library—a big first step toward making the IRIS Graphics Library the industry standard.

Also in 1988, Silicon Graphics introduced amid much fanfare a new line of entry level graphics workstations, which it called Eclipse. Although it dominated the more expensive end of the graphics workstation market, the company needed to broaden its customer base if it expected to maintain sales growth. The Eclipse was designed to bring 3-D graphics to people who had previously regarded IRIS workstations as unaffordable. Eclipse lacked the speed and processing power of more expensive machines, but initial versions sold for less than $20,000—as little as one-fifth of the cost of higher-end machines. Eclipse scored a major success soon after its release when Chrysler announced that it would buy a large number of the machines to go with the IRIS workstations that it was already using to help design its automobiles.

Although Eclipse put Silicon Graphics into more direct competition with its rival workstation manufacturers, who began to chip in with their own low-end 3-D workstations, it also succeeded in expanding the company's customer base. In 1990 sales volume topped $420 million. The move into the lower priced, high-volume end of the market worked well enough for Silicon Graphics that in 1991 the company released an even less expensive product line—the IRIS Indigo, a 3-D graphics workstation so compact that the company called it the first personal computer to use RISC architecture. The Indigo offered many features found on more expensive models, as well as digital audio and video processing capability, and the base model sold for less than $10,000.

During this time, Silicon Graphics scored several major coups on the business side. In 1991 the company granted a license to software giant Microsoft for the IRIS Graphics Library. Microsoft intended to use the IRIS Graphics Library in its New Technology operating system for personal computers. Also in 1991, Compaq Computer agreed to acquire a 13 percent stake in Silicon Graphics for $135 million, giving Silicon Graphics a much-desired infusion of capital. Furthermore, Compaq agreed to invest $50 million in a joint workstation development project with Silicon Graphics. Together, these moves provided software developers with greater incentive to write programs for Silicon Graphics machines and also broadened the company's customer base even further.

In 1992 Silicon Graphics agreed to acquire MIPS Computer Systems, which had run into financial difficulties, in a stock swap valued at $230.8 million. The cost of assimilating MIPS forced Silicon Graphics to post a loss of $118.4 million that year, but it also secured the company's long-term supply of MIPS's RISCs, which had become a crucial piece of technology.

In January 1993 Silicon Graphics announced a new computer that would use RISC architecture to achieve supercomputer power at relatively affordable prices. The Power Challenge, as it was called, would link multiple RISCs in a single machine to provide unprecedented processing capability in a computer of that price. Whereas traditional supercomputers like those made by IBM and Cray Research typically sold for millions of dollars, the Power Challenge would sell for between $120,000 and $900,000. The new product was announced over a year in advance of its anticipated shipping date to give targeted customers, such as government agencies and universities previously unable to afford supercomputers, time to include it in their budgets. Observers pegged Power Challenge as a sudden move into the faltering field of supercomputer manufacturing, but in fact the company's ever more powerful workstations were approaching the level of supercomputers anyway, and the company had already established contacts with customers at whom the Power Challenge would be aimed.

In April 1993 Silicon Graphics and Industrial Light and Magic, the famed special effects division of Lucasfilm, announced that they had joined forces to create a high-tech entertainment special effects laboratory. The joint venture was called Joint Environment for Digital Imaging—the acronym JEDI recalled the Jedi Knights of Lucasfilm chair George Lucas's *Star Wars* trilogy—and grew out of the fact that Industrial Light and Magic had been using Silicon Graphics workstations since 1987. The liquid metal cyborg featured in the film *Terminator 2,* the dinosaurs in *Jurassic Park,* special effects in *The Hunt for Red October* and *The Abyss,* and animation in *Beauty and the Beast* were all created on Silicon Graphics computers. For Lucas and Industrial Light and Magic, JEDI was expected to yield both financial and aesthetic benefits: digital manipulation of images cost about one-tenth as much as models and drawings, and, according to Lucas, would "change motion pictures from a photographic process to more of a painterly process," enabling greater authorial control over a film's appearance. For its part, Silicon Graphics hoped that alliance with an entertainment industry partner would help push the leading edge of its technological development forward.

The entertainment industry was also a growing interest of James Clark's at the time. On the heels of the announcement of the JEDI alliance, reports surfaced that Silicon Graphics had entered into talks with communications giant Time Warner to explore the possibilities of interactive home entertainment and other advanced cable television technologies. The company would not comment on the reports, but Clark and some of his executives had made it known publicly that Silicon Graphics was interested in developing a computer that would provide interactive services, including networked 3-D video games, for users through cable television hookups.

Silicon Graphics' interest in entertainment-related technologies is perhaps particularly apropos since the company was founded by a man whom *The Business Journal–San Jose* once described as looking like "Hollywood's idea of a successful entrepreneur"—tall, blond, and clad in "expensive Italian suits with bright Italian knit-silk ties." While some have suggested that the move into entertainment technology represents the deliberate attempts of Clark and McCracken to lead Silicon Graphics away from academia, others have maintained that the company has simply refused to remain in the small niche in which it developed. Instead, Silicon Graphics has made a lot of money in its short history by delivering the technology that made it distinctive to as many people as need and enjoy it.

Principal Subsidiaries: Silicon Graphics International Inc. (Barbados); Silicon Graphics Ltd. (U.K.); Nihon Silicon Graphics K.K. (Japan); Silicon Graphics Pte Ltd. (Singapore); Silicon Graphics AB (Sweden); Silicon Graphics S.A. (Switzerland); Silicon Graphics Gmbh (Germany); Silicon Graphics Canada Inc.; Silicon Graphics World Trade Corp.; Silicon Graphics Ltd. (Israel); Silicon Graphics Ltd. (Hong Kong); Silicon Graphics S.A.R.L. (France); Silicon Graphics S.p.A. (Italy); Silicon Graphics B.V.(Netherlands); Silicon Graphics Pty Ltd. (Australia); Silicon Graphics Federal Sales Corp.; Silicon Graphics Computer Systems Ltd. (Israel); Silicon Graphics Manufacturing S.A. (Switzerland); Silicon Graphics Applications Systems Ltd. (U.K.); Silicon Graphics A/S (Norway); Silicon Graphics A/S (Denmark); Silicon Graphics N.V./S.A. (Belgium); Silicon Graphics OY (Finland); Silicon Graphics S.A. (Spain); Silicon Graphics Computer Systems Gmbh (Austria).

Further Reading:

Hof, Robert, and Jeffrey Rothfeder. "This Machine Just Might Eclipse Apollo and Sun," *Business Week,* October 10, 1988.
Hof, Robert D. "Is Silicon Graphics Busting Out of Its Niche?" *Business Week,* April 22, 1991.
Koland, Cordell, "Graphics Firm Leader Combines Technical, Managerial Skill," *The Business Journal—San Jose,* December 14, 1987.
Yamada, Ken. "Silicon Graphics Aims to Be Supercomputer Contrarian," *The Wall Street Journal,* January 27, 1993.

—Douglas Sun

Society Corporation

127 Public Square
Cleveland, Ohio 44114
U.S.A.
(216) 689-3000
Fax: (216) 689-5115

Public Company
Incorporated: 1958
Employees: 7,919
Assets: $24,978.3 million
Stock Exchanges: New York
SICs: 6712 Bank Holding Companies; 6021 National
   Commercial Banks; 6022 State Commercial Banks; 6099
   Functions Related to Deposit Banking, Nec; 6091
   Nondeposit Trust Facilities; 6082 Foreign Trade and
   International Banking Institutions; 6211 Security Brokers,
   Dealers and Flotation Companies, 6311 Life Insurance

Headquartered in Cleveland, Ohio, Society Corporation is one of the fastest-growing and most innovative bank holding companies in the United States. The corporation is focused in the Great Lakes Basin, but also has subsidiaries in Florida, New York, Missouri, Colorado, and Texas. Society Corp.'s primary business activities include general banking and associated financial services for consumer, business, and commercial markets. Society Corp. grew quickly by avoiding such banking pitfalls as bad foreign, agricultural and leveraged buyout loans that were common in the 1980s. In that decade, it was able to boast an almost unparalleled decade of consecutive earnings-per-share improvements. Society Corp. emerged from the late 1980s and early 1990s banking dilemmas as the United States' 29th largest bank holding company and one of the country's largest and best performing trust departments. Society Corp. has the highest return on assets figure, at 1.4 percent, of all the country's major banks.

The Society for Savings was founded by Samuel H. Mather as a mutual savings bank in Cleveland, Ohio in 1849. Within three years, Mather's part-time business had collected deposits of $150,000; by 1857, Society had become Mather's full-time job. Ten years later, the bank built its first headquarters, a three-story building on Cleveland's Public Square. Society outgrew that building by 1890, when the bank erected Cleveland's first "skyscraper," a ten-story stone structure that featured two

massive murals depicting the story of "the goose that laid the golden egg." At the time, the Society for Savings was the tallest structure between New York and Chicago.

The bank earned a reputation for security and conservatism during its first half-century in business by surviving four depressions and financial panics before the turn of the century. It emerged from the Great Depression's federally mandated bank holiday as one of Cleveland's four largest banks, with deposits of over $100 million. By the time Society celebrated its centenary in 1949, it was the largest mutual savings bank west of the Allegheny Mountains. Although it still had only one office, Society had garnered 200,000 depositors and over $200 million in deposits.

Society National Bank was formed in 1955 as a commercial bank of the National Banking Association. Society National acquired the assets and liabilities of the Society for Savings mutual bank in 1958. The terms of the merger also made Society a public company. Voting certificates were issued to depositors of record at the end of 1958 at $500 each. Society Corporation was then created and became the first entity in Ohio formed under the 1956 federal Bank Holding Company Act. Before 1960, Society National became the first commercial bank in the United States to use on-line teller terminals, one of the decade's newest electronic data systems.

Society Corp.'s adoption of the holding company structure enabled it to grow rapidly between 1958 and 1978, when it acquired 12 community banks, including: Fremont Savings Bank, Western Reserve Bank of Lake County, Springfield Bank, Xenia National Bank, Erie County Bank, Farmers National Bank & Trust Co., Tri-County National Bank, Second National Bank of Ravenna, Peoples Bank of Youngstown, 1st State Bank & Trust, and American Bank, and First National Bank of Clermont County. The subsidiary banks had combined assets of over $500 million in 1972.

Society Corp.'s history as a mutual savings bank was often derided by analysts, but by the mid-1970s, the heritage was recognized as an advantage. Savings accounts, a source of strength and stability, represented 65 percent of the bank's $1.5 billion in total deposits. In 1979, when Ohio's banking laws were revised to permit banks to establish branches in counties contiguous to the home office's county, Society Corp. was poised for its second growth spurt. The expansion was accomplished through dozens of small acquisitions and four billion-dollar mergers from 1979 to 1989.

Society Corp.'s opening salvo in its acquisitions spree occurred in 1979 with the acquisition of Canton, Ohio's largest bank, Harter BanCorp. Harter entered Society Corp.'s 12-bank stable second only to Society Corp.'s flagship Society National Bank, adding $400 million in assets to the holding company's $1.8 billion. Society Corp. acquired five smaller banks over the next three years. Second National Bank of Bucyrus, with assets of $34.6 million, was purchased in 1980 for $5.2 million. Second National helped fill a gap between Society Corp.'s northern Ohio banks and its Dayton and Columbus affiliates, thereby giving the corporation access to counties that it had not been able to reach in the past. Later that year, Society Corp. acquired Community National Bank (Mount Gilead, Ohio) and merged its $15 million assets and customers with Second National of Bucyrus. The new entity was renamed Society National Bank of Mid-Ohio. In 1981, Society Corp. purchased First National Bank of Carrollton and merged it with Harter BanCorp.'s flagship Harter Bank & Trust. Lancaster National Bank's $30 million in assets and three branch offices were added to Society Corp.'s roster at a cost of $2.78 million later that year. The acquisition of Citizens Bank of Hamilton for $10.7 million in cash and notes closed Society Corp.'s first round of relatively small acquisitions.

The corporation regrouped over the next two years by reorganizing its top management structure and consolidating its bank holdings. Early in 1982, a tripartite management team was formed, with J. Maurice Struchen, chairman and chief executive officer of Society Corp., Robert W. Gillespie, vice chairman of Society Corp. and chief operating officer of Society National Bank, and Gordon E. Heffern, president and chief operating officer of Society Corp., sharing the corporation's top responsibilities. The team concept helped coordinate policy-making, planning, and operating between the holding company and its largest subsidiary. It also helped Society Corp.'s management prepare for interstate banking and inter-industry acquisitions.

Later in 1982, Society Corp. merged three of its northwest Ohio banks—Society National Bank of Northwest Ohio, Fremont Savings Bank and American Bank in Port Clinton—to form a $250 million, 15-office, five-county bank. Society Corp. also joined with three other banks, National City Corp. (Cleveland), Fifth Third Bancorp. (Cincinnati), and Third National Bank of Dayton, to form an automatic teller machine (ATM) network of 400 machines. The virtually statewide network gave over one million customers access to accounts in most major Ohio cities.

By the end of 1983, Society Corp. had net earnings of $8.01 million on total assets of $4.3 billion, and was poised for another major acquisition. In the spring of 1984, Society Corp. merged with Interstate Financial Corporation, parent of Third National Bank in Dayton. The acquisition increased Society Corp.'s assets to $5.1 billion and gave the corporation a stronger foothold in Dayton metropolitan area banking, where Interstate was the second-largest bank. Interstate's subsidiary, North Central Financial Corp., had offices in Ohio, Indiana, Virginia, Maryland, and Florida, and held $1.1 billion in mortgage loans.

Within a little over a year, Society Corp. would make an even larger acquisition, but in the meantime, the corporation contented itself with the purchase of BancSystems Association, a regional bank card processor headquartered in suburban Cleveland. BancSystems was formed as a not-for-profit association in 1969 by National City Bank, Society Corp., and Central National Bank. National City Bank sold its interest in the association to Society Corp. after it acquired BancOhio National Bank in Columbus, which had its own card processing facility. BancSystems provided MasterCard and Visa credit and debit card processing for 140 banks and savings and loan associations, and employed over 300 people. The acquisition helped Society Corp. diversify its income base into more non-interest sources, giving it over 1.4 million credit card accounts and annual volume of $2.3 billion in processed transactions. Later in 1984, Society Corp. set up barriers to a takeover by prohibiting

two-tier pricing and establishing a two-thirds majority in case a takeover vote was called.

The corporation further shored up its takeover defenses with the purchase of Centran Corp., a holding company of Cleveland's fourth-largest bank, Central National, in 1985. Society Corp. offered Centran's stockholders a choice of cash or stock totalling $220 million for its assets of $3.1 billion and 82 offices in northern and central Ohio. The acquisition made Society Corp. one of the state's top five banks. But the merger had some drawbacks. Centran carried with it the vestiges of ill-advised bond investments made in 1980, an unsuccessful attempt to expand into consumer finance that lost another $20 million, and problems with international loans. Centran lost $70 million on the bad bonds and had to be bailed out by Marine Midland Banks, Inc., which held influential stock in the company. Society Corp. offered Marine Midland $26 million in cash and $50 million in non-voting adjustable-rate perpetual preferred stock, thereby limiting this bank's voice in the merged company.

Society Corp. reorganized statewide to accommodate its growing Columbus affiliate. It set up a separate region, which was centered in the state capitol, to control $700 million in assets. Society Corp. later added its $100 million-asset Scioto Bank offices and Central National's Columbus-area branches to the newly organized, 36-unit region. Society Corp. scaled back in northwest Ohio, selling two banks with 18 offices and $275 million in assets to Toledo Trustcorp, Inc. for cash, then spent most of the next two years rationalizing Centran's corporate culture, computer systems, branches, and top management. Two task forces were formed: one worked to combine the holding companies, and the other merged flagship banks Society National and Central National. The company instituted a hiring freeze and eliminated excess personnel, primarily through attrition. Centran sold 18 Akron offices to First National Bank of Akron for $21 million, and Society Corp. closed 13 branches in Cleveland and Akron to eliminate overlapping territories. Society Corp. chairman Gordon E. Heffern continued as chair and CEO, and Wilson M. Brown Jr., chairman, president, and CEO of Centran, became president and chief administrative officer of Society Corp. Robert W. Gillespie, president and chief operating officer of Society Corp., became deputy chairman and chief operating officer. All three combined to maintain the tripartite "office of the chairman."

The merger was deemed a success when the positive results started pouring in as early as 1985: both Society Corp. and Centran chalked up record earnings for the year, and once their two primary banks were integrated, Society National Bank ranked second in Cleveland. Society Corp.'s assets reached $9 billion, up from $6.1 billion before the acquisition, while the company saved $28 million in annual operations in the process of the merger. Society Corp. became Ohio's third-largest bank holding company, next to National City Corp. (Cleveland), with $12 billion in assets, and Banc One Corp. (Columbus), with $9.6 billion in assets. Society Corp. had 250 bank branches statewide and about 6,500 employees. One of the reasons for the bank's continuing success was its tradition of conservatism. The company's executives were proud of the fact that it had avoided most of the decade's banking pitfalls: agricultural, energy, and foreign loans, and especially the financing of leveraged buyouts.

In 1987, Society Corp.'s Gordon E. Heffern retired and was succeeded as CEO by Robert W. Gillespie, who, at 42, became the youngest chief executive in Ohio's top-ten bank holding companies. The promotion gave Gillespie a total of four titles: CEO and president of Society Corp. and CEO and president of Society National Bank. Gillespie had spent his entire career at Society Corp., starting out as a part-time teller while in graduate school at Case Western Reserve University. Also in 1987, Society Corp. was able to set earnings records by repurchasing some of its stock after the October 1987 stock market crash. Profits rose to $89 million, and the stock appreciated almost $10 per share within less than a year.

Ohio's interstate banking legislation opened the state to banks from virtually any other state with similar legislation in October 1988. By 1990, new state laws enacted around the country had made old federal laws against interstate banking irrelevant, and in the summer of 1989, a federal thrift reform law that permitted the purchase of savings and loans was passed.

The country had entered an era of "super-regional banks," like NBD Bancorp of Detroit, PNC Financial Corp of Pittsburgh, and Banc One Corp. of Columbus. To prepare for the increased competition that would come from these powerful banks, Society Corp. began to consolidate its holdings. Society Bank of Eastern Ohio was merged into Society National Bank, creating a bank with assets of $7.5 billion and 132 offices. Society National was then reorganized into nine districts to take advantage of the growing bank's economies of scale. Late in the year, Society Corp. increased its impact in Central Ohio with the purchase of 13 branches of Citizens Federal Savings and Loan Association. The acquisition increased Society Corp.'s number of offices in the Columbus area by 50 percent, and raised the assets of the newly-merged bank to $2.75 billion. Society Corp. sold BancSystems Association Inc. to Electronic Data Systems Corp. of Dallas to garner an estimated $6 million profit late in 1989.

Society Corp. entered the 1990s with two major acquisitions that placed it among the area's super-regional banks. In 1990, the purchase of Toledo's Trustcorp, Inc. through an exchange of $430 million in stock gave Society Corp. operations in Ohio, Michigan, and Indiana and raised its total assets to almost $16 billion, thereby ranking the company among the United States' 40 largest banks. Trustcorp's BB credit rating pulled Society Corp.'s A-plus down to an A because of several loan losses on downtown Toledo real estate projects. Society Corp. was also obliged to settle a $5.6 million shareholder lawsuit against Trustcorp and assign extra funds to reserves that would cover any defaulted loans. But by the fall of 1991, Society Corp. had turned its newest subsidiary around and renamed its affiliates Society Bank & Trust; Society Bank, Indiana; Society Bank, Michigan.

Society Corp. worked to pare down its non-interest expenses during the recession of the early 1990s that slowed loan demand and cut into profits. In March 1990, it repurchased Marine Midland's interest in the corporation for $49.25 million, thereby saving the preferred dividends paid on the stock. That spring, Society Corp. vowed to cut about ten percent, or $40 million, from its $390 million in annual non-interest expenses.

In September 1991, Society Corp. announced the largest bank acquisition in Ohio history. It merged with Cleveland's Ameritrust Corporation. The tax-free agreement called for an exchange of $1.2 billion in Society Corp. stock, and created a new corporation with combined assets of $26 billion. The addition of Ameritrust's retail and trust locations throughout Ohio, Indiana, Michigan, Texas, Florida, Missouri, Colorado, New York, and Connecticut made Society Corp. the largest bank in Cleveland and the 29th-largest in the country. The two banks' trust departments became the 15th-largest in the country in terms of revenues. Merging Ameritrust and Society Corp. required the elimination of about 2,000 positions and closing or selling 90 branches. Society Corp. also had to divert about $46 million to Ameritrust's reserve against problem loans. An integration team was formed late in 1991 to coordinate the merger.

In 1992, Society Corp. launched a carefully planned advertising campaign to "reintroduce" itself to customers. The multimedia campaign featured the theme, "Where to grow," in radio, television, print, and outdoor outlets. Society Corp.'s acquisitions in 1992 and 1993 were modest, compared to the purchases made in the first two years of the decade, but they expanded the Great Lakes corporation geographically. In 1992, the corporation purchased First of America Bank-Monroe (Michigan), a $149-million bank, from First of America Bank Corporation. And early in 1993, Society Corp. completed its purchase of First Federal Savings and Loan Association of Fort Myers, a $1.1 billion thrift with 24 branch offices in central and southwestern Florida.

In October of 1993, Society purchased Scaenen Wood & Associates Inc., a privately held investment management firm based in New York. While Society Corp. concentrated on relatively small acquisitions and customer relations, the holding company's leader, Robert W. Gillespie, predicted more large mergers in the near future. He noted that the desire to increase earnings and simultaneously cut costs fueled the corporation's drive to consolidate. Meanwhile there seemed to be a lull in Society Corp.'s acquisition fervor in the early 1990s, although it appeared to be only a matter of time before a major merger was announced. Indeed, on October 4, 1993, Society Corporation and KeyCorp of Albany, New York, announced the signing of a definitive agreement to merge. The transaction, which requires approval of shareholders of both Society and KeyCorp, as well as the receipt of regulatory approval, was expected to close in early 1994.

Principal Subsidiaries: Society National Bank; Society National Bank, Indiana; Society National Bank, Michigan; Society Capital Corporation; Society Community Development Corporation; Society Equipment Leasing Corporation; Society First Federal Savings Bank; Society Life Insurance Company; Society Management Company; Society National Trust Company; Society Trust Company of New York; St. Joseph Insurance Agency, Inc.; Trustcorp Financing Service; A.T.-Sentinel, Inc.; Schaenen Wood & Associates, Inc.; Society Asscst Management, Inc.; Society Investments Inc.; SocietyLease Inc.; Society Mortgage Company; Society Shareholder Service, Inc.; Society Venture Capital Corporation.

Further Reading:

Clark, Sandra, "Society Opens Ad Campaign," *Plain Dealer* (Cleveland), September 22, 1992, p. 2F.

Ferguson, Rodney, "Deal Expected to Pass Muster," *Plain Dealer* (Cleveland), September 14, 1991, p. 1F.

Fuller, John, "Society, Interstate Merger Is Approved," *Plain Dealer* (Cleveland), February 10, 1984, p. 9C.; "Society Seeks Centran Merger," *Plain Dealer* (Cleveland), September 25, 1984, p. 1A; "A Tale of Two Bankers," *Plain Dealer* (Cleveland), September 30, 1984, p. 1E.

Hill, Miriam, "Society to Buy 13 Branches," *Plain Dealer* (Cleveland), December 8, 1989, p. 9C; "Society Aims to Trim Expenses," *Plain Dealer* (Cleveland), April 18, 1990, p. 1E; "Society to Take Over Ameritrust," *Plain Dealer* (Cleveland), September 14, 1991, pp. 1A, 4A; "Society Chief Sees Fewer Big Banks," *Plain Dealer* (Cleveland), February 25, 1993, p. 1C.

Mahoney, Mike, "Merger Looks Bright for Banks," *Plain Dealer* (Cleveland), July 14, 1985, pp. 1D, 2D; "Deregulation Will Test New Leaders of Banks Here," *Plain Dealer* (Cleveland), October 13, 1987, p. 1E.

" 'Old Stone Bank' Is 88 this Week," *Plain Dealer* (Cleveland), June 13, 1937, p. 29A.

Phillips, Stephen, "Merger Means Layoffs, Consolidation of Services," *Plain Dealer* (Cleveland), September 14, 1991, pp. 1A, 5A.

"Society Corp. Reports Green Light on Merger with Harter BanCorp," *Plain Dealer* (Cleveland), June 9, 1979, p. 9B.

—April S. Dougal

Sprint Communications Company, L.P.

8140 Ward Parkway
Kansas City, Missouri 64114
U.S.A.
(913) 624-3000
Fax: (913) 624-5655

Wholly Owned Subsidiary of the Sprint Corporation
Incorporated: 1986 as US Sprint Communications Company,
    L.P.
Employees: 20,000
Sales: $6.0 billion
SICs: 4813 Telephone Communications Except
    Radiotelephone

Sprint Communications Company, L.P., is the third-largest long distance telephone company in the United States and the principal subsidiary of the Sprint Corporation. The often confusing relationship between the two entities stems from the frequent changes in ownership of the long distance provider that occurred during the 1980s. United Telecommunications, Inc., a parent company of local telephone companies, acquired control of Sprint in 1989 and subsequently adopted the name of its new subsidiary as its own.

Sprint Communications has its origin with the Southern Pacific Communications Corporation, a division of the Southern Pacific Railroad. During the early years of electronic communication, it was common for railroads to install telegraph wire on poles along its tracks. This enabled dispatchers to monitor trains and relay track conditions to locomotive engineers. With the advent of telephony, these wires were converted to voice communications. The complex nature of railroad communications necessitated the installation of telephone switches and multiplexing equipment, which allowed several conversations to be carried over the same pair of wires. By the 1940s, these railroads had established enormous long distance networks that were independent of the Bell System and other telephone companies.

The Southern Pacific Railroad operated its telephone system as an independent company, called the Southern Pacific Communications Corporation, or SPCC. Like all telephone systems, this network used copper wire as its transport medium. But by the late 1950s, the Southern Pacific and other railroads started to use radio systems, which eliminated the need to maintain thousands of miles of aerial wire and enabled dispatchers to communicate directly with engineers. SPCC continued to operate its ''switched private network'' for official interoffice communications. But during the 1970s maintenance costs for the wireline system became uneconomic.

In 1983 the GTE Corporation offered to purchase SPCC, which included a satellite company and the Switched Private Network Telecommunications group, known as ''Sprint.'' GTE, parent company of General Telephone, the United States's largest non-Bell telecommunications company, hoped to add the system to its own toll office network to form the backbone for a new long distance unit to compete with AT&T. Federal antitrust action obliged AT&T to divest itself of its 22 local Bell companies by 1984. In addition, AT&T's long distance monopoly was ended, clearing the way for competition.

GTE knew that a long distance network would be relatively simple to create and extremely profitable once in operation. It had the engineering and switching capability, but lacked the long distance corridors in which it could install wiring. While Sprint came with a dilapidated wire network, it offered hundreds of miles of open easements between major cities. GTE completed its acquisition of SPCC later in 1983, rechristening the operation GTE Sprint Communications.

A year earlier, a second non-Bell telephone company called United Telecommunications began development of its own long distance company, United Telecom Communications, later called US Telecom. Unlike Sprint, US Telecom was a satellite-based system designed to handle commercial data communications. By 1984, hundreds of long distance companies had emerged, each looking for just a piece of AT&T's hugely profitable business. Few of these actually operated alternative networks, choosing instead to simply aggregate traffic over AT&T's high-capacity data lines.

GTE Sprint installed fiber optic cable along its routes—a process begun by SPCC—because the transmission medium operated at extremely high frequencies, used virtually incorruptible digital signals, and was impervious to electronic interference. A single cable, the size of a common electrical cord, could carry as many calls as a three-foot thick copper cable.

The technology wasn't lost on US Telecom, whose president, Bill Esrey, announced that the company would construct its own nationwide fiber optic network and fight for a position in the long distance market along with GTE, MCI, and AT&T. To bolster the small network, United Telecom purchased U.S. Telephone Communications, a fledgling Dallas-based long distance carrier, and easements along key routes of the Consolidated Rail Corporation between cities in New England, and mid-Atlantic and Midwestern states.

Esrey's plan for a long distance company was denounced as impossible by experts quoted in *Telephony, TE&M,* and other trade publications. The critics would probably have been proven correct—the costs of assembling such a network were astronomical. But Esrey, who was named president and CEO of United Telecom in 1985, believed his goal could be attained—before competitors gained a lock on the market—by taking on a partner. In GTE Sprint, Esrey saw a well-capitalized partner with an identical strategy and a largely complementary network. He organized discussions with GTE, and in 1986 announced the merger of US Telecom and GTE Sprint. The 50–50 joint venture (technically a limited partnership) was created on July 1, 1986, under the name US Sprint. Commensurate with the creation of US Sprint, the company introduced its distinctive logo, a diamond split by a series of horizontal lines. The lines, reportedly meant to represent fiber optic channels, become thicker from left to right.

Because United Telecom and GTE operated hundreds of local exchanges, they had to guarantee that their customers would have equal access to AT&T and MCI. This would prevent US Sprint from gaining a long distance monopoly among United Telecom and GTE customers. In October of that year, the new company introduced an imaginative advertising campaign, featuring a tiny pin that was dropped on a table in front of a telephone handpiece. As it hit, the "ting" could be heard on a phone thousands of miles away. The ad maintained that this clarity was made possible by US Sprint's fiber optic network, implying that it was superior to AT&T's wireline system and MCI's microwave network. The image in the advertisement was so powerful and the campaign so successful that the tiny pin came to symbolize the superiority of US Sprint's network.

Within nine months, US Sprint had doubled its number of customers. But the company was ill-prepared for this growth. Bell companies, which dominate the nation's population centers, were slow to establish equal access to US Sprint, MCI, and other competitors of AT&T. Often, customers had difficulty using US Sprint. Many who got through reportedly received wildly inaccurate bills. These problems took months to iron out, inspiring AT&T to launch a massive ad campaign to woo customers back.

United Telecom and GTE channeled more than $2 billion into US Sprint, mostly for construction and marketing. The company issued millions of "F NCards" (for Fiber Optic Network), containing dialing instructions that would enable callers to gain access to US Sprint from any telephone. The company also built a National Operations Control Center in Kansas City, joining another in Atlanta. The NOCC managed call routing nationwide and enabled US Sprint to offer the nation's first non-AT&T long distance operator services. US Sprint equipped its network almost entirely with switches built by Northern Telecom—also a major competitor of AT&T, but in the manufacturing market.

In planning its long distance network, US Sprint adopted a flat architecture in which calls were passed from center to center, and routed around congested switching offices. By contrast, AT&T's network used a hierarchical design, in which calls of only a few dozen miles were routed over a bottom-tier network. Calls of a few hundred miles were passed along to a higher-tier network, and calls of a thousand miles or more were carried on yet another network.

The simplicity of US Sprint's network enabled engineers to make changes in its switching software instantaneously. AT&T's system required a series of staggered cutovers. One of the changes US Sprint made was the conversion in 1988 to Signaling System 7, a highly efficient routing technology that improved network management and speeded call completion. The system also enabled US Sprint to begin offering its own 800 services in competition with AT&T.

In a spirited demonstration of the obsolescence of the microwave networks operated by AT&T and MCI, US Sprint blew up one of the last of its own microwave towers in February of 1988. This action inspired AT&T and MCI to speed efforts to convert their systems over to fiber optic cable. By May of that year, US Sprint completed the last cutover of traffic from the old US Telecom and GTE Sprint networks to the fiber optic system. The company was now 100-percent fiber optic.

In November of 1988 US Sprint completed construction of its third transcontinental route. This helped US Sprint to win a contract to handle 40 percent of the federal government's long distance business, through a system called FTS2000. While AT&T won the remaining 60 percent, the division ensured that the government could maintain long distance communications in the event either company suffered a network failure. The government became US Sprint's largest customer. Companies such as Grumman, Calvin Klein, Elizabeth Arden, Chesebrough-Pond's, and National Starch also became major US Sprint accounts.

In April of 1989, US Sprint won its battle to gain access to millions of Bell company telephones whose long distance service could be provided only by AT&T. U.S. District Court Judge Harold Greene, who presided over the break-up of the Bell System, ordered pay phone franchisees to select a long distance company or be assigned one at random. This provided US Sprint with an opportunity to gain thousands of new accounts, handling long distance calls placed from Bell company pay phones. Also in April, US Sprint reported its first profitable quarter, earning $27.5 million.

GTE, however, had encountered financial difficulties resulting from a battle with another party for control of options on US Sprint. The company also needed cash to pay down debts and finance other areas of its business. GTE's chairman Rocky Johnson announced that his company wanted out of US Sprint. United Telecom purchased a 30.1 percent interest in US Sprint from GTE in July of 1989, leaving Johnson's company with a 19.9 percent stake until such time that United Telecom could generate the funds to complete the buyout.

In August US Sprint acquired Long Distance/USA, a Honolulu-based company whose bilingual agents handled calls between Hawaii and Japan. The acquisition left US Sprint with a 50 percent market share of call traffic out of Hawaii. Telenet, a satellite communications division that evolved from the SPCC's original satellite operations, was merged with US Sprint's international voice services in January of 1990 and renamed Sprint International.

Expanding its presence in the global telecommunications market, US Sprint purchased a 50 percent interest in PTAT-1, a transatlantic fiber optic cable system run in conjunction with Britain's Cable & Wireless. The relationship was later expanded to allow US Sprint to engage in joint marketing efforts in Britain with Cable & Wireless. The company established another marketing arrangement with Maryland National Bank (later called MBNA America) to issue Visa and MasterCard charge cards. The "Priority" Card provided all the features of the F NCard, while enabling users to build bonus rebates from credit purchases. It was also intended to match a similar card from AT&T.

US Sprint launched a new advertising campaign in October of 1990, featuring the actress Candice Bergen, star of the television series *Murphy Brown*. Bergen's effectiveness as a spokesperson grew with the show's popularity, eventually making her the most valuable spokesperson in advertising.

By 1991, US Sprint had garnered a seemingly small nine percent of the nation's long distance business, placing it behind MCI, with 14 percent, and AT&T, with 64 percent. This was, however, nine percent of a $70 billion market, and it provided United Telecom with about half of its total annual revenue. Hard-earned market share gains of only a tenth of a percent represented $70 million in revenue.

To win those bits and pieces of the market, US Sprint inaugurated its Priority marketing program, extending discounts to customers with monthly billing of $20 or more. But much of the company's efforts were concentrated in the business market. US Sprint operated more than 1,200 videoconferencing centers, enabling business customers to conduct visual presentations without having to fly and lodge their participants. In addition, US Sprint was the first major carrier to offer public frame relay data service, a high-speed digital transmission service unencumbered by standard error-correction, thus allowing more information to be transmitted in less time. This was followed by worldwide virtual private network services, in which a customer could communicate between offices in different countries as easily as between offices in the same building.

Continuing its international growth, US Sprint was licensed to construct a fiber optic network in the United Kingdom, using canal and river routes owned by the British Waterways Board. It began planning partnership agreements for several more submarine cable projects spanning the Atlantic and Pacific Oceans and the Caribbean. The company branched into Canada and established interconnection arrangements with TelMex, the Mexican telephone authority, and the Russian telephone network. US Sprint also entered the Unisource partnership with Swedish and Dutch firms, enabling it to win over another major customer, Unilever.

United Telecom completed its acquisition of US Sprint from GTE in 1992. The long distance group's revenues dwarfed those of United Telecom's other operations, necessitating a corporate reorganization.

Bill Esrey led an effort to drop "US" from the Sprint name, in order to better reflect the globalization of the company. He also suggested changing United Telecom's name to Sprint, thereby making more efficient use of promotional budgets. Thus, US Sprint became Sprint Communications, and United Telecom was renamed the Sprint Corporation. Later that year the parent company successfully bid to acquire Centel, a company with local telephone operations in 13 states and numerous cellular properties. The Centel operations were folded into Sprint.

While Sprint Communications was now part of a company with extensive local, long distance, and cellular operations, it remained the company's largest and best-known division. Still the nation's third-largest long distance company, with a fairly static ten percent of the market, Sprint Communications is likely to reap its greatest growth in international markets.

Further Reading:

"Let's Celebrate!," *Sprint Monthly,* July 1991, pp. 14–17.
"The Sprint Network: A Technical Overview," "United Telecom/ Sprint Profile," "Sprint Corporate Milestones," "Sprint Corporate Profile," Company Documents.
Sprint Technical Report, April 1992.

—John Simley

Standard Federal Bank

2600 West Big Beaver Road
Troy, Michigan 48084
U.S.A.
(313) 643-9600
Fax: (313) 637-2782

Public Company
Incorporated: 1893 as Standard Savings & Loan Association
Employees: 2,000
Assets: $9.8 billion
Stock Exchanges: New York
SICs: 6035 Federal Savings Banks

Standard Federal Bank stands as the largest thrift institution in the Midwest and the seventh largest in the United States. Founded in 1893, the bank survived the Great Depression of the 1930s and the savings and loan crises of the 1980s to enter 1993 with strong growth and assets of approximately $10 billion. The bank operates a retail franchise of over 150 banking centers, over 200 automated teller machines (ATMs), and over seven loan production offices throughout southern Michigan, northern Indiana, and northwestern Ohio. Although its primary lending activity is single-family mortgage lending—approximately $4.18 billion in home mortgage loans were closed in 1993—Standard Federal provides a full range of retail banking services, including checking and savings accounts, consumer loans, certificates of deposit, money market accounts, IRAs, and discount brokerage services.

On April 25, 1893, Standard Savings & Loan Association was established in downtown Detroit, taking over the charter of the Workman's Savings and Loan Association and building off assets of $31,000 to fund thrift services and affordable home ownership. After steady growth, the business moved to larger headquarters in 1914. By 1927, with assets surpassing $10 million, Standard Savings constructed its own headquarters. The new location, at the corner of Griswold and Jefferson, held symbolic importance as the site of Detroit's first building, Ste. Anne's Church, built in 1701.

Contending with the hard times of the 1930s, Standard Savings reinforced the credibility of its old slogan, "Safety For Saving Since 1893." The thrift managed to weather the Crash of '29 and the subsequent Great Depression. Having collected a large store of cash, Standard Savings was able to avoid a serious "run" on its offices and managed to keep its doors open even through the torrential bank closings of 1933.

After the Depression, Standard Savings was in a secure position to excel though World War II and the postwar boom years. In 1942 the company began sales of war bonds. By 1948, business had expanded enough to warrant multiple facilities, and the first branch office was opened in northwest Detroit. In 1950, Standard was issued a federal charter and changed its name to Standard Federal Savings & Loan Association. In 1957, with total assets at $100 million, the first branch offices outside Detroit city limits were opened. Steady success in the postwar years helped the company mold an identity and a set of standards that distinguished it from other savings and loan organizations and yielded sustained success into the 1990s.

A substantial part of the company's distinct character derived from three executives who steered the company from the 1950s into the 1990s. Thomas R. Ricketts served as Standard's president for 20 years starting in 1973 and also served as CEO from 1981 into the 1990s. His career with Standard Federal began in 1956 as a management trainee. His predecessor, Robert J. Hutton, started working at the company in October of 1929 and contributed to efforts at resisting the downward pull of the Crash. Hutton eventually served as president from 1962 to 1973 and as chairman from 1973 to 1981. Setting the precedent for both these company leaders, Walter J. L. Ray joined the company as a bookkeeper in 1908 and rose to serve as president from 1946 to 1962 and chairman from 1962 to 1973.

In the 1970s Standard Federal took a course of rapid expansion through mergers and acquisitions. In 1970, Birmingham (Michigan) Federal Savings merged with Standard Federal and main offices were moved to Birmingham. By 1973 the enlarged company had attained $1 billion in total assets and moved into larger headquarters in Troy, Michigan. Assets continued to climb with other mergers: Wayne (Michigan) Federal Savings merged with Standard Federal in 1975; First Federal Savings of Niles (Michigan) merged with the company in 1980; Landmark Savings and Loan (Saginaw/Bay City, Michigan) and First Savings Association of Dowagiac (Michigan) merged with Standard Federal in 1981; and Peoples Federal Savings of Detroit joined the bandwagon in 1982.

The year 1982 marked a temporary gap in Standard Federal's pattern of upward growth. That year the thrift suffered a loss of $331.6 million. Most of that loss, however, was attributed to $1 billion of low-yielding loans that were sold in a restructuring effort. Standard Federal implemented a wholesale banking strategy to increase profitability and position itself strongly for stock conversion. Standard Federal's pattern of healthy growth was quickly restored and continued through the 1980s. In 1984 the firm achieved assets in excess of $5 billion. In 1985 Standard Federal adopted a mutual savings bank charter, shifting from its status as an "association" to become Standard Federal Bank. In 1987 the bank converted from a mutual company to a publicly owned stock company listed on the New York Stock Exchange. The move represented one of the largest stock conversions by dollar amount in the history of the thrift industry, with the issuance of 30.4 million shares of common stock.

In addition to assuming a bank charter and going public in the 1980s, Standard Federal continued to grow through mergers and acquisitions. In 1983, the firm completed the largest merger in its history, joining forces with four Indiana thrifts simultaneously: American Federal Savings of Fort Wayne, First Federal Savings of Fort Wayne, Fort Wayne Federal Savings, and South Bend Federal Savings. The year 1988 saw the acquisition of Tower Federal Savings of South Bend (Indiana), adding eight branch offices to Standard Federal's growing list. Finally, the stream of 1980s mergers was capped in 1989 by Standard Federal's mergers with two prominent Michigan institutions: First Federal Savings and Loan of Kalamazoo and Peoples Savings of Monroe. The First Federal deal involved the acquisition of 1,812,910 shares of common stock for $29 per share, valued at approximately $54 million. Peoples had 2,200,000 shares of common stock acquired at $20 per share and amounting to an overall value of $44.7 million.

Another strategy to augment business growth in the 1980s involved renting space in K Mart retail stores to provide a full array of consumer banking and lending services at convenient shopping centers. In 1984 K Mart Corporation began a shotgunning effort to identify new markets for consumer banking and lending services in its stores. In 1984 the retailer began a one-year test of limited-service banking in eight Florida and Texas K Marts, of which four in Florida were operated by Standard Federal. In a series of December 1984 court decisions, K Mart beat down legal challenges to its new financial services and thereby paved the way for banker's services in 29 Florida stores. In 1985 the new strain of "retailer" banking moved north, with Standard Federal setting up financial service centers in four South Bend Indiana K Mart stores. The bank was thus able to bring checking accounts, passbook savings accounts, money market accounts, and consumer lending services directly to consumers.

Combining public relations with a vested interest in home ownership, in 1987 Standard Federal introduced a program titled, "Unique Realtor Services." The program was designed to provide consultation to real estate salespersons and ultimately to better inform consumers about home financing and other real estate matters. The services included "Sixty Minute" realtor seminars for local realtor boards and half-day sales training seminars for top sales associates. Such seminars were attended by more than 6,500 real estate sales people in 1992 alone. Standard Federal also engaged the noted real estate authority Thomas Ervin by sponsoring his weekly newspaper column, "Let's Talk About Real Estate," and by helping distribute his booklet, "How to Use the Services of a Realtor When Buying or Selling a Home."

Serving the needs of sellers and buyers of residential real estate through Unique Realtor Services was just one of the methods by which Standard Federal promoted home ownership and otherwise reinvested in the communities it served. In 1990, for example, the bank received $309,775 from the Federal Home Loan Bank (FHLB) of Indianapolis to finance two affordable housing projects in Michigan and Indiana. The funds were used to subsidize financing for the Historic Dunbar Corner Project in South Bend, Indiana, and the Gladstone Transitional Housing Project in Detroit. The entire concept was an indirect result of the Financial Institutions Reform, Recovery, and Enforcement

Act of 1989, by which regional FHLB organizations were to allot specified portions of their annual net income to Affordable Housing Program participants investing in low- to moderate-income programs. Standard Federal was distinguished as the only financial institution to receive funds for more than one project from the FHLB of Indianapolis during the 1990 period. By 1992, Standard Federal had won approval on 13 Affordable Housing Program applications, totaling approximately $1 million in funds, more than any other thrift in its FHLB district.

In conjunction with the city of Detroit, the regional builder's association, and local community groups, Standard Federal also co-sponsored HOMEARAMA Detroit, the city's first new subdivision of single-family homes in over 40 years. The first phase of the project opened at Victoria Park and was completely sold out by the end of 1992, signaling new hopes for single-family homes in a beleaguered real estate market. In a May 1993 interview for *Corporate Detroit* magazine, Thomas Ricketts, Standard Federal's chairman and president, expressed optimism for the project's second phase and for the benefits of such projects in general: "What we thought is, rather than have a house here and a house there, really to help rejuvenate Detroit, you have to take a mass of an area. And then if that can be outwardly grown, I think it can make a difference."

In 1992 Standard Federal also expanded its Community Home Buyers Program, which was co-sponsored by GE Capital and the Federal National Mortgage Association. The program enabled low- and moderate-income borrowers to purchase homes with as little as a three percent down payment. It also featured educational seminars and alternative credit sources to widen the pool of qualified applicants without substantially increasing risk.

In addition to new programs for mortgage lending and community reinvestment in the 1990s, Standard Federal continued its track of growth through acquisitions. In 1991 United Home Federal Savings of Toledo (Ohio) was acquired. The 1992 acquisition of First Federal Savings and Loan Association of Lenawee County added four new offices in southeastern Michigan, providing impetus for future growth in that market area. In 1993 Standard Federal acquired InterFirst Bankcorp, Inc., of Ann Arbor, Michigan, with five full-service offices serving the residents of Washtenaw County and a wholesale mortgage division serving 31 states in the United States. That same year Standard Federal established a presence in the Flint–Bay City–Saginaw area and northern Michigan with the acquisition of Taylor-based Heritage Bankcorp for $110.7 million in cash.

Standard Federal's success from the late eighties onward stood out in visible relief against a backdrop of major failures affecting other banks and thrifts. The firm seemed to be thriving on the very conditions that were driving other institutions out of business in scores. In 1992 Standard Federal established new records for profitability, loan closings, and total deposits: net income for the year totaled $95.6 million, a 45 percent increase over 1991 net income; the bank made $3.61 billion in residential mortgage loans, a 117 percent increase over 1991; and assets reached $9.5 billion, with $6.5 billion in deposits. An analyst for Shearson Lehman Hutton Inc., New York, attributed Standard Federal's success to its efficiency of operations, strict underwriting standards, and "a favorable match between earning assets and costing liabilities," in a November 1988 article for *American Banker*. Painting a broader picture of his company's successful character, Ricketts told stockholders in a 1992 annual report: "The Bank does not have significant loan concentrations to any one borrower, has no foreign loans, and does not make loans to borrowers engaged in highly leveraged transactions. The Bank has never purchased 'junk bonds' or other high-risk securities for its investment portfolio." One consequence was an extremely low level of nonperforming assets—0.75 percent of total assets—compared to an industry average of over 4 percent.

Standard Federal also benefited from falling interest rates in the early 1990s, riding a boom in home-mortgage refinancing. In January of 1992, for example, the bank reported the largest volume of single-family mortgage loan activity in its history, with 7,699 mortgage loan applications received as compared to 1,470 applications in January of 1991. In an October 1991 *Crain's Detroit Business* article, Standard Federal's chief financial officer, Joseph Krul, stressed the need for prudent management of the bank's loan portfolio to protect against the possibility of rising interest rates. "We're managing our interest-rate profile such that we're not going to end up with the same profile as the early eighties. Forty percent of our assets are either adjustable-rate or extremely short-term, like 90 day. In the early eighties, that figure was close to zero."

In order to further reduce risks of changing interest rates for mortgage financing, and to increase operating efficiencies in general, Standard Federal developed highly automated operating systems. The efficiencies of such systems dramatically reduced operating costs and produced good customer service. Moreover, the productivity improvements of automated mortgage application systems alleviated the need to hedge with futures and options contracts, according to William Murray, senior vice president of corporate planning, in a February 1990 article for *National Mortgage News*. "The whole idea of options and forwards is that time is money. And the longer you sit there with something that is in process, the greater interest rate risk you bear," explained Murray. The average time for Standard Federal to receive and close an application for a mortgage loan was 18 days in 1989, Murray pointed out. In addition, the company could sell the mortgages it originated to the secondary market—the Federal Home Loan Mortgage Corp. or the Federal National Mortgage Association—in 24 hours flat.

On April 25, 1993, Standard Federal observed its centennial anniversary with cause for celebration. Over its 100-year history, it had grown into the Midwest's largest thrift and still showed little fatigue of old age. Low interest rates continued to lower interest payments on savings accounts and to spur record-breaking lending activity in 1993. In addition, implementation of a consultant's recommendations had cut 1992 operating costs by $6 million. On May 6, 1993, the Office of Thrift Supervision (OTS) awarded Standard Federal its "Outstanding" rating, the highest rating granted to financial institutions for performance in the area of community lending and reinvestment. In all, the bank seemed poised for continued success well beyond the 1990s.

Nor did CEO and President Thomas Ricketts lack enthusiasm for the future. In a May 1993 article for *Corporate Detroit,* he explained: "I love my work, I really do. I really feel we are doing something important. I mean, we are putting Americans into housing, and I don't know anything that's nicer. We've got a product that everybody wants—money to get a home. We want to be the most successful financial institution in America."

Principal Subsidiaries: Standard Financial Corp.; Standard Service Corp.; Standard Insurance Agency, Inc.; Tower Service Corp.; Standard Brokerage Services, Inc.; Eureka Service Corp.

Further Reading:

"K-Mart Widens Financial Services to Up Traffic, Profit," *Discount Store News,* February 18, 1985, p. 3.

Matthews, Gordon, "Michigan Savings Bank Wins Praise for Efficiency," *American Banker,* November 4, 1988, p. 2.

Ringer, Richard, "Very Slow Start for MBS Futures," *National Mortgage News,* February 26, 1990, p. 11.

Roush, Matt, "Big Interest in Falling Rates," *Crains Detroit Business,* October 7, Sec. 1, p. 3.

"Standard Federal Bank Experiences Greatest Lending Month in Its History," *PR Newswire,* February 14, 1992.

"Standard Federal Bank and Interfirst Bankcorp, Inc., Execute Definitive Merger Agreement," *PR Newswire,* July 16, 1993.

"Standard Federal Bank Receives Funds to Assist in Two Affordable Housing Projects," *PR Newswire,* August 13, 1990.

"Standard Federal Bank Sponsors Unique Realtor Services," *PR Newswire,* July 8, 1987.

Waldsmith, Lynn, "Capitalizing on the American Dream: Standard Federal Bank CEO Thomas Ricketts Does Things the Old Fashioned Way," *Corporate Detroit,* May 1993, Sec. 1, p. 7.

—Kerstan Cohen

Sunbeam®-Ōster®

Sunbeam-Oster Co., Inc.

2100 New River Center
200 East Las Olas Blvd.
Fort Lauderdale, Florida 33301-2100
U.S.A.
(305) 767-2100
Fax: (305) 767-2105

Public Company
Incorporated: 1989
Employees: 9,400
Sales: $1 billion
Stock Exchanges: New York
SICs: 3634 Electric Housewares & Fans; 3596 Scales &
   Balances, except Laboratory; 3631 Household Cooking
   Equipment; 2844 Toilet Preparations; 3999 Manufacturing
   Industries; 3421 Cutlery; 3873 Watches, Clocks,
   Watchcases, and Parts

Sunbeam and Oster are consumer brand names recognizable from coast to coast, and by all generations of Americans. Although the Sunbeam-Oster Company is a relatively new entity, formed in 1989, its brand names predate the present company by many decades. Currently the company manufactures and markets a wide variety of high quality Sunbeam and Oster products via its four principal operations: Outdoor Products, led by barbecue grills with a 50 percent market share, and outdoor aluminum furniture with better than 60 percent market share; Household Products, led by market-leading warming blankets and heated throws; Specialty Products, led by personal care items used by barbers and beauticians; and the International division, which markets Sunbeam and Oster products in over sixty countries, primarily Canada and Latin America. Twenty percent of the company's billion-dollar sales derive from the increasingly important foreign market. Sunbeam-Oster is the only small appliance manufacturer in the United States whose brand names are known worldwide.

The Sunbeam-Oster Company emerged from the stormy bankruptcy proceedings of Allegheny International in 1989. Prior to their merger, Sunbeam and Oster were separate firms within the sprawling Allegheny International (AI) group of companies. Only five years before the establishment of Sunbeam-Oster, this group of companies within AI had a workforce of 40,000 worldwide and was engaged in dozens of different enterprises. Hit hard by the recession of 1981–82, over extended and out of touch with the market, AI was compelled to sell off its businesses one by one, until all that remained were the profitable Sunbeam and Oster firms.

In 1898, in the heyday of steel making, the Allegheny Steel and Iron Company (which changed its name five years later to the Allegheny Steel Company, and after World War II became Allegheny Ludlum Industries) was incorporated in Pennsylvania, with headquarters in Pittsburgh. Over the next few decades, Allegheny Ludlum Industries acquired numerous businesses, most notably the Chemetron Corporation and the Wilkinson Sword Group. When Sunbeam was purchased in 1981, the transformation of Allegheny into Allegheny International, Inc. was complete.

Sunbeam originated in 1897 as the Chicago Flexible Shaft Company, a maker of electrical appliances. So successful were the range of its products, from toasters to irons to mixers, that the company changed its name to Sunbeam Corporation in 1946. When AI purchased Sunbeam in 1981 (whereupon it became the Sunbeam Appliance Division), Sunbeam had sales of well over one billion dollars and was already the best known brand of small electrical appliances in the country.

The Oster brand was named after John Oster Sr., who organized the John Oster Manufacturing Company in Racine, Wisconsin in 1924. The company primarily catered to the barber and beauty salon supply market. Increasingly, Oster expanded its product range to include massage equipment and other beauty care items. During World War II, the company switched from beauty care products to the production of small electric motors for military planes. While the company returned to civilian production at the war's end, its experience as a manufacturer of small machines did not go to waste. A year after the war, the Oster company took its first tentative steps into the housewares products arena with a blender it called the Osterizer, which quickly became a household word. The success of this product led to expansion into other related businesses. In the 1950s, Oster acquired the Northern Electric Company, which produced such consumer items as electric blankets and mattresses, vaporizers, thermostats and humidifiers, a variety of hair dryers, hair setters, and mirrors.

In 1980, however, the Oster Company was acquired by the Sunbeam Corporation, which a year later found itself part of the Allegheny International group of companies. As part of AI, the Sunbeam division included the John Zink Company, manufacturer of air pollution control devices, and Hanson Scale, manufacturer of bathroom scales and other balance machines.

By the mid-1980s, Allegheny International's four principal divisions, Sunbeam/Oster, Sunbeam Leisure, Northern Electric and Almet/Lawnlite, had entered a period of steep decline in sales revenues. Nearly half of AI's manufactures derived from its most important division, the Sunbeam/Oster group of companies. Neither their products nor the famous Sunbeam and Oster brands were in jeopardy; rather, problems centered around over-extension, poor morale in the workforce, and an unusually high turnover in management. Stockholders in 1986 accused Chairman and CEO Robert J. Buckley of mismanagement and a lavish lifestyle at company expense.

Buckley's successor, Oliver S. Travers, who had been head of AI's consumer products group, energetically set about to downsize the firm, ridding it in due course of no less than twenty-four diverse business operations. By 1988, AI essentially consisted of Sunbeam and Oster. One third of AI's workforce was let go and managers' salaries were frozen. Nonetheless, the decline continued, accelerated by the stock market crash in October, 1987. Four months later, AI filed in court for re-organization under Chapter 11 bankruptcy. The court approved re-organization was expected to put AI back on its feet.

Instead, the entity that would emerge from the wreckage, Sunbeam-Oster Corp., was entirely distinct from its predecessor. In the fall of 1989, an investment group calling itself Japonica Partners purchased the remains of AI for a $250 million, which market analysts considered a textbook example of well thought out bankruptcy investment. Only two years later, the investment yielded a billion dollars in sales revenues.

As the major stockholders of the bankrupt AI, Japonica Partners had created a new company, Sunbeam-Oster Company, Inc., reflecting the name recognition and abiding market strengths of these well regarded brands. AI was dissolved; the youthful Paul B. Kazarian was appointed CEO and chairman, and under his aggressive (some said domineering) management, Sunbeam-Oster emerged from the doldrums a dynamic and profitable firm.

Much of the downsizing and trimming of the former AI's operations had been accomplished by AI's last chairman, Oliver Travers, who had rid the ailing firm of half of its former businesses. Nonetheless, Mr. Kazarian set about streamlining a dozen diverse operations into four coordinated businesses: Outdoor Products, Household Products, Specialty Products and International sales. Layers of management inherited from the former AI were pared down, marginally profitable products were discontinued, and total spending was reduced a hefty 17 percent. The firm's headquarters also were re-located from Pittsburgh to Providence, Rhode Island. These and other changes occurred during the worst period of the 1990s recession. By late 1991, however, Sunbeam-Oster's sales had increased seven percent and totaled nearly a billion dollars, enabling it to make the list of Fortune 500 companies.

The new stockholders at the same time approved a coordinated business strategy that emphasized the manufacture of new products; quick distribution by means of electronic communication with the customer; working closely with retailers to promote efficiency and service; and lastly, the promotion of brand name marketing, the company's greatest strength. Advertising would be continuous and year round. The budget for advertising increased nine million dollars from 1991 to 1992, to $59 million. Promotions focussed on making consumers aware of the ''Made In America'' labels on many Sunbeam and Oster products.

The new Sunbeam-Oster company, with its historic old brands, was a success in a very short time. Though Chairman Kazarian's accomplishments were notable, his manner so antagonized the majority of company stockholders that they dismissed him in early 1993. Under his successor, interim Chairman and CEO Charles J. Thayer, the company continued its record growth, as well as its expansion into international markets. The four operating divisions of Sunbeam-Oster pursue the strategy put into effect at the company's founding, with each business segment holding dominant market shares in their respective products. Outdoor Products, which accounts for approximately one third of total sales and manufactures an array of barbecue grills and other products, has at least a 50 percent market share in grill commodities as well as in outdoor aluminum furniture. Household Products, which account for another third of company sales, manufactures and sells a huge variety of small electrical appliances, and holds a leading market share in such items as warming blankets and throws, heating pads, mixers and blenders. Specialty Products, which produces a variety of beauty and personal care products such as hair dryers, curlers, and scales, holds a number one market share in weather stations and thermometers, as well as in hair clippers for human and animal hair. This division generates around ten percent of company revenues.

The international division accounts for nearly one quarter of company sales, and while most of these sales are generated in Canada and Latin America, the company is making efforts to expand in the United Kingdom, the Middle East and Eastern Europe. In Latin America, Sunbeam and Oster are the most popular small appliance brands, and the company holds number one market positions in small kitchen appliances in Peru and Venezuela. While most Sunbeam-Oster products are made in the United States, the company has some manufacturing facilities in Mexico, Venezuela, and Peru. Sales and distribution of Sunbeam-Oster products in Canada have been extremely strong for decades, with market shares mirroring those in the United States. Sunbeam-Oster plans to expand its international presence by building on its brand name recognition and marketing an increasing number of products that hitherto had been sold mainly in the United States and Canada, such as outdoor folding furniture and barbecue grills. International markets will play an increasingly important role in the fortunes of Sunbeam-Oster.

In August of 1993 Sunbeam-Oster elected Roger W. Schipke as chairman and CEO. Schipke brought to the company recognized leadership in the consumer products industry. He joined Sunbeam-Oster from the Ryland Group, where he served as chairman and CEO. Prior to joining Ryland in 1990, Schipke spent 29 years with General Electric, ultimately serving on the GE Corporate Executive Council as senior vice-president in charge of General Electric's Appliances Division. He grew the Appliances Division over an eight-year period from approximately $2 billion in revenues with primarily a domestic focus to an approximately $5.5 billion global consumer products business with manufacturing facilities around the world.

The company's greatest strengths in the future will remain its widespread brand recognition, which is synonymous with quality and durability, as well its huge variety of products. A steady stream of new products continuously appear on Sunbeam-Oster's assembly lines, some, such as the unique warming blanket that adjusts heat by sensing the body's temperature, requiring high technological proficiency. The list of new products is grows steadily, and includes an automatic shut-off iron, large print bath scales, an angled toothbrush and side burner grills. Approximately one quarter of company sales derive from new products that have come on the market over the past few years.

Traditional and new products are sold in such large discount stores as Wal-Mart, K-Mart, Target, Sears, and Best Products.

Further Reading:

Allegheny International: A New Global Business Enterprise, New York: Newcomen Society, 1983.

''Peanuts' Linus to Blanket Media for Sunbeam-Oster,'' April 19, 1993, p. 6.

Ratliff, Duke, ''Sunbeam-Oster Shaking Up Massager Field,'' *HFD: The Weekly Home Furnishings Newspaper,* May 17, 1993, p. 54.

Rothman, Matt, ''Keeping the Faith in Allegheny International,'' *Business Week,* January 18, 1988, pp. 74–75.

Schifrin, Matthew, ''Hidden Value,'' *Forbes,* May 11, 1992, pp. 60, 64.

Schroeder, Michael, ''Allegheny's Battle to Come Back from the Abyss,'' *Business Week,* June 26, 1989, pp. 130, 134.

Silver, A. J., ''Sunbeam-Oster Co., Inc. Company Report,'' *Dillon, Read & Co.,* September 10, 1992.

''Sunbeam-Oster Plans to Post 48 Percent Increase in Second Period Net,'' *Wall Street Journal,* July 28, 1993, p. A8.

—Sina Dubovoj

Suzuki Motor Corporation

300, Takatsuka-cho
Hamamatsu-shi
Shizuoka-ken 432-91
Japan
(53) 440-2111
Fax: (53) 456-0002

Public Company
Incorporated: 1920 as Suzuki Loom Manufacturing
    Company
Employees: 12,757
Sales: ¥1.24 trillion
Stock Exchanges: Tokyo Osaka Nagoya Fukuoka Amsterdam
SICs: 3711 Motor Vehicle and Passenger Car Bodies; 3714
    Motor Vehicle Parts & Accessories; 3751 Motorcycles,
    Bicycles & Parts

Suzuki Motor Corporation is best known in the United States and Europe as a manufacturer of small, fuel-efficient automobiles and trucks and powerful motorcycles. In its home market of Japan, however, the company is the leading maker of "midget" cars—a classification almost unknown outside Japan. These tiny subcompact automobiles are popular because of the tremendous overcrowding in Japanese cities, where a larger car cannot be purchased legally until the owner can show proof that he or she has a parking spot. Until the early 1990s, no such proof was required for a midget cars, which are smaller than a Yugo or Ford Fiesta and are comparable to the British Mini.

In the market for two-wheeled vehicles, approximately 80 percent of Suzuki's domestic output is mopeds, or motor-driven bicycles. The company also makes marine outboard motors, generators, water pumps, and even motorized wheelchairs. In addition, through its network of foreign assembly plants, Suzuki is adept at turning out millions of car parts.

Suzuki's growth has been predicated on its domestic and international strategies. Domestically, the company owes its success to its high-quality engines, around which it designs a wide variety of vehicles for special or emerging niche markets. Internationally, Suzuki has traditionally targeted developing countries with growing populations, including Cambodia, India, China, Egypt, Hungary, and Pakistan. Suzuki's policy in these markets is to find a local partner to sell simple, more affordable vehicles, taking advantage of the small margins on huge vol-

umes of sales. In the U.S. market, Suzuki's strategy is an extension of its domestic plan. While Ford Motor Company, General Motors Corporation (GM), Toyota Motor Corporation, and Chrysler Corporation battle for leadership in mass markets, Suzuki excels in the quirky niches between jeep and utility vehicle and between compact and subcompact.

Suzuki Motor Corporation was founded by Michio Suzuki in 1909 as a manufacturer of weaving machines. From its base in Hamamatsu, the Suzuki Loom Works, as it was then known, supplied weaving equipment to hundreds of small fabrics manufacturers in and between Tokyo, Yokohama, and Nagoya. At the time, textile manufacturing was one of Japan's biggest industries. It provided a growing and stable market for the Suzuki enterprise. In 1920 Michio Suzuki took his company public and named the new firm Suzuki Loom Manufacturing Company.

Suzuki continued to manufacture weaving machines exclusively throughout the 1920s and until the mid-1930s. At that time a militarist clique gained control of the government and began a massive mobilization program called the "quasi-war economy." Companies throughout the country were asked to begin planning for a conversion to armaments manufacturing. Suzuki was an especially attractive supplier because it was in the business of equipping other factories. In addition, the company was located far away from major industrial centers that would become primary bombing targets.

By 1937 Suzuki had begun production of a variety of war-related materials, which may have included vehicle parts, gun assemblies, and armor. For its part in Japan's World War II effort, Suzuki, like thousands of other companies, was requisitioned for war production and probably had no intention of becoming a manufacturer of military implements. Nevertheless, the company continued to manufacture weaving machines for the duration of the war. Fortunately, the Suzuki factory and the city of Hamamatsu escaped the ravages of U.S. bombing campaigns. The company was capable of resuming production after the war, but the economy and supply networks were in ruins.

Suzuki reestablished production of textile manufacturing equipment soon after World War II. Japan, however, was so impoverished that there was little demand for new woven products. As a result, few companies could afford to purchase new looms. By 1947 the pace of investment continued to be slow, prompting Suzuki to make a major change in its business. That year the company moved to a new headquarters building and, relying on the manufacturing experience it had gained during the war, began design work on motorized vehicles. The prospects were favorable; Japan was a nation of nearly 100 million people, nearly all of whom lacked access to basic transportation.

The heart of the new Suzuki product line was a small 36cc engine that could be used to motorize bicycles. Production of the moped, called the Power Free, began in 1952, prompting Suzuki to abandon weaving equipment entirely. In conjunction with the introduction of the new product line, the company changed its name to the Suzuki Motor Company in 1954, the same year it introduced its first line of motorcycles. The following year, Suzuki graduated from two-wheeled vehicles to a light passenger sedan called the Suzulight, powered by a 360cc engine. In the process, Suzuki gained valuable experience in developing larger internal combustion engines, vehicle frames, gear systems, and steering mechanisms.

Suzuki developed an improved moped, named the Suzumoped, in 1958. And in 1959, the company began production of a revolutionary delivery van, much smaller than conventional delivery trucks then in use and more appropriately suited to many motorized businesses.

Suzuki banked on the fact that, as its customers' operations grew, so would their needs. Therefore, it would be pointless for the company to squander hard-won loyalty by neglecting to offer its customers a properly diverse product line. Having gained an important foothold in various sectors of the Japanese vehicle market, Suzuki cleverly used these beachheads for further expansion. The popular delivery van of 1959 convinced the company to develop a light truck, called the Suzulight Carry FB, in 1961.

The single event that gained Suzuki its greatest international recognition occurred the following year, when a Suzuki motorcycle won the 50cc-class Isle of Man race. It was the first of many victories for Suzuki motorcycles, victories that firmly established the previously unknown company model as a world leader. By 1970, demand for more powerful motorcycles would prompt Suzuki to develop its first line of four-stroke engine motorcycles. This preserved Suzuki's position of leadership in the market.

Suzuki had difficulty expanding into domestic automobile markets that were dominated by Toyota, Honda, and Nissan. As a result, it was unable to develop a more sophisticated product line. In its search for growth, Suzuki turned instead to export markets that were in the same economic condition Japan had been in 10 or 15 years earlier. The most promising market was Thailand, a country that historically had close ties with Japan. In 1967 Suzuki established a factory in Thailand to assemble a variety of vehicles whose parts were made in Japan. By providing local employment and inviting Thai investment in the venture, Suzuki skirted import restrictions that locked out other manufacturers. Later, Suzuki duplicated the export development formula in Indonesia and the Philippines.

Still unable to reach sales goals for domestic vehicles, however, Suzuki began a diversification campaign. The company's small engines were fitted to electrical generators, yielding an entirely new line of portable power sources. In addition, the company dabbled in housing, an initially successful but short-lived venture.

The 1973 Organization of Petroleum Exporting Countries (OPEC) oil embargo drastically changed the automobile market. Faced with skyrocketing fuel prices, consumers showed interest in more efficient cars. But while Suzuki's little cars and trucks sipped gasoline, they were underpowered when compared to competing models from Japan's big three. The company's domestic auto sales slid further during a 1974 recession resulting from the oil crisis. That year, total sales of minicars—Suzuki's prime automobile segment—fell by more than 65 percent from 1970.

Suzuki began a major export campaign soon afterward, commencing full motorcycle production in Thailand, Indonesia, and Taiwan. In addition, it sent automobiles to the United States for the first time. The product was a bit unusual in the U.S. market, where the roads were dominated by enormous, heavy cars. Suzukis were introduced in the United States in small numbers but were refreshingly fuel efficient, capable of using half or even a third as much gasoline as some American models. Suzuki, however, entered the U.S. market well behind Toyota, Honda, Nissan, and even Mazda and Subaru. Furthermore, by 1978, fuel prices had fallen, and demand for Suzuki's "economy cars" was evaporating. Oil prices would shoot up again briefly in 1979, following the Iranian Revolution, but by then many of Suzuki's most promising markets had enacted tough laws restricting imports from Japan.

Returning to the development strategy it had begun in Thailand in 1967, Suzuki negotiated a number of foreign investment deals, agreeing to locate production facilities in several countries in return for access to their markets. In 1982 the company established a Pakistani production firm called PACO and a similar operation in India called Maruti Udyog, Ltd. Suzuki also established a partnership in Spain with Land Rover known as Land Rover Santana S.A. Two years later Suzuki set up new marketing operations in New Zealand and France.

In the United States, Suzuki's largest market outside Japan, the company signed a series of marketing and production contracts with General Motors and rival Isuzu Motors in 1981. As part of the deal, GM purchased a 5.2 percent interest in Suzuki. The companies planned to share production facilities and handle marketing of each other's products. In 1983 Suzuki began production of its Swift subcompact, selling the cars through GM as the Chevy Sprint and later as the Geo Metro. Another one of the results of Suzuki's arrangements with GM was the creation of a joint subsidiary in Canada, called CAMI Automotive, in 1986. This plant went into production in 1989 and manufactured Sprints, Metros, and Suzuki Sidekicks, also marketed as Geo Trackers.

While Suzuki's joint venture with GM was off to a good start, Suzuki had considerably more trouble of its own. Shortly after establishing a U.S. subsidiary at Brea, California, in 1986, the company was accused by *Consumer Reports* of producing an unsafe vehicle, the Samurai. Specifically, the magazine noted that the Samurai's high center of gravity could cause it to flip over while negotiating turns even at low speeds. Suzuki launched its own investigation and took remedial measures, but the damage had already been done. Worse for Suzuki, the company's entire U.S. executive team resigned—a gesture of atonement that was misinterpreted as an abandonment of the company's commitment to the product and to the U.S. market in general.

Domestically, Suzuki developed several new models during the 1980s, including the Cultus subcompact in 1983 and the four-wheel drive Escudo in 1988. Also in 1988, Suzuki agreed to handle sales of Peugeot automobiles in Japan. The following year, the company rolled out the Cultus Esteem, which shared the same 1600cc engine as the Escudo. And shoring up revenues, motorcycle sales, which had been in decline since 1982, recovered by 1990.

With the Samurai debacle behind it, Suzuki initiated a subtle campaign to reestablish the vehicle's promising U.S. franchise. The high-riding Samurai was popular with younger adults who favored a more rugged jeep-like buggy that was impervious to off-road obstacles. Above all, it was fun to drive and made a strong statement about its owner.

Suzuki also continued its push at globalization, opening a plant in Great Britain in 1986 that turned out 15,000 microvans annually. The company established a partnership with the Egyptian company Modern Motors SAE, called Suzuki Egypt SAE, to build compact cars and the Super Carry truck and van line in that country. Suzuki licensed manufacture of its Swift/Forsa model through Colmotores SA in Columbia. The Pakistani venture was also expanded to include automobile manufacture under a new company, Pak Suzuki Motor Company, Ltd. In April of 1991 Suzuki established a joint venture with C. Itoh, the start-up Hungarian auto manufacturer Autokonzern RT, and the International Finance Corporation. The enterprise, called Magyar Suzuki Corporation, began production of the Suzuki Swift in Hungary the following year. In addition to putting up $230 million in capital for the new company, Suzuki flew each of its Hungarian workers to Japan for training in its production methods.

Also in 1991 Suzuki Motor Company adopted the more international name Suzuki Motor Corporation. That year and in 1992, however, the company suffered reverses in its largest enterprise, midget cars with engines under 550cc. This was due to two factors: new laws that extended parking restrictions to cars of that class and a worsening recession in Japan. Suzuki's losses were partially offset by an increase in motorcycle sales. But because revenues from auto manufacturing are nearly five times greater than motorcycle sales, the company's overall growth rate slowed substantially.

A promising area for Suzuki is its place under the umbrella of General Motors' international ventures. Through teaming agreements, Suzuki has been designated GM's *de facto* small car division, developing automobiles for the American company under the Geo nameplate. Elsewhere in Suzuki's U.S. business, sales of the Samurai recovered to 20,000 in 1992, and the company projected revenues of the Samurai would exceed 50,000 by 1995.

Globally, Suzuki remains primarily a niche manufacturer. The company derives 71 percent of its income from sales of automobiles, including the Cervo, Alto and Swift car models, the Samurai jeep, Carry van, and Escudo off-road vehicle, which is sold in the United States as the Sidekick. Suzuki is Japan's leading minicar manufacturer, a position it has held for 20 years. Motorcycles, though, which comprise 15 percent of Suzuki's business, make up a considerably more glorious area for the company. Its motorcycle products range from 50cc scooters to 1100cc touring bikes. In addition, outboard motors contribute three percent of Suzuki Motor Corporation sales, with the balance supplied by parts sales.

Principal Subsidiaries: American Suzuki Motor Corp. (United States); Suzuki Canada, Inc.; Suzuki Motor de Columbia SA; Suzuki Australia Pty., Ltd.; Suzuki New Zealand Ltd.; Suzuki Motor GmbH. Deutschland (Germany); Suzuki France S.A.; Suzuki Motor España, S.A. (Spain); Suzuki Philippines, Inc.; Suzuki Italia S.p.A. (Italy); Suzuki Transport and Packaging Co., Ltd.; Suzuki Real Estate Co., Ltd.; Suzuki Parts Manufacturing Co., Ltd.; Suzuki Marina Hamanako Co., Ltd.; Suzuki Oil Co., Ltd.; Suzuki Special Products Manufacturing Co., Ltd.

Further Reading:

Suzuki, The Corporation, Suzuki Motor Corporation.

—John Simley

TALISMAN
E N E R G Y

Talisman Energy

Suite 2400
855 2nd Street S.W.
Calgary, Alberta
Canada T2P 4J9
(403) 237-1123
Fax: (403) 237-1027

Public Company
Incorporated: 1925 as Supertest Petroleum Corporation
Employees: 1,450
Sales: $195.7 million
Stock Exchanges: Toronto Montreal Vancouver

Talisman Energy is a natural resource company engaged in exploration and drilling for crude oil, natural gas, and sulfur in western Canada. It also has oil and gas exploration and marketing interests in the country's eastern half. The company in 1992 took over the operations of the former BP Canada operation after its parent, the British Petroleum Company, sold its 57 percent interest in the Canadian concern.

Talisman's roots can be found in the Supertest Petroleum Corporation, established on December 17, 1925, with the opening of a corner gas station in London, Ontario. The company immediately began building a network of gas stations, and in 1926 it bought the gas and oil interests of Ensign Oil Company, based in Montreal. Growth for Supertest was slow during the economic depression of the 1930s, when unemployment and persistent economic downturns affected the ability of Canadians to buy and drive cars.

In 1953, the rival BP company made its first large foray into the Canadian market. BP, headquartered in London, England, had its earliest roots in the Middle East, where extensive gas and oil interests were found and exploited, in Iran and Saudi Arabia in particular. As early as 1926, the company considered expanding outside of the Middle East. Specifically, Arnold Wilson, who succeeded F. G. Watson as managing director of D'Arcy Exploration Company, a division of BP, told company directors that disappointment with drilling in Asia and Africa led him to consider drilling opportunities in Canada or South America. As it happened, BP did much to explore new opportunities before it entered the Canadian market in a substantial way. Between 1927 and 1930, company geologists showed considerable interests in possible fields in British Columbia, New Brunswick, and Alberta. However, the geologists could not agree on whether potential gas and oil reserves in the Canadian hinterland warranted further investment towards drilling.

In 1953, BP bought a minority stake in Triad Oil Company, a small exploration company based in Calgary with large exploration holdings in western Canada. Four years later, BP entered the Quebec market. By 1960, when the company's first refinery opened for business in Montreal, BP had over 800 service stations in the French-speaking province. Now operating as rivals, both companies expanded during the 1950s and 1960s. Earlier, in 1959, Supertest merged into its own operations those of Reliance Petroleum Ltd., also based in Calgary. In 1964, BP bought the eastern Canadian interests of Cities Service, comprising 750 retail gas stations and a refinery at Oakville, Ontario. This acquisition brought to just under 1800 the number of retail gas stations that BP had in Ontario and Quebec and added to its sales and service teams for home heating and the agricultural, commercial, marine, and aviation industries.

In 1969, BP's holding company in Canada was renamed BP Canada, and the principal marketing company was renamed BP Oil Ltd. Put another way, BP's Canadian operations now had two arms, an upstream—that is, oil and gas exploration and production—arm, and a downstream—refining and marketing—arm. A year later, all BP's marketing and refining interests in western Canada were put under the corporate umbrella of BP Oil and Gas Ltd., including the interests of the former Triad Oil Company.

The discovery in August 1969 of giallt oil reserves at Prudhoe Bay, Alaska, convinced BP headquarters in London that it had a significant future in northern Canada. In August 1971 BP Canadian Holdings Ltd., then BP Canadian Ltd., and a division of BP in Britain offered to buy a controlling interest in Supertest. The British parent exchanged for shares all of its petroleum marketing, refining, and exploration interests in Canada. These entailed all the outstanding stock of BP Oil Ltd.—an associate company mainly engaged in marketing and refining in eastern Canada—and a 65.9 percent interest in BP Oil and Gas Ltd. The BP offer was accepted by Corlon Investments Ltd., which then held an 83.7 percent stake in Supertest. It sold its entire stake for $10 a share. By November of that year, BP had bought 97.8 percent of Supertest, having paid $16.50 per share for that holding.

Immediately upon buying Supertest, the new company, BP Canada Ltd., set about securing new oil and gas acreage holdings in the Arctic Islands region of Canada. The idea was to explore for possible oil and gas reserves in the regions adjoining the 1969 Alaskan oil and gas discoveries. Once located, substantial oil and gas reserves would be extracted from the earth via drilling rigs, and then refined downstream before being sold to consumers through a network of gas stations. Other oil companies tended to be specific about identifying and taking aim at specific oil targets. BP Canada, on the other hand, had a "shotgun", as opposed to a "rifle", approach. It explored in many places in search of leads and eventual discoveries.

Total acreage in 1970 for BP Canada amounted to 26.7 million gross acres, up from 19.3 million gross acres held a year earlier. Of particular interest was a 1.2 million permit acre tract of property purchased for exploration on Vanier, Emerak, and Prince Patrick Islands where actual drilling was to commence in 1971. BP Canada's net production of crude oil and natural gas in 1970 amounted to 18,582 barrels daily, up 17 percent on production a year earlier. Sales of natural gas had jumped 24 percent to an average of 62.4 million cubic feet per day, compared with production in 1969. In 1971, the company drilled its first Arctic well on Vanier Island, and labeled it "BP et al Panarctic Hotspur J-20". It then added two more, one on Prince Patrick Island ("BP et al Panarctic Satellite F-68") and the other on Graham Island ("BP et al Graham C-52"). BP Canada also purchased considerable acreage holdings in northern Alberta and British Columbia for possible exploration and drilling in those regions.

A year later, the former offices of Supertest Investments and Petroleum in Calgary had been closed as management of the new company was moved to the Montreal-based headquarters of BP Oil and Gas Ltd. Production for the company jumped substantially in 1972. Sales of petroleum products averaged 94,400 barrels daily, whereas production of crude oil and natural gas was posted at an average 22,132 barrels daily. To accommodate this increased production, the company announced plans in 1972 to add a further 40,000 barrels per day of refining capacity at its Trafalgar Refinery facility in Oakville, Ontario. Products produced there would be marketed under the BP and Supertest brand names.

In April 1972, just months after the Supertest merger, company president Derek Mitchell, who had initially come to the position in 1966, outlined his business strategy to shareholders in the company's 1971 annual report: "Your company is now firmly established as a major marketer and refiner of petroleum products in Ontario and Quebec, is well placed as a producer of oil and gas in Western Canada, and has an important stake in the exploration activity rapidly gaining momentum in Canada's frontier areas." BP Canada was establishing up-stream exploration and production facilities in western Canada to serve key downstream markets in Ontario and Quebec, where oil and gas products could be sold directly to consumers.

By late 1972, the company was beginning to feel the effects of higher world prices for a barrel of oil, caused by the efforts of the Organization of Petroleum Exporting Countries (OPEC) cartel. Essentially, a higher price paid for imported crude oil forced BP Canada to pay more for the energy reserves it required to replace petroleum products sold earlier downstream in the marketplace.

This trend worried Mitchell, who said in March 1973 in the company's 1972 annual report: "The comparative stability of the 1960s is giving way to a decade likely to be characterized by rising prices for petroleum and growing government interest in the industry's affairs, both at the political and at the technical levels." Mitchell's words were to prove prophetic. Throughout 1973, OPEC instigated production cutbacks and embargoes among its customers, which played havoc with the global oil industry. The price of oil on the global market went up, and the world supply seemed to be shrinking.

Turmoil and confusion gripped the oil industry. Responding, BP Canada began moving crude oil from western Canada to Montreal through the St. Lawrence Seaway, and later through the Panama Canal during the winter freeze-up. A thorn in the company's side was the growing involvement in the domestic oil industry by the Canadian government in Ottawa. Specifically, the government was calling on the industry to hold down anticipated price rises for Canadian oil products, which would grow costlier as they were affected by the rising world oil prices charged by OPEC member countries. Such restraint was meant to allow the government to develop a Canadian pricing policy to cushion the impact on consumers from rising world oil prices and provide an incentive for the domestic oil industry to develop new energy sources.

As a measure of the growing spread between domestic and world oil prices, a barrel of Canadian crude oil rose by 85 cents to around $4.50 in Toronto in the 12 months leading up to January 1, 1974. During that same period, the cost of imported crude oil rose by some $8 to over $11 a barrel in Montreal. BP Canada was making increased profits from selling petroleum products to consumers at higher prices, but it had to restore energy reserves it had sold off by buying imported crude oil at around twice the December 1973 level. According to the company, it was under-recovering its cost of crude oil by some $300,000 a day in the second half of 1973.

BP Canada might have been trading in crisis-ridden conditions in 1974, but it still managed to see profits rise 82 percent to $39.5 million that year. Even so, the company still found grounds to complain in its 1975 annual report about growing royalties and income taxes owed to Canada's provincial and federal governments. What is more, by the end of 1974, world oil prices had risen to five times the mid-1973 level. The unprecedented price hikes had led to increased production, and ultimately a glut in the world oil market. The net result: lower margins for BP Canada products in an ever more competitive market.

In 1975, the company began exploring for oil off Newfoundland, on Canada's easternmost seaboard. Also that year, the expansion of the Trafalgar Refinery was completed, but only after delays and cost overruns. A year later, BP Canada bought the remaining 65 percent stake in British Columbia Oil Sands Ltd. to take full control of the company. Paying $20 per share in the transaction, the company gained ownership of oil and gas acreage in the Yoyo, Kotcho, Cabin, and Louise gas fields of northeastern British Columbia. Cost-cutting measures that year included reducing the number of retail outlets selling BP petroleum brand products in Ontario and Quebec from just over 3000 to around 1800. The company also introduced BP No-Lead gasoline at its remaining retail outlets.

Early in 1977, BP Canada signed an agreement with the Alberta Oil Sands Technology and Research Authority that would see the government body contribute half the $18 million cost of testing a sequential steam heating system to extract heavy crude oil (thick sludge used as highway asphalt) in the Wolf Lake area of Alberta. These tar-like deposits are filled with impurities but can be upgraded to light, valuable crude oil; the process is worthwhile if there is a $3 to $5 spread between the light and heavy crude oil variants. At the time, the price of oil on the world market was rising at too fast a rate compared with the price for domestically produced oil to fully justify the development of heavy oil upgraders. The Wolf Lake project was noteworthy for its incentives to develop new sources of oil and gas in Canada. Companies like BP Canada often had to extract heavier crude oil reserves at greater than average expense and longer than usual lead times before it could deliver a refined product to consumer markets in a light crude form.

BP Canada in the 1970s continued its thrust into the rugged terrain of the Monkman area in northeastern British Columbia. It now held interests from 25 to 64 percent in 204,000 acres and 100 percent of 94,000 acres in the region, which was thought to hold vast natural gas reserves. The British Columbia Petroleum Corporation announced plans to build a pipeline and plant facilities to bring the Monkman area natural gas to market in 1980.

In 1978, BP Canadian saw its profits rise over the $40 million mark for the first time. However, this record was reached at a time when the industry as a whole was experiencing a market glut due to excess refining capacity and reduced consumer demand for petroleum products due to the unexpected success of conservation measures. The Iranian revolution in 1979 caused yet another jump in the price of oil on the world market. BP Canada saw its off-shore supply drop substantially due to embargoes. To replace the shortfall, the company arranged to send Canadian crude oil from western Canada to northern-tier U.S. refiners, who in turn would divert their imported oil to the Montreal refinery.

At this time, BP Canada also faced a glut in the natural gas market, then a key earner for the company. Production in 1979 was 109.5 million cubic feet per day, down from 122.7 million cubic feet per day a year earlier. Purchasers had essentially been unable to take all the gas they had contracted to buy. Sales of natural gas continued slowly in 1980, but the company did manage to post profits of $63.1 million for fiscal 1979, up 93 percent from the year before. A jump like that had company chairman and CEO Mitchell defending the company's performance, given its persistent calls for less government control over the oil industry. Suspicions abounded in the 1970s that the oil industry as a whole was manipulating the OPEC crisis for their own profitable ends.

Speaking to shareholders, Mitchell repeated his company's call for regulatory restraint in the company's 1980 annual report: "Their is no doubt that given appropriate policies—higher crude oil prices, a fair and stable tax and royalty system which will allow adequate netbacks to the industry, a commitment to allow companies to reap the fruits of their endeavors, and the encouragement of fuels substitution and energy conservation— Canada can again become self-sufficient in oil." If Mitchell sought government restraint, he ended up with greater intervention still. The Conservative government, entering the 1980 federal election, had proposed an 18-cent-a-gallon gasoline tax, whose revenues were to subsidize more expensive oil imports. That proposed excise tax in part led to the Conservative government's downfall at the polls. The incoming Liberal government introduced the National Energy Program in October 1980. It painted foreign oil companies as profit-hungry conglomerates and gave support to Canadian-owned companies like Petro-Canada.

Company chairman Mitchell complained in March 1981 in the company's 1980 annual report: "The government is now hellbent on putting on a circus for the benefit of the media and the public. . . . The principal purpose will, doubtless, be to try to justify by propaganda and by 'trial' in the media the federal government's already well-demonstrated xenophobic prejudices against one of Canada's vital and most successful industries."

Although the Liberal government became a foul word in the BP Canada boardroom, the company's fortunes did not suffer. For the first time in 1980, gas from the Sukunka-Bullmoose area of northeastern British Columbia reached the market after many years of exploration. It was also announced that year that BP Canada's headquarters would move from Montreal to Toronto. The move served two purposes: it would remove the company from the separatist tensions then developing in Quebec and would place the headquarters in Ontario, where 70 percent of the company's assets were.

Profits for 1980 were posted at $104.3 million, a 56 percent jump on 1979. The rate of return on investment was 17.3 percent, a company record. Despite the government's aim to restrain foreign oil companies in Canada and support the domestic sector, the multinationals were doing better than ever.

Company chairman Mitchell died suddenly on October 29, 1981, and was replaced by R. Hanbidge as president and CEO. A year later, BP Canada shelved plans to proceed with developing the Sukunka coal mine in northeastern British Columbia. Low coal prices on the world market accounted for the strategic move. The company in 1984 completed work on its Wolf Lake project, which came on stream five months ahead of schedule and with a price tag of $110 million. Full production of 1,100 cubic meters of fuel per day was achieved in September 1985, and expanded production at Wolf Lake was forecast at 5,600 cubic meters per day by the end of the decade.

The falling price of oil on the world market hit BP Canada's earnings in 1985. Cash flow fell by 17 percent, and net profits fell by 55 percent to $20 million, compared with results for the year earlier. Continuing success at energy conservation during the 1980s also cut into production at BP Canada. In 1985, sales of light and medium oil were down by 10 percent on sales a year earlier, and 15 percent of production was lost during the first quarter of 1987. Also that year, production at the Wolf Lake project stood at 1,140 cubic meters per day, not far above production figures when the project came on stream in 1984.

For these reasons, the company attempted to curb its operating costs to maintain profitability. M. A. Kirkby, president of BP Canada told shareholders in the 1987 annual report: "While we cannot control the worldwide prices of oil, gas and metals, we are constantly working to reduce our costs and to improve our netbacks within the market." Cost-cutting measures helped boost BP Canada's net profits to $44.6 million in 1987, an all-time high. But the very next year, net profits were down to $10.3 million. The main reason: world oil prices fell by 27 percent in 1988.

In 1989, David Claydon replaced M. A. Kirkby as president of BP Canada. That year, he ordered environmental audits of all BP Canadian operations in response to growing concerns about possible environmental damage from oil exploration and refining. The company also announced plans to boost its natural gas exploration and reserves, recognizing that natural gas was a clean-burning fuel considered more environmentally sound by consumers than oil or coal.

In 1991, mounting debt and losses prompted a management shuffle and a worldwide review of operations by the head office of British Petroleum in London. By mid-1992, BP announced it would sell off its 57 percent stake in BP Canada through a secondary offering of shares. The *Financial Times of Canada* reported that Canadian employees responded with a burst of applause on hearing the news. To sell its stake in a highly profitable company with prospects that greatly encouraged Canadian and American investors, BP in London clearly had priorities elsewhere.

Upon being sold in June 1992, Talisman's share price stood at C$13.00. At the end of July 1993, the share price had climbed to C$26.50. The company now had Jim Buckee at its helm as president and CEO. The British-born businessman, Oxford-educated and with a PhD in astrophysics, transformed Talisman into a smaller, more focused company in the 1990s. For example, the company sold its Wolf Lake oil sands assets to Amoco Canada Petroleum Company in April 1992. Talisman then bought Encor Inc., which held the oil and gas assets that once belonged to TransCanada PipeLines Ltd. The purchase price comprised C$239 million worth of treasury shares.

Talisman achieved impressive growth in the early 1990s. The company saw promising signs of the world oil price creeping upwards, perhaps a go-ahead for continued exploration and drilling in Canada's north. Talisman suggested it would explore gas plays in Alberta and British Columbia and even announced in 1992 that it had entered into two joint ventures with companies involved in exploration in Cuba. Given the company's record of innovation and business savvy, it is likely that Talisman will remain among Canada's best performing oil companies.

Principal Subsidiaries: Encor Inc.

Further Reading:

"BP Canada Cut Loose as British Parent Sells Stake," *Globe and Mail,* May 13, 1992.
"BP Plans Further Cutbacks," *Globe and Mail,* May 6, 1992.
"Free of Stodgy Parents and Gushing Profits," *Financial Times of Canada,* July 31, 1993.
"Talisman in a Flurry of Changes," *Globe and Mail,* April 14, 1993.

—Etan Vlessing

 **Telephone and Data Systems, Inc.**

Telephone and Data Systems, Inc.

30 North LaSalle Street
Suite 4000
Chicago, Illinois 60602
U.S.A.
(312) 630-1900
Fax: (312) 630-1908

Public Company
Incorporated: 1969
Employees: 3,803
Sales: $456.1 million
Stock Exchanges: American
SICs: 4813 Telephone Communications Except
Radiotelephone; 4812 Radiotelephone Communications

Telephone and Data Systems, Inc., or TDS, is one of the most highly praised telecommunications enterprises in the United States. While only a fraction the size of General Telephone Corporation and the Baby Bell companies, TDS has consistently grown at twice the rate of its larger counterparts, and it is the ninth largest non-Bell telephone company in the United States. TDS was founded in 1967 by LeRoy T. Carlson. Since that time, the company has grown into a holding company for more than 90 small rural telephone companies. Included in its operations are printing, computer services, paging, and cellular communications subsidiaries serving customers in markets across the United States. The company is divided into seven main operating units, including TDS Telecom, American Paging, and United States Cellular Corporation.

Earlier in his career, Carlson had been a product development director for Acme Steel. In 1950 he acquired the Suttle Equipment Company, a small supplier of business forms, equipment, and other supplies for independent telephone companies. Through his sales efforts, Carlson was well acquainted with many of these small, primarily rural companies and the difficulties they faced. In 1956 a business associate suggested that Carlson consider buying a small telephone company in Calvert City, Kentucky that had 218 customers. When he learned that Southern Bell was about to take over the company, Carlson quickly examined the situation and, over the course of a weekend, bought the company. He subsequently purchased a hodgepodge of other small telephone companies, a directory publisher, and some manufacturing operations, assembling them

into a minor conglomerate called Telephones, Inc. The publicly listed common shares of the holding company were sold to Continental Telephone Company in 1964, but Carlson continued to dabble in the market by buying and selling several other small telephone companies.

By 1967 Carlson decided to play a bolder role in the industry. Driven by the rewards of investment in new technologies and economies of scale, he began searching for telephone properties located adjacent to one another. The task was made harder by the fact that the large independents—General, United Telephone, and Continental—had already snapped up many of the best prospects. Carlson and his associates concentrated their search on Wisconsin, where they identified several rural companies that together would provide the critical mass for an efficient operation.

Negotiations were often difficult for Carlson, who was forced to make his pitch to busy owners who were farmers, store keepers, and struggling rural entrepreneurs, but the extraordinary effort paid off. Beginning with the Central State Telephone Company in September 1967, Carlson acquired nine more companies over the next 14 months. He set up an operations group in Madison and a corporate staff in his home town of Chicago. With help from his father-in-law, a corporate attorney, the new company was incorporated on January 1, 1969, as Telephone and Data Systems, Inc. Carlson's son, Ted Carlson, was a member of the original board.

Certain that the future growth of his company would turn on its reputation, Carlson invested heavily on improvements for his 25,000 customers. TDS eliminated multiparty service, installed new electronic switching systems, and introduced direct distance dialing. It preserved the local flavor of each company and built on their established goodwill by maintaining local managements, who were well known in each community and provided valuable public relations counsel. In 1969 TDS bought out six more companies, five of which were in Wisconsin. Suddenly, TDS was the third largest telephone company in the state and was beginning to encounter mounting, potentially disastrous opposition from General, Continental, and other established holding companies. For these reasons, TDS abruptly shifted its acquisition activity to the Northeast, and during 1970 snapped up five companies in New Hampshire, Vermont, and Maine. In each case, state regulatory commissions noted the company's good reputation for service improvement.

TDS companies benefitted from centralized purchasing and standardized systems and engineering, but it quickly outgrew the capabilities of its small organization and was obliged to establish specialized subsidiaries to provide management and engineering services. The company also outgrew its financial resources and in 1971 issued more than $4 million in long term debentures. But with the rise of the consumerist movement, TDS found itself increasingly unable to push rate increases past state regulators. These increases made network improvements harder to fund, and made it difficult to float debentures and other investment papers. Carlson personally spearheaded his company's case in rate proceedings and often produced favorable results, earning a reputation as a formidable negotiator. He also won a favorable arrangement with the Bell System that would provide more equitable distribution of interconnection fees.

Between 1971 and 1973, TDS added 19 more companies in the Northeast and Midwest as well as in Oregon, Idaho, North Carolina, Alabama, and Mississippi. The geographical diversity of TDS was further enhanced in 1974 and 1975 when eight more companies were added in Virginia, Pennsylvania, and Tennessee, bringing TDS its one-hundred-thousandth customer. By that time, even with 503 employees, it became impossible to properly administer the growing TDS system. In July of 1974 the company reorganized into groups comprising the Wisconsin, Northeast, Southeast, and Mid-Central regions, and an "Assigned" group for companies outside those regions. In 1976 TDS created a computer services subsidiary to implement centralized, automated bill processing. The company also acquired Carlson's old Suttle equipment company, and transferred its operations from Lawrenceville, Illinois, to Waunakee, north of Madison, Wisconsin.

LeRoy Carlson was active in regulatory policy proceedings and emerged as a strong opponent of the Justice Department's attempts to break up the Bell System. He argued that the task of providing affordable telephone service to everyone in the United States could be completed only through subsidies from American Telephone and Telegraph Company's (AT&T) long distance revenues. The position of AT&T and other monopoly providers, however, gradually eroded. Even TDS began to experience competition in its key systems and PBX sales from companies that were not obligated to do business in unprofitable areas. Nevertheless, TDS finished 1978 as the twelfth largest telephone company in the United States, serving 173,500 customers. It operated 52 telephone companies and recorded $33.7 million in revenue, ten times the figure it recorded in 1969.

That year, TDS switched the focus of its expansion from acquiring individual companies to taking over franchises from other independents. TDS acquired several companies from United and Continental, including Tennessee Telephone, a company with 15 exchanges serving 39,000 customers. These acquisitions helped TDS to amass more than 250,000 customers in 22 states by 1983. They also necessitated the creation of a new Tennessee operating division. As great as the company's strides had been, it remained a regulated company earning a prescribed rate of return. To achieve greater rates of growth, TDS needed to expand into a range of unregulated services. Such a move required additional financing. Having gained a listing on the American Stock Exchange in 1981, TDS distributed four million new common shares, raising $25 million dollars.

TDS became involved with paging services in Wisconsin in 1972. After battling to win the right to serve more populous adjacent communities where it did not provide telephone service, TDS built up a highly profitable paging service territory that included Madison, Green Bay, Milwaukee, and all the areas in between. Spurred on by the Bell companies' reluctance to develop paging systems, TDS later won the right to offer paging services in Chicago, Miami, San Antonio, and Tucson, and established a special subsidiary called American Paging to operate these franchises.

Another area TDS developed was cable television. The company acquired its first cable franchise in April of 1975, when it took over the Calhoun City Telephone Company in Mississippi. Additional systems were added later as TDS acquired other telephone companies that also operated cable franchises. By 1978 it had become apparent that cable television companies could develop the capability to displace telephone companies by offering switched voice connections, as well as television service, over their coaxial networks. TDS quickly applied for licenses and cross-ownership waivers to set up cable television systems within its other existing telephone service territories.

In many cases, TDS's staff lacked the experience to properly administer these new ventures. A separate cable television operation was thus established. Carlson, who turned 65 in 1981, relinquished his post as president to his son Ted, who bolstered the company's engineering group by hiring experienced cable television and radio systems managers. He also expanded the managerial hierarchy to accommodate the company's growing range of interests. Cable operations were centralized in 1984 under the newly created TDS Cable Communications Company. By the next year, the company operated 16 cable systems serving more than 30,000 homes. Meanwhile, a new, much more promising technology was emerging.

Cellular telephones were first tested by Illinois Bell in 1979. But while the Bell companies were slow to develop cellular service, hundreds of other companies—including TDS—saw tremendous new opportunities for the technology. The company quickly planned to establish a series of cellular communications networks, beginning with an application to serve Indianapolis. The Federal Communications Commission, which granted cellular licenses, was overwhelmed by the tremendous number of applications it received and a myriad of challenges to its rulings. To speed the process, the FCC asked the hundreds of applicants to work out their own partnership agreements before applying for a license. TDS eventually abandoned its bid for Indianapolis in favor of a five percent stake in the Los Angeles market. TDS spent a quarter million dollars on its first filing, developing detailed business and engineering plans, but later applications brought the average cost to below $10,000.

Unable to handle its growing cellular activities, TDS established a new subsidiary called United States Cellular Corporation on December 23, 1983. The small company was frequently steamrollered by larger companies. The arrogance of these companies raised the ire of LeRoy Carlson, who fought tenaciously for United States Cellular, and often prevailed. Through an industry-wide agreement, the company was awarded licenses for cellular networks in Knoxville and Tulsa. TDS made the development of its cellular unit a major priority in March 1985, when it decided to sell its cable television holdings and devote its full attention to United States Cellular Corporation. The cellular market promised considerably higher growth and rates of return than cable, and it also posed a greater threat to wireline services than cable. TDS generated $41 million from the sale of its cable systems, the last of which was disposed of in November 1986.

By 1987 United States Cellular Corporation was highly influential in the cellular industry. The company applied for more than 70 additional licenses and won franchises in Peoria, Des Moines, and Poughkeepsie. The same year, TDS diluted its control of United States Cellular Corporation by issuing additional shares in the unit to Coditel, a Belgian cable television company. It planned to sell an additional block of shares to the public. However, the sale had to be postponed until May of 1988, after the Black Monday stock market collapse. More than three million shares were distributed, reducing TDS's interest in United States Cellular Corporation to just over 80 percent. In 1988 United States Cellular Corporation was active in 31 regions, including Wichita, Atlantic City, and Columbia, Missouri. Meanwhile, TDS greatly expanded its American Paging business, and was serving 127,600 customers in 31 major metropolitan areas, including San Francisco, St. Louis, and Pittsburgh.

When LeRoy Carlson turned 70 in 1986, he relinquished the title of chief executive officer to his son Ted. The elder Carlson retained his position as chairman of the board, and remains active in the development of the company's strategies.

The TDS Telecom wireline division resolved to register an annual growth rate of seven percent in access lines, through internal growth and acquisitions. As existing systems provided only about four percent growth, TDS continued on the acquisition trail. Between 1989 and 1992, TDS Telecom brought the number of telephone companies it operated up to 88. Over the previous 20 years, however, TDS and companies such as Rochester Telephone and Century Telephone had purchased so many independent companies that the number of remaining prospects had dwindled considerably. TDS Telecom was forced to look for new companies in areas well outside its established operating territories. Still, the geographical remoteness of some companies did not preclude them from the taking advantage of the centralized purchasing, engineering, and billing services that had made TDS's existing companies able to operate so much more efficiently.

Again, to fund the company's expansion, TDS issued more shares, diluting the existing shareholder base by 24 percent over just 18 months. Because financial demands were even greater in the cellular market, the number of United States Cellular Corporation shares grew by 61 percent over the same period. Meanwhile, TDS held its ownership in United States Cellular Corporation at 82.3 percent, which meant that it took on four-fifths of all the new shares in United States Cellular Corporation that were issued. Due to the high start-up costs associated with cellular systems, the investments had a profound effect on TDS's earnings growth. Once these investments were made,

however, the way was clear for a steady return from United States Cellular. This growth was first realized in 1992, when United States Cellular Corporation registered a 58 percent increase in the number of subscribers, to 182,500. The number of subscribers rose above 260,000 in 1993.

The same year, the company's American Paging group registered 36 percent growth, serving 321,000 customers. The division's strength was due mainly to excellent marketing and customer retention efforts, as well as the introduction of enhanced-function paging systems. In 1993 American Paging served more than 433,000 units. Within TDS's core wireline business, TDS Telecom, the customer base grew by nearly six percent to 321,700 access lines in 1992. TDS Telecom acquired five additional telephone companies during 1992, bringing the total number of TDS telephone companies to 90. In 1993 the customer base rose to 350,600 and the number of telephone companies to 92. This made TDS the ninth largest non-Bell local telephone company in the country, with a presence in 28 states. The consolidated customer units of TDS topped one million in 1993.

TDS maintained a reputation for superior customer service and the technological upgrade of rural and small town systems. This stemmed from the company's commitment to the rural economies it served, and its dedication to ensuring that the telecommunications infrastructure contributed to the growth of these markets. This philosophy has remained intact ever since LeRoy Carlson first organized TDS, and it served to dissuade potential competitors from any attempt at raiding its markets.

Principal Subsidiaries: TDS Telecommunications Corporation; American Paging, Inc.; United States Cellular Corporation (82.3%); TDS Computing Services, Inc.; American Communications Consultants, Inc.; Suttle Press, Inc.; Answer Madison Telemessaging Center, Inc.

Further Reading:

August, K. C., *TDS: The First Twenty Years,* Madison, WI: Telephone and Data Systems, Inc., 1989.
''Company Watch,'' *Financial World,* September 15, 1992, pp. 12–13.
''TDS,'' *Telephone News,* April 14, 1985, p. 8; September 9, 1989, p. 1.

—John Simley

TEXTRON Lycoming

Textron Lycoming Turbine Engine

550 Main Street
Stratford, Connecticut 06497
U.S.A.
(203) 385-2000
Fax: (203) 385-3122

Wholly owned subsidiary of Textron, Inc.
Incorporated: 1920 as Lycoming Motor Corporation
Employees: 2,600
Sales: $670.0 million
SICs: 3724 Aircraft Engines and Engine Parts; 4581 Airport
  Fields & Terminal Services

Textron Lycoming Turbine Engine is the aircraft engine manufacturing division of Textron, Inc. Acquired by Textron in 1985,
Lycoming has a long and distinguished history in engine building, and was for many years the primary manufacturing entity
of Avco, one of the largest aviation conglomerates of the first
half of the twentieth century.

The company originated in the Lycoming Foundry and Machine
Shop, established in 1908 in Williamsport, the seat of government for Lycoming County, Pennsylvania. The company was
an early developer of internal combustion engines and later
built a variety of models for industrial and automotive markets.
This business expanded so rapidly that on April 20, 1920 the
company established a separate engine-building entity called
the Lycoming Motor Corporation.

In 1923 Lycoming acquired the operations of the Standard
Heater Company, a manufacturer of heating appliances and
systems for industrial and automotive markets. Lycoming established separate motor and heating divisions on May 5, 1924,
and changed Standard to the Spencer Heater Company. During
the early years, Lycoming's primary line of business was automobile, industrial, and marine engines. The company supplied
motors for a variety of manufacturers, including Cord, Dusenberg, and International Harvester. Eventually, the Auburn Automobile Company took over Lycoming.

Lycoming was drawn into the aircraft engine business during
the late 1920s, when hundreds of airframe builders sprung up,
hoping to build better craft for mail delivery. Experienced with
the small engines that were demanded for these new, light
aircraft, Lycoming quickly established a name for itself among
airplane builders. Its most promising aviation product was the
nine-cylinder R680 radial engine. Rated at 215 horsepower, this
engine was standard on many civilian and military aircraft.

Charles Lindbergh's solo flight across the Atlantic in 1927
created such investor enthusiasm for aviation stocks that by
1929, approximately $9 billion had been poured into the indus-
try. Several organizations took advantage of this demand by
patching together vertical monopolies that included airframe
and engine manufacturing, airline services and airport management. One of these conglomerates was the Aviation Corp. of
the Americas, or Avco.

Avco was established on March 1, 1929. Under the leadership
of railroad magnate Averell Harriman, Avco stitched together
several air services, including Colonial Airways, Universal Aviation, Embry-Riddle Aviation, Southern Air Transport, and
Interstate Airlines to form American Airways, the forerunner of
American Airlines. Separately, Avco also amassed a small
interest in Pan American Airways.

After the stock market crashed in October of 1929, many of the
backers of aviation companies were ruined. Many of the original founders of Avco were forced to sell their interests in the
company to cover other losses. As a result, Avco went up for
grabs, and a lengthy battle for control ensued. The company
eventually fell into the hands of E. L. Cord, whose empire
included Auburn, Dusenberg, Columbia Axle, Checker Cab,
Stinson Aircraft, Lycoming, and the New York Shipbuilding
Corporation.

With a steady stream of income from carrying air mail, and
aided by the depression in share values, Cord moved Avco into
the field of manufacturing. The company consolidated Stinson,
and took over the Airplane Development Corporation (later
called Vultee Aircraft) and Smith Engineering. On November
30, 1934, Avco acquired the aircraft engine and propeller manufacturing business of the Lycoming company, which subsequently operated as a division of Avco's aircraft subsidiary, the
Aviation Manufacturing Corporation. Earlier that year, however, a Congressional investigation led by Senator Hugo Black
resulted in legislation that forced the aviation combines to
divest either their manufacturing operations or their airlines.
Avco spun off its airlines, and in 1937 Cord sold his interest in
the company to a utilities financier named Victor Emmanuel.

Lycoming engineers developed a four-cylinder piston engine in
1938 called the O145. This model was the company's first to go
into mass-production, and it was used in 1939 to power the first
helicopter, the Vought-Sikorsky VS-300. In addition to its line
of engines, Lycoming held a joint patent with Smith Engineering for a revolutionary variable pitch propeller that enabled
pilots to alter their air speed without changing the speed of their
engines.

Aided by the proceeds from the divestiture of Cord's 45-
company empire, Emmanuel engineered Vultee's takeover of
Consolidated Aircraft Corporation. As the nation geared up for
World War II, Avco was enlisted to build a wide variety of war
implements. Emmanuel negotiated contracts to build 33,000
airplanes from Consolidated Vultee, and the engines to run
them from Lycoming. In addition, Avco's shipbuilding unit
won contracts to build nine aircraft carriers and even the battle-
ship South Dakota.

Long before the war's end, Emmanuel began planning for the postwar conversion to a civilian economy. Even before the shooting stopped, Emmanuel directed Avco into the manufacture of several types of consumer products, including household appliances, refrigerators, washers, and radios, which were marketed under the Crosley, Shelvador, and Bendix brand names. Because few of these items had anything to do with engine building, Avco units other than Lycoming conducted the manufacturing. For its part, Lycoming emerged from the war as a small but important aircraft engine builder.

The company, however, was ill-prepared for the industry's switch to jet engines. The armed forces already were awash in surplus piston engines, so there were few orders for new engines from Lycoming. To make matters worse, in Avco's rush to get into civilian markets, it virtually abandoned critical investments in technology at Lycoming.

With the outbreak of war on the Korean Peninsula in 1950, the company was once again pressed into action for the armed forces. Emmanuel hired James R. Kerr, a former air force official, to rebuild Avco as a defense supplier. In 1951, Lycoming received permission to take over a 1.8-million-square foot plant at Stratford, Connecticut. Formerly owned by Chance Vought Aviation, and shuttered since the end of the war, the plant became Avco's Stratford Lycoming Division and its new headquarters for aircraft engine development.

Lycoming had already been eclipsed in aircraft technology by Pratt & Whitney, Allison, and the newcomer General Electric. Management at Lycoming realized that niche markets were the key to survival. Dr. Anselm Franz was place in charge of developing a new gas turbine engine for helicopters in 1952. The result was the T53, a light, powerful design that became Lycoming's most popular engine. T53s later drove the Bell UH-1 Huey and AH-1 Cobra helicopters and Grumman OV-1 Mohawk reconnaissance aircraft.

Avco, meanwhile, encountered problems within its aircraft division, now called Convair. The company had only turboprop commercial aircraft under development at a time when Boeing Co. and Douglas had jetliner designs well under way. On the military side, Convair had built hundreds of B-36 bombers for the Air Force and was a leader in the development of delta-wing jet bombers.

Avco, strapped for cash and apparently unwilling to carry a company so dependent on defense contracts, sold Convair to the Atlas Corporation, and was subsequently acquired by General Dynamics Corp., leaving Lycoming as Avco's one remaining aircraft enterprise. In typical fashion, the flamboyant Emmanuel chose to invest the proceeds of the Convair divestiture in a completely new line of business. He purchased Delta Acceptance and a string of other finance companies in an effort to turn Avco into a financial services conglomerate.

Lycoming had less and less to do with Avco during this period. After demonstrating its success with missile technologies— Lycoming successfully tested the first re-entry vehicle in 1959—the company won additional contracts in engine propulsion. In 1954 Lycoming won a contract to develop a slightly more powerful gas turbine for similar applications. This engine, the T55, was employed aboard the Boeing CH-47 Chinook and Bell 214A helicopters. Later that year, Victor Emmanuel

brought Dr. Arthur Kantrowitz to Avco to develop missile systems for Lycoming. His work led to contracts for the re-entry vehicles for the Titan and Minuteman missiles, and firmly established Avco as a leading research-oriented company.

Emmanuel retired, turning over Avco's reins to Kendrick Wilson and James Kerr. Avco continued its diversification into a dizzying array of businesses, including television, motion pictures, credit cards, insurance, real estate development and farm equipment. Rather than bolster Avco's earnings, the diversification only bled the company of its strengths. Fortunately, Lycoming avoided the distractions at Avco and kept its eye intently on its market.

During the early 1960s, the company invested heavily in a new jet engine, the PLF-1A turbofan. This engine incorporated a wide fan which, driven by a jet engine, produced high amounts of thrust with relatively low fuel consumption. Not suitable for supersonic jet propulsion, the turbofan was intended primarily for non-combat service. By virtue of its compact design, it was perfect for small and medium size aircraft, including small transports. Pratt & Whitney and General Electric, which by now dominated the jet engine business, also had turbofan designs under development, but these were huge engines intended for freighters and jumbo jets. Lycoming's smaller PLF-1A, tested in February of 1964, set the trend in efficient turbofan propulsion.

Lycoming's parent company continued to be driven down by a series of bad investments and poor management. It fared poorly in its attempt at the financial services industry, which was heavily dependent on interest rates. When rates soared in the late 1960s, drying up investment demand, Avco took tremendous hits on its earnings. Avco suspended dividend payments in 1970, and by 1974 had amassed more debt than equity. Shares in the company, which had been as high as $49, plunged to $2. The company's board ultimately took out its frustration on Kendrick Wilson, who was demoted and replaced as chairman by James Kerr.

In the midst of this managerial malaise, Avco made one last attempt to re-establish itself in the aircraft market by manufacturing wings for Lockheed's L-1011 Tristar jetliner. The Tristar, however, was doomed by problems with its Rolls-Royce engines, which ultimately cost Lockheed its position in the commercial jetliner market and plunged Rolls-Royce into bankruptcy. Avco managed only a small profit from its wing building venture.

The end of the Vietnam War in 1975 severely curtailed the demand for Lycoming helicopter engines. The energy crisis, however, created new demand for helicopters in servicing offshore oil platforms, providing some relief. Meanwhile, Kerr began a concerted effort to clean house at Avco. He sold and closed the company's money-losing ventures, made operations more rational, and reduced debt.

These measures took some pressure off Lycoming, whose helicopter business was booming. The company's engines had won a place on several helicopter models from Bell, Aerospatiale, and Augusta. In addition, Lycoming had a contract to maintain a fleet of helicopters for the Shah of Iran. In late 1978, however, a populist revolutionary Islamic faction overthrew the Shah. In reaction to the bitterly anti-American clerics that took control, the U.S. government suspended all commercial agreements between American companies and Iran.

Soaring interest rates resulting from the five-year reign of OPEC stifled demand for corporate and private aircraft and the Lycoming engines that powered them. During this time, the U.S. government's support for missile activities carried the company. In May of 1977, Lycoming won an important contract to develop a gas turbine engine for the Army's new main battle tank, Chrysler's M1 Abrams. The AGT1500 engine weighed half as much as a diesel powered engine, and promised to provide greater power and speed. After successful testing, more than 11,000 AGT1500s were delivered. In addition, Lycoming won a contract to develop the LT101 turbine, a 650 shaft horsepower engine designed for use on coast guard helicopters. The company also introduced its TF turbine series, designed for marine applications, such as hovercraft and boat propulsion, pumping, and power generation.

For commercial markets, Lycoming was working on a follow-on to its PLF-1A, an improved turbofan called the ALF502. This engine, capable of generating up to 7,500 pounds of thrust, was chosen to power the Canadair CL600 Challenger business jet. The 502 was the only engine in its class suitable for commuter jetliners, specifically the four-engine BAe 146 being developed by British Aerospace plc. When British Aerospace began the promising production run for the 146, it chose Lycoming's 502 engine.

Kerr retired as chairman in November of 1981, and Robert Bauman, a former General Foods executive, took his place. By the time Bauman took over Avco, the company had extended its wing building business to Rockwell's B-1 bomber, and the engine business looked more promising than ever. In fact, the ten years that James Kerr had spent cleaning up Avco's operations and balance sheet made the company an extremely enticing takeover target. Corporate raiders might easily consume Avco and profit from selling the company's remaining divisions.

Joseph Steinberg and Irwin Jacobs began separate plays for Avco in 1984. At this point, Textron chairman Beverly Dolan contacted Bauman, announcing his company's interest in Avco. Rather than risk Avco's acquisition by a mere profiteer, Bauman decided to accept Dolan's $1.4 billion offer. Almost as an afterthought, it occurred to Dolan and Bauman what a perfect match Textron would be for Avco. Textron was a similarly diversified conglomerate with strong interests in aviation (through its Bell Helicopter subsidiary, a customer of Lycoming), financial services, and manufacturing. By acquiring Avco, in 1985 Textron could assume additional debt that would repel any remaining corporate raiders.

Due to the suspension of business between the United States and Iran, Bell had suffered the same type of losses as Lycoming. The cooling oil industry also contributed to diminished profits. Textron opted to service its debt from asset sales rather than operating income. The company sold off several subsidiaries, eliminating much of the debt that it had counted on as protection. Ultimately, no hostile bids were launched for Textron.

Avco Lycoming, as the engine group had been known, was now called Textron Lycoming. The division suffered several reverses in the late 1980s. The ALF502 engine initially had frequent reduction gear failures and problems with cracks on the spacer rings between turbine disks. To make matters worse, Lycoming had little experience with commercial customers who, unlike the military, demanded strong after-market support. The lowest point came when Canadair decided to switch over to a competing engine from General Electric for its Challenger. The engine's problems were corrected, but Lycoming had difficulty living down the engine's reputation. Eventually, the 502 gained high marks in the field, where it exhibited superior resilience in the face of frequent short-haul takeoffs and landings.

In 1989 the coast guard's mounting problems with the HH-65A helicopter were traced to failures with their Lycoming LTS101 turboshaft engines. While the coast guard began testing a replacement design from Allison-Garrett, the Justice Department charged Lycoming with fraud. Eventually, Avco settled the suit out of court for $17 million.

Lycoming's former parent, the Avco Corporation, became Textron's Aerostructure division. The unit won additional contracts to build the fuselage for the Lockheed C-5 Galaxy and the wings for the Airbus A330. Bell Helicopter remained one of Lycoming's better customers, and because few of its designs competed with those of Lycoming's other customers, there was no appreciable decline in engine sales.

Lycoming, once the engine division of a major aviation conglomerate, has survived fifty years of consolidation in the industry to emerge as the engine division of yet another aviation conglomerate. Whether Textron can build Lycoming into an engine powerhouse like Pratt & Whitney or General Electric is doubtful. Nevertheless, Lycoming is in a stronger position as a result of its association with Textron.

Further Reading:

"Avco: Back From the Brink," *Forbes,* November 1, 1976, pp. 63–64.
"Avco Made its Mistakes Early," *Business Week,* August 22, 1964, pp. 131–36.
"Aviation Corporation," *Moody's Manual of Investments, 1943,* p. 1118.
"Being a Conglomerate Is Not All Bad," *Forbes,* December 11, 1989, pp. 40–41.
"Coast Guard Weighs Replacing Troubled Textron Lycoming Engines," *Aviation Week & Space Technology,* May 15, 1989, pp. 19–20.
"The Corporate Faddist," *Forbes,* April 1, 1974, pp. 23–24.
"Isn't Anybody Listening?" *Forbes,* April 2, 1979, pp. 58–62.
"Lycoming to Pay U.S. $17.9 Million in LTS-101 Performance Settlement," *Aviation Week & Space Technology,* July 16, 1990, pp. 24–25.
"Prodigal Son," *Forbes,* December 7, 1981, pp. 125–27.
"Textron's Aerospace Group Gets Lift From Avco Buy," *Business Marketing,* May 1988, p. 111.
"Textron and Avco Look Made for Each Other," *Business Week,* December 17, 1984, p. 34.
"Textron Lycoming Building Larger Engines on ALF502 Core," *Air Transport World,* October 1988, pp. 82–85.
"Two For the Price of One?" *Forbes,* December 31, 1984, pp. 76–77.

—John Simley

Thiokol Corporation

2475 Washington Blvd.
Ogden, Utah 84401-2398
U.S.A.
(801) 629-2270
Fax: (801) 629-2420

Public Company
Incorporated: 1890
Employees: 11,200
Sales: $1.32 billion
Stock Exchanges: New York
SICs: 3764 Space Propulsion Units and Parts; 2911
   Petroleum Refining

The Thiokol Corporation is involved in the engineering and manufacture of rocket boosters and other parts for the aerospace industry. The company regained its independence from the salt and chemicals conglomerate Morton in 1989, when Thiokol's rocket boosters were cited as the cause of the 1986 *Challenger* space shuttle explosion. Thiokol had been acquired by Morton in 1982 as part of that company's attempt to bolster itself from unwelcome takeover attempts and diversify into markets unrelated to its core salt and chemical operations.

Thiokol was founded during the Great Depression by two chemists, J. C. Patrick and Nathan Mnookin, who were trying to invent an inexpensive antifreeze. In the course of an experiment involving ethylene dichloride and sodium polysulfide, they created a gum whose outstanding characteristic was a terrible odor. The substance clogged a sink in the laboratory, and none of the solvents used to remove it were successful. Then the frustrated chemists realized that the resistance of the material to any kind of solvent was a useful property. They had invented synthetic rubber, which they christened "Thiokol," from the Greek words for rubber and sulfur.

Mnookin and Patrick initially negotiated with Standard Oil to develop the product, but they could not reach an agreement. Finally, a salt merchant named Bevis Longstreth provided the financial support for the construction of a plant in Kansas City, Missouri. However, the plant produced an odor so obnoxious that local residents asked the mayor to remove the company from the area. As a result, Thiokol Inc. was forced to move to New Jersey.

At the onset of World War II the company hoped that the rubber shortage would increase demand for Thiokol, but organic rubber was recycled instead. Thiokol Inc. was thus relegated to making hoses for specialized uses during the wartime period. Dow Chemical purchased 30 percent of Thiokol in 1948, and later sold its share of the company on the open market in 1953, when, according to Wall Street analysts, Thiokol was not a promising takeover candidate. In 1944, when Bevis Longstreth died, no one on the board of directors was willing to replace him; Joseph Crosby, a department head, ended up in Longstreth's position.

When it was brought to Crosby's attention that the jet propulsion laboratories at the California Institute of Technology were buying large quantities of the company's solvent resistant polymer, he decided to talk to some of the Institute's scientists. There he learned that the polymer was the best rocket fuel the scientists had ever used.

In the 1950s, the first rockets were powered by liquid fuel. This required heavy tanks to hold not only the fuel and the oxidizer, but also the binding agent that held them together. Rocket fuel was so dangerous that one part fuel was mixed with four parts oxidizer to reduce flammability. Thiokol's polymer began attracting attention because it was fuel and binding agent in one.

Management at Thiokol decided to go straight to the military with its product, and the U.S. Army agreed to finance a laboratory. Research began even before the building was finished. The company's research director recalled mixing propellant late at night in a room illuminated by his car's headlights before any electric lights had been installed.

The Korean War benefited Thiokol considerably. Solid rocket fuel began to displace liquid, and the company's solvent resistant sealants were selling very well. During this time Thiokol began to design and manufacture rocket engines, and with a 70 percent share of the solid rocket fuel market the company achieved a significant measure of success.

During the 1960s the company worked on the propulsion systems for the Minuteman 3 rocket, the Poseidon submarine, and the Sam-D missile. It also provided flares and other pyrotechnic devices for the war in Vietnam. Almost two-thirds of the company's business came from the government; in fact, Crosby spent as much time in Washington as he did at the company's headquarters in Trenton, New Jersey.

Although Thiokol conducted most of its business with the government at this time, during the 1960s it also became involved in several humanitarian projects. Thiokol's educational division operated training programs for the unemployed, including Native Americans. Housing programs for low income residents of Gulfport, Mississippi, and Raleigh, North Carolina, were also administered by Thiokol. The company's extensive contact with the military gave it an edge in the competition for these educational and housing programs, which were government funded.

While government contracts were lucrative, they were also undependable, since programs were funded according to the policies of the political party in power. To ensure its continued success, Thiokol used its income from aerospace contracts to diversify into specialty chemicals, fibers, off-road vehicles, and household products such as Spray-n-Wash. While the market for these products was somewhat cyclical, demand was not linked in any direct way to the political climate, which influenced the size and number of the government programs that Thiokol depended on. The need to partially disassociate itself from the U.S. government became clear in 1970 when fewer government contracts caused sales to drop from $245 million to $205 million. After the market for synthetic fibers declined in 1975, Thiokol again reappraised its situation and decided to rely on specialty chemicals as the division that would provide the company with financial stability in case aerospace contracts were discontinued. The fiber and off-road operations were sold.

In the 1970s Thiokol experienced a 20 percent annual growth rate. The specialty chemicals and the Texize household products divisions were performing well, while the military contracts remained lucrative. Towards the end of the decade Thiokol became a prime candidate for merger with Morton Industries, which had embarked on a diversification program and was attracted to Thiokol's control of 40 percent of the solid rocket fuels market, as well its lucrative Texize household products division. Morton's interest in Thiokol came out of necessity—it needed debt on its balance sheet to repel takeover bids. In addition, the company's previous attempts at diversification showed only mixed results. In Thiokol, Morton also saw a company concentrated in the rapidly growing defense industry. Propelled by feverish expansion under the Reagan administration, Thiokol stood to benefit greatly from its established role as a special-purpose rocket builder. Morton considered it possible to invest the vast profits from its salt and chemical businesses into highly lucrative new Thiokol rocket systems. Indeed, Thiokol's place as the supplier of rockets to America's ambitious space shuttle program positioned it well for work in Reagan's strategic defense initiative.

Morton completed its takeover of Thiokol in 1982. One year later a severe disagreement arose between the upper management of each company. As a result, the top management at Thiokol walked out. Among the defectors was Robert Davies, president of Thiokol, considered one of the brightest executives in the aerospace and chemical industries. Four other high level executives with experience in aerospace either retired or quit when Davies left. Consequently, Morton's Charles Locke was given complete control of both companies.

Despite these defections, few industry analysts questioned the wisdom of the Thiokol-Morton merger. In the first year after the merger the company posted record earnings. Two years later earnings per share increased 26 percent. Morton's and Thiokol's specialty chemicals divisions worked well together, and the new company offered chemical purification products, electronics and metal recovery chemicals, coatings, polymers, and chemicals for the electronics industry.

The household products division saw many of its items, including Glass Plus, Yes Detergent and Spray & Wash, achieve a ten to 20 percent market growth in a crowded and highly competi-

tive field. To further strengthen its position in the household products market, Morton Thiokol began to manufacture its own packaging materials, becoming one of the first companies in the industry to do so. In 1985 the household products division was sold to Dow Chemical Company in order to prevent an attempted takeover by that chemical firm.

In the mid-1980s, Morton Thiokol's staff of engineers won a contract to produce rocket boosters for NASA's space shuttle *Challenger*. On January 28, 1986 NASA engineers reportedly asked Morton Thiokol engineers for their approval to go ahead with the launch of the shuttle *Challenger*, despite temperatures that had dipped below freezing. Company executives, who knew that the shuttle's boosters were not rated for operation below 40 degrees, were not consulted. Just over a minute after launch, a flare of fire from one of the boosters ignited the shuttle's external fuel tank, destroying the orbiter and killing its seven astronauts.

While Locke ordered an investigation of the accident, he failed to handle the public relations crisis that followed. At one point after the blast he told the *Wall Street Journal* that "the shuttle thing will cost us ten cents a share." While quoted out of context, Locke nonetheless came across as a callous and tactless. In a demonstration of good faith, Locke conducted more than $400 million of redesign work on the boosters, working at cost.

The company suffered further damage in December 1987 when an explosion at its MX missile plant killed five employees. Furthermore, work on the boosters revealed new design flaws that had to be corrected. In 1989, despite performing $400 million worth of redesign work at cost and the resumption of shuttle flights, Morton Thiokol lost a bid for a new booster design to Lockheed. At this point, Locke decided to spin off the Thiokol division.

Before dividing the companies, Locke transferred Thiokol's chemical businesses to the Morton side of the company. Morton also retained Thiokol's promising automotive airbag business. The companies were officially split on July 1, 1989, when Locke offered stockholders shares in Morton International, with options to trade them for Thiokol shares. Morton International, with $1.4 billion in sales and 8,000 employees, remained concentrated mostly in chemicals and salt, while investing nearly $100 million in its airbag business.

Utah-based Thiokol emerged as a $1.1 billion company with 12,000 employees. However, its profitable chemicals and airbag businesses had been carved away by Morton—all that remained was rockets. With greatly relaxed tensions between the United States and the Soviet Union, defense spending began to fall. Thiokol's new president Edwin Garrison found himself in charge of a company with a declining market and the prospect of losing the shuttle booster business to Lockheed.

During this time, however, NASA was strapped for funds, and, unwilling to carry the development costs of Lockheed's trouble-plagued booster, the agency expressed interest in extending its contract with Thiokol and its proven boosters. Thiokol also began looking for commercial markets, finding a new customer in Motorola, whose 77-satellite Iridium system would provide seamless, worldwide cellular telephone service. Motorola hoped to use Thiokol's Castor rockets to get its system into orbit.

Late in 1991, Thiokol purchased the Huck Manufacturing Corporation for $150 million as part of an effort to diversify. Huck, based in California, made high grade rivets, lock bolts, and other fasteners, mostly for non-defense markets. Despite the *Challenger* disaster and a spin-off that robbed it of some of its best operations, Thiokol survived its association with Morton and appears well positioned to remain a major rocket manufacturer.

Principal Subsidiaries: Omneco, Inc.

Further Reading:

''After an Aerospace Spin-off, Morton is Ready for an Upswing,'' *Chemical Week,* May 23, 1990, pp. 14–19.
''Life Beyond Challenger,'' *Forbes,* September 21, 1987, p. 44.
''Morton Thiokol Completes Spinoff,'' *Journal of Commerce,* July 6, 1989.
''Morton Thiokol is to Spin Off Chemical Line, *Wall Street Journal,* February 28, 1988, p. A3.
''Morton Thiokol: Reflections on the Shuttle Disaster,'' *Business Week,* March 14, 1988, pp. 82–91.
''Tough Assignment,'' *Forbes,* March 16, 1992, p. 126.

—John Simley

Thomas Cook Travel Inc.

100 Cambridge Park Dr.
Cambridge, Massachusetts 02140
U.S.A.
(617) 868-9800

Private Company
Incorporated: 1965
Employees: 2,700
Revenues: $1.7 billion
SICs: 4724 Travel Agencies

Thomas Cook Travel Inc. is the third largest travel agency in the United States, with revenues of more than $1.7 billion annually. Although Thomas Cook Travel is independently owned, it is part of the global network of Thomas Cook Group Ltd, which issued the American company license to use the Cook name.

Thomas Cook Travel's roots date back to 1841 in Victorian England, when Thomas Cook organized his first chartered excursion aboard an English train. Cook began his travel career at the age of 33, while he was secretary of the Leicester Temperance Society. He convinced his employer to allow him to charter a special train to take members of the society to Loughborough for a temperance rally. He then appealed to the Midland Counties Railway Company for a chartered train.

The railroad—which was in need of new passengers since rail travel was new, and the public was skeptical about its safety and put off by high fares—agreed to charter a train for Cook at a reasonable cost on Cook's promise that he could fill it. Cook heavily promoted the train ride and the rally with posters on walls and fences throughout the area. This first Thomas Cook excursion was an overwhelming success: the train was filled, as the rally in Loughborough attracted 2,000 people, many of whom were clearly not advocates of temperance so much as they were anxious to participate in Cook's adventure.

In 1845, Cook decided to begin arranging tours for the general public as a commercial enterprise. His first tour was to Liverpool, England's gateway to North Wales and North America at that time. He convinced four railways to let him charter trains at a reduced rate. He also arranged for side tours, wrote and printed a guide book for the trip, and visited hotels and restaurants in Liverpool ahead of time so that he could personally recommend accommodations to his travelers. This first trip was

an overwhelming success with the 350 first and second class tickets completely sold out. Cook's next trip, to Glasgow, Scotland, again sold out the 350 available tickets. Over the next ten years, Cook arranged more tours in Britain as excitement about travel and tourism grew throughout the country.

In 1851 London hosted the Great Exhibition to impress foreign markets with British products and industry as well as to tout the progress brought about through the Industrial Revolution. An opportunity for the country to inspire its own workers with the technological advances being made, the Great Exhibition was also a great impetus for Cook's travel business. Cook heavily promoted the Great Exhibition among workers and their employers as a unique educational opportunity. He also traveled to London and made arrangements for accommodations affordable to working class travelers. When the fare he arranged with Midland Railway was bettered by a competing rail company, Cook had to renegotiate a lower fare with a guarantee of more passengers.

Soon Cook was looking to the Continent for new destinations. He was also looking to the professional class of teachers, doctors, and clergy as a new market for his travel services. One of the earliest Cook foreign excursions was a trip to the Paris Exhibition in 1855. When the Brighton and South Coast Railway refused to charter a train for Cook, he arranged for his group to travel via a circuitous route through Harwich, Antwerp, and Cologne, and then down the Rhine river to Paris.

The International Exhibition of 1862 in London was an opportunity to recreate the success of the exhibition of 1851. This time, however, Midland Railways decided to handle rail traffic itself, cutting Cook out of the tour business to the event. Undaunted, Cook focused on hotel accommodations for travelers to the event, once again meeting with great success. He was also busy promoting trips to a newly popular destination— the seashore.

Having resolved his difficulties with the Brighton and South Coast Railway, the tours to Paris were more direct, and Cook was ready to announce a tour to Switzerland. Soon, he was arranging tours to Italy as well. Although he did not speak Italian, he managed to convince railway companies and hotels to provide the necessary services and to honor his ticket and coupon system. The Italian tours quickly became his most popular service.

In 1864, Cook entered the guide book business, producing comprehensive guides to his various destinations. The following year, Cook moved his headquarters from Leicester to a building he purchased in London. On the first floor Cook maintained an office and shop, where he sold a wide array of travel products, such as guide books, luggage, telescopes, and footwear. He also ran an advertising agency for provincial and London newspapers. Upstairs were the family living quarters and a Temperance Hotel that he and his wife ran.

As a youth and teenager, John Mason Cook, Cook's son, had helped out on tours, but had remained in Leicester as a printer when the family moved to London. When Cook and his wife needed help they summoned him to join them. John Mason was reluctant, as he and his father had different views on how the business should be run, but he eventually moved to London to become manager of the London travel office. The London office was a great success. Londoners were eager to book tours on Cook's Tour and Excursion systems. Railway and hotel managers and owners were also approaching Cook to promote their services.

Cook also began plans for excursions to the United States. He traveled to North American only months after the U.S. Civil War had ended and toured such cities as Detroit, Chicago, Springfield, Cincinnati, Philadelphia, Washington D.C., and Baltimore, as well as several cities in Canada. He became convinced that the time was right for a Thomas Cook excursion of English travelers to America. In 1865, the first American tour left England, picking up passengers from several departure points, with John Mason in charge. The trip included a tour of Civil War battlefields.

In 1871, Cook went into partnership with an American, forming Cook, Son and Jenkins, and the company continued its American tours for the English. However, the relationship between John Mason and Jenkins eventually soured, in part because the younger Cook did not approve of Jenkins's handling of company finances and was convinced that Jenkins's lavish spending could destroy the company. When John Mason accused the American partner of embezzlement, the partnership was dissolved, and Jenkins brought a legal suit against Cook and his son. Jenkins won the suit and was awarded the grand total of six cents.

The opening of the Suez Canal in 1869 had opened up travel to India and the Far East, and the first Cook tour around the world was conducted in 1871 with an international group of eleven tourists, including American, British, Scottish, Russian, and Greek travelers. This first tour started with an Atlantic crossing, then a journey across the United States to San Francisco, where the tour caught a ship to Japan, China, and then India and the Red Sea. It then joined up with other Cook tours operating between Cairo and London.

Trips to Egypt had proved quite popular, with tours bringing travelers across Europe by train and then on to Port Said by steamer. There was steady traffic by civil and military personnel as well as British tourists curious to see this country newly available to them. Because Middle East tours usually included a trip to the Holy Land, where there were few hotels and transportation was unreliable, Cook organized his own luxury camps to accommodate his travelers. His caravans moved across the desert with pack animals carrying tourists, supplies, and equipment that included bedsteads and mattresses, carpets for tent floors, and tables and chairs. By the 1890s, business to Egypt was booming. Thomas Cook and Son soon became the largest employer in the country, maintaining office staff, staff for the desert camps, crews on the Nile steamers, attendants for the animals, men at shipbuilding yards to assemble steamers brought in pieces from Britain, and people to grow vegetables and raise chickens to be served to tourists.

Upon his return from a year's tour around the world in the 1870s, Thomas Cook had a serious disagreement with his son that led to Thomas's semi-retirement from the company. The relationship between father and son had always been strained, and John Mason finally gave his father an ultimatum stating that he would leave unless his father gave him sole leadership. Thomas, now in his seventies, realized that his son was the better businessman and did as his son demanded. John Mason's sons, Frank, Ernest, and Thomas, joined the firm in the late 1870s. The three brothers traveled all over the world, and by 1880 they had helped the company expand to 60 offices worldwide. Five years later, there were 120 Cook offices.

John Mason Cook ruled the company autocratically. Running a worldwide company was particularly difficult in those days when travel and communication were slow and arduous. Nevertheless, profits continued to increase, and the Cooks had more business than they could handle. Soon competition in the industry arose, particularly from the firm of Dean and Dawson, which later would become a Cook subsidiary.

By 1876 the company had become particularly familiar to Americans, having established a presence at the American Centennial celebration in Philadelphia. The Cook pavilion was a popular attraction at the Centennial. By the 1880s, most Americans had heard of Thomas Cook and Son's travel company. In addition to its U.S. and European excursions, the company had begun offering Circular Notes, an early form of travelers' checks, which became popular as a safe way for Cook's customers to carry money. The number of hotels that would cash these notes grew steadily, and by 1880, almost 1,000 hotels would cash the checks for tourists in Europe and the United States. During this time, the company also arranged for special immigrant fares to Canada and the United States. Some fares even included a small plot of land on which the new immigrants could build a home. By 1896 Cook's American business was offering travel arrangements to the Klondike for both Americans and Europeans with gold fever.

The company also developed sea tours. These first "cruises" departed and returned to the same port; travelers spent a holiday at sea with the ship as their hotel. The first such tour was the Midnight Sun Voyage to the North Cape in Scandinavia with the Bergen line of ships in 1875. By the 1890s, shipboard holidays were very popular. After World War I cruise business showed the most growth because the large number of spare ships available allowed ship lines to offer trips at bargain prices. The popularity of cruises continued until World War II erupted.

Thomas Cook died in 1892, and John Mason Cook died only eight years after his father. John Mason's three sons carried on the family business, and, during their stewardship, Cook began offering the latest mode of travel—flight. Their first venture into air tourism was in 1911 when they made an agreement to sell tickets for excursions of an airship around Lucerne and around Burgenstock and the Righi. Cook received a six percent commission for each passenger booked. In 1919, its first advertisement for airplane flights appeared in *The Times,* simply offering the opportunity to experience flight. The next year, however, Cook was offering business or pleasure flights aboard converted war-time planes. The company printed a brochure informing travelers that air travel aboard these planes was safe and reliable and that the flight to Paris took just less than three hours. Although competition among the new airlines was fierce, passengers were few. Airlines began offering incentives such as limousine service to the airfield. Gradually, they also started offering food in flight, and by 1927, a full menu was available.

The Cooks set out to make airline contracts all over the world. Passenger flying had begun in the United States in 1926, and the Cooks made contracts there with three airlines. Cook provided passengers and booked reservations, while the airline was responsible for maintaining the planes and providing safe transport.

By 1928, all three of John Mason's sons had retired from the company, which was then sold to the Belgian *Compagnie des Wagons-Lits et des Grands Express Europeens,* a company formed by George Nagelmackers in the 1870s to construct and develop the use of sleeping and restaurant cars on trains and which also had established the Orient Express and several luxury hotels.

Under its new ownership, Cook began offering an increasing number of motor tours, including an automobile trip to the desert and the Oasis of Bou-Saada in Algeria. Air traffic also grew in popularity because of the travel time it saved. Although planes could not compete on the transatlantic crossing because they could not carry enough fuel, German zeppelins ran regular flights to Rio de Janeiro and North America. Cook, always at the forefront of travel, advertised these journeys of the Graf Zeppelin which traveled to America and the Middle East and even made a round-the-world flight in 1929. The explosion of the hindenburg at Lakehurst, New Jersey, however, once again virtually eliminated attempts at transatlantic flight. Airplane flights from England to the Middle East and to South Africa were routine as they could be undertaken in stages.

Imperial Airways and Pan American began experimenting with flying boats in the early 1930s, and by 1939 Cook was advertising a round-the-world tour with the Yankee Clipper carrying passengers across the long ocean stretches of the journey. World War II brought an end to travel in many areas of the world, and Cook downsized. However, the company still offered holidays in areas outside the war zones. During the war, Cook operated a letter service through Portugal for people left behind the enemy lines and helped lead evacuations of children after the air raids started. It also lent its Egyptian shipyards for servicing and repairing ships of all kinds and allowed ships from the East Africa war operations to use its workshops for repairing vehicles.

During World War II when the Germans occupied Brussels and Paris, Thomas Cook and Son passed into the hands of the Custodian of Enemy Property. After the war, however, the tourism trade was back in full swing. The British government arranged for the company to be purchased by several British railway companies. When the railways were nationalized in 1948, Thomas Cook also became state-owned.

In 1958, a Boeing 707 crossed the Atlantic. This not only meant the opening of a new mode of transatlantic travel, but it also meant that new, more reliable aircraft were available to tourists, who had until then been reluctant to fly. Accordingly, Thomas Cook faced a new era and increased competition. While Cook had become an institution in England, a new, younger consumer market looked to modern travel companies that could provided

unique opportunities. As a state-owned agency, Cook was unable to obtain money for new ventures, such as purchasing its own airline, as some rivals did.

Thomas Cook was sold to Midland Bank in 1974. The following year, Midland Bank sold the U.S. operation to Dun & Bradstreet as a result of federal banking regulations. Under an agreement with Thomas Cook Group Ltd., Dun & Bradstreet continued to use the Cook name and remained part of a network membership agreement. In 1988, Dun & Bradstreet put the business up for sale in order to concentrate only on its traditional services of marketing, credit risk, finance, and directory information.

Publishing magnate Robert Maxwell bought Thomas Cook the next year and renewed the licensing agreement to use the Cook name. Thomas Cook Travel Inc. generated business of about $365 million. It had 60 full service locations, including nine regional reservation centers. Although industry members speculated that Maxwell would sell the company, since his main business activity was publishing, he maintained that he had big plans to make Thomas Cook a dominant force in the U.S. travel business through the acquisition of other companies.

In 1989 Thomas Cook joined forces with Crimson/Heritage Travel to form a $1.3 billion company and instantly jumped in rankings to become the third largest travel company in the United States. Maxwell and David Paresky, founder and president of Crimson Travel, each owned a 50 percent share of the new Thomas Cook Travel. Paresky became president, chairman, and chief executive officer of the newly-merged company. He relocated company headquarters to Cambridge, Massachusetts, from New York City.

When Maxwell died suddenly in 1991, his 50 percent share of Thomas Cook was eyed by many potential buyers, including Midland Bank, which had made itself eligible by selling the bank that conflicted with further U.S. operations. However, Paresky had the right of first refusal, and in 1993, he and his wife Linda, vice-chairwoman of the company, purchased the Maxwell share.

Thomas Cook Travel, the U.S. operation, had about 700 offices in 45 states and Washington, D.C. in 1993 and had become predominantly a corporate agency, handling the travel of some of the largest companies in the country. Business travel revenues accounted for 84 percent of the company's revenues that year. The company also operated a franchise program with more than 40 locations.

Further Reading:

Golden, Fran, ''Industry Weighs Impact of Crimson/Heritage-Thomas Cook Merger,'' *Travel Weekly,* December 28, 1989, p. 17–18.
——. ''Maxwell to Buy Thomas Cook Travel,'' *Travel Weekly,* February 16, 1989, p. 1.
——. ''Thomas Cook Joins Forces with Crimson,'' *Travel Weekly,* December 18, 1989, p. 1.
Swinglehurst, Edmund, *Cook's Tours: The Story of Popular Travel,* Dorset, England: Blandford Press, 1982.
——. *The Romantic Journey: The Story of Thomas Cook and Victorian Travel,* New York: Harper & Row, 1974.

—Wendy J. Stein

Torchmark Corporation

2001 Third Avenue South
Birmingham, Alabama 35233
U.S.A.
(205) 325-4200
Fax: (205) 325-4157

Public Company
Incorporated: 1929 as Liberty National Insurance Company
Employees: 6,242
Sales: $2.05 billion
Stock Exchanges: New York London
SICs: 6311 Life Insurance; 6321 Accident & Health
   Insurance; 6331 Fire, Marine & Casualty Insurance; 6719
   Holding Companies, Nec; 6282 Investment Advice

Torchmark Corporation is an insurance and diversified financial services holding company. Most of the company's history involves a single corporate entity, Liberty National Insurance Holding Co., but in the 1980s the company entered a period of aggressive acquisition. By 1993, Torchmark controlled ten principal subsidiaries, branching out into individual life and health insurance; funeral, fire, and property insurance; financial planning; mutual funds; and investment management services. Torchmark's subsidiaries held leading positions in their industry segments in the early 1990s.

The company's roots extend back to the turn of the twentieth century, when the Heralds of Liberty was incorporated in Huntsville, Alabama. Although the entity purported to be a fraternal benefit society, it was actually a front for another company, headquartered in Philadelphia. The fraternal charter limited the Alabama Insurance Department's ability to oversee the Heralds of Liberty, enabling the parent to circumvent state insurance regulations. The parent company's officers used a variety of schemes to embezzle funds from the fraternity. The officers sold it worthless bonds, borrowed money on insufficient collateral, and had the Heralds make "payments" to the parent. After 20 years of these illicit practices resulted in a backlog of unpaid claims, the Alabama Insurance Department took over the fraternity in June of 1921.

The state agency assigned deputy insurance commissioner Robert Park Davison to the case. He proceeded to "clean house" at the Heralds of Liberty. He forced all of the fraternity's officers and directors to resign and was made "Supreme Commander"

of the group. Frank Park Samford, Davison's colleague and cousin, was elected "Supreme Recorder." The unusual titles reflected the group's origins as a secret society. Davison and Samford went to the parent's headquarters in Philadelphia to begin reformation of the Heralds of Liberty. They found that the group was insolvent: unpaid claims amounted to $80,000, but the firm held only $1,410 cash. The Heralds had no reserves, and premiums on the policies that existed were insufficient to meet financial demands. Davison and Samford discovered that the only policy the Heralds had sold was a lottery-type plan, or "Joint Life Distribution Plan." The scheme divided policyholders into classes by age. When a policyholder died, his beneficiary and the holder of the lowest certificate number in each class were both paid. Although the Heralds had tried to eliminate these policies through exchanges and introduction of new insurance plans, the parent company was dependent on this business for financial support and was compelled by the nature of the plan to continue to place new policies in the existing classes. It took the new officers until the mid-1930s to rid itself of these policies.

Davison and Samford worked during the 1920s to raise premiums, sell legal life insurance policies based on an adequate reserve, pay past-due claims, and build up a team of trustworthy agents. By 1927, the year the headquarters of the reformed company moved to Birmingham, Alabama, it had 26 employees and one new officer, an assistant secretary. In order to build up a reserve fund, Davison and Samford made the company's first stock offering in 1929 under its new name, Liberty National Life Insurance Co. Many officers and agents borrowed money in order to purchase shares of the $325,000 offering. The stock offering was supplemented with an additional assessment on Heralds of Liberty policyholders. Liberty National's officers feared that many clients would cancel their policies, but by July 1929 the company appeared to have endured its transformation into a legitimate insurer.

Disaster struck again when the stock market crashed that year. Many of those who had borrowed to capitalize the new company were stuck with debts that exceeded the value of their collateral. To make matters worse, the cash generated by the initial stock issue had been deposited with the Southern Bank and Trust Company as trustee, and before Liberty National had a chance to invest, it became apparent that the money could not be withdrawn without breaking the bank. Unlike many other banks during this crisis, Southern managed to stay open, and Liberty National was able to withdraw its funds in small increments over the next few months.

Liberty National struggled over the next five years to endure the Great Depression. Income from premiums declined as customers were forced to cancel their policies, and losses were sustained when banks failed and debtors defaulted on their bonds. Cost-cutting helped the company survive losses during the depression, and Liberty National even invested $95,000 to acquire the distribution system of a failing competitor. Circumstances compelled Liberty to use creative financing to remain solvent in the early years of the decade. In 1931 the company purchased a 70 percent interest in a headquarters building, then claimed it as an asset in order to maintain an adequate surplus. Davison and Samford even offered to surrender some of their stock to the company in 1932 in order to subsidize Liberty

National's surplus, but that drastic step was not necessary. In fact, Liberty National paid its first cash dividend the following year. The insurance company's officers perceived that its shareholders doubted the continued viability of Liberty National, and felt that the $21,000 dividend would restore investor confidence. That first payment started a custom that was followed every year in the company's history.

When Davison died in 1934, Samford was elected president and chief executive officer, more traditional administrative titles than "Supreme Commander." Liberty National enjoyed a period of growth and prosperity after that year, and worked to build a dependable base of financial strength. Innovative policies helped the company compete successfully with its older and larger rivals. Liberty National made its first acquisition in 1944 through an interesting series of events. Late in 1943, Rufus Lackey, the principal stockholder of the Brown-Service Insurance Company, offered to sell his share of the Alabama insurer to Liberty National for $5 million, provided the transaction was completed by the end of the year. Liberty National had the will, but neither the cash nor the borrowing power to make the acquisition on such short notice. Samford and the company's general counsel secured personal loans with their Liberty National stock as collateral, purchased the stock themselves, and Brown-Service merged with Liberty National in 1944.

Brown-Service, a successful regional company, specialized in burial insurance plans. Liberty National utilized the subsidiary's large agency force to accomplish the greatest market penetration ever achieved by a life insurance company. Although Liberty National later discontinued the sale of burial insurance policies, the plan provided substantial savings to many citizens of Alabama and helped Liberty National build a highly efficient and profitable operation. In the 1960s, over 80 percent of white Alabamans held Brown-Service policies. Even as late as the mid-1980s, almost half of the people who died in Alabama each year were insured under a Brown-Service policy.

Liberty-National progressed steadily after 1945. The company made several relatively minor acquisitions, expanded geographically, and introduced numerous new insurance products. Beginning in 1952, the company began recording consecutive annual increases in both earnings and dividends that went unmatched by any other member of the New York Stock Exchange.

In 1958 Liberty National altered Birmingham's skyline by placing a one-fifth-sized replica of the Statue of Liberty atop its Birmingham headquarters. During the 1950s and 1960s, the insurer grew to become America's second-largest publicly owned provider of so-called industrial insurance. This type of policy was renewed weekly, and had been discontinued by most other major insurers, but Liberty National was reluctant to abandon these policies, which were popular with the company's rural customers. By the end of the 1960s, it ranked eighteenth in regular coverage, and had expanded its geographical service area to include Georgia, Florida, Tennessee, and California. In 1968 Liberty National sold more than $1 billion in new policies for the first time.

Frank P. Samford, Jr., replaced his father as president and chief executive officer of Liberty National in 1967. He served in that position until 1985. The younger Samford brought Liberty National's policyholders more modern coverage. In the late 1960s, for example, the company introduced an estate plan and a special program for college students. The company's agents continued to take a very personal approach to life insurance, however. In 1975 its 2,500 agents still sold monthly life insurance door-to-door. And while other, more urban, companies had abandoned these low-premium policies, Liberty National continued to earn profit margins of 15 percent on the old-style coverage.

In 1979 Liberty National undertook an agenda of expansion and diversification through acquisition. Prior to that time, most of the company's investments were concentrated in mortgages, bonds, and a limited number of stocks, but by the mid-1980s, the company had grown from a regional life insurance firm into a diversified national insurance and financial services corporation. From 1980 to 1982, the company spent over half a billion dollars to purchase several insurance and investment businesses. In 1980 the company bought Globe Life And Accident Insurance Company. Headquartered in Oklahoma City, Globe was founded in 1951 by John Singletary and Ralph Reese. Although the company was established with borrowed money, it had grown into a consistently profitable firm through the use of innovative marketing techniques such as direct mail. When Singletary died in 1977, Ronald K. Richey was elected president and CEO. In 1979 the company underwent a crisis when the executor of Singletary's estate sought to sell his 36 percent share. Liberty National purchased the company in a friendly takeover, and made Richey a director of the parent. He succeeded Samford as president and CEO in 1986.

Liberty National was reorganized as a holding company in 1980. The new entity made two major acquisitions in 1981: Continental Investment Corporation and United American Insurance Company of Dallas. Continental owned Waddell & Reed and United Investors Life Insurance Company, two businesses that would become primary subsidiaries of Liberty National. Waddell & Reed (W&R) was created as a sales and distribution division for United Mutual Funds and was named for the fund's founders, Chauncey Waddell and Cameron Reed. United Funds became the first mutual fund group to be registered under the Investment Company Act of 1940, the legislation that brought funds under the jurisdiction of the Securities and Exchange Commission.

Waddell & Reed (W&R) hoped their group of mutual funds would make it easier for middle-income Americans to participate in the investing process. United Investors Life Insurance Company was created as an outgrowth of W&R in 1961. Its term insurance product soon accounted for a major part of Continental Investment Company's income. Problems in the national economy and the stock market, as well as difficulties stemming from Continental's ownership of Waddell & Reed, combined to force W&R into bankruptcy reorganization in the 1970s. The firm emerged from the crisis with new leadership and new products: financial planning seminars and services. By the early 1980s, W&R was a leading American financial planner. Liberty National purchased W&R's parent, Continental Investment Corporation, for $155 million in 1981.

The United American Insurance Company of Dallas, Liberty National's other major acquisition of 1981, was founded in 1947 by Casey Dunlap and Russ Donovan. This company had pioneered the employment of independent health insurance agents in the mid-1950s. It parlayed this new sales system into a nationwide system that extended into Canada by the time it was acquired by Liberty National for $138 million.

Liberty National's expansion into mutual funds, health insurance, and financial services rendered its formal name, Liberty National Insurance Holding Co., too limiting. The company adopted the name Torchmark Corporation in 1982. Torchmark combined the Statue of Liberty's torch and the word "hallmark" to form a unique name that drew upon the company's long history, yet reflected its new components.

While many other insurance providers were lured into the high-return, high-risk junk bond and commercial real estate markets of the 1980s, Torchmark maintained three-fourths of its invested assets in reliable, government-guaranteed securities and short-term investments. When the bottom fell out of the junk bond and real estate markets in the late 1980s, Torchmark emerged unscathed. Torchmark's conservative investment strategies earned its primary subsidiaries the industry's highest ratings. The national scandals, however, did affect the company, in the form of increased contributions to the federal guaranty fund to bail out insolvent insurers.

In the 1990s the company planned to limit acquisitions to niche companies with specialized services like pre-need, fire, and cancer insurance. Torchmark continued to focus on home service and term insurance, mutual funds, and asset management as its core businesses. Growth vehicles included Medicare supplemental insurance, variable insurance, and direct mail products.

In 1992 Torchmark recorded its forty-first consecutive year of increased per-share earnings and dividends. The company's stock had appreciated by an incredible 1,675 percent since 1980. These figures helped the holding company's subsidiaries maintain leading positions in their industry segments—leadership they were not likely to relinquish in the near future.

Principal Subsidiaries: United Investors Management Company (83%); Liberty National Life Insurance Company; United American Insurance Company; Globe Life and Accident Insurance Company; Family Service Life Insurance Company; Liberty National Fire Insurance Company; United Investors Life Insurance Company; Waddell & Reed, Inc.; Torch Energy Advisors Incorporated.

Further Reading:

"A Dying Business," *Forbes,* April 15, 1975, p. 61.
"Industrial Insurance Profitable Line for Liberty National Life," *Barron's,* July 29, 1968, pp. 33, 35.
Samford, Frank P., Jr., *Torchmark Corporation: History of a New Company,* Princeton University Press, 1985.

—April S. Dougal

Totem Resources Corporation

1100 Olive Way
Suite 1100
Seattle, Washington 98124
U.S.A.
(206) 628-4343
Fax: (206) 628-9245

Private Company
Incorporated: 1982
Employees: 1,153
Sales: $200 million
SICs: 6719 Holding Companies Nec; 4424 Deep Sea
  Domestic Transportation of Freight

Totem Resources Corporation is the holding company of Totem Ocean Trailer Express, Inc. (TOTE), Foss Maritime Co., and Interocean Management Corp. Operating with almost no infrastructure, Totem Resources was formed in 1982 to enable the purchase of TOTE, a steamship company operating oceangoing containerships between Washington and Alaska. Subsequent acquisitions garnered the corporation a shipyard, tugboat bases along the West Coast, cargo terminals in Seattle and Tacoma, Washington, and entrance into the business of vessel maintenance management. During its short history, Totem Resources has evolved into a dominant force in the Northwest's maritime industry.

During the early 1970s, Sun Oil Company, a Philadelphia-based energy corporation, began looking for an entry into the rapidly growing Alaskan market. The construction of Alaska's oil pipeline had bolstered the state's wealth and its population, and Sun Oil saw an opportunity to capitalize on the region's growth potential by providing high speed ocean carrier service to transport consumer goods and equipment to the area. While rich in oil, Alaska lacked many of the items necessary to support its subsistence. Clothes, food, books, building materials, automobiles, and any of the sundry goods a burgeoning population required had to be imported into the state. To accomplish this, cargo had to be shipped via the 1,500 miles of water separating Alaska from the contiguous United States. Gauged by weight, 99 percent of everything exported to Alaska arrived by water, a lifeline Sun Oil sought to tap. Sun Oil ordered its subsidiary, Sun Shipbuilding & Dry Dock Inc., to design and build a vessel

capable of transporting cargo along the route, and by 1975 a 790-foot trailership, the *S. S. Great Land,* was completed.

Able to haul the equivalent of 386 40-foot trailers and 126 vehicles, the *Great Land,* weighing 31,762 displacement tons, was a giant even among the massive cargo vessels of its time. Powered by steam and capable of maintaining a cruising speed of 24 knots, the ship could complete the voyage to Alaska in between 62 and 66 hours, a trip that formerly took several times as long. Quick and large, the *Great Land* also possessed another enviable characteristic and one crucial to the efficiency and profitability of a cargo carrier—the ability to load and unload cargo quickly. Designed as a roll on/roll off carrier, known in the maritime industry as RO/RO, the *Great Land* did not require special equipment to transfer cargo from truck trailer to ship container and back to truck trailer. Semitrailers could simply be driven up ramps onto the ships, then driven off once the ship arrived at its destination. The RO/RO system afforded several benefits, one being that perishable goods such as produce, meat, and dairy products were less subject to spoilage because they were loaded and removed quickly. By removing a step from the loading process, cargo could be received up to 30 minutes before sailing, and the shorter transition period while at port allowed a greater number of service runs.

With its modern carrier ready to begin service, Sun Oil formed TOTE as a subsidiary to oversee the operation of the *Great Land.* TOTE, 70 percent of which was owned by Sun Oil and the remaining 30 percent belonging to Sun Shipbuilding, established its terminal at the Port of Seattle and launched the *Great Land* on its maiden voyage to Anchorage in September 1975.

TOTE's first few years were difficult, as the fledgling company grappled with problems associated with its youth. It upgraded its trailer fleet, provided better training for its maintenance personnel, and established sales offices away from the Seattle-Anchorage shipping route to cultivate additional business. During the peak summer months, however, business was brisk, prompting the company to lease an additional carrier, *El Taino,* as a temporary response to increased demand in 1976. That year, contract negotiations with the Port of Seattle soured, and TOTE relocated its docking facilities to the Port of Tacoma, approximately 30 miles south of Seattle. By the following year, Sun Shipbuilding had constructed an exact copy of the *Great Land,* the *S. S. Westward Venture,* which was added to TOTE's Tacoma-Anchorage shipping run. Now with two sailings per week, TOTE had readied itself for the expected continuation of growth in Alaska. The addition of the *Westward Venture* also affirmed the esteem TOTE's clients had for the RO/RO concept. The only other oceangoing carrier fleet operating between Washington and Alaska, Sea-Land Services, transported its cargo in containers adapted to trailer chassis, requiring deck personnel to hitch and unhitch containers before loading and unloading. Given a choice, many had opted for the greater flexibility and speed offered by the RO/RO method, earning TOTE additional business during these early years it would have otherwise missed.

TOTE's estimate of Alaska's future growth, however, fell short of expectations. The boom created by the oil pipeline began to wane by 1977, and Alaska's economy consequently began to suffer. TOTE, whose success was so closely tied to the fate of

Alaska's economy, felt the effects of the decline, and business for the shipper also dipped. The other two major shippers operating between Washington State and Alaska, Sea-Land Services and Alaska Hydro-Train, also incurred a drop in business, and the ensuing struggle to maintain their diminished market share touched off a rate war between the three shippers in 1978. Prior to 1978, the three companies charged the same rate for their services, but in a bid to increase its business, Sea-Land proposed to lower its rates. The Interstate Commerce Commission (ICC) halted the attempt, however, and Sea-Land withdrew its proposal. Alaska Hydro-Train, which transported its shipments by tugboat-towed barges, responded by offering an "incentive rate" for large shipments, to which the ICC gave approval. Next, Sea-Land, feeling the pressures of a drop in revenues, asked the ICC to allow it to raise its rates. The ICC allowed the company to raise its rates by eight percent, and TOTE followed suit. But Alaska Hydro-Train surprised the other two shippers by not raising its rates in kind. Consequently, Sea-Land and TOTE were forced to roll back their prices, causing their revenues to fall. While each of the companies suffered as a result of this fracas, Sea-Land and TOTE incurred the greater damage. Each controlled 40 percent of the market, by far outdistancing the smaller Alaska Hydro-Train, but meeting the costs of securing that lead demanded the higher revenues thwarted by Alaska Hydro-Train. Sea-Land's aging fleet required extensive maintenance expenditures, and TOTE needed the additional cash to pay for its two new vessels. Alaska Hydro-Train, on the other hand, was less troubled by the curtailment of rate increases and emerged from the dispute with a small, if somewhat costly, victory.

Although revenues dropped, and some of TOTE's shipping runs left the docks only 50 percent full, the rollback of rates helped sustain its share of the market. The question of TOTE's future solvency lay not so much in the outcome of the rate war, but in the recovery of the Alaskan market. As always, the success of TOTE hinged on the growth of consumer and industrial demand for goods in Alaska. Fortunately for TOTE and its anxious competitors, the Alaskan economy rebounded in 1981. An upsurge in housing construction and an increase in the demand for consumer goods invigorated shipping to the region, as oil revenues once again helped lift the state's economy. TOTE's business activity had once again reached the levels that had initially encouraged Sun Oil to enter the market six years earlier. Sailings continued into the winter months, usually a slow period of the year, with both the *Great Land* and the *Westward Venture* delivering shipments of automobiles, building materials, oil-field equipment, groceries, and other merchandise. According to TOTE's management, now led by Robert B. McMillen, prospects for the future looked encouraging. The vitality of Alaska's economy was expected to continue into the future, a forecast that, if true, would fill the coffers of not only TOTE's two ships, but TOTE itself.

At this point, in 1982, TOTE's management, perhaps encouraged by what the future held in store, decided to purchase a controlling interest in TOTE from Sun Oil. Led by McMillen, a group of investors from the Pacific Northwest formed Totem Resources Corporation to facilitate the purchase. Sun Oil agreed and, although the energy corporation would continue to exert its influence as a substantial and active stockholder, TOTE now took charge of its own destiny.

Shipping between Alaska and Washington flourished for the next several years, evidenced by TOTE's construction of a new 33-acre, $10.5 million terminal in 1984. But as its shipping route between became more lucrative, it also began to attract the attention of other shipping companies. Marine Power and Equipment, emboldened by the success of TOTE and its competitors, formed Seaway Express in 1984, which began shipping runs with the area's first high capacity, triple-decked barge. Crowley Maritime, the owner of Alaska Hydro-Train, responded by adding an additional deck to one of its barges, sparking a wave of capacity and service increases by other shipping companies. Soon, before the summer of 1984 was over, a crisis had developed.

The shipping market had quickly become saturated, with ships and barges along the route operating at 30 percent below capacity, which ignited another rate war. Freight rates for some items, such as lumber, were halved, as the plethora of shipping companies fought for business. Hardest hit by the renewed battle over prices were Sea-Land and TOTE, whose faster vessels cost more to operate than the slower, cheaper barges. Given the choice between cheaper rates or quicker service, many opted for the former, and TOTE was forced to relegate itself to transporting the more time-sensitive shipments, such as fresh produce. Furthermore, the growth in Alaska's economy began to subside just as the carriers were slashing their rates and jockeying for business. With the conditions exacerbated by yet another demonstration of the cyclicality of Alaska's economy, the competition for freight intensified, and Totem Resources began to look for a solution to the situation through diversification.

While the Pacific Northwest maritime community struggled with the decline in Alaska's economy and the overabundance of carriers, Totem Resources announced its plans to purchase Lykes Brothers Steamship Co., Inc., a steamship company owned by Florida-based Interocean Steamship Company. One of the nation's largest steamship companies, Lykes' recent history paralleled TOTE's. Senior Lykes officials formed Interocean in 1982 to purchase Lykes from LTV Corporation, the same year TOTE's management formed Totem Resources to purchase TOTE. In size, however, Lykes had the advantage. With a fleet of 32 American flagships serving five continents and operating out of U.S. ports on the Gulf Coast, West Coast, and the South Atlantic, Lykes dwarfed TOTE.

The fluctuations in the Alaskan market that TOTE had experienced during its ten years of operation had demonstrated to Totem Resources' management the inherent problems of focusing solely on TOTE's service to Alaska. Totem had other investment besides TOTE, but TOTE was the only operating entity of the corporation. This, however, would change with the acquisition of Lykes. The diversification into other shipping areas than the Alaska routes would lessen the corporation's reliance on the vacillating Alaskan economy; a move that many of TOTE's competitors had already made.

However, the acquisition never occurred. Lykes, as a company operating American flagships involved in international trade, received subsidization from the U.S. government, so competing steamship companies, Sea-Land and Crowley Maritime included, protested the acquisition. They argued that Totem Resources' purchase of Lykes would violate a maritime law prohibiting federally subsidized steamship companies and their affiliates from engaging in domestic shipping activities. Although Totem Resources had planned to operate the two companies as separate entities, protesters maintained that profits earned by Lykes would benefit the operation of TOTE's two carriers. Rather than face litigation that could have taken up to a year to resolve, Totem Resources withdrew its proposal in late 1985 and searched for another way to broaden its maritime interests.

Two years later, Totem Resources found Foss Maritime Co., a Seattle-based company with a fleet of 65 tugboats and barges, that had been operating in the Puget Sound area for nearly a century. In 1889, Thea Foss, a Norwegian immigrant, purchased a rowboat for $5, refurbished it, then sold it at a profit and bought additional rowboats to sell. After several years, Foss had accumulated a fleet of rowboats which she rented from a dock in Tacoma, Washington. In 1912, she and her husband, Andrew, purchased their first tugboat, adding a fleet of tugboats five years later with their purchase of Tacoma Tug Boat Co. Eventually, the company, named Foss Launch Co., became a key maritime operator in the Pacific Northwest. It expanded by purchasing tugboat companies from neighboring ports, and it established a barge service to Alaska, which became an integral segment of its business. By 1987, the company, now named Foss Maritime and owned by San Francisco-based Dillingham Holdings Inc., operated a tugboat and barge fleet, a towing and salvage firm in southern California, a shipyard in Seattle, and an environmental division involved in the clean-up of oil spills and other maritime pollution problems. For Totem Resources, the addition of Foss Maritime met the diversification needs it had attempted to fulfill with Lykes; Foss Maritime would strengthen its service to Alaska, while other ventures the tugboat and barge company was involved with tempered the effects of the cyclical Alaskan economy. The company was purchased in 1987 for an undisclosed sum from Dillingham Holdings, and another operating entity was added to Totem Resources.

The volume of cargo shipped to Alaska continued to decline from the early 1980s levels after the acquisition, but the addition of Foss Maritime's interests outside the shipping route assuaged what would have otherwise been a bleak period for Totem Resources. Although the corporation preferred not to divulge financial figures, it maintained that both of its companies were profitable ventures, with revenues evenly divided between the two. TOTE still held a commanding control of the Alaskan market, and Foss Maritime profited from its diverse capabilities, such as its contribution to the clean-up of the Alaskan shore after the Exxon *Valdez* oil spill in 1989.

That year, Totem Resources made another move toward diversification by purchasing, for an undisclosed sum, Interocean

Management Corp., a Philadelphia-based company that managed the maintenance and operation of ships. Interocean fit well with the other two companies; the *Great Land* and the *Westward Venture* were both client vessels of Interocean before the acquisition, and Foss Maritime's ability to move and repair ships provided services to Interocean it had previously hired other companies to supply.

By the early 1990s, shipments to Alaska once again began to rise. Totem Resources purchased another ship, the *S. S. Puerto Rico*, in 1991 and renamed it the *S. S. Northern Lights* to spell TOTE's two other carriers while undergoing maintenance. During the winter of 1991, an additional 90 feet was added to the ship, making her identical to the *Great Land* and the *Westward Venture*. The *S. S. Northern Lights* was slated to begin regular sailings to Alaska in the summer of 1993.

Totem Resources' future success rests on the vitality of the maritime market in the Northwest. Although its reliance on the fickle Alaskan market remained considerable, through the diversification of the late 1980s, this dependence was decreased. The question of whether the demand for trade in the area justified the corporation's extensive holdings depended entirely on the future conditions of the market, but, whatever conditions developed, Totem Resources was poised to garner a substantial portion of the maritime business in the area.

Principal Subsidiaries: Totem Ocean Trailer Express, Inc.; Foss Maritime Co.; Interocean Management Co.

Further Reading:

Cushing, William, "A Shipping War," *Seattle Post-Intelligencer,* September 24, 1978, p. B8.

Nogaki, Sylvia, "Protests Sink Proposed Buyout of Lykes By Totem Resources." *The Seattle Times,* December 31, 1985, p. D3.

——. "Shippers Wait for End to Industry Shakeout," *The Seattle Times,* October 20, 1985, p. E1.

——. "Totem Resources to Buy Foss Maritime," *The Seattle Times,* June 27, 1987, p. D8.

——. "TOTE to Buy Big Steamship Firm," *The Seattle Times,* November 6, 1985, p. E12.

"Shipping to Alaska Remains Strong," *The Seattle Times,* November 2, 1981, p. D10.

"Totem Northwest Corp. Formally Acquires TOTE," *Seattle Daily Journal of Commerce,* October 19, 1982, p. 16.

"TOTE's Westward Venture Sails North May 25," *Seattle Daily Journal of Commerce,* April 23, 1976, p. 7.

Wilhelm, Steve, "Totem Makes Waves With Almost No Infrastructure," *Puget Sound Business Journal,* July 3, 1989, p. 18A.

"World's Largest Trailership Off To Good Start," *Shipping Digest,* November 17, 1975, p. 10.

—Jeffrey L. Covell

Tridel Enterprises Inc.

4800 Dufferin Street
Downsview, Ontario
Canada
M3H 5V9
(416) 661-9290
Fax: (416) 661-6971

Public Company
Incorporated: 1981
Employees: 1980
Sales: C$391 million (1991; US$311 million)
Stock Exchanges: Toronto Montreal

Tridel Enterprises Inc. is a residential real estate developer that builds and sells condominiums in the Toronto metropolitan area. The company has developed approximately 40 condominium projects in the Toronto area, including the Skymark Place development in North York, 130 Carlton in downtown Toronto, and the Greencroft Estates development in Etobicoke. Through its Construction Technology Division, Tridel also develops, sells, and leases shoring, forming, scaffolding, and concrete construction accessories, systems, and equipment throughout North America.

The company that became Tridel was founded by a stonemason named DelZotto from Fruili, Italy, who moved to Canada in 1934 to work in the Sudbury nickel mines of northern Ontario. DelZotto eventually moved to Toronto for its milder climate, built his own home, raised enough capital to build two more, and developed a thriving residential construction business. In the early 1950s DelZotto's company was taken over by his three sons, Angelo, Elvio, and Leo, and named Tridel, for "the three DelZottos."

In 1968 Tridel branched into the field of construction technology by entering into a joint venture with Alcan Aluminum, based in Montreal, to found Aluma Systems Corp Among Aluma's first products was an extruded aluminum form for the pouring of concrete for construction, a system that saved time and money because the forms did not have to be taken apart and reassembled to be moved between floors. The venture proved successful, and in the early 1970s Tridel bought out Alcan's share of Aluma.

The DelZotto brothers incorporated Tridel Enterprises Inc. in 1981. In 1986—the same year in which the company went public—Tridel completed a series of share exchanges in which AEL Ventures Ltd. purchased all the shares of the DelZotto brothers' business. Tridel, in turn, acquired from AEL Ventures the entire stock of Trilan Developments Ltd., a residential property development company and owner of a residential housing bank. Tridel also acquired the entire stock of Hominal Developments Inc., in exchange for 500 common shares of Tridel. At the same time, AEL Ventures Ltd. transferred its common stock in Tridel Enterprises to a wholly owned subsidiary, Tridel Financial Corp. The shift gave the DelZotto Brothers a controlling 85 percent interest in Tridel.

The series of deals was meant to acquire funds for Aluma Systems, the construction technology side of the business. The DelZotto brothers felt that they needed to prepare for the day when Toronto's bustling condominium market would slow. Speculating that after the end of the Cold War governments would move to stimulate a faltering economy by spending heavily on infrastructure rather than military expansion, Tridel sought to position itself to capitalize on the shift.

To implement this plan, the DelZotto brothers bought several small construction companies using funds generated from their residential real estate activities. This added to Aluma's marketability as a supplier of scaffolding, cement, and other building trade equipment.

The strategy seemed to work, as evidenced by Tridel's posted profits of $16.2 million on revenues of $410 million in 1987. Compared with profits of $8.5 million in 1986 on revenues of $183 million, the company was enjoying unprecedented expansion. In January 1988 Aluma Systems purchased Shepler Equipment Co., a Houston, Texas, supplier of concrete forming systems. Later that year, Burke Scaffolding Co.—a newly created Tridel U.S. subsidiary bought two years earlier for $27.6 million—bought GKN Kwidform Inc. of Orange County, California. The $12 million company provided equipment to raise and dismantle scaffolding to the construction and assembling sectors.

Later in the same year, Tridel's leadership ceased buying land in Toronto, believing that the real estate market had peaked. Rather, the company sold off $100 million of land, or 40 percent of its standing inventory. The strategy was intended to reduce the company's debt load and, perhaps more importantly, to avoid holding property that had been acquired at peak prices.

In 1989 Aluma continued to acquire other companies, buying Anthes Industries Inc.'s construction equipment division, for $63.4 million. Also that year, Aluma formed two joint ventures in the Soviet Union, which was then undergoing fundamental economic reform to a free-market economy.

Tridel had been investing heavily in Aluma Systems in preparation for an anticipated recession, and its forecasts proved correct in the late 1980s. Far from spending to stimulate their lagging economies, the governments of Canada and the United States cut spending to reduce debt levels. What spending there was on infrastructure proved minimal.

Fortunately, condominium sales did not decline as sharply as the DelZotto brothers initially predicted either. By 1990 the company's assets had grown to over $1 billion for the first time, and revenues that year surpassed $650 million. Had it not been for Aluma's losses, the company would have achieved a profit rather than the posted loss of $14.2 million for fiscal 1991.

Nevertheless, in response to the difficult economic conditions, in 1991 Tridel reduced its labor force by 240 employees. The company's sales force was also offered sales incentive programs that stressed company profits rather than sales volume. Tridel's marketing team worked to increase the company's name recognition to complement its on-site advertising of residential developments. This effort included the launch of a major marketing publication to publicize Tridel developments to existing owners and prospective buyers. Also, Tridel re-emphasized after-sales service by instituting a quality awareness program for its employees.

Despite their efforts, Tridel's Aluma subsidiary was hit hard by the weak economy, and by April 1992 Aluma had breached the terms of its loan agreements. A $45 million loan was quickly arranged to meet obligations to Aluma lenders, and plans were announced for Tridel to buy and resell some of Aluma's manufacturing operations and other non-core assets. Tridel president Elvio DelZotto announced in June that Aluma would be taken public once it was returned to health.

In October 1992, Tridel asked its lenders to reschedule interest and principal payments on the approximately $200 million debt owed by Aluma Systems. The company admitted that it did not have the cash to repay outstanding loans if the lenders avoided rescheduling and demanded instant repayment.

Far from keeping Tridel above water during the recession, Aluma Systems now threatened to pull the DelZotto empire down. Austin Page, Aluma's president and Tridel's chief financial officer, explained the predicament to the *Globe and Mail* at the time: "Aluma still has too much equipment, too much debt and too much overhead. This has been the toughest recession I've ever seen, especially for the construction industry."

By 1992 the complicated system of guarantees and pledges of collateral between the DelZotto companies forced Tridel to negotiate for extended terms with its own creditors.

The situation became critical in April 1993 when Tridel's three principal creditors threatened to force Aluma into bankruptcy court. A month earlier, the lenders had begun legal action in Toronto to drive another Tridel subsidiary, Umacs of Canada Inc., into bankruptcy court. The move was considered necessary due to the financing agreements between Umacs and Aluma. These twin threats prompted a spate of resignations from the Tridel board.

Tridel's chief financial officer, Austin Page, told the *Globe and Mail* in April 1993 that he had successfully negotiated the broad outlines of an agreement with the company's creditors that would avoid bankruptcy proceedings. "We have a memorandum of understanding between all the lenders. It's a draft understanding that is equitable and fair that all the lenders have worked hard to bring about." Tridel's lenders were careful not to signal that they might initiate bankruptcy proceedings for fear that negative publicity might further undermine confidence in the company.

The question for Tridel in late 1993 became whether the company's officers could successfully forge a conclusive restructuring plan with lenders, especially in light of the fact that the banking community was taking few risks with property companies after numerous recent real estate failures.

Industry analysts maintained that Tridel had endured the worst of its credit problems, and were cautiously optimistic that if an agreement could be reached, Tridel could rebound despite a sluggish condominium market. As one commentator stated: "Tridel has been an astute survivor in an unpredictable market. Tridel has been the dominant player in the Toronto high-rise market for many years and they're magnificently positioned to serve that market. They know their customers, they know what their customers want and they've consistently led the way with innovative designs and leading-edge marketing programs."

Principal Subsidiaries: Aluma Systems Corp.; The Burke Company; Burke M & E Inc.; Trilan Developments Limited; Umacs of Canada Inc.; Beaverbrook Estates Inc. (75%).

Further Reading:

"Financing Deadline Looms for Tridel," *Globe and Mail,* April 3, 1993.
"Tridel Director Quits Board," *Globe and Mail,* April 3, 1992.
"Tridel Unit Breaches Loan Pact," *Globe and Mail,* April 30, 1992.
"Aluma May Push Tridel into a Loss This Year," *Globe and Mail,* June 18, 1992.

—Etan Vlessing

U.S. Robotics Inc.

8100 North McCormick Blvd.
Skokie, Illinois 60076-2999
U.S.A.
(708) 982-5010
Fax: (708) 982-5235

Public Company
Incorporated: 1976
Employees: 866
Sales: $189.2 million (1993)
Stock Exchanges: NASDAQ
SICs: 3661 Telephone and Telegraph Apparatus

U.S. Robotics is one of America's most promising manufacturers of high-tech equipment for computers. In the early 1980s, U.S. Robotics was involved in the manufacture of modems—devices that translate digital computer signals into analog signals for transmission over conventional telephone lines. Once considered a minor part of the computer, modems enable users to communicate with other computers, including large data bases and mainframes—in effect, giving the simple desktop device computing capabilities well beyond its own capacity. U.S. Robotics eventually evolved from being mainly a modem manufacturer to an important maker of internetworking equipment. It established a strategic partnership with Advantis (a joint venture between Sears Technology Services, Inc., and IBM) to supply Wide Area Network (WAN) this technology.

U.S. Robotics was started principally by Casey Cowell, a native of Detroit who completed his degree in economics at the University of Chicago in 1975. He then pursued a doctorate in economics at the University of Rochester, where a friend informed him that after he graduated he'd be the only person in the unemployment line who knew exactly why he was there.

Cowell, age 23, dropped out of the doctoral program, moved back to Chicago, and re-established contact with former classmates Paul Collard and Steve Muka, who had an interest in computers. Eventually, the group grew to five men who pooled $200 and laid out plans to build a keyboard and acoustic coupler for communication over phone lines.

At the time, computers consisted of huge mainframes, and four-function calculators were expensive novelties. FCC regulations would not permit direct connection of any device not built by

AT&T into the telephone network. While modems could translate digital signals into tones, these tones could only be fed mechanically into an AT&T handset.

In need of a name for the enterprise, one of Cowell's partners suggested a moniker from Isaac Asimov's 1950 science fiction novel *I, Robot,* which featured a company called U.S. Robot and Mechanical Men, Inc. Dropping the reference to mechanical men, the group settled simply on U.S. Robotics. Initially, the name was problematic, proving unfamiliar and therefore difficult for many people to spell. Furthermore, the name suggested that the company made robots.

Nevertheless, Cowell liked the name because it connoted advanced technology at a time when he and his partners were unsure what product the company would eventually produce. As it turned out, they perfected an acoustic coupler before the keyboard and, in need of cash, decided to begin marketing the device immediately.

Cowell later told the Chicago paper the *Reader* that, to his surprise, the city was replete with small factories that supplied plastic compounds, vacuum molding materials, electronic parts, and people willing to share their expertise with him. The first couplers were cast in mahogany molds, and the assembly line was located in Cowell's tiny Hyde Park apartment.

U.S. Robotics garnered sales initially through word of mouth. In time, customers started inquiring which terminal systems were recommended for use with the coupler. It soon occurred to Cowell that the company could generate additional revenue by distributing terminal connections made by other companies.

A range of equipment made by DEC, Teletype, General Electric, Applied Digital Data Televideo, and Perkin-Elmer was added to the U.S. Robotics product line. By the end of the first year, the company cleared $50,000 in sales, about half of which resulted from its distribution business.

The company launched its second product, a modem, in 1979, after FCC regulations were changed to allow non-AT&T equipment to be connected directly with the telephone network. The modem was operated by homemade circuit boards, created by silk screening paint over a copper-plated board, then immersing the board in an acid bath where all but the painted surfaces were dissolved. Cowell took out a classified ad in *Byte* magazine, and soon orders for the modems began rolling in. With its increased cash flow, Cowell rented manufacturing space west of Chicago's Loop.

In the early 1980s Cowell approached the investment community for the first time in search of capital, most importantly for a new manufacturing facility. In addition to being small, the west Loop facility had no shipping door, forcing workers to hand boxes through doorways and pack palettes on a makeshift loading dock. The search for funding was successful, and in 1984 U.S. Robotics relocated to a large factory space, formerly a pharmaceutical building, in Skokie, a suburb north of Chicago. The modem became U.S. Robotics' only product. Through research and development, modems were by now eight times faster than they had been only a few years earlier. Rather than sending a page of text every minute, the devices could shuttle through nearly ten.

The company encountered a market dominated by three major competitors, Hayes Microcomputer Products and Motorola's Codex and UDS divisions. Nevertheless, U.S. Robotics held several advantages over these competitors. Most importantly, the company manufactured its own "data pump," the computer chip that controlled the modem's transmission features. As a result, U.S. Robotics modems were built to its own specifications, not those of Rockwell and other chip manufacturers that supplied Hayes and Motorola. This allowed U.S. Robotics to develop faster modems and get them to market more quickly than its competitors.

While modems operating at a rate of 1,200 baud (signal variations per second) were once considered fast, by 1990 rates of 9,600 bits per second were becoming common. These systems multiplied the number of variations by using different forms of modulation on the signal. In 1990 the standard was known as V.32, or "V-dot 32." During this time, U.S. Robotics began development of a much faster modem system that could deliver 14.4 kilobits per second. Nevertheless, when the international standard, called "V.32bis," was adopted, U.S. Robotics also had a product meeting these specifications ready for manufacture.

The modem made it possible to send and receive information much more quickly, which was both a convenience for the computer user and, more importantly, a cost savings, involving less time that a user needed to keep expensive long distance telephone lines engaged. For many, the new modem represented a tremendous savings in operating expenses. While maintaining third place in the general modem market, with an 8.3 percent share, U.S. Robotics dominated the high-speed sector of the market, capturing a 43 percent share.

The risky but successful coup in the high end of the market did much to further the legitimacy of the U.S. Robotics name. Companies previously unfamiliar with U.S. Robotics became customers and, in doing so, identified themselves for future marketing efforts.

U.S. Robotics has also expanded into foreign markets; its first acquisition was Miracom Technology, Ltd. (later called U.S. Robotics Ltd. UK), with which the company established EEC sales and manufacturing capabilities, in 1989. In 1991, U.S. Robotics' sales and marketing concern, U.S. Robotics, s.a., was established in Europe. Two years later, the company acquired P.N.B., s.a., a designer and manufacturer of data communications products for IBM-compatible personal computers and workstations and other pcmcia products. This overseas presence not only gave U.S. Robotics access to international market intelligence and standards, but enabled the company to maintain the same level of local market support worldwide that it had in North America.

In 1993 U.S. Robotics changed the face of the personal communications market through aggressive pricing moves and an expanded retail presence with its Sportster line of modems. Capitalizing on the low-cost digital signal processor (DSP)-based architecture—developed for the company's line of Courier organizational modems—the company's brand image as a technical leader and its well-known quality, allowed U.S. Robotics to become the dominant modem supplier to the personal communications market.

U.S. Robotics also serves its worldwide corporate customers with three product lines: Courier organizational desktop modems; Shard Access local area network (LAN) communications servers; and Total Control, analog and digital WAN Hubs.

Courier was the first modem on the market to include industry-standard V.32bis 14,000 bps data transmission. U.S. Robotics motherboard/daughterboard architecture enhances the Courier's functionally, and allows the company to offer the first modem with a field upgrade to the upcoming V.34 28, 800 bps architecture.

U.S. Robotics' two WAN hubs serve distinct markets. The Enterprise Network Hub serves the corporate market, which requires high-speed, error-free data transmission for applications such as file transfer and electronic mail. The Transaction Processing Hub provides the quick connections and multiple protocols needed for applications such as credit card verification, point of sale terminals and inquiry response.

Additional areas in which U.S. Robotics planned for future product introduction in 1994 included an even faster modem system run on the "V.Fast" protocol, and a cellular modem system called HST Cellular (for "high speed technology"). This system would allow data transmissions over a cellular telephone network, again with adaptive speed leveling, even while traveling between cell sites at 60 miles per hour.

U.S. Robotics raised $28.3 million through an initial public offering, in which 2,380,000 shares of common stock were offered by the company. U.S. Robotics hoped to avoid excessive debt, keep a lean operation centered on customer needs, and maintain a generous research and development budget. The company planned to go private in 1994.

Principal Subsidiaries: U.S. Robotics, Ltd. (UK); U.S. Robotics S.A. (France); P.N.B., s.a. (France).

Further Reading:

"The Disenchanted Professor," *Industry Week,* August 19, 1985, p. 49.
"How to Succeed in High Tech, Without Really Knowing What You're Doing," *Reader,* April 13, 1990, p. 1.
"Making the Right Calls at U.S. Robotics," *Business Week,* December 21, 1992, p. R86.
"U.S. Robotics Has High Aspirations for Lowly Modem," *Wall Street Journal,* July 27, 1993.
"U.S. Robotics Not Shy About Plans," *Chicago Tribune,* March 17, 1991, Sec. 20, p. 5.

—John Simley

Union Carbide Corporation

39 Old Ridgebury Road
Danbury, Connecticut 06817
U.S.A.
(203) 794-2000
Fax: (203) 794-7031

Public Company
Incorporated: 1917 as Union Carbide & Carbon Corp.
Employees: 15,000
Sales: $5 billion
Stock Exchanges: New York Amsterdam Basel Brussels
    Frankfurt Geneva Lausanne London Paris Zurich
SICs: 2869 Industrial Organic Chemicals Nec; 2821 Plastics
    Materials & Resins; 2813 Industrial Gases; 6719 Holding
    Companies Nec

Union Carbide Corporation is the world's largest producer of
ethylene glycol, commonly used as antifreeze, and is a leading
manufacturer of the world's most widely used plastic, polyethylene. In spite of a massive fatal disaster at its Bhopal, India,
pesticide plant in 1984 and a devastating takeover attempt that
followed, the corporation remained one of top twenty exporters
in the United States in the early 1990s. Union Carbide pioneered the petrochemicals industry and introduced the first two
modern plastics. The company became known as "chemist to
the chemical industry and metallurgist to the metals industry"
because of its production of many of the building blocks of
those two industries.

The Union Carbide & Carbon Corp. (UCC) was formed in 1917
from the combination of four companies: Union Carbide Co.
(incorporated 1898), Linde Air Products Co. (incorporated
1907), National Carbon Co., Inc. (incorporated 1899), and
Prest-O-Lite Co., Inc. (incorporated 1913). The new entity was
organized as a holding company, with its four members acting
relatively autonomously and cooperating where their businesses
converged.

The merger combined what had often been competing interests
to form an industrial chemicals powerhouse. The oldest member
of the quartet, Union Carbide, had been formed to manufacture
calcium carbide, which was used in the production of metal
alloys. A by-product of alloying calcium carbide with aluminum was acetylene, a gas that company executives hoped would
prove useful for street and household lighting. But when

Thomas Edison's electric incandescent light bulbs proved more
practical for most lighting, it looked as if Union Carbide's
acetylene lighting business was obsolete. Luckily, a French
researcher discovered that acetylene could be burned in oxygen
to produce a hot, metal-cutting flame. A whole new market for
the gas emerged, and UCC was ready to take advantage of it.

The company continued to manufacture calcium carbide at
plants in Sault Ste. Marie, Michigan, and Niagara Falls, New
York, and by 1900 the Union Carbide's capital stock stood at $6
million. Union Carbide combined America's first commercial
high-carbon ferrochrome process, which had been developed by
company founder Major James T. Moorhead in the late 1890s,
with a metal alloying business acquired in 1906. The subsidiary
created a line of metals composed of iron and one or more other
metals, known in the industry as ferroalloys. Ferroalloys made
the production of alloy steels more efficient, because they could
be incorporated more easily with steel to create new metals with
specific properties. Union Carbide's low-carbon ferrochrome,
for example, was a precursor of modern stainless steel.

Union Carbide had been involved with the Linde Air Products
Co. through joint acetylene experiments for about six years
before the formation of the UCC holding company. As one of
America's first oxygen-producing concerns and (after 1917)
part of one of the country's largest chemical companies, Linde
soon became the world's largest producer of industrial gases
like acetylene, hydrogen and nitrogen. These gases formed the
foundation of the petrochemical industry. The Prest-O-Lite
Company had been one of Union Carbide's primary competitors for most of the two companies' histories, but three years of
cooperative acetylene experiments among UCC, Prest-O-Lite,
and Linde made the merger more smooth. Before the turn of the
century, National Carbon Co. had produced the first commercial
dry cell battery and offered it under the Eveready trademark.
The well-known brand would be a UCC staple for the next
seven decades.

With combined research efforts and a national push for new
technologies to help win World War I, new developments came
in rapid succession at Union Carbide. New products included
batteries for portable radios and corrosion and heat-resistant
ferroalloys that strengthened the steel used to build skyscrapers,
bridges, and automobiles. The government's need for ethylene
during "the great war" also generated interest in hydrocarbon
byproducts. These substances were made from calcium carbide
and would later become the raw materials for the production of
plastics, synthetic rubber, fibers, solvents, explosives, and industrial chemicals. In 1919 the first production of synthetic
ethylene began. Ethylene would develop into the industry's
most important industrial hydrocarbon, eventually used in polyethylene (plastics), polystyrene (styrofoam), and antifreeze,
among other products. Union Carbide's Prestone brand ethylene glycol soon became the top-selling antifreeze, a position it
held throughout the twentieth century.

The new corporate structure enabled UCC to leverage the combined assets of its four primary subsidiaries and embark on an
acquisitions spree that wasn't even halted by the Great Depression. In 1919 alone, the company acquired an acetylene manufacturer, created Canadian subsidiaries of National Carbon Co.
and Prest-O-Lite, and purchased a new headquarters at 42nd

Street and Madison Avenue in New York City. This new home served the company until the late 1970s. During the 1920s, Union Carbide expanded its overseas interests with the acquisition of a Norwegian hydroelectric plant in 1925 and a calcium carbide/ferroalloy plant in that same country in 1929. The holding company added to its battery business with the purchase of Manhattan Electrical Supply Co. in 1926. UCC annexed two domestic industrial gases interests in 1928 and strengthened its industrial electric furnace business with the acquisition of the Acheson Graphite Corporation in 1928.

One of UCC's most vital acquisitions of the 1920s was the purchase of U.S. Vanadium Co.'s Colorado mine, mill, and reduction plant in 1926. Carbide's subsequent vanadium research was a truly corporate venture that coordinated several of the company's subsidiaries and eventually involved the company in the government's atomic energy program. Uranium-bearing materials were located and provided by U.S. Vanadium. UCC scientists demonstrated that gaseous diffusion could be used to separate quantities of uranium-235 and contracted with the federal government in 1943 to operate the Oak Ridge Gaseous Diffusion Plant. After intensive research, UCC's Linde Company perfected a refining process for treating uranium concentrates. A plant was built and operated by the Electro Metallurgical Company (acquired in 1922) to provide extensive metallurgical research, and manufacture uranium. Finally, Union Carbide and Carbon Research Laboratories contributed to the development of the atomic weapon itself.

In 1939 UCC acquired the Bakelite Corporation, which developed the first modern plastic, phenol formaldehyde. And in 1941, Carbide made permanent-press fabrics possible with its development of glyoxal.

Union Carbide earned a reputation for developing raw materials for the chemical and metals industries during World War II. Since natural rubber was in very short supply during the war, the company resumed its experiments with butene, a hydrocarbon that was developed into a synthetic rubber. Modern neoprene is a familiar example of butene's application.

Postwar prosperity camouflaged nagging problems at UCC: the company was chalking up a bad track record of discovering new substances and processes, but not capitalizing on them. For example, UCC pioneered urethanes, but didn't commit enough financial resources to the new field in time to profit. The company also made permanent-press fabrics possible with its development of glyoxal, but couldn't come up with a consumer product that maximized its profit potential. It often ended up riding the coattails of movements it had spawned. Union Carbide's program of internal promotion engendered company loyalty, but also stifled creativity. The company started a slide into relative mediocrity that, with few exceptions, would consume the next three decades.

A succession of well-meaning chief executives kept UCC in "turnaround mode." Under the direction of CFO Morse G. Dial, Carbide absorbed its major operating subsidiaries and formally relinquished its holding company status in 1949. Dial hoped to reverse the excessive autonomy at UCC by creating a "President's Office" composed of the corporation's division heads. The company name was changed to Union Carbide

Corporation in 1957 to reflect its reorganization from a holding company to a diversified corporation. By that time, Union Carbide and Carbon Corporation had established some 400 plants in the United States and Canada, in addition to overseas affiliates. The company went from having 18 autonomous divisions to just four primary domestic groups: Union Carbide Chemicals Co., Linde Co., Union Carbide Plastics Co., and Union Carbide Consumer Products Co. Even though these corporate segments were technically divisions, the retention of the word "company" in each section's name represented the perpetuation of the decentralized management structure of a holding company, and its detrimental effect on Union Carbide continued.

Polyethylene, a plastic used in squeeze bottles (high-density polyethylene), as well as in films and sheeting (low-density polyethylene), became Union Carbide's largest dollar-volume product after World War II. An olefins division was set up in the 1950s to supply low-cost raw materials for the chemicals and plastics industry in the 1950s. For several years the company sold these plastics to other manufacturers. But Carbide finally capitalized on this discovery in 1964, when Glad branded plastic wraps, bags, and straws were introduced. Within just four years, Glad became the leading brand in its market.

By the 1960s, Union Carbide occupied the top spot in many of its primary fields, including industrial gases, carbon electrodes for industrial electric furnaces, batteries, atomic energy, polyethylene plastic, and ferroalloys. In 1965 the conglomerate's sales topped $2 billion for the first time. And from 1956 to 1966, Union Carbide parlayed a few plants in a dozen countries into 60 major subsidiary and associated companies with plants in 30 countries serving over 100 markets. International operations of the conglomerate contributed 29 percent of its annual sales, and mid-decade the company name was changed to Union Carbide International Co. to reflect its increased global presence.

But in spite of consistently rising sales (which doubled from 1960 to 1970 to $3 million) Union Carbide's profits plummeted and stayed low from 1966 to 1971. Carbide could claim leading market shares, but top shares of low-margin commodities still equaled low profits. Industry-wide overcapacity in ferroalloys ran as high as 70 percent in the early 1960s, and prices for these products fell 25 percent. The company was compelled to cut its ferroalloys work force by 40 percent and close a major plant at Niagara Falls. To make matters worse, the market for low-density polyethylene stagnated for the first time in over 20 years.

Union Carbide was still the United States' second-largest chemical producer, but it invariably lagged behind most of its competitors in terms of growth and profitability during this period. Misguided investments in petroleum, pharmaceuticals, semiconductors, mattresses, and undersea equipment, combined with a $1 billion petrochemicals complex at Taft, Louisiana, which ran in the red for the last three years of the 1960s, further tarnished Union Carbide's standing. Not surprisingly, the conglomerate's stock dropped from $75 in 1965 to $45 in 1968 as the company "earned a reputation for aimless fumbling," according to *Business Week*.

Unfortunately for Union Carbide, environmental complaints about the company's Marietta, Ohio, ferroalloy plant came to a head in 1971, when consumer champion Ralph Nader brought a decade of local residents' complaints into the national spotlight. For four years, the conglomerate had largely ignored public and government efforts to make it clean up several plants that were polluting the air over West Virginia. Union Carbide's resistance to outside influence gave it the public image of a reactionary bully concerned only with profits and scornful of the environment, a stigma that would haunt the company for years to come. In 1971, UCC capitulated to federal orders that it immediately use more expensive low-sulphur coal to reduce noxious sulfur dioxide emissions by 40 percent. The company was given a fall 1974 deadline to install $8 million in advanced emissions scrubbers.

The bad news continued, as the recession of 1970–71 hammered commodities companies like UCC, with the chemicals and plastics markets entering another cycle of overcapacity. From 1968 to 1973, UCC's sales grew by only 4 percent annually, well below the industry average. CFO and president F. Perry Wilson, who had been promoted to those offices in 1971, made his bid to turn Union Carbide around. His restructuring plan included three primary changes. First, he tried to pare back peripheral activities and focus on plastics and chemicals. Among the businesses sold were a bedding company, most of UCC's oil and gas interests, a pollution-monitoring devices business, a plastic container line, a fibers business, a jewelry line, and an insect repellant business. Second, he worked to shift the corporate focus from market share to profitability. Finally, Wilson tried to plan capital and capacity investments so that UCC could avoid the inefficiencies and plummeting prices that had accompanied industry-wide overcapacity in the past.

A New Business Development Department was formed in 1970 to coordinate the three areas outside of chemicals and plastics that Wilson didn't sell: Biomedical Systems, Marine Foods, and Agricultural Systems. Another key organizational change was the disbanding of the Consumer & Related Products Division, which had contributed 22 percent of UCC's annual revenues. The Eveready business was split off into a Battery Products Division, while Glad and Prestone were coordinated in a division with the production of their raw materials. Despite the fragmentation of the Consumer Products Division, Wilson said that he hoped that consumer products would contribute 50 percent of UCC's revenues in the future. He recognized that these relatively stable, high-margin product lines sustained Union Carbide through economic downturns.

For a few years, it looked as if the new strategy was working. From 1973 to 1981, earnings per share rose 100 percent. UCC increased productivity dramatically during the late 1960s and early 1970s to keep its corporate head above water. From 1967 to 1973, physical output of chemicals and plastics rose 60 percent, while per-pound production costs were cut by one-third. William S. Sneath continued these trends when he became chairman and CEO in 1977. Still, the company found itself increasingly strapped for cash. Steadily rising expenses in Europe resulted in a $32 million loss in 1978, which forced Carbide to divest virtually all of its European petrochemicals and plastics operations. That same year, UCC was forced by its creditors to retire $292 million in long-term debt, which forced it to borrow another $300 million in 1979. That year, Carbide's

Standard & Poor's credit rating fell from AA to A +, and its stock fell as low as 42 percent below its $61 book value.

Chairman Sneath embarked on another round of cost-cutting in 1980, pruning the executive staff by 1,000 and divesting a total of 39 businesses. Sneath retained six primary businesses: graphite electrodes, batteries, agricultural products, polyethylene, and industrial gases. By 1980, Carbide had 116,000 employees at over 500 plants, mines, and laboratories in 130 countries, bringing in over $9 billion in annual sales. Sneath embarked on a plan to invest profits into high-margin consumer goods and specialty chemicals.

The massive disaster at Union Carbide's pesticide plant in Bhopal, India, in December 1984 struck the corporation just as it was beginning to make lasting strides toward profitability. UCC had established battery plants in India as early as the mid-1920s, and had seven plants with 5,000 employees there by 1967. India's chronic food shortages precipitated a government-sponsored "Green Revolution" in the 1960s, with the country's socialist government eager to join Union Carbide in establishing pesticide and fertilizer plants. In 1975 the Indian government granted Union Carbide a license to manufacture pesticides, and a plant was built on the sparsely populated outskirts of the regional capital of Bhopal. The plant drew more than 900,000 people to Bhopal by 1984. Union Carbide officials estimated that at least five tons of methyl isocyanate (MIC) seeped out of the plant in just 30 minutes one day in December 1984. The accident killed over 2,300 people and permanently injured another 10,000. *Newsweek* magazine called the incident "the worst industrial accident in history."

Five senior Indian executives of Union Carbide were arrested. The Indian government charged Warren Anderson, chairman of Union Carbide's board, with "corporate and criminal liability" and accused the Union Carbide management of "cruel and wanton negligence." Many class action suits were filed against Union Carbide on behalf of the victims. In April 1988, a court in India ordered Carbide to pay $192 million in "interim" damages. Union Carbide and the Indian government reached a much-criticized settlement for $470 million in 1989.

In addition to the human toll, the tragedy set off a chain reaction at Carbide: by 1985, the company's market value dropped by two-thirds to less than $3 billion, and GAF Corp.'s Samuel Heyman accumulated enough stock to mount a hostile takeover bid of $5.3 billion. After working for two decades to expand its consumer products lines, Carbide was forced to sell off its Consumer Products Division, a profitable group that included Glad trash bags, Eveready batteries, Prestone, and STP automotive products, for $840 million. The corporation borrowed $2.8 billion, raised a total of $3.6 billion in asset sales, and repurchased $4.4 billion in stock to repulse Heyman's attack.

Carbide scaled back to the three main business lines—chemicals and plastics, industrial gases, and carbon products—that were once its strength, and benefitted from sharply reduced interest rates and falling costs of petrochemical feedstocks. But the company had lost the safety net provided by its consumer products. Union Carbide's debt stood at 63 percent of capital and its equity was cut to a quarter of its former value. Income rose 78 percent in 1987 to $232 million, but high debt service made it hard for the company to develop and introduce new products. In 1988 UCC reduced its debt by more than $400 million and increase equity by almost $600 million.

By 1988, Union Carbide's corporate identity had begun to take clearer shape. Sales hit $8.3 billion (one-third below the 1981 peak), profits were up to more than $300 million, and the company had a new CEO, Robert D. Kennedy. His goals for the company included growth—an ambitious prospect in the face of depleted finances. His solution was to trim operating expenses and generate profits. Between 1984 and 1988, payroll was reduced from 98,000 employees to 43,000, while Carbide set up joint ventures with British Petroleum Co. and Allied-Signal Corp. and made a few modest acquisitions.

In 1989 Carbide advanced slightly on its long journey toward financial recovery. Net income was $573 million. Profits in the chemicals and plastics divisions put Carbide in the number two spot on the list of the top ten publicly traded companies in America. The company succeeded in reducing its debt-to-capital ratio to below 50 percent, and invested $181 million in research and development. That year, the company introduced its proprietary LIHDE Oxygen Combustion System, which used pure oxygen to burn organic wastes.

Carbide's fate was far from settled. A $3.3 billion debt stymied both diversification and overseas expansion. Carbide's sales were dependent on cyclical commodities such as polyethylene, and as the chemical industry stumbled, earnings declined. Net income decreased 46 percent from 1990. The brightest prospects were in the industrial gas unit—Carbide remained number one in North America in that industry, with $2.4 billion in sales.

The company launched a "work simplification program" in the early 1990s. The program had a cost reduction goal of $400 million a year by the end of 1994. Carbide progressed toward this goal by repurchasing 20 million shares, spinning off two small businesses, and selling 50 percent of its carbon business in 1990.

As a fitting mark to Union Carbide's 75th anniversary in 1992, the company had the year's best-performing stock on the Dow Jones list of 30 industrials. Carbide was half way to achieving its $400 million cost reduction goal, and had endured a loss of $187 million. The dramatically smaller corporation had shifted its focus from diversification to becoming a low-cost leader in basic chemicals. This strategy included uncharacteristic environmentalism: Carbide anticipated "inevitable government mandates on waste reduction and recycling" when it started reprocessing plastic bottles in 1992. After Bhopal, UCC's efforts helped raise industry performance standards and levels worldwide, and the company was praised for its "Responsible Care" efforts.

Sales showed a slight gain in the 1993 first quarter, closing at $1.19 billion. The sale of Union Carbide's OrganoSilicon business for $220 million completed Kennedy's program to divest $500 million in assets. Although some Wall Street analysts predicted that Union Carbide Corporation would be subsumed by another firm, others characterized it as a "surprisingly potent company."

Principal Subsidiaries: Amerchol Corporation; Amko Service Company; Bayox, Inc.: Beaucar Minerals, Inc.; BEK III Inc.; Be-Kan, Inc.; Bentley Sales Co. Inc.; Blue Creek Coal Company, Inc.; Catalyst Technology, Inc.; Cellulosic Products, Inc.; Chemicals Marine Fleet, Inc.; Dexter Realty Corporation; Gas Technics Gases and Equipment Centers of Eastern Pennsylvania, Inc.; Gas Technics Gases and Equipment Centers of New Jersey, Inc.; Gas Technics Gases and Equipment Centers of Ohio, Inc.; Global Industrial Corporation; Hampton Roads Welders Supply Company, Inc.; Harvey Company; Innovative Membrane Systems, Inc.; International Cryogenic Equipment Corporation; Iweco, Inc.; Karba Minerals, Inc.; KSC Liquidation, Inc.; XTI Chemicals, Inc.; Linde Homecare Medical Systems, Inc.; Linox Welding Supply Co.; London Chemical Company, Inc.; Media Buyers Inc.; Merritt-Holland Company; Mon-Arc Welding Supply, Inc.; Nova Tran Corporation; Paulsboro Packaging Inc.; Phoenix Research Corporation; Polysak, Inc.; Prentiss Glycol Company; Presto Hartford, Inc.; Presto Welding Supplies, Inc.; Seadrift Pipeline Corporation; Soilsery, Inc.; South Charleston Sewage Treatment Company; UCAR Capital Corporation; UCAR Energy Services Corporation; UCAR Interam, Inc.; UCAR Louisiana Pipeline Company; UCAR Pipeline Incorporated; UCORE Ltd.; Umetco Minerals Exploration; Umetco Minerals Sales Corporation; Unigas, Inc.; Union Carbide Africa and Middle East, Inc.; Union Carbide Canada Ltd. (74.5%); Union Carbide Caribe, Inc.; Union Carbide Communications Company, Inc.; Union Carbide Engineering and Hydrocarbons Service Company, Inc.: Union Carbide Engineering and Technology Services; Union Carbide Ethylene Oxide/Glycol Company; Union Carbide Europe, Inc.; Union Carbide Films-Packaging, Inc.; Union Carbide Grafito, Inc.; Union Carbide Imaging Systems, Inc.; Union Carbide Industrial Services Company; Union Carbide Inter-America, Inc.; Union Carbide International Capital Corporation; Union Carbide International Sales Corporation; Union Carbide Polyolefins Development Company, Inc.; UNISON Transformer Services, Inc.; Vametco Minerals Corporation; V.B. Anderson Co. (85.33%); Welders Service Center of Nebraska, Inc.; Wolfe Welding Supply Company, Inc. The company also lists subsidiaries in the following countries: Australia, Austria, Belgium, Bermuda, Brazil, Canada, Colombia, Costa Rica, Ecuador, Egypt, France, Ghana, Greece, Guatemala, Hong Kong, India, Indonesia, Iran, Italy, Japan, Kenya, Malaysia, Malawi, Mexico, Netherlands, Netherlands Antilles, New Zealand, Nigeria, Pakistan, Panama, Philippines, Puerto Rico, Singapore, South Africa, South Korea, Spain, Sri Lanka, Sweden, Switzerland, Taiwan, Thailand, Turkey, United Kingdom, U.S. Virgin Islands, Venezuela, West Germany, and Zimbabwe.

Further Reading:

"Carbide Lays Out Its Strategy through 1983," *Chemical Week,* v. 125, September 19, 1979, 49.

"A Corporate Polluter Learns the Hard Way," *Business Week,* February 6, 1971, 52–56.

"The Cure for a Chemical Giant," *Business Week,* July 14, 1973, 88–92.

Everest, Larry, *Behold the Poison Cloud: Union Carbide's Bhopal Massacre,* Chicago: Banner Press, 1986.

"Giant with a (Giant) Headache," *Forbes,* December 1, 1968, 24–26.

Hoffman, Charles B. "Union Carbide Formula Calls for Higher Net," *Barron's,* v. 53, April 16, 1973, 31, 39.

"How Union Carbide Has Cleaned up Its Image," *Business Week,* August 2, 1978, 46.

Lappen, Alyssa A., "Breaking Up Is Hard to Do," *Forbes,* December 10, 1990, p. 102.

Levy, Robert. "The Man from Uncarb," *Dun's Review & Modern Industry,* v. 87, July 1966, 46–48.

Menzies, Hugh D. "Union Carbide Raises Its Voice," *Fortune,* v. 98, September 25, 1978, 86–88.

Norman, James R., "Carbide Saves Itself—But Was It Worth It?" *Business Week,* January 20, 1986, p. 26.

"Turnaround Year for Union Carbide?" *Financial World,* January 5, 1972, 5, 23.

"A New Union Carbide Is Slowly Starting to Gel," *Business Week,* April 18, 1986, p. 68.

"Union Carbide: Revolution without the 'R'," *Forbes,* November 1, 1963, 22–26.

—by April S. Dougal
updated by Marinell Landa

Union Texas Petroleum

Union Texas Petroleum Holdings, Inc.

1330 Post Oak Boulevard
P.O. Box 2120
Houston, Texas 77252-2120
U.S.A.
(713) 623-6544
Fax: (713) 968-2771

Public Company
Incorporated: 1982
Employees: 1,000
Sales: $714.01 million
Stock Exchanges: New York Pacific
SICs: 1311 Crude Petroleum and Natural Gas

Union Texas Petroleum Holdings, Inc. is one of the largest independent oil and gas producing companies in the United States. Also engaged in oil and gas exploration overseas, the company conducts its principal operations in the United Kingdom sector of the North Sea, Indonesia, and Pakistan. Union Texas is also engaged in the manufacturing of petrochemicals.

Union Texas traces its corporate history to the Union Sulphur Company, a sulphur-mining firm founded in southern Louisiana in 1896. In 1926 Union Sulphur entered the oil business, completing its first oil well in Louisiana and then extending its exploration activities into the Rio Grande Valley of Texas. In 1953 the company discovered one of its first major oil finds in the Lake Aurthur South field in Louisiana, which soon became the company's biggest domestic oil producing property.

In 1960 the company—then called Union Oil & Gas Corporation—merged with Texas Natural Gas Corporation, combining the oil and gas production operations of Union Oil and the natural gas liquids processing and marketing facilities of Texas Natural Gas under the name Union Texas Natural Gas Corporation. The operations of the new company included oil and gas production facilities in the United States, Canada, Venezuela, and Argentina, as well as the propane marketing operations of Texgas, the former Texas Natural subsidiary. A year after the merger Union Texas Natural Gas expanded its oil and gas activities when it purchased an oil refinery and pipeline system from Anderson-Prichard Oil Corporation.

In 1962 Allied Chemical Corporation acquired the two-year-old Union Texas Natural Gas, renaming it the Union Texas Petroleum Division. In the transaction two former Union Texas Natural Gas executives, J. Howard Marshall, president, and A.M. Burden, chairperson, became directors of Allied Chemical's board. Over the next 23 years Union Texas Petroleum operated in the form of unincorporated divisions or wholly owned subsidiaries of Allied.

Union Texas expanded its principal business lines during the 1960s, participating in the joint venture construction of an ethylene manufacturing plant in Louisiana, broadening its propane operations through the acquisition of Southern Propane Company, and participating in joint venture exploration programs in the North Sea. During the 1970s Union Texas laid a foundation for long term activities overseas when it became actively engaged in exploration operations not only in the United Kingdom North Sea, but also in Indonesia, Pakistan, and Argentina.

In 1972 Union Texas and its partners became active in Indonesia and discovered a sizable gas field in East Kalimantan. During the early 1970s Union Texas and its exploration partners also made significant United Kingdom North Sea discoveries, including the Piper oil field and the Claymore oil field. Union Texas entered Pakistan in 1977 after receiving a government concession to explore for, develop, and produce oil and gas on a tract of land in southeastern Pakistan. Two years later Union Texas and its partners won a 25-year contract to develop oil fields in Argentina.

Between 1978 and 1980—with the overseas operations of Union Texas expanding—Allied began selling off domestic pipeline operations which had been losing money because of long term, fixed price contracts. In 1978 the 328-mile intrastate Winnie pipeline system was sold, and two years later two gas pipelines subsidiaries in Louisiana were sold.

In 1979 Allied, looking for new leadership, recruited Edward L. Hennessy Jr. to serve as its chair and chief executive. Hennessy—who would move Allied in and out of over 50 different businesses during the next decade—took over the corporation at a time when more than 70 percent of the diversified company's profits were coming from oil and gas, while Allied's chemical businesses were either losing money or barely breaking even.

By 1980 the Union Texas division was participating in oil and gas ventures worldwide, operating a few gas processing facilities in Texas and neighboring states and serving as a retail and wholesale marketer of liquified petroleum gas in the eastern United States. In 1980 Union Texas launched a program to enlarge its natural gas processing operations, and during the next two years the company expanded its existing plants and acquired several other gas processing systems in Texas, Louisiana, and Oklahoma. During this period of expansion the company focused its domestic gas exploration activities in Texas and Louisiana, where the company made a number of discoveries between 1980 and 1982.

International operations also continued to expand during the early 1980s, and between 1980 and 1981 the company made oil and gas discoveries in the Canadian provinces of Alberta and

British Columbia. In 1981 Union Texas acquired an exploration tract offshore the Ivory Coast, and a Union Texas-operated venture discovered the company's first oil in Pakistan. Union Texas solidified its presence in Indonesia in early 1982 when it signed a production sharing contract with the Indonesian state oil company.

In 1982 world oil prices began to decline, and while Allied began cutting corporate costs, it continued to pump increasing amounts of money into oil and gas exploration and development. In April 1982 Union Texas further expanded its domestic operations, acquiring a joint venture interest in Supron Energy Corporation, which substantially increased Union Texas's exploration leaseholds in the western United States. Before the end of 1982, Union Texas Petroleum was incorporated as a wholly owned, Houston-based gas and oil subsidiary of Allied.

In 1983 A. Clark Johnson was named president and chief operating officer of Union Texas. A year later Johnson was named to the additional post of chief executive, succeeding William D. Geitz, who remained chairperson. Beginning in 1983 Union Texas—seeking additional natural gas sales— began pursuing spot or short-term sales of natural gas to local distribution companies and major end-users.

During the mid-1980s Union Texas continued expanding and maximizing its interest in exploration ventures in Indonesia and Pakistan. In 1984 the company participated in a joint acquisition which brought Union Texas a 50 percent interest in ENSTAR Corporation, a lucrative Indonesian oil and gas company. Between 1984 and 1985 the company made several discoveries in the southeastern area of Pakistan, where Union Texas had initially uncovered natural gas in the 1970s. During the mid-1980s Union Texas began placing an increasing emphasis on offshore domestic operations and securing federally leased tracts in the Gulf of Mexico. These operations were facilitated by the company's development of a semisubmersible offshore drilling rig earlier in the decade.

In July 1985 Union Texas Petroleum Holdings, Inc. became an independent company, after Allied—in the throes of refocusing its principal business operations—sold a 50.3 percent interest in the oil and gas company through a leveraged buyout valued at $1.7 billion. At the time of the sale about one-third of Allied's profits were coming from oil and gas.

The Union Texas stake was acquired by an investor group comprised of the New York investment firm Kohlberg, Kravis, Roberts & Company (KKR) and Union Texas's top management. This collective acquired the stake in Union Texas with $250 million in cash and an additional $1.15 billion borrowed against Union Texas's assets from a group of banks and institutional investors. Following the leveraged buyout Allied and KKR each owned a 49.7 percent interest in Union Texas, while Union Texas managers owned the remainder of the company's stock. A. Clark Johnson retained his post as chief executive and also became chair of Union Texas, heading up a board of directors which included five members each from both Allied and KKR.

Union Texas's domestic production capacity was significantly boosted in 1986 with the startup of various Gulf of Mexico operations. However, a dramatic drop in crude oil prices forced Union Texas to cut its expenses, and in 1986 the company sold its subsidiary Texgas and abandoned several undeveloped lease tracts, raising more than $325 million through the sale of assets. Despite the company's 1986 cost-cutting moves, which included slashing its workforce by more than 12 percent for the second straight year, Union Texas lost $57.5 million in 1986 on revenues of $1.25 billion.

By 1987 Union Texas had reduced the amount of bank debt it had carried into the leveraged buyout by more than $375 million. With investor interest in oil stocks climbing, Union Texas, then the nation's largest independent oil and gas company, announced plans to go public. Allied and KKR initially agreed to each sell a 17 percent stake in Union Texas. However, just days prior to the late September 1987 offering, the two shareholding companies pulled out of the sale after market for oil stocks softened due to an excess of oil production by the Organization of Petroleum Export Countries (OPEC).

Union Texas scaled down its planned debut on the New York Stock Exchange, reducing its public offering from 29 million to 18 million common shares, diluting previously owned common stock, and reducing the ownership of Allied and KKR to about 39 percent each. Union Texas raised $236 million through the stock sale, which helped push the company back into the black and earn $56 million in 1987 on revenues of $1.25 billion.

The following year Union Texas, in response to a growing local demand, announced plans for a $71 million expansion of its jointly-owned ethylene plant. During the late 1980s Union Texas also boosted its interest in domestic and Gulf of Mexico projects as well as its production activities in areas where it had a history of success, including the North Sea, Pakistan, Indonesia, and Argentina.

In July 1988 an explosion at the Piper Alpha field production platform in the North Sea—operated by one of Union Texas's partners, Occidental Petroleum—killed 167 workers and shut down a sizable portion of Union Texas's North Sea operations. Business interruption insurance covered the company's loss of sales, and eventually Union Texas received a $228 million insurance settlement. Despite the loss of Piper field production, the company's earnings jumped 96 percent to $109.3 million on revenues of $1.28 billion.

The company's financial picture continued to improve in 1989, due in part to an 89 percent increase in offshore production in the Gulf of Mexico and an oil discovery at the Saltire field in the North Sea. For the year Union Texas earned $173 million on sales of $1.16 billion.

Union Texas entered 1990 committed to focusing on and expanding its core nondomestic operations overseas, while also initiating new overseas ventures. In 1990 the company signed a 20-year extension agreement with the national oil company of Indonesia, solidifying its presence in that country until 2018. Early that year Union Texas also signed an agreement for a new venture to explore 4.4 million acres offshore Argentina. Moreover, the company began a development project in Egypt, conducted seismic studies on a tract offshore Spain, and acquired a 20 percent interest in a petroleum prospect license awarded by the government of Papua New Guinea.

In May 1990 Union Texas announced that it would put itself up for sale in order to increase shareholder benefits. However, after seven months on the block, the company took itself off the market after failing to get the price it wanted for the entire company. For the year Union Texas earned $116 million on revenues of $1.33 billion.

In 1991 the company began aggressively expanding its exploration activities into several frontier ventures, including those in Papua New Guinea and offshore Argentina. The company also launched a program to identify coal basins in Europe with high potential for yielding methane gas and was awarded two permits in Spain to explore for natural gas in coal beds using a methane recovery technology. In the North Sea, Union Texas focused on completing a new production platform to replace the Piper Alpha platform, dedicating $136 million in 1991 to the redevelopment of Piper field and the development of the nearby Saltire field.

Despite its decision not to sell the company as a whole, Union Texas entered 1991 with plans to sell the majority of its North American operations, and by the end of the year the company had sold its domestic offshore oil and gas business for $475 million, its North American oil and gas business, excluding Alaskan operations, for $260 million, and its domestic natural gas processing business, including 12 gas processing plants, for $135 million. For 1991 Union Texas earned $333 million—including a one-time gain of $203 million stemming from the sale of businesses—on revenues of $1.08 billion.

After selling its U.S. assets, Union Texas entered 1992 free from exposure to the cyclical domestic natural gas market. The divestitures also left Union Texas a more sharply-focused company, with activities in the United Kingdom North Sea, Indonesia, and Pakistan serving as cornerstones of its business.

During 1992 the company launched several new exploration programs, highlighted by a crude oil discovery offshore northern Alaska. The company's overseas joint ventures in Indonesia and Pakistan set production records, and Union Texas entered the French gas market after securing a permit to explore for oil and gas in France using coalbed methane technology.

In November 1992 Allied—in the throes of its own restructuring and consolidation program—sold its 39 percent stake in Union Texas in a secondary public offering of more than 33 million shares. Union Texas received no proceeds from the sale, which left about 61 percent of the company in the hands of the general public. That year Union Texas earned $109 million on revenues of $714 million. As a result of the sale of its domestic assets, Union Texas was listed by *Fortune* as having the biggest 1992 sales decrease among Fortune 500 Companies, with divestitures leading to a 34 percent drop in sales from a year earlier.

While continuing to depend on its more established operations, Union Texas entered 1993 placing increasing emphasis on other territories such as Alaska—where the company began actively pursuing and exploring new leaseholds—as well as Papua New Guinea and offshore Argentina. Coalbed methane projects continued to grow as well, and in early 1993 the company received a license to explore for coalbed methane in Great Britain.

In early 1993 production at the Piper oil field resumed at a reduced rate, with full production expected by 1994. With the redevelopment of the Piper field, Union Texas moved towards the mid-1990s in a mode geared towards restaking its claim in the North Sea. At the same time the company looked to maintain its solid presence in Pakistan and Indonesia, secure a growing foothold in Alaska, Argentina, and Papua New Guinea, and expand its foundation in Europe through coalbed methane explorations.

Principal Subsidiaries: Union Texas Petroleum Limited (England); Union Texas Petroleum Europe & Middle East, Inc. (England); Union Texas South East Asia Inc. (Indonesia); Union Texas Pakistan, Inc.; Union Texas Asia Corporation (Singapore); Union Texas Espana, Inc. (Spain); Unistar, Inc.; Union Texas Exploration Corporation; Union Texas Petroleum First Financial Corporation.

Further Reading:

Byrne, Harlan S., "Allied-Signal Inc.: The Shuffling Over, It Nurtures a Profitable Blend of Businesses," *Barron's,* June 18, 1990, pp. 49–50.

Calkins, Laurel Brubaker, "Union Texas Petroleum Cancels Proposal to Sell Entire Company," *Houston Business Journal,* December 24, 1990, p. 13.

Frazier, Steve, "Union Texas Petroleum Plans Initial Offering," *The Wall Street Journal,* August 5, 1987, p. 8.

Hager, Bruce, "Taking an Ax to Allied," *Business Week,* November 4, 1991, p. 70.

Koen, A. D., "U.S. Petroleum Industry Adjusts to Tough Economy," *Oil and Gas Journal,* July 13, 1992, pp. 14–17.

Kurylko, Diana T., "The Corporate Chameleon," *Business Journal of New Jersey,* October, 1988, p. 50.

Naj, Amal Kumar, "Allied-Signal Inc. Will Sell Its Interest in Union Texas, Raising $955 Million," *The Wall Street Journal,* September 24, 1992, p. A4.

Percefull, Gary, "Oxy to Redevelop North Sea Oil Field," *Tulsa World,* December 1, 1989, p. B7.

Solomon, Caleb, and Patricia Ann McKanic, "Union Texas Petroleum Cuts Price, Size of Offering as Large Holders Pull Out," *The Wall Street Journal,* September 25, 1987, p. 6.

Solomon, Caleb, "Union Texas Petroleum Expects to Post Surge in 2nd-Quarter Operating Profit," *The Wall Street Journal,* July 10, 1989, p. A5.

———. "Union Texas Putting Itself on the Block," *The Wall Street Journal,* May 1, 1990, p. A4.

—Roger W. Rouland

United HealthCare Corporation

300 Opus Center
9900 Bren Road East
Minnetonka, Minnesota 55343
U.S.A.
(612) 936-1300
Fax: (612) 939-7752

Public Company
Incorporated: 1977
Employees: 3,200
Sales: $1.44 billion
Stock Exchanges: New York
SICs: 6324 Hospital and Medical Service Plans; 8099 Health
    Allied Services

United HealthCare Corporation is a national leader in health care management programs, serving about two million health plan enrollees through about 20 locally based health maintenance organizations (HMOs) the company owns or manages. The company also serves about 20 million people in all 50 states through other managed-care specialty services, including preferred physician organizations (PPOs), pharmaceutical cost management services, managed mental health and substance abuse services, workers compensation/casualty services, employee assistance services, Medicare and managed care programs for the elderly, health care evaluation services, health care information systems, and administrative services.

United HealthCare Corporation informally traces its roots to the development of the HMO as a model for organized health care. The HMO's leading spokesperson, Dr. Paul Ellwood, helped develop several HMO companies in Minnesota and nearly single-handedly thrust managed health care onto the national stage during the early 1970s. In 1970 Ellwood—who later became known as the "Father of the HMO"—founded the Minnesota-based health care think tank, Interstudy, and later succeeded in getting congressional approval for his HMO model. In 1971 Ellwood hired Richard Burke to help put the HMO model to practice. Three years later Burke founded United HealthCare as a Minnetonka, Minnesota-based for-profit company organized to manage the newly created Physicians Health Plan of Minnesota, which under Minnesota's HMO law at the time was required to be a non-profit company.

In January 1977 the company was incorporated as United HealthCare Corporation. Through acquisitions and expansion of its management services United grew steadily as an owner and manager of HMOs, and by 1984 the company was running 11 HMOs in ten states.

With plans to step up expansion and acquisition efforts, United HealthCare went public in 1984 and began trading as an over-the-counter stock. Soon thereafter the company launched an ambitious national expansion program, which included starting new HMOs and acquiring multi-state HMO companies.

In June 1985 United HealthCare made its first major acquisition since going public, acquiring Share Development Corporation, an Indiana-based multi-state HMO through a stock swap valued at nearly $60 million. Share Development increased United HealthCare's health plan membership by 167,000 enrollees, and by the end of the year United HealthCare and its subsidiaries were active in 22 states, covering 822,400 members through company owned or managed health plans.

In November 1986 United HealthCare paid $83 million to acquire the Colorado-based Peak Health Care Inc., a four-state HMO network with 104,000 enrollees. By the end of the year United HealthCare owned or managed health care plans serving about 1.6 million people. The expansion efforts paid short-term dividends, and for the year the company earned $7.2 million on revenues of more than $216 million, which was more than double the company's 1985 revenues and more than six times United HealthCare's 1984 revenues.

In April 1987 Kenneth Simmons, the former president of Peak Health Care, was named chief operating officer of United HealthCare, succeeding Robert Ditmore, who remained president. Seven months later Simmons was named to replace Richard Burke as chief executive in order to pacify Physician Health Plan (PHP) doctors who were balking at Burke's management style. Burke, who remained chairperson, also gave up his post as chief executive of PHP in November 1987 and lost his status as the company's largest shareholder that month when United HealthCare—with finances strained by rapid expansion—turned to the New York investment group Warburg, Pincus Capital Company L.P. for an infusion of cash. With an annual loss looming as a result of unprofitable and marginally profitable HMO startups, Warburg agreed to purchase $9.8 million worth of newly issued preferred voting stock and acquire a 39.5 percent stake in the company.

Although United HealthCare doubled its revenues in 1987 to more than $440 million, its operating expenses had grown at a faster rate, and the company lost $15.8 million for the year while its stock value fell from a 1986 high of $15.88 to $4.25 by the end of 1987. Unsteady market conditions, excessive administrative costs and price competition battles with traditional insurance companies led United HealthCare to abandon several health plans, including HMO startups in six large cities and another well-established HMO operation in Phoenix.

In 1988 United HealthCare completed its restructuring program, selling several unpromising businesses in areas where it had entered highly competitive markets too late. In another restructuring move designed to shore up its relationship with PHP, United agreed to a new five-year contract in April 1988, which gave the PHP board of directors the power to appoint its own chief executive and other key officers.

In September 1988 United sold its interest in Peak Health Care Corporation for $41.5 million and raised an additional $31.6 million through a secondary public stock offering. Despite revenues, which reached nearly $440 million that year, the company lost $36.7 million, bringing the cost of its extensive two-year restructuring to $53 million.

Nevertheless, the restructuring program eventually returned United to profitability, and by the end of 1989 it was one of the largest publicly traded HMOs in the United States, serving about one million people in 15 states. The company was not only managing PHP, the largest HMO in Minnesota, but it was also managing Share Health Plan, the state's fourth largest HMO. For the year, United HealthCare earned $13.6 million on revenues of $412 million.

With its restructuring completed, the company began buying up specialty companies designed to control some of the most exorbitant medical costs, including companies that managed programs for the aged, prescription drugs, mental health treatments, and organ transplants. At the same time, the company launched a new expansion and acquisition plan under the direction of Dr. William McGuire, a former Peak Health Care president who was promoted to United HealthCare president in 1989. The new program focused on geographic markets where the company was already operating.

In March 1990 United HealthCare held a secondary public offering of three million shares, adding about $100 million to the $60 million the company had at its disposal for acquisitions and operations. That month United HealthCare acquired Prime-Care Health Plan Inc., a Milwaukee-based HMO and the second largest HMO in Wisconsin with 103,000 members. The acquisition was designed to complement the services of a growing United HealthCare subsidiary, Diversified Pharmaceutical Services, Inc. (DPS), a provider of managed-care drug services to about 200,000 members of several Wisconsin HMOs. The acquisition also sent a signal to the business world that United HealthCare was ready to spend more of its resources to continue expanding its core business.

In July 1990 United became the first managed health care company to go after clients already associated with other HMOs, offering three types of health care services separately rather than in a package. The new services were designed to attract customers who already belonged to an HMO but wanted programs to further contain exorbitant medical costs. The services included: United Resource Network, a program designed to manage the delivery of high cost, low volume procedures such as organ transplants; Healthmarc, a program offering health care utilization review and case management services for workers' compensation claims; and Employee Performance Design, a group of employee assistance programs offering financial, personal, legal, and other advice to workers.

By the close of 1990 United HealthCare, with about 1.5 million members enrolled in its health plans, was serving more patients than any other independent HMO company. The company's members included those belonging to United HealthCare-owned HMOs in Chicago, Atlanta, Salt Lake City, Des Moines,

and Milwaukee, as well as members belonging to HMOs United HealthCare was contracted to manage in other areas.

In capitalizing on the growing trend towards managed health care and the monitoring of medical expenses and claims procedures, United HealthCare's net income surged from $13.7 million 1989 to $33.9 million in 1990, as revenues rose from $412 million to $605.5 million. Pacing the revenue growth was the increasing numbers of customers served by HMOs that United HealthCare owned or managed, as well as the company's growing list of specialty programs, particularly DPS.

In February 1991 McGuire was named to the additional positions of chair and chief executive, succeeding Burke and Simmons. In April 1991 United acquired the Institute of Human Resources (IHR), a Rockville, Maryland-based employee assistance company operating of one of the largest networks of employee counselors in the United States and providing phone counseling services to workers with mental health, drug abuse, or alcohol problems. United HealthCare's own employee assistance operation, Employee Performance Design, was merged into IHR with the combined operation comprising 2,650 mental health and employee assistance professionals working in 15 separate specialist networks in various regions of the United States.

In July 1991 two of the largest HMOs United HealthCare was managing, PHP and Share Health Plan, were merged into a single company, bringing more than 480,000 Minnesota medical plan enrollees together under one HMO. The merger allowed the new company, Medica, to provide for a wider range of health care benefit packages offered by a single company and also served to shore up the Share Health Plan organization, which had been experiencing financial difficulties and was losing members. As a result of the merger, PHP was renamed Medica Choice, and Share Health became Medica Primary.

In July 1991 United purchased the Wauwatosa, Wisconsin-based Samaritan Health Plan Insurance Corporation, one of the first hospital-sponsored HMOs in the country. Four months later Samaritan was merged into PrimeCare, creating the second largest HMO in the Milwaukee area with a total 157,000 members. The following month United expanded its presence in New England when it acquired Ocean State Physicians Health Plan, a Rhode Island-based HMO previously managed by United HealthCare. By the time United HealthCare closed its books on 1991 it was trading on the New York Stock Exchange and had more than doubled its previous year's income to $74.8 million on revenues of $847.1 million.

In January 1992 United HealthCare paid $84 million to acquire Physicians Health Plan of Ohio, a Columbus-based HMO with 154,000 members. In March United HealthCare staged another secondary public offering, generating $200 million. Then, in July, United HealthCare acquired the assets of HealthPro, Inc., a Massachusetts-based benefits management company providing utilization management and medical review services to government agencies, labor union health and welfare funds, and corporations. One month later United HealthCare agreed to acquire a 50 percent stake in Physicians Health Plan of North Carolina, a 50,000-member health plan.

By end of 1992 United HealthCare was considered an industry leader in product diversification among managed health care companies, as well as an HMO force in Minneapolis, and a growing HMO factor in Milwaukee, Ohio, and Rhode Island. Acquisitions, enrollment growth, and increased sales in specialty operations all contributed to significant financial gains, and for 1992 United HealthCare's revenues leaped 70 percent to $1.4 billion, while income rose 54 percent to $111.5 million.

In early 1993 United HealthCare became Ohio's preeminent HMO when it paid $100 million to acquire Western Ohio Health Care Corporation, a 185,000-member health plan and the largest HMO in Dayton, Ohio. The deal was the fifth and largest acquisition of an HMO by United HealthCare since 1991 and gave United HealthCare 338,000 HMO members in Ohio, or 20 percent of the state's HMO enrollment.

In March 1993 DPS reconfigured its product lines in order to become more competitive and began targeting the public sector market, including state and federal government health insurance programs. In May United agreed to acquire HMO America Inc. in an exchange of stock valued at more than $370 million. HMO America was the second largest HMO in Chicago, owning and operating a 300,000-member plan, Chicago HMO Ltd. This operation was combined with United HealthCare's Share Illinois company, a 97,300-member plan, to form the largest managed-care health system in the Chicago area. That month, on the heels of the HMO America deal, United HealthCare agreed to make its first divestiture since 1987, selling its Des Moines-based health plan with about 26,000 members.

As it moved towards the mid-1990s United HealthCare appeared financially prepared for additional HMO acquisitions and growth in major market areas. The company anticipated that the demand for its specialty services, particularly DPS and those designed to contain low volume, high cost medical expenses, would continue to grow rapidly. In late 1993, with health care reform hitting the national spotlight, United Health-Care appeared poised to take advantage of increasing numbers of public and private sector customers and providers.

Principal Subsidiaries: United Behavioral Systems, Inc.; Diversified Pharmaceutical Services, Inc.; UHC TPA, Inc.; United Health and Life of New England, Inc.; UHC Management Company, Inc.

Further Reading:

Booth, Michael, "The Latest From the Father of the HMO," *Corporate Report Minnesota,* October 1991, p. 28.

Freudenheim, Milt, "Market Place: Picking Winners Among H.M.O.'s," *New York Times,* April 27, 1992, p. D6.

Gold, Jacqueline S., "Future Doc?: Meet the Current Health-Care Darling," *Financial World,* November 10, 1992, pp. 25–26.

Hirschman, Carolyn, "United HealthCare to be Ohio's Largest HMO," *Business First-Columbus,* January 25, 1993, p. 3.

Howatt, Glenn, "United HealthCare Corp. to Buy Chicago-Based HMO America," *Star Tribune,* May 14, 1993.

Nissen, Todd, "United HealthCare Adds Three Divisions," *Minneapolis-St. Paul CityBusiness,* July 30, 1990, p. 8.

——. "United HealthCare Again Looking to Buy," *Minneapolis-St. Paul CityBusiness,* December 11, 1989, p. 6.

——. "With an M.D. as CEO, Firm Hopes for Health Growth," *Minneapolis-St. Paul CityBusiness,* March 18, 1991, p. 1.

"Pact Is Signed to Sell Stake To Warburg Pincus Capital," *The Wall Street Journal,* November 17, 1987, p. 5.

Reilly, Lucy, "Health Probe Leads to Baltimore Indictments," *Washington Business Journal,* October 3, 1988, p. 18.

Stocker, Susan J., "Despite Conviction, Felon Remains on State Board," *Washington Business Journal,* March 13, 1989, p. 6.

Straumanis, Andris, "United HealthCare: Not Just an HMO Manager," *Corporate Report Minnesota,* February 1991, p. 60.

Tooher, Nora Lockwood, "Local HMO Parent Has Big Plans to Extend Reach, *The Providence Journal-Bulletin,* September 29, 1991, p. F1.

"United HealthCare Says Charge to Result In Loss for 3rd Period," *The Wall Street Journal,* November 4, 1987, p. 59.

Valentine, Paul W., "D.C. Clinic Kickbacks Admitted: Md. Executive Guilty In 2 Health Schemes," *Washington Post,* March 8, 1989, pp. C1, C7.

—Roger W. Rouland

United States Cellular Corporation

8410 West Bryn Mawr Avenue
Suite 700
Chicago, Illinois 60631
U.S.A.
(312) 399-8900
Fax: (312) 399-8936

Public Company
Incorporated: 1983
Employees: 1,175
Sales: $164 million
Stock Exchanges: American
SICs: 4812 Radiotelephone Communications

United States Cellular Corporation is one of the country's smaller cellular communications companies. It is also one of the fastest growing companies in the industry and is distinguished by its exceptional tenacity in acquiring operating licenses and participating in cellular partnerships. United States Cellular Corporation, or USCC, as the company is commonly referred to, is largely controlled by Telephone and Data Systems, Inc., an independent telephone holding company based in Chicago. Originally established as the cellular communications division of TDS, USCC maintains a close relationship with its parent company.

TDS was established in 1968 by Chicago entrepreneur LeRoy T. Carlson who, over a period of years, assembled a small rural telephone conglomerate consisting of fifty independent companies. TDS realized tremendous economies through centralized purchasing and system standardization. The policy of collecting companies in adjacent areas, along with consistent growth in rural areas, amplified these benefits.

By 1982 TDS had invested heavily in cable television services, operating 16 individual cable companies. The diversification was spurred by a fear that cable companies might one day usurp traditional telephone companies by offering their own telephone services. At the time, cable companies were unwilling to develop telephone services out of their own fear that such a move would provide justification for the huge Bell companies to storm into the cable television industry.

By 1982 cellular communication, still in its embryonic stages, was beginning to emerge as a much more serious and immediate threat to the business of wireline telephone companies. One of the first companies to recognize this was TDS, whose senior management quickly devised plans to establish its own cellular communications franchises. There was no shortage of companies willing to compete for licenses to provide cellular service. Start-up costs were high, but economies of scale were extremely impressive, particularly in metropolitan areas. The Federal Communications Commission (FCC), which granted the licenses, established a bidding process for the thirty most populous market service areas (MSAs), and proclaimed that only two companies would be licensed to compete in each one. The first license was reserved for the local wireline company (most often a Bell company), while the second would be awarded to another bidder.

The FCC was monumentally ill-prepared to handle the deluge of applications it received. While TDS applied for a license to serve Indianapolis, a fierce turf battle erupted throughout the industry. Because MSAs often covered several different wireline franchises, dozens of perplexing questions arose over the FCC's as-yet-unofficial definitions. The commission finally asked its vast pool of applicants to hammer out their own partnership agreements prior to requesting a license. As a result, TDS opted to abandon its bid for Indianapolis in favor of a five percent stake in the hugely profitable Los Angeles MSA. Because it was obliged to provide detailed engineering and market surveys, TDS poured a quarter million dollars into its first application. By the time the second set of 30 MSAs was put up for grabs, however, the company had become experienced in such matters, and soon the average application cost fell below $10,000.

No longer able to support its growing activities in the cellular industry by itself, TDS created a separate subsidiary called United States Cellular Corporation. The new company began operations on December 23, 1983, with Rudy Hornacek, a TDS executive, as its president.

The FCC's call for pre-arranged agreements among applicants eliminated years of comparative studies and appeals processes. It also emboldened the larger, predominantly metropolitan Bell companies into running roughshod over smaller companies. Such cavalier disregard for companies such as US Cellular hit a nerve with LeRoy Carlson. He took such an aggressive position in negotiations that larger companies were forced to make room for US Cellular. One bemused representative complained that Carlson didn't realize how small his company really was. As the process rambled on, the public grew more vocal and critical of the FCC's seemingly endless formalities. Finally, the commission decided to award remaining licenses through a series of lotteries.

In a separate agreement signed by the Bell companies, TDS, and other independents, TDS was allowed to operate cellular networks in Knoxville and Tulsa. In October 1984, before the FCC formally granted the licenses, USCC began to assemble its management team. This team was responsible for the selection of cell sites, construction of towers, installation of operating systems, establishment of business offices, and staffing. Accordingly, USCC moved its operations out of TDS headquarters and into a new building in Park Ridge, near Chicago's O'Hare Airport.

By March 1985 the senior management of TDS had become convinced that the cellular industry was poised for tremendous growth. The company decided to make the development of its cellular unit a major priority. In order to be a more serious bidder, the company needed access to greater investment funding. Rather than raising the necessary financing through additional debt or selling additional shares to an equity partner, USCC turned to TDS. At that time, the parent company elected to abandon the cable television market and devote the proceeds of the sales of its systems to USCC. In addition, funding that was earmarked for the development of new cable systems was diverted to cellular investments.

TDS decided to concentrate on the cellular industry, at the expense of cable television, because cellular promised considerably higher growth and rates of return. Moreover, cellular communications posed a greater threat to TDS's established wireline services than cable, since the technologies needed to provide telephone service over cable systems had not been developed. TDS disposed of its cable operations during 1985, and sold its last system in November 1986.

USCC's Knoxville system commenced in June 1985, and its Tulsa system went on line in August. Meanwhile, the Los Angeles system, which was activated the previous year, turned its first profit in October. That year, the company filed applications for five of the nation's largest markets, and applications for seventy more in smaller markets. The licenses for smaller MSAs were important because they covered areas adjacent to larger existing systems or formed corridors along heavily traveled highway routes.

In addition to the two MSAs USCC operated in 1986, the company was a minority partner in an additional nine. The following year, it completed eight more cellular networks, including systems in Peoria, Des Moines, and Poughkeepsie. To meet the company's growing organizational demands, USCC established five operating regions in 1987, including a Midwest Region headquartered in Davenport, Iowa; a Southeast Region in Knoxville; a Southwest Region in Tulsa; and a North Central Region located in Minneapolis. That year, Don Nelson, head of operations at USCC, succeeded Hornacek as president of the company and took on the title of CEO as well.

In an effort to derive additional revenue from its systems, USCC negotiated numerous roaming agreements with other cellular providers, which allowed customers to continue calls even if they strayed outside their provider's service area. In addition, the company began implementation of enhanced "vertical" services, such as voice mail and information services. By 1987 USCC had been recognized as a formidable player in the cellular communications industry. Clearly in a position to win additional licenses, the company had exhausted its credit lines and would be unable to maintain its growth without a sizable issue of equity capital. The company therefore sold 6.2 percent of its capital stock to Coditel, a Belgian cable television company, for $10 million.

Late in the summer of 1987, USCC planned a public stock offering to raise additional capital. While the company was preparing its prospectus and working with the Securities and Exchange Commission to make the offering, the stock market took an enormous plunge. The date, October 19, became known as Black Monday. The Dow Jones Industrial Index fell by more than 500 points, to about 1700 points. The collapse of confidence in the markets not only torpedoed USCC's prospective share offering, it ruined public offerings of at least three other cellular companies. The company finally went forward with its public share offering on May 4, 1988. Three million shares were distributed, mostly in the United States, at $15 per share, and the company was listed on the American Stock Exchange. The share offering diluted TDS's control of USCC to just over 80 percent.

By December 1988, USCC was active in 31 MSAs, including Wichita, Atlantic City, and Columbia, Missouri. This rapid growth forced the company to move out of its Park Ridge offices and into a larger facility in Chicago. To bolster its identity in the increasingly crowded industry, USCC adopted a new logo and promotional materials that included the no-nonsense tag line "Mobile Telephone Network."

To augment its growth in the market, USCC began issuing additional blocks of shares. During one 18-month period, the number of USCC shares increased by 61 percent. TDS maintained its ownership in USCC at 82.3 percent. Due to the high start-up costs associated with cellular systems, investments in new franchises had severely hampered TDS's earnings potential. USCC was a constant drain to TDS, but these investments were necessary to ensure that USCC had a good position in the industry. If the company did not invest in new systems while they were available, it risked losing opportunities to build the enterprise.

When the cellular market had been exhausted of the most desirable franchises, the market value of existing licenses began to climb. In fact, USCC bought into the market at relatively low prices. Later, the value of its cellular properties climbed so dramatically that if it were to sell the licenses it had acquired, it would realize a tremendous gain.

After USCC secured the necessary licenses and completed the establishment of new networks, it prepared to collect on its substantial investments. A portion of the earnings from these operations was channeled back toward the servicing or retirement of debt and the settlement of obligations to TDS. A second, but rapidly growing portion of USCC's operating income was distributed to its shareholders, the largest of which was TDS. As a result, TDS began collecting an increasingly large dividend from USCC, which registered a 58 percent increase in subscribers, to 182,500, in 1992. TDS used its share of the earnings to retire its own debt and finance new investment opportunities, including additional wireline franchises.

Between 1989 and 1992, USCC expanded from interests in 33 cellular systems to 129. Forty percent of this growth occurred in areas where TDS had a presence in the wireline market, or through settlements with other companies. The remaining licenses were acquired directly through acquisitions of licenses awarded to TDS and other companies.

As the supply of available cellular licenses continued to dwindle, and the prices increased, USCC was faced with the possibility of actually making money. As the investment stage of the company's development drew near an end, positive cash flow was likely to follow. The primary beneficiary of this profitability would be TDS, whose shares were favored over those of USCC because its business was more thoroughly diversified. In 1993 USCC had interests in 193 cellular systems, 129 of which it had a hand in managing. Of that number, the company maintained a majority interest in 91 franchises. This makes USCC the eighth-largest non-Bell cellular company in the United States.

Further Reading:

August, K. C., *TDS: The First Twenty Years,* Telephone and Data Systems, Inc.: Madison, Wisconsin, 1989.
''Company Watch,'' *Financial World,* September 15, 1992, pp. 12–13.
''TDS,'' *Telephone News,* April 14, 1985, p. 8; September 9, 1989, p. 1.

—John Simley

Univar
CORPORATION

Univar Corporation

6100 Carillon Point
Kirkland, Washington 98033
U.S.A.
(206) 889-3400
Fax: (206) 889-4100

Public Company
Incorporated: 1966 as VWR United Company
Employees: 3,325
Sales: $1.80 billion
Stock Exchanges: New York Pacific
SICs: 5169 Chemicals & Allied Products Nec; 5191 Farm
    Supplies; 8741 Management Services

Univar Corporation is a leading, international distributor of a broad range of industrial chemicals, which it distributes through its three subsidiaries: Van Waters & Rogers Inc. in the United States, Van Waters & Rogers Ltd. in Canada, and Univar Europe N.V. Chemicals distributed by Univar are purchased from manufacturers and then resold by Univar to various industries. Serving an estimated $27 billion market, Univar quickly established a considerable presence in the chemical distribution industry, both in North America and abroad, with approximately 150 distribution offices located throughout the United States, Canada, and Europe.

In 1966, the merging of two Seattle-based companies formed what is now known as Univar. While this date marks the formal creation of Univar, the essence of the corporation begins with the driving force behind the 1966 merger: Van Waters & Rogers. The history of Van Waters & Rogers began with a bridge game in Seattle in 1924.

The card game brought together for the first time two individuals who would figure prominently in Univar's history—George Van Waters and Nat S. Rogers. Van Waters had arrived in Seattle four years earlier to work for the P. W. Patterson Company, distributors of cotton linters, linseed oil, tallow, and cotton seed oil. After two years, Van Waters had earned enough money to buy the company's Seattle territory. During this time, Rogers decided to leave his studies at the University of Washington in 1921 and began working as a chemist for a plywood adhesives firm. When the two men met in 1924, they decided to enter into business together and, before the summer was over, Van Waters & Rogers had been incorporated.

Each of the hopeful entrepreneurs, both in their mid-twenties, contributed $2,500 to start the business, which initially sold paint, cotton linters, raw materials, and naval supplies at wholesale from a small sales office they had rented. Van Waters, the more effective salesman of the budding team, sold the products over the telephone, while Rogers assumed the administrative duties. By the end of their first year of business, which now included selling laundry and industrial chemicals, Van Waters and Rogers had parlayed their initial investment of $5,000 into $80,000 in revenues. Van Waters—who developed the curious habit of sticking his head under his desk while speaking long distance on the telephone, yet sat upright if the call was local—proved to be an effective salesperson, while Rogers, with his experience in chemistry, astutely led the company toward diversification and expansion in the industry.

By 1926, the company had added soap, bleach, and allied products to its line and had also established a laundry supplies department. Two years later, the partners made their first acquisition, purchasing Bourret Kirkwood Company, a laundry and dry cleaning supply firm, after which their revenues doubled. Van Waters and Rogers next began a series of acquisitions that expanded the company's presence southward. In 1932, they purchased S.L. Abbott Co. in Portland, Oregon, and, four years later, they purchased a cotton linters sales company in Los Angeles. In 1939, Van Waters and Rogers set their sights east of Seattle and purchased the Arthur Pittack Company in Spokane, Washington, thereby creating the company's feed and fertilizer department. That year, encouraged by their success at selling almost any product they took on, the partners entered into the upholstery supply and textile field.

By the late 1930s, the company had opened offices in Portland, Oregon, and Spokane, Washington, and had offered ownership in the business to its key personnel. Department and branch managers had been granted almost full autonomy, the only stipulation being that they succeed in whatever they chose to market. Since its inception the company had operated in the black, posting profits throughout the Great Depression. This success, coupled with considerable freedom and responsibility given to the sales managers, led to a somewhat incongruous pattern of diversification, first evidenced by the company's move into industrial textiles. This wide-ranging style would continue for many years and would be indicative of Univar's disparate business concerns throughout much of its history. In this sense, the late 1930s and the early 1940s were defining years for both Van Waters & Rogers and Univar. Perhaps the most illustrative example of this rather haphazard style of growth occurred as World War II was ending, when a department manager purchased a carload of extra-large men's pajama tops. Clearly well beyond the parameters of Van Waters & Rogers' product line, the tops, without matching bottoms, were sold for use as rags to a company in the machine tool industry.

For the first 26 years of its existence, Van Waters & Rogers grew by purchasing small companies. In 1950 the company made its first major purchase, acquiring San Francisco-based Braun-Knecht-Heimann (B-K-H). Twenty years earlier, Van Waters & Rogers had been awarded a contract for the Northwest sales of the chemicals distributed by B-K-H. This arrangement eventually evolved into an agreement that granted Van Waters & Rogers the exclusive distributing rights for B-K-H chemicals. As part of the B-K-H purchase, Van Waters & Rogers obtained a 50 percent stock interest in Scientific Supplies Company, a Seattle-based scientific apparatus distribution company; they purchased the remaining percentage three years later.

In 1951 Van Waters & Rogers secured a foothold in Canada by purchasing Industrial Materials Ltd. in Vancouver, British Columbia. Established as Van Waters & Rogers Ltd., the Canadian subsidiary spread across the country, acquiring chemical distribution companies that eventually lent considerable strength to Van Waters & Rogers North American presence.

By the early 1950s, the core of Van Waters & Rogers' product line, which Univar would inherit, had been established. In the remaining years before the 1966 merger, Van Waters & Rogers continued to expand, acquiring companies in Los Angeles, Dallas, and St. Paul, Minnesota.

The other player in the Univar merger, a company that began as United Pacific Corporation, had been operating in Seattle for almost as long as Van Waters & Rogers, but had experienced a more tumultuous history. In 1925, two bankers from Tacoma, Washington, Ben S. Ehrlichman and Roscoe Drumheller, decided to enter into the investment banking business and formed Drumheller & Ehrlichman. Four years after its inception, the company, newly named United National Corporation, purchased United Pacific Insurance Company, United Pacific Realty, and Ferris & Hargrove, an investment banking company. For a young corporation beginning with $25,000 in capital, these three acquisitions, with a combined net worth of over $18 million, represented a bold move that earned the two partners a national reputation as prudent and shrewd investors.

However, their business acumen was put to a test in the same year, as the stock market crashed. Believing their holdings would withstand the economic turmoil that swept through the country, Ehrlichman and Drumheller, whose investments included the ownership of several commercial buildings in Seattle, continued to augment their real estate holdings. When a majority of the tenants reneged on their lease agreements, the results were catastrophic. The company's preferred stock plummeted from $50 a share to 25 cents, and Drumheller withdrew from the business. The corporation teetered on the brink of failure, but survived, making a slow recovery during World War II.

In 1958, United National Corporation became United Pacific Corporation. Ehrlichman relinquished his controlling interest in the corporation to a group of Seattle area businessmen, one of whom was Nat S. Rogers. In 1964, With Rogers as a board member, United Pacific, underwent a complete restructuring. As part of this process, in which some subsidiaries were sold and others established as independent operating entities, United Pacific began to invest in Van Waters & Rogers. This confluence of Nat Rogers' business concerns led to the merger of United Pacific and Van Waters & Rogers two years later, in 1966, creating VWR United Company.

The formation of the new company—which retained the VWR United name until 1974 when it was renamed Univar—brought together two disparate forces with divergent operating philosophies and business interests. Since it first opened for business,

Van Waters & Rogers had aggressively expanded, acquiring companies and broadening its product line at a brisk rate. United Pacific, on the other hand, had a history of cautious growth, engendered by a conservative investment policy that was largely the result of Ehrlichman's nearly disastrous experience during the Great Depression. When these two contrary business strategies came under one leader, the result resembled Van Waters & Rogers much more than United Pacific. Indeed, the newly formed VWR United was, in effect, Van Waters & Rogers with a new name and a larger capital base. In this respect, the merger created a more powerful Van Waters & Rogers, a company with an enhanced ability to expand and diversify.

This new strength was put to use throughout the 1970s and early 1980s, as VWR United acquired a substantial array of chemical and scientific supply companies. Acquisitions during this period included Will Scientific in Rochester, New York; Penick & Ford Ltd., a subsidiary of R.J. Reynolds Industries; and Trek Photographic, a division of Eastman Kodak. While these acquisitions bolstered the company's chemical and scientific holdings, additional purchases stretched the parameters of its business interests. In 1976, Univar purchased the Great Western Malting Company, the largest maltster on the West Coast.

By the early 1980s Univar had become a diverse chemical and scientific distributor involved in graphic arts, fabrics, and agricultural processing, as well as a supplier to furniture and interior design industries. Expansion and diversification, undertaken to counteract any recessive periods suffered by a particular Univar product line, had created a company with a broad spectrum of business interests and revenues of over $900 million. For Univar's management, this spectrum had become too broad by the beginning of the 1980s, and the corporation began divesting itself of certain segments of its business, forming them into separate, independent companies.

First to undergo this process, in 1984, were the corn, potato, and barley processing operations obtained through the purchase of Great Western Malting Co. and Penick & Ford Ltd. The new, independent company, PENWEST, LTD., manufactured brewer's malt for breweries, produced treated starches for the textile and paper industries, and served as the model for another spin-off two years later. VWR Corporation was formed when Univar was effectively divided into two corporations of roughly equal size. The removal of VWR Corporation's product lines stripped Univar of what its management had determined were peripheral business interests, enabling the corporation to concentrate solely on the distribution of industrial and textile chemicals and pest-control supplies through its two subsidiaries, Van Waters & Rogers Inc. and Van Waters & Rogers Ltd.

The removal of Univar's grain processing operations and its laboratory and non-chemical distribution business, however, also removed an appreciable portion of Univar's revenues. Penick & Ford and Great Western Malting had accounted for $127 million before their departure, and the revenues now collected by VWR Corporation nearly matched those of Univar, which, after the two spin-offs, stood at $543 million. In order to recoup the losses and increase its size, Univar began looking for an acquisition consistent with its renewed commitment to the industrial chemical distributing business.

In 1986, a suitable company was found. The acquisition of McKesson Corp.'s chemical distribution operations, McKesson Chemical Co., more than made up for the loss of PENWEST and VWR Corporation. With 65 branch offices and sales of over $600 million, the addition of San Francisco-based McKesson doubled Univar's revenues, making it North America's largest chemical distributor. Univar's rise to the top, however, came with a hefty price tag and a complex purchasing arrangement that ceded an approximately 31 percent interest in Univar to a Dutch holding company. In order to reach the $76 million required to purchase McKesson, Univar arranged for Royal Pakhoed N.V., a 350-year-old Dutch company providing chemical storage, transportation, and distribution services, to capitalize a U.S. subsidiary with $26 million. Univar then loaned the subsidiary $50 million to purchase McKesson. After the subsidiary purchased the chemical company, Pakhoed transferred its ownership to Univar in exchange for approximately three million shares of Univar's stock, leaving the Dutch company with a sizable interest in Univar.

Two years passed before Univar was able to overcome the expenditures made in the McKesson acquisition. After posting $693 million in sales in 1987, revenues leapt to $1.12 billion in 1988, marking the first time the corporation had reached the $1 billion plateau. That year, Univar formed a national waste management service, called Chemcare, to operate as a unit under Van Waters & Rogers Inc. Through Chemcare, Univar began collecting and transporting hazardous waste produced by client businesses to qualified treatment, storage, and disposal facilities.

Once the extensive transformation of the 1980s was completed and the benefits of the McKesson acquisition were fully realized, Univar once again set its sights on acquiring additional companies. The company's position in the U.S. market had been strengthened by the McKesson purchase, especially in the East and Midwest, so Univar looked toward Canada and Europe for potential companies. In 1991, as the corporation's earnings suffered from a worldwide economic recession, Univar purchased Hacros Chemicals Canada Inc., which further solidified the corporation's standing as the largest chemical distributor in Canada. Hacros' $90 million in sales boosted Van Waters & Rogers Ltd. total revenues to $325 million, the majority of which was reaped from the western regions of the country.

Earlier in the same year, Univar entered the European chemical distribution market for the first time through a partnership with the corporation's Dutch facilitator in the McKesson acquisition, Pakhoed Holding, N.V. Pakhoed's investment company, Pakhoed Investeringen B.V., joined with Univar to form Univar Europe N.V. as a subsidiary. Through Univar Europe, 51 percent of which was owned by Univar and the remaining 49 percent by Pakhoed Investeringen, Univar acquired Beijer In-

dustrial Distribution Group, a Swedish company with $380 million in sales at the time of the purchase, from Beijer Industries. Beijer, the fourth largest chemical distribution company in Europe, operated through 17 European offices in Scandinavia, the United Kingdom, Switzerland, and Italy. As with the McKesson acquisition, the purchase of Beijer was funded through the sale of Univar's stock—1.9 million shares to The Dow Chemical Company, representing $30.9 million—and, again like McKesson, the addition of Beijer substantially affected the scope of Univar's operations. Considering that the European chemical distribution market was larger than the North American market, this initial foray into Europe represented a significant step toward Univar's bid to increase its global presence.

As Univar planned for the future, the corporation's prospects for further expansion were beginning to brighten as it slowly recovered from the economic recession of the early 1990s. After recording a net income loss of $5.6 million in fiscal 1992, Univar returned to posting a profit of $5.1 million in fiscal 1993, largely as a result of an upsurge in business during the final two quarters. Additional acquisitions in Europe were also expected, providing that expansion remained an economically sound option. Within the estimated $11 billion chemical distribution market in Europe in 1993, Univar Europe posted sales of $290 million compared with the $1.2 billion Van Waters & Rogers Inc. recorded in the $14.5 billion U.S. market. Univar hopes to ameliorate this disparity in market share in the years ahead.

Principal Subsidiaries: Van Waters & Rogers Inc.; Van Waters & Rogers Ltd.; Univar Europe N.V. (51%).

Further Reading:

Brockington, Langdon, "Bernard Takes a Long-Term Outlook," *Chemical Week,* October, 26, 1988, pp. 34–36.

Dunphy, Stephen, H., "Univar . . . Putting Some Spin On Things," *The Seattle Times,* June 29, 1986, p. E1.

Flynn, Dan, "Despite Size, Univar Gets Little Attention in This Area," *Seattle Business Journal,* June 20, 1983, p.8.

Gilje, Svein, "Univar to Serve Small Businesses with Waste-Management," *The Seattle Times,* May 19, 1988, p. B3.

Heberlein, Greg, "Univar Purchase to Double Its Size," *The Seattle Times,* September 22, 1986, p. D9.

Morris, Gregory, DL, "North American Operations Weather the Storm," *Chemical Week,* August 5, 1992, pp. 28–29.

"$2,500 in 1924 Started Van Waters & Rogers," *Washington Purchaser,* July 1975, pp. 21–24.

"Univar Corp. Planning to Spin Off Two Units," *The Wall Street Journal,* September 15, 1983, p. 15.

"Univar Planning to Set Up Another Spin-Off Company," *The Seattle Times,* December 5, 1985, p. D5.

"Univar Sells Stake To Fund Acquisition," *The Seattle Times,* April 4, 1991, p. E1.

—Jeffrey L. Covell

Circus Foods, a candy bar and nut products manufacturer. However, the market was already dominated by Planters, according to Louis Bantle, UST's chief executive officer from 1972 to 1992. Shortly after that, UST purchased pet food company B.A. Bernard and marketed Cadillac dog food. According to Bantle, UST was a few years too late with that venture as well, since Alpo already had established itself as the top premium dog food company.

W. H. Snyder & Sons, a Pennsylvania cigar company, became a subsidiary of UST in 1965. It was later merged into Wolf Brothers Cigar Co., and the name was changed to House of Windsor, Inc. In 1981, UST acquired the assets of Havano Cigar Corp. of Tampa, Florida, and transferred its operations to House of Windsor. House of Windsor, however, was sold to its employees in 1987. UST continued to produce and market Don Tomas premium cigars, handmade in Honduras, in the early 1990s.

In 1969, United States Tobacco acquired Henry, Leonard & Thomas Inc., which manufactured Dr. Grabow pre-smoked pipes. UST added to its pipe business in 1974 by acquiring Mastercraft Pipes, Marxman Imports, Inc., and Manhattan Briar Pipes, Ltd. UST continues to market Borkum Riff, the best-selling brand of imported tobacco in the United States, as well as Dill pipe-cleaners.

While UST had been testing the waters in outside industries for decades, the 1980s saw both further diversification and the divestiture of incompatible businesses. In 1980, UST acquired WPBN-TV and WTOM-TV but five years later sold these broadcast holdings. A year later, UST bought Heritage Health, which operated 14 drug- and alcohol-abuse clinics in hospitals. A few years later, however, UST turned around and sold it because it was not consistent with the company's core business. It also sold its interests in its pen and pencil company and its cigar company. UST considered its diversification into the premium wine business a good complement to its core tobacco business, and kept its ownership of Washington state wineries Chateau St. Michelle and Columbia Crest and California's Conn Creek and Villa Mt. Eden.

UST's top brand, Copenhagen, the world's best-selling brand of moist smokeless tobacco, is one of the oldest packaged consumer brands in the United States, according to the company. Skoal, a wintergreen-flavored moist smokeless tobacco and UST's other flagship brand, was launched in 1934. While United States Tobacco Company had been making inroads into new regional markets, it wasn't until the last half of the 1970s that moist smokeless tobacco use and UST sales soared. Between 1974 and 1979, sales had increased by more than ten percent annually, bringing 1979 United States Tobacco sales to more than $233 million, with 60 percent of that total coming from sales of moist smokeless tobacco products Happy Days, Skoal, and Copenhagen. Its earnings were $32 million, up 15 percent from the year 1978. Most of the company's growth was from sales to young men between the ages of 18 and 35. According to a University of Nebraska study, snuff use increased 30 percent between 1988 and 1992 and one in five male high school seniors used the smokeless tobacco product.

UST Inc.

100 West Putnam Avenue
Greenwich, Connecticut 06830
U.S.A.
(203) 661-1100
Fax: (203) 863-7235

Public Company
Incorporated: 1986, as UST Inc., a holding company for U.S. Tobacco Company; originally incorporated as Weyman-Bruton Co., 1911
Employees: 3,569
Sales: $1.04 billion
Stock Exchanges: New York
SICs: 2131 Tobacco and Snuff; 2121 Cigars

UST Inc., considered the United States' most profitable firm because of its top-rated return on assets, is a holding company for four subsidiaries: United States Tobacco Company, International Wine & Spirits Ltd., UST Enterprises, Inc., and UST International Inc. United States Tobacco Company is the country's leading producer of moist smokeless tobacco products and is the central business of UST.

Although health concerns cut down on growth in the rest of the tobacco industry, snuff sales were increasing during the first part of the 1990s. Snuff is pulverized tobacco that is placed between the cheek and gums. Snuff, practically a UST monopoly, was the fastest growing segment of the U.S. tobacco industry, increasing at three to five percent a year. UST controls between one-third and one-half the oral tobacco market, which includes chewing tobacco, dry tobacco, moist snuff, and several other products.

The formation of the United States Tobacco Company dates back to 1911, when the U.S. government dissolved the tobacco monopoly of James Buchanon Duke. From that dissolution, several cigarette companies, including as R.J. Reynolds, Liggett & Myers, and Lorillard, as well as several smaller tobacco concerns, including Weyman-Bruton Co., were formed. Weyman-Burton Co., a snuff manufacturer in 1911, eventually became United States Tobacco Company and came to control about 85 percent of the U.S. snuff market.

Although oral tobacco products have been UST's mainstay, it has been in and out of many businesses. In 1958, it acquired

According to CEO Louis F. Bantle, the company's primary markets had been "Chicago through North and South Dakota, Minnesota, Montana out to Washington state." UST had not even introduced its products to the Southwest until 1950 or to the Southeast until the mid-1960s. Between 1974 and 1979, sales in the Southeast and Southwest leaped 145 percent and 108 percent respectively. Bantle told *Forbes,* "If you go to high school in Texas and you don't have a can of snuff in your pocket, you're out." The company growth strategy included ads featuring sports and rodeo stars attesting to the sense of "individuality" expressed by snuff users. Since then, the tobacco industry agreed to stop using athletes in advertising and smokeless tobacco has been banned at some levels of pro baseball and in some college conferences. Some major league teams banned distribution of free samples in their clubhouses.

Research showed that in the 1970s the moist tobacco market was comprised mostly of men whose work or activities made cigarette smoking inconvenient or even hazardous. Users were miners, lumberjacks, and petroleum workers—men who had to keep their hands free for their work or for whom a burning cigarette could cause fire or explosion. This was a small market compared to the cigarette industry's market, but UST practically had a monopoly on this smokeless market. Bantle predicted that the snuff market would increase to 100 million pounds by the turn of the century and that most of the users would be people who had quit smoking but could not give up tobacco use. By 1992, males in the Southeast, Mountain/Plain, and Southwestern regions had per capita use of more than ten cans of smokeless tobacco annually. The Northeast region had a per capita use of only two cans. UST had an 85 percent share of the moist smokeless tobacco market, the largest segment of the smokeless tobacco market.

In 1983, UST introduced Skoal Bandits, small, "tea-bag" pouches of wintergreen-flavored tobacco designed for novice snuff users. Its four-week $2-million ad campaign for New York City touted the Bandits as an alternative to smoking and invited potential users to "take a pouch instead of a puff." By 1990, Bandits comprised five percent of UST's business.

According to *FDA Consumer,* moist smokeless tobacco use caught on among teens because of UST's aggressive ad campaigns, which specifically targeted them. The campaigns featured popular sports heroes, including Yankee pitcher Catfish Hunter, Houston Oilers running back Earl Campbell, and Dallas Cowboys running back Walt Garrison. *FDA Consumer* claimed that with this campaign, "smokeless tobacco became a socially acceptable symbol of virility, machismo and coolness." The article added that UST attracted teens with free samples of low-nicotine and fruit-flavored tobaccos. Although UST had been accused of promoting Skoal and Copenhagen among minors, UST denied the allegation. Walt Garrison also denied the charge.

Like other tobacco products, snuff and chewing tobacco have been criticized as menaces to health. In 1986, Betty Ann Marsee brought a $147-million lawsuit against UST. Marsee claimed her son's death at age 19 from mouth cancer was the direct result of his use of UST's smokeless tobacco. The trial was closely covered by the national news media, bringing the issue of the safety of smokeless tobacco to the public's attention even though Marsee's lawyers were unable to prove that UST was liable for her son's health problems.

Snuff had been touted by UST as a safe alternative to cigarettes, capitalizing on the growing evidence that smoking was responsible for many life-threatening conditions. The 1986 Smokeless Tobacco Act, passed during the same spring the Marsee trial occurred, ended snuff's exemption from the restrictions placed on cigarettes in the 1960s and 1970s. The 1986 law called for three rotating labels warning that the products could cause mouth cancer; that they could cause gum disease and tooth loss; and that smokeless tobacco is not a safe alternative to cigarette smoking.

The 1986 legislation enacted an excise tax on smokeless tobacco of about two cents a can, although a nine-cent tax had been proposed by some legislators and anti-tobacco lobbyists. Senate Majority Leader Robert Dole of Kansas promised a hike would be considered if a forthcoming Surgeon General's report on smokeless tobacco was unfavorable. Despite a Surgeon General's report that concluded that "smokeless tobacco can cause cancer and a number of noncancerous oral conditions and can lead to nicotine addiction," the tax remained at two cents until several years later, when it was raised about one cent per can. State excise taxes varied widely, from 65 percent of wholesale price per can in Washington to no tax in a majority of states. Meanwhile, health officials called for an excise tax comparable to that on cigarettes as well as an extra $1 or $2 per can to discourage teen use of the products.

The 1986 law also imposed a ban on broadcast ads for smokeless products, a tactic popular since the 1950s. However, the act did not allocate sufficient funds to finance the anti-smokeless tobacco campaign that the act legislated. In 1993, Congress did allocate slightly more than $10 million for public education about snuff and other smokeless products. In 1991 alone, however, UST had spent $14 million to distribute free samples of its products. According to company officials, the individual approach is important because novices need a personal introduction to use of snuff since they usually need instruction as to its use. In addition, UST spent millions of dollars annually on political contributions and lobbying in Washington to block anti-snuff legislation. Bantle called legislation and taxes the greatest threats to his company and the industry.

Since the Marsee case, the threat of litigation against UST diminished. A ruling by the National Academy of Sciences concluded that there was no epidemiological or clinical data that proved that moist smokeless tobacco caused cancer. While this ruling was reassuring to investors, it also was likely to deter users or their families from filing suit against the company. A recent Supreme Court ruling that said cigarette companies could not be sued for failure to warn was also likely to be a deterrent to litigation against UST, which now included warnings on its products.

UST expected to benefit from the growing trend towards banning smoking in public places and office buildings. Of the oral tobacco market, which included chewing tobacco, dry tobacco, and moist snuff, moist snuff was the only product showing sales increases. UST controlled half the oral tobacco market through its 85 percent share of the moist snuff market. UST marketed ten products in its Skoal line, but Copenhagen was responsible for 50 percent of sales.

The company continued to rely on its core business for its success, with relatively modest contributions from its wine subsidiary and its other smaller concerns, including Dr. Grabow Pre-Smoked pipes, Dill's pipe cleaners, and Cabin Fever Enterprises, which developed, produced and marketed video programming with an American theme.

In the early 1990s, exports to countries other than Canada accounted for about one percent of sales. Moist smokeless tobacco products were little known outside of the United States and Sweden, where it originated. Several nations had imposed stiff restrictions on snuff, including Australia, Hong Kong, Ireland, Israel, New Zealand, Saudi Arabia, Singapore, Tasmania, Thailand, the United Kingdom, and other European nations. However, Bantle considered the international market, especially the countries of Eastern Europe, UST's greatest opportunity for growth. Louis Bantle announced he would retire at the end of 1993 after 20 years as CEO. During this period UST sales grew from $100 million to just over $1 billion.

Principal Subsidiaries: United States Tobacco Company; International Wine & Spirits Ltd.; UST Enterprises, Inc.; UST International Inc.

Further Reading:

Deveny, Kathleen, "With Help of Teens, Snuff Sales Revive," *Wall Street Journal,* May 3, 1990, p. B1.

Loeffelholz, Suzanne, "Raider Bait," *Financial World,* September 20, 1988, pp. 24–25.

Mintz, Morton, "The Artful Dodgers," *Washington Monthly,* October 1986, pp. 9–16.

"When Diversification Doesn't Pay," *Institutional Investor,* August 1990, pp. 39–40.

White, Larry C., "Tobacco on Trial," *Merchants of Death,* New York: William Morrow, 1988, pp. 88–115.

—Wendy J. Stein

Visa International

900 Metro Center
Foster City, California 94404
Mailing Address: P.O. Box 8999
San Francisco, California 94128
U.S.A.
(415) 432-3200
Fax: (415) 432-3856

Private Company
Incorporated: 1970
Billings: $500 billion
Employees: 1,500
SICs: 6153 Payment Cards, Travelers Cheques, and Travel
  Vouchers

Visa International has grown from a credit card company into
the largest full-service consumer payment system in the world.
With over 300 million cards issued, the Visa payment card is the
most widely recognized general purpose payment card in the
world. Worldwide consumer purchases made with Visa exceeded $500 billion in 1993. In the United States, Visa com-
mands approximately 50 percent of the market in transactions
made with credit cards, equal to American Express, Master-
Card, Discover, Diner's Club, and Carte Blanche combined.

The driving force behind Visa's explosive growth was Dee
Ward Hock. Born in 1930, the son of a lineman for Utah Power
& Light Company, Hock was raised in North Ogden, Utah. He
attended a local junior college, married his childhood sweet-
heart soon after school, and worked in a slaughterhouse and for
a brick mason. In the early 1950s, Hock joined the consumer
finance department of Pacific Finance Company and soon became a local branch manager.

In 1965 Hock began working for National Bank of Commerce
in Seattle, eventually becoming assistant vice-president. At the
same time, Bank of America was in the process of licensing
BankAmericard, its credit card operation, to other banks. National Bank became one of BankAmericard's first licensees, and
Hock was promoted to manager of the bank's credit card program. However, many of the new licensee banks complained of
delayed payment transfers and lack of adequate measures to
prevent user fraud. At a meeting of over 100 bank licensees in
1968, Hock prodded the members to restructure the entire credit

card operation. Hock was elected head of the committee to
resolve recurring problems.

Hock influenced an industry with a history dating back to 1914
when the first customer charge card was issued by Western
Union. This card provided many different services, including
deferred payment for preferred customers. Over the years, a
variety of hotels, gasoline companies, and department stores
issued their customers charge cards, but the first card accepted
by a number of different merchants, the Diners Club Card, was
introduced in 1950. Merchants were reimbursed for transactions
made with the Diners Club Card by deducting a small fee.
Customers were billed monthly for the charges they incurred on
the card, and were required to pay the full amount of the invoice
upon receipt.

In 1951 Franklin National Bank on Long Island issued the first
bank-based charge card. The card was accepted only by local
merchants, but soon more than 100 other banks were issuing
cards. Merchants were charged a fee by the issuing bank for any
transaction made with the card, and no fee or interest was
charged to cardholders who paid the entire bill upon receipt.
However, since these early bankcard systems only served a
bank's local area, profits remained low.

Bank of America issued its BankAmericard in 1958. The card
was successfully marketed throughout the entire state of California. One new factor essential to its success was the credit
service. BankAmericard provided its customers with the option
of paying the balance of the account in installments, with a
monthly finance charge on the remaining balance, rather than
requiring a full payment upon receipt of the bill. Of course, the
customer could still pay the full balance of the account for the
month without any finance charge.

Soon Bank of America was forming licensing agreements with
banks outside of California which allowed them to issue the
BankAmericard. At approximately the same time, a consortium
of banks from Illinois, California, and a number of East Coast
states established another bankcard association and began to
issue Master Charge. In light of the success of these two
bankcard licensing associations, most local and regional banks
terminated their independent bankcard programs and joined either BankAmericard or Master Charge. By 1970, over 1,400
banks offered one of the two cards, and total consumer charges
on the cards amounted to $3.8 billion.

The success of Bank of America's credit card operation was
accompanied by problems, which Hock, in his capacity as head
of the banks' committee, was responsible for solving. He urged
the member banks to take control of the BankAmericard program, and in 1970 they created National BankAmericard Inc.
(NBI), a consortium of banks that issued the BankAmericard.
This independent, non-stock membership corporation purchased the entire bankcard operation from Bank of America
over the next few years, and then began to administer and
develop the BankAmericard system. Hock was chosen to lead
the new organization.

Hock headed an entirely domestic bankcard system. Outside the
United States, BankAmericard was issued by Bank of America's licensee banks in over 15 countries. In 1974 Hock negotiated the sale of all foreign credit card operations held by Bank

of America to IBANCO, a group of bank licensees that formed a multinational, non-stock corporation to administer and develop the international operations of the BankAmericard program. He then made the entire domestic BankAmericard system a subsidiary of IBANCO, and served as this group's chief executive officer.

When it came to Hock's attention that in many foreign countries there was resistance to issuing a card associated with Bank of America, despite the fact that the association was nominal only, he decided to change the name of the card and the company. In 1977 BankAmericard was renamed the Visa card. Hock chose the name "Visa" because it implied no national identification, it was relatively easy to pronounce in any language, and it made no reference to a bank, which Hock thought might limit how customers perceived they could use the card. Concurrently, NBI was rechristened Visa U.S.A., and IBANCO became Visa International.

Under Hock's leadership, customer billings for the Visa card rose dramatically, and worldwide name recognition grew at an astronomical rate. The first Visa Classic card was issued in 1977, and in 1979 Visa Traveler's Checks were introduced. Also in 1979, Visa management began to encourage merchants to use an electronic transaction-authorizing system whenever a purchase was made with the card. Visa terminals read a magnetic strip on the card and automatically requested authorization, thereby reducing retail store fraud by almost 85 percent. The Visa Premiere card was introduced in 1981, and in 1983 the Visa Classic card was redesigned to include a hologram for added security against user fraud. In 1977 Visa's market share of the bank card business was 40 percent and Master Card International's was 60 percent. By 1983, the market share proportions of each company had reversed, with Visa's billings amounting to $59 billion and MasterCard's billings at $42 billion.

In 1983 Hock implemented one of the most important and far-reaching services known in the credit card industry: a global network of automated teller machines (ATMs) that allowed Visa cardholders to obtain cash at locations far away from the banks or credit unions that originally issued them the card. The network provided a cash-dispensing service for travelers carrying the Visa card; after inserting the card into an ATM, the customer received cash from a bank account or from a previously established line of credit. Most of the ATMs were situated initially in places convenient for travelers, such as airports and tourist attractions, but soon ATMs were placed in banks themselves, gas stations, grocery stores, and innumerable other locations.

Visa's ATM network was not well received by the banking industry, since many banks operated their own network of automated teller machines. The Plus System Inc., located in Denver, was owned by 34 banks, all of which were Visa members, and had approximately 950 various financial institutions which operated ATMs that only accepted the Plus card. The banks each invested up to $150,000 in order to exclude customers who banked with competitors. Thus, while the Plus System and other similar ATM networks worked hard to ensure exclusivity for their members, Hock was implementing a net-

work that would be accessible to customers of all 15,000 member banks of Visa.

Dee W. Hock retired as president of Visa in 1984 and was succeeded by Charles T. Russell, vice-president and longtime employee of the company. Russell immediately defused the animosity between Visa and its member banks over the ATMs. During that year, the Visa ATM network was the first to complete a transnational transaction.

Visa continued its phenomenal growth under the leadership of Russell. In 1986 Visa and Mastercard took a 73 percent share of the $275 billion worldwide charge card market, and their combined transactions totalled $3.9 billion, far more than any other financial services company.

In January of 1987 Visa won a contract to operate Interlink, the largest retailer, or point-of-sale (POS), network that accepted debit cards in restaurants and stores in the United States. Already managing the California-based Interlink network of transactions since 1984, Visa was ahead of the competition in the burgeoning point-of-sale business. In February of the same year, it reached an agreement to pay $5 million for a 33 percent share in the Plus System of ATMs. By adding the 13,000 machines from Plus, the second largest ATM network in the nation, Visa provided its cardholders with access to almost one-third of the 68,000 ATMs in the United States. The Plus System was acquired completely by Visa in 1993.

One of Russell's most important strategies to maintain Visa's market share involved a commitment to improving the company's communications network. Having started VisaNet in 1972, a comprehensive communications and data processing network, Russell directly supervised a $16 million transformation of the system from a credit card transaction system to a general-purpose electronic payment system, capable of dealing with most any type of consumer banking transaction. Aware that the continued success of Visa was dependent upon the connection between its electronic mail systems and data processing networks, Russell initiated a comprehensive redesign of the company's data centers. In 1992 Visa converted its Basingstoke, England, and McLean, Virginia, data centers into global "supercenters" capable of processing worldwide volume from either location. This setup was made possible because Visa incorporated transoceanic fiber-optic cables to upgrade its international communications network. As a result of these improvements, a significant increase in volume occurred while the cost per transaction decreased. In 1992 the number of transactions on VisaNet reached a record 807 per second. The network is capable of processing 1,100 transactions per second at less than a penny per transaction.

By 1992, Visa's Gold Card, previously the Premiere Card, had become the most widely used and best recognized credit card in the world. Indeed, by all measures of success, 1993 was a banner year for Visa. The company's total worldwide billings amounted to over $500 billion; more than 300 million cards were issued to customers around the world; more than six billion card and cheque transactions were made, with travelers cheques alone growing to a worldwide sales volume of more than $16 billion; and Visa operated more than 160,000 ATMs in 60 nations.

An aggressive marketing campaign conducted against Visa by MasterCard in 1991 and 1992 appeared to pay off by March 1993. For the first time in 14 years, MasterCard reported a gain in its U.S. market share for charge-card spending, up to 26.8 percent, while Visa's market share decreased from 45.3 percent to 45.1 percent. The competition between Visa and MasterCard, however, is friendly since almost all the banks that own the MasterCard association also belong to the Visa association, and no one bank benefits from a gain in market share by one at the expense of the other.

Visa's primary competitor for both the U.S. and international market is American Express. While the Diners Club card holds a 2.2 percent market share of U.S. charge-card spending, and the Sears Discover card a 6.5 percent share, American Express maintains a 19.4 percent share and is working hard to increase it. Both Visa and American Express have intensified the competition for a larger U.S. market share by using the concept of "ambush advertising" in their commercials. Visa, as one of the major sponsors of the 1992 Olympics, used its television ads to remind viewers that the Visa card is more widely accepted than American Express. American Express, on the other hand, featured an Olympic theme while using a clever play on the word "visa" to promote its own card at Visa's expense.

In the mid-1990s, Visa's focus was on developing its foreign operations, increasing its debit activity, and improving its technological infrastructure. If past accomplishments are indicative, Visa will continue to serve as the world's largest full-service consumer payment system.

Further Reading:

Garfield, Bob, "AMEX vs. Visa—Round 2: The Agony of Ambushing," *Advertising Age,* July 20, 1992, p. 44.
Louis, Arthur M., "Visa Stirs Up the Big Banks—Again," *Fortune,* October 3, 1983, pp. 196–203.

—Thomas Derdak

Washington Natural Gas Company

815 Mercer Street
Seattle, Washington 98109-4714
U.S.A.
(206) 622-6767
Fax: (206) 382-7875

Wholly Owned Subsidiary of Washington Energy Company
Incorporated: 1955
Employees: 1,679
Sales: $277.4 million
Stock Exchanges: New York
SICs: 4924 Natural Gas Distribution

Washington Natural Gas Company, the largest natural gas utility in the State of Washington, is one of the fastest growing natural gas utilities in the United States. Serving 425,000 customers in five counties, Washington Natural's customer base is primarily residential, with industrial and commercial clientele composing about ten percent of total customers, but accounting for 61 percent of the total volume of natural gas distributed by the company. In 1978, a holding company, Washington Energy Company, was formed to enable the diversification into energy related businesses. Washington Natural Gas is the largest subsidiary and the primary focus of the holding company's business, which also includes oil and gas exploration and production operations, sales of home energy and security products, a partnership in a railroad company, and a partnership in a coal mining venture.

The roots of Washington Natural Gas may be traced back to the introduction of gas lighting in Seattle, Washington. For the 2,000 residents residing in the young and growing town, New Year's Eve of 1873 was the first time that gas lamps lit 42 private homes and five public streets. The company responsible for this historic moment was Seattle Gas Light Company, a recently formed utility founded by Seattle's first banker, Dexter Horton; one of the town's founders, Arthur Denny; and the city's mayor, John Collins. The gas for the region's first private utility was manufactured from coal and distributed to the company's limited customers through hollowed-out fir logs, a rudimentary system that, nevertheless, effectively carried what was considered to be a quality of gas equal to the fuel distributed by more sophisticated systems in the western United States.

Seattle Gas grew over the years, adding customers who could afford the luxury of gas lighting and collecting revenues from supplying the gas to light Seattle's streets. In 1889, a new form of energy attracted the attention of Seattle Gas' founders, as Seattle became the fourth city in the world to operate an electric streetcar system. Horton, Denny, and Collins foresaw the possibilities in electricity for Seattle and created another utility company, Seattle Gas and Electric Light Company, which generated electricity from steam.

Shortly after the creation of Seattle Gas and Electric Light, an enormous blaze, the Great Seattle Fire of 1889, swept through the city, consuming nearly every building and residence and destroying the electric and gas facilities used by the two utilities. After the fire, the founders of the two companies created a new utility, with the somewhat unwieldy name of Seattle Gas, Electric Light and Motor Company. This newly formed utility operated until 1892, when investors from the East purchased a controlling interest in the utility's stock and reorganized it as Seattle Gas and Electric Light Company. By this time the utility served roughly 1,200 customers and produced 96,000 cubic feet of gas per day—a small amount of fuel compared to the 525 million cubic feet the company's successor would distribute in one day nearly a century later—but as the uses of gas multiplied, Seattle Gas' volume of gas increased. As Seattle's residents celebrated the arrival of a new century, gas was used not only to fuel lamps, but also to power appliances and heat water. Gas was heralded as the energy source of the modern age, and many Seattle residents responded by equipping their homes with machines that relied on gas.

Gas continued to attract customers until the mid-1930s when high manufacturing costs increased the competition between Seattle Gas and alternative energy source utilities. One such energy source, natural gas, had begun to entice utility companies in other parts of the country as a cheaper, more profitable fuel to distribute, the availability of which had been made easier by the development of thin-walled, large-diameter steel pipe. The advent of the steel pipe encouraged business leaders and public officials to initiate a campaign in the early 1950s to bring natural gas to the Pacific Northwest. In anticipation of the fuel's arrival, Seattle Gas and Electric Light Company, which by this time had been renamed Seattle Gas Company, merged with Washington Gas & Electric Co., a utility based in Tacoma, Washington, in 1955, to form Washington Natural Gas Company.

The following year, when the two merged gas manufacturers completed the conversion of their facilities to distribute natural gas, the new fuel was brought to the Pacific Northwest through a pipeline operated by Pacific Northwest Pipeline Co. With 48,500 customers and revenues of $7 million, Washington Natural Gas entered a new era of business, confident that natural gas would generate greater revenues and attract more customers. To this end, Washington Natural Gas' management was not disappointed. In four years, revenues nearly tripled to $20.4 million, earnings more than quintupled to $1.6 million, and the number of customers swelled to 76,000. Natural quickly became the new fuel of the modern age in the Pacific Northwest, attracting many residential, commercial, and industrial consumers impressed by its cheaper cost and the several advantages its usage offered. For industrial users, natural gas required no storage facilities, possessed greater combustion efficiency, and could be utilized in a number of ways. It was also a cleaner burning fuel that could be heated in more compact furnaces, enabling residential customers to convert areas surrounding their furnaces into living space. Washington Natural Gas soon added to its rapidly rising revenues by selling natural gas appliances, a side business that generated significant revenue for the company. With these synergistic sales and rental programs augmenting Washington Natural Gas' burgeoning distribution business, the company had achieved remarkable results in a short time and stood ready to capitalize on what promised to be a lucrative business.

The robust growth the company experienced during its first several years of distributing natural gas continued into the 1960s, invigorated by favorable economic conditions in the Pacific Northwest. The population in the region was rapidly increasing, by far eclipsing the national rate of population growth, as industrial and commercial expansion persuaded many out-of-state residents to relocate within Washington Natural's area of service. Of these new homes, many were connected to Washington Natural Gas' distribution system. By the beginning of 1963, the company had connected its 100,000th customer, adding a minimum of 10,000 customers annually in the first three years of the decade. Revenues also continued their exponential rise, reaching nearly $26 million by the end of 1962, which represented a 132 percent increase since the utility had converted to natural gas. To keep pace with the growing demand for natural gas, Washington Natural Gas had increased the mileage of its distribution network by 52 percent since 1956, requiring 2,806 miles of transmission line by 1962, the same year in which over $10 million were spent on capital expenditures.

With projections for the remainder of the decade calling for a similar rate of population growth, future demand for natural gas appeared secure. However, some uncertainties concerning the supply of natural gas to the Pacific Northwest were beginning to develop by the mid-1960s. Washington Natural Gas' primary supply of natural gas came from the pipeline owned by Pacific Northwest Pipeline Co., which by this time had been purchased by El Paso Natural Gas Co. The relationship between Washington Natural Gas and Pacific Northwest Pipeline had always been mutually beneficial, before and after El Paso assumed control. Pacific Northwest Pipeline had access to ample supplies of natural gas from Canada and the San Juan Basin fields in New Mexico and Colorado, which had proven sufficient to meet Washington Natural Gas' needs and those of other utilities in the region. However, when the U.S. Supreme Court ordered El Paso Natural to relinquish control of Pacific Northwest Pipeline, some doubts were raised as to whether the pipeline would be allocated a sufficient supply of fuel. Although Washington Natural Gas never suffered from the change of the pipeline's ownership, as did several utilities operating in the Pacific Northwest, the anxiety evoked by the uncertainty of supply led the company's management to seriously consider developing ancillary sources of natural gas. Some efforts had been directed toward this objective before the El Paso Natural divestiture, including a joint venture with Washington Water Power Company and El Paso Natural to develop an underground storage facility for natural gas in the southern end of Washington Natural's service area, but the incident did serve as a reminder

of Washington Natural's vulnerability. In 1965, the utility completed a propane air gas plant, which, combined with the underground storage facility, provided a supplementary source of natural gas to be utilized during periods of heavy demand.

While the issue of natural gas availability was being debated, the full ramifications of which were not decided until the end of the decade, Washington Natural Gas continued to add customers and increase its profits at the same vigorous rate as the late 1950s and early 1960s. By 1968, Washington Natural Gas served 164,183 customers, and its earnings had reached $4.5 million, a twelvefold increase in ten years. A large part of this growth was still attributable to the booming population within the company's service area, which increased 32 percent from 1965 to 1970 compared to a national increase of six percent over the same span of time. However, the company's growth was also attributable to the utility's success in persuading customers to use natural gas for a multitude of energy needs. Three of its competitors in the energy market—Seattle City Light, Tacoma City Light, and Puget Sound Power and Light—sold fewer BTUs of energy to their 600,000 customers than Washington Natural Gas sold to customers representing only one-fourth the combined total of the other utilities. Encouraged by this success, Washington Natural Gas management allocated over $75 million to be spent by 1972 for capital expenditures in anticipation of increasing the number of its customers by 90,000.

As it entered the 1970s, Washington Natural Gas initiated a more concerted effort toward developing supplementary supplies of natural gas and began diversifying into non-utility ventures. Its supply of natural gas from Pacific Northwest Pipeline was still ample and stable, enough for a 20-year supply, compared to a national average among utility companies of ten years. However, the utility's dependence on the pipeline and particularly its reliance on Canadian gas prompted it to invest in natural gas exploration and mining ventures to ameliorate its position.

Washington Natural Gas received nearly 70 percent of its natural gas from Canada, a source that had proven advantageous for several reasons, including Canada's large supply of gas and its geographic proximity. Canada had enough natural gas to supply users for a projected 25 years, and this supply was expected to increase since Canada paid producers of newly acquired natural gas a higher price than the United States did, which encouraged natural gas exploration. However, water seepage into key Canadian natural gas fields in 1973, as well as increased Canadian demand, demonstrated to Washington Natural Gas the inherent danger of depending on one source for a majority of its gas.

Although Washington Natural customers connected to firm, or consistent, supplies of fuel did not experience any interruption of service, those users connected to interruptable lines did suffer from a reduced supply as a consequence of the production difficulties in Canada. From 1974 to 1977, sales to interruptible consumers were curtailed for an average of approximately 80 days per year, further underscoring the need for Washington Natural Gas to develop alternative sources of natural gas. Accordingly, through its newly formed subsidiary, Thermal Exploration Inc. (now Washington Energy Resources Co.), Washington Natural Gas engaged in several joint ventures to explore and develop new natural gas reserves in the United States, specifically in Colorado and Montana, where the utility held an interest in a total of 345,000 acres. Washington Natural Gas also became involved in coal mining ventures in Montana to explore the possibility of converting coal to gas. The technology for the gasification of coal had been available for a considerable length of time, but the process was prohibitively expensive. However, Washington Natural Gas' management believed that energy prices would rise sufficiently within the next decade to make the gasification of coal an economically feasible substitute for natural gas.

By 1977, Washington Natural Gas investments in ventures unrelated to natural gas distribution led the utility to form a holding company to reorganize its operations and separate its other interests into distinct subsidiaries. In addition to Washington Natural Gas, operating within the holding company, named Washington Energy Company, were Thermal Energy, Inc., Thermal Exploration, Inc., and Thermal Efficiency. These three wholly owned subsidiaries were involved in the distribution of energy conservation equipment, oil and gas exploration, and the development of coal reserves—businesses that would add revenues to the company and help mitigate the cyclicality of the company's distribution operations. Although natural gas usage per customer had decreased during the 1970s, and the price of Canadian gas had risen, Washington Natural continued to increase its revenues during this period, albeit at a slower rate than in the 1960s. By the end of the decade, revenues had swelled to over $300 million, representing a 17 percent compounded annual increase since the beginning of the decade. Moreover, the utility's number of customers had topped 240,000, finally reaching the level forecasted by Washington Natural's management in 1968.

Washington Natural Gas' dependence on Canadian gas began to diminish in the 1980s. As Canadian natural gas became increasingly expensive, the company began to rely more on the alternative sources created by its subsidiaries, and by 1982, only half of the utility's supply came from Canada. In 1979, the Washington Utilities and Transportation Commission withdrew its permission for Washington Energy Co. to fund oil and natural gas exploration by charging expenses to customers. Nevertheless, the holding company continued to direct its subsidiary to explore for oil and gas through joint ventures. By 1985, Washington Natural Gas had become the 47th largest natural gas distributor in the United States, with 266,349 customers. Although

revenues sagged after the record year of 1985, by the end of the decade the utility had once again returned to posting enviable financial figures. In 1989, the utility added customers three times faster than the national average, largely due to the enormous price advantage natural gas had over electricity. Through aggressive marketing, Washington Natural Gas served 96 percent of the single-family market within its distribution area, reaching a total of 324,222 customers.

In 1990, Washington Natural Gas recorded $292 million in revenues and $20.6 million in net income. The following year, revenues climbed to $303 million, and net income increased to nearly $31 million. Anticipating similar results in 1992, Washington Natural's management was disappointed by a year of unusually warm weather, which impeded revenue growth. For the year, revenues dropped to $277 million and net income plummeted to $14 million.

Further Reading:

"The Executive's Corner," *Wall Street Transcript,* June 17, 1968, pp. 13,605–606.

"The Fair Is Officially Over But Its Effects Linger On," *Investment Dealers' Digest,* March 4, 1963, p. 30.

Holland, Sidney M., "Washington Natural Gas Co.," *Investment Dealers' Digest,* August 12, 1963, p. 17.

Neurath, Peter, "Washington Energy Keeps Stretching Its Energy Base," *Puget Sound Business Journal,* February 19, 1990, p. 2.

——. "WECO Bucking a Trend in Oil, Gas Exploration," *Puget Sound Business Journal,* March 13, 1989, p. 11.

Warren, Gail, "Gas Showed the Way," *Puget Sound Business Journal,* April 3, 1989, p. 6.

"Washington Energy Company," *Wall Street Transcript,* March 16, 1981, p. 60,854.

"Washington Energy Venture," *The Wall Street Journal,* April 16, 1980, p. 20.

"Washington Natural Gas Company," *Capital Changes Reports,* 1990, p. 2,074.

"Washington Natural Gas Company," *Wall Street Transcript,* August 23, 1976, p. 44,528.

"Washington Natural Gas Company," *Wall Street Transcript,* January 27, 1969, pp. 15,623–15,624.

"Washington Natural Marks Growth," *Investment Dealers' Digest,* July 24, 1961, p. 42.

"Washington Natural Realigns, Forms Washington Energy Co.," *Pipeline & Gas Journal,* October 1976, p. 7.

—Jeffrey L. Covell

Waxman

INDUSTRIES INC. [UU]

Waxman Industries, Inc.

24460 Aurora Road
Bedford Heights, Ohio 44146
U.S.A.
(216) 439-1830
Fax: (216) 439-1262

Public Company
Incorporated: 1971
Employees: 1,805
Sales: $397.6 million
Stock Exchanges: New York
SICs: 5074 Plumbing and Hydronic Heating Supplies; 5063
   Electrical Apparatus & Equipment; 5072 Hardware

Waxman Industries, Inc., a company based in suburban Cleveland, Ohio, has grown from a small family concern to one of the largest full-line suppliers of plumbing, electrical, and hardware products for the do-it-yourself market. Waxman and its subsidiaries market products in the United States and Canada through home improvement centers, warehouse home centers, mass merchandisers, hardware stores, lumber yards, wholesalers, and mail order catalogs. The company serves its customers from packaging and distribution facilities located throughout the United States, Canada, Taiwan, and mainland China.

The business was founded in 1934 by Stanley Waxman, a Russian immigrant who sold used sinks, bathtubs, and other plumbing equipment in inner-city Cleveland. By the time Stanley handed over the family business to sons Armondand Melvin in 1965, Waxman Industries had expanded into the do-it-yourself business. The company concentrated on assembly, packaging, and distribution, rather than manufacturing. The brothers made their first acquisition, Rex Supply, in January 1970, and took the company public in 1971. The Waxman family retained a controlling interest in their namesake company.

The 1970s were a decade of trial and error for the growing business. Two business strategies in particular jeopardized the company's progress. First, the Waxmans attempted to expand into northern California's intensely competitive building supplies market in 1974 by acquiring plumbing and electrical distributors. The two businesses had solid sales but meager profits, and soon began to detract from Waxman's other operations. Then, in 1977, Waxman launched six retail Handi-Fix stores in Indianapolis. The stores, located primarily in strip malls, had to be closed in mid-1979.

At the same time, high interest rates during the inflationary 1970s battered the highly-leveraged company. Waxman's earnings declined in five out of seven years during the decade, and in 1977 the company suffered a net loss of $1.2 million on sales of $23.7 million. To make matters worse, Handy City, one of Waxman's primary customers, canceled its accounts in 1980. As a result, the company was forced to close a major Atlanta distribution center that year. Sales and earnings declined again in 1981, and the company reached the nadir of its downward spiral in 1982: net income plummeted 83 percent, from $301,000 in 1981 to $51,000.

Although the 1970s had challenged Waxman Industries, the company's co-CEOs learned valuable lessons from their experiences. Armond, the company's acquisitions chief, arrived at a specific set of criteria for new purchases. Candidates for acquisition would have to be profitable, have distribution capabilities, a reliable management team, and a customer or product base that correlated to Waxman's customers and products. All acquisitions were financed with cash or debt, not stock. Melvin Waxman would manage the growing operations acquired by his brother during the 1980s.

Waxman Industries began to emerge from the doldrums of the 1970s in the early years of the following decade. In 1981, the company acquired Medal Distributing Co., of Sharon, Pennsylvania, and in 1982, the company expanded to the East Coast with the purchase of Singer Hardware & Supply Co. and its affiliate, Shalin Sales, Inc. Both businesses were located in New Jersey.

The company began a growth spurt in mid-decade, with acquisitions that propelled it to the forefront of the highly fragmented do-it-yourself-supply market. Waxman had endured the industry's slow climb from a volume of $8 billion in 1972 to $40 billion by 1983. The expansion of this industry was fueled, in part, by the high cost of professional plumbers and electricians. Industry observers also noted that many people appreciated the sense of satisfaction they got from doing their own home repairs. Analysis of the do-it-yourself industry showed that, by 1984, 75 percent of all single-family homes had at least one do-it-yourselfer. Waxman got a leg up in this market by "assuming their customers were dopes and providing instructions with their goods that the least handy consumer could follow," according to *Forbes*. These user-friendly products earned customer loyalty early.

Waxman established several brands of best-selling products in the early 1980s. The company's Plumbcraft plumbing parts constituted the bulk of annual sales volume. Plumbcraft stock ranged from household chemicals to kitchen and bathroom accessories. Electrical products were sold primarily under the Electracraft name. Waxman introduced its Fancraft ceiling-fan accessories in 1983. Within a few years, ceiling fans went from being energy-related products to a useful and basic household appliance. Fancraft soon became one of the company's primary lines. The company's TelCraft line of telephone accessories was introduced at about the same time. It satisfied demands for connecting devices after the breakup of AT&T and the proliferation of phone manufacturers encouraged self-installation and maintenance of home telephones. Waxman brands were promoted with print advertisements, point-of purchase displays, and colorful packaging. The company also sponsored in-store how-to clinics to promote its products, which pleased retailers and consumers alike.

Waxman's acquisitions in the 1980s increased sales volume, broadened the company's customer base, and expanded its geographical reach. The company made its first major acquisition of the decade, Barnett Brass & Copper Inc. of Jacksonville, Florida, for $12.5 million in cash and credit in 1984. Barnett's $28 million annual sales gave Waxman a foothold in markets served by major hardware cooperatives and supermarkets, as well as the mail-order market. Mail-order sales helped Waxman increase its geographical distribution without having to open distant warehouses, and Barnett doubled its mail-order offerings by supplementing its product line with Waxman supplies. Waxman augmented Barnett's line of imported plumbing items with a packaging facility established in Taiwan in 1984. The overseas operations were part of the company's efforts to be a low-cost supplier, and by 1989, 25 percent of Waxman's products came from Taiwan.

Waxman's acquisition program continued in 1985, with the $3.7-million cash purchase of LeRan Copper & Brass Inc., a Coldwater, Michigan supplier of copper tubing and fittings, brass valves and fittings, and other specialty products. LeRan contributed $25 million in annual sales to Waxman's profits, and increased the parent's customer base by almost 8,000 customers. The company's successes of the first half of the decade permitted a 3-for-2 stock split in 1985.

Select-Line Industries joined the roster of companies the following year. This Cleveland company supplied plumbing and electrical products to do-it-yourself retailers, and had about $8 million in annual sales. Waxman also acquired Keystone Franklin, Inc., a manufacturer of Sears, Roebuck & Co.'s Craftsman label, for $4 million in 1986. Pennsylvania-based Keystone Franklin was founded in 1927 and had estimated sales of $22 million at the time of its purchase. About half of that subsidiary's business was with Sears and other major retailers. The merger of Waxman and Keystone products expanded the latter company's private label plumbing program with Sears by two-thirds, increasing the number of products it supplied to the mass merchandiser to 375 items.

Waxman's profits more than doubled in each of the three years from 1983 to 1986, culminating in record earnings. Later that year, the Waxmans won approval of a plan that helped keep control of the company in the family through the creation of two classes of common stock with separate voting rights. The plan, effectively a 2-for-1 stock split, helped the Waxman brothers maintain their 45 percent share of the company.

By 1987, Waxman Industries topped $100 million in annual sales with a diversified customer base of do-it-yourselfers and professionals. The sales were made through a variety of venues: warehouse home centers, mass merchandisers, lumberyards, and neighborhood hardware stores. No one customer group or retail situation accounted for more than seven percent of total sales, which sheltered the company from downturns in specific markets.

Debt remained the company's only problem. In 1987, Waxman offered $25 million in long-term convertible bonds through Drexel-Burnham-Lambert and used the proceeds to retire $13.7 million in face value of 10-year senior subordinated notes sold in 1985. At the same time, Waxman made its first purchasing foray outside the United States with the acquisition of H. Belanger Plumbing Accessories, Ltd., of Montreal Quebec. The buy pushed Waxman's long-term debt to $41 million from $22 million, bringing the ratio of long-term debt to equity to almost 2-to-1. Although some industry observers were wary of Waxman's debt load, the co-CEOs characterized it as a necessary evil.

Waxman acquired Madison Equipment Co., of Cleveland, and the plumbing products and floor care business of the Stanley Works Co., of New Brittan, Connecticut, in 1988. That year, the parent made a 3-for-1 stock split and secured a $100-million, three-year, unsecured revolving credit agreement with its banks to help fund yet another acquisition. That August, Waxman acquired U.S. Lock, a distributor of professional locksmiths' supplies, including locksets, deadlocks, padlocks, door closers, exit devices, and key blanks. U.S. Lock marketed over 3,200 products under its namesake trademark, as well as over 7,700 products supplied by other security hardware manufacturers. This Edgewood, New York company had annual sales of about $20 million. Waxman wrapped up the decade with its largest-ever acquisition: the Ideal Group of Companies. Waxman took on more debt to purchase Canada's third-largest distributor of plumbing and heating products, but the parent's sales nearly doubled with the addition of Ideal's $205-million annual volume.

Waxman's acquisitions of the 1980s contributed to almost a decade of phenomenal growth for the company. From 1982 to 1989, sales grew from $36 million to $238.9 million, and profits increased from about $400,000 to $7.3 million over the same period. The growth was based partially on internal expansion, but stemmed primarily from savvy acquisitions. Wall Street recognized the difference between the 1970s and 1980s at Waxman, too: the company's stock appreciated 2,846.4 percent over the decade, from $.28 per share on December 31, 1979 to $8.25 at the end of 1989. The company ranked 152nd on *Financial World's* list of America's 500 fastest-growing companies.

In the early 1990s, Waxman slowed its rate of growth through acquisitions to concentrate on internal growth and debt reduction. The company's sole acquisition in the first two years of the decade extended its reach across the United States' southern border. Waxman purchased Western American Manufacturing, a manufacturing and packaging operation in Tijuana, Mexico that was founded in 1966 to make WAMI brand pipe nipples (lengths of pipe with threads at both ends). Internal growth got a boost in 1991 when K-Mart chose Waxman to supply its packaged plumbing to 2,300 stores nationwide. The mass merchandiser was the United States' largest plumbing retailer, and brought $10 million of new business to Waxman during the first year of the agreement. Sales in the early 1990s declined annually, due more to a deep recession in Canada than the economic slowdown in the United States. Waxman hoped to increase its growing mail order and telemarketing business as the two countries recovered from the economic downturn.

Waxman's efforts at debt reduction started in 1991 with the sale of $50 million in bonds in a private placement with institutional investors. The bonds offered the outstanding stock of Barnett Brass & Copper as collateral. Debt restructuring continued the following year, when Waxman repurchased over $12 million in long-term debt, reducing the company's debt levels by about five percent. The company also completed a public offering of 2.2 million shares of common stock, netting $9.8 million and enabling Waxman to retire even more debt. By the end of fiscal year 1992, Waxman had improved its debt-to-equity ratio from 6.2-to-1 to 5.4-to-1.

Further Reading:

"Do-it-yourself Business Raises Waxman Earnings," *Plain Dealer* (Cleveland), January 21, 1988, p. 2C.

Gerdel, Thomas W., "Net Income Falls 32 Percent at Waxman," *Plain Dealer* (Cleveland), November 4, 1992, p. 2D.

——, "Waxman Agrees to Acquire Canadian Distribution Firm," *Plain Dealer* (Cleveland), March 3, 1989, p. 8C.

——, "Waxman Brothers' Firm Grows," *Plain Dealer* (Cleveland), August 21, 1984, p. 7D.

——, "Waxman Weighs New Facility for China Venture," *Plain Dealer* (Cleveland), January 18, 1989, p. 2C.

Gleisser, Marcus, "If You Only Knew Then. . . Waxman Industries Topped All Cleveland Firms in Past Ten Years," *Plain Dealer* (Cleveland), January 8, 1990, pp. 1D, 6D.

——, "K-Mart Picks Waxman as Plumbing Supplier," *Plain Dealer* (Cleveland), October 1, 1991, p. 6D.

——, "Waxmans Grow on Opportunity in Acquisitions," *Plain Dealer* (Cleveland), August 1, 1988, p. 9B.

——, "Waxman Industries Buys Company," *Plain Dealer* (Cleveland), November 29, 1990, p. 2D.

——, "Waxman Uses Stock-sale Proceeds to Cut Debt Load," *Plain Dealer* (Cleveland), June 3, 1992, p. 2E.

Gordon, Mitchell, "Close to Home: Acquisitions, K-Mart Chain Pace Waxman's Profits," *Barron's,* March 24, 1986, pp. 47–48.

——, "Pulling for K-Mart: It's a Big Customer of Waxman, Home-repair Supplier," *Barron's,* August 17, 1987.

Karle, Delinda, "Waxman Industries Acquires U.S. Lock," *Plain Dealer* (Cleveland), July 2, 1988, p. 10A.

Mahoney, Mike, "Waxman OKs Plan to Convert Stock," *Plain Dealer* (Cleveland), December 19, 1986, p. 17B.

Montgomery, Leland, and Alexandra Ourusoff, "The Top 500 Growth Companies," *Financial World,* August 7, 1990, pp. 46–48.

Morgenson, Gretchen, "Back from the Brink," *Forbes,* June 15, 1987, pp. 109–110.

"Three More Acquisitions Noted," *Plain Dealer* (Cleveland), November 2, 1985, p. 8C.

Troxell, Thomas N., "Handyman Special: Waxman Looks for Profit Boost from Mail-order Unit," *Barron's,* October 29, 1984, p. 59.

—April S. Dougal

Wegmans

Wegmans Food Markets, Inc.

P.O. Box 844
Rochester, New York 14692-0844
U.S.A.
(716) 328-2550
Fax: (716) 464-4626

Private Company
Incorporated: 1931
Employees: 18,000
Sales: $1.64 billion
SICs: 5411 Grocery Stores

Wegmans Food Markets, Inc. is a privately held, family-run corporation that operates 47 supermarkets, 14 Chase-Pitkin Home and Garden stores, and a child development center in upstate New York. With headquarters in Rochester, New York, Wegmans' primary operating area is that city and surrounding Monroe County; it is one of the top five employers in the Rochester area. Wegmans also has four stores in adjoining counties, nine supermarkets in the Syracuse and Auburn area, five in Buffalo, five in the southern tier, and one in Erie, Pennsylvania.

Wegmans was founded as the Rochester Fruit and Vegetable Company in 1916, a small food store run out of the front of the Wegman family's house in Rochester. After six years of selling groceries from home, brothers Walter and Jack Wegman moved their enterprise to a small, full-scale grocery store featuring canned goods, produce, a bakery, and even a cafeteria.

The two brothers became known as innovators in the grocery business, and in the early 1930s, they opened a self-service grocery, a new concept that would revolutionize food shopping. The new store was incorporated in 1931 as Wegmans Food Markets, Inc. The Wegmans store became a successful operation as well as a tourist attraction, featuring self-service and several other innovations, including vaporized water spray for vegetables and fruits, refrigerated food display windows, home-made candy, and a cafeteria that seated 300 people.

In 1950, Robert Wegman, son and nephew of the founders, became president of Wegmans stores, and the company began to invest in businesses that would enhance its central focus. Wegman acquired an egg farm and developed an on-site meat processing center and a central bakery. He also formed Weg-

mans Enterprises, Inc. to handle real estate development, leasing, and property management for the company. In 1969 he was named chairman and CEO of Wegmans.

In the late 1960s, Wegmans expanded outside of Monroe County, building stores in Syracuse, New York. The 1970s brought new 40,000-square-foot stores that were intended to incorporate the ''mall in a store'' concept. These new stores included gift cards, floral products, and pharmaceutical departments and were open 24 hours. Wegmans also became the third chain in the country to use electronic cash registers when it installed an optical scanner system in a Rochester store in 1972.

In 1973, Robert Wegman capitalized on the growing demand for do-it-yourself home improvement products, opening his Home Improvement Center next to one of its Rochester groceries. The following year, Wegmans purchased Bilt-Rite Chase-Pitkin, Inc., a retail operation that sold lumber, hardware, millwork, garden and landscape materials, and building supplies. Wegmans soon began expanding this chain and building Chase-Pitkin stores next to existing Wegmans stores. Robert Wegman's son Danny assumed the presidency of Wegmans in 1976.

The company began carrying its own store brand items in 1979, and the line became so popular that by the early 1990s, Wegmans was carrying 1,000 items under its own name, including a line of soda. In 1983 Wegmans became one of the first chains to install automated teller machines connected to local banks. The ATMs were profitable for the store because Wegmans owned the machines and charged fees to the bank for providing all the front-line services including replenishing cash and receipt forms. Other developments included the 1986 establishment of the Wegmans Federal Credit Union for company employees. Four years later, the company opened one of the first child care services offered by a private company with its Wegmans Child Development Center in the town of Greece, New York.

Wegmans prided itself on its contributions to the communities in which it operated, noting its donations of damaged packaged goods and perishables to local food banks as well as its sponsorship of local events, donations of foods to charitable activities, and contributions to community projects. Wegmans has been nationally recognized several times throughout its history. In 1987, *Fortune* magazine named Wegmans the best U.S. supermarket in terms of customer service. In 1991, Wegmans' work scholarship program was awarded a ''Points of Light Award'' by President George Bush. The company was also listed in the 1993 publication of *The 100 Best Companies to Work for in America*.

Wegmans received the American Business Press competition, ''Points of Light,'' for its community service through its Work/Scholarship Connection program. The Wegmans program, started in 1987, helped mostly 14- and 15-year-old children at risk of dropping out of school. The store gave these participating students part-time jobs and assigned a mentor to each of them. The mentor, an adult co-worker, helped the student on the job and with schoolwork. Students who stayed on the job and stayed in school to graduate from high school also won a $5,000 college scholarship to the school of his or her choice.

The Wegmans entry in *The 100 Best Companies to Work For in America* cited the company's child and development center, medical and vacation benefits for part-time workers, scholarship program and Work-Scholarship Connection, job security, and opportunities for promotion. Wegman's was one of only two supermarket businesses included in the *100 Best Companies* listing.

Benefits for employees of Wegmans included medical and life insurance and prescription plans for full-time employees after 90 days of service and for part-time employees after one year, profit-sharing for full-timers after one year, tuition scholarships up to $1,500 for both full and part time employees, a 401K plan, and paid vacations. Full-time cashiers, as of January 1993 were paid $6.70 per hour and part-timers $4.50 per hour. Department managers earned annual salaries of between $30,000 and $40,000, while store managers earned $50,000 to $80,000 a year.

Nevertheless, Wegmans had its share of controversy and critics. The company came under attack from consumer groups as well as the New York State Attorney General's office for its alleged refusal to adhere to the state's item pricing laws. Wegmans' stores violations of state item pricing laws dated back to 1986, but the company argued that item pricing increased consumer costs because of the expense of pricing each item. Wegmans continued to stand by its electronic scanner pricing, claiming it was more accurate than price stickers and refused to pay fines levied against it for violations of the unit pricing regulations. Wegmans won the Attorney General's lawsuit, and the item pricing law in question subsequently expired in 1991.

Wegmans also faced protests from environmental groups when it launched a campaign to decrease paper bag use in favor of plastic. Environmentalists claimed that Wegmans was misleading the public with its claim that plastic bags were better for the environment than paper bags. The critics argued that for Wegmans the main issue was cost: paper bags cost $41 per 1,000 while plastic cost $18.50 per thousand. According to Wegmans, however, paper bags did not disintegrate in modern dumps any more quickly than plastic, and production of plastic was more energy and resource efficient. Wegmans finally responded to protests by letting each customer decide how he or she wanted purchases bagged. Furthermore, the company established bins for customers to deposit plastic bags for recycling, as part of a trial program with Mobil Chemical Company for recycling plastic. Wegmans also began using paper bags made from recycled paper.

Wegmans also felt criticism commonly directed at companies that experience periods of growth and operation expansion. The needs of the company, it was felt, in some cases conflicted with the needs and interests of local residents when Wegmans sought to enlarge existing stores, requiring the purchase of surrounding properties and development of new traffic control patterns.

By 1993, the largest Wegmans stores were 120,000 square feet, three times the size of the "mall-in-a-store" facilities established 20 years earlier. New Wegmans superstores included cafes with Chinese food, pizza and pasta bars, as well as cappucino and coffee bars. Wegmans promoted itself as a strong advocate of health and nutrition, launching series of bulletins called "Strive for Five," prepared by a registered dietician and featuring information and recipes for fruits and vegetables. Furthermore, in the early 1990s, Wegmans launched a line of diet foods, called "Just Help Yourself," featuring frozen, prepackaged meals comparable to those offered by diet centers.

In 1993, Wegmans employed more than 18,000 people and continued to grow as it expanded many of its existing stores, opened its first store outside of New York State, in Erie, Pennsylvania, and contemplated building other stores in Pennsylvania. That year, its Chase-Pitkin chain had ten locations in Rochester, one in Canandaigua, one in Buffalo, and two in Syracuse. In 1993, Wegmans Enterprises, the company's real estate division, owned most of the property on which its stores were situated. About 1.1 million of the division's 4.6 million square feet of shopping plaza retail space was leased to tenants, including small shops as well as major department store facilities.

Further Reading:

Khermouch, Gerry, "Wegmans Builds its Local Base with Private Label," *Brandweek,* March 8, 1993, p. 23.

Uttal, Bro, Bill Saporito, and Monci Jo Williams, "Companies That Serve You Best," *Fortune,* December 7, 1987, p. 98.

"Wegmans Community Scrapbook," Rochester, NY: Wegmans Food Markets, Inc., 1993.

"A Winning Day at the White House," *Supermarket Business,* November 1991, p. 9.

—Wendy J. Stein

Westin Hotel Co.

2001 Sixth Avenue
Seattle, Washington 98121
U.S.A.
(206) 443-5000
Fax: (206) 443-5096

Wholly Owned Subsidiary of Aoki Corporation (Japan)
Incorporated: 1930 as Western Hotels Inc.
Sales: $1.3 billion
Employees: 35,000
SICs: 7011 Hotels & Motels

Westin Hotel Co., the oldest hotel management company in North America, is the operating company for all the hotel assets of its parent company, Aoki Corporation. With more than 35,000 hotel rooms in South America, North America, Europe, and Asia, Westin books roughly 2.2 million rooms a year. Throughout its history, the company has pioneered many hotel innovations adopted by the industry worldwide.

In the late 1920s, hotel ownership in the Pacific Northwest included several key figures. Severt W. Thurston arrived in Seattle in 1903 to pursue a career as a vaudeville acrobat. According to legend, Thurston's brief career behind the stage lights came to an ignoble end when, as the top man on a human pyramid, he was thrown off balance and into the orchestra pit by one of his human supports whose sobriety was in question. Thurston quickly left show business and took a job as a porter in a local hotel. The hotel owner's son, Harold E. Maltby, became friends with Thurston and, eventually, they decided to enter the hotel business, forming the Maltby-Thurston Corporation in 1910.

At roughly the same time the Maltby-Thurston partnership was created, Nebraska native Frank A. Dupar was working in Seattle as a plumber. After several years, Dupar became the owner of Palmer Supply Co., a wholesale plumbing and supply firm, and promoted apartment houses and hotels in the area with his younger brother Harold. The Dupars initially contracted to lay the plumbing for hotels and apartments, obtaining the materials from their supply business, but then, as their work earned the esteem of the local building community, they began contracting for the construction of entire hotels. Ownership of one particular hotel, the Cascadian, fell into their hands as a result of the stock market crash in 1929. A majority of the investors who were to supply equity funds for the hotel were stripped of their assets by the collapse of the stock market, so the Dupars hired a stock promoter to sell enough shares in the hotel to meet costs, and the two brothers found themselves owning the 130-room hotel.

The following year, in 1930, Frank Dupar and Severt Thurston were seated at different tables in a coffee shop in a small town east of Seattle called Yakima. Both hotel owners were in the area looking to expand their hotel business. As competitors, Dupar and Thurston recognized each other and ended up sitting together. In the course of their discussion in the coffee shop, they talked of the advantages of pooling their efforts toward expansion and decided to include two other hotel owners in their proposed union who were also vying for expansion in Yakima, Adolph and Peter Schmidt. The Schmidts, forced to close their beer distillery, the Olympia Brewing Company, in accordance with prohibition laws, owned five hotels in the Puget Sound area. A meeting was arranged and, as a protective measure from the depressed economic climate pervading U.S. business at the time, the three groups of owners decided to unite their hotels under a single management umbrella. The joint venture, called Western Hotels Inc., was formed as a management corporation. Rather than owning the hotels, Western Hotels signed management agreements with local hotel owners and provided accounting, advertising, and referral services to the owners, as well as the hotel's personnel, whose salary was paid by the owners. As recompense, Western received one percent of the gross receipts from each of the hotels it managed. And so, with Peter Schmidt as the chairperson, Severt W. Thurston as president, Harold E. Maltby and Adolph Schmidt as vice-presidents, and Harold E. Dupar as treasurer, the odd combination of a former vaudeville acrobat, a plumber, and two displaced brewers formed the foundation of what would later become Westin Hotels & Resorts.

In its first year of operation, Western Hotels operated 18 hotels containing 3,137 rooms. All of the hotels were located in Washington, with the exception of one in Boise, Idaho. The following year, in 1931, Western assumed the management of its first property outside U.S. borders by adding Vancouver, British Columbia's Georgia Hotel to its consortium of hotels. That year, Western concluded a pivotal deal with the Multnomah Hotel in Portland, Oregon. The Multnomah, a prestigious 500-room hotel, was suffering severe losses during the early 1930s, recording monthly losses of up to $20,000. For the first time, Maltby, Thurston, Dupar, and the Schmidts entered into a joint purchase of the property. Under Western management, the lobby and the rooms were refurbished, and the failing hotel began producing profits within 90 days.

News of its success with the Multnomah earned Western the reputation as a management team that could produce profits for properties even during the harsh economic times of the Great Depression. Capitalizing on this reputation, the company assumed managerial control of six additional hotels by the end of the decade, one of which, the Baronof in Juneau, extended Western's presence into Alaska. Western's dramatic turnaround of the Multnomah also showed those in charge of the company that success could sometimes be achieved quickly. Often, Western managed a hotel for only a short time, reviving a floundering property, then withdrawing its control. The company maintained this fluid method of managerial control well into the future, constantly acquiring new contracts to replace those that were dissolved. Contracts were terminated with six of Western's original 18 hotels by the end of the decade, and over half of the properties managed by the company in the 1930s would operate in the 1940s without Western's assistance.

In its first decade of business, Western achieved considerable success in the Pacific Northwest. With the exception of the three hotels in Idaho, Oregon, and Alaska, all of Western's hotel concerns were located in Washington. As the company entered the 1940s, it sought to expand its interests outside of the region and, in 1941, an opportunity arose in California. Conrad Hilton owned the Sir Francis Drake, a 438-room hotel in San Francisco, but when Hilton settled a local strike, the city's businessmen became enraged, causing the hotel's clientele to shrink, and Hilton decided to sell the hotel. He sold it to a local industrialist and financier, E. B. Degolia. When Degolia attempted to get a mortgage for the property, his insurance company suggested he hire a professional hotel management firm to operate the hotel. The insurance company recommended Western, and DeGolia began negotiations with Thurston and Dupar (the Schmidts had returned to brewing beer when prohibition was repealed in 1933). Thurston and Dupar agreed to manage the hotel, provided they receive an equity share in the hotel. DeGolia agreed and, by the end of the year, Western had assumed managerial control over the Sir Francis. Additional California properties came under control of Western later in the decade. In 1949, Western gained the stewardship of the Maurice Hotel in San Francisco and the Mayfair Hotel in Los Angeles.

As the expansion of the 1940s increased Western's territory of operations to Los Angeles in the south and Utah to the east, issues of lasting importance were being discussed among the company's senior management. In 1941, manager at a meeting in Seattle began to precisely describe the role of Western in relation to the hotels it managed. Virtual autonomy of the various hotels was decided as the best stance to assume. Managers were to be given full responsibility and authority in their particular hotel, guided generally by the operating policies of Western. Western's influence over the hotels was to be downplayed in all publicity, with the hope that the individual hotels would not be perceived as units of a hotel chain, a modern, corporate concept many found distasteful.

By 1946, however, Western had begun a gradual shift toward assuming a more prominent image within its hotels. During another manager's meeting in Portland, Oregon, the first such meeting since the gathering in Seattle five years earlier, Western's strategists decided to hire an advertising firm and to produce an employee handbook and publication. The company also decided to affix its logo on stationery, matchbooks, soap wrappers, and other items.

The decision to adopt a more visible role was consistent with several innovative services Western introduced that hinted of a larger administrative structure than an individual hotel would likely possess. In 1946, the company issued the first guest credit cards, enabling patrons of Western hotels to charge their rooms, food, and beverage bills to a single account. The introduction of the paper cards was followed the next year by the establishment of "Hoteltype," the industry's first reservations system. Before

the implementation of Hoteltype, reservations were booked by mail, telegram, or telephone, and often resulted in lost or forgotten reservations. The new teletype machines, however, enabled instantaneous confirmation of reservation requests.

The 1940s also witnessed the emergence of Western's "specialty rooms," as management discovered the profits that could be garnered by devoting more energy and investing more money in their hotels' coffee shops, lounges, and dining facilities. During Western's early years, little attention had been paid to providing a place for hotel guests to eat and drink inside the hotel, but, as the years progressed, and after a survey of its hotels, Western discovered that the greatest earnings per square foot were gleaned from the coffee shops and cocktail lounges, and the smallest profits were produced by the more formal dining rooms. Greater care was given to providing livelier and more intimate eating and drinking facilities, as Western created an assortment of distinctive motifs for each hotel. Cocktail lounges and dining areas were decorated in a motifs replicating various geographical locations and historical periods. With names such as the "Matador Room," "The Outrigger," and the "Hitching Post," the lounges and dining rooms experienced increased revenues and were greatly augmented when Idaho and Washington legalized the sale of liquor by the drink in 1949.

Western continued to expand in the 1950s, adding 22 hotels located throughout California, Arizona, Colorado, Montana, and Washington. In 1956, the company began managing the massive, 1,200-room Hawaiian Village in Honolulu and, by the end of the decade, had assumed control of four hotels in Guatemala. As the number of Western hotels proliferated, further guest service innovations made their debut. In 1952, Western's "Family Plan" was introduced, allowing children under the age of 14 to stay without charge in their parent's room. Seven years later, the company made a long-standing promise to honor confirmed reservations, paying for the room if the guest had to be relocated to another hotel. That year, Western also made available the hotel industry's first 24-hour room service.

In the late 1950s and early 1960s, new management took the reins of Western from the company's founders. The core of this new leadership, Lynn P. Himmelman, Edward E. Carlson, and Gordon M. Bass, was drawn from inside the Western organization, establishing Western's tradition of promoting from within. The early working years of these men paralleled the modest beginnings of their predecessors, Thurston and Dupar. Himmelman, a fourth generation hotelier whose father was an early investor in the Maltby-Thurston Corporation, started his hotel career as a room clerk at the Multnomah. After serving as the manager of Seattle's Benjamin Franklin Hotel in 1946, he became Western's executive vice-president in 1960 and chief executive officer ten years later. Carlson, who would eventually become chair and chief executive officer of UAL, Inc., started as a page boy at the Benjamin Franklin in 1929, then became the hotel's elevator operator and bellhop. In 1946, he accepted a position as Thurston's assistant and steadily rose through the ranks, becoming Western's president in 1960. Bass also got his start at the Benjamin Franklin, working as a cashier for Himmelman's father. After managing the Multnomah, he was named vice-president of Western in 1951, executive vice-president in 1965, and president in 1971.

With this infusion of new management, Western experienced a fantastic surge in growth in the 1960s, adding 57 hotels to its management contracts, 36 of which were located outside of the United States. The company had become a genuine international concern, with hotels in Mexico, Guatemala, Venezuela, Ecuador, Australia, Japan, and Hong Kong. To better reflect this dramatic entry into foreign countries, Western changed its name in 1963 to "Western International Hotels."

As Western's business expanded internationally, it also entered into a new arena within the hotel industry—building its own hotels. Its first such venture was the construction of the 332-room Bayshore Inn in Vancouver, British Columbia. This was followed by the construction of Calgary, Alberta's Calgary Inn, in 1964, the 800-room Century Plaza in Los Angeles two years later, and Colorado Springs' Antlers Plaza in 1967. Building projects for the decade ended in 1969 with the construction of the Washington Plaza in Seattle. These projects proved successful, evidenced by the vigorous construction Western embarked upon in the next decade. Of the 30 hotels added to Western's management group in the 1970s, over half were built by Western.

Physical growth translated into fiscal growth over the next few years. From 1965 to 1970, the company's gross revenues doubled from $45 million to $90 million, and its net earnings jumped from $750,000 to $3 million. This success had not gone unnoticed. During the late 1960s, United Airlines had been searching for an entry into the hotel business to complement its international transportation service. Airlines had just recently begun to seek control of hotels as a solution to the sometimes limited, sometimes overcrowded accommodation facilities offered by the various destination cities the airlines served. For United, Western's chain of international hotels seemed a perfect match; 78 percent of Western's hotel rooms were located in cities served by United. In order to facilitate its proposed diversification into the hotel industry, United formed a holding company, UAL, Inc., in 1969, and began negotiations with Western. Carlson, Western's chairman and chief executive officer, foresaw the additional opportunities an affiliation with United would create. In 1970, negotiations were concluded and United and Western merged, with Western operating as an autonomous, wholly owned subsidiary, keeping its management and headquarters in Seattle. Five months after the merger, Carlson became president and chief executive officer of UAL, Inc. and Lynn Himmelman became chief executive officer of Western.

Although Western had aggressively expanded almost throughout its history, its expansion during the 1970s was unique. Instead of managing hotels with 300 or 400 rooms, Western assumed control of much larger hotels, many of which were constructed by Western, such as the 1,500-room Hotel Bona-

venture in Los Angeles. While the company continued to manage smaller hotels, it had begun to focus on the massive hotel complexes that were becoming popular in the industry. Expansion also took the Western name to new areas of the world during the company's fifth decade of operation. In 1970, a 525-room hotel was opened in Bangkok and, a year later, a hotel of similar size was opened in Singapore, both of which were constructed by Western. Two other Western-built hotels brought the company into South Africa and Norway, with the opening of Johannesburg's Carlton in 1972 and the Hotel Scandinavia three years later in Oslo.

In 1981, Western changed its name to Westin Hotels, and then four years later to Westin Hotels & Resorts. The company continued to aggressively pursue additional management contracts during the early 1980s to counterbalance the termination of contracts with hotels no longer deemed profitable. By the late 1980s, however, Westin's capability to expand or even to plan for the future was in doubt. United Airlines' strategy to develop a vertically integrated travel empire, which had begun with its merger with Westin, had proved unsuccessful and, by 1987, United was looking to divest the hotel chain. An interested party, the Aoki Corporation of Japan, began negotiations with United and, in 1988, Aoki Corp.—a diversified international corporation with major lines of business in engineering, construction, and hotels—purchased Westin for $1.53 billion. The acquisition proved mutually beneficial; Aoki Corp. constructed the hotels, and Westin assumed the management of the new buildings. Three years after the acquisition, Westin became the operating company for all the hotels owned by Aoki Corp., including Caesar Park Hotels, the Hotel Vier Jahreszeiten in Hamburg, Germany, and The Algonquin Hotel in New York.

Westin's projections for growth in the 1990s were optimistic. The company planned to double its size during the decade and intended to aggressively pursue international properties, especially in Europe where the company's presence was limited. With over 60 years of experience to draw from and the strength of Aoki Corp. as a partner, Westin management was likely to continue to oversee the operation of many of the world's hotels.

Further Reading:

Copeland, Sid, *The Story of Western International Hotels,* Seattle: Western International Hotels, 1976.
Del Rosso, Laura, "Westin Moves Into Area With Management of Former Doubletree," *Travel Weekly,* April 27, 1992, p. C14.
Ellis, James E., "The Allegis Experiment Turns Into A Bonanza," *Business Week,* November 9, 1987, pp. 123, 126.
Rismond, Maureen, "Magnan Heads Banquet Table He Once Waited On," *Puget Sound Business Journal,* January 29, 1990, pp. A4–A5.

—Jeffrey Covell

Weyerhaeuser

Weyerhaeuser Company

33663 Weyerhaeuser Way
Federal Way, Washington 98003
U.S.A.
(206) 924-2345
Fax: (206) 924-3543

Public Company
Incorporated: 1900 as Weyerhaeuser Timber Company
Employees: 39,022
Sales $9.22 billion
Stock Exchanges: Midwest New York Pacific Tokyo
SICs: 2611 Pulp Mills; 2631 Paperboard Mills; 2421
   Sawmills & Planing Mills—General; 6552 Subdividers &
   Developers Nec

Weyerhaeuser Company is the world's largest private owner of timber and the world's largest pulp and paper company. This diversified forest products company owns 5.6 million acres of timberland in the United States and license for 18.8 million acres in Canada. In 1990, with Weyerhaeuser's stock selling below breakup value and earnings below the industry average, the company reviewed its corporate strategy and reaffirmed its commitment to its historic strengths in paper and wood.

Weyerhaeuser Timber Company, headquartered in Tacoma, Washington, was incorporated in 1900 as a joint venture in Pacific Northwest timber by James J. Hill, railroad magnate, and Frederick Weyerhaeuser, joint owner of Weyerhaeuser & Denkmann, a midwestern lumber company that relied on forests in Wisconsin and Minnesota. Weyerhaeuser remained privately owned, primarily by the Weyerhaeuser family, until 1963.

Prior to World War I, the company was run by Frederick Weyerhaeuser. A German-born immigrant to the Midwest before the Civil War, his business philosophy evolved over his lifetime and became the operating philosophy for the new company. Weyerhaeuser felt that "The way to make money is to let the other fellow make some too."

Timber holdings doubled in the period preceding World War I. The company opened a sawmill to produce lumber and soon had the nation's first all-electric lumber mill, in 1915. Company plans to market lumber on the east coast, using the new Panama Canal, were delayed until the end of World War I.

Although demand for lumber for railroad cars declined during World War I as steel was utilized, demand for lumber for military planes and other military uses increased. In the early days of the lumber mill, itinerant single men formed the core of the mill's laborers. Represented by the International Workers of the World (the Wobblies), they pushed for better working conditions, including an eight-hour work day. A struggle resulted, and labor unrest threatened the war effort. To ensure a steady supply of lumber for war material, the federal government established a union for the industry, something never done before or since. The union, the Loyal Legion of Loggers and Lumbermen, prevailed in its demand for the eight-hour day and 40-hour week. The hours changed the work force; family men then constituted the core of workers in lumber.

The surplus of naval vessels at the end of the war allowed Weyerhaeuser to purchase ships at a reasonable cost to transport lumber to the east coast through the Panama Canal. Weyerhaeuser Sales Company had been established in 1916 to promote this postwar expansion of markets.

John P. Weyerhaeuser, eldest son of the founder, led the company during the war and through the 1920s. He relied heavily, as had his father, on George Long, general manager from 1900 to 1930. Long, an early proponent of reforestation, approached the federal government before the war to lobby for cooperative forest fire prevention and for lower property taxes for timberland to make reforestation economically viable. This lobbying led to the Clark-McNary Act in 1924, which addressed these issues and expanded the national forest. The act also encouraged changes in taxation policies at the state level to promote reforestation. Weyerhaeuser responded by creating the Logged Off Land Company in 1925 to handle the sale of "logged off" land, to study reforestation, and to lobby at the state level for lower timberland taxes.

By the end of the 1920s, Weyerhaeuser was the largest private owner of timber in the United States. At the beginning of that decade, the company had produced its first national advertising campaign, promoting the lumber industry. By the decade's end, the company's advertisements focused on the recently upgraded quality of its lumber, by trademarking and grademarking lumber, as well as by taking more care in handling the lumber during shipment to market.

The Great Depression produced hard times for the company, as few businesses or homes were being built. The depression in the lumber market would have been devastating if not offset by the company's diversification into pulp in 1931. By 1933 profits from pulp offset losses from lumber. The New Deal's Civilian Conservation Corps assisted in reforestation of logged off land during this period. State tax laws in the Pacific Northwest were amended to provide lower taxes for timberland, promoting reforestation. In 1940 the company started the first tree farm in the United States, near Gray's Harbor in Washington.

In 1935 the kidnapping of George Weyerhaeuser, the nine-year-old son of CEO John P. Weyerhaeuser Jr., catapulted the Weyerhaeuser family to national attention. The Weyerhaeuser kidnapping ended happily, the child safe, the ransom recovered, and the kidnappers apprehended. George Weyerhaeuser grew up to become president of his family's company.

In 1940 the company expanded its lumber business to include plywood and paneling. The Lend-Lease Program to assist the British prior to U.S. entry into World War II found Weyerhaeuser transport ships utilized to carry lend-lease material to the British in Egypt. During the war itself, the company served as an agent of the War Shipping Administration, directing 68 freighters and troop ships, of which two were sunk in combat.

Rapid technological and commercial changes in the lumber industry after the war affected Weyerhaeuser. The hand operated whipsaw was replaced by the power chain saw, and truck hauling replaced hauling by rail. Pent-up demand in construction, from the 1930s and early 1940s, led to greatly increased sales of lumber in this postwar era.

However, the company's organizational structure, highly informal and fraternal, was altered to accommodate rapid postwar expansion: more formal programs and reports were instituted, and subsidiaries were absorbed. A philanthropic foundation was established, and the Weyerhaeuser Real Estate Company replaced the Logged Off Land Company.

Under continued leadership of the Weyerhaeuser family, the company expanded into particle board production, ply-veneer, hardboard, and hardwood paneling in the 1950s. Timberland holdings expanded beyond the Pacific Northwest for the first time, as land was purchased in Mississippi, Alabama, and North Carolina.

In 1958 Weyerhaeuser Sales Company, established in 1916, was absorbed into the parent company, and Weyerhaeuser International S.A. was created to expand into foreign markets. The company dropped "Timber" from its official name to become Weyerhaeuser Company, and adopted its current trademark, a triangular tree over the word "Weyerhaeuser."

In 1960, for the first time in company history, the presidency of Weyerhaeuser passed out of the family to Norton Clapp. Under Clapp, the company went public in 1963. It expanded into the Japanese market as a result of surplus lumber involuntarily "logged" by Typhoon Frieda's 150-mile-per-hour winds in 1962. Weyerhaeuser's first overseas office was opened in Tokyo in 1963. In 1964 and 1965 European offices were opened in France and Belgium, respectively. The company acquired a wood products distribution firm in Australia, and it entered into a joint venture for bleached kraft pulp in Canada.

Clapp was succeeded as CEO in 1966 by George Weyerhaeuser, who served until 1988. Growth per year in the high-yield forestry program doubled, while the company contracted its first long-term debt. By the end of the 1960s, annual sales exceeded $1 billion.

The 1970s were years of phenomenal growth, with sales surpassing the $2 billion mark in 1973. Sales doubled in five years and doubled again before the end of the decade. Weyerhaeuser entered the disposable diaper business in 1970 and centralized research in Tacoma in 1975. At the decade's end, the company concluded an agreement with China to work there on the world's largest reforestation effort. In 1979 company sales were $4.4 billion.

If the 1970s were a boom decade, the early 1980s were a bust, with tight credit in housing leading to a depression in lumber similar to that of the 1930s. The volcanic eruption of Mount Saint Helens in May 1980 was also a blow to the company. Weyerhaeuser's Saint Helens Tree Farm was just below the mountain's dome, and the company lost 68,000 acres of timberland. Fortunately, the eruption took place on a Sunday, and fewer workers were in the path of the devastation. As a result of the eruption timberland values in the Northwest fell 75 percent. The company maintained dividends by diversifying into real estate and financial services. In 1986 Weyerhaeuser became the first U.S. forest products company listed on the Tokyo Stock Exchange, and soon became the third most traded foreign stock there.

In response to difficult economic conditions, downsizing and economizing became company emphases in the 1980s. In one dramatic example, Weyerhaeuser instiued saftey measures that reduced workers' compensation claims from $30 million to $10 million by 1990. In order to cut production costs still further, the company introduced a plant-wide computer integrated manufacturing system.

In 1988 John Creighton became president of Weyerhaeuser, and George Weyerhaeuser became chairman. Creighton re-evaluated the company's diversification into areas outside of forest products. During the 1980s, the company had become involved in insurance, home building, mortgage banking, garden products, pet supplies, and disposable diapers. While these businesses contributed greatly to the company's sales volume, they added very little to profits. As the head of Weyerhaeuser's nursery operations noted in the *Wall Street Journal* several years later, after the divestiture of his unit, "Weyerhaeuser was darn good at growing trees, but they sure didn't know anything about garden supplies."

Creighton reorganized Weyerhaeuser to focus the company's priorities and develop a coherent long-term strategy, selling off less profitable businesses and returning to a focus on forest products. As part of the restructuring program, Creighton altered the company's incentive system to reward each mill for profitability rather than the amount of product it manufactured. He also whittled Weyerhaeuser's product lines to concentrate on high-quality, higher-margin products such as white papers and high-grade lumber. By 1990 the company had sold or closed operations that had previously accounted for nearly $1 billion in sales. The loss of this revenue, however, affected virtually none of its profits.

As the restructuring program was gaining momentum in 1989, an economic recession loomed. After posting a record high of over $10 billion in sales in 1989, Weyerhaeuser's sales dipped to $9 billion in 1990 and profits fell by 35 percent. The decline was attributed to decreased housing and other construction projects as banks grew more reluctant to lend money, and also to an oversupply of pulp and paper in the market that lowered the price of paper. In 1991 the financial situation did not improve. Sales fell to $8.7 billion, and the company recorded a loss of $162 million compared to a profit of $565 million three years earlier.

Although significant, the losses suffered by Weyerhaeuser were not as large as those incurred by the rest of the forest industry. Beyond the damaging effects of the recession, other companies also sustained losses due to the protection of federal timberlands that reduced their supply of wood. With 5.5 million acres of federal timberland cordoned off in the Pacific Northwest, lumber prices soared, and Weyerhaeuser was able to reap the benefits, harvesting timber on land it owned. This enviable position resulted in greater earnings for the company, and it was able to rebound from 1991's disastrous year. Profits in the first quarter of 1991 jumped 81 percent and, for the year, the company recorded earnings of $372 million.

By 1992 the company had closed 50 plants—representing roughly 20 percent of its operating facilities—as part of its restructuring program, and continued the divestiture of businesses that did not support the company's core business strategy. In 1993 Weyerhaeuser's diaper business was sold for $215 million; GNA Corp., Weyerhaeuser's consumer finance unit, was sold for $525 million, which represented the largest divestiture ever made by the company. In addition to shedding businesses that no longer fit the company, Weyerhaeuser strengthened its core businesses through the purchase of two pulp mills, several sawmills, and approximately 175,000 acres of timberland in Georgia from Proctor & Gamble Co. in 1992 for $600 million.

In 1993 the company continued to face challenges, as public opinion built in favor of protecting Sockeye salmon runs in the Pacific Northwest, which critics claimed were stilted up by heavy logging, and as a movement grew to ban timber exports, which accounted for 26 percent of the company's profits. However, as Weyerhaeuser completed its restructuring program to solidify its position as one of the premier forest products companies in the world, company management remained optimistic about its future.

Principal Subsidiaries: Weyerhaeuser Real Estate Company; Weyerhaeuser Financial Services, Inc; Weyerhaeuser International Inc.; Weyerhaeuser Venture Co, Inc.; Weyerhaeuser Canada, Ltd.

Further Reading:

Carlton, Jim, ''Weyerhaeuser Outbids Georgia-Pacific To Acquire P&G Assets for $600 Million,'' *Wall Street Journal,* August 21, 1992, p. A3.

Ferguson, Tim W., '' 'Timmm Burrr!' Could Remain the Northwest's (Muffled) Cry,'' *Wall Street Journal,* July 9, 1991, p. A17.

Lipin, Steven, ''GE Capital to Buy GNA Corp. Unit Of Weyerhaeuser,'' *Wall Street Journal,* January 7, 1993, p. A5.

Patrick, Ken L., ''Weyerhaeuser Brings High-Tech Pulp Mill Online at Mississippi Complex,'' *Pulp & Paper,* December 1990, p. 79.

Richards, Bill, ''Silver Lining: Owls, of All Things, Help Weyerhaeuser Cash in on Timber,'' *Wall Street Journal,* January 24, 1992, pp. A1, A6.

Taylor, John H., ''Rip Van Weyerhaeuser,'' *Forbes,* October 28, 1991, pp. 38–40.

Where the Future Grows, Tacoma, Washington: Weyerhaeuser Corporation, 1989.

—Ellen NicKenzie Lawson
updated by Jeffrey L. Covell

WISCONSIN PUBLIC SERVICE

Wisconsin Public Service Corporation

700 North Adams Street
P.O. Box 19001
Green Bay, Wisconsin 54307-9001
U.S.A.
(414) 433-1598
Fax: (414) 433-1526

Public Company
Incorporated: 1883 as Oshkosh Gas Light Company
Employees: 2,619
Sales: $634.8 million
Stock Exchanges: Midwest New York
SICs: 4931 Electric & Other Services Combined

Wisconsin Public Service Corporation is one of the larger public utilities in the Midwest. It supplies electricity and natural gas to customers in northeastern Wisconsin and part of the Upper Peninsula of Michigan. The company's largest urban markets are the cities of Green Bay, Oshkosh, Wausau, and Stevens Point.

Wisconsin Public Service traces its origins to Oshkosh Gas Light Company, the successor company to a franchise that had been taken out in 1868 to sell coal gas, which was used for lighting, to the citizens of Oshkosh. The franchise had lain dormant for about five years when E. P. Sawyer, a businessman whose previous experience had been in the lumber industry, acquired it in 1883 and reincorporated it under the name Oshkosh Gas Light. In 1885 the company received a franchise to sell electricity in Oshkosh, putting it into direct competition with Oshkosh Electric Light and Power. The two companies merged in 1907.

In these early years, the electrical utility industry in the United States little resembled its current state, in which a relatively small number of large companies are granted state-regulated franchises to produce and sell power in large geographic areas. Instead, a bewildering array of strictly local companies took out franchises to provide electricity and coal gas to small areas on a small scale. But, as the merger between Oshkosh Gas Light and Oshkosh Electric Power suggests, this began to change after the turn of the century, when the industry underwent a period of rapid consolidation and centralization of power.

In 1911 a Milwaukee engineer named Clement Smith joined with his brother-in-law, utility lawyer George Miller, to found Wisconsin Securities Company with the purpose of operating it as a utilities holding company. They quickly acquired Green Bay Gas and Electric Company, Green Bay Traction Company, and Northern Hydro-Electric Power Company. In 1922 Wisconsin Securities acquired Oshkosh Gas Light from the estate of E. P. Sawyer, changed its name to Wisconsin Public Service Corporation, and merged it with the other companies that it had acquired, which by now included Sheboygan Gas Light Company, Calumet Service Company, and Manitowoc and Northern Traction Company. Wisconsin Securities had also founded Peninsula Service Company to supply electricity to Door County in 1920, and it, too, was merged into Wisconsin Public Service.

This rapid consolidation among electrical utilities did not escape notice and drew fire from some reform-minded journalists. *New Republic,* for instance, published two books during the 1920s critical of current trends in the industry, one of which mentioned Wisconsin Public Service as a brief example. However, the desire to gain monopolistic control of regional markets for electrical power was not the sole factor at work, perhaps not even the most important one. The attrition rate for the small power companies that characterized the early days of the industry was quite high. Nor were those small companies likely to have the capital to invest in new power plants. In the case of Wisconsin Securities, the owners of Green Bay Gas and Electric, Green Bay Traction, and Northern Hydro-Electric Power asked Clement Smith and George Miller for help after cost overruns from a hydro-electric plant they were building threatened to bankrupt them. Thus, a certain amount of consolidation was not only inevitable, but healthy for the industry and necessary for maintaining consistency of service.

More mergers and acquisitions followed the creation of Wisconsin Public Service. In 1924 the company bought small electric companies operating in the towns of Brillion, Mishicot, and DePere. The next year it acquired all the assets of Northeastern Power Company, including its subsidiaries Riverview Motor Bus Company; Oslo Power and Light Company; Denmark Power and Light Company; Green Bay Park Railway Company; Northern Light, Heat, and Power Company of Suring; and Wabeno Lighting Company.

As some of the names of the acquired Northeastern Power subsidiaries suggest, Wisconsin Public Service operated public transportation at this time, in addition to supplying electricity. Electric companies had long been in this line of business, a natural consequence of the fact that they produced the electricity that made trolley cars run. After World War I, street railways were widely replaced by buses, which were more flexible and less expensive to operate. From the 1920s through World War II, Wisconsin Public Service operated transportation systems in Green Bay, Wausau, Merrill, and, briefly, in Menominee and Marinette.

Just after the Northeastern Power acquisition, Wisconsin Public Service was itself acquired by H. M. Byellsby, an electrical engineer who had worked for the Edison and Westinghouse Electric Corporation before going into business himself, designing and building power stations and hydro-electric plants for utility companies. Byellsby immediately turned over control of

Wisconsin Public Service to Standard Gas and Electric, a public utility holding company that he had founded in 1910. As a result of the move, Clement Smith stepped down as president in 1926.

In 1927 Standard Gas and Electric acquired another large electrical utility, Wisconsin Valley Electric Company. Like Wisconsin Public Service, Wisconsin Valley Electric had grown rapidly through a series of mergers and acquisitions, and was selling electricity to the towns of Merrill, Stevens Point, Tomahawk, Antigo, Rhinelander, and Waupaca when Standard Gas and Electric won a bidding war to acquire it. Though a successful and growing company, Wisconsin Valley Electric operated hydro-electric plants exclusively and ran into trouble in winter because of ice and low water on the Wisconsin River. In 1933 Standard Gas and Electric decided to merge its two main subsidiaries, so that Wisconsin Public Service's steam turbine plants could pick up Wisconsin Valley Electric's wintertime slack.

During World War II, Wisconsin Public Service's public transportation systems saw increases in ridership due to gas rationing and reduced automobile production. However, wartime shortages also made running bus lines difficult, despite the increases in business. For instance, the company's fleet in Green Bay was forced to bring an old 1925 Reo bus out of mothballs and press it into service. It was christened the *Queen Marie,* and a slogan painted on her side declared that she would be retired again, "when the clock strikes peace!" After the clock did, in fact, strike peace, bus ridership declined as gasoline rationing ended and private cars returned to the roads. In 1951 Wisconsin Public Service divested its bus lines in Wausau and Merrill, and they began independent operation under the name Wausau Transit Lines.

Wisconsin Public Service also gained independence of a sort in the 1950s; in 1952 Standard Gas and Electric divested its entire stake in the company. Common stock was distributed to Wisconsin Public Service's preferred stockholders. The following year, Wisconsin Public Service was listed on the Midwest and New York Stock Exchanges for the first time.

In the 1960s natural gas became an increasingly important fuel source, and Wisconsin Public Service responded by expanding its operations in that area. The company had been selling natural gas to its customers since 1950, just after the first pipeline from the Hugoton Field in the Oil Patch of Oklahoma and Texas to the Upper Midwest was built. In 1961 it made a move to control the means of distribution when it acquired two natural gas franchises, Merrill Gas Company and Oneida Gas Company. By 1963 over half of the homes in Wisconsin Public Service's service area were heated with gas, and by the mid-1970s natural gas sales would account for about 30 percent of the company's operating revenues.

In 1967 Wisconsin Public Service acquired the electrical distribution system for the municipality of Kewaunee, which had been owned by the city. That year, the company also took its first plunge into the age of nuclear energy when it broke ground on a nuclear plant nine miles south of Kewaunee, on the shores of Lake Michigan. The Kewaunee nuclear plant, which did not begin operation until 1974 (once safety and environmental concerns had been assuaged), was built and operated by Wisconsin Public Service, but was, in fact a joint venture between three

Wisconsin utility companies. Wisconsin Public Service owned 41.2 percent, with Wisconsin Power and Light Company holding 41 percent and Madison Gas and Electric Company 17.8 percent.

In 1970 the company consolidated its corporate offices. True to its roots as an amalgamation of many small, local companies, Wisconsin Public Services had long operated out of offices scattered among the cities of Green Bay, Milwaukee, and Oshkosh. For decades, Wisconsin Public Service had used a stately old mansion in Milwaukee as one of its headquarters—which made little sense, since the city lay outside the company's operating area, except that Clement Smith had acquired the house from his brother-in-law. In 1970, the old Milwaukee mansion was vacated, and operations were consolidated at a new corporate headquarters in Green Bay.

In 1973 Wisconsin Public Service left the public transportation business entirely. Its Green Bay lines had been losing money since the 1950s, and the company finally sold its operations to the city of Green Bay that year. Its Green Bay bus system notwithstanding, Wisconsin Public Service prospered during the 1970s. In 1975 it posted revenues of $219.9 million, its best sales year ever. Its most important customer was the paper industry, which accounted for 15 percent of the company's electricity sales, and renewed strength among paper companies operating mills in northeastern Wisconsin meant increased demand for Wisconsin Public Service's main product. The company's reliance on the paper industry continued to serve it well into the 1980s, giving it a solid base of industrial demand.

In 1992 Wisconsin Public Service's contacts with the paper industry resulted in a joint venture seeking to find an efficient, ecologically sound way to generate electricity. That year, the company signed an agreement with Rhinelander Paper Company to build a 90 to 100 megawatt power plant that would be fueled by low-sulfur coal and paper mill waste. Wisconsin Public Service began using more low-sulfur coal in its power plants in the 1990s in order to comply with state and federal air pollution laws.

Wisconsin Public Service has performed well financially, especially in recent years; its revenues tripled between 1975 and 1992. This record of growth is impressive, considering that the relatively modest city of Green Bay is its largest urban market. It has benefited from the presence of large industrial customers in its area of operations, and it has shown that an electrical utility can prosper and grow large by hanging around small towns.

Principal Subsidiaries: WPS Communications, Inc.

Further Reading:

Campanella, Frank W., "Profits Generator," *Barron's,* March 29, 1982.
Hillert, Mark, and Paul Davis, *Wisconsin Public Service Corporation: 100 Years—1883–1983—A Century of Service,* Green Bay: Wisconsin Public Service Corporation, 1983.
"Wisconsin Public Service Generating Higher Net," *Barron's,* August 30, 1976.

—Douglas Sun

INDEX TO COMPANIES AND PERSONS

Listings are arranged in alphabetical order under the company name; thus Eli Lilly & Company will be found under the letter E. Definite articles (The) and forms of incorporation that precede the name (A.B. and N.V.) are ignored for alphabetical purposes. Company names appearing in bold type have historical essays on the page numbers appearing in bold. Updates to entries that appeared in earlier volumes are signified by (upd.). The index is cumulative with volume numbers printed in bold type.

Bank of New England Corporation, II 213–15
Bank of New Queensland, II 188
Bank of New South Wales, II 188–89, 388–90
Bank of New York and Trust Co., II 218
Bank of New York Company, Inc., II 192, 216–19, 247
Bank of New York, N.B.A., II 217–18
Bank of Nova Scotia, II 220–23, 345; **IV 644**
Bank of Nova Scotia Trust Co., II 221
Bank of Ontario, II 210
Bank of Osaka, II 360
Bank of Ottawa, II 221
Bank of Pasadena, II 382
Bank of Queensland, II 188
Bank of Scotland, II 422; III 360; V 166
Bank of Spain, II 194, 197
Bank of the People, II 210
Bank of the United States, II 207, 216, 247
Bank of the West, II 233
Bank of Tokyo, Ltd., II 224–25, 276, 301, 341, 358; **IV 151**
Bank of Toronto, II 375–76
Bank of Upper Canada, II 210
Bank of Western Australia, II 187
Bank of Winterthur, II 378
Bank Powszechny Depozytowy, IV 119
Bank voor Handel en Nijverheid, II 304
BankAmerica Corporation, II 226–28, 436; **8 45–48 (upd.)**, 295, 469, 471. *See also* Bank of America *and* Bank of America National Trust and Savings Assoc.
Bankers and Shippers Insurance Co., III 389
Bankers Co., II 230
Bankers Investment, II 349
Bankers Life Association, III 328
Bankers Life Co., III 328–30
Bankers Life Equity Management Co., III 329
Bankers Life Equity Services Corp., III 329
Bankers National Bank, II 261
Bankers National Life Insurance Co., II 182
Bankers Trust Co., II 229–30
Bankers Trust Co. of South Carolina, II 337
Bankers Trust New York Corporation, I 601; II 211, 229–31, 330, 339; III 84–86
Bankhaus IG Herstatt, II 242
Bankhead, Tallulah, II 155
Banks, David R., III 76–77
Banks, Howard, I 95
BankVermont Corp., II 208
Banner Life, III 273
Banque Belge et Internationale en Egypte, II 295
Banque Belge pour l'Etranger, II 294
Banque Belgo-Zairoise, II 294
Banque Bruxelles Lambert. *See* Bank Brussels Lambert.
Banque Commerciale du Maroc, II 272
Banque Commerciale-Basle, II 270
Banque d'Anvers/Bank van Antwerpen, II 294–95
Banque de Bruxelles, II 201–02, 239
Banque de Credit et de Depot des Pays Bas, II 259
Banque de l'Indochine et de Suez, II 259

Banque de l'Union Européenne, II 94
Banque de l'Union Parisienne, II 270; IV 497, 557
Banque de la Construction et les Travaux Public, II 319
Banque de la Société Générale de Belgique, II 294–95
Banque de Louvain, II 202
Banque de Paris, II 259
Banque de Paris et des Pays-Bas, II 136, 259
Banque de Reports et de Depots, II 201
Banque du Congo Belge, II 294
Banque Européenne pour l'Amerique Latine, II 294
Banque Française et Espagnol en Paris, II 196
Banque Francaise pour le Commerce et l'Industrie, II 232, 270
Banque Génerale des Pays Roumains, II 270
Banque Générale du Luxembourg, II 294
Banque Indosuez, II 429
Banque Internationale à Luxembourg, II 239
Banque Internationale de Bruxelles, II 201–02
Banque Italo-Belge, II 294
Banque Italo-Francaise de Credit, II 271
Banque Lambert, II 201–02
Banque Nationale de Crédit, II 232
Banque Nationale de Paris S.A., II 232–34, 239; III 201, 392–94; **9 148**
Banque Nationale Pour le Commerce et l'Industrie, II 232–33
Banque Nationale pour le Commerce et l'Industrie (Afrique), II 232
Banque Nordique du Commerce, II 366
Banque Orea, II 378
Banque Paribas, II 192, 260; IV 295
Banque Rothschild, IV 107
Banque Sino-Belge, II 294
Banque Stern, II 369
Banque Transatlantique, II 271
Banque Worms, III 393
Banquet Foods Corp., II 90, 494
Bantam Books, Inc., III 190–91
Bantam Doubleday Dell Publishing Group, IV 594
Bantle, Louis F., 9 533–34
Banyu Pharmaceutical Co., I 651
BAPCO, III 745
Barach, Philip G., V 208
Barat. *See* Barclays National Bank.
Barbakow, Jeffrey, II 149–50
Barbanson, Gustave, IV 24
Barber (Lord), II 358
Barber, Anthony, III 739
Barber, Charles, IV 33
Barber, Nicholas, 6 417
Barber, Red, III 52
Barber, Walter C., V 753
Barbera, Joe, II 148
Barberet & Blanc, I 677
Barbero, Ronald D., III 340
Barbier, Aristide, V 236
Barclay & Co., Ltd., II 235
Barclay & Fry, I 604–05
Barclay Group, I 335
Barclay, James, II 235
Barclay, Kenneth, 8 544–45
Barclay, Robert, I 604
Barclays American Corp., II 236
Barclays Bank (Canada), II 244

Barclays Bank (D.C.O.), II 236
Barclays Bank (Dominion, Colonial & Overseas), II 236
Barclays Bank International, II 236; IV 23
Barclays Bank of California, II 236, 383
Barclays Bank of New York, II 236
Barclays Bank S.A., II 237
Barclays, Bevan & Tritton, II 235
Barclays de Zoete Wedd, II 237, 429
Barclays Merchant Bank Ltd. de Zoete, II 237
Barclays National Bank, II 237; IV 23
Barclays PLC, I 604; II 202, 204, 235–37, 239, 308, 319, 333, 422; III 516; **IV 722; 7 332–33; 8 118**
Barclays, Tritton, Ransom, Bouverie & Co., II 235
Bard, Charles Russell, 9 96
Bard, Thomas, IV 569
Barden Cablevision, IV 640
Bardot, Brigitte, III 46
Bardou, Jean-Pierre, I 188
Barell, Emil C., I 642–43
Barents, Brian, 8 315
Barfoot, Henry Charles, III 334
Baring Brothers, III 699
Baring, Francis, III 372
Barker & Dobson, II 629
Barklay, Norman A., I 483
Barlow, Charles, I 422–23
Barlow, Ernest (Maj.), I 422
Barlow Rand Ltd., I 288–89, 422–24; IV 22, 96
Barlow, Robert, I 604–05
Barlow, William (Sir), III 434
Barmer Bankverein, II 238, 241
Barnato, Barney, IV 64; 7 121
Barnato Brothers, IV 21, 65; 7 122
Barnes Group, III 581
Barnes, J. David, II 316
Barnes, James E., IV 459
Barnes, Leslie O., V 505
Barnes, Robert J., 9 203
Barnes-Hind, III 56, 727
Barnet, Herbert, I 277
Barnetson, William (Lord), IV 686
Barnett Banks, Inc., 9 58–60
Barnett Banks of Florida, Inc., 9 58
Barnett, Bion, 9 58
Barnett Brass & Copper Inc., 9 543
Barnett Equity Securities, 9 59
Barnett First National Bank of Jacksonville, 9 58
Barnett, Frank, V 531
Barnett, Hoares and Co., II 306
Barnett National Securities Corporation, 9 58
Barnett, William Boyd, 9 58
Barnett, William D., 9 58
Barnette, Curtis H., 7 51
Barnetts, Hoares, Hanbury and Lloyds, II 306
Barnevik, Percy, II 2–4; IV 204
Barney, Ashbel H., II 381
Barney, Danforth N., II 380–81, 395
Barney, Hiram, II 239
Barney, J.W., IV 601
Barney, Lawrence D., I 643
Baron, Stanley Wade, I 219, 255, 270, 292
Baroncini, Gino, III 208
Barr & Stroud Ltd., III 727
Barr, David W., IV 645
Barr, John J. (Jack), 6 443
Barr, Kenneth J., 7 107–08

Commercial & General Life Assurance Co., **III** 371

Commercial Alliance Corp. of New York, **II** 289

Commercial Aseguradora Suizo Americana, S.A., **III** 243

Commercial Assurance, **III** 359

Commercial Bank of Australia Ltd., **II** 189, 319, 388–89

Commercial Bank of London, **II** 334

Commercial Bank of Tasmania, **II** 188

Commercial Banking Co. of Sydney, **II** 187–89

Commercial Bureau (Australia) Pty., **I** 438

Commercial Credit Company, 8 117–19

Commercial Credit Corp., **III** 127–28

Commercial Exchange Bank, **II** 254; **9** 124

Commercial Filters Corp., **I** 512

Commercial Insurance Co. of Newark, **III** 242

Commercial Life, **III** 243

Commercial Life Assurance Co. of Canada, **III** 309

Commercial National Bank, **II** 261

Commercial National Bank & Trust Co., **II** 230

Commercial National Bank of Charlotte, **II** 336

Commercial Ship Repair Co., **I** 185

Commercial Union plc, II 272, 308; **III** 185, **233–35**, 350, 373; **IV** 711

Commerz- und Credit-Bank, **II** 257

Commerz- und Disconto-Bank, **II** 256–57

Commerz- und Privatbank, **II** 256

Commerzbank A.G., II 239, 242, **256–58**, 280, 282, 385; **IV** 222; **9** 283

Commerzbank Bankverein, **II** 257

Commerzfilm, **IV** 591

Commes, Thomas A., **III** 745

Commodore Business Machines Ltd., **7** 95

Commodore Computers, **II** 6; **III** 112; **7** 532

Commodore Corporation, **8** 229

Commodore International Ltd., 6 243–44; **7 95–97**; **9** 46

Commodore Portable Typewriter Co., Ltd., **7** 95

Commonwealth & Southern Corporation, **V** 676

Commonwealth Aluminium Corp., Ltd., **IV** 122. See also Comalco Ltd.

Commonwealth Bank, **II** 188, 389

Commonwealth Board Mills, **IV** 248

Commonwealth Edison, II 28, 425; **III** 653; **IV** 169; **V 583–85**; **6** 505, 529, 531

Commonwealth Hospitality Ltd., **III** 95

Commonwealth Industries, **III** 569

Commonwealth Insurance Co., **III** 264

Commonwealth Land Title Insurance Co., **III** 343

Commonwealth Life Insurance Co., **III** 216–19

Commonwealth Mortgage Assurance Co., **III** 344

Commonwealth National Financial Corp., **II** 316

Commonwealth Oil Refining Company, **II** 402; **7** 517

Commtron, **V** 14, 16

Communication Services Ltd. See Hongkong Telecommunications Ltd.

Communications Data Services, Inc., **IV** 627

Communications Properties, Inc., **IV** 677

Communicorp, **III** 188

Community Direct, Inc., **7** 16

Community HealthCare Services, **6** 182

Community Hospital of San Gabriel, **6** 149

Community Medical Care, Inc., **III** 245

Community National Bank, **9** 474

Community Power & Light Company, **6** 579–80

Community Public Service Company, **6** 514

Community Savings and Loan, **II** 317

Comnet Corporation, **9** 347

Compactom, **I** 588

Compagnia di Assicurazioni, **III** 345

Compagnia di Genova, **III** 347

Compagnie Auxiliaire de Navigation, **IV** 558

Compagnie Bancaire, **II** 259

Compagnie Belge pour l'industrie, **II** 202

Compagnie Continentale, **I** 409–10

Compagnie d'Assurances Générales, **III** 391

Compagnie d'assurances Mutuelles contre l'incendie dans les départements de la Seine Inférieure et de l'Eure, **III** 210

Compagnie d'Investissements de Paris, **II** 233

Compagnie de Compteurs, **III** 617

Compagnie de Five-Lille, **IV** 469

Compagnie de Mokta, **IV** 107–08

Compagnie de Navigation Mixte, **III** 185

Compagnie de Reassurance Nord-Atlantique, **III** 276

Compagnie de Recherche et d'Exploitation du Pétrole du Sahara, **IV** 545

Compagnie de Saint-Gobain, **8** 395, 397

Compagnie de Saint-Gobain S.A., II 117, 474–75; **III 675–78**, 704

Compagnie de Suez, **III** 677

Compagnie de Transport Aerien, **I** 122

Compagnie des Glaces, **III** 675

Compagnie des Machines Bull S.A., II 40, 42, 70, 125; **III 122–23**, 154; **IV** 600

Compagnie des Messageries Maritimes, **6** 379

Compagnie des Produits Chimiques d'Alais et de la Camargue, **IV** 173

Compagnie des Produits Chimiques et Électrométallurgiques d'Alais, Froges et Camargue, **IV** 173–74

Compagnie du Midi, **III** 209, 211

Compagnie du Nord, **IV** 108

Compagnie Européenne de Publication, **IV** 614–15

Compagnie Financiere Alcatel, **9** 10

Compagnie Financiere de Paribas, II 192, **259–60**; **III** 185

Compagnie Financiere de Paris et des Pays-Bas, **II** 259

Compagnie Financière de Suez, **III** 394

Compagnie Française de Distribution en Afrique, **IV** 559

Compagnie Française de Raffinage, **IV** 558–60

Compagnie Française des Lubricants, **I** 341

Compagnie Française des Minerais d'Uranium, **IV** 108

Compagnie Française des Mines de Diamants du Cap, **IV** 64; **7** 121

Compagnie Française des Pétroles, **II** 259; **IV** 363–64, 423–24, 454, 466, 486, 504, 515, 544–46, 557–60; **7** 481–83

Compagnie Française des Produits d'Orangina, **I** 281

Compagnie Française du Méthane, **V** 626

Compagnie Française Thomson-Houston, **I** 357; **II** 116

Compagnie Générale d'Électricité, I 193; **II 12–13**, 25; **IV** 174, 615; **9** 9–10

Compagnie Generale de Cartons Ondules, **IV** 296

Compagnie Generale de Radiologie, **II** 117

Compagnie Generale de Telegraphie Sans Fils, **II** 116

Compagnie Générale des Eaux, **V** 632–33; **6** 441

Compagnie Générale des Établissements Michelin, V 236–39

Compagnie Générale Maritime (CGM), **6** 379–80

Compagnie Générale Maritime et Financière, 6 379–81

Compagnie Générale Transatlantique (Transat), **6** 379–80

Compagnie Industriali Riunite S.p.A., **IV** 587–88

Compagnie Internationale de l'Informatique, **III** 123

Compagnie Internationale Pirelli S.A., **V** 249

Compagnie Navale Des Pétroles, **IV** 558

Compagnie Parisienne de Garantie, **III** 211

Compagnie Pneumatique Commerciale, **III** 426

Compagnie Tunisienne de Ressorts a Lames, **III** 581

Companhia Brasileira de Aluminio, **IV** 55

Companhia Brasileira de Mineracão e Siderugica, **IV** 54

Companhia de Diamantes de Angola, **IV** 21

Companhia de Minerales y Metales, **IV** 139

Companhia de Pesquisas Mineras de Angola, **IV** 65; **7** 122

Companhia de Seguros Argos Fluminense, **III** 221

Companhia Siderúrgica de Tubarao, **IV** 125

Companhia Siderúrgica Mannesmann S.A., **III** 565–66

Companhia Siderúrgica Nacional, **II** 199

Companhia Uniao Fabril, **IV** 505

Companhia Vale do Rio Doce, IV 54–57

Compañia Arrendataria del Monopolio de Petróleos Sociedad Anónima, **IV** 396–97, 527–29

Compañia de Investigacion y Exploitaciones Petrolifera, **IV** 397

Compañia de Líneas Aéreas Subvencionadas S.A., **6** 95

Compañia Española de Petroleos S.A., IV 396–98, 527

Compañia Minera La India, **IV** 164

Compañia Nacional Minera Petrólia del Táchira, **IV** 507

Compañia Telefónica Nacional de España S.A., **V** 337

Compaq Computer Corporation, II 45; **III** 114, **124–25**; **6** 217, **221–23 (upd.)**, 230–31, 235, 243–44; **9** 42–43, 166, 170–71, 472

Compass Group, plc, **6** 193

Competition Tire East, **V** 494

Competition Tire West, **V** 494

Compex, **II** 233

Northrup King Co., **I** 672
Northwest Airlines Inc., **I** 42, 64, 91, 97, 100, 104, **112–14**, 125, 127; **6** 66, 74, 82 **103–05 (upd.)**; **9** 273
Northwest Benefit Assoc., **III** 228
Northwest Engineering Co. *See* Terex Corporation.
Northwest Industries, **I** 342, 440; **II** 468 **8** 367. *See also* Chicago and North Western Holdings Corporation.
Northwest Instruments, **8** 519
Northwest Orient, **6** 123. *See also* Northwest Airlines, Inc.
Northwest Paper Company, **8** 430
Northwest Telecommunications Inc., **6** 598
Northwestern Bell Telephone Co., **V** 341
Northwestern Benevolent Society, **III** 228
Northwestern Expanded Metal Co., **III** 763
Northwestern Industries, **III** 263
Northwestern Manufacturing Company, **8** 133
Northwestern Mutual Life Insurance Company, **III** 321–24, 352; **IV** 333
Northwestern National Insurance Co., **IV** 29
Northwestern Public Service Company, **6** 524
Northwestern States Portland Cement Co., **III** 702
Northwestern Telephone Systems, **6** 325, 328
Norton, Charles H., **8** 396
Norton Company, **III** 678; **8** **395–97**
Norton Emery Wheel Company, **8** 395
Norton, Eugene, **IV** 81; **7** 185
Norton, Frank, **8** 395
Norton Opax PLC, **IV** 259
Norton Simon Inc., **I** 446; **IV** 672; **6** 356
Norton Stone Ware, F.B., **8** 395
Norwegian Assurance, **III** 258
Norwegian Globe, **III** 258
Norwegian Petroleum Consultants, **III** 499
Norwest Publishing, **IV** 661
Norwich Pharmaceuticals, **I** 370–71; **9** 358
Norwich Union Fire Insurance Society, Ltd., **III** 242, 273, 404; **IV** 705
Norwich Winterthur Group, **III** 404
Norwich Winterthur Reinsurance Corp. Ltd., **III** 404
Norwich-Eaton Pharmaceuticals, **III** 53; **8** 434
Nottingham Manufacturing Co., **V** 357
Nouvelles Messageries de la Presse Parisienne, **IV** 618
Nova, an Alberta Corporation, **V** 674
Nova Corporation of Alberta, **V** **673–75**
Novak, William, **I** 145
Novell Data Systems. *See* Novell, Inc.
Novell, Inc., **6** 255–56, 260, **269–71**; **9** 170–71
Novello and Co., **II** 139
Novo Industri A/S, **I** **658–60**, 697
Nowell Wholesale Grocery Co., **II** 681
Nox Ltd., **I** 588
Noxell Corporation, **III** 53; **8** 434
Noyce, Robert, **II** 44–46
Noyes, John Humphrey, **7** 406
Noyes, Pierrepont Burt, **7** 406–07
Nozaki, Hirota, **IV** 655
NS. *See* Norfolk Southern Corporation.
NS Petites Inc., **8** 323
NSG America, Inc., **III** 715
NSG Foreign Trade, **III** 715
NSG Information System Co., **III** 715

NSG Materials Service Co., **III** 715
NSG-Taliq, **III** 715
NSK. *See* Nippon Seiko K.K.
NSK Bearings Europe, **III** 589
NSK Corp., **III** 589
NSK do Brasil Industria e Comercio de Rolamentos, **III** 589
NSK Kugellager, **III** 589
NSK-Torrington, **III** 589
NSMO. *See* Nederlandsche Stoomvart Maatschappij Oceaan.
NSP. *See* Northern States Power Company.
NTCL. *See* Northern Telecom Canada Ltd.
NTN Bearing Corp. of America, **III** 595
NTN Bearing Corp. of Canada, **III** 595
NTN Bearing Manufacturing Corp., **III** 595
NTN Bearings-GKN, **III** 595
NTN Bower Corp., **III** 596
NTN Corporation, **III** **595–96**, 623
NTN de Mexico, **III** 596
NTN Driveshaft, **III** 596
NTN France, **III** 595
NTN Kugellagerfabrik, **III** 595–96
NTN Manufacturing Canada, **III** 595
NTN Manufacturing Co., Ltd., **III** 595
NTN Sales, **III** 595
NTN Suramericana, **III** 596
NTN Toyo Bearing Co., **III** 595–96
NTN Trading-Hong Kong, **III** 595
NTN Wälzlager Europa, **III** 595
NTT. *See* Nippon Telegraph and Telephone Corp.
NTT International Corporation, **V** 305–06
NTTI. *See* NTT International Corporation.
NTTPC. *See* Nippon Telegraph and Telephone Public Corporation.
NU. *See* Northeast Utilities.
Nuclear Electric, **6** 453
Nucoa Butter Co., **II** 497
Nucor Corporation, **7** **400–02**
Nucorp Energy, **II** 262, 620
NUG Optimus Lebensmittel-Einzelhandelgesellschaft mbH, **V** 74
Nugent, D. Eugene, **7** 420
Nugent, Frank, **III** 738
Nugget Polish Co. Ltd., **II** 566
Numerax, Inc., **IV** 637
Nuovo Pignone, **IV** 420–22
NUR Touristic GmbH, **V** 100–02
Nurad, **III** 468
Nursefinders, **6** 10
Nusbaum, Aaron, **V** 180
NutraSweet Company, **II** 463, 582; **8** **398–400**
Nutrena, **II** 617
Nutrilite Co., **III** 11–12
Nutt, Roy, **6** 227
NVH L.P., **8** 401. *See also* NVR L.P.
NVHomes, Inc., **8** 401–02. *See also* NVR L.P.
NVR Finance, **8** 402–03
NVR L.P., **8** **401–03**
NVRyan L.P., **8** 401. *See also* NVR L.P.
NWA Aircraft, **I** 114
NWK. *See* Nordwestdeutsche Kraftwerke AG.
NWL Control Systems, **III** 512
Nya AB Atlas, **III** 425–26
Nybom, F.K., **II** 302
Nydqvist & Holm, **III** 426
Nye, David E., **I** 168
Nye, Gerald, **I** 57
Nyers, Howard, **IV** 673; **7** 527

Nyhamms Cellulosa, **IV** 338
NYK. *See* Nihon Yusen Kaisha.
NYK. *See* Nippon Yusen Kabushiki Kaisha *and* Nippon Yusen Kaisha.
Nylex Corp., **I** 429
Nyman & Schultz Affarsresbyraer A.B., **I** 120
NYNEX Corporation, **V** **311–13**; **6** 340
Nyrop, **I** 113
Nyrop, Donald, **6** 104
Nysco Laboratories, **III** 55
NYSEG. *See* New York State Electric and Gas Corporation.
NZI Corp., **III** 257

O'Brien, John, **IV** 306
O'Brien, John J., **V** 711
O'Brien, Morgan, **III** 247
O'Brien, Raymond F., **V**, 433; **6** 390
O'Brien, Robert, **I** 185, 286
O'Brien, Thomas H., **II** 342
O'Brien, William, **II** 381
O'Connor, Flannery, **IV** 622
O'Connor, John, **III** 471
O'Donnell, William T., **III** 430–31
O'Donnell-Usen Fisheries, **II** 494
O'Gorman and Cozens-Hardy, **III** 725
O'Green, Fred, **I** 485
O'Hagan, Henry Osborne, **III** 669
O'Hagan, William D., **7** 361
O'Hara, J.B., **9** 177
O'Hare, Dean R., **III** 221
O'Hare, Don R., **7** 504
O'Keefe, Bernard J., **8** 163–65
O'Malley, Shaun F., **9** 424
O'Malley, Thomas, **7** 538
O'Neal, Edward, **I** 366; **9** 356
O'Neil, Jerry, **8** 207; **9** 248
O'Neil, John, **9** 248
O'Neil, John P., **9** 134
O'Neil, Thomas, **9** 248
O'Neil, William, **8** 206–07; **9** 247–48
O'Neil, William F., **8** 212–14
O'Neill, John, **III** 673
O'Neill, Paul, **IV** 16
O'Neill, Peter L., **II** 607
O'okiep Copper Compny, Ltd., **7** 385–86
O'Reilly, Anthony J.F., **II** 508
O&Y. *See* Olympia & York Developments Ltd.
O.B. McClintock Co., **7** 144–45
Oahu Railway & Land Co., **I** 565–66
Oak Farms Dairies, **II** 660
Oak Industries, **III** 512
Oakes, C. Gordon, **I** 714
Oakley, Jonas, **III** 240
Oakville, **7** 518
OASIS, **IV** 454
Oates, James, Jr., **III** 248
Oates, Keith, **V** 126
Oats, Francis, **IV** 65
ÖBB. *See* Österreichische Bundesbahnen GmbH.
Obbola Linerboard, **IV** 339
Ober, Edgar B., **8** 369
Ober, John, **I** 499
Oberkotter, Harold, **V** 534
Oberrheinische Bank, **II** 278
Oberschlesische Stickstoff-Werge AG, **IV** 229
Oberusel AG, **III** 541
Oberwinder, J. F., **6** 21
Obunsha, **9** 29
Occidental Chemical Corp., **IV** 481–82

Tetley Inc., **I** 215
Tetley Tea, **I** 215
Tetra Plastics Inc., **V** 374; **8** 393
Teutonia National Bank, **IV** 310
Tevis, Lloyd, **I** 527; **II** 381
Tex-Star Oil & Gas Corp., **IV** 574; **7** 551
Texaco, **7** 172
Texaco Canada, **IV** 439
Texaco Chemical Co., **IV** 552–53
Texaco Inc., **I** 21, 360; **II** 31, 313, 448;
  III 760; **IV** 386, 403, 418, 425, 429,
  461, 464, 466, 472–73, 479–80, 484,
  488, 490, 510–11, 530–31, 536–39,
  545, **551–53**, 560, 565–66, 570, 575; **7**
  280, 483; **9** 232
Texada Mines, Ltd., **IV** 123
Texas Air Corporation, **I** 97, 100, 103,
  118, **123–24**, 127, 130; **6** 82, 129
Texas Butadiene and Chemical Corp., **IV**
  456
Texas Co., **III** 497; **IV** 386, 400, 464, 536,
  551; **7** 352
Texas Co. of California, **IV** 552
Texas Co. of Delaware, **IV** 551–52
Texas Commerce Bankshares, **II** 252
Texas Corp., **IV** 551–52
Texas Eastern Corp., **6** 487
Texas Eastman, **III** 475; **7** 161
Texas Electric Service Company, **V** 724
Texas Fuel Co., **IV** 551
Texas Gas Resources, **IV** 395
Texas Gypsum, **IV** 341
Texas Industries, Inc., **8** 522–24
Texas Instruments, **8** 157
Texas Instruments Incorporated, **I** 315,
  482, 523, 620; **II** 64, **112–15**; **III** 120,
  124–25, 142, 499; **IV** 130, 365, 681; **6**
  216, 221–22, 237, 241, 257, 259; **7** 531;
  9 43, 116, 310
Texas International, **IV** 413
Texas International Airlines, **I** 117, 123; **II**
  408
Texas Life Insurance Co., **III** 293
Texas Metal Fabricating Company, **7** 540
Texas Oil & Gas Corp., **IV** 499, 572, 574;
  7 549, 551
Texas Overseas Petroleum Co., **IV** 552
Texas Pacific Coal and Oil Co., **I** 285–86
Texas Pacific Oil Co., **IV** 550
Texas Pipe Line Co., **IV** 552
Texas Power & Light Company, **V** 724
Texas Public Utilities, **II** 660
Texas Super Duper Markets, Inc., **7** 372
Texas Trust Savings Bank, **8** 88
Texas United Insurance Co., **III** 214
Texas Utilities Company, **V** 724–25
Texas Utilities Electric Company, **V**
  724–25
Texas Utilities Fuel Company, **V** 724–25
Texas Utilities Mining Company, **V** 725
Texas Utilities Services, Inc., **V** 725
Texas-New Mexico Power Co., **6** 580
Texas-New Mexico Utilities Company, **6**
  580
Texasgulf, **IV** 546–47
Texboard, **IV** 296
Texize, **I** 325, 371
Texkan Oil Co., **IV** 566
Texstar Petroleum Company, **7** 516
Texstyrene Corp., **IV** 331
Textile Paper Tube Company, Ltd., **8** 475
Textron Inc., **I** 186, **529–30**; **II** 420; **III**
  66, 628; **8** 93, 157, 315, 545; **9** 497, 499

**Textron Lycoming Turbine Engine, 9
497–99**
TF-I, **I** 563
TFN Group Communications, Inc., **8** 311
TGEL&PCo. *See* Tucson Gas, Electric
  Light & Power Company.
Th. Pilter, **III** 417
Thackeray, William Makepeace, **IV** 617
Thai Airways Company. *See* Thai Airways
  International Ltd.
Thai Airways International Ltd., **I** 119;
  II 442; **6 122–24**
Thai Aluminium Co. Ltd., **IV** 155
Thalberg, Irving, **II** 148
Thalhimer Brothers, **V** 31
Thames Board Ltd., **IV** 318
Thames Television Ltd., **I** 532
Tharsis Co., **IV** 189–90
Thatcher Glass, **I** 610
Thatcher, Margaret, **I** 34, 51, 83, 94, 556;
  III 336, 753; **IV** 38, 40, 380, 452,
  641–42; **7** 332, 532
Thayer, Charles J., **9** 485
Thayer Laboratories, **III** 55
Thayer, W. Paul, **I** 490–91
Theis, Fran, **6** 395
Theo H. Davies & Co., **I** 470
Theo Hamm Brewing Co., **I** 260
Theobald, Thomas, **II** 262
Théraplix, **I** 388
Therm-o-Disc, **II** 19
Therm-X Company, **8** 178
Thermacote Welco Company, **6** 146
Thermo Electron Corporation, **7** 520–22
Thermodynamics Corp., **III** 645
Thermogas Co., **IV** 458–59
Thermoplast und Apparatebau GmbH, **IV**
  198
Thieme, Carl, **III** 183, 299–300
Thierry, Jacques, **II** 201–03
Thies, Wes, **9** 434
Thiess, **III** 687
Thiess Dampier Mitsui, **IV** 47
Thimont, Bernard, **7** 217
Think Entertainment, **II** 161
Thiokol Chemical Corporation, **8** 472
Thiokol Corporation, **9** 358–59, **500–02**
  (upd.)
Thiokol Inc., **I** 370
Third National Bank, **II** 291
Third National Bank of Dayton, **9** 475
Third National Bank of New York, **II** 253
Thistle Group, **9** 365
Thom McAn, **V**, 136–37
Thomas & Betts, **II** 8
Thomas & Howard Co., **II** 682
Thomas and Hochwalt, **I** 365
Thomas, Bailey, **7** 316
Thomas Barlow, **IV** 22
Thomas Barlow & Sons (South Africa)
  Ltd., **I** 422
Thomas Barlow & Sons Ltd., **I** 288, 422
Thomas, Bert L., **II** 683
Thomas, Charles, **I** 126, 366; **9** 355
Thomas Cook Travel Inc., 9 503–05
Thomas, Edward, **7** 234
Thomas, Edwin J., **V** 246
Thomas Firth & Sons, **I** 573
Thomas, Grant, **IV** 92
Thomas Jefferson Life Insurance Co., **III**
  397
Thomas, John, **III** 720
Thomas, Joseph, **I** 484
Thomas, Ken W., **V** 523–25

Thomas Linnell & Co. Ltd., **II** 628
Thomas Nationwide Transport Limited, **V**
  523
Thomas Nelson & Sons, **8** 526
Thomas, O. Pendleton, **V** 233
Thomas, Peter, **III** 114
Thomas, Philip E., **V** 438
Thomas, Philippe, **IV** 174
Thomas, R. David, **8** 563–65
Thomas, Robert E., **IV** 458–59
Thomas, Rubel, **6** 134
Thomas, S.B., **II** 498
Thomas, S.G., **IV** 24
Thomas Tilling plc, **I** 429
Thomas, Watson, **6** 250
Thomas Y. Crowell, **IV** 605
Thomasville Furniture Industries, **III** 423
Thomopoulous, Anthony, **II** 149
Thompson, Adam, **I** 94
Thompson, David, **II** 513–14
Thompson, David, **V** 80
Thompson, Edward K., **IV** 674; **7** 527
Thompson, Glenn W., **8** 38–39
Thompson, Harry, **6** 585
Thompson, J.J., **II** 24
Thompson, J. Walter, **I** 19–20
Thompson, Jack, **I** 400
Thompson, James S., **IV** 635–36
Thompson, Jere W., **II** 661; **7** 491
Thompson, Joe C. "Jodie", **7** 490
Thompson, John F., **IV** 111
Thompson, John P., **7** 490–91
Thompson, John P., **II** 660–61
Thompson, John S., **III** 303
Thompson, Joseph C., **II** 660; **7** 491
Thompson, Julian Ogilvie, **IV** 68; **7** 125
Thompson, Kay, **IV** 672
Thompson, M.B., **II** 505
Thompson, Peter, **6** 413–14
Thompson Products Co., **I** 539
Thompson, Rupert, **I** 529
Thompson, W. Reid, **6** 553–54
Thompson, William, **I** 132
Thompson, William Boyce, **7** 287, 385
Thompson-Ramo-Woolridge, **I** 539
Thompson-Werke, **III** 32
Thomson, Alexander, **IV** 263
The Thomson Corporation, **IV** 651, 686;
  7 390; **8 525–28**
Thomson, Cy, **II** 505–05
Thomson, Elihu, **II** 27
Thomson family, **IV** 263–64
Thomson, Kenneth, **V** 80; **8** 525–67
Thomson, Logan, **IV** 263
Thomson, Peter, **IV** 263–64
Thomson, Richard Murray, **II** 376
Thomson, Roy, **8** 525–27
Thomson, Roy (Lord of Fleet), **IV** 651
Thomson S.A., **I** 411; **II** 31, **116–17**; **7** 9
Thomson, S.C., **IV** 164
Thomson, Spencer, **III** 360
Thomson T-Line, **II** 142
Thomson, William Thomas, **III** 359–60
Thomson-Bennett, **III** 554
Thomson-Brandt, **I** 411; **II** 13, 116–17; **9**
  9
Thomson-CSF, **II** 116–17; **III** 556
Thomson-Houston Co., **II** 27
Thomson-Houston Electric Co., **II** 27, 116,
  330
Thomson-Lucas, **III** 556
Thoreau, Henry David, **IV** 661
Thorley, Gerald (Sir), **IV** 712
Thorn Apple Valley, Inc., 7 523–25

INDEX TO INDUSTRIES

Index to Industries

SmithKline Beckman Corporation, I
Squibb Corporation, I
Sterling Drug, Inc., I
Syntex Corporation, I
Takeda Chemical Industries, Ltd., I
The Upjohn Company, I; 8 (upd.)
Warner-Lambert, I
The Wellcome Foundation Ltd, I

ELECTRICAL & ELECTRONICS

ABB ASEA Brown Boveri Ltd., II
Advanced Technology Laboratories, Inc., 9
Alps Electric Co., Ltd., II
AMP, Inc., II
Atari Corporation, 9
Avnet Inc., 9
Bicoastal Corporation, II
Compagnie Générale d'Électricité, II
Cooper Industries, Inc., II
Digi International Inc., 9
E-Systems, Inc., 9
Emerson Electric Co., II
Fuji Electric Co., Ltd., II
General Electric Company, II
General Electric Company, PLC, II
General Signal Corporation, 9
GM Hughes Electronics Corporation, II
Harris Corporation, II
Honeywell Inc., II
Hubbell Incorporated, 9
Intel Corporation, II
Itel Corporation, 9
KitchenAid, 8
KnowledgeWare Inc., 9
Koor Industries Ltd., II
Kyocera Corporation, II
Loral Corporation, 9
Lucky-Goldstar, II
Matsushita Electric Industrial Co., Ltd., II
Mitsubishi Electric Corporation, II
Motorola, Inc., II
National Semiconductor Corporation, II
NEC Corporation, II
Nokia Corporation, II
Oki Electric Industry Company, Limited, II
Omron Tateisi Electronics Company, II
N.V. Philips Gloeilampenfabrieken, II
Pittway Corporation, 9
The Plessey Company, PLC, II
Premier Industrial Corporation, 9
Racal Electronics PLC, II
Raychem Corporation, 8
Raytheon Company, II
RCA Corporation, II
Reliance Electric Company, 9
Sanyo Electric Company, Ltd., II
Schneider S.A., II
SCI Systems, Inc., 9
Sharp Corporation, II
Siemens A.G., II
Silicon Graphics Incorporated, 9
Sony Corporation, II
Sumitomo Electric Industries, Ltd., II
Sunbeam-Oster Co., Inc., 9
Tandy Corporation, II
TDK Corporation, II
Tektronix, Inc., 8
Texas Instruments Incorporated, II
Thomson S.A., II
Victor Company of Japan, Ltd., II
Westinghouse Electric Corporation, II
Zenith Electronics Corporation, II

ENGINEERING & MANAGEMENT SERVICES

The Austin Company, 8
CDI Corporation, 6

CRSS Inc., 6
Day & Zimmermann Inc., 9
EG&G Incorporated, 8
Foster Wheeler Corporation, 6
Jacobs Engineering Group Inc., 6
JWP Inc., 9
McKinsey & Company, Inc., 9
Ogden Corporation, 6
The Parsons Corporation, 8
Susquehanna Pfaltzgraff Company, 8
United Dominion Industries Limited, 8
VECO International, Inc., 7

ENTERTAINMENT & LEISURE

Asahi National Broadcasting Company, Ltd., 9
Blockbuster Entertainment Corporation, 9
British Broadcasting Corporation, 7
Cablevision Systems Corporation, 7
Capital Cities/ABC Inc., II
CBS Inc., II; 6 (upd.)
Central Independent Television plc, 7
Cineplex Odeon Corporation, 6
Columbia Pictures Entertainment, Inc., II
Comcast Corporation, 7
Continental Cablevision, Inc., 7
Granada Group PLC, II
Home Box Office Inc., 7
Japan Broadcasting Corporation, 7
King World Productions, Inc., 9
Ladbroke Group PLC, II
MCA Inc., II
Media General, Inc., 7
MGM/UA Communications Company, II
National Broadcasting Company, Inc., II; 6 (upd.)
Orion Pictures Corporation, 6
Paramount Pictures Corporation, II
Promus Companies, Inc., 9
Rank Organisation PLC, II
Tele-Communications, Inc., II
Television Española, S.A., 7
Thomas Cook Travel Inc., 9
The Thomson Corporation, 8
Touristik Union International GmbH. and Company K.G., II
Turner Broadcasting System, Inc., II; 6 (upd.)
Twentieth Century Fox Film Corporation, II
Viacom International Inc., 7
Walt Disney Company, II; 6 (upd.)
Warner Communications Inc., II

FINANCIAL SERVICES: BANKS

Algemene Bank Nederland N.V., II
American Residential Mortgage Corporation, 8
Amsterdam-Rotterdam Bank N.V., II
Australia and New Zealand Banking Group Ltd., II
Banca Commerciale Italiana SpA, II
Banco Bilbao Vizcaya, S.A., II
Banco Central, II
Banco do Brasil S.A., II
Bank Brussels Lambert, II
Bank Hapoalim B.M., II
Bank of Boston Corporation, II
Bank of Montreal, II
Bank of New England Corporation, II
The Bank of New York Company, Inc., II
The Bank of Nova Scotia, II
Bank of Tokyo, Ltd., II
BankAmerica Corporation, II; 8 (upd.)
Bankers Trust New York Corporation, II
Banque Nationale de Paris S.A., II
Barclays PLC, II

Barnett Banks, Inc., 9
Bayerische Hypotheken- und Wechsel-Bank AG, II
Bayerische Vereinsbank A.G., II
Beneficial Corporation, 8
Canadian Imperial Bank of Commerce, II
The Chase Manhattan Corporation, II
Chemical Banking Corporation, II
Citicorp, II; 9 (upd.)
Commercial Credit Company, 8
Commerzbank A.G., II
Compagnie Financiere de Paribas, II
Continental Bank Corporation, II
Crédit Agricole, II
Crédit Lyonnais, 9
Crédit National S.A., 9
Crédit Suisse, II
Credito Italiano, II
The Dai-Ichi Kangyo Bank Ltd., II
The Daiwa Bank, Ltd., II
Deutsche Bank A.G., II
Dime Savings Bank of New York, F.S.B., 9
Dresdner Bank A.G., II
First Chicago Corporation, II
First Fidelity Bank, N.A., New Jersey, 9
First Interstate Bancorp, II
First of America Bank Corporation, 8
Fleet Financial Group, Inc., 9
The Fuji Bank, Ltd., II
Generale Bank, II
Great Lakes Bancorp, 8
H. F. Ahmanson & Company, II
The Hongkong and Shanghai Banking Corporation Limited, II
The Industrial Bank of Japan, Ltd., II
J.P. Morgan & Co. Incorporated, II
Japan Leasing Corporation, 8
Kansallis-Osake-Pankki, II
KeyCorp, 8
Kredietbank N.V., II
Lloyds Bank PLC, II
Long-Term Credit Bank of Japan, Ltd., II
Manufacturers Hanover Corporation, II
Mellon Bank Corporation, II
Midland Bank PLC, II
The Mitsubishi Bank, Ltd., II
The Mitsubishi Trust & Banking Corporation, II
The Mitsui Bank, Ltd., II
The Mitsui Trust & Banking Company, Ltd., II
National Westminster Bank PLC, II
NCNB Corporation, II
Nippon Credit Bank, II
Norinchukin Bank, II
Northern Trust Company, 9
NVR L.P., 8
PNC Financial Corporation, II
Pulte Corporation, 8
The Royal Bank of Canada, II
The Ryland Group, Inc., 8
The Sanwa Bank, Ltd., II
Seattle First National Bank Inc., 8
Security Pacific Corporation, II
Skandinaviska Enskilda Banken, II
Société Générale, II
Society Corporation, 9
St. Paul Bank for Cooperatives, 8
Standard Chartered PLC, II
Standard Federal Bank, 9
State Street Boston Corporation, 8
The Sumitomo Bank, Ltd., II
The Sumitomo Trust & Banking Company, Ltd., II
Svenska Handelsbanken, II
Swiss Bank Corporation, II
The Taiyo Kobe Bank, Ltd., II

Knight-Ridder, Inc., IV
Kodansha Ltd., IV
Maclean Hunter Limited, IV
Macmillan, Inc., 7
Maxwell Communication Corporation plc,
  IV; 7 (upd.)
McGraw-Hill, Inc., IV
Mirror Group Newspapers plc, 7
Moore Corporation Limited, IV
National Geographic Society, 9
The New York Times Company, IV
News Corporation Limited, IV; 7 (upd.)
Nihon Keizai Shimbun, Inc., IV
Pearson plc, IV
R.R. Donnelley & Sons Company, IV; 9
  (upd.)
The Reader's Digest Association, Inc., IV
Reed International P.L.C., IV
Reuters Holdings PLC, IV
Simon & Schuster Inc., IV
Southam Inc., 7
The Thomson Corporation, 8
The Times Mirror Company, IV
Toppan Printing Co., Ltd., IV
Tribune Company, IV
United Newspapers plc, IV
Valassis Communications, Inc., 8
The Washington Post Company, IV
West Publishing Co., 7

REAL ESTATE

Bramalea Ltd., 9
Cheung Kong (Holdings) Limited, IV
The Edward J. DeBartolo Corporation, 8
The Haminerson Property Investment and
  Development Corporation plc, IV
Hongkong Land Holdings Limited, IV
JMB Realty Corporation, IV
Kaufman and Broad Home Corporation, 8
The Koll Company, 8
Land Securities PLC, IV
Lend Lease Corporation Limited, IV
Lincoln Property Company, 8
Melvin Simon and Associates, Inc., 8
MEPC plc, IV
Mitsubishi Estate Company, Limited, IV
Mitsui Real Estate Development Co., Ltd.,
  IV
New World Development Company Ltd.,
  IV
Olympia & York Developments Ltd., IV; 9
  (upd.)
Perini Corporation, 8
Slough Estates PLC, IV
Sumitomo Realty & Development Co.,
  Ltd., IV
Tokyu Land Corporation, IV
Trammell Crow Company, 8
Tridel Enterprises Inc., 9

RETAIL & WHOLESALE

Ames Department Stores, Inc., 9
Au Printemps S.A., V
AutoZone, Inc., 9
Belk Stores Services, Inc., V
Bergen Brunswig Corporation, V
Best Buy Co., Inc., 9
The Boots Company PLC, V
The Burton Group plc, V
C&A Brenninkmeyer KG, V
Campeau Corporation, V
Carter Hawley Hale Stores, Inc., V
Circuit City Stores, Inc., 9
Coles Myer Ltd., V
Comdisco, Inc., 9
Costco Wholesale Corporation, V
Cotter & Company, V

County Seat Stores Inc., 9
Crate and Barrel, 9
The Daiei, Inc., V
The Daimaru, Inc., V
Dayton Hudson Corporation, V
Dillard Department Stores, Inc., V
Dixons Group plc, V
Eckerd Corporation, 9
El Corte Inglés Group, V
Federated Department Stores Inc., 9
Fingerhut Companies, Inc., 9
Florsheim Shoe Company, 9
Fred Meyer, Inc., V
Galeries Lafayette S.A., V
The Gap, Inc., V
GIB Group, V
The Great Universal Stores P.L.C., V
Hankyu Department Stores, Inc., V
Hertie Waren- und Kaufhaus GmbH, V
The Home Depot, Inc., V
Home Shopping Network, Inc., V
Hudson's Bay Company, V
The IKEA Group, V
Isetan Company Limited, V
Ito-Yokado Co., Ltd., V
J.C. Penney Company, Inc., V
John Lewis Partnership PLC, V
JUSCO Co., Ltd., V
Karstadt Aktiengesellschaft, V
Kaufhof Holding AG, V
Kingfisher plc, V
Kmart Corporation, V
Kohl's Corporation, 9
Kotobukiya Co., Ltd., V
Lands' End, Inc., 9
The Limited, Inc., V
The Littlewoods Organisation PLC, V
Longs Drug Stores Corporation, V
Lowe's Companies, Inc., V
Marks and Spencer p.l.c., V
Marui Co., Ltd., V
Matsuzakaya Company Limited, V
The May Department Stores Company, V
Melville Corporation, V
Mercantile Stores Company, Inc., V
Merry-Go-Round Enterprises, Inc., 8
Mitsukoshi Ltd., V
Montgomery Ward & Co., Incorporated, V
Musicland Stores Corporation, 9
Nagasakiya Co., Ltd., V
National Intergroup, Inc., V
Nichii Co., Ltd., V
Nordstrom, Inc., V
Office Depot Incorporated, 8
Otto-Versand (GmbH & Co.), V
Pay 'N Pak Stores, Inc., 9
Petrie Stores Corporation, 8
The Price Company, V
Quelle Group, V
R.H. Macy & Co., Inc., V; 8 (upd.)
Revco D.S., Inc., V
Riklis Family Corp., 9
Rite Aid Corporation, V
Sears plc, V
Sears, Roebuck and Co., V
Seibu Department Stores, Ltd., V
The Seiyu, Ltd., V
Service Merchandise Company, Inc., V
Stinnes AG, 8
Stride Rite Corporation, 8
Takashimaya Co., Limited, V
The TJX Companies, Inc., V
Tokyu Department Store Co., Ltd., V
Toys "R" Us, Inc., V
The United States Shoe Corporation, V
Uny Co., Ltd., V
W H Smith Group PLC, V
W.W. Grainger, Inc., V

Wal-Mart Stores, Inc., V; 8 (upd.)
Walgreen Co., V
Wickes Companies, Inc., V
Woolworth Corporation, V

RUBBER & TIRE

The BFGoodrich Company, V
Bridgestone Corporation, V
Carlisle Companies Incorporated, 8
Compagnie Générale des Établissements
  Michelin, V
Continental Aktiengesellschaft, V
Cooper Tire & Rubber Company, 8
General Tire, Inc., 8
The Goodyear Tire & Rubber Company, V
The Kelly-Springfield Tire Company, 8
Pirelli S.p.A., V
Sumitomo Rubber Industries, Ltd., V
The Yokohama Rubber Co., Ltd., V

TELECOMMUNICATIONS

Alltel Corporation, 6
American Telephone and Telegraph
  Company, V
Ameritech, V
Ascom AG, 9
BCE Inc., V
Belgacom, 6
Bell Atlantic Corporation, V
Bell Canada, 6
BellSouth Corporation, V
British Columbia Telephone Company, 6
British Telecommunications plc, V
Cable and Wireless plc, V
Centel Corporation, 6
Century Telephone Enterprises, Inc., 9
Chris-Craft Industries, Inc., 9
Cincinnati Bell, Inc., 6
DDI Corporation, 7
Deutsche Bundespost TELEKOM, V
Directorate General of
  Telecommunications, 7
France Télécom Group, V
GTE Corporation, V
Hong Kong Telecommunications Ltd., 6
Koninklijke PTT Nederland NV, V
LDDS-Metro Communications, Inc., 8
LIN Broadcasting Corp., 9
McCaw Cellular Communications, Inc., 6
MCI Communications Corporation, V
Mercury Communications, Ltd., 7
Nippon Telegraph and Telephone
  Corporation, V
Northern Telecom Limited, V
NYNEX Corporation, V
Österreichische Post- und
  Telegraphenverwaltung, V
Pacific Telecom, Inc., 6
Pacific Telesis Group, V
Posti- ja Telelaitos, 6
QVC Network Inc., 9
Rochester Telephone Corporation, 6
Schweizerische Post-, Telefon- und
  Telegrafen-Betriebe, V
Scientific-Atlanta, Inc., 6
Società Finanziaria Telefonica per Azioni,
  V
Southern New England
  Telecommunications Corporation, 6
Southwestern Bell Corporation, V
Sprint Communications Company, L.P., 9
Swedish Telecom, V
Telecom Australia, 6
Telecom Eireann, 7
Telefonaktiebolaget LM Ericsson, V
Telefónica de España, S.A., V
Telephone and Data Systems, Inc., 9

WASTE SERVICES

NOTES ON CONTRIBUTORS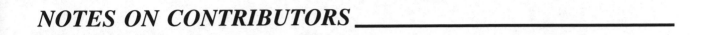

Notes on Contributors

BOHN, Thomas. Free-lance writer.

BRENNAN, Carol. Free-lance writer in Chicago.

BROWN, Susan Windisch. Free-lance writer and editor.

COHEN, Kerstan. Free-lance writer and French translator; editor for *Letter-Ex* poetry review.

COLLINS, Cheryl L. Free-lance writer and researcher.

COVELL, Jeffrey L. Free-lance writer and corporate history contractor.

DERDAK, Thomas. Free-lance writer and adjunct professor in philosophy at Loyola University of Chicago; former executive director of the Albert Einstein Foundation.

DOUGAL, April S. Archivist and free-lance writer specializing in business and social history in Cleveland, Ohio.

DUBOVOJ, Sina. History contractor and free-lance writer; adjunct professor of history, Montgomery College, Rockville, Maryland.

GRANT, Tina. Free-lance writer and editor.

HECHT, Henry. Editorial consultant and retired vice-president, editorial services, Merrill Lynch.

HEDBLAD, Edna. Free-lance writer and elementary school teacher.

HEDDEN, Heather Behn. Business periodical abstractor and indexer, Information Access Company, Foster City, California. Senior staff writer, *Middle East Times* Cairo bureau, 1991-92.

JACOBSON, Robert R. Free-lance writer and musician.

KERNS, Jennifer. Free-lance writer and editor in Paris.

KIELTYKA, Carol. Free-lance writer.

LANDA, Marinell. San Francisco–based writer and editor specializing in business and health-care topics.

LEWIS, Scott M. Free-lance writer and editor; contributing editor, *Option.* Staff editor, *Security, Distributing and Marketing,* 1989-90.

MARTIN, Jonathan. Free-lance writer.

MCNULTY, Mary. Editor, American Association of Law Libraries; contributor to the Chicago *Tribune.*

PEDERSON, Jay P. Free-lance writer and editor.

PENDERGAST, Sara. Free-lance writer and copyeditor.

PENDERGAST, Tom. Free-lance writer and graduate student in American studies at Purdue University.

ROULAND, Roger. Free-lance writer whose essays and journalism have appeared in the *International Fiction Review*, Chicago *Tribune*, and Chicago *Sun-Times.*

ROURKE, Elizabeth. Free-lance writer.

SALTER, Susan. Free-lance writer for reference series including *Contemporary Authors*, *Newsmakers*, and *Major Authors and Illustrators for Children and Young Adults.*

SARICH, John A. Free-lance writer and editor. Graduate student in economics at the New School for Social Research.

SCHOOLMAN, Martha. Free-lance writer in Chicago.

SCHUSTEFF, Sandy. Marketing and communications consultant; adjunct professor, Lake Forest Graduate School of Management, Lake Forest, Illinois.

SIMLEY, John. Professional researcher and corporate issues analyst. Former research editor for *International Directory of Company Histories;* contributor to *Encyclopedia of Consumer Brands.*

STEIN, Wendy. Free-lance writer and editor. Writer of reports, manuals, public relations materials, and catalogs for Dal Pos Architects, Oneida Ontario Company, Mahar Insurance Company, and Laubach Literacy International. Former managing editor of periodicals department, New Readers Press. Former reporter for Syracuse *Herald-Journal* and *Herald-American.*

SUN, Douglas. Assistant professor of English at California State University at Los Angeles.

SWARTZ, Mark. Manuscript editor for the journals division of the University of Chicago Press.

TROESTER, Maura. Free-lance writer based in Chicago.

VLESSING, Etan. Free-lance writer and editor. Former editor of *Insight;* news editor, *Financial Weekly.*

WOLF, Gillian. Free-lance writer specializing in corporate history, biography, music, and gardening.

WOODWARD, Angela. Free-lance writer.

THE
Complete
Middle
Eastern
COOKBOOK

THE Complete Middle Eastern COOKBOOK

TESS MALLOS

hardie grant books
MELBOURNE · LONDON

CONTENTS

ÍNTRODUCTION

Cooking should be an enjoyable experience. It should also open doors to many cultures and creeds, and its acceptance and appreciation should not be clouded by politics or prejudice. Middle Eastern cooking, as presented here, is open to controversy, but not for these reasons.

First the selection of the countries is controversial, as the area covered includes Greece, Cyprus, Turkey and Armenia. More correctly, perhaps, the title should have been *Near and Middle Eastern Cookbook*, though Greece and Turkey are regarded as the eastern boundaries of Europe. There seemed to be only one course open to me – to delve into the region's early history and justify the inclusion of certain countries from that viewpoint. Pure geography has also played a part, as the area covered fits rather neatly between longitudes 20°E and 70°E, and between latitudes 15°N and 45°N.

The region encompasses the birthplace of civilisation and its history goes back as far as 3500 BCE with a pre-history dating back to 10,000 BCE. The Mesopotamian, Assyrian, Ancient Egyptian, Phoenician, Hebrew, Minoan, Mycenaean, Ancient Greek and Persian civilisations all flourished within this area, and their contributions to world knowledge cannot be disputed. In pre-history humans first learned to harness nature, and farming had its tenuous beginnings in the area now known as Kurdistan, stretching from south-east Turkey across to northern Iran.

It is on this basis that the countries have been selected, for Middle Eastern cookery has evolved over several thousand years.

The second area of controversy relates to the actual recipes. Which dish really originated in which particular country? Again, history can solve this in part; however, there has been so much interchange of culture through trade, migration, colonisation, invasion and counter-invasion that even this presents difficulties. So many similar recipes turn up in the culinary repertoire of a number of countries that to trace the source of many of them is virtually impossible. There are *dolmas* with variations in both name and ingredients stretching from Greece to Afghanistan and south to the Arab Gulf States; *keftethes* in Greece gradually change in name and character to *kofta* in Afghanistan; a sweet preserve made from green walnuts is made in Greece and Cyprus and the same delicacy is prepared in Iran, but nowhere else in between; there are variations on the Greek *kourabiethes* and the Gulf States *ghiraybah* in every other country of the region.

Do not assume that the book is a collection of a group of recipes with countless variations – I have avoided this as far as possible – for the scope of Middle Eastern cooking surprised me as much as it will probably surprise you.

Food and its preparation around the world have almost come full circle. (I say almost, for many aspects have of course changed, and will continue to do so – this is the essence of civilisation. There has been change in the manner of cultivation and the raising of livestock, though there are areas in the region where primitive methods are still employed; and there has been change in cooking methods.)

People have realised that highly refined foods are responsible for a number of their ailments; nutrition experts now advocate a diet based on simple, natural foods – meats, fish, poultry, less refined cereals, pulses, vegetable oils, pure butter and ghee, vegetables, fruit, nuts, yoghurt and cheese. And these, along with herbs and spices, are what Middle Eastern cooking is all about – a diet basically unchanged for thousands of years.

Western kitchen appliances – the electric blender, food processor, grinder, mixer and juicer – cut down on preparation time considerably. Many ingredients you will already have or be familiar with; the others are readily available at Middle Eastern, Greek and Armenian food stores, and at specialised food stores such as those stocking natural foods. The glossary will assist you greatly as it gives the various names for particular ingredients, and which substitutes, if any, may be used for unusual or hard-to-come-by ingredients.

Now let us mount the magic carpet for a culinary tour of the mystical, exotic world of Homer, the Arabian Nights and Omar Khayyam. *Ahlan wasah'lan!* (Welcome!)

Tess Mallos

BASICS OF MIDDLE EASTERN COOKING

Many foods are common to most Middle Eastern countries. Though most recipes give full details of their preparation, here is some basic information for easy reference.

Preparation of vegetables

Okra

Wash well, handling the okra gently. Trim the stem end without cutting the pod. If desired, trim around the conical stem attached to the pod, removing a thin layer. This is the correct way to prepare okra, but it is time consuming and only serves to remove the fine brown ring just above the pod and the outer layer of the stem. Middle Eastern cooks prefer to do this as the whole vegetable is then edible.

Fuzz can be removed if desired by rubbing the pod gently with a fine nylon scourer. Do this under running water. If the okra is young, there is no need to remove fuzz. Dry the okra well in a cloth, or spread out and leave until dry.

Place in a bowl and pour 125 ml (4 fl oz/½ cup) vinegar over each 500 g (1 lb 2 oz) okra. Toss gently using your hands so that the vinegar coats the okra. Leave for 30 minutes, drain and rinse well. Dry and use as directed in recipes. The vinegar treatment stops the okra becoming slimy during cooking.

FREEZING OKRA

As fresh okra are available for only a short time, it is worthwhile freezing some if tinned or frozen okra are not readily available.

Method I: Prepare as directed above, then dry. In a deep saucepan, heat 2 tablespoons olive oil for each 500 g (1 lb 2 oz) okra. Fry the okra for 5 minutes, tossing gently with a wooden spoon. Cool, place in freezer bags, expel the air, then seal and label. Place in the freezer.

Method II: Prepare as above. Bring a large saucepan of water to the boil. Have ready a bowl of iced water. Place the prepared okra in a frying basket and lower into the boiling water. Boil for 3 minutes, timed from when the water returns to the boil. Lift out and place in iced water for 3 minutes. Drain well, pack and store in the freezer.

Globe artichokes

Have ready a large bowl of cold water, with the juice of 1 lemon and some lemon slices added. If desired, stir in 2–3 tablespoons plain (all-purpose) flour, as this is quite effective in preventing discolouration.

Wash the artichokes well and cut off the stem close to the base. As each artichoke is prepared to requirements, rub the cut surfaces with a lemon slice from the bowl and place in the bowl until all are prepared. Cook as soon as possible after preparation.

Whole artichokes: Remove the tough outer leaves and trim carefully around the base, just enough to neaten. Cut off 3 cm (1¼ inches) from the top and trim the remaining leaf ends with scissors. If the artichokes are of a good shape and quality, it is not necessary to trim the leaf ends.

Artichoke hearts: As for whole artichokes, only remove three or four layers of leaves, until the tender inner leaves remain. Scoop out the hairy choke and pink thorny leaves from the centre, using a spoon or melon ball scoop. Leave whole, or cut in half.

Artichoke bases (fonds): Pull off all the leaves. Remove the hairy choke and trim the base into a neat cup shape. Do not over-trim, as you will lose too much of the best part of the artichoke.

Eggplant (aubergine)

Recipes give details of preparation in most instances. However, as a general rule, leave the skin on, removing the green stem for general usage.

The stem is left on if baking or grilling as it provides a convenient handle.

Slice, cube or slit the eggplant as directed in the recipe. While it has always been my habit to salt eggplant for many recipes, I have found that if I choose them carefully, salting is not required. When eggplant is required for frying, choose eggplant about 400 g (14 oz) in weight. Look at the base: the little 'navel' should be oval in shape, not round.

BAKED EGGPLANT FOR PURÉES

Recipes give detailed instructions, as methods vary in different countries. However, a microwave oven is an excellent means of cooking whole eggplant. Pierce it in several places with a fork or fine skewer, place on a suitable dish and cook for 3–5 minutes, according to size. The flesh becomes soft and creamy and remains light in colour.

Whichever way eggplant is baked, the skin must be removed quickly and the flesh combined with some lemon juice or vinegar from the recipe to avoid discolouration.

Spinach and silverbeet (Swiss chard)

Spinach should not be confused with silverbeet — the two vegetables are not even related botanically. Spinach is native to Iran, and widely used there and in other countries of the region. As spinach has a short season, from mid-winter to late spring, frozen leaf spinach may be substituted at other times.

Silverbeet can be used instead of spinach, but in some recipes the result is not quite the same, particularly for Iranian recipes. However, there are instances where silverbeet is the desired vegetable, with spinach an impractical substitute. Individual recipes indicate whether one can be substituted for the other. Whether spinach or silverbeet is being prepared, it is preferable to cook either vegetable in a stainless steel or enamelled pan as aluminium can cause discolouration.

As bunch sizes vary, I have given a weight as the amount required for a recipe. If your bunch is above the weight given, the success of the recipe will not be affected if the whole bunch is used. Some recipes give amounts in cups of shredded spinach leaves, or the number of silverbeet leaves.

Preserving grape vine leaves

Pick leaves early in their growth period — that is, early summer — when vines are well covered with leaves.

Choose leaves of medium-light colour, not too young. If the vines have been sprayed, wait for the period recommended for general harvest by the insecticide manufacturer. When picking leaves, snip off the stem.

Wash the leaves and stack them in piles of 24, shiny side up. Roll up and tie with string.

Bring 2 litres (68 fl oz/8 cups) water to the boil with 3 tablespoons salt. Drop in one four-leaf bundle at a time, return to the boil and blanch for 3 minutes, turning the rolls over so they blanch evenly. Lift out and drain.

Make a brine by boiling 2 litres (68 fl oz/8 cups) water with 315 g (11 oz/1 cup) rock salt. Pack the rolls upright into warm sterilised jars and pour the hot brine over the leaves. Remove air bubbles and seal when cold.

The brine should be sufficient for 20 bundles of leaves. Adjust according to the quantity being preserved.

Parsley

In all recipes flat-leaf parsley (sometimes called Italian parsley) is used. Curly parsley may be used as a garnish.

Pulses or legumes

Pulses are the edible seeds of leguminous plants. The glossary lists them individually with their botanical names, as well as the names by which they are known in the various countries of the region. Following is a general run-down on their basic preparation.

To soak or not to soak? Some require pre-soaking, some do not, just as some cooks prefer to pre-soak while others do not. It all depends on the nature of the seed and on its age. A dried bean less than a year old cooks more quickly than one that has aged somewhat in the pantry or store. As pulses are more readily available, and stores turn over stocks more frequently because of higher demand, the ones you are likely to encounter are relatively fresh. However, as a general guide, I have categorised them.

Lentils, split peas and mung beans

There is no need to pre-soak these unless a recipe specifically calls for it. Brown lentils are often soaked for certain recipes so that the skin can be removed before cooking (see 'Skinning pulses' right).

As a general rule, place the required amount in a sieve and rinse well under cold running water. If it looks as though small stones have been left in after processing, spread the dried peas, beans or lentils on a tray, remove any stones and discoloured seeds, then rinse.

Black-eyed, cannellini, haricot (navy), red kidney beans and butterbeans (lima beans)

Pick over the beans and wash well under cold running water. To each cup of beans, add 750 ml (25 fl oz/3 cups) cold water and bring slowly to the boil. Allow to boil for 2 minutes, then cover, remove from heat and set aside until the beans are plump. Cook as specified in the recipe, using the liquid in which they were soaked.

If overnight soaking is preferred, wash the beans well and use 750 ml (25 fl oz/3 cups) water for every cup of beans. If the weather is warm, place them in the refrigerator to soak. Often beans soaked overnight at room temperature ferment — reason enough for not recommending this method for the beans listed above.

Another method I use — particularly for the quicker-cooking black-eyed, lima and haricot beans — is to wash them, then soak them in very hot water. In 2 hours they are plump enough for cooking.

Dried broad beans (fava beans) (large and small varieties) and chickpeas

Wash the beans or chickpeas well and add 750 ml (25 fl oz/3 cups) cold water for every cup of beans. Soak for 12–48 hours, in a refrigerator in warm weather. Soaking time depends on the recipe.

Skinning pulses

After soaking chickpeas or green or brown lentils, take a handful and rub them with the palms of both hands so that the seeds actually rub against one another. Drop them back into the bowl and take up another lot. Skim off the floating skins as they accumulate.

Another method for skinning chickpeas is to place the drained peas in a shallow dish in a single layer and roll a bottle or rolling pin over them, exerting considerable pressure. Add water so that the skins float, skim them off, pour off the water, and repeat until all are skinned.

There is no shortcut to removing skins from large broad (fava) beans — none that I know of anyway. After soaking for 48 hours, squeeze each bean firmly: it should pop out of its skin easily. If not, slit the skin with a fingernail or the point of a knife, then squeeze. Sometimes these beans are available already skinned — ask for skinned *ful nabed* if the storekeeper is confused.

I am not an advocate of the long soak-drain-and-cook method unless absolutely necessary for the success of the dish. The reason is simple: as well as containing proteins and minerals, pulses are a good source of certain vitamins, in particular B group vitamins such as niacin, riboflavin and thiamine. These are water soluble; by soaking and throwing the water away you are losing valuable nutrients. As the cooking liquid in most pulse recipes forms an integral part of the dish, I advocate thorough washing before soaking so that the soaking water can form part or all of the liquid in the finished dish.

For the same reason I do not recommend the addition of bicarbonate of soda (baking soda) when soaking — this also destroys nutrients.

Rice

In many countries of the Middle East, rice is as important a part of the daily diet as it is in Asia. However, one rice dish you will never find in a Middle Eastern household is plain boiled rice.

In its simplest form, rice is light and fluffy, tinged with a golden hue from the butter, ghee or oil in which it is coated, each grain glistening separately from the other. This is the *riz* or *timman* of the Arab world, the *pilav* of Turkey, the *pilafi* of Greece, the *chelou* of Iran and the *chalau* of Afghanistan.

Then there are the exotic *polous* and *palaus* of Iran and Afghanistan; the more elaborate versions of *timman* and *roz*, and numerous other rice dishes of the Arab world; the imaginative and flavourful *pilavs* and *pilafis* of Turkey, Armenia, Greece and Cyprus.

One point all countries have in common is that you will rarely find two cooks agreeing on which is the right way to cook a particular rice dish. However, on one point they do all agree: to wash the rice well until the water runs clear. From that point on there is controversy.

In testing rice recipes, I looked for the simplest methods to give the required results. As to the washing of the grain, in most recipes it is necessary, but there are exceptions; I find rice produced in the West is as clean as you could wish it to be, and some dishes benefit from the extra starch not lost in the rinsing process. As to the soaking of the grain before cooking, I found in comparing results that there is no detectable benefit to be derived from soaking. Many cooks believe it to be absolutely necessary and refuse to prepare a rice dish without a pre-soaking time ranging from 10 minutes to several hours.

Not all countries are particular about the type of rice used. Greece, Cyprus and Egypt are flexible in their choice of grain, with a general preference for short-grain rice. Turkey prefers long-grain rice of good quality for *pilavs*, but uses any available grain in *dolmas*, soups and puddings.

Most of the Arabic countries use only high-quality, aromatic long-grain rice: the basmati rice of Pakistan. Any good-quality long-grain rice can be used successfully, though others lack that special fragrance of basmati.

In Iran, rice is of such importance in the daily diet that none of the rice produced is exported. It is said to be the finest of all the rices — delicate in flavour and aroma, and hard of grain.

Irrespective of the variety, rice is available in three main qualities — Berenje Domsiah, Berenje Sadri and Berenje Champa. The first is the whole, long slender grain; the second is grain slightly broken in the polishing process; the third consists of broken grains.

Basmati or any good-quality long-grain rice may be used successfully for Iranian rice dishes.

Nuts

Middle Eastern cooking calls for plenty of nuts: nuts in pastries, nuts in cakes, nuts in sauces, stuffings and rice dishes — nuts, nuts and more nuts.

Almonds

Purchase almonds in their shells or, for easier storage, already shelled (but not blanched if they are to be stored for a while). The skin prevents the kernel drying and losing flavoursome oils. Store in a sealed container, in the refrigerator during summer when certain nut-loving insects decide to multiply.

To blanch: Pour boiling water over the kernels, leave for 2–3 minutes and drain. When cool enough to handle squeeze the nut and the kernel will pop out of its skin.

To split almonds: Separate the two halves with a fine-bladed knife.

To sliver almonds: Let them soak a little longer when blanching to soften the kernel, then cut into three or four slivers. (If the almonds are very crisp, slivers break in the wrong places.) Dry out slivers in the oven at 150°C (300°F).

To chop: Use a nut chopper, food processor or blender and chop to degree required.

To grind: Use a nut grinder or food processor. A blender is likely to cause oils to separate. Almonds should be dry and crisp for grinding finely.

Walnuts

For peak flavour, purchase walnuts in shells, or buy them ready-shelled from a reputable retailer. If walnut halves are required, it is best to purchase these prepared in this way — as any frustrated walnut-cracker will confirm. Store, chop and grind as for almonds.

Pistachio nuts

Unsalted pistachios are the ones required for cooking; they are usually purchased in the shell. Break them open and remove the kernel. Store, blanch, chop and grind as for almonds.

Hazelnuts

Hard nuts to crack! Buy these ready-shelled. Blanch as for almonds and dry off in a low oven. Alternatively, place in a 180°C (350°F/Gas 4) oven for 15–20 minutes, then rub in a tea towel (dish towel) to remove the skins. Store, chop and grind as for almonds.

Bread

This most ancient of foods has sustained humans from time immemorial. It is said that bread — or the lack of it — makes history. A profound statement. However, it is not my intention to expound on its history, only on the basics of bread-making so that your efforts to produce Middle Eastern breads will be successful. Actually these principles are worth applying to the baking of any bread.

The flour

Wheat flour is the most widely used, varying from white to wholemeal (also called whole-wheat or wheatmeal). The gluten in the flour is the protein which, when worked by mixing and kneading, becomes an elastic network to hold in the gases generated by the yeast.

The percentage of gluten in flour varies; the higher the percentage, the better the flour for bread-making. As flours are rarely labelled with relevant information, your only guide to high gluten content is where the flour was milled, which is usually close to where it was grown.

Wheat grown in the warmer regions of your state or country has a harder grain and is therefore higher in gluten content, so look for flours milled in such areas.

If in doubt you can increase the gluten content by adding 1 teaspoon gluten (available from specialist food stores) to each 150 g (5 oz/1 cup) flour. Sift together twice to blend thoroughly.

The yeast

For convenience, a long shelf life and consistently good results, I have used active dried yeast granules in recipes; 1 sachet is equivalent to 7 g (¼ oz or 2 teaspoons) of granules if purchased loose, rather than in sachets.

Compressed yeast may be substituted for the active dried yeast in the proportion of 30 g (1 oz) for each sachet.

Where cake yeast is available, it should not be confused with compressed yeast; 1 yeast cake (a little over 10–15 g/½ oz) may be used in place of 1 sachet.

Whatever yeast is used, it should be dissolved in warm water first — lukewarm for cake or compressed yeast, 30°C (85°F), and a little warmer for active dried yeast, but no more than 45°C (115°F). Do not cream cake or compressed yeast with sugar as the sugar slows down the yeast action. Add the balance of the liquid to the dissolved yeast, then add the sugar if used, and pour into the flour. Stir a little of the flour into the yeast liquid and leave covered for 10–15 minutes in a warm place until frothy, to speed up the rising process.

Where fat is used, adding it to the yeast liquid retards the action — it is better to add it after some of the flour has been incorporated; better still, blend the yeast liquid into the flour and work the fat in afterwards.

If you follow these guidelines, your doughs will rise much more quickly.

TESTING YEAST FRESHNESS

If you are unsure about the freshness of the yeast, dissolve it in 60 ml (2 fl oz/¼ cup) warm water, stir in 2 teaspoons flour, then cover and leave in a warm place. If there is no sign of activity in 15 minutes, the yeast is stale.

Baking flat breads

Basically there are two types of flat breads — those with a pocket, and those without. To form a pocket, bread must be rested for a period after shaping and before baking, and it has to be baked in the hottest part of the oven. The heat must be even, otherwise the bread does not puff properly. If the oven heat is uneven, an electric frying pan may be used with good results. The recipes give further details.

For bread without a pocket, prick the shaped dough with a fork or pinwheel, or during cooking press the bread with a folded cloth. Again recipes give details.

Some breads have a higher water content than normal, in order to give a characteristic chewy texture. Flour with a high gluten content is necessary, and as beating must be prolonged so that the water may be absorbed, a high-powered electric mixer with a dough hook attachment is recommended. My 12-year-old mixer coped very well indeed with the rigours of the long beating necessary.

Storing flat breads

When baking flat breads it is worth preparing enough bread to freeze for later use. Package cooled breads in freezer bags, sealing well. To use, individually wrap frozen breads in foil and reheat in the oven at 200°C (400°F) for 10 minutes.

Fillo pastry

Fillo is the Greek name for this delicate, tissue-thin pastry. Frequently it is spelled 'phyllo', which perhaps is a closer transliteration of the Greek word meaning 'leaf'; however, I prefer the simplified spelling.

The Turks call the pastry *yufka*, and in the Arab countries it is generally known as *ajeen*, which can be rather confusing, as *ajeen* is any dough or pastry.

Fillo pastry is available commercially either fresh (chilled) or frozen. If properly sealed, fresh pastry can be stored in the refrigerator for several weeks, but must never be frozen. Frozen fillo pastry is more readily available at supermarkets. It varies slightly from fresh fillo, a different formula being used to withstand the rigours of freezing. For thawing, follow the directions on the packet.

Both types of fillo should be left in their packaging and brought to room temperature for 2 hours before using. If opened out while chilled, the pastry could break apart at the folds and can be difficult to handle.

Handling fillo pastry for cooking

Remove fillo from the wrapping and open out. Spread the leaves on a folded dry tea towel (dish towel) and cover with another folded dry tea towel. Moisten a third tea towel with water and wring it well to make it evenly damp. Spread over the top tea towel.

Remove one sheet at a time, re-covering the fillo with cloths. If the recipe requires pastry to be cut to size, cut all the sheets, then stack and cover. Fillo dries out very quickly in the heat of the kitchen, so it is essential to cover it, particularly if shaping individual pastries takes time.

Rolling pastry or dough thinly

Many recipes require the pastry to be rolled out thinly. As doughs are often elastic, normal rolling methods can prove very frustrating. This method, widely practised in Greece, Turkey, Armenia and Iran, is referred to in recipes, and is a skill worth developing. A length of wooden dowelling 60 cm (24 inches) long and 1 cm (½ inch) in diameter is required, although the dowel used for rolling fillo may also be used.

Shape the dough into either a ball or a square. Dust your work surface and dough with flour and roll out to a 20 cm (8 inch) round or square using a rolling pin.

Dust your work surface and dough again with flour. Place the dowel on the dough end nearest you. Roll the pastry onto the dowel, pressing down firmly as you roll to the end. Unroll carefully, turn the pastry around 180 degrees and dust your work surface and pastry again with flour. Roll up again onto the dowel, then unroll carefully.

The pastry is now ready for use. Be guided by the dimensions given in the recipes, and roll a third time if very thin pastry is required.

Do not grip the dowel as you would a rolling pin. Place the palms of your hands on the dowel, on each side of the pastry, letting the dowel roll under your hands. Move your hands outwards as the pastry stretches on the dowel.

Perhaps it is worth mentioning another method — a variation on the one just given.

Roll the pastry onto the dowel to within 5 cm (2 inches) of the end of the pastry. Place the palms of your hands, fingers spread out, on top of the pastry, then roll back and forwards with four or five quick movements, moving your hands outwards along the pastry as you roll. Roll up to the end of the pastry, then unroll carefully. Turn the pastry around 180 degrees, dust again with flour and roll again.

The advantage of this method is that pastry can be rolled very thinly, and it is a good way to stretch fillo pastry; the disadvantage is that the centre can become much thinner than the edges, and is often creased in the process. I call this the 'rock and roll' method — this might give you an indication of the kind of movement involved.

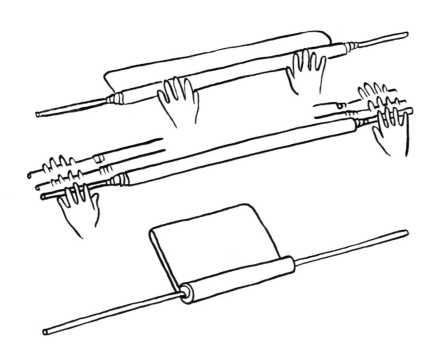

Homemade fillo pastry

Equipment required: Large work surface, large cloth, mixing bowl, plastic wrap, greaseproof (parchment) paper, rolling pin, wooden dowel no less than 60 cm (24 inches) long and 2 cm (¾ inch) in diameter.

Sift 600 g (1 lb 5 oz/4 cups) plain (all-purpose) flour and 1 teaspoon salt into the mixing bowl. Add 335 ml (11½ fl oz/1⅓ cups) tepid water with 60 ml (2 fl oz/¼ cup) olive, corn or peanut oil. Stir to a soft dough, then knead in the bowl with your hands for 10 minutes, using a kneading action similar to how you would knead for bread-making. It is easier to do this sitting down with the bowl placed in your lap. The dough will feel sticky at first, but with kneading the gluten in the flour is developed and the dough becomes smooth and satiny.

Wrap the pastry in plastic wrap and leave to rest at room temperature for 1 hour or longer. If all the dough is not to be used, wrap the unused portion and refrigerate for up to 1 week. Bring to room temperature before rolling out.

Divide pastry into 12 even portions, shaping each into a smooth ball. Cover with a cloth.

Take a ball of pastry and shape it into a square. Place on a lightly floured work surface and dust the top with flour. Roll out to a 15 cm (6 inch) square. Dust again with flour.

Place the dowel on one end of the pastry. Roll the pastry neatly onto the dowel, pressing firmly as you roll, keeping your hands on each side of the pastry.

Unroll the pastry and dust the work surface and pastry again with flour. Roll up again from the opposite side of the pastry, again exerting pressure. Unroll carefully. After the second rolling, the pastry should be about 25 × 30 cm (10 × 12 inches) in size.

Using the backs of your hands (remove any rings), place your hands under the pastry and gently stretch it, moving your hands to stretch it evenly, working towards the edges. The edges can be given a final stretch with your fingertips. You will end up with a piece of fillo about 36 × 46 cm (14 × 18 inches) in size. Place on a cloth, cover with greaseproof (parchment) paper and fold a cloth over the top.

Repeat with the remaining pastry, laying each completed sheet on top of the previous one, with greaseproof paper in between. Use the pastry soon after making, as directed in recipes. For pies and layered pastries where a number of sheets are required, use half the number of homemade fillo sheets to those given in recipes.

Don't be concerned if the pastry tears during stretching. Tears may be mended as the fillo is being used, or avoided if cutting the pastry into pieces or strips.

Cutting and shaping techniques

Many recipes refer to cutting foods into diamond shapes for serving. This can be done whether the dish is round, square or rectangular.

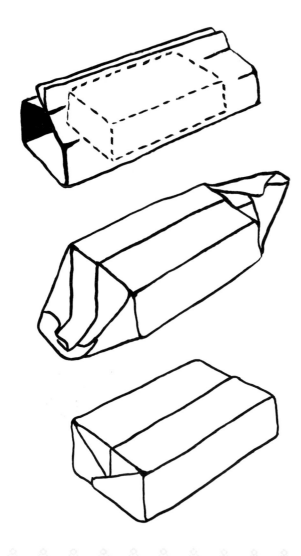

In special recipes, I refer to the chemist or druggist fold, as it gives an interesting finish to individual, fillo-wrapped packages (Arnaki se Fillo, page 71, and Talas Kebap, page 196).

The shaping of pastries in triangles or rolls, though described in recipes, is perhaps clarified with these step diagrams.

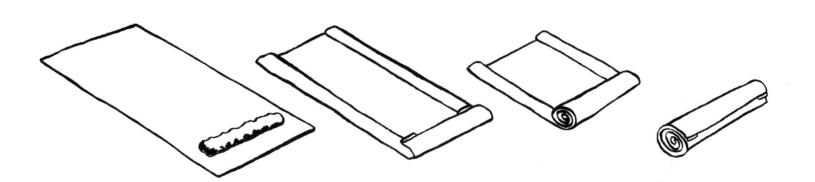

Syrups

Syrups are widely used for fruit preserves, pastries and cakes. The recipes are self-explanatory, but it is helpful to know the basics.

Use a heavy-based saucepan and dissolve the sugar in water over medium heat, stirring occasionally. Boiling should begin only after all the sugar crystals have been dissolved. Once boiling, do not stir, as the syrup will become cloudy or even crystallise. When a thick syrup is required, you can usually judge this by the nature of the bubbling. As the syrup boils, the bubbles become smaller and the sound of the bubbling changes; the sides of the pan become peppered with minute drops of syrup.

If you have a sugar thermometer, the temperature of a thin syrup should be 105°C (220°F); for thick syrup, 110°C (230°F).

Experienced cooks have their own favourite methods of determining when a syrup is right. Putting a drop on the thumbnail or a cold saucer: the drop does not spread when the syrup is thick enough. Dropping it off the end of a spoon: when thick enough, the last drop clings to the end of the spoon. Spooning a tablespoon of syrup onto a saucer and cooling it quickly by spooning it up with a small spoon, then dropping it back until cool.

When testing the syrup, first remove it from the heat, so you don't risk overcooking the syrup if it happens to be of the right thickness.

The food processor

If there is one modern appliance tailor-made for Middle Eastern cooking, the food processor must be it. Though the processor container might not be large in capacity, preparation time is so abbreviated that even if it is necessary to process food in separate portions, you are still way ahead. Where applicable, recipes give details on using both the food processor and the blender, as well as the conventional method.

Use your food processor for chopping and grinding nuts to whatever degree required, from coarsely chopped to finely ground; for crumbing bread; for chopping large amounts of herbs and onions; for grating cheese and vegetables; for grinding or chopping meat; for grinding pulses, whether soaked and still raw, or cooked; and for puréeing anything that requires puréeing.

The food processor makes the best taramasalata, the finest baba ghanoush or *melitzanosalata*, the creamiest tahini and *tarator* sauces, and is a great time and effort-saver when making *kibbi*. Anyone tackling Middle Eastern cookery should consider using this whizz of an appliance.

Yoghurt

To the Middle Eastern cook, the making of yoghurt is a necessary daily routine. Because it is made so frequently and the art is so developed, each batch is as good as the last; the traditional method always produces a good yoghurt in the Middle Eastern kitchen.

As the Western cook might not use yoghurt as frequently I have given a second method, which ensures a constant good result, minimising the varied results obtainable if following traditional methods in the Western kitchen.

Yoghurt I

(*Yaourti, yogurt, madzoon, laban, mast, maust, yurt, leben hamid*)

Combine 1.5 litres (51 fl oz/6 cups) whole milk and 75 g (2½ oz/¾ cup) full-cream or skim milk powder in a saucepan and bring to the boil. Remove from the heat and leave to cool until a little above body temperature. The favoured method for testing temperature is to insert a little finger into the milk for a count of 10 before the sting of the heat is felt. It is wise to check with a thermometer: 45°C (115°F) is the desired temperature.

Blend 60 ml (2 fl oz/¼ cup) of the warm milk with 60 g (2 oz/¼ cup) of starter (fresh, commercially made yoghurt). Gently stir the starter into the milk and pour into

a casserole dish or deep bowl. Cover with the lid or a plate, then wrap in thick towels or a blanket. Leave undisturbed for at least 6 hours at room temperature and away from draughts. Remove the covers and test: the yoghurt is ready when it is set like a junket. For a more tart flavour, yoghurt may be left in its wraps for up to 12 hours.

Remove the wraps, place in a covered container in the refrigerator and chill for 2 hours before using. If using this yoghurt as a starter for a new batch, the starter should be used within 3 days, otherwise the balance of the bacteria in the culture alters, causing variable results.

Yoghurt II

Equipment required: 1.5 litre (51 fl oz/6 cup) jar; either six sterilised 250 ml (8½ fl oz/1 cup) jars, or three 500 ml (17 fl oz/2 cup) jars; thermometer; preserving pan or large pot; blanket or thick towels.

Blend 75 g (2½ oz/¾ cup) full-cream or skim milk powder and 1.5 litres (51 fl oz/6 cups) whole milk, preferably homogenised.

Pour into a clean 1.5 litre (51 fl oz/6 cup) jar, cover with a lid and stand in a saucepan of water. Heat the water until the milk temperature is 80°C (180°F). Remove the jar from the hot water bath and cool to 45°C (115°F).

Remove 60 ml (2 fl oz/¼ cup) of the warm milk and blend it with 60 g (2 oz/¼ cup) fresh, commercially made yoghurt. Stir the mixture into the milk in the large jar, then pour into smaller jars. Seal the jars with their lids and stand them in the preserving pan.

Add water to the pan to come up to the necks of the jars. Heat until the water temperature reaches 50°C (120°F), then remove from the heat.

Cover the pan with a lid, then wrap in thick towels or a blanket. Leave undisturbed for 3 hours. Remove the jars, screw the lids on tightly and store in the refrigerator.

Yoghurt made this way will keep in good condition for 7–10 days, with little change in the balance of the culture. Use some of this for your next yoghurt. After making three or four batches, it is advisable to begin with a fresh starter.

A thermostatically controlled yoghurt-maker is a good investment for those who make yoghurt frequently, as it is so simple to use and produces good results.

Low-fat yoghurt

Use skimmed milk and skim milk powder instead of whole milk and full-cream powdered milk. Follow the directions given in either Yoghurt I or Yoghurt II.

Drained yoghurt

Recipes often call for drained yoghurt. Simply place yoghurt in a cheesecloth or a doubled piece of muslin (cheesecloth), tie it up with string and suspend it from a fixed object over a receptacle to collect the draining liquid.

Leave for 2–4 hours, depending on the initial thickness of the yoghurt.

When drained, the yoghurt should have the consistency of softened cream cheese.

Sterilising jars

Pickles, preserves and spoon sweets should be packed into sterilised jars to ensure they keep well.

Wash the jars well in hot soapy water, then rinse and drain. Stand the jars upright on a baking tray and place in a cold oven. Close the door and set the oven temperature to 140°C (275°F/Gas 1).

Once this temperature is reached, switch off the oven and leave the jars in the oven until required for filling.

As a general rule, pack hot foods into hot jars, and cooled foods into cooled jars, so the jars don't crack.

Greece

GREECE

Having cut my first tooth on a *paximathi* and coped with many a childhood illness fortified with bowls of *avgolemono soupa*, I had taken Greek cooking for granted. When friends returned from a visit to Greece with a grand passion for Greek cooking, I began to look at it through the eyes of my non-Greek friends. And what did I see? I saw a cuisine shaped through over 3000 years of history; through the geography and climate of a country lolling in azure blue seas; through sloping mountains thrusting upwards to the heavens where humans and nature vie for control; through the people of the land whose joy for life is evident every evening at the quaysides, in the tavernas, in town squares at the *kafenia*.

Such vast differences in geography and climate have given Greek cookery an infinite variety, but there are still some dishes that are universally prepared and loved: *avgolemono*, the delightfully tangy egg and lemon combination used in sauces to bathe meats, fish and vegetables, and as a soup with chicken, lamb or fish stock, recognised as the crowning glory of Greek cooking; *taramosalata*, the caviar of Greece, so symbolic of the sea and its importance to the Greek; *moussaka*, the marrying of eggplant, lamb and a cheese-topped béchamel sauce; octopus and squid, regarded in horror by those who have not dared to taste them, and relished by those who have; *spanakopita*, a delightful combination of spinach, herbs, eggs and cheese, but with regional variations and adaptations; and many, many more.

While there are no taboos regarding any particular food, fasting is an important part of the Orthodox faith, and after the fasting, there is feasting! During periods of fasting, no animal products — meat, butter, cheese, milk or eggs — may be taken, so Greek cuisine offers many dishes for those who prefer to reduce the amounts of such foods in their diet.

Spanakopita is a most popular, very typically Greek pie; and not to be denied its enjoyment when fasting, it is prepared similarly to the Spanakopita Peloponnisos recipe (page 29), though its final shape could be a roll, smaller rolls, or a flat pie, depending on the mood of the cook. This is a favourite of Chantal Countouri, a well-known Greek–Australian actress from the 1970s whose family came from the southern Peloponnese. Chantal frequently adds eggs and feta cheese, for yet another variation of spinach pie.

The permutations and combinations of Greek cooking are endless. If any recipe seems to be omitted, the basic recipe could be included under another name. For example, if you have tried *trigona* in Greece, a sweet pastry filled with walnuts, then it is a simple

matter to adapt the *baklava* recipe. Just cut the pastry into strips, butter them, put on some of the filling and fold into triangles (see page 17 for pastry shaping techniques). Baking is quicker and the cooled syrup is poured on the hot pastries. If you prefer *floyeres* (almond pipes), use almonds instead of walnuts, and roll the strips into cylinders. Actually, *floyeres* are similar to the *sarigi burma* that you'll find in the chapter on Turkey, using the alternative shaping at the end of that recipe. Indeed, any other Greek recipe you might be looking for could be in the Turkey, Cyprus or Armenia chapters.

THE FLAVOURS OF GREEK FOOD

The flavours of Greek foods tend to be subtle rather than overpowering. Favourite herbs are parsley — always the flat-leaf variety — rosemary, dill, fennel, bay leaves, mint, rigani (a wild marjoram, not to be confused with oregano) and celery leaves. Basil always grows in Greek gardens, but was seldom used in cooking in the past, though its addition to the Greek cooking pot is increasing of late. It is of religious significance, as the Greeks claim that basil grew on the site of the Cross. A sprig is always handed to visitors on their departure as a gesture of goodwill.

Of the spices, cinnamon, cloves, nutmeg, *masticha* and *mahlepi* (*mahlab*, the kernel of the black cherry stone, imported from Syria) are the most frequently used; all but masticha and mahlepi feature in both savoury and sweet dishes.

For sweet preserves, the leaf of the rose geranium imparts a particular fragrance and often is used instead of cinnamon and lemon rind. These sweet preserves, called *glyka*, are made from orange, lemon or grapefruit peel; little green figs; grated quince preserve and quince jelly; watermelon rind; or green walnuts. There is even one similar to a vanilla fondant. *Glyka* are an important aspect of Greek hospitality: a guest is offered a glass of cold water into which the *glyka* is placed, adhering to a spoon. The guest sucks small mouthfuls and sips the water alternately.

Among the fruits, the lemon reigns supreme. A Greek garden without a lemon tree is unthinkable. Seafoods and vegetables without lemon? Well, almost never. Even lamb is not spared. The rind makes a superb sweet preserve and is used in most other preserves, together with the juice to prevent the sugar crystallising. Then, of course, there would be no *avgolemono* without the lemon — nothing can substitute for it, though it is believed that the sour sauce of Ancient Greece used the juice of the citron, since lemon was not introduced until much later.

On second thoughts, the lemon does not reign alone, for without the olive, would there be a Greece? For countless centuries the olive tree has been an enduring symbol of Greek life. The fragrant oil, from earliest times, has sustained the people, been used in trade and has given Greek cooking its essence.

MEALS GREEK STYLE

Greece is a country established in the European cultural traditions, and with a lifestyle similar to that of most countries bordering the Mediterranean; eating is a very social occasion, reminiscent of the symposiums of Ancient Greece.

To the Greek, food is incidental. What is important is enjoying the company of friends, discussing a wide variety of topics with much gesticulating — with the occasional pause to dip a piece of bread into *taramosalata* or pop an olive into the mouth and sip an ouzo or a beer. From midday onwards, this scene is enacted in a wide variety of locations. It could be at an outdoor restaurant, in the town square, in the colourful Plaka in the old part of Athens, or at a waterfront tavern anywhere in Greece. Such occasions can extend far into the early hours of the morning. This basically is how the Greek regards eating, as just part of the happy business of living.

The main meal of the day is taken at midday and the food is served in a Western manner; that is, at a table spread with a cloth, with china, cutlery and glassware. The food is placed in its dishes on the table at the beginning of the meal. There could be a roast leg of lamb with potatoes that were cooked in the same dish to absorb the flavours of the meat with its rigani, lemon and olive oil. A Greek salad — a mixture of sweet red tomatoes, crisp cucumbers and capsicums (peppers), feta cheese and olives — would accompany the meat course. Bread is served with every meal and is used to soak up the salad dressing or meat juices. A wine, more often than not a retsina, accompanies the meal. Quite often other dishes could be served, such as one of the vegetable stews for which the Greeks are famous.

Dessert is seldom served; if it is, it could be a simple bowl of yoghurt or *rizogalo* (creamed rice). Fresh fruit and cheese complete the meal. In summer lunch is taken outdoors on the terrace, patio or balcony or in the garden.

After lunch it is time for siesta, and even if there are guests present they are offered pyjamas and a bed. Very hospitable! After siesta is the time when the exotic sweets and pastries are likely to be eaten, if not at home then at the local *zaharoplastio*, which is similar to the French *patisserie*.

Early evening sees a repeat of the symposium-type gathering described earlier, which often suffices as the evening meal. The variety of *mezethakia* served in Greece is limited only by the imagination of the cook and the availability of ingredients.

Where an evening meal is served, it could be taken at any time from 8 to 11 p.m. and is generally a lighter meal. More often than not, particularly in the summer months, it is taken at a restaurant or taverna. Early bedtime for children during summer vacation is seldom demanded, and even more seldom obeyed — there is too much living to do.

COOKING METHODS

Greece is more Western than Eastern, and even the humble village home has a modern stove. Even so, sometimes in cities as well as rural and island villages people take the midday meal — ready prepared in its *tapsi* (round baking dish) or *tsoukali* (casserole dish) — to the local bakery so that the kitchen will not become hot from the heat of the stove: a very popular practice during the summer months. Women who hold a job also take advantage of the baker's oven and deliver the prepared food on their way to work, to be collected at midday. The baker tends, checks, stirs and turns the food. After the early morning's bake, the food cooks slowly in the residual heat of the oven — a marvellous service for little cost. Slow cookers will never take off in Greece while the baker is so obliging.

Kitchen equipment is as modern as any, though you'll find traditional items such as the pestle and mortar, a *briki* for making coffee, *tapsi* and *tsoukalia* (mentioned previously), *saganaki* (two-handled frying pan), a long piece of wooden dowel used as a rolling pin for pastry, and perhaps a *kakavi*, a large copper pot once hung over the hearth for cooking, now seldom used except for ornamentation.

INGREDIENTS FOR GREEK COOKING

Fortunately, you can buy anything you might need at your usual market, and any particularly Greek ingredient is available at Greek, Armenian and Middle Eastern food stores. Rigani is a must, as are feta cheese, olive oil, fillo pastry, macaroni and pulses (dried beans, lentils and peas). But why list them here? The recipes are self-explanatory and the introductory passages and Glossary will fill in the gaps. It is evident that you do not need to chase around for the ingredients for Greek cooking — you probably use most of them already.

PRONUNCIATION

Recipe names have been transliterated from the Greek. Pronounce each syllable with equal emphasis, for example *do-ma-tes*, with 'o' as in *ought*, 'a' as in *past*, and 'es' as in *esteem*. Pronounce 'e' as in *egg*, 'ou' as in *soup*, 'i' as in *sit* and 'y' as 'i' when between consonants, and as in *yes* or *your* when followed by a vowel.

TOMATA PELTES
Tomato paste
MAKES: APPROXIMATELY 1 KG (2 LB 3 OZ)

5 kg (10 lb 15 oz) tomatoes
2 tablespoons salt
olive oil, for sealing

Choose ripe, sound tomatoes; do not use any with signs of decay. Wash well, core out the stem end and slice the tomatoes into a large preserving pan. Cover and heat gently until the tomatoes are soft. Rub them through a sieve.

Return the juice to the pan and leave over medium–low heat, uncovered, until reduced by half (it will be a tomato purée at this stage).

Pour the mixture into two large dishes (baking dishes will do) and place in the sun; protect with a covering of gauze. Dry in the sun for 2–4 days, stirring the paste now and then.

Alternatively, place the dishes in a 100°C (210°F/Gas ½) oven and let the purée evaporate; this will take 4–6 hours.

When the paste is the consistency of the type available commercially (a soft paste, or concentrated purée), stir in the salt, then transfer to sterilised jars. Pour a layer of oil on top of the paste and seal. Store in a cool place.

Once a jar of paste has been opened, store it in the refrigerator.

SALTSA AVGOLEMONO
Egg and lemon sauce
MAKES: 625 ML (2 FL OZ/2½ CUPS)

375 ml (12½ fl oz/1½ cups) stock
1 tablespoon cornflour (cornstarch)
3 eggs, separated
juice of 1 lemon
salt and freshly ground white pepper, to taste

Bring the stock to the boil in a saucepan. Mix the cornflour to a paste with a little cold water and add it to the stock, stirring until thickened and bubbling. Let it boil for 1 minute.

In a bowl, beat the egg whites until stiff, then add the egg yolks and continue beating until light and fluffy. Gradually add the lemon juice, beating constantly. Slowly pour in the boiling, thickened stock, beating constantly.

Return the sauce to the pan and cook over low heat, stirring constantly, for 1–2 minutes to cook the egg. Do not allow the sauce to boil. Remove from the heat and continue to stir for 1 minute. Season to taste with salt and pepper.

Serve immediately with poached fish, boiled or steamed vegetables, meat and chicken dishes.

❊ *Note: Choose a stock to complement the dish with which it is to be served: fish stock for poached fish, chicken stock for boiled or steamed vegetables — or use the cooking liquid from the dish with which it is to be served.*

MAYONNEZA
Mayonnaise

MAKES: 375 G (13 OZ/1½ CUPS)

Yes, this is a French recipe. Nicholas Tselementes was a Greek who trained in Vienna and worked in many hotel kitchens in Europe and the US, especially New York, during the early part of last century. Returning to Greece, he wrote a large tome on Greek cookery, including many French recipes. This is one of them, taught to me by my mother.

- 2 egg yolks
- 1 small garlic clove, crushed
- ½ teaspoon mustard powder
- ½ teaspoon sugar
- salt and freshly ground white pepper, to taste
- 1–2 tablespoons lemon juice
- 250 ml (8½ fl oz/1 cup) olive oil

Remove all traces of egg white from the yolks using a piece of egg shell. Place the yolks in a small mixing bowl and stir them well with the garlic, mustard, sugar, about ½ teaspoon of salt and some pepper. Beat until light and smooth, using a wooden spoon or balloon whisk, or the small bowl of an electric mixer.

Add 2 teaspoons of the lemon juice and about one-quarter of the oil, a drop at a time. Mix in the remaining lemon juice and oil alternately, this time adding the oil in a thin trickle.

When the mayonnaise is thick, adjust the flavour and seasoning with more lemon juice, salt and pepper if necessary.

Finally, beat in 1 tablespoon boiling water so that the mayonnaise will not separate if it is to be stored in a cool place for a while before use.

Serve with steamed fish, cooked lobster and prawns (shrimp), or as directed in recipes.

❀ *Note: If the mayonnaise curdles, begin again with an egg yolk beaten in a clean bowl. Gradually add the curdled mayonnaise and the mixture will begin to emulsify immediately. And a special tip: use olive oil, not extra virgin olive oil, as it is too strong in flavour.*

MIZITHRA
Cottage cheese

MAKES: ABOUT 600 G (1 LB 5 OZ)

Given modern-day packaging and health concerns regarding fat content, whole, unhomogenised milk may be difficult to obtain. Homogenised milk can be used instead, as can fortified milk with a low fat content. If using either of these alternatives, double the amount of rennet to 4 tablets. Skim milk that has not been fortified with skim milk powder is not recommended.

- 2.5 litres (85 fl oz/10 cups) whole unhomogenised milk
- 3 teaspoons salt
- 2 rennet (junket) tablets

Heat the milk in a heavy-based saucepan until lukewarm. Stir in the salt and remove from the heat.

Crush the rennet tablets in a small bowl, add 1 tablespoon cold water and stir until dissolved.

Slowly pour the rennet liquid into the milk, stirring gently. Cover the pan with a lid and leave it at the side of the stove, undisturbed, for 30 minutes.

When the liquid has set, break up the curds by stirring with a whisk or spoon. Let the curds settle.

Line a colander or large sieve with a double layer of muslin (cheesecloth). Ladle the curds into this. Collect the whey in a bowl if required (see note below).

Let the curd drain for a while, then scrape down the cheese on the sides of the cloth and tie the ends of the cloth together. Suspend from a fixed object and leave to drain for another 6 hours at room temperature, then suspend from a shelf in the refrigerator with a dish underneath to gather the remaining whey. Leave for another 12 hours to drain thoroughly.

Turn the cheese out of the cloth and store in a sealed container in the refrigerator. It will keep for 4–5 days.

❀ *Note: The whey may be used for making a whey cheese such as anari, a cheese from Cyprus normally made after making haloumi cheese. The Syrians also make a whey cheese called* kareeshee bi limoun. *Another use for whey is for storing feta cheese in the home (see the Glossary entry for feta on page 520).*

MELITZANOSALATA
Eggplant dip
MAKES: ABOUT 500 G (1 LB 2 OZ/2 CUPS)

1 large or 2 medium oval eggplants (aubergines),
    about 500 g (1 lb 2 oz) in total
1 garlic clove
½ teaspoon salt
60 g (2 oz/1 cup) soft white breadcrumbs
60 ml (2 fl oz/¼ cup) lemon juice
125 ml (4 fl oz/½ cup) olive oil
1 small onion, grated
3 tablespoons chopped flat-leaf parsley
salt and freshly ground black pepper, to taste

Place the whole, unpeeled eggplant on a baking tray and cook in a 180°C (350°F/Gas 4) oven for 30–50 minutes, depending on size, until it is soft to the touch. While it is hot, remove the skin and chop the flesh roughly. Drain off excess moisture.

While the eggplant is baking, crush the garlic with the salt using a mortar and pestle.

Gradually add the warm eggplant to the mortar, alternating with the breadcrumbs. Add the lemon juice and olive oil alternately, working the mixture thoroughly with the pestle. Mix in the onion, parsley, and salt and pepper to taste.

Transfer to a bowl, cover and refrigerate; the mixture thickens when thoroughly chilled.

Garnish with black olives and serve with crackers, toast fingers or crusty bread.

❀ *Note: Eggplant discolours quickly once exposed to air, so mixing it with the other ingredients straight away is important. You can also use a blender or food processor to make the dip. Add all the ingredients except the oil to the processor. Blend until smooth, then gradually add the oil; this makes a smoother dip.*

❀ *Variation: Add 1 large peeled, chopped ripe tomato to the garlic mixture with the eggplant.*

OKTAPOTHI TOURSI
Pickled octopus
SERVES: 6–8

1 octopus, about 1.5 kg (3 lb 5 oz)
1 garlic clove, crushed
125 ml (4 fl oz/½ cup) olive oil
60 ml (2 fl oz/¼ cup) vinegar
salt and freshly ground black pepper, to taste

For serving
lemon wedges
flat-leaf parsley

To clean the octopus, pull off the tentacles and remove the intestines and ink sac. Cut out the eyes and beak. Remove the skin and rinse well.

Place the body and tentacles in a large saucepan without any liquid. Cover and simmer the octopus in its own juices over low heat until it turns deep pink and is tender — about 45–60 minutes.

Drain the octopus. When cool enough to handle, strip off the suckers from the tentacles if desired. Cut the head and tentacles into bite-sized pieces and place in a bowl.

Combine the garlic, oil, vinegar, salt if necessary, and pepper to taste in a small bowl and pour over the octopus. Mix well, then cover and leave to marinate in the refrigerator for 12 hours before using. Stir occasionally.

To serve, lift the octopus out of the marinade, pile into a dish and garnish with lemon wedges and parsley. Supply cocktail sticks for your guests' convenience.

SPANAKOPITA PELOPONNISOS
Peloponnese spinach rolls
SERVES: 6–8

The Greek Orthodox religion has many fast days during the year, but the 40-day Lenten fast is the most important. Home cooks try to prepare interesting meals without meat and other animal products. Very strict adherents even deny themselves olive oil. This recipe is easy to adjust to dietary restrictions.

500 g (1 lb 2 oz) spinach

85 ml (3 fl oz/⅓ cup) olive oil

1 onion, chopped

1 leek, white part only, chopped

8 spring onions (scallions), chopped

small handful chopped flat-leaf parsley

3 teaspoons chopped dill or fennel

¼ teaspoon ground nutmeg

salt and freshly ground black pepper, to taste

8 sheets fillo pastry

olive oil or melted butter, for brushing

Preheat the oven to 180°C (350°F/Gas 4).

Wash the spinach well and cut off any coarse stems. Chop the leaves roughly and place in a large saucepan. Cover and place over medium–low heat for 7–8 minutes, shaking the pan now and then or turning the spinach with a fork. Heat just long enough to wilt the spinach so that the juices can run out freely. Drain well in a colander, pressing occasionally with a spoon.

Heat the oil in a frying pan and gently fry the onion for 10 minutes. Add the leek and spring onion and fry gently for a further 5 minutes, or until translucent.

Place the well-drained spinach in a mixing bowl and add the onion mixture, herbs and nutmeg. Mix thoroughly, adding salt and pepper to taste.

Place a sheet of fillo pastry on your work surface and lightly brush with oil or melted butter. Top with three more sheets of pastry, brushing each with oil or melted butter.

Brush the top layer lightly with oil or butter. Place half the spinach mixture along the length of the pastry towards one edge, leaving 4 cm (1½ inches) clear on each end.

Fold the bottom edge of the pastry over the filling. Roll once, fold in the ends, then roll up. Place a hand at each end of the roll and push it in gently like a concertina. Repeat with the remaining pastry and filling.

Place the rolls in an oiled baking dish, leaving space between the rolls. Brush the tops lightly with oil or melted butter and bake for 30 minutes, or until golden.

Serve hot, cut into portions.

SPANAKOPITA
Spinach pie

SERVES: 8 AS AN APPETISER, 6 AS A LIGHT MEAL

While I use butter for the fillo sheets, olive oil may be used if desired. A spray can of olive oil is a time saver – but use it sparingly.

500 g (1 lb 2 oz) spinach

125 ml (4 fl oz/½ cup) olive oil

1 onion, chopped

8 spring onions (scallions), chopped

small handful chopped flat-leaf parsley

2 teaspoons chopped dill or fennel

¼ teaspoon ground nutmeg

125 g (4 oz/½ cup) Mizithra (page 27) or ricotta cheese

150 g (5 oz/1 cup) well-crumbled feta cheese

25 g (¾ oz/¼ cup) finely grated kefalotiri or parmesan cheese

4 eggs, lightly beaten

salt and freshly ground black pepper, to taste

melted butter, for brushing

10 sheets fillo pastry

Preheat the oven to 180°C (350°F/Gas 4).

Prepare the spinach as directed in the Spanakopita Peloponnisos recipe (page 29).

Heat the oil in a frying pan and gently fry the onion for 10 minutes. Add the spring onion and cook for a further 5 minutes or until translucent.

Transfer the onion mixture to a large mixing bowl. Add the drained spinach, herbs, nutmeg, cheeses and eggs and stir to combine. Check the saltiness of the mixture, then season to taste with salt and pepper.

Brush a 25 × 30 cm (10 × 12 inch) baking dish with melted butter and line it with a sheet of fillo pastry. Top with another four sheets, brushing each with butter.

Spread the filling over the pastry and top with the remaining fillo, brushing each sheet again with butter. Trim the edges if necessary and tuck the pastry in on all sides.

Brush the top lightly with more butter. Lightly score the top layer of pastry into squares, using a sharp knife or stanley knife. Sprinkle a little cold water on top to prevent the pastry curling up.

Bake for 45 minutes, or until puffed and golden brown. Remove from the oven and allow to sit for 5 minutes before cutting into portions for serving.

SPANAKOPITES APO TI SAMOS
Spinach pies from Samos
MAKES: 20

500 g (1 lb 2 oz) fresh spinach, or 2 × 250 g (9 oz)
   packets of frozen leaf spinach
60 ml (2 fl oz/¼ cup) olive oil, plus extra for brushing
8 spring onions (scallions), finely chopped
300 g (10½ oz/2 cups) crumbled feta cheese
3 tablespoons finely chopped dill or fennel
2 eggs, beaten
¼ teaspoon ground nutmeg
salt and freshly ground pepper, to taste
10 sheets fillo pastry

Preheat the oven to 190°C (375°F/Gas 5).

Prepare the fresh spinach as directed in the Spanakopita Peloponnisos recipe (page 29). If using frozen spinach, let it thaw, then drain well and chop if necessary. Place the spinach in a mixing bowl.

Heat the oil in a frying pan and gently fry the spring onion until soft. Add the mixture to the spinach, along with the cheese, herbs, eggs and nutmeg. Mix well to combine, then season with salt and pepper.

Open out the fillo pastry sheets and cut them in half, so that you have pieces approximately 20 × 30 cm (8 × 12 inches) in size. Stack them and cover with a cloth.

Take a sheet of fillo pastry and brush it lightly with oil. Fold it in half to make a strip about 10 cm (4 inches) wide. Brush it again with oil and spread about 2 tablespoons of the filling across one long edge, leaving the ends clear of filling. Fold in the ends, then roll up firmly. Bend the roll round into a coil and place it in an oiled baking dish. Repeat with the remaining ingredients.

Brush the tops lightly with oil and bake for 25 minutes, or until golden brown. Serve hot as an appetiser or light meal.

TIROPITAKIA
Cheese triangles
MAKES: ABOUT 60

375 g (13 oz/2½ cups) crumbled feta cheese
250 g (9 oz/1 cup) ricotta cheese or Mizithra (page 27)
3 tablespoons finely chopped flat-leaf parsley
2 teaspoons finely chopped mint, optional
freshly ground black pepper, to taste
2–3 eggs
375 g (13 oz) fillo pastry
185 g (6½ oz/¾ cup) butter, melted

Preheat the oven to 190°C (375°F/Gas 5).

Combine the feta and ricotta or mizithra cheese in a mixing bowl. Mash finely with a fork to mix thoroughly. Add the parsley, the mint if using, and pepper to taste.

Lightly beat two of the eggs and stir into the cheese — the mixture should be soft, but still hold its shape. If it is too stiff, add another egg.

Cut each fillo pastry sheet into three strips, each approximately 13 × 30 cm (5 × 12 inches) in size. Stack them on a dry cloth and cover with another folded, dry cloth. Place a moistened cloth on top.

Take a strip of fillo and brush it lightly with melted butter. Fold it in half lengthways and brush it again with butter. Place a generous teaspoon of the cheese mixture towards the bottom edge of the strip. Fold the end of the strip diagonally over the filling, so that the bottom edge is in line with the folded edge, forming a triangle. Fold up once, then fold diagonally to the opposite side. Continue to fold in a triangle to the end of the strip (see illustrations on page 17). Repeat with the remaining ingredients.

Place the pastries on lightly greased baking trays and brush the tops lightly with more butter. Bake for 20 minutes, or until puffed and golden. Serve hot.

TIROPITA
Cheese pie

SERVES: 12 AS AN APPETISER, 6 AS A LIGHT MEAL

Pies such as this one are prepared in villages and cooked in the home wood-fired oven after the weekly bread baking. A tray of sesame rings may also be baked, along with slices of the previous week's bread to make rusks, a breakfast staple.

500 ml (17 fl oz/2 cups) milk

60 g (2 oz/½ cup) fine semolina (farina)

40 g (1½ oz) butter

125 g (4 oz/1 cup) coarsely grated sharp cheddar cheese

150 g (5 oz/1 cup) crumbled feta cheese

35 g (1 oz/⅓ cup) grated kefalotiri or parmesan cheese

3 eggs

¼ teaspoon ground nutmeg

2 tablespoons finely chopped flat-leaf parsley, optional

salt and freshly ground white pepper, to taste

10 sheets fillo pastry

125 g (4 oz/½ cup) butter, melted

Preheat the oven to 220°C (430°F/Gas 7).

Combine the milk and semolina in a heavy-based saucepan. Add the 40 g (1½ oz) butter and stir constantly over medium—high heat until thickened and bubbling. Reduce the heat and let the mixture boil gently for 2 minutes.

Add the cheeses and stir until well combined. Remove from the heat and leave to cool, stirring occasionally.

Beat the eggs well and stir into the cheese sauce. Add the nutmeg, the parsley if using, and salt and pepper to taste.

Butter a 25 × 30 cm (10 × 12 inch) baking dish, then line it with half the fillo pastry sheets, brushing each sheet with melted butter.

Spread the filling in the dish, then top with the remaining pastry sheets, again brushing each with melted butter. Brush the top with the remaining butter and tuck the edges under to hold in the filling.

Score the top sheets in squares or diamonds with a stanley knife, according to the servings required — small for appetisers and snacks, larger for a light meal or first course.

Sprinkle the top lightly with cold water to prevent the pastry curling. Bake for 30 minutes, or until puffed and golden.

Leave to cool in the dish for 10 minutes. Cut into portions and serve hot or warm.

❧ *Note: Shortcrust pastry or home-made Fillo Pastry (pages 13–14) may be used instead of fillo pastry sheets.*

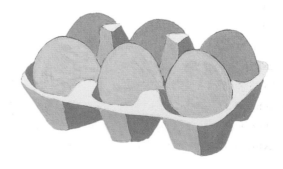

TARAMOSALATA
Fish roe purée
MAKES: ABOUT 500 G (1 LB 2 OZ/2 CUPS)

Tarama is the salted and cured roe of the grey mullet or cod, the basis of this popular and delicious Greek *meze*. As there are various types available, you might have to experiment to find one to your liking, and adjust the recipe accordingly.

The best *tarama* to my mind is the one imported from Greece. Usually available in bulk or in jars, it is a very firm, dusty-pink paste. Sometimes a retailer 'improves' it by softening the *tarama* (with what I do not know) and brightening it with food colouring. Avoid this variety.

Small tins of locally produced *tarama* are more widely available and handy to have in the refrigerator. This is a firm, orange-coloured paste and just a little bitter to my taste, though this lessens considerably if the *taramosalata* is refrigerated a day or two before serving.

Avgotaraho – salted, dried, amber-coloured roe – is often available at fishmongers and delicatessens. This makes an excellent *taramosalata*, but choose one that is not too hard. You can also prepare your own Avgotaraho (see page 36).

The strong-flavoured *tarama* must be broken down with crustless stale white bread, preferably from a Greek or continental-style loaf. Equal proportions by weight of these two ingredients is a good rule of thumb. Some cooks add mashed potato instead of the bread, or a combination of the two, to the detriment of the final *taramosalata*.

4–5 thick slices of crustless stale white bread,
    about 150 g (5 oz)
125 g (4 oz/½ cup) *tarama*
1 small garlic clove, crushed
½ small onion, finely grated or ground
60 ml (2 fl oz/¼ cup) lemon juice, strained
1 egg yolk, plus 1 egg white if needed
165 ml (5½ fl oz/⅔ cup) olive oil, plus extra for drizzling

For serving
black olives, to garnish
crusty bread and crackers
raw vegetables such as radishes, celery and cucumber sticks

Soak the bread in cold water and then squeeze dry. Add to a food processor with the tarama, garlic, onion and half the lemon juice. Process until smoothly combined.

Add the egg yolk and beat well, then slowly add 125 ml (4 fl oz/½ cup) of the oil. Taste and add more lemon juice if the mixture is too salty. Gradually add the remaining oil until the *tarama* is light and creamy. If it is very stiff, add the egg white and beat in well. (Some *taramas* will take the egg white, while others have a satisfactory consistency without it.)

When completed, the *taramosalata* should hold its shape; chilling will thicken it further. Store it in a sealed container in the refrigerator until required.

To serve, pile the *taramosalata* in a deep bowl and garnish with olives. Serve with crusty bread, assorted crackers and a dish of crisp celery pieces, radish and cucumber sticks. The vegetable accompaniment is not traditional, but a joy to eat with the *taramosalata* spread onto the pieces.

AVGOTARAHO
Dried mullet roe (Boutargo)

One of my most persistent childhood memories is of my mother preparing *avgotaraho*. For the uninitiated, this is the salted and dried roe of the mullet, rich amber in colour and a delight to eat, though its one annoying characteristic is that it rather clings to the teeth. At least the taste lingers for longer!

First of all you need to be on good terms with your fishmonger, particularly if he has a large Greek clientele. Cultivate the friendship so that it is ripe by early autumn or fall, wherever you happen to live. This is when the mullet is about to spawn, and some of the catch will yield trembling pairs of yellow roe. A good fishmonger knows how to gut the fish so as not to cut into the roe. However, my father preferred to do this himself at the fishmongers.

> fresh mullet roe, in pairs
> good-quality pure cooking salt
> beeswax or paraffin wax, optional

Remove any red veins on each roe by carefully scraping with the back edge of a spoon. The spoon edge should not be sharp, as this could break the fine skin. Leave the roe in pairs.

Cover a flat dish with a layer of salt. Arrange the fish roe side by side on the salt, sprinkle thickly with more salt and place another layer of roe on top if you have a good supply. Top with more salt, adding enough to completely cover the roe. Leave for 6 hours at room temperature.

Have a large bowl of cold water ready. Dip each pair of roe into the water, lift out immediately and place flat on a rack. Smooth the roe with your fingers and leave to drain for 10 minutes.

Place the drained roe flat on a clean wooden board, then carefully place another board on top. If the top board is not very heavy, weigh it down with a heavy object. Leave for another 30 minutes.

Transfer the roe to a stainless steel or plastic-coated rack.

Dry in an airy, shaded place for 1 week, turning the roe once each day. Cover them lightly with muslin (cheesecloth) to protect them. After drying, the roe will be firm and an amber shade, varying in depth according to the original colour.

Store the roe in a cool place, but not in a sealed container. The longer they are stored, the firmer they become; they will keep for up to 6 months.

To store them longer, dip the roe in melted beeswax or paraffin wax, place them on flat trays and leave them until set. This protects the roe more, but the roe will not dry out as much as the uncoated roe. Connoisseurs prefer very firm roe.

To eat, remove any wax coating and the fine skin, and slice the roe thinly. It is excellent as an appetiser with crusty bread and butter, or drizzle it with olive oil and add a squeeze of lemon juice and a grinding of black pepper.

The dried roe may also be used to make Taramosalata. Grate the amount required, mix well with a little lemon juice and leave until it softens. Then follow the recipe directions for Taramosalata on page 35.

AGINARES ME AVGOLEMONO
Artichokes with Egg and Lemon Sauce
SERVES: 6

Egg and Lemon Sauce marries perfectly with globe artichokes, which grow wild in rural Greece and on the islands. In this dish, they are used in a vegetable stew.

juice of 1 lemon
1 tablespoon olive oil
6 globe artichokes
Egg and Lemon Sauce (page 26)
chopped fresh dill or parsley, to garnish, optional

Add the lemon juice and oil to a saucepan of salted water and bring to the boil. Prepare the whole artichokes (see page 8), add them to the boiling water and cook for 30 minutes, or until tender. Test by pulling a leaf — if it comes away easily, the artichokes are done.

Lift the artichokes out with a slotted spoon and invert them to drain. Place in a serving dish and keep hot.

Make the Egg and Lemon Sauce using chicken stock, or half stock and half cooking liquid from the artichokes. Pour the sauce over the artichokes and sprinkle with dill or parsley if desired. Serve as a first course or a light meal.

❀ *Variation: Instead of artichokes you can also use asparagus, broccoli, brussels sprouts or celery hearts. Steam or boil according to the vegetable used, and make the sauce with chicken stock.*

AGINARES ME ANITHO
Artichokes with dill
SERVES: 8 AS AN APPETISER, 4 AS A LIGHT MEAL

12 globe artichokes
60 ml (2 fl oz/¼ cup) olive oil
60 g (2 oz/½ cup) chopped spring onions (scallions),
    white part only
juice of 1 lemon
salt and ground freshly ground white pepper, to taste
2 tablespoons finely chopped dill, plus extra to garnish
3 teaspoons cornflour (cornstarch)
2 eggs

Prepare the artichokes as directed on page 8 and cut each one in half.

Heat the oil in a large saucepan and gently fry the spring onion until soft. Add half the lemon juice and 750 ml (25 fl oz/3 cups) water. Season generously with salt and pepper and bring to the boil.

Drain the artichokes and add them to the pan with the dill. Return to a slow simmer, then cover and simmer gently for 30 minutes, or until the artichokes are tender.

Lift the artichokes out with a slotted spoon and keep them hot in the oven, at 150°C (300°F). Strain the cooking liquid into another saucepan and boil until it has reduced by half.

Mix the cornflour to a paste with a little cold water and stir it into the simmering liquid. Stir until thickened and bubbling and leave to simmer gently.

Beat the eggs in a mixing bowl until light and frothy and gradually add the remaining lemon juice. Gradually pour in the simmering stock, beating constantly. Return the mixture to the pan and stir it over low heat for a minute or two to cook the egg.

Pile the artichokes on a warm platter. Drizzle with the sauce and sprinkle with a little more dill. Serve as a first course or a light meal.

SPANAKOPITAKIA
Spinach pastries
MAKES: 15 TRIANGLES

Use half the quantity of spinach filling from the Spanakopita recipe on page 31. Shape into triangles or rolls as directed in the Tiropitakia recipe on page 32, or the Bourekakia Apo Tiri recipe to the right.

✿ *Note: To freeze cheese and spinach pastries, prepare the pastries ready for baking and place on foil-lined baking trays. Brush the tops lightly with melted butter and place in the freezer only until firmly frozen. Remove them carefully and pack into freezer containers, placing plastic wrap between the layers. Seal and store in the freezer. To serve, transfer the frozen pastries to greased baking trays and bake in a preheated 190°C (375°F/Gas 5) oven for 20–25 minutes, or until golden brown and puffed.*

BOUREKAKIA APO TIRI
Cheese rolls
MAKES: 8 ROLLS

Preheat the oven to 190°C (375°F/Gas 5).

Use the same ingredients as for the Tiropitakia recipe on page 32. Cut the pastry sheets in half, so that you have strips of fillo about 25 × 30 cm (10 × 12 inches) in size. Brush the strips with melted butter and fold in half lengthways. Brush them again with butter.

Spread about a tablespoon of filling along the bottom edge, keeping the sides clear. Turn the end of the pastry over the filling and fold in the sides along the length of the strip to contain the filling. Roll up firmly and place on greased baking trays, with the fold underneath.

Bake for 20–25 minutes, or until golden brown and puffed.

✿ *Note: The filling for the Tiropita recipe on page 33 may be used instead of the cheese filling given in the Tiropitakia recipe on page 32. Use 2 eggs so that the filling is firmer and easier to work with.*

PSOMI
Greek bread

MAKES: 2 LOAVES

This is the crusty, torpedo-shaped bread available at Greek and continental delicatessens. The moist atmosphere in the oven and spraying the bread with water produces a thick, crisp crust.

900 g (2 lb/6 cups) plain (all-purpose) flour

1 tablespoon active dried yeast

2 teaspoons salt

3 teaspoons sugar

1 tablespoon olive oil or melted warm butter

1 tablespoon fine semolina (farina)

Sift the flour into a heatproof mixing bowl and warm it in a low oven.

Dissolve the yeast in 60 ml (2 fl oz/¼ cup) warm water. Stir in 440 ml (15 fl oz/1¾ cups) warm water, the salt and sugar.

Remove about 300 g (10½ oz/2 cups) flour from the bowl and set aside. Make a well in the remaining flour and pour in the yeast mixture.

Stir in a little of the flour until the liquid is thick. Cover and leave in a warm place until frothy — about 10 minutes.

Stir the rest of the flour into the liquid, gradually adding the oil or butter. Beat with a wooden spoon or by hand until smooth for 10 minutes, or in an electric mixer with a dough hook for 5 minutes.

Gradually knead in the reserved flour; only knead in enough to stop the dough sticking. The dough is ready when it is satiny and the surface has a wrinkled texture. Shape into a ball.

Put the dough in a lightly oiled bowl, then turn it over so that the top is oiled. Cover the bowl with plastic wrap and place in a warm place for 1–1½ hours, or until the dough has doubled in size.

Punch down the dough and divide in half. Turn out onto a floured board and form each half into a torpedo-shaped loaf.

Grease a baking tray and sprinkle it with the semolina. Place the loaves well apart on the baking tray and make four diagonal slashes across the top of each loaf. Cover them with a cloth and leave in a warm place until they have doubled in size — about 1 hour.

Meanwhile, preheat the oven to 190°C (375°F/Gas 5).

Place a dish of boiling water on the floor or the lowest shelf of the oven. Spray the bread lightly with water and bake for 35–40 minutes. After the first 15 minutes, spray the loaves again with water, then again 10 minutes later.

Cool on a rack near an open window.

FASSOULATHA
« Bean soup
SERVES: 6–8

400 g (14 oz/2 cups) dried haricot (navy), cannellini, butterbeans (lima beans) or black-eyed beans

1 large onion, finely chopped

375 g (13 oz/1½ cups) chopped, peeled tomatoes

2 tablespoons tomato paste (concentrated purée)

140 g (4¾ oz/1 cup) chopped celery, including leaves

155 g (5 oz/1 cup) diced carrot

3 tablespoons chopped flat-leaf parsley, plus extra to garnish

85 ml (3 fl oz/⅓ cup) olive oil

½ teaspoon sugar

salt and freshly ground black pepper, to taste

Wash the beans well in several changes of water. Place them in a large saucepan with 2 litres (68 fl oz/8 cups) water and bring to the boil. Leave to boil for 2 minutes, remove from the heat and leave the pan covered until the beans become plump. The time varies according to the size of the beans, with the smaller beans plumping in 1 hour; larger beans take about 2 hours.

Add the remaining ingredients, except for salt, which will stop the beans softening. Bring to the boil, then cover the pan, reduce the heat and simmer gently for 1 hour.

Add salt to taste. Cook for a further 30–60 minutes, or until the beans are tender — the actual time depends on the beans.

Serve hot in soup plates, sprinkling some more chopped parsley on each serve. Crusty bread, black olives, cheese and wine can accompany *fassoulatha* for a complete meal.

AVGOLEMONO SOUPA
Egg and lemon soup
SERVES: 6

1.5 litres (51 fl oz/6 cups) chicken or fish stock

75 g (2½ oz/⅓ cup) short-grain white rice or small soup noodles

3 eggs, separated

juice of 1 large lemon

salt and freshly ground white pepper, to taste

Bring the stock to the boil and add the rice or noodles and salt. Stir until the stock returns to a slow boil, then cover and simmer gently for 20 minutes, or until the rice or noodles are tender. Skim off any froth during cooking.

In a mixing bowl, beat the egg whites until stiff. Add the egg yolks and beat until light and creamy. Gradually beat in the lemon juice.

Ladle about one-quarter of the simmering soup into the eggs, whisking constantly.

Gradually add the egg mixture to the soup, stirring vigorously. Remove the soup from the heat.

Keep stirring for 1 minute. Adjust the seasoning with salt and pepper and serve immediately.

✿ *Note: This soup does not reheat satisfactorily, so must be prepared just before serving. Only the stock can be prepared beforehand. The rice or noodles must also be cooked in the stock just before serving.*

MAYERITSA
Easter soup
SERVES: 6–8

The Paschal lamb, so much a part of the Greek Easter Sunday celebrations, usually comes with head and edible innards. The head is left on and it secures the lamb to the spit more successfully. The innards are used for making either *mayeritsa* or Kokoretsi tis Souvlas (page 72). Often extra ingredients are obtained for making both.

A bowl of *mayeritsa* is the first meal served after the Lenten fast and follows the Saturday midnight service of the Resurrection.

As you are unlikely to purchase a lamb with all its spare parts, the recipe is given with ingredients easily obtained from your butcher.

500 g (1 lb 2 oz) lamb tripe

2 lamb lungs

1 lamb heart

1 lamb liver

juice of 1 lemon

60 g (2 oz/¼ cup) butter

240 g (8½ oz/2 cups) chopped spring onions (scallions)

2 tablespoons chopped flat-leaf parsley

2 teaspoons chopped dill

salt and freshly ground white pepper, to season

75 g (2½ oz/⅓ cup) short-grain white rice

To finish

3 eggs

juice of 1 lemon

Rinse the tripe well, place in a saucepan and cover with cold water. Bring to the boil, then drain.

Put the scalded tripe in a deep saucepan and add 2 litres (68 fl oz/8 cups) cold water. Bring to the boil, then reduce the heat, cover and simmer for 1 hour.

Meanwhile, rinse the lungs, heart and liver. Place in a bowl, cover with cold water and add the lemon juice. Leave to soak for 30 minutes, then drain.

Add the lungs, heart and liver to the pan and simmer gently, uncovered, for a further 10 minutes, skimming as required.

Lift out all the meats, reserving the stock. Cut the meat into very small pieces, discarding any tubes from the heart and liver. Set aside.

Melt the butter in a frying pan and gently fry the spring onion until translucent. Add the chopped meats and stir over medium heat for 5 minutes.

Transfer the pan contents to the saucepan of hot stock. Add the parsley and dill, and season with salt and pepper. Cover and simmer gently for 2 hours, or until meats are tender.

Rinse the rice and add to the pan. Boil, uncovered, for a further 20 minutes, adding a little more water if necessary.

To finish, beat the eggs in a bowl until foamy. Gradually beat in the lemon juice. Ladle about 500 ml (17 fl oz/2 cups) of the boiling stock into the egg mixture, beating constantly. Pour the mixture back into the soup and stir over low heat for a minute or two to cook the egg. Do not let the soup boil again.

Remove the pan from the heat so that the heat of the pan does not curdle the egg. Keep stirring for a further minute and serve immediately.

❀ *Note: The soup may be prepared and cooked for 2 hours, or until the meats are tender, then removed from the heat before the rice is added. When required for serving, return to the boil, add the rice and complete the cooking.*

BAMYES TIGANITES
Fried okra
SERVES: 6

500 g (1 lb 2 oz) okra
60 ml (2 fl oz/¼ cup) olive oil
salt, to season
lemon wedges, to serve

Prepare the okra as directed on page 8. Dry very well with paper towels or a cloth.

Heat the oil in a large frying pan with a lid to fit. Add the okra and fry over medium heat, turning the okra carefully using blunt-ended tongs so it browns evenly.

When lightly browned, reduce the heat to low and cover the pan with the lid. Cook for 10 minutes, or until the okra are tender. Sprinkle lightly with salt.

Serve hot as a vegetable accompaniment, with lemon wedges for squeezing over the okra. Cooked this way, okra tastes like asparagus.

TOMATES YEMISTES
Stuffed tomatoes
SERVES: 6

12 ripe tomatoes
sugar, for sprinkling
salt and freshly ground black pepper, to taste
125 ml (4 fl oz/½ cup) olive oil
1 large onion, chopped
40 g (1½ oz/¼ cup) pine nuts, optional
330 g (11½ oz/1½ cups) short-grain white rice
75 g (2½ oz/½ cup) currants
2 tablespoons chopped flat-leaf parsley
2 tablespoons chopped mint
water or dry white wine

Preheat the oven to 180°C (350°F/Gas 4).

Slice the tops from the tomatoes and reserve. Scoop out the pulp and place in a saucepan. Sprinkle the cavities with a little sugar and set aside.

Add ½ teaspoon sugar to the tomato pulp and season with salt and pepper. Simmer until soft, then press through a sieve, reserving the pulp.

Heat half the oil in a saucepan and gently fry the onion until translucent. Add the pine nuts, if using, and cook for a further 5 minutes. Stir in 375 ml (12½ fl oz/1½ cups) hot water. Add the rice, currants, parsley, mint and salt and pepper to taste.

Bring to the boil, then cover and reduce the heat. Simmer gently for 10 minutes, or until the rice has absorbed the liquid.

Spoon the mixture into the tomato cavities, allowing room for the rice to swell. Replace the tops and stand the tomatoes in a baking dish.

Pour the puréed tomato pulp and an equal quantity of water or white wine into the baking dish. Spoon the remaining oil over the tomatoes.

Bake, uncovered, for 30 minutes. Serve hot or cold.

❧ *Note: This makes a pleasant luncheon dish, or an attractive accompaniment to main meals.*

AGINARES ALA POLITA
« Braised artichokes
SERVES: 6

12 globe artichoke hearts

4 spring onions (scallions), chopped

500 g (1 lb 2 oz) baby carrots, scraped

12 small onions, peeled

12 small new potatoes, scraped

juice of 1 lemon

185 ml (6½ fl oz/¾ cup) olive oil

chicken stock or water

salt and freshly ground black pepper, to season

1 tablespoon chopped dill or flat-leaf parsley,
    plus extra to garnish

1 tablespoon cornflour (cornstarch)

Prepare the artichoke hearts as directed on page 8.

Line a wide-based saucepan with the spring onions. Arrange the artichoke hearts and other vegetables on top.

Add the lemon juice, oil and enough water or chicken stock to barely cover. Season with salt and pepper and sprinkle the dill or parsley over the vegetables.

Cover and simmer gently for 30 minutes, or until the vegetables are tender.

Remove the vegetables to a heated platter with a slotted spoon, arranging them attractively. Keep them hot.

Mix the cornflour to a paste with a little cold water and stir it into the liquid in the pan. Let it boil gently for 2 minutes, until thickened.

Pour the sauce over the vegetables and serve sprinkled with some more chopped herbs.

BRIAMI
Vegetable casserole
SERVES: 6

1 kg (2 lb 3 oz) zucchini (courgettes)

500 g (1 lb 2 oz) potatoes

2 green capsicums (peppers)

2 onions

2 garlic cloves, crushed

500 g (1 lb 2 oz/2 cups) chopped, peeled tomatoes

½ teaspoon sugar

salt and freshly ground black pepper, to season

2 tablespoons chopped flat-leaf parsley,
    plus extra to garnish

2 teaspoons chopped dill or fennel,
    plus extra to garnish

125 ml (4 fl oz/½ cup) olive oil

Preheat the oven to 180°C (350°F/Gas 4).

Cut the zucchini and potatoes into 1 cm (½ inch) slices. Wash the capsicums and remove the stems, seeds and white membrane, then slice the flesh. Slice the onions.

Mix together the garlic, tomatoes and sugar.

Oil a baking dish and arrange some onion slices on the base. Add a layer of zucchini, potato and capsicum, then top with some of the tomato mixture. Season with salt and pepper and sprinkle with some of the herbs and oil. Repeat with a few more layers until all the ingredients have been used, finishing with the herbs and oil.

Cover and bake for 1–1½ hours, or until the vegetables are tender, removing the lid or foil for the last 15 minutes.

Garnish with some more chopped herbs and serve immediately as a course on its own, or as an accompaniment to roasted or grilled meats, fish or meat patties.

❧ *Variation: Reduce the zucchini to 500 g (1 lb 2 oz) and add an equal quantity of eggplant (aubergine), sliced thickly and salted for 30 minutes. Rinse and dry before using.*

KOUKIA TIGANITA
Fried broad beans
SERVES: 6

500 g (1 lb 2 oz) very young broad beans (fava beans)
    (fava beans)
plain (all-purpose) flour, for coating
olive oil, for pan-frying
lemon wedges, to serve

Wash the broad beans well. Remove the tops and tails, pulling off the strings as they are removed. Leave whole.

Drop the beans into boiling salted water and boil rapidly for 5 minutes. Remove and drain well. Leave until dry.

Roll the beans in flour to coat. Heat enough oil in a frying pan to coat the base. Fry the beans over medium–high heat until golden brown, turning to brown them evenly.

Serve hot, with lemon wedges for squeezing over.

SPANAKORIZO
Spinach pilaff
SERVES: 6

750 g (1 lb 10 oz) spinach
125 ml (4 fl oz/½ cup) olive oil
120 g (4 oz/1 cup) chopped spring onions (scallions)
1 leek, white part only, chopped, optional
440 g (15½ oz/2 cups) short-grain white rice
60 ml (2 fl oz/¼ cup) lemon juice
2 tablespoons chopped flat-leaf parsley
1 teaspoon chopped dill
salt and freshly ground black pepper, to taste

Remove the roots and any damaged leaves from the spinach. Wash the spinach well in several changes of water, then drain. Tear the leaves into pieces and chop the stalks.

Heat the oil in a deep saucepan and gently fry the spring onion and leek, if using, until soft.

Wash the rice, drain well and add to the pan. Cook for 5 minutes, stirring frequently.

Add the remaining ingredients and 750 ml (25 fl oz/3 cups) water and bring to the boil. When the mixture is boiling, add the spinach, stir well and cover tightly with a lid. Reduce the heat and simmer gently over low heat for 15 minutes.

Remove the pan from the heat, leaving it tightly covered, and allow to stand for 5–10 minutes before serving.

Serve hot as an accompaniment to main meals, particularly grilled meats and fish. It is also good served cold.

❧ *Note: Silverbeet (Swiss chard) may be used instead of spinach. Remove the stalks, wash the better stalks and chop finely. Parboil the stalks for 5 minutes in salted water, drain, then add to the rice with the chopped leaves.*

SALATES
Salads

To the Greeks, salads range from the puréed Taramosalata (page 35) and Melitzanosalata (page 28), through to a variety of boiled vegetable salads simply dressed with olive oil and lemon juice and usually served lukewarm, to the traditional salads made from raw ingredients.

The cooked and raw vegetable salads require dressings and these are given with serving suggestions. Use them for Cypriot cooking as well.

LATHOXITHO
Oil and vinegar dressing
MAKES: ABOUT 200 ML (7 FL OZ)

Pepare as for Latholemono (see right), but substitute wine vinegar for the lemon juice and add ½ teaspoon mustard powder. Serve with any raw vegetable salad, or cooked dried bean, potato, and beetroot salads.

LATHOLEMONO
Oil and lemon dressing
MAKES: ABOUT 200 ML (7 FL OZ)

125 ml (4 fl oz/½ cup) olive oil

60 ml (2 fl oz/¼ cup) lemon juice

2 teaspoons chopped oregano or flat-leaf parsley, optional

1 garlic clove, crushed, optional

½ teaspoon salt

freshly ground black pepper, to taste

Combine the ingredients in a bowl and beat well with a fork, or place in a screw-top jar, seal and shake well.

Beat or shake again just before using.

❋ *Note: This dressing can be used in a variety of ways. Pour it over hot boiled vegetables such as green beans, endive, zucchini (courgettes) — which are particularly good if their blossom is still attached — broccoli, globe artichokes, cauliflower, cabbage, spinach, silverbeet (Swiss chard), and wild greens such as dandelion and amaranth (vlita). Either serve hot, or let the vegetables cool to room temperature. You can also brush the dressing onto fish, shellfish, lamb or chicken when grilling. It is excellent served with lobster and prawns (shrimp).*

SALATA ELINIKI
« Greek salad

The ingredients and the quantities you use in this salad are up to you. The greens, feta and olives are mandatory, and many would not regard it a Greek salad without the anchovies. The combination depends on what is available and the meal it is to accompany – choose a plain salad for rich meals, and a salad with a variety of ingredients for plain meals such as grilled meats, chicken and fish.

> salad greens such as cos (romaine), imperial or
>   iceberg lettuce
> onion rings
> sliced radishes
> tomato wedges
> cucumber slices
> green capsicum (pepper) strips
> feta cheese
> black olives
> anchovy fillets
> chopped flat-leaf parsley
> pickled capers
> Lathoxitho (page 47)
> dill sprigs or fennel fronds, to garnish, optional

Wash the greens well, shake off the excess moisture and wrap them in a tea towel (dish towel). Place in the refrigerator for 1–2 hours to dry the greens and make them crisp.

Break up the greens, or shred them coarsely using a very sharp knife (this is the Greek method and it is a good one, as the greens are less likely to be bruised).

Place the greens in a bowl and add any other ingredients desired. Add the dressing just before serving and toss at the table. Garnish as desired.

SALATA HORIATIKO
Village salad
SERVES: 6

> 4 tomatoes
> 2 slender, young green cucumbers
> 1 green capsicum (pepper)
> 2 red onions
> 125 g (4 oz) feta cheese
> 60 g (2 oz/½ cup) black olives
> Lathoxitho (page 47)

If peeled tomatoes are desired, score a cross in the base of each one, place in a heatproof bowl and cover with boiling water. Leave for 30 seconds, then transfer to cold water and peel the skin away from the cross.

Cut the tomatoes into wedges. Peel the cucumbers thinly, halve them lengthways, then cut into 1 cm (½ inch) slices.

Wash the capsicum and remove the stem, seeds and white membrane, then cut into thick strips. Slice the onion and separate into rings.

Place the prepared ingredients in a salad bowl. Dice the feta and scatter over the top with the olives. Pour on the dressing just before serving.

GARÍTHES YIOUVETSI
Baked prawns

SERVES: 6

1 kg (2 lb 3 oz) large raw prawns (shrimp)
125 ml (4 fl oz/½ cup) olive oil
1 onion, finely chopped
120 g (4 oz/1 cup) chopped spring onions (scallions)
2 garlic cloves, crushed
500 g (1 lb 2 oz/2 cups) chopped, peeled tomatoes
125 ml (4 fl oz/½ cup) dry white wine
3 tablespoons chopped flat-leaf parsley
½ teaspoon dried rigani or oregano
salt and freshly ground black pepper, to taste
125 g (4 oz) feta cheese
crusty bread, to serve

Shell the prawns, leaving the last segment of the shell and the tail intact. Devein the prawns and rinse them. Dry with paper towels and refrigerate until required.

Heat the oil in a saucepan and gently fry the onion until translucent. Add the spring onion and garlic and cook for a further 2 minutes. Add the tomatoes, wine, most of the parsley, the rigani or oregano and salt and pepper to taste. Cover and simmer gently for 30 minutes, or until the sauce is thick.

Meanwhile, preheat the oven to 250°C (480°F/Gas 9).

Spoon half the sauce into six individual baking dishes or one large baking dish. Add the prawns and spoon the remaining sauce over them. Coarsely crumble the feta cheese and sprinkle over the top.

Bake for 10–12 minutes, or until the prawns are pink and the feta has melted and is lightly browned. Sprinkle with the remaining parsley and serve immediately as a first course with crusty bread.

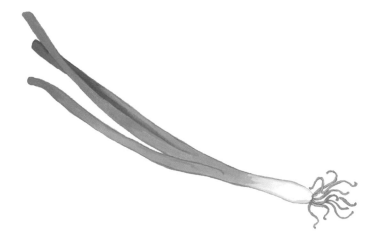

OKTAPOTHI KRASATO
Octopus in red wine

SERVES: 5-6

1 octopus, about 1 kg (2 lb 3 oz), plus the ink sac, optional
60 ml (2 fl oz/¼ cup) olive oil
1 large onion, chopped
2 garlic cloves, crushed
125 ml (4 fl oz/½ cup) dry red wine
375 g (13 oz/1½ cups) chopped, peeled tomatoes
salt and freshly ground black pepper, to season
2 tablespoons finely chopped flat-leaf parsley

Clean the octopus as directed in the Oktapothi Toursi recipe on page 28. Reserve the ink sac if still present.

Place the body and tentacles in a saucepan without any liquid, then cover and simmer for 15 minutes — the octopus will exude its own juice. Drain and leave to cool a little.

Cut the body and tentacles into small pieces, stripping off the suckers if desired.

Heat the oil in a separate saucepan and gently fry the onion until translucent. Add the garlic and octopus pieces and stir over medium heat for 5 minutes longer. Add the wine and cook until most of the wine has evaporated.

Reduce the heat and add the ink from the sac, if using. Add the tomatoes and season with salt and pepper. Cover and simmer gently over low heat for 1½ hours, or until the octopus is tender. Add water during cooking if the mixture looks like it may be scorching.

Stir in most of the parsley, then cook for a further minute. Sprinkle with the remaining parsley and serve hot, with boiled pasta or rice.

❊ *Note: The ink from the octopus can also be used as a bread dip: sizzle it in olive oil in a frying pan and combine it with lemon juice. Delicious!*

PILAFI ME MYTHIA
« Mussel pilaff

SERVES: 6

1.5 kg (3 lb 5 oz) fresh mussels

60 ml (2 fl oz/¼ cup) olive oil

60 g (2 oz/¼ cup) butter

1 large onion, finely chopped

125 ml (4 fl oz/½ cup) dry white wine

1½ teaspoons salt

freshly ground black pepper, to season

440 g (15½ oz/2 cups) short-grain white rice

3 tablespoons chopped flat-leaf parsley, plus extra
    to garnish

lemon wedges, to serve

Scrub the mussels with a stiff brush, scraping the shells with a knife blade to clean them thoroughly. Tug the beard towards the pointed end to remove.

Place the mussels in a bowl of lukewarm salted water until they open. If any are open to begin with, tap the shell — if the mussel does not close, discard it. While the mussels are open, run lukewarm water into the bowl so that any sand can be expelled from the mussels. Drain.

Heat the oil and butter in a deep saucepan and gently fry the onion until translucent. Add the mussels, then cover and cook for 5 minutes, or until the shells open. If any do not open, discard them.

Pour in 750 ml (25 fl oz/3 cups) cold water. Add the wine and salt and season with pepper. Cover and bring to a slow simmer. Leave to simmer gently for 10 minutes, then remove the mussels with a slotted spoon.

Wash the rice until the water runs clear, then add to the liquid in the pan with the parsley. Bring to the boil, stirring occasionally. Reduce the heat, cover the pan tightly and cook over low heat for 15 minutes.

While the rice is cooking, scoop most ot the mussels from their shells and reserve. Keep six mussels in their shells to decorate the finished dish.

Put the shelled mussels on top of the rice. Place two paper towels over the rim of the pan and fit the lid on firmly. Leave over low heat for a further 5 minutes, then remove the pan to the side of the stove and leave to sit for 10 minutes.

Mix the mussels through the rice with a fork. Pile the *pilafi* into a dish. Serve garnish with the reserved mussels, some more parsley and lemon wedges.

❀ *Note: For a different flavour, replace 125 ml (4 fl oz/½ cup) of the cooking water with 125 ml (4 fl oz/½ cup) tomato passata (puréed tomatoes).*

PILAFI ME GARITHES
Prawn pilaff

Follow the basic ingredients and method for Pilafi me Mythia (left), replacing the mussels with 1 kg (2 lb 3 oz) raw prawns (shrimp). Rinse the prawns well and cook them gently in their shells until they turn pink. Shell the prawns and devein them, reserving six in their shells as a garnish.

Follow the remainder of the method for Pilafi me Mythia, adding the shelled prawns to the rice instead of the mussels. Tomato passata (puréed tomatoes) may also replace some of the cooking water in this pilaff.

SOUPIES ME SPANAKI
Cuttlefish with spinach
SERVES: 6

Soupies (cuttlefish), as distinct from *kalamaria* (squid), are preferred for this dish, though either may be used. Cleaning cuttlefish can be a rather messy business as these marine molluscs have an ink sac (from which the pigment sepia is obtained). The sac ruptures easily and is usually ruptured by the time you purchase the cuttlefish, so don't be put off by their colour – the ink rinses off easily.

750 g (1 lb 10 oz) cuttlefish or squid

85 ml (3 fl oz/⅓ cup) olive oil

salt and freshly ground black pepper, to season

750 g (1 lb 10 oz) spinach

8 spring onions (scallions), chopped

juice of ½ lemon

Rinse the cuttlefish or squid and remove the head, tentacles and intestines. Discard the intestines. Pull out the cuttle bone, or the fine translucent bone if squid is being used. Pull off the fine skin and rinse. Remove the eyes and beak from the head, leave the head attached to the tentacles, and pull or rub off as much skin as will easily come off from the tentacles.

Slice the hood or body into strips. If the squid are large, slice the head and tentacles; cuttlefish tentacles are usually small and these are left intact.

Place the cuttlefish or squid in a saucepan over medium heat. Cover and cook for 15 minutes in its own juices.

Add half the oil and just enough water to cover. Season with salt and pepper. Cover and simmer gently for 45 minutes, or until tender.

Meanwhile, trim the spinach and wash thoroughly. Drain well and coarsely chop the leaves and stalks.

Heat the remaining oil in a large frying pan and gently fry the spring onion until soft. Add the spinach and stir until it wilts.

Add the spinach mixture to the cuttlefish or squid with the lemon juice. Adjust the seasoning to taste.

Cover and simmer for a further 10–15 minutes. Serve hot.

HINA YEMISTI ME KASTANA
Roast goose with chestnut stuffing
SERVES: 8–10

500 g (1 lb 2 oz) chestnuts
100 g (3½ oz) butter
1 small onion, chopped
5 cooking apples
1 goose, about 4 kg (8 lb 12 oz)
salt and freshly ground black pepper, to season
½ lemon
white wine

Preheat the oven to 180°C (350°F/Gas 4).

Cut through the shell of each chestnut at each end, cover with water and boil for 10 minutes. Remove from the water a few at a time and peel off the shell and inner covering on the nut. Break half the chestnuts in half to use in the stuffing; leave the rest whole as a garnish and set aside.

Melt 60 g (2 oz/¼ cup) of the butter in a frying pan and gently fry the onion until soft. Add the broken chestnuts and cook for a few minutes longer, then remove from the heat. Peel, core and dice four of the apples and add to the sautéed chestnut mixture. Mix well and set aside.

Remove the fat from the cavity of the goose. Dry well inside and out and sprinkle the cavity with salt and pepper. Fill with the chestnut mixture, secure the opening and truss. Rub the goose with the cut lemon and season well.

Place on a rack in a roasting tin and roast for 3½ hours, or until tender. Place the goose on a warm platter and leave to rest in a warm place for 20 minutes.

Skim the fat from the pan juices and dilute with a little wine. Reheat, adjust the seasoning and strain into a sauceboat.

Meanwhile, melt the remaining butter in a frying pan. Slice the remaining apple, gently fry until golden and remove from the pan. Gently fry the reserved whole chestnuts in the butter.

Garnish the goose with the apple and chestnuts and serve.

KOTOPOULO KAPAMA
Braised chicken
SERVES: 6

1 chicken, about 2 kg (4 lb 6 oz)
60 g (2 oz/¼ cup) butter
1 onion, finely chopped
1 garlic clove, crushed
375 g (13 oz/1½ cups) chopped, peeled tomatoes
1 tablespoon tomato paste (concentrated purée)
125 ml (4 fl oz/½ cup) dry white wine
1 bay leaf
2 pieces of cinnamon bark
½ teaspoon sugar
salt and freshly ground black pepper, to season

Cut the chicken into serving pieces and wipe dry. Melt the butter in a heavy-based saucepan or flameproof casserole dish and brown the chicken in batches on all sides. Remove to a plate.

Reduce the heat and gently fry the onion and garlic until the onion is translucent. Add all the remaining ingredients, except the chicken. Mix well, then cover and simmer for 20 minutes.

Return the chicken to the pan. Cover and simmer gently for a further 45 minutes, or until the chicken is tender. Remove the bay leaf and cinnamon.

Serve with boiled macaroni or spaghetti and grated cheese.

❀ *Note: The chicken may also be cooked in a 160°C (320°F/Gas 2-3) oven for 1–1½ hours.*

KOTOPOULO STIFATHO
Chicken with onions

Follow the Kotopoulo Kapama recipe (opposite). When returning the browned chicken pieces to the sauce, add 3 cloves and 750 g (1 lb 10 oz) peeled small whole onions (with a cross cut into the root ends to stop the centres popping out). Cook for 45-60 minutes. Remove the cloves and serve with mashed potato and a boiled green vegetable or a tossed salad.

KOTOPOULO ME BAMYES
Chicken with okra

Proceed as for Kotopoulo Kapama (opposite). Prepare 500 g (1 lb 2 oz) okra as directed on page 8 and dry very well with paper towels or a cloth. Lightly brown the okra in a little butter. Add to the chicken 20 minutes before the end of the cooking time. Serve with whole boiled or mashed potatoes.

PSITO KATSAROLAS LEMONATO
Pot roast with lemon
SERVES: 6

1 boned shoulder of lamb or veal, about 1.5 kg (3 lb 5 oz)
85 ml (3 fl oz/⅓ cup) lemon juice
salt and freshly ground black pepper, to season
2 teaspoons dried rigani or oregano
60 ml (2 fl oz/¼ cup) olive oil
2 garlic cloves, crushed

If using lamb, first trim away the excess fat. Open out the shoulder and rub the meat with some of the lemon juice. Sprinkle with salt and pepper and about ½ teaspoon of the rigani or oregano. Roll up and tie securely with kitchen string.

Rub the outside of the meat with more lemon juice, salt, pepper and rigani.

Heat the oil in a heavy-based saucepan and brown the meat on all sides. Reduce the heat and add the garlic and the remaining lemon juice and rigani.

Cover the pan tightly and simmer over low heat for 2½ hours, or until the meat is tender. Turn the meat occasionally during cooking.

Remove the string and slice the pot roast to serve. Pour the juices into a bowl and serve separately.

❉ *Note: 750 g (1 lb 10 oz) small potatoes, peeled and browned in a little olive oil, may be added to the roast 1 hour before the end of cooking time.*

LAMBRATIS ANDROS
Easter lamb or kid, Andros style
SERVES: 20

The major problem with preparing this Easter lamb speciality from the lovely island of Andros is having an oven large enough for the lamb. Perhaps an obliging restaurateur or baker in your area might let you use their oven at a convenient time.

In Andros they use a special cover made of baked clay to keep the lamb moist and succulent. Foil is a reasonable substitute, but has to be removed to give the browning effect naturally produced with the traditional covering.

1 baby lamb or kid, about 10–12 kg (22–26½ lb)
juice of 2 lemons
salt and freshly ground black pepper, to season
60 g (2 oz/¼ cup) butter, melted
60 ml (2 fl oz/¼ cup) olive oil

Spinach and feta stuffing
2.5 kg (5 lb 8 oz) spinach
185 ml (6½ fl oz/¾ cup) olive oil
12 spring onions (scallions), chopped
220 g (8 oz/1 cup) short-grain white rice, washed
1.5 kg (3 lb 5 oz) feta cheese
3 tablespoons chopped dill
3 tablespoons chopped mint
salt and freshly ground black pepper, to taste

Preheat the oven to 180°C (350°F/Gas 4).

Wipe the lamb or kid inside and out with a damp cloth. Rub the cavity and the outside with some of the lemon juice, salt and pepper. Cover and set aside while making the stuffing.

Trim the roots from the spinach, if present, and remove any discoloured and damaged leaves. Wash the spinach in several changes of water, drain well and chop roughly.

Heat the oil in a large heavy-based (non-aluminium) saucepan and gently fry the spring onion until soft. Add the spinach and stir until it wilts. Stir in the washed rice, then cover and cook over low heat for 10 minutes, or until most of the liquid has been absorbed. Remove from the heat and cool.

Break the feta into small chunks and add to the spinach mixture with the herbs. Mix well, taste, then add salt if necessary and a generous grinding of pepper. Mix thoroughly.

Partly sew up the lamb or kid cavity with kitchen string. Pack the stuffing in through the opening and finish sewing up the cavity. Push the foreshanks back towards the body and tie them in position, passing string over the back of the carcass. Tie the back legs, leaving them a little apart — tying them will stop them splaying outwards.

Rub the outside again with lemon juice, salt and pepper and place on a rack set in a large catering-size baking dish.

Combine the melted butter with the oil and brush half the mixture over the meat. Cover the dish with large sheets of foil, sealing the joins with double folds. Press the foil under the edges of the dish to seal it completely.

Roast for 2 hours. Lift the foil and brush the meat with more of the butter and oil mixture. Roast for a further 1½–2 hours, remove the foil and brush again.

Roast, uncovered, for a further 30 minutes, or until the meat is cooked through and browned — depending on its size, it may need a final 30 minutes or so.

Remove from the oven and cover with the foil and a thick cloth. Leave to rest for 30 minutes before carving.

Lift the meat onto a large wooden board. Remove the string and spoon the stuffing onto a platter.

Turn the meat on its back and chop along the backbone from the inside with a cleaver. Then chop each half into chunks and pile them onto platters. The meat on the legs may be carved into slices.

PASTITSO
Macaroni and meat pie

SERVES: 12 AS A FIRST COURSE, 6–8 AS A MAIN COURSE

Meat sauce

40 g (1½ oz) butter

1 large onion, chopped

1 garlic clove, crushed

750 g (1 lb 10 oz) minced (ground) beef

60 g (2 oz/¼ cup) tomato paste (concentrated purée)

125 ml (4 fl oz/½ cup) dry red or white wine

125 ml (4 fl oz/½ cup) stock

2 tablespoons chopped flat-leaf parsley

½ teaspoon sugar

salt and freshly ground black pepper, to taste

Pasta mixture

500 g (1 lb 2 oz) long macaroni

90 g (3 oz/⅓ cup) butter

75 g (2½ oz/¾ cup) grated kefalotiri or parmesan cheese

¼ teaspoon grated nutmeg

salt and freshly ground black pepper, to taste

3 eggs, lightly beaten

Cream sauce

90 g (3 oz/⅓ cup) butter

75 g (2½ oz/½ cup) plain (all-purpose) flour

750 ml (25 fl oz/3 cups) milk

¼ teaspoon grated nutmeg

salt and ground freshly ground white pepper, to taste

1 egg, lightly beaten

To make the meat sauce, melt the butter in a large saucepan and gently fry the onion and garlic until the onion is soft. Increase the heat and add the beef. Stir well and cook until the meat begins to brown. Add the remaining ingredients, then cover and simmer over a gentle heat for 40 minutes.

Meanwhile, preheat the oven to 180°C (350°F/Gas 4) and prepare the pasta mixture. First cook the macaroni in a saucepan of boiling salted water until just tender. Drain and return to the pan. Melt the butter in a saucepan until golden brown and pour over the macaroni. Add two-thirds of the cheese, the nutmeg and salt and pepper to taste. Toss well and leave until cool. Add the eggs and toss again. Set aside.

To make the cream sauce, melt the butter in a saucepan, stir in the flour and cook gently for 2 minutes. Add the milk all at once and bring to the boil, stirring constantly. Simmer gently for 1 minute. Add the nutmeg, season to taste with salt and freshly ground white pepper and allow to cool a little before stirring in the egg.

Stir 125 ml (4 fl oz/½ cup) of the cream sauce into the cooked meat sauce.

To assemble the *pastitso*, butter a 23 × 33 × 8 cm (9 × 13 × 3¼ inch) baking dish. Spoon half the pasta mixture evenly over the base, then top with the meat sauce. Cover with the remaining pasta mixture, levelling the top.

Pour on the cream sauce and spread it to completely cover the macaroni. Sprinkle the remaining cheese on top and bake for 50 minutes, or until golden brown.

Let the *pastitso* stand for 10 minutes before cutting it into squares to serve.

STIFATHO
Braised beef and onions

SERVES: 5–6

1 kg (2 lb 3 oz) braising beef

60 g (2 oz/¼ cup) butter or oil

1 onion, finely chopped

2 garlic cloves, crushed

125 ml (4 fl oz/½ cup) tomato passata (puréed tomatoes)

125 ml (4 fl oz/½ cup) red wine

2 tablespoons wine vinegar

1 bay leaf

2 pieces of cinnamon bark

4 cloves

1 teaspoon sugar

salt and freshly ground black pepper, to season

750 g (1 lb 10 oz) small pickling onions

2 tablespoons currants, optional

Prehead the oven to 150°C (300°F).

Cut the beef into 3 cm (1¼ inch) cubes. Heat half the butter in a frying pan and brown the meat, placing one layer of meat in the pan at a time. Transfer the browned meat to a casserole dish.

Add the onion and garlic to the pan with the remaining butter and fry gently until the onion is soft.

Add the tomato passata, wine and wine vinegar, and stir to dislodge any cooked-on bits on the base of the pan. Pour the juices over the meat in the casserole.

Stir in the bay leaf, spices and sugar and season with salt and pepper. Cover and bake for 1 hour.

Meanwhile, remove the tops and roots from the onions. Cut a cross into the root ends to stop the centres popping out during cooking. Place the onions in a heatproof bowl and cover with boiling water. Leave for 2 minutes, then drain and slip off the skins — they will now slip off easily.

Add the onions to the casserole with the currants, if using, and bake for a further 1–1½ hours, or until the meat and onions are tender and the sauce is thick. Remove the cinnamon.

Serve with mashed potato or pilaff.

❧ *Note: This dish may also be cooked slowly on top of the stove.*

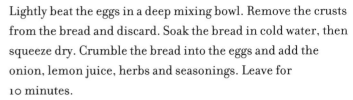

KEFTETHES
Meat patties
SERVES: 6

These delicious meat patties are a family favourite. Since the introduction of the food processor, I have developed the recipe so that the meat mixture can be made very quickly.

2 eggs
4–5 slices of stale white bread
1 large onion, grated
juice of 1 lemon
2 tablespoons chopped flat-leaf parsley
1–2 teaspoons chopped mint, optional
1½ teaspoons salt
freshly ground black pepper, to season
1 kg (2 lb 3 oz) finely minced (ground) beef or lamb
plain (all-purpose) flour, for coating
oil, for pan-frying

Lightly beat the eggs in a deep mixing bowl. Remove the crusts from the bread and discard. Soak the bread in cold water, then squeeze dry. Crumble the bread into the eggs and add the onion, lemon juice, herbs and seasonings. Leave for 10 minutes.

Add the meat and mix lightly and thoroughly, using your hands if necessary. Cover and refrigerate for 1 hour.

With moistened hands, shape the meat into balls about the size of small eggs. Roll them in flour, then flatten each one to a thick patty. Working in batches, pan-fry the patties in hot oil for 3–4 minutes on each side, until nicely browned. Drain on paper towels.

Place the patties in a serving dish as they are cooked and drained, and keep them hot until all the patties are done.

Serve hot with a boiled green vegetable and mashed potato, or with a tossed salad and fried potatoes.

If you wish, make Tomato Sauce (page 109), omitting the cinnamon, and pour over the patties before serving.

❀ *Note: If using a food processor, combine the well-squeezed, soaked bread in the processor with the roughly chopped onion and herbs. Blend until puréed, then add the lemon juice, eggs, salt and pepper. Process until combined, then add a handful of the beef or lamb and process briefly. Add the mixture to the remaining meat and mix thoroughly with your hands. Cover and refrigerate, then shape and cook as above.*

KEFTETHAKIA

Cocktail meatballs

Follow the recipe for Keftethes (page 62) substituting
1 tablespoon ouzo for the lemon juice. Shape the meatballs to
the size of small walnuts, coat with flour and deep-fry in hot
oil, a few at a time. Drain and serve hot or cold as an appetiser.
Garnish with lemon wedges and parsley and supply cocktail
sticks for your guests' convenience.

KEFTETHES APO TON PONTOS
Meat patties from Ponti

SERVES: 5–6

500 g (1 lb 2 oz) veal stewing meat
250 g (9 oz) pork stewing meat
3 thick slices of stale bread, crusts removed
1 onion, finely chopped
1 garlic clove, finely chopped
3 tablespoons chopped flat-leaf parsley
1 teaspoon chopped mint
1 teaspoon chopped basil
1 tomato, peeled and chopped (see page 528)
1 egg
1 tablespoon vinegar
1 teaspoon bicarbonate of soda (baking soda)
salt and freshly ground black pepper, to season
plain (all-purpose) flour, for coating
oil, for pan-frying

Grind the veal and pork finely, leaving some fat on the pork.
Alternatively, ask a butcher to do this for you.

Soak the bread in cold water, then squeeze it dry and
crumble it into a mixing bowl. Add the onion, garlic, herbs,
tomato, egg and vinegar. Mix in the bicarbonate of soda and
season with salt and pepper.

Add the veal and pork and mix lightly and thoroughly, using
your hands if necessary. Cover and refrigerate for 1 hour.

Roll about 2 tablespoons of the mixture at a time into balls.
Moisten your hands occasionally. Roll the balls in flour, then
flatten them into rounds about 5 cm (2 inches) in diameter.

Working in batches, pan-fry the patties in hot oil for
4–5 minutes on each side. The patties will puff up, so turn
them carefully with a spatula or tongs. Drain on paper towels.

Place the patties in a serving dish as they are cooked and
drained, and keep them hot until all the patties are done.

Serve hot with fried potatoes and vegetables or salad.

MELITZANES MOUSSAKA
Eggplant moussaka

SERVES: 6-8

1 kg (2 lb 3 oz) eggplants (aubergines)
salt, for sprinkling
olive oil, for brushing

Meat sauce

2 tablespoons olive oil
1 large onion, chopped
2 garlic cloves, crushed
1 kg (2 lb 3 oz) minced (ground) beef or lamb
250 g (9 oz/1 cup) chopped, peeled tomatoes
2 tablespoons tomato paste (concentrated purée)
125 ml (4 fl oz/½ cup) white wine
2 tablespoons chopped flat-leaf parsley
1 teaspoon sugar
¼ teaspoon ground cinnamon
salt and freshly ground black pepper, to season

Béchamel sauce

60 g (2 oz/¼ cup) butter
50 g (2 oz/⅓ cup) plain (all-purpose) flour
500 ml (17 fl oz/2 cups) milk
⅛ teaspoon ground nutmeg
25 g (¾ oz/¼ cup) grated kefalotiri or parmesan cheese
salt and freshly ground black pepper, to taste
1 egg, lightly beaten

Wash the eggplants. Leaving the skin on, cut them into 5 mm (¼ inch) slices. Sprinkle the slices with salt and leave for 1 hour. Dry with paper towels.

Place a layer of the eggplant on an oiled baking tray and brush with oil. Lightly brown under a hot grill (broiler); turn, brush again with oil and brown the other side. (Alternatively, the eggplant may be pan-fried in oil; however, the grilling method stops the eggplant absorbing excessive oil.) Stack the slices on a plate when cooked.

To make the meat sauce, heat the oil in a large saucepan and gently fry the onion and garlic for 10 minutes. Add the meat and brown over high heat, stirring well. Add the remaining ingredients, then cover and simmer gently for 30 minutes.

Meanwhile, preheat the oven to 180°C (350°F/Gas 4).

To make the béchamel sauce, melt the butter in a saucepan, stir in the flour and cook gently for 2 minutes. Add the milk all at once and bring to the boil, stirring constantly. Let the sauce bubble gently for 1 minute. Remove from the heat, stir in the nutmeg and 1 tablespoon of the cheese. Season to taste. Cover the top of the sauce with buttered greaseproof (parchment) paper if not required immediately.

Grease a 23 × 33 × 5 cm (9 × 13 × 2 inch) baking dish. Place a layer of eggplant slices in the base, then top with half the meat sauce. Add another layer of eggplant, then the remaining meat sauce. Finish with a third layer of eggplant.

Stir the beaten egg into the béchamel sauce and spread it over the *moussaka*. Sprinkle with the remaining cheese and bake for 1 hour.

Allow the *moussaka* to stand for 10 minutes before cutting into squares to serve.

ARNI FRICASSE
Lamb fricassee
SERVES: 4–6

40 g (1½ oz) butter

1 large onion, chopped

1 kg (2 lb 3 oz) lean boneless lamb, cubed

2 tablespoons chopped flat-leaf parsley, plus extra to garnish

1 teaspoon chopped dill or fennel, optional

salt and freshly ground black pepper, to season

your choice of prepared vegetable (see note)

Egg and Lemon Sauce (page 26)

Melt the butter in a heavy-based saucepan or flameproof casserole dish. Gently fry the onion until translucent. Increase the heat to medium–high and add the lamb. Cook, stirring constantly, until the meat juices evaporate — the meat should not brown.

Reduce the heat and pour in 250 ml (8½ fl oz/1 cup) hot water. Stir in the herbs and season with salt and pepper. Cover and simmer gently for 1–1½ hours.

Add your choice of vegetable and continue to cook until the lamb and vegetable are tender.

Carefully drain the liquid from the pan into a measuring jug. Add enough hot water or stock to make 375 ml (12½ fl oz/ 1½ cups) sauce. Keep the sauce contents hot.

Meanwhile, pour the Egg and Lemon Sauce over the lamb mixture. Cover and leave at the side of the stove for 5 minutes.

Arrange the lamb and vegetables in a serving dish and sprinkle with more chopped parsley. Serve immediately with crusty bread and a chilled white wine.

❁ Note: Add any one of the following vegetables to the fricassee:

- 8–12 small globe artichoke hearts, prepared as directed on page 8. Add to the meat after 1 hour and cook for a further 30–45 minutes.
- 500 g (1 lb 2 oz) celery stalks, cut into 8 cm (3¼ inch) lengths and blanched in boiling salted water for 5 minutes. Drain, add to the meat after 1 hour and cook for a further 45 minutes. Pork can be used instead of lamb with this vegetable.
- 4 heads of endive, washed well and trimmed of any coarse leaves. Slit the heads in half lengthways and blanch them in boiling salted water for 2 minutes. Drain, add to the meat after 1½ hours and cook for a further 15 minutes.
- 4 small firm heads of lettuce, washed well and quartered. Place in a colander and scald with boiling water. Add after 1½ hours and cook for a further 15 minutes.

ARNI LEMONATO
« Roast lemon lamb
SERVES: 6–8

1 leg of lamb, about 2 kg (4 lb 6 oz)

2–3 garlic cloves

juice of 2 lemons

salt and freshly ground black pepper, to season

1 teaspoon dried rigani or oregano

40 g (1½ oz) butter

Preheat the oven to 180°C (350°F/Gas 4).

Wipe the lamb with a damp cloth, then cut small slits into the lamb. Cut the garlic cloves into slivers and insert them in the slits. Rub the entire surface of the lamb with lemon juice and season with salt and pepper. Sprinkle with the rigani or oregano.

Place the lamb in a roasting tin and roast for 1 hour.

Drain off the fat and add 250 ml (8½ fl oz/1 cup) hot water to the roasting tin. Spread the butter over the lamb and return it to the oven. Roast for a further 1½ hours, or until the lamb is cooked to taste. Turn during cooking to brown it evenly.

Allow the lamb to rest in a warm place for 15–20 minutes before carving.

Skim off the excess fat from the pan juices. Reduce it by simmering it in a saucepan if necessary and serve with the lamb.

✿ *Note: 1 kg (2 lb 3 oz) peeled and quartered potatoes may be cooked with the lamb during the last hour. Sprinkle the potatoes with some extra lemon juice, rigani or oregano, salt and pepper.*

PAÏTHAKIA ALA HASAPIKO
Lamb chops butcher's style
SERVES: 6

1 kg (2 lb 3 oz) lamb shoulder chops

60 ml (2 fl oz/¼ cup) olive oil

salt and freshly ground black pepper, to season

½ teaspoon rigani or oregano

4 tomatoes

2 onions, sliced

500 g (1 lb 2 oz) potatoes, peeled and sliced

Preheat the oven to 180°C (350°F/Gas 4).

Trim the excess fat from the lamb chops. Brush a baking dish with 1 tablespoon of the oil and place the chops in a single layer in the dish. Season with salt and pepper and sprinkle on the rigani or oregano.

Score a cross in the base of each tomato. Place in a heatproof bowl and cover with boiling water. Leave for 30 seconds, then transfer to cold water and peel the skin away from the cross. Slice the tomatoes.

Arrange the onion slices on top of the chops and cover with a layer of sliced tomatoes. Season the tomatoes lightly. Pour on the remaining oil and bake for 1 hour.

Top with the potatoes, season lightly and brush with a little more oil. Bake for a further 30 minutes.

Serve hot with a green vegetable, salad and crusty bread.

✿ *Variation: Add a sliced carrot to the dish with the onions, and a cup of shelled peas with the potatoes for a complete one-dish main course.*

SKEMBE YAHNI
Tripe stew
SERVES: 4–5

750 g (1 lb 10 oz) tripe

juice of 1 lemon

40 g (1½ oz) butter

1 large onion, chopped

3 tablespoons chopped flat-leaf parsley, plus extra to garnish

60 g (2 oz/¼ cup) tomato paste (concentrated purée)

125 ml (4 fl oz/½ cup) dry white wine

salt and freshly ground black pepper, to season

Wash the tripe well and drain. Cut into small squares or fingers and place in a dish. Add the lemon juice, stir and leave for 1 hour.

Place the tripe in a saucepan, add water to cover and bring to the boil. Drain off the water and remove the tripe to a plate.

Clean the saucepan and add the butter. Melt over medium heat and gently fry the onion until translucent.

Stir in the parsley and fry for 1 minute. Add the tomato paste, 250 ml (8½ fl oz/1 cup) water and the wine. Season with salt and pepper and bring to a slow simmer.

Return the tripe to the pan. Cover and simmer gently for 2 hours, or until the tripe is tender. To test for tenderness, take out a piece and pull — if it breaks apart easily, the tripe is cooked.

Place in a serving dish, garnish with parsley and serve hot with pilaff and a tossed salad.

ARNI SOUVLAKI
Skewered lamb
SERVES: 6–8

1 leg of lamb, about 2 kg (4 lb 6 oz), boned

125 ml (4 fl oz/½ cup) olive oil

125 ml (4 fl oz/½ cup) dry white wine

juice of 1 lemon

2 teaspoons dried rigani or oregano

2 garlic cloves, crushed or chopped

3–4 bay leaves, torn

salt and freshly ground black pepper, to season

flat-leaf parsley, to garnish

lemon wedges, to garnish

Cut the lamb into 4 cm (1½ inch) cubes and place in a glass or ceramic dish. Add the remaining ingredients, except the garnishes. Mix well to coat the meat. Cover and marinate in the refrigerator for 12–24 hours, stirring the meat occasionally.

Lift the lamb out of the marinade and thread onto metal skewers, placing pieces of bay leaf between the lamb cubes.

Cook under a hot grill (broiler) or over glowing barbecue coals for 15 minutes, or until cooked to taste, turning and basting frequently with the marinade.

Place on a platter and garnish with parsley and lemon wedges. Serve hot.

YAHNI ME KOUKIA
Meat stew with broad beans

SERVES: 5–6

1 kg (2 lb 3 oz) boneless beef or lamb stewing meat

2 tablespoons olive oil, or 40 g (1½ oz) butter

1 large onion, finely chopped

2 garlic cloves, crushed

70 g (2½ oz/½ cup) chopped celery

1 carrot, sliced

250 g (9 oz/1 cup) chopped, peeled tomatoes

60 g (2 oz/¼ cup) tomato paste (concentrated purée)

60 ml (2 fl oz/¼ cup) dry red wine

3 cloves

1 bay leaf

3 tablespoons chopped flat-leaf parsley

½ teaspoon sugar

salt and freshly ground black pepper, to season

500 g (1 lb 2 oz) very young broad beans (fava beans);
  (see note)

Trim the meat and cut into 3 cm (1¼ inch) cubes.

Heat half the oil or butter in a heavy-based saucepan. Add a single layer of meat to the pan at a time and brown quickly on each side. Remove to a plate.

Reduce the heat and add the remaining oil to the pan. Gently fry the onion until translucent. Add the garlic, celery and carrot and fry for a few minutes longer.

Stir in the tomatoes, tomato paste, wine, cloves, bay leaf, most of the parsley and 250 ml (8½ fl oz/1 cup) water. Return the meat to the pan. Add the sugar and season with salt and pepper. Cover and simmer gently for 45 minutes for lamb, or 1¼ hours for beef.

Wash the broad beans well, then top and tail them, pulling off the strings at the same time. Cut into 8 cm (3¼ inch) lengths, then add them to the stew. Cover and simmer for a further 30–45 minutes, or until the meat is tender.

Sprinkle with the remaining parsley. Serve hot with a tossed salad and crusty bread.

❀ *Note: Any one of the following vegetables can be used instead of broad beans. Use the same quantity unless otherwise specified.*

· Green beans: Top, tail and string if necessary.

· Green peas: Shell 1 kg (2 lb 3 oz) fresh green peas, or use 310 g (10¾ oz/2 cups) frozen peas.

· Celery: Omit celery from the basic recipe. Cut ½ bunch celery into 8 cm (3¼ inch) lengths and blanch in boiling salted water for 5 minutes.

· Zucchini (courgettes): Top and tail, then cut into 1 cm (½ inch) slices.

· Cauliflower: Break 1 small head of cauliflower into florets. Soak in salted water, drain and rinse.

· Potatoes: Peel 750 g (1 lb 10 oz) potatoes. Cut into quarters.

· Okra: Prepare as directed on page 8.

ARNAKI SE FILLO
Lamb in fillo
SERVES: 6

This is one of the ways in which a basic Greek recipe can be revamped to produce a really superb dish. Basically it is Ami Palikari (Lamb Bandit Style).

Traditionally, the food was wrapped in paper before cooking so that the cooking aromas would not betray the presence of the bandits. Nowadays foil has replaced the paper.

This recipe goes one step further and makes the individual parcel totally edible by using fillo pastry. Many Greek restaurateurs make use of fillo in this way in similar recipes.

6 boneless lamb leg steaks, about 2 cm (¾ inch) thick

freshly ground black pepper, to season

40 g (1½ oz) butter, or 2 tablespoons oil

2 onions, sliced

1 garlic clove, crushed

12 sheets fillo pastry

125 g (4 oz/½ cup) butter, melted

salt, to season

3 tomatoes, peeled (see page 528) and sliced

1 teaspoon rigani or oregano

125 g (4 oz) feta cheese, cut into 6 slices

flat-leaf parsley sprigs, to garnish

Preheat the oven to 200°C (400°F/Gas 6).

Trim the steaks of most of the fat and shape them neatly — the trimmings can be used in a minced (ground) lamb dish. Season with pepper.

Heat the butter or oil in a large frying pan and brown the steaks quickly on each side — do not cook them through. Lift them out into a dish and leave until cool.

Add the onion to the pan and gently fry until translucent. Add the garlic and remove from the heat.

Brush a sheet of fillo pastry with the melted butter and place another sheet on top, brushing again with butter. Fold the sheet in half to make almost a square. Put it aside and cover with a dry tea towel (dish towel), then one dampened with warm water. Repeat with remaining fillo to give six squares.

Leaving the remaining pastry covered, take one square and brush the top with butter.

Place a lamb steak in the centre and season lightly with salt. Top with the onion mixture and cover with two tomato slices. Sprinkle with a little rigani or oregano and some salt and pepper. Place a slice of feta on top.

Bring up the ends of the pastry and double-fold them over the top. Fold in the ends as you would a package, then tuck the ends underneath; this is known as the 'chemist's (druggist's) fold'. Place the parcel on a greased baking tray. Repeat with the remaining ingredients.

Brush the tops and sides of the parcels lightly with more melted butter and bake for 15 minutes.

Serve immediately if possible, though they will survive in the oven with the heat turned off for about 10 minutes.

Garnish with parsley and serve with green beans or zucchini (courgette) dressed with olive oil and lemon juice.

❦ *Note: Medallions of lamb cut from a trimmed loin can be used instead of the steaks. If cut from a small lamb, you will require 12, placing two in each package.*

KOKORETSI TIS SOUVLAS
Skewered variety meats
SERVES: 6, MORE AS AN APPETISER

This is an everyday version of the *kokoretsi* prepared and cooked on Easter Sunday, using lamb innards. Normally other innards are added, but they are omitted here as they are not readily available.

250 g (9 oz) lamb sweetbreads

1½ lemons

500 g (1 lb 2 oz) lamb liver

2 lamb hearts

2 lamb kidneys, cut in half

sausage casings

Marinade

1 small onion, grated

juice of 2 lemons

125 ml (4 fl oz/½ cup) olive oil

4 bay leaves, each torn into 3 pieces

1 teaspoon dried rigani or oregano

2 tablespoons chopped flat-leaf parsley

1 teaspoon salt

freshly ground black pepper, to season

Rinse the sweetbreads, place in a saucepan and cover with cold water. Add the juice of ½ lemon. Bring to the boil, then drain.

Place the liver, hearts and kidneys in a bowl. Cover with cold water and add the juice of 1 lemon. Soak for 30 minutes, then drain.

Remove the skin from the liver and trim the larger tubes from the liver and heart. Cut out the fatty core from the kidneys. Cut the meats and sweetbreads into 3 cm (1¼ inch) pieces and place in a glass or ceramic bowl.

Combine the marinade ingredients and pour over the meats. Cover and marinate in the refrigerator for at least 2 hours. Meanwhile, soak the sausage casings in cold water.

Thread the meats alternately onto six skewers, adding 2 bay leaf pieces to each skewer among the meats. Drain the sausage casings and wind a length of casing around the meats on each skewer, tucking the ends in to keep the casings in place.

Grill slowly over glowing barbecue coals for 15–20 minutes, turning the skewers frequently and brushing occasionally with the marinade. During this time, you may need to adjust the height of the barbecue grill or move the skewers to a cooler part of the fire so they cook slowly. Serve hot.

KREATOPITA
Lamb pie

SERVES: 6

450 g (1 lb/3 cups) plain (all-purpose) flour
pinch of salt
125 g (4 oz/½ cup) butter
1 small egg
1 tablespoon milk
sesame seeds, for sprinkling

Filling

60 g (2 oz/¼ cup) butter
1 large onion, finely chopped
1 kg (2 lb 3 oz) lean boneless lamb, from the leg,
    cut into 2 cm (¾ inch) cubes
salt and freshly ground black pepper, to season
250 g (9 oz/1 cup) Mizithra (page 27) or ricotta cheese
75 g (2½ oz/½ cup) crumbled feta cheese
3 tablespoons chopped flat-leaf parsley
1 teaspoon chopped dill

Sift the flour and salt into a bowl and rub in the butter with your fingertips until the mixture resembles fine crumbs. Sprinkle in 185 ml (6½ fl oz/¾ cup) water and mix to a soft, workable dough. Knead until smooth, then cover and leave to rest while making the filling.

Melt the butter in a saucepan and gently fry the onion until translucent. Increase the heat to high, add the lamb and stir for 5 minutes, or until the meat loses its red colour.

Reduce the heat to low. Stir in 250 ml (8½ fl oz/1 cup) cold water and season with salt and pepper. Cover and simmer gently for 45 minutes. There should be little liquid left in the pan; if necessary, remove the lid and simmer until reduced.

Meanwhile, preheat the oven to 200°C (400°F/Gas 6).

Turn the lamb into a bowl and mix in the cheeses and herbs. Adjust the seasoning with salt and pepper.

Divide the pastry into two portions, one slightly larger than the other. Roll out the larger piece and use it to line a 23 cm (9 inch) greased pie plate. Spread the filling in the pastry.

Roll out the remaining pastry to fit the top. Moisten the edges of the pastry with water and lift it in place, over the top of the pie. Press the edges to seal, then trim the pastry and crimp the edge.

Beat the egg with the milk and brush it over the top of the pie. Sprinkle with sesame seeds and bake for 30 minutes, or until golden brown. Serve hot, cut into wedges.

YEMISTA ME LAHANO
« Stuffed cabbage leaves

SERVES: 6

1 tablespoon olive oil

1 large onion, finely chopped

1 kg (2 lb 3 oz) minced (ground) beef or lamb

75 g (2½ oz/⅓ cup) short-grain white rice

1 tomato, peeled (see page 528) and chopped

2 tablespoons chopped flat-leaf parsley

1 teaspoon chopped dill or mint, plus extra to garnish

⅛ teaspoon ground cinnamon

salt and freshly ground black pepper, to season

24 cabbage leaves

500 ml (17 fl oz/2 cups) hot stock or water

1 tablespoon butter

1 tablespoon cornflour (cornstarch)

2 eggs, separated

juice of 1 lemon

Heat the oil in a frying pan and gently fry the onion until soft. Tip the onion into a bowl and add the meat, rice, tomato, herbs and cinnamon. Season with salt and pepper and mix well using your hands. Divide into 24 portions.

Blanch the cabbage leaves in a saucepan of boiling salted water for 5 minutes, or until softened. Drain until cooled. Cut out the thick centre of the larger leaves, and cut any very large leaves in half.

Working with one leaf at a time, place one portion of the meat mixture on the base of the leaf. Turn up the base, fold in the sides and wrap firmly into a neat roll. Repeat with the remaining ingredients.

Line a deep saucepan with the trimmings from the cabbage leaves. Pack the rolls in close together, seam side down. Add the stock and butter and season with salt and pepper.

Invert a heavy plate on top of the rolls and cover the pan tightly. Simmer gently for 1½ hours.

Carefully drain off the stock, into a small saucepan. Reduce the stock to 375 ml (12½ fl oz/1½ cups) over medium–high heat. Mix the cornflour to a paste with a little cold water. Stir it into the stock and boil for 1 minute, until thickened.

Beat the egg whites in a bowl until stiff. Add the egg yolks and beat thoroughly. Gradually beat in the lemon juice, then the boiling stock.

Return the sauce to the saucepan, place over low heat and stir constantly until the egg is cooked — do not allow to boil.

Arrange the rolls on a heated serving dish and spoon some of the sauce over them. Garnish with chopped dill or mint and serve the remaining sauce separately. Serve with mashed potatoes.

❀ *Note: Grape vine leaves may be used instead of cabbage. You will need about 40, as they are smaller and will hold less filling.*

KOLOKITHAKIA YEMISTA
Stuffed zucchini

Follow the recipe for Yemista Me Lahano (left), substituting 24 zucchini (courgettes) for the cabbage leaves. Cut off the stems, wash the zucchini and cut 1 cm (½ inch) off the stem end. Reserve the ends. Scoop out the centres with a small spoon or zucchini corer, then fill with the meat mixture. Use the reserved ends as corks and press one in each opening. Layer them in the saucepan and cook as directed.

MELOPITA
Honey pie
SERVES: 8–10

225 g (8 oz/1½ cups) plain (all-purpose) flour
pinch of salt
1 tablespoon caster (superfine) sugar
90 g (3 oz/⅓ cup) butter, cubed
1 egg, separated
2 teaspoons lemon juice
ground cinnamon for dusting

Filling

500 g (1 lb 2 oz/2 cups) Mizithra (page 27) or ricotta cheese
175 g (6 oz/½ cup) honey
1 tablespoon caster (superfine) sugar
3 eggs
2 teaspoons lemon juice
1 teaspoon ground cinnamon

Sift the flour, salt and sugar into a mixing bowl. Rub in the butter with your fingertips until the mixture resembles fine crumbs.

Beat together the egg yolk, lemon juice and 2 tablespoons cold water. Add to the flour mixture and mix through using a knife. When the dough clings together, knead lightly until smooth. Cover and leave to rest for 30 minutes.

Meanwhile, preheat the oven to 200°C (400°F/Gas 6).

To make the filling, beat the cheese in a mixing bowl until smooth, then gradually beat in the honey and sugar. Beat in the eggs, lemon juice and cinnamon.

Roll out the pastry on a lightly floured work surface to a 30 cm (12 inch) circle. Line a greased 25 cm (10 inch) springform tin or pie plate with the pastry. Lightly beat the egg white and brush a little over the pastry.

Pour the filling into the pastry case and smooth the top. Transfer to the oven and bake for 15 minutes.

Reduce the oven temperature to 170°C (340°F/Gas 3) and bake for a further 30 minutes, or until the filling has set.

Turn off the heat and open the oven door slightly. Leave the pie in the oven until cool.

Dust with the cinnamon and serve cut into wedges, or in traditional diamond-shaped pieces.

Store in a covered container in the refrigerator and bring back to room temperature before serving.

GALATOBOUREKO
Milk pie

SERVES: 12

1 litre (34 fl oz/4 cups) milk

165 g (5½ oz/¾ cup) sugar

90 g (3 oz/¾ cup) fine semolina (farina)

60 g (2 oz/¼ cup) butter

grated zest of ½ lemon

1 piece of cinnamon bark

pinch of salt

5 eggs, lightly beaten

1 teaspoon vanilla essence

10 sheets fillo pastry

185 g (6½ oz/¾ cup) unsalted butter, melted

Syrup

220 g (8 oz/1 cup) sugar

1 piece of cinnamon bark

2 teaspoons lemon juice

Preheat the oven to 180°C (350°F/Gas 4).

Mix together the milk, sugar, semolina, butter, lemon zest, cinnamon and salt in a heavy-based saucepan. Heat until thickened, stirring constantly. Let the custard bubble gently over low heat for 5 minutes.

Remove from the heat and remove the cinnamon. Cover the custard with a piece of buttered greaseproof (parchment) paper to prevent a skin forming. When cooled, mix in the eggs and vanilla.

Butter a 23 × 33 cm (9 × 13 inch) baking dish. Place half the fillo pastry sheets in the dish, brushing each sheet with the melted butter.

Pour in the custard and top with the remaining pastry sheets, again brushing each with butter as you place them in position. Brush the top with the remaining butter. Using a sharp knife or stanley knife, score through the top three sheets in 8 cm (3¼ inch) squares or diamonds. Sprinkle the top lightly with water and trim the edges.

Bake for 45 minutes, or until the pastry is golden brown and the custard is set when tested with a knife. Remove from the oven and leave to completely cool in the dish.

To make the syrup, dissolve the sugar in 185 ml (6½ fl oz/¾ cup) water over low heat, then increase the heat to medium and bring to the boil. Add the cinnamon and lemon juice and boil for 10 minutes.

Cool the syrup to lukewarm before straining and pouring over the cool pie. Leave until cold before serving.

KATAIFI ME KREMA I
« Shredded pastry with custard I
SERVES: 8

Kataifi is made by pouring a batter through a perforated plate onto a hot surface. The resulting pastry strands dry sufficiently for handling and they are scooped off immediately. When cooked, *Kataifi* looks rather like shredded wheat. It is available from Greek and Lebanese delicatessens.

500 g (1 lb 2 oz) kataifi pastry (see page 521)
185 g (6½ oz/¾ cup) unsalted butter, melted

Custard
1 litre (34 fl oz/4 cups) milk
90 g (3 oz/¾ cup) cornflour (cornstarch)
4 eggs, beaten
pinch of salt
110 g (3¾ oz/½ cup) sugar
1 teaspoon vanilla essence

Syrup
440 g (15½ oz/2 cups) sugar
1 thin strip of lemon rind
1 piece of cinnamon bark
3 teaspoons lemon juice

Preheat the oven to 190°C (375°F/Gas 5).

To make the custard, combine the milk and cornflour in a heavy-based saucepan. Blend in the eggs and add the salt and sugar. Place over medium heat and stir constantly until thickened and bubbling. Remove from the heat and stir in the vanilla. Cover the top of the custard with buttered greaseproof (parchment) paper to prevent a skin forming.

Place the *kataifi* in a large bowl and gently separate the strands with your fingers.

Grease a 20 × 28 cm (8 × 11 inch) baking dish with some of the melted butter. Put half the *kataifi* in the base, pressing it down to make it compact. Drizzle 60 g (2 oz/¼ cup) of the melted butter evenly over it.

Pour the custard filling over the *kataifi*, spreading it evenly. Top with the remaining *kataifi*. Spread evenly and pat down gently. Pour the remaining melted butter evenly over the top.

Bake for 45 minutes, or until golden brown. Remove from the oven and leave until cool.

To make the syrup, dissolve the sugar in 375 ml (12½ fl oz/ 1½ cups) water over medium heat. Add the lemon rind and cinnamon and bring to the boil. Add the lemon juice and boil over medium heat for 15 minutes, skimming when necessary. Do not stir once the syrup is boiling.

Strain the hot syrup over the cooled pastry and leave until cold. Cut into diamond shapes to serve.

KATAIFI ME KREMA II
Shredded pastry with custard II
SERVES: 8

The previous recipe is the traditional way in which this dessert is made. As the custard and syrup soften the *kataifi*, many good cooks use the following method for a crisp finish.

Preheat the oven to 190°C (375°F/Gas 5). Prepare the syrup as in the previous recipe and leave until cool.

Place the *kataifi* in a bowl and loosen the strands. Pour on 125 g (4 oz/½ cup) melted unsalted butter and mix with your fingers to coat the strands. Spread the *kataifi* in two buttered 20 × 28 cm (8 × 11 inch) straight-sided baking dishes and press down to make it compact. Bake for 20–25 minutes, or until golden, taking care it does not become too brown.

Remove from the oven and pour the cooled syrup evenly over the hot *kataifi* in each dish. Cover each dish with a tea towel (dish towel) so the *kataifi* softens slightly; otherwise it will be difficult to cut.

Make the custard as directed in the previous recipe. While it is still hot, pour the custard onto the *kataifi* in one dish. Invert the other dish of *kataifi* on top of the custard.

Leave uncovered until cool, then cut into diamond shapes to serve.

KATAIFI
Shredded nut pastries

MAKES: 40 PIECES

500 g (1 lb 2 oz) kataifi pastry (see page 521)
250 g (9 oz/1 cup) unsalted butter, melted

Nut filling

115 g (4 oz/1 cup) coarsely ground walnuts
100 g (3½ oz/1 cup) coarsely ground almonds
115 g (4 oz/½ cup) caster (superfine) sugar
1 teaspoon ground cinnamon
¼ teaspoon ground cloves
1 egg white, lightly beaten
1 tablespoon brandy

Syrup

440 g (15½ oz/2 cups) sugar
1 thin strip of lemon rind
1 teaspoon lemon juice
4 cloves
1 piece of cinnamon bark
1 tablespoon honey

Preheat the oven to 180°C (350°F/Gas 4).

Take one-eighth of the pastry strands and spread them out on a board to make an 18 × 25 cm (7 × 10 inch) rectangle, with the strands running roughly lengthways. Using a pastry brush, dab some melted butter over the strands.

Combine the nut filling ingredients and spread about 2 tablespoons of filling along one narrow edge of the pastry strands. Roll up firmly into a neat roll. Repeat with the remaining ingredients.

Place the rolls close together in a 20 × 30 cm (8 × 12 inch) slab cake tin or baking dish. Brush the top with the remaining butter. Bake in the oven, one shelf above the centre, for 50–55 minutes, or until golden brown.

Meanwhile, make the syrup. Dissolve the sugar in 375 ml (12½ fl oz/1½ cups) water over medium heat. Add the lemon rind and juice, cloves and cinnamon. Boil over medium heat for 10 minutes. Stir in the honey, then strain and cool.

Pour the cooled syrup over the hot pastries and place a folded cloth on top. Leave until cool.

Cut each roll diagonally into five pieces if desired.

❀ *Note: For an alternative shaping, take a small handful of pastry strands and spread out fairly compactly on the board, with the strands running towards you as much as possible. Dab with melted butter. Mould a tablespoon of nut filling into a short sausage shape and place on one end. Roll up firmly into a neat roll and place in a baking dish. Repeat with the remaining ingredients. Make about 30 rolls, each about 5 cm (2 inches) long, then bake and finish with syrup as before.*

THIPLES
Fried rosettes
MAKES: 30

3 eggs

1 tablespoon caster (superfine) sugar

pinch of salt

225 g (8 oz/1½ cups) plain (all-purpose) flour,
  plus extra for dusting

peanut or corn oil, for deep-frying

warmed honey, for drizzling

toasted sesame seeds, for sprinkling

ground cinnamon, for dusting

In a mixing bowl, beat the eggs until frothy, then add the
sugar and salt and beat until thick. Sift the flour and gradually
stir into the eggs with a wooden spoon — the dough should
be slightly sticky. Turn the dough onto a lightly floured work
surface, dust with flour and knead lightly.

Divide the dough into two balls. Place one ball of dough on
a floured surface, dust the top with flour and roll out thinly
as instructed on page 15. Using a fluted pastry wheel or sharp
knife, cut the dough into strips 2.5 cm (1 inch) wide and 50 cm
(20 inches) long.

Working with one strip of pastry at a time, pinch the sides
together at 2 cm (¾ inch) intervals to form little boat-shaped
depressions. On a flat surface, shape the strip into a flat coil,
beginning at the centre. Shape the coil loosely and pinch the
pastry strip firmly together at intervals to hold the shape.
Repeat with the remaining dough.

Meanwhile, heat your deep-frying oil to 200°C (400°F), or
until a cube of bread dropped into the oil browns in 5 seconds,
in a deep-fryer or heavy-based saucepan.

Fry the rosettes two at a time in the hot oil until lightly
golden, placing them in the oil upside down and turning to
cook evenly. Drain on paper towels.

Place a layer of pastries on a platter and drizzle the honey
into the depressions, letting it fall off the end of a fork.
Sprinkle with the sesame seeds and dust with cinnamon. Pile
more pastries on top, finishing each layer with honey, sesame
seeds and cinnamon. Serve warm or cold.

PASTELLI
Sesame and honey candies
MAKES: 30

220 g (8 oz/1 cup) sugar

350 g (12 oz/1 cup) honey

310 g (10¾ oz/2 cups) sesame seeds

Combine the sugar and honey in a heavy-based saucepan with
60 ml (2 fl oz/¼ cup) water. Stir occasionally over low heat
until the sugar has dissolved.

Increase the heat to medium and bring to the boil. Allow to
boil for about 15 minutes, until the mixture reaches the soft
ball stage — when a small amount dropped into cold water
forms a soft ball. If you have a sugar thermometer, cook to
115°C (240°F).

Stir in the sesame seeds and return to the boil. Allow to boil
for 15 minutes, or until the seeds turn golden and a little of the
syrup dropped into water forms a hard ball — 130°C (265°F) on
a sugar thermometer. Take care not to overcook or the sesame
seeds will brown too much, spoiling the flavour.

Pour into an oiled 18 × 28 cm (7 × 11 inch) slab cake tin, or
onto an oiled marble slab, shaping the mixture into a rectangle
of that size with a spatula.

When almost cool, cut into squares, triangles or fingers.

Cut again when completely cold and wrap pieces in waxed
paper or cellophane.

BAKLAVA
Baklava

MAKES: 30 PIECES

185 g (6½ oz/¾ cup) unsalted butter, melted

20 sheets fillo pastry

250 g (9 oz/2 cups) finely chopped walnuts

155 g (5 oz/1 cup) finely chopped almonds

55 g (2 oz/¼ cup) caster (superfine) sugar

2 teaspoons ground cinnamon

⅛ teaspoon ground cloves

Syrup

330 g (11½ oz/1½ cups) sugar

90 g (3 oz/¼ cup) honey

thinly peeled strip of lemon rind

1 small piece of cinnamon bark

3 cloves

2 teaspoons lemon juice

Preheat the oven to 160°C (320°F/Gas 2–3).

Take a 23 × 33 × 5 cm (9 × 13 × 2 inch) baking dish and brush the base and sides with melted butter. Place nine sheets of fillo pastry one at a time into the dish, brushing each with melted butter.

Mix together the nuts, sugar and spices, then spread half the mixture over the pastry. Top with another two sheets of fillo, brushing each with butter. Spread the remaining nuts on top and finish with the remaining fillo, brushing each sheet as before.

Trim the pastry edges and brush the top with butter. Using a sharp knife, cut the baklava into diamond shapes, cutting through to the base. Sprinkle the top lightly with water to prevent the top layers curling upwards.

Bake on the centre shelf of the oven for 30 minutes. Move up one shelf and bake for a further 30 minutes. Cover with greased brown paper or foil if the top colours too quickly — the pastry must be allowed to cook thoroughly.

When the baklava goes into the oven, make the syrup. Place the sugar and honey in a heavy-based saucepan with 375 ml (12½ fl oz/1½ cups) water. Stir over medium heat until the sugar has dissolved. Add the remaining syrup ingredients, bring to the boil and boil for 15 minutes. Strain and cool.

Spoon the cooled syrup evenly over the hot baklava. Leave for several hours before cutting into serving portions.

HALVAS FOURNO
Semolina cake

SERVES: 8

125 g (4 oz/½ cup) butter

170 g (6 oz/¾ cup) caster (superfine) sugar

grated zest of 1 lemon

3 eggs

185 g (6½ oz/1½ cups) fine semolina (farina)

150 g (5 oz/1 cup) plain (all-purpose) flour

1 tablespoon baking powder

125 ml (4 fl oz/½ cup) milk

80 g (3 oz/½ cup) finely chopped almonds, toasted

blanched split almonds, for decorating

Syrup

550 g (1 lb 3½ oz/2½ cups) sugar

2 tablespoons lemon juice

Preheat the oven to 180°C (350°F/Gas 4).

Cream the butter, sugar and lemon zest until light and fluffy. Beat in the eggs one at a time.

Sift the semolina, flour and baking powder twice, then fold into the butter mixture alternately with the milk. Mix in the chopped almonds.

Spread the batter into a buttered 18 × 28 cm (7 × 11 inch) slab cake tin. Arrange the split almonds in rows on top of the batter. Bake for 50 minutes, or until the cake is golden and shrinks slightly from the sides of the tin.

Meanwhile, dissolve the sugar in 750 ml (25 fl oz/3 cups) water over low heat. Add the lemon juice and bring to the boil. Boil over medium heat for 20 minutes, then leave until cool.

Pour the cooled syrup over the hot cake; the syrup will penetrate more evenly if the cake surface is pricked with a fine skewer before pouring the syrup over.

Leave in the tin until cool, then cut into squares or diamond shapes for serving.

KARITHOPITA
Walnut cake

SERVES: 8

125 g (4 oz/½ cup) butter

170 g (6 oz/¾ cup) caster (superfine) sugar

4 eggs, separated

225 g (8 oz/1½ cups) plain (all-purpose) flour

1 tablespoon baking powder

1 teaspoon ground cinnamon

pinch of salt

250 g (9 oz/2 cups) finely chopped walnuts

Syrup

330 g (11½ oz/1½ cups) sugar

1 piece of cinnamon bark

1 teaspoon lemon juice

1 tablespoon brandy

Preheat the oven to 180°C (350°F/Gas 4).

Cream the butter and sugar until light and fluffy. Add the egg yolks and beat in well.

In a separate bowl, beat the egg whites until stiff.

Sift the flour, baking powder, cinnamon and salt twice. Fold into the butter mixture, then mix in about one-third of the beaten egg white. Fold in the walnuts. Lastly, fold in the remaining egg white, using a metal spoon to combine the mixture evenly and quickly.

Spread the batter evenly into a buttered 23 × 30 cm (9 × 12 inch) baking dish. Bake for 45 minutes, or until a skewer inserted in the centre of the cake comes out clean.

Meanwhile, dissolve the sugar in 375 ml (12½ fl oz/1½ cups) water over low heat. Add the cinnamon and lemon juice and bring to the boil. Allow to boil for 10 minutes, then remove from the heat. Stir in the brandy, cool and strain into a jug.

Pour the cold syrup evenly over the hot cake and leave until cool. Cut into squares or diamond-shaped pieces to serve. Delicious served with whipped unsweetened cream.

TAHINOPITA
Tahini cake

SERVES: 8–10

This cake is frequently made during Lent as it contains no animal products. Peanut butter – the smooth, creamy variety – may be used instead of tahini.

1 tablespoon vegetable margarine or peanut oil

270 g (9½ oz/1 cup) tahini

230 g (8 oz/1 cup) caster (superfine) sugar

grated zest of 1 orange

185 ml (6½ fl oz/¾ cup) strained orange juice

335 g (11½ oz/2¼ cups) plain (all-purpose) flour,
    plus extra for dusting

3 teaspoons baking powder

½ teaspoon bicarbonate of soda (baking soda)

½ teaspoon ground allspice

pinch of salt

60 g (2 oz/½ cup) finely chopped walnuts

60 g (2 oz/½ cup) sultanas (golden raisins)

Preheat the oven to 180°C (350°F/Gas 4).

Grease a 20 cm (8 inch) tube tin (bundt tin) or a 20 × 30 cm (8 × 12 inch) slab cake tin with melted margarine or oil. Chill in the refrigerator until required.

Beat the tahini, sugar and orange zest in a mixing bowl for 10 minutes. Gradually beat in the orange juice.

Sift the flour, baking powder, bicarbonate of soda, allspice and salt twice, then fold into the tahini mixture. Mix in the walnuts and sultanas.

Dust the chilled cake tin with flour. Spoon the cake batter into the tin, spreading it evenly. Knock the base of the tin on the work surface to settle the batter.

Bake for 55–60 minutes if using a tube tin, or about 45 minutes if using a slab tin. When cooked, invert the cake in its tin onto a cake rack and leave for 2–3 minutes before lifting the tin from the cake.

Cool the cake and store in a sealed container. Cut into slices or squares to serve.

KOPENHAI
Copenhagen almond torte
MAKES: 28–30 PIECES

185 g (6½ oz/¾ cup) butter

55 g (2 oz/¼ cup) caster (superfine) sugar

grated zest of 1 orange

2 egg yolks

375 g (13 oz/2½ cups) plain (all-purpose) flour

pinch of salt

Almond filling

6 eggs, separated

115 g (4 oz/½ cup) caster (superfine) sugar

¼ teaspoon almond essence

35 g (1¼ oz/¼ cup) plain (all-purpose) flour

½ teaspoon baking powder

200 g (7 oz/2 cups) ground almonds

pinch of salt

To finish

8 sheets fillo pastry

60 g (2 oz/¼ cup) unsalted butter, melted

440 g (15½ oz/2 cups) sugar

1 thinly peeled strip of orange rind

1 thinly peeled strip of lemon rind

2 teaspoons lemon juice

2 pieces of cinnamon bark

Preheat the oven to 190°C (375°F/Gas 5).

Cream the butter and sugar with the orange zest until light and fluffy; beat in the egg yolks. Sift the flour and salt and stir into the butter mixture to form a soft dough.

Lightly grease a round 30 cm (12 inch) dish (a *tapsi*) or a 25 × 30 cm (10 × 12 inch) baking dish. Roll out the pastry on a floured work surface and place in the dish to line the base and sides. As this pastry moulds easily, any tears can be pressed together. An alternative is to put the pastry in the dish without rolling, and press it over the base and sides with your fingers; even it out by rolling over it with a straight-sided glass.

Bake for 15–20 minutes, or until lightly coloured. Remove from the oven and leave to cool.

Reduce the oven temperature to 180°C (350°F/Gas 4).

To make the almond filling, beat the egg yolks, sugar and almond essence until thick and light. Sift the flour with the baking powder and mix in the ground almonds. Lightly fold the mixture into the beaten egg yolks.

Beat the egg whites and salt until stiff, but not dry, then lightly fold into the almond mixture. Pour into the pastry-lined dish.

To finish, brush a fillo pastry sheet with melted butter. Top with another sheet and more butter. Continue until all the sheets are used, leaving the top sheet unbuttered. Lift the sheets over the almond filling and trim the fillo edges in line with the pastry crust, using kitchen scissors.

Brush the top with the remaining butter. Using a sharp knife or stanley knife, make slits through the top two or three sheets, running the length of the dish and about 4 cm (1½ inches) apart. Bake for 45 minutes, or until the top is golden and the filling set.

Meanwhile, dissolve the sugar in 250 ml (8½ fl oz/1 cup) water over medium heat. Add the fruit rinds, lemon juice and cinnamon and bring to the boil. Allow to boil for 10 minutes, then strain and leave to cool.

When the torte is cooked, cut through the slits in the pastry, down to the bottom crust. Pour the cooled syrup over the hot torte, and leave to cool. Cut diagonally to give diamond-shaped pieces for serving.

KOURABIETHES
Shortbread cookies or almond shortbreads

MAKES: 40

250 g (9 oz/1 cup) unsalted butter

3 tablespoons icing (confectioners') sugar, sifted

1 egg yolk

1 tablespoon brandy

80 g (3 oz/½ cup) finely chopped toasted blanched almonds

375 g (13 oz/2½ cups) plain (all-purpose) flour

1 teaspoon baking powder

To finish

40 cloves

250 g (9 oz/2 cups) icing (confectioners') sugar

Preheat the oven to 160°C (320F°/Gas 2–3).

Melt the butter in a saucepan until the bubbles subside and the sediment is golden brown — do not allow to burn. Pour the butter and sediment into a mixing bowl.

When the butter has solidified, add the icing sugar and beat with electric beaters until light and fluffy. Add the egg yolk and brandy and beat well.

Stir in the almonds. Sift the flour and baking powder twice, then mix lightly into the butter mixture. Knead by hand until smooth.

Break off small pieces of the dough the size of large walnuts. Shape into crescents, or roll into balls. Place on a flat surface and pinch the tops twice, making four indentations, and at the same time flattening the cookies slightly.

To finish, insert a clove in the top of each cookie. Place on ungreased baking trays and bake for 20 minutes, or until lightly coloured but not browned. Leave to cool on the baking trays for 10 minutes.

Sift some icing sugar over greaseproof (parchment) paper and lift the warm cookies onto this. Sift more icing sugar over the top and sides.

When cool, transfer the cookies to a container and sift the remaining sugar over the top. Seal and store for 2 days before serving to improve the flavour.

❀ *Note: The melting and light browning of the butter is not traditional, but it does give a delightful flavour to the cookies. Many excellent Greek cooks use this method, but omit this step if you wish.*

KOULOURAKIA
Butter cookies

MAKES: 70

Every Greek home has a container of *koulourakia* on hand. They are dipped into the morning coffee and served up to any visitors who might drop in. My mother used to make hers shaped into rings and sprinkled with sugar. We would take a tin of them to school on cake sale days; we called them doughnuts (influenced by American movies – who would argue with us?) and they were a sell-out.

- 250 g (9 oz/1 cup) butter
- 230 g (8 oz/1 cup) caster (superfine) sugar
- 1 teaspoon vanilla essence
- 3 eggs, beaten
- 750 g (1 lb 10 oz/5 cups) plain (all-purpose) flour
- 3 teaspoons baking powder
- ½ teaspoon ground cinnamon
- ½ teaspoon ground cloves
- 60 ml (2 fl oz/¼ cup) milk, plus extra for glazing
- 80 g (3 oz/½ cup) toasted sesame seeds

Cream the butter and sugar with the vanilla until light and fluffy. Reserve 1 tablespoon of the beaten eggs for glazing the cookies; add the remainder gradually to the butter mixture, beating well.

Sift the flour, baking powder, cinnamon and cloves twice. Stir into the butter mixture alternately with the milk to form a soft dough. Knead lightly until smooth. If the dough is sticky, cover it and refrigerate for 1 hour.

Preheat the oven to 190°C (375°F/Gas 5).

Scatter the sesame seeds lightly over a work surface. Form pieces of the dough into thick pencil shapes and roll them over the sesame seeds to lightly coat. Double the dough over and twist, or form into rings, figure eights or coils.

Place on greased baking trays and glaze with the reserved egg, beaten with a little milk.

Bake for 15–20 minutes, or until golden brown. Cool on a wire rack and store in an airtight container.

❀ *Variation: Roll the dough in sugar instead of sesame seeds, and glaze lightly with milk.*

MELOMAKARONA
Honey-dipped cookies

MAKES: 60

These are the most delicious of Greek cookies. You do not need to use the nut filling – in fact, when I make them now, I press a walnut quarter into the centre of each and reshape them into ovals.

250 g (9 oz/1 cup) butter

170 g (6 oz/¾ cup) caster (superfine) sugar

grated zest of 1 orange

185 ml (6½ fl oz/¾ cup) corn or peanut oil

900 g (2 lb/6 cups) plain (all-purpose) flour

1 tablespoon baking powder

185 ml (6½ fl oz/¾ cup) orange juice

Nut filling, optional

1 tablespoon honey

1–2 teaspoons orange juice

1½ teaspoons ground cinnamon

185 g (6½ oz/1½ cups) finely chopped walnuts

2 drops of almond essence

Syrup

220 g (8 oz/1 cup) sugar

90 g (3 oz/¼ cup) honey

1 piece of cinnamon bark

2 teaspoons lemon juice

Preheat the oven to 180°C (350°F/Gas 4).

Beat the butter and sugar with the orange zest until creamy. Gradually add the oil and continue beating until the mixture is very light and fluffy.

Sift the flour with the baking powder, then stir into the butter mixture alternately with the orange juice. Knead the dough lightly with your hands for 1 minute.

To make the nut filling, thin the honey with orange juice and mix with the remaining nut filling ingredients.

Take a scant tablespoon of dough at a time and flatten it a little. Place a teaspoon of the nut filling in the centre and fold the dough over to enclose. Shape into ovals, pinching the ends to a point. Decorate the tops with tines of a fork, or by crimping the cookies diagonally across the top in three rows with a special crimper (see note below).

Place on lightly greased baking trays and bake for 25–30 minutes, or until golden. Cool on wire racks.

To make the syrup, combine the sugar and honey in a saucepan with 250 ml (8½ fl oz/1 cup) water and stir over low heat until dissolved. Bring to the boil, add the cinnamon and lemon juice, then boil for 10 minutes over medium heat.

Dip the cookies into the boiling syrup, four at a time, turning them once; only those that are to be served immediately should be dipped. Leave them in the syrup for 10 seconds in all, or a little longer if well-soaked cookies are preferred. Lift out onto a wire rack set over a baking tray and leave until cool. During dipping, the syrup becomes thick after a while, so thin it with a little water.

If not using the nut filling, sprinkle the tops with some crushed walnuts or toasted sesame seeds and cinnamon.

Store the undipped cookies in an airtight container and dip when required. The syrup can be kept in a jar in the refrigerator.

❧ *Note: Icing crimpers will be familiar to many pastry cooks and cake decorators who work with icing (frosting). If you do not own a crimper, have the family handyman cut a piece of tin or aluminium plate, measuring 2.5 × 10 cm (1 × 4 inches). Bend the metal in half over a thin rod and cut six to eight evenly spaced saw-like teeth on the narrow edges. Curl the 'teeth' slightly inwards.*

FINIKIA
Semolina honey cookies

MAKES: 60

125 g (4 oz/½ cup) butter

115 g (4 oz/½ cup) caster (superfine) sugar

grated zest of 1 orange

125 ml (4 fl oz/½ cup) corn or peanut oil

375 g (13 oz/2½ cups) plain (all-purpose) flour

1 tablespoon baking powder

185 g (6½ oz/1½ cups) fine semolina (farina)

1 teaspoon ground cinnamon

pinch of ground cloves

125 ml (4 fl oz/½ cup) orange juice

toasted sesame seeds or chopped walnuts,
   for sprinkling

Syrup

220 g (8 oz/1 cup) sugar

175 g (6 oz/½ cup) honey

1 piece of cinnamon bark

2 teaspoons lemon juice

Preheat the oven to 180°C (350°F/Gas 4).

Cream the butter and sugar with the orange zest until light and fluffy. Gradually add the oil and continue to beat at high speed until the mixture thickens to a whipped-cream consistency.

Sift the flour and baking powder twice, then combine with the semolina and spices. Gradually add to the butter mixture, alternately with the orange juice. When combined, knead with your hands to form a firm dough.

Shape tablespoons of the dough into ovals. Place them on ungreased baking trays and pinch the ends to form torpedo shapes.

Bake for 25 minutes, or until golden brown and firm. Cool on the baking trays.

To make the syrup, combine the sugar and 250 ml (8½ fl oz/1 cup) water in a saucepan and stir over low heat until the sugar has dissolved. Add the honey, cinnamon and lemon juice and bring to the boil. Allow to boil over medium heat for 10 minutes, then remove the cinnamon.

Dip the cookies into the boiling syrup, three at a time; only those that are to be served immediately should be dipped. Turn them over in the syrup using two forks, then transfer to a wire rack placed over a baking tray. Sprinkle the dipped cookies with sesame seeds or chopped walnuts and serve.

Store the remainder in a sealed container for later dipping. The syrup can be kept in a jar in the refrigerator.

AMIGTHALOTA
Almond pears

MAKES: 30

Amigthalota are a speciality of the island of Hydra. Flavouring these almond delicacies with rose or orange flower water is a matter of taste. If you like these scented flavours, then omit the lemon zest from the recipe. Whatever flavouring is used, *amigthalota* make an excellent accompaniment for after-dinner coffee. Serve in petit-four cases.

butter, for greasing
300 g (10½ oz/3 cups) ground almonds
60 g (2 oz/½ cup) icing (confectioners') sugar
60 ml (2 fl oz/¼ cup) egg whites (about 2),
    lightly beaten
2 drops of almond essence
½ teaspoon grated lemon zest, optional
30 cloves

To finish
250 g (9 oz/2 cups) icing (confectioners') sugar
rose or orange flower water, optional

Preheat the oven to 160°C (320F°/Gas 2–3). Butter and flour a baking tray.

Combine the ground almonds and icing sugar. Add the lightly beaten egg whites, almond essence and lemon zest, if using. Mix to a firm dough with your hands.

Clean your hands and rub them with a little butter to stop the dough sticking while shaping. Break off small pieces of dough the size of walnuts and form them into pear shapes. Insert a whole clove in the top of each shape to resemble a stem, then place upright on the baking tray.

Bake for 20 minutes, covering the tops with brown paper if they begin to brown.

To finish, sift the icing sugar into a bowl and dip the hot *amigthalota* into it; you may brush a little rose or orange flower water onto the *amigthalota* before dipping them into the icing sugar. Place on a wire rack to cool.

Sift the remaining sugar from the bowl into a container and arrange the cooled almond pears upright in a single layer.

Sift more sugar thickly over the tops and sides. Seal and store for a day or two before serving to improve the flavour.

VASILOPITA
New Year bread
SERVES: 12

New Year bread is traditionally cut at midnight on New Year's Eve. After baking, a coin is inserted through a slit in the base. The person who finds the coin will have luck in the New Year. Long ago the coin was a gold one, and it was inserted into the dough before baking. Nowadays, because of the nickel content of coins, it is undesirable to bake a coin in the cake.

2 teaspoons active dried yeast

185 ml (6½ fl oz/¾ cup) lukewarm milk

3 eggs, beaten

1½ teaspoons grated orange zest

170 g (6 oz/¾ cup) caster (superfine) sugar

675 g (1 lb 8 oz/4½ cups) plain (all-purpose) flour

¼ teaspoon salt

½ teaspoon ground cinnamon

¼ teaspoon ground masticha (see page 522)

125 g (4 oz/½ cup) butter, melted

1 egg, beaten, for glazing

blanched split almonds, for decorating

Follow the same mixing, kneading and rising directions as for the Easter Bread recipe (page 95).

When the dough has doubled in size, punch it down and turn out onto a lightly floured work surface. Knead lightly and shape into a round loaf. Place on a large greased baking tray or in a greased 25 cm (10 inch) deep cake tin. Cover and leave to rise in a warm place until doubled — about 1½–2 hours.

Preheat the oven to 190°C (375°F/Gas 5).

Brush the bread with the beaten egg. Arrange the almonds in numbers on top, to denote the new year, pressing in lightly.

Bake for 45 minutes, or until the bread is golden brown and sounds hollow when tapped on the base. If it is browning too quickly, cover with a piece of greased brown paper.

Cool on a wire rack, then store in a sealed container.

PASKALINA AVGA
Red-dyed Easter eggs
MAKES: 12

Dyeing eggs is a ritual in every Greek and Cypriot Greek Orthodox household on the day before Good Friday. This is performed without great attention to detail by many cooks, and the eggs can end up cracked, rendering them useless for the ritual game on Easter Sunday morning of who can crack whose eggs, a game children delight in. Also, uneven dyeing frequently occurs with the usual method of boiling the eggs in the dye bath, so I suggest hard-boiling them first, then giving them a brief boil in the dye.

12 eggs, at room temperature

½ teaspoon powdered red dye (from Greek food stores)

125 ml (4 fl oz/½ cup) white vinegar

oil, for rubbing

Carefully place the eggs in a saucepan and cover with cold water. Place over gentle heat and bring slowly to the boil so the eggs don't crack. Leave to boil, uncovered, over medium heat for 15 minutes.

Meanwhile, place the dye in a heatproof bowl. Boil 1 litre (34 fl oz/4 cups) water in a saucepan large enough to hold all the eggs in a single layer. Pour 125 ml (4 fl oz/½ cup) of the boiling water over the dye and dissolve it, then pour it back into the saucepan. Add the vinegar and allow the dye to boil until the eggs are ready.

Lift the hot eggs into the dye bath using a slotted spoon. Increase the heat and let the eggs boil steadily for 2 minutes, stirring gently now and then so that the dye will take evenly.

Lift the eggs out with a slotted spoon and place them on folded paper towels to dry. Allow them to cool a little, then rub the eggs with an oil-soaked cloth to give a pleasant sheen.

❀ *Note: Another six eggs may be dyed in the same dye bath — add 2 tablespoons extra vinegar to the dye mixture.*

TSOUREKI TOU PASKA
Easter bread

SERVES: 10

2 teaspoons active dried yeast

125 ml (4 fl oz/½ cup) warm milk

2 eggs, beaten

1 teaspoon grated lemon zest

115 g (4 oz/½ cup) caster (superfine) sugar

525 g (1 lb 2½ oz/3½ cups) plain (all-purpose) flour

¼ teaspoon salt

1 teaspoon ground mahlepi or allspice

125 g (4 oz/½ cup) butter, melted

1 egg, beaten, for glazing

sesame seeds, for sprinkling

Dissolve the yeast in 60 ml (2 fl oz/¼ cup) of the milk. Add the remaining milk, eggs, lemon zest and sugar.

Sift 450 g (1 lb/3 cups) of the flour into a warm bowl with the salt and spice. Make a well in the centre. Pour in the yeast mixture, then stir to mix in a little flour to make a thin batter. Cover and leave in a warm place for 15 minutes, or until bubbles begin to form. Gradually add the warm melted butter.

Mix the dough with your hands until it comes away from the side of the bowl. Turn out onto a floured surface and knead until smooth and elastic, adding the remaining flour as required. Knead for 10 minutes.

Place the dough in a clean bowl brushed with melted butter. Turn the dough over to coat the top with butter. Cover the bowl with a cloth or plastic wrap and leave to rise in a warm place until doubled in size.

Punch down the dough and turn out onto a floured work surface. Knead lightly, then tear into three equal portions. Roll each into a rope about 30 cm (12 inches) long. Press the ends together and plait (braid) them loosely; press the ends together and tuck them under the loaf.

Place the dough on a greased baking tray, cover with a cloth and leave to rise in a warm place until doubled in size — about 1–2 hours, depending on the ambient warmth.

Preheat the oven to 190°C (375°F/Gas 5).

Brush the bread with the beaten egg and sprinkle with sesame seeds. Bake for 30 minutes, or until the bread is golden brown and sounds hollow when tapped on the base.

Cool on a wire rack, then store in a sealed container.

❀ *Variation: Proceed as above, but make each rope of dough about 50 cm (20 inches) long. Plait and shape them into a ring, pressing the two ends together. Place on a greased baking tray and press four Paskalina Avga (red-dyed eggs; see recipe on page 94) at intervals into the braid. Leave to rise, then glaze and bake as directed; the sesame seeds may be omitted.*

KYTHONI PELTES
Quince jelly

This method might seem complicated. Peels and cores are boiled separately to extract the pectin, which is necessary for setting. Of course, you can cook the quince together with the peels and cores with a lot less fuss, but the Greeks waste nothing: the pulp left after making the jelly makes a delightful confection called Kythonopasto (quince paste; page 98) — so it is worthwhile keeping the pulp free of peels and cores for this purpose.

1 kg (2 lb 3 oz) quinces

sugar

125 ml (4 fl oz/½ cup) lemon juice

2 unsprayed rose geranium leaves

Wash the quinces well to remove their fuzz, then peel and core them. Slice the quinces into a preserving pan and add 500 ml (17 fl oz/2 cups) water. Set aside, but do not be concerned if the quince discolours.

Place the peels and cores in a saucepan with another 500 ml (17 fl oz/2 cups) water and boil for 30 minutes. Strain, then top the liquid up to 500 ml (17 fl oz/2 cups) with more water. Now add this liquid to the sliced quinces in the preserving pan.

Bring to the boil and simmer gently for 1 hour, or until the quince flesh is very tender.

Scald a large piece of doubled muslin (cheesecloth), wring it out and drape it over a deep bowl.

Pour the quince and liquid into the cloth and gather up the ends. Tie with string and suspend over a bowl. Secure to a fixed object so that the juice can drip slowly into the bowl. Leave for 24 hours. Do not squeeze the bag to hasten dripping as this will make the jelly cloudy.

Measure the quince juice into a clean preserving pan. For each cup of juice, add 220 g (8 oz/1 cup) sugar. Stir over medium heat until the sugar has dissolved. Add the lemon juice and washed geranium leaves and bring to the boil.

Boil rapidly for 25 minutes, skimming frequently. Remove the pan from the heat while you test the jelly, so it doesn't overcook. Test the jelly by dripping a teaspoonful onto a cold saucer. Leave to cool, then run your finger across the jelly: setting point is reached when the surface wrinkles.

When setting point is reached, remove the geranium leaves and ladle the hot jelly into hot sterilised jars (see page 19). Seal when cold.

KYTHONOPASTO
Quince paste

quince pulp from the Kythoni Peltes (page 97)
sugar
bay leaves
caster (superfine) sugar

Purée the quince pulp by pressing it through a sieve or blending it in a food processor.

Measure the purée into a heavy-based saucepan. For each cup of pulp, add 220 g (8 oz/1 cup) sugar and 60 ml (2 fl oz/¼ cup) water.

Place over medium–low heat and stir occasionally until the sugar has dissolved. Bring to the boil, then boil steadily for 60–80 minutes, stirring occasionally so that the paste cooks evenly. As the paste is thickening, it has a tendency to scorch, so watch it carefully.

When cooked, the paste will come away from the side of the pan and will be dark red in colour. While it is still hot, spread it into an oiled slab cake tin to a thickness of 2 cm (¾ inch). Leave it in the tin at room temperature for 2–3 days, lightly covered with muslin (cheesecloth).

When the paste is dry and firm, cut it into small diamond shapes with an oiled knife. Lift the pieces out and place them in a container with bay leaves between the layers. Seal tightly.

When serving, dip the tops lightly into caster sugar to give the pieces a fine coating.

Kythonopasto keeps indefinitely stored at room temperature, and is traditionally served in place of a spoon sweet, accompanied by a glass of iced water.

KYTHONI XYSTO
Grated quince preserve

1 kg (2 lb 3 oz) quinces
880 g (1 lb 15 oz/4 cups) sugar
2 strips of thinly peeled lemon rind
1 piece of cinnamon bark, or 2 unsprayed rose
    geranium leaves
30 g (1 oz/¼ cup) blanched split almonds, toasted
2 tablespoons lemon juice

Wash the quinces well to remove their fuzz, then peel them, cut into quarters and remove the cores. Place the peels and cores in a saucepan with 500 ml (17 fl oz/2 cups) water. Boil, covered, for 30 minutes.

Grate the quince quarters into a heavy preserving pan. Pour in 750 ml (25 fl oz/3 cups) water and set aside until the peels are boiled. Do not be concerned if the quince discolours.

Strain the liquid from the peels into a measuring jug and top the liquid up to 500 ml (17 fl oz/2 cups) with more water. Now add this liquid to the grated quince. Add the sugar, lemon rind strips and cinnamon or washed geranium leaves. Place over medium heat and stir occasionally with a wooden spoon until the sugar has dissolved.

Bring to the boil and allow to boil fairly rapidly for 1 hour, or until the mixture gels when tested on a cold saucer.

Remove the cinnamon or geranium leaves, stir in the almonds and lemon juice and boil for 1 minute longer.

Ladle into hot, sterilised jars and seal when cold.

✿ *Note: As the peel and core contain pectin — the setting ingredient for jellies and preserves — it is advisable that these be boiled to extract the pectin.*

PORTOKALI GLACE
Glacé orange peel

4 large thick-skinned oranges
880 g (1 lb 15 oz/4 cups) sugar
2 tablespoons liquid glucose, or 60 ml (2 fl oz/¼ cup)
   light corn syrup

Prepare the orange peel into strings of rolls as in the
Glyko Portokali recipe on page 99.

Dissolve the sugar in 500 ml (17 fl oz/2 cups) water over
medium heat. Add the glucose or corn syrup and bring to the
boil. Add the strings of rolls and return to the boil.

Boil gently for 10 minutes, skimming when necessary.
Transfer to a bowl and leave for 24 hours so that the peel can
absorb the sugar.

Drain the syrup back into a saucepan. Bring to the boil over
medium heat and boil for 10 minutes.

Remove the threads from the rolls and pour the syrup over
the rolls in the bowl. Invert a plate onto the rolls to keep them
submerged in the syrup. Leave for a further 24 hours.

Drain the syrup back into a saucepan. Bring to the boil and
boil for 5 minutes. Add the rolls, return to the boil and boil for
a further 5 minutes.

Return the rolls to a bowl, submerging them as before.
Leave for a further 24 hours.

Place a wire rack over a dish and place the rolls on the rack
to drain. Leave to dry in a warm place for 48 hours.

When dry, store in a sealed container.

GLYKO PORTOKALI
Preserved orange rolls

6 large, thick-skinned oranges
660 g (1 lb 7 oz/3 cups) sugar
1 tablespoon lemon juice

Lightly grate the entire surface of each orange. Deeply score
the peel into six segments, from the stem end to the base.
Carefully remove the peel.

Tightly roll up the peel, passing a needle and long
thread through each roll, and tying the others to the first roll.
When 12 rolls are threaded, tie the ends together to form a
circle of rolls. Repeat with the remaining rolls.

Put the rolls in a saucepan of cold water. Bring to the boil
and drain immediately. Repeat the boiling and draining
process twice more to remove the bitterness from the peel.

Cover the rolls with more fresh cold water and return to the
boil. Leave to boil gently for 45–60 minutes, or until tender.
Drain and place on paper towels to dry.

In a clean saucepan, dissolve the sugar in 750 ml (25 fl oz/
3 cups) water and bring to the boil. Add the lemon juice and
boil the syrup for 5 minutes. Add the strings of orange rolls
and boil for 10 minutes, timed from when the preserve returns
to the boil. Skim when necessary.

Remove from the heat, cover and leave overnight.

Next day, bring the pan contents back to the boil and cook
gently for 15–20 minutes, or until the syrup is thick when
tested on a cold saucer.

Leave to cool a little, then remove the threads and place the
rolls and syrup into sterilised jars (see page 19). Seal when
cold and store in a cool place.

GLYKO KARPOUZI
Watermelon rind preserve

1 kg (2 lb 3 oz) watermelon rind
660 g (1 lb 7 oz/3 cups) sugar
2 small pieces of cinnamon bark
1 strip of thinly peeled lemon rind
90 g (3 oz/¼ cup) honey
2 tablespoons lemon juice
60 g (2 oz/½ cup) blanched split almonds, toasted

Cut off all traces of pink from the watermelon rind. Peel off the green skin. Cut the firm white flesh into 2 cm (¾ inch) cubes.

Place the white flesh in a preserving pan and cover with cold water. Bring to the boil, then reduce the heat and simmer for 1 hour, or until translucent. Drain.

Pour 750 ml (25 fl oz/3 cups) water into a saucepan. Add the sugar, cinnamon, lemon rind strip, honey and 1 tablespoon of the lemon juice. Stir over medium heat until the sugar has dissolved. Bring to the boil, skimming when necessary.

Add the drained watermelon, return to the boil and leave to boil gently for 15 minutes. Remove from the heat, cover and leave for 12 hours or overnight.

Return the mixture to the boil over medium heat. Boil until the syrup is thick when tested on a cold saucer. Remove the cinnamon and lemon rind.

Add the remaining lemon juice and toasted almonds. Boil for 1 minute, then ladle into warm, sterilised jars (see page 19). Seal when cold.

FRAPA GLYKO
Preserved grapefruit rolls

Substitute 4 thick-skinned grapefruit for the oranges in the Glyko Portokali recipe on page 99. After grating, cut the peel into sixths or eighths, depending on the size of the fruit. Follow the same cooking instructions, but this time be sure to boil the rolls four times, instead of three.

LEMONI GLYKO
Preserved lemon peel

Follow the recipe for Glyko Portokali on page 99, substituting 6 thick-skinned lemons for the oranges. Cut the peel into quarters after grating, then cut each quarter in half, giving eight triangles of peel from each lemon. There is no need to roll and thread the lemon peels, but otherwise follow the method for Glyko Portokali.

Alternatively, if you want to make the rolls, boil and drain the quarters as they are peeled from the fruit. They will then be soft enough to roll up and thread.

FRAPA GLACE
Glacé grapefruit rolls

Follow the recipe for preparing Portokali Glacé on page 100, using 3 grapefruit. Boil and change the water four times, before boiling the peel until tender. Then follow the remaining directions for the Portokali Glacé.

LEMONI GLACE
Glacé lemon peel

Follow the recipe for preparing Portokali Glacé on page 100, using 4–6 thick-skinned lemons, depending on size.

Leave in triangular segments as instructed in the Lemoni Glyko recipe on page 100.

Cyprus

CYPRUS

With my parents hailing from the Greek island of Kythera, I have always felt an affinity with the people of Cyprus, as both Kythera and Cyprus, through legend, lay claim to the goddess Aphrodite. Legend has it that Aphrodite rose from the sea and went to Kythera, and then to Cyprus. The Cypriots tell it differently. For the romantic among you, Cyprus is regarded as the Island of Aphrodite, and for an island so endowed with beauty, there could hardly be a more appropriate symbol.

Before I visited Cyprus, I was under the mistaken impression that Cypriot and Greek cooking were much the same. I was proved wrong and pleasantly surprised. One of Cyprus's most interesting dishes would have to be *afelia*. The basic food can be either pork, new potatoes, mushrooms or globe artichoke hearts, and it is cooked with crushed coriander seeds and red wine. Irrespective of the food used in the dish, it is still called *afelia*, so I have numbered the variations later in this chapter and depend on the English translation to distinguish between them.

I was also pleased to find that stuffed vine leaf rolls were not called *dolmathakia* as they are in Greece. They go by the delightful name of *koupepia* — meaning little cigars.

Cypriot cooking seems to be a happy mixture of Greek, Lebanese–Syrian and Turkish cuisines, with an unmistakable mark that makes it Cypriot. Naturally with my heritage, Greek cooking is the best known to me and I was happy to be able to add more Greek recipes through the pages of Cyprus, although both Greece and Cyprus have a great variety of dishes, perhaps because of their history and proximity to Europe. Nevertheless, the recipes in this chapter are very much Cypriot in execution, as Cypriots have a great passion for certain ingredients, such as cinnamon and coriander (cilantro).

Perhaps to really experience the Cypriot cuisine and its adaptation of recipes from other countries, a visit to a taverna best proves the point. One we visited in Nicosia only serves meze (snacks or appetisers, known as *mezethakia*) — 25 in all. They came in steady procession throughout the course of the evening. *Koupepia*, *koupes*, feta and haloumi cheese, olives, tabbouleh, hummus, *tahinosalata*, *talattouri*, *souvlakia*, *miala*, *lounza* (cured pork fillet, grilled and topped with melting haloumi), *stifatho*, *tavas*, *marides* (fried small fish), *panjaria salata*, raw artichoke hearts, celery sticks, cucumber, tomato, octopus in wine ... We were informed that we could have a grilled fillet steak afterwards! You will find recipes for most of these *mezethakia* in various chapters as well as this in chapter. The description given should suffice for the remainder.

A trip to the local market in Nicosia gave me further insight into the uniqueness of Cypriot food. Our guide, though claiming that she was not a good cook, filled me in on the preparation of vegetables. One that particularly intrigued me was *kolokassi* (taro) — more about that on page 151.

The Cypriot fondness for pork is evident in their meat markets. They make a ham called *hiromeri*, very similar to Italian prosciutto, and *lounza*, cured, smoked pork fillet. My previous description of *lounza* with haloumi cheese is virtually the recipe itself, and *lounza* is available at Greek and Cypriot food stores.

In the little village of Kakopetria I was told how to make Cypriot sausages. The village method calls for days of soaking the pork and spices in red wine — at room temperature! With regard to your health, the recipe I have given is one used by Cypriot butchers, which you can prepare with confidence.

The same cook gave me her recipe for making green walnut preserves. The process involved is lengthy, but well worth trying. A friend of ours recalls his boyhood days in Cyprus when he and his friends would be commandeered to peel the walnuts. They thought it great fun to go round for days with blackened hands. It happened to me — but I did not regard it as fun! Rubber gloves are strongly advocated.

Cypriot breads, though similar to Greek breads, have some interesting variations. Haloumopsomi (page 126) is filled with chunks of haloumi. This cheese can be made in the home and I have given a recipe for making your own on page 108; however nowadays, such is its popularity that haloumi is widely available in supermarkets and delicatessens, as well as Greek and Cypriot food stores. The same cheese is combined with cheddar and edam cheeses as well as a few other ingredients and used as a filling for Flaounes (Easter cheese pies, page 119), the pie crust being a yeast dough. Elioti (page 126) is another typically Cypriot bread, with onions and black olives baked in it.

THE FLAVOUR OF CYPRIOT FOODS

While olive oil is almost as widely used as in Greece, the Cypriot cook prefers corn oil for the preparation of many dishes. Butter is considered something of a luxury and is used only in the making of Greek pastries and cakes. Typical Cypriot cakes and cookies often use lard or corn oil, for example Lokoumia Parayemista (page 157), similar to the *ma'amoul* of Lebanon (page 301), which are made in huge quantities, especially for pre-wedding festivities. In Cyprus these are made with lard, but expatriate Cypriots prefer to use butter, and so do I.

While cassia bark is widely used in Greece instead of cinnamon, in Cyprus the more delicately flavoured cinnamon bark is preferred. This is sold in sticks or quills, the kind generally used in Western cooking. A good Cypriot cook prefers to pound the bark to a powder rather than buy it already ground.

Coriander, native to southern Europe, is a most popular flavouring ingredient. Both the leaves and the dried seeds are used extensively.

The Cypriots take pride in being self-sufficient and in rural areas they prepare their own *pourgouri* (burghul), haloumi and *anari* cheese, ham and a pasta called *trahana*. The latter is made with soured milk and ground wheat. It is a lengthy process and ends up as small, square noodles. *Trahana* forms the basis of winter soups, cooked in chicken broth with perhaps a little tomato to flavour it, and with cubes of haloumi cheese stirred in just before it is removed from the fire. *Trahana* is also made in Greece, with semolina (farina) instead of the ground wheat. *Trahana* is readily available at Greek and Cypriot stores.

EATING CYPRIOT STYLE

With such a history, it is natural for the Cypriots to take their meals in a Western manner, though it is not served in separate courses. A meat, fish or poultry dish will form the basis of the meal, perhaps preceded by a soup. When fasting, a vegetable dish such as Polypikilo (page 134), Louvana (page 130) or Louvia Mavromatika Me Lahana (page 133) could replace the meat or poultry. A salad — either a cooked green vegetable with an oil and lemon dressing, or a combination of raw vegetables — would be served as an accompaniment. Olives, cheese, pickles, bread, fresh fruit and wine complete the meal.

The Cypriot lifestyle is very similar to that of Greece and Turkey. One delightful custom practised in both Cyprus and Greece is the serving of *glyko* (spoon sweets). These delightful fruit preserves are lovingly prepared by Greek and Cypriot women, using fruits in season. When a visitor calls, the *glyko* is served in small glass or silver dishes with a spoon. It is accompanied by a glass of iced water — certainly necessary as they are very sweet — and after this formality, coffee is served, perhaps with a selection of sweet pastries.

COOKING METHODS

For Cypriot cooking, a Western kitchen needs little extra in the way of equipment, as any pot, pan or casserole dish can be used. In Cyprus the kitchen can be as up to date as your own, or a farm-style kitchen with an open hearth where sausages and hams can be smoked in the chimney, with large pots for preparing Zalatina (page 149) and haloumi cheese, and *talaria*, woven baskets for draining the curds. In rural areas where they make their own pickles, breads, *trahana*, sweet preserves and cured olives, every kitchen would be equipped with large utensils and large storage jars, usually of glazed or unglazed pottery, depending on their use.

The *tapsi*, a round baking dish, is used for roasting meats and baking sweets; a *tava*, an unglazed terracotta casserole dish, is used for preparing a dish by the same name (page 144); a *saganaki*, a two-handled frying pan for cooking mezes, can be taken directly to the table. Any baking dish, casserole or frying pan can be used instead.

For rolling pastry, a long length of dowel is a definite advantage, as the Cypriot cook prepares pastries in great quantities, and dowel makes the process so much simpler.

INGREDIENTS FOR CYPRIOT COOKING

The recipes are self-explanatory, and ingredients readily available. Burghul (bulgur), rice, pulses, pasta, semolina, cinnamon, coriander leaves and seeds, and haloumi are necessary ingredients. You can see it would not be difficult to prepare Cypriot food in your kitchen.

HALOUMI
Haloumi cheese
MAKES: 250 G (9 OZ)

Haloumi is a favourite cheese in Cyprus, Greece and Lebanon. In Cyprus it is frequently made in the home when plenty of milk is available. Sheep's milk is traditionally used, but cow's milk gives a satisfactory result. This is a typical Cypriot version and it is quite different to the haloumi available from supermarkets.

The Cyprus home cheese-maker uses reed baskets called *talaria* for draining the curds. A colander lined with muslin (cheesecloth) works just as well.

While the haloumi is draining, before its final heating and shaping, the whey is used for making cottage cheese, or *anari* (see opposite page).

The quantity produced with 2 litres (68 fl oz/8 cups) of milk is quite small for the effort entailed; however, if you have copious amounts of milk available, use one rennet tablet to each litre of milk, or four tablets to each imperial or US gallon.

For Lebanese-style haloumi, sprinkle the cheese with black cumin seeds instead of dried mint after salting.

3 rennet (junket) tablets
2 litres (68 fl oz/8 cups) whole milk
35 g (1¼ oz/¼ cup) good-quality cooking salt,
    plus an extra 2 tablespoons salt
1 tablespoon dried mint

Crush the rennet tablets in a small bowl. Add 2 tablespoons cold water and stir to dissolve.

Place the milk in a large saucepan and warm to body temperature, or no more than 38°C (100°F). Add the dissolved rennet and stir gently for a few seconds only. Cover the pan and leave in a warm place, undisturbed, for 30 minutes, or until set.

Using a whisk, gently stir the set milk to break up the curds. Leave until the curds settle.

Line a colander with a doubled piece of muslin (cheesecloth) and set it over a deep bowl. Ladle the curds into the colander, collecting the whey in the bowl.

When well drained, lift the cloth with the curds onto a clean chopping board set on the sink top. Shape the curds by hand into a square about 2 cm (¾ inch) thick. Fold the cloth over the top and press gently with your hand. Raise one end of the board so that the remaining whey can drain. Leave for 1½–2 hours. Return the collected whey to the pan and put on to boil.

When the curd is well drained and compact, cut it into four pieces and carefully place them in the boiling whey. Cook until the cheese floats. Now remove from the heat and leave for 5 minutes.

Place the cooking salt on a plate. Crumble the mint into coarse flakes.

Lift out each piece of cheese with a spatula and place on a board. While still hot, press the pieces with your hand to flatten them a little. Dab dry with paper towels. Dip the pieces on each side in the salt, then sprinkle some mint on one side. Fold each in three to enclose the mint and press with your hand to keep the cheese in shape. This step must be carried out while the cheese is warm and pliable.

Pack the cooled cheese into a sterilised jar (see page 19). Dissolve the 2 tablespoons salt in 500 ml (17 fl oz/2 cups) of the whey, then pour over the cheese. Seal and store in a cool place.

The cheese may be eaten when freshly made, or allowed to mature in the salty whey for up to 6 weeks.

ANARI
Cottage cheese

whey from making Haloumi (page 108)
1 litre (34 fl oz/4 cups) whole milk
1 tablespoon strained lemon juice

Prepare the whey from the Haloumi recipe (opposite). Bring to the boil and add the milk and lemon juice.

Return to the boil, stirring constantly with a whisk. Curds will form on top of the whey. If the milk does not develop curds, add a little more lemon juice. Remove from the heat and set aside for 10 minutes.

Strain through a colander lined with a doubled piece of muslin (cheesecloth), collecting the whey in a bowl.

When most of the whey has drained out, scrape down the curds from the sides of the cloth. Gather the ends and tie the cloth with string. Hang the bag over a sink for 2 hours or more to drain completely.

When well drained, turn the cheese into a bowl, cover and refrigerate. Use within 3 days.

You can now return the reserved whey to the saucepan and proceed with the Haloumi recipe. It may be necessary to skim fine milky curds from the top of the whey after making the *anari* and before returning the haloumi to the whey.

❀ *Note: Anari is a whey cheese similar to Italian ricotta. In Cyprus, when haloumi is made at home, the whey is used for making* anari *while the haloumi is draining, before the final heating of the haloumi.*

SALTSA TOMATA
Tomato sauce
MAKES: 500 ML (17 FL OZ/2 CUPS)

60 g (2 oz/¼ cup) butter, or 60 ml (2 fl oz/¼ cup) corn oil
1 large onion, finely chopped
250 g (9 oz/1 cup) chopped, peeled tomatoes
125 g (4 oz/½ cup) tomato paste (concentrated purée)
1 teaspoon sugar
250 ml (8½ fl oz/1 cup) stock or water
1 bay leaf
1 large piece of cinnamon bark
salt and freshly ground black pepper, to season

Heat the butter or oil in a heavy-based saucepan and gently fry the onion until translucent. Add the tomatoes and cook them until soft.

Stir in the tomato paste, sugar and stock. Add the bay leaf and cinnamon and season with salt and pepper. Bring to a gentle simmer, then cover and simmer gently for 20 minutes.

Remove the lid and simmer for a further 10 minutes, so that some of the liquid can evaporate to thicken the sauce.

Remove the bay leaf and cinnamon.

Serve hot on boiled pasta, or as directed in recipes.

ELIES TSAKISTES
Cracked green olives
MAKES: 1 JAR OR SEVERAL JARS

When we were in our teens, my two sisters and I had the chore of cracking the olives so that our mother could preserve them. While olives would not grow in our semi-tropical climate, we would receive a case from an aunt who lived in the south of our state. Our olive oil would come from there as well, especially during the Second World War.

fresh green olives
rock salt — 105 g (3½ oz/⅓ cup) rock salt for every 1 litre
   (34 fl oz/4 cups) water
grape vine leaves, washed
lemon slices

For serving
juice of 1 lemon
1 garlic clove, crushed
25 g (¾ oz/¼ cup) coriander seeds,
   coarsely pounded
60 ml (2 fl oz/¼ cup) olive oil

Crack the olives by hitting each one separately with a mallet or smooth stone. Only the flesh has to be cracked, so do not hit too hard as the seed should remain intact.

Place the cracked olives in a large jar (or jars) and cover with cold water. Keep the olives submerged using a small heavy plate or clean flat stone. Change the water every 24 hours. Do this four times in all.

Measure the last amount of water poured from the olives before discarding. Now measure the same amount of fresh water into a large saucepan and add 105 g (3½ oz/⅓ cup) rock salt to each litre (34 fl oz/4 cups) water. Stir over low heat until the salt has dissolved.

(When the brine is cool you can check the strength of it with a fresh egg. The right saltiness is reached when the egg floats, with an area about 2.5 cm (1 inch) in diameter breaking the surface of the water.)

Transfer the olives to a sterilised jar or jars (see page 19). Pour the brine over the olives, place the grape vine leaves and lemon slices on top and seal. Leave in a cool, dark place for at least 3 weeks; the olives may be kept like this for a few months.

When required, take out about 350 g (12 oz/2 cups) olives. Any growth on top is of no importance, so long as the olives are not soft and do not show signs of decay. If the olives are soft, discard them — it may be that only those at the top are affected. Remove any fungus.

Rinse the olives under cold water, drain well and place in a bowl. Sprinkle the lemon juice over the olives. Add the garlic, coriander seeds and oil. Stir well and leave for 1–2 hours for the flavours to develop.

Serve as an appetiser with bread, or as an accompaniment to meals.

SKORTHALIA
Garlic sauce

MAKES: 375 ML (12½ FL OZ/1½ CUPS)

4–5 garlic cloves, halved
60 ml (2 fl oz/¼ cup) white vinegar
½ teaspoon salt
125 g (4 oz) crustless stale white bread
50 g (2 oz/½ cup) ground almonds
125 ml (4 fl oz/½ cup) olive oil
1 tablespoon lemon juice
salt and freshly ground black pepper, to taste

Soak the garlic in the vinegar for 10 minutes. Remove the garlic and place in a mortar; reserve the vinegar. Add the salt to the garlic and using a pestle pound it to a paste.

Soak the bread in cold water and squeeze dry. Crumble the bread into small particles and gradually blend into the garlic, adding a little of the reserved vinegar to smooth the mixture.

When well pounded and smooth, transfer the mixture to a bowl if the mortar is too small. Gradually beat in the ground almonds and oil alternately with the remaining vinegar.

Beat in the lemon juice and add salt and pepper to taste. If the mixture is very thick, beat in a little more oil or lemon juice, depending on the flavour balance. The mixture should be the consistency of stiff mayonnaise.

Turn into a serving bowl and serve with fried fish, squid, fried or boiled vegetables, or as directed in recipes.

❁ *Note: If using a food processor or blender, soak the garlic as above. Process or blend all the ingredients except the oil until smooth, then gradually beat in the oil. Adjust the seasoning, flavour and consistency as above and blend until smooth. Do not overbeat, as the mixture could heat and curdle.*

AGINARES OMA
Raw artichokes

In Cyprus the globe artichoke is enjoyed more often raw than cooked. Use young artichokes and remove three or four layers of leaves to expose the hearts. Cut off the top section of the leaves and trim carefully around the base to neaten. Cut into quarters and remove the choke with a spoon.

Drop the artichokes into a bowl of water, to which the juice of two lemons has been added.

When ready to serve, drain well and serve with crisp celery sticks as a meze.

Lemon wedges can be added for squeezing to individual taste, or the artichokes may be dipped into Bakdounis Bi Tahini (page 253), a parsley and tahini sauce that in Cypress is known as *tahinosalata*.

MIALA ME LEMONI
Marinated brains
SERVES: 6

6 sets of lamb brains
2 tablespoons white vinegar
1¼ tablespoons salt
1 garlic clove, peeled but left whole

Dressing
juice of 1 lemon
85 ml (3 fl oz/⅓ cup) olive oil
salt and freshly ground black pepper, to taste
2 tablespoons finely chopped flat-leaf parsley

Place the brains in a bowl and cover with cold water. Add 1 tablespoon each of the vinegar and salt. Soak for 15 minutes.

Drain and remove the skin if possible. This is difficult if the brains have been frozen, and it might be necessary to leave the skin on. Any veins should be removed.

Place the brains in a saucepan with fresh water to cover. Add the garlic clove and the remaining salt and vinegar. Bring to just below the boil, cover the pan and simmer gently for 15 minutes, or until the brains are tender. Do not allow to boil.

Drain the brains well, cut into cubes and place in a bowl.

Beat the dressing ingredients together and pour over the brains. Cover and leave to marinate in the refrigerator for 2 hours or longer.

Serve in the dressing, as a meze.

MIALA TIGANITA
Fried brains
SERVES: 6

Prepare and gently simmer the brains as directed in the Miala Me Lemoni recipe (left).

Drain the brains, dry well with paper towels and cut into 1 cm (½ inch) slices.

Dip them in flour to coat, then pan-fry in hot corn oil or butter until golden brown.

Serve hot with lemon wedges, as a meze.

KOUPEPIA
Stuffed grape vine leaves
SERVES: 8 AS AN APPETISER, 6 AS A MAIN COURSE

375 g (13 oz) preserved vine leaves, or 60 fresh leaves

2 tablespoons lemon juice

1 tablespoon butter

500 ml (17 fl oz/2 cups) light stock

parsley sprigs, to garnish

lemon slices, to garnish

Filling

2 tablespoons corn oil

1 onion, finely chopped

500 g (1 lb 2 oz) finely minced (ground) lamb

250 g (9 oz) finely minced (ground) veal

110 g (3¾ oz/½ cup) short-grain rice

2 tablespoons finely chopped flat-leaf parsley

2 teaspoons finely chopped mint

1 teaspoon salt

freshly ground black pepper

Egg and lemon sauce

40 g (1½ oz) butter

2 tablespoons plain (all-purpose) flour

375 ml (12½ fl oz/1½ cups) chicken or lamb stock

2 eggs

1–2 tablespoons lemon juice

salt and freshly ground white pepper, to taste

Rinse the grape vine leaves (fresh or preserved) in cold water. Add them to a saucepan of boiling water in three or four batches and blanch each batch for 2 minutes. Using a slotted spoon, remove the leaves to a basin of cold water, then into a colander to drain.

To make the filling, heat the oil in a frying pan and gently fry the onion until soft. Tip the onion into a mixing bowl, add the remaining ingredients and season with pepper. Mix lightly until well combined.

Place a vine leaf, shiny side down, on a work surface. Snip off the stem, if there is one. Place about 1 tablespoon of the filling near the stem end, fold the end and sides over the filling, then roll up firmly. Repeat with the remaining leaves and filling; the filling is sufficient for about 48 rolls. Reserve any damaged leaves for lining the pan.

Use six vine leaves to line the base of a heavy-based saucepan. Pack in the *koupepia* close together, in layers. Sprinkle each layer with a little of the lemon juice.

Cover the top of the rolls with the remaining vine leaves. Add the butter and the stock to the pan with any remaining lemon juice. Invert a heavy plate on top of the rolls so they keep their shape during cooking.

Cover the pan and place over medium heat. Bring to just below boiling, then simmer gently over low heat for 1½ hours.

To make the sauce, melt the butter in a small saucepan and stir in the flour. Cook for 2 minutes without browning, then stir in the stock. Stir constantly until the sauce thickens and bubbles.

Beat the eggs in a bowl until frothy, then beat in 1 tablespoon lemon juice. Gradually pour the hot sauce into the eggs, beating constantly. Return the sauce to the pan and stir over gentle heat for 2 minutes to cook the egg, taking care not to curdle the sauce. If this happens, sprinkle a little cold water into the sauce and beat with a balloon whisk.

Drain the cooked *koupepia* and arrange on a hot serving dish. Garnish with parsley and lemon slices. Serve the sauce in a separate sauceboat.

❀ *Note: The* koupepia *may be served cold as an appetiser, without the sauce. Serve with a bowl of yoghurt on the side.*

KOUPES
Cigars (meat-filled burghul shells)

MAKES: ABOUT 35

350 g (12 oz/2 cups) fine burghul (bulgur)
oil, for deep-frying

Filling
1 tablespoon corn oil
250 g (9 oz) minced (ground) lamb or beef
1 large onion, finely chopped
3 tablespoons finely chopped flat-leaf parsley
pinch of ground cinnamon
salt and freshly ground black pepper, to season

It is not necessary to wash the burghul, but do so if you wish. If you've washed the burghul, drain it well in a fine sieve, then press with the back of a spoon to extract the excess moisture.

Place the burghul in a bowl with 375 ml (12½ fl oz/1½ cups) boiling water. Stir well, cover and set aside for 2–3 hours.

Meanwhile, make the filling. Heat the oil in a frying pan, then add the meat and onion and stir over high heat until the juices evaporate and the meat begins to brown. Add the parsley and cinnamon and season with salt and pepper. Remove from the heat and leave to cool.

Knead the burghul well to form a coarse-textured dough. With moistened hands, break off a piece about the size of a walnut and squeeze the dough together, moulding it into an oval cigar shape. Wet a forefinger and push it into one end of the oval, to make a hole. Meanwhile, work the other hand around the outside of the dough to make the wall of the *koupa* as thin as possible. A long forefinger is a definite advantage!

Fill the hollow with about a teaspoon of the filling. Close the opening, moistening the dough with a little water to seal. Any breaks can be sealed by dabbing with water. Smooth the *koupa* with moistened hands and place on a tray. Repeat with the remaining ingredients.

Deep-fry six or eight *koupa* at a time in a saucepan of hot oil (180°C/350°F), or until a cube of bread dropped in the oil browns in 15 seconds, approximately 10 cm (4 inches) deep, for a minute or so before turning. Keep frying and turning each batch for 6–8 minutes, or until deep golden brown and crisp. Drain on paper towels.

Serve hot, as an appetiser.

TALATTOURI
Yoghurt and cucumber salad

SERVES: 6

2 slender green cucumbers

3 teaspoons salt

500 g (1 lb 2 oz/2 cups) thick drained yoghurt (page 19)

2 garlic cloves, crushed

2–3 teaspoons dried mint, finely crushed

1–2 tablespoons olive oil

mint sprigs, to garnish

Peel the cucumbers and cut into quarters lengthways. Slice thinly and place in a bowl. Mix in the salt and leave to stand for 1 hour.

Drain the cucumbers well. Mix them into the yoghurt with the garlic, and mint to taste. Add salt to taste, if necessary.

Stir in the oil a little at a time, adding as much as needed to make a thick, creamy mixture. Chill well.

Serve in a deep bowl, garnished with mint sprigs, as a meze with raw artichokes (page 112), crisp celery sticks, fried smelts and sardines, and crusty bread.

Talattouri also makes an excellent sauce for fried fish.

MOUNGRA
Pickled cauliflower

Moungra is traditionally prepared in the households of the devout for serving on Pure Monday, the first day of the 40-day Lenten fast, although it is also enjoyed during the year.

2 teaspoons active dried yeast

225 g (8 oz/1½ cups) plain (all-purpose) flour

1¼ tablespoons salt

1 cauliflower, about 1.5 kg (3 lb 5 oz)

3 tablespoons white mustard seeds

Dissolve the yeast in 60 ml (2 fl oz/¼ cup) warm water, then add 185 ml (6½ fl oz/¾ cup) warm water.

Put the flour and 1 teaspoon of the salt in a large mixing bowl. Stir in the yeast mixture until combined, then beat until smooth. Cover with plastic wrap and leave for 3 days at room temperature to ferment.

Separate the cauliflower into florets and soak in cold salted water for 10 minutes. Drain.

Half-fill a large saucepan with water, add the remaining salt and bring to the boil. Add half the cauliflower, return to the boil, then lift the cauliflower out with a slotted spoon. Place immediately into a bowl of cold water to cool, then drain. Repeat with the remaining cauliflower.

Bring 2 litres (68 fl oz/8 cups) water to the boil. Cool a little, then gradually pour into the fermented dough, stirring well to form a thin, milky liquid.

Pound the mustard seeds just enough to crack them, then sprinkle a little in the base of a large stone crock or a sterilised glass jar (see page 19). Place some cauliflower in the jar and sprinkle with more mustard seeds. Repeat until all the ingredients have been used.

Pour the milky liquid over the contents, covering the cauliflower completely. Cover with a lid or plastic wrap.

Each day, turn the cauliflower pieces with your hand (wash your hand and forearm well first). Do this for 8 days. The cauliflower is then ready for eating. *Moungra* will keep for 1 month if the cauliflower is turned every 2 days.

FLAOUNES
Easter cheese pies
MAKES: ABOUT 30

These pleasant cheese pies are prepared in enormous quantities to be eaten on Easter Sunday morning. The recipe given to me by a good Cypriot cook began with 6 pounds (2.7 kg) cheddam, 3 pounds (1.35 kg) haloumi cheese and 3 or 4 dozen eggs. You can imagine the proportions of the rest of the recipe! She has a large family, and would certainly need some helpers to prepare the pies. I have scaled the recipe down considerably.

Cypriot cooks abroad find that 'cheddam' cheese – a combination of cheddar and edam cheeses – is a good substitute for the cheese used in Cyprus. Should this not be available, try the Greek *kasseri* cheese, or use a mild-flavoured cheddar combined with edam.

The flavouring of the cheese mixture also varies. Some cooks use the easily available dried mint, others insist on fresh mint, and others still substitute sultanas for the mint. I prefer the mint flavour.

900 g (2 lb/6 cups) plain (all-purpose) flour

2 teaspoons active dried yeast

250 ml (8½ fl oz/1 cup) milk

1 teaspoon salt

2 teaspoons sugar

60 ml (2 fl oz/¼ cup) corn oil

1 tablespoon melted butter

1 egg, beaten

sesame seeds, for sprinkling

Cheese filling

250 g (9 oz) cheddam cheese (see introductory note above)

125 g (4 oz) haloumi cheese

1 tablespoon fine semolina (farina)

1 teaspoon baking powder

4 eggs, lightly beaten

1 tablespoon crushed dried mint, or 2 tablespoons finely chopped fresh mint

Sift the flour into a mixing bowl and warm it in a low oven.

Dissolve the yeast in 60 ml (2 fl oz/¼ cup) warm water, then add another 185 ml (6½ fl oz/¾ cup) warm water, the milk, salt and sugar. Stir well.

Remove and reserve about 300 g (10½ oz/2 cups) of flour from the bowl. Pour the yeast mixture into the centre of the bowl and stir in a little flour from the side to thicken the liquid. Cover and leave for about 10 minutes, or until frothy.

Gradually stir in the rest of the flour in the bowl. Combine the oil and melted butter, then slowly add to the flour. Beat by hand, or using the dough hook of an electric mixer, for 10 minutes, gradually adding half the reserved flour.

Sprinkle a work surface with more of the remaining flour and turn out the dough. Knead for 5–10 minutes, using as much flour as the dough will take. When smooth and satiny, shape into a ball. Place in a lightly oiled bowl and turn to coat with the oil. Cover with plastic wrap and leave in a warm place for 1–1½ hours, or until the dough has doubled in size.

Meanwhile, preheat the oven to 220°C (430°F/Gas 7).

To make the filling, coarsely grate the cheeses into a bowl. Sift the semolina with the baking powder and work in with a wooden spoon to soften the cheese and mix the ingredients to a thick paste. Gradually stir in the eggs and mint, and mix to a fairly stiff paste; it may be necessary to hold back a little egg, as cheeses vary in moistness and the mixture must hold its shape.

Punch down the dough and turn out onto a lightly floured work surface. Divide into two and shape into balls. Roll out each ball of dough until 5 mm (¼ inch) thick, then cut into 10 cm (4 inch) rounds. Place the rounds on a cloth and keep covered until all the dough is shaped.

Place a generous tablespoon of filling in the centre of a round of dough, spreading it slightly. Pull the dough up at three points to make a triangle, or four points to make a square. About 2 cm (¾ inch) of dough should overlap the filling all around. Press the points of the triangles or squares to seal the edges, using your fingers or the tines of a fork. Brush the dough overlap with beaten egg and sprinkle with sesame seeds.

Bake on greased baking trays for 12–15 minutes, until the filling is puffed and the *flaounes* are golden. Serve warm or cold.

·119·

SAGANAKI HALOUMI
Fried haloumi
SERVES: 4

250 g (9 oz) haloumi cheese
flour, for coating, optional
olive or corn oil, for pan-frying
1 lemon, cut in half, plus extra lemon wedges to serve
crusty bread, to serve

Cut the cheese into 5 mm (¼ inch) slices and coat them with flour if desired.

Heat enough oil in a small, two-handled frying pan (*saganaki*) to cover the base to a depth of 5 mm (¼ inch). Fry the cheese over medium – high heat for about 1 minute each side. Squeeze lemon juice to taste onto the cheese.

Place the pan on a heatproof plate and take immediately to the table. Serve with additional lemon wedges and eat with crusty bread dipped into the lemon-flavoured oil in the pan — a tasty meze that is very quick to prepare.

SAGANAKI ALA PEREA
Fried prawns and artichokes
SERVES: 2

Years ago I tried this delicious combination at the White Towers Restaurant in London, run by John Stais, a Greek Cypriot. This version is very close to the White Towers version, if my memory serves me well.

4 globe artichoke bases
250 g (9 oz) raw prawns (shrimps)
125 g (4 oz) small mushrooms
60 ml (2 fl oz/¼ cup) olive oil
1 tablespoon lemon juice
60 ml (2 fl oz/¼ cup) dry sherry
salt and freshly ground black pepper, to taste
1 tablespoon finely chopped flat-leaf parsley
crusty bread, to serve

Prepare the artichoke bases as directed on page 8 and cut them in half. Cook in a saucepan of boiling salted water for 15 minutes, or until tender. Drain well and leave until dry.

Shell and devein the prawns, then rinse and dry. Wipe and trim the mushrooms and leave them whole.

Heat the oil in a small, two-handled frying pan (*saganaki*) and add the artichokes. Quickly fry over medium–high heat until lightly browned on each side. Push the artichokes to one side of the pan and add the prawns, mushrooms and lemon juice. Fry, stirring continually, just until the prawns turn pink — do not overcook them.

Stir the artichokes into the prawn mixture and add the sherry. Reduce the heat to low, season with salt and pepper and simmer gently for 1 minute.

Sprinkle with the parsley and serve at once, taking the pan to the table on a heatproof plate.

Serve with crusty bread as an appetiser.

❧ *Note: To serve more than two people, use a large frying pan to hold a larger quantity of ingredients. Serve in heated individual ramekins, placed on heatproof plates.*

KOLOKETES
Pumpkin pies

MAKES: 30

600 g (1 lb 5 oz/4 cups) plain (all-purpose) flour
pinch of salt
185 ml (6½ fl oz/¾ cup) peanut oil or corn oil
3 teaspoons lemon juice
1 egg, beaten with a little milk, for glazing

Pumpkin filling

450 g (1 lb/3 cups) diced butternut pumpkin (squash)
2 tablespoons coarse burghul (bulgur)
1 onion, chopped
60 ml (2 fl oz/¼ cup) peanut or corn oil
½ teaspoon ground cinnamon
pinch of ground cloves
1½ teaspoons salt
freshly ground black pepper, to season

Start by making the filling. Peel the pumpkin, remove the seeds and cut the flesh into 5 mm (¼ inch) cubes. Weigh the diced pumpkin and place in a bowl. Add the remaining filling ingredients, stir to combine, then cover and leave for 12 hours, or overnight.

Sift the flour and salt into a mixing bowl. Rub in the oil with your fingertips until distributed evenly. Add the lemon juice and 125 ml (4 fl oz/½ cup) cold water and mix to a firm dough. Knead lightly, then cover and leave to rest for 30 minutes.

Meanwhile, preheat the oven to 200°C (400°F/Gas 6).

Roll out the dough thinly — about the thickness of a normal pie crust — and cut into 15 cm (6 inch) rounds. Take a round of pastry and moisten the edge with a little water. Place a good tablespoonful of filling in the centre, fold the pastry over and press the edges well to seal. Flute the edge with your fingers, or press with the tines of a fork. Repeat with the remaining pastry rounds and filling.

Place the pies on lightly greased baking trays and glaze the tops with the beaten egg. Bake for 10 minutes.

Reduce the oven temperature to 180°C (350°F/Gas 4) and bake the pies for a further 20 minutes. Serve hot or cold.

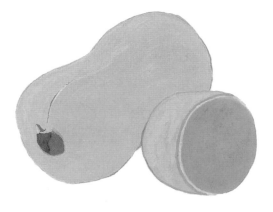

RAVIOLES
Boiled cheese-filled pasta

SERVES: 6

It could well be that *ravioles* and Kaloyrka (page 144) are Venetian legacies to Cyprus from the Venetian occupation of the island (1489–1571). Then again, somewhat similar pasta dishes are to be found in Armenia, Iran and Afghanistan.

The origin of pasta is shrouded by history, but can be traced back to China. My money is on the Mongol influence (in the 13th and 14th centuries), which could have filtered down from Persia or the Caucasus. The name, *ravioles*, could well be modern Italian influence in Cyprus as elsewhere, but the dish is as much a part of Cyprus cookery today as *afelia*, Koloketes (page 121) and so on.

Dough

450 g (1 lb/3 cups) plain (all-purpose) flour

1 teaspoon salt

2 eggs, lightly beaten

Cheese filling

225 g (8 oz/1½ cups) grated haloumi cheese

250 g (9 oz/1 cup) Anari (page 109) or ricotta cheese

2 eggs

1–2 teaspoons dried mint, crushed

To finish

125 g (4 oz/½ cup) butter, melted

grated haloumi or kefalotiri cheese, or a mixture

To make the dough, sift the flour and salt into a bowl. Add the eggs and about 125 ml (4 fl oz/½ cup) cold water. Mix to a soft dough, adding more water if necessary. Turn out onto a floured work surface and knead for 10 minutes, or until elastic and smooth, adding a little flour if the dough still sticks. Cover and leave to rest for 1 hour.

Meanwhile, thoroughly combine the cheese filling ingredients, adding crushed mint to taste. The mixture should be fairly stiff.

Divide the dough into two equal portions and roll each one out thinly, as instructed on page 15.

Cut the dough into strips 8 cm (3¼ inches) wide. Spread a strip on a work surface and place a teaspoon of cheese filling at 4 cm (1½ inch) intervals on one side of the centre of the strip.

Using a pastry brush dipped in water, lightly moisten the pastry around one side of the filling. Fold the pastry over the filling, pressing well between the mounds of filling and along the edge.

Cut the *ravioles* into crescents, using a 5 cm (2 inch) biscuit cutter. Press the edges again with the tines of a fork to seal well, then place on a cloth and cover. Repeat with the remaining ingredients, rolling out and using the pastry trimmings as well.

Cook 15 *ravioles* at a time in a large saucepan of boiling salted water for 15–20 minutes, or until tender. Remove each batch with a slotted spoon, to a colander set over simmering water to keep them warm while cooking the remainder.

When all *ravioles* are cooked, turn them into a dish and drizzle with the melted butter. Sprinkle with grated cheese and serve hot.

❀ *Note: Cooked* ravioles *may be refrigerated in a sealed container and heated in a colander over boiling water before serving.*

KANELLONIA
Meat-filled pancakes

SERVES: 6–8

Pancakes

150 g (5 oz/1 cup) plain (all-purpose) flour
¼ teaspoon salt
4 eggs
375 ml (12½ fl oz/1½ cups) milk
oil, for greasing

Meat filling

40 g (1½ oz) butter
1 small onion, finely chopped
500 g (1 lb 2 oz) finely minced (ground) beef or veal
1 tablespoon finely chopped flat-leaf parsley
½ teaspoon ground cinnamon
salt and freshly ground black pepper, to season
1 tablespoon plain (all-purpose) flour
125 ml (4 fl oz/½ cup) milk
1 egg, beaten

To finish

1 cup Saltsa Tomata (page 109)
35 g (1¼ oz/¼ cup) grated haloumi or kefalotiri cheese

To make the pancake batter, sift the flour and salt into a mixing bowl. Break the eggs into the centre and gradually stir the flour into the eggs. When half the flour is blended in, add half the milk. Mix to a smooth batter and beat with a wooden spoon for a few minutes. Stir in the remaining milk, then cover the batter and leave to stand for 30 minutes.

Meanwhile, prepare the filling. Melt half the butter in a saucepan and gently fry the onion until soft. Increase the heat to high, add the meat and stir until the juices evaporate and the meat is crumbly.

Reduce the heat and add the parsley, cinnamon and 125 ml (4 fl oz/½ cup) water. Season with salt and pepper. Cover and simmer gently for 20 minutes, or until the liquid evaporates. Set aside.

Melt the remaining butter in a small saucepan. Add the flour and stir over medium heat for 2 minutes, without allowing the flour to colour. Pour in the milk, stirring constantly until thickened and bubbling. Stir the sauce into the meat mixture, leave to cool a little, then blend in the beaten egg.

Preheat the oven to 180°C (350°F/Gas 4).

Heat a 15 cm (6 inch) frying pan or pancake pan and grease with a wad of paper towels dipped in oil. Using a jug, pour in 2–3 tablespoons of the pancake batter and tilt the pan to coat the base evenly. Cook until browned on the bottom, then turn and cook for a further minute. Remove to a plate. Cook the remaining pancakes and stack them on a plate.

Place about 2 tablespoons of the filling along the centre of each pancake and roll up. Place in rows in a greased baking dish and pour the Saltsa Tomata on top. Sprinkle with grated cheese and bake for 15–20 minutes, or until the cheese has melted.

Serve as a first course or as a light meal.

KOULOURA
Bread ring
MAKES: 1 LOAF

450 g (1 lb/3 cups) plain (all-purpose) flour

2 teaspoons active dried yeast

125 ml (4 fl oz/½ cup) warm milk

1 teaspoon salt

2 teaspoons sugar

2 tablespoons oil

sesame seeds, for sprinkling

Sift the flour into a mixing bowl and warm it in a low oven.

Dissolve the yeast in 60 ml (2 fl oz/¼ cup) warm water, then add another 60 ml (2 fl oz/¼ cup) warm water, the milk, salt and sugar. Stir well.

Remove and reserve about 150 g (5 oz/1 cup) of flour from the bowl. Pour the yeast mixture into the centre of the bowl and stir in a little flour from the side to thicken the liquid. Cover and leave for about 10 minutes, or until frothy.

Stir in the rest of the flour in the bowl, adding the oil gradually. Beat by hand using a wooden spoon for 10 minutes, or using the dough hook of an electric mixer for 5 minutes.

Knead in the reserved flour by hand, either in a bowl or on a board; only knead in enough flour to stop the dough sticking. Keep kneading for about 10 minutes, or until smooth and satiny. Shape into a ball.

Place in a lightly oiled bowl and turn to coat with the oil. Cover with plastic wrap and leave in a warm place for 1–1½ hours, or until the dough has doubled in size.

Punch down the dough and turn out onto a lightly floured work surface. Flatten out into a circle, then roll up firmly. Roll back and forth with the palms of your hands so that it forms a thick rope 50 cm (20 inches) long, tapering in at each end.

Lift onto a greased baking tray and form into a ring. Overlap the ends and tuck them under the loaf. Cover with a cloth and leave to rise in a warm place.

Preheat the oven to 190°C (375°F/Gas 5).

Brush the dough with water and sprinkle with sesame seeds. Bake for 30 minutes, or until golden brown and cooked. Remove from the oven and cool on a wire rack.

❁ *Note: This is also a popular Greek bread.*

ELIOTI
Olive bread
MAKES: 1 LOAF

According to religious traditions, during periods of fasting, meat, eggs and dairy products should not be eaten. One way of adding interest to meals is to serve olive bread. It is so delicious you will want to make and serve it often, whether fasting or not – unless you are fasting to reduce weight.

1 quantity Kouloura dough (page 125)
1 tablespoon olive oil, plus extra for brushing
1 onion, finely chopped
125 g (4 oz/1 cup) pitted black olives
oil, for glazing

Make the dough according to the directions on page 125, replacing the milk in the recipe with warm water if necessary. Leave to rise in a warm place until doubled in size.

Heat the oil in a frying pan and gently fry the onion until translucent. Stir in the olives and leave until cool.

Punch down the dough and turn it out onto a lightly floured surface. Press it out to a rectangle about 1 cm (½ inch) thick.

Spread the onion and olive mixture over the dough, leaving the sides clear. Roll the dough up firmly from the longer side and shape into a loaf. Press the ends to seal.

Place on a greased baking tray and make four shallow diagonal slashes across the top with a sharp knife. Cover with a cloth and leave in a warm place until doubled in size.

Meanwhile, preheat the oven to 190°C (375°F/Gas 5).

Brush the top of the loaf lightly with some extra oil. Bake for 35–40 minutes, or until the loaf is golden and sounds hollow when tapped on the base. Cool on a wire rack and serve warm or cold.

HALOUMOPSOMI
Haloumi cheese bread
MAKES: 1 LOAF

1 quantity Kouloura dough (page 125)
250 g (9 oz) haloumi cheese, cut into 1 cm (½ inch) cubes
milk or beaten egg, for glazing
sesame seeds, for sprinkling

Make the dough according to the directions on page 125. Cover and leave to rise in a warm place until doubled in size.

Punch down the dough and turn out onto a lightly floured work surface. Press it out to a rectangle about 1 cm (½ inch) thick. Place the cheese cubes on the dough, leaving the sides clear. Roll the dough up firmly from the longer side and press the ends to seal, forming the loaf into an oval shape.

Carefully place the loaf onto a greased baking tray. Make four shallow, diagonal slashes across the top with a sharp knife. Cover with a cloth and leave in a warm place until doubled in size.

Meanwhile, preheat the oven to 190°C (375°F/Gas 5).

Brush the top and sides of the loaf lightly with milk, or an egg beaten with a little water. Sprinkle with sesame seeds.

Bake for 35–40 minutes, or until the loaf is golden and sounds hollow when tapped on the base. Cool on a wire rack and serve warm or cold.

PĀTCHA
Lamb's head soup
SERVES: 6

Patcha is not only a Cypriot dish; Turkey, Iraq and the Gulf States all have their versions, but they all use lamb feet. As these are not readily available in Western countries for hygiene reasons, only the Cypriot version is given. Again the head is not always available, so the recipe has been modified to overcome this problem, with the result being similar to the traditional dish.

1 kg (2 lb 3 oz) lamb soup bones

6 lamb tongues

salt, to season

3 sets of lamb brains

60 ml (2 fl oz/¼ cup) vinegar

To finish

60 g (2 oz/¼ cup) butter

35 g (1¼ oz/¼ cup) plain (all-purpose) flour

1 small garlic clove, crushed

2 eggs

2 tablespoons lemon juice

6 slices of dry toast

1½ tablespoons white vinegar

Put the lamb bones in a large saucepan and cover with cold water. Scrub the tongues and add to the pan. Place over medium heat and bring to the boil, skimming when necessary.

When the liquid is well skimmed and boiling, season it with salt. Cover and simmer gently for 1½ hours, or until the tongues are tender when tested with a skewer inserted into the root end.

Meanwhile, soak the brains in the vinegar and enough cold water to cover for 30 minutes. Drain and remove the skin if possible. This is difficult if the brains have been frozen, and it might be necessary to leave the skin on. Any veins should be removed.

When the tongues are tender, add the brains to the pan. Cover and simmer very gently for 15 minutes, or until cooked; do not allow to boil.

Lift the tongues and brains from the stock. Skin the tongues and remove any gristle and the bone from the root end. Cut the tongues and brains into thick slices, place in a dish and spoon over a little stock to keep them moist. Cover the dish and keep warm.

Strain 500 ml (17 fl oz/2 cups) of the stock into a measuring jug. Strain the remaining stock into a small saucepan and keep it at a simmer.

Melt the butter in a saucepan and stir in the flour. Cook for 2 minutes, without allowing the roux to colour. Add the garlic, cook for a few seconds, then pour in the stock from the jug, stirring constantly. Keep stirring until the sauce boils and thickens. Reduce the heat and let the sauce bubble gently while preparing the eggs.

Beat the eggs in a bowl until foamy, then gradually beat in the lemon juice. Pour the thickened stock onto the eggs, beating constantly. Return the mixture to the pan and heat for 2–3 minutes, or until the sauce begins to bubble. The flour will prevent the sauce curdling.

Place a slice of toast in each of six deep plates, then sprinkle with 1 teaspoon vinegar. Pour 60 ml (2 fl oz/¼ cup) of the reserved hot stock onto each slice of toast. Arrange the sliced tongue and brains on the toast. Pour the hot egg and lemon sauce on top and serve immediately.

PSAROSOUPA AVGOLEMONO
« Egg and lemon fish soup
SERVES: 6

2 kg (4 lb 6 oz) fish heads, backbones and trimmings

2 small onions, peeled

4 small carrots, scraped and quartered

70 g (2½ oz/½ cup) chopped celery, including leaves

3 tablespoons coarsely chopped flat-leaf parsley

2 teaspoons salt

freshly ground black pepper, to season

75 g (2½ oz/⅓ cup) short-grain white rice

3 eggs

juice of 1 lemon

extra virgin olive oil, for drizzling

Wash the fish heads and trimmings in cold water and place in a large saucepan. Add 2 litres (68 fl oz/8 cups) water and bring to the boil, skimming when required.

Add the onions, carrots, celery, parsley and salt. Season with pepper, then cover and simmer gently for 1½ hours.

Strain the stock into a bowl and discard all the vegetables. Return the stock to the cleaned saucepan, adjust the seasoning with salt and pepper and bring to the boil.

Wash and drain the rice, then stir into the soup. Boil, uncovered, for 20 minutes, or until the rice is tender.

Beat the eggs in a bowl until foamy, then gradually beat in the lemon juice. Ladle about 500 ml (17 fl oz/2 cups) of the boiling stock into the egg mixture, beating constantly, then stir the mixture back into the gently boiling stock.

Keep stirring over low heat for 1 minute. Remove the pan from the heat, so the heat of the pan will not curdle the eggs, then stir for a further minute. Serve immediately with a drizzle of olive oil.

YOURVARLAKIA AVGOLEMONO
Meatball soup
SERVES: 6

500 g (1 lb 2 oz) finely minced (ground) lamb

1 small onion, finely chopped

1 egg, beaten

75 g (2½ oz/⅓ cup) short-grain white rice

2 tablespoons finely chopped flat-leaf parsley, plus extra to garnish

1 teaspoon finely chopped mint, optional

salt and freshly ground black pepper, to season

plain (all-purpose) flour, for coating

1.25 litres (42½ fl oz/5 cups) light stock

1 tablespoon butter

2 eggs

juice of 1 lemon

Mix the lamb in a bowl with the onion, egg, rice, parsley and mint, if using. Season with salt and pepper. Shape into meatballs the size of small walnuts and coat lightly with flour.

Bring the stock to the boil in a large saucepan. Season if necessary, then drop in the meatballs. Add the butter, cover and simmer gently for 1 hour.

In a mixing bowl, beat the eggs until light and foamy, then gradually beat in the lemon juice. Slowly add about 500 ml (17 fl oz/2 cups) of the simmering stock, beating constantly.

Pour the egg mixture into the soup and stir constantly over low heat for 2 minutes to cook the egg. Remove the pan from the heat, so the heat of the pan will not curdle the eggs, then stir for a further minute.

Ladle the soup into deep soup plates and sprinkle with a little extra chopped parsley. Serve with crusty bread.

LOUVANA
Split pea purée
SERVES: 6

440 g (15½ oz/2 cups) yellow split peas
60 ml (2 fl oz/¼ cup) olive oil
2 onions, sliced
2 potatoes, peeled and cut into small cubes
salt, to taste

To serve
lemon wedges
olive oil, for drizzling
black olives
crusty bread

Pick over the split peas, discarding any that are discoloured. Wash well in several changes of cold water. Place in a deep, heavy-based saucepan and pour in 1.25 litres (42½ fl oz/ 5 cups) water.

Bring to the boil over medium heat, skimming when necessary. Reduce the heat to low, then cover and simmer gently for 1 hour, without stirring.

Heat the oil in a small frying pan and gently fry the onion until lightly flecked with brown. Add the onion mixture to the split peas, along with the potato. Cover and simmer for 1 hour, or until the peas and potatoes are very soft. Do not stir during cooking as this causes scorching.

Stir in salt to taste. Beat until puréed, or process in small batches in a blender or food processor and reheat in the pan.

Serve in deep plates, with lemon wedges. Additional olive oil is usually poured onto the purée.

Serve with black olives and bread. Often a salad of tomatoes, cucumber, green or red capsicums (peppers) and onion is also served on the side.

FAKES XITHATI
Sour lentil soup
SERVES: 6

370 g (13 oz/2 cups) brown lentils

8 finely chopped spring onions (scallions)

3 tablespoons finely chopped coriander (cilantro) leaves
    or flat-leaf parsley, or a mixture

85 ml (3 fl oz/⅓ cup) olive oil

1 garlic clove, crushed, optional

1 tablespoon plain (all-purpose) flour

60 ml (2 fl oz/¼ cup) vinegar, or to taste

salt and freshly ground black pepper, to taste

Wash the lentils in several changes of cold water, or place in a sieve and run water through them. Drain.

Place the lentils in a large saucepan with the spring onion, herbs, oil and garlic, if using. Pour in 2 litres (68 fl oz/8 cups) water. Bring to the boil, cover and simmer over low heat for 1 hour, or until the lentils are soft.

Put the flour in a screw-top jar with 60 ml (2 fl oz/¼ cup) cold water. Seal and shake until thoroughly combined (this prevents lumps forming).

Gradually pour the flour mixture into the boiling soup, stirring constantly, until thickened slightly.

Add the vinegar, and salt and pepper to taste. Return to the boil, then allow to boil gently for 5 minutes before serving.

PANJARIA SALATA
Beetroot salad
SERVES: 6–8

6 beetroot (beets), with leafy tops

1 quantity Skorthalia (page 112), optional

Dressing, optional

85 ml (3 fl oz/⅓ cup) olive oil

2 tablespoons wine vinegar

1 tablespoon finely chopped coriander (cilantro) leaves,
    optional

Wash the beetroot well. Cut off the tops, leaving about 3 cm (1¼ inches) attached to the beetroot. Reserve the tender, undamaged leaves of the beetroot, discarding the remainder.

Place the beetroot in a saucepan, with salted water to cover. Boil for 30–45 minutes, or until tender.

Meanwhile, boil the reserved tops in a separate saucepan of salted water for 15 minutes.

Peel the beetroot, then slice or dice into a salad bowl. Drain the tops and either add them to the bowl, or serve in a separate bowl.

Either serve at room temperature with the Skorthalia, or pour the combined dressing ingredients over the hot beetroot and leaves and allow to cool before serving.

LOUVIA MAVROMATIKA ME LAHANA
Black-eyed beans with silverbeet

SERVES: 6

Although a simple dish, the combination of black-eyed beans and silverbeet is delicious. Dressed with olive oil and lemon juice, it is often enjoyed as a main meal, served with crusty bread, some cheese and a glass of wine.

400 g (14 oz/2 cups) black-eyed beans

1 kg (2 lb 3 oz) silverbeet (Swiss chard)

salt, to taste

2 garlic cloves, optional

125 ml (4 fl oz/½ cup) olive oil

juice of 1 lemon

lemon wedges, to serve

Wash the dried beans well and place in a large saucepan. Cover with 1.5 litres (51 fl oz/6 cups) water and bring to the boil.

Boil, uncovered, for 2 minutes, then remove from the heat. Cover and leave for 2 hours, or until the beans are plump.

Place the pan back over the heat and bring to a slow simmer. Cover and simmer for 1 hour, or until the beans are just tender.

Wash the silverbeet, changing the water several times. Trim the stems, then cut the stems into 1 cm (½ inch) pieces and add to the beans. Add salt to taste, then cover and cook for a further 10 minutes.

Shred the silverbeet leaves roughly and add to the beans. Cover and cook for a further 15 minutes, or until the beans and silverbeet are tender. Drain well and turn into a deep bowl.

If using the garlic, crush it with a little salt. Mix it into the combined oil and lemon juice and pour over the hot bean mixture. Toss well.

Serve hot or warm, with lemon wedges so diners can adjust the flavour to their individual taste.

VEGETABLES

POLYPIKILO
Vegetable potpourri
SERVES: 6

2 eggplants (aubergines)
salt, for sprinkling
500 g (1 lb 2 oz) potatoes
500 g (1 lb 2 oz) zucchini (courgettes)
6 ripe tomatoes
185 ml (6½ fl oz/¾ cup) corn oil
40 g (1½ oz/½ cup) soft white breadcrumbs
3 garlic cloves, finely chopped
1 small handful finely chopped flat-leaf parsley
salt and freshly ground black pepper, to season

Wash the eggplants, remove the stems and cut into 1 cm (½ inch) slices. Sprinkle with salt and leave for 30 minutes. Rinse and dry well with paper towels.

Meanwhile, preheat the oven to 170°C (340°F/Gas 3).

Peel and slice the potatoes thinly. Cut the zucchini into 1 cm (½ inch) slices. Peel the tomatoes (see page 528) and slice them thinly.

Pour some of the oil over the base of a large baking dish. Add half the breadcrumbs, garlic and parsley.

Layer the eggplant, potatoes, zucchini and tomatoes in the dish, seasoning lightly with salt and pepper. Repeat the layers, finishing with the tomatoes.

Pour the remaining oil over the vegetables and add 125 ml (4 fl oz/½ cup) water. Season the tomatoes with salt and pepper and sprinkle the remaining garlic, parsley and breadcrumbs over the top.

Bake for 1½ hours, or until the vegetables are tender. Check during the latter part of cooking and add a little water if necessary – *polypikilo* should be fairly moist.

Serve hot or at room temperature.

POURGOURI PILAFI
Burghul pilaff
SERVES: 6

60 ml (2 fl oz/¼ cup) corn oil or butter
1 onion, finely chopped
810 ml (27 fl oz/3¼ cups) chicken stock or water
350 g (12 oz/2 cups) coarse burghul (bulgur)
salt, to taste
yoghurt, to serve

Heat the oil or butter in a deep saucepan and gently fry the onion until translucent. Add the stock or water and bring to the boil.

Place the burghul in a sieve and wash quickly under cold running water. Add the burghul to the boiling stock, with salt to taste. Stir until boiling again, then reduce the heat, cover and simmer gently for 20 minutes, or until the liquid has been absorbed.

Remove from the heat, place a cloth or two paper towels over the rim of the pan and replace the lid. Allow to stand for 15 minutes.

Serve with yoghurt, as an accompaniment to Afelia dishes (page 137), mixed vegetable dishes, *keftethes* (meatballs), or any dish normally served with rice pilaff.

✽ *Note: Often vermicelli is added for variety. Add 50 g (2 oz/½ cup) crumbled vermicelli noodles to the pan with the onion and fry until golden. Add an additional 250 ml (8½ fl oz/1 cup) stock or water after frying the onion.*

YEMISTA
Stuffed vegetables

SERVES: 6

6 long eggplants (aubergines)

6 green capsicums (peppers)

6 tomatoes

Stuffing

2 tablespoons corn oil

1 large onion, finely chopped

1 kg (2 lb 3 oz) finely minced (ground) lamb or beef

125 ml (4 fl oz/½ cup) tomato passata (puréed tomatoes)

110 g (3¾ oz/½ cup) short-grain white rice

2 tablespoons chopped flat-leaf parsley

1 teaspoon dried mint, optional

salt and freshly ground black pepper, to season

Tomato sauce

125 ml (4 fl oz/½ cup) tomato passata (puréed tomatoes)

1 small piece of cinnamon bark

60 ml (2 fl oz/¼ cup) corn oil, or 60 g (2 oz/¼ cup) butter

½ teaspoon sugar

salt and freshly ground black pepper, to taste

Wash the vegetables. Remove the stalks from the eggplants, cut off 2 cm (¾ inch) from the stem end and set aside. Scoop out the eggplant flesh, leaving a 5 mm (¼ inch) border of flesh. Place the eggplants in salted water and soak for 20 minutes. Rinse and drain.

Meanwhile, cut the tops off the capsicums and reserve. Remove the core, seeds and white membrane from the capsicums, then rinse and drain.

Cut the tops off the tomatoes (the stem end) and set aside. Scoop out the tomato pulp with a spoon and keep it separate. Drain the tomatoes.

Preheat the oven to 180°C (350°F/Gas 4).

To make the stuffing, heat the oil in a large frying pan and gently fry the onion until translucent. Add the meat and stir constantly over high heat, until the meat is crumbly and the colour changes. Reduce the heat and add the remaining stuffing ingredients. Cover and simmer until the liquid has been absorbed.

Fill the vegetables with the stuffing, leaving a little room for the filling to expand, then replace the reserved tops. Arrange in rows in a large baking dish.

Place the reserved tomato pulp in a saucepan and cook until soft. Blend in the remaining sauce ingredients, then pour over the vegetables in the baking dish.

Cover with foil and bake for 30 minutes. Remove the foil and baste the vegetables with the sauce.

Bake for a further 15–20 minutes, or until the vegetables are tender. Serve hot, with crusty bread and salad.

❀ *Note: Zucchini (courgettes), silverbeet (Swiss chard) leaves, blanched cabbage leaves and artichokes may also be filled with the meat stuffing mixture. The zucchini may be oven baked, but the other vegetables are best cooked in a large saucepan on top of the stove, in a light stock instead of the tomato sauce. When prepared this way, the tomato passata in the stuffing mixture should be omitted and a little lemon juice added instead. Finish with an Egg and Lemon Sauce, following the directions given in the Koupepia recipe (page 115).*

AFELIA I
« Potatoes with coriander

SERVES: 6

The next three recipes are all called *afelia*, though the vegetable used differs in each one. *Afelia* is a Cypriot style of cooking vegetables or pork with coriander seeds and red wine. More detail is given later in this chapter, on page 150.

1 kg (2 lb 3 oz) small new potatoes, of an even size
60 ml (2 fl oz/¼ cup) corn oil
125 ml (4 fl oz/½ cup) dry red wine
salt and freshly ground black pepper, to season
3 teaspoons crushed coriander seeds

Wash the potatoes well and dry with paper towels. Crack the potatoes by hitting each one sharply with a mallet.

Heat the oil in a large frying pan that has a lid to fit. Add the potatoes and fry over high heat to brown them lightly, turning the potatoes frequently by shaking the pan.

Reduce the heat. When the potatoes are cooking less vigorously, add the wine and season the potatoes with salt and pepper. Cover and simmer gently over low heat for 20–25 minutes, or until the potatoes are tender, shaking the pan occasionally.

Sprinkle the coriander seeds over the potatoes. Cover and simmer for 2 minutes longer.

Serve hot, as a vegetable accompaniment to grilled or roast lamb, pork, veal or chicken.

AFELIA II
Mushrooms with coriander

Follow the recipe at left, substituting 500 g (1 lb 2 oz) mushrooms for the potatoes. Trim the mushrooms and wipe them clean with a dry cloth — do not wash.

Fry the whole mushrooms in the oil until the juices evaporate. Reduce the heat, add the wine, and salt and pepper to taste. Cover and simmer for 10 minutes. Add the coriander seeds, then cook for a further 2 minutes and serve.

AFELIA III
Artichoke hearts with coriander

Substitute 12 artichoke hearts for the potatoes, preparing them as instructed on page 8.

Drain and dry well, then cut each heart into quarters. Fry in the oil until lightly browned.

Reduce the heat, add the wine and season with salt and pepper. Cover and simmer for 15–20 minutes, or until tender. Add the coriander seeds and cook a little longer. Serve hot.

KALAMARIA PARAYEMISTA
Stuffed squid

SERVES: 4 AS A MAIN, OR 5–6 AS AN APPETISER

1 kg (2 lb 3 oz) small squid, with hoods about 10–12 cm
   (4–5 inches) long

coarse salt, for rubbing, optional

125 ml (4 fl oz/½ cup) corn oil

1 onion, finely chopped

110 g (3¾ oz/½ cup) short-grain white rice

125 ml (4 fl oz/½ cup) tomato passata (puréed tomatoes)

1 small piece of cinnamon bark

2 cloves

salt and freshly ground black pepper, to season

125 ml (4 fl oz/½ cup) dry white wine

To clean the squid, pull off the heads and attached tentacles. Cut out the eyes and beaks and discard. Clean the dark skin from the head and tentacles by pulling it off, or rubbing it off with a cloth dipped in coarse salt.

Clean out the hoods (bodies) and remove the transparent backbone from inside the hoods. Pull or rub off the skin. Rinse well, drain and dry.

Chop three or four squid into small pieces and reserve. Set the rest aside.

Heat 1 tablespoon of the oil in a saucepan and gently fry the onion until translucent. Add the rice and stir for 2 minutes.

Add the passata, cinnamon, cloves, chopped squid and 60 ml (2 fl oz/¼ cup) water. Season with salt and pepper. Cover and simmer over low heat for 10 minutes, or until the liquid has been absorbed. Remove the cinnamon and cloves.

Fill the squid hoods with the rice mixture, packing it in loosely, as the rice will expand and the hoods will contract during cooking. Close the tops of the hoods with wooden cocktail sticks, or sew together with strong thread.

Heat the remaining oil in a deep saucepan and fry the squid rolls until lightly coloured, turning them frequently.

Reduce the heat and add the wine. Cover and simmer gently over low heat for 1 hour, or until the squid is tender. Add a little water to the pan if necessary during cooking.

Serve hot or warm, as a main dish or a meze.

OKTAPOTHI STIFATHO
Braised octopus and onions
SERVES: 6

1 octopus, about 1 kg (2 lb 3 oz)

60 ml (2 fl oz/¼ cup) corn oil

1 onion, chopped

2 garlic cloves, finely chopped

250 ml (8½ fl oz/1 cup) tomato passata (puréed tomatoes)

60 ml (2 fl oz/¼ cup) dry red wine

60 ml (2 fl oz/¼ cup) wine vinegar

2 cloves

1 large piece of cinnamon bark

salt and freshly ground black pepper, to season

750 g (1 lb 10 oz) small whole onions

Pull the tentacles from the octopus and set aside. Remove and discard the intestines, ink sac, eyes and beak. Wash the head and tentacles and pull the skin off the head.

Place the head and tentacles in a saucepan. Cover and cook over medium heat for 10 minutes, or until the juices have exuded. Drain, cool and cut into small pieces.

Heat the oil in a heavy-based saucepan and gently fry the chopped onion until translucent. Add the garlic and chopped octopus and fry over medium heat for 5 minutes.

Add the passata, wine, vinegar, cloves and cinnamon. Season with salt and pepper, then cover and simmer over low heat for 30 minutes.

Peel the small onions, then cut a cross in the root end of each onion so the centres don't pop out during cooking. Add them to the pan. (If desired, the peeled onions may be blanched in boiling water for 5 minutes, then drained, before adding them to the octopus.)

Cover and cook for a further 1 hour, or until the octopus is tender. Remove the cloves and cinnamon, then adjust the seasoning to taste.

Serve with a plain rice pilaff.

PSARI STO FOURNO
Baked fish
SERVES: 6

2 whole baking fish, each about 1.5 kg (3 lb 5 oz)

juice of 1 lemon

salt and freshly ground black pepper, to season

125 ml (4 fl oz/½ cup) corn or olive oil

40 g (1½ oz/½ cup) soft white breadcrumbs

3 garlic cloves, finely chopped

1 small handful finely chopped flat-leaf parsley

3 large tomatoes, peeled (see page 528) and sliced

2 large potatoes, peeled

Clean and scale the fish if necessary. Wipe them dry, then rub each one inside and out with the lemon juice and some salt and pepper. Cover and refrigerate for 1–2 hours.

Preheat the oven to 180°C (350°F/Gas 4).

Oil a baking dish large enough to accommodate the fish. Sprinkle the breadcrumbs over the base, then top with the garlic and most of the parsley.

Place the fish in the baking dish and drizzle with a little of the oil. Arrange the tomato slices over the fish.

Peel the potatoes and cut into thick finger-length chips. Place them around and between the fish. Season the tomatoes and potatoes with salt and pepper, then pour the remaining oil over all the ingredients in the dish.

Cover with foil and bake for 15 minutes. Remove the foil and bake for a further 20–25 minutes, or until the fish and potatoes are cooked.

Serve hot, sprinkled with the remaining parsley.

PSARI SAVORO
« Fried fish with rosemary and vinegar
SERVES: 6

In both Cyprus and the Greek islands, an abundance of fish is prepared with vinegar-based sauces, which are used as marinades to preserve fried fish for a few days. This recipe, Psari Savoro, has a simple sauce of garlic, rosemary, vinegar and wine; Psari Marinato (right) adds the ubiquitous tomato, plus a few more herbs. Both sauces are well worth trying.

1 kg (2 lb 3 oz) small whole fish, fish fillets or fish steaks, suitable for pan-frying

salt, for sprinkling

plain (all-purpose) flour, for coating

olive or corn oil, for pan-frying

3 garlic cloves, finely chopped

1 teaspoon fresh or dried rosemary

60 ml (2 fl oz/¼ cup) brown vinegar

60 ml (2 fl oz/¼ cup) dry white wine

salt and freshly ground black pepper, to taste

Clean and scale the fish if necessary. Rinse and pat dry. Sprinkle with salt, then cover and leave for 20 minutes.

Coat the fish with flour.

Pour oil into a frying pan to a depth of 5 mm (¼ inch) and place over medium–high heat. Fry the fish in the hot oil until golden brown on both sides and cooked through. Drain and arrange the fish on a platter.

Pour all but 60 ml (2 fl oz/¼ cup) of the oil from the pan. Add the garlic and rosemary to the pan and cook for a few seconds. Sprinkle in 3 teaspoons flour and stir over medium heat until lightly coloured.

Remove from the heat and pour in the vinegar — take care as vinegar sizzles. Stir in the wine and return to the heat, stirring until bubbling. Add salt and pepper to taste, then pour the sauce over the fish.

Serve hot, or cover and refrigerate until cold.

PSARI MARINATO
Fish with tomato herb sauce
SERVES: 6

Ingredients as for Psari Savoro (left)

Additional sauce ingredients

1 bay leaf

2 tablespoons finely chopped flat-leaf parsley

125 ml (4 fl oz/½ cup) tomato passata (puréed tomatoes)

salt and freshly ground black pepper, to taste

½ teaspoon sugar

Prepare and fry the fish as directed in the Psari Savoro recipe (left), placing the fish in a dish.

Drain the oil from the pan, then clean out the pan. Return 60 ml (2 fl oz/¼ cup) of oil to the pan, or more if necessary. Add the garlic and 2 tablespoons flour and stir over medium heat until the flour colours.

Stir in the vinegar, wine and rosemary as before, but this time also adding the additional bay leaf, parsley, passata and 250 ml (8½ fl oz/1 cup) water.

Bring to the boil, stirring constantly. Let the sauce bubble gently over low heat for about 5 minutes.

Add the sugar and adjust the seasoning with salt and pepper. Pour the sauce over the fish and serve hot or cold.

GALLOS YEMISTOS
Roast stuffed turkey

SERVES: 8–10

1 turkey, about 4 kg (8 lb 12 oz)

1 lemon

salt and freshly ground black pepper, to season

125 ml (4 fl oz/½ cup) corn oil or melted butter

2 small pieces of cinnamon bark

Stuffing

40 g (1½ oz) butter

1 onion, finely chopped

70 g (2½ oz/½ cup) chopped celery

250 g (9 oz) minced (ground) veal

1 turkey liver, chopped

220 g (8 oz/1 cup) short-grain white rice

125 ml (4 fl oz/½ cup) dry white wine

250 ml (8½ fl oz/1 cup) chicken stock

75 g (2½ oz/½ cup) currants

60 g (2 oz/½ cup) blanched slivered almonds

½–1 teaspoon ground cinnamon

salt and freshly ground black pepper, to season

Wipe the turkey inside and out with paper towels. Cut the lemon into quarters and rub the cavities with the cut lemon. Sprinkle the turkey lightly with salt and pepper.

To make the stuffing, melt the butter in a saucepan and gently fry the onion and celery for 10 minutes. Add the veal and liver and stir for 5 minutes. Stir in the rice, wine and stock, then cover and cook for 10 minutes. Remove from the heat and mix in the remaining stuffing ngredients.

Meanwhile, preheat the oven to 180°C (350°F/Gas 4).

Fill the turkey neck and body cavities with the stuffing. Secure the openings with a trussing needle or skewer and truss the rest of the turkey (wings and legs).

Place the turkey in a roasting tin and drizzle with the oil or melted butter. Add the cinnamon and 125 ml (4 fl oz/½ cup) water to the roasting tin.

Cover the turkey with foil and roast for 3 hours, basting every 30 minutes with the pan juices.

Remove the foil to allow the turkey to brown. Roast for a further 1 hour, basting with the pan juices halfway through.

Transfer the turkey to a warm platter. Skim the pan juices and strain into a sauceboat to serve on the side.

YIOUVETSI
Lamb casserole with pasta
SERVES: 6

6 lamb leg or shoulder chops (cutlets),
    cut about 4 cm (1½ inches) thick

60 ml (2 fl oz/¼ cup) corn oil or melted butter

1 large onion, finely chopped

250 ml (8½ fl oz/1 cup) tomato passata (puréed tomatoes)

250 g (9 oz/1 cup) chopped, peeled tomatoes

3 cloves

1 large piece of cinnamon bark

salt and freshly ground black pepper, to season

1–1.25 litres (34–42½ fl oz/4–5 cups)
    boiling stock or water

440 g (15½ oz/2 cups) orzo or *kritharaki*
    (rice-shaped pasta)

25 g (¾ oz/¼ cup) grated kefalotiri or
    parmesan cheese

70 g (2½ oz/½ cup) diced haloumi or
    feta cheese

Preheat the oven to 180°C (350°F/Gas 4).

Place the lamb chops in a baking dish and drizzle the oil or melted butter on top. Bake for 20 minutes.

Add the onion to the dish and bake for a further 10 minutes.

Add the passata, chopped tomatoes, cloves and cinnamon and season with salt and pepper. Baste the lamb with the tomato mixture and cook for a further 1 hour, or until the lamb is tender, adding a little of the boiling stock if necessary.

When the lamb is tender, add the boiling stock and stir in the pasta. Bake for a further 20 minutes, stirring occasionally, and adding a little more liquid if the mixture looks dry.

When the pasta is tender, sprinkle the cheeses over the pasta and bake for a further 5 minutes to melt the cheese.

Serve immediately.

✤ *Note: This is a popular restaurant dish in Greece, Cyprus and Egypt. After the initial cooking, the ingredients are transferred to individual casserole dishes before the cooking is completed. In the home I suggest dividing the meat and pasta after it is cooked, and just before adding the cheese. Return to the oven to melt the cheese.*

TAVAS
Lamb and cumin casserole
SERVES: 6

This dish is named after the dish in which it is cooked. A *tava* is made of unglazed terracotta, with a snug-fitting lid. Before the advent of the home oven, the *tava* was placed on glowing embers in a hole in the ground, with earth packed around and on top of the dish. The lamb is cooked slowly to mouth-watering tenderness. Though you might not find a Cypriot *tava*, numerous terracotta casseroles are now available.

In Cyprus the *tava* is never washed in detergent suds — just wiped clean, rinsed with hot water, dried and left to air in the cupboard until next time.

Only this particular dish is prepared in the *tava*.

1.5 kg (3 lb 5 oz) boneless lamb shoulder or leg
3 large onions, sliced
750 g (1 lb 10 oz/3 cups) chopped, peeled tomatoes
2 teaspoons cumin seeds, plus extra pounded cumin
    seeds, to serve
salt and freshly ground black pepper, to season
Pourgouri Pilafi (page 134), to serve

Preheat the oven to 150°C (300°F/Gas 2).

Cut the lamb into 3 cm (1¼ inch) cubes. Place in a deep casserole dish, preferably one made of unglazed terracotta. Add the onions and tomatoes.

Crush the cumin seeds using a mortar and pestle and sprinkle into the dish with salt and pepper to season. Stir well, then add 125 ml (4 fl oz/½ cup) water.

Cover tightly and bake for 2½–3 hours, or until the lamb is tender and the sauce is thick. After 1½ hours, check the dish and add more water if required, though this should not be necessary — it depends on how tightly the lid fits.

Serve at the table from the dish, with Pourgouri Pilafi and additional pounded cumin seeds to add according to individual taste.

KALOYRKA
Boiled meat-filled pasta
SERVES: 6

1 quantity Ravioles dough (page 123)
1 quantity Saltsa Tomata (page 109)

Meat filling
2 tablespoons corn oil
500 g (1 lb 2 oz) finely minced (ground) lamb or beef
1 large onion, finely chopped
3 tablespoons finely chopped flat-leaf parsley
salt and freshly ground black pepper, to taste

Prepare the dough as directed in the Ravioles recipe on page 123, to the point of dividing it into two equal portions.

To make the filling, heat the oil in a frying pan, add the meat and onion and stir over high heat until the meat changes colour and is crumbly. Reduce the heat, add the parsley, salt and pepper to taste and 250 ml (8½ fl oz/1 cup) water. Cover and simmer for 30 minutes, or until the liquid evaporates. Remove from the heat and leave to cool.

Prepare the Saltsa Tomata as directed in the recipe on page 109 and keep it hot.

Meanwhile, roll out the dough, then cut, fill and shape the *kaloyrka* as directed in the Ravioles recipe.

Cook the pasta in a large saucepan of boiling salted water, 15 at a time, for 15–20 minutes, or until tender. Remove to a colander set over simmering water, using a slotted spoon. Cook the remaining *kaloyrka* in the same way.

Turn into a serving dish and cover with the hot Saltsa Tomata. Serve immediately.

Grated cheese may be served on the side if desired.

ARNI PSITO
Roast lamb
SERVES: 6

1 leg of lamb, about 2 kg (4 lb 6 oz)

2 garlic cloves

salt and freshly ground black pepper, to season

1 kg (2 lb 3 oz) potatoes

juice of 1 lemon

2 large onions, sliced

375 g (13 oz/1½ cups) chopped, peeled tomatoes

1 bay leaf

1 small piece of cinnamon bark

125 ml (4 fl oz/½ cup) stock or water

60 ml (2 fl oz/¼ cup) red or white wine

40 g (1½ oz) butter

Preheat the oven to 180°C (350°F/Gas 4).

Dry the lamb with paper towels and cut slits in the surface. Cut the garlic into slivers and insert them into the slits. Season the lamb with salt and pepper and place in a roasting tin. Roast for 1 hour, then drain off the fat.

Peel the potatoes, halve them lengthways, then cut partway down through the rounded side of each half. Arrange the potatoes around the lamb, with the rounded sides up. Sprinkle with the lemon juice and more salt and pepper. Top the potatoes with the onion and tomatoes.

Add the bay leaf, cinnamon, stock and wine to the dish. Dot the lamb with the butter and roast for a further 1½ hours, turning the lamb occasionally to brown evenly. Remove the lamb to a carving platter and keep it warm.

Skim the excess fat from the roasting tin. (Reserve this fat for mixing through hot spaghetti.)

Carve the lamb and serve with the potatoes, the sauce from the roasting tin and a side salad or green vegetable.

HIRINO ME MELITZANES
Pork with eggplant
SERVES: 5–6

1 kg (2 lb 3 oz) pork stewing meat, from the shoulder

60 ml (2 fl oz/¼ cup) corn or peanut oil

1 large onion, chopped

1 garlic clove, crushed

500 g (1 lb 2 oz/2 cups) chopped, peeled tomatoes

salt and freshly ground black pepper, to season

2 eggplants (aubergines)

finely chopped flat-leaf parsley, to garnish

Preheat the oven to 170°C (340°F/Gas 3).

Trim the pork and cut into fairly large cubes, reserving some of the pork fat.

Grease a heated frying pan with some of the reserved pork fat and brown the pork on all sides. Transfer to a casserole dish and drain off the fat from the pan.

Heat 1 tablespoon of the oil in the pan and gently fry the onion and garlic until the onion is translucent. Add the tomatoes and season with salt and pepper. Stir well to dissolve the browned sediment and bring to the boil.

Pour the mixture over the pork. Cover with a lid and bake for 1½ hours.

Meanwhile, wash the eggplants, remove the stems and cut lengthways into quarters. Place in a colander and sprinkle the cut surfaces liberally with salt. Leave for 30 minutes. Rinse and dry with paper towels.

Heat the remaining oil in a clean frying pan and brown the eggplant pieces on all sides.

Skim the fat from the casserole and place the eggplant on top of the pork. Cover and bake for a further 1 hour.

Sprinkle with parsley and serve from the casserole dish, with mashed or fried potatoes and a tossed salad.

LOUKANIKA
Pork sausages
MAKES: ABOUT 1 KG (2 LB 3 OZ)

1 kg (2 lb 3 oz) boneless pork, from the shoulder (see note)

60 ml (2 fl oz/¼ cup) port wine

1 teaspoon whole black peppercorns

½ teaspoon ground black pepper

1½ teaspoons ground coriander

¼ teaspoon ground cinnamon

¼ teaspoon whole cumin seeds

2 teaspoons salt

2 garlic cloves, crushed

grated zest of 1 orange

sausage casings

Cut the pork into cubes, leaving on a good deal of the fat. Process the pork in short bursts in a food processor, so that it is not chopped too finely. Alternatively, pass it through a meat grinder using a coarse screen.

Place the pork in a glass or ceramic mixing bowl and add the wine, spices, salt, garlic and orange zest. Mix until thoroughly combined. Cover and leave in the refrigerator for 1 day, stirring occasionally.

Place the sausage casings in cold water to loosen them. Remove each length as required.

Fill the casings using a meat grinder and a special attachment, or use a large funnel with a long nozzle, pushing the skin onto the nozzle and easing it off as it fills. Push the meat through the casings using the handle of a wooden spoon. Knot the end of the skin just as the meat begins to come through the nozzle.

When filled, twist the sausages into 15 cm (6 inch) lengths, twisting the first one way, the second in the opposite direction and so on. Knot the other end.

Cover the sausages loosely and store in the refrigerator until required.

To serve, fry the sausages in a little pork fat until cooked through. The cooked sausages can also be served as an appetiser, cut into small pieces and skewered with cocktail sticks.

❀ Note: The pork should have about 20 per cent fat. If the pork is purchased with the skin (rind) on, use a little more pork than the amount specified, as the rind must be removed.

SHEFTALIA
Barbecued sausages
MAKES: 50

The essential ingredient for these tasty sausages is *panna*, the caul fat from a pig (the outer covering of the paunch). When purchased, caul fat looks like long strips of creamy pink pork fat. Opened out, it is attractively patterned with lacy threads of fat on very fine membrane, finer than sausage casings.

The simply flavoured meat mixture is wrapped in pieces of *panna*, forming small sausages.

Sheftalia must be cooked over glowing charcoal – once cooked, the only evidence of the covering is the delicious flavour imparted to the contents.

500 g (1 lb 2 oz) finely minced (ground) fatty pork
500 g (1 lb 2 oz) finely minced (ground) veal or lamb
1 large onion, finely chopped or grated
1 small handful finely chopped flat-leaf parsley
2 teaspoons salt
freshly ground black pepper, to season
250 g (9 oz) *panna* (the caul fat from a pig)

Combine all the meat in a mixing bowl with the onion, parsley, salt and a generous grinding of black pepper.

Dip the *panna* into a bowl of warm water for a minute or two. Remove and carefully open out a piece at a time, laying it flat on a work surface. Cut with kitchen scissors into pieces about 10 cm (4 inches) square.

Take a good tablespoonful of the meat mixture and shape it into a thick sausage about 5 cm (2 inches) long. Place it towards one edge of a piece of *panna*, fold the end and sides over the meat, then roll up firmly. Repeat with the remaining *panna* and meat mixture.

Thread the sausages onto flat, sword-like skewers, leaving space between them. (The number of sausages on each skewer will depend on the length of the skewers.)

Cook over glowing charcoal, turning frequently. Do not place them too close to the heat — *sheftalia* must cook fairly slowly, so that the inside is well cooked and the outside nicely browned, without being burnt. The *panna* melts during cooking, keeping the meat moist and adding flavour.

Excessive flaring of the fire can be controlled with a sprinkle of water on the coals.

Serve *sheftalia* as an appetiser or main course.

ZALATINA
Brawn
MAKES: 16–20 SLICES

Traditionally this is made with a pig's head. As this part of the animal is not often available, and if the thought of cooking one is intolerable, you can make a perfectly good brawn with other parts of the carcass. Trotters or veal shanks will supply the necessary gelatinous properties, as will the rind (skin) and bones of the pork shoulder.

2 veal shanks, cracked

2 pig's trotters (knuckles), cracked

1 kg (2 lb 3 oz) fresh pork shoulder, cut into 4–5 pieces

2–3 pig or lamb tongues

1 teaspoon cracked black peppercorns

1 large piece of cinnamon bark

2–3 fresh or dried hot chillies

3 teaspoons salt

85 ml (3 fl oz/⅓ cup) white vinegar

125 ml (4 fl oz/½ cup) lemon juice

salt and freshly ground black pepper, to season

Wash the meats, place in a large saucepan and cover with cold water. Bring slowly to the boil, skimming when necessary. When well skimmed and boiling, add the peppercorns, cinnamon, chillies and salt. Cover and simmer gently for 3 hours, or until all the meat is very tender.

Remove the meat and trim. Discard the bones, fat and skin. Cut the meat into small cubes and set aside. Skin the tongues and cut into cubes.

Boil the stock until about 1.5 litres (51 fl oz/6 cups) remain, skimming as required. Strain through a sieve lined with muslin (cheesecloth), into a clean saucepan. Add the cubed meat and tongue, the vinegar and lemon juice. Adjust the seasoning with salt and pepper.

Bring back to the boil, then pour into two loaf tins or moulds. Cover and refrigerate until set.

To release the brawn, dip the moulds in fairly hot water for a few seconds. Run a knife around the inside of the moulds to loosen the brawn. Place a flat plate over each mould, then invert the moulds and shake downwards to free the brawn.

Slice and serve as part of a cold buffet, or as an appetiser.

❁ *Note: You can garnish the brawn with bay leaves, herb sprigs, sliced hard-boiled eggs, red and green capsicum (pepper) strips or sliced olives, alone or in combination. Pour a little of the cooled stock into the base of each mould, set in a dish of iced water. When thickened, arrange the selected garnish in a pleasing pattern and spoon a little more stock on top. Leave in iced water until set, then carefully fill with the cooled brawn mixture.*

AFELIA

Cypriots say if a dish has coriander seeds in it, then it is Cypriot. Many would disagree, but it is true Cypriots are inordinately fond of this spice. Coriander (cilantro) is native to southern Europe and the Mediterranean, its use dating back to 1552 BCE.

Afelia is a name applied to pork and vegetable dishes that feature cracked coriander seeds. Whether it is pork with coriander, mushrooms with coriander or a combination, the dish is still called *afelia*. Pork *afelias* follow here; you will also find vegetable *afelias* on page 137.

To Cypriot tastes, I might be a little conservative with my quantities of coriander – add more if you so desire.

AFELIA I
Fried pork with coriander

SERVES: 4

750 g (1 lb 10 oz) boneless pork shoulder, leg or loin
250 ml (8½ fl oz/1 cup) dry red wine
1 teaspoon salt
freshly ground black pepper, to season
2 tablespoons corn oil, or 40 g (1½ oz) butter
2–3 teaspoons crushed coriander seeds
Pourgouri Pilafi (page 134), to serve

Cut the pork into 2 cm (¾ inch) cubes, removing any skin if present, but leaving the fat. Place in a glass or ceramic bowl and add the wine, salt and a good grinding of pepper. Mix well, then cover and marinate in the refrigerator for several hours, stirring occasionally.

Drain the pork, reserving the marinade. Heat the oil or butter in a heavy-based frying pan and fry the pork over high heat, stirring frequently, until browned and just cooked through. Remove to a plate.

Cook the marinade in the pan until reduced to about 60 ml (2 fl oz/¼ cup). Add the pork, sprinkle with the coriander seeds and toss until heated through. Serve immediately, with Pourgouri Pilafi and a tossed salad or green vegetable.

AFELIA II
Braised pork with coriander

SERVES: 4–5

750 g (1 lb 10 oz) pork fillet, leg or loin pork
60 g (2 oz/¼ cup) butter
500 g (1 lb 2 oz) new potatoes, peeled
250 g (9 oz) small mushrooms, trimmed and wiped clean
250 ml (8½ fl oz/1 cup) red wine
salt and freshly ground black pepper, to season
2 teaspoons crushed coriander seeds

Cut the pork into 3 cm (1¼ inch) cubes, leaving some fat on the meat as this is desirable.

Heat half the butter in a heavy-based saucepan and brown the potatoes all over. Remove to a plate.

Add the remaining butter and brown the pork on all sides, then push the pork to the side of the pan. Add the mushrooms and quickly fry them in the pan, next to the pork. Stir to combine, then reduce the heat to low.

Pour in the wine and season with salt and pepper. Place the potatoes on top and sprinkle with the coriander seeds. Cover and simmer over low heat for 45 minutes, or until the pork and potatoes are tender.

Serve with a tossed green salad.

HIRINO ME KOLOKASSI
Pork with taro

SERVES: 6

When I was introduced to *kolokassi* in Cyprus I did not recognise it. The locals informed me *kolokassi* was Cyprus sweet potato and only available there – and indeed it does look like a very large sweet potato. As it happens the Egyptians use it also, but it is unknown elsewhere in the region.

The preparation of *kolokassi* is accompanied by a certain amount of ritual. Scrub the root, dry it well, peel, do not wet once peeled – if you do happen to wet it, dry it well again.

Chip off pieces – do not chop into it. To do this, slice into the root at an upwards angle, then break pieces off in thin wedges. As the root is large in circumference, work your way around it, ending up with pieces rather like apple wedges.

This is all to stop the taro becoming slimy during cooking.

The whole matter of the *kolokassi* intrigued me, until I found out that it was the taro (*Colocasia esculenta*) native to the Pacific Islands – a long way from home!

1 kg (2 lb 3 oz) boneless stewing pork

60 ml (2 fl oz/¼ cup) corn oil

1 large onion, chopped

185 g (6½ oz/1½ cups) thickly sliced celery

250 ml (8½ fl oz/1 cup) tomato passata (puréed tomatoes)

2 teaspoons salt

freshly ground black pepper, to season

1 kg (2 lb 3 oz) taro (*kolokassi*)

juice of ½ lemon

Cut the pork into 2 cm (¾ inch) cubes, leaving some fat on the meat.

Heat half the oil in a heavy-based saucepan and brown the pork over medium–high heat, removing each batch to a plate.

Reduce the heat and add the remaining oil. Gently fry the onion and celery until the onion is translucent. Add the passata and bring to the boil, stirring to dissolve the browned sediment from the base of the pan.

Return the pork to the pan. Season with the salt and a good grinding of pepper. Cover and simmer for 45 minutes.

Scrub the taro, dry well with paper towels and peel. If the taro is soiled during peeling, rinse it and dry well. Chip off pieces as described in the introduction to the recipe.

Place the taro on top of the pork and sprinkle with the lemon juice. Tilt the pan so that liquid runs over the taro, adding a little water if necessary.

Cover tightly and simmer for a further 30–45 minutes, or until the pork and taro are tender. Do not stir once the taro has been added.

Tilt the pan and skim off the excess fat. Adjust the seasoning and serve.

KOLOKASSI VRASTO
Boiled taro

The large taro root is simply scrubbed and boiled in its skin until tender. When cooked, peel off the skin, cube the flesh and combine it in a bowl with sliced celery, lemon juice, olive oil, salt and pepper. Serve warm.

POULLES TIGANITES
Fried taro shoots

The taro grown in Cyprus produces small torpedo-shaped offshoots. These are simply scrubbed and peeled, again keeping the root dry, except for a final rub with lemon juice. The shoots are then fried slowly in hot oil until golden brown and tender. Lemon juice and salt are sprinkled on at the table.

They are delicious served with Skorthalia (page 112), and are often served alongside boiled beetroot (beets).

THAKTILA KYRION
Ladies' fingers

MAKES: ABOUT 48

Pastry

450 g (1 lb/3 cups) plain (all-purpose) flour
¼ teaspoon salt
60 ml (2 fl oz/¼ cup) corn oil or peanut oil

Nut filling

155 g (5 oz/1 cup) finely chopped almonds
2 tablespoons caster (superfine) sugar
½ teaspoon ground cinnamon

Syrup

330 g (11½ oz/1½ cups) sugar
2 teaspoons lemon juice
2 tablespoons honey
1 teaspoon orange flower water, optional

To finish

500 ml (17 fl oz/2 cups) corn or peanut oil, for deep-frying
chopped toasted almonds, to serve

To make the pastry, sift the flour and salt into a mixing bowl. Stir the oil into the flour, then rub in with your fingertips to distribute the oil evenly. Add 185 ml (6½ fl oz/¾ cup) cold water and mix to a soft dough. Knead until smooth, then cover the pastry and leave to rest for 1 hour.

Meanwhile, make the syrup. Put the sugar and 185 ml (6½ fl oz/¾ cup) water in a heavy-based saucepan over medium heat and stir occasionally to dissolve the sugar. Add the lemon juice and honey and bring to the boil. Allow to boil rapidly, without stirring, for 5 minutes. Stir in the orange flower water, if using, then leave the syrup to cool.

Combine the nut filling ingredients in a mixing bowl.

Knead the pastry lightly on a floured work surface and divide into three. Roll out one portion very thinly, then cut into 8 cm (3¼ inch) squares.

Place a teaspoon of the nut filling along one edge of the pastry, keeping the filling away from the sides. Fold over three times, then press the join and press each end firmly to seal. Press the ends with the tines of a fork to decorate them. Place the finished pastries on a cloth-lined tray and keep them covered. Repeat with the remaining pastry and filling.

To cook the pastries, heat the oil in a deep saucepan to 160°C (320°F), or until a cube of bread dropped into the oil browns in 30–35 seconds, and deep-fry a few pastry fingers at a time for 1–2 minutes, turning them to brown evenly. Cook until golden, lift out with a slotted spoon and place immediately in the cold syrup. Turn the pastries in the syrup, leave for 1 minute, then lift out onto a wire rack to drain. Repeat with the remaining pastries.

Sprinkle the cold pastries with chopped toasted almonds.

The pastries keep well in a sealed container in a cool place.

BOUREKIA TIS ANARIS
Fried cheese pastries
MAKES: ABOUT 72

Pastry
450 g (1 lb/3 cups) plain (all-purpose) flour

¼ teaspoon salt

60 ml (2 fl oz/¼ cup) corn oil or peanut oil

Cheese filling
375 g (13 oz/1½ cups) soft curd cottage cheese, such as ricotta,
    Anari (page 109), or Mizithra (page 27)

55 g (2 oz/¼ cup) caster (superfine) sugar

1 egg, lightly beaten

1½ teaspoons ground cinnamon

To finish
corn oil, for deep-frying

sifted icing (confectioners') sugar, for sprinkling

To make the pastry, sift the flour and salt into a mixing bowl. Pour the oil into the centre, then gradually work in the flour until the mixture is crumbly, using your fingertips to rub the oil evenly into the flour. Add 185 ml (6½ fl oz/¾ cup) cold water and mix to a soft dough. Knead until smooth, then cover the pastry and leave to rest for 1 hour.

To make the filling, cream the cottage cheese with the sugar and gradually blend in the beaten egg and cinnamon.

Roll out half the pastry as thinly as possible, using a rolling pin, or better still, a 60 cm (24 inch) length of wooden dowelling — an authentic and very effective Cypriot and Greek method.

Cut the pastry into 8 cm (3¼ inch) rounds using a pastry cutter. Roll and cut the remaining pastry, as well as the pastry trimmings. Stack the rounds and cover with a cloth.

Moisten the edge of a pastry round with water. Place a teaspoon of cheese filling in the centre, fold over, then press around the edge with a fork to seal. Place on a cloth-lined tray and repeat with the remaining dough rounds and filling.

Heat the oil in a large saucepan to 180°C (356°F), or until a cube of bread dropped into the oil browns in 20 seconds.

Fry the pastries a few at a time, turning to brown evenly — they should cook in about 2 minutes. Lift out with a slotted spoon and drain on paper towels.

Serve warm, sprinkled with sifted icing sugar.

Any pastries not required immediately should be refrigerated in an airtight container and reheated in a 180°C (350°F/Gas 4) oven for 5 minutes before serving.

KAFES
Cypriot Coffee

Somehow precise measures sound odd for the Cypriot and Greek way of making coffee, so I have departed from my usual style.

You will require a *briki* (a long-handled coffee pot, wide at the base and tapering in at the top) or a small saucepan, and demitasse or small espresso cups.

To each demitasse cup of cold water measured into the pot, add 1 heaped teaspoon of powdered (not instant) coffee, and sugar to taste.

For sweet coffee (*glykos*) add the same amount of sugar; for moderately sweet coffee (*metrios*) add a level teaspoon of sugar; or no sugar, if that is your preference (*sketos*).

Stir over the heat only until the sugar has dissolved and bring to the boil. The coffee forms a creamy froth on top called *kaimak*. As the froth turns in from the sides and the coffee begins to rise in the pot, remove from the heat at once. Pour a little into each cup to distribute the froth, then fill your cups.

GLYKO KARITHI
Green walnut preserve

The first requirement for this preserve is a walnut tree. Though the preparation is lengthy, the preserve is well worth trying, as it is superb. Incidentally, a similar preserve, but flavoured with cardamom, is made in Iran, where it is called *morabaye gerdu*.

The walnuts must be picked very early in the summer when the green fruit are not yet full size and the inner shell is still soft. Test a nut by pricking it deeply in several places with a darning needle, paying particular attention to the long crease on one side; this indicates the join of the forming shell and is the part of the shell that hardens first. If there is no hint of resistance, cut the nut in half to check again. You will see the thick outer green covering progressing to white. The actual nut meat should be apparent – if it is clear and gelatinous, then the nuts are ready for the preserving pan. If the nut meat is not visible, try again in a few days.

2 kg (4 lb 6 oz) green walnuts (about 50 nuts)
½ cup slaked lime (food-grade pickling lime)
1.32 kg (2 lb 14 oz/6 cups) sugar
thinly peeled rind of 1 lemon
1 large piece of cinnamon bark
3 cloves
60 ml (2 fl oz/¼ cup) lemon juice
90 g (3 oz/¼ cup) honey

It is advisable to wear rubber gloves when preparing the walnuts as they contain iodine, which stains the hands black — a stain that is very stubborn to remove, though it does wear off eventually.

Peel the walnuts thinly with a sharp knife, placing them in a bowl. Cover with cold water and leave for 8 days, changing the water daily.

Put the slaked lime in 500 ml (17 fl oz/2 cups) water and stir to dissolve. Add the drained walnuts and sufficient cold water to cover. Stir, then leave for 4 hours.

Drain the walnuts and rinse well, changing the water several times. Tip the walnuts into a colander and run cold water through them to remove all traces of lime. This treatment firms the outer covering on the nuts; otherwise they will disintegrate during cooking.

Place the walnuts in a preserving pan and cover with cold water. Bring to the boil and leave to boil gently, uncovered, for 1–1½ hours, or until tender. Test with a needle, as described in the recipe introduction.

Drain the walnuts. Wearing rubber gloves for protection, pierce each walnut in several places so that the syrup can penetrate into them.

Layer the walnuts in a clean preserving pan, sprinkling 220 g (8 oz/1 cup) of the sugar over each layer. Cover with water and leave for 2 hours, so the sugar can dissolve slowly.

Add the lemon rind, cinnamon and cloves to the pan. Heat gently, shaking the pan to help dissolve the remaining sugar crystals. Bring to the boil, then add the lemon juice and allow to boil for 5 minutes. Remove from the heat, cover and leave for another 24 hours.

Add the honey to the pan and return to the boil. Allow to boil over medium heat for 10 minutes without stirring. Skim when necessary. When the syrup is very thick — the consistency of honey when a little is cooled on a cold saucer — the preserve is ready.

Remove the lemon rind, cinnamon and cloves. Ladle into hot sterilised jars (see page 19) and leave until cold before sealing. Store at room temperature.

LOKOUMIA PARAYEMISTA
Nut-filled semolina cookies

MAKES: ABOUT 45

560 g (1 lb 4 oz/4½ cups) fine semolina (farina)

375 g (13 oz/1½ cups) butter, either salted or unsalted, melted

1 large piece of cinnamon bark

2 teaspoons orange flower water

Nut filling

150 g (5 oz/1½ cups) coarsely ground almonds

55 g (2 oz/¼ cup) caster (superfine) sugar

1½ teaspoons ground cinnamon

To finish

60 ml (2 fl oz/¼ cup) orange flower water

icing (confectioners') sugar, for sprinkling

Put the semolina in a mixing bowl, add the melted butter and mix well with a wooden spoon, until the butter is distributed evenly. Cover the bowl with plastic wrap and leave for 6–8 hours, or overnight.

Preheat the oven to 200°C (400°F/Gas 6).

Put the cinnamon in a small saucepan with 250 ml (8½ fl oz/ 1 cup) water and bring to the boil. Remove the cinnamon and pour the boiling water onto the semolina. Add the orange flower water and mix until well blended. Leave for a few minutes to cool down, then knead until smooth. The dough should be firm; if crumbly, add a little more water.

Combine the nut filling ingredients in a mixing bowl.

Break off pieces of dough the size of large walnuts and mould each piece into an oval shape. Make a hole with your forefinger through the centre from one end, then enlarge the hole by turning the dough in your hand and working your finger inside the dough. Fill with a generous teaspoon of filling and close the end. Alternatively, press the dough flat in the palm of your hand, put the filling in the centre and close the dough around the filling, then remould the dough into an oval shape.

Place the cookies on ungreased baking trays and bake for 20–25 minutes, or until cooked but only lightly coloured.

As the hot cookies are removed from the oven, finish them off by brushing them with orange flower water.

Sift icing sugar onto a large piece of greaseproof (parchment) paper and place the hot cookies on the icing sugar. Sift more icing sugar thickly over the tops and sides and leave until cold. Store in a sealed container.

When serving the cookies, sift more icing sugar over the top to give a smooth finish.

Turkey

TURKEY

Istanbul stands majestically astride Europe and Asia, symbolic of the nature of Turkish cuisine. Two bridges straddle the Bosphorus, linking two culinary heritages, though each has in itself evolved through centuries of history.

In the 1920s, Mustafa Kemal Atatürk determined to Westernise all that is Turkey, including the country's cuisine. I am so glad that he did not complete this part of his project, though fried pastries using a choux pastry base and *dondurmas* (water ices) certainly suggest attempts were made.

A tour of the Topkapi Palace in Istanbul, once the home of sultans, princes, their wives and concubines, gives further insight into Turkish cooking. Just a look at the names of the recipes emphasises the romantic, exotic era when Turkey's cuisine was being developed: Hünkâr Beğendi (sultan's delight), Kadin Göbeği (ladies' navels), Kadin Budu (ladies' thighs), Dilber Dudaği (lips of the beauty), Hanim Parmaği (dainty fingers), Imam Bayildi (swooning Imam).

The sea and its gifts play a large part in the lifestyle and food of Turkey. One favourite dish, Kiliç Şiş (skewered swordfish, page 189), is a Turkish delicacy long remembered by visitors. The aroma of fish cooking over glowing charcoal or by other means permeates the air around the shores of the Bosphorus — Sardalya Sarmasi (sardines in grape vine leaves, page 169), Midye Dolmasi (stuffed mussels, page 187), Balik Plaki (baked fish, page 186) and many more. A favourite sauce served with many seafoods is *tarator*, a delectable combination of ground nuts, garlic, olive oil and vinegar. Though hazelnuts are generally used, almonds, pine nuts and walnuts are sometimes substituted.

DONER KEBAP

This famous Turkish speciality is found throughout Turkey and other countries of the region, though it is definitely Turkish in origin. As it is impractical for home preparation, a description will have to suffice.

Even-sized rounds of boneless lamb, taken from a whole carcass, are marinated for 24 hours in a mixture of olive oil, vinegar, onion, parsley, thyme, oregano or other combinations of herbs. A long, very heavy spit is loaded with the meat, layers interspersed with slices of fat from the tail of the lamb. The bottom of the spit is fitted with a disc to keep the meat in place, and the top is finished with a whole green capsicum (pepper) and a tomato for colour. The loaded spit is then placed before a vertical fire of charcoal or electrically heated elements. It is motor-driven so that the kebab revolves to cook evenly. As the lamb cooks on the outside, it is deftly sliced off into a special pan and served immediately in *pide* (flat bread) with salad. The doner kebap (or 'doner kebab') is now prepared in many

Western cities by ethnic groups, since it is as popular in Lebanon, Syria, Greece and Iraq as it is in its native Turkey. It is called *chawarma* in Lebanon and Syria, *grass* in Iraq and *gyros* in Greece.

THE FLAVOUR OF TURKISH FOOD

Turkey's cuisine, coloured by its history, is a mixture of Oriental and Byzantine influences, with the subtlety of Western cuisine softening the impact. Yoghurt would have to be one of the most important elements, its use stretching back into pre-history. While mostly enjoyed in its simplest form, with perhaps a dash of salt or a sprinkling of sugar, it is added to soups, becomes a sauce with little effort, and imparts a delicious flavour to cakes and desserts.

Perhaps the next pillar of Turkish cooking would be *pilavlar* (pilaff), renowned in world cuisine and worthy of its place. In researching, writing and testing the recipes I became aware that no matter how they were formulated, there would be some cooks who would agree and others who would strongly disagree with my methods. This is the beauty of Turkish cooking; a dish is a reflection of the cook, their love of food, and dedication to its preparation for the pleasure of the family.

Herbs are subtly used in Turkish cooking, predominantly parsley, dill, mint, bay leaves and, to a lesser extent, thyme and oregano. In spicing, pepper, *bahar* (allspice), cinnamon and paprika are the most widely used. A favourite Turkish garnish for foods is paprika steeped in oil. Çerkes Tavüğü (Circassian chicken, page 193) goes one step further: a dedicated cook will painstakingly extract the oil from walnuts to blend with paprika for the garnish. It is without doubt one of the most delicious chicken dishes I have ever tasted.

Turkey produces a wide variety of fruit and vegetables, all excellent in their season, but tomatoes in summer are a special joy. A good Turkish cook would prefer to use fresh tomatoes rather than tomato paste (concentrated purée), but certainly uses the latter when tomatoes are out of season.

The lemon is almost as popular in Turkey as it is in Greece and Cyprus; indeed many Turkish recipes using lemon juice are similar to Greek recipes, particularly when combined with egg.

Terbiye, *terbiyeli tavuk suyu* and *terbiyeli kofte* are similar to the egg and lemon sauce, soup and meatball soup of Greece and Cyprus.

Olive oil and butter are favoured for cooking above all other oils and fats, though peanut or corn oil can be used for general frying, particularly for pastries. Olive oil is essential for vegetable dishes, not only for its flavour, but also because such dishes are often eaten cold and other oils coagulate on cooling.

EATING TURKISH STYLE

The early days of the Ottoman Empire saw Istanbul (then called Constantinople) as a cosmopolitan city of Turks, Greeks, Armenians, Bulgars, Circassians, Venetians, Genoese, Jews, Serbs and Arabs. With such a beginning, is it any wonder that confusion exists as to what is Turkish and what is not?

The point is that Turkish cuisine, as with most cuisines, has been shaped by its history, but the people of the country through ensuing generations have marked it indelibly so that it is now a cuisine with its own national character.

Perhaps Istanbul today is the epitome of all that is Turkish. The streets are thronged with vendors selling *şiş kebaps* and kofta in *pide* (Turkish flat bread) with crisp cucumbers, capsicums (peppers) and tomatoes or *simit*, crusty bread rings smothered with sesame seeds; with lemonade and *visine* (sour cherry drink) vendors, laden with highly polished glass tanks with brass ornamentation strapped to their backs or slung across their bodies; and with the typical Turkish coffee vendor, a gleaming brass urn on his back, a pile of handle-less cups in his hand which he continually flings up and down, their jingling and his cry heralding his presence.

If a Turk wants refreshment, whether bought from an itinerant vendor or from a shop or store, the opportunity is ever present.

The coffee house is a favourite meeting place, a predominantly male domain, with coffee drinking an extremely popular pastime. Coffee was introduced to Turkey by the Arabs, and Turkey in turn introduced it to Europe.

The pastry shops are a delight to the eye and a threat to the waistline. Lokum (Turkish delight, page 203) is made in huge quantities with an unbelievable assortment of flavours, varying from the typical pink-coloured and rosewater-flavoured confection to one so filled with chopped nuts and dried fruit that the *lokum* in the mixture just serves to hold the gelatinous mass together.

One feature of entertaining in a Turkish home is the serving of an assortment of mezes. These are served en masse on the one table, called a *raki* table. Of course *raki*, a potent aniseed-flavoured spirit of Turkey, is always served at such a gathering. And though the occasion might appear at first to resemble a Western cocktail party, it could continue until the early hours of the morning, with an ever-changing assortment of hot and cold mezes being served.

While the serving of Turkish meals differs from house to house and between the city and rural dweller, it is basically the same. Meals are served Western style at a table, with all the dishes for the meal placed on the table at the same time. Meat or chicken is generally combined with vegetables for a casserole or baked dish; if kebap or a kofta is prepared, a separate vegetable accompaniment would be served. A salad, either an elaborate assortment or a simple combination of one or two ingredients, plus pickles and yoghurt and the inevitable pilaff, are always present. Cheese, bread and fresh fruit complete the meal. The beverage is usually *ayran* (yoghurt drink), particularly in summer.

When a Turk wishes to entertain in a grand manner, the range of recipes is such that a banquet to delight any gourmet can be prepared. It is not unusual to find Turks entertaining in such a way, particularly those who have a high social status.

COOKING METHODS

While the household might have a modern stove, cooking on a charcoal fire is still very much preferred. The Western barbecue, of whatever type, will serve you most satisfactorily. For food preparation, the mortar and pestle is an essential item of kitchen equipment.

Cooking saucepans and pans are either tin-lined copper or aluminium, with a variety of pottery dishes for oven cooking. Any Western cooking utensil can be used for Turkish cooking, with the addition of a food processor or blender to replace the mortar and pestle, though using the latter does give the cook a great deal of satisfaction.

For making Turkish coffee a small, long-handled coffee pot, called a *jezve*, is essential, and these are readily available in Middle Eastern stores. A small saucepan really does not give the same results.

INGREDIENTS FOR TURKISH COOKING

There are few, if any, ingredients used in Turkish cooking which are difficult to obtain. Cosmopolitan influences have been felt in most Western countries and such foods are commonplace. One vegetable, the eggplant (aubergine), which is so much a part of Turkish cooking, is now widely available; however, recipes using this vegetable detail the Turkish methods for its preparation. The preferred variety of eggplant is the long purple fruit, but as this particular eggplant is only available during the summer, you will have to choose the smallest possible oval eggplants at other times to produce dishes such as Imam Bayildi (swooning Imam, page 185).

The introductory chapter and Glossary give further details on foods for Turkish cooking and the recipes are self-explanatory.

PRONUNCIATION

The Arabic script was discontinued in the 1920s. The written language of Turkey now includes accents. A guide to assist you with pronunciation of recipe names follows.

Â/â as in 'past' (used only in words originating from the Ottoman Turkish)
A/a as in 'past'
E/e as in 'egg'
I/ı as the second vowel in 'valid'
İ/i as in 'pit'
Ö/ö as the vowel in 'err'
O/o as in 'over'
Ü/ü as in 'unit'
U/u as in 'put'
Ç/ç as 'ch' in 'chair'
Ş/ş as 'sh' in 'ship'
Ğ/ğ is a soft, slightly aspirate 'g', always between vowels

The Turkish alphabet contains no Q, W or X.

YOGURT SALÇASI
Yoghurt sauce
MAKES: 250 G (9 OZ/1 CUP)

1–2 garlic cloves
½ teaspoon salt
250 g (9 oz/1 cup) yoghurt

Pound the garlic and salt using a mortar and pestle. Alternatively, use a garlic press and combine the garlic with salt.

Mix the garlic into the yoghurt, then cover and refrigerate until required.

Serve with fried vegetables, kebabs, and as directed in recipes.

TARATOR
Hazelnut sauce
MAKES: 600 G (1 LB 5 OZ/2 CUPS)

140 g (4 ¾ oz/1 cup) hazelnuts
80 g (3 oz/1 cup) soft white breadcrumbs
3 garlic cloves, crushed
250 ml (8½ fl oz/1 cup) olive oil
125 ml (4 fl oz/½ cup) white wine vinegar
1 teaspoon salt

Blanch the hazelnuts if desired. Place in a bowl, cover with boiling water and leave for 5 minutes. Drain and peel off the skins. (This is not necessary, but I find it improves the flavour and appearance of the sauce.)

Grind the hazelnuts in a blender, food processor or nut grinder, or pound in a mortar and pestle. If using a grinder or mortar and pestle, transfer the nuts to a bowl as they are pulverised.

Add the breadcrumbs, garlic and 1 tablespoon water. Process or beat by hand while adding the oil in a thin stream. Gradually add the vinegar, beating well until smooth. Stir in the salt. The blender gives the smoothest sauce; other methods give a textured sauce.

Transfer to a serving bowl, then cover and chill.

Serve with seafood, fried vegetables and plain cooked vegetable salads, or as directed in recipes.

❀ *Note: Although the true Turkish tarator is almost always prepared with hazelnuts, walnuts are sometimes used, as well as blanched almonds or pine nuts, in which case add lemon juice instead of vinegar.*

HAMOUR
Shortcrust pastry
MAKES: 500 G (1 LB 2 OZ)

375 g (13 oz/2½ cups) plain (all-purpose) flour
½ teaspoon salt
125 g (4 oz/½ cup) cold butter
1 egg yolk

Sift the flour and salt into a mixing bowl. Cut the butter into small pieces and rub into the flour using your fingertips, until the mixture resembles fine breadcrumbs.

Beat the egg yolk lightly and add to the flour mixture with 85 ml (3 fl oz/⅓ cup) cold water. Mix to a soft dough, then knead lightly until smooth.

Cover and leave to rest for 20–30 minutes, before using as directed in recipes.

BÖREKLER
Savoury pastries

These delicate pastries are filled and shaped in various ways. Though you might like to try your hand at making your own pastry, the readily available fillo pastry (*yufka* in Turkish) is the ideal pastry as nothing can match its crisp, light flakiness. However, you will need homemade pastry for certain *böreks*.

Fillings are listed separately from the final shaping, as the shape of the *börek*, rather than the filling, determines the name.

The role of the *börek* in Turkish cuisine is not merely as an appetiser or first course; they are often served as an accompaniment to light soups, and the more substantial versions containing meat or chicken fillings are served as main courses. You will find the latter in the Meat and Poultry sections of this chapter.

KIYMA
Meat filling

MAKES: ABOUT 600 G (1 LB 5 OZ)

40 g (1½ oz) butter
1 large onion, finely chopped
500 g (1 lb 2 oz) finely minced (ground) lamb or beef
1 small handful finely chopped flat-leaf parsley
salt and freshly ground black pepper, to season

Heat the butter in a frying pan and gently fry the onion until translucent. Increase the heat, add the meat and stir frequently until the meat is crumbly. Fry until the juices evaporate and the meat begins to brown.

Remove the pan from the heat, add the parsley and season with salt and pepper. Use as directed in recipes.

BEYAZ PEYNIR
White cheese filling

250 g (9 oz) feta cheese
1 egg, lightly beaten
1 small handful finely chopped flat-leaf parsley
freshly ground black pepper

Crumble the cheese into a bowl using your fingers or a fork. Mix in the egg, parsley and a good grinding of black pepper.

Use as directed in recipes.

ISPANAK
Spinach filling

750 g (1 lb 10 oz) fresh spinach, or 250 g (9 oz) packet of frozen chopped spinach
2 tablespoons olive oil
1 onion, finely chopped
75 g (2½ oz/½ cup) crumbled feta cheese
1 egg, beaten
3 tablespoons finely chopped flat-leaf parsley
salt and freshly ground black pepper, to taste

If using fresh spinach, clean it well, removing any discoloured leaves, roots and any coarse or damaged stems. Wash well in several changes of water and shake the leaves to remove the excess moisture. Chop coarsely. If using frozen spinach, thaw it according to the packet instructions.

If using fresh spinach, place it in a large saucepan, then cover and cook over medium heat for 7–8 minutes, tossing occasionally. Cook only until wilted.

Place the wilted or thawed spinach in a sieve and press with the back of a spoon to extract the moisture. Transfer to a bowl.

Heat the oil in the saucepan and gently fry the onion until translucent. Add the mixture to the spinach, along with the cheese, egg and parsley. Combine thoroughly, seasoning to taste with salt and pepper. Use as directed in recipes.

PATLICAN KIZARTMASI
Eggplant fritters

SERVES: 6

3 long eggplants (aubergines), each about 250 g (9 oz)
salt, for sprinkling
1 quantity Beer Batter (see page 191)
oil, for pan-frying

For serving
Yogurt Salçasi (page 164) or Tarator (page 164)

Remove the stems from the eggplants and wash well. Peel off
1 cm (½ inch) strips lengthways at intervals to give a striped
effect. Cut the eggplants lengthways into 5 mm (¼ inch) slices
and spread on a tray. Sprinkle liberally with salt and leave for
30 minutes. Dry with paper towels.

Make the Beer Batter as directed on page 191.

Dip each eggplant slice into the batter and pan-fry over
medium–high heat in hot oil until tender and golden brown
on both sides. The slices cook in about 3 minutes. Drain on
paper towels.

Serve hot with Yogurt Salçasi or Tarator as an appetiser, or
as a side dish to main meals.

HAVUÇ KIZARTMASI
Carrot fritters

Substitute 750 g (1 lb 10 oz) large carrots for the eggplants in
the Patlican Kizartmasi recipe (left). Scrape the carrots, then
slice diagonally into 5 mm (¼ inch) pieces.

Cook the carrot slices in boiling salted water for 5 minutes,
or until just tender. Drain and dry, then dip in the batter and
fry as directed in the recipe.

KABAK KIZARTMASI
Zucchini fritters

Substitute 750 g (1 lb 10 oz) zucchini (courgettes) for the
eggplants in the Patlican Kizartmasi recipe (left).

Trim the zucchini and cut into 5 mm (¼ inch) slices
lengthways or diagonally, depending on how they are to be
served. Salt them if you like, but this softens them and they are
better if slightly firm when cooked.

Pat dry, then dip in the batter and continue as directed.

PIRASAPIDE
Leek pie

SERVES: 6–8

1 quantity Hamour pastry (page 164)

4–5 leeks

1 tablespoon salt

150 g (5 oz/1 cup) crumbled feta cheese

3 tablespoons finely chopped flat-leaf parsley

¼ teaspoon ground hot chilli or chilli pepper

85 ml (3 fl oz/⅓ cup) olive oil

4 eggs

milk, for brushing

Make the pastry as directed on page 164. Cover and set aside.

Remove the roots and discoloured leaves from the leeks. Cut off most of the green tops, leaving about 8 cm (3¼ inches). Halve the leeks lengthways and wash well to remove the soil between the leaves.

Cut out the root core, then slice the leeks fairly thinly. If the leeks are small, measure them, as you will require 600–700 g (1 lb 5 oz – 1 lb 9 oz/6–7 cups) sliced leeks. Prepare more if necessary.

Place the leeks in a colander and wash again to ensure all the soil has been removed. Drain well, then sprinkle with the salt, rubbing it through the leeks with your hands. Leave for 15–20 minutes, until the leeks are limp. Now press the leeks well so that the moisture drains out.

Meanwhile, preheat the oven to 220°C (430°F/Gas 7).

Combine the leeks in a mixing bowl with the feta, parsley, chilli and oil. Beat the eggs, set 2 teaspoons of the egg aside, and add the remainder to the leek. Stir well to combine.

Divide the pastry in two, making one piece slightly larger than the other. Roll out the larger piece on a floured work surface and place in a 30 cm (12 inch) round baking dish, or a 25 × 30 cm (10 × 12 inch) baking dish.

Spread the leek filling in the pastry and moisten the pastry edges with water. Roll out the remaining pastry and place over the top. Press the edges to seal well, then trim and crimp around the edge.

Beat the reserved egg with a little milk and brush the top of the pastry. Cut small slits into the top of the pie, to allow steam to escape. Bake for 30 minutes, or until golden brown.

Allow the pie to stand for 10 minutes, before cutting into serving portions.

❉ *Note: Instead of the Hamour pastry you can use 10 fillo pastry sheets. Line the dish with five sheets, brushing each with melted butter. Add the filling and top with the remaining sheets, again brushing each with butter. Trim the edge and butter the top sheet. Score the top layers lightly in serving portions, using a sharp knife or stanley knife. Sprinkle the top lightly with water to stop the pastry curling during baking.*

SARDALYA SARMASI
Sardines in grape vine leaves
SERVES: 6

24 fresh sardines
salt, for sprinkling
24 fresh or preserved grape vine leaves
85 ml (3 fl oz/⅓ cup) olive oil
freshly ground black pepper, to season
lemon wedges, to serve

Twist the heads off the sardines, gut them and rinse under cold running water. Drain and dry with paper towels.

Spread the sardines on a dish and sprinkle each side with salt. Cover and leave for 20–30 minutes.

Rinse the vine leaves in cold water, then drain and pat dry with paper towels. Remove any stems if present.

Spread a vine leaf on a work surface, shiny side down, and brush with olive oil. Lay a sardine across the base of the leaf, sprinkle the sardine with pepper and dab with a little oil. Roll up firmly and place on a hinged barbecue grill basket. Repeat with the remaining sardines and vine leaves.

Close the grill basket and brush the outside of the rolls with oil. Cook over glowing charcoal for 2–3 minutes each side.

Arrange on a platter and serve immediately, with plenty of lemon wedges.

The sardine is unwrapped and lemon juice squeezed on to taste. The vine leaves are not eaten — they are used to impart a pleasing and unusual flavour to the fish.

❁ *Note: If no hinged grill basket is available, you can cook the rolls under a hot grill (broiler). Secure the leaves with wooden cocktail sticks that have first been soaked in cold water for 30 minutes.*

CİĞER TAVASI
Fried liver bits
SERVES: 10–12

500 g (1 lb 2 oz) lamb or calf liver
plain flour, for coating
olive oil, for pan-frying
salt and freshly ground black pepper, to season
4 spring onions (scallions), chopped
3 tablespoons finely chopped flat-leaf parsley

Soak the liver in salted water to cover for 30 minutes. Remove the fine skin and larger tubes and cut the liver into 2 cm (¾ inch) cubes. Drain well.

Toss the liver cubes in flour to coat.

Pour oil to a depth of 5 mm (¼ inch) into a frying pan and heat well over a high heat. Adding only a single layer of diced liver to the pan at a time, fry the liver quickly, browning on all sides, and turning the liver with tongs. Take care not to overcook it.

Remove each batch to a warm serving dish with a slotted spoon, then sprinkle with salt and pepper.

Garnish the hot liver with the spring onion and parsley and serve immediately, providing cocktail sticks for convenience.

SIGARA BÖREĞI
« Fried cigarette pastries
MAKES: 75

20 sheets fillo pastry
1 quantity meat, cheese or spinach filling (page 165)
oil, for deep-frying

Open out the pastry sheets and place them in an even stack on a board. Using a stanley knife and a ruler, cut the stack into three strips, each about 14 cm (5½ inches) wide and 28 cm (11 inches) long.

Stack the strips on a dry cloth, folding the cloth over the top of the pastry, then covering with another folded dry cloth so they don't dry out as you work with them.

Place a strip of pastry on a work surface with the narrow edge towards you. Thinly spread 2 teaspoons of filling towards the edge, keeping a 2 cm (¾ inch) border. Turn the end of the pastry over the filling, then fold in the sides, pressing the fold along the length of the pastry. Brush the folded sides and the top edge of the pastry lightly with water. Roll up firmly, so that the finished pastry is as slender as possible.

Repeat until all the ingredients have been used, placing the pastries on a cloth-lined tray, seam side down.

Deep-fry the pastries a few at a time in a saucepan of hot oil, approximately 10 cm (4 inches) deep, for 4 minutes or until golden, turning to brown evenly. Lift out with a slotted spoon and drain on paper towels.

Serve hot as an appetiser, or as an accompaniment to light soups.

❀ *Note: The finished pastries may be reheated in a moderate oven (180°C/350°F/Gas 4) if necessary.*

BURMA BÖREK
Baked pastry rolls
MAKES: 30

10 sheets fillo pastry
125 g (4 oz/½ cup) butter, melted
1 quantity meat, cheese or spinach filling (page 165)

Preheat the oven to 190°C (375°F/Gas 5).

Open out the pastry sheets and cut each sheet into strips as directed in the Sigara Böreği recipe (left). Stack them and cover with a cloth.

Take a strip of pastry and brush it lightly with melted butter. Spread a generous tablespoon of filling towards the narrow edge, keeping the filling clear of the sides. Fold in the sides and roll up. Repeat with the remaining ingredients, placing the finished rolls on a buttered baking tray, seam side down.

Brush the rolls lightly with butter and bake for 20 minutes, or until golden. Serve hot.

❀ *Note: Smaller cocktail-sized rolls may be made by cutting pastry sheets into quarters. Use less filling and the yield is greater.*

PiYAZ
« White bean salad

SERVES: 6–8

400 g (14 oz/2 cups) dried haricot (navy) beans,
    or other white beans

salt, to taste

1 garlic clove

2 small onions

60 ml (2 fl oz/¼ cup) lemon juice

1 tablespoon white vinegar

60 ml (2 fl oz/¼ cup) olive oil

60 ml (2 fl oz/¼ cup) good salad oil

3 tablespoons chopped flat-leaf parsley

1 teaspoon chopped mint

2 teaspoons chopped dill

To finish

1 green capsicum (pepper), diced

3 hard-boiled eggs

Wash the beans in several changes of cold water and place in a large saucepan. Cover with 1.5 litres (51 fl oz/6 cups) cold water and bring to the boil. Allow to boil for 2 minutes, then remove from the heat. Cover and leave for 2 hours, or until the beans are plump. (Alternatively, soak the beans in cold water overnight, in the refrigerator if the weather is warm.)

Return the beans to the boil in their soaking water. Cover and simmer gently over low heat until tender, but still intact. The cooking time will vary according to the bean used, but about 2 hours should be sufficient. After 1½ hours cooking, add salt to taste. When tender, drain well and put the beans into a bowl.

Crush the garlic with a little salt. Cut the onions in half from top to bottom, then slice each half into semi-circles. Add to the hot beans with the lemon juice, vinegar and combined olive and salad oils. Leave until cool.

Gently mix in the chopped herbs and chill for 1–2 hours.

Serve in a deep bowl garnished, with the capsicum and sliced or quartered hard-boiled eggs.

DOMATES SALATASI
Tomato salad

SERVES: 6–8

4 firm tomatoes

2 long, young cucumbers

60 ml (2 fl oz/¼ cup) lemon juice

1 tablespoon white wine vinegar

60 ml (2 fl oz/¼ cup) olive oil

1 teaspoon finely chopped mint

1 tablespoon finely chopped flat-leaf parsley

salt and freshly ground black pepper, to taste

black olives, to serve

Peel the tomatoes if desired (see page 522). Slice them fairly thinly and arrange in two rows on an oval platter.

Peel the cucumbers and score the flesh with the tines of a fork. Slice thinly and arrange on one side of the tomatoes.

Beat together the lemon juice, vinegar, oil and herbs, then add salt and pepper to taste. Pour the dressing over the tomatoes and cucumbers. Cover and chill until required.

Just before serving, place the drained olives on the other side of the tomatoes.

This salad accompanies most meals, particularly in summer, when tomatoes are at their best.

İSKEMBE ÇORBASI
Tripe soup

SERVES: 5–6

500 g (1 lb 2 oz) tripe

1 small onion, quartered

1 teaspoon salt

1 teaspoon freshly ground white pepper

60 g (2 oz/¼ cup) butter

35 g (1¼ oz/¼ cup) plain (all-purpose) flour

125 ml (4 fl oz/½ cup) milk

2 egg yolks

2 tablespoons lemon juice

2 teaspoons paprika

1 tablespoon oil

3–4 garlic cloves, crushed

85 ml (3 fl oz/⅓ cup) white vinegar

Wash the tripe and place in a saucepan. Cover with cold water and bring to the boil. Pour off the water, then add 1.25 litres (42½ fl oz/5 cups) fresh cold water. Add the onion, salt and pepper. Cover and simmer gently for 2 hours, or until tender.

Remove and discard the onion. Lift out the tripe, reserving the liquid, and cut it into small strips.

Melt the butter in a small saucepan. Stir in the flour and cook gently for 1 minute, without allowing the flour to colour. Stir in the milk and 750 ml (25 fl oz/3 cups) of liquid from the tripe. Stir constantly until thickened and bubbling, then leave over a low heat to simmer gently.

Beat the egg yolks in a heatproof bowl, then beat in the lemon juice. Pour in the thickened sauce, stirring constantly.

Return the tripe to the tripe cooking liquid remaining in the saucepan. Pour in the egg mixture, stirring constantly. Still stirring, cook over gentle heat until the soup bubbles gently. Adjust the seasoning and remove from the heat.

Mix the paprika into the oil and set aside. Combine the garlic and vinegar.

Serve the soup in bowls, with a little paprika oil floated on top as a garnish. Diners can add the garlic vinegar mixture according to individual taste.

DÜĞÜN ÇORBASI
Wedding soup

SERVES: 6–8

500 g (1 lb 2 oz) boneless lamb stewing meat

500 g (1 lb 2 oz) lamb soup bones

1 onion, quartered

1 carrot, quartered

salt and freshly ground black pepper, to season

90 g (3 oz/⅓ cup) butter

75 g (2½ oz/½ cup) plain (all-purpose) flour

3 egg yolks

2–3 tablespoons lemon juice

2 tablespoons melted butter

2 teaspoons paprika

Place the lamb meat and bones in a large saucepan and pour in 2 litres (68 fl oz/8 cups) water. Add the onion and carrot. Bring to a slow simmer, skimming when necessary. Season with salt and pepper, cover and simmer gently for 1½ hours, or until the meat is tender.

Remove and discard the bones. Lift out the meat and cut it into small pieces. Strain the stock, return it to the pan and let it simmer gently.

Melt the butter in a large saucepan. Stir in the flour and cook gently for 2 minutes, without allowing the flour to colour. Gradually add the hot soup stock, stirring constantly. When smooth and bubbling, leave it to simmer gently.

Beat the egg yolks in a heatproof bowl and gradually add the lemon juice, holding a little back. Gradually beat in about 500 ml (17 fl oz/2 cups) of the thickened stock, then pour the mixture into the soup. Stir over gentle heat and add the lamb meat. Heat gently, still stirring, until the egg is cooked.

Adjust the flavour with lemon juice and add more salt if necessary. Remove from the heat.

Combine the melted butter and paprika. Serve the soup in deep bowls, with a little paprika butter floated on top of each as a garnish.

PiLAV
Pilaff

The *pilavlar* of Turkey have an established place in world cuisine; even so we have only been exposed to a few variations. The possible permutations and combinations of the *pilav* are endless. The recipes given here are indicative of the various ways in which *pilav* is prepared; once you have mastered *pilav* cooking you can devise your own variations.

The Turkish cook soaks rice in hot, salted water for 10-30 minutes; with the rices available today, this is not necessary. However, washing is necessary if you are to achieve the right result. Place the rice in a bowl, add cold water and stir. Pour off the water, then add fresh water. Do this until the water runs clear. Another method is to place the rice in a sieve.

Move the grains constantly with your fingers so that the starch is released as the cold water runs through.

As rice grains vary in hardness according to the variety, you may find the directions given need slight modification for the type you are using. You might require more or less liquid, and the cooking time may need to be extended or reduced. Make a note of any alterations necessary for that particular brand of rice.

To serve *pilav*, either fluff it up with a fork and pile it on a serving dish, or press the hot *pilav* into an oiled mould and turn it out onto a serving dish. A little of the sauce from the accompanying food may be spooned on top as an additional garnish.

iC PiLAV
Liver pilaff

SERVES: 6

400 g (14 oz/2 cups) long-grain white rice
250 g (9 oz) chicken or goose livers
90 g (3 oz/⅓ cup) butter
40 g (1½ oz/¼ cup) pine nuts
8 spring onions (scallions), white part only, chopped
¼ teaspoon ground allspice
3 tablespoons currants
750 ml (25 fl oz/3 cups) chicken stock
2 teaspoons salt
freshly ground black pepper, to taste
3 tablespoons finely chopped flat-leaf parsley or dill

Wash the rice until the water runs clear, then leave to drain well.

Clean the livers, then slice finely or dice.

Heat half the butter in a small frying pan and fry the pine nuts until golden. Remove to a plate using a slotted spoon.

Add the spring onion to the pan and fry gently until translucent. Add the liver and stir over medium heat until the colour changes; do not overcook. Stir in the allspice and set aside in the pan.

Heat the remaining butter in a deep, heavy-based saucepan. Add the drained rice and stir over medium heat until the grains change from translucent to opaque, without colouring. Stir in the currants, then add the stock, salt, and pepper to taste. Stir occasionally until boiling, then reduce the heat to low. Cover and simmer for 15 minutes.

Remove the lid and add the reserved pine nuts, liver mixture, and the parsley or dill. Gently stir through the rice with a wooden spoon.

Place two paper towels over the rim of the pan and fit the lid on tightly. Cook over low heat for a further 10 minutes.

Remove from the heat and leave to stand for 10 minutes before serving. This *pilav* is an excellent accompaniment for roast poultry or lamb.

PATLICANLI PiLAV
Eggplant pilaff
SERVES: 6

2 oval eggplants (aubergines), about 500 g
    (1 lb 2 oz) in total
salt, for sprinkling
85 ml (3 fl oz/⅓ cup) olive oil
1 large onion, cut in half lengthways, then sliced
500 g (1 lb 2 oz/2 cups) chopped, peeled tomatoes
1½ teaspoons salt
freshly ground black pepper, to season
2 tablespoons chopped flat-leaf parsley
2 teaspoons chopped mint
400 g (14 oz/2 cups) long-grain white rice
625 ml (21 fl oz/2½ cups) light stock or water
yoghurt, to serve

Cut the eggplants into large cubes, leaving the skin on.
Place in a colander, sprinkle liberally with salt and leave
for 30 minutes. Rinse and dry with paper towels.

Heat 60 ml (2 fl oz/¼ cup) of the oil in a heavy-based
saucepan and fry the eggplant in batches until lightly browned.
Remove to a plate.

Add the remaining oil to the pan and gently fry the onion
until translucent. Add the tomatoes, salt, pepper, herbs and
fried eggplant. Bring to the boil.

Wash the rice until the water runs clear. Drain and place on
top of the eggplant mixture. Pour in the stock or water, then
bring to the boil without stirring.

Reduce the heat, cover and leave to simmer gently for
20 minutes. Turn off the heat, place a cloth or two paper towels
over the rim of the pan and fit the lid on tightly. Remove from
the heat and leave to stand for 10 minutes before serving.

Stir gently and turn into a heated dish. Serve with yoghurt.

TÜRKiSTAN PiLAVI
Turkistan carrot pilaff
SERVES: 5–6

400 g (14 oz/2 cups) long-grain white rice
60 g (2 oz/¼ cup) butter
310 g (10¾ oz/2 cups) coarsely grated carrots
½ teaspoon whole black peppercorns
1 teaspoon sugar
875 ml (29 fl oz/3½ cups) chicken stock
salt, to taste

Wash the rice until the water runs clear. Drain well.

Melt the butter in a heavy-based saucepan. Add the carrot
and peppercorns and fry over medium heat for 3 minutes,
stirring often. Sprinkle in the sugar towards the end of frying.

Add the rice and fry for a further 2 minutes, stirring
constantly. Pour in the stock and add salt to taste. Stir until
boiling, then reduce the heat to low. Cover and cook for
25 minutes.

Turn off the heat, place a cloth or two paper towels over
the rim of the pan and fit the lid on tightly. Remove from the
heat and leave to stand for 10 minutes before serving.

Excellent with roast chicken or the Tavuk Yufka Içinde
recipe on page 192.

BEYAZ PiLAV
White pilaff

SERVES: 6

400 g (14 oz/2 cups) long-grain white rice

60 g (2 oz/¼ cup) butter

875 ml (29 fl oz/3½ cups) chicken stock

salt, to taste

Wash the rice until the water runs clear. Drain well.

Melt the butter in a heavy-based pan and add the drained rice. Stir over medium heat for 5 minutes.

Add the stock and salt to taste, stirring occasionally until boiling. Reduce the heat, cover and simmer for 20 minutes. Test a grain to gauge when the rice is cooked — the grain should be firm to the bite, but evenly tender.

Turn off the heat, place a cloth or two paper towels over the rim of the pan and fit the lid on tightly.

Remove from the heat and leave to stand for at least 10 minutes before removing the lid. The *pilav* may be left for as long as 30 minutes without spoiling, depending on the quality of the grain.

Fluff up the rice with a fork and serve, or spoon into an oiled mould, press firmly and turn out onto a serving dish.

DÜĞÜN PiLAV
Wedding pilaff

Use the same ingredients and method as for the Beyaz Pilav recipe (left), with the addition of 40 g (1½ oz/¼ cup) pine nuts or blanched pistachio nuts, and substituting meat stock for chicken stock. Fry the nuts with the rice and continue the recipe as directed.

DOMATESLI PiLAV
Tomato pilaff

Use the same ingredients and method as for the Beyaz Pilav recipe (left), adding 375 g (13 oz/1½ cups) chopped, peeled tomatoes halfway through frying the rice. Chicken or meat stock may be used, reducing the quantity to 625 ml (21 fl oz/2½ cups) if tinned tomatoes have been used. Add salt and pepper to taste.

TURKEY

RICE

YUFKALi PiLAV
Pilaff in pastry

SERVES: 8–10

400 g (14 oz/2 cups) long-grain white rice

60 g (2 oz/¼ cup) butter

60 g (2 oz/½ cup) slivered almonds

1 large onion, finely chopped

155 g (5 oz/1 cup) coarsely grated carrot

250 g (9 oz) lean boneless lamb, cut into
    1 cm (½ inch) cubes

185 g (6½ oz/1 cup) chopped dried apricots

1 teaspoon ground allspice

1½ teaspoons salt

freshly ground black pepper, to season

875 ml (29 fl oz/3½ cups) light stock or water

100 g (3½ oz/1 cup) crumbled vermicelli noodles

To finish

6–8 sheets fillo pastry, or 1 quantity Hamour pastry
    (page 164)

90–125 g (3–4 oz/⅓–½ cup) butter, melted

Wash the rice until the water runs clear. Leave to drain.

Melt half the butter in a deep saucepan. Fry the almonds until golden, then remove to a plate with a slotted spoon.

Add the remaining butter to the pan and gently fry the onion until translucent. Add the carrot and fry for 5 minutes longer. Increase the heat and add the lamb. Stir until the lamb changes colour, then add the apricots, allspice, salt and a good grinding of pepper.

Stir in 250 ml (8½ fl oz/1 cup) of the stock or water. Reduce the heat, cover and simmer gently for 15 minutes.

Add the remaining liquid and return to the boil, then stir in the vermicelli and rice. Bring back to the boil over medium heat, stirring occasionally. Cover and reduce the heat to low. Cook slowly for 20 minutes, or until the liquid is absorbed and the rice is just tender. Set aside with the lid on.

Preheat the oven to 190°C (375°F/Gas 5). Brush a 2 litre (68 fl oz/8 cup) pudding basin or square casserole dish with melted butter.

Brush a sheet of fillo pastry with melted butter and place another on top. Set aside and butter the remaining pastry sheets in pairs in the same way. You will need three pairs of buttered sheets for a pudding basin, four for a casserole dish.

Place one pair of pastry sheets in the dish, positioning it across the base and up the sides, with the ends hanging well over the edge. Butter the pastry in the dish, then arrange the remaining pastry in the same way, so that the dish is covered with pastry, with a generous overlap. If you are using Hamour pastry, roll it out to fit the basin or dish, with enough overlap to cover the finished pie.

Stir the almonds through the pilaff and place in the dish, spreading evenly. Pour 60 g (2 oz/¼ cup) of melted butter over the pilaff, then fold the pastry across the top to cover, buttering the top of each layer as it is put into place. Brush the top with butter.

Bake for 30 minutes. Invert onto a serving platter and cut the pie into wedges. Serve as a light meal, as part of a buffet, or as a first course.

HÜNKÂR BEĞENDİ
Sultan's delight

SERVES: 6

500 g (1 lb 2 oz) small eggplants (aubergines)
1 tablespoon lemon juice
60 g (2 oz/¼ cup) butter
35 g (1¼ oz/¼ cup) plain (all-purpose) flour
185 ml (6½ fl oz/¾ cup) milk
40 g (1½ oz/½ cup) soft white breadcrumbs, optional
60 g (2 oz/½ cup) grated *kashkaval* or *kasseri* cheese
salt and freshly ground black pepper, to taste
finely chopped flat-leaf parsley, to garnish
Tas Kebap, to serve (page 196)

Grill the eggplants over glowing charcoal, or impale on a fork and hold over a gas flame. Alternatively, place on an electric hotplate set to medium heat. Turn frequently until soft to the touch and the skin is charred to a certain degree. Another alternative is to char the skin only, then bake the eggplants at 200°C (400°F/Gas 6) for 10–20 minutes, depending on size.

Rinse off any burnt skin under cold water, then peel off the remaining skin. Purée the flesh in a blender or food processor, adding the lemon juice to keep it light in colour.

Melt the butter in a heavy-based saucepan. Stir in the flour and cook gently for 2 minutes, without letting it colour. Add the milk, stirring constantly until thickened and bubbling.

Add the eggplant purée and leave over gentle heat for 20 minutes, or until reduced a little and very thick, stirring occasionally. If desired, fine breadcrumbs may be stirred into the purée to thicken it further. Remove from the heat.

Stir in the cheese and beat well until smooth, then add salt and pepper to taste.

Pile the purée around the edge of a serving dish and sprinkle with chopped parsley. Fill the centre with Tas Kebap, or serve hot with roast lamb or chicken dishes.

❋ *Note: You can cook the eggplant in a microwave oven. Char the eggplant as described, pierce the skin in several places with a fine skewer, then microwave for 3–5 minutes, depending on size.*

KARNIBAHAR KIZARTMASI
Fried cauliflower

SERVES: 6

1 cauliflower
juice of ½ lemon
2 teaspoons salt, plus extra to season
2 eggs
freshly ground white pepper, to season
fine dry breadcrumbs, for coating
oil, for deep-frying
Yogurt Salçasi (page 164) or Tarator (page 164), to serve

Break the cauliflower into florets, cover with salted water and leave for 10 minutes to release any insects. Rinse well.

Bring 1.5 litres (51 fl oz/6 cups) water to the boil in a saucepan with the lemon juice and the 2 teaspoons salt. Drop the cauliflower florets in the boiling water and boil rapidly, uncovered, for 8–10 minutes, or until just tender.

Drain the cauliflower and spread out on paper towels to dry.

Beat the eggs and season with salt and white pepper. Dip the florets in the egg, then roll in breadcrumbs to coat completely. Place on a tray until all the florets are prepared.

Deep-fry a few at a time in a saucepan of hot oil, approximately 10 cm (4 inches) deep, for 4 minutes or until golden, turning to brown evenly. Lift out with a slotted spoon and drain on paper towels.

Serve hot as an appetiser with Yogurt Salçasi or Tarator, or as a vegetable accompaniment.

ZEYTiNYAĞLi PiRASA
Braised leeks
SERVES: 6

6 leeks
125 ml (4 fl oz/½ cup) olive oil
1 onion, sliced
2 tablespoons tomato paste (concentrated purée)
125 ml (4 fl oz/½ cup) light stock or water
½ teaspoon sugar
3 tablespoons finely chopped flat-leaf parsley
salt and freshly ground black pepper, to season
juice of ½ lemon
1 teaspoon chopped dill
extra parsley or dill sprigs, to garnish
lemon slices, to garnish

Remove the coarse outer leaves from the leeks. Trim the roots while leaving the base intact so that the leeks hold together. Cut off most of the green tops. Cut the leeks in half lengthways, then wash well to remove all traces of soil. Set aside to drain.

Heat the oil in a deep frying pan and gently fry the onion until translucent. Stir in the tomato paste, mixed with the stock or water. Add the sugar and half the chopped parsley. Season with salt and pepper and bring to the boil. Reduce the heat to low, then cover and simmer for 10 minutes.

Add the leek and lemon juice, then spoon the liquid over the leeks. Cover and simmer gently for 15–20 minutes, or until the leek is tender.

Remove to a serving dish and sprinkle with the remaining parsley and the chopped dill.

Serve at room temperature or chilled, garnished with herb sprigs and lemon slices.

HAVUÇ PLAKiSi
Braised carrots
SERVES: 6

750 g (1 lb 10 oz) carrots
2 onions
60 ml (2 fl oz/¼ cup) olive oil
1 teaspoon sugar
3 tablespoons finely chopped flat-leaf parsley
salt and freshly ground black pepper, to season
1 teaspoon lemon juice

Wash and scrape the carrots, then cut diagonally into 5 mm (¼ inch) slices. Cut the onions in half from top to bottom, then slice each half into semi-circles.

Heat the oil in a deep frying pan and gently fry the onion until translucent. Add the carrot and fry for a further 5 minutes, stirring frequently.

Add 250 ml (8½ fl oz/1 cup) water, the sugar and half the parsley. Season with salt and pepper, cover the pan tightly and simmer over low heat for 15–20 minutes, or until tender. Add the lemon juice and transfer to a dish.

Leave to cool at room temperature, or chill if preferred. Serve sprinkled with the remaining parsley.

Serve as a vegetable accompaniment.

GÜVEÇ or TÜRLÜ
Vegetable casserole

SERVES: 6

There is some confusion about the name of this dish. To the Turks, *türlü* is a vegetable casserole containing lamb or chicken. In other countries of the region, *türlü* is prepared as an all-vegetable casserole, with cooks admitting to it being a Turkish dish. *Güveç*, on the other hand, is a casserole of meat or poultry and vegetables, or vegetables on their own.

2 long eggplants (aubergines) or 1 oval eggplant

salt, for sprinkling

4 small zucchini (courgettes)

3 small green capsicums (peppers)

250 g (9 oz) okra, optional

250 g (9 oz) green beans

4–5 small ripe tomatoes, peeled (see page 528)

125 ml (4 fl oz/½ cup) olive oil

3 small onions, sliced

2 garlic cloves, crushed

salt and freshly ground black pepper, to season

1 handful chopped flat-leaf parsley

Remove the stems from the eggplants and wash well. Peel off 1 cm (½ inch) strips of skin lengthways at intervals to give a striped effect. Cut long eggplants into 1 cm (½ inch) slices; an oval eggplant should be quartered lengthways, then cut into chunky pieces.

Spread the eggplant on a tray and sprinkle liberally with salt. Leave for 30 minutes, then pat dry with paper towels.

Meanwhile, preheat the oven to 180°C (350°F/Gas 4).

Trim the zucchini and cut into 4 cm (1½ inch) pieces. Quarter the capsicums and remove the stem, seeds and white membrane. If using okra, prepare them as directed on page 8. String the beans if necessary and slit in half (French cut). Slice the tomatoes.

Heat half the oil in a frying pan and fry the eggplant until lightly browned. Remove the eggplant to a plate and reserve the oil.

Add the remaining oil to the pan and gently fry the onion until translucent. Stir in the garlic, cook for 1 minute, then remove the pan from the heat.

Place a layer of eggplant in the base of a casserole dish. Top with some of the zucchini, capsicum, okra, if using, and beans. Spread some onion mixture on top and cover with tomato slices. Sprinkle with salt, pepper and some of the parsley. Repeat until all the ingredients have been used, reserving some tomato slices and parsley.

Place the prepared okra on top, if using, and cover with the last of the tomato. Sprinkle with the remaining parsley and some salt and pepper. Pour in 125 ml (4 fl oz/½ cup) water and the reserved oil drained from the eggplant.

Cover and bake for 1–1½ hours, or until the vegetables are tender. Serve from the casserole dish as an accompaniment to roasted or grilled meats and poultry.

This dish is often served as a light meal on its own, with bread and feta cheese.

ISPANAKLI YUMURTA
Spinach and eggs

SERVES: 2 AS A LUNCHEON DISH, 4 AS A FIRST COURSE

300 g (10½ oz) fresh spinach, or 250 g (9 oz)
　　packet frozen spinach
40 g (1½ oz) butter
1 onion, finely chopped
salt and freshly ground black pepper, to season
50 g (2 oz/⅓ cup) coarsely crumbled feta cheese
4 eggs

If using fresh spinach, clean it well, removing any discoloured leaves, roots and any coarse or damaged stems. Wash well in several changes of water and shake the leaves to remove the excess moisture. Shred the leaves.

Frozen spinach may be heated in a covered saucepan over low heat. Turn the spinach occasionally until thawed.

Melt the butter in a frying pan and gently fry the onion until translucent. Add the shredded spinach, if using, and stir over medium heat until the leaves wilt and the liquid runs out. Continue to cook until there is just enough liquid to cover the base of the pan.

Alternatively, add the thawed spinach to the onion and bring to a simmer.

Season the spinach mixture with salt and pepper and stir in the cheese. Make four depressions in the mixture and break an egg into each.

Cover and cook over medium heat until the eggs have set. Serve immediately.

❀ *Note: To serve attractively as a first course, divide the spinach mixture among four individual ovenproof dishes and heat in the oven. Add an egg to each dish, drizzle a little melted butter over each and bake until set.*

FASULYE PLAKISI
White bean stew

SERVES: 6–8

400 g (14 oz/2 cups) dried haricot (navy) beans,
　　or other small white beans
125 ml (4 fl oz/½ cup) olive oil
2 large onions, chopped
2 garlic cloves, chopped
155 g (5 oz/1 cup) diced carrot
125 g (4 oz/1 cup) sliced celery, including leaves
60 g (2 oz/¼ cup) tomato paste (concentrated purée)
½ teaspoon sugar
pinch of ground hot chilli or chilli pepper
juice of ½ lemon
3 tablespoons chopped flat-leaf parsley
salt, to taste

Wash the beans in several changes of cold water and place in a large saucepan. Cover with 1.5 litres (51 fl oz/6 cups) cold water and bring to the boil. Allow to boil for 2 minutes, then remove from the heat. Cover and leave for 2 hours, or until the beans are plump. (Alternatively, soak the beans in cold water overnight, in the refrigerator if the weather is warm.)

Heat the oil in a frying pan and gently fry the onion until translucent. Add the garlic, carrot and celery and fry for 5 minutes, stirring often. Set aside.

Return the beans to the boil in their soaking water. Cover and boil gently for 30 minutes. Stir in the fried vegetables, tomato paste, sugar and chilli. Cover and simmer for a further 1½ hours, or until the beans are tender, but still intact.

Add the lemon juice, half the parsley, and salt to taste. Cook for 10 minutes longer.

Serve in a deep bowl, sprinkled with the remaining parsley. May be served hot or cold.

MENEMEN
Vegetable omelette
SERVES: 4

1 green capsicum (pepper)

1 red capsicum (pepper)

1 large onion

60 g (2 oz/¼ cup) butter, or 60 ml (2 fl oz/¼ cup) oil

250 g (9 oz/1 cup) chopped, peeled tomatoes

salt and freshly ground black pepper, to season

6 eggs

75 g (2½ oz/½ cup) crumbled feta cheese

3 tablespoons chopped flat-leaf parsley

Halve the capsicums and remove the stem, seeds and white membrane. Cut the flesh into short strips.

Cut the onion in half from top to bottom, then slice each half into semi-circles.

Heat the butter or oil in a large frying pan and gently fry the capsicum and onion until the onion is translucent, stirring often.

Stir in the tomatoes, season with salt and pepper and bring to the boil. Simmer gently for a few minutes, until the vegetables are soft.

Beat the eggs lightly, then pour into the pan. Gently stir into the vegetable mixture until creamy.

Combine the cheese with 2 tablespoons of the parsley, add to the eggs and fold in gently.

Serve immediately, sprinkled with the remaining parsley.

İMAM BAYILDI
Swooning Imam
SERVES: 4–8

8 long eggplants (aubergines)

3 onions

125 ml (4 fl oz/½ cup) olive oil

4 garlic cloves, chopped

3 tomatoes, peeled (see page 528) and chopped

3 tablespoons chopped flat-leaf parsley

salt and freshly ground black pepper, to taste

2 tablespoons lemon juice

pinch of sugar

Remove the stems from the eggplants and wash well. Peel off 1 cm (½ inch) strips lengthways at intervals to give a striped effect. On one side of each eggplant, cut a deep slit lengthways, stopping short of the top and base. Place the eggplants in a large bowl of cold, well-salted water and leave for 30 minutes. Drain, squeeze out the moisture and dry with paper towels.

Halve the onions lengthways, then cut into slender wedges. Heat half the oil in a heavy-based saucepan and gently fry the onion until translucent. Add the garlic and cook for 1 minute, then transfer the mixture to a bowl. Mix in the tomatoes and parsley, and salt and pepper to taste.

Heat the remaining oil in the pan and fry the eggplants over high heat until lightly browned, but still rather firm. Remove the pan from the heat and turn the eggplants so that the slit faces up.

Spoon the vegetable mixture into the slits, forcing in as much filling as possible. Spread the remaining filling on top. Add the lemon juice, sugar and 125 ml (4 fl oz/½ cup) water and cover the pan tightly.

Cook over gentle heat for 45 minutes, or until the eggplants are tender. Add more water only if necessary, as eggplants release a lot of moisture.

Leave to cool to room temperature. Serve as an appetiser or as a light meal with bread, or chill and serve as a salad accompaniment.

BALIK PLAKİ
Baked fish

SERVES: 6

6 fish steaks
salt and freshly ground black pepper, to season
2 onions
85 ml (3 fl oz/⅓ cup) olive oil
2 garlic cloves, finely chopped
70 g (2½ oz/½ cup) chopped celery, including leaves
80 g (3 oz/½ cup) thinly sliced carrot
375 g (13 oz/1½ cups) chopped, peeled tomatoes
lemon slices, to garnish
chopped flat-leaf parsley, to garnish

Preheat the oven to 180°C (350°F/Gas 4).

Season the fish with salt and pepper, then cover and set aside while preparing the vegetables.

Cut the onions in half from top to bottom, then slice each half into semi-circles.

Heat the oil in a frying pan and gently fry the onion with the garlic, celery and carrot until the onion is translucent. Add the tomatoes, 125 ml (4 fl oz/½ cup) water, and salt and pepper to taste. Cover and simmer gently for 20 minutes.

Spoon some of the tomato mixture into the base of a baking dish. Add the fish steaks and top with the remaining tomato mixture. Bake for 30 minutes, or until the fish flakes easily when tested with a fork.

Serve hot or cold, garnished with lemon slices and parsley.

BALIK KÖFTESİ
Fish balls

SERVES: 8–10 AS AN APPETISER

750 g (1 lb 10 oz) white fish fillets
2 spring onions, finely chopped
3 tablespoons chopped flat-leaf parsley
1 teaspoon chopped dill
120 g (4 oz/1½ cups) soft white breadcrumbs,
    plus extra if needed
1 egg
1 teaspoon salt
freshly ground black pepper, to season

To finish
plain (all-purpose) flour, for coating
oil, for deep-frying
lemon wedges, to serve

Remove any skin from the fish fillets and also remove any bones. Chop the fish roughly and combine in a bowl with the spring onion, parsley and dill.

Pass the fish mixture through a food grinder using a fine screen, or process to a paste in two batches in a food processor, using a steel blade.

Turn the mixture into a bowl. Add the breadcrumbs, egg and salt and season with pepper. Mix to a firm paste, adding some more breadcrumbs if necessary; the quantity depends on the type of fish used.

Using moistened hands, shape the mixture into balls the size of walnuts. Cover and chill until firm.

Coat the fish balls with flour and deep-fry eight at a time in a saucepan of hot oil, approximately 10 cm (4 inches) deep, for 3–4 minutes, turning to brown evenly.

Drain on paper towels and serve hot, with lemon wedges.

HAMSİ KIZARTMASI
Fried brislings or sprats

SERVES: 6 AS AN APPETISER

500 g (1 lb 2 oz) brislings, sprats or other tiny fish

salt, for sprinkling

plain (all-purpose) flour, for coating

250 ml (8½ fl oz/1 cup) oil

For serving

flat-leaf parsley sprigs, to garnish

lemon slices, to garnish

Limon Salçasi (page 189)

Wash and drain the fish; there is no need to clean the insides unless you wish to. Leave the fish intact. Drain, sprinkle with salt and leave for 10 minutes.

Coat the fish with flour. Take four or five fish, moisten the tails with water, then press the tails together to form a fan, dusting the tails again with flour.

Heat the oil in a frying pan over medium–high heat. Fry the fish in batches for about 1 minute each side, or until golden brown and crisp. Drain on paper towels.

Serve hot, garnished with parsley and lemon slices, and with a bowl of Limon Salçasi on the side.

MİDYE DOLMASI
Stuffed mussels

SERVES: 8–10

40 large mussels

250 ml (8½ fl oz/1 cup) fish stock or water

flat-leaf parsley sprigs, to garnish

lemon wedges, to serve

Tarator (page 164), to serve

Filling

85 ml (3 fl oz/⅓ cup) olive oil

1 large onion, finely chopped

3 tablespoons pine nuts

135 g (4½ oz/⅔ cup) long-grain white rice, washed

2 tablespoons chopped flat-leaf parsley

½ teaspoon ground allspice

250 g (9 oz/1 cup) chopped, peeled tomatoes

250 ml (8½ fl oz/1 cup) fish stock or water

salt and freshly ground black pepper, to taste

To make the filling, heat the oil in a frying pan and gently fry the onion until translucent. Add the pine nuts and fry for 2 minutes. Stir in the rice, parsley, allspice, tomatoes and stock. Add salt and pepper to taste, then cover and simmer gently for 15 minutes, until the rice has absorbed the liquid.

Prepare the mussels as directed in the note on page 191.

Place a generous teaspoon or two of filling in each mussel and close the shell as much as possible. Arrange in a heavy-based saucepan in even layers. Invert a heavy-based plate on top to keep the mussels closed.

Pour in the stock, bring to a simmer, then cover and simmer gently for 30 minutes. Turn off the heat and leave the mussels in the pan until cool.

Lift out the mussels and wipe dry with paper towels. For a glossy appearance, you can rub the shells with a cloth dipped in oil. The mussels may be served chilled or at room temperature, so refrigerate them if not needed immediately.

Serve on a platter, garnished with parsley and lemon wedges, with a bowl of Tarator on the side.

KILIÇ ŞİŞ
Skewered swordfish

SERVES: 6

1 kg (2 lb 3 oz) swordfish fillets, cut 3 cm
    (1¼ inches) thick
Beyaz Pilav (page 177), to serve

Marinade
60 ml (2 fl oz/¼ cup) lemon juice
2 tablespoons olive oil
1 small onion, sliced
1 teaspoon paprika
1 teaspoon salt
freshly ground black pepper, to season
2 bay leaves, crumbled

Limon salçasi
60 ml (2 fl oz/¼ cup) olive oil
60 ml (2 fl oz/¼ cup) lemon juice
3 tablespoons finely chopped flat-leaf parsley
salt and freshly ground black pepper, to taste

Remove the skin from the swordfish, if present, and cut the fillets into 3 cm (1¼ inch) cubes.

Combine the marinade ingredients in a glass or ceramic bowl. Add the fish, turn to coat with the marinade, then cover and refrigerate for 1–2 hours, turning the fish occasionally.

Thread the fish onto six metal skewers and cook over glowing charcoal for 10–12 minutes, turning the skewers frequently and brushing occasionally with the marinade.

Combine the Limon Salçasi ingredients in a screw-top jar, seal and shake until combined.

Serve the hot fish skewers with Beyaz Pilav, with the Limon Salçasi served separately.

❁ *Note:* Limon Salçasi *(lemon sauce) is used as a dressing for grilled, fried, boiled and baked fish, as well as salads and vegetables.*

MiDYE TAVASI
Fried mussels

SERVES: 6

40 mussels
plain (all-purpose) flour, for coating
oil, for deep-frying

Beer batter
150 g (5 oz/1 cup) plain (all-purpose) flour
1 teaspoon salt
185 ml (6½ fl oz/¾ cup) beer,
   approximately

For serving
lemon wedges
chopped flat-leaf parsley
Tarator (page 164)

To make the beer batter, sift the flour and salt into a mixing bowl. Pour in the beer and mix to a smooth batter, adding a little more beer if necessary.

If the mussels are in their shells, prepare them as directed below. Release the mussels from their shells with the point of a knife. Drain the mussels on paper towels.

Toss the mussels in flour to coat them lightly. Dip them in the batter and deep-fry a few at a time in a saucepan of hot oil, approximately 10 cm (4 inches) deep, turning to brown evenly. Remove with a slotted spoon and drain on paper towels.

Serve hot, garnishing the platter with lemon wedges and parsley, with the Tarator in a separate bowl. Provide cocktail sticks for convenience.

❈ *Note: To prepare the mussels, scrub them well with a stiff brush, scraping the shells with a knife to remove any marine growth. Tug the beards towards the pointed end and remove them. To open the mussels easily, place them in warm salted water. As each one opens, insert the point of a knife between the two shells and slide it towards the pointed end, to sever the fine white ligament near the hinge. For stuffing, take care not to separate the shells; the shells may be separated if removing mussel meat for other recipes.*

TAVUK YUFKA İÇİNDE
Chicken in pastry

SERVES: 6

90 g (3 oz/⅓ cup) butter

1 kg (2 lb 3 oz) chicken breast fillets

4 small onions

1 large ripe tomato, peeled (see page 528) and chopped

salt and freshly ground black pepper, to taste

To finish

12 sheets fillo pastry

90 g (3 oz/⅓ cup) butter, melted

flat-leaf parsley sprigs, to garnish

Preheat the oven to 190°C (375°F/Gas 5).

Melt half the butter in a frying pan and brown the chicken over medium heat, turning frequently. Cook for 10 minutes, or until just cooked through. Remove to a plate.

Cut the onions in half from top to bottom, then slice each half into thin semi-circles. Heat the remaining butter in the pan and gently fry the onion until translucent.

Add the tomato and salt and pepper to taste. Stir in 185 ml (6½ fl oz/¾ cup) water and cook gently until the moisture evaporates. The mixture should look oily.

Cut the chicken breasts into strips about 5 cm (2 inches) long, then stir gently into the tomato mixture. Remove from the heat.

Brush a sheet of fillo pastry with melted butter. Top with another sheet, butter it, then fold the pastry in half, to form almost a square shape. Brush again with butter.

Place one-sixth of the filling towards the centre and slightly towards one corner. Fold this corner over the filling, then fold the adjacent corners on top and finish like a parcel, tucking the last corner underneath the package. Place on a lightly buttered baking tray. Repeat with the remaining ingredients.

Brush the top of each pastry parcel lightly with butter, then bake for 15 minutes, or until golden.

Serve immediately, garnished with parsley. Turkistan Pilavi (page 176) is a good accompaniment.

ÇERKES TAVÜGÜ
Circassian chicken

SERVES: 6

1 chicken, about 1.5 kg (3 lb 5 oz)
1 large onion, quartered
1 carrot, quartered
2 flat-leaf parsley sprigs
1½ teaspoons salt
freshly ground white pepper, to taste
3 slices of stale white bread, crusts removed
170 g (6 oz/1½ cups) finely ground walnuts
½ teaspoon paprika
1 garlic clove, crushed, optional

For serving
½ teaspoon paprika
1 tablespoon walnut oil (see note)
finely chopped flat-leaf parsley, optional

Place the chicken in a saucepan with the onion, carrot, parsley sprigs and 750 ml (25 fl oz/3 cups) cold water. Bring to a slow simmer, skimming when necessary. Add the salt, and white pepper to taste. Cover and simmer gently for 1½ hours, but do not allow to boil, as this makes the flesh stringy.

Allow to cool a little, then remove the chicken from the pan. Strip off the flesh and reserve. Return the skin and bones to the pan, then boil the stock with the bones and skin until reduced by half. Strain and reserve the stock.

Cut the chicken meat into 5 cm (2 inch) strips and place in a bowl. Moisten with 2 tablespoons of the stock, then cover and refrigerate.

Soak the bread in a little chicken stock, then squeeze and crumble into a bowl. Mix in the walnuts, paprika and garlic, if using. Pass the mixture through a food grinder using a fine screen, or process in a food processor or blender using a steel blade.

Slowly beat in 250 ml (8½ fl oz/1 cup) of the warm chicken stock, skimmed of any fat, adding a little more if necessary to make a smooth, thick sauce. Adjust the seasoning with salt and white pepper.

Gently mix one-third of the walnut sauce into the chicken. Shape the chicken mixture into a neat mound on a shallow dish and spread the remaining walnut sauce over it. Cover lightly with plastic wrap and chill.

To serve, steep the paprika in walnut oil for 10 minutes or longer, and drizzle over the chicken just before serving.

Garnish with chopped parsley if desired. Serve cold, with salad accompaniments.

❊ *Note: Walnut oil is available from some health food stores and is usually very expensive. See page 529 for details on how to prepare your own.*

İZMİR KÖFTESİ
« Meatballs in tomato sauce
SERVES: 5–6

750 g (1 lb 10 oz) finely minced (ground) lamb or beef

1 garlic clove, crushed

1 small onion, finely grated

2 thick slices of stale white bread

1 egg

1 teaspoon ground cumin

2 tablespoons finely chopped flat-leaf parsley

salt and freshly ground black pepper, to season

plain (all-purpose) flour, for coating

60 g (2 oz/¼ cup) butter, or 60 ml (2 fl oz/¼ cup) oil

Tomato sauce

375 g (13 oz/1½ cups) chopped, peeled tomatoes

80 g (3 oz/½ cup) finely chopped green capsicum (pepper)

½ teaspoon sugar

salt and freshly ground black pepper, to taste

In a mixing bowl, combine the meat, garlic and onion. Soak the bread in cold water, squeeze dry and crumble into the bowl. Add the egg, cumin and parsley and season with salt and pepper. Mix thoroughly to a smooth paste.

Using moistened hands, shape tablespoons of the meat mixture into oval, sausage-like shapes. Coat them lightly with flour.

Heat the butter or oil in a deep saucepan. Fry the meatballs in batches until lightly browned on all sides, removing each batch to a plate with a slotted spoon.

To make the tomato sauce, add the tomatoes and capsicum to the pan and stir over medium heat for 5 minutes. Add the sugar and salt and pepper to taste, then stir in 125 ml (4 fl oz/ ½ cup) water. Bring to the boil and return the meatballs to the pan. Bring to a slow simmer.

Cover and simmer gently for 1 hour, until the meatballs are tender and the sauce is thick. Serve with pilaff.

ŞİŞ KEBAP
Skewered lamb and vegetables
SERVES: 6

1 kg (2 lb 3 oz) boneless lamb, from the leg

juice of 1 large lemon

60 ml (2 fl oz/¼ cup) olive oil

1 onion, thinly sliced

1 bay leaf, crumbled

½ teaspoon dried thyme

freshly ground black pepper

To finish

12 small onions

1 red capsicum (pepper)

1 green capsicum (pepper)

salt, to season

Beyaz Pilav (page 177), to serve

Cut the lamb into 3 cm (1¼ inch) cubes and place in a glass or ceramic bowl. Add the lemon juice, oil, onion slices, bay leaf and thyme. Season with pepper, but do not add salt until after cooking, as it tends to draw out the meat juices.

Cover and marinate in the refrigerator for 4–6 hours, turning the meat occasionally.

Peel the whole small onions and parboil in a saucepan of salted water for 5 minutes. Drain.

Wash the capsicums and remove the stems, seeds and white membrane. Cut into 3 cm (1¼ inch) squares. Lift the lamb from the marinade and thread onto six long skewers, alternating with the onions and capsicum pieces.

Cook over glowing charcoal for 10–12 minutes, turning frequently and brushing with the marinade when required. After sealing the meat, remove the skewers to a cooler part of the fire or raise the grill, otherwise the vegetables will burn.

Serve hot, on a bed of Beyaz Pilav. The rice may be coloured with ½ teaspoon turmeric, added when frying the rice in the butter.

TAŞ KEBAP
Braised lamb

SERVES: 6

1 kg (2 lb 3 oz) boneless lamb stewing meat

60 g (2 oz/¼ cup) butter

2 onions, finely chopped

40 g (1½ oz/¼ cup) chopped green capsicum (pepper), optional

375 g (13 oz/1½ cups) chopped, peeled tomatoes, or 60 g (2 oz/¼ cup) tomato paste (concentrated purée)

½ teaspoon ground allspice

salt and freshly ground black pepper, to season

3 tablespoons chopped flat-leaf parsley

For serving
Hünkâr Beğendi (page 180), or Beyaz Pilav (page 177)

Trim the meat and cut into 2 cm (¾ inch) cubes.

Melt half the butter in a heavy-based saucepan. Working in batches, brown the meat quickly on each side, transferring each batch to a plate.

Melt the remaining butter in the pan and gently fry the onion and capsicum, if using, until the onion is translucent.

Add the tomatoes or tomato paste. Pour in 250 ml (8½ fl oz/1 cup) water if using tomatoes, and more if using tomato paste. Stir well to dissolve any browned sediment. Add the allspice, most of the parsley, and salt and pepper to taste.

Return the lamb to the pan. Cover and simmer gently for 1½ hours, or until the lamb is tender and the sauce has thickened.

Pile in the centre of a dish of Hünkâr Beğendi; if serving with Beyaz Pilav, press the cooked pilaff into an oiled ring mould and turn it out onto a serving platter. Spoon some of the sauce over the rice and place the meat in the centre of ring.

Sprinkle the meat with the remaining parsley and serve hot.

TALAŞ KEBAP
Lamb in pastry

SERVES: 4

750 g (1 lb 10 oz) boneless lamb, from the shoulder

40 g (1½ oz) butter

1 small onion, finely chopped

250 g (9 oz/1 cup) chopped, peeled tomatoes

2 tablespoons chopped flat-leaf parsley

salt and freshly ground black pepper, to season

8 sheets fillo pastry

90 g (3 oz/⅓ cup) butter, melted

Trim the lamb and cut into 1 cm (½ inch) cubes.

Melt the butter in a heavy-based saucepan. Add the lamb and brown over high heat, stirring often. Reduce the heat to medium, add the onion and cook with the lamb for 10 minutes, stirring occasionally.

Stir in the tomatoes and parsley and season with salt and pepper. Cover and simmer gently for 1 hour. Remove the lid and increase the heat to reduce the liquid to a thick sauce if necessary. Remove from the heat.

Preheat the oven to 180°C (350°F/Gas 4).

Brush one sheet of fillo pastry with melted butter and place another sheet on top. Brush the top with more butter and fold the pastry in half, to give almost a square shape. Cover with a cloth and assemble the remaining pastry similarly.

Take one lot of pastry and brush the top with butter. Spread one-quarter of the lamb mixture towards one end, leaving the sides clear. Fold the end of the pastry over the filling, roll once, fold the sides in, then roll up. Place on a buttered baking tray, seam side down. Repeat with the remaining pastry and lamb.

Brush the top of the pastries with more butter. Bake for 30 minutes, or until puffed and golden. Serve immediately.

❁ *Note: Commercial puff pastry may be used instead of fillo; 375 g (13 oz) is sufficient. Roll out thinly, then cut into four 15 × 20 cm (6 × 8 inch) rectangles. Moisten the sides and press to seal, instead of folding the sides over the filling. Bake at 230°C (450°F/Gas 8) for 10 minutes, then at 180°C (350°F/Gas 4) until puffed and golden.*

DÜĞÜN ETİ
Wedding meat
SERVES: 6

Another wedding feast dish. Ingredient quantities have been scaled down considerably – even the Turks don't wait for a wedding just to prepare this spicy lamb dish.

6 lamb shoulder chops, cut 4 cm (1½ inches) thick
60 g (2 oz/¼ cup) butter
2 onions, chopped
375 g (13 oz/1½ cups) chopped, peeled tomatoes
1½ teaspoons ground cinnamon
½ teaspoon whole allspice, crushed
3 cloves
salt and freshly ground black pepper, to season

For serving
grilled tomato slices
Düğün Pilav (page 177)

Trim the chops if necessary. Melt half the butter in a heavy-based saucepan and brown the meat on each side, in batches if necessary. Remove to a plate.

Melt the remaining butter in the pan and gently fry the onion until translucent. Add the tomatoes, spices and 250 ml (8½ fl oz/1 cup) water, stirring well to dissolve the browned sediment. Bring to the boil, then reduce the heat.

Return the lamb to the pan and season with salt and pepper. Cover and simmer over low heat for 1½ hours, or until the meat is tender. Remove the cloves if desired.

Arrange the lamb on a warm platter, with the grilled tomato slices around the lamb. Pour the sauce over the meat and serve hot, with Düğün Pilav.

KADIN BUDU
'Ladies' thighs' croquettes
SERVES: 6

750 g (1 lb 10 oz) finely minced (ground) lean lamb or beef
185 g (6½ oz/1 cup) boiled long-grain white rice
1 onion, finely chopped
75 g (2½ oz/½ cup) crumbled feta cheese
3 tablespoons finely chopped flat-leaf parsley
1 teaspoon finely chopped dill
2 large eggs
salt and freshly ground black pepper, to season
oil, for pan-frying
plain (all-purpose) flour, for coating

Combine the meat, rice, onion and cheese in a mixing bowl. Pass the mixture through a meat grinder using a fine screen, or process in a food processor using a steel blade.

Add the herbs and 1 lightly beaten egg; season with salt and pepper. Mix by hand to a smooth paste.

Using moistened hands, take a generous tablespoon of the mixture and form it into an elongated egg shape, wider at one end than the other, or into a simpler torpedo shape. Place each one in a dish, side by side, as each one is finished.

Pour oil into a frying pan to a depth of 1 cm (½ inch). Heat the oil over high heat. Meanwhile, beat the remaining egg well and pour over the croquettes, then turn them over in the dish to coat them evenly with a film of egg. Place about 75 g (2½ oz/½ cup) flour on a plate.

Roll the croquettes in the flour, one at a time, placing them into the hot oil as they are coated. Use one hand for rolling them in the flour; keep the other hand dry for moving them to the pan.

Fry over high heat until golden brown, turning the croquettes frequently with tongs so they keep their shape. Drain on paper towels.

Serve hot, with a vegetable or salad accompaniment.

KUSYUVASI
Bird's nest pastries

MAKES: 20

20 sheets fillo pastry

185 g (6½ oz/¾ cup) unsalted butter, melted

Syrup

550 g (1 lb 4 oz/2½ cups) sugar

thinly peeled rind of ½ lemon

juice of ½ lemon, strained

Nut filling

235 g (8½ oz/1½ cups) finely chopped blanched
    almonds

65 g (2¼ oz/½ cup) finely chopped blanched
    pistachio nuts

2 tablespoons caster (superfine) sugar

To make the syrup, put the sugar and 375 ml (12½ fl oz/ 1½ cups) water in a heavy-based saucepan over medium heat, stirring occasionally to dissolve the sugar. Bring to the boil, then add the lemon rind and lemon juice. Allow to boil, without stirring, for 15 minutes. Cool and strain into a jug, then chill until required.

Preheat the oven to 180°C (350°F/Gas 4).

To make the nut filling, combine the almonds and pistachios in a bowl. Set aside about one-third of the mixture, then stir the sugar into the remainder.

Open out the fillo sheets and place between two dry cloths. Cover the top with a lightly dampened cloth to prevent the pastry drying out.

Spread one sheet of pastry out on a work surface. Brush with melted butter and fold in half lengthways, to give almost a square shape. Brush again with butter and sprinkle 1 tablespoon of the nut filling near the folded edge. Turn the pastry over the filling, fold in 1 cm (½ inch) on each side, and roll up to within 4 cm (1½ inches) of the other edge.

Lift the pastry up by the rolled edge, with the flap hanging towards you, and twirl it into a ring, curling it away from you. Tuck the loose pastry under, into the centre of the ring, to form a nest. Repeat with the remaining ingredients.

Place the pastries in a buttered baking dish and brush the tops lightly with butter.

Bake for 20 minutes, then reduce the oven temperature to 150°C (300°F/Gas 2) and bake for a further 15 minutes, so that the pastry cooks through without over-browning.

Pour half the cold syrup over the hot pastries. Leave until cool, then sprinkle some of the reserved nuts over the centre of each pastry.

Remove to a serving platter and serve the remaining syrup in a jug, for adding to individual taste.

KADIN GÖBEĞİ
Ladies' navels
MAKES: ABOUT 20

The name and the finished dish are colourfully Turkish, while the basic dough is very definitely French. Though the ingredient proportions differ from the traditional formula, it is choux pastry nonetheless, prepared in the Turkish manner.

oil, for shaping and frying

whipped cream or Ushta (clotted cream, page 296)

35 g (1¼ oz/¼ cup) finely chopped, blanched
    pistachio nuts

Syrup
440 g (15½ oz/2 cups) sugar

juice of ½ lemon, strained

Choux pastry
150 g (5 oz/1 cup) plain (all-purpose) flour

¼ teaspoon salt

60 g (2 oz/¼ cup) butter

2 large eggs, lightly beaten

⅛ teaspoon almond essence

To make the syrup, put the sugar and 375 ml (12½ fl oz/1½ cups) water in a heavy-based saucepan over medium heat, stirring occasionally to dissolve the sugar. Bring to the boil, then add the lemon juice. Allow to boil rapidly, without stirring, for 15 minutes. Leave the syrup to cool in the pan.

To make the pastry, sift the flour and salt onto a square of stiff paper. In another heavy-based saucepan, heat the butter and 250 ml (8½ fl oz/1 cup) water until boiling. Pour in the flour all at once, stirring constantly with a wooden spoon or balloon whisk. Keep stirring until the mixture leaves the side of pan, then cook over low heat, stirring occasionally, for a further 5 minutes.

Remove the roux from the heat and tip it into a bowl. Cool for 2 minutes, then gradually beat in the eggs. Add the almond essence and beat until smooth and satiny. A balloon whisk will break up lumps, while a wooden spoon is better for beating to a smooth finish, so use both.

Oil your hands and take pieces of dough the size of walnuts. Roll into smooth balls and place on an oiled tray. Flatten into rounds about 5 cm (2 inches) in diameter, then press an oiled forefinger into the centre of each to make a hole. Keep your hands oiled during the shaping so that the dough will not stick.

Pour oil into a large electric frying pan to a depth of 1 cm (½ inch). Heat until just warm. Place half the doughnuts in the oil. As soon as they are added, increase the heat to 200°C (400°F). When they rise to the surface and are puffed, turn them over. Fry them for 15 minutes in all, timed from when they are first placed into the pan; turn frequently during the last half of the cooking time so they brown evenly.

When cooked, remove them from the oil with a slotted spoon and drain briefly on paper towels. Place them in the syrup, turn them to coat, then leave for 5 minutes before removing to a plate.

Turn off the frying pan and allow the oil to cool down before adding the second batch of doughnuts.

Arrange the doughnuts on a flat platter and place a dollop of whipped cream or Ushta in the centre. Serve sprinkled with the pistachios.

❀ *Note: If you don't have an electric frying pan, use a large frying pan set on a thermostatically controlled hot plate or burner. Otherwise, use an ordinary burner, start at low and increase the heat to midway between the medium and high settings.*

DİLBER DUDAĞI
Lips of the beauty

Follow the Kadin Göbeği recipe on page 200, until the roux has been prepared. Oil your hands, take pieces of dough the size of walnuts and roll into balls. Flatten each ball of dough in your hand to a 6 cm (2½ inch) round, then fold the dough over so that the pastries resemble lips on their curved edge. Place on an oiled tray until all are shaped. Fry and finish as instructed. Serve plain, or with whipped cream or Ushta (page 296).

HANIM PARMAĞI
Dainty fingers

Follow the Kadin Göbeği recipe on page 200, to the stage where the eggs are beaten into the roux. Instead of shaping the dough into balls, shape about 2 teaspoons of the dough into fingers about 8 cm (3¼ inches) long. Keep your hands oiled, and place the finished shapes on an oiled tray.

Heat the oil for deep-frying to 200°C (400°F/Gas 6) and deep-fry eight to ten at a time for 10 minutes, turning to brown evenly. Drain briefly on paper towels and place in the syrup. Leave for 5 minutes to soak, then lift out and serve warm, piled on a platter. Sprinkle with finely chopped walnuts or pistachio nuts if desired.

KESKÜL
Almond custard

SERVES: 6

115 g (4 oz/¾ cup) whole blanched almonds

1 litre (34 fl oz/4 cups) milk

30 g (1 oz/¼ cup) ground white rice

¼ teaspoon salt

55 g (2 oz/¼ cup) sugar

4 drops of almond essence

chopped pistachio nuts or toasted slivered almonds, to garnish

pomegranate seeds, to garnish, optional

Grind the almonds finely in a food processor or blender, or pass through a food grinder two or three times using a fine screen. Tip into a bowl, then knead to a firm paste with your hand.

Heat 250 ml (8½ fl oz/1 cup) of the milk to boiling point. Pour onto the almonds and stir with a wooden spoon until well combined. Set aside to steep.

In a large bowl, mix together the ground rice and another 60 ml (2 fl oz/¼ cup) of the milk. Heat the remaining milk in a heavy-based saucepan, preferably one with a non-stick coating. Bring to the boil, then pour the milk into the ground rice mixture, stirring constantly, then return all the mixture to the pan.

Bring to the boil, add the salt and boil gently for 10 minutes, stirring occasionally.

Strain the almond milk through a fine sieve set over a bowl, pressing on the almonds with the back of a spoon. Discard the almonds. Pour the almond milk into the saucepan and stir well to combine. Add the sugar and boil gently for a further 10 minutes.

Stir in the almond essence and pour into individual dessert bowls. Serve garnished with chopped nuts, and pomegranate seeds if available.

LOKUM
Turkish delight

MAKES: ABOUT 1 KG (2 LB 3 OZ)

It is very important that the right cornflour (cornstarch) be used. There are two types available in some countries – one is made from corn/maize; the other is made from wheat and called wheaten cornflour. Use the one made from corn, otherwise your *lokum* will not remain thick during the lengthy cooking.

880 g (1 lb 15 oz/4 cups) sugar

1 teaspoon lemon juice

125 g (4 oz/1 cup) cornflour (cornstarch; see note above)

1 teaspoon cream of tartar

1–2 tablespoons rosewater

red food colouring

80 g (3 oz/½ cup) chopped, toasted unblanched almonds, optional

To finish

60 g (2 oz/½ cup) icing (confectioners') sugar

30 g (1 oz/¼ cup) cornflour (cornstarch; see note above)

Combine the sugar, lemon juice and 375 ml (12½ fl oz/ 1½ cups) water in a heavy-based saucepan. Stir over low heat until the sugar has dissolved, brushing the sugar crystals off the side of the pan with a bristle brush dipped in cold water.

Bring the syrup to the boil. Allow to boil to the 'soft ball' stage, when a small spoonful of the syrup forms a ball when dropped into a bowl of very cold water — 115°C (240°F) on a sugar thermometer. Remove from the heat.

In another heavy-based saucepan, mix together the cornflour, cream of tartar and 250 ml (8½ fl oz/1 cup) cold water until smooth.

Boil 500 ml (17 fl oz/2 cups) water and stir into the cornflour mixture. Place over the heat and stir constantly until the mixture thickens and bubbles; use a balloon whisk if any lumps form.

Gradually pour the hot syrup into the cornflour mixture, stirring constantly. Bring to the boil, then allow to boil gently for 1¼ hours. Stir occasionally with a wooden spoon and cook until the mixture is a pale golden colour. Stirring is essential during this time.

Stir in the rosewater to taste, and a few drops of red food colouring to tinge it a pale pink. Mix in the nuts, if using, and remove from the heat.

Pour into an oiled 23 cm (9 inch) square cake tin and leave for 12 hours to set.

To finish the Turkish delight, combine the icing sugar and cornflour in a flat dish. Cut the Turkish delight into squares with an oiled knife, then gently toss in the icing sugar mixture.

Store in a sealed container, with the remaining icing sugar mixture sprinkled between the layers.

❉ *Variations*

Crème de menthe lokum: *Replace the rosewater and red food colouring with 2 tablespoons crème de menthe liqueur and a little green food colouring. Omit the nuts.*

Orange lokum: *Use 1–2 tablespoons orange flower water instead of rosewater; use orange food colouring.*

Vanilla lokum: *Use 2 teaspoons vanilla essence instead of rosewater and colouring, and stir in 80 g (3 oz/½ cup) toasted chopped almonds or chopped walnuts. Do not blanch the almonds.*

SARIĞI BURMA
Sultan's turbans
MAKES: 24

This dish is also prepared in Lebanon and Syria, where it goes under the delightful name of *zind es sitt* (ladies' wrists). It is important to have very fresh, pliable fillo pastry sheets, as the roll has to be crumpled up; brittle pastry breaks. If you find early attempts fail, then shape the remainder of the ingredients as directed at the end of the method. For tips on handling fillo sheets, see page 13.

24 sheets fillo pastry

185 g (6½ oz/¾ cup) unsalted butter, melted and warm

Syrup

440 g (15½ oz/2 cups) sugar

1 tablespoon lemon juice

1 small piece of cinnamon bark

2 cloves

Nut filling

200 g (7 oz/2 cups) finely ground almonds or walnuts

55 g (2 oz/¼ cup) caster (superfine) sugar

1 teaspoon ground cinnamon

To make the syrup, put the sugar and 375 ml (12½ fl oz/1½ cups) water in a heavy-based saucepan over medium heat, stirring occasionally to dissolve the sugar. Bring to the boil, then add the lemon juice, cinnamon and cloves. Allow to boil rapidly, without stirring, for 15 minutes. Skim if required, then strain and cool.

Meanwhile, preheat the oven to 180°C (350°F/Gas 4).

Combine the nut filling ingredients in a bowl. Have a length of wooden dowel on hand — one about 5 mm (¼ inch) in diameter and 50 cm (20 inches) long.

Spread a sheet of pastry on a work surface, with the longer edge towards you. Brush lightly and evenly with warm melted butter. (To keep the butter warm, have it in a heatproof bowl, sitting in a saucepan of hot water.)

Evenly sprinkle 2 tablespoons of the filling across the lower third of the pastry, keeping 3 cm (1¼ inches) clear of the base and just a little in from the sides.

Fold the bottom edge over the filling and place the wooden dowel along the edge. Roll the pastry with the filling firmly over the dowel, to the end of the sheet. Make sure the end of the pastry sticks on firmly; if not, brush again with a little warm melted butter.

Grip the dowel at each end of the pastry and push your hands gradually towards each other, crumpling up the pastry evenly as you push. When evenly crumpled and with the pastry roll less than half its original length, slip the pastry roll off the dowel, onto the work surface. Trim the ends, then twist into a flat snail-like coil.

Repeat with the remaining ingredients, taking care that the pastry does not dry out, otherwise shaping will be difficult.

Place the completed coils close together in a buttered baking dish. Brush lightly with melted butter and bake for 25–30 minutes, until light golden brown.

Pour the cooled thick syrup over the hot coils. Leave in the baking dish until cold before serving, or store in a sealed container at room temperature.

✿ *Note: For an alternative shape, assemble and roll the pastry on the dowel prior to crumpling, then slide the pastry onto a work surface. Using a sharp knife, cut the roll into 10 cm (4 inch) lengths. Place in a greased baking dish, brush lightly with melted butter and finish as directed above.*

AŞURE
Noah's pudding

SERVES: 12–16

The credit for this dish goes back a long, long way. Of course it is pure speculation, but it illustrates the romantic nature of the Turks. It is said that on the last day on the Ark, the women used up all the remaining foods and came up with *aşure*.

In Turkey today, this pudding is prepared with great ceremony during the month of Muharrem, also known as the Month of Aşure. Usually a vast quantity is made so that some may be given to friends and relatives. It is considered impolite not to give *aşure* to any person who may catch the cooking aroma.

As the right wheat for *aşure* is difficult to find outside the Middle East, the recipe is usually made with coarse burghul (bulgur) elsewhere.

110 g (3¾ oz/½ cup) chickpeas

100 g (3½ oz/½ cup) dried haricot (navy) beans

175 g (6 oz/1 cup) coarse burghul (bulgur)

110 g (3¾ oz/½ cup) short-grain white rice

330 g (11½ oz/1½ cups) sugar

½ teaspoon salt

375 ml (12½ fl oz/1½ cups) milk

90 g (3 oz/¾ cup) sultanas (golden raisins)

35 g (1¼ oz/¼ cup) currants

95 g (3¼ oz/½ cup) chopped dried apricots

95 g (3¼ oz/½ cup) chopped dried figs

80 g (3 oz/½ cup) chopped blanched almonds

60 g (2 oz/½ cup) chopped walnuts

40 g (1½ oz/¼ cup) pine nuts

60 ml (2 fl oz/¼ cup) rosewater

pomegranate seeds, blanched almonds or
    pistachio nuts, to garnish

Wash the chickpeas and beans well and place in separate bowls. Cover each with 375 ml (12½ fl oz/1½ cups) cold water and leave overnight in a cool place.

Rinse the burghul and rice and place in separate bowls. Add 1 litre (34 fl oz/4 cups) cold water to the burghul, and 250 ml (8½ fl oz/1 cup) water to the rice. Leave overnight.

The next day put the chickpeas and beans, with their soaking water, in separate saucepans. Cook for 1½–2½ hours, or until tender — the chickpeas will take longer to cook than the beans.

Place the burghul with its soaking water in a large heavy-based saucepan. Pour in an additional 750 ml (25 fl oz/3 cups) water. Drain the rice and add to the pan. Place over low heat and cook gently, uncovered, for 40–50 minutes, or until the mixture is very soft, with a porridge-like consistency.

Drain the chickpeas and beans and add to the saucepan with another 250 ml (8½ fl oz/1 cup) water. Leave over low heat, uncovered, for 30 minutes, stirring occasionally, until the liquid is well reduced and the mixture is thick.

Stir in the sugar, salt and milk and cook for 15 minutes longer. Stir in the fruits and nuts and remove from the heat. Add the rosewater and stir well, then pour into a large bowl or individual dessert bowls.

Cool to room temperature, or cover and chill in the refrigerator.

Serve decorated with pomegranate seeds if available, otherwise decorate with blanched almonds or pistachio nuts.

YOĞURT TATLISI
« Yoghurt cake
SERVES: 10–12

185 g (6½ oz/¾ cup) butter

grated zest of 1 lemon

230 g (8 oz/1 cup) caster (superfine) sugar

5 eggs, separated

250 g (9 oz/1 cup) yoghurt

335 g (11½ oz/2¼ cups) plain (all-purpose) flour

2 teaspoons baking powder

pinch of salt

½ teaspoon bicarbonate of soda (baking soda)

Syrup
220 g (8 oz/1 cup) sugar

1 thin lemon rind strip

1 tablespoon strained lemon juice

Preheat the oven to 180°C (350°F/Gas 4). Grease and flour a 20 cm (8 inch) ring cake tin.

Cream the butter, lemon zest and sugar in a bowl until fluffy. Add the egg yolks separately, beating well after each addition, then mix in the yoghurt.

Sift the flour, baking powder, salt and bicarbonate of soda together, then fold into the creamed butter mixture.

Beat the egg whites until stiff, then fold into the cake batter. Spoon into the cake tin and bake for 50–55 minutes.

Meanwhile, make the syrup. Combine the sugar and 185 ml (6½ fl oz/¾ cup) cold water in a heavy-based saucepan over medium heat, stirring occasionally to dissolve the sugar. Bring to the boil, then add the lemon rind strip and lemon juice. Allow to boil over medium heat, without stirring, for 10 minutes. Remove the lemon rind strip and leave the syrup to cool in the pan.

Cool the cake in the tin for 5 minutes, then turn out onto a serving dish.

Spoon the cold syrup over the cake, letting it seep slowly into the cake. Serve warm, cut into thick slices, with whipped cream or Ushta (page 296).

İNCİR COMPOSTU
Figs in syrup
SERVES: 6–8

500 g (1 lb 2 oz) dried figs

blanched almonds, for stuffing

165 g (5½ oz/¾ cup) sugar

1 thin lemon rind strip

juice of 1 lemon

90 g (3 oz/¼ cup) honey

For serving
chopped almonds, pistachio nuts or walnuts

whipped cream or yoghurt

Wash the figs well and cover with 1 litre (34 fl oz/4 cups) cold water. Leave for 8 hours, or until plump. Drain the soaking liquid into a heavy-based saucepan.

Insert an almond into each fig, from the base. Set aside.

Add the sugar to the water in the pan and heat, stirring occasionally, until the sugar has dissolved. Add the lemon rind strip, lemon juice and honey and bring to the boil.

Add the stuffed figs and return to the boil. Allow to boil gently, uncovered, for 30 minutes, until the figs are tender and the syrup is thick. Remove the lemon rind strip.

Arrange the figs upright in a bowl. Pour the syrup over the figs, leave to cool, then cover and chill.

Sprinkle with chopped nuts and serve with whipped cream or yoghurt.

DONDURMA ÇİLEKLİ
Strawberry water ice
SERVES: 6–8

Flavoured water ices are another Western dessert adapted into Turkish cuisine. Turkey has wonderful fruit, and the climate is conducive to cooling desserts such as these.

450 g (1 lb/3 cups) whole strawberries
1 teaspoon strained lemon juice
60 ml (2 fl oz/¼ cup) milk
red food colouring

Syrup
220 g (8 oz/1 cup) sugar
2 teaspoons lemon juice

To make the syrup, put the sugar in a heavy-based saucepan with 500 ml (17 fl oz/2 cups) water and stir over medium heat until the sugar has dissolved. Add the lemon juice and bring to the boil. Allow to boil for 5 minutes, skimming when necessary, then leave until cool.

Wash the strawberries, drain well and remove the hulls. Purée the strawberries in a food processor; you should end up with about 500 ml (17 fl oz/2 cups) strawberry purée.

Combine the purée with the cooled syrup, lemon juice and milk. Stir in a few drops of food colouring. Pour into a freezer tray or loaf tin and freeze.

Spoon into chilled dessert glasses and serve immediately.

If desired, the ice can be flaked with a fork before spooning it into glasses.

DONDURMA LİMONLU
Lemon water ice
SERVES: 6–8

4 lemons
220 g (8 oz/1 cup) sugar
1 egg white
yellow food colouring, optional

Wash the lemons well. Thinly peel the rind from each lemon, so that there is little or no white pith left on the rind.

Place the rind in a saucepan with 750 ml (25 fl oz/3 cups) water and bring slowly to the boil. Boil, uncovered, for 10 minutes. Strain into a measuring jug and discard the rind. If necessary, make up the liquid to 500 ml (17 fl oz/2 cups) with water. Return the liquid to the pan.

Add the sugar to the pan and dissolve over medium heat, stirring occasionally. Bring to the boil, then leave to boil over medium heat for 5 minutes. Leave until cool.

Juice the lemons and strain. Measure 185 ml (6½ fl oz/ ¾ cup) of the juice and add to the cooled syrup. Pour into a bowl and place in the freezer. Leave until the mixture is half-frozen, then stir well to break up any ice crystals.

Beat the egg white until stiff. Combine thoroughly into the half-frozen syrup, with a little yellow food colouring if desired. Return to the freezer and leave until just firm.

Remove from the freezer and beat well until smooth and light. Pour into a loaf tin, cover with foil and freeze until very firm — about 3 hours or longer.

To serve, draw a metal spoon across the *dondurma* and place the flaky curls into chilled sweet glasses. Alternatively, scoop it out with an ice-cream scoop.

DONDURMA PORTAKAL
Orange water ice

SERVES: 6–8

thinly peeled rind of 2 oranges
thinly peeled rind of 1 lemon
220 g (8 oz/1 cup) sugar
250 ml (8½ fl oz/1 cup) orange juice
60 ml (2 fl oz/¼ cup) lemon juice

Put the orange and lemon rinds in a saucepan with 750 ml (25 fl oz/3 cups) water. Boil, uncovered, for 10 minutes.

Strain the liquid into a measuring jug and discard the rind. If necessary, make up the liquid to 500 ml (17 fl oz/2 cups) with water. Return the liquid to the pan.

Add the sugar to the pan and dissolve over medium heat, stirring occasionally. Bring to the boil, then leave to boil over medium heat for 5 minutes. Leave until cool.

Add the orange and lemon juice to the sugar syrup, then pour into a bowl. Freeze for 3 hours, or until firm. Flake with a fork and pile the flakes into chilled sweet glasses.

❀ *Note: Orange food colouring may be added to the syrup if desired.*

DONDURMA KIRAZ
Cherry water ice

Use the same method as for the Dondurma Çilekli recipe on page 208, substituting 500 ml (17 fl oz/2 cups) cherry purée for the strawberry purée.

To make cherry purée, wash and pit about 600 g (1 lb 5 oz/ 3 cups) cherries and purée in a food processor or blender. Measure and add to the syrup with the lemon juice, milk and red food colouring if necessary.

Freeze and serve in chilled sweet glasses.

TÜRK KAHVESİ
Turkish coffee

Turkish coffee is prepared in a small, long-handled pot tapering at the top, called a *jezve*. The purist (and *all* Turks are, when it comes to making coffee) would grind the beans to a fine powder just before brewing. Turkish brass coffee mills are sold throughout the Middle East.

When offered a cup, you will be asked if you like it *sade* (unsweetened), *orta* (moderately sweetened) or *sekerli* (very sweet). Ideally, Turkish coffee is made one cup at a time, or three at the most.

Measure one demitasse cup of cold water into a *jezve* and add 1 heaped teaspoon of powdered Turkish coffee; and sugar if desired — a level teaspoon for *orta*, a heaped teaspoon or more for *sekerli*. Stir and place over medium–low heat.

When the coffee rises in the pot, immediately remove the pot from the heat, then spoon the froth into a cup. Return the pot to the heat and cook until the coffee rises again. Remove and fill the cup.

Some prefer to heat the coffee three times in all, though twice is sufficient, particularly if only making one cup. With the repeated heating method, a little froth is spooned into each cup each time it is removed from the heat, as a good cup of *kahve* must have creamy foam floating on top.

ÇİLEK REÇELİ
« Strawberry jam

1 kg (2 lb 3 oz) strawberries
juice of 2 lemons
770 g (1 lb 11 oz/3½ cups) sugar

Wash the strawberries, drain well and remove the hulls. Cut in half and place in a preserving pan with the lemon juice.

Place over medium heat, cover the pan and bring to the boil. Reduce the heat to low and simmer gently for 20–30 minutes, or until the fruit is very soft.

Remove the pan from the heat and stir in the sugar. Place back over medium heat, stirring again to dissolve the sugar.

Bring to the boil, then allow to boil over medium heat for 15 minutes, or until the jam sets when a little is tested on a cold saucer — see the Kayisi Reçeli recipe (right) for more detail on testing.

Cool the jam a little, then ladle into hot, sterilised jars (see page 19).

Seal while hot and store in a cool place.

GÜL REÇELİ
« Rose petal jam

4 cups fragrant rose petals
660 g (1 lb 7 oz/3 cups) sugar
juice of ½ lemon

Snip off the white base of each rose petal with kitchen scissors and discard. Wash the petals gently in cold water and drain.

Layer the petals in a bowl, sprinkling 2 tablespoons of the sugar on each layer. Leave overnight.

The next day, put the remaining sugar and 500 ml (17 fl oz/ 2 cups) water in a heavy-based saucepan and set over medium heat. Stir occasionally until the sugar has dissolved, then bring to the boil. Add the lemon juice and boil for 5 minutes without stirring. Remove the syrup from the heat and cool to lukewarm.

Stir the rose petals and their liquid into the syrup and return the pan to the heat. Bring slowly to the boil, then allow to boil gently for 15 minutes, or until the syrup is thick when tested on a cold saucer (see recipe below).

Cool the jam a little, then ladle into hot, sterilised jars (see page 19).

Seal while hot and store in a cool place.

KAYISI REÇELİ
Apricot jam

360 g (12½ oz/2 cups) dried apricots
juice of 1 lemon
660 g (1 lb 7 oz/3 cups) sugar
60 g (2 oz/½ cup) blanched, split almonds, optional

Wash the apricots very well in cold water. Chop into small pieces and place in a bowl with 750 ml (25 fl oz/3 cups) cold water. Leave to soak for 12 hours.

Put the fruit and the soaking liquid in a preserving pan. Add the lemon juice and bring to the boil. Cover and boil gently for 30 minutes, or until the apricots are very soft.

Add the sugar and stir to dissolve. Return to the boil and boil quickly, stirring often.

Boil for 15 minutes, then test a little jam on a cold saucer. Draw a finger across the surface of the cooled jam — it is ready when the surface wrinkles. (Remember to remove the jam from the heat while testing.) Return to the heat if necessary and test the jam again after another 5 minutes.

Stir in the almonds, if using.

Cool the jam a little, then ladle into hot, sterilised jars (see page 19).

Seal while hot and store in a cool place.

Armenia

ĂRMENIA

Proclaimed a Soviet Republic in 1920, Armenia regained its nationhood in 1991, after the collapse of the Soviet Union. During the years of oppression, the nationalistic spirit lived on, both in the people of the Armenian Soviet Socialist Republic and in those who, through the events of history, found a home elsewhere. They have shown that while adversity altered their fate, it has never altered their spirit. It is to their credit that, in spite of insurmountable odds, they have preserved their language, religion, customs and traditions.

To really understand the evolvement of a cuisine, one must know something of a country's history. I doubt if there ever has been a country that has undergone such upheavals as Armenia, and about which the world knows so little. Perhaps knowing something of Armenia's history will shed light on many aspects of Middle Eastern cooking. Tradition has it that the kingdom of Armenia was founded by Haig, a descendant of Noah, in the Near East region of Lake Van. For centuries it was ruled by Haig's successors. There followed invasions by Assyrians, Medes and Persians; it was conquered by Alexander the Great and passed on to the ancient Syrian King, Seleucus I. Independence was finally declared in 189 BCE. This was short-lived, however, and Armenia was eventually made a protectorate of Rome. Nero confirmed a Parthian prince as King of Armenia in 66 CE. Christianity was introduced in the first century, and Armenia now has the distinction of being the oldest Christian state. Peace reigned for the next 300 years or so and then a succession of invasions followed for the next 1500 years, with brief periods of independence.

While Byzantium was at its zenith, Armenian Orthodox church leaders and many Armenians were centred in Constantinople, as were numbers of Greeks, and it was during this era, the pre-Ottoman era, that the exotic cuisine of Byzantium was developed, influencing Armenian and Greek and eventually Turkish cooking. It must also be noted that the Armenian boundaries through history have expanded and contracted considerably, accounting for so many similarities to Turkish dishes.

Mongol hordes swept across India, Afghanistan, Persia and Armenia into Russia in the 13th century, and though their mission was not one of goodwill, it is believed that they introduced pasta and noodles, almost a hundred years before Marco Polo's return from China. An Armenian noodle-type dish called *mante* also features in Russian cooking in a slightly varied form; it is a speciality of Uzbrek on the eastern side of the Caspian Sea, and both areas were once under Mongol influence. In Turkish cooking, *mante* is known as *Tartar boregi* (the Mongols, in their surge, were joined by other peoples and became

known collectively as Tartars). It is only through similar clues that one might hope to piece together the jigsaw of culinary origins.

THE FLAVOUR OF ARMENIAN FOOD

True Armenian cooking is relatively simple fare, often of a kind necessary in a cold climate. It is subtly herbed and spiced with overtones of the colourful era of Byzantium. The combination of rice, currants, onions and pine nuts is a legacy from that era — a legacy that in fact belongs to those of the Orthodox faith, be it Armenian, Greek or Eastern. Fasting is a very important requirement of the religion, and the ingenuity of the Armenians in preparing dishes without any animal products is evident in recipes. Many such recipes in other chapters are also used in Armenian cooking.

To illustrate their staunch upholding of tradition, the founder of Armenia is immortalised in the recipes *haigagan parak hatz* and *haigagan keteh*. The former is a bread similar to the flat breads of Persia and Lebanon, cooked a little longer so that it dries out. Try the Khoubiz recipe (page 264), but cook it straight after it is shaped, sprinkling the breads with sesame seeds. Bake for 6–7 minutes, long enough to dry it. This keeps well and is served as a dry bread or moistened with water. *Haigagan keteh* is the same as Glor Keteh (page 226), with the circle folded in on itself, then pressed flat rather than rolled into a rope and coiled.

Another recipe worthy of mention is *topig*, one dating back to the days of Byzantium. His Grace, the Armenian Bishop of the Diocese of Sydney, is not only renowned among Sydney's Armenian community as a cook of great standing, he is also remembered for his culinary achievements in Los Angeles and Washington. His *topig* and his *oologantch litzk* are the envy of every Armenian cook in these three cities. The Topig recipe (page 221) I have given does not quite follow his Grace's in that I refuse to soak the chickpeas for the length of time he recommends (my comments on this matter are documented in the section on pulses at the beginning of this book). Investigation and testing found that I did not need to cook the *topig* for quite as long he recommends either. My taste testers, members of his congregation, assured me that it was a very good *topig*, not quite as good as His Grace's, but near enough, and just like their mothers used to make. Perhaps I should give you details of the famous *topig* so that you might judge for yourself.

Apparently the secret is to soak the chickpeas for three days, changing the water daily and letting them ferment, as he claims this is necessary for the success of the dish. By then the peas are much easier to skin. His method is to wrap the peas in a cloth and rub vigorously. The skins come off easily. Put the peas in a bowl of water and skim off the floating skins. Grind the drained peas in a food grinder, or process in a food processor using a steel blade. The onions should be boiled in a generous amount of water and drained, reserving the water. Regarding the filling, we both agree on that point, so mix the onions with the remaining ingredients listed. Now, to prevent the water penetrating the cloth used for boiling, it should be soaked in the reserved onion water, and wrung out well. Spread out one-quarter of the ground pea mixture (mixed with mashed potato) on the cloth in a very thin square — as thin as you can make it. Fill as described, then fold the corners over,

sealing the joins. Knot the cloth and prepare the remaining *topigs* in the same way. Boil them in salted water for 1 hour. Drain and leave them in the cloths until completely cold before removing. Now you know.

The Oologantch Litzk recipe (page 234) is also His Grace's, minus three onions.

AN ARMENIAN MEAL

Rather than describe Armenian meals as served today in the Republic of Armenia, it is preferable to describe the usual way in which Armenians, wherever they may live, may take a meal following tradition. Meals are served in the Western manner; that is, with Western table appointments. All the prepared dishes for the meal are placed on the table at the one time so that the diners may take what they wish. In cooler weather the meal could begin with a bowl of soup, probably spiced with mint and thickened with yoghurt. Then follows a meat, chicken or fish dish, and vegetable, rice or pasta accompaniment, salad, bread and pickles. *Tan* (yoghurt drink) accompanies every meal served in the Armenian tradition. When fasting, the meal could feature fish or one of their delicious dishes made from dried beans, peas or burghul (bulgur). The full range of foods, from meats to desserts, could be Armenian, but they are just as likely to be from any of the Arabic countries, Greece or Iran — in fact from countries where they or their parents sought a new home.

COOKING METHODS

Armenians, particularly in the United States, are renowned for their success in the food industry. They operate speciality food stores, delicatessens, restaurants and bakeries, and while Armenian foods feature in their commercial endeavours, their affinity with food extends to preparing dishes from any nation. Perhaps it is an inherited gift; to be able to adapt to a situation is either born with us or thrust upon us. It has been thrust upon the Armenians for generations and it has held them in good stead. In other words, it is difficult to say that the Armenian uses this pot or that method of cooking, for it could be anything you might be using yourself.

An Armenian kitchen would be well stocked and well equipped with all the items necessary for producing good, wholesome food. You would not find cupboards filled with tins, or freezers filled with TV dinners, but you would be likely to find pantry shelves lined with jars of pickles and preserves, with perhaps a *basderma* hanging. I tested the latter recipe but I am afraid that I cannot advise you to prepare this pungent, spiced meat at home, as it requires days of hanging in the open air to dry it. I would prefer you to patronise your local Armenian or Greek food store and buy it ready prepared, as its commercial preparation is carried out under controlled conditions. *Basderma* is similar to the Romanian pastrami, except that a large quantity of fenugreek is included in the garlic and spice coating.

INGREDIENTS FOR ARMENIAN COOKING

There is hardly an ingredient in Armenian cooking with which the Western cook would not be familiar. Harissa (page 222) is made in Armenia with a special wheat unavailable outside the Near and Middle East. Pearl barley is a more than reasonable substitute; consequently, in this recipe barley has been given as the ingredient.

Chickpeas are usually preferred without the skin. These are available at Armenian and Greek food stores but are difficult to find elsewhere. It may be necessary for you to follow the instructions on page 10 for removing the skins.

Sumac is a coarse powder with a sour flavour, prepared from the dry red berries of a species of the sumac tree. It is also used in Iran and other countries of the region.

NIVIK
« Chickpeas with spinach

SERVES: 6

330 g (11½ oz/1½ cups) chickpeas

60 ml (2 fl oz/¼ cup) olive oil

1 large onion, chopped

60 g (2 oz/¼ cup) tomato paste (concentrated purée)

salt and freshly ground black pepper, to season

1 teaspoon sugar

750 g (1 lb 10 oz) spinach

lemon wedges, to serve

Wash the chickpeas well, place them in a bowl and cover them with 1.125 litres (38 fl oz/4½ cups) cold water. Leave to soak overnight, in a cool place if the weather is warm.

The next day, put the chickpeas and soaking water in a deep saucepan and bring to the boil. Cover and simmer gently for 2 hours, or until tender.

Heat the oil in a frying pan and gently fry the onion until translucent. Stir in the tomato paste, some salt, a generous grinding of black pepper and the sugar, then add to the cooked chickpeas.

Wash the spinach well, removing the roots and discoloured leaves. Chop the leaves and stems roughly and stir them through the chickpea mixture.

Simmer, uncovered, for a further 20 minutes, adding more water only if necessary. Nivik should be moist, but not too liquid. Serve with lemon wedges, bread, salad and pickles as an appetiser or light meal. Also good served cold.

YEREPOUNI
Brain fritters

SERVES: 4 AS AN APPETISER

As the recipe name suggests, these delicately flavoured brain fritters are from Yerevan, the capital and largest city of Armenia.

6 sets of lamb brains

2 tablespoons vinegar

3 teaspoons salt, plus extra to taste

2 egg yolks

1 tablespoon finely chopped dill

30 g (1 oz/¼ cup) finely grated kasseri cheese

olive or corn oil, for pan-frying

lemon wedges, to serve

Cover the lamb brains with water, adding the vinegar and 2 teaspoons of the salt. Leave for 15–20 minutes, then drain. Remove the skin and any veins. If the brains have been frozen, it is very difficult to remove the skin — this does not matter so much, but do cut out any veins present, as the blood discolours the brains.

Place the brains in a saucepan with fresh water to cover, add the remaining salt and bring almost to the boil. Cover and simmer gently over low heat for 15 minutes, or until tender.

Drain the brains well and turn them into a mixing bowl. Mash them finely with a fork and leave to cool.

Add the egg yolks, dill and cheese. Mix to a soft paste and add more salt to season if necessary.

Add the oil to a frying pan, to a depth of 5 mm (¼ inch). Place six egg-poaching rings in the oil, turning them to oil the surfaces.

Heat the oil over medium–high heat. Spoon a generous tablespoon of the brain mixture into each ring and fry until golden brown on each side. Once the mixture is set, the rings may be removed.

Drain on paper towels and add the remaining mixture to the rings in the pan. Serve hot or warm as an appetiser, with lemon wedges.

DEREVE PATTOUG
Stuffed grape vine leaves
MAKES: 80

80 fresh or preserved grape vine leaves

1 lemon, thinly sliced

60 ml (2 fl oz/¼ cup) olive oil

lemon wedges, to serve

yoghurt, to serve

Rice filling

125 ml (4 fl oz/½ cup) olive oil

2 large onions, finely chopped

220 g (8 oz/1 cup) short-grain white rice

40 g (1½ oz/¼ cup) pine nuts

35 g (1¼ oz/¼ cup) currants

1 teaspoon ground allspice

2 tablespoons finely chopped dill

salt and freshly ground black pepper, to season

To make the rice filling, heat the oil in a frying pan and gently fry the onion until translucent. Add the rice and stir for 5 minutes. Add the pine nuts, currants, allspice and dill, and season with salt and pepper. Cover and cook over gentle heat for 5 minutes. Remove from the heat and set aside.

Blanch the fresh or preserved vine leaves in boiling water for 3 minutes, adding them in three batches. As each batch is blanched, remove it to a bowl of cold water, then drain well.

Spread a vine leaf on a work surface, shiny side down. Snip off the stem and place a heaped teaspoon of the rice filling towards the stem end. Roll once, fold in the sides, then roll into a neat package. Repeat with the remaining ingredients.

Line the base of a heavy-based saucepan with four vine leaves. Place the rolls, seam side down, in closely packed rows. As each row is completed, place three thin lemon slices on top before beginning the next row.

When all the rolls are in the pan, top them with another three lemon slices and cover with the remaining vine leaves. Pour the oil and 500 ml (17 fl oz/2 cups) water over the rolls, then invert a heavy plate on top of the rolls so they keep their shape during cooking.

Bring to a slow simmer, reduce the heat and cover the pan. Simmer gently for 50 minutes. Remove the pan from the heat and leave until cool.

Carefully transfer the rolls to a serving dish, discarding the lemon slices. Serve at room temperature, or cover the dish and chill before serving.

Serve with lemon wedges and a bowl of yoghurt.

TOPIG
Lenten chickpea kofta

SERVES: 8–12

440 g (15½ oz/2 cups) chickpeas
2 small potatoes, boiled in their jackets
1½ teaspoons salt
freshly ground white pepper, to season

Filling

3 large onions, halved and sliced
¼ teaspoon ground allspice
½ teaspoon ground cumin
50 g (2 oz/⅓ cup) pine nuts
50 g (2 oz/⅓ cup) currants
205 g (7 oz/¾ cup) tahini
salt and freshly ground black pepper, to season

To finish and serve

1 tablespoon salt
olive oil
ground cinnamon or paprika
lemon wedges
parsley sprigs

Soak the chickpeas in 1.5 litres (51 fl oz/6 cups) cold water for 24 hours, in a cool place if the weather is warm. Remove the skins by either of the methods described under 'Skinning pulses' on page 10. Drain well.

Pass the skinned chickpeas through a food grinder twice, using a fine screen. Alternatively, process them to a paste in two batches in a food processor, using a steel blade.

Peel the boiled potatoes, place in a mixing bowl and mash finely with a fork. Add the ground chickpeas, salt and a generous pinch of white pepper. Mix thoroughly and set aside.

To make the filling, place the onion in a saucepan with 2 tablespoons water. Cover and steam over medium heat for 10 minutes, then remove the lid and allow the moisture to evaporate. Tip the onion into a bowl and cool.

Add the allspice, cumin, pine nuts and currants to the onion. Combine well, then mix in the tahini, and season to taste with salt and pepper.

Take four pieces of muslin (cheesecloth), each about 50 cm (20 inches) square, and scald them in boiling water. Cool them a little, then wring them out well.

Open out a square of cloth on a work surface and place one-quarter of the chickpea paste in the centre. Spread the paste evenly with a spatula to a 20 cm (8 inch) square, then place one-quarter of the filling in the centre, spreading it a little.

Bring each corner of the paste over the filling by lifting up the corners of the cloth. The paste should enclose the filling in envelope fashion. Smooth the joins to seal them well.

Make a single tie with each pair of diagonally opposite corners of cloth, then tie a second time.

Complete another three *topigs* in the same way.

Half-fill a large saucepan with water, bring to the boil and add the 1 tablespoon salt.

When the water is briskly boiling, lower the prepared *topigs* into the pan and return to the boil. Cover the pan and allow it to boil steadily for 12–15 minutes, or until the *topigs* float and feel firm to the touch.

Lift out the *topigs* immediately and place them on a tray, draining off the water that collects in the tray.

Untie and invert the *topigs* on a platter and leave until cool.

When ready to serve, pour a little olive oil over each *topig* and dust lightly with cinnamon or paprika. Garnish with lemon wedges and parsley.

To serve, cut each *topig* in half, then slice into thick pieces. Add olive oil and lemon juice to individual taste.

❧ *Note: Ready-skinned chickpeas are available at some Armenian and Greek food stores. These look like split peas, but are larger and nut-coloured.*

HARISSA
Meat and barley purée
SERVES: 6–8

There are versions of harissa in various countries of the region. The Armenians use a special wheat that is unavailable outside the Middle East, so this version uses barley instead. Harissa is traditionally served on the first day after New Year.

330 g (11½ oz/1½ cups) pearl barley

1 kg (2 lb 3 oz) chuck steak

salt and freshly ground black pepper, to season

90 g (3 oz/⅓ cup) butter

1 teaspoon ground cinnamon

1 teaspoon ground cumin

Wash the barley well under cold running water. Place in a bowl and add cold water to cover. Leave to soak overnight.

Place the barley and soaking water in a heavy-based saucepan. Place over medium heat and bring to the boil. Reduce the heat, then cover and simmer gently for 1½ hours, or until the barley is just tender.

Meanwhile, preheat the oven to 170°C (340°F/Gas 3).

Cut the steak into 3 cm (1¼ inch) cubes and place in a separate saucepan with water to cover. Bring slowly to the boil, skimming as required.

Place the barley and steak, together with their simmering liquids, into a large casserole dish. Season with salt and pepper. Transfer to the oven and bake for 3 hours, stirring occasionally during cooking, and adding water if the mixture looks like scorching.

In a small frying pan, heat the butter until browned, then stir in the cinnamon and cumin. Remove from the heat.

When the meat is very tender and falling apart, remove the casserole from the oven and beat the mixture with a wooden spoon until puréed. The meat should break up into stringy pieces and combine with the barley.

Spread on a heated serving platter, smoothing the surface. Make indentations over the surface with the back of a spoon and fill with the melted butter mixture.

Serve with bread and salads.

CHROD BOUREK
Water-dipped pastry with cheese filling
SERVES: 12 AS AN APPETISER, 6 AS A MAIN COURSE

Occasionally during the compilation of this book I almost resorted to coin-tossing to decide which chapter I should place some recipes in – such as this particular gem, which both the Turks and the Armenians lay claim to.

As the Armenian *mante* uses a noodle-type dough, its origin probably dating from the influence of the Mongols, it is possible this water-dipped pastry was developed around the same time.

Cheese filling

300 g (10½ oz/2 cups) crumbled feta cheese

250 g (9 oz/1 cup) cottage or ricotta cheese

125 g (4 oz/1 cup) grated *kasseri* cheese

4 eggs, lightly beaten

3 tablespoons finely chopped flat-leaf parsley

2 tablespoons chopped dill

freshly ground black pepper, to taste

Water-dipped pastry

450 g (1 lb/3 cups) plain (all-purpose) flour,
   plus extra for kneading and rolling

1 teaspoon salt

3 eggs, beaten well

125 g (4 oz/½ cup) butter, melted, for brushing

To make the cheese filling, finely mash the feta in a mixing bowl, using a fork. Combine with the remaining filling ingredients and refrigerate until required.

To make the pastry, sift the flour and salt into a bowl and make a well in the centre. Add the eggs to the centre of the flour with 125 ml (4 fl oz/½ cup) lukewarm water. Gradually stir the flour into the liquid to form a soft dough.

Thoroughly knead the dough in the bowl. If it is still sticky, gradually add a little more sifted flour until the dough is smooth and comes away cleanly from the side of the bowl. The amount of flour depends on the size of the eggs and the flour's absorption qualities. Shape the dough into a ball, then cover the bowl with plastic wrap. Rest for 30 minutes.

Divide the dough into 10 even-sized balls. On a lightly floured work surface, shape one ball of dough into a square, dust it with flour and roll it out thinly, following the directions in the 'Rolling pastry thinly' section on page 15. The final pastry sheet should be about 28 × 33 cm (11 × 13 inches) in size. Stack and cover as directed as each sheet is rolled. All but two sheets of pastry are to be boiled.

Preheat the oven to 180°C (350°F/Gas 4).

Three-quarters fill a large saucepan with water and bring to the boil. Have a large bowl of cold water next to the pan, and spread a large, folded cloth next to this.

Lift up one pastry sheet and lower it gradually into the boiling water. Boil for 1 minute, then scoop it out carefully with a large sieve, guiding the pastry into the sieve with a wooden spoon. Plunge the pastry into the cold water, leave it for 2 minutes, lift it out and drain it over the bowl. Turn the pastry onto the cloth and open it out carefully to drain and dry a little. Boil another three sheets, laying them separately on the cloth to drain. Any sheets that tear may still be used.

Brush a 25 × 30 cm (10 × 12 inch) baking dish with melted butter and spread one uncooked pastry sheet in the dish. Brush it with butter and place the four boiled sheets of pastry on top, brushing each with butter as it is positioned. Spread the cheese filling evenly in the dish.

Boil another four sheets of pastry as described above, using a dry cloth for draining. Place them on top of the filling, buttering each layer as it is placed in the dish. Top with the last uncooked pastry sheet, then trim the edges with a sharp knife, level with the top of the dish. Brush the top of the pie with the remaining butter.

Bake for 1 hour, or until the top is golden brown and crisp. The centre sheets will be soft and tender. Rest the pie for 10 minutes before cutting it into serving portions. Serve hot as an appetiser, or as a main course for a light meal.

❧ *Note: Spinach, meat or chicken fillings may be used with this pastry. See 'Savoury pastries' in the index.*

KHARENI TTVASH
Armenia pickles

½ small cauliflower

2–3 celery stalks

1 green capsicum (pepper)

1 red capsicum (pepper)

2 carrots

2 green tomatoes

cooking salt, for sprinkling

Brine mixture

80 g (3 oz/¼ cup) rock salt

250 ml (8½ fl oz/1 cup) white vinegar

3 teaspoons sugar

To finish

1–2 garlic cloves

1–2 hot fresh or dried chillies

1–2 dill sprigs, optional

Wash the vegetables well. Break the cauliflower into florets; cut the celery into 5 cm (2 inch) lengths. Core and seed the capsicums, then cut into wide strips. Peel the carrots and cut into 5 mm (¼ inch) slices. Cut the tomatoes into thick wedges.

Layer the vegetables in a bowl, sprinkling each layer with about 2 tablespoons cooking salt. Leave for 5–6 hours, then rinse well and drain.

To prepare the brine mixture, heat 1 litre (34 fl oz/4 cups) water and the rock salt in a stainless steel or enamelled saucepan, stirring until the salt has dissolved. Add the vinegar and sugar and bring to the boil. Remove from the heat and leave until cool.

Pack the vegetables into one or two sterilised jars, arranging them attractively. To each jar add a cut garlic clove, a whole chilli and a sprig of dill among the vegetables.

Pour the cooled brine over the pickles and seal with glass or plastic lids. Store in a cool, dark place for 1 week before using, or up to 2–3 months. Once opened, store in the refrigerator.

LOUPIA TTVASH
Green bean pickles

1. 5 kg (3 lb 5 oz) stringless green beans, thoroughly washed

cooking salt, for sprinkling

1 quantity Brine Mixture; see Khareni Ttvash recipe (left)

2 fresh or dried hot chillies

2 garlic cloves

Top and tail the beans. Cut diagonally into 8 cm (3¼ inch) lengths, or leave whole if desired. Layer the beans in a bowl, sprinkling each layer with about 2 tablespoons cooking salt. Leave for 6 hours, then rinse well and drain.

Make the brine mixture as directed and leave until cool.

Pack the beans into two sterilised jars, placing a chilli and a cut garlic clove in each jar. Pour the cooled brine over the pickles and seal. Store in a cool, dark place for 1 week before using, or up to 2–3 months. Refrigerate after opening.

DZAGHAGAGHAMPI TTVASH
Cauliflower pickles

1 quantity Brine Mixture; see Khareni Ttvash recipe (left)

1 cauliflower, thick stems removed, broken into florets

1–2 hot chillies

1–2 garlic cloves

Make the brine mixture as directed and leave until cool.

Soak the cauliflower in a bowl of cold salted water for 15–20 minutes. Rinse well and drain.

Blanch the cauliflower in a large saucepan of boiling water in two batches, for 3 minutes each batch, timed from when the water returns to the boil. Drain well.

Pack into one large or two smaller sterilised jars, adding a chilli and a cut garlic clove to each jar. Pour the cooled brine over the pickles and seal. Store in a cool, dark place for 1 week before using, or up to 2–3 months. Refrigerate after opening.

GIOR KETEH
Butter-flaked breads

MAKES: 6 BREADS

2 teaspoons active dried yeast

600 g (1 lb 5 oz/4 cups) plain (all-purpose) flour

250 ml (8½ fl oz/1 cup) warm evaporated milk

1 egg, beaten

1 teaspoon salt

1 tablespoon caster (superfine) sugar

60 ml (2 fl oz/¼ cup) melted unsalted butter

To finish

125 ml (4 fl oz/½ cup) melted unsalted butter

1 small egg, beaten

sesame seeds or black cumin seeds

Soak the yeast in 60 ml (2 fl oz/¼ cup) warm water and stir to dissolve. Sift the flour into a mixing bowl. Remove and reserve about 150 g (5 oz/1 cup) of the flour.

Mix the evaporated milk with the beaten egg; add the salt and sugar and stir until dissolved. Pour the yeast liquid and evaporated milk into the centre of the flour. Stir in a little flour to thicken the liquid, then cover and leave in a warm place for 10 minutes, or until frothy.

Mix in the remaining flour in the bowl. Beat by hand for 2 minutes, then gradually beat in the warm, melted butter with a little of the reserved flour. Beat the dough for a further 5 minutes by hand, or in an electric mixer fitted with a dough hook.

Knead in the reserved flour, adding as much as the dough will take. Knead for 10 minutes, or until the dough is smooth and satiny. Form into a ball.

Grease a clean bowl with a little butter, then add the dough and turn to coat it with butter. Cover the bowl with plastic wrap and leave the dough to rise in a warm place for 1 hour, or until it has doubled in size.

Punch down the dough and turn it out onto a lightly floured work surface. Knead until smooth, divide into six even portions, and roll each portion into a ball. Cover with a cloth.

Dust the surface and one ball of dough with flour, then roll the dough into a large, thin circle about 40 cm (16 inches) in diameter.

To finish, brush the dough evenly with some of the melted butter. Roll it up into a long rope. Take each end and swing it up and down, letting the dough hit the work surface; you want to stretch the rope to twice its original length.

Coil the rope into a round, with the ends of the dough on top. Press the ends onto the coil and flatten them a little.

Shape the remaining dough in the same way.

When all are shaped, press firmly with your hands and flatten each into an 18 cm (7 inch) round — use a rolling pin if you prefer. Place the rounds on greased baking trays. Cover and leave for 45 minutes, or until they have doubled in size.

Meanwhile, preheat the oven to 190°C (375°F/Gas 5).

Glaze the breads with the beaten egg and sprinkle with sesame or cumin seeds. Bake for 12–15 minutes, or until golden brown and cooked.

Serve warm, with fruit preserves or cheese.

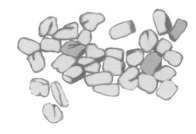

MANTIABOUR
Lamb pasta and yoghurt soup
SERVES: 6

Shades of Italy again? No – more likely a descendant from the *man-ton* of the nomadic Mongolians, and a relative of the *manty* of Russia. Here, *mante* is served in a satisfying soup. You will also find *mante* as a lamb pie on page 238.

300 g (10½ oz/2 cups) plain (all-purpose) flour

½ teaspoon salt

1 egg

Filling

200 g (7 oz) finely minced (ground) lamb (choose lamb
  that is not too lean)

1 onion, grated

3 tablespoons finely chopped flat-leaf parsley

salt and freshly ground black pepper, to season

To finish

2 teaspoons salt

1.25 litres (42½ fl oz/5 cups) chicken stock

250 g (9 oz/1 cup) drained yoghurt (see page 19)

1 garlic clove, crushed, optional

2 teaspoons dried mint

Sift the flour and salt into a mixing bowl. Using a fork, beat the egg in a cup measure and make up to 125 ml (4 fl oz/½ cup) with cold water. Pour into the flour and mix to a firm dough, adding a little more water if necessary. Knead until smooth, then cover and rest for 20–30 minutes.

Meanwhile, place the filling ingredients in a mixing bowl, season with salt and pepper and thoroughly combine.

Roll out half the dough as thinly as possible on a floured work surface. Cut it into 4 cm (1½ inch) squares, then stack the squares and cover them while rolling and cutting the remaining dough.

Place a teaspoon of the filling in the centre of a square of dough; fold the dough over into a triangle, then press the edges well to seal. Bring the two narrow angles of the triangle together and press well, making a shape resembling the Italian tortellini. Place on a cloth-lined tray and cover while preparing the remaining *mante*.

To finish, bring 2 litres (68 fl oz/8 cups) water to the boil in a large saucepan and add the salt. Add about 20 *mante*, return the water to the boil and leave to boil for 10 minutes. Remove the *mante* with a slotted spoon and place in a colander while boiling the remainder. (The *mante* may be kept in a sealed container in the refrigerator if not required immediately.)

When ready to serve, bring the stock to the boil in a large saucepan. Add the *mante* and boil gently for 10 minutes.

Add the yoghurt and garlic, if using. Stir gently over the heat for 2–3 minutes, without allowing the soup to boil. Rub the mint into a powder and stir into the soup.

Serve immediately.

VOSBOV ABOUR
« Lentil soup
SERVES: 6

1 quantity lamb stock; see Dzedzadz Tanabour recipe (right)

250 g (9 oz/1 cup) red lentils, washed

3 onions

60 g (2 oz/¼ cup) butter

salt and freshly ground black pepper, to taste

To finish

paprika, for sprinkling

herbs, such as chopped parsley, to garnish

olive oil, for drizzling

Make the stock as directed and strain it into a measuring jug. Add water if necessary to make it up to 1.5 litres (51 fl oz/ 6 cups). Pour the stock into a deep saucepan and bring to the boil. Add the lentils and return to the boil, skimming when necessary. Partially cover with a lid and boil gently while preparing the onions.

Finely chop two of the onions. Heat half the butter in a frying pan and fry the onions until lightly browned.

Stir the fried onions into the lentils. Cover the pan tightly and simmer for 1 hour, or until the lentils are tender. Add salt and pepper to taste.

Cut the remaining onion in half from top to bottom, then slice each half into semi-circles. Melt the remaining butter in the frying pan and fry the onion until golden brown.

Serve hot, garnished with the fried onion, a sprinkling of paprika and herbs, and a drizzle of oil.

DZEDZADZ TANABOUR
Yoghurt and barley soup
SERVES: 6

110 g (3¾ oz/½ cup) barley, washed

750 g (1 lb 10 oz/3 cups) yoghurt

1 egg

1 tablespoon dried mint

40 g (1½ oz) butter, optional

Lamb stock

1.5 kg (3 lb 5 oz) lamb soup meat, with bones (neck, breast, shank)

2 carrots, quartered

1 onion, quartered

leafy top of 1 celery stalk

salt and freshly ground black pepper, to taste

To make the lamb stock, rinse the lamb pieces, place them in a large saucepan and pour in water to cover. Add the remaining stock ingredients, except any salt, and bring to the boil. Skim off any froth before the liquid boils. When well skimmed and boiling gently, season with salt and pepper, then cover and simmer over low heat for 1½ hours.

Strain the stock into another saucepan; discard or reserve the stock ingredients for another use.

Add the barley to the stock and stir occasionally until boiling. Cover and simmer over low heat for 1½ hours, or until the barley is very soft and the soup is thick.

Beat the yoghurt with the egg, then stir it into the simmering soup. Crush half the dried mint to a coarse powder and stir it through the soup as well. Return to a slow simmer, stirring occasionally, but do not allow to boil.

Ladle into bowls and serve hot, sprinkled with the remaining mint — or you can heat the butter in a frying pan, stir in the remaining mint and drizzle this over each soup.

ARAPGIRI TOPIG
Burghul and potato balls
SERVES: 6

6 potatoes, about 750 g (1 lb 10 oz) in total,
 scrubbed clean
130 g (4½ oz/¾ cup) fine burghul (bulgur)
110 g (3¾ oz/¾ cup) plain (all-purpose) flour
salt and freshly ground black pepper, to taste
oil, for deep-frying

Filling
2 onions, chopped
¼ teaspoon ground allspice
40 g (1½ oz/¼ cup) pine nuts
35 g (1¼ oz/¼ cup) currants
90 g (3 oz/⅓ cup) tahini
salt and freshly ground black pepper, to taste

In a large saucepan, boil the potatoes in their jackets until tender. Drain the potatoes and leave to cool slightly. Remove the skins, place in a bowl and mash.

Meanwhile, soak the burghul in a bowl of cold water for 5 minutes. Drain it through a fine sieve, pressing well with the back of a spoon to squeeze out all the moisture.

Add the burghul to the mashed potato, along with the flour. Season to taste with salt and pepper and combine thoroughly to a paste.

To make the filling, place the onion in a saucepan with 2 tablespoons water. Cover and steam over medium heat for 10 minutes, then remove the lid and allow the moisture to evaporate. Tip the onion into a bowl and add the remaining filling ingredients. Season to taste with salt and pepper and mix until thoroughly combined.

Using moistened hands, shape a scant tablespoon of the burghul mixture at a time into balls. Flatten a ball in your hand, put a generous teaspoon of filling in the centre, then close the burghul mixture over the filling, moulding it into a smooth oval shape. Repeat with the remaining burghul mixture and filling.

Heat 10 cm (4 inches) of oil in a deep saucepan over medium heat to 160°C (320°F). Deep-fry six balls at a time for 6–8 minutes each batch, turning to brown evenly. When golden brown, remove with a slotted spoon and drain on paper towels. Serve hot or warm.

SHEHREHI YEGHINTZ
Rice with vermicelli
SERVES: 6

60 g (2 oz/¼ cup) butter
100 g (3½ oz) fine vermicelli noodles, lightly crushed
300 g (10½ oz/1½ cups) long-grain white rice
875 ml (29 fl oz/3½ cups) chicken or vegetable stock
1½ teaspoons salt

Melt the butter in a heavy-based saucepan. Add the noodles and stir over medium heat for 5 minutes, or until the noodles are golden brown.

Add the rice and cook, stirring, for 5 minutes. Stir in the stock and salt and bring to the boil. Reduce the heat to low, then cover and cook gently for 15 minutes.

Turn off the heat and leave covered for 5 minutes before serving.

HARSANIK YEGHINTZ
Spiced lamb pilaff
SERVES: 6

250 g (9 oz) lean boneless lamb
1 onion
½ teaspoon saffron threads
60 g (2 oz/¼ cup) butter
30 g (1 oz/¼ cup) blanched slivered almonds
½ teaspoon ground allspice
1 litre (34 fl oz/4 cups) lamb or chicken stock
1 teaspoon salt
freshly ground black pepper, to taste
400 g (14 oz/2 cups) long-grain white rice

Cut the lamb into thin strips 4 cm (1½ inches) long. Halve the onion lengthways and cut it into slender wedges. Pound the saffron threads and leave them to steep in 2 tablespoons hot water.

Melt the butter in a heavy-based saucepan and brown the lamb and onion over high heat, stirring constantly. Add the almonds and fry for 2 minutes longer. Reduce the heat and stir in the allspice.

Add 250 ml (8½ fl oz/1 cup) of the stock, the salt and a good grinding of black pepper. Cover and simmer gently for 20 minutes. Increase the heat, pour in the remaining stock and bring to the boil.

Wash the rice well and drain, then add it to the boiling stock. When it returns to the boil, reduce the heat to low, cover the pan with paper towels and a lid and simmer for 20 minutes.

Pour the saffron liquid over the rice, then cover and cook for a further 5 minutes. Turn off the heat and leave covered for 5 minutes before serving.

HAVGOTOV SHIOMIN
« Eggs with spinach

SERVES: 6

750 g (1 lb 10 oz) spinach
4 small onions
85 ml (3 fl oz/⅓ cup) olive oil, plus extra for drizzling
salt and freshly ground black pepper, to taste
6 eggs
yoghurt, to serve

Trim any roots and discoloured leaves from the spinach.
Wash the spinach in several changes of water and drain well.
Coarsely chop the leaves and stalks.

Place the spinach in a large non-aluminium saucepan,
then cover and cook over medium heat for 15 minutes, stirring
occasionally. There is no need to add water to the pan as the
moisture on the leaves will be sufficient for cooking. Drain
the spinach in a colander, pressing with the back of a spoon to
extract the moisture.

Meanwhile, preheat the oven to 180°C (350°F/Gas 4).

Cut the onions in half from top to bottom, then slice each
half into semi-circles. Heat the oil in a frying pan and gently
fry the onions until translucent and lightly browned. Add the
spinach and stir over the heat for a few minutes. Season to
taste with salt and pepper.

Tip the spinach mixture into a large, shallow baking dish,
or six smaller ramekins. If using one large dish, make six
depressions in the spinach with the back of a spoon; if using
six ramekins, make a depression in each one. Break an egg
into each depression, then drizzle a little oil on top of each egg.

Bake for 10 minutes, or until the eggs are set. Serve hot as a
light meal, with a small bowl of yoghurt.

ZADIG AGHTZAN
Spinach salad

SERVES: 6

750 g (1 lb 10 oz) spinach
750 g (1 lb 10 oz/3 cups) drained yoghurt (see page 19)
1 garlic clove
½ teaspoon salt
1 small handful finely chopped flat-leaf parsley
pinch of sugar

Remove the roots and coarse stems from the spinach. Wash
the leaves well, shake off as much moisture as possible, then
shred the leaves quite thinly.

Place the spinach in a large non-aluminium saucepan,
then cover and cook over medium heat for 10 minutes,
stirring occasionally. When just cooked, drain the spinach
in a colander, pressing with the back of a spoon to extract
the moisture. Leave until cool.

Place the yoghurt in a mixing bowl. Crush the garlic with the
salt, then stir into the yoghurt with the cooled spinach, parsley
and sugar. Check the seasoning and add more salt and sugar to
taste. Cover and chill well before serving.

OOLOGANTCH LITZK
Stuffed mussels
SERVES: 8–10

Many cooks have trouble closing mussels after filling them with the rice mixture. Near the pointed end of the mussel, close inspection reveals a fine white ligament. Sever this and the mussel can be closed easily after filling — but do take care as you can completely unhinge it.

60 large mussels

olive oil, for rubbing

lemon wedges, to serve

Filling

125 ml (4 fl oz/½ cup) olive oil

3 large onions, finely chopped

220 g (8 oz/1 cup) short-grain white rice, washed

50 g (2 oz/⅓ cup) pine nuts

50 g (2 oz/⅓ cup) currants

½ teaspoon ground allspice

1 tablespoon chopped dill

salt and freshly ground black pepper, to taste

To make the rice filling, heat the oil in a frying pan and gently fry the onion until translucent. Stir in the remaining filling ingredients and set aside.

Scrub the mussels well with a stiff brush, scraping the shells with a knife to remove any marine growth. Tug the beards towards the pointed end and remove them. To open the mussels easily, place them in warm salted water. As each one opens, insert the point of a knife between the two shells and slide it towards the pointed end, to sever the fine white ligament near the hinge, taking care not to separate the shells.

Place two generous teaspoons of filling in each mussel. Close each one up and arrange them in layers in a deep saucepan. Invert a heavy plate on top of the mussels to keep them intact during cooking. Pour in 500 ml (17 fl oz/2 cups) water and place over medium heat. Bring to the boil, then cover and simmer gently over low heat for 35–40 minutes.

Remove the pan from the heat and leave the mussels to cool in the pan.

Remove the mussels from the pan. Wipe them dry with paper towels, then rub the shells with a cloth dipped in oil for a glossy appearance.

Arrange on a serving dish and garnish with lemon wedges. Serve at room temperature, or chilled.

SEMPOOGI YEV MISOVGHOROVATZ
Baked eggplant with lamb

SERVES: 4 AS A MAIN COURSE, 8 AS AN APPETISER

8 long eggplants (aubergines), each about 250 g (9 oz)

salt, for sprinkling

500 g (1 lb 2 oz) finely minced (ground) lamb

1 onion, finely chopped

2 tablespoons finely chopped flat-leaf parsley

1 green capsicum (pepper)

¼ teaspoon ground allspice

1 teaspoon salt, plus extra to taste

freshly ground black pepper, to season

60 g (2 oz/¼ cup) tomato paste (concentrated purée)

40 g (1½ oz) butter

Remove the stems from the eggplants. Cut the eggplants crossways at 2 cm (¾ inch) intervals, almost all the way through. Sprinkle salt liberally into the cut surfaces and leave for 30 minutes.

Meanwhile, preheat the oven to 180°C (350°F/Gas 4).

Rinse the eggplants in cold water and squeeze them dry by pushing the ends of each eggplant together.

Combine the lamb, onion and parsley in a mixing bowl. Core and seed the capsicum, keeping a quarter of it aside, and chop the remainder finely. Add to the lamb with the allspice, salt and a generous grind of black pepper. Mix together thoroughly.

Stuff some meat mixture into each slit in the eggplants, filling them generously. Place the eggplants in a baking dish.

Mix the tomato paste with 185 ml (6½ fl oz/¾ cup) water and add salt and pepper to taste. Pour over the eggplants and place the reserved piece of capsicum in the liquid. Dot the tops with the butter.

Bake, uncovered, for 45 minutes, basting with the juices during cooking. Serve hot, with salad and bread.

ARMENIA

MEAT

235

KHARENI LITZK BULGHOUROV
Vegetables stuffed with lamb

SERVES: 6 AS A MAIN COURSE, OR MORE IN A BUFFET

6 long eggplants (aubergines), or 3 oval eggplants

6 green capsicums (peppers)

6 tomatoes

3 tablespoons sumac

1 tablespoon tomato paste (concentrated purée)

1½ teaspoons salt

1 teaspoon sugar

Stuffing

750 g (1 lb 10 oz) finely minced (ground) lamb
(not too lean)

1 small onion, finely chopped

250 g (9 oz/1 cup) chopped, peeled tomatoes

60 g (2 oz/¼ cup) tomato paste (concentrated purée)

40 g (1½ oz/¼ cup) finely chopped green capsicum (pepper)

55 g (2 oz/¼ cup) short-grain white rice

90 g (3 oz/½ cup) coarse burghul (bulgur), rinsed

pinch of hot chilli powder

1½ teaspoons salt

Wash the vegetables. Remove the stalks from the eggplants, cut off 2 cm (¾ inch) from the stem end and set aside. Scoop out the eggplant flesh, leaving a 5 mm (¼ inch) border of flesh. Place the eggplants in salted water and soak for 20 minutes. Rinse and drain.

Meanwhile, cut the tops off the capsicums and reserve. Remove the core, seeds and white membrane from the capsicums, then rinse and drain.

Cut the tops off the tomatoes (the stem end) and set aside. Scoop out the tomato pulp with a spoon and keep it separate. Set the tomatoes upside down to drain off the juices.

Combine the stuffing ingredients in a bowl and mix together thoroughly.

Spoon the stuffing into the vegetables, but don't fill them completely as the rice needs room to expand. Put the reserved tops back on the capsicums and tomatoes. For the eggplants, pare down the reserved ends to form a cork.

In a saucepan, mix the sumac with 500 ml (17 fl oz/2 cups) water and bring to the boil. Drain the liquid through a fine sieve, into a jug. Discard the sumac. Make the liquid back up to 500 ml (17 fl oz/2 cups) with water if necessary.

Spread the tomato pulp in the base of a deep, heavy-based saucepan. Arrange the stuffed capsicums upright in the pan. Lay the eggplants on top of the capsicums, placing them on their sides. Place the tomatoes upright on top of the eggplants.

Combine the sumac liquid with the tomato paste, salt and sugar and pour over the vegetables. Cover the pan tightly and bring to the boil, then reduce the heat to low and simmer gently for 1¼ hours.

Arrange the vegetables in a serving dish and keep warm. Boil the liquid in the pan to reduce it a little and pour over the vegetables. Serve hot or warm.

MANTE
Lamb pie

SERVES: 4–5

300 g (10½ oz/2 cups) plain (all-purpose) flour
½ teaspoon salt
60 ml (2 fl oz/¼ cup) oil
melted butter, for brushing
250 ml (8½ fl oz/1 cup) hot chicken stock
yoghurt, to serve

Filling

1 tablespoon oil
1 small onion, finely chopped
500 g (1 lb 2 oz) finely minced (ground) lamb
   (not too lean)
2 tablespoons finely chopped flat-leaf parsley
salt and freshly ground black pepper, to season

Sift the flour and salt into a mixing bowl. Add the oil and rub it into the flour with your fingertips. Add 125 ml (4 fl oz/½ cup) cold water, mix to a soft dough and knead lightly until smooth. Cover and rest for 30 minutes.

Meanwhile, preheat the oven to 180°C (350°F/Gas 4).

To make the filling, heat the oil in a frying pan and gently fry the onion until translucent. Tip the onion into a mixing bowl and add the lamb and parsley. Season with salt and pepper and mix together thoroughly.

Roll out one-third of the pastry to fit the top of a buttered 25 × 30 cm (10 × 12 inch) baking dish. Set aside and cover with a cloth.

Thinly roll out the remaining pastry, then cut it into 4 cm (1½ inch) squares. Place a teaspoon of the filling in the centre of each, fold up the sides and press the ends together to seal them — the finished pastries will look like miniature canoes, with the meat filling showing.

Place the pastries side by side in rows in the baking dish. Top with the reserved sheet of pastry, tucking the edges in neatly. Brush with melted butter and bake for 45 minutes.

Pour the hot chicken stock over the pastry and bake for a further 10–15 minutes, or until most of the stock has been absorbed.

Cut into squares and serve with yoghurt.

❈ *Note: Sometimes this is prepared without the top covering of pastry, but it is more attractive with the pastry. If not covering the pie with pastry, brush the meat filling with butter before baking.*

AGHTZIVADZ KEDNAHUNZOUR
Lamb sausages with potatoes

SERVES: 6

As with many Armenian recipes, this cumin-flavoured lamb dish also features in Turkish and Greek cookery (Turkish, *izmir kbftesi*; Greek, *souzoukakia*). While the sausage-shaped meatballs are browned first in the Turkish and Greek versions, then simmered in tomato sauce, the Armenians arrange them in a baking dish alternately with pieces of potato, then pour the sauce over them and bake them for a one-dish main course.

750 g (1 lb 10 oz) finely minced (ground) lamb

3 slices of stale white bread, crusts removed

2 garlic cloves, crushed

1 tablespoon chopped flat-leaf parsley

1 teaspoon ground cumin

salt and freshly ground black pepper, to season

750 g (1 lb 10 oz) potatoes

60 g (2 oz/¼ cup) melted butter

Tomato sauce

60 g (2 oz/¼ cup) tomato paste (concentrated purée)

½ small green capsicum (pepper), chopped

½ teaspoon sugar

salt and freshly ground black pepper, to season

Preheat the oven to 180°C (350°F/Gas 4).

Place the lamb in a mixing bowl. Soak the bread in cold water, squeeze it dry and crumble it over the lamb. Add the garlic, parsley and cumin, and season with salt and pepper.

If you have a meat grinder, pass the mixture through it once, using a fine screen; alternatively, process the mixture in a food processor using a steel blade, then knead it to a paste. (If you have neither, just knead the mixture by hand until it is thoroughly combined and paste-like in consistency.)

Using moist hands, shape generous tablespoons of the lamb mixture into oval sausage-like rolls. Set aside.

To make the tomato sauce, combine the tomato paste with 250 ml (8½ fl oz/1 cup) water. Add the capsicum and sugar, and season with salt and pepper.

Peel the potatoes and cut them in half so that the pieces are about the same size and shape as the meatballs.

Brush a baking dish with some of the melted butter. Arrange the meatballs in rows in the dish, placing pieces of potato, cut side down, between the meatballs. Brush with more melted butter. Pour the tomato sauce mixture evenly over the top.

Bake, uncovered, for 10 minutes, basting occasionally with the sauce in the dish.

Reduce the oven temperature to 160°C (320°F/Gas 2–3), then cover the dish with foil and cook for a further 1 hour, adding a little more water to the dish if necessary.

Serve hot with a green vegetable or salad accompaniment and pickles.

ANOUSHABOUR
« Christmas pudding
SERVES: 8–10

220 g (8 oz/1 cup) pearl barley
1 small piece of cinnamon bark
220 g (8 oz/1 cup) sugar

To serve
ground cinnamon
blanched almonds and hazelnuts
chopped walnuts
sultanas (golden raisins)
rosewater, optional

Wash the barley well, place in a bowl and cover with 1 litre (34 fl oz/4 cups) cold water. Soak overnight.

Next day, combine the barley, soaking water and cinnamon in a heavy-based saucepan and bring to the boil. Reduce the heat, leave uncovered and gently boil for about 2 hours, or until the barley is very soft and porridge-like in consistency. Remove the cinnamon.

Stir in the sugar and cook for a further 10 minutes. Ladle into individual bowls and sprinkle with ground cinnamon. Decorate with nuts and sultanas.

Serve warm or chilled, with a little rosewater stirred through, if desired.

TAHINOV HATZ
Tahini cookies
MAKES: ABOUT 60

125 g (4 oz/½ cup) butter
270 g (9½ oz/1 cup) tahini
230 g (8 oz/1 cup) caster (superfine) sugar
115 g (4 oz/½ cup firmly packed) brown sugar
1 egg
375 g (13 oz/2½ cups) plain (all-purpose) flour
1½ teaspoons baking powder
pinch of salt
125 g (4 oz/1 cup) finely chopped walnuts

Preheat the oven to 180°C (350°F/Gas 4).

Beat the butter, tahini and sugars until light and creamy. Add the egg and beat well.

Sift the flour, baking powder and salt twice, then fold into the tahini mixture with the walnuts.

Roll portions of the dough into balls the size of small walnuts and place on greased baking trays. Lightly press each one with the tines of a fork to flatten slightly and give a decorative finish.

Bake for 15 minutes, or until lightly coloured. Leave to cool on the baking trays for 5 minutes, then lift onto wire racks to cool completely. Store in an airtight container.

KHORSHAAF
Dried fruit compote
SERVES: 6

220 g (8 oz/1 cup) pitted prunes
180 g (6 oz/1 cup) dried apricot halves
125 g (4 oz/1 cup) sultanas (golden raisins)
110 g (3¾ oz/½ cup) sugar
thin strip of lemon rind
2 cloves
¼ teaspoon ground allspice, optional
chopped walnuts, to serve

Wash the dried fruits well and place in a saucepan. Pour in enough cold water to cover and bring to the boil. Reduce the heat to low, then cover and simmer for 15 minutes.

Add the sugar, lemon rind, cloves and allspice, if using. Stir to dissolve the sugar, and add a little more water to cover the fruit if necessary. Leaving the lid off, simmer gently until the syrup is thick, and the fruit is soft but not mushy. Remove the lemon rind and cloves.

Spoon the compote into a bowl and chill well. Serve in dessert glasses, sprinkled with chopped nuts.

DARTCHINOV TEY
« Cinnamon tea
MAKES: 2 TEACUPS

4 pieces of cinnamon bark, each 8 cm (3¼ inches) long
sugar, to serve

Leave the cinnamon bark intact and place in a long-handled coffee pot with 375 ml (12½ fl oz/1½ cups) water.

Bring to the boil, then reduce the heat and leave to boil gently for 15 minutes.

Remove the cinnamon bark and pour the tea into teacups. Serve the sugar separately.

TAN
Yoghurt drink
MAKES: ABOUT 750 ML (25 FL OZ/3 CUPS)

In many countries in the region, a yoghurt beverage is served with meals. It is most refreshing, particularly in summer. In Turkey and Iran it is called *ayran* and *abdug* respectively; in Lebanon, Syria and Jordan it is *ayraan* when salt is used, and *laban bi sikkar* when sweetened with sugar. *Tan* accompanies every Armenian meal.

500 g (1 lb 2 oz/2 cups) yoghurt
pinch of salt

Beat the yoghurt in a blender or bowl until smooth.

Gradually add 250 ml (8½ fl oz/1 cup) water, beating constantly. If the yoghurt is too thick, add a little more water, as yoghurts vary in consistency.

Beat in the salt and chill well before serving.

Syria, Lebanon, Jordan

ṢYRIA, LEBANON, JORDAN

In writing this book I was faced with many a dilemma. This chapter was one of them. Should I treat each country separately, or place them together? So many dishes, though different in name, are basically the same, and are claimed by each nation. In the interests of avoiding repetition it seemed best to put them together. You will find a mixture of Arabic dialects in the names because recipes were given to me by Lebanese, Syrians, Jordanians and Palestinians.

The area which is now Lebanon, Syria and Jordan has played a significant part in history for thousands of years, a trading link with East and West and a melting pot of Arabic cultures and creeds. Their dishes have been developed through the wide variety of foods available and the diverse nature of the people in the cities, towns and the remotest desert areas. Collectively this has produced a cuisine that epitomises the Arabic people, adopted by other nations in the region, and that has in turn adopted dishes from its neighbours.

THE FLAVOUR OF ARABIC FOODS

In my time I have tried many a kibbeh, some excellent, others good, and an occasional disappointing one. The excellence of an Arabic cook is measured by their kibbeh, and in trying to find out how a cook goes about making an excellent kibbeh or a *kibbeh bil sanieh*, I was left thoroughly bewildered, since no two cooks seemed to agree. Keep the mixture cold, I was told; it doesn't matter, said someone else. Use only hogget, not lamb, for cooked kibbeh; lamb is fine if it is not too young. Bake it for a long time; bake it for a short time. What confusion! Try my Kibbeh Bil Sanieh (page 285) and you can start on the merry-go-round of kibbeh-making! I am dizzy!

One modernisation that will probably have traditional kibbeh-makers throw their hands up in horror is the use of the food processor. But try it before you condemn its use. Though I enjoy using a mortar and pestle, I lack the stamina to use it for making kibbeh. Furthermore, I doubt if many cooks do use one away from their native home, as even the hand-operated food grinder makes light of the task in comparison.

Following kibbeh in popularity is tabbouleh, the delicious parsley and burghul (bulgur) salad of the region. Again there will be those who disagree with my recipe — more about that in the introduction to the recipe on page 257.

Parsley, mint, the understated spiciness of cinnamon and allspice, the somewhat acidic flavour of yoghurt, the refreshing tartness of lemon, the fruitiness of olive oil, the earthiness of burghul, tahini, eggplant (aubergine), dried beans, rice — these are the flavours of the cuisine of this region. Never overpowering, subtly blended, a delight to the palate.

Arabic hospitality is frequently expressed with the offering of meze, a variety of appetisers only limited by the availability of ingredients and the capacity of the cook to prepare them. Hummus bi Tahini (page 255), Baba Ghanoush (page 256) and Bakdounis bi Tahini (page 253) are three bread dips that are almost always on hand for meze as they keep very well in the refrigerator. With the food processor, these dips can be prepared very quickly and efficiently.

More time-consuming in their preparation, but nevertheless prepared frequently, are *mihshi warak enib* (stuffed grape vine leaves). Recipes for these most popular morsels are found in the chapters on Armenia and Cyprus; these are similar to the Arabic versions.

A diligent cook prepares pastries and stores them in the freezer, to be reheated at a moment's notice. *Fatayer*, *sfiha* and *lahm bi'ajeen* — delicious spinach pies and flat or shaped lamb pies and rolls — are piled on platters and served with yoghurt or lemon wedges. Khoubiz bread dough, a kind of shortcrust pastry, or the fine fillo pastry can form the basis of the pies and rolls. You can take short cuts by using frozen bread dough for some of them, if it is available in your region, and the advantages of fillo pastry are already well known.

Other mezes include Labneh Makbus (yoghurt cheese balls, page 251); Tabbouleh (page 257), a good salad to have on hand for any situation; Falafel (dried bean croquettes, page 263), and fried or baked kibbeh balls. All these can be prepared ahead: store labneh and tabbouleh as directed in the recipes; falafel and kibbeh balls freeze well and may be defrosted and heated in a 180°C (350°F/Gas 4) oven. With modern refrigeration, freezers and food preparation appliances, the Arabic cook has a much easier task entertaining than their predecessors had, even in their native land.

All meze are served with Khoubiz (page 264), the Lebanese flat bread now so widely available to the Westerner. Even if your local store does not keep it in stock, you will find the recipe given quite easy to follow, particularly if you bake bread. The Lebanese *khoubiz sorj*, and the Palestinian and Jordanian *shirak* are one and the same. The same dough is rolled and stretched as thinly as possible without breaking it, and baked on a large metal dome called a *sorj*. The *sorj* is heated curved side up over a fire until very hot, and the bread draped over it. Cooking time is short — about 3 minutes — and after cooking the bread is wrapped in a cloth to keep it soft. The *sorj* is available in varying sizes, but I have found that a good iron Chinese wok inverted over a charcoal fire works very well, even if the breads are not as large as they should be. Bread sheets, as they are commonly called, are cut into squares and rolled up with grilled meats and salad ingredients for an Arabic-style hamburger. Khoubiz bread has a convenient pocket for the same kind of filling, or anything you would conceivably put between two slices of bread.

Tahini is a most important ingredient in the Arabic cooking of the region. It is a paste made from toasted sesame seeds; sometimes a little experimentation is required to find a blend to your liking, as they do vary in quality. I have found considerable variation between tahinis, though they all separate to some degree. Store the unopened jars upside down for some time before use; this way the blending usually required is minimised considerably.

The making of yoghurt is an art handed down from mother to daughter and is almost a daily occurrence in traditional homes. Instructions have been given in the introductory chapter of the book, with two methods detailed. It is through the cooking of this region that I learned how to stabilise yoghurt, and for those who might be watching their saturated fat intake, cooked skim milk yoghurt, Laban Mutboukh (page 252), is an excellent substitute for sour cream. The people of the region never, ever, serve yoghurt with fish. I really do not know why; the different reasons I have been given have varied considerably.

The pastries of the region are renowned worldwide: every Western city now has Lebanese or Syrian pastry shops. I have always made it a practice to patronise such shops as I have found their pastries superb. My favourite version of baklava is the Lebanese Baklawa Be'aj (page 300). In my quest to find and develop this recipe for the home I had a problem finding a name for it. Though to me the shape resembles the petals of a flower, it seems that the Lebanese or Syrian is reminded of a cloth-wrapped bundle called a be'aj, and this is the name they give this pastry, though it is generally referred to as baklawa. The other version of baklawa I have given, Kul'wa'shkur (page 304), has a delightful translation, which describes the pastry admirably — 'eat and praise'.

EATING IN THE STYLE OF THE REGION

With such a diverse group of peoples, it is difficult to give a general method of serving a meal, as the meal could be taken in a city home, a village dwelling or a desert tent. As I describe the traditional Arabic feast as served in a tent in the Gulf States chapter, I shall concentrate on the city or village meal service.

Once again foreign influences have been felt widely in the area and Beirut is considered a very Western city, though still with an essentially Arabic character. The meal is likely to be set on a conventional table spread with a cloth, or it could be set up on a large, low, brass table, depending on the atmosphere that the hosts wish to create. The one single feature of any meal is abundance, with a large variety of foods served at the meal. There could be kibbeh prepared in one of the many ways, tabbouleh, perhaps a fish dish, rice, a vegetable stew, crisp cos (romaine) lettuce, and other salad ingredients, khoubiz, pickles, olives and fresh fruit. Individual serving plates, cutlery and glassware are part of the table appointments. The setting could be as refined as any Western dining room, or colourfully Arabic in flavour. After the meal, coffee is taken in a separate room, perhaps with sweets,

though these are more likely to be eaten at a later time. With coffee comes conversation and sharing the *narghile*, the water pipe of the area.

COOKING METHODS

The *jorn* and *madaqqa*, the mortar and pestle of the region, is a necessary piece of cooking equipment. The mortar is usually very large and made of stone for kibbeh-making, with smaller versions in stone or brass for hummus and other purées, and for pounding spices. A *sanieh* — large, round baking tray — is an ideal cooking utensil for the oven and readily available at Middle Eastern food stores. For shaping *ma'amoul*, a *tabi* can also be obtained from such stores, though I have given a means of shaping using equipment you will have on hand. Coring zucchini (courgettes) is an art that requires an implement more slender than an apple corer, and zucchini corers are also available.

For general cooking, standard pots and pans may be adapted, though I recommend heavy-based pans, particularly for thick soups and dishes containing yoghurt.

INGREDIENTS FOR ARABIC COOKING

Stock up on fine and coarse burghul, tahini, dried beans, chickpeas, dried mint and a spice mix called *za'tar*, used as a topping with oil on khoubiz bread before baking. Flat-leaf parsley is used in abundance, and it is worthwhile having a sizeable patch in your herb garden. The favoured fats are olive oil and Samneh (clarified butter, page 253), though substitutes can be used in many recipes. Where a recipe's flavour is dependent on the right oil or fat, no substitute is given.

Rosewater and orange flower water are required for flavouring syrups and pastries; and you will need walnuts, almonds and pine nuts, with the occasional use of unsalted pistachio nuts. Salted nuts, and toasted and salted chickpeas and pumpkin seeds, are favoured for nibbling with *arak*, the potent aniseed-flavoured spirit of the region, and no Arabic household of this region would be without them.

Dibs (carob syrup) is also very much part of the cuisine. It is mixed with tahini and spread on khoubiz.

LABNEH
« Yoghurt cheese
MAKES: ABOUT 500 G (1 LB 2 OZ/2 CUPS)

Yoghurt made from full-cream milk must be used when making *Labneh*.

1.5 kg (3 lb 5 oz/6 cups) *Laban* (yoghurt I, pages 18-19)
2 teaspoons salt

Measure the yoghurt into a bowl and stir in the salt.

Place the yoghurt in the centre of a doubled-over piece of muslin (cheesecloth), or a piece of soft cotton cloth. Gather up the corners and tie them securely.

Suspend the bundle from a fixed object over a bowl and leave to drain for at least 10 hours. It is best to do this at night when it is cooler.

When well drained and the consistency of ricotta cheese, transfer the cheese to a bowl. Cover and store in the refrigerator.

Use as directed in recipes, or as a spread on Khoubiz (page 264) or other flat bread.

Labneh is a popular breakfast food; it is spread on bread with a drizzle of olive oil and eaten with olives.

LABNEH MAKBUS
« Yoghurt cheese balls
MAKES: ABOUT 500 G (1 LB 2 OZ)

1 quantity Labneh (left)
olive oil, to cover

Make the Labneh as directed in the recipe (left). When well drained, take a tablespoonful at a time and roll into smooth balls. Place the balls side by side on a tray.

Chill the cheese balls in the refrigerator for several hours, or until firm. When firm and a little dried, pack them into a sterilised jar (see page 19) and cover with olive oil. Seal and store at room temperature.

When serving as an appetiser or for spreading on flat bread, serve in a bowl with a little of the oil, so that the oil may be used to soften the cheese.

LABAN MUTBOUKH
Cooked yoghurt
MAKES: ABOUT 500 G (1 LB 2 OZ/2 CUPS)

Yoghurt is used in Lebanese and other Middle Eastern dishes in much the same way as sour cream is used in Western cuisine. If goat's milk yoghurt is available, it may be added as it is to any dish that requires yoghurt to be cooked for a time.

However, the yoghurt generally available (or made at home) is made with cow's milk. This curdles when heated for a long period, so it has to be stabilised beforehand.

Cow's milk yoghurt can be added to a cooked dish just before serving without being previously stabilised, providing the sauce is not allowed to boil.

500 g (1 lb 2 oz/2 cups) yoghurt
1 egg white
2 teaspoons cornflour (cornstarch)
1 teaspoon salt

Place the yoghurt in a heavy-based saucepan.

Beat the egg white with a fork until frothy, then stir it into the yoghurt with the cornflour and salt. Stir in the same direction until thoroughly combined.

Place the pan over medium heat and stir constantly with a wooden spoon. Heat until the yoghurt begins to boil, stirring continuously in the same direction. This is important.

Reduce the heat and leave to simmer gently, uncovered, for 3–5 minutes, until thick.

Use as required in recipes.

KAREESHEE
Cottage cheese

This is the Syrian version of the Greek Mizithra, and as there is little difference, simply follow the directions for making Mizithra on page 27.

However, if you wish to make Kareeshee bi Limoon (below) – a whey cheese similar to the Italian ricotta cheese – be sure to collect all the whey.

KAREESHEE BI LIMOON
Whey cheese

whey from making Kareeshee (above)
1 litre (34 fl oz/4 cups) whole milk
juice of 1 lemon, strained

Heat the whey in a large saucepan over low heat until lukewarm. Pour in the milk and continue to heat until the milk rises to the surface, keeping the heat low.

Add the lemon juice and leave until the cheese thickens, with the pan still over low heat. This takes about 15 minutes.

Line a colander or large sieve with a doubled-over piece of muslin (cheesecloth), set it over a bowl and ladle the cheese into it. Leave until well drained, scraping down the sides of the muslin occasionally.

Gather the ends and tie them securely. Suspend the bundle from a fixed object over a bowl and leave until completely drained.

Remove the cheese from the cloth and store in a sealed container in the refrigerator until required. It will keep for up to 1 week.

Use as for ricotta cheese in recipes.

SAMNEH

While ghee is popularly used in place of *samneh*, the flavour is not quite the same as the clarified or drawn butter prepared by the Arabic cook.

Melt salted or unsalted butter in a saucepan over low heat. When the froth rises, skim it off — it contains some of the milk solids, and the salt if salted butter is used.

Line a sieve with a doubled-over piece of muslin (cheesecloth). Pour the clear oil through the sieve into a container, leaving the milk solids in the pan. These can be combined with the froth for adding to meat and chicken stews, or tossed through vegetables not prepared in the Middle Eastern tradition.

BAKDOUNIS BI TAHINI
Parsley and tahini sauce
MAKES: ABOUT 400 G (14 OZ/1½ CUPS)

Follow the directions for the Taratour bi Tahini recipe (right), adding 1 large handful finely chopped flat-leaf parsley after the 60 ml (2 fl oz/¼ cup) water and all the lemon juice has been blended into the tahini. Beat well and add more water only if it is necessary.

At the end, add coarsely chopped parsley to the food processor or blender and process just long enough to chop it finely; the parsley must still be visible.

Serve as a dip as part of a meze, or as an accompaniment to simple fish dishes.

❋ *Note: In Cyprus this sauce is known as* tahinosalata.

TARATOUR BI TAHINI
Tahini sauce
MAKES: ABOUT 350 G (12 OZ/1¼ CUPS)

2 garlic cloves
½ teaspoon salt
135 g (4½ oz/½ cup) tahini
125 ml (4 fl oz/½ cup) lemon juice

Crush the garlic cloves with the salt in a mixing bowl. Gradually add the tahini and beat well with a wooden spoon.

Beat in a little water and lemon juice alternately. The water thickens the mixture, and the lemon juice thins it. Add all the lemon juice and enough water to give the desired consistency, thick or thin, depending on its intended use; you will need about 60–125 ml (2–4 fl oz/¼–½ cup) water in total.

Add more salt to taste; the sauce should be tart in flavour. Use as directed in recipes.

❋ *Note: If using a food processor or blender, blend or process the tahini and garlic for a few seconds to crush the garlic. Add the lemon juice and water alternately, a little at a time, until the desired consistency is reached. Blend in salt to taste.*

HUMMUS BI TAHINI
Chickpea and sesame purée
MAKES: ABOUT 660 G (1 LB 7 OZ/3 CUPS)

Even if you use a modern appliance for making this popular dish, the chickpeas must first be separated from their skins for a successful hummus. Preparation time can be shortened by removing the skins either after the initial soaking, or after boiling. See page 10 for more details.

220 g (8 oz/1 cup) dried chickpeas

1½ teaspoons salt

90 g (3 oz/⅓ cup) tahini

125 ml (4 fl oz/½ cup) lemon juice

2 garlic cloves, crushed

For serving

olive oil, for drizzling

chopped flat-leaf parsley

paprika or cayenne pepper, for sprinkling

Wash the chickpeas well, cover with 750 ml (25 fl oz/3 cups) water and soak for 12 hours, or overnight.

Drain the chickpeas, reserving the soaking water. Place the chickpeas and soaking water in a saucepan. Bring to the boil, then reduce the heat and leave to boil gently for 2 hours.

Add 1 teaspoon of the salt and cook for a further 1 hour, or until the chickpeas are very tender.

Drain, reserving some of the cooking liquid and 1 tablespoon of the chickpeas.

Press the chickpeas through a sieve or food mill, adding about 2 tablespoons of the cooking liquid to separate the last of the chickpeas from the skins.

Slowly stir the tahini and most of the lemon juice into the purée.

Crush the garlic with the remaining ½ teaspoon of salt using a mortar and pestle and add to the purée. Adjust the flavour and consistency with lemon juice or cooking liquid and add more salt if necessary. Hummus should be thick and smooth.

Spread in a shallow serving dish, swirling it with the back of a spoon. Serve drizzled with olive oil and garnished with the reserved chickpeas, chopped parsley and a sprinkling of paprika or cayenne pepper.

❋ *Note: If you are using a blender or food processor, first soak the chickpeas to separate the skins (see recipe introduction). Add the soaked chickpeas to the processor with the remaining ingredients, holding back some lemon juice and salt to adjust the flavour. Blend or process until thick and smooth.*

BABA GHANOUSH
Eggplant and sesame purée

SERVES: 4–6

1 eggplant (aubergine), about 375 g (13 oz)

60 ml (2 fl oz/¼ cup) lemon juice

65 g (2¼ oz/¼ cup) tahini

2 garlic cloves

2 teaspoons salt, or to taste

1 tablespoon olive oil

3 tablespoons finely chopped flat-leaf parsley

Grill the eggplant over a charcoal fire for 30–40 minutes, turning frequently. Alternatively, place on the centre shelf of a preheated 200°C (400°F/Gas 6) oven and cook until soft, again turning often.

Peel off the skin while the eggplant is still hot. Remove the stem, and the end of the eggplant, if firm.

Chop the flesh and pound to a purée using a mortar and pestle, or purée using a blender or food processor. Blend in most of the lemon juice and gradually add the tahini.

Crush the garlic to a paste with 1 teaspoon of the salt and add to the eggplant. Beat well and adjust the flavour with more lemon juice and salt. Beat in the oil and parsley.

Spread in a shallow serving dish, swirling it with the back of a spoon. Garnish with parsley and serve with Khoubiz (page 264) as an appetiser.

❧ *Note: If using a food processor or blender, use about 4 parsley sprigs instead of the chopped parsley. Add towards the end and blend until the parsley is chopped, but still visible. If making the dish ahead, store it in a sealed container in the refrigerator and bring to room temperature before serving.*

LSANAT MTABBLI
Lamb tongue salad

SERVES: 6–8

10 lamb tongues

3 teaspoons salt

1 garlic clove, halved

1 quantity Fattoush dressing (page 269), or ½ quantity Bakdounis bi Tahini (page 253)

2 tablespoons finely chopped flat-leaf parsley

Wash the lamb tongues well, scrubbing if necessary. Place in a saucepan, cover with cold water and bring to the boil.

Add the salt and garlic. Reduce the heat to low, then cover and simmer for 1½–2 hours, or until the tongues are tender when tested with a skewer.

Drain the tongues and cool a little. Take off the skin and gristle and remove the bone from the root end. Cut the meat into 2 cm (¾ inch) cubes and place in a serving bowl.

Pour the Fattoush dressing or Bakdounis bi Tahini over the tongues and toss well.

Serve sprinkled with the parsley, at room temperature or chilled, as an appetiser or part of a main meal.

TABBOULEH
Burghul and parsley salad
SERVES: 6–8

I once prepared this salad on my television cookery show and received much criticism from members of the Lebanese community in Sydney. It was said that I used far too much burghul (bulgur) and should have mixed the tomato through the salad, not just used it as a garnish. I concede the latter point, with one reservation. If you wish to have the salad on hand for a few days in the refrigerator for convenience, then leave the tomato out and add it to the portion being served.

As to the former criticism, I still believe tabbouleh should have a large proportion of burghul to flat-leaf parsley. While in the Middle East I spoke with many excellent exponents of Lebanese cookery, and found they agreed with me.

If you beg to differ, then reduce the burghul to 45 g (1½ oz/¼ cup) and increase the chopped parsley to 3 large handfuls or more.

130 g (4½ oz/¾ cup) fine burghul (bulgur)

1 large bunch flat-leaf parsley

60 g (2 oz/½ cup) finely chopped spring onions (scallions)

3 tablespoons finely chopped mint

60 ml (2 fl oz/¼ cup) olive oil

2 tablespoons lemon juice

1½ teaspoons salt

½ teaspoon freshly ground black pepper

2 firm ripe tomatoes

For serving

crisp lettuce leaves

60 ml (2 fl oz/¼ cup) lemon juice, mixed with
½ teaspoon salt

Place the burghul in a bowl and cover with 500 ml (17 fl oz/2 cups) cold water. Leave to soak for 30 minutes.

Drain the burghul through a fine sieve, pressing with the back of a spoon to extract the moisture. Spread over a cloth and leave to dry further.

Meanwhile, prepare the parsley. Wash well, shake off the excess moisture and remove any thick stalks. Wrap in a tea towel (dish towel) and place in the refrigerator to crisp and dry.

Put the burghul in a mixing bowl and add the spring onion. Squeeze the mixture with your hands so the burghul absorbs the onion flavour.

Chop the parsley fairly coarsely, then measure it (you need 2 cups) and add it to the burghul with the mint.

Beat the oil with the lemon juice and stir in the salt and pepper. Add to the salad and toss well.

Peel the tomatoes (see page 528), then remove the seeds and dice the flesh. Gently mix through the salad. Cover and chill for at least 1 hour before serving.

Serve in a salad bowl lined with crisp lettuce leaves. Serve the lemon juice and salt mixture separately in a jug so that it may be added according to individual taste.

ZAYTUN MSABBAH
« Spiced olives

fresh green olives
105 g (3½ oz/⅓ cup) rock salt per 1 litre
   (34 fl oz/4 cups) water
3 small, dried hot chillies for each 1 kg (2 lb 3 oz) olives

Either leave the olives as they are, or cut three or four slits in each with a fine-bladed stainless steel knife or stanley knife. Discard any damaged olives.

Pack the olives into a sterilised glass jar or jars (see page 19) and cover with cold water. Soak for 3 days, changing the water each day. Measure the last amount of water.

Measure the same amount of fresh water into a saucepan and add the appropriate amount of rock salt — 105 g (3½ oz/ ⅓ cup) to each litre (34 fl oz/4 cups) water. Heat and stir until the salt dissolves. Leave to cool.

Pack the chillies into the jar or jars, placing them among the olives. Pour the cooled brine on top, filling the jars. Remove any air bubbles by inserting a fine skewer down the side of a jar and seal with a plastic lid. Store in a cool, dark place for 5 months before using.

To serve, remove the required amount of olives, rinse them under cold water, then drain and place in a bowl. Squeeze the juice of a lemon over the olives and drizzle with 60 ml (2 fl oz/¼ cup) olive oil. Stir to combine and leave for 1–2 hours before serving.

KABES EL KARNABEET
Pickled cauliflower

1 cauliflower
40 g (1½ oz/⅓ cup) pickling salt or table salt
750 ml (25 fl oz/3 cups) white vinegar
1 beetroot (beet), optional
2 garlic cloves
2 hot chillies

Break the cauliflower into florets and place in a bowl of salted water to remove any insects. Leave for 10 minutes, then drain and rinse well. Drain again.

Heat 500 ml (17 fl oz/2 cups) water in a saucepan with the pickling salt until the water is boiling and the salt has dissolved. Leave to cool, then add the vinegar.

Peel the beetroot, if using. Cut into slices, then cut the slices in half.

Pack the cauliflower into two sterilised jars (see page 19), placing slices of beetroot between the layers, if using, and adding 1 garlic clove and 1 hot chilli to each jar.

Fill the jars with the pickling solution and seal with glass or plastic lids. Store in a cool place for 1 week before using.

Once opened, store in the refrigerator. Unopened pickles can be kept in a cool, dark place.

FATAYER SBANIKH
Triangle spinach pies
MAKES: ABOUT 30

½ quantity Khoubiz dough (page 264)

Spinach filling

750 g (1 lb 10 oz) spinach

85 ml (3 fl oz/⅓ cup) olive oil

1 large onion, finely chopped

80 g (3 oz/½ cup) pine nuts, or 60 g (2 oz/½ cup)
   chopped walnuts

¼ teaspoon ground nutmeg

60 ml (2 fl oz/¼ cup) lemon juice

salt and freshly ground black pepper, to season

Make the Khoubiz dough as directed on page 264, using the full amount of yeast specified, even though making half the quantity. Cover and leave to rise.

Meanwhile, make the filling. Remove the roots and any damaged leaves from the spinach. Wash the spinach well in several changes of water, then shake off the excess moisture. Chop the leaves and stalks fairly finely.

Place the spinach in a deep non-aluminium saucepan and cook over medium heat, uncovered, for 5–8 minutes, or until the leaves are wilted and the juices run out. Toss with a fork during cooking.

Tip the spinach into a colander and press with the back of a spoon to remove as much moisture as possible.

Heat the oil in a heavy-based saucepan and gently fry the onion until translucent. Add the spinach and fry for 5 minutes, stirring frequently.

Add the nuts, nutmeg and lemon juice and season with salt and pepper. Cook for a further 5 minutes, or until the moisture has evaporated. Leave to cool.

Preheat the oven to 200°C (400°F/Gas 6).

Punch down the dough and roll out on a lightly floured work surface until 5 mm (¼ inch) thick. Cut into 10 cm (4 inch) rounds. Place the rounds on a cloth and cover with another cloth.

Place a tablespoon of the spinach filling in the middle of each round, then bring up the sides at three points to form a triangular shape. Press the edges very firmly with your fingertips to seal the pies completely. Take care not to let the oily juices of the filling seep onto the edge of the dough. If this happens, dip a finger in flour and dab it onto the dough before sealing.

Place the pies close together on a lightly oiled baking tray and bake for 15 minutes, or until lightly coloured and cooked. For a golden brown top, place briefly under a hot grill (broiler). Serve hot or warm.

ARDISHAWKI MIHSHI
Stuffed artichokes

SERVES: 4

8 large globe artichokes

juice of 1 lemon

1 tablespoon olive oil

1 onion, finely chopped

40 g (1½ oz/¼ cup) pine nuts

500 g (1 lb 2 oz) finely minced (ground) lamb

1 tablespoon finely chopped flat-leaf parsley

2 teaspoons salt

freshly ground black pepper, to season

40 g (1½ oz) butter

2 tablespoons plain (all-purpose) flour

Wash and prepare the artichokes following the directions for whole artichokes on page 8.

Open them carefully with your fingers to expose the choke and remove it with a teaspoon. Drop the prepared artichokes into a bowl of cold water with half the lemon juice.

Heat the oil in a frying pan and gently fry the onion until translucent. Add the pine nuts and stir until lightly browned.

Tip the mixture into a bowl and add the meat, parsley and 1 teaspoon of the salt. Season with pepper and mix well.

Drain the artichokes and fill the centres with the meat mixture, forcing in as much as they will take, and mounding the meat on top.

Arrange the artichokes upright in a large saucepan, in a single layer if possible. Add 500 ml (17 fl oz/2 cups) water and the remaining 1 teaspoon salt. Sprinkle the remaining lemon juice over the artichokes.

Cover and bring to just below the boil. Simmer gently for 45–60 minutes, or until the artichokes are tender.

Drain off the liquid into a measuring jug and top it up to 375 ml (12½ fl oz/1½ cups) with water, if needed. Keep the artichokes hot.

Melt the butter in a small saucepan and stir in the flour. Cook for 1 minute, then add the reserved cooking liquid, stirring constantly. Bring to the boil, still stirring, then boil gently for 2 minutes.

Arrange the artichokes on a platter and drizzle with the sauce. Serve hot.

FALAFEL
Dried bean croquettes

MAKES: ABOUT 35

175 g (6 oz/1 cup) dried broad beans (fava beans)

220 g (8 oz/1 cup) dried chickpeas

1 onion, roughly chopped

2 garlic cloves, crushed

1 small handful finely chopped flat-leaf parsley

pinch of ground hot chilli or chilli pepper

1 teaspoon ground coriander

½ teaspoon ground cumin

½ teaspoon bicarbonate of soda (baking soda)

salt and freshly ground black pepper, to season

oil, for deep-frying

Put the beans in a bowl and cover with 750 ml (25 fl oz/3 cups) cold water. Leave to soak for 48 hours, changing the water once each day, or twice in hot weather.

Meanwhile, soak the chickpeas in 750 ml (25 fl oz/3 cups) cold water for 12–15 hours, in a cool place.

Drain the beans and chickpeas. Remove the skins as directed on page 10, in the section 'Skinning pulses'. The skin may be left on the chickpeas.

Combine the uncooked beans and chickpeas with the onion and garlic. Pass through a food grinder twice, using a fine screen, or process in two batches in a food processor using a steel blade.

Combine the mixture with the parsley, spices and bicarbonate of soda. Season with salt and pepper and knead together well, then leave to rest for 30 minutes.

Shape 1 tablespoon of the mixture at a time into balls, then flatten into thick patties 4 cm (1½ inches) across. Place on a tray and leave for 30 minutes at room temperature.

Heat 10 cm (4 inches) of oil in a deep saucepan to 170°C (338°F). Deep-fry in hot oil, six to eight at a time, and cook for 5–6 minutes, turning to brown evenly. When well browned, remove and drain on paper towels.

Serve hot as an appetiser with Taratour bi Tahini (page 253), or in split Khoubiz (page 264) with the Taratour bi Tahini and salad vegetables.

KHOUBIZ
Lebanese flat bread
MAKES: 8 FLAT BREADS

Of all the Middle Eastern breads, this is the most widely known. In recent years its popularity has increased enormously as Western tastes become more adventurous.

Though widely available, *khoubiz* is easily made in a domestic oven or electric frying pan. Though the home product is not as evenly browned, it has a better flavour and finer texture. Traditionally, *khoubiz* contains no shortening, but I find a little oil in the dough improves the flavour and texture. Many Lebanese cooks also add oil.

You will find more details on baking, storing and serving Khoubiz in the 'Bread' section on pages 12–13.

900 g (2 lb/6 cups) plain (all-purpose) flour

2 teaspoons active dried yeast

1½ teaspoons salt

1 teaspoon sugar

2 tablespoons oil

Sift the flour into a large mixing bowl and warm in a low oven.

Dissolve the yeast in 60 ml (2 fl oz/¼ cup) warm water. Add another 440 ml (15 fl oz/1¾ cups) warm water and stir in the salt and sugar.

Remove and reserve about 300 g (10½ oz/2 cups) flour from the bowl. Pour the yeast liquid into the centre and stir in some flour from the side of the bowl to make a thick liquid. Cover with a cloth and leave in a warm place until frothy.

Stir in the flour remaining in the bowl, adding the oil gradually. Beat until smooth, either by hand for 10 minutes, or with an electric mixer using a dough hook for 5 minutes.

Sprinkle some of the reserved flour onto a surface. Turn out the dough and knead for 10 minutes, using more flour as required. The dough is ready when it is smooth and satiny, with a slightly wrinkled texture. Shape the dough into a ball.

Put the dough in an oiled bowl, then turn it over to coat the top with oil. Cover with plastic wrap and leave to rise in a warm place for 1–1½ hours, or until almost doubled in size.

Preheat the oven to 250°C (480°F/Gas 9).

Punch down the dough and turn it out onto a lightly floured work surface. Knead for a minute or so, then divide into eight equal pieces, rolling each into a ball.

Roll each ball into a 25 cm (10 inch) circle and place on a lightly floured cloth. Cover with another cloth and leave for a further 20 minutes.

Heat a large baking tray or flat griddle on the lowest shelf of an electric oven; in a gas oven, select the section of the oven with the most even heat, probably near the top.

Place a round of dough on a lightly floured baking tray with one flat edge, or on a piece of plywood, spreading it evenly. Shake to ensure that it will slide off easily.

Rub the heated baking tray or griddle with a wad of paper towels dipped in oil, then slide the dough onto it.

Bake for 4–5 minutes, or until the dough puffs up like a balloon. If you would like it browned on top, turn the bread quickly and leave for a minute.

Remove the bread from the oven and wrap in a cloth to keep it warm and soft. Bake the remaining rounds in the same way.

❀ *Note: To bake the flat breads in an electric frying pan — a good alternative if your gas oven does not heat evenly — preheat the frying pan on the highest setting with the metal lid on, vent closed. When heated, oil the base quickly and slide the dough onto the base. Cover and cook for 3 minutes, then remove the lid and turn the bread over. Cover and cook for a further 2 minutes.*

MNA'ISH BI ZA'TAR
Seasoned flat bread
MAKES: 8 FLAT BREADS

Make the Khoubiz dough as directed on page 264, but do not
rest it for 20 minutes after shaping the rounds. Flute the edge
of each round with your fingertips and generously brush each
round with olive oil. Sprinkle 2 tablespoons Za'tar spice mix
(see page 523) evenly over the 8 rounds and bake as for
Khoubiz. Do not turn it over; brown the top under a hot grill
(broiler) if desired.

RIZ MUFALFAL
Plain rice
SERVES: 5–6

400 g (14 oz/2 cups) good-quality
    long-grain white rice

2 tablespoons Samneh (page 253) or ghee

2 teaspoons salt, or to taste

Place the rice in a bowl and cover with cold water. Stir with
your fingers to loosen the starch, then drain. Rinse under
running water, then drain thoroughly.

Heat the Samneh in a heavy-based saucepan. Add the rice
and stir over medium heat for 2 minutes, or until the grains
are well coated with fat.

Pour in 750 ml (25 fl oz/3 cups) hot water and add the salt.
Stir occasionally until boiling, reduce the heat, cover the pan
tightly and leave over low heat for 25 minutes.

Turn off the heat and leave for 10 minutes before serving —
the rice may be left longer if desired.

Fluff up the grains with a fork before serving.

ADAS BIS SILQ
Lentil and silverbeet soup
SERVES: 5–6

280 g (10 oz/1½ cups) brown lentils

8–10 leaves silverbeet (Swiss chard)

60 ml (2 fl oz/¼ cup) olive oil

1 large onion, finely chopped

3 garlic cloves, finely chopped

15 g (½ oz/¼ cup) chopped fresh coriander
    (cilantro) leaves

60 ml (2 fl oz/¼ cup) lemon juice

salt and freshly ground black pepper, to taste

lemon wedges, to serve

Khoubiz (left), to serve

Wash the lentils well and place in a heavy-based saucepan
with 1.5 litres (51 fl oz/6 cups) cold water. Bring to the boil,
skimming if necessary, then cover and simmer gently for
1 hour, or until the lentils are soft.

Meanwhile, wash the silverbeet well and cut off the stems.
(The stems may be used as a separate vegetable in other
meals.) Slit the leaves down the middle, then shred coarsely.

Heat the oil in a heavy-based saucepan and gently fry the
onion until translucent. Stir in the garlic and cook for a few
seconds longer. Add the shredded silverbeet and fry, stirring
often, until the leaves wilt.

When the lentils are soft, add the onion and silverbeet
mixture. Stir in the coriander and lemon juice and season
to taste with salt and pepper. Cover and simmer gently for a
further 15–20 minutes.

Serve the soup in deep plates, with lemon wedges for
squeezing into the soup according to individual taste.

Khoubiz or other bread is a necessary accompaniment.

SHURABĀT AL KIBBEH
« Kibbeh soup
SERVES: 6

½ quantity Kibbeh mixture (page 283)

50 g (2 oz/⅓ cup) pine nuts

60 g (2 oz/¼ cup) Samneh (page 253)

1 large onion, finely chopped

1 small piece of cinnamon bark

110 g (3¾ oz/½ cup) short-grain white rice,
   washed

salt and freshly ground black pepper, to taste

3 tablespoons finely chopped flat-leaf parsley

Khoubiz (page 264), to serve

Make the Kibbeh as directed on page 283 and shape into balls
the size of walnuts. Make a hole in each ball, insert ½ teaspoon
of the pine nuts in each, then re-form into balls.

Heat the Samneh in a large frying pan and brown the kibbeh
balls, shaking the pan so they keep their round shape and
brown evenly. Remove to a plate, leaving the Samneh in the
frying pan.

Gently fry the onion in the Samneh until translucent and
soft, stirring often. Add 250 ml (8½ fl oz/1 cup) water and
bring to the boil, stirring to dissolve the browned sediment.

Tip the pan contents into a deep saucepan. Add 1.25–
1.5 litres (42½–51 fl oz/6–7 cups) water, the cinnamon and
rice, and season with salt and pepper. Bring to the boil,
stirring occasionally. Cover and simmer for 10 minutes.

Add the kibbeh balls, then cover and simmer for a further
20 minutes. Ladle into bowls, sprinkle with the parsley and
serve with warm Khoubiz or other flat bread.

SHURABĀT MOZAĀT
Meat soup
SERVES: 6

1 kg (2 lb 3 oz) lamb soup bones

500 g (1 lb 2 oz) lamb stewing meat, cubed

salt and freshly ground black pepper, to season

1 small piece of cinnamon bark

3 small carrots, quartered

70 g (2½ oz/½ cup) chopped celery

125 g (4 oz/½ cup) chopped, peeled tomatoes

110 g (3¾ oz/½ cup) short-grain white rice,
   or 100 g (3½ oz/1 cup) fine noodles, crushed

3 tablespoons finely chopped flat-leaf parsley

Rinse the bones and place in a large saucepan. Add the meat,
cover with 2 litres (68 fl oz/8 cups) water and bring to the boil,
skimming when necessary.

When well skimmed, add the cinnamon and season with
salt and pepper. Cover and simmer for 45 minutes.

Add the vegetables, then cover and cook for a further
30 minutes. Remove and discard the soup bones.

Stir in the washed rice or crushed noodles and adjust the
seasoning. Cover and simmer for a further 20–25 minutes.
Remove the cinnamon.

Serve in soup bowls, sprinkled with the parsley.

SYRIA, LEBANON, JORDAN

SOUPS

267

FATTOUSH
« Toasted bread salad

SERVES: 6

1 Khoubiz (page 264)

6 cos (romaine) lettuce leaves, or
    4 other lettuce leaves, crisped

1 slender green cucumber

2 tomatoes

60 g (2 oz/½ cup) chopped spring onions (scallions)

3 tablespoons finely chopped flat-leaf parsley

3 tablespoons chopped mint

155 g (5 oz/1 cup) chopped green capsicum (pepper)

60 g (2 oz/1 cup) purslane (ba'le or chickweed), optional
    (see page 525); choose the leaves near the top
    of the stalks and the young leafy ends

Salad dressing

1 garlic clove

1 teaspoon salt

125 ml (4 fl oz/½ cup) lemon juice

125 ml (4 fl oz/½ cup) olive oil

freshly ground black pepper, to taste

Toast the Khoubiz under a hot grill (broiler) until golden brown. Break into small pieces, or cut into small squares using kitchen scissors. Set aside.

Shred the lettuce or break into small pieces. Peel the cucumber, cut into quarters lengthways, then cut into chunks. Cut the tomatoes into small cubes.

To make the dressing, crush the garlic in a bowl with the salt and mix to a paste. Stir in the remaining dressing ingredients and beat thoroughly with a fork.

Put all the salad vegetables and herbs in a salad bowl, with the bread on top. Pour over the dressing, toss well and serve.

BATATA MTABBLI
Potato salad

SERVES: 6

8 potatoes

1 onion, finely chopped

1 small handful finely chopped flat-leaf parsley

½ teaspoon dried mint

salt and freshly ground black pepper, to season

1 quantity Fattoush salad dressing (left)

Scrub the potatoes, then cook them in their jackets in a saucepan of boiling salted water until tender. Drain and cool slightly, then peel and cut into 2 cm (¾ inch) cubes.

Place the potatoes in a bowl with the onion and parsley. Sprinkle with the mint, rubbing it to a powder. Season with salt and pepper.

Make the salad dressing as directed in the Fattoush recipe (left) and pour over the potatoes. Toss and serve at room temperature.

SHURABAT AL KISHK
Soup with kishk

SERVES: 6

The preparation of *kishk* is a once-a-year effort when the wheat crop is harvested. Villagers, particularly in isolated areas, depend on *kishk* for nutritious winter breakfasts, and add it to soups for substance.

Basically *kishk* is burghul (bulgur) fermented with milk and yoghurt, a long process which all together takes 2 weeks. After the fermentation process, the mixture is salted, spread on cloth and allowed to dry thoroughly, then rubbed to a fine powder.

Middle Eastern food stores sell *kishk*, and although it is expensive, a little goes a long way. It is also used in Iran.

1 tablespoon Samneh (page 253) or oil
250 g (9 oz) lean minced (ground) lamb
1 large onion, finely chopped
3 garlic cloves, finely chopped
1 cup kishk
salt and freshly ground black pepper,
   to taste

Heat the Samneh in a heavy-based saucepan and stir the lamb and onion over high heat until the meat loses its pink colour and is crumbly. Add the garlic and cook until the juices evaporate.

Stir in the kishk and cook over medium heat for 3 minutes, stirring constantly. Remove the pan from the heat and gradually add 1 litre (34 fl oz/4 cups) cold water, stirring constantly. Season to taste with salt and pepper.

Return to medium heat and stir constantly, until thickened and bubbling. The consistency should be that of a thick cream soup; add a little more water if necessary.

Remove from the heat and serve immediately.

❀ *Note: This soup can be served at any time. For breakfast in Syria and Lebanon, it is often prepared without the meat and garlic.*

KIBBEH BATATA BI SANIEH
Potato kibbeh

SERVES: 6–8

6 potatoes, about 750 g (1 lb 10 oz) in total
265 g (9½ oz/1½ cups) fine burghul (bulgur)
1 onion, grated
1 small handful finely chopped flat-leaf parsley
1 teaspoon dried mint
½ teaspoon ground cinnamon
2–3 teaspoons salt
freshly ground black pepper, to taste
75 g (2½ oz/½ cup) plain (all-purpose) flour, optional

To finish

1 large onion, halved, and sliced
185 ml (6½ fl oz/¾ cup) olive oil

Scrub the potatoes, then cook them in a saucepan of boiling salted water until tender. Drain and cool, then peel and mash.

Place the burghul in a fine sieve and rinse with cold water. Press with the back of a spoon to extract the moisture, then tip into a large bowl and leave for 15 minutes.

Meanwhile, preheat the oven to 200°C (400°F/Gas 6).

Add the potato to the burghul, along with the onion, parsley, mint, cinnamon and 2 teaspoons salt. Season with pepper and mix together. Taste and add more salt if necessary.

Knead well by hand, moistening the mixture occasionally with water. If the mixture is too soft, add enough flour to make a firm paste, kneading well.

To assemble the dish, spread the onion slices in a 25 × 30 cm (10 × 12 inch) baking dish, or a 30 cm (12 inch) round dish. Drizzle with half the oil. Dot the potato paste over the onions, then spread evenly with a spatula. Deeply score the top into diamond shapes using a sharp oiled knife. Drizzle the remaining oil evenly over the top.

Bake for 40 minutes, or until golden brown. Cool in the dish for 10 minutes if serving hot, otherwise serve at room temperature with salad.

MIHSHI MALFUF BI ZAYT
Meatless cabbage rolls

SERVES: 6

1 cabbage, to give 24 leaves

3 garlic cloves

1 teaspoon salt

1 teaspoon dried mint

60 ml (2 fl oz/¼ cup) lemon juice

125 ml (4 fl oz/½ cup) olive oil

Rice and chickpea stuffing

60 ml (2 fl oz/¼ cup) olive oil

180 g (6 oz/1½ cups) chopped spring onions (scallions)

200 g (7 oz/1 cup) long-grain white rice

200 g (7 oz/1 cup) drained, tinned chickpeas

15 g (½ oz/½ cup) finely chopped flat-leaf parsley

250 g (9 oz/1 cup) chopped, peeled tomatoes

½ teaspoon ground allspice

salt and freshly ground black pepper, to taste

Start by making the stuffing. Heat the oil in a frying pan and gently fry the spring onion for 2–3 minutes. Tip into a bowl and add the remaining stuffing ingredients. Season to taste with salt and pepper.

Carefully separate the leaves from the head of cabbage. You will need 24 leaves, although larger leaves may be counted as two. Blanch the leaves in two or three batches in a large saucepan of boiling water for 5 minutes, or until limp — do not overcook.

Drain the leaves, then cut out and remove the larger end of the white centre rib in each leaf. Cut the larger leaves in half down the centre. Line the base of a deep saucepan with the ribs and any torn leaves.

Working one at a time, place a generous tablespoon of the stuffing on the base of each leaf. Roll up once, fold in the sides, then roll up into a firm package. Repeat with the remaining ingredients.

Crush the garlic with the salt and mix in the crumbled mint and lemon juice.

Pack the rolls in the lined pan, seam side down, close together, stacking them in layers, and sprinkling some of the garlic–lemon mixture and oil between each layer.

Invert a plate on top of the rolls to keep them intact during cooking. Pour in enough cold water to just cover the rolls and put the lid on firmly.

Bring to the boil over medium heat, then reduce the heat to low and simmer gently for 45 minutes.

Remove from the heat and set aside for 30 minutes. Serve lukewarm or cold.

WARAK MIHSHI BI SILQ
Stuffed silverbeet leaves

Follow the Mihshi Malfuf bi Zayt recipe (left), substituting 1½ cups (300 g /10½ oz) cooked brown lentils for the chickpeas in the stuffing.

Instead of cabbage leaves, use silverbeet (Swiss chard) leaves, halved lengthways and cut into 10 cm (4 inch) squares. You will require about 50 squares.

Dip the leaves briefly in boiling water, or just run hot tap water over to soften them enough for handling. Drain, then place the squares shiny side down on a work surface.

Use one scant tablespoon of stuffing for each square and roll them up into small, neat rolls.

Finish as for the Mihshi Malfuf bi Zayt, omitting the dried mint and increasing the lemon juice to 125 ml (4 fl oz/½ cup).

KOUSA MIHSHI BI LABAN
« Stuffed zucchini with yoghurt
SERVES: 6–8 AS AN APPETISER, 4–5 AS A MAIN COURSE

1 kg (2 lb 3 oz) evenly sized zucchini (courgettes); choose
    ones that are either small or medium in size

1 quantity Laban Mutboukh (page 252)

2 garlic cloves, crushed

1 teaspoon dried mint

Stuffing

1 tablespoon Samneh (page 253) or oil

1 onion, finely chopped

1 tablespoon pine nuts, optional

250 g (9 oz) minced (ground) lamb or beef

55 g (2 oz/¼ cup) short-grain white rice

1 tablespoon chopped flat-leaf parsley

½ teaspoon ground allspice

1 teaspoon salt

freshly ground black pepper, to season

Wash the zucchini well and cut off the stem end. Using a vegetable or apple corer, hollow out each zucchini, leaving the rounded end intact. Try not to puncture the skin. Soak in salted water for 10 minutes, then drain.

Heat the Samneh or oil in a frying pan and gently fry the onion until translucent. If using pine nuts, add them to the pan after 10 minutes, and cook with the onions for at least another 5 minutes, stirring occasionally.

Tip the mixture into a bowl. Add the remaining stuffing ingredients and 60 ml (2 fl oz/¼ cup) water. Season with pepper and thoroughly combine.

Fill the zucchini with the stuffing. Although the rice expands during cooking, the meat shrinks, so there is no need to allow room for expansion.

Arrange the zucchini in layers in a heavy-based saucepan, sprinkling the layers lightly with salt. Pour in 300 ml (10 fl oz/1¼ cups) cold water. Invert a heavy plate on top of the zucchini and bring to a slow simmer. Cover and simmer gently for 1 hour, or until tender.

Meanwhile, prepare the Laban Mutboukh as directed on page 252. When it begins to boil, stir in the crushed garlic and boil for 2 minutes, then remove from the heat.

When the zucchini are cooked, remove the plate and pour the Laban Mutboukh over them. Boil gently, uncovered, over medium heat for 10 minutes, or until the sauce is thick.

Crush the dried mint to a coarse powder and sprinkle it over the zucchini. Remove from the heat, cover and stand for 10 minutes before serving.

For a main course, serve the zucchini and sauce with mashed potatoes or steamed rice.

❀ *Note: Middle Eastern food suppliers usually stock a special corer for preparing vegetables for stuffing. It is not as wide as an apple corer, and much longer.*

KOUSA MIHSHI BI BANDOURA
Stuffed zucchini with tomato sauce

Prepare and stuff the zucchini (courgettes) as directed in the Kousa Mihshi bi Laban recipe (left), using the same stuffing mixture. Set aside.

To make the tomato sauce, heat 60 g (2 oz/¼ cup) Samneh or oil in a frying pan and gently fry 1 large chopped onion until translucent. Add 2 finely chopped garlic cloves and cook for a few seconds. Stir in 250 g (9 oz/1 cup) chopped peeled tomatoes, 60 g (2 oz/¼ cup) tomato paste (concentrated purée), 250 ml (8½ fl oz/1 cup) water and ⅛ teaspoon cinnamon. Season with salt and pepper and bring to the boil.

Pour one-quarter of the sauce into a heavy-based saucepan. Arrange the filled zucchini in layers in the pan, spooning the remaining sauce over each layer. Cover and simmer gently for 1¼ hours. Serve hot or warm, with the sauce.

LUBYI BI ZAYT
« Green beans in oil
SERVES: 6

500 g (1 lb 2 oz) green beans
60 ml (2 fl oz/¼ cup) olive oil
1 onion, chopped
2 garlic cloves, chopped
250 g (9 oz/1 cup) chopped, peeled tomatoes
1 tablespoon tomato paste (concentrated purée)
½ teaspoon sugar
salt and freshly ground black pepper, to taste
2 tablespoons chopped flat-leaf parsley

Wash the beans well, then top and tail and remove the strings, if present. Cut into 5 cm (2 inch) lengths, or slit them lengthways (French cut). Set aside.

Heat the oil in a heavy-based saucepan and gently fry the onion until translucent. Add the garlic and cook for a few seconds longer.

Add the tomatoes, tomato paste, sugar and 125 ml (4 fl oz/½ cup) water. Season to taste with salt and pepper, then cover and simmer for 15 minutes.

Stir in the beans and parsley. Cover and simmer for a further 15–20 minutes, or until the beans are tender.

Serve hot or lukewarm in the traditional way. The beans are also very good served chilled.

BAMYI BI ZAYT
Okra in oil
SERVES: 6

Substitute 500 g (1 lb 2 oz) okra for the beans in the Lubyi bi Zayt recipe (left); prepare the okra as directed on page 8.

Heat the oil in a frying pan and fry the okra quickly, stirring carefully so as not to break them. Remove to a plate with a slotted spoon and set aside.

Make the tomato and onion sauce as directed and simmer for 15 minutes. Add the okra and 3 tablespoons chopped coriander (cilantro) leaves instead of the parsley. Cover and simmer for 20 minutes, or until tender.

Pour 60 ml (2 fl oz/¼ cup) lemon juice over the okra, then cover and cook for a further 5 minutes. Serve hot or lukewarm.

❀ *Note: Tinned or frozen okra may be used instead of fresh okra. Do not fry them in the oil.*

KARNABIT BI TAHINI
Cauliflower with tahini sauce
SERVES: 6

1 cauliflower
salt
270 g (9½ oz/1 cup) Taratour bi Tahini (page 253)

Break the cauliflower into florets and place in a bowl of salted water to remove any insects. Leave for 10 minutes, then drain.

Cook the cauliflower in a saucepan of rapidly boiling salted water, without a lid, for 10–12 minutes, or until just tender and still a little crisp. Drain.

Place the cauliflower in a serving bowl and spoon half the tahini sauce evenly over it. Serve hot or cold, with the remaining tahini sauce in a separate bowl for adding to individual taste.

LABAN BIL BAYD
Eggs in yoghurt garlic sauce
SERVES: 6

1 quantity Laban Mutboukh (page 252)
2 garlic cloves
½ teaspoon salt
2 teaspoons dried mint
60 g (2 oz/¼ cup) Samneh (page 253)
6 eggs

Preheat the oven to 200°C (400°F/Gas 6).

Make the Laban Mutboukh as directed on page 252 and leave to simmer gently, uncovered.

Crush the garlic with the salt and mix in the mint, crumbled to a coarse powder.

Heat the Samneh in a small frying pan and add the garlic mixture. Fry for 5 minutes, stirring often.

Pour the hot Laban Mutboukh into a shallow baking dish. Break the eggs on top, spacing them evenly.

Pour the garlic Samneh mixture over the eggs. Bake for 15–20 minutes, or until the eggs are set hard. Serve hot.

✿ *Note: For an interesting first course, divide the yoghurt mixture among six individual dishes, break an egg into each dish and top with the garlic Samneh mixture. Bake as above.*

'IGGIT AN NUKHAAT
Brain omelette
SERVES: 4–5

4 sets of lamb brains
salt, to season
1 garlic clove
juice of 1 lemon
60 g (2 oz/¼ cup) Samneh (page 253)
1 onion, finely chopped
6 eggs
4 tablespoons chopped flat-leaf parsley
freshly ground black pepper, to season

Cover the brains with cold salted water and leave to soak for 20 minutes. Drain and remove the skin if possible. This is difficult if the brains have been frozen, and it might be necessary to leave the skin on. Any veins should be removed.

Place the brains in a saucepan with water to cover. Add the garlic clove and lemon juice and season with salt. Bring to a slow simmer, then simmer, uncovered, for 15 minutes, or until tender. Drain the brains and cut into tiny pieces.

Heat the Samneh in a frying pan and gently fry the onion until translucent. Remove the onion to a bowl, and drain the Samneh back into the pan. Cool.

Break the eggs into a bowl with the onion and beat lightly with a fork. Add the parsley and brains and season with salt and pepper. Stir to combine.

Reheat the frying pan over medium heat, then pour in the egg mixture. Cover and cook over low heat for 10–15 minutes, or until the eggs are set and puffed.

Serve hot, cut into wedges.

SAMKE BI TARATOUR
Fish with tahini sauce

SERVES: 6–8

1 snapper or other fish suitable for baking,
    weighing about 2 kg (4 lb 6 oz)

juice of ½ lemon

salt, to season

60 ml (2 fl oz/¼ cup) olive oil

double quantity Taratour bi Tahini (page 253)

3 tablespoons finely chopped flat-leaf parsley

To garnish

thinly peeled cucumber skin

olives

parsley sprigs

pomegranate seeds, if available

1 tablespoon pine nuts, pan-fried in 1 tablespoon
    olive oil until golden

lemon wedges or slices

Clean and scale the fish if necessary. Leave the head on but remove the eyes. Rinse the fish and pat dry with paper towels. Make three slashes into the skin on each side of the body.

Rub the fish inside and out with the lemon juice and salt. Cover and refrigerate for 1 hour.

Meanwhile, preheat the oven to 180°C (350°F/Gas 4).

Oil a large baking dish. Lay the fish in it and pour the remaining oil over the top. Bake for 30 minutes, or until the fish is cooked when tested at its thickest part. Baste the fish occasionally with the pan juices during baking, and do not overcook.

Carefully lift the fish onto a platter, cover with plastic wrap and chill. Alternatively, leave it to cool a little, then neatly cut off the head and tail and reserve. Remove the side fins and lift the flesh from the body in two sections from each side. Take off the skin and remove any bones. Discard the backbone and fins. Rearrange the fish in its original shape on a clean platter, then cover and chill.

Make the Taratour bi Tahini as directed on page 253, using enough water to give a thick sauce. Spread half the sauce over the fish, leaving the head and tail uncovered. Smooth the sauce with a small spatula.

Decorate as desired, with whatever garnish ingredients are available or appeal. Cucumber skin can be used to simulate fins; make fringe-like cuts along the length of the strips. Use an olive or a parsley sprig for the eye. Cover and chill again until ready to serve.

Garnish the platter with lemon slices or wedges and parsley sprigs. Stir most of the chopped parsley into the remaining sauce, place in a bowl and sprinkle with the remaining chopped parsley.

Serve as part of a buffet spread, or as a first course.

SAMKE HARRAH AL-SAHARA
Baked fish with hot chilli sauce

SERVES: 4

Many versions of this famous Lebanese fish dish exist. Even pronunciations and the resultant transliteration vary considerably. The regional Arabic for fish is *samke* (singular) and *samek* (plural), the 'a' pronounced as the 'u' in 'up', and the 'e' as in 'end'. Thus spellings vary from *samke*, *sumke*, *sumki* to *samek*, *samak* and *sumak*.

This delicious version was graciously provided by Mrs Laudy Jammal and Mr Jimmy Antoun of the popular Al-Sahara Lebanese restaurant in Chatswood, a Sydney suburb, so I have just as graciously used their translation.

1 snapper or other fish suitable for baking,
    weighing about 2 kg (4 lb 6 oz)
salt, for sprinkling
100 ml (3½ fl oz) olive oil

Hot chilli sauce
4–6 garlic cloves
1 teaspoon salt
3 tablespoons finely chopped coriander (cilantro) leaves
270 g (9½ oz/1 cup) tahini
125 ml (4 fl oz/½ cup) lemon juice
¼–½ teaspoon ground hot chilli or chilli pepper

To garnish
1 tablespoon pine nuts, pan-fried in 1 tablespoon
    olive oil until golden
lemon wedges
coriander (cilantro) leaves

Clean and scale the fish if necessary. Leave the head on but remove the eyes. Slash the body diagonally in two places on each side. Sprinkle inside and out with salt, then cover and refrigerate for 1–2 hours.

Meanwhile, preheat the oven to 180°C (350°F/Gas 4).

Pat the fish dry. Heat the oil in a large frying pan and fry the fish over high heat for a few minutes each side. Do not cook it through. Remove the pan from the heat, then lift the fish out and place in a baking dish.

To make the hot chilli sauce, pound the garlic cloves with the salt, then mix in the coriander. Tip most of the oil out of the frying pan, leaving about 2 tablespoons. Heat the oil and add the garlic mixture; fry quickly until the mixture is crisp, but not burnt. Remove from the heat and cool.

Place the tahini in a bowl, beat well, then gradually add 125 ml (4 fl oz/½ cup) water, beating constantly. The mixture will thicken. Gradually beat in the lemon juice, then stir in the garlic mixture and chilli to taste. Add more salt if necessary.

Pour the sauce over the fish, covering it completely. Bake for 30–35 minutes, or until the fish is cooked through and the sauce is bubbling.

Lift the fish onto a platter and spoon the sauce over the top. Sprinkle with the pan-fried pine nuts and garnish the platter with lemon wedges and coriander. Serve hot.

KIBBEH SAMAK
Fish kibbeh

SERVES: 6

Fish kibbeh

525 g (1 lb 2¾ oz/3 cups) fine burghul (bulgur)

1 kg (2 lb 3 oz) white fish fillets

1 large onion, chopped

3 tablespoons finely chopped coriander
   (cilantro) leaves

3 tablespoons finely chopped flat-leaf parsley

grated zest of 1 orange

3 teaspoons salt

freshly ground black pepper, to season

Filling

60 ml (2 fl oz/¼ cup) olive or other oil

50 g (2 oz/⅓ cup) pine nuts

2 large onions, halved and sliced

To finish

125 ml (4 fl oz/½ cup) olive or other oil

Preheat the oven to 200°C (400°F/Gas 6).

Put the burghul in a fine sieve and rinse under cold running water. Press out the moisture with the back of a spoon. Set aside.

Remove the skin and any bones from the fish. Roughly chop the flesh.

Pass the fish and onion through a food grinder using a fine screen, or process in a food processor using a steel blade.

Combine the fish and onion with the burghul, coriander, parsley, orange zest and salt. Season with pepper, then knead to a firm paste. (The mixture may be processed in a food processor in four batches.)

To make the filling, heat the oil in a frying pan and fry the pine nuts until golden brown. Remove with a slotted spoon. Then gently fry the onion in the pan until translucent. Return the pine nuts to the pan and remove from the heat.

Grease a 25 × 30 cm (10 × 12 inch) baking dish with some of the remaining oil. Add half the fish kibbeh, spreading it out evenly. Top with the onion and pine nut mixture.

Dot the remaining fish kibbeh over the filling, spreading it evenly with a spatula, to keep the filling in place. Deeply score the top into diamond shapes using a sharp oiled knife. Drizzle the remaining oil evenly over the top.

Bake for 30–35 minutes, or until golden brown.

Serve hot or cold.

MOUSAKHAN
Chicken roasted with bread

SERVES: 8

Mousakhan is a Palestinian speciality that calls for a very thin flat bread called *shirak*. This bread requires considerable expertise in making the dough paper thin, and also should be baked on a large metal dome (*sorj*) over a charcoal fire. Mousakhan is well worth trying, so I have given a substitute bread.

2 chickens, each about 1 kg (2 lb 3 oz)

salt and freshly ground black pepper, to season

85 ml (6½ fl oz/⅓ cup) olive oil

3 onions, sliced

3 teaspoons sumac

2 Khoubiz (page 264)

Preheat the oven to 180°C (350°F/Gas 4).

Pat the chickens dry with paper towels. Rub inside and out with salt and pepper. Tie the legs together and tuck the wings under the body.

Heat half the oil in a large frying pan and fry the chickens over medium heat until lightly browned, turning them often. Remove to a plate and set aside.

Add the remaining oil to the pan and gently fry the onion until translucent, stirring often. Sprinkle in the sumac and cook for a further 2 minutes. Remove from the heat.

Split each Khoubiz horizontally into two, to give four flat pieces of bread. Place two pieces slightly overlapping in the base of a baking dish.

Place a mound of the onion mixture in the centre of each piece of bread, using about one-quarter of the onion mixture. Put a chicken on top of each mound, then spread the remaining onion mixture over the top of each chicken. Pour the oil from the pan over the chicken and bread.

Cover the chickens with the remaining bread pieces, laying the white surface of the bread face down. Sprinkle the bread lightly with water.

Bake for 1½ hours, or until the chickens are tender and thoroughly cooked. If the bread begins to burn, cover the top with a piece of foil. The bread covering keeps the chickens moist, while the bread in the base of the dish absorbs the flavoursome juices.

Serve cut into portions, with a piece of bread for each serving.

KASBI MISHWI BI TOUM
Grilled liver with garlic
SERVES: 4–6

500 g (1 lb 2 oz) lamb liver
3–4 garlic cloves
½ teaspoon dried mint, finely crumbled
60 ml (2 fl oz/¼ cup) olive oil
salt and freshly ground black pepper, to season
lemon wedges, to serve

Soak the liver in cold salted water for 20 minutes. Drain, remove the skin, then cut the liver into 1 cm (½ inch) slices. Cut the slices into roughly 2 cm (¾ inch) squares. Pat dry with paper towels.

Crush the garlic and combine with the mint. Spread each side of the liver pieces with the garlic paste and place in a dish. Sprinkle with the oil and season with salt and pepper. Cover and leave for 30 minutes.

Thread the liver pieces onto skewers, passing them through the sides of the squares so that the liver is flat on the skewers.

Cook over a glowing charcoal fire for 1–2 minutes each side, taking care not to overcook, and brushing with the oil from the dish during cooking.

Serve hot with lemon wedges. Serve as a meze or main meal.

KIBBEH NAYYE
Raw kibbeh
SERVES: 10–12 AS AN APPETISER OR FIRST COURSE

1 quantity Kibbeh (page 283)
60 ml (2 fl oz/¼ cup) olive oil
65 g (2¼ oz/1 cup) sliced spring onions (scallions), including the green tops
2 cos (romaine) lettuce
lemon wedges, to serve
4–6 Khoubiz (page 264), cut into quarters

Make the Kibbeh according to the directions on page 283, using only 350 g (12 oz/ 2 cups) burghul (bulgur).

After the final kneading, place the kibbeh on a large oval platter and spread it out flat. Dip your hand in iced water and round the edges and smooth the top. Make a depression in the centre with your thumb. With the side of your forefinger, make two grooves along and across the kibbeh, to the edges. Alternatively, shape the kibbeh on individual dishes.

Place the kibbeh in the refrigerator, uncovered. Chill for about 1 hour, or until the colour of the kibbeh changes to a pleasant red (the cold plus the oxygen brings up the colour).

If not serving immediately, cover with plastic wrap. If using individual plates, do not stack them, otherwise the colour will change.

To serve, drizzle the oil in the centre depression and along the grooves. Garnish with a ring of spring onion around the edge. Place the washed and crisped lettuce leaves in a bowl, the lemon wedges in another bowl, and the Khoubiz in a basket.

The kibbeh is scooped up with either lettuce leaves or bread, and lemon juice squeezed on if desired.

❧ *Note: Kibbeh Nayye should be eaten the day it is made. Any leftovers should be used for a cooked kibbeh dish.*

KIBBEH
Minced lamb and burghul

SERVES: 6–10

The preparation of kibbeh, virtually the national dish of both Lebanon and Syria, is an exercise in patience and stamina. Or rather this was the case, and still is for the purists of Middle Eastern cookery. Modern appliances can replace the traditional *madaqqa* and *jorn* (mortar and pestle) for the tedious preparation – the kibbeh will be just as good and the cook far less exhausted.

Two essential principles of kibbeh-making are to have the right meat, and to keep the mixture cool. Ideally hogget (yearling mutton) should be used; if you cannot obtain this, lamb may be used, provided it is not too young. Look for lamb with a deep pinky-red colour and a good fat cover. Very young lamb is a definite pink in colour, very lean and velvety in texture, and may be used for the making of Kibbeh Nayye (left) only. Beef topside (US bottom round) may be used as a last resort, providing it is prime quality.

Whatever the meat, it must be trimmed of all fat and gristle before preparation, so allow for this trimming when purchasing your meat.

In cities with large Lebanese and Syrian communities, it is sometimes possible to find a butcher who specialises in providing ready minced (ground) kibbeh meat. A Lebanese or Syrian acquaintance might know of such a butcher.

525 g (1 lb 2¾ oz/3 cups) burghul (bulgur)

1 kg (2 lb 3 oz) lean lamb or hogget (yearling mutton), from the leg

1 large onion, chopped

3 teaspoons salt

1 teaspoon freshly ground black pepper

1 teaspoon ground allspice

125 ml (4 fl oz/½ cup) iced water or ice chips

Food grinder method

Place the burghul in a bowl, cover with cold water and leave to soak for 10 minutes. Drain in a sieve and press with the back of a spoon to remove as much moisture as possible. Tip into a flat dish, spread out and chill for 1–2 hours. This also dries the burghul further.

Trim all the fat and fine skin from the meat and cut it into cubes. Chill for 1 hour if not very cold.

Pass the meat through the meat grinder twice, using a fine screen. Grind the onion twice and combine with the meat, burghul, salt, pepper and allspice.

Pass the mixture through the grinder again twice, adding a little iced water or ice chips if the mixture feels warm.

Knead to a smooth, light paste with your hands, adding iced water or ice chips when necessary. Cover and chill until required.

Food processor method

Prepare the burghul and meat as above. Using a steel cutting blade, process a quarter of the meat cubes at a time until paste-like in consistency. Transfer to a large bowl. Process the onion to a thick liquid and add to the meat. Combine the meat with the onion, seasoning, allspice and burghul. Process again in six lots, adding a tablespoon of iced water or ice chips to each lot. Combine again in a bowl and give a final knead by hand. Cover and chill until required.

KIBBEH BIL SANIEH
Baked stuffed kibbeh in a tray

SERVES: 6–10

60 g (2 oz/¼ cup) Samneh (page 253) or oil

2 onions, finely chopped

40 g (1½ oz/¼ cup) pine nuts

250 g (9 oz) coarsely minced (ground) lamb
    or veal

salt and freshly ground black pepper, to season

¼ teaspoon ground cinnamon

1 quantity Kibbeh (page 283)

To finish

185 ml (6½ fl oz/¾ cup) melted Samneh (page 253),
    ghee or olive oil

pine nuts, to garnish, optional

Preheat the oven to 180°C (350°F/Gas 4).

Heat the Samneh or oil in a frying pan and gently fry the onion until translucent. Add the pine nuts and fry until the nuts are lightly browned.

Increase the heat and add the meat. Stir and cook until the juices evaporate and the meat begins to brown. Remove from the heat, season with salt and pepper and add the cinnamon.

Make the Kibbeh mixture as directed on page 283 — there is no need to chill it, unless making ahead of time.

To assemble the dish, brush a 28 × 33 cm (11 × 13 inch) baking dish, or a 35 cm (14 inch) round dish, with some of the melted Samneh or ghee. Press a little less than half the kibbeh mixture onto the base, smoothing it with a wet hand.

Top with the meat and nut mixture, spreading it evenly. Dot the top with mounds of the remaining kibbeh mixture, then carefully press it out evenly, to keep the filling in place. Smooth the top.

Run a knife blade around the edge of the dish, then deeply score the top into diamond shapes. Press a pine nut into the centre of each diamond if desired.

Mix the remaining melted Samneh or ghee with 2 tablespoons cold water. Pour it over the top, making sure some runs down between the sides of the dish and the kibbeh.

Bake for 30 minutes; to brown the top, sprinkle lightly with water three or four times during cooking.

Cut through the scored sections and serve hot or cold with yoghurt, salads and Khoubiz (page 264).

❧ *Note: Use oil if planning to serve the dish cold. It may also be cooked without the filling. Spread the kibbeh evenly in a dish, without the meat and pine nut filling. Score the top as required and pour on the melted Samneh or oil. Bake as above.*

KIBBEH MISHWEY OR KIBBEYET
Stuffed kibbeh balls
SERVES: 6

Use the same ingredients as for the Kibbeh bil Sanieh recipe on page 285, replacing the 185 ml (6½ fl oz/¾ cup) melted Samneh, ghee or olive oil with sufficient oil for deep-frying.

Take lumps of Kibbeh (page 283) the size of small eggs and shape into balls.

Dip your hands in cold water, roll a ball of kibbeh in your palms until smooth, then make a hole in the ball with your forefinger. Work your finger round in the hole until you have a shell of even thickness. Fill the hole with the filling mixture and close the opening. Moisten with cold water to seal well. If any breaks appear in the shell, close them with wet fingers.

Complete the shape to resemble either a torpedo, pointed at each end, or a spinning top, rounded at one end and pointed at the other. Place the finished kibbeh shells on a tray.

Heat the oil in a frying pan and deep-fry a few at a time until they become a deep brown colour, without being burnt, turning them to brown evenly. Lift out with a slotted spoon and drain on paper towels. Keep warm in a low oven until the remainder are cooked.

Alternatively, place the shaped kibbeh side by side in a large greased baking dish, brush well with the melted Samneh or oil, and bake in a preheated oven at 180°C (350°F/Gas 4) for 20–25 minutes.

Serve hot or cold with salads, yoghurt and Khoubiz (page 264) or other flat bread.

❧ *Note: Torpedo-shaped* kibbeyet *are usually fried in oil. The ones shaped like spinning tops can be cooked over a glowing charcoal fire or baked in the oven.*

KIBBEH BI LABAN
Kibbeh balls in yoghurt
SERVES: 6

½ quantity Kibbeh Mishwey (left)
double quantity Laban Mutboukh (page 252)
1 garlic clove
½ teaspoon salt
2 teaspoons dried mint
60 g (2 oz/¼ cup) Samneh (page 253)

Make the kibbeh balls as directed (left), filling with the stuffing and shaping them into torpedo shapes. Do not cook the finished balls. Set aside.

Prepare the Laban Mutboukh as directed on page 252, adding 125 ml (4 fl oz/½ cup) water after the mixture has simmered for 3–5 minutes. Bring to the boil and simmer, uncovered, for a further 5 minutes.

Add the kibbeh balls and simmer, uncovered, over low heat while preparing the garlic mint mixture.

Crush the garlic with the salt and stir in the crushed mint. Heat the Samneh in a small saucepan, add the garlic mixture and fry for 2–3 minutes.

Gently stir the mixture through the kibbeh balls, stirring only in one direction. Add more salt to taste.

Leave to simmer gently, uncovered, for 15 minutes. Do not stir again. When the kibbeh are cooked, the yoghurt sauce should be thick; if not, leave to simmer for a further 5 minutes.

Serve hot, with Riz Mufalfal (page 265).

MANSAAF
Spiced lamb in yoghurt
SERVES: 6

Apparently it is a popular misconception to regard *mansaaf* as a Jordanian feast. I have been assured by Jordanian friends that *mansaaf* is actually a *dish* served at feasts. The Palestinians also prepare this, calling it *mansi*.

As a favour to my friends, I shall now set the record straight, and give you the recipe. Of course in Jordan they would probably use a whole lamb, though it is scaled down for normal meals.

- 1.5 kg (3 lb 5 oz) lamb shoulder, on the bone, cut by your butcher into 6 evenly sized pieces, or 1.5 kg (3 lb 5 oz) thickly cut lamb shoulder chops
- salt and freshly ground black pepper, to season
- 60 g (2 oz/¼ cup) Samneh (page 253) or ghee
- 40 g (1½ oz/¼ cup) pine nuts
- 1 large onion, chopped
- 1½ teaspoons ground turmeric
- ½ teaspoon ground allspice
- 1 small piece of cinnamon bark
- 1 quantity Laban Mutboukh (page 252)

Place the lamb in a saucepan and add just enough cold water to cover. Bring slowly to the boil, skimming as required. When well skimmed and boiling, season with salt and pepper, then cover and simmer gently for 30 minutes.

Heat the Samneh in a frying pan and fry the pine nuts until golden. Remove the pine nuts to a plate, draining the Samneh back into the pan.

Add the onion to the pan and gently fry until translucent. Stir in the turmeric, allspice and cinnamon and cook for a further 2 minutes. Stir this mixture into the simmering lamb.

Meanwhile, make the Laban Mutboukh according to the directions on page 252 and set aside.

After the lamb has been simmering for 1 hour, remove the lid and reduce the liquid until it half covers the lamb.

Now add the Laban Mutboukh, shaking the pan to combine it evenly with the liquid. Leave to simmer gently over low heat until the lamb is tender and the sauce is thick. If the sauce must be stirred, only stir in one direction.

Remove the cinnamon and add salt and pepper to taste.

Serve piled on a serving platter, sprinkled with the pine nuts. Serve hot, with Riz Mufalfal (page 265).

❀ *Note: To serve in the traditional manner, line the serving platter with split Khoubiz (page 264) as a substitute for the paper-thin shirak bread of Jordan. Pile on the rice (Riz Mufalfal, page 265) and cover with the lamb and yoghurt mixture. Sprinkle with pine nuts.*

MIHSHI MALEUF
Cabbage rolls
SERVES: 6

1 large cabbage

4 garlic cloves, chopped

salt, for sprinkling

60 ml (2 fl oz/¼ cup) lemon juice, or
   3 teaspoons pomegranate molasses

1 teaspoon dried mint

Filling

40 g (1½ oz) Samneh (page 253), or 2 tablespoons oil

1 onion, finely chopped

750 g (1 lb 10 oz) finely chopped or coarsely
   minced (ground) lamb shoulder

220 g (8 oz/1 cup) short-grain white rice,
   washed and drained

½ teaspoon ground allspice

salt and freshly ground black pepper,
   to season

Core the cabbage and carefully remove the leaves. The heart may be reserved for making salad. Blanch the leaves in a saucepan of boiling salted water, a few at a time, until limp. Drain.

Cut the larger leaves in half, removing the thick white central rib. Cut the thicker part of the rib from the smaller leaves. Line a deep pan with the ribs and any torn leaves.

To make the filling, heat the Samneh or oil in a frying pan and gently fry the onion until translucent and soft. Tip into a bowl, add the remaining filling ingredients and season with salt and pepper. Combine thoroughly.

Place a tablespoon of filling on the bottom edge of each leaf. Roll up, tucking in the sides to contain the filling. Press with your hand into a neat sausage shape.

Pack the finished rolls, seam side down, in the lined saucepan. Place them close together in layers, sprinkling each layer with a little garlic, salt and lemon juice; if using pomegranate molasses instead of lemon juice, mix it into 60 ml (2 fl oz/¼ cup) water before sprinkling onto the rolls.

Crush the remaining garlic and mix with the coarsely powdered mint. Scatter over the final layer of rolls and add enough water to the pan to just cover the rolls.

Invert a heavy plate on top of the rolls, then cover the pan and bring to a simmer. Leave to simmer over low heat for 1 hour. Serve hot or warm.

❀ *Note: Lean lamb bones may be used to line the base of the pan instead of the cabbage trimmings. Another alternative is to simmer the rolls in lamb stock instead of water.*

LAHM BI'AJEEN
Lamb-filled pastry rolls

MAKES: ABOUT 60

These delicate pastries often appear on restaurant menus as 'ladies fingers'. Sometimes they are called *sambusik bi lahm*, but any combination of lamb and pastry or dough is usually called *lahm bi'ajeen* or similar, literally meaning 'meat with dough'.

As there is another recipe by this name in this chapter (page 291), I am depending on the translation to indicate the difference.

15 sheets fillo pastry
125–185 g (4–6½ oz/½–¾ cup) Samneh
   (page 253), melted

Filling

2 tablespoons Samneh (page 253) or ghee
80 g (3 oz/½ cup) pine nuts
500 g (1 lb 2 oz) finely minced (ground) lean lamb
1 large onion, finely chopped
¼ teaspoon ground cinnamon
salt and freshly ground black pepper, to season
3 tablespoons finely chopped flat-leaf parsley
1 tablespoon finely chopped fresh mint

To make the filling, heat the Samneh or ghee in a frying pan and fry the pine nuts until golden. Remove to a plate with a slotted spoon.

Add the lamb to the pan and stir over medium–high heat until the colour changes and the lamb is crumbly. Add the onion and gently fry until the onion is translucent.

Reduce the heat, add the cinnamon and season with salt and pepper. Cover and simmer for 15 minutes, or until the juices evaporate, stirring occasionally. Stir in the parsley and mint, remove from the heat and leave covered until cool. Add the pine nuts.

Meanwhile, preheat the oven to 200°C (400°F/Gas 6).

Take a sheet of fillo pastry and brush it lightly with melted Samneh. Fold it in half, to give almost a square shape. Brush again with Samneh and place about 2 tablespoons of filling towards the edge of the longer end of the pastry. Fold the pastry over the filling, fold in the sides to contain the filling, then roll up firmly so the finished pastry looks like a long cigar, about the thickness of a finger.

Repeat with the remaining ingredients, keeping the finished pastries covered.

Place the rolls on baking trays lightly greased with melted Samneh. Brush the rolls lightly with more Samneh.

Using a sharp knife, make shallow slits across the top of each roll, about 8–10 cm (3¼–4 inches) apart, so that the rolls are evenly marked. This helps when cutting the finished rolls into finger lengths, as fillo pastry shatters easily when cooked.

Bake the rolls for 12–15 minutes, or until golden brown.

Cut into finger lengths and serve hot, piled on platters.

❖ *Note: Smaller rolls can also be made. Shape as directed on pages 16–17, using pastry strips 12 cm (5 inches) wide.*

SFIHA, LAHM BI'AJEEN
Flat lamb pies
MAKES: ABOUT 30

Sfiha is the Syrian equivalent of Lahm bi'Ajeen (page 289), a flat lamb pie popular throughout this region – an area known as the Fertile Crescent (which also includes Iraq). Khoubiz dough is used in Syria for *sfiha*.

The Lebanese cook often uses a pie-crust or short-crust pastry base for a more tender and crisp crust, and a lot less fuss.

½ quantity Khoubiz dough (page 264), optional

Pie-crust pastry, optional
600 g (1 lb 5 oz/4 cups) plain (all-purpose) flour
1 teaspoon salt
250 ml (8½ fl oz/1 cup) melted Samneh (page 253),
    or other shortening

Lamb filling
1 tablespoon oil
500 g (1 lb 2 oz) minced (ground) lamb
1 large onion, finely chopped
50 g (2 oz/⅓ cup) pine nuts
¼ teaspoon ground cinnamon
¼ teaspoon ground allspice
¼ teaspoon freshly ground black pepper
¼ teaspoon freshly ground white pepper
salt, to season
125 g (4 oz/½ cup) chopped, peeled tomatoes
3 teaspoons pomegranate molasses or lemon juice

To finish
oil, for brushing
pomegranate seeds, lemon wedges or yoghurt, to serve

If using the Khoubiz dough option, make the dough as directed on page 264, using the full amount of yeast, even though making the half quantity of dough. Cover and leave to rise.

Alternatively, make the pie-crust pastry. Sift the flour and salt into a bowl, add the cool melted Samneh and rub it thoroughly and lightly into the flour with your fingertips. Have 185 ml (6½ fl oz/¾ cup) warm water ready. Sprinkle in most of the water and mix to a pliable dough, adding more water if necessary. Knead lightly until smooth. Cover with plastic wrap and leave to rest for 30 minutes.

To make the filling, heat the oil in a frying pan, add the lamb and stir over medium–high heat until the colour changes and the meat is crumbly. Add the onion and gently fry until the onion is translucent and soft. Add the pine nuts and spices and season with salt. Fry for 1 minute longer, then stir in the tomatoes. Cover and cook over low heat for 10 minutes, or until the tomato softens.

Stir in the pomegranate molasses or lemon juice. Remove from the heat and leave to cool. The mixture should be moist, but not liquid.

Meanwhile, preheat the oven to 200°C (400°F/Gas 6).

Punch down the pie-crust dough, if using.

Roll out the dough or pastry on a lightly floured work surface until 5 mm (¼ inch) thick, then cut into 10 cm (4 inch) rounds. Alternatively, take balls of dough the size of eggs and press each into a round by hand.

Cut out or shape the trimmings too. Place the rounds on a cloth, covering them with another cloth.

Take a round of dough and flute the edge with your fingertips. Spread a tablespoon of filling onto the dough and place the pies close together on oiled baking trays. Brush the meat and crust lightly with oil.

Bake the pies for 12–15 minutes. Serve hot or warm, sprinkling with a few fresh pomegranate seeds if available. Lemon wedges for squeezing onto the pies, or yoghurt for drizzling over them, may also be served.

FATAYER
Triangular lamb pies
MAKES: ABOUT 30

½ quantity Khoubiz dough (page 264)
Lamb Filling (see Sfiha, page 291)
oil, for brushing

For serving
lemon wedges or *Laban* (yoghurt I, pages 18–19)

Make the Khoubiz dough as directed on page 264, using the full amount of yeast, even though making the half quantity of dough. Cover and leave to rise.

Prepare the lamb filling according to the directions on page 291, making the filling a little drier than for the Sfiha.

Meanwhile, preheat the oven to 200°C (400°F/Gas 6).

Punch down the dough and turn out onto a lightly floured work surface. Roll out until 5 mm (¼ inch) thick, then cut into 10 cm (4 inch) rounds. Alternatively, roll the dough into balls the size of eggs and flatten them out with your hand or a rolling pin.

Working with one round at a time, place a tablespoon of the lamb filling in the centre. Moisten the edge of the dough with a little water, then bring up the sides at three points to form a triangular shape. Press the edges firmly to seal, leaving the top of the pie open a little to show the filling.

Place the pies on oiled baking trays and brush with oil. Bake for 15 minutes, or until golden and cooked.

For a golden brown top, place the pies under a hot grill (broiler) for a few seconds.

Serve hot or warm, with lemon wedges so that the juice may be squeezed into the centre of the pie.

Alternatively, serve with a bowl of yoghurt on the side.

SHISHBARAK
Lamb pastries in yoghurt sauce
SERVES: 6

300 g (10½ oz/2 cups) plain (all-purpose) flour

½ teaspoon salt

60 ml (2 fl oz/¼ cup) melted Samneh (page 253)

Filling

2 tablespoons Samneh (page 253)

40 g (1½ oz/¼ cup) pine nuts

500 g (1 lb 2 oz) finely minced (ground) lean lamb

1 large onion, finely chopped

¼ teaspoon ground allspice

pinch of ground cinnamon

salt and freshly ground black pepper, to season

Yoghurt sauce

1.25 kg (2 lb 12 oz/5 cups) yoghurt

1 tablespoon cornflour (cornstarch)

1 egg white, lightly beaten

2 teaspoons salt

To finish

2 garlic cloves

½ teaspoon salt

60 g (2 oz/¼ cup) Samneh (page 253)

1 tablespoon dried crushed mint

Riz Mufalfal (page 265), to serve

Sift the flour and salt into a mixing bowl, add 185 ml (6½ fl oz/¾ cup) cold water and mix to a soft dough, adding a little more flour if necessary. Knead lightly until smooth, then cover the dough with plastic wrap and rest for 30 minutes.

Meanwhile, make the filling. Heat half the Samneh in a pan and fry the pine nuts until golden brown. Lift out with a slotted spoon and set aside.

Heat the remaining Samneh in the pan and stir the meat over high heat until the meat changes colour and is crumbly. Add the onion and fry for a further 10 minutes, or until the onion is translucent. Stir in the spices and season with salt and pepper. Add the pine nuts and leave to cool.

Meanwhile, preheat the oven to 180°C (350°F/Gas 4).

Roll out the pastry on a lightly floured work surface and cut into 5 cm (2 inch) rounds. Place a teaspoon of meat filling in the centre and fold the pastry over into a crescent. Press the edges to seal, then crimp with your fingers or the tines of a fork. Wrap the crescent around your finger and press the two points together to give a hat shape. Place on baking trays greased with some of the melted Samneh. When the pastries are filled and shaped, brush with the remaining Samneh.

Bake for 10–15 minutes, or until lightly browned; the pastries do not have to be completely cooked.

To make the yoghurt sauce, place the yoghurt in a large heavy-based saucepan and stir until smooth. Blend the cornflour into 375 ml (12½ fl oz/1½ cups) water and stir into the yoghurt with the egg white and salt. Stir constantly in one direction over medium heat, until thickened and bubbling.

Add the pastries to the bubbling yoghurt, stir gently, then cook, uncovered, over medium–low heat for 10 minutes. Stir twice more during cooking.

To finish, crush the garlic with the salt. Heat the Samneh in a small saucepan, add the garlic and fry gently for a few seconds. Stir in the mint and remove from the heat.

Pour the garlic mixture into the *shishbarak*. Stir gently and cook for 2–3 minutes longer.

Serve hot in deep plates, with Riz Mufalfal.

SHEIKH AL MIHSHI
Stuffed eggplant

SERVES: 6

12 small long eggplants (aubergines),
    or 6 oval eggplants

60 g (2 oz/¼ cup) Samneh (page 253),
    or 60 ml (2 fl oz/¼ cup) oil

250 ml (8½ fl oz/1 cup) tomato passata (puréed tomatoes)

salt and freshly ground black pepper, to season

Meat filling

2 tablespoons oil

500 g (1 lb 2 oz) finely minced (ground) lamb or beef

1 large onion, finely chopped

1 garlic clove, finely chopped

40 g (1½ oz/¼ cup) pine nuts

¼ teaspoon ground cinnamon

¼ teaspoon ground allspice

3 tablespoons finely chopped flat-leaf parsley

salt and freshly ground black pepper, to season

Preheat the oven to 190°C (375°F/Gas 5).

Remove the stalks from the eggplants, then peel off 1 cm (½ inch) strips lengthways at intervals to give a striped effect.

Heat the Samneh or oil in a frying pan and brown the eggplants lightly on all sides, in batches if necessary. Remove to a plate.

To make the filling, heat the oil in the pan and fry the meat, onion and garlic, stirring often, until the juices evaporate. Add the pine nuts, spices and parsley. Season with salt and pepper and remove from the heat.

Cut a deep slit along one side of each eggplant. Fill the slits with the meat mixture.

Arrange the eggplants in a baking dish and pour the passata over the top. Season with salt and pepper.

Bake for 30 minutes, adding water to the baking dish during cooking if necessary, and basting the eggplants occasionally with the sauce mixture.

USHTA
Clotted cream
MAKES: ABOUT 375 G (13 OZ/1½ CUPS)

Where buffalo milk is available in the Middle East you will find *ushta*. The rich milk is boiled and left to stand until the cream on the top becomes solid. It is so thick it can be cut with a knife. The cream is enjoyed with certain pastries, used as a filling for pancakes ('Ataif, page 297) as it does not melt on heating, or enjoyed on its own with sweet preserves or honey.

As the flavour of the genuine *ushta* is rather strong, it is an acquired taste. This version uses dried cow's milk to make the flavour more widely acceptable. If you have access to rich milk fresh from the cow, it is possible to make clotted cream; Devonshire cream is a good substitute where available.

Ushta (sometimes transliterated as *kishta* with a deep guttural sound for the 'k') is the Arabic name for the region covered in this chapter. In Turkey it is known as *kaymak*, and in Iraq, *gaimer*.

200 g (7 oz/2 cups) full-cream powdered milk

Thoroughly combine the powdered milk with 625 ml (21 fl oz/ 2½ cups) water, beating if necessary to break up lumps.

Pour the mixture into a heavy-based 23 cm (9 inch) frying pan, preferably one with a non-stick coating, so the milk will not scorch. Place over medium–low heat and bring slowly to a gentle simmer — do not allow to boil.

When a skin forms on the top, pull it to one side of the pan with a large spoon. Lift the skin out, pouring any liquid in the spoon back into the pan. Place the skin in a bowl.

Every 10 minutes or so, for the next 2–2½ hours, remove the skin as it forms. At the end, only a thin layer of thick milk will remain in the pan. This may be discarded or used in cooking.

Process the collected cream in a blender or food processor and process until smooth. Pour back into the bowl and chill thoroughly. The cream sets solidly and, if kept covered, will keep in the refrigerator for 1 week or more. Use as directed in recipes, or with stewed fruits and desserts.

'ATAR I
Scented syrup
MAKES: ABOUT 625 ML (21 FL OZ/2½ CUPS)

660 g (1 lb 7 oz/3 cups) sugar
1 teaspoon lemon juice
1–2 tablespoons rosewater or orange flower water

Dissolve the sugar in 625 ml (21 fl oz/2½ cups) cold water in a heavy-based saucepan over medium heat, stirring occasionally. Bring to the boil and add the lemon juice. Allow to boil over medium heat, without stirring, for 12 minutes, or until the syrup is thick when tested on a cold saucer.

Add rosewater or orange flower water to taste, then boil for 1 minute longer. When cool, the consistency should be similar to thin honey.

Strain, cool and store in a sealed container in the refrigerator until required.

❧ *Note: Once the syrup has begun to boil, do not stir it again, as this makes the syrup cloudy.*

'ATAR II
Syrup
MAKES: ABOUT 625 ML (21 FL OZ/2½ CUPS)

660 g (1 lb 7 oz/3 cups) sugar
1 tablespoon lemon juice
1 piece of cinnamon bark

Dissolve the sugar in 625 ml (21 fl oz/2½ cups) cold water in a heavy-based saucepan over medium heat, stirring occasionally. Bring to the boil and add the lemon juice and cinnamon.

Boil over medium heat, without stirring, for 12 minutes, or until the syrup is thick when tested on a cold saucer; when cool, the consistency should be similar to thin honey.

Strain, cool and store in a sealed container in the refrigerator until required.

'ATAIF
Pancakes
MAKES: 16–18

2 teaspoons active dried yeast
1 teaspoon sugar
225 g (8 oz/1½ cups) plain (all-purpose) flour
pinch of salt
melted ghee or oil, for brushing

For serving
cold 'Atar I or II (left)
Ushta (left), or thick whipped cream

Dissolve the yeast and sugar in 60 ml (2 fl oz/¼ cup) lukewarm water. Stir in another 250 ml (8½ fl oz/1 cup) warm water.

Sift the flour and salt into a warm mixing bowl and make a well in the centre.

Pour the yeast mixture into the centre, then gradually stir in the flour with a wooden spoon until smoothly combined. If the batter is lumpy, stir with a balloon whisk until smooth.

Cover the bowl with a cloth and leave in a warm place for 1 hour, or until the batter has risen and the surface is bubbly.

Heat a heavy-based frying pan and grease it with a paper towel dipped in melted ghee or oil. Medium heat should be sufficient for cooking the pancakes.

Using a ladle, pour in about 1½ tablespoons of the batter in one lot and tilt the pan immediately so that the batter spreads a little into a circle about 10 cm (4 inches) in diameter. If the batter is too thick, stir in another 60 ml (2 fl oz/¼ cup) water — the pancakes should be thick, but should spread a little.

Cook until golden brown on the underside, then flip over and cook the other side. Lift out and stack on a plate.

Dip the pancakes into the 'Atar syrup and pile onto a plate. Serve with Ushta or thick whipped cream.

❧ *Note: Flours vary in their absorbing quality, so hold back some of the liquid and adjust the consistency before cooking.*

'ATAIF MIHSHI
Stuffed pancakes
MAKES: 16–18

1 quantity 'Ataif batter (left)
250 ml (8½ fl oz/1 cup) cold 'Atar I or II (page 296)
corn oil or peanut oil, for deep-frying

Nut filling, optional
185 g (6½ oz/1½ cups) finely chopped walnuts
55 g (2 oz/¼ cup) sugar
1½ teaspoons ground cinnamon

Cheese filling, optional
250 g (9 oz/1 cup) Kareeshee (page 252), or
  Italian ricotta cheese

Make the pancakes as directed in the 'Ataif recipe (left), cooking them on one side only for about 3 minutes, until the top loses all trace of whiteness. Stack the pancakes on a plate.

Prepare your chosen filling — either combine the nuts, sugar and cinnamon in a bowl, or mash the cheese with a fork to soften it.

Place 2 generous teaspoons of filling in the centre of each pancake, on the uncooked side. Fold the pancake over and pinch the edges well together to seal.

Heat the oil in a deep saucepan to 200°C (400°F), or until a cube of bread dropped into the oil browns in 5 seconds.

Deep-fry the stuffed pancakes three or four at a time for 2–3 minutes, turning to brown them evenly. Lift out with a slotted spoon and drain on paper towels.

While they are hot, dip the pancakes into the 'Atar syrup and pile onto a plate. Serve warm or cold.

❧ *Note: Ushta (page 296), a thick clotted cream, may be used as a filling for these pancakes. However, do not be tempted to use any other cream as it will melt.*

MUHALLABIA
« Almond cream pudding
SERVES: 6

35 g (1¼ oz/¼ cup) rice flour

750 ml (25 fl oz/3 cups) milk

pinch of salt

55 g (2 oz/¼ cup) sugar

80 g (3 oz/¾ cup) ground almonds

1 tablespoon rosewater

pistachios or almonds, to serve

pomegranate seeds, to serve, optional

Mix the rice flour in 185 ml (6½ fl oz/¾ cup) of the milk.

Bring the remaining milk to the boil in a heavy-based saucepan. Stir in the rice flour mixture, salt and sugar.

Stir constantly with a wooden spoon over medium heat until the mixture bubbles gently.

Reduce the heat and simmer gently for 5 minutes, stirring often; it is important that the mixture cooks slowly.

Stir in the ground almonds until smoothly combined. Stir in the rosewater and remove from the heat.

Stir occasionally until the mixture cools a little, then pour into a serving bowl or six individual dishes.

Chill the pudding or puddings and serve garnished with nuts, and pomegranate seeds if available.

K'NAFI JIBNI
Shredded pastry with cheese
SERVES: 10–12

500 g (1 lb 2 oz) konafa (kataifi) pastry
 (see page 521)

250 g (9 oz/1 cup) Samneh (page 253), melted

1 quantity cold 'Atar I or II (page 296)

Filling

500 g (1 lb 2 oz/2 cups) ricotta cheese or Mizithra (page 27)

1 tablespoon sugar

grated zest of 1 lemon

Preheat the oven to 180°C (350°F/Gas 4).

Loosen the pastry by pulling it gently with your fingers. Place in a large bowl and pour the melted Samneh over. Toss the pastry shreds so that they are evenly coated with Samneh, using a fork or your fingers.

Place half the strands in a 25 × 30 cm (10 × 12 inch) baking dish, or in a 25 cm (10 inch) round baking dish. Press down to make the pastry layer more compact.

Combine the filling ingredients in a mixing bowl and beat until softened. Evenly spread the filling over the pastry in the baking dish, then top with the remaining pastry.

Bake for 45 minutes, or until golden brown.

Remove from the oven and pour the 'Atar syrup over. Leave until cold, then serve cut into squares or diamonds. Store any remaining *k'nafi* in a covered container in the refrigerator.

BAKLAWA BE'AJ
Nut pastries

MAKES: ABOUT 40

500 g (1 lb 2 oz) fillo pastry
185 ml (6½ fl oz/¾ cup) melted Samneh (page 253) or
    unsalted butter
65 g (2¼ oz/½ cup) chopped pistachio nuts, optional

Nut filling
2 egg whites
115 g (4 oz/½ cup) caster (superfine) sugar
230 g (8 oz/2 cups) coarsely ground walnuts
200 g (7 oz/2 cups) coarsely ground almonds
1 teaspoon rosewater

Syrup
440 g (15½ oz/2 cups) sugar
1 teaspoon lemon juice
1 teaspoon orange flower water
1 teaspoon rosewater

Preheat the oven to 180°C (350°F/Gas 4).

Stack 10 sheets of fillo pastry on a flat surface, keeping the remainder covered with a dry tea towel (dish towel), with a damp tea towel on top.

Brush the top sheet of the stack with melted Samneh or butter. Lift the sheet and replace it on the stack, buttered side down. Brush the top with butter, lift the top two sheets and turn over on the stack. Repeat until all 10 sheets are buttered, lifting an extra sheet each time. The top and bottom of the finished stack should remain unbuttered.

Using kitchen scissors, cut the buttered stack of fillo into approximately 10 cm (4 inch) squares. Stack and cover. Prepare the remaining fillo pastry as before. Depending on the size of the fillo sheets, you may have fewer than 10 left at the end, so halve the sheets if necessary to give 10 layers.

To make the filling, beat the egg whites until stiff, then gradually beat in the sugar. Fold in the nuts and rosewater.

Butter the top of a fillo square and place a tablespoon of nut mixture in the middle. Gently squeeze into a lily shape, with the four corners of the square as petals, and the filling in the centre. Place in a buttered 25 × 33 cm (10 × 13 inch) baking dish.

Repeat with the remaining ingredients, placing the finished pastries close together in the dish. Bake for 30 minutes.

Reduce the oven temperature to 150°C (300°F/Gas 2) and bake for a further 15 minutes.

Meanwhile, make the syrup. Dissolve the sugar in 375 ml (12½ fl oz/1½ cups) cold water in a heavy-based saucepan over medium heat. Add the lemon juice and orange flower water and bring to the boil. Allow to boil for 15 minutes without stirring, then stir in the rosewater and cool.

Spoon the syrup over the hot pastries and leave until cool. Sprinkle pistachio nuts in the centre of the pastries if desired.

❀ *Note: If you are not used to working with fillo pastry, fill and shape the first stack of buttered squares before working with the next lot. The butter firms fairly quickly and it may be difficult to shape the pastries if the buttered sheets are left for a time.*

MA'AMOUL B'JOWZ
Easter walnut cakes

MAKES: 45

560 g (1 lb 4 oz/4½ cups) fine semolina (farina)

115 g (4 oz/½ cup) caster (superfine) sugar

250 g (9 oz/1 cup) butter

250 ml (8½ fl oz/1 cup) milk

½ teaspoon bicarbonate of soda (baking soda)

icing (confectioners') sugar, for coating

Walnut filling

170 g (6 oz/1½ cups) coarsely ground walnuts

55 g (2 oz/¼ cup) caster (superfine) sugar

1 teaspoon ground cinnamon

Combine the semolina and sugar in a mixing bowl.

Melt the butter in a frying pan and heat until bubbling. Pour over the semolina and sugar and mix with a wooden spoon until the butter is evenly distributed.

Heat the milk in a heavy-based saucepan until bubbles begin to rise. Remove from the heat and stir in the bicarbonate of soda, then pour into the semolina mixture. Mix with a wooden spoon to a soft dough.

When the mixture cools a little, knead it lightly by hand. Cover the bowl with plastic wrap to make an airtight seal. Leave for at least 5 hours, or overnight.

Mix the walnut filling ingredients together in a bowl.

Knead the dough again to make it pliable. Roll a tablespoonful of dough at a time into balls the size of large walnuts. Flatten a ball of dough in your palm, then push up the sides to make a bowl shape. Fill the hollow with a generous teaspoonful of nut filling, then mould the dough over the filling. Press the edges to seal well and roll into a ball again.

Press into a decorated mould (a *tabi*) and tap out on a board. Place on an ungreased baking tray. Alternatively, place the ball of dough on a tray, flatten slightly and press the tines of a fork obliquely around the sides to give the cakes a slightly conical shape. Press the top with a fork.

Repeat with the remaining ingredients.

Meanwhile, preheat the oven to 230°C (450°F/Gas 8).

Transfer the cakes to the preheated oven. Now reduce the oven temperature to 180°C (350°F/Gas 4) and bake the cakes for 20–25 minutes, or until lightly coloured. Remove from the oven and cool on the trays for 10 minutes.

Sift icing sugar onto a sheet of greaseproof (parchment) paper. Place the cakes on the sugar and sift more sugar on top to coat thickly. When cool, store in an airtight container.

❀ *Note: Traditionally,* ma'amoul *are shaped using the same technique as the Stuffed Kibbeh Balls (page 286).*

SAMBUSIK
Date crescents
MAKES: 30

375 g (13 oz/2½ cups) plain (all-purpose) flour

½ teaspoon ground *mahlab*, optional
   (see page 522)

60 g (2 oz/¼ cup) butter, melted

85 ml (3 fl oz/⅓ cup) milk

55 g (2 oz/¼ cup) sugar

60 ml (2 fl oz/¼ cup) olive oil or nut oil

Date filling

250 g (9 oz) dates

60 g (2 oz/¼ cup) butter

1 teaspoon rosewater

Preheat the oven to 180°C (350°F/Gas 4).

Sift the flour into a mixing bowl with the *mahlab*, if using. Rub in the butter until evenly distributed.

Heat the milk and sugar in a heavy-based saucepan and stir until the sugar has dissolved. Leave until lukewarm.

Pour the milk mixture into the flour, then add the oil and mix to a soft dough. Knead until smooth.

To make the filling, chop the dates and place in a heavy-based saucepan with the butter. Stir over medium heat until the mixture is combined and has a paste-like consistency.

Remove from the heat and stir in the rosewater.

Roll out the dough on a lightly floured board until 5 mm (¼ inch) thick. Cut into 5 cm (2 inch) rounds.

Working with one piece at a time, place a teaspoon of the date filling in the middle of each round, then fold the pastry over the filling to form a crescent. Crimp the edge with your fingers, or press with the tines of a fork to seal.

Place the crescents on ungreased baking trays and bake for 20–25 minutes, or until lightly coloured.

Remove from the oven and cool on the trays for 5 minutes, then lift onto a wire rack to cool completely.

When cool, store in an airtight container.

❀ *Note: A walnut filling may be used instead of dates. Use the filling from the Ma'amoul b'Jowz recipe on page 301.*

KUL'WA'SHKUR
Almond pastry ('Eat and praise')
MAKES: 40 PIECES

185 g (6½ oz/¾ cup) Samneh, melted (page 253) or
    unsalted butter, melted

500 g (1 lb 2 oz) fillo pastry

65 g (2¼ oz/½ cup) chopped pistachio nuts,
    optional

Almond filling

300 g (10½ oz/3 cups) coarsely ground almonds

230 g (8 oz/1 cup) caster (superfine) sugar

1 egg white

1½ teaspoons orange flower water

2 drops of almond essence

Syrup

440 g (15½ oz/2 cups) sugar

2 teaspoons lemon juice

2 teaspoons rosewater

Preheat the oven to 180°C (350°F/Gas 4).

Brush a 25 × 33 cm (10 × 13 inch) baking dish with the Samneh or melted butter. Place a sheet of fillo pastry in the dish. Brush the fillo with butter and top with another sheet. Butter the sheet and repeat until half the fillo sheets are used.

To make the almond filling, combine the almonds and sugar in a bowl. Beat the egg white in a separate bowl until stiff, then fold in the nuts, orange flower water and almond essence.

Spread the nut filling over the pastry in the baking dish.

Place a sheet of fillo on top, butter it, then repeat until all the remaining fillo sheets are used.

Brush the top sheet with butter. Using a sharp knife, cut through the pastry layers in diamond shapes (see the diagram page 17). Sprinkle the top lightly with cold water.

Bake on the middle shelf of the oven for 30 minutes.

Raise the shelf one notch above the centre and bake the pastry for a further 30 minutes.

Meanwhile, make the syrup. Dissolve the sugar in 375 ml (12½ fl oz/1½ cups) cold water in a heavy-based saucepan over medium heat, stirring occasionally. Add the lemon juice and bring to the boil. Allow to boil over medium heat, without stirring, for 15 minutes, or until the syrup is thick when tested on a cold saucer. Stir in the rosewater and leave until cool. The syrup should be the consistency of thin honey when cool.

Pour the cooled syrup over the hot pastry and leave until cold. Sprinkle with chopped pistachios if desired.

Cut through the pastry again and lift out the pieces with a spatula. Store in a sealed container at room temperature.

QAHWI
Coffee

Coffee-making in this part of the world is taken as seriously as it is in Turkey and the Gulf States. Every household has its *rakwi* (long-handled coffee pot) and *tahrini* (brass coffee grinder).

To impress your Arabic host or your guests, use the right coffee term — *murrah* for sugarless coffee, *mazboutah* for medium-sweet and *hilweh* for very sweet.

Coffee is always served in tiny, bowl-shaped, handle-less cups, sometimes placed in decorative brass holders. The *rakwi* is usually made of brass and attractively worked; very old pieces have a lid to keep the coffee hot. The *rakwi* is often taken to the coffee drinkers with the cups. Speed in transferring the coffee from the stove to the serving area is necessary as the grounds must not be given time to settle in the pot. When drinking coffee, however, you must allow a little time before drinking it to allow the grounds to settle.

To each Arabic coffee cup measure of water, add a level teaspoon of sugar for medium-sweet, and a heaped teaspoon for very sweet. Stir the sugar in the water over the heat until dissolved and boiling. Add 1 heaped teaspoon of pulverised coffee (usually a dark roasted coffee) for each cup of water, stir well and cook until the foam rises to the top of the pot. The pot is removed from the heat and the base rapped on a flat surface to reduce foaming. Heat twice more, with raps in between. Pour immediately into the cups.

To flavour the coffee, either grind cardamom pods with the coffee beans (three or four with each 250 g/9 oz beans), or add one pod to the pot for each four cups of coffee being brewed, though this is the particular flavouring of the Arab Gulf countries. Traditionally a little silver urn of rosewater or orange flower water would accompany the coffee so that a few drops may be added to individual taste.

SHARAB EL WARD
« Rosewater syrup

440 g (15½ oz/2 cups) sugar
strained juice of ½ lemon
pink food colouring
85 ml (3 fl oz/⅓ cup) rosewater

Put the sugar and 250 ml (8½ fl oz/1 cup) water in a heavy-based saucepan and stir over medium heat until the sugar has dissolved. Bring to the boil and add the lemon juice.

Boil, without stirring, for 10 minutes, skimming when necessary.

Add a few drops of colouring to the syrup to achieve a deep pink — it will be lighter when diluted later.

Add the rosewater and boil for 3 minutes longer. Remove from the heat, leave to cool, then bottle and seal.

To serve, pour 2–3 tablespoons of the syrup into a glass and fill with iced water.

GHERFER or AINAR
Spiced tea with nuts
SERVES: 4

4 large pieces of cinnamon bark
40 g (1½ oz/⅓ cup) finely chopped walnuts
sugar, to taste

Put 500 ml (17 fl oz/2 cups) water into a long-handled coffee pot (*rakwi*). Add the cinnamon and bring to the boil.

Boil gently for 5 minutes, then remove the cinnamon.

Put 2 teaspoons walnuts in each of four tea glasses. Pour the tea into the glasses and add sugar to taste.

Serve with a spoon.

SYRIA, LEBANON, JORDAN

DRINKS

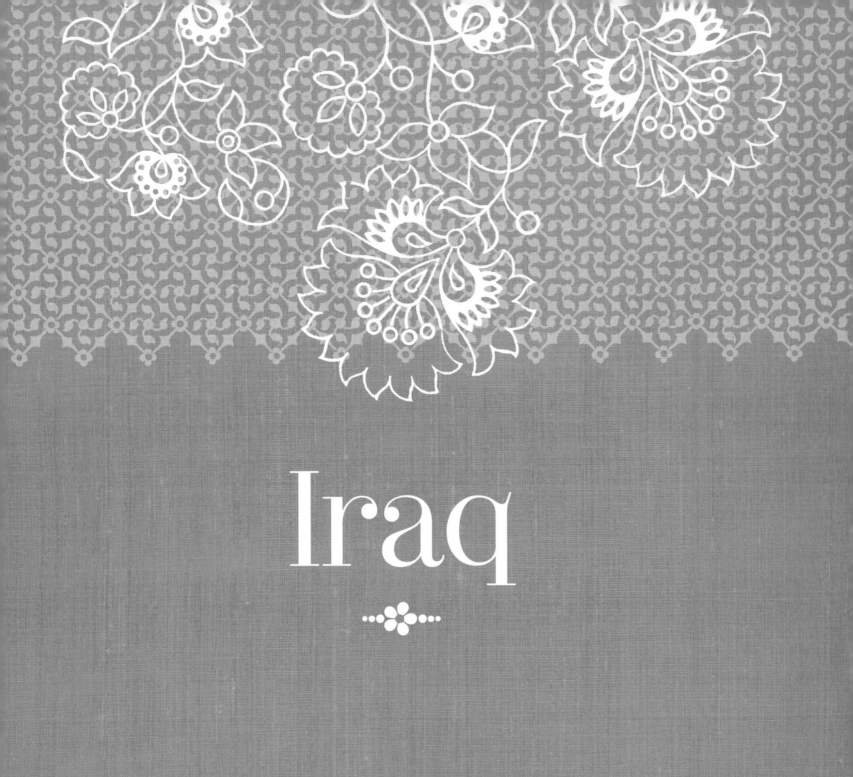

Iraq

IRAQ

In northern Iraq lies Kurdistan, an area stretching across to southern Turkey and western Iran. It is here that humans first began farming, planting grain crops and raising livestock in order to control food production.

The fertile valley between the Tigris and Euphrates Rivers saw the birth of the Sumerian civilisation before 5000 BCE. Called Mesopotamia by the Ancient Greeks, this area is regarded as the birthplace of Western civilisation. Towards the southern part of the valley, Babylon and Ur grew, flourished and died around 500 BCE, leaving a legacy for civilisations to come.

After the unification of the Arab people under the banner of Islam some 1300 years later, the region came under Arab rule, with Baghdad succeeding Damascus as the capital of the Islamic world. Baghdad became the centre of Arabic culture and trade, with caravans bringing foods and spices from China, India and Persia (Iran).

In the courts of the caliphs of Baghdad, the art of cooking thrived, with a strong Persian influence — a legacy of Persian civilisation. Arabic cooking and food tastes flourished and expanded with the vast variety of foods brought from Asia. As the Arabs swept westward, spreading Islam, they took with them the foods to which they had become accustomed — saffron from Asia Minor; citrus fruits, almonds, rice and sugar cane from Asia — many to be planted in their conquered lands, thus introducing new foods to Europe.

The Mongols, then the Ottoman Turks, swept into Baghdad and the political power of the city diminished, but the culinary glories spread far and wide, influencing the cuisine of the Arab world in general. That influence is still evident today.

THE FLAVOUR OF IRAQI FOOD

One usually enters a country with preconceived ideas about their foods. Though I expected an extension of Arabic cuisine, all I could associate with Iraq was the Lion of Babylon dates I had been buying for years, and I wondered in what other ways the date was used on its home ground.

When dates are being dried for export and for use throughout the remainder of the year, a thick dark amber syrup is exuded from the fruit. It is used in Hamuth Heloo (page 323), a lamb and dried fruit dish reminiscent of Iranian meat and fruit combinations, but with a flavour more sweet than sweet–sour. *Marees* is a combination of date syrup and butter, heated and blended with squares of *khoubiz* (bread) and eaten with *gaimer*, the thick buffalo cream of the area, similar to the *ushta* and *kaymak* of neighbouring countries. The Kurds in the north of Iraq use a raisin syrup for *marees*.

For a simple date sweetmeat, try Holwah Tamar (page 332), or the more intricate Murabba Tamar (pages 331 and 332) and Klaicha (page 329), for a mouth-melting pastry filled with dates and perfumed with rosewater or orange flower water.

Iraqi date varieties dried for export are *kahastawari*, *khadrowi* and *zhehdik*, the first two being the varieties exported to the West. *Baban* and *berhi* are delicate dates best eaten fresh, though they freeze very well. *Baban* is a black date with a fairly firm skin — when squeezed gently the flesh pops out and literally melts in the mouth. *Berhi*, a light golden date with a tender skin, is not skinned before eating. It is stringy, sweet and delicious, with a slightly peppery undertone, and the texture of fresh sugar cane. If left too long, *berhi* dates become overripe and squashy, rather like bananas do.

The rice dishes of Iraq, though not extensive in range, are somewhat similar to those of Persia: Timman (page 317) — steamed rice very similar to *chelou* — and Timman Z'affaran (page 316), a rice dish reminiscent of Persian *polous*, with the spiciness of the Gulf Arabic cooking, but essentially Iraqi in concept and presentation.

Dolmas are as popular here as elsewhere and I was fascinated with Mumbar (page 321), basically a *dolma* meat filling in a sausage casing. A long length of the casing is filled and coiled into a pan and given a long, slow simmering; the *mumbar* is then sliced into portions and served as an appetiser.

Though potatoes are relative newcomers to Middle Eastern cooking, and in Iraq not readily available all year round, the Iraqis make the most of the potato when it is in season, using it for delightful potato cakes called *batata charp*, filled with a spicy meat or a tomato and parsley stuffing.

In discussing foods with our Iraqi contact, I would frequently ask how a particular dish was served. His reply was always 'as part of a feast', giving me the impression that Iraqis are always feasting. After visiting his home unexpectedly, I found that every meal indeed is a feast, with huge quantities served. It was at this meal that another side of Arabic hospitality was revealed. Our host did not eat while we were his guests, as it is the custom for the host to look after their guests' needs exclusively; his needs were not considered until after our departure. I was impressed and amazed at his self-control in not even venturing to take a nibble during the many hours we enjoyed his hospitality. However, he did take care of his thirst with a few glasses of beer — Australian beer at that.

One typically Iraqi dish, and a speciality of Baghdad outdoor restaurants bordering the Tigris, is *masgoof*. It is a dish that is seldom prepared in the home, though it is possible to do so. The Tigris River teems with a vast variety of freshwater fish — very large, firm-fleshed and flavourful. The fish is gutted and slit, opened out and impaled on two green sticks secured in the earth and set alongside a fire of fragrant woods. As the fish is rather oily, it needs little attention from the cook, except perhaps light seasoning with salt, pepper and paprika before cooking. The fish is barbecued slowly with the inner flesh exposed to the heat. After almost an hour's cooking in this way, the fish is removed from the sticks and thrown skin side down on top of the now-glowing embers to complete the cooking. It is served on a platter with sliced onion and tomato, and plenty of bread. The right way to eat *masgoof* is with your fingers, so that you may feel the bones — it makes a lot of sense. While

the variety of fish is large, the most popular fish for *masgoof* is the *shabboot*, though *booni* and *theka* are also available and equally good (local alternatives include Murry River carp or golden carp). The diner is given a choice of which fish to have prepared, as they are all kept in a tiled pond on the premises for your selection. There is certainly no doubt about the freshness.

Beautiful parks and gardens stretch along the banks of the Tigris, with bronzed statues set in groups, the tableaux depicting tales from the Arabian Nights, a reminder of the glorious days of the caliphs of Baghdad and their contribution to the art and culture of the Arabic world. Zlabiya (page 335), a kind of sweet, syrupy pastry rosette and a favourite of the Iraqis, is immortalised in the stories of the Arabian Nights: 'Of sweet *zlabiya* chain I hung a necklace around her neck. From its delicious loops I made a ring on her ears.' The same confection is prepared in neighbouring countries to the west and as far east as India, but its home is Iraq.

One particular dish served at feasts — that is, real feasts — is *khouzi*. A version that I found fascinating, *khouzi khasibi*, needs very special facilities for its preparation. A rice is prepared similar to Timman Z'affaran, but with little cooking of the grain. The lamb is steamed beforehand in a conventional oven until half done. It is then skewered with two green ribs from palm branches passing through the leg and shoulder on each side. The rice is placed in a deep tray on top of a bed of glowing coals set in the base of a *tannour* oven. The lamb is lowered head down into the *tannour*, with the fat tail of the lamb at the top of the carcass so that the meat is basted as the fat melts. The opening of the oven is crisscrossed with green palm leaves, and wet clay is packed on top to seal the opening completely. The lamb cooks slowly, the juices dripping onto the rice below, and when the clay seal begins to crack, the lamb is cooked. The use of the green palm ribs is all part of the flavour of the whole dish as these begin to smoulder towards the end of cooking, imparting a special fragrance to the meat. The *khouzi* of the city-dweller is prepared in a similar way to the *khouzi* of Saudi Arabia, and you may find that recipe easier to duplicate for an Arabic feast.

Khoubiz, the flat bread of Iraq, is similar to the Mafrooda Burd (page 347) of the Gulf States and the Nane Lavash or *taftoon* (page 437) of Iran. There is also a recipe for Khoubiz on page 264, in the chapter on Syria, Lebanon and Jordan. *Samoon* is a diamond-shaped thick loaf similar to the Barbari (page 439) of Iran, but only a quarter of its size. *Khoubiz* is served with every meal; *samoon* is a popular bread for breakfast.

EATING IRAQI STYLE

A meal in a town house is served on a dining table spread with a cloth, with china and cutlery. All the dishes for the meal are placed on the table at the one time. Soup is seldom, if ever, served. Rice is always part of the meal and served with Murag (page 327), a meat stew with *bamia* (okra), eggplant (aubergine), green peas or beans. A roast chicken could also be served with a platter of *batata charp*, a large bowl of salad containing cos (romaine) lettuce, crisp cucumbers, tomatoes, onion rings and a cress-like herb called *barbeen*. Another herb which could be included is *rashad*, resembling coarse dill and with the peppery flavour of cress. Date vinegar is used as the dressing on salads, with a little salt and pepper. The beverage is more than likely to be beer, and when one recalls the area's earliest history

it is understandable because beer was made by the Sumerians as far back as 3000 BCE. At the conclusion of the meal, coffee — prepared in the Turkish manner — and sweet pastries are served in another room. If you are a guest, on your departure your hostess sprinkles the top of your head with rosewater dispensed from a long silver decanter fitted with a perforated top. The significance is to carry the pleasure of the visit away with you, the lingering fragrance serving as a reminder.

INGREDIENTS FOR IRAQI COOKING

Favourite meats are lamb, beef and chicken. The rice preferred is the basmati rice of Pakistan. You will need Baharat (page 344), the spice mix popular in the Gulf States, although the Iraqi cook is quite likely to substitute ground allspice, adding a little pepper and paprika for added heat and colour. Flat-leaf parsley is essential, and watercress for salads in place of the *rashad* and *barbeen* which are difficult to obtain outside the region. Dried dates are essential and, if you can get them, fresh dates for preserves and sweets; rosewater, orange flower water, saffron, almonds, walnuts and dried fruits also feature heavily. The dried lime of the Gulf States and Iran is also used in Iraq, where it is called *noomi basra*. Basra is a seaport on the Arabian Gulf, and as the dried limes would arrive from there the locals added the name of the seaport to the name for the lime. I have referred to the lime as *noomi* in the Iraqi recipes, although it is elsewhere known as *loomi*; the directions for preparing your own dried limes can be found on page 345.

PRONUNCIATION OF ARABIC NAMES

Pronounce ʿaʾ as in *past*; ʿeʾ as in *egg*; ʿehʾ as in *egg*, slightly aspirated; ʿouʾ as in *soup*; ʿiʾ as in *pit*; ʿuʾ as in *put*; an inverted comma (ʿ) before a vowel is a barely perceptible ʿkʾ (Lebanon, Syria and Jordan only).

This guide serves for all Arabic-speaking countries: Iraq, Lebanon, Syria, Jordan, the Gulf States, Yemen and Egypt, and for Iran and Afghanistan.

BATATA CHARP I
« Potato cakes with meat filling
MAKES: 40

1 kg (2 lb 3 oz) potatoes

1 large egg, beaten

35 g (1¼ oz/¼ cup) plain (all-purpose) flour,
    plus extra for coating

salt and freshly ground black pepper, to season

oil, for pan-frying

Meat filling

1 tablespoon oil

1 onion, finely chopped

1 garlic clove, finely chopped

250 g (9 oz) finely minced (ground)
    lamb or beef

1 teaspoon Baharat (page 344)

125 g (4 oz/½ cup) chopped, peeled tomatoes

3 teaspoons chopped flat-leaf parsley

salt, to taste

Scrub the potatoes and boil them in their jackets until tender. Drain, peel and mash to a smooth purée. Leave to cool, then mix in the egg and flour. Season with salt and pepper and set aside.

To make the meat filling, heat the oil in a frying pan and gently fry the onion until translucent. Add the garlic and meat and stir over high heat until the mixture is crumbly and the meat begins to brown. Stir in the Baharat, tomatoes and parsley and season with salt. Reduce the heat, cover and simmer for 15 minutes — the mixture should be fairly dry.

Take about a tablespoon of the potato mixture and flatten it in the palm of your hand. Put a teaspoon of meat filling in the centre and close the potato around the filling. Roll into a ball and place on a tray. While shaping the potato cakes, moisten your hands with water to prevent the potato sticking.

Roll the balls in some extra flour and flatten them slightly to make thick cakes.

Pour oil into a frying pan to a depth of 5 mm (¼ inch). Heat well and fry the potato cakes until golden brown on each side — about 3 minutes in all. Drain on paper towels and serve hot, piled on a plate.

BATATA CHARP II
Potato cakes with vegetable filling
MAKES: 40

2 tablespoons oil

1 large onion, finely chopped

1 teaspoon turmeric

2 large ripe tomatoes

1 small handful finely chopped flat-leaf parsley

salt and freshly ground black pepper, to taste

Prepare the potato mixture as for Batata Charp I (left).

Heat the oil in a frying pan and gently fry the onion until translucent. Add the turmeric and fry for a further 1 minute. Remove from the heat.

Score a cross in the base of each tomato. Place in a heatproof bowl and cover with boiling water. Leave for 30 seconds, then transfer to cold water and peel the skin away from the cross.

Slice the tomatoes in half crossways and remove the seeds and juice. Chop finely and place in a bowl. Add the onion mixture and parsley, and salt and pepper to taste.

Make the potato cakes as instructed in Batata Charp I, using the vegetable filling in place of the meat filling.

TIMMAN Z'AFFARAN
Saffron rice
SERVES: 5–6

400 g (14 oz/2 cups) basmati rice

½ teaspoon saffron threads

2 tablespoons rosewater

85 g (3 oz/⅓ cup) ghee, or 85 ml (3 fl oz/⅓ cup) oil

40 g (1½ oz/⅓ cup) blanched split almonds

1 onion, finely chopped

250 g (9 oz) minced (ground) lamb or beef

½ teaspoon Baharat (page 344)

½ teaspoon salt, plus extra to season

30 g (1 oz/¼ cup) sultanas (golden raisins)

750 ml (25 fl oz/3 cups) chicken stock

Place the rice in a sieve and wash well until the water runs clear. Cover with cold water and leave to soak for 30 minutes.

Meanwhile, pound the saffron threads and place in a small bowl. Add the rosewater and leave to steep until required.

Heat half the ghee or oil in a frying pan, add the almonds and fry until golden. Remove to a plate with a slotted spoon and set aside.

Add the onion to the pan and fry gently until translucent. Increase the heat, add the meat and cook, stirring often, until the meat is crumbly. Fry until the juices evaporate, then add the Baharat, salt and sultanas. Fry for 1 minute longer, then remove the pan from the heat. Cover and set aside.

Heat the remaining ghee or oil in a deep, heavy-based saucepan. Add 2 teaspoons of the saffron mixture and the chicken stock. Bring to the boil.

Drain the rice and add to the boiling stock with salt to taste. Stir occasionally until the stock returns to the boil, then reduce the heat to low and cover the pan tightly. Simmer gently for 30 minutes.

Fold the meat mixture gently through the rice. Cover the rim of the pan with a cloth or two paper towels and set the lid on tightly. Leave over low heat for 5 minutes. Remove from the heat and leave for another 5 minutes, or longer if necessary. The rice should not spoil, though this depends on its quality.

Pile the rice in a serving dish or platter and sprinkle with the almonds and the remaining saffron–rosewater mixture.

Excellent served with roast chicken and lamb, or as part of a buffet.

TIMMAN
Steamed white rice
SERVES: 5–6

Iraqi steamed rice is rather like the *chelou* of neighbouring Iran, but there is sufficient difference in the preparation to warrant its inclusion. As with *chelou*, it can be just steamed to a light fluffy grain, or cooked in such a way as to achieve a crisp golden rice crust on the base of the saucepan.

400 g (14 oz/2 cups) basmati, or other good-quality long-grain white rice
85 g (3 oz/⅓ cup) ghee, or 85 ml (3 fl oz/⅓ cup) oil
2 tablespoons salt

Wash the rice well in cold water. Drain well.

Heat 1 tablespoon of the ghee or oil in a heavy-based saucepan and add the rice. Stir over high heat for 2 minutes, then add 2 litres (68 fl oz/8 cups) warm water and the salt. Bring to the boil, stirring occasionally. Boil for 5 minutes, then drain.

Heat another tablespoon of the ghee or oil in the same pan. Add the drained rice and spread evenly. Pour the remaining ghee on top of the rice.

Cover tightly with a lid. For rice without a crust, cook over constant low heat for 40 minutes. For rice with a crust, cook over medium heat for the first 10 minutes, then reduce the heat to low and cook for a further 30 minutes.

To remove the crust easily, place the pan in cold water for 5 minutes to loosen the rice from the base. Otherwise, fluff up the rice with a fork and pile it into a serving dish. If the crust is present, break it into pieces and place it on the dish around the rice.

TASHREEB DIJAJ
Pot-roasted chicken
SERVES: 6

1 chicken, about 1.7 kg (3 lb 12 oz)
1 lemon
salt and freshly ground black pepper, to season
2 tablespoons ghee or oil
1 garlic bulb, left whole and unpeeled
Timman (left) or Timman Z'affaran (page 316), to serve

Clean the chicken and wipe dry with paper towels. Cut half the lemon into quarters and rub them over the chicken, inside and out. Season the cavity and the outside of the chicken with salt and pepper and leave for 30 minutes to absorb the flavours.

Remove the outer dry layers from the garlic bulb, exposing the cloves, but leaving them unpeeled and attached to the root. Wash well and set aside.

Heat the ghee or oil in a heavy-based saucepan and brown the chicken on all sides. Add the garlic bulb to the pan. Reduce the heat to low, then cover and cook for 10 minutes.

Juice the remaining lemon half and add to the pan with 250 ml (8½ fl oz/1 cup) water. Cover the pan tightly and simmer gently over low heat for 2 hours, turning the chicken twice during cooking.

When tender, remove the chicken to a platter and keep hot. Skim the fat from the juices in the pan; remove and discard the garlic. Cook the juices over high heat until reduced by half, then adjust the seasoning.

Cut the chicken into serving portions and pour the juices over the chicken. Serve with Timman (left) or Timman Z'affaran.

DIJAJ ALA TIMMAN
Roast stuffed chicken

SERVES: 6

1 chicken, about 1. 7 kg (3 lb 12 oz)

salt and freshly ground black pepper, to season

60 g (2 oz/¼ cup) butter or ghee

125 ml (4 fl oz/½ cup) light stock or water

Rice stuffing

100 g (3½ oz/½ cup) basmati, or other
   good-quality long-grain white rice

60 g (2 oz/⅓ cup) ghee

1 small onion, finely chopped

40 g (1½ oz/¼ cup) pine nuts or slivered almonds

30 g (1 oz/¼ cup) chopped walnuts

30 g (1 oz/¼ cup) sultanas (golden raisins)

½ teaspoon Baharat (page 344) or ground allspice

salt and freshly ground black pepper, to taste

Preheat the oven to 180°C (350°F/Gas 4).

To make the rice stuffing, wash the rice in a sieve until the water runs clear, then drain well and set aside.

Heat the ghee in a frying pan and gently fry the onion until translucent. Stir in all the nuts and the rice and fry for 5 minutes, stirring often.

Add the sultanas, Baharat, 250 ml (8½ fl oz/1 cup) water, and salt and pepper to taste. Stir well, then cover and cook over low heat for 10 minutes, or until the water has been absorbed. Remove from the heat and leave to cool.

Clean the chicken and wipe dry with paper towels. Fill the cavity with the rice stuffing then truss the chicken. Rub the chicken with salt and pepper.

Melt the butter or ghee in a baking dish. Put the chicken in the dish and baste well. Pour the stock or water into the dish.

Roast the chicken for 2 hours, basting often with the juices in the dish.

Serve the chicken cut into portions, with the stuffing piled in the centre of the platter. Though not usual, the juices in the dish may be skimmed, diluted with a little stock, brought to the boil and served separately in a sauceboat.

HABEET I
Stewed lamb
SERVES: 6

1.5 kg (3 lb 5 oz) lamb shoulder, cut into
   6 pieces on the bone
1 *noomi* (dried lime; see page 345), or thinly
   peeled rind of ½ lemon
salt and freshly ground black pepper, to season
6 garlic cloves, chopped
125 ml (4 fl oz/½ cup) cider or malt vinegar

Place the lamb in a large saucepan and cover with cold water. Add the dried lime, pierced twice with a skewer, or the lemon rind.

Bring slowly to the boil, skimming frequently as the froth rises. When well skimmed and simmering, add about 2 teaspoons salt, a good grinding of pepper, the garlic and vinegar.

Cover and simmer gently for 2½–3 hours, or until the liquid is reduced to a thick sauce and the meat falls off the bones.

Remove the bones and the lime or lemon rind. Serve on a platter with flat breads.

HABEET II
Spiced stewed lamb
SERVES: 6

Reduce the garlic in the recipe for Habeet I (above) to 3 cloves and omit the pepper and vinegar. When the broth is well skimmed, add some salt, the chopped garlic, 1 teaspoon ground turmeric and 1 tablespoon Baharat (page 344). Cover and simmer as before. Serve with Timman (page 317).

KHOUZI ALA TiMMAN
Lamb shanks and rice
SERVES: 6

A restaurant speciality in Baghdad, this dish is a scaled-down version of the festive Arabic *khouzi* (whole lamb stuffed with rice). The cooking method and the stuffing vary according to the region; see page 364 for *khouzi* as prepared in the Gulf States. Although the lamb is not stuffed in this recipe, the final dish has the basic components of *khouzi*.

6 lamb shanks, cracked
1 *noomi* (dried lime; see page 345), or thinly
   peeled strip of lemon rind
60 ml (2 fl oz/¼ cup) oil
1 large onion, finely chopped
1 teaspoon Baharat (page 344)
½ teaspoon ground turmeric
500 g (1 lb 2 oz/2 cups) chopped, peeled tomatoes
2 teaspoons salt
2 teaspoons freshly ground black pepper
Timman (page 317) or Timman Z'affaran (page 316), to serve

Rinse the lamb shanks in cold water and place in a large saucepan. Pour in enough cold water to just cover the meat. Add the dried lime, pierced twice with a skewer, or lemon rind and bring slowly to the boil, skimming as required.

Heat the oil in a frying pan and gently fry the onion until translucent. Add the Baharat and turmeric and fry for a further 1 minute. Add the tomatoes, salt and pepper.

When the lamb shank liquid is well skimmed and simmering, add the tomato mixture. Cover and simmer gently for 1½–2 hours, or until the meat is very tender. Towards the end of cooking, place the lid at an angle so the liquid can reduce to a thick sauce.

Arrange the lamb shanks on a bed of Timman or Timman Z'affaran and pour the sauce over.

Serve with salad and flat breads.

MUMBAR
Lamb and rice sausage

SERVES: 6–8

Mumbar is another Iraqi innovation, popular during winter when the variety of available vegetables is limited.

Lamb filling

1 kg (2 lb 3 oz) finely minced (ground) lamb,
   with a little fat
3 garlic cloves, finely chopped
1 small onion, finely chopped
3 tablespoons chopped flat-leaf parsley
60g (2 oz/¼ cup) tomato paste (concentrated purée)
100 g (3½ oz/½ cup) long-grain white rice, washed
1 teaspoon Baharat (page 344)
salt and freshly ground black pepper, to season

To finish

750 g (1 lb 10 oz) lamb breast (riblets)
1 *noomi* (dried lime; see page 345), optional
salt and freshly ground black pepper, to season
thick lamb or beef sausage casing, about 60 cm
   (24 inches) long

Combine the lamb filling ingredients in a mixing bowl. Mix thoroughly, then cover and refrigerate until required.

If the lamb breast is in one piece, cut it into strips between the bones. Place in a large saucepan and cover with cold water. Bring slowly to the boil, skimming as required.

When the broth is well skimmed and simmering, add the dried lime, pierced twice with a skewer, if using. Season with salt and pepper. Cover and simmer for 30 minutes.

Rinse the sausage casing and leave in one piece. Open the casing under running water and slip it onto the end of a large funnel. Push the length of the casing onto the funnel.

Place the filling in the funnel and push it through using the end of a wooden spoon. As the filling comes through, pull the end of the casing over it and make a knot. Fill the casing as evenly as possible.

When filled, run your hands along the casing to distribute the filling evenly, then knot the other end.

Remove the pan of lamb from the heat. Coil the *mumbar* into the pan on top of the lamb, keeping the coil flat. Invert a heavy plate on top to keep the *mumbar* in place.

Place the pan back over low heat. Cover and simmer for a further 1½ hours. Check the liquid after 30 minutes and add water if necessary to just cover the *mumbar*.

When cooked, set the pan to one side for 15 minutes, then remove the *mumbar* to a plate. Slice into 4 cm (1½ inch) pieces and serve with Murag (page 327) and Timman (page 317).

DOLMAS
Stuffed vegetables

MAKES APPROXIMATELY 60

Dolmas are as popular in Iraq as in other countries of the region. The filling given for Mumbar (left) is used in the Iraqi version of *dolma*, along with the usual vegetables — eggplant (aubergine), tomatoes, capsicums (peppers), zucchini (courgettes), cabbage, grape vine and silverbeet (Swiss chard) leaves. The Iraqis, still the innovators in Arabic cuisine as they were centuries ago, also fill egg shells with any meat mixture left after preparing the vegetables. These are placed on top of the vegetables for cooking.

Use the lamb filling as for the Mumbar recipe (left). Prepare the vegetables as directed in the Khareni Litzk Bulghourov recipe in the Armenia chapter (page 237), then fill with the lamb filling.

Place in an oiled baking dish, brush with oil, cover with foil and bake in a 180°C (350°F/Gas 4) oven for 30 minutes. Remove the foil and bake for a further 20–30 minutes.

HAMUTH HELOO
Lamb with dried fruits

SERVES: 5–6

When dates are being dried, they exude a thick, molasses-like syrup. The Iraqi cook adds some of this syrup when making this dish, but the addition of brown sugar gives a somewhat similar flavour.

1 kg (2 lb 3 oz) boneless stewing lamb

60 g (2 oz/¼ cup) ghee, or 60 ml (2 fl oz/¼ cup) oil

1 onion, chopped

1 small piece of cinnamon bark

1 *noomi* (dried lime; see page 345), or thinly
    peeled rind of ½ lemon

salt, to season

80 g (3 oz/½ cup) chopped dates

135 g (4½ oz/¾ cup) dried apricots

185 g (6½ oz/¾ cup) chopped pitted prunes

30 g (1 oz/¼ cup) sultanas (golden raisins)

2 tablespoons brown sugar

Timman (page 317), to serve

Cut the lamb into 2 cm (¾ inch) cubes. Heat half the ghee or oil in a large, heavy-based saucepan and brown the lamb over medium–high heat, in batches if necessary.

Return all the lamb to the pan and push to one side. Add the onion and cook for 5 minutes. Add 250 ml (8½ fl oz/ 1 cup) water, the cinnamon, and the dried lime, pierced twice with a skewer, or lemon rind. Season with salt, then reduce the heat, cover and simmer for 45 minutes.

Meanwhile, place the dates in a small saucepan with 250 ml (8½ fl oz/1 cup) water and heat until the dates soften. Press through a sieve to purée.

Add the date purée to the stew with the apricots, prunes, sultanas and sugar. Stir, then cover tightly and simmer for a further 1 hour, or until the lamb is tender. Check during cooking to ensure the fruit does not stick to the pan, adding a little more water if necessary.

Remove the cinnamon and lime or lemon rind. Serve hot, with a dish of Timman.

LAHAM AJEEN
Flat lamb pies
MAKES: 24

Many Middle Eastern countries have their favourite version of these pies. In Iraq they are made in great quantities and sold as between-meal snacks. As I rather enjoyed these in Baghdad, this is the version I have chosen to include.

These pies freeze well, so it is worthwhile having a quantity on hand for the lunchbox or picnic hamper, as they are equally good served cold. Another way to present them is to make smaller versions and serve them hot as a finger food with pre-dinner drinks.

750–900 g (1 lb 10 oz–2 lb/5–6 cups) plain (all-purpose) flour

2 teaspoons active dried yeast

2 teaspoons sugar

2 teaspoons salt

2 tablespoons oil

Lamb topping

2 tablespoons oil

1 large onion, finely chopped

2 garlic cloves, finely chopped

500 g (1 lb 2 oz) finely minced (ground) lamb

375 g (13 oz/1½ cups) chopped, peeled tomatoes

200 g (7 oz/1½ cups) grated zucchini (courgette)

2 tablespoons chopped flat-leaf parsley

½ teaspoon dried thyme

1 small red chilli, seeded and finely chopped

salt and freshly ground black pepper, to season

Sift the flour into a large mixing bowl and warm in a low oven.

In a bowl, dissolve the yeast in 60 ml (2 fl oz/¼ cup) warm water. Stir in another 500 ml (17 fl oz/2 cups) warm water with the sugar and salt.

Remove about 300 g (10½ oz/2 cups) of the flour from the warmed bowl and set aside. Pour the yeast mixture into the centre of the warmed bowl and mix in a little of the flour to thicken the liquid. Cover with a cloth and leave until frothy.

Stir in enough of the remaining flour to make a soft dough, gradually adding the oil. Beat by hand for 10 minutes, or use an electric mixer with a dough hook for 5 minutes.

Turn out onto a work surface dusted with flour and knead until smooth and elastic, using just enough flour to stop the dough sticking. Shape into a ball. Place in an oiled bowl and turn the dough over to oil it all over. Cover the bowl with plastic wrap and leave the dough in a warm place until doubled in size — about 1 hour.

Meanwhile, make the lamb topping. Heat the oil in a saucepan and gently fry the onion until translucent. Add the garlic. Increase the heat to high, add the lamb and stir until the juices evaporate and the meat begins to brown.

Stir in the remaining topping ingredients. Cover and simmer over gentle heat for 30 minutes, removing the lid towards the end of cooking so that the excess moisture can evaporate — the mixture should be thick. Leave to cool.

Preheat the oven to 220°C (430°F/Gas 7).

Punch down the dough and turn it out onto a floured surface. Knead for 2 minutes, then divide into 24 equal portions, shaping each into a ball.

Roll out each ball to a 12 cm (5 inch) round and place on greased baking trays. Spread a generous tablespoon of topping on each. Bake for 12–15 minutes, or until cooked.

Serve hot or cold.

TASHREEB
Stewed lamb shanks and tripe
SERVES: 6

For a genuine *tashreeb*, lambs' feet are required. As these are difficult to obtain, often being prohibited from sale by health regulations, I have used lamb shanks instead. This is just one version of *tashreeb* as prepared in Iraq.

500 g (1 lb 2 oz) tripe

4 lamb foreshanks, cracked

110 g (3¾ oz/½ cup) dried chickpeas, soaked overnight, then drained

2 *noomi* (dried limes; see page 345), or the thinly peeled rind of ½ lemon

1 garlic bulb, left whole and unpeeled

60 g (2 oz/¼ cup) ghee, or 60 ml (2 fl oz/¼ cup) oil

1 large onion, finely chopped

500 g (1 lb 2 oz/2 cups) chopped, peeled tomatoes

2 teaspoons Baharat (page 344)

salt and freshly ground black pepper, to season

2 large flat breads

Wash the tripe well and cut into 3 cm (1¼ inch) squares. Place in a large saucepan with the lamb shanks and chickpeas, cover with cold water and bring to the boil. Drain off the water.

Add enough fresh water to the pan to just cover the tripe and lamb shanks. Add the dried limes, each pierced twice with a skewer, or the lemon rind.

Wash the garlic bulb well and strip off the outer layers of papery skin, leaving the unpeeled cloves exposed. Leave the garlic intact and add to the pan. Bring to a slow simmer, skimming as required.

Meanwhile, heat the ghee or oil in a frying pan and gently fry the onion until translucent. Add the tomatoes and Baharat.

When the lamb mixture is well skimmed and simmering, add the tomato mixture and season with salt and pepper. Cover and simmer gently for 2–2½ hours, or until the lamb and tripe are tender.

Remove and discard the garlic bulb and the limes or lemon rind. Lift out the lamb shanks and strip the meat from the bones. Cut the meat into pieces and return to the pan. Bring to the boil to reheat the meat.

Cut the bread into squares and place in the base of a deep serving dish or casserole. Pour the liquid from the stew over the bread, then top with the stew. Serve hot, in deep plates.

MURAG
Meat stew
SERVES: 5–6

Though the literal translation of *murag* is sauce or gravy, it is the Iraqi version of the popular Middle Eastern meat stew. A vegetable is usually added – green beans, peas, eggplant (aubergine) or okra being the most popular. When *murag* is served with rice, as it almost always is, the dish is then called *timman murag*.

1.5 kg (3 lb 5 oz) boneless stewing beef or lamb

60 ml (2 fl oz/¼ cup) oil

2 large onions, finely chopped

500 g (1 lb 2 oz/2 cups) chopped, peeled tomatoes, or
    60 g (2 oz/¼ cup) tomato paste (concentrated purée)

1 teaspoon sugar

1 teaspoon Baharat (page 344), optional

salt and freshly ground black pepper, to season

your choice of prepared vegetable (see note)

Timman (page 317) or Timman Z'affaran (page 316), to serve

Trim the meat and cut into 4 cm (1½ inch) cubes. Heat half the oil in a heavy-based saucepan and brown the meat in batches over high heat. Remove to a plate.

Reduce the heat, add the remaining oil and gently fry the onion until translucent. Add the tomatoes or tomato paste. If using tomatoes, also add 250 ml (8½ fl oz/1 cup) water; if using tomato paste, add 375 ml (12½ fl oz/1½ cups) water.

Stir in the sugar, and Baharat if using. Season with salt and pepper and bring to the boil. Reduce the heat and return the meat to the pan. Cover and simmer for 45 minutes for lamb, or 1¼ hours for beef.

Add your choice of vegetable, then cover and simmer for a further 1 hour, or until the meat is tender. Serve with Timman or Timman Z'affaran, flat breads and pickles.

❀ *Note:* Add any one of the following vegetables to the stew:
- 500 g (1 lb 2 oz) green beans, topped, tailed and cut in half
- 500 g (1 lb 2 oz) okra, prepared as directed on page 8; also add 2 chopped garlic cloves when frying the onion
- 310 g (10¾ oz/2 cups) shelled green peas
- 500 g (1 lb 2 oz) eggplant (aubergine), cubed, salted for 30 minutes, then rinsed.

MURABBA TRINGE
Citron peel in syrup

2 citrons (or lemons or limes)
660 g (1 lb 7 oz/3 cups) sugar
1 tablespoon lemon juice

Lightly grate the entire surface of each citron. Deeply score the peel, from the stem end to the base, into six or eight segments, depending on the size of the citrons. Carefully remove the peel.

Cut each segment into three pieces. As the piece from the centre will be square, cut it in half diagonally so that all the pieces are triangular.

Place the peel in a saucepan and cover with cold water. Bring to the boil, then pour off the water.

Cover with fresh cold water, then boil again and drain.

Do this five times in all, then cover with more fresh cold water and leave to stand for 6–8 hours.

Drain and cover again with fresh cold water. Bring to the boil and boil gently until tender — about 45 minutes. Drain again and spread out on paper towels to dry.

In a clean saucepan, dissolve the sugar in 750 ml (25 fl oz/ 3 cups) cold water over medium heat, stirring occasionally. When dissolved, bring to the boil and add the lemon juice. Boil without stirring for 5 minutes.

Add the citron peel to the syrup and bring back to the boil. Leave to boil over medium heat for 10 minutes, skimming when necessary. Remove the pan from the heat, then cover and leave overnight.

The next day, bring the pan contents back to the boil and boil gently for 15–20 minutes, or until the syrup is thick when tested on a cold saucer.

Cool a little, then ladle the peel and syrup into warm, sterilised jars (see page 19). Seal when cold and store in a cool, dark place.

Serve as a confection in small dishes with a spoon.

KLAICHA
Date-filled pastries
MAKES: 30

Klaicha dough
450 g (1 lb/3 cups) plain (all-purpose) flour
115 g (4 oz/½ cup) caster (superfine) sugar
250 g (9 oz/1 cup) unsalted butter
3 teaspoons orange flower water or rosewater

Date filling
250 g (9 oz) dried pitted dates
40 g (1½ oz) butter

To make the Klaicha dough, sift the flour and sugar into a large mixing bowl. Cut the butter into pieces and rub into the flour with your fingertips until distributed evenly.

Combine the orange flower water or rosewater with 60 ml (2 fl oz/¼ cup) water and sprinkle onto the flour mixture. Mix to a firm dough, then knead lightly until smooth. Rest the dough for 30 minutes.

Meanwhile, make the date filling. Chop the dates and place in a saucepan with the butter. Heat gently until the dates soften, stirring often. Remove from the heat and set aside.

Preheat the oven to 170°C (340°F/Gas 3).

Roll the dough into balls the size of large walnuts.

Working one at a time, flatten a ball of dough in the palm of your hand and place a teaspoon of the date filling in the centre. Mould the dough around the filling and reshape it into a ball.

Press the ball into a carved mould, similar to a *tabi* (a Lebanese mould for shaping pastries), and place on an ungreased baking tray. Alternatively, place the filled pastries on a tray, flatten slightly, then press the tines of a fork obliquely around the sides and across the top, giving a slightly conical shape.

Bake for 30–35 minutes, until lightly browned.

Leave to cool on a tray; the pastries will become firm and crisp on cooling. Store in a sealed container when cool.

❋ *Note: For an alternative shape, divide the pastry into three equal portions and roll each portion into a rectangle 1 cm (½ inch) thick and 10 cm (4 inches) wide. Put one-third of the date mixture, shaped in a long roll, along one pastry edge and roll up to enclose the filling. Press the edges and ends to seal. Place the rolls, seam side down, on an ungreased baking tray. Decorate the top with a pastry crimper or any other means to make a design. Bake as above, then cool and slice at an angle to serve. Store in a sealed container.*

MURABBA TĀMAR I
Dates in syrup

Cooking dates are required for this confection. The fresh dates available in non-date growing countries are table varieties, usually imported frozen. These are too soft to be prepared in the traditional way. If these are the only dates available, then follow the directions for Murabba Tamar II on page 332.

> 750 g (1 lb 10 oz) fresh cooking dates
> walnut halves, for filling the dates
> 660 g (1 lb 7 oz/3 cups) sugar
> 1 thin strip of lemon rind
> juice of ½ lemon, strained
> 4 cloves
> small piece of cinnamon bark

Wash the dates and remove the stems. Peel off the skin using a sharp knife. Place the dates in a saucepan and cover with cold water. Bring to the boil, then boil gently for 15 minutes, or until the dates are tender. Drain, reserving the cooking liquid.

When the dates are cool enough to handle, push the date seeds out with a chopstick.

Cut the walnut halves in half to give quarters, about the size of the date seed. Insert a piece of walnut in each date.

Place the filled dates in a bowl in layers, sprinkling the sugar generously between each layer and over the top. Leave for 12 hours, or overnight.

Measure the reserved date cooking liquid and make up to 500 ml (17 fl oz/2 cups) with water if necessary. Pour over the dates and leave for 2 hours to dissolve the sugar, shaking the bowl contents occasionally.

Drain the sugar liquid into a heavy-based saucepan and bring to the boil. Add the lemon rind and juice, the cloves and cinnamon. Boil, uncovered, over medium heat for 10 minutes without stirring. Skim off any froth as required.

Add the dates and return to the boil. Boil for 10 minutes, or until the syrup is thick when tested on a cold saucer.

Remove the lemon rind and cinnamon. Pack the dates into sterilised jars (see page 19) and pour the syrup over them. Seal when cold and store at room temperature.

Serve in small dishes with a spoon, or as a sweetmeat.

MURABBA TAMAR II
Table dates in syrup

Use the same ingredients as for the Murabba Tamar I recipe on page 331, substituting table dates for the cooking dates. Leave the dates unpeeled and wash well. Either push the date seeds out with a chopstick and insert walnut pieces in each date, or slit the side of the date to remove the seed and then insert a walnut piece.

Combine 500 ml (17 fl oz/2 cups) water with the sugar and dissolve over medium heat, stirring occasionally. Add the lemon rind, juice and spices and boil, uncovered, for 10 minutes without stirring. Add the prepared dates and return to the boil, then remove from the heat and set aside for 12 hours.

Remove the dates from the syrup and place in a heatproof bowl. Bring the syrup to the boil, then boil without stirring for 10 minutes, skimming when necessary. Strain the syrup over the dates and leave until cool.

Pack into sterilised jars (see page 19), seal and store in the refrigerator.

HOLWAH TAMAR
Date sweetmeat

500 g (1 lb 2 oz) dried pitted dates
60 g (2 oz/¼ cup) ghee
250 g (9 oz/2 cups) walnut pieces
2 tablespoons toasted sesame seeds

Chop the dates roughly and place in a heavy-based saucepan with the ghee. Cook over medium heat, stirring often, until the dates soften and are combined with the ghee.

Spread half the date mixture in a 23 cm (9 inch) square cake tin. Sprinkle the walnut pieces over the dates, pressing them in lightly. Place the remaining date mixture on top, spreading it evenly.

Sprinkle the top with the sesame seeds, pressing them on lightly. Leave until cold, then cut into small squares or diamond shapes.

Store in a sealed container and serve as a sweetmeat.

MANAISAMA
Walnut-filled pastries
MAKES: 30

Klaicha dough (page 329)
icing (confectioners') sugar, for dusting

Walnut filling
230 g (8 oz/2 cups) coarsely ground walnuts
55 g (2 oz/¼ cup) caster (superfine) sugar

Make the dough as directed in the Klaicha recipe and leave to rest for 30 minutes.

Combine the walnut filling ingredients, kneading by hand to form a coarse paste.

Preheat the oven to 170°C (340°F/Gas 3).

Roll the dough, a tablespoon at a time, into balls the size of large walnuts. Working one at a time, flatten them out in the palm of your hand and put a generous teaspoon of nut filling in the centre. Close the dough around the filling, sealing well.

Press the ball into a carved mould, similar to a *tabi* (a Lebanese mould for shaping pastries), and place on an ungreased baking tray. Alternatively, place the filled pastries on a tray, flatten slightly, then press the tines of a fork obliquely around the sides and across the top, giving a slightly conical shape.

Bake for 30–35 minutes, or until very lightly browned. Leave to cool on the baking tray for 10 minutes.

Sift a layer of icing sugar onto a sheet of greaseproof (parchment) paper and place the pastries on the sugar. Sift more icing sugar on top to coat them thickly.

Leave the pastries until thoroughly cooled, then store in a sealed container.

ZLABIYA
Fried sweet rosettes

MAKES: ABOUT 30

2 teaspoons active dried yeast

375 g (13 oz/2½ cups) plain (all-purpose) flour

½ teaspoon salt

2 teaspoons sugar

corn or peanut oil, for deep-frying

Syrup

440 g (15½ oz/2 cups) sugar

2 teaspoons lemon juice

2 teaspoons rosewater or orange flower water

Dissolve the yeast in 60 ml (2 fl oz/¼ cup) warm water.

Sift the flour into a bowl and make a well in the centre.

Add the salt and sugar to the yeast mixture, along with 375 ml (12½ fl oz/1½ cups) warm water. Pour the yeast mixture into the centre of the flour. Gradually stir in the flour to form a thick liquid batter, then beat vigorously for 10 minutes. (This can be done using ordinary electric beaters.)

Cover the batter and leave to rest in a warm place for 30 minutes.

Meanwhile, make the syrup. Dissolve the sugar in 375 ml (12½ fl oz/1½ cups) water in a saucepan over medium heat. Bring to the boil, add the lemon juice and boil briskly for 15 minutes. Add the rosewater or orange flower water, boil for 1 minute longer, then set aside to cool.

Beat the batter again for 5 minutes, then let it rest for a further 30 minutes.

Heat enough oil for deep-frying in a wide saucepan — a depth of 4 cm (1½ inches) is sufficient. Heat the oil to 190°C (375°F), or until a cube of bread dropped into the oil browns in 10 seconds; the pastries must fry without colouring too much.

Beat the batter again briefly. Spoon some of the batter into a piping bag fitted with a 5 mm (¼ inch) plain nozzle. Hold a finger over the nozzle while filling the bag.

Squeeze the batter into the oil in a 10 cm (4 inch) circle, and fill in the circle with a lacy pattern of squiggles or zig-zags, ensuring that the batter touches the outer circle in places. The finished pastry must look like a rough, lacy rosette.

Fry for about 3 minutes, turning once to cook evenly. When golden, lift out the rosette with a slotted spoon, drain briefly, then place into the cooled syrup.

Using a second spoon or a fork, turn the pastry in the syrup and lift it out onto a plate. (A second pair of hands will make the process much less complicated.)

Continue cooking and turning the rosettes in the syrup until all the batter is used.

Serve the rosettes piled on a plate. They will remain crisp for some time if the syrup is very thick.

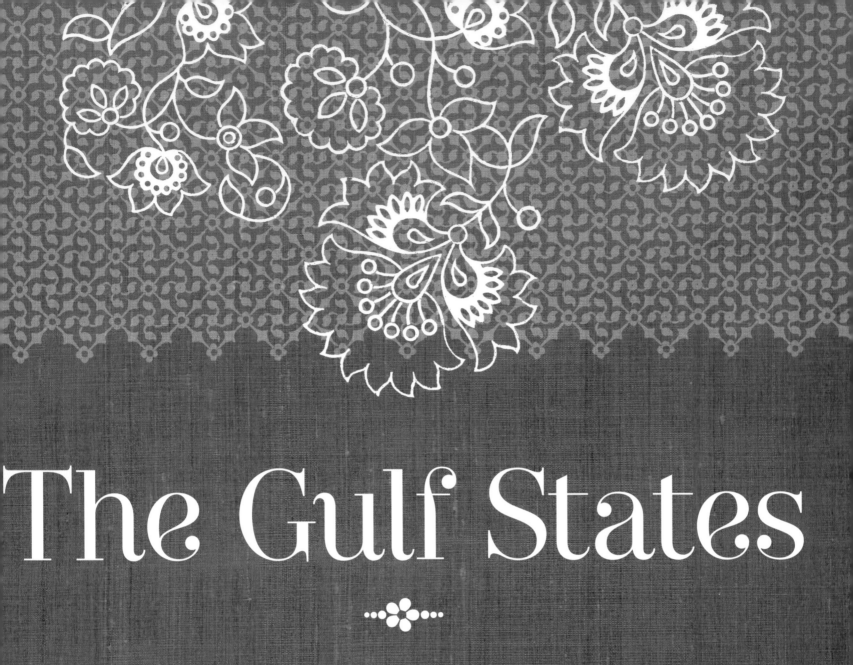

The Gulf States

·•❖•·

THE GULF STATES

UNITED ARAB EMIRATES, SAUDI ARABIA, BAHRAIN, KUWAIT, QATAR, OMAN

While the United Arab Emirates, Saudi Arabia, Bahrain, Kuwait, Qatar and Oman are separate countries, the collective grouping in one chapter is necessary as their cooking is very similar. One can trace the origin of certain recipes to one particular place, but you would also find the same dish prepared in the other countries.

The aspect of Arabic life that impresses one most is their hospitality, and the single food — if it could be called such — with which this is expressed is coffee. The coffee pot is ever present, though nowadays coffee is likely to be prepared early in the day and kept hot in a vacuum flask ready in case a guest should drop in.

There are certain rules that should be observed if ever you are offered coffee in this region. First, do not refuse a cup; to do so is an insult to the host. Your cup will be replenished a second time and a third, and more if you do not indicate to the host that you are satisfied. A simple little jiggle of your empty cup from side to side indicates that you have had sufficient. Only a small portion of coffee is served — a third of a cup is poured each time, and the handle-less cups are very small. Coffee is always served unsweetened and flavoured with cardamom. Taking three cups of coffee is expected of you, rather than just one.

The first impressions of the food of the Gulf States — particularly in the *souk* (market) — quash any notion originally held that the staple diet is boiled meat (lamb, mutton or camel) served on a huge mound of spiced rice. While this might be true of the nomadic Bedouin, camped far from places which could provide anything else, it is not so of the food of townspeople. The variety of fresh vegetables, fruits, spices, meat, fish and poultry from which to choose would delight any serious cook and amaze at the same time, as an aerial view of the region with its vast, arid landscape does not indicate abundance — not of the edible kind anyway.

THE FLAVOUR OF ARABIC COOKING

The Gulf Arabs are very fond of skewered meats, either succulent cubes of lamb similar to the kebabs of other Middle Eastern countries, or Kabab Mashwi (page 359), a meat paste moulded onto flat skewers and grilled over coals. These are often served folded into *khoubiz* (flat bread) together with salad ingredients.

Their rice dishes are of the kind one would expect, knowing the colourful history of the Arabs, as it was the Arabs who opened the spice routes to India and the East, and to the West, trading their cardamom, coriander seeds and cumin for cinnamon, nutmeg, cassia, ginger, pepper, turmeric and cloves. The most popular spicing is a mixture of most of these, called Baharat (page 344), and it is used in rice, soups, fish, poultry and meat dishes, usually with the addition of whole spices to emphasise certain flavours, and turmeric or saffron for colour. Often the saffron is steeped in rosewater and poured over the dish towards the end of cooking, or as it is, served for a final dash of colour and fragrance.

Shades of near-Indian cooking are to be expected, with the historical links probably going even further back than those already documented. The Indus Valley civilisation mysteries have yet to be unravelled, but recent archaeological finds in Bahrain and elsewhere in the Gulf region reveal seals similar to those found in the Indus Valley.

Machbous (page 355) is a particularly interesting dish of meat, fish, prawns (shrimp) or chicken, cooked in spices with rice. The rice itself must be basmati as the Arab refuses any other substitute. Basmati is an aromatic rice from Pakistan, hard of grain, which holds up to the long cooking involved. However, cooking times have been shortened in the recipes, in anticipation of possible substitutes.

One ingredient that intrigued me is the *loomi* (dried lime). In the Gulf region it is used extensively, either whole or pounded into a powder, and it imparts an interesting and unusual flavour to foods. It is difficult to give a substitute, but in some recipes the thinly peeled rind of a lemon may be used instead. The lime itself is dried naturally on the tree; it is grown in Oman and also imported from Thailand. *Loomi* is also to be found in Iran and Iraq, where it is called *limu omani* and *noomi* respectively, but in these countries it is only used whole. I have given details in this chapter on how to prepare your own dried limes.

The cucumbers of the Gulf are much loved by the people, and after tasting them I could understand why. The familiar long green cucumber is picked before it reaches maturity, and this is when cucumbers are at their best. One other variety, a long slender cucumber with a dark green and deeply grooved skin, is available in Western countries under a variety of names. In the Gulf it is called *trooh*; the locals claim that when the moon is full one can hear the cucumber groaning as it twists itself into the circles and other squiggly shapes in which it comes.

The waters of the Gulf are teeming with prawns (shrimp) and an infinite variety of fish. The most popular fish for the table are *gugurfan* and *shehen* (similar to bream), *wahar* (called flathead in the waters of Australia), *beyah* (mullet), *chanad* (mackerel) and a popular Kuwaiti fish called *zubaidi* (pomfret). Generally, fish is cooked over glowing coals, oven-baked, fried or stewed.

The *khoubiz* of the area is made in a similar way to the Iranian *nane lavash* and *taftoon*. Although the general term is *khoubiz*, the breads are known as Mafrooda (page 347) and Mafrooda Burd (page 347), depending on the flour used. Quite often Iranian bakers run the bakeries, and the same ovens and equipment are used as in Iran. Samouli (page 347), a white bread similar to long French baguettes, is baked in a conventional oven.

EATING ARABIC STYLE

Today the region, while still keeping its traditions, is likely to cater also to Western tastes. A town house is likely to have a living room with one part furnished with floor and wall cushions for Arabic visitors, and a table and seating for Western visitors, emphasising the innate hospitality of the Arab.

Whether served on a cloth spread over a carpet on the floor or on a dining table, the food is presented in the same way. All the components of the meal are placed in dishes and platters, with plates, spoons, forks and glassware. Only in a Bedouin tent is one likely to have the experience of eating from a communal platter, using the fingers of the right hand.

The main dish could be meat, fish or chicken, either cooked in a rich sauce, or roasted, baked or grilled. Muhammar (sweet rice; page 348), Mashkoul (rice with onions; page 349) or Muaddas (rice with lentils; page 349) is served separately, unless rice is incorporated with the meat dish. A dish of fresh salad is always served, consisting of cos (romaine) lettuce, crisp firm cucumbers, tomatoes, green or red capsicums (peppers), radishes and a cress-like green herb. The salad is simply dressed with vinegar. Bowls of yoghurt and pickles accompany the meal and bread is always served.

If you want to serve a meal with all the exotic elements of a feast in a desert sheikh's tent, then the dish to prepare is Khouzi (page 364). While *khouzi* is prepared throughout the Gulf States and other Arabic countries, the Saudi Arabian *khouzi* reigns supreme. First you require a whole lamb, including the head. A rice stuffing, redolent with nuts, onions, sultanas and spices, is prepared. Some of this is packed into a chicken with shelled hard-boiled eggs; then the chicken is placed in the cavity of the lamb with the bulk of the rice mixture. The cavity is sewn up and the lamb trussed. Although frequently roasted on the spit, it is traditionally placed in a large tray, with the ribs of palm leaves serving as a rack. Water is added to the tray and a lid is sealed over the tray with a flour-and-water paste. It is then oven-baked to succulent perfection. The lamb is cooked until it is so tender that the meat comes away from the bones easily. The stuffing is removed and spread on a serving platter with the lamb resting on top.

The *khouzi* is served with great ceremony. Servants present pitchers and bowls for guests to wash their hands before the meal. All the components of the meal are spread on a cloth over a colourful and usually expensive carpet, with cushions scattered around. The guests sit in their places with the most important guest seated next to the host, and the host delights in selecting the most succulent pieces of lamb to offer to the principal guest. The most highly regarded parts of the lamb are the eyes, which the Arabs consider great delicacies. I should imagine it would be somewhat like tackling your first oyster. To serve such a feast in the traditional manner would of course mean that only men would be present, but this problem is overcome by proclaiming any woman guest to be an honorary male. (There are most reputable precedents for this: the Queen of England was accorded this honour during a visit to Saudi Arabia in 1979.) At feasts of this type, eating is regarded as a serious business and there is little, if any, conversation. When the meal is finished hands are washed again, and the guests adjourn to another area for coffee, conversation and the water pipe.

INGREDIENTS FOR GULF COOKING

Basmati rice is a necessary ingredient for authentic Gulf cooking. The meat is usually lamb, but now that more food is imported, beef is gaining in popularity. Coarsely ground coffee (preferably *moccha*), cardamom, saffron, turmeric, flat-leaf parsley, coriander seeds, rosewater, *loomi* and dates are frequently used. Tamarind is still used in certain dishes, though tomato has replaced tamarind to a great extent. A large quantity of onions should be on hand, as they are much used in Gulf cooking. The recipes, Glossary and recipe notes give more detail on Gulf foods.

ACHAR LEFET
« Pickled turnips

80 g (3 oz/¼ cup) rock salt

1 kg (2 lb 3 oz) small white turnips (about 8)

1 small beetroot (beet)

1 garlic clove, peeled and cut in half lengthways

250 ml (8½ fl oz/1 cup) white vinegar

Put the salt in a saucepan with 500 ml (17 fl oz/2 cups) water. Bring to the boil, stirring until the salt has dissolved. Cool.

Peel the turnips and cut into quarters or sixths. Peel the beetroot and cut into thick strips.

Pack the turnips in a large sterilised jar (see page 19), placing the beetroot strips and garlic between the layers.

Stir the vinegar into the cooled brine and pour over the turnips. Remove the air bubbles by inserting a fine skewer down the sides of the jar. Seal with a glass or plastic lid; if using a metal lid, place a doubled piece of plastic wrap over the top of the jar before securing the lid.

Leave in a cool place for at least 3 weeks before opening. Once opened, store in the refrigerator. Unopened pickles will keep in a cool, dark place for up to 3 months.

ACHAR TAMAT
« Pickled tomatoes

1 kg (2 lb 3 oz) firm, ripe, small or medium tomatoes

80 g (3 oz/¼ cup) rock salt

3 teaspoons freshly ground black pepper

3 teaspoons paprika

2 teaspoons ground coriander

6 garlic cloves, halved lengthways

750 ml (25 fl oz/3 cups) white vinegar

Choose tomatoes with no sign of decay; wash them well. Cut a slit almost halfway through each tomato at the stem end, then fill the slits with salt. Place upright in a bowl and leave for 3 days. Drain off the liquid as it accumulates.

Invert the tomatoes in a colander to drain the excess liquid.

Combine the pepper, paprika and coriander and sprinkle about ½ teaspoon of the mixture into each tomato.

Pack the tomatoes into sterilised jars (see page 19), adding the garlic pieces between the layers. Fill the jars with the vinegar and seal with glass or plastic lids; if using metal lids, place a doubled piece of plastic wrap over the top of the jars before securing the lids.

Leave for 1 week before opening. Use within 6 weeks.

ACHAR FILEIL
« Pickled peppers

500 g (1 lb 2 oz) green or red capsicums (peppers)

80 g (3 oz/¼ cup) rock salt

500 ml (17 fl oz/2 cups) white vinegar

2 garlic cloves, halved

1 hot chilli, washed and trimmed

Wash the capsicums well and dry them. Trim the stems, but do not remove. Cut a long slit in each capsicum.

Put the salt in a saucepan with 500 ml (17 fl oz/2 cups) water. Bring to the boil, stirring until the salt has dissolved. Add the vinegar and return to the boil.

Pack the capsicums into a warm sterilised glass jar (see page 19), adding the garlic and chilli. Pour the boiling hot brine mixture over the capsicums, filling the jar to overflowing. Let them absorb the brine, then top the jar up when they settle. Remove the air bubbles by inserting a fine skewer down the sides of the jar.

Seal the jar with a glass or plastic lid; if a metal lid is used, place a doubled layer of plastic wrap over the top of the jar before securing the lid.

Leave in a cool place for 3 weeks before opening. Once opened, store in the refrigerator. Unopened pickles will keep in a cool, dark place for 3–4 months.

BAHARAT
Mixed spices

MAKES: ABOUT 225 G (8 OZ)

70 g (2½ oz/½ cup) black peppercorns

25 g (¾ oz/¼ cup) coriander seeds

10 g (½ oz/¼ cup) cassia bark

20 g (¾ oz/¼ cup) cloves

35 g (1¼ oz/⅓ cup) cumin seeds

2 teaspoons cardamom seeds

4 whole nutmegs

50 g (2 oz/½ cup) paprika

Grind the peppercorns, coriander seeds, cassia, cloves, cumin and cardamom seeds to a powder in a blender. (It may be necessary to combine all the ingredients, then grind about ½ cup of the mixture at a time.)

Grate the nutmeg and blend it into the spices with the paprika. Store in an airtight jar and use as directed in recipes.

❁ *Note: You can also use the same quantities of ready-ground spices. Four nutmegs yield approximately 20 g (¾ oz/½ cup) ground nutmeg. It will yield a greater amount of spice mix than the quantity above.*

DUKKOUS AL-ṬAMAṬ
Tomato sauce

MAKES: ABOUT 375 ML (12½ FL OZ/1½ CUPS)

1 tablespoon oil

4–6 garlic cloves, crushed

750 g (1 lb 10 oz) ripe tomatoes, peeled (see page 528) and chopped

salt, to season

1½ teaspoons Baharat (left)

Heat the oil in a saucepan, add the garlic and cook for a few seconds only.

Add the tomatoes and season with salt. Cover and leave to simmer on low heat for 30 minutes.

Stir in the Baharat and cook with the lid off for 2–3 minutes.

Serve with rice, or as directed in recipes.

The sauce may be stored in a sealed jar in the refrigerator and heated for use as required.

DUKKOUS AL-BADINJAN
Eggplant sauce

MAKES: ABOUT 375 ML (12½ FL OZ/1½ CUPS)

2 oval eggplants (aubergines), each about 250 g (9 oz)

4 garlic cloves

1 teaspoon salt

2 tablespoons oil

¼–½ teaspoon ground hot chilli or chilli powder

1 teaspoon paprika

Preheat the oven to 180°C (350°F/Gas 4). Place the eggplants on a baking tray and bake for 30 minutes, or until soft.

Crush the garlic with the salt using a mortar and pestle. Alternatively, crush it in a garlic press and mix it with the salt.

While the eggplants are still hot, peel off the skin and place the flesh in a bowl. Roughly chop the flesh, then mash with a fork. Stir in the crushed garlic mixture and remaining ingredients. Taste and adjust the spices if necessary.

Serve warm with Muaddas (page 349) or other rice dishes.

LOOMI
Dried limes

Gulf cooks use dried limes (*loomi*) either whole or powdered, but in Iran and Iraq they are only used whole. When using intact *loomi*, they must be pierced with a skewer on each side so the cooking liquid can travel through the lime to take the flavour. In the dry heat of the Middle East the limes are very brittle and the holes can be made by simply pressing with a finger. I live in a humid climate and find that the humidity toughens the lime, so more forceful means of piercing and powdering need to be adopted. To powder *loomi*, pound them using a mortar and pestle, or process in a blender.

As *loomi* are not readily available outside the Middle East, instructions for preparing them are given below. The species of lime used alters the flavour a little, but it is still a most interesting spice. A sprinkling of powdered *loomi* also does wonders for steaks — rub some in before grilling or pan-frying!

small fresh limes, preferably Tahitian limes

1 tablespoon salt

Leave the limes whole, but if they are very large they can be halved to speed the drying process.

Put the limes in a saucepan of boiling water with the salt. Return to the boil, then allow to boil rapidly for 3–5 minutes, depending on size. Drain.

Spread the limes on a wire rack and place them in the sun to dry. This takes up to a week, depending on the strength of sun. Turn the limes daily.

If there is insufficient heat in the sun (which could be the case, as limes are a late autumn and winter fruit), it might be necessary to resort to other means. In this case place the rack of limes in the oven, set on the lowest possible heat. Place the rack in the coolest part of the oven and leave for 3–4 days. A warming drawer would be even better — or if you can get one, use an electric food dryer.

The limes are ready when they are dark and the flesh is completely dehydrated, but take care not to leave them until they are too dark. Store in an airtight container.

KHOUBIZ
« Flat bread

Although *khoubiz* is a general term for bread in the Arabian Gulf region, there are more precise names for the various breads. As there are so many similar bread recipes already given, it will suffice to give the names and tell you which bread recipe to follow to make them Gulf-style breads.

MAFROODA
White flat bread

Mafrooda is a white flat bread without a pocket. Follow the Khoubiz recipe on page 264, but do not rest the bread after shaping, and instead prick it with a fork or pinwheel.

Bake on a hot griddle or baking tray for 4 minutes, pressing the bread with a cloth if it looks as though a pocket is forming. Turn to brown the other side after 2 minutes, or brown under a hot grill (broiler) after baking.

MAFROODA BURD
Wholemeal flat bread

Follow the same directions as for Mafrooda (below left), using 600 g (1 lb 5 oz/4 cups) wholemeal (whole-wheat) flour and 300 g (10½ oz/2 cups) white flour.

SAMOULI
White bread

This is similar to the French baguette, and comes in sizes ranging from short sticks to very long ones. The top is glazed with water or egg glaze and sprinkled with coarse salt, sesame seeds or caraway seeds.

Follow the Kouloura recipe on page 264, and roll the dough into a 40 cm (16 inches) circle. Cut the circle into quarters. Beginning at the curved side, roll up to the point of the section. Put the loaves on baking trays, cover with a cloth and leave in a warm place until doubled in size. Glaze with beaten egg or water, sprinkle with coarse salt, sesame or caraway seeds, then sprinkle lightly with cold water.

Bake in a 190°C (375°F/Gas 5) oven for 15 minutes, or until the loaves sound hollow when tapped.

MUHAMMAR
Sweet rice

SERVES: 5–6 (1 IF YOU ARE DIVING)

Known as the Bahraini pearl divers' rice, *muhammar* is one of those recipes that falls into the 'necessity is the mother of invention' category.

Though early pearl divers were doubtlessly not aware of the physiological implications of diving, at some stage they must have found they could dive more frequently and with less ill-effect if they ate sweet foods (which maintained blood sugar levels) and sustaining foods (carbohydrates and fats). The combination of date juice, rice and fat in this dish fulfilled these requirements.

Diving enthusiasts might be interested in the skills of these intrepid men. Using a rope to guide them, they would rapidly descend to a depth of up to 40 metres (130 feet) with a weight tied to their toes. They would stay down for 10–15 minutes, scoop up any oysters in sight, then ascend.

Diving at such a depth even with modern scuba gear has its hazards, let alone with no breathing apparatus at all. Needless to say the mortality rate was high, with sharks, sea snakes and jellyfish adding to the dangers involved.

¼ teaspoon saffron threads

3 cardamom pods, cracked

2 tablespoons rosewater

400 g (14 oz/2 cups) basmati rice

1 tablespoon salt

55–75 g (2–2½ oz/¼–⅓ cup) sugar or honey

60 g (2 oz/¼ cup) ghee or butter

Add the saffron and cardamom to the rosewater and set aside to steep.

Pick over the rice, place in a sieve and wash under cold running water until the water runs clear. Drain.

Bring 1.5 litres (51 fl oz/6 cups) water to the boil in a heavy-based saucepan. Add the salt and rice and stir occasionally until the water returns to the boil. Leave uncovered and boil for 8 minutes. Strain and place in a bowl.

Pour the sugar or honey over the hot rice and mix through with a fork.

Heat the ghee or butter in the same pan in which the rice was cooked. Add the sugared rice and sprinkle the rosewater mixture over the top. Make three holes in the rice with the end of a wooden spoon.

Cover the rim of the pan with a paper towel and place the lid on tightly. Cook over low heat for 20–25 minutes, or until the rice is tender.

Serve with grilled fish and roast lamb.

MASHKOUL
Rice with onion

SERVES: 5–6

400 g (14 oz/2 cups) basmati or other good-quality
    long-grain white rice

1 tablespoon salt

60 g (2 oz/¼ cup) ghee, or 60 ml (2 fl oz/¼ cup) oil

1 large onion, finely chopped

Pick over the rice, place in a sieve and wash under cold
running water until the water runs clear. Drain.

Bring 1.5 litres (51 fl oz/6 cups) water to the boil in a large
saucepan. Add the rice and salt and return to the boil, stirring
occasionally to keep the grains separate. Boil for 8 minutes,
then strain into a large sieve.

Heat the ghee or oil in a heavy-based saucepan and gently
fry the onion until translucent. Increase the heat and fry until
the onion is crisp and lightly coloured. Remove half the onion
and ghee mixture and set aside.

Add the strained rice to the pan and toss with a fork to mix
the onion through the rice. Spread the reserved onion and
ghee on top of the rice. Cover the pan tightly and cook over low
heat for 35–40 minutes, or until the rice is tender.

Fluff up the rice with a fork and serve piled on a platter.

Mashkoul is a standard accompaniment to most Gulf meals.

MUADDAS
Rice with lentils

SERVES: 6

400 g (14 oz/2 cups) basmati or other good-quality
    long-grain white rice

95 g (3½ oz/½ cup) brown or green lentils

60 g (2 oz/¼ cup) ghee, or 60 ml (2 fl oz/¼ cup) oil

1 large onion, finely chopped

2 teaspoons salt

Pick over the rice, place in a sieve and wash under cold
running water until the water runs clear. Drain well.

Pick over the lentils to remove any small stones and
discoloured seeds. Place in a bowl of water and remove any
that float. Wash the lentils well and drain thoroughly.

Heat the ghee or oil in a heavy-based saucepan and
gently fry the onion until translucent and lightly flecked
with brown. Add the rice and lentils and stir over medium
heat for 3 minutes.

Add 1 litre (34 fl oz/4 cups) boiling water and the salt.
Return to the boil, stirring occasionally. Reduce the heat to
low, then cover and simmer gently for 45 minutes.

Remove the pan from the heat. Take off the lid and place
two paper towels over the rim of the pan. Replace the lid and
set aside for 10–15 minutes before serving.

Serve as a rice accompaniment to meat and fish dishes,
or as directed in recipes.

SHAURABAT ADAS
Lentil soup

SERVES: 6

375 g (13 oz/1½ cups) small red lentils

60 g (2 oz/¼ cup) ghee, or 60 ml (2 fl oz/¼ cup) oil

1 large onion, finely chopped

4–5 garlic cloves, crushed

2 teaspoons Baharat (page 344)

500 g (1 lb 2 oz/2 cups) chopped,
   peeled tomatoes

2 *loomi* (dried limes; see page 345), or thinly peeled
   rind of ½ lemon

100 g (3½ oz/1 cup) crushed fine noodles,
   optional

salt, to taste

Pick over the lentils, place in a sieve and rinse under cold running water. Tip into a large large saucepan and pour in 1.5 litres (51 fl oz/6 cups) water. Bring to the boil, skimming if necessary.

Meanwhile, heat the ghee or oil in a frying pan and gently fry the onion until translucent, but not brown. Stir in the garlic and Baharat, cook for a few seconds, then add the tomatoes.

Once the lentils have come to the boil, add the onion mixture to the pan. Pierce each dried lime twice with a skewer and add them to the pan.

Return to the boil and allow to boil gently, uncovered, for 40 minutes. Add the noodles, salt to taste, and a little more water if the soup looks too thick.

Simmer gently for a further 25–30 minutes, uncovered, stirring occasionally, until the lentils and noodles are tender.

Serve hot in deep bowls with Khoubiz (page 264), salad and pickles (page 343).

MAZZA BISHURBA
Lamb knuckle soup

SERVES: 6

4 lamb shanks (knuckles)

1 *loomi* (dried lime; see page 345)

1 large onion, finely chopped

40 g (1½ oz) ghee or 2 tablespoons oil

1 tablespoon Baharat (page 344)

2 small pieces of cinnamon bark

375 g (13 oz/1½ cups) chopped, peeled tomatoes

salt and freshly ground black pepper,
   to season

100 g (3½ oz/½ cup) good-quality long-grain
   white rice, preferably basmati

Wash the lamb shanks if necessary, place in a large saucepan and pour in 2 litres (68 fl oz/8 cups) cold water. Pierce the dried lime on each side with a skewer and add to the pan.

Bring to a slow simmer over medium heat, skimming frequently as the scum rises. When well skimmed and almost boiling, cover and simmer over low heat for 30 minutes.

Heat the ghee in a frying pan and gently fry the onion until translucent. Add the Baharat and cinnamon and fry for a further 3 minutes. Add the onion mixture to the soup.

Stir in the tomatoes and season with salt and pepper. Cover and simmer for 1½ hours.

Remove and discard the lime and cinnamon. Lift out the lamb shanks and trim off the meat. Cut the meat into small pieces and return to the soup.

Pick over the rice, wash well and stir into the soup. Cover and simmer gently for a further 30 minutes, or until the rice is very tender.

Serve hot, with Khoubiz (page 264).

SAMAK QUWARMAH
Fish curry
SERVES: 6

750 g (1 lb 10 oz) fish steaks or fillets

salt, to season

40 g (1½ oz) ghee, or 2 tablespoons oil

2 onions, chopped

1 teaspoon grated fresh ginger

2 garlic cloves, crushed

½ teaspoon ground hot chilli or chilli powder

1 teaspoon Baharat (page 344)

1 teaspoon ground turmeric

1 small piece of cinnamon bark

2 *loomi* (dried limes; see page 345), or thinly peeled
   rind of ½ lemon

250 g (9 oz/1 cup) chopped, peeled tomatoes

For serving

Muhammar (page 348) or Mashkoul (page 349)

Wipe the fish dry with paper towels, cut into serving pieces and sprinkle lightly with salt. Cover and set aside in a cool place.

Heat the ghee or oil in a heavy-based saucepan and gently fry the onion until translucent. Add the ginger, garlic, chilli, Baharat, turmeric and cinnamon and stir for 2 minutes.

Pierce each dried lime twice with a skewer and add them, or the lemon rind to the pan. Add the tomatoes and 125 ml (4 fl oz/½ cup) water, season with salt and bring to a slow simmer. Cover and simmer gently for 15 minutes.

Place the fish pieces in the sauce, then cover and simmer gently for 15–20 minutes, or until the fish is cooked through.

Lift the fish onto a bed of Muhammar or Mashkoul. Remove the cinnamon and limes or lemon rind from the sauce and spoon the sauce over the fish.

SAMAK MAHSHI
Fried stuffed fish
SERVES: 4–6

1 kg (2 lb 3 oz) small whole fish, scaled and gutted

1 teaspoon salt

40 g (1½ oz) ghee or 2 tablespoons oil

1 large onion, finely chopped

2 garlic cloves, finely chopped

½ teaspoon ground *loomi* (dried lime; see page 345),
   or grated zest of ½ lemon

1½ teaspoons Baharat (page 344)

½ teaspoon ground turmeric

To finish

oil, for pan-frying

flour, for coating

flat-leaf parsley sprigs, to garnish

lemon wedges, to serve

Rub the cavity of the fish with a wad of paper towels dipped in salt to clean it thoroughly. Rinse the fish and dry well.

Heat the ghee in a frying pan and gently fry the onion and garlic until lightly browned. Stir in the ground *loomi* and 1 teaspoon of the Baharat. Season with salt and remove from the heat.

Stuff the fish with the onion mixture, placing a small wad of greaseproof (parchment) paper or foil in the opening to keep the stuffing in.

Combine the remaining Baharat with the turmeric and the 1 teaspoon salt. Rub the spice mixture over the fish, then set aside for 15 minutes to absorb the flavours.

Heat 1 cm (½ inch) oil in a large frying pan over medium heat. Coat the fish lightly in flour and shallow-fry until cooked through.

Drain on paper towels and garnish with parsley. Serve hot, with lemon wedges.

❧ *Note: In Bahrain, curry powder is often used instead of* baharat.

CHEBEH RUBYAN
Prawn balls

SERVES: 4–6

1 kg (2 lb 3 oz) raw prawns (shrimp)

25 g (¾ oz/¾ cup) coriander (cilantro) leaves

½ teaspoon ground turmeric

½ teaspoon ground *loomi* (dried lime; see page 345),
    optional

150 g (5 oz/¾ cup) rice flour

1 teaspoon salt

Filling

40 g (1½ oz) ghee or 2 tablespoons oil

1 large onion, finely chopped

1 teaspoon Baharat (page 344)

½ teaspoon ground *loomi* (dried lime; see page 345),
    or grated zest of ½ lemon

Tamarind sauce

1 piece of tamarind paste, the size of a small egg

1 small onion, finely chopped

20 g (¾ oz) ghee or 1 tablespoon oil

1 large tomato, peeled (see page 522) and chopped

1 teaspoon Baharat (page 344)

¼–½ teaspoon ground hot chilli or chilli powder

2 teaspoons sugar

salt, to season

For serving

cooked prawns (shrimp), to garnish

coriander (cilantro) sprigs, to garnish

Muhammar (page 348)

Shell and devein the prawns, then rinse and dry well. Combine the prawns and coriander leaves and pass through a food grinder using a fine screen, or process to a paste in a food processor using a steel blade.

Empty the prawn mixture into a mixing bowl and sprinkle with the turmeric, ground *loomi*, if using, and rice flour. Add the salt and mix well with your hands until thoroughly combined. Cover and refrigerate until required.

To make the filling, heat the ghee in a frying pan and gently fry the onion until translucent. Stir in the Baharat and ground *loomi*, or lemon zest. Remove from the heat and set aside while making the tamarind sauce.

Soak the tamarind in 250 ml (8½ fl oz/1 cup) warm water for 10 minutes, then rub with your fingers. Pass the mixtre through a sieve, pressing the pulp through with the back of a spoon. Reserve the tamarind liquid.

In a large, heavy-based saucepan, gently fry the onion in the ghee until translucent. Stir in the tamarind liquid, 250 ml (8½ fl oz/1 cup) warm water, the tomato, spices, sugar and salt to season. Cover and simmer gently for 15–20 minutes.

While the sauce is simmering, make the prawn balls. Take about 1 tablespoon of the prawn paste and flatten it in a moistened palm. Place 1 teaspoon of the filling in the centre and close it up, shaping it into a ball. Keep your hands moist during the shaping. Repeat with the remaining prawn mixture and filling.

Drop the prawn balls into the simmering sauce, then cover and simmer gently for 35–40 minutes. The prawn balls will swell during cooking.

Garnish with some cooked prawns and coriander sprigs and serve hot, with Muhammar.

MACHBOUS
Spiced prawns and rice

SERVES: 4–5

1 kg (2 lb 3 oz) raw prawns (shrimp)

40–60 g (1½–2 oz) ghee or 2–3 tablespoons oil

2 garlic cloves, chopped

1 large onion, chopped

2 teaspoons Baharat (page 344)

1 teaspoon ground turmeric

375 g (13 oz/1½) cups chopped, peeled tomatoes

1 tablespoon chopped flat-leaf parsley

1 teaspoon chopped coriander (cilantro) leaves

2 teaspoons salt

freshly ground black pepper, to taste

400 g (14 oz/2 cups) basmati or other good-quality
    long-grain white rice

Shell the prawns and devein them if necessary.

In a large, heavy-based saucepan, heat 20 g (¾ oz) of the ghee with the garlic. Add the prawns and stir over medium–high heat until the prawns stiffen and turn pink — there is no need to cook them through. Lift them out of the pan and set aside.

Add the remaining ghee to the pan and gently fry the onion until translucent and lightly browned.

Stir in the Baharat and turmeric and fry for 1 minute.

Add the tomatoes, herbs and salt and season to taste with pepper. Bring to the boil and pour in 625 ml (21 fl oz/2½ cups) water. Cover and boil over medium heat for 5 minutes.

Place the rice in a sieve and wash under cold running water until the water runs clear. Stir the rice into the sauce and bring to the boil. Cover and leave to boil for 10 minutes. Reduce the heat to low.

Stir the pan contents, then place the prawns on top of the rice, stirring them in gently. Cover and simmer gently over low heat for 20 minutes, stirring halfway through cooking.

Stir again, then take the pan off the heat and leave covered for 5 minutes.

Serve with Khoubiz (page 264), pickles (page 343) and salad.

SAMAK MASHWI
Barbecued fish with dates

SERVES: 6

The traditional Gulf way to grill fish is in a special cut-away dome-shaped clay barbecue with glowing coals in the base. The fish is impaled on a firm stick, with the stick passing through the mouth and into the body.

The end of the stick protruding from the mouth is stuck into the earth under the bed of coals, at a 45 degree angle. Perhaps you could try a similar method, using a fire beneath a low grill, with galvanised iron set around three sides to deflect the heat.

The dates give the fish a very pleasant flavour.

180 g (6 oz/1 cup) dried pitted dates
6 whole firm-fleshed fish, each about
    375 g (13 oz), gutted
salt, for sprinkling
2 large onions, finely chopped
2 garlic cloves, crushed, optional
1½ teaspoons Baharat (page 344)
1 teaspoon ground turmeric

Cover the dates with cold water and leave to soak for 30 minutes, or until soft. At the same time, soak six wooden skewers or about 18 cocktail sticks in cold water for 30 minutes to stop them scorching.

Meanwhile, rinse the fish cavities and dry with paper towels. Sprinkle with salt, inside and out, and leave for 15 minutes or longer.

In a mixing bowl, combine the onion, garlic, if using, and the spices. Add a little water and mix together well.

Fill the fish cavities with the onion mixture and close the cavities with the soaked wooden skewers or cocktail sticks.

Rub the dates through a sieve to purée them, adding some of the soaking water, or purée in a blender or food processor, adding enough soaking liquid to make a soft paste.

Spread the date purée on each side of each fish and leave on a wire rack for 10 minutes.

Cook the fish over glowing charcoal for 4–5 minutes each side, depending on the thickness of the body.

Serve hot. The skin, with the scales attached, is removed before eating.

❁ *Note: Choose a fish suitable for barbecuing, preferably a round-bodied variety such as red mullet. Do not have them scaled — the scales keep the flesh intact during grilling.*

QUWARMAH ALA DAJAJ
Curried chicken

SERVES: 5–6

1 chicken, about 1.5 kg (3 lb 5 oz), jointed

salt, for sprinkling

1½ teaspoons Baharat (page 344)

1 teaspoon ground turmeric

60 g (2 oz/¼ cup) ghee or 3 tablespoons oil

2 large onions, finely chopped

2 garlic cloves, crushed

1 teaspoon grated fresh ginger

1 small piece of cinnamon bark

¼–½ teaspoon ground hot chilli or chilli powder

2 *loomi* (dried limes; see page 345), or thinly peeled rind of ½ lemon

250 g (9 oz/1 cup) chopped, peeled tomatoes

For serving

Muhammar (page 348) or Mashkoul (page 349)

Cut the chicken joints into smaller pieces if desired. Wipe them dry and sprinkle with salt. Combine the Baharat and turmeric and rub half the mixture over the chicken pieces. Leave to absorb for 15 minutes.

Heat the ghee in a large, heavy-based saucepan. Working in batches if necessary, brown the chicken pieces on each side, removing each batch to a plate.

Add the onion to the pan and gently fry until translucent. Add the garlic, ginger, remaining spice mixture, cinnamon, and chilli to taste. Fry for 5 minutes, stirring often.

Pierce each dried lime twice with a skewer and add them, or the lemon rind to the pan. Add the tomatoes, 185 ml (6½ fl oz/¾ cup) water and salt to taste, then bring to the boil.

Add the chicken pieces, reduce the heat to low and cover the pan tightly. Simmer very gently for 1½–2 hours, or until chicken is tender and the sauce is thick.

Serve hot with Muhammar or Mashkoul.

MACHBOUS ALA DAJAJ
Spiced chicken and rice

SERVES: 4–5

40 g (1½ oz) ghee or 2 tablespoons oil

2 large onions, chopped

1 tablespoon Baharat (page 344)

1 teaspoon ground turmeric

1 chicken, about 1.5 kg (3 lb 5 oz), jointed

375 g (13 oz/1½ cups) chopped, peeled tomatoes

3 cloves

½ teaspoon ground *loomi* (dried lime; see page 345), or grated zest of ½ lemon

2 pieces of cinnamon bark

6 cardamom pods

3 teaspoons salt

400 g (14 oz/2 cups) basmati or other good-quality long-grain white rice

2 tablespoons chopped coriander (cilantro) leaves

2 tablespoons chopped flat-leaf parsley

Heat the ghee or oil in a large heavy-based saucepan and gently fry the onion until translucent. Stir in the Baharat and turmeric and cook for 2 minutes longer.

Add the chicken pieces and turn in the onion mixture over medium heat to brown lightly. Add the tomatoes, cloves, ground *loomi*, or lemon zest, cinnamon, cardamom pods and salt, stirring well to combine.

Pour in 625 ml (21 fl oz/2½ cups) water, then cover and simmer over gentle heat for 45 minutes.

Pick over the rice to remove any discoloured grains. Place in a bowl and wash with cold water until the water runs clear. Drain. Stir the rice gently into the stew, add the herbs and bring back to a slow simmer.

Cover and simmer over low heat for 35–40 minutes, or until the chicken is tender, stirring gently once or twice during cooking. Remove from the heat and leave for 10 minutes.

Pile the mixture onto a large platter, arranging the chicken pieces in the centre. Serve hot with pickles (page 343), salad and Khoubiz (page 264).

KABAB MASHWI
Minced meat kebab

SERVES: 8

It is quite a sight to see these flavoursome kebabs being prepared in the Gulf States, with many shops and food stalls specialising in them.

Lightning-quick hands shape the herbed and spiced meat paste onto long, flat skewers. Iron troughs running the length of the shop glow hotly with their charcoal fires ready to cook the kebabs quickly to juicy tenderness. The skewers sit across the top of the troughs in neat formation, with the cooks working their way up and down the passageway between, turning the skewers or removing them when cooked.

The finished kebab is deftly slid off the skewer onto soft, flat *khoubiz*; shredded lettuce, sliced tomato, chopped onion and cucumber are added and it is handed to the waiting customer. Hamburger Gulf style!

1 kg (2 lb 3 oz) minced (ground) lamb or beef

1 handful coarsely chopped flat-leaf parsley

2 large onions, chopped

2 teaspoons salt

2 teaspoons Baharat (page 344)

oil, for brushing

To serve

Khoubiz (page 264)

cos (romaine) lettuce, in leaves or shredded

sliced tomatoes

sliced cucumber

finely chopped onion or spring onions (scallions)

In a mixing bowl, combine the meat, parsley, onion, salt and Baharat. Pass the mixture through a meat grinder twice, using a fine screen; alternatively, process the mixture in four batches in a food processor, using a steel blade.

Turn the mixture into a bowl. If a meat grinder was used, knead the mixture to a smooth paste by hand; if the mixture was processed, knead it to combine the flavours evenly.

Moisten your hands with water. Take generous tablespoons of the paste and mould it around flat, sword-like skewers, in finger shapes about 10 cm (4 inches) long. Place two such shapes on long skewers, or just one shape if the skewers are short. Keep your hands moistened during shaping.

As the skewers are prepared, set them across a baking dish, with the ends of the skewers resting on each side.

Have a charcoal fire at the glowing stage and remove the grill if possible. A rectangular barbecue such as the Japanese *hibachi* is an advantage here, as medium-length skewers will fit across it without the need for a grill.

Brush the kebabs lightly with oil and grill for 2–3 minutes, turning frequently. If it is impossible to cook the kebabs without a grill, then try to place the skewers so the meat lies between the grill bars.

Remove the cooked kebabs from the skewers and serve immediately in warmed Khoubiz, with salad ingredients.

They may also be served on a plate with a vegetable or salad accompaniment.

THARYD
Braised meat and potatoes

SERVES: 5–6

1 kg (2 lb 3 oz) boneless lamb or beef stewing meat

40 g (1½ oz) ghee, or 2 tablespoons oil

2 large onions, chopped

2 teaspoons Baharat (page 344)

1 garlic clove, crushed

500 g (1 lb 2 oz/2 cups) chopped, peeled tomatoes

60 g (2 oz/¼ cup) tomato paste (concentrated purée)

2 teaspoons salt

½ teaspoon freshly ground black pepper

3 teaspoons chopped flat-leaf parsley, plus extra to garnish

750 g (1 lb 10 oz) potatoes

Khoubiz (page 264)

Trim the meat and cut into cubes. Set aside.

Heat the ghee or oil in a heavy-based saucepan and gently fry the onion until translucent. Increase the heat and add the meat. Stir until the meat loses its red colour, then add the Baharat and garlic and cook for 1 minute.

Add the tomatoes, tomato paste, salt, pepper and parsley. Cover and simmer very gently for 1½ hours.

Peel the potatoes, and halve them if large. Add them to the pan, then cover and simmer for a further 1 hour.

Cut the Khoubiz into small pieces and place in a serving dish. Ladle the meat, potatoes and sauce over the top and sprinkle with some extra chopped parsley.

Serve hot with salad and pickles (page 343).

LAHM BIL BAYD
Minced meat with hard-boiled eggs

SERVES: 3–6

500 g (1 lb 2 oz) minced (ground) lamb

1 small onion, chopped

3 tablespoons finely chopped flat-leaf parsley

40 g (1½ oz/½ cup) soft breadcrumbs

salt and freshly ground black pepper, to taste

To finish

6 hard-boiled eggs

1 egg white

1 egg

100 g (3½ oz/1 cup) dry breadcrumbs

oil, for deep-frying

Dukkous al-Tamat (page 344), to serve, optional

Combine the lamb with the onion and pass it through a meat grinder twice using a fine screen; alternatively, process to a paste in a food processor, using a steel blade.

Turn the mixture into a bowl and add the parsley and breadcrumbs. Season with salt and pepper and knead to a fairly soft paste. Divide into six equal portions.

Shell the hard-boiled eggs. Beat the egg white and egg in separate small bowls; spread the breadcrumbs on a small plate.

Coat the eggs with the beaten egg white. Shape a portion of the meat paste around each egg, moulding it on smoothly.

Now brush the meat-coated eggs with the beaten whole egg, then roll them in the breadcrumbs to coat.

In a large saucepan, heat about 10 cm (4 inches) of oil to 160°C (320°F) or until a cube of bread dropped into the oil browns in 30-35 seconds. Deep-fry the meat-coated eggs, cooking for 5–7 minutes in all, and turning to brown evenly. Do not have the oil too hot, or it will brown the outside before the inside is cooked.

Cut in half and serve hot with Dukkous al-Tamat, if desired, or cold with salad.

KUBA AL-AISH
Stuffed meat rolls

SERVES: 4

500 g (1 lb 2 oz) lean lamb or mutton

280 g (10 oz/1½ cups) boiled and strained
    short-grain white rice

2 garlic cloves, chopped

1½ teaspoons Baharat (page 344)

1½ teaspoons salt

1 egg, beaten

oil, for pan-frying

Filling

55 g (2 oz/¼ cup) yellow split peas, washed

20 g (¾ oz) ghee

2 onions, finely chopped

30 g (1 oz/¼ cup) sultanas (golden raisins)

¼ teaspoon ground cardamom

½ teaspoon Baharat (page 344)

salt, to season

To make the filling, gently boil the split peas in a small saucepan with 250 ml (8½ fl oz/1 cup) water for 45 minutes, or until tender. Drain.

Meanwhile, heat the ghee in a frying pan and gently fry the onion until translucent and beginning to brown. Stir in the sultanas and spices.

Add the split peas, season with salt and set aside.

Chop the meat into small pieces and combine in a mixing bowl with the rice, garlic, Baharat and salt. Pass the mixture through a meat grinder twice, using a fine screen; alternatively, process the mixture in two batches in a food processor, using a steel blade. If a grinder was used, beat the mixture to a paste-like consistency.

Take a lump of the meat mixture, about the size of a small egg. Coat your palms with the beaten egg and shape the meat smoothly into a ball. Using a thumb, make a hollow in the ball, moulding the meat to a fairly thin shell. Fill with the filling, then press the opening firmly to close. Reshape into either an oval or an oblong shape with rounded edges. Place on a tray and repeat with the remaining meat mixture and filling.

Heat about 1 cm (½ inch) oil in a frying pan over medium heat. Fry the rolls for about 5 minutes each side. Drain on paper towels.

Serve hot with salad and flat bread.

BASAL MAHSHI
Stuffed onions

SERVES: 6–8 AS A MAIN COURSE, 12 AS AN APPETISER

1 walnut-sized piece of tamarind paste

5 large onions

1 tablespoon oil or melted ghee

salt, for sprinkling

2 teaspoons sugar

Stuffing

750 g (1 lb 10 oz) minced (ground) beef or lamb

100 g (3½ oz/½ cup) long-grain white rice, rinsed

1½ teaspoons Baharat (page 344)

½ teaspoon ground turmeric

125 g (4 oz/½ cup) chopped, peeled tomatoes

2 tablespoons tomato paste (concentrated purée)

2 tablespoons chopped flat-leaf parsley

1 tablespoon oil

salt and freshly ground black pepper, to season

Soak the tamarind in 125 ml (4 fl oz/½ cup) warm water for 30 minutes. Strain into a bowl, pressing with the back of a spoon to separate the pulp. Reserve the liquid and discard the seeds and fibres.

Peel the onions and carefully cut out the root with a pointed knife. Slit the onion on one side through to the centre, cutting from the top to the root end.

Drop the onions into a saucepan of boiling water and boil gently for 8–10 minutes, or until softened. Drain and cool.

In a mixing bowl, thoroughly combine the filling ingredients and season with salt and pepper.

Carefully separate the onion layers. The outer layers may be cut in half; leave the inner layers intact.

Place about a tablespoonful of the filling on each onion layer, then roll each one up firmly.

Grease a heavy-based saucepan with the oil or melted ghee. Pack the rolls in the pan, seam side down, lightly sprinkling each layer with salt.

Combine the reserved tamarind liquid with the sugar and 125 ml (4 fl oz/½ cup) warm water, then pour over the rolls. Invert a heavy plate on top of the rolls to keep them intact during cooking. Cover and bring to a simmer over medium heat.

Reduce the heat to low and simmer gently for 1½ hours.

Serve hot with salads, pickles (page 343) and Khoubiz (page 264), or lukewarm as an appetiser.

KHOUZI
Baked whole lamb

SERVES: 20

1 small lamb, about 10–12 kg (22–26 lb)

salt, for rubbing

2 tablespoons Baharat (page 344), plus extra for the chicken,
   if using

1 teaspoon ground turmeric, plus extra for the chicken,
   if using

1 small chicken, about 1 kg (2 lb 3 oz), optional

3 shelled hard-boiled eggs, optional

125 g (4 oz/½ cup) ghee, melted

Rice stuffing

2 teaspoons saffron threads, pounded

125 ml (4 fl oz/½ cup) rosewater

1 kg (2 lb 3 oz/5 cups) basmati or other good-quality
   long-grain white rice

125 g (4 oz/½ cup) ghee

3 large onions, finely chopped

2 tablespoons Baharat (page 344)

1 teaspoon ground turmeric

salt, to taste

155 g (5 oz/1 cup) blanched almonds or
   cashew nuts

80 g (3 oz/½ cup) pine nuts

75 g (2½ oz/½ cup) pistachio nuts

60 g (2 oz/½ cup) sultanas (golden raisins)

Wipe the lamb inside and out with a damp cloth. Rub the
cavity and outer surface with salt, the Baharat and turmeric.

If a chicken is being used, wipe it dry with paper towels and
rub the cavity and skin with a little extra Baharat, turmeric and
salt. Insert the shelled hard-boiled eggs in the chicken cavity.

Set the lamb and chicken aside while preparing the
rice stuffing.

Soak the pounded saffron in the rosewater for 10 minutes.
Pick over the rice, place in a sieve and wash well under cold
running water. Drain and set aside.

Melt the ghee in a large saucepan and gently fry the onion
until translucent. Stir in the Baharat and turmeric, then add
the rice and stir over medium heat for 5 minutes.

Pour in 1.25 litres (42½ fl oz/5 cups) water and bring to the
boil, stirring occasionally. Add salt to taste, reduce the heat,
then cover and simmer over low heat for 10 minutes.

Fold the nuts and sultanas through the rice, then sprinkle
with half the rosewater mixture. Cover and leave off the heat
for 10 minutes, until the liquid has been absorbed.

Meanwhile, preheat the oven to 180°C (350°F/Gas 4).

Spoon some of the rice stuffing into the chicken, filling it
loosely. Secure the opening with wooden skewers.

Sew up the cavity of the lamb halfway with kitchen string and
leave the thread hanging. Fill the cavity with some of the rice
stuffing, put the chicken in, if using, and fill with the
remaining stuffing. Finish sewing up the cavity.

Place the lamb on a large rack over a very large catering-size
baking dish. Brush the lamb with the melted ghee. Cover the
dish with large sheets of foil, sealing the joins with double
folds. Press the foil under the edge to seal completely.

Transfer to the oven and bake for 2 hours. Baste the lamb
with the juices in the dish and pour the remaining rosewater
mixture over the lamb.

Cover and bake for a further 2–3 hours, or until very tender,
basting twice more with the baking juices, and removing the
foil 30 minutes before the end of cooking.

Lift the lamb onto a large platter. Remove the string and
spoon the stuffing out onto the platter. Set the chicken, if used,
on top of the stuffing. The lamb can be carved — but it is much
more fun to break off very soft tender chunks of meat.

Enjoy your feast and feel like a sheikh!

❁ *Note: Kid may be used instead of lamb.*

KEBAT AL BATATIS WAL BURKUL
Burghul and potato cakes with lamb and apricot filling
SERVES: 6

4 potatoes, about 500 g (1 lb 2 oz) in total, scrubbed

130 g (4½ oz/¾ cup) fine burghul (bulgur)

35 g (1¼ oz/¼ cup) plain (all-purpose) flour

1 egg, beaten

salt and freshly ground black pepper, to season

oil, for deep-frying

Lamb and apricot filling

40 g (1½ oz) ghee, or 2 tablespoons oil

1 large onion, finely chopped

500 g (1 lb 2 oz) finely minced (ground) lamb

40 g (1½ oz/¼ cup) chopped almonds

90 g (3 oz/½ cup) chopped dried apricots

½ teaspoon Baharat (page 344), optional

salt and freshly ground black pepper, to season

Boil the potatoes in their jackets until tender. Drain, allow to cool, then remove the skins. Place in a mixing bowl and mash.

Meanwhile, place the burghul in a bowl and cover with 500 ml (17 fl oz/2 cups) cold water. Soak for 15 minutes. Strain through a fine sieve, pressing with the back of a spoon to extract the moisture.

Add the burghul to the potato, along with the flour and egg. Season with salt and pepper and mix thoroughly to a paste. Moisten your hands and shape tablespoons of the mixture into balls. Set aside.

To make the filling, heat the ghee or oil in a frying pan and gently fry the onion until translucent. Increase the heat, add the lamb and cook over high heat, stirring often, until the lamb is crumbly and begins to brown.

Reduce the heat to low, stir in the remaining filling ingredients and season with salt and pepper. Stir in 60 ml (2 fl oz/¼ cup) water. Cover and simmer over low heat for 10 minutes, then remove from the heat and cool a little.

Flatten a ball of the potato mixture in the palm of your hand and place a generous teaspoon of filling in the centre. Close up the potato mixture and reshape into a ball, then flatten to a thick cake. Repeat with the remaining ingredients.

Heat approximately 10 cm (4 inches) of oil in a saucepan to (180°C/356°F) or until a cube of bread dropped into the oil browns in 15 seconds. Deep-fry the cakes six at a time for 7–8 minutes, turning to brown evenly. Drain on paper towels and serve hot.

MARAQ AL-BAMIYA
« Meat with okra

SERVES: 5–6

1 walnut-sized piece of tamarind paste

1 kg (2 lb 3 oz) beef or lamb stewing meat

60 ml (2 fl oz/¼ cup) oil

2 large onions, chopped

3 garlic cloves, crushed

375 g (13 oz/1½ cups) chopped, peeled tomatoes

2 teaspoons Baharat (page 344)

2 teaspoons sugar

salt, to season

500 g (1 lb 2 oz) okra

Mashkoul (page 349), to serve

Soak the tamarind in 125 ml (4 fl oz/½ cup) warm water.

Trim the meat and cut into 2 cm (¾ inch) cubes. Heat half the oil in a heavy-based saucepan and brown the meat in batches, removing each batch to a plate.

Heat the remaining oil in the pan and gently fry the onion until translucent. Add the garlic, cook for a few seconds, then stir in the tomatoes, 125 ml (4 fl oz/½ cup) water, the Baharat and sugar. Season with salt.

Return the meat to the pan, then cover and simmer for 1–1½ hours, or until the meat is almost tender. The time will depend on the type of meat used.

Prepare the okra as directed on page 8. Rub the tamarind to separate the pulp from the seeds and fibres, then pass through a sieve, reserving the liquid.

Arrange the okra on top of the meat and pour the tamarind liquid over the top. Cover and simmer for a further 30 minutes, or until the meat and okra are tender. Do not stir once the okra is added — just shake the pan gently to distribute the flavours.

Serve with Mashkoul or another simple rice dish.

MACHBOUS
Spiced lamb and rice

SERVES: 4–5

40 g (1½ oz) ghee

2 large onions, chopped

1 tablespoon Baharat (page 344)

1 teaspoon ground turmeric

1.5 kg (3 lb 5 oz) lamb shoulder, on the bone, cut into 4–5 pieces

375 g (13 oz/1½ cups) chopped, peeled tomatoes

3 cloves

½ teaspoon ground *loomi* (dried lime; see page 345) or grated zest of ½ lemon

2 pieces of cinnamon bark

3 cardamom pods

3 teaspoons salt

3 teaspoons chopped flat-leaf parsley or coriander (cilantro)

400 g (14 oz/2 cups) basmati or other good-quality long-grain white rice

Heat the ghee in a heavy-based saucepan and gently fry the onion until translucent and beginning to brown. Stir in the Baharat and turmeric and cook for 2 minutes longer.

Add the lamb pieces and turn them in the onion mixture over medium heat, lightly browning the meat. Add the tomatoes, spices and salt, stirring well to combine. Cover and simmer for 10 minutes.

Add 625 ml (21 fl oz/2½ cups) water and the parsley or coriander. Cover and simmer over gentle heat for 2–2½ hours, or until the meat is fork tender.

Pick over the rice if necessary, then place in a bowl or sieve and wash until the water runs clear. Drain and stir gently into the stew. Return to the boil, reduce the heat and cover tightly.

Simmer for 20 minutes, stirring once or twice during cooking. When the rice is cooked, stir carefully once more, then cover and leave off the heat for 5 minutes.

Pile the mixture onto a large platter, arranging the meat pieces in the centre. Serve hot with pickles (page 343), salad and Khoubiz (page 264).

TAMAR
Dates

Not so long ago the date palm was the fountain of life to the people of the Gulf region – their fruit for trade and sustenance, the palm itself for building materials, household and personal articles, and for fuel. Indeed it is still revered by many today.

In Oman the date is enjoyed in simple ways, which is all this nectar-sweet fruit requires. Fresh dates are dipped in Samneh (clarified butter; page 253) or ghee, or eaten with camel milk curds. The date molasses gathered after drying the fruit also features in Omani cooking, for making a sweetbread (right) or adding to Muhammar (page 348).

To enjoy the date all year round, various sweetbreads are made. The simplest is dates formed into a ball and rolled in ash as a protection against insects. Other date recipes also follow.

TAMAR AL GIBNA
Dates with white cheese
SERVES: 6

750 g (1 lb 10 oz) fresh dates
500 g (1 lb 2 oz) Mizithra (page 27), Anari (page 109) or
   ricotta cheese, or 500 g (1 lb 2 oz/2 cups) yoghurt

Pit the dates and place in individual dishes. Serve with the cheese or yoghurt.

AL BATHEETH
Date sweetbread
MAKES: 20

150 g (5 oz/1 cup) wholemeal (whole-wheat) flour
60 g (2 oz/¼ cup) ghee or Samneh (page 253)
1 cardamom pod, bruised
160 g (5½ oz/1 cup) chopped dates
½ teaspoon ground ginger
icing (confectioners') sugar, for sprinkling

Place the flour in a heavy-based saucepan and stir over medium heat until lightly browned — about 10 minutes.

While the flour is browning, heat the ghee or Samneh in a small saucepan with the cardamom pod. Heat for 5 minutes and leave aside.

Add the dates to the flour and heat for 2 minutes, stirring constantly, until the dates feel soft.

Remove the cardamom pod from the ghee and add the ghee to the date mixture. Sprinkle with the ginger and stir until the ghee is evenly distributed — the mixture will be crumbly. Remove from the heat and leave until cool enough to handle.

Take about a tablespoonful of the mixture at a time and knead by hand, tossing from one hand to the other. When the mixture holds together, squeeze it into an oval shape, moulding it smoothly. Place on a plate and repeat with the remaining mixture.

Leave until cool, then pack in an airtight container.
Serve sprinkled with icing sugar.

RANGINA
Fresh date sweet

SERVES: 6

500 g (1 lb 2 oz) fresh dates
125 g (4 oz/½ cup) butter
110 g (3¾ oz/¾ cup) plain (all-purpose) flour
1 teaspoon ground cardamom

Pit the dates and arrange them in individual dessert dishes.

Melt the butter in a heavy-based saucepan and stir in the flour. Cook over medium heat, stirring constantly, until the flour turns golden brown — take care not to burn it.

Remove from the heat and stir in the cardamom. Leave to cool a little, stirring occasionally as it cools.

Pour the warm butter mixture over the dates. Allow to cool to room temperature before serving.

❀ *Note: Stirring chopped walnuts into the browned flour will add a delightful taste and texture.*

NASHAB
Fried nut rolls

MAKES: ABOUT 40

10 sheets fillo pastry
ghee or oil, for deep-frying

Nut filling
100 g (3½ oz/1 cup) finely ground cashew nuts
115 g (4 oz/1 cup) finely ground walnuts
115 g (4 oz/½ cup) caster (superfine) sugar
1–1½ teaspoons ground cardamom

Combine the nut filling ingredients in a mixing bowl, adding the cardamom to taste.

Cut the pastry sheets into quarters, into pieces about 15 cm (6 inches) wide and 20 cm (8 inches) long. Stack them and cover with a cloth.

Take a strip of pastry and place it on a work surface, with the narrow edge towards you. Thinly sprinkle 2 teaspoons of the nut filling across the base of the strip, keeping 1 cm (½ inch) of pastry clear of the filling at the sides and base.

Moisten the sides of the strip with water. Fold the sides over the filling, pressing the folds along the length of the sides. Roll up firmly to within 5 cm (2 inches) of the end of the strip. Moisten this section lightly and evenly with water, then complete the roll.

Repeat using the remaining ingredients, placing the completed rolls on a cloth.

Heat the oil or ghee in a deep saucepan to 180°C (356°F), or until a cube of bread dropped into the oil browns in 15 seconds.

Deep-fry the rolls, five at a time, for 2–3 minutes, turning to brown evenly. When the rolls are deep golden brown, remove with a slotted spoon and drain on paper towels.

Allow to cool before serving. Store in a sealed container at room temperature.

AL-SALOOQ
« Fried cardamom sweetbreads
MAKES: 24

125 ml (4 fl oz/½ cup) milk
300 g (10½ oz/2 cups) plain (all-purpose) flour
1 teaspoon baking powder
½ teaspoon ground cardamom
125 g (4 oz/½ cup) butter, melted
oil, for deep-frying
sifted icing (confectioners') sugar, for sprinkling

Bring the milk to the boil, then leave to cool.

Sift the flour, baking powder and cardamom into a mixing bowl. Add the melted butter and stir with a wooden spoon until combined and crumbly.

Pour in the cooled milk and mix to a soft dough. Knead lightly for 1 minute, or until smooth.

Roll the dough into walnut-sized balls. Roll them into thick fingers, then press each one around a forefinger to make a crescent shape.

Heat the oil to 180°C (356°F), or until a cube of bread dropped into the oil browns in 15 seconds. Add six *salooq* at a time and fry for 5 minutes, turning to brown evenly.

Lift out with a slotted spoon and drain on paper towels.

After two batches are cooked, place the *salooq* in a bag of icing sugar and shake to coat. Lift them out.

Cook and coat the remaining *salooq*. Serve warm or cold.

GHIRAYBAH
Shortbread cookies
MAKES: 35–40

250 g (9 oz/1 cup) Samneh (page 253)
125 g (4 oz/1 cup) icing (confectioners') sugar, sifted
375 g (13 oz/2½ cups) plain (all-purpose) flour

The Samneh needs to be firm, so chill it in the refrigerator if it is soft. Place the firm Samneh in a mixing bowl and beat until light. Gradually add the icing sugar, beating until very creamy and light.

Sift the flour and fold it into the Samneh mixture. Knead lightly until smooth. If your kitchen is hot, chill the dough in the refrigerator for 1–2 hours.

Meanwhile, preheat the oven to 170°C (340°F/Gas 3).

Roll the dough into walnut-sized balls and place on ungreased baking trays. Press a thumb into the centre of each ball to make a dimple and to flatten the dough slightly. Flour your thumb lightly if necessary.

Bake for 20–25 minutes, or until very lightly coloured. Allow to cool on the baking trays.

Store the biscuits in a sealed container. These biscuits are very delicate and must be handled carefully.

❀ *Note: These cookies are prepared in most countries of the Middle East. Sometimes they are topped with pine nuts or a blanched almond instead of being dimpled; cooks in other areas prefer not to let the cookies colour at all; others finish them with a dusting of icing sugar. Outside the Gulf States, caster (superfine) sugar is often used in the mixture rather than icing sugar.*

SAMBOOSA HOLWAH
Fried nut triangles
MAKES: ABOUT 60

Samboosa holwah should be very tiny and literally bulging with sugar and nuts. You might find it difficult to contain the nut filling in the narrow confines of the pastry strip as it is folded. Push the filling in during the first two or three folds — if you go off-course with the shaping, do not be concerned, as the final shape will be near enough to a triangle.

Try one or two strips before cutting all the pastry. If it proves too difficult, cut the remaining strips 5 cm (2 inches) wide, using the same amount of filling.

10 sheets fillo pastry
ghee or oil, for deep-frying

Nut filling
100 g (3½ oz/1 cup) coarsely ground raw cashew nuts
55 g (2 oz/½ cup) coarsely ground walnuts
115 g (4 oz/½ cup) caster (superfine) sugar
½–1 teaspoon ground cardamom

Combine the nut filling ingredients in a mixing bowl, adding the cardamom to taste. Add 2 teaspoons cold water and knead well by hand until the mixture clings together in a coarse paste.

Cut the pastry sheets into 4 cm (1½ inch) strips, across the width of the sheet. The strips may be a little longer or shorter, according to the size of the sheet. Cover the strips with a cloth.

Take a strip of pastry and place a teaspoon of filling on one end of the strip. Fold the pastry diagonally over the filling, forming a triangle, then fold it straight over, followed by another diagonal fold in the opposite direction to the first fold (see diagrams on page 17). Continue folding to the end of the strip. Moisten the end of the pastry with water and press together to seal.

Repeat using the remaining ingredients, placing the finished pastries on a cloth.

Heat 10 cm (4 inches) of ghee or oil in a deep saucepan to 180°C (356°F), or until a cube of bread dropped into the oil browns in 15 seconds.

Deep-fry the triangles, 10 at a time, for about 2–3 minutes, turning to brown evenly. The pastries must not cook too quickly, as the inner layers must cook before the outside becomes too brown.

When the pastries are a deep golden brown, remove them with a slotted spoon and drain on paper towels. Leave until cold before serving.

The pastries will keep crisp for a number of days, stored in an airtight container at room temperature.

SABB AL-GAFSHA
Sweet puffs

MAKES: ABOUT 40

2 teaspoons active dried yeast

80 g (3 oz/¾ cup) chickpea flour

75 g (2½ oz/½ cup) plain (all-purpose) flour

3 teaspoons ground rice

5 large eggs, at room temperature

½ teaspoon ground cardamom

¼ teaspoon saffron threads, pounded

60 g (2 oz/¼ cup) ghee, melted and cooled

oil, for deep-frying

Syrup

440 g (15½ oz/2 cups) sugar

2 tablespoons strained lemon juice

½ teaspoon ground cardamom

¼ teaspoon saffron threads, pounded

Add the yeast to 2 tablespoons warm water. Leave to soak, then stir to dissolve.

Sift the chickpea flour, plain flour and ground rice into a mixing bowl and make a well in the centre.

Beat the eggs well and stir in the cardamom, saffron and yeast mixture. Add the mixture to the dry ingredients, pour in the cooled ghee and gradually mix into a thick batter, beating until smooth.

Cover the bowl with plastic wrap and leave in a warm draught-free place for at least 4 hours.

To make the syrup, dissolve the sugar in 500 ml (17 fl oz/ 2 cups) water in a heavy-based saucepan over medium heat, stirring occasionally. Bring to the boil, add the lemon juice, cardamom and saffron and boil for 15 minutes, stirring occasionally. Remove from the heat and leave until cool.

Heat 10 cm (4 inches) of ghee or oil in a deep saucepan to 180°C (356°F) or until a cube of bread dropped into the oil browns in 15 seconds. Stir the dough, then drop teaspoonfuls into the hot oil, pushing it off the end of the spoon with a round-bladed knife. Drop 10–12 balls in at a time and fry for 3–4 minutes, turning to brown evenly.

When golden brown and cooked through, lift the puffs out with a slotted spoon and place in the cooled syrup.

When all the puffs are cooked, stir them in the syrup to coat evenly, then lift out with a slotted spoon and pile onto a plate. Serve warm.

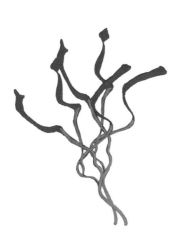

QAHWAT
« Arabic coffee

SERVES: 8

6 cardamom pods
20 g (¾ oz/¼ cup) coarsely pulverised
dark roast coffee

Bruise the cardamom pods by hitting them with a mallet, or pounding them briefly using a mortar and pestle.

Pour 250 ml (8½ fl oz/1 cup) cold water into a long-handled coffee pot and add the cardamom pods and coffee. Bring to the boil, then reduce the heat to low. Leave to simmer over low heat for 20 minutes, so that the coffee grounds settle.

Pour the coffee into Arabic coffee cups, only half-filling the cups. It is traditionally served without sugar.

QAHWAT AL-HILO
Sweet Arabic coffee

SERVES: 6

Although called a coffee, there is no coffee in this exotic brew. It is actually a spice infusion!

3 whole cardamoms
3 teaspoons saffron threads
sugar, to taste

Pound the saffron using a mortar and pestle. Add the cardamom pods and briefly pound them to bruise them.

Transfer the mixture to a small saucepan or large long-handled coffee pot. Add 375 ml (12½ fl oz/1½ cups) water, and sugar to taste. Stir to dissolve the sugar, then leave over low heat for 30 minutes, or until reduced and thickened.

Serve in Arabic coffee cups, filling them to the top.

Yemen

⋯❀⋯

YEMEN

Once known as North and South Yemen, and later as the Arab Republic of Yemen and the Democratic People's Republic of Yemen, the two countries put aside their ideological differences and merged in 1990, becoming the Republic of Yemen. Yemeni hospitality is typically Arabic; indeed, many years ago in a remote part of the Hadramaut to the south, one Yemeni host would be so incensed if travellers passed by without calling that he would shoot over their heads. Perhaps that was going a little too far!

THE FLAVOUR OF YEMENI FOOD

Hot, spicy foods are particularly loved by the Yemenis, so be warned when tackling a recipe calling for chillies.

Zhug (page 382), a hot relish fired with chillies and pepper and flavoured with cardamom, caraway, fresh coriander (cilantro) and garlic, is used as a bread dip. Breads and cereals are the staples of the Yemeni diet, and *zhug*, together with a fenugreek-based mixture called Hilbeh (page 381), add flavour and interest to these foods. *Hilbeh* is used in southern Yemen, while another version called Hulba (page 381) is used in the north. Though the basic ingredients are the same, the preparation is slightly different.

The basic sauce is combined with bone stock and placed on a small fire close to where the meal is eaten. At the end of the meal, any remaining food, such as rice, vegetables, lentils and meat, is added to the pot. The pot is heated and stirred and the resultant hash is scooped up with fresh-baked flat bread, usually Khobz (page 385) or Malvj (page 386). I have given a version in the recipes following as it is a good way to use up leftovers — rather like a Middle Eastern meal of bubble and squeak.

The Yemeni cook makes quite a variety of breads, some leavened with yeast, others somewhat similar to the Indian *chapatti*. One bread much loved by the Yemenis is Malvj, a barley bread, and though recipes vary considerably you will find my version on page 386 an easy bread to make and quite delicious.

Bint-al-Sahn (page 392) is a fine-textured yeast bread formed into very thin 'leaves' and smothered with *samneh* (ghee or clarified butter). The 'leaves' are placed one on top of the other, forming dough cakes, then baked. They are served hot from the oven with more *samneh* and honey, and served at the beginning of a meal on festive occasions and on Fridays, the Muslim holiday. In the early days honey was frequently poured over meat and rice; however, the men allowed this luxury only to themselves, as honey was considered an aphrodisiac and it was thought improper for the womenfolk to partake.

While yoghurt is used in large towns and cities, the Yemenis in remote rural areas use sour milk instead. There is little difference in flavour and no doubt the Yemenis have their particular utensils set aside for making the sour milk. It is impossible for Westerners to make an equivalent, as Western milk is usually pasteurised, a process that kills the bacteria essential for the souring process. I have used yoghurt in these recipes.

Meat and chicken are popular foods, but so little is available that the Yemenis, particularly the poorer ones, would have meat perhaps once a week or even less. However, they do tend to use a lot of bones for basic stock.

Though Mocha is renowned for its coffee, few Yemenis can afford it. Instead they grind the husks and make a very pleasant brew called *qishr* with ground ginger.

EATING YEMENI STYLE

Of all the countries in this book, Yemen has been the least touched by Western customs. Generally, the men eat first and the women and children have their meal afterwards or in another room. A cloth is spread on a carpet and cushions are placed on the floor and around the walls. All the food is placed in pots, platters or bowls, with no separate plates for individual diners. Hands are washed before the meal, which is eaten using the fingers of the right hand. The food is likely to include boiled rice, a cereal dish made of ground sorghum or flour, a soup, cooked and raw vegetables, a hot relish such as *zhug*, and plenty of bread. Fruits are included, when available: though parts of the country are fertile and can grow a variety of fruits such as grapes, mangoes and bananas, the land is not fully productive.

After the meal, any food left is put into the *hulba* dish and heated on the small wood burner, called a *mauqad*, and then scooped out with fresh bread. Soup is passed around in a ladle so that each diner may sip from it to cleanse the palate.

The meal is eaten with little or no conversation and as soon as a person has had enough to eat, he leaves the table and retires to the *mafraj*, a sitting room furnished with carpets and cushions. Here coffee is taken, the *mada'a* (water pipe) shared, and conversation flows.

COOKING METHODS

Much of the cooking is done on fires out of doors. Bread is baked on the sides of a beehive-shaped oven, or on a flat iron over the fire. While traditional cooking vessels were made of iron or carved out of stone, aluminium saucepans and pottery vessels are more likely to be used today. The traditional shape is rather shallow, with a ridge halfway up the side of the vessel, forming two handles, rather like a shallow casserole dish. You will need a heavy-based frying pan or griddle for cooking breads.

INGREDIENTS FOR YEMENI COOKING

Wholemeal (whole-wheat), barley and white flour for breads; dried beans and lentils; beef or lamb; any vegetable used in Middle Eastern cooking; fresh coriander (cilantro), hot chillies, fenugreek, cardamom, black cumin, caraway seeds, turmeric and saffron — with these foods you will be able to duplicate Yemeni cooking. As you probably will not be able to obtain coffee husks, use finely ground mocha coffee for making Qishr (page 393).

HULBA
Fenugreek paste

SERVES: 6

In this recipe you can substitute whatever you have on hand for some of the ingredients, such as diced boiled potatoes for rice, or cooked dried beans for lentils.

3 tablespoons ground fenugreek

2–4 hot chillies, to taste

salt, to taste

1 tomato, peeled (see page 528) and chopped

3 tablespoons chopped onion or spring onions (scallions)

2 garlic cloves, crushed

⅓ teaspoon Hawayij (page 382)

175 g (6 oz/1 cup) finely chopped boiled lamb or chicken

185 g (6½ oz/1 cup) boiled lentils (see note)

185 g (6½ oz/1 cup) boiled rice

1 tablespoon chopped coriander (cilantro) leaves

2 tablespoons oil or 40 g (1½ oz) ghee

bone or chicken stock, for moistening

flat breads, to serve

❀ *Note: To yield 185 g (6½ oz/1 cup) cooked lentils, simmer 125 g (4 oz/½ cup) red lentils in 375 ml (12½ fl oz/1½ cups) water for 15–20 minutes, until thick.*

Place the fenugreek in a bowl and add 250 ml (8½ fl oz/1 cup) cold water. Leave to soak for 5 hours. Pour off the excess water, then beat the fenugreek with a fork until frothy.

Remove the stalks and seeds from the chillies and chop finely — take care in handling them. Mix into the fenugreek paste with salt to taste and place in a saucepan. (This mixture is the actual *hulba*.)

Stir in the remaining ingredients, except the stock, then stir in enough stock to moisten. Place over medium heat and cook, stirring occasionally, until bubbling and thick. Add a little more stock during heating if necessary.

Adjust the seasoning with salt. Serve in a deep bowl, or in individual bowls if preferred, with flat breads such as Khobz (page 385), Malvj (page 386) or pitta breads for scooping up the mixture.

HILBEH
Fenugreek and coriander paste

SERVES: 4

2 teaspoons fenugreek seeds

2 garlic cloves

1 handful chopped coriander (cilantro) leaves

½ teaspoon salt

2 teaspoons lemon juice

1 small hot chilli, seeded (optional)

Soak the fenugreek seeds in 125 ml (4 fl oz/½ cup) cold water for 12–18 hours, until a jelly-like coating is evident on them. Drain off the water.

Transfer the fenugreek seeds to a blender. Add the garlic and coriander and blend to a coarse purée, adding the salt, lemon juice and chilli, if using, and enough cold water to draw the ingredients over the blades.

Empty the paste into a sterilised jar (see page 19); seal and store in the refrigerator. Use as a bread dip or as directed in recipes.

ZHUG
Hot relish

3 cardamom pods
1 teaspoon black peppercorns
1 teaspoon caraway seeds
4–6 hot chillies, to taste
2 handfuls coriander (cilantro) sprigs,
   washed and drained
6 garlic cloves
½ teaspoon salt

Place the cardamom pods, peppercorns and caraway seeds in a blender and blend to a coarse powder.

Cut the stems from the chillies, leaving the rest of the chilli intact. Add to the blender with the remaining ingredients and 60 ml (2 fl oz/¼ cup) cold water. Blend to a coarse purée.

Empty the purée into a small saucepan and bring to the boil. Simmer, uncovered, for 10 minutes.

Spoon the relish into a sterilised jar (see page 19); seal and store in the refrigerator. Use as a bread dip, or as directed in recipes.

HAWAYIJ
Spice mix

6 teaspoons black peppercorns
3 teaspoons caraway seeds
1 teaspoon saffron threads
1 teaspoon cardamom seeds
2 teaspoons ground turmeric

Pound the peppercorns, caraway seeds, saffron and cardamom seeds to a coarse powder using a mortar and pestle, or in a spice grinder. Stir in the turmeric.

Store the spice mix in a clean sealed jar and use as directed in recipes.

SALUF BI HILBEH
Flat breads with fenugreek and coriander paste

MAKES: 12 ROUNDS

2 teaspoons active dried yeast

300 g (10½ oz/2 cups) plain (all-purpose) flour

300 g (10½ oz/2 cups) wholemeal (whole-wheat) flour

½ teaspoon salt

oil or ghee, for greasing

Hilbeh (page 381)

Dissolve the yeast in 60 ml (2 fl oz/¼ cup) lukewarm water.

Sift the flours into a mixing bowl, then remove about 150 g (5 oz/1 cup) of flour and set aside.

Mix the salt into the yeast mixture with 375 ml (12½ fl oz/1½ cups) warm water, then pour the yeast mixture into the flour. Mix in a little of the flour to thicken the liquid. Cover and leave in a warm place for 10–15 minutes, or until frothy.

Work in the remaining flour in the bowl, then beat by hand for 10 minutes, or with an electric mixer using a dough hook for 5 minutes.

Turn out onto a floured work surface and knead in enough of the reserved flour to make the dough smooth and satiny. Return the dough to the bowl and sprinkle the top lightly with flour. Cover with plastic wrap and leave the dough in a warm place until doubled in size — about 30 minutes.

Preheat the oven to 220°C (430°F/Gas 7).

Place a heavy flat griddle or baking tray on the centre shelf of the oven and leave to heat for 10 minutes. Grease with a wad of paper towels dipped in oil or ghee.

Punch down the dough and turn it out onto a surface. Knead it a little, then divide into 12 equal portions.

Roll out each portion to a 15 cm (6 inch) round and prick with a fork. Brush the top lightly with oil or ghee and spread on 1 teaspoon *hilbeh*.

Cooking two breads at a time, lift two rounds onto a lightly floured, flat-edged baking tray or plywood board, then slide them onto the heated griddle or baking tray.

Bake for 4 minutes; the tops may be lightly browned under a hot grill (broiler).

As the breads are removed, wrap them in a cloth to keep them warm and soft. Serve warm.

❀ *Note: If the breads begin to puff up during cooking, press the top down with a folded cloth. The breads should be bubbly, but should not form a pocket.*

LAHUH
Sourdough flat breads
MAKES: ABOUT 10 ROUNDS

This sourdough bread is cooked in a frying pan, as you would cook pancakes. It is favoured during Ramadan and other Muslim feasts when enormous quantities of food are prepared and consumed. No doubt its popularity lies in the simplicity of its ingredients and preparation.

300 g (10½ oz/2 cups) wholemeal (whole-wheat) flour
1 teaspoon salt
oil, for pan-frying

Sift the flour and salt into a mixing bowl. Add 375 ml (12½ fl oz/1½ cups) water and stir to make a thin batter.

Cover with plastic wrap and leave at room temperature for 2–3 days, until the batter is fermented. The length of time depends on the temperature. You will know it is fermented when bubbles pepper the surface and the batter has a sour smell.

Pour just enough oil into a heavy-based frying pan to finely coat the base and place over medium heat.

When the oil is heated, stir the batter, then pour about 85 ml (3 fl oz/⅓ cup) into the pan, shaping it into a round with the back of a spoon.

Cook for 2–3 minutes, or until the batter has browned and the surface looks dry. Turn over and cook for a further 2–3 minutes. Lift the bread out and place on a plate.

Repeat with the remaining batter, stacking the breads on the plate as they are cooked, and adding more oil to the pan as required.

Serve warm, either as an accompaniment to Yemeni meals, or drizzled with melted butter and honey.

KHOBZ
Wholemeal flat breads
MAKES: 12 ROUNDS

450 g (1 lb/3 cups) wholemeal (whole-wheat) flour
1 teaspoon salt
oil, for pan-frying

Combine the flour and salt in a mixing bowl. Pour in 250 ml (8½ fl oz/1 cup) tepid water and mix to a soft dough.

Knead in the bowl for 10 minutes. The dough will feel slightly sticky at first, but will become smooth as it is kneaded. Form it into a ball. Cover with plastic wrap and leave to rest for 2 hours, or even longer.

Divide the dough into 12 even portions, each the size of a large egg. Roll out to rounds 15 cm (6 inches) in diameter. The dough can be shaped without flour — but if it sticks, dust the work surface and dough very lightly with white flour.

Place the rounds side by side on a cloth. Cover and leave to rest for 20 minutes.

Heat a heavy-based frying pan or flat griddle over medium–high heat. The cooking surface is hot enough when a little sprinkled water bounces off it. Rub the pan using a cloth dipped in oil.

Add a round of dough and cook for about 1 minute, pressing the top lightly with a folded cloth to encourage even bubbling. When it is browned on the base, turn it over and cook for a further 1 minute, or until the bread looks cooked.

Cook the remaining breads in the same way, wrapping them in a cloth to keep them soft and warm, and rubbing the cooking surface occasionally with the oiled cloth.

MALUJ
Barley bread
MAKES: 8 BREADS

1 teaspoon active dried yeast

125 g (4 oz/½ cup) skim milk yoghurt, at
    room temperature

½ teaspoon bicarbonate of soda (baking soda)

125 g (4 oz/1 cup) barley flour

150 g (5 oz/1 cup) wholemeal (whole-wheat) flour

½ teaspoon salt

oil, for greasing

Dissolve the yeast in 60 ml (2 fl oz/¼ cup) warm water.

Stir the yoghurt until smooth, then mix in the bicarbonate of soda — the yoghurt will froth.

Combine the flours and salt in a mixing bowl. Add the yeast mixture and the yoghurt and stir to a soft dough. Knead the dough by hand for 10 minutes.

Cover with plastic wrap and leave the dough in a warm place for 1–1½ hours, or until almost doubled in size.

Turn the dough out onto a work surface and knead it a little. Divide into eight equal portions, then roll into balls. Press or roll each ball into a flat 15 cm (6 inch) round. Place the rounds on a cloth, then cover and rest for 20 minutes.

Heat a griddle or electric frying pan to medium–high heat. Rub the pan with a wad of paper towels dipped in oil. Add one round of dough. After a few seconds, press the dough with a folded cloth to encourage small bubbles. (If the dough is not pressed, the bread forms a pocket.)

Cook for 1½ minutes, then turn and cook for a further 1 minute, or until done — the bread will have a slightly moist appearance around the edges.

Cook the remaining breads in the same way, wrapping them in a cloth to keep them soft and warm, and rubbing the cooking surface occasionally with more oil. Serve warm.

FATUT
Fried bread with eggs
SERVES: 4

60 g (2 oz/¼ cup) ghee

2 Khobz (page 385), or pitta breads,
    broken into small pieces

4 eggs, lightly beaten

salt, to season

Heat the ghee in a large frying pan. Add the broken bread pieces and stir over medium heat until the bread is beginning to crisp and lightly brown.

Pour in the eggs. Season with salt and stir over the heat for 2 minutes, as you would for scrambled eggs. When the egg is just set, pile it onto plates and serve hot.

This is a great breakfast dish — scrambled eggs and toast from the one pan!

FATUT BIL HULBA
Fried bread with eggs and fenugreek
SERVES: 4

This is a combination of Fatut (above) and the Hulba from page 381. Make the basic fenugreek paste (hulba) with the chillies and salt as directed in the Hulba recipe, to the end of paragraph 2. Stir 500 ml (17 fl oz/2 cups) chicken stock into the hulba, then pour it into the pan with the cooked fatut. Bring to the boil and serve in bowls with lemon juice added to taste.

SHOURBA BILSEN
Thick lentil soup

SERVES: 6

250 g (9 oz) beef or lamb soup bones

370 g (13 oz/2 cups) dried brown lentils, rinsed

60 ml (2 fl oz/¼ cup) oil

1 large onion, finely chopped

3 garlic cloves, chopped

500 g (1 lb 2 oz/2 cups) chopped, peeled tomatoes

3 tablespoons coriander (cilantro) leaves

salt and freshly ground black pepper, to taste

Rinse the bones and place them in a saucepan with 1.75 litres (59 fl oz/7 cups) cold water. Bring to a slow simmer, skimming when necessary. When the broth is well skimmed and boiling, add the lentils and return to the boil.

Meanwhile, in a separate saucepan, heat the oil and gently fry the onion until soft and lightly browned. Add the garlic and cook for a further 1 minute. Stir in the tomatoes, coriander, and salt and pepper to taste.

Remove the bones from the broth pan and discard. Add the onion mixture to the lentils, then cover and simmer gently for a further 1 hour, or until the lentils are thickened. Take care that the soup does not catch on the base of the pan.

Serve hot in small bowls, with flat bread and salad.

SHOURBA FUL
Dried bean soup

Follow the Shourba Bilsen recipe (left), but use 400 g (14 oz/ 2 cups) dried haricot (navy) beans instead of lentils. First rinse the beans and place in a saucepan with 1.75 litres (59 fl oz/ 7 cups) cold water. Bring to the boil and boil for 2 minutes, then remove from the heat and leave until the beans are plump.

Rinse the bones and add them to the pan. Return to the boil, skimming as required. When the broth is well skimmed and boiling, cover and simmer for 1 hour.

Now continue with the Shourba Bilsen recipe, frying the onion and finishing the soup as described.

YEMEN

SOUPS

BANADURA SALAT A BIL KIZBARA
« Tomato and coriander salad
SERVES: 6

6 firm tomatoes
1 small handful chopped coriander (cilantro) leaves
1 small hot chilli, or freshly ground black pepper
juice of ½ lemon
1 teaspoon salt
60 ml (2 fl oz/¼ cup) olive oil

Score a cross in the base of each tomato. Place in a heatproof bowl and cover with boiling water. Leave for 30 seconds, then transfer to cold water and peel the skin away from the cross.

Slice the tomatoes into a bowl and sprinkle with the chopped coriander.

If using the chilli, cut off the stalk, slit it open and remove the seeds. Take care not to put your fingers near your eyes or mouth after handling the chilli. Chop the chilli finely.

Combine the chopped chilli or plenty of black pepper with the lemon juice and salt. Beat in the olive oil.

Pour the dressing over the tomatoes and leave for 15 minutes before serving.

SHAWAYUH
Spiced charcoal-grilled meat
SERVES: 6

Though very little meat is available for the Yemeni diet, when it is possible to obtain meat suitable for grilling, these cuts are spiced with *hawayij* and cooked over glowing charcoal. If the meat is tough, it is simmered after the grilling in a little water flavoured with onion or spring onion (scallion). We are more fortunate in that we can choose suitable cuts of meat.

6 thickly cut grilling steaks or lamb chops
2–3 teaspoons Hawayij (page 382)
oil, for basting
salt, to taste

Slit the fat selvedge on the steaks or chops to prevent the meat curling while cooking. Sprinkle the meat on each side with the *hawayij* and leave for 30 minutes at room temperature.

When your barbecue coals are red-hot, dab the meat with oil and place it over the fire. Cook until seared on each side, then move the meat to a cooler part of the barbecue.

Continue to cook until done to your taste, though the Yemeni prefer well-done meat. Brush occasionally with oil during cooking. Season with salt and serve immediately.

HOR'EE
« Stewed beef shank

SERVES: 5–6

1.5 kg (3 lb 5 oz) beef foreshanks, on the bone

2 large onions, quartered

6 garlic cloves

500 g (1 lb 2 oz/2 cups) chopped, peeled tomatoes

2 teaspoons Hawayij (page 382)

salt and freshly ground black pepper, to season

1–2 hot chillies, optional

Ask your meat retailer to cross-cut the foreshanks on the bone, into thick slices.

Place the meat in a large saucepan and just cover with cold water. Bring slowly to the boil, skimming when necessary. When well-skimmed and boiling, add the onion, garlic, tomatoes and *hawayij*. Add salt and plenty of pepper or 1–2 whole chillies, depending on how hot a dish you enjoy.

Cover and simmer gently for 4 hours, or until the meat is very tender and the liquid is reduced to a thick sauce. Serve hot.

AKUW'A
Oxtail stew

SERVES: 5–6

2 oxtails, jointed

500 g (1 lb 2 oz/2 cups) chopped, peeled tomatoes

3 small onions, peeled

4–5 garlic cloves

2 teaspoons Hawayij (page 382)

salt, to season

Wash the oxtail and place in a large pan. Cover with cold water and bring to a slow simmer, skimming when necessary. When boiling gently and well skimmed, add the tomatoes, whole onions, garlic, *hawayij* and salt. Cover and simmer gently for 3–3½ hours, or until the meat is tender and the liquid reduced.

Serve hot, with rice or boiled potatoes, flat bread and salad.

KIRSHUH
Stewed liver and kidney

SERVES: 5–6

Though *kirshuh* is usually made with a selection of variety meats (offal), depending on what is available to the Yemeni cook, it is just as good using liver and kidney – or liver and lung, if you don't mind the sound of lung frying.

500 g (1 lb 2 oz) lamb liver

2 lamb kidneys

60 ml (2 fl oz/¼ cup) oil

1 large onion, finely chopped

3 garlic cloves, finely chopped

1 teaspoon ground turmeric

250 g (9 oz/1 cup) chopped, peeled tomatoes

1 teaspoon ground coriander seeds

½ teaspoon ground cumin

2 cardamom pods

salt and freshly ground black pepper, to taste

1 tablespoon finely chopped coriander (cilantro) leaves
   or flat-leaf parsley

Soak the liver in cold salted water for 30 minutes. Drain, dry with paper towels and pull off the fine skin. Cut into 2 cm (¾ inch) cubes, removing any large tubes.

Skin, core and dice the kidneys, rinse briefly under cold running water, then drain and dry with paper towels.

Heat the oil in a deep saucepan and gently fry the onion until translucent. Add the garlic and turmeric, cook for 2 minutes longer, then add the liver and kidney. Increase the heat and fry quickly until the colour changes, stirring often.

Reduce the heat and add the tomatoes, ground coriander, cumin and cardamom pods. Stir in 125 ml (4 fl oz/½ cup) water and season with salt and pepper. Cover and simmer gently over low heat for 1–½ hours, or until the liver and kidneys are tender. As the mixture should be thick, add more water only if the stew looks like scorching.

Stir in the chopped coriander or parsley and serve hot.

BINT-AL-SAHN
Dough cake with honey

SERVES: 8

2 teaspoons active dried yeast

450 g (1 lb/3 cups) plain (all-purpose) flour

1 teaspoon salt

4 eggs

185 g (6½ oz/¾ cup) ghee, melted

melted butter, for drizzling

warm honey, for drizzling

Dissolve the yeast in 60 ml (2 fl oz/¼ cup) warm water.

Sift the flour and salt into a mixing bowl and make a well in the centre. Beat the eggs well and pour into the flour with the yeast mixture. Stir to combine, then knead well.

Gradually add 60 ml (2 fl oz/¼ cup) of the ghee (this should be just warm), kneading well into the dough. Keep kneading until the dough is smooth and fairly elastic. If the dough looks too dry, add a little water; this depends on the size of eggs used.

With floured hands, divide the dough into 16 balls, each the size of a large egg, placing them on a tray.

Take a ball of dough, place on a lightly floured work surface and form a very thin round shape by working the heel of your hand in a rotary motion on the dough. (I am right-handed, and I find that I can best do this with my left hand, using the right hand to move the dough around in order to flatten it evenly.) If you have any trouble flattening it, resort to a rolling pin.

Brush a baking tray well with some of the remaining ghee and place the completed round on one side of this. Brush the top of the dough generously with more ghee.

Shape another seven balls of dough and place them on top of the first round. As each round is placed on the previous round, press the edges with your fingertips, then brush generously with more ghee.

Shape the remaining eight balls of dough in the same way and stack them on the baking tray in another pile, pressing the edges together and brushing with ghee as before. The top layers should also be coated with ghee.

Leave the dough in a warm place for 45 minutes.

Meanwhile, preheat the oven to 190°C (375°F/Gas 5).

Bake the cakes for 25–30 minutes, or until lightly golden and cooked. Tap the base of the tray — it should sound hollow when the cakes are cooked.

Serve the cakes hot on a platter, drizzled with melted butter and warm honey — the amount should be generous, but depends on your taste.

The Yemenis break the cake off in flakes with their fingers, dipping pieces in the butter–honey mixture on the platter. You may serve it cut in wedges if preferred, with butter and honey from the platter spooned on top.

QISHR
Coffee with ginger

SERVES: 6 IN ARABIC COFFEE CUPS, 4 IN DEMITASSE CUPS

Though coffee is a major export from Mocha in the Republic of Yemen, the locals can rarely afford it. They generally use the ground coffee husks and flavour it with ground ginger. As you are unlikely to have access to ground coffee husks, the recipe given uses coffee and ground ginger for a delightfully different brew.

1½ tablespoons ground coffee
1½ tablespoons sugar
2 teaspoons ground ginger

Pour 250 ml (8½ fl oz/1 cup) cold water into a long-handled coffee pot. Add the coffee, sugar and ginger and stir well to combine. Place over medium heat and bring to the boil.

Remove from the heat until the bubbling subsides, then return to the boil. Do this three times in all.

Pour into Arabic coffee or demitasse cups and serve.

YEMEN

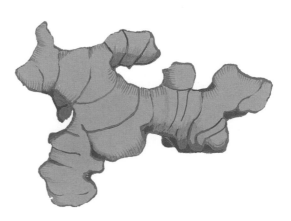

DRINKS

Egypt

EGYPT

With a history so ancient and so awesome in its magnificence, perhaps too much is expected of Egypt's foods. Last century saw a more cosmopolitan Egypt, with culinary influences of the French, Italians, Turks and Greeks. However, the new Egypt has loosened her links with the West and regained her national identity and food preferences.

Bread stands out as the most important component of the Egyptian diet. Vendors, flat wicker baskets piled high with *aish* and perched precariously on their heads, wind their way through the crowded streets of Cairo to their favourite selling spots. *Aish*, the flat bread of Egypt, is usually made from a combination of plain (all-purpose) and wholemeal (whole-wheat) flour with sufficient leavening to form a pocket and a soft crust, its basic character unchanged by the passage of millennia, and a constant reminder of the role Ancient Egypt played in developing the staff of life.

Barley, millet and wheat were the principal grains of earliest civilisations. Bread baked during these times was hard and chewy, as barley and millet do not contain adequate amounts of the gluten-forming proteins essential for making a light-textured bread. Wheat, on the other hand, does contain these proteins, but their nature can be altered if heat is applied at the wrong stage of preparation. The early wheat strains had to be heated before threshing so that the husk could be removed, so destroying these essential properties in the grain and giving wheat bread characteristics similar to those of barley and millet.

The Ancient Egyptians developed a strain of wheat that could be threshed without the preliminary heating. Whether by accident or by design, they also found a means to leaven bread made from this wheat. Because of the shortage of the new grain, some centuries passed before other civilisations were introduced to leavened bread.

THE FLAVOUR OF EGYPTIAN FOOD

Even expatriate Egyptians living in countries where vast varieties of food are constantly available will still yearn for the nostalgic bean dishes of their homeland. They are likely to remember the vendors of their native homeland with their huge *idras* of *ful* — tiny broad beans (fava beans) — simmering day and night, ready to provide a satisfying breakfast, a midday meal, or just a snack at any time. Ful Medamis (page 406), the brown bean purée made with *ful*, is served as a mazza, or as a substantial meal with hard-boiled eggs mashed into it, tart with lemon, pungent with garlic, subtly flavoured with cumin, crowned with golden olive oil and topped with a generous sprinkling of parsley. This simple peasant dish is of a kind that Westerners now endeavour to duplicate. Flat or crusty bread is a must and a variety of salad vegetables may be served with it, plus Salata Tahina (page 402). Similar foods that will equally stir the Egyptian far from home are Tameya (broad bean patties;

page 401), Ful Nabed (page 408) and Besara (page 399), a soup and a purée respectively, both made with skinned broad beans. A prized vegetable is okra (*bamia*), mostly favoured in meat and vegetable stews.

Many of Egypt's favoured recipes also appear in the cuisines of other countries, so if you are looking for a particular dish you may find it in another chapter, under another name. For example, the popular *lissan al assfourthe* is known as *yiouvetsi* in Cyprus and Greece (see recipe on page 143). If you can buy specially raised pigeons and wish to try an Egyptian recipe using them, then prepare the Farroog Mahshi recipe (page 413) using four pigeons instead of the two chickens specified. The stuffing for this particular recipe is usually made with a green wheat called *fireek* or freekah, available from specialist food stores. Coarse burghul (bulgar) or barley are substitutes, burghul the best for this recipe.

Whatever the occasion, *aish* is served with all meals. Aish is similar to the *saluf* of Yemen. Follow the Saluf recipe on page 383, omitting the potent *hilbeh* topping. Allow the shaped bread to rise for 15 minutes before baking and do not prick it with a fork; this ensures that a pocket forms when cooked. Even if you include the *hilbeh* topping, you will not be far from the flavour of Egyptian food, as *hilbeh* is used as a bread dip in Alexandria.

EATING EGYPTIAN STYLE

The Western influence is still in evidence in Egypt. The dining table is spread with a cloth and all the components of the meal are placed in their dishes and set on the table at the beginning of the meal. Individual plates or bowls are set out, with knives, forks and spoons. The meal could comprise a soup, chicken, fish or meat stew such as Bamia (417), rice, pickles, olives, salad and bread. If a bean purée or soup is served, then lemon wedges, chopped onions, salad vegetables and Salata Tahina (page 402) accompany it. Quite often such a meal is served without other foods — except plenty of bread, of course.

COOKING METHODS

In many homes, a single burner is often the only means by which to cook. For making Ful Medamis (page 406), the Egyptians use a small electric hotplate. This keeps a constant low heat and is just large enough to take the small *idra* — a special pot that tapers at the top, in which the beans are cooked slowly for several hours. A casserole dish with a wide base tapering to a narrow opening will substitute for the *idra*. For any other Egyptian cooking, modern pots, pans and casserole dishes can be used successfully.

INGREDIENTS FOR EGYPTIAN COOKING

The dried beans, *ful* and *ful nabed*, are available at Greek and Middle Eastern food stores and specialist food stores. Broad beans (fava beans), are now available already skinned, and are also called ful beans. These look white (the unskinned ones are green to almost purple) and should be used for Besara (page 399), Ful Nabed (page 408) and Tameya (page 401), which will save considerable time. A shorter soaking time is required, and though your yield will be greater, you can still use the quantities given in the recipes, adjusting the flavourings slightly. Ground cumin, dried mint, fresh dill, flat-leaf parsley and garlic are the principal flavour-givers, with butter and olive oil the favoured fats.

TA'LEYA I
Garlic sauce
SERVES: 2–4

This is more of a condiment to be added to cooked dishes than a sauce in the accepted sense. I have given a somewhat modified version – usually six or seven garlic cloves are used in Egypt for adding to a dish that serves six or so.

As garlic increases in pungency when cooked as directed, be warned and decrease the number of cloves even further if you wish. Of course, it depends on the size of the garlic cloves used and the pungency of the variety.

3–4 garlic cloves
¼ teaspoon salt
2 tablespoons ghee
1 teaspoon ground coriander
pinch of ground hot chilli or chilli powder

Crush the garlic with the salt using a mortar and pestle. Alternatively, crush it in a garlic press and mix it with the salt.

Heat the ghee in a small saucepan and add the garlic. Cook, stirring constantly, until golden brown, then remove the pan from the heat and stir in the coriander and chilli.

Use sizzling hot, as directed in recipes.

TA'LEYA II
Onion sauce
SERVES: 2–4

2 large onions
60 ml (2 fl oz/¼ cup) olive oil
1–2 garlic cloves, finely chopped

Cut the onions in half from top to bottom, then slice each half into thin semi-circles.

Heat the oil in a frying pan and fry the onion over medium heat until golden brown.

Add the garlic and cook for a minute longer.

Use hot, as directed in recipes.

BESARA
Broad bean purée

SERVES: 5–6

Large dried broad beans (fava beans) (*ful nabed*) are used for this purée. Those sold skinless are creamy white and are well worth using if you can find them. Soak the skinned beans for 24 hours in a cold place and use the soaking water in the cooking. The beans with skin intact require longer soaking, so that the tough seed covering can be removed (see skinning directions on page 10).

Use a stainless steel, tin-lined copper or an enamelled cooking vessel if possible, as an aluminium one is likely to discolour the purée.

The *melokhia* in the recipe is optional; it imparts a green colour to the purée without affecting the flavour.

525 g (1 lb 2½ oz/3 cups) dried broad beans (fava beans)
3 teaspoons dried mint
1 teaspoon dried melokhia, optional
salt and freshly ground black pepper, to taste

For serving
Ta'leya II (page 398)
olive oil, for drizzling
chopped onions
lemon wedges

Cover the beans well with cold water and soak for 48 hours, changing the water two or three times. Remove the skins.

Place the beans in a saucepan with 1.25 litres (42½ fl oz/5 cups) water and bring to a slow simmer. Cover and simmer gently for 1½ hours, or until very soft.

Pass the beans through a sieve, or purée in a blender and return to the pan. Rub the dried mint into the beans, and the well-rubbed *melokhia*, if using. Season to taste with salt and pepper. Gently cook without the lid on until bubbling.

Serve hot in small bowls, garnishing each with Ta'leya. Have on hand some olive oil, chopped onions and lemon wedges so that these may be added to individual taste.

Serve with flat bread or crusty bread.

TAMEYA
Broad bean patties
MAKES: 30

Dried broad beans (fava beans) (*ful nabed*) are normally used for these patties, but the lengthy soaking takes time, as does removing the skins. Fortunately dried skinned broad beans are available at Middle Eastern and Greek food stores – ask for these as they will save a lot of preparation time. They are creamy in colour.

350 g (12 oz/2 cups) dried broad beans (fava beans)

120 g (4 oz/1 cup) chopped spring onions (scallions)

3 tablespoons chopped flat-leaf parsley

2 tablespoons chopped coriander (cilantro) leaves

3 garlic cloves

1½ teaspoons salt

¼ teaspoon ground hot chilli or chilli powder

¼ teaspoon bicarbonate of soda (baking soda)

freshly ground black pepper

sesame seeds, optional

oil, for deep-frying

Place the skinned beans in a bowl and cover well with cold water. Leave to soak for 2 days in a cool place, changing the water two or three times.

Drain the beans but do not cook them. Place in a food processor and blend to a paste. Add the spring onion, parsley, coriander, garlic, salt, chilli and bicarbonate of soda. Season with black pepper and process again to a thick paste, scraping down the side of the bowl. Let the mixture rest for 30 minutes.

With wet hands, shape about a tablespoon of the mixture at a time into thick patties about 4 cm (1½ inches) in diameter. Dip each side in sesame seeds if desired. Place on a tray and leave at room temperature for 20 minutes.

Heat the oil to 170°C (338°F), or until a cube of bread dropped in the oil browns in 20 seconds. Fry the patties a few at a time until deep golden brown, turning to brown evenly; each batch should take about 5 minutes to cook. Drain on paper towels.

Serve hot, with flat bread such as Khoubiz (page 264), Salata Tahina (page 402) and assorted salad vegetables such as tomato, cucumber, sweet capsicums (peppers) and lettuce.

SALATA TAHINA
Tahini salad
MAKES: ABOUT 500 G (1 LB 1 OZ/2 CUPS)

2 garlic cloves
½ teaspoon salt
205 g (7 oz/¾ cup) tahini
1 tablespoon white vinegar
juice of 1 lemon
½ teaspoon ground cumin
1 small handful chopped flat-leaf parsley

Crush the garlic with the salt using a mortar and pestle. Alternatively, crush it in a garlic press and mix it with the salt.

Place the tahini in a mixing bowl and beat well. This preliminary beating reduces the strong flavour of the tahini.

Beat in the garlic mixture and vinegar. Gradually add the lemon juice alternately with 125 ml (4 fl oz/½ cup) water. (To make a creamy salad of good consistency, add enough lemon juice to make the tahini very thick before adding water. This way you have more scope in adjusting the flavour and consistency of the sauce.)

Add more salt to taste, and more lemon juice if a sharper sauce is required. Mix in the cumin and parsley, then cover and chill until required.

Serve as a mazza or as directed in recipes.

ROZ
Boiled rice
SERVES: 6

400 g (14 oz/2 cups) long-grain white rice, or 440 g
    (15½ oz/2 cups) short-grain white rice
2 teaspoons salt
40 g (1½ oz) ghee or butter

Place the rice in a sieve and wash under running water. Tip into a bowl and sprinkle with 1 teaspoon of the salt. Cover with cold water, soak for 10 minutes, then drain in the sieve. Do this well ahead of the time required for cooking so that the grains can dry. Spread them out in a dish if you like.

Heat the ghee or butter in a heavy-based saucepan and add the rice. Stir over medium heat for 2 minutes, or until the grains are well coated. Pour in 875 ml (29 fl oz/3½ cups) water and the remaining 1 teaspoon salt and bring to the boil, stirring occasionally.

Reduce the heat to low. Cover the pan tightly and leave to simmer for 15–20 minutes.

Turn off the heat and leave the lid on for a further 5–10 minutes. Fluff up the grains with a fork and serve.

❋ *Note: For an alternative cooking method, drain the rice after soaking – no need to let the grains dry. In a heavy-based saucepan, combine the ghee or butter, the 2 teaspoons salt and 875 ml (29 fl oz/ 3½ cups) water; bring to the boil and add the rice. Return to the boil, stirring once or twice, reduce the heat, cover and finish as above.*

COUSCOUS
Couscous

SERVES: 4

Though couscous is the national dish of Morocco, Tunisia and Algeria, it is also popular in Egypt. The other North African nations serve steaming mounds of couscous with their flavoursome stews; in Egypt it is generally prepared as a dessert, and only occasionally makes an appearance with stews.

While couscous is now widely available, I have given directions for making your own. Allow plenty of time and give yourself lots of space. Once you have mastered the art, increase the ingredients proportionately to make a larger quantity and store in an airtight container.

125 g (4 oz/1 cup) fine semolina (farina)
35–50 g (1¼–2 oz/¼–⅓ cup) plain (all-purpose) flour
¼ teaspoon salt

Place the semolina in a large round baking dish or a basin with a flat base. Form into a circle, leaving the centre clear.

Pour 2 tablespoons cold water into the centre, flick the semolina into the water with your fingers, then work with the palm of your hand in a circular motion to moisten the semolina evenly.

Mix the flour with the salt and sprinkle half of this over the semolina. Work it into the semolina, again using the palm of your hand and circular movements. Add a little more water and flour so that small, round grains about the size of sesame seeds begin to form. The aim is to coat the semolina grains with flour.

Turn the mixture into a wide, medium-meshed wire sieve (a wooden-framed sieve is ideal), set over a large cloth. Sieve the grains and return them from the cloth to the dish or basin, leaving any large lumps in the sieve. The smaller grains in the sieve are the couscous; tip these into a bowl.

Work a little more flour and water into the dish or basin contents. Sieve, sort and work again until the ingredients are formed into pellets of couscous, adding more flour and water as required. No more than 50 g (2 oz/⅓ cup) flour and 85 ml (3 fl oz/⅓ cup) water should be used per 125 g (4 oz/ 1 cup) semolina.

Line the top section of a couscousier or a colander with a piece of muslin (cheesecloth) and spread the couscous in it evenly.

Bring about 750 ml (25 fl oz/3 cups) water to the boil in the bottom section of the couscousier or a deep saucepan, then place the container with the couscous on top. If using a colander that does not fit snugly, drape a cloth around the edge so that steam does not escape. The container with the couscous must not touch the water. Cover the couscous with a lid and steam for 10 minutes.

Turn the couscous onto a cloth and break up any lumps with your fingers. Spread it out and leave for several hours in an airy place to dry thoroughly.

Store in an airtight container and use as directed in recipes.

KOUSHARI
Lentils, macaroni and rice in oil
SERVES: 6

This is classed as an 'oil' dish by Coptic Egyptians, and is prepared during periods of fasting when animal products cannot be eaten. You may cook the lentils, macaroni and rice simultaneously in three saucepans – or if, like me, you prefer to keep pans to a minimum, use the method given.

185 g (6½ oz/1 cup) brown lentils

1 tablespoon salt

155 g (5 oz/1 cup) small macaroni noodles

220 g (8 oz/1 cup) short-grain white rice

2 tablespoons olive oil

1 quantity Ta'leya II (page 398)

250 ml (8½ fl oz/1 cup) tomato passata (puréed tomatoes)

Place the lentils in a sieve and wash well under running water. Tip them into a large saucepan. Add 750 ml (25 fl oz/3 cups) water and 1 teaspoon of the salt. Bring to the boil, then reduce the heat and simmer, uncovered, for 1 hour, or until the lentils are tender but still intact. Drain and set aside.

Clean out the pan and pour in 1 litre (34 fl oz/4 cups) water. Bring to the boil and add another 2 teaspoons of the salt and the macaroni. Stir constantly until the water returns to the boil. Now cook, uncovered, for 15 minutes, or until the macaroni is tender, stirring occasionally. Drain and set aside. Clean out the pan again and dry.

Place the rice in a sieve, wash well under running water, then drain. Heat the oil in the saucepan and fry the rice over medium heat for 2–3 minutes, stirring to coat with the oil. Add 500 ml (17 fl oz/2 cups) water and the remaining 1 teaspoon salt and bring to the boil, stirring occasionally. Reduce the heat to low, cover and simmer for 15 minutes, or until tender. Remove from the heat and leave the lid on for 5 minutes to allow the grains to separate.

Prepare the Ta'leya following the directions on page 398, then add the passata and bring to the boil.

Add the lentils and macaroni to the cooked rice and toss together lightly with a fork. Pour the hot Ta'leya and tomato mixture on top, toss again and cover the pan. Leave over low heat for a final 10 minutes.

Serve hot with salads, grilled fish or prawns (shrimp).

FUL MEDAMIS
Simmered broad beans

SERVES: 6

Ful medamis, Egypt's national dish, is also enjoyed in other countries of the region. In Egypt the *ful* – small broad beans (fava beans) – are cooked very slowly in an *idra*, a special pot that tapers to a narrow neck. The shape ensures that the small amount of water used in the cooking is not lost: as steam condenses on the upper sloping sides, it drops back into the pot. There are casserole dishes with a somewhat similar design, and these may be used successfully for preparing *ful*. Otherwise use a heavy-based saucepan with a tight-fitting lid.

175 g (6 oz/1 cup) dried small broad beans (fava beans)
    185 g (6½ oz/¾ cup) red lentils, optional
3 garlic cloves
salt and pepper, to taste
pinch of ground cumin

For serving
6 hard-boiled eggs, optional
finely chopped flat-leaf parsley
lemon wedges
olive oil, for drizzling
freshly ground black pepper, to taste

Wash the beans well, then cover with 1 litre (34 fl oz/4 cups) cold water. Leave to soak overnight, in a cool place if the weather is warm.

Place the beans and their soaking water in a heavy-based saucepan; add the lentils if using. Cover tightly and simmer very gently for 5–6 hours. Alternatively, place the ingredients in a casserole dish with tapering sides, cover tightly and cook in a 120°C (250°F/Gas ½) oven for 6 hours.

Check the beans occasionally, and add a little water if they look dry. Do not stir during cooking, as this will cause them to stick to the pot.

Crush the garlic with a little salt and add to the beans. Add the cumin and additional salt to taste. If desired, the beans may be passed through a sieve to purée them; otherwise, serve them as they are.

Serve in soup bowls, adding a quartered hard-boiled egg if desired, and a sprinkling of chopped parsley to each. Each diner squeezes on lemon juice and adds olive oil and pepper to individual taste. The beans and egg are then usually crushed with a fork and the bowl contents combined.

Serve with flat or crusty bread, crisp salads and Salata Tahina (page 402).

❀ *Note: To serve as an appetiser, purée the beans, add the garlic, salt, pepper and cumin and mix in the lemon juice and olive oil to taste. Serve spread on a dish, with a good sprinkling of parsley; offer flat bread on the side, cut into quarters.*

SEMIT
Sesame bread rings

MAKES: ABOUT 18

2 teaspoons active dried yeast

600 g (1 lb 5 oz/4 cups) plain (all-purpose)
    flour

125 ml (4 fl oz/½ cup) milk, boiled and
    cooled to lukewarm

1 teaspoon salt

2 teaspoons sugar

2 teaspoons olive oil

1 small egg, beaten

sesame seeds, for sprinkling

Soak the yeast in 60 ml (2 fl oz/¼ cup) warm water and
stir to dissolve.

Sift the flour into a mixing bowl. Remove and reserve
about 150 g (5 oz/1 cup) of the flour.

Add the warm milk and 125 ml (4 fl oz/½ cup) warm water
to the yeast with the salt and sugar. Stir to dissolve the sugar.

Pour the liquid into the centre of the flour and stir in a little
of the flour to thicken the liquid. Cover and leave in a warm
place for 10 minutes, or until the liquid is frothy.

Mix in the flour remaining in the bowl, then beat until
smooth. Beat by hand for 10 minutes, or use an electric mixer
with a dough hook for 5 minutes. Gradually beat in the oil,
adding a little of the reserved flour.

Turn out onto a floured work surface and knead in as much
of the reserved flour as the dough will take. Knead for 10
minutes, or until smooth and satiny. Shape into a ball.

Oil a bowl lightly, add the dough and turn it in the bowl to
oil the whole ball. Cover the bowl with plastic wrap and leave
the dough in a warm place for 30 minutes, or until doubled
in size.

Punch down the dough and turn it onto a lightly floured
surface. Knead a little, then break off pieces the size of a
small egg.

Roll a piece of dough into a rope 1 cm (½ inch) thick and
20 cm (8 inches) long. Form the rope into a ring, overlapping
the ends and pressing to seal. Make about five rings, then glaze
with the beaten egg and dip the tops in a dish of sesame seeds.
Place on a lightly oiled baking tray.

Shape the remainder of the dough into rings, five at a time,
finishing each batch with egg glaze and sesame seeds.

Cover the bread rings with a cloth and leave in a warm place
for about 30 minutes, until they double in size.

Meanwhile, preheat the oven to 220°C (430°F/Gas 7). Place
a baking dish of hot water on the bottom shelf of the oven.

Bake the bread rings on the centre shelf of the oven for
15 minutes, or until they sound hollow when tapped on
the base.

Brush the hot bread rings with water and leave on the
baking trays to cool; this crisps the crust.

❀ *Note: Normally each bread ring is shaped, glazed and coated
separately, but preparing them in small batches speeds up the job.
However if you shape all of them before glazing, the first ones you
make will begin to rise and will be more difficult to handle.*

SHOURBA ADS
Lentil soup
SERVES: 6

375 g (13 oz/1½ cups) red lentils
1.5 litres (51 fl oz/6 cups) meat or chicken stock,
    or water
1 onion, grated
1 teaspoon ground cumin
salt and freshly ground black pepper,
    to taste
1 tablespoon lemon juice

For serving
Ta'leya II (page 398)
lemon wedges
olive oil, for drizzling

Place the lentils in a sieve and wash under running water.

Bring the stock or water to the boil in a large saucepan and add the lentils and onion. Return to a slow boil, cover and simmer over low heat for 45–60 minutes, or until the lentils are tender. Do not stir during cooking.

By now the lentils should have formed a purée; for a finer texture, pass them through a sieve, or purée in a blender.

Add the cumin and season to taste with salt and pepper. If a thinner soup is required, add water to achieve the desired consistency. Stir in the lemon juice and heat gently until bubbling.

Serve hot in deep bowls, topping each serving with Ta'leya. Add more lemon juice according to individual taste. Have olive oil on hand, as the amount in the Ta'leya may not be sufficient for some tastes.

FUL NABED
Broad bean soup
SERVES: 6

525 g (1 lb 2 oz/3 cups) dried broad beans (fava beans)
1 teaspoon ground cumin
60 ml (2 fl oz/¼ cup) olive oil
1 tablespoon lemon juice
salt and freshly ground black pepper, to taste

For serving
finely chopped flat-leaf parsley
lemon wedges

Cover the beans well with cold water and soak for 48 hours, changing the water two or three times. Remove the skins as directed in the preparation instructions on page 10.

Place the beans in a large saucepan with 1.5 litres (51 fl oz/6 cups) water and bring to a slow simmer. Cover and simmer gently for 1½ hours, or until very soft.

Press the beans through a sieve, or purée in a blender. Return them to the pan and add the cumin, oil and lemon juice, and salt and pepper to taste. Stir over gentle heat until bubbling.

Serve hot in deep bowls, garnished with chopped parsley. Lemon juice is squeezed on according to individual taste.

Flat bread or other bread should accompany this soup.

FATA
Lamb and bread soup

SERVES: 6

750 g (1 lb 10 oz) lean boneless lamb
1 large onion, finely chopped
salt and freshly ground black pepper, to season
1 clove or pinch of ground mastic, optional
110 g (3¾ oz/½ cup) short-grain white rice
½ teaspoon salt
20 g (¾ oz) ghee or butter

To finish
60 g (2 oz/¼ cup) ghee or butter
2–3 garlic cloves, crushed
60 ml (2 fl oz/¼ cup) vinegar
2 rounds Khoubiz (page 264), toasted
finely chopped flat-leaf parsley

Cut the lamb into small cubes and place in a large saucepan with 1.5 litres (51 fl oz/6 cups) cold water. Slowly bring to the boil, skimming when necessary. Add the onion and season with salt and pepper. If you find the aroma of boiling lamb unpleasant, add a clove or mastic (I find it unnecessary).

Cover and simmer gently for 1½ hours, or until the lamb is tender, but not falling apart.

Meanwhile, place the rice in a sieve, wash well under running water, then drain.

In a separate saucepan, bring 250 ml (8½ fl oz/1 cup) water to the boil. Add the salt, ghee and rice and return to the boil, stirring occasionally. Cover and simmer over low heat for 15–20 minutes, or until the rice is tender.

Lift the cooked lamb from the soup with a slotted spoon and allow to drain briefly.

To finish the dish, melt 20 g (¾ oz) of the ghee or butter in a frying pan. Add the lamb and fry until lightly coloured; remove from the pan and keep hot.

Melt the remaining ghee or butter in the frying pan and fry the garlic until lightly coloured. Take the pan off the heat and pour in the vinegar, then place back over the heat and boil for a few seconds. Set aside.

Place a round of toasted bread in a large tureen or casserole dish; you can first cut it into quarters if you like. Spoon a little of the garlic mixture over the bread and top with half the cooked rice. Pour on some of the soup and add another layer of bread and the remaining rice.

Arrange the lamb on top and spoon the remaining garlic mixture over. Pour in the remaining soup and garnish with chopped parsley before serving.

❀ *Note: To simplify the rather complex preparation of this dish, the rice may be boiled in the soup after the meat has been removed.*

MELOKHIA
« Green herb soup
SERVES: 6

Though in Egypt a stock made from any available vegetables is often used in this soup, it is preferable to use lamb, beef or chicken stock. If chicken is used, the bird is roasted with butter after the initial boiling and served separately as part of the meal. Egyptians living abroad find our mass-produced chickens lack flavour, and many add a stock (bouillon) cube so that the end result is just like 'back home'. For more information on *melokhia*, see the Glossary (page 522).

1.5 litres (51 fl oz/6 cups) chicken or meat stock, flavoured with onion, strained

1 chicken stock (bouillon) cube, optional

salt and freshly ground black pepper, to taste

45 g (1½ oz/1½ cups) dried *melokhia* leaves

2 silverbeet (Swiss chard) leaves

1 quantity Ta'leya I (page 398)

For serving

chopped onion

vinegar or lemon juice

Bring the stock to the boil in a large saucepan. If using chicken stock, crumble in the stock cube. Adjust the seasoning with salt and pepper to taste.

Finely crumble the *melokhia* leaves and add to the boiling stock. Remove the white stalks from the silverbeet. Chop the leaves finely and add to the stock. Return almost to the boil, then reduce the heat and simmer, uncovered, for 10 minutes. The *melokhia* swells and stays suspended in the stock.

Prepare the Ta'leya following the directions on page 398. Stir it into the soup, then cover and simmer for 2 minutes.

Serve piping hot, with a bowl of chopped onion bathed in vinegar or lemon juice, to be added to individual taste.

❀ *Note: If a whole chicken has been simmered for the stock, oven-roast with butter and serve it at the same meal, with plain boiled rice (Roz; see page 402).*

SAYYADIAH
Fish with rice
SERVES: 4

4 whole fish, each about 375 g (13 oz), scaled and gutted

juice of 1 lemon

salt and freshly ground black pepper, to season

2 tablespoons olive oil

2 onions, finely chopped

400 g (14 oz/2 cups) long-grain white rice

3 garlic cloves, finely chopped or crushed

1 teaspoon ground cumin

flour, for coating

oil, for pan-frying

parsley sprigs, to garnish

lemon wedges, to serve

Rinse each fish and wipe dry. Leaving the heads on, rub the surfaces and cavities with the lemon juice and season with salt and pepper. Cover and set aside for 30–45 minutes.

Heat the oil in a deep saucepan and gently fry the onion for 15–20 minutes, or until very soft and golden. Wash the rice, drain and add to the pan. Stir over medium heat for 2–3 minutes, or until coated.

Pour in 875 ml (29 fl oz/3½ cups) hot water and bring to the boil. Reduce the heat to low, then cover the rice and gently cook for 20 minutes.

Mix the garlic with the cumin. Make three or four deep slits on each side of each fish, fill the slits with the garlic and cumin mixture and coat the fish with flour. Coat a large frying pan with oil and place over medium–high heat. Pan-fry the fish in the hot oil for 4–5 minutes on each side or until golden brown and cooked.

Remove the fish and keep hot.

Add about 2 tablespoons of the oil in which the fish was cooked to the cooked rice. Stir it through with a fork, cover the pan and leave the rice for 5 minutes.

Pile the rice on a platter and arrange the fish on top. Garnish with parsley sprigs and serve with lemon wedges.

FARROOG MAHSHI
Roast stuffed chicken

SERVES: 6

2 chickens, about 1 kg (2 lb 3 oz) each; keep the
    livers, hearts and other giblets, or use an extra
    125 g (4 oz) chicken livers
salt and freshly ground black pepper, to season
60 g (2 oz/¼ cup) butter, melted

Stuffing

175 g (6 oz/1 cup) coarse burghul (bulgur)
livers and hearts from the chickens
40 g (1½ oz) butter
1 large onion, finely chopped
2 tablespoons finely chopped flat-leaf parsley
1 teaspoon dried mint, rubbed to a powder
salt and freshly ground black pepper
250 ml (8½ fl oz/1 cup) chicken stock, made
    from the remaining giblets

Wipe the chickens with paper towels and season inside and out with salt and pepper. Cover and refrigerate until required.

To make the stuffing, place the burghul in a bowl, cover with water and soak for 5 minutes. Strain in a sieve, pressing with the back of a spoon to extract all the moisture.

Meanwhile, clean the chicken livers and hearts, then finely chop. (Use the 125 g/4 oz chicken livers if you don't have the hearts.) Melt the butter in a frying pan and gently fry the onion until translucent. Add the chopped liver and heart and fry just long enough for the colour to change. Remove the pan from the heat.

Stir in the drained burghul, parsley, mint, and salt and pepper to taste. Add the stock, then cover and cook over low heat for 5 minutes. Allow the stuffing to cool.

Preheat the oven to 180°C (350°F/Gas 4).

Fill the chickens with the stuffing, then truss.

Pour the melted butter into a baking dish. Add the chickens, breast side up, and baste them with the melted butter. Bake for 1½ hours, turning the chickens on their sides during cooking, then breast side up during the last 10 minutes to complete the browning.

Remove the chickens to a plate and spoon the stuffing onto a serving platter. Joint the chickens and place the pieces on top of the stuffing. Keep hot.

Dissolve the browned cooking juices in the baking dish with a little hot water. Bring to the boil and served strained over the chicken.

KOLKAS
Meat with taro
SERVES: 6

Of all the countries of the Middle East, only Egypt and Cyprus use the root vegetable taro, which is indigenous to the Pacific region. The Egyptians call the root *kolkas*, and call the dish they use it in by the same name (see page 528 of the Glossary for more detail on taro). Just remember not to wet the root once it has been peeled and cut, as it can go slimy. The Egyptians do not chip off the pieces as they do in Cyprus.

1 kg (2 lb 3 oz) boneless beef or lamb stewing meat

60 g (2 oz/¼ cup) butter

2 teaspoons salt

freshly ground black pepper, to season

1 kg (2 lb 3 oz) taro

juice of ½ lemon

15 silverbeet (Swiss chard) leaves

1 tablespoon finely chopped coriander (cilantro) leaves

2 garlic cloves, crushed

Trim the meat and cut it into cubes. Melt 20 g (¾ oz) of the butter in a deep heavy-based saucepan and lightly fry the meat — just enough for it to lose its red colour. Do not brown.

Add 375 ml (12½ fl oz/1½ cups) water and the salt. Season with pepper, then cover and simmer gently for 1 hour, or until the meat is half-cooked.

Wash the taro and dry well. Peel and cut it into squarish pieces about 2 cm (¾ inch) thick. Add to the stew with the lemon juice, making sure the taro is totally immersed in the liquid, otherwise it could discolour. Cover and simmer for a further 1 hour, or until the meat is tender. Do not stir once the taro is added.

Wash the silverbeet well and strip the leaves from the white stalks (the stalks can be used as a vegetable for later meals). Drain the leaves.

Melt the remaining butter in a large frying pan and add the silverbeet leaves. Stir over medium heat until they are well wilted and darkened in colour. Chop finely while in the pan. Add the coriander and garlic and stir over the heat for 1 minute.

Stir the silverbeet mixture into the stew. Cover the pan and leave off the heat for 5 minutes before serving.

Serve with bread.

KORUMB MAHSHI
Cabbage rolls

SERVES: 6

24 cabbage leaves

250 ml (8½ fl oz/1 cup) tomato passata (puréed tomatoes)

125 ml (4 fl oz/½ cup) meat stock

juice of ½ lemon

2 garlic cloves, chopped

½ teaspoon sugar

salt and freshly ground black pepper, to season

40 g (1½ oz) butter

Stuffing

40 g (1½ oz) butter

1 onion, finely chopped

750 g (1 lb 10 oz) finely minced (ground) beef

110 g (3¾ oz/½ cup) short-grain white rice

1 tablespoon chopped dill

½ teaspoon ground cumin

60 ml (2 fl oz/¼ cup) tomato passata (puréed tomatoes)

salt and freshly ground black pepper, to season

If the cabbage leaves are large, halve them and count as two leaves. Bring a large saucepan of salted water to the boil and blanch a few cabbage leaves at a time for 3–5 minutes each batch, or until softened enough to roll. Drain the leaves in a colander.

Remove the hard centre rib from the cabbage leaves. Line the pan with these cabbage ribs and add extra leaves if needed to fill any gaps.

To make the stuffing, melt the butter in a frying pan and gently fry the onion until soft. Tip the onion into a mixing bowl and add the remaining stuffing ingredients. Season with salt and pepper and mix together well.

Place a generous tablespoon of filling on one edge of a cabbage leaf. Roll it into a neat package, folding in the sides. Repeat with the remaining leaves and stuffing, placing the rolls in the lined pan, seam side down.

Combine the passata with the stock, lemon juice, garlic and sugar; add salt and pepper to taste. Pour the mixture over the rolls and add the butter to the pan.

Invert a heavy plate on top of the rolls. Cover and bring to a slow simmer over medium heat. Reduce the heat to low and simmer for 1 hour. Serve hot.

BAMIA
Lamb and okra casserole
SERVES: 5–6

1 kg (2 lb 3 oz) boneless lamb or beef stewing meat

40 g (1½ oz) ghee or butter

1 large onion, finely chopped

½ teaspoon ground cumin

250 g (9 oz/1 cup) chopped, peeled tomatoes

2 tablespoons tomato paste (concentrated purée)

125 ml (4 fl oz/½ cup) stock or water

½ teaspoon sugar

salt and freshly ground black pepper

Roz (page 402), to serve

To finish

500 g (1 lb 2 oz) fresh okra

20 g (¾ oz) ghee

1 quantity Ta'leya I (page 398)

Preheat the oven to 150–160°C (300–320°F/Gas 2–3).

Trim the meat and cut into 3 cm (1¼ inch) cubes. Melt the ghee or butter in a heavy-based saucepan and brown the meat on all sides, adding a single layer of meat to the pan at a time. Transfer to a casserole dish.

Reduce the heat, add the onion to the pan and fry gently until translucent. Add the cumin, tomatoes, tomato paste and stock and stir well to dissolve the browned sediment.

Pour the mixture over the lamb. Add the sugar and season with salt and pepper. Cover tightly and bake for 1½ hours.

To finish the dish, prepare the okra as directed on page 8. Dry very well with paper towels or a cloth. Melt the ghee in a frying pan, add the okra and fry over medium heat for 3 minutes, tossing gently.

Arrange the okra over the stew, then cover and bake for a further 40 minutes, or until the meat is tender.

Prepare the Ta'leya following the directions on page 398, and pour while hot over the okra.

Serve from the casserole dish, with a separate dish of Roz.

BASBOUSA
« Semolina cake
SERVES: 8–10

125 g (4 oz/½ cup) butter, preferably unsalted

170 g (6 oz/¾ cup) caster (superfine) sugar

1 teaspoon vanilla essence

2 eggs

250 g (9 oz/2 cups) fine semolina (farina)

1 teaspoon baking powder

½ teaspoon bicarbonate of soda (baking soda)

185 g (6½ oz/¾ cup) plain yoghurt

blanched split almonds

Syrup
440 g (15½ oz/2 cups) sugar

1 tablespoon lemon juice

Preheat the oven to 180°C (350°F/Gas 4). Grease a 20 × 30 cm (8 × 12 inch) slab cake tin.

Cream the butter, sugar and vanilla until light and fluffy. Add the eggs one at a time and beat well after each addition. Sift the semolina, baking powder and bicarbonate of soda twice, then fold into the butter mixture alternately with the yoghurt.

Spread the batter into the cake tin. Evenly arrange the almonds in rows on top of the cake, placing four rows across and seven down — so that when the cake is cut, an almond will be centred on each piece.

Bake for 30–35 minutes, or until a skewer inserted into the centre of the cake comes out clean.

Meanwhile, make the syrup. In a saucean, dissolve the sugar in 375 ml (12½ fl oz/1½ cups) water over medium heat. Add the lemon juice and bring to the boil, then allow to boil rapidly for 10 minutes. Cool the syrup by standing the pan in cold water.

Spoon the cooled syrup over the hot cake. Allow the cake to cool thoroughly.

To serve, cut into diamond shapes or squares. Serve with thick whipped cream if desired.

COUSCOUS BI SUKKAR
Sweet couscous with nuts
SERVES: 6–8

370 g (13 oz/2 cups) couscous (page 403)

125 g (4 oz/½ cup) unsalted butter, melted

For serving
icing (confectioners') sugar, for sprinkling

toasted peanuts or almond slivers

Place the couscous in a bowl and cover with cold water. Stir with your fingers, then drain off the water. Leave the couscous to stand for 15 minutes. The grains will swell.

Place the couscous in the top section of a couscousier and set over 1 litre (34 fl oz/4 cups) boiling water. Alternatively, place the couscous in a fine sieve or muslin (cheesecloth)-lined colander that fits snugly over a deep saucepan of boiling water, ensuring that the bottom of the sieve or colander does not touch the water.

Drape a cloth over the top of the couscous container and fit the lid on, bringing the ends of the cloth over the top of the lid. Steam for 15 minutes, then tip the couscous into a bowl.

Break up any lumps with your fingers or a fork and sprinkle with 2 tablespoons cold water. Fluff up the couscous with a fork and return it to the steaming container, adding more boiling water if necessary.

Cover as before and steam for 30 minutes, regulating the heat so that the water boils gently. When the cooking is completed, the couscous should be tender but not mushy.

Tip the couscous into a bowl and fluff it up with fork, breaking up any lumps. Add the melted butter and toss through to coat the grains evenly.

Serve warm, piled in individual sweet dishes, and sprinkled with icing sugar and peanuts or almonds.

Iran

İRAN

While Iran is its official name, I cannot help referring to the country as Persia, as this seems to me to be an expression of the essence of the country and its people. Do not be confused with my Irans and Iranians, Persias and Persians: they are all one and the same. Most countries of the Middle East were influenced in one way or another by Persia, particularly in terms of cuisine. The *dolmeh* of Persia, for instance, became the *dolma* and other sundry variations of Iraq, Turkey, Greece, Cyprus, Armenia, Lebanon, Syria and the Gulf States.

THE FLAVOUR OF PERSIAN FOOD

One of the most popular dishes in Tehran is *chelou kebab*, and there are restaurants that specialise in its preparation. It is simple, and its success depends on the quality of the basic elements, which are melded into a culinary delight with a simple stir of the diner's fork.

My first taste of *chelou kebab* won me over to Persian cooking, for in it I could see the true art and dedication of the Persian cook. To behold, it is a dish of rice and grilled lamb. But once tasted it is much, much more. Only the best portion of the lamb will do — the tender, lean eye of the rib, trimmed so that not a trace of fat or gristle mars its purity, sliced thinly and marinated in lemon and onion juice to melt-in-the-mouth tenderness. Charcoal-grilled only seconds before, it is served nestling in a pile of steaming hot *chelou* (rice), with a tomato or two for colour. Pats of butter, a generous dusting of sumac and raw egg yolk accompany it, to be stirred into the rice for an amalgamation of subtle flavours complementing the lamb. The rice is the most important element of the dish; Persian rice is aromatic, hard-grained and almost without equal. Pakistan's basmati rice is the nearest and certainly the best substitute. Once you make *chelou* and taste it, you will never cook plain rice any other way again.

Polous (another rice dish) are an extension of *chelous* and are well worth trying. The imaginative use of fruits is another high point in Persian cooking, with sweet–sour flavours the Western palate has learned to appreciate. Fruits are frequently combined with meats in Iran's *polous*. Persian cooks, like their Western counterparts, do take shortcuts, and if you find *chelous* and *polous* are too time-consuming in their preparation, then try Kateh (page 445) in place of *chelou*, and Dami (pages 445 and 448) instead of *polous*. The most important factor is using the right rice. Experiment by trying basmati rice first, so you have a yardstick against which to measure the success of future efforts using another more readily available long-grain white rice. The quantities of rice have been trimmed to suit Western tastes and appetites, but the essence of the dishes has not suffered.

The Persian *khoresh*, loosely translated as 'sauce', is a combination of meat or poultry with vegetables, fruits, herbs and spices, to make a substantial 'sauce' for serving with rice dishes. *Abgusht*, on the other hand, is a meat stew that can become, with the addition of more liquid, a substantial meat-based soup, while *aashe* is always regarded as a soup.

The fruits of Persia are highly regarded and are served during the day, preceding meals. The cucumber is regarded as a fruit — and if you have ever tasted a Persian cucumber you will understand why.

Herbs are an important part of Persian cooking. Sabzi Khordan (page 427) is a platter of mixed herbs served with Nane Lavash bread (page 437), *panir* (goat's milk cheese) and Mast Va Khiar (yoghurt and cucumber salad, page 431) as a refreshing start to a meal. More detail is given in the recipe on page 427.

Spinach is native to Persia; how it came to be known as English spinach I cannot say. It features in salads, stews and *kuku* (egg casseroles or omelettes).

Sweet—sour flavours are essentially Persian in character, with dishes featuring fruit such as pomegranates, peaches, sour cherries, apples and quinces, and lime or lemon juice added for good measure. Verjuice — the juice of green (unripened) grapes — is widely used in Iran for a really sour flavour.

The *samovar* is an essential item in every Persian household, as tea ranks with *abdug* (yoghurt drink) as Persia's principal beverage. Tea is taken in small, slender glasses and served with lumps of sugar. To drink it in the Persian way, one must hold the lump of sugar between the teeth and sip the tea through it. The sugar can be conventional cube sugar or small 'cushions' of clear white toffee.

NOW ROOZ

Though Iran is predominantly a Muslim country, their most joyous feast has its origins long before Islam, in the time of the prophet Zoroaster and the great kings of Ancient Persia. It is the celebration of Now Rooz, the Persian new year, actually beginning on the first day of spring, 21 March. The new year means new life, and this celebration places constant emphasis on the newness of life. About two weeks before Now Rooz, wheat or other grain is sown in a sandy bed. By Now Rooz Eve the green shoots are well in evidence and the clump is usually divided according to the number of family members. Each piece is tied with a colourful ribbon and set on the *haft seen* (seven S's) table, symbolic of the roots of life. Altogether, seven food items whose names begin with an 's' must be placed on the table. The number seven probably relates to the seven days of the week, or the seven planets of the solar system. Apples (*sib*), garlic (*sir*), sumac (a kind of spice), herbs (*sabzi*), vinegar (*sarkh*), coin (*sekeh*), and a *samanoo* (a sweet pudding made with a special wheat) are the usual items. The table would also have a bowl of water with a green leaf floating in it, fresh fruit, eggs, meat, fish, fowl, sweetmeats, pastries, grains and nuts — in other words a harvest festival in miniature. These are the raw foods used for meals throughout the holiday period.

We arrived in Iran on the thirteenth day of Now Rooz. On that day every person who is able leaves their home and travels as far away as possible so that their bad luck can be left behind. Persians love picnics and this is one massive picnic day. Food is packed along

with the *samovar* to supply the copious amounts of tea consumed. A clump of green shoots is placed jauntily on the bonnet, roof or trunk of the family car, and during the picnic it is thrown into a running stream. In Tehran, the deep gutters that carry the spring water from the mountains behind the city were dotted with these clumps, as those who cannot get to the country, picnic instead at one of the city's beautiful parks or gardens. Now Rooz celebrations last for about two weeks.

PERSIAN BREADS

Bread is the staff of life: in Iran, as in most other Middle Eastern countries, you are constantly aware of the importance of this most ancient of foods.

As Persia has influenced the bread-making of so many of the countries surrounding it, a description of the process should be part of this chapter.

Bread is still baked traditionally, though the oven is more likely to be heated by oil-fed burners than by wood.

One bakery we visited in Shiraz was baking *nane lavash*. In one room was the dough-maker, tending the modern breadmixer in the centre. Along the full length of three walls ran a waist-high bench structure made of a stone compound, with straight-sided holes 50 cm (20 inches) in diameter formed into the structure. There were at least thirty of these proving vats, each with softly rounded cushions of dough gently billowing above the level of the bench. We were looking at just one of the three 'bakes' of the day.

Next door was a room filled with cream-coloured flour, shovel at the ready. Then came the bakehouse. The heat exuding from this area was sufficient to keep the proving room warm enough for the dough to rise, though with the flat breads the rising of the dough is not necessary.

The procedure in the bakehouse goes something like this: one person breaks off lumps of dough from the huge mass on his table, shaping them into balls. These are rolled out to an oval shape by another worker. A more experienced baker takes the rolled-out dough, expertly throws it back and forth across the backs of his hands, enlarging it even further, runs a *jella* (a spiked wheel on a handle) across the dough three times, then throws it onto the *manjak* — a slightly domed oval cushion about 60 cm (24 inches) long and 30 cm (12 inches) across. After all the rolling, throwing and tossing, the sheet of now-thin dough covers this cushion completely. The baker then slips his hand into a pocket in the back of the *manjak*, takes it up and presses the dough deftly onto the scorching hot wall of the *tannour*, the beehive clay oven of the Middle East and India. In 30–40 seconds the bread bubbles and cooks to golden brown crispness. Another baker, armed with a *mengash* (a long rod finished with a metal hook), pulls off the cooked bread and flicks it through a waist-high opening into the actual shop, where it is sold immediately.

The whole procedure is carried out with rhythmic precision and at a pace so rapid that the onlooker almost becomes mesmerised. The aroma of the baking bread alone is enough to keep one in a state of euphoria.

Other breads baked in Iran are:

Taftoon: Similar to *nane lavash* in preparation and baking, but round and slightly smaller. Usually made with flour resembling wholemeal (whole-wheat) flour with the bran removed.

Sangyak: About 75 cm (30 inches) long and 30 cm (12 inches) wide. The top is oiled and well indented by fingertips. Baked in a traditional oven on a bed of hot pebbles, it is a bubbly, crisp flat bread, usually made with wholemeal (whole-wheat) flour. At its best when warm.

Barbari: Shaped in long loaves about 60 cm (24 inches) long, 25 cm (10 inches) wide and 4 cm (1½ inches) thick when cooked. The top is oiled, and four grooves running the length of the bread are made with the fingers. Baked on trays in a traditional oven, it is the most popular breakfast bread. Excellent when warm, but not as pleasant cold as the texture is rather coarse. Plain (all-purpose) flour is used for *barbari*.

EATING PERSIAN STYLE

The midday and evening meals are almost identical, with the same variety of foods served.

The Persians serve their meals on carpets. The carpet is spread with a leather cover called a *sofreh*, which serves as protection and provides a firm base for the dishes. This is covered with a white cloth *sofreh* and the carpet is surrounded with cushions for seating. China dinner plates are set out with spoons and forks, which have now replaced the traditional method of eating from the fingers of the right hand. A rice dish, either *chelou*, *polou*, *dami* or *kateh*, is always served with a *khoresh*. *Abgusht*, either as a soup or as a stew, could also be served, or perhaps a baked chicken or fish. A *borani* (salad), if made with a yoghurt base, often replaces the *khoresh*, particularly in summer. A mixed green salad with cos (romaine) lettuce, cucumber, tomatoes, radishes and herbs, and dressed with olive oil and vinegar, is frequently included. Yoghurt, pickles, flat bread and fresh fruit complete the meal. *Abdug* (yoghurt drink) is usually served as the beverage.

Tea, *sharbat* (fruit sherbet) and *sekanjabin* (a sweet–sour mint-flavoured beverage) are usually taken as refreshments between meals. *Kuku* (an egg casserole or omelette) is often included at the table, particularly for festive occasions, or served as the main dish for a light meal. *Kababs* and *kuku* are favourite picnic foods.

INGREDIENTS FOR PERSIAN COOKING

Basmati rice or a suitable substitute is a must for Persian cooking. The meats that are generally preferred are lean lamb, veal, venison if available, lean beef and poultry. Though recipes may list a particular meat and may give two choices, often any other of these meats may be used. Turmeric, cinnamon, saffron, sumac and dried mint are the popular spices and seasonings. For cooking, ghee (clarified butter) is preferred, though oil, butter or margarine may be substituted. *Limu omani* (dried lime) is used whole in Persian cooking, generally when the cook wishes to remove strong flavours from meats. Directions for preparing your own dried limes are given in the chapter on the Gulf States (see the Loomi recipe on page 345).

SABZI KHORDAN
Mixed herb platter

Herbs feature prominently in Iranian cuisine. Sabzi Khordan is a popular appetiser, often served at the beginning of a meal. In many restaurants in Iranian cities this platter is placed on the table as soon as you are seated, whether you order it or not. I found it delightfully refreshing and appetite-stimulating, and certainly most welcome. The plates are left during most of the meal for between-course nibbles.

Herbs

flat-leaf parsley

mint sprigs

tender radish leaves

spring onion (scallion) tops

chives or garlic chives (*tareh*)

tarragon

coriander (cilantro) leaves

watercress or *shahat*

fenugreek

Serve with

***panir* (Iranian goat's milk cheese)**

Mast Va Khiar (page 431), optional

Nane Lavash (page 437) or other flat bread

Select a variety of herbs from those listed. Wash them well and remove any coarse and discoloured leaves. Cut the bladed herbs into finger lengths; break the other herbs into small sprigs; separate the radish leaves. Drain and wrap in a cloth. Place the leaves in a plastic bag and refrigerate for 3–4 hours to crisp them.

Arrange the herbs attractively on a platter or in a flat basket. Dice the cheese and place in a bowl. Prepare the Mast Va Khiar, if using, as directed on page 431, then place in a bowl and chill.

Cut the flat bread into 8 cm (3¼ inch) squares and place in a napkin-lined basket. Arrange the ingredients on the table before guests are seated. Alternatively, serve with pre-dinner drinks.

❀ *Note: To eat Sabzi Khordan, wrap a selection of herbs and a piece of cheese in bread; if desired, add a little Mast Va Khiar. Panir is the goat's milk cheese of Iran, similar to feta.*

NANO DOK
Spicing mix
MAKES: 30–60 ML (1–2 FL OZ)

Persian cooks frequently spice their soups and *boranis* (yoghurt salads) just before serving. Nano Dok is a favourite, and one I found to my liking. Sometimes this basic mix is combined with crisp fried onion, and where this is the case I have included the spicing within the recipe, as the onion is often used both in and on top of the prepared dish.

Another popular seasoning for soup is a combination of dried mint, cinnamon and pepper (no ghee), but as these ingredients are often used in the soup, the Nano Dok given here is the one I recommend for a final dash of colour and fragrance to soups and *boranis*.

1–3 tablespoons ghee
1 teaspoon ground turmeric
1½ teaspoons dried mint

Heat the ghee in a small saucepan, stir in the turmeric and cook for a few seconds, until the turmeric turns golden brown.

Crush the mint, add to the pan, stir and immediately remove from the heat. The heat in the pan will be sufficient to bring out the flavour of the mint.

❀ *Note: Use the amount of ghee according to the recipe the Nano Dok is accompanying — the smaller amount if a lot of ghee has been used in the soup, and for* boranis; *the larger amount if only a little ghee has been used in the soup.*

BORANIS

These simply prepared, cooling Persian salads are most versatile. While they may replace the traditional salad at a meal, they also serve as appealing appetisers. In this role the only accompaniment necessary is a flat bread, such as Nane Lavash (page 437) or Nane Sangyak (page 436), or the readily obtainable *khoubiz*, the Arabic flat bread (see also the recipes for Khoubiz on pages 264 and 347). Cut the bread into manageable squares for scooping up the *borani*.

The other role of *boranis*, popular in summer, is as a substitute for a *khoresh* when serving a full Persian meal; they also make an interesting 'sauce' for *polous* and *kababs* served with *chelou*.

Always be sure to use a thick, drained yoghurt (see page 19) when preparing *boranis*.

BORANI ESFANAJ
Spinach salad
SERVES: 6

750 g (1 lb 10 oz) spinach

1 tablespoon oil

1 onion, finely chopped

2 garlic cloves, crushed

1 teaspoon salt

freshly ground black pepper, to taste

500 g (17 oz/2 cups) drained yoghurt (page 19)

Nano Dok (page 428)

Trim the roots and coarse stalks from the spinach. Wash the leaves well, discarding any that are discoloured or damaged. Drain and shred them coarsely.

Heat the oil in a frying pan and gently fry the onion until translucent. Add the spinach and toss over medium heat until wilted. Cook until the moisture evaporates. Add the garlic, salt and pepper to taste. Remove from the heat and cool a little.

Pour the yoghurt into a mixing bowl and add the spinach mixture. Toss well and adjust the seasoning.

Prepare the Nano Dok as directed on page 428, using a small amount of ghee.

Turn the *borani* into a serving dish and drizzle with the Nano Dok. Serve at room temperature.

BORANI CHOGONDAR
Beetroot salad
SERVES: 6–8

3 cooked or pickled beetroot (beets)

500 g (1 lb 2 oz/2 cups) drained yoghurt
    (page 19)

salt and freshly ground black pepper,
    to taste

vinegar or lemon juice, optional

1 tablespoon chopped fresh mint, or
    1 teaspoon dried mint

fresh or dried mint, to garnish

Peel and cool the beetroot if freshly cooked. Cut the fresh or pickled beetroot into 1 cm (½ inch) cubes.

Reserve about 35 g (1¼ oz/¼ cup) of the diced beetroot. Place the remainder in a bowl, gently mix in the yoghurt and season to taste with salt and pepper. If using freshly cooked beetroot, it may be necessary to add a little vinegar or lemon juice to sharpen the flavour.

Mix in the mint; if using dried mint, first rub it to a coarse powder. Cover and chill.

Place the salad in a serving bowl. Garnish with the reserved beetroot, and some mint leaves or powdered dried mint.

BORANI BADEMJAN
« Eggplant salad
SERVES: 6–8

2 large, oval eggplants (aubergines),
    each about 375 g (13 oz)
salt, for sprinkling
125 ml (4 fl oz/½ cup) oil
500 g (1 lb 2 oz/2 cups) drained yoghurt
    (page 19)
2 garlic cloves, crushed
freshly ground black pepper, to taste
chopped walnuts, to garnish, optional

Cut the eggplants in half lengthways, then slice crossways to
5 mm (¼ inch) thick. Sprinkle the slices liberally with salt,
stacking them if necessary. Leave for 30 minutes, then rinse
and dry with paper towels.

Heat half the oil in a large frying pan. Fry the eggplant in
batches, over medium heat, until golden brown on each side,
adding more oil to the pan as required. Drain on paper towels.

Mix the yoghurt and garlic with salt to taste.

Place a layer of cooled eggplant in a serving dish,
overlapping the slices a little. Season with pepper and spread
some yoghurt mixture on top. Repeat the layers, finishing with
a layer of yoghurt.

Cover and chill. Serve garnished with chopped walnuts
if desired.

❁ Note: Borani Bademjan may be layered in individual dishes
to serve as a first course. If serving in place of a khoresh, dice the
eggplant, fry until cooked through, and fold into the yoghurt with the
other ingredients.

MAST VA KHIAR
Yoghurt with cucumber and sultanas
SERVES: 6–8

This dish is classed as a *borani*. Another version of this recipe
is served as a soup (see page 440).

2 slender, firm green cucumbers
500 g (1 lb 2 oz/2 cups) drained yoghurt (page 19)
2 spring onions (scallions), finely chopped
60 g (2 oz/½ cup) sultanas (golden raisins),
    washed if necessary
30 g (1 oz/¼ cup) chopped walnuts, optional
salt and freshly ground white pepper, to taste
1 tablespoon finely chopped fresh mint, or
    1 teaspoon dried mint

Peel the cucumbers and halve them lengthways. If they are
very seedy, remove the seeds with the end of a teaspoon. Slice
the cucumber thinly and leave to drain.

Combine the cucumber and yoghurt in a bowl. Stir in the
spring onion (including some of the green tops), sultanas and
walnuts, if using. Season to taste with salt and white pepper.

Mix in the mint; if using dried mint, first rub it to a coarse
powder. Cover and chill for at least 1 hour.

Serve with flat bread, cut into squares.

TORSHI HOLU
Peach pickles

375 ml (12½ fl oz/1½ cups) wine vinegar
   or cider vinegar
500 g (1 lb 2 oz) fresh peaches
1 tablespoon grated fresh ginger
3 teaspoons ground coriander
3 garlic cloves, crushed
1½ teaspoons tamarind paste
110 g (3¾ oz/½ cup) sugar
¼ teaspoon ground hot chilli or chilli pepper
¼ teaspoon salt
¼ teaspoon freshly ground black pepper

Pour 250 ml (8 ½ fl oz/1 cup) of the vinegar into a preserving pan. Peel and slice the peaches, placing the slices in the vinegar as they are prepared. Add the ginger, coriander and garlic.

Dissolve the tamarind paste in the remaining vinegar, then add to the preserving pan with the remaining ingredients.

Bring slowly to the boil, stirring gently until the sugar has dissolved. Boil gently for 5 minutes.

Ladle the pickles into warm, sterilised jars (see page 19). Seal with glass or plastic lids and leave for 1 week before opening.

❀ *Note: You can also use 250 g (9 oz) dried peaches instead of fresh peaches. Rinse them well in cold water, then drain and chop. Soak them overnight in 250 ml (8½ fl oz/1 cup) wine vinegar or cider vinegar and proceed as directed in the recipe.*

TORSHI BADEMJAN
Eggplant pickles

1 kg (2 lb 3 oz) eggplants (aubergines)
500 ml (17 fl oz/2 cups) cider vinegar
1 piece of dried tamarind (pulp), the size of an egg
1 tablespoon white mustard seeds
1 tablespoon coriander seeds, toasted
2 teaspoons fennel seeds
4–6 garlic cloves
1 teaspoon chopped fresh ginger
½ teaspoon ground hot chilli or chilli pepper
2 teaspoons freshly ground black pepper
2 teaspoons salt

Preheat the oven to 200°C (400°F/Gas 6).

Pierce the eggplants with a fork and place them directly on an oven shelf. Place a dish underneath to catch the juices. Bake for 20 minutes, or until soft.

Holding onto the stem, peel the skin from the eggplants, then remove the stems. Chop the flesh into a bowl and immediately mix in 125 ml (4 fl oz/½ cup) of the vinegar to stop the eggplant discolouring.

Soak the tamarind in 125 ml (4 fl oz/½ cup) hot water for 10–15 minutes, or until softened. Rub with your fingertips to separate the pulp, then press it through a sieve, into the eggplant.

In a blender, combine another 125 ml (4 fl oz/½ cup) of the vinegar with the mustard, coriander and fennel seeds, garlic and ginger. Blend to a smooth paste.

Stir the paste through the eggplant mixture, along with the chilli, pepper and salt. Mix in the remaining vinegar.

Ladle the pickles into sterilised jars (see page 19). Seal with glass or plastic lids and store in a cool place.

TORSHI KHRAMLU
Persimmon pickles

1 kg (2 lb 3 oz) ripe persimmons

2 dried limes (Loomi, page 345)

2 teaspoons black peppercorns

4 cloves

3 teaspoons white mustard seeds

1 teaspoon cardamom seeds

3 teaspoons toasted coriander seeds

1 teaspoon fennel seeds

2 small pieces of cinnamon bark

10 garlic cloves, cracked

12 fresh or dried dates, pitted and halved

750 ml (25 fl oz/3 cups) white vinegar

55 g (2 oz/¼ cup) sugar

2 teaspoons salt

Wash the persimmons and dry them well. Remove the stems and core using a pointed knife. Cut them in half, then slice into wedges.

Break the dried limes into small pieces.

Grind the peppercorns, cloves and mustard, cardamom, coriander and fennel seeds to a coarse powder using a spice grinder or mortar and pestle.

Place some persimmon wedges in a large, sterilised jar (see page 19). Add a piece of cinnamon. Add a few pieces of dried lime and two garlic cloves. Add a few date halves and some of the ground spices. Repeat in layers until all the ingredients have been used, placing the second piece of cinnamon near the top of the jar.

Combine the vinegar, sugar and salt in a saucepan and bring to the boil, stirring to dissolve the sugar.

Pour the hot vinegar mixture into the jar. Remove any air bubbles by inserting a fine skewer down the sides of the jar.

Seal with a glass or plastic lid and leave for 1 week before opening. Use within 3 months of making.

KŌTAH DOLMEH
Fried dough with lentils

MAKES: 72

185 g (6½ oz/1 cup) brown lentils
90 g (3 oz/⅓ cup) ghee
2 large onions, finely chopped
salt, to season
2 tablespoons brown sugar
oil, for deep-frying

Dough

2 teaspoons active dried yeast
2 teaspoons rosewater
525 g (1 lb 2½ oz/3½ cups) plain
   (all-purpose) flour
1 teaspoon salt
½ teaspoon ground cardamom
60 ml (2 fl oz/¼ cup) melted, cooled ghee or oil

To make the dough, dissolve the yeast in 60 ml (2 fl oz/¼ cup) warm water. Add another 185 ml (6½ fl oz/¾ cup) warm water and the rosewater.

Sift the flour, salt and cardamom into a mixing bowl, then set aside 75 g (2½ oz/½ cup) of the flour mixture.

Add the yeast liquid to the flour and mix to a soft dough. Work in the ghee or oil with the reserved flour, then knead for 10 minutes, or until smooth and elastic. Cover and leave in a warm place for 1 hour, or until doubled in size.

Meanwhile, wash the lentils well, place them in a saucepan and add 750 ml (25 fl oz/3 cups) cold water. Bring to the boil, then cover and simmer over low heat for 1–1¼ hours, or until the water is absorbed and the lentils are soft. Mash with a fork.

Heat the ghee in a frying pan and gently fry the onion until translucent and lightly browned. Add the lentils and fry for a further 5 minutes. Season with salt and stir in the sugar. Leave to cool.

Punch down the dough and divide it into two portions. Thinly roll out each portion to a 45 cm (18 inch) circle, as described on page 15.

Cut the dough into 8 cm (3¼ inch) rounds with a biscuit cutter. Place a generous teaspoon of the lentil mixture in the centre of each round. Moisten the edge of the dough lightly with water, fold over and press firmly to seal. Press around the edge with the tines of a fork.

Heat the oil in a deep saucepan to 160°C (320°F) or until a cube of bread dropped in the oil browns in 30 seconds. Beginning with the dough pieces that were shaped first, deep-fry six to eight pieces at a time for 3 minutes, or until golden brown and puffed, turning to brown evenly. Lift out with a slotted spoon and drain on paper towels.

Serve hot or warm as a snack, or as part of a meal, particularly a picnic.

PERSIAN BREADS

With patience, and a high-powered mixer with a dough hook attachment (or a strong arm), it is possible to achieve acceptable results when making these delicious breads.

In bakers' language, Persian breads are classed as 'lean' – that is, not of definite flavour – as their role is to aid the eating of other foods, rather than being enjoyed for their own sake. Personally, I find the breads absolutely delicious on their own, but I like mine buttered – in Iran this is never done.

You will need a little extra equipment, such as a small cushion wrapped in a tea towel (dish towel) and fastened on one side with a safety pin. The other side should be smooth, as the dough has to be placed on this. A cast iron or aluminium smooth-surfaced griddle is also necessary, as the bread has to cook as quickly as possible.

The bread freezes and reheats well, so once you have mastered the art, you can attempt larger quantities when you feel in the mood for bread-making.

SANGYAK
Pebble-baked wholemeal bread

The ingredients and method for making this fascinating bread are the same as for Nane Lavash (opposite). Instead of the griddle, you will require enough well-washed blue metal baking trays to cover the base of a large, shallow baking dish. Brush the blue metal with peanut oil when first making this bread. Once a few loaves have been cooked on it, the metal absorbs enough oil for further bakings.

Place the blue metal in its dish on the lowest shelf in the oven and heat the oven to 250°C (480°F/Gas 9). If using a gas oven, the centre shelf may be a better position, as these ovens do not have the advantage of having a heating element directly under the dish.

Divide the dough into six equal portions. Roll one piece out to an oval shape, or as near to oval as you can; do not roll too thinly. The rolled-out dough should not rest before being baked, so prepare each round just before you are ready to bake it.

Place a dough round on the cushion and turn onto the hot blue metal. Bake for 1 minute, then press the dough with the cushion. Bake for a further 3 minutes, then turn over and bake for 2 minutes more, or until the bread is cooked.

Remove from the oven and pull off any pieces of blue metal, returning them to the dish. (After a few breads have been baked, the metal is less likely to stick.) Wrap the bread in a cloth as it comes out of the oven.

If the bread has not browned sufficiently, place it under a hot grill (broiler) for a few seconds on each side.

Bake the remaining dough rounds in the same way, allowing the oven temperature to return to the set heat before baking the next dough round.

NANE LAVASH or TAFTOON
Wholemeal flat bread
MAKES: 6 ROUNDS

The only difference between *nane lavash* and *taftoon* is their size. *Nane lavash* is the better known of the Persian breads, but it is a very large bread and impossible to cook in the domestic oven because of its size. *Taftoon* is the same dough shaped in a smaller round, so you will be making *taftoon*. Call it *nane lavash* if you like.

150 g (5 oz/1 cup) plain (all-purpose) flour
450 g (1 lb/3 cups) wholemeal (whole-wheat) flour
2 teaspoons active dried yeast
1½ teaspoons salt
oil, for greasing

Sift the flours into a large mixing bowl, discarding any husks left in the sieve.

Dissolve the yeast in 60 ml (2 fl oz/¼ cup) warm water, then add another 375 ml (12½ fl oz/1½ cups) water and the salt. Pour the yeast mixture into the centre of the flour and gradually work in the flour.

Beat by hand for 20–30 minutes, or use the dough hook of an electric mixer and beat for 20 minutes, gradually beating in 185 ml (6½ fl oz/¾ cup) water, or as much of that amount as the dough will take. As the dough is beaten, its ability to absorb water increases.

Preheat the oven to 250°C (480°F/Gas 9) and place the griddle on the centre shelf for 10 minutes to heat. When hot, rub with a wad of cloth dipped in oil.

As there is no need to prove this dough, turn it out of the bowl onto an oiled work surface when the oven is ready.

Oil your hands and divide the dough into six equal portions, shaping each into a ball. The rolled-out dough should not rest before being baked, so prepare each round just before you are ready to bake it.

Roll out one ball of dough as thinly as possible with an oiled rolling pin. Prick it well all over with a fork, or run a pinwheel three or four times across the surface. Flip the dough across the backs of your hands to stretch it a little. Place it on the smooth side of your cushion.

Pull out the oven rack with the heated griddle, quickly turn the cushion over and press the dough onto the griddle. Close the oven and bake for 1 minute, then pat the dough down again with the cushion to stop the bread puffing up.

Bake for 3 minutes, or until the surface is bubbly, then turn the bread over and cook for 2 minutes more. Remove the bread from the oven and wrap it in a cloth.

Let the oven temperature return to the set heat before baking the next dough round.

BARBARI
White bread

MAKES: 4 LOAVES

2 teaspoons active dried yeast

1½ teaspoons salt

750 g (1 lb 10 oz/5 cups) plain
   (all-purpose) flour

1 tablespoon oil, plus extra for brushing

Dissolve the yeast in 60 ml (2 fl oz/¼ cup) warm water, then add another 440 ml (15 fl oz/1¾ cups) water and the salt.

Sift the flour into a large mixing bowl, holding back 150 g (5 oz/1 cup) of the flour. Make a well in the centre and add the yeast mixture. Stir in a little of the flour to slightly thicken the liquid, then cover and leave in a warm place for 10 minutes, or until frothy.

Mix in the flour remaining in the bowl, then beat by hand for 20 minutes, gradually adding 1 tablespoon of oil and the reserved flour. Knead in the flour when the dough becomes too stiff for beating, only adding enough to stop the dough sticking. Alternatively, beat with an electric mixer using a dough hook for 15 minutes, adding the oil gradually, then the reserved flour.

Cover and leave to rise in a warm place for 30–60 minutes, or until doubled in size.

Turn the dough out onto an oiled work surface and divide it into four equal portions. Oil your hands and a rolling pin. Roll each portion into a ball. Shape each one into a rectangle, then lightly roll each into a long strip about 12 cm (5 inches) wide and 30 cm (12 inches) long. Each loaf should be about 1 cm (½ inch) thick.

Place the loaves on lightly oiled trays, cover with cloths and leave in a warm place for 15–20 minutes.

Meanwhile, preheat the oven to 220°C (430°F/Gas 7).

Brush the tops of the loaves with oil. Using the side of your forefinger, make four parallel grooves in each loaf, running the length of the loaf, and beginning and finishing 2 cm (¾ inch) in from the ends.

Bake the loaves on the centre shelf of the oven for 15 minutes, or until cooked and golden brown.

AASHE JOE
Barley soup
SERVES: 8–10

110 g (3¾ oz/½ cup) dried chickpeas

105 g (3½ oz/½ cup) dried red kidney beans

750 g (1 lb 10 oz) lamb neck or shoulder, with the bone, chopped into chunky pieces by your butcher

165 g (5½ oz/¾ cup) pearl barley, rinsed

45 g (1½ oz/¼ cup) brown lentils, rinsed

salt and freshly ground black pepper, to season

1 small handful chopped flat-leaf parsley

1–2 tablespoons chopped coriander (cilantro) leaves

60 g (2 oz) chopped garlic chives or spring onion (scallion) leaves

30 g (1 oz/1 cup) chopped watercress

20 g (¾ oz) ghee

1 large onion, halved, then sliced

1 teaspoon ground turmeric

1 teaspoon dried mint

Wash the chickpeas and kidney beans and place in a bowl. Cover with 750 ml (25 fl oz/3 cups) water and soak overnight.

Rinse lamb in water and place it in a large saucepan. Add 2 litres (68 fl oz/8 cups) water, the chickpeas, beans and their soaking water. Bring slowly to a simmer, skimming when necessary. Cover and simmer gently for 1 hour.

Add the barley and lentils and season with salt and pepper. Cover and simmer for a further 1½ hours, or until the meat is tender and the beans are soft.

Remove the meat from the pan and strip the flesh from the bones. Cut into small pieces and return to the pan with the herbs and greens. Cover and leave over low heat for 15 minutes.

Meanwhile, heat the ghee in a frying pan and gently fry the onion until golden. Sprinkle with the turmeric and fry until the onion is crisp, ensuring it doesn't burn. Rub the mint to a powder, stir it through the onion and remove from the heat.

Stir half the onion mixture into the soup. Serve with flat bread as a main meal, garnished with the remaining onion.

MAST VA KHIAR
Cold yoghurt soup
SERVES: 6

2 green cucumbers

750 g (1 lb 10 oz/3 cups) yoghurt

3 spring onions (scallions), including the green tops

60 g (2 oz/½ cup) sultanas (golden raisins), washed if necessary

1 tablespoon finely chopped flat-leaf parsley

1 tablespoon finely chopped dill

2 shelled hard-boiled eggs, finely chopped

60 g (2 oz/½ cup) finely chopped walnuts, optional

salt, to taste

250 ml (8½ fl oz/1 cup) iced water

extra flat-leaf parsley and/or dill, to garnish

Peel the cucumbers thinly, then grate coarsely. Place the cucumber flesh and juice in a bowl with the yoghurt.

Thinly slice the spring onions, leaving on some of the green tops. Add to the yoghurt with the sultanas, herbs, egg and walnuts, if using. Season to taste with salt.

Mix in enough iced water to give a thick cream consistency, and adjust the flavour with more salt if necessary. Cover and chill for at least 2 hours.

Serve in bowls, garnished with additional chopped herbs or herb sprigs.

AASHE ANAR
Pomegranate soup
SERVES: 6

2 lamb or veal foreshanks, cracked

55 g (2 oz/¼ cup) yellow split peas, rinsed

1 small beetroot (beet), peeled and diced

1 small onion, finely chopped

salt and freshly ground black pepper, to season

40 g (1½ oz/1 cup) finely chopped spinach

1 small handful finely chopped flat-leaf parsley

2 tablespoons finely chopped coriander
(cilantro) leaves, optional

2 tablespoons chopped garlic chives

60 g (2 oz/½ cup) chopped spring onion
(scallion) tops

75 g (2½ oz/⅓ cup) short-grain white rice, washed

375 ml (12½ fl oz/1½ cups) pomegranate juice
(see page 525)

sugar, to taste

1–2 tablespoons lemon or lime juice

1 quantity Nano Dok (page 428)

Rinse the meat and place it in a saucepan with 1.5 litres
(51 fl oz/6 cups) water. Add the split peas and bring to a slow
simmer, skimming when necessary.

When well skimmed and beginning to boil, add the beetroot
and onion, and season with salt and pepper. Cover and simmer
over low heat for 1½–2 hours, or until the meat is very tender.

Remove the shanks from the pan and strip the meat from
the bones. Chop the meat into small pieces and return to the
soup with the spinach, herbs, garlic chives, spring onion and
rice. Add the sugar and lemon or lime juice to taste — the soup
should have a tart but slightly sweet flavour. Cover and simmer
for a further 30 minutes.

Meanwhile, prepare the Nano Dok as directed on page 428,
using a larger amount of ghee. Stir half of it into the soup.

Ladle the soup into bowls, drizzling the remaining Nano
Dok on top of each.

ABGUSHTE MIVEH
Dried fruit soup
SERVES: 6

500 g (1 lb 2 oz) lean lamb or beef stewing meat

500 g (1 lb 2 oz) lamb or beef soup bones

1 dried lime (Loomi, page 345), optional

salt and freshly ground black pepper, to season

40 g (1½ oz) ghee or butter

1 large onion, finely chopped

2 teaspoons ground turmeric

220 g (8 oz/1 cup) pitted prunes

90 g (3 oz/½ cup) dried apricot halves

90 g (3 oz/½ cup) chopped dried peaches

80–115 g (3–4 oz/⅓ –½ cup) firmly packed brown sugar

1–2 tablespoons lemon or lime juice

Cut the meat into small cubes and place in a saucepan with the
bones and 1.75 litres (59 fl oz/7 cups) water. If using a dried
lime, pierce the top and base using a skewer and add it to the
pan. Bring slowly to the boil, skimming when necessary.
Season with salt and pepper.

Cover and simmer gently for 1½ hours, or until the meat is
almost tender. Remove the bones and dried lime.

Heat the ghee or butter in a frying pan and gently fry the
onion until translucent. Stir in the turmeric and cook until
lightly browned. Add the mixture to the soup with the dried
fruits (these may be washed if necessary, but do not require
soaking). Cover and simmer for 30 minutes.

Add the sugar and lemon or lime juice to taste, so that the
soup has a pleasant sweet–sour flavour. Serve hot.

❧ *Variation: Follow the directions above, replacing the dried fruits
with 525 g (1 lb 2½ oz/3 cups) of chopped, peeled and cored quince.
After the browned onion and turmeric have been added to the soup,
heat another 2 tablespoons of ghee in the pan and fry the quince
gently for 10 minutes, stirring often. Add to the soup, then cover and
simmer for 30–45 minutes, or until the quince is tender. Adjust the
sweet–sour flavour at end of cooking.*

ESHKANEH
Onion soup
SERVES: 6

Many versions of this soup are prepared in Iran. Basically it is a meatless soup with onion and a sour juice – lime, lemon, pomegranate or verjuice (the juice of unripened grapes) – as the principal ingredients, with the tartness counterbalanced by the addition of sugar. Sometimes apricots or sour cherries are used instead of fruit juice. Walnuts, spinach or diced potatoes are added to give substance.

In other words, the soup is composed of ingredients the cook might have on hand; once you have tried this version, experiment with other combinations.

The eggs, prepared in either of the two ways mentioned in the recipe, are essential.

5 onions

90 g (3 oz/⅓ cup) ghee

50 g (2 oz/⅓ cup) plain (all-purpose) flour

½ teaspoon ground turmeric

60 g (2 oz/½ cup) finely chopped walnuts, or
　　130 g (4 oz/2 cups) finely chopped spinach,
　　or 360 g (12½ oz/2 cups) diced potatoes

125 ml (4 fl oz/½ cup) lime or lemon juice

95 g (3½ oz/½ cup) lightly packed brown sugar,
　　approximately

salt and freshly ground black pepper, to taste

1 quantity Nano Dok (page 428)

2–6 eggs

Cut the onions in half from top to bottom, then slice each half into semi-circles.

Heat 1 tablespoon of the ghee in a heavy-based saucepan over medium–high heat. Add about 80 g (3 oz/½ cup) of the onion slices and fry until brown and crisp. Remove and set aside for garnishing.

Heat the remaining ghee in the pan and gently fry the remaining onion until translucent. Stir in the flour and cook until golden.

Add the turmeric, and your choice of walnuts, spinach or potatoes. Cook for 2 minutes, stirring often. Stir in 1.25 litres (42½ fl oz/5 cups) water and cook until thickened and bubbling, stirring occasionally. Cover and simmer for 20 minutes.

Add the lime or lemon juice and the sugar. Season with salt and pepper. Cover and simmer for a further 15 minutes.

Meanwhile, prepare the Nano Dok as directed on page 428. Stir the Nano Dok into the soup.

Lightly beat two eggs and slowly pour them into the soup, stirring gently until the eggs set in shreds. Alternatively, break six eggs into the simmering soup, one at a time, and simmer gently until the eggs have set.

Ladle the soup into bowls; if using whole eggs, add one to each bowl. Garnish with the reserved browned onions and serve with flat bread.

CHELOU
Steamed rice
SERVES: 6

400 g (14 oz/2 cups) basmati or other
    good-quality long-grain white rice
2 tablespoons salt
60 g (2 oz/¼ cup) butter or ghee

Remove any discoloured grains and stones from the rice. Place the rice in a sieve and wash well under running water until the water runs clear. Drain.

Bring 2 litres (68 fl oz/8 cups) water to the boil in a heavy-based saucepan. Add the salt and rice and stir until the water returns to the boil. Allow the rice to boil for 5 minutes, then drain immediately.

In a small saucepan, heat the butter with 60 ml (2 fl oz/¼ cup) water until bubbling. Pour half the mixture into the saucepan in which the rice was cooked, swirling to coat the base and side. Spread half the partly cooked rice in the pan and even it out with the back of a spoon.

Spoon the remaining rice on top in a mound. Make a hole in the centre with the end of a wooden spoon, then pour the remaining butter mixture on top.

Cover the rim of the pan with a doubled-over tea towel (dish towel) and put the lid on firmly. Cook over medium–low heat for 10 minutes. Reduce the heat to low and cook for a further 35 minutes. The cloth absorbs the steam and makes the rice fluffy and light.

Stir the rice gently with a fork to distribute the butter evenly. Serve with *kababs* and *khoreshes*, and use as a basis for *polous*.

CHELOU TA DIG
Steamed crusty rice
SERVES: 6

This is the rice dish by which the expertise of a Persian cook is gauged. While plain *chelou* gives a rice so light and fragrant, each grain glistening separately, *chelou ta dig* is all this, plus crusty, crunchy golden-brown rice for a completely new rice-eating experience – except to the Persians, of course.

Follow the basic Chelou method (left), to the stage where you have drained the partly cooked rice. Combine about 185 g (6 oz/1 cup) of the rice with a beaten egg yolk or 60 g (2 oz/¼ cup) yoghurt, then spread it in the butter-swirled saucepan.

Spoon the remaining rice on top in a mound, and continue with the basic Chelou method, until you come to the cooking.

Cook over medium heat for 15 minutes, then reduce the heat to medium–low for a further 30 minutes. By this time the bottom of the rice should be golden brown and crisp.

Place the pan on a cold surface for a few minutes to loosen the rice from the base.

Spoon the fluffy rice into a heated dish. Break up the crusty layer into pieces and arrange around the rice, browned side up. Serve with *kababs* and *khoreshes*.

KATEH
Rice cake

SERVES: 6

This method of cooking rice is popular in the Caspian Sea region of northern Iran, where much of Iran's rice is grown. It is a simplified version of Chelou Ta Dig (page 444), unmoulded like a cake and served cut into wedges.

Basmati rice is best for this dish.

400 g (14 oz/2 cups) basmati rice
2 teaspoons salt
60 g (2 oz/¼ cup) ghee or butter

Remove any discoloured grains and stones from the rice. Place the rice in a sieve and wash well under running water until the water runs clear. Drain.

Place the rice in a heavy-based saucepan, preferably one with a non-stick coating. Add 875 ml (29 fl oz/3½ cups) water and the salt.

Bring to the boil over medium heat, stirring occasionally. Cover, reduce the heat a little and cook for 25 minutes, or until the water is absorbed.

Stir the ghee or butter through, using a wooden spoon. Even out the top of the rice, pressing lightly. Cover and return to medium–low heat for 30 minutes. Move the pan over the hotplate or burner from time to time, so the base becomes evenly browned.

Remove the pan from the heat and place in cold water for 10 minutes. Run a spatula or knife around the side of the rice to loosen it, then invert a plate on top. Holding the plate firmly to the saucepan, turn the pan upside down, so that the rice cake comes out cleanly.

Cut into wedges and serve with *khoreshes*. The rice cake is often served cold in summer.

DAMI
Boiled rice

SERVES: 6

Here is yet another method for cooking rice. It is similar to Kateh (left), except that the heat is kept lower once the rice begins to boil, and the rim of the pan is covered with a cloth or two paper towels before the lid is placed in position.

After 30 minutes, pour the melted ghee or butter over the rice, replace the lid without the cloth, and leave over low heat for a further 30 minutes.

Fluff up the rice with a fork. Serve as an accompaniment to *khoreshes*, or mix with other ingredients before or halfway through cooking.

ESTANBOLI POLOU
Potato-crusted rice with lamb

SERVES: 6

For this recipe I have used a method that can be applied to other *polous*. Akhtar Ostowari, an Iranian residing in Sydney, Australia, makes many of her *polous* in this way. She has found that straight-sided utensils with a non-stick coating always ensure perfect unmoulding of any crusted *polou*, without the need to place the utensil on a cold surface to loosen the contents.

With the potato lining used in this recipe, a straight-sided pan of heavy-gauge aluminium works just as well. You can use the potato-crusted rice method for other *polou* recipes.

750 g (1 lb 10 oz) lean boneless lamb or beef,
    suitable for braising

60 g (2 oz/¼ cup) ghee or butter

1 large onion, finely chopped

½ teaspoon ground cinnamon

1 teaspoon paprika

250 g (9 oz/1 cup) tomato passata (puréed tomatoes)

salt and freshly ground black pepper,
    to season

Potato-crusted rice

400 g (14 oz/2 cups) basmati or other
    good-quality long-grain white rice

2 tablespoons salt

3–4 potatoes

90 g (3 oz/⅓ cup) ghee

Trim the meat and cut into 3 cm (1¼ inch) cubes. Heat half the ghee or butter in a saucepan and brown the meat on all sides. Transfer to a plate.

Heat the remaining ghee in the pan and gently fry the onion until translucent. Sprinkle in the cinnamon and paprika and return the meat to the pan. Add the passata and 125 ml (4 fl oz/½ cup) water and season with salt and pepper. Cover and simmer gently for 1 hour, or until the meat is just tender.

Meanwhile, prepare the potato-crusted rice. Remove any discoloured grains and stones from the rice. Place the rice in a sieve and wash well under running water until the water runs clear. Drain.

Bring 2 litres (68 fl oz/8 cups) water to the boil. Add the rice and salt and stir occasionally until the water starts boiling again. Allow to boil, uncovered, for 8 minutes, then drain.

Meanwhile, peel the potatoes and cut into 5 mm (¼ inch) slices. Place them in cold salted water and leave to soak until the meat is cooked.

Drain the potatoes and dry well. Melt half the ghee in a heavy-based saucepan. Coat the potato slices in the ghee and arrange them around the base and side of the pan.

Add half the rice, spreading it evenly, and top with the cooked meat mixture. Spread the remaining rice on top and pour the remaining melted ghee evenly over the rice.

Cover the rim of the pan with two paper towels or a cloth and put the lid on tightly. Cook over high heat for 3 minutes, then reduce the heat to medium and cook for 30 minutes.

Reduce the heat to medium–low and cook for a further 30 minutes. Move the pan on the hotplate or burner from time to time so that the potatoes brown evenly.

Run a knife around the rice to loosen it, then carefully invert it onto a serving platter. Cut into wedges to serve.

MIVEH DAMI
Rice with fruit
SERVES: 6

400 g (14 oz/2 cups) basmati or other
    good-quality long-grain white rice

60 g (2 oz/¼ cup) ghee or butter

1 small onion, finely chopped

250 g (9 oz) lean lamb or veal stewing meat, diced

½ teaspoon ground cinnamon

300 g (10½ oz/1½ cups) pitted sour cherries

60 g (2 oz/½ cup) chopped walnuts

35 g (1¼ oz/¼ cup) currants

40 g (1½ oz/¼ cup) chopped dried apricots

2 teaspoons salt

freshly ground black pepper, to season

Remove any discoloured grains and stones from the rice. Place the rice in a sieve and wash well under running water until the water runs clear. Drain.

Heat the ghee in a heavy-based saucepan and gently fry the onion and meat until lightly browned. Stir in the cinnamon, cherries, walnuts, currants and apricots. Add the salt and season with pepper.

Add the drained rice and stir to combine. Pour in enough cold water to cover the rice by 2 cm (¾ inch).

Cover the rim of the pan with a cloth or two paper towels and put the lid on tightly. Cook over very low heat for 50 minutes.

HAVIJ POLOU
Rice with carrots
SERVES: 6

1 kg (2 lb 3 oz) chicken breasts, or 1 whole chicken

500 g (1 lb 2 oz) carrots

185 g (6½ oz/¾ cup) ghee or butter

salt and freshly ground black pepper, to season

1 large onion, finely chopped

1 teaspoon ground turmeric

60 ml (2 fl oz/¼ cup) lemon juice

55 g (2 oz/¼ cup) firmly packed brown sugar

1 quantity Chelou (page 444)

Cut the chicken breasts into quarters; if using a whole chicken, joint the chicken and cut the larger pieces in half. Scrape the carrots and cut into batons 5 mm (¼ inch) thick and 5 cm (2 inches) long.

Heat half the ghee in a frying pan and brown the chicken pieces on each side, in batches if necessary. Remove to a plate and season with salt and pepper.

Heat the remaining ghee in the pan and gently fry the onion until translucent. Sprinkle in the turmeric, add the carrots and cook, stirring often, for a further 5 minutes.

Add the lemon juice, sugar and 125 ml (4 fl oz/½ cup) water and stir to dissolve the browned sediment. Return the chicken to the pan, then cover and simmer gently for 10 minutes. Remove the chicken and set aside.

Meanwhile, prepare the Chelou recipe as directed on page 444, to the point where the rice is boiled for 5 minutes and drained. Swirl half the butter mixture from the Chelou recipe around the pan, then spread half the rice evenly over the base. Place the chicken pieces on top of the rice, then spread the carrot mixture over the chicken. Spread the remaining rice over the carrots, then add the remaining butter mixture from the Chelou recipe.

Cover the rim of the pan with two paper towels. Put the lid on tightly and cook over medium–low heat for 40 minutes. Alternatively, you can layer the *polou* in a casserole dish and bake in a 170°C (340°F/Gas 3) oven for 30 minutes.

KADO POLOU
Rice with pumpkin
SERVES: 4–5

500 g (1 lb 2 oz) finely minced (ground) lamb,
    beef or veal

1 small onion, grated

½ teaspoon ground cinnamon

¼ teaspoon ground nutmeg

1 teaspoon salt

freshly ground black pepper, to season

500 g (1 lb 2 oz) butternut pumpkin (squash)

1 large onion

60 g (2 oz/¼ cup) butter or ghee

1 quantity Chelou (page 444)

3 teaspoons brown sugar

Combine the meat in a mixing bowl with the onion, cinnamon, nutmeg, salt and pepper and mix thoroughly. Shape into balls the size of large walnuts, then flatten into thick patties.

Peel the pumpkin and cut into slices 1 cm (½ inch) thick.

Halve the onion lengthways and slice thinly.

Heat half the butter or ghee in a frying pan and gently fry the onion until translucent and lightly browned. Take care not to burn it. Remove from the pan and set aside.

Add the remaining butter to the pan and brown the meat patties on each side. Remove from the pan and set aside.

Meanwhile, prepare the Chelou recipe as directed on page 444, to the point where the rice is boiled for 5 minutes and drained. Swirl half the butter mixture from the Chelou recipe around the pan, then spread half the rice evenly over the base. Place the meat patties on top of the rice, cover with half the onion, then all the pumpkin. Sprinkle with the sugar, salt and pepper and top with the remaining onion. Spread the remaining rice over the top, then add the remaining butter mixture from the Chelou recipe.

Cover the rim of the pan with two paper towels, close the lid tightly and cook over medium for 10 minutes. Reduce heat to low and cook for 30 minutes, until the pumpkin is tender.

Alternatively, you can layer the *polou* in a casserole dish and bake in a 180°C (350°F/Gas 4) oven.

MORGH POLOU
Rice with chicken
SERVES: 4–5

1 chicken, about 1.5 kg (3 lb 5 oz), jointed

salt and freshly ground black pepper, to season

60 g (2 oz/¼ cup) butter or ghee

1 large onion, finely chopped

75 g (2½ oz/½ cup) chopped dried apricots

60 g (2 oz/½ cup) sultanas (golden raisins)

½ teaspoon ground cinnamon

½ teaspoon saffron threads

1 quantity Chelou (page 444)

Wipe the chicken dry with paper towels. Season all the pieces with salt and pepper.

Heat half the butter in a frying pan and brown the chicken pieces on all sides, in batches if necessary. Remove to a plate.

Heat the remaining butter in the pan and gently fry the onion until translucent. Add the apricots and sultanas and cook for a further 5 minutes. Stir in the cinnamon and a little water to dissolve the browned sediment.

Meanwhile, prepare the Chelou recipe as directed on page 444, to the point where the rice is boiled for 5 minutes and drained. Swirl half the butter mixture from the Chelou recipe around the pan, then spread half the rice evenly over the base. Place the chicken pieces on top of the rice. Spread the apricot mixture over the chicken. Spread the remaining rice over the top, then add the remaining butter mixture from the Chelou recipe.

Cover the rim of the pan with two paper towels, put the lid on tightly and cook over low heat for 50 minutes, or until the chicken is tender.

While the *polou* is cooking, boil two tablespoons of water and mix it with the saffron. Set aside to steep.

Just before serving, sprinkle the saffron liquid over the rice and gently stir it in. Serve piled on a platter.

MOHI POLOU
Fish with herbed rice

SERVES: 6

750 g (1 lb 10 oz) fish steaks

salt, for sprinkling

60 g (2 oz/¼ cup) ghee

1 teaspoon ground turmeric

1 quantity Chelou (page 444)

120 g (4 oz/1 cup) chopped spring onion (scallion) tops

95 g (3½ oz/1½ cups) chopped spinach

3 tablespoons chopped coriander (cilantro) leaves

3 tablespoons chopped flat-leaf parsley

2 tablespoons chopped dill

freshly ground black pepper, to season

Pat the fish dry with paper towels. Sprinkle lightly with salt and leave for 15 minutes.

Heat the ghee in a frying pan and quickly brown the fish steaks on each side — it is not necessary to cook them through. Transfer to a plate.

Add the turmeric to the ghee remaining in the pan. Fry for 2 minutes, then remove from the heat.

Prepare the Chelou recipe as directed on page 444, to the point where the rice is boiled for 5 minutes and drained. Tip the drained rice into a bowl, add the chopped vegetables and herbs and season with salt and pepper. Toss until thoroughly combined.

Swirl half the butter mixture from the Chelou recipe around the pan, then spread half the rice and herb mixture evenly over the base. Place the fish steaks on top of the rice, then pour the turmeric-flavoured ghee over the fish. Spread the remaining rice and herb mixture over the top, then add the remaining butter mixture from the Chelou recipe.

Cover the rim of the pan with two paper towels, put the lid on tightly and cook over low heat for 45 minutes.

Spoon the rice from the top of the dish around the edge of a serving platter. Lift the fish onto a plate. Spoon the remaining rice into the centre of the platter and arrange the fish on top. Serve hot, garnished with herb sprigs if desired.

SHEVID BHAGALA POLOU
Rice with lamb, broad beans and dill
SERVES: 6

60 g (2 oz/½ cup) ghee or butter

1.5 kg (3 lb 5 oz) lamb shoulder chops, cut 4 cm
(1½ inches) thick

1 large onion, finely chopped

½ teaspoon ground turmeric

salt and freshly ground black pepper, to season

600 g (1 lb 5 oz/3 cups) basmati or other
good-quality long-grain white rice

2 tablespoons salt

300 g (10½ oz) fresh shelled broad beans (fava beans),
skins removed (see note)

1 handful chopped dill

Heat 1 tablespoon of the ghee in a heavy-based saucepan. Working in batches, brown the lamb chops on each side, removing each batch to a plate.

Heat another tablespoon of ghee in the pan and gently fry the onion until translucent. Add the turmeric and cook for 2 minutes longer.

Stir in 250 ml (8½ fl oz/1 cup) water, return the lamb to the pan and season with salt and pepper. Cover and simmer gently for 1 hour, or until the lamb is tender but not falling apart.

Preheat the oven to 180°C (350°F/Gas 4).

While the lamb is cooking, bring 2 litres (68 fl oz/8 cups) water to the boil in a large saucepan. Add the well-washed rice and the 2 tablespoons salt. Stir until the water returns to the boil, then allow to boil, uncovered, for 5 minutes. Drain immediately.

Mix the broad beans and dill in a bowl. Add half the hot rice, toss to combine and season with salt.

Melt the remaining ghee in a large casserole dish and add 1 tablespoon water. Swirl to coat the side of the dish, then pour most of the ghee into a container.

Place the remaining plain rice in the casserole dish and even it out. Top with the lamb mixture, including the juices. Spread the broad bean and rice mixture on top. Pour half the reserved ghee evenly over the rice. Cover and bake for 35–40 minutes, or until the beans are tender.

Spoon the broad bean and rice mixture from the top and arrange around the edge of a serving platter. Remove the lamb pieces to a plate. Spoon the rice from the bottom of the dish in the centre of the platter and top with the lamb pieces.

Pour the ghee from the dish over the lamb and rice. Serve with yoghurt and pickles.

❋ *Note: Fresh shelled broad beans are skinned similarly to dried soaked broad beans, as described on page 10. Fennel can be substituted for the dill in this recipe.*

KUKU

These delicious egg dishes feature prominently in Persian menus because of their versatility. Cut into small squares they can be served with pre-dinner drinks; with yoghurt and bread they make an excellent luncheon or supper dish; for dinner in the Western tradition they make an excellent first course, and are almost always part of the menu for a Persian dinner. As they are just as delicious served cold, prepare one for the picnic hamper, as they do in Iran.

The usual method of cooking is in the oven, a relatively recent adaptation, since ovens were seldom part of the early Persian kitchen. The other and more authentic method is to cook the *kuku* in a frying pan on the stovetop. The finished *kuku* should resemble a cake when served, lightly browned and crisp all over, so your choice of cooking utensil and cooking method can be determined by the equipment you have on hand.

Modern Persian cooks have been quick to see the advantage of non-stick cookware for many of their dishes – in particular for certain rice dishes and for *kukus*.

For oven cooking, choose a smooth-surfaced casserole dish, or a Dutch oven or cake tin with a non-stick coating. The straighter the sides, the better.

For stovetop cooking, a well-seasoned heavy-based frying pan, or one with a non-stick coating, should be used. An omelette pan is far too small, unless you halve the recipe.

Where initial cooking of the vegetables is required, use any pan, keeping your special pan for finishing the *kuku*.

To present the *kuku* for serving, it always looks better with the top uppermost. If unmoulding from an oven dish, invert the *kuku* onto a plate, then place the serving plate on top and turn it upright.

Of course you can serve it straight from the dish it was cooked in if you find your *kuku* has stuck!

KUKUYE SIBZAMINI
Potato omelette
SERVES: 4–6

500 g (1 lb 2 oz) potatoes

2 onions, grated

1 teaspoon ground turmeric

salt and freshly ground black pepper, to taste

6 eggs

60 g (2 oz/¼ cup) ghee

Cook the potatoes in a saucepan of boiling water. Drain them well and mash to a purée. Mix in the onion and turmeric and season with salt and pepper. Leave until cold.

Meanwhile, preheat the oven to 180°C (350°F/Gas 4).

Break the eggs into a bowl. Beat with a whisk, then gradually stir into the potato mixture. Mix thoroughly and season with salt and pepper.

Melt the ghee in a 20 cm (8 inch) casserole dish, non-stick Dutch oven or cake tin in the oven. Swirl the melted ghee around the dish to coat the base and side, then pour in the egg mixture.

Bake for 30 minutes, or until set and lightly browned on top. If insufficiently browned, place under a hot grill (broiler) for a few seconds.

Turn out onto a serving dish and serve cut into wedges.

Note: Alternatively, the kuku *may be cooked in a frying pan on a stovetop. Cover and cook over medium heat until set, then brown the top under a hot grill (broiler). Loosen the* kuku *and slide onto a serving dish.*

KUKUYE BADEMJAN
« Eggplant omelette

SERVES: 4

500 g (1 lb 2 oz) eggplants (aubergines)

90 g (3 oz/⅓ cup) ghee, or 85 ml (3 fl oz/⅓ cup) oil

2 spring onions (scallions), chopped

6 eggs

1 teaspoon salt

freshly ground black pepper, to season

20 g (¾ oz) ghee

yoghurt and flat bread, to serve

Peel the eggplants and cut into large cubes.

Heat the ghee or oil in a frying pan and fry the eggplant over medium heat until lightly browned and tender.

Pour the pan contents into a bowl, mash with a fork and add the spring onion. Leave until cool.

Meanwhile, preheat the oven to 180°C (350°F/Gas 4).

Break the eggs into a bowl, then beat well with a fork or whisk. Season with salt and pepper and add to the eggplant.

Melt the ghee in a 23 cm (9 inch) round casserole dish or cake tin in the oven. Swirl the melted ghee around the dish to coat the base and side, then pour in the egg mixture.

Bake for 40 minutes, or until firm and lightly browned on top. If insufficiently browned, place under a hot grill (broiler) for a few seconds.

Serve hot, cut into wedges, with yoghurt and flat bread. It is also good served cold.

KUKUYE KADOU HALVAII
Pumpkin squash omelette

SERVES: 4

Follow the Kukuye Sibzamini recipe on page 453, using 500 g (1 lb 2 oz) butternut pumpkin (squash) or similar yellow firm pumpkin (winter squash) instead of the potatoes.

Boil and drain, return to the heat and let the excess moisture evaporate. Mash to a purée, add a little sugar and continue as directed in the recipe.

KUKUYE KADOU
Zucchini omelette

SERVES: 6

4–5 zucchini (courgettes), preferably the
    light-skinned variety

60 g (2 oz/¼ cup) ghee

1 large onion, grated or finely chopped

1 teaspoon ground turmeric

1 teaspoon salt

1 teaspoon sugar

freshly ground black pepper, to taste

6 eggs

20 g (¾ oz) ghee, or 1 tablespoon oil

yoghurt and flat bread, to serve

Wash and trim the zucchini and cut into 5 mm (¼ inch) slices.

Heat the ghee in a frying pan and gently fry the onion until translucent. Add the zucchini, increase the heat to medium–high and cook for 15 minutes, stirring occasionally, until the vegetables are lightly coloured and any moisture has evaporated.

Remove from the heat. Stir in the turmeric, salt and sugar. Season with pepper and leave until cooled.

Meanwhile, preheat the oven to 180°C (350°F/Gas 4).

Break the eggs into a bowl. Beat with a whisk and season lightly. Stir in the cooled zucchini mixture.

Heat the 1 tablespoon of ghee or oil in a 20 cm (8 inch) non-stick casserole dish, Dutch oven or cake tin in the oven. Swirl the ghee or oil around the dish to coat the base and side. Pour in the egg mixture.

Bake for 30 minutes, or until set, puffed and lightly browned on top. If insufficiently browned, place under a hot grill (broiler) for a few seconds.

Unmould onto a plate. Serve hot or cold, cut into wedges, with yoghurt and flat bread.

❀ *Note: To cook the* kuku *in a frying pan, heat 1 tablespoon ghee in the pan and swirl to coat the side. Pour in the egg mixture, then cover and cook over medium heat for 10–15 minutes, or until set and puffed in the centre. Place under a hot grill (broiler) to brown the top. Loosen the egg, tilt the pan and slide the* kuku *onto a serving platter.*

KUKUYE SABZI
Herb omelette
SERVES: 4–6

For this dish, the vegetables and herbs must be well washed and dried before chopping and measuring. The chopping can be done very speedily and efficiently in a food processor. Accurate measuring of greens is not essential to the success of this dish.

130 g (4½ oz/2 cups) finely chopped spinach
180 g (6 oz/1½ cups) finely chopped spring onions
    (scallions), including the green tops
1 small handful finely chopped flat-leaf parsley
1 small handful finely chopped coriander
    (cilantro) leaves
1 tablespoon chopped dill
1 tablespoon chopped tarragon, optional
2 tablespoons chopped garlic chives
1 tablespoon plain (all-purpose) flour
1 teaspoon salt
freshly ground black pepper, to season
8 eggs
60 g (2 oz/¼ cup) ghee or butter
yoghurt and flat bread, to serve

Preheat the oven to 180°C (350°F/Gas 4).

Combine the greens and herbs in a bowl. Season the flour with the salt and a good grinding of pepper, sprinkle over the greens and toss well.

Break the eggs into a bowl. Beat until frothy, then pour over the greens. Stir well to combine.

Melt the butter in a 23 cm (9 inch) round casserole dish or deep cake tin in the oven. Swirl the melted butter around the dish to coat the base and side, then pour in the egg mixture.

Place in the oven, one shelf above the centre. Bake for 45–50 minutes, or until set and lightly browned on top. If insufficiently browned, place under a hot grill (broiler) for a few seconds.

Serve hot, cut into wedges, with yoghurt and flat bread.

KUKUYE MOHI
Fish omelette
SERVES: 4–6

500 g (1 lb 2 oz) skinless white fish fillets
salt, for sprinkling
90 g (3 oz/⅓ cup) ghee
1 small onion, finely chopped
½ teaspoon ground turmeric
1 tablespoon finely chopped coriander
    (cilantro) leaves
1 tablespoon plain (all-purpose) flour
6 eggs
freshly ground black pepper, to season

Pat the fish dry with paper towels. Sprinkle lightly with salt and leave for 10 minutes.

Meanwhile, preheat the oven to 180°C (350°F/Gas 4).

Heat 60 g (2 oz/¼ cup) of the ghee in a frying pan and fry the fish quickly on each side until cooked through; it does not have to brown. Remove the fish to a plate and flake it with a fork, removing any bones. Tip the fish into a bowl.

Gently fry the onion until translucent, in the ghee remaining in the pan. Stir in the turmeric and cook for 2 minutes. Add the mixture to the fish, along with the coriander and flour, and mix to combine.

Break the eggs into a bowl. Beat well with a fork and add to the fish mixture. Season with salt and pepper and mix thoroughly.

Melt the remaining ghee in a 20 cm (8 inch) non-stick cake tin, casserole dish or Dutch oven. Swirl the melted ghee around the dish to coat the base and side, then pour in the egg mixture.

Bake for 30 minutes, or until set. If insufficiently browned, place under a hot grill (broiler) for a few seconds.

Unmould onto a serving platter. Serve hot or cold, cut into wedges.

MOHI SHEKUMPOUR
Stuffed baked fish

SERVES: 4–5

1 whole fish suitable for baking,
    weighing about 1.5 kg (3 lb 5 oz)
salt and freshly ground black pepper, to season
60 g (2 oz/½ cup) finely chopped spring onions
    (scallions)
100 g (3½ oz/2 cups) chopped mixed fresh herbs,
    such as flat-leaf parsley, coriander (cilantro),
    dill and watercress
juice of 1 lemon
60 ml (2 fl oz/¼ cup) olive oil
herb sprigs, to garnish
lemon wedges, to garnish
Chelou (page 444), to serve

Preheat the oven to 190°C (375°F/Gas 5).

Clean and scale the fish if necessary. Rub it inside and out with salt and pepper and set aside.

In a mixing bowl, combine the spring onion and herbs with 1 tablespoon of the lemon juice and 1 tablespoon of the oil. Season lightly and toss together.

Fill the cavity of the fish with the herb mixture. Secure the opening with wooden cocktail sticks or a fine metal skewer. Cut three diagonal slashes on each side of the fish. Place it in a well-oiled baking dish and pour the remaining lemon juice and oil over the top.

Bake for 40–50 minutes, or until the fish flakes easily when the thickest part is tested with a fork. During cooking, baste the fish with the juices in the baking dish.

Lift the fish carefully onto a serving platter. Garnish with fresh herb sprigs and lemon wedges. Serve with Chelou and a *borani* (Persian salad).

If desired, serve a small bowl of yoghurt on the side, drizzled with olive oil and paprika.

IRAN

SEAFOOD

KHORESHE FESENJAN
Duck in walnut and pomegranate sauce
SERVES: 4

1 duck, about 2 kg (4 lb 6 oz), cleaned

salt and freshly ground black pepper, to season

40 g (1½ oz) ghee or butter

1 large onion, finely chopped

115 g (4 oz/1 cup) finely ground walnuts

60 g (2 oz/½ cup) coarsely ground walnuts

375 ml (12½ fl oz/1½ cups) pomegranate juice
   (see page 525)

3 tablespoons brown sugar

2 pieces of cinnamon bark

1 tablespoon lime or lemon juice, optional

For serving

30 g (1 oz/¼ cup) coarsely chopped walnuts

pomegranate seeds, if available

Chelou (page 444) or Chelou Ta Dig (page 444)

Remove the pin feathers from the duck. Remove the excess fat from the cavity. Wipe the duck dry with paper towels, then truss. Season with salt and pepper.

Heat half the ghee in a large heavy-based saucepan and brown the duck on all sides over medium heat. Remove to a plate. Drain the fat from the pan.

Heat the remaining ghee in the pan and gently fry the onion until translucent. Add the walnuts, pomegranate juice, sugar and cinnamon and bring to the boil.

Return the duck to the pan and spoon the sauce over it. Cover and simmer gently for 2–2½ hours, or until tender, basting the duck occasionally during cooking. Also adjust the seasoning of the sauce during cooking, adding lime or lemon juice if the pomegranate juice lacks tartness.

Lift the duck onto a platter and keep it hot.

Skim the excess oil from the sauce, then return the sauce to the boil.

To serve, spoon the sauce over the duck and garnish with the walnuts. Add a dash of colour with pomegranate seeds, if available.

Carve the duck into four portions and serve with *chelou*.

❀ *Note: A whole chicken or chicken pieces may also be used instead of duck.*

KHORESHE HOLU
Peach sauce with chicken

SERVES: 5–6

1.5 kg (3 lb 5 oz) chicken pieces, such as breasts,
    legs and thighs, or 1 jointed whole chicken

salt and freshly ground black pepper, to season

60 g (2 oz/¼ cup) ghee or butter

1 onion, chopped

1 teaspoon ground turmeric

1 small piece of cinnamon bark

3 firm peaches

60 ml (2 fl oz/¼ cup) lemon or lime juice

2 tablespoons brown sugar

Chelou Ta Dig (page 444), to serve

Cut the chicken pieces if they are large. Pat the pieces dry with paper towels, then season with salt and pepper.

Heat half the ghee in a heavy-based saucepan and brown the chicken pieces in batches. Remove to a plate.

Using the fat in the pan, gently fry the onion until translucent. Sprinkle with the turmeric and fry until the onion begins to brown. Add 250 ml (8½ fl oz/1 cup) water and stir to dissolve the browned sediment.

Return the chicken to the pan and add the cinnamon. Cover and simmer gently for 45 minutes, or until almost tender.

Peel and stone the peaches, then slice into wedges. Heat the remaining ghee and fry the peaches until lightly coloured.

Arrange the peaches on top of the chicken. Sprinkle with the lemon juice and sugar, then cover and simmer for a further 20–25 minutes. Check the flavour and add salt and pepper if needed.

Serve hot, with Chelou Ta Dig.

❉ Note: When peaches are not in season, use 350–400 g (12–14 oz/ 1½–2 cups) frozen peach slices or drained tinned peaches. Omit the sugar if using tinned peaches, then adjust the flavour if necessary before serving.

MORGH SHEKUMPOUR
Stuffed chicken

SERVES: 5–6

90 g (3 oz/⅓ cup) ghee or butter

1 onion, finely chopped

125 g (4 oz/½ cup) chopped pitted prunes

30 g (1 oz/¼ cup) sultanas (golden raisins)

90 g (3 oz/½ cup) dried apricot halves

1 apple, peeled, cored and diced

1 teaspoon ground cinnamon

salt and freshly ground black pepper, to season

brown sugar, to taste

1 chicken, about 1.5 kg (3 lb 5 oz)

½ lemon

Chelou (page 444), to serve

Preheat the oven to 190°C (375°F/Gas 5).

Heat half the ghee or butter in a frying pan and gently fry the onion until translucent. Add the prunes, sultanas and apricots and stir for 2 minutes. Add 60 ml (2 fl oz/¼ cup) water, then cover and simmer for 10 minutes, or until the fruit is plump and the liquid is absorbed. Stir in the apple and cinnamon and season with salt, pepper and sugar.

Check the cavity of the chicken and clean further if needed. Pat the chicken inside and outside with paper towels; washing the chicken removes valuable juices and is not necessary.

Stuff the chicken with the fruit mixture; close the cavity and truss the legs. Rub the skin with the cut lemon and season with salt and pepper.

Place the chicken in a greased roasting tin and spread the remaining ghee or butter over the top. Roast for 2 hours, or until cooked through. Baste the chicken frequently during cooking, and turn it so it browns evenly.

Before carving the chicken, remove the stuffing and place it on top of the Chelou. Mix it through just before serving.

If desired, ½ teaspoon saffron threads may be soaked in a little hot water for 10 minutes and spooned over the Chelou.

❉461❉

JOOJEH KABAB
Skewered grilled chicken
SERVES: 6

2 chickens, each about 1 kg (2 lb 3 oz)

125 ml (4 fl oz/½ cup) lemon juice

1 large onion, grated

2 teaspoons salt

freshly ground black pepper, to season

60 g (2 oz/¼ cup) ghee or butter, melted

1 teaspoon paprika

Chelou (page 444), to serve

blistered cherry tomatoes, to garnish (see Note)

Halve the chickens and remove the backbone. Cut each half into six pieces of fairly even dimensions — halve the breast pieces and thighs, chop off the bony end of the leg, and leave the wings intact.

Combine the lemon juice, onion, salt and a good grinding of pepper in a glass or ceramic dish. Add the chicken pieces, turning them in the marinade to coat. Cover and marinate for 3–4 hours in the refrigerator, turning occasionally.

Thread the chicken pieces onto six long flat skewers, placing the thicker pieces in the centre, and placing them all close together. Combine the melted ghee or butter with the paprika, then brush over the chicken.

Cook over glowing charcoal for 12–15 minutes — or grill (broil) the skewers, initially cooking them under high heat, then reducing the heat to medium.

Turn the skewers often during cooking, and baste them frequently with the ghee mixture; concentrate the heat on the centre pieces towards the end of cooking.

Remove the chicken from the skewers if desired. Garnish with blistered cherry tomatoes and serve with Chelou.

❀ *Note: To blister cherry tomatoes, cut a cross on the rounded end of each tomato, brush with butter and grill (broil) under high heat or over glowing charcoal until the skin blisters and browns lightly.*

KHORESHE ALU
Prune and meat sauce
SERVES: 4–5

750 g (1 lb 10 oz) boneless lamb or beef stewing meat

20 g (¾ oz) ghee, or 1 tablespoon oil

1 large onion, chopped

½ teaspoon ground turmeric

pinch of ground cinnamon

salt and freshly ground black pepper, to season

220 g (8 oz/1 cup) pitted prunes

2 teaspoons lemon juice

1 tablespoon brown sugar

Chelou (page 444), to serve

Trim the meat and cut into 2 cm (¾ inch) cubes.

Heat the ghee or oil in a heavy-based saucepan and gently fry the onion until translucent, adding the turmeric and cinnamon while the onion cooks.

Increase the heat and add the meat. Stir frequently until the meat begins to brown. Pour in 375 ml (12½ fl oz/1½ cups) water and season with salt and pepper.

Bring to a slow simmer. Reduce the heat, then cover and simmer gently for 1 hour.

Rinse the prunes if necessary and add them to the meat with the lemon juice and sugar. Cover and simmer for a further 45 minutes.

Serve hot, with Chelou.

KHORESHE ALBALOO
Sour cherry and meat sauce

SERVES: 6

Sour black cherries are not readily available in many areas. However, table cherries can give almost the same flavour with the addition of more lime or lemon juice, making this *khoreshe* possible. Perhaps the flavour will not be quite the same, but it will be just as enjoyable.

Morello cherries, though not the same as the sour black cherries of Persia, may be used with less adjustment to the tartness of the dish; the Morello is thought to be a descendant of the Albaloo, the Persian sour cherry.

If one wishes to be pedantic, when using the sweet table cherry, the name of the dish should be Khoreshe Guillass. However, a Persian would not have heard of such a dish!

500 g (1 lb 2 oz) lean lamb or veal stewing meat

60 g (2 oz/¼ cup) ghee, or 60 ml (2 fl oz/¼ cup) oil

1 large onion, finely chopped

½ teaspoon ground turmeric

½ teaspoon ground cinnamon

salt and freshly ground black pepper, to season

250 g (9 oz/1¼ cups) pitted black cherries,
    preferably a sour variety

1–3 tablespoons lime or lemon juice

brown sugar, to taste

Trim the meat and cut into 2 cm (¾ inch) cubes.

Heat half the ghee or oil in a heavy-based saucepan and brown the meat on each side. Remove to a plate.

Using the ghee or oil remaining in the pan, gently fry the onion until translucent. Stir in the turmeric and cook for a further 2 minutes.

Return the meat to the pan and add 125 ml (4 fl oz/½ cup) water. Add the cinnamon and season with salt and pepper. Cover and simmer gently for 40 minutes.

Add the cherries and simmer for 10 minutes to release their flavour. Taste the sauce. If the cherries are sufficiently sour, add 1 tablespoon of the lime or lemon juice and enough brown sugar to give a pleasant sweet–sour flavour; if sweet cherries are used, add more lime or lemon juice, and a little sugar if necessary to balance the flavour.

Cover and simmer for a further 20 minutes, or until the meat is tender.

Serve with Chelou (page 444), Kateh (page 445) or a *polou* (pages 447–452).

IRAN

MEAT

463

KHORESHE GORMEH SABZI
« Green vegetable and meat sauce
SERVES: 6

750 g (1 lb 10 oz) boneless lamb or beef stewing meat

185 g (6½ oz/¾ cup) ghee, or 185 ml (6½ fl oz/¾ cup) oil

1 large onion, finely chopped

1 teaspoon ground turmeric

60 ml (2 fl oz/¼ cup) lemon juice

salt and freshly ground black pepper, to season

270 g (9½ oz/1½ cups) diced potatoes

60 g (2 oz/1 cup) chopped spring onion (scallion) tops

95 g (3½ oz/1½ cups) chopped spinach

1 small handful chopped flat-leaf parsley

3 tablespoons chopped coriander (cilantro) leaves, optional

3 tablespoons chopped garlic chives, optional

Trim the meat and cut into 2 cm (¾ inch) cubes.

Heat half the ghee or oil in a heavy-based saucepan and gently fry the onion until translucent. Add the turmeric and fry for 2 minutes longer.

Increase the heat, add the meat and stir over high heat until the meat changes colour and begins to brown. Reduce the heat.

Add 375 ml (12½ fl oz/1½ cups) water and the lemon juice. Season with salt and pepper and stir to dissolve any browned sediment. Cover and simmer gently for 1–1½ hours, or until just tender. The time depends on the type of meat used.

Heat the remaining ghee or oil in a large frying pan and fry the potatoes over high heat until lightly browned. Add to the meat mixture, leaving the fat in the pan. Cover and simmer for 10 minutes.

Add the greens and herbs to the frying pan and fry over medium heat until wilted. Add to the meat mixture, then cover and simmer for a further 15–20 minutes, or until the meat and potatoes are tender.

Adjust the seasoning and serve.

KHORESHE SIB
Apple and meat sauce
SERVES: 6

Follow the directions for the Khoreshe Alu recipe on page 462, substituting 4 apples for the prunes. Peel, core and slice the apples and gently fry in 2 tablespoons ghee or butter for 5 minutes, or until lightly coloured.

When you add the water, salt and freshly ground black pepper, allow the sauce to simmer for 1½ hours, then add the apples and simmer for 10–15 minutes to heat through, keeping the slices intact. Add the lemon juice and sugar to achieve a pleasant sweet–sour flavour.

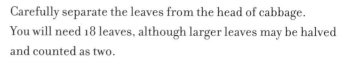

DOLMEH KALAM
Stuffed cabbage leaves with sweet-sour sauce

SERVES: 6

1 cabbage, to give 18 leaves

750 g (1 lb 10 oz) finely minced (ground)
   beef or lamb

1 large onion, finely chopped

55 g (2 oz/¼ cup) short-grain white rice

3 tablespoons finely chopped flat-leaf parsley

2 tablespoons finely chopped coriander (cilantro)

1 teaspoon ground turmeric

1½ teaspoons salt

freshly ground black pepper, to season

95 g (3½ oz/½ cup) lightly packed brown sugar

125 ml (4 fl oz/½ cup) cider vinegar

Carefully separate the leaves from the head of cabbage. You will need 18 leaves, although larger leaves may be halved and counted as two.

Blanch the leaves in a large saucepan of boiling water for 5 minutes, or until limp — do not overcook. Drain, then cut away the lower portion of the thick, white central rib.

Combine the meat in a mixing bowl with the onion, rice, herbs and turmeric. Season with salt and pepper. Divide the mixture into 18 portions.

Spread a cabbage leaf flat on a work surface and place one portion of the filling on the base of the leaf. Roll once, fold in the sides, then roll up into a firm package. Repeat with the remaining ingredients.

Line a heavy-based saucepan with the cabbage trimmings or a well-washed outer leaf. Pack the rolls in close together, satcking them in layers. Add 250 ml (8½ fl oz/1 cup) cold water and invert a heavy plate over the rolls. Cover, bring to simmering point, then simmer gently for 45 minutes.

Combine the sugar and vinegar and add to the pan. Tilt the pan to blend the liquids. Cover and cook for a further 30 minutes.

Serve with Chelou (page 444) or flat bread.

DOLMEH BEH
Stuffed quinces
SERVES: 6

60 g (2 oz/¼ cup) ghee or butter

1 onion, finely chopped

500 g (1 lb 2 oz) lean minced (ground) beef or veal

2 tablespoons uncooked white rice

½ teaspoon ground cinnamon

salt and freshly ground black pepper,
    to season

6 quinces

2 teaspoons sugar

60 ml (2 fl oz/¼ cup) cider vinegar or
    lemon juice, approximately

45 g (1½ oz/¼ cup) lightly packed brown sugar,
    approximately

Heat half the ghee or butter in a frying pan and gently fry the onion until translucent. Add the meat and stir over high heat until the juices evaporate and the meat begins to brown. Stir in 60 ml (2 fl oz/¼ cup) water and the rice and cinnamon. Season with salt and pepper and remove from the heat.

Wash the quinces well, rubbing off the fuzz, then dry them. Cut off and reserve the tops (stem end). Scoop out the core and most of the quince flesh with a melon baller, leaving a cavity of reasonable size in each. Sprinkle the cavities with the sugar and fill with the meat mixture. Replace the tops.

Pour 250 ml (8½ fl oz/1 cup) water into a deep saucepan large enough to hold the quinces side by side. Arrange them upright in the pan. Top each quince with a knob of the remaining ghee. Place about a cup of the quince flesh around the quinces.

Place two paper towels on the rim of the pan and cover tightly with the lid. Set over medium heat, bring to a simmer, then lower the heat and cook gently for 1 hour.

Add the vinegar or lemon juice and sugar to the liquid. Tilt the pan to blend the liquids, then baste the quinces with the sauce. Cook for a further 45 minutes, or until the quinces are tender, basting occasionally during cooking.

Carefully remove the quinces to a serving dish and keep them hot. Pass the liquid and quince pulp through a sieve and return to the pan. Cook until reduced by half, then adjust the sweet–sour flavour with a little more sugar and vinegar or lemon juice if needed.

Pour the sauce over the quinces and serve with flat bread as a first course.

DOLMEH SIB
Stuffed apples
SERVES: 6

Follow the directions for the Dolmeh Beh recipe (left), using 12 apples in place of the quinces. Arrange the stuffed apples in a baking dish, adding half the apple pulp to the water. Dot the apples with the butter, cover the dish with foil and bake in a preheated 180°C (350°F/Gas 4) oven for 30 minutes.

Remove the foil. Add the vinegar or lemon juice and sugar to the liquid. Tilt the dish to blend the liquids, then baste the apples with the sauce. Cook, uncovered, for a further 15–20 minutes, or until the apples are tender.

❈ *Note: Eating apples are less likely to disintegrate during cooking. Choose a variety with a tart flavour.*

LULEH KABAB
Minced lamb on skewers

SERVES: 4–6

500 g (1 lb 2 oz) lean boneless lamb
1 large onion
1 teaspoon salt
freshly ground black pepper, to season
½ teaspoon ground cinnamon, optional
melted ghee or butter, for basting
4–6 small tomatoes

For serving

1 quantity Chelou (page 444)
4–6 egg yolks, in their half-shells
4–6 knobs of butter
sumac, for sprinkling
salt and freshly ground black pepper,
    for sprinkling

Pass the lamb through a meat grinder twice, using a fine screen, then grind the onion. Alternatively, process in a food processor, using a steel blade.

Mix in the salt, pepper and cinnamon, if using. Beat well to a paste, using a wooden spoon.

Divide the mixture into 12 equal portions. Shape the portions around long, moistened sword-like skewers, making thin sausage shapes about 12 cm (5 inches) long. Moisten your hands frequently to mould the mixture more easily.

Cook over a glowing charcoal fire, placing the skewers across supports so that the meat does not touch the grill — remove the grill if possible. Turn the skewers frequently to brown the meat evenly. Cook for about 5–7 minutes, basting occasionally with melted ghee or butter.

Meanwhile, cut a cross into the rounded end of each tomato. Thread the tomatoes onto a skewer and brush with melted ghee. Grill next to the *kababs* for about 4 minutes, until the skin blisters.

Slide the *kababs* off the skewers. Serve immediately on individual plates of hot Chelou, with a tomato as garnish for each serve. Each diner places an egg yolk in the centre of their hot Chelou and stirs it into the rice. Butter, sumac, salt and pepper are then stirred into the rice before eating.

CHELOU KABAB
Grilled lamb with rice

SERVES: 6

3 lamb loins (6 ribs), each about 20 cm
   (8 inches) long (see Note)
155 g (5 oz/¾ cup) grated or minced onion
185 ml (6½ fl oz/¾ cup) lemon juice
freshly ground black pepper, to season
6 small tomatoes
melted ghee, for brushing

For serving
Chelou (page 444)
6 egg yolks, in their half-shells
6 knobs of butter
sumac, for sprinkling
salt and freshly ground black pepper,
   for sprinkling
yoghurt, optional

Remove the fillets from the loins. Trim all fat and gristle from the main muscles (the 'eye'). Slice each piece lengthways, with the grain, into three, giving strips of lamb about 8 cm (3¼ inches) wide, 20 cm (8 inches) long and 8 mm (⅜ inch) thick. Split each fillet without cutting right through, then open each one out.

Lightly hammer the meat with a heavy-bladed knife to make fine, shallow incisions along the length of the meat.

Place the onion in a sieve over a bowl and press to extract as much juice as possible. Discard the pulp. Add the lemon juice and season with pepper. Place the lamb in this marinade, stirring to coat. Cover and refrigerate for 12 hours, or longer, turning the meat occasionally.

Pass a flat, sword-like skewer through the length of each lamb strip. Cut a cross into the rounded end of each tomato, then thread the tomatoes onto a skewer.

Lightly brush the meat and tomatoes with melted ghee. Cook the meat over a glowing charcoal fire for about 5 minutes, turning frequently; grill the tomatoes next to the *kababs* for about 4 minutes, until the skin blisters. The meat will flop somewhat at the beginning of cooking. As it cooks it flattens out — a good indication it is ready. It should be lightly browned and just cooked through.

Slide the lamb off the skewers. Serve on individual plates of hot Chelou, with a tomato as garnish for each serve. Each diner places an egg yolk in the centre of their hot Chelou and stirs it into the rice. Butter, sumac, salt and pepper are then stirred into the rice before eating. Yoghurt can be added, if desired.

Speed is the essence of a good Chelou Kabab meal, as it is more enjoyable when very hot.

❈ *Note: Ask your butcher to remove the backbones from the loins, or do this yourself with a boning knife. This dish may be prepared more economically with lamb leg, although it will be slightly less authentic. Bone the leg and trim off all fat and fine sinew; cut the meat into 8 cm (3¼ inch) squares instead of long strips. Lightly hammer with a sharp knife to make shallow incisions. Thread four pieces onto each skewer, to serve 8.*

TAH CHIN
Yoghurt, lamb and rice
SERVES: 6

1 kg (2 lb 3 oz) lean lamb, from the leg

625 g (1 lb 6 oz/2½ cups) yoghurt

4 tablespoons salt

1 teaspoon ground turmeric, or ½ teaspoon
    pounded saffron threads

freshly ground black pepper, to season

600 g (1 lb 5 oz/3 cups) basmati or other
    good-quality long-grain white rice

2 egg yolks

60 g (2 oz/¼ cup) ghee or butter, melted

Cut the lamb into 3 cm (1¼ inch) cubes. Combine in a bowl with 500 g (1 lb 2 oz/2 cups) of the yoghurt, half the salt and the turmeric or saffron. Add a good grinding of pepper and turn to coat. Cover and marinate in the refrigerator for 6 hours, or overnight.

Preheat the oven to 160°C (320°F/Gas 2–3).

Pick over the rice and wash it well until the water runs clear. Bring 2 litres (68 fl oz/8 cups) water to the boil in a large saucepan. Add the remaining 2 tablespoons salt and the rice, stir and return to the boil. Allow to boil, uncovered, for 5 minutes, then drain the rice.

Beat the egg yolks in a bowl. Stir in the remaining yoghurt and half the partly cooked rice.

Place the melted ghee and 1 tablespoon hot water in a 2.5 litre (85 fl oz/10 cup) casserole dish or Dutch oven. Swirl to coat the base and side. Spread the egg, yoghurt and rice mixture evenly over the base. Arrange half the lamb on top and drizzle with some of the yoghurt marinade. Add another layer of rice, the remaining lamb mixture, and all but 125 ml (4 fl oz/½ cup) of the marinade. Top with the remaining rice and spread the reserved yoghurt marinade on the top.

Cover and bake for 1½ hours.

Spoon the rice and lamb mixture into the centre of a serving dish. Lift off the crusty layer from the bottom of the dish and break it into large pieces. Arrange around the edge of the dish.

Alternatively, if you are using a Dutch oven, place it on a cold surface or in cold water for 5–10 minutes. Run a knife round the edge of the contents and invert a serving dish on top. Tip the pan upside down so that the contents come out like a cake. Cut into wedges to serve.

ABGUSHT

The literal translation of *abgusht* is 'the water of the meat'. In Persian cookery, this can be a substantial soup or a stew. In fact, what might begin as a stew may end up as a soup if unexpected guests arrive. Then again, it may serve as two courses from the one pan, with the flavoursome liquid ladled into bowls and served as soup, leaving enough liquid in the saucepan for the remainder to be served as a moist stew.

Whichever *abgusht* is being made, the essence is in the long slow cooking. Though my cooking times are considerably shorter than those in Iran, I have taken into account the nature of the ingredients available to the Western cook. Our lamb and beef are considerably more tender, dried beans and fruit take less time to cook than in the past – and we usually tend to hurry things up considerably.

However, with the era of slow cooking upon us once more, *abgusht* simmered in a slow cooker takes on excitingly different dimensions. For a guide to using a slow cooker, see the Note at the end of the recipe below.

ABGUSHTE LUBIA GHERMEZ
Lamb and bean stew
SERVES: 6

210 g (7½ oz/1 cup) dried red kidney beans

60 g (2 oz/¼ cup) ghee or butter

1.5 kg (3 lb 5 oz) lamb shoulder on the bone, chopped into 6 pieces, or 6 lamb foreshanks, cracked

1 large onion, finely chopped

1 teaspoon ground turmeric

125 ml (4 fl oz/½ cup) tomato passata (puréed tomatoes)

1 dried lime (Loomi, page 345), or 1 tablespoon lemon juice

salt and freshly ground black pepper, to taste

Wash the kidney beans well and place them in a saucepan with 750 ml (25 fl oz/3 cups) water. Bring to the boil and leave to boil for 2 minutes. Cover and leave off the heat for 30 minutes, or until the beans are plump.

Heat half the ghee or butter in a deep, heavy-based saucepan and brown the meat on all sides. Remove each batch to a plate.

Heat the remaining ghee in the pan and gently fry the onion until translucent. Stir in the turmeric and cook for 2 minutes.

Return the lamb to the pan and add the beans and their soaking liquid and the passata. If using a dried lime, pierce it twice with a skewer, then add to the stew. Alternatively, add the lemon juice. Pour in another 500 ml (17 fl oz/2 cups) water and bring to the boil.

Cover and simmer over low heat for 1 hour. Season with salt and pepper and cook for a further 1 hour, or until the meat and beans are tender. Remove the dried lime, if used.

Serve in deep plates, with a piece of lamb in each. Pickles, fresh herbs, chopped onion, radishes and flat bread should be served as accompaniments.

✿ *Note: If you are using a slow cooker, instead of returning the lamb to the pan with the onion and turmeric, place all the ingredients in a slow cooker and cook on low for 9–10 hours, or on high for 5–6 hours. Use a little less water and add more only if necessary, as less liquid evaporates when using this appliance.*

ABGUSHTE BADEMJAN
Lamb and eggplant stew
SERVES: 6

Follow the Abgushte Lubia Ghermez recipe (left), omitting the kidney beans and soaking water. Cut 2 eggplants (aubergines) into chunky pieces, leaving the skin on. Sprinkle liberally with salt and leave for 30 minutes. Pat dry with paper towels and fry in additional ghee until lightly coloured. Set aside. Return the lamb to the pan with all the remaining ingredients and season with salt and pepper. Cook for 1½ hours, add the eggplant and cook for a further 30 minutes, or until the meat and eggplant are tender. Add more water only if necessary. If using a slow cooker, add the eggplant after cooking for 8 hours on low, or after 4 hours on high.

BAQLAWA
Almond and cardamom pastry

MAKES: ABOUT 40 PIECES

Though baklava is regarded as a Greek pastry, its popularity extends throughout the Middle East. The Persian version differs considerably in that it uses a greater proportion of nuts, and is perfumed with rosewater and flavoured with cardamom.

Baqlawa and the celebration of Now Rooz (New Year) go hand in hand. It is one of the special foods prepared in abundance for this joyful celebration.

For the best flavour, use freshly ground or pounded cardamom, unless the quality of the ready-ground product is very good.

300 g (10½ oz/3 cups) ground almonds

155 g (5 oz/1 cup) finely chopped almonds

230 g (8 oz/1 cup) caster (superfine) sugar

1 teaspoon ground cardamom

185 g (6½ oz/¾ cup) clarified butter or
    ghee, melted

10 sheets fillo pastry

Syrup

440 g (15½ oz/2 cups) sugar

1 teaspoon lemon juice

½ teaspoon ground cardamom

1 tablespoon rosewater

Preheat the oven to 180°C (350°F/Gas 4).

Combine the ground and chopped almonds in a bowl with the sugar and cardamom.

Brush a 25 × 33 cm (10 × 13 inch) baking dish with the melted clarified butter or ghee. Place three fillo pastry sheets in the dish, brushing each sheet with butter, including the top. Sprinkle one-third of the nut mixture over the top.

Add two more pastry sheets, again buttering each sheet. Repeat with another two layers of nut mixture, with two buttered pastry sheets between each layer.

Top the last layer of nuts with three sheets of fillo, buttering each sheet as before, including the top.

Trim the edges with a sharp knife. Carefully cut through the pastry and nut layers in diamond shapes. Drizzle the remaining melted butter over the top, letting it run into the cuts and around the sides of the *baqlawa*. Place on the centre shelf of the oven and bake for 30 minutes. Raise the shelf one notch above the centre and bake for another 5–10 minutes, or until the pastry is a pale golden brown.

Meanwhile, prepare the syrup. In a heavy-based saucepan, dissolve the sugar in 375 ml (12½ fl oz/1½ cups) water over medium heat, stirring occasionally. Bring to the boil, add the lemon juice and cardamom then boil rapidly for 15–18 minutes without stirring, or until the syrup is thick when a little is tested on a cold saucer. Stir in the rosewater and remove from the heat. Set aside until the pastry is cooked.

Remove the *baqlawa* from the oven and pour the warm syrup evenly over the hot pastry. Leave for at least 2 hours before cutting again and removing from the dish.

The pastry may be left in the dish, covered lightly with a fine cloth to protect it from dust, and will remain crisp for 3–4 days. Any left after serving may be stored in a sealed container for several days, though the crispness will decrease. Do not refrigerate.

KHARBOOZEH VA HOLOO MAKHLOOT
Melon and peach dessert
SERVES: 8

1 Persian or honeydew melon

1 rockmelon (cantaloupe)

115 g (4 oz/½ cup) caster (superfine) sugar

½ teaspoon salt

4 firm, ripe peaches

60 ml (2 fl oz/¼ cup) lemon juice

2–3 tablespoons rosewater

shaved or crushed ice, to serve

Cut each melon in half. Scoop the seeds into a sieve set over a bowl. Let the juice drip into the bowl, then discard the seeds.

Working over the bowl, scoop the melons into neat balls with a melon ball scoop, letting the juices fall into the bowl with the melon balls. Add the sugar and salt and stir gently to combine.

Peel the peaches, halve them and slice them into a bowl containing the lemon juice. As each peach slice is added to the bowl, stir gently to coat it with the lemon juice, to prevent discolouration.

Add the peaches and lemon juice to the melon balls. Stir gently and add rosewater to taste. Cover and chill for several hours.

To serve, pile into individual dessert glasses and top with a little shaved or crushed ice. Serve immediately.

HALVAYE SHIR
Milk pudding
SERVES: 5–6

60 g (2 oz/¼ cup) ghee or unsalted butter

90 g (3 oz/½ cup) rice flour

375 ml (12½ fl oz/1½ cups) milk

55 g (2 oz/¼ cup) sugar

3 teaspoons rosewater

¼–½ teaspoon ground cardamom

40 g (1½ oz) chopped blanched almonds or
    pistachio nuts

Melt the ghee or butter in a heavy-based saucepan, preferably one with a non-stick coating. Stir in the rice flour and cook over medium heat, stirring often, for 3 minutes, without allowing the ground rice to colour.

Add the milk, stirring constantly until the mixture has thickened and is bubbling. Stir in the sugar, rosewater and cardamom to taste. Stir for a further 5 minutes.

Pour into small bowls, sprinkle with the nuts and serve warm or at room temperature. Alternatively, pour into a lightly buttered 20 cm (8 inch) square cake tin, sprinkle with the nuts, leave until cold and serve cut into squares.

SHIR BERENJ
Rice pudding
SERVES: 6

110 g (3¾ oz/½ cup) short-grain white rice

1 litre (34 fl oz/4 cups) milk

pinch of salt

55 g (2 oz/¼ cup) sugar

½ teaspoon ground cardamom

2–3 teaspoons rosewater

honey, for drizzling, optional

Rinse the rice only if necessary. Place in a heavy-based saucepan with 375 ml (12½ fl oz/1½ cups) cold water and bring to the boil, stirring occasionally. Boil gently, uncovered, for 15 minutes, or until the water has been absorbed.

Stir in the milk, add the salt and bring to a slow simmer. Simmer gently, uncovered, for 40 minutes, or until the pudding is thick. Stir occasionally with a wooden spoon and take care that the pudding does not scorch.

Stir in the sugar, cardamom and rosewater to taste. Spoon into small bowls. Serve warm or chilled, with a little honey drizzled on top if desired.

KALUCHEH BERENJ
Rice cookies
MAKES: 60

250 g (9 oz/1 cup) butter

125 g (4 oz/1 cup) icing (confectioners') sugar, sifted

2 egg yolks

440 g (15½ oz/2½ cups) rice flour

½–1 teaspoon ground cardamom

1 egg white, lightly beaten

65 g (2¼ oz/½ cup) finely chopped pistachio nuts or almonds

Preheat the oven to 180°C (350°F/Gas 4).

Cream the butter and icing sugar in a bowl until light and fluffy. Gradually add the egg yolks, beating well. Sift the rice flour with the cardamom and fold into the butter mixture to form a soft dough. Knead for 2 minutes, then cover and allow the dough to rest for 1 hour.

Shape generous teaspoonfuls of the dough into balls, placing them on ungreased baking trays. Using a thimble, make three crescent shapes on each cookie.

Brush the cookies very lightly with the egg white and lightly sprinkle with the chopped nuts. Bake for 15 minutes, but do not let the tops colour; the bases should be golden brown.

Leave the cookies on the baking trays for 5 minutes, then lift onto wire racks to cool completely.

Store in a sealed container.

LAUZE BADAM
« Almond sweetmeat
MAKES: ABOUT 45 PIECES

Sweetmeats are much appreciated in Iran, and their making
is a long and ancient art. To assure success for the Western
cook, I have followed basic candy-making principles, without
sacrificing the Persian flavour of the sweetmeat. The following
recipes use a base so similar to a cooked fondant that I have
given the basic fondant as the basis from which to work.

Fondant
440 g (15½ oz/2 cups) sugar
¼ teaspoon cream of tartar

To finish
200 g (7 oz/2 cups) finely ground almonds
½ teaspoon vanilla essence

Pour 125 ml (4 fl oz/½ cup) water into a heavy-based
saucepan, add the sugar and place on a very low heat so that the
sugar dissolves slowly — do not stir.

When the sugar has completely dissolved, bring to the boil,
add the cream of tartar and allow to boil for 20–25 minutes,
or until the mixture reaches the 'soft ball' stage, when a small
spoonful of the syrup forms a ball when dropped into a bowl of
very cold water — 115°C (240°F) on a sugar thermometer.

Place 180 g (6 oz/1¾ cups) of the ground almonds in a
heatproof bowl; sprinkle half the remaining almonds over the
base of an 18 cm (7 inch) square cake tin.

Pour the syrup over the ground almonds in the bowl and
leave for 15 minutes, or until a skin begins to form around
the edge. Take a spatula and work the mixture together in a
figure-8 movement, until it begins to grain. Add the vanilla
during this process.

When the mixture is cool enough to handle, knead it into a
ball. Press the fondant out flat on a work surface, then place it
in the cake tin, pressing it into the shape of the tin. Sprinkle
with the remaining almonds, pressing them into the fondant.

Leave for about 3 hours, or until firm. To serve, cut into
small diamond-shaped lozenges using an oiled knife.

LAUZE NARJEEL
« Coconut sweetmeat
MAKES: ABOUT 45 PIECES

Follow the Lauze Badam recipe (left), replacing the ground
almonds with 180 g (6 oz/2 cups) desiccated coconut.

LAUZE TOOT
« Mulberry sweetmeat
MAKES: ABOUT 45 PIECES

The shape, rather than the ingredients, gives this confection
its name. Follow the Lauze Badam recipe (left), using all the
ground almonds in the fondant mixture. When the mixture
is cool enough to handle, shape it into small pieces the size
and shape of a mulberry, then roll them in sugar. Insert a
sliver of blanched pistachio nut in the top of each one to
resemble a stem.

SHARBAT ALBALOO
Cherry sherbet
SERVES: 4–6

The black sour cherries of Iran are used for this sherbet. If sour cherries such as Morello are unavailable, use the table varieties and increase the lemon juice to give the characteristic sharp tang.

500 g (1 lb 2 oz) sour or other cherries

sugar

juice of ½ lemon

Wash the cherries and remove the stems and seeds. Place in a saucepan with 375 ml (12½ fl oz/1½ cups) water and bring to the boil. Cover and simmer over low heat for 15 minutes, or until the cherries are soft.

Strain the cherries through a sieve, set over a bowl. Leave for 30 minutes to drain thoroughly.

Measure the juice back into the saucepan and add an equal volume of sugar — 220 g (8 oz/1 cup) of sugar to each 250 ml (8½ fl oz/1 cup) of juice.

Add the lemon juice and bring to the boil over medium heat, stirring occasionally to dissolve the sugar. Allow to boil, uncovered, for 8–10 minutes without stirring, skimming when necessary.

Leave to cool, then pour into a sterilised bottle (see page 19). Store at room temperature.

To serve, pour 2–3 tablespoons of the syrup into a glass and add ice cubes and cold water to taste. Stir gently and serve.

SHARBAT BEH
Quince sherbet
SERVES: 4–6

Traditionally this sherbet is made by grating the fruit into water. Lemon juice is rubbed on the fruit and added to the water to stop the fruit discolouring. It seems like such a lot of trouble when the resultant juice is cooked anyway. The method given here works just as well, and gives a better colour to the syrup.

2 large quinces

sugar

juice of ½ lemon

Peel the quinces, remove the cores and chop the flesh into small pieces. Place in a stainless steel or enamelled pan and add 500 ml (17 fl oz/2 cups) water. Bring slowly to the boil, then simmer gently for 40 minutes, or until the quince is very soft and has coloured to a pinky orange.

Place a doubled-over piece of muslin (cheesecloth) in a bowl, draping the ends over the side. Pour the fruit and juice into the centre of the cloth, gather the ends and tie with string. Lift the bag up and suspend it over the bowl. Leave it to drip for several hours, as you would for jelly-making.

Measure the juice back into the saucepan and add an equal volume of sugar — 220 g (8 oz/1 cup) of sugar to each 250 ml (8½ fl oz/1 cup) of juice.

Add the lemon juice and bring to the boil over medium heat, stirring occasionally to dissolve the sugar. Allow to boil, uncovered, for 8–10 minutes without stirring, skimming when necessary.

Leave to cool, then pour into a sterilised bottle (see page 19). Store at room temperature.

To serve, pour 2–3 tablespoons of the syrup into a glass and add ice cubes and cold water to taste. Stir gently and serve.

❧ *Note: The quince pulp may be used in the Quince Paste recipe on page 98.*

SEKANJABIN
Sweet-sour mint syrup
MAKES: ABOUT 375 ML (12½ FL OZ/1½ CUPS)

The Persian penchant for sweet-sour flavours extends to desserts and beverages. Sekanjabin, a sweet-sour syrup with a flavour reminiscent of mint sauce, plays a number of roles in the Persian household. It may be served as a dip for crisp cos (romaine) lettuce leaves for an unusual dessert. With bread as an accompaniment to the lettuce and syrup, it becomes a light meal. With water or soda water and ice it makes a refreshing drink. With grated cucumber, soda water and ice, a very pleasant punch can be made, though this last innovation bears Western influence. Persians in the past treated jaundice attacks with a diet of Sekanjabin and lettuce — no bread — until the patient recovered.

> 440 g (15½ oz/2 cups) sugar
> 125 ml (4 fl oz/½ cup) white vinegar
> juice of ½ lemon
> 6 large mint sprigs

Put the sugar and 250 ml (8½ fl oz/1 cup) water in a saucepan and stir over medium heat until the sugar dissolves. Bring to the boil, add the vinegar and lemon juice, and return to a steady boil. Allow to boil over medium heat for 15–18 minutes, or until thick, skimming as required. Test a little on a cold saucer: when cool, it should have a thin honey consistency.

Add the mint sprigs to the boiling syrup. Boil for 1 minute, then remove from the heat and leave until cool. Strain into a sterilised bottle (see page 19) and store at room temperature.

To serve as a dessert, pour some syrup into a shallow bowl and float a mint sprig on top. Serve with crisp cos (romaine) lettuce leaves, for diners to fold and dip into the syrup.

To serve as a beverage, one-third fill a glass with the syrup, add ice cubes and top with water or soda water. Stir gently and float a mint sprig on top.

To serve as a punch, coarsely grate a young, peeled cucumber into a punch bowl. Add 1 quantity of the syrup, plenty of ice cubes and soda water to taste. Garnish with mint sprigs and thin cucumber slices.

MORABAYE HENDEVANEH
Watermelon rind preserve

> 750 g (1 lb 10 oz) watermelon rind
> 660 g (1 lb 7 oz/3 cups) sugar
> 1 tablespoon lemon juice
> 1 teaspoon cardamom seeds

Peel the green skin from the watermelon rind and remove any pink flesh. Weigh after peeling, or cut into 2 cm (¾ inch) cubes and measure. You will require four cups of diced rind.

Place the watermelon rind in a preserving pan and cover with cold water. Bring to the boil, then simmer gently for 1 hour, or until the rind is tender and translucent. Drain.

Place the preserving pan back over medium heat. Add the sugar and 500 ml (17 fl oz/2 cups) water and stir to dissolve the sugar. Add the lemon juice and bring to the boil. Add the drained rind and return to the boil. Allow to boil for 15 minutes, skimming when necessary.

Crush the cardamom seeds using a mortar and pestle and stir into the preserve. Boil for 1 minute, then remove from the heat. Cover and leave for 12 hours, or overnight.

Remove the lid and place the pan over medium heat. Bring to the boil and leave to boil gently for 15–20 minutes, or until the syrup is thick when tested on a cold saucer.

Ladle into warm, sterilised jars (see page 19), leave to cool, then seal.

Afghanistan

ÄFGHANISTAN

In early history Alexander the Great conquered Afghanistan on his way to India; the country was plundered by Genghis Khan and his Mongol hordes in their surge to the Middle and Near East; and it served as a route for Marco Polo on his journey to China. It is the land of the Khyber Pass, which features in the annals of military history in Britain's attempts to maintain her colonies in India. Babur, founder of the Moghul Empire in India and a direct descendant of Genghis Khan, began his rise to power in Kabul and returned there to die.

Being a land-locked country, as one might expect, the foods of Afghanistan reflect those of its neighbours, Pakistan, India and Iran. Though the country shares a border with Russia, there is little evidence that Russia has influenced the cuisine of Afghanistan.

THE FLAVOUR OF AFGHAN FOOD

The Pakistan–Indian influence is prevalent in Afghan spices and *palaus*. Garam masala is a popular spice blend, with saffron, cinnamon, cloves, peppers and hot chillies echoing the same influence; cardamom, dill, mint, cumin and coriander reflect the Persian and Arabic influences. *Gashneez*, fresh coriander (cilantro), is referred to as Afghan parsley and is used extensively. Though history shows that Persia influenced cooking in India in early times, Afghanistan seems to have taken the best of both worlds. The Mongol influence can be seen in noodle-type dishes such as *aushak* and *aush*, though it is possible that any grain-producing area could have conceived the noodle without outside influence.

Maust (yoghurt) is a necessary part of Afghan cooking and is frequently drained to make a thick, cream cheese–like substance called *chakah*. Yoghurt or sour milk is drained and dried for a cheese called *quroot*, which is then painstakingly dissolved in water to reconstitute it; you will find instructions for making a similar-tasting cheese condiment in the recipes (page 488).

The breads of Afghanistan are similar to those of Pakistan, India and Iran, though they are prepared a little differently. *Naun* and *lawash* are two different breads, *naun* being similar to the Punjabi (North Indian) *naan*, and *lawash* similar to the *nane lavash* of Iran. This perhaps shows clearly the influences of each of the countries on the others' cooking.

The *chalau* and *palau* of Afghanistan are again similar to the rice dishes of both Iran and Pakistan or India. Basmati rice is used in Afghanistan, though another good-quality long-grain white rice may be substituted.

The *korma* (meat sauce) of Afghanistan has a parallel in the korma of India, though it is not as spicy, and *khoreshe gormeh sabzi* is a related dish from Persia (now Iran). Here again, another similarity is apparent. The *sabzee* and *sabzi* of Afghanistan and Iran can also be found in Pakistan–Indian cooking. Persian *sabzi* refers to green herbs, Afghan *sabzee* to spinach, and Pakistan–Indian *sabzi* to a variety of vegetables. The point is, of course, that the Indo–Iranian sub-family of languages is the basis of the languages spoken in these four countries. Language aside, their foods are closely linked in many areas.

The *kabaub* is a convenient way to cook cubes of meat and Afghans like to serve them between pieces of *lawash*. Favoured meats are beef and lamb, though occasionally goat or camel meat is used. As much of the meat is rather tough, minced (ground) meat is used extensively, either in sauces or made into *kofta kabaub*.

The fat from the tail of the Awassi sheep is highly favoured and added to minced meat, or diced and placed between meat cubes when preparing *kabaubs*. For a somewhat similar flavour, use lamb with a proportion of fat – lamb shoulder is a good choice. The Afghans like their foods to be oily, either from the lamb fat or from the use of rather large amounts of vegetable oil or ghee.

The latter is the preferred fat, but in short supply in Afghanistan. The amounts of these fats have been reduced in recipes to cater for Western tastes, and may be reduced even further if necessary.

A wide variety of vegetables is used in cooking, with leeks being particularly popular, fired with chilli and used as a filling for boiled and fried doughs for *aushak* and *boolawnee*. Vegetables are frequently combined with meats for *korma*, with spinach, turnip, potato and carrot being the most popular. Though I have called such recipes Korma Sabzee (page 489), Korma Zardak (page 489) and so on, when the *korma* is served with *chalau* the correct titles become *sabzee chalau* or *zardak chalau* – rather confusing, but this is how the Afghans refer to them.

Yellow split peas are frequently used to thicken sauces and soups. The use of mung beans in *maushawa* interested me, as this is the only recipe I have ever encountered using the whole mung bean. Usually these beans are used for the Chinese bean sprouts, or ground into a flour for Asian sweet-making.

Chai, the tea of Afghanistan, is ever present. It is usually served black, very strong, sometimes flavoured with cardamom, and can be taken with or without sugar. Afghans are renowned for their hospitality, and when serving a guest with tea they are likely to add copious quantities of sugar. If your tea is served very, very sweet, you can count yourself as a very honoured guest indeed. Generally tea is served at the end of a meal, with each person being provided with their own teapot, cup and a bowl for the tea dregs. Tea with milk, *sheer chai*, is usually served on more formal occasions, green tea being used for this brew.

EATING AFGHAN STYLE

The food is served on large platters or in pots, and placed on a cloth spread over a mat or carpet. Sometimes individual plates or bowls are provided, though this varies according to location, whether in a house or a tent. Cushions are provided for seating and the food is generally eaten with the fingers of the right hand, after the traditional hand-washing. A *chalau* or *palau* is always served, usually with *korma*. *Kabaub*, chicken or *aushak* plus a thick soup could also be served, particularly if the occasion is festive. The Afghans are noted for serving foods in large quantities. Vegetables, salad, pickles, yoghurt and bread are always served. The bread is used to scoop up soft foods. *Dug* (yoghurt drink) or *murgh* (buttermilk) is often served as the beverage during the meal. Fresh fruit is plentiful and very good and is always part of the meal. Puddings or sweet pastries frequently follow the meal, with tea being served quite some time later.

COOKING METHODS

Rice is cooked in a traditional pot called a *degh* and stirred and served with a *gafgeer*. Cooking over the embers of a wood fire is a popular method for *kabaubs*, the same fire also being used to cook the other components of the meal. The oven for bread-making is the *tandour* — the beehive oven of Iran, Iraq and Asia — and as this is not suitable for baking pastries, the sweet tooth of the Afghan is satisfied with copious amounts of fried pastries, though baklava and *kalucheh berenj*, the rice cookies of Iran, are available at pastry shops. One fried pastry that intrigued me considerably was the *abraysham kabaub*, actually a kind of sweet omelette. You might enjoy tackling the recipe I have given.

INGREDIENTS FOR AFGHAN COOKING

There are few ingredients that you might not already have on your pantry shelf or in your vegetable storer. Fresh coriander is a must and can be grown from seed. Pick it before flowering. Coriander is a delicate herb and if it is washed, allowed to dry well, then packed loosely into a plastic bag, it should keep in the refrigerator for four days or so.

You will require lots of garlic, onions and dried mint, and a few hot chillies for flavouring; leeks for special recipes; and plenty of yoghurt – try making your own (see the instructions on pages 18–19). Spices required are cinnamon, cloves, nutmeg, cardamom, cumin, black cumin and garam masala (see page 487), although you can use ready-made if you would rather not make your own. For sweet pastries, you will need saffron threads, rosewater, unsalted pistachio nuts, almonds and walnuts. Use ghee or vegetable oil for cooking. Fresh limes and lemons are also necessary.

CHATNI GASHNEEZ
« Coriander chutney
MAKES: 350 G (12 OZ/1¼ CUPS)

50 g (2 oz/1 cup) roughly chopped coriander
    (cilantro) leaves
2 garlic cloves
1 green chilli
60 g (2 oz/½ cup) coarsely chopped walnuts
60 ml (2 fl oz/¼ cup) lemon juice or vinegar
salt, to taste

Pack the chopped coriander firmly into a cup to measure.
Peel the garlic and chop roughly; slit the chilli, remove the
seeds and chop roughly.

Place the prepared ingredients and walnuts in a blender
or food processor and process to a textured paste, adding the
lemon juice or vinegar gradually while processing.

Add salt to taste, place in a bowl and chill until required.
Serve with *kabaubs*.

❧ *Note: If you have no processor or blender, pass the ingredients
through a food grinder using a fine screen, or chop the ingredients
finely, then pound using a mortar and pestle. Gradually stir in the
lemon juice or vinegar and add salt to taste.*

GARAM MASALA
Fragrant spice mix
MAKES: 50 G (2 OZ/½ CUP)

5 cardamom pods
2 pieces of cinnamon bark,
    each about 8 cm (3¼ inches) long
½ teaspoon cloves
2 tablespoons cumin seeds
1 teaspoon black cumin seeds
½ whole nutmeg, grated

Combine all the spices except the nutmeg in a small frying
pan and roast over medium heat, stirring occasionally, until
the spices smell fragrant. Remove to a plate and cool.

Remove and discard the pods from the cardamom. In a
blender, process the cardamom seeds and roasted spices to
a fine powder.

Grate the nutmeg and add to the ground spices. Store in
a sealed jar.

QUROOT
Yoghurt cheese
MAKES: 550 G (1 LB 3½ OZ/2½ CUPS)

Quroot is a ball of very dry Afghan cheese made from drained, salted and dried yoghurt. To prepare *quroot* for serving with particular dishes, the cheese ball is soaked in hot water in a special bowl containing a stone. The *quroot* is then rubbed against the stone and the sides of the bowl, and gradually worked into the water to form a thick sauce.

Afghans living abroad have found a substitute by combining *chakah* (drained yoghurt) and mature cheddar cheese. The cheddar provides the tang associated with ripened cheese.

Another substitute is a combination of undrained yoghurt, mature cheddar and sour cream.

500 g (1 lb 2 oz/2 cups) drained yoghurt
  (see page 19)
60 g (2 oz/½ cup) finely grated mature
  cheddar cheese
salt, to taste

Mix a little of the yoghurt into the grated cheese, working the mixture with the back of a wooden spoon to blend the ingredients. Gradually stir in the remaining yoghurt and add salt to taste. Pile into a small bowl or serve as directed in recipes.

Alternative mixture

250 g (9 oz/1 cup) undrained yoghurt
60 g (2 oz/½ cup) grated mature
  cheddar cheese
250 g (9 oz/1 cup) sour cream
salt, to taste

Prepare as before, mixing the yoghurt into the cheese, then adding the sour cream and salt to taste.

KORMA
Meat sauce

SERVES: 6

750 g (1 lb 10 oz) lean beef or lamb stewing meat
125 ml (4 fl oz/½ cup) oil
1 large onion, finely chopped
2 garlic cloves, crushed
55 g (2 oz/¼ cup) yellow split peas, washed
1 teaspoon ground cumin
¼–½ teaspoon hot chilli powder
salt and freshly ground black pepper, to season
2–3 tablespoons chopped coriander (cilantro) leaves
Chalau (page 495), for serving

Cut the meat into 2 cm (¾ inch) cubes.

Heat the oil in a heavy-based saucepan, add the onion and fry gently until translucent. Increase the heat, add the garlic and meat and fry, stirring often, until the juices evaporate and the meat begins to brown.

Stir in 375 ml (12½ fl oz/1½ cups) water, the washed split peas, cumin and chilli powder, to taste. Season with salt and pepper and bring to a slow simmer. Cover the pan and simmer gently for 1–1½ hours, until the meat is tender. The time depends on the cut of meat used.

Add the coriander and cook for a further 10 minutes.

Mound the Chalau on a platter and spoon some of the sauce on top. Serve the remaining sauce in a separate bowl.

KORMA SABZEE
Meat and spinach sauce

Prepare the basic Korma (see left), omitting the split peas. Add 120 g (4 oz/3 cups) chopped fresh spinach with the coriander. Cook for a further 10–15 minutes.

KORMA SHULGUN or KORMA KACHALO
Meat and turnip sauce or meat and potato sauce

Prepare the basic Korma (see left), omitting the split peas. About 20 minutes before the meat is cooked, add 3 white turnips or 3 potatoes, peeled and cut into 2 cm (¾ inch) cubes. When the meat and vegetables are tender, add the coriander and cook for a further 10 minutes.

KORMA ZARDAK
Meat and carrot sauce

Prepare the basic Korma (see left) with the Korma Shulgun variation above, but adding 310 g (10½ oz/2 cups) diced carrots instead of turnips.

BOOLAWNEE
Fried leek pastries
MAKES: ABOUT 32

Pastry
300 g (10½ oz/2 cups) plain (all-purpose) flour
½ teaspoon salt

Leek filling
2 leeks (to make 405 g/14 oz/3 cups chopped)
2 teaspoons salt
¼ teaspoon hot chilli powder
3 teaspoons vegetable oil

To finish
oil, for deep-frying

Sift the flour and salt into a bowl, make a well in the centre and add 185 ml (6½ fl oz/¾ cup) cold water. Mix to a firm dough and knead for 5 minutes until elastic, dusting with more flour if necessary. Wrap in plastic wrap and leave to rest for 30 minutes.

Cut off and discard most of the green tops from the leeks. Halve them lengthways and rinse well to remove all traces of soil between the leaves. Remove the roots and dry the leeks with paper towels. Place the leeks flat on a board, cut along the length at 5 mm (¼ inch) intervals, then across to dice. Measure in cups and place in a bowl.

Add the salt and chilli powder and knead by hand to soften the leeks. Stir in the oil.

Roll pieces of the dough into balls the size of large hazelnuts, then roll thinly into a 10 cm (4 inch) circle. Alternatively, roll out the dough and cut into 10 cm (4 inch) rounds.

Place about 2 teaspoons of the leek filling in the centre of each circle, moisten the pastry halfway round the edge of the circle and fold the pastry over the filling. Press the edge to seal well and, using the edge of a thimble (the traditional method), or a coffee spoon, make little crescent-shaped marks around the edge, or press with the tines of a fork.

Fry three or four at a time in hot oil until golden brown, turning to brown evenly. Drain on paper towels and serve hot or warm.

MAUSHAWA
Bean and meatball soup

SERVES: 6

105 g (3½ oz/½ cup) dried red kidney beans,
   washed and soaked overnight
110 g (3¾ oz/½ cup) yellow split peas
110 g (3¾ oz/½ cup) mung beans
110 g (3¾ oz/½ cup) short-grain white rice
2 teaspoons salt

Meatballs
250 g (9 oz) finely minced (ground) beef or lamb
½ teaspoon salt
½ teaspoon freshly ground black pepper
¼ teaspoon hot chilli powder
¼ teaspoon ground cinnamon

To finish
60 ml (2 fl oz/½ cup) vegetable oil
1 large onion, finely chopped
125 g (4 oz/½ cup) chopped, peeled tomatoes
1 tablespoon chopped dill
250 g (9 oz/1 cup) yoghurt

Place the kidney beans in a large saucepan with their soaking water. Bring to the boil, cover and simmer gently for 1 hour.

Wash the yellow split peas and mung beans and add to the beans with 500 ml (17 fl oz/2 cups) water. Return to the boil and simmer for 30 minutes.

Wash the rice and add to the pan with the salt. Simmer for a further 30 minutes, until the ingredients are soft.

Combine the meat with the seasonings and shape into balls the size of hazelnuts.

Heat the oil in a large heavy-based saucepan and fry the onion until translucent and lightly browned. Add the meatballs and fry, stirring often, until browned. Stir in 250 ml (8½ fl oz/1 cup) water and the tomatoes, then cover and simmer for 30 minutes.

Add the cooked bean mixture, another 500 ml (17 fl oz/2 cups) water and the dill. Bring to the boil, then add the yoghurt, stirring over low heat until almost boiling.

Adjust the seasoning with salt and more chilli powder if desired. Serve hot in deep plates with Lawash (page 494) or Naun (page 494).

BOURANEE BAUNJAUN
Eggplant with yoghurt sauce
SERVES: 6

4 eggplants (aubergines), about 1 kg (2 lb 3 oz)

salt, for sprinkling

oil, for frying

2 onions, sliced

1 green capsicum (pepper), seeds removed,
    sliced into rings

2 large ripe tomatoes, peeled and sliced

¼ teaspoon hot chilli powder

Chakah (yoghurt sauce)

500 g (1 lb 2 oz/2 cups) drained yoghurt
    (see page 19)

2–3 garlic cloves, crushed

salt, to taste

Cut the stems from the eggplants, but leave the skin on. Cut the eggplants into slices 1 cm (½ inch) thick. Spread on a tray and sprinkle the slices liberally with salt. Leave for 30 minutes, then dry well with paper towels.

Pour enough oil into a deep frying pan (with a lid to fit) to cover the base well. Fry the eggplant until lightly browned on each side, but do not cook completely. Lift onto a plate when browned. Add more oil to the pan as required for the remaining slices.

As the oil drains out of the eggplant on standing, return it to the pan and add the onion. Fry gently until translucent, then remove to another plate.

Place a layer of eggplant back into the pan. Top with some sliced onion, capsicum rings and tomato slices. Repeat using the remaining ingredients and adding a little salt and the chilli powder between the layers. Pour in any remaining oil from the eggplant and onion and add 60 ml (2 fl oz/¼ cup) water. Cover and simmer gently for 10–15 minutes, until the eggplant is tender.

Combine the Chakah ingredients and spread half of the Chakah into the base of a serving dish. Top with the vegetables, lifting the eggplant carefully to keep the slices intact. Leave some of the juices in the pan.

Top the vegetables with the remaining Chakah and drizzle the vegetable juices over it. Serve with *kabaubs* and Lawash (page 494).

AFGHAN BREADS
Afghanistan

The breads of Afghanistan are similar to those of neighbouring Iran on one side, and India on the other. Basically two breads are widely eaten: one is the large, flat *lawash* or *parakee* baked on the wall of a beehive oven called the *tandour*; the other is *naun*, similar to the Punjabi naan in shape. Wholemeal (whole-wheat) flour is generally used, and the bread is leavened with a fermented starter. As you really have to know how to handle such a starter, it is better to use conventional yeast, though the flavour is not quite the same.

LAWASH
Wholemeal (whole-wheat) flat bread

Follow the recipe for Nane Lavash (page 437) in the chapter on Iran. Use as directed in recipes, or as an accompaniment to foods. The readily available Lebanese pitta bread may be used instead. When Lawash is required in the serving of food, split a Lebanese bread and use the two rounds separately to replace the Lawash. Although the flavour is not the same, the basic effect is there.

To warm Lawash, wrap it in foil and heat in the oven at 180°C (350°F/Gas 4) for 5 minutes.

NAUN
Wholemeal (whole-wheat) bread
MAKES: 8 LOAVES

2 teaspoons active dried yeast
450 g (1 lb/3 cups) wholemeal (whole-wheat) flour
300 g (10½ oz/2 cups) plain (all-purpose) flour
1½ teaspoons salt
oil, for shaping

Dissolve the yeast in 60 ml (2 fl oz/¼ cup) warm water.

Put the flours and salt in a mixing bowl and stir well with a balloon whisk to combine — this is just as effective as a sieve and the flakes from the wholemeal flour are retained. Remove about 150 g (5 oz/1 cup) of the flour and set aside.

Add 440 ml (15 fl oz/1¾ cups) warm water to the yeast mixture and pour into the centre of the flour. Stir a little flour into the liquid to thicken it slightly, cover the bowl and leave it in a warm place for 10 minutes, or until the liquid is frothy.

Stir in the remaining flour, then beat by hand for 20 minutes, gradually kneading in the reserved flour towards the end of this time. Alternatively, beat the dough for 15 minutes using an electric mixer with a dough hook, gradually adding as much of the reserved flour as the mixture will take.

Cover the bowl and leave the dough in a warm place to rise until it has doubled in size — 30 minutes to 1 hour.

Preheat the oven to 220°C (430°F/Gas 7). With oiled hands, divide the dough into eight equal portions, then roll into balls.

Lightly oil your hands and, working on an oiled work surface, press a ball of dough into a tear shape, about 1 cm (½ inch) thick. Place the shaped loaves on baking trays, cover with cloths and leave for 15 minutes.

Dip a forefinger in oil and make three parallel grooves in each loaf, about 2 cm (¾ inch) in from the edge, by pressing the side of the finger along the length of the bread. You will end up with ridged, tear-shaped loaves, each with three grooves, the middle groove longer than those on either side.

Bake the loaves on the middle shelf of the oven for 15 minutes, or until the loaves are lightly browned and cooked. Wrap in a cloth as they come out of the oven.

CHALAU
Steamed rice

SERVES: 6–8

600 g (1 lb 5 oz/3 cups) basmati or other
    good-quality long-grain white rice
60 ml (2 fl oz/¼ cup) vegetable oil
2 teaspoons salt

Pick over the rice if necessary and place in a sieve. Wash under cold running water until the water runs clear. Leave to drain for 30 minutes.

Heat the oil in a heavy-based saucepan and add the rice. Stir over medium heat for 5 minutes.

Add cold water to a level 2 cm (¾ inch) above the surface of the rice — reaching up to the first joint of your forefinger is a reliable indication of the level required. Stir in the salt.

Bring to the boil, stirring occasionally until boiling, then reduce the heat to low. Cover the rim of the pan with a cloth or two paper towels and fit the lid on tightly.

Cook gently for 30 minutes over low heat. Fluff up the rice grains with a fork and mound on a platter to serve.

Alternative method

Wash the rice only if necessary. Bring 2 litres (68 fl oz/8 cups) water to the boil in a heavy-based saucepan, then add the rice and 1 tablespoon of salt. Stir until the water comes to the boil, then boil, uncovered, for 8 minutes. Drain.

Place the rice in a large casserole dish, add the oil and toss to coat the grains with oil. Add 1 teaspoon salt and 125 ml (4 fl oz/½ cup) cold water.

Cover the rim of the casserole with a cloth or two paper towels and fit the lid on tightly. Cook in a preheated oven at 150°C (300°F/Gas 2) for 30 minutes.

ZARDA PALAU
Sweet rice with orange and chicken

SERVES: 5–6

thinly peeled rind of 2 oranges

220 g (8 oz/1 cup) sugar

60 g (2 oz/¼ cup) ghee, or 60 ml (2 fl oz/¼ cup)
   vegetable oil

60 g (2 oz/½ cup) slivered almonds

1 kg (2 lb 3 oz) chicken breast fillets, quartered

salt and freshly ground black pepper, to season

1 onion, sliced

1 tablespoon salt

400 g (14 oz/2 cups) basmati or other
   good-quality long-grain white rice, washed

½ teaspoon saffron threads

35 g (1¼ oz/¼ cup) blanched pistachio nuts, optional

Cut the orange rind into fine shreds about 3 cm (1¼ inches) long. Boil them in 500 ml (17 fl oz/2 cups) water for 5 minutes to remove any bitterness, then drain and rinse.

Dissolve the sugar in 250 ml (8½ fl oz/1 cup) water. Add the orange rind shreds and boil gently for 5 minutes, or until the syrup is thick. Remove from the heat and set aside.

In a frying pan, heat 1 tablespoon of the ghee or oil, add the almonds and fry gently until golden. Remove from the pan and set aside.

Heat the remaining ghee or oil in the frying pan and brown the chicken pieces on all sides. Remove the chicken, leaving the fat in the pan. Season the chicken with salt and pepper.

Add the onion to the frying pan and fry gently until soft and slightly browned. Add 250 ml (8½ fl oz/1 cup) water and stir to lift the browned juices. Return the chicken to the pan, cover and simmer gently for 20 minutes.

Meanwhile, preheat the oven to 150°C (300°F/Gas 2).

Bring 2 litres (68 fl oz/8 cups) water to the boil in a large saucepan. Add the washed rice and 1 tablespoon of salt. Bring back to the boil, then boil for 8 minutes and drain.

Tip the rice into a bowl and strain the syrup from the orange rind shreds over the rice, reserving the rind. Toss the rice and spread half over the base of a greased casserole dish.

Arrange the chicken pieces on top with the onion and half the cooking liquid. Sprinkle with half the shredded rind and half the browned almonds.

Spread the remaining rice on top, then pour the remaining chicken liquid evenly over the rice. Cover the casserole, transfer to the oven and bake for 40 minutes.

Meanwhile, pound the saffron threads and steep them in 2 tablespoons hot water.

When the *palau* is cooked, remove the top layer of rice and arrange it around the edge of a warm serving platter. Put the chicken pieces aside and place the bottom layer of rice in the centre of the platter. Top with the chicken pieces and garnish with the reserved orange rind shreds and almonds.

Sprinkle with the pistachio nuts, if using. Pour the saffron liquid over the rice border and serve immediately.

KABAB-E-MURGH
Roast chicken

SERVES: 5–6

1 chicken, about 1.5 kg (3 lb 5 oz)
1–2 garlic cloves, crushed
salt and freshly ground black pepper, to season
125 ml (4 fl oz/½ cup) melted ghee or vegetable oil
1 onion, finely chopped
250 g (9 oz/1 cup) chopped, peeled tomatoes

For serving
2 Lawash (page 494)
3 hard-boiled eggs, peeled and sliced
coriander (cilantro) leaves

Preheat the oven to 190°C (375°F/Gas 5).

Check the cavity of the chicken and clean further if necessary. Wipe the chicken inside and out with paper towels.

Season the cavity with salt and pepper. Rub crushed garlic and more salt and pepper over the skin. Truss if desired.

Brush the chicken all over with some of the ghee or oil and place in a roasting tin. Roast for 1½ hours, basting occasionally with more ghee. Turn to brown evenly.

Meanwhile, gently fry the onion in 1 tablespoon of the ghee until soft, add the tomatoes and season to taste. Simmer, uncovered, for 15 minutes, then pass the mixture through a sieve or food mill.

Combine the tomato mixture with the last of the ghee and frequently brush it over the chicken during the last 30–45 minutes of roasting.

To serve, cut a Lawash into pieces, place around the edge of a platter and place the chicken in the middle. Garnish with the egg slices and the coriander leaves and top with a second Lawash. Carve or joint the chicken at the table.

❁ *Note: If you have a rotisserie, place the chicken on the spit and cook, basting with the ghee, then later with the tomato sauce mixture.*

KABAUB
Lamb kebabs with yoghurt marinade
SERVES: 5–6

Traditionally this *kabaub* uses pieces of lean lamb alternated on skewers with similar-sized pieces of lamb tail fat. As this kind of lamb, the Awassi or fat-tailed sheep, is not available outside the Middle East, I have used lamb shoulder. The cubes will contain fat either running through the meat or on one side, to give the desired effect. The fat flavours and moistens the meat.

750 g (1 lb 10 oz) boneless lamb shoulder

250 g (9 oz/1 cup) yoghurt

2 garlic cloves, crushed

1 teaspoon salt

freshly ground black pepper, to taste

For serving

5–6 Lawash (page 494) or other flat bread

sliced tomatoes

sliced onions

lemon wedges

coriander (cilantro) sprigs

Cut the lamb into 3 cm (1¼ inch) cubes.

Combine the yoghurt, garlic, salt and a generous grind of pepper in a glass or ceramic bowl. Add the meat, stir to coat, then cover and refrigerate for 4–5 hours, or overnight.

When ready to cook the *kabaubs*, thread five or six pieces of lamb onto five or six skewers, leaving a little space between the cubes. Brush off the excess marinade — the meat should be coated with a thin film.

Cook the skewers over a glowing charcoal fire. If possible, remove the grill from the barbecue and rest the skewers across the sides of the barbecue, so that the meat is not directly on the grill. Turn the skewers frequently during cooking.

Push the meat off the skewer onto one half of each flat bread. Add some tomato and onion slices. Fold the bread over the top to keep the meat warm and serve immediately, garnished with lemon wedges and coriander.

AUSH
Noodles with pulses, meat and yoghurt

SERVES: 6

Aush dough

300 g (10½ oz/2 cups) plain (all-purpose) flour,
   plus extra as needed

1 teaspoon salt

1 tablespoon vegetable oil

80 g (3 oz/2 cups) finely chopped fresh spinach

Pulse mixture

110 g (3¾ oz/½ cup) yellow split peas

250 g (9 oz/1 cup) tinned red kidney beans,
   with liquid

2 teaspoons salt

Keema (meat sauce)

125 ml (4 fl oz/½ cup) vegetable oil

1 onion, finely chopped

750 g (1 lb 10 oz) minced (ground) lamb or beef

125 ml (4 fl oz/½ cup) tomato passata (puréed tomatoes)

salt and freshly ground black pepper, to season

Chakah (yoghurt sauce)

375 g (13 oz/1½ cups) drained yoghurt (see page 19)

3 teaspoons dried mint, rubbed

¼–½ teaspoon hot chilli powder, to taste

3 tablespoons finely chopped coriander (cilantro) leaves

salt, to taste

To make the dough, sift the flour and salt into a bowl and add 165 ml (5½ fl oz/⅔ cup) cold water. Mix to a firm dough, adding more flour if necessary. Divide into two balls and wrap in plastic wrap. Rest for 30 minutes.

On a floured work surface, roll out each ball of dough very thinly. Cut into 5 mm (¼ inch) noodles, either while the dough is flat,
or after rolling up each sheet of dough.

Place the noodles on a floured cloth, dust with flour and leave to dry for about 30 minutes.

To prepare the pulse mixture, wash the split peas well and place in a saucepan with 375 ml (12½ fl oz/1½ cups) cold water. Bring to the boil, then boil gently for 30 minutes, or until tender. Add the kidney beans and their liquid and keep warm.

In a large saucepan, bring 2 litres (68 fl oz/8 cups) water to the boil. Add the salt and oil. Put the noodles in gradually, stirring after each addition. Return to the boil and cook, uncovered, for 5 minutes. Add the spinach and cook for a further 5 minutes. Drain, then return to the pan.

Add the split pea mixture to the noodles. Toss lightly and keep hot, over low heat.

To make the Keema, heat the oil in a heavy-based saucepan and gently fry the onion until soft. Add the meat and stir over high heat until the juices evaporate and the meat browns lightly. Stir in the passata and 125 ml (4 fl oz/½ cup) water and season with salt and pepper. Cover and simmer for 10 minutes, then remove the lid and let the moisture evaporate. The sauce should be oily.

Combine the Chakah ingredients, add to the noodle mixture and toss well; the mixture should be moist.

Place the noodle mixture in a deep dish and top with the Keema. Stir at the table and serve in deep plates.

KOFTA KABAUB SURKH SHUDA
Fried ground lamb kebab

SERVES: 6

1 kg (2 lb 3 oz) boneless lamb stewing meat

2 onions, chopped

110 g (3¾ oz/½ cup) yellow split peas

2 teaspoons salt

3 tablespoons chopped coriander (cilantro) leaves

1 garlic clove, chopped, optional

½ teaspoon Garam Masala (page 487)

1 egg, beaten

salt and freshly ground black pepper,
   to taste

35 g (1¼ oz/¼ cup) wholemeal
   (whole-wheat) flour, approximately

oil, for pan-frying

4 potatoes, each peeled and cut into 8 wedges

For serving

2 Lawash (page 494), optional

lemon or lime wedges

coriander (cilantro) leaves

Cut the lamb into cubes and place in a saucepan with 500 ml (17 fl oz/2 cups) water. Add 1 chopped onion and bring slowly to the boil, skimming when necessary. Cover and simmer for 30 minutes.

Rinse the split peas and add them to the pan with the salt. Cover and cook for a further 30 minutes, or until the lamb and split peas are tender and the water has been absorbed. Leave the lid off the pan and cook over medium heat for a few minutes to evaporate some of the moisture.

Allow to cool a little, then stir in the remaining chopped onion, and the coriander and the garlic, if using. Pass the mixture through a meat grinder using a fine screen, or process in a food processor using a steel blade.

Turn the mixture into a bowl and leave until cold. Mix in the garam masala, egg, and salt and pepper to taste. Add enough flour to make a manageable paste.

Using moistened hands, shape about 2 tablespoons of the paste at a time into sausage shapes about 10 cm (4 inches) long.

Heat enough oil to cover the base of a frying pan to a depth of 5 mm (¼ inch). Fry the *kabaubs* in batches until golden brown on all sides. Drain and keep hot.

While the *kabaubs* are cooking, deep-fry the potatoes in another pan until golden brown and cooked through. Drain.

To serve, arrange the *kabaubs* on one Lawash placed on a platter; garnish with lemon or lime wedges and coriander. Top with the second Lawash and arrange the potatoes on another platter.

If not using the Lawash, arrange the *kabaubs*, potatoes and garnishes on a platter and serve with another flat bread.

KHABLI PALAU
Spiced lamb pilaf

SERVES: 4–5

60 g (2 oz/¼ cup) ghee, or 60 ml (2 fl oz/¼ cup)
    vegetable oil

2 onions, chopped

500 g (1 lb 2 oz) boneless lamb, cut into 2 cm
    (¾ inch) cubes

½ teaspoon Garam Masala (page 487)

¼ teaspoon ground cardamom

¼ teaspoon ground cinnamon

¼ teaspoon freshly ground black pepper

1½ tablespoons salt

40 g (1½ oz/⅓ cup) slivered almonds

60 g (2 oz/¼ cup) butter or ghee

2 carrots, cut into matchstick lengths

125 g (4 oz/1 cup) seedless raisins

2 teaspoons sugar

400 g (14 oz/2 cups) long-grain white rice

Heat half the ghee or oil in a deep, heavy-based saucepan. Add the onion and fry over medium heat for 15 minutes, or until translucent and golden brown. Remove and set aside.

Add the lamb to the pan with the remaining ghee and fry over high heat until browned, stirring often. Sprinkle with the spices and 1 teaspoon of the salt. Stir over heat for 1 minute, add 375 ml (12½ fl oz/1½ cups) water, then return the onion to the pan. Cover and simmer for 1 hour.

While the meat is cooking, lightly brown the almonds in a frying pan in the butter or ghee. Remove from the pan and set aside, leaving the fat in the pan.

Add the carrots to the frying pan and fry over medium heat until lightly coloured, stirring often. Add the raisins and continue to fry, stirring until the raisins become plump. Sprinkle with the sugar and set aside.

Wash the rice well and strain. In a saucepan, bring 1.5 litres (51 fl oz/6 cups) water to the boil with another 1 tablespoon of the salt. Add the rice, return to the boil, then boil for 6 minutes. Strain.

Remove the cooked lamb and about 125 ml (4 fl oz/½ cup) liquid from the saucepan. Stir the rice and the remaining 1 teaspoon of salt into the juices still remaining in the pan. Make three or four holes in the rice with the end of a wooden spoon. Place the lamb mixture over one half of the rice, and place the carrot and raisin mixture over the rest of the rice. Spoon the reserved meat juices all over the top.

Place two paper towels over the pan and cover tightly with a lid. Cook over medium heat for 5 minutes, then reduce the heat to low and cook for a further 25 minutes. Remove from the heat and keep covered for 5 minutes.

Pile the lamb pieces in the centre of a platter and top with the carrot and raisin mixture. Fluff up the rice grains with a fork and mound the rice around the edge of the dish. Sprinkle with the reserved browned almonds and serve.

SAMBOSAY GOSHTI
Fried meat triangles

MAKES: 40

Filling

500 g (1 lb 2 oz) lean beef or lamb
1 teaspoon salt
60 ml (2 fl oz/¼ cup) vegetable oil
1 small onion, finely chopped
½ teaspoon Garam Masala (page 487)
salt and freshly ground black pepper, to season

Pastry

300 g (10½ oz/2 cups) plain (all-purpose) flour
1 teaspoon salt
60 g (2 oz/¼ cup) butter or ghee
1 egg
oil, for deep-frying

Cut the meat into cubes and place in a saucepan with the salt and 250 ml (8½ fl oz/1 cup) water. Bring slowly to the boil, then simmer for 1–1½ hours, or until the meat is tender.

Lift the meat from the liquid, reserving the liquid. Allow to cool slightly, then chop finely, or pass through a meat grinder using a coarse screen.

Heat the oil in a frying pan and gently fry the onion until translucent. Add the meat, increase the heat and fry until lightly browned; add a little of the reserved cooking liquid to moisten. Stir in the garam masala and season lightly with salt and pepper. Remove from the heat and cool.

To make the pastry, sift the flour and salt into a bowl. Add the butter or ghee and lightly rub into the flour with your fingertips until well distributed. Lightly beat the egg, then add enough cold water to make up the liquid to 125 ml (4 fl oz/½ cup).

Pour the liquid into the flour mixture and mix to a soft dough. Cover with plastic wrap and leave to rest for 15 minutes.

Thinly roll out half the pastry, using the method described on page 15. The circle should be about 50 cm (20 inches) in diameter.

Fold the pastry back on itself in 8 cm (3¼ inch) pleats, so that you finish with a strip of that width, and the length of the circle's diameter. Press lightly with a rolling pin, then cut the strip in half for easier handling.

Roll each strip lengthways, so each is about 75 cm (30 inches) long and 9 cm (3½ inches) wide, then cut each into squares and stack. Repeat with the remaining pastry.

Working one at a time, place a generous teaspoon of filling in the centre of each square of pastry; moisten two adjacent edges with water and fold over to form a triangle. Press the edges to seal, then press with the edge of a thimble in crescents, or with the tines of a fork. Place the finished pastries on a tray.

Deep-fry three or four at a time in hot oil, turning to cook evenly. Fry until golden brown, then lift out and drain on paper towels. Serve hot.

AUSHAK
Boiled leek pastries with yoghurt and meat sauce

SERVES: 6

It is popularly believed that Marco Polo introduced noodles to Italy from China. Some 50 years before his travels, Arabs and Indians were eating noodles, called *rishta* in Arabic (a name still used today and derived from the Persian word for 'thread'), and *sevika* in India. As Afghanistan was the natural land route from one area to the other, it's anybody's guess where *rishta*, *sevika* or *aush* (page 501) originated.

All this preamble because the usual English description of *aushak* is leek 'ravioli' with yoghurt and meat sauce! With all respect to the Italians, to prevent confusion I have refrained from using Italian words. This recipe is of ancient origin, and without doubt Afghan. Only the tomato is a recent introduction and probably replaced tamarind or some such acid ingredient.

1 quantity Aush Dough (page 501)

2 leeks (to make 405 g/14 oz/3 cups chopped)

¼ teaspoon hot chilli powder

2 teaspoons salt

2 tablespoons vegetable oil

2–3 teaspoons dried mint

Keema (meat sauce)

125 ml (4 fl oz/½ cup) vegetable oil

1 large onion, finely chopped

500 g (1 lb 2 oz) lean minced (ground) lamb or beef

125 ml (4 fl oz/½ cup) tomato passata (puréed tomatoes)

salt and freshly ground black pepper, to season

Chakah (yoghurt sauce)

500 g (1 lb 2 oz/2 cups) drained yoghurt (see page 19)

3–4 garlic cloves, crushed

1 teaspoon salt

Make the dough as directed on page 501, wrap in plastic wrap and rest for 30 minutes.

Cut off and discard most of the green tops from the leeks. Halve them lengthways and rinse well to remove all traces of soil between the leaves. Remove the roots and dry the leeks with paper towels. Finely chop the leeks and measure in cups.

Combine the leek in a bowl with the chilli powder, 1 teaspoon of the salt and 1 tablespoon of the oil. If desired, the leek may be fried gently in oil until soft.

Divide the dough in two and roll out very thinly on a lightly floured work surface. Cut into 5 cm (2 inch) rounds or squares. Stack and cover them as the shapes are made; roll out the trimmings and cut to shape.

Working one at a time, place a teaspoon of the leek filling in the centre of the dough. Moisten the edge with water and fold over to make semi-circles; fold squares into triangles. Seal the edges by pressing with the edge of a thimble or the tines of a fork. Put each pastry on a cloth-lined tray and keep covered with another cloth.

To make the Keema, heat the oil in a saucepan and gently fry the onion until translucent. Increase the heat, add the meat and stir until crumbly. Cook until the juices evaporate and the meat browns. Reduce the heat and stir in the passata and 250 ml (8½ fl oz/1 cup) water. Season with salt and pepper. Cover and simmer gently for 20 minutes, then remove the lid and cook until the moisture evaporates and the mixture is oily. Keep hot.

Combine the Chakah ingredients in a bowl and set aside.

Bring 2 litres (68 fl oz/8 cups) water to the boil in a large saucepan. Add the remaining 1 teaspoon salt and 1 tablespoon oil. Drop in about 20 pastries and boil for 10 minutes. Remove with a slotted spoon to a colander set over simmering water. Cover and keep warm while cooking the remaining pastries.

Spread half the Chakah on an oval platter. Top with the hot pastries and cover with the remaining Chakah. Rub the dried mint to a powder and sprinkle over the Chakah. Top with the hot Keema and serve immediately.

KECHEREE QUROOT-E-KOFTA
Rice and mung beans with meatball and yoghurt sauce

SERVES: 6

750 g (1 lb 10 oz) finely minced (ground) lamb

1 onion, grated

1 teaspoon ground coriander

1 teaspoon ground cumin

½ teaspoon hot chilli powder

1½ teaspoons salt

125 ml (4 fl oz/½ cup) vegetable oil, or
    125 g (4 oz/½ cup) ghee

1 large onion, finely chopped

375 g (13 oz/1½ cups) chopped,
    peeled tomatoes

Kecheree (rice and mung beans)

110 g (3¾ oz/½ cup) mung beans

330 g (11½ oz/1½ cups) short-grain white rice

125 g (4 oz/½ cup) ghee

2 onions, chopped

2 teaspoons salt

freshly ground black pepper, to season

½ teaspoon Garam Masala (page 487)

1 teaspoon dried mint, rubbed

For serving

60 g (2 oz/¼ cup) ghee or butter

3 garlic cloves, finely chopped

Quroot (page 488)

Combine the lamb with the grated onion, spices and salt. Shape into walnut-sized balls.

Heat the oil or ghee in a saucepan and gently fry the chopped onion until lightly browned. Add the tomatoes, 250 ml (8½ fl oz/1 cup) water and some more salt to taste. Bring to the boil and add the meatballs, then cover and simmer for 30 minutes. Remove the lid and cook until most of the liquid has evaporated, stirring occasionally.

Meanwhile, prepare the Kecheree. Wash the mung beans and rice separately; drain and set aside. Heat the oil or ghee in a heavy-based saucepan and gently fry the onion until lightly browned. Add 1 litre (34 fl oz/4 cups) water and bring to the boil, then stir in the mung beans. Return to the boil and simmer, covered, for 10 minutes.

Stir in the rice, salt, pepper, garam masala and mint. Bring back to the boil, then reduce the heat to low. Cover the pan tightly with a cloth and a lid and simmer gently for 30 minutes.

Mound the Kecheree onto a platter, hollowing the centre. Fill the hollow with some of the meatballs and sauce. Place the remaining meatballs in a bowl beside the platter.

To finish, heat the ghee or butter in a small saucepan and gently fry the garlic until lightly coloured. Put the Quroot in a bowl and pour the hot garlic mixture over it. Serve the Quroot immediately with the other dishes, so that it may be added to individual taste.

ABRAYSHAM KABAUB
Silk kebab

MAKES: ABOUT 30 PIECES

This fascinating sweet is actually a sweet omelette cooked in a most unusual way. Afghan cooks differ about how the silken-thread omelette should be prepared. I have given the method that works best for me – once you have the idea you might devise a simpler method.

This is regarded as one of the great delicacies of Afghan cooking, but the 'kebab' part of the name is rather confusing. Perhaps it is because the final pieces resemble kebab meats; personally I cannot see it.

Syrup
330 g (11½ oz/1½ cups) sugar
1 teaspoon lemon juice
¼ teaspoon saffron threads, optional

Omelette
8 eggs
pinch of salt

To finish
500 ml (17 fl oz/2 cups) vegetable oil
100 g (3½ oz) finely chopped pistachio nuts or walnuts
½ teaspoon ground cardamom

To make the syrup, dissolve the sugar in 250 ml (8½ fl oz/ 1 cup) water in a heavy-based saucepan over medium heat. Bring to the boil, add the lemon juice and saffron, if using, and boil for 10 minutes. Cool and strain into a 25 cm (10 inch) pie plate, then set aside.

To make the omelette, break the eggs into a flat-based dish about 20 cm (8 inches) in diameter; the size of the dish and the flat base are important. Add a pinch of salt and mix the eggs with a fork until the yolks and whites are thoroughly combined — but do not beat, as the eggs must not be foamy.

Heat the oil in an electric frying pan to 190°C (375°F), or in a 25 cm (10 inch) frying pan placed on a temperature-controlled hot plate or burner.

Have ready a long skewer, the plate of syrup, a baking tray and the nuts mixed with the cardamom. A bowl of water and a cloth for drying your hands are also necessary.

Hold the dish with the eggs in one hand, next to and slightly above the pan of oil. Put a hand into the egg, palm down, so the egg covers the back of the hand. Lift out your hand, curling your fingers slightly inwards, then open out over the hot oil, fingers pointing down. Move your hand across the oiled surface so the egg falls in streams from your fingertips. Dip your hand in the egg again and make more strands across those already in the pan. Repeat three or four times, until about an eighth of the egg is used. There should be a closely meshed layer of egg strands about 20 cm (8 inches) across. Work quickly so the last lot of egg is added not long after the first lot.

Quickly rinse your hand and dry it. Slide the skewer under the bubbling omelette, lift it up and turn it over to lightly brown on the other side. The first side will be bubbly, the underside somewhat smoother. When the omelette is golden brown, lift it out with the skewer and drain over the pan.

Place the omelette flat in the syrup, spoon over the syrup and lift it out with a skewer onto a baking tray. Roll it up with the bubbly side inwards. The finished roll should be about 3 cm (1¼ inches) in diameter. Sprinkle with nuts and set aside.

Repeat with the remaining egg, making seven or eight rolls in all. Although the depth of the egg reduces, you will become so adept that somehow you will get it into the pan in fine strands.

When cool, cut the rolls into 4–5 cm (1½–2 inch) pieces and serve. These keep well in a sealed container in a cool place.

HALWAU-E AURD-E SUJEE
« Semolina sweetmeat
SERVES: 6–8

This *halwau* is very similar in preparation to a Greek *halva* I have been making for years. The ghee, cardamom and rosewater give it a typically Oriental flavour.

220 g (8 oz/1 cup) sugar
185 g (6½ oz/¾ cup) ghee
125 g (4 oz/1 cup) semolina (farina)
35 g (1¼ oz/¼ cup) pistachio nuts
30 g (1 oz/¼ cup) slivered almonds
½–1 teaspoon ground cardamom
1–2 teaspoons rosewater
additional pistachio nuts or almonds, to decorate

Combine the sugar and 500 ml (17 fl oz/2 cups) water in a saucepan. Stir occasionally over medium heat until the sugar has dissolved. Bring to the boil, then boil briskly for 5 minutes without stirring. Remove from the heat and set aside.

Meanwhile, heat the ghee in a deep, heavy-based saucepan. Add the semolina and stir over medium heat for 5 minutes, without allowing the semolina to colour.

Pour the hot syrup into the semolina, stirring constantly. When smoothly combined, reduce the heat a little and leave to cook, uncovered, until the liquid has been absorbed. The mixture should be thick, but still moist at this stage. Stir in the nuts, and the cardamom and rosewater to taste.

Cover the pan with a cloth or two paper towels, put the lid on tightly and leave over low heat for 5 minutes. Turn off the heat and leave the pan undisturbed for 10 minutes.

Spread the *halwau* on a flat, lightly oiled platter and decorate it with nuts. Serve warm or cold, cutting pieces into diamond shapes or squares (see page 16 for cutting techniques).

FIRNEE
Almond and cardamom cream pudding
SERVES: 6–8

750 ml (25 fl oz/3 cups) milk
pinch of salt
75 g (2½ oz/⅓ cup) sugar
60 g (2 oz/½ cup) cornflour (cornstarch)
80 g (3 oz/½ cup) slivered almonds, or chopped blanched almonds
¼ teaspoon saffron threads, pounded
¼–½ teaspoon ground cardamom
35 g (1¼ oz/¼ cup) finely chopped pistachio nuts

Pour all but 125 ml (4 fl oz/½ cup) of the milk into a heavy-based saucepan and add the salt and sugar. Heat gently, stirring to dissolve the sugar.

Blend the cornflour with the reserved milk and 60 ml (2 fl oz/¼ cup) cold water. Pour the mixture into the warm milk, stirring constantly. Add the almonds and keep stirring until the mixture thickens and bubbles — use a whisk if the mixture becomes lumpy.

Add the pounded saffron, and cardamom to taste. Cook over low heat for 5 minutes, letting the pudding simmer very gently, and stirring occasionally.

Pour into six or eight individual dishes. Sprinkle the pistachios around the edge of each dish.

❀ *Note: To serve* firnee *in the traditional manner, the pudding should be poured into two deep plates, decorated with pistachios, cut into quarters and served in wedges.*

GOSH FEEL
« Elephant ear pastries
MAKES: ABOUT 40

2 eggs

2 teaspoons caster (superfine) sugar

¼ teaspoon salt

125 ml (4 fl oz/½ cup) milk

1 tablespoon vegetable oil

½ teaspoon ground cardamom

375 g (13 oz/2½ cups) plain (all-purpose) flour,
    plus 35 g (1¼ oz/¼ cup) for kneading

oil, for deep-frying

To finish

125 g (4 oz/1 cup) icing (confectioners') sugar

½ teaspoon ground cardamom, optional

130 g (4½ oz/1 cup) finely chopped blanched pistachio nuts,
    or 55 g (2 oz/½ cup) finely chopped walnuts

Beat the eggs until frothy, then beat in the sugar and salt.
Stir in the milk, oil and cardamom. Sift the flour, add half to
the egg mixture and mix in with a wooden spoon. Gradually
stir in the remaining flour, holding back about 75 g
(2½ oz/½ cup).

Turn out onto a floured work surface and dust with some
of the reserved flour. Knead for 10 minutes, until smooth and
glossy, using more flour as required; the dough will still be
slightly sticky. Cover with plastic wrap and rest for 2 hours.

Take a piece of dough about the size of a large hazelnut and
roll out on a floured surface to a circle about 8–10 cm
(3¼–4 inches) in diameter. Gather up the dough on one side
and pinch, forming a shape resembling an elephant ear. Place
on a cloth and cover. Repeat with the remaining dough.

Deep-fry one at a time in oil heated to 190°C (375°F),
turning to cook evenly. Fry until golden; do not over-brown.
As the dough is rather elastic, the pastry tends to contract with
handling, so just before dropping each pastry into the hot oil,
pull it out lightly with your fingers to enlarge.

Drain the pastries on paper towels.

To finish, sift the icing sugar with the cardamom, if using,
and dust the pastries with the mixture. Sprinkle with the nuts
and serve warm or cold. Store in a sealed container.

 *Note: For an alternative topping, make a syrup using 220 g
(8 oz/1 cup) sugar and 125 ml (4 fl oz/½ cup) water. Bring to the boil
when the sugar has dissolved and boil for 5 minutes. Drizzle the syrup
onto warm pastries and sprinkle with cardamom and nuts.*

SAMBOSAY SHEEREEN
Fried sweet pastries
MAKES: 40

1 quantity Sambosay Goshti pastry (page 505)

60 g (2 oz/½ cup) icing (confectioners') sugar

55 g (2 oz/½ cup) ground pistachio nuts, optional

oil, for deep-frying

Filling

115 g (4 oz/1 cup) ground walnuts

160 g (5½ oz/1 cup) chopped seedless raisins

Make the pastry as directed, up to the point of filling.
Combine the icing sugar and pistachio nuts and set aside.

To make the filling, combine the walnuts and raisins to
form a coarse paste.

Working one at a time, place a generous teaspoon of filling
in the centre of the pastry squares. Moisten two adjacent edges
and fold the pastries diagonally to form a triangle. Press the
edges to seal, then press with a thimble in crescents, or with
the tines of a fork. Place the finished pastries on a tray.

Deep-fry three or four pastries at a time in hot oil, turning
to brown evenly. Cook until golden brown, then lift out and
drain on paper towels.

Sprinkle the warm pastries with the icing sugar and nut
mixture and serve warm or cold. Store the remaining pastries
in a sealed container.

GLOSSARY

ALLSPICE

Botanical name: *Pimenta officinalis*
Family name: *Myrtaceae*
Arabic: *bhar hub wa na'im, bahar*
Turkish: *yeni bahar*

Although it is a spice from the New World, allspice has been adopted in Middle Eastern cooking for its similarity to the combined flavours of clove, cinnamon and nutmeg. Commonly referred to as *bahar*.

BAHAR

See Allspice.

BAHARAT

A mixture of spices used in Gulf Arabic and Iraqi cooking, it is a combination of cinnamon, cloves, nutmeg, cumin, coriander and pepper, with paprika added for colour.

BAKALIAROS

Dried salt cod. A favourite in Greece and Cyprus. Requires soaking for several hours, changing the water often. It is usually par-boiled, coated with batter and fried, with garlic sauce an essential accompaniment. Also used in stews or rissoles.

BAY LEAF

Botanical name: *Laurus nobilis*
Family name: *Lauraceae*
Arabic: *warak al gar*
Greek: *thaphne*
Turkish: *dafne yapregi*

Used in Greek, Turkish and Cypriot cooking as a flavouring herb in meat stews, and in marinades for lamb and fish. Pieces of bay leaves are frequently placed on skewers between food pieces. Occasionally used in Arabic cooking.

BEANS, DRIED

See individual entries under Black-eyed beans, Broad beans and Mung beans. Only the lesser known dried beans are detailed.

BLACK-EYED BEANS

Botanical name: *Vigna unguiculata*
Family name: *Leguminosae*
Arabic: *lubyi msallat*
Greek: *fassoulia mavromatica*
Greek Cypriot: *louvi mavromati*

The black-eyed bean is a variety of the cowpea, and native to Central Africa. It should not be confused with the dried bean of *Vigna sesquipedalis*, which, when immature, is the yard-long asparagus or snake bean so popular in Mediterranean countries. Black-eyed beans have a pleasant, slightly sweet flavour and cook more quickly than other dried beans. Though they discolour the liquid in which they are cooked, I prefer these beans to any other for making *fassoulatha* (bean soup).

BROAD BEANS (FAVA BEANS)

Botanical name: *Vicia faba*
Family name: *Leguminosae*
Arabic: *ful nabed*
Greek: *koukia*
Iranian: *bhagala*
Turkish: *fava*

Used fresh in Greek, Cypriot, Turkish and Arabic cooking. When very young, the whole bean is used — topped, tailed and strings removed. Mature beans are shelled and used in most countries of the region. They are very good when cooked with globe artichoke hearts. In Iranian cooking the skin is removed from the fresh, shelled beans. Frozen broad beans are a good year-round standby and are easily skinned.

Dried broad beans vary in colour from olive green to a purplish hue. The green beans are usually new season's beans and take less soaking and cooking than the darker beans. Used in Egyptian and Arabic cooking for *ful nabed*, *tameya* and *falafel*.

See page 10 for instructions on soaking and skinning. Sometimes available ready skinned; when skinned, the beans are white.

BROAD BEANS, SMALL

Botanical name: *Vicia faba var. minor*
Family name: *Leguminosae*
Arabic: *ful*
Greek: *fava*
Turkish: *bakla*

Also called Egyptian brown beans, tick, horse, fava and ful beans, these are only used dried. They are essential for the Egyptian *ful medamis*, a dish popular throughout most of the region, though the name varies occasionally. They range in colour from beige to purple and require soaking and long, slow cooking. Native to the Mediterranean region, their use as a food goes back to pre-history.

BURGHUL

Arabic: *burghul, bulkar*
Greek: *pourgouri*
Turkish: *bulgar*

Burghul is hulled wheat, steamed until partly cooked, then dried and ground. It is available in fine and coarse grades. Recipes specify which grade to use. It has a nut-like flavour, making it a popular food for those following natural food diets. It is widely used in Lebanon, Syria and neighbouring countries. You will find it in Middle Eastern, Greek and Armenian grocers, speciality food stores and health food shops.

CAPSICUM

Botanical name: *Capsicum spp.*
Family name: *Solanaceae*
Arabic: *felfel, felfel bard*
Armenian: *ganantch biber*
Greek: *piperies*
Iranian: *felfel sabz*

Also known as bell peppers, sweet peppers and pimento, these green summer vegetables ripen to a deep red, with a change in flavour when ripe. The spice paprika is made from the ripe capsicum. Though native to tropical America, they are very popular throughout the Middle East.

CARDAMOM

Botanical name: *Elettaria cardamomum*
Family name: *Zingiberceae*
Afghan: *hale*
Arabic: *hell, hail*
Iranian: *hell*

An expensive spice, but necessary to Gulf Arabic, Iranian and Afghan cooking. Available in pods, as seeds or ground. Where ground cardamom is required, a better flavour is obtained with freshly ground seeds, particularly for sweet recipes. It is also a necessary spice for Arabic coffee.

CAROB

Botanical name: *Ceratonia siliqua*
Family name: *Leguminosae*
Arabic: *kharrub*

An evergreen tree native to the Mediterranean region, yielding long fleshy pods. The dried pods are sold in the Middle East as a snack food; the slightly sweet, chocolate flavour appeals, particularly to children. In carob, the Western natural food advocates have found a substitute for chocolate — one with far less fat.

See also Dibs.

CASSIA

Botanical name: *Cinnamomum cassia*
Family name: *Lauraceae*
Arabic: *darseen, kerfee*
Greek: *kanella*

Also known as Chinese cassia, this spice is considered an inferior form of cinnamon. The thick pieces of bark are widely used in Arabic and Greek cooking in savoury dishes and sweet syrups, and although cinnamon is specified in recipes, either cassia or cinnamon may be used.

CHESTNUTS

Botanical name: *Castanea sativa*
Family name: *Fagaceae*
Arabic: *kestani, abu / arwe*
Greek: *kastana*
Turkish: *kestane*

Native to Mediterranean regions, chestnuts have been used from ancient times. The chestnut-sellers with their charcoal braziers ply their trade in cities around the Mediterranean, but are a less frequent sight today, as crops are dwindling due to fungus diseases affecting the trees. Chestnuts are used in stuffings for poultry; in Greece chestnut purée is a favourite dessert, and the *zaharoplasti* (sweet-maker) excels in preparing glacé chestnuts.

To prepare chestnuts for cooking, cut through the shell at each end, cover with water and boil for 10 minutes. Remove a few at a time and peel off the shell and inner covering on the nut. To roast, cut a cross on one side of the shell, then cook in a moderate oven (180°C/350°F) for 10–15 minutes. Peel while hot.

CHICKPEAS, GARBANZO BEANS

Botanical name: *Cicer arietinum*
Family name: *Leguminosae*
Arabic: *hummus*
Armenian: *siser-noghud*
Greek: *revithia*
Iranian: *nakhod*
Turkish: *nohut*

Used as a food from ancient times in Egypt and Greece, chickpeas are popular throughout the region. They must be soaked before cooking, and some recipes require the removal of the skins (see page 10). Armenian food stores sometimes stock ready-skinned chickpeas.

They are also sold roasted as a snack food.

CHILLI

Botanical name: *Capsicum frutescens*
Family name: *Solanaceae*
Afghan: *murgh*
Arabic: *felfel, bisbas*

The long, slender green or red hot chilli is favoured in Gulf and Yemeni cooking. Frequently the whole pod is used, including the seeds, but as the seeds are very hot indeed it is better to remove them. Take care when handling chillies, keeping fingers away from the mouth and eyes. Dried chillies or ground hot chilli pepper may be substituted.

Remove the seeds from dried chillies and soak the chillies in hot water for 5 minutes before using.

Use ground hot chilli or chilli pepper cautiously, adding a small amount at a time, and tasting until the desired heat is obtained.

CINNAMON

Botanical name: *Cinnamomum zeylanicum*
Family name: *Lauraceae*
Afghan: *dolchini*
Arabic: *darseen, kerfee*
Armenian: *dartchin*
Greek: *kanella*
Iranian: *derchin*
Turkish: *tarcin*

A popular spice for both savoury and sweet dishes; either ground cinnamon or pieces of bark are used. It is an essential ingredient in the *baharat* of the Gulf States and Iraq, and the garam masala of Afghanistan and India. Fine sheets of the inner layer of the cinnamon bark are dried and interleaved to form sticks or quills. In recipes, a small piece of bark refers to a stick about 4 cm (1½ inches) long, while a large piece is twice as long; however, there is no need to be very accurate in measuring.

CLOVES

Botanical name: *Syzygium aromaticum or Eugenia aromatica*
Family name: *Myrtaceae*
Afghan: *kala*
Arabic: *habahan, gharanful-mesmar*
Greek: *garifala*
Iranian: *nebos*
Turkish: *karinfil*

The dried flowerbud of an evergreen tree native to tropical Asia is used in both savoury and sweet dishes. A clove is sometimes added to simmering chicken to remove unwanted flavours, perhaps necessary for range-fed chickens or boiling fowls, but not for specially raised birds.

Cloves are claimed to sweeten the breath after eating garlic. In the Gulf States they are infused for a spicy tea.

CORIANDER (CILANTRO)

Botanical name: *Coriandrum sativum*
Family name: *Umbelliferae*
Afghan: *gashneez*
Arabic: *kazbarah*
Greek Cypriot: *koliandros*
Iranian: *geshniez*
Turkish: *kis nis*

Both the green leaves and seeds of this parsley relative are widely used in the Middle East. The flavour of the leaves is an acquired taste; the name of this pungent herb comes from the Greek *koris*, meaning 'bug', indicative of its aroma. However, it is also similar to the aroma of dried orange peel, a more acceptable comparison. Known as cilantro in the US, it is used in the cooking of Afghanistan, Iran, the Gulf States, Yemen and Cyprus.

Ground coriander seeds are also widely used and feature in the *baharat* of the Gulf States and Iraq. The crushed seeds are also an essential ingredient in the *afelias* of Cyprus.

CORNFLOUR

Also called cornstarch: a white starch used for thickening milk puddings, and essential in Turkish delight. Not to be confused with yellow cornflour.

CRESS

Botanical name: *Arabis caucasica*
Family name: *Cruciferae*
Arabic: *barbeen*
Iranian: *shahat*

A green herb much used in Iran, Iraq and the Gulf States as a salad herb. In Iran it is also used for the pot. Very similar to watercress in appearance and flavour, though the leaves are larger and more closely bunched on the stems.

CUMIN

Botanical name: *Cuminum cyminum*
Family name: *Umbelliferae*
Afghan: *zeera*
Arabic: *kamoon*
Armenian: *kimion*
Greek: *kimino*
Iranian: *zire*
Turkish: *cemen*

Native to Egypt, the seeds have been widely used as a spice from ancient times in Egyptian and Eastern Mediterranean cooking. In Cyprus a seed called *artisha* is used in *tavas*, and though similar in appearance and flavour to cumin, it is claimed to be different by the Cypriots and is rarely available outside Cyprus. Some herbs and spices do vary in flavour when grown in different climates and soils; perhaps this can explain the difference.

CUMIN, BLACK

Botanical name: *Nigella sativa*
Family name: *Ranunculaceae*
Afghan: *kala zeera*
Arabic: *habet el sauda*
Armenian: *shoushma*
Greek: *mavrokoko*

This small black aromatic seed bears no relationship to cumin. It is used on sweet yeast breads and cakes in Cyprus, Lebanon, Syria and Armenia; for flavouring haloumi cheese in Lebanon; and is one of the spices in the garam masala of Afghanistan.

DIBS

A syrup made from the carob pod, which has a chocolate flavour. Popular in Lebanon and Syria, where it is mixed with tahini as a spread for bread.

DIBS ROMAN

Pomegranate molasses or syrup, used in Lebanese and Syrian cooking. See Pomegranate.

DILL

Botanical name: *Anethum graveolens*
Family name: *Umbelliferae*
Afghan: *shabit*
Armenian: *samit*
Greek: *anitho*
Turkish: *dereotu*

Native to the Mediterranean region, dill was much favoured as a medicinal herb in ancient times. The feathery leaves are blue-green in colour and give a distinctive, slightly aniseed flavour to meat, vegetable and rice dishes and pickles. An excellent herb for globe artichokes. Fennel may be substituted.

DRIED LIMES

Arabic: *loomi, noomi, noomi besra*
Iranian: *limu omani*

Also called black limes, these are available in the Gulf States, either light grey-brown in colour or almost black. In Iran and Iraq, the lighter limes are used. They come from Oman and also from Thailand, and are dried on the trees. As they are not readily available to the Westerner, directions are given to make your own on page 345.

FENUGREEK

Botanical name: *Trigonella foenum-graecum*
Family name: *Leguminosae*
Arabic: *hulba, hilbeh*
Armenian: *chaiman*
Iranian: *shambalileh*

Though indigenous to the Eastern Mediterranean countries, the fawn, three-sided seed is used in Yemeni cooking for a potent paste called *hulba* or *hilbeh*, according to the dialect of the region; it is also a principal ingredient for *pastourma* (dried, spiced beef). The seeds have a slightly bitter flavour and are an essential ingredient in Indian curry blends.

The small, oval leaves are used in Iran in dishes such as *sabzi khordan*, *kukuye sabzi* and *khoreshe gormeh sabzi*. Though some recipes do not include the herb because it is not readily available, add a small quantity if you have it on hand.

FETA

Greek in origin, feta is a soft, crumbly, white cheese made from goat's or ewe's milk. Turkey's *beyaz peynir* and Iran's *panir* are both feta-style cheeses, and as these are not exported, feta is the only substitute.

Feta is made in many other countries, and the quality varies according to the milk used. Greek, Bulgarian and Romanian fetas are the best for serving as appetisers or in salads. Firmer fetas are made from cow's milk; usually less expensive, these are suitable for cooking purposes.

To keep feta for a considerable time, take a wide-necked jar with you when purchasing so that the cheese may be covered with the whey in which it is packed. Alternatively, reserve the whey when making *mizithra* (page 27), then boil it, leave to cool and pour over the feta. Seal the container and store in thc rcfrigerator.

FLOUR

The plain flour used in these recipes is known in North America as all-purpose flour; wholemeal flour is known as whole-wheat or wheatmeal flour.

Unbleached plain (all-purpose) flour can be used in recipes if preferred, especially for bread. See also the 'Bread' section on pages 12—13.

FUL, FUL MEDAMIS

See Broad beans, small.

GARBANZO BEANS

See Chickpeas, garbanzo beans.

GARLIC

Botanical name: *Allium sativum*
Family name: *Liliaceae*
Afghan: *seer*
Arabic: *tum*
Armenian: *sekhdor*
Greek: *skortho*
Iranian: *sir*
Turkish: *sarimsak*

Known and used from ancient times for the medicinal properties attributed to it, garlic is essential to Middle Eastern dishes and should not be omitted from recipes using it. Remember that the flavour of garlic becomes more pronounced if browned, so avoid browning if a strong flavour is not desired. Raw garlic, finely chopped, is often mixed through boiled greens. Any recipe using raw garlic will leave you with unpleasant breath. Chewing on a clove or drinking milk are favourite antidotes.

GARLIC CHIVES

Botanical name: *Allium tuberosum*
Family name: *Liliaceae*
Iranian: *tareh*

This flat-bladed green herb is used extensively in Iranian cooking and has a garlic-like flavour. If unavailable, it may be omitted from the ingredients, or add onion-flavoured chives and half a crushed garlic clove.

GHEE

Afghan: *roghan*
Arabic: *samneh*
Iranian: *roghani kare*

Ghee is pure butter fat. Because of the absence of milk solids, ghee can be heated to high temperatures without burning, and imparts a special fragrance to foods. When ghee is heated a degree of oxidation occurs, evident in the white colour of the ghee when it solidifies. Food laws in some countries are not as stringent as in others, and ghee often includes other fats or vegetable oils; for this reason clarified butter is given as the alternative in recipes where the flavour of ghee is necessary.

HALOUMI

This salty, sheep's milk cheese is made in Cyprus and Lebanon, and matured in whey. It is string-like in texture, as it is kneaded after the drained curd is boiled in the whey. Cyprus haloumi is flavoured with dried mint; the Lebanese haloumi uses black cumin. The cheese can be made in the home using cow's milk; see page 108 for details.

HALVA

Halva, with its many variations in spelling, generally means sweet, and is frequently a thickened pudding or sweetmeat. The confection called *halva* is made from ground raw sesame seeds; as its preparation requires cooking under pressure and the skill of a professional confectioner, it is not possible to duplicate the process in the home. Halva often contains almonds or pistachio nuts. It is a delicious confection, and though high in calories, it has good nutritive value and is highly recommended if you wish to gain weight.

KASSERI

A Greek sheep or goat's milk cheese, creamy white, firm textured with a few very small holes. It is a good table cheese, is excellent fried in butter or olive oil and served with a squeeze of lemon juice, and is frequently used diced on top of lamb stews. *Kaser*, a Turkish cheese, and *kashkaval*, a Romanian cheese, may be used instead.

KATAIFI

Arabic: *konafa, k'nafi*
Greek: *kataifi*
Turkish: *kadaif*

A shredded pastry which looks rather like slightly soft vermicelli noodles. A dough, somewhat similar to fillo dough, is forced through a finely perforated metal plate. The fine pastry strands are dropped onto a solid, heated metal plate, cooked briefly, then scooped off while still pliable. *Kataifi* is usually packaged in plastic and keeps well in the refrigerator or freezer, providing the package is sealed, and overwrapped if stored in the freezer. It has a longer storage life than fillo pastry. Bring it to room temperature, in its package, before attempting to loosen the strands. It is available from Greek and Middle Eastern food stores and pastry shops.

KEFALOTIRI

A popular Greek grating cheese, whose name literally means 'head cheese'. The Italian parmesan cheese may be substituted.

KISHK

Burghul fermented with milk and yoghurt, in a very lengthy process. After fermentation it is salted, spread on a cloth to dry, then ground to a fine powder and stored for winter use. Cooked with water, *kishk* becomes a nourishing breakfast; it is also added to soups for extra nourishment. It is used in Lebanon and Syria, and to a lesser extent in Iran, where it is called *kashk*. It is available from Middle Eastern food stores.

LOOMI

See Dried limes.

MAHLAB

Greek: *mahlepi*

A Syrian spice from the kernel of the black cherry stone, with a sweet spicy fragrance. The spice is always sold whole and is a small, husked seed, pale brown in colour and a little smaller than a coriander seed. Pound using a mortar and pestle before using to flavour sweet yeast breads.

MASTICHA

Botanical name: *Pistacia lentiscus*
Family name: *Anacardiaceae*
Arabic: *mistki*
Greek: *masticha*

Mastic is a resin from a small evergreen tree, with most of the world's supply coming from the Greek island of Chios. From ancient times it has been used as a chewing gum. The powdered resin is used to flavour sweet yeast breads and a Greek liqueur of the same name. In Egypt, a small piece of *masticha* is often added to boiling chicken to remove unwanted flavours.

MELOKHIA

Botanical name: *Corchorus olitorius*
Family name: *Tiliaceae*

This is a secondary source of jute grown in Egypt and India. In Egypt the younger shoots are harvested and the oval leaves, 4–8 cm (1½–3¼ inches) long, are stripped from the long stalks and used as a pot herb for a soup of the same name. The herb has the viscous properties of okra, and it is favoured more for this than for its flavour. *Melokhia* sometimes makes its appearance in Western city markets during late spring and summer. Strip the leaves from the stalks, wash well, then drain and shred very finely, using about 500 g (1 lb 2 oz) leaves in place of the 1½ cups dried leaves given in the recipe on page 399. Dried *melokhia* is available at Greek and Middle Eastern food stores.

MINT

Botanical name: *Mentha spicata* or *M. viridis*
Family name: *Labiatae*
Afghan: *nauna*
Arabic: *na'na*
Armenian: *ananoukh*
Greek: *thiosmos*
Iranian: *nano*
Turkish: *nane*

The mint most favoured throughout the region is spearmint, both in fresh and dried form. Used in meat and vegetable dishes, and fragrant when fried in butter or ghee for or a final touch to yoghurt, soups and salads, mint gives Middle Eastern cooking a distinct and appealing flavour. Dried mint is readily available at any store carrying a wide range of dried herbs.

MUNG BEANS

Botanical name: *Vigna radiata*
Family name: *Leguminosae*
Afghan: *maush*

Also known as green beans, golden gram or green gram, mung beans have been cultivated in Asia for centuries. While mainly used for bean sprouts or ground to a flour for Asian sweets, they are used whole in Afghan cooking. Mung beans do not require pre-soaking as they cook quickly.

NOOMI

See Dried limes.

NUTMEG

Botanical name: *Myristica fragrans*
Family name: *Myristicaceae*
Arabic: *josat al teeb*
Greek: *mostokaritho*
Turkish: *kucuk hindistancevizi*

The hard inner kernel of the fruit of a tropical tree grown in the West Indies, Sri Lanka and South-East Asian countries. An essential ingredient in the *baharat* of the Gulf States. In Greek cooking, a small quantity of ground nutmeg is added to cream and meat sauces and spinach pie fillings.

OKRA

Botanical name: *Abelmoschus esculentus* or *Hibiscus esculentus*
Family name: *Malvaceae*
Arabic: *bamia*
Greek: *bamye*
Turkish: *bamya*

Also called ladies' fingers and gumbo. Native to Africa, okra is an angular pod, tapering to a point. Young okra are preferred. The vegetable has viscous properties, and while it is used for these properties in Western cooking, the preparation of the vegetable in the Middle East, particularly in Greece, is so devised that these properties are lessened (see page 8 for preparation). If you like the glutinous texture, do not use the vinegar treatment given, though a brief blanching will firm the vegetable.

Okra is also available dried, tinned and frozen.

OLIVES

Botanical name: *Olea europaea*
Family name: *Oleaceae*
Arabic: *zaytun*
Greek: *elies*
Turkish: *zeytin*

Native to Eastern Mediterranean regions, the olive has been enjoyed as a fruit and for its oil from ancient times. The fresh fruit is bitter and must be treated to make it edible. Though recommended methods use a lye solution initially, home-cured olives are prepared in other ways. Ripe olives are dry-salted in wicker baskets and left for several days until the bitter juices have run out, then placed in wooden casks to mature, giving olives a wrinkled appearance. Another method for both ripe and green olives requires water-soaking for 3–7 days (the longer period for green olives), with water changed daily; they are then left in brine to mature. Splitting or cracking the fruit hastens curing.

Oil is extracted by pressing, the first pressing yielding the finest oil, which is greenish in colour. The pulp is treated and subsequent pressings give oil of gradually lessening quality. Better-quality oils keep the longest.

If you find high-quality oil strong in flavour, blend a small amount at a time with a bland salad oil.

ORANGE FLOWER WATER

Arabic: *ma'ez zahr*
Greek: *neroli*
Turkish: *portakal cicegi suyu*

A fragrant liquid distilled from orange blossoms, used to flavour syrups and pastries. Available at Middle Eastern and Greek food stores. Chemists (pharmacies or drug stores) sell a concentrated essence; if this is all you can obtain, use in drops rather than the teaspoon or tablespoon measures given.

ORZO

Flat, oval noodles with a shape similar to rice grains. Used in soups or for *yiouvetsi*.

PARSLEY

Botanical name: *Petroselinum crispum neapolitanum*
Family name: *Umbelliferae*
Arabic: *bakdounis*
Armenian: *azadkegh*
Greek: *maidano*
Iranian: *jafari*
Turkish: *maydanoz*

Only the flat-leaf parsley is used in the region, being regarded as more flavoursome than its curly-leafed cousin. Where small quantities are given in recipes, use the curly-leaf variety if that is all you have, adding some finely chopped stalks for more flavour. For dishes such as tabbouleh, and Iranian recipes using large quantities of herbs, the flat-leaf variety is essential. It is now very widely available, and is easily grown from seed.

PASTOURMA

Armenian: *basderma, arboukht*
Greek: *pastourma*
Turkish: *pastirma*

Dried, highly spiced beef popular in Turkey, Greece and Armenia. *Pastourma* is the most widely used term, as it is generally available at Greek food stores. Fenugreek, garlic, paprika, black pepper and chilli pepper are the main ingredients used in the thick, spicy coating. Slice it very thinly and eat with bread, or fry in butter and serve with fried eggs.

PEPPERS, SWEET

See Capsicum.

PINE NUTS

Botanical name: *Pinus pinea*
Family name: *Pinaceae*
Arabic: *snoober*
Greek: *koukounaria*
Turkish: *cam sistigi*

Also called pignolia nuts, these are the kernels from the cones of the stone or umbrella pine, native to the Mediterranean region. Pine nuts are evenly oval and slender. There is another nut sold as pine nuts; it is tear-shaped, and is actually the pinon (pronounced *pi'nyon*) nut from pines native to north-west America. Pinon nuts are less expensive.

POMEGRANATE

Botanical name: *Punica granatum*
Family name: *Punicaceae*
Arabic: *roman*
Iranian: *anar*

A fruit known from ancient times and native to south-western Asia. The fruit will keep for months in a cool, dry place if picked before full maturity. It is much used in the cooking of Iran, where its sour juice is highly favoured. As some varieties are not very sour, the addition of lime or lemon juice may be necessary. In Lebanon and Syria the juice is used in cooking, and the colourful seeds are a popular garnish.

To juice the fruit, wrap a handful of seeds at a time in some muslin (cheesecloth) and squeeze the juice into a bowl. Freeze in ice-cube trays, then pack the frozen cubes in plastic bags and store in the freezer. The seeds also freeze well if required as a garnish. If fresh pomegranate juice is not available, use pomegranate molasses or syrup (see Dibs roman), available from Middle Eastern food stores.

Use 3–4 teaspoons dibs roman in 250 ml (8½ fl oz/1 cup) water for 250 ml (8½ fl oz/1 cup) pomegranate juice.

The syrup grenadine is made from pomegranates, but cannot be used in savoury dishes.

PURSLANE, PURSLEY

Botanical name: *Portulaca oleracea*
Family name: *Portulacaceae*
Arabic: *ba'le, bakli, farfhin*
Armenian: *perper*
Greek: *glystiritha*

A wild green with fleshy leaves, popular as a salad ingredient for the *fattoush* of Syria and Lebanon. In Armenian cookery it is added to yoghurt with cucumber for a refreshing salad; in Greece and Cyprus it is used in raw vegetable salads. Pick the young leaves and tender leafy tips from the reddish-coloured stalks.

RIGANI

Botanical name: *Origanum vulgare*
Family name: *Labiatae*

A pungent Greek herb and an essential flavouring for many Greek lamb dishes. It is wild marjoram, made that little more pungent because of the hot, dry climate. Picked when the flowers are in bud, the herb is dried before use. Though oregano grown elsewhere, picked at the bud stage and dried, is a reasonable substitute, it lacks the special, pleasantly pungent flavour of that grown in Greece. Available from Greek food stores, either in dried bunches or stripped from the stalks.

ROSEMARY

Botanical name: *Rosmarinus officinalis*
Family name: *Labiatae*
Greek: *thendrolivano*
Turkish: *biberiye*

Widely used in ancient times, being regarded as beneficial to the head, in ways ranging from curing headaches to aiding the memory. Occasionally used in Greek, Turkish and Cypriot cooking, in lamb or fish dishes.

ROSEWATER

Arabic: *ma'el ward*
Iranian: *golab*
Turkish: *gul suyu*

Distilled from fragrant rose petals, rosewater is used for both savoury and sweet dishes. As the strength varies according to the quality, when using a new brand add it cautiously and taste to judge how much is required. Price is usually indicative of quality, with the more expensive brands being stronger. Rosewater essence is a concentrate available from chemists (pharmacists or drug stores); it should be used in drops rather than spoon measures. Rosewater is available from Middle Eastern and Greek food stores.

SAFFRON

Botanical name: *Crocus sativus*
Family name: *Iridaceae*
Afghan: *zaffaron*
Arabic: *zaffaran*
Iranian: *zaffaron*

When it takes the stamens of almost a quarter of a million blooms to produce 500 g (1 lb 2 oz) of saffron, is it any wonder that saffron is the world's most expensive spice? The use of saffron originated in Asia Minor in ancient times. Buy a reliable brand, as there are cheaper versions sold that are not true saffron. Pound the saffron threads using a mortar and pestle and soak it in the specified liquid to bring out the fragrance and colour.

SALEP

Arabic: *sahlab*
Greek: *salepi*
Iranian: *neshasteh*
Turkish: *salep*

A fawn-coloured powder made from the dried tubers of various species of *Orchis*. It has a gelatinous quality, similar to cornflour (cornstarch) or arrowroot. In Greece and Turkey it is made into a hot beverage with milk and sugar (1 teaspoon *salep* to 1 cup cold milk; stir and heat until boiling), served with a dusting of cinnamon.

In Lebanon and Syria it is the thickener for the custard base for *buza* (ice cream). The *falooda* of Iran is a cream pudding thickened with *salep*, chilled and served with fruit syrup and crushed ice.

SESAME SEEDS

Botanical name: *Sesamum indicum* or *S. orientate*
Family name: *Pedaliaceae*
Arabic: *simsum*
Armenian: *sousma*
Greek: *sousame*
Turkish: *susam*

Pale cream seeds of a plant widely grown in tropical regions. Sesame seeds are oily and highly nutritious and used since ancient times in the Middle East. The seeds are used on breads and cookies; for *pastelli*, a confection made with honey; for another confection called halva; and for tahini (see Glossary entries for the last two).

SPRING ONIONS

Botanical name: *Allium cepa*
Family name: *Liliceae*

Also known as scallions and green onions, these are the long green shoots of an immature onion. Unless otherwise specified in the recipe, use some of the tender green tops as well as the white section.

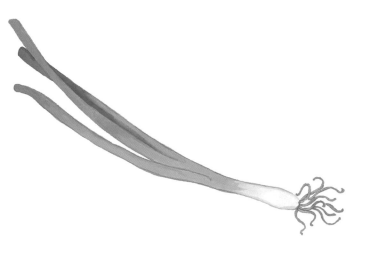

SUMAC

The dried, crushed red berries of a species of sumach tree. It has a pleasant sour taste, rather lemony in flavour. As many trees of related species are poisonous, I have deliberately omitted the botanical name – it is advisable that sumac be purchased at Middle Eastern and Armenian food stores.

TAHINI

Also called *tahina* in some countries, this oily paste is made from toasted sesame seeds. The flavour of different brands varies, so it might be necessary to try various tahinis to find one to your liking. Smooth peanut butter is frequently given as a substitute; though it is a good substitute in cakes and cookies, only tahini should be used for any other recipes. Tahini separates on standing for a considerable time and requires blending before use. Storing unopened tins or jars upside down for some days makes blending easier.

TAMARIND

Botanical name: *Tamarindus indica*
Family name: *Leguminosae*
Arabic: *sbar, tamar hindi*

The word tamarind comes from the Arabic, and literally means 'date of India'. The large bean pod of this tropical tree is favoured for its strongly acid quality. Dried pods, compressed and packaged, are available at Asian food stores and require soaking and straining to separate the pulp from the seeds and fibres. Tamarind is used in the Gulf States and Iraq for dishes that include okra, as well as in other Gulf dishes. Tamarind pulp is also combined with a syrup for a cooling beverage popular in Egypt.

TARO

Botanical name: *Colocasia esculenta*
Family name: *Araceae*
Arabic: *kolkas*
Greek Cypriot: *kolokassi*

Though there are species of *Colocasia* native to tropical Asia and Africa, the *kolokassi* used in Cyprus is the same species as that of the Pacific Islands. It is a large, starchy tuber with side tubers or corms. The taro is toxic if eaten raw; heating destroys the toxicity.

TOMATOES

Some recipes call for fresh tomatoes to be peeled before using. To do this, score a cross in the base of the tomato, place in a heatproof bowl and cover with boiling water. Leave for 30 seconds, then transfer to cold water and peel the skin away from the cross. To seed tomatoes, cut the tomato in half and scoop out the seeds with a teaspoon.

TOMATO PASTE (CONCENTRATED PURÉE)

A thick concentrated paste made from tomatoes, also known as tomato purée in the UK. The tomato passata (puréed tomatoes) used in recipes, however, refers to a thick, pourable tomato concentrate, which is thicker than tinned tomato juice but thinner than tomato paste; it is available in tins and bottles.

See also recipe for Tomato Paste, page 26.

TROUMIS

Botanical name: *Lupinus luteus*
Family name: *Leguminosae*

Certain lupins have been used as foods in the Mediterranean region from 2000 BCE. With the wide variety of pulses available today, lupins are now used only as a snack food. *Troumis* is the Arabic for dried white lupins, and as these look rather like dried butterbeans (lima beans) (though close inspection reveals differences), an explanation is necessary. As they are bitter, *troumis* should not be prepared similarly to other pulses. Soak for 4 days in cold water, changing the water twice daily. Boil until tender, adding salt after 1½ hours. Drain and serve cold with olive oil and lemon juice as an appetiser.

TURMERIC

Botanical name: *Curcuma domestica*
Family name: *Zingiberaceae*
Afghan: *zarchoba*
Arabic: *kurkum*
Iranian: *zarchubeh*

Though often regarded as a spice for colouring food rather than flavouring it, turmeric does impart a pleasant, mildly pungent aroma to foods. It is used only in small quantities in Gulf Arabic and Iranian cooking for both colour and flavour, and is an essential ingredient in Indian curry blends.

WALNUT OIL

Walnut oil is available commercially, but it is very expensive. To extract the oil from walnuts, roughly chop shelled walnuts and press a few pieces at a time in a garlic press. For 1 tablespoon oil, you will require 6–7 walnuts. In Turkey the chopped nuts are enclosed in muslin (cheesecloth) and squeezed — but the garlic press is much easier.

Walnut oil is used as a garnish combined with paprika for *cerkes tavugiu*. A bland salad oil may be substituted for this particular garnish.

YOGHURT DRINK

Afghanistan: *dugh*
Arabic: *aryaan, laban bi sikkar*
Armenia: *tan*
Iranian: *abdug*
Turkish: *ayran*

Yoghurt blended with cold water, usually 2 parts yoghurt to 1 part water, though this varies according to the thickness of the yoghurt.

Salt is usually added, although in Lebanon, Syria and Jordan, sugar is sometimes used (*laban bi sikkar*). In Iran, *abdug* is prepared commercially, being carbonated and bottled.

ZA'TAR

A blend of powdered herbs, including thyme, marjoram and sumac, with salt added. Sprinkle on oiled *khoubiz* (page 264) before baking for a flavourful flat bread; it is occasionally used as a flavouring spice mix in cooked meat dishes. *Za'tar* also refers to the herb thyme.

INDEX

ACKNOWLEDGEMENTS

Writing a book such as this could not be possible without support from many quarters. Organisations and numerous individuals assisted me and thanking each and every one of them is the least I can do.

It is to my family that I owe deep and heartfelt gratitude. John and I have enjoyed over half a century of partnership, and nothing can test its strength more than writing a book of this magnitude. If this book symbolises anything, then it has to be the strength of the family bond. With the constantly taxing effort involved in testing, research and writing I barely had time to be part of my family, but they were always there, encouraging, supportive, loving and very willing taste-testers — maybe that willingness stemmed from pure hunger!

My sincere gratitude to:

For her valuable assistance in working with me and overseeing the many changes in this latest edition, my heartfelt thanks and love to my daughter Suzanne.

The Australian Meat and Live-stock Corporation and their representatives in Middle Eastern countries, without whose valuable assistance and advice much of this research would not have been possible.

The Ethnic Communities Council of New South Wales was wholeheartedly behind my task and gave me contacts in the various ethnic groups of Sydney.

The late Stirling Macoboy, long-time friend and author of garden books, for his assistance with the botanical details necessary for the Glossary. The Dondurmas in the Turkish chapter are dedicated to him.

To my publishers for having faith in my ability to prepare such a book.

My thanks also to those who advised me regarding various countries, their foods, names of ingredients and general information.

Greece: Much of my knowledge of Greek cooking has come through a lifetime of contact with excellent Greek cooks beginning with my mother, Kaliope Calopades, then my mother-in-law Marika Mallos. My sister, Eleni Argyriou, gave me much information. Sylvia Glytsos, Efthalia Serafim, Koula Simos and Zoe Kominato for correcting my Greek transliteration.

Cyprus: Tatia Phillipides of Nicosia; Sophia Agathocleous, Olga Constantine, Erato Christoforou, Anna Adamon, Socrates Andoniou, Chris Jacovides and Dimitra Rose.

Turkey: Gulcin Incekara for a great deal of invaluable assistance, and Ayse Oztunc.

Armenia: Chake and Berdj Sebefdjian, Anny and Joyce Tshaglassian.

Lebanon: Len Obeid and George Habib of Lebanese Import Export, distributors of Middle Eastern foods, for answering innumerable queries about the foods they sell, and Evelyn Bobb.

Syria: Jimmy Antoun and Laudy Jammal of the Al-Sahara Restaurant, Chatswood, Sydney, and Rene Jammal.

Jordan: Idlid Arida and her brother-in-law Nazih Arida.

Iraq: Claire Truscott, who, as a diplomat's wife, spent many years in the Middle East.

Yemen: Zdenka Underwood of Perth, WA, who worked for two years in North Yemen with her husband, Dr Peter Underwood. Zdenka was made an honorary male, enabling her to be present at many special feasts, so gaining further insight into the manners and customs of the Yemenis. Doreen Ingrams' book *A Time in Arabia* was a source of many anecdotes and much information regarding South Yemen.

Egypt: Solange Mattar and Nargus Youssof.

Iran: Akhtar Ostowari, an excellent cook with a vast knowledge of Iranian foods, although she has lived in other countries for much of her life. Helen and Keith Weymouth, who spent ten years in Iran, were most helpful in providing information and props for photographs.

Afghanistan: Faizi and Fahima Seddiq; Anwar and Pari Afzali of the Shah Restaurant, Manhattan Beach, California.

For general assistance, and for lending props and treasures for photography, my thanks to Sydney Fresh Seafood, Manly, Afghan Interiors, Newtown, and Piggot's Store, Woollahra.

TESS MALLOS

⊕ Tess Mallos passed away at the conclusion of this project. She generously shared her recipes with the world and was an inspiration to generations of cooks.

Completely revised and updated in 2012
First published in 1979

Published in 2012 by Hardie Grant Books

Hardie Grant Books (Australia)
Ground Floor, Building 1
658 Church Street
Richmond, Victoria 3121
www.hardiegrant.com.au

Hardie Grant Books (UK)
Dudley House, North Suite
34–35 Southampton Street
London WC2E 7HF
www.hardiegrant.co.uk

A Cataloguing-in-Publication entry is available from the catalogue of the National Library of Australia at www.nla.gov.au
The Complete Middle Eastern Cookbook
ISBN 978 1 74270 492 0

Publishing Director: Paul McNally
Project Editors: Lucy Heaver and Helen Withycombe
Editors: Writers Reign and Katri Hilden
Design Manager: Heather Menzies
Design Concept: Clare O'Loughlin
Typesetter: Megan Ellis
Photographer: Alan Benson
Stylist: Michelle Noerianto
Production Manager: Todd Rechner

Colour reproduction by Splitting Image Colour Studio
Printed and bound in CHINA by 1010 Printing International Limited

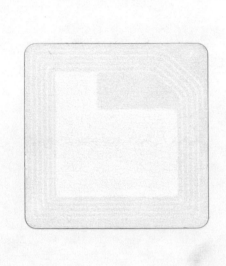